Dictionary of World Biography

The 19th Century

Dictionary of World Biography

Dictionary of World Biography

Volume 6
The 19th Century
K–Z

Frank N. Magill, *editor*

Christina J. Moose, *managing editor*

Alison Aves, *researcher and bibliographer*

Mark Rehn, *acquisitions editor*

FITZROY DEARBORN PUBLISHERS
CHICAGO • LONDON

SALEM PRESS
PASADENA • HACKENSACK, NJ

Dictionary of World Biography is a copublication of Salem Press, Inc. and Fitzroy Dearborn Publishers

For information, write to:

SALEM PRESS, INC.
P.O. Box 50062
Pasadena, California 91115

or

FITZROY DEARBORN PUBLISHERS
919 North Michigan Avenue, Suite 760
Chicago, Illinois 60611
USA

or

FITZROY DEARBORN PUBLISHERS
310 Regent Street
London W1R 5AJ
England

The paper used in this volume conforms to the American National Standard for Permanence of Paper for Printed Library Materials, Z39.48-1992.

Library of Congress Cataloging-in-Publication Data
Dictionary of world biography / editor, Frank N. Magill ; managing editor, Christina J. Moose ; researcher and bibliographer, Alison Aves ; acquisitions editor, Mark Rehn.
     v. cm.
     A revision and reordering, with new entries added, of the material in the thirty vols. comprising the various subsets designated "series" published under the collective title: Great lives from history, 1987-1995.
     Includes bibliographical references and indexes.
     Contents: v.6. The nineteenth century, entries K–Z.
     ISBN 0-89356-319-6 (v. 6: alk. paper)
     ISBN 0-89356-317-X (v. 5-6 set: alk. paper)
     ISBN 0-89356-273-4 (v. 1-10 set: alk paper)
     1. Biography. 2. World history. I. Magill, Frank Northen, 1907-1997. II. Moose, Christina J., 1952- . III. Aves, Alison. IV. Great lives from history.
CT104.D54   1998
920.02—dc21
97-51154
CIP

British Library Cataloguing-in-Publication Data is available.
Fitzroy Dearborn ISBN 1-57958-045-9
First Published in the U.K. and U.S., 1999
Printed by Braun-Brumfield, Inc.

Cover design by Peter Aristedes.

First Printing

CONTENTS

LIST OF ENTRANTS

KAMEHAMEHA I

Born: c. 1758; Halawa, North Kohala, the island of
Hawaii, Hawaiian Islands
Died: May 8, 1819; Kailua, Hawaii
Areas of Achievement: Government and politics,
and military affairs
Contribution: Through his prowess, astute leadership in battle, and adroit use of European advisers, ships, and weapons, Kamehameha overcame his adversaries and united the Hawaiian Islands for the first time in their history. In the process, he made himself their king and founded a dynasty.

Early Life

Since Kamehameha ("the lonely one" or "the silent one"; born Paiea, or "soft-shelled crab") was born before the European discovery of the Hawaiian Islands and therefore before there were any written records, scholars have been forced to rely on native tradition for information about his birth. Estimates of his birth year vary from 1736 to 1758, but today the consensus favors 1758. Kamehameha's mother was Kekuiapoiwa, and his father was Keoua, although there is a story that his real father was Kahekili, king of Maui.

Kamehameha was described by European contemporaries as being well over six feet tall, athletically built, and savage in appearance. He was a member of the chiefly caste, the *alii*, who ruled despotically over the common people. The *alii* were considered to have descended directly from the gods and possessed varying degrees of divinity. The highest *alii* were those who were born to a high-ranking chief and his sister—a system reminiscent of ancient Egypt. Hawaiians worshipped a number of gods, including Kane, the god of creation; Ku, the war god; and Lono, the fertility god. Life was governed by many prohibitions and strict rules for behavior known as the *kapu* (taboo). A priestly caste had charge of worship in the *heiau*, or open stone temples.

Kamehameha's father, Keoua, died young, and from then on Kamehameha was reared at the court of his uncle, Kalaniopuu, the king of Hawaii. It was during this period that Captain James Cook happened upon the Hawaiian Islands, which he called the Sandwich Islands in honor of John Montagu, fourth earl of Sandwich. Cook came first to Kauai and Niihau in 1778, and in 1779 entered Kealakekua Bay near Kailua on the lee side of Hawaii. The Hawaiians at first considered Cook to be the god Lono, but an unfortunate series of events disillusioned them, and he was killed in a skirmish on the shore of Kealakekua Bay. Kamehameha accompanied Kalaniopuu during a visit to one of Cook's ships and even spent the night there, but he seems not to have been present when Cook died.

Life's Work

When Kalaniopuu died, he left the kingship to his son Kiwalao, who undertook a system of land distribution unfavorable to Kamehameha and the other chiefs of Kona. After a bloody battle at Mokuohai in 1782 in which Kiwalao was killed, and with the assistance of an eruption of the volcano Kilauea that wreaked havoc with other opposing forces and showed them that Pele (the goddess of volcanoes) was against them, Kamehameha gained control over all of Hawaii.

When King Kahekili died in 1794, he controlled all the islands of the Hawaiian chain except Hawaii, Kauai, and Niihau. With the assistance of foreign ships and weapons, Kamehameha soon conquered Maui, Molokai, Lanai, and Kahoolawe. In 1795 he proceeded to Oahu—which now had Kalanikupule, Kahekili's brother, as its king—and landed his forces at Waikiki and Waialae. They drove Kalanikupule's forces up the Nuuanu Valley and forced the bulk of them to fall to their deaths from cliffs. Kalanikupule escaped but was later captured and sacrificed to the war god Kukailimoku.

Kamehameha now ruled all the Hawaiian Islands except for Kauai. He soon started preparations for an invasion of Kauai, and in the spring of 1796, he headed toward the island with a large flotilla of canoes. However, rough seas forced him to turn back and postpone his invasion. Hearing that a rebellion was taking place in Hawaii, he returned there to squelch it. He spent the next six years in Hawaii, during which time he assembled a formidable fleet of double canoes and a number of small schooners constructed by European carpenters. With these ships and a large supply of European weapons, he sailed to Oahu in 1804. However, his invasion plans were frustrated again, this time by a terrible plague (probably cholera) that was brought by foreign ships. The population of Oahu was decimated, and large numbers of Kamehameha's army also succumbed. Kamehameha himself was stricken but managed to survive.

Kamehameha continued to plan his invasion of Kauai and even acquired a large ship, the *Lelia Byrd*, to lead the assault. He also entered into negotiations with the island's king, Kaumualii, to solve the problem without battle. An American captain, Nathan Winship, persuaded the two kings to meet on board his ship, the *O'Cain*, and Kaumualii submitted to Kamehameha's sovereignty on the condition that he could retain his position until death.

Now Kamehameha reigned over all the islands, apparently the first to do so. He was an absolute dictator but used his power wisely. He divided up the lands in such a way that no chief had enough power to be tempted to rebel and appointed governors to administer each island. He issued decrees that made life safer and often worked at menial tasks to set an example for his people to follow. He appointed a Hawaiian named Kalanimoku (known as Billy Pitt after the British prime minister William Pitt) as chief executive officer.

During Kamehameha's lifetime, foreign visitors to the Hawaiian Islands became increasingly numerous. The first ships to appear after Cook's unfortunate visit were those captained by George Vancouver, who had been a member of Cook's crew. Vancouver visited the islands in 1792, 1793, and 1794. He brought cattle and goats and other commodities to the islands but refused to provide any arms. He persuaded Kamehameha to cede the Hawaiian Islands to Britain, although Kamehameha apparently believed that he was entering into a defensive alliance in the hope that he would get help against his enemies. In any event, Britain made no effort to follow through, but a close connection between Britain and the "Sandwich Islands" continued. This is symbolized by the Hawaiian flag, which bears the Union Jack in the upper left corner.

Although most of the ships that visited Hawaii during this period were traders searching to replenish their ships, there were occasional visits of a different stripe. Anton Schäffer, a German surgeon in the employ of the Russian-American Company, was sent to Hawaii to recover or receive compensation for a Russian cargo lost from a ship wrecked off Kauai. Schäffer got grandiose ideas and attempted, with the help of Kaumualii, to establish Russian outposts in Kauai and Oahu. He was repulsed by the Hawaiians with the assistance of the Americans in Honolulu and was forced to make his escape by hiding on a ship to Canton.

When the Europeans first visited the Hawaiian Islands, they were able to obtain valuable goods from the natives for baubles or for small pieces of iron, which were especially prized because they could be made into fishhooks or daggers. Fresh water, hogs, and other food items were needed. As time went by, the Hawaiians became aware of the value of their commodities, and prices went up accordingly. Kamehameha himself secured great amounts of goods in barter and even large amounts of hard money, which he retained in storehouses in Kailua, Lahaina, and Honolulu.

Kamehameha had a total of twenty-one wives, but his favorite was Kaahumanu, by whom he had no children. Kamehameha married Keopuolani for dynastic purposes when she was about thirteen years old. Keopuolani and Kamehameha had three children who survived, one of whom, Liholiho, was designated as the heir to the kingdom. Kamehameha spent most of his last years in Kailua, although he occasionally traveled to the other parts of his realm. In 1819, he contracted a malady that no one could cure, and on May 19, he died. His body was treated in the usual way for *alii*: His bones were stripped of their flesh and hidden somewhere in a cave by one of his faithful retainers.

Summary

Only a few monarchs in world history have received the appellation "great." Kamehameha, by uniting all of the Hawaiian Islands under his sway and keeping his land independent of foreign dominance, probably deserves such a title. He was flexible enough to adapt to the changing times but still retained his way of life under the taboo system. If he was sometimes harsh and cruel by contemporary standards, he was also kind and generous. During his brief reign as Kamehameha II, his son Liholiho, upon the urging of Kaahumana (a *kuhina nui*, or prime minister), put a dramatic end to the taboo system by publicly eating with the women, which had been strictly forbidden. After Liholiho's death (by measles during a trip to England), Kaahumanu remained as regent until Liholiho's brother came of age, and she saw to it that the remnants of the taboo system were destroyed. In 1819, the same year that Kamehameha died, the missionaries came to Hawaii and transformed Hawaiian life forever.

Bibliography

Daws, Gavan. *Shoal of Time: A History of the Hawaiian Islands*. New York: Macmillan, 1968.

Daws's book, the best one-volume history of Hawaii, contains an excellent section on Kamehameha and his times, starting with Cook's discovery of the islands. It is very readable, with copious endnotes and an excellent bibliography.

Kuykendall, Ralph S. *The Hawaiian Kingdom 1778-1854: Foundation and Transformation.* Honolulu: University of Hawaii Press, 1938. This first volume of Kuykendall's monumental history of Hawaii contains extensive account of Kamehameha's life and the history of Hawaii since Cook's appearance there. The book also includes an appendix discussing Kamehameha's controversial birth year.

Malo, David. *Hawaiian Antiquities.* Translated by Nathaniel B. Emerson. 2d ed. Honolulu: Bishop Museum Press, 1951. This volume, written by a native Hawaiian in the Hawaiian language, was translated in 1898 by one of the great experts on Hawaiian culture. It contains a wealth of information about virtually every aspect of Hawaiian life before the European discovery, including old Hawaiian folktales and chants.

Mellen, Kathleen Dickenson. *The Lonely Warrior: The Life and Times of Kamehameha the Great of Hawaii.* New York: Hastings House, 1949. This is a well-researched and readable biography. Mellen used oral sources of Hawaiian traditions along with written sources and was aided in her work by Kawena Pukui, a distinguished scholar of Hawaiian culture and language employed by the Bishop Museum. The book contains several useful maps, including one denoting the battle on Oahu that ended at Nuuanu Pali.

Mrantz, Maxine. *Hawaiian Monarchy: The Romantic Years.* Honolulu: Aloha Graphics, 1973. This booklet (47 pages) gives a quick summary of the monarchy by providing short biographies of all of the monarchs from Kamehameha I to Liliuokalani. It also contains portraits of all the monarchs, as well as other interesting photographs.

Tregaskis, Richard. *The Warrior King: Hawaii's Kamehameha the Great.* New York: Macmillan, 1973. Tregaskis relies too heavily on unauthenticated sources and his own imagination to write what amounts to a fictionalized biography. Still, the main facts are there, and the book contains genealogical tables, a map of the Hawaiian Islands, sixteen pages of reproductions of contemporary paintings, and a useful bibliography.

Henry Kratz

EDMUND KEAN

Born: November 4, 1787?; London, England
Died: May 15, 1833; Richmond, England
Area of Achievement: Theater
Contribution: Kean's capacity to identify deeply and sympathetically with the characters he portrayed and his ability to communicate passion to his audiences established him as the foremost tragic actor of his day and assured the dominance of Romantic over classical acting techniques on the nineteenth century British stage.

Early Life

Considerable uncertainty exists about Edmund Kean's date of birth. November 4, 1787, is the most frequently mentioned possibility, but March 17, 1789, has also been suggested, and both may be incorrect. Some doubt exists, too, about Kean's parentage, but the consensus is that his mother was Ann "Nance" Carey, an untalented actress and part-time street vendor, and that his father was Edmund Kean, at various times a surveyor's clerk, an architect, an amateur orator, a professional mime, a drunkard, and a madman. The great actor himself often speculated that he was the son of his sometime guardian, Charlotte Tidswell, and Charles Howard, the eleventh Duke of Norfolk, but this appears to be romantic fantasy. Contemporary testimony points with near unanimity to Nance Carey as Kean's mother, and the actor's physical and temperamental resemblance to the dark-eyed, darkhaired, alcoholic, unstable Edmund suggests, although it does not quite prove, the elder Edmund's paternity.

Since both the Carey and the Kean families had strong connections with the theater, it is hardly surprising that the younger Edmund Kean became a performer. In addition to Nance, her father, George Saville Carey, appeared on the stage both as an actor and an impersonator of figures from the entertainment world. George's father, Henry Carey, was a writer of ballad operas whose one claim to fame, other than being Edmund Kean's grandfather, is his composition of the song "Sally in Our Alley." Like George Carey, with whom he occasionally performed, Moses Kean, the actor's uncle and a man of considerable theatrical renown, was an impersonator of public figures.

Although the details of his childhood are almost as sketchy as the facts of his birth, it appears that Kean was primarily cared for not by his parents but by a Mrs. Price, his father's sister, and by Charlotte

Tidswell, an actress who was Moses Kean's mistress for a time. Young Kean may also have been negligently attended by a professional nurse for a short while, resulting in health problems which required his temporarily wearing leg braces, but again the biographers contradict one another on this point.

What the biographers agree on, however, is that Kean began his stage career early and experienced a long and often frustrating apprenticeship in his craft. The earliest playbill which mentions him by name is dated June 8, 1796, and announces him as Robin in a Drury Lane production of *The Merry Wives of Windsor* (1597), but he is reputed to have played a goblin in a presentation of *Macbeth* (1606) as early as April 21, 1794, when the new Drury Lane first opened its doors, and his actual debut may have occurred still earlier. Separating fact from myth for this first stage of Kean's theatrical life is nearly impossible, but what emerges from the various accounts is the portrait of a gifted, undereducated, rebellious child performing sporadically in the major and minor theaters and entertainment halls of London and beyond while being shunted from guardian to exploitative mother to guardian. The young Kean is likely to have been experienced in every form of theatrical entertainment, from singing to tumbling to Shakespearian recitation, by the time he was announced on May 18, 1802, at Covent Garden as "the celebrated Master Carey."

The above billing suggests that Kean was exhibited as a child prodigy, an assumption strengthened by the oft-repeated claim that he was capable, perhaps even before entering his teens, of reciting *The Merchant of Venice* (1596-1597) in its entirety from memory. Whatever the truth, Kean, despite his small stature, could hardly have passed for a prodigy beyond his mid-teens, and by 1804, he was working as a journeyman actor at a weekly wage of fifteen shillings for Samuel Jerrold, an organizer of a provincial touring troupe. Kean played a wide variety of roles for several companies during the next decade, spent mainly in the provinces, and while mastering an impressive dramatic repertoire, he waited with growing impatience for the opportunity to prove himself before an audience at London's Drury Lane or Covent Garden. Compounding his troubles during this period of comparative obscurity were the attractions of alcohol and the financial

responsibilities which accompanied his marriage to Mary Chambers on July 17, 1808, and the births of his sons Howard Anthony Kean, on September 13, 1809, and John Charles Kean, who eventually became a distinguished actor in his own right, on January 18, 1811.

Life's Work

One of the terrible ironies of Kean's life is that his beloved Howard Anthony died during the complex contract negotiations which led to Kean's first London successes. The son died on November 22, 1813, and the father premiered at Drury Lane as Shylock on January 26, 1814. Reviewers for only two of the London papers, the *Morning Chronicle* and the *Morning Post*, were present for the historic performance, but both praised Kean's innovative, passionate, sardonic interpretation of Shakespeare's familiar Jew. The *Morning Chronicle*'s William Hazlitt, who was to become Kean's foremost champion and most insightful critic, was especially impressed with the variety of emotion Kean infused into the too-often predictable role.

After several performances of *The Merchant of Venice*, the patrons of Drury Lane, still uncertain of Kean's potential, looked forward with considerable anticipation to his appearance on February 12 as Richard III. This time, a full retinue of reviewers was present. The Richard to which London audiences were accustomed was the carefully cadenced, classically restrained Richard of John Philip Kemble. Kean's Richard, by contrast, was emotionally complex, unpredictable, electrifying; his gestures and vocal intonations were subtle at one moment and fiery at the next. This Richard was not simply a character played by a skillful actor with a mellifluous voice; this was the moody, richly varied human being as he might really have been. For those who would accept nothing but Kemble's declamatory style, the evening was disconcerting, but for the rest, the performance was a revelation, and Kean's success was assured. Kean's subsequent performances of *Richard III* (1592-1593) filled Drury Lane to capacity and restored the financially ailing house to solvency. His appearance as Hamlet on March 12, although not quite the success that his Richard had been, was received well enough to confirm him as Kemble's primary rival for preeminence on the English stage and to raise the public's hope that Kean might become as great as the immortal David Garrick. His triumphs also ended the financial privations of his family. The provincial player who had so recently been earning a few shillings a week was now the most lionized actor in London, under contract to Drury Lane Theater for five years at the princely sum of eighty pounds a month.

The extraordinary season continued with Kean's portrayal on May 5 of Othello and, in the immediately following performance, of Iago. His Othello, eventually recognized as one of his greatest roles, at first received lukewarm reviews, but his Iago was immediately acknowledged as masterful. As generally happened when Kean performed, what the critics noted were the subtleties of gesture, the nuances of expression which set his version of the character apart from all others. Kean's voice lacked the grandiloquent music of that of Kemble, but he could communicate emotion with a glance, with some bit of body movement which no previous actor had thought to attempt, and he could shift the emphasis of a familiar dramatic line in such a way that it became startlingly new and the character astonishingly human.

Kean followed up his London successes with well-received performances in Dublin, Gloucester, and Birmingham. He returned to London in the fall of 1814, and in addition to repeating the roles which had made his reputation during his first London season, he played Macbeth, Romeo, Richard II, and various forgettable non-Shakespearian parts. Although his Richard II was widely admired and his Macbeth profitable, the season, which ran from October, 1814, through July, 1815, was not quite the dazzling triumph that the previous one had been. Nevertheless, Kean remained a vastly admired man, and he thoroughly immersed himself in the life which his recent fame and wealth had made possible. His friendship was cultivated by Lord Byron, and he began developing eccentricities which rivaled Byron's own. He sometimes startled his guests by introducing them to his pet lion, often rode after dark at full gallop through the countryside on a black horse, and, most ominously, spent interminable hours drinking in the Coal Hole Tavern with his cronies of the Wolf Club, a notorious organization of his own founding.

By the season of 1815-1816, Kean was advising in the management of Drury Lane, with Byron and four others, and he continued to be the theater's major attraction. His performances were generally well attended, but when he added new roles to his previous successes, the public, having been disappointed by a number of his previous efforts to diversify, was slow to respond. Three new parts, however, were well received: Florez in Douglas Kinnaird's *The Merchant of Bruges: Or, Beggar's Bush* (1815), Sir Giles Overreach in Philip Massinger's *A New Way to Pay Old Debts* (1621-1622?), and Bertram in the play of that name by Charles Robert Maturin. Overreach, one of his very finest portrayals, illustrates his genius for representing evil. During the final scene of the January 12, 1816, premiere, one of the supreme moments of his career, Kean rendered Overreach's culminating madness with such passionate conviction that his fellow actors were astounded, the pit enthralled, and the susceptible Lord Byron quite literally thrown into a convulsive fit. Needless to say, the play was profitably repeated for many nights thereafter.

Unfortunately, Kean's drinking problem was increasing, and his first missed performance at Drury Lane, occurring on March 26, 1816, is probably attributable to drunkenness. He recovered well from this first misstep, however, and the season's end and the subsequent summer tour of the provinces were successful. All appeared prosperous as the

1816-1817 season began, but soon matters took a troublesome turn, with Drury Lane receipts falling disastrously and Kean's homelife threatening to deteriorate. Furthermore, despite the retirement of Kemble at the end of the season, Kean's preeminence among English tragedians was still insecure because of the appearance of two new rivals, Junius Brutus Booth and William Charles Macready. Booth, father of the great actor Edwin Booth and the infamous assassin John Wilkes Booth, was soon overcome, but Macready remained a thorn in Kean's side to the very end.

The 1817-1818 and the 1818-1819 seasons were again mediocre, and Kean's health, which had already shown signs of decline, began growing worse under the various pressures of his intense acting and his equally intense carousing. He was also alienating many of his fellow actors through the ruthlessness with which he eliminated rivals to his theatrical fame. Booth was the most illustrious of Kean's victims, but there were others. In addition, Kean became entangled in disputes over which plays were to be performed at Drury Lane, and on more than one occasion, he helped to scuttle the hopes of an aspiring playwright by resisting the inclusion of a particular play in the season's schedule or by putting little effort into the performance of a role which did not provide him with any likelihood of further glory.

Because of various managerial difficulties, a number of them aggravated by Kean, control of Drury Lane was handed over at the beginning of the 1819-1820 season to an old theatrical enemy, Robert William Elliston, for whom Kean at first refused to work. The combination of a threatened lawsuit for breach of contract and various flattering promises soon changed his mind, and the season included Kean's London debut as King Lear, seen first on April 24, 1820, and repeated twenty-five times by May 27. That Kean, despite his five-foot, seven-inch frame, could succeed as Lear, perhaps the most formidable of all dramatic roles, is a clear indication of his continuing power as an actor.

Kean spent the 1820-1821 season in the United States, dividing his time between New York, Philadelphia, Boston, and Baltimore. All went well until May 25, 1821, when he refused to perform before a Boston audience which he judged to be insultingly small. The ensuing national furor cut short his intended tour, and on June 6, he set sail for home. His return to Drury Lane was greeted enthusiastically, but his health failed him, as it would more and more frequently in the future, and he took several weeks off. The rest of the 1821-1822 season brought no new triumphs, and it was only through the shrewd introduction by Elliston of a rival tragedian, Kemble's heir apparent Charles Young, into the Drury Lane company that Kean was once more inspired to act to his full potential. During the 1822-1823 season, both Young and Kean played to large houses, and when they played together, especially in *Othello, the Moor of Venice* (1604), the theater was packed. The 1823-1824 season saw Young at Covent Garden and Kean and Macready at Drury Lane, but nothing like the previous year's rivalry developed. Kean's performances were usually quite profitable, but provincial touring and sporadic bad health kept him frequently away from Drury Lane.

As the 1824-1825 season began, Kean's tempestuous personal life became even more the subject of scandalous rumor than it had formerly been. Town gossip alleged that a liaison had long existed between Kean and the wife of a close family friend and that the aggrieved husband, one Robert Cox, was about to seek damages for the insult to his marriage. When, on January 17, 1825, the suit actually materialized, resulting in a judgment of eight hundred pounds against Kean, the English and American newspapers gave the matter their full attention, and several of Kean's audiences reacted with predatory delight. His performance as Richard III on January 24 was shouted down, and disruptive behavior marred two or three of his subsequent appearances, but the Drury Lane patrons gradually shifted their sympathies back to Kean, and his London career survived the crisis. Unfortunately, his long-abused marriage did not. Although there was no divorce, he and Mary were permanently estranged. Problems continued, too, during various performances away from Drury Lane. Partially because of public disapproval of his personal life and partially because of his own belligerence and more and more noticeable drunkenness on the stage, a tour of the provinces and a second North American tour, this time including Canada, were stormy. They were not without their triumphant moments, however; Kean's star was rapidly declining, but it had not quite set.

Kean's January 8, 1827, return to Drury Lane in *The Merchant of Venice* was a tumultuous success, but the Cox scandal still haunted him, and he escaped his sorrows through spectacular indulgences in liquor and women. The cumulative effect on his health, physical and mental, was disastrous, and he

soon found it nearly impossible to memorize new roles. He failed miserably, for example, in the May 21, 1827, premiere of Thomas Colley Grattan's *Ben Nazir* (1827), only a few lines of which he was able to deliver correctly. He then quarreled with Stephen Price, the new manager of Drury Lane, deserted to Covent Garden for the 1827-1828 season, and found himself competing with his own inexperienced son, with whom he was also quarreling and whom the sly Price had signed straight from the amateur theatricals of Eton.

The final period of Kean's career is an odd mixture of the pathetic and the heroic, as Kean continued to act—sometimes badly, sometimes with a return of the old fire—despite continual announcements of his impending retirement. His final performance occurred on March 25, 1833, at Covent Garden, where he played Othello opposite the Iago of his son Charles, with whom he had since been reconciled. He collapsed into his son's arms halfway through the presentation and was taken to his home in Richmond, where he died on May 15.

Summary

Edmund Kean was the quintessential Romantic actor, capable of stirring a depth and variety of emotion unmatched by the best of his contemporaries and perhaps unequaled in the history of the English theater. He was the perfect actor for his time, a period in which theaters were large and audiences attuned to the stormy emotive power of which Kean was the acknowledged master. Although the ephemeral nature of the performing arts, at least before the next century's audio and video recording, makes it impossible to know with certainty what a performance by Kean was like, contemporary accounts suggest that classical polish gave way entirely to passion and psychological exploration when Kean was on the stage. Laurence Olivier's brooding Heathcliff and John Barrymore's eccentric Svengali, rather than John Gielgud's regal Hamlet, are the lineal descendants of the characters brought to vivid life by Kean. That dexterity of face and body which Kean developed during his long, obscure apprenticeship served him well in his years of triumph, and though his voice was not the sonorous, cadenced instrument of a John Philip Kemble, it was capable of both the subtlety and the projective power needed to stir the soul of the furthest spectator at Drury Lane.

As the comments of such writers as William Hazlitt and John Keats, another of Kean's admirers, make clear, Kean was capable of identifying so completely with his role that all distinction between actor and character disappeared. The intensity which was displayed by Kean both on the stage and in his tempestuous private life destroyed him, as it has destroyed other actors like him, but it created some of the most inspired moments in world theater and made the Romantic rather than the classical ideal the standard which English-speaking actors most frequently sought to emulate for decades following his untimely death.

Bibliography

Booth, Michael R., et al. *The Revels History of Drama in English*. Vol. 6. London: Methuen, 1975; New York: Routledge, 1996. A wide-ranging history invaluable for understanding the complex theatrical world in which Kean flourished. Volume 6 covers the years 1750 to 1880. The direct commentary on Kean's acting contrasts the passion of his technique with the classical restraint of that of John Philip Kemble. An evenhanded account of both Kean's strengths and weaknesses is presented through references to many of the roles with which Kean was most closely associated.

Cornwall, Berry. *The Life of Edmund Kean*. 2 vols. London: Edward Moxon, and New York: Harper, 1835. This earliest full-length biography of Kean has the advantage of direct access to those who knew him but is unreliable in many details. Less fanciful than Hawkins but should still be read with caution.

Davis, Tracy C. " 'Reading Shakespeare by Flashes of Lightning': Challenging the Foundations of Romantic Acting Theory." *ELH* 62, no. 4 (Winter 1995). Discusses Kean's acting style, which was likened to "flashes of lightning" by Samuel Taylor Coleridge. The origin and later quotations of this metaphor are explored.

FitzSimons, Raymund. *Edmund Kean: Fire from Heaven*. London: Hamilton, and New York: Dial Press, 1976. A popular biography which makes use of all preceding biographical material as well as some newly discovered documents. A vivid account of both the private and public lives of the great actor which leans a bit too strongly toward the credulous. Contains an extremely useful bibliography.

Hawkins, F. W. *The Life of Edmund Kean from Published and Original Sources*. 2 vols. London: Tinsley, 1869; New York: Blom, 1969. One of the more influential and unreliable of the nineteenth century biographies. A repository of mingled fact and myth which has led many later researchers astray.

Hazlitt, William. *Hazlitt on Theatre*. Edited by William Archer and Robert Lowe. New York: Hill and Wang, 1957. Fully one-third of the essays in this volume are reviews of particular performances by Kean directly witnessed by Hazlitt. An invaluable depiction by Kean's greatest champion and most astute critic of what Kean's acting was like. Hazlitt emphasizes the naturalness and the emotive power of Kean's stage presence.

Hillebrand, Harold Newcomb. *Edmund Kean*. New York: Columbia University Press, 1933. This is the definitive scholarly account of Kean's public life. A valuable resource, too, for some details of Kean's private life. Any serious research on Kean should begin with this volume.

Playfair, Giles. *Kean*. London: Bless, and New York: Dutton, 1939. A revision of Playfair's widely respected 1939 study. Playfair has the advantage of familiarity with Hillebrand's work and improves on Hillebrand's treatment of the private life.

Robert H. O'Connor

JOHN KEATS

Born: October 31, 1795; London, England
Died: February 23, 1821; Rome, Italy
Area of Achievement: Literature
Contribution: Keats, whose works explore the significance of beauty, joy, and imagination in a world of suffering and death, was one of the great poets of the Romantic era and is generally acknowledged to be among the finest writers of personal correspondence in English.

Early Life

John Keats, the eldest child of Thomas Keats and the former Frances Jennings, was born on October 31, 1795, in the living quarters of the family business, the Swan and Hoop Stables, in London, England. He had three brothers, George, Thomas, and Edward (who died in childhood), and a sister, Frances Mary. By all accounts, the family was lively and affectionate, and John's earliest years were probably happy. Unfortunately, the Keats family fortunes received a disastrous shock with the death of John's father following a riding accident in April of 1804. John's mother, in desperate haste, married an unpropertied bank clerk, William Rawlings, on June 27, 1804, and left him soon thereafter, thus forfeiting everything she had inherited from her first husband.

The children had moved into the home of their grandparents, John and Alice Jennings, even before this second marriage, and it was there that their mother ultimately rejoined them. She lived on only until March of 1810, succumbing to what was almost certainly tuberculosis, the disease which would eventually kill both young Thomas and her favorite son, John. John is reported to have nursed her through some of the worst stages of her illness, thereby getting a foretaste of what he himself would experience a decade later. Even before this, on March 8, 1805, the grandfather had died, leaving a will which provided fifty pounds annually for his daughter Frances and lump sums of 250 pounds plus interest for each of her children when they came of age, none of which was paid out during the poet's lifetime. Additional money, placed as a trusteeship in the hands of Richard Abbey by Alice Jennings several years before her death in December of 1814, was mishandled, perhaps criminally, and the poet spent much of his life on the brink of poverty, partially because his obsession with poetry brought him little income but also because Abbey, his legal guardian, gave him only a portion of the money which was rightfully his. Despite the various deaths and the family's financial problems, the Keats siblings remained close, maintaining their affectionate relationship through visits and regular correspondence after the breakup of the household.

During the summer before his father's death, Keats had entered the academy of schoolmaster John Clarke at Enfield, where the future poet was a student until his mid-teens. Although quick-tempered and often involved in fights, the result of boyish high spirits rather than malice, he formed friendships easily and was a favorite among his schoolmates. Despite his curly hair, rather delicate features, and diminutive stature—he stood less than five-foot-one at his full growth—Keats experienced little of the adolescent persecution which so plagued his contemporary, Percy Bysshe Shelley. Keats possessed the same sensitivity and generosity as Shelley, but he was more pugnacious and down-to-earth than the ethereal pacifist, and this gritty, bantam element made him more compatible with his peers. Indeed, throughout his short life, he had a talent for friendship exceeded only by his talent for poetry.

With the encouragement of John Clarke and his son Charles Cowden Clarke, Keats developed a passion for reading during his final years at Enfield, especially an interest in books of Greek mythology. After leaving the school in 1811 to become an apprentice apothecary-surgeon with Thomas Hammond of nearby Edmonton, Keats continued his reading, visiting the schoolmaster's son several times a month to discuss books and authors. On one memorable occasion, the young Clarke introduced Keats to Edmund Spenser's *The Faerie Queen* (1590, 1596). The eventual result of Keats's enthusiasm for the Elizabethan poet was his first poem, "Imitation of Spenser," written in 1814, when he was approaching his nineteenth birthday; that age was comparatively advanced for a poet who was to become one of the most important in the English (or any) language, especially when one considers how little time Keats had left to live. Although the conclusion of his apprenticeship with Hammond was still ahead, plus several months of study at Guy's Hospital in London, Keats's growing fascination with poetry would assure that he would never make significant use of the apothecary's license granted him in 1816.

Life's Work

Keats successfully completed his apothecary's examination on July 25, 1816, after which he vacationed in Margate with his ailing brother Tom. Following his return to London in September, he sought out Clarke, who had recently moved to London from Enfield, and the two read George Chapman's translation of Homer together. By the next morning, Keats had written the sonnet "On First Looking into Chapman's Homer," the first of his poems which bears the undeniable stamp of genius. Shortly thereafter, Clarke introduced Keats to Leigh Hunt, a fellow poet and the influential editor of the ultraliberal *Examiner*, where Keats's poem "To Solitude" had been published during the previous May. The two became immediate friends, and while visiting Hunt again later in the year, Keats wrote a large part of "Sleep and Poetry," a work which explicitly announces his dedication to the poetic life.

Through Hunt, whose stylistic influence is evident in much of Keats's early work, not always happily, Keats became acquainted with the poets, artists, and intellectuals of London. At various times, Hunt's circle included such figures as the literary parodist Horace Smith, the political philosopher William Godwin, the painter Benjamin Robert Haydon, the critic William Hazlitt, the essayist Charles Lamb, and the poets John Hamilton Reynolds and Shelley. Haydon, with whom he discussed the grandeur of William Shakespeare and the beauty of the Elgin marbles; Hazlitt, many of whose ideas on the poetic imagination he borrowed; and Reynolds, to whom he addressed several of his profoundest letters, were to be especially important to his future.

Hunt recommended Keats to his many friends as a gifted young writer and published an article in praise of Reynolds, Shelley, and Keats in the December 1, 1816, *Examiner*. The lure of poetry was now so great that Keats announced to the angry Abbey that he was giving up plans to earn his surgeon's license and turning his full attention to establishing himself as a poet. His first volume, a generally undistinguished collection which he dedicated to Hunt, was published by Charles and James Ollier on March 3, 1817. Within a few weeks, Keats had left London to work on a much more ambitious project, the sprawling poetic allegory of the questing imagination, *Endymion*. By late November, having moved restlessly from the Isle of Wight to Margate to Canterbury to Hastings back to London and finally to Oxford, he had the four-thousand-line poem ready for final revision. By April of 1818, *Endymion* had been published by the firm of Taylor and Hessey.

Keats spent several weeks of the period between completing the draft and seeing the final printed version of *Endymion* in London, where he met William Wordsworth, whose egotism offended him, and heard several lectures on poetry by Hazlitt, one of which gave him the inspiration for the grotesque verse romance drawn from Giovanni Boccaccio's "Isabella: Or, The Pot of Basil." He then visited his brother Tom in Teignmouth, Devonshire, and was troubled by Tom's obviously declining health. During the brothers' return to London, Tom, who had only a few months to live, experienced serious hemorrhaging. His brother George, meanwhile, had become engaged to marry Miss Georgiana Wylie and had committed himself to emigration to America.

George and Georgiana were married in late May and left England the following month, after which Keats and a new friend, Charles Brown, made a walking tour of the English Lake District and Scotland. Having written a bundle of poetic impressions of his journey, Keats returned in mid-August, feverish and susceptible to further infection, only to discover that Tom's tubercular symptoms had become much aggravated. To make matters worse, as Keats began the melancholy and dangerous task of nursing his brother through his last weeks of life, critical attacks on *Endymion* appeared in three conservative periodicals: *Blackwood's Edinburgh Magazine*, the *Quarterly Review*, and the *British Critic*. The particularly vicious and snobbish article in *Blackwood's Edinburgh Magazine*, probably written by John Gibson Lockhart, lumped Keats with Hunt and several others into the "Cockney School" of poetry, a condemnation by association echoed in John Wilson Croker's critique in the *Quarterly Review*. Although these attacks did not, as some have claimed, hasten Keats's death, they made an already unpleasant period of his life even less pleasant.

On December 1, 1818, nineteen-year-old Tom Keats died, leaving John with memories of suffering and death that would cast their shadow over much of his remaining poetry and add profundity to what had previously been beautiful, sometimes brilliant, but too often shallow and naïve. He had already begun the Miltonic fragment "Hyperion," a poem which he would later rework as *The Fall of Hyperion: A Dream* (1856), thereby making even more explicit his theme of the growth of the imagination that follows the human fall into full knowledge of the entwined joys and agonies of earthly life.

Deepening his sense of this inevitable entanglement of joy and sorrow was his love for the beautiful young Fanny Brawne, whom he had first met during Tom's final weeks of life and to whom many of his most passionate short lyrics were addressed. Often driven frantic by Fanny's flirtatiousness, Keats nevertheless won her pledge, late in 1819, to marry him, but their union was made impossible by his own impending death. On February 3, 1820, after months of uncertain health, he spat up a quantity of arterial blood which he immediately recognized as evidence of his doom.

What occurred between Tom's death and that terrible day on which he foresaw his own demise, however, was a flowering of poetic genius unmatched in English literary history. During his *annus mirabilis*, in addition to continuing "Hyperion" and working on *The Fall of Hyperion*, Keats wrote "The Eve of St. Agnes," "La Belle Dame Sans Merci," "Ode to a Nightingale," "Ode on a Grecian Urn," "Ode on Melancholy," "Lamia," and "To Autumn," as distinguished a manifestation of lyric power as any poet has ever produced. Peripatetic as ever, Keats composed "The Eve of St. Agnes" during a visit to Chichester and Bedhampton early in 1819; "La Belle Dame Sans Merci," "Ode to a Nightingale," "Ode on a Grecian Urn," and probably "Ode on Melancholy" during a spring interlude at Wentworth Place in the Hampstead area of London; the first part of "Lamia" during a summer stay on the Isle of Wight; and the second part of "Lamia" as well as the whole of "To Autumn" in August and September at Winchester.

Tragically, when most of these poems, plus a handful of others, were published by Taylor and Hessey during June of 1820 in Keats's third volume of poetry, his poetic career had already ended. In a vain effort to recover his health, Keats had left England for Italy in September of 1820 with the painter Joseph Severn. He died in Rome on February 23, 1821, where he was buried, at his own request, under the inscription, "Here lies one whose name was writ in water."

Summary

John Keats's personality and his poetry can best be understood through a careful reading of his letters, perhaps the most insightful written by any English poet. What emerges from his correspondence is the portrait of a charming, generous, surprisingly levelheaded young man who loves the world of the five senses with consummate intensity and who believes passionately in the power of poetry to create essential beauty from the unrefined ore of human experience. During the earliest phase of Keats's career, this artistic intensity, this "gusto" as Hazlitt frequently referred to it, manifested itself as a power to suspend his own ego and to identify imaginatively and nonjudgmentally with objects and events beyond himself. Although he never lost this power of empathy, the intoxicated pastoralism which it frequently produced gradually gave way to a darker and, at the same time, more satisfying vision of human life, a vision in which our earthly existence is portrayed as an unresolvable mixture of bliss and pain whose mingled ecstasies and purgatorial trials fashion our souls. At its most mature, Keats's poetry never denies that the world is a place of suffering and death, but it courageously affirms that the sorrows of life must be embraced if life's beauty is to be realized. For Keats, the rejection of life is the worst of all possible errors.

Bibliography

Bate, Walter Jackson. *John Keats*. Cambridge, Mass.: Harvard University Press, 1963; London: Oxford University Press, 1967. For the advanced and the ambitious intermediate student of Keats, this Pulitzer Prize-winning critical biography is the place to begin. Bate analyzes the intellectual and artistic life of Keats with scrupulous scholarly care, weaving copious comments on the poetry and the more important letters into his account of the poet's everyday life.

Finney, Claude Lee. *The Evolution of Keats's Poetry*. Cambridge, Mass.: Harvard University Press, 1936. Finney's impressive study of the development of Keats's poetry is recommended for the advanced and intermediate student rather than the beginner. Emphasis is on the impact of Keats's experiences and of the world in which he lived on his creative output. Still of great value.

Gittings, Robert. *John Keats*. London: Heinemann, and Boston: Little Brown, 1968. With access to certain British resources unavailable to the American biographers, Gittings expands on the work of Finney, Bate, and Ward. A valuable supplement to the earlier studies.

————. *John Keats: The Living Year, 21 September 1818 to 21 September 1819*. Cambridge,

Mass.: Harvard University Press, 1954; London: Heinemann, 1962. This critical biography limits its attention to the *annus mirabilis*, the period in which nearly all of Keats's important poetry was written. Especially good for its detailed tracing of the impact of Keats's reading and day-to-day experiences on his poetic imagery.

Hirst, Wolf Z. *John Keats*. Boston: Twayne, 1981. Like the other volumes in the Twayne series, this study is an excellent starting point for the beginner. Contains a convenient capsule biography, a helpful chapter on the letters, good critical assessments of the poems, and an extensive annotated bibliography.

Keats, John. *The Letters of John Keats, 1814-1821*. 2 vols. Edited by Hyder Edward Rollins. Cambridge, Mass.: Harvard University Press, 1958. This is the definitive collection of Keats's extensive correspondence. No thorough understanding of Keats as a poet or a man is possible without reading these extraordinary letters. Presented with meticulous editorial care.

————. *The Poems of John Keats*. Edited by Jack Stillinger. London: Heinemann, and Cambridge, Mass.: Harvard University Press, 1978. Stillinger's edition of the poetry supersedes all previous collections. The extensive textual notes are an invaluable source of information on the sometimes tortuous history of the individual poems.

Motion, Andrew. *Keats*. London: Faber and Faber, 1997; New York: Farrar, Straus, 1998. The author provides a discerning account of Keats's life in the context of the social and political worlds in which he lived. Motion's main source is the poet's own letters.

O'Neill, Michael. *Keats: Bicentenary Readings*. Edinburgh: Edinburgh University Press, 1997. A collection of essays by leading Romanticists on Keats's style, career, and his poetry's relationship to history.

Rollins, Hyder Edward, ed. *The Keats Circle: Letters and Papers and More Letters and Poems of the Keats Circle*. 2 vols. 2d ed. Cambridge, Mass.: Harvard University Press, 1965. Rollins' edition of the Harvard collection of Keatsiana is an excellent supplement to the Keats letters. These glimpses of Keats from the perspective of his friends, relatives, and acquaintances help to complete the picture of Keats's complex personality. Valuable biographical sketches of many of the people important in Keats's life are included in volume 1.

Stillinger, Jack. "John Keats." In *The English Romantic Poets: A Review of Research and Criticism*, edited by Frank Jordan. 4th ed. New York: Modern Language Association of America, 1985. For the student of Keats who wishes to explore studies of the poet not mentioned in this bibliography, Stillinger's evaluation of available scholarship is definitive.

Ward, Aileen. *John Keats: The Making of a Poet*. Rev. ed. New York: Farrar, Straus, 1986. Ward's much-admired study attempts to analyze the complex psychological forces which produced Keats the poet. Usually, but not always, convincing.

Robert H. O'Connor

LORD KELVIN
Sir William Thomson

Born: June 26, 1824; Belfast, Ireland
Died: December 17, 1907; Largs, Scotland
Area of Achievement: Physics
Contribution: Kelvin contributed fundamentally to the mid-nineteenth century revolution in physics.

Early Life

William Thomson was born June 26, 1824, in Belfast. His father, James, was an Irishman who had been graduated from Glasgow University and who was teaching mathematics in Belfast at the time of William's birth. Thomson's mother, née Margaret Gardner, the daughter of a wealthy Glasgow merchant, died when William was six years old. In 1832, James Thomson took his motherless family of six children to Glasgow, where he had been appointed the professor of mathematics at Glasgow University. William's life was to be centered in Glasgow.

Thomson was a prodigy with a father who knew how to cultivate genius. James Thomson educated his children himself, and at the remarkably young age of ten, William became a student at Glasgow University. His older brother, James (1822-1892), later a professor of engineering at Glasgow University, entered the university at the same time. The Thomson brothers generally placed at the top of their classes, usually William first and James second. Along with ancient languages, mathematics, and moral philosophy, William studied chemistry and natural philosophy (that is, physics) at Glasgow. The broad natural philosophy course covered heat, electricity, magnetism, optics, and astronomy. At the age of seventeen, William published his first paper, a successful defense of work by a leading French mathematician against charges from the professor of mathematics at Edinburgh University. William's father arranged for the publication of the paper, which appeared anonymously. The paper was published about the time that Thomson left Glasgow to enroll at Cambridge University, the leading British university for studies of mathematics and mathematical theories of astronomy and optics. Since Thomson was already an accomplished mathematician, it is debatable how much mathematics he actually learned at Cambridge. Nevertheless, his stellar performance as an undergraduate there confirmed that he was a mathematician to be reckoned with. His abilities were also confirmed by the original papers in mathematical physics which he published as an undergraduate, while his fellow students were preparing for examinations.

Shortly after Thomson took his degree at Cambridge in 1845, the professorship of natural philosophy became vacant at Glasgow. With his father's guidance, Thomson successfully applied for the post, being appointed in 1846 at twenty-two years of age. The influential father and his talented son enjoyed membership in the same university faculty for only three years, for James died of cholera in 1849. William retained his position at Glasgow until he retired in 1899.

Thomson's early publications were mathematical studies of heat, electricity, and magnetism, which combined a Glasgow emphasis on those subjects with a Cambridge-like emphasis on high-level mathematics. Even early in his career, Thomson's exuberant brilliance readily drew others into his research program. He offered the most advanced physics instruction available in Great Britain in the late 1840's; he had established a laboratory where his students did experimental work in support of his own scientific and engineering research. He also worked closely at this time with the experimental physicists James Prescott Joule and Michael Faraday, collaborations that did much to transform the science of physics.

Life's Work

Thomson's easy-flowing genius spilled over into numerous areas of science and engineering. He wrote some 650 papers, coauthored a major physics textbook that helped establish the new science of thermodynamics, and took out some seventy patents. His research on heat in the 1840's and 1850's is embodied in what is now known as the Kelvin temperature scale and brought him into conflict with geologists over estimates of the age of the earth. In the 1850's and 1860's, his inventions and his applications of mathematical physics to telegraphy problems were keys to the success in 1866 of the Atlantic Cable, a submarine telegraph from Europe to North America. For his efforts, he was knighted the next year, becoming Sir William Thomson. Later, his love of sailing led to patents for improved ships' compasses and methods of taking

deep-sea soundings. Most momentous of all, however, was Thomson's lifetime of speculative thinking in physics: He brought together different approaches and different subjects in a highly original conceptualization that deeply influenced the course of physical thought. In recognition of all of his accomplishments, he was raised to the peerage in 1892. He chose the name Baron Kelvin of Largs, after both the River Kelvin that runs through Glasgow and the seaside town of Largs, where he had built a mansion financed from the proceeds of his patents.

To understand Kelvin's contributions to physics, one must see the science as Kelvin first saw it. The great success of early nineteenth century physics had been the establishment of the wave theory of light, according to which light consisted of waves in a rarefied form of matter called the luminiferous ether. New experimental results and sophisticated mathematical analysis of wave motion had combined to bring this theory to an advanced state. Heat, electricity, and magnetism, on the other hand, were not as well understood; experimental results in those areas had not yet been fit into a satisfactory mathematical theory comparable to the

wave theory of light. Furthermore, the best mathematical physicists in the early nineteenth century were Frenchmen. In Great Britain, the most interesting work in physics tended to be done by experimentalists, such as Joule and Faraday, who knew little of high-level mathematics. Thoroughly familiar with French mathematical physics (as indicated by his first publication), Kelvin was able to deal with Joule's and Faraday's results in heat, electricity, and magnetism in ways that they could not.

Joule claimed that his experiments proved that heat was not "conserved," that the total amount of heat in the world did not remain constant but could be created and destroyed in physical processes. Contemplating Joule's arguments, which he at first rejected, Kelvin was led to publications at midcentury which were instrumental in founding the science known as thermodynamics. Now, it was energy, not heat, that was understood to be conserved. Different forms of energy (electrical, thermal, and magnetic) could be converted into one another (so that the total amount of heat, for example, could change), but in such conversions the total amount of energy remained the same. That was the first law of thermodynamics, the conservation of energy. The second law, in Kelvin's words, involved a "dissipation" of energy. In an example given by Kelvin, the potential energy of a rock was converted into the kinetic energy of motion as it fell. As it accelerated toward the ground, it lost potential energy but gained kinetic energy in such a way that their sum was constant. Upon impact with the ground, the rock's kinetic energy was converted not only into energy of sound but also into energy of heat, as the rock and the ground around it were slightly warmed. The energy, though constant, had "dissipated," for the sound and heat were not as usable as was the initial potential energy of the rock. Thermodynamics was a unifying science, because heat and other forms of energy were understood to be convertible into one another.

Faraday's experiments in 1845 had shown that the plane of polarization of polarized light was rotated by a magnetic field under certain circumstances. Experiments by Faraday and others had already demonstrated that there were mutual influences between magnetism and electricity, and in this context Faraday's findings of 1845 gave Kelvin a case of what he later called his half century of "ether dipsomania." Time and again over the decades, Kelvin tried to figure out how—just as light consisted of waves within the ether—all physical phenomena could be reduced to activity of one kind or another in the ether. The overall strategy was to use analogies with ordinary matter to visualize properties of the ether and then to seek correlations between resultant theories of the ether with experimental results. For example, Faraday's experiment with polarized light suggested to Kelvin that magnetism must involve microscopic rotational motions that could influence the direction of the ethereal vibrations of light. Kelvin's seminal results rendered highly influential his view of all physical phenomena unified in ethereal activity. The view eventually led Kelvin's younger colleague, James Clark Maxwell, a fellow Scot and Cambridge graduate, to his electromagnetic theory of light in the 1860's. Indeed, Maxwell's particular solution to the general problem prevailed over Kelvin's and remains as a part of modern physics. Kelvin himself never formulated a satisfactory theory of the ether, and pursuit of his own insights prevented him from accepting most of Maxwell's electromagnetic theory.

The drive toward unification, exemplified in Kelvin's theories of ether and energy, reached its greatest extent in Kelvin's vortex-atom theory, published in 1867. Kelvin imagined material particles themselves to be microscopic whirlpools in a frictionless fluid, analogous to ordinary smoke rings. Experiments showed that smoke rings bounced off one another just as it seemed reasonable to suppose that atoms would. Moreover, Faraday's 1845 experiments had shown the importance of rotational motion in nature. In addition, Kelvin argued that many of these fluid whirlpools packed together and repelling one another would possess the kind of elasticity that allowed the ether to transmit light waves. If successful, the vortex-atom theory would, therefore, have reduced both ordinary matter and the ether to the same underlying frictionless fluid. All physical phenomena would then be reduced to states of potential and kinetic energy within this cosmic fluid. Though Maxwell and others were highly impressed by the theory, the mathematics of such rotational motion were difficult to work out. Kelvin himself finally decided that the theory was physically implausible, and in the early years of the twentieth century it gave way to quite a different conception of matter. Yet, during its late nineteenth century lifetime, Kelvin's theory directed the research and imagination of many physicists and, indeed, represented the essence of the Victorian concept of physical nature.

Summary

Rejecting Maxwell's electromagnetic theory, which guided so much of late nineteenth century research, Lord Kelvin was somewhat at odds with the physics community in the last decades of his life. So profound had his influence been, however, that a leading British physicist was correct when he declared in 1889 that he lived in a "Thomsonian era." Thermodynamics and Maxwell's Kelvin-inspired electromagnetic theory of light survive as integral parts of physics. Yet physicists abandoned much of the "Thomsonian" worldview, especially that involving the ether, during the early twentieth century revolution in physics associated with relativity and quantum mechanics. This constant updating of theories inevitably occurs in the history of science, however, and it should not diminish appreciation of the power of Kelvin's physical insight. In fact, at a fundamental level, there is considerable continuity between Kelvin's views and those of the modern physicist, for both sought a unified physical theory to be expressed mathematically and supported by precise experimental results.

Bibliography

Burchfield, Joe D. *Lord Kelvin and the Age of the Earth*. London: Macmillan, and New York: Science History Publications, 1975. Burchfield discusses Kelvin's various calculations of the age of the earth, their impact on geological thought, and their eventual downfall. Relying especially on thermodynamics, Kelvin estimated the earth to be about one hundred million years old, far younger than uniformitarian geologists of the day thought. Kelvin convinced them that he was right, but modern discoveries in radioactivity have undermined Kelvin's calculations, extending the earth's age to a few billion years.

Cardwell, D. S. L. *From Watt to Clausius: The Rise of Thermodynamics in the Early Industrial Age*. Ithaca, N.Y.: Cornell University Press, and London: Heinemann, 1971. Examines the growth of thermodynamics, especially as it related to technology. Thermodynamics successfully explained the operation of steam engines, so essential for the Industrial Revolution and the development of railway technology.

Dunsheath, Percy. *A History of Electrical Engineering*. London: Faber, and New York: Pitman, 1962. Dunsheath gives an overview of the history of electrical engineering, placing Kelvin's contributions in their technical context.

Harman, P. M. *Energy, Force, and Matter: The Conceptual Development of Nineteenth-Century Physics.* Cambridge and New York: Cambridge University Press, 1982. Provides an introductory survey of nineteenth century physics with an excellent discussion of Kelvin's various researches.

———. *Wranglers and Physicists: Studies on Cambridge Mathematical Physics in the Nineteenth Century.* Manchester and Dover, N.H.: Manchester University Press, 1985. Brings together several advanced essays, most of which concern Kelvin and Maxwell—their education, their physics, their disagreements, their influence.

King, Elizabeth. *Lord Kelvin's Early Home.* London: Macmillan, 1909. Describes the domestic life of James Thomson's large family, written by Kelvin's sister.

Thomson, Silvanus P. *The Life of William Thomson, Baron Kelvin of Largs.* 2 vols. London: Macmillan, 1910. Explores Kelvin's entire life, often in year-by-year fashion, but also provides a good analysis of Kelvin's search for a "great comprehensive theory."

Weaire, Denis. "Froths, Foams and Heady Geometry." *New Scientist* 142, no. 1926 (May 21, 1994). The challenge of solving the geometry of foams comprised of random bubbles of different sizes is discussed, including the lattice approach suggested by Lord Kelvin.

Wilson, David B. *Kelvin and Stokes: A Comparative Study in Victorian Physics.* Bristol: Adam Hilger, 1987. Compares Kelvin to another major physicist, concentrating on physics education, science and religion, ether theories, and Kelvin's reasons for rejecting modern theories of atomic structure.

David B. Wilson

FANNY KEMBLE

Born: November 27, 1809; London, England
Died: January 15, 1893; London, England
Areas of Achievement: Theater and drama and social reform
Contribution: Kemble was one of the finest actresses on the British and American stage. Her *Journal of a Residence on a Georgian Plantation in 1838-1839* is one of the best firsthand accounts of slavery in the United States.

Early Life

Frances Anne Kemble was born on November 27, 1809, into the most famous acting family in Great Britain. Her father, Charles Kemble, had succeeded his brother John as the manager of the Covent Garden theater in London, and two of her aunts were well-known actresses. Her mother, Maria Therese De Camp, was an actress who appeared on the London stage with her husband.

Frances, known as Fanny, was largely reared by her aunt, Adelaide ("Dall") De Camp, but because of her excitable temperament she was sent to France for her elementary schooling. Her antics soon caused the school's neighbors to refer to her as "*cette diable* Kemble" (that devil Kemble). She returned to France for a finishing-school education in Paris. She became fluent in French, developed a lifelong interest in religion, and began to read Lord Byron and Sir Walter Scott. She was a natural bookworm despite her excitable nature. During her years in Paris, Fanny also discovered her histrionic ability when acting in a school production.

Aside from singing and piano lessons, she spent the next three years in England pondering the question of a career, finding herself drawn to writing except for the uncertainness of the income. Perhaps a career on the stage would provide the income for her to pursue her literary aspirations. Her enthusiasm for the theater evaporated, however, when she pondered how much it had cost other members of the Kemble family.

Life's Work

Fanny Kemble's return to London in 1829 marked a dramatic change in her life's work. She found her family in dire financial circumstances because of the burden of managing Covent Garden, which was covered with bills of sale. Although Kemble disliked the theater and had never had any dramatic training, her mother enlisted her to learn the role of Juliet in William Shakespeare's *Romeo and Juliet* (c. 1595-1596). On October 5, 1829, Kemble made her debut, was an overnight success, and soon became the darling of the British theater crowd. Two other important events happened in this two-year period: Kemble's play *Francis I* was published, and Kemble met the woman who would be her lifelong friend and correspondent, Harriet St. Leger of Ireland. For two years, Kemble performed in London and the provinces and made enough money to keep the Covent Garden in business. The great economic and political crisis of the 1830's, however, finally caused Charles Kemble to abandon the Covent Garden and to take Fanny Kemble and her Aunt Dall to America in the hope of recouping the family fortunes.

Fanny Kemble determined to keep a journal of her sea voyage and the tour of America. She was a good writer and a keen observer of the American scene, which she recorded in what others would later see as very blunt and unkind language that was unsuitable for a lady.

The tour of America was all that they had hoped it would be. She was as popular in the United States as she had been in Great Britain, and American dollars flowed into the family purse. Although Kemble found being an actress distasteful, she believed that it was her duty to help her parents, and that was the only way that she could do so. As she had in Great Britain, Kemble met in the United States famous and about-to-be famous people, including John Quincy Adams, Dolley Madison, Andrew Jackson, Nathaniel Hawthorne, and Charles Sumner, to list but a few. She also came under the influence of William Ellery Channing, the spiritual leader of the Unitarians and abolitionists in New England.

During this two-year tour of the United States, two important changes in her life occurred: She met and was ardently pursued by Pierce Mease Butler of Philadelphia, and her beloved Aunt Dall died as a result of a coach accident. Some of Kemble's biographers opine that if her Aunt Dall had not died in April of 1834, Kemble might not have been so quick to marry Pierce Butler that June. Her marriage meant that Kemble was saying goodbye to both her father and her country. Her last act of filial duty was to arrange to turn over to her father the monies she expected to receive from the publication of her travel journal.

To
Mrs Charles Kemble
with Sir Thos Lawrence's Respects

Although Pierce Butler was well aware of Kemble's independent ways, he soon endeavored to make her over into the submissive wife that he wanted, a wife who would not embarrass him or his family by expressing her own ideas. His attempts resulted in failure and ultimately in the end of the marriage.

At the time of his marriage, Butler was heir, along with his brother, to a Georgia plantation that grew sea-island cotton tended by approximately seven hundred slaves. The Butler family had become one of the wealthiest Philadelphia families with the riches acquired from the absentee ownership of the very lucrative slave property.

At the time of her marriage, Fanny Kemble knew nothing of the source of the Butler wealth—a circumstance which was not at all unusual. By the same token, Pierce Butler was unaware that his new wife had decidedly antislavery views that had been formed in the agitation that had only recently resulted in the abolition of slavery in England. To Fanny, to be anything but antislavery would have been a disowning of her English heritage.

Once Kemble was aware of the source of the Butler money, the overwhelming concern of her life was slavery and how she could convince her husband to free the slaves. During these early days of her marriage, Kemble devoted herself to reading, writing, and elaborating her thoughts on slavery, which soon caused disagreements between husband and wife. The first battle was over the travel journal, which was published in 1835 as the *Journal*. Kemble proposed to include in this travel journal a treatise against Negro slavery. Although Butler was unsuccessful in convincing the publisher to suppress the *Journal*, he did succeed in keeping Kemble from including the tirade against slavery by throwing the offending manuscript into the flames.

Fanny Kemble's opinions about slavery were strengthened when she read William Ellery Channing's *Slavery* (1835) in 1836 and adopted his idea that the slave owner must be won to repentance. Kemble accepted that her duty was to become Pierce Butler's conscience and mentor. In order to accomplish this goal, she needed to go to the Butlers' Georgia plantation. After much resistance, Butler took her there in 1838 when he had to assume the running of the plantation. As she was accustomed to do, Kemble kept a journal of her experiences while living in Georgia for fifteen weeks.

The state of Georgia had one of the densest slave populations of any state. When Kemble arrived, the residences for both the Butler family and the slaves were in wretched condition. The slaves were in poor physical condition, especially the women, who were sent back to the fields immediately after giving birth. This resulted in high infant mortality as well as many gynecological problems that were not treated. Kemble soon sought to remedy some of these conditions. Despite the fact that the slave owner's wife traditionally served as a "doctor" to the slaves, Butler interpreted his wife's interest as female meddling. Anyone who complained to Kemble was promptly flogged. Although Butler sometimes showed compassion—for example, by buying a slave's children from another owner so that the family could remain together—he soon tired of Kemble's complaints. In retaliation, she began to teach slaves to read, which was a serious crime, and to pay them for doing tasks for her.

When the couple returned to Philadelphia, their marriage was already breaking apart, although it would be almost ten years before Pierce secured a divorce. In 1849, the marriage formally ended, and the two Butler children, Sarah and Fan (Fanny), were given into the custody of their father.

For some years, Kemble spent her time between the United States and Europe; eventually, she found herself back in England during the American Civil War. There was much interest in England in the war because of the question of the recognition of the Confederacy as an independent nation. The one thing that might prevent that recognition was slavery. She tried to give an accurate picture of slavery to British authorities she knew, such as Charles Grenville, the diarist, and Lord Clarendon, a liberal peer. Her lack of success led Kemble to publish her journal of the time spent in Georgia. *Journal of a Residence on a Georgian Plantation in 1838-1839* appeared in May of 1863, when recognition of the Confederacy was being debated in Parliament. There is no indication that it had any effect. It was brought out in the United States in July of 1863, shortly after the dual Union victories of Gettysburg and Vicksburg. The book did serve to fan the antislavery fire in what by then were war-weary Northerners.

During her years as a divorcée, Fanny Kemble earned her living by doing dramatic readings, which had become more popular than plays. She was very successful at this and toured both the British Isles and the United States. Upon the death of her husband in 1867, Kemble was able to reestablish contact with her two daughters. As she entered old age, she wrote her autobiographies based on the letters that she had sent to St. Leger and that St. Leger now returned to her. She died at her daughter Sarah's home in England in 1893.

Summary

Fanny Kemble's impact on her time rests on two factors: her acting and her writing. Despite the fact that she did not like acting, she is acknowledged as one of the finest actresses that England has ever produced. Her craft, whether acting or doing dramatic readings, brought the pleasures of Shakespeare and other writers to people throughout the British Isles and the United States. Her most significant written work, *Journal of a Residence on a Georgian Plantation in 1838-1839*, effectively gave the lie to the southern claim that slavery had been a benign institution. Its publication ensured that Northerners would not lose heart in the struggle to end the Civil War and see that the slaves would be freed by the Thirteenth Amendment. Despite efforts to discredit it in the post-Civil War period, it remains the best available firsthand account of slavery in the United States. Kemble had indeed accomplished her goal of being a writer.

Bibliography

Booth, Alison. "From Miranda to Prospero: The Works of Fanny Kemble." *Victorian Studies* 38, no. 2 (Winter 1995). Examines Kemble's three competing roles in Victorian life as revealed in her writings: Miranda, a woman controlled by her race, class, and gender; Caliban/Ariel, an artist who valued freedom; and as Prospero in a political environment.

Driver, Leota Stultz. *Fanny Kemble*. Chapel Hill: University of North Carolina Press, 1933. Provides portraits, pictures from Butler's island, a bibliography, notes, and an index. Contains interesting facts not recorded in other biographies, but the reader must beware of the author's opinions and her use of emotional terms.

Furnas, J. C. "Extrapolating Shakespeare." *American Scholar* 67, no. 3 (Summer 1998). Discussion of Shakespearean productions by Kemble and William Hazlitt including background on both and examples of their work.

———. *Fanny Kemble: Leading Lady of the Nineteenth-Century Stage*. New York: Dial Press, 1982. Well illustrated with copious notes and a good bibliography. Provides in-depth coverage of Kemble's life up to the publication of *Journal of a Residence on a Georgian Plantation in 1838-1839*. At times, the author exhibits a male bias.

Kemble, Frances Anne. *Journal of a Residence on a Georgian Plantation in 1838-1839*. Edited by John A. Scott. London: Cape, and New York: Knopf, 1961. Scott's introduction provides a short biography of Kemble up to the publication of the journal in 1863. Evaluates the importance of the journal.

Marshall, Dorothy. *Fanny Kemble*. London: Weidenfeld and Nicolson, 1977; New York: St. Martin's Press, 1978. Written from an English viewpoint. Includes many illustrations of family and friends not found in other biographies. Accepts as fact that Kemble was mentally imbalanced.

Wise, Winifred E. *Fanny Kemble: Actress, Author, Abolitionist*. New York: Putnam, 1967. Places Kemble's life in historical context by identifying persons whom other biographers simply name. Provides little information about the second half of her life.

Wright, Constance. *Fanny Kemble and the Lovely Land*. New York: Dodd, Mead, 1972; London: Hale, 1974. The best of the Kemble biographies. Places Kemble in her historical setting by explaining the historical importance of the various people in Kemble's life. A good bibliography and many illustrations are included.

Anne Kearney

JAMES KENT

Born: July 31, 1763; Fredericksburg, New York
Died: December 12, 1847; New York, New York
Area of Achievement: Law
Contribution: Kent acquired renown as a legal scholar of profound intellect from his law lectures, written judicial opinions, and four-volume *Commentaries on American Law* (1826-1830). His work set the standard by which subsequent legal and constitutional scholarship in the United States was measured.

Early Life

James Kent was born in Fredericksburg, New York, on July 31, 1763. His mother, née Hannah Fitch, was the daughter of a physician. His father, Moss Kent, the son of a noted Connecticut Presbyterian minister, had been educated at Yale College and had become a successful lawyer. It was natural, as he was born into an educated and socially prominent family, that James would be sent to the best private schools and tutors available. Beginning at age five, he studied the traditional college preparatory curriculum for that era. He had a happy childhood, notwithstanding the loss of his mother at age seven and the troubles and loss of home during the early days of the American Revolution.

At fourteen, James Kent entered Yale College, where he excelled as a student, being accepted into Phi Beta Kappa in his senior year. In 1779, he had to flee Yale when the British threatened to march through New Haven, Connecticut, and the college was closed down. During this brief interruption of his college studies, Kent discovered his father's four-volume set of William Blackstone's *Commentaries on the Laws of England* (1765-1769). He found the clear and eloquent prose of the *Commentaries* so profound that it turned his interest toward law.

By the time he was graduated from Yale at age eighteen in 1781, Kent had become a scholar and a gentleman. He was considered a handsome youth, slight of build and just under average height, with a high forehead and a friendly face. He was somewhat shy, but throughout his life he made friends easily. Kent was ambitious and understood that preferment often came to those who were respectful of their superiors. By 1781, Kent had acquired life-long beliefs in caution and conservativism, hard work and honesty, and a sense of duty to soci-

ety in return for his position as a member of the country's elite upper class.

Because there were no law schools in the United States before 1784, the only way for Kent to become a lawyer was to "read for the law" while working for a practicing attorney or judge. He secured a clerk's position with New York's attorney general, Egbert Benson, in Poughkeepsie, New York. He soon reestablished his reputation for diligence, spending most of his own time reading and studying the classics in law by Hugo Grotius, Samuel von Pufendorf, John Locke, Blackstone, and Edward Coke, among others. By January of 1785, he easily passed the oral examination admitting him to the bar. While clerking for Benson, he lived with John Bailey and fell in love with his daughter Elizabeth. They were married on April 3, 1785, just after he had joined Gilbert Livingston, a prominent Poughkeepsie lawyer, as a partner. He was twenty-one and she was sixteen. It was to be a long and very happy union with four children, three of whom survived to adulthood.

Life's Work

The events surrounding the adoption of the United States Constitution drew Kent into a short political career and brought him to the attention of prominent politicians. He was keenly interested in the proposed new federal constitution, attending as a spectator all sessions of New York's special convention to decide whether to adopt it. His interest was so piqued, he ran for and was elected to the New York Assembly in 1790 and reelected in 1792 as a delegate of Poughkeepsie. Although his voting record clearly aligned him with the more conservative Federalists, he gained the trust and admiration of all factions for his hard work and knowledge of law. In 1792, the governorship was also being contested. John Jay, the Federalist candidate, was defeated by George Clinton. Kent gained the recognition of Jay and the Federalist leadership of New York when he led the fight during that election to expose some questionable campaign practices by the Clinton forces. Jay and other leading Federalists persuaded Kent to run for the United States House of Representatives in 1793, a race he lost.

With a rare lapse of good grace, Kent moved his family to New York City and opened his own law office, saying Poughkeepsie was too provincial. In

November of 1794, he also began teaching law at Columbia College. The lectures written for the course were very well researched and systematically covered all areas of American law. They later were published and then expanded into his famous, four-volume *Commentaries on American Law*. The professorship lasted only four years. The course seemed to have been too demanding for undergraduate students to be popular.

In 1795, John Jay ran again for the governorship and won, but he did so just as the news broke of the very unpopular treaty with England he had just negotiated for President Washington. Kent entered the public debate to defend Jay by writing and publishing several pamphlets and essays. Jay rewarded Kent in 1796 by appointing him one of the two masters in chancery for New York City. A year later, Jay also appointed Kent as recorder of the City of New York. These two appointments, held simultaneously, made keeping a private practice unnecessary, an outcome which Kent welcomed. Although he had proved himself to be a fine courtroom lawyer, Kent had learned that he did not like arguing against other attorneys.

In 1798, Jay promoted Kent to associate justice of the New York State Supreme Court, a position he held until 1804 when he became chief justice. The new position required him to move to the state capital, Albany, and did not pay particularly well. Neither proved a problem, however, since he and Elizabeth had come to dislike the squalor and noise of the city and Kent had made some wise real estate investments that had paid off handsomely. Wealth was never Kent's ambition, for he sought instead respect as a scholar and man of principle. Kent was an intellectual. In Albany he found time for the further study of law and literature, and his library increased considerably.

The majority of the five-man New York State Supreme Court were Democratic-Republicans (that is, Jeffersonians), a political orientation Kent wholeheartedly despised. He perceived in their philosophy a plot by the lower classes to plunder the wealth and property of the upper classes. This, he thought, was the worst threat to liberty facing the United States. That Kent was successful in becoming the leading justice on the court was a testament to his congenial personality as well as his scholarship. A major problem before the court, and all state and federal courts at this time, was whether English common law was still in force. Federalists such as Kent thought the answer was yes, while Democratic-Republicans favored developing an American common law spiced with French doctrines as needed. The contest in New York was decisively won by English common law and Kent was largely responsible. Drawing on his profound learning and using his extensive powers of logic and persuasion, Kent carried his colleagues. This situation did not go unnoticed in the press, which praised Kent for his clarity, impartiality, and precision. As chief justice after 1804, Kent arranged to have all of the Court's opinions written and published, an effort which spread his influence throughout the nation.

Kent did not embrace English common law wholly and without question. There were times when he found it either unsuited to a republican environment or contrary to his sense of justice. He was then willing to amend or alter English precedent. The result was that by the time he left the New York Supreme Court in 1814, a fair body of logically consistent judicial doctrine was in place as a heritage for New York's future. This included laying the foundations for free enterprise capitalism and the defense of rights such as the free press.

In the latter case Kent argued, contrary to English common law, that truth with legitimate intent was an acceptable defense against libel.

In 1814, in recognition of his eminence as a jurist, Kent was appointed chancellor of New York, a judicial office that has since fallen into disuse in the United States. A chancery court was a court of equity which heard cases where the injustice claimed was not covered by statutory law. Such cases were decided on the basis of rules of equity developed by the equity courts over the years. The object of these rules was to render each man his due and make justice and right-dealing prevail in the regulation of people's affairs. Each case was an ethical rather than legal issue and required a wise and learned judge.

Kent approached his new position with characteristic vigor and scholarly acumen and was soon gaining renown in New York and throughout the nation for the quality of his decisions. As he had done before, Kent began the practice of written decisions which were then published in book form periodically. He became particularly famous for defending property and contract rights. Chancellor Kent did not, however, favor the wealthy, as some claimed. His decisions often provided relief for the poor, and he was known for being hard on those who violated the trusts of widows, orphans, and the feebleminded.

Chancellor Kent was reversed by the New York Court of Errors only on occasion and his reputation for honesty, fairness, high professionalism, and incorruptibility became legend. Many famous lawyers and politicians consulted him on difficult points of law. Chancellor Kent wanted to continue on as chancellor as long as he was physically and mentally able, but New York's Constitution mandated retirement at age sixty, an age Chancellor Kent reached in 1823.

After retiring, Kent moved back to New York City to open a law office and became a very successful lawyer's lawyer. Columbia College again asked him to accept a professorship of law. Kent reworked his old lectures, and in the process began his greatest work, the *Commentaries on American Law*, published between 1826 and 1830. Kent's retirement turned out to be the most important period of his life. Five editions of his *Commentaries* were published during his lifetime and he had finished the sixth just before he died. In the years following his death, further editions under various editors were also published; the fourteenth, in 1896, was the last. The *Commentaries* were the first effort by anyone to study the American laws and the Constitution in a systematic and scholarly manner. Judges, lawyers, and law students throughout the nation bought and used these books. Every copy of every edition published during the chancellor's lifetime (indeed until nearly the last edition) was sold. Although the *Commentaries* reflect Kent's conservative bias, his careful scholarship and intellectual integrity made the books of great value to everyone regardless of their political philosophy. It is probable that, until about 1900, the number of American lawyers unfamiliar with Chancellor Kent's *Commentaries* were few.

Besides his professional work, Kent spent his declining years traveling and enjoying the company of his wife, children, and grandchildren. He seemed especially to enjoy the many banquets held to honor him. He remained alert and vigorous until nearly the end of his life. Besides old age, a touch of arthritis was all that seemed to bother him. He died quietly at home in his sleep December 12, 1847, at the age of eighty-four.

Summary

As a New York Supreme Court justice and then chancellor, Kent left a legacy of written opinions of exceptional merit and scholarly precision that had influence far beyond the state's borders. During Kent's tenure on these courts, only the United States Supreme Court was more highly respected or more frequently cited as precedent in the decisions of other courts. Kent set standards for the entire American legal profession and was studied even in Europe. Kent respected the power of justice to maintain a stable and free society, and through his writings helped teach this respect to American lawyers. He also helped significantly in creating the aura of impartiality, justice, and wisdom that typically surrounds American judges and inspires the individual judge himself to live up to that standard.

Kent's *Commentaries* were often used as texts in colleges and law schools, teaching law to generations of American lawyers. More important, the four volumes also taught by example how to study the law. Some might disagree with some of Kent's conclusions and ideas, but few could fault the manner by which he arrived at them. The *Commentaries* stressed the significance of the unique American doctrine of judicial review. Kent believed that this doctrine, which allowed courts to declare actions by other branches of government unconstitutional, was the keystone of liberty and justice. Through the courts' exercise of judicial review, the power of the state could be confined to legitimate uses. This would both preserve the principles of the Constitution and build public faith and trust in government. Further, Kent, unlike many Jeffersonians, never questioned that the final arbiter of constitutional issues was the United States Supreme Court. He had lived through the years of the Articles of Confederation and understood that America could not long survive with a weak and powerless national government. Kent's *Commentaries* also contributed to the intellectual tradition favoring an indivisible union, based on the principles of the Constitution, with a national government strong enough to preserve those principles. When the crisis of secession came, it was this tradition that preserved the United States.

Bibliography

Ferguson, Robert A. *Law and Letters in American Culture*. Cambridge, Mass.: Harvard University Press, 1984. Interesting and perceptive discussion of the impact of law and lawyers on American culture from the Revolution to the Civil War, an era during which lawyers were perhaps the most respected professionals. Mentions Kent only briefly.

Horton, John Theodore. *James Kent: A Study in Conservatism, 1763-1847*. New York and London: Appleton, 1939. Not particularly profound, but the only published biography. What is lacking is insight into Kent's personality and any real appreciation of his impact on the American legal profession.

Horwitz, Morton J. *The Transformation of American Law, 1780-1860*. Cambridge, Mass.: Harvard University Press, 1977; Oxford; Oxford University Press, 1992. Mentions Kent in a number of places. Probably the best legal history of the era to date. Emphasis is on the transformation of English law in the Colonies into a modern national legal system, and how this transformation aided economic development.

Kent, James. *Commentaries on American Law*. Edited by Oliver Wendell Holmes, Jr. 12th ed. 4 vols. Boston: Little Brown, 1864. The fifth and sixth editions are considered by many the best produced by Kent personally, although any of the fourteen will suffice. The twelfth, by Oliver Wendell Holmes, Jr., is considered the most definitive edition.

————. *Memoirs and Letters of Chancellor James Kent*. Compiled by William Kent. Boston: Little Brown, 1898. Compiled by Kent's eldest son. For readers interested in more personal details of Kent's life and his correspondence with other famous people of his day. The selection is a bit biased in Kent's favor.

Langbein, John H. "Chancellor Kent and the History of Legal Literature." *Columbia Law Review* 93, no. 3 (April 1993). Discusses Kent's influence on the development of law as a body of precedent based on published, written opinions.

Newmyer, R. Kent. *The Supreme Court Under Marshall and Taney*. New York: Crowell, 1968. The best short discussion of the great legal and constitutional questions of Kent's era from the viewpoint of the Supreme Court. Although Kent is mentioned only briefly, this work is an excellent introduction to the important issues Kent had to face.

Richard L. Hillard

FRANCIS SCOTT KEY

Born: August 1, 1779; Frederick County (now Carroll County), Maryland

Died: January 11, 1843; Baltimore, Maryland

Areas of Achievement: Law and music

Contribution: Key is most widely known as the author of the song "The Star-Spangled Banner," which became the national anthem of the United States in 1931.

Early Life

Francis Scott Key was born on August 1, 1779, on his family's estate in Frederick County (now Carroll County), Maryland. He was the son of John Ross Key, who owned a plantation, and Ann Phoebe Charlton. At the age of ten, Key was sent to Annapolis, Maryland, to live with his grandmother, Ann Ross Key. While in the state capital, Key attended St. John's College, where he received the modern equivalent of a high school and university education at the same institution.

Following his graduation from college in 1796, Key decided to become a lawyer. In the days before law schools, students had to find an established attorney who owned a law library. Key found a patron in the form of Judge J. T. Chase and was allowed to read and study the law, as well as be tutored by Judge Chase, until he was prepared to take the bar examination. He succeeded in 1801 and immediately opened his own practice in the town of Frederick, Maryland.

On January 19, 1802, Key married Mary Tayloe Lloyd, the daughter of Colonel Edward Lloyd of Annapolis, Maryland. Shortly thereafter, the newlywed couple moved to Georgetown in the District of Columbia. The Keys remained residents of Georgetown for the next twenty-eight years. During that time they raised eleven children—six boys and five girls. Key quickly established a successful law practice by specializing in federal court cases. He was also active at St. John's Episcopal Church in Georgetown and was known for his keen intellect and speaking ability.

Life's Work

The events that led to Key's writing of "The Star-Spangled Banner" began in 1814 during the War of 1812. The United States and Great Britain had been at war with each other for more than two years when Key was approached with an urgent request for his help. Dr. William Beanes, a popular doctor and town leader from Upper Marlboro, Maryland, had been arrested by the British. Beanes's friends went to Key to gain his help in securing the doctor's release.

Beanes's ordeal began with the British invasion of the Chesapeake Bay area in the summer of 1814. On August 23, the English troops under the command of Major General Robert Ross passed through Upper Marlboro, a town in Maryland located southeast of Washington, D.C. Beanes, one of the few residents who did not evacuate during the invasion, was forced to open his home to Ross and Rear Admiral George Cockburn for an overnight stay. The following day, the British entered Washington, D.C., and Ross ordered his troops to put the nation's capital to the torch. Beanes responded to the burning of Washington by helping to organize a vigilante group that jailed British soldiers who became separated from the rest of the invasion force. When news of Beanes's actions reached Ross, the British commander ordered his men to arrest the doctor.

The friends of Dr. Beanes succeeded in retaining Key to attempt to win the doctor's release. Although Key had no experience with negotiating the release of prisoners of war, he did have experience fighting the British. Key had been involved in the war effort as the aide-de-camp to General Walter Smith, commander of the militia protecting the District of Columbia. When Key agreed to help Beanes, he was granted permission by President James Madison to approach the British. Because Key had no experience in this area of diplomacy, the War Department sent John S. Skinner, an American prisoner-of-war exchange agent, to assist Key in the negotiations.

On September 6, Key and Skinner boarded the HMS *Royal Oak*. The Americans were told that Beanes, along with Ross and Cockburn, were aboard the HMS *Tonnant*, a British warship that was anchored off the coast of Tangier Island near the mouth of Chesapeake Bay. On the following day, much to the surprise of everyone aboard the *Royal Oak*, the ship carrying Beanes was spotted heading right for them under full sail. Key and Skinner were transferred to the *Tonnant*, where they learned that Beanes was to be released. Not long after boarding the British man-of-war, the Americans were also told that the *Tonnant* was en route to Baltimore, where it would join the rest of

the British fleet for a full-scale assault on the largest and most prosperous city in the state of Maryland. In order to keep the operation a secret, Key, Skinner, and Beanes would be held until the end of the invasion. They were transferred to the HMS *Surprise*, a larger warship, and the fleet headed north for Baltimore.

Clearly, the invasion of Baltimore did not remain a secret for long as the movement of so many enemy vessels in the Chesapeake Bay alarmed residents along the way. Word spread quickly among the people on shore. When the British assault began in the early morning hours of September 13, 1814, the people of Baltimore were prepared. Fort McHenry, the star-shaped fortification guarding Baltimore's inner harbor, was stocked with fifty-seven cannons and nearly one thousand men.

The British attack on Baltimore began at 5:00 A.M. on September 13, and artillery fire from both U.S. and British guns continued for the next twenty-three hours. The primary target of the enemy's guns was Fort McHenry because the English warships could not proceed until the heavily fortified arsenal was captured and its guns silenced.

Throughout the day, Key, Skinner, and Beanes observed the battle through a spyglass from the deck of the *Surprise*, which was anchored eight miles away from the fighting. Key and his colleagues knew that as long as Fort McHenry withstood the invasion, Baltimore would not fall into enemy hands. Because they were so far away from the fighting, the only way they could be sure was to see the large red, white, and blue flag of the United States flying over the fort. As the fighting continued after nightfall, Key could see the flag still flying over Fort McHenry through the glare of bombs and rockets exploding in and around the arsenal.

At 4:00 A.M. the following day, the fighting finally ended. The American prisoners aboard the British warship wondered if the assault on Baltimore had succeeded. They anxiously waited until daybreak, only to discover that the heavy haze of smoke from the artillery fire obscured their view. When the smoke cleared, Key and his friends were relieved to see that the U.S. flag was still flying over Fort McHenry. The signal was given for the British fleet to withdraw, thereby ending the battle. Key was so moved by the sight of the flag that he scribbled a few phrases on an envelope that he carried in his pocket.

On the evening of September 16, the British deposited Key, Skinner, and Beanes at Hughes' Wharf in Baltimore. The men were taken immediately to the Indian Queen Hotel in order to rest and recuperate from their recent ordeal as prisoners of war. Key, however, found it impossible to sleep. The images of the recent battle—the blasts of cannon fire and the shrieking of shells cutting through the dark sky—still swirled in his head. He returned to the series of phrases that he had written on the envelope. Key completed the poem, then borrowed the melody from a popular British drinking song of the day titled "To Anacreon in Heaven" to complete his composition. The next day he showed the song to his family and friends.

Although it is not known exactly who was responsible for releasing the song to the public, someone passed the composition to the publisher of the *American and Commercial Daily Advertiser*, a small local newspaper produced in Baltimore. The song was printed on handbills under the title "Defence of Fort M'Henry," and the following week the song appeared in the *Baltimore Patriot and Evening Advertiser*. On September 27 it became a national sensation after being published in the *Daily National Intelligencer* of

Washington, D.C. Several more weeks passed before the title of the song was changed to "The Star-Spangled Banner."

Summary

Following the War of 1812, Francis Scott Key resumed his law practice. In 1833, President Andrew Jackson appointed him to negotiate a treaty with the Creek Indians in Alabama. At the time, the Jackson administration was beginning preparations for removal of the remaining Native American tribes from the southeastern United States to areas west of the Mississippi River. In the same year, Key was selected to be the United States district attorney for the District of Columbia, a position he held for eight years. He died from a lung disease called pleurisy on January 11, 1843, at the home of his daughter in Baltimore.

Key was a successful attorney throughout his life, but he will forever be known as the composer of "The Star-Spangled Banner." Although the song became popular almost immediately after it was written, it did not become the national anthem until Congress passed a resolution in 1931. As for the flag that inspired Key to write his song, it still hangs in the Smithsonian Institution in Washington, D.C.

Bibliography

Hickey, Donald R. *The War of 1812: A Forgotten Conflict*. Urbana: University of Illinois Press, 1989. One of the best sources on the War of 1812. Contains only a few pages on Key, but provides a thorough study of the British operations in the Chesapeake Bay.

Lord, Walter. *The Dawn's Early Light*. London: Hamilton, and New York: Norton, 1972. Lord provides a lengthy and interesting explanation of how Key was inspired to write his song.

Patterson, Lillie. *Francis Scott Key: Poet and Patriot*. Champaign, Ill.: Garrard Publishing, 1963. A short study of Key written for middle school students.

Quaife, Milo M., Melvin J. Weig, and Roy E. Appleman. *The History of the United States Flag: From the Revolution to the Present*. New York: Harper, 1961. Contains information on Key and instructions for the use and display of the U.S. flag.

Tucker, Glenn. *Poltroons and Patriots: A Popular Account of 1812*. Indianapolis, Ind.: Bobbs-Merrill, 1954. Tucker's study provides information on Key as well as the British invasion of the Chesapeake Bay area.

Jonathan M. Jones

SØREN KIERKEGAARD

Born: May 5, 1813; Copenhagen, Denmark
Died: November 11, 1855; Copenhagen, Denmark
Areas of Achievement: Philosophy and religion
Contribution: Kierkegaard's challenge to neat systems of philosophical thought, such as that propounded by Georg Wilhelm Friedrich Hegel, has highlighted his philosophical influence. His predominant assumption, that existence is too multiform to be systematized, created the fabric around which existentialism, and indeed much of Continental philosophy, have been woven.

Early Life

Søren Aabye Kierkegaard was the last of seven children born to Michael Pedersen Kierkegaard and his second wife, Ane Sørensdatter (Lund); she had been the maid of Michael's first wife, who died childless after two years of marriage. The elder Kierkegaard, an affluent businessman, had himself been born in poverty and virtual servitude, rising by dint of hard work and good fortune to the comfortable status the family enjoyed at Søren's birth.

Despite such prosperity, the Kierkegaard household was haunted by early death. Two of Søren's siblings died before he was nine; his mother and three more siblings died in a span of less than three years before his twenty-first birthday. Michael was never able to overcome the belief that these deaths were punishment for the unpardonable sin he committed when, as a boy of eleven, tending sheep and bitter at his lot, he cursed God.

The influence of the somber elder Kierkegaard upon his gifted son is certain, but the extent to which it permeated Kierkegaard's character and influenced his writings throughout his life is difficult to estimate. A key passage from Kierkegaard's journals suggests that his father's inadvertent revelation of some past misdeeds permanently altered their relationship:

> An affair between the father and son where the son finds everything out, and yet dare not admit it to himself. The father is a respectable man, God-fearing and strict; only once, when he is tipsy, he lets fall some words which arouse the most dreadful suspicions. Otherwise the son is never told of it and never dares to ask his father or anybody else.

Regarding this incident, Frederick Sontag says that it thrust Kierkegaard into a "period of dissipation and despair," causing him for a time to neglect completely his theological studies at the university.

In addition to his father's influence, Kierkegaard was indelibly marked by his engagement to Regina Olsen. He met her for the first time at a party, when she was fourteen. She was captivated by his intellectual sagacity; he later admitted that that had been his design. They both endured a difficult period of waiting until she was nearly eighteen before they became engaged. Yet, having endured such a lengthy period of waiting, within days after the engagement had been effected Kierkegaard was convinced that it was a mistake. Some years after he had broken the engagement, he wrote in his journal:

> I said to her that in every generation there were certain individuals who were destined to be sacrificed for the others. She hardly understood what I was talking about. . . . But just this spontaneous youthful happiness of hers, set alongside my terrible melancholy, and in such a relationship, must teach me to understand myself. For how melancholy I was I had never before surmised; I possessed no measure for conceiving how happy a human being can be.

In 1841, not long after breaking his engagement, Kierkegaard successfully defended his doctoral thesis and departed for Berlin, where he stayed for several months attending lectures. Within two years, he published his first books, the product of an intense period of creativity, and his career was fully launched.

Life's Work

Kierkegaard was a powerful and prolific writer. The bulk of his corpus was produced within a period of about seven years, spanning 1843-1850. Appreciative readers of Kierkegaard's writings can be thankful for the voluminous groundswell of production which came in his early thirties, for he died a young man of forty-two. During the course of his writing career, he pursued several recurring themes; it would be misleading, however, to treat his work as though he had systematically moved from one arena to another in a planned, orderly fashion.

Indeed, Kierkegaard's decided distrust of the systematizing of Hegel had pushed him in the direction of an existential methodology which would be expressive of his whole personality. Rather than creating a system for the whole of reality which

was necessarily linked by chains of reasoning, Kierkegaard created in his writings psychological experiments centered on persons confronting life situations. By so doing, he avoided both the strict rationalism and the Idealism so characteristic of analytic philosophers, and pulled his readers into existential consideration of life's dilemmas.

Kierkegaard considered his life and cojointly his works as an effort to fulfill a divinely appointed task. This conviction had led to his breakup with Regina because of what he called his destiny "to be sacrificed for the others." It also led him to the realization that his vocation was to confront his contemporaries with the ideal Christian life. He saw that as his purpose in life and consequently chose to lay aside every weight that would hinder him from "willing that one thing."

Denmark had appropriated Hegelianism as the proper mode of informed thinking. Indeed, Kierkegaard's countrymen had even allowed Christianity to be absorbed into the Hegelian system. Hence, the Christian ideal of individuals choosing Christ was lost: Every person in Denmark was nominally a Christian. When applied to the Church, the totalizing attempt prefigured in Hegel made everyone a Christian by birth. It was within this context, and for the purpose of confronting this attitude, that Kierkegaard arose to do battle in print. He described himself as a "midwife," helping to bring forth authentic individuals. His goal was nothing short of arousing his age from its complacence. Whereas Hegelianism might encourage rigors of thought, it made things easy through its promise of certainty. Kierkegaard, on the other hand, made things difficult by thrusting the individual into the fray, thereby teaching him what it truly means "to become a Christian."

An important aspect of many of Kierkegaard's works had to do with his method. For his philosophical works, he used a variety of often-flamboyant pseudonyms, such as Victor Eremita, Constantine Constantius, Virgilius Haufniensis, Johannes Climacus, and Anti-Climacus. At the same time, under his own name, he produced a number of devotional works and religious meditations. Kierkegaard's indirect communication has caused not a little bewilderment. He himself addressed what he referred to as his "polynymity" rather than "pseudonymity" in an appendix to *Afsluttende uvidenskabelig Efterskrift til de Philosophiske Smuler: Mimisk-pathetisk-dialektisk Sammenskrift, existentielt Indlæg* (1846; *Concluding*

Unscientific Postscript, 1941, 1968). Given his consistent and unwavering emphasis upon "choice," it is reasonable to assume that Kierkegaard believed that this method of presentation enhanced his ability to confront the reader. As long as pseudonyms were used, his readers were not free to see what "Kierkegaard the authority" had to say about the issues. The reader would thus be thrown back upon himself, having to choose an interpretive stance for himself.

Since Kierkegaard was a difficult writer, ahead of his time, he received little income from his writings, depending largely on his substantial inheritance. Moreover, as a brilliant, acerbic, and uncompromising critic of his society, he was frequently embroiled in controversy; in his later years, he worked in great isolation. Near the end of his life, Kierkegaard wrote several books which dealt explicitly with Christianity. *Til Selvprøvelse* (1857; *For Self-Examination*, 1940) challenged his readers to view themselves in the light of New Testament descriptions of Christianity rather than simplistically accepting the terms which the established church was propounding. His final book, *Hvad Christus dømmer om officiel Christendom* (1855; *What Christ's Judgment Is About Official Christianity*, 1944), views the relationship between the state and Christianity. He shows that the official Christianity of which every Dane partook was far from New Testament Christianity.

On October 2, 1855, Kierkegaard collapsed while walking in the street. The nature of his final illness is not certain. He was hospitalized, accepting his fate with tranquillity. He died on November 11, 1855.

Summary

At the time of his death, and for a long period thereafter, Søren Kierkegaard's works were little known outside Denmark. Both his striking originality and the fact that he wrote in Danish delayed recognition of his achievement. By the early twentieth century, however, a wide diversity of thinkers reflected his influence, which has continued to grow since that time; he is often hailed as "the father of existentialism."

Even Kierkegaard's most explicitly philosophical writings, it should be noted, bear an undeniable theological character. In *Philosophiske Smuler: Eller, En Smule Philosophi* (1844; *Philosophical Fragments: Or, A Fragment of Philosophy*, 1936, 1962), he plumbs the epistemological depths of how a historical consciousness can confront an eternal consciousness and come away with what one might call "knowledge." In other words, to what degree can eternal truth be learned within the categories of time or space? In *Concluding Unscientific Postscript*, he confronts the objective problem of the truth of Christianity. The issue involved here is often referred to as "Lessing's ditch." Gotthold Ephraim Lessing believed that there exists an intellectually impossible leap from the contingent truths of history to the necessary truths of divine revelation. Kierkegaard looked at this problem and concluded that "a leap of faith" was required for the individual bound by finiteness and historical necessity to encounter eternal truth. This assertion has caused most to claim that Kierkegaard equated truth with subjectivity.

Bibliography

Blackham, H. J. "Søren Kierkegaard." In *Six Existentialist Thinkers*. London: Routledge, 1951; New York: Macmillan, 1952. A brief but incisive treatment of Kierkegaard's championing of individuality and inwardness as opposed to Hegel's notion of abstract system building. Emphasizes Kierkegaard's claim that any true philosophy confronts the intellectual, the aesthetic, and the ethical arenas in terms of the existing individual's life situations. Further alludes that faith is a fourth category, not to be confused with any of the others.

Duncan, Elmer H. *Søren Kierkegaard*. Waco, Tex.: Word Books, 1976. Surveys Kierkegaard's thought for the stated purpose of "making him more accessible to all of us." Ties the theme of Kierkegaard's corpus to traditional problems of philosophy. Emphasizes Kierkegaard's lasting contribution of categories, such as "absolute paradox," "absurdity," and "angst," which have been used by the main voices of existentialism, as well as the key figures of contemporary theology.

Evans, C. Stephen. *Kierkegaard's "Fragments" and "Postscript": The Religious Philosophy of Johannes Climacus*. Atlantic Highlands, N.J.: Humanities Press, 1983. Provides a thorough and serious conceptual look at Kierkegaard's writings through the two books that he pseudonymously attributed to Johannes Climacus. Its intent is that of a "companion" to the two works. Provides as much elucidation as would a good commentary.

Lowrie, Walter. *Kierkegaard*. 2 vols. New York: Harper, 1962. This is a definitive biography of Kierkegaard, written by one of the most prominent translators of his writings. Follows Kierkegaard's life chronologically, providing a list of dates for major events and publications. Also includes a helpful fifteen-page synopsis of Kierkegaard's works.

Rae, Murray A. *Kierkegaard's Vision of the Incarnation: By Faith Transformed*. New York: Oxford University Press, and Oxford: Clarendon Press, 1997. Rae concentrates on Kierkegaard's thoughts on Christian faith and conversion, in particular, conversion by revelation.

Ree, Jonathan and Jane Chamberlain. *Kierkegaard: A Critical Reader*. Oxford and Malden, Mass.: Blackwell, 1998. Collection of challenging interpretations of Kierkegaard's work and ideas including previously published and new essays from experts such as Jacques Derrida and Paul Ricoeur.

Rudd, Anthony. *Kierkegaard and the Limits of the Ethical*. New York: Oxford University Press, and Oxford: Clarendon Press, 1993. Rudd discusses Kierkegaard's central concepts and relates them to contemporary arguments on ethics, religion, and other issues. The book has received critical acclaim as useful to scholars, undergraduates, and graduate students.

Sontag, Frederick. *A Kierkegaard Handbook*. Atlanta, Ga.: John Knox Press, 1979. Sontag provides for Kierkegaard's works what Kierkegaard himself conscientiously avoided: a systematic approach. Sontag intended this dialectical study of key concepts as a companion reader for the student of Kierkegaard's corpus.

Stephen M. Ashby

RUDYARD KIPLING

Born: December 30, 1865; Bombay, India
Died: January 18, 1936; London, England
Area of Achievement: Literature
Contribution: The author of several books of extraordinary insight about the realm of childhood, as well as some stirring popular poetry sympathetic to the British soldier, Kipling's greatest accomplishment was his depiction of life in India at the close of the nineteenth century.

Early Life

Rudyard Kipling was born in 1865 in India, one year after his father had accepted a position as a teacher of architecture in Bombay. His parents both came from prominent but not wealthy families, and the promise of a reliable source of income was sufficient inducement for the Kiplings to leave England. Rudyard Kipling always recalled his childhood in India as a time of exceptional happiness, a paradisiacal existence in an Edenic setting where he was treated like a young god by a loving family and many friendly local servants. This idyll came to an end in 1871, when his parents, in accordance with British cultural expectations about hygiene, social status, and racial purity, sent him to England to board with a retired sea captain in Southsea. For the next six years, Kipling lived in what he called "The House of Desolation," severely disciplined by the captain's widow. The only pleasure he had during this time was his holiday visits to the home of his uncle Edward Burne-Jones, the renowned Pre-Raphaelite painter, in whose "magical domain" Kipling learned the stories of the "Arabian Nights" from family group readings, and from whom he developed an appreciation for games of language and wit, for stories of invention and surprise, and for the eclectic decor of the Burne-Jones home.

In 1875, Kipling's father became curator of the museum in Lahore, a considerable advancement in status and financial remuneration. This promotion permitted Kipling to enter the United Services College, a very new, very minor public school with an unusual headmaster (Cormell Price) who shared the radical public views of William Morris and recognized Kipling's need for encouragement in his idiosyncracies of character. Incompetent at and disdainful of the social-entry games of cricket and soccer, Kipling nevertheless became close friends with two other individualistic boys (the trio became the basis for the heroes of *Stalky & Co.*, 1899) who shared his early interest in writing, debating, and exotic gestures such as decorating their study with Japanese fans, old china, and glass from second-hand shops. Avidly pursuing a program of self-education, the boys read and discussed all the modern poets, including Walt Whitman, whom Kipling defended against attacks by the English master. Kipling was editor of the school magazine but otherwise an ordinary student, and he could not qualify for a scholarship at Oxford, a necessity since his parents could not afford to pay his tuition. With no other prospects immediately apparent, his parents used their social connections to make an arrangement for him to return to India as a reporter for *The Civil and Military Gazette* of Lahore. In 1882, Kipling accepted this position and returned to India, three months before his seventeenth birthday.

Life's Work

Kipling's return to the land of his birth gave him a renewed access to places and situations which fired his imagination and gave a direction to his tremendous latent creative energy. From his parents' place in Anglo-Indian society, he was able to get a clear picture of the workings of the British colonial administration. His journalistic assignments enabled him to learn about the daily life of the British soldiers "at the ready," and his desire to learn about Indian culture took him on excursions across much of the subcontinent. In 1885, in collaboration with his parents and his sister, he published *Quartette*, including his first major short story, "The Strange Ride of Morrowbie Jukes," a powerful evocation of the fears of the rulers who recognized the precariousness of their position in a country torn by mutiny only twenty years before. In 1886, the year of his majority, he published *Departmental Ditties*, poems primarily about life among the civil servants based in Simla, the summer home for the Viceroy of India. Kipling's stories had become a regular feature of *The Civil and Military Gazette*, and the pace of his work drove him to the limits of his energy. Between November, 1886, and June, 1887, thirty-nine stories appeared. In 1888, the volume *Soldiers Three* was published. It contained many of the best stories of three "typical" British privates whose farcical adventures in a picaresque

milieu gave Kipling a frame to probe the barracks' world of adultery, treachery, bullying, and even murder, and then to probe further into the brooding interior landscape of the soldier's life, a harsh existence relieved only by the deep, close friendship of the men.

In autumn, 1887, Kipling was transferred to the senior paper of the syndicate, *The Pioneer*, where his astute but opinionated political commentary led to the threat of a lawsuit, attempted assault, and the grievance of some high government officials. As Kipling was becoming increasingly famous in English literary circles, with his parents' encouragement he decided to test his skills as a free-lance writer in London. In March, 1889, he left Calcutta, returning only once more to India to visit his parents in 1891. For the remainder of his life, the cultural and psychic landscape of India haunted his dreams; it had already become the foundation for his finest work.

Kipling established himself in London as a kind of tentative bohemian bachelor. Generally reserved and no self-promoter, his ambition was still quite clear. Above the door in his rooms, he declared, "To Publishers, A classic while you wait." Many others agreed, and his reception in London was very encouraging, beginning with a London *Times* leading article in March, 1890. The style of his life is captured in the description by Kay Robinson, his editor at *The Pioneer*, who wrote in 1896 about a man in a white cotton vest and trousers who suggested a Dalmatian because of the mass of inkspots that covered him. Robinson saw him as mildly eccentric, with a "mushroom-shaped" hat and a fox terrier that looked like a "nice clean sucking pig." In later years, Kipling tended to look more formal, a smallish man of soldierly bearing with glasses and a cartoonist's delight of a mustache, a high forehead, and, quite often, a hat when out in public. His first years in London saw the publication of the finest stories of his early period, *The Courting of Dinah Shadd and Other Stories* (1890), the two versions of *The Light That Failed* (1890, 1891), both in American editions, and *Barrack-Room Ballads and Other Verses* (1892), which included poems such as the very well known "Danny Deever." Kipling's visits to London music halls seem to have been instrumental in the development of the insistent jaunty rhythms which he fitted to poems of military life.

In spite of his success, Kipling was not entirely comfortable with the world of letters in London. Its innate conservatism in literary matters did not really suit his temperament or aesthetic principles. In addition, his usual regimen of constant, intensive writing and a continuing feeling of displacement or homelessness had brought him to the verge of a breakdown. Part of his course of recovery included a long sea voyage to Calcutta to visit his supportive family, and another part included his marriage to Caroline Balestier, the sister of his agent and a member of a prominent American family from Brattleboro, Vermont. By way of a kind of extended honeymoon, Kipling and his bride traveled extensively in the United States, where Kipling met Mark Twain, a favorite author. In 1893, Kipling and his wife settled in southern Vermont on five acres of land purchased from her family and lived there until 1895. The distance from India may have given Kipling the perspective he needed to shape his experiences and impressions of India into literature, because it was in Vermont that he produced the Mowgli stories, publishing *The Jungle Book* in 1894 and *The Second Jungle Book* in 1895. He wrote the second half of *Barrack-Room Ballads and Other Verses* in Vermont, and began work on *Kim* (1901), his great visionary epic of India. During this time he also made several trips to the whaling port of Gloucester, Massachusetts, to do research for *Captains Courageous* (1897). Several factors combined, however, to end his stay in the United States. His once-harmonious relationship with his wife's younger brother deteriorated into litigation, he feared that the Cleveland Administration would draw the United States into war with Great Britain over a minor dispute in Venezuela, and he felt hounded by American reporters who pursued him for his celebrity without giving him the peace to continue the writing that produced it.

The Kiplings returned to England in time for the Jubilee of 1897, and Kipling contributed to the carnival atmosphere with his memorable poem "Recessional," which was published in the London *Times* after a family friend retrieved it from the wastebasket where Kipling had discarded it. Many people read their own political feelings into the poem, often missing its negative view of the imperial creed, but the poem contributed considerably to Kipling's reputation. Oxford granted him an honorary degree, compensating for the disappointment of his inability to matriculate there ten years earlier, and he was elected to the very exclusive Athenaeum Club, a tribute considered "one of the greatest professional-class establishment honors of late

Victorian England." The publication of "The White Man's Burden" (also in *The Times*) in 1898, with its explicitly racist title, was Kipling's statement of resistance to foreign tyranny and anarchy, two *bêtes noires* of his belief in the necessity of an ordered existence. While visiting South Africa during the winter of 1898, he met and was captivated by Cecil Rhodes, and became a firm supporter of Rhodes's empire-building ideas, thus further developing an ideology particularly repugnant even to many people who much admired his other work. Perhaps more significantly, during his stay in South Africa he journeyed along the Limpopo River, a crucial part of his inspiration for the *Just So Stories* (1902), which he composed in a comfortable house made available on Rhodes's estate.

After returning from the United States, the Kipling family had lived in close proximity to various relatives in Rottingdean, in Sussex, from 1897 to 1902. Kipling completed *Kim* in this setting and pulled the Stalky stories together, as well as finishing the last of the *Just So Stories*, "The Elms." The death of his young daughter Josephine in New York City in 1899, however, spoiled the charm of the home in which she had been reared. Kipling purchased a house in Burwash, in the country of East Sussex, in 1902, and there spent the remainder of the time he was in England. The failure of the British imperial venture in South Africa distressed him, and the ascendancy of the Liberal Party to power in 1906 made him feel like a member of the rejected Tory old guard. He believed that his cherished concept of "order," the foundation of his faith in existence, was now threatened by such new forces as "cosmopolitanism," "egalitarianism," and "individualism," unconventional ideas which, he thought, undermined England's "world-civilizing mission." With his fabled India fading into the oblivion of memory, the deaths of both his parents in the winter of 1910-1911 cut him off from the possibility of recall in conversation, and he felt compelled to find a new locus for his faith. To some extent, he found it in the lush, unspoiled Sussex countryside which he established as a constant source of value in his cyclical stories of renewal set in medieval times, *Puck of Pook's Hill* (1906). Paradoxically, just as he was retreating from public life, he was named the first British laureate by the Nobel Committee (1907).

England's entry into World War I drew Kipling back into active public life, and the death of his son John in October, 1915, led him into two large-scale projects to combat his sorrow. As a kind of memorial for his son, he compiled *The Irish Guards in the Great War* (1923), interviewing many of his son's fellow officers, and he accepted an appointment to be Commissioner of War Graves, a post that took him to Gallipoli, Mesopotamia, Palestine, and other sites where British forces fell in battle. His last two collections of stories deal primarily with the psychological effects of war on combatants and emphasize themes of compassion and healing. A striking exception to this, however, was his continuing hatred of everything German, which found expression in some virulent anti-Kaiser poetry and in the famous story "Mary Postgate," in which a German airman dies in agony. Through the 1930's, Kipling continued to criticize the Germans, and with the rise of Nazism, acting with typical consistency in personal as well as political affairs, he removed the Indian "ganesh" sign from his publications because of its resemblance to the swastika.

Kipling's health had been declining for some time when, in 1922, he suffered a serious gastrointestinal attack (the result of an undiagnosed duodenal ulcer). This moved him further into what Angus Wilson called "an ever-growing introspective meditative frame of mind." During his later years, Kipling and his wife spent considerable time abroad, particularly in France, with Kipling writing occasional stories, verse, essays, and an interesting and revealing autobiography, *Something of Myself: For My Friends Known and Unknown* (1937). He died in January, 1936, just as England was beginning to respond to the Nazi menace about which he had warned. Kipling was buried in Poets' Corner, Westminster Abbey, near the ashes of Charles Dickens, who had died the year before Kipling arrived in England.

Summary

The passage of time has not been particularly kind to Rudyard Kipling. His strong political opinions earned for him the enmity of many people in Great Britain, the United States, Canada, and India during his lifetime, and while such eminent critics as Edmund Wilson and George Orwell paid him the compliment of taking him seriously, their attacks on his ideas and his art have contributed to a general attitude that Kipling is either a historical curiosity, a local colorist, a Tory bully, or, at best, the writer of cliché-ridden, jangling verse and a few charming children's books. Ezra Pound's caustic assessment, beginning "Rudyard the dudyard/

Rudyard the false measure . . .," suggests how simple it is to dismiss Kipling in the style of his own poetry, how close he is to parody even at his best.

Yet Pound, probably because he detested Kipling's politics, missed one of Kipling's greatest strengths, something that Pound himself (in *The ABC of Reading*, 1934) prescribes as an essential component of poetry: the sheer, unforgettable rhythmic musicality of Kipling's best work. There is a primal power of language in poems such as "Gunga Din" and "Mandalay" which has pressed them into the memory of at least three generations in the United States and the British Commonwealth, where they can be easily recalled and recited with evident sensual delight. Kipling instinctively sensed the energy of the popular song and knew how to seize and use it, though it is not only the sound of the best poems that is so compelling. Some of his most familiar lines—"East is East and West is West," "Somewheres East of Suez," "The female of the species is more deadly than the male," and "He travels fastest who travels alone"—have been incorporated into the collective subconscious as aphoristic folk wisdom.

Even if Pound were right about Kipling's politics—a bizarre anomaly in the light of Pound's own political theories—the chauvinistic, semiracist, cryptofascist declarations are distortions of some quite sensible and thoughtful political formulations. Kipling's idea of The Law is akin to Ernest Hemingway's famous "Code" in that it was not a rigid social contract but a method of maintaining personal integrity amid the forces of chaos, and a doctrine designed to ensure maximum individual freedom amid a cooperative social system. Because Kipling was so easily unsettled by personal demons, he tended to overcompensate by supporting what he hoped were organizational principles which would guarantee some stability in what he knew was a fragile world even for the strongest of men and women. A careful reading of Kipling's stories and poems will reveal a very subtle mind.

While his children's stories have been highly praised, they have also been appreciated *only* as children's stories. As Angus Wilson points out:

> . . . the elusive magic which lies at the heart of most of his best work . . . came from the incorporation into adult stories and parables of two of the principal shapes which are to be found in the imaginative world of children. The first is the transformation of a small space into the whole world which comes from the in-

tense absorption of a child. The second is the map-making of hazards and delights which converts a child's smallest journey into a wondrous exploration.

That aspect of the adult psyche that remains permanently tied to childhood has rarely been touched and projected as well as in Kipling's writing.

Finally, Kipling's sense of India, especially the Anglo-Indian world that he loved, gave him a subject and a sense of place from which a powerful literary vision could be drawn. Kim, the "Ariel of Kipling's magic kingdom," is one of the true originals of English literature. His delight in life, his openness to people and things, make him a wonderful guide to Kipling's own India, and his story, as Wilson perceptively explains, is "an allegory of that seldom portrayed ideal, the world in the service of spiritual goodness." By contrast, the more ordinary but still complex mortals of his songs and stories are dreadfully human in their faults and limits, but the soldiers, civil servants, and their families that he wrote about are the subject of a kind of compassion and empathy surprising in a man regarded as an aloof defender of class and caste. If the worst of Kipling is caught in the crumbling of an obsolete empire, the best is preserved in the art of a man who understood how tenuous life is and how valiant the human struggle can be.

Bibliography

Bodelsen, C. A. *Aspects of Kipling's Art.* Manchester: Manchester University Press, and New York: Barnes and Noble, 1964. A superior interpretation of Kipling's writing, with attention to his symbols.

Cornell, Louis L. *Kipling in India.* London: Macmillan, and New York: St. Martin's Press, 1966. Contains a considerable amount of important information about Kipling's early career, as well as an incisive interpretation of the crucial aspect of India as a visionary concept in Kipling's writing.

Dobrée, Bonamy. *Rudyard Kipling.* Rev. ed. London: Longman, 1965. An early examination of Kipling from the perspective of a professional soldier turned professor who provides a balanced view of Kipling's ideas.

Henn, T. R. *Kipling.* London: Oliver and Boyd, and New York: Barnes and Noble, 1967. Brief but succinct discussion of Kipling and his writing, including a survey of criticism and a list of the short stories.

Hopkirk, Peter. *Quest for Kim: In Search of Kipling's Great Game.* London: Murray, 1996; New York: Oxford University Press, 1997. The author examines the mysteries of Kipling's tale of Indian life involving the power struggle between Russia and Great Britain.

Kemp, Sandra and Lisa Lewis, eds. *Kipling, Rudyard: Writings on Writing.* Cambridge and New York: Cambridge University Press, 1996. Discusses Kipling's opinions on writing and writers as expressed in previously unpublished letters and papers.

Kipling, Rudyard. *Something of Myself.* London: Macmillan, 1936; New York: Doubleday, 1937. An underrated, candid, and revealing account of Kipling's life from the artist's own point of view. Important as a complement to any other study of Kipling.

Rutherford, Andrew, ed. *Kipling's Mind and Art.* Stanford, Calif.: Stanford University Press, and London: Oliver and Boyd, 1964. Includes the historical views of Lionel Trilling, George Orwell, and Edmund Wilson, as well as more recent essays of particular sensitivity that cover the full spectrum of modern criticism.

Stewart, J. I. M. *Rudyard Kipling.* London: Gollancz, and New York: Dodd, Mead, 1966. A biographical and critical study of Kipling's writing and his personality.

Wilson, Angus. *The Strange Ride of Rudyard Kipling.* London: Secker and Warburg, and New York: Viking Press, 1977. A prominent novelist's quirky, passionate, and highly knowledgeable study of Kipling's life and writing, grounded in very thorough scholarship and guided by a most sympathetic, individualistic series of insights. Indispensable for anyone interested in Kipling.

Leon Lewis

HEINRICH VON KLEIST

Born: October 18, 1777; Frankfurt an der Oder, Prussia

Died: November 21, 1811; Wannsee bei Potsdam, Prussia

Areas of Achievement: Literature and drama

Contribution: Kleist was one of the most important literary figures in the development of the German *Novellen* of poetic realism. Although he is better known in Germany than in English-speaking countries, he is usually acknowledged to have been ahead of his time, a forerunner of the modern literature of the grotesque, usually associated with Franz Kafka a century later.

Early Life

Heinrich Wilhelm von Kleist was born on October 18, 1777, in Frankfurt an der Oder, the first son of a Prussian officer, Joachim Friedrich von Kleist, and his second wife, Juliane Ulrike Pannwitz. By the time he was fifteen, both of his parents had died and he, without much enthusiasm, had become a soldier. Although little is known about his childhood, what evidence there is available from letters and other sources indicates that he was bored and unhappy with his life as a soldier; although he was promoted to lieutenant, he resigned from the army in 1799 to enter the University of Frankfurt. While there for three semesters, Kleist threw himself wholeheartedly into his studies of mathematics, physics, and philosophy.

Also while at the university, Kleist met and became engaged to Wilhelmine von Zenge, the daughter of an army officer. His letters from this period suggest that he was an extremely serious young man, introspective and concerned with finding fulfillment in his life by means of intellectual pursuits. Even his love affair with Wilhelmine was characterized by his efforts to make her into a kind of idealized soul mate, an embodiment of intellectual and moral beauty. In letters to his sister and his fiancée, he talks of his "life plan," a rational pursuit that would prevent him from being merely a puppet at the mercy of fate.

Yet Kleist's hopes for a purely rational plan of life were crushed in 1801 by what his biographers refer to as his "Kantian crisis." In a letter to Wilhelmine, he declared that as a result of reading Immanuel Kant all of his faith in rationality as a basis for leading a purposeful life had been destroyed, and his anguish at facing a life governed by chance, fate, and meaninglessness had become almost unbearable. In what some have called an attempt to escape his intellectual torment, Kleist left Frankfurt and began traveling, first to Paris and then to Switzerland, where he became fascinated with ideas learned from Jean-Jacques Rousseau about leading the "natural life." Because his fiancée refused to go along with his new enthusiasm to lead the simple life of a peasant, their engagement was broken the following year. It was while living in Switzerland that Kleist began writing and thus launched his short-lived career.

Life's Work

Some of his biographers suggest that Kleist's literary career began because he was attempting to compensate for his failure to achieve his intellectual goals by succeeding immediately as a writer. While living on a small island on the Lake of Thun in Switzerland, he completed his drama *Die Familie Schroffenstein* (1803; *The Schroffenstein Family*, 1916) and began work on *Der zerbrochene Krug* (1808; *The Broken Jug*, 1930) and *Robert Guiskard* (1808; English translation, 1962). Although he began two of his best-known short fictions at this time, "Die Verlobung in St. Domingo" (1811; "The Engagement in Santo Domingo," 1960) and "Das Erdbeben in Chili" (1807; "The Earthquake in Chile," 1946), he had been greatly encouraged to continue his work on *Robert Guiskard* by the high praise for an early fragment of the play received from Christopher Martin Wieland, one of the most respected literary figures in Germany at the time.

For reasons known only to the tormented mind of Kleist, when he returned to Paris he burned the fragment of *Robert Guiskard*, which Wieland had said was worthy of Sophocles and William Shakespeare. Stung by his own self-imposed sense of failure, he joined Napoleon I's forces, which were ready for an invasion of England, perhaps hoping, as some biographers suggest, that death in battle would redeem his failure in a glorious way. Shortly thereafter, however, he was sent back to Germany and hospitalized for a nervous breakdown.

After recovering, Kleist obtained a post with the government in the Ministry of Finance. During this time, he continued to write, finishing *The Broken Jug*, drafting both plays *Amphitryon* (1807; English translation, 1962) and *Penthesilea* (1808; English translation, 1959), and beginning his best-known fiction, *Die Marquise von O . . .* (1810; *The Marquise of O . . .*, 1960). He suffered, however, from both depression and physical ailments that made it necessary for him to take an indefinite leave from his government job.

While on a trip to Dresden with two friends in January, 1807, Kleist was arrested by French authorities in Berlin on suspicion of being a spy and sent to prison in France. For several months during his imprisonment, he continued to work on his plays, especially *Penthesilea*. After being cleared and released, Kleist returned to Dresden to enjoy literary success as the author of *Amphitryon*, which had been published during his incarceration.

His newly raised hopes for a successful literary career seemed dashed when *The Broken Jug* was poorly received by drama critics and when a literary journal he had begun to edit had to be sold for lack of sufficient subscribers. At first seemingly undeterred by these setbacks, Kleist continued his writing, reconstructing the destroyed *Robert Guiskard* fragment, finishing *The Marquise of O . . .* , and beginning another great novella, *Michael Kohlhaas* (1810; English translation, 1844).

Kleist traveled to Austria in 1809 and attempted to start a patriotic journal in support of Germany's efforts against Napoleon; however, that too failed, and during this time he once again suffered depression and physical illness. There were even rumors that he had died. Nevertheless, he returned to Dresden, in good health, although penniless, in 1810. His play *Das Käthchen von Heilbronn: Oder, Die Feuerprobe* (1810; *Cathy of Heilbronn: Or, The Trial by Fire*, 1927) was staged in Vienna to an approving audience, and he now was making plans to stage *Prinz Friedrich von Homburg* (1821; *The Prince of Homburg*, 1875), which he had completed during his travels to Austria. Yet a planned performance of the play in the private theater at the palace of Prince Radziwill was canceled; the publisher of *Cathy of Heilbronn* refused to honor his promise to publish the work; and the director of the Prussian National Theater refused to allow the play to be staged. Again, Kleist's hopes for a literary career seemed dashed.

Kleist's next effort to support himself in the literary world was to become editor of the *Berliner Abendblätter*, the first daily newspaper to be published in Germany. Although the newspaper was popular with the public, it was somewhat too daring in its political editorials for the Prussian government censors. Although Kleist made strong pleas for freedom of the press, even to Prince Wilhelm, he was ignored. Despite the fact that the newspaper was forbidden from publishing what the government considered radical political ideas, it did publish Kleist's famous essay on the marionette theater, as well as some of his short fictions. Also during 1810, a second volume of his short fiction was published. The newspaper, however, was doomed to failure; the last issue of the *Berliner Abendblätter* was published on March 31, 1811.

At this time, Kleist was alone and without means of support; a request for a position with the government was ignored; his family, in a reunion at Frankfurt in October, was reluctant to support him. During this period, he met the young wife of a government official, Henrietta Vogel, who, biographers suggest, was suffering from an incurable illness. Together they made a suicide pact, and on November 21, 1811, near Berlin, Kleist shot Henrietta Vogel and then himself.

Summary

Heinrich von Kleist remains a mysterious figure in the history of literature. Relatively little is known about his tragic life, and his art and ideas have not been discussed in the United States or Great Britain to the extent that they have in Germany. The major focus of the criticism of Kleist's work has been on its philosophical content, although some studies (mostly in German) have been made on his narrative technique. Despite the fact that critical attention on Kleist has shifted to structural and textual analyses of his *Novellen* and plays, the primary emphasis is still on the mysterious tension in his work between the nature of consciousness and the nature of external reality.

Kleist is an important German Romantic writer, who represents the significant intellectual shift in the early nineteenth century from an earlier dependence on rational, intellectual assumptions and structures to a new approach to reality based on the individual's own perception. He is often referred to as a precursor to twentieth century existential thought in his emphasis on the tension between the individual's desire for meaning and unity and the cold and unresponsive external world.

Bibliography

Brown, Hilda Meldrum. *Heinrich von Kleist: The Ambiguity of Art and the Necessity of Form.* New

York: Oxford University Press, and Oxford: Clarendon Press, 1998. Brown provides a new view of Kleist's dramas and prose with emphasis on the theatrical and visual aspects of his work.

Ellis, John M. *Heinrich von Kleist: Studies in the Character and Meaning of His Writings*. Chapel Hill: University of North Carolina Press, 1979. Contains detailed analyses of Kleist's most mature works. Based on these discussions, Ellis provides a summary chapter on the general nature of Kleist's fiction, primarily its typical themes.

Gearey, John. *Heinrich von Kleist: A Study of Tragedy and Anxiety*. Philadelphia: University of Pennsylvania Press, 1968. A helpful and readable general study of the major short fictions and the plays. According to Geary, the basic tension in Kleist's works is not simply between rationality and emotion or even self-consciousness and the external world. More basically, his works focus on the general nature of opposition itself.

Guenther, Beatrice M. *The Poetics of Death: The Short Prose of Kleist and Balzac*. Albany: State University of New York Press, 1996. Assesses of the use of death by Balzac and Kleist and places their writings in historical context.

Helbling, Robert E. *The Major Works of Heinrich von Kleist*. New York: New Directions, 1975. A general introduction which surveys previous Kleist criticism, provides a brief biographical sketch, and then argues that Kleist's vision is tragic, not pathological. The predominant theme of Kleist's works is the conflict between the individual consciousness and the unresponsive external world.

Maass, Joachim. *Kleist: A Biography*. Translated by Ralph Manheim. London: Secker and Warburg, and New York: Farrar, Straus, 1983. Maass's workmanlike biography, the first full-length account of Kleist's life available in English, was first published in German in 1957 and was reissued in a revised version in 1977, the basis for the English translation. Includes brief discussions of Kleist's major works. Illustrated, with indexes but no notes or bibliography.

McGlathery, James M. *Desire's Sway: The Plays and Stories of Heinrich von Kleist*. Detroit, Mich.: Wayne State University Press, 1983. The primary focus of this relatively brief and highly documented critical study is the tension in Kleist's characters between their devotion to lofty ideas and their outbursts of passion—a tension which McGlathery says is typical of comedy.

March, Richard. *Heinrich von Kleist*. New Haven, Conn.: Yale University Press, and Cambridge: Bowes and Bowes, 1954. Perhaps the best introduction to Kleist's life and art. Although this is only a brief (fifty pages) pamphlet, it provides a concise biographical sketch as well as an informed introduction to the basic themes in Kleist's work.

Charles E. May

ROBERT KOCH

Born: December 11, 1843; Clausthal, Prussia
Died: May 27, 1910; Baden-Baden, Germany
Areas of Achievement: Bacteriology and medicine
Contribution: Koch was a pioneer bacteriologist and the first to prove definitively that specific microorganisms cause specific diseases. He identified the bacterium that caused cholera, enabling the virtual elimination of that disease in the Western world. He isolated the causative agent of tuberculosis, eventually leading to the containment of that once-deadly scourge, and he discovered the reproductive cycle of anthrax, providing for the successful combating of that disease.

Early Life

Robert Koch was born in the mining country of the Harz Mountains in central Germany and was one of thirteen children of Hermann Koch and his wife, Mathilde Biewend. Hermann was a mining official and reasonably well-off, although provision for a large family taxed his resources. A timely promotion assisted him in educating Robert, a precocious child drawn to the study of nature, who was able to excel at the local *Gymnasium*, or academic preparatory school. He went on to study at the nearby University of Göttingen. After a year of science and math, young Koch abandoned the idea of a teaching career and in 1863 transferred to the medical school at Göttingen, hoping that that field would allow him to pursue his love of science and travel. Koch's greatest scientific mentor was Jacob Henle, an anatomy professor who had published on disease causation and who speculated that infection might be transmitted by living organisms. At that time, however, no medical school in the world offered courses in bacteriology.

In 1866, at age twenty-three, Koch received his M.D. degree, passed his medical examination, and went to Berlin, where for a few months he attended lectures by the famous Rudolf Virchow, author of the notion that disease is the result of disturbance of cell function in the body tissues. Koch, from the very beginning of his career, was no mere medical practitioner concerned with diagnosis and treatment of disease but was a scientist interested in its very causes.

After a brief internship at Hamburg General Hospital, where he learned about cholera at first hand, he returned home and in July, 1867, married Emmy Fraatz, a daughter of the mining superintendent of Clausthal. Koch and his wife then lived for about a year at Langenhagen, Hanover, where he served at a hospital for mentally handicapped children while he practiced medicine privately in the community. By the time the couple's only child, Gertrud, was born in September of the following year, they were living at Niemegk, near Berlin. The young doctor's practice did not flourish there, and Koch moved his family to Rakwitz, near Posen, where he became a successful country doctor.

During the Franco-Prussian War, Koch entered the Prussian Army Medical Corps and served in 1870 and 1871 in France, working both with the wounded and with soldiers afflicted with typhoid. He left the army and returned briefly to his patients at Rakwitz, but in 1872 he secured appointment as district physician for Wollstein, another small town in the province of Posen. It was from that area of lakes, woods, and fields that Koch moved into national and international acclaim. A ruralist would have called the setting idyllic; Koch's later friend and admirer Élie Metchnikoff, a city-dweller, referred to Wollstein as "a God-forsaken hole in Posen." Nevertheless, it was the very rurality of Wollstein that provided Koch with his first great opportunity.

Life's Work

Koch had become a mature physician with a lengthy and varied record of civilian and military experience. A smallish man with a bristling beard and round spectacles, he was the stereotypical Germanic scientist, and he longed to do more actual research than he could perform by examining algae and lesions with a hand glass. A good microscope would have enabled him to peer more deeply into diseased tissue, but he believed that he could not afford such an instrument. His wife, Emmy, however, saved coins in a beer mug and surprised Koch with the money: The right man and the right research tool had come together at last. Like all men of genius, however, Koch was a driven man and made a poor companion. Emmy was neglected while her husband devoted most of his spare time to his laboratory, where he began by investigating the cause of anthrax—a very rural disease, a malady of grazing animals, primarily, but sometimes an ailment that could infect humans.

In the 1860's, the French physician-researcher Casimir-Joseph Davaine had discovered that a bacterium was the cause of anthrax. He called the rod-like microorganism "bactéridie" (later known to science as *Bacillus anthracis*), but he was not able to ascertain how the disease was transmitted or how the bacteria, which did not seem to be very long-lived, managed to survive between hosts.

Koch first verified Davaine's work by using sterilized wood splinters to inject anthrax bacilli into the tails of mice which he kept in cages in his laboratory. When the first mouse died, a drop of its blood was injected into a second mouse, and so on, until after eight mice the conclusion had to be reached that the poison was a living, self-perpetuating entity. A chemical poison would eventually have become so attenuated as to lose its potency. To grow his anthrax bacilli without contamination from other bacteria, Koch invented the hanging-drop technique. He ground out a depression in a thick glass slide, put a drop of blood containing anthrax microbes on a thin glass coverslip, put sealant around the edges of both sterile slides, placed the thick one over the thin one, and quickly invert-

ed the pair, causing the drop to hang suspended over the depression. As a culture medium for the bacilli, he used liquid from the interior of the eye.

Only about one hundred miles from Wollstein was the large university city of Breslau in Silesia, and there the renowned botanist Ferdinand Julius Cohn had been working with bacteria. He had predicted that anthrax bacilli might form small eggs or spores. Koch clearly observed the spores, as he had been keeping his slides at body temperature, thus allowing the bacteria to develop through their life cycle though outside a host. Koch noted that, in the inert or spore stage, anthrax bacilli, normally quick to perish when not in a warm host, could survive for years and only be destroyed by burning. He found that the spores formed only when the host died but was still warm.

Koch wrote to Cohn at Breslau in 1876 and arranged to demonstrate his techniques and findings. Koch packed his equipment and animals and treated Cohn and other scientists to a history-making exhibition, during which the pathologist Julius Cohnheim was said to have rushed from the room in great excitement to summon his students to see the masterful work being demonstrated. Though self-taught, Koch handled his equipment like a master scientist, and his three-day re-creation of his experiments left no room for doubt that he had discovered the true etiology of anthrax. He was the first to prove that a microscopic one-celled organism caused a disease.

Cohn and Cohnheim became Koch's champions in the academic community. Cohn, in his biology journal, published Koch's paper on anthrax, and Koch's fame began to spread. While the Breslau scientists tried to find government support for Koch, he had to continue his researches in his tiny laboratory—a laboratory that Koch could hardly suspect would one day be turned into a museum. Koch, meanwhile, was making a definitive record of his observations by purchasing a special camera that he fitted to his microscope—a pioneer technique on which he wrote in 1877 in another article in Cohn's journal of biology. In the same article, he touted the use of the still fairly new aniline dyes for staining bacterial cultures on slides to make organisms contrast with the background. He had not been the first to employ the technique, but he was one of the earliest to advocate it.

By that time, the news of Koch's work had spread not only around Germany but also over all the world. Even the hidebound German bureaucracy began to pay attention. In 1879, Koch was given a post at Breslau, but it had an insufficient salary so the Koch family returned to Wollstein. Finally, the following year, Cohnheim succeeded in having Koch named as government counselor to the Imperial Bureau of Health in Berlin. A country doctor no more, Koch was given a laboratory, two assistants, and financial support.

It was after moving into his new laboratory in the capital city that Koch innocently made a rather rural discovery: He saw bacterial colonies growing on a slice of leftover boiled potato. Several different kinds were on the slice, and it struck Koch that a solid medium would provide an excellent way to keep separate the bacteria he was culturing. After a while, he abandoned cooked potato slices and employed a mixture of gelatin and beef broth, which he allowed to set in petri dishes. Louis Pasteur, who always cultured microorganisms in a souplike mixture, had a difficult time separating the desired microbes.

In Berlin, Koch concentrated on finding the agent causing tuberculosis, a slow but usually fatal endemic disease that was at its height in the late nineteenth century. Tubercle bacilli are much smaller and harder to grow than those of anthrax, but Koch persisted and produced a special blood-serum jelly to culture tuberculosis outside the body. Although he did prove that the tubercle bacillus caused the disease, Koch's vaunted tuberculin, a serum designed to cure tuberculosis in nonterminal patients, proved ineffective. Nevertheless, tuberculin can be used to diagnose the disease and is thus quite valuable.

Koch's greatest success story was the discovery of the cause of cholera—a horrible and usually fatal disease whose deadly epidemics were the terror of nineteenth century Europe and America. In 1883, cholera spread into Egypt and threatened to cross into Europe. To prevent this, the governments of France and Germany sent their best scientists to Alexandria: a French team consisting of Pasteur's top men and a German squad led by Koch himself. They searched for a microbe guilty of causing the feared cholera, and Koch was rather sure that he had located it. Then the epidemic left Egypt as mysteriously as it had come, and Europe was temporarily safe, but no one knew why. Back in Berlin, Koch asked the government to send him to Calcutta, eastern India, to find the disease in its permanent home. There, Koch and his assistants in early 1884 positively identified the vibrio bacillus as the cause and found that it was transmitted by water and other substances polluted with fecal matter. When the German scientists arrived home in May, they were greeted as conquering heroes. With lavish ceremony, the German Emperor William I personally decorated Koch with the Order of the Crown, with Star, while the Reichstag voted the scientist a large monetary gift.

Summary

Robert Koch shares with Pasteur the honor of founding modern medical bacteriology, but, in employment of solid culture media, discovery of improved sterilization by steam, use of staining techniques, and other innovations, he built the modern bacteriological laboratory. Koch's name is permanently associated with the conquest or taming of anthrax, cholera, and tuberculosis, but he did much other work. He always had a yearning to travel, frustrated in earlier years by family responsibilities. Leaving his perennial and only partially successful work on tuberculosis, Koch worked on malaria in Italy, rinderpest in South Africa, sleeping sickness and tick fever in German East Africa, and bubonic plague in northern India. He identified the rat and its flea as vectors of the plague, but it remained for Koch's Japanese disciple Shibasaburo Kitasato to isolate the actual microbe.

Koch scandalized Victorian mores in 1892 when, his marriage failing, he divorced his first wife and married a young actress, Hedwig Freiburg. Many of his biographers deliberately omitted any mention of the occurrence, as they themselves were scandalized—a comment on the strict middle-class morality of the late nineteenth century. Koch was awarded the Nobel Prize in Physiology or Medicine in 1905, primarily for his work on tuberculosis. It was an ultimate vindication for great efforts that bore fruit in many different ways that he was given such recognition for a disease that he had not managed to kill.

Bibliography

De Kruif, Paul. *Microbe Hunters*. New York: Harcourt Brace, 1926; London: Cape, 1927. This readable yet detailed account has a lengthy chapter on "Koch: The Death Fighter." De Kruif's entertaining style makes the sometimes arcane world of microbiology accessible to the general reader.

Dubos, René. *The Unseen World*. New York: Rockefeller Institute Press, 1962. This work has a large section on Koch's life and contributions, including several interesting photographs. The book is an excellent and easily understandable introduction to microbiology and gives great credit to Koch as a founder of the science.

Fox, Ruth. *Great Men of Medicine*. New York: Random House, 1947. This book has a lengthy, thorough, and entertaining chapter on Koch. Fox concentrates on the early and middle portions of of the pathologist's career.

Fry, William F. "Prince Hamlet and Professor Koch." *Perspectives in Biology and Medicine* 40, no. 3 (Spring 1997). Discusses "Koch's Postulate," Koch's method of proving the causal relationships between microorganisms and disease and suggests that it may have been influenced by "The Tragedy of Hamlet, Prince of Denmark."

Metchnikoff, Élie. *The Founders of Modern Medicine*. New York: Walden, 1939. This outstanding volume by a man who was himself a famous medical scientist and who knew Koch personally provides a rare and valuable look at Koch's scientific and personal lives.

Riedman, Sarah R., and Elton T. Gustafson. *Portraits of Nobel Laureates in Medicine and Physiology*. London and New York: Abelard-Schuman, 1963. Contains an excellent chapter on Koch plus a considerable amount of discussion of him in other chapters relating to researchers who were indebted to or in contact with him.

Stevenson, Lloyd G. *Nobel Prize Winners in Medicine and Physiology, 1901-1950*. New York: Henry Schuman, 1953; London: Abelard-Schuman, 1966. This volume concentrates on and gives a very good account of Koch's work on tuberculosis, as Koch's labor in this area was what won for him the Nobel Prize.

Sutter, Morley C. "Assigning Causation in Disease: Beyond Koch's Postulates." *Perspectives in Biology and Medicine* 39, no. 4 (Summer 1996). Discusses the limitations of "Koch's Postulate" and the importance of controlled experimentation.

Allan D. Charles

ALFRED KRUPP

Born: April 26, 1812; Essen, Grand Duchy of Berg
Died: July 14, 1887; Essen, Germany
Areas of Achievement: Business, industry, and technology
Contribution: During the period of Germany's unification into one of the most powerful nations in Europe, Krupp expanded his family's steelmaking concern into one of the most powerful industrial enterprises of the nineteenth century.

Early Life

The son of Friedrich Krupp, the founder of the family steelmaking business, Alfred Krupp was born in the Ruhr River valley town of Essen only five months after Friedrich had founded the firm in 1812. When Alfred was fourteen, his father died and Alfred, along with his widowed mother, Therese, was left in charge of the business. Alfred had already been removed from school, largely because of his father's inability to make enough money to pay for his eldest son's education. As Krupp was to say in later life, his education came at an anvil, not a school desk.

As befitting a boy who had the responsibility of both a family and factory thrust upon him, Krupp became consumed with work. His family and friends at the time described him as tall, slim, and delicate-looking, but at the same time stoic and resolute. When Krupp inherited the family concern, the factory was almost bankrupt. Only seven men remained on the payroll, and wages had not been paid for several weeks. Moreover, few orders for steel products—the firm specialized in cutlery—were placed during the next several years. As Krupp later acknowledged, his mother held the family together during those lean times by sheer industriousness, a trait in himself which Krupp attributed to his mother's influence. From 1826 until he reached full adulthood, Krupp devoted every waking hour to the firm—helping either on the foundry floor or in the bookkeeper's office. Instead of playing with the other boys his age, young Krupp became obsessed with making steel.

Life's Work

For the next twenty years, Krupp endured a perpetual grind of hard work and impending financial collapse. The chief problem lay in competing with foreign producers. As late as 1848, steel from England still dominated the Prussian market. What little profit Krupp made during this time he put back into the firm, constantly attempting to expand and improve the foundry works. He was not above telling potential customers outright lies to gain a contract, nor was he reluctant to steal useful ideas from competitors. Finally, in 1834 Krupp steel was united with a force which was to transform the company as well as the map of Europe. This force was the kingdom of Prussia. Three years after the 1815 peace eliminated Napoleon I and restored the balance and power of Europe, the Prussian government abolished all hindrances to trade among its scattered provinces. On January 1, 1834, other German states joined Prussia in an economic union, the *Zollverein*, which extended to cover most of German-speaking Europe, with the exception of Austria and Hanover. Krupp was among the first businessmen to exploit this new advantage. By the end of 1834, he had traveled to all parts of the customs union and increased his orders for steel threefold. A year later, he again doubled his production, was employing seventy workmen, and had purchased a steam engine to power his foundry tools.

In 1847, the Krupp firm cast its first steel cannon, a small three-pound field gun, which attracted interest, but few orders. The foundry still specialized in the production of fine steel suitable for dies and machine tools. The big break came in 1851, however, at the London Exhibition. Krupp was determined to gain international renown for his firm by taking to London the best example of steel casting ever produced. The result, a flawless two-ton steel ingot, representing a giant step forward in metallurgy, caused a sensation and advertised Krupp's skill as no other demonstration could have. Following the London Exhibition, orders flowed in from around the world. The next step in the Krupp concern's development centered on mass production. By the late 1850's, Krupp had fully converted to the new production system. With his adoption of two new methods for steel manufacturing, which both lowered costs and increased production—the Bessemer and Siemens-Martin processes—Krupp was able to achieve such innovations as the seamless railroad wheel. This wheel revolutionized the railroad industry and made a fortune for Krupp; three interlocking wheels were chosen as the company emblem.

In 1858, large-scale armaments orders from the Prussian government began to dominate the firm's business. Krupp steel cannons became world-re-

nowned after they helped Prussia defeat both Austria and France between 1866 and 1871. As a result, Krupp became a close associate of both Kaiser William I, who dubbed Krupp the "Cannon King," and German Chancellor Otto von Bismarck.

By 1871, Krupp employed sixteen thousand men in numerous foundries and workshops. Ever the paternalistic proprietor, Krupp furnished an elaborate social-welfare program for his workers, including low-cost housing, free medical care, pensions, and consumer cooperatives. Workers' unions, however, were vigorously opposed, and Krupp deemed any flirtation with unions a personal affront to him. Krupp became a leader of the other Ruhr industrialists in opposing workers' organizations, and he helped finance strident anti-union and antisocialist campaigns. Most of the Krupp employees remained loyal to the firm, however, and the majority enjoyed referring to themselves as "Kruppianer."

In the 1860's, Krupp pioneered the development of vertically integrated industry by his acquisition of coal mines and railroads. By the 1870's, Krupp had amassed one of the largest fortunes in Europe. The associated Krupp steel and coal companies employed more than twenty thousand men. The German elite, including the royal family, were frequent guests at Krupp's colossal mansion in Essen, the Villa Huegel, a Renaissance-style house built entirely of stone and Krupp steel. On July 14, 1887, Krupp died at Villa Huegel, attended by his family and mourned by the kaiser. Krupp's eldest son, Friedrich Alfred, continued the Krupp family's sole control over its steel empire until his death, when the firm became a corporation.

Summary

With the death of his father, the founder of the Krupp steelmaking dynasty, Alfred Krupp saved the firm from near collapse and built it into an industrial giant by making use of the newest metallurgical techniques, by instilling tough discipline, and by obsessive hard work. Krupp began by making machine tools, coin dies, and steel cutlery, but his fame emerged with his production of steel cannons for the Prussian army in the 1860's and 1870's. By 1887, the name Krupp was world famous for the manufacture of quality steel, especially steel cannons for the Prussian army, which became the standard for comparison throughout the world. As an industrial empire builder, Krupp pioneered vertical integration by acquiring a variety of mining, power, and transportation concerns. An avowed opponent of socialism and labor unions, Krupp nevertheless was one of the first modern industrialists to provide full welfare services, including health insurance, pension benefits, and low-cost housing for his workers. Krupp served as a model for the nineteenth century aggressive, innovative, and paternalistic industrialist.

Bibliography

Batty, Peter. *The House of Krupp*. London: Secker and Warburg, 1966; New York: Stein and Day, 1967. Batty's survey of the Krupp dynasty from its founding to the post-World War II period is less ambitious than Manchester's, but it provides the most readable and concise study. Batty thoroughly investigates Krupp's youth, and the author is especially adroit at displaying the youthful factors which later played a role in Krupp's direction of the firm.

Henderson, William Otto. *The Rise of German Industrial Power, 1834-1914*. London: Smith, and Berkeley: University of California Press, 1975. The author concentrates on the role of unification in the rise of Germany as an industrial power. Krupp and the development of the Krupp firm from near bankruptcy to world acclaim is placed in the context of Germany's overall economic growth in the nineteenth century.

Kitchen, Martin. *The Political Economy of Germany, 1815-1914*. London: Croom Helm, 1978. The book addresses the relationship between the growth of German industry and the creation of an industrialist class. While the discussion centers largely on the political debate over tariffs and taxes, the Krupp dominance of German armaments is given partial credit for the direction of nineteenth century German foreign policy.

Manchester, William. *The Arms of Krupp, 1587-1968*. London: Joseph, 1964; Boston: Little Brown, 1968. The standard popular biography of the Krupp dynasty. A major section of the work concerns Krupp and his career as proprietor of the firm. Of special interest is Manchester's investigation of Krupp's private life and eccentricities, including the construction of the Villa Huegel. The work is careless in some of the details of the Krupp family saga.

Showalter, Dennis E. *Railroads and Rifles: Soldiers, Technology, and the Unification of Germany*. Hamden, Conn.: Archon Books, 1975. This work provides a close study of Krupp's role in the unification of Germany. The author focuses on Krupp's early years of business and his successful association with the Prussian government through the acquisition of government contracts.

Especially well covered are Krupp's armaments contracts during the critical period of German unification in the 1860's and 1870's.

William G. Ratliff

MIKHAIL ILLARIONOVICH KUTUZOV

Born: September 16, 1745; St. Petersburg, Russia

Died: April 28, 1813; Bunzlau, Silesia (now Boleslawiec, Poland)

Area of Achievement: Military affairs

Contribution: An innovative Russian military commander, Kutuzov is best known for defeating Napoleon during the French invasion of Russia in 1812 after having lost to him at Austerlitz in 1805.

Early Life

Born in St. Petersburg, Russia's capital and "Window on the West," Mikhail Illarionovich Kutuzov was the son of Illarion Matveevich Kutuzov, a lieutenant general of the army corps of engineers who had married well and enjoyed the Empress Elizabeth's patronage. Following his mother's early death, young Mikhail was raised in the country by his maternal grandmother but eventually spent time at his father's house in the capital, where he acquired the social graces necessary to function among the high nobility.

At age twelve, Kutuzov was sent to military engineering school, where he compiled a stellar academic record. By 1761 he attained the rank of ensign and entered military service. Promoted to captain in 1762, he was posted to Astrakhan, serving under Colonel Aleksandr Suvorov, who would become Russia's most revered military leader. Later the same year, Kutuzov was transferred to Reval to serve as aide-de-camp to the Estonian military governor. An accomplished horseman, Kutuzov first saw action in cavalry sorties against Polish patriots in 1768.

In 1770 Kutuzov, now a major, moved south to serve with Count Pyotr Rumyantsev's army against the Turks near Bucharest. Although he distinguished himself in battle and earned a position on the count's staff, he was transferred in disgrace in 1772 for mimicking his commander. Thereafter Kutuzov would be less open and trusting and more prone to suspicion and keeping his own counsel. His subsequent service with the Second Army in the Crimea introduced him to operational service with Cossacks. Nearly fatally wounded near the eye during an assault on Alushta in 1773, he returned to St. Petersburg for convalescence. After sustaining a nearly identical wound inflicted years later, he retained his sight but suffered recurring bouts of pain and displayed a disfiguring scar. In 1774 Kutuzov began a tour of Western Europe in search of medical help. Over the following two years, he travelled in Prussia, Holland, Britain, Austria, and Italy. In London he developed an interest in the American Revolution, especially George Washington's later leadership of the Continental Army.

In 1776 Kutuzov returned to the Crimea, once again serving under Suvorov. From Rumyantsev he had learned the importance of maneuvering his army to avoid unfavorable conditions for battle, even retreating to gain an advantage; from Suvorov he would gain a deep respect for the bravery and endurance of the Russian soldier, learn the necessity of leading by example, and cultivate a common-sense approach to training and managing his army. During his decade in the Crimea, he was promoted to brigadier general (1782) and married Ekaterina Il'inichna Bibikova, who presented him with five daughters and a son who died prematurely. Renewed hostilities took his unit to the Turkish border

in 1787. In 1790 Kutuzov won commendations and promotion to lieutenant-general following his heroism in the storming of the stronghold of Ismail, of which Suvorov appointed him commandant.

Between 1792 and 1802 Kutuzov served Russia as a diplomat or administrator in Poland, Istanbul, Berlin (where he acquired an appreciation of the superiority of the new French battle tactics and of the backwardness of the Prussian military), Vilna (where he served as governor-general), and St. Petersburg (also as governor-general). In this last post he was implicated in the assassination of Paul III, the "mad czar," and exiled from the capital by the new czar, Alexander I. After three years on his estates, Alexander recalled Kutuzov to assume command of the Russian forces in the War of the Third Coalition (August, 1805).

Life's Work

Despite a notable career to 1805, the world knows Kutuzov as the opponent of Napoleon. The highly influential Prussian military theorist Carl von Clausewitz, an observer in Kutuzov's army, declared that "the wily Kutuzov was [Napoleon's] most dangerous adversary." In their two main encounters, Kutuzov was able to utilize the lessons learned from Rumyantsev and Suvorov to good effect, always concentrating on maneuvering and preserving his army rather than rashly committing it to possible destruction.

During the 1805 campaign, the Russians and Austrians combined forces near the Danube River for an assault on the Rhine region as the southern arm of a giant pincer designed to wrest Germany from French control. Napoleon, having concentrated the French army in Boulogne, France, in preparation for an invasion of England, was supposed to be caught off guard. The Austrians under Baron Karl Mack von Leiberich proceeded westward too rapidly, however, and the Russians never caught up. Napoleon discovered the plan and, with fabled speed, caught the Austrians in a trap near Ulm on the Danube and forced their surrender. Kutuzov now stood between Napoleon and Vienna, awaiting reinforcements from Russia. Despite political pressure to shield Vienna, he maneuvered his army north and eastward away from it, using tributaries of the Danube as obstacles to the pursuing French vanguard. Though Kutuzov knew that this would doom Vienna, it would also overextend French supply and communication lines and increase the likelihood of Russian reinforcement. He feigned a

stand at St. Polten and gained additional time by making the French commander believe an armistice had been signed. Enraged at the ruse, General Joachim Murat furiously attacked the Russian rear at Schöngraben, but Kutuzov's strategic withdrawal continued. Finally, the Austrian and Russian emperors intervened and forced Kutuzov to engage Napoleon near Austerlitz.

Both overall command and the plan of battle were Austrian, however, and Kutuzov, in his customary plain gray tunic and battered peaked hat, commanded only the center. Rankling at the subordination, he nonetheless chose to stay with his troops for the sake of morale; he often referred to them as his "children" and never shirked his responsibility to them. In the ensuing battle on December 2, 1805, the French annihilated the allied army of ninety-five thousand men, inflicting thirty thousand casualties. Perhaps Kutuzov's principal achievement was his management of the orderly withdrawal of the Russian units under his command.

Understandably, if not justifiably, Kutuzov was passed over for the Russian command during the Prussian-French War and remained in Kiev until the spring of 1807. He then returned to garrison duty along the Turkish front, serving under the unstable and extremely suspicious Prince Prozorovski. Suspected of intrigue, Kutuzov was removed to Vilna in 1809 to serve as the military governor of the Lithuanian province. Meanwhile, the French stepped up operations in the east, and the Turks once again became restive, while Alexander strengthened his western armies. Kutuzov returned to the Turkish frontier in March, 1811, with orders to strike a swift and decisive blow. He gathered scattered garrison units into an army at Rustchuk and countered a Turkish attack. Waiting until the Turks split their forces while crossing the Danube in late September, Kutuzov surrounded and besieged their army of fifty thousand men. Despite demands for action by Alexander, Kutuzov refused to attack and only lifted the siege in May with the signing of the Treaty of Bucharest. Although rewarded with the title "most illustrious Prince," Kutuzov had incurred Alexander's displeasure and was sent to Vilna, a fine vantage point from which to view the growing French menace to the Russian frontier.

On June 23, 1812, France's Grand Armee crossed the Nieman River, headed for Smolensk and Moscow. Mikhail Barclay de Tolly commanded the Russian army while Kutuzov recruited and trained men for the campaign. Barclay proved indecisive and ineffective, but Alexander's disdain for Kutuzov delayed his appointment as Barclay's replacement until Napoleon had captured Smolensk in mid-August. Although Kutuzov suffered from rheumatism, corpulence, and severe headaches, he was extremely popular with both civilians and the military. The army's morale, if not its fortunes, soon rose, and leaders now expected a fight. Under Barclay, the First and Second armies had lost one-quarter of their men, and Kutuzov had received only fifteen thousand of a requested eighty-thousand-man reserve when he began to deploy near Borodino on September 3.

Napoleon faced the Russian army of 128,000 men and 640 cannons with 130,000 men and 587 guns of his own. Initial clashes on September 5 cost each side five thousand casualties. Napoleon used September 6 to prepare for his assault on the Russian redoubts—well-chosen and heavily fortified positions from which the Russians could inflict heavy losses. Typically pragmatic, Kutuzov's idea of preparation for battle was a good night's rest for all. Next day, as the French assault slowly forced the Russian lines back, both commanders seemed detached and lost in their own thoughts; Kutuzov was accused of lethargy and apathy by his enemies. Whatever his mental state, he refused to abandon the field of battle and at day's end dressed his line where his baggage train had been posted earlier. He declared victory and prepared to fight again, a ploy that heightened his men's morale and convinced them of their success.

His declaration also encouraged the Muscovites. At the council of war (September 13) held at Fili on the outskirts of Moscow, however, Kutuzov decided to abandon the capital: "The loss of Moscow is not the loss of Russia. My first obligation is to preserve the army." He would retreat through Moscow to draw the French forces into the city, then withdraw to the southeast toward Ryazan. Though neither "scorched earth" nor the burning of Moscow were Kutuzov's ideas, his armies benefitted from both, which deprived Napoleon of badly needed supplies. The Russian withdrawal to the southeast turned abruptly westward after reaching Bronniski, south of the Pakra River. Murat's pursuing cavalry, however, was shielded from this maneuver and led farther south, while Kutuzov headed west and then southwest to Tarutino, eighty kilometers southwest of Moscow. This strategic point allowed him to block French movement to southern supply depots in Kaluga and Tula and placed him in a position to intercept or harry a French retreat westward. He was also able to consolidate and augment his forces (from 85,000 to 120,000) and organize partisan detachments that would prove brutally effective.

On October 18, Kutuzov attacked Murat at Chernishna, west of Tarutino, which brought the Grand Armee out of Moscow. Napoleon decided to strike toward Kaluga, a potential gateway to Russia's southwestern agricultural heartland, but was checked in a furious battle at Maloyaroslavets on October 24. The next day he decided to abandon his invasion and retreat westward along the Moscow-Smolensk road. Kutuzov had his army shadow the French along their horrific winter exodus. Though he planned several major attacks on the bedraggled columns, only minor actions resulted.

Kutuzov continued into Prussia on January 9 and was named commander of the Russian-Prussian coalition army at a meeting at Kalisch. Soon attacked by cold and fever, he died in Bunzlau on April 28 and was interred in St. Petersburg's Kazan Cathedral.

Summary

Russian poet Alexander Pushkin considered Kutuzov the "Savior of Russia," and many Russians would agree. Though he enjoyed high company, he eschewed military glory, preferring patience to rashness and striking when he held the advantage. Though Czar Alexander disdained him, Kutuzov's men knew that he understood them, and they proved fiercely loyal. Such loyalty was vital in the aftermaths of Austerlitz and Borodino and during the abandonment of Moscow. "General Winter" indeed battered the remnants of the Grand Armee, but only because Kutuzov's Tarutino maneuver cut it off from the resources of the south. Kutuzov always considered retention of the integrity of his army more important than victory in battle, a philosophy that served him well in the Patriotic War of 1812.

Bibliography

Bragin, Mikhail. *Field Marshal Kutuzov*. Moscow: Foreign Languages Publication House, 1944. Written in the midst of the Soviet repulsion of the Nazi invasion of the Soviet Union, this is an uncritical and unreliable treatment of Kutuzov's life.

Duffy, Christopher. *Austerlitz 1805*. London: Seeley, and Hamden, Conn.: Archon, 1977. Detailed military history of the Austerlitz campaign with maps and illustrations.

————. *Borodino and the War of 1812*. London: Seeley, and New York: Scribner, 1972. Excellent account of the battle, including aftermath. Nicely illustrated.

Palmer, Alan. *Napoleon in Russia*. London: Deutsch, and New York: Simon and Schuster, 1967. Standard military history of the 1812 campaign that balances French and Russian viewpoints. Includes excellent notes on sources.

Parkinson, Roger. *The Fox of the North: The Life of Kutuzov, General of War and Peace*. London: Davies, and New York: McKay, 1976. The only critical full biography in English of Kutuzov, it places him firmly in the context of his time while giving him the benefit of every doubt.

Tolstoy, Leo. *War and Peace*. New York: Penguin Classics, and London: Hern, 1996. This great novel is the only introduction most people have to Kutuzov; a portrayal firmly grounded in reality and colored by Tolstoy's admiration.

Joseph Byrne

JOSEPH LANCASTER

Born: 1778; London, England
Died: October 24, 1838; New York, New York
Area of Achievement: Education
Contribution: An advocate of mass education, Lancaster devised an intricate educational system which was economical and replicable, thus promoting its adoption by numerous countries.

Early Life

Joseph Lancaster was born in 1778 (the exact date is not recorded) in Southwark, London. Though his parents' names are unknown, his father was a sieve maker and a soldier in the war against the American Colonies. Both parents were Nonconformists who intended their son for the ministry.

Lancaster's own mystical bent appeared when he was very young: At the age of fourteen, he was compelled to walk to Bristol, intending to board a ship bound for Jamaica, where he would "teach the poor blacks the word of God." In Bristol, Lancaster realized that he was without funds to embark on a voyage, so, with characteristic impulsiveness, he volunteered to serve in the British navy. After one voyage, he was released from his obligation through the intervention of friends. He left the ship after delivering an impassioned sermon to the crew.

Lancaster returned to London, where he soon joined the Religious Society of Friends (Quakers), which shared his avid interest in the education of the poor. He then served as an assistant schoolmaster at two schools before securing his father's permission, in 1798, to bring home a few poor children to teach. As well as teaching reading, writing, and arithmetic, the young man often provided clothing and food for his students. While his generosity was much appreciated by the children, it was not matched by prudence: Lancaster's financial irresponsibility would be a leading cause of his later downfall.

His great enthusiasm and aptitude for teaching won for him many students, however, and in 1801, at the age of twenty-three, Lancaster rented a large room in Borough Road, a site which was to become internationally renowned as the home of the Lancasterian monitorial school system. Over the door he had inscribed, "All who will may send their children and have them educated freely, and those who do not wish to have education for noth-ing may pay for it if they please." In an age in which the education of the poor was considered by the aristocracy to be dangerous, Joseph Lancaster not only championed the right to education for the masses but also devised an economical and coherent system which made such education possible.

Life's Work

The Borough Road school proved so popular that young Lancaster soon had three hundred pupils. Turning to some Quaker philanthropists for aid, he was able to provide for some of his pupils' material needs, but he still lacked funds to pay salaries for assistant teachers. He therefore adopted a strategy cited by several other previous and contemporary educators: the use of pupil-teachers, or monitors. While Lancaster did not "invent" this system, he was responsible for popularizing it. His enthusiasm, his talent for fundraising, and public speaking, and his gift for meticulous systematizing (curious in an otherwise impulsive and extravagant person), quickly won for him many supporters.

Imbued with the nineteenth century's faith in the goodness of technology, Lancaster brought the virtues of standardization, uniformity, and technology to the classroom. By employing monitors—older boys who taught younger ones—Lancaster could divide his three hundred students into groups of ten of roughly the same ability in a subject area (reading, writing, or arithmetic). Lessons were conducted in the manner of a spelling bee, with each group gathered in a semicircle around their monitor and each pupil competing to better his standing. This afforded direct attention and immediate reinforcement from the monitor—not possible in the traditional system in which the entire class recited lessons *en masse* to one teacher. In the Lancasterian system, each pupil's progress (or lack of it) was duly noted in meticulous logs kept by the monitors, who were also supposed to be learning according to the classical dictum "he who teaches learns." The regimented system lent itself favorably to comparisons with the military and with factories, since each placed emphasis on the system rather than the individual: Monitors, like officers or machine parts, were replaceable in a smoothly running system. Because the system was easily copied, many monitors went out to establish their own schools elsewhere.

Lancaster's fascination with efficient technology led him also to invent ingenious cost-cutting and time-saving devices and methods for his monitorial system of education. For example, he realized that the use of textbooks was inefficient, because only one page of the book could be used at one time, and by only one student. Therefore, he made large lesson cards on which to display each lesson. These could be read simultaneously by all ten boys in the group, and, since they were not handled except by the monitors, the cards would last indefinitely. Lancaster also invented time-saving routines for taking roll, checking on truants, and almost every other activity occurring in the school day.

In an age when students were often beaten for not learning their lessons, Lancaster's psychology offered some improvement. Although whippings were still considered an option, he advised adherents of his system that even the most unruly child responds better to encouragement than to punishment. Thus, he devised an intricate system of rewards, wherein prizes could be won by the most accomplished students. (It should be noted that Lancaster also invented cages in which boys could be hung from the ceiling and advocated some other strategies which relied on humiliation for effectiveness. While it may be argued that such tactics might be less cruel than corporal punishment, these ideas are also indicative of Lancaster's increasing mental instability.)

One of the most important features of the Lancasterian system was its nondenominational religious training. Lancaster promoted "scriptural education," which consisted solely of readings from the Scriptures without providing any doctrinal interpretations, thus encouraging individual interpretations, a practice advocated by Nonconformists and Quakers. At first, even the powerful Church of England supported this program, but this was to change as Lancaster's monitorial schools met with increasing success.

By 1805, the twenty-seven-year-old teacher was famous, having won the approval of George III and attracted international attention to his Borough Road School. Despite his increasing personal problems—he was deemed by some to be "thriftless, impulsive, extravagant, and sadly deficient in ordinary self-control"—Lancaster inspired many followers to begin Lancasterian schools elsewhere.

At this point, conservatives grew alarmed at Lancaster's success. The Church of England and various conservative leaders attacked the Lancasterian system as an attempt to undermine the High Church by educating the masses with a neutral point of view about religion. Andrew Bell, who had established his own (earlier) form of monitorial school in India, was persuaded to come out of retirement to lead this opposition. The ensuing Bell-Lancaster controversy, which raged over the next twenty years, was centered on this difference in religious perspective. That the debate really had its basis in politics is evident in the conservatives' objections to an educated underclass. Bell wrote, "It is not proposed that the children of the poor be educated in an expensive manner, or even taught to write and to cypher." Lancaster's advocates denounced this as elitism, and Lancaster himself declared that he was precluded from offering an even more extensive curriculum by expense only.

Lancaster's largess, devoid of prudence, quickly became a major problem. In 1807, a small group of benefactors had to step in to rescue him from his large debt. Recognizing signs of his increasing mental instability, they agreed in confidence that "the prudent management of J. L. was the first and great object" of their organization. In 1811, this group became the Royal Lancasterian Society, which solicited public funds and defended the movement from attack by the conservative Bellites, as well as promoting the movement abroad.

Although the Lancasterians dreamed of a national system of education, it was never to be in their homeland. The monitorial schools met with varying degrees of success in many foreign countries, however, including Ireland, France, Denmark, Sweden, Spain, Russia, Greece, the West Indies, and various nations in Latin America.

By 1814, Joseph Lancaster's shortcomings had overshadowed the strengths he had to offer his own educational movement. Burdened by a mentally ill wife and his own serious psychological problems—he was paranoid, deluded that he was being persecuted, even by those who most wanted to help him—Lancaster finally alienated even his most loyal supporters. He was "read out" (expelled) from the Society of Friends for his financial irresponsibility, and the British and Foreign School Society (previously the Royal Lancasterian Society) pressured him into resigning, following an incident in which he had apparently beaten some of his monitors for pleasure. As philanthropist Samuel Whitbread told Lancaster grimly, "If we have to choose between the man and the system, we shall save the system and reject the man." Ironically, Lancaster's success in creating an educational system in which individuals were replaceable had made him obsolete.

At only thirty-six, Lancaster had passed the apex of his career and was destined for misfortune the rest of his life. Although he always commanded audiences wherever he went, his delusions of martyrdom precluded his being able to hold a position at monitorial schools in Philadelphia, Baltimore, Caracas, Trenton, or Montreal. Always inspired by visions of the great things he would do next, Lancaster was incapable of working responsibly in the present. His autobiographical sketch entitled *Epitome of Some of the Chief Events and Transactions in the Life of Joseph Lancaster* (1833) reveals the extent of his mental aberration. Still convinced of his persecution, he died in 1838 in New York City, having been trampled by a runaway horse.

Summary

Joseph Lancaster himself was not a major figure in education, but he is notable for his good fortune in capturing the spirit of the age—the enthusiasm for the Industrial Revolution—in a manner which benefited the advocates of education for the masses. Whereas the opposers of public education cited exorbitant cost and unfeasibility as obstacles, Lancaster provided a systematized plan for the monitorial schools which was not only cheap but also relatively efficient. His genius lay in his ability to detail every aspect of the pedagogy so minutely that any follower could implement the system.

Although later generations derided the monitorial schools as being "factories," the fact that they were efficient is evidenced in the presence of many Lancasterian elements in our schools today, such as emphasis on discipline, routine, and pride in the school community.

The reliance on a chain of command, wherein authority lay in an office rather than a person, had both advantages and disadvantages. Advantages included the clarity of organization and the regularity of discipline, the individualized attention, and the psychological motivation provided by competition and prizes; the disadvantages included the damage done by any incompetent monitors and the rigidity of the teaching. These weaknesses were quickly identified and were in part responsible for the movement toward the professionalization of teaching in subsequent decades. While Lancaster enjoyed personal acclaim only from 1804 to 1814, his monitorial school system continued to influence the rise of mass education internationally, until its decline in the 1840's.

Bibliography

Cohen, Sol, ed. "Joseph Lancaster's Monitorial System (1805)." In *Education in the United States: A Documentary History*, edited by Fred L. Israel and William P. Hansen, vol. 2. New York: Random House, 1974. Contains excerpts from Lancaster's *Improvements in Education, as It Respects the Industrious Classes of the Community* (London, 1803), affording a firsthand look at the educator's philosophy, as well as his methods of teaching and discipline.

Dickson, Moira. *Teacher Extraordinary: Joseph Lancaster, 1778-1838*. London: Book Guild, 1986.

Fouts, Gordon E. "Music Instruction in Early Nineteenth-century American Monitorial Schools." *Journal of Research in Music Education* 22 (Summer 1974): 112-119. Discusses the contributions of Bell and Lancaster to music education by describing Ezra Barratt's fifty-six page *Sabbath School Psalmody*, prepared expressly for use in monitorial schools.

Jones, Rufus M. *The Later Periods of Quakerism*. Vol. 2. London: Macmillan, 1921; Westport, Conn.: Greenwood Press, 1970. Chapter 17, "Friends in Education," provides brief biographies of Lancaster and other Quakers influential in the rise of public education.

Kaestle, Carl F., ed. *Joseph Lancaster and the Monitorial School Movement: A Documentary History*. New York: Teachers College Press, 1973. An informative collection of documents, including excerpts from the writings of Joseph Lancaster, his advocates, and his detractors. Kaestle provides a lengthy and highly informative overview of the monitorial movement, the Bell-Lancaster controversy, and the international spread of the Lancasterian system in his introduction.

Rayman, Ronald. "Joseph Lancaster's Monitorial System of Instruction and American Indian Education, 1815-1838." *History of Education Quarterly* (Winter 1981): 395-409. Gives background on how Lancaster's plan was seized as the most efficient way to achieve the white settlers' goals of Indian education and cultural assimilation. The federally funded Brainerd School and the Choctaw Academy, supposedly model Lancasterian schools, soon abandoned any educational ideals in favor of manual labor. An extensive bibliography is included.

Read, Julie. "Working-Class Hall of Fame Reopens." *Times Educational Supplement,* no. 4288 (September 4, 1998). Discusses an exhibition in Hitchin, Hertfordshire, which depicts and describes Lancaster's educational system in detail.

Leslie Todd Pitre

SAMUEL PIERPONT LANGLEY

Born: August 22, 1834; Roxbury, Massachusetts

Died: February 27, 1906; Aiken, South Carolina

Areas of Achievement: Astronomy, aviation and space exploration, and invention and technology

Contribution: Through pioneering research, Langley discovered new portions of the infrared spectrum, while his invention of the bolometer aided in spectral measurements of solar and lunar radiation. He also established the principles of flight and demonstrated the practicability of mechanical flight with self-propelled, heavier-than-air machines.

Early Life

Samuel Pierpont Langley was born the son of Samuel Langley, a Boston merchant of English descent, and Mary Sumner Williams. The family background included intellectuals as well as skilled mechanics and artisans. As a boy, Langley played with his father's telescope and, with his brother John, built a new telescope and made astronomical observations. In addition to astronomy, the flight of birds fascinated the young boy. Langley read extensively throughout his life and studied science, literature, and history. He was well read in the classics in several languages, including English, French, and German. Langley attended the Boston Latin School and Boston High School. He had a gift for drawing and an interest in mathematics so, upon graduation in 1851, he turned his attention to civil engineering and architecture.

Rather than attending a university, Langley went to work for an architectural firm in Boston. In 1857 he moved west and worked as an architect and civil engineer for several years in both Chicago, Illinois, and St. Louis, Missouri. In 1864 he returned to New England where he built a larger telescope with his brother from the ground up. He and his brother also went to Europe for one year and visited observatories, museums, and art galleries.

With this varied background and without university training, Langley began a career as a self-taught astronomer. Upon his return to the United States in 1865, the director of the Harvard College Observatory asked Langley to become an assistant. In 1866 Langley became an assistant professor of mathematics at the Naval Academy in Annapolis, Maryland, although his primary responsibility was as director of their observatory. In 1867 he became a professor of astronomy and physics at Western University in Pittsburgh, Pennsylvania, where for twenty years he taught and was the director of the Allegheny Observatory.

Life's Work

Langley did most of his original scientific investigations during his years in Pittsburgh. To get funding for the Allegheny Observatory, he tried to make astronomy practical and profitable. He convinced the Pennsylvania Railroad Company that he could produce an accurate time-keeping system for their train personnel. At that time, these personnel had to change time every forty or fifty miles along the railroad lines. The observatory sent out a signal two times per day based on astronomical observations that gave the accurate time to all Pennsylvania Railroad stations. This arrangement provided complete funding for the Allegheny Observatory for many years and established a practice of standard time that later became universal.

During his tenure at Allegheny Observatory, Langley determined that current measuring instruments were not precise enough for his astronomical work. From 1879 to 1881 he developed and invented the bolometer, an instrument that accurately measures heat in small increments and enables astronomers to study the infrared region of the solar spectrum. The bolometer is basically an electrical thermometer. The sensitive element is a thin, blackened metallic tape adapted to absorb radiation in very narrow bands of the spectrum and with precision to one ten-millionth of a degree Centigrade.

Langley undertook many survey expeditions and investigated eclipses, sun spots, and other astronomical phenomena. He also studied the solar spectrum. One of his most important expeditions was to Mount Whitney in California, the highest point in the United States at that time (1881). His team measured the energy of solar radiation with the bolometer and discovered infrared areas of the solar spectrum that were far beyond the spectral limit that was recognized at that time.

Langley's research at the Allegheny Observatory also encompassed many fields: the distribution of radiation over the sun's surface and in sun spots, the solar energy spectrum and its extension into the infrared, the lunar energy spectrum, spectra of terrestrial sources and determination of unmeasured wave lengths, absorption of the radiation of the sun by the earth's atmosphere, and the determination of the solar constant of radiation. This research contributed to what was originally known as the "new astronomy" and is now called astrophysics. Rather than investigating the existence and position of astronomical bodies, Langley studied their physical characteristics—heat, light, and radiant energy.

In 1887 Langley also began research into aerodynamics. He formulated Langley's Law, which states that the faster a body travels through the air the less energy is required to keep it aloft. Langley's experiments showed that the work of the wind aided soaring flight, just as buoyancy aided swimming. He discovered principles of lift and resistance for rapidly moving surfaces in air.

In January, 1887, Langley joined the staff of the Smithsonian Institution as assistant secretary in charge of exchanges, publications, and the library. This position interested Langley because he had been somewhat isolated in western Pennsylvania. His move to the Smithsonian brought him to the center of the scientific community in the United States. By November, 1887, Langley had become

the third secretary of the Smithsonian, a position he held until his death in 1906. Under his leadership, the Smithsonian expanded its areas of research with the National Zoological Park in 1890 and the National Gallery of Art in 1904. The museum also added a "children's room" for science education. Langley's key contribution to the Smithsonian as an institution was the founding of the Smithsonian Astrophysical Observatory in 1890, where he continued his work on solar radiation during the 1890's.

Aerodynamics also continued to fascinate Langley. He built what he called an "aerodrome"—an unmanned flying machine with wide-spreading wings to sustain its flight while it was driven along by a gasoline-fueled, steam-powered engine. It had a wingspan of about 14 feet patterned after a four-winged dragonfly. On May 6, 1896, Langley sent up aerodrome model number 5, which landed safely after flying over one-half mile (3000 feet) for about 90 seconds. On November 28 of the same year, a larger model traveled about three-quarters of a mile (4000 feet). The two flights proved the practicability of mechanical flight and were the first sustained free flights of power-propelled, heavier-than-air machines.

Although Langley showed the scientific feasibility of mechanical flight, he wished to leave further development to commercial applications. However, under pressure from the U.S. government, he pursued experimentation on a model large enough to carry a human. In 1898 the U.S. War Department, with the Spanish-American War looming, allotted $50,000 to Langley to develop, construct, and test a large aerodrome. The Smithsonian added another $20,000 to the project. Langley intended to simply build a larger version of the models already flown and add a different engine. He eventually used an engine based on a design by Stephen Balzer and modified by Charles Manly, who had been working with Langley over the previous few years. Manly tested the manned machine himself.

On August 8, 1903, a 14-foot model flew without a pilot for about 1000 feet. However, two tests of the full-sized, manned machine failed on October 7 and December 8 of 1903. In both cases, failure occurred during the launch rather than during flight. In scaling up the models, Langley had not accounted for the fact that the drag would increase exponentially. Langley's last trial preceded the successful flight of the Wright brothers by only nine days. Langley's tests were well publicized in newspapers, unlike those of the Wright brothers, and the reporters called the machines "Langley's Folly." Less than two years after the failed tests, in November, 1905, Langley had a stroke. For rest and convalescence, he traveled to South Carolina in early February, 1906. He suffered a second stroke there and died on February 27, 1906.

Summary

Samuel Pierpont Langley's work in aerodynamics followed a different technical path than that of the Wright brothers, but his work was key to aviation development. The notion of heavier-than-air flight by humans had been ridiculed, but Langley's research provided a scientific basis for experimentation in mechanical flight. As a prominent member of the scientific community, Langley's beliefs carried weight. In addition, Manly's improvements to Langley's engine turned it into the world's first radial engine designed for flight, and it was the same basic engine used in aircraft through World War II.

Langley's primary contributions were in the field of astrophysics, where he developed new apparatus and techniques for the measurement of radiation. With his invention of the bolometer, it became possible not only to identify radiant energy but also to measure it. Langley used the instrument to discover and explore new portions of the solar spectrum and measure the heat of sunspots, various parts of the sun's disk, and the temperature of the moon. His experiments aided in determining the distribution of radiation in the solar spectrum, the transparency of the atmosphere to different solar rays, and the enhancement of their intensity at high altitudes. In 1947 his name was given to a new unit of measurement: The "langley" is defined as a unit of illumination used to measure temperature equal to one gram calorie per square centimeter of irradiated surface.

Langley also contributed to the institutionalization and popularization of American science, particularly astronomy. His administration at the Smithsonian Institution also expanded the exchange and distribution programs for scientific research. Langley gave many public lectures and wrote essays on astronomical subjects in popular magazines of his day, including *Popular Science Monthly*, *Atlantic Monthly*, *Century Magazine*, and *McClure's*. He also wrote a book called *The New Astronomy* (1888). Langley not only advanced science but also diffused and distributed new scientific knowledge to both specialists and the public.

Bibliography

Barr, E. Scott. "Infrared Pioneers—III. Samuel Pierpont Langley." *Infrared Physics* 3 (1963): 195-206. Contains detailed information on Langley's work in solar astrophysics and minor details on aeronautical and other research. Includes technical details and a selected list of Langley's publications.

Berliner, Don. *Aviation: Reaching for the Sky.* Minneapolis: Oliver Press, 1997. Contains a chapter on Langley and the aerodrome, while chapters on other aviation pioneers provide context for his aeronautical research. Includes illustrations, a glossary, and a chronology of aviation advances.

Crouch, Tom D. *A Dream of Wings, Americans and the Airplane, 1875-1905.* New York: Norton, 1981. Covers developments in American aviation, including several chapters on Langley. This work is the most complete research on Langley's aeronautical contributions and includes an extensive bibliography.

Eddy, John A. "Founding the Astrophysical Observatory: The Langley Years." *Journal for the History of Astronomy* 21 (February 1990): 111-120. Contains a short, general biography of Langley with major emphasis on his astronomical research and administrative duties at the Smithsonian.

Jones, Bessie Zuban. *The Golden Age of Science, Thirty Portraits of the Giants of 19th-Century Science.* New York: Simon and Schuster, 1966. Contains a chapter on Langley and provides context for his research.

Meadows, A. J. *Early Solar Physics.* Oxford and New York: Pergamon Press, 1970. Contains an overview of the development of the new astronomy from 1850 to 1900, including Langley's accomplishments. Also includes the writings of contemporary astrophysicist and a reference list with technical and scientific details.

Oehser, Paul Henry. *Sons of Science: The Story of the Smithsonian Institution and Its Leaders.* New York: Schuman, 1949. Includes a chapter on Langley that contains information on all of his various activities and accomplishments. Includes a selected bibliography.

Vaeth, J. Gordon. *Langley: Man of Science and Flight.* New York: Ronald Press, 1966. Short but complete biography of Langley written for nonspecialists. Includes a short bibliographical essay on sources.

Linda Eikmeier Endersby

SIR EDWIN RAY LANKESTER

Born: May 15, 1847; London, England
Died: August 15, 1929; London, England
Areas of Achievement: Zoology and natural history
Contribution: After studying invertebrates, Lankester systematized the field of embryology, and he researched major groups of living and fossil animals. He wrote more than one hundred scientific essays, mostly dealing with comparative anatomy and paleontology, and his series of books made scientific matters understandable and interesting to laypersons.

Early Life

Sir Edwin Ray Lankester was born on May 15, 1847, in London, England. His father, Edwin Lankester, M.D., served as a coroner, and he also lectured and wrote articles about natural history, diseases, and foods. Also interested in science, Lankester's mother, née Phebe Pope, assisted her husband with his scientific articles and wrote her own on botany and on health.

When he was eleven years old, Lankester entered St. Paul's School, where he earned several classical prizes and won cups for sculling and the long jump. At the age of seventeen, he entered Downing College, Cambridge, on a scholarship, but he transferred to Christ Church, Oxford, in his second year and won a scholarship there for his junior year.

In 1868, Lankester was graduated from Oxford with first-class honors in natural science and was given a scholarship in geology. With this and the Radcliffe Traveling Fellowship granted him in 1870, he studied at Vienna, Leipzig, and Naples. He returned to Oxford to teach for two years and then became a professor of zoology and comparative anatomy at University College, London, until 1889.

He was welcomed to London by Thomas Huxley, a British biologist and surgeon, and other scientists who had known him since childhood. Lankester's personal charm earned for him the respect and affection of these men as well as a wider circle of friends. He was sincere, unprejudiced, and tolerant of differences in method and opinion. Especially kind to young workers, he listened sympathetically to others and was gentle and affectionate. His wit and anecdotes made him a delightful companion as guest or host. He enjoyed golf, cards, country walks, and fireside chats.

Although he had many close friends, Lankester never married. Robust in appearance and able to handle stress, his health nevertheless was delicate, and he suffered several illnesses. As he grew older he experienced problems with indigestion, bronchitis, and depression.

As a professor he quickly became known by the success of his lectures and the results of investigations by his students and himself. His clear and skillful illustrations instilled in his students his own enthusiasm for science.

Life's Work

After his graduation from Oxford, Lankester assisted his father in editing the *Quarterly Journal of Microscopical Science*. Two years later, he became the editor and held that position until his death sixty years later. During that time he became one of England's most noted zoologists and received major honors in his field.

These honors recognized his varied activities, his energy in teaching, and his philosophical thinking. His work benefited because of his principle that speculation should be the servant, not the master, of the biologist. In 1875, Lankester was accepted as a member of the Royal Society, a scientific association which supports and promotes scientific research. He was Royal Medalist in 1885 and served as the society's vice president from 1882 to 1896. In 1884, Lankester founded the Marine Biological Association and served as its president in 1892. The association's laboratory has aided in the training of British biologists.

Lankester was appointed Linacre Professor of Comparative Anatomy at Oxford in 1890. In addition to teaching, he reorganized the University Museum to make it useful in teaching and beneficial to the educational community. This experience proved invaluable when he became director of the British Museum (Natural History) in 1898, resigning from his Oxford post. Conflicts with the museum committees and opposition from the trustees frustrated his plans for the museum, however, and he resigned his post in 1907, the year he was knighted.

Despite his varied duties, Lankester was first a professional zoologist. His curiosity about nature, his observations of living creatures, his skill in dissection and microscopy, and his patience in acquiring facts combined to give him a wide interest in zoology and detailed knowledge of many of its branches. He wrote well, and the ability to coordinate and arrange facts made his scientific writings easy to understand. He loved to teach zoology to beginners and laypersons, and he could encourage researchers with criticism and praise in any area.

Lankester's brilliance and abilities in science were not matched by great success with officialdom. Often in defending a cause he would act impulsively and even violently, never bothering to apologize or rectify his mistakes. His character and intelligence made it almost certain that he was promoting the best course of action, but his impetuous behavior ruined his arguments and position; officials saw his conduct, not his wisdom. A misunderstanding with the University of Edinburgh, a lawsuit with Oxford University, and his poor relationships with the committees of the Natural History Museum all occurred because of disputes accentuated by his imprudence.

Some of Lankester's best work was in the area of morphology, the study of the form and structure of plants and animals, without regard to function. He saw beauty in the varieties of animal form, and he arranged them in categories, explaining them clearly. His essays on classification and natural history were illuminating, and he contributed to almost every branch of zoology.

Lankester wrote widely about zoology and more general problems of science. His books included *On Comparative Longevity in Man and the Lower Animals* (1870), *The Advancement of Science* (1890), *The Kingdom of Man* (1907), and *Great and Small Things* (1923). These and other writings were read widely by the general public as well as the scientific community.

In addition to his work in zoology, Lankester studied and promoted Neo-Darwinism and followed Gregor Mendel's work in hybridizing cultivated plants. He had a keen interest in the application of bacteriology and protozoology to preventive medicine, and through his Royal Society work he encouraged the investigations into sleeping sickness and other tropical diseases. Close friends with Louis Pasteur and Elie Metchnikoff, the institute's director, he often visited the Pasteur Institute in Paris and was proud to have contributed to medical knowledge and theory.

Lankester was highly respected by the scientific community, and this respect was demonstrated by the honorary degrees given him by Leeds, Exeter, and Christ Church College. He was still writing and studying when he died in London on August 15, 1929, after a short illness.

Summary

The scientific discoveries of the eighteenth and nineteenth centuries revolutionized life and awakened a hope that man might master nature. This hope fostered a faith in science and an enthusiasm for learning. Sir Edwin Ray Lankester's books, which conveyed his zeal and knowledge in the layperson's language, were popular in this atmosphere because they made scientific achievements and information accessible to the public. The *Quarterly Journal of Microscopical Science*, which he edited, held an international reputation, and his encyclopedia articles were widely read.

Because of his own enthusiasm for comparative anatomy, Lankester inspired numerous students and colleagues to continue their own study and research. His most distinguished pupil, Edwin Goodrich, continued Lankester's work in zoology and spread his teaching.

He brought order to an entire branch of biology when he studied the structure and embryos of invertebrates, systematized the field of embryology, and invented new technical terms to describe his discoveries. Adding greatly to man's knowledge of comparative anatomy, he researched major groups of living and fossil animals, from protozoa to mammals. He then showed the basic similarities in structure and close relationships among spiders, scorpions, and horseshoe crabs.

Scientists in the nineteenth century were using science for the power it gave to man through mechanical and electrical devices, military weapons, food preservation, and control over disease. They discovered that science could lead to profit as well as to knowledge. Lankester, on the other hand, still saw the value of science in its gathering of information, its observations of nature, and its satisfaction to man's inner being. Pure science was, for Lankester, a thing of beauty.

Bibliography

Darwin, Charles. *The Illustrated Origin of Species*. Abridged and introduced by Richard E. Leakey. London: Faber, and New York: Hill and Wang, 1979. An abridgment of Darwin's *On the Origin of Species* (1859) which explains his theory of evolution, a theory which Lankester advocated, although he later supported the school of Neo-Darwinism. In his introduction, Leakey discusses Darwin's work and its problems, as well as the work of other scientists in that era.

Dubos, Rene J. *Louis Pasteur: Free Lance of Science*. Boston: Little Brown, 1950; London: Gollancz, 1951. This biography of Lankester's friend and contemporary sheds light on the work of other scientists of that period, and it includes background on previous scientific philosophy.

Lankester, Sir Edwin Ray. *Diversions of a Naturalist*. New York: Macmillan, and London: Methuen, 1915. A collection of essays and illustrations about nature suitable for reading by the general public. Contains articles previously written for *The Daily Telegraph*.

————. *Great and Small Things*. London: Methuen, and New York: Macmillan, 1923. A miscellaneous collection of short articles related to the study of living things. The articles cover such varied subjects as the gorilla, the liver fluke, and human eyes.

————. *Science from an Easy Chair*. London: Methuen, 1910; New York: Macmillan, 1911. A collection of brief essays on a variety of scientific subjects, written for the layperson in common language. Readers are then encouraged to do further research on ideas that interest them. Includes illustrations.

————. *Science from an Easy Chair: A Second Series*. London: Adlard, 1912; New York: Holt, 1913. An assortment of essays, originally written for *The Daily Telegraph*, to interest the layperson in scientific matters. Includes subjects such as elephants, smells and perfumes, museums, and parasites.

Metchnikoff, Olga. *Life of Elie Metchnikoff: 1845-1916*. Boston: Houghton Mifflin, and London: Constable, 1921. This biography, with a preface by Lankester, describes Metchnikoff's life, research, and studies in medicine, including his work at the Pasteur Institute. Lankester and Metchnikoff were close friends and interested in each other's research.

Elaine Mathiasen

PIERRE-SIMON LAPLACE

Born: March 23, 1749; Beaumont-en-Auge, Normandy, France

Died: March 5, 1827; Paris, France

Areas of Achievement: Astronomy, mathematics, and physics

Contribution: Laplace made groundbreaking mathematical contributions to probability theory and statistical analysis. Using Isaac Newton's theory of gravitation, he also performed very detailed mathematical analyses of the shape of Earth and the orbits of comets, planets, and their moons.

Early Life

Pierre-Simon Laplace was born into a well-established and prosperous family of farmers and merchants in southern Normandy. An ecclesiastical career in the Church was originally planned for Laplace by his father, and he attended the Benedictine secondary school in Beaumont-en-Auge between the ages of seven and sixteen. His interest in mathematics blossomed during two years at the University of Caen, beginning in 1766. In 1768, he went to Paris to pursue a career in mathematics; he remained a permanent resident of Paris or its immediate vicinity for the rest of his life. Soon after his arrival in Paris, he sought and won the patronage of Jean Le Rond d'Alembert, a mathematician, physicist, and philosopher with great influence among French intellectuals. D'Alembert found Laplace employment teaching mathematics to military cadets at the École Militaire, and it was in this position that Laplace wrote his first memoirs in mathematics and astronomy. In 1773, Laplace was elected to the Academy of Sciences as a mathematician. This achievement, at the relatively young age of twenty-four, was based upon the merits of thirteen memoirs he had presented to academy committees for review. Some of Laplace's earliest mathematical interests involved the calculation of odds in games of chance. At a time when there was not yet a field of mathematics devoted to the systematic study of probability, Laplace played a major role in carrying the early development of this topic beyond the rules of thumb of gambling and the preliminary conclusions of earlier mathematicians. In addition, Laplace emphasized the relevance of probability to the analysis of statistics. He believed that, since all experimental data are imprecise to some extent, it is important to be able to

calculate an appropriate average or mean value from a collection of observations. Furthermore, this mean value should be calculated in such a way as to minimize its difference from the actual value of the quantity being measured.

Statistical problems of this type inspired Laplace's initial interest in astronomy. He became intrigued by the process through which new astronomical data should be incorporated into calculations of probabilities for future observations. In particular, he concentrated on the application of Sir Isaac Newton's law of gravitation to the motions of the comets and planets. Laplace's interest in physics thus had a very mathematical orientation. Throughout his career, he retained his early concentration on the solution of problems suggested by the mathematical implications of physical laws; he never devoted himself to extensive experimental investigation of new phenomena. Laplace's primary motivation was a deep conviction that, even if human limitations prevent an exact knowledge of natural laws and experimental conditions, it is still possible progressively to eliminate error through increasingly accurate approximations.

Very little is known about Laplace's personal life during these early years. He does not seem to have stimulated strong friendship or animosity. In 1788, he married Marie-Charlotte de Courty de Romanges, who was twenty years younger than himself, and they had two children. Laplace established and maintained comfortable but disciplined living habits, and he retained an undiminished mental clarity to the moment of his death.

Life's Work

Although a brief summary of Laplace's life's work requires some classification by topics and an emphasis on final results rather than chronology, the highly integrated and developmental nature of his research should not be forgotten. For example, mathematical techniques that he invented for the solution of problems in probability theory often were immediately applied to similar problems in physics or astronomy. Since Laplace was particularly interested in approximate or probable solutions and the analysis of error, he repeatedly revised his mathematical techniques to accommodate new data.

Laplace's contributions to probability theory were both technical and philosophical. This twofold concern is expressed in the titles of the influen-

tial volumes in which he summarized his work, *Théorie analytique des probabilités* (1812; analytic theory of probability) and *Essai philosophique sur les probabilités* (1814; *A Philosophical Essay on Probabilities*, 1902). The *Théorie analytique des probabilités* was the first comprehensive treatise devoted entirely to the subject of probability. Laplace provided a groundbreaking, although necessarily imperfect, characterization of the techniques, subject matter, and practical applications of the new field. He relied on the traditional problems generated by games of chance, such as lotteries, to motivate his mathematical innovations, but he pointed toward the future by generalizing these methods and applying them to many other topics. For example, since the calculation of odds in games of chance so often requires the summation of long series of fractions in which each term in the series differs from the others according to a regular pattern, Laplace began by reviewing some of the methods he had discovered to approximate the sums of such series, particularly when very large numbers are involved. He then proceeded to state what has since come to be called Bayes's theorem,

after an early predecessor of Laplace. This theorem states how to use partial or incomplete information to calculate the conditional probability of an event in terms of its absolute or unconditional probability and the conditional probability of its cause. Laplace was one of the first to make extensive use of this theorem; it was particularly important to him because of its relevance to how calculations of probability should change in response to new knowledge.

The *Théorie analytique des probabilités* includes Laplace's applications of his mathematical techniques to problems generated by the analysis of data from such diverse topics as census figures, insurance rates, instrumentation error, astronomy, geodesy, election prognostication, and jury selection. In particular, he gave an important statement of what has since been called the least square law for the calculation of a mean value for a set of data in such a way that the resulting error from the true value is minimized.

A Philosophical Essay on Probabilities has been one of Laplace's most widely read works; it includes the conceptual basis upon which Laplace constructed his mathematical techniques. Most important, Laplace stated and relied upon a definition of probability that has been a source of considerable philosophical debate. Given a situation in which specific equally possible cases are the results of various processes (such as rolling dice) and correspond to favorable or unfavorable events, Laplace defined the probability of an event as the fraction formed by dividing the number of cases that correspond to or cause that event by the total number of possible cases. When the cases in question are not equally possible (as when dice are loaded), the calculation must be altered in an attempt to include this information. Laplace's definition thus calls attention to his treatment of probability as an application of mathematics made necessary only by human ignorance. In one of the most famous passages in *A Philosophical Essay on Probabilities*, Laplace expresses this view by describing a supreme intelligence with a complete knowledge of the universe and its laws at any specific moment; for such an intelligence, Laplace believed that probability calculations would be unnecessary since the future and past could be calculated simply through an application of the laws of nature to the given perfectly stipulated set of conditions. Since knowledge of natural laws and the state of the world is always limited, probability is an essential feature of all human affairs. Nevertheless, Laplace's emphasis was not on the negative aspect of this conclusion but on the mathematical regularities to which even seemingly arbitrary sequences of events conform.

The domain in which Laplace saw the closest human approach to the knowledge of his hypothetical supreme intelligence was the application of Newton's theory of gravitation to the solar system. Since Newton's publication of his theory in 1686, mathematicians and physicists had reformulated his results using increasingly sophisticated mathematics. By Laplace's time, Newton's theory could be stated in a type of mathematics known as partial differential equations. Laplace made major contributions to the solution of equations of this type, including the famous technique of "Laplace transforms" and the use of a "potential" function to characterize a field of force.

Laplace made remarkably detailed applications of Newton's results to the orbits of the planets, moons, and comets. Some of his most famous calculations involve his demonstration of the very long-term periodic variations in the orbits of Jupiter and Saturn. Laplace thus contributed to an increasing knowledge of the stability and internal motions of the solar system. He also applied gravitation theory to the tides, the shape of Earth, and the rings of Saturn. His hypothesis that the solar system was formed through the condensation of a diffuse solar atmosphere became a starting point for more detailed subsequent theories.

Newtonian gravitation theory became Laplace's model for precision and clarity in all other branches of physics. He encouraged his colleagues to attempt similar analyses in optics, heat, electricity, and magnetism. His influence was particularly strong among French physicists between 1805 and 1815. By his death in 1827, however, this attempt to base all physics upon short-range forces had achieved only limited success; aside from the mathematical methods he developed, Laplace's conceptual contributions to physics were not as long-lasting as his more fundamental insights in probability theory.

Summary

Pierre-Simon Laplace's cultural influence extended far beyond the relatively small circle of mathematicians who could appreciate the brilliant technical detail in his work. In several ways he has become a symbol of some important aspects of the rapid scientific progress that took place during his career as a result of his role in institutional changes in the scientific profession and the implications that have been drawn from his conclusions and methods.

Laplace was very active within the highly centralized French scientific community. As a member of the French Academy of Sciences, he served on numerous research or evaluative committees that were commissioned by the French government. For example, following the French Revolution in 1789, he was an influential designer and advocate of the metric system, which has become the most widely used international system of scientific units. The academy was disbanded during the radical phase of the Revolution in 1793, but in 1796 Laplace became the president of the scientific class of the new Institute of France. Highly publicized institute prizes were regularly offered for essays in physics and mathematics, and Laplace exerted a powerful influence on French physics through the attention he devoted to choice of topic and support for his preferred candidates. He also played an important part in the early organization of the École Polytechnique, the prestigious school of engineering founded in 1795. Although Laplace lived through turbulent political changes, he remained in positions of high scientific status through the Napoleonic era and into the Bourbon Restoration, when he was raised to the nobility as a marquis. Laplace seems to have held few strong political views, and he thus is sometimes cited as an example of a powerful scientist indifferent to social or political conditions.

Aside from his work in probability and statistics, which has quite direct impact on modern societies, other aspects of Laplace's work have contributed to general perceptions of the goals, limitations, and methods of science. With Newton's theory of gravitation as his paradigmatic example, Laplace was convinced that, although human knowledge of nature is always limited, there are inevitable regularities that can be expressed approximately with ever-increasing accuracy. Laplace thus has become a symbol of nineteenth century scientific determinism, the view that the uncertainty of the future is only the result of human ignorance of the natural laws that determine it in every detail. When Napoleon I asked Laplace why God did not play a role in Laplace's analysis of the stability of the solar system, Laplace replied that he had had no need for such a hypothesis. Laplace thus contributed to a growing association of the scientific tradition with atheism and materialism. Finally, Laplace's style of mathematical physics has become a primary example of a reductionistic research strategy. Just as the gravitational effect of a large mass is determined by the sum of the forces exerted by all of its parts, Laplace expected all phenomena to reduce to collections of individual interactions. His success in implementing this method contributed to widespread perceptions that this is a necessary component of scientific investigation.

Bibliography

Arago, François. "Laplace." In *Biographies of Distinguished Scientific Men.* London: Longman, 1857; Boston: Ticknor and Fields, 1859. Arago was a student and colleague of Laplace for many years. His essay discusses only Laplace's work in astronomy and concentrates on his study of the stability of the solar system.

Fox, Robert. "The Rise and Fall of Laplacian Physics." *Historical Studies in the Physical Sciences* 4 (1974): 89-136. This is an excellent summary of Laplace's efforts to direct French physics according to a research program based upon short-range forces.

Gillispie, Charles C. et al. *Pierre-Simon Laplace, 1749-1827: A Life in Exact Science.* Princeton, N.J.: Princeton University Press, 1997. Covers the development of Laplace's research program and his work with the Academy of Science. The three authors cover different aspects, including biographical information from a scientific point of view; Laplace's efforts to gather young physicists who would work with the Newtonian model in physics; and an overview of the Laplace Transform.

Gillispie, Charles Coulston, Robert Fox, and Ivor Gratton-Guiness. "Pierre-Simon Marquis de Laplace." In *Dictionary of Scientific Biography*, vol. 15. New York: Scribner, 1970. This chronological survey of Laplace's scientific career combines discussion of significant concepts with summaries of important mathematical derivations.

Hahn, Roger. *Laplace as a Newtonian Scientist.* Los Angeles: Williams Andrew Clark Memorial Library, 1967. This short essay describes the philosophical debate concerning the status of laws of nature that occurred during Laplace's formative period at the University of Caen and his early years in Paris. Laplace's convictions about the law-governed structure of the universe are traced to his reading of d'Alembert and Marquis de Condorcet.

Todhunter, Isaac. *A History of the Mathematical Theory of Probability from the Time of Pascal to that of Laplace.* London: Macmillan, and New York: Chelsea, 1965. Chapter 10 provides a quite technical chronological account of the chief results and some of the derivations found in Laplace's publications on probability theory.

James R. Hofmann

FERDINAND LASSALLE

Born: April 11, 1825; Breslau, Prussia

Died: August 31, 1864; Geneva, Switzerland

Areas of Achievement: Political science and economics

Contribution: Lassalle was one of the founders of the German labor movement and the most important advocate of scientific socialism in Germany after the Revolution of 1848. His theory of evolutionary socialism eventually triumphed within the German Social Democratic Party.

Early Life

Ferdinand Lassalle was born on April 11, 1825, in Breslau, Prussia, the modern Polish city of Wrocław. He was the only son of Heymann Lassal, or Loslauer, a well-to-do Jewish silk merchant. Although admitted to the synagogue at thirteen, the young Lassalle never took his ancestral faith seriously. Lassalle lived at home until he was fifteen. Much of his time as a teenager was spent playing cards or billiards for spending money. Not a particularly bright student, Lassalle was expelled from the classical high school (*Gymnasium*) for forging his parents' signatures to his grade reports, an offense he committed repeatedly.

In May, 1840, Lassalle's father enrolled him in the Commercial Institute in Leipzig. His father had hopes that his son would eventually take over the family business, but Ferdinand was not willing. He announced his intention to study history, "the greatest subject in the world. The subject bound up with the holiest interests of mankind. . . ." After having passed his examinations in 1843, he was enrolled at the University of Breslau.

At the university, Lassalle studied history, archaeology, philology, and philosophy. It was while an undergraduate at Breslau that he was introduced to the works of the German philosopher Georg Wilhelm Friedrich Hegel. Hegel's dialectic soon became the cornerstone of Lassalle's worldview. This dialectic was for him, as it was also for Karl Marx, the key to understanding and interpreting the flow of human history. Like Marx, Lassalle came to believe that the future new order in society would be an inevitable product of the historical dialectic. Unlike Marx, who held to the necessity of revolution to move the dialectic forward, Lassalle came to understand it as a peaceful, evolutionary process.

In 1844, Lassalle entered the University of Berlin, where he continued studying philosophy. Although his interests extended to other philosophers such as Ludwig Feuerbach and the French Utopian thinkers, Hegel remained his primary influence. He would often rise at four in the morning to begin the day with readings from Hegel's works. He also began work on his doctoral thesis, a Hegelian interpretation of the Greek philosopher Heracleitus. From 1845 to 1847, Lassalle lived in Paris, where he met and was influenced by the French socialist and anarchist philosopher Pierre-Joseph Proudhon and the German poet Heinrich Heine. It was also during his stay in Paris that he changed the spelling of his last name from "Lassal" to "Lassalle."

In 1846, Lassalle met the Countess Sophie von Hatzfeldt, who was seeking a divorce from her husband, one of the wealthiest and most influential noblemen in northwestern Germany. Although not a lawyer, Lassalle took up her cause. Between 1846 and 1854, he conducted thirty-five lawsuits on behalf of the countess before eventually win-

ning her case. The countess rewarded Lassalle with a lifelong pension that made him financially independent. It was also the beginning of a lifelong relationship that both positively and negatively affected his political career.

Life's Work

Lassalle's career as a labor organizer and political agitator began in earnest during the Revolution of 1848. He was living in Düsseldorf, an emerging industrial center in the Prussian-ruled Rhineland. In November, 1848, Lassalle was arrested for making an incendiary speech, calling upon the populace and the militia to rise up in armed revolt. The occasion for the speech was a meeting called by Friedrich Engels, Marx's chief collaborator. Lassalle's relationship with Marx was not a smooth one. When they first met during the Revolutions of 1848, Lassalle had not yet read *Manifest der Kommunistischen* (*The Communist Manifesto*, 1850), first published in 1848. Many scholars believe that many of Lassalle's theoretical assumptions, which were later harshly criticized by Karl Marx, were in fact borrowed from Marx's early writings, and may be found in *The Communist Manifesto*.

When the Revolutions of 1848 collapsed, most of the revolutionary leaders fled the Continent. Marx settled in London. After his release from prison in July, 1849, Lassalle chose to remain in Germany. It was a choice that no doubt helped him in his subsequent bid for leadership of the German labor movement.

During the 1850's, and until their final estrangement in 1862, Marx and Lassalle remained hospitable toward each other, at least publicly. Marx looked to Lassalle for help in getting his books and articles published in Germany. He also called upon Lassalle for financial support. Yet as Marx's own thought matured over the years, he became increasingly critical of Lassalle's writings and obviously jealous of Lassalle's emergence as the leader of the German working class.

The tension between Marx and Lassalle was the result in large part of the differing historical roles to which each was called. Marx was basically an intellectual, addressing a small international audience of highly educated intellectuals like himself. He was a theorist, constructing the guiding principles of a future society. Lassalle, on the other hand, was a man of action. He was addressing the uneducated, illiterate, and backward German working class. He was attempting to shake them out of their

political lethargy and mold them into a major political force. For Lassalle, unlike Marx, the future new order in society was immediately obtainable.

Toward the end of 1861, Lassalle made two speeches in which he called upon the working class to form its own political party. He believed that once the workers became a formidable political force, it would have the effect of altering the power relationships in the state. Since he believed that the written constitution of necessity reflects the true power-ratio in society, Lassalle called upon the workers to organize and agitate for universal direct suffrage in all the German states.

In December of 1862, Lassalle was approached by the executive committee of the Central Committee to Convoke a General Congress of German Workers. They asked him to draw up a program for the congress. Lassalle's affirmative response marked the beginning of the final and most important phase in his life's work. Lassalle's response took the form of a pamphlet entitled *Offnes Antwortschreiben an das Central-Comité zur Berufung eines Allgemeinen Deutschen Arbeitercongresses zu Leipzig* (*Lassalle's Open Letter to the National Labor Association of Germany*, 1879), published in March, 1863. It contained his advice on what policies should be adopted by the working-class movement. Marx criticized the pamphlet as a vulgarization of his own ideas, but Lassalle's clarion call to action was well received by the workers. It led directly to the founding of the General German Workers' Association (Allgemeiner Deutscher Arbeiterverein) in Leipzig on May 23, 1863. Its chief goal, as stated in its bylaws, was to achieve justice for the German working class "through establishment of universal, equal, and direct suffrage."

Although Lassalle was a socialist, he was also a Prussian nationalist. He also felt the intellectual's usual frustration with the sluggishness of the working class. His attitude toward the workers was aristocratic and paternalistic, and his administrative style was authoritarian. He saw to it that the president of the association, the office he held, possessed dictatorial powers. "Otherwise," he said, "nothing will get done."

Being a nationalist, Lassalle did not find it necessary for the state to wither, as Marx did. In a letter to the Prussian prime minister Otto von Bismarck, in which he enclosed a copy of the association's bylaws, Lassalle said that the working class was instinctively inclined toward a dictatorship. He believed that the workers would prefer a monarchy, if only the king would look after their interests. Lassalle's willingness to consider the idea of a monarchical welfare state provided a common ground for his discussions and correspondence with Bismarck during late 1863 and early 1864. At that time, the prime minister was searching for allies in his struggle with the liberals in the Prussian parliament. The Bismarck-Lassalle talks came to nothing, however, in part because of Lassalle's presumptuousness and in part because of Bismarck's growing preoccupation with the unification of Germany.

By late spring, 1864, Lassalle was disappointed with the association's failure to increase its membership as rapidly as he had expected. He was also physically exhausted. His exhaustion was in part the result of his having contracted syphilis in 1847, when he was twenty-two. By the early 1860's, the disease was in the secondary stage, and the bones in one of his legs were deteriorating. In July, 1864, he decided to go to Switzerland for a rest.

In Geneva, Lassalle acted out the final chapter in his life as a romantic revolutionary. He had always pursued the conquest of women with the same enthusiasm as politics. He met and began courting passionately Helene von Dönniges. When he proposed marriage, he encountered opposition from her father and from her former fiancé, Yanko von Racowitza. In response to a challenge from Lassalle, a duel between Lassalle and Racowitza was fought on August 28, in a forest outside Geneva. Lassalle was mortally wounded and died three days later on August 31, 1864.

Summary

After Ferdinand Lassalle's death, Karl Marx and Friedrich Engels praised his memory in public, while continuing to criticize him in their correspondence with each other. Engels admitted that Lassalle had been politically "the most important fellow in Germany." In a letter to the Countess Hatzfeldt, Marx noted Lassalle's abilities, then added, "I personally loved him." He went on to lament the fact that they had drifted apart.

The General German Workers' Association continued to grow. By the late 1860's, it had split into two factions: the orthodox Marxists, who in 1869 founded the Social Democratic Labor Party (Sozialdemokratische Arbeiterpartei), and the Lassalleans, who were viewed by the former as reformist heretics. The two factions united in 1875 to form the Socialist Labor Party of Germany (Sozialistische Arbeiterpartei Deutschlands). The new party's program was largely based on theories and slogans associated with Lassalle.

In 1891, the party changed its name to the Social Democratic Party of Germany (Sozialdemokratische Partei Deutschlands), or SPD. The SPD was Marxist in theory, rather than Lassallean, but in practice it was becoming a mass parliamentary and reformist party, which is what Lassalle had advocated. The SPD became the largest and most influential socialist party in Europe prior to World War I. It was not until 1959, however, that the SPD formally abandoned all its Marxist ideology.

Much of what Lassalle had called for was later enacted by the German state under Bismarck's leadership. Perhaps, as some believe, Bismarck was only trying to win the workers away from socialism. In any case, speaking before the Reichstag in 1878, Bismarck said of Lassalle: "He was one of the most intelligent and likeable men I had ever come across. He was very ambitious and by no means a republican. He was very much a nationalist and a monarchist. His ideal was the German Empire, and here was our point of contact."

In 1866, Bismarck granted universal suffrage in elections to the Reichstag. In 1881, he began enacting a comprehensive social security program that included accident, health, and old age insurance. Bismarck's brand of "state socialism" may have been influenced by his earlier conversations with Lassalle. In any event, the German welfare program, inspired by Lassalle and initiated by Bismarck, served as a model for all other Western nations.

Bibliography

Bernstein, Edward. *Ferdinand Lassalle as a Social Reformer.* London: Sonnenschein, and New York: Scribner, 1893. A sympathetic but critical study by the father of revisionism in German social democracy. Bernstein was the most important figure in the SPD from Lassalle to the Nazi seizure of power in 1933. Bernstein also edited the party's official publication of Lassalle's collected works.

Footman, David. *The Primrose Path: A Life of Ferdinand Lasalle.* London: Cresset Press, 1946; as *Ferdinand Lassalle: Romantic Revolutionary.* New Haven, Conn.: Yale University Press, 1947. A very well-written and highly readable biography. It is the best book on Lassalle in English, and the place to begin a more detailed study. Footman believes that Lassalle's romantic nature is important for understanding his role in the birth of the German labor movement.

Gay, Peter. *The Dilemma of Democratic Socialism: Edward Bernstein's Challenge to Marx.* New York: Collier Books, 1962. Chapters 1 and 4 discuss Lassalle's influence on Bernstein and thus establish his place in the revision of Marxism that resulted in the modern SPD.

Meredith, George. *The Tragic Comedians: A Study in a Well-Known Study.* London: Chapman and Hall, 1880; New York: Scribner, 1898. Lassalle's final days in Geneva, including his courtship of Dönniges, is the subject of this romantic novel. The story is based largely on Dönniges' own account. It is considered to be a creditable attempt at making history come alive.

Wilson, Edmund. *To the Finland Station: A Study in the Writing and Acting of History.* London: Secker and Warburg, and New York: Doubleday, 1940. A popular study of the revolutionary tradition in European history from the beginning of the nineteenth century to the triumph of the Communist Revolution in Russia. Chapter 13, "Historical Actors: Lassalle," provides a brief account of Lassalle's life and thought, and tries to define his contributions to the rise of socialism in Europe.

Paul R. Waibel

BENJAMIN HENRY LATROBE

Born: May 1, 1764; Fulneck, England
Died: September 3, 1820; New Orleans, Louisiana
Areas of Achievement: Architecture and engineering
Contribution: Latrobe was the founder of the architectural profession in the United States as the country's first professional architect-engineer.

Early Life

Benjamin Henry Boneval Latrobe was born May 1, 1764, in Fulneck, Yorkshire, England (near Leeds). Exiled French Protestants, originally named de La Trobe, the family of Benjamin Henry Latrobe (as he usually signed himself) had been distinguished in religious, cultural, and business circles in Ireland, England, and Holland. His father, Benjamin Latrobe, was educated at the University of Glasgow as well as in Europe. Converted from the Baptist faith to that of the Moravians (United Brethren), the senior Latrobe was an internationally recognized preacher and teacher, a Moravian leader whose headquarters at one time were in Fulneck. There, he married Anna Margaretta Antes. A Pennsylvanian with honored Revolutionary War ancestors and a wealthy, landowning father, she traveled to Fulneck at fourteen to deepen her own Moravian learning. The sociability, cosmopolitanism, learned values, and interesting familial contacts surrounding young Benjamin were augmented by his parents' Moravian belief in directing education toward the broadening of childrens' individuality and tastes.

Thus, Latrobe's father, who returned to London to direct church interests better for the remainder of his life, placed Benjamin in Fulneck's Moravian school. Between the ages of four and fourteen, he acquired there a basic classical education: Latin, Greek, algebra, and geometry, as well as religious instruction. Then, following the example of an older brother and because of his father's dismay with the outbreak of the Revolution in 1776, Benjamin was sent to Moravian schools in Niesky and Barby in German Silesia.

Little documentation exists of the seven years he spent in Europe. What is known is that, having established himself in London in 1783, Latrobe was fluent in French, German, and Italian and was proficient in Hebrew and Spanish as well. He also exhibited a knowledge and love of music. He had completed a translation of a popular German work on Frederick the Great, indicated an interest in military engineering, and manifested superior literary and artistic skills. Behind him, too, were invaluable friendships and acquaintances with European scholars and connoisseurs, which had led him deeply into philosophy, logic, ethics, a mastery of mathematics, sidereal navigation, and surveying.

At the age of twenty, Latrobe was a dark-haired, handsome, muscular young man, six feet, two inches in height. In addition to being privileged with an extraordinary background, he was ambitious, impetuous, childishly vivacious, and charming. He was also subject in young adulthood and throughout his life, however, to abnormal sensitivities, severe headaches, and sometimes debilitating depressions. Notwithstanding, he was remarkably accomplished and clearly gifted.

Life's Work

Technically, Latrobe was employed in the London Stamp Office from 1784 to 1794. Yet the commencement of his lifetime career proceeded unhindered by a civil service post, for within two years he began working with John Smeaton. Smeaton, though trained as a lawyer, was in fact a renowned instrument maker and the designer and builder of, among other engineering feats, the famed Eddystone Lighthouse. He was the first Englishman to designate himself as a "civil engineer"; as an acknowledged master, he founded Great Britain's first organization of civil engineers. Smeaton wrote extensively, was a friend of James Watt and a respected acquaintance of most upcoming architects and engineers; indeed, a whole generation of engineers sprang from association with him. Smeaton assigned Latrobe to work with his chief assistant, a master in his own right, William Jessop, chief inventor of the "edge rail," as well as the designer-builder of numerous canals, docks, and other harbor facilities. From 1786 into 1789, Latrobe served under Jessop on Rye Harbor's improvements and on construction of the Basingstoke Canal, both major engineering assignments.

Thanks to his achievements and his family and professional connections, Latrobe skipped the usual lengthy apprenticeships and joined the office of Samuel Pepys Cockerell, Cockerell being the founder of his own dynasty of great architects and officials. There, between 1789 and 1792, Latrobe variously helped design the Admiralty Building in

Whitehall and took on private commissions, in the process making lifelong friends such as First Lord of the Admiralty, Sir Charles Middleton.

Briefly, London was good to him. In 1792, he was able to establish his own architectural office. He became "surveyor" (designer) of London's police offices and conducted surveys for the Chelmer and Blackwater Navigation improvement. He also married Lydia Sellon and started his own family. Unhappily, Lydia died giving birth to their third child, and Latrobe suffered a nervous breakdown. That and a series of financial reverses shortly left him bankrupt and, in a sense, a professional failure. Only lands bequeathed to him by his mother in the United States allowed a way out of a sad situation. Further spurred on by a romantic, liberal attachment to American Revolutionary principles and republican values, he abandoned England, landing in Norfolk, Virginia, in March, 1796.

Assisted by splendid references, Latrobe designed his first American house in Norfolk within months after landing and worked busily in Virginia until the end of 1798. He surveyed the upper Appomattox River for commercial navigational purposes, served as engineering consultant to the Dismal Swamp Land Company, and, receiving a gubernatorial appointment, he designed and built the Virginia State Penitentiary in Richmond, which drew acclaim for the liberal philosophy of penology that it embodied. Finally, he designed a novel Richmond theater complex. During his Virginia years, Latrobe became a friend of Thomas Jefferson and Bushrod Washington and struck close acquaintances with George Washington and his family at Mt. Vernon, with the Madisons, Randolphs—indeed, with most important social and political figures in Virginia. Moreover, keen observer that he had always been, he kept an exceptional journal and sketches of his journeys through the state.

Residing in Philadelphia until 1807 despite serious struggles and misfortunes, Latrobe reached new heights in his career. In 1800, he started his second family with his marriage to Mary Elizabeth Hazlehurst. With this stability and a genius for combining architecture and engineering skills possessed by no one else in the country, he designed many of his masterworks. By tapping the Schuylkill River and ingeniously utilizing steam power for pumping and distribution of purified water, he sanitized a basic service while masking his work behind beautiful buildings. With private and public commissions, he designed splendid private homes and completed designs for a national military academy, a monument to Washington, and the Chestnut Street Theater. He was chosen both engineer and contractor of the Susquehanna River Survey; he restored Nassau Hall at Princeton University. He designed Transylvania College for Henry Clay (and Clay's home) in Lexington, Kentucky, and the main buildings of Dickinson College, Carlisle, Pennsylvania, and he helped Jefferson with design of the University of Virginia. Three of his masterworks in Philadelphia were the Bank of Pennsylvania, the Bank of Philadelphia, and the University of Pennsylvania Medical School, while two others in nearby Baltimore were the first Roman Catholic cathedral in the United States and the Baltimore Exchange. He also surveyed, then served as chief engineer of, the great Chesapeake and Delaware Canal enterprise. Meanwhile, he designed a covered naval dry dock in Washington for Jefferson and accepted his appointment as the surveyor of the public buildings.

Since Latrobe enjoyed federal commissions or appointments during all but four of his twenty-four years in the United States, he was drawn to Washington in 1807. There, besides building the Washington Navy Yard and the Washington Canal, he designed, helped construct, and—after its destruction by the British—helped reconstruct the national Capitol, which was the subsequent standard for hundreds of American public buildings. He continued scores of other architectural interests: close association with Nicholas Roosevelt and Robert Fulton, among others, on the uses of steam power, development of public works, and contributions to learned societies. In 1819, he moved his family to New Orleans, drawn by son Henry's death (which occurred while he was working on a lighthouse of his father's design) and by the prospect of new commissions such as the Louisiana Bank, the Customs House, the unfinished lighthouse, and other private projects. Like his son, he died in New Orleans, on September 3, 1820, of yellow fever.

Summary

Latrobe's genius encompassed nearly every area of classical architecture, though he is most noted for his Greek revival influences. Indeed, his work was marked by considerable originality and restrained and novel interpretations in the use of columns, domes, and masonary vaults and penditives. He founded and, through family and pupils, perpetuated professional architecture in the United States.

Throughout his career, he was plagued by personal and political hostilities and by chronic financial difficulties, in addition to the philosophy of impermanence and cheap construction that seemed an American style, yet his living was made almost entirely from his architectural and engineering works. Few aspects of civil engineering escaped his touch: surveys, canals, tunnels, waterworks, beach conservation, public buildings, universities, bridges, lighthouses, arsenals, and naval and port facilities. Before the professionalization of mechanical engineering, he joined with other pioneers in the design and use of steam power in manufactures, utilities, and land and water locomotion. His legacy also included journals, papers, drawings, and designs of the highest merit. Of great importance, his breadth of learning helped bridge the technological and artistic gap between the best British and European work and their adaptation to young republican America.

Bibliography

Calhoun, Daniel H. *The American Civil Engineer, 1792-1843.* Cambridge, Mass.: MIT Press, 1960. Emphasis upon professionalization of civil engineering in the United States. Influences of West Point and state and federal sponsorship of public works are dealt with more extensively than the work of individuals such as Latrobe, who by mid-century would be eclipsed by task-oriented specialists. Excellent scholarly context for understanding the strengths and weaknesses of Latrobe's generation of architect-engineers with classical and continental educations.

Carter, Edward C., II, with Darwin H. Stapleton and Lee W. Formwalt. *Benjamin Henry Latrobe and Public Works: Professionalism, Private Interest, and Public Policy in the Age of Jefferson.* Washington, D.C.: Public Works Historical Society, 1976. Excellent, if brief, analysis of conflicting elements confronting early architect-engineers by foremost experts on Latrobe's journals and papers.

Condit, Carl W. *American Building: Materials and Techniques from the First Colonial Settlements to the Present.* 2d ed. Chicago: University of Chicago Press, 1982. Chapter 5 is particularly pertinent to masonry and to Latrobe's and his contemporaries' employment of it.

―――. *American Building Art: The Nineteenth Century.* New York: Oxford University Press, 1960. Chapter 1 puts Latrobe's work in context of previous American experience and later nineteenth century architectural and building directions.

Hamlin, Talbot. *Benjamin Henry Latrobe.* New York: Oxford University Press, 1955. The most thorough, scholarly, and personalized appreciation of Latrobe in all of his dimensions. Well written and an expert critical analysis of the great architect-engineer's trials, successes, and failures.

Latrobe, Benjamin Henry. *The Correspondence and Miscellaneous Papers of Benjamin Henry Latrobe.* Vol. 1. Edited by John C. Van Horne and Lee W. Formwalt. New Haven, Conn., and London: Yale University Press, 1986. The editors and Latrobe himself have made this an intriguing and readable volume of keen observations and literary merit.

Stapleton, Darwin H. "Benjamin Henry Latrobe and the Transfer of Technology." In *Technology in America: A History of Individuals and Ideas,* edited by Carroll W. Purcell, Jr. 2d ed. Cambridge, Mass.: MIT Press, 1990. Focuses upon an important aspect of Latrobe's contribution to American architecture and engineering as a result of his British and Continental training.

Clifton K. Yearley
Kerrie L. MacPherson

FIRST BARON LAWRENCE

Born: March 4, 1811; Richmond, Yorkshire, England

Died: June 26, 1879; London, England

Area of Achievement: Colonial administration

Contribution: Lawrence was one of the builders of British India. His efforts were crucial to the successful establishment of the administration of the Punjab and to the defeat of the great Indian mutiny of 1857. He was viceroy from 1864 to 1869.

Early Life

John Laird Mair Lawrence, the first Baron Lawrence, was born March 4, 1811, at Richmond, Yorkshire, in England, the eighth of twelve children of Lieutenant Colonel Alexander Lawrence. A family friend was a director of the East India Company and, in 1827, he obtained an appointment in the company's civil service for John as he had earlier obtained military appointments for three of his brothers. At the time, instead of ruling India directly, the British government left its administration to the East India Company under a charter going back to the seventeenth century.

Lawrence spent two years in the company's training school at Maileybury, finishing in May, 1829. He sailed for India with his brother Henry, arriving in Calcutta in February, 1830. After studying Urdu and Persian at the College of Fort William, he was posted to Delhi. For the next fourteen years he served in civil posts in the area around Delhi as a magistrate and financial officer. He worked energetically and established himself as a competent administrator.

In 1839, a severe fever, which was almost fatal, interrupted his career and sent him home on invalid leave. Returning to England in 1840, he regained his health, traveled in Ireland and on the European continent, and, in August, 1841, was married to Harriet Catherine Hamilton, the daughter of a clergyman in Donegal. Though he was again sick with fever and was warned not to return to India, he disregarded the advice with characteristic stubbornness, resuming his career in the spring of 1843. His absence had not improved his position in the civil administration, where up to this time he had progressed only modestly.

Life's Work

In 1845, for the first time, Lawrence was able to bring his abilities to the attention of the governor general and to make some professional progress in a substantial way. The new governor general, Lord Hardinge, had just come out to India. The British had annexed the large province of Sind and were consequently at war with the neighboring Sikhs in the Punjab. Hardinge was eager to consolidate the rather shaky British position, and he called on Lawrence to supply the army with much-needed ammunition. Lawrence's determined energy won for him Hardinge's approval as he organized a great convoy of bullock-drawn carts and moved enough ammunition from Delhi to secure a victory which closed the First Sikh War decisively.

Lawrence's reward in 1846 was a post as administrator of one of the newly annexed provinces. His brother Henry, who had risen further than any of his brothers in the military service, was appointed the company's principal resident at Lahore. During his brother's absence from the post, Lawrence acted in his stead as the chief administrator of the entire area. In March, 1848, he held his province secure during the Second Sikh War, though he was attacked by sizable irregular forces. At the successful conclusion of the war, he urged that the entire Punjab be annexed quickly to prevent future trouble. This was done and the highest level of administration was left to a board of three, to which Lawrence was appointed, his brother being named president.

The newly conquered Punjab, an area as large as France, had not even the rudiments of European-style administration, and all the structure of modern government, from roads to tax collection agencies, had to be created, a huge undertaking. To complicate the task, the military administrator, Sir Charles Napier, was critical of the civil administration, and the governing board could not agree within itself because Henry and John Lawrence, both men of strong views and fierce tempers, quarreled frequently. John was also attacked repeatedly by bouts of fever, which made the work no easier. At last, in 1853, the governor general, Lord Dalhousie, while acknowledging their success, dissolved the board and made John Lawrence the chief administrator of the Punjab.

Although Lawrence cautioned the government against being drawn into the affairs of Afghanistan during the Crimean War, the government decided on a formal treaty with the emir and Lawrence was sent in March, 1855, to negotiate it. On the successful conclusion of the negotiation, he was rewarded with a knighthood. Having established a relationship with the emir, he was sent, early in 1857, to negotiate a second treaty.

Like many of the company's senior civil servants at the time, Lawrence saw no warning of the underlying discontents which produced the great mutiny of 1857; he applied for leave from his post only a few weeks before the subcontinent erupted in the most serious challenge British authority in India ever faced.

Lawrence's greatest moments came in the desperate danger of the weeks and months that followed. Mutineers besieged Delhi and the Punjab was cut off. Lawrence was on his own, having to hold the province against the rebels and to mobilize its resources in suppressing the uprising elsewhere. With great coolness he collected all the reliable men he could find, striking swiftly at the mutineers and quieting much of the area. After a brief respite, he bent his efforts toward supplying the regular forces outside Delhi, seeing that that was the crucial situation. If Delhi fell, Lawrence would be unable to hold the territory, however vigorously he acted, for the whole province would rise against British rule. By August, the tide had turned and with the lifting of the siege of Delhi, the heart went out of the mutiny.

In the aftermath of the uprising, which had been crushed with great ferocity, bitterness lingered. Lawrence acted as a moderating figure, advising against further harsh reprisals, though during the fighting he had not hesitated to act with the greatest severity. Despite his own deeply evangelical temperament, he firmly opposed suggestions that the Indian administration be purged of all non-Christians, understanding that the only prudent course, if Great Britain were to continue to govern India, was to seek whatever accommodation could be made with the Indian people.

Lawrence's health had deteriorated seriously under the strain of the mutiny, and he returned to England, amid considerable popular acclaim for his heroism. When the furor was over, he settled down to work at the India Office in London as a member of the newly created Indian Council, although he did not find it satisfying employment, for it conferred no real power. He was offered the governorship of Bombay in 1860 but declined it. In November, 1863, on the death of the viceroy, Prime Minister Lord Palmerston offered Lawrence the position, and he accepted immediately. Only once before in the century had a civil servant been offered the highest position in the Indian government. For Lawrence it was the crowning moment of his long career.

Lawrence was viceroy for five years, from January, 1864, to January, 1869. Compared to the heroic years in the Punjab, they must have been frustrating. There were no great victories to be won, only the humdrum battles of successful administration. His predecessor had allowed government expenses to outrun revenues considerably, and Lawrence undertook to redress the balance by cutting back on expenditure. Though the deficit continued throughout his administration, he was harshly criticized by official India for the constraints imposed by his parsimony. There was a terrible famine in Orissa which he was unable to alleviate and a war in Bhutan which he could not avoid. His long experience governing the Punjab had taught him the wisdom of caution on the northwestern frontier. He resisted firmly pressures for expansion and meddling in the affairs of Afghanistan. Again, for this reluctance, he was criticized with some rancor. In an age in which many believed fervently in the desirability of expanding the Empire, his was not a popular position, however sensible. In the long term, his judgment, that the natural limits of British power in that area had been reached, was sustained by history. Afghanistan proved indigestible and remained for another century the buffer zone between Russia and India.

In January, 1869, Lawrence left office and returned home to England, where he was finally awarded his peerage. He continued to play a significant part in politics in the 1870's as a member of the House of Lords. Though a reluctant speaker, he spoke often and to good effect, whenever the subject was India, and his judgment was respected, if not always heeded. His caution about imperial expansion meant that he often voted with the Liberals, though he was not a partisan. He was particularly active in the late 1870's in opposing the Conservative government's policy which led to the Afghan War of 1878-1879.

Though he kept active, serving on the boards of a number of charitable and public organizations, Lawrence's health deteriorated markedly, and the onset of blindness limited what he could do. He continued to speak in the House of Lords to the very end, dying only a week after his last speech, on June 26, 1879. He was buried in Westminster Abbey as a national hero.

Summary

The first Baron Lawrence played a crucial part at one of the great turning points in the history of British rule in India. That history is, for the most part, the story of a small number of British soldiers and civil administrators governing a vast subcontinent of people whose languages, cultures, and values they neither shared nor fully understood. The consolidation and expansion of British power seemed inevitable in an age of empire, but the explosion of 1857 showed how tenuous British control in India might be if the people of India chose to resist. Lawrence understood this fact clearly. The continuation of British rule depended on Great Britain's ability to understand the needs of India's people and to provide for them better than the traditional system and its rulers had been able to do. While Lawrence showed that he could be as firm, and as ruthless, as any in putting down opposition, it was his own lifelong effort to understand India sympathetically that made it possible for him to rule successfully, both in the Punjab and then over the whole British Raj. In the end, it was as much his good sense as his heroic energy and courage which accounted for that success.

Bibliography

The Cambridge History of India. 6 vols. Cambridge and New York: Cambridge University Press, 1922-1932. The standard work on Indian history. Despite its age, still provides a detailed overview, though the interpretation is naturally outdated.

Herbert, John Alexander. "John Laird Mair Lawrence." In *Dictionary of National Biography,* edited by Sir Leslie Stephen and Sir Sidney Lee, vol. 11. Oxford and New York: Oxford University Press, 1885-1900. The standard biographical dictionary of British history. The article on Lawrence provides a concise summary of the Victorian literature on the man, from works usually available only in major research collections. There is no full-scale modern biography.

Smith, Vincent A. *The Oxford History of India.* 4th ed. New York: Oxford University Press, 1981. A good general guide to Indian history and its literature.

Spear, Perceval. *India: A Modern History.* Ann Arbor: University of Michigan Press, 1961. An excellent, concise account of Indian history.

Wolpert, Stanley. *A New History of India.* 5th ed. New York: Oxford University Press, 1997. A recent study, providing a general review of Indian history and incorporating much new work.

Woodruff, Philip [Philip Mason]. *The Men Who Ruled India: The Founders.* London: Cape, 1953. The first volume of a two-volume work by a member of the Indian Civil Service under British rule. The third section is relevant. The focus is on individuals, but they are put nicely in context. An appreciative and sympathetic commentary on British administration in India in the early nineteenth century.

————. *The Men Who Ruled India: The Guardians.* New York: St. Martin's Press, 1954. Second and concluding volume of the preceding work. The first half of the book covers 1858-1909 and, like the first volume, focuses generally on individuals. Contains much of interest about Lawrence, his brother Henry, and the conditions under which the administrators struggled to work.

S. J. Stearns

EMMA LAZARUS

Born: July 22, 1849; New York, New York
Died: November 19, 1887; New York, New York
Areas of Achievement: Literature and social reform
Contribution: Lazarus began writing poems as a girl and published volumes of poetry, plays, translations, a novel, and many influential essays in *Century* magazine and in the American Jewish press. She is best remembered for her sonnet "The New Colossus," which is engraved on the base of the Statue of Liberty.

Early Life

On July 22, 1849, Emma Lazarus was born into an American Jewish family that had lived in New York for generations. One of her ancestors was a Sephardic Jew from Portugal who had fled the Spanish Inquisition and emigrated to the West Indies. Emma's father, Moses Lazarus, was a successful sugar merchant and one of New York's wealthiest men. He was a founder of the Knickerbocker Club and belonged to the influential Spanish-Portuguese Synagogue. Emma's mother, Esther Nathan Lazarus, belonged to a prominent New York family whose members were distinguished in the legal profession.

Emma, the fourth daughter born to the family, was named for one of the novelist Jane Austen's heroines. A boy and two more girls followed. The family enjoyed summers in fashionable Newport, Rhode Island. Emma and her older sisters were educated at home by private tutors; Emma in particular was considered too frail for schooling outside the house. She had a gift for languages and learned French, Italian, and German. She also immersed herself in children's stories and then in the volumes of her father's library. She was particularly taken with Walter Scott, the Scottish novelist and poet, and with Greek and Roman mythology.

When the Civil War broke out, Emma was only eleven, but she was aware of the uncles and male cousins, dressed in Union blue, who arrived at her home at all hours to say tearful goodbyes to her parents. She wrote poems on war and on nature themes, and translated French and German poets. Her father retired in 1865 at the age of fifty-two and devoted himself to his children. When he saw Emma's notebooks, he was taken with her thirty original poems as well as with her translations of Heinrich Heine and Victor Hugo. He decided to

have the manuscript printed for private circulation. *Poems and Translations by Emma Lazarus. Written Between the Ages of Fourteen and Sixteen* appeared in 1866. The book was received enthusiastically and, with the addition of ten new poems, was reprinted the following year for general circulation. To crown the events of her eighteenth year, Moses Lazarus introduced Emma to Ralph Waldo Emerson, who was then in his sixties. Emerson, one of the most influential poets and writers of his time, asked the young poet to send a copy of her book to him in Concord, Massachusetts. He praised the book and offered constructive criticism, which led to a long and fruitful correspondence. He was to be an important influence on her work.

Life's Work

In the next few years, Emma Lazarus pursued nature, classical, and Jewish themes in her poetry. She wrote one of her best-known poems, "In the Jewish Synagogue at Newport," drawing on the historical resonance of the oldest synagogue in the United States and patterning it after Henry Wadsworth Longfellow's "The Jewish Cemetery at Newport." "Admetus," a long, romantic poem with scenes from Greek mythology, was accepted by *Lippincott's*, the leading literary magazine of the day, and became the title poem of her second collection. Emerson praised *Admetus and Other Poems*, and Lazarus dedicated it to him over his objections. Published in 1871, the book was well received in the United States and earned rave reviews in England, where one critic compared Lazarus favorably to Robert Browning, one of the most erudite living English poets.

Lazarus' next project was a romantic novel titled *Alide*, based on a love incident in the life of Johann Wolfgang von Goethe, the great German writer whose work she had translated. When *Alide* was published in 1874, Lazarus sent a copy to Ivan Turgenev, a world-famous Russian novelist whom she revered. His response was reserved but positive; he praised her grasp of the German spirit and admired her depiction of character. Lazarus treasured his letter, and it may have offered her some comfort when *Parnassus*, a poetry anthology edited by her friend Emerson, appeared shortly afterward. It was an important anthology in which English and American poets were published together for the

first time. When she found that she was omitted from *Parnassus* despite Emerson's years of praise for her work, Lazarus was deeply wounded. She wrote him a proud letter questioning his sincerity, but he did not answer.

Lazarus' mother died early in 1876, breaking up an unusually close-knit family circle and prompting new poems on the theme of mother love. The following summer, after a year and a half of silence, Emerson and his wife invited Lazarus to visit them in Concord. It was a great adventure for the twenty-seven-year-old poet. She was immediately taken with Mrs. Emerson and developed a friendship with Emerson's daughter Ellen, who was ten years her senior. Among the people she met there was the poet and biographer William Ellery Channing, who took Lazarus to Henry David Thoreau's cottage at Walden Pond and presented her with the pocket compass that his old friend Thoreau had carried on his walks.

Lazarus returned to her literary life in New York, interspersed with summers in elegant Newport. Her poems continued to appear, and her name became widely known as her activities branched out into critical essays, book reviews, and profiles of prominent artists. Lazarus now began to recognize the limitations of her knowledge of the world and started to question the importance of her work. At about that time, Gustave Gottheil, a New York rabbi, asked her to translate some medieval Jewish hymns from German. These were the first of many that she was to translate from German, Spanish, and Hebrew sources and that were to appear over the years in the *Jewish Messenger*. She next wrote a long, ambitious work titled *The Dance to Death*. This powerful verse-drama in five acts chronicles the martyrdom of the Jews of Nordhausen in 1349, when they were accused of causing the Black Plague and were sentenced to be burned to death. At the time, Lazarus neither showed it to anyone nor submitted it for publication. Her interest in her Jewish heritage found a new outlet in the life and work of the German Jewish poet Heinrich Heine. She translated many of his poems and wrote others based on Heine's notes that were found after his early death in 1856. A book grew from these endeavors, *Poems and Ballads of Heinrich Heine*, which included Lazarus' biographical study of the German poet.

The early years of the 1880's were marked by historical events that were to have a profound effect on Lazarus' work. A series of bloody riots against the Jewish population in Russia had caused hundreds of thousands of destitute Jews to flee to the United States. Lazarus visited the refugees at Ward's Island in the East River, where they were temporarily housed. The first task was to resettle the refugees, and she immediately started to raise funds for that purpose from her wide circle of acquaintances. In April of 1882, *Century* magazine carried an article by a Russian historian that justified the pogroms by vilifying Jews. Incensed, Lazarus wrote an answering essay that appeared in the May issue. She had found her cause, and with it, a new voice.

She wrote many new poems on Jewish themes and sent them to Philip Cowen, editor of the *American Hebrew*. She also sent him *The Dance to Death*, which he published in installments. In September of 1882, the verse-drama was published together with new poems in *Songs of a Semite*. Lazarus continued to visit the refugees on Ward's Island, occasions that stimulated new perspectives. In a burst of energy, Lazarus wrote "An Epistle to the Hebrews," which grew into fifteen articles that appeared in the *American Hebrew* between November, 1882, and February, 1883. The work was an appeal to American Jews to reflect upon their history and try to retain their special identities. "An Epistle" provoked great controversy, particularly in its support for the establishment of a Jewish state in Palestine.

Her reputation preceded her when Lazarus sailed to England in the spring of 1883 with her younger sister Annie. She was showered with invitations from the artistic elite of British society. She returned home in the autumn, and shortly after, she received an appeal from a fund-raising committee for the gigantic new Statue of Liberty to be erected on Bedlow Island in New York Harbor. The committee requested an original manuscript to sell at an auction along with manuscripts by Henry Wadsworth Longfellow, Walt Whitman, and Mark Twain. In reply, Lazarus wrote the sonnet "The New Colossus," a poem that was to ensure her immortality in a world of changing tastes and fashions.

The following year Lazarus fell ill, but she persevered in her work, writing a long poem that was intended to sum up her beliefs about the Jews. Influenced by Walt Whitman, she chose a new form: a cycle of lyrics made up of long, sprawling lines, which became "By the Waters of Babylon." Lazarus had apparently recovered from her illness when her father died in May of 1885. It was a numbing shock, and eight weeks later she departed for a tour of Europe with her sister Josephine. Lazarus spent two years abroad, although she was an invalid for much of that time. She finally returned to New York in 1887, where she died of cancer at the age of thirty-eight.

Summary

Emma Lazarus' popular fame rests on her sonnet on the Statue of Liberty. Ironically, the author never assigned any particular importance to the poem. Only through the efforts of a friend, Georgiana Schuyler, was "The New Colossus" inscribed on a plaque on the base of the Statue of Liberty in 1903, sixteen years after the author's death. During her lifetime, hers was a strong and eloquent voice advancing provocative ideas on the history and future of the Jews. At a time when anti-Semitism was widespread, she wrote convincingly of the proud Jewish spirit. An ardently patriotic American, she had no difficulty reconciling this patriotism with her ethnic loyalty. She was one of the first Americans to take up the cause of a Jewish homeland, an idea that was not welcomed by the American Jews of her time.

Quiet, almost withdrawn, Emma Lazarus became an influential writer and intellectual who was admired by major contemporary figures. It cannot be known what Emma Lazarus might have accomplished if she had lived, but in her thirty-eight years she became a widely known artist and important public advocate for causes whose time had not yet arrived.

Bibliography

Gordh, George. "Emma Lazarus: A Poet of Exile and Freedom." *The Christian Century* 103 (November 19, 1986): 1033-1036. In a careful reading of Lazarus' poetry, Gordh compared her early, romantic verse with the later work, which he finds imbued with a religious sensibility. "The New Colossus" is discussed at length.

Jacob, Heinrich E. *The World of Emma Lazarus.* New York: Schocken Books, 1949. Jacob uses a Freudian model to understand Lazarus, concluding that the major influence on her life was her father. This study is fanciful but interesting.

Lichtenstein, Diane. "Words and Worlds: Emma Lazarus's Conflicting Citizenships." *Tulsa Studies in Women's Literature* 6, no. 2 (Fall 1987): 247-263. Lichtenstein demonstrates that Lazarus used her writing to achieve a resolution between her American and Jewish identities in the last decade of her life. The article also raises the issue of the poet's gender, another form of marginality that Lazarus forged into her unique identity.

Merriam, Eve. *Emma Lazarus: Woman with a Torch.* New York: Citadel Press, 1956. This biography studies Lazarus' life as it was reflected in her work. Merriam traces the poetry from the early focus on history and myth to its later engagement with events of her own time.

Vogel, Dan. *Emma Lazarus.* Boston: Twayne, 1980. This work, one of a standardized series of monographs, offers the general reader a well-organized, concrete overview of the poet's life and work.

Young, Bette Roth. "Emma Lazarus and Her Jewish Problem." *American Jewish History* 84, no. 4 (December 1996). Profile of Lazarus and her fight against anti-Semitism as evidenced in her work.

————. *Emma Lazarus in Her World: Life and Letters.* Philadelphia, Pa.: Jewish Publication Society, 1995. The author presents over one hundred letters by Lazarus that illuminate both her life and personality and clarify her devotion to the cause of Jewish renewal.

Sheila Golburgh Johnson

ROBERT E. LEE

Born: January 19, 1807; Stratford, Virginia
Died: October 12, 1870; Lexington, Virginia
Area of Achievement: The military
Contribution: Perhaps the finest army tactician of his generation, Lee, by his brilliant command of the Army of Northern Virginia, prolonged the life of the Confederacy during the Civil War.

Early Life

Last in the long line of the famous Lees of Virginia and fifth of seven children, Robert Edward Lee was born at the family estate of Stratford. His father, Colonel Henry "Light Horse" Harry Lee, had served with distinction as a cavalryman in the Revolutionary War and later as governor of Virginia, although he was financially insecure. His mother, Anne Hill Carter Lee, belonged to another aristocratic Virginia family. The family moved to Alexandria in Robert's fourth year, and he attended the local schools there. Because of the long absences and then the death of his father, Robert gradually took over the major care of his invalid mother. This intimate relationship shaped young Lee's character as one of quiet dignity, high moral integrity, and personal strength.

Desiring to emulate his father and to obtain a free education, Lee attended the United States Military Academy at West Point, where he performed as an outstanding cadet and was graduated second in a class of forty-six in 1829. Entering the engineer corps, he built and maintained coastal fortifications and river works. In June, 1831, he married his childhood friend Mary Anne Randolph Custis, the great-granddaughter of the wife of George Washington, at the opulent Custis estate at Arlington. Their marriage strengthened Lee's deep roots in his native state, though his devotion to his country enabled him to resist the temptation to settle down to the life of a country squire at Arlington, which he managed even while posted elsewhere, and where his seven children were reared. He ably performed the mundane tasks of a peacetime army engineer and held the rank of captain at the outbreak of the Mexican War in 1846.

Life's Work

Lee's genius as a field officer emerged during the Mexican War and placed him in the public eye. He received the brevet rank of major for his performance as a staff officer in the early campaigns, after which he transferred to the staff of General Winfield Scott for the major invasion of central Mexico. Lee contributed materially to the capture of Vera Cruz in April, 1847; through his ability and bravery in placing artillery and reconnoitering in several battles, he was promoted to brevet lieutenant colonel. After the attack on Chapultepec, in which he was wounded, he became brevet colonel.

Soon, however, Lee returned to routine duties, constructing fortifications near Baltimore and then, during 1852-1855, improving the course of study at West Point as superintendent. His reward was a transfer out of engineering to the Second Cavalry Regiment, with the rank of lieutenant colonel, policing the Indians in west Texas. In July, 1857, he assumed the colonelcy of the regiment. Home on leave during the fall of 1859, Lee was ordered to subdue John Brown's force, which had occupied the armory at Harpers Ferry (then part of Virginia) in Brown's stillborn attempt to incite a slave uprising in the South. After accomplishing the task, Lee returned to his regiment and, in 1860, assumed command of the Department of Texas.

A mild-mannered, even gentle officer with an excellent physique and devoted to the army and the flag, Lee dutifully obeyed his orders to return to Washington upon the secession of Texas from the Union in February, 1861. The next month, he was made colonel of the First Cavalry. By any measure the most able officer in the army, he was the logical choice to command the forces necessary to subdue the Southern rebellion, a command offered him by the Lincoln Administration upon the outbreak of the Civil War in mid-April, 1861. Following the secession of Virginia and considerable soulsearching, however, Lee decided that his loyalty rested with his home state, whereupon he resigned his commission on April 23. He was given command of the Virginia militia and was soon appointed brigadier general in the new Confederate Army. Within months, his normal dark hair and mustache would be replaced by a full beard and hair completely grayed, the result no doubt of his awesome responsibilities.

Promoted to the full rank of general during the summer, one of five initially appointed, Lee first advised President Jefferson Davis in organizing the Confederate Army. He took command of the forces attempting to hold West Virginia in the

Confederacy in August, but was soundly defeated the next month at Cheat Mountain. Early in November, he assumed command of the coastal defenses of South Carolina, Georgia, and eastern Florida. Shortages of troops there led him to establish an in-depth defense against potential Union naval and amphibious penetrations. His strategy was faulty, however, because the Union had no intention of invading the interior in that quarter and instead attacked and successfully occupied key coastal positions merely for use as blockading stations for the navy.

Lee was recalled early in March, 1862, to help Davis organize the defenses of Richmond against the advance of General George B. McClellan's army in the Peninsular Campaign. When the commander of the defending army, General Joseph E. Johnston, was wounded at Fair Oaks, Lee was given command on June 1, and he quickly reorganized his forces into the Army of Northern Virginia, a name he created. He masterfully countered McClellan's forces in the Seven Days' Battles, concluded on July 1, then swung north to defeat the army of General John Pope at the Second Battle of Bull Run in late August. Crossing the Potomac, Lee attempted to gain the support of Marylanders but was stopped by McClellan in the Antietam campaign in September. He concluded the year by repulsing the bloody Union assaults on his well-placed army at Fredericksburg in December.

Lee's true genius in tactics lay in erecting field fortifications and in his remarkable ability to operate from the interior position—that is, to shift his forces between different points in his lines that were threatened by the larger numbers of the opposing Union armies. This tactic was best demonstrated in his stunning victory at Chancellorsville in May, 1863, when his army was half the size of that of the enemy. His greatest gamble occurred when he invaded Pennsylvania a month later. Frustrated from trying to turn the Union flanks at Gettysburg in July, he tried a frontal assault—"Pickett's charge"—that was virtually annihilated by the Army of the Potomac under General George G. Meade. As a result of this defeat, Lee was thereafter confined to the strategic defensive.

Lee fought a steadily losing battle against the vastly greater numbers and better-equipped troops of General Ulysses S. Grant's armies in the Wilderness Campaign during the spring of 1864. Lee's men, inspired largely by his towering leadership, stopped every bloody assault, but Lee was obliged to retreat each time, lest the larger Union forces turn his flank and cut him off from Richmond. As a result, Lee withdrew into the defenses of that city and adjacent Petersburg, to withstand what turned out to be a nine-month-long siege. Near its end, in February, 1865, he was finally made general in chief of all Confederate armies. It was, by this time, too late. He placed Johnston in command of the only other remaining major army, in the Carolinas, then, in April, attempted to escape a fresh Union offensive at Petersburg to link up with Johnston. Grant cut him off at Appomattox Court House in Virginia, where Lee surrendered on April 9, effectively ending the Civil War. His three sons were with him, two of them major generals, one a captain.

Having lost his home at Arlington, which became the national cemetery, Lee assumed the presidency of Washington College at Lexington, Virginia, in October, 1865. For the next five years, in weakened health, he served effectively not only as a college administrator but also as a quiet symbol of reunion and restoration, burying the passions of the wartime bitterness and thereby setting an example for the defeated South. Following his death, the college was renamed Washington and Lee in his honor.

Summary

Robert E. Lee became a legend in his own time, first to the embattled peoples of the South and, eventually, to the nation at large. He symbolized the plain fact that, rather than treason, the cause of the Confederacy had represented the playing out of the final contradiction of the American nation. North and South, geographically, economically, and socially distinct, could no longer coexist within the fabric of the Constitution. The Southern plantation aristocracy, agrarian and founded upon slavery, had become an anachronism in the modern, industrialized Western world. Its ultimate survival could be obtained only by arms, in which contest Lee had been the supreme champion. His stately character, bearing, and professionalism represented the ideal of Southern society. Though he had opposed slavery, secession, and even war as a final political solution, like so many of his generation, he had had to make the tragic, fateful decision to stand by his neighbors in defense of the only way of life they knew. In defeat, he accepted the course of history without rancor.

The contrast between Lee's conduct and that of his Union counterparts reflected the great shift in social values marked by the Civil War. He ordered his troops to abstain from plundering civilian property, failing to understand—unlike Grant, William T. Sherman, and Philip H. Sheridan—that the modern war which they were all waging was a harbinger of a new age of mass conflict, aimed at breaking civilian resistance with the use of modern industrialized machine weapons, thus destroying the very socioeconomic institutions of an enemy. No better example of the adage that the Civil War was the last great war between gentlemen could be found than in the person of Robert E. Lee himself, the perfect gentleman of the long-past Age of Reason that had spawned his noble family.

His achievements on the field of battle, however, established Lee as one of the greatest army commanders in history. Not merely an inspiring leader, he made correct, informed judgments about his enemy, then struck decisively. As a theater strategist defending his beloved Virginia, he became a master of the mobile feint, thanks largely to several able lieutenants. Stonewall Jackson's fast-moving so-called foot cavalry thrust into the Shenandoah Valley to draw away troops from McClellan during the Peninsular Campaign. J. E. B. Stuart's cavalry rode circles around the Union armies in every campaign. Yet both these men were killed, in 1863 and 1864, respectively. Jubal A. Early's drive up the valley the latter year might have succeeded but for the determined riposte of Grant and Sheridan. In grand strategy, however, Lee was not adept, having misjudged Union intentions along the South Atlantic coast early in the war and never having the authority to mastermind Confederate fortunes until near the end of the struggle. Nor did he attempt to influence Davis beyond the Virginia theater.

Still, had Lee not been outnumbered most of the time, one can only conjecture what might have been the outcome of the war: As a tactician, he had no match in the Union army. The fatal flaw lay in the nature of the Confederacy itself, a politically loose grouping of rebelling states, devoid of effective central leadership. After Gettysburg, observed one of Lee's generals on the eve of Appomattox, the men had been fighting simply for him.

Bibliography

Connelly, Thomas L. *The Marble Man: Robert E. Lee and His Image in American Society.* New York: Knopf, 1977. An excellent interpretative analysis of Lee's reputation as a Southern and national hero during and since the Civil War.

Dowdey, Clifford. *Lee.* London: Gollancz, and Boston: Little Brown, 1965. The best one-volume treatment of Lee's career, adding new materials and interpretations of Lee's performance at Gettysburg.

Flood, Charles Bracelen. *Lee: The Last Years.* Boston: Houghton Mifflin, 1981. The best analysis of Lee's actions and achievements during the last five years of his life, including his reactions to the late war.

Freeman, Douglas Southall. *Lee's Lieutenants.* 3 vols. New York: Scribner, 1942-1944. A masterwork of Lee's subordinate commanders, revealing his inability to disagree with them, notably James Longstreet.

———. *R. E. Lee.* 4 vols. New York and London: Scribner, 1934-1935. The definitive biography, which dissects Lee's career with such detail and careful interpretation as to become the standard work for all students of Lee.

Gallagher, Gary W., ed. *Lee the Soldier.* Lincoln: University of Nebraska Press, 1996. Covers all facets of Lee's military leadership. Includes essays, unpublished accounts of campaigns by Lee himself, an annotated bibliography, and a section emphasizing Gettysburg.

Johnson, Robert Underwood, and Clarence Clough Buel, eds. *Battles and Leaders of the Civil War.* 4 vols. New York: Century, 1887. The most comprehensive and reliable source of reminiscences of key Civil War leaders, including many of Lee's subordinates and opponents, with complete lists of the opposing armies and navies, down to the regimental and ship level. Excellent maps and illustrations.

Lee, Robert E. *Recollections and Letters of General Robert E. Lee by His Son Capt. Robert E. Lee.* New York: Doubleday, 1905. An invaluable memoir, especially useful for insights into Lee's family relationships.

———. *The Wartime Papers of R. E. Lee.* Edited by Clifford Dowdey and Louis Manarin. Boston: Little Brown, 1961. Primary source material drawn from official records and private sources which offer insights into Lee's character and abilities as a commander.

Long, Armistead L. *Memoirs of Robert E. Lee.* New York: Stoddart, and London: Sampson Low, Marston, 1886. Perhaps the best of many postwar reminiscences by officers under Lee's command, Long having served on his staff and as a commander of artillery.

Sanborn, Margaret. *Robert E. Lee*. 2 vols. Philadelphia: Lippincott, 1966-1967. A sound popular history based on the usual abundant primary and secondary sources.

Thomas, Emory M. *Robert E. Lee: A Biography*. New York: Norton, 1995. A balanced, fair, and personal account of Lee's life.

Clark G. Reynolds

ÉTIENNE LENOIR

Born: January 12, 1822; Mussy-la-Ville, Belgium
Died: August 4, 1900; La Varenne-Saint-Hilaire, France
Areas of Achievement: Invention and technology
Contribution: Lenoir invented a number of useful processes and devices, the most famous being an internal-combustion engine. The quality and significance of his engine are still matters of controversy, but there is little doubt that it stimulated the efforts of the other pioneers of internal-combustion-engine design.

Early Life

Although born in the French-speaking region of Belgium, Étienne Lenoir spent all of his productive life in France. He went to his adopted country at the age of sixteen in 1838 to begin work as a metal enameler. Within a few years, he had several inventions to his credit. In 1847, he patented an enameling process, in 1851 an electroforming process, in 1853 an electric-railway brake, and in 1865 an automatic telegraph that printed messages on a ribbon of paper. This telegraph was thus a forerunner of the ticker-tape machine. On January 24, 1860, he received a patent for his most famous invention—an internal-combustion engine.

Interest in internal-combustion engines was as old as the discovery of atmospheric pressure in the seventeenth century. Experiments and demonstrations that showed the power of atmospheric pressure working against or into a vacuum inspired a number of people to imagine an engine that could be powered by having atmospheric pressure drive a piston into a vacuum chamber. The difficulty in creating such an engine was in producing the vacuum—not once, but in rapid succession, since the piston must have continuous up-and-down motion. An obvious solution was to use gunpowder to burn the air in a chamber and to create a vacuum by allowing the resulting gas to cool. Christiaan Huygens actually constructed such engines, but they were impractical because of the incompleteness of the vacuum. The solution was the steam engine, as steam could drive the air from a chamber without an explosion and then be reduced to only one seventeen-hundredth of its original volume when converted to water.

There were suggestions for engines' employing heated air rather than steam in the late eighteenth century, and some were in use by the end of the century. The real impetus for an internal-combustion engine came, however, from the work of Sadi Carnot in the 1820's. Among the ideas about thermodynamics that Carnot established was the concept of a heat engine. He demonstrated that a steam engine was basically inefficient, because little of the heat produced to power it was actually used. He believed that an air engine would be much more efficient because more heat could be utilized.

By the time Lenoir appeared in Paris, the idea of an internal-combustion engine was widespread and a number had been built, but none proved practical enough to be offered commercially. In addition to the familiarity of the idea, the stage was further set for Lenoir by the ready availability of natural gas for the gas lighting that was becoming common in Paris.

Life's Work

Lenoir's gas engine was the first internal-combustion engine practical enough to be offered for sale

in significant numbers. It ran on the natural gas piped into factories and businesses for lighting purposes or distillates of petroleum similar to modern gasoline. In 1897, Lenoir claimed in *France Automobile* that he used the engine to power a vehicle of some sort—probably a farm cart—for several trips between Joinville-le-Pont and Paris in 1863. The Automobile Club of France conducted an investigation in 1900 and concluded that he had made the world's first automobile trip in May, 1862, between Paris and Vincennes. It has been observed that the discrepancy in dates is rather suspicious. These claims came at a time when there was controversy about who had invented the automobile, involving French and German inventors as well as their champions. Even if one assumes that Lenoir powered a vehicle with an internal-combustion engine in 1862 or 1863, it was hardly more than a publicity stunt similar to the motorboat trips made on the Seine using his engine. He did nothing to develop a practical horseless carriage for his own use or for sale.

Although his engine was sold commercially and, in that sense, may be regarded as a success, there have been questions about the importance of his accomplishment. The most telling criticism of his work is that he did not understand the fundamental requirement for a truly successful internal-combustion engine, namely that the gas must be compressed before firing. A further complaint is that he thought of his engine as nothing more than an advanced steam engine. In his patent application he stated:

> My engine cannot be classed among gas engines. Indeed, the functions of the gas I employ do not consist in detonating or exploding it, thereby impelling the piston, as this has heretofore been done or suggested, but in the use of gas as a fuel that can be instantaneously and regularly ignited, and without producing any shock, for the purpose of heating the air that is mixed with it. The air thus dilated or expanded will act on the piston in the same manner as steam would in ordinary steam engines.

Despite his patent claims to have produced a gas engine unlike others, a company advertising brochure of 1864 pointed out that his engine was closely linked to those of previous inventors. It was stated that the Lenoir engine used Robert Street's piston with Philippe Lebon's double action, an ignition like that of Isaac de Rivas, and a cooling system similar to Samuel Brown's. Perhaps these claims and denials, as well as the similarity in appearance of the engine to stationary steam engines,

were meant to reassure a buying public dubious about the idea of gas explosions.

Whether owing to the conservative buying habits of potential customers, design inadequacies, or both, the engine was not a commercial success. Lenoir had done engineering work for Gautier and Company of Paris and apparently convinced its proprietors of the merits of his design. This company backed him in forming the Société des Moteurs Lenoir in 1859. Some four thousand stocks were issued in the new company but no dividends appear ever to have been paid. The Parisian Gas Company took control of the engine in 1863 and paid Lenoir a pension in his old age.

Most of the engines were built under license from Lenoir's company. The Reading Iron Works in England built about one hundred. Two German companies built some, and the Lenoir Gas Engine Company of New York sold some at a cost of five hundred dollars for the half horsepower model and fifteen hundred dollars for the four horsepower version. The Marinoni and Lefebvre companies of Paris produced more than any of the foreign manufacturers, but, all told, fewer than five hundred were made.

The Lenoir engine resembled a stationary, double-acting, horizontal steam engine. With power being produced on each side of the piston, it was, in effect, the equivalent of a two-cylinder engine. Sliding valves connected to the crankshaft by rods that covered and uncovered ports to admit fuel and exhaust-spent fumes. The ignition system was electric. A battery provided power to an induction coil with a vibrating contact to provide a primary spark, and a sliding distributor alternated delivery of current between the two spark plugs. The electrical system was changed at least twice, as it never worked satisfactorily. The final version used a rotary distributor with the rotor driven by the crankshaft. An unusual feature by comparison with later engines was that air and gas were admitted to the combustion chamber separately. This was the basis of Lenoir's claim that he had not produced an ordinary gas engine. He believed that the air should remain separate from the gas, at least in part, to provide a cushion between the explosion of gas and the piston head. Unfortunately, the exhaust ports opened before the expansion was complete, and much of the heat produced was lost to the cooling water in violation of Carnot's principles. The loss of heat also meant that there were problems with overheating and that a huge radiator was necessary. The company suggested a radiator capacity of one hundred gallons for the half horsepower model.

The engine was uneconomical for industrial applications. It consumed about one hundred feet of gas per hour in the half horsepower model, and it had maintenance problems. Overheating caused the valves to stick, there was no self-contained means of recharging the batteries, and the spark plugs required frequent cleaning. Later versions of this type of engine, such as that of Pierre Hugon, provided for the injection of a spray of water into the cylinder to help in cooling, but the improvement was not enough to rescue the design. A steam engine of comparable size was as economical to operate and much less troublesome.

Carnot had observed that the most obvious way to produce a great change of temperature, as required in an efficient engine, was to compress the air used in the engine. Since compression was the key to success, Lenoir's noncompressing engine was out of production by the late 1860's, but he tried again in the 1880's with a four-cycle compression engine. It had poppet valves and other advances over his earlier model, including a 300 percent improvement in fuel consumption rates. This engine was produced for a while by the Mignon and Rouart Company.

Lenoir made no substantial profits from any of his inventions, but he did receive several honors. For his engine, he received a prize at the London Exposition of 1862 and several French prizes including that of the Marquis d'Argenteuil, which brought him twelve thousand francs, in 1886. His most prestigious award was the Legion of Honor, which he received in 1881 for the invention of the teletype machine in 1865. He died in relative obscurity and poverty in 1900.

Summary

Even if Étienne Lenoir had not built an engine, his teletype machine and other inventions would have gained for him a respectable place in the story of modern technological development. It is, however, his production of the first commercial engine and, especially, his connection with the automobile, that has brought him more attention than the other engine designers who were his contemporaries. He was not the first to build an internal-combustion engine. In fact, by his own admission, his design depended almost entirely on the work of predecessors. Several hundred of his engines were built and

sold, but, by all accounts, they were not very suitable. It is on the automobile connection that his fame primarily rests.

Assessment of Lenoir's achievements is made difficult by the controversies surrounding the invention of the automobile. As indicated, national pride and the championing of personal favorites has made this a hotly debated subject. Moreover, the difficulty in defining exactly what constitutes the first automobile probably means that there will never be a clear ranking of its inventors.

The claims and counterclaims in France and Germany as to who invented the automobile brought some attention to Lenoir at the end of his life, but it was the Selden Patent Case that did the most to bring him to the attention of the English-speaking world. George Baldwin Selden obtained a United States patent on automobiles in 1895. Although he never built any automobiles, the Association of Licensed Automobile Manufacturers was formed to exploit the patent by selling the right to manufacture to other companies. Henry Ford challenged the patent, and in the subsequent trials, which lasted from 1903 to 1911, the Ford Company maintained that Selden's patent was invalid because practical automobiles predated the patent by a number of years. A significant part of the Ford case was the claim that Lenoir had constructed an automobile in 1860. The Ford lawyers cited an article describing a self-propelled vehicle built by Lenoir that appeared in the June 16, 1860, edition of *Le Monde illustré*. There is no other evidence that this vehicle was ever built. Even Lenoir never claimed that he had built an automobile as early as 1860. The claims made for and by him in the late 1890's were also placed into evidence. When the Selden attorneys imported British experts to deny that an automobile could be powered by a non-compressing engine, the Ford Company actually built a copy of Lenoir's engine and used it to drive a Ford automobile. The attention drawn to Lenoir's name in this case has done much to establish him in the list of automobile pioneers.

Whatever one's opinion about Lenoir's importance as an inventor of the automobile, his engine stimulated the production of better engines and, ultimately, automobiles. All the pioneers of automobile design studied his engine. Those uninterested in automobiles were encouraged to build better stationary engines for industrial use, and Lenoir played a significant role in the transition from the age of steam to the age of oil.

Bibliography

Bishop, Charles W. *La France et l'automobile*. Paris: Librairies-Techniques, 1971. Gives considerable space to advocating Lenoir's importance and priority in developing engines and automobiles. The author carefully explains the invalidity of all complaints made against Lenoir or his engine. He is convinced that Lenoir invented the automobile and that others, such as Carl Benz and Gottlieb Daimler, were inspired by his inventions.

Cardwell, D. S. L. *From Watt to Clausius: The Rise of Thermodynamics in the Early Industrial Revolution*. London: Heinemann, and Ithaca, N.Y.: Cornell University Press, 1971. Gives the early history of the effort to develop an efficient heat engine.

Cummins, C. Lyle, Jr. *Internal Fire: The Internal Combustion Engine*. Rev. ed. Warrendale, Pa.: Society of Automotive Engineers, 1989. This is a history of the internal-combustion engine. Although Lenoir's work is covered only in a portion of one chapter, it is one of the best accounts of his activities in English. Contains technical details, graphs, and illustrations of the engine.

Field, D. C. "Internal Combustion Engines." In *A History of Technology*, edited by Charles Singer et al., vol. 5. London and New York: Oxford University Press, 1958. Details the general development of the internal-combustion engine and dismisses the value of Lenoir's engine except for the observation that its limited commercial appeal encouraged others to attempt improvements.

Mott-Smith, Morton. *The Concept of Energy Simply Explained*. New York: Dover, 1964. Presents the concepts of heat engines as well as major scientists who have dealt with the subject and their theories. Contains very little mathematics, and the author does a good job of explaining theories simply without being simplistic.

Philip Dwight Jones

LEO XIII

Vincenzo Gioacchino Pecci

Born: March 2, 1810; Carpineto Romano, Italy

Died: July 20, 1903; Rome, Italy

Areas of Achievement: Religion and church reform

Contribution: Leo XIII, considered to be one of the greatest leaders of the Roman Catholic church during a period of crisis, tried to maintain the strength and power of the Church in a world changing through industry, colonization, and governmental upheaval. The fact that he was not always successful is not as significant as the fact that he was a pioneer, aware of the needs of the modern Roman Catholic church.

Early Life

Leo XIII was born Vincenzo Gioacchino Pecci in the hills south of Rome in Carpineto Romano, in central Italy. His parents, Colonel Ludovico Pecci and Anna Prosperi Buzi, were patrician, but neither wealthy nor of great nobility. The sixth in a family of seven children, Pecci began his education in Viterbo at the Jesuit college from 1818 to 1824. He was a brilliant student, with what became lifelong scholarly achievement in Latin. He continued his studies in Rome from 1824 to 1832 at the Roman College and in 1832 was admitted to the Academy of the Noble Ecclesiastics. He completed his religious studies at the University of the Sapienza between 1832 and 1837, concentrating in theology and civil and canon law. He was ordained in 1837.

In the same year, he was appointed a domestic prelate, and in 1838 he was named governor or apostolic delegate of Benevento by Pope Gregory XVI, who had praised Pecci's courageous service during the cholera epidemic of 1837. His success in this position, especially in reducing banditry and eliminating the inroads being made by liberals, led to his appointment in 1841 to the same position in Perugia. While this area had similar problems to solve, Pecci went beyond his previous successes and improved the economy by building roads, establishing a farmers' savings bank, and gaining great popularity among the residents.

With these achievements, Pecci was sent to Belgium as nuncio, the pope's representative, in January, 1843, after having been consecrated titular Archbishop of Damietta. Pecci spent three difficult years in Belgium, which finally ended when

King Leopold requested of the pope that Pecci be recalled. The king and his Prime Minister Nothomb had been seeking to confer the right to name members of the university juries to the government. In this matter, crucial to the educational system of Belgium, Pecci sided with the bishops and Catholic politicians in opposition to the king. Even though the Catholic side won, the victory was empty for Pecci. While this period appears to have been a failure, Pecci gained experience that helped form his future conservatism. During this time, his only extended observation of the more industrialized, liberal areas of Europe, he saw the behavior of a liberal political regime toward Catholics and learned to oppose it. As he fought against unionism, the compromise and agreement between Catholics and moderate liberals in Belgium, he came to be wary of liberal hands extended in compromise.

Life's Work

When Pecci left Belgium, he returned to Perugia, where he served as archbishop until 1878 and further solidified many of the ideologies which would serve him during his pontificate. Along with his brother Joseph, a Jesuit seminary professor, he worked to increase the numbers of clerics; modernize the curriculum at the seminaries; revive Thomism, the medieval Scholasticism based on the Aristotelianism of Thomas Aquinas; and establish the Academy of Saint Thomas in 1859. As a result of these activities, Pecci was named a cardinal in 1853.

During the period that he was archbishop in Perugia, Pecci was politically prudent and reserved. He protested the annexation of Perugia by the kingdom of Sardinia in 1860; on the other hand, he would not join Cardinal Giacomo Antonelli, the Secretary of State to Pope Pius IX, in his methods of government and involvement in conflicts. Consequently, Antonelli considered Pecci an enemy and kept him from Rome. Following his moderate views as a Catholic, Pecci wrote his pastoral letters of 1874-1877, recommending that the Catholic church make conciliatory gestures toward contemporary society. Self-evident as it may seem, he recognized that the Church did not exist in a void, but rather in the quickly changing world of the late nineteenth century. These letters, in addition to his other achievements, gained for him the respect of Pius, and, when Antonelli died in 1877, Pecci was summoned to serve as camerlengo in the Roman curia, the chamberlain who oversees the Church when the pope dies.

When Pius died in 1878, Pecci was in a good position to be elected pope. Since this was the first conclave since the Holy See had lost its temporal power, Pecci's role as the leading moderate was important. He was indeed elected on the third ballot with forty-four of the sixty-one votes, after having received a plurality on the first ballot of nineteen votes, thirteen more than the second most favored candidate.

When he became Pope Leo XIII, Pecci was sixty-eight years old and in fragile health. These facts, combined with his delicate appearance, all indicated that his would be, at best, a brief transitional appointment. Yet he was popular. Because the Italian government feared demonstrations in his support in St. Peter's Square and all over Rome, his crowning took place in private on March 3 in the Sistine chapel so that he would not appear publicly on the loggia to bless the people as he wished to do.

His acts on the evening of his coronation, however, foreshadowed the theme of Leo's reign: He wrote letters to the German emperor, the Swiss president, and the Russian czar announcing his election and offering hope that the Church might come to better accord with their governments. While doctrinally conservative, he sought to maintain a strong role for the Church in the modern world.

In the course of his papacy, Leo wrote numerous encyclicals on subjects ranging from traditional piety to social issues. He wrote eleven encyclicals to the Blessed Virgin Mary and the Rosary, two each to the Eucharist and the redemptive work of Christ, and one to the renewal of the Franciscan Third Order. In the Jubilee Year of 1900, he consecrated the entire human race to the Sacred Heart of Jesus, an initiative begun by Pius, and in 1893 instituted a feast of the Holy Family. Becoming more conservative in the final few years or his life, he published new norms for censorship in 1897 and a new Index in 1900, and he set up a permanent Biblical Commission in 1902 after writing the encyclical to Bible study, *Providentissimus Deus* (1893; *On the Study of the Scriptures*, 1894).

That Leo was able to align such conservative piety to a new recognition of modern states is quite remarkable. It was accomplished, however, not with statements of accord with government, but rather, with statements only of recognition. In 1878, the year of his coronation, Leo attacked socialism, communism, and nihilism in *Quod apostolici muneris* (*Concerning Modern Errors, Socialism, Communism, Nihilism*, 1895), and, in 1884, he wrote similarly on Freemasonry. He also acted to increase centralization within the Church, much to the disappointment of progressives. At the same time, however, he wrote encyclicals to the relationship of the Church to sociopolitical order: *Diuturnum illud* (1881; *On Civil Government*, 1942) recognized the existence of democracy in God's world; *Immortale Dei* (1885; *On the Christian Constitution of States*, 1885) defined the spiritual and temporal spheres of power; and *Libertas praestantissimum* (1888; *Human Liberty*, 1895) viewed the Church as the true source of liberty. Most important was *Rerum novarum* (1891; *The Condition of Labor*, 1891), which advocated private property rights, fair wages, workers' rights, and trade unionism, while, predictably, condemning socialism and economic liberalism. Because of the positions presented in this encyclical, Leo came to be known as "the workers' pope."

In addition to these, Leo wrote encyclicals to social and intellectual issues. *Arcanum divinae sapientia* (1880; *On Christian Marriage*, 1880) is a highly conservative statement on marriage, identical in tone and thought to writings of his predecessors. On intellectual matters, however, he was more open to new ideas than the revival of old ones. Following his lifelong respect for and study of Thomism, he encouraged Catholics to incorporate fully Thomist metaphysics into Catholic philosophy in *Aeterni patris* (1879; *Scholastic Philosophy*, 1879). Leo also bridged the gap between Catholicism and the natural sciences by encouraging Catholics to study astronomy and the other natural sciences. He urged complete objectivity in all areas of scholarship done by Catholics; in an unprecedented ecumenical spirit, he opened the Vatican libraries to scholars of all faiths in 1883. This was begun in 1879, when he allowed the German historian Ludwig Pastor access to the secret archives of the Vatican.

In many ways, Leo was a far more political pope than was his successor, yet while he and his four secretaries of state had many diplomatic successes, he failed in matters closest to home, such as the achievement of accord with the Italian government. By 1887, Leo was willing to accept a compromise in which Italy would be entirely unified under the House of Savoy; the Papal States, a sixteen-thousand-square-mile area in central Italy, would be given to Italy; and an indemnification or compensation therefore, offered under the Law of Guarantee, would be received from Italy. The Italian government, however, wanted the abdication of the pope's sovereignty, which would lead inevitably to limited freedom for Leo himself and future popes. He made a counterrequest for a repeal of the anticlerical laws and restoration of papal rule for Rome, but it was denied. Thus, Leo was unable to achieve any resolution of conflict with the Italian government. None, indeed, was attained until the Lateran Treaty of 1929.

France, too, presented problems for the pope. With its republican government, France sought the separation of church and state and secular, social, and educational systems. Catholics within France were not enthusiastic in their support for the Church against their government. Soon, government recognition of all religious groups was required or the groups were to be disbanded. In 1880, the Jesuits

were dissolved, followed in 1900 by the Congregation of the Assumptionists. Teaching orders went into exile, and the pope was unable to turn the tide, which became a crisis for his successor, Pius X.

Relations with England remained unchanged. At the beginning of his reign, Leo initiated a study seeking possible reconciliation with the Anglican church. When such a unification proved impossible, he issued an apostolic letter in 1896, discouraging any move in this direction; yet he was responsible for the cardinalship of John Henry Newman in 1878.

Leo actively sought a reunion with the Oriental and Slavic Catholic churches, going so far as to praise the work of Saint Cyril and Saint Methodius in the encyclical *Grande munus* (1880) and to discuss rites and reunion in the apostolic letter of 1894. Again, he was unable to make concrete advances in this direction.

More satisfactory were Leo's efforts in Belgium, Germany, and Russia. He negotiated agreements with Belgium in 1884 and with Russia in 1894. In 1886-1887, he successfully achieved the repeal of the anticlerical laws in Germany (the Kulturkampf) and, in his sole diplomatic success, he mediated in Germany's dispute with Spain over the possession of the Caroline Islands in the Pacific Ocean in 1885. He was, however, unsuccessful in his attempt to keep Germany and Austria from joining Italy in the Triple Alliance in 1887. Nor was he invited to the Hague Peace Conference of 1899, because of the intransigence of the Italian government.

In other areas of the world Leo recognized the importance of colonialism to Christian evangelism, and he approved 248 sees, forty-eight vicarates or prefectures, and two patriarchates in Scotland, North Africa, India, Japan, and the United States. Although he criticized "Americanism," which would have attempted to modernize Catholicism, in a letter of 1899, he named the first apostolic delegate to the United States in 1892.

The twenty-five years of Leo's reign ended in 1903 with his death at the age of ninety-three. He far exceeded expectations in the longevity, the social concern, and the intellectual strength of his service to the Church.

Summary

It was fortunate for the Catholic church that Leo XIII became the pope when the Western world was experiencing great turmoil. A brilliant man, he was able to steer the Church into a role in society which at once showed an awareness of the modern world but did not stray far from traditional church doctrine. The English writer Thomas Carlyle called him a great "reconciler of differences." Leo's was a strong voice against the growing popularity of socialism in Europe; yet he accepted democracy and advocated the rights of workers in the growing industrialized world. Within his own church, he was able to create a clear role of spiritual leadership for the pope to replace the recently lost temporal powers of the Papacy. While some scholars consider his learning antiquated, restricted, and perhaps obsessively concerned with Thomism, his intellectual breadth, strength of character, and devotion to service have brought him great praise. Even with his many failures, he is generally considered the greatest pope in three hundred years. Leo said of himself, "I want to set the church so far forward that my successor will not be able to turn back." As a pioneer whose ideas shone even more brightly after his death, he clearly achieved this goal.

Bibliography

Bokenkotter, Thomas. "Social Catholicism and Christian Democracy." In *A Concise History of the Catholic Church*. New York: Doubleday, 1927. A scholarly and detailed narrative of the political world into which Leo was thrust at his ordination. Leo's charitable piety is shown as it affected the changing governments and economies of the entire Western world.

Fortin, Ernest L. " 'Sacred and Inviolable': 'Rerum Novarum' and Natural Rights." *Theological Studies* 53, no. 2 (June 1992). Examines Pope Leo XII's encyclical "Rerum novarum," of 1891, which views the right to private property as "sacred and inviolable," a concept incompatible with the premodern thought Leo advocated in the encyclical.

Gargan, Edward T., ed. *Leo XIII and the Modern World*. New York: Sheed and Ward, 1961. A series of nine essays by various scholars preceded by an introductory essay and followed by an extensive bibliography on Leo and his period in history. The essays stress Leo's theological contributions, especially as a Thomist, and his impact on the European and American political worlds of the late nineteenth century.

Lefevere, Patricia. "Anglicans, Catholics Discuss Holy Orders; Centenary of Leo's Bull Brings No Rejoicing." *National Catholic Reporter* 31, no. 28 (May 12, 1995). Reports on the efforts of an Episcopalian/Catholic coalition working for the repeal of Pope Leo XIII's "Apostolicae Curae," which bars the Catholic Church from recognizing the ordination of Anglican clergy.

McCabe, Joseph. "Leo XIII." In *Crises in the History of the Papacy*. New York and London: Putnam, 1916. An objective appraisal of the life and accomplishments of Leo, which assesses him as the best pope in three hundred years but a failure in gaining influence upon the thoughts or actions of Western society.

Miller, J. Martin. *The Life of Pope Leo XIII*. Philadelphia: National Publishing, 1903. A five-hundred-page biography written in praise of Leo that was begun before his death, containing several drawings and photographs. The author writes conversationally and quaintly, quoting letters and relating anecdotes in dialogue. His purpose is the veneration of Leo and nearly one-third of the book is devoted to a detailed description of Leo's final illness and death.

Wallace, Lillian Parker. *Leo XIII and the Rise of Socialism*. Durham, N.C.: Duke University Press, 1966. A presentation of the juxtaposition of two major antagonistic ideologies of the nineteenth century, held on the one side by Leo and his church and on the other by Karl Marx and his followers. This 464-page volume shows Leo's power as he stems the tide of Marxism in Europe with his intellectual and compassionate approach to the social problems of the industrial world.

Vicki Robinson

MIKHAIL LERMONTOV

Born: October 15, 1814; Moscow, Russia
Died: July 27, 1841; Pyatigorsk, Russia
Area of Achievement: Literature
Contribution: Lermontov left an impressive legacy as a poet during the Russian Romantic period, writing both lyric and narrative verse of lasting significance. He was also a dramatist and a novelist whose major work, *A Hero of Our Time*, presaged the great realistic psychological novels of Leo Tolstoy and Fyodor Dostoevski.

Early Life

Mikhail Yuryevich Lermontov's father was a poor army officer, the descendant of a Scottish mercenary who had come to Russia in the early seventeenth century. He claimed relation to the twelfth century Scottish bard known as Thomas the Rhymer. A major success in his life was his marriage to seventeen-year-old Marya Arsenieva, the only daughter of the widowed Elizaveta Arsenieva, a member of the rich and powerful Stolypin family and the owner of a large estate, Tarkhany, in central Russia.

The death of Marya Lermontova in 1817, when the future poet was only three years of age, caused a one-sided power struggle for his custody between his grandmother and his father. Elizaveta Arsenieva desperately wanted to keep her young grandson in her household. She threatened to disinherit the child should he be removed from her and promised his disfavored father both money and the forgiveness of a previous debt if he would leave young Mikhail with her. Yury Lermontov therefore surrendered his son's custody and had only sporadic or indirect contact with him thereafter.

Lermontov's grandmother showered attention on the precocious boy. She hired foreign tutors, who taught him French and gave him the rudiments of Greek and Latin. He was given music lessons so that he was later able to compose tunes to accompany his own lyrics and was able to impress his contemporaries with his ability on the piano and on the violin. He was encouraged to draw and to paint, taking lessons from the artists A. S. Solonitsky and P. E. Zabolotsky, and his talent was so developed that his graphic oeuvre, consisting of more than four hundred oil paintings, aquarelles, sketches, and caricatures, is roundly praised by modern critics. It was Lermontov's early love of poetry, however, that was most thoroughly in-

dulged. Having read Vasily Zhukovsky's translations of George Gordon, Lord Byron's verse, he desired to learn English so that he could read Byron's work in the original. Thus, when Lermontov was in his teens, a special tutor was engaged to impart this knowledge to him.

In addition to a remarkable home education, young Mikhail Lermontov received the benefit of three exciting journeys, made at ages three, five, and ten, to the Caucasus Mountains in the extreme south of Russia. The reasons for these journeys were both to avoid imminent visits at the Tarkhany estate by his father and to bolster his precarious health. Rheumatic fever and measles left him very frail, and he developed a stoop-shouldered posture and sickly pallor, which later caused him considerable ridicule from his schoolmates, who nicknamed him "the frog."

The spectacular scenery and the unsubjugated tribes of the Caucasus Mountains made a lasting impression on Lermontov, an impression of adventure and romance in an exotic locale which found its way into many of his later works, both poetry and prose. He gained there an appreciation for freedom as an ideal apart from that of civilization, which he came to regard as corrupt.

In 1827, Arsenieva moved with Mikhail to Moscow. The next year, she enrolled him in an elite preparatory school attached to Moscow State University, the Nobles' Pensionate, which employed a number of prominent university professors as faculty. There, Lermontov read and discussed the works of such contemporary Russian poets as Zhukovsky, Konstantin Batyushkov, and especially Alexander Pushkin, whose work Lermontov zealously admired. During this period, Lermontov began his own literary activity, having one of his poems accepted for publication by the journal *Atheneum* in 1830. Thereafter, he wrote almost continually, entering into his notebooks epigrams, commentary, drafts of a drama, and a number of lyrics on nature, death, and love.

Life's Work

In 1830, Lermontov enrolled in Moscow University's department of ethics and politics, from which he soon transferred to the department of literature. His classmates in the university included a constellation of later luminaries of Russian social and political dissidence: Vissarion Belinsky, the social lit-

erary critic; Aleksandr Herzen, the seminal socialist thinker and editor of radical émigré publications; Nikolai Stankevich, the social philosopher and organizer of radical salons; and Ivan Goncharov, the prominent novelist. Lermontov, however, held himself aloof from these future stars, regarding himself as superior not only to them but to the faculty as well. He took part in one major scandal, in which an unpopular professor was driven out of the classroom, and he quarreled with one of his examination committees severely enough that, in 1832, he left the university, intending to move to the capital and to enroll at St. Petersburg University. The paperwork required by such a transfer was more than Lermontov's patience could endure, however, and he instead enlisted in the army—a move unpleasantly surprising to his grandmother, who used her influence to have him enrolled in the School of Ensigns of the Guards and Cavalry Cadets.

The literary production of Lermontov's university years is highlighted by the remarkable poem "Angel," which evokes the blissful prenatal memories of an earthbound soul. Prominent also is "Parus" ("The Sail"), in which Lermontov gives a symbolic

portrait of a revolutionary. It is at this time too that Lermontov began his ten years of work on the romantic narrative poem "Demon," which remained unpublished in his lifetime as the result of censorship. A fallen angel's love for a mortal woman is related amid sparkling descriptions of Caucasian natural splendor. The university years also produced a cycle of poems connected with Lermontov's unreturned love for a young woman.

In the army, Lermontov tried to find acceptance among his fellow cadets by posturing as a daredevil and a womanizer. The highly affected social life of St. Petersburg increased his cynicism and his bitterness at his intellectual estrangement from his compatriots. He did pen some ribald songs and some bawdy verse but for the most part turned his attention to drama and prose. The best of his five plays, *Maskarad* (1842; *Masquerade*, 1973), reflects, through his moody villain Arbenin, his disillusionment with St. Petersburg society. Influenced by the popular prose of Sir Walter Scott, he explored the genre of historical novel by beginning the unfinished *Vadim* (1832-1834; English translation, 1982), a contorted tale of unrequited love intertwined with the historical events of Russia's Pugachov Rebellion of 1773-1774. This work signaled the beginnings of Lermontov's work in prose, which continued through the unfinished society novel *Knyaginya Ligovskaya* (1836; *Princess Ligovskaya*, 1965) to the maturity of his masterpiece, *Geroy nashego vremeni* (1840; *A Hero of Our Time*, 1854). Before he was commissioned an officer in Czar Nicholas I's Life Guard Hussars in 1834, Lermontov began a lifelong attachment to Varvara Lophukhina, the attractive daughter of family friends. Although Lermontov never married, his attachment to Lophukhina survived even her marriage to a man much her senior, of whom Lermontov disapproved. The relationship with her caused him considerable despair, which infused his verse thereafter with a note of brooding melancholy over the impossibility of love and happiness.

Lermontov's poetic response to the death by duel of Pushkin in 1837 earned for him instant fame. His poem "Smert poeta" ("The Death of a Poet") was circulated throughout the St. Petersburg literary salons. It blamed the capital society and its authorities for inciting Pushkin to the duel which caused his death. Largely as a result of this poem, Lermontov was arrested, tried, and sentenced to serve among the frontline troops fighting wild tribesmen in the Caucasus. The intercession of his grandmother and the publication of his patriotic poem about the victory over Napoleon I at Borodino softened the czar's attitude, however, and he was allowed to return to the capital.

The years 1838-1841 found Lermontov at the height of his popularity. His verse frequently appeared in the leading literary journals. It was during this time that his poems "Kazachia kolybelnaia pesnia" ("Cossack Lullaby") and "Vykhozhu odin ya na dorogu . . ." ("I Walk Out Alone onto the Road . . .") were published, providing the lyrics to well-known Russian songs. His Byronesque narrative poem "Mtsyri" ("The Novice") extolls the freedom experienced just before death by a native child pledged as a novice monk by his captors.

In 1840, *A Hero of Our Time* was published in book form. The protagonist, Pechorin, epitomizes the emotional isolation and intellectual frustration of his generation. Pechorin is the archetypical superfluous man later to be found in many Russian literary portrayals. His intellect tells him that he brings others only hardship and tragedy, but he lacks the moral certitude to change his ways. There is much autobiography in Lermontov's depiction of Pechorin, and it is a depiction in which every succeeding generation has found relevance.

A duel with the son of the French ambassador, in which only Lermontov was lightly wounded, caused him to he reassigned by the czar to frontline duty in the Caucasus. Lermontov so distinguished himself in battle that he was recommended for citation. He wrote a poem about the Battle of Valerik. On a self-granted furlough to the spa city of Pyatigorsk, he tormented a former cadet schoolmate, Nikolai Martynov, who challenged him to a duel. Outside the city, at the foot of Mount Mashuk, the duel took place. Martynov shot first, killing Lermontov outright. Thus, before the age of twenty-seven, Lermontov had inherited both Pushkin's literary fame and his personal fate.

Summary

Western evaluations of Mikhail Lermontov's impact on world literature are often confined to discussing the influence of A Hero of Our Time on subsequent novels by Ivan Turgenev, Dostoevski, and Tolstoy, and on the stories of Anton Chekhov and Maxim Gorky, authors whose own influence is better established and more familiar. This discussion focuses on the addition of psychological examination, an inner dialogue of thought, to the realistic portrayal of the characters' actions.

Questions of good and evil are left unresolved, at least in surface interpretations, much as Lermontov left unresolved in the minds of his readers the question of whether his main protagonist, Pechorin, is to be positively or negatively regarded, that is, is he seriously, or only ironically, to be considered a hero of our time? In literature of the previous Romantic period, good characters and evil characters were clearly delineated. In this, Lermontov's work is transitional and therefore important.

Russian evaluators of Lermontov's significance invariably foreground his contributions as a poet. His verse is well woven into the fabric of Russian society. Mothers sing his lullaby to their children. Children sing the words of his patriotic "Borodino" to Modest Mussorgsky's music in school. In a nation of poetry lovers, Lermontov's popularity is unmatched by any poet except Pushkin. Subsequent poets, such as Boris Pasternak, have dedicated works to Lermontov as if he were still alive. The permanence of his poetic legacy stems from the musicality of his verse—the sound of which so pleases the ear that memorization is effortless—and its direct appeal to primary emotions, feelings of love, freedom, and patriotism.

In sum, Lermontov was a person with severe problems relating to others. Early bereft of his parents, spoiled by his guardian, failed in academic credentials, restricted and hampered by authorities, he died before he was truly mature. Yet his desire to find a soul mate, a confidant, became literary in method and, in the power and excellence of his still-developing talent, resulted in lasting achievement.

Bibliography

Eikhenbaum, Boris M. *Lermontov.* Translated by Ray Parrot and Harry Weber. Ann Arbor, Mich.: Ardis, 1981. A seminal study by the renowned Soviet scholar on Lermontov's poetic method, focusing on the literary precedents of his figures of speech. Includes a multitude of citations of poetry from Lermontov's Russian predecessors and contemporaries. A last chapter is included which examines Lermontov's prose in the light of the development of Russian as a literary language.

Kelly, Laurence. *Lermontov: Tragedy in the Caucasus.* London: Constable, 1977; New York: George Braziller, 1978. A biography of Lermontov which delves thoroughly into the influence on Lermontov's work of his time spent in the Caucasus Mountains. Both the childhood trips and the adult military sojourns are well treated. Appendices include treatments of the relationship of Byron and Lermontov, an essay on Lermontov's poetry, and "The Official Report on the Death of Lieutenant Lermontov."

L'Ami, C. E., and Alexander Welikotny. *Michael Lermontov: Biography and Translation*. Winnipeg, Canada: University of Manitoba Press, 1967. An older-style biography, replete with the reminiscences of Lermontov's contemporaries as to his character. A general outline of Russian history forms a significant part of this treatment. The second part of the book contains more than one hundred of Lermontov's poems in rhymed English translation as well as a small sample of prose.

Lavrin, Janko. *Lermontov*. London: Bowes and Bowes, and New York: Hillary House, 1959. The first widely available biographical treatment of Lermontov in English, introducing the reader not only to the personage of Lermontov but also to Russian history and Russian society of the early nineteenth century. Lermontov is seen as a key link in the historical development of Russian literature between the imitative eighteenth century and the world-leading literature of Russia's nineteenth century. Alexander Pushkin's influence is thoroughly treated.

Lermontov, Mikhail. *Major Poetical Works*. Translated with a biographical sketch, commentary, and an introduction by Anatoly Liberman. London: Croom Helm, and Minneapolis: University of Minnesota Press, 1983. A thorough detailing of Lermontov's life which takes good advantage of the previous works together with translations of more than one hundred of Lermontov's poems, not all of which have appeared in English previously. The translations have won much professional praise for their surprising poeticality which does not compromise accuracy. The text includes more than fifty illustrations and is wonderfully annotated and indexed.

Mersereau, John, Jr. *Mikhail Lermontov*. Carbondale: Southern Illinois University Press, 1962. A very concise biography which manages to include much valuable detail. The focus is distinctly on Lermontov's development of a prose style, with more than half of the book devoted to an examination of *A Hero of Our Time*.

Lee B. Croft

FERDINAND DE LESSEPS

Born: November 19, 1805; Versailles, France
Died: December 7, 1894; La Chênaie, France
Areas of Achievement: Diplomacy and entrepreneurship
Contribution: Having initiated his career in diplomacy, Lesseps, though never trained as an engineer, is best known for his entrepreneurial abilities that led to the construction of the Suez Canal and the commencement of the transisthmian Panama Canal.

Early Life

Ferdinand-Marie Vicomte de Lesseps was born into a family of diplomats on November 19, 1805, literally within a few meters of the great architectural expression of French monarchism, the Palaces of Versailles, France. For several generations, the men of the family had been distinguished by their cultivation, vigor, belief in progress, extravagant life-styles, and womanizing. Long before Ferdinand's birth, his granduncle, Dominique, had been ennobled for his public services, namely for his extraordinary around-the-world adventures which resulted in his presentation to Louis XVI as a national hero; Ferdinand's grandfather, Martin, had served as a diplomat at the Russian court of Catherine the Great; and his father, Mathieu, a friend of the great statesman Talleyrand, performed with distinction in Franco-Egyptian relations and, while posted to the United States, negotiated France's first commercial treaty with that country. Thus, there was a firm foundation for adventure, valor, and endurance in the family, all of which characterized Ferdinand's life and career.

Ferdinand's mother was the daughter of a prosperous French vintner who had settled in Spain, where she spent her life until her marriage, so that Ferdinand grew up speaking Spanish as well as French. He would later claim that his Spanish temperament led Panama to "seduce" him. Although his family reputedly was wealthy, in fact money was generally scarce. His mother's jewelry was often pawned and his father died bankrupt. Ferdinand himself, while later to marry well and affect the high life, never enjoyed real wealth either.

Against this family background, Lesseps moved naturally into a diplomatic career, and while he had studied some law he was apprenticed, when he was nineteen, to an uncle then serving as France's am-bassador to Portugal. Subsequently, he refined his diplomatic apprenticeship, serving with his father until his death in 1832 in Tunis, after which appointments received were his own.

Life's Work

Lesseps' diplomatic career had come naturally, and he enjoyed it, as did his ravishing Parisian wife, Agnes, who not only bore him five sons (two lived to maturity) but also was a marvelous asset to the sociability expected of her diplomat husband. They were indeed a handsome couple, he well formed and dark eyed, with a memorable smile. The first seven years of his official work were spent in Egypt, then, variously, in Rotterdam, the Netherlands, Malaga, Spain, and finally as France's minister to Spain in 1843.

Lesseps' interest in Suez was not born of interests in engineering; he enjoyed no training whatever along that line. Rather, it emerged from his partial adherence to the philosophy of Comte de Saint-Simon, who believed that private property and nationalism ought to be abolished and the world made over by scientists, engineers, industrialists, and artists.

Lesseps had met a coterie of French Saint-Simonian engineers during his duty in Egypt in the 1830's. This group, led by Prosper Enfantin, hoped to abolish war, end poverty, and generally reorder the world by great public improvements—railways, highways, and both a Suez and a Panamanian canal. For four years, perhaps with some financial assistance from Lesseps, Enfantin and his group labored to dig the canal but were ultimately defeated; indeed, their ranks were decimated by cholera. While little had been accomplished, many Europeans continued to hope for a canal.

A career crisis diverted Lesseps once again from Suez. He was dispatched on a diplomatic mission to Italy. Lesseps was reprimanded for exceeding instructions and fired in 1848. By 1850, Napoleon III, by *coup d'état*, had made himself Emperor of the Second Empire, had married one of Lesseps' distant cousins, and, surrounded by Saint-Simonians, had again urged great projects upon France. Meanwhile, political upheaval in Egypt had brought a new viceroy into power, Mohammed Said, whom Lesseps had befriended when Said was a boy. His diplomatic career finished and with Agnes dead the previous

year, in 1854 Lesseps left his home at La Chênaie to join his old friend. Said, hopeful of launching his regime with some great enterprise, asked for Lesseps' advice: It was to dig a Suez Canal.

Tirelessly, meticulously watching details, and above all incessantly scurrying about the world raising or borrowing funds (half the money came from Frenchmen, the rest from Said and his successor), he justified a reputation as one of the nineteenth century's greatest entrepreneurs: patient, untiring, an imaginative propagandist, at times deceptive, and very much a shrewd actor-diplomat. On November 17, 1869, amid lavish fanfare, the 160-kilometer, sea-level canal opened. While, at most stages of its construction, Lesseps could have sold his rights and garnered great wealth, he was uninterested in money: The Suez had been dug for the good of humanity.

While being richly honored, lionized, and feted, he married the stunning young daughter of a wealthy friend and instantly started two great projects: founding what became a family of six sons and six daughters and planning a number of grandiose undertakings: a railway linking Paris, Moscow,

Bombay, and Peking and the flooding of vast areas of the Sahara, among them. Before the Parisian Geographical Society in 1875, he proposed elaboration of plans for an interoceanic isthmian canal. To that end, he helped form the Société Civile Internationale du Canal Interocéanique de Darien, the so-called Türr Syndicate. Both the syndicate as well as Lesseps' role in it would be, and remain, controversial. The intent of Parisian Geographical Society was a binational effort composed of leading international scientists, ensuring an objective analysis of sites and possible problems; however, the Türr Syndicate agreed to handle everything. It did indeed make several expeditions; by 1882, it had contracted with the Colombian government in detail for a ninety-nine-year lease, financing, land concessions, rights of the syndicate to transfer its holdings to other individuals (or syndicates) but not to foreign countries, and distribution of profits.

Meanwhile, an international congress for the study of the isthmian canal convened in Paris in May, 1879. After much disappointing information, some disinformation, and intelligent conjecture, without consensus, Lesseps, who initially had seemed ineffectual, won his audience by declaring that for all insurmountable obstacles there existed men of genius to master them. Later in the day, another genius, a great engineer and the head of France's famed Corps de Ponts et Chaussees (bridges and highways), the only person present who had experience with construction in tropical America, warned of the deadly menaces of endemic, epidemic disease and of the impossibility of the sea-level canal (one without locks) upon which Lesseps was determined. Lesseps ultimately carried the day. His victory in the congress would shortly cost tens of thousands of lives, the loss of millions by investors, ruin of the syndicate, scandals which historians have not yet entirely unraveled, judicial probes, and eventually the then-greatest real estate transaction in history when the United States bought the remnants of Lesseps' efforts under dubious circumstances.

Yet Lesseps was magnificent in pursuit of his great objective: a Panamanian canal. He bought out the Türr Syndicate; created his own company; mesmerized general publics throughout Europe and the United States; and raised funds from a vast range of sources. He visited the Panama site, declared, with aplomb, that there were no insurmountable difficulties; hired a remarkable team of French engineers, whose general repute had been singular for nearly two centuries; mustered the great excavators necessary to gnaw their way through the terrain; provided the best housing and medical facilities then known for the protection of his aides, engineers, and workers; and launched the great dig in 1881. Before disease and natural obstacles made obvious the impossibility of a sea-level canal, and before Americans undertook construction of a lock canal, Lesseps' crews had excavated nearly a third of the distance between Colon, on the Caribbean, and Panama City, on the Pacific: if not the most difficult portion, a sterling achievement nevertheless. Yet by 1889, Lesseps' losses in life and money were too great. His grand enterprise was failed, bankrupt. Old, under financial pressures, he remained only vaguely aware of the press and judicial trials with which irate investors were crushing members of his family and colleagues, unaware that "Panama" had become a term of national opprobrium. Through his wife's protective care, the great adventurer sat at home in a seaman's peacoat, with his smoking cap and with his knees blanketed, wasting away, oblivious to the storms raging around his devastated enterprise. He died on December 7, 1894, at La Chênaie, and was quietly buried in Paris' Pére Lachaise Cemetery.

Summary

Ferdinand de Lesseps was the complex scion of a distinguished family. A successful diplomat, he was shamelessly duped by the state he served, only to turn about and become the driving force behind two immensely important undertakings: the Suez and the Panama Canals. At one he succeeded, at one he failed. Yet his success at Suez, certainly in global economic terms, far outweighed the financial disaster, and perhaps even the thousands of lives lost in Panama. For all of his deceptions, he was a heroic romantic, an inspired entrepreneur, suffused with the Saint-Simonian urge to remodel the world. In no technical or scientific sense did he qualify as an expert, and in an age in which the engineer and scientist became the forces with which to reckon, he relied upon his own fixations, rhetoric, and manipulations to launch his great enterprises. It had been the wisdom of Lesseps' father that he forget his great Panama scheme and settle for the undying fame earned at Suez. Yet hubris and heroism are usually intertwined. It remains sufficient that his accomplishment, against great odds at Suez, matched his daring but partial failure at Panama—partial because it finally moved the Americans to complete that singularly remarkable construction.

Bibliography

Beatty, Charles. *Ferdinand de Lesseps: A Biographical Study*. London: Eyre and Spottiswoode, and New York: Harper, 1956. An eminently readable, well-researched biography of genuine quality on one of the more vital personalities of the nineteenth century. Contains a fine bibliography, a chronology, and a very useful double-columned index.

Cameron, Ian. *The Impossible Dream: The Building of the Panama Canal*. London: Hodder and Stoughton, and New York: Morrow, 1971. A competent study, which while focused chiefly on the American effort, deals with Lesseps and the initial French enterprise, though it is less generous than other works on the real difficulties and progress made by the French. Contains a select bibliography and an adequate index.

Farnie, D. A. *East and West of Suez: The Suez Canal in History, 1854-1956*. Oxford: Clarendon Press, 1969. A large scholarly study which helps place the importance of Lesseps' work in perspective of the canal's subsequent history. Scholarly and well written, this work has several graphs, statistical tables, maps, a fine, extensive bibliography, and a superb index.

Fitzgerald, Percy. *The Great Canal at Suez*. 2 vols. London: Tinsley, 1876; New York: AMS Press, 1978. Delightful reading, lending an ambience to the great event hard to find elsewhere. While documentation is inserted in the text, there are no notes, bibliography, illustrations, or index.

McCullough, David. *The Path Between the Seas: The Creation of the Panama Canal, 1870-1914*. New York: Simon and Schuster, 1977. While detailed treatment of Lesseps occupies only a portion of this marvelous work—winner of many prizes—it is easily the most readable and most thoroughly researched study of the wonder that is the canal. Contains great photographs, an extensive and first-rate bibliography of primary and secondary sources, and a useful index.

Schonfield, Hugh J. *The Suez Canal in Peace and War, 1869-1969*. Rev. ed. London: Vallentine, and Coral Gables, Fla.: University of Miami Press, 1969. A readable, competent, and scholarly study, the first six chapters of which cover Lesseps' planning and work. Contains seven useful appendices. The index is full and useful.

Clifton K. Yearley

MERIWETHER LEWIS and WILLIAM CLARK

Meriwether Lewis

Born: August 18, 1774; Albemarle County, Virginia
Died: October 11, 1809; Grinder's Stand, Tennessee
Area of Achievement: Exploration
Contribution: Lewis was coleader of the Lewis and Clark Expedition, the first party of white men to cross the North American continent from the Atlantic to the Pacific coast within the geographical limits of the present United States.

Early Lives

Meriwether Lewis was born August 18, 1774, on a plantation in Albemarle County, Virginia. Meriwether's father was William Lewis, who married Lucy Meriwether, for whom the explorer was named. Meriwether had an older sister and a younger brother. The first Lewises in America, who were Welsh, migrated to Virginia in the mid-seventeenth century, where the family became planters. Meriwether's father was a lieutenant during the Revolutionary War, but he drowned while on leave in 1779. Six months later, Lucy married Captain John Marks. After the war, the Marks family moved to Georgia, but Meriwether soon went back to Virginia to live with his relatives. There he attended several small schools taught by parsons and received some tutoring, but his chief interest and delight was in rambling in the woods, hunting, and observing nature. Although rather stiff and awkward as a child, Meriwether grew up to be a handsome young man.

When John Marks died in 1791, his widow returned to Virginia. She brought with her, besides Meriwether's brother and sister, a son and daughter she had borne her second husband.

A short time after his mother's return, Lewis became a soldier, as he was to remain most of his life. In 1794, he enlisted in the Virginia militia to help suppress the Whiskey Rebellion in western Pennsylvania. Liking this taste of military life, Lewis stayed in the militia until May, 1795, when he became an ensign in the United States Army. A few months thereafter, he was assigned to the "Chosen Rifle Company" which William Clark commanded, and during the short time that the two men were together, they became fast friends. Later that year, Lewis joined the First Infantry Regiment and for the next four years was engaged in a number of noncombatant duties, mainly on the Western fron-

William Clark

Born: August 1, 1770; Caroline County, Virginia
Died: September 1, 1838; St. Louis, Missouri
Areas of Achievement: Exploration and Native American affairs
Contribution: After serving as coleader of the Lewis and Clark Expedition, Clark was for three decades one of the most important administrators of Indian affairs in the nation's history.

tier. In December, 1800, he was promoted to captain and became regimental paymaster.

It was while he was thus occupied that, in February, 1801, President-elect Thomas Jefferson wrote to invite Lewis to become his private secretary, probably with a view to naming him to command a transcontinental exploring expedition. Jefferson had thought about, and even planned for, such an undertaking since the United States had won its independence in 1783. In 1792, Lewis, then only eighteen years old, had volunteered for the assignment. Jefferson chose someone else, however, who failed to go.

Soon after coming to Washington, Lewis, under the president's direction, began to plan and prepare for the expedition. He obtained scientific and technical training from members of the faculty of the University of Pennsylvania, collected, with their advice, various kinds of equipment and supplies, and gathered information on his proposed route. Following congressional approval and funding of the mission and his formal designation as its commander, Lewis, early in 1803, with Jefferson's concurrence, invited his friend William Clark, with whom he had maintained contact since they served together in the army, to be its coleader.

Clark was born August 1, 1770, on his family's plantation in Caroline County, Virginia. He was the youngest of six sons and the ninth of ten children of John and Ann (Rogers) Clark. The Clarks had emigrated from England some time in the seventeenth century and, like the Lewises, had become planters. When the Revolution came, the Clarks were staunch patriots, and all of William's older brothers fought as officers in the War for Independence. The most famous was Brigadier General George Rogers Clark, who was the conqueror of the Illinois Country. William, who was too young to fight, stayed home. He received a little formal schooling and acquired the rudiments of learning, but mainly he developed the skills of a frontiersman: the ability to ride, hunt, and shoot.

When he was fourteen years old, Clark moved with his family to a new plantation near the Falls of the Ohio at Louisville. As a young Kentucky frontiersman, Clark, a big, bluff redhead, served with the militia in several campaigns against the hostile Indian tribes living north of the Ohio River. In March, 1792, he was commissioned a lieutenant in the United States Army and two years later fought under General Anthony Wayne in the famous battle of Fallen Timbers. In July, 1796, however, Clark resigned his commission and returned home, where for the next seven years he managed his aged parents' plantation. It was there that, in July, 1803, he received Lewis' invitation to join him in leading a transcontinental exploring expedition and quickly accepted it.

Lives' Work

About the time Clark received his letter, Lewis, in the East, completed his preparations for the expedition and received final detailed directions from the president. The mission's purpose, as stated by Jefferson, was to explore the Missouri River up to its source in the Rocky Mountains and descend the nearest westward-flowing stream to the Pacific in order to extend the American fur trade to the tribes inhabiting that vast area and to increase geographical knowledge of the continent. With these instructions, Lewis left Washington for Pittsburgh. Descending the Ohio River by boat, he picked up Clark at Louisville, in late summer 1803. Together with a few recruits for the expedition, the two men proceeded to Wood River, Illinois, opposite the mouth of the Missouri, where they encamped early in December. During the next five months, Lewis and Clark recruited and trained their party and finished their preparations for the journey.

With everything in readiness, the expedition set out on May 14, 1804, for the Pacific. Lewis, still a captain in the First Infantry, was the expedition's official commander. Although commissioned only a second lieutenant of artillerists, on the expedition Clark was called "captain" and was treated in every way as Lewis' equal. During the journey, Lewis, a rather intense, moody introvert, spent much of his time alone, walking on shore, hunting, and examining the country. Because Lewis was better-trained scientifically and the more literate of the two officers, he wrote most of the scien-

tific information recorded in the expedition's journals. Clark, a friendly, gregarious individual, spent most of his time with the men in the boats. He was the expedition's principal waterman and mapmaker, and he was better able to negotiate with the Indians. Together, the two officers' dispositions, talents, and experience complemented each other superbly. Despite the differences in their personalities, they seem always to have enjoyed the best of personal relations.

In its first season's travel, the expedition advanced some sixteen hundred miles up the Missouri and went into winter quarters in a small fort, named Mandan for the nearest Indian tribe, situated in modern North Dakota. The following spring the expedition proceeded to the headwaters of the Missouri, made a portage of the Rocky Mountains, and descended the nearest westward-flowing tributaries of the Columbia as well as the Columbia itself. Lewis and Clark reached the Pacific by mid-November, 1805. After wintering a few miles from the ocean, in a post they called Fort Clatsop, for a nearby tribe, in March, 1806, the explorers set out for home and arrived in St. Louis in September, having long since been given up for lost by virtually everyone but Jefferson.

As rewards for their great achievement, the president appointed Lewis governor of Louisiana Territory and Clark its principal Indian agent and brigadier general of the territorial militia. Detained in the East by business related to the expedition and other matters, Lewis did not actually assume the governorship of the territory until March, 1808. He soon proved to be unsuited for the office by temperament and experience and quickly ran into trouble. He quarreled with Frederick Bates, the territorial secretary, and became unpopular with many of the people of the territory. He seldom reported to his superiors in Washington and failed to consult them on his policies and plans. As a result, he fell under their severe criticism, and he probably would not have been appointed to a second term of office had he survived the first.

In September, 1809, after only about a year and a half in office, Lewis left St. Louis for Washington, in order to try to straighten out his affairs with the government and to renew his efforts to get the expedition's journals published. On the way, while stopping at a tavern on the Natchez Trace, he was either murdered or committed suicide. Although the evidence is inconclusive, there is reason to believe, as did Clark and Jefferson, that Lewis died

Meriwether Lewis

by his own hand. Thus at the age of thirty-five ended the life of this great pathfinder.

Clark, in the meantime, was mainly concerned
with improving relations and promoting trading activities with the Indian tribes of the territory and
protecting the white settlers against the tribes of
the Upper Mississippi who were allied with the
British in Canada. Following Lewis' death, he was
offered the governorship of Louisiana, but he declined it because he felt he lacked political experience. In June, 1813, however, the governorship of
the Territory of Missouri, as the Louisiana Purchase was called after 1812, again became available, and this time Clark accepted it. During the
War of 1812, which was then raging, Clark's chief
responsibility was to defend the territory against
the hostile Indians of the Upper Mississippi. After
the war, Indian relations and the economic and political needs of the white settlers pouring into Missouri absorbed his time and interest.

Following Missouri's admission to the Union in
1821, Clark (an unsuccessful candidate to be the
state's first governor), was appointed superinten-

dent of Indian affairs at St. Louis and retained responsibility for the tribes of the Missouri and Upper
Mississippi. Clark held this office until his death on
September 1, 1838. As superintendent of Indian affairs, he played a major role in effecting the removal of Indians living east of the Mississippi and in
Missouri to new lands in modern eastern Kansas.

Unlike Lewis, who never married, Clark was an
affectionate family man. In 1808, he married Julia
Hancock, with whom he had five children. Following Julia's death, in 1821 he married her cousin
Harriet Kennerly Radford, a widow, who bore him
two sons. Four of his sons lived to manhood.

Summary

Lewis and Clark's fame rests almost entirely on the
success of their great expedition, one of the most
extensive explorations undertaken in their time.
They and their companions were the first American citizens to cross the continent and the first
white men to traverse it within the area of the modern United States. During a journey that lasted a
little more than twenty-eight months, the expedition traveled more than eight thousand miles. On
the entire trip, only one man, Sergeant Charles
Floyd, lost his life, and he died from a cause almost
certainly unrelated to his exploring activities. In
their contacts with thousands of Indians, they had
only one minor encounter, which cost the lives of
two Indians. The total expense of the undertaking
was a little less than forty thousand dollars. Although Lewis and Clark did not find a commercially feasible route across the continent, as Jefferson
hoped they would, they did make a significant contribution to the existing knowledge of the geography of a great part of North America. They also
took a historic step toward opening the Trans-Mississippi West to American trade and subsequently
to American settlement, thus providing the basis
for one of the United States' strongest claims to the
Oregon Country. Their great achievement stimulated the pride of the American people and served to
make Americans aware of the vastness of the continent on which they lived.

Although Lewis' career after the expedition was
short and hardly noteworthy, Clark's was long and
eminently successful. In three decades of dealing
with the tribes of the Upper Mississippi and the
Trans-Mississippi West, he carried out the policies
of the federal government faithfully and effectively, helping to adjust relations peacefully between
the native Americans and the whites. In doing so,

by the standards of his own time, he treated the Indians fairly and sympathetically and, in return, had their respect and confidence.

Bibliography

Bakeless, John. *Lewis and Clark: Partners in Discovery.* New York: Morrow, 1947; London: Constable, 1996. This is a readable and relatively well-researched study, but its treatment of Lewis, and especially Clark, after the expedition is brief and sketchy.

Cutright, Paul Russell. *Lewis and Clark: Pioneering Naturalists.* Urbana: University of Illinois Press, 1969. This volume contains a wealth of detailed information on the scientific and technical aspects of the expedition, including fauna and flora discovered, topographic features discovered or named, and Indian tribes encountered.

Dillon, Richard. *Meriwether Lewis: A Biography.* New York: Coward-McCann, 1965. The only noteworthy biography of Lewis, this somewhat sentimental and romantic work provides a relatively comprehensive treatment of the subject with emphasis on the expedition.

Duncan, Dayton. "If Lewis and Clark Came Back Today." *American Heritage* 48, no. 7 (November 1997). Examines the changes that have occurred in the Louisiana Territory covered by Lewis and Clark in 1804.

Fisher, Ron. "Lewis and Clark." *National Geographic* 194, no. 4 (October 1998). Discusses a multivolume work by the University of Nebraska Press that analyzes in depth the explorations of Lewis and Clark.

Jackson, Donald D., ed. *Letters of the Lewis and Clark Expedition, with Related Documents: 1783-1854.* Urbana: University of Illinois Press, 1962. This is a comprehensive collection of meticulously edited letters, memoranda, and other documents dealing with all aspects of the expedition gathered from widely scattered sources.

Lewis, Meriwether, and William Clark. *The Journals of Lewis and Clark.* Edited by Bernard De Voto. Boston: Houghton Mifflin, 1953. Based on the eight-volume Thwaites edition of *The Original Journals of the Lewis and Clark Expedition.* Edited by Rubengold Thwaites. 8 vols. New York: Dodd, Mead and Co., 1904-1905. This single volume provides a good, readable narrative of that great enterprise that retains its flavor.

Ronda, James P. *Lewis and Clark Among the Indians.* Lincoln: University of Nebraska Press, 1984. An important, sophisticated, and engaging ethnohistorical study, this work chronicles the daily contact between the explorers and Indians and shows that the expedition initiated important economic and diplomatic relations with them.

Steffen, James O. *William Clark: Jeffersonian Man on the Frontier.* Norman: University of Oklahoma Press, 1977. Steffen sketches selectively and very briefly Clark's life, making an occasional reference to the intellectual framework which he believes explains it.

John L. Loos

LI HUNG-CHANG

Born: February 15, 1823; Ho-fei, Anhwei, China
Died: November 7, 1901; Tientsin, China
Areas of Achievement: Government and the military
Contribution: Li played a leading role in the Ch'ing Dynasty, instituting reforms based on a moderate policy of Westernization known as self-strengthening, while in foreign affairs he adopted a firm, but conciliatory attitude.

Early Life

Li Hung-chang came from a wealthy and successful literati family. His father, Li Wen-an, was the holder of the highest imperial degree and had achieved that great status in 1838, along with Tseng Kuo-fan. Li Wen-an sent his son to Peking to study with Tseng; in 1847, Li Hung-chang also acquired the highest degree. He began service in the Hanlin Academy and was being groomed as an important high official. Li's career underwent a dramatic shift in 1853, when he and his father returned home to raise a local militia to protect their region from the Taiping rebels. Through his connections with Tseng, Li entered into the top ranks of the anti-Taiping forces in Anhwei Province. He served with great success in Anhwei and Kiangsi provinces until 1861. During this period, however, he had difficulties with his superiors, including Tseng, all of whom he believed were too cautious in taking the offensive.

Li was an unusually tall man for his time, more than six feet in height. As a young man, he was powerful and courageous; photographs taken in his sixties show a dignified, alert, and energetic man dressed self-assuredly in his official robes and with a small white beard. Li acquired enormous wealth in official service; at his death, his estate was estimated to be worth at least 500,000 Chinese ounces of silver, or several hundred million dollars. He used his wealth to sustain his political and family power; personally, he lived a plain and temperate life. Li had five brothers and six sons who profited from his prominence, both politically and financially, but none was as capable as he.

Life's Work

From 1860 to 1870, Li emerged from the ranks of Tseng's lieutenants to become a key regional official in the Lower Yangtze River valley and commander of his own regional force, the Huai Army (so named after a region within Li's home province,

Anhwei, from which the army was raised). When Tseng assumed overall command of the anti-Taiping forces in 1860, he gave Li and the Huai Army a key role. Li joined in the campaign coordinated by Tseng that destroyed the Taipings in 1864. Three years later, still under Tseng's leadership, Li and his Huai Army implemented the offensive that destroyed the Nien rebellions in Shantung.

During the defense of Shanghai in 1862, Li incorporated into his forces the foreign-led and armed "ever victorious army" and became an advocate of Western military technology. Cooperating with Tseng, Li played an important role in the establishment of small-arms factories in 1863-1864, the Kiangnan Shipyard in Shanghai in 1865, and the Nanking Arsenal in 1867. These early self-strengthening projects were arms factories operated as official state enterprises and thus incorporated the nepotism and inefficiency typical of the Ch'ing bureaucracy. All were headed by foreign technical experts, who were to train Chinese technicians while producing modern arms.

The production of these arsenals was available to Li's own regional forces, further increasing his power. Unlike Tseng, Li did not disband his provincial forces following the Taipings' defeat. He and a few others continued to command independent regional armies, a characteristic that gives a special feudal flavor to the late Ch'ing period (1860-1911), in which militarily strong officials such as Li are seen as the precursors of China's twentieth century warlords.

Li's early regional effort at military modernization is important because it was more effective than another program directed from Peking by Prince Kung, a brother of the Hsien-feng emperor. Kung understood the significance of Western military technology after the sacking of the Summer Palace at Peking by an Anglo-French force in 1860, but his modernization efforts encountered delays and setbacks. Then Kung's power declined after the death of his brother, the emperor. The Empress Dowager Tz'u-hsi consolidated her power behind the new child emperor T'ung-chih, and she viewed Kung as a rival. By the 1870's, Kung was no longer a significant figure in Ch'ing politics.

In 1870, when a crisis arose in Tientsin following a riot in which foreigners were killed, the dynasty turned to Tseng. Tseng's health was poor, so he recommended Li, who was then appointed

Governor General of Chihli and Commissioner of the Northern Sea. Li quickly settled the Tientsin incident and proceeded during the next quarter century to wield enormous power from his posts at Tientsin, which combined control of military, trade, and diplomatic affairs for the whole of China north of Shanghai. Li also held several key positions in the central bureaucracy at Peking, such as grand secretary (1872-1901), which further magnified his power.

Li maintained his positions through a combination of ability and political guile. He had relied upon Tseng until Tseng's death in 1872. Li cultivated Kung in the 1860's, when the prince's star was ascendant in Peking. In 1875, he helped Tz'u-hsi ensure the enthronement of her infant nephew as the Kuang-hsu emperor, and he became an important supporter of her long domination of the dynasty's fortunes. Li's penchant for modernization put him at odds with more conservative officials, and his willingness to compromise in the face of foreign threats of force brought him into disrepute with hot-blooded young officials who hoped to best the foreigners in war. Thus, while enormously powerful, Li was both dependent upon a short-sighted and narrow empress dowager and open to challenge by other officials on a wide variety of grounds.

From 1870 to 1895, while based at Tientsin, Li followed a three-pronged foreign policy which combined moderate accommodation of foreign demands; construction of new Ch'ing military power, especially a modern navy; and extension of Ch'ing influence through the new diplomatic forms emerging in East Asia. Li assumed that the Ch'ing Empire, like other ruling dynasties before, would continue to dominate all states in the region, including Russia and Japan, as well as the new trading powers such as Great Britain, France, Germany and the United States. Although similar to European conceptions of a diplomacy based on a balance of power, Li's ideas derived from traditional Chinese notions of international politics, in which the foreigners' advantages are turned against themselves and China plays various foreign powers' ambitions against one another.

Li's diplomatic record from 1870 to 1895 is not distinguished by great successes. He was forced to accept extensions of Japanese power in the Ryukyu Islands and Taiwan, Russian power in the far western Ili valley, and the assertion of French power into Vietnam in the period from 1870 to 1885. Li was strongly criticized by more aggressive officials at the time for his role in these affairs as well as by later, nationalistic historians, who often cast Li as a venal traitor. Still, aside from the defeat in the Sino-French War in 1884-1885, a war Li knew the dynasty should have avoided, the Ch'ing did not suffer any major defeats during this period.

The Sino-French War destroyed much of the Ch'ing's military and naval modernization efforts south of Shanghai and had the effect of further increasing the weight of Li's Peiyang (Northern Sea) commissionership. Li undertook modernization programs in his region after 1870 that included the China Merchants' Steam Navigation Company, the K'ai-p'ing Coal Mines, textile factories, a telegraph system from Shanghai to Tientsin, new arsenals, a railroad at Tientsin, and a major naval base on the Liaotung peninsula. Some of these mark a continuation of his pre-1870 pattern of military modernization; others included new forms of transportation and communication with commercial, diplomatic, and military advantages. Li also approved innovative forms of industrial operation involving less state control, a more active role for merchants, and greater opportunities for personal wealth for both the Chinese entrepreneurs involved and the Chinese officials, including himself.

In the late 1880's, Li undertook a diplomatic offensive in response to Japanese interest in extending their power into Korea. The complex machinations among the Koreans, the Ch'ing Dynasty, and the Japanese unraveled in the fall of 1894 and produced the First Sino-Japanese War (1894-1895). In this war, Li's Northern Sea fleet was destroyed, his armies were disgraced, and Japan won a massive victory. Li's career never recovered from these defeats. Still, he was dispatched to Japan to negotiate a settlement and while there was wounded in an assassination attempt. Ashamed, the Japanese agreed to impose slightly less humiliating terms on the Ch'ing.

As the distasteful peace with Japan was being concluded, Li became involved in a remarkable diplomatic maneuver known as the Triple Intervention. Seeking to offset Japanese power in Manchuria, Li concluded an agreement with Russia, Germany, and France to intervene and force Japan to give up the special privileges it had won from China in the First Sino-Japanese War. Japan grudgingly conceded to the international pressure but then was incredulous as the Ch'ing Dynasty proceeded to bestow on Russia special privileges, including railway and naval-base rights, in Manchuria. Li conducted negotiations on some of these matters in Europe and is believed to have accepted bribes from the Russian government for his favor to their interests in Manchuria. This charge of personal venality, combined with his compromise of Ch'ing sovereignty in Manchuria, has sealed the unfavorable judgment of Li held by most historians of modern China. Li's late diplomacy in Manchuria began the rivalry between Japan and Russia over control of this region of China. That rivalry led to the Russo-Japanese War of 1905 and later produced the 1931 Japanese takeover of Manchuria, one of the critical steps on the way to World War II in the Pacific.

Li had no role in either the Reform movement of 1898 or the Boxer Uprising of 1900. He appeared on the dynasty's behalf in 1901 to negotiate the settlement of the Boxer incident. He had little leverage because foreign armies occupied Peking and the empress dowager and emperor were in self-imposed exile away from the court, while Li himself was known to be out of favor and devoid of real power. Li died before agreement was reached on the final terms.

Summary

The failure of Li Hung-chang's efforts and the disgrace of his policies was much more than a great personal defeat. Li represented the best possibility that the Ch'ing Dynasty had to accommodate itself to the rapidly changing world of the post-1850 era. He understood the need for China to adapt itself to an altered political and military situation in Asia and made some of the most enlightened efforts to encourage moderate modernization. These efforts were more successful than those of other Manchu and Chinese leaders but still fell far short of what was necessary.

Personally, Li was a decisive, innovative official, who learned to act with restraint. His accommodation of Tz'u-hsi can be interpreted either as a necessary compromise to the reality of court politics or as tragic misjudgment that doomed to failure all Li's carefully laid projects and plans. Whatever weaknesses that Li's stewardship contained, they remained largely unrecognized until the First Sino-Japanese War, when all of his authority and glory were swiftly destroyed by the force of Japanese

arms. Li's conception of what would happen to the dynasty and to China after this war remains a mystery, as does the full motivation behind his diplomatic maneuvers after 1895. The collapse of Li's own career by 1897 reflects the true decline of the Ch'ing Dynasty's power and authority.

Bibliography

Bland, J. O. P. *Li Hung-chang*. New York: Holt, and London: Constable, 1917. A biography of Li. Bland was a reporter in China, and his account contains much of the foreign community's gossip about Li.

Chu, Samuel C. and Kwang-Ching Liu, eds. *Li Hung-Chang and China's Early Modernization*. Armonk, New York: Sharpe, 1994. A collection of thirteen essays exploring Hung-Chang as a modernizer, diplomat, and national official and attempting to restore his name despite historical accusations of illegal financial activities and nepotism.

Folsom, Kenneth E. *Friends, Guests, and Colleagues: The Mu-fu System in the Late Ch'ing Period*. Berkeley: University of California Press, 1968. A rich and useful study of Li and his staff that contains many details about Li's life and career.

Hsu, Immanuel C. Y. *The Rise of Modern China*. 5th ed. New York: Oxford University Press, 1998. The author of this standard text is an authority on the self-strengthening period; the section entitled "Self-strengthening in an Age of Accelerated Foreign Imperialism" puts Li's career into context.

Liu, K. C. "Li Hung-chang in Chihli: The Emergence of a Policy, 1870-1875." In *Approaches to Modern Chinese History*, edited by Albert Feuerwerker et al. Berkeley: University of California Press, 1967. Liu, who is a leading authority on Li, outlines Li's policies during his first years as governor-general and Northern Sea commissioner at Tientsin.

Spector, Stanley. *Li Hung-chang and the Huai Army*. Seattle: University of Washington Press, 1964. An important study that emphasizes Li's role in creating the system of regionally based military power in China after 1860.

David D. Buck

JUSTUS VON LIEBIG

Born: May 12, 1803; Darmstadt
Died: April 18, 1873; Munich, Germany
Area of Achievement: Chemistry
Contribution: Liebig was one of the most important chemists of the nineteenth century. In addition to pioneering experimental research that transformed the basis of modern organic chemistry, his studies on agriculture led to the development of agricultural chemistry, and his systematic processes for training students became institutionalized within the German research university.

Early Life

Born the second of nine children to Johann Georg and Maria Karoline Moserin Liebig, Justus von Liebig, the son of a dealer in pharmaceuticals and paint supplies, developed an interest in chemistry and experimentation at an early age. As a young boy, Liebig was especially fascinated with the explosive properties of silver fulminate, and his experiments with this material resulted in an explosion that prematurely ended his career as an apothecary apprentice. After returning home for a short time, Liebig enrolled at the University of Bonn in 1820, where he studied under the chemist Wilhelm Gottlob Kastner. Later in life, Liebig was particularly critical of Kastner's inability to teach him chemical analysis and the lack of adequate laboratory equipment, but Liebig followed Kastner from Bonn to the University of Erlangen, where he received a doctorate in 1822. It was at Erlangen that Liebig became convinced of the need to study abroad, and he successfully persuaded the Grand Duke Louis I of Hesse to award him a grant to pursue his chemical education in Paris from 1822 to 1824.

In Paris, Liebig received the chemical training that proved to be decisive and pivotal in his professional career. He attended the lectures of Louis-Jacques Thénard, Pierre-Louis Dulong, and Joseph-Louis Gay-Lussac and also gained entrance into the latter's laboratory through the intervention of Alexander von Humboldt. Liebig would leave Paris thoroughly trained in critical thinking, in chemical analysis, and in the experimental methods necessary for making careful physical measurements, all hallmarks of the "new" chemistry first articulated by Antoine-Laurent Lavoisier at the close of the eighteenth century.

Life's Work

Liebig returned to Germany in 1824 as extraordinary professor of chemistry at the University of Giessen; his appointment was the result of Humboldt's successful efforts in convincing Louis I that the young chemist had exceptional promise. Although his laboratory initially consisted of only one room surrounded by benches along its walls with a coal stove at its center, Liebig would quickly rise from these humble beginnings to become Europe's most distinguished chemist, the consequence of his personal charisma, scientific skills, and technical ingenuity.

Until the time of Liebig, organic chemistry was for the most part an inexact descriptive science based upon a hodgepodge of conflicting observations and personal opinions. There existed no viable classificatory scheme for organic substances, and there was little consensus concerning the fundamental building block of these materials, the molecule. Further, it was generally thought that a vital force arising from life itself was necessary for

the synthesis of an organic compound. These uncertainties and others related to organic chemistry were ultimately explained by Liebig and his students using data gained from chemical analyses derived from the use of his combustion apparatus. This simple glass triangle consisted of several bulbs filled with potash, and it enabled the chemist to determine the percentage of carbon in a compound with great accuracy, precision, and relative ease. The combustion apparatus proved to be at the heart of Liebig's success, revolutionizing both organic chemistry and nineteenth century chemical education.

The use of exact analysis did much to elucidate the nature of chemical compounds such as alcohols, aldehydes, ethers, and ketones during the late 1820's and 1830's. In the Giessen laboratory, where much of this compound characterization was done, large numbers of students, admitted on their talents and attracted by the low cost, flocked to the charismatic Liebig. While their training encompassed both theoretical and practical chemistry, the combustion apparatus was an integral part of a systematic curriculum that enabled even the average worker to make valuable contributions. Typically, the beginning student first sat in on Liebig's lectures on introductory chemistry and then was initiated in laboratory practices by doing qualitative analysis in which one characterizes a series of unknown compounds. Subsequently, a varied set of quantitative analyses were performed, followed by exercises in preparative chemistry in which certain substances were synthesized. After successfully completing these stages, the student was permitted to pursue independent research, often using the combustion apparatus to explore the reactions and compositions of organic substances. Since Liebig was editor of his own journal, *Annalen der Chemie und Pharmacie*, his students often had no problem in rapidly publishing their findings to a scientific community that by the 1840's recognized Giessen as the Mecca of organic chemistry.

Without doubt, Liebig's scientific reputation resulted in the best and brightest students in chemistry coming to study with him at Giessen during the second quarter of the nineteenth century. Among his students were August Wilhelm von Hofmann, discoverer of aniline and the first director of the British Royal College of Chemistry; Friedrich August Kekule von Stradonitz, whose structural interpretation of benzene was crucial to development in structural organic chemistry; James Muspratt of England, who was a leader in the late nineteenth century British chemical industry; and Oliver Wolcott Gibbs, who was a key figure within the emerging chemical community of nineteenth century America. Indeed, Liebig's influence was truly international, as by the 1850's most important academic positions in Western Europe were filled by his former students.

Liebig's fame among his contemporaries and especially the public was perhaps not so much the result of his students and their work as the result of his opinions and writings on agricultural chemistry. In 1840, Liebig, weary after more than a decade of debate with the French chemist Jean-Baptiste André Dumas over the nature of organic molecules, gave a series of lectures on agricultural chemistry in Glasgow, Scotland, that subsequently would be the basis of *Die organische Chemie in ihrer Anivendung auf Agricultur und Physiologie* (1840; *Organic Chemistry in Its Applications to Agriculture and Physiology*, 1840). This work, which dealt with the uses of fertilizers, plant nutrition, and fermentation was seriously flawed in its analysis but was so popular that by 1848 it appeared in seventeen editions and in nine languages, proving to be a powerful stimulus to the agricultural station movement in Europe and the United States. In addition to his views on agriculture, Liebig also extended into the area of physiology and in 1842 expressed his views on nutrition and the chemical changes taking place within living organisms in *Die Thier-Chemie: Oder, Die organische Chemie in ihrer Anwendung auf Physiologie und Pathologie (Animal Chemistry: Or, Organic Chemistry in Its Applications to Physiology and Pathology*, 1842). Like his agricultural chemistry, Liebig's animal chemistry aroused criticism that ultimately was crucial to the late nineteenth century development of modern physiological chemistry.

In 1852, Liebig left Giessen for a modern, well-equipped laboratory in Munich, where he would continue to research and write on aspects of organic chemistry. Although the latter stages of his career were not as fruitful as those early years at Giessen, his legacy in terms of ideas and of followers was crucial to the shaping of modern civilization.

Summary

Justus von Liebig perhaps did more than any other nineteenth century chemist in creating the modern synthetic world of the twentieth century.

His reliance upon exact knowledge based upon chemical analysis resulted in the emergence of the discipline of organic chemistry, a field that has provided modern society with myriad synthetic products, including polymeric materials such as polyvinyl chloride, polypropylene, and synthetic rubber. Yet Liebig did far more than influence the internal aspects of science, for his work on agricultural chemistry had enormous consequences in influencing what would become an ongoing agricultural revolution, and his speculations on physiology reoriented the course of medical research. Finally, his ideas on chemical education—ideas that continue to be practiced in universities today—mark perhaps his most lasting contribution, for most chemists trace their educational heritage to a small laboratory in Giessen and to its master, Justus von Liebig.

Bibliography

Beer, John J. *The Emergence of the German Dye Industry.* Urbana: University of Illinois Press, 1959. One important legacy of Liebig is in the creation of a modern synthetic world, the ultimate fruit of his many students working in industrial research laboratories during the last quarter of the nineteenth century. Beer's study carefully traces the emergence of the science-based dye industry and the role of Liebig's ideas in influencing its organizational development.

Brock, William. *Justus von Liebig: The Chemical Gatekeeper.* Cambridge and New York: Cambridge University Press, 1997. Discusses Liebig's contributions to the field of organic chemistry including his advocation of recycling sewage and replacing nutrients in the soil.

Foster, John Bellamy and Fred Magdoff. "Liebig, Marx, and the Depletion of Soil Fertility: Relevance for Today's Agriculture." *Monthly Review* 50, no. 3 (July-August 1998). Discusses the efforts of Liebig and Marx in the field of soil fertility.

Ihde, Aaron J. *The Development of Modern Chemistry.* New York: Harper, 1964. This survey work in the history of chemistry is excellent in characterizing the nature of organic chemistry during Liebig's lifetime. Discusses Liebig's contributions to organic, agricultural, and physiological chemistry as well as to the field of chemical education.

Lipmann, Timothy O. "Vitalism and Reductionism in Liebig's Physiological Thought." *Isis* 58 (1967): 167-185. A superb article that serves as a model for scholarship in the history of science. Lipmann demonstrates that while Liebig did not believe in the doctrine of vitalism as applied to organic compounds, he did adhere to the notion that a living force (*Lebenskraft*) was an essential part of physiological processes and necessary for the building up of organized structures in living bodies.

Morrell, J. B. "The Chemist Breeders: The Research Schools of Liebig and Thomas Thomson." *Ambix* 19 (1972): 1-47. A penetrating study that examines the pioneering contributions of Liebig in establishing the first modern scientific research school. Morrell analyzes Liebig's charismatic personality, the significance of the combustion apparatus, his ability to control the field of organic chemistry with *Annalen der Chemie und Pharmacie*, and his ability to secure financial and institutional resources.

Rossiter, Margaret W. *The Emergence of Agricultural Science: Justus Liebig and the Americans, 1840-1880.* New Haven, Conn.: Yale University Press, 1975. Traces the diffusion of Liebig's ideas on agriculture from Europe to the United States during the nineteenth century. By the conclusion of the Civil War, a powerful movement to establish agricultural experiment stations emerged and Rossiter particularly focuses on the influence of Liebig on those scientists working at the Connecticut Station.

John A. Heitmann

WILHELM LIEBKNECHT

Born: March 29, 1826; Giessen, Hesse-Darmstadt
Died: August 7, 1900; Berlin, Germany
Areas of Achievement: Government and politics
Contribution: Liebknecht was a founding member of the German Social Democratic Party and an extreme critic of authoritarian government in Germany. He was a delegate to the German Reichstag and editor of the Social Democratic Party newspaper *Vorwärts*. His most important contribution was an effort to promote the ideals of democracy in the nineteenth century European socialist movement.

Early Life

Wilhelm Liebknecht was born in Giessen, a small town near Marburg in Hesse-Darmstadt. Liebknecht's father was a government registrar, and the family was considered middle class by the standards of the early nineteenth century. One of three surviving children, Liebknecht benefited from his father's study of post-Napoleonic Enlightenment thought, and from an early age he was interested in social justice. By December, 1832, however, both of his parents were dead and the six-year-old orphan was reared by Karl Osswald, a theologian, who had been a close friend of the family. By the time Liebknecht had reached his tenth birthday, what was left of his father's estate had disappeared. Although the sudden deaths of his parents and the descent into poverty must have made a lasting impression on him, Liebknecht seldom wrote of his childhood. His only lasting memories were of his uncle, the Reverend Friedrich Ludwig Weidig, a liberal democrat and author of fiery revolutionary tracts. Repeatedly jailed for his antimonarchist writings, in February, 1837, Weidig was apparently murdered in prison in Darmstadt. Although Liebknecht rarely referred to his uncle's death, evidence suggests that at this time he began to identify the authoritarian state as the source of his own bereavement and the problems of society.

Although reduced in circumstances, Liebknecht was still able to attend school, and it was education rather than hardship which pushed him in the direction of radical politics. In the autumn of 1845, Liebknecht left for Berlin to enroll at the university. Berlin was already an industrial city with a population approaching half a million, and the condition of the city's industrial workers, who were forced to live in appalling slums and to suffer brutal working conditions, made an instant impression on the young student. Indeed, Liebknecht's course of study at the university perfectly complemented his introduction to working-class life. His major interests lay in philosophy and economics, and he read avidly in the works of the French socialist Claude Henri de Saint-Simon. As Liebknecht himself admitted, however, his real grounding in socialist thought began with his reading of Friedrich Engels' *Die Lage der arbeitenden Klasse in England* (1848; *The Condition of the Working Class in England in 1844*, 1887). This work persuaded Liebknecht to join the struggle against capitalism, and he cut his education short to join the liberal-democratic Revolution of 1848. The collapse of the revolutionary movement in 1849 forced Liebknecht to flee Germany.

Life's Work

Liebknecht's post-1848 travels took him to Switzerland and then to Great Britain. During his migration, he became acquainted with both Karl Marx and Engels. In 1850, he joined the Union of Communists and became a dedicated exponent of socialist political and economic theory. A proclamation of amnesty permitted Liebknecht to return to Berlin in 1862. He worked as a correspondent for various democratically oriented German and foreign newspapers and became a founding member along with Ferdinand Lassalle of the General German Workers' Association, an organization which favored workers' cooperatives financially supported by the state, universal suffrage, and a program of social legislation regulating wages and hours. In 1869, however, Liebknecht helped to create a new workers' party, the German Social Democratic Labor Party, a more radical organization which emphasized the class struggle and which demanded the abolition of class privileges in Prussia.

In the late 1860's, the two rival groups became parliamentary parties and sent representatives to the assembly of the North German Confederation, which had been created following the Prussian defeat of Austria in 1866. Liebknecht served as a Social Democratic delegate from 1867 to 1870 and vigorously attacked the reactionary policies of the Prussian Junker class and denounced Prussian militarism. Along with August Bebel, Liebknecht opposed the Franco-Prussian War of 1870-1871, fought against the annexationist plans of the Prussian government, and appealed for working-class solidarity with the Paris Commune of 1871. For his opposition to Germany's annexation of Alsace and Lorraine, Liebknecht was brought to trial in 1872 for treason against the state and sentenced to two years' imprisonment.

The Franco-Prussian War, however, led to increased cooperation between the Social Democrats and Lassalle's Workers' Association. Many factional disputes disappeared with the unification of Germany and, by 1875, the two socialist parties resolved to join forces against capitalism and Prussian militarism. At the Socialist Congress at Gotha in May, 1875, a new German Social Democratic Labor Party was founded, and Liebknecht became one of the most influential party leaders, along with Lassalle and Bebel. The Gotha Program reflected Liebknecht's democratic tendencies and was far from a radical socialist agenda. The party program called for such socialist measures as the abolition of "wage slavery" through the establishment of state-supported workers' cooperatives, but it also advocated many commonly held liberal-democratic policies, including universal suffrage, the secret ballot, guaranteed civil liberties, free public education, freedom of speech and assembly, and government-mandated social legislation. The republican nature of the Gotha Program engendered criticism from more doctrinaire socialists, including Marx. In 1875, Marx published his *Randglossen zum Gothaer Partei Programm* (1875; *Critique of the Gotha Program*, 1938), a scathing ideological attack on the German Social Democrats. Nevertheless, Liebknecht repudiated Marx's denunciation, and the new party achieved impressive electoral gains in 1877. The party's moderate-democratic approach allowed it to increase its popular vote by 40 percent and helped it to capture twelve seats in the German Reichstag.

Following the Gotha meeting, however, German Chancellor Otto von Bismarck took steps to prevent any further growth of socialism in Germany. As a result of Liebknecht's and other socialist leaders' opposition to Prussian policies during the Franco-Prussian War, Bismarck was inclined to regard all Social Democrats as enemies of the state. Therefore, in 1878, Bismarck persuaded the Reichstag to pass a series of antisocialist laws which suppressed all political and economic associations of the German socialists. Technically the German Social Democratic Party was not illegal, but party effectiveness was practically destroyed by curtailments in electoral funding and the harassment of party leaders. Liebknecht retained his democratic philosophy during this period and helped to retain party unity until the antisocialist legislation lapsed in 1890.

In 1890, Liebknecht became editor in chief of *Vorwärts*, the central organ of the Social Democratic Party. During this period, and until his death in 1900, Liebknecht's socialist beliefs centered on the issue of the legitimacy of parliamentary activity in the context of the class struggle against capitalism and militarism. Liebknecht's position held that the workers' interests would be more effectively served by sending deputies to the Reichstag who would use the democratic system to achieve social, political, and economic reform. Liebknecht, Bebel, and other moderates helped mold the German Social Democratic movement into a responsible parliamentary party, defending workers' interests and political liberalism. Liebknecht was especially responsible for formulating specific policies aimed at promoting social legislation, reducing the military budget, and eliminating economic protectionism. By the late 1890's, however, Liebknecht's position as party leader had diminished, largely as a result of his inexpert handling of intraparty strife. On the morning of August 7, 1900, Liebknecht suffered a fatal stroke while working at his office in Berlin. His leadership of the German Social Democrats fell to Bebel, Karl Kautsky, and Eduard Bernstein, but Liebknecht was eulogized as one who had helped to elevate a struggling socialist faction into the world's largest and most effective socialist party.

Summary

Wilhelm Liebknecht's achievement was to help to establish the world's first mass-based Marxist political party. He was a nineteenth century social democrat whose political philosophy was formed in the nexus of liberal-democracy, Marxism, and nationalism. He was noted as being tolerant, humanitarian, and democratic. While he did not excel as a statesman or political revolutionary, he was a master at political organization. His advocacy of revolutionary change was tempered with his abjuration of violence. He encouraged open discussion within his party, and he defended the right to hold dissenting viewpoints. In reaching decisions, he preferred persuasion and open voting to intimidation and deference to an elite party leadership. He rejected any form of conspiratorial action by a minority and based his socialism on the basic premise of mass participation. Liebknecht argued that the basic tool of working-class revolution remained education. Voluntary and enlightened mass participation in the revolutionary process was Liebknecht's aim. For him, the manipulative dictatorship of the proletariat always remained an incongruous part of Marxism. While most nineteenth century socialist movements indulged in sectarian debates and self-defeating intraparty rivalries, the German Social Democrats, largely as a result of Liebknecht's efforts, crystallized the socialist movement and forestalled party schism until 1917. Overall, Liebknecht's leadership molded the German socialists into a respected and effective workers' party and ultimately inspired the creation of modern European social democracy.

Bibliography

Braunthal, Julius. *History of the International.* Translated by Henry Collins and Kenneth Mitchell. 2 vols. London: Collins, 1966; New York: Praeger, 1967. This standard work on the Socialist International includes a discussion of Liebknecht's efforts in attracting German workers' attention to the First International. Places Liebknecht in the context of the early days of European socialism.

Dominick, Raymond H., III. *Wilhelm Liebknecht and the Founding of the German Social Democratic Party.* Chapel Hill: University of North Carolina Press, 1982. Dominick provides the standard biography of Liebknecht. His focus is on the philosophical struggle inherent in the founding of the German Social Democratic Party. He attributes to Liebknecht the party's emphasis on participatory democracy. Liebknecht is given credit for retaining party unity in the face of Prussian repression and ideological disputes within European socialism.

Hall, Alex. *Scandal, Sensation, and Social Democracy: The SPD Press and Wilhelmine Germany, 1890-1914.* Cambridge and New York: Cambridge University Press, 1977. The author examines in detail the workings of such major Social Democratic organs as *Vorwärts* and provides a detailed discussion of Liebknecht's direction of the paper during the 1890's. Liebknecht is given credit for maintaining his democratic principles in the face of severe criticism from both the government and his own party's radical elements.

Lidtke, Vernon L. *The Outlawed Party: Social Democracy in Germany, 1878-1890.* Princeton, N.J.: Princeton University Press, 1966. This study is devoted largely to the struggle of the German Social Democratic Party during the period of Bismarck's antisocialist laws. Early chapters, however, deal in depth with Liebknecht's role in the founding of the party. The author emphasizes the impact of Liebknecht's liberalism in the formulation of party ideology.

Pelz, William, ed. *Wilhelm Liebknecht and German Social Collections: A Documentary History.* Translated by Erich Hahn. Westport, Conn.: Greenwood Press, 1994. Presents Liebknecht through a sampling of his most renowned work. Whenever possible, the writings are included unedited, and each offering is preceded by an introduction placing the piece in context. Also included are essays by colleagues and those who knew Liebknecht personally.

Roth, Guenther. *The Social Democrats in Imperial Germany: A Study in Working-Class Isolation and National Integration.* Totowa, N.J.: Bedminster Press, 1963. This work is basically a sociological view of the integration of the German working class into German society. The author attacks party leaders, including Liebknecht, for denying strict Marxism in favor of watered-down liberalism. Credit is given, however, for Liebknecht's criticism of militarism and other evils of Prussian authoritarianism.

William G. Ratliff

LILIUOKALANI

Born: September 2, 1838; Honolulu, Hawaii
Died: November 11, 1917; Honolulu, Hawaii
Area of Achievement: Government and politics
Contribution: The last monarch of Hawaii, Liliuokalani witnessed the end of the Hawaiian kingdom and the beginning of the islands' annexation as a territory of the United States.

Early Life

Liliuokalani was born into Hawaii's royal family. She was the daughter of a chief named Kapaakea and his wife Keohokalole, who was one of the fifteen counselors of the king, Kamehameha III. Immediately after her birth, she was adopted into another family. A woman named Konia was her foster-mother, and her foster-father was a chief named Paki. This practice of adoption was the custom among the leading families of Hawaii; it was a way to cement alliances among the chiefs, who were the nobility of Hawaii. All of Liliuokalani's ten brothers and sisters were also adopted into and reared by other families.

When she was four years old, the little princess was enrolled in the Royal School, a boarding school run by American missionaries. The students of this school were all members of the royal extended family, which was made up of the families of the king and chiefs. In this school, Liliuokalani learned English and was taken to church every Sunday, but she said that she never got enough to eat.

The school closed in 1848, when she was ten years old, and after that she attended a day school also run by American missionaries. Learning was very important to Liliuokalani throughout her life.

After Paki's death in 1855, Liliuokalani continued to live in his home, along with her sister Bernice and Bernice's husband, Charles R. Bishop. The Bishops were to be a major influence on Liliuokalani's life.

Although at one time she was engaged to be married to Lunalilo (also known as Prince William), who would become king in 1873, she ultimately was married to the son of an Italian-born sea captain and a New England woman. The man was named John O. Dominis, and the marriage took place on September 16, 1862. The couple began their married life at Washington Place, the estate built by the groom's father for his family. This was to remain Liliuokalani's private residence throughout her life.

Much of Liliuokalani's adulthood before her accession as queen was spent on benevolent work for native Hawaiians. She was also a composer of music, and she wrote several Christian hymns as well as the famous Hawaiian song "Aloha Oe." In 1887, she attended Queen Victoria of England's Jubilee celebration as an honored guest. She never had any children.

Life's Work

A year after Liliuokalani's marriage, King Kamehameha IV died, on November 30, 1863. Since the young king had recently lost his only son to illness, there was no direct heir to the throne. According to the Hawaiian Constitution of 1852, the king's brother was elected as the new monarch by the cabinet, the privy council, and the *kuhina nui* (the queen, who served as coruler with the Hawaiian king). He became known as Kamehameha V. When he died in 1872, a new constitution had been passed (in 1864) that gave the king the right to choose his own successor. The successor he had named, however, his sister Princess Victoria, had died in 1866, and he had named no one else.

Now it was up to the Hawaiian legislature to elect a new king from among the nobility. This was when Liliuokalani's former fiancé, Lunalilo, ascended the throne. He lived only a year longer, however, and also died without naming an heir. This time, Liliuokalani's brother Kalakaua was elected, and in 1877 she was chosen as heiress to the throne. She served as regent from January to October of 1881 while the king was making a trip around the world, which gave her a taste of what it would later be like to be queen. She took this role again in 1890 and 1891 while the king was in California on a trip meant to restore his failing health. He died in January of 1891, however, leaving his sister Liliuokalani as queen.

Liliuokalani was proclaimed queen on January 29, 1891, at the age of fifty-two. She inherited a government that had been, throughout the nineteenth century, a mixture of Hawaiian tradition, British constitutional ideals, Victorian influence, and American interference brought by missionaries, adventurers, and politicians. Symbolic of this mixture were the combinations of names held by

the Hawaiian nobility. (Liliuokalani was also known as Lydia Kamekaeha Paki and Mrs. John O. Dominis.) This mixture was strengthened by the frequency of intermarriage between Hawaiians and people of European-American extraction, of which Liliuokalani's own marriage was an example.

Liliuokalani's brother, influenced by American businessmen, had led Hawaii on a course toward ruin by trying to return to a more despotic form of government. This led to revolution in 1887 and to increased American influence, since in the new constitution of that year members of the nobility were to be elected by voters of large income and property, which in practice meant large numbers of Americans and others of foreign birth or ancestry. Hawaii was also under the grip of an economic depression as a result of the McKinley Tariff Act, which removed tariffs on other importers of sugar to the United States. Since sugar had become the center of Hawaii's economy, this act devastated the island nation.

This was the situation the new queen faced: political turmoil and economic difficulty. Her solution was to strengthen the monarchy. Liliuokalani was firmly opposed to the Constitution of 1887, which was far more democratic than previous constitutions had been. At the same time, the political strife and economic difficulties in the islands made the idea of annexation by the United States look rather appealing to some Hawaiians, and by 1892 there were secret organizations working toward that end.

After an attempt by the queen to promulgate a new constitution giving the monarchy more power, in January, 1892, a revolutionary committee took over the government and ended the monarchy, setting up a provisional government until a union with the United States could be worked out. The queen assented against her will, in order to avoid bloodshed, and retired to Washington Place. A treaty of annexation by the United States was drawn up and signed by the provisional government on February 14, 1893. It had not been acted upon, however, by the Senate of the United States by the time Grover Cleveland became president a few days later. Cleveland, a friend of Liliuokalani, had received a letter from her about the coup d'état. After his inauguration, he withdrew the treaty from the Senate's consideration and launched a lengthy investigation into the matter. Meanwhile, the provisional government remained in power.

When it became clear that annexation was not imminent, a constitutional convention in 1894 set up what was to be the Republic of Hawaii. Liliuokalani protested to both the United States and Great Britain, but to no avail. An attempt to restore the monarchy was quickly squelched, leading to Liliuokalani's arrest and conviction on charges of treason. She was imprisoned in the Iolani Palace and forced to sign abdication papers. Hawaii was officially annexed to the United States on August 12, 1898, but the Republic continued to govern the islands under the authority of the president of the United States.

Liliuokalani was pardoned in 1896, and in that year she traveled to the United States to visit her late husband's relatives, trying to forget her sorrows over recent events. She returned in August of 1898, her enthusiastic welcome home showing how much support she still retained among both native-born and foreign-born Hawaiians.

While in the United States, she wrote her autobiography, *Hawaii's Story by Hawaii's Queen* (1898), as well as translating an ancient Hawaiian poem. Liliuokalani died on November 11, 1917, in Honolulu, Hawaii.

Summary

Although her reign was Hawaii's last as an independent nation, Liliuokalani's impact on Hawaii's history cannot be denied. Because she was part of a tradition in which women played important roles, she never questioned her right to rule. Although she believed in a strong monarchy, Liliuokalani organized institutions for the improvement of the health, welfare, and education of her native Hawaiian compatriots. She was an educated woman who valued learning, and she was both an author and a composer. A native Hawaiian, she was also an enthusiastic participant in the Victorian-inspired society of her times. Her downfall was her accession to the throne at a time when her tiny kingdom, influenced as it was by both European and American values and politics, could no longer remain independent. Although she resigned herself to Hawaii's annexation to the United States, she never agreed with the idea, always remaining convinced of the value of national autonomy for her islands.

Liliuokalani is something of a tragic figure. Trained and educated as a potential ruler, passionate about her country and her people, a woman of cosmopolitan learning and taste, she nevertheless came to power at a time when her method of rule came into conflict with the movement of history.

Bibliography

Kuykendall, Ralph S., and A. Grove Day. *Hawaii: A History, from Polynesian Kingdom to American State*. Rev. ed. Englewood Cliffs, N.J.: Prentice-Hall, 1961. The parts of this book labeled books 3 and 4 (chapters 11 through 12) give a very helpful chronicle of the events of the latter years of the Hawaiian kingdom. They help the reader understand the background to the situation that Liliuokalani inherited, as well as the outcome of her own reign.

Liliuokalani. *Hawaii's Story by Hawaii's Queen*. Boston: Lee and Shepard, 1898. The queen's autobiography is the best source for learning about her early life. Although it is somewhat rambling, it is invaluable in that it gives Liliuokalani's perspective on events in her own words. It ends with her return from the United States in 1898.

Loomis, Albertine. *For Whom Are the Stars?* Honolulu: University Press of Hawaii, 1976. A highly readable and sympathetic account of the end of the Hawaiian monarchy, discussing the revolution and events leading up to it, the first failure to annex Hawaii to the United States, the founding of the Republic, the rebellion of 1895, and the queen's arrest and trial.

Russ, William Adam, Jr. *The Hawaiian Republic, 1894-98, and Its Struggle to Win Annexation*. Selinsgrove, Pa.: Susquehanna University Press, 1961; London: Associated University Presses, 1992. This book follows up on Russ's earlier book (below). This volume analyzes the years of the Hawaiian Republic, between the time of Liliuokalani's abdication and Hawaii's annexation by the United States.

———. *The Hawaiian Revolution, 1893-94*. Selinsgrove, Pa.: Susquehanna University Press, 1959; London: Associated University Presses, 1992. Analyzes in readable detail the events of the revolution that deposed Queen Liliuokalani. It also examines the involvement of the United States and American interests in the overthrow of Hawaiian autonomy.

Tate, Merze. *The United States and the Hawaiian Kingdom: A Political History*. New Haven, Conn.: Yale University Press, 1965. This book focuses on the period of Hawaiian history that included Liliuokalani's life and work: 1864 to 1898. Chapters 4 through 7 deal specifically with various events of her reign: her attempt to change the constitution, the Revolution of 1893, and annexation by the United States.

Young, Lucien. *The Real Hawaii: Its History and Present Condition*. New York: Doubleday, 1899. An eyewitness account of the Revolution of 1893 and the events that followed. The author was on a ship stationed at Honolulu at the time. Written to discount the reports of James H. Blount, the envoy of Liliuokalani to President Cleveland, the book gives an account of Hawaiian culture, history, and economy as well as of the revolution and its aftermath.

Eleanor B. Amico

LIN TSE-HSÜ

Born: August 30, 1785; Hou-kuan, Fukien, China
Died: November 22, 1850; Ch'ao-chou, Kwang-
tung, China
Areas of Achievement: Government and politics
Contribution: A respected scholar-official serving
the Manchu Ch'ing Dynasty, Lin led the effort to
eradicate the sale of opium by foreigners at Can-
ton, a successful campaign that led to the Opium
War (1839-1842) and the ignominious 1842
Treaty of Nanking.

Early Life

Lin Tse-hsü was the second child born in 1785 to
Lin Pin-jih, a poor scholar. His father, hoping to
emulate earlier family members by entering the
government bureaucracy through the civil service
exam system, could not rise beyond the initial *hsiu-
ts'ai* (cultivated talent) degree and at forty-one
gave up his quest for the provincial level *chü-ren*
(recommended man) degree to run a private school
to support his growing family (ultimately three
sons and eight daughters). The young Lin Tse-hsü
grew up in a loving but impoverished family environment. His education began at home under his
father's tutelage, and he entered school at age four.
During his youth, he helped sell his mother's em-
broidery to make ends meet. A bright student, he
entered the local academy at nine and won the
hsiu-ts'ai degree when fourteen. In an oral test to
choose the best of the exam entrants, he bested a rival candidate many years his senior.

At twenty, he passed the *chü-ren* exams, which
entitled him to go to Peking to take the capital
tests, but he could not afford to do so. Instead, he
entered the local yamen (government office) as a
clerk-scribe. When a New Year's greeting he wrote
caught the attention of Chang Shih-ch'eng, the
Fukien provincial governor, Lin was summoned to
neighboring Foochow to serve for three years on
Chang's staff.

Seven years after achieving *chü-ren* status, Lin finally went to Peking to take the highest-level exams. He attained *chin-shih* (presented scholar) rank
and entered the Hanlin Academy. His nine-year stay
in Peking gained for him considerable experience in
handling the myriad governmental concerns
brought to the attention of the six ministries at the
top of the Ch'ing bureaucracy. He also made valuable, lifelong contacts within the power structure,
connections important for career advancement.

In 1819, Lin was sent to Yunnan in the southwest
to be head examiner in the provincial exams. This
was a stepping stone to his first major appointment
as intendant of the administrative circuit (*tao*) in the
Hangchow area. In 1822, Lin went to Peking and
had an audience with the newly enthroned Tao-
kuang emperor. The emperor praised Lin's work in
the Hangchow region and permitted Lin to return
there. In succession, he was given posts in Kiangsu
(intendant) and Chekiang (salt monopoly controller)
provinces. In 1823, he became surveillance commissioner of Kiangsu. By cleaning up a backlog of judicial cases with great impartiality and reforming the
penal system, he earned the epithet "Lin as Clear as
the Heavens" (Lin Ch'ing T'ien). The following
year, his mother died, requiring a return to his hometown for a custom-dictated three years of mourning.
This period was interrupted twice, first to help in
flood relief in Kiangsu along the Yellow River, and
then to work in the salt monopoly administration.
After a visit to Peking in 1827, he was assigned to
Sian in Shensi; there he became familiar with military affairs as a result of a nearby Muslim rebellion
being quashed by the Ch'ing military.

While Lin was serving as financial commissioner
in Nanking, his father died en route to joining him.
This again necessitated a three-year absence from
government service for official mourning in his native village. In 1830, Lin was back in the capital,
awaiting a new assignment. During this stay, Lin renewed and made friendships with middle-echelon
bureaucrats, men on the periphery of power yet
close enough to the real problems to be concerned
about the dynasty's ossifying rule. Lin was part of a
coterie (often meeting socially as the Hsüan-nan
Poetry Society) of younger degree-holders, inspired
by their study of "modern text" (*chin-wen*) Confucian writings to seek practical solutions to problems
of governing. When Lin received his next set of assignments, he left the capital, invigorated with ideas
shared by a nascent group of intellectual-adminis-
trators devoted to practical statecraft.

In the next twenty months, Lin was given five different assignments: provincial administration commissioner, in turn, of Hupei, Hunan, and Chiangn-
ing, followed by that of water conservancy director-
general in Shantung and Honan, and, in 1832, governor of Kiangsu. He stayed in the latter post for five
years. His tenure in Kiangsu under his friend Governor-General T'ao Shu added to his reputation. A

new problem he encountered was the outflow of local silver used to pay for opium distributed into the hinterland from foreign sources at Canton.

Life's Work

At age fifty-two, Lin was appointed governor-general of Hupei and Hunan. Increasingly, much of his time came to be concentrated on a matter that was by this time a major local and national concern—opium control. Trade between the Western powers and China, begun in the mid-1700's, originally was in China's favor, since European and American demand for tea leaves, raw silk, rhubarb, chinaware, and lacquer items far exceeded Chinese interest in Western woolens, tin, lead, furs, and linen. The anticommercial Manchu rulers only begrudgingly tolerated this trade, despite its profitability, and confined it to the southern port of Canton, where foreigners could not easily press on the dynasty their demands for diplomatic recognition.

The import of tea to England was lucrative to the Crown as a result of a 100 percent excise duty, but, since it could not be paid for only by the sale of Indian cotton to the Chinese, Britain had to bring in silver bullion from Mexico and Peru to pay its bills. A triangular trade among England, India, and China operated through the "Canton system" whereby foreign ships, stopping first at the Portuguese enclave Macao, would proceed with Chinese permission to Canton and sell their cargoes at a waterfront warehouse enclave through the *co-hong* trade guild run by Chinese merchants supervised by the *hoppo* (customs official).

The British and the other foreigners tolerated this inconvenient system because it was lucrative. The trade imbalance in China's favor began to change with the export by the East India Company of opium from Bengal to Canton, starting in the 1770's. Opium was originally used for its reputed medicinal and aphrodisiac qualities, and, even though the Chinese repeatedly had outlawed its use, it became a popular drug, inhaled by pipe. The East India Company, to protect itself legally, consigned the opium transport and sale to private traders not bound by the intricacies of the formalistic Canton system. In 1834, the company's China trade monopoly was ended by the British parliament's response to domestic demands for free trade. The resulting free-for-all among opium dealers dramatically increased sales to the Chinese, and by the late 1830's anywhere from two to ten million Chinese had become addicted. In addition, the outflow of Chinese silver

and the worsening exchange ratio between silver and Chinese copper coins (a problem Lin had confronted earlier) created economic havoc.

In China, a debate raged between those wanting to legalize the opium trade in order to control it and those favoring an end to it. The Tao-kuang emperor sided with the officials who opposed legalization, and Governor-General Teng T'ing-chen cracked down on the Canton opium trade between 1836 and 1838. He was successful in dealing with the Chinese end of the problem but had difficulty with the foreign merchants. After the East India Company's monopoly ended, the Chinese, preferring to deal with a formal middleman rather than a host of competing foreign interests, asked the British to designate someone to be *taipan* (head merchant). The British, wanting official Chinese diplomatic recognition, sent, in 1833, Lord William John Napier, assisted militarily by Captain Charles Elliot.

In one stroke the British put a government official in a position formerly occupied by the East India Company, thus making trade, originally a private arrangement between the company and the *co-hong* merchants, the official concern of the Crown. Increasingly, questions of commercial interests and national honor coalesced as the British, using commerce as a wedge, continued to attempt to persuade the Chinese to recognize their representative on a government-to-government basis.

Teng's anti-opium campaign was very successful. To preclude Teng from carrying out his threat to end all trade, the foreigners eventually reluctantly cooperated in the opium-suppression efforts. Smuggling by illegal profiteers, however, continued in the waters surrounding Canton. In Peking, pressure increased for the complete eradication of opium. Lin, successful in curbing opium use in his jurisdiction, was among the hard-liners. The emperor consulted with him personally and was impressed by his opium-elimination measures in Hupei and Hunan. On December 31, 1838, Lin was appointed imperial commissioner to eradicate the opium trade.

Lin arrived in Canton on March 10, 1839. The foreign community took his arrival calmly, viewing his subsequent crackdown on Chinese opium sellers and users as a continuation of the government's toughened policy. Lin's tack in dealing with the foreigners was to try to establish jurisdiction by getting them to accept Chinese legal rights and to convince them of the immorality of their actions. With imperial permission, he drafted two letters addressed to Queen Victoria, appealing to her moral propriety and common sense. Pointing out that opium smoking was a crime in England, he asked why her government promoted its use in his land and urged her to control her subjects' actions. These letters were widely circulated, for effect, among the foreign residents. A ship captain agreed to take a copy to England, but the foreign office refused to accept it.

On March 18, Lin ordered the surrender, through the hong merchants, of all opium in the foreigners' possession and required all to sign a bond pledging, on penalty of death, no longer to engage in this trade. A token 1,036 chests were turned in. Dissatisfied, Lin attempted to coerce Lancelot Dent, a major opium supplier, to surrender himself to Chinese authority. Dent refused, and Elliot, fearing the worst, left Macao for Canton, arriving on the day before Lin enacted a total trade embargo and ordered all Chinese help out of the foreigners' compound, thus imposing a siege on the 350 foreigners trapped there. The standoff ended after six weeks on Elliot's promise to have the foreigners turn over all of their opium to Lin. This was readily done, since there no longer was a market and Elliot promised reimbursement. The forfeited 21,306 chests were emptied into a huge pit and the opium was dissolved in seawater and lime, ending up in the ocean. Lin was victorious; however, by making his demands of Elliot, he now was dealing directly with a representative of the British government.

On May 24, all the British evacuated Canton for Macao. News of their confinement had infuriated the British public, and foreign secretary Lord Palmerston was bombarded with traders' petitions to be compensated for their losses. The British refugees thought they were secure in Portuguese Macao. The killing of a Chinese peasant on July 12 by some drunken British sailors at Kowloon, however, led to Lin's demand that the perpetrators be turned over to Chinese jurisdiction. This was refused. Lin had supplies to Macao cut off and ordered troops to surround it. The Portuguese evicted the British, who now sailed for Hong Kong. They were prevented from landing to replenish supplies. Elliot then ordered his ships to fire on some Chinese junks after being refused water and food.

By the fall of 1839 some British traders, aware that Americans were taking over their lucrative business in Canton, broke ranks with Elliot and decided to sign Lin's bond. On November 3, as some British traders were preparing to give in, a naval skirmish occurred at Ch'uan-pi. Losing several ships, the Chinese retreated. On December 6, Lin

ordered the end of all trade with the British. Unaware of this last event and responding to earlier provocations, the British Parliament, after an acrimonious debate between Tories opposing a war to support opium smugglers and prowar politicians prodded by a strong China lobby with vested interests, voted by a narrow margin to retaliate.

A large British expeditionary force under Elliot's uncle arrived in Chinese waters in June, 1840. Anticipating this reaction, Lin fortified the Canton area. Coastal batteries at the Bogue were augmented with foreign-purchased guns, war-junks surrounded Canton waters, and chain blockades were put across the Pearl River. Peasant militia were mobilized in Kwangtung Province. Martial arts fighters and Taoist magicians were also mustered. Lin wrote to the emperor that the large British warships were incapable of sailing up the Pearl River, adding that foreign soldiers, inept at fighting with swords and fists, could easily be routed.

Lin patiently waited for the British attack, but the fleet under Elliot's command, after blockading Canton, proceeded northward to deliver written ultimatums from Henry John Temple, Viscount Palmerston, directly to the court. After being refused at several ports, which were then blockaded, the British arrived in late August at the Peiho River near the Taku forts, protecting the approach to Peking. The court was shocked that the local problem of Canton was now brought to its doorstep. Palmerston's letter of demands, putting most of the blame on Elliot's personal nemesis, Lin, was accepted. The emperor now saw Lin as a convenient scapegoat. On July 1, 1841, Lin was ordered into exile in remote I-li in Central Asia.

Lin's dismissal was merely an interlude in what became known as the Opium War. Diplomatic efforts to prevent further military action failed, and Elliot's military campaigns in the Canton delta eventually gave the British the upper hand. Sir Henry Pottinger, commanding a punitive naval force sent from India and England, followed up in 1841 with attacks on major Chinese ports. The Chinese reluctantly agreed on August 29, 1842, to the Treaty of Nanking, requiring the payments of a war indemnity and reparations for seized opium, the opening of five coastal cities to trade and diplomatic residence, the abolishment of the co-hong monopoly, and the ceding of Hong Kong.

Though in official disgrace, Lin was still a faithful servant to the dynasty. On his way to exile he was asked to fight a break in the Yellow River dykes at Kaifeng. While banished in I-li, he directed irrigation projects which reclaimed much land for farming. In 1845, he was recalled to service as acting Governor-General of Shensi and Kansu, followed by posts in Shensi and Yunnan. His final task was imperial commissioner to fight the T'ai-p'ing rebels in the Kwangsi region. He died on November 22, 1850, en route to this last assignment.

Summary

Lin Tse-hsü was a victim of two cultures; his Confucian upbringing and fidelity to the Ch'ing required him to deal with the opium problem in an administrative and moralistic way that was outdated in the face of British might and the Western concept of foreign relations that denied China her self-assumed superiority. The Opium War, and Lin's role in it, marked a watershed in Chinese history. The "Middle Kingdom" would never recover from the burden of the "unequal treaties" begun at Nanking and the Western powers were not appeased by this first of many concessions to be extracted over the ensuing century. This happened despite Lin, not because of him.

Chinese Marxist historians use the Opium War as the beginning event in the history of modern China, the story of a collapsing feudal system ravished by foreign imperialism. Irrespective of ideology, Chinese everywhere respect Lin as a patriot who stood up to foreign aggression and the venal opium trade that symbolized it. His loyalty, though, was misplaced. It would take nationalism and revolution in the twentieth century to replace Lin's form of parochial dynastic allegiance before the Chinese would be able to reclaim their destiny for themselves.

Bibliography

Chang, Hsin-pao. *Commissioner Lin and the Opium War.* Cambridge, Mass.: Harvard University Press, 1964. The most thorough study of the events leading to the Opium War are examined in the context of Lin's role in them. Uses Chinese and Western sources to give a well-rounded account, analyzing, from respective perspectives, the positions of the English and the Chinese. Portrait of Lin faces the title page. Includes copious notes, a glossary, and a bibliography.

Compilation Group for the "History of Modern China" Series. *The Opium War.* Peking: Foreign Language Press, 1976. A booklet based on research by history professors at the University of Futan and Shanghai Teachers' University depicting Lin as one of "the capitulationists of the landlord class" who appeased Western imperialists in the Opium War; useful for understanding the Chinese Marxist historiographical approach.

Fairbank, John K., ed. *The Cambridge History of China.* Vol. 10, *Late Ch'ing, 1800-1911, Part 1.* Cambridge and New York: Cambridge University Press, 1978. Includes "The Canton Trade and the Opium War" by Frederic Wakeman, Jr., concisely narrating and analyzing the events before and after the war, including Lin's participation.

Teng, Ssu-yü, and John K. Fairbank. *China's Response to the West: A Documentary Survey, 1839-1923.* Cambridge, Mass.: Harvard University Press, 1954. Lin's famous 1839 letter to Queen Victoria admonishing the British for their moral double-standard in opium dealing and a short 1842 letter to a friend concerning the military superiority of the West are given in translation.

Waley, Arthur. *The Opium War Through Chinese Eyes.* London: Allen and Unwin, and New York: Macmillan, 1958. Uses Chinese documentary sources, Lin's diaries, and other writings to present the Opium War from a Chinese point of view.

William M. Zanella

ABRAHAM LINCOLN

Born: February 12, 1809; near Hodgenville, Kentucky

Died: April 15, 1865; Washington, D.C.

Areas of Achievement: Civil rights and government

Contribution: Lincoln is generally considered to have been the outstanding figure responsible for the preservation of the federal Union.

Early Life

Abraham Lincoln was born February 12, 1809, on the Sinking Spring Place, a farm three miles south of Hodgenville, Kentucky. His mother was the former Nancy Hanks, and his father was Thomas Lincoln, both natives of Virginia whose parents had taken them into the Kentucky wilderness at an early age. Thomas Lincoln was a farmer and a carpenter. In the spring of 1811, they moved to the nearby Knob Creek Farm.

The future president had a brother, Thomas, who died in infancy. His sister, Sarah (called Sally), was two years older than he. Much has been made in literature of his log-cabin birth and the poverty and degradation of Lincoln's childhood, but his father—a skilled carpenter—was never abjectly poor. The boy, however, did not aspire to become either a farmer or a carpenter. A highly intelligent and inquisitive youth, he considered many vocations before he decided upon the practice of law.

In Kentucky during his first seven years, and in Indiana until he became an adult, Lincoln received only the rudiments of a formal education, about a year in total. Still, he was able to read, write, and speak effectively, largely through self-education and regular practice. He grew to be approximately six feet, four inches tall and 185 pounds in weight. He was angular and dark-complected, with features that became familiar to later generations.

Moving with his family to Spencer County, Indiana, in December, 1816, Lincoln learned to use the American long ax efficiently on the Pigeon Creek Farm, where his father constructed another simple log cabin. He grew strong physically, and, largely through books he was able to borrow from neighbors, he grew strong mentally as well. The death of his mother from "the milk sick" in the summer of 1818 left both the boy and his sister emotionally depressed until the arrival of their stepmother, Sarah Bush Johnston Lincoln, from Elizabethtown, Kentucky. This strong and resourceful widow brought love and direction back to Lincoln's life and introduced him to her lively children, Elizabeth, Matilda, and John D. Johnston, then aged twelve, eight, and five, respectively.

While in Indiana, Lincoln was employed in 1827 as a ferryman on Anderson Creek and on the Ohio River into which it flowed. Then, in cooperation with Allen Gentry and at the behest of Gentry's father, he took a flatboat full of goods down the Mississippi River to New Orleans in 1828. Another childhood companion of this time was Lincoln's cousin, Dennis Hanks, who, in his later years, would relate many colorful stories about the future president's boyhood.

In March, 1830, the family moved to central Illinois, where Thomas Lincoln had heard that the farming was superior. They situated their cabin on a stretch of prairie in Macon County, some ten miles west of Decatur. There Lincoln split many rails for fences, although not as many as would later be accredited to the Rail-splitter. Another nickname he earned in Illinois which would serve him well in his later political career was Honest Abe. His honesty in business dealings became legendary.

Again, in the spring of 1831, Lincoln took a flatboat laden with supplies down the Mississippi River to New Orleans, this time commissioned by Denton Offutt and in the company of John Hanks and John D. Johnston. Hanks would later claim that the sight of a slave auction on this visit to the busy Southern city stirred in Lincoln his famous opposition to slavery, but historians now discredit this legend. Upon his return, Lincoln, having reached maturity, struck out on his own for the village of New Salem, Illinois.

Life's Work

Lincoln had been promised a store clerk's position in New Salem by Offutt and worked at this task for almost a year before the store "winked out." Then, in the spring of 1832, he served as a captain of volunteers in the Black Hawk War for thirty days. This service was followed by twenty days under Captain Elijah Iles and thirty days under Captain Jacob M. Early as a mounted private seeking to discover the whereabouts of the Indian leader for whom the war was named. While he saw no action, the war soon ended, and Lincoln returned home something less than a war hero.

Immediately upon returning to New Salem, Lincoln threw himself into an election for the lower house of the Illinois state legislature but, having no reputation, failed to win the seat. He was a loyal supporter of Henry Clay for president and therefore a Whig, but Clay failed also. In desperation, Lincoln became a partner in a store with William Berry, but its failure left him with an eleven-hundred-dollar "national debt." In 1834, however, and in 1836, 1838, and 1840 as well, Lincoln won consecutive terms in the state house of representatives. He also served as postmaster of his village from 1833 to 1836 and as deputy county surveyor from 1833 to 1835. Effective in these roles and being groomed for a leadership position in the legislature by Whigs such as John Todd Stuart, Lincoln studied law and passed the state bar examination in 1836.

New Salem was too small a village to sustain a lawyer, and Lincoln moved to the new capital city of Springfield in April, 1837, to join the law firm of Stuart and Lincoln. This firm was successful, and Lincoln won more cases than he lost, but Stuart wanted to devote more time to his political career. In 1841, the partnership was dissolved, and Lincoln joined, again as junior partner, with the master lawyer Stephen T. Logan. Finally, in 1844, he formed his last partnership, taking on young William H. Herndon as his junior partner.

In 1839, Lincoln met his future wife, Mary Todd, at the home of her sister, Mrs. Ninian Edwards. Lincoln and Edwards were already Whig leaders and members of the influential Long Nine. Lincoln and Todd intended to marry in 1841, but on January of that year, he suffered a nervous breakdown, broke the engagement, and then cemented it again. Their marriage took place at the Edwards home on November 4, 1842. From this union would be born four children: Robert Todd (1843), Edward Baker (1846), William Wallace (1850), and Thomas, called Tad (1853). Lincoln was always a kind and caring husband and father. Their home, purchased in 1844, was located at Eighth and Jackson streets.

When Clay again ran for president in 1844, Lincoln campaigned energetically on his behalf, but Clay was defeated once again. Two years later, Lincoln canvassed the district on his own behalf and won his sole term in the United States House of Representatives over the Democrat Peter Cartwright. During this term, which ran from 1847 to 1849, the Mexican War was still in progress, and Lincoln followed the Whig leadership in opposing it. For this decision, he suffered among the voters at home and had to content himself with the single term. Before leaving Washington, however, he patented a device for lifting riverboats over the shoals.

In the early 1850's, Lincoln concentrated upon his legal practice, but perhaps his most famous legal case came much later, in 1858, when he defended Duff Armstrong successfully against a charge of murder. Lincoln was a friend of Duff's parents, Jack and Hannah, and took the case without charging a fee. His use of an almanac in this case to indicate the brightness of the moon on the night of the purported murder is justly celebrated in the annals of courtroom strategy.

The passage of the Kansas-Nebraska Act in 1854 and the Supreme Court decision in the Dred Scott case in 1856 aroused Lincoln's antislavery fervor and brought him back into active politics. In 1855, he campaigned as an Anti-Nebraska (later Republican) candidate for the United States Senate but was compelled to stand aside in favor of his friend Lyman Trumbull, the eventual victor. A year later, Lincoln campaigned on behalf of presidential candidate John C. Frémont. Then, in 1858, he contended with his archrival, Stephen A. Douglas, for another Senate seat.

Before engaging in the famous debates with Douglas, Lincoln gave his most famous speech to date at Springfield, in which he proclaimed, "A house divided against itself cannot stand . . . this government cannot endure permanently half slave and half free." This House Divided Speech set the tone for his antislavery attacks in the debates that followed. Lincoln was a Free-Soiler and was truly outraged by Douglas' amoral stance on slavery. Many observers thought that Lincoln had won the debates, but largely because of a pro-Democratic apportionment, Douglas won reelection. Still, the fame Lincoln achieved through these debates assured his consideration for a presidential nomination in 1860.

The Republican Convention of that year was held in Chicago, where Lincoln was especially popular. Then, too, the original leading candidates, William Seward and Salmon Chase, detested each other; accordingly, their delegates turned to Lincoln as a "dark horse" when their favorites destroyed each other's chances. The Democrats then split their support with the dual nominations of Stephen A. Douglas and John C. Breckinridge. What was left of the old Whig Party split the South further by nominating as the Constitutional Union nominee John Bell of Tennessee.

Lincoln grew the dark beard associated with him during his campaign. He did not campaign actively but was elected over his divided opposition with 173 electoral votes, while Breckinridge amassed seventy-two, Bell thirty-nine, and Douglas merely twelve. Lincoln had the necessary majority of the electoral college but did not have a majority of the popular votes—no one did. The division in the country at large was made even more coldly clear when seven Southern states seceded over his election.

Inaugurated March 4, 1861, Lincoln took a strong stand against secession; when newly armed Confederate troops fired upon and captured Fort Sumter on April 12-13, 1861, he announced the start of the Civil War by calling for seventy-five thousand volunteers and a naval blockade of the Southern coast. Four more states then seceded, and the War Between the States began in earnest, lasting four years.

During the war, President Lincoln often visited the fighting front, intercepted telegraphic messages at the War Department, and advised his generals as to strategy. He was a remarkably able wartime leader, but Lincoln was deeply dissatisfied with his highest-ranking generals in the field until he "found his general" in Ulysses S. Grant.

In the midst of the struggle, Lincoln drafted his Emancipation Proclamation, calling for the freedom of the slaves. A few months later, in 1863, he wrote and delivered his most famous speech, the Gettysburg Address. This speech summed up the principles for which the federal government still fought to preserve the Union. Upon being reelected in 1864, over Democratic nominee General George B. McClellan, the president gave another stirring speech in his Second Inaugural Address. Final victory was only achieved after the defeat of Confederate General Robert E. Lee's Army of Northern Virginia at Appomattox Court House on April 9, 1865. Less than a week later, on April 14, Lincoln was assassinated by the Southern partisan actor John Wilkes Booth at Ford's Theatre in Washington, expiring the following morning. Secretary of War Edwin Stanton then was heard to say: "Now he belongs to the ages."

Summary

More books have been written about Lincoln and more legends have been told about him than about any other individual in American history. This sixteenth president often is regarded as the greatest leader America has yet produced or is likely to produce, yet he came from humble stock and little was given him that he had not earned.

He was the first Republican president, was twice elected, had to fight a cruel war yet remained sensitive, humble, and magnanimous to the end. It was his intention, had he lived, to "bind up the nation's wounds" with a speedy and liberal method of reconstruction. His death assured the opposite, or Radical Reconstruction.

His greatest achievements were the preservation of the federal Union and the liberation of the slaves. The former was achieved with the cessation of fighting in the South, which came only days after his death. The latter was brought about at last by the Thirteenth Amendment to the Constitution a few months later. Yet the nobility and simple dignity he brought to the nation's highest office are also a part of his legacy.

Bibliography

Brooks, Noah. *Lincoln Observed: Civil War Dispatches of Noah Brooks.* Michael Burlingame, ed. Baltimore, Md.: Johns Hopkins University Press, 1998. Brooks had almost daily access to Lincoln during the last two years of the war and was too be Lincoln's personal secretary during his second term. This book offers Brooks' own candid accounts of Lincoln and his relationships with family, friends, generals, and many others.

Herndon, William H. *Herndon's Lincoln: The True Story of a Great Life.* 3 vols. Chicago: Belford, Clarke, 1889. The color and dash of Lincoln's law partner almost make up for his lack of objectivity. Herndon is strongest when he speaks from experience, weakest when he deals with Lincoln's early years and personal relationships.

Kunhardt, Philip B., Jr. *A New Birth of Freedom.* Boston: Little Brown, 1983. A concentrated examination of the background and circumstances of Lincoln's greatest speech, the Gettysburg Address. Vivid in the memory of a nation, this speech was considered a failure at the time by the president himself. Well written and beautifully illustrated, the book itself is one of the more important works dealing with a segment of Lincoln's life.

Lamon, Ward Hill. *The Life of Abraham Lincoln.* Boston: Osgood, 1872. Lincoln's longtime friend, fellow attorney, and marshal of the District of Columbia knew him well but was not very particular about his sources. Certainly he relied too heavily upon Herndon's fulminations about the Ann Rutledge love affair (a myth) and Lincoln's stormy marriage to the former Mary Todd.

Nicolay, John G., and John Hay. *Abraham Lincoln: A History*. 10 vols. New York: Century, 1890. This major production is based upon Lincoln's personal papers but is rather laudatory. There is, perhaps, too much detail and too little insight in these volumes.

Oates, Stephen B. *With Malice Toward None*. New York: Harper, 1977; London: Allen and Unwin, 1978. The best scholarly biography available, this work reflects much new research. It is well written and well documented.

Sandburg, Carl. *Abraham Lincoln: The Prairie Years*. 2 vols. New York: Harcourt, Brace, and London: Cape, 1926.

————. *Abraham Lincoln: The War Years*. 4 vols. New York: Harcourt Brace, 1939. These two sets are beautifully poetic but lacking in historical accuracy at times. Many readers have started with Sandburg, gained a sense for the subject, and gone on to develop a profound love of Lincolniana.

Stevens, Walter B., and Michael Burlingame. *A Reporter's Lincoln*. Lincoln: University of Nebraska Press, 1998. Reproduction of a book published in 1916 of Walter B. Stevens' 1886-1909 interviews with people who had known Lincoln personally. This version is supplemented with additional Stevens articles omitted from the earlier version. Provides personal information on Lincoln the man, Mary Todd Lincoln, and their family traditions.

Thomas, Benjamin. *Abraham Lincoln*. New York: Knopf, 1952; London: Eyre and Spottiswoode, 1953. This is probably the finest biography of Lincoln available which is a balanced scholarly-popular work in one volume. It is a must for any shelf of Lincoln books.

Vidal, Gore. *Lincoln*. New York: Random House, and London: Heinemann, 1984. The most celebrated novel yet written about Lincoln's presidential years. Well worth reading by those who would gain an understanding of his actions. Without psychoanalysis or unfettered pathos, Vidal has portrayed Lincoln and his wartime contemporaries with exceptional accuracy, taking only a few liberties with history.

Joseph E. Suppiger

JENNY LIND

Born: October 6, 1820; Stockholm, Sweden
Died: November 2, 1887; Wynds Point, Hereford-
  shire, England
Area of Achievement: Music
Contribution: Through perseverance, hard work,
  and her unique charismatic personality, Lind,
  known as the "Swedish Nightingale," became
  the most famous female singer of the nineteenth
  century, an internationally successful touring
  star, and a role model for her generation.

Early Life

Jenny Lind was born Johanna Maria Lind in Stockholm, Sweden, on October 6, 1820, to Anne-Marie
Fellborg and Niclas Jonas Lind, who lived together
but did not choose to marry until their daughter
was fifteen. For this reason, she was placed in a
foster home. Although considerate of her parents
in later years, she was more devoted to her grandmother, who had instilled in her the spiritual values
that became so much a part of her life.

After Lind's precocious singing ability was discovered by a member of the Swedish Royal Opera,
she was admitted to the court theater school at age
nine. Her first major role was the part of Agathe in
Carl Maria von Weber's opera *Der Freischütz*
(1821; the marksman) at the Stockholm Opera on
March 7, 1838. In 1840 Lind became a member of
the Royal Swedish Academy of Music with the rank
of court singer. Recognizing that her voice needed
more extensive and better training, however, in 1841
she left to study in Paris, France, with vocal instructor Manuel García, Jr., brother of the famous early
nineteenth century diva Maria García Malibran and
son of the singer and impresario who had introduced
Italian opera to the United States in 1825. After one
year of intensive training with García, who was considered the world's greatest teacher of singing, Lind
returned home and resumed her operatic career,
which would last nineteen years.

Life's Work

In 1844 Lind began an extensive and successful
European tour that included performances in Berlin, Hamburg, Cologne, Vienna, Copenhagen, and
London. In addition to being a technically brilliant
coloratura soprano with a range of two and three-
quarters octaves and having perfect pitch, she impressed almost all of her contemporaries with her
piety, simplicity, and instinctive dislike of celebri-

ty. Her generous donations to charity wherever she
performed also made her a unique symbol of virtue
and goodness. The public had found a new heroine,
and Lindomania soon swept Europe. Despite enthusiastic accounts by the press and large crowds
wherever she appeared, Lind grew tired of theatrical life and chose to retire from the operatic stage
in May, 1849, after more than six hundred performances in thirty operas. For the more than thirty
years remaining in her professional life, she sang
in oratorios and concerts.

Lind was not a beautiful woman; although she
had typical Nordic blond hair and blue eyes, she
had plain features with a broad mouth and wide
nose. Some of her portraits were even enhanced to
make her appear more romantically appealing.
However, her remarkable charismatic stage presence transcended mere physical attractiveness.
Dressed simply in blue or white and carrying flowers, this rather ordinary looking young woman
seemed to many concertgoers to become an angelic
being as soon as she began to sing. Along with a

magnificent voice, she possessed a unique ability to make an emotional connection to her audiences.

In 1850 American impresario Phineas Taylor Barnum persuaded Lind to undertake a tour of the United States and Cuba. Despite his career as a showman of curiosities such as the midget Tom Thumb and overt frauds such as the Feejee Mermaid (a combination of a dead monkey and a fish), Barnum appreciated culture and genuinely admired Lind, and his offer was generous. For each concert, Lind would receive one thousand dollars plus all her expenses; she would choose the music to be performed and was allowed give charity concerts when she wished. Barnum also agreed to manage her publicity, secure her lodgings and concert sites, and make other technical arrangements. Along with his potential profits, Barnum would gain respectability and even admiration as the man who brought Europe's greatest singer to the United States. The contract was signed in January, 1850, and on August 21, Lind and her entourage of eight, including a companion, her secretary, her pianist and musical director, servants, and her pet dog, left Liverpool, England, to begin a concert tour that lasted until May 27, 1852.

Enthralled by the sometimes fanciful accounts of her life in newspapers and literary magazines, a crowd of about thirty thousand people was waiting on the pier when Lind's party reached New York on September 1, 1850. She toured the city and gave concerts during most of September; the profits from two of these performances, a sum of more than ten thousand dollars, were designated for charity. Lind then moved on to Boston and Philadelphia, where again she sang to capacity crowds.

At each stop, Barnum had arranged for the first few tickets to the opening performance to be auctioned to the highest bidders, a scheme that pitted individuals and even cities against each other; it was a publicity ploy that Lind disliked. The highest bidder in Philadelphia, for example, paid $625 for his ticket, although most seats could be purchased for three to seven dollars each. In Boston a young working girl purchased one of the cheaper tickets, declaring, "there goes half a month's earnings, but I am determined to hear Jenny Lind." On being told this, Lind asked her secretary to give her admirer a twenty-dollar gold piece. Similar acts of kindness in other cities and her well-publicized charity concerts illustrated not only Lind's generosity but also Barnum's media skills. He also approved of the marketing of a variety of items with her name, including Jenny Lind coats, hats, sewing machines, singing tea kettles, cigars, pianos, sofas, and bed frames.

To appeal to large general audiences, Lind's concerts were a blend of several different types of music, a tradition that dated from at least the late eighteenth century. Along with overtures and arias from her popular operatic roles—including Vincenzo Bellini's *La sonnambula* (1831; the sleepwalker) and *Norma* (1831), Gaetano Donizetti's *Lucia di Lammermoor* (1835), Giacomo Meyerbeer's *Robert le Diable* (1831), Weber's *Der Freischütz*, and Wolfgang Amadeus Mozart's *Don Giovanni* (1787) and *Le nozze di Figaro* (1786; the marriage of Figaro)—were excerpts from sacred works, especially George Frideric Handel's *The Messiah* (1742) and Franz Joseph Haydn's *Die Schöpfung* (1798; the creation). Light popular songs such as "Home, Sweet Home," "Echo Song," and settings of Robert Burns' "John Anderson, My Jo," and "Comin' thro' the Rye" were always part of her programs. Lind knew instinctively that these simpler pieces would be more meaningful to many in her audience, however splendidly the classical works displayed the remarkable qualities of her voice.

In 1850 and 1851 Lind gave concerts in Baltimore; Washington; several southern cities, including Richmond, Charleston, and New Orleans; Havana, Cuba; and the Midwest, including St. Louis, Louisville, and Cincinnati. Her last (and ninety-fifth) performance before she terminated her contract with Barnum to develop her own touring schedule was held in Philadelphia's National Theater on June 9, 1851.

Now independent, Lind reorganized her troupe and revisited a number of cities in the North, Midwest, and New England. In December, however, news of her mother's death temporarily halted the concert series. On February 5, 1852, she married her pianist and musical director Otto Goldschmidt, whom she had first met while touring in Europe. Though her concerts had brought her increased wealth, much of which she continued to give to charity, she was growing tired of travelling; after three final concerts in New York in May, 1852, the couple returned to Europe in early June.

With Lind's marriage, the adulation of the press became more subdued, but her international popularity remained. The Goldschmidts lived briefly in Dresden but in 1856 settled permanently in England. They had three children, one of whom wrote a biography of her mother (1926). Lind gave her last concert in 1880. Like many retired performers of the time, she became a teacher. Beginning in 1876, she devoted her energies to the Bach Choir founded and directed by her husband, and from 1883 to 1886, she was professor of singing at London's Royal College of Music. After a long illness, Lind died on November 2, 1887.

Summary

Although Jenny Lind was the nineteenth century's most famous vocal star and was admired by millions of people, she was not above criticism. She was occasionally faulted for high ticket prices and her association with Barnum, and a few critics thought that her concert choices lacked originality or that she was excessively religious. Though shy and prone to stage fright, she was resolute where her performances were concerned; she won over a hostile audience who hissed her first Havana concert, and after a drunken crowd outside the performance hall spoiled her first visit to Pittsburgh, she returned for a successful second engagement.

No one disputed her commercial success. Barnum, with Lind's somewhat reluctant help, launched the first successful large-scale promotion of a performer. Music publishers profited handsomely from her fame, and several later singers began their careers as "new" Jenny Linds. Her programs of arias by composers she preferred, balanced by Scottish, British, and Swedish folk melodies, reinforced a long English and American tradition of shared popular culture that could be enjoyed by rich and poor alike. A hallmark of her success was that Lind was more than a splendid singer; she was a person with whom ordinary individuals could identify and whose lifestyle they could genuinely respect.

Bibliography

Barnum, Phineas Taylor. *Struggles and Triumphs: Or, Forty Years' Recollections of P. T. Barnum.* Buffalo, N.Y.: Warren, Johnson, 1871; London: Abrahams, 1889. Ever the showman, Barnum tells a good story, and it is useful to read his version of his relationship with Lind since he was frequently accused of exploiting her for commercial purposes.

Dizikes, John. *Opera in America: A Cultural History.* New Haven, Conn.: Yale University Press, 1993. This comprehensive (612 pages) history of opera and its influence on American culture includes a chapter on Lind's American tour as well as references throughout the work. Dizikes' book is particularly helpful in placing the singer within the context of her time. It contains bibliographical notes and numerous illustrations.

Saxon, A. H. *P. T. Barnum: The Legend and the Man.* New York: Columbia University Press, 1989. In dealing specifically with Lind's career in relationship to Barnum, this biography is more critical than most of the singer's personality, motivations, and failings, therefore providing a corrective to other more complimentary accounts. It contains valuable annotated notes and illustrations.

Shultz, Gladys Denny. *Jenny Lind, the Swedish Nightingale.* Philadelphia: Lippincott, 1962. This pleasantly written account deals not only with Lind's successes but also with the hardships in her early life and how she managed to overcome them. However, some aspects of the singer's life have been fictionalized, thus marring an otherwise interesting study.

Wagenknecht, Edward Charles. *Jenny Lind.* Boston: Houghton Mifflin, 1931. This brief (231 pages) biography considers Lind not only as a performer but also as a woman whose primary motivation was her spiritual life, for which she left the operatic stage to devote herself to concerts, oratorios, and eventually her marriage. It contains an extensive bibliography of articles and books about Lind.

_____. *Seven Daughters of the Theater.* Norman: University of Oklahoma Press, 1964. Lind's biography is the first in this series of famous women singers, actors, and dancers. Although Wagenknecht's account of Lind includes much material from his earlier full-length study, its juxtaposition with six related biographies provides a valuable study in contrasts.

Ware, W. Porter, and Thaddeus C. Lockard, Jr. *P. T. Barnum Presents Jenny Lind: The American Tour of the Swedish Nightingale.* Baton Rouge: Louisiana State University Press, 1980. This laudatory biography is one of the more recent studies of the singer. Focusing primarily on Lind's reception in America, it includes a number of useful reviews and descriptions of her and her concerts by contemporaries.

Dorothy T. Potter

JOSEPH LISTER

Born: April 5, 1827; Upton Park, Essex, England
Died: February 10, 1912; Walmer, Kent, England
Area of Achievement: Medicine
Contribution: Combining skill as a laboratory scientist with great technical ability at surgery, Lister developed and helped to propagate antiseptic surgery.

Early Life

Joseph Lister was born on April 5, 1827, at Upton Park, just east of London. His parents, Joseph Jackson and Isabella Lister, were Quakers, and the family—there were six children—was unusually close. Lister's father owned a prosperous wine business and was a scientist in his own right. His development of the achromatic lens made a significant improvement in the microscope, and he became a Fellow of the Royal Society. Paternal example helped Lister develop an interest in and skill at scientific investigation.

After his primary education in Quaker schools, Lister entered University College, London, the only option for non-Anglicans interested in medicine. Unlike most mid-nineteenth century medical students, Lister first studied for an arts degree. Then, following a brief bout with nervous problems, he began the study of medicine, taking his degree in 1852. He won a number of prizes for scholarship, served as House Physician and Surgeon at University Hospital, and became a Fellow of the Royal College of Surgeons of England. Lister's decision to be a surgeon was an unlikely one, for with anesthesia being then only recently developed and the problems of infection still ill-understood, surgery was a brutal and little-respected specialty.

Two professors had significant influence on Lister. Wharton Jones, who did important work on blood circulation and inflammation, inspired an interest in the nature of inflammation that was important in the eventual understanding of infection. William Sharpey, one of the first modern physiologists, not only gave the young Lister a solid foundation in his field but also, when asked about the best way to get more experience, suggested visits to Edinburgh and the Continent. He also provided an introduction to James Syme, whose work at Edinburgh had made him the most distinguished surgeon in Great Britain and perhaps all of Europe.

Lister's visit to Edinburgh, planned for a month, lasted seven years, a period during which he completed his apprenticeship and began his career in earnest. His relationship with Syme was quickly one of friendship and mutual respect. He accepted a position as Syme's house surgeon, an unusually modest post for a man of his credentials. His willingness to serve as Syme's assistant seems to have reflected Lister's sincere desire to learn more, humility arising from his Quaker background, and perhaps some personal inclination. He not only found Syme extremely congenial but also married Syme's daughter, Agnes, in 1856. The match proved excellent. Agnes Syme Lister was better educated than most Victorian women, and she discussed and even helped her husband with his scientific work. The two, though sorry that they never had children, were devoted to each other until her death during an 1893 European tour.

In 1856, a year after Lister was made Lecturer on Surgery at the Edinburgh School of Medicine,

he was appointed assistant surgeon at the Royal Infirmary. Scottish medicine had for years been at the intellectual forefront of the field, and so for Lister maturing in that country was, if not socially a plus, an excellent opportunity.

The mature Lister was taller than average, well built, and strong. As he aged, he tended to stoutness and wore "mutton-chop" whiskers, shaving his chin and around his mouth. Contemporaries reported that he always gave an impression of health and vigor. In manner he was reserved and proper. Although he was unusually thoughtful of and kind to patients, his students gave him the nickname "the Chief" and did not find him particularly approachable. His manner appears to have been a mixture of his Quaker heritage—although he left the Society of Friends when he married outside it—and a natural shyness. His personality, combined with a strict forthrightness, did not help win supporters for his antiseptic theory.

Life's Work

Although identified with his later development of antiseptic surgery, Lister began serious scholarly work promptly after graduation—he published his first article in 1853—and continued research while working with Syme. In 1857, he made a presentation concerning inflammation to the Royal Society, though he had not yet begun to include infection as part of this work. Such experimentation was very unusual for surgeons of the period.

In 1860, Lister, with eleven published research papers to his credit, was appointed surgeon at the Glasgow Royal Infirmary and elected a Fellow of the Royal Society. His research expanded to the coagulation of blood, about which he gave a major address to the Royal Society in 1863. Over the next two years, the theory that was to dominate the rest of his life was developed. He became acquainted with the work of the French chemist Louis Pasteur concerning fermentation. This led to experiments testing whether putrefaction occurred in substances which air could not reach and the conclusion that hospital infections such as gangrene were caused by microbes in the air or on the hands and instruments of doctors and nurses. He decided that the cycle could be broken by the introduction of a proper antiseptic, and knowing that carbolic acid had been used to purify sewers at Carlisle, he decided to try a dilute mixture on the first appropriate case that came under his care.

Lister first used antiseptics on compound fractures. Such injuries were routinely treated by amputation because setting them almost inevitably resulted in blood poisoning and/or gangrene, and though the stump left after amputation almost always became infected, because the wound could drain, the patient sometimes survived. Using carbolic acid first directly in the wound and later increasingly as part of the dressing to exclude germs, Lister found that such fractures could be treated usually with no infection at all. Between March and July of 1867, *Lancet* carried in five installments the report of Lister's initial antiseptic treatments. Because of Lister's modest claims and the profession's conservatism about innovation, antiseptic surgery was initially taken as a method for the specific treatment of compound fractures rather than a general principle.

Over the next twenty years, Lister struggled to refine the antiseptic procedure and convince his skeptical and sometimes self-serving colleagues to adopt it. His work ranged from such physiological studies as the importance of blood clots in healing to investigation of ligatures to replace the previously used silk and linen, which had to be pulled out of the wound once ulceration loosened them, often causing secondary hemorrhaging. He found that catgut treated with carbolic acid to prevent the passage of infection into the wound was absorbed by the body. In 1869, Lister returned to Edinburgh to replace Syme, who was ill and going into retirement, as Regius Professor of Clinical Surgery at the University of Edinburgh and Surgeon to the Royal Infirmary.

In the early 1870's, Lister began to use a spray made with carbolic acid to keep the air clean any time a wound was exposed and began to search for dressings that would be an effective barrier to infection. By the late 1880's, he had settled on gauze impregnated with cyanide of mercury and zinc. Although the spray was unpleasant and soon lost favor—Lister dropped it himself in 1887—its use coincided with increasing reduction of the use of carbolic acid in the wound itself, presaging the development of aseptic surgical techniques in the twentieth century.

Lister's wards were the healthiest in Edinburgh, as healthy as they had been in Glasgow, and he continued to expand his repertoire of operations. He was successfully applying surgical treatments to cases that would not have even been accepted into hospitals only a few years before. It is sad to note that his fame spread on the Continent—his wards were being visited by European surgeons by 1872—long before his British colleagues gave his techniques much more than scorn. James Simpson, well-known and respected for his introduction of anesthesia into the British Isles, had concluded that hospital infections could best be prevented by frequent replacement of facilities. He advocated quickly built wooden hospitals that could be abandoned when infections became rampant, and he acquired his considerable prestige not only in advancing his own ideas but also in deprecating those of Lister. Poorly conducted experiments with antiseptics, of course, failed, and the annoyed Lister resisted publication of much of his work lest it lead to more harm than good. Students and others who worked closely with Lister personally began slowly to spread the corrected antiseptic technique.

In 1877, Lister was invited to become Professor of Clinical Surgery at King's College in London. He was reluctant to leave Edinburgh, where he had become popular—his students organized a petition begging him to remain—and his fame was secure, but he felt duty-bound to go because London was the professional center of the country. Success in London would mean that his antiseptic techniques would gain a wide audience in short order, and thus he accepted the position, also becoming Surgeon to King's College Hospital. Within a decade, he was a dominant figure in British medicine. Honors followed thick and fast. In 1883, he was created a baronet, and in 1897, he was raised to the peerage as Baron Lister. He retired from teaching in 1892 and private practice in 1896 but served as president of the Royal Society from 1895 to 1900. In 1896 and 1897, he helped reorganize the Jenner Institute of Preventive Medicine, which he had helped to found and which was later renamed the Lister Institute of Preventive Medicine. In 1902, Lister was selected as an original member of the Order of Merit, founded by King Edward VII, but in the following year he fell ill and was an invalid until his death in February 10, 1912.

Summary

In many ways, Joseph Lister typified the Victorian era. Driven by the Nonconformist ethic calling for hard work and service, he also had the British genius for technology. Choosing to be a surgeon at a time when surgeons' most prized skill was speed at completing a procedure before the shock of the operation killed the unanesthetized patient and when infection killed many of those who survived surgery, he transformed the profession. Lister recognized the value of anesthesia and was among the first to slow his operations, preferring precision to speed. He then took advantage of scientific discoveries—his own but to a greater degree those of Pasteur—to develop antiseptic surgical techniques. The nineteenth century was a time when British manufacturers were preeminent in applying science to practice in the name of profit; Lister, in much the same way, applied it to the easing of human suffering.

Bibliography

Cartwright, Frederick Fox. *Joseph Lister: The Man Who Made Surgery Safe*. London: Weidenfeld and Nicolson, 1963. Well written but based largely on secondary sources.

Cheyne, Sir William W. *Lister and His Achievement*. London and New York: Longman, 1925. Written by a house surgeon and admirer of Lister. Includes a summary of Lister's life and a longer appendix appraising his work.

Fisher, Richard B. *Joseph Lister*. London: Macdonald, and New York: Stein and Day, 1977. A scholarly, well-researched biography, though a bit dry in style.

Godlee, Sir Rickman John. *Lord Lister*. 3d ed. Oxford: Clarendon Press, 1924. A typical late-Victorian biography written by Lister's nephew. Includes much of Lister's correspondence.

Leeson, John R. *Lister as I Knew Him*. London: Balliere, and New York: William Wood, 1927. Reminiscences by a student and assistant of Lister. The style is chatty and personal, but the author did not know Lister intimately.

Turner, A. Logan, ed. *Joseph, Baron Lister: Centenary Volume, 1827-1927*. London: Oliver and Boyd, 1927. A collection of essays, including a biographical sketch, mostly by contemporaries, colleagues, and friends of Lister.

Woodward, John. *To Do the Sick No Harm: A Study of the British Voluntary Hospital System in 1875*. London and Boston: Routledge, 1974. A useful and scholarly study. Excellent background for the study of Lister's work.

Fred R. van Hartesveldt

FRANZ LISZT

Born: October 22, 1811; Raiding, Hungary
Died: July 31, 1886; Bayreuth, Germany
Area of Achievement: Music
Contribution: Liszt revolutionized the art of piano playing and thus established the vogue of the recitalist. As a composer, he attempted to reconcile the trends of French and German Romanticism, created the musical genre of the symphonic poem, founded new innovations in harmony and form, and in his late works anticipated many devices of twentieth century music.

Early Life

Franz Liszt was born in Raiding, near Sopron, in the province of Burgenland. His father, Ádám Liszt, was a clerk in the service of Prince Nikolaus Esterházy, the Hungarian noble family that had supported Joseph Haydn. An amateur cellist, Ádám Liszt had played in orchestras under Haydn and Ludwig van Beethoven and was his son's first teacher in piano.

Young Liszt showed phenomenal gifts for music as a child and began to study piano in his sixth year. His debut concerts in Sopron and Bratislava at the age of nine enabled him to acquire the support of several Hungarian nobles to finance his musical studies in Vienna under Karl Czerny and Antonio Salieri. Liszt soon acquired a reputation as a formidable sight reader. He published his first composition, a variation on a waltz by Anton Diabelli, in 1822, and in the following year made his debut in Vienna. The often-repeated story that Beethoven attended the concert and kissed the boy after the boy afterward cannot be proved, but it is certain that Liszt met Beethoven at his apartment and forever cherished the meeting.

Liszt continued his musical eduation in Paris. Denied admission to the Paris Conservatory because of his foreign citizenship, he studied privately with Anton Reicha and Ferdinando Paer. In 1824, he began his concert tours of England; until 1847, he was best known as a virtuoso pianist who revolutionized the art of playing that instrument and who was a pioneer in giving solo recitals performed from memory; he even invented the term "recital," to describe his solo programs in London in 1840.

The death of his father in 1826 and the rejection of his suit of Caroline de Saint-Cricq by her noble family brought about a period of depression when he contemplated entering the priesthood. In the early 1830's, he came under the influence of the Saint-Simonian movement and the liberal Catholicism of the Abbé Hughes-Félicité-Robert de Lamennais; both placed art in a central place in society. Liszt's first mature compositions, the *Apparitions* (1834), were written under Lamennais' influence, whereas his piano piece *Lyon* was influenced by a silk-weavers' strike there in 1834.

Life's Work

Liszt compensated for his lack of formal education by extensive reading and by seeking the company of writers. He was introduced to the Countess Marie d'Agoult, of German descent, who left her husband and children in 1835 to live with Liszt in Switzerland and Italy. The musical results of the sojourn were the first two volumes of the *Années de pèlerinage* (1835-1877; years of pilgrimage), featuring, in the first volume, nature scenes in Switzerland and, in the second, the art and literature of Italy. D'Agoult guided Liszt in his reading and interested him in the visual arts. They had three children. Blandine and Daniel died while in their twenties, but Cosima lived until 1930, to become the wife first of the pianist-conductor Hans von Bülow and then of the composer Richard Wagner.

Liszt's decision to return to concert playing in 1839 placed a strain on his relationship with d'Agoult, which ended in 1844 during a hectic period of concertizing all over Europe, performing as far afield as Portugal, Ireland, and Turkey, traveling under primitive conditions, and being subject to the kind of adulation given to modern rock stars. The main works of this period were his songs for voice and piano (highly expressive and unjustly neglected) and his opera paraphrases and transcriptions for the piano. The transcriptions are reproductions of the vocal music, but the paraphrases are virtual recompositions of the opera based on its main tunes; the most famous of these is the *Réminiscences de Don Juan* (1841), based on Wolfgang Amadeus Mozart's opera *Don Giovanni* (1787). During his tours of Hungary, he was able to hear authentic Gypsy music and re-created these sounds in his Hungarian Rhapsodies (1839-1847).

On his last concert tour in 1847, he met in Poland the Princess Carolyne de Sayn-Wittgenstein, with whom he began a lengthy relationship; be-

Franz Liszt, third from left, with religious leaders and nobleman from his native country, Austria

cause the Czar of Russia would not grant her a divorce, she could not marry Liszt but was able to flee Russia with most of her money. Liszt, in turn, accepted an offer to become musical director of the court at Weimar and was able to abandon his career as a touring piano virtuoso in 1847 to devote himself to musical composition. He and Carolyne moved there during the following year.

During Liszt's thirteen years in Weimar, he revised most of his earlier compositions for publication and embarked on many ambitious musical projects which he had sketched earlier, such as his two piano concerti. During these years, Liszt invented the symphonic poem, an extended programmatic work for orchestra. His first two works in this genre, the so-called Mountain Symphony (begun 1848) and *Tasso* (begun 1849-1854), required assistance from others as Liszt was learning how to write for orchestra, but the next work, *Les Préludes* (1854), his best-known symphonic poem, shows his complete mastery of both form and instrumentation. Among the best of the remaining nine are

Orpheus (1853-1854) and *Hamlet* (1858). The culmination of his orchestral works is his monumental *A Faust Symphony* (1854-1861), composed of three movements, character portrayals of the three main personages in Johann Wolfgang von Goethe's drama: Faust, Gretchen, and Mephistopheles. The less conventional *A Symphony to Dante's "Divina Commedia"* (1855-1856) was originally intended to accompany a stage performance with dioramas and does not follow normal symphonic form. A work of "absolute music" without an overt program is the Sonata in B Minor (1852-1853) for piano, the culmination of Liszt's experiments in harmony, form, and the construction of a large-scale work from a few ideas which are extensively developed and transformed.

While in Weimar, Liszt continued his altruistic gestures that got the music of his contemporaries performed. Earlier he had played the large piano works of Robert Schumann and Frédéric Chopin when their composers were physically unable to do so, and widened the audience for Beethoven's symphonies and Schubert's songs by arranging them for the piano. Now he devoted his energies to organizing and conducting performances of the operas of Richard Wagner, who was in exile in Switzerland after his participation in the abortive revolt in Dresden in 1849. Though Liszt had abandoned concertizing except for benefits and charities, he had a large number of piano students whom he taught without charge, and a coterie of ardent musical disciples. Disappointed at the lack of support he was receiving in Weimar from the new grand duke, who preferred the theater to music, Liszt resigned as musical director in 1858 and made it effective after a music festival in 1861, when he moved to Rome to join Carolyne.

The wedding of Liszt and Carolyne was to have taken place on the composer's fiftieth birthday, but it was abruptly canceled; the reasons have yet to be revealed. Shortly thereafter, Liszt took the initial steps toward entering the priesthood; though he dressed in clerical clothes and was known as "Abbé Liszt," he did not complete the final stages of holy orders and thus could not say Mass or hear confessions. Not until 1865 was his entry into the religious life generally known. During this period, he wrote principally religious music, especially choral works such as the *Missa Choralis* (1865), two large oratorios, *Die Legende von der heiligen Elisabeth* (1857-1862) and *Christus* (1855-1866), the "Legends" for piano (1863), and the *Totentanz* (1849, revised 1853, 1859; dance of death) for piano and orchestra, a paraphrase of the *Dies Irae* (day of wrath) chant from the Requiem Mass.

In 1869, Liszt was reconciled with the Grand Duke of Weimar and began his *vie trifurquée* (three-pronged life) between Rome, Weimar, and Budapest. The third book of his *Années de pèlerinage* reflects his journeys, especially to Rome and Hungary. The best known of the works in this set is "The Fountains of the Villa d'Este" in Rome, where Liszt often stayed; this piece anticipates many of the impressionistic harmonic and coloristic effects of Claude Debussy and Maurice Ravel.

In Weimar and Budapest, Liszt held master classes in which he trained a new generation of pianists. His style of composition also changed to a very spare, attenuated style, avoiding extensive developments or repetitions and using often unusual harmonic sonorities which he treated in unconventional ways. Many of these last pieces are extremely short, beginning and ending abruptly, without the extensive introductions or closes of his Weimar works. Publishers rejected these compositions, nearly all of which were published long after Liszt's death. Best known of these late works are the short piano pieces, such as "Unstern" (evil star) and "Nuages gris" (gray clouds) from the 1880's, and the *Via Crucis* (1879; the way of the cross) for chorus and organ.

Liszt's death in 1886 came, after an extensive tour of Belgium and England, in Bayreuth, Germany, where he had attended a festival of operas by his son-in-law Richard Wagner. The cause of death was pneumonia; he had earlier suffered from edema.

Summary

Franz Liszt was a man of immense personal magnetism and charisma, as attested by the immense acclaim he received during his years as a virtuoso and reflected in later years during his charity concerts and appearances as a conductor. He attracted a devoted coterie of students, and though he failed to found a school of composition, he influenced virtually every composer of the second half of the nineteenth century and anticipated many of the devices and techniques of the twentieth.

A man of formidable energy, he composed about thirteen hundred works. He was one of the leading letter writers of the century, and, though he did not write the many books and essays attributed to him, he dictated their ideas, edited the text, and assumed responsibility for their final form. If one had to choose a single composer whose works sum up the nineteenth century's achievements, innovations, and also weaknesses, Liszt would be the most likely candidate.

Bibliography

Fay, Amy. *Music-Study in Germany*. Chicago: Jansen, McClurg, 1881; London: Macmillan, 1887. This engagingly written firsthand account of Liszt's teaching in Weimar was written by one of his few American pupils; her study also gives an incisive view of Germany shortly after unification.

Journal of the American Liszt Society. 1960- . This journal, edited since 1987 by Michael Saffle, is principally devoted to articles dealing with Liszt's musical style. Also contains numerous investigations of Liszt's life, works, students, associates, and ambience.

László, Zsigmond, and Béla Mátéka. *Franz Liszt: A Biography in Pictures*. London: Barrie and Rockliff, 1968. This series of pictures and facsimiles of manuscripts and documents is arranged to provide a chronological account of Liszt's life, achievements, and circle of friends and students. An extensive commentary explains and connects the various illustrations.

Liszt, Franz. *Franz Liszt: Selected Letters.* Edited and translated by Adrian Williams. New York: Oxford University Press, and Oxford: Clarendon Press, 1998. A collection of Liszt's letters, many translated here for the first time, which flesh out the composer's character and his relationships with the art, literary, and religious communities.

Longyear, Rey M. "Ferenc (Franz) Liszt." In *Nineteenth-Century Romanticism in Music.* 3d ed. Englewood Cliffs, N.J.: Prentice-Hall, 1988. A brief survey of Liszt's musical style, emphasizing the Weimar and late works, which relates Liszt's music to that of the century as a whole. Liszt is also presented as a seminal composer for the twentieth century.

Merrick, Paul. *Revolution and Religion in the Music of Liszt.* Cambridge and New York: Cambridge University Press, 1987. This interesting and controversial study emphasizes Liszt's music with religious import, particularly the choral works; the author tends to overstate his case in seeking hidden religious programs in some of the instrumental works.

Searle, Humphrey. *The Music of Liszt.* London: Williams and Norgate, 1954; New York: Dover, 1966. A still-valuable survey of this prolific composer's works. Not too technically oriented for the person with limited musical background. Searle's book was a landmark in restoring Liszt's works to musical respectability after decades of neglect and disdain.

Searle, Humphrey, and Sharon Winklhofer. "Franz Liszt." In *The New Grove Early Romantic Masters I: Chopin, Schumann and Liszt,* edited by Nicholas Temperley. London: Macmillan, and New York: Norton, 1985. A concise study, balanced between Liszt's life and his music, derived from Searle's article in *The New Grove* and revised by Sharon Winklhofer. The list of Liszt's approximately thirteen hundred compositions is particularly valuable.

Walker, Alan. *Franz Liszt.* Vol. 1, *The Virtuoso Years, 1811-1847.* Rev. ed. Ithaca, N.Y.: Cornell University Press, 1987.

—————. *Franz Liszt.* Vol. 2, *The Weimar Years, 1848-1861.* New York: Knopf, 1986. Walker's two-volume study is the most complete biography of Liszt. Though the focus is on his biography, some often insightful discussion is given to his music. Volume 2 provides the definitive account of his most productive years and shows Liszt not only as the musical director at Weimar but also as a composer, teacher, administrator, and writer on music.

Walker, Alan. *Franz Liszt.* Vol. 3: *The Final Years, 1861-1886.* New York: Knopf, 1996. Walker, a noted Liszt scholar, completes the third volume of the definitive Liszt biography.

Rey M. Longyear

SECOND EARL OF LIVERPOOL

Robert Banks Jenkinson

Born: June 7, 1770; London, England
Died: December 4, 1828; London, England
Areas of Achievement: Politics and government
Contribution: As prime minister from 1812 to 1827, Liverpool led Great Britain to victory over Napoleon, rode out the domestic strife of the postwar years, and directed the economic recovery and liberal legislation of the 1820's.

Early Life

Robert Banks Jenkinson, who would become the second Earl of Liverpool, was born in London on June 7, 1770. His mother, née Amelia Watts, daughter of an ex-governor of Fort William in Bengal, died a month after the birth. He was thus reared by his father, Charles Jenkinson, first Baron Hawkesbury and first Earl of Liverpool, who was an adviser of George III, secretary at war under Lord North, and president of the Board of Trade under William Pitt the Younger. Jenkinson was educated at Charterhouse and Christ Church, Oxford, emerging as an excellent classicist and historian, well versed in international affairs and political economy. While on the Grand Tour in 1789, he witnessed the storming of the Bastille, an experience which bred in him a lifelong distrust of mobs.

Jenkinson was elected to Parliament in 1790 but, declining to sit as a minor, waited until 1792 to deliver his maiden speech, a well-received defense of Great Britain's handling of the Oczakov crisis. In 1793, his usefulness to the Tory government was demonstrated further by speeches answering Whig criticisms of the French war and demands for parliamentary reform, and Pitt rewarded him by appointment to the Indian Board of Control. For some years, he attended Parliament irregularly because of obligations in the Kentish militia, which he joined at the outbreak of war, and affairs of the heart. In 1795, he married the Earl of Bristol's daughter, Louisa Theodosia Hervey, to whom he remained utterly devoted until her death. Despite his absences, Lord Hawkesbury (the courtesy title he assumed when his father received an earldom in 1796) was a valued supporter of the government. In 1799, he was made Master of the Mint, an appointment which gave membership of the Privy Council and a clear signal that Pitt had marked him out for further advancement.

Portraits of Hawkesbury reveal an ungainly figure with a long neck, awkward posture, and untidy appearance. He was a shy, sensitive man, respected in political circles for his modesty, integrity, and sound judgment. Although not a scintillating orator, his speeches were typically clear, well prepared, and effective, and it is understandable that Pitt, whose front bench was short of able speakers, should view him with favor. Nevertheless, appointment to the cabinet came unexpectedly early. After resigning over the Catholic question in 1801, Pitt persuaded Hawkesbury to support Henry Addington, who, desperate for the assistance of another minister in the Commons, gave him the Foreign Office at the age of thirty.

Life's Work

In the decade after joining the cabinet, Hawkesbury occupied all three secretaryships of state. As foreign secretary between 1801 and 1804, he negotiated the abortive Peace of Amiens (1802), a policy which was vehemently criticized by his predecessor, William Wyndham Grenville. In 1803, to help counter such attacks, he was raised to the House of Lords, where he led the Tories—initially as Baron Hawkesbury and, after his father's death in 1808, as Earl of Liverpool—until retiring from politics. From 1804 to 1806, he was Pitt's home secretary and, after the latter's death, rejected a royal offer of the premiership because the cabinet had decided not to continue without its leader. Subsequently, he served as home secretary under the Duke of Portland and secretary at war under Spencer Perceval, acquiring a reputation as a conciliator and a skilled administrator. By 1812, he was far more experienced than any of his ministerial colleagues, who elected him leader when Perceval was assassinated. The prince regent, after approaching a number of other politicians, endorsed this decision by making Liverpool prime minister on June 8, 1812.

At the time of its formation, there was little reason to expect Liverpool's administration to prove more resilient than any of its five predecessors in the previous eleven years. The most immediate threat was the issue of Catholic emancipation. Although personally opposed to the proposal that political rights be given to Catholics, Liverpool adopted a position of government neutrality on the question. This device maintained cabinet unity in 1812 and became a permanent feature of his policies. In the following three years, the government won immense popularity as a result of its contributions to Napoleon's defeat and the subsequent peace negotiations, and in 1814, Liverpool was made Knight of the Garter for his services to the country.

The period from 1815 to 1821 was the most difficult of Liverpool's career. During these years, he grappled with economic and social problems brought on by the end of the war; the government experienced continuous budgetary problems resulting from its reluctant abandonment of the wartime income tax. More obviously, the ministry's responsibility was the Corn Law of 1815, prohibiting importation until the domestic price reached eighty shillings a quarter. Viewed by Liverpool as a temporary measure to facilitate the agricultural sector's transition to peacetime conditions and reduce dependence upon foreign supply, the act provoked widespread outbursts against a self-interested landowning Parliament. Discontent was aggravated by economic distress, itself popularly attributed to the government's extravagance, and produced unprecedented calls for parliamentary reform, which culminated in the unfortunate "Peterloo Massacre" of 1819. Lacking adequate information, Liverpool believed that there was an organized revolutionary movement and determined upon decisive action to maintain order. In 1817, habeas corpus was suspended, in 1819 the notorious Six Acts increased magistrates' powers against sedition, and a small number of suspects was jailed. These relatively mild measures silenced the radicals briefly but intensified their bitterness. After the accession of George IV in 1820, opposition rose to fever pitch around the figure of his adulterous wife, Caroline, whose return from the Continent obliged Liverpool to introduce a divorce bill and severely compromised him. On the one hand, he was vilified as the lackey of a licentious husband brutally attacking an innocent woman. On the other, his inability to carry the bill almost led to dismissal by the disgruntled monarch. By the time the affair was ended by Caroline's death in 1821, it appears to have taken a considerable personal toll of Liverpool, for afterward his

characteristic good temper gave way increasingly to testiness and intolerance. His spirits were lowered further in 1821 by the death of Louisa, a devastating loss only partly cushioned by marriage to her close friend, Mary Chester, niece of Lord Bagot, in 1822.

Fortunately, Liverpool's public life took a favorable turn in the early 1820's as economic recovery dispelled social unrest and facilitated more constructive policies. In conjunction with able colleagues such as William Huskisson, Sir Robert Peel, and Frederick Robinson, he sought to eradicate discontent by reducing economic instability and implementing moderate liberal reforms. In 1821, the Bank of England resumed cash payments, which had been suspended with inflationary consequences since 1797. In 1826, the volatility of provincial credit was tackled by a statute prohibiting country bank notes under five pounds and permitting the erection of large joint-stock banks and Bank of England branches outside London. Similarly, to meet the population's need for steadier food supply and employment, the government attempted to regularize commerce by loosening trade restrictions and lowering duties on a broad range of imports. In addition, it passed a series of law reforms, including statutes which repealed the combination acts, halved the number of capital offenses, regulated judicial incomes, and improved provincial prisons. The government's liberalism was reflected also in its foreign policy, conducted until 1822 by Lord Castlereagh and afterward by George Canning. While pursuing the national interest, both vehemently opposed the efforts of the reactionary European powers to suppress revolutionary activity, and Canning in particular stirred patriotic spirit when he supported liberal and nationalist movements in Greece, Portugal, and South America.

By the mid-1820's, the government had regained its popularity but was seriously threatened by the perennial corn and Catholic questions. In 1826, in defiance of the agriculturalists, Liverpool prepared a corn bill replacing import prohibition below eighty shillings a quarter with a sliding scale of duties which would decline as the price rose. This was passed in a slightly altered form in 1828 and remained in force until 1846. The Catholic issue had become urgent because of Irish agitation and growing cabinet opposition to governmental neutrality. Liverpool believed that pro-Catholic aggression might destroy his ministry during the

1827 session. He suffered a cerebral hemorrhage on February 17 of that year, however, and played no further part in politics before his death on December 4, 1828. As he died without issue, he was succeeded as Earl of Liverpool by his half brother, Charles Cecil Cope Jenkinson.

Summary

As prime minister for fifteen years, a period exceeded only by Robert Walpole and William Pitt, the second Earl of Liverpool exerted a profound influence on the development of British politics and public policy. Determined to enhance the authority of his office, he resisted both royal interference with the cabinet and the independent leanings of its members. After appointment by the premier, ministers were given considerable administrative scope but general policy and major decisions were formulated in conjunction with him. Government was conducted in accordance with Liverpool's own moral code, a fact that helped to raise the public image of politicians and their expected standards of behavior. It also reflected his personal views, which represented, to a remarkable degree, the contradictory currents of early nineteenth century opinion and made him acceptable to both conservative and liberal wings of his party. In particular, Liverpool's reverence for the traditional constitution was shared by the large, influential group of orthodox Tories. After he was replaced by the pro-Catholic Canning in 1827, their defection threw the party into chaos, and within five years the legislature had enacted Catholic emancipation and parliamentary reform. In contrast, Liverpool was progressive on other issues. Guided by the principles of political economy, he sought to promote industry and commerce, if necessary at the expense of the landed interest. His ministry's tariff policies inaugurated the Free Trade movement, which, after a hiatus under the Whigs in the 1830's, was resumed by Peel and came to be viewed as the basis of mid-Victorian prosperity. Similarly, the banking legislation laid the groundwork for Peel's later measures, and the law reforms paved the way for the radical work of Henry Brougham in the 1830's. In sum, although Liverpool is a little-known historical figure, his achievements were diverse and substantial. After leading Great Britain to victory over Napoleon and through the postwar troubles, he implemented constructive reforms which were to have important, long-term consequences.

Bibliography

Brady, Alexander. *William Huskisson and Liberal Reform.* London: Oxford University Press, 1928; New York: Kelley, 1967. Dated but still useful essay on the nature and purposes of economic reforms. Particularly helpful on commercial legislation.

Brock, William Ranuf. *Lord Liverpool and Liberal Toryism, 1820 to 1827.* 2d ed. Hamden, Conn.: Archon Books, and London: Cass, 1967. Stimulating analysis of Liverpool's final years, especially valuable on his ideas and administrative methods. The second edition eliminates factual errors in original.

Cookson, J. E. *Lord Liverpool's Administration: The Crucial Years, 1815-1822.* London: Chatto and Windus, and Hamden, Conn.: Archon Books, 1975. Excellent narrative of the government's reactions to events in the troubled years after Waterloo. Exposes the increasing influence of public opinion on policy and contains suggestive comments on Liverpool's administration as a whole.

Gash, Norman. *Lord Liverpool.* London: Weidenfeld and Nicolson, and Cambridge, Mass.: Harvard University Press, 1984. A brilliant, superbly written portrait, good on all aspects of Liverpool's life, particularly his character and personal relations. Skillfully traces continuities between Liverpool's policies and those of Peel in the 1840's. Essential reading.

Hilton, Boyd. *Corn, Cash, Commerce: The Economic Policies of the Tory Governments, 1815-1830.* Oxford and New York: Oxford University Press, 1977. Penetrating, controversial account of leading politicians' views on economic policy, based on parliamentary debates and private papers. Stresses the influence of pragmatic rather than doctrinal considerations.

Petrie, Sir Charles. *Lord Liverpool and His Times.* London: Barrie, 1954. The only modern biography before that by Gash, this book provides an outline of Liverpool's career. Dwells excessively on background events and largely neglects economic matters.

Plowright, John. "Lord Liverpool and the Alternatives to 'Repression' in Regency England." *History Review,* no. 28, (September 1997). Discusses varying views of Lord Liverpool's efforts to maintain order during the period of unrest (1815-1820) in the United Kingdom.

———. *Regency England: The Age of Lord Liverpool.* London and New York: Routledge, 1996.

Comprehensive treatment of the period prior to the Great Reform Act of 1833. Discusses Liverpool's abilities as Prime Minister and public unrest in the early nineteenth century.

Yonge, Charles Duke. *The Life and Administration of the Second Earl of Liverpool.* London: Macmillan, 1868. A three-volume biography with little analysis, but extensive quotations from Liverpool's papers reveal his reactions to specific events.

Ian Duffy

DAVID LIVINGSTONE

Born: March 19, 1813; Blantyre, Scotland

Died: May 1, 1873; Chitambo's village near Lake Bangweulu, Central Africa

Areas of Achievement: Exploration and religion

Contribution: Although Livingstone is often thought of primarily as a missionary, in truth he was singularly unsuccessful in this endeavor. His actual importance was as an explorer whose travels, together with moving appeals asking Britons to do something about the slave trade in the African interior, focused the eyes of the civilized world on the "dark continent."

Early Life

David Livingstone, the son of an impoverished tea vendor who was more interested in distributing religious tracts than selling tea, was born in Blantyre, near Glasgow, on March 19, 1813. Although he grew up in a very large family under adverse economic circumstances, Livingstone managed, even though he began working in a cotton mill at the age of ten, to secure a solid education. He accomplished this by studying in every spare moment, and, while still in his teens, he determined to become a medical missionary.

His preparations for such a career were successful, and when he completed his medical studies and became Dr. Livingstone in 1840, he was already unusual: It was simply unheard-of for a factory boy from a poverty-stricken background to achieve such educational heights. Livingstone's original intention had been to serve in China, but the outbreak of the Opium War effectively ended this plan. Instead, he sought and won an assignment from the nondenominational London Missionary Society in South Africa. He reached Cape Town on March 14, 1841, and from there made his way into the interior to the mission station of Kuruman, Bechuanaland. This isolated outpost had been established by Robert Moffat, and a few years later, in 1845, Livingstone would marry Moffat's daughter, Mary.

Life's Work

For most of the first decade that he spent in southern Africa, from 1841 to 1849, Livingstone devoted himself to the type of labors that were expected from missionaries. Livingstone founded three separate mission stations—Mabotsa, Chonuane, and Kolobeng—in the interior to the north of Kuruman.

Yet he quarreled incessantly with other missionaries and his superiors, and the sole convert he made, a chieftain named Sechele, soon lapsed. By 1849, frustrated with the routine of mission station life and increasingly attracted by the vast unexplored region to the north, he began traveling as a sort of itinerant missionary.

In truth, his religious duties were increasingly subordinated to exploration, and it was in the field of discovery that Livingstone made his real mark. Between 1849 and 1852, he made three journeys, with the noted big-game hunter William Cotton Oswell as a companion, which altered the entire course of his career. They explored Lake Ngami and the upper reaches of the Zambezi River, and during these travels, Livingstone came to recognize the extent of the internal slave trade.

He sent his wife and children, whom he regarded as impediments to his exploring ambitions, back to Great Britain in 1852, and following their departure, he continued his travels on the Zambezi. Between 1853 and 1856, he crossed the entire southern interior of Africa, traveling first to the port of Luanda, Angola, on the west coast and then later following the course of the Zambezi to Quelimane, Mozambique, on the Indian Ocean. During the latter journey, which had commenced at Linyanti, he discovered the massive falls which he named Victoria, in honor of his queen. After the completion of this journey, he returned to England for the first time since he had originally traveled to Africa.

Livingstone was already something of a geographical celebrity, thanks to contacts he had established with Sir Roderick I. Murchison, the president of the Royal Geographical Society, and articles he had written for the society's journal. It was the appearance of his great book, *Missionary Travels and Researches in South Africa* (1857), however, which brought Livingstone national fame. He completed the book shortly after returning home, and its appearance caused a sensation. He described his travels in detail and depicted the South African interior as a region which offered a fertile field for his countrymen to pursue the laudable and interconnected goals of commerce, Christianity, and civilization. So compelling was his book, together with a series of lectures that he made in England, that he secured government support for an exploratory mission on the Zam-

bezi. Its primary purpose was to open the interior for parties of settlers who would bring British commerce and the benefits of their advanced society to the region.

Severing his formal ties with the London Missionary Society, in 1858 Livingstone returned to Africa as head of the Zambezi Expedition. This undertaking was a fiasco from start to finish. Far from being the navigable river that Livingstone had imagined it to be, the Zambezi posed all sorts of obstacles as a potential highway to the interior. The Anglican missionaries who followed him suffered greatly from the climate, and Livingstone proved woefully inadequate as a leader in the conduct of the Zambezi Expedition. He quarreled with the other members of his party, death and disease took a heavy toll on the Universities' Mission which he had encouraged to come to the region, and his wife died en route to join him. Ultimately, the British government, under growing protest, recalled him in 1863. Livingstone returned to England by way of India and arrived home on July 23, 1864.

He was no longer the conquering hero he had been in 1857, but Livingstone's ill-fated Zambezi Expedition had added appreciably to geographical knowledge of Africa. By this juncture, he had become fascinated with the controversy surrounding attempts to discover the sources of the Nile, and thenceforth he abandoned all pretense of being a missionary. He rested in England in 1865 and wrote, in collaboration with his brother Charles, a book entitled *Narrative of an Expedition to the Zambezi and Its Tributaries* (1865).

Shortly after the book was published, he made his way back to Africa, and by early 1866, Livingstone was once more in the interior. Although his announced goals were to end the slave trade and advance Christianity, he had become virtually obsessed by the watershed of the Nile. The remaining seven years of his life would be spent in an unsuccessful search for the Nile's sources, and during most of this time, he would travel without European companions.

From 1866 to 1871, Livingstone traveled in the area of Lake Nyasa and the upper reaches of the Congo (modern Zaire) River. Among his discoveries were Lakes Mweru and Bangweulu, but these years cost him dearly in health. Indeed, when the journalist Henry Morton Stanley found him at Ujiji on Lake Tanganyika late in 1871, he was near death. With the medicines and supplies proffered by Stanley, Livingstone quickly recovered. Together they explored portions of Lake Tanganyika and ascertained that the reservoir was not a part of the Nile system.

The few weeks he spent with Livingstone influenced Stanley profoundly, and he did his best to convince the aging man to leave Africa. Livingstone refused, but he did open himself up to his traveling companion in a way that he had never done with any other person. He told Stanley of the horrible massacre of Africans by Arab slave traders that he had witnessed a few months earlier, and he shared his dreams of what he desired for the continent's future. Eventually, Stanley's anxiety to let the outside world know that he had "found" Livingstone led to his departure. The two separated at Unyanyembe (near the modern city of Tabora, Tanzania), with Livingstone determined to continue his explorations for the Nile's sources.

Livingstone's health, already seriously affected by recurrent bouts of malaria and years of unconcern for his physical state, degenerated rapidly. Tragically, Livingstone's instruments had also been damaged in transit, and in his final days, he was for all practical purposes lost. After days of being carried by the handful of "faithfuls" who continued to accompany him and being in a coma much of the time, Livingstone died in the pre-dawn hours of May 1, 1873. Death came at a small village on the shores of Lake Bangweulu. His native companions eviscerated his body and embalmed it as best they could before beginning the long journey back to the East African coast with it. Once the party reached Zanzibar, Livingstone's remains were turned over to British authorities. Eventually, his body was taken to England and interred in Westminster Abbey on April 18, 1874.

Summary

David Livingstone was a difficult, complex individual who was always surrounded by controversy. There can be little doubt that he was an abysmal failure as a missionary, husband, and father. He lacked the patience to pursue the daily drudgery required of missionaries to Africa in his era, and he was so lacking in sympathy and understanding for his wife that he drove her into the depths of alcoholism. Similarly, at least some of his children were disillusioned by Livingstone's total lack of parental concern. Against these shortcomings stand Livingstone's compassion for Africans and his almost superhuman determination as an explorer and exponent of Great Britain's civilizing mission on the African continent.

There is no disputing Livingstone's profound influence in directing British attention to what he called the "open, running sore" of the internal slave trade in Africa. Similarly, his writings, speeches, and the very nature of this controversial man captured the public imagination. In particular, his "last journey"—the final seven years he spent in Africa—fascinated the British public. There was something exceptionally poignant about the aging, ill man, struggling against all odds and frequently incommunicado as he sought to discover the sources of the Nile.

In the aftermath of his death, Livingstone came to be viewed almost as a saint. Modern observers realize that this was a misconception. Nevertheless, he exerted a profound influence on what came to be known as "the opening up of Africa." His death inspired Stanley to complete his unfinished geographical travels, and the attention he directed to Africa—both official and otherwise—loomed large in the "scramble" of the late 1870's and 1880's. Livingstone remains a frequently misunderstood figure who has attracted scores of biographers yet who still awaits a definitive biography. Thanks to the massive Livingstone Documentation Project launched in connection with the centenary celebrations of 1973, the wherewithal now exists at the National Library of Scotland for such a study.

Bibliography

Casada, James A. *Dr. David Livingstone and Sir Henry Morton Stanley: An Annotated Bibliography*. New York: Garland, 1976. A detailed analytical bibliography of works by and relating to Livingstone.

Clendennen, Gary W., and I. C. Cunningham, comps. *David Livingstone: A Catalogue of Documents*. Edinburgh: Livingstone Documentation Project, 1979. A full listing of all known extant Livingstone documents, with a description and their location, which is invaluable for any serious study of the man. Cunningham prepared a supplement which was published in 1985.

David Livingstone and the Victorian Encounter with Africa. London: National Portrait Gallery, 1996. Published in connection with exhibits in London and Edinburgh, this volume includes almost two hundred photographs of exhibited items (portraits, artifacts, and early photos) and six essays covering Livingstone's artifacts, his place in history, and more.

Holmes, Timothy. *David Livingstone: Letters and Documents, 1841-1872, The Zambian Collection at the Livingstone Museum*. Bloomington: Indiana University Press, and London: Currey, 1990. Includes 140 items, mostly letters, which are published here for the first time.

Jeal, Tim. *Livingstone*. London: Heinemann, and New York: Putnam, 1973. Although characterized by a certain overemphasis on debunking the Livingstone myth, Jeal's is perhaps the fullest, and certainly the most readable, of the many modern biographies of Livingstone.

Ransford, Oliver. *David Livingstone: The Dark Interior*. London: Murray, and New York: St. Martin's Press, 1978. A detailed, carefully researched biography which is marred by the author's insistence that all Livingstone's life and actions can be explained by a disease which led to wide swings in mood ranging from deep depression to great elation.

Seaver, George. *David Livingstone: His Life and Letters*. London: Lutterworth, and New York: Harper, 1957. A solid life notable primarily for reprinting a number of interesting Livingstone letters.

James A. Casada

NIKOLAY IVANOVICH LOBACHEVSKY

Born: December 1, 1792; Nizhny Novgorod, Russia

Died: February 24, 1856; Kazan, Russia

Area of Achievement: Mathematics

Contribution: Lobachevsky was the boldest and most consistent founder of a post-Euclidean theory of real space. His persistence in holding open his revolutionary line of inquiry into the reality of geometry helped to set the stage for the radical discoveries of twentieth century theoretical physics.

Early Life

Nikolay Ivanovich Lobachevsky, whose parents were a minor government clerk and an energetic woman of apparently no education, was a member of what most nearly corresponded to a middle class in preemancipation Russia. As a government-supported student, he was recorded in school as a *raznochinets* (person of miscellaneous rank—not a noble, a peasant, or a merchant). Despite the early marriage of his mother, Praskovya, to the collegiate registrar Ivan Maksimovich Lobachevsky, the evidence strongly suggests that Nikolay and his two brothers were the illegitimate sons of an army officer and land surveyor, S. S. Shebarshin. Ivan Maksimovich Lobachevsky died when Nikolay, the middle son, was only five years old. The widowed Praskovya left Nizhny Novgorod and moved eastward along the Volga to the provincial center of Kazan. She enrolled all three boys in the local *Gymnasium* (preparatory school). Nikolay attended the school between 1802 and 1807.

Lobachevsky's student years at Kazan University (1807 to 1811) were a time when Russia was eager to learn from the West and to give more than it had received. Lobachevsky was awarded Kazan's first master's degree for his thesis on elliptic movement of the heavenly bodies. He worked closely with Johann Martin Bartels, who had earlier discovered and taught Carl Friedrich Gauss, a great mathematician of the day.

Lobachevsky taught at Kazan University from 1811 until his mandated but most unwilling retirement in 1846. The tenure of Mikhail Magnitskii as curator from 1819 to 1826 was the school's most difficult period. A religious fanatic who attempted to give this particularly science-oriented university the atmosphere of a medieval monastery, Mag-

nitskii was imprisoned in 1826 for his gross incompetence. He was particularly suspicious of the philosophy of Immanuel Kant. All the distinguished German professors left; for a time, the young Lobachevsky carried the burden of providing all the advanced lectures in mathematics, physics, and astronomy alone. His own development and integrity were only strengthened during this phase. It did Lobachevsky no harm that he too was anti-Kantian; he completely disagreed with Kant's view that Euclidean geometry was proof of the human mind's inborn sense of lines, planes, and space.

Life's Work

As a young professor in 1817, Lobachevsky was intrigued by the problem of Euclid's fifth postulate, which implies the possibility of infinitely parallel lines. More technically, one may draw a single line through a given point on a given plane that will never intersect another given line on the same plane. On the one hand, this is not a simple axiom that has no need of proof. On the other, it cannot be proved. Two thousand years of general satisfaction with Euclidean geometry had seen many vain attempts to prove the fifth postulate and thereby give this geometry its final perfection. Such attempts became particularly frenzied in the eighteenth century. A rare few thinkers began to entertain the idea that the postulate was wrong, but they denied it even to themselves.

From 1817 to 1822, Lobachevsky made repeated attempts to prove the fifth postulate, already resorting to non-Euclidean concepts such as an axiom of directionality. Once he perceived the hidden tautology of even his best attempts, he concluded that the postulate must be wrong and that geometry must be put on a new foundation.

In addition to the resistance of intellectual tradition, Lobachevsky could expect little support in a country whose ruling house saw itself as the very embodiment of stability and conservatism. The unsettling implications of losing true parallelism and rocking the foundations of classical geometry were as unwelcome in czarist Russia as they could possibly have been anywhere in the world. This resistance makes Lobachevsky's boldness all the more impressive. Simultaneously and independently, two leading mathematicians of the day—Gauss in Germany and János Bolyai in Hungary—were facing

the same conclusion as Lobachevsky. Despite their secure reputations, both refrained from pursuing the implications of negating the fifth postulate, correctly assessing that the world was not ready for it.

To exacerbate the radicalism of his approach in a highly religious country, Lobachevsky, though not an atheist, was a materialist in a most fundamental and original sense of the word. In his mathematical syllabus for 1822, he made the extraordinary statement: "We apprehend in Nature only bodies alone; consequently, concepts of lines and planes are derived and not directly acquired concepts, and therefore should not be taken as the basis of mathematical science."

In 1823, Lobachevsky's full-length geometry textbook *Geometriya* was submitted to school district curator Magnitskii, who sent it to the St. Petersburg Academy of Sciences for review. The text was emphatically rejected, and Lobachevsky's difficulties with the academy began. A subsequent manuscript, "O nachalakh geometrii" (1829-1830; on the elements of geometry), was also submitted to the academy. Not only did the academy reject the manuscript but also an academician's flawed

critique was fed to the popular press, which turned it into a lampoon of Lobachevsky.

The date February 7, 1826, marks the official debut of Lobachevskian geometry as an independent theory. On that day, Lobachevsky submitted to his department his paper entitled "Exposition succincte des principes de la géométrie avec une démonstration rigoureuse du théorème des parallèles." It was rejected for publication, as his colleagues ventured no opinion on it. Other major works continued to be largely ignored.

Nevertheless, the new school district curator who replaced Magnitskii, Count Mikhail Musin-Pushkin, was sufficiently impressed with Lobachevsky to make him rector of Kazan University in 1827. Thus began Lobachevsky's dual life as a brilliantly successful local administrator and a frustrated intellectual pioneer kept outside the pale of the St. Petersburg establishment. During his tenure as rector, Lobachevsky built Kazan University into an outstanding institution of high standards. He founded the scientific journal *Uchenye zapiski*, in which he published many of his works and which has flourished to the present day.

In 1846, Lobachevsky's life in the sphere of action fell apart, as he received a succession of blows: Musin-Pushkin was transferred to the St. Petersburg school district; the request to forestall Lobachevsky's mandatory retirement was denied; his eldest son, Aleksei, died of tuberculosis at nineteen; his wife became seriously ill; his wife's half brother, dispatched to handle the sale of two distant estates, gambled away both the Lobachevskys' money and all of his own; and Lobachevsky's eyesight began to deteriorate. In the last year of his life, he was virtually blind, yet he dictated his best and strongest work, *Pangéométrie* (1855-1856). His views had evolved from rejection of Euclidean parallelism into a vision of reality that anticipated theories of the curvature of space and was validated by Albert Einstein's general theory of relativity.

Summary

When Nikolay Ivanovich Lobachevsky's ideas first caught the imagination of a wide audience in the late nineteenth century, he was dubbed "the Copernicus of geometry," partly because of his Slavic origin (Nicolaus Copernicus was Polish), but far more because of the profound reorientation of thought that he set in motion. Lobachevsky forced the scale of earthly dimension as the measure of the universe off its pedestal, as Copernicus had earlier shattered the illusory status of Earth as the center of the solar system. This upheaval, which initially met with great resistance, forced the mind to focus on awesome phenomena that were not so much abstract as invisible to the human eye. Lobachevsky promoted bold and fruitful speculation about the nature of reality and space.

In *Pangéométrie*, his crowning work, Lobachevsky opens: "Instead of beginning geometry with the line and plane, as is usually done, I have preferred to begin with the sphere and the circle. . . ." For this geometry, there are no straight lines or flat planes, and all lines and planes must curve, however infinitesimally. Yet, while pointing to modern concepts of the curvature of space, Lobachevsky does not abolish Euclidean geometry. In some areas, his geometry and Euclid's coincide. Yet the latter is a limited case, whose relative certainties hold true on a merely earthly scale. In the conclusion to *Pangéométrie*, Lobachevsky correctly predicted that interstellar space would be the proving ground for his theory, which he saw not as an abstruse logical exercise but as the real geometry of the universe.

Bibliography

Bonola, Roberto. *Non-Euclidean Geometry: A Critical and Historical Study of Its Development*. Translated by H. S. Carslaw. New York: Dover, 1955. Very up-to-date for its time, and still relevant to the general reader. Focuses on a basic exposition of Lobachevsky's theories without the highly sophisticated applications thereof. Contains several relevant appendices.

Kagan, Veniamin Fedorovich. *N. Lobachevsky and His Contributions to Science*. Moscow: Foreign Languages, 1957. A solid, basic account by one of the chief Russian experts on Lobachevsky. Omits most of the human-interest material to be found in Kagan's 1944 biography. Includes a bibliography, necessarily of primarily Russian materials.

Kulczycki, Stefan. *Non-Euclidean Geometry*. Translated by Stanisław Knapowski. Oxford and New York: Pergamon Press, 1961. Another introduction for the general reader, which updates but does not supplant Bonola.

Shirokov, Pëtr Alekseevich. *A Sketch of the Fundamentals of Lobachevskian Geometry*. Edited by I. N. Bronshtein. Translated by Leo F. Boron and Ward D. Bouwsma. Groningen, the Netherlands: Noordhoff, 1964. Written in Russian in the 1940's, it appears to have been aimed at the secondary-school mathematics student.

Smogorzhevskii, A. S. *Lobachevskian Geometry*. Translated by V. Kisin. Moscow: Mir, 1982. Partly accessible to the general reader but of particular interest to the serious student of mathematics. Emphasizes specific mathematical applications of Lobachevsky's theories.

Vucinich, Alexander. "Nikolay Ivanovich Lobachevsky: The Man Behind the First Non-Euclidean Geometry." *Isis* 53 (December 1962). A substantial, well-written article, abundantly annotated to point the reader in the direction of all the basic sources, which are primarily in Russian. Highlights some avenues not mentioned elsewhere, such as Lobachevsky's role in the mathematization of science. Includes a balanced account of Lobachevsky's life.

D. Gosselin Nakeeb

BELVA A. LOCKWOOD

Born: October 24, 1830; Royalton, New York
Died: May 19, 1917; Washington, D.C.
Areas of Achievement: Law, women's rights, and peace advocacy
Contribution: Lockwood obtained passage of federal legislation giving women equal pay for equal work in government service, became the first woman to be granted the right to plead cases before the U.S. Supreme Court, and was a committed activist for women's rights.

Early Life

Belva Ann Bennett, the second of the five children of Lewis Bennett and Hannah Green Bennett, was born on October 24, 1830, in Niagara County, New York. She attended country schools and completed her education by the age of fifteen. Her father's opposition to her educational ambitions, as well as a lack of funds, led her to begin a career in teaching. She taught school for four years before marrying Uriah McNall, a local farmer. The young couple moved to the country near Gasport, where Belva gave birth to a daughter, Lura. When her husband died in a sawmill accident in 1853, Belva returned to school to further her education in order to support herself and her child.

Belva McNall sold the farm and entered Gasport Academy. She also continued to teach school. As a teacher, she experienced at first hand inequities toward women when she was offered half the salary paid to male teachers. Angry and upset, she left her daughter with her parents and entered Genessee College, where she studied law, political economy, and the U.S. Constitution. On June 27, 1857, she received a bachelor of science degree from the college that was to become Syracuse University.

In 1857, Belva McNall became headmistress of Lockport Union School, where her daughter studied. For the next four years, she supervised the staff, taught courses, and, despite conservative disapproval, encouraged gymnastics, public speaking, nature walks, and skating for young women. She also taught at the Gainesville Female Seminary and later became proprietor of the Female Seminary in Oswego, New York. In 1866, while in her middle thirties, Belva McNall, with her daughter Lura, left for Washington, D.C. Her profession was still teaching, but she had political ambitions that would eventually take her far beyond the classroom.

In 1867, Belva McNall opened a school of her own. On March 11, 1868, she married Ezekiel Lockwood, a dentist and former Baptist minister. Their only child, Jessie, died in infancy. Ezekiel Lockwood assumed the administrative duties of his wife's school so that she could pursue a law degree. Denied admission to Columbia, Georgetown, and Harvard because she was not only a woman but a married one, Lockwood was finally accepted at the National University Law School. She completed her studies in 1873 but was awarded her diploma only after she petitioned President Ulysses S. Grant, the school's ex officio president, to intervene on her behalf. Her husband, who had continued to supervise her school in Washington, was finally forced to close it because of his ill health. He died in 1877.

Life's Work

After judicial rules were changed and women were allowed to practice law in the District of Columbia, Belva Lockwood was admitted to the bar on Sep-

tember 24, 1873. At the age of forty, she embarked on a distinguished career in law. When one of her cases came before the Federal Court of Claims that winter, Lockwood was refused, because she was a woman, the right to plead a case. Her petition for admission to the Supreme Court of the United States (1876) was denied on the basis of custom, but Lockwood would not admit defeat. She petitioned Congress to pass a Declaratory Act or Joint Resolution "that no woman otherwise qualified, shall be debarred from practice before any United States Court on account of sex." Reasoning that if women had the right to practice law they were entitled to pursue legal matters through the highest courts in the country, Lockwood pushed enabling legislation through Congress. By means of energetic lobbying, and with the support of such pro-suffrage senators as Aaron A. Sargent of California and George F. Hoar of Massachusetts, Lockwood secured the passage of the Lockwood Bill, which permitted women to practice before the Supreme Court. On March 3, 1879, she became the first woman to be admitted to the Bar of the United States Supreme Court. Three days later, she was admitted to the U.S. Court of Claims.

A year later, on February 2, 1880, in a striking demonstration of her commitment to racial equality, Belva Lockwood appeared before the Supreme Court of the United States and made a motion that Samuel R. Lowery, an African American, be allowed to practice before the Supreme Court. Lowery, who was the principal of the Huntsville Industrial University in Alabama, became the first southern African American to practice law before the Supreme Court of the United States.

Belva Lockwood became a familiar sight in Washington as she pedaled throughout the city on "Challenge No. 2," an English tricycle that she introduced to the nation's capital. She rode the vehicle to the Capitol, the courts—wherever her work led her. By 1890, Belva was well established in her law career, specializing in pension and claims cases against the U.S. government. It was this specialty that led her to one of the greatest legal triumphs of her career. The Cherokee Indian Nation secured Lockwood to represent it in claims against the U.S. government related to an 1891 treaty involving the sale and purchase of more than eight million acres of land known as the Cherokee Outlet. Lockwood was entrusted with defending nearly fifteen thousand Cherokee clients. After reviewing the numerous treaties and

statutes that governed the history of the Cherokees, she filed a petition to uphold the claim of her Indian clients.

On March 20, 1905, the case of the Eastern and Emigrant Cherokees against the United States was decided before the Court of Claims. Following an impassioned argument by Lockwood, the Chief Justice agreed that the United States had broken and evaded the letter and spirit of its agreement with the Cherokees. Nevertheless, although he decreed that the Cherokees recover certain amounts due in the account rendered by the government, he could not bring himself to allow the full interest on those amounts. The case was appealed to the Supreme Court, where, on April 30, 1906, Lockwood again argued for the Indians and their rights. The court agreed and awarded the Cherokees five million dollars.

As a feminist, Lockwood did much to further women's rights. In 1867, she was one of the founders of Washington's first suffrage group, the Universal Franchise Association. During the 1870's and early 1880's, she was active in the Washington conventions of the National Woman Suffrage Association (NWSA). In January, 1871, Belva Lockwood presented a memorial to the United States Senate on "The Right of Women to Vote."

She addressed congressional committees and drew up innumerable resolutions and bills that would help bring equality to women in the United States. She circulated a petition at the meetings of the National and American Woman Suffrage Associations in New York that hastened the passage, in 1872, of legislation giving women government employees equal pay for equal work. In 1873, she represented a woman in a divorce case, charging the defendant with drunkenness, cruel treatment, desertion, and refusal to support. She won the case for her client, obtaining the decree of divorce and alimony with costs. Later, in 1896, as a member of a committee of the District Federation of Women's Clubs, she helped Ellen Spencer Mussey and others secure passage of a law liberalizing the property rights of married women and equal guardianship of their children in the District of Columbia. In 1903, she proposed the inclusion of woman suffrage clauses in the statehood bills for Oklahoma, Arizona, and New Mexico, which were then under consideration.

In 1872, Belva Lockwood spoke at Cooper Union in New York on behalf of Victoria Woodhull's candidacy for president of the United

States. Lockwood herself was nominated for president in 1884 by women representing the National Equal Rights Party. Her platform reflected her commitment to civil rights, temperance, and feminism. She encompassed equal rights for all, including African Americans, Indians, and immigrants. She advocated curtailment of the liquor traffic, reform in marriage and divorce laws, and universal peace. She flourished a banner inscribed on one side with the words "Women's Rights" and on the other with the word "Peace." Although her campaign alienated many members of the organized suffrage movement, including Susan B. Anthony, it generated much public interest. Astonishingly, she won the electoral vote of Indiana, half that of Oregon, nearly captured New Hampshire, and made a respectable showing in New York. A second campaign four years later was less successful. Her political aptitude was recognized by President Grover Cleveland, who sent her as the U.S. delegate to the Congress of Charities and Correction in Geneva, Switzerland.

Increasingly committed to the cause of world peace, Lockwood put much of her energy into peace organizations after the 1880's. One of the earliest members of the Universal Peace Union, Lockwood served at various times in the 1880's and 1890's on the union's executive committee and the editorial board of its paper, the *Peacemaker*, as a corresponding secretary and vice president, and as one of the union's chief lobbyists. She was the union's delegate to the International Peace Congress of 1889 and its successors; served as the American secretary of the International Bureau of Peace, founded in Berne in 1891; and served on the nominating committee for the Nobel Peace Prize. In all these organizations, she agitated for the arbitration principle as a means of settling world problems.

Belva Lockwood remained politically active into her later years. She continued lecturing well into her eighties, and at the age of eighty-seven she campaigned for Woodrow Wilson. In 1909, she was awarded an honorary LL.D. degree by Syracuse University, and in 1913, she was presented with an oil portrait of herself by the women of Washington, D.C. The portrait now hangs in the Art Gallery of the National Museum.

Following the death of her daughter Lura in 1894, Lockwood's financial fortunes collapsed, and her last years were spent in ill health and relative poverty. She died at George Washington University Hospital in 1917 and was buried in the Congressional Cemetery in Washington. The funeral service held in the Wesley Chapel of the Methodist Episcopalian Church recalled the triumphs of her life, and the newspapers recorded her history. A scholarship was established in Lockwood's name, and a bust of Lockwood was unveiled by the Women's Bar Association of the District of Columbia to commemorate the seventy-fifth anniversary of her admission to the Supreme Court.

Summary

Legally and socially, Belva A. Lockwood scored important victories for women. Marriage, she concluded, should be a civil contract in which property rights were equal. She rebelled against the law in the District of Columbia that could compel a man to support his illegitimate child but could not compel him to support his wife and his legitimate children. She worked for the reform of probate law and recognition of the rights of widows and orphans. Single-handedly, Lockwood moved the U.S. Congress to open the highest court to women lawyers. She fought for civil rights for all Americans. Up to the day she died, she worked for world peace.

Over the years of her practice, Lockwood gave aid, advice, and encouragement to women from all parts of the country who were attempting to become attorneys-at-law. Belva Lockwood's hard-won battles, confidence, and fortitude are an inspiration to women throughout the world.

Bibliography

Curti, Merle. *Peace or War*. New York: Norton, 1936. Curti discusses Lockwood's pacifism and her efforts to advance peace on the national and international scenes.

Fox, Mary Virginia. *Lady for the Defense: A Biography of Belva Lockwood*. New York: Harcourt Brace, 1975. A useful, relatively recent treatment of Lockwood's life and work.

Stanton, Elizabeth Cady, et al. eds. *History of Woman Suffrage*. Rochester, N.Y.: Anthony, 1881. Contains informative accounts of the NWSA's Washington conventions, 1870 to 1874, in volumes 2 through 4 (1882-1902) and useful chapters on the District of Columbia in volumes 3 and 4.

Stern, Madeleine. *We the Women*. New York: Schulte, 1963. This work contains the most complete account available of Belva Lockwood's life. Stern discusses, at length, Lockwood's most celebrated court cases, including her own quest to practice before the Supreme Court. This is the best source to consult regarding Lockwood's commitment to women's rights, civil rights, and pacifism.

Whitman, Alden, ed. *American Reformers*. New York: Wilson, 1985. A brief but fairly thorough account of Lockwood's life, highlighting her women's rights and peace activism.

Diane C. Vecchio

SIR JOSEPH NORMAN LOCKYER

Born: May 17, 1836; Rugby, Warwickshire, England

Died: August 16, 1920; Salcombe Regis, Devonshire, England

Areas of Achievement: Science publishing and astrophysics

Contribution: Lockyer was a pioneering, self-educated astrophysicist who founded in 1869, and edited throughout its first fifty years, the weekly journal *Nature*, which is the world's premier general science periodical.

Early Life

Joseph Norman Lockyer was born May 17, 1836, in Rugby, Warwickshire, England. His mother, née Anne Norman, was the daughter of the squire of a Warwickshire village near Rugby; his father, Joseph Hooley Lockyer, was a surgeon-apothecary in Rugby. Norman, as he was called, had a younger sister. His father had broad scientific interests and had been a founding member of the Rugby Literary and Scientific Institution. As a teenager, Lockyer's principal interest at school was not science but languages, especially Latin and Greek. In 1856, at the age of twenty, he went to the Continent for a year to study French and German. Upon his return to England, Lockyer obtained a temporary position at the War Office in May, 1857. In February of the following year he was appointed to a permanent clerkship in the War Office and appeared destined for a career in the civil service. In the same year he married Winifred James, whose father, William, had an important role in the early development of English railroads. Winifred possessed, as did her husband, an excellent knowledge of the French language, and after her marriage she became known as a translator of French scientific texts.

The Lockyers' first home was in the village of Wimbledon, an easy commute by train to London and the War Office. The Lockyers had nine children, seven boys and two girls, before Winifred died in 1879. Twenty-four years later, in 1903, Lockyer married Thomasine Mary Brodhurst, the fifty-year-old widow of a surgeon. She outlived Lockyer and after his death published a volume on Lockyer's life and work.

Lockyer was an energetic and forceful personality of medium height, somewhat thickset, who did not shrink from controversy. He was ambitious and an exceedingly hard worker, driving himself on several occasions to the point where he required a complete respite from work; nevertheless, he also enjoyed a variety of leisure activities, particularly golf, for which he coauthored *The Rules of Golf* (1896).

Life's Work

Lockyer's transformation from obscure War Office clerk to internationally known editor and scientist began in Wimbledon, where, influenced by new acquaintances, he took up astronomy as a hobby, purchasing a three-and-three-quarters-inch refracting telescope and becoming a Fellow of the Royal Astronomical Society in 1861. On May 10, 1862, the *London Review* published his account of his observations of the transit of the shadow of Saturn's moon Titan across the planet's disc. The *London Review's* editor subsequently invited Lockyer to submit an article each month under the title "Face of the Sky." Lockyer regarded this series as the beginning of his literary work. He also became science editor and writer for the *Reader*, a new literary and scientific journal. When the *Reader* foundered after only a few years, Lockyer envisioned a weekly journal devoted exclusively to science. His idea appealed to the publisher Alexander Macmillan, and *Nature* was launched on November 4, 1869. *Nature* experienced financial difficulties in its early years, but thanks to Lockyer's enthusiasm and Macmillan's continued support it survived, showing a profit for the first time in 1899 and going on to become the world's most respected general scientific journal in the twentieth century and Lockyer's most lasting contribution. Lockyer was its editor throughout its first fifty years.

When in 1870 the British government named a Royal Commission on Scientific Instruction and the Advancement of Science, Lockyer was delighted to be summoned from the War Office to be its secretary, a position he held until the commission issued its final report in 1875. The experience gave him a comprehensive knowledge of the strengths and weaknesses of science in Great Britain. Throughout his adult life he was an advocate of the state support of science. Upon the completion of the commission's work, Lockyer did not return to the War Office, being appointed instead to the government's Science and Art Department with responsibility for arranging an exhibition of significant laboratory and scientific teaching apparatus at London's South Kensington Museum. Held in 1876 and opened by Queen Victoria, the exhibition was a great success. In addition to arranging the exhibition, Lockyer was expected by the department to continue his by then significant astrophysical researches, and so he established a small government observatory, soon to be known as the Solar Physics Observatory. When in 1878 the government created a Solar Physics Committee, Lockyer sat on it as representative of the Science and Art Department. Nine years later, the committee became an advisory and supervisory board for the Solar Physics Laboratory still directed by Lockyer. Since 1881, Lockyer had taught astronomy at the Normal School of Science and the Royal School of Mines (renamed the Royal College of Science in 1890) in London. He was promoted to professor of astronomical physics in 1887.

While earning his livelihood in these various positions, Lockyer had from the 1860's pursued, frequently in his spare time, his research interests in the new field of astrophysics. In 1859, Robert Bunsen and Gustav Robert Kirchhoff, professors of chemistry and physics, respectively, at the University of Heidelberg in Germany, had founded spectrum analysis on the principle that each element has its characteristic spectrum. During the following year Kirchhoff had given an explanation of the dark, or Fraunhofer, lines in the solar spectrum, thereby revealing the chemical composition of the sun and at the same time initiating the science of astrophysics. Lockyer quickly became attracted to this new branch of astronomy—which utilized the new instrument the spectroscope, and also the camera, together with the traditional telescope—and just as quickly began to make his mark in it. In the early 1860's, a dispute had arisen concerning whether spots on the sun were hotter or cooler than the surrounding solar surface. Lockyer devised a means of spectroscopically examining the light from individual sunspots, as opposed to the entire solar disc, and established that the spots are cooler than their surroundings. He then turned to a study of solar prominences, bright clouds of matter which were observed during solar eclipses to rise from the sun's surface into its corona, or atmosphere. Employing the method that he had devised for examining individual sunspots, Lockyer demonstrated in 1868 that prominences could be studied with the spectroscope at times other than solar

eclipses, and, further, that, because of their bright line spectra, prominences were clouds of hot gas. Unknown to Lockyer, this conclusion had been independently reached by the French astrophysicist Pierre Jules César Janssen, using a similar method, a few weeks earlier. The French government honored Janssen's and Lockyer's simultaneous discovery by striking a medal with their portraits on it. On the strength of his original contributions to solar physics, Lockyer was elected a Fellow of the Royal Society, Great Britain's most prestigious scientific society, in 1869.

Lockyer's further spectroscopic and astrophysical researches led him to formulate two bold hypotheses for which he became widely known. The first hypothesis concerned the dissociation of matter. At the time, in the 1870's, the concepts of atom and molecule (a combination of two or more atoms) were found to be useful in chemistry and certain branches of physics. For example, gaseous hydrogen was regarded as being composed of hydrogen molecules, each consisting of two hydrogen atoms; the two spectra found in the laboratory to be characteristic of hydrogen, a band spectrum and a line spectrum, were attributed to the molecular and atomic forms of hydrogen respectively. It was believed that as the temperature of the hydrogen gas was increased the molecules of hydrogen became dissociated into atoms, and so the band spectrum became replaced by the line spectrum. In the astrophysical realm, red stars, believed to be of relatively low temperature, exhibited band spectra; yellow stars, of higher temperature, such as the Sun, exhibited the line spectra of numerous elements, including the heaviest; and white stars, believed to be of yet higher temperature, displayed the line spectrum of the simplest element of all, hydrogen. From these and from other observations, Lockyer hypothesized in 1873 that with increasing stellar temperature heavier elements became dissociated into lighter ones and their common constituents. In considering the constitutions of elemental atoms, Lockyer suggested an analogy with the composition of members of a hydrocarbon series which organic chemists had shown could be built up through successive additions of the radical, CH2. Earlier in the nineteenth century, a British physician, William Prout, had hypothesized that the hydrogen atom might be the building block of all other atoms. At the annual meeting of the British Association for the Advancement of Science in 1879, Lockyer announced that he had been suc-

cessful in partially decomposing several elements into hydrogen in the laboratory. Chemists were not convinced, however, and even though astrophysicists continued to support the dissociation hypothesis during the 1880's, by the end of the century they, too, had concluded that it was untenable. About that time a quite different view of atomic composition was beginning to take shape following Joseph John Thomson's discovery in 1897 of the astonishingly small particle, some two thousand times smaller than the hydrogen atom, soon to be known as the electron. In *The Chemistry of the Sun* (1887) Lockyer summarized his ideas on dissociation and answered criticisms of the dissociation hypothesis. He published a revised version of the hypothesis in *Inorganic Evolution as Studied by Spectrum Analysis* (1900).

In connection with the dissociation hypothesis, Lockyer had been unable to determine the constituents of atoms, but with the much grander meteoritic hypothesis he specified that meteors were the building blocks of the visible universe. As he claimed, "all self-luminous bodies in the celestial spaces are composed either of swarms of meteor-ites or of masses of meteoritic vapour produced by heat." In 1866, two striking astronomical phenomena, a nova and the Leonid shower of meteors, greatly impressed Lockyer. He speculated that the phenomena might be related, that a nova might result from the collision of showers of meteors. Later, in 1874, in viewing Coggia's comet Lockyer adopted the idea, not original with him, that a comet consists of a shower of meteors whose frequent, mutual collisions cause the comet's luminosity. The spectroscopic study in the laboratory of available meteorites strengthened Lockyer's belief in the meteoritic nature of comets. When in 1877 the first nova to be examined systematically using the spectroscope developed a spectrum characteristic of a nebula, Lockyer argued that the observed spectroscopic changes could be interpreted as the result of a gradual cooling of meteors from the intense heat of their impact to the cooler state of a nebula. Hitherto, Lockyer had, like others, assumed nebulas to be the hottest bodies in the universe, which in cooling developed into stars which continued to fall in temperature over time. Now, on spectroscopic grounds, Lockyer argued that nebulas developed into *cool* stars which, on condensing, rose in temperature before becoming cool once more. He was aware that the teaching of the accepted view of stellar evolution, that stars are born hot and cool throughout their lives, ran against his argument. Principally because of this disagreement with the prevailing view, the meteoritic hypothesis lost support among astrophysicists and perished. Lockyer published his views on stellar evolution in *The Meteoritic Hypothesis* (1890) and his further development of the meteoritic hypothesis in *The Sun's Place in Nature* (1897). *Inorganic Evolution as Studied by Spectrum Analysis* (1900) was the last of Lockyer's books to deal with both the meteoritic and the dissociation hypotheses.

During a visit to Greece and Turkey early in 1890, Lockyer became curious about the orientations of ancient temples. Later, in studying Egyptian temples, to which most of the available data referred, he argued that if their orientations had an astronomical basis, then determination of the orientations could lead to establishing the dates of construction of the temples. Lockyer determined that several temples at Karnak were oriented toward either the rising or the setting solstitial sun, while the pyramids and temples at Giza were oriented toward the equinoctial sun. He calculated that the temple of Amen-Ra at Karnak had been built about 3700 B.C. Lockyer found that some temples were not oriented toward the sun, but instead toward bright stars, including Sirius. Lockyer went on to apply his ideas on orientation to Stonehenge and other ancient stone monuments in Great Britain. He concluded that they could be arranged in an evolutionary order: Avenues and cromlechs came first, and stone circles, representing a more advanced state of astronomical knowledge, came later. He believed that the sunrise orientations used in the earlier stage were related to the appearance of new vegetation in May, whereas those of the later stage were related to the summer solstice in June. In dealing with both Egyptian temples and British monuments, Lockyer made speculative, and controversial, excursions into mythology and folklore. His conclusions regarding the orientations of Egyptian temples were published in *The Dawn of Astronomy: A Study of the Temple Worship and Mythology of the Ancient Egyptians* (1894) and his views on British stone structures in *Stonehenge and Other British Monuments Astronomically Considered* (1906).

In 1901, Lockyer was obliged to retire from the Royal College of Science because of age regulations, but he continued as director of the Solar Physics Laboratory until 1911, when it was decided, to his profound disappointment and against his vigorous opposition, to transfer the observatory to Cambridge University. Lockyer's response to the transfer was to build an observatory at Sidmouth in Devonshire, which he directed until his death in 1920.

Summary

Joseph Norman Lockyer was a self-educated and widely known man of broad interests, including scientific publishing, astrophysics, ancient astronomy, meteorology, education, the state support of science, and golf. During his busy life he played many roles, including those of civil servant, secretary to a royal commission on science, professor of astronomy, director of astronomical observatories, Fellow of the Royal Society, president of the British Association for the Advancement of Science, and founder of the British Science Guild. Finally, he made substantial contributions: He was a leading astrophysicist, a sound experimentalist, and a bold theorizer, and he founded and edited *Nature*, which remains the world's foremost general scientific periodical. Lockyer's positive influence was felt by international scientists, British scientific institutions, the field of astrophysics, science in general, and even scholars and fields outside science. In recognition of his services to science in Great Britain, Lockyer was knighted in 1897.

Bibliography

Clerke, Agnes M. *A Popular History of Astronomy During the Nineteenth Century.* Edinburgh: Black, 1885; New York: Macmillan, 1886. The second part, "Recent Progress of Astronomy," provides useful accounts of various aspects of astrophysics during its first twenty-five years.

Lockyer, T. Mary, and Winifred L. Lockyer, with the assistance of Prof. H. Dingle. *Life and Work of Sir Norman Lockyer.* London: Macmillan, 1928. This volume consists of a chronology of Lockyer's life by Dingle based on materials gathered by Lockyer's second wife, Mary, and younger daughter, Winifred, and a series of useful essays on aspects of Lockyer's work, for example the dissociation hypothesis, not explained in the chronology.

McGucken, William. *Nineteenth-century Spectroscopy: Development of the Understanding of Spectra, 1802-1897.* Baltimore: The Johns Hopkins University Press, 1969. The second chapter, "Atoms and Molecules and the Further Extension of the Principle of Spectrum Analysis," includes a detailed discussion of Lockyer's dissociation hypothesis.

Meadows, A. J. *Early Solar Physics.* Oxford and New York: Pergamon Press, 1970. Provides a good account of the development of solar physics during the second half of the nineteenth century; also reproduces original papers, including several by Lockyer, that contributed to that development.

————. *Science and Controversy: A Biography of Sir Norman Lockyer.* Cambridge, Mass.: MIT Press, and London: Macmillan, 1972. This is the better of the two accounts of Lockyer's life and work. Although the author occasionally lapses into a chronological account, he enables the reader to see Lockyer within the context of his times. He also presents a fuller, more critical account of Lockyer the man.

William McGucken

HENRY WADSWORTH LONGFELLOW

Born: February 27, 1807; Portland, Maine
Died: March 24, 1882; Cambridge, Massachusetts
Area of Achievement: Literature
Contribution: Besides working to establish the study of modern languages and comparative literature in the United States, Longfellow became the most popular of all living poets during his time.

Early Life

The second of Stephen and Zilpah Wadsworth Longfellow's eight children, Henry Wadsworth Longfellow was born on February 27, 1807, in Portland, Maine, while Maine was still a part of Massachusetts. As a member of a loving, prosperous, and distinguished Unitarian family, the future poet seems to have had a happy childhood that included the scenes he would describe in "My Lost Youth." He was a gentle, precocious boy who started school when he was three. At the age of six, he enrolled in the Portland Academy, where he was still a student when, on November 17, 1820, "The Battle of Lovell's Pond," his first published poem, appeared in the *Portland Gazette* with merely "Henry" given as the author's name. His work did not receive unanimous acclaim: That evening, he heard a family friend disparage the poem.

In 1821 Longfellow passed the entrance examination for Bowdoin College; however, maybe because of his age, he remained at the Portland Academy another school year while working for college credit. It was not until the fall of 1822 that Longfellow, with his older brother, left home to study on the campus in Brunswick, Maine. While at Bowdoin, he studied hard, read avidly, joined a college literary club known as the Peucinian Society, had poems published in several off-campus periodicals, and, in 1825, graduated fourth in a class of thirty-eight.

As graduation approached, Longfellow feared that he would have to follow his practical-minded father's wish and study law instead of pursuing a literary career, but the Bowdoin trustees offered him the new professorship of modern languages, provided that he study in Europe at his own expense to prepare himself for the job. Having accepted the opportunity gladly, Longfellow sailed from New York on May 15, 1826, at the age of nineteen.

Life's Work

When his ship docked in France one month later, Longfellow began acquiring a knowledge of modern European languages and literature that would serve him well as a widely read author and translator. Although his intellect was hardly provincial before the voyage, his long, early visit to Europe made him a literary man of the world. His method of study was mainly one of informal immersion in the ordinary life of the countries he visited: France, Spain, Italy, Austria, Germany, the Netherlands, Belgium, and England.

Beginning his duties at Bowdoin in the fall of 1829, Longfellow became one of the first professors of modern languages in any U.S. college, since the traditional emphasis in languages had been on Latin and ancient Greek. As an innovative, enthusiastic teacher who could not find suitable materials, he had to translate or edit textbooks for his classes, trying to make modern European literature interesting for his students. During this period at Bowdoin, Longfellow put aside his ambition for fame as a creative writer and devoted himself more to scholarly articles than to poems and prose stories. His interest turned also to courtship, and on September 14, 1831, he married Mary Potter, an educated, intelligent, nineteen-year-old girl from his hometown.

Even before his wedding, Longfellow had grown dissatisfied with teaching at Bowdoin. By 1832 he was applying for other jobs, including ones outside the field of higher education. Then Longfellow, talented as he was, again had the sort of good luck that had let him avoid life as a lawyer: George Ticknor, who taught modern languages at Harvard, resigned his position and recommended Longfellow as his replacement. The Harvard administration accepted Ticknor's recommendation, with the inclusion of their own recommendation that Longfellow travel again to Europe, this time to enrich his knowledge of German. Having resigned from Bowdoin, Longfellow, with his wife and two of her friends, sailed across the Atlantic and docked in England on May 8, 1835.

After a stay in London, where Longfellow arranged for the British publication of *Outre-Mer: A Pilgrimage Beyond the Sea* (1833-1834), his new prose collection based on the journal he had kept during his first European tour, he and his party sailed for northern Germany, from which they traveled through Denmark to Sweden, where he studied the Swedish and Finnish languages. In the fall, they went to the Netherlands, where, in Amster-

dam, Mary, who had been enduring a difficult pregnancy, suffered a miscarriage. After awhile, when her health seemed better, they traveled to Rotterdam, forty miles away; there, on November 29, 1835, Mary died.

In his grief, Longfellow still believed he should continue his European studies and decided not to return to the United States with his wife's body but to study in Heidelberg, Germany. In the summer of 1836, while on a vacation in the Alps, Longfellow met Frances "Fanny" Appleton, who, still in her late teens, was a smart, pretty, and charming woman from a rich Boston family. A mutual attraction soon developed. However, the time that Longfellow had available for his second visit to Europe had almost expired, and in October he sailed for the United States.

Settling in Cambridge, Massachusetts, Longfellow began his official duties as Smith Professor of Modern Languages at Harvard, delivering his first lecture on May 23, 1837. In effect, he chaired a small academic department, besides teaching in the same attention-getting way he had taught at Bowdoin. He also wrote, but, unlike his writing during his stay at the smaller college, his writing at Harvard was more imaginative and autobiographical than scholarly. His loosely built novel *Hyperion*, published in the summer of 1839, tells in only slight disguise of his courtship of Appleton, who had rejected his marriage proposal in 1837. Still romantically interested in her, he sent her a copy of the book, apparently not realizing that she would object to having the courtship made so nearly public. It was not until 1843 that she encouraged Longfellow's attention, and on July 13 of that year they married, receiving as a gift from the bride's father Craigie House, the historic Cambridge mansion where Longfellow had been renting rooms.

Meanwhile, a few months after *Hyperion*, Longfellow's first volume of poetry, *Voices of the Night* (1839), was published; it contained "The Psalm of Life," which became one of his best-known poems, and marked the beginning of his immense popularity with critics and ordinary readers. In 1841 Longfellow published *Ballads and Other Poems*, which included "The Skeleton in Armor," "The Village Blacksmith," and "Excelsior." The next year, while sailing home after a stay in Germany, he wrote eight short abolitionist poems published as *Poems on Slavery* (1842). After Longfellow married Frances in 1843, his literary productivity continued. Although he published one more novel, *Kavanagh* (1849), his big success came in poetry, not only in such short poems as "The Arsenal at Springfield" and "The Building of the Ship" but also in long narrative poems, especially *Evangeline* (1847), *The Song of Hiawatha* (1855), and *The Courtship of Miles Standish* (1858). In 1854, when Longfellow resigned his position at Harvard to give his full professional attention to writing, the president, accepting the resignation with regret, praised Longfellow for the fame he had brought the college.

No famous writer has ever had a happier marriage. Tragedy, however, struck suddenly on July 9, 1861. While Frances was heating wax to seal locks of her daughters' hair, her dress caught fire. She raced to her husband in a nearby room, but he could not put out the flames in time, and she died the next day. Longfellow, badly burned on his hands and face, never fully recovered from her death. His sonnet "The Cross of Snow," written in 1879, suggests the emotional scar, and, with shaving difficult because of his facial scars, he grew the white beard that his admirers came to associate with him.

When Longfellow eventually resumed writing after his second wife's death, he produced the long collections of related poems *Tales of a Wayside Inn* (1863), which included "Paul Revere's Ride," and *Christus: A Mystery* (1872). He also wrote such separate long poems as *Aftermath* (1873), *The Hanging of the Crane* (1874) and *Morituri Salutamus* (1875). Furthermore, from 1867 to 1869, he added Dante Alighieri's monumental fourteenth century Italian poem *Divina Commedia* (1321; *The Divine Comedy of Dante Alighieri*) to his impressive list of translations. Working almost until the end of his life, Longfellow added a last stanza to his own poem "The Bells of San Blas" on March 15, 1882. On March 24, having been sick only a short time, he died at Craigie House, forty-five days after an admiring nation had celebrated his seventy-fifth birthday.

Summary

As Longfellow's friend George Washington Greene said, no poet ever received such acclaim while he was living. In North America and in Europe, Longfellow triumphed both popularly and critically. In 1868, while he was on his last visit to England, Queen Victoria invited him to Windsor Castle. That in itself was a high honor, but even more indicative of Longfellow's fame was that some of the Queen's servants, ordinarily nonchalant about seeing the powerful and the celebrated, hid in the halls to watch Longfellow as he walked by.

Amid all the praise, Longfellow lived like a gentleman, not merely in the sense that, with his second wife's fortune and the money from his books, he could keep an ample store of wine at Craigie House, but also in the sense that he gave himself graciously. Reserved though he normally was, his many friends loved him, and they included such well-known men as the English novelist Charles Dickens, the American novelist Nathaniel Hawthorne (who had been one of Longfellow's Bowdoin classmates), and the abolitionist senator of Massachusetts, Charles Sumner. Having become an institution, Longfellow found himself besieged at Craigie House by uninvited strangers and by unknown letter writers; yet he remained polite, even when the visitors and correspondents were boorish.

Almost inevitably, such a high reputation had to fall. Although some readers voiced objections to his poetry during his lifetime and shortly after his death, the outcry arose with the general anti-Victorianism that began during World War I. Among other features of his poems, critics targeted his notion of propriety in diction and subjects, his sentimentality, and his overt didacticism. Yet a cry of protest against the harshest of the criticism eventually arose as well, and by the end of the twentieth century the mainstream critical opinion was that besides his contribution as an innovative professor in a new discipline, Longfellow enriched American literature. While his rank among nineteenth century American poets is lower than that of Walt Whitman and Emily Dickinson and he belonged to what hostile sociological critics denounce as a privileged class, he remains important not only for what his contemporaries thought of him but also for what he wrote.

Bibliography

Arvin, Newton. *Longfellow: His Life and Work.* Boston: Little Brown, 1963. Seeing Longfellow as a significant minor poet, Arvin is most helpful when he critically examines many of the works and explains why Longfellow's reputation fell.

Hirsh, Edward L. *Henry Wadsworth Longfellow.* University of Minnesota Pamphlets on American Writers 35. Minneapolis: University of Minnesota Press, 1964. This booklet contains ten pages of biography, thirty pages of well-balanced criticism of Longfellow's poetry and prose, one page about his reputation, and a three-page selected bibliography without annotation.

Longfellow, Samuel, ed. *Life of Henry Wadsworth Longfellow, with Extracts from His Journals and Correspondence.* 2 vols. Boston: Ticknor, and London: Kegan Paul, 1886. This biography, prepared by a younger brother, withholds some information but has proved indispensable to all subsequent authors of full-scale biographies. For the most part, the author allows Henry Longfellow to speak for himself. Includes illustrations and an index.

_____, ed. *Final Memorials of Henry Wadsworth Longfellow.* Boston: Ticknor, and London: Kegan Paul, 1887. Printed in 1891 as the third volume of *Life of Henry Wadsworth Longfellow,* this book provides letters and journal entries to supplement the 1886 biography, especially for the poet's last fifteen years.

Wagenknecht, Edward. *Henry Wadsworth Longfellow: Portrait of an American Humanist.* New York: Oxford University Press, 1966. After a short narrative biography, Wagenknecht presents Longfellow topically as a Christian humanist, analyzing the man rather than his writings.

Williams, Cecil B. *Henry Wadsworth Longfellow.* Twayne's United States Authors Series 68. New York: Twayne, 1964. After a chronology and a chapter on Longfellow's "Image and Actuality," Williams devotes four chapters to biography, three to a sympathetic study of the works, and one to "Longfellow in Literary History and in Literature." The selected bibliography is annotated.

Victor Lindsey

SIR CHARLES LYELL

Born: November 14, 1797; Kinnordy, Kirriemuir, Scotland
Died: February 22, 1875; London, England
Area of Achievement: Geology
Contribution: Lyell gave shape to the emerging science of geology with his theory of Uniformitarianism, explaining past change from currently observable causes.

Early Life

Sir Charles Lyell was born on November 14, 1797, into a substantial London mercantile and naval family on a Scottish estate, Kinnordy. The family spent the years of young Charles's boyhood in the south of England, where his father, also Charles, engaged in the gentlemanly pursuit of botanical collecting, especially of mosses. His father was a member of the Linnean Society and corresponded with many of the leading scientific men of the time. Young Charles, sickly as a boy, received a private grammar school education and matriculated at Exeter College, Oxford, in 1816. He acquired a standard classical education, receiving his B. A., with second-class honors, in 1819. In the same year, he moved to London to read law at Lincoln's Inn. He was called to the bar in 1822 and practiced law intermittently during the remainder of the 1820's. In London, he made a name for himself in broader intellectual circles as a regular contributor to the *Quarterly Review.* In 1826 alone, he provided examinations of the English university question, scientific institutions, and reviews of geology. Of medium height, with a large forehead and a slim build, he presented the gentlemanly exterior of proper dress and the demeanor of a young man of society, although his lifelong problem with weak eyes forced him to wear a squinting quizzical expression.

Lyell's geological reviews in the *Quarterly Review* reveal the increasingly central role that geology was playing in his life. His interest, aroused by William Buckland's mineralogy and geology lectures at Oxford in 1817 and 1818, had been supplemented by bits of geologizing with family friends, in Scotland, the south of England, and the Swiss Alps in 1818. Graduation from Oxford and his move to London brought him membership in the Geological Society of London and the Linnean Society in 1819.

Gradually, as Lyell's interest in geology changed from an avocation to a committed vocation, he became secretary of the Geological Society from 1823 to 1826 and in 1826 was elected a fellow of the Royal Society. Visits to France and geologizing in the Paris Basin with Constant Prévost in 1823, and Prévost's return visit in 1824, brought Lyell closer to the heart of specialized geology. It also led to his first Geological Society paper in 1824, in which he noted the equivalency of freshwater limestones in the Paris Basin to new limestones deposited in Scottish lakes. In his 1826 articles in the *Transactions of the Geological Society* in the *Quarterly Review*, he tentatively began theorizing about the nature of geological change.

In the 1820's, an amateur making original contributions to geology was not unusual. Geology was still in its Baconian, gentlemanly tradition of collecting and observing, with plenty of room for the gifted amateur. While little theoretical framework for geology was accepted or recognized, a consensus existed that the Earth's geological past could be unraveled and ordered. This stratigraphic ordering was based on the agreement that superposition, the sequence or succession of rock strata appearing in the order in which they were deposited, the youngest at the top and the oldest at the bottom, indicated the relative age of each stratum. This stratigraphic concept was combined with the ideas of William Smith and his map of 1816, showing that each stratum's different characteristic fossils also indicated relative age. The Geological Society of London had been founded in 1807 on the basis of this empirical, rather than theoretical, consensus, consciously shunning theorizing and stressing observation. Most geologists agreed that the science had been hindered by the extravagant assertions of systems-builders, such as Abraham Gottlob Werner in Germany and James Hutton of Scotland, who seemed to place theory above field experience.

By the late 1820's, Lyell was planning a popular "Conversations on Geology" to satisfy his geological and monetary needs. When he reviewed George Scrope's *Memoir on the Geology of Central France* (1827), however, the book focused his attention on the Auvergne in Central France, where a complex series of lava flows seemed to offer a unique key to geological forces and successions. In 1828, Lyell visited the Auvergne with Roderick Murchison, a retired army officer and amateur geologist who had taken up geology in part to satisfy his craving for outdoor activity and to supplement his passion for hunting. Viewing the continually re-excavated river beds and successive lava flows suggested to Lyell analogies between past and present geological actions. From France, on "the best and longest geological tour which I ever made . . . which made me what I am in theoretical geology," he traveled to Italy with Murchison and then alone to Southern Italy and Sicily. Struck by the number of fossil shells of living Mediterranean species, Lyell realized that one could order the Tertiary, or most recent, rocks according to the proportional relationship of living to extinct species. He also saw that past changes in land levels in the area of volcanic Mount Etna could be explained by analogy to present forces. The Italian trip forced him to change the scope of "Conversations on Geology" from a brief popular exposition to a major work.

Life's Work

By January, 1830, Lyell had clarified his ideas and published the first volume of *Principles of Geology*. This work presents a picture of the geological past as essentially uniform and explicable by analogy to currently operating forces. Lyell found no need for extravagantly violent alterations in forces and rejected the explanation adopted by the Catastrophists, who relied on irregular major convulsive change. Part of the basis of Catastrophism was the need to fit the biblical flood, or deluge, into geological history (thus their alternative designation, Diluvialists). Lyell instead offered a picture of gradual, cumulative change in a uniform process; thus, his doctrine is called Uniformitarianism. He rejected any effort to explain the beginnings of the world, returning to the famous dictum of Hutton that no vestige of a beginning could be found.

To present a convincing argument, Lyell had to solve a number of problems, the first of which was climatic change. Most older fossils seemed to indicate a past tropical climate much warmer than the climate of Lyell's England. Most geologists explained the anomaly through the central heat theory, referring to an Earth formed out of fire and then cooling, such that the climate as a whole was slowly cooling over time. Lyell argued that climate was a local and variable phenomenon, dependent on relations of land and sea masses, showing that as the proportion of land and sea varied with uplifting and subsidence of land, climate varied around a stable norm, providing quite different climates and physical environments over time.

Volume 1 of *Principles of Geology* was an immediate popular success, with more than half the

original edition sold by November, 1830. It met with less enthusiasm from the Catastrophists. Adam Sedgwick, in his 1831 presidential address to the Geological Society, pointed to the recent theory of Élie de Beaumont of France that mountain chains had been thrown up in parallel lines by great convulsions. Sedgwick then dismissed Lyell's theories and supported those of de Beaumont, since Lyell's work seemed to set out from deductive assumptions rather than empirical fieldwork.

In the second volume of *Principles of Geology*, which appeared in January, 1832, Lyell examined patterns left by living forms over geological time. If the stratigraphic record was to be intimately tied to the fossil record, then changes in life forms over time had to be explained for fossils to be accurately used as indices. Since each successive formation displayed a gradually changing mix of different fossils, Lyell had to explain how the characteristic life forms of each geological epoch had changed. He argued that species were discrete entities and rejected Lamarck's idea of continual transmutation and plasticity in favor of regular and periodic extinction of species. Then, as land forms and environments altered over time, some species would become extinct from the loss of suitable environment. Changing methods of rock deposition in marine or fresh waters and thus differing environments could explain gaps in the fossil record without reference to periodic catastrophes. The problem of the replacement of extinct species by new and different species remained an unsolved puzzle for Lyell.

The third volume of *Principles of Geology* appeared in 1833. While Lyell addressed some of his critics, the bulk of the volume was devoted to the direct application of the principles of the first two volumes to the rocks of the Tertiary. To divide the Tertiary, he introduced a new terminology, based on the proportional relationship of extinct to existing fossil forms. He also offered the names Eocene (dawn, recent), Miocene (less, recent), and newer and older Pliocene (more, larger, recent) to identify the succeeding epochs.

Principles of Geology propelled Lyell into the public and scientific eye. Revising it became the work of a lifetime. "Indeed," he once wrote, "I sometimes think I am in danger of becoming perpetual editor to myself." Over the next forty years, twelve editions appeared, each thoroughly revised and updated to reflect Lyell's own work and the work of his colleagues. In 1838, he published *Elements of Geology*, a work based on the theory of *Principles of Geology* but emphasizing the descriptive and practical. *Elements of Geology* became the first true geological textbook. With most of the purely descriptive material relegated to *Elements of Geology*, *Principles of Geology* remained his theoretical tour de force.

In 1832, in the forefront of his specialty, Lyell became professor of geology at King's College, London. He delivered only two series of lectures before resigning in 1834. The pressure of constant fieldwork and controversy prevented sufficient attention to the university. He made trips to the Pyrenees in 1830 to examine de Beaumont's theory of mountain building and to Sweden in 1834 to investigate the uplift of the lands of Scandinavia.

In 1832, Lyell married Mary Elizabeth Horner, daughter of Leonard Horner, a fellow of the Geological Society. A marriage tour of the Rhine, Switzerland, and France showed that he had married a woman with a fascination for and insight into geology. She became a skilled conchologist who helped him in his work, especially because of his weak eyes, often writing for him. Recognition and honors were heaped upon Lyell. In 1834, he re-

ceived the Royal Medal of the Royal Society. From 1834 to 1836, and again in 1849, he served as president of the Geological Society. In 1848, Lyell was knighted by Queen Victoria and through his friendship with Prince Albert was named a commissioner of the Great Exhibition of 1851.

In 1841, Lyell stepped onto a new stage. He sailed for the first of four trips to North America. In the United States, he presented the Lowell Lectures in Boston, visited Benjamin Silliman at Yale, and toured New York State with James Hall of the New York Geological Survey. He was particularly struck by Niagara Falls and the possibility that the recession of the falls presented for explaining the passage of geological time. Along the border of New York and Pennsylvania, he was able to study the Devonian rocks, subject of a controversy then raging in England. After touring in the Southern states, Lyell attended the spring, 1842, meeting of the American Association of Geologists and Naturalists in Boston. Finally, a tour of British North America took him through the St. Lawrence Valley and ended in the coal fields of Nova Scotia, where he met an enthusiastic young geologist, John William Dawson. Lyell's collaboration with and encouragement of Dawson would help him become one of the two greatest geologists of nineteenth century Canada. The trip was capped by the appearance of his two-volume work *Travels in North America with Geological Observations on the United States, Canada, and Nova Scotia* in 1845.

Lyell returned to North America in 1845, concentrating his attention on the Tertiary rocks of the South. His observations were published in *Second Visit to the United States of North America* in 1849. Lyell briefly visited a third time in 1852, when he worked in the South Joggins coal formations of Nova Scotia with Dawson. His final visit was in 1853 when he served as one of the British commissioners to the New York Industrial Exhibition, working closely again with Hall.

After an 1853-1854 visit to the island Madeira, Lyell concentrated on the species question. While studying the Madeira fossils, he was struck by the large number and variety of species, a discovery analogous to Charles Darwin's at the Galápagos Islands. Noting that every species must have come into existence near in time and place to closely allied species, Lyell began a series of seven notebooks solely devoted to the subject.

This new focus brought him back into intimate contact with Darwin. In 1836, after Darwin had returned from his expedition on the *Beagle*, a working and personal friendship developed with Lyell. Initially, the relationship was one of Lyell as mentor and Darwin as student, for Darwin had used a copy of *Principles of Geology* on his expedition. Darwin's first published work after his return explicitly used and expanded Lyell's ideas. In his 1837 presentation to the Geological Society, Darwin argued for the elevation of South America through successive earthquake and volcanic action rather than a single convulsive upheaval. At the same time, Darwin presented a new theory of coral reefs, applying Lyellian principles, as the remnants of subsiding mountains, rather than Lyell's specific theory that they represented the tops of submerged volcanoes. This forced Lyell to alter his ideas, for as he wistfully recognized, "I must give up my volcanic crater theory for ever, though it costs me a pang at first, for it accounted for so much."

By 1856, Lyell consulted regularly with Darwin and urged him to publish his ideas promptly on the transmutation of species though natural selection, particularly after the revelation that Alfred Russell Wallace had come independently to the idea of natural selection and might forestall Darwin. Lyell and Joseph Hooker were instrumental in presenting both Darwin's and Wallace's ideas to the Linnean Society in July, 1858, and in impelling Darwin to publish his *On the Origin of Species* in 1859.

Although the Madeira species caused Lyell to accept tentatively Darwinian ideas of transmutation, he was unwilling to commit himself to the theory. Discovery of mammal remains in the supposedly reptile-dominated rocks of the Secondary epoch raised doubts about the change in species. Moreover, discovery of human-crafted implements in the later Pliocene deposits of France, shell mounds in Denmark, Lake Dwellings in Switzerland, and an apparently human skull at Neanderthal in Germany all focused Lyell's attention on the specific question of human origins. His investigations culminated in 1863 with the publication of *The Geological Evidences of the Antiquity of Man.* In a tightly argued exposition, Lyell presented the evidence for a common parentage for mankind and the long period of time necessary for his development. He presented the evidence and then left his readers to reach their own conclusions; while the book offered a powerful argument in support of Darwin, Lyell did not make his support for Darwin explicit. Darwin was disappointed in the lukewarm support, but as Lyell explained to him in an 1863

letter, "I have spoken out to the utmost extent of my tether, so far as my reason goes, and farther than my imagination and sentiment can follow, which I suppose has caused occasional incongruities." By 1864, however, Lyell expressed his full and unalloyed support for Darwin. The tenth edition of *Principles of Geology*, which appeared in 1868, was revised around a specifically Darwinian explanation for the transmutation of species.

Summary

Sir Charles Lyell died on February 22, 1875, and was interred in Westminster Abbey, the final recognition for an illustrious career. The last years of his life had been marked by continuing honors, as in 1864 he was made a baronet and elected president of the British Association for the Advancement of Science. His honors included the Royal and Copley medals of the Royal Society and the Wollaston Medal of the Geological Society.

Lyell had provided the broad intellectual framework within which geology progressed in the nineteenth century. *Principles of Geology* is an enduring landmark in geology. In arguing for a geological past that changed through small, cumulative change, Lyell had defeated his Catastrophist opponents who supposed that nature changed primarily through violent and discontinuous means. His Uniformitarian geology had provided a flexible model for research, as he demonstrated through his constant revision of *Principles of Geology*. He never abandoned the principles of Uniformitarianism yet demonstrated a remarkable willingness to alter specific conclusions when presented with contradictory evidence.

Lyell always stood somewhat outside the geological establishment of Great Britain, with its central concern for the Baconian tradition. While Murchison and Sedgwick were crafting their Devonian, Silurian, and Cambrian systems in a practical, hands-on way within the stratigraphic consensus, Lyell was building his Uniformitarian system.

Lyell also served as a link between British and North American geology, cross-fertilizing both. Lyell had brought the best of British geology directly to North America, which was then only beginning geological surveys and investigations. Through his books and papers for the Geological Society, he brought the new phenomena of North America back to Great Britain.

Fostering, aiding, and abetting Darwin, first as mentor and then as follower, Lyell contributed to a momentous scientific development in the nineteenth century. The personal scientific relationship was fruitful for both men, while Lyell's Uniformitarian geological framework and analysis of fossil life changes were key to Darwin's hypothesis.

Bibliography

Gillispie, Charles Coulston. *Genesis and Geology.* Cambridge, Mass.: Harvard University Press, 1951. Classic study of the "biblical" geology against which Lyell argued. May overstate the depth of biblical geology, but well worth studying for the interaction of science and religious views.

Gould, Stephen Jay. *Time's Arrow, Time's Cycle: Myth and Metaphor in Discovery of Geological Time.* Cambridge, Mass.: Harvard University Press, 1987. A revisionist account by the popular science writer, showing that Lyell's conception of geological time was essentially static, in contrast to the modern sense of "deep" time with its unimaginable immensity. Scholarly but accessible, and engagingly written. Illustrated.

Lyell, Charles. *Elements of Geology.* London: Murray, 1838; Philadelphia: James Kay, 1839. Six editions down to 1865. Lyell's basic textbook, not a useful introduction to his thought.

———. *The Geological Evidences of the Antiquity of Man with Remarks on Theories of the Origin of Species by Variation.* London: Murray, and Philadelphia: Childs, 1863. Four editions down to 1873. Clearly written and argued. Although it does not explicitly support Darwin, the evidence seems to do so.

———. *Life, Letters, and Journals of Sir Charles Lyell.* Edited by K. M. Lyell. 2 vols. London: Murray, 1881; New York: AMS Press, 1983. A classic Victorian life-and-letters approach, filled with fascinating insights. Lyell's combative and epigramatic style is allowed to come through.

———. *Principles of Geology, Being an Attempt to Explain the Former Changes of the Earth's Surface by Reference to Causes Now in Operation.* 3 vols. London: John Murray, 1830-1833; New York: Johnson Reprint, 1960. Twelve editions down to 1875, in various formats and numbers of volumes. Widely available in many British and American editions, each of which is worth examining for his general theories. Remarkably easy to read, and written with an open and accessible style.

———. *Travels in North America with Geological Observations on the United States, Canada, and Nova Scotia.* 2 vols. London: Murray, 1845; *A Second Visit to the United States of North America.* 2 vols. London: John Murray, 1849. Filled with fascinating comments on the American social and political scene, particularly on the slavery question, as well as geological observations. Interesting for the observations of an intelligent British tourist.

North, Frederick J. *Sir Charles Lyell: Interpreter of the Principles of Geology.* London: Baker, 1965. Popular, brief biography that deals with the essential facts and ideas clearly. A good introduction to the subject.

Rudwick, Martin, J. S. *The Great Devonian Controversy: The Shaping of Scientific Knowledge Among Gentlemanly Specialists.* Chicago: University of Chicago Press, 1985. Densely factual history of an important geological controversy which provides a context for the geological atmosphere in which Lyell was working. Worth plowing through.

Silliman, Robert H. "The Hamlet Affair: Charles Lyell and the North Americans." *Isis* 86, no. 4 (December 1995). Examines Lyell's time in the United States and the criticism and suspicion leveled by Americans who questioned his motives.

Wilson, Leonard G. *Charles Lyell, the Years to 1841: The Revolution in Geology.* New Haven, Conn. and London: Yale University Press, 1972. The first of a projected three-volume definitive biography. Detailed and a gold mine of information.

Wilson, Leonard G. *Lyell in America: Transatlantic Geology, 1841-1853.* Baltimore, Md.: Johns Hopkins University Press, 1998. Important contribution to the work on Lyell including for the first time material from Lyell's wife Mary's correspondence from the United States. Provides a more complete view of Lyell's opinions on slavery and other social issues, as well as his scientific views on the origins of species.

William E. Eagan

MARY LYON

Born: February 28, 1797; Buckland, Massachusetts
Died: March 5, 1849; South Hadley, Massachusetts
Area of Achievement: Educations
Contribution: Combining a strong religious faith with a firm belief in the necessity of advanced training for women, Lyon served as the impetus for the creation of Mount Holyoke Female Seminary (later Mount Holyoke College). Insisting on a permanent endowment, she founded what has become the oldest continuing institution of higher learning for women in the United States.

Early Life

Mary Mason Lyon was born February 28, 1797, in Buckland, Massachusetts. The sixth of eight children, she was the daughter of Aaron Lyon and Jemima Shephard Lyon, both of whom were descended from old New England stock. Mary Lyon's father, a veteran of the American Revolution and a struggling small farmer in western Massachusetts, died in 1802. Shortly after her husband's death, his widow made the decision to continue working the family farm with her children. While still a child, Lyon learned to perform many household chores; she also attended nearby one-room schools.

Upon her mother's remarriage in 1810, Lyon remained on the family farm in order to keep house for her brother, who paid her a salary of a dollar a week. This she saved for her education. In 1814, Lyon began to teach in summer schools for local children; she "boarded round," as was the custom. As she matured, Lyon turned into a sturdy, well-built woman who possessed blue eyes, auburn hair, and a fine complexion. Apparent from her youth was her warmth, great physical energy, and selfless concern for others.

In 1817, Mary Lyon drew upon her small inheritance and meager earnings and enrolled in Sanderson Academy, a new coeducational institution in Ashfield, Massachusetts. This school introduced her to such advanced subjects as astronomy and Latin. While at Sanderson, Lyon made the acquaintance of Thomas White, whose daughter Amanda became a close personal friend. Throughout Lyon's life, White acted as a confidant and supporter; he also carefully managed her money, serving eventually as executor of her estate.

In 1821, Lyon and Amanda White attended the Byfield (Massachusetts) Female Seminary. This school was headed by the Reverend Joseph Emerson, who firmly believed that permanent institutions of higher learning should be created for women. At Byfield, Lyon formed a lifelong friendship with Zilpah Grant, a teacher at the Academy. At that time, Lyon, who had been brought up in a religious household, became concerned about the state of her soul. In March, 1822, she was baptized and received into the Congregational Church. For the duration of her life, Lyon would remain a devout Christian.

By the mid-1820's, Mary Lyon could be found teaching and studying in a variety of institutions in Massachusetts and New Hampshire. It was not unusual for her to teach at one school during the fall and spring terms, and then to teach at another during the summer. In 1828, however, Lyon suffered from a severe case of typhoid fever. She decided that henceforth she would devote herself completely to one institution, the Ipswich (Massachusetts) Female Seminary. Her friend Zilpah Grant served as principal of the school.

Her experiences at Ipswich proved instructive for Lyon. The Seminary had been founded with no endowment; she quickly realized that any successful educational institution had to be based on continuing funding which could ensure permanence. Also while she was at Ipswich, Lyon came to the conclusion that her goal in life was to be a teacher of teachers. This meant that, in the future, she would insist on minimum age requirements for her students, the study of sciences, and a curriculum which excluded such ornamental courses as conversational French or painting.

During the summer of 1833, in the midst of her Ipswich years, Lyon traveled through New York, Pennsylvania, and the Midwest. She visited numerous schools and colleges along her route. Urged to do so by generous local citizens, she seriously considered establishing a female seminary in Detroit, Michigan. After prayerful deliberation, Lyon decided against the Detroit plan. She returned to the East, where she became determined to create her own academy.

Life's Work

Although still teaching at the Ipswich Female Seminary, in 1834 Lyon began to meet with benevolent men such as Thomas White. These individuals supported her in her belief that what needed to be created was a new school for women which would be run by a disinterested board of trustees. Lyon hoped that in this proposed institution, teachers could be persuaded to accept low salaries and that students would do domestic work in a dormitory atmosphere. Such policies would help keep tuition low so that even girls of modest means could attend the school. The goal of the institution would be to educate women teachers.

During the next three years, Lyon worked unceasingly to make her dream a reality. Remaining humble and self-effacing, she exhibited a remarkable determination. For the most part, Lyon relied on wealthy male trustees to fund her institution. As these men raised the school's endowment, Lyon traveled throughout New England collecting money from women on farms and in small towns. It was her hope that the dormitory rooms of her students could be furnished from contributions made by such women.

After lengthy negotiations, Lyon's trustees made the decision to establish her school in South Hadley, which had made the best offer for it with a contribution of eight thousand dollars. The new institution would be named Mount Holyoke Female Seminary, after a nearby mountain. The Commonwealth of Massachusetts granted the school a charter in 1836. Soon thereafter, construction commenced. Lyon closely supervised this process.

On November 8, 1837, the barely completed seminary opened its doors to the eighty eager students who had been accepted for admission. According to Mary Lyon's original plans, all of her pupils were over seventeen, and everyone was required to engage in domestic work. The curriculum consisted of a three-year program which called for the concentrated teaching of courses over a short period of time. Science was emphasized, and guest lecturers such as Edward Hitchcock of Amherst College frequently came from nearby institutions. Public oral examinations proved to be a highlight of the end of each school year. Students also received religious training, a requirement upon which Lyon insisted. She hoped that all of her students would be "saved"; she frequently held religious meetings in her quarters to further this goal. The Seminary directed much attention to foreign missions; it was not uncommon for students to enter this field of endeavor upon graduation. Lyon herself made a plea for increased missionary work when she published a short book, *A Missionary Offering*, in 1843.

Mount Holyoke Female Seminary quickly flourished. By the mid-1840's, enrollment had climbed to more than two hundred students. Because of the expanding size of the student body, new additions had to be made to the Seminary's building. The curriculum also expanded in size; it became increasingly sophisticated with the introduction of such subjects as Latin and human anatomy. As the years passed, Lyon did less and less teaching. That job was performed by a handpicked group of recent graduates. Lyon herself acted as an administrator who oversaw all operations of Mount Holyoke. Increasingly, she seemed unable to delegate responsibility; the strain of many years of arduous effort were taking their toll. Having long suffered from lung problems which weakened her resistance to other illnesses, Lyon died at Mount Holyoke of erysipelas in March, 1849. She was buried on the Seminary's grounds.

Although Lyon's death dealt a severe blow to Mount Holyoke, it did not destroy it. For several years the institution foundered as its leadership remained uncertain. By the mid-1850's, however, this problem was solved and the school continued along on its path to permanence.

Summary

Typical of many other early nineteenth century reformers, Lyon possessed a vision of how life could be improved for society as a whole. A woman of extraordinary enthusiasm, selfless determination, and loving compassion, she refused to be discouraged by adversity and she eagerly pursued her goal of providing a first-rate higher education for American women.

From her experiences in a variety of small New England institutions, Lyon learned that often a school's existence depended upon the health and good fortune of a single founder or teacher. To her, this was wrong. What she hoped to create with Mount Holyoke was an endowed and financially sound seminary whose control would be vested in a self-perpetuating board of trustees; these men would oversee the continuance of the institution through changes in leadership.

Furthermore, Lyon desired to prove that young women were as intellectually able as men, and that, like men, they were capable of doing advanced academic work. She dreamed that once Mount Holyoke achieved intellectual prominence, the American public would understand the advantages of educating women and go out and found other such institutions. To a great extent, this visionary plan came true, for by the late nineteenth century numerous "daughter" schools had been created which emulated Mount Holyoke's success. Yet unlike its more secular counterparts, the Seminary proved to be a deeply religious institution which was devoted to Christian piety and evangelism. In this respect, Lyon and Mount Holyoke were representative of the religiously motivated reform movements of the Second Great Awakening.

Whether consciously or unconsciously, Lyon also served to improve the quality of elementary and secondary education in the United States. As Mount Holyoke's fame spread, greater efforts were made by local teachers to prepare their students for the stiff entrance examinations which were required for entrance to the Seminary. In addition, graduates of Mount Holyoke quickly came into demand as teachers in the United States and elsewhere in the world. Well-trained instructors inevitably improved the level of training in schools throughout the world.

What is amazing about Lyon's accomplishments is that they were carried out by a conservative individual who refused to challenge the prevailing social mores of her era. Unlike some of her more vocal contemporaries, Lyon avoided the limelight; she insisted upon achieving her goals through maintaining her ladylike composure and never stepping outside her prescribed sphere. This meant that, while she routinely relied on male benefactors for advice and financial support, she refused to appear before them at any meetings of her board of trustees. Thus, she never spoke publicly to mixed audiences, and most of her personal pleas for money were reserved for rural New England women.

The result of Lyon's efforts was the successful operation of Mount Holyoke Female Seminary, an institution which would achieve collegiate status in 1888. With a permanent endowment, secure leadership, low tuition, and a carefully structured living and learning environment, Mount Holyoke served as the model of women's higher education for generations to come.

Bibliography

Cole, Arthur Charles. *A Hundred Years of Mount Holyoke College: The Evolution of an Educational Ideal.* New Haven, Conn.: Yale University Press, and London: Oxford University Press, 1940. The best historical account of the first century of Mount Holyoke's existence. Approximately one-third of the volume is devoted to an explanation of the activities of Lyon.

Fiske, Fidelia. *Recollections of Mary Lyon with Selections from Her Instructions to the Pupils of Mt. Holyoke Female Seminary.* Boston: American Tract Society, 1866; as *Mary Lyon: Recollections of a Noble Woman,* London: Morgan and Scott, 1899. Badly dated as a biography, this work is valuable for contemporary reminiscences of Lyon. Also included are selections from Lyon's lectures and Sabbath services.

Gilchrist, Beth Bradford. *The Life of Mary Lyon.* Boston: Houghton Mifflin, 1910. A traditional biography which is important for revealing early twentieth century attitudes toward Lyon.

Goodsell, Willystine. *Pioneers of Women's Education in the United States.* New York and London: McGraw-Hill, 1931. Placing Lyon in the company of Emma Willard and Catherine Beecher, Goodsell provides a brief biographical sketch and includes lengthy excerpts from Lyon's writings.

Green, Elizabeth Alden. *Mary Lyon and Mount Holyoke: Opening the Gates.* Hanover, N.H.: University Press of New England, 1979. The definitive biography of Lyon. Providing a clear, concise, and balanced narrative, the volume shows the results of impressive research in primary and secondary sources.

Hitchcock, Edward, comp. *The Power of Christian Benevolence Illustrated in the Life and Labors of Mary Lyon.* Northampton, Mass.: Hopkins, Bridgman, 1851. A complimentary account of Lyon's work as perceived by a close friend. The volume has historical importance as it is partially based on letters from Lyon which were later destroyed.

Howe, Mark Anthony DeWolfe. *Classic Shades: Five Leaders of Learning and Their Colleges.* Boston: Little Brown, 1928. This volume contains an uncritical biographical sketch of Lyon which rates her achievements in the field of education with those of such men as Timothy Dwight of Yale and Charles William Eliot of Harvard.

Lyon, Mary. *Mary Lyon Through Her Letters.* Edited by Marion Lansing. Boston: Books, 1937. An account of Lyon's life which was published to coincide with the one hundredth birthday of Mount Holyoke. Complimentary in tone, the book combines a narrative with excerpts from Lyon's letters.

Sklar, Kathryn Kish. "The Founding of Mount Holyoke College." In *Women of America: A History*, edited by Carol Ruth Berkin and Mary Beth Norton. Boston: Houghton Mifflin, 1979. An article-length account of Lyon's activities. Sklar emphasizes the role of evangelical religion in the founding of Mount Holyoke.

Woody, Thomas. *A History of Women's Education in the United States*. New York: Science Press, 1929. The classic work on its subject. Although dated in some of its interpretations, it is useful for placing Lyon's activities in their proper historical context.

Marian E. Strobel

THOMAS BABINGTON MACAULAY

Born: October 25, 1800; Rothley Temple, Leicestershire, England

Died: December 28, 1859; Holly Lodge, Kensington, England

Areas of Achievement: Politics, literature, and historiography

Contribution: Macaulay was a prominent Whig politician and popular essayist, but his greatest achievement was *The History of England from the Accession of James the Second*, a work of enduring popularity and influence.

Early Life

Thomas Babington Macaulay was born on October 25, 1800, in Rothley Temple, Leicestershire, England, the first child of Zachary Macaulay, a descendant of Scottish highland chiefs, a merchant, a ship owner, a member of the Clapham Sect of Evangelical Anglicans, and a campaigner against the slave trade. Macaulay grew up in an atmosphere of stifling religious observance and self-examination which he rejected in later years, although still maintaining conventional Christian morality. He was a child prodigy who began to read voraciously at the age of three, thus beginning early to accumulate that vast array of facts with which he delighted his friends and belabored his enemies. He entered Trinity College, Cambridge, in 1818, and proceeded to win debating triumphs in the University Union and numerous academic prizes, including an award for his "Essay on the Life and Character of William III," who was to be the great hero of his historical masterpiece. After graduation, Macaulay studied law and was called to the bar in 1826, but he never put much effort into becoming a practicing lawyer.

In 1825, Macaulay began to contribute to *The Edinburgh Review*, the prestigious quarterly journal for intellectual Whigs. His second essay, discussing the poet John Milton and defending his radical politics during the English Civil War, made him an instant celebrity and star guest at Holland House, the very center of Whig society. Over the next twenty years, Macaulay wrote thirty-six articles for *The Edinburgh Review*, most of them ostensibly beginning as book reviews, but soon turning into long and independent essays. Macaulay at twenty-five had mastered the style he was to wield for the rest of his life. The essays were vigorous and assertive, abounding in paradox and contrast,

intimidating in their command of facts, confident in judgment, and exciting to read. His literary fame brought him some unexpected rewards. In 1828, Lord Lyndhurst made him a Commissioner of Bankruptcy, and in 1830, Lord Lansdowne used a pocket borough, Calne, which was under his control, to send the young Macaulay to Parliament.

Macaulay the public figure seemed assured and successful, but the private man was sometimes troubled and uncertain. He never married and concentrated his emotions completely on two younger sisters, Hannah and Margaret. By the 1820's, Macaulay's father, at one time very wealthy, had lost most of his money, and thereafter, Macaulay, though sometimes short of funds himself, felt obliged to help. He was, for a time, in much demand at fashionable dinner tables, and yet he often failed to impress at first sight. Many described him as a short, squat man with vulgar, though energetic, features, who talked interminably. He was also unusually clumsy and often had trouble tying his cravats properly or shaving without drawing blood.

Life's Work

Macaulay entered Parliament as a Whig, a member of the party of moderate reform, led by liberal aristocrats, proud of their descent from the families of the Glorious Revolution of 1688-1689, which had overthrown King James II, brought in William III, and asserted parliamentary supremacy. Macaulay was a man of the political center, or slightly left of center, but he asserted his moderate views with combative zeal. He delivered his maiden speech in April, 1830, in defense of a bill to remove civil disabilities from Jews. In March, 1831, he gave the first of a series of powerful orations supporting the Whig Reform Bill, which abolished many rotten or pocket boroughs (seats with very few inhabitants, such as Calne, for which Macaulay sat), created new parliamentary districts, and gave the vote to most of the middle class, though not to the working class. It was a very limited reform but was bitterly opposed by the Tories as threatening the social order. The very reverse was true, argued Macaulay. The refusal to reform when reform was needed would create a justified discontent that would bring on revolution. "Reform," urged Macaulay, "that you may preserve." In June, 1832, the Reform Bill became law, and Macaulay returned to Parliament for one of the new constituencies, Leeds. He was

acknowledged as a great orator and rising statesman. In December, 1833, he became the legal
member of the newly created four-man Supreme
Council of India at the amazing salary of ten thousand pounds a year. He planned to stay in India for
five or six years, live splendidly on five thousand
pounds a year (in fact he spent much less), and
then return to England a rich man, able to follow
his political and literary interests without financial
concerns.

In February, 1834, Macaulay sailed for India accompanied by a small library of the Greek and Latin classics and by his adoring sister Hannah. His
other favorite sister, Margaret, had, much to his
distress, married the year before. Before the year
was over, Hannah married Charles Trevelyan, a
brilliant young official of the East India Company,
and Macaulay received news that Margaret had
died of scarlet fever. Hannah was to remain his
closest friend and intimate, although she could not
be as close as before. Macaulay felt lonely and
devastated. He saved himself by rereading a good
portion of Greek and Latin literature and by entering into hard and controversial work. He was fortu-

nate in enjoying the backing of a reforming governor-general, but still had to fight harsh opposition
in convincing the Supreme Council to abolish
press censorship and to end certain privileges held
by Englishmen appearing in Indian courts. He became president of the General Council of Public
Instruction, which was bitterly split between the
Orientalists, who wished to continue subsidizing
native schools teaching traditional learning in Arabic, Persian, and Sanskrit, and the Anglicists, who
wished to support only European learning taught in
English. With his usual vigor and with even more
than his usual intolerance of folly, Macaulay argued for English. In his famous "Minute on Indian
Education" of February 2, 1835, he summed up Indian learning as: ". . . Astronomy, which would
move laughter in girls at an English boarding
school—History, abounding with Kings thirty feet
high, and reigns thirty thousand years long—and
Geography, made up of seas of treacle and seas of
butter." Macaulay despised Indian culture, but he
did not despise Indians. He believed that Indian
students could master the same curriculum as English students. His position became policy, and before the end of the century, several hundred thousand Indians were studying modern subjects in
English. In May, 1835, Macaulay became head of
the Law Commission which proceeded in two
years to draw up a new, rational, and humane penal
code, in large part composed by Macaulay, to replace the jumble of different systems in the various
regions of India. The code was not put into operation until January of 1862, after the death of its creator, but it has remained the basis for Indian criminal law ever since. The rather inactive English
barrister had become the lawgiver for India.

Macaulay returned to England in June, 1838. An
uncle had left him a legacy of ten thousand pounds
in 1836, which meant that Macaulay was able to
accumulate the sum he was aiming at more quickly
than he had expected. While in India, he had written his longest and one of his most celebrated essays for *The Edinburgh Review*, a defense of Francis Bacon, whom Macaulay extolled as one of the
fathers of inductive reasoning and experimental
science. He also began to plan a large-scale history
of England from 1688 to 1830. He began to write
the history in March, 1839, but returned to Parliament in September as M.P. for Edinburgh and entered Lord Melbourne's cabinet as secretary at war.
The government fell in August, 1841, and Macaulay, while still in Parliament, now had more time to

write. In 1842, he published *Lays of Ancient Rome*, vigorous ballads, written as if they were ancient Roman poems. Like all of his writings, they were an instant success. In 1843, he published *Critical and Historical Essays*, which brought together most of his articles from *The Edinburgh Review* and which sold several hundred thousand copies in England and in the United States in the next few decades. In 1846, the Whigs again formed a government, and Macaulay accepted the post of paymaster general because it would not take much time. In July, 1847, Macaulay lost his seat and decided to leave politics.

In 1849, Macaulay published the first two volumes of *The History of England from the Accession of James the Second* (1849-1855) to the acclaim of scholars and the appreciation of general readers. He had said earlier, "I shall not be satisfied unless I produce something which shall for a few days supersede the last fashionable novel on the tables of young ladies." Tens of thousands of copies were sold within months and several hundred thousand before the end of the century. In 1852, Macaulay, with great reluctance, allowed the Whigs of Edinburgh to return him to Parliament, but he refused to take office again. He suffered a heart attack soon after, gave only a few speeches in the next few years, and resigned from Parliament in January, 1856. In December, 1855, volumes 3 and 4 of his historical study appeared. His publisher presented him with a check for twenty thousand pounds, well over one million dollars in today's currency. Honors of all sorts showered upon him, and, in September, 1857, he became Baron Macaulay of Rothley, though he never spoke in the House of Lords. Macaulay did not live to complete his masterpiece. He died December 28, 1859, at Holly Lodge, Kensington, and was buried in Westminster Abbey. His sister, Hannah, now Lady Trevelyan, put together his final chapters to form volume 5, which appeared in 1861, and brought the story up to the death of King William III in 1702.

Summary

Thomas Babington Macaulay was an important essayist, politician, and parliamentary orator. He achieved lasting importance, however, by providing India with an educational system and a law code, while he earned fame and recognition by writing *The History of England from the Accession of James the Second*. It is, first, an extraordinary work of literature. The characters, both heroes and villains, come alive as if in a novel. His battle scenes—Sedgemoor, Killiecrankie, Londonderry, the Boyne—are virtually refought as one reads them. The sympathetic reader, moreover, can almost believe that he is at the deathbed of Charles II, in the court rooms of the ferocious Judge Jeffries, at the trial and execution of the noble Argyle, and in the crowd which welcomes William of Orange as he enters Exeter. Yet Macaulay did more than write extremely well. His research was on a far more thorough scale than that of English historians before him. He sought out new archives and walked over old battlefields. Macaulay's work also is an analysis of important political actions, their causes, and their consequences, written with the acute understanding of a man who had spent time in cabinet meetings as well as libraries. Macaulay did indeed see politics as central, but in the famous chapter 3, he devotes more than one hundred pages to the state of England in 1685, its towns, clergy, roads, stage coaches, highwaymen, inns, newsletters, wages of workers, female education, and much else. Much has been written on these topics since Macaulay, but no one before him had attempted anything as comprehensive. Macaulay, who has sometimes been criticized as too political in his interests, virtually invented social history.

Macaulay writes Whig history. It is sometimes Whig in a narrow and partisan sense as when Macaulay favors the Whigs, the Liberal aristocrats who drove James II from the throne, and attacks the Tories who so often opposed them. It is also Whig history in the broader sense which traces, explains, and celebrates progress in human societies. It looks to the past for the origin of what men value in the present. Macaulay linked men and causes of the present with those of the past and brought new significance to both. In his history, Macaulay only reached the year 1702, but he had planned to go to 1830, the eve of the battle over the Reform Bill in which the Whigs, this time with Macaulay among them, saved the nation once again producing the right kind of fundamental constitutional change. Macaulay often refers in the multivolume study to later and even contemporary events. Thus, at the very conclusion of the first two volumes which appeared in December, 1848, the end of the year in which revolutions had broken out in most of Europe, Macaulay states triumphantly, "Now, if ever, we ought to be able to appreciate the whole importance of the stand which was made by our forefathers against the House of Stuart. All around us the world is convulsed by the agonies of great nations." England, in contrast, has been at peace. "It is because we had a preserving revolution in the seventeenth century that we have not had a destroying revolution in the nineteenth."

Macaulay had critics in his day and afterward. He painted in primary colors. He was vigorous but not subtle and never appeared to doubt or even hesitate before pronouncing judgment on men and causes. At times, Macaulay was as partisan in writing history as when delivering parliamentary speeches. This lent passion to his work but sometimes produced bad judgments. He was clearly unfair to the Jacobite Viscount Dundee, the Quaker William Penn, and the great General Marlborough. Macaulay's critics have found flaws, but none that seriously diminishes the work. There are blemishes, but blemishes on a still great and imposing structure.

Bibliography

Beatty, Richmond Croom. *Lord Macaulay: Victorian Liberal.* Norman: University of Oklahoma Press, 1938. A good middle-sized biography (almost four hundred pages); friendly, but critical.

Clive, John. *Macaulay: The Shaping of the Historian.* New York: Knopf, 1973. A magnificent full-scale biography covering Macaulay up to his return from India. It is both appreciative and critical. The definitive study for the early years.

Firth, Sir Charles. *A Commentary on Macaulay's History of England.* London: Macmillan, 1938; New York: Barnes and Noble, 1964. A full-length book, based on a series of university lectures, that evaluates and comments on Macaulay's history. Respectful, but critical.

Hamburger, Joseph. *Macaulay and the Whig Tradition.* Chicago: University of Chicago Press, 1976. An interesting though not always convincing study of Macaulay's political thought which asserts that he was too pessimistic to be a true Whig.

Levine, George. *The Boundaries of Fiction: Carlyle, Macaulay, Newman.* Princeton, N.J.: Princeton University Press, 1968. About a third of the book is a thoughtful analysis of Macaulay's history as imaginative literature.

Macaulay, Thomas Babington. *Critical and Historical Essays.* 2 vols. London: Longman, 1850; New York: Sheldon, 1860.

———. *The History of England from the Accession of James the Second.* 4 vols. London: Longman, and New York: Harper, 1850.

———. *The Letters of Thomas Babington Macaulay.* Edited by Thomas Phinney. 6 vols. Cambridge: Cambridge University Press, 1974-1981.

Millgate, Jane. *Macaulay.* London and Boston: Routledge, 1973. An excellent short biography and analysis of the major writings.

Paget, John. *The New "Examen."* Manchester: Haworth Press, 1934. This is an unusual book which was first published in 1861, though some parts appeared in the last two years of Macaulay's life. It is a vigorous and extended attack on Macaulay for misusing evidence in order to blacken William Penn, Viscount Dundee, and the Duke of Marlborough, and to whitewash William III of responsibility for the Glencoe massacre. Paget goes too far, but he does score some valid points.

Trevelyan, George Otto. *The Life and Letters of Lord Macaulay.* 2 vols. London: Longman, and New York: Harper, 1876. An important and basic book, written by the son of Macaulay's beloved sister Hannah, who was himself a good historian. It is admiring and uncritical, limited naturally enough by familial piety.

Trevor-Roper, Hugh. Introduction to Macaulay's *Critical and Historical Essays.* London: Collins, 1965.

———. Introduction to Macaulay's *History of England.* London and New York: Penguin, 1980. Two excellent introductory essays by a distinguished historian of the seventeenth century.

Melvin Shefftz

CYRUS HALL McCORMICK

Born: February 15, 1809; Rockbridge County, Virginia

Died: May 13, 1884; Chicago, Illinois

Areas of Achievement: Invention and philanthropy

Contribution: McCormick revolutionized American agriculture through his invention of the reaper and through his marketing innovations. He also shaped American theological development by his patronage of a Northwest seminary.

Early Life

Cyrus Hall McCormick was born February 15, 1809, in his family's home, Walnut Grove, which was situated in the Virginia Valley. His father, Robert McCormick, and his mother, Mary Ann Hall, came from strong Scotch-Irish stock, and they represented two of the most influential families in the community. Cyrus was the eldest of eight children born to Robert and Mary Ann McCormick, two of whom died in their infancy.

His education was gained in a field school where he was taught the three R's, geography, and religion. At home he was daily instructed in the Shorter Catechism. Although Washington College (founded in 1782) was located at nearby Lexington, neither he nor any of his brothers received higher education. His constant instruction in the principles of the Bible and Calvinism molded his thought and faith throughout his life. He attended New Providence Church, eight miles from his home, and for several years led the congregation in singing. In 1834, he joined that church. Three years later he moved his membership to the Mt. Carmel Presbyterian Meeting House at Steele's Tavern, it being closer to home.

Both of McCormick's parents were about five feet, eight inches in height. Cyrus was just under six feet tall. He was of powerful physique. This permitted him to work almost tirelessly in his later years, much to the dismay of associates who were obliged to follow him through the day. He once described himself thus: "My hair is a very dark brown,—eyes dark, though not black, complexion fresh and health good, 5 ft. 11 1/2 inc. high, weighing 200 lbs." Much of his good health and strong physical condition he attributed to his refusal to drink alcoholic beverages and his disdain for smoking tobacco. Even as a youth he abstained from many of the debilitating habits of his peers. In 1857, at the age of forty-eight, he married Nancy Fowler. Up to this point he had eschewed feminine companionship. She entered into his work, serving as a secretary who copied all his letters. Their marriage endured for twenty-six years and produced seven children.

Life's Work

McCormick's first reaper was demonstrated on the fields of Walnut Grove. It was a workable horse-powered reaper with a reciprocating cutting blade protected by metal fingers, a reel to bring the grain against the blade, a divider to separate the grain to be cut from the grain in the field, and a platform to catch the felled grain. In 1840, McCormick began to manufacture and sell his reapers locally. His first models exhausted the horses that pulled them, and they were constantly breaking down. So expensive were the repairs that hand reaping still remained the most economical way to harvest. In 1844, seeking increased sales, McCormick visited the Northwest. The large, flat fields of that region proved more conducive to his machinery than the small, rocky fields of Virginia. He moved his manufacturing operations to Chicago in 1847, and by 1850 he was producing McCormick reapers in his own factories.

Harvesting machinery thus became practicable through McCormick's inventions and those of Obed Hussey, a New Englander, who constructed a successful reaper in Cincinnati and obtained a patent in 1833, a year before McCormick received his; it is quite probable, however, that the latter's invention preceded Hussey's. The ensuing rivalry between the two inventors over patents and markets was long, bitter, and led to considerable controversy and numerous court battles.

McCormick's 1840 machine, in spite of its weaknesses, proved superior to Hussey's. As sales expanded, his reaper proved revolutionary. With only two men the McCormick machine could do ten times the work of two scythe or cradle harvesters. The reaper's entrance into the Midwest made extensive wheat growing possible, and it further encouraged frontier migration. William Seward once commented that McCormick pushed the line of civilization westward at least thirty miles per year.

McCormick entered the field of merchandising, and by 1856 more than four thousand McCormick reapers were being sold annually on the installment plan. On the eve of the Civil War, between eighty thousand and ninety thousand reapers were in use, primarily in Midwest farms. McCormick improved the method of harvesting hay. In 1856, he patented a two-wheeled mower with a flexible cutter bar. This permitted operation on rough, uneven ground. By 1860, a variety of types of mowing machines similar to modern mowers were on the market, for it was very easy for inventors to make minor alterations to any of McCormick's machines—a practice which also involved him in numerous court suits.

McCormick's inventions contributed indirectly to the ultimate Northern success in the Civil War, increasing the amount of grain and forage for human and animal consumption. His inventions permitted more men to leave the farm either to go into the army or to the city to work in factories which produced war materiel. The South, with its paucity of factories for civilian consumption, in addition to its hilly, rocky terrain, simply could not produce the necessary quantity of field-grown foodstuff.

McCormick entered the international trade scene with his reaper. He was awarded numerous prizes and medals for this invention, and in 1878, for the third time, he received a grand prize at the French Exposition for his reaping and self-binding machine. The rank of officer in the Legion of Honor was also conferred upon him. At that time he was elected a corresponding member of the French Academy of Sciences, "as having done more for the cause of agriculture than any other living man." Reverdy Johnson remarked in 1859 that the McCormick reaper alone contributed an annual income of fifty-five million dollars to the whole country.

His religious training and discipline remained a part of McCormick's entire life. His Calvinistic philosophy was a source of comfort in the midst of his failures, and a beacon of direction through success. The greatest monument to his devotion to the Church is the seminary which bears his name: McCormick Theological Seminary, located in Chicago. He stands in the company of men such as John D. Rockefeller, John Wanamaker, Jay Cooke, and W. H. Vanderbilt: successful businessmen who contributed liberally to the institutions of their respective churches—institutions which now bear witness to their dedicated commitment.

McCormick represented that portion of the Presbyterian Church denominated the "Old School." His move to Chicago brought him into a strong New School community. His move to that city stirred within him religious pride to the point that he wanted more than merely an Old School congregation in which to worship, he desired a school of the prophets to train men to convert the Northwest to Old Schoolism.

A floundering seminary in New Albany, Indiana, attracted him, and it was primarily because of his beneficence that it was moved to Chicago in 1859. He ultimately endowed the seminary—the Presbyterian Seminary of the Northwest—with $100,000, a figure sufficient to underwrite four chairs. As the shadows of war began to creep across the Presbyterian horizon, none pleaded more than he that the Church should not divide. When the war was over, he was in the front ranks of those who called for a reunion of the Old School wings, North and South, rather than a union of the Old School North with the New School, whose doctrinal soundness he questioned. He also contributed generously to several of the institutions of the Southern Presbyterian Church in the days of reconstruction, helping them to get back on their feet.

At the Seminary of the Northwest—renamed the McCormick Seminary in 1886—he fought to acquire and retain scholars from the Old School. For a time he appeared willing to tolerate a degree of liberalization within the seminary in order to increase financial support from other sources. When this additional financial support did not materialize, however, McCormick's financial contributions, and consequently his influence upon the seminary, increased. As a result, the Seminary dominated the rapidly growing Midwestern portion of the church, and exerted a large, if not decisive, influence on the Church's theological history at a critical point in the twentieth century. McCormick remained active in the Presbyterian Church until his death on May 13, 1884.

Summary

The genius of Cyrus Hall McCormick lay in his unrelenting dedication to improving his inventions and his personal commitment to the Presbyterian Church; in him, vocation and faith were blended. He revolutionized agricultural economics. He initiated the installment plan, whereby ordinary farmers could afford to buy large machines. He made possible a more rapid expansion of America's drive to the West, and he presented his Church with a valuable tool for the conversion of that portion of America. The Shorter Catechism, on which Mc-

Cormick was nurtured as a youth, begins by asking: "What is the chief end of man?" McCormick's life was directed by the answer he learned by heart: "To glorify God and to enjoy Him forever."

Bibliography

Hounshell, David A. "Public Relations or Public Understanding?: The American Industries Series in *Scientific American.*" *Technology and Culture* 21 (1980): 589-593. Points out that the article regarding the McCormick Harvesting Machine Co. which appeared in a series of the *Scientific American* (May 14, 1881) was actually written and paid for as an advertisement.

Hutchinson, William T. *Cyrus Hall McCormick.* 2 vols. New York and London: Century, 1930-1935. The definitive biography of McCormick. Thoroughly documented and based primarily on material in the McCormick Historical Association Library (Chicago).

Loetscher, Lefferts A. *The Broadening Church: A Study of Theological Issues in the Presbyterian Church Since 1869.* Philadelphia: University of Pennsylvania Press, 1954. Discusses the theological developments that emerged following the reunion of the Presbyterian Old School and New School in 1869. Presents McCormick's efforts to establish in Chicago a seminary grounded on Old Schoolism.

McClure, James G. K. *The Story of the Life and Work of the Presbyterian Theological Seminary Chicago Founded by Cyrus H. McCormick.* Chicago: Lakeside Press, R. R. Donnelley, 1929. Traces the history of the McCormick Theological Seminary, emphasizing the role of McCormick in establishing it in Chicago.

McCormick, Cyrus. *The Century of the Reaper: An Account of Cyrus Hall McCormick, the Inventor of the Reaper; of the McCormick Harvesting Machine Company, the Business He Created; and of the International Harvester Company, His Heir and Chief Memorial.* Boston: Houghton Mifflin, 1931. As the author states in the foreword, "It must be obvious that I, his grandson, am not in a position to write a coldly impartial account of his contribution to history." Written on the occasion of the centennial celebration of McCormick's invention of the reaper. Weaves together the technological accomplishments with McCormick's religious propensities. Contains thirty-one illustrations.

Wendel, Charles H. *One Hundred Fifty Years of International Harvester.* Sarasota, Fla.: Crestline Publishing, 1981. A study of McCormick's business enterprises. Essentially a photographic essay, with a brief biography of McCormick. Contains short accounts of the numerous companies that joined to form the International Harvester Co. Its purpose was to celebrate the sesquicentennial of McCormick's first reaper and to "show the evolution of the farm implement industry."

Harold M. Parker, Jr.

SIR JOHN ALEXANDER MACDONALD

Born: January 11, 1815; Glasgow, Scotland
Died: June 6, 1891; Ottawa, Ontario, Canada
Areas of Achievement: Government and politics
Contribution: Macdonald not only had a major role in drawing up the British North American Act, which created the Dominion of Canada, but also, as Canada's first prime minister, brought about the new nation's territorial and political expansion from sea to sea. Within the British community, he paved the way for Canadians to determine their own foreign affairs and foreshadowed the British Commonwealth of Nations.

Early Life

John Alexander Macdonald was born on January 11, 1815, in Glasgow, Scotland. His mother, Helen Shaw, hailed from a family of military professionals. After several generations of farmers, his father, Hugh John Macdonald, was the first to earn a living from business. Ultimately, however, his business failed in Glasgow, and he, his wife, and children—John Alexander (then five years old), Margaret, Louisa, and James—traveled to Kingston, Upper Canada, to join Hugh John's in-laws, Lieutenant Colonel Donald Macpherson and his family, who had retired there. Macpherson helped the Macdonald family to get settled, and the two families remained close.

After receiving the best education the local schools offered, at fifteen years of age the young Macdonald was apprenticed to a Kingston lawyer, George Mackenzie. For a year or two, Macdonald worked as a messenger, a clerk, and a stenographer. At night he studied British law. Since Macdonald was advancing rapidly in his studies, Mackenzie put him in charge of a branch office. Macdonald then took over the law practice of his sick cousin, L. P. Macpherson. The latter recovered, and in 1835, with Mackenzie's death, Macdonald opened his own law office in Kingston. In the next year he was admitted to the bar.

Early in his legal career, Macdonald helped put down the 1837 insurrection. In the next year he participated in the capture of Americans who had invaded Canada. Even thought it might have damaged his career, Macdonald defended these men, as well as a man accused of raping a child. Macdonald provided them with the best legal advice,

but he lost the cases. The men were hanged. Macdonald would continue in the practice of law, specializing in commercial law, first at Kingston and then at Toronto, with various partners, until his death in 1891. His clients were businessmen and corporations.

Macdonald entered politics at the grass-roots level, serving first as secretary for a local school board, then as alderman for Kingston. While serving in the latter office, he was elected to represent Kingston in the Canadian legislature. The British government had recently united Upper Canada and Lower Canada into Canada West (Ontario) and Canada East (Quebec) in the Act of Union of 1840. In one of his first addresses, Macdonald stated that the British Crown must be maintained in Canada. He never deviated from that stance, which remained his guiding principle.

Macdonald was nearly six feet tall, slender, and looked much like his English contemporary Benjamin Disraeli. He was not a good-looking man: His large nose dominated his face, and he became fair game for caricaturists. These "ugly" physical features were overcome by his natty dress, his keen sense of humor, his excellent memory for persons' faces and names, and his ease at making and keeping friends. Nevertheless, he was also noted for a caustic tongue and bad temper. He was never an orator, but rather a debater who made best use of the quick retort and the penetrating question. Though a clever tactician, Macdonald was a practical man who used practical means to achieve his goals. At times he was accused of being devious and unscrupulous.

In his early twenties, Macdonald often was ill. He became worse with the death of his father in 1841. To recuperate, he traveled to England and Scotland. In the latter country he met his cousin, Isabella Clark. After his return to Kingston, Isabella followed him. They were married soon afterward, in September of 1843. Within two years of the marriage, Isabella fell ill. She spent the rest of her life bedridden. Seeking a cure, Macdonald took her first to New York, then to Savannah, Georgia. He returned in six months; she stayed three years. In spite of her life-threatening illness, she gave birth to two sons, John Alexander (1847), who died at the age of thirteen months, and Hugh John (1850). Her illness, Macdonald's being deprived of her company, the huge medical bills, and later the

additional pressures from the demands placed upon Macdonald by his constituency and his parliamentary obligations led Macdonald to become a heavy drinker. His alcoholism resulted in his having a number of short-term political reverses. He almost always turned those defeats into victories, however, through quick thinking and political machination.

Life's Work

During his wife's long years of illness (from 1845 until her death in December, 1857), Macdonald endured "the great struggle for power and place," as he defined it. In the Conservative government, he was receiver general from 1847 to 1848. The Conservatives and Macdonald were out of power from 1848 to 1854. In those years, "Responsible Government" was established by the Reformers (Liberals), with political power resting in the prime minister. It had been vested in the Governor-General for Queen Victoria, Canada's monarch.

The Conservative Party almost destroyed itself in 1849. The Empire's old economic organization was eroding with Great Britain's adoption of free trade. Politically, the government's Rebellion Losses Bill signified the end of the old imperial government. The result was that the Ultra-Conservatives went on a rampage in 1849, burning the Parliament building and demanding an end to the British connection and Canada's annexation to the United States. They came to their senses, but damage had been done. The parliamentarians moved the capital's site from Montreal, but since no permanent location could be decided on, it would alternate between Quebec and Toronto.

Macdonald disavowed himself of the Ultra-Conservatives. He helped form the British America League to work for confederation of all the provinces, for strengthening the British connection, and for adoption of a national commercial policy. Macdonald embraced Responsible Government. He worked within his party to destroy the Ultra-Conservatives—the Tory, Anglican, and Loyalist oligarchy (the family compact)—who had for so long dominated politics in Toronto, the capital of old Upper Canada.

Macdonald formed his own government by organizing a new political coalition once the Reformers (Liberals) left office in 1854. The Conservatives, along with the existing alliance of Upper Canadian Reformers, joined with the French majority political bloc. The coalition became a permanent political party, eventually the Progressive Conservative Party, known as the Liberal-Conservative Party, one of Canada's great political parties. Macdonald was the party's parliamentary leader. As attorney general, he established an elected legislative council, or upper house, in the provincial parliament. With the removal of the aged prime minister, Sir Allan McNabb, Macdonald became co-prime minister with Étienne P. Tache. Macdonald finally had power and place. Later George Étienne Cartier joined the cabinet, replacing Tache as co-prime minister. The partnership would end with Cartier's death in 1873.

Macdonald was an able, skillful, and clever politician. He proved it more than once. In 1858, he and Cartier had Queen Victoria select Canada's permanent capital; she chose Ottawa. The decision was presented to the legislature by Macdonald. The vote taken on the issue defeated the government. The Liberals under George Brown formed a new government. By law, all new cabinet appointees, including the prime minister, had to seek reelection. Macdonald refused to agree to a recess. While they were temporarily absent from Parliament,

Macdonald, leader of the opposition, obtained a vote of no confidence in Brown's government. By ingenious political maneuvering, Macdonald secured his party's return to government, having been out of power for only two days.

In the mid-1850's, Brown introduced a new issue into the political scene. Representation in the legislature was shared equally by Canada West and Canada East, even though Canada West now had the greater population. Brown, from Canada West, demanded representation by population. In the Union, Canada West was stymied in matters of education, westward expansion, railway subsidies, and taxation. Macdonald stayed in power only with French Canadian bloc support. The latter was determined not to promote Canada West; the legislature as then constituted was a guarantee of their French Canadian identity. Regional and racial conflicts threatened destruction of the Canadian union.

The raging American Civil War exacerbated matters: During the war, serious disputes arose between Great Britain, British North America, and the United States. Since Great Britain was in charge of Canadian foreign affairs, any one of these disputes could have involved Great Britain and British North America (Canada) in war. For five long years, Macdonald believed that the Americans could (and would) invade his country and conquer it. Great Britain expected Canada to provide some contribution to defense. Macdonald and Cartier agreed. The Militia Bill's passage through the assembly failed. Conservative French Canadians refused to support their government. Macdonald, imbibing excessively, failed to provide the necessary leadership. His mother's death in October, 1862, had stripped him of any incentive he might have had.

Macdonald's government fell following an adverse vote in the legislature. He considered retiring from public life, but the Liberal government's ineptness changed his mind. When he knew the government was doomed, he got the assembly to vote no confidence in it. To save his government, the new prime minister, John Sandfield Macdonald, received a called general election. The results returned the administration, but opposition and government were too evenly matched in the legislature—the Union of Canada was deadlocked.

To solve the constitutional dilemma, Macdonald accepted Brown's proposal for a new coalition to include Upper Canadian Reformers to bring about a federal union of all British North American provinces. Macdonald accepted leadership in drawing up a new constitution. In its drafting, he presided over meetings at Charlottestown, Quebec, and in London, England, where representatives of the Crown joined them. The British Parliament passed the resultant British North America Act in 1867, creating the Dominion of Canada to replace the Union of Canada.

In London, Macdonald married Susan Agnes Bernard, even though he barely knew her. Her brother was a member of the Office of the Attorney General, Canada West, and had once roomed with Macdonald. They had one daughter, Mary (1869-1933), who was confined from infancy to a wheelchair.

Before confederation was realized on July 1, 1867, Macdonald was disturbed by Fenian invasions from the United States, the American abrogation of the 1854 Reciprocity Treaty, and the Maritime Provinces' resistance in joining the Dominion. In 1867, however, Nova Scotia and New Brunswick came into the confederation. Macdonald followed through on a pledge given earlier to link the Maritime Provinces to Quebec by the building of the Intercolonial Railway.

The new federal Parliament met in Ottawa in 1867 with Macdonald, its first prime minister. A host of challenges faced the new government: the diverse claims of the French and English Canadians, the provinces' determination to maintain their rights, and the need for a continued British connection. In spite of these obstacles, Macdonald persevered, handling each problem as it arose. He was the Canadian representative among the British delegation that settled problems arising out of the American Civil War. From that time on, whenever Canadian interests were involved with a foreign country, Great Britain would include Canadians in any discussion or settlement.

Macdonald worked hard to enlarge the territorial boundaries of Canada from sea to sea. To forestall any American settlement of the western region, Macdonald arranged to purchase rights of the Hudson's Bay Company to the Northwest Territories, including the prairies. The Métis Red River rebellion under Louis Riel delayed its acquisition for several months. The rebellion, even though put down by military force, quickened Macdonald's decision to create the province of Manitoba (1870) and take it into the Dominion earlier than planned. He feared American intervention and the possibility of American annexation of the prairies.

Macdonald made possible the entry into the Dominion of British Columbia (1871) and Prince Edward Island (1873). British Columbia demanded as her price the construction of a transcontinental railway across the empty plains and through the Canadian Rockies to the east. Macdonald's Quebec leader, Cartier, accepted, during the 1872 general election, campaign monies in return for a charter for the Pacific Railway Company. In the midst of the ensuing Pacific Scandal of 1873, Cartier died. Even though Macdonald proved that he had known nothing about the deal, he was forced to resign from the government. A new election was called, returning the Liberals to office, which they held from 1873 to 1878, a period of depression; they adopted free trade. In 1878, Macdonald returned to political power on the basis of the "National Policy," a system of protection of Canadian manufacturers through imposition of high tariffs on foreign imports, especially American imports. The National Policy appealed to anti-Americans and Canadian nationalists and became a permanent part of Canadian economic and political life.

Macdonald's last years in office were politically difficult ones. He secured for a new Canadian Pacific Railway a charter in 1880. In spite of hardships encountered in its construction (Parliament had to appropriate funds far beyond original estimates), the line was in operation in the fall of 1885. As in 1870, the Indians and the Métis under Riel tried to stop western settlement. Canadian military forces—one of the soldiers was Macdonald's son, Hugh John—once again defeated them. Riel turned himself in. He was tried for treason, found guilty, and hanged, Macdonald refusing to pardon him. The French Canadians thought of Riel as great hero; to the English Canadians he was a murderer. Several years before, he and his Métis had executed an Ontario Orangeman, Thomas Scott. Riel's death intensified racial and religious tensions, severely hurt the Conservative Party in Quebec, and led to the French Canadian "nationalist" movement.

Macdonald wanted a strong national government. The federal power's right of disallowance over provincial legislation was challenged through the legal system. Great Britain's Privy Council often decided matters on appeal in favor of the provinces, resulting in a federal system much more decentralized than Macdonald wanted. In the face of provincial opposition, however, he had no choice. Macdonald's National Policy was successful during the first years of his return to power. With the return of depression, the opposition (Liberals) worked for its abandonment in favor of unrestricted reciprocity with the United States and their own return to political power. To Macdonald, unrestricted reciprocity meant total surrender to the United States—loss of Canadian commercial autonomy, loss of fiscal freedom, and eventually the Dominion's annexation to the United States. The general election of 1891 was fought on this issue, and Macdonald and the Conservatives were victorious. Macdonald was pleased to see his son, Hugh John, a lawyer, elected to Parliament from Winnepeg, Manitoba. In the election, Macdonald overexerted himself. He died from heart failure in Ottawa, on June 6, 1891, and was buried in Kingston.

Summary

For forty-seven years, Sir John Alexander Macdonald sat in a Canadian parliament. His cabinet experience encompassed forty-four years. In his life-time he held seven cabinet posts, served as prime minister in the Union of Canada, and was singularly honored with his election as the first Prime Minister of the Dominion of Canada. He witnessed and, as prime minister, had a large role in the economic and political evolution of Canada, from its earliest years until it became an industrialized nation. More than any other single person, Macdonald "made" Canada and provided its character. As first Prime Minister of the Dominion of Canada, his greatest achievement was that he set forth the policy goals in domestic and external affairs for all future Canadian political leaders. If Macdonald was not Canada's greatest political leader, he certainly is numbered among her greatest.

Bibliography

Creighton, Donald Grant. *John A. Macdonald*. Vol. 1, *The Young Politician*. Boston: Houghton Mifflin, 1953. The first extended biography of Macdonald was written from contemporary sources by one of Canada's best historians. It portrays the life and times of Macdonald from his arrival in Kingston as a five-year-old boy from Scotland to the time he became the architect of the Dominion of Canada. Its one failing is that too much attention is given to provincial matters.

———. *John A. Macdonald*. Vol. 2, *The Old Chieftain*. Boston: Houghton Mifflin, 1955. This book (also based on contemporary sources) is the definitive study of Macdonald and the history of the Dominion of Canada from its inception in 1867 to Macdonald's death in 1891.

Pope, Joseph. *Memoirs of the Rt. Honourable Sir John Alexander Macdonald, G.C.B., First Prime Minister of the Dominion of Canada.* 2 vols. London: Arnold, 1894. This biography was the first to be based entirely on Macdonald's private papers and was the standard biography until Creighton's work. Pope was Macdonald's private secretary for a number of years and became his literary executor; Pope's account is highly partial to Macdonald and the Conservatives.

Swainson, Donald. *The Rt Honourable Sir John A. Macdonald.* Toronto: Pagurian Press, 1968.

Written in journalistic style, this work briefly narrates Macdonald's family background, his education, and his entrance into law, with the greater part dealing with his life's work in politics and his "creating" the Dominion of Canada. Macdonald's failings are not glossed over, but are considered in their proper context.

Waite, P. B. *Macdonald: His Life and World.* Toronto and New York: McGraw-Hill Ryerson, 1975. This work, as the title indicates, treats Macdonald's life and his world, with the emphasis on his world. Very few works written about Macdonald address the places with which he was associated.

Kathleen E. Dunlop

WILLIAM HOLMES McGUFFEY

Born: September 23, 1800; Washington County, Pennsylvania

Died: May 4, 1873; Charlottesville, Virginia

Area of Achievement: Education

Contribution: As an early nineteenth century college president, professor, and Presbyterian clergyman in the Ohio Valley, McGuffey compiled the most famous series of school textbooks in American history. His six *Eclectic Readers* sold more than 122 million copies between 1836 and 1920, and impressed upon young Americans the virtues of individual morality, thrift, hard work, and sobriety.

Early Life

William Holmes McGuffey was born September 23, 1800, on his mother's family farm in Washington County, Pennsylvania. He was the second child and the eldest son of Alexander and Anna Holmes McGuffey, who had seven children before she died in 1829. His grandfather William McGuffey (1742-1836) and grandmother Ann McKittrick (1747-1826) had emigrated from Wigtown, Gallowayshire, Scotland, in 1774, sailing on the stormy Atlantic for thirteen weeks before landing in Philadelphia. His father was only seven years old when the family came to America, on the eve of the Revolutionary War. After a short stay in the city, the McGuffeys moved due west to carve out a farm in York County on the edge of the Appalachian mountains, which was their wartime home. Like thousands of other Scottish immigrants, who traditionally disliked the British, the elder William McGuffey enlisted in the Pennsylvania regiments and served under General George Washington until the defeat of General Lord Cornwallis at Yorktown in 1781. In 1789, the family moved to the western edge of Pennsylvania, settling along Wheeling Creek in Washington County, south of Pittsburgh. Living among English and Scotch-Irish immigrants, the war veteran became known as "Scotch Billy." His son Alexander, nicknamed "Sandy," became a skilled frontiersman with his rifle, and with a friend, Duncan McArthur, became a scout and soldier in the Indian wars of the 1790's. They marched with General Anthony Wayne to drive the Indians out of the Ohio Territory.

After returning from the Miami Valley, Alexander married Anna Holmes in 1797, and they lived with her family in Pennsylvania, where three children were born: Jane (in 1799); William Holmes (in 1800); and Henry (in 1802). When Ohio entered the Union in 1803, Alexander moved his family directly north from West Alexander and across the Pennsylvania state line into Trumbull (modern Mahoning) County, near Youngstown, Ohio, where he had erected a windowless log cabin. There, four more daughters and one son, Alexander, Jr., were born. As the oldest boy, William worked long hours on the Ohio farm to support the growing family. After he had left home, his mother died there at the age of fifty-three in 1829. Two years later, his father was remarried, to Mary Dickey, and in 1836, after the birth of three more daughters, he moved his family and father back to the Keystone state, where "Scotch Billy" died at the age of ninety-four.

McGuffey's early education began in the family's log cabin, where his mother taught her children the three R's. Local "subscription schools," generally taught by a young man or minister, provided further education. Like Abraham Lincoln in western Kentucky amid similar wilderness conditions, young McGuffey borrowed books from neighbors, memorized portions of the Bible and sermons, read before the fireplace, and taught his younger brothers and sisters. His father crafted an adjustable wooden candlestand that provided better light for his love of learning. Before his fourteenth birthday, "Master McGuffey" advertised opening his own school at West Union (modern Calcutta, Ohio), with a four-month term starting in September, 1814; forty-eight pupils paid two dollars each for his instruction.

He attended the Reverend William Wick's boarding school in Youngstown for a year or two, then took his high school level studies at the Old Stone Academy in Greersburg (modern Darlington), Pennsylvania, under the tutoring of Presbyterian minister and principal Thomas E. Hughs. From Greersburg he acquired sufficient command of classical languages for admission in 1820 to Washington College in Washington, Pennsylvania, near his birthplace. He found lodging with the head of the school and daily walked six miles to and from the college with President Andrew Wylie. McGuffey majored in philosophy and languages, learning Latin, Greek, and Hebrew. During his senior year, with most of his classwork completed,

McGuffey accepted a teaching position near Paris, Kentucky, for 1825-1826. On a visit to Lexington, the first president of Miami University, Robert Hamilton Bishop, happened to meet McGuffey and promptly offered him a professorship in languages at the Oxford, Ohio, land-grant college, at a salary of six hundred dollars per year. He accepted, and Washington College graduated him with honors at the end of the school year.

McGuffey began his ten-year career at Miami University at the age of twenty-six in the fall of 1826. The new professor impressed observers with his penetrating blue eyes, swarthy complexion, and dark hair. His rugged features were characteristically Scottish, and his height was average.

His younger brother, Alexander Hamilton McGuffey (1816-1896), rode to Oxford with his brother and attended the village school before enrolling in William's language classes. At fifteen, Alexander entered Washington College, and he was graduated in 1836; that fall, he became a professor of languages at Woodward College in Cincinnati. He studied law at the Cincinnati Law School and was admitted to the Ohio bar as a lawyer in 1839.

During his first year on the faculty, William met Harriet Spining, a daughter of Judge Isaac Spining of Dayton, Ohio, when she was visiting her brother, Charles, a merchant in Oxford. They were married at her family home on April 3, 1827, and lived in a boardinghouse until McGuffey bought a four-acre corner lot with a frame house across the street from the college campus. By 1833, he had built a two-story, six-room red brick house onto the frame house to create the finest house in town. (It was sold to Miami University in 1958 and has been the McGuffey Museum since 1963.)

Four McGuffey children were born there: Mary Haines (in 1830), who married Dr. Walker Stewart of Dayton; Henrietta (in 1832), who married the Reverend Andrew D. Hepburn; William Holmes (in 1834), who lived only two weeks; and Charles Spining (in 1835). A fifth child, Edward Mansfield (born in 1838), was born in Cincinnati and died in Athens.

Life's Work

McGuffey's career encompassed teaching at four colleges, serving as president of two, preaching as an ordained Presbyterian minister, lecturing on educational topics, fighting for state common school

systems in Ohio and Virginia, and compiling the first volumes of the famous McGuffey *Eclectic Readers* (1836-1837).

To meet the need for textbooks for the rising number of tax-supported public schools in the Mississippi Valley, the publishing house of Truman and Smith in Cincinnati began issuing common school books during the 1830's. In April, 1833, McGuffey entered into a contract with the firm to develop a series of texts—a primer, four readers, and a speller to rival Noah Webster's. Drawing on his knowledge of languages (he had mastered seven), and with the help of his wife and neighborhood children, he selected and graded reading materials by testing them with pupils gathered around a revolving octagonal table. The first and second readers were published in 1836, the third and fourth followed in 1837, and the McGuffey speller appeared in 1838. Dr. William E. Smith of Miami University wrote the most concise summary of the contents of the original editions and revisions:

The *First Reader* introduced children to the code of ethics which ran through the four *Readers*—promptness, truthfulness, kindness, and honesty. . . . For the

Second Reader, he chose stories about the heavens and the earth beneath, stories about table manners, fear of God, and behavior toward parents, teachers, and the poor. . . . The *Third Reader*, published in 1837, was much like other third readers of the time. Method and content were more formal than in the *Second Reader*. Rules were introduced for oral reading. Its fifty-seven lessons were made up of such stories as "The Moss-Covered Bucket," "The Dying Boy," and "George's Feast"—stories that readers never forgot. . . . The objective of McGuffey's *Fourth Reader* (1837) was "reading aloud with sense, clearness, and appreciation." This *Reader*, introducing good prose and poetry, completed the *Eclectic Series*. McGuffey frequently used selections from the Bible and apologized for not using more.

. . . In 1838, the *Readers* were improved and enlarged. In 1844 the *Rhetorical Guide* by Alexander Hamilton McGuffey was placed on the market. It became the *Fifth Reader* in the *Eclectic Series*. . . . Later selections in the *Fourth* and *Fifth* were put in the *Sixth Reader*. . . . The late Dean Harvey C. Minnich and others have estimated that, on an average, each *Reader* was used by ten pupils before it was worn out or laid aside. Except the Bible, no other book or set of books has influenced the American mind so much.

McGuffey's contract for the original set allowed him a royalty of ten percent on sales up to a limit of one thousand dollars. Beyond that the story is that the publisher annually sent him a barrel of smoked hams. Eventually, in the Civil War years, the publisher, then a millionaire, had the company grant McGuffey an annuity until his death.

In August, 1836, McGuffey resigned from Miami to accept the presidency of the revived Cincinnati College. His publisher was in Cincinnati, his brother Alexander had accepted a professorship at Woodward College, and Cincinnatians promised financial support. The panic of 1837, however, ruined the school, and in 1839 McGuffey accepted the presidency of Ohio University at fifteen hundred dollars a year. Friction with landowners and with students led to his resignation in 1843, and he returned from Athens to Cincinnati to teach at Woodward College. In 1845, elected to the chair of moral philosophy and political economy at the University of Virginia, McGuffey moved to Charlottesville, where he taught until his death in 1873. His wife Harriet died in 1850, and the next year he married Laura Howard; their child, Anna, died in Charlottesville at age five.

Summary

The tremendous impact of McGuffey's readers upon American youth in more than 150 years, with more than 135 million copies in print, ranged even wider and deeper than numbers indicate. At least three generations of nineteenth century citizens were indoctrinated by the moral truths and personal values learned from literary selections of the *Eclectic Readers*. As a Presbyterian minister and as a professor, McGuffey perpetuated the Calvinistic virtues of hard work, thrift, and sobriety, commonly referred to as the Protestant ethic, through his extracts from English and American literature. His textbooks inculcated the character traits that upheld the ideal family, community, and nation. Honesty, industry, diligence, obedience, piety, and frugality were applauded; the evil consequences were clearly noted for those who ignored these lessons. Public schools soon shared in character-building along with the family and church.

McGuffey and his readers taught native and foreign-born Americans how to read and pronounce English words, how to read aloud and to speak effectively, and how to write and spell correctly. During the century of great immigration and an age when the written word predominated as the method of communication via newspapers, books, and magazines, the readers perpetuated the English language in the United States.

Admirers of McGuffey have long delighted in extolling the virtues of his textbooks as a Western product that brought enlightenment to rural and frontier folk; since 1960, scholars of history and sociology have declared that his lessons instilled the very virtues which industrial and urban societies needed among the working class in shops and factories of modern America. Critics of American common schools suggest that his textbooks served the rising middle classes but ignored the needs and traditions of the immigrants, the poor, and minorities in America's pluralistic culture.

Bibliography

Crawford, Benjamin F. *William Holmes McGuffey: Schoolmaster of the Nation*. Delaware, Ohio: Carnegie Church Press, 1963. A short 105-page book that summarizes much of other authors' findings on McGuffey. Crawford's best contribution is the title he gave his book.

Lindberg, Stanley W. *The Annotated McGuffey: Selections from the McGuffey Eclectic Readers,*

1836-1920. New York: Van Nostrand Reinhold, 1976. A splendid sampling of the entire collection of materials in the readers with a brief but significant introduction describing the publisher's expertise, which the editor declares had much to do with the success of the series. Lindberg details how fortunate was the use of the word "eclectic" in the name of the series and how cleverly the publisher got the textbooks installed in the Confederate schools during the Civil War, where they captured the market thereafter.

Minnich, Harvey C. *William Holmes McGuffey and His Readers*. New York: American Book Company, 1936. Written by the dean of the School of Education of Miami University, this remains the best comprehensive McGuffey biography.

Ruggles, Alice McGuffey. *The Story of the McGuffeys*. New York: American Book Co., 1950. Written by the granddaughter of Alexander Hamilton McGuffey, who wished to relate the human side of the authors of the readers, this is a very readable, nonscholarly narrative of her distinguished relatives. Published by the same company that had printed the readers, this volume will be found in more libraries than any of the other biographies cited here.

Smith, William E. *About the McGuffeys: William Holmes McGuffey and Alexander H. McGuffey*. Oxford, Ohio: Cullen Printing, 1963. As historian and dean of the Graduate School of Miami and director of the McGuffey Museum Library, Smith worked with Harvey Minnich to honor McGuffey by founding the National Federation of McGuffey Societies; this twenty-eight-page booklet is the best introduction to the teamwork of the McGuffey brothers in the production of the readers. Smith also deftly describes the content of the various readers, the primer and speller, and the later revisions.

Westerhoff, John. *McGuffey and His Readers: Piety, Morality and Education in Nineteenth Century America*. Nashville: Abingdon Press, 1978. Harvard Divinity School professor John Westerhoff provides a reassessment of the religious worldview undergirding the teaching McGuffey incorporated in his readers. A very readable volume which contains many other original writings of McGuffey that were not related to the textbooks.

Paul F. Erwin

JOAQUIM MARIA MACHADO DE ASSIS

Born: June 21, 1839; Rio de Janeiro, Brazil
Died: September 29, 1908; Rio de Janeiro, Brazil
Area of Achievement: Literature
Contribution: Because of his uniquely modern and boldly experimental contribution to narrative form and technique, as well as the universal appeal of his works, Machado is considered the greatest figure in nineteenth century Brazilian literature and a world master of the short story.

Early Life

Joaquim Maria Machado de Assis' father, Francisco José de Assis, was a native of Rio de Janeiro, the son of free mulattoes, and a housepainter by trade. His mother, Maria Leopoldina Machado da Câmara, was a Portuguese woman from the Island of São Miguel in the Azores. His mother could read and write, and similarities observed between her handwriting and that of her son indicate that she may have taught her son how to read and write as well.

Machado had a younger sister, Maria, who died of measles in 1845; his mother died of tuberculosis in 1849, when he was ten years of age. His father remarried Maria Ignez da Silva on June 18, 1854, but he died ten years later, on April 22, 1864. While the exact circumstances of the boy's early life as well as his relationship with his stepmother are matters of speculation among his biographers, it is believed that Machado did not get along with his stepmother or her family. Although one of his early poems is dedicated to a cousin, Henrique José Moreira, nothing else is known about this or any other relative.

It is believed that when he was ten years of age, Machado went to live with a priest who provided the boy with a primary education; Machado never attended secondary school. Largely self-taught, the young man was an avid reader, who educated himself by spending his free time at the Library of the Portuguese Cabinet of Reading. Nothing further is known of Machado until his fifteenth year, when one of his poems was published in the magazine *A Marmota*. Henceforth, his professional activities, at least, are well known. At the age of seventeen, he was a typesetter; at the age of nineteen, he was a proofreader; and at the age of twenty-one, he was on the editorial staff of the republican newspaper *Diário do Rio de Janeiro*.

By 1860, Machado had begun to gain recognition with theater criticism, articles, poems, and stories. At the age of twenty-five, he published a first volume of verse, *Chrisalides poesias* (1864). The young man continued writing poems, more or less successfully—columns of clever and insightful commentary on current events, translations from French and English, and drama—but soon realized that fiction was the genre in which he was most proficient.

Machado was short and slight; his facial features were strong, although he was not considered handsome, and he was pronouncedly nearsighted. He was extremely conscious of his appearance and suffered from a lifelong inferiority complex because of his racial heritage. He was a victim of epilepsy; the illness was particularly pronounced during his early years and the last four years of his life—after the death of his wife.

Machado married Carolina Augusta Novaes (sister of the Portuguese poet Faustino Xavier de Novaes) on November 12, 1869, and in the same year became the assistant director of *Diário do Rio de Janeiro*, a post which he held until 1874. Machado and his wife remained devoted to each other throughout their marriage. During his lifetime, Machado never even ventured more than a few miles beyond the city limits of his native Rio. From 1873, his meager income as a writer was augmented by a position at the Ministry of Agriculture, where he served until his death in 1908. An exemplary civil servant, Machado never missed a day at the office.

During the period of Machado's novelistic production—his career as a novelist began in 1872 with the publication of *Resurreicão* (resurrection)—romanticism was still flourishing, but the incursions of naturalism were soon apparent. In general, Brazilian Romanticism is characterized by lyric poetry, Indianism, poetry of the *mal du siècle*, and sociopolitical literature concerned with events such as abolition. The movement included the expansion of literary genres and was based on a veneration of nature and the observation and analysis of customs and characteristic types.

From the beginning of his novelistic career, Machado outlined an experimental literary form which contained some Romantic elements but was not strictly representative of the movement. While his earlier novels utilize some Romantic devices,

1444

they also demonstrate many of the features to be found in his later works. In breaking with the movement, Machado freed himself not only from the school of Sir Walter Scott but also from all literary schools. With the publication of the novel *Yayá Garcia* (1878; *Iaia Garcia*, 1977), Machado ended the first phase of his literary career.

Life's Work

When he was already forty-two, Machado published his first great novel *Memórias póstumas de Bráz Cubas* (1881; *The Posthumous Memoirs of Brás Cubas*, 1951; better known as *Epitaph of a Small Winner*, 1952). The appearance of this work marks the beginning of the second, more powerful phase of the author's career. In this period Machado violently attacked the naturalist movement, which he referred to as *realismo* (naturalism applied a scientific objectivity to the representation of reality). His advice to young writers in Portugal and Brazil was not to be lured into a movement which, despite its novelty, was already obsolete.

Machado took from the reigning schools, Romanticism and naturalism, only those elements which he chose to incorporate into his own aesthetic. In *Epitaph of a Small Winner*, he announced that he would make no concessions to popular literary fashion, despite the limited number of readers that the book would probably have. In that novel, Machado first introduced in his work archaic literary techniques of the eighteenth century. Yet his archaism is surprisingly modern in, among other things, its formal fragmentation, use of ellipsis, and irony.

In one sense, Machado's fiction can be seen as a continuation of the work of the Brazilian writer José de Alencar. Yet at a time when Alencar was still struggling to rid himself of Romantic attitudes and methods, Machado, quickly and with apparent ease, abandoned Romanticism, and Alencar, in the incredible maturity of *Epitaph of a Small Winner*. Whereas Alencar represented the clash and conflict of sharply delineated characters in concrete settings and in a series of well-staged confrontations, Machado developed the art of ambiguity and understatement. Instead of the social criticism that in Alencar bordered on satire, he chose irony. Machado's characters are always plagued by their own demons: They are caught in a web of their own fears and dreams, and their vision of reality is entirely subjective.

Machado was deeply indebted to such British writers as Laurence Sterne. In the major works of both writers, the story is never presented directly to the reader but always through a first-person narration by the protagonist. The narrator, who is usually the main actor as well as the storyteller, becomes an unreliable witness. He is also so often compelled to discuss his own version of the facts that the novels become exercises in a new type of self-reflexive fiction. The text itself ultimately emerges as the protagonist.

In this second phase of Machado's writing, in addition to the short stories collected in *Histórias sem data* (1884; timeless stories) and *Várias histórias* (1896; stories), he wrote other novels. In the next twenty years he would complete a kind of trilogy with *Epitaph of a Small Winner, Quincas Borba* (1891; *Philosopher or Dog?*, 1954), and *Dom Casmurro* (1899; English translation, 1953). Before his death, he completed two extremely subtle novels, *Esaú e Jacob* (1904; *Esau and Jacob*, 1965) and *Memorial de Ayres* (1908; *Counselor Ayres' Memorial*, 1973).

Machado died in his native city of Rio in 1908. The Chamber of Deputies, in a special session, voted to hold a state funeral with civil and military honors. This was the first time in the history of Brazil that a literary man of humble origins was buried like a hero. The author was eulogized throughout Brazil, and in France a memorial service was held in his honor at the Sorbonne, with Anatole France presiding.

Summary

A master of realistic and accurately detailed portrayal, Joaquim Maria Machado de Assis so subtly distorted the proud self-image of his generation that the brilliance of his critical eye was almost a century in being appreciated. In presenting the follies and foibles of his contemporaries, he was not only a faithful portraitist but also a judge. Yet, while Machado's writing reveals a bitter disillusionment with mankind, it exhibits the serenity of one who has learned to laugh at his own lost illusions and broken dreams.

Machado has achieved a unique place in Brazilian literature, above and beyond all artistic schools and cultural movements. Besides demonstrating insight, simplicity, and subtlety, his work reveals a spirit that animated the new generation of modernism. Yet his novels about life in Rio are realistic psychological studies set in a middle-class milieu. No writer in Latin America has embraced as much and as varied a terrain as has this Brazilian author.

Many honors in recognition of his writing were bestowed on him, the first by the emperor in 1867. Finally, when the Brazilian Academy of Letters was founded in 1897, he was elected its first president and perpetually was reelected. Thus, although he was not widely known outside Brazil, his talents were appreciated and acknowledged during his lifetime. This acknowledgment has continued through the years.

Bibliography

Bettencourt Machado, José. *Machado of Brazil: The Life and Times of Machado de Assis, Brazil's Greatest Novelist.* New York: Bramerica, 1953. This rather sentimental study focuses primarily on the life of Machado and secondarily on his work. Since little factual information exists on Machado's early life, and since Bettencourt does not reveal the sources of his information, his interpretation is interesting, although largely a matter of speculation. Includes a bibliography of primary and secondary works.

Caldwell, Helen. *Machado de Assis: The Brazilian Master and His Novels.* Berkeley: University of California Press, 1970. In this well-written and informative work of literary analysis, Caldwell discusses, after an introductory chapter, Machado's first four novels. Then follows a chapter on *Epitaph of a Small Winner*, one on *Philosopher or Dog?* and *Dom Casmurro*, and a concluding chapter on the writer's last two novels. Contains extensive footnotes and a brief biographical epilogue.

Machado de Assis, Joaquim Maria. *The Posthumous Memoirs of Bras Cubas.* Gregory Rabassa, trans. New York: Oxford University Press, 1997. This de Assis' story is told as a memoir delivered after death. Exhibits the author's disdain for the upper class through the main character's view that his bourgeois life is mediocre, at best.

Nist, John. *The Modernist Movement in Brazil.* Austin: University of Texas Press, 1967. In this work, Nist attempts to describe and illustrate the modern spirit in Brazilian poetry and fiction. In the section devoted to Machado, Nist discusses the author's antiromantic temperament and aesthetics in the context of the new social and political order in Brazil, assesses the writer's contribution to modernism, and praises the universality of his works. Nist's book contains a bibliography of general works on the Brazilian modernist movement.

Nunes, Maria Luisa. *The Craft of an Absolute Winner: Characterization and Narratology in the Novels of Machado de Assis.* Westport, Conn.: Greenwood Press, 1983. This brief but insightful work maintains that the most important element of Machado's art was his exploration of character. It is also the first study in English to apply systematically a philosophical and aesthetic critical apparatus to the texts of Machado, specifically that of narratology. Includes a bibliography of primary and secondary works.

Putnam, Samuel. *Marvelous Journey: A Survey of Four Centuries of Brazilian Writing.* New York: Knopf, 1948. In this survey, Putnam's purpose is to acquaint English-speaking readers with the main figures and currents in Brazilian literature of the past four centuries. In a rather lengthy chapter devoted to a discussion of Machado's work, "Machado de Assis and the End-of-the-Century Realists," Putnam places Machado's writing in the literary and social context of nineteenth century Brazil, and highlights the rebelliousness, originality, and universality of the author's work. Contains extensive footnotes, a bibliography, chronological tables, and reading lists.

Schwartz, Roberto. "The Historical Meaning of Cruelty in Machado de Assis." *Modern Language Quarterly* 57, no. 2 (June, 1996). Analysis of the works of de Assis and the emphasis he placed on oppression by the Brazilian upper class.

Genevieve Slomski

WILLIAM LYON MACKENZIE

Born: March 12, 1795; Springfield, Dundee, Forfarshire, Scotland

Died: August 28, 1861; Toronto, Canada

Areas of Achievement: Politics and journalism

Contribution: Mackenzie sought to establish for English Canada a political entity independent of British colonialism and devoted his life to a critique of English political authority in Canada and a demand for redress of grievances by English Canadians.

Early Life

William Lyon Mackenzie was the only child of Daniel and Elizabeth (née Chalmers) Mackenzie. His mother, an austere, demanding, and strong-willed adherent of the Presbyterian faith, was in her forties when she married. His father was in his mid-twenties, a weaver by trade with a reputation for carousing and pursuing life's pleasures. They were married on May 8, 1794, at Dundee, and three weeks after the birth of their only child, after having become blind, Daniel died, on April 9, 1795. William Mackenzie's mother instilled in her son great pride in his family, tracing it back to the wars of the clans and participation with Charles Edward Stuart (the Young Pretender) in the critical battle at Culloden which culminated in English domination of Scotland. Both paternal and maternal grandfathers were named Colin Mackenzie, and William Lyon carried with him the belief that his family was specially endowed, but that its fortunes had been denied because of the English dominance following 1745. Throughout his life, he cultivated an attachment to the farmers and working classes while presuming a status equal to the well-born and wealthy.

His father's untimely death pushed Mackenzie's mother into poverty, compelling her to sell personal items from her dowry and the clothing of her late husband. Nevertheless, she sustained a fierce independence and faith in her religion, and strove for the education of her son. The youthful Mackenzie, always small in stature and reckless in nature, became a rowdy while at the same time he was a resolute student. He mimicked his teachers and haunted libraries and bookstalls. He pushed himself vigorously to gain attention throughout his life. From the age of five, when he entered school, until the day he died, Mackenzie found himself fighting the odds. In his early teens, he became a regular in the commercial reading room of the Dundee *Advertiser*, where he was the youngest member. He began to list by topic, number, and description all the works that he read. This reading continued until he arrived in Canada at the age of twenty. Divinity, geography, history and biography, poetry and drama, science and agriculture, and 352 novels, all were included in his 957-book reading list. Even his mother registered concern that his continual reading might disturb him. Nevertheless, Mackenzie persisted with his eclectic studies throughout his life, and his habit of filing away information and ideas was to sustain him in his newspaper work and in political debate.

At a scientific society, Mackenzie met and became friends with Edward Lesslie and his son James, both of whom were to become associated with him at various times and in various enterprises in Canada. With some help from friends, Mackenzie and his mother operated a store and lending library in the village of Alyth just north of Dundee, but the business failed and they returned to Dundee. Mackenzie also found time to travel to London and to France, where he did some work with newspapers, living a somewhat dissipated life of gambling and drinking and fathering an illegitimate son. The child, named James, was taken in by Mackenzie's mother, who brought him along when she later joined her son in the Americas. Mackenzie was later to marry a former schoolmate, Isabel Baxter, who would bear him thirteen children, only seven of whom survived childhood. The family, including his first son, was always central to Mackenzie's life and work.

In 1820, Mackenzie traveled to Canada with the prospect of setting up a business. Mackenzie had sworn off gambling and loose living and served notice to his creditors that he would make good his accounts, a promise which he kept. Arriving in Quebec, he immediately took a job as an accountant in Montreal, where he worked only for several weeks. He proceeded to set up a pharmacy and bookstore with a partner in the town of York and shortly thereafter opened a general store as a second enterprise in the town of Dundas, farther west. This second business also included a circulating library, and Mackenzie felt comfortable enough economically to marry. Given the dearth of women in frontier Canada, the choice of a bride was probably

encouraged by his mother, who escorted Isabel to Canada.

The ambitions of Mackenzie were still not realized, however, and he chose to end his business partnership and open a store of his own. His alert, agile mind did not seem suited to the mercantile life, for despite a fetish for efficiency and careful accounting, the mundane demands of a storekeeper's duty did not satisfy him. Mackenzie decided that his perceptions of society and government needed to reach an audience that could never be reached by a shop owner, despite the material comforts such a business guaranteed. Canada in the early 1800's was not a country that rewarded men of enterprise and ideas; in fact, British Canada was developing the same class structures as those found in Great Britain. Those who had fought in the Napoleonic Wars or the War of 1812 on the British side had been granted land and economic privileges in Canada that set them apart from immigrants such as Mackenzie. The town of York, which was to become the city of Toronto, was the capital of British Upper Canada, and, despite its small size, it was the center of English rule in North America.

The privileged families of Canada were a small and immensely powerful group perhaps best symbolized by the St. James Church and its powerful parishioners, which included the lieutenant governor of Upper Canada, Major General Sir Peregrine Maitland. Maitland's father-in-law was the Duke of Richmond, governor in chief of all the colonies in North America. Presiding over the church was John Strachan, the first bishop of Toronto, who took seriously the obligation that the church was the center of Great Britain in Canada. Lands, schools, marriages, customs, and laws were subject to his administrative guidance. The leaders of both court and Parliament in Upper Canada were integral parts of the force of the church in the perpetuation of the Family Compact.

Dissenters from this conservative British contract of vested power did exist. Some, such as Dr. William Baldwin, stood in opposition politically while accepting Anglicanism as their faith. Men such as Mackenzie, a Presbyterian, however, were privy to neither the authority of that faith nor the economic, social, and political power. Had the dominant society of the day accepted him as one of its own, his rebellious career would never have developed. Given Mackenzie's background and the conditions he confronted in a developing colony that seemed to hold great promise for intelligent, aggressive, and ambitious settlers, his later actions can be understood. At the top, British rule in Upper Canada, aside from the lieutenant governor, consisted of an appointed Executive Council of leading citizens who held acceptable ideas as to the direction the colony should take and whose advice generally guided their patron in Great Britain. This council was not responsible to the public or to any legislative body. Members were selected carefully and almost never asked to resign. As in Great Britain, British Canada had an upper house called the Legislative Council (modeled after the House of Lords), whose members were appointed by the lieutenant governor for life. Some members, such as Bishop Strachan, were members of both the Executive and the Legislative councils. The House of Assembly, the lower house, was the forum for the common citizens and encouraged avenues for dissent. This dissent, however, was often negated by the power of the government to distribute funds to various troublesome areas. Though the sympathies of the majority of the people might lie with their elected delegates to the lower house, the conservatives still dominated Canada's policy. Expenditures were controlled by forces over which the lower house had no control. This condition allowed for the abuse of authority by the dominant Tory elements who were not accountable to any constituency and for the irresponsibility of critics and reformers who could eschew responsibility for promises which they had no power to fulfill. The paternal rule of the governing class became the focus of Mackenzie's new crusade.

The ending of Mackenzie's business partnership was not easy, and Mackenzie found it difficult to survive at first when he moved in 1823 to Queenston, in southern Ontario. He again started a store and attracted the help of Robert Randall, a member of the Assembly. In Queenston, Mackenzie began the publication of his first and most outstanding newspaper, the *Colonial Advocate*, on May 18, 1824. The paper sought to influence elections to the Assembly by comparing American political practices and institutions with those of Upper Canada. Though Mackenzie did not challenge the British controls directly, agencies of the government, such as the post office, worked against him. Mackenzie immediately transferred his operations to York, and in November of 1824, he escalated his attacks against the Tory authority. His paper had some immediate success, but a competitive newspaper was begun, *Canadian Freeman*, which supported a more moderate approach to reform. Some historians believe that this paper was funded by conservative elements hoping to destroy Mackenzie's influence. Mackenzie, undaunted, purchased new equipment and continued his forays against the establishment, which in turn escalated its pressure to remove Mackenzie. In the spring of 1826, he left Canada for Lewiston, New York, to avoid arrest for debt. During his absence, a gang of influential Tory citizens dressed as Indians destroyed his office and press in broad daylight. The magistrates did nothing to protect Mackenzie's property, and Mackenzie returned from New York to file suit and win compensation. With his settlement, he immediately paid off his creditors while capitalizing on his role as a martyr to free speech. The Tories, though chastened, resumed their harassment.

Mackenzie next took up the cause of American immigrants in Canada who sought the same rights as English settlers. Randall carried Mackenzie's petitions to London in 1827, an act which influenced the Colonial Office to order the upper legislature to guarantee full rights to Americans living in Canada. In the same year, Mackenzie joined forces with a Methodist leader to protest attempts by Strachan to use funds from the sale of clergy lands to build his proposed King's College. Mackenzie declared his candidacy for the Assembly and engaged in direct correspondence with reform elements in both England and Lower Canada. Mackenzie used his newspaper effectively, publishing what he called a "black list" of his opponents. He won election on the Reform ticket which controlled the Assembly but missed being elected Speaker. He now had a forum from which he could attack monopoly and vested interests. He argued against corporations dependent on public monies, against the practice of having an Anglican as chaplain of the Assembly, and against the increasing indebtedness of the government. In 1829, he found time to go to the United States, where he observed at first hand the enthusiasm surrounding the election of Andrew Jackson and the anticipation for an enlarged democracy. Mackenzie was struck by the economy of government in the United States and even admired the use of party patronage, which he hoped might be a means to revamp the Family Compact. He met Jackson personally and was intrigued by the twin ideas of hard money and anti-banking monopolies. The success of a radical politician such as Jackson seemed to represent encouraged Mackenzie.

Life's Work

After that visit to the United States, Mackenzie's career took a new direction. Upon his return to Canada in 1830, he soon found that the legislature was dissolved because of the death of King William IV. A new governor of Upper Canada had replaced Maitland, and this new English leader, Sir John Colborne, worked to increase the numbers of English by financed immigration. He used the upper house to block legislation sought by the Assembly which in turn weakened Mackenzie's reform group. In the 1830 elections, the Mackenzie forces lost their majority, gaining but twenty of the fifty-one seats. Dismayed by what he regarded as tampering with the democratic process, Mackenzie gave up any pretense of association with conservative tradition. He challenged the church-state relationship while joining St. Andrews Presbyterian Church, which ironically had been established by Presbyterian Tories who also attended St. James, as was expected of members of the government. Mackenzie constantly attacked the government, which was in some disarray internally because of the governor's attempts to change the upper house without the support of either the Executive Council or Strachan. Mackenzie was joined by other reformers in trying to gain control of certain revenues. Attempts were made to remove Mackenzie while he traveled throughout Upper Canada with petitions listing grievances against the government, communicated again with reform elements in Lower Canada, which enraged Upper Canadian Tories, and encouraged the participation of new immigrants—especially the Americans and the Irish, who were enthusiastic about the attention he brought to them. His *Colonial Advocate* attacked conservative privilege; the Tories countered with petitions of their own and voted to expel him from the Assembly. Hundreds of people stormed the Assembly demanding that the governor dissolve Parliament. They were refused, but the people gained their revenge in a by-election which gave Mackenzie an overwhelming victory in January of 1832. Five days later, the Tories expelled him once again, and the province was in civil disarray. Opposing groups clashed physically in the streets, meetings were disrupted, religious groups clashed openly, and in Hamilton a band of hoodlums was hired by a magistrate to attack Mackenzie. He decided to travel to Great Britain in the spring of 1832 to present his view of the situation to British authorities. While there, he wrote several articles for the London *Morning Chronicle* and drew up a document called *Sketches of Canada and the United States* (1833) for presentation to the people of Great Britain.

Mackenzie had once again been returned to the Assembly, and while he was abroad, the Tories again expelled him for a third time. This time he was reelected by acclamation, much to the rage of his enemies. Their anger was heightened further when Lord Goderich, British colonial secretary, sent the governor a dispatch advising financial and political reform and an end to the Tory crusade against Mackenzie. The upper house refused to receive the dispatch, placing them in the difficult position of rejecting their superiors. In the Assembly, a close vote on the issue was approved, but Mackenzie was deprived of his vote and a call for a new election was refused. Learning of this, the colonial secretary dismissed both the attorney general and the solicitor general over Governor Colbourne's objections. The Mackenzie family now left London in triumph to tour Scotland, England, and France. It was a short-lived victory, however, for in April,

1833, a more conservative colonial secretary came into power and all that Mackenzie had accomplished was undone. Frustrated and in despair, he dropped the word "colonial" from his newspaper's title. He returned to Canada in late summer and in December he was again expelled from the Assembly, only to be returned later in the same month.

Mackenzie now took advantage of the incorporation of York as the new city of Toronto by leading a slate of reformers to victory in the city elections. Elected as alderman and gaining a majority over the Tories, the redoubtable Mackenzie was chosen as the first mayor of Toronto. The Tory opposition sought to unseat him from that post and succeeded in early 1835, but meanwhile, in the fall of 1834, Mackenzie and the reformers again won a majority in the Assembly, despite his publication of a letter which all but called for colonial independence. In November, Mackenzie stopped publication of the *Advocate*, turning over its assets to a fellow reformer in the Assembly. He then took on a committee assignment and in three months compiled a devastating record of grievances against past government administrations and a list of proposed remedies. A larger problem was a new lieutenant governor, Sir Francis Bond Head, whose conservatism was a throwback to the 1820's. He clashed openly with reformers in the Assembly, dissolved the legislature, and openly campaigned on the issue of loyalty to the Crown. In July, 1836, Mackenzie met defeat at the polls.

Enraged at the injustice and corruption that he discovered following the election, Mackenzie immediately started another newspaper, called the *Constitution*. Given the circumstances, this paper was not overly radical, as it called only for specific constitutional change in Canada. This moderation was to change dramatically in the early months of 1837. Great Britain had begun to tighten its grip on Lower (French) Canada with new resolutions which took away all powers that the Assembly in that region had over the executive authority of the governor. Mackenzie foresaw the same thing happening to Upper Canada and now began an outright protest. He moved about the province making speeches, raising funds, rallying people against the tyranny of the government, and proposing an alliance of the two Canadas in a common front. Some of his adherents began military training, while the Tories and the Orange Order to which many belonged harassed and physically attacked Mackenzie and his growing constituency.

Mackenzie counted on two things to work in favor of a successful revolution: the absence of the military, which had been sent to Lower Canada, and the belief that the mere threat of a massive assault on the government would avoid hostilities and bring capitulation. Lower Canada's rebellion was successfully under way, but Mackenzie had little communication with their movement. Nevertheless, he suggested a common rebellion against Great Britain. The date was set for the march on Toronto, and on November 15, Mackenzie published a constitution for the new government. He hired a former colonel, Anthony Van Egmond, to head the revolutionary army and wrote a declaration of independence to be distributed prior to the march. It was not lost on Mackenzie that Upper Canada was far more conservative, despite the general dissatisfaction with conservative rule, than Lower Canada. He planned to use large demonstrations of possible force to compel the government to capitulate. His plans began to unravel on the eve of the march because of a lack of communication with the various groups. Unanticipated resistance from conservative riflemen also threw the movement into disarray. In the end, the grand citizen rebellion dissipated into the countryside and many participants made their way to the United States.

After an abortive attack by the regrouped forces failed, despite some American help, Mackenzie was joined by his wife in Buffalo, where he was arrested for violating American neutrality. Seeing the futility of further hostilities, he brought the rest of his family to the United States and settled in New York. Old friends sent him what money they could, but poverty haunted his family at every turn. In 1839 he was found guilty on the neutrality violation and sentenced to a fine of ten dollars and a term of eighteen months in prison. He was still in the newspaper business, having founded the *Mackenzie's Gazette*, and tried to run the paper from his Monroe County prison cell. The death of his mother while he was in prison was especially difficult. He believed that he had lost a guide and an anchor. He was pardoned in the spring of 1840 and gave up his paper.

Mackenzie's fierce independence demanded that any return to Canada be on his terms, and his old associates kept him informed of the changing conditions in the province. He took advantage of the new amnesty extended to the rebels of 1837 by the reform-minded government of Robert Baldwin in 1851. He wrote for his old friend James Lesslie's paper and also for the Niagara *Mail* while trying to make up his mind about returning permanently. Mackenzie took up residency, and in the spring of 1851 he was elected to the provincial parliament. He defeated one of the future powerbrokers in Canadian politics, George Brown. In office, Mackenzie was still effective in galvanizing attention against patronage, corruption, monopoly, sales of church lands, and use of public monies for church colleges. Ironically, his investigations forced the fall of the Baldwin government and he joined Lesslie in an attack on phony reformers. He alienated associates by exposing their culpability in passing legislation that increased debt. He even broke temporarily with Lesslie over attempts to edit a critical letter dealing with Crown Lands policy.

Mackenzie was still a figure to be reckoned with, and reformers sought him out to lead a true reform party. Mackenzie insisted on independence of thought and action, even turning down general editorship of his paper, the *Message* with two others because stock ownership would be shared with investors who might compromise him. His work was an inspiration to his colleagues, who began to raise a Homestead Fund in his honor. Thomas D'Arcy McGee called him "the oldest living sentinel of public liberty in Canada." Mackenzie's newspaper began to take on a more conciliatory tone in his old age as he turned away from the idea of creating an independent constitutional state. He resigned his seat in the legislature, declined offers to run for the Legislative Council, and further refused to run for the mayor's office of Toronto. He began to renew friendships with old adversaries and shortly before his death, on August 28, 1861, entertained the notion of running again for the legislature.

Summary

William Lyon Mackenzie stood as the conscience of a country which was not ready to realize the independence of people, place, and political institutions. The things Mackenzie sought for Canada would have reordered the status of Canada and perhaps accomplished an eventual unity of British and French regions. Mackenzie was a radical in every sense of the word. Within him there was a curious admixture that might be regarded as the birthright of the Scots—a durable distrust of the British, an intense devotion to Scotland, and a detached view of Europe. It is not certain whether Mackenzie ever shared his countrymen's concern for the United States. Mackenzie trusted the spirit of democracy that he observed in the age of Andrew Jackson. Mackenzie's identification with the American politics of democracy was generally unacceptable, despite the real concerns for the corruption and the venality of the colonial administration and the Family Compact system. Mackenzie's words and actions struck at the heart of the issue of national identity. Being American to him meant more than mere geography. His life was consumed with the matter of what it meant to be a Canadian. Mackenzie was an important and even uncomfortable presence in Canada's struggle from colony to nation. He will endure as one of its true giants of democracy.

Bibliography

Craig, Gerald. *Upper Canada: The Formative Years*. Toronto: McClelland and Stewart, and New York: Oxford University Press, 1963. One of the first serious studies of the Family Compact and English colonial tradition. Critical of Mackenzie while praising conservative principles.

Dent, John Charles. *The Story of the Upper Canada Rebellion*. 2 vols. Toronto: C. B. Robinson, 1885. Particularly harsh on Mackenzie; a debunking of all that Mackenzie represented.

Flint, David. *William Lyon Mackenzie: Rebel Against Authority*. Toronto: Oxford University Press, 1971. Provides the broad chronology of Mackenzie's career but does not develop much of the politics or philosophy of the man. Has a useful bibliography.

Kilbourn, William. *The Firebrand: William Lyon Mackenzie and the Rebellion in Upper Canada*. London: Cape, 1958. Perhaps the most readily available work on Mackenzie. Centers on interpreting the character of the protagonist rather than assessing all areas of controversy surrounding the man and his times.

LeSueur, William Dawson. *William Lyon Mackenzie: A Reinterpretation*. Toronto: Macmillan, 1979. Harshly critical of Mackenzie's career. Le Suer was a conservative in the Victorian tradition who opposed representative government as being nothing but partisan party-oriented and antithetical to the national concerns of Canada.

Lindsey, Charles. *The Life and Times of William Lyon Mackenzie*. Philadelphia: Bradley, 1862. Defends Mackenzie, portraying him as a valiant reformer and promoter of an independent Canadian tradition.

Mackenzie, William Lyon. *1837: Revolution in the Canadas*. Edited by Greg Keilty. Toronto: N. C. Press, 1974. Both protagonist and editor join to establish that the Rebellion of 1837 was more than a passing phase in Canada's history. Views the rebellion as a joint struggle of Lower and Upper Canada against both the privileged entities of property and patronage and the oppressive British colonial rule.

Jack J. Cardoso

WILLIAM McKINLEY

Born: January 29, 1843; Niles, Ohio
Died: September 14, 1901; Buffalo, New York
Areas of Achievement: Government and politics
Contribution: By strengthening the powers of the presidency, McKinley's administration prepared the way for forceful executives of the twentieth century such as Woodrow Wilson, Theodore Roosevelt, and Franklin D. Roosevelt. His expansionist policies brought new overseas territories such as Puerto Rico, the Philippines, Guam, and Hawaii into the American empire.

Early Life

William McKinley, Jr., was born January 29, 1843, in Niles, Ohio. His mother, née Nancy Allison, was descended from pious Scottish ancestors; his father, William McKinley, Sr., of Scotch-Irish and English Puritan descent, was an iron founder in Pennsylvania and Ohio. The elder McKinley's iron furnace brought only a meager living. The son grew up in a rural environment and attended the Methodist Church faithfully with his parents. When the family moved to the larger town of Poland, near Youngstown, Ohio, William was able to attend the academy there in preparation for college. He was able to complete only one term during 1860 at Allegheny College in Meadville, Pennsylvania; family financial reverses prevented resumption of his studies. Young McKinley had proved himself to be a good public speaker and a diligent, if not brilliant, student.

Because of his short stature—five feet six inches tall—erect posture, and somber countenance, McKinley's physical appearance has often been compared to that of Napoleon Bonaparte. His gray, penetrating eyes gazed intently from a pale, serious face. McKinley did not have a sophisticated or cosmopolitan upbringing, yet he had a manner that was sedate and dignified. Those who knew him well were also aware of his good sense of humor and very kindly disposition. He was abstemious, almost prudish in behavior. In early life, he disdained smoking, drinking, dancing, and gambling. In his middle years, however, he became addicted to the use of tobacco.

At the outset of the Civil War (1861), he enlisted as a private in the Twenty-third Ohio Volunteer Infantry. He participated in many of the major battles of the conflict, including the clash at Antietam. He rose rapidly through the ranks during his four years, attaining the rank of captain by 1864. He demonstrated impressive administrative abilities while serving on the staff of General Rutherford B. Hayes. His growing friendship with Hayes would serve him well in his later political career. He was mustered out of the service in 1865, with the brevet rank of major, a title that would often be used with his name.

After the war, McKinley studied law briefly at the Albany (New York) Law School and was admitted to the bar and set up his practice at Canton, Ohio, in 1867. This northeastern Ohio town became his home for the remainder of his life. In 1871, he married Ida Saxton, a young woman from a wealthy home. Unfortunately, the couple enjoyed only two tranquil years of marriage before a severe nervous illness struck down Ida. Many of her later years were spent as a virtual invalid. William McKinley seemed to show infinite and unending compassion and devotion to his sick wife. He always found time during even his presidential years to minister to her needs.

Life's Work

William McKinley served twelve years as a Republican member of the United States House of Representatives, from 1877 to 1891, a period interrupted briefly by his loss of the 1882 election. The loss came from one of the periodic Democratic gerrymanders that plagued his career in Congress. He quickly became one of the leading proponents of protectionism in the House. His knowledge of the tariff issue and industrial questions helped him to secure a place on the Ways and Means Committee, a position which allowed him a major influence over revenue matters. He became chairman of the committee in 1889, after having lost in a battle for Speaker of the House to Thomas B. Reed. His most important achievement in the Congress was the successful passage, in 1890, of a highly protectionist tariff that came to be known as the McKinley Act. The bill provided for a reciprocal lowering of the tariffs of two countries when a treaty to accomplish this could be negotiated. Several European states did enter into such arrangements with the United States. McKinley's tariff also reduced the excess revenue from the tariff which had been swelling the treasury. Sugar was placed on the free list, and American producers were compensated for this loss of protection by a subsidy of two cents a pound, paid to refiners. What had seemed to be McKinley's moment of triumph soon became abysmal defeat, however, when a storm of criticism from consumers brought about the defeat of many Republican congressmen in the 1890 elections, including McKinley himself.

The defeat in McKinley's district of Ohio in 1890 had been partly a result of another Democratic gerrymander rather than a wholesale repudiation of the candidate. His reputation still intact in Ohio, McKinley, with the backing of the wealthy Cleveland industrialist Marcus A. Hanna, won the governorship in 1891 and 1893. In 1892, Hanna tried to engineer the nomination of McKinley for president, but McKinley refused to encourage the movement because of his conviction that the Republican Party should stand by its incumbent president, Benjamin Harrison.

By 1896, when McKinley was ready to accept his party's nomination, a new issue had begun to overshadow the tariff question. Grover Cleveland's term (1893-1897) had been an era of severe depression and suffering, especially for the farmers. Many of those at the lower economic level began to see some hope in a new panacea. The monetization of silver would allow for inflation of the currency, bringing relief to debtors and a hoped for increase in agricultural prices. Such ideas were anathema to financiers and industrialists. The eastern aristocracy of wealth stood foursquare for the gold standard. Although the "standpatters" had faith in McKinley as the apostle of protectionism, his record on the currency issue was less encouraging. He had in fact voted for overriding Hayes's veto of the Bland-Allison Act in 1878, a bill providing for the issuing of a moderate number of silver certificates. McKinley now took a position more reassuring to business. He favored a gold standard until such time as the other nations agreed to an international bimetallic (silver and gold) standard. It was not expected by most businessmen that such an international agreement was likely.

In the election of 1896, McKinley ran against the prosilver candidate of the Democrats, William Jennings Bryan. In the campaign, McKinley stayed at his home in Canton, Ohio. He would appear on his front porch to make campaign speeches to supporters who were brought in by train for his rallies. The dignified campaign was in sharp contrast to the whirlwind tour of Bryan, who spoke from the rear of his train in numerous hamlets and towns along his path. To many, Bryan seemed a dangerous demagogue, while McKinley appeared to be an experienced and sane candidate who would restore prosperity and confidence. McKinley won by a comfortable margin.

One of McKinley's most important abilities as an administrator was a talent for choosing gifted men to work with him. Yet he did choose a few men to serve in his first cabinet who proved unequal to the task. The elderly John Sherman was physically unable to carry on the duties of secretary of state at a time when international affairs were moving toward a critical stage. He served slightly more than a year. Later, McKinley chose such able men as John Hay, secretary of state; Philander Knox, attorney general; and Elihu Root, secretary of war. During McKinley's first year as president, Congress passed a tariff which continued the high protectionist policies advocated by the president, the Dingley Act. The president sent emissaries to England to begin the process of sounding out other nations on the prospects for international bimetalism. The industrial nations had very little interest in this proposal. The currency question would not be settled for McKinley until 1900, when the Congress passed the Gold Standard Act which declared that gold would be the only standard of value for the dollar. The debt-ridden farmers failed to receive the relief they sought. Yet new discoveries of gold around the world did increase the supply of the precious metal slightly, and during McKinley's first term, the economy increased so markedly that most of the agrarian protest agitation died out.

The most significant theme of McKinley's presidency involved foreign affairs. Although McKinley came out of the Civil War with a strong aversion to war, events and pressures around him seemed to be carrying the nation toward war with Spain. In 1895, the Cuban people had begun a guerrilla war aimed at securing independence from Spain. The Spanish government appeared adamant in its determination to hold on to the last relics of empire in the New World. The United States found its interests inextricably involved in the fortunes of the rebels. The island's geographic proximity and its close economic ties made its destiny a major concern. The brutal treatment of Cubans in what were called "reconcentration" areas provoked sympathy and concern. William Randolph Hearst's New York *Journal* and Joseph Pulitzer's New York *World* found the Cuban atrocities a ready-made source for the kind of sensational stories that could build up newspaper circulation. To the cry of the yellow journals were soon added the chorus of angry congressmen and senators. McKinley preferred the quiet path of diplomacy as a means of settling the issues between Spain and the United States, but an increase of pressure and tension in 1898 convinced him to submit the issue to a Congress already determined upon war. In February, 1898, the destruction of the American battleship *Maine*, probably because of an internal explosion, incited further angry demands for war. The assumption that the Spanish had intentionally destroyed an American vessel was a highly unlikely one, but many Americans rashly made that assumption.

McKinley took a direct hand in guiding the conduct of the war that lasted only from April through August of 1898. Only the office of president was available to coordinate the activities of the war and navy departments. The war was primarily a naval affair fought in Manila Bay in the Philippines and near Santiago in Cuba. The navy demonstrated that it had finally achieved the modernity expected of a major power. It won decisive battles in both theaters. McKinley had entered the war for the avowed purpose of liberating Cuba from Spain, but during the course of the conflict, he made a decision to send troops to Manila to follow up the defeat of the Spanish fleet in the bay. The decision indicated a shift in direction, an apparent decision to use the conflict as a means of acquiring territory. McKinley directed the American representatives at Paris to secure a peace treaty which included the acquisition from Spain of Puerto Rico, Guam, and the Philippine Islands.

The president easily defeated Bryan in the election of 1900. The slogan "a full dinner pail" reflected the reality that the agricultural crisis had eased and that workers were again finding employment. Yet McKinley served only a half year of his second term before being succeeded by his vice president, Theodore Roosevelt. An anarchist, Leon Czolgosz, shot the president while he was attending the Pan-American Exposition at Buffalo. McKinley lived eight more days. Death came on September 14, 1901.

Summary

As president, McKinley led the United States toward the creation of an overseas empire. Grover Cleveland had rejected an attempt to annex the Hawaiian Islands, but McKinley, fearing that Japan might gain a foothold, pressed for action. Congress annexed the islands by joint resolution in July, 1898. In 1899, McKinley acquired a settlement by treaty with Germany that recognized American control over a part of the Samoan Islands. The agreement granted Pago Pago to the United States, thus providing a strategically important South Pacific base for the navy. The Treaty of Paris of 1898, which ended the war with Spain, brought Puerto Rico, Guam, and the Philippines into the empire. Although Cuba was set free, it became a protectorate of the United States. McKinley's secretary of state, John Hay, began the process of removing barriers to the United States' building a canal. Negotiations to remove Britain's objections were begun but not finished before McKinley's death.

While McKinley is usually not placed on most historians' list of the greatest American presidents, he did prepare the way for an increase in presidential influence and power in the twentieth century. He did not stand by idly while Congress conducted its business apart from the executive branch. He actively sought to influence legislation by suggesting the possibility of special sessions and by utilizing the veto threat. McKinley's direct guidance of the war effort also exemplifies his use of power in the fashion of a twentieth century president. While he did not always explain his actions publicly, he seems to have been acting effectively and purposefully in his conduct of diplomacy. At the outset of his administration, he had to assert some control of foreign affairs because of the ineptness of the aged John Sherman. During McKinley's presidency, it became clear that the United States had reached great power. The power of the navy, demonstrated by the brief and spectacular victories of the Spanish-American War, dictated that the United States would have to be accepted as one of the major forces in international politics.

The strengthening of industry, trade, and the economy of the United States was McKinley's major domestic aim throughout his career. He tried to accomplish this aim primarily through the tariff and by avoiding policies that would be injurious to the business community. Later economic experience seems to show that the nation might have profited from freer trade and a slight inflation of the currency. Just before his death, McKinley seems to have been intimating that he was reconsidering the tariff issue himself.

Bibliography

Chandler, D. Aaron. "A Short Note on the Expenditures of the McKinley Campaign of 1896." *Presidential Studies Quarterly* 28, no. 1 (Winter 1998). Chandler looks at the finances of the 1896 presidential campaign of McKinley, including his relationship with Mark Hanna who raised and spent between $3 and $16 million on the election.

Glad, Paul W. *McKinley, Bryan, and the People.* Philadelphia: Lippincott, 1964. A brief study of the election of 1896 and its two main antagonists. The book provides a summary of the issues that led to the dramatic contest between Bryan and McKinley. It offers an analysis and contrast of the two men.

Gould, Lewis L. *The Presidency of William McKinley.* Lawrence: University Press of Kansas, 1981. Gould argues effectively that McKinley was the first modern president. Many historians have seen McKinley as Hanna's puppet and as being too weak to resist the pressures for war. This book is especially useful in that it offers a carefully reasoned alternative to the traditional view. Gould believes that McKinley was an effective administrator who increased the powers of the presidency and thus prepared the way for the imperial presidency of the twentieth century.

Leech, Margaret. *In the Days of McKinley.* New York: Harper, 1959. This book combines scholarship and an entertaining writing style. The work is carefully researched and provides details of McKinley's personal life. It is one of the best full-length biographies of McKinley available. Leech is generally sympathetic to McKinley.

Morgan, Howard Wayne. *America's Road to Empire: The War with Spain and Overseas Expansion.* New York: Wiley, 1965. This is a brief work but a useful one for insights on McKinley's diplomacy, leading up to the Spanish-American War. It suggests that McKinley did not rush impetuously into war as pressures built up in the nation. There had been a patient and sincere diplomatic offensive aimed at preventing conflict, but this effort had been beset by Spanish temporizing.

————. *William McKinley and His America.* Syracuse, N.Y.: Syracuse University Press, 1963. This book, along with Leech's work, is one of the two most important full-length biographies of McKinley. Morgan's chief contribution is his in-depth understanding of the political background of the Gilded Age. Morgan is known as a revisionist on the era. He disagrees with those who view the period as little more than a generation of political, social, and economic degeneracy.

Ranson, Edward. "Electing a President, 1896." *History Today* 46, no. 10 (October, 1996). Discussion of the platforms and oratory styles of Bryan and McKinley, the politics of the period, and the 1896 election results.

Richard L. Niswonger

DANIEL AND ALEXANDER MACMILLAN

Daniel Macmillan

Born: September 13, 1813; Island of Arran, Buteshire, Scotland   *Died:* June 27, 1857; Cambridge, England

Alexander Macmillan

Born: October 3, 1818; Irvine, Ayrshire, Scotland   *Died:* January 26, 1896; London, England

Area of Achievement: Publishing

Contribution: Starting as booksellers, the Macmillans, in 1844, founded Macmillan and Company, which would eventually become one of the world's major publishing enterprises.

Early Lives

The Macmillan brothers were of Scottish stock, sons of Duncan and Katherine Crawford Macmillan, who had a dozen children. Born in 1766, Duncan lived on the Island of Arran. He succeeded his father-in-law in running a small farm. On this farm Daniel Macmillan was born in 1813. By 1816, the family had moved to Irvine in Ayrshire, where Alexander was born in October of 1818.

Duncan's death in 1823 left the family hardpressed. The eldest son, Malcolm, a schoolmaster who later became a Baptist clergyman, at twenty-five became head of the family and did what he could to help keep it solvent. Nevertheless, financial exigencies forced Daniel, only three months past his tenth birthday, to become self-supporting. He was apprenticed to Maxwell Dick, a local bookseller, for seven years and was paid a small wage.

Young Daniel was so dependable that when Dick went to London on business in 1828, he was able to leave his teenage apprentice in charge. Daniel learned from Dick how to buy, sell, and bind books. Dick also taught Daniel how to handle and groom horses. The apprenticeship was largely a positive experience for Daniel, a frail child, of normal height, perilously thin, whose lungs were weak.

Alexander, the younger brother, attended Irvine Academy, where he enjoyed the more vigorous games his classmates played. He and Daniel both were accustomed to seeing their mother, a woman of intellect, read voraciously, and they both early developed a similar love of books.

When Daniel's apprenticeship ended, the seventeen-year-old was in bad health. After working for booksellers in Stirling and in Glasgow, in 1833, Daniel sailed for London, a sixty-three-hour jour-

ney, to seek his fortune. He sought work there as a bookseller but found a more compatible job in a Cambridge bookstore, where he went at half the salary that Simpkin's in London had offered him. He remained for three years in Mr. Johnson's Cambridge bookshop.

In 1836, a year after his mother had died, Daniel returned to Scotland. Alexander by this time had an ill-paying job as usher in a school and was destitute. When Daniel was offered a job in London at Seeley's in Fleet Street, he took it, and three years later, in 1839, he had arranged for Alexander to work in the same bookstore. Daniel, who shared lodgings with Alexander, assiduously promoted the younger man's education.

By late 1842, the two brothers could think of opening their own bookstore, which they did in Aldersgate Street early the following year. Because of the shop's out-of-the-way location, it did not show a profit, although it attracted some of London's most prestigious intellectuals. By June, 1843, the brothers had the chance to buy Mr. Newby's shop in Cambridge and did so. Alexander kept his job at Seeley's for a while to assure them of a secure income. Daniel left Seeley's to devote full time to running the bookstore. Alexander was as active in the new venture as his job at Seeley's permitted.

Before long, the brothers began a small publishing operation in connection with the new bookshop. By November 10, 1843, the first book bearing the Macmillan imprint was in the British Museum Library. By this time, both brothers were deeply in debt. Daniel had lung problems against which he constantly struggled. Then, early in 1844, he had a life-threatening hemorrhage, brought on by the long hours his new enterprise required.

Life's Work

Before Daniel moved to Cambridge, he had become friends with Archdeacon Julius Charles Hare, to whom he had written about one of Hare's religious books. Through Hare, Daniel came to meet some of the notable writers of his day, among them F. D. Maurice, whose religious books had gained considerable celebrity. Religious books were best-sellers in that era, so it was commercially prudent for publishers to have as many of them as possible on their lists of offerings.

The archdeacon and his brother helped finance the Macmillans when they bought Newby's bookshop in Cambridge, lending them five hundred pounds at four percent interest. Despite Daniel's continued ill health, the shop prospered. The most notable intellectuals from Cambridge University flocked to it, as did Cambridge students, who looked upon it as a second university.

Daniel was aware early of the need for re-editions of books by some notable writers, including Jeremy Taylor, John Donne, Henry Moore, and John Milton. He was too much in debt to do much about publishing these new editions, although in 1844 he published an edition of William Law's 1723 answer to Bernard de Mandeville's *Fable of the Bees* (1714, 1723), with a preface by Maurice.

At about this time, the Macmillans had the opportunity to buy for six thousand pounds a bookselling business, run by Thomas Stevenson, that had flourished in Cambridge for almost a century. The challenge of expanding in this way was great, and the only way the brothers could meet it was to take on a partner, a wholesale drug merchant.

In 1845, the brothers moved their enterprise to 1 Trinity Street, and it is there that William Wordsworth, William Makepeace Thackeray, and Charles Kingsley were their guests. The Macmillans were becoming a force in British publishing. Both brothers were charming and patient. They made writers believe that the Macmillans had their best interests at heart and understood what they wanted to accomplish in their writing. An aura of trust and mutual understanding surrounded the brothers' dealings with writers.

Alexander, a man of impeccable intellect and firm ideas, could respect people at odds with his thinking if their reasoning was sound. He had strong persuasive gifts and avoided intellectual confrontation; he took the arts seriously, and creative artists immediately sensed the depth of his devotion to the arts; and he stood ready to defend his authors. These qualities served him admirably as a publisher. When Cambridge University took Maurice's professorship from him in 1853, Alexander lent Maurice his support and kept his controversial books in print.

Through Maurice, the Macmillans published the work of Charles Kingsley, the first author to bring them considerable financial success. Within a decade of their first venture in publishing, the Macmillans had published scores of books, many of them translations from the classics, for which a ready market existed. One of their enduring successes was the publication in 1852 of John Llewellyn Davies and David James Vaughan's translation of Plato's *Republic*, a book that went into countless editions and still sold well a century after it first appeared. Kingsley's *Phaethon* and Isaac Todhuner's *Differential Calculus* appeared in 1852 and were dependable sellers for years to come. In 1855, Macmillan press issued a reprint of Maurice's 1853 book, *Prophets and Kings of the Old Testament*, which sold briskly.

On September 4, 1850, Daniel had married Frances Orridge. A desperately ill man, Daniel continued to live for only a little more than six years. During his brief marriage, he fathered four children. By 1852, however, it was necessary for him to be away from Cambridge frequently to breathe the sea air that gave him some relief from his illness. He and Alexander carried on a voluminous business correspondence during Daniel's absences. Despite his illness and absence from the Macmillan Publishing Company, Daniel continued to be intimately involved in forming its policies, in soliciting manuscripts, and in directing the course those manuscripts took.

In the early 1850's, Great Britain's uncertain economic climate placed the Macmillans under financial pressure. Nevertheless, they had faith in their basic business policies, knowing that their company could survive periods of economic instability. Daniel, although ill, had worked from 1854 with Kingsley as Kingsley wrote *Westward Ho!* (1855), which proved to be one of Macmillan's continuing windfalls, its earnings proliferating markedly after 1889, when the sixpenny edition of the work appeared.

When Daniel died, on June 27, 1857, Kingsley's current novel, *Two Years Ago*, was breaking sales records, and the Macmillans, while not yet wealthy, were in a financially promising position. Upon Daniel's death, Alexander, who had run the day-to-day operations of the company, became its head.

Shortly after Daniel's death, Alexander opened a branch of the company in London. His nephew, Robert Bowes, who had worked for the company since 1846, ran this operation. Alexander routinely went to London on Thursdays and stayed overnight. During these visits, London's literati flocked to the Henrietta Street offices in Covent Garden, where Alexander was at home to all comers. It was during these bristling sessions that the idea of *Macmillan's Magazine* (1859-1907) was incubated. Alexander launched the magazine, and it became a force in establishing the course of both British and American writing during the nearly fifty years of its existence.

By 1863, Alexander was appointed Publisher to the University of Oxford. He had moved his prosperous publishing company from Cambridge to London. Some of the most notable authors of the nineteenth century wrote for Macmillan, which by then had published Thackeray, Walter Pater, Alfred, Lord Tennyson, Mrs. (Margaret) Oliphant, Thomas Hardy, Thomas Hughes, Christina Rossetti, and Cardinal John Henry Newman.

In 1867, Alexander made his first trip to the United States and was well received. Although he had not gone abroad to establish an American Macmillan, the idea now seemed feasible to him. Daniel's sons and his own were of an age that they would soon be entering the business, and an American branch provided just the sort of testing ground they needed. By November, 1869, the company had an American branch. Macmillan books printed after 1870 listed both London and New York on their imprint.

Summary

Daniel and Alexander Macmillan established one of the most influential and diverse publishing companies in the world. They were good businessmen, well seasoned in their trade. Their chief skill, however, was their ability to identify and nurture talent. They had endless patience in their dealings with authors. They were willing to take risks by publishing works that might not sell, but by doing so, they achieved some of their most remarkable successes.

These two men, rising from humble origins and working against substantial economic and personal handicaps, helped establish the intellectual tone of the age in which they lived by making available to readers the most exciting and controversial ideas of their day. Their company, now in its second century, still affects the intellectual direction of the English-speaking world.

Bibliography

Foster, James. *A Bibliographical Catalogue of Macmillan and Company's Publications from 1843 to 1880*. London and New York: Macmillan, 1891. This comprehensive list shows the broad range of books that issued from Macmillan and Company during the days when Daniel and Alexander had their most direct influence upon it.

Graves, Charles L. *The Life and Letters of Alexander Macmillan*. London: Macmillan, 1910. Although not comprehensive, Graves's edition of the letters has an interesting interspersion of biographical data. The letters are well chosen and illuminate the early history of Macmillan and Company.

Macmillan, Alexander. *The Letters of Alexander Macmillan*. Edited by George Macmillan. Glasgow: University Press, 1908. These letters reflect both the range of authors with whom Alexander Macmillan dealt and the careful attention he lavished on them.

Morgan, Charles. *The House of Macmillan: 1843-1943*. London and New York: Macmillan, 1944. This book remains the comprehensive history of the founding of the Macmillan company and provides a detailed biographical background of both of its founders as well as valuable information about other members of the Macmillan family.

Packer, Lona Mosk, ed. *The Rossetti-Macmillan Letters*. Cambridge: Cambridge University Press, and Berkeley: University of California Press, 1963. This collection of 133 letters written to Alexander Macmillan and other officials of Macmillan and Company by Dante Gabriel, William Michael, and Christina Rossetti, between 1861 and 1889, reveals Alexander's gentle and understanding handling of one of his notable authors and demonstrates the cordiality of the Rossettis' relationship with their publisher.

R. Baird Shuman

WILLIAM CHARLES MACREADY

Born: March 3, 1793; London, England
Died: April 27, 1873; Cheltenham, England
Area of Achievement: Theater
Contribution: The mid-nineteenth century's most influential actor-manager, Macready laid the foundations for reform in the theater, helping to forge the modern theater; restored uncorrupted Shakespeare texts to the stage; and gave solid encouragement to the contemporary "new drama."

Early Life

William Charles Macready was born March 3, 1793, the son of an actress and daughter of a respectable surgeon, and an improvident, womanizing actor-manager and son of a Dublin upholsterer, whose personal and theatrical tastes and notorious example were to influence his son profoundly: The seeds were sown early of Macready's lifelong professional caution and private propriety.

The delusions of genteel grandeur of the elder Macready led to his son's entering Rugby school in 1803. There Macready gained both a liking of his own for polite society and a taste for the classics. By 1808, stimulated by the intellectual rigor of his studies, he had formed hopes of going to Oxford and preparing for the bar, but these were forever and bitterly dashed when his father's near-bankruptcy forced the sixteen-year-old Macready to undertake the comanagement of his company. This baptism of fire in theatrical business was supplemented by a visit to London in 1809 to learn fencing and study the reigning stars of his profession.

On June 7, 1810, Macready made his first stage appearance, playing Romeo in white silk stockings and dancing pumps, a costume not calculated to flatter an actor of only medium height and rather heavy on his feet, who possessed (in addition to a noble brow) not only the large blue eyes but also the flat face and irregular features of the Irish. Nevertheless, his success was considerable, and continued so for six prosperous provincial years.

Life's Work

On September 16, 1816, Macready finally stepped onto the stage of a London theater. His Covent Garden debut, delayed by his caution, occasioned many favorable and some perceptive reviews:

Mr. Macready strikes us as having a better conception of his Author's meaning [than Kean]. He trusts more to plain delivery and proper emphasis—and consequently has less occasion for starting—pointing—and slapping his forehead.

The instant comparison to Edmund Kean, the great and well-established romantic actor of the age, anticipated the jealous rivalry that swiftly developed. Also of interest is the immediate critical recognition of the more natural style of acting that Macready brought to the stage. There are indications, too, of why the more intellectual Macready would become the preeminent actor-collaborator of the 1830's and 1840's, working directly and with success with authors.

For three years after this auspicious beginning, however, to his own disgust, Macready was relegated to playing a selection of gothic and melodramatic "heavies." His luck turned in 1819, when his Richard III caught the public's fancy. Then, in 1820, a poverty-stricken and eccentric first-time playwright named Sheridan Knowles sent Macready a manuscript. He decided at once to stage it. *Virginius*, with its combination of sensibility with a plea for the rights of man, caught the spirit of its age, and eminently suited the talents of its star. Macready's success as the noble centurion raised him to the top of his profession.

In a few short years, however, his relationship with the Covent Garden management had soured sufficiently for his contract to be canceled. Thus, on October 13, 1823, he made his first appearance at Drury Lane, where he was to stay for thirteen years which did little to enhance his reputation, and during which Kean refused to act with him. His unhappiness was somewhat mitigated in 1823 by his marriage (prudently later in life), in 1826 by the first of several trips to the United States.

In 1835 occurred a famous incident. Macready's sense of angry frustration at the low status of tragedy in the theater (reduced to a mere part of a miscellaneous entertainment) boiled over. On April 29, focusing this anger on the figure of the Drury Lane manager, money-minded Alfred Bunn, he called him a "damned scoundrel" and knocked him down. It says much for the nature of the audiences of the period that Macready's popularity increased after this outrageous assault.

The later 1830's saw Macready premiering several of Bulwer-Lytton's highly acclaimed historical dramas, Sir Thomas Noon Talfourd's *Ion* (1836), another influential major play of the "new drama," and Robert Browning's *Strafford* (1837), written for Macready at his own request. As often in Macready's career, this last was a critical rather than a popular success, and yet another factor in the cementing of his friendships with these eminent literary figures, as well as John Forster and Charles Dickens (who dedicated to Macready his *Nicholas Nickleby*, 1838-1839).

On September 20, 1837, Macready opened the Covent Garden season (1837-1838) for the first time as manager, himself playing Leontes in a restored text of *The Winter's Tale*. He gathered about him a powerful company, together with a troupe of pantomimists—crucial in the recouping of the three thousand pounds he was said to have lost by Christmas. In February, he had a remunerative hit with Edward Bulwer-Lytton's *The Lady of Lyons: Or, Love and Pride*. In his second season as manager (1838-1839), the most notable performances were of *The Tempest* (an elaborate revival); of Bulwer-Lytton's *Richelieu: Or, The Conspiracy*, which took the town by storm; and of *Henry V* (with staging supervised by Bulwer-Lytton, Dickens, Forster, W. J. Fox, and the artists Daniel Maclise and Clarkson Stanfield)—another resounding success.

The next highlight in Macready's career was his second period of management, again for two seasons, this time at Drury Lane. The hit of the 1841-1842 season was *Acis and Galatea*, a pantomime by W. H. Oxberry, with Stanfield's scenery and George Frideric Handel's music. Macready himself scored a great personal success in the title role in another restored "problem" Shakespeare play, *King John*, on October 24, 1842. On June 14, 1843, he appeared for the last time as manager, in his "keynote" role of Macbeth. After this high point, remunerative and well-received trips to the United States and Paris aside, he played mostly in the provinces, returning to London on November 22 to play his last new part, Philip Van Artevelde, in his own somewhat botched adaptation of Henry Taylor's play, regarded by contemporaries as a species of nineteenth century *Hamlet*.

At the end of 1848, however, came the low point of his career, in one sense, when his last trip to the United States ended in tragedy. Poor reception of the highly popular American actor Edwin Forrest in England, and American discontent with recent

unflattering portraits of the country by Mrs. Frances Trollope and Dickens, erupted into a full-scale riot at the Astor Place Opera House in New York, during a Macready performance as Macbeth on May 10, 1849. Troops were called in, and twenty-two people were left dead. Macready himself, whose characteristic lack of tact had not helped the situation, was ignominiously smuggled away and sent back to England.

Macready's farewell to the stage came in 1851, shortly after the death of a daughter, the first of many domestic tragedies: Only three of his twelve children outlived him. He left the stage, by choice, while he was still near the height of his powers and resisted the temptation of a comeback. On February 28, he played Macbeth for the last time, at Drury Lane. On March 1, a public dinner for six hundred, hosted by Bulwer-Lytton, with speeches by Dickens and William Makepeace Thackeray, paid him the tribute his age believed was his due. He withdrew to the gentleman's residence he had purchased in Dorset, and later to Cheltenham (with a second wife, married 1860), where he died at eighty-one, on Sunday, April 27, 1873.

Summary

In his farewell address, William Charles Macready asked his last theater audience to give him credit for two things: his efforts "to establish a theatre, in regard to decorum and taste, worthy of our country, and to have in it the plays of our divine Shakespeare fitly illustrated." He succeeded. In the words of the sonnet Alfred, Lord Tennyson wrote for his farewell dinner: "Thine is it that our drama did not die,/ Nor flicker down to brainless pantomime."

Macready by no means banished money-spinning pantomime from the theater (although he did draw the line at trained lions and prostitutes); what he did was disentangle it from serious drama. Other aspects of his management similarly combined practicality with principle: preeminent among his reforms, crucial to the development of modern theater, was his insistence on regular full rehearsals. Also influential was his concept of the play as a coherent artistic whole.

His other great achievement lies in the support he gave the legitimate theater of his time. Bulwer-Lytton declared of him: "He has identified himself with the living drama of his period, and by so doing he has half created it." The playwrights wrote for him, visualizing Macready as their Virginius, Ion, Richelieu, or Strafford: What Tennyson called his "moral, grave, sublime" stage persona was the heroic type of the period.

Indeed, even in his limitations, the essence of Macready's era was distilled. His popularity is evidence of a public preference for the domestic over the sublime. He was a self-made businessman with social ambitions, an "eminent Victorian" before his time. For William Hazlitt, even his Macbeth was "a mere modern, agitated by common means and intelligible motives." For Leigh Hunt, Macready was proto-Victorian respectability itself: "Violent or criminal pains he makes simply violent and criminal. Nothing remains to him, if his self-respect, in the ordinary sense of the word, is lost."

Yet Macready's limitations are insignificant compared to his personal failings. Had he not been humorless and prone to ungovernable and childish rages and sulks, less egocentric, and better able to attract the loyalty and best efforts of his companies, there is no doubt that his periods of management would have been longer, more successful, and more influential in reviving a degraded theater. As it was, company members were treated with a snobbish and haughty contempt that can be traced to Macready's fundamental dislike of what he saw, in quintessentially Victorian terms, as his dirty trade, as such diary entries as this, for April 26, 1843, testify:

> [My] darling children acted Comus in the drawing room after dinner, interesting and amusing me very much; they recited the poetry very well indeed, and only gave me a fear lest they should imbibe a liking for the wretched art which I have been wasting my life upon. God forbid!

Bibliography

Agate, James Evershed, ed. *These Were Actors: Extracts from a Newspaper Cutting Book, 1811-1833.* London and New York: Hutchinson, 1943. This absorbing collection of contemporary reviews gives pride of place to Macready's great rival, Kean, and bitingly witty short shrift to the "eminent tragedian" himself. Well worth reading for context, balance, and sheer enjoyment.

Archer, William. *William Charles Macready.* London: Kegan Paul, and New York: Longman, 1890. Still brilliantly readable and reliable. Focuses on the four crucial seasons of management.

Downer, Alan S. *The Eminent Tragedian: William Charles Macready.* Cambridge, Mass.: Harvard University Press, 1966. Lively and well documented. Locates Macready in his theatrical context; analyzes the "Macready style" and contribution to the stage. Final chapter is an "ideal" reconstruction of Macready's famed *Macbeth* in performance, drawing on his heavily annotated prompt books, reminiscences, and reviews.

Macready, William Charles. *Macready's Reminiscences, and Selections from His Diaries and Letters.* Edited by Sir Frederick Pollock. London and New York: Macmillan, 1875. Macready's autobiographical account of his life until 1826, followed by a slightly circumspect but nevertheless fascinating selection from the actor's diaries. Alternately frankly self-lacerating and pompously self-centered.

Rowell, George. *The Victorian Theatre: A Survey.* London and New York: Oxford University Press, 1956. The standard work on the theater from 1792 to 1914, with solid but never stolid coverage of the "new drama" of the 1830's and 1840's. Invaluable thirty-page bibliography.

Shattuck, Charles H., ed. *Bulwer and Macready: A Chronicle of the Early Victorian Theatre.* Urbana: University of Illinois Press, 1958. Correspondence covering the years of collaboration between the actor-manager and the lionized author. Excellent sixteen-page introduction.

Southern, Richard. *The Victorian Theatre: A Pictorial Survey*. Newton Abbot: David and Charles, and New York: Theatre Arts Books, 1970. Concise information on theatrical scenery, staging and architecture, Victorian audiences and Victorian "stars" and shows; supplements a wealth of photographs, drawings, paintings, and diagrams.

Trewin, J.C. *Mr. Macready: A Nineteenth Century Tragedian and His Theatre*. London: Harrap, 1955. A more personal, psychological account; thorough, with illustrations and a helpful bibliography.

————, ed. *The Pomping Folk in the Nineteenth Century Theatre*. London: Dent, 1968. A survey in the words of actors Macready, Helen Faucit, and Fanny Kemble; dramatist Bulwer-Lytton and authors Thackeray and Dickens; managers Edward Stirling and Alfred Bunn (from *The Stage: Both Before and Behind the Curtain*, 1840); drama critics Clement Scott and Henry Morley (from *The Journal of a London Playgoer*); and others.

Joss Marsh

DOLLEY MADISON

Born: May 20, 1768; Guilford County, North Carolina

Died: July 12, 1849; Washington, D.C.

Areas of Achievement: Government and politics

Contribution: First Lady Dolley Madison's popularity and social acumen made her a political asset to President James Madison. The leading social figure in the capital city for years, she was arguably the most beloved and important woman of her times and later became a role model for many First Ladies in the United States.

Early Life

John and Mary Coles Payne moved to Piedmont, North Carolina, from Virginia. It was there that their daughter Dolley Payne was born in 1768. The following year, the Payne family moved back to their native Virginia. In 1783, after freeing his slaves, John again moved his family, this time to Philadelphia, Pennsylvania, where the Paynes raised their eight children in the strict disciplinary tradition of the Quaker Society of Friends. Dolley was also raised modestly, as her father had failed in business.

In 1790 Dolley married John Todd, Jr., a successful lawyer and Quaker. Dolley and John had two sons: John Payne in 1790 and William Temple in 1792. Tragedy struck when the yellow fever epidemic hit Philadelphia in 1793 and claimed the lives of Dolley's husband, both of his parents, and Dolley's son William, leaving her a young widow with an infant child. The strong-willed Dolley was determined to persevere and make something of herself. Among her many courters at this time was the "Father of the Constitution" and author of the Bill of Rights, Representative James Madison of Virginia. They seemed to make an unlikely couple, as the longtime bachelor James was seventeen years Dolley's senior. He was also unlike most of the dashing gentlemen of his time, since he had not been a soldier, did not dance, and did not ride horses. However, Dolley eventually fell for the intelligent but dour James. They were married on September 15, 1794, and enjoyed a happy but childless marriage. After abandoning her Quaker roots for James's Episcopalianism, she was disowned by the Quakers.

Life's Work

Dolley appears to have completely shed her conservative Quaker upbringing after her second marriage and developed a love of music, gardens, and socializing. She also acquired a taste for fashion that could not have been further from the social standards of the day that included bright colors, scandalously low-cut dresses, and a bold hairstyle of large curls. Incredibly, for much of the early nineteenth century she was at the center of social life in Washington, D.C. During this time, Dolley was quite possibly the most widely known and beloved woman in the country. A highly capable woman, Dolley managed the Madison family plantation when James was away in Washington, D.C. Admired for her outgoing, pleasant personality, her legacy belongs to her famous social events. Even among present-day First Ladies, Dolley is widely considered to have been the most talented social hostess in the history of the White House. In this endeavor she was aided by what appears to have been a deep, selfless, and genuine love of people and a knack for remembering everyone's name.

In 1801, newly elected President Thomas Jefferson appointed James as his secretary of state. As a widower, Jefferson asked James's wife Dolley to help serve as the White House's social hostess. For eight years she presided over the social affairs of the Jefferson White House. This was followed by another eight years during which her husband was president of the United States from 1809 to 1817. It was Dolley who presided over the nation's first inaugural ball in 1809.

Among the Washington social crowd and much of the nation, Dolley was hailed as "Queen Dolley," "Lady Presidentress," or the "Queen of Washington City." Her socials were the events of the social season, and all of Washington awaited an invitation. Breaking with tradition, she served American dishes for dinner (even contacting people all over the country for recipes), rearranged rooms to better accommodate her guests, and defied convention by sitting at the head of the table at dinners. Dolley set a precedent for future First Ladies when she renovated and redecorated the White House. Strategically, she invited members of Congress to the White House so they could see the poor condition of the building; after securing congressional funding for the renovation project, she even worked with the supervising architect. She successfully blended European flair with American homespun simplicity in her entertaining and invited a wide array of guests to the White House. Although the historical record is far from complete, she seems to have made a positive impression on almost every visitor to the White House. She also emerged as a fashion trendsetter as the nation took a keen interest in her taste for European attire, jewels, bird plumes, and even what became known as "the Dolley Madison turban." Details of her social events and attire were reported in newspapers.

Along with her successful social role, she was the perfect political partner for James. In comparison with his subdued seriousness, she was funny, talkative, and engaging. As was the norm for women of the eighteenth and nineteenth centuries, Dolley had very little formal education and was not as well read or intellectual as her predecessor, Abigail Adams. She had been tutored at her childhood plantation home in Virginia and had received some education at a Quaker school in Pennsylvania. Yet, in an era during which women rarely spoke publicly and took no interest in politics, Dolley functioned as an advisor to her husband on both social and political matters. She traveled with him, campaigned with him, and appeared in public with him. James was proud of his wife's accomplishments. He appears to have recognized her social abilities and his limited interpersonal skills. He often sought and took her advice, appreciating her political astuteness, warm personal touch, and legendary tact.

Even though James had been the secretary of state, it was Dolley who was the diplomat. She took no formal or public role in politics and claimed to not be interested in political affairs. However, her actions revealed her many political contributions to James's presidency. Many historical accounts exist of Dolley disarming her husband's political opponents, charming his potential supporters, and captivating statesmen, dignitaries, and other White House guests. Dolley made sure she invited every member of Congress to dinner at least once during legislative sessions. In doing so, she was a century ahead of her time as the first presidential spouse to blend White House social events with political agendas. She also held socials in honor of U.S. accomplishments, including the capture of British ships during the War of 1812.

When the British sacked the capital city and set the White House ablaze during the War of 1812, Dolley was among the very last Americans to leave. The president and cabinet had already evacuated the city. Refusing pleas to abandon the capital city, Dolley watched the approach of the British

through a spy glass. Unconcerned about her own safety, she thought to load as many White House archives as possible (including official papers, china, and silver, as well as such artifacts as the famous Gilbert Stuart portrait of George Washington) onto a wagon while the British army literally marched into the city. With a wagon full of priceless items, she fled to Virginia at the last possible moment. Her courageous act inspired a nation stung by the defeat and the August 24, 1814, burning of the White House. After the war an unfazed but heroic Dolley continued entertaining in her temporary quarters in a private home on Penn Avenue in Washington, D.C. She proclaimed to a cheering city, "We shall rebuild Washington!"

Summary

After James's second term as president ended in 1817, he and Dolley returned to Montpelier, their plantation home in Virginia, where they enjoyed a comfortable retirement highlighted by the many visitors and guests who attended Dolley's parties. Dolley continued to support her husband's political work by taking dictation for him through his failing health during the last years of his life. James Madison died in 1836 and, in the autumn of 1837, Dolley returned to the capital city to live. She moved into a small home that James had built some years earlier. Back in Washington, Dolley returned to the social and political life, enjoying an honorary seat on the Senate floor, attending social events, and receiving lifetime franking privileges from Congress. She wisely sold James's official papers to the government for $30,000 to both assure their preservation and provide for herself financially. She remained a central figure until her death in 1849.

Dolley Madison loved living in the White House and was perhaps the first presidential spouse as well as one of the few women prior to the twentieth century to develop an identity of her own beyond that of her husband. She fashioned the social side of the office of First Lady and consequently became a role model for many future First Ladies. On her death, President Zachary Taylor aptly described her as "Our First Lady for a half-century."

Bibliography

Anthony, Carl Sferrazza. *First Ladies: The Saga of the Presidents' Wives and Their Power, 1789-1961.* New York: Morrow, 1990. Contains a chapter on each First Lady, including Dolley. Anthony provides both personal and political details of Dolley's life.

Arnett, Ethel Stephens. *Mrs. James Madison: The Incomparable Dolley.* Greensboro, N.C.: Piedmont Press, 1972. A source for Dolley's life before meeting James Madison and later in the White House. Examines her personality and character.

Gould, Lewis L., ed. *American First Ladies: Their Lives and Their Legacy.* New York: Garland, 1996. Contains a chapter on each First Lady that includes an examination of their contributions to the presidency. Includes a helpful bibliography.

Hunt-Jones, Conover. *Dolley and the "Great Little Madison."* Washington, D.C.: American Institute of Architects Foundation, 1977. Hunt-Jones explores the Madison's marriage, their long life together, and Dolley's influence on her "Great Little Madison."

Ketcham, Ralph. *James Madison: A Biography.* New York: Macmillan, 1971. Insights on the life and presidency of the fourth president. Dolley is discussed periodically, but it also benefits one studying Dolley to know James Madison, his times, and life in the Madison White House.

Quackenbush, Robert. *James Madison and Dolley Madison and Their Times.* New York: Pippin Press, 1992. A children's book that is appropriate for elementary and middle school students.

Truman, Margaret. *First Ladies: An Intimate Group Portrait of White House Wives.* New York: Random House, 1995. Contains numerous discussions of Dolley's sense of style, famous social events, renovation of the White House, and heroism during the War of 1812. The book is written in a conversational, nonacademic style and is very readable.

Robert P. Watson

THOMAS ROBERT MALTHUS

Born: February 13, 1766; the Rookery, near Dorking, Surrey, England

Died: December 23, 1834; Claverton, Bath, England

Area of Achievement: Economics

Contribution: The original professor of political economy, Malthus will be forever linked to discussions of the population problem. Terms such as "Malthusian economics" and "neo-Malthusianism" have achieved a permanent place in the English language and suggest the high level of controversy which his work engendered.

Early Life

Thomas Robert Malthus was born on February 13, 1766, at his father's estate, the Rookery, near Dorking, England. Some biographies incorrectly list February 14, the day of his baptism, as his birthdate. His father, Daniel Malthus, was an Oxford-educated lawyer and a gentleman of some means, as well as an intellectual of the Enlightenment and a devotee of the French thinker Jean-Jacques Rousseau.

Malthus grew up in a genteel, intellectually invigorating environment provided by his father, who was caught up in the exciting ideas of the Age of Reason and the French Revolution. Indeed, Malthus' great work was initially a reaction to many of those ideas, especially the notion that through the use of reason, humankind could achieve perfection. Privately educated under a series of tutors, Malthus entered Jesus College of Cambridge in 1784 when he was eighteen. There he won prizes in Latin and English grammar, but his chief study was, as his father had suggested, mathematics. In that area, he was graduated as Ninth Wrangler (high honors) and was awarded a fellowship.

Upon graduation, Malthus took religious orders in 1788 and became a pastor in the Church of England, taking charge of the rectory in the village of Surrey in 1793. In 1804, he gave up his fellowship and married Harriet Eckersall, his cousin and eleven years his junior. A devoted family man, his home life appears to have been quite stable, and his wife was reputed to have been a charming hostess. He sired three children—two sons and a daughter who died when she was seventeen, the one note of tragedy in his personal life.

Malthus was a handsome man, with an aristocratic nose, sharp eyes, and a high forehead. He dressed as a gentleman of the day and wore his curly hair short with sideburns. Contemporary sources generally indicate that his personality, despite the heated controversy which ensnared him, was genuinely amiable and pleasant. Even his worst enemies frequently noted his sincerity and fairness. He was, by all reports and in spite of the terrible things which have been said about him, a gentle man.

Life's Work

In 1805, Malthus received an appointment as professor of history and political economy at the newly founded East India College, the purpose of which was to train civil servants for work in India. This was the first such professorship established, and Malthus retained it until his death. He was a dedicated teacher, called "Pop" by his students.

By the time he left religious work for education, Malthus had already written the book which resulted in his historical significance: *An Essay on the Principle of Population, as It Affects the Future Improvement of Society, with Remarks on the Speculations of Mr. Godwin, M. Condorcet, and Other Writers* (1798). Despite his other contributions, it was this work which marked him as a man of controversy. The original work was fairly short and published anonymously, but it became widely read, quickly sold out, and generated considerable discussion, not all of it positive. From 1799 to 1802, Malthus traveled widely throughout Europe, going as far as Russia, collecting additional data on his theory that the growth of population will always outstrip the production of food. The second edition, of 1803, was greatly expanded, and while critics still quote from the first edition, it is the 1803 version which represents the fuller accounting of Malthusian principles. During his lifetime, *An Essay on the Principle of Population* went through six editions, and extracts and complete renditions remain in print.

Malthus was both attacked and admired in his day. In 1819, he was elected a Fellow of the Royal Society, and in 1821 he became a charter member of the Political Economy Club, along with David Ricardo, his close friend, and James Mill. In 1824, he received admission as a royal associate into the

Royal Academy of Literature. Also a member of the French Institute and the Royal Academy in Berlin, in 1834 he became a Charter Fellow of the Statistical Society. During the Christmas vacation of 1834, he and his family visited his father-in-law at Claverton, Bath. There, on December 23, Malthus died of a heart attack. He is buried in Bath Abbey. His wife survived him by thirty years.

Students of Malthus and Malthusian economics can easily become confused by the controversy surrounding Malthus and particularly by arguments advanced in his name that actually bear no relation to the man or his ideas. It is best to begin by asking how did Malthus come to write *An Essay on the Principle of Population* and what did he say in it? As the subtitle suggests, Malthus wrote in response to certain ideas put forth by the reforming Englishman William Godwin and the equally perfectionistic Frenchman, the Marquis de Condorcet. Simply stated, Godwin and Condorcet believed that with the use of reason and education there could be no end to human progress. They both foresaw continued physical, intellectual, and moral advancement until a perfect society resulted. In

discussing these ideas with his father, Malthus entered certain objections to such a happy view, and his father suggested that he put them in writing. Thus came about the first *An Essay on the Principle of Population*.

Like so many of his contemporaries, Malthus admired science and mathematics, and he believed in a natural law which would inevitably prevent human perfection. The secret lay in the mathematical ratios which he understood to govern the growth of population and the production of food. Population, he said, increased geometrically, while food or agriculture could be increased only arithmetically. Thus, human population would increase by the following ratio: 1, 2, 4, 8, 16, 32, 64, 128, and so forth. Food, however, would increase thus: 1, 2, 3, 4, 5, 6, 7, 8. To many in this early age of science, and an age so eager to discover natural laws, the simple proof that Malthus offered seemed inescapable: There would never be enough food to feed the world's population.

To the question of what could be done about this situation, Malthus had little in the way of encouraging answers. In his day, there were no dependable methods of birth control (which was at any rate regarded as immoral), and abortion was illegal. The only natural limits to population growth appeared to lie in war, disease, and poverty. This depressing situation gave rise to attacks on Malthus and to his being called the Dismal Parson and to political economy becoming known as the Dismal Science. There were simply no checks on population that Malthus could find which did not come under the heading of either vice or misery. In the second edition in 1803, Malthus introduced the notion that a possible curb on population growth might rest in what he called "moral restraint," by which he meant the social responsibility to bear no more children than parents could properly maintain. While the addition of moral restraint is the greatest change that Malthus made in his theory, the inherent weakness of this restriction, since it depends on individual control, is and was obvious.

Viciously attacked during his lifetime, Malthus and his ideas actually became even less popular in the second half of the nineteenth century. Marxists were particularly bitter in finding that Malthusian economics was merely a tool of the capitalist society to keep the poor oppressed. Humanitarians found the theory hard-hearted and mean-spirited and rejected it vigorously. More important, the mathematical analysis employed by Malthus simply did not withstand rigorous scrutiny. Food, critics observed, was organic, and thus it also increased geometrically. Additionally, technological advances made in agriculture seemed almost to eliminate hunger. By 1900, Malthus was generally dismissed as a pseudoscientist who had leaped to a gross generalization. The only school of thought which continued to embrace Malthus was that of some Social Darwinists (and, indeed, Charles Darwin had been influenced by Malthus) who found the population theory acceptable in the light of their emphasis on the struggle for survival.

In the twentieth century, however, Malthus emerged as an important symbol in a concept known as neo-Malthusianism. Ironically, this movement advocated birth control, which Malthus opposed as immoral. Nevertheless, after World War II it became apparent that in many areas of the world, particularly in underdeveloped countries, population was growing at an alarming rate. As the prospect, and often the reality, of famine loomed in Africa and Asia, calls for government-sponsored birth-control programs mounted. Some attempts were made in India and China. The problem, however, continues, as does the image of Malthus in this monumentally important issue.

Summary

Whatever the flaws of his analysis, Thomas Robert Malthus must be regarded as the father of demographic studies. In addition, he was an important and influential figure in the development of early nineteenth century economic thought. His influence on Darwin was certainly of enormous importance, as was his work on the diminishing returns of agricultural production. The Malthusian legacy is most evident in the continued use and misuse of his name, which has become synonymous with population studies and the population problem.

Bibliography

Dupaquier, Jacques, et al., eds. *Malthus Past and Present*. London and New York: Academic Press, 1983. A selection of papers presented in 1980 at the International Conference on Historical Demography. Contains useful information on the influences on Malthus, the conditions of his time, and the neo-Malthusian movement.

Gilbert, Geoffrey, ed. *Malthus: Critical Responses*. 4 vols. London: Routledge, 1997; New York: Routledge, 1998. This unusual collection brings together responses to Malthus' work by scientists, economists, and literary figures in Europe and the United States between 1798 and 1900. Although the bulk of the collection deals with his thoughts on population, essays also touch on the political economy.

Hollander, Samuel, ed. *An Essay on Population: The Six Editions*. 11 vols. London: Routledge, 1996. Examines Malthus' controversial 1798 "Essay on Population" and the six versions executed in the 28 subsequent years. The revisions show Malthus' reactions to negative comments leveled at the piece.

James, Patricia. *Population Malthus: His Life and Times*. London and Boston: Routledge, 1979. An excellent biography.

Malthus, Thomas Robert. *An Essay on the Principle of Population, Text Sources and Background Criticism*. Edited by Philip Appleman. New York: Norton, 1976. Contains selections from Condorcet, Godwin, and the two important editions of *An Essay on the Principle of Population*, as well as responses, positive and negative, from the nineteenth and twentieth centuries.

Marx, Karl, and Friedrich Engels. *Marx and Engels on Malthus: Selections from the Writings of Marx and Engels Dealing with the Theories of Thomas Robert Malthus*. Edited and translated by Ronald L. Meek. London: Lawrence and Wishart, 1953; New York: International Publishers, 1954. The Marxist condemnation of Malthus in the nineteenth century.

Petersen, William. *Malthus*. Cambridge, Mass.: Harvard University Press, 1979. An intellectual biography that properly sets the work of Malthus into the context of early nineteenth century thought.

Pullen, J. M. *T. R. Malthus: Unpublished Papers in the Collection of Kanto Gakuen University*. Cambridge and New York: Cambridge University Press, 1998. A collection of documents by and about Malthus that were previously unpublished and only recently discovered. Included are letters, essays, sermons, and lecture notes illuminating Malthus' personal and private relationships.

Turner, Michael, ed. *Malthus and His Time*. London: Macmillan, and New York: St. Martin's Press, 1986. Further selections, somewhat more technical, from the 1980 international conference on historical demography.

Wood, John Cunningham, ed. *Thomas Robert Malthus*. 4 vols. London and Dover, N.H.: Croom Helm, 1986. A detailed and quite helpful overview of the work and importance of Malthus, including selections from contemporary sources to the 1980's.

Roy Talbert, Jr.

ÉDOUARD MANET

Born: January 23, 1832; Paris, France
Died: April 30, 1883; Paris, France
Area of Achievement: Art
Contribution: In a relatively short career of just over twenty years, Manet challenged the conventions of European art by creating a body of paintings, drawings, and etchings manifesting novel approaches both to form and to content. His works and his career were the focal points of the struggle for artistic independence waged by a generation of French artists and writers in the mid-nineteenth century.

Early Life

Édouard Manet was born in Paris at 5 rue de Grands Augustins, a street bordering the Seine, not far from the Cathedral of Nôtre Dame. His father, Auguste Manet, was a high official in the Ministry of Justice. At the time of Édouard's birth, his mother, Eugénie-Désirée Manet, was twenty years old, fourteen years her husband's junior. The family was prosperous from the beginning, and in keeping with its social status Eugénie Manet held twice-weekly receptions for the influential associates of her husband; Auguste, nevertheless, preferred the company of scholars and ecclesiastics to that of his colleagues.

From the ages of six to eight, Édouard attended the Institut Poiloup in Vaugirard; in his twelfth year, he began studies at a boarding school, the Collège Rollin, where he befriended Antonin Proust, who later wrote about his childhood friend. During these school years, Manet and Proust frequently visited the Louvre, accompanied by the former's maternal uncle, Captain Édouard Fournier, who encouraged his nephew's interest in art by paying for drawing lessons. Though Édouard excelled at drawing and soon expressed his wish to follow an artistic career, Auguste Manet's ambition for his eldest son was that he become a lawyer (Édouard's brothers, Eugène and Gustave, born in 1833 and 1835, were to become civil servants). Since his teachers at the Collège Rollin had found him "distracted" and "slightly frivolous," in July, 1848, Auguste Manet proposed a compromise in which Édouard would apply to the École Navale, or naval school. Failing the entrance examination, he embarked on a training ship instead, sailing on December 8 for Rio de Janeiro, Brazil. He is re-ported to have found the cruise boring; after his return to France in June, 1849, having again failed the entrance examination, he was finally allowed to study for an artistic career. By January of 1850, he had registered as an art student to copy paintings in the Louvre, and in September he and Antonin Proust joined the studio of Thomas Couture, a noted painter of innovative, though not revolutionary, sympathies.

Soon after his return from the sea voyage, Édouard and his brother Eugène began to take piano lessons from a young Dutch woman, Suzanne Leenhoff. It seems clear that his association with Suzanne quickly blossomed into love, and when she became pregnant in the spring of 1851, Manet, who was still required to obtain his father's permission to go out at night, succeeded in keeping his liaison a secret from him. The child born to Suzanne Leenhoff was registered as the son of a probably fictitious Koëlla but was presented socially as Suzanne's younger brother, Léon. It was not until 1863, more than a year after the death of Auguste Manet, that Suzanne Leenhoff and Manet were married.

Living in his parents' home, and with their financial support for his study of art, Manet continued working at the studio of Couture during the early 1850's. His relationship with his teacher was frequently stormy, and Manet acquired a reputation as a rebellious pupil, but Couture was in many ways a good choice of teacher. He represented a middle ground between the academic side of French art, with its often-rigid adherence to tradition, and the experimental, individualistic tendencies of artists such as Honoré Daumier and Gustave Courbet. Manet was, by nature, a somewhat conservative personality—he was always well dressed, even fashionable, and he enjoyed the civil pleasures of bourgeois life—but as an artist he challenged from the outset many of the conventions of painting, even as he learned from the masters of the past.

Life's Work

After leaving Couture's studio in 1856, Manet occasionally brought his works to the master for criticism, a circumstance that must have been more than a polite gesture. Manet's interest in tradition was profound, but his studies of the past were undertaken to achieve a personal understanding of the

old masters rather than to emulate their styles. Like many young Parisian artists, Manet often copied paintings in the Louvre and elsewhere. He was particularly attracted to Spanish masters such as Diego Velázquez but also copied works by Peter Paul Rubens and Eugène Delacroix, from whom he personally requested permission to copy *The Barque of Dante*. Equally important for his future as an artist, however, was Manet's devotion to recording the life of the Paris boulevards, where he daily observed the activities of all levels of society. Despite his comfortable family background, Manet had an instinctive appreciation for the urban poor, and in 1859 he submitted his painting *The Absinthe Drinker* to the Salon, a biennial exhibition of art which was judged by the established painters of the day. *The Absinthe Drinker* is based in part upon Manet's observation of a ragpicker named Collardet, part of a legion of characters who were increasingly visible as a result of the redevelopment of Paris begun in 1853 under the direction of Baron Eugène Haussmann. Although such a subject was considered appropriate for the popular press, it was thought too vulgar for the Salon, and Manet's painting was re-

jected. In 1861, however, two of his works were accepted into the exhibition; one of them, *The Spanish Singer*, received an honorable mention.

At this time in his career, Manet's art had been noticed appreciatively by a few knowledgeable critics, but his audience was comparatively small. An event in 1863 changed not only Manet's relationship to the public but also that of a generation of French artists. This was the Salon des Refusés, an exhibition held by order of the Emperor Napoleon III, which was to include all of the work rejected by the jury from the regular Salon of 1863. The emperor's decree invited the public to be the final judge of the quality of the art rejected, and the public responded with tumultuous curiosity and derision. Manet's principal submission, *Déjeuner sur l'herbe* (luncheon on the grass), while appreciated by a discerning few, was taken by many visitors to the exhibition to be the flagship of artistic revolt. The work shows a nude woman with two fashionably dressed men in a modern parklike setting, and although the painting is based upon various historical prototypes, its broad, painterly technique and contemporary setting seem intended to challenge the public's artistic taste and its moral standards. *Déjeuner sur l'herbe* marks the beginning of a widespread but often-hostile interest in the dissident claims of modern art; the polarization of the art world into "academics" and the "avant-garde" had begun.

In Manet's paintings of the early 1860's, one sees the influence of his friend the poet Charles Baudelaire. In an essay written years earlier, Baudelaire had called for an art based upon "the heroism of modern life" which would show "how great and how poetic we are with our neckties and our varnished boots." Manet's emphasis on clothes, costume, fashion, and other aspects of everyday life, rather than giving a trivial view of society, shows urban life as a complex network of signs which require a skilled interpreter. The emergence of the city as the fulcrum of modern culture is one of the implicit themes of Manet's art, though this is seen more often in his graphic works than in his paintings.

Manet caused another public outcry at the Salon of 1865 with his *Olympia*, which depicts a nude courtesan, attended by a black servant and a cat, looking impudently toward the viewer. One critic advised that "women on the point of giving birth and proper young girls would be well-advised to flee this spectacle," and two guards were stationed by the painting, which had already been removed to an obscure and dishonorable location within the immense exhibition. The audacity of *Olympia* far outdistanced that of *Déjeuner sur l'herbe*, and in addition to suffering criticism on account of the theme, Manet came under attack for the structure and technique of the painting. Courbet said that it looked flat, like a playing card, and a newspaper critic accused Manet of "an almost childish ignorance of the fundamentals of drawing." It is clear that Manet, though not systematically courting the disfavor of the public, was willing to suffer incomprehension both of his treatment of subjects and of his style. He was fully capable of painting appealing subjects in a more traditional manner, but for complex reasons he ruled out forms of compromise which might have gained for him a higher level of public esteem. He subsequently painted popular pictures, such as *The Good Glass of Beer* (1873), and though he wished for broad acceptance of his art he was never inclined to pursue it.

In many of his works of the 1870's Manet sought an increasing naturalism by emphasizing lighter colors and more varied surfaces. In paintings made in 1874 at Argenteuil, a few miles northwest of Paris, Manet drew close to the group which became known that year as the Impressionists. He borrowed the light and color of his younger friends Claude Monet and Pierre-Auguste Renoir, but his canvases are more deliberately composed and are much less extraverted than theirs of the same period. Some critics who had been sympathetic to Manet's work, including the novelist Émile Zola, considered Manet's technical gifts unequal to his ambition of painting in the open air; others recognized that these works were, in part, the result of exacting formal experimentation. In a famous remark made in 1890, the painter Maurice Denis asserted that "a painting—before it is a battle horse, a nude woman, or some anecdote—is essentially a flat surface covered with colors assembled in a certain order." To a significant extent, Manet's work of the 1870's is a precocious fulfillment of this concept, particularly in a work such as *The Rue Mosnier with Pavers* (1878), which brings the spontaneous brushwork, subtle coloration, light, and movement of the Argenteuil paintings back to the streets of Paris. Manet had by this time developed fully a means of drawing with strokes of paint which both represents objects in space and unifies the painting as an assemblage of shapes and colors.

In late 1878, Manet began to have trouble with his leg, and by September of the following year he was seeking treatment for it. The precise nature of his ailment has never been specified, but it seems likely that he was suffering from the advanced stages of a syphilitic infection contracted in his youth. During his last three years, he was in pain, and small drawings and oil paintings began to take the place of larger works, reflecting his diminished mobility. There are a number of fine portraits and still lifes dating from 1880 through 1882, and there is also one major subject painting, *A Bar at the Folies-Bergère*. This work, which is about three feet high by four feet wide, is widely considered to be one of Manet's finest works. It shows a barmaid at the celebrated Paris "café-concert," standing behind a marble counter on which have been placed bottles of ale and champagne, a compote with mandarin oranges, and a glass holding two pale roses. Behind the melancholy and distracted young woman, a mirror reflects a brightly lit crowd which seems unaware of a trapeze artist whose green-slippered feet are whimsically shown in the upper left-hand corner of the painting. There are many subtle, calculated ambiguities concerning things viewed either directly or in reflection. Manet seems to have decided, at the end of an artistic career often criticized for a lack of psychological insight, to address the human element in one final, haunting but luminous canvas. In early April, 1883, as Manet's health precipitously declined, he briefly considered taking lessons in miniature painting from a friend, but by April 20 his condition required that his left leg be amputated, and on April 30 he died.

Summary

Édouard Manet has been celebrated as a rebellious artist who was rejected by his own time; however, such a stereotyping of his career ignores not only the complexities of his personality and artistic production but also the varieties of response which his work elicited from his contemporaries and from the generation that followed. For years, many critics and art historians fostered the notion of a noble, progressive lineage of art which was engaged in perpetual conflict with a defensive, static "establishment" art supported by reactionary social forces; Manet, quite understandably, was installed as the great progenitor of the progressive trend. As the discipline of art history established a broader foundation of fact and methodology during the first half of the twentieth century and the issues of mid- and late-nineteenth century art became both clearer and more intricate, the assessment of Manet's achievement in particular came to be seen more as a problem in defining the changing relationship of artists and audiences than of arriving at objectively valid, stabilized conclusions about his paintings.

Manet was somewhat conservative by temperament, but he was also creatively independent. Though many of his images involved adaptations of ideas and images borrowed from the past, and thus appealed to aspects of public taste, other elements of his work were vibrantly novel and challenged both the visual imagination and social consciousness of his contemporaries. These contrasting elements in Manet dictated that he could not rely on conventional taste to provide him with a constituency; his success was one that might be earned only by tremendous labor and courage. Finally, it was a largely posthumous success. In his later career, he frequently despaired at the inconsistency with which his work was received, believing, perhaps somewhat naïvely, that it should suffice for an artist to present sincere work. Like many of his contemporaries, he hoped that the public would be able to recognize and value sincerity and commitment and would reward it at least as strongly as virtuosity and predictability. In hoping for this kind of relationship with an ever-expanding mass audience, Manet presents to history a modernity of outlook in keeping with the adventurousness of his finest paintings.

Bibliography

Adler, Kathleen. *Manet*. Oxford: Phaidon Press, 1982. An excellent source of collateral illustrations concerning Manet's life and times, as well as of his art and its sources. The text emphasizes the eclectic nature of the artist's work and provides an integrated view of modern scholarship concerned with Manet's place in nineteenth century art.

Bareau, Juliet W. *Manet, Monet, and the Gare Saint-Lazare*. New Haven, Conn.: Yale University Press, 1998. Discussion of Manet's "Gare Saint-Lazare" based on new research that identifies precisely the site used in the painting. Also includes accounts of Manet's relationships with poet/critic Stephane Mallarme.

Bataille, Georges. *Manet*. London: Macmillan, and New York: Rizzoli, 1983. Françoise Cachin, in her introduction to this reprinting of Bataille's 1955 essay, shows how the author's view of Manet was colored by his close association with the artistic trends of his own time. Nevertheless, she concedes, Bataille's essay has "unusual penetration and appeal."

Blunden, Maria, and Godrey Blunden. *Impressionists and Impressionism*. New York: Rizzoli, 1976; London: Macmillan, 1980. Manet is accorded only his share of attention in this survey volume, but contemporary photographs and documents, many of which are seldom reproduced, vividly reveal the artist and his contemporaries. Text and images are presented in a loosely integrated but nevertheless effective manner.

Cachin, Françoise, Anne Coffin Hanson, et al. *Manet: 1832-1883*. New York: Metropolitan Museum of Art, 1983. This large, indispensable volume was issued in connection with a major international exhibition organized to commemorate the one hundredth anniversary of the painter's death. There are several fine essays, and the book is illustrated with hundreds of exemplary color and black-and-white plates, most of which are discussed in some detail by accompanying text.

Fried, Michael. *Manet's Modernism or The Face of Painting in the 1860's*. Chicago: University of Chicago Press, 1998. Discusses Manet's work and its place in art history.

Hamilton, George Heard. *Manet and His Critics*. New Haven, Conn.: Yale University Press, 1954; London: Yale University Press, 1986. This book is a chronological study of the criticism published about Manet and his art during his lifetime, with some mention of critical material appearing after his death. The mediocre illustrations are suitable only for reference.

Mauner, George. *Manet, Peintre-Philosophe: A Study of the Painter's Themes*. University Park: Pennsylvania State University Press, 1975. The author is one of many who have sought to provide a corrective to a once-prevalent view of Manet as a painter obsessed with structural matters and indifferent to meaning; his scholarly arguments are involved but clearly stated. The lack of color plates does not diminish the book's interest.

Rewald, John. *The History of Impressionism*. 4th ed. New York: Museum of Modern Art, and London: Secker and Warburg, 1973. This masterly chronological study of the Impressionists does full justice to nine artists in addition to Manet, but Manet's art is unquestionably the author's touchstone. There is an excellent annotated calendar covering the years 1855-1886, as well as an extensive bibliography and an index.

Schneider, Pierre. *The World of Manet, 1832-1883*. New York: Time-Life Books, 1968. The popular format of this book should not be allowed to obscure the fact that it contains a wealth of information. The quality and variety of its reproductions are matched by an intelligent, readable text.

Sloane, Joseph C. "Manet." In *French Painting Between the Past and the Present: Artists, Critics, and Traditions from 1848 to 1870*. Princeton, N.J.: Princeton University Press, 1951. The author's emphasis is upon the reaction of critics and the public to Manet's paintings of the 1860's, and he shows why the artist's innovations were met with resistance. Includes an excellent bibliography.

Tucker, Paul H. *Manet's "Le Dejeuner sur l'Herbe."* Cambridge and New York: Cambridge University Press, 1998. A collection of essays by noted scholars in French modern art providing six readings of Manet's controversial work.

Wadley, Nicholas. *Manet*. London: Hamlyn, 1967. This survey of the artist's paintings is valuable principally for its good color plates, which are briefly annotated. A modest essay is complemented by a chronology and extensive quotations from Manet and his contemporaries.

C. S. McConnell

HENRY EDWARD MANNING

Born: July 15, 1808; Copped Hall, Totteridge,
  Hertfordshire, England
Died: January 14, 1892; London, England
Areas of Achievement: Religion and social reform
Contribution: Manning combined a deep Christian
  faith with an active Christian conscience. As an
  Anglican cleric he was an avid reformer and the
  leader of the Oxford Movement. In 1851, Manning converted to the Roman Catholic faith and
  continued his careers as theologian, reformer,
  and philanthropist. Manning contributed greatly
  to the rebirth of Roman Catholicism in England.

Early Life

Henry Edward Manning was born on July 15,
1808, at Copped Hall, Totteridge, Hertfordshire,
England. He was the third and youngest son of
William Manning, a West Indian merchant and parliamentarian, and his second wife, Mary, the
daughter of Henry Leroy Hunter. The Hunter family claimed Italian extraction, "Hunter" being a
translation of "Venature." As a youngster, Manning
was educated at Harrow, and on April 2, 1827, he
matriculated at Balliol College, Oxford. While
Manning was at Balliol, his father suffered severe
financial problems that eliminated any possibility
of Manning's pursuing a career in Parliament. Instead, Manning applied himself to his studies and
received a first-class degree in 1830. He then obtained a post in the colonial office. At the suggestion of Miss Favell Lee Bevar, an evangelical Anglican, he considered a career in the Church and
then returned to Oxford at Merton College to study
for the priesthood. On December 23, 1832, he was
ordained and at once took a curateship at Wollav-
ington-cum-Graffham, Sussex. In 1833, he received his M.A. and was installed as rector, and in
the same year he married Caroline Sargeant, the
late Rector John Sargeant's third daughter.

As a parish priest, Manning was deeply loved by
his parishioners and devoted to their care. He successfully rebuilt the churches in his parish. Manning participated in the Ecclesiastical commission
of 1835 and was active on the diocesan boards of
the National Society for Promoting the Education
of the Poor.

In 1837, Manning was appointed to the rural
deanery of Midhurst. It was there that Mrs. Manning died of tuberculosis on July 24, 1837. Manning was deeply sorrowed by his wife's death. His
marriage, although childless, had been extremely
happy. Manning's affection for his wife can be
seen in the fact that he observed the anniversary of
her death until he died.

In 1840, Manning was advanced to the Archdeaconry of Chichester. Manning's appointment was
hailed as a "blessing for the church" by *The Christian Remembrance.* Advancement to a bishopric or
an even higher post seemed assured. At this point,
as an important figure in the Church of England,
Manning showed no sympathy toward the Church
of Rome. Indeed, he preached against papal power.
Yet Manning not only believed in one holy, catholic, and apostolic Church but also espoused baptismal regeneration, apostolic succession, and Richard Hooker's theory of the Eucharist. He also hated
the idea of the Erastian state and deplored the decline of the church parliament of convocation. Still,
Manning was not active in the Tractarian, or Oxford, Movement until the secession to Rome of
Newman and W. G. Ward. At that point, Manning
became one of the leaders of the movement. He
was liked and trusted by most of his colleagues in
the Church.

Life's Work

The year 1847 was a momentous one for Manning,
marking a decisive turning point in his life. A tour
of the Continent impressed him with the vitality of
the Roman Catholic Church and the difficulty of
explaining the Anglican position to foreigners.
Upon his return to England, Manning resumed his
activities. The year 1850, however, brought Manning to a decision. In that year, George Gorham, a
Calvinist theologian, was refused appointment to a
living because of his holding that divine grace was
not imparted at baptism. The bishop's refusal was
reversed on an appeal to the Judicial Committee of
the Privy Council, an action which invited controversy. A protest was circulated which stated that to
regard an article of faith as a debatable question
meant that the Anglican church could not assure its
members the grace of the sacraments and the re-
mission of sins. Manning signed the protest but,
significantly, his good friend William Ewart Gladstone did not. At this point, Manning was asked to
consider the founding of an Anglo-Catholic "free
church" but declined on the grounds that "three
hundred years ago we [England] had left a good
ship for a boat. I am not going to leave a boat for a

tub." On top of this decision, the bull reestablishing a Roman Catholic hierarchy in England caused 1850 to be dubbed the year of papal aggression. Thousands of meetings were held protesting papal authority, including one in Chichester Cathedral on November 22, 1850. This was Manning's last official act in the Anglican church. He renounced his archdeaconry and withdrew to London, where he was a communicant at St. Paul's, Knightsbridge.

On April 6, 1851, Passion Sunday, Manning was received into the Church of Rome at the Jesuits church, Mayfair, London. He was confirmed by Cardinal Nicholas Wiseman on April 11, tonsured on April 29, admitted to four minor orders on April 30, admitted to the subdiaconate on May 25 and to the diaconate on June 8, and ordained to the priesthood on June 15.

The fall of 1851 saw Manning at the Academie di Nobili Ecclesiastici in Rome. He spent the next three years studying at the college and summering in England and Ireland. Pope Pius IX took great interest in Manning and from the beginning saw him frequently on a private basis. On January 24, 1854, he was given the degree of doctor of divinity by the Pope and made provost of the chapter at Westminster. On May 31, 1857, he was installed as superior of the Congregation of the Oblates of St. Charles at St. Mary's Church, Bays Water, which he had founded.

For the next eight years, Manning devoted his time to preaching, to teaching in the slums of Westminster, and to the defense of the temporal power of the Pope. In 1860, he received the title of monsignor.

Upon the death of Cardinal Wiseman on February 23, 1865, Manning preached the funeral sermon. On April 30, 1865, the Pope appointed Manning to the vacant see of Wiseman over three other candidates. He was consecrated archbishop on June 8, 1865, in the largest Catholic assembly seen since the Reformation. On September 29, 1865, Pius IX conferred the pallium on Manning.

As archbishop, Manning made full use of his powers, and he continued to do so after he became a cardinal ten years later. For the rest of his life, he devoted his time not only to theological writings but also to humanitarian causes. He was not interested in building a Catholic cathedral in London, although in 1903 the Catholic Westminster Cathedral was opened on ground Manning had acquired. Manning was active in improving and expanding the Catholic school system. He established a diocesan seminary of St. Thomas at Hammersmith. From 1880 to 1887, he served on the Royal Commission of Education and was responsible for much of the work in the Education Act of 1891 that dealt with voluntary schools. He also advocated temperance and abstained from alcohol for the last twenty years of his life. He campaigned for restrictive legislation on the alcohol traffic and founded the temperance society known as the League of the Cross. Manning was active also in the Irish nationalist movement, favoring home rule, reform of the land laws, and disestablishment of the Irish church. On the labor front, Manning sat on the royal commission of 1884-1885 for improving working-class housing. He was interested in workers' rights, child-labor laws, better housing, better education, and relief for the starving poor. In the famous London Dockers' Strike of August, 1889, it was Manning's exceptional powers as a diplomat and advocate of labor rights that ended the strike peacefully on September 16—hence the name for the strike's resolution, "the Cardinal's peace."

In his theological writing, Manning was an Ultramontane for his support of the supremacy of papal power and the doctrine of infallibility. He wrote in defense of communion in onekind, the doctrine of the Sacred Heart, and on the Holy Spirit. Despite his deep devotion to papal power, Manning remained devoted to England and the growth of ecumenism. He worked with the Nonconformists on education bills. Again and again, Manning held the position that England had never deliberately rejected the Roman Catholic faith but rather had been robbed of it by her rulers. He believed that Protestanism would eventually become extinct because of its accommodations to modern rationalism, and he hoped for England's return to the Roman fold. He did not live to see it, for he died on January 14, 1892, from bronchitis. Manning was buried in St. Mary's Cemetery, Kensal Green. His net worth was less than three thousand pounds because of his devotion to charity.

Summary

Henry Edward Manning's early career reflected the spiritual complexities of the Oxford Movement. His search for spiritual peace and his growing disillusionment with the true significance of state control were feelings with which many Anglicans could identify. Moreover, although Manning had regarded his submission to Rome as the end of his career as a cleric, this did not prove so. Manning, unlike Newman, retained the affection of most Anglicans while being deeply appreciated by members of the Roman Catholic Church. Under Manning's leadership, the Roman Catholic Church in England grew in numbers and influence. At the same time, Manning continued his devotion to all the humanitarian causes for which he had worked throughout his clerical career. He was a hero to the poor and the working class regardless of their religious affiliation.

Manning was not, however, simply an ecclesiastical statesman. He was a prolific theological writer, although much of his work was polemical in regard to papal power. He believed that Roman Catholicism was most concerned with the predicament of the worker in the modern state. In this, he presaged modern Catholic views of the world and the Church as being one sphere.

Manning's influence lies in his deep contribution to the revival of Roman Catholicism within England during the nineteenth century. Less obvious is the impact of his commitment to the welfare of the common man. In his humanitarian efforts, Manning served England well as both an Anglican and a Catholic.

Bibliography

Fitzsimons, John. *Manning: Anglican and Catholic*. London: Burns and Oates, 1951; Westport, Conn.: Greenwood Press, 1979. An excellent account of Manning's conversion to Roman Catholicism. Emphasizes Manning's belief that the Church of England was the closest approximation to a perfect church but that only Rome could sustain his intellectual, sentimental, and emotional nature.

Gray, Robert. *Cardinal Manning: A Biography*. London: Weidenfeld and Nicolson, and New York: St. Martin's Press, 1985. Gives a detailed description of Manning's High Church background and belief in good works. Shows that the estrangement between Gladstone and Manning after his conversion was a result of Gladstone's fear of papal political power. A valuable study of Manning's dedication to humanitarian causes, which stemmed from his belief that the Church must stand in contrast with the uncaring modern state system.

Leslie, Sir Shane. *Cardinal Manning: His Life and Labours*. London: Burns and Oates, 1921; New York: Kenedy, 1954. The thesis of this biography is that Manning was a theologian who, although

born into Anglicanism, was by nature destined for Rome. An interesting undercurrent of this book is its examination of how prominent Victorians were disillusioned by the Church of England's apathy toward the social problems of the day. Valuable for its insights into Manning's contemporaries as well as for its account of his life and thought.

McClelland, Vincent Alan. *Cardinal Manning: His Public Life and Influence, 1865-1892*. London and New York: Oxford University Press, 1962. A detailed study of Manning's career as the head of the Roman Catholic Church in England. Stresses Manning's contributions to the lives of workers in England. Provides a clear picture of Manning's working habits, his differences with Newman, and his contributions to the social history of nineteenth century England.

Newsome, David. *The Convert Cardinals: John Henry Newman and Henry Edward Manning*. London: Murray, 1993. Dual biography of Manning and Newman, the two most famous converts to Catholicism.

―――. *The Wilberforces and Henry Manning: The Parting of Friends*. Cambridge, Mass.: Harvard University Press, and London: Murray, 1966. A detailed, scholarly examination of Manning's relationship with his cousin William Wilberforce and the other Wilberforces. Stresses that the estrangement between them was a result of the Wilberforces' unwillingness and/or inability to understand why he left the Church of England. Newsome contends that the basis of this difference concerned the role of the Church—Anglican or Roman Catholic—in modern society.

Pereiro, James. *Cardinal Manning: An Intellectual Biography*. New York: Oxford University Press, and Oxford: Clarendon Press, 1998. Pereiro follows Cardinal Manning's intellectual development within the historical context that affected his thought. Based on Manning's published works (many of which have not been used previously) and unused manuscript sources.

Reynolds, E. E. *Three Cardinals: Newman, Manning, and Wiseman*. London: Burns and Oates, and New York: Kenedy, 1958. This book, although only partly concerned with Manning, is important for the insight it gives on the development of his spiritual thought. Reynolds contends that Manning was most influenced by the thought of St. Thomas Aquinas and Richard Hooker, and that Manning became a Roman

Catholic not by conversion but because of what he believed as an Anglican.

Strachey, Lytton. *Eminent Victorians*. London: Chatto and Windus, and New York: Harcourt Brace, 1918. A dated and acerbic minibiography of Manning and other prominent Victorians; ex-aggerates Manning's egotism and minor weaknesses. Strachey's biting if not vindictive style reveals, however, how deep a loss the Church of England believed Manning to be.

Rose Ethel Althaus Meza

DANIEL MANNIX

Born: March 4, 1864; Charleville, County Cork, Ireland

Died: November 6, 1963; Melbourne, Victoria, Australia

Areas of Achievement: Politics, religion, and government

Contribution: Mannix became the hero of working-class Catholics for his articulate and outspoken views in favor of Ireland and against British and Protestant influences in Australia which he believed threatened their rights to equality and justice.

Early Life

Daniel Mannix was born March 4, 1864, at Deerpark Farm in Charleville, County Cork, Ireland. His mother was the former Ellen Cagney and his father, Timothy Mannix, was a prosperous tenant farmer. Daniel was the first of eight children, of whom three died in infancy and another died as a young man in New York. Educated at first at the parish school and then by the Christian Brothers, at twelve Mannix enrolled at a classical school, a preliminary to entering the priesthood. A studious lad, while later boarding at St. Colman's College, Fermoy, he won a scholarship to Maynooth Seminary, where from 1882 his academic achievements set a standard by which all other students came to be measured.

Resembling his tall, slim mother in appearance, Mannix was ordained on June 8, 1890, and, after a year's postgraduate study, taught logic, metaphysics, and ethics at Maynooth. Qualifying for a doctorate of divinity in 1895 and receiving rapid promotion, first to the chair of higher philosophy and then, at the age of thirty-one, to the chair of moral theology, he also became a contributing editor to the *Irish Ecclesiastical Record.* By 1903, Mannix was college president.

During this time, Mannix acquired a reputation as a cold, abstemious, but competent administrator, a disciplinarian who held himself apart from the Gaelic revival then in progress. His main achievement was to gain affiliation for Maynooth to the Irish National University (established in 1908) and a seat on the senate for himself.

Life's Work

Mannix was forty-eight and president of Maynooth. The future looked very promising. Some imagined that he would succeed Archbishop William Walsh of Dublin. The Vatican, however, agreed to the request of Archbishop Thomas Carr of Melbourne that Mannix be appointed his coadjutor and his successor. A former vice president of Maynooth, a recognized scholar, and a firm believer in the value of a Catholic-run school system, Carr had held the archbishopric since 1886. He never consulted Mannix about his coming to Melbourne, and Mannix never questioned his appointment.

On his arrival in Melbourne on March 23, 1913, Mannix was incensed to find a policy of compulsory, free, and secular education in operation. In 1870, state aid to church schools had been abolished and continuing attempts, especially by Catholics and Anglicans, to have it restored were unsuccessful. Convinced that secular education was a "great stain upon the statute books of this free and progressive land," Mannix made its removal a paramount objective. Though state aid was not reinstated in his lifetime, he never ceased to confront politicians with the issue.

In the 1911 census only three percent of the Australian population were recorded as Irish born but more than twenty-two percent were Catholics, most of Irish descent. Surprisingly few approved of the Irish rebellion (the Easter Rising) in 1916; their sympathy was aroused, however, at Great Britain's tough response. Although official church policy was to stay on the sidelines, Mannix opposed Labour prime minister William Morris Hughes's proposal to introduce conscription for overseas service when recruiting numbers started to fall during World War I. Mannix argued, among other things, that by removing troops from Ireland, Great Britain would have enough men to continue the fight against Germany without drawing on more Australians.

Although in favor of supporting Great Britain in the war, Australians narrowly rejected conscription for overseas service in a referendum held on October 28, 1916. Expelled from the Labor Party for contravening the spirit of its platform, which was opposed to compulsion, Hughes led a "Win the War" party to victory at elections held the following May. Yet, despite a bitter campaign in December, a second referendum was lost by an increased margin. Once in favor, this time Victoria was opposed.

It is difficult to know how important Mannix's role was. Hundreds of thousands attended mass rallies to hear him exercise his renowned sarcastic wit, and yet a majority in the more populous state of New South Wales voted no in both referenda without Mannix to lead them. Hughes was not quite the ogre Mannix painted him. He had privately intervened on Irish demands for independence with British prime minister David Lloyd George, and he had quickly given assurances that Australia would not follow New Zealand's lead by requiring priests to argue for exemption before a magistrate. There is no doubt, Professor Patrick O'Farrell writes, that Catholic influence was much stronger in the Labor Party after the expulsion of Hughes and his followers: Only three out of twenty-four federal M.P.'s who left the party were Catholics. This did not result, however, in the more Catholic-minded party that Mannix desired.

Despite Vatican displeasure, Mannix continued his attack on Great Britain's Irish policy. In mid-1920, he was feted in the United States for his views, appearing at Madison Square Garden in New York City with the Irish Republican leader, Eamon de Valera. Mannix's planned visit to Ireland, however, was aborted by the British government. In a dramatic move, he was taken from the passenger steamer en route and landed by destroyer in England. Thus thwarted, he went on to Rome, where he persuaded Pope Benedict XV to censure British conduct in Ireland. Mannix never faltered in his support of de Valera and the republican cause. By 1925, when he was able to enter Ireland freely, he was said to be the only episcopal supporter of de Valera in all of Ireland and Australia.

During World War II, Mannix defended Irish neutrality, but by that time Communism, not the British, absorbed most of his attention. Again he went on the attack. In line with Vatican policy, in 1937 the Australian National Secretariat of Catholic Action had been established. A decision was taken in September, 1945, by Australian bishops to expand its political wing, the Catholic Social Studies Movement, which became known simply as the Movement. One of its founders was his protégé, Bartholomew Augustine Santamaria, who proposed that the Movement copy its enemy's organizational methods by creating cells with which to infiltrate the Labor movement and counter Communist elements. Once its existence became public in the mid-1950's, the activities of the Movement caused a rift among Catholics and a split in the Labor Party far more damaging than that of 1916-1917.

Summary

Daniel Mannix was not a humble man. During his presidency at Maynooth he got into a dispute with Father Michael O'Hickey, professor of Irish language studies since 1896, who wanted Irish to be made compulsory for university entrance. Postgraduate students supporting Hickey became so rebellious that Mannix closed the center and expelled five students, all ordained priests. Dismissed from his post, Hickey appealed to the Rota in Rome. By the time the tribunal concurred with Mannix that the matter was one only of seminary discipline, he had departed for Melbourne.

The rector of the Irish College in Rome, who was not consulted about Mannix's appointment, believed in 1912 that Australia should direct its own destiny. The Vatican unwittingly, however, sent a man who came to believe that being Irish was almost synonymous with being Catholic.

From 1820, successive colonial governments had allowed the gradual establishment of a Catholic church hierarchy in Australia. Its early members were actually paid from the public purse. A shortage of English priests meant that the majority of priests were recruited in Ireland, and so by the 1890's, powerful English Benedictine forces in Sydney had been silenced. From 1914, however, priests trained at St. Patrick's College in Manly, Sydney, were outspokenly in favor of Rome's policy of a native-born, locally trained clergy, and from 1930, Manly-trained priests were made bishops.

While allowing Catholic laity a greater say in church affairs, Mannix favored Irish-trained, preferably Maynooth, clergy. He was rude to the apostolic delegate Archbishop John Panico, whose arrival in March, 1936, was seen as a further attempt by the Vatican to limit Irish influence in the Australian church. In February, 1937, a Manly product, Justin Simonds, became the first Australian-born archbishop on his appointment to Hobart, Tasmania; in 1943, this was followed by the elevation of Sydney-born Norman T. Gilroy to the archbishopric of Sydney. Mannix remained, however, an unrepentant Irishman, a self-confessed supporter of the Sinn Féin.

Coming to Australia apparently crystallized Mannix's Irishness. Whereas at Maynooth he was prepared to receive royalty, in Melbourne during the visit of Queen Elizabeth II in 1954 he would not relax his rule of declining invitations to government house. He widened the rift between Catholics and Protestants by refusing to allow Catholic participation in any ceremonies including a religious segment. Partly because of his determination, the religious component was dropped from the trooping of the colors ceremony at military colleges and the traditional Anzac Day (April 25) service at Melbourne's Shrine of Remembrance. Even on the death of his old antagonist, Dr. Frederick W. Head, the Anglican archbishop, he would not enter St. Paul's Cathedral, waiting outside to join his funeral procession.

Mannix seemed to completely disregard the effect of his much-publicized anticonscription activities on the welfare of the ordinary Catholic worker, whom he claimed to represent. Discrimination by employers and landlords against those with German connections gradually embraced Catholics, who came to be regarded by some as disloyal, partly understandably at least in Victoria, where their archbishop made practically no concessions to the fact that he lived in a country where most were still happy with the British connection, nearly eighty percent were non-Catholic, and (even among Catholics) republican sentiments were minute. He accused others of sectarianism but constantly indulged in its practice himself. He did mellow in some ways: In 1937 he made conciliatory gestures to Hughes which resulted in the regular exchange of birthday greetings. He never gave way, however, on the big issues.

Despite his time at Maynooth and his acknowledged intellectual abilities, Mannix wrote (or at least published) no great works, not even any polemics on his strongly held beliefs. On the contrary, he destroyed almost all of his private papers that may have helped one to understand the man. It is interesting to contrast Mannix with his contemporary in Brisbane, Archbishop James Duhig. Duhig was also Irish-born; he became archbishop the same year as Mannix. He came to Australia at the age of thirteen, however, after his family first moved to Yorkshire, England, and then to Queensland. Perhaps that is why the more moderate position Duhig adopted was in many ways more attuned to the Australian way of thinking. Unlike Mannix, he took part in community activities and fostered good relations with other religious groups.

Like Mannix, he never received a cardinal's cap. Both experienced disappointment when in 1946 the cardinalship went to Archbishop Gilroy. Admirers believed it a tremendous insult to Mannix, but their efforts to achieve this honor for him were unsuccessful. With his death, the great Irish influence on the Catholic church declined.

Bibliography

Garden, Don. *Victoria: A History*. Melbourne: Nelson, 1984. A good general history of Victoria, helpful for putting Mannix and his activities into the Victorian setting.

Gilchrist, Michael. *Daniel Mannix: Priest and Patriot*. Melbourne: Dove Communications, 1982. Gilchrist uses sectarian and state aid controversies to highlight Mannix's role as priest and uses the issues of conscription, Ireland, and Communism to show him as a patriot.

McKernan, Michael. "Catholics, Conscription, and Archbishop Mannix." *Historical Studies* 17 (April, 1977): 299-314. McKernan shows the division among Catholic attitudes toward Mannix's conscription stand.

Murphy, Jeffrey J. "The Lost (And Last) Animadversions of Daniel Mannix." *Quadrant* 42, no. 10 (October, 1998). Opinion piece on Mannix, his theology, and church and state issues.

O'Farrell, Patrick. *The Catholic Church and Community in Australia: A History*. Melbourne: Nelson, 1977. Written by a well-regarded Catholic historian, this general history includes a substantial and diverse bibliography.

————. *The Irish in Australia*. Rev. ed. Kensington: New South Wales University Press, 1993. This study complements O'Farrell's history of the Catholic Church in Australia (see above).

Santamaria, B. A. *Daniel Mannix: The Quality of Leadership*. Melbourne: Melbourne University Press, 1984. By a leading Melbourne Catholic conservative who from the 1930's worked closely with Mannix and led the Catholic Social Studies Movement in its campaign against Communism.

Annette Potts
E. Daniel Potts

ALESSANDRO MANZONI

Born: March 7, 1785; Milan, Lombardy
Died: May 22, 1873; Milan, Italy
Area of Achievement: Literature
Contribution: Among his writings in various genres, Manzoni authored the great Romantic historical novel *The Betrothed*, an acknowledged world masterpiece and much-beloved expression of Italian culture that contributed to the unification of Italy and to the Italian language.

Early Life

Alessandro Manzoni was born into the aristocratic liberal circles of late eighteenth century Milan, which, influenced by the Enlightenment, was the leading political and intellectual center of preunification Italy. His maternal grandfather was Cesare Beccaria, an economist and jurist whose lectures anticipated the theories of Adam Smith and Thomas Malthus and whose influential work *Dei delitti e delle pene* (1764; *An Essay on Crimes and Punishments*, 1767) reformed thinking on penology. Beccaria introduced the modern view that punishments should be for the purpose of protecting society, not for taking vengeance on criminals. Among Beccaria's close friends were such writers as Giuseppe Parini and the brothers Pietro and Alessandro Verri. The young Manzoni idolized his grandfather and his grandfather's friends, who provided him with role models and a liberal outlook.

Young Manzoni seriously needed such role models, since his parents took little interest in his upbringing. His mother, Giulia Beccaria Manzoni, unfortunately resembled her mother, Teresa de' Blasco Beccaria, a lovely but scandalous lady who caused discord between Cesare Beccaria and his family and friends and who finally died of venereal disease. Young Giulia became involved in an affair with Giovanni Verri, the pleasure-seeking younger brother of Pietro and Alessandro Verri. In an attempt to end the affair, Pietro Verri arranged her marriage to Pietro Manzoni, a stolid middle-aged member of the Lecco landed gentry. The marriage was a disaster from the beginning, but then young Manzoni was born (no one is sure whether Pietro Manzoni or Giovanni Verri was his actual father). With no talent or taste for motherhood, Giulia farmed him out to a wet nurse, a peasant woman who cared for him in her home. Eventually, Giulia and Pietro Manzoni separated, and Giulia fled to London and then Paris with a rich Milanese banker, Carlo Imbonati.

Manzoni spent his childhood and youth in a series of boarding schools. From 1791 to 1798, he attended schools in Merate and Lugano run by the Somaschi friars, and from 1798 to 1801 he was at schools in Magenta and Milan run by the Barnabite fathers. A sensitive child, he longed for his mother (he and Pietro Manzoni never cared for each other), endured the bullying of headmasters and other students, and led a miserable existence. Besides reducing him to a shy, withdrawn individual prone to assorted lifelong paranoias, one notable result of his religious schooling was to turn him into a youthful atheist. When he was sixteen, Manzoni's formal education ended, and he moved into a Milan townhouse with an aunt (a former nun), who introduced him to a life of dissipation, which included gambling and women. At the age of sixteen, Manzoni also wrote his first surviving verse, including the unpublished four-quarto poem "Il trionfo della Libertà" ("The Triumph of Liberty").

In 1805, his mother and Carlo Imbonati invited him to join them in Paris, but before Manzoni arrived, Imbonati died, leaving Manzoni's mother a fortune. While Manzoni consoled her, she introduced him to the literary salons of Paris. There Manzoni absorbed the brilliant conversations of writers, philosophers, and politicians that, combined with his avid reading of French literature, made him extremely fluent in French. He became friends with a number of French intellectuals, particularly the literary and historical scholar Claude-Charles Fauriel, who remained a lifetime friend and correspondent. Gradually, however, events began to occur that would draw Manzoni away from Paris. In 1807, Pietro Manzoni died, leaving Manzoni the family estate in Lecco. Then in 1808 Manzoni married Henriette Blondel (who changed her name to Enrichetta), a sixteen-year-old Swiss Calvinist, and in 1810 Enrichetta, Manzoni, and his mother all converted to Catholicism and returned to Italy.

Life's Work

Most commentators cite Manzoni's conversion as the turning point in his life, but a more propitious event might have been his marriage to Blondel, who probably influenced his conversion. Gentle,

masterpiece, the long historical novel *I promessi sposi* (1827, 1840-1842; *The Betrothed*, 1828, 1951). Manzoni then spent the next fifteen years rewriting, revising, and polishing *The Betrothed*.

Aside from his literary publication, Manzoni led a retiring and tranquil life on his farm among his family. He needed such a placid life, since he still suffered from phobias (for example, he reputedly weighed his clothes several times a day) and nervous disorders that occasionally left him incapacitated. The various portraits of Manzoni suggest his nervous disposition through his slimness and his long, thin nose that seemed to grow sharper with age. Otherwise, the portraits show a man with regular, almost handsome features whose dark hair and sideburns gradually turned white over the years.

Manzoni's tranquillity was disturbed only by a series of deaths in his family. One child died in 1811, another in 1823, and in 1833 the most shattering blow of all occurred, his beloved wife died. Before Manzoni could recover from her death, their eldest child, Giulia, died in 1834. Needing the supportive companionship of a wife, Manzoni in 1837 married a widow, Teresa Borri Stampa, who brought along stepchildren. The intermittent deaths of his many children continued, and Manzoni outlived all except two. These somber events may help account for Manzoni's turning away from poetry and fiction in his later life to take up the study of history, literary theory, and language. Manzoni published an account of the seventeenth century Milan plague, *Storia della colonna infame* (1842; *The Column of Infamy*, 1845), appended to the final version of *The Betrothed*. Later writings included *Del romanzo storico* (1845), which theorized about historical novels; *Dell'invenzione* (1850), a theoretical work concerning creativity; and *Dell'unità della lingua e dei mezzi di diffonderla* (1868), a report on the Italian language commissioned by the government.

As this last work indicates, Manzoni received much official recognition during his later years. In 1860, the newly unified Italy granted him a pension and made him a senator; he was visited by foreign government dignitaries and by other writers. Most satisfying, however, was the unofficial veneration heaped upon him by the Italian people. Few writers have lived to see such adoration. His death on May 22, 1873, was considered a national tragedy. Giuseppe Verdi's *Messa da requiem* (*Requiem Mass*) was composed and performed in Manzoni's honor the following year.

loving, and strong, she provided Manzoni with the family life and stability that he had never had before. With Manzoni's mother, they settled near Milan on the Brusuglio estate that his mother had inherited from Carlo Imbonati (in 1813 Manzoni also purchased a home in Milan and in 1818 sold the Lecco estate). They proceeded to have a houseful of children while Manzoni practiced agronomy and wrote.

Among the first fruits of his conversion were the *Inni sacri* (1812-1815; *The Sacred Hymns*, 1904), followed by an essay defending Catholicism, *Osservazioni sulla morale cattolica* (1819; *A Vindication of Catholic Morality*, 1836). Then, however, Manzoni turned to history for inspiration in writing two verse tragedies, *Il conte di Carmagnola* (1820; the count of Carmagnola) and *Adelchi* (1822), which, like most Romantic dramas, are hardly suited for the stage, although *Adelchi* was performed. He also wrote an ode on the death of Napoleon, "Il cinque maggio" (1821; "The Napoleonic Ode," 1904), and *Lettre à M. *** sur l'unité de temps et de lieu dans la tragédie* (1823) defending Romantic drama. His next work was the first version of his

Summary

The writing of *The Betrothed* presented Alessandro Manzoni with a unique problem that most modern writers face only in translation. That is, at the time Manzoni wrote, not only was Italy divided into different states ruled by various rulers, but also Italians spoke provincial dialects. There was no unified or standard Italian language. Like other Italian writers at the time, Manzoni briefly considered writing his novel in French, but patriotic sentiments prevailed: How could the great Italian novel be written other than in Italian? Manzoni wrote the first version of *The Betrothed* in his native Lombardy dialect, sometimes called Milanese, but he was dissatisfied with the first version as soon as it appeared. He decided to rewrite the whole novel in the Tuscan dialect, which Dante had used for his *La divina commedia* (c. 1320; *The Divine Comedy*), and which Manzoni considered the purest and most graceful Italian dialect. For purposes of learning the Tuscan dialect, Manzoni made several visits to Florence and grilled any Florentine visitors. Experts in the Italian language still find Lombardisms in *The Betrothed*, but the novel gained such immense popularity that, together with Dante's *The Divine Comedy*, it is credited with establishing the Tuscan dialect as standard Italian.

The unification of the Italian language only begins to account for Manzoni's achievements in *The Betrothed*. By balancing the good-hearted but shrewd Italian peasant against the disorder and tyranny of Spanish rule in seventeenth century Lombardy, *The Betrothed* fueled the nineteenth century Risorgimento movement which was still trying to throw off foreign rule and unify Italy. It is no wonder that when unification came about Manzoni was hailed as both poet and patriot. Religious readers also found cause for praise in Manzoni's theme of divine Providence working through history. Finally, a reader looking for a good story was bound to be enthralled by the novel's long, suspenseful plot, its memorable characters, and its climax during the Milan plague. When Manzoni gratefully acknowledged the influence of Sir Walter Scott on *The Betrothed*, Scott generously replied that it was by far the best novel Manzoni had ever written.

Bibliography

Barricelli, Gian Piero. *Alessandro Manzoni*. Boston: Twayne, 1976. A competent and useful source containing a brief biography followed by a critical survey of Manzoni's writings, concentrating on *The Betrothed*. Includes an annotated bibliography.

Caserta, Ernesto G. *Manzoni's Christian Realism*. Florence: Olschki, 1977. Focuses on Manzoni as a Christian writer. Begins with an examination of his aesthetic theory, then traces his development as a Christian writer from the *Inni sacri* through *The Betrothed*.

Chandler, S. B. *Alessandro Manzoni: The Story of a Spiritual Quest*. Edinburgh: Edinburgh University Press, 1974. Another competent critical survey of Manzoni's writings, concentrating on *The Betrothed*. Includes a fairly extensive bibliography.

Colquhoun, Archibald. *Manzoni and His Times*. London: Dent, and New York: Dutton, 1954. The best biography of Manzoni in English, written by the translator of the definitive English version of *The Betrothed*. Provides a context of extensive social and family background and includes sixteen pages of photographs.

De Simone, Joseph Francis. *Alessandro Manzoni: Esthetics and Literary Criticism*. New York: Vanni, 1946. A dull but informative source, originally a Columbia University Ph.D. thesis. The first part traces Manzoni's aesthetics through three phases—classicism, Romanticism, and "negation of his poetic work"—while the second part surveys Manzoni's critical opinions of other writers, primarily French and Italian.

Ginzburg, Natalia. *The Manzoni Family*. Translated by Marie Evans. New York: Seaver, 1987; London: Paladin, 1989. A translation of *La famiglia Manzoni* (1983). Using letters and other old documents, the author constructs a loose account of Manzoni's family from 1762 to 1907, concentrating on his mother, his two wives, his friend Claude Fauriel, and his children.

Godt, Clareece G. *The Mobile Spectacle: Variable Perspective in Manzoni's "I Promessi Sposi."* New York: Lang, 1998. Examines Manzoni's use of variable perspective, a technique that allows a work to transcend time.

Lindon, John. "Alessandro Manzoni and the Oxford Movement: His Politics and Conversion in a New English Source." *The Journal of Ecclesiastical History* 45, no. 2 (April, 1994). Discusses Manzoni's dedication to Italy's fight for independence and his conversion to Catholicism.

Matteo, Sante, and Larry H. Peer, eds. *The Reasonable Romantic: Essays on Alessandro Manzoni*. New York: Lang, 1986. An anthology of seventeen original essays (a few using deconstruction techniques) written by new and established Manzoni scholars to introduce Manzoni. The first section is a general introduction, followed by sections on Manzoni and Romanticism, language, history, and religion.

Reynolds, Barbara. *The Linguistic Writings of Alessandro Manzoni: A Textual and Chronological Reconstruction.* Cambridge: Heffer, 1950. Originally a University of London Ph.D. thesis. A bit of scholarly detective work that uses Manzoni's published and unpublished writings to reconstruct his changing theories on language, particularly on how to achieve a standard Italian language.

Wall, Bernard. *Alessandro Manzoni.* New Haven, Conn.: Yale University Press, and Cambridge: Bowes and Bowes, 1954. A short introduction to Manzoni's life and works, marred by its brevity and stereotypical thinking, but still useful.

Harold Branam

JOHN MARSHALL

Born: September 24, 1755; Germantown, Virginia
Died: July 6, 1835; Philadelphia, Pennsylvania
Area of Achievement: Law
Contribution: During his long tenure as chief justice of the United States Supreme Court, Marshall used his considerable intelligence, personal charm, and political skills to make the Supreme Court the chief arbiter of constitutional doctrine, thereby establishing what had been the weakest branch of the national government as an equal with Congress and the executive.

Early Life

John Marshall was born September 24, 1755, to Thomas and Mary Randolph Keith Marshall in Germantown (modern Midland), Virginia. He was the eldest of fifteen children. His father was a planter of moderate means who in time became a wealthy leading citizen of Virginia and later of Kentucky, serving in numerous official capacities in both states. Through Mary, the Marshall family was connected to most of the important families of Virginia. Growing to manhood among the landed gentry molded John Marshall's character, yet his too casual and occasionally sloppy appearance was at odds with his background. John Marshall's education was a typical blend, for the sons of Southern Colonial gentry, of intermittent and limited formal instruction by tutors in the classics and informal instruction by his parents in reading, writing, and elementary mathematics. The few books in the family library included several on law and served as Marshall's introduction to the subject; from his family's participation in state and local government, he learned about politics.

Only nineteen in 1774, when the chain of events beginning with the Boston Tea Party led to the American War of Independence, John Marshall followed his father's example and enthusiastically took the patriots' side in the quarrel with England. He was a popular first lieutenant in the local militia when the fighting started but followed his father into the Continental army as soon as it was formed. He served with distinction until independence was nearly won, rising to the rank of captain and becoming something of a hero. He fought in several battles, was wounded, and was with George Washington at Valley Forge. During a lull, while stationed in Virginia, he studied law and other subjects for three months at the College of William and Mary in Williamsburg. His law teacher was George Wythe, one of the most respected Colonial lawyers, with whom Thomas Jefferson, Marshall's cousin, had also studied. While short, Marshall's legal education was better than most, since there were no law schools in America. The College of William and Mary was one of the few to offer any law classes as part of the undergraduate curriculum. Most lawyers learned only by self-study while working as a clerk in a practicing attorney's office. During these months of study, he also met and began courting Mary Willis Ambler, known all of her life as Polly.

Marshall had passed the bar examination and received his license to practice from Governor Thomas Jefferson in August of 1780. He returned to Oak Hill in Fauquier County, the family estate, to begin his career. In April of 1782, Marshall was elected to represent his county in the House of Delegates. In the state capital, Richmond, Marshall was introduced to a world beyond that of the country lawyer and landed gentry, and his ambition to be part of it was fired. Marshall renewed his courtship of Polly Ambler, whose family now lived in Richmond, and they were married on January 3, 1783, when he was twenty-seven and she was nearly seventeen. Marshall decided to move to Richmond to practice and became a leading member of the bar within three years.

Life's Work

The man who had joined the mainstream of Virginia's affairs was a commanding, lean figure, six feet in height, black-haired, with a nearly round face and strong, penetrating black eyes, complimented by a smile that seemed to disarm everyone. Honest, capable of sustained hard work, and possessed of a probing intellect, Marshall was also a gregarious man who loved games and athletic activity and who radiated a captivating friendliness. By nature, he was a gracious person, although he did not have a polished manner. As happened with so many patriots who actively participated in the military and political events of the War of Independence, Marshall had acquired a deep sense of nationalism from his travels through the former Colonies and the comradeship of men from all parts of the emerging nation. That this new nation should survive and prosper became a concern of Marshall for the remainder of his life.

Marshall worked hard to build his Richmond practice. He held various official positions with the state and local governments but refused any that would seriously interfere with his private law work. A major reason was Polly's poor health after 1786. Their second child died shortly after birth, and then Polly miscarried a few months later. The shock of these two tragedies brought on a nervous breakdown from which Polly never totally recovered. For the remainder of their long married life and through the eight children yet to come, Polly could not abide crowds or noise. It was necessary to have servants to perform the routine household duties, and Marshall personally did the family marketing.

The condition of the nation worried Marshall throughout the 1780's. He thought the national government was too weak to protect the new nation from foreign threats or to restrain state governments from abuses of power. For this reason, he wholeheartedly supported the work of the Constitutional Convention of 1787 to create a "more perfect union." Elected as delegate to Virginia's special convention to decide whether to adopt the new national constitution, he spoke strongly for it. Once the issue was favorably resolved, however, and the new national government instituted under the leadership of his idol, George Washington, Marshall's attention returned to the practice of law.

He refused all offers of appointment to national office, including the Cabinet, until 1797, when he accepted what he thought would be a short-term diplomatic appointment from President John Adams. When Marshall returned to the United States in July of 1798, he was feted as a national hero for his part in what had become known as the XYZ affair. George Washington persuaded him to capitalize on his public recognition and run for a seat in the House of Representatives. Washington had persuaded him to agree to leave his lucrative private practice by convincing him that the Republic was in danger from the development of political factionalism. Marshall, in the conventional wisdom of his day, believed that political factions were a threat to the smooth and stable operation of a republican government. Factionalism stirred up the masses to interfere in the affairs of government, best left to the better educated and propertied gentry, who alone could be expected to function from motives of civic virtue and on the basis of practical common sense. While willing to fight for fundamental principle, Marshall was a man who other-wise believed in moderation and compromise on matters of policy; he saw that political polarization, if unchecked, would eventually destroy the nation. In Congress, he became the leading House spokesman for President Adams' moderate Federalist administration. In recognition of his service he was promoted to secretary of state in 1800, and, when the Federalists lost the election that year, to Chief Justice of the United States Supreme Court in 1801. He would remain chief justice until 1835, the year he died.

The Supreme Court in 1801 had serious problems with low public esteem, low pay, poor morale, and rapid turnover of justices. The Court had developed no corporate sense of identity. Marshall's first innovation was to convince the justices not to give their written opinions *seriatim*—that is, each justice writing his own. Instead, in most cases Marshall persuaded the justices to confer until they reached a consensus so that a single opinion could be issued for the majority. Marshall correctly reasoned that the Court's decisions would be much more authoritative if the majority spoke with one voice. The institution of this practice was the single most important reason for the rise of the Supreme Court to equality with the other branches of government. To facilitate the development of collegiality, he also encouraged the justices to lodge at the same Washington, D.C., inn during the one-to-two-month yearly sessions.

The single most distinctive feature of the American system of government is the power of its courts to declare actions by other parts of the government unconstitutional. This power, called judicial review, had not yet been exercised except by some state courts (with mixed results) when Marshall became chief justice. The first instance of the power's use arose out of the fury of President Jefferson and his party over the famous Midnight Appointments of President Adams in 1801, in the case of *Marbury v. Madison* (1803). The case involved a request that the Supreme Court issue a writ of *mandamus* (a court order) to Secretary of State James Madison. The Court's decision, written by Marshall, first lectured Jefferson and his party on their failing in the practice of principles of good government and then announced that the writ of *mandamus* requested in this case could not be issued because section 13 of the Judiciary Act of 1789, which gave the Court the power to issue the writ, was unconstitutional. This self-denial by the Court was a shrewd political maneuver. In its first big

MARSHALL

constitutional case under Marshall, the Court had exercised judicial review and declared an act of Congress unconstitutional, and there was nothing anyone could do about it. It was also a brave act in the face of the enormous antijudiciary bias of the Jeffersonians. Although the Court did not declare another act of Congress or the president unconstitutional during Marshall's tenure, it did so for state laws on a number of occasions. Thus, the practice as well as the principle of judicial review was established.

After 1805, the political pressure on the Court decreased, partly because the government's attention was increasingly focused on foreign affairs and partly because, under Marshall, the Court had acquired greater respect and, therefore, greater independence. The work of the Court now centered more on two objectives: the supremacy of the national government and the preservation and protection of rights. The two were directly related in Marshall's view. The point in establishing the supremacy of the federal Constitution, statutes, and treaties over the states was to counter the threat to inalienable rights from abuses of power by the states. Marshall perceived this as the most serious threat of all. For example, the Constitution prohibited the states from interfering with the obligations of the parties to a contract, yet many states were doing just that in numerous ways. In a long line of cases interpreting the "contract clause," Marshall's court fashioned from it a powerful defense of the private citizens' right to whatever property they had come by honestly. In the famous trial of Aaron Burr for treason, Marshall interpreted the Constitution to prevent the charge of treason from becoming an instrument to punish political enemies. In *Gibbons v. Ogden* (1824), Marshall's court struck down a law creating a steamboat monopoly, not only because it infringed on federal power to regulate interstate commerce, but also because the constitutional framers had given the commerce power to Congress in order to establish the whole of the United States as a free trade area and the steamboat monopoly violated freedom of commerce. The issue of slavery presented a serious problem for Marshall; on the one hand, the slave owner's property right had to be protected, like any other property right, but on the other hand, Marshall thought that black slaves had the same rights as white people. It seemed to him that the only solution to this dilemma was the American Colonization Society. This organization hoped to remove all black slaves from America to Liberia, Africa.

The Jackson years disheartened Marshall. He hated the viciously partisan character assassinations of the Jackson campaign, and he feared that universal manhood suffrage, a major Jacksonian goal, could only result in politicians pandering to the prejudices of the common people. He also believed the states' rights orientation of the Jackson appointees to the Court threatened all of his work to establish the supremacy of the Constitution, guarantees of rights, and the restraint of state uses of power. As he increasingly saw himself as a relic of the past, he found it necessary to compromise on some issues to save at least something of his work. When Polly died in 1831, he was desolate and felt very much alone. There were, however, some positive moments. When Jackson stood up for the supremacy of the national government in 1832 against South Carolina's attempt to nullify a national tariff, Marshall relented somewhat in his dislike of the old general. Although unable to stop Georgia from brutally removing the Cherokee Indians from the state and humiliated at seeing the state of Georgia flout the Supreme Court's decision forbidding the removal—the Court had no means of enforcing it and the president would not—a remedy was provided. President Jackson's Force Bill, passed by Congress in connection with the Nullification Crisis, provided the Court with its own officials to enforce future decisions.

He was seventy-nine in 1835, when, in a stagecoach accident, he suffered a spinal injury from which he never fully recovered. He also suffered from serious liver trouble. When told that his time was short, Marshall put his affairs in order and, on July 6, 1835, he died.

Summary

Marshall built better than he knew. He was mistaken in his beliefs about political parties and the superior governing abilities of the gentry, but practices he established for the Court and many of his judicial doctrines are still important. Supreme Court majorities continued after Marshall generally to speak with one voice. His example of collegial leadership remains the standard for chief justices. The defense of property rights based on the contract clause and his interpretation of the commerce clause contributed significantly to the legal environment necessary for the free enterprise economic system to flourish. Treason remains only a crime and not a weapon against the enemies of whatever politicians are in power.

In raising the visibility and authority of the Supreme Court to a position of equality with the other branches, Marshall created a potent force for political stability within the American system of government. This was his most important achievement. The government's ability to correct its mistakes through the Supreme Court's exercise of the power of judicial review inspires confidence and trust in all levels of the system. The Supreme Court became the guardian and final arbiter of the Constitution, establishing the primacy of the constitutional principles of the Founding Fathers. In 1801, when John Marshall became chief justice, none of this was certain to evolve, but the fundamentals were all in place when he left, thirty-four years later. During that time, he wrote 519 of the Court's 1,106 opinions, including thirty-six of the sixty-two involving major constitutional questions. John Marshall had a major hand in creating the most balanced and equable judicial system in the world.

Bibliography

Baker, Leonard. *John Marshall: A Life in Law*. New York and London: Macmillan, 1974. A good biography of Marshall's professional life; includes some private matters as well. Explains many of the details on how Marshall and the legal system in his time worked. Also explains his reasoning in his Supreme Court decisions.

Baxter, Maurice G. *Daniel Webster and the Supreme Court*. Amherst: University of Massachusetts Press, 1966. A superb and scholarly examination of the relationship between Daniel Webster, one of the leading constitutional lawyers of his day and a Marshall supporter, and the development of judicial doctrine by the Supreme Court during much of Marshall's tenure as chief justice.

Beveridge, Albert J. *The Life of John Marshall*. 4 vols. Boston: Houghton Mifflin, 1916-1919; Cambridge: Riverside Press, 1947. Detailed and wonderfully told story, yet sadly lacking in balance, making Marshall seem a heroic savior of his nation against arch-villains. Even so, these four volumes are still the starting point for Marshall scholarship.

Faulkner, Robert K. *The Jurisprudence of John Marshall*. Princeton, N.J.: Princeton University Press, 1968. Definitive examination of the political philosophy of Marshall. Traces the origins to a mix of the theories of John Locke, American nationalism, and the respect for landed gentry typical of the classical Romans, especially Cicero.

Horwitz, Morton J. *The Transformation of American Law: 1780-1860*. Cambridge, Mass.: Harvard University Press, 1977; Oxford: Oxford University Press, 1992. Mentions Marshall only briefly. Probably the best one-volume legal history of the era to date. Emphasis is on the transformation of English law in the Colonies into a modern national legal system and how this transformation aided economic development.

Newmyer, R. Kent. *The Supreme Court Under Marshall and Taney*. New York: Crowell, 1968. A succinct but thorough and perceptive study of the Marshall Court in the context of the people and events of the times. The Marshall chapters concentrate on Marshall as chief justice, and little of his personal life is included.

Rudko, Frances H. *John Marshall and International Law: Statesman and Chief Justice*. New York: Greenwood Press, 1991. Examines Marshall's years prior to the Supreme Court (1793-1801) and the knowledge he gained during those years in the area of international law. The author focuses on four events during this period that shaped Marshall's understanding of international law.

Shevory, Thomas C. *John Marshall's Law: Interpretation, Ideology, and Interest*. Westport, Conn.: Greenwood Press, 1994. Study examining Marshall's contributions to law and political philosophy providing new insight into his decisions on matters of debt, property, and contracts, which were affected by his pragmatism.

Stites, Francis N. *John Marshall: Defender of the Constitution*. Boston: Little Brown, 1981. This is an excellent short biography of Marshall. Well researched and carefully written, it brings together in a reasonable synthesis the voluminous scholarship available on Marshall.

Richard L. Hillard

KARL MARX

Born: May 5, 1818; Trier, Prussia
Died: March 14, 1883; London, England
Areas of Achievement: Economics and philosophy
Contribution: Marx's ideas concerning modes of economic distribution, social class, and the developmental patterns of history have profoundly influenced theories in philosophical and economic thought and have helped shape the political structure of the modern world.

Early Life

Karl Marx was born into a Jewish family in the city of Trier in the southern Rhineland area. When the Rhineland was rejoined, after the Napoleonic Wars, to Protestant Prussia in 1814, his father, a public lawyer, had converted to Christianity. In 1830, the young Marx entered the Trier secondary school and pursued the traditional humanities curriculum. In the fall of 1835, he entered the University of Bonn as a law student but left the following year to enroll at the University of Berlin. His studies were concentrated on law, history, and the works of the then-leading philosophers Johann Gottlieb Fichte and Georg Wilhelm Friedrich Hegel.

Marx was graduated in 1841, after writing his doctoral dissertation, and returned to Bonn, where he became involved with his friend Bruno Bauer in left-wing politics and in the study of the materialist philosophy of Ludwig Feuerbach. In April, 1842, he began writing radical articles for the *Rheinische Zeitung* (Rhenish gazette), and he assumed its editorship in Cologne that October. He married in June, 1843, and moved to Paris that October.

In August, 1844, Marx met Friedrich Engels in Paris, and the two began a productive collaboration. Marx's articles had angered the Prussian government, and in February, 1845, he moved to Brussels. In 1848, the year of revolutions in many European countries, Marx was ordered to leave Brussels; he returned to Paris and then to Cologne. He was again compelled to leave in 1849 and went to London, where he would remain for the rest of his life.

Life's Work

Marx's lifelong critique of capitalist economy began in part as an analysis of the then-dominant Hegelian system of philosophical Idealism. Influenced to a degree by Feuerbach's materialism, Marx rejected Hegel's metaphysical vision of a *Weltgeist*, or Absolute Spirit. It was not metaphysical Spirit that governed history but rather material existence that determined consciousness. The ways in which an individual was compelled to seek physical necessities such as food, shelter, and clothing within a society profoundly influenced the manner in which a person viewed himself and others. As Hegel (and others) suggested, the course of history was indeed a dialectical process of conflict and resolution, but for Marx this development was determined to a great extent by economic realities. Whereas Hegel saw dialectical process (thesis/antithesis/synthesis) as one of ideas, for Marx it was one of class struggle. Hence Marx's position is called dialectical materialism. He stood in staunch opposition to the prior philosophical tradition of German Idealism and thinkers such as Immanuel Kant, Fichte, and Hegel. German philosophy, he believed, was mired in insubstantial theoretical speculation when concrete and practical thought about the relationship between reality—especially economic and political realities—and consciousness was needed. In general, Marx was a synthetic thinker, and his views represent a mixture of German materialist philosophy such as that of Feuerbach; the French social doctrines of Charles Fourier, Comte de Saint-Simon, and Pierre-Joseph Proudhon; and British theories of political economy such as those of Adam Smith and David Ricardo.

Marx's philosophical position of a dialectical materialism suggests a comprehensive view of social organization—which is, broadly speaking, a dimension of human consciousness—in all its manifestations. The determinant of all societal forms is its economic base (*Basis*), that is, the means of production and the distribution of its produced wealth. All aspects of human social interaction, what Marx called the superstructure (*Überbau*), are influenced and shaped by the economic base and its consequent relationships of power among social classes. The superstructure ultimately involves a society's educational, legal, artistic, political, philosophical, and scientific systems. The nature of the economic base—above all the power relationships of the classes—tends to be reproduced in an overt or covert fashion in the various dimensions of the societal superstructure. The pedagogical curriculum of the school system, for example, might reproduce or reinforce in some unconscious manner the inequality of the social classes upon which the mode of production is based. Various aspects of the artistic or cultural dimensions of a society (a novel, for example) might also incorporate in symbolic expression the nature of the economic base. Thus Marx's economic theories provide an account for a wide variety of phenomena.

In capitalist political economy, the individual must sell his physical or intellectual labor, must sell himself as a commodity, in order to survive. Thus, Marx's early writings, such as *Ökonomische und philosophische Manuskripte* (1844; *Economic and Philosophic Manuscripts of 1844*, 1947), deal with the pivotal concept of alienation (*Entfremdung*) as a central aspect of the worker's experience in capitalism. Since the worker is reduced to an exploited commodity or object, this is above all a condition of dehumanization (*Entmenschlichung*). The individual is alienated or divorced from his full potential as a human being. Committed to long hours of labor in a factory, the worker—and this means man, woman, and child—has no time to develop other facets of the personality. In a capitalist society, individuals are estranged not only from aspects of their own selves but also from others in that the labor market is a competitive one, and workers must outdo one another in order to survive. In its crudest form, capitalist economy, Marx would assert, is a kind of Darwinian "survival of the fittest," in which the weak—those who cannot work—must perish.

In his *Die deutsche Ideologie* (1845-1846; *The German Ideology*, 1938), Marx discusses earlier forms of social organization, such as tribal or communal groups, in which the estrangement of the individual in industrialist society was not yet a crucial problem. His vision of an ideal socialist state would be one in which the individual might, for example, manufacture shoes in the morning, teach history in the afternoon, and play music in an orchestra in the evening. In other words, a person would be free to utilize or realize all dimensions of the self. This idealized notion of social organization in the writings of the young Marx indicates the utopian influence of romantic thought upon his initial critique of capitalist society.

In 1848, after the Paris revolts of that same year, Marx and Engels published *Manifest der Kommunistischen Partei* (*The Communist Manifesto*, 1850), a booklet that has become the best-known and most influential statement of Marxist ideology.

It presents a brief historical sketch of bourgeois society and suggests that capitalism will eventually collapse because of its inherent pattern of cyclical economic crises and because of the worsening situation of the worker class, or the proletariat, in all capitalist nations. The proletariat has become, they argue, more conscious of its situation, and a worker revolution is inevitable. The international communist party presents a revolutionary platform in which the workers are the ruling class in charge of all capital production. Marx and Engels call for a worker revolt to overthrow the "chains" that bind them.

Marx wrote and published *Zur Kritik der politischen Ökonomie* (1859; *A Contribution to a Critique of Political Economy*, 1904), which became a preliminary study for the first volume of his and Engels' planned multivolume analysis of capitalist political economy, *Das Kapital* (1867, 1885, 1894; *Capital: A Critique of Political Economy*, 1886, 1907, 1909, better known as *Das Kapital*). Marx actually completed only the first volume; the second and third were edited from his notes by Engels, who was helped on the third by Karl Kautsky.

This work is a more technical economic analysis of the capitalist mode of production with the intention of revealing "the economic law of motion" that underlies modern (industrial) society.

It would be beyond the scope of this study to provide a detailed summary of this complex work, but a few words of general explanation may be given. Marx discusses economic issues such as the labor theory of value and commodities, surplus value, capital production and accumulation, and the social relations and class struggles involved in capital production. Capital accumulation, the central goal and justification of the system, is beset by certain internal contradictions, such as periodic episodes of moderate to extreme market inflation and depression and a tendency toward monopoly. These inherent conditions usually have their most deleterious effects upon the wage laborer. Such cycles will eventually lead to economic collapse or revolutionary overthrow by the proletariat. In general, Marx's analyses were flawed—especially the labor theory of value upon which much of this work is based—and could not account for adaptive changes in the capitalist system.

In December, 1881, Marx's wife, Jenny, died, and his daughter died the following year. Marx himself, after a life of overwork and neglect of his health, died in 1883.

Summary

Karl Marx was a critical social and economic philosopher whose materialist analyses of bourgeois capitalist society initiated a revolution that has had profound effects on the development of human civilization. Despite some of the later ideological, and at times quasi-religious and fanatical, adaptations of his thought, the basic philosophical assumptions of Marx's approach remain humanistic and optimistic; they are based upon fundamental notions of the European Enlightenment, that is, that human reason can successfully alleviate the problems of life. Alienation is, for example, in Marx's view (as opposed to modern existential thought) a historical and societal phenomenon that can be overcome through a change in the social-economic order. Marxism has remained a vital intellectual position and therefore possesses much relevance to the modern world.

Subsequent developments of Marxist thought have resulted in Communist Party revolutions in a number of countries such as that led by the ideologue Vladimir Ilich Lenin (1870-1924) within czarist Russia in 1917 or that of the popular leader Mao Tse-tung (1893-1976) in the Republic of China in 1949. Unfortunately, these revolutions have involved pogroms and mass executions of certain segments of the population, usually elements of the landed bourgeoisie. This was the case under the rule of Joseph Stalin (1879-1953) in Soviet Russia. These socialist governments have become reified, for the most part, at the intermediate stage of a party dictatorship rather than the essentially free state of the people that Marx had ideally envisioned.

Marx's philosophy has led to fruitful thought in areas other than social and economic thought. The notion that the power relationships of the economic base effect in various ways the manifestations of the societal superstructure has produced an analytical mode called ideological criticism, in which the hidden dimensions of class ideology are revealed in their social expressions. This has been especially productive in the field of literature and the arts. Marxist analyses of literary texts have yielded new insights into the nature of literary production and its relationship to society at large. The Hungarian critic Georg Lukács (1885-1971), for example, wrote many excellent books and essays on the history of European literature, establishing a new model of Marxist interpretation and criticism.

Bibliography

Bottomore, Tom, ed. *Karl Marx.* Englewood Cliffs, N.J.: Prentice-Hall, 1973; Oxford: Blackwell, 1979. An excellent collection of essays by prominent scholars on various aspects of Marx's thought. Contains a selected bibliography.

Brudney, Daniel. *Marx's Attempt to Leave Philosophy.* Cambridge, Mass.: Harvard University Press, 1998. The author discusses Marx's exclusion of philosophy and metaphysics from his writings and rhetoric.

Henry, Michel. *Marx: A Philosophy of Human Reality.* Translated by Kathleen McLaughlin. Bloomington: Indiana University Press, 1983. An important critical work by a French scholar who gives close readings/interpretations of Marx's key texts.

Lapides, Kenneth. *Marx's Wage Theory in Historical Perspective: Its Origins, Development and Interpretation.* Westport, Conn.: Praeger, 1998. The author examines Marx's views on labor and wages and the financial analysis that shaped his theory of the labor movement. Placed in proper historical context, we see the sources Marx used, which have been gleaned from his own writings.

Love, Nancy S. *Marx, Nietzsche, and Modernity.* New York: Columbia University Press, 1986. Examines the teachings of Marx and Nietzsche with respect to the nature of man and their resulting theories on history.

McLellan, David. *Karl Marx: His Life and Thought.* New York: Harper, and London: Macmillan, 1973. An excellent critical biography of Marx by a prominent Marxist scholar. Contains a good bibliography.

————. *Marx Before Marxism.* New York: Harper, and London: Macmillan, 1970. An excellent study of Marx's important early years as a student and the development of his initial ideas. Contains a selected bibliography.

Singer, Peter. *Marx.* Oxford and New York: Oxford University Press, 1980. A brief but informative introduction to Marx's life and major ideas. Contains suggestions for further reading.

Suchting, W. A. *Marx: An Introduction.* New York: New York University Press, and Brighton: Wheatsheaf, 1983. A good critical biography of Marx presented chronologically and by topic. Contains helpful guide for further reading.

Thomas F. Barry

VINCENT MASSEY

Born: February 20, 1887; Toronto, Canada
Died: December 30, 1967; London, England
Areas of Achievement: Government and politics
Contribution: Massey's career, which culminated in his appointment as the first native-born governor-general in Canadian history, illustrates his constant striving to make Canadian nationalism compatible with continued Canadian ties to Great Britain and the Commonwealth.

Early Life

Vincent Massey was born February 20, 1887, in Toronto, Canada. His father, Chester D. Massey, was associated with the farm implement manufacturing company which, in the 1890's, merged with a competitor to become the Massey-Harris Company. His American-born mother, Anna Vincent, died when he was sixteen. Growing up within a politically conservative circle, and inculcated with stern Methodist teachings, Massey did not break out from the family mold until he attended University College at the University of Toronto. With history as his speciality, he pursued a literary and artistic bent which was unusual for a scion of the Massey family. His interest in the theater was shared by his younger brother Raymond, whose successful career in theater and films took him to London and Hollywood.

Though Vincent Massey was said to be an excellent actor, his interests were more diverse. Earning his B.A. from Toronto in 1910, he went on to Balliol College, Oxford, where he received another B.A. in 1913 and an M.A. in 1918. While completing his master's, he lectured in modern history at the University of Toronto from 1913 to 1915. Massey's marriage to Alice Parkin in 1915 began a partnership which lasted until her death in 1950. The two shared an interest in the arts which led to a lifetime of contributions to Canadian cultural life. Their initial foray as patrons of the arts came through Massey's appointment as administrator of his grandfather Hart Massey's trust. Acting with the advice of his cousin George Vincent, president of the Rockefeller Foundation in the United States, Massey in 1918 turned the trust into Canada's first foundation. The Massey Foundation then financed Hart House, a student union on the University of Toronto campus, personally planned by Vincent and Alice Massey. Of special interest to them was the Hart House Theatre, where Massey produced, directed, and often performed, and the Hart House Quartet.

Thus, a devotion to the arts and education appeared central to Massey's life at this time. Although he served on the staff of a military district in the Toronto area from 1915 to 1918, and was associate secretary of the War Committee of the cabinet in 1918 and director of the Government Repatriation Committee, 1918-1919, a political career did not yet appear on the horizon—though his interest was whetted. Immediately, the family business called, and Massey became president of Massey-Harris Company from 1921 to 1925. His future interests were by then apparent. Never consumed by the acquisitive instincts of many fellow businessmen, Massey was content with his family fortune. Not an aggressive president, Massey preferred to focus on such issues as government foreign trade policy and labor relations. He traveled widely, including a visit to the newly created Soviet Union.

Life's Work

In 1925, Massey's political career began in earnest, as he resigned his position with Massey-Harris to throw in his lot with the government of Liberal prime minister William Lyon Mackenzie King. Massey seemed a good catch for the Liberals, whose ranks were short of millionaire Toronto industrialists, especially ones who would accept the Liberal low tariff policy. King offered Massey not only a seat in Parliament but also immediate entrance into his cabinet as a minister without portfolio. Until King's retirement in 1948, Massey's career would be linked not only to the fortunes of King and his Liberal Party but also to the mercurial temperament of King himself. At this early stage in their relationship, King found Massey and his wife to be soulmates, who shared his appreciation of "spiritual" qualities.

Massey had to win an election, however, in order to serve as a Member of Parliament, and his failure to win in a hand-picked constituency, followed by failure to find any other constituency that sought him as their M.P., marked an end to an elective political career. After serving in the cabinet for only a few weeks, Massey was forced to revert to a behind-the-scenes position. One reporter described the Masseys as being part of King's "kitchen cabinet," spending election eve with him receiving reports on the 1926 Liberal victory.

Hoping that a diplomatic success might make him more appealing as a political candidate, Massey accepted King's offer of a diplomatic post—Canadian Minister to the United States. Since the British North America Act of 1867 had created the Dominion, Great Britain had retained some control over Canada's foreign policy. To do otherwise was seen by imperialists in Canada and Great Britain as a breaking of the last imperial tie, since Canada would then have all the attributes of sovereignty and be, in effect, an independent nation. Though World War I had revealed the inadequacies of conducting Canadian diplomacy through the British Foreign Office, no Canadian diplomat had yet been accredited to a foreign capital. As the constitutional issues were slowly resolved, one concrete problem remained: Who would the first diplomat be? Massey was available, and King needed a suitable appointive job for him.

As minister in Washington from 1926 to 1930, Massey resolved no major diplomatic issue. The St. Lawrence waterway was still being "studied," as it would be for more than twenty more years, and talk of a higher American tariff—which came to fruition in 1930—constantly bedeviled the Massey mission. Yet Massey's public relations role was unexcelled. His acting experience and excellent voice made his speechmaking chores most productive, as he reminded his American audiences of Canada's existence and of her differences from the United States. Socially, Massey revealed both the desire and ability to mingle with the rich and famous, as he and Alice entertained in their new half-million-dollar legation on Massachusetts Avenue. Precisely this aristocratic side of Massey was the one which so frequently offended King.

Though next appointed by King to the position he most desired, high commissioner to Great Britain, Massey found himself with no appointment when King's government lost the 1930 election. Richard B. Bennett, the new Conservative prime minister, would neither confirm Massey in the London post nor keep him in Washington. Massey continued his benefactions via the Massey Foundation, traveled widely, and contemplated a variety of posts. At King's urging, the position that Massey took in 1932 was president of the newly created National Liberal Federation, an attempt to give some respectability to a Liberal Party smarting

from scandal. Seeing this as a means to bring his own liberal vision to the party and to induce the progressive third party, the Cooperative Commonwealth Federation, to join the Liberals, Massey was soon at odds, once again, with King. Wanting Massey's respectability and hoped-for fund-raising ability, King found Massey attempting to move the party to a more leftish, New Deal-style social philosophy while ignoring fund-raising.

Massey did, however, support King in the 1935 parliamentary elections, and the platform of "King or Chaos" brought victory over Bennett's Tories. Massey soon received his appointment as high commissioner in London. Not a truly diplomatic job, this euphemistic title had been created in 1880 as a way for a mother country and its dominion to exchange representatives without utilizing diplomats, as two foreign countries would do. This proved troublesome to Massey, however, because again his conception of his role differed from that of King's. Wanting to be a diplomat and policymaker, rather than a salesman for Canadian products, Massey was stymied until the outbreak of war made it impossible to ignore his talents.

As in Washington, Massey at first focused on social events, speechmaking, and cultural affairs. His aristocratic bearing made it easy for him to be taken into the bosom of the English ruling class. Like those in power, Massey was relatively unquestioning about the virtues of appeasement. His secretary during these years described him as having "the austere visage of an Indian chief belied by [a] small, frail-appearing form." Though shorter and slighter of build than his actor brother, he shared the craggy facial appearance which made Raymond so successful portraying Abraham Lincoln on stage and screen.

War brought approval from Ottawa for Massey to meet regularly with the other dominion high commissioners, though they always found themselves struggling for information from the British government. Massey was particularly influential in creating the British Commonwealth Air Training Plan and organizing services for Canadian servicemen in England, such as the Beaver Club and the Canadian Officers' Club, as well as a convalescent hospital. His interest in art led him to promote a war artists' program, and resulted in his appointment as trustee, and later chairman, of the British National Gallery of Art. Among his responsibilities was preserving England's art treasures from wartime destruction.

After eleven years at the London post, Massey returned to Canada in 1946. The war years had not diminished the frequent Massey-King quarrels. Indeed, King had gone so far as to accuse Massey of "self-aggrandizement" while in London. King had no intention of providing further appointive office to Massey, at least not the type of office Massey would accept. With no suitable political or diplomatic office available, Massey accepted the position of chancellor of the University of Toronto in 1947. Massey quickly discovered that it did not allow him the policy-making role that he desired in all of his posts. King's retirement, however, paved the way for Prime Minister Louis St. Laurent in 1949 to appoint Massey head of the Royal Commission on National Development in the Arts, Letters and Sciences. Massey was an ideal choice: A renowned Canadian, Massey's knowledge of most fields of artistic endeavor enabled him to be far more than a figurehead chairman. An early postwar manifestation of Canadian nationalism, this would be the first of several Royal Commissions studying foreign (United States) penetration of the Canadian culture and economy. All of its major recommendations were ultimately adopted by the government, such as continued support for the Canadian Broadcasting Corporation, federal aid to universities, and the creation of a Canada Council to provide government patronage of the arts. Its 1951 report was aptly titled the Massey Commission Report.

From 1952 to 1959, Massey embodied another "first" for Canada: He became the first Canadian-born governor-general since the Dominion had been created. The last major link with the Crown, this post by the 1950's had little but symbolic importance. In an era when the maple leaf flag was created, and separate Canadian citizenship established, the symbolism of a Canadian-born governor-general was no minor event. Massey's love of pomp and ceremony could now reach its fulfillment in executing the ceremonial duties of office. Not only did he travel throughout Canada, but an airplane ride over the North Pole was included in his itinerary as well.

In retirement, Massey continued his philanthropic activities, building Massey College at the University of Toronto. He turned to memoir writing, publishing *What's Past Is Prologue* in 1963. On a visit to his beloved London, he died on December 30, 1967.

Summary

Without doubt, Vincent Massey was an Anglophile. His natural inclinations in this direction were reinforced by his wife, who had grown up in England. Massey cherished all those honors that he received from the Crown, and deeply regretted Prime Minister John Diefenbaker's refusal to allow his acceptance of the Order of the Garter. Yet his imperialistic loyalty to the mother country and Crown was not a nineteenth century, unquestioning faith. He was also a Canadian nationalist who sought to develop a distinctively Canadian culture and maintain Canadian diplomatic and political prerogatives. These goals could still be compatible, he believed, with continued ties to the mother country and to the British Commonwealth of Nations. Massey's biographer, Claude Bissell, describes Massey's vision of Canada as "a European country in a North American environment." If European was synonymous with British in Massey's mind, he was not without some consideration for French Canadians. He studied French during his absence from office in 1930, and brushed up on his French again prior to assuming the position of governor-general.

In Washington, Massey worked closely with the British ambassador to downplay the potentially revolutionary aspects of his role. As high commissioner, and especially as governor-general, he continued to stress the importance of Commonwealth bonds, often to the displeasure of King, whose sentimental sympathy for Great Britain was at times displaced by irritation and suspicion. For Massey, the Crown "is not something reposing in the Tower of London but the very symbol of our own nationality, which helps to give us our individual character and draws all parts of Canada together." Without it, the Canadian chief executive would soon become indistinguishable from the American president, and Canada would then become a republic.

Massey's passion for associating with the powerful and famous, however, along with his aristocratic manner, offended not only associates such as King but also many of his fellow Canadians and even some Englishmen. One story retold by Massey's biographer has two proper Englishmen discussing the high commissioner from Canada. Though agreeing that Massey had many excellent qualities, one concluded: "But damn it all, the fellow always makes one feel like a bloody savage." While an exaggeration, the tale helps explain Massey's failure to win elective office, since a genuine appeal to the common man seemed even beyond his acting ability.

Bibliography

Bissell, Claude T. *The Young Vincent Massey.* Toronto: University of Toronto: University of Toronto Press, 1981.

———. *The Imperial Canadian: Vincent Massey in Office.* Toronto: University of Toronto Press, 1986. These two volumes are the authorized biography of Massey. Bissell, who knew Massey in his later years, had sole access to the Massey diaries and papers. The volumes are divided at the year 1935.

Denison, Merrill. *Harvest Triumphant: The Story of Massey-Harris.* London: Falcon Press, and New York: Dodd, Mead, 1949. An official history of the firm, describing Massey's ancestors and explaining how the family fortune was created.

Massey, Vincent. *What's Past Is Prologue: The Memoirs of the Right Honorable Vincent Massey, C.H.* London: Macmillan, 1963; New York: St. Martin's Press, 1964. Since Massey's papers are unavailable, these memoirs, along with Bissell's two-volume biography, provide the most complete account of his life.

Ritchie, Charles. *The Siren Years: A Canadian Diplomat Abroad, 1937-1945.* London: Macmillan, 1974. An account of Massey's London mission by his secretary during the war years.

Skilling, Harold Gordon. *Canadian Representation Abroad: From Agency to Embassy.* Toronto: Ryerson Press, 1945. Provides the context of Massey's Washington mission, along with one chapter on the mission itself.

Martin B. Cohen

GUY DE MAUPASSANT

Born: August 5, 1850; Château de Miromesnil,
    near Dieppe, France
Died: July 6, 1893; Passy, Paris, France
Area of Achievement: Literature
Contribution: Maupassant was one of the major lit-
    erary figures at the end of the nineteenth century
    to help move short fiction away from the primi-
    tive folktale form to the short story of psycho-
    logical realism. His most significant
    contributions to the form may be found in such
    affecting realistic stories as "Boule de Suif" and
    such powerful tales of psychological obsession
    as "The Horla."

Early Life

Henri-René-Albert-Guy de Maupassant was born
on August 5, 1850. He was the first son of Laure
Le Poittevin and Gustave de Maupassant, both
from prosperous bourgeois families. When Maupassant was eleven and his brother Hervé was five,
his mother, an independent-minded woman, risked
social disgrace to obtain a legal separation from
her husband. With the father's absence, Maupassant's mother became the most influential figure in
the young boy's life.

At age thirteen, he was sent to a small seminary
near Rouen for classical studies, but he found the
place unbearably dreary and yearned for home, finally getting himself expelled in his next-to-last
year. He returned home to the influence of his
mother, as well as her brilliant brother Alfred and
his student and friend Gustave Flaubert. At age
eighteen, Maupassant was enrolled at the Lycée de
Rouen, and he began law studies soon afterward in
Paris, only to have these studies interrupted by the
Franco-Prussian War, for which he enlisted. After
the war, he gained a position in the Naval Ministry, but under the tutelage of Flaubert he began to
publish poetry and stories in various small journals. He also became part of a group of literary
figures, including Alphonse Daudet, Émile Zola,
and Ivan Turgenev, who met regularly at the home
of Flaubert.

Life's Work

Maupassant's first published story, "La Main
d'écorché" (1875; "The Skinned Hand," 1909),
which was reworked in 1883 as simply "La Main"
or "The Hand," belongs to a tradition of supernatural short fiction that is as old as legend itself; in re-

working the story, however, Maupassant grounded
it in the revenge-tale tradition popularized by his
countryman Prosper Mérimée and at the same time
managed to make the story an ironic comment on
supernatural fictions.

With the publication of "Boule de Suif" (1880;
English translation, 1903), a tale which Flaubert
praised extravagantly, Maupassant ceased working
for the government and devoted himself to a career
as a writer, excelling especially in the genre of the
conte, or short story, which was quite popular at
the time in periodical magazines and newspapers.
Before achieving this initial success, however,
Maupassant contracted syphilis, which was to take
his life after a relatively brief writing career of ten
years.

After the success of "Boule de Suif," the touching story of the prostitute who reluctantly goes to
bed with a Prussian officer in order to procure the
release of her traveling companions, only to be
scorned by them, Maupassant began to write anecdotal articles for two newspapers, the practice of
which served as preparation for writing the short
stories that were to make him famous.

His first full volume of short fiction appeared in
1881 under the title of his second important story,
"La Maison Tellier" (1881; "Madame Tellier's Establishment," 1903), a comic piece about a group
of prostitutes who attend a First Communion. After
the success of this book, Maupassant published numerous stories in newspapers and periodicals.
These stories were reprinted in volumes containing
other Maupassant stories. Many of his stories created much controversy among the French critics of
the time because he dared to focus on the experiences of so-called lowlife characters.

In addition to the realistic stories of the lower
classes, Maupassant experimented with mystery
tales, many of which are reminiscent of the stories
of Edgar Allan Poe. Instead of depending on the
supernatural, these stories focus on some mysterious dimension of reality which is justified rational-
ly by the central character. As a result, the reader is
never quite sure whether this realm exists in actuality or whether it is a product of the narrator's obsessions.

After having published as many as sixty of Maupassant's stories, the newspaper *Gil-Blas* began the
serialization of his first novel, *Une Vie* (*A Woman's
Life*, 1888), in February, 1883, which was pub-

lished in book form two months later. The year 1884 also saw the publication of Maupassant's most famous short story and his most widely read novel. The story, "La Parure" (1884; "The Necklace," 1903), has become one of the most famous short stories in any language. Indeed, it has become so famous that it is the story which most commonly comes to mind when Maupassant's name is mentioned, despite the fact that most critics agree that Maupassant's creation of tone and character in such stories as "Boule de Suif" and "La Maison Tellier" is much more representative of his genius than this ironically plotted story about a woman who wasted her entire life working to pay back a lost necklace, only to discover that it was fake.

"Le Horla" (1887; "The Horla," 1890), a story almost as famous as "The Necklace," is often referred to as the first sign of the syphilis-caused madness that eventually led to Maupassant's death. As a story of psychological horror, however, it is actually the pinnacle of several stories of madness with which Maupassant had previously experimented. The story focuses on the central character's intuition of a reality which surrounds human life but remains imperceptible to the senses. Told by means of diary entries, the story charts the protagonist's growing awareness of his own madness as well as his lucid understanding of the process whereby the external world is displaced by psychic projections.

What makes "The Horla" distinctive is the increasing need of the narrator to account for his madness as the result of something external to himself. Such a desire is Maupassant's way of universalizing the story, for he well knew that human beings have always tried to embody their most basic desires and fears in some external but invisible presence. "The Horla" is a masterpiece of hallucinatory horror because it focuses so powerfully on that process of mistaking inner reality for outer reality—a process which is the very basis of hallucination. The story is too strongly controlled to be the work of a madman.

Moreover, those who argue that with the writing of "The Horla" Maupassant was already going mad cannot explain the fact that the following year he published the short novel *Pierre et Jean* (1888; *Pierre and Jean*, 1890), which is one of his best-conceived and best-executed works. This work was his last major contribution, however, for after its publication his intensive production of

stories slowed almost to a halt, and he began to complain of migraine headaches, which made it impossible for him to write. His eyesight began to fail, his memory faded, and he began to suffer from delusions.

Just after the first of the year in 1892, Maupassant had to be taken to a sanatorium in a straitjacket after having slashed his own throat in a fit of what he himself called "an absolute case of madness." In the sanatorium, he disintegrated rapidly until he died on July 6, 1893.

Summary
Guy de Maupassant is one of those writers whose contribution to literature is often overshadowed by the tragic facts of his life and whose unique experimentation is often ignored in favor of his more popular innovations. Too often it is his promiscuity and profligate Parisian lifestyle that receive the most attention from the casual reader. As if to provide evidence for the payment Maupassant had to make for such a lifestyle, these readers then point to the supposed madness-inspired story "The Horla" as a fit ending for one who not only wrote about

prostitutes but also paid for their dangerous favors with his life. Yet Maupassant's real place as a writer belongs with such innovators of the short-story form as Anton Chekhov, Ivan Turgenev, Ambrose Bierce, and O. Henry. Too often, whereas such writers as Turgenev and Chekhov are admired for their so-called lyricism and realistic vignettes, such writers as Bierce and O. Henry are scorned for their so-called cheap narrative tricks. Maupassant falls somewhere in between. On the one hand, he mastered the ability to create the tight, ironic story that depends, as all short stories do, on the impact of the ending. On the other hand, he had the ability, like Chekhov, to focus keenly on a limited number of characters in a luminous situation. The Soviet short-story writer Isaac Babel has perhaps paid the ultimate tribute to Maupassant in one of his stories by noting that Maupassant knew the power of a period placed in just the right place.

Maupassant had as much to do with the development of the short-story genre in the late nineteenth century as did Chekhov, although in somewhat different ways. Yet, because such stories as "The Necklace" seem so deceptively simple and trivial, his experiment with the form has often been ignored.

Bibliography

Hottell, Ruth A. "The Delusory Denouement and Other Strategies in Maupassant's Fantastic Tales." *The Romantic Review* 85, no. 4 (November, 1994). Examines de Maupassant's ability to merge the natural and supernatural ("Le Horla," "L'Auberge," and so on), drawing the audience into the work and providing a creative connection between writer and reader.

Ignotus, Paul. *The Paradox of Maupassant.* London: University of London Press, 1966; New York: Funk and Wagnalls, 1968. A biographical and critical study that focuses much more on the unsavory aspects of Maupassant's life than it does on the excellence of his fiction. Ignotus insists, with little evidence to support his arguments, that Maupassant was primarily driven by his sexual appetites, perversions, and immoralities.

Lerner, Michael G. *Maupassant.* London: Allen and Unwin, and New York: Braziller, 1975. Primarily a biographical study, although discussion of the publication of Maupassant's work is often accompanied by some brief discussion of how his novels and stories are influenced by and in turn reflect his own social milieu.

Steegmuller, Francis. *A Lion in the Path.* New York: Random House, 1949; London: Macmillan, 1972. Not only the best biographical study of Maupassant but also one of the most perceptive critical estimates of Maupassant's works; it is the one indispensable book on Maupassant by an excellent biographer and critic who clearly understands the important role that Maupassant plays in the history of French literature.

Stivale, Charles J. *The Art of Rupture: Narrative Desire and Duplicity in the Tales of Guy de Maupassant.* Ann Arbor: University of Michigan Press, 1994. The author notes that de Maupassant's work exhibits an undercurrent of "fundamental masculine fear" of various issues which are usually represented in the literature by a woman. Men put up defenses through "the art of rupture." Stivale presents examples from de Maupassant's short fiction and analysis.

Sullivan, Edward D. *Maupassant: The Short Stories.* London: Arnold, and Great Neck, N.Y.: Barron's, 1962. Although little more than a pamphlet-length introduction to some of Maupassant's basic themes and story types, this valuable study can serve to orient the reader to Maupassant's contribution to the short-story form. Particularly helpful is Sullivan's attempt to place Maupassant's short stories within their proper generic tradition.

―――. *Maupassant the Novelist.* Princeton, N.J.: Princeton University Press, 1954. A study of the basic themes and technique of Maupassant's novels, as well as an attempt to synthesize his aesthetic and critical ideas from his essays and newspaper articles. Sullivan admits that Maupassant was a "natural" short-story writer but argues that a study of his novels provides an opportunity to study Maupassant's creative process.

Wallace, A. H. *Guy de Maupassant.* New York: Twayne, 1973. A conventional biographical and critical study that adds little to Steegmuller's earlier work. Wallace focuses on Maupassant's use of fictional themes and obsessions taken from his own life, primarily the cuckoldry of his father, the women in his life, and his madness.

Charles E. May

FREDERICK DENISON MAURICE

Born: April 29, 1805; Normanston, Suffolk, England

Died: April 1, 1872; London, England

Areas of Achievement: Religion and education

Contribution: Maurice was the one of the most respected theologians in an age when religious crisis was a part of almost every person's life. His efforts to support educational and social reforms, specifically his involvement with the movement known as Christian Socialism, had significant beneficial impact on the working classes.

Early Life

Born on the English coast on April 29, in the year Admiral Horatio Nelson defeated the French in the Battle of Trafalgar, John Frederick Denison Maurice (he dropped his first name early in his adult life) was the only surviving son of Unitarian minister Michael Maurice and his wife, Priscilla. Frederick and his five sisters, along with two cousins who moved in with the family while Frederick was quite young, grew up in a deeply religious household whose history was, by any standards, most unusual. Originally, the family adhered to the father's strict Unitarian beliefs. In a hectic period beginning in 1814, however, the family members began to fall away from that creed. Maurice's older sisters, and then his mother, adopted a Trinitarian stance influenced strongly by Calvinism and Evangelicalism. Though the younger children were reared Unitarian, the tense atmosphere that existed in the household was certainly in part responsible for Frederick's eventual decision to accept the notion of the divinity of Christ and to move closer toward Anglicanism, a faith he ultimately embraced in 1831.

Maurice was educated by his father to prepare for admission to Cambridge, where he matriculated in 1823. There, though he was not ready to subscribe to the Thirty-nine Articles (a condition required for receiving a degree), he pursued studies that would eventually prepare him for a career in law. He studied under Julius Hare, a compassionate and learned tutor who helped him explore various academic and theological questions. From Hare, he learned of the idea of Absolute Truth, and he was taught that it was each man's responsibility to search for it. While at Cambridge, Maurice took the lead in forming a club for undergraduates who met periodically to discuss important political,

philosophical, and literary subjects: the Apostles Club, perhaps the most famous of such societies, which eventually numbered among its members John Sterling, Arthur Henry Hallam, and Alfred, Lord Tennyson.

In 1826, Maurice left Cambridge without taking a degree and went to London to continue his study in law. There, he actually spent considerable time in literary activities, including service as editor for two separate periodicals. Maurice also worked on a novel, *Eustace Conway*, which was eventually published in 1834. Religious questions continued to plague him, however, and to "discipline" himself, as he put it, in his studies he decided to renew his formal education; this time, however, he enrolled in the more conservative Oxford University, where he associated with such men as the young William Ewart Gladstone. He received a bachelor of arts degree from Oxford in 1831.

The years 1831-1834 were crucial in Maurice's spiritual development and hence in determining his future. In 1831, after years of contemplation and study, he converted to Anglicanism. Three years later, he took orders, embarking on a career that would bring him to prominence within a short time.

Life's Work

Maurice began his ministry firmly convinced that the traditional view of religion based on the notion of the Fall was wrongheaded, for men had spent too much time wrangling over the problems of sin and damnation and had given too little attention to the fact that the essence of Christian theology was the presence (or potential presence) of Christ in every man. Maurice had been heavily influenced by theologians Edward Irving and Thomas Erskine, as well as by the religious writings of Samuel Taylor Coleridge. His studies and his reading of the Bible led him to believe that faith must be based on God's revelation of himself to men; men must, he thought, come to know God intimately, as a friend. That view he preached in his first curacy at Bubbenhall and for years while serving as chaplain at Guy's Hospital, a post he assumed in the fall of 1835.

By 1835, Maurice had come to recognize that the Thirty-nine Articles were no inhibition to a man's personal search for God; certainly the requirement that young men subscribe to them was no cause for anyone to stay away from the universities. To support his position, Maurice published *Subscription No Bondage* (1835), in which he argued that the Articles simply provided a framework within which theological inquiry could proceed; they were not, he claimed, a set of rules that limited one's exploration for the truth. This position seemed to place him in alignment with members of the Oxford Movement, but Maurice was not ready to go as far as the most extreme thinkers of that group. He broke with them openly over the question of the nature of Baptism, which he saw as a sign of the continuing relationship God has with every man.

Growing increasingly dissatisfied with such tenets as the Oxford Movement proposed and with other issues with which he found himself continually at odds, Maurice decided to outline his own theological beliefs in a series of "Letters to a Quaker." These sermons he published in 1838 as *The Kingdom of Christ*, a volume he revised in 1842 in order to clarify his basic beliefs. In that work, Maurice displayed his dissatisfaction with the Tractarians of Oxford and affirmed his notion that man is saved through a personal relationship with Christ. For Maurice, the Kingdom of Heaven already exists—in every man who has established this relationship.

During the 1830's, Maurice's friendship with Sterling led to marriage for the theologian. Though shy and unassuming by nature, Maurice was not without passion, and during 1837 he found a woman who stirred feelings of love within him: Anna Barton, Sterling's sister-in-law. The two were married on October 7, 1837, and were soon blessed with two sons. Unfortunately, Anna Maurice did not live to see her children grow up or her husband bring to fruition many of the projects and publications for which he is most remembered; she died of illness in March, 1845.

Maurice was selected to serve as professor of English literature and modern history at King's College, London, in 1840. Not a strong lecturer, he nevertheless captivated audiences with the sincerity of his presentations and remained popular and influential in the various professorships he held throughout his career.

When, in 1846, King's College established a program of religious studies, Maurice was given an additional appointment as professor of theology, a position that permitted him to influence young men who were themselves training for the clergy. The

same year, he was appointed chaplain at Lincoln's Inn, where his weekly sermons were well received by the young men studying for the bar. During the same period, he was asked to deliver several lecture series. As the Boyle Lecturer, he pioneered the study of comparative religions; as the Warburton Lecturer, he spoke eloquently on St. Paul's Epistle to the Hebrews.

During the 1840's, Maurice began to attract a following, both through his teaching and especially through his writings. In 1844, influenced by his reading of *The Kingdom of Christ*, author and social worker Charles Kingsley began a lifelong friendship with Maurice. They were joined by J. M. Ludlow, a more radical Socialist, in an effort to help improve the living conditions and the education of the London poor; their movement became known as Christian Socialism. Ludlow pressed for more radical solutions to current ills, but Maurice held out to effect such reforms within existing social and political structures.

The trio engaged in several schemes, including publication of several journals, to assist the working poor and to raise the conscience of their countrymen to the plight of the less fortunate. In 1848, Maurice and his followers were first encouraged and then dismayed by the rise and subsequent collapse of the Chartist movement.

By the end of the 1840's, Maurice's personal life took a new turn. He had always been close to his old tutor, Julius Hare, who had married Maurice's sister Esther in 1844. In 1848 and 1849, Maurice was finding another reason to visit the Hare family: Julius' sister Georgiana. They became engaged early in 1849 and were married July 4 of that year.

Since his appointment at King's College, Maurice had devoted much of his life to education. That commitment went beyond his lecturing; for example, in 1848 he was instrumental in establishing Queen's College to educate young women. As early as 1850, Maurice was working to promote education for working men as a means of bettering their lot. His first efforts were directed at assisting various Working Men's associations to conduct independent programs, but it was not long before he found himself at the center of a movement to establish the Working Men's College. Perhaps he would not have been as heavily involved as he eventually became had it not been for a change in his fortunes at King's College.

Maurice was freed of his commitment to King's College in 1853—but not because he had sought release. On the contrary, he was dismissed from his professorships, largely through the efforts of the principal of the college, Dr. Jelf, and conservative members of the Board of Trustees, who objected to his position on eternal punishment, published in his *Theological Essays* (1853). Though his prose was never crystal-clear to even the most discerning reader, Maurice seemed to suggest in *Theological Essays* that he could not accept the notion of eternal punishment. To theologians educated in a system that stressed the significance of the Fall and the ever-present threat of eternal damnation, such an idea appeared heretical. Despite objections from some board members, including Gladstone, the trustees voted to oust Maurice from the college.

That dismissal proved fortunate in some ways, since it permitted Maurice to become principal of the Working Men's College, which opened in 1854. Men who labored by day in London's factories and trade shops attended classes in the evenings. The college offered instruction in a number of subjects and attracted a faculty of noteworthy educators and intellectuals, including John Ruskin, who taught drawing.

Though he was no longer a professor of theology after 1853, Maurice continued to be an important voice on theological issues for the next decade and to cause consternation among those who opposed what they considered to be Maurice's unorthodox views. His appointment to St. Peter Vere Chapel in 1860, made by the Crown through the Board of Public Works, caused quite a stir; the editors of the *Record*, a paper long opposed to Maurice, lobbied to have the appointment canceled. Maurice continued to publish his own theology in volumes and pamphlets, the most important of which were *What Is Revelation?* (1859), *The Claims of the Bible and of Science* (1863), and *Moral and Metaphysical Philosophy* (1850-1862). These works, and his criticisms of the works of others, showed the essentially conservative bias of his thinking, despite his liberal notions about Hell. He objected strongly to the controversial collection of radical religious writings *Essays and Reviews* (1860), which argued that the Bible should be criticized in the same fashion as other books. Similarly, he took issue with Bishop John Colenso over the publication of the bishop's study *The Pentateuch and Book of Joshua Critically Examined* (1862-1879), because Colenso argued that some of the writings were forgeries.

In 1866, Maurice finally regained a position within the traditional academic community when

Cambridge University appointed him Knightsbridge Professor of Casuistry, Moral Theology and Moral Philosophy. He held the appointment until his death. Failing health caused him to reduce his work as the decade turned; he finally succumbed on April 1, 1872, and was buried in the family plot at Highgate.

Summary

No theologian in the nineteenth century was more committed to the idea that the Church should be one than was Frederick Denison Maurice. His constant attempts to show that sectarian division was artificial and against the will of God influenced many in his lifetime and became an important source of inspiration for later theologians and clergy. Even more significant was Maurice's insistence on the personal relationship that exists between God and man, a commitment that led him to pronounce that the Kingdom of God exists in every man who comes to know his maker personally. Not only in theology, though, has Maurice's impact been felt in England: The Christian Socialist movement was important in the steady progress that liberalism made during the century to improve the lot of the poor and the working classes and to promote the dignity of the individual. Modern British democracy owes a debt to Maurice for his work in this area.

Bibliography

Brose, Olive J. *Frederick Denison Maurice: Rebellious Conformist*. Athens: Ohio University Press, 1971. A scholarly study of Maurice, focusing on the influence he exerted on Victorian theological issues. Assesses his stature in the history of Christian thought. Especially detailed analysis of Maurice's conversion to Anglicanism and its impact on his life and opinions.

Courtney, Janet E. *Freethinkers of the Nineteenth Century*. New York: Dutton, and London: Chapman and Hall, 1920. This book includes a brief biographical sketch of Maurice as well as similar sketches of other important intellectuals in nineteenth century England.

Davies, W. Merlin. *An Introduction to F. D. Maurice's Theology*. London: S.P.C.K., 1964. Largely based on Maurice's important work, *The Kingdom of Christ*, this study presents a summary of his theology, making a strong case for the primacy of Maurice's belief in Christ and his personal relationship with God as an underpinning of his work as a social and educational reformer.

Higham, Florence. *Frederick Denison Maurice*. London: SCM Press, 1947. A brief, conversationally written biography that highlights Maurice's movement toward acceptance of Christian Socialism as a necessary consequence of his theological inquiry. Contains a good discussion of his association with Working Men's College and with such figures as Richard Trench, John Sterling, Charles Kingsley, J. M. Ludlow, and F. J. Furnivall.

Maurice, Frederick. *The Life of Frederick Denison Maurice*. 2 vols. New York: Scribner, and London: Macmillan, 1884. Lengthy biography compiled by Maurice's son from letters, family papers, and reminiscences provided by friends. Contains hundreds of important excerpts from Maurice's letters. A primary source of information for scholars and for others interested in Maurice's life and opinions.

Vidler, Alec R. *Witness to the Light: F. D. Maurice's Message for To-day*. New York: Scribner, 1948. An extensive analysis of Maurice's theological views, relying heavily on excerpts from Maurice's own writings. Contains a chapter on Maurice's views of Christian Socialism, including his assessment of the relationship between individual nations and established religions.

Wood, H. G. *Frederick Denison Maurice*. Cambridge: Cambridge University Press, 1950. A series of lectures outlining Maurice's theological position, examining his critique of Newman's writings and statements, and commenting on Maurice's study of comparative religion.

Laurence W. Mazzeno

MATTHEW FONTAINE MAURY

Born: January 14, 1806; Spotsylvania County, Virginia

Died: February 1, 1873; Lexington, Virginia

Areas of Achievement: Oceanography, meteorology, and physical geography

Contribution: A universal scientist, Maury did not limit his endeavors to one area of science; instead, he researched the land, sea, and air and showed how they are inextricably linked to one another. Maury brought the study of physical geography and oceanography into the modern age.

Early Life

Matthew Fontaine Maury, a descendant of French Huguenots, the fourth son in a family of five sons and four daughters, was born on a farm in Spotsylvania County, Virginia, near Fredericksburg, on January 14, 1806. Matthew's father, Richard, was an unsuccessful tobacco farmer who was forced, before Matthew reached the age of five, to move his family to Tennessee in search of better land. Matthew's mother, née Diana Minor, was from a prominent Virginia family of Dutch descent.

Young Matthew grew up in a very strict household. His father was a disciplinarian who believed that children must never question an order from a parent and should never speak unless spoken to. The elder Maury wanted his son to become a farmer and could not understand Matthew's passionate love for books and learning. In 1818, at age twelve, the young boy was enrolled in Harpeth Academy for a formal education and studied there until 1825. He proved to be an excellent student in all subjects and showed a particular aptitude for languages. Disappointed by the lack of books at school and at home, Matthew spent much time at his uncle Abram's nearby house, where books were plentiful. There, Matthew met John Bell, a future United States senator, and Sam Houston, a future governor of Tennessee and military hero. These contacts were to help young Maury later in his naval career.

In 1823, Matthew's eldest brother, John, contracted yellow fever and died at sea. The twenty-eight-year-old naval lieutenant had served as a role model for Matthew. John's death caused the grief-stricken father to forbid Matthew to enter West Point, as the young man had desired. Instead, in 1825, Maury contacted then Congressman Houston and requested help in obtaining a naval com-

mission. Richard Maury was so angered that he refused to communicate with his son for many years.

Life's Work

Matthew was assigned as a midshipman on the frigate *Brandywine*, bound for France. He had hoped to improve his education aboard the vessel but soon found that he would have to teach himself navigation, since the teacher aboard became impatient with the midshipmen's lack of interest. During the voyage, Maury realized how inadequate and outdated the navy's navigational materials were.

In August, 1826, the *Brandywine* departed New York for a three-year tour around South America. In Chile, Maury was transferred to the *Vincennes*, which patrolled the western coast of South America in response to the political unrest created in several countries by the wars for independence being waged against Spain. In July, 1828, the *Vincennes* received orders to circumnavigate the globe, the first American naval vessel to accomplish that two-year mission.

Although Maury loved the life of a sailor, he longed to marry and rear a family. Years before, Maury had fallen in love with Ann Herndon, a distant cousin. They were engaged in the summer of 1831, but the wedding was postponed until 1834, since Matthew received orders to leave on another three-year voyage. (He and his wife had seven children, three boys and four girls.) It was on this passage that he wrote the first of many articles, "On the Navigation of Cape Horn," published in the *American Journal of Science and Arts* in July, 1834. He also started writing a new navigation textbook that explained the mathematical principles behind the formulas used to derive longitude. This concept was a departure from the rote method then used to learn navigation. In April, 1836, his book *A New Theoretical and Practical Treatise on Navigation* was published. It soon became the official textbook for instructing midshipmen in navigation techniques. Partly as a result of the acclaim that this publication received, Maury was promoted to the rank of lieutenant in June, 1836.

Maury was anxious to return to sea duty, but at that time, there were too many officers and not enough ships in the navy. Finally, in 1838, the young sailor was assigned to a vessel surveying

harbors on the North Carolina and Georgia coasts. When the survey was completed, Maury was given leave to visit his aging parents. On October 17, 1839, returning to active duty, Maury received a severe fracture of his leg when the stagecoach in which he was riding overturned. The injury ended Maury's sailing duties, since it permanently crippled him. During a long period of recovery, he turned to writing articles for the highly respected *Southern Literary Messenger*, exposing what he considered to be the deteriorating condition in the United States Navy. The articles written in 1840 and 1841, under the pen name "Harry Bluff," called for a revision in the promotion ranks, a four-year naval academy stressing a curriculum that included languages, the sciences, international law, and mathematics in order to educate properly future naval officers. He also stressed greater efficiency in ship construction. In 1845, the United States Naval Academy was established, a result, in part of Maury's articles. The true identity of Harry Bluff became known, and Maury received praise as well as criticism for the publicity he had brought to the navy.

Photographs of Maury show him as a stocky individual, five feet six inches tall. He was described as having a soft voice with a Southern accent, and as a meticulous dresser who walked with a slight limp.

In 1842, Maury was appointed as superintendent of the Depot of Charts and Instruments in Washington, D. C. He was responsible for maintaining the accuracy of the navigational instruments and charts issued to departing navy ships. He soon discovered that most of the navigation charts used by the navy had been compiled by foreigners and were outdated. He therefore began the monumental task of examining old ship logs and calculating prevailing winds, currents, and water temperature conditions for various sailing routes. By 1847, he was able to publish the *Wind and Current Chart of the North Atlantic*. This work provided such accurate navigational information and so reduced the sailing times on commercial sea routes that other nations began requesting copies of Maury's charts. To keep his charts current, he obtained abstract logs from American navy and merchant captains, which contained the latest meteorological observations. Later, he compiled a chart that provided information on the migration patterns and habits of sperm and right whales.

In 1844, Maury was appointed as the first superintendent of the new Naval Observatory in Washington, D. C. The observatory studied and recorded astronomical, hydrographical, and meteorological data and phenomena. Maury's reputation as a scientist had grown greatly, and even though he had not received a college education, the University of North Carolina bestowed an honorary master of arts degree upon him in May, 1847, to honor his contributions to scholarship. In July of 1853, Maury received an honorary LL.D. degree from Columbian College (modern George Washington University).

The year 1853 marked the start of the successful Brussels Conference. This meeting was called by the United States to seek the cooperation of the major seafaring nations in a project to exchange marine meteorological data, which Maury used to make new charts of the world's oceans.

In 1854, Cyrus Field consulted Maury regarding the feasibility of laying a transatlantic telegraph cable. Maury had conducted deep-sea soundings and told Field that the project would be possible. After two failures, a short-lived cable did link Europe and the United States, but it was not until 1866 that a final link across the Atlantic was achieved.

By 1854, Maury's publisher suggested that he should consider writing a popular treatment of his studies of the oceans in order to take advantage of commercial possibilities. In 1855, the first addition appeared under the title *Physical Geography of the Sea*. It appealed to the general reader and included material on the winds and currents of the sea, temperature data, theories on the circulation of ocean waters, and descriptions of the flora and fauna of the oceans.

For all of Maury's scientific achievements and fame, both at home and abroad, there was to occur an event that was to spell an end to his scientific research and association with the United States Navy. His home state, Virginia, passed an ordinance of secession on April 17, 1861, five days after forces of the Confederate States of America fired upon Fort Sumter. Maury resigned from the navy on April 20, 1861, offered his services to the governor of Virginia, and was immediately appointed to the Governor's Executive Council.

Maury started working on plans for the construction of electric and mechanical "torpedoes" (mines) that could be used to break the Union naval blockade of Virginia ports. By July, 1861, Maury had experimented with powder charges and fuse devices that could be used in the construction of mines. On the night of July 7, Maury led a small raiding party in an attack upon the Union blockading fleet in Hampton Roads. The effort did not succeed in sinking any Union ships, since the fuse device would not detonate the two-hundred-pound powder charge in the mine. In June, 1862, however, Maury mined the James River below Richmond with electrically detonated torpedoes, discouraging Union gunboat movement below that city.

In August, 1862, Maury was sent on a successful secret mission to Europe in order to secure ships and munitions for the Confederacy. He also attempted to influence European public opinion to favor the Southern cause. While abroad, Maury continued his investigations of electrical torpedoes. In May, 1865, Maury was ordered back to the South with torpedoes to be used in the defense of Galveston, Texas. Before he reached Confederate soil, he was informed that the war was over. Maury decided to sail to Mexico and offer his services to Maximilian, the French-supported emperor, since he could not be assured of receiving an amnesty from the United States. He planned to establish a colony for displaced Confederates in Mexico, but the scheme did not succeed. In March, 1866, Mau-

ry traveled to England for a reunion with his wife and decided not to return to Mexico. While in England, he received a doctor of laws degree from Cambridge University. He was offered academic positions at universities in Tennessee and Virginia. (During the war, he had refused offers from Russia and France.) In 1868, he finally accepted a position at the Virginia Military Institute as professor of physics and superintendent of the Physical Survey of Virginia, a project designed to investigate the natural resources of that state and utilize them to improve Virginia's depressed economic condition. On several occasions after he took the position, other universities attempted to hire Maury away from Virginia, but he remained loyal to his home state, even in peacetime.

By January, 1873, Maury's health had seriously deteriorated. He attempted to continue a speaking tour, calling for the establishment of a national weather bureau and crop reporting system to aid farmers, but his strong will alone was not enough to sustain his failing body. He died peacefully on February 1, 1873, at his home in Lexington, Virginia.

Summary

During his lifetime, Maury embodied the spirit of nineteenth century America. A zeal for inquiry, discovery, and improvement may be said to have characterized Maury's America. Yet he was, perhaps, a man with even stronger commitments and goals than the average person. His inquiring mind spoke of his commitment to discovery. His desire to share his discoveries with ordinary citizens spoke of his commitment to the dissemination of knowledge. His loyalty to Virginia in war and strife spoke of his commitment to a principle, an ideal. Maury's concern for education was mirrored in the publication of his school geographies and wall maps, designed for elementary school use, and in his attempt to establish an agricultural college at the Virginia Military Institute.

He was a self-made man in an era of self-made men. He had no college education in the sciences and was criticized by some university-trained scientists for his lack of formal schooling. (Foreign governments and kings showered Maury with honors and memberships in many learned societies for his efforts in charting the oceans.) Yet he possessed the gift of observation and an experimentation-oriented intellect that allowed his successes to surpass those of many of his more formally educated critics.

Maury was not afraid to dream. Goals that some would have thought impossible or too difficult to achieve, Maury readily accomplished. He was a nineteenth century American possessing those attributes that made this country unique among the nations. By showing that determination, patience, and hard work, even in the face of adversity, could bring achievement, his example for Americans of any century should not be ignored.

Bibliography

Bulloch, James D. *The Secret Service of the Confederate States in Europe: Or, How the Confederate Cruisers were Equipped.* 2 vols. London: Bentley, 1883; New York: Putnam, 1884. Maury is only mentioned briefly in connection with his secret service mission to Europe during the Civil War. Yet the book still provides a firsthand account by the Confederate States' naval representative in England of efforts to buy and arm ships for the Confederate navy.

Corbin, Diana Fontaine Maury. *A Life of Matthew Fontaine Maury, U.S.N. and C.S.N.* London: Sampson Low, Marston, 1888. This laudatory book by one of Maury's daughters contains much personal history of Maury and his family. Includes letters to and from Maury. Unfortunately, there are many factual errors throughout the work.

Hawthorne, Hildegarde. *Matthew Fontaine Maury: Trail Maker of the Seas.* New York: Longman, 1943. Written more in the style of a historical novel, this very readable work is a good introduction to Maury's life. It suffers, though, from a lack of documentation and does not have the benefit of new archival material drawn upon by later works.

Jahns, Patricia. *Matthew Fontaine Maury and Joseph Henry: Scientists of the Civil War.* New York: Hastings House, 1961. This work presents a not-too-flattering and possibly overly critical treatment of Maury. It does, however, point out some of his faults and personality clashes with other scientists of the era that earlier biographers glossed over.

Lewis, Charles Lee. *Matthew Fontaine Maury: The Pathfinder of the Seas.* Annapolis: United States Naval Institute, 1927. General overview of Maury's life. Not much about his personal life but contains a good chapter on how his family and friends viewed him before the Civil War. The best early biography, but lacks documentation or bibliography.

Lewis, J. M. "Winds over the World Sea: Maury and Koppen." *Bulletin of the American Meteorological Society* 77, no. 5 (May, 1996). Examines the contributions of Maury and Wladimir Koppen to sea travel through creation of wind and current charts for the world's oceans.

Wayland, John Walter. *The Pathfinder of the Seas: The Life of Matthew Fontaine Maury.* Richmond, Va.: Garrett and Massie, 1930. This highly readable book is particularly good on Maury's Tennessee years; it has been superseded by later biographies but still provides an enjoyable introduction to its subject.

Williams, Francis Leigh. *Matthew Fontaine Maury: Scientist of the Sea.* New Brunswick, N.J.: Rutgers University Press, 1963. The best and most accurate biography, based on primary sources in the Library of Congress, National Archives, and the Maury Collection at the University of Virginia. Contains excellent bibliography and is well documented. The fullest account of Maury's scientific achievements. Valuable list of published works of Maury is included.

Charles A. Dranguet, Jr.

JAMES CLERK MAXWELL

Born: June 13, 1831; Edinburgh, Scotland
Died: November 5, 1879; Cambridge, England
Area of Achievement: Physics
Contribution: Both a theoretical and an experimental physicist as well as a notable mathematician, Maxwell founded modern field theory and statistical mechanics, mathematically describing interactions of electrical and magnetic fields that produce radiant energy, thus confirming the existence of electromagnetic waves that move at light speed. He also elaborated theories of the mechanics and kinetics of gases and a theory of Saturn's rings.

Early Life

James Clerk Maxwell was born in Edinburgh, Scotland, on June 13, 1831. An only child, he was reared by devout Episcopalian parents who, in a generally impoverished Scotland, enjoyed the comforts of Middlebie, a modest landed estate, and other small properties. Though rarely practiced, his father's profession was law. Between his parents and grandparents, James was a descendant of middle-level government officials, landed developers of small mines and manufactories, and acquaintances of such famous Scotsmen as Sir Walter Scott and the great geologist John Hutton, although none of Maxwell's immediate kin displayed unusual drive or distinction.

Maxwell's boyhood was that of a happy, unusually observant, and well-loved child to whom were imparted clear religious and moral precepts that prevailed throughout his life. His health was sometimes delicate, and between his fourteenth and sixteenth years he learned that he was nearsighted and afflicted with a persistent ear infection. Regardless of whether these infirmities were contributory, he manifested a shyness and reserve, a superficial impression of dullness, though not unfriendliness, that remained permanent characteristics.

In his earliest years, Maxwell had no formal education. Clearly, despite his affection for the outdoors, his mother introduced him to John Milton's works, as well as other classics, and he became a catholic, voracious reader prior to his entrance into the prestigious Edinburgh Academy in 1841. There, for six years, if at first unenthusiastically, he pursued a classical curriculum. Equally important, James's father introduced him into the meetings of the Edinburgh Society of Arts and the Royal Soci-

ety, where he met D. R. Hay, a decorative painter interested in explaining beauty in form and color according to mathematical principles. Stimulated by his own prior interest in conic forms, James was encouraged to pursue such inquiries seriously, one result being his receiving of the academy's Mathematical Medal (he also took first prize in English verse) in 1846. A second consequence stemmed from his introduction to Dr. James D. Forbes, of Edinburgh University, subsequently a lifelong friend, for Forbes sent the young Maxwell's ". . . Description of Oval Curves, and Those Having a Plurality of Foci" to be included in the *Proceedings of the Edinburgh Royal Society* the same year. At fifteen, Maxwell, in sum, was already recognized by Forbes and other mentors as an original, proficient, and penetrating mind, confirmation of this coming with publication by the Royal Society of two additional papers in 1849 and 1850, one dealing with the theory of rolling curves, the other with the equilibrium of elastic solids. These achievements came while Maxwell attended the

University of Edinburgh, steeping himself in natural philosophy (a Scottish intellectual specialty of great logical rigor), mathematics, chemistry, and mental philosophy.

Life's Work

Precocious, already credited with natural genius, Maxwell entered Cambridge University (first Peterhouse but soon Trinity College) in 1850. There, he swiftly came under the direction of William Thomson, popularly known for helping lay the Atlantic cable but academically to gain fame as Lord Kelvin, expert on the viscosity of gases and collaborator with James Joule in experiments on properties of air, heat, and electricity and in thermodynamics. Maxwell's superb tutor, William Hopkins, simultaneously brought discipline and order to Maxwell's incredible range of knowledge. Graduated in 1854, Maxwell shortly was made a Fellow of Trinity College and was authorized to lecture. By 1856, however, he accepted a professorship in natural philosophy at Marischal College, whose reorganization as the University of Aberdeen in 1860 caused him to move to King's College, London, still professing natural philosophy. He took with him to London the daughter of Marischal's principal, Katherine Dewar, whom he had married in 1858. They were to have no children.

Maxwell remained at King's until 1865. From students' perspectives, he was a poor instructor; his voice, mirroring his shyness, was husky and monotonal; his explanations were pitched beyond their grasp, particularly when he was lecturing workingmen. In addition, both his wife's health and his own seemed precarious. Upon arrival at King's, he had been infected with smallpox, and in 1865 a riding accident resulted in erysipelas, which seriously drained him. Perhaps persuaded by these circumstances, he retired to the family farm at Glenair until 1871, when Cambridge University offered him a new chair in experimental physics. Since the university's chancellor had presented funds to it for a modern physical laboratory, subsequently the world-famous Cavendish Laboratory, Maxwell devoted himself to designing and equipping it, alternating between spending academic terms there and summers at Glenair. He completed this task in June, 1874.

Contrary to superficial appearances, Maxwell's theoretical and experimental work proceeded steadily from his entrance into Trinity College until his death. Before completion of the Cavendish, he had converted his London home into an extensive laboratory, and the results of his investigations were both continuous and impressive. They basically fell into seven seemingly disparate but actually related areas: experiments in color vision and optics, which later had important consequences in photography; studies in elastic solids; explorations in pure geometry; mechanics; Saturn's rings; electromagnetism and electricity, which began with Michael Faraday's lines of force and eventuated in Maxwell's theory of the electromagnetic field, in the electromagnetic theory of light, and, among other electrical investigations, in establishing standards for the measurement of resistance for the British Association.

Maxwell published in each of these seven areas, but he is undoubtedly best known for his works on electricity and magnetism. His papers "Faraday's Lines of Force" and "Physical Lines of Force," presented between 1855 and 1861, were seminal studies. Originally confessing little direct knowledge of the field in which Michael Faraday worked, Maxwell nevertheless sought to demonstrate mathematically that electric and magnetic behavior was not intrinsic to magnetic bodies or to conductors, that rather, this behavior was a result of vaster changes in the distribution of energy throughout the ether, albeit by unknown means. In 1864, he further demonstrated in a paper, "On a Dynamical Theory of the Electromagnetic Field," that electromagnetic forces moved in waves and that the velocity of these waves in any medium was the same as the velocity of light, thus paving the way for an electromagnetic theory of light. In connection with his many published papers, Maxwell also wrote a textbook, *Theory of Heat* (1871), a study in dynamics, *Matter and Motion* (1876), and gathered and edited the *Electrical Researches of Henry Cavendish* (1879). His own *An Elemental Treatise on Electricity* was published posthumously, in 1881. Unfortunately, while he recovered from his erysipelas and remained in good health until 1877, though in his prime, he fell ill again with painful dyspepsia. For nearly two years, Maxwell treated himself and kept silent on his illness. By 1879, when he acknowledged it to physicians, his disease was diagnosed as terminal, and he died at Cambridge on November 5, 1879.

Summary

James Clerk Maxwell is probably the only nineteenth century physicist whose reputation has grown greater in the twentieth century than it was in his own. Rarely have such capacities for inventiveness, exposition, experiment, and mathematical descriptiveness been brought to bear by one man in the physical sciences. He gave new direction and substantiation to Faraday's work and effected a bridge to the investigations of Heinrich Hertz, who did in fact measure the velocity of electromagnetic waves, confirm that these waves indeed behaved precisely like light, and showed therefore that light and electromagnetic waves were one and the same. Practical evidence of the importance of this work is manifest in modern electronics, in radio, television, and radar. Maxwell was the effective founder of field theory and of statistical mechanics, with enormous implications for theoretical and tabletop physics, not only for questions which he clarified but also for those which he raised. Similarly, his curiosity about the rings of Saturn led him productively into study of the kinetic theory of gases, adding to the work of John Herapath, Rudolf Clausius, and Joule, by treating the velocities of molecules statistically. His conclusions about the nature of light made physical optics a branch of electricity, providing a basis for the study of X-rays and ultraviolet light. Even in metallurgy, he was credited with the invention of an automatic control system. In short, his inquiries ranged from the macrocosm to the microcosm and were ultimately knit together and described mathematically in the tradition of Newton.

Bibliography

Brush, Stephen G. "James Clerk Maxwell and the Kinetic Theory of Gases: A Review Based on Recent Historical Studies." *American Journal of Physics* 39 (June, 1971): 631-640. Assesses Maxwell's four major papers relating to kinetic theory and statistical mechanics in the light of subsequent research. Available in science libraries.

Campbell, Lewis, and William Garnett. *The Life of James Clerk Maxwell.* London: Macmillan, 1882; New York: Johnson Reprint, 1969. This remains the most detailed and accurate nineteenth century view of Maxwell. Maxwell's letters added in the second edition of 1884. Lifelong friends and associates, the authors supply a full account of his personal life and a detailed review of his scientific contributions as they were understood in the 1880's. Though in need of intelligent editing, this is an extremely informative study. Readily available in major libraries.

Domb, Cyril, ed. *Clerk Maxwell and Modern Science.* London: Athlone Press, 1963. Six commemorative essays by scientists who place Maxwell's contributions in twentieth century perspective. Excellent for general readers; reflective and instructive. Readily available in major science libraries.

Fuller, A. T. "Clerk Maxwell's London Notebooks: Extracts Relating to Control and Stability." *International Journal of Control* 30 (1979): 729-744. Fascinating account of Maxwell's 1868 paper "On Control," which Norbert Wiener labeled the first significant study on feedback mechanisms. Based on Maxwell's notebooks at King's College between 1860 and 1865. Requires understanding of math and physics and therefore not for the general reader.

Garber, Elizabeth. "James Clerk Maxwell and Thermodynamics." *American Journal of Physics* 27 (February, 1969): 146-155. Excellent, readable scholarly analysis of Maxwell's anticipation and subsequent stimulation of Willard Gibbs's work in thermodynamics. Readily available in most science libraries.

Harman, P. M. *The Natural Philosophy of James Clerk Maxwell.* Cambridge and New York: Cambridge University Press, 1998. A scientific biography that introduces the reader to Maxwell's physics, philosophy and contributions to theoretical physics.

Larsen, Egon. *The Cavendish Laboratory.* London: Ward, and New York: Watts, 1962. Places Maxwell's preparation and subsequent work at this remarkable research laboratory in perspective. Readable. Availability limited to major libraries.

Maxwell, J. C. *The Scientific Letters and Papers of James Clerk Maxwell.* Volume 1: *1846-1862.* Edited by P. M. Harman. Cambridge and New York: Cambridge University Press, 1989. The first volume of an extensive work that covers Maxwell's scientific letters and manuscripts. Harman provides commentary and annotations of the manuscripts, many published for the first time, and a fuller understanding of the development of Maxwell's work.

———. *The Scientific Letters and Papers of James Clerk Maxwell.* Volume 2: *1862-1873.* Edited by P. M. Harman. Cambridge and New York: Cambridge University Press, 1990. The second volume of Harman's presentation of Maxwell's letters and manuscripts. This volume includes Maxwell's work on statistical molecular theory, field physics, and his correspondence with Lord Kelvin, G. G. Stokes, and P. G. Tait.

Clifton K. Yearley
Kerrie L. MacPherson

GIUSEPPE MAZZINI

Born: June 22, 1805; Genoa, Ligurian Republic
Died: March 10, 1872; Pisa, Italy
Areas of Achievement: Philosophy, politics, and government
Contribution: Mazzini was the most influential leader of the Risorgimento—the Italian national unification movement. His political activities and philosophy were carried beyond Italy and inspired fledgling nationalist and democratic reform movements throughout the world.

Early Life

Giuseppe Mazzini was born in 1805, the son of a well-to-do Genoese family. A sickly but precocious child, he could scarcely walk until the age of six. His mother, Maria Drago, practiced the morally rigorous Catholic doctrine of Jansenism and provided the young Mazzini with Jansenist tutors. His political education began at home under the influence of his father, Giacomo—a renowned physician and a professor at the University of Genoa. Mazzini's father, like many educated Italians, had embraced the nationalist and democratic ideas of the French Revolution. These ideas endured even after the Napoleonic Wars, when authoritarian rule had been restored to the various Italian states. Giacomo and other Italian patriots nurtured hopes for democratic reform, independence from foreign rule, and ultimately a united Italy.

As a young man, Mazzini was deeply moved by the suffering of others and was recklessly generous in his charity. He tended to be melancholy, always dressed in black—as if in mourning—and enjoyed long, solitary walks. At the University of Genoa, he studied law, but his real interest was in history and literature. He organized a student group to study censored books and wrote provocative essays for several literary journals. The Italian universities in the 1820's were a conduit for subversive political organizations. During his student years, Mazzini became involved with a secret revolutionary society—the Carbonari. The July Revolution of 1830 in France inspired the Carbonari to plot insurrections in Piedmont and other Italian states. Government officials uncovered the conspiracy and arrested hundreds of suspects, including Mazzini. He defended himself successfully in court, but the Piedmontese authorities forced him into exile. At the age of twenty-six, he left Genoa for France.

Life's Work

The failure of the Carbonari insurrections during 1830-1831 led Mazzini to organize his own secret society, Young Italy. Through this group, he hoped to bring a youthful energy and idealism to the movement for Italian independence and unification. His sincerity and the quiet strength of his convictions won for him a devout following. His agents distributed the newspaper *Young Italy* and established affiliated societies throughout the Italian peninsula. In 1833, Mazzini joined with nationalists from other countries to found Young Europe. This organization embodied the aspirations of many European nationalities seeking to break free of the Austrian and Russian empires and to establish their own independent states with democratic institutions. Mazzini's European network of secret societies made him a notorious figure. The Austrian government considered him an international terrorist, a threat to the entire European order. Yet to the peoples of Europe who chafed under authoritarian rule, he appeared as a symbol of liberty.

The insurrections organized in the 1830's by Mazzini and his followers failed to ignite a popular uprising in Italy. For his subversive activity, he received the death sentence in absentia from a Piedmontese court in 1833. His life in exile took him from France to Switzerland to Great Britain. He traveled like a fugitive—under the constant threat of arrest and imprisonment. To survive these difficult years in exile, he relied on the loyalty of his followers and the generous financial support from his mother. Once in London, he devoted his time to writing for popular journals and to publishing his own newspaper. His most notable work during his years in exile was *Doveri dell'uomo* (1860; *The Duties of Man*, 1862). Through his many editorials, essays, commentaries, and correspondence, he shaped and refined his political philosophy. He became a celebrated figure among intellectuals and reformers in Great Britain and the United States. At the same time, he generated international sympathy for the Italian cause.

Mazzini based his philosophy on a profound belief in God, in human progress, and in the fundamental unity and cooperation of mankind. The banner of Young Italy best summarized his thought: "Liberty, Equality, Humanity, Unity." These words had universal application. For Mazzini, liberty meant the elimination of all despotism, from tyranny in Italy to slavery in the American South. His belief in equality extended to women as well as men, and for this he won the admiration and devotion of many women's rights advocates in Europe and the United States. His faith in humanity was expressed in the Latin epithet: *Vox populi, vox Dei* (the voice of the people is the voice of God). He believed that the Italian unity would be forged through a spontaneous, general uprising of the Italian people. Mazzini's call for unity transcended national boundaries. He envisioned no less than a brotherhood of nations, beginning with a new federation of European states—a United States of Europe—with the new Italy in the vanguard.

Mazzini's religious faith bordered on mysticism. Yet despite his religious convictions and his Catholic education, he had no room for the authority of the pope, either as civil ruler of the Papal States or as the spiritual leader of the Christian world. Although sympathetic to the plight of the working class, he rejected the materialist, atheistic character of socialist philosophy and avoided emphasizing class conflict as the Marxists would later do. Instead, he advocated worker-aid associations and a spirit of cooperation between labor and capital. He sought to extend the Christian ethic from the home to the workplace to the halls of government and spoke more of duties and responsibilities than of rights and privileges.

The popular revolts in Europe during 1848-1849 gave Mazzini the opportunity to return to Italian soil. He arrived in Milan in April, 1848, shortly after the city's heroic five-day uprising against Austrian rule. Despite the generous welcome extended to the exiled patriot, Mazzini represented only one of several political factions vying for leadership. He left Milan after a failed attempt to organize the city's defenses against the returning Austrian army.

His second opportunity to create a new Italy came in November, 1848, when the populace of Rome revolted, drove Pope Pius IX from the city, and established a republican government in the Papal States. Mazzini entered Rome as an elected leader and immediately implemented his reform program. Church lands were confiscated and redistributed to the peasants, church offices became shelters for the homeless, and public works provided labor for the unemployed. The new republic lasted only a few months. In response to the pope's plea for intervention, the French government dispatched an army to central Italy. The French occupied the Papal States and won control of Rome,

despite a tenacious, monthlong defense of the city led by Giuseppe Garibaldi. Mazzini, devastated by the turn of events, left Rome and once again went into exile.

Mazzini's direct influence on Italian politics waned after the failed Revolutions of 1848. The work of Italian unification passed to the hands of the Piedmontese prime minister Count Cavour, who preferred international diplomacy to popular uprisings to achieve his goals. Mazzini maintained contacts with republican groups who attempted several unsuccessful, sometimes tragic, insurrections during the 1850's. These failures provoked public criticism even from his supporters. He made several secret trips to Italy and in one instance was arrested and imprisoned briefly near Naples.

Mazzini held stubbornly to his republican principles. Elected to the Italian parliament in 1865, he refused his seat because of the required oath of allegiance to the monarch. He also rejected the general amnesty offered to him by the king in 1871. He spent his last years in Pisa and lived to see Italy unified with Rome as its capital. His political legacy was continued by his followers, many of whom championed further democratic reforms in the parliamentary politics of postunification Italy.

Summary

Giuseppe Mazzini was the international spokesman for Italian unification and the Italian people. Ironically, he knew little of his own country. He spent much of his life in exile and, before 1848, had never traveled in central or southern Italy. Much of his knowledge of Italy came from history texts and secondhand reports from visitors, and he did not have many contacts with working-class Italians. His concept of "the people" was a middle-class intellectual's romanticized notion, far removed from the brutish existence of the Italian peasant.

Mazzini was not a profound philosopher; many of his writings are characterized by vagaries, inconsistencies, and temperamental ramblings. Despite these shortcomings, his life had a mythical, heroic quality, and his political philosophy had universal appeal. He personified the idealism, optimism, and faith in humanity that motivated many nineteenth century reformers in Europe and the United States. Even Indian and Chinese nationalists invoked Mazzini's name in their efforts to create new democratic nations. They all found inspiration in his life and in his thoughts on political

freedom, social equality, economic cooperation, and the brotherhood of nations.

Many of Mazzini's ideas seemed unrealistic in his own time, but some had a prophetic ring, and others have become even more relevant in the twentieth century. His hopes for an Italian republic were finally realized in 1946. His proposals for worker associations and a reconciliation between labor and capital proved far more constructive than did Karl Marx's vision of unmitigated class conflict, and his dream of a United States of Europe anticipated the post-World War II movement toward a unified European community.

Bibliography

Biddiss, Michael. "Nationalism and the Moulding of Modern Europe." *The Journal of the Historical Association* 79, no. 257 (October, 1994). Discusses the idea of a unified Europe which was proposed in 1850 by Mazzini and the preservation of cultural identity within unity.

Griffith, Gwilym O. *Mazzini: Prophet of Modern Europe*. London: Hodder and Stoughton, and New York: Harcourt Brace, 1932. The best writ-ten of the English biographies, this work offers an uncritical study with emphasis on Mazzini's theology.

Hales, Edward E. Y. *Mazzini and the Secret Societies*. New York: Kenedy, and London: Eyre and Spottiswoode, 1956. A critical study of Mazzini's early years. Hales highlights the climate of conspiracy to which the young Mazzini was drawn and describes the making of the Mazzini "myth." Contains a helpful annotated bibliography.

Hinkley, Edyth. *Mazzini: The Story of a Great Italian*. London: Allen and Unwin, and New York: Putnam, 1924. This sympathetic biography emphasizes Mazzini's profound religious convictions and the universal character of his philosophy.

King, Bolton. *Mazzini*. London: Dent, and New York: Dutton, 1902. The first serious English study of Mazzini. King offers a very generous portrayal of Mazzini as a historical agent of political and moral progress. Includes an appendix containing several of Mazzini's letters and a bibliography listing many of Mazzini's writings published in English during the nineteenth century.

Lovett, Clara M. *The Democratic Movement in Italy, 1830-1876*. Cambridge, Mass.: Harvard University Press, 1982. Places Mazzini in the broader context of a complex and diverse democratic political movement.

Mazzini, Giuseppe. *Life and Writings of Joseph Mazzini*. 6 vols. London: Smith, Elder, 1864-1870. A comprehensive collection of Mazzini's writings available in English.

Salvemini, Gaetano. *Mazzini*. Translated by I. M. Rawson. London: Cape, 1956; Stanford, Calif.: Stanford University Press, 1957. An English translation of Salvemini's study, originally published in 1905 and revised in 1925. His commentary provides a good, critical introduction to Mazzini's thought and writings but contains very little biographical information.

Smith, Denis Mack. *Mazzini*. New Haven, Conn.: Yale University Press, 1994; London: Yale University Press, 1996. Smith presents Mazzini, one of the lesser-known figures in the mid-nineteenth-century Italian unification movement. Arguing that he was often misunderstood, Smith notes that Mazzini's approach was exaggerated by his critics and not as "revolutionary" as advertized.

Michael F. Hembree

SECOND VISCOUNT MELBOURNE
William Lamb

Born: March 15, 1779; Brocket Hall, Hertfordshire, England

Died: November 24, 1848; Brocket Hall, Hertfordshire, England

Areas of Achievement: Government and politics

Contribution: A man of wit, urbanity, and cynicism, Melbourne was the stereotype of the aristocratic Whig politician. As prime minister in
1834 and from 1835 to 1841, he helped set the
pattern for governmental reforms. He also was a
crucial influence on the young Queen Victoria.

Early Life

William Lamb, second Viscount Melbourne, was
born March 15, 1779, at his family home, Brocket
Hall in Hertfordshire. His father, Peniston Lamb,
squandered the family fortune but secured a title of
nobility by means of his loyalty to the ministry of
Lord North and his friendship with the Prince of
Wales (later George IV). His mother, née Elizabeth
Milbanke, brought a fortune to the marriage and
took a deep interest in her son's education. After
tutoring at home, Melbourne studied at Eton, at
Trinity College, Cambridge, at Lincoln's Inn
(where he qualified as a lawyer), and as a private
student of history, economics, and political science
in Glasgow. An intelligent and well-read man, he
had only begun his career in law when, at the death
of his elder brother in 1805, he became heir to the
family title. He gave up the law for politics, as was
the duty of a man in his position.

Melbourne sat in the House of Commons from
1806 to 1812 and again from 1816 to 1829; he entered the House of Lords upon his father's death in
1829. At first an advanced Whig who opposed the
war against France, Melbourne moderated his
opinions as he moved into the orbit of George Canning, the leader of the moderate Conservatives. Although Melbourne rarely spoke in debates, Canning and the Prince Regent liked him; when
Canning became prime minister in 1827, Melbourne was appointed Irish secretary. At that time,
the Conservative domination of British politics was
beginning to break up under the pressures of the
movements to abolish slavery, to give Roman
Catholics political rights, and to reform the electoral system. Melbourne followed the liberal followers of Canning into opposition, and when Earl
Grey formed a Whig ministry in 1830, Melbourne
was named home secretary.

As home secretary (1830-1834), Melbourne was
responsible for maintaining public order in England and Ireland. This was no small task, for the
kingdom seemed on the verge of revolution. Daniel
O'Connell's Catholic Association held mass rallies
to demand home rule for Ireland; factory workers
marched to demand a ten-hour working day; agricultural laborers burned hayricks and tried to organize a union. Middle-class Nonconformists wanted
to crush the power of the Church of England and
the landed gentry. Philosophical Radicals advanced
Prussian or French centralization as the model for
Great Britain to follow in reforms. As home secretary, Melbourne sought to find a middle ground
among these competing voices, mediating differences between factory owners and workers, members of the Church of England and Nonconformists, Whigs and Radicals. As a minister of state, he
was a reasonably efficient man of business who
paid attention to the actions of his civil servants
and was evenhanded within the limits of his political views. (Although he is remembered by left-
wing historians as the man responsible for exiling
to Australia the Tolpuddle Martyrs, who had tried
to organize a farm workers' union, Melbourne opposed both legislation to repress the free exercise
of dissent and the use of police spies to infiltrate
working-class movements.) Whiggish in his toleration for religious dissent, he exhibited a healthy
skepticism for reformers who did not have to bear
the responsibility for the practical consequences of
their theoretical radicalism. His politics were as
moderate as his demeanor was affable.

A handsome and sophisticated man, Melbourne
was known for his cynical flippancy and religious
skepticism. He was reputed to be lazy, both personally and politically, but that was a pose. He liked
attractive women and was cited as a correspondent
in several divorce actions, most notably that of
Mrs. Caroline Norton. Melbourne's marriage to
Lady Caroline Lamb (née Ponsonby) was an unhappy one. Lady Caroline had many affairs, and
her liaison with the poet Lord Byron was an open
scandal. The couple separated in 1825; that their
only child, a son, was retarded only added to Melbourne's domestic unhappiness. Thus Mel-

bourne's cynicism, flippancy, and skepticism concealed inner pain.

Life's Work

Melbourne was prime minister from July to November of 1834, and again from April, 1835, to August, 1841. (In the interval, the Conservative Sir Robert Peel held office.) Melbourne faced two great problems during his premiership: the pressure for reforms of institutions in church and state, and the accession to the throne of the eighteen-year-old Queen Victoria.

The coming to power of the Whigs in 1830 and the reform of Parliament in 1832 had opened the floodgates for reform. All sorts of political, economic, social, and religious groups, representing important divisions within British society, expected the reformed Parliament to be attentive to their desires. Taken together, their desires, had they been gained, would have resulted in a radical restructuring of British institutions. Religious Nonconformists objected to the Anglican Established Church's right to collect local taxes (tithes) and its monopoly on higher education; some wanted to separate church and state. Industrialists and merchants wanted an end to protective tariffs and the abolition of all government restrictions on the way that they did business. Workers wanted the state to protect them from their powerful employers by limiting the length of the working day and by inspecting factories to uncover hazardous working conditions. Humanitarians wanted the state to help the West Indian slaves, the children, and the poor. The middle classes wanted to increase their political power at the expense of the landed gentry.

The Whigs, especially Lord Melbourne, were moderate liberals. On the one hand, they believed in religious freedom, in the classical economics of Adam Smith and David Ricardo, and in the paternalistic duty of those better able to help others. On the other hand, the Whigs also believed that democracy led to social disorder and tyranny, either of a dictator (as revolutionary France showed) or of a fickle and ignorant majority (as the republican United States showed). Moreover, they were practical politicians who wanted to gain power and, once having gained power, remain in power. The Whigs understood that they had to balance all competing demands, giving something to each, but not enough to all, if government was to proceed. They charted a careful and moderate path in such matters as the New Poor Law, the Municipal Corporations Act, state aid to education, the tithe question, Irish grievances, and the civil registration of births, marriages, and deaths.

As prime minister, Melbourne presided over a cabinet of Whig grandees, some of whom were able, and all of whom thought highly of themselves. Melbourne was able to keep the peace by acting as mediator and by restraining some of the more activist ministers, although in a genial way. When necessary, however, he could be firm, as in the case of Lord Brougham, the brilliant but erratic Lord Chancellor. Melbourne excluded Brougham from his second ministry, but did it in a way that minimized Brougham's anger.

In his relationship with Queen Victoria, Melbourne did three very important things. First, he taught her the ins and outs of politics, of the great questions of the day, and of the personalities of public figures. This tutoring was invaluable for a young, inexperienced monarch. Second, he helped Albert of Saxe-Coburg-Gotha adjust to his role as prince consort and Victoria's husband. This task was extremely delicate, for Albert as husband broke up the close personal relationship between queen and prime minister. Nevertheless, Melbourne not only made room for Albert, but also introduced him to the art of British politics. Third, Melbourne helped the queen understand the role of the monarch in a constitutional system. The queen tried to maintain contact with him after he went into opposition in 1841, but he resisted this unconstitutional relationship and helped Peel, the new prime minister, establish a good working relationship with the monarch.

Melbourne led the Whig opposition until he suffered a stroke in 1842. Thereafter he withdrew gradually from active politics and spent more and more time at Brocket Hall, his country estate in Hertfordshire, where he died on November 24, 1848.

Summary

A skeptic, rationalist, and epicure, very much in the mold of the eighteenth century, the second Viscount Melbourne served in and later presided over the Whig ministries of the 1830's, a time that historians call "the decade of reform." A believer in moderation, consensus, and reasonable reform, he charted for the Whigs a middle course, between the pressures of Nonconformists and middle-class Philosophical Radicals on the left and the reaction of Anglicans and Conservatives on the right. The moderate nature of his party's programs allowed the liberal Conservatives, led by Peel, to pursue a policy rather more reformist than their right wing would otherwise have accepted. This circumstance promoted stability and evolutionary tendencies in British politics.

In his relationship with Queen Victoria, Melbourne contributed greatly to the Hanoverian monarchy's adjustment to the more parliamentary and responsible constitutional system of the nineteenth century, a system in which the monarch was expected to support, or at least not to oppose actively, that politician whose party commanded a parliamentary majority gained through honest elections. Melbourne, then, contributed to the stability of the British monarch and to its ability to survive into the twentieth century.

Bibliography

Arnstein, Walter L. *A History of England*. Vol. 4, *Britain Yesterday and Today: 1830 to the Present*. 7th ed. Lexington, Mass.: Heath, 1996. A very readable survey of English history; useful for background.

Brown, Lucy M., and Ian R. Christie. *Bibliography of British History, 1789-1851*. Oxford: Clarendon Press, 1977. A superb bibliography of writings on British history for this period. Organized by subject and well indexed.

Cecil, David. *Melbourne*. New York: Grosset and Dunlap, 1954; London: Reprint Society, 1955. A beautifully written study by one of the masters of the art of biography.

Finlayson, Geoffrey B. A. M. *England in the Eighteen Thirties: Decade of Reform*. London: Arnold, 1969. A brief but thoughtful, clear, and succinct analysis of the reform tendencies of the day.

Gash, Norman. *Politics in the Age of Peel: A Study in the Technique of Parliamentary Representation, 1830-1850*. London and New York: Longman, 1953. This and the following study are essential reading for anyone concerned with the politics of the 1830's and 1840's.

———. *Reaction and Reconstruction in English Politics, 1832-1852*. Oxford: Clarendon Press, 1965; Westport, Conn.: Greenwood Press, 1981. An overview of the forces that determined how politics functioned, written by the dean of the political historians who study the 1830's and 1840's.

Melbourne, W. L. *Lord Melbourne's Papers*. Edited by Lloyd C. Sanders. London and New York: Longman, 1889. A reasonably accurate edition of Melbourne's political correspondence, the originals of which are at the Royal Archives at Windsor Castle.

Mitchell, Austin. *The Whigs in Opposition, 1815-1830*. Oxford: Clarendon Press, 1967. A scholarly study of how the Whigs conducted themselves in opposition and prepared for taking office in 1830.

Mitchell, L. G. *Lord Melbourne, 1779-1848*. Oxford and New York: Oxford University Press, 1997. The first biography of Lord Melbourne in twenty years. Using the Melbourne family papers, the author fleshes out the man versus the politician.

Southgate, Donald. *The Passing of the Whigs, 1832-1886*. London: Macmillan, and New York: St. Martin's Press, 1962. Seeks to show how the Whigs emerged from the late eighteenth century with a coherent party program, but ultimately failed to attract the mass electorate of the late nineteenth century.

Ziegler, Philip. *Melbourne: A Biography of William Lamb, Second Viscount Melbourne*. London: Collins, and New York: Knopf, 1976. An excellent biography, well grounded in documentary sources, that convincingly links Melbourne's personal life and political style.

D. G. Paz

HERMAN MELVILLE

Born: August 1, 1819; New York, New York
Died: September 28, 1891; New York, New York
Area of Achievement: Literature
Contribution: With great power and insight into man's ambiguous nature, Melville helped prove that American literature could equal that of England.

Early Life

Herman Melville was born August 1, 1819, in New York City, the second son of Allan and Maria Gansevoort Melvill. (The final *e* was added after Allan's death in 1832, perhaps to indicate the family's connection with the aristocratic Melville clan of Scotland.) He grew up in the shadow of his older brother, Gansevoort, for whom the family had high expectations. In contrast, his mother found seven-year-old Herman "very backward in speech and somewhat slow in comprehension." The Melvills wanted all of their children to excel because of the family's prominence. Maria's father was considered the richest man in Albany, New York, a Revolutionary War hero after whom a New York City street was named, and Allan's father participated in the Boston Tea Party. Allan Melvill did his best to keep up the appearance of prosperous respectability, moving several times to larger and more comfortable houses in better Manhattan neighborhoods, yet this surface prosperity belied his problems with his business, importing fine French dry goods. In 1830, he closed his shop and moved the family to Albany, leaving unpaid bills behind.

Allan's worries about his new Albany business drove him mad just before he died in January, 1832, and his two oldest sons had to go to work. (Maria was left with four sons and four daughters.) While sixteen-year-old Gansevoort took over his father's fur store and factory, Herman became a bank clerk. He wanted more than a career in commerce, however, and quit the bank in 1835 to work in the family store while attending the Albany Classical School. In 1837, he qualified to be a teacher and was in charge of a one-room school near Pittsfield, Massachusetts, for one term.

After his family moved to Lansingburgh, New York, in 1838, Melville studied engineering and surveying at the Lansingburgh Academy. After failing to obtain a job on the Erie Canal, he, like many restless young men from families with financial problems, went to sea, sailing on the *St. Lawrence*

with a cargo of cotton to Liverpool in June, 1839. Despite presenting this trip as a miserable experience in *Redburn: His First Voyage* (1849), Melville thrived on the freedom from family responsibilities. The only negative aspect of the journey was his horror at the poverty of the Liverpool slums. He returned home that fall to teach at the Greenbush Academy near Lansingburgh and contributed a gothic horror sketch to the local newspaper. He made another important trip in the summer of 1840 along the Great Lakes and the Mississippi and Ohio rivers.

Unable to secure a profitable or interesting position on land, Melville sailed for the Pacific on the whaler *Acushnet* in January, 1841. Life on this ship was unpleasant, so Melville and a shipmate ran away in the Marquesas and spent twenty-six days in the valley of the Typees, who were alleged to be cannibals. He then signed on the *Lucy Ann*, an Australian whaler, in August, 1842. This time, conditions were even worse than those on the *Acushnet*, and Melville was put ashore in Tahiti and briefly held as a mutineer. He joined another whaler, the *Charles and Henry*, that November. Discharged in Hawaii, he worked as a clerk and bookkeeper at a Honolulu general store.

Throughout these travels, Melville was appalled at the way supposed civilization was being imposed upon the natives, primarily by missionaries. Having seen enough of the exotic and of the depravities of his fellow white men, he enlisted in the navy in August, 1843, so that he could sail to Boston on the *United States*. His cynicism about civilized behavior was further hardened on this voyage as he saw 163 seamen and apprentices flogged.

Life's Work

Back home, because travel literature, especially that about the South Seas, was in vogue, Melville began writing a book. Realizing that he could not rely completely upon his memory and untested descriptive skills, he read numerous books about voyages to the Pacific. Such researches into factual material to support his stories continued throughout his career.

The result of Melville's labors was *Typee: A Peep at Polynesian Life* (1846). He combined his experiences and his reading with his imagination to produce a romantic adventure which was rejected by the first publisher to whom it was submitted be-

cause it could not possibly be true. Gansevoort, in London as secretary to the American legation, showed his brother's manuscript to John Murray, who agreed to publish it, and an American publisher was also soon found. Gansevoort became ill and died a few months later, creating an additional pressure on Melville to succeed.

Typee received praise from both American and British critics, including, in unsigned reviews, Margaret Fuller, Nathaniel Hawthorne, and a then-unknown Walt Whitman. The American edition sold an impressive 5,753 copies in its first year. Melville based his second book, *Omoo: A Narrative of Adventures in the South Seas* (1847), on his *Lucy Ann* and Tahiti experiences, again borrowing material from other sources. *Omoo* sold as well as *Typee*, but both were attacked in religious journals for their unflattering view of missionaries.

During this time, Melville had met and fallen in love with a Boston friend of his sister Helen. Elizabeth Shaw was the daughter of Lemuel Shaw, chief justice of Massachusetts and a boyhood friend of Melville's father. Elizabeth may have been attracted to Melville, who stood five feet, nine and a half inches, had a stocky build, oversized ears, small blue eyes—and later a big black beard—because his experiences and prospects as an artist seemed romantic to someone who had led a relatively tame existence. They were married August 4, 1847, and began sharing a Manhattan house with his mother, sisters, and brother Allan and his new wife.

Melville started his third novel intending simply to repeat his formula of blending his seagoing experiences and his research, but his reading of German romances and the poetry of Lord Byron, John Keats, and Percy Bysshe Shelley, together with his affection for his young wife, turned *Mardi and a Voyage Thither* (1849) into a whimsical Polynesian romance. He injected philosophy and political commentary in *Mardi* as well, presenting a theory of history in which American freedoms are not the products of the country's institutions but are made possible by the geographical fact of a constantly diminishing frontier. Melville also wanted the United States to refrain from meddling in European affairs and from imperialism in its own hemisphere. Throughout his career, he criticized the ways in which American society fell short of the ideals it professed.

Melville had hoped *Mardi* would be a popular success, but reviewers were unfriendly, one calling it "a transcendental *Gulliver*, or *Robinson Crusoe*

run mad." Because his first child, Malcolm, had just been born, he felt compelled to delay the more ambitious work he wanted to do. Since something commercial was called for, he planned "a plain, straightforward, amusing narrative of personal experience—the son of a gentleman on his first voyage to sea as a sailor—no metaphysics, no conic-sections, nothing but cakes and ale." *Redburn* was written to this prescription, quickly followed by a similar novel, *White-Jacket: Or, The World in a Man-of-War* (1850), based on his duty on the *United States* (*White-Jacket* is said to have contributed to ending flogging in the United States Navy). His expectations for the novels were rewarded when both were well received by critics and the public.

Melville believed that these five books had exhausted the interesting incidents in his life, so he went to Europe in the autumn of 1849 hoping to collect material he could use in new books. Returning to America, he planned to write about an American exile in Europe, but Richard Henry Dana, Jr., suggested that he do for the whaling industry what he had done for the navy in *White-Jacket* and what Dana had done for the merchant marine in *Two Years Before the Mast* (1840). Melville agreed and promised Dana "a strange sort of book," though not as strange as *Mardi*.

Feeling cramped living with his relatives in New York, Melville moved his wife and son in 1850 to a 145-acre farm near Pittsfield, where he met Hawthorne at a gathering of leading literary figures. Melville spoke to his fellow writers of the potential greatness of American literature, and in reading Hawthorne's *Mosses from an Old Manse* (1846) soon afterward, he found confirmation of American genius. Melville interrupted his work on *Moby Dick: Or, The Whale* (1851) to write "Hawthorne and His Mosses," in which he argued that the literature of America could rival that of England, that an American writer with the intellectual capacity of Hawthorne could create art on Shakespearean levels. Melville deliberately tried for this kind of greatness in *Moby Dick*, his ambition matching Captain Ahab's obsession with the white whale.

Although some reviewers perceived the originality and power of *Moby Dick*, many misunderstood and attacked it. *United States Magazine and Democratic Review* found it full of "bad rhetoric, involved syntax, stilted sentiment and incoherent English." *Southern Quarterly Review* considered the parts not dealing with the white whale "sad stuff, dull and dreary, or ridiculous." Even Melville's close friend and staunchest supporter, Evert Duyckinck, a prominent editor and critic, disliked the novel.

Acknowledging that the reading public was predominantly female, Melville decided to direct his next book toward feminine tastes. He was further motivated by having received an average of only twelve hundred dollars for his books and by being in debt to Harper's, his American publisher. In attempting to create a gothic romance in the manner of Hawthorne's *The House of the Seven Gables* (1851), however, Melville became recklessly carried away as he had with *Mardi* ignoring his commercial judgment in his effort to "find out the heart of a man."

Pierre: Or, The Ambiguities (1852), a story of love, murder, and suicide, with overtones of incest, was rejected by Melville's English publisher and almost unanimously vilified by reviewers for its "impurity." When only 283 copies were sold during the first eight months after publication, Melville finally began to be discouraged by his prospects as a writer. His family thought there was a danger of his work affecting his mental health and set out to find for him a more profitable and less demanding occupation, such as a foreign consulship. Melville was hardly ready to abandon his writing and turned much of his attention to well-paying magazine stories, the best of which are "Bartleby the Scrivener" (1853) and "Benito Cereno" (1855). He was encouraged enough by this success to write his long-planned American-exile novel, *Israel Potter: His Fifty Years of Exile* (1855), keeping what he had learned about the interests of magazine readers constantly in mind. This satirical look at the Revolutionary War and its aftermath sold well and brought Melville, who had four children by then, closer to financial security than he had ever been.

His next book, however, *The Piazza Tales* (1856), a collection of stories, was unsuccessful, and his family believed that the writing of *The Confidence Man: His Masquerade* (1857) was ruining his health. They decided that he needed a vacation, and Judge Shaw paid for him to go to Europe and the Holy Land. Melville hoped to have some sort of simple religious faith restored on this trip but found the Holy Land more unattractive and uncomfortable than inspiring.

He returned home to find *The Confidence Man*, a satirical allegory based upon his Mississippi River trip years before, a critical and commercial failure.

His brother-in-law, Lemuel Shaw, Jr., felt it belonged to "that horribly uninteresting class of nonsensical books he is given to writing," the view of most of his relatives of most of his work. Melville chose not to write any further, since doing so would upset his family.

Instead of writing, Melville took to the lecture circuit, speaking on statuary in Rome and the South Seas throughout the Northeast and Midwest in 1857-1859, but these lectures were only moderately successful. He next turned to poetry, but he had no illusions about popular success, creating his art simply to satisfy himself, especially since no publishers were interested in his poems.

After failing to obtain a consulship, Melville traded his farm for the Manhattan house of his brother Allan. He also began writing Civil War poems based upon newspaper accounts and one visit to the front lines. He paid for the publication of *Battle-Pieces and Aspects of the War* (1866) and lost four hundred dollars on the venture.

In 1867, he submitted to his family's wishes and became a deputy customs inspector in New York for four dollars a day, later reduced to $3.60. He continued writing poetry, and Peter Gansevoort, his uncle, gave him twelve hundred dollars to publish *Clarel: A Poem and Pilgrimage in the Holy Land* (1876), his most significant poetry. After its publication, he settled into a daily routine of work, family obligations, and the frequent illnesses associated with age.

Contrary to legend, Melville's novels were not completely forgotten. They sold about one hundred copies yearly during 1876-1880 and twice that many in 1881-1884, and W. Clark Russell, the popular English writer of sea stories, praised him as "the greatest genius" America had produced. At sixty-five, Melville found himself without financial worries for the first time, primarily because of money his wife inherited from her parents, and he retired from the customhouse in December, 1885.

Melville privately published two collections of poems during this time of leisure: *John Marr and Other Sailors* (1888) and *Timoleon* (1891). In 1888, after neglecting fiction for thirty years, he started a long-planned project based upon a famous case in which a sailor was perhaps unjustifiably hanged at sea. (A cousin of Melville presided over the court-martial.) He may also have been exploring his feelings about the apparent suicide of his son Malcolm in 1867 and the death in 1886 of his other son, the unhappy, wandering Stanwix. He completed *Billy Budd, Foretopman* before dying of enlargement of the heart of September 28, 1891. This short novel was not published until 1924 after biographer Raymond M. Weaver discovered it in 1919, concealed in a tin breadbox.

Summary

New editions of *Typee, Omoo, White-Jacket,* and *Moby Dick* were published in 1892 and, surprisingly, found a market, going through forty-four editions in the United States and Great Britain by 1919, when Melville's work began to be widely rediscovered and reassessed. The Melville revival exploded in the 1920's with several books and articles, led by Weaver's 1921 biography. By this time, readers were more accustomed to symbolism and psychological fiction and recognized the originality and power of Melville's writing, with many proclaiming *Moby Dick* the Great American Novel for its insight into the contradictory motives underlying so much of American experience. Equally important is what D. H. Lawrence describes as "the peculiar, lurid, glamorous style which is natural to the great Americans" and which stems "from the violence native to the American Continent, where force is more powerful than consciousness." *Moby Dick* is, in Alfred Kazin's words, "a hymn to the unequalled thrust that lifted America to the first rank."

Melville's famous skepticism and cynicism resulted from a very American restlessness of the intellect and the spirit. As Hawthorne wrote of his friend, "He can neither believe, nor be comfortable in his unbelief; and he is too honest and courageous not to try to do one or the other." Melville was more bitter about not making money as a writer than about not receiving the recognition he deserved. He would have been content, as he was in his last years, simply to write for himself. He even described himself as "a happy failure."

Melville had integrity as an artist, an inherent inability to be satisfied with giving superficial readers what they wanted. *Moby Dick* is a masterpiece because its author dared to attempt so much. As he wrote Evert Duyckinck in 1849, "I love all men who *dive.* Any fish can swim near the surface, but it takes a great whale to go down stairs five miles or more." More than anything, Melville stands for the courage to risk failure.

Bibliography

Anderson, Charles R. *Melville in the South Seas.* New York: Columbia University Press, 1939. Lengthy, detailed account of the most important period of Melville's life, with analysis of how he used these experiences in his art. Attempts to separate fact from fiction.

Arvin, Newton. *Herman Melville.* London: Methuen, and New York: Sloane, 1950. Combines a biography with a psychoanalytical view of Melville's personality. Presents the writer in conflict with himself.

Gilman, William H. *Melville's Early Life and "Redburn."* New York: New York University Press, 1951. Most detailed account of Melville's life from 1819 to 1841, with the emphasis on his voyage to Liverpool.

Howard, Leon. *Herman Melville: A Biography.* Berkeley: University of California Press, 1951. Standard Melville biography, based upon material assembled by Jay Leyda. Attempts to understand Melville as a product of his times.

Kazin, Alfred. *An American Procession.* New York: Knopf, 1984; London: Secker and Warburg, 1985. Study of American literature from 1830 to 1932 places Melville's work in the context of a literary tradition and offers a good, brief sketch of Melville as writer and man.

Levine, Robert S., ed. *The Cambridge Companion to Herman Melville.* Cambridge and New York: Cambridge University Press, 1998. A collection of essays commissioned for this book that provide an overview of Melville's career and works.

Leyda, Jay. *The Melville Log: A Documentary Life of Herman Melville, 1819-1891.* 2 vols. New York: Harcourt Brace, 1951. Amazingly complete document based on letters to, from, and about Melville, journals, publishers' files, newspaper articles, Melville's marginalia in the books he read, and similar sources. Arranged in a day-by-day chronology. Supplemented in 1969.

Miller, Edwin Haviland. *Melville.* New York: Braziller, 1975. Psychoanalytical biography offers the most complete view of the Melville-Hawthorne friendship.

Mumford, Lewis. *Herman Melville.* New York: Harcourt Brace, 1929. Interpretation of Melville's life based on his writings, including letters and notebooks. Concerned more with the writer's view of his world than with the details of his life.

New, Elisa. "Bible leaves! Bible leaves! Hellenism and Hebraism in Melville's 'Moby Dick.'" *Poetics Today* 19, no. 2 (Summer 1998). Discusses symbolism and religious metaphors in Melville's *Moby Dick*.

Sealts, Merton M., Jr., comp. *The Early Lives of Melville: Nineteenth-Century Biographical Sketches and Their Authors*. Madison: University of Wisconsin Press, 1974. Compiles biographical material by those who knew Melville, including his wife and granddaughters. Reveals how he was perceived in his time.

Weaver, Raymond M. *Herman Melville, Mariner and Mystic*. New York: Doran, and London: Oxford University Press, 1921. First book-length biography of Melville by the scholar who virtually discovered him. Weakened by treating Melville's fiction as fact and by saying very little about the last thirty years of his life.

Michael Adams

GREGOR JOHANN MENDEL

Born: July 22, 1822; Heinzendorf, Austria
Died: January 6, 1884; Brno, Austria
Area of Achievement: Genetics
Contribution: Mendel demonstrated the rules governing genetic inheritance with his statistical approach to experiments in plant hybridization.

Early Life

Gregor Johann Mendel's father, Anton, was a peasant, and his mother was the daughter of a village gardener. They had five children. Two of Mendel's sisters died, but Veronica, born in 1820, and Theresia, born in 1829, survived. The Mendel lineage included other professional gardeners. Fortunately for his future career, Mendel went to a village school where the teacher taught the children about natural science. Mendel was exposed early to the cultivation of fruit trees, at the school as well as at home, where he helped his father with the family orchard. Mendel attended secondary school in the year 1833 and then spent six years in the *Gymnasium* in Troppau, where he did well overall.

His nervous physical reaction to stress, which partially determined Mendel's choices and possibilities in later life, became evident when he was a student. Initially, when Mendel's father, unable to work because of serious injuries, had to give his son-in-law control of the farm in 1838, Mendel gave private lessons to make money. The stress affected him to such a degree that he had to miss several months of his fifth year at the *Gymnasium* in order to recover. He started a philosophy course at the Philosophical Institute at Olmütz in 1840 but was unable to find tutoring jobs. He fell ill again and spent a year with his parents. His sister Theresia offered to support him out of her dowry so he could continue his studies. With her aid, Mendel completed the two-year course in philosophy, physics, and mathematics, which would have led to higher studies. He did well enough that one of his professors, who had lived in an Augustinian monastery for nearly twenty years, recommended Mendel to the same monastery.

Life's Work

Mendel entered the Augustinian monastery, taking the name Gregor, on October 9, 1843, out of sheer financial necessity. It proved, however, to be a fruitful decision. Though he felt no great vocation to be a monk, he found himself in the environment most conducive to his studies; it was at the monastery that Mendel was able to concentrate on those studies in meteorology and, more significant, plant reproduction that made him a pioneer in genetics.

The abbot of the monastery was actively involved in encouraging agricultural studies, so Mendel was surrounded by other scholars and researchers. The nervous disposition which had affected him as a student continued to plague him, for he would become ill when he visited invalids. Useless as a pastor, he was assigned instead to the *Gymnasium* in Znaim as a substitute teacher. In this capacity, Mendel was successful and was encouraged to become a teacher permanently, if he could pass the required examinations for a license.

Ironically, this careful researcher never made much headway in official academic circles, though his education was crucial to shaping the course of his experiments. He failed to pass all the examinations to become a permanent teacher and was sent to the University of Vienna to study natural science more thoroughly. From October, 1851, to August, 1853, Mendel was in the intellectually stimulating company of men such as Franz Unger, a professor of plant physiology, who asserted that the plant world was not fixed but had evolved gradually—a view that caused much controversy. From Christian Doppler and Andreas von Ettingshausen, both physicists, Mendel most likely acquired the technique of approaching physical problems with mathematical analysis. He served as a demonstrator at the Physical Institute in Vienna and became adept at the physicist's approach to a problem. In 1855, Mendel took the teachers' examination again but fared even worse; he became sick after writing the first answer and was apparently so ill subsequently that his father and uncle came a long way to visit him. Because he never tried the examinations again, Mendel remained a substitute teacher for sixteen years, kind, conscientious, and well liked.

In 1856, he began his experiments with garden peas. It was known at the time that the first generation reproduced from hybrids tended to be uniform but that the second generation reverted to the characteristics of the two original plants that had been crossbred. Such facts were observable, but the explanations remained unsatisfactory. In *An Introduction to Genetic Analysis* (1976, 1981) the authors note that before Mendel, the concept of blending inheritance predominated; that is, it was assumed that offspring were typically similar to the parents because the essences of the parents were contained in the spermatozoon and the egg, and these were blended at conception to form the new offspring. Mendel's work with pea plants suggested another theory, that of particulate inheritance; this theory postulated that a gene passes from one generation to the next as a unit, without any blending.

As several historians of science have noted, Mendel approached this problem of heredity in hybrids as a physicist would, and this may account for some of the suspicion surrounding the success of Mendel's famous experiments with garden peas. Instead of making many observations of natural life and then looking for the general pattern, as was the conventional approach of biologists, Mendel determined the problem first, devised a solution to the problem, then undertook experiments to test the solution. Mendel prepared the groundwork for his experiments by testing thirty-four varieties of peas to find the most suitable varieties for research. From these, he picked twenty-two to examine for two different traits, color and texture. He was then able to trace the appearance of green and yellow seeds, as well as round and wrinkled ones, in several generations of offspring. By literally counting the results of his hybridization, he found the ratio of dominant genes to recessive ones: 3 to 1. In effect, he demonstrated that there was a rule governing inheritance.

When he finished his experiments with peas in 1863, Mendel was well aware that his conclusions were not what the scientific knowledge of the time would have predicted. To confirm his findings, he experimented with the French bean and the bush bean, crossed the bush bean with the scarlet runner, and got the same 3:1 ratio, though in the last case, he could not obtain the same ratio for the white and red colors. He spoke about his work at two meetings of the Naturforschenden Verein (natural science society) and was asked to publish his lecture in 1866. Only a few of the forty copies made have been recovered: One of the most important recipients was Carl von Nägeli, a leading botanical researcher who had written about the work of preceding experimenters. Nägeli found it impossible to accept Mendel's explanation but did engage in discussion with him; the two corresponded from 1866 to 1873. Nägeli's influence was not altogether salutary, for he set Mendel on a futile track ex-

perimenting with *Hieracium*, which, as was established later, breeds slightly differently.

In 1868, Mendel was promoted to abbot of the monastery. He became involved in a controversy about taxes on the monastery and eventually, in 1871, abandoned his studies of hybrids. A heavy smoker toward the end of his life, Mendel developed kidney problems, which led to a painful illness. Theresia, the sister who had helped him pay for his education with her dowry, was also there for his last days, taking care of him until he died in January of 1884.

Summary

Gregor Johann Mendel's work was not rediscovered for thirty years, by which time three other researchers—Hugo de Vries, Carl Erich Correns, and Erich Tschermak von Seysenegg—had, working independently, drawn some of the same conclusions. Thus, Mendel's work in itself did not directly influence the history of science, for it was not well known. Even his original explanations of meteorologic phenomena, particularly of a tornado which struck Brno in 1870, was ignored. He died without achieving the full recognition he deserved.

The explanation for his contemporaries' lack of appreciation for his work can only be speculative. For example, Mendel's successor destroyed his private papers; furthermore, scientists at the time considered Mendel's experiments to be a hobby and his theories the "maunderings of a charming putterer." In part, Mendel's use of numerical analysis, so different from the conventional working procedures of biologists up to that time, may have been suspect. Mendel's personal qualities, which enabled him to reduce a puzzling problem to its bare essentials, may also have been a contributing factor to his obscurity. Though widely read in scientific literature and an active participant in the affairs of his community, he was a modest and reticent man, who compressed twenty years of scientific work into four short papers.

This lack of fanfare concerning his discoveries was not rectified until a young priest discovered Mendel's official documents, preserved in monastery archives, in the first decade of the twentieth century. Only then were Mendel's conscientious, careful, painstaking work and the results that he achieved fully appreciated. As L. C. Dunn notes, there had been several experiments with hybridization before Mendel. Among his predecessors, Josef Gottlieb Kölreuter was an important figure, for it was he who produced the first plant hybrid with a planned experiment in 1760.

What Mendel did that no one else thought to do was to apply statistical analysis to an area of study which had not habitually conceptualized problems numerically. By so doing, he was able to discover specific and regular ratios. With this apparently simple technique, Mendel was able to formulate the rules of inheritance and thus give birth to the science of genetics.

Bibliography

Dunn, L. C. *A Short History of Genetics: The Development of Some of the Main Lines of Thought, 1864-1939.* New York: McGraw-Hill, 1965. As indicated in the subtitle, this is a study of the development of the main lines of thought in genetic studies from 1864 to 1939. Contains chapters on Mendel and on the aftermath of Mendelism. Includes photographs, a glossary, a bibliography, and an index.

Iltis, Hugo. *Life of Mendel.* Translated by Eden Paul and Cedar Paul. London: Allen and Unwin, and New York: Norton, 1932. Researched and written by the man who helped to rediscover Mendel and preserve his remaining papers. One of the best biographies of Mendel. Includes illustrations, color plates, and an index.

Mendel, Gregor. *Experiments in Plant-Hybridisation.* Foreword by Paul C. Mangelsdorf. Cambridge, Mass.: Harvard University Press, 1936. Reprinted to celebrate the centennial of Mendel's lectures on his groundbreaking experiments. The foreword contains a concise explanation of the experiments and their significance.

Olby, Robert C. *Origins of Mendelism.* 2d ed. Chicago: University of Chicago Press, 1985. Places Mendel's work in the context of those who came before him. Starts with Kölreuter and his hybridization experiments, includes a discussion of Charles Darwin's genetics, and concludes with the work of the three who replicated Mendel's work independently. Contains an appendix, an index, plates, and suggested readings at the end of each chapter.

Rodgers, Joann. "What Mendel Wrought." *Mosaic* 22, no. 3 (Fall 1991). Discusses Mendel's work with pea plants and the resulting theories regarding inheritance of traits from parents.

Sturtevant, Alfred H. *A History of Genetics.* New York: Harper, 1965. Provides a historical background of genetics from before Mendel through the genetics of mankind. Lively discussion of the controversy over Mendel's near-perfect results. Includes a chronology of genetics history, a bibliography, and an index.

Suzuki, David T., Anthony J. F. Griffiths, and Richard C. Lewontin. *An Introduction to Genetic Analysis.* 4th ed. San Francisco: Freeman, 1989. A chapter on Mendelism provides a clear explanation of Mendel's experiments, using contemporary terminology. Includes problems, with answers, a glossary, a bibliography, and an index.

Shakuntala Jayaswal

DMITRY IVANOVICH MENDELEYEV

Born: February 8, 1834; Tobolsk, Siberia, Russia
Died: February 2, 1907; St. Petersburg, Russia
Area of Achievement: Chemistry
Contribution: Although he did important theoretical work on the physical properties of fluids and practical work on the development of coal and oil resources, Mendeleyev is best known for his discovery of the periodic law, which states that the properties of the chemical elements vary with their atomic weights in a systematic way. His periodic table of the elements enabled him to predict accurately the properties of three unknown elements, whose later discovery confirmed the value of his system.

Early Life

Dmitry Ivanovich Mendeleyev was born in 1834 at Tobolsk (modern Tyumen Oblast), an administrative center in western Siberia. He later recalled that he was the seventeenth child, although a sister claimed that he was the sixteenth and many scholars state that he was the fourteenth. His mother, Marya Dmitrievna Kornileva, came from an old merchant family with Mongolian blood. She became deeply attached to her youngest son and played an influential role in shaping his passionate temperament and directing his education. His father, Ivan Pavlovich Mendeleyev, was a principal and teacher at the Tobolsk high school, but shortly after his son's birth he became totally blind. The modest disability pension he received did not allow him to support his large family, and so Marya, a remarkably able and determined woman, reopened a glass factory that her family still owned in a village near Tobolsk. She ran it so successfully that she was able to provide for her family and complete her younger children's education.

In the Tobolsk schools, young Dmitry, an attractive curly-haired, blue-eyed boy, excelled in mathematics, physics, geography, and history, but he did poorly in the compulsory classical languages, Latin in particular. Tobolsk was a place for political exiles, and one of Dmitry's sisters wedded an exiled Decembrist, one of those who tried unsuccessfully in December, 1825, to overthrow Czar Nicholas I. He took an active interest in Dmitry, taught him science, and helped form his political liberalism.

Toward the end of Dmitry's high school education, a double tragedy occurred: His father died of tuberculosis and his family's glassworks burned to the ground. By this time, the older children had left home, leaving only Dmitry and a sister with their mother, who decided to seek the help of her brother in Moscow. After Dmitry's graduation from high school in 1849, Marya, then fifty-seven years old, secured horses and bravely embarked with her two dependent children on the long journey from Siberia. In Moscow, her brother, after first welcoming them, refused to help his nephew obtain an education on the grounds that he himself had not had one. Marya angrily left Moscow for St. Petersburg, where she again encountered difficulty in getting her son either into the university or into the medical school. Finally, through a friend of her dead husband, she secured a place for Dmitry in the faculty of physics and mathematics of the Main Pedagogical Institute, the school his father had attended. Three months later, Marya died, and not long afterward her daughter succumbed to tuberculosis. Mendeleyev, who also suffered from tuberculosis, later wrote that his mother instructed him by example, corrected him with love, and, in order to consecrate him to science, left Siberia and spent her last energies and resources to put him on his way.

Mendeleyev received a good education at the Pedagogical Institute. One of his teachers had been a pupil of Justus von Liebig, one of the greatest chemists of the time. In 1855, Mendeleyev, now qualified as a teacher, was graduated from the Pedagogical Institute, winning a gold medal for his academic achievements.

Worn out by his labors, he went to a physician, who told him that he had only a short time to live. In an attempt to regain his health, he was sent, at his own request, to the Crimea, in southern Russia. He initially taught science at Simferopol, but when the Crimean War broke out, he left for Odessa, where he taught in a local lyceum during the 1855-1856 school year and where, aided by the warm climate, his health improved. In the autumn of 1856, he returned to St. Petersburg to defend his master's thesis. He succeeded and obtained the status of privatdocent, which gave him the license to teach theoretical and organic chemistry at the University of St. Petersburg.

Life's Work

In his teaching, Mendeleyev used the atomic weights of the elements to explain chemistry to his students. This did not mean that he believed that chemistry could be completely explained by physics, but his work on isomorphism and specific volumes convinced him that atomic weights could be useful in elucidating chemical properties. To improve his understanding of chemistry, he received in 1859 a stipend for two years' study abroad. In Paris, he worked in the laboratory of Henry Regnault, famous for his studies on chlorine compounds, and at the University of Heidelberg, where he had the opportunity to meet Robert Bunsen, Gustav Kirchhoff, and other notable scientists. Because his weak lungs were bothered by the noxious fumes of sulfur compounds in Bunsen's laboratory, Mendeleyev set up a private laboratory to work on his doctoral thesis on the combination of alcohol and water. In the course of his research at Heidelberg, he discovered that for every liquid there existed a temperature above which it could no longer be condensed from the gas to the liquid form. He called this temperature the absolute boiling point (this phenomenon was rediscovered a decade later by the Irish scientist Thomas Andrews, who called it the "critical temperature," its modern descriptor). In September, 1860, Mendeleyev attended the Chemical Congress at Karlsruhe, Germany, and met the Italian chemist Stanislao Cannizzaro, whose insistence on the distinction between atomic and molecular weights and whose system of corrected atomic weights had a great influence on him.

Upon his return to St. Petersburg, Mendeleyev resumed his lectures on organic chemistry. Because he lacked a permanent academic position, he decided to write a textbook on organic chemistry, which became a popular as well as a critical success. In 1863, he began to act as a consultant for a small oil refinery in Baku. In this same year he was married to Fezova Nikitichna Leshcheva, largely because one of his sisters insisted that he needed a wife. The couple had two children, a boy, Vladimir, and a girl, Olga. The marriage was not happy, however, and quarrels were frequent. Eventually, Mendeleyev and his wife separated. He continued to live in their St. Petersburg quarters, while his wife and children lived at their country estate of Boblovo. In 1864, Mendeleyev agreed to serve as professor of chemistry at the St. Petersburg Technical Institute while continuing to teach at the university. A year later, he defended his doctoral thesis on alcohol and water, arguing that solutions are chemical compounds indistinguishable from other types of chemical combination.

A turning point in Mendeleyev's career occurred in October, 1865, when he was appointed to the chair of chemistry at the University of St. Petersburg. While teaching an inorganic-chemistry course there, he felt the need to bring to this subject the same degree of order that had characterized his earlier teaching of organic chemistry. Since he could find no suitable textbook, he decided to write his own. The composing of this book, eventually published as *Osnovy khimii* (1868-1871; *The Principles of Chemistry*, 1891), led him to formulate the periodic law. It was also one of the most unusual textbooks ever written. Unlike most textbooks, it was not a recycling of traditional material. It had instead a novel organization and an abundance of original ideas. It was also a curious blend of objective information and personal comment in which footnotes often took up more space than the text.

In organizing his ideas for the book, Mendeleyev prepared individual cards for all sixty-three elements then known, listing their atomic weights and properties, which showed great dissimilarities. For example, oxygen and chlorine were gases, whereas mercury and bromine were liquids. Platinum was very hard, whereas sodium was very soft. Some elements combined with one atom, others with two, and still others with three or four. In a search for order, Mendeleyev arranged the elements in a sequence of increasing atomic weights. By moving the cards around, he found that he could group certain elements together in already familiar families. For example, in the first table that he developed in March of 1869, lithium, sodium, potassium, and the other so-called alkali metals formed a horizontal row. In some groups he left empty spaces so that the next element would be in its proper family.

Mendeleyev's analysis of his first arrangement convinced him that there must be a functional relationship between the individual properties of the elements and their atomic weights. One of the many interesting relationships he noticed concerned valence, the ability of an element to combine in specific proportions with other elements. He observed a periodic rise and fall of valence—1, 2, 3, 4, 3, 2, 1—in several parts of his arrangement. Because valence and other properties of the elements exhibited periodic repetitions, he called his arrangement in 1869 the periodic table. At the same time he formulated the periodic law: Elements organized according to their atomic weights manifest a clear periodicity of properties. He had been thinking about information relevant to the periodic law for fifteen years, but he formulated it in a single day. Mendeleyev would spend the next three years perfecting it, and in important ways he would be concerned with its finer points until his death.

When his paper was read by a friend at the Russian Chemical Society meeting in 1869, the periodic table did not evoke unusual interest. Its publication in German met with a cool reception. Mendeleyev's opponents, who were especially censorious in England and Germany, were suspicious of highly imaginative theoretical schemes of the elements; many scientists before Mendeleyev had proposed such systems, which resulted in little of practical benefit for chemists.

Mendeleyev believed that if he could convince scientists of the usefulness of his system, it would attract followers. Therefore, he tried to show how his table and periodic law could be used to correct erroneously determined atomic weights. More significant, he proposed in an 1871 paper that gaps in his table could be used to discover new elements. In particular, he predicted in great detail the physical and chemical properties of three elements, which he called eka-aluminum, eka-boron, and eka-silicon, after the Sanskrit word for "one" and the name of the element above the gap in the table. These predictions were met with great skepticism, but when, in 1875, Paul Lecoq de Boisbaudran discovered eka-aluminum in a zinc ore from the Pyrenees, skepticism declined, especially after chemists learned that the element's characteristics had been accurately foretold by Mendeleyev. When, in 1879, Lars Nilson isolated eka-boron from the ore euxenite, even fewer skeptics were to be found. Finally, in 1879, when Clemens Winkler in Germany found an element in the ore argyrodite which precisely matched Mendeleyev's predictions for eka-silicon, skepticism vanished. In fact, Winkler used Mendeleyev's predictions of a gray element with an atomic weight of about 72 and a density of 5.5 in his search (he found a grayish-white substance with an atomic weight of 72.3 and a density of 5.5). These new elements were given the names gallium (1875), scandium (1879), and germanium (1886), and their discovery led to the universal acceptance of Mendeleyev's periodic law.

In addition to campaigning for his periodic system, Mendeleyev during the 1870's spent time on his technological interests. He was a patriot who wanted to see such Russian resources as coal, oil, salt, and metals developed properly. With this in

mind, he visited the United States in 1876 to study the Pennsylvania oil fields. He was critical of the American developers' concentration on the expansion of production while ignoring the scientific improvement of industrial efficiency and product quality. Upon his return to Russia, he was sent to study his country's oil fields, and he became very critical of the way they were exploited by foreign companies. He urged Russian officials to develop native oil for the country's own benefit. From his experience in the oil fields, Mendeleyev developed a theory of the inorganic origin of petroleum and a belief in protective tariffs for natural resources.

In the year of his American trip, Mendeleyev underwent a domestic crisis. At a sister's home he had met Anna Ivanovna Popov, a seventeen-year-old art student, and fallen desperately in love with her. Anna's family opposed the relationship and made several attempts to separate the pair, resorting finally to sending her to Rome to continue her art studies. Mendeleyev soon followed her, leaving behind a message that if he could not wed her, he would commit suicide. She was mesmerized by this passionate man who, with his deep-set eyes and patriarchal beard, looked like a biblical prophet. She agreed to return to Russia and wed him, but the couple discovered that, according to the laws of the Russian Orthodox church, Mendeleyev could not be remarried until seven years after his divorce. He eventually found a priest who was willing to ignore the rule, but two days after the marriage the priest was dismissed and Mendeleyev was officially proclaimed a bigamist. Despite the religious crisis, nothing happened to Mendeleyev or his young wife. As the czar told a nobleman who complained about the situation: "Mendeleyev has two wives, yes, but I have only one Mendeleyev." The second marriage proved to be a happy one, and the couple had two sons and two daughters. Anna Ivanovna introduced her husband to art, and he became an accomplished critic and an astute collector of paintings.

During the 1880's and 1890's, Mendeleyev became increasingly involved in academic politics. Ultimately, conflict with the minister of education prompted him to resign from the University of St. Petersburg. At his last lecture at the university, where he had taught for more than thirty years, the students gave him an enthusiastic ovation. His teaching career at an end, Mendeleyev turned to public service, where he was active in many areas.

When the Russo-Japanese War broke out in February, 1904, Mendeleyev became a strong supporter of his country's efforts, and Russia's defeat disheartened him. By this time, Mendeleyev was not only the grand man of Russian chemistry but also, because of the triumph of the periodic law, a world figure. In 1906, he was considered for a Nobel Prize, but the chemistry committee's recommendation was defeated by a single vote, mainly because his discovery of the periodic law was more than thirty-five years old. Though he missed winning the Nobel Prize, he was showered with many awards in Russia and in many foreign countries. His end came early in 1907, when he caught a cold that developed into pneumonia. His chief consolation during his final illness was the reading of *A Journey to the North Pole* by Jules Verne, his favorite author.

Summary

Dmitry Ivanovich Mendeleyev's name has become inextricably linked with the periodic table, but he was not the first to attempt to develop a systematic classification of the chemical elements. Earlier in the century, Johann Döbereiner, a German chemist, had arranged several elements into triads—for example, calcium, strontium, and barium—in which such properties as atomic weight, color, and reactivity seemed to form a predictable gradation. John Newlands, an English chemist, arranged the elements in the order of atomic weights in 1864 and found that properties seemed to repeat themselves after an interval of seven elements. In 1866, he announced his "law of octaves," in which he saw an analogy between the grouping of elements and the musical octave. Several other attempts at a systematic arrangement of the elements were made before Mendeleyev, some of which were known to him. Many scholars credit the German chemist Lothar Meyer as an independent discoverer of the periodic law, since in 1864 he published a table of elements arranged horizontally so that analogous elements appeared under one another. Other scholars, however, contend that Mendeleyev's table was more firmly based on chemical properties than Meyer's and it could be generalized more easily. Furthermore, Mendeleyev was a much bolder theoretician than Meyer. For example, he proposed that some atomic weights must be incorrect since their measured weight caused them to be placed in the wrong group of the table (Meyer was reluctant to take this step). In most instances Mendeleyev's proposals proved to be correct (although the troublesome case of iodine and tellurium was not resolved until the discovery of isotopes). Finally and most notably, Mendeleyev was so impressed with the periodicity of the elements that he took the risk of predicting the chemical and physical properties of the unknown elements in the blank places of his table. Although his table had imperfections, it did bring similar elements together and help make chemistry a rational science and the periodic law an essential part of chemistry.

The periodic table grew out of the theoretical side of Mendeleyev's scientific personality, but he also had a practical side. He made important contributions to the Russian oil, coal, and sodium-carbonate industries. He served the czarist regime in several official positions. Nevertheless, he did not hesitate to speak out against the government's oppression of students, and his sympathy for the common people led him to travel third-class on trains. Though he held decidedly liberal views, it is wrong to see him as a political radical. Perhaps he is best described as a progressive, since he hoped that the czarist government would correct itself and evolve into a more compassionate regime.

Had Mendeleyev lived a few more years, he would have witnessed the complete and final development of his periodic table by Henry Moseley, whose discovery of atomic number by interacting X rays with various elements led to the use of the positive charge of the nucleus as the true measure of an element's place in the periodic table. Throughout the twentieth century, the periodic table, which owed so much to Mendeleyev, continued to be enlarged by the discovery of new elements. It was therefore appropriate that a new element (atomic number 101), discovered in 1955, was named mendelevium, in belated recognition of the importance of his periodic law.

Bibliography

Farber, Eduard, ed. *Great Chemists*. New York: Wiley, 1961. This collection of more than one hundred biographies of chemists contains an excellent short biography of Mendeleyev. Nontechnical and contains ample references to both primary and secondary literature.

Ihde, Aaron J. *The Development of Modern Chemistry*. New York: Harper, 1964. Ihde traces the development of chemistry largely through its disciplines, for example, inorganic chemistry, organic chemistry, physical chemistry, and the like. Discusses Mendeleyev's life and work in a chapter on the classification of elements. Contains an excellent and extensive annotated bibliography.

Jaffe, Bernard. *Crucibles: The Lives and Achievements of the Great Chemists*. New York: Simon and Schuster, 1930; London: Jarrolds, 1931. This book tells the story of chemistry through the lives of some of its greatest practitioners. The approach is popular, uncritical, and accessible to young readers and those with little knowledge of chemistry. The chapter on Mendeleyev contains a good basic treatment of his life and his discovery of the periodic law.

Rouvray, Dennis. "Elementary, My Dear Mendeleyev." *New Scientist* 141, no. 1912 (February 12, 1994). Examines the periodic table of elements developed by Mendeleyev and proposals for its expansion.

Van Spronsen, Johannes W. *The Periodic System of Chemical Elements: A History of the First Hundred Years*. Amsterdam and New York: Elsevier, 1969. Several books have been written about the periodic system of chemical elements and its history, but this one, written to commemorate the hundredth anniversary of the periodic system, is the best. Spronsen analyzes Mendeleyev's achievement in great detail. Based on original sources, the book requires some knowledge of chemistry for a full understanding of the analysis. Generously illustrated with diagrams, photographs, and graphs.

Weeks, Mary Elvira. *Discovery of the Elements*. 7th ed. Edited by Henry Leicester. Easton, Penn.: Journal of Chemical Education, 1968. This book, which has served chemists as a rich source of information about the elements—chemical, technical, historical, and biographical—has been made even more valuable by this new edition prepared by Leicester. The material on Russian chemists, including Mendeleyev, has been expanded. Extensively illustrated and thoroughly understandable to readers with a modicum of chemical knowledge.

Robert J. Paradowski

FELIX MENDELSSOHN

Born: February 3, 1809; Hamburg
Died: November 4, 1847; Leipzig, Saxony
Area of Achievement: Music
Contribution: Mendelssohn was one of the great composers of the Romantic period. His music is noted for its exceptionally melodic qualities and its ability to capture a mood. It has been continually performed and studied.

Early Life

Felix Mendelssohn was an unusually gifted and precocious child musically and was the most prominent member of an exceptionally talented family. He worked long and diligently, absorbed in his music, aware of his subtle talent and discernment in music. He loved taking walks in the woods and often wrote down the notes he heard the birds singing. His first musical influence was his mother, Leah, an expert pianist and vocalist. When Felix was only four years old, she gave him five-minute piano lessons, soon extended as the music capivated Felix's imagination. At age eight, Felix began music lessons with Karl Friedrich Zelter, the director of Berlin's Singakademie. Before long, the young musical genius was composing fugues, songs, operettas, violin and piano concerti, and piano quartets. He performed Sunday concerts in his home and even conducted a small orchestra.

Abraham Mendelssohn, Felix's father, was a prominent German banker, and his fashionable home was one of the intellectual and musical centers of Berlin. The excitement of learning reigned in Felix's "childhood castle," a home bustling with activity, servants, and tutors. Rebecka sang, Paul played the violoncello, and the eldest child, Fanny, played the piano almost as well as Felix. The children wrote their own newspaper, called at first "The Garden Paper" and, later, "The Tea and Snow Times." They made paper lanterns to decorate the trees in the garden for dances. Felix particularly loved the park, where he rode his horse. He played billiards and chess and practiced the piano, organ, and violin. He learned landscape drawing and calligraphy.

Felix, a gentle, cheerful, kindly person, was handsome, self-confident, and even-tempered. His hair was dark black and his eyes, dark brown. He dressed elegantly, was very sociable, and loved good meals and stimulating companionship. He was sharply critical of his own work, revising five or six times pieces that had already been performed successfully.

Life's Work

In a sense, Mendelssohn began his life's work before he was ten years old, inasmuch as he was already busily composing music by that age. It was, however, the composition of his early masterpiece, *A Midsummer Night's Dream* (1826), at the age of seventeen that launched him into a serious career as a composer.

An early extended trip throughout Germany and Switzerland gave Mendelssohn a love of travel. He visited most of the beautiful, historical, cultural, and scenic places of Europe, carrying his sketchbook with him. His first visit to England and Scotland in 1829, at the age of twenty, began his lifelong attraction to English culture. The English were similarly enchanted with both Mendelssohn and his music. Even on this first visit he conducted the London Philharmonic.

Also in 1829, Mendelssohn helped to revive the singing of Johann Sebastian Bach's *Saint Matthew Passion*, which he had studied for years. Beginning in 1827, Mendelssohn and his friends assembled a small, dependable choir which met one evening a week for practice of rarely heard works. They secured permission to present the work at the Berlin Singakademie. Mendelssohn shortened the work drastically. He omitted many of the arias and used only the introductory symphonies of others. He edited passages for greater brevity. The performance was a historic success. The chorus numbered 158 and the orchestra included many from the Royal Orchestra. The king was in the royal loge with members of his court. And twenty-year-old Mendelssohn conducted without a score, as he knew the music and lyrics from memory. The historical effect was a Bach revival in Europe.

Despite his many musical activities, Mendelssohn had a very active social life and was often invited by families with girls of marriageable age. He was wealthy, cultured, courteous, handsome, of good moral character, and had a promising future. Mendelssohn chose for his wife Cécile Jeanrenaud, the daughter of a leading Huguenot minister in Frankfurt, who had died in 1819. Mendelssohn became acquainted with Cécile on one of his extended musical engagements in Frankfurt and finally realized that he was in love with this beautiful, charming girl, nine years his junior. Cécile and Mendelssohn were married on March 28, 1837, in the Reformed French Church in Frankfurt. The ceremony was performed in French. A friend wrote special music for the wedding; Mendelssohn's "Wedding March" from *A Midsummer Night's Dream* had yet to come into fashion. The couple spent their honeymoon in the upper Rhine valley and in the Black Forest. It was a wondrous and creative time: Mendelssohn sketched the outlines of half a dozen works. Mendelssohn was a devoted and content husband and Cécile an ideal wife. She loved her domestic life and was an excellent and charming hostess and a cheerful companion to her husband. She was a pious and orthodox Protestant, as was Mendelssohn. The couple had five children, one of whom died at the age of nine.

In 1833, Mendelssohn wrote the *Italian* Symphony and his oratorio on the life of the Apostle Paul. In 1835, he became conductor of the Leipzig Gewandhaus Orchestra and continued in that post for the rest of his life. Mendelssohn loved the Psalms and set many of them to music. In 1840, he finished *Hymn of Praise* (Second Symphony), with its delicate melodic contrasts so characteristic of Mendelssohn. The choral movement is mostly from scripture, "Let everything that hath life and breath praise the Lord!" Mendelssohn also wrote the melody for "Hark, the Herald Angels Sing," and his *Reformation* Symphony (Fifth Symphony) expands on Martin Luther's "A Mighty Fortress Is Our God." In 1846, Mendelssohn completed and directed his oratorio *Elijah* to enthusiastic response. He soon began the opera *Lorelei* and his oratorio on the life of Christ, *Christus*, but he was unable to complete either. In May of 1847, his sister Fanny suddenly died. Mendelssohn lived only six months longer and died of a cerebral hemorrhage on November 4, 1847, at the age of thirty-eight.

Summary

Felix Mendelssohn excelled in Romantic musical scene painting. His two most important symphonies are geographically identified: the *Italian* and the *Scotch*, which was dedicated to Queen Victoria, whom he met during his concert tours of England. The *Italian* pictures the spirited and sunny, vibrant south, while the *Scotch* has its own peculiar northern beauty. His works *The Hebrides* (1830-1832) and *Meeresstille und glückliche Fahrt* (1828-1832; calm sea and prosperous voyage) continue to influ-ence musical seascapes. The listener can almost hear the sounds of the sea. Mendelssohn in fact listened to the waves and the gulls and ships and the water rushing into Fingal's Cave and recorded the sounds he heard in musical transcription, just as he had recorded the songs of birds in the gardens of his boyhood home.

It was no doubt an advantage to Mendelssohn to be born into a family of wealth so that he could concentrate unreservedly on his art. He worked exceptionally hard, however, and was motivated by a sense of duty and a desire to excel. He was Jewish by birth but had been baptized into the Christian faith. His philosophy of life, morals, and music all reflected a sincere orthodox faith. Mendelssohn agreed with Bach's philosophy of sacred music, that music should "form an integral part of our service instead of becoming a mere concert which more or less evokes a devotional mood."

How is music different from verbal communication? When someone asked Mendelssohn the meanings of some of his songs in "Songs Without Words," he responded: ". . . genuine music . . . fills the soul with a thousand things better than words. . . . Only the song can say the same thing, can arouse the same feelings in one person as in another, a feeling which is not expressed . . . by the same words." Mendelssohn's music continues to evoke strong feelings.

Bibliography

Blunt, Wilfrid. *On Wings of Song: A Biography of Felix Mendelssohn*. London: Hamilton, and New York: Scribner, 1974. A particularly interesting biography because of the many illustrations, anecdotes, and quotations from primary sources. An excellent introduction for the general reader. Includes cultural and scenic descriptions by Mendelssohn himself during his early nineteenth century travels in Switzerland, Germany, and Scotland.

David, Hans T., and Arthur Mendel, eds. *The Bach Reader: A Life of Johann Sebastian Bach in Letters and Documents*. Rev. ed. London: Dent, and New York: Norton, 1966. Valuable for a study of Mendelssohn because of the chapter on Mendelssohn's revival of the *Saint Matthew Passion*. Part of the eleven-page account is Edward Devrient's first-person account of the revival.

Kaufman, Schima. *Mendelssohn: "A Second Elijah."* New York: Crowell, 1934. This occasionally laudatory biography contains some dated material. Alludes to Mendelssohn's masterpiece, *Elijah*, and considers Mendelssohn himself to have called Western civilization from "Baal-worship of the false," the banal, and the cacophony and confusion of "mere sound" that passed for music.

Kupferberg, Herbert. *The Mendelssohns: Three Generations of Genius*. London: Allen, and New York: Scribner, 1972. Places Mendelssohn in historical context by giving a one-hundred-page biographical sketch of his father, Abraham Mendelssohn, and his grandfather Moses Mendelssohn. Kupferberg also gives brief sketches of the lives of many others in the Mendelssohn family and shows them to be, men and women, a remarkable clan. The last chapter follows the Mendelssohns into the twentieth century. Includes a genealogical chart.

Marek, George R. *Gentle Genius: The Story of Felix Mendelssohn*. New York: Funk and Wagnalls, 1972; London: Hale, 1973. A very interesting biography. The lengthy quotations from the Mendelssohn correspondence and the many pictures enhance the book's value. Some of Mendelssohn's charming landscape drawings are also reproduced. "A Mendelssohn Calendar" is included.

Mendelssohn, Felix. *Letters*. Edited by G. Sheldon-Goth. New York: Pantheon, 1945. A fascinating collection of personal letters. Indispensable in giving insights into the personality, character, and thinking of Mendelssohn.

Mendelssohn, Felix, and Cecille Mendelssohn. *The Mendelssohns on Honeymoon: The 1837 Diary of Felix and Cecille Mendelssohn Bartholdy, Together with Letters to Their Families*. Translated and edited by Peter W. Jones. Oxford and New York: Oxford University Press, 1997. The first publication of the joint diary kept by Mendelssohn and his wife during their honeymoon and early marriage. Covers their travels and includes watercolors by Mendelssohn.

Radcliffe, Philip. *Mendelssohn*. London and New York: Dent, 1954. A standard biography for many years. Quite technical, but brief. Includes excerpts of musical scores and a catalog of Mendelssohn's works.

Todd, R. Larry. *Mendelssohn, "The Hebrides" and Other Overtures: A Midsummer Night's Dream, Calm Sea and Prosperous Voyage, the Hebrides (Fingal's Cave)*. New York: Cambridge University Press, 1993. Argues that the overtures "A Midsummer Night's Dream," "Calm Sea and Prosperous Voyage," and "The Hebrides" were conceived by Mendelssohn before he was twenty years of age. Support is offered based on analysis of primary documents.

————, ed. *Mendelssohn Studies*. Cambridge and New York: Cambridge University Press, 1992. A collection of ten essays covering recent Mendelssohn research and based on primary sources including correspondence and autograph manuscripts. Topics include his relationships with contemporaries, individual works, and critical response in his time.

Werner, Eric. *Mendelssohn: A New Image of the Composer and His Age*. Translated by Dika Newlin. London: Free Press of Glencoe, 1963; Westport, Conn.: Greenwood Press, 1978. The longest and most complete biography of Mendelssohn. Includes detailed technical and artistic discussions of all Mendelssohn's major works, including musical scores as examples.

William H. Burnside

MENELIK II
Sahle Mariam

Born: August 17, 1844; Ankober, Shoa

Died: December 12, 1913; Addis Ababa, Ethiopia

Areas of Achievement: Monarchy, government, and politics

Contribution: Menelik II unified Ethiopia after centuries of political fragmentation, consolidated the ancient Christian heritage against the growth of Muslim influence, and saved Ethiopia from European colonialism. He laid the foundations for Ethiopia's transformation from a medieval, feudal empire to a modern state.

Early Life

Menelik II was born Sahle Mariam in the court of his father, Haile Malakot, a leading prince of the province of Shoa. Chronicles and oral tradition reflect some uncertainty as to the details of the birth: Sahle Mariam may have been born out of wedlock, possibly the result of Haile Malakot's infatuation with a concubine. Yet the traditional sources, while almost ignoring Sahle Mariam's father—whose reign appears to have been less than illustrious—often make much of the piety and reputation of the child's mother. In Ethiopia, where the nobility put much importance on genealogy, these were matters of enormous concern for Sahle Mariam's career. These concerns caused Haile Malakot's father, the mighty Sahle Selassie who had led the resurgence of the Christian, Amharic-speaking nobles in Shoa earlier in the nineteenth century, to intercede. Sahle Selassie and his influential queen, Bezzabbesh, saw that the parents of Sahle Mariam were married in a civil ceremony shortly after the child's birth. In order to erase any further question of Sahle Mariam's pedigree, Sahle Selassie rechristened the child Menelik II. He prophesied that Menelik would restore the empire of Ethiopia to the ancient greatness wrought by Menelik I, the offspring of a legendary union between Solomon, the King of ancient Israel, and Sheba, Queen of south Arabia.

In Menelik's youth, however, there were others with similar aspirations. Ethiopia was just emerging from the *Zamana Masafent* (age of the princes), a long period of disunity and internal chaos. The most notable of the early unifiers was Theodore, ruler of the province of Gonder. In 1856, Theodore's forces defeated the Shoan levies and incorporated the province. Menelik's father died of

malaria during the final campaign against Theodore. Menelik himself, now the designated heir to the throne of Shoa, became a ward of Theodore at his fortress capital of Magdela. There, Menelik received the favored treatment and education due a noble. He completed religious training and developed excellent military skills. Above all, Menelik obtained the practical experience necessary for success as a ruler and statesman in his own right. He also formed lasting alliances with other noble children from far-flung parts of Ethiopia.

Theodore's enterprise began with great promise. He envisioned an Ethiopia of law and order and of conciliation between Muslims and Christians. As his reign progressed, however, he resorted increasingly to force, infuriated by the resistance of Muslim principalities and deeply suspicious of intrigue. Theodore may well have been demented in his final years. After 1864, he executed members of the court on a whim and imprisoned members of the British diplomatic mission. The latter indiscretion brought a British military expedition; Theodore committed suicide as it was about to storm Magdela in 1868.

Life's Work

The disintegration of Theodore's authority set the stage for Menelik's emergence. In 1865, the Shoan nobles revolted and beseeched Menelik to return. He escaped Magdela under cover of darkness to return to Ankober. By 1866, Menelik was firmly in command in Shoa. From the moment of his return, Menelik dreamed of succeeding where Theodore had failed, in ruling a united Ethiopian empire.

In 1872, after four years of intrigue and dynastic struggles, Yohannes IV was crowned Emperor of Ethiopia at the ancient capital of Aksum in the north. Yohannes managed to hold together the tenuous unity imposed by Theodore. Only Menelik's homeland of Shoa remained outside the empire.

Menelik's ambitions—indeed his durability as an independent ruler—required outside support. Theodore's notoriety, and the British punitive expedition of 1868, had shattered Ethiopia's isolation and exposed the country to outside pressures. The opening of the Suez Canal in 1869 greatly increased European interest in the countries along the Red Sea. Egypt, ruled by the ambitious mod-

ernizer Ismail Pasha, pushed its authority deep into the Sudan, west of Ethiopia, and in 1865 occupied the old Turkish port of Mesewa on the Ethiopian coast. Menelik cultivated an alliance with the Egyptians in the hope of forcing Yohannes IV to divide his attention between two opponents rather than concentrate on Shoa. The Egyptians, however, were decimated by Yohannes' forces when they attempted to move inland in 1875. Yohannes' predominantly Greek advisers urged him to articulate a pan-Christian front in the Middle East against both Egyptian and Turkish ambitions. Yohannes also had reached an understanding with the British, who were alarmed at the pace of Egyptian expansion in northeast Africa.

In 1883, tribes in the Sudan rose in rebellion against Egyptian rule. Under the leadership of a Muslim cleric who styled himself as *Mahdi* (savior), tens of thousands of Sudanese Muslims invaded western Ethiopia in 1887 and sacked Gonder, massacring its inhabitants. Yohannes retaliated the following year by butchering sixty thousand Mahdist troops, but he was wounded in the battle and died shortly thereafter.

The throne now went to Menelik II, and his reign proved among the greatest in Ethiopian history. Menelik immediately set about pushing Ethiopia's frontiers west toward the Nile and south toward Lake Victoria. He incorporated vast quantities of trade into the empire, thus filling his usually extended exchequer. Menelik departed from the crusading ways of his predecessors by restoring religious liberty and ending the persecution of Muslims and pagans. His method of establishing a dominant culture in Ethiopia was economic and diplomatic rather than military. When new regions were added to the empire, he sowed them with strategically placed settlements of lesser Amhara nobles and Christian clergy, whose increasing control of commerce provided an incentive for the Christianization of many areas. Even tribes who remained Muslim adopted the trappings of Christian, Amhara noble etiquette and fashion.

One of Menelik's most lasting contributions to modern Ethiopia was the establishment of a new capital at Addis Ababa (new flower) in a relatively sheltered location on the central plain. The region around Addis Ababa contained many of the oldest and most venerated Christian monasteries in the country. Founding the capital there not only reiterated Menelik's commitment to the Christian tradition of Ethiopia but also brought to an end the practice of changing capitals each time a new dynastic line or regional nobility assumed power. Eucalyptus trees, imported by Menelik to provide shade for government buildings in Addis Ababa, soon spread throughout Ethiopia and helped reforest some of the barren and denuded hillsides of the country. Telegraph communication, and later the beginnings of a telephone system, tied together the outlying regions of the huge, mountainous country. In 1897, a French firm completed a direct railway link between Addis Ababa and the Red Sea coast at Djibouti.

Menelik is best known for transforming Ethiopia's role in international affairs from that of potential prey of European colonialism to that of a factor in the regional balance of power. He did so by successfully confronting Italy's bid to incorporate Ethiopia into its colonial domain. In 1882, the Italians purchased the port of Aseb from a private trading company and began to expand along the Red Sea coast. Italian ambitions triggered British occupation of northern Somalia and a French landing at Djibouti in 1885. At first, Menelik deferred to the Italians. Under the Treaty of Uccialli of May,

1889, Menelik recognized Italian sovereignty on the coast and agreed to link his foreign policy with that of Italy. Four years later, however, with Italian columns steadily pushing inland and nearby provincial governors calling for assistance, Menelik prepared for war. After several inconclusive skirmishes, the decisive battle came at Adwa on March 1, 1896, where the Ethiopian army crushed an Italian force.

The news of Adwa electrified the world; it was a stunning reverse of the forces of colonialism hitherto judged irresistible. Within months, a new treaty finalized the Italian colonial frontier with Ethiopia. Emboldened, Menelik pushed his borders westward, joining with France in 1898 in an effort to control the Upper Nile by planting his flag alongside the French at Fashoda (modern Kodok). Ethiopia thus became a factor in a major Anglo-French diplomatic crisis. In 1902, Menelik agreed to the Treaty of Addis Ababa, in which Great Britain and Ethiopia, negotiating on equal terms, reached agreement on placement of the western frontier.

Menelik grew frail in his final years. In 1909, he relinquished the government to a regency in the name of his grandson, Lij Yasu, whose Muslim leanings led to renewed strife and political intrigue. Menelik's new imperial administration and cultural latticework of Christian-Amhara tradition survived the crisis, however, and continued to support Ethiopia as a nation.

Summary

Menelik II ruled Ethiopia at a crucial time in its history, when the country was emerging from its own dark age and opening itself up to the world. He accomplished the rarest of feats in assimilating the military and technological advances of Europe while turning religion, tradition, and an antiquated class structure toward productive ends. In doing so, he saved Ethiopia from the fate of the rest of Africa, which fell under European rule. For nearly a century, the culture, economy, and political system of Ethiopia bore his stamp.

Bibliography

Abir, Mordechai. *Ethiopia: The Era of the Princes, the Challenge of Islam, and the Reunification of the Christian Empire, 1769-1855*. London: Longman, and New York: Praeger, 1968. Analyzes the crucial period of disunity from the mid-eighteenth to the mid-nineteenth century, when the power of the traditional Christian nobility was in decline and Ethiopia faced the challenge of a revitalized Islam. Excellent on the importance of trade expansion and fiscal control.

Berkeley, George Fitz-Hardinge. *The Campaign of Adowa and the Rise of Menelik*. London: Constable, 1902; New York: Negro Universities Press, 1969. A reprint of a 1902 edition which examines the enormous impact of the Ethiopian victory at Adwa, and the consequent rise of the country's international prestige on the intellectual and political environment of Afro-American society.

Caulk, Richard A. "Minilik II and the Diplomacy of Commerce." *Journal of Ethiopian Studies* 17 (1984): 63-76. Discusses the emperor's commercial and diplomatic aplomb in gaining control of the productive means of his country and in balancing the opportunities and dangers of increased trade with Europeans.

Darkwah, R. H. Kofi. *Shewa, Menilek, and the Ethiopian Empire, 1813-1889*. London: Heinemann, and New York: Holmes and Meier, 1975. Monographic coverage of the period with emphasis on the later portion. Extensive coverage of agriculture and other economic issues, suppression of the slave trade, and military organization. Contains a useful bibliography.

Fellman, Jack. "The Birth of an African Literary Language: The Case of Amharic." *Research in African Literatures* 24, no. 3 (Fall 1993). Examines the contributions made by Menelik II toward the adoption of Amharic as the most commonly used language in Ethiopia.

Holly, Susan. "Feature: the United States and Ethiopia, 1903." *U.S. Department of State Dispatch* 3, no. 8 (February 24, 1992). Profile of Menelik II, his reputation and the American-Ethiopian relationship established by diplomat Robert P. Skinner.

Horvath, R. J. "The Wandering Capitals of Ethiopia." *Journal of African History* 10 (1969): 205-219. Discusses the locations of the capital in various periods; also useful as a brief synopsis of Ethiopian politics and society prior to the nineteenth century.

Marcus, Harold G. "Ethio-British Negotiations Concerning the Western Boundary with Sudan, 1896-1902." *Journal of African History* 4 (1963): 81-94. Reveals changed British attitudes toward Ethiopia in the wake of Adwa, which led to the bilateral Treaty of Addis Ababa in 1902.

———. *The Life and Times of Menelik II of Ethiopia: 1844-1913.* Oxford: Clarendon Press, 1975; Lawrenceville, N.J.: Red Sea Press, 1995. The primary focus is on Menelik's relations with Ethiopian noble dynasties and European powers. Extensive political narrative. Excellent bibliography.

Rosenfeld, Chris Prouty. *A Chronology of Menilek II of Ethiopia, 1844-1913.* East Lansing, Mich.: African Studies Center, 1976. A diary of the life and reign of Menelik gleaned from many different sources. Major foreign developments correlated with those in Ethiopia. A must for research on the period.

Ronald W. Davis

OTTMAR MERGENTHALER

Born: May 11, 1854; Hachtel, Germany
Died: October 28, 1899; Baltimore, Maryland
Area of Achievement: Printing technology
Contribution: Mergenthaler invented Linotype, the most prominent typesetting device before the advent of computerized photocomposition, thus revolutionizing the production of printed matter.

Early Life

Ottmar Mergenthaler was born into a family of schoolteachers in Hachtel, Württemberg, in what was to become Germany. Born May 11, 1854, Ottmar was the third of five children born to Johann George and Rosine (Ackermann) Mergenthaler. After an unexceptional grade school education in Ensingen, to which his family had moved, his father attempted to enroll him in a seminary in preparation for a career as a teacher. His early interest in engineering, however, and his skill at repairing all kinds of mechanisms, including the village clock, overcame his father's desire. Mergenthaler rejected the seminary, opting instead for an apprenticeship with a maker of watches and clocks.

Mergenthaler was fourteen when he began his apprenticeship with Louis Hahl in Bietigheim. He completed his apprenticeship in 1872, having shown himself to be a talented and ambitious mechanic. These were difficult times in Mergenthaler's homeland. Soldiers returning from the Franco-Prussian War were flooding the labor market. Economic reforms were disrupting established patterns of everyday life. In order to avoid military service himself and to further his career, he arranged to emigrate to the United States to work for Hahl's son, August, who was already an established instrument maker in Washington, D. C.

Although Washington was more of a governmental center than a manufacturing city, its skilled mechanics benefited from their proximity to scientific agencies and the patent office. August Hahl's shop concentrated on making electrical and meteorological apparatus, and Mergenthaler distinguished himself as an ingenious and dexterous mechanic. Curious and sensitive to a fault, he was also anxious to prove his competence and to make a success of himself in his adopted homeland. Bearded, with a high forehead, wavy dark hair, and deep-set eyes, he conveyed an intense, almost brooding presence.

The United States into which Mergenthaler arrived was different in several respects from the Germany he left. Mergenthaler grew up in a society in which precision and pride in craft were highly valued. In the United States, economic gain and productivity were more evident priorities. Germany had a more rigid class system and was developing a strong tradition of centralized state interference in the economy. In the United States, careers tended to be more open to the talented, and there was relatively greater opportunity for individual entrepreneurship. Mergenthaler seemed to be in his element.

Life's Work

Mergenthaler's introduction to the printing trade came in 1876, after Hahl's shop had been moved to Baltimore because it was more of an industrial center than Washington. Ironically, it was a Washington court reporter, James O. Clephane, who envisioned a means of transferring a printed page by means of a new kind of typewriter. He took his idea to an inventor, Charles Moore, who had developed a prototype. Moore brought his device to Hahl's shop for refinement. Mergenthaler was entrusted with the job of perfecting this machine and determining if it would serve its purposes. After three years of work, he decided that neither this idea nor a subsequent papier-mâché process would ever succeed. He also became obsessed with the idea that he could develop a successful machine to compose type automatically.

Mergenthaler became Hahl's partner in 1878 and continued there until 1883, when he established his own instrument-making and machine shop in Baltimore. From 1876 until his death in 1899, wherever Mergenthaler worked, it was the perfection of mechanical type composing that held his attention. Clephane continued to encourage him and found financial backing for his early endeavors.

In 1883, Mergenthaler produced a machine that used relief figures on long bands to make a papier-mâché mold of a line of type from which a metal line could be cast. In 1884, he developed a second so-called band machine, which aligned recessed dies on the bands from which a metal type line could be directly cast. Mergenthaler recognized that using individual brass molds for each character would improve the quality of the cast line and the machine's ability to redistribute molds for re-use. Despite the opposition of his financial backers, organized into the National Typographic Company, Mergenthaler worked on developing this new machine rather than producing the band model.

In 1885, Mergenthaler tested his new machine, and in the summer of 1886 the first one was installed at the *New York Tribune*. Whitelaw Reid, the *New York Tribune* editor and a financial backer of the machine, is reputed to have given the machine its name by exclaiming his amazement at the "line o' type" produced.

Several newspaper publishers formed a syndicate to support Mergenthaler's device, and they immediately sought to encourage its production for use on their papers. Mergenthaler opposed their efforts to move rapidly into manufacturing because he felt that significant improvements were needed. Nevertheless, the machine went into production, with Mergenthaler making improvements along the way. By 1888, disputes between Mergenthaler and his business partners reached a crisis and he resigned from the company, reorganized in 1885 as the Mergenthaler Printing Company.

Mergenthaler set up his own company to build parts and assemble machines for the syndicate that controlled the rights to the invention. He continued to make dozens of patented improvements on the Linotype. In 1890, he developed a new model Linotype that was more efficient and more reliable. In 1891, he was induced to rejoin the syndicate, re-named this time the Mergenthaler Linotype Company. He resigned in anger again in 1895 after the company president unsuccessfully requested that Mergenthaler's name be removed from the title.

Struck by tuberculosis in 1894, Mergenthaler spent the last years of his life perfecting his invention, battling for recognition and financial reward, and struggling to regain his health. He moved with his wife and three surviving children to New Mexico in 1897 but soon returned to Baltimore, where he died on October 28, 1899.

As completed, the Linotype combined the processes of composing text, casting type, and redistributing the molds. Type molds, called matrices, were held in a magazine. By working on a keyboard, the operator assembled in sequence individual matrices for letters, numbers, or marks. The line of assembled matrices was automatically spaced to the desired length by expanding wedges. Then it was held in front of a casting mechanism as molten type metal was forced into the molds. The completed line of type, called a slug, was then dropped into a galley, ready to be joined by the next line. Finally, after casting, the matrices were automatically carried back to the magazine and distributed to their original places to be reused. When the galley was full, the slugs were taken away to be prepared and arranged for printing.

The machine provided several advantages over handset type. First, it was about four to five times as fast as hand composition. Second, it allowed each publication to be printed from what was, in essense, new, unworn type. Third, composed matter could be stored for later printing without tying up expensive foundry type and depriving compositors of type to use on other jobs.

The Linotype faced a number of competitors, a few of which had been in limited use for years while others were introduced almost simultaneously with Mergenthaler's invention. In 1891, the American Newspaper Publishers Association invited the makers of fourteen machines to compete in a typesetting machine contest. Only four machines were eventually tested and, although not considered the best, the Linotype performed well enough to encourage several newspaper publishers to place orders.

Not surprisingly, the Linotype caused concern among skilled printing workers. During the 1890's, no fewer than twelve thousand journeymen printers, most often older men or those without a permanent job, lost their positions. Their union, the International Typographical Union, developed a set of policies to bring the machine predominantly under the control of the union rather than attempting to oppose its introduction. It thus set a precedent followed by many other American trade unions in response to technological innovations.

The Linotype's influence spread beyond the printing office itself. Newspaper publishers began to insist that reporters and editors use typewriters so that Linotype operators would not be slowed by unreadable manuscript. American type founders quickly learned that the Linotype was cutting into orders for new type. A group of them responded in 1892 by forming a new corporation, the American Type Founders Company, to benefit from economies of scale, reduced competition, and promotional activities.

The Linotype rapidly overwhelmed its competition in machine typesetting. About two hundred of the initial model, the Blower, were manufactured by 1890; between 1890 and 1892, more than 350 of the improved model were made; and more than seven thousand of the perfected Model 1 were in use by 1901. More than ninety thousand of the machines had been produced in the United States by 1971, when domestic production ended, and another forty thousand had been produced in foreign factories. Nearly all American daily and even weekly newspapers were produced on Linotypes in the early 1960's, when the shift to computer-based technologies began in earnest.

Summary

Ottmar Mergenthaler's single contribution to American, indeed world, culture came in the form of a perfected machine for automatically composing printing type. This invention transformed the printing trade and contributed to increasing the amount and speed with which printed material reached the public. It reduced the labor costs of employing printers and increased their ability to produce large quantities of text in a short time. This was particularly important in the newspaper trade, where time was of the essence. Although initially more appropriate for producing text than advertisements, the Linotype increased the total size of papers and encouraged more advertising. Although it imposed some limits on typefaces and page design, it was sufficiently flexible to meet the aesthetic needs of most publishers.

In some ways, Mergenthaler epitomized the ironies of American industrial history. An immigrant who saw America as a land of opportunity, Mergenthaler achieved a significant level of success and acclaim, having contributed materially to his adopted homeland, yet he was unwilling to compromise his craftsman's principles in the face of economic pressures and was unable to create a practical balance between technical and business affairs.

Bibliography

Barnett, George E. *Chapters on Machinery and Labor.* Cambridge, Mass.: Harvard University Press, 1926. Includes Barnett's seminal essay on the economic and labor aspects of the Linotype's introduction. Provides the best conceptual discussion of the pace of introduction and its impact.

Chappell, Warren. *A Short History of the Printed Word.* 2d ed. Point Roberts, Wash.: Hartley and Marks, 1998. An accessible, generally reliable history of printing in world context. Covers intellectual, aesthetic, and technical aspects of printing. Places the mechanization of typesetting into the context of other nineteenth century changes in the book trades.

Huss, Richard E. *The Development of Printers' Mechanical Typesetting Methods: 1822-1925.* Charlottesville: University Press of Virginia, 1973. A chronological survey of typesetting devices, particularly strong on technical descriptions of their mechanisms. Includes 294 individual items with illustrations of most.

Jennett, Sean. *Pioneers in Printing.* London: Routledge, 1958. A series of biographies of influential individuals in the book trades. Places Mergenthaler's work in the context of others working on mechanical typesetting. Gives a good, brief introduction to the complex business arrangements surrounding the Linotype.

Kelber, Harry, and Carl Schlesinger. *Union Printers and Controlled Automation.* London: Macmillan, and New York: Free Press, 1967. A thorough discussion of the impact of the Linotype and subsequent technological changes on printing labor. Contains a complete analysis of the development of attitudes toward technology by the International Typographical Union.

Mengel, Willi. *Ottmar Mergenthaler and the Printing Revolution.* Brooklyn, N.Y.: Mergenthaler, 1954. Produced for the centenary anniversary of Mergenthaler's birth, this volume relies heavily upon Mergenthaler's autobiography for its discussion of the Linotype. Also includes helpful material on earlier efforts to mechanize typesetting.

Mergenthaler, Ottmar. *Biography of Ottmar Mergenthaler and History of the Linotype.* Baltimore: Author, 1898. Written in the third person, this publication was pulled together by Mergenthaler just before his death after an original manuscript and notes were destroyed in a fire. The biography is an indispensable source, full of information and insights unavailable elsewhere. It is marred, however, by an understandably one-sided and frequently bitter perspective.

Thompson, John S. *The Mechanism of the Linotype; History of Composing Machines.* 2 vols. Chicago: Inland Printer, 1902-1904. Originally published as serials in a trade journal, these two works constitute a basic source written by a former Mergenthaler employee. Contains a complete technical description of the Linotype and its operation and maintenance, as well as comparisons with other typesetting devices.

William S. Pretzer

METTERNICH

Born: May 15, 1773; Coblenz, Archbishopric of Trier

Died: June 11, 1859; Vienna, Austro-Hungarian Empire

Areas of Achievement: Diplomacy, government, and politics

Contribution: As Europe's preeminent champion of post-French Revolution conservatism, Metternich was the chief architect in the reconstruction of the European map after the fall of Napoleon I. As minister of foreign affairs, and, later, as state chancellor to the Austrian emperor, Metternich presided for more than three decades over the political and diplomatic workings of the continent he had restored until the Revolutions of 1848 swept him from power and ushered in a new generation of leaders.

Early Life

Clemens Wenzel Nepomuk Lothar von Metternich was born, not within the vast hegemonous region that comprised the Austro-Hungarian Empire, but in the small German state of Trier, ruled by prince-bishops, one of whom, in the early seventeenth century, had been a Metternich. His father, Count Franz Georg Karl von Metternich, had represented the elector of Trier at the Imperial Court of Vienna, and, at the time of his son's birth, had reversed that role and was representing the Austrian emperor in his homeland. As a result, young Clemens was reared in the Rhineland, and he remained fond of this region all of his life. His mother, Countess Beatrix Kagenegg, was a woman of considerable culture, intelligence, and charm, whose sophistication and elegance were more French than Germanic. These qualities she passed on to her son, who was always more at home with the language and Old World manners of the country of his greatest adversary, Napoleon I, then he was with his own.

In 1788, at the age of fifteen, he was sent to study diplomacy at the University of Strasbourg. There, he studied under a celebrated professor, Christoph Wilhelm Koch, who was an ardent proponent of creating a conservative counterbalance that would oppose the growing nationalist sentiment in Europe. The following year saw the outbreak of the French Revolution, which spread to Strasbourg in 1790. Abhorring the destructive violence of the Revolution, Metternich left Strasbourg for Mainz, where he enrolled in the university. He abandoned that city before the arrival of the French revolutionary troops to join his father in Brussels, where the count was prime minister of the Austrian Netherlands. From there, young Metternich was sent on a minor diplomatic mission to England in 1794, the first of his career. Upon his return later that year, he rejoined his family in Vienna, where they had fled after the ever-growing fury of the French Revolution had deprived them of their position in Brussels and their home in Coblenz.

In September, 1795, Metternich married Eleonore von Kaunitz, but it was not a love match. While a student at Mainz, Metternich had been initiated into the erotic privileges of a young nobleman, and he was to show a lifelong predilection for the company of a great variety of attractive women that his steadily increasing political status made available to him, even using some of these amorous liaisons to great diplomatic advantage. His was not merely a marriage of convenience but of opportunity as well, for his bride was the granddaughter of the powerful Wenzel von Kaunitz, state chancellor to the late Empress Maria Theresa. By marrying into this family of tremendous political and social prestige, Metternich at last had entrée into the exclusive imperial inner circle of influence from which he could make his bid for high office.

Life's Work

During his first ten years of service as an ambassador for the Austrian emperor, Metternich witnessed the final dissolution of the ancient Holy Roman Empire, whose (by this time) symbolic and powerless crown had traditionally rested on the head of the reigning Habsburg monarch in Vienna. After serving as Austrian minister to the Saxon court in Dresden and the Prussian court in Berlin, where his anti-French efforts were thwarted, Emperor Francis I placed his young ambassador in the front ranks of the battle, and in 1806 Metternich presented his credentials to France's newly self-declared emperor, Napoleon, at Saint Cloud.

In Paris, he became very well informed as to the internal workings of the French Empire through his many important connections and his vast network of spies, which became legendary. For all of these advantages, his initial diplomatic efforts with the brilliant French tyrant proved to be a costly failure to his own country. Overestimating the effect of the 1808 Iberian uprising against the Bonapartes, he precipitated Austria into a war against France that ended disastrously for the Austrians in the Battle of Wagram (1809). Recalled to Vienna by the emperor, Metternich was appointed minister of foreign affairs, in which capacity he bought time for an exhausted Austria by giving Napoleon one of Francis' daughters as a bride. The match with the Archduchess Marie Louise (ironically a grandniece of Louis XVI's tragic queen, Marie Antoinette) was a calculated psychological maneuver to flatter Napoleon, whose character Metternich had closely studied during his tenure in Paris. Austria could now remain independent from the seemingly invincible French Empire, preserving the autonomy it needed to recoup its losses.

While Napoleon turned his attention and his Grande Armée from Austria to Russia, Austria quietly rearmed and Metternich tried to preserve the shaky balance of power in Europe, striving to keep the momentary status quo he had bought at so high a price. Austria now needed France to remain strong. Fearing the creation of a Prussian empire after French assault had awakened a dormant sense of German nationalism, and mindful of the threat of a Russian invasion of Europe if France collapsed, Metternich needed to counterbalance these threats with French power until Austria was again fit to face its dangerous adversary.

Metternich found his moment with France's catastrophic and surprising defeat in Russia in 1812. Confident of Austria's rejuvenation, he concluded a treaty with Russia and Prussia in June, 1813. Metternich negotiated with France for a separate peace treaty, but Napoleon hesitated, and in August of that year Austria declared war on France. That October, Francis bestowed on his most illustrious subject the hereditary title of prince. Holding close the South German states as allies to block any Russo-Prussian aggrandizement during this final conflict with France, Metternich arrived in Paris in May, 1814, after Napoleon's defeat at Waterloo and subsequent abdication, with the upper hand to sign the Treaty of Paris and open the way to the Congress of Vienna (September, 1814, to June, 1815).

Employing his own great charm and worldliness along with the music for which Vienna is legendary, Metternich attracted Europe's most powerful and glamorous figures to the Austrian capital for the "Congress that Danced," giving that city for the first and only time in its history the distinction of being the center of European politics. It was a

splendid social occasion with an unending round of balls and festivities. It was also the most important political congress in a generation, and Europe's future hinged on the negotiations that took place there during those nine months.

Conservative by temperament, upbringing, and education, Metternich was further persuaded by the horror of two decades of pan-European war to restore the Continent to its pre-Napoleonic form. Additionally, he sought to replace the Habsburgs' traditional but meaningless role as the preeminent monarchs of Europe by establishing for them a very real leadership over loose confederations of German and Italian states. To this end he proposed the creation of an imperial German title to be borne by the Austrian emperor. Furthermore, he wanted to restore France to its pre-Revolutionary status with the old royal house of Bourbon, giving it equal footing with its conquerors to counter the threat of Russian dominance. Metternich failed in Germany and in Italy, primarily through the archconservatism of his own emperor. Francis embraced the idea of power in Italy, where Austria was initially welcomed with enthusiasm, but he mishandled it and only succeeded in agitating the feeling of national unity that his foreign minister had thereby tried to avoid; he refused the title of German emperor, leaving Austrian influence in the German states on an equal footing with Prussia. With France, Metternich was successful. France's Talleyrand and England's Castlereagh concluded an alliance with Metternich to keep in check the Russo-Prussian pact that had taken place.

That was the essential balance of power when the Congress broke up, and it established a European order that lasted well into the middle of the century. During most of that time Metternich was custodian of that order, making him the virtual prime minister of Europe. With patience, insight, and an uncanny ability to see through the heated rhetoric and quickly shifting currents of the time, Metternich triumphed over the more imposing figures of his generation, yet he was unable to defeat the new ideas that they had helped unleash. With England withdrawn from continental politics, republican restlessness in France, and nationalistic fervor in the German and Italian states, Metternich, by now Austrian state chancellor, could not prevent in 1848 the eruption of revolutions that swept through the great European capitals. Hated by now as a reactionary and the leading figure of repressive government, Metternich was forced to resign on March 13, 1848. He went into exile in England for three years but returned to Vienna, where he died in 1859 in his eighty-sixth year.

Summary

A cursory investigation of Metternich's many and varied achievements could give the impression that the subject was a genius. This, however, would do him an injustice because, though he may have possessed a kind of genius, the genius of his day was Napoleon and Metternich was his enemy. Although Metternich and his ilk eventually triumphed over Napoleon, it was the more prosaic qualities of patience, industry, and levelheadedness that won for him the war after losing most of the battles. He was not a visionary, but a practical man. Imagination, great style, and charm he did possess; indeed, he often depended on these qualities. Beyond this, however, Metternich was built to last long after the dust had settled and there was work still to be done. He saw his age through to its end and beyond, living long enough to see himself vilified by the very generation whose future he had striven to preserve. The conservatism he reimposed on Europe lasted nearly forty years until it was swept away forever by men such as Napoleon III, Giuseppe Garibaldi, and Otto von Bismarck, who were, if not his political heirs, certainly his successors. Seen from a modern, liberal perspective, it is easy to label those four decades as reactionary and oppressive. They were also four decades of a desperately needed peace, perhaps the longest such period that Europe has ever known.

Bibliography

Bertier de Sauvigny, G. de. *Metternich and His Times*. Translated by Peter Ryde. London: Longman, 1962. Written one hundred years after its subject's death, this biography is a good introduction to Metternich and his world. Most of this work is devoted to the comments of Metternich himself and his contemporaries, while the author serves as a guide to the Austrian minister's life.

Cecil, Algernon. *Metternich, 1773-1859: A Study of His Period and Personality*. London: Eyre and Spottiswoode, and New York: Macmillan, 1933. A thorough and engaging biography of Metternich and his times. The great statesman's life is recounted with an imagination that counterbalances its frequently difficult scholarly approach. Inaccessible to the lay reader, this book of moderate length is a good in-depth account of Metternich's professional life.

Haas, Arthur G. *Metternich, Reorganization, and Nationality, 1813-1815: A Story of Foresight and Frustration in the Rebuilding of the Austrian Empire*. Knoxville: University of Tennessee Press, 1964. For those interested in a detailed, documented, blow-by-blow account of the crucial negotiations and renegotiations that followed the resettlement of Europe after Napoleon's fall, this book is thorough and easy to understand.

Kissinger, Henry A. *A World Restored: Metternich, Castlereagh, and the Problems of Peace, 1812-22*. Boston: Houghton Mifflin, and London: Gollancz, 1957. A biography of a celebrated nineteenth century statesman by a celebrated twentieth century statesman before the latter was well known. This is a good, if somewhat dry, introduction to Europe after Napoleon.

Liang, Hsi-Huey. *The Rise of Modern Police and the European State System from Metternich to the Second World War*. Cambridge and New

York: Cambridge University Press, 1992. The author questions the development of various police forces in Europe such as the SS and Gestapo and the issues that have caused history to brand them as out of control. Includes Metternich's theories on maintaining European equilibrium.

Metternich, Prince Clemens von. *Memoirs of Prince Metternich, 1773-1835.* 5 vols. Edited by Prince Richard Metternich. Translated by Mrs. Alexander Napier and Gerard W. Smith. New York: Scribner, and London: Bentley, 1880-1884. Completed in 1844 by Metternich himself and brought to publication twenty years after his death by his son, Prince Richard, here is an account of his life from his birth to the Congress of Vienna. Recounted with the clarity and arrogance for which he was well known. Contains important documents and correspondence.

Schroeder, Paul W. *Metternich's Diplomacy at Its Zenith, 1820-1823.* Austin: University of Texas Press, 1962. An account of Metternich's years of diplomatic supremacy following the Congress of Vienna. Using maps to help illustrate this history, Schroeder describes the first years of Metternich's chancellory when his plan for Europe was most successful.

Sofka, James R. "Metternich's Theory of European Order: A Political Agenda for 'Perpetual Peace.'" *Review of Politics* 60, no. 1 (Winter 1998). Profile of Metternich focusing on his involvement with the Enlightenment and its affect on his foreign policies. Includes Metternich's Vienna Treaty of 1815 and its impact on international politics in the nineteenth century.

Pavlin Lange

JULES MICHELET

Born: August 21, 1789; Paris, France
Died: February 9, 1874; Hyères, France
Areas of Achievement: Historiography and philosophy
Contribution: Michelet was France's greatest national historian and one of the guiding forces of modern historical writing.

Early Life

Jules Michelet was the only child of a poor Parisian printer. His early life was one of material privation but deep familial love. Forced to work in his father's establishment from an early age, the youth lived a solitary life and experienced few of the common joys of childhood. His only pleasure came from his long walks after hours in the famous cemetery, Père Lachaise, and his occasional visits to Lenoir's Museum. It was from the latter that he first experienced a vivid realization of history and a fascination with the past.

Michelet's antagonism toward the Church and toward monarchy, which would loom so large in his later writings, stemmed, in part, from his youth. The family of the future historian, already in dire poverty, was reduced to absolute destitution during the Reign of Terror as Robespierre's henchmen combed the streets of Paris, jailing and executing men whose manuscripts his father had published. Fearing for his life, the elder Michelet first curtailed his printing projects and was finally forced to terminate his business by the government. Unemployment led to debts for which his father was arrested in 1808 and incarcerated for nearly a year. The collapse of his father's occupation and his ensuing imprisonment engendered in Jules a hatred of Napoleon I, clerics, and the empire that endured to his death. In his last work, *Histoire du XIXᵉ siècle* (1872-1875; history of the nineteenth century), he continued to spew forth the vitriolic opinions inculcated during his childhood.

Although financial problems led to marital strife, both parents agreed on one thing; Jules should be formally educated whatever the cost. After being tutored in Latin by a family friend, Michelet entered Lycée Charlemagne in 1812, which proved to be socially disastrous. His life of solitude had not prepared him for the competitive academic world, and the small, sensitive, shy lad became the object of endless verbal and physical abuse. The owl in daylight, as one source described him, endured the abuse and, capitalizing on his native intelligence, innate writing skills, and untiring work habits, became the top student in his class.

His brilliant academic career won for him a teaching position at the Collège Sainte-Barbe in 1822. In 1827, he published a translation of Giambattista Vico's *Principi di scienza nuova d'intorno alla comune natura delle nazione* (1744; *The New Science*, 1948) that brought him both public acclaim and an appointment to teach history and philosophy at the École Normale Supérieure, a position he held until 1838, when he accepted a chair at the Collège de France. In addition to his academic positions, he served as head of the history section of the National Archives from 1830 to 1852.

Life's Work

The philosophical foundation for Michelet's seventeen-volume *Histoire de France* (1833-1867; partial translation as *The History of France*, 1844-1846) and the seven-volume *Histoire de la Révolution française* (1847-1853; *History of the French Revolution*, 1972), his life's work, slowly evolved in 1827 as he came under the influence of German Romanticism. Vico, the little-known Neapolitan philosopher, taught Michelet that all history was universal, constantly in motion, and that humanity was the common element unifying all ages. Men die, but humanity, the receptacle for human wisdom, lives on. The still-embryonic scholar first expressed his historical philosophy in *Introduction à l'histoire universelle* (1831; introduction to universal history), maintaining that history was nothing more than the story of liberty: man's ongoing struggle to free himself from nature and fatality. As history was constantly in motion, he likened it to the movement of the sun. It rose in the east, in India, moved westward to Persia, Greece, Rome, and culminated in France. In his typically unabashed, chauvinistic manner, Michelet explained that France was superior to the rest of Europe in culture and civilization and, being such, was the new apostle of liberty. Along this line of reasoning, France became synonymous with humanity, and France alone would control the destiny of mankind. Thus, in Vico, Michelet found both a philosophy of history and a mission. His life's work would be to show how the French people fostered and nourished the spirit of liberty.

The History of France filled seventeen volumes, took thirty-four years to write, and was a labor of love. Of the seventeen volumes, only the first six merit serious consideration. These six, written between 1833 and 1844, are based on primary sources, contain no obvious bias, and reflect a unique historical method. Michelet's objective was to treat the "whole of the parts"—the land, its people, events, institutions, and beliefs—but it was the people who were the important element. The remaining eleven volumes (written between 1854 and 1867), covering the end of the Middle Ages to the Revolution, are inferior, as Michelet was forced to write them without full benefit of manuscripts and documentation. Michelet, having been relieved of his professorship and archival position for refusing to swear an oath of allegiance to Napoleon III, voices in volumes seven through thirteen his hostility toward the monarchy and toward Christianity.

In the interval that divided his work on *The History of France*, Michelet turned his attention to the French Revolution. Using the turmoil of 1789 as a backdrop, he painted a gloomy picture of the state of affairs in France; he maintained that the Church, supported by the monarchy, was threatening education, which had been an essential reform of the Revolution. In both *History of the French Revolution* and *Le Peuple* (1846; *The People*, 1846), he maintained that France was once again suffering under the tyranny of Christian monarchy and it was time for the people to sally forth and rekindle the light for justice and liberty. In *History of the French Revolution*, the voice is that of a revolutionary as Michelet becomes one of the common people who won the triumph for law and justice in 1789. His objective was to stir the masses. So effective was his effort that he has been credited with being instrumental in instigating the Revolution of 1848, which, in addition to his refusal to swear allegiance to Napoleon, cost him his academic post at the Collège de France as well as his archival position.

Deprived of rank and income, Michelet was forced to move to the countryside with only the company of his young wife, Athenais, to comfort him. As his own suffering paralleled his father's at the hands of the government, it is not surprising that when he resumed work on *The History of France* an obvious bias against the government ran through the remaining volumes. In January, 1874, the great historian fell ill, and a month later, on February 9, 1874, he died of a heart attack. Al-

though initially interred at Hyères, France, in May, 1875, his body was later exhumed, and, before thousands of public officials, students, and friends, he was buried a second time at Père Lachaise, where he had spent his happiest moments as a child.

Summary

Jules Michelet was a product of the Romantic movement, the world of color, passion, and poetry, but his love for France became excessive. So intense were his emotions that he could not see life as it was. As his patriotism turned into idolatry and as he deified the French people and the Revolution, it became impossible for him to explain the terror of the age. While his work must be admired for its novelty and beauty, it must be scorned for its mysticism. Yet his labors were not without merit. He was the first to use the term "Renaissance" to refer to a specific period in history. He was the first to insist that geography was a determining factor in shaping a state. He was the first to make widespread use of artifacts in interpreting the past. He was the first to assign a major role to the common man as the molder of his own destiny. If his excessive love for France distorted his analysis, his historical method was destined to play a major role in inspiring future historians to view the past in its totality.

Bibliography

Geyl, Pieter. *Debates with Historians*. London: Batsford, 1955; New York: Philosophical Library, 1956. Provides good balance to Gooch's work, as Geyl is very critical of Michelet. Although attention is given to both *The History of France* and *History of the French Revolution*, the latter is emphasized. The major criticism is Michelet's attempt to use emotionalism and sentimentality to make wrong appear right.

Gooch, G. P. *History and Historians in the Nineteenth Century*. 2d ed. New York: Barnes and Noble, and London: Longman, 1952. The best work on nineteenth century historiography in English. Gives one of the more favorable views of Michelet. Gooch notes the historian's bias toward the monarchy, his anticlerical position, and his excessive adoration of France.

Hooper, John. "Changing Perceptions of Jules Michelet as Historian: History between Literature and Science, 1831-1874." *Journal of European Studies* 23, no. 91 (September, 1993). Examines the mid-nineteenth-century perceptual division of literature and history into separate disciplines and how the writings of Michelet were classified over time.

Kippur, Stephen A. *Jules Michelet: A Study of Mind and Sensibility*. Albany: State University of New York Press, 1986. The only full biography of Michelet in English. The work considers Michelet's childhood, social status, and intellectual development as they contributed to Michelet's work as a historian and professor. Kippur examines Michelet's ideas on France, religion, and "the people." Gives a good analysis of Michelet's major works and is a balanced account.

Mitzman, Arthur. "Michelet and Social Romanticism: Religion, Revolution, Nature." *Journal of the History of Ideas* 57, no. 4 (October, 1996). Examines Michelet's migration from liberalism to social romanticism.

Orr, Linda. *Jules Michelet: Nature, History, and Language*. Ithaca, N.Y.: Cornell University Press, 1976. Orr provides excellent coverage of Michelet's nonhistorical writings. Gives particular attention to his writings on natural science. Traces Michelet's search for patterns of coherence in nature, which influenced his historical works. Draws upon Michelet's journal to provide fascinating insight into the personal aspects of his private life.

Thompson, J. W. *A History of Historical Writing*. Vol. 2. New York: Macmillan, 1942. This good source gives a chronological account of the major aspects of Michelet's life. Particularly good on the problems leading to Michelet's anticlerical stance in his history of the Revolution. Advocates dividing Michelet's works into two categories for analysis.

Wayne M. Bledsoe

ALBERT A. MICHELSON

Born: December 19, 1852; Strelno, Prussia
Died: May 9, 1931; Pasadena, California
Area of Achievement: Physics
Contribution: Michelson was the first American to win a Nobel Prize for Physics, which he received for determining the length of the standard meter in terms of wavelengths of light. His significant contributions to physics and optics include measurement of velocity of light, of the ether drift, of the rigidity of earth, and of the diameter of stars, as well as development of the interferometer.

Early Life

Albert Abraham Michelson was born December 19, 1852, at Strelno (modern Strzelno), which was Polish in population and tradition but was located in German territory at that time. His mother, Rosalie Przlubska, was the daughter of a businessman, and the effect of her early teachings made Albert resist the lure of easy money all of his life. At the time of Albert's birth, his father, Samuel Michelson, was the proprietor of a dry-goods shop. Political upheavals in Europe in 1848 accelerated anti-Semitism there, and late in 1855, the Michelsons decided to emigrate to California. They traveled by steamer to Panama; made the laborious trip across the Isthmus by muleback, canoe, and train; and boarded another boat to San Francisco, where Samuel's sister and brother-in-law, Belle and Oscar Meyer, were living. The Michelsons settled in Murphys, a mining town in the heart of the gold country, where Samuel opened a store. Young Albert took violin lessons from a local prospector who was a fine musician. Albert's parents realized that he was very bright and decided that he needed a better education than was available in the mining town. They boarded him with his cousins in San Francisco to finish the last two years of grammar school, and he matriculated to San Francisco Boys High School. The principal, Theodore Bradley, recognized the boy's exceptional mechanical abilities and took him into his own home. While Albert was in high school, his father moved the family to Virginia City, Nevada, and opened a business there. After graduation at sixteen, Albert went to the famous mining town and took the competitive examination for the United States Naval Academy at Annapolis at the Storey County Court House. He lost the appointment to the son of a man who had been injured in the Civil War. Undaunted, the young man solicited letters of recommendation and made the long train trip alone across the country, determined to petition the president for an appointment. Arriving in Washington, he learned that President Ulysses S. Grant walked his dogs at a regular hour. Young Michelson waited on the White House steps and approached the president with his petition. The president advised him that the appointments-at-large had been filled, but Michelson implored the president to consider another appointment. Impressed with the young man who would not take no for an answer, the president suggested that Albert visit Annapolis. Three days later, President Grant named him the eleventh appointee-at-large. This characteristic of attempting the impossible became a pattern in Michelson's life.

Michelson entered Annapolis in June, 1869. He made a striking figure clad in his naval uniform with his chiseled features, jet-black hair, and deep-set hazel eyes. He appeared taller than his five feet seven or eight inches because of an elegant and dignified bearing. While at the academy, he excelled in optics, acoustics, and drawing but always had time for fencing, boxing, music, and painting. His spirited independence and youthful exuberance were not evident in gunnery class, and a superior officer scolded that he might eventually be of some use to his country if he paid more attention to his gunnery than to science. No one knew at that time that this ensign would become one of America's greatest scientists.

Upon graduation, Albert served for two years at sea and then returned to the academy as an instructor in the department of physics and chemistry headed by Admiral William T. Sampson. He met the admiral's niece, Margaret Heminway, and they married in 1877 and had two sons and a daughter.

Life's Work

The speed of light had interested scientists for centuries, including Galileo Galilei, Armand-Hippolyte-Louis Fizeau, and Jean-Bernard-Léon Foucault. This was to become the all-consuming question of Michelson's life. Anxious to use demonstrations in his physics class, he gathered crude pieces of apparatus lying about the laboratory, spent ten dollars of his own money, and modified Foucault's earlier experiment. The young ensign was able to make a more accurate measurement of the speed of light than had ever before been achieved. The superintendent of the United States Navy's nautical almanac office, Simon Newcomb, appointed Michelson to a position in a government-sponsored project to determine the velocity of light. Albert quickly surpassed his peers and even his seniors, as he had an uncanny ability to devise experimentation techniques.

In 1880, Michelson secured a leave of absence from the navy and spent two years in Europe studying under Hermann von Helmholtz at the University of Berlin, Georg Hermann Quincke at Heidelberg University, and Marie Alfred Cornu at the Collège de France and the École Polytechnique in Paris. Scientists of the nineteenth century believed that light was propagated through a luminiferous ether which filled all space around the earth. The inquisitive Michelson wondered whether the existence of this luminiferous ether could be proved or disproved. This was a big idea, but big ideas appealed to him. He began studying light interference patterns and reasoned that an instrument was needed for measuring distances that would be far beyond the range of the most powerful microscope invented. In 1881, he developed this delicate instrument, which became known as the Michelson interferometer, and performed his first ether-drift experiment in Europe. He calculated a negative result on the motion of the ether relative to the earth, but scientists at that time hesitated to accept this challenge to their belief.

Michelson decided to devote his life to science, reasoning that staying in the navy would thwart this career. He resigned to become professor of physics at Case School of Applied Science in Cleveland, Ohio. He was appointed corresponding member of the British Association for the Advancement of Science in 1884, named associate fellow of the American Academy of Arts and Sciences in 1885, and received his first honorary Ph.D. from Western Reserve University the following year. In 1885, he met Professor Edward Williams Morley, a well-established chemist. Michelson must have learned much from this versatile scientist, and Morley's influence on Michelson's work has not been adequately acknowledged. They collaborated on light experiments, and Michelson worked day and night, neglecting food and rest. He reached the point of nervous exhaustion and had to take time away from the experiments. When he returned, Michelson and Morley submitted a joint paper to the *American Journal of Science* reporting

negative results from the ether-drift experiment. In 1887, they conducted an experiment to see if light traveled in the same velocity in any direction and discovered no observable difference. Scientists of the nineteenth century had reasoned that since the earth moves around the sun at approximately eighteen miles per second, the speed of a light beam traveling with the earth's orbital motion should be greater than that of a beam traveling in the opposite direction. The negative result of the Michelson-Morley experiment provided the raw material which stimulated the theory of relativity. It proved that there were not different velocities of light. This discovery was catastrophic to the mechanical theory of science, which had received support since the time of Sir Isaac Newton. The two scientists worked together until 1889.

Michelson left Case Institute to teach at Clark University between 1889 and 1892. His first sojourn into astronomy began at this time when he took his equipment to Lick Observatory in California and actually measured Jupiter's satellites. In 1892, he moved to the University of Chicago and assumed the position as head of the department of physics but continued working on experiments in astronomy, spectroscopy, geophysics, and optics. He also lectured to graduate students. By the end of the nineteenth century, he was considered to be one of the twelve greatest scientists in the world, yet he was very modest: When Michelson was teaching, he gave credit to all the scientists for their contributions, but the students noticed that when he started describing current experiments and results which were clearly more significant than the preceding ones, he neglected to cite the author. The puzzled students questioned another instructor about this strange behavior. The instructor laughingly resolved the problem. The mysterious experiments had been those of Albert Abraham Michelson, and the renowned scientist had not wanted to call undue attention to his own work.

Michelson was more interested in his scientific work than in a social life, and his first marriage ended in divorce in 1897. Some sources present an austere, forbidding, overwrought picture of him at that time, but in December, 1899, he married Edna Stanton, a former student, and life with his second wife and their three daughters seemed to be happier.

Michelson continued to be very productive during this period of time and developed an echelon spectroscope with high enough resolution to indicate optical evidence of molecular motion associated with temperature. By 1905, he had completed a ruling engine which had 110,000 lines on a six-inch square of glass, which he referred to as the "she-devil." This instrument was later used by astronomers to discover the innermost secrets of the atom.

In 1907, Michelson received the Nobel Prize for Physics for establishing the length of the meter in terms of cadmium light. A few years earlier, the International Conference on Weights and Measures had made the metric system standard and deposited a platinum-iridium bar in a well-guarded vault at Severes. The Franco-Prussian War brought to the forefront the idea that the bar, which established the length of the meter, would be lost. Scientists suggested that measurement of a length of light wave would be more permanent. Michelson attempted this experiment, as he was able to measure the wavelengths of various gases with his versatile interferometer. After experimenting with sodium and mercury, he settled for the bright red line of cadmium light. He announced that 1,553,163.5 wavelengths of the red line of the metal cadmium were equal to the length of the platinum-iridium standard. The Nobel Prize was awarded to him for accomplishment in precision measurements.

Michelson was also very interested in zoology. He related the phenomenon of the iridescent colors of hummingbirds, butterflies, and beetles to interference and reflection of light. In his book *Studies in Optics* (1927), he noted that the diamond beetle had diffraction grating ruled on its wings as fine as two thousand to the inch.

Michelson remained active in naval affairs throughout his life. He commanded the Illinois Naval Militia for years. During World War I, he served as a lieutenant commander and patented five optical range-finders for naval vessels.

Ever reaching for new planes, he used his interferometer to indicate the substance of the earth's interior, and, in 1920, he was the first to measure the angular diameter of a distant star. The Royal Astronomical Society of England recognized this achievement by presenting its gold medal to him, but this was only one of numerous medals and prizes from scientific societies which he was awarded. Michelson received six honorary Ph.D.'s during his lifetime. Although he disliked publicity, he did realize the value of promotion in obtaining money for his projects, and was very gracious in his dealings with people.

In his later years, Michelson still held himself erect, maintaining the quiet demeanor of his youth. His hair was white, and he wore a close-cropped gray mustache. He enjoyed tennis, bridge, chess, and billiards. He would discuss these subjects socially, but he preferred to keep his science and art, which were so dear to his heart, in the laboratory and the studio.

Michelson always believed that his greatest experiment was still ahead of him. He considered it great fun to do the arduous work involved in setting up experiments and overseeing the technical difficulties. When he was in his seventies, he once again determined to measure the velocity of light. He worked with George Ellery Hale at Mount Wilson Observatory on five sets of light measurements between 1924 and 1927. He was dissatisfied with these tests because of the obstruction of valley haze and smoke and constructed an experiment in a vacuum tube where light could travel in empty space. He was directing this work when he became ill, but the dedicated man, then in his late seventies, carried on the work from his sickbed. He dictated the introduction of a scientific paper to astronomer Francis Pease, and when the report was published posthumously, the title was "On a Method of Measuring the Velocity of Light," the same title of his first paper when he was an ensign in the navy. He died May 9, 1931, of a cerebral hemorrhage.

Summary

Albert Abraham Michelson obtained world attention for American science at a time when European scientists were inclined to characterize Americans as lacking in scientific capabilities. It is evident that his contributions helped forward the theory of relativity, though it would be an overstatement that Albert Einstein's theory was a generalization of the Michelson-Morley experiment or that the theory of relativity could not have been arrived at without this experiment. Michelson has often been called "the man who measured the stars," but he was more than this. His major contributions include precision optical measurements of the velocity of light, of the ether drift, of the length of the standard meter, of the angular diameters of stars, and of the rigidity of the earth; developmental experimentation in the young field of spectroscopy; and invention of the harmonic analyzer, in addition to the Michelson interferometer. His efforts extended to the precision of measurement represent an extraordinary contribution to scientific knowledge.

Michelson always had the greatest respect for the navy, where he received his start. The navy did not forget him and, in 1948, honored his memory with the construction of a laboratory for basic and applied research at the United States Naval Ordnance Test Station at China Lake in the Mojave Desert. In 1969, Michelson Hall, housing the science department, was dedicated at Annapolis in honor of its graduate of the class of 1873. The building stands over the area of the old seawall where Michelson made his earliest measurements of the speed of light. His papers, accumulated over a period of thirty years by Ted McAllister, curator of Michelson Museum at the Naval Weapons Center at China Lake, have been transferred to this facility.

Very few Americans are chosen for the Hall of Fame. Michelson was selected to receive this honor; the tribute ceremony and unveiling of the bust took place on October 21, 1973, at the Hall of Fame for Great Americans at New York University. His own words were chosen as the inscription on the bronze tablet which accompanies the sculpture:

"It seems to me that scientific research should be regarded as the painter regards his art, as the poet his poems, and the composer his music." Michelson was a splendid scientist, a fine naval officer, a talented artist, and an honored educator. He will be remembered for his significant contributions to physics and optics.

Bibliography

Bennett, Jean M., D. Theodore McAllister, and Georgia M. Cabe. "Albert A. Michelson, Dean of American Optics: Life, Contributions to Science, and Influence on Modern Day Physics." *Journal of Applied Optics* 12 (October, 1973): 2253. Excellent article which not only summarizes Michelson's life but also details his scientific experiments in a readable fashion. Compiled by the curator of the Michelson Museum, who spent thirty years compiling the Michelson papers. One of the most concise sources available. Well documented. Thorough bibliography.

Holton, Gerald. *Thematic Origins of Scientific Thought.* Rev. ed. Cambridge, Mass.: Harvard University Press, 1988. Systematically attacks any relationship between Einstein, Michelson, and the "crucial" experiment. Persuasive that the Michelson-Morley experiment had no effect on Einstein's theory of relativity.

Jaffe, Bernard. *Men of Science in America.* Rev. ed. New York: Simon and Schuster, 1958. Jaffe has done a considerable service for students of the history of science in this assortment of materials dealing with scientists in the United States. Sound and scholarly, the book presents Michelson's participation as a catalyst in the revolution of modern physics.

————. *Michelson and the Speed of Light.* New York: Anchor Books, 1960; London: Heinemann, 1961. A well-balanced biography of Michelson. Includes descriptions of his experiments. Designed for popular reading but contains relatively few errors. Excellent bibliography. Thematic approach correlated chronologically.

Livingston, Dorothy Michelson. *The Master of Light: A Biography of Albert A. Michelson.* New York: Scribner, 1973. An admirable book which falls short of being a scientific biography as it lacks the critical analysis of scientific and technical matters essential in such a work. Written by Michelson's daughter, it gives a picture of the man rather than the scientist.

Ronan, Colin A. *Science: Its History and Development Among the World Cultures*. New York: Facts on File, 1982. Mentions Michelson in passing but provides a detailed account of the events, in chronological order, in the fields of science during Michelson's life. Relates to the Michelson-Morley experiment.

Swenson, Loyd S., Jr. *Genesis of Relativity: Einstein in Context*. New York: Franklin, 1979. Good detail of the Michelson-Morley experiment and its contribution to the theory of relativity. Readable and within reach of the average student. A valuable study.

Evelyne L. Pickett

JAMES MILL

Born: April 6, 1773; Northwater Bridge, Logie
   Pert, Forfarshire, Scotland
Died: June 23, 1836; Vicarage Place, Kensington,
   England
Areas of Achievement: Historiography, philosophy,
   and economics
Contribution: A utilitarian propagandist and theo-
   rist, Mill shattered neat boundaries of modern
   special scholarship with his intellectual and
   practical interests.

Early Life

James Mill was born April 6, 1773, in the parish of
Logie Pert, Forfarshire, in Scotland. His father,
James, was a poor shoemaker, and his mother, Isabel Fenton, was the daughter of an originally
wealthy farmer. Both parents were stern Puritans,
but James's mother was ambitious and tried to
bring up her son to be a gentleman and a minister.
He was educated at Montrose Academy, after
which he met Sir James and Lady Jane Stuart, who
made it possible for him to attend Edinburgh University. Mill entered there in 1790 and stayed for
seven years, living with the Stuarts and tutoring
their only child, Wilhelmina.

At Edinburgh, Mill became interested in Greek
thought, particularly Plato and the Socratic method
he would later use on his own son John. Dugald
Steward, a professor of moral philosophy, gave
James a taste for studies and a moral consciousness
that were to stay with him for life. Here he also met
Henry Peter Brougham and Francis Jeffrey—later
literary associates—and Thomas Thomson, a fine
scientist who became Mill's lifelong friend.

Mill was licensed to preach in 1798, but his sermons were unsuccessful and he received no parish
call. In 1902, he accompanied Sir John Stuart to
London and the Parliament, where he observed the
House of Commons and developed his interest in
politics. Probably because of later opposition to religion and the aristocracy, Mill chose to forget his
early days, and even though he later became an advocate of the free press, he maintained one's young
life was not for public knowledge.

In the early 1800's, Mill began to write for journals, the *Anti-Jacobin Review*, the *Literary Journal*, which he helped establish with his Scottish
friends, and the *St. James Chronicle*. In this new
setting, he wrote two essays that signaled his future
thought, one on the corn trade (1804), in which he
defended landholders who profited from the export
of grain, and the other a translation of Charles
François Dominique de Villers' *Essay on the Spirit
and Influence of the Reformation* (1805) wherein,
with the help of Thomson, he championed the
progress of the human mind following an age of religious faith.

In 1805, Mill married Harriet Burrow and settled
in Pentonville. Contrary to the thinking of Malthus,
whom Mill would eventually support, he fathered
nine children, educating the oldest, John Stuart, in
his own philosophy to eventually became the
spokesman of utilitarianism. After his literary jobs
failed, Mill struggled to survive economically, adding to his own debts those of his bankrupt father.
Hoping to free himself financially, Mill began
work on his *History of British India*, but that was
to take twelve years until it was published in 1817.
In the meantime, in 1808, he met Jeremy Bentham,
a man who was to determine the tone and character
of the rest of his life.

Life's Work

Almost immediately, Mill became the devoted disciple of Bentham, whose philosophy of utilitarianism—promoting the greatest good for the greatest
number—needed practical application. Bentham
wanted Mill close at hand, so he provided housing
at Queen's Square and supported him financially.
Unlike the fanciful Bentham, Mill was stern and
rigid, but the two conversed almost daily and, with
the exception of a major quarrel in 1814, agreed
that they needed each other if their thinking was to
have a lasting effect.

Able from his family training and schooling to
speak and write clearly and forcefully, Mill began
to use the press and the public forum to further
Bentham's goals. By 1810, he had dropped his theology and became an open critic of the established
church. He began to write for the *Edinburgh Review*, and though Brougham's and Jeffrey's editing
concealed Mill's connections to Bentham, Mill still
was able to externalize utilitarian views in many
areas—emancipation, foreign affairs, economics,
and penal reform. In his article "Commerce Defended" he reversed his earlier defense of wealthy
landowners to become an overt opponent of the aristocracy.

Mill was also interested in education. John Stuart Mill in his *Autobiography* (1873) speaks of how

his father brought him up to be a rigorous rationalist at the expense of both feeling and sentiment. In the 1810's, Mill championed the Lancasterian theory of education (teaching the poor to read and write, and having students help each other learn), as opposed to the church schools, which dwelt on the study of the catechism. He later espoused Bentham's chrestomathic method (adult education in utilitarian tendencies), but generally his efforts to promote a lasting method failed.

Mill was more fortunate in the area of governmental reform. Supporting the Radicals, he was instrumental in increasing their representation in Parliament and promoted the consequent changes in government policy. Mill was able to work with men of vastly different persuasions—William Allen, a Quaker, and the Evangelical Zachary Macaulay—to accomplish such things as prison reform and legislation abolishing the slave trade. He continued to write, publishing articles on freedom of the press and governmental reform in the supplement to the *Encyclopaedia Britannica* from 1815 to 1824. His thinking on democratic government was rooted, not in human rights but on the utilitarian principle that it best served the interests of all classes.

Between 1806 and 1818, Mill worked on his *History of British India*, which was to become the definitive work on that country. In his history, he focused on the importance of democratic government run as in England, not by the natives. Mill knew little of the class system in India, but he used that factor as an argument for objectivity. This work not only established Mill as an authority on India but also brought him employment with the East India House, thus securing his financial future for life; it also gave him the freedom to pursue the goals of utilitarianism and the Radical Party.

By the middle of the 1820's the Radicals had become a major power in England, and there were many good men who supported the cause because of Mill—names such as David Ricardo, Francis Place, and George Grote. It was at that time that Mill's brilliant son assumed the leadership of the group, leaving the older Mill with the opportunity to write and pull strings in the background. When the Radical magazine *Westminter Review* began publication in 1824, Mill for the first time was free to write without the restraints placed upon him by other publications.

In 1832, the Reform Bill passed the English Parliament, enabling the country to accomplish democratic reform without the violence of the French Revolution. Though the Whigs claimed victory and the Tories were thankful that bloodshed had been averted, it was the Radicals who provided a solid theoretical and practical basis for the historic bill. Mill had advocated middle-class governance rather than aristocratic control, progress through political reform rather than violent takeover, education through the press rather than religious indoctrination, and these were the factors that prevailed. Having suffered from lung disease for several months, Mill died of bronchitis on June 23, 1836. He was buried in Kensington Church.

Summary

James Mill was at the height of his intellectual powers when England was undergoing a most significant time of unrest and change. Basically, he was a propagandist and a reformer, with philosophical underpinnings in the British empiricists. Unlike Thomas Hobbes, however, he was not an egoistic hedonist but believed in the perfectibility of man quite apart from divine grace. For him, morality was more important than religion, though he based his morality on utilitarian principles rather than on any inherent right or the goodness of mankind.

In Bentham, Mill found a mentor and a rational basis for cultural change. These two met in the context of Bentham's interest in legal reform, but their mutual concerns spread to many fields—economics, government, psychology, ethics, and education. For the Utilitarians, the Church of England was spiritually dead and the aristocracy inherently selfish. Hence the importance of democratic (by which Mill meant middle class) control to best satisfy the greatest number of people.

Sometimes called the last great eighteenth century man, Mill, mostly because of his Scottish past, was well-educated and highly disciplined. It was in England, however, that he became convinced that the intellect was man's greatest asset. Mill rejected Romantics, such as Samuel Taylor Coleridge, for he was unimaginative himself, and thoroughly distrustful of feelings. Nor was he inclined to socialism, as were William Cobbett and Robert Owen, who believed that government, rather than any class, should be responsible for the just treatment of the people.

Perhaps Mill's greatest gift, apart from his skillful pen and ability to articulate precise positions, was his propensity in work for common goals with people of widely differing points of view and to persuade others to go along with utilitarian ends. Harriet Grote (wife of the future historian) said of Mill:

> Before many months ascendancy of James Mill's powerful mind over his younger companion made itself apparent. George Grote began by admiring his wisdom, the acuteness, the depth of Mill's character. Presently he found himself enthralled in the circle of Mill's speculations, and after a year or two of intimate commerce there existed but little difference in point of opinion between master and pupil.

Even Thomas Macaulay, the champion of Whig politics and industrial progress, who had attacked the *Encyclopaedia Britannica's* "Essay on Government," came to admire Mill in the end.

Mill was not an original thinker, but he held his intellectual convictions with vigor. By the mid 1820's, when his son began to lead the Radicals, it became evident that Mill was a success. John Stuart Mill would eventually go beyond his father, incorporating the importance of feeling and imagination into his vision of the world, but he saw in James Mill, if not a good husband and father, certainly a disciplined teacher who gave him an intellectual advantage few parents pass on to their children.

The Reform Bill was perhaps the single most significant event of the first half of the nineteenth century in England, and James Mill had a giant's part in its conception and passage. Though few agree with him now, he championed a philosophy that had an enormous impact in the shaping of Western civilization and perhaps still remains a subconscious, if not conscious, part of us all.

Bibliography

Bain, Alexander. *James Mill: A Biography.* London: Longman, and New York: Holt, 1882. Dated, but still the most thorough account of Mill's life.

Halevy, Elie. *The Growth of Philosophical Radicalism.* Translated by Mary Morris. 3 vols. London: Faber, and New York: Kelley, 1928. Traces the evolution of utilitarianism from its philosophical roots in John Locke and David Hume, details the changes in Mill and Bentham as they worked together, and captures the essence of Mill's debates leading up to the Reform Bill. A good reference book from a Continental perspective.

Hamburger, Joseph. *James Mill and the Art of Revolution.* New Haven, Conn.: Yale University Press, 1963. A book about radical strategy: how Mill employed extraparliamentary means—the press, petitions, public meetings—to change the English constitution. A scholarly work that gives a larger picture for understanding Mill's time.

Mill, James. *The Collected Works of James Mill.* 7 vols. London: Routledge, 1992. This seven volume set offers Mill's most important thoughts on utilitarianism, psychology, economics, philosophy, and education.

————. *Selected Economic Writings.* Edited by Donald Winch. Chicago: University of Chicago Press, 1966. Best biographical sketch; relates Mill's life to his economic and political contributions. Includes bibliography of Mill's works, some of which are reprinted with interesting introductions that trace the development of his thought.

Mill, John Stuart. *Autobiography and Literary Essays.* Edited by John M. Robson and Jack Stillinger. London: Routledge, and New York: Penguin, 1981. Mill recounts the place of Bentham in his father's life and the rationalistic education he got during the time James was closest to Bentham. Short and moving in parts. The essay "Utilitarianism" in this volume is more wordy but represents John's defense of his father's philosophy of life.

Plamenatz, John. *The English Utilitarians.* Oxford: Blackwell, 1949. A succinct and thoughtful study of how Hume, Bentham, and James and John Stuart Mill each contributed to utilitarianism. Chapter 6 is a pithy analysis of James Mill and his accomplishments.

Stephen, Leslie. *The English Utilitarians.* 3 vols. London: Duckworth, and New York: Putnam, 1900. Scholarly but readable study of a complex time. Volume 2 is a thematic analysis of Mill's involvement in politics, economics, legal changes, and church reform. Other chapters explain his relationship to movements (Whiggism and socialism) as well as key personalities (Thomas Robert Malthus and Ricardo). A good source book.

Thomas Matchie

JOHN STUART MILL

Born: May 20, 1806; London, England
Died: May 8, 1873; Avignon, France
Areas of Achievement: Philosophy and economics
Contribution: Desiring the greatest possible happiness for individual men and women and an England of the greatest possible justice and freedom, Mill questioned all assumptions about knowledge and truth and made what was observed the starting point of his discussions.

Early Life

John Stuart Mill was the eldest of nine children born to James Mill and Harriet Burrow. James Mill, the son of a shoemaker, with the help of his patron, Sir John Stuart, attended the University of Edinburgh, where he studied philosophy and divinity. He qualified for a license to be a preacher, but soon lost his belief in God. In 1802, in the company of Sir John Stuart, who was then a Member of Parliament, James Mill went to London to earn his living as a journalist.

Two years after the birth of John Stuart Mill, James Mill began his association with Jeremy Bentham, twenty-five years older and the founder of utilitarianism. James Mill became Bentham's disciple and the principal disseminator of utilitarianism; along with free trade, representative government, and the greatest happiness of the greatest number, another major belief of utilitarianism is that through education the possibilities for improving mankind are vast. The association between James Mill and Bentham, therefore, was to have a profound effect on the childhood, and indeed on the entire life, of John Stuart Mill, for he became the human guinea pig upon whom Bentham's ideas on education were acted out. Under the direction of his father, John Stuart Mill was made into a Benthamite—in John's own words, "a mere reasoning machine."

James Mill began John's education at the age of three, with the study of Greek, and it was not long before the boy was reading Aesop's Fables. By the time he was eight and began the study of Latin, he had read a substantial body of Greek literature, including the whole of the historian Herodotus and much of Plato. In the opening chapter of the *Autobiography* (begun in 1856 but published posthumously in 1873), Mill gives a detailed account of his prodigious feats of reading. Much of his studying was done at the same table at which his father did his writing. On the morning walks on which he accompanied his father, Mill recited the stories about which he had read the day before. In the *Autobiography*, he states: "Mine was not an education of cram. My father never permitted anything which I learnt to degenerate into a mere exercise of memory." The purpose of the education was to develop the greatest possible skills in reasoning and argumentation. Those skills then were to be used for the improvement of humanity.

In the year of John's birth, James Mill began to write a work that would be eleven years in the making, his *History of British India* (1818). In the *Autobiography*, John tells of his part in the making of that formidable work, reading the manuscript aloud while his father corrected the proof sheets. He goes on to say that the book was a great influence on his thinking. The publication of the *History of British India* led directly to James Mill's appointment to an important position in the East India Company, through which he was able to have a considerable impact upon the behavior of the English in India.

The final episode in James Mill's education of his son was the work they did with David Ricardo's treatise *On the Principles of Political Economy and Taxation* (1817). On their daily walks, the father gave lectures to the son drawn from Ricardo's work. On the following day, the son produced a written account of the lecture, aimed at clarity, precision, and completeness. From these written accounts, James Mill then produced a popularized version of Ricardo, *Elements of Political Economy* (1821); this exercise in the thinking of Ricardo also formed the basis of one of John Stuart Mill's great works, the *Principles of Political Economy* (1848). When he and his father finished with Ricardo, John was fourteen and was allowed to be graduated from James Mill's "academy."

John then spent a year living in France with Samuel Bentham, brother of Jeremy. When he returned to England, he began the study of law with John Austin, a lawyer who was a friend of his father and Bentham. It was during this period that Mill had one of the greatest intellectual experiences of his life, the reading of one of Bentham's great works, which, edited and translated into French by Bentham's Swiss disciple Étienne Dumont, has come to be known as the *Traité de législation civile et pénale* (1802). Mill was exhilarated by

Bentham's exposure of various expressions, such as "law of nature" and "right reason," which convey no real meaning but serve to disguise dogmatisms.

Mill also was greatly impressed by the scientific statement in this work of the principle of utility. Reading Bentham's statement of the principle "gave unity to my conceptions of things." Mill says in the *Autobiography* that at this time all of his ideas came together: "I now had opinions; a creed, a doctrine, a philosophy." He had been transformed: "When I laid down the last volume of the *Traité*, I had become a different being."

In 1823, James Mill obtained for his son a position in the same department as the one in which he worked at the East India Company. For the next thirty-five years of his life, John Stuart Mill worked in the office of the Examiner of India Correspondence. This was for Mill his "professional occupation and status." He found the work wholly congenial and could think of no better way to earn a steady income and still be able to devote a part of every day to private intellectual pursuits.

Life's Work

It was in the *London and Westminster Review*, founded by Bentham, that Mill's first writings of significance appeared in 1824 and 1825. Among others were essays on the mistaken notions of the conservative *Edinburgh Review* and on the necessity of absolute freedom of discussion. In 1826, however, at the age of twenty, Mill became seriously depressed and experienced what has come to be known as his "mental crisis," a period in his life discussed in detail in the *Autobiography*. Mill explains that at twenty he suddenly found himself listless and despairing and that he no longer cared about the purpose for which he had been educated. He had to confess to himself that if all the changes in society and in people's attitudes were accomplished for which he, his father, and Bentham were working, he would feel no particular happiness. He had been taught that such accomplishments would bring him great happiness, but he realized that on a personal level he would not care. Thus, he says, "I seemed to have nothing to live for."

The *Autobiography* tells of his dramatic recovery. He read of a boy who, through the death of his father, suddenly had the responsibility for the well-being of his family thrust upon him. Feeling confident that he was capable of doing all that was expected of him, the boy inspired a similar confidence in those who were dependent on him. Mill claimed that this story moved him to tears: "From this moment my burden grew lighter. The oppression of the thought that all feeling was dead within me, was gone. I was no longer hopeless: I was not a stock or a stone." He says further that he learned two important things from his mental crisis. First, asking whether you are happy will cause you to be happy no longer. Second, stressing right thinking and good behavior is not enough; one must also feel the full range of emotions.

It is thought that the intensity of his relationship with his father was the main cause of Mill's crisis. He adored and worshiped James Mill, and thus found it impossible to disagree with him. In recognizing the value of feeling, however, the son was rejecting his father's exclusion of feelings in determining what is desirable. As John came out of his depression, he let himself take an interest in poetry and art; William Wordsworth's poetry was a medicine to him, bringing him joy, much "sympathetic and imaginative pleasure." He was further helped in his emotional development with the beginning, in 1830, of his platonic love affair with Harriet Taylor and, in 1836, by the death of his father.

In 1830, Mill began to commit to paper the ideas that were to go into his first major work, *A System of Logic* (1843). Mill had come to believe that sound action had to be founded on sound theory, and sound theory was the result of sound logic. He was aware of too much argumentation that was not based on clear thinking; in particular, what were no more than habitual beliefs were frequently represented as truths. The subtitle of *A System of Logic* helps to explain Mill's intention: "Being a Connected View of the Principles of Evidence and the Methods of Scientific Investigation."

While Mill and the utilitarians regarded experience or observation as the exclusive determinant of truth, of considerable influence in both Great Britain and on the Continent were those who believed that truth could be known through intuition. Those who started with intuition, Mill believed, started with nothing more than prejudices, and these prejudices then provided justification for untrue doctrines and harmful institutions. In *A System of Logic*, Mill attempted to combat what he considered prejudices with philosophy by establishing a general theory of proof. Insisting that "facts" were facts only if they could be verified by observation, Mill argued the necessity of ascertaining the origins of individual ideas and belief systems.

The publication of *A System of Logic* established Mill as the leader of his school of thought, now known as Philosophical Radicalism. *A System of Logic* became the most attacked book of its time, and Mill responded by revising to take account of the attacks; over the remaining thirty years of his life, Mill took the book through eight editions. His response to the criticisms of *Principles of Political Economy* was similar; he saw that treatise through seven editions.

As *A System of Logic* was an attempt to overthrow the dominance of the intuitionalists, *Principles of Political Economy* was an attempt to liberate economic thinking from his own utilitarian predecessors, especially his father and David Ricardo. In the preliminary remarks, Mill says:

> It often happens that the universal belief of one age of mankind—a belief from which no one *was*, nor without an extraordinary effort of genius and courage, *could* at that time be free—becomes to a subsequent age so palpable an absurdity, that the only difficulty then is to imagine how such a thing can ever have appeared credible.

By 1848, the descriptions of economic activity by his predecessors had gained the status of natural law among the newly dominant middle class; to behave otherwise than to sell as dearly as possible and to buy as cheaply as possible, including human services, was to violate natural law. Mill thought it necessary to consider the effects of economic behavior on individuals and on society. He refused to accept the idea that there must be no interference with the playing out of economic forces.

Unlike his predecessors, Mill saw feasible alternatives to the system of laissez-faire and private property. He refused to accept the idea that there was nothing to be done about the suffering and injustices wrought by the system. He could not passively accept a system in which remuneration dwindles "as the work grows harder and more disagreeable, until the most fatiguing and exhausting bodily labour cannot count with certainty on being able to earn even the necessaries of life." He would consider communism as an alternative if there were no possibility of improving the system then at work. He insists, though, that a comparison with communism must be made "with the regime of individual property, not as it is, but as it might be made." Thus, Mill comes to advocate that the "Non-Interference Principle," sacred to his predecessors, must not be regarded as inviolable.

One of the markets in which interference by government is justified is education, which, as governed by the free market, was to Mill "never good except by some rare accident, and generally so bad as to be little more than nominal." Yet education is the key to elevating the quality of life, for well-educated persons would not only understand that true self-interest depends upon the advancement of the public interest; they also would be thoroughly impressed with the importance of the population problem. Mill was a whole-hearted Malthusian and believed that there could be no permanent improvement of society unless population be under "the deliberate guidance of judicious foresight." Another of the many high points of *Principles of Political Economy* is the chapter on the stationary state, in which Mill rejects the desirability of indefinitely pursuing higher rates of economic development. Mill was "not charmed with the ideal of life held out by those who think that the normal state of human beings is that of struggling to get on, that the trampling, crushing, elbowing, and treading on each other's heels are the most desirable lot of human kind." The ideal economic state of society for Mill is that in which "no one is poor, no one desires to be richer, nor has any reason to fear being thrust back, by the efforts of others to push themselves forward."

On Liberty (1859) is one of the most influential works in all of Western literature. It is a justification of the value of individuality, to the individual and to the individual's society. Written during a period of rigid, although informal, social control, *On Liberty* is an encouragement for the individual to do and say whatever he or she wishes to do or say. The work consists of five chapters, the first of which is a history of the contention between liberty and authority. The objective of this introductory chapter is to show that whereas limiting political tyranny used to be a foremost goal, in his own time and country it is the tyranny of public opinion that must be withstood and limited. The tyranny of the majority is an evil against which society must guard, for the tendency of the majority is to coerce others to conform to its notions of proper behavior and right thinking. Mill asserts that the "engines of moral repression" are growing and that a "strong barrier of moral conviction" must be raised against them.

In the chapter "Of the Liberty of Thought and Discussion," Mill argues the necessity of providing freedom for the expression of any and all opinions. Preventing an opinion from being expressed is an evil act against all humanity; even if the opinion happens to be false, the truth could be strengthened by its collision with the false opinion. If, however, the silenced opinion happens to be true, an opportunity to move toward truth has been lost. Only when it is possible to hear one's own opinions contradicted and disproved can one feel confidence in their truth. Throughout history, the most eminent of persons have believed in the truth of what turned out to be foolish notions or have engaged in conduct that later appeared to have been irrational. Yet progress has been made; fewer people are prone to holding foolish opinions and behaving irrationally. That has happened because errors are correctable. People learn from experience, but they also learn from discussion, especially discussion on how experience is to be interpreted. "Wrong opinions and practices gradually yield to fact and argument: but fact and argument, to produce any effect on the mind, must be brought before it."

"Of Individuality, As One of the Elements of Well-Being" is perhaps *On Liberty's* most potent chapter. In it, Mill argues that both the highest development of the individual and the good of society require that the individual human being be free to express his or her individuality. Mill regards individuality as a "necessary part and condition" of civilization, instruction, education, and culture. Different modes of living need to be visible in a society; where there is no individuality, there is no impetus for either other individuals or the society as a whole to improve. The visible individuality of some forces others to make choices, and it is only in making choices that various human faculties are developed—"perception, judgment, discriminative feeling, mental activity, and even moral preference." Where there are no opportunities to choose, the feelings and character are rendered "inert and torpid, instead of active and energetic." Human beings must be free to develop themselves in whatever directions they feel the impulse, and the stronger the impulses the better. Should eccentricity be the result, then it should be remembered that "the amount of eccentricity in a society has generally been proportional to the amount of genius, mental vigor, and moral courage which it contained." The chief danger of the time is that so few dare to be eccentric. "Every one lives as under the eye of a hostile and dreaded censorship." This suppression of individuality can make a society stagnant.

Soon after the appearance of *On Liberty*, Mill began work on *Utilitarianism* (1863). About half

the length of the former, it is, despite its title, a great humanistic work. Mill stretches Bentham's very limited concept of human motivation from the absolutely egotistic or selfish to include the altruistic. Bentham believed that experiences fell into one of two categories, pleasurable or painful, and that within each category there were quantifiable differences in such qualities as intensity and duration; Mill believed that in regard to pleasure there are two different kinds, higher and lower. The higher pleasures, which include knowledge, the experience of beautiful objects, and human companionship, Mill asserts, are more valuable than the lower, animal pleasures. Mill felt it necessary to make this distinction because whenever he came across the term "utilitarianism" the term seemed to sanction the lower pleasures and excluded the higher. Mill wished to rescue the term from the "utter degradation" into which it had fallen.

Rather than encouraging degradation, utilitarianism encourages the development of nobility. Truly noble persons always have the effect of making other people happy. Utilitarianism, therefore, could only attain its end—the greatest happiness of the greatest number—through the general cultivation of nobleness of character, not selfishness. Indeed, Mill insists, "In the golden rule of Jesus of Nazareth we read the complete spirit of the ethics of utility. To do as you would be done by, and to love your neighbor as yourself, constitute the ideal perfection of utilitarian morality."

Doing as one would be done to is at the heart of Mill's discussion of relations between the sexes in *The Subjection of Women* (1869). Centuries-old customs and laws have subordinated women to men, but the test of true virtue is the ability of a man and woman to live together as equals. One reason why they often do not is that the law favors men. That is seen particularly when the law returns women to the custody of the very husbands who have physically abused them. Another reason they do not usually live together as equals lies in what women are taught is proper behavior toward men. Women are taught to be submissive and to make themselves attractive, but men are not taught to behave similarly toward women. Such an imbalance in the way men and women relate to each other is doomed: "this relic of the past is discordant with the future and must necessarily disappear." Throughout his life, Mill sought equality and justice for women, not only because he believed strongly in the abstractions "equality" and "justice" but also because he believed that equality and justice in their relationships would improve and make happier both men and women. Hill's last years were devoted to public service. A few months before his death he was involved in beginning the Land Tenure Reform Association, for which he wrote in *The Examiner* and spoke publicly. Mill died at Avignon on May 8, 1873.

Summary

In the nineteenth century, John Stuart Mill was England's most thoughtful and most wide-ranging writer on the subjects of how truth could be determined, what was good for the individual human being, and what was good for society as a whole. As a result of his consideration of these questions, he is known as a great champion of fundamental civil liberties and an opponent of all forms of oppression. He is one of the two great defenders in English, along with John Milton, of the necessity of the freedoms of thought, expression, and discussion.

For the most part, Mill's discussions in print are dispassionate and disinterested; he sincerely sought knowledge and truth, regardless of the sources from which ideas came. Without preconceptions of how it must have been, he sought to understand the past. Without contempt, he listened to and read his philosophical opponents in order to find and make use of whatever germs of truth there might be in their positions. He was always open to modifying and correcting what he had said previously. Aware of the brutality in mankind's past, he was never cynical about human nature nor pessimistic about humanity's long-term future. He was optimistic about the desire and capacity of men and women to make themselves better persons, not all people certainly, but enough to have the net effect of improving society. He respected the complexity of human nature and human behavior. Never quick to rush to judgment, he saw that even an immoral action might have a sympathetic side or have qualities of beauty to it. John Stuart Mill was a very wise man, the nineteenth century's Socrates. Generations of students have been nourished on his works, and rightly so.

Bibliography

Ellery, John B. *John Stuart Mill*. New York: Twayne, 1964. A book of one hundred pages that efficiently highlights and connects "the rare spirit of the man," the ideas of the man, and the spirit and ideas of the age in which he lived.

Glassman, Peter. *J. S. Mill: The Evolution of a Genius*. Gainesville: University of Florida Press, 1985. A fascinating analysis of Mill's life and writings from a psychoanalytic point of view. Glassman argues that long into adulthood Mill was struggling to repair the damage done to his emotional life and imagination by his father's domination.

Mazlish, Bruce. *James and John Stuart Mill: Father and Son in the Nineteenth Century*. London: Hutchinson, and New York: Basic Books, 1975. A very thorough discussion of the entangled personalities and ideas of the two Mills.

Mill, John Stuart. *Essays on Politics and Culture*. Edited by Gertrude Himmelfarb. New York: Doubleday, 1962. Contains eleven lesser-known essays, including the two seminal works "Bentham" and "Coleridge." In a twenty-page introduction, Himmelfarb discusses Mill's "peculiar brand of conservatism."

———. *John Stuart Mill: A Selection of His Works*. Edited by John M. Robson. New York: Odyssey Press, 1966. Contains all of *On Liberty* and *Utilitarianism*, selections from the *Autobiography, A System of Logic*, and *The Subjection of Women*, and passages from eighteen other essays. Robson's twenty-page introduction is excellent.

———. *John Stuart Mill's Social and Political Thought: Critical Assessments*. 4 vols. Edited by G. W. Smith. London: Routledge, 1998. Four volume set examining Mill's work in political and social theory.

Packe, Michael St. John. *The Life of John Stuart Mill*. London: Secker and Warburg, and New York: Macmillan, 1954. Especially good on Mill's relationship with Harriet Taylor, the woman with whom Mill had a platonic love affair for twenty years while she was married and whom he married in 1851, two years after her husband's death.

Riley, Jonathan. *Mill on Liberty: A Defense*. Edited by John Gray. London and New York: Routledge, 1998. Includes the full text of *Mill on Liberty* plus a comprehensive piece by the editor defending the original interpretation of Mill, but suggesting criticism of Millian and other liberalism.

Robson, John M. *The Improvement of Mankind*. Toronto: University of Toronto Press, and London: Routledge, 1968. A comprehensive examination of Mill's social and political thought by a sympathetic critic who writes excellent prose.

Ryan, Alan. *J. S. Mill*. London and Boston: Routledge, 1974. Focuses on seven of Mill's major works; summarizes them and relates them to the issues of the time that gave Mill the impetus to write.

Skorupski, John, ed. *The Cambridge Companion to Mill*. Cambridge and New York: Cambridge University Press, 1998. Organized, contemporary look at Mill's thought and its influence on modern culture. Important both for those seeking an introduction to Mill and those looking for updated interpretations of his work.

Paul Marx

THEODOR MOMMSEN

Born: November 30, 1817; Garding, Schleswig
Died: November 1, 1903; Charlottenburg, Germany
Area of Achievement: Historiography
Contribution: Mommsen transformed the study of
Roman history by correcting and supplementing
the literary tradition of the ancient historians
with the evidence of Latin inscriptions. Going
beyond the usual focus on the generals and emperors, Mommsen championed study in all aspects of ancient societies.

Early Life

Now considered a German historian, Theodor
Mommsen was born a Danish subject in Garding,
Schleswig, on November 30, 1817. The eldest son
of a poor Protestant minister, Mommsen was
reared in Oldesloe, where he was educated by his
father until 1834, when he attended school in Alto-
na, outside Hamburg. In 1838, he entered the University of Kiel to study jurisprudence, which at the
time involved a thorough grounding in Roman law.
Under the influence of Friedrich Karl von Savigny's writings on the interrelationship of law and
history, Mommsen's interest shifted to Roman history by the time he completed his doctorate in
1843. Equally influential were Otto Jahn's lectures
on epigraphy, the study of inscriptions, which convinced Mommsen of the need for a complete collection of Latin inscriptions.

With a grant from the Danish government,
Mommsen traveled through Italy from 1844 to
1847, collecting inscriptions and studying ancient
Italian dialects. At the suggestion of the Italian
scholar Bartolomeo Borghesi, he concentrated on
Naples, and his subsequent monograph, *Inscriptions regni Neapolitani Latinae* (1852; inscriptions of the Latin Neopolitan kingdom), impressed scholars with its philological method and
organization.

When Mommsen returned to take a post in Roman law at the University of Leipzig in 1848,
Schleswig was agitating for union with Prussia.
An ardent German patriot, Mommsen was caught
up in the revolutionary nationalism, and his academic career was momentarily interrupted.
Slightly injured in a street riot, Mommsen stayed
behind when his brothers took up arms against the
Danish crown, and instead he furthered the cause
as editor and writer for the *Schleswig-Holstein-
ische Zeitung.*

In the reaction after the failed uprising, Momms-
en was eventually dismissed from his teaching post
in 1851. After a period of what he termed exile in
Zürich, he returned to Germany in 1854 to teach at
the University of Breslau, before settling permanently in Berlin, first with the Berlin Academy of
Sciences and then with the University of Berlin.

Life's Work

Nineteenth century scholars, Germans in particular, applied scientific methods to the humanities in
the belief that just as Charles Darwin had demonstrated the laws of natural selection, they could
discover the laws of historical and social evolution. Unfortunately, some scholars were led by the
evolutionary analogy, with its emphasis on the
survival of the fittest, to dismiss questions of morality in their desire to establish the inevitability of
historical development. This was especially true in
Germany, where the nationalistic yearning for a
unification had been building ever since Napoleon
I's power over the German states was broken.
Consequently, German scholars often found it
easy to let supposedly objective science serve political ends.

Mommsen never overtly subverted scholarship
to nationalism; however, the tendency was manifest in his most famous work, *Römische Geschichte* (1854-1856; *The History of Rome,* 1862-1866),
which covers Roman history up to the end of the
Republic. Never intending to write for a general
audience, Mommsen was approached in 1851 by
his future father-in-law, the publisher Carl Reimer,
who convinced him to undertake the project.

Immediately famous, even notorious, *The History of Rome* was not only the first comprehensive
survey of Roman history but also a passionate narrative of the rise and fall of the Republic, brought
to life by Mommsen's vivid and partisan portraits
of historical personalities. With a dynamic, jour-
nalism-influenced style, Mommsen drew on familiar political and historical incidents and presented
even abstract ideas in concrete imagery to make
Roman history accessible to a wide audience.

The History of Rome impressed the scholarly
community with its rigorous questioning of the ancient historians, but it was faulted for not citing
sources or acknowledging any possible differences
in interpretation. Moreover, many believed that he
went so far in his demythologizing that he falsely

recast Roman history in terms of his biased perspective of German politics.

These critics feared that *The History of Rome*'s adulatory depiction of Julius Caesar as the savior of Rome dangerously glorified power and buttressed Prussian militarism. Despite a belief in the generally progressive and civilizing effect of the emergence of powers such as Rome or Germany, Mommsen was not authoritarian so much as elitist, believing that the best government was that of an intellectual aristocracy in support of an enlightened leader such as Caesar. Because the closest example in German history was Prussian leadership in the tradition of Frederick the Great, Mommsen initially supported Prussia's central role in German unification.

Yet when other Germans surrendered to, even welcomed, outright domination, masterfully managed by the German Chancellor Otto von Bismarck, Mommsen felt betrayed. He opposed the extralegal and self-interested ambitions of Bismarck in Germany and of Napoleon III in France, though *The History of Rome* was often used to justify their actions. Mommsen served in both the Prussian and German legislatures, where he resisted Germany's colonial and economic policies. When he denounced protectionism as a swindle, Mommsen was brought into court by Bismarck on a charge of libel. Though acquitted, Mommsen largely withdrew from politics after 1884.

It was in the calmer arena of the university that Mommsen made his more important though less famous contributions to scholarship. Mommsen's collection of Neapolitan inscriptions had made it obvious that he was the man to undertake a more comprehensive cataloging of all Latin inscriptions, a project already begun by the Berlin Academy. He was appointed editor in 1858 and worked on the project the rest of his life, demonstrating the highest standards of scholarly and organizational brilliance. To eliminate any possibility of forgery or error, he insisted on the examination of the actual inscriptions instead of secondhand reports. With the first volume of the monumental *Corpus inscriptionum Latinarum* (1863-1902; collection of Latin inscriptions), Mommsen transformed Roman historiography by providing it with an extensive factual basis. At the time of Mommsen's death, *Corpus inscriptionum Latinarum* comprised 130,000 inscriptions in fifteen volumes, six of which he edited himself.

Though this would have been the life's work of other men, Mommsen also reconstructed Roman

law in *Römisches Staatsrecht* (1871-1888; Roman constitutional law) and *Römisches Strafrecht* (1899; Roman criminal law). In the tradition of Savigny, Mommsen examined Roman law not as an abstract system but as a cultural and historical development determined by power struggles in the Roman Republic and Empire.

Despite reiterated plans to continue *The History of Rome*, Mommsen did almost no work on a narrative history of the Empire. Instead, he published *Das Weltreich der Caesaren* (1885; *The Provinces of the Roman Empire from Caesar to Diocletian*, 1886), which, though termed a continuation of his *The History of Rome* and accessible to the non-scholar, is very different from the earlier work. Nonnarrative and nonpartisan, *The Provinces of the Roman Empire* is a study based on the Latin inscriptions gathered from the areas that were once under Roman domination, revealing the Empire to have been far more stable than the traditional focus on dynastic struggles suggested.

Over the years, Mommsen became a well-known character in Berlin. Active up to his death at eighty-five, he worked late each night but arrived at the university each morning at eight, even using the tram ride to read. Although he was neither a graceful man nor, with his shrill voice, a particularly good lecturer, he commanded absolute respect. Mesmerized by his piercing blue eyes and intellectual authority, his students sat in total silence as Mommsen raced through prepared lectures. Rigorous in his criticism, he was equally generous in his assistance to his former students and left a lasting legacy with the generation of scholars he trained to his own exacting standards of research. At a time when solitary labor was still normal for scholars, Mommsen contributed to many cooperative efforts, started several international journals, and helped found the International Association of Academies in 1901.

Said by some to be intolerant of equals, Mommsen was no recluse, surrounding himself with students, friends, and a large family. Marie Reimer, to whom Mommsen was married in 1854, bore him sixteen children and for nearly fifty years provided her husband with a comfortable and supportive domestic life.

Summary

Theodor Mommsen is universally acknowledged as one of the nineteenth century's most important historians. In his own lifetime, Mommsen's eminence was recognized when he was awarded the Nobel Prize in 1902. Because so much of his work dealt with matters of interest only to scholars, however, his fame is overshadowed by that of the great narrative historians, such as Leopold von Ranke.

With his amazing capacity for work, Mommsen put his name to more than a thousand published articles in his nearly sixty-year career. Highly regarded for an imaginative handling of voluminous statistics and detail as well as memorable epigrams and pithy summations, most of Mommsen's writing is still of interest mainly to specialists. Except for his *The History of Rome*, he wrote little narrative history, focusing instead on gathering and interpreting the inscriptions on stone and coins left by the Romans and correcting the less reliable written tradition. The *Corpus inscriptionum Latinarum*, which continues to grow, is indispensable for Roman studies, as are his studies of Roman law; yet much of his other work was superseded even in his own lifetime as others built on his pioneering work and methodology.

Throughout his career, Mommsen represented the very best in humanistic scholarship. Dedicated to putting all studies on the most rigorous scientific footing, Mommsen never lost sight of the human element, which transcends national and racial considerations. Despite the controversy still surrounding *The History of Rome*, Mommsen's positive estimation of Caesar is shared by most scholars today, and his animated style exerted a beneficial influence on later German writing. His emphasis on the nonliterary sources encouraged scholars to shift their attention away from dynastic history to many areas of ancient societies. Welcoming innovative ideas and methods regardless of their political or personal consequences, Mommsen was always more interested in forwarding scholarship than in preserving his preeminence.

Bibliography

Broughton, T. Robert S. Introduction to *The Provinces of the Roman Empire*, by Theodor Mommsen. New York: Scribner, and London: Bentley, 1886. Provides biography with an overview of Mommsen's major works and a discussion of reasons for his not finishing *The History of Rome*. Examines Mommsen's innovative scholarship and traces his influence on historiography into the mid-twentieth century. Contains a bibliography.

Bruhns, Hennerk. "Theodor Mommsen: A Fiery Patriot." *UNESCO Courier* (April, 1990). Profile of Mommsen with emphasis on his *History of Rome*, for which he won the 1902 Nobel Prize for Literature.

Gooch, George Peabody. "Mommsen and Roman Studies." In *History and Historians in the Nineteenth Century*. 2d ed. London and New York: Longman, 1913. Chronological overview of Mommsen's life and his major work, detailing his many interests and activities along with contributions to the work of others. Conceding Mommsen's historical biases and tendency to esteem the victorious too highly, Gooch ranks Mommsen along with Ranke for demythologizing Roman history and encouraging new trends in scholarship. Contains valuable bibliographical footnotes.

Haverfield, F. "Theodor Mommsen." *The English Historical Review* 19 (January, 1904): 80-89. An obituary assessing Mommsen's character and contribution. In a review of Mommsen's main works, Haverfield analyzes the historian's remarkable combination of imagination, hard work, and organizational brilliance. Stresses

Mommsen's pioneering use of inscriptions and cooperative projects in scholarship.

Kelsey, Francis W. "Theodore Mommsen." *Classical Journal* 14 (January, 1919): 224-236. A comprehensive biographical and character sketch with attention to the influences of Mommsen's teachers and colleagues. Argues that Mommsen was not so much an innovator as a brilliant and diligent realizer of the innovations of others. Details Mommsen's helpfulness as a teacher and includes a portrait of his happy domestic life.

Mommsen, Theodor. *A History of Rome under the Emperors*. Demandt, Alexander and Barbara Demandt, eds. London and New York: Routledge, 1996. Mommsen's treatise on the Roman quest for power and land. Valuable publication in classic historiography.

Thompson, James Westfall, and Bernard J. Holm. *A History of Historical Writing*. Vol. 2. New York: Macmillan, 1942. Contends that through mastery of scholarship and a scientific approach to evidence, Mommsen revolutionized the study of Roman history. Examines Mommsen's elitist views and adulation of Caesar, dismissing their connection to German militarism and anti-Semitism. Includes a biographical sketch, a physical description, and a good bibliography.

Philip McDermott

JAMES MONROE

Born: April 28, 1758; Westmoreland County, Virginia

Died: July 4, 1831; New York, New York

Areas of Achievement: Government and politics

Contribution: As President of the United States and author of the Monroe Doctrine, Monroe set forth one of the basic principles of American foreign policy

Early Life

James Monroe was born April 28, 1758, in Westmoreland County, Virginia. He came from a good but not distinguished family of Scottish origin. His father was Spence Monroe, and his mother was Elizabeth Jones Monroe, sister of Judge Joseph Jones, a prominent Virginia politician. James was the eldest of four children. His formal education began at the age of eleven, at a private school operated by the Reverend Mr. Archibald Campbell, which was considered the best school in the colony. At the age of sixteen, after the death of his father, Monroe entered the College of William and Mary upon the advice of his uncle, Judge Jones, who was to have a very formative influence upon Monroe's life.

At the College of William and Mary, the Revolutionary War intruded, and Monroe, with his education unfinished, enlisted, in the spring of 1776, as a lieutenant in a Virginia regiment of the Continental Line. Slightly more than six feet tall, with a large, broad-shouldered frame, the eighteen-year-old was an impressive figure. He had a plain face, a rather large nose, a broad forehead, and wide-set, blue-gray eyes. His face was generally unexpressive, and his manners were simple and unaffected. He fought in the battles at Harlem and White Plains, and he was wounded at Trenton. During 1777 and 1778, he served as an aide, with the rank of major, on the staff of William Alexander, Lord Stirling. As an aide, Monroe mingled with the aides of other commanders and other staff officers, among them Alexander Hamilton, Charles Lee, Aaron Burr, and the Marquis de Lafayette. This interlude broadened his outlook and view of the ideals of the Revolution, which he carried with almost missionary zeal the remainder of his life. After participating in the battles of Brandywine, Germantown, and Monmouth, Monroe resigned from Stirling's staff in December, 1778, and returned to Virginia to apply for a rank in the state line. Unable to secure a position, Monroe, upon the advice of Judge Jones, cultivated the friendship of Governor Thomas Jefferson, and he formed a connection as a student of law with Jefferson that continued until 1783. This was the beginning of a long and valuable relationship, especially for Monroe. In 1782, Monroe was elected to the Virginia legislature, thus beginning a political career that lasted for more than forty years and brought him eventually to the highest office in the land.

Life's Work

In 1783, Monroe was elected to the Congress of the Articles of Confederation. He was an active and useful member, and he gained invaluable experience. He cultivated a friendship with James Madison, who was introduced to him by Jefferson. Monroe was identified with the nationalists, but his strong localist and sectional views made him cautious. He was particularly opposed to John Jay's negotiations with Don Diego de Gardoqui, the first Spanish minister to the United States, which threatened the western navigation of the Mississippi River. Monroe helped to defeat the negotiations, thereby gaining great popularity in the Western country, which lasted all of his political life.

Monroe's congressional service expired in 1786. He returned to Virginia intending to become a lawyer. By this time, he had married Elizabeth Kortright, the daughter of a New York merchant, on February 16, 1786. She was attractive but formal and reserved. Years later, she proved to be a marked contrast to her predecessor as hostess of the White House, Dolley Madison.

Monroe set up a law practice at Fredericksburg, Virginia, but he was not long out of politics. He was again elected to the Virginia legislature. He was also a delegate at the Annapolis Conference, but he was not chosen for the Federal Convention. In 1788, Monroe was elected to the Virginia convention for ratification of the Constitution. Here he joined with the opponents of the Constitution, fearing that the government would be too strong and would threaten Western development.

Monroe soon joined the new government, however, after losing a race for the House of Representatives against James Madison. He was elected to the United States Senate in 1790 and served there until May, 1794. He took an antiadministration stand, opposing virtually all of Secretary of the

Treasury Alexander Hamilton's measures. It was a surprise, therefore, when he was selected as the new United States minister to France in June, 1794. Relations between the United States and France were at a low ebb. President George Washington apparently believed that Monroe, whose pro-French attitude was well-known, would improve relations as well as appease the Republican Party at home.

Moved by his sympathies and a desire to satisfy the French, Monroe addressed the French National Convention in a manner that brought a rebuke from Secretary of State Edmund Randolph. Monroe was unable to defend Jay's treaty to the French, and he was considered too pro-French in the United States. In 1796, he was recalled by the new secretary of state, Timothy Pickering. When he returned, Monroe responded to innuendoes about his conduct with a nearly five-hundred-page pamphlet entitled *A View of the Conduct of the Executive, in the Foreign Affairs of the United States* (1797), revealing his belief that he had been betrayed by the Administration. Although attacked by Federalists, among Westerners and his friends, his reputation was enhanced.

Monroe's diplomatic career was not finished. After an interlude as governor of Virginia (1799-1802), Monroe was chosen to return to France to assist Robert R. Livingston in negotiations to purchase New Orleans. Monroe always believed that his arrival in France was the decisive factor in convincing Napoleon Bonaparte to shift his position and offer the entire Louisiana Territory to the United States. Livingston had, however, already opened the negotiations and, with Monroe's assistance, closed the deal.

In 1804, Monroe went to Spain to "perfect" the American claim that the Louisiana Purchase included West Florida. The Spanish would not budge, and Monroe returned to England in 1805. In London, Jefferson matched Monroe with William Pinkney to negotiate with the British to end the practice of impressments and other disputes which had arisen between the two countries. The Monroe-Pinkney Treaty of December, 1806, gained few concessions but apparently satisfied the two American ministers. President Jefferson and Secretary of State Madison, however, rejected the treaty, and Jefferson did not submit it to the Senate.

Monroe returned to the United States in December, 1807, in an angry mood. He allowed his friends to present him as a presidential contender against Madison. Although Monroe's ticket was swamped in Virginia, ending his effort, he still had support in Virginia, for he was elected to the Virginia legislature in 1810, and the next year, to the state's governorship.

In 1811, Monroe and Madison were reconciled. Monroe accepted the offer of secretary of state. Relations between the United States and Great Britain had so deteriorated that Monroe concluded, as had Madison, that war must result. Monroe sustained the president's policy and the declaration of war on June 18. As secretary of state, Monroe supported Madison's decision to enter negotiations with the British and helped him select an outstanding negotiating team. Thereafter, Monroe had little influence upon the negotiations that resulted in the Treaty of Ghent, which ended the War of 1812.

Monroe emerged from the war with his reputation generally unscathed, and he was a leading contender for the presidency. The congressional caucus in 1816, however, partially influenced by a prejudice against the Virginia dynasty, accorded him only an eleven-vote margin to win the nomination. The discredited Federalists offered only token opposition, and Monroe won easily. His years in the presidency (1817-1825) are often referred to as the Era of Good Feelings. The Federalist Party gradually disappeared and offered no opposition. Monroe was reelected in 1820, only one vote short of a unanimous vote. He sought to govern as a president above parties. He took two grand tours, one to the North and the other to the South, and was well received wherever he went. Monroe also appointed some Federalists to office.

The outward placidity of these years, however, was belied by ferment below the surface. The question of slavery was raised to dangerous levels in the debate over restrictions upon the admission of Missouri to statehood. Monroe did not interfere in the debate, and he readily signed the compromise measure. Other issues during his presidency revealed the dissension within his party—for example, the debate over Jackson's invasion of Florida, army reduction, and internal improvements.

Diplomatic successes included neutralizing the Great Lakes, arbitrating the fisheries question, establishing the northern boundary of the Louisiana Purchase as the forty-ninth parallel, and joint occupation of Oregon with Great Britain. Much of the success of these negotiations was a result of Monroe's able secretary of state, John Quincy Adams. After Jackson's foray into Florida, Adams got

Spain to transfer Florida to the United States and to settle the border extending to the Pacific Ocean.

The Monroe Doctrine, issued in 1823, capped off these diplomatic successes. It arose out of American fears that European nations would intervene to subdue the newly independent countries in South America. Invited by the British to join in a statement warning against intervention, Monroe, at the urging of Adams, issued a unilateral statement warning Europe not to interfere in the affairs of the Western Hemisphere.

In 1824, the unity of the party was shattered by a contest between several strong rivals for the presidency. William H. Crawford, Monroe's secretary of the treasury, secured the caucus nomination from a rump group of congressmen, but other contenders, including Adams, Jackson, and Henry Clay, threw the vote into the House of Representatives. Clay threw his support to Adams, who won the presidency. In the aftermath, new coalitions were formed and eventually another two-party system emerged.

Monroe did not exert any political leadership during this period. It was not his temperament to operate in the new style of politics emerging as the Age of the Common Man. In many ways, he was obsolete when he left the presidency. His last years were spent making claims upon the government for past service. He received $29,513 in 1826, and he got an additional $30,000 in 1831, but this did not stave off advancing bankruptcy. In 1830, upon the death of his wife, he moved to New York City to live with a daughter and her husband. He died there on July 4, 1831.

Summary

Monroe, the third of the Virginia triumvirate, has generally been ranked below his two predecessors in intellectual ability, although he has been ranked higher than either for his administrative skills. Monroe was more narrowly partisan and sectional, but he tried to be a president of all the people. The question has been raised, however, as to what extent he understood the role of the president as a party leader. It is to be noted that the party disintegrated under his presidency, but that may be a result, in part, of the decline of the Federalist Party as a viable opposition.

During his last years, Monroe was much concerned about his reputation. His concern reflects the essentially political cast of his mind. His letters throughout his life concerned almost exclusively political matters. An experienced and even a sensitive politician, he was an anachronism by the end of his presidency. The last representative of the generation of the Founding Fathers, his idea of government by consensus was out of place in the new democratic politics of the era of the common man.

Monroe's legacy was his Americanism. If he was at times narrow and sectional, he was always an American. His Monroe Doctrine aptly expressed the feelings of his fellow Americans that the Western Hemisphere was where the principles of freedom would be worked out and show the way to Europe and the rest of the world. His career was long and successful, and his public service, if not brilliant, was useful to his country.

Bibliography

Ammon, Harry. *James Monroe: The Quest for National Identity*. New York: McGraw-Hill, 1971. The most comprehensive biography. This book is well researched and well written. The interpretations are favorable to Monroe.

Burstein, Andrew. "Jefferson's Madison vs. Jefferson's Monroe." *Presidential Studies Quarterly* 28, no. 2 (Spring 1998). Examines Monroe, Thomas Jefferson, and James Madison and their styles and approaches to common goals.

Cresson, William P. *James Monroe*. Chapel Hill: University of North Carolina Press, 1946. Until Ammon's book, this was the standard biography. Engagingly written, it lacks rigorous analysis. The point of view of the author is also favorable to Monroe.

Dangerfield. George. *The Era of Good Feelings*. New York: Harcourt Brace, 1952; London: Methuen, 1953. Brilliantly written, this work, though superficial in many places, is still the best account of Monroe's presidency.

Gawalt, Gerard W. "James Monroe, Presidential Planter." *The Virginia Magazine of History and Biography* 101, no. 2 (April, 1993). Discusses Monroe's plantations, his management of them, and ultimate loss of many of them to creditors.

Monroe, James. *The Autobiography of James Monroe*. Edited by Gerry Stuart Brown. Syracuse, N.Y.: Syracuse University Press, 1959. Monroe's own view of his early career (the narrative extends only to 1805). Partly written to advance his claims upon the government, and partly to leave his own record of his career, Monroe's narrative does not always achieve objectivity.

Morgan, George. *The Life of James Monroe*. Boston: Small, Maynard, 1921. Entertainingly written, but thin on analysis and weak on some subjects. The book is also marred by the biases of the author in favor of Monroe.

Perkins, Dexter. *Hands Off: A History of the Monroe Doctrine*. Rev. ed. Boston: Little Brown, 1955; London: Longman, 1962. In part a summary of a three-volume study by the same author and the considered judgment of the authority on the Monroe Doctrine.

Schoenherr, Steven E. "James Monroe, Friend of the West." *Journal of the West* 31, no. 3 (July, 1992). Focuses on Monroe's efforts in bringing the West into the Union and touches on his roles in the Louisiana Purchase and avoidance of war with Spain over Florida.

Styron, Arthur. *The Last of the Cocked Hats: James Monroe and The Virginia Dynasty*. Norman: University of Oklahoma Press, 1945. Less a biography than a collection of the author's favorable opinions of Monroe. Written in a spritely manner, but there is more style than substance.

C. Edward Skeen

DWIGHT L. MOODY

Born: February 5, 1837; Northfield, Massachusetts

Died: December 22, 1899; Northfield, Massachusetts

Area of Achievement: Religion

Contribution: In mass evangelistic campaigns, Moody preached a message of salvation and brought spiritual revival to the United States and England.

Early Life

Dwight Lyman Moody was born February 5, 1837, in Northfield, Massachusetts, the sixth of nine children. His father, Edwin Moody, died when Dwight was four, leaving the family with no provision for their future. With determination, hard work, and assistance from others, Dwight's mother, Betsey Holton Moody, kept the family together and reared them in a strict, loving, devout home. Because he was impatient with school and needed to work, Moody had very little formal schooling. Always conscious of this lack, he was for many years hesitant to speak in public and only gradually attained the ability to preach.

At the age of seventeen, Moody left Northfield and obtained work as a shoe salesman in the store of his uncle, Samuel Holton. Ambition, boundless energy, natural wit, and unorthodox selling methods made him an unusually successful salesman.

As a condition of employment, Moody had to attend Holton's church, the Mount Vernon Orthodox Congregationalist Church. Reared as a Unitarian, Moody had never heard the message that was preached at Mount Vernon: that Jesus Christ had died for all men, risen from the dead, and lived to be the Savior and friend of all who trusted Him. Moody resisted this idea for some time, but when his Sunday-school teacher asked him privately for a response, Moody gave himself and his life to Christ. From that date forward, April 21, 1855, Moody had a new purpose in life.

In 1856, Moody moved to Chicago and within two years was earning more than five thousand dollars a year. His ambition was to succeed in business and accumulate the wealth to support his philanthropic work.

Needing an outlet for his energy and Christian zeal, Moody started a mission Sunday school in 1858. In two years, the regular attendance grew to 450 children. By 1864, the school had outgrown two buildings, and members wanted to form a church. The Illinois Street Church was founded that year, later becoming Moody Memorial Church.

In 1860, Moody resigned his business position to devote himself full time to Christian work. He joined the fledgling Young Men's Christian Association (YMCA) and, in 1865, became its president. Through the years, he was one of the foremost fund-raisers for YMCA buildings and activities. During the Civil War, the YMCA held evangelistic services for the soldiers, and though still unpolished, Moody became an effective and practiced preacher. He also visited personally with the soldiers.

In 1862, Moody married Emma Revell, a beautiful and well-educated girl of nineteen. They differed sharply in personality traits. While Emma Moody was poised, retiring, and conservative, her husband loved publicity and practical jokes and was impulsive, quick-tempered, and outspoken. Though she suffered from poor health, he was robust and was always active. Practical and orderly, she handled most of her husband's correspondence and the family's finances. He depended on her good judgment and learned self-discipline from her. With all of his brusqueness, he was warm, tenderhearted, and sensitive to others. Humble and peace-loving he was quick to apologize when he had wronged another. Under his wife's influence, Moody mellowed and improved in manners and speech.

In the 1860's, the YMCA expanded its work among the poor of Chicago. The association set up a distribution system for food and clothing using Moody's mission staff as workers. Moody organized literacy and Americanization classes. Also, the YMCA sponsored evangelism of the poor and, under Moody's leadership, citywide distribution of religious tracts.

As president of the YMCA, Moody became responsible for traveling to national conventions. At the same time, he participated in Sunday-school conventions and interdenominational "Christian conventions." Since he played a prominent role in YMCA work and the Sunday-school movement, Moody was well-known as a colorful and effective speaker. At a convention Moody heard Ira Sankey sing and persuaded Sankey to leave his home and business and to join him as an associate. This partnership led Moody in a new direction.

Life's Work

After much prayer and soul-searching, Moody concluded that God was calling him to full-time evangelism. In June, 1873, Moody and Sankey sailed for England. After an inauspicious beginning, the two met with minor success in Newcastle and then preached to huge crowds in Edinburgh and Glasgow.

Throughout 1874, Moody moved slowly through Scotland and Ireland and reached England in 1875. Moody would select a local person to coordinate plans for the campaign, and he insisted on cooperation among the local churches. He encouraged people to hold prayer meetings to pray for his work.

Attendance at the revivals required a huge building and, at times, a special temporary structure was built. Meetings were publicized in circulars and through home visitation.

As the evangelists approached London, the question was whether London would accept this uneducated preacher with his simple and direct messages. Short and heavy set, he wore a full beard on his round, ruddy face. Good-humored with a rich, full laugh, he walked quickly and spoke loudly. De-

spite criticism from the press, Moody's popularity seemed assured from the beginning of his London meetings. It was estimated during the four-month campaign that Moody spoke to more than two million people.

Moody returned to the United States as an international figure, receiving numerous requests for speaking engagements. After a short time at Northfield, Moody and Sankey held campaigns in Brooklyn, Philadelphia, and New York. After these campaigns, a visit to the South and a tour of the Midwest brought the two evangelists back to Chicago. In the fall of 1876, they began a revival in Chicago that lasted until mid-January, 1877. Following this revival, they held campaigns in Boston, Baltimore, St. Louis, Cleveland, and San Francisco.

Moody proved to be a sought-after speaker for the remainder of his life, and he traveled in North America and Britain with his message of revival. Recognizing a need for trained laymen to work in the churches, he established schools to instruct new converts. The Northfield School for Girls opened in 1879, followed by the Mount Hermon School for Boys in 1881. Their purpose was to provide a preparatory school education that would encourage the development of Christian character and prepare the students for Christian service. Moody did not consider himself an educator; rather, he obtained funds, facilities, and personnel for his schools.

In 1880, Moody held the first summer Bible conference at Northfield, with his friends and himself as speakers. The goal was to give laymen increased understanding of the Bible and to foster spiritual renewal. These laymen would then return to work in their churches with greater power. In 1886, the conference was expanded to include college students.

Chicago was the setting for another of Moody's ventures into education. Friends had long hoped for a permanent school there, and Miss Emma Dryer, with Moody's encouragement, had founded a small training school. Under Moody's direction, the Chicago Bible Institute officially opened on September 26, 1889. The school's purpose was to train Christian workers and equip them to serve in city missions. After Moody's death, the name was officially changed to Moody Bible Institute.

In 1894, Moody became convinced that masses of people could be reached if Christian books were available in inexpensive editions. A colportage department was begun at the Chicago Bible Institute, with students often distributing the books. In his later years, Moody developed a concern for prisoners, and books from the institute's colportage line were provided to prison libraries.

Moody had continued his revival preaching from 1878 to 1899, and he was speaking at Kansas City when his fatal illness struck. He hastened home to Northfield, and there he died on December 22, 1899.

Summary

A man of incredible energy and authority, Moody was an evangelist to the masses and brought spiritual renewal to urban centers, both in the United States and abroad. The most significant religious leader of the Gilded Age, he instituted new strategies and techniques in mass evangelism that have been used by later evangelists. These included his methods of planning, organization, and publicity. By enlisting cooperation among the churches, he proved that evangelism could be above denominationalism.

Living in the midst of a change from traditional conservatism to a liberal outlook in theology, Moody nevertheless maintained a deep belief in a literal interpretation of the Bible and its fundamental creeds. His message typified the thought of the evangelical Protestant movement. Out of the millions who heard him speak, many became converted and carried on his message.

In Moody's era, Christian elementary and secondary schools had not come into existence. The schools he established at Northfield were innovative in their approach as Christian education. The Chicago Bible Institute was the second significant Bible school started up in the United States and became the impetus for others. His use of lay people in his work—Moody himself was never ordained—and his Christian schools ushered in the age of the lay worker in the Church.

Moody's influence was felt in evangelical circles long after his death. Probably more than his theology, his personality and fierce concern for mankind have inspired others to continue his work. His compassion, humility, and earnest message of salvation remain an example for other evangelists.

Bibliography

Evensen, Bruce J. " 'Expecting a Blessing of Unusual Magnitude:' Moody, Mass Media, and Gilded Age Revival." *Journalism History* 24, no. 1 (Spring 1998). Provides an excellent look into Moody's life.

Findlay, James F., Jr. *Dwight L. Moody: American Evangelist, 1837-1899.* Chicago: University of Chicago Press, 1969. The single best scholarly biography. Includes an analysis, though inadequate, of Moody's personality, theology, and techniques of evangelism. Examines critical shifts in the social and religious thought of the nineteenth century, placing Moody in historical perspective. A review of Moody's home life and later accomplishments is included.

Getz, Gene A. *MBI: The Story of Moody Bible Institute.* Rev. ed. Chicago: Moody Press, 1986. Getz details the early history of the Moody Bible Institute and describes Moody's role in its beginnings and early years. A comprehensive account of the growth and expansion of the institute and its varied ministries.

Gundry, Stanley N. *Love Them In.* Chicago: Moody Press, 1976. Balanced, comprehensive evaluation of Moody's theology and how it related to his evangelistic campaigns. Within the historical context, Gundry considers Moody's doctrine in matters such as Calvinism, perfectionism, speaking in tongues, and the life of the believer. He stresses how Moody viewed the Gospel and its message of salvation.

Hopkins, C. Howard. *History of the Y.M.C.A. in North America.* New York: Association Press, 1951. A valuable resource as it examines the interplay of influences between Moody and the YMCA. Details the work Moody did for the YMCA in organization, fund-raising, and evangelism.

McLoughlin, William G., Jr. *Modern Revivalism: Charles Grandison Finney to Billy Graham.* New York: Ronald Press, 1959. Attempting to explain the significance of revivalism in the social, intellectual, and religious life of America, McLoughlin examines the lives of major revivalists, including Moody. He analyzes their social environment and their effect on American life. Includes a description of the work of Moody's associate, Ira Sankey.

Moody, William R. *Dwight L. Moody.* Rev. ed. New York: Macmillan, 1930. Just before his death, Moody commissioned his son to write this official biography. Though eulogistic, it is complete and invaluable in any study of Moody's life.

Pollock, John. *Moody.* Chicago: Moody Press, 1983. A readable, inspirational biography. Although it is not a theological analysis, Moody's personality is illuminated, and the detailed story gives information not found in other biographies.

Sankey, Ira D. *My Life and the Story of the Gospel Hymns.* Chicago: Bible Institute Colportage Association, 1907; London: Harper, 1928. Since Ira Sankey was Moody's associate in his evangelistic campaigns, his autobiography gives insight into the way Moody conducted services. Also included are anecdotes which further aid in the understanding of Moody's personality.

Elaine Mathiasen

J. P. MORGAN

Born: April 17, 1837; Hartford, Connecticut
Died: March 31, 1913; Rome, Italy
Areas of Achievement: Banking and philanthropy
Contribution: As an extraordinarily successful investment banker and a conspicuous philanthropist, and one of the most prominent art collectors of his day, Morgan symbolized an era of aggressive capitalism.

Early Life

John Pierpont Morgan had remarkable parents: Junius Spencer Morgan (1813-1890) owned part of a large mercantile house in Hartford, advanced to a larger one in Boston, and finally became partner, then successor to the very wealthy George Peabody, an American who made his career banking in London. Junius settled there in 1854 and lived in England for the remainder of his life. Morgan's mother, Sarah Pierpont, came from the family of a brilliant preacher in Boston, much given to abolitionism and other reforms. Young Morgan received his formal education in Hartford, in Boston, in Vevey, Switzerland, and at the University of Göttingen. Seriously ill as a teenager, he had a long and successful convalescence in the Azores. At age twenty, he began his career as a clerk in Duncan, Sherman, and Company in New York. Two years later, while traveling in the Caribbean to study the sugar and cotton markets, he bought, without authorization, a cargo of unwanted coffee with a draft on his employers. They complained but accepted the profit of several thousand he earned by wholesaling the coffee in New Orleans.

In 1860, Morgan set up his own company. He had plenty of business from his father in London and also took advantage of many opportunities to buy and sell in the booming commercial city of New York. In 1861, he married Amelia Sturges, after courting her for several years. She was clearly in the advanced stages of tuberculosis, but Morgan, daring in love as well as in business, gave up all commercial activities and took his stricken bride to Algiers and then to Nice, hoping to cure her. He failed, returning to the United States as a widower in 1862. He formed a partnership with his cousin, Jim Goodwin, and called the firm J. P. Morgan and Company, Bankers.

Writers hostile to Morgan claim that he selfishly pursued profit during the Civil War years, trading in gold against the government's fluctuating greenbacks, buying a substitute for three hundred dollars under the Conscription Act, and on one occasion buying obsolete arms from the federal government in the East and then selling them to General John C. Frémont in the West at an enormous profit. Morgan never apologized for his own actions, but writers friendly to him have argued that recurrent fainting spells, from which he suffered as a young man, made him unfit for military duty, that he served the Union cause well as an agent for Junius Morgan, who was staunchly pro-Union and placed United States bonds in England, and, finally, that two other men arranged and carried out the affair of the arms. Morgan was involved only as their banker, extending a short-term loan. Furthermore, the weapons were improved by rifling the barrels, and the young entrepreneurs, whatever their motives, did what the disorganized Department of the Army could not manage: They delivered arms at a reasonable price to the desperately needy Western army. On one point, however, there is no dispute: Morgan spent that part of the war that followed his disastrous first marriage in making money as rapidly as he could. In September, 1864, he took in new partners and reorganized as Dabney, Morgan and Company. At twenty-seven, he was a leader in the financial life of the United States' largest city. Yet he was already launched in his career of philanthropy, helping to raise money for the wounded and widowed and working effectively to establish and enlarge the Young Men's Christian Association (YMCA). In 1865, he married Frances Tracy, one of the six daughters of attorney Charles Tracy. The Tracys were fellow communicants at St. George's Episcopal Church in the Bowery, which Morgan had joined in 1861 and attended for the remainder of his life.

Largely free, at this point, of the illnesses and spells that had marred his youth, Morgan stood well over six feet, with powerful shoulders, penetrating eyes, and the air of one born to command. In later life, he would grow portly and suffer painfully from acne rosacea, an inflammation of the skin which settled especially in his nose. He doted on his and Frances' four children, Louisa, Jack (John Pierpont Morgan, Jr.), Juliet, and Anne. In the summer of 1869, Morgan and his wife, accompanied by two relatives, rode the new transcontinental railroad to Utah and to California, where they toured extensively by stagecoach and horse-

back. Returning East, the Morgans occupied a comfortable new home at Six West Fortieth Street. In 1871, troubled by nervous disorders, Morgan briefly considered retiring. Instead, he accepted a new partnership with the powerful Drexels of Philadelphia. He would be a full partner and would head their New York office under the title of Drexel, Morgan, and Company.

Life's Work

To understand the later fame of Morgan, the investment banker, one must first understand how and why he became involved with the railroads of the United States. From their earliest beginnings around 1830 to the Civil War, American railroads were generally small affairs, connecting neighboring cities or connecting cities with important rivers or seaports. Most companies supposed that they could not manage more than five hundred miles of track. The two systems which thoroughly refuted this thinking, the New York Central and the Pennsylvania, were quite exceptional until Congress, offering large land grants, encouraged the building of transcontinental railroads. Some firms can begin business with very little capital investment and grow on earnings; others, including railroads and electric power systems, are expensive to build and cannot be put into operation or earn money until everything is in place, including the employees. Thus, the quantities of federal land given to the Western railroads were not the source of huge profits that they have been claimed to be. The railroads had to be built and operating, and the land had to be well along toward settlement, before any of those lands were salable. Railroads, the most important and transforming feature of the American economy in the nineteenth century, relied entirely on borrowed capital for their construction and initial operation. Furthermore, they had to be public corporations, their stock for sale in markets throughout the world; otherwise, the enormous sums required would not be forthcoming. This feature led inevitably to the separation of management from stockholders, too numerous and too scattered to exercise a coherent will on railroad affairs. Yet stockholders all had one thing in common: They wished to protect their investments. It was therefore logical that investment bankers, whose income derived largely from marketing stocks and bonds, would wish to protect their own business positions by assuring the quality of the stocks and bonds being sold. Morgan was thus drawn into railroad af-

fairs by a desire, born of necessity, to see that railroads were properly and efficiently managed, so that the stockholders and bondholders would be properly rewarded for their investments. Furthermore, he clearly saw what Cornelius Vanderbilt, Thomas A. Scott, and Jay Gould had seen earlier: The future of American railroading lay in building large, integrated systems, in which a single corporation controlled not only trunk lines but also feeders and operated without competition.

His first adventure was a colorful skirmish with the most notorious railroad pirates of the age, Gould and Diamond Jim Fisk, in a battle for the control of the Albany and Susquehanna. There is a legend that Morgan kept control of a crucial stockholders meeting by hurling the burly Fisk down a flight of stairs, scattering his henchman as though they were tenpins. If true, this was the only time Morgan gained control of a railroad by hand-to-hand combat. In 1879, he performed a more sedate but much more lucrative feat in marketing William Vanderbilt's 250,000 shares (eighty-seven percent of those in existence) of New York Central Stock without suffering any depreciation or exciting any move to displace the railroad's management.

The year 1880 brought another enormous challenge, converted into enormous profits, not because Drexel, Morgan, and Company charged high brokerage fees but because they were handling so much money. In this case, it was a question of marketing forty million dollars in bonds for the improvement of the Northern Pacific, a transcontinental that had suffered bankruptcy and reorganization in the Panic of 1873. Great though his resources were, Morgan could not finance such enormous sales of stocks and bonds entirely through his own and his father's partnerships. He brought in other major banking houses, in the United States and abroad, discreetly organized in syndicates. To help protect the investments so arranged, Morgan, or one of his trusted partners or friends, became director of the refinanced railroad. Morgan later helped to finance and manage dozens of railroads.

Morgan was involved in the finances of the federal government on four major occasions. With other leading bankers, he helped refinance the federal debt under President Ulysses S. Grant. In the summer of 1877, Morgan committed another of his unexpected and extraordinary moves: He loaned the army money with which to pay its troops, largely engaged in the Western Indian wars, after a distracted Congress had adjourned without renewing their appropriation. Since the army was not authorized to borrow, Morgan had paid out more than two million dollars at his own risk; Congress, however, appropriated funds to repay the banker. Much more effort was required to save the United States Treasury's gold reserve in the depression of 1893. A combination of laws, more popular than wise, had forced the Treasury to sell gold until it was on the brink of bankruptcy; the Panic of 1893 had further started a general flight of gold back to Europe. To save the situation, Morgan had to form a syndicate of American and European bankers both to loan gold to the government at acceptable rates and to check the flow of gold from the Treasury out of the country. Furthermore, Grover Cleveland, whose party was rapidly coming under the control of Populists and Bryanites, was extremely reluctant to accept help from the only people who could give it, the "monied interests of Wall Street."

Morgan's greatest triumphs and defeats came at the end of his life. In 1901, he formed a combination to buy out Andrew Carnegie and merge his steel colossus with several other companies. The resulting United States Steel Corporation, the first "billion dollar corporation," renewed charges of monopoly and chicanery. Morgan then turned to a merger of the Northern Pacific with its regional rival, the Great Northern, by means of a holding company, the Northern Securities Company. Theodore Roosevelt, the Progressive president, ordered a prosecution which the government won in 1904, and the merger fell apart. Morgan, however, ever the patriot, returned in 1907 to lead yet another syndicate of bankers to prevent a financial panic. One of the New York banks saved on that occasion had chiefly working people for its depositors; Morgan ordered his company to save them even if he lost money; in fact, he did. In the last year of his life, Morgan was summoned before the Pujo Committee, which charged him with destroying competition by controlling all the large banks, railroads, and steel companies of the United States through interlocking directorships and stock proxies. Morgan stoutly denied the charge, claiming that his methods guaranteed the proper management of business by men of high character.

At St. George's Church, Morgan led the vestry in hiring W. S. Rainsford, an Emerson-inspired Progressive who introduced a community center, a house for Deaconesses (Episcopal women doing social work, in this case), an industrial school, a summer camp, and a seaside resort for working-class women and children, all of which Morgan helped plan and most of which he financed. He also helped maintain the church near his summer home, served on the committee that planned the cathedral, and attended every national triennial convention of his church until his death.

Always something of a collector, Morgan began buying rare and old works of art on a stupendous scale after the death of his father. As a collector, Morgan displayed the decisiveness and flair that had characterized his business career. A trustee of the Metropolitan Museum from its fledgling days, he became its most active member in the last fifteen years of his life and left it priceless collections of paintings, ceramics, armor, and other objets d'art. For his collection of rare manuscripts and books, he built his own library next to the home at 219 Madison Avenue which he had built in 1881. It would later be administered as a public reference library. Collecting art went nicely with Morgan's lifelong habit of traveling abroad. He spent almost every summer in England, France, Italy, and, on several occasions, Egypt, where he often visited archaeological digs. He died during one of his periods of travel in Rome, Italy, on March 31, 1913.

Summary

J. P. Morgan's power grew because of the unusual combination of boldness and good sense, ruthlessness and responsibility, that made up his complex personality. The failure of the American people, between 1836 and 1913, to have any sort of central bank created rare opportunities for investment bankers with strong connections to foreign centers of capital. Hating waste, inefficiency, and conflict, Morgan used his growing financial power to impose order on the railroad and steel industries, inevitably reducing competition and calling into question the Adam Smith economics that most educated people took seriously. Democrats also feared the growing power of rich men who appeared responsible to no one but themselves. Morgan, thus, stirred up controversy and antagonism; yet, on his death in 1913, he left a legacy of responsibility in business and civic affairs and a priceless collection of art for the enjoyment of, literally, millions.

Bibliography

Allen, Frederick Lewis. *The Great Pierpont Morgan*. London: Gollancz, and New York: Harper, 1949. The most readable of the biographies and the only one that does justice to Morgan while stating the full case against him.

Canfield, Cass. *The Incredible Pierpont Morgan: Financier and Art Collector*. London: Hamilton, and New York: Harper, 1974. Richly illustrated and with superb color plates, this is a delightful book on Morgan.

Chandler, Alfred D., Jr. *The Visible Hand: The Managerial Revolution in American Business*. Cambridge, Mass.: Belknap Press of Harvard University Press, 1977. A comprehensive business history, placing Morgan exactly in context.

Chernow, Ron. "Blessed Barons." *Time* 152, no. 23 (Dec 7, 1998). Profiles three American business tycoons: Morgan, John D. Rockefeller, and Andrew Carnegie. Discusses the contributions of each towards U.S. industrial leadership and their well-known philanthropic efforts.

De Long, J. Bradford. "What Morgan Wrought." *Wilson Quarterly* 16, no. 4 (Autumn 1992). Examines Morgan's influence on U.S. corporate financial structure, including the Congressional inquiry into Morgan's Money Trust and the sphere of his firm's influence.

Gras, N. S. B., and Henrietta Larson. "J. P. Morgan: 1837-1913." In *The Coming of Managerial Capitalism: A Casebook on the History of American Economic Institutions*, edited by A. D. Chandler and R. S. Tedlow, 257-288. Homewood, Ill.: Irwin, 1985. An outstanding short treatment of Morgan's business affairs and their significance.

Hoyt, Edwin P., Jr. *The House of Morgan*. New York: Dodd, Mead, and London: Muller, 1966. This is uniquely valuable in tracing the careers of four generations of Morgans.

Hughes, Jonathan. *The Vital Few: American Economic Progress and Its Protagonists*. London and Boston: Houghton Mifflin, 1966. A splendid interpretive history with a graceful chapter on Morgan.

Rainsford, W. S. *The Story of a Varied Life: An Autobiography*. New York: Doubleday, 1922. Rainsford was Rector of Morgan's church for twenty-two years and, for all of his spiritual condescension, the only informed witness to Morgan's strenuous service.

Satterlee, Herbert L. *J. Pierpont Morgan: An Intimate Portrait*. New York: Macmillan, 1939. A narrative chronicle by Morgan's son-in-law, in whose eyes the financier was a great and good man. Dull, but full of family information not available elsewhere.

Sinclair, Andrew. *Corsair: The Life of J. Pierpont Morgan*. London: Weidenfeld and Nicolson, and Boston: Little Brown, 1981. A stylishly written book in the muckraking tradition, slightly marred by the repetition of the unlikely theory that Morgan resented his rich and powerful father right up to the old gentleman's death in 1890.

Tomkins, Calvin. *Merchants and Masterpieces: The Story of the Metropolitan Museum of Art*. London: Longman, and New York: Dutton, 1970. Richly illustrated, this work places Morgan's collecting and ambitions for the museum in proper context.

Robert McColley

LEWIS HENRY MORGAN

Born: November 21, 1818; Aurora, New York
Died: December 17, 1881; Rochester, New York
Areas of Achievement: Anthropology and natural history
Contribution: Extending kinship studies, first among the Iroquois, then to cultures around the world, Morgan devised a theory of social and cultural evolution that provided both a theoretical paradigm for late nineteenth century anthropology and a theory of early family evolution that Karl Marx used in his interpretation of history.

Early Life

Lewis Henry Morgan was born November 21, 1818, in Aurora, New York, to Harriet Steele and Jedediah Morgan. Morgan's father, a wealthy landholder, died when Morgan was eight, and the farm's operation was placed in the hands of young Morgan's older brothers. After receiving an education at the Cayuga Academy in Aurora and being graduated from Union College in 1840, Morgan decided to pursue a career in law. In Aurora, while reading for his bar exams, Morgan joined a secret men's organization called the Grand Order of the Iroquois. Morgan's participation and leadership in this organization proved to be the beginning of his ethnological career. In order to model the order after the political organization of the six Indian nations of New York, known as the Iroquois Confederacy, Morgan and other members of the club made trips to several Iroquois reservations to study their history and culture.

Later, Morgan took an active role in protesting the loss of Iroquois land, specifically reservations of the Seneca—one of the six Iroquois nations—to a land company, and he even traveled to Washington to present a petition to the president and the Senate on behalf of the Seneca. For his support of the Seneca Indians in this matter and his continuing interest in their culture, the Seneca adopted Morgan as a member of the Hawk clan.

In 1844, Morgan moved to Rochester, New York, and opened a law office. This career move did not deflect Morgan from his preoccupation with Indian studies. Not only did he supply Indian artifacts to the Regents of the University of New York, for what would later become a collection of the New York State Museum, but he also wrote a series of articles that appeared under the title "Letters on the Iroquois Addressed to Albert Gallatin," published in the *American Whig Review* (1847-1848). These letters he later revised and expanded into *League of the Ho-dé-no-sau-nee, or Iroquois* (1851), now considered the first full ethnography of an American Indian group. Morgan dedicated the book to Ely S. Parker, a Seneca Indian whom Morgan met in an Albany bookstore and who was instrumental in helping Morgan collect Seneca data. If Morgan never lived among the Indians, as some writers have claimed, neither was he an armchair ethnologist. He read what books he could find on the Iroquois and then complemented this reading with extensive fieldwork. Indeed, Morgan proved to be one of the first ethnologists to rely heavily on data collected in the field for the construction of ethnological theories.

The publication of Morgan's work on Iroquois history and culture drew the attention of others in the new science of ethnology, including the Indian agent, historian, and ethnographer Henry Rowe Schoolcraft and archaeologist Ephraim George Squier. After the publication of his book on the Iroquois, Morgan hoped to put aside his study of Indians and devote himself to his career in law. His marriage to his cousin Mary Elisabeth Steele, in 1851, strengthened his desire to succeed in his law career.

Life's Work

Morgan's early law career in Rochester proved unspectacular. Unknown and without influential friends, Morgan supported himself on local collection cases and occasional criminal cases. In time, he became known more for his public lectures at the Mechanic's Institute and at the Rochester Athenaeum than as a trial lawyer. These lectures, as well as his book on the Iroquois, eventually introduced Morgan to the elite society of Rochester. Through these contacts, he invested in railroad and mining companies in the Upper Peninsula of Michigan. By the late 1850's, through wise investments, he had acquired a modest fortune that allowed him to retire from legal practice in the early 1860's. Except for brief stints in the New York assembly in 1861 and the New York senate from 1868 to 1869, Morgan devoted the remainder of his life to ethnology.

Morgan's return to anthropological studies really began in 1857. In 1856, Morgan attended the meetings of the American Association for the Advancement of Science. Impressed with the papers he heard, Morgan decided to return the following year and deliver a paper on Iroquois kinship. This paper grew out of Morgan's earlier research and his discovery that the Iroquois determined kinship differently from the way of Anglo-Americans. Morgan suspected that other Indian tribes exhibited similar kinship patterns, but he had no opportunity to test this theory until the summer of 1858, while traveling in upper Michigan. There, Morgan met some Ojibwe Indians and was excited to discover that their system of kinship was essentially the same as that of the Iroquois. It occurred to Morgan that kinship systems might be linked to a people's economy. Morgan noted that North American Indian kinship systems, which he termed classificatory, seemed to be associated with a hunting-gathering horticultural economy. Assuming that kinship systems changed slowly and then only when a people's economy changed, Morgan believed such systems to be quite old. If they were ancient and if similar systems could be found in other parts of the world, Morgan believed that this would constitute proof of the migration of American Indians from the Old World.

Because the origin of the American Indian remained an important question throughout the first half of the nineteenth century, Morgan believed that discovering an Old World connection would be a major contribution to the young science of ethnology. Seeking an answer to these questions, Morgan made four trips, between 1859 and 1862, to Indian tribes west of the Mississippi River to collect kinship information. On these trips, he interviewed missionaries, schoolteachers, merchants, government agents, Indian traders, and steamboat captains, checking and rechecking the data he received from his talks with Indians from various reservations. He also sent questionnaires to missionaries and government agents around the world to learn how other non-European cultures determined kinship. Out of these travels and research came his *Systems of Consanguinity and Affinity of the Human Family* (1871). Discovering that the method of designating kinship which he first found among the Iroquois Indians also existed in Asia, Morgan became convinced of the Old World origin of the American Indians.

Morgan's trips to the West and his examination of conditions in various Indian communities made him sharply critical of the federal government's

handling of Indian affairs. His shock and frustration over educational and health facilities available to Indians poured out in a series of articles triggered by the public outcry at the deaths of General George A. Custer and his troops at Little Big Horn. In "Factory Systems for Indian Reservations," "The Hue and Cry against the Indians," and "The Indian Question," all published in the *Nation*, Morgan castigated the government for its treatment of Indians and blamed Custer's death on the government's long-standing mismanagement and indifference to reservation administration. Morgan claimed that Indians could not be civilized quickly and that teaching them farming might not be the best approach to changing their behavior. Change would take time, and American society would have to be patient in their expectations for the Indian.

Along with many others, Morgan sharply criticized government Indian policy. His reputation, however, rests not on these attacks but on his study of Indian kinship, which led him to theorize about the history and nature of the family. His evidence convinced him that the family had evolved through gradual stages from promiscuity to monogamy.

This idea contributed to the development of Morgan's theory of human social and cultural evolution through stages of savagery, barbarism, and civilization. He developed these ideas in his next and best-known work, *Ancient Society: Or, Researches in the Lines of Human Progress from Savagery through Barbarism to Civilization* (1877). After the publication of *Ancient Society*, Morgan published little. A section on the evolution of house architecture and home life originally intended for *Ancient Society* and deleted by the publishers because of its length, was published separately as *Houses and House-Life of the American Aborigines* in 1881.

Although Morgan's primary contribution to American scholarship came through his work in anthropology, he also made contributions to natural history. Intrigued by the question of whether animals operated through instinct or reason, Morgan set out to investigate this question through an extensive study of the American beaver. Through his thorough examination of beaver behavior, Morgan concluded that beaver, in particular, and animals, in general, did indeed use reason. With the publication of *The American Beaver and His Works* (1868), Morgan became the foremost authority on the beaver. The study impressed both famed Harvard zoologist Louis Agassiz and English evolutionist Charles Darwin.

Summary

Morgan began writing at a time when American ethnology still stressed collection and classification, with little emphasis on the interpretation of these accumulating data. His evolutionary theory moved American ethnology beyond mere classification to a larger consideration of humankind and their place in space and time. By placing American Indian ethnology into the larger context of human social evolution or human history, Morgan proved a pioneer in the development of the science of anthropology.

Morgan's legacy to anthropology is considerable. His studies of kinship and theories of social evolution became the paradigm for anthropological study in the second half of the nineteenth century and influenced, in both Europe and the United States, the development of social anthropology into the twentieth century. His accomplishments were recognized by Charles Darwin, Henry Adams, Francis Parkman, and Karl Marx. Morgan's election to membership in the American Academy of Arts and Sciences, the National Academy of Science, and the American Association for the Advancement of Science, in which he served as president, indicates the esteem in which he and his ideas were held by the scientific community.

The work of Lewis Henry Morgan embodied much of the optimistic spirit that prevailed in nineteenth century America, a spirit that enthusiastically emphasized laws of progress for both the individual and society. Morgan's theory of social evolution—the evolution of society through levels of savagery and barbarism to civilization—well expressed this fundamental belief in progress.

Bibliography

Bieder, Robert E. *Science Encounters the Indian, 1820-1880: The Early Years of American Ethnology.* Norman: University of Oklahoma Press, 1986; London: University of Oklahoma Press, 1989. Contains a chapter on Morgan discussing his views on Indians and considering his influence on American anthropology.

Eggan, Fred. *The American Indian: Perspectives for the Study of Culture Change.* Chicago: Aldine, 1966; London: Weidenfeld and Nicolson, 1967. A series of lectures given by Eggan at the University of Rochester's Morgan Lectures, which focused on Morgan's contributions to the study of American Indian social organization.

Fortes, Meyer. *Kinship and the Social Order: The Legacy of Lewis Henry Morgan.* Chicago: Aldine, 1969; London: Routledge, 1970. Also lectures in the University of Rochester's Morgan Lecture series. Fortes explores the larger scope of Morgan's ideas on kinship and social order in contemporary anthropology.

Michaelson, Scott. "Ely S. Parker and Amerindian Voices in Ethnography." *American Literary History* 8, no. 4 (Winter 1996). Focuses on the correspondence between Morgan and Native American Ely Samuel Parker concerning their collaboration on Morgan's "League of the Hode'-no-sau-nee, Iroquois." The two men were opposed in their approaches to differing cultures.

Morgan, Lewis Henry. *Lewis Henry Morgan: The Indian Journals, 1859-1862.* Edited by Leslie A. White. Ann Arbor: University of Michigan Press, 1959. Morgan's journals of his four trips, relating experiences among the Western Indians.

———. *Pioneers in American Anthropology: The Bandelier-Morgan Letters, 1873-1883.* Edited by Leslie A. White. Albuquerque: University of New Mexico Press, 1940. A collection of letters between Morgan and his foremost American disciple.

Resek, Carl. *Lewis Henry Morgan: American Scholar*. Chicago: University of Chicago Press, 1960. A brief but well-written biography of Morgan.

Stern, Bernhard Joseph. *Lewis Henry Morgan: Social Evolutionist*. Chicago: University of Chicago Press, 1931. A dated but still useful biography of Morgan, written by a sociologist and social theorist.

Stocking, George W. *Race, Culture, and Evolution: Essays in the History of Anthropology*. New York: Free Press, 1968; London: Macmillan, 1971. Contains a chapter in which Morgan's anthropological theories are considered, along with those of his English contemporaries E. B. Tylor and Herbert Spencer.

Tooker, Elizabeth. *Lewis H. Morgan on Iroquois Material Culture*. Tucson: University of Arizona Press, 1994. The author discusses Morgan's impressive collection of over five hundred Iroquois artifacts and his research methods, which are often overlooked.

Robert E. Bieder

WILLIAM MORRIS

Born: March 24, 1834; Walthamstow, near London, England

Died: October 3, 1896; Hammersmith, near London, England

Areas of Achievement: Art, architecture, literature, publishing, and politics

Contribution: Morris' influence on book design has been almost as profound as his impact on the decorative arts and the course of modern design; his key contribution to the growth of modern British socialism was practical, financial, and philosophical; he was also a powerful force in the revival of narrative poetry and the rediscovery of Norse literature, and an influential romantic and utopian writer.

Early Life

Future Socialist William Morris was born into upper-middle-class comfort on March 24, 1834, the son of a nondescript Evangelical mother and a businessman father. He was brought up in a series of semirural residences near Epping Forest, where he acquired a love of natural form that would later manifest itself in his designs. At Marlborough public school, from January, 1848, until December, 1851, he benefited not from studying (since the school, then newly founded, was rather lax and rough) but from having free access to beautiful countryside and the wealth of historic buildings in the area. This resulted in his coming to know, as he later said, "most of what was to be known about English Gothic."

In 1853, he entered Exeter College, Oxford. In 1854, he made the first of several summer trips abroad that expanded his conception of art and architecture. During this period, the writings of essayist and reformer John Ruskin proved to be a revelation to Morris, clarifying his unconventional beliefs. Also critical to his development was Thomas Carlyle's upholding of the virtues of the medieval past over the vices of the present. Also at Exeter, Morris made two friendships that would last his lifetime and inform his work. Most important, the idealistic enthusiasm for things medieval of future painter Edward Burne-Jones confirmed Morris' own. The two gathered about them a group of friends, the "Brotherhood," dedicated to a "Crusade and Holy Warfare against the age"; for the twelve months of 1856, they published the *Oxford*

and Cambridge Magazine (largely funded by Morris, who in 1855 came into an income of nine hundred pounds a year). At the same time, after taking his degree, in January, 1856, Morris articled himself to George Edmund Street, one of the most prominent architects of the revived English Gothic. In his Oxford office, he met and became friends with young architect Philip Webb.

Another major influence of the Oxford years was the Pre-Raphelite painter-poet Dante Gabriel Rossetti, who swayed Morris toward painting and away from architecture: Crucially, Rossetti's painting was medieval in inspiration and tended to emphasize the decorative. The influence is apparent in one of Morris' few extant paintings, a mural executed at the new Oxford Union Debating Hall in 1857. His model was seventeen-year-old Jane Burden, daughter of an Oxford groom: In 1859, in the teeth of Victorian convention, Morris married her. In a poem in his first volume, *The Defence of Guenevere* (1858), he pays tribute to the beautiful and enigmatic Jane; it points, too, at the loneliness he would later suffer in this marriage. Her great "mournful" eyes "[are] most times looking out afar,/ Waiting for something, not for me/ *Beata mea Domina!*"

Life's Work

Anticipating the birth of two daughters in 1861 and 1862, in 1860 Morris joined with Webb to build himself a house. At this moment, Morris' path started to unroll before him. "Red House," so called for the color of its brick, left uncovered in defiance of architectural convention, has been said to have initiated plain, unostentatious modern domestic design. The problem of what to do about aesthetically satisfying interior decoration and furniture led directly to the formation of Morris and Company.

The aim of "the Firm," which involved painters Rossetti and Ford Madox Brown as well as Webb and Burne-Jones, was to reinstate decoration as one of the fine arts. As its prospectus stated, it was concerned with everything from paintings "down to . . . the smallest work susceptible of . . . beauty." It was so successful that by 1866, only four years after the first Morris wallpaper, "Daisy," the Firm was decorating rooms at St. James's Palace. Gradually, as he mastered each craft, Morris expanded its scope to include, besides painted windows and mural decoration, furniture, metal and glassware, cloth and paper wall-hangings, embroideries, jewelry, dyed and printed silks and cottons, and carpets and tapestries. He created more than six hundred designs for the Firm, basing his designs on natural forms, primarily flowers, but always retaining a structural pattern. His designs are characterized by his firm calligraphic line (anticipating the style of art nouveau) and suggestions of movement, growth, and fullness.

At the height of these activities, in 1869, Morris was visited by Henry James, who remembered the bearded and still somewhat bohemian designer as "short, burly and corpulent, very careless and unfinished in his dress. . . . He has a very loud voice and a nervous restless manner and a perfectly unaffected and business-like address." As a younger man, Morris had been rather poetically beautiful, though not when in the throes of his occasional childish rages, during which he would bang his head on the walls.

There had been a lull in poetic production between *The Defence of Guenevere* and publication of Morris' next major works, *The Life and Death of Jason* in 1867 and *The Earthly Paradise*, a series of intricately interweaved narrative poems, in 1868-1870. These brought Morris instant success and popularity. Meanwhile his first translations of Icelandic sagas were published in 1869; their influence is apparent in much of his writing after the lonely and escapist *The Earthly Paradise*, most powerfully in his acclaimed epic *Sigurd the Volsung* (1876), the immediate cause of his being considered for the prestigious post of professor of poetry at Oxford: He declined to be considered (as later he would decline to be nominated for the post of poet laureate upon the death of Alfred, Lord Tennyson, in 1892).

By 1881, when the Firm moved to larger premises, there was essentially very little difference between Morris the businessman and any other Victorian capitalist. Contrary to eulogizing tradition, he did not entirely spurn machines (spurning instead "the great intangible machine of commercial tyranny"). Although he provided rather better pay and conditions, work in the Firm was boring: Certainly, it did not reach Morris' Ruskinian, medieval-Gothic ideal of delight and self-expression in work. Once he had become a committed Socialist, Morris was even more aware of the ironies of his position, as well as its benefits, such as his ability to fund Socialist activities and the Socialist

press: Yet he operated the way his society dictated he must in order to operate at all.

What Morris called his "conversion" to radical political activism came about gradually from 1876, in protest against the "dull squalor" of his civilization. By the early 1880's, he had openly committed himself to socialism, and despite some problems within the Socialist League, which he helped to found in 1884, he remained faithful to this cause until he died, not only writing political poetry (*Chants for Socialists*, 1883-1886; *The Pilgrims of Hope*, 1885), pamphlets, and tales, but also editing the League's journal *Commonweal*, from 1885 to 1890, selling it on the streets, speaking at workingmen's clubs and on street corners throughout the country, and braving arrest during the "free-speech" disturbances of 1886.

Philosophically, socialism gave Morris an analysis that provided firmer foundations for his belief that art has its roots in the social and political body, and will wither if that body is not in good health. High Victorian capitalist society, as his reading of the works of Karl Marx impressed upon him, was sick; nothing less than revolution was needed, and accordingly he would work for it. From the late 1870's, Morris went on to express these beliefs in the many lectures and publications, often spin-offs from his design work, on which rests his reputation as a pivotal figure in the development of the modern conception of culture. His analysis was deepest and most eloquently expressed in *A Dream of John Ball* in 1886 (a mix of romance and the philosophy of history) and in the Utopian Socialist vision *News from Nowhere* in 1890. Between 1889 and his death in 1896, Morris also published eight prose romances, set in a semimythological past, which prefigure the fantasies of C. S. Lewis and J. R. R. Tolkien.

The third of these tales, *The Story of the Glittering Plain*, was the first book to be published, in 1890, by the Kelmscott Press. Morris' great "typographical adventure" that revitalized English printing, then at a low ebb, stimulating experimentation and a proliferation of private presses. His insistence that the best books are "always beautiful by force of the mere typography" led to his designing two alphabets and producing more than six hundred designs for initials, borders, and ornaments. Between 1891 and 1898, when his executors wound up the Press, fifty-two books were produced; his 1896 Kelmscott edition of the works of Geoffrey Chaucer has been pronounced the finest book ever produced. Morris lived long enough to see it finished, but the punishing round of his many activities took its toll at last, and he died at age sixty-two.

Summary

The greatest pattern designer of the nineteenth century, William Morris has had a lasting effect upon the look and thought of the modern world because of his attempt to uphold in practice his Ruskinian belief in truth to nature, his respect for his materials, his fight for quality workmanship in a world already engulfed by shoddy mass-production, and the protofunctionalism he came to advocate, expressed in his famous dictum: "Have nothing in your house that you do not know to be useful or believe to be beautiful."

Yet beyond even this, Morris was one of the most searching, and certainly the most well-rounded critic of English society and culture in the nineteenth century. He made in action, in his own life, the kind of links between poetry, politics, art, and society that are usually left to academics. His work was unified and therefore made more influential by a core of essentially simple ideas: to make life more worth living, less complicated, and more beautiful for more people. As he wrote in an 1894 article, "How I Became a Socialist": "Apart from the desire to produce beautiful things, the leading passion of my life has been and is hatred of modern civilization." He refused to believe, he added, that all the beauty of the world was destined to end "in a counting-house on the top of a cinder heap."

Bibliography

Hough, Graham. *The Last Romantics*. New York: Barnes and Noble, 1947; London: Duckworth, 1949. Seminal work tracing the influence of Ruskin on the visual arts and literature through the Pre-Raphaelites, Morris, and Walter Pater to the *fin de siècle* and W. B. Yeats.

Mackail, J. W. *The Life of William Morris*. London and New York: Longman, 1899. The standard, authorized biography, written at the request of Burne-Jones, with unhampered access to papers of the family and the Firm. A skillful patchwork of extracts from Morris' own writings, diaries, and letters; Mackail's own narrative is quietly elegant and highly readable.

Morris, May, ed. *William Morris: Artist, Writer, Socialist*. London: Blackwell, 1936; New York: Russell and Russell, 1966. The invaluable insights of Morris' beloved and politically sympathetic daughter, also the editor of the twenty-four volumes of *The Collected Works of William Morris* (1910-1915).

Morris, William. *The Collected Letters of William Morris*. Edited by Norman Kelvin. 2 vols. Princeton, N.J.: Princeton University Press, 1984; Guildford: Princeton University Press, 1987. Excellent edition: solid introduction, chronology, more than thirty illustrations per volume (including reproductions of letters, plus designs, places, and people), indexes of subjects and correspondents, unobtrusive footnoting.

———. *Journalism: Contributions to Commonweal 1885-90*. Edited and introduced by Nicholas Salmon. Bristol, Avon: Thoemmes Press, 1996. Focuses on Morris' own articles in *Commonweal*, the most influential socialist journal of the time, founded by Morris. These articles, most previously unpublished, show Morris to be a perceptive journalist.

———. *Political Writings: Contributions to Justice and Commonweal 1883-1890*. Edited and introduced by Nicholas Salmon. Bristol, Avon:

Thoemmes Press, 1994. This volume includes all of Morris' important political essays written between 1883 and 1890 and sheds new light on his philosophy.

————. *Selected Writings and Designs*. Edited by Asa Briggs. London and Baltimore: Penguin, 1962. Includes two short autobiographical pieces; helpfully organized under the headings of "Romance" (including his best poetry), "Commitment," "Socialism," and "Utopia" (the first half of *News from Nowhere* is printed in full). Excellent but overshort introduction by Briggs and good interleaved central section on Morris as designer by Graeme Shankland (twenty-four plates).

Naylor, Gillian. *The Arts and Crafts Movement: A Study of Its Sources, Ideals, and Influence on Design Theory*. Cambridge, Mass.: MIT Press, and London: Studio Vista, 1971. More than one hundred illustrations, nine in color: designs, fabrics, furniture, household objects. Morris takes his place in a well-organized survey leading from Augustus Pugin through to Frank Lloyd Wright and the modern "efficiency" style.

Pevsner, Nikolaus. *Pioneers of Modern Design: From William Morris to Walter Gropius*. Rev. ed. London: Penguin, 1960. First published in 1936. A compelling case for the crucial influence of Morris, despite his medievalism, for the modern movement. Makes clear the connections between interior and pattern design, architecture (including the work of Webb), and painting. Heavily illustrated.

Stansky, Peter. *William Morris*. Oxford and New York: Oxford University Press, 1983. This excellent brief study in the Past Masters series is less a collection of the essential facts than a reflective essay upon the essential Morris. Thoroughly readable and frequently witty.

Thompson, E. P. *William Morris: Romantic to Revolutionary*. London: Lawrence and Wishart, 1955; New York: Monthly Review Press, 1962. A monumental, primarily political study by the author of the classic work, *The Making of the English Working Classes* (1963). Traces how Morris' intense romanticism came to unite with his political idealism.

Vallance, Aymer. *William Morris: His Art, His Writings, and His Public Life, a Record*. London: Bell, 1897; Boston: Milford House, 1971. Draws extensively on contemporary reviews, criticism, and opinions. Heavily and attractively illustrated.

Joss Marsh

SAMUEL F. B. MORSE

Born: April 27, 1791; Charlestown, Massachusetts
Died: April 2, 1872; New York, New York
Areas of Achievement: Telegraphy and invention
Contribution: Persevering through the trials of experimentation and the sluggishness of public approval, Morse developed and implemented a system of electric communication which revolutionized the availability of information and forever changed the sense of world distances.

Early Life

In the shadow of Boston, a center for politics and communications, was born Samuel Finley Breese Morse, whose life and work would revolutionize those pursuits. First son of the young Calvinist minister Jedidiah Morse and his New Jersey wife Elizabeth Breese, "Finley," as the child was called, was born on April 27, 1791, in Charlestown, Massachusetts. Three years later, a brother, Sidney Edwards, was born, and the next year, Richard Cary followed.

The Morses had great expectations of their sons, who were born into a family with a strong history of education: Their mother's grandfather had been president of Princeton College, and their father, Pastor Morse, earned a degree from Yale and wrote the first geography text in America. When the boys started school, however, they showed distinctly different aptitudes for study. Their father characterized Finley as the hare, quick to lose interest and change paths; Sidney, he said, was the tortoise of the family, stubborn and steadfast; Richard, the youngest Morse to survive birth, was more like Sidney than he was like Finley. Though the younger siblings were of different temperaments, they would often later come to the aid of their older brother: easing his financial woes, caring for his children after his first wife's death, offering an editorial forum for discourses on the telegraph.

Morse's parents believed that the discipline of education would benefit their firstborn. They sent him off to Phillips Academy in Andover, Massachusetts, at the tender age of seven. His aptitude in the classroom was not legendary, though his aptitude for drawing proved somewhat greater and was encouraged by the family. By the time he studied at Yale, Morse was able to sponsor his affinity for cigars and wine with miniature portraits on ivory. Further encouragement from a meeting with the artist Washington Allston, whom Morse would lat-

er credit as his mentor, prompted him to set some goals. Young Morse yearned to go abroad to study painting with Allston and Benjamin West. With some persuasion, his parents agreed to send him to England. There, at the Royal Academy of London, he learned to work in other media: charcoal, marble, oils. West lent his work a critical eye and often turned the callow artist back to finish works he had thought completed. Soon, England recognized his talent and diligence with a gold medal from the Adelphi Society of Arts for his sculpture of the dying Hercules.

Morse returned to the United States (via a nearly two-month voyage), convinced of the historical genre's preeminence as "the intellectual branch of art." Commissions of such works were not readily available, however, and he had to resort to portrait work for subsistence. His pursuit of commissions took him up and down the Eastern seaboard. In Concord, Massachusetts, he met his bride-to-be, Lucretia Pickering Walker. The wedding was postponed until he could save enough money to set up winter housekeeping in Charleston, South Carolina, where he had been awarded a commission for a portrait of President James Monroe.

Charleston, however, was only a temporary residence, and eventually Morse was forced by impecunity to leave his wife in New Haven, where his entire family seemed to be toiling without benefit of regular salary. He traveled continually to paint and dreamed of the means to live in the same house as his wife and children. That dream was never realized while Lucretia lived. In fact, he learned of Lucretia's death days after the event, while he was in Washington to paint the Marquis de Lafayette.

The Lafayette portrait, which hangs in New York's City Hall, is not without critical acclaim. At least one art historian deems it worthy of nomination to the Golden Age of American portrait painting. Portrait painting, especially for civic commission, offered a regular income, but the two large-scale historical works Morse hoped to exhibit for profit did not. Morse conceived of these historical pieces in a grand manner. The one, *Congress Hall*, otherwise known as *The Old House of Representatives*, shows the National Hall during a session of Congress and includes likenesses of the congressmen, achieved from individual sittings, as well as Jedidiah Morse, Benjamin Silliman, and a Pawnee chief. The other, *The Louvre*, shows a room at the museum, the Salon Carré, complete with more than forty great paintings. When he thought of these works initially (nearly ten years apart), Morse wanted to create something which would appeal to the common man, though the historical genre was to his mind the most elevated of art forms. With *Congress Hall*, Morse thought each man would at least recognize his representative and have an interest in seeing him at work. *The Louvre*, he thought, would open the treasures of the Old World to Americans, who were rarely privileged to see these masterpieces.

Morse dreamed of an additional historical commission to decorate panels at the new Capitol, but the commission went to someone else; in this case, perhaps, art's loss directly contributed to science's gain.

Life's Work

When there is a question of who was the first to invent a machine or a process, research often shows more than one person working with similar ideas, though the one has no knowledge of the others' works. Such was the case with the invention of the telegraph. In 1832, while Morse was returning from Europe aboard the packet ship *Sully*, isolated from libraries, laboratories, and scientific journals, he formulated his first hypotheses regarding the possibility of transmitting information by electric impulses.

His only formal education in matters of electricity had been lectures during his junior year at Yale when Silliman and Jeremiah Day gave demonstrations there. Morse himself experimented with electricity in the basements of Yale, apparently for reasons of native curiosity. Outside the classroom, Silliman, who was Morse's neighbor, and James Dwight Dana, an acquaintance with more than passing knowledge of electromagnetism, rounded out Morse's knowledge of electricity.

Long out of Yale by 1832, Morse had not read current scientific journals and was not aware that, at the same time, there were men experimenting in England with semaphore telegraphs—that is, those which worked with visual signals. On board the *Sully*, he was inspired in a conversation on electromagnetism with Dr. Charles T. Jackson to note that information could be sent electrically. With that grain of thought he began investigating possibilities for transforming the potential into a reality.

Morse's shipboard sketch pad shows his early ideas for a code based on dots and dashes and for devices to send and record messages. Upon his arrival at his brother's house in New York City, he began work on a prototype. With an old canvas stretcher and saw-tooth type that he had forged at his sister-in-law's hearth, he produced a rudimentary model of a machine which would make electricity useful to mankind. The forces which had confronted Morse as artist, however, now played upon Morse the inventor: The initial stroke of genius demanded systematic revisions and fresh income if it were to be developed fully. Nevertheless, Morse was too active to be incapacitated by despair over lack of remuneration for his art or invention. He was busy running the National Academy of Design (he was among its founders), running for mayor of New York, and accepting the first art professorship at New York University (NYU).

To further his telegraphic work, Morse contracted several partners. These partners agreed that any new discoveries made to the telegraph would become public under Morse's name. The original partners, Leonard Dunnell Gale, Alfred Vail, and that cantankerous man, most often cast as a villain in stories of the telegraph, F. O. J. "Fog" Smith, contributed money and ideas to development of the telegraph.

Two crucial contributions by scientists made Morse's telegraph work. A professor, Joseph Henry, had discovered a principle that, though made public in 1831, did not come to Morse's attention until after he had made preliminary investigations. Henry discovered that increasing the number of turns in a coil increased the power of the current. Morse's partner Gale, who brought Henry's law to Morse's attention, was responsible for persuading Morse to change his primitive battery, designed for quantity, into one of intensity. This factor, with Morse's concept of an electric relay, enabled the telegraph to be effective over great distances.

Morse continued wrapping wires around and around his NYU studio, testing and demonstrating his remarkable new device. In 1837, he applied for his first telegraph patent in the form of a caveat to protect his preliminary inventions. They included a code of dots and dashes (to become, eventually, the "Morse code"), a mechanism for sending information and another for receiving, a method of laying wire, and a code dictionary. That same year, Morse began petitioning Congress to accept and implement his system on a national basis.

Congress let the initial telegraph offer pass them by as Morse set sail for Europe to secure foreign

patent rights. Europe, though enthusiastic about the abilities of the electromagnetic telegraph, would not bless it with the official sanction of patent.

This European excursion, however, was not completely futile. Morse learned the newly discovered photographic process of Louis-Jacques-Mandé Daguerre and resorted to it as a means to gain additional funds for his research concerning the telegraph. His trained artistic eye and his direct knowledge of the process from study with Daguerre in France made him an ideal teacher. In time, the success of Morse's students, who literally kept him from the brink of starvation, earned for him the epithet "Father of Photography."

Physically, Morse showed the effects of years of struggle. He looked haggard, and his clothes were shabby with wear. In this condition Morse returned to Washington, D. C., wooing Congress with demonstrations. At last, Congress awarded him money to build a line between Baltimore and Washington in 1843. This line reported to the Capitol the results of the national presidential conventions held in Baltimore and broadcast the first formal message, "What hath God wrought?"

Once financial remuneration was forthcoming with the spread of lines across the country, Morse became the subject of suit and countersuit as others tried to claim rights of invention and expansion in this new and as yet unregulated field. Morse energetically fought off these attacks. His mind was active with thoughts of a transatlantic cable, a new wife, and a home in the country that he could share with his children. After the trials and disappointments of his earlier years, Morse lived to enjoy universal approbation and financial success. At the time of his death, on April 2, 1872, his invention was in use throughout the world.

Summary

Morse lived at the vanguard of a communications revolution. Trained as a painter, he combined knowledge of composition that would convey a message without words with the technology of Daguerre's picture-taking method to train the men who would record the Civil War through the eye of the camera. The photographic images, along with the news of the war transmitted instantly by telegraph, reported the immediate and shocking news of the war to the folks at home. This ability to unite and make useful abstract theories is a trademark of the American inventor.

Morse as a communicator, through his portraits and historical genre paintings, through working on the public relations of trying to fund experimentation, and in having the foresight and magnanimity to encourage Congress to establish this new machine under the auspices of the postal system, was always ready to serve. Even when pressed with other responsibilities, he ran for mayor of New York City, appeared at the statue erection in Central Park, and helped found the National Academy of Design. In each case, his motivation was the desire to contribute to society rather than to promote himself.

Though Morse was a nativist, he worked to make the telegraph a force for international communication, and his success in making the world much smaller was clearly demonstrated in the memorial services held upon his death: Telegrams arrived at the nation's capital from as far as Egypt and from all over the United States as well.

Bibliography

Boorstin, Daniel J. *The Americans: The Democratic Experience*. New York: Random House, 1973;

London: Cardinal, 1988. Includes an examination of the spirit and character peculiar to the American innovator-entrepreneur.

Gordon, John Steele. "Technology of the Future." *American Heritage* 44, no. 6 (October, 1993). Short piece on the telegraph and Morse's accomplishments.

Harlow, Alvin F. *Old Wires and New Waves*. New York and London: Appleton, 1936. A comprehensive look at long-distance communication via signal, from Trojan War signal fires to the American telephone.

Larkin, Oliver W. *Art and Life in America*. Rev. ed. New York: Holt Rinehart, 1960. Though not as specific as the author's *Samuel Morse and American Democratic Art*, published in 1954 in Boston by Little, Brown and Co., this text seems more readily available. Explores Morse's standing among other artists of the period. Very good on the contrasts between pursuit of the arts in the New World and the Old.

Mabee, Carleton. *The American Leonardo: A Life of Samuel F. B. Morse*. New York: Knopf, 1944. The standard Morse biography. Mabee writes a unified account of a man whose varied interests are a delight and challenge to follow.

————. *Memorial of Samuel Finley Breese Morse, Including Appropriate Ceremonies of Respect at the National Capitol and Elsewhere*. Washington, D.C.: Government Printing Office, 1875. One measure of a man's life is the mourning of his passing. The ceremonies described here were particularly modern, uniting electronically virtually the entire world in a common bond of gratitude and sorrow.

Morse, Samuel F. B. *Samuel F. B. Morse: His Letters and Journals*. 2 vols. Edited by Edward Lind Morse. Boston: Houghton Mifflin, 1914. Begins with Morse's first thoughts of telegraphic communication while aboard the packet ship *Sully*.

Staiti, Paul. *Samuel F. B. Morse*. Cambridge and New York: Cambridge University Press, 1989. A landmark study of Morse's achievements in technology and art which combines an intellectual biography, interpretation of his works, and accounts of his work on the electromagnetic telegraph.

Vail, Alfred. *The American Electro Magnetic Telegraph*. Philadelphia: Lea and Blanchard, 1845. Explains the workings of the telegraph, illustrated with fully labeled diagrams.

Ellen Clark

WILLIAM THOMAS GREEN MORTON

Born: August 9, 1819; Charlton, Massachusetts
Died: July 15, 1868; New York, New York
Areas of Achievement: Dentistry and anesthesiology
Contribution: Morton discovered anesthesia by ether inhalation. Rival claims to priority resulted in the most acrimonious debate in the history of medicine.

Early Life

William Thomas Green Morton was born to James Morton, a farmer of Scottish descent, and his wife, Rebecca Needham, a native of Charlton. A sternly religious upbringing, a wholesome and plain family life, and a boyhood filled with farm tasks formed Morton's character. His father insisted on a proper education, enrolling him in several country academies from the age of twelve. The boy wanted to become a physician, but his hopes vanished when a business venture undertaken by his father failed.

In 1836, Morton moved to Boston, making a living as a clerk and salesman for several firms. He hated the drudgery and crassness of business life, choosing a career in dentistry with the opening of the first American dental school, the Baltimore College of Dental Surgery, in 1840. One year later, he apprenticed himself to Horace Wells, a young dentist from Hartford, before establishing his own practice in Farmington, Connecticut. In 1842, he met Elizabeth Whitman, daughter of a prominent Farmington family. The Whitmans were disturbed by their daughter's interest in him, the owner of no property and a dentist, dentists then being regarded as ignorant "tooth-pullers." Determined to marry, Morton convinced them that dentistry was a temporary occupation; he intended to become a physician. The marriage took place in May of 1844; the first of the Mortons' children, William James Morton, became an important neurologist and a pioneer in the use of X rays.

Morton was a tall, dark-haired, handsome man, neat and methodical, mild and agreeable in manner. He maintained his dignity and composure through the long years of the bitter ether controversy, never attempting to retaliate against his enemies despite the relentless attacks on his character.

Life's Work

Prior to his marriage, Morton had formed a partnership in Boston with Wells in order to exploit the development of a noncorrosive dental solder for attaching false teeth to plates. Artificial teeth were hinged monstrosities set over the roots of old teeth, leaving the face swollen, the solder coloring and corroding the teeth. The two young dentists devised enameled teeth which they attached with their new solder to a hingeless plate. To fit the plate snugly in the mouth, however, required the removal of the roots of the old teeth. No one would accept their innovations unless they found a means to overcome the extremely painful extractions.

By the end of 1843, the partnership failed for lack of patients. Wells returned to Hartford, Morton remained in Boston, both intent on succeeding in dentistry. During their development of the solder, they sought the advice of an expert chemist, Charles T. Jackson, a European-trained physician, chemist, and geologist. In 1844, Morton became Jackson's private student, boarding in his house, first alone and then with his wife, hoping to prepare himself for entrance into Harvard Medical School.

During 1844-1845, his dental practice flourished, and his income enabled him to buy a farm in West Needham (modern Wellesley) near Boston. Morton became a specialist in prosthetic dentistry and prospered by his thoroughness and his skill in excavating and filling cavities.

During the summer of 1844, Morton discussed with Jackson the need to control pain. He had tried many pain remedies, but none was satisfactory. Jackson gave him a bottle of ether and urged him to try his "toothache drops" as a local painkiller for filling teeth. He also learned from Jackson that physicians used ether as an inhalant in treating respiratory ills, believing it to be a possible cure for tuberculosis and other lung diseases.

Morton used the ether drops, finding that he could remove tooth decay and fill cavities painlessly. He noticed that often the region near the tooth became numb and wondered whether ether had wider possibilities. Morton wanted to experiment with ether. What happens upon inhaling it? Was it dangerous? Might it be an effective painkiller for all aspects of dentistry, including the extraction of the stumps and roots of old teeth? He experimented with ether inhalation into 1846, using animals of all kinds, including his pet spaniel.

In August of 1846, Morton purchased a new supply of ether in Boston. His two apprentices submitted to ether inhalation but became excited rather than quieted. He sought Jackson's advice on September 30, careful not to tell him about his inhalation experiments but only about the problems he was having with different samples of ether. Jackson informed him that ether varied considerably in quality and that he must use only pure, highly rectified ether.

Events happened swiftly on September 30; obtaining the best-quality ether, Morton induced unconsciousness in himself for about seven minutes, recovering with no ill effects. That same day, a patient, Eben Frost, came to him with a painful toothache. Morton persuaded him to have his tooth extracted under ether.

During the next two weeks, he successfully etherized about one hundred patients, developing an inhaler in the form of a glass globe that had two necks to allow both ether and air to be inhaled. Suddenly, his horizons widened beyond dentistry. A young surgeon, Henry Jacob Bigelow, appeared at his office, having become aware of his ether experiments and wanting to observe some painless tooth extractions. Through Bigelow, Morton arranged a public demonstration at Massachusetts General Hospital on October 16, 1846. John Collins Warren, the preeminent surgeon in Boston and founder of Massachusetts General and of the *New England Journal of Medicine*, agreed to perform surgery on an etherized patient.

Warren removed a three-inch tumor from the neck of a young man, Gilbert Abbott, with Morton administering the inhalant. Before a large audience, the hitherto exceedingly painful operation proceeded smoothly, with no cry or struggle from Abbott, the first public demonstration that ether could prevent the pain of surgery. Anesthesia quickly became routine at Massachusetts General. (The Boston physician Oliver Wendell Holmes introduced the name "anesthesia" in November.) The very newness of the procedure caused concern, however, and the case records of etherized patients at the hospital never mentioned anesthesia; only after its general acceptance were the records altered to record that it had been used.

Prior to the surgical demonstration, Morton visited Richard M. Eddy, patent commissioner in Boston, to inquire whether his painless tooth extraction method could be patented. The visit reveals his determination to secure a monopoly; he planned to sell licenses for the use of ether and gain a royalty on the price of all inhalers. On October 21, Eddy

informed him that the process was patentable but that Jackson should be included, since he had provided essential information. Jackson knew Eddy and convinced him that he had been essential to the discovery. While Morton did not share their opinions, he agreed to an arrangement whereby Jackson received ten percent of the profits, while turning over the responsibility of the patent to Morton. He received the patent on November 12.

Morton failed to appreciate the professional opposition to his scheme of licenses and royalties. Bigelow, in a hectic meeting, told him that he should give his discovery to the world for the relief of human suffering. Morton, however, believed that he had to control his procedure to prevent its misuse, granting licenses only to qualified people, and candidly admitted that he wanted to make a living from his discovery. He did convince Bigelow of his good intentions and expressed his willingness to surrender the patent if the government would take it over and reward him for the discovery.

Problems began immediately. Morton had just received a bill for one thousand inhalers when he learned that they were inferior to a simple bell-shaped sponge saturated with ether. The Massachusetts Medical Society protested the procedure because it was for private profit and a secret remedy. (Morton had disguised the nature of the agent by adding a red dye and calling it "Letheon.") He soon saw his hopes of controlling anesthesia and gaining a financial reward dashed. As physicians realized that the readily available ether was the active agent, there was no need to buy a patented preparation.

Morton may have been disappointed by the turn of events, but surgeons were not. Surgical anesthesia spread with unprecedented speed, far more rapidly than earlier innovations as vaccination or later ones as antisepsis. Bigelow was once again the key figure in alerting physicians to the discovery. His detailed report in the *Boston Medical and Surgical Journal* was the first in a professional journal, copies of which spread the news throughout the United States and Europe. Etherization was in use in American, English, and French hospitals by the year's end. By 1848, anesthetics were in use in dentistry, obstetrics, and therapeutics, as well as in surgery.

The ugliest aspect of the ether controversy was the dispute between Morton and Jackson. In mid-November of 1846, Jackson was claiming full

credit for the discovery of anesthesia. He asserted that he had been experimenting with ether since 1841, had discovered its anesthetic properties, and had instructed Morton in how to use it in his dental practice and in how to seek a surgical demonstration. Jackson used his prestige and influence to press his case in both the popular press and professional journals and before such bodies as the American Academy of Arts and Sciences and the French Academy of Sciences.

For the remainder of his life, Morton had to face attacks on his character and ability, Jackson using Morton's faulty education and the fact that he was a mere dentist to make him out to be an unscrupulous profit-seeker and fraud. His life became exceedingly troubled. He lost his dental practice, and creditors demanded payments on loans; he was ruined financially. Supporters petitioned Congress to give adequate compensation for his discovery of anesthesia. In the 1850's, Congress introduced two bills appropriating $100,000, but active supporters of Jackson, Wells (who successfully used nitrous oxide for tooth extractions), and several other

claimants prevented any appropriation. A direct appeal by Morton to President Franklin Pierce led to a promise of a reward, but the presidential promise proved worthless. With the coming of the Civil War, the cause was lost. During that war, Morton served with distinction as an anesthetist in field hospitals.

In 1868, Morton went to New York in an agitated state over a pro-Jackson article in the *Atlantic Monthly*, determined to defend himself with a reply. While there, he suffered a fatal stroke. Following his interment, Boston citizens donated a monument bearing a moving tribute to him as the inventor of anesthetic inhalation. In 1873, Jackson visited the site; still obsessed with Morton, he began to scream and flail wildly. He had to be restrained, and he remained confined to a mental institution until his death in 1880.

Summary

Anesthesia is America's greatest contribution to nineteenth century medicine. Until 1846, all surgical operations were done without anesthesia: The patient was strapped or held down, struggling in agony over the cutting, speed being the prime requisite of a surgeon. Anesthesia freed the patient of pain, while giving the surgeon the gift of time.

The ether controversy reflected the medical profession's disarray in the 1840's: full of disputes over causes and cures with no central authority to confer legitimacy to an innovation. In addition, Morton violated four norms of the medical profession. He patented his "Letheon," patented pain cures being synonymous with quackery. He indulged in promotional advertising. He was a dentist, dentists being regarded with mistrust as mere empirics. Last, he engaged in a bitter, unprofessional quarrel over priority which tarnished both the image of anesthesia among physicians as well as whatever reputation the disputants possessed.

Despite the violation of these taboos, Morton's discovery spread with remarkable speed, because the benefits of ether were so evident. It did prevent pain. Leading surgeons saw ether as primarily benevolent and humane; it relieved human suffering, hence its rapid, general acceptance.

Bibliography

Davis, Audrey B. "The Development of Anesthesia." *American Scientist* 70 (September, October,

1982): 522-528. A superb essay by a historian of science, relating the development of anesthesia to the context of nineteenth century surgery and dentistry.

Fülöp-Miller, René. *Triumph over Pain*. Translated by Eden Paul and Cedar Paul. New York: Literary Guild of America, and London: Hamilton, 1938. A comprehensive study of the search for pain relief, focusing on the American discovery of anesthesia. Not a scholarly work, but absorbing reading.

Ludovici, L. J. *The Discovery of Anaesthesia*. New York: Crowell, 1962. A fine biography of Morton. More concerned with the personalities of the characters and why they behaved as they did than other works.

MacQuitty, Betty. *Victory over Pain: Morton's Discovery of Anaesthesia*. New York: Taplinger, 1971. A clear, dramatic story of Morton and his career set against life in pre-Civil War America.

Well written, with an emphasis on Morton's struggle to secure recognition.

Pernick, Martin S. *A Calculus of Suffering: Pain, Professionalism, and Anesthesia in Nineteenth-Century America*. New York: Columbia University Press, 1985. A brilliant book. Pernick goes beyond a history of surgical anesthesia to consider how the medical profession confronted the discovery and the implications of anesthesia for society. Social history at its finest.

Woodward, Grace Steele. *The Man Who Conquered Pain: A Biography of William Thomas Green Morton*. Boston: Beacon Press, 1962. The most vivid, elegantly written biography of Morton. Woodward's study was based on hitherto unavailable letters and other unpublished material of the Morton family. Very good at describing the medical atmosphere of early nineteenth century Boston.

Albert B. Costa

LUCRETIA MOTT

Born: January 3, 1793; Nantucket, Massachusetts
Died: November 11, 1880; near Philadelphia, Pennsylvania
Areas of Achievement: Social reform and women's rights
Contribution: An eloquent advocate of the abolition of slavery and of equality for women, Mott devoted her life to working toward these goals.

Early Life

Lucretia Coffin was the daughter of the master of a whaling vessel. Her parents, Thomas and Anna Folger Coffin, were hard-working Quakers. Although public education was not available, Lucretia learned to read and write as a young child, probably attending Quaker schools. In 1804, Thomas Coffin, who had lost his ship, moved the family to Boston, where he became a successful merchant. Here the children could be educated, and when Lucretia showed particular talent, she was sent to Nine Partners Boarding School, a Quaker academy in Southeast New York. She became an academic success, met James Mott—her future husband—and got a lesson in discrimination when she discovered that James was paid five times as much as a woman with the same title at the school.

In 1809, the Coffin family moved to Philadelphia, and James Mott followed, taking a job in the family business. In 1811, James and Lucretia were married. They experienced several years of hard times because of the depression that followed the War of 1812, but eventually they settled in Philadelphia, where James established a successful business. Lucretia, despite having two small children, took a job teaching. Four more children followed, but Mott's son Thomas died in 1817. As the children began to spend time at school and her husband prospered, Mott had time to read many books, including Mary Wollstonecraft's *Vindication of the Rights of Women* (1792), which had a strong influence on her. Mott began to speak in Quaker meetings and in the early 1820's was approved as a Quaker minister.

Life's Work

For Lucretia Mott, faith was always important, and it led her to desire justice for all, including slaves and women. Although she always wanted to avoid controversy, when issues she cared about arose, she was often very outspoken. In the early 1830's,

she befriended William Lloyd Garrison, a leading abolitionist who founded the New England Anti-Slavery Society. When women's groups were called for, Mott helped found the Philadelphia Female Anti-Slavery Society and held some office for virtually every year of its existence. Mott was soon a leader in the Anti-Slavery Convention of American Women, and when its 1838 meeting was met by riots and arson in its meeting hall, it was the Mott home at which convention leaders reconvened.

Mott soon found equality an issue within the abolitionist movement. In 1838, the Massachusetts branch of the Anti-Slavery Society gave women the right to vote. A decision on the issue was blocked at a regional meeting, and a debate began at the 1839 national convention. After the five sessions adjourned without a decision, Garrison managed to get agreement that the organization's roll would include all persons, but a number of leading abolitionists were opposed, maintaining that the organization was being diverted from the issue of slavery. In 1840, the British and Foreign Anti-Slavery Society issued invitations for a world convention, and Mott was elected as one of the American delegates. The British group had indicated that women were not wanted, and Mott arrived to find that the credentials of female delegates were not being honored. Despite an angry debate, the decision stood, and Mott had to sit in the visitors' gallery, where she was joined by Garrison and the other American delegates. Mott did not speak at the convention, preferring to defer to proper authority even when it was mistaken.

After the convention Mott traveled in Britain—it was her one trip abroad—and visited such luminaries as Harriet Martineau. In Scotland, it was suggested that she address the Glasgow Emancipation Society, but the directors demurred. The city's Unitarian church, however, welcomed her, and she gave her address there. During this trip, she also began a friendship with Elizabeth Cady Stanton, with whom she would fight discrimination against women. The two were close until Mott's death in 1880.

Mott's attitude about slavery was quite clear: It was unmitigated evil and should be ended forthwith. She rejected any idea of compensation for slave owners as adding to the immorality, and urged abolitionist groups to stop debating the ethical and philosophical implications of the institution—for her, these were settled anyway—and stick to the practical question of ending it. She argued for "free produce"—that is, refusing to conduct any trade in goods produced by slaves—but Northern economic interests in Southern goods and commerce were too large for such a boycott to win many friends even among abolitionists. In theory, she rejected colonization and even flight as solutions to slavery because the numbers who escaped did not even equal the natural increase of the enslaved population. In practice, however, she supported the Underground Railroad, freely opening her home to fugitives. She was an active supporter of many escapees, including Henry "Box" Brown, who had himself nailed into a packing box and shipped to her friend Miller McKim.

In the early years of the 1840's, Mott was often ill. Her husband, however, had become prosperous enough to give up his business so that the family could pursue other interests. The Mott home was known for its hospitality to its many guests, including Garrison, Theodore Parker, Frederick Douglass, and Sojourner Truth. As her health allowed, Mott continued her preaching, mostly at Quaker and Unitarian meetings. Having rejected orthodox Quaker theology in 1827, she faced charges of heresy as well as denunciations for daring, as a woman, to speak in church. Never ruffled, she spoke to hostile audiences—including slave owners—forthrightly and firmly.

Although she never gave up her work toward abolition, in the later 1840's Mott became more and more involved in the crusade for women's rights. In 1845, she made her first public call for woman suffrage in a speech to the Yearly Meeting of Ohio Quakers. Three years later, in an address to the American Anti-Slavery Society entitled "The Law of Progress," she lamented the lack of improvement in the condition of women. It was after this speech that Mott fell in with a suggestion by Elizabeth Cady Stanton that there should be a women's rights convention.

The future stars of the women's movement, Stanton and Susan B. Anthony, were virtually unknown, so the much better known Mott emerged as the person in the public eye at the first Women's Rights Convention, which met at Seneca Falls, New York, July 19 to 20, 1848. Mott and others drew up a Declaration of Sentiments modeled on the Declaration of Independence, but the women were so unsure of themselves that they asked

James Mott to preside at their meeting. The convention then debated the Declaration paragraph by paragraph, ultimately passing them all unanimously. Mott had been somewhat reluctant to press the issue of suffrage, but, urged on by Stanton and Frederick Douglass, she agreed to it. In the end, she was the most frequent speaker at Seneca Falls. At a follow-up meeting two weeks later in Rochester, New York, she responded to critics who asserted that the women were ignoring St. Paul's injunction that they be subservient to their husbands by noting that most of the complainers had ignored the saint's advice not to marry. The 1853 convention met in Philadelphia only to be so disrupted by hostile demonstrations that Mott, the presiding officer, was forced to adjourn it. An invitation to move to Cleveland was accepted, and despite some tension, the meeting was completed without interruption.

Although she was beginning to experience some physical decline in the 1850's, Mott made many efforts on behalf of the abolitionist and women's rights crusades. In 1849, she agreed to make a speech to counter the traditional misogynist position taken by Richard Henry Dana during a lecture series in Philadelphia. Her "Discourse on Women," tracing the history of women's achievements and reiterating her position that female inferiority was a function of systematic repression and denial of opportunity, was printed. A second edition appeared in 1869 in response to requests from feminists in England. In the early 1850's, she confronted Horace Mann and the new National Education Association on the issue of equal pay for women teachers, though without much immediate success. She also continued to speak for the abolitionist cause, traveling as far south as Maysville, Kentucky, where, despite some significant hostility, she presented her case for freedom. Although she took no public position on John Brown's raid on Harpers Ferry—Quaker principles of pacifism overrode even the urgency of freeing slaves—she did shelter Mrs. Brown while she was trying to visit her husband in the weeks before his execution.

In 1857, the Mott family moved to Roadside, a comfortable estate between New York and Philadelphia. The move was intended in part to get Lucretia away from the stress of her numerous commitments. Although her health was somewhat restored by rest, she was sixty-four years old and beginning increasingly to feel her age. A pacifist, she was torn by the Civil War, but after the conflict she tried to preserve the antislavery society to support the freedmen. She was also active in the Free Religious Association, which had been formed in 1867 to encourage an end to sectarian strife. She also continued her activities with the Equal Rights Convention.

When that organization began to split in the 1870's, Mott tried vainly to heal the breach. The feminists divided into the National Woman Suffrage Association, led by Elizabeth Cady Stanton and Susan B. Anthony, and the American Woman Suffrage Association, headed by Lucy Stone and Julia Ward Howe. Mott remained with her longtime friends Stanton and Anthony but deeply regretted the split. Mott's activities decreased steadily throughout the late 1860's and 1870's. She died on November 11, 1880, at Roadside.

Summary

Lucretia Mott was an unusual woman. In an age when most people objected to women ministers, she was an eloquent advocate for her faith. Not only did she speak effectively within Quaker meetings, but she also had the confidence to challenge the leadership on points of theology. Her preaching and erudition won the respect of many, although no woman in the first half of the nineteenth century could have achieved full acceptance in the pulpit. Believing that she was in the right, she was unruffled by criticism and continued to speak as she deemed appropriate.

Mott was less unusual in the ranks of the abolitionists, which included many women, white and black. Nevertheless, her dignified mien and public speaking ability gave her a leadership role. The strength of her conviction led her to take risks, speaking out in the 1830's when the antislavery position was far from popular and going into hostile areas—even the South. She fought diligently for her view that the antislavery forces should insist on total abolition immediately and should use the economic weapon of refusing to trade in products produced by slave labor. Although she was unsuccessful in winning support for the latter position, she provided the abolitionist movement with one of its best examples of idealism and principle.

Faced with serious sexual discrimination within the ranks of the abolitionists, Mott emerged as a champion of women's rights. At a time when most of the eventual champions of the feminist movement were young and unknown, Mott was a respected and respectable leader. If Elizabeth Cady Stanton and Susan B. Anthony, in 1848, could be dismissed as part of a radical fringe, Lucretia Mott could not. As a minister whose knowledge and conviction were well established and as a mainstay of the abolitionist movement, she gave the fledgling women's movement a credibility that would have taken much time and effort to gain without her leadership. She did not live to see the triumph of equal rights for women, but she did much to give the movement the impetus necessary to obtain them.

Bibliography

Bernikow, Louise. "What Really Happened at Seneca Falls." *Ms.* 9, no. 1 (July-August, 1998). Focuses on the women's rights convention of 1848 in Seneca Falls, N.Y., including information on Mott and Elizabeth Cady Stanton.

Burnett, Constance. *Five for Freedom: Lucretia Mott, Elizabeth Cady Stanton, Lucy Stone, Susan B. Anthony, Carrie Chapman Catt.* New York: Abelard Press, 1953. This is an effective and well-written biography that gives a thorough account of Mott's life and career.

Carlson, A. Cheree. "Defining Womanhood: Lucretia Coffin Mott and the Transformation of Femininity." *Western Journal of Communications* 58, no. 2 (Spring 1994). Focuses on Mott's use of "bridging devices" as a means of surmounting divisions in a social order. In her "Discourse on Woman," Mott employs the Quaker idea of "inner light" to lessen the conflict between a conservative society and her liberal goals. Carlson suggests Mott's approach is useful today for feminists wishing to unite women of varying cultural backgrounds.

Cromwell, Otelia. *Lucretia Mott.* Cambridge, Mass.: Harvard University Press, 1958. A scholarly, well-researched biography that sets Mott's life and activities in the context of nineteenth century America, this work is somewhat lacking in critical analysis of the subject.

Hallowell, Anna. *James and Lucretia Mott: Life and Letters.* 5th ed. Boston: Houghton Mifflin, 1896. An early biography made particularly valuable by the inclusion of correspondence. Oversupportive of the Motts.

Mott, Lucretia. *Lucretia Mott: Her Complete Speeches and Sermons.* Edited by Dana Greene. New York: Mellen Press, 1980. A convenient source of much of Mott's writing that provides an excellent means of gaining an understanding of her philosophy and ideas.

Stewart, James B. *Holy Warriors: The Abolitionists and American Slavery.* Rev. ed. New York: Hill and Wang, 1996. A useful survey of abolitionism that is extremely valuable in setting Mott's work and views in the context of the movement as a whole.

Fred R. van Hartesveldt

MUHAMMAD 'ALĪ PASHA

Born: 1769; Kavala, Macedonia

Died: August 2, 1849; Alexandria, Egypt

Areas of Achievement: The military and government

Contribution: By applying strong-arm techniques so as to assure central-government control, Muhammad transformed Egypt from its eighteenth century status as an ungovernable and unproductive province of the Ottoman Empire into a largely autonomous state supported by an impressive military apparatus. That was done by combining Ottoman "new order" reform priorities with European technical contributions, especially in the areas of military and agricultural modernization.

Early Life

Although Muhammad 'Alī Pasha's family originated in Albania, it was in the Ottoman Turkish province of Macedonia (in modern Greece) that the first biographical information concerning him was recorded. His father's position as a ranking Ottoman bureaucrat serving the sultanate of Selim III (who ruled between 1789 and 1808) was very significant for the future career of Muhammad. One of Selim's main goals was to use loyal servants of the state to create, in the place of the by then severely inefficient Janissary corps and imperial administrative system, an army and government of "the new order" (*nizam-ul Cedid*). Without actually being members of the new order elite military unit which Selim had consciously copied from contemporary European models, both his father and the young Muhammad were heavily influenced by the visible efficiency of new order Ottoman institutions.

When the sultan needed a capable lieutenant to accompany a force of irregular Albanian troops sent to reoccupy the Ottoman province of Egypt (after the retreat of Napoleon I's famous 1798-1802 expeditionary force on the Nile), he chose Muhammad. The future governor of Egypt entered history in early adulthood, not as an Albanian and certainly not as an Egyptian, but as a loyal Ottoman military officer.

Life's Work

Muhammad's rise to power as an Ottoman governor and then a virtually independent ruler of Egypt between 1805 and 1848 was tied to his ability to centralize (in typical Ottoman new order fashion) governmental control over military, bureaucratic, and economic functions. He began this process in Egypt by befriending rival local groups and playing each against the others. Then he gradually and systematically reduced each of his temporary allies to dependence on his sole will. In stages, for example, the army under the new governor's command ceased to be Albanian and was replaced by trainees under new order officer candidates selected by Muhammad. Some of those selected to take the place of Albanian irregulars and residual (pre-1798) *mamluk* (foreign slave elite) military grandees were already Ottoman professionals. Others were retrained *mamluks*. Any elements likely to resist Muhammad's restructuring of the province's military forces were eliminated either by being reassigned (the case of Albanians sent to combat Wahhabi tribes in Arabia after 1811) or by being mercilessly killed (the fate of many *mamluk* beys in 1811).

Once he was in firm political and military control over Cairo's governorate, Muhammad proceeded to introduce a series of major internal reforms which would help strengthen his position. First, Egypt's old *mamluk*-dominated tax farm system (*iltizamat*) was replaced by a single tax (*ferda*) collected by direct salaried agents of the governor. Proceeds from taxes were used not only to expand and train the new military establishment (by bringing more professionals, including, after 1815, retired Napoleonic officers) but also to invest in publicly sponsored agricultural innovations. These included new irrigation canals engineered to increase productivity during the low Nile season and the introduction of new internationally marketable crops. The latter, especially silk and cotton, were brought under cultivation according to strictly controlled governmental terms.

By the early 1820's, the effectiveness of Muhammad's authority as Governor of Egypt was so obvious that his sultanic sovereign, Mahmud II, called on him (in 1826-1827) to send troops to help subdue Greek insurrectionists. Had this expedition been successful, Muhammad might well have been named to the high imperial post of Ottoman grand vizier. Instead, the Concert of Europe powers, worried about Ottoman repression of the Greek independence movement but also very seriously concerned about Muhammad's dominant, monopolistic control over the conditions of cash-

crop trade (especially cotton) in Egyptian ports, intervened militarily at Navarino in 1827 and forcibly removed him from the Ottoman theater. Sultan Mahmud was thus robbed of the possibility of having a grand vizier and military commander capable of reversing Istanbul's obvious decline.

The result was that Muhammad redoubled his determination to make Egypt strong. State monopolistic controls over agricultural production methods and marketing were increased (in a specifically agricultural-labor code, or *ganun al filahah*, in 1829), and the army was expanded to include, for the first time, large numbers of Egyptian peasant recruits. In 1831, this army, under the command of Muhammad's son Ibrahim, seized control of Mahmud's Syrian province, including the key Levant trade subzones of Lebanon and Palestine. Egypt's governor then extended to Syria the same ironhanded controls over taxes, agricultural production, and trade that applied in Egypt, creating a sort of mini-empire, this time at Mahmud's expense.

For eight years, Muhammad and Ibrahim reigned supreme over this expanded Arab state of Egypt, Greater Syria, and the Red Sea coast province of Arabia. By 1839, it was clear that the European powers that had intervened at Navarino in 1827 were determined that an even greater show of force against Muhammad might be necessary. When the Battle of Nezib occurred in June, 1839, the Ottomans were so roundly defeated that Mahmud's successor Abulmecid might very well have been removed by Muhammad. That would have made it possible to put the revolutionary reform methods of the latter in place throughout the Ottoman Empire. To avoid this, the London Convention of 1840 produced an international ultimatum to Muhammad: either withdraw to a hereditarily guaranteed Egyptian governorate and abandon commercial monopolies over the Levant zone as a whole or confront a joint European force.

Muhammad's decision to save his Egyptian governorate (which eventually became the hereditary possession of his family, a situation that ended only with the overthrow of King Faruk in 1952) saved him from a nearly certain military disaster in 1840. The terms which the Ottoman sultan imposed on Cairo during the last eight years of his rule, however, made it clear that the new order principles that had built Muhammad's power would not survive long. Egypt's cotton monopoly was dismantled and its army cut back to a mere eighteen thousand men. By the time of his death in 1849, Muhammad had begun to rely on practices of ruling patronage (private land grants for privileged political supporters and members of the ruling family, decentralization of taxation with benefits for privileged elements, and the like) that would characterize Egypt's decline and eventual chaotic drift toward foreign colonial domination in the third quarter of the nineteenth century.

Summary

Muhammad 'Alī Pasha's governorate in Egypt represented a successful application of Ottoman imperial new order reform priorities to a single regional province. Once the old forms of inefficient military and fiscal organization were removed and restored state authority became unchallenged, the productive potential of Egypt became very promising. Because of what proved to be possible in Egypt under the right conditions, future prospects for the eastern Mediterranean basin as a whole took on new importance. From a position of relative unimportance until 1798, Egypt emerged in the brief span of twenty years, between 1820 and 1840, to occupy a key position of international strategic importance that it would hold throughout the nineteenth and into the twentieth century.

Muhammad's strongly autocratic reforms may have been necessary to assure the maintenance of order and expanded productivity in the local context of the Egyptian province. When they were expanded beyond this local context, however, it became apparent that parties who were accustomed to the Ottoman status quo prior to 1798, especially where open trade in Levantine agricultural and transit trade products were concerned, were not keen to see other areas of the empire fall under Muhammad's control. The effects of his expanded governorate over Syria and Lebanon proved to be very controversial, both for the interests of internal social and economic subgroups (especially the Maronite Christians) and, ultimately, for the foreign powers who drafted the 1840 London Convention on the "Egyptian crisis." Once the latter decided to intervene to reverse Muhammad's gains, a pattern was set for the future intermingling of foreign imperial priorities and vested (if not to say reactionary) local interest groups leery of centrally imposed government reform priorities.

Bibliography

Abdel-Rahim Mustafa, Ahmed. "The Breakdown of the Monopoly System in Egypt After 1840."

In *Political and Social Change in Modern Egypt*, edited by Peter M. Holt. London and New York: Oxford University Press, 1968. Deals specifically with the internal and international consequences of the Concert of Europe's decision, in 1840, to force free-market conditions on Muhammad's governorate. Particularly useful for its discussion of the terms of the Anglo-Ottoman Commercial Treaty of 1838, which became after 1840 the basis for European dealings, not only in cotton but also in other agricultural products which Muhammad's monopoly system had defined as the basis of a nationalistic (or protectionist) economy for the Egyptian province as early as the 1820's.

Baer, Gabriel. *A History of Landownership in Modern Egypt, 1800-1950*. London and New York: Oxford University Press, 1962. Baer's study contains perhaps the best-documented examination of the pre-Muhammad decentralized tax farm (*iltizam*) system and its linkages with land ownership and patterns of cultivation. The chapter on Muhammad's reforms examines his success not only in boosting administrative efficiency by replacing the *iltizams* but also in the effect such changes had on agricultural productivity.

Fahmy, Khaled. *All the Pasha's Men: Mehmed Ali, His Army and the Making of Modern Egypt*. Cambridge and New York: Cambridge University Press, 1997. The author challenges traditional views and argues that Muhammad fortified the Egyptian army to support his own desires rather than the effort to gain independence for Egypt.

Gammer, Moshe. "The Imam and the Pasha: A Note on Shamil and Muhammad Ali." *Middle Eastern Studies* 32, no. 4 (October, 1996). Examines the alliance between Muhammad and Shamil, Imam against Russian forces which garnered fame for both men.

Holt, Peter M. *Egypt and the Fertile Crescent, 1516-1922*. Ithaca, N.Y.: Cornell University Press, and London: Longman, 1966. Deals with the general history of Egypt and its relations with surrounding Ottoman provinces. Contains a chapter on Muhammad's governorate in part 3: "The Last Phase of Ottoman Rule." Because both Syria and Lebanon are part of Holt's general history, this book makes it possible to place the phenomenon of the Egyptian occupation of 1831-1841 in a comparative historical context.

Hunter, F. Robert. *Egypt Under the Khedives, 1805-1879*. Pittsburgh: University of Pittsburgh Press, 1984. Part 1 of this book is devoted to a concentrated analysis of Muhammad's reign, which the author characterizes as "the emergence of the new power state." In addition to its concise synopsis of Muhammad's governorate, this work contains the most comprehensive coverage, in one book, of the reigns of his immediate successors, Abbās the Great, Sa'īd Pasha, and Ismā'īl Pasha. The study of these successors is important in order to gauge the long-term effects, both positive and negative, of what Muhammad had accomplished, both in the area of political institutions and in their supporting social and economic structures.

Sayyid-Marsot, Afaf Lutfi. *Egypt in the Reign of Muhammad Ali*. Cambridge and New York: Cambridge University Press, 1984. Deals not only with the close circles of elites, both Egyptian and foreign, who had a hand in the construction of Muhammad's state system but also with the measurable effects of the changes which he introduced. Very valuable, for example, for its investigation of the industrial and commercial sectors of Egypt's economy under Muhammad, which complemented developmental efforts in agriculture.

Byron D. Cannon

JOHN MUIR

Born: April 21, 1838; Dunbar, Scotland
Died: December 24, 1914; Los Angeles, California
Areas of Achievement: Exploration and conservation
Contribution: Combining his skills as a scientist, explorer, and writer, Muir played a significant role in the conservation movement and in the development of the United States National Park system.

Early Life

John Muir was born April 21, 1838, in Dunbar, Scotland. His mother, Ann Gilrye Muir, would give birth to three sons and five daughters, John being the eldest son and the third child. She married Daniel Muir, who as a child grew up under the harshest poverty imaginable. He eventually gained stature as a middle-class grain merchant and became a Presbyterian of severe Fundamentalist religious beliefs. He worshiped a God of wrath who found evil in almost every childish activity. Typically, John and his playmates would leave the yard, and his tyrannical father would fly into a rage and punish the innocent lad. When his father did not have the total devotion of his entire family, he would punish them with the greatest severity.

In 1849, at age eleven, John and his family immigrated to the United States in search of greater economic opportunity. The Muirs moved to Portage, Wisconsin, an area that had a fine reputation for wheat growing, where they purchased farmland. John marveled at the beauty of the countryside. He kept busy with farm chores and read at night when he was thought to be asleep. He also developed an early love of machinery and began the practice of waking at one in the morning to go to his cellar workshop to build things out of scraps of wood and iron. His father considered his inventions a waste of time, but John built a sawmill, weather instruments, waterwheels, and clocks. In 1860, at age twenty-two, he displayed his inventions at the state fair in Madison. His gadgets were well received, but his dour father only lectured him on the sin of vanity.

At this juncture in his life, John decided to leave home to make his own way. First, he moved to nearby Madison and attended the University of Wisconsin. He followed no particular course of study; he took classes that interested him. He seemed more concerned with learning than with earning a degree. Muir excelled in the sciences and also enjoyed the outdoor laboratory of nature. A tall, disheveled, bearded man with penetrating, glacial-blue eyes, Muir eventually grew tired of the regimentation of college. He liked books, but he loved experience more. Some men from the university were leaving to fight in the Civil War. Muir was twenty-five years old and in his junior year of school, but he decided to leave also.

From Madison, he journeyed into Canada to take odd jobs and to study the botany of the area. Later, he turned up in Indianapolis, Indiana, working in a carriage shop. With his inventive mind, he proved a success in the factory environment until one day he suffered an eye injury while working on a machine. The puncture wound effected both eyes, and soon he lost his eyesight. After a month of convalescence in a darkened room, his vision slowly returned. With a new lease on life and his eyesight fully restored, Muir decided to abandon the factory world and enjoy nature.

Life's Work

In September of 1867, Muir began a walking tour that would take him from Louisville, Kentucky, to the Gulf Coast of Florida. He found the wildlife and plants of the South fascinating. His travels took him through Kentucky, Tennessee, Georgia, and Florida, until he reached the Gulf at Cedar Key. He had no particular route planned, other than to head south. He was not disappointed in what he found on his four-month trek and decided to continue his journey. He had often read the exciting travel accounts of Alexander von Humboldt, who had explored widely in South America. That was Muir's dream also, but it was interrupted by a three-month bout with malaria. When he was almost recovered, he set off for Cuba, but, upon reaching that tropical island and after waiting for a southbound ship for a month, he settled on a new destination.

Muir believed that California offered the best climate for his malarial disorder and also afforded an environment of substantial botanical interest. He made the long journey to the West and settled in beautiful Yosemite Valley, which was snuggled in the Sierra Nevada. At times, he worked as a sheepherder and at a lumber mill, but he spent most of the time exploring the beautiful countryside, taking notes of his findings, and looking for one more glorious site of the wondrous Sierra. In 1869, Muir and a friend built a one-room cabin of pine logs near Yosemite Falls, and this became his home. He had famous visitors such as Asa Gray, the Harvard botanist, the novelist Therese Yelverton, and the renowned Transcendentalist, Ralph Waldo Emerson. With all, he shared the exhilarating scenes of the high country.

After four years in Yosemite Valley, Muir moved to San Francisco and dreamed of other trips. He traveled up the coast to Oregon and Washington and climbed Mount Shasta and Mount Rainier. He also made six excursions to Alaska, where he climbed mountains and studied glaciers. His favorite area was Glacier Bay in southern Alaska, but he loved any place where he could find a mountain to climb. During his stay in Alaska, he also studied the customs of the Tlingit Indians.

Muir also found time for romance. A friend introduced him to Louisa Strentzel, daughter of horticulturalist Dr. John Strentzel and owner of a large fruit ranch east of San Francisco, near the town of Martinez. Louisa and John were married on April 14, 1880. At the same time, he became the overseer of the Strentzel ranch and introduced changes that brought production to peak efficiency. Muir grafted one hundred varieties of pears and grapes onto the best strains. His effective management of the ranch provided him with economic security. For the next ten years, he neglected his writing and mountain climbing, but he and his wife grew reasonably prosperous and reared their two daughters, Wanda and Helen.

Nine years after his marriage, Muir took an important trip back to Yosemite. With him was Robert Underwood Johnson, an old friend and editor of the influential *The Century.* The two were dumbfounded by the changes that had taken place in the Sierra during such a short time. Sheep and lumberjacks had created great devastation in the valley and high country. Forest land was bare and grass root structures were severely damaged by the sharp hoofs of the sheep. Johnson was moved to action. He promised to lobby influential congressmen, and he encouraged Muir to convince the American public of their conservationist cause and the need to take action before it was too late. Muir accepted the challenge and, in two well-argued articles published in *The Century,* he convinced many readers of the desperate need to preserve some of the natural wonders of the California highlands.

In 1890, the federal government rewarded the efforts of Muir, Johnson, and other conservationists by creating Yosemite National Park. Other victories followed when Congress established Mount Rainier, the Grand Canyon, the Petrified Forest, and parts of the Sierra as national preserves. The following year, Muir worked for the passage of legislation that eventually allowed President Benjamin Harrison to set aside thirteen million acres of forest land and President Grover Cleveland, twenty-one million acres more. Muir continued the conservationist cause by helping to create the Sierra Club in 1892. He became the club's first president, and the members vowed to preserve the natural features of the California mountains.

With the total support of his wife, Muir decided to abandon the ranch work and concentrate on furthering his writing career. In 1894, he published *The Mountains of California* and followed it with *Our National Parks* (1901), *Stickeen* (1909), *My First Summer in the Sierra* (1911), *The Yosemite* (1912), and *The Story of My Boyhood and Youth* (1913). In these works, he richly illustrated the growth of a conservationist mind and presented forceful arguments for preservation and ecological protection.

In his last years, Muir traveled to Europe, South America, and Africa, always learning and experiencing what he could. Seventy-six years of life and accomplishment came to an end in December of 1914, when Muir died in Los Angeles on Christmas Eve.

Summary

For John Muir, it had been a full life. Forced to make a decision at an early age between machines and inventions on the one hand and nature and conservation on the other, he chose the path of mountains, flowers, and preservation. In nature, he found his cathedral, and there he preached the gospel of conservation, preservation, and ecology. He walked the wilderness paths with Ralph Waldo Emerson and Theodore Roosevelt; in the end, he convinced many of his contemporaries of the rightness of his ideas.

He lived at a time when the United States was becoming a great industrial leader in the world. Still, he was able to point to the wisdom of preserving many natural wonders of the American West. While an earlier generation had plundered the East, his efforts and those of others helped to save significant portions of the West, to create large national parks and forest preserves, and to protect the ecological systems so necessary for the survival of nature.

Bibliography

Badè, William Frederic. *The Life and Letters of John Muir.* 2 vols. New York: Houghton Mifflin, 1924. The best collection of Muir's letters.

Cohen, Michael. *The Pathless Way: John Muir and the American Wilderness.* Madison: University of Wisconsin Press, 1984. Although there is much biographical information in this book, it is mostly an intellectual history of Muir and his ideas as he expressed them in his writings.

Fox, Stephen R. *John Muir and His Legacy: The American Conservation Movement.* Boston: Little Brown, 1981. This is a biography of Muir, a chronological history of the conservation movement from 1890 to 1975, and an analysis of what conservation means in historical terms.

Melham, Tom. *John Muir's Wild America.* Washington, D.C.: National Geographic Society, 1976. A good place to begin the study of Muir. Beautiful illustrations and sound background history.

Nash, Roderick. *Wilderness and the American Mind.* 3d ed. New Haven, Conn.: Yale University Press, 1982. This work traces the idea of wilderness from an early view as a moral and physical wasteland to its present acceptance as a place to preserve. John Muir emerges as one of many significant figures in this intellectual transformation.

Smith, Herbert F. *John Muir.* New York: Twayne, 1965. Approaches Muir through his writings as literary works and places him in the context of Transcendentalist literature.

Smith, Michael B. "The Value of a Tree: Public Debates of John Muir and Gifford Pinchot." *The Historian* 60, no. 4 (Summer 1998). Discusses the conflict between Muir and Pinchot with respect to use and misuse of natural resources. Muir helped develop the U.S. National Park system while Pinchot paved the way for logging on public lands.

Turner, Frederick. *Rediscovering America: John Muir in His Time and Ours.* New York: Viking Press, 1985. A good, sound coverage of Muir's life in the context of his times and the development of the United States.

Wilkins, Thurman. *John Muir: Apostle of Nature.* Norman: University of Oklahoma Press, 1995. Profile of Muir, his efforts in the area of conservation, and the influence he still has with the public through the Sierra Club.

Wolfe, Linnie Marsh. *Son of the Wilderness: The Life of John Muir.* New York: Knopf, 1945. A well-written biography based on solid research that shows the many-faceted dimensions of Muir's personality.

John W. Bailey

MODEST MUSSORGSKY

Born: March 21, 1839; Karevo, Pskov, Russia
Died: March 28, 1881; St. Petersburg, Russia
Area of Achievement: Music
Contribution: Mussorgsky, a major figure in the Russian national school, was the most original composer among the so-called Mighty Five. He excelled in creating dramatic works and songs in which natural speech inflections determined the vocal line, thus creating a striking realism, or naturalism.

Early Life

Modest Petrovitch Mussorgsky was descended from wealthy landowners. Modest's father, Peter, and his mother, Julia Chirikova, had four sons. The first two died in infancy; the third, Filaret, survived the youngest, Modest, by some twenty years. Much of what is known about the composer's early years is drawn from some drafts (one in Russian, two in poor French) which he wrote himself and from the scattered recollections of his brother. Mussorgsky's familiarity with Russian folklore is attributed to the family nurse, while his skill at the piano is credited to the lessons he took from his mother and, during the period 1849-1854, from Anton Herke in St. Petersburg. Mussorgsky, according to his own account, was able to play some small pieces by Franz Liszt by age seven and a concerto by John Field at age eleven.

In August, 1849, Modest and Filaret were taken by their father to St. Petersburg. There, Modest entered a preparatory school while studying with Herke; in 1852, he followed Filaret to the School for Cadets of the Guard. In this environment, the embryonic military man was exposed to a life of drinking, gambling, dancing, and debaucherie. Although serious study was not a highly prized virtue at the institution, Mussorgsky seems to have taken an interest in history and German philosophy. His musical inclinations resulted in the dedication of a piano piece, *Porte-Enseigne Polka*, to his fellow students; it was published at the expense of his proud father, who died in 1853. Mussorgsky participated in the school choir and made a cursory study of old Russian church music, including some of the works of Dmitri Bortnyanski, though he did little composition.

In 1857, however, a year after leaving the cadet school, he met Aleksandr Dargomyzhski and César Cui; through them, he became acquainted with Sta-sov and Mili Balakirev. At musical gatherings of these men and other artists, Mussorgsky was exposed to the music of such luminaries as Hector Berlioz, Franz Liszt, Robert Schumann, and Mikhail Ivanovich Glinka, much of it performed on the piano. He then sought Balakirev as a teacher of composition. Shortly thereafter, he resigned his commission. Under Balakirev's guidance, the youthful creator produced various early pieces, some of which were later lost.

Nervous disorders, at least in part attributed to excessive drinking, appeared as early as 1858. A visit to the estate of family friends near Moscow in 1859 for a rest resulted in a turn from a cosmopolitan outlook to a Russian orientation. On January 23, 1860, Anton Rubinstein conducted the orchestral version of Scherzo in B-flat Major, thus marking Mussorgsky's public debut as a composer. Another nervous crisis ensued, but after spending the summer at the estate of friends, the composer pronounced himself cured of the "mysticism" with which he had been afflicted.

Life's Work

In 1861, an imperial decree declared the emancipation of the serfs, and Mussorgsky was immediately enmeshed in family difficulties associated with the change in the social order. Over the next two years, he was obliged to spend considerable time aiding his brother in managing the family estate. Mussorgsky, however, was not musically inactive during this period. The *Intermezzo in modo classico* (1860-1861) for piano and such songs as "Tsar Saul" (1863) manifest a musical maturity. The opera *Judith* by composer-critic Aleksandr Serov, performed on May 28, 1863, and a reading of Gustave Flaubert's *Salammbô* (1862) that autumn, impelled the composer to to write a libretto based on *Salammbô*. Mussorgsky's mélange of verse, with liberal borrowings from Russian poets and from Heinrich Heine, took its stage directions from Flaubert's work. The accompanying music, which occupied his attention until 1866, contains borrowings from his earlier piece *Oedipus in Athens*, and some portions of *Boris Godunov* are prefigured.

In December of 1863, as a consequence of a major downturn in his financial status, Mussorgsky took a position as collegiate secretary in the engineering department of the Ministry of Communications, and, on February 1, 1864, he was elevated to the post of assistant head clerk in the barracks section of the same department. In December, 1866, Mussorgsky was made titular councilor, but, on May 10, 1867, he was fired. In late 1863, the composer joined a commune with five other young men, lived together with them in a flat, and engaged in discussions on life and art. The group was strongly influenced by the novel *Chto delat'?* (1863; *What Is to Be Done?*, c. 1863), by Nikolai Chernyshevski, written during the author's imprisonment in the fortress of St. Petersburg. The burning issue with which Mussorgsky wrestled from this point onward was the subordination of art to life, as proposed by Chernyshevski. Musical works which exemplify this turn in his creative thinking are the two-piece *From Memories of Childhood* and *Rêverie* (both compositions dating from 1865). That year was, indeed, a pivotal one. Following his mother's death, Mussorgsky's alcoholism became so serious that a case of delirium tremens caused the severing of his ties with communal life. His recovery at his brother's flat allowed him to resume work, but the seeds of destruction were sown.

Salammbô was abandoned, probably because Mussorgsky had come to grips with his technical deficiencies and his lack of empathy, at the time, for the Eastern coloration the work demanded; however, in January, 1867, *The Destruction of Sennacherib* for chorus and orchestra was completed, and, late in 1866, such songs as "Darling Savishna," "You Drunken Sot," and "The Seminarist" flowed from his pen. Naturalism and irony were by then mainstays of the composer's vision, and, as he provided his own texts to each of these three efforts, there is a distinctly personal level embodied therein. A modest degree of recognition was bestowed on the beleaguered artist when, with the earlier "Tell Me Why" (1858), "Darling Savishna," and "Hopak" were published in 1867, Mussorgsky's first creative efforts to appear in print since the youthful *Porte-Enseigne Polka*.

In 1866, Mussorgsky, who had for some years been interested in Nikolai Gogol's tale "St. John's Eve" even to the point of considering it for an opera, wrote a piece based on the tale as a tone poem for orchestra. This work became *Night on Bare Mountain* (popularized in the film classic *Fantasia*, 1940). The unusual tonalities, intentionally "foul and barbarous," disturbed the sensibilities of his more conventional contemporaries, and the work was never performed in Mussorgsky's lifetime. During this same period, an orchestral setting of

the *Intermezzo in modo classico* (with an added trio) and an unfinished tone poem inspired by the Pan-Slav Congress, *King Poděbrad of Bohemia*, give witness to the several directions in which Mussorgsky was moving.

After a hiatus of several years, Mussorgsky returned to the Dargomyzhski circle at a time when "Dargo" was working on *The Stone Guest*, based on Aleksander Pushkin's play. By this time, he was officially a member of what Vladimir Stasov called "The Mighty Handful," known familiarly as "The Five." He also rejoined the ranks of the employed by accepting an appointment as assistant head clerk in the forestry department in the Ministry of Imperial Domains. Early in 1868, he busied himself with song composition, composing "The Orphan" and "Eremushka's Lullaby." In June of 1868, he set the first act of Gogol's comedy *The Marriage*, and a few months later he commenced composition on *Boris Godunov*, based in part on a play by Pushkin, and with a libretto fashioned by the composer. Unlike the usual fits and starts that accompanied many of his large-scale works, Mussorgsky's energy and intensity were such that *Boris Godunov* was completed by December 15, 1869. Although Dargomyzhski died on January 5 of that year, his influence is notable. The Imperial Theatre rejected *Boris Godunov* for its "extraordinary modernism": The piece departed from custom and operatic tradition; for example, it lacked a major female character. Undeterred, Mussorgsky set about to revise by excising politically objectionable material and by adding two "Polish Scenes" that included a female character, Marina, and a closing "Revolutionary Scene." Individual portions, such as the "Coronation Scene" and the "Polonaise," received favorable receptions, but the Committee of the Theater remained implacable in their shortsightedness. On February 17, 1873, Eduard Nápravník directed the "Inn Scene" and the "Polish Act" at the Marinsky Theatre. Cui reported that the ovations were unprecedented. A full production was finally mounted on February 8, 1874, with Nápravník again on the podium. While the public was enthusiastic (Mussorgsky took some thirty curtain calls), the critics were, for the most part, unmoved. The composer could take solace in that the public had at last recognized his immense talent. The realism and the intensity of the drama struck a nerve in the audience of the time that set into motion a new way of thinking about opera.

While *Boris Godunov*'s travails occupied several years of his lifetime, Mussorgsky, nevertheless, busied himself with other grand projects. During much of 1873 and 1875-1876, he devoted his attention to *Khovanshchina*, another historial opera; sustained periods of heavy drinking prevented uninterrupted work, however, and his last efforts on this work date from 1880. Nikolay Rimsky-Korsakov completed the work in 1886.

During the summer of 1873, Mussorgsky began to share living quarters with a distant relative, the amateur poet Count Arseny Golenishchev Kutuzov. The latter provided the texts to two song cycles, *Sunless* (1874) and *Songs and Dances of Death* (1875-1877). The six *Sunless* songs, reflecting a morbid text, contain much of Mussorgsky's characteristic melodic recitative, but with increased attention to subtle shadings in harmony reflective of changes in mood. The piano is used in a most original manner to evoke or to suggest the appropriate atmosphere. In the *Songs and Dances of Death*, there emerges a series of vividly painted dramas in cameo. The vocal declamation, now at a level of perfection, is blended with a melodic line that grips and sustains the listener's attention. Golenishchev-Kutuzov provided the texts for two more individual songs, "Forgotten" (1874) and "The Vision" (1877). Mussorgsky wrote the texts to his remaining songs, "Epitaph" (1874), "The Nettle Mountain" (1874), and "Sphinx" (1875); only the latter was actually completed.

Stasov, who was growing increasingly alarmed at Mussorgsky's dementia, encouraged the latter to visit Liszt, who had made known his admiration for *The Nursery*, a song cycle published in 1872. Mussorgsky declined; instead, he devoted his energy both to composition and to his civil service position. In June of 1874, he created the piano suite *Pictures from an Exhibition*, inspired by the architectural drawings and paintings of his friend Victor Hartmann, who had died only the year before. The musical depiction of such drawings as *The Gnome, The Old Castle, The Hut of Baba-Yaga*, and the concluding *Great Gate at Kiev*, unified by a recurring "Promenade" theme, include bold and unconventional harmonies which unsympathetic critics referred to as "crude" and "barbaric."

Mussorgsky and Glinka's sister were involved in the jubilee celebrations for Osip Petrov, the bass whose role of Varlaam in *Boris Godunov* set the standard for others to follow; during this general time frame (spring 1876), the composer returned to a projected comic opera based on Gogol's "Sorochintsy Fair," which he had begun two years earlier. By 1878, he had abandoned the work once again. Another regression in his battle with the bottle caused Stasov to intercede with the state controller for the purpose of transferring Mussorgsky to his own control department. As the state controller was a devotee of folk songs and an admirer of "The Five," he complied willingly with the entreaty; furthermore, he gave Mussorgsky permission to take a three-month leave in order to accompany the contralto Darya Leonova on a concert tour through central Russia and the Crimea. Delighting in the scenery, Mussorgsky composed some pleasant but inconsequential piano pieces and the popular "Song of the Flea."

In November, 1879, Rimsky-Korsakov conducted excerpts from *Khovanshchina* in St. Petersburg. As the new year began, however, Mussorgsky was relieved of his duties in the Control Department. Friends came to his rescue by providing funds, with the stipulation that he complete *Khovanshchina* and *Sorochintsy Fair*. Neither composition was completed. Leonova provided him with employment as her accompanist and as a teacher of theory and arranger of duos, trios, and quartets for use by students in her singing school. At her summer residence at Oranienbaum, Mussorgsky conceived a plan for a suite for orchestra with harp and piano based on motives from folk tunes he had collected on his tours.

On February 15, 1881, Mussorgsky received the applause of the audience at a performance of *The Destruction of Sennacherib* given by Rimsky-Korsakov at the Free School of Music. Only eight days later, he suffered an apparent stroke on a visit to Leonova, and, on the following day, he was taken unconscious to the Nikolaevsky Military Hospital. Periods of lucidity enabled the noted portrait painter, Ilya Repin, to produce, in four sittings, the most frequently reproduced painting of the unruly genius; in it, he appears haggard and disheveled. According to Repin, a misguided attendant gave Mussorgsky a bottle of brandy to help celebrate his impending birthday. Craving the alcohol, Mussorgsky disobeyed doctor's orders and, at five in the morning on March 28, 1881, he died.

Summary

In his last year of life, Mussorgsky provided a statement of his artistic principles: "Art is a means of communicating with people, not an aim in itself." Only artist-reformers, he stated, such as Giovanni Palestrina, Johann Sebastian Bach, Christoph Gluck, Ludwig van Beethoven, Berlioz, and Liszt, create art's laws, but these laws are not immutable. Art for its own sake was anathema to Mussorgsky; he believed that art should reflect life and communicate the common experiences of the human condition. Mussorgsky had particular empathy for the peasant class, despite his privileged early years; this earthiness, in fact, becomes a distinguishing feature of some of his most profound musical utterances.

During Mussorgsky's formative years, the many and varied influences of Glinka, Balakirev, Schumann, and Liszt, among others, are readily identifiable, as are the technical deficiencies which created a host of detractors and which caused Rimsky-Korsakov and others to rework some of Mussorgsky's pieces. Later, Mussorgsky aimed at the musical representation of human speech, but, from time to time, elements of Russian folk song are discernible, and they establish the lyrical quality which gives his work its unique blend of antipodal musical forces. His gift for satire is most observable in the songs, revealing Mussorgsky as a keen observer of all aspects and stations of life. His extraordinary talent for penetrating the inner recesses of the soul is nowhere better demonstrated than in *Boris Godunov*; because of this ability, the harmony, which would otherwise appear to be amateurish, seems perfectly suited to the requirements of dramatic expression.

Starting with the best intentions, "the fixers," such as Rimsky-Korsakov, were determined to complete, to reorchestrate, and to revise much of Mussorgsky's corpus. It has been argued that these refurbishings made the compositions accessible to audiences at large and contributed to their publication; however, the prettification of such masterworks as *Boris Godunov* and *Night on Bare Mountain* have stripped them of their raw, rough-hewn strength. Now that the original versions are available, there is no justification for automatically opting for the well-known revisions.

Bibliography

Brown, Malcolm Hamrick, ed. *Musorgsky: In Memoriam, 1881-1981*. Ann Arbor, Mich.: UMI Research Press, 1982. A collection of essays dealing with various aspects of Mussorgsky's life and music. Among the most informative and revelatory are "Musorgsky and the Populist Age," by Richard Hoops; "Musorgsky's Interest in Judaica," by Boris Schwarz; "Musorgsky's Choral Style," by Vladimir Morosan; "Editions of *Boris Godunov*," by Robert William Oldani; and "Musorgsky and Shostakovitch," by Laurel E. Fay.

Calvocoressi, Michael D. *Modest Mussorgsky, His Life and Works*. London: Rockliff, and Boston: Crescendo, 1956. A major biographical study, this work contains musical illustrations, portraits of "The Five," and a catalog of Mussorgsky's compositions. A chronological account of the composer's life and works is followed by two excellent chapters devoted to "Technique and Style."

———. *Mussorgsky*. London: Dent, and New York: Dutton, 1946. This book, part of Dent's Master Musicians series, presents the salient facts about Mussorgsky and his music. There are fine musical illustrations to highlight the descriptive analyses of important compositions. The appendices are of practical value; they include a calendar of Mussorgsky's life with an adjoining column relating to contemporary musicians.

Emerson, Caryl, and Robert W. Oldani. *Modest Musorgsky and* Boris Godunov: *Myths, Realities, and Reconsiderations*. Cambridge: Cambridge University Press, 1994. This book is a collaboration between a specialist in literature and a music historian for the study and analysis of Mussorgsky's opera *Boris Godunov*. Includes criticism, photographs, bibliography, and a discography.

Leyda, Jay, and Sergei Bertensson, eds. *The Musorgsky Reader: A Life of Modest Petrovich Musorgsky in Letters and Documents*. New York: Norton, 1947. Essentially, this valuable source is a life of Mussorgsky in letters and documents. They are presented in chronological order and appear in their entirety in English translations. The footnotes provide excellent explanatory data.

Montagu-Nathan, M. *Moussorgsky*. London: Constable, 1916; New York: Duffield, 1917. This book, part of the Masters of Russian Music series, is divided into four parts: career, Mussorgsky as operatic composer, choral and instrumental works, and songs. Emphasis is placed on what the author perceives as the high points in the composer's career. A brief commentary is provided on all the major works.

Orlova, Alexandra. *Musorgsky's Days and Works.* Edited and translated by Roy J. Guenther. Ann Arbor, Mich.: UMI Research Press, 1983. This work contains an exhaustive day-by-day account of Mussorgsky's life; it is, in effect, a biography in documents. Material is drawn from letters, diaries, newspaper and journal articles, and reviews, and the like. Sheds much new light on Mussorgsky's travels with Darya Leonova.

Riesemann, Oskar von. *Moussorgsky.* Translated by Paul England. New York and London: Knopf, 1929. This popular biography encompasses all aspects and phases of the composer's life. Despite occasional errors in small details, the book has much to admire, and the material is presented in a logical and orderly manner.

Russ, Michael. *Musorgsky:* Pictures at an Exhibition. Cambridge and New York: Cambridge University Press, 1992. Discusses Mussorgsky's *Pictures at an Exhibition* in the context of Russian cultural life. The author provides information on the works of Victor Hartman, the artist whose work inspired this piece.

David Z. Kushner

NAPOLEON I

Born: August 15, 1769; Ajaccio, Corsica
Died: May 5, 1821; Saint Helena Island
Areas of Achievement: Government, politics, and the military
Contribution: One of the greatest generals in history, Napoleon I also made lasting contributions to the laws and civil administration of France and other lands. His darker legacy is to have developed a dictatorial rule that is the precursor of modern Fascism.

Early Life

Although a native of Corsica, Napoleon Bonaparte was sent to French military schools in Brienne and Paris, where he became known as "the little corporal" because of his small stature. Commissioned to the artillery in 1785, he later took part in fighting on behalf of the French Revolution. In 1793, he was promoted to brigadier general, but he was imprisoned the next year when the forces in power changed from the radical Jacobins to Thermidorean reactionaries intent on stopping the reign of terror that had made the Revolution turn on its own members. He was soon released, however, and back in favor in October, 1795, when he dispersed a Parisian mob threatening the government.

A politically helpful marriage and victories in the field, especially in northern Italy, increased Napoleon's prestige. Other spectacular victories in Egypt, coupled with a weak government at home that was overthrown in 1799, led to his elevation as first consul in the new government. A plebiscite was held confirming his enormous popularity, and by 1801 (the year in which he made peace with the Roman Catholic church, one of the Revolution's greatest enemies) he was the supreme dictator of France.

Napoleon's remarkable early success was in part a matter of good fortune and in part the product of an unconquerable will and energy that took the maximum advantage of every political and military opportunity. Given the chaos of the revolutionary years, it is not surprising that a military man with political prowess should do so well. With France under siege and surrounded by hostile powers, Napoleon's victories could be viewed (rather romantically) as having saved the Revolution from destruction. At the same time, his own steadiness of purpose prevented warring factions from destroying the Revolution from within.

Life's Work

Napoleon I was to keep France in the paramount position to which he had brought it in only a few years. If France were to be secure, it had to dominate the European continent. Thus Napoleon intervened successfully in Austria, Italy, and Germany—all enemies of the Revolution. England, with its control of the sea, was a major target, but Napoleon repeatedly failed in attempts to destroy British military power in Egypt and on the European continent.

By 1804, Napoleon had himself proclaimed emperor. What had once been a man of humble origins, whose energies and talents had been released by revolutionary actions, now increasingly became an individual identifying his personal successes with the glory of the state. England, Austria, Russia, and Sweden formed an alliance against him, but on December 26, 1805, he overwhelmingly defeated their armies at Austerlitz. By 1808, he was master of the Continent, with only the sea power of England to thwart his imperial plans.

Although Napoleon had made significant legal reforms in France, he relied increasingly on the force of his own personality to rule. Rather than developing some kind of governmental structure that might perpetuate his rule or forming a strong general staff that could carry through with his military plans, he relied almost exclusively on his own genius. As a tireless worker and supremely organized person, he counted on being able to switch rapidly from one issue to another or from one field of battle to another. He had a detailed grasp of both civil and military matters that was awesome, and he refused to delegate the authority that accrued from his command of the components of power.

Napoleon thought, mistakenly, that he could use members of his own family as extensions of his will. Thus he conferred the thrones of Holland and Westphalia on his brothers Louis and Jerome. He made his stepson, Eugène, a viceroy of Italy and his third brother, Joseph, King of Naples and later of Spain. Few of these familial appointments were successful, either because his relatives were incompetent or because they acted independently of his wishes. Yet he continued to act as though he could invent a royal line for himself, having his marriage to Joséphine (who was unable to bear his child) annulled in 1809 so that he could marry the daughter of the Austrian emperor Francis II, Marie-Louise, who bore him a son.

Between 1808 and 1814, Napoleon continued to triumph in war, but at great cost to his country. A defeat he suffered in May, 1809, in a battle with the Archduke Charles at Aspern, demonstrated his vulnerability. Yet he drove his forces on, invading Russia in June, 1812, with an army of 500,000 men, the largest collection of troops ever mobilized in Europe. Although he made it to Moscow, the Russians had devastated their own country along the route of his advance, depriving him of the sustenance of the land and exacerbating his problems with supply lines that became overextended. With winter overtaking him, the Russians struck back, reducing his huge army to one-fifth of its original size, so that he had to hasten back to Paris to prepare a defense against an invasion. When Paris fell on March 31, 1814, Napoleon abdicated and was exiled to Elba.

A much lesser man might have accepted the verdict of history. It was a measure of the esteem Napoleon could still compel that he was able to escape and rally France once more. In his effort to reconstruct his empire, he liberalized certain features of the French constitution, but, before he could truly mobilize public opinion, he was forced into battle at Waterloo (June 12-18, 1815), the decisive defeat of his career. In exile on Saint Helena Island, Napoleon assiduously built up the myth of himself as the Revolution's man, the conqueror who had meant to liberate Europe from reactionary elements.

Summary

Napoleon I's impact on his time and on subsequent events has been extraordinary. First, there was his conceit that Europe could be unified under the rule of one man. Napoleon established a cult of the personality, a disturbing phenomenon that would be repeated in the bloody rules of Joseph Stalin and Adolf Hitler in the twentieth century. Hitler, in particular, suffered from delusions of grandeur that had their precedent in Napoleon. Both leaders, in fact, were bold military strategists who imagined that if only they took over the details of command the world could be shaped according to their desires. Napoleon established the modern model for the world-historical individual who believes in the triumph of his will.

The great Marxist critic Georg Lukács has argued that Napoleon's movement of masses of men across a continent resulted in the development of a historical consciousness in which millions of men suddenly saw their fate linked to the fate of millions of others. Even when Lukács' Marxist bias is discounted, his evocation of Napoleon's ability to motivate millions of people takes on an inspiring and frightening aspect. Napoleon took the ideas of democracy, of popular rule, and of government by the majority and turned them into another tool of the dictator. At the height of his own popularity, at crucial periods in his career, Napoleon used plebiscites to legitimate his military and imperial ambitions.

Historians of various biases continue to argue over Napoleon's significance, for they recognize in his example a powerful lesson on personality and politics. At the beginning of his career, Napoleon was seen as the outcome of a revolutionary movement and as the very type of man the forces of history had shaped to rule. Yet by the end of his career, large parts of Europe regarded him only as a dictator who camouflaged his tyranny in the rhetoric of the Revolution.

The comparison with Hitler is, again, apposite. There is virtually nothing in Hitler's record that can be salvaged, no vision of a united Europe worth contemplating. The difference between him and Napoleon can be gauged by imagining what would have happened if each man had been able to conquer all of Europe. Hitler's ideology was founded on excluding and exterminating various groups of people. Napoleon's ideology was based on the principle of inclusion. Armies were defeated in the field, and, though civilian populations also suffered in the Napoleonic Wars, the emperor had no final solution, no master plan, to rid Europe of undesirable elements. If Napoleon did betray much of the Revolution, he also left a code of law and an enviable legacy of civil administration. He is not the monster Hitler was precisely because Napoleon evolved from the context of a revolution, which in practice he may have subverted but which he also supported in a way that still influences scholars of this period.

Bibliography

Broers, Michael. *Europe under Napoleon 1799-1815*. London: Arnold, and New York: St. Martin's Press, 1996. Examines the Napoleonic Empire from the perspective of the people of Europe. Innovative treatment of the period.

Cronin, Vincent. *Napoleon Bonaparte: An Intimate Biography*. London: Collins, 1971; New York: Dell, 1972. As the title suggests, this biography aims to give a close-up view of the man. Written in a clear, conversational style, this is by no means one of the classic works on Napoleon, but it is an accessible way of studying a figure who has been layered with so many different interpretations. The notes and the index sections are helpful guides to further research.

Gates, David. *The Napoleonic Wars, 1803-1815*. London and New York: Arnold, 1997. Departing from past volumes on the Napoleonic Wars, Gates takes a new approach focusing on individual facets of the wars. Gates divides his analysis into sections on the social, economic, intellectual, and diplomatic factors that affected the wars' operations.

Geyl, Pieter. *Napoleon, For and Against*. London: Cape, and New Haven, Conn.: Yale University Press, 1949. This study by a great Dutch historian is essential reading. With great clarity and impartiality he relates the various reactions to Napoleon that still govern writing on him today. Geyl is an acute student of nationalism and shows how nationalistic reactions to Napoleon color much of the writing that has been done on him.

Hobsbawm, E. J. *The Age of Revolution: Europe, 1789-1848*. London: Weidenfeld and Nicolson, and New York: New American Library, 1962. Napoleon cannot really be understood apart from his age. This classic history by one of the most important British historians of the century brilliantly evokes a sense of the historical period and of social and political change.

Jones, R. Ben. *Napoleon: Man and Myth*. London: Hodder and Stoughton, and New York: Holmes and Meier, 1977. Should be read after consulting one of the standard biographies of Napoleon. Divided into chapters on historical background, Napoleon's civil and military career, and the impact of his myth, this is a very useful study that includes maps, bibliographies, and chronologies of important periods and events.

Kircheisen, F. M. *Napoleon*. London: Howe, 1931; New York: Harcourt Brace, 1932. One of the standard biographies of Napoleon, condensed in this edition from nine volumes and more than five thousand pages of text. Based on extensive archival research and reading in sources in many languages, but still a readable and informative study. Well indexed with maps and illustrations.

Lefebvre, Georges. *Napoleon: From 18 Brumaire to Tilsit, 1799-1807*. London: Routledge, and New York: Columbia University Press, 1969.

————. *Napoleon: From Tilsit to Waterloo, 1807-1815*. London: Routledge, and New York: Columbia University Press, 1969. These volumes are a translation of what is generally considered to be the greatest biography of Napoleon. While it focuses on the man, the biography opens with a first chapter that helpfully situates him in the context of his revolutionary times.

Palmer, R. R. *The Age of Democratic Revolution: A Political History of Europe and America, 1760-1800*. 2 vols. Princeton, N.J.: Princeton University Press, 1959-1964. This is a particularly lucid overview of the Napoleonic period. Palmer's balanced prose and helpful bibliography are essential and should be read in conjunction with Hobsbawm's classic study.

Simms, Brendan. *The Impact of Napoleon: Prussian High Politics, Foreign Policy and the Crisis of the Executive, 1797-1806*. Cambridge and New York: Cambridge University Press, 1997. Presents a fresh picture of pre-1806 Prussia and its response to Napoleon's expansionism.

Stendhal. *The Red and the Black*. Translated by C. K. Scott Moncrieff. New York: Modern Library, 1929; London: Everyman, 1997. Stendhal served in Napoleon's army and was his great admirer. In this novel, his masterpiece, he traces the career of Julien Sorel, a young man of Napoleonic ambitions. There is no finer source for appreciating the power of Napoleon's myth on his generation and on the generations to follow.

Thompson, J. M. *Napoleon Bonaparte: His Rise and Fall*. Oxford: Blackwell, and New York: Oxford University Press, 1952. A standard biography relying extensively on Napoleon's correspondence. It is somewhat unusual for being structured in chapters strictly devoted to the many countries on which Napoleon had an impact. Contains notes and an index.

Tolstoy, Leo. *War and Peace*. Translated by Constance Garnett. London: Heinemann, and New York: McClure, Phillips, 1904. No student of Napoleon should overlook this great novelist's attack on the "great man" theory of history. The novel is an epic view of Napoleon's invasion of Russia and of the inexorable historical forces in which Tolstoy's characters find themselves immersed.

Carl Rollyson

NAPOLEON III

Born: April 20, 1808; Paris, France
Died: January 9, 1873; Chislehurst, Kent, England
Areas of Achievement: Government and politics
Contribution: Napoleon III, nephew of Napoleon I, was President of the Second French Republic from 1848 to 1852 and Emperor of the Second Empire from 1852 to 1870. He was one of the key figures, sometimes unwittingly, in the political unification of both Italy and Germany, and was also greatly responsible for the rebuilding of Paris.

Early Life

Louis Napoleon Bonaparte was born in Paris in 1808. His father, also Louis Napoleon, was a younger brother of Napoleon I, and his mother, Hortense, was the daughter of the emperor's first wife, Josephine, from an earlier marriage. The marriage of Louis Napoleon and Hortense was not a success, and rumors persisted regarding the child's paternity. After Waterloo and the exile to St. Helena, all the Bonapartes were forced out of France. Hortense, having separating from her husband, settled in Switzerland, where Louis Napoleon was educated to the dual heritage of the French Revolution and the imperialism of Napoleon I. Both traditions formed his character.

As a young man, Louis Napoleon was a romantic figure. Of average height for the day, about five feet, five inches, he had a pale complexion and dark, curly hair. Women were greatly attracted to him, perhaps because of his name. It is impossible to ascertain when his own political ambitions first matured, though it is probable that he saw himself as a man of destiny at a very early age. Louis Napoleon's older brother died in 1831, and Napoleon I's son by his second wife, the so-called Duke of Reichstadt, died in 1832, leaving Louis Napoleon as the political head of the Bonaparte family. In 1836, he attempted his first *coup d'état* against the French government of King Louis-Philippe. It failed ignominiously, and after his arrest he was exiled, first to the United States and then, after his mother's death, to London.

In 1840, the British government consented to the return of Napoleon I's body to France from St. Helena, where he had died in 1821. Hoping to take advantage of the Bonaparte legend, Louis Napoleon again attempted a coup against Louis-Philippe. It, too, utterly failed, and he was sentenced to imprisonment for life. During the next few years, Louis Napoleon wrote and studied. He authored various works, identifying himself with the heritage of Napoleon I. In 1844, he published "Extinction du paupérisme" (the extinction of poverty), which, contrary to the laissez-faire ideology of the times, advocated government intervention in the economy. In 1846, he escaped from prison and within a few hours was back in England, but no closer to power.

Life's Work

The year 1848 was a revolutionary year in Europe and in France. In February, Louis-Philippe was overthrown. Initially, Louis Napoleon was unable to profit by the change, but after a working-class uprising in May and June, which alarmed the middle and upper classes, his opportunity came. Abandoning the monarchy, the French established the Second Republic, and Louis Napoleon was elected president, receiving almost 75 percent of the vote. His uncle's reputation, his own activities against the former regime, his economic program, the divisions among his opponents, and perhaps merely the times made Louis Napoleon President of France.

The government of the Second Republic was modeled after the American presidential system rather than the parliamentary form of England. Louis Napoleon lacked a political party of his own and the newly elected French assembly owed him little loyalty. In addition, the presidential term was for four years with no immediate reelection allowed. Finally, there were Louis Napoleon's own ambitions and his heritage. Those factors guaranteed still another revolution, this time, ironically, by Louis Napoleon against his own government. "Operation Rubicon" was successful, in December, 1851, but at the cost of many arrests, 370 lives lost, and twenty thousand exiled, damaging the legitimacy of his rule. Yet, in a carefully worded plebiscite, the voters approved the *coup d'état*, and a year later, in another plebiscite, they overwhelmingly voted to abolish the Second Republic and replace it with the Second Empire, with Louis Napoleon as Emperor Napoleon III.

The creation of the Second Empire caused considerable fear among other European governments as possibly portending the revival of the military imperialism of Napoleon I. Napoleon III, however, publicly stated that his empire would be an empire of peace; as president, he had proposed to the British and Prussian governments that naval and land armaments be reduced, although nothing came of it. Early in his reign, Russian pressure on the Turkish Ottoman Empire ignited the fears of both France and England about Russia's territorial ambitions and its perennial quest for warm-water ports. The result was war in the Crimea in 1854. For Napoleon, the determining factor was his desire for an alliance with England, the old enemy, more than fear of Russia. The war itself was a standoff, but the emperor reaped credit for his diplomacy which led to peace.

In the nineteenth century, national unification was perceived by many to be both logical and necessary. Napoleon was sympathetic toward Italian unity. Yet it was easier for Napoleon to become involved in Italian affairs than to get out of them. In 1849, he had alienated both Italian nationalists and Catholics when he intervened in Roman affairs. Expecting to be welcomed, instead the French were opposed both by liberals on the Left, who had recently established a republic in Rome, and by conservative Catholics on the Right. In spite of Napoleon's support of Italian national aspirations, for some Italian patriots he moved too slowly, and in 1858 there was an attempt to assassinate him. Napoleon supported Sardinia's aim of eliminating Austria from Italy, but he envisioned not a strong united Italy but a federated state which would look to France and himself for guidance. His decision to wage war against Austria was risky, lacking as it did the support of most European governments, and after initial victories, Napoleon agreed to peace. Sardinia was not pleased, but France obtained Savoy and Nice as a result of the newest Napoleon's imperialism. Italian unification remained for the future, and Napoleon's intervention had failed to satisfy any of the participants.

Perhaps the major accomplishment of the Second Empire was the rebuilding of Paris. Here, too, Louis Napoleon was inspired by his uncle's accomplishments. Even as late as 1848, Paris was in many ways a medieval city, but, with the assistance of Georges Haussmann, Napoleon made Paris into one of the first modern and planned cities in Western civilization. The Seine River was no longer a public sewer, the city streets were widened, trees planted, parks provided, and gaslights added, making Paris the famous City of Lights. Undoubtedly, the emperor wished to create a monument to his rule—he saw himself as a second Caesar Augustus building a new Rome—but there were economic and strategic considerations. Jobs would be created, and the wider, straighter streets would make it more difficult for the Parisians to rebel against his regime.

As emperor, Napoleon faced the responsibility of providing an heir. After canvassing several European princesses, the imperial eye fell upon Eugenie de Montijo, daughter of a Spanish nobleman and his part-Scottish wife. For Napoleon, it was a love match, unpopular with many of his advisers; yet Eugenie, for all of her beauty and charm, was ultimately not a suitable consort. She gave birth to a son, the prince imperial, in 1856, but she and the emperor were not close and Eugenie often pursued policies independent of those of Napoleon. In particular, she was a strong supporter of the Papacy during the era of Italian unification, and she was the energetic sponsor of French adventure in Mexico whereby the Austrian Archduke Maximilian was placed on the throne of that unwilling country. In time, Maximilian's position became untenable, and the Austrian was executed by his Mexican subjects.

The 1860's saw a change in policy as the emperor slowly began moving toward the creation of a more liberal empire. The earlier high tariff policies, which had benefited French industrialists, were modified and freer trade with Great Britain instituted. The assembly was given additional powers, and in elections republican and Royalist opponents of the imperial regime, although still in the minority, improved their numbers. Napoleon III had claimed to be a socialist, and in the 1860's he allowed the development of labor unions, but his policies and approaches were more paternalistic than democratic. By the end of the decade, the empire was more liberal than at its beginning but in reality still more despotic than democratic. If given sufficient time, Napoleon's empire might have evolved into something approximating the constitutional monarchy of Victorian England, but it faced many obstacles. Its violent birth in 1851 and its opposition from both the Left and the Right— from republicans and from Royalists—created problems which were difficult to surmount. Napoleon's advisers were often marginal political figures who lacked prominence and political stature. Napoleon's health was poor, and his own personality was more suited to the seeking of power than to the wielding of it. He remained more the conspirator than the statesman.

It was Napoleon's ultimate misfortune to face one of the most astute statesman of modern European history. Otto von Bismarck of Prussia desired a united Germany, a Germany created by blood and iron. In 1866, Prussia defeated the Austro-Hungarian Empire in only six weeks, which led the northern German states into a federation. In 1870, Bismarck turned his talents against Napoleon. The vacant Spanish throne was offered to a Catholic prince of the Protestant ruling house of Prussia. The French feared that they would find themselves encircled by Germans. Napoleon's government demanded that the Prussian king apologize for the affair, but Bismarck made the diplomatic conversations appear that the Prussian rejection of the French demand was harsher and more dismissive than it was in reality. The French public, including Eugenie, demanded war with Prussia, and against his own inclinations Napoleon weakly succumbed. War was declared in 1870. It was an unmitigated disaster. Napoleon III was captured by the Prussians and soon abdicated. The Second Empire was over.

Summary

Napoleon III chose exile in England. In France, the war against Prussia continued briefly, but ultimately Germany prevailed and the French were forced to surrender the provinces of Alsace and Lorraine. The Second Empire was replaced by the Third Republic. Napoleon III died in his English exile in 1873. His son and heir, the prince imperial, the hope of the Bonaparte dynasty, joined the British army in South Africa. He was killed in action against the Zulus in 1879. Eugenie survived until 1920; she lived long enough to see Alsace and Lorraine restored to republican France after World War I.

Although Napoleon's diplomatic accomplishments were sometimes significant and his economic policies showed vision, the ease with which he was swept away in the events of 1870 suggests that his hold upon France was extremely superficial. He ruled for more than twenty years—longer than his famous uncle—but other than on Paris, his ultimate impact was slight. He remained the political adventurer and the dreamer to the end.

Bibliography

Bury, J. P. T. *Napoléon III and the Second Empire*. London: English Universities Press, 1964; New York: Harper, 1968. Bury, also a biographer of Leon Gambetta, a leading republican opponent of Napoleon III, has here written one of the best introductions to the Second Empire.

Corley, T. A. B. *Democratic Despot: A Life of Napoleon III*. London: Barrie and Rockliff, and New York: Potter, 1961. This study notes two of the elements found in Napoleon, the popular and the autocratic, and the emperor's attempt to reconcile them. The author takes Napoleon's intellectual attempts seriously, arguing that he was the first modern politician but failed as a statesman.

Gooch, Brison D., ed. *Napoleon III, Man of Destiny: Englightened Statesman or Proto-Fascist?* Gloucester: Smith, and New York: Holt Rinehart, 1963. This volume is a compendium of excerpts by various historians of Napoleon, allowing the reader to sample differing interpretations of the emperor and his regime. The subtitle captures its scope.

McMillan, James. *Napoleon III*. London and New York: Longman, 1991. Focuses on Napoleon III's use of power.

Pinkney, David H. *Napoleon III and the Rebuilding of Paris*. Princeton, N.J.: Princeton University Press, 1958. The author concentrates upon the creation of modern Paris under the leadership of the emperor and Georges Haussmann. The City of Lights is perhaps the major monument to the Second Empire, showing both its strengths and its weaknesses.

Price, Roger D. *Napoleon III and the Second Empire*. London and New York: Routledge, 1997. The author evaluates the nineteenth-century conditions that led to Napoleon's election as president. Includes discussions of Napoleon's objectives, his abilities as a ruler and his influence on social, political and economic conditions.

Thompson, J. M. *Louis Napoleon and the Second Empire*. Oxford: Blackwell, 1954; New York: Noonday Press, 1955. This analysis of Napoleon ultimately finds the emperor lacking the necessary qualities to succeed in the inheritance left to him by Napoleon I. Suggesting the author's interpretation, each chapter begins with a quote from *Hamlet*.

Eugene S. Larson

JAMES NASMYTH

Born: August 19, 1808; Edinburgh, Scotland
Died: May 7, 1890; London, England
Areas of Achievement: Mechanical engineering and invention
Contribution: Nasmyth developed and successfully marketed a pioneering class of industrial metalworking machines, principally the steam hammer, contributing to Great Britain's role as the fountainhead of the Industrial Revolution.

Early Life

James Hall Nasmyth was born in Edinburgh, into a family of Scottish artists, on August 19, 1808, the youngest of nine children of Alexander Nasmyth, a prominent Edinburgh painter, and Barbara Foulis, a member of the Scottish aristocracy. As a child, James assisted in his father's studio, mixing paints and working wood and metal on the family's foot-powered lathe. Together with five of his brothers and sisters, James developed skills as a graphic artist that were to remain with him throughout his working life.

In 1821, Nasmyth entered the Edinburgh School of Arts while receiving more intensive technical training from his father. The fine arts and the applied arts of metallurgy, draftsmanship, and mathematics worked together in Nasmyth's upbringing. In frequent visits to the forges, foundries, and factories of industrial Edinburgh, Nasmyth sharpened a keen interest in the methods of machine manufacture, building his own stationary steam engine by the age of seventeen.

With his father's assistance, Nasmyth secured a position in 1829 as personal assistant to Henry Maudslay, one of England's most noteworthy mechanical engineers. In his London shops, Maudslay built steam engines and many pioneering machines for the working of wood and metal. Several of the country's most prominent machine-tool builders received their initial exposure to engineering practice in Maudslay's shops, including Joseph Clement, William Muir, Joseph Whitworth, and Richard Roberts. After three years with Maudslay, Nasmyth returned to Edinburgh to manufacture the machines that he would need to set up practice as an independent manufacturer of metalworking machines. By 1834, he had accumulated sufficient goods and capital to establish himself in Manchester, at the heart of the Lancashire manufacturing industry.

Nasmyth's shop stood on the first floor of a former cotton mill, where his success in building heavy tools and steam engines for the surrounding mills quickly taxed the limited quarters. In late 1835, Nasmyth undertook a search for a new site to satisfy his growing needs for proper space, for access to better transport, and for greater prominence among Lancashire factory owners in need of new machinery.

Life's Work

At Patricroft, a short distance west of Manchester, Nasmyth found a site offering all the advantages he sought: a large plot of land at the intersection of the Bridgewater Canal and the main road and railway connecting Manchester with Liverpool. With the financial backing of a Manchester investment firm and various other sources of capital, Nasmyth set about the construction of the Bridgewater Foundry. Unlike his Manchester shop, this new enterprise was to include the entire range of workshops necessary to execute all classes of heavy work from their inception to delivery.

By 1838, Nasmyth was overseeing the operation of a complete machinery-design department, iron and brass foundries, machine and erecting shops, forge shop, pattern shop, and various other lesser shops, the whole connected by a network of rail transport. Aided by the business skills of his brother, George, and his partner Holbrook Gaskell, Nasmyth began a rapid climb to the upper reaches of British industrial enterprise. Between 1838 and his retirement from the firm in 1856, the Bridgewater Foundry produced the full range of heavy machine tools then in use: lathes, planers, shapers, slotters, boring mills, and drilling machines. Many of Nasmyth's own machinery designs were incorporated into the output. Also produced at Bridgewater were steam locomotives, hydraulic presses, stationary and marine steam engines, and pumps. While the considerable business success of the Bridgewater Foundry was the key element in Nasmyth's own prosperity, it was the production of the steam hammer that created his reputation as one of the preeminent British engineers of the Victorian age.

The steam hammer appeared at a time when the hammering or forging of iron had reached the limits of existing technology. By the 1830's, blacksmiths could not effectively produce such large iron forgings as engine shafts or ships' anchors without considerable labor and time spent at water-powered trip hammers, frequently reheating the piece and gradually working the iron up into its rough form.

Although the first practical use of the steam hammer occurred in France in 1841, at the Schneider works in Le Creusot, in 1838 Nasmyth had conceived the general form such a machine would take and the needs it could fill. With the addition of controls designed by his works manager, Robert Wilson, the steam hammers that Nasmyth began producing in 1843 became symbolic as well as immensely practical giants of the industrial age, towering structures with ponderous steam-driven hammerheads that would crash down on red-hot iron masses to rough out enormous piston rods, crankshafts, anchors, and cannon. The great force exerted by each blow of the hammer both reduced the forging time dramatically and produced a metallurgically superior product. Nasmyth's tight control over the patented features of his hammers, along with Bridgewater's production capacities, ensured a steady demand for steam hammers produced there until well after his departure in 1856.

By the end of the century, steam hammers would give way to hydraulic presses in producing large forgings of greater strength and integrity. Nevertheless, Nasmyth hammers remained in use in factories throughout the world, their quick action and powerful blows rendering them invaluable to the production of many industrial goods.

Largely on the strength of his steam-hammer sales, Nasmyth had amassed a considerable fortune by the age of forty-eight, when he chose to leave the firm and devote himself to private scientific pursuits. Astronomical studies became one of his chief interests, and he coauthored an account of his observations of the moon in 1874. As with many other men of his age who left behind a life of busy industrial pursuits, Nasmyth began to seek answers to some of the ancient riddles of the day: the origin of the pyramids, early alphabets, and various astrological speculations. He also traveled widely, took up photography, and resumed his interest in painting.

A portion of Nasmyth's retirement was spent defending his claim to the invention of the steam hammer, a campaign that had developed into a nationalistic debate between advocates of French and British engineering practice. Although most popular accounts of the hammer's appearance still credit Nasmyth as its originator, contemporary records do

indicate that French engineers independently conceived, built, and used a steam hammer prior to its construction by Nasmyth. The autobiography which Nasmyth completed in 1883 established his reputation among his countrymen, a reputation he rightly deserves as the steam hammer's chief advocate and one of Great Britain's most successful machine-tool innovators.

Summary

Mirroring the careers of many self-taught British engineers before the professionalization of the field, James Nasmyth had early been trained in the handicrafts that were an essential foundation of all engineering. His skills as a machinist and his knowledge of machine design and steam engineering are well documented. Of his forty-three mechanical innovations, he patented nineteen, including a safety foundry ladle, cotton press, rolling mill, pile driver, and iron-making process.

As the head of a major industrial works, Nasmyth sought to retain shop-floor control of his workforce of several hundred men, to resist union demands, and to introduce machinery that would limit the degree of skill needed to operate it. A principal feature of the machine tools Nasmyth developed and used at the Bridgewater Foundry was the automatic motion, or feed, of their cutting tools, reducing the need for experienced machinists. Less knowledgeable machine tenders, often young boys, could operate such machines with ease.

Nasmyth's opposition to organized labor, including its system of apprenticeship, resulted in several labor actions against his firm and may have played a role in his early retirement. His view of skill as a marketable product subject to agreement solely between employer and employee did not fare well in the early period of the industrial workers' rights movement but did allow Nasmyth to compile a highly successful record as a builder of revolutionary industrial machinery.

Bibliography

Briggs, Asa. *Iron Bridge to Crystal Palace: Impact and Images of the Industrial Revolution*. London: Thames and Hudson, 1979. A richly illustrated treatment of the sweeping influences of industrialization in Great Britain from 1779 to 1851, this thin volume depends less on authoritative research than it does on more than two hundred visual impressions of industry selected from popular literature, technical publications, and art galleries.

Cantrell, John A. *James Nasmyth and the Bridgewater Foundry*. Manchester and Dover, N.H.: Manchester University Press, 1985. This thorough study of the economic and technical history of Nasmyth's Bridgewater years dispells many of the excessively heroic notions associated with the man and his principal product, the steam hammer. The author uses business records and correspondence to unravel the actual roles played by Nasmyth and his contemporaries in the success of the business.

Clayre, Alasdair, ed. *Nature and Industrialization*. Oxford and New York: Oxford University Press, 1977. In his later years, Nasmyth was saddened by the damaged landscapes wrought by industry. This anthology of British prose and poetry confronts many of industry's social side effects—good and evil. The words of Charles Dickens, William Wordsworth, Alfred, Lord Tennyson, and Thomas Carlyle are used extensively.

Karwatka, Dennis. "James Nasmyth and the Steam-Powered Forge." *Tech Directions* 55, no. 5 (December, 1995). A profile of Nasmyth that includes his influence on nineteenth-century manufacturing, his work on the steam-driven piston, and other achievements.

Landes, David S. *The Unbound Prometheus*. London: Cambridge University Press, 1969. The broad sweep of European industrialization from 1750 to the late twentieth century is examined in this textbook study. Landes attempts to explain why Europe was industrialized first by studying the processes of industrial growth in Great Britain, France, and Germany.

Mayr, Otto, and Robert C. Post, eds. *Yankee Enterprise: The Rise of the American System of Manufactures*. Washington, D.C.: Smithsonian Institution Press, 1981. The proceedings of a symposium held at the Smithsonian, this collection of essays from distinguished historians of technology examines the reasons that industrialization emerged so rapidly and successfully in the United States, specifically in the manufacture of interchangeable parts.

Nasmyth, James Hall. *James Nasmyth, Engineer: An Autobiography*. Edited by Samuel Smiles. London: Murray, and New York: Harper, 1883. Written in part to refute allegations that there was French precedent to Nasmyth's invention of the steam hammer, this self-appraisal edited by Samuel Smiles glorifies Nasmyth's personal attributes in explaining his engineering and business success. Many statements are clarified by Cantrell, above.

Rolt, Lionel Thomas Caswell. *Tools for the Job*. London: Batsford, 1965. A technical history of the five major machine-tool groups (turning, drilling, planing, milling, and grinding), this study places Nasmyth's metal-cutting innovations in their British and American contexts.

Smiles, Samuel. *Industrial Biography: Iron Workers and Tool Makers*. London: Murray, 1863; New York: Kelley, 1967. Smiles uses the biographies of several commercially successful British engineers, including Nasmyth, to highlight the benefits of self-reliance and hard work in improving one's economic welfare. His romantic accounts of engineering enterprise found large audiences in Victorian England and helped establish the popular image of Nasmyth as the sole inventor of the steam hammer.

David Shayt

THOMAS NAST

Born: September 27, 1840; Landau, Germany
Died: December 7, 1902; Guayaquil, Ecuador
Areas of Achievement: Art and politics
Contribution: As one of the greatest American cartoonists, Nast created lasting works of art that expressed his personal and political convictions while reflecting the hopes and dreams of a generation.

Early Life

Thomas Nast was born September 27, 1840, in army barracks in Landau, Germany. His father, also called Thomas, was a musician in the Ninth Regiment Bavarian Band. The elder Nast and his wife, Apollonia Apres, had three children before Thomas was born. Two boys died at a very early age, so that Nast's only playmate was an older sister. In 1846, the Nast family decided to move to the United States, because of the father's political affiliations and the threat of revolution in Germany. While the elder Nast served in the French and American navies, his family moved to New York. He joined them four years later.

Young Thomas Nast had by this time developed considerable artistic talent. His crayon drawings thrilled fellow students and teachers, but Nast did not enjoy school. Finally, his parents allowed him to take art classes instead, first with Theodore Kaufmann and later, Alfred Fredericks. Nast's formal education soon ended, when he showed some of his work to Frank Leslie, publisher of *Frank Leslie's Illustrated Newspaper*. Leslie was impressed with the boldness, if not talent, of this short, round-faced, pudgy, fifteen-year-old German with dark hair and olive skin. After Nast's successful completion of a difficult assignment, Leslie hired him at four dollars a week.

Nast worked diligently for *Leslie's Illustrated Newspaper* over the next four years, receiving much technical training from Sol Eytinge, a co-worker and good friend. Nast's drawings during this early period frequently reflected his humorous personality in their subject matter and his study of the English illustrators, John Leech, Sir John Gilbert, and Sir John Tenniel, in methodology. Perhaps most significant for the future, however, was Nast's first battle with corruption. Frank Leslie discovered that while dairy owners sold "swill milk" from diseased cows, New York city officials were looking the other way. With Nast's vivid depictions of the squalid conditions in these dairies, *Leslie's Illustrated Newspaper* brought the issue to the forefront of the news and created a public outcry, which quickly defeated the promoters of the contaminated milk. In this first campaign against corruption, Nast learned that his art could have tremendous political power—a lesson he would not forget.

When Nast left *Leslie's Illustrated Newspaper* in 1859, to work for the *New York Illustrated News*, he covered events such as the funeral of John Brown and the John Heenan-Tom Sayers fight in England. Then, hearing of Giuseppe Garibaldi's invasion of Italy, Nast left England to join the great liberator. While witnessing and recording only a few skirmishes, Nast found upon his return home in February, 1861, that his reputation had grown considerably. Later that year, on the day before his twenty-first birthday, a dignified looking Nast with a recently grown mustache (which became his trademark) married the refined and lovely Sarah Edwards. She would become not only the mother of his five children but also the author of many of the captions for his artwork. Their Niagara Falls honeymoon was a pleasant escape from the realities of a country torn by the Civil War.

Life's Work

At the outbreak of the Civil War, Nast determined to do what he could for the sacred Union. A more devoted patriot could not be found, especially one with his battlefield experience. Consequently, *Harper's Weekly*, a pictorial newspaper begun in 1857, hired Nast to illustrate the events of the war. This association with *Harper's Weekly* would provide Nast the perfect forum for the expression of his ideas and the development of his art.

Nast soon began to create imaginative works which aroused the patriotism and commitment of his Northern audience, pictures which made the Confederate soldier the embodiment of evil and the Union soldier the defender of justice. Nast's fervent support of the Union was recognized by President Abraham Lincoln, who called Nast his best recruiting sergeant.

After the Civil War, Nast used his art to support the Republican Party, which to him represented freedom and equality for the slaves and punishment of the treasonous South. Thus, when President Andrew Johnson adopted a lenient Recon-

struction policy for the South, Nast retaliated with his first use of caricature, the comic distortion of identifiable men. In 1868, Nast used this art form in the campaign to elect Ulysses S. Grant, the hero of the war, to the presidency. With his satiric caricatures of the Democratic presidential candidate from New York, Governor Horatio Seymour, Nast not only helped Grant but also established a national reputation for himself.

The following year marked the beginning of Nast's most widely acclaimed political battle. In his crusade against the corrupt Tweed Ring of New York City, Nast's work matured in technique, composition, and power. Nast's enemies were the Tammany Hall Democrats who controlled the New York state legislature, the immigrants, the courts, the police, and, to some extent, organized crime. Nast made the four Tweed Ring leaders—city boss William Marcy Tweed, Peter Barr Sweeny, Richard Connolly, and A. Oakey Hall—famous with his caricatures. A cartoon entitled "Shadows of Forthcoming Events" (June 4, 1870) revealed the areas of corruption—schools, elections, street cleaners, the fire department, the board of health, saloons—and the men who were responsible for these conditions.

For two years, Nast bombarded the enemy with artistic accusations. His most viciously direct cartoon indicating ring members was "Who Stole the People's Money?" (April 19, 1871), in which corrupt officials stood in a circle, pointing to one another and proclaiming, "Twas Him." Ring members became so frightened over this cartoon that Tweed tried to stop Nast's attacks by threats and then bribery. Nast, true to his principles, vowed not only to continue his fight but also to put the Ring leaders behind bars. With increased public awareness and an honest tabulation of the ballots, the Tweed Ring was defeated in the 1871 election. Although Nast did not win a single-handed victory over the Tweed Ring, one of his caricatures of Tweed did help officials in Spain identify and capture the American fugitive, who died in jail in 1878.

During the early 1870's, Nast continued to support the Republican Party and its candidates, especially Grant, his hero. Nast even created the symbol for the Republican Party, the Republican elephant, and popularized the Democratic donkey in his cartoons. For his assistance in the 1876 campaign of Rutherford B. Hayes, the Republican Party offered Nast ten thousand dollars, but he refused to accept money for expressing his convictions.

Nast became disillusioned with the Republican Party, however, when President Hayes restored home rule to the South in the Compromise of 1877. By 1884, Nast's political dilemma had reached its climax. He could not back James G. Blaine, Republican presidential candidate, since Blaine sponsored Chinese exclusion, a policy contrary to Nast's belief in equality. Nast therefore abandoned the Republicans for the Democratic candidate, Grover Cleveland, whose fiscal policy and personal and political philosophies were more acceptable. Yet, even though Cleveland won the election, Nast's political influence would never be the same. In 1886, the forty-six-year-old Nast ended his fruitful career with *Harper's Weekly*.

Though Nast continued free-lance work and even tried to establish his own paper with the motto Principles, not Men, he soon realized that only one area of his work remained popular—his Christmas sketches. For more than twenty-five years, the Christmas issue of *Harper's Weekly* had contained Nast's drawings of Santa Claus, the jolly, fat, fur-clad, white-bearded legend whom Americans still recall at the holiday season. Nast's inspiration for the character came from his childhood memories of Pelze-Nicol—the local name for the German

Saint Nicholas who awarded good children with toys and bad ones with switches. Appropriately, Nast's last publication was a Christmas drawing for *Leslie's Weekly* in 1901.

Summary

Thomas Nast more completely represents life in late nineteenth century United States than most prominent men of his day, for he not only lived it, but he also captured its essence in his artistic creations. His career began at a time when intense nationalism was of primary importance to his country; his Uncle Sam became the symbol of patriotic feeling. After the Civil War, an era of political Reconstruction caused heated debates among American politicians. Nast became a pictorial contributor to these debates as a Radical Republican. Wherever he saw a threat to American democracy, he pounced on it—whether it took the form of the Ku Klux Klan in the South or the Tweed Ring in New York.

Nast's caricatures and cartoon symbols were given life by the intensity of his principles. The popularity of his Tammany tiger, empty dinner pail, and rag baby of inflation reveals more about society in this period than any political speech or statistical study. For twenty-five years, Nast was a molder of public opinion, intuitively sensing the public mood and responding with drawings which stirred the public mind to thought or action.

Yet by the 1890's, things had changed. The public had grown tired of moral and political crusades. Nast's popularity decreased rapidly, his finances dwindled, and, in 1902, he was forced to accept a gift from his beloved country—a consulship in Ecuador, where he died from yellow fever.

Nast's death indicated the end of an era, but he left a powerful legacy of images: the Republican elephant, the Democratic donkey, Uncle Sam, and the jovial figure who spreads happiness to all mankind, Santa Claus. Moreover, he left the story of a dedicated American whose pursuit of a perfect society with liberty and justice for all could never end.

Bibliography

Gopnik, Adam. "The Man Who Invented Santa Claus: Thomas Nast's Eye for Who's Been Naughty and Who's Been Nice." *The New Yorker* 73, no. 39 (December 15, 1997). Profile of Nast, including his emigration from Germany, his life in the United States, and his illustrations of Santa Claus, which became the icon's model image.

Harper's Weekly, 1859-1886. The original publications of Nast's drawings are an essential source of information in tracing his development and analyzing his contribution.

Keller, Morton. *The Art and Politics of Thomas Nast*. London and New York: Oxford University Press, 1968. Shows how Nast's work reflected the post-Civil War belief that society can be reformed. Weak regarding Nast's artistic techniques.

Levy, Alan. "Thomas Nast's Triumphant Return to Germany." *Art News* 78 (March, 1979): 118-119, 122-123, 125. Details the discovery of Nast's work in his native land. Noting the great success of the 1977 Nast Festival in Landau, Levy suggests that Nastomania has gripped Germany.

Murrell, William. *A History of American Graphic Humor*. New York: Macmillan, 1933-1938. An early work showing the evolution of cartoons from Nast's day to Walt Disney's. Chapter 3 is devoted to Nast. Helpful in placing Nast's work in the appropriate context.

Nast, Thomas. *Thomas Nast's Christmas Drawings*. Introduction by Thomas Nast St. Hill. New York: Dover, 1978. A reprint of the work published by Harper and Brothers in 1890, which compiled Nast's Christmas drawings of almost thirty years. Three illustrations and the introduction by Nast's grandson have been added.

Paine, Albert Bigelow. *Th. Nast: His Period and His Pictures*. New York and London: Macmillan, 1904. Nast selected Paine to write this comprehensive biography. Provides sympathetic insight into Nast's personal life while presenting the history of an era. Used by all subsequent biographers.

Provenzo, Eugene F., Jr. "Thomas Nast and the Church/State Controversy in Education (1870-1876)." *Educational Studies* 12 (Winter, 1981-1982): 359-379. An informative article discussing Nast's fight against funding for parochial schools, especially Catholic ones.

Rawlings, Kevin. "Christmas in the Civil War." *Civil War Times Illustrated* 37, no. 6 (December, 1998). Focuses on Nast's illustrations for the Christmas edition of *Harper's Weekly* in 1893.

Vinson, J. Chal. *Thomas Nast: Political Cartoonist*. Athens: University of Georgia Press, 1967. A scholarly work that condenses the Paine biography, concentrating on those aspects of Nast's career that made him a powerful influence on the politics of his day.

Alice Taylor

CARRY NATION

Born: November 11, 1846; Garrard County, Kentucky

Died: June 9, 1911; Leavenworth, Kansas

Area of Achievement: Social reform

Contribution: An activist in the temperance and women's rights movements, Nation gained international notoriety by smashing saloons. She demonstrated the strength and place of women in temperance reform.

Early Life

Born to George Moore and Mary Campbell Moore, Carry (written in her illiterate father's hand in the family Bible using this spelling) Amelia Moore grew up in the slave culture of Kentucky. Her father was a prosperous planter and stock trader; her mother suffered from a delusionary mental illness and assumed she was Queen Victoria, demanding the appropriate degree of respect from those around her.

At age ten, Carry was converted at a Campbellite revival, an event that had a profound effect on her spiritual development. Her early secular education was limited because her family moved at least a dozen times between Kentucky, Missouri, and Texas before she was sixteen. She did manage, however, to attend a teacher's college in Missouri, where she earned a teaching certificate.

Her father lost his slaves and land as a result of the Civil War, and took his family back to Missouri, settling in Belton. Carry met and fell in love there with a young army physician, Charles Gloyd. They were married on November 21, 1867; however, because of Gloyd's alcoholism and fierce devotion to the Masonic Lodge, the marriage deteriorated soon after the nuptials. Despite her love for Charles, she never persuaded him to stop drinking, which he did in the company of his fellow Masons, and within two years of their marriage he was dead, leaving Carry with an infant daughter, Charlien, who may have grown up insane, an elderly mother-in-law, and an intense dislike for both alcohol and secret societies. For several years, Carry supported herself, her daughter, and her mother-in-law by teaching in a primary school in Holden, Missouri. In 1877, she married David Nation, an attorney, minister, and editor who was nineteen years her senior. They had little in common, and for Carry it proved to be an unhappy match. They lived for several years in Texas, where Carry supported the family by running a hotel. In 1890, they moved to Medicine Lodge, Kansas, where David became a minister and then left the pulpit to practice law. His practice grew large enough to free Carry from the necessity of supporting the family, and as a result, she became active in the temperance movement as well as in religious and civic reform. Because of her interest in charitable activities, the residents of Medicine Lodge called her Mother Nation. Her second marriage also deteriorated, however, and in 1901 Carry's husband divorced her.

Life's Work

Before David and Carry Nation moved to Kansas, a constitutional amendment adopted in 1880 had made it a dry state. This occurred nearly half a century before the passage of the Eighteenth Amendment and fifty years after the beginning of the temperance movement in the United States. In Kansas, a legal technicality allowed liquor in its original container to be served. Carry, believing that she had a divine mission to stop the drinking of alcoholic beverages, organized a chapter of the Women's Christian Temperance Union (WCTU) with the intention of driving out the "wets" (those who drank). Her first major confrontation took place in 1899, when, in the company of several other WCTU members, she managed through nonviolent means to shut down seven liquor distributors. During the following year, she changed her tactics when she traveled twenty miles by buggy to smash three "joints," or saloons, using rocks and brickbats, in Kiowa, Kansas. Carry rationalized that because those establishments were illegal, they had no protection under the law; therefore, she had the right to destroy them. From Kiowa she went to Wichita, where she used a hatchet to destroy the bar in the Hotel Carey. This venture resulted in several thousand dollars of property damage for the saloon owner and seven weeks in jail for Nation. From there it was on to Enterprise and then the state capital, Topeka, for several days of bar chopping. Each incident earned for her more time in the local jail, usually for disturbing the peace.

Prior to her appearance in Topeka, Nation's activities had been of the hit-and-run variety. She would typically break up a few saloons and then either leave town or go to jail. Realizing that she could not single-handedly close down all the offending liquor establishments in Kansas, she intended to use Topeka as a focal point for an organization that, she hoped, would achieve her goal.

After holding an unsuccessful meeting with the governor of Kansas, Carry Nation set about to organize her mostly feminine supporters into an army of Home Defenders. Led by General Nation, who was ably supported by assistant generals, the force numbered several hundred. Nation accepted numerous speaking engagements to spread her message that the only way to close the joints was to increase the agitation against them. In keeping with her message, she took her Home Defenders on the offensive, smashing the ritzy Senate Saloon. In the melee, Nation, who was often in physical danger, received a nasty cut on the head. Despite the destruction, the bar reopened within hours, selling beer, whiskey, and souvenirs from the wreckage.

Carry Nation's actions exacerbated the split in the temperance movement: on the one hand, between the sexes, and on the other hand, between those who supported such violence as necessary and those who took a more passive and traditional approach to the liquor control issue. Nation helped to focus the issue of prohibition in Kansas. Generally, the Prohibitionists, who represented the more radical fringe, supported her tactics, while the Women's Christian Temperance Union leadership, made up mostly of Republicans or Populists, opposed them. Those who opposed Nation disliked her taking the law into her own hands, and they rejected her argument that the joint owners, being lawbreakers themselves, deserved to be put out of business violently.

Nation supported herself and paid her fines by means of lecturing, stage appearances, and the sale of souvenir miniature silver hatchets. For a time, she earned as much as $300 a week. To help with her finances, she employed a management firm, and she later hired her own manager, Harry C. Turner. Unfortunately, Nation had little business sense, giving away most of her money to the poor and to temperance groups, not all of which were legitimate.

Nation also took on a few publishing ventures to spread the word. At varying times, *The Smasher's Mail*, *The Hatchet*, and *The Home Defender* appeared. While in Topeka, she wrote her autobiography, *The Use and Need of the Life of Carry A. Nation* (1905).

Although she spent the majority of her time in the temperance crusade in Kansas, she did venture to the East Coast, where she visited both Yale and Harvard. Unfortunately, on both occasions she allowed herself to be portrayed as a buffoon, thus adding to the negative image surrounding her. She later toured England, where again her welcome was less than expansive.

Physically, Carry Nation was a large woman. Nearly six feet tall, she weighed approximately 175 pounds and was extremely strong. When she and her minions broke up the Senate Saloon, she lifted the heavy cash register, raised it above her head, and smashed it to the ground.

After less than a decade in the public spotlight, however, her health failed, and she retired to a farm in the Ozark Mountains of Arkansas. She spent the last several months of her life in a Leavenworth, Kansas, hospital and died there on June 9, 1911. After her death, friends erected a monument at her gravesite with the inscription "She hath done what she could."

Summary

Carry Nation's impact is both real and symbolic. She did show the nation that direct action can help to focus attention on a moral issue. When, in 1901, Nation went to speak to the Kansas legislature, she told them that since she was denied the vote, she would have to use a stone, and use the stone (or hatchet, to be more specific) she did. The joints she smashed were not significant in terms of her impact on temperance and prohibition. In fact, at least a few of them reopened within hours or days of her visit. Her impact had to do with her ability to rally support to her cause. She focused attention on the issue of alcohol consumption. Representing the views of a majority of Kansans, she showed them that one individual could make a difference.

Nation also had a significant impact on women's rights. She certainly broke with the traditional roles of woman as wife and mother, although she did fulfill both roles. At a time when few women engaged in public protest, Nation was at the cutting edge of that activity. She opened a home in Kansas City for women who had suffered at the hands of male alcoholics. She determined that her activity had been made necessary by a male-dominated world—as a woman, she did not have access to political power. As time went on, however, Nation ap-

peared to be moving toward nonviolent direct action and away from saloon smashing. The masthead of her newspaper *The Hatchet* (1905) encouraged women to seek the vote instead of resorting to the hatchet.

Carry Nation has been badly treated by most of her biographers. In part, she was responsible for her own bad reputation. In her autobiography, she perhaps revealed too much of her personal and religious life, thus exposing herself to criticism. She played into the hands of her critics when she made outrageous statements or visited college campuses where she should have expected to be placed in a bad light. Her methods appeared unfeminine in a decade when feminine virtue was extolled. She also became the victim of the eastern press, which delighted in poking fun at the crude ways of westerners by mocking Nation as a social misfit and a religious freak.

Carry Nation died almost a decade before the passage of the Eighteenth Amendment, which outlawed the manufacture, distribution, sale, and consumption of alcoholic beverages. Whether people remembered her in 1919 is not of great importance; the amendment passed in part at least because she focused the attention of many Americans on the issue of prohibition. Whether one was for or against temperance, it would have been difficult in the first decade of the twentieth century to ignore the issue, especially when Carry Nation went storming into bars with hatchet in hand.

She also died a decade before the passage of the Nineteenth Amendment, which granted women the right to vote. Her statements to the Kansas legislature, as well as her newspaper's masthead, indicate that Carry Nation well knew the power of the ballot and the importance of working for the right of women to vote.

Bibliography

Asbury, Herbert. *Carry Nation.* New York: Knopf, 1929. This older biography paints Nation as a social misfit.

Bader, Robert Smith. *Prohibition in Kansas.* Lawrence: University Press of Kansas, 1986. This general history of prohibition in Kansas contains a very positive chapter on Carry Nation and her contribution to the temperance movement.

Boring, Mel. "Carry Nation's Hatchetations." *Cobblestone* 14, no. 8 (October, 1993). Profile of Nation and her efforts as a prohibitionist.

Day, Robert. "Carry from Kansas Became a Nation All Unto Herself." *Smithsonian* 20, no. 1 (April, 1989). Examines Nation's strengths and weaknesses.

Flexner, Eleanor. *Century of Struggle: The Woman's Rights Movement in the United States.* Rev. ed. Cambridge, Mass.: Belknap Press of Harvard University Press, 1975. Provides an excellent starting point for anyone interested in the women's rights movement.

Gusfield, Joseph. *Symbolic Crusade: Status Politics and the American Temperance Movement.* 2d ed. Urbana: University of Illinois Press, 1986. An interesting and useful history of the temperance movement from its nineteenth century roots to the passage of the Eighteenth Amendment.

Lewis, Robert Taylor. *Vessel of Wrath: The Life and Times of Carry Nation.* New York: New American Library, 1966. A relatively recent biography written in negative terms.

Nation, Carry. *The Use and Need of the Life of Carry A. Nation, Written by Herself.* Rev. ed. Topeka, Kans.: Steves, 1905. Nation's autobiography sets the negative tone for her biographers.

Duncan R. Jamieson

LORD NELSON

Born: September 29, 1758; Burnham Thorpe, Norfolk, England

Died: October 21, 1805; off Cape Trafalgar, Spain

Area of Achievement: The military

Contribution: Nelson's innovative tactics in battle and his determination to achieve total victory over the enemy made him the most famous admiral in British history and helped to establish the tradition of British perseverance until final victory could be won.

Early Life

Horatio Nelson was born in the Anglican parsonage at Burnham Thorpe, England, in the county of Norfolk, on September 29, 1758, the sixth of eleven children born to his parents, Edmund and Catherine Nelson. Edmund Nelson, a very devout, educated man, was a minister in the Church of England and was following his father's occupation, although without much financial reward. Catherine Nelson came from a family that owned much land and occupied a respected position on the social ladder; her father was the prebendary of Westminster, and her maternal grandmother was the sister of Sir Robert Walpole, the first prime minister in English history. The Walpoles resided nearby, at Houghton, and the second Lord Walpole of Wolterton acted as godfather to young Nelson when he was christened.

As a young boy, Nelson was sent by his father to three separate schools in Norfolk, but some of his major personal beliefs he developed at home. Although his mother died when he was only nine years old, Nelson remembered that it was from her that he became aware that France was England's ancient enemy. From his father, he learned about piety and obedience to God, and throughout his naval career he often expressed his pleasure at being able to serve God as well as his country.

Young Nelson was always very sensitive to criticism, and he displayed his emotions publicly. In future years, as an officer in the fleet, he continued to display these same feelings, even though it was a tradition for naval officers to keep their feelings well hidden from their men. This practice, however, coupled with an unusually large measure of common sense, a genuine interest in the welfare of his men, and a willingness to lead his crew personally into battle, helped to produce the feelings of awe, respect, and loyalty that his men always held

for him. Nelson received many serious injuries in the line of duty, and members of his crew, who were the most likely to be injured or killed in close combat with the enemy, trusted him as an officer who would actually lead them into battle and not simply watch their actions from a safe distance.

In the meantime, after the death of Catherine Nelson it was increasingly difficult for Edmund Nelson to provide proper care for all of his children, and they gradually left home to obtain independent positions. For Horatio, an interest in the sea had been slowly developing. From his hometown, he could easily catch sight of the North Sea and the ships that sailed its waters almost constantly, and on occasion he would sail some of his paper boats down one of the streets of Burnham Thorpe. His desire to go to sea, however, seemed to represent a most unlikely choice for a boy of his physical build: His rather thin face was highlighted by a large, protruding nose and piercing blue eyes, and he possessed a frail body that would attain a height of less than five feet and six inches by adulthood. Throughout his life, he would be plagued by a constant cough, and he often had difficulty sleeping at night. Fits of depression troubled him from time to time, and occasionally he was unable to keep his food down. Later in life, he would be afflicted with seasickness if forced to remain for long on a small vessel.

These problems notwithstanding, Nelson, at the age of twelve, sought to go to sea. His father registered no objections, and his uncle, Maurice Suckling, who held the position of post-captain in the navy at the time, agreed to obtain a position for his young nephew on his own ship, the *Raisonnable*, in spite of his personal doubts about Nelson's physical qualifications.

Suckling's ship was to sail to the Falkland Islands to defend Great Britain's position in a dispute with Spain over the ownership of those islands. This voyage, which was Nelson's first at sea, ended peacefully, and subsequently the young man was placed with John Rathbone, an officer who had served under Suckling during the Seven Years' War and who was now commanding a ship for the trading firm of Hibbert, Purrier, and Horton. Under Rathbone's guidance, the young Nelson sailed on a voyage to the West Indies, and it was this voyage that convinced him that he wanted to spend the rest of his life in the British navy.

Life's Work

Nelson's naval career began in 1773, when he served as a coxswain on a scientific expedition to the Arctic. He subsequently was assigned as a midshipman in the waters off India, and by the age of nineteen, he was commissioned with the rank of lieutenant. Throughout his career as an officer, Nelson worked hard to keep morale high on his ship. He regularly invited other officers to fine dinners in his quarters and tactfully inquired as to the welfare of the members of their families. While he expected absolute obedience, he never forgot the basic needs of his men; their living quarters were equipped with stoves to prevent dampness, and in the evenings, they were allowed to play music and to dance.

At the time Nelson was commissioned, the American Revolution was in progress, and he spent much of the war on duty in the West Indies. After the war ended, Nelson, now a post-captain, remained in the islands until 1787. It was on this peacetime tour that he met Frances Nesbit, the widowed niece of John Herbert, the president of the island of Nevis. On March 11, 1787, Nelson married the woman he said would keep him happy for the rest of his life.

During his courtship, however, Nelson aroused the ire of the local planters and merchants by refusing to allow them to trade with ships from the United States. Although the Board of Trade defended Nelson's actions, he became so unpopular that he returned to England two months after his marriage in 1787. From 1787 to 1793, Nelson lived quietly with his family in Burnham Thorpe, a virtual social outcast because of the many complaints from the wealthy residents of the West Indies. When war with France appeared imminent in 1793, however, his unpopularity faded and he was assigned to the Mediterranean fleet under Admiral Samuel Hood.

On this tour of duty, Nelson saw military action around Corsica. As was his custom, he took little precaution for safety and was standing right up at the batteries outside Calvi on July 12, 1794, when he was hit in the right eye by sand and rocks from a French shell. As a result of this injury, he permanently lost the use of his eye, although it was never removed.

After a brief period of recuperation, Nelson was eventually assigned to the command of Admiral John Jervis, who commanded a fleet of fifteen ships of the line and was known for his strict discipline. On February 14, 1797, off Cape St. Vincent,

Jervis attacked a Spanish fleet of twenty-seven ships of the line by moving his ships in a line between the leading and the trailing Spanish columns. Nelson, however, realized that the enemy segments would be able to join before the British move could be completed, and without orders he pulled his own ship out of the line and blocked the advance of the Spanish flagship. In the fierce fighting that followed, Nelson personally boarded and captured two Spanish ships. When the battle ended, the Spanish had lost four ships of the line, while the British had lost none. For Nelson, who had risked a court-martial by breaking naval tradition, Jervis had only words of praise. Both men were subsequently rewarded; Jervis became the Earl of St. Vincent, and Nelson was promoted to the rank of rear-admiral and became a Knight of the Bath.

St. Vincent, convinced by now of Nelson's abilities, next sent him to capture a Spanish treasure ship in the harbor of Santa Cruz, on the island of Teneriffe, in the Canary Islands. On July 24, 1797, Nelson, in typical fashion, led the attack himself, but a musket ball shattered his right arm. Within hours, surgeons amputated the arm just above the elbow, and Nelson's tour of duty had come to an end.

After a brief recuperation in England, Nelson was sent to watch the French fleet at Toulon. When this fleet sailed for Egypt in May, 1798, he gave chase and finally came upon it in late July in Aboukir Bay, just east of Alexandria. Admiral Francis Brueys, the French commander, had placed his thirteen ships of the line very close to the shoals offshore, so that only the seaward side of his ships could be attacked by Nelson. Because of his strong position, Brueys did not bother to clear his guns on the landward side of his ships, and he was caught completely by surprise on August 1, 1798, when Nelson sent five of his thirteen ships of the line between the French fleet and the shoals offshore. Panic broke out among the French as they were fired on from two sides at once, and although Nelson himself was wounded in the forehead, his victory in the Battle of the Nile was assured when Brueys's flagship, *L'Orient*, exploded. By dawn of the next day, only two of the French ships had escaped; Nelson had not lost a single ship, and for his efforts he was made Baron of the Nile.

From Egypt, Nelson sailed to Naples, where his famous affair with Lady Emma Hamilton led to the birth of a daughter, Horatia. This affair, however, severely damaged Nelson's reputation; when he returned to England in 1799, he found himself rejected by both society and his wife. In January, 1801, Horatio and Frances Nelson permanently separated.

The Admiralty, however, still needed Nelson's services, and he was assigned as second in command to Sir Hyde Parker on an expedition to detach Denmark from the League of Armed Neutrality. Parker, who fought by the book, cautiously agreed to Nelson's plan to attack the harbor of Copenhagen at its least defended point by sailing through a very narrow, shallow water-way that was considered impassable for ships of the line. Nelson attacked on April 2, 1801, but when the Danes put up unexpected resistance Parker ordered him to withdraw. In response, Nelson placed his telescope to his blind eye, reported that he could see no such order, and scored a major victory within the hour. Once again, Nelson had disobeyed the orders of a superior officer, but he was praised by Sir Thomas Masterman Hardy, Nelson's flag captain, and was made a viscount for his victory.

Lord Nelson subsequently remained in England until 1803, when war with France was renewed.

Now a vice-admiral, he was named commander in chief for the Mediterranean Fleet and began to cover the fleet of Admiral Pierre de Villeneuve at Toulon. Villeneuve made various efforts to join up with other ships of the French fleet, but Nelson pursued him closely and eventually engaged him in battle off Cape Trafalgar on October 21, 1805. In this action, Nelson's twenty-seven ships broke the enemy line of thirty-three in two places, in the rear and in the center. Typically, Nelson led the attack on the center himself, but about one hour and twenty minutes after the battle had begun, a musketeer in the rigging of the French ship *Redoutable* fatally wounded Nelson, who fell with a bullet through his spine. Before he died, however, he learned that eighteen of the enemy ships had been destroyed or captured and that not one of his own vessels had been lost. With his last words, he thanked God that he had been able to do his duty.

Nelson's body was returned to England, where on January 9, 1806, it received one of the most impressive funerals in all British history. According to his wishes, Nelson was buried in St. Paul's Cathedral.

Summary

Even before his death, Lord Nelson was regarded as a legend, and the circumstances surrounding his funeral merely added to that mystique. Captain Benjamin Hallowell of the *Swiftsure* had given his commander, as a victory souvenir, a beautiful wooden coffin fashioned out of part of the main mast of *L'Orient* after the Battle of the Nile, and it was in this coffin that the famous admiral was buried.

Memories of the funeral faded, but people never forgot that Nelson was the first British commander to seek not merely victory but also total destruction of the enemy fleet. The victory at Trafalgar ended Napoleon's hopes for an invasion of Great Britain and became a symbol of British inspiration in the dark days when Adolf Hitler was putting forth every effort to conquer the island kingdom.

Nelson's legacy is well represented by preservation of his last ship, the *Victory*, a ship of the line of one hundred guns that became a national monument. Nelson himself is also remembered in London's Trafalgar Square, where his statue stands as a constant reminder of the man who saved Great Britain from one of the greatest threats in its long history.

Bibliography

Bowen, Marjorie. *Patriotic Lady.* New York and London: Appleton, 1936. A useful work that presents much detailed information about the personalities of Nelson and Hamilton. The coverage of Hamilton's first meeting with Frances Nelson is particularly interesting. Well researched, the work includes a good index and a helpful bibliography.

Cowie, Leonard W. *Lord Nelson, 1758-1805: A Bibliography.* London and Westport, Conn.: Meckler, 1989. A comprehensive, annotated bibliography on the life and career of Lord Nelson.

Hattersley, Roy. *Nelson.* London: Weidenfeld and Nicolson, and New York: Saturday Review Press, 1974. The style is very easy to follow, and many drawings and portraits are included. While he covers Nelson's major victories, Hattersley also takes time to bring out the personality behind those victories. The index is most helpful for the general reader.

Howarth, David. *Trafalgar: The Nelson Touch.* London: Collins, and New York: Atheneum, 1969. One of the most readable of all books about Nelson, this work concentrates upon the admiral's last campaign. Howarth provides specific details; he also covers Nelson's close relations with the men who served under him. An excellent index and many maps and drawings enhance the scholarly nature of this work.

Mahan, Alfred T. *The Influence of Sea Power upon History, 1660-1783.* London: Sampson, Low, Marston, and Boston: Little Brown, 1890. A standard work in the field, Mahan's book helps the reader to understand why control of the sea is so important during wartime. Nelson's tactics at Aboukir Bay and Trafalgar are analyzed, and his general manner in battle is also discussed.

———. *The Influence of Sea Power Upon the French Revolution and Empire, 1793-1812.* 2 vols. London: Sampson, Low, Marston, and Boston: Little Brown, 1892. A famous work in the field, featuring maps, drawings, explanatory footnotes, and an extremely complete index. Contains helpful coverage of Nelson's campaigns in detail, with emphasis upon the tactics that he introduced.

Marcus, Geoffrey J. *The Age of Nelson: The Royal Navy, 1793-1815.* London: Allen and Unwin, and New York: Viking Press, 1971. An excellent, well-researched work complete with maps, many illustrations, footnotes, and a thorough list of sources for additional reading. Quite helpful in its discussion of Nelson's relations with Jervis.

Pope, Dudley. *The Great Gamble.* London: Weidenfeld and Nicolson, and New York: Simon and Schuster, 1972. A complete account of the Copenhagen campaign, Pope's work provides footnotes, maps, and a full bibliography. Discussion of the contrast in the personalities of Nelson and Parker is especially helpful. Virtually any fact that the reader desires to know about the Copenhagen campaign may be found in this book.

Warner, Oliver. *Nelson's Battles.* London: Batsford, and New York: Macmillan, 1965. Warner provides detailed information about Nelson's major engagements; an appendix lists all the ships and captains who served with Nelson at Aboukir Bay, Copenhagen, and Trafalgar. Excellent maps, many portraits, and frequent quotations from Nelson and his contemporaries.

———. *Victory: The Life of Lord Nelson.* Boston: Little Brown, 1958. A well-written, very detailed life of Nelson in which considerable emphasis is placed upon personalities as well as major campaigns. Includes an extensive bibliography and a most complete index.

David W. Krueger

SIMON NEWCOMB

Born: March 12, 1835; Wallace, Canada
Died: July 11, 1909; Washington, D.C.
Area of Achievement: Science
Contribution: Combining intellectual prowess and organizational ability, Newcomb, the best-known American scientist at the turn of the century, revolutionized dynamical astronomy.

Early Life

Although primarily of New England stock, Simon Newcomb was born in Wallace, Nova Scotia, Canada, on March 12, 1835, the elder son of John Burton Newcomb, an itinerant country schoolteacher, and Emily Prince, the daughter of a New Brunswick magistrate. He spent his youth traveling with his father from village to village in Nova Scotia and Prince Edward Island. On reflection, he believed that he had had relatively little formal education, although he had attended his father's schools on occasion. (Newcomb later claimed that scientific geniuses were born, not created through formal education; he may have had his own experience in mind.)

At sixteen, Newcomb was apprenticed to a Dr. Foshay for five years of training in medical botany. After only two years, Newcomb ran away to the United States, having concluded that Foshay was an uneducated quack. Newcomb found employment as a country schoolteacher and tutor in Maryland. A frequent visitor to Washington, D. C., he became acquainted with Joseph Henry, secretary of the Smithsonian Institution, and J. E. Hilgard of the United States Coast Survey. He impressed them with his intellectual prowess; less evident at this point were his abrasiveness and sense of self-importance. Through their recommendations, he gained an audience with the Nautical Almanac Office in Cambridge, Massachusetts. In early 1857, he was appointed astronomical computer with the almanac on a trial basis, entering what he would later call in his autobiography the "world of sweetness and light."

Life's Work

During the next four years, Newcomb increased his sophistication as a mathematical astronomer. Taking advantage of his location and the relatively undemanding responsibilities of a computer, he studied mathematics at Harvard University with Benjamin Peirce, gaining a B.S. degree in 1858. Thereafter, he continued his efforts at self-education. He gained a reputation for industry and the ability to grasp material quickly. A sign of his maturing as a scientist was his election to membership in the American Association for the Advancement of Science in 1859.

Two years later, Newcomb left Cambridge to assume a professorship in mathematics in the United States Navy and an assignment at the Naval Observatory. His initial duty was to take observations with a transit instrument and then to reduce his observations and those of the other astronomers using the instrument. He soon discovered that the Naval Observatory lacked a uniform system of reducing data, making Newcomb's task of combining the data more difficult. This confusing situation revealed to Newcomb the importance of organization to the efficient completion of a scientific endeavor.

During the next sixteen years, Newcomb investigated a number of research problems regarding the sun, moon, and planets, concentrating on the orbit theory. In 1866, he published his theory of Neptune's motion; his tables of the motion of Uranus appeared in 1874, and his treatise on the moon in 1878.

This was also a period of personal and professional change. In 1863, Newcomb married Mary Caroline Hassler. His growing family (he would eventually have three daughters) and the realization that he preferred theoretical mathematical research to observation led him to contemplate a career change. He alternately attempted to become superintendent of the Naval Observatory and to obtain an appointment as a theorist in the Nautical Almanac Office. The navy blocked the former efforts because it wanted a naval officer to run the observatory. His superior at the observatory, having no desire to lose him, offered a compromise: In 1869, Newcomb was relieved of his responsibilities for routine observations so that he could concentrate on the tables of lunar motion. In 1870, he was sent to Europe by the United States government to observe a solar eclipse and to collect additional data from European observations on lunar motion. Newcomb's consultations with some of Europe's leading astronomers confirmed both the significance of the problems he was investigating and the quality of his own work. In September, 1877, he was appointed superintendent of the Nautical Almanac Office, which had, by this time, moved to Washington, D. C.

His major research program for the Nautical Almanac Office was the development of new theories and tables for planetary motion. At first, he funded the program by restructuring the *American Ephemeris and Nautical Almanac*, the primary product of the Nautical Almanac Office, so that it required less calculation, thus freeing up staff. Later, he persuaded Congress to support the research directly. Newcomb divided the program into three separate parts: the four inner planets, Jupiter and Saturn (which were given to George W. Hill), and Uranus and Neptune (which was only an updating of Newcomb's earlier work). It was not until 1895 that the program was essentially completed.

Photographs of the mature astronomer show a large head and a graying beard, usually in need of a trim. Contemporaries describe him as a dominating presence at a scientific meeting. They had many opportunities to see him. He belonged to numerous organizations, astronomical societies, and academies, including the National Academy of Sciences and the American Astronomical Society; he was elected the first president of the latter.

Newcomb authored hundreds of items, among them some widely read popular astronomical works, a text on spherical astronomy, mathematics texts (in the 1880's and 1890's, he taught mathematics at The Johns Hopkins University, becoming a professor in 1884), and papers on psychic research (he was a skeptic) and economics. He even wrote three novels.

In 1897, at the age of sixty-two, he was automatically retired by the navy with the rank of captain, although he continued to work for the Nautical Almanac on a consulting basis. He was promoted to the rank of rear admiral (retired) in 1906. He died on July 11, 1909, in Washington, D. C., and was buried with military honors in Arlington National Cemetery.

Summary

Simon Newcomb began his scientific career at an opportune time. The American scientific community was sufficiently mature and large so that there were jobs available for bright young men, but not so mature or large as to exclude mathematical astronomers who lacked formal educational credentials. For a man of Newcomb's background, the 1850's were the ideal time to start a career.

Newcomb was lucky also because his chosen field of endeavor was reaching the peak of its importance. The predicted discovery of Neptune in 1846 had demonstrated the great power of celestial mechanics. Astronomers were concerned with predicting and determining the position of stars, planets, and the moon. Newcomb was involved in the central astronomical research problem. By the end of the century, however, it was the "new" astronomy, astrophysics, which was the important field. The essential question had become the composition of the stars and planets. Newcomb's work became relatively peripheral.

There was yet a third way in which Newcomb's timing was perfect. With the death of Joseph Henry in 1878, the American scientific community lost its leader. There was no obvious successor. A void had developed which Newcomb consciously attempted to fill over the years, with great success—the product of his visibility as a scientist, his extensive popular writings, and his international reputation.

According to the traditional American success story, the individual who is poor and self-educated gains success through hard work and dedication.

Normally, however, the success is in the fields of business or politics. Simon Newcomb proved that it could happen in science.

Bibliography

Clerke, Agnes M. *A Popular History of Astronomy During the Nineteenth Century.* 4th ed. London: Black, 1902; St. Clair Shores, Mich.: Scholarly Press, 1977. Still the best overview of the astronomical research of the period. This edition provides a sense of Newcomb's position in international astronomy just prior to the completion of his major research program at the Nautical Almanac.

Dupree, A. Hunter. *Science in the Federal Government: A History of Policies and Activities to 1940.* Cambridge, Mass.: Harvard University Press, 1957; London: Johns Hopkins University Press, 1986. The best survey of scientific activity in the federal government. It places Newcomb's career and the history of the institutions he worked for in a larger context.

Moyer, Albert. *A Scientist's Voice in American Culture: Simon Newcomb and the Rhetoric of Scientific Method.* Berkeley: University of California Press, 1992. In this, the first serious biography of Newcomb, Mayer pays particular attention to Newcomb's adherence to the scientific method, which is linked by the author to the pragmatic traditions of C. S. Peirce and William James.

———. "Simon Newcomb: Astronomer with and Attitude." *Scientific American* 279, no. 4 (October, 1998). Examines Newcomb and his work in astronomy and celestial navigation. Includes Newcomb's belief in the use of the scientific method in scientific, cultural, and social endeavors.

Newcomb, Simon. *The Reminiscences of an Astronomer.* Boston: Houghton Mifflin, and London: Harper, 1903. Still the basic source of information on Newcomb's early life.

Norberg, Arthur L. "Simon Newcomb's Early Astronomical Career." *Isis* 69 (1978): 209-225. A scholarly analysis of Newcomb's life and work through 1870.

———. "Simon Newcomb's Role in the Astronomical Revolution of the Early Nineteen Hundreds." In *Sky with Ocean Joined: Proceedings of the Sesquicentennial Symposia of the U.S. Naval Observatory.* Edited by Steven J. Dick and LeRoy E. Doggett, 74-88. Washington, D.C.: United States Naval Observatory, 1983. Focuses on Newcomb's research program on planetary tables.

Weber, Gustavus A. *The Naval Observatory: Its History, Activities and Organization.* Baltimore: The Johns Hopkins University Press, 1926. Although badly dated, this is the only general history of this institution which covers the entire period of Newcomb's life. It provides unique insight into the bureaucratic structure within which Newcomb functioned.

Marc Rothenberg

JOHN HENRY NEWMAN

Born: February 21, 1801; London, England
Died: August 11, 1890; Edgbaston, England
Area of Achievement: Religion
Contribution: A leading figure in the Oxford Movement, which brought religious issues to the forefront of the Victorian consciousness, Newman, after his conversion to Catholicism, became the leading Catholic figure in Great Britain, writing eloquently about religion and education and influencing the course of theological and administrative practices within the Catholic church in Great Britain and throughout the world.

Early Life

The eldest of six children, John Henry Newman grew up in a close-knit family and was educated at Dr. Nicolas' school at Ealing. At age fifteen, shortly before he matriculated at Oxford, Newman underwent a period of extreme mental crisis, which he later described as his conversion, and became deeply religious, convinced that God had destined him for a high calling. His reading during this period led him to appreciate the early church fathers and to fear the Roman Catholic church's influence in the modern world.

In the fall of 1816, Newman's father took his son to Oxford and enrolled him at Trinity College. Newman did not actually move to the university until the following summer, when he began a period of intense study in the classics and mathematics. His performance during his first year earned for him a prestigious scholarship, but he was bitterly disappointed in 1820 when he failed to gain a coveted first in either classics or mathematics.

Believing that his performance at Trinity did not truly represent his abilities, Newman applied for a fellowship at Oriel College. The examiners found him clearly the best applicant, and in April, 1822, he joined the college, where he was to achieve fame and then notoriety. At Oriel, he became acquainted first with Edward Pusey, Edward Copleston, Richard Whately, and Edward Hawkins, and later with Richard Hurrell Froude and John Keble. In 1825, Newman was ordained an Anglican priest. For the next several years he combined duties as an educator at the college and at Alban Hall, with priestly functions as vicar of St. Mary's Church, Oxford.

An extended trip through Sicily led to a serious illness, which forced Newman into a lengthy period of convalescence on the Continent. He returned to Oxford in time for his friend John Keble's famous sermon on national apostasy, which initiated what came to be known as the Oxford Movement.

Life's Work

Newman and his Oxford colleagues took advantage of the outcry generated by Keble's sermon to bring before the public their thoughts on the proper role of the Church. In September, 1833, Newman published his thoughts on Apostolic Succession in a small pamphlet, or tract, which he had delivered all over Great Britain. This first pamphlet was followed by dozens of others during the next eight years, written by various Tractarians, as Newman's group was called. Intended to establish the right of the Anglican church to the title of "catholic," *Tracts for the Times* eventually led many to believe that the Church of Rome, not that of Canterbury, was the only body to preserve the true spirit of early Christianity. Newman's polemical *Tract Ninety*, in which he argued that even Roman Catholics could subscribe to the Thirty-nine Articles, caused such a stir that the tracts were terminated. Newman himself had grown to believe that the Anglican church was not a "via media," as he had once argued so eloquently. In 1841, he left Oxford to reside at the parish house in nearby Littlemore where he spent four years agonizing over his own religious future. Finally, he broke openly with the Church of England: On October 9, 1845, he was baptized into the Roman Catholic church.

The Anglican church hierarchy was shaken by this move; the Roman Catholic community was elated. Within two years, Newman completed his studies in Rome and was ordained a priest, receiving from the Pope a commission to establish in Great Britain an Oratory like those of Saint Philip Neri. Newman established his community in 1848, in Birmingham, bringing into it several men who had converted at or about the same time.

The move into the bosom of Rome had ironic consequences. In the Anglican church, Newman had been one of the chief spokesmen for conservative values; as a Roman Catholic, he found himself immediately cast as the champion of liberalism. Newman's belief in individual intellectual inquiry

and in participation by the laity in the government of the Church set him at odds with numerous bishops and priests who viewed centralization of all authority as essential to the health of the "one true Church." These differences of opinion caused Newman considerable difficulty for almost two decades. Even within his own community at Birmingham he faced controversy. Several of the Oratorians, recent converts to Roman Catholicism, had found great solace in practicing the extreme forms of worship common in Italian churches. These men were disillusioned with Newman's moderate tone toward non-Catholics. Eventually, the community split, with a group establishing a separate Oratory in London under Frederick William Faber, one of Newman's most trusted friends and followers.

Newman was not anxious to challenge openly the Church of England; rather, he wanted to lead British Catholics to the Church of Rome through conciliatory measures. That plan was made especially difficult almost from the outset when, in 1850, the Pope decided to reestablish bishops in residence in Great Britain; since the sixteenth century, the country had been a "mission" for the Catholic church, without a designated diocesan headquarters. To make matters worse, Nicholas Wiseman, first archbishop of Westminster, inflamed public opinion by suggesting that the Catholic church was "reclaiming" England. Protestants rallied against this "papal aggression," and Newman found himself explaining to both Catholics and Protestants that the Church had no temporal aims.

In the early 1850's, the Irish bishops, wanting to establish an independent university to provide Catholics with an education not influenced by the Protestant institutions of higher learning, sought out Newman to found a Catholic university in Dublin. Initial efforts were promising. In 1852, Newman delivered a series of lectures in Ireland, outlining his plans for the school, which were later collected under the title *The Idea of a University Defined and Illustrated* (1852). Newman wanted to build a university on the model of Oxford, where classical and scientific learning were the cornerstones of education. The bishops wanted little of such independent thinking; instead, they had hoped that the new colleges would indoctrinate students in Catholicism. Newman tried for several years to compromise and bring the school into existence; the effort eventually failed, and in 1858 he resigned.

During this period, Newman found himself embroiled in a lawsuit, brought against him by a former priest, Giacinto Achilli. Having fled to Great Britain, Achilli entertained Protestants by railing against the Church of Rome; in response, Newman, knowing Achilli to be a philanderer, castigated him in print. When Achilli sued, Newman was unable to obtain from Rome or from Archbishop Wiseman the documents he needed for a defense. Though a friend went to Rome and brought back witnesses against Achilli, Newman was still found guilty and ordered to pay a fine. Public outcry against what appeared to be Protestant injustice brought Newman considerable support, financial as well as moral; with the excess funds which were sent to him by well-wishers Newman was able to build a church for the university in Dublin.

Almost immediately after he resigned from his position at the University in Dublin, Newman found himself at the center of another controversy over the *Rambler*, a monthly Catholic lay magazine which often questioned church authorities. To quell growing dissatisfaction, Newman agreed to become the editor, but his own practices were not acceptable to the bishops, who had originally objected. Newman was forced to resign almost immediately after he had assumed the editorship, but not before he published an influential article, "On Consulting the Faithful in Matters of Doctrine." His liberal ideas on the role of the laity—ideas based on his study of the Church and its early history— caused him to be accused of heresy and left him under a cloud with those in Rome.

Vindication for Newman came slowly and began not within the church he had adopted but rather within his country. The publication of an article by Charles Kingsley in 1864, in which Kingsley accused Newman of condoning lies as a means of promoting the Catholic faith, forced Newman to clear his reputation by explaining his conversion. The series of letters Newman published in the spring of 1864 were collected into a volume that became the most important religious autobiography of the century: *Apologia Pro Vita Sua*. The work was praised by both Protestants and Catholics for its sincere presentation of a man's search for truth. After its publication, Newman became reconciled with several of the friends whom he had abandoned when he converted two decades earlier. *Apologia Pro Vita Sua* was followed in 1870 by *An Essay in Aid of a Grammar of Assent*, which explains how one can find assurances in faith that go beyond the merely intellectual.

In 1870, Newman was invited to the First Vatican Council to help determine an important and controversial issue: papal infallibility. He declined. He believed in the doctrine but feared that the council would declare the Pope infallible in all of his pronouncements. He need not have been concerned. The council adopted a more circumscribed definition, that the Pope spoke infallibly only on matters of faith and morals.

In 1878, Oxford honored Newman when officials of Trinity College elected him as the first Honorary Fellow. Not until Leo XIII became pope, however, did Newman gain the ecclesiastical recognition he deserved. One of the new pope's first acts was to make Newman a cardinal. After some initial concern, and an attempt by Henry, Cardinal Manning, of Westminster to thwart the appointment, Newman eventually accepted the honor, and he was elevated to the cardinalate in May, 1879. The Pope allowed Newman to retain his residence at the Oratory in Birmingham, where he died on August 11, 1890.

Summary

John Henry Newman's influence on the Catholic church in England during the nineteenth century cannot be overestimated. His own conversion was the catalyst that led dozens of others to adopt the Roman rule. Within the Church, he served as a constant voice for liberalism, stressing the dignity of individuals and the importance of the laity. Many of his ideas about the role of the laity formed the basis for later decisions of the Second Vatican Council in 1965, seven decades after his death.

Similarly, Catholic education has accepted a number of Newman's ideas. His influence on Catholic colleges and universities both in Great Britain and in America has been significant. As Newman had urged, while most Catholic institutions of higher learning offer a liberal education that includes the study of theology, they also teach secular subjects and allow students to confront the evils of the world directly, offering guidance rather than trying to isolate students from life's challenges.

Though Newman was a poet of some merit, his major contributions to British letters are his volumes of prose, especially his spiritual autobiography, his analysis of the nature of belief, and his writings on education. In an eloquent yet accessible style, he explored his subjects with great erudition and sincerity. His works continue to be read as examples of the essay at its best.

Bibliography

Bouyer, Louis. *Newman: His Life and Spirituality.* Translated by J. L. May. London: Burns and Oates, and New York: Kenedy, 1958. Detailed biography illuminating the complex psychology of its subject. Excellent analysis of Newman's motives for his conversion, his belief in the importance of the laity, and his insistence on the need for intellectual inquiry for all Catholics. Makes extensive use of Newman's diaries and letters.

Culler, A. Dwight. *The Imperial Intellect: A Study of Newman's Educational Ideal.* New Haven, Conn.: Yale University Press, and Oxford: Oxford University Press, 1955. Well-researched study of Newman's life, focusing primarily on his thinking, writing, and action concerning education. Excellent discussions of *The Idea of a University,* and of Newman's efforts to found such an institution.

Dessain, Charles Stephen. *John Henry Newman.* 3d ed. Oxford and New York: Oxford University Press, 1980. Brief biography by the editor of Newman's letters. Concentrates on Newman's religious life and the controversies surrounding his conversion and his dealings with the hierarchy in Rome. Excellent analysis of Newman's lifelong quest to understand and propagate the notion of revealed religion.

Hollis, Christopher. *Newman and the Modern World.* London: Hollis and Carter, 1967; New York: Doubleday, 1968. Biographical sketch which examines Newman's ideas and contributions to religion as they affected his contemporaries and the subsequent actions and pronouncements of the Roman Catholic church. Good source of information about both the major events of Newman's life and the impact his writings have had on the changes brought about by the Second Vatican Council.

Ker, Ian, ed. *Newman and Conversion.* Notre Dame, Ind.: University of Notre Dame Press, 1997. This volume was published in conjunction with a conference held at Oxford in 1995 commemorating the 150th anniversary of Newman's conversion to Catholicism. Contributors include Ker, Cyril Barrett, Avery Dulles, Ronald Begley, and more.

Martin, Brian. *John Henry Newman: His Life and Work*. London: Chatto and Windus, and New York: Oxford University Press, 1982. Brief, highly readable biographical sketch, profusely illustrated. Provides short analyses of Newman's major works, including his novels. Stresses the difficulties Newman had in dealing with the conservative party within the Catholic church.

Rothblatt, Sheldon. *The Modern University and Its Discontents: The Fate of Newman's Legacies in Britain and America*. Cambridge and New York: Cambridge University Press, 1997. Rothblatt uses Newman's "The Idea of a University" as the basis for his study of the modern university and the manner in which the past has shaped its development.

Trevor, Meriol. *Newman*. Vol. 1, *The Pillar of the Cloud;* Vol. 2, *Light in Winter*. London: Macmillan, and New York: Doubleday, 1962. The standard biography. Provides well-documented sources, illustrations, and an extensive index.

Ward, Wilfrid. *The Life of John Henry Cardinal Newman*. 2 vols. London and New York: Longman, 1912. First major biography of Newman; makes extensive use of personal correspondence and private papers, as well as anecdotes from those who knew him. Despite the title, deals almost exclusively with the years Newman spent as a member of the Roman Catholic church.

Yearley, Lee H. *The Ideas of Newman: Christianity and Human Religiosity*. University Park: Pennsylvania State University Press, 1978. Scholarly study that analyzes Newman's attitudes toward man's innate need for religion. Contains a good bibliography.

Laurence W. Mazzeno

MICHEL NEY

Born: January 10, 1769; Saarlouis, France
Died: December 7, 1815; Paris, France
Area of Achievement: The military
Contribution: Ney was arguably the most celebrated of the twenty-six marshals who served Napoleon I and the French Empire throughout the 1804-1815 period. Ney is primarily remembered for his leadership during the retreat from Moscow and at Waterloo.

Early Life

Michel Ney was born in the French city of Saarlouis in 1769, twenty years before the outbreak of the French Revolution. Michel was the second son of Pierre Ney, a barrel cooper, and Marguerite Grevelinger. Michel received training as a notary public and as an overseer of mines but discovered that his inclinations lay in martial pursuits. In 1788, one year before the Revolution, he joined the light cavalry and from 1789 fought in the French republican armies.

Ney underwent his baptism of fire from 1792 to 1794, when he rose to the ranks of sergeant major and subsequently of captain. The tall, sturdily built, blue-eyed Ney was already a superb horseman and swordsman and was skilled in drill and maneuver. He had also acquired the reputation for reckless courage and a hot temper, which, combined with his flaming red hair, earned for him the nickname of "Le Rougeaud," or "the red-headed one."

From 1794 to 1799, Ney advanced steadily to the rank of general of division. His military talent was complemented by an immense personal charisma. He led his men from the front rank, an exposure to danger that endeared him to the soldiery of France. Already, he had been wounded three times and had been temporarily captured. In 1800, Ney contributed to the French victory at Hohenlinden. Thereafter, the future Emperor of France, Napoleon, took an interest in him. In 1802, Ney was further connected to Napoleon through marriage to Aglaé Louise Auguié, a friend of Napoleon's wife. When Napoleon was crowned in 1804, he elevated Ney to the distinguished position of marshal.

Life's Work

From 1804 to 1815, the French Empire under Napoleon fought successive wars against seven coalitions of enemies. The foundation of Napoleon's rule was the military, and at the top of the military

was his personally created body of twenty-six marshals. Ney was France's most celebrated marshal and the one most remembered by posterity, even if he was not its most consistently talented member. During the 1805-1807 campaigns in Central Europe, Ney demonstrated both his talents and his weaknesses. One of his greatest victories was the Battle of Elchingen, during which he surrounded an Austrian army at Ulm. Ney then subdued the Austrian Tyrol. Against the Prussians at Jena, however, he attacked too precipitously, nearly cutting off his VI Army Corps. The impetuous Ney then provoked a foraging incident in eastern Prussia in January, 1807, which developed into the Battle of Eylau. Eylau was the first real check to Napoleon's Imperial Grand Army, but Ney partially redeemed himself by staving in the Russian right flank and causing their withdrawal. Ney's redemption was completed after the Battle of Friedland, wherein his advance led to a decisive defeat of the Russian army and directly to the Treaty of Tilsit. Out of gratitude, Napoleon created Ney Duke of Elchingen in June, 1808.

Ney's years in Spain, from August, 1808, to March, 1811, were less happy. Spain, the scene of a bloody guerrilla war, damaged many French officers' reputations, and Ney's was no exception. Initially, Ney led his VI Army Corps to minor victories, and in 1810 he participated in the invasion of Portugal under Marshal André Masséna. Ney captured the fortress of Ciudad Rodrigo and fought, indecisively, at Bussaco. The French high-water mark was reached at Torres Vedras, and, thereafter, the British, Spanish, and Portuguese armies slowly rolled back the French. Ney's gallantry and inspiration held the exposed rear guards together, but another side to his personality was revealed: a general lack of cooperation with his fellow marshals and with his superior. That resulted in his being dismissed by Masséna in 1811.

Napoleon, however, was seldom disturbed when his marshals drew daggers against one another, and he lost no time in appointing Ney head of the military camp of Boulogne, a post he held from August, 1811, to February, 1812. In April, 1812, Ney was put in charge of the III Army Corps in the greatest French army yet assembled, which was preparing to invade Russia and bring Czar Alexander I back into an economic line more favorable to Napoleon's continental system. Instead, it was the French who were brought to heel in the beginning of the end for the French Empire.

Conversely, however, Ney's reputation prospered. On August 17, Ney was the first to go into Smolensk, where he was again wounded; at Borodino, on September 7, he pushed back Prince Pyotr Ivanovich Bagration's troops. The French occupied Moscow a week later. Yet the Russian field army had not been decisively beaten, and the czar would not come to terms. Moreover, a mysterious fire in Moscow robbed the French of their winter quarters. The cataclysmic French retreat began on October 19. As in Spain, Ney was placed in command of the dangerous rear guard. There, amid snows, harassed by Cossacks, and low on supplies, Ney led by such heroic personal example and élan that Napoleon respectfully named him "the bravest of the brave." Ney was reportedly the last Frenchman to have left Russian soil. Next to Napoleon, Ney had emerged the most renowned soldier of France. In recognition, Napoleon created Ney Prince of the Moskowa, in March, 1813.

After the disaster in Russia, much of Europe rallied against the French, and Ney fought a series of battles in German states in 1813. After receiving yet another wound and achieving an indecisive victory at Lützen, Ney blundered at Bautzen, where he had been in command of several corps. Briefly recovering at Dresden, Ney was defeated at Dennewitz and failed to take Berlin. His critics would note that his effective span of control was one corps and that he was not usually successful with a larger body. Defeated at last in 1813, Napoleon and Ney fell back on France, engaging in some of their most classic if smaller battles in an effort to keep their country from being overrun. Sensing the end, Ney was one of the first marshals to call for Napoleon's abdication. That set the stage for Ney's increasing political involvement, which went so much against his temperament and natural ability.

When Napoleon was exiled to Elba, the returned Royalist government under Louis XVIII eagerly employed such a preeminent marshal as Ney on its own behalf. Complicating events, Napoleon escaped in February, 1815, and began raising a new army with which to conquer France and, ultimately, Europe. That put Ney in a terrible quandary, for he owed Napoleon his career and owed nothing to the aristocrats, who looked upon him as a mere upstart. Although Napoleon's chances seemed dim, Ney could see that the army rank and file largely longed for a return to the former days of glory. Ney

deserted to Napoleon, an act for which he would later pay with his life.

During the Waterloo Campaign in June, 1815, Ney commanded the left wing in the Battle of Quatre-Bras. Uncharacteristically, Ney's actions on June 16 were dilatory. He incorrectly assessed the situation and failed to take the strategic crossroads. Napoleon's own choice of ground at the Battle of Waterloo on June 18 was unfortunate, and his method of frontal attack was equally so. Further, even though Ney's capabilities in the grander scale had already been tested and found not to be his strongest feature, Napoleon chose to entrust to him the conduct of the main assault at Waterloo. Repeatedly and courageously, Ney charged against the well-prepared British defenses, exhausting the French cavalry. Unable to break through to Brussels, the French were themselves struck in the right flank by the Prussians. As a word, "Waterloo" has become synonymous with defeat. Napoleon was exiled to the remote island of St. Helena, and Ney was tried and executed by the Bourbon Royalists on December 7, 1815. Out of respect for France's hero, "the bravest of the brave" was allowed to conduct his own firing squad beside the wall of the tranquil Luxembourg Gardens in Paris.

Summary

Michel Ney's life may be considered a failure if one only reflects that the cause he served failed. If, above all, the age symbolized the drift away from monarchy, the seeds had at least been planted. From a personal view, Ney's career was spectacular. Few have risen from completely obscure origins to become a marshal and a prince. Ney was a successful man before Napoleon chose him as one of the elect, but Ney largely owes his historical reputation to his service in Napoleon's French Empire while under the banner of the Imperial Grand Army. Had there been no Napoleon, Ney might well have been marked by posterity as no more than one of the many newly promoted republican generals.

Ney's career as a marshal of France was made more because of his outstanding bravery than from any qualified skill as a military strategist. That is not to belittle Ney's overall martial talent. Ney's personal example, energy, charismatic inspiration, and willingness to share risks made him an exceptional leader of men and France's greatest period soldier second only to Napoleon.

From 1815 to 1848, France struggled between her traditions of monarchy and her increasingly republican leanings. The Bourbons understandably forbade the erection of a statue to Ney's memory, until their own downfall in 1848. In 1852, however, the nephew of Napoleon secured by plebiscite the mantle of hereditary emperorship, and the following year a statue of Ney was commissioned. The statue stands in the Carrefour de l'Observatoire in Paris as an eternal tribute to a national military hero of France.

Bibliography

Chandler, David G. *The Campaigns of Napoleon.* New York: Macmillan, 1966; London: Weidenfeld and Nicolson, 1967. This work is the best single-volume work on the period. Ney appears in the index, and his name covers an entire column of entries. Invaluable for understanding Ney's position in the Imperial Grand Army. Excellent maps indicate where Ney fought. Although it is appreciative of Ney's role throughout, the chapters concerning Russia and Waterloo are especially rewarding.

―――. *Dictionary of the Napoleonic Wars.* London: Arms and Armour, and New York: Macmillan, 1979. The entry on Ney fills approximately two pages and includes a picture. The subject is covered chronologically. Key events are set off by asterisks, which permit cross-referencing and therefore a more complete explanation.

―――, ed. *Napoleon's Marshals.* London: Weidenfeld and Nicolson, and New York: Macmillan, 1987. This is the best account of the twenty-six marshals so far published. Each marshal is presented in a separate section authored by a separate period scholar and includes a picture of the subject. Ney is covered by Peter Young. A map and analysis of the Battle of Elchingen sheds light on Ney as a commander. His talents may be easily compared and contrasted to those of his fellow marshals.

Delderfield, R. F. *The March of the Twenty-Six: The Story of Napoleon's Marshals.* London: Hodder and Stoughton, 1962. The book is illuminating because it deals with the interactions of the marshals in a chronological sequence. Thus, it is complementary to works that adopt a sectional subject approach. Ney is indexed throughout the text.

Esposito, Vincent J., and John Robert Elting. *A Military History and Atlas of the Napoleonic Wars.* London: Faber, and New York: Praeger, 1964. The atlas is without doubt the best military atlas on the Napoleonic period and, because of the rising cost of publication, may stand indefinitely as the definitive work. The maps offer a complete understanding of Ney's positions during the campaigns. Coverage is comprehensive, and each map is supported by an oversize page of linking narrative.

Marshall-Cornwall, Sir James. *Napoleon as Military Commander.* London: Batsford, and Princeton, N.J.: Van Nostrand, 1967. This book offers a literate exposition that is well illustrated with detailed maps and a chronological table. Presents a balanced account of Napoleon's career. Ney is frequently referenced in the index and may be briefly related against the larger background of his leader.

Morton, John Bingham. *Marshal Ney.* London: Barker, 1958. Only two chapters cover the 1812-1815 period. Three chapters review the politics of the second restoration or the events surrounding Ney's trial. The work adequately portrays the ineptitude of Ney in the climate of shifting politics.

Young, Peter. *Napoleon's Marshals*. New York: Hippocrene Books, 1973. The section on Ney is not as comprehensive or informative as Young's section in Chandler's edited *Napoleon's Marshals*. Four pictures of Ney and a color plate of the marshal in uniform provide the finest single, illustrative coverage, but the Chandler book is to be preferred in most respects.

David L. Bullock

NICHOLAS I
Nikolay Pavlovich

Born: July 6, 1796; Tsarskoye Selo, Russia
Died: March 2, 1855; St. Petersburg, Russia
Areas of Achievement: Government and politics
Contribution: As Czar of the Russian Empire, 1825-1855, Nicholas I partially succeeded in restoring the historic power and position of the autocracy in Russian life and European affairs. His reign marks the high point of Russian conservative reaction to the French Revolution, Napoleonic Europe, and the Decembrist Revolt.

Early Life

Nikolay Pavlovich, known in the West as Nicholas I, was born on July 6, 1796, in Tsarskoye Selo, the third surviving son of Emperor Paul I and Empress Maria Fyodorovna, a former Princess of Württemberg. Being the third son, Nicholas was not expected to rule in his own right but rather to serve one of his elder brothers, the future Czar Alexander I or the Grand Duke Constantine Pavlovich. Consequently, Nicholas was not initially prepared to rule but rather was given a traditional, conservative, military education. What liberal training Nicholas did receive probably came from one of his tutors, the German economist Heinrich Storch. Nicholas proved to have no mind for abstraction; he was interested in science and technology and was especially talented in mathematics. Like his father before him, he took a strong interest in military affairs.

Nicholas' natural conservatism was profoundly deepened during the last years of Alexander's reign, after 1812-1814, and as a result of the Decembrist Revolt in 1825. After he returned from the Congress of Vienna, Alexander—and Russia through him—came under the sway of conservative German mystical Romanticism from the West. Opposition arose from young reform-minded noble military officers and civil servants, who staged demonstrations in St. Petersburg to influence the new czar, Constantine, upon the somewhat sudden death of the childless Alexander in 1825. Unbeknown to the Decembrists, however, Constantine secretly had renounced his right to succeed in 1822, in favor of Nicholas, when he had married a Roman Catholic Polish aristocrat. When they realized that Nicholas was the new emperor, the Decembrists went into rebellion in St. Petersburg and

Kiev. The Decembrist Revolt was thoroughly crushed, and Nicholas I saw it as a manifestation of the liberal treason of much of the nobility, an attitude which set the tone for his entire reign at home and abroad.

Life's Work

Not only did the Decembrist Revolt strengthen Nicholas' conservative resolve, but also it forced him to rebuild the historic power of the Russian autocracy and concentrate on internal affairs over foreign relations throughout most of his reign. To do this he surrounded himself with reasonably talented conservative and reactionary advisers in key positions, many of whom came from military backgrounds. Together they created and enforced the state ideology of official nationalism, with its four-pronged attack: autocracy, orthodoxy, nationality, and legitimacy. Autocracy meant the historic direct, divine-right absolutism of the czar; orthodoxy reaffirmed Russian Orthodoxy as the one true faith and condoned the persecution of all dissenters, especially Roman Catholics, Muslims, and Jews; nationality called for the protection of the unique Russian character from the decadence of the West; and legitimacy was a guide for foreign policy, allowing for intervention abroad to preserve the anti-revolutionary status quo.

To create a degree of bureaucratic efficiency, Nicholas did not reform the bureaucracy as such; rather, he added yet another layer, His Majesty's Own Imperial Chancery, which was more directly responsible to him. It contained six sections: Sections 1 and 6 dealt with charity and welfare, respectively. Section 2, under Count Michael Speransky, very successfully carried out the codification and some modernization of Russian law from 1833 to 1835, a prelude to the judicial reforms to come under the reign of Alexander II in 1864. Section 4 managed the conquest of the Caucasus Mountains region, which began under Nicholas and continued in the reigns that followed. Part of Armenia was secured in a war with Persia in 1826-1828 and the eastern shore of the Caspian Sea in a war with Turkey in 1828-1829. Section 5, under General Paul Kiselyov, considered the reform of serfdom. Nicholas wanted to do something about this pressing problem, which had kept Russia economically and socially backward, had in large part precipitated the Decembrist Revolt, and had constantly fueled debate and dissent in the Russian Empire. As with so many important matters, however, he never committed himself to doing anything about it.

The most infamous of these sections, though, was the third, the secret police, under General Alexander Benckendorff. Based on French Revolutionary and Napoleonic models, it was a modern, professional police establishment through which Nicholas controlled dissent, monitored public opinion, propagandized his people, and otherwise enforced his will. Through the third section, censorship was maintained, and famous troublesome intellectuals such as Peter Chaadayev, Alexander Pushkin, Nikolai Gogol, Vissarion Belinsky, and Aleksandr Herzen were hounded and controlled. Nevertheless, under Nicholas, dissent (especially that dissent inspired by the West) continued to grow.

Nicholas did not see art as propaganda but believed that it was able to portray attitudes; he was therefore determined that the attitudes portrayed be the correct ones. He fancied himself as an artist and an architect, and he played a personal role in the rebuilding of the Winter Palace and the completion of St. Isaac's Cathedral in St. Petersburg.

Section 3 acted and reacted efficiently and helped Russia to suppress the Polish uprisings of 1830-1831 and move against Russian dissidents to prevent trouble in 1848; Russia and Great Britain were the only two major European countries not to experience upheavals in 1848. Nicholas' Russia even sent troops abroad to quell a rebellion in Hungary in 1848. With section 3, Nicholas laid the basis for the modern Russian and Soviet police states. In this regard, Nicholas eventually came to be known as the "gendarme of Europe."

Nicholas reenergized the pattern of "defensive modernization" for the Russian Empire first set by Czar Alexei Mikhailov and his son Peter the Great in the late seventeenth and early eighteenth centuries. Russia did not have an original industrial revolution, and Nicholas believed it necessary for Russia to modernize cautiously to protect itself from the aggressive tendencies of the West and to avoid coming under the sway of Western decadence. Western expertise and capital therefore were allowed to come into Russia only very slowly and selectively. For example, under Nicholas the first railroad in Russia was completed in 1838, not

primarily to foster internal economic development but to move troops more efficiently between Moscow, St. Petersburg, and Kiev to control possible social disorder.

Meanwhile, intellectuals of opposing Slavophile and Westernizer groupings debated the past, present, and future of Russia and sought to influence the czar and his policies. Slavophiles such as Sergei Khomyakov and the Aksakovs usually were supportive, while Westernizers such as Belinsky were much more critical. Through its control of government spending, it was really the Ministry of Finance under the reactionary Count Yegor Kankrin that was in charge of modernization and reform during much of Nicholas' reign.

A haphazard commitment to improve education also was made. A heavy emphasis was placed on science and technology. New schools and curricula were established and the older ones expanded by Minister of Public Instruction Sergei Uvarov in the years 1833-1848, marking the end of the period of reaction to the Decembrist Revolt. Soon, however, the educational system, especially as manifested by the universities, was seen as responsible for stimulating the development of a radical intelligentsia. The universities came to be distrusted, greater centralized control was instigated, and the period of post-1848 reaction ensued.

Despite the efforts at reform and modernization, the Russian defeat in the Russian-provoked Crimean War (1854-1856) at the end of Nicholas' reign showed how far the Russian Empire had declined from great power status and how backward it was. The defeat spurred Nicholas' son and successor, Alexander II, to initiate a major era of reform, beginning with the emancipation of the serfs in 1861.

Summary

Nicholas I was the last Russian czar to embody the historical definition of the autocrat. Through the strength of his conservative character and the power of his will, he reconstructed the autocracy of Ivan the Great, Ivan the Terrible, and Peter the Great in his own image. Unfortunately, in the process of this atavistic quest he retarded and often hurt Russia and its people. His stifling of progressive development, furthering of bureaucratic absolutism, expensive militarism and foreign adventurism, and general lack of progressive accomplishment left those who followed in his footsteps with a growing number of aggravated problems with which to cope.

Yet, while Nicholas did not stop Russia's slide from greatness, he did prepare the way for some of the accomplishments of his successors. The addressing of the problems of serfdom and the codification of law facilitated the later reforms of Alexander II. He furthered the march of the Russian Empire across Eurasia and into China. Defensive modernization helped bring on the Russian Revolution, and modernization continues through the Soviet period of Russian history to the present. Nicholas was a strong ruler but not a positive one, and his antireform reactionary conservatism was out of step with the needs of his country, the times in which it existed, and the modern world. In trying to strengthen the Russian Empire, Nicholas actually weakened it severely.

Bibliography

Blackwell, William L. *The Beginnings of Russian Industrialization, 1800-1860*. Princeton, N.J.: Princeton University Press, 1968. Largely a study of the very important period under Nicholas in the history of Russian industrialization prior to the actual Russian industrial revolution. Very good on the role of the state in stimulating Russian industrialization and modernization.

Golovin, Ivan. *Russia Under the Autocrat Nicholas the First*. London: Colburn, 1846; New York: Praeger, 1970. A critical account of the first two decades of Nicholas' reign written by a member of one of Russia's more important aristocratic families. A valuable primary source on the life and times of Nicholas and his Russia.

Grunwald, Constantin de. *Tsar Nicholas I*. Translated by Brigid Patmore. London: Saunders, 1954; New York: Macmillan, 1955. Somewhat romanticized and very traditional, but for years the standard biography of Nicholas. Stresses foreign affairs.

Ingle, Harold N. *Nesselrode and the Russia Rapprochement with Britain, 1836-1844*. Berkeley: University of California Press, 1976. Centering on the activity of Nicholas' principal foreign minister, Count Karl Nesselrode, this work addresses the Cold War relationship that developed between Russian and Great Britain in the nineteenth century. A good study of Nicholas' unsuccessful attempt to transfer his conservative values to European affairs.

Kohn, Hans, ed. *The Mind of Modern Russia: Historical and Political Thought in Russia's Great Age*. New Brunswick, N.J.: Rutgers University Press, 1955. Commentary and documents on Russian intellectual history in the nineteenth century. The first seven chapters deal with the reign of Nicholas. A classic text.

Leatherbarrow, W. J., and D. C. Offord, eds. *A Documentary History of Russian Thought: From the Enlightenment to Marxism*. Ann Arbor, Mich.: Ardis, 1987. In many ways an expanded modernization of Kohn, but sadly lacking in his commentary and insight. Parts 2, 3, and 4 center on the activities during the years of Nicholas.

Lincoln, W. Bruce. *Nicholas I: Emperor and Autocrat of All the Russias*. London: Lane, and Bloomington: Indiana University Press, 1978. Largely synthetic, but very good and readable. A definitive and up-to-date standard biography of Nicholas.

Monas, Sidney. *The Third Section: Police and Society Under Nicholas I*. Cambridge, Mass.: Harvard University Press, and Oxford: Oxford University Press, 1961. Excellent on the third section and its various activities and on the early modern Russian police state of Nicholas. An unmatched standard.

Pintner, Walter McKenzie. *Russian Economic Policy Under Nicholas I.* Ithaca, N.Y.: Cornell University Press, 1967. A study of Russian "defensive modernization" under Nicholas I. Especially good on the philosophy and activities of Nicholas' Minister of Finance, Count Kankrin.

Riasanovsky, Nicholas V. *Nicholas I and Official Nationality in Russia, 1825-1855.* Berkeley: University of California Press, 1959. An excellent study that concentrates on the construction of the conservative Russian state ideology of official nationality by Nicholas and his advisers. Reveals in part the complex personality of Nicholas I.

Roberts, Ian W. *Nicholas I and the Russian Intervention in Hungary.* London: Macmillan, and New York: St. Martin's Press, 1991. Roberts, a former British diplomat stationed in Budapest, offers a comprehensive account of the Russian intervention in Hungary in 1849 and relates this event and its history to the Crimean War.

Dennis Reinhartz

BARTHOLD GEORG NIEBUHR

Born: August 27, 1776; Copenhagen, Denmark
Died: January 2, 1831; Bonn, Prussia
Areas of Achievement: History and philology
Contribution: An extraordinarily able historian, Niebuhr, through meticulously researched as well as voluminous books and published lectures, founded the modern German school of critical historical scholarship, one objective of which was regeneration of the Prussian state.

Early Life

Son of the noted German philologist and Arabian traveler Karsten Niebuhr, Barthold Georg Niebuhr was born on August 27, 1776, in Copenhagen, Denmark. Despite the appearance of being Danish, the Niebuhrs regarded themselves as German by virtue of having lived in Denmark's Dithmarschen district, where for centuries Germans maintained separate, nearly independent rights, within the disputed duchies of Schleswig-Holstein. Self-described, Barthold's childhood was that of a physically weak, almost chronically ill, and dreamy boy who lived in worlds of his own imaginative creation, which throughout life he regarded as dangerous to thought, justice, and morality. Indeed, from child to adult, he remained short, thin, and constitutionally nervous and excitable. Not surprisingly, having seldom passed beyond his house and garden, and being the only son of a then-famous father, he was precociously studious by disposition almost from infancy. He evinced predilections for ancient and modern languages, mathematics, geography, history, and political economy. Yet, until he was an adolescent ready for university he received his education at home.

Already formidably equipped intellectually, Barthold entered the University of Kiel eager to avoid narrow specialization and to master everything available in Kiel's curriculum, from philosophy to mathematics, physics, chemistry, natural history, additional languages, Roman law, European constitutions, and antiquities. The purpose of this ambitiously catholic intellectual immersion was preparation for public service: Niebuhr wanted to become, on his father's advice, not an academician but a man of practical affairs.

Life's Work

Impatient to get on, Niebuhr thus abandoned the university in January, 1796, to serve as secretary to the Danish minister of finance, a post for which he seemed well adapted, considering his early and continuing interest in Danish-German land tenures (hence finance), curiosities that bent increasingly toward Europe's classical origins. After two years' service at the ministry, Niebuhr left to spend 1798-1799 between London and Edinburgh. These were years that generated interesting, if superficially critical, observations on British life and institutions to his father and the Moltke family. Although Niebuhr later developed immense admiration for most things British, particularly their practicality and liberties, his encounters at the time left him feeling that the quality of German conversation and thought was far superior.

Consequently Niebuhr returned to Denmark, married in 1801, and resumed various high-status official positions: assessor in the East Indies Company's commerce department and director of the Copenhagen Royal Bank as well as of the Commercial Company of the East Indies. The great Prussian statesman-reformer Freiherr vom Stein soon drew him into Prussian service, initially to negotiate Dutch and English loans (essential during Prussian participation in the Napoleonic Wars), then as Frederick William III's privy councillor during the Saxony campaign of 1813, and finally, from 1816 to 1822, as Prussian ambassador to Rome.

Although Niebuhr's responsibilities in Prussia's wartime officialdom were complex and onerous, his relations with Stein and State Chancellor Karl von Hardenberg became strained. Stein had misread Niebuhr both as a practical man of affairs and as a politician; accidentally, Stein had recruited a pedant. "Niebuhr," Stein remarked, "is no use save as a dictionary whose leaves one turns over." Yet these were mismatches made in Heaven, for Niebuhr, a staunch Protestant, regarded Hardenberg as immoral and complained repeatedly that he detested the public duties that he executed for Stein. Essentially what he preferred all along was an exclusive devotion to historical scholarship.

Time and fortune favored him. Selecting faculty for the newly founded University of Berlin in 1810, Prussia's distinguished philologist, educational reformer, and, at the time, Minister of Education Wilhelm von Humboldt appointed Niebuhr professor of ancient history, a position with singular requirements for philological genius. Although dedicated to free research, the university's faculty was also dedicated to Prussia's internal reformation and enhancement of the state's power against the powerful menace posed by France under Napoleon I. Niebuhr was second to none in his advocacy of these objectives. Prussia's great field marshal Helmuth von Moltke described young Niebuhr as a true representative of the Prussian mind.

Popular as a lecturer with students, savants, and colleagues alike, Niebuhr, drawing upon years of previous research, converted these lectures into the first two volumes of the *Römische Geschichte* (1811-1812; *The Roman History*, 1827). Combined, the brilliance of his lectures and the fresh contributions of his first major publications solidly established his professional reputation. In these works, Niebuhr was the first scholar to attack the arcane problems of ancient Italian ethnology; to illuminate the lasting importance of the legends of ancient kings passed down to the Roman historian Livy, not as historically evidential but, through his novel philological, legal, and religious evidence, as persisting social beliefs among subsequent generations of Rome's plebeian populace; and to concentrate upon the social consequences of economic and political questions such as the Roman state's agrarian problems: that is, to unravel the complexities of Rome's agrarian laws, thereby differentiating public from private ownership uses and rights. Perhaps equally important were his efforts, born of intense empathy with his materials, to perceive interrelationships between ancient institutions and to develop a pragmatic sense for their everyday operations.

Outstanding as a historian, Niebuhr nevertheless returned to public life in 1813, reassuming a role in financial negotiations with the Dutch, witnessing Prussia's humiliation at the passage of Napoleon's troops through Berlin and defeat at the Battle of Bautzen, and suffering exhaustion as well as the burden of his wife's serious illness.

Prompted in 1815 by the deaths of his wife and father and the nearly simultaneous settlement of Napoleon's fate at Waterloo, he quickly remarried and, through appointment as Prussian ambassador to the Vatican, left Berlin for Italy which, though central to his scholarship, he had never visited. Though loathing Italians generally, much as he did the French, he vastly enriched his scholarship during his seven-year "exile" in Italy. At Verona Cathedral, he unearthed the manuscript find of a lifetime: the corpus of the legal textbook by second century Roman legist Gaius, from which subsequent knowledge of early Roman law derives. Similarly, despite the chaos of the Vatican Library, he found and published fragments of Marcus Tullius Cicero's speeches. With such professional triumphs and a growing, happy family life, he cheerfully abandoned Italy in 1823 for a resumption of professorial duties in Bonn, where, despite occasional commands from Berlin for consultations, he established residence. There he revised and republished two volumes of his Roman history, plus, in three volumes, his *Vorträge über die römische Geschichte* (1828-1830; *Lectures on Roman History*, 1850), and delivered what became his three-volume *Vortäge über altbekannt Geschichte* (1829-1830; *Lectures on Ancient History*, 1852). Drawn into the December cold of 1830 to seek late news on the French revolt—and deposition—of Charles X, Niebuhr, who had lived in fear of Napoleon's revolutionary France, contracted pneumonia and died in Bonn on January 2, 1831.

Summary

Notwithstanding his precocious erudition as applied to the attempts of Stein and Hardenberg to strengthen Prussia in confrontations with the aggressive expansions of Napoleon's revolutionary France and not discounting his successful and complex financial, consultative, and diplomatic services to Prussia, Barthold Georg Niebuhr was too passionate, excitable, physically vulnerable, and moral to earn renown in the political arena. A supporter of liberal reformers in the Prussian sense, Niebuhr, like those whom he served, mistrusted the general public's capacities either to strengthen the state or to contribute directly to German unification under the aegis of Prussia. Rather, unlike the popular origins of revolutions in France, which Niebuhr and most liberal Germans abhorred, he believed that a strong, unified Prussian state would have to extend liberalism from above.

In this context, the focus of his historical work on classical societies, on Rome particularly, was not entirely fortuitous. Rome and its institutions had been a great unifying force in Western civilization; thus, to dissect and explore Rome's evolution, strengths, and weaknesses was to instruct—or remind—intelligent Germans how better they might proceed with their own nation-building. In that didactic sense, his work would be followed by many of his colleagues, disciples, and immediate successors.

Unquestionably, Niebuhr's critical historical methodology and his penchant for solid documentation and detailed philological scrutiny of the ancient institutions upon which his work was focused distinguished him from his predecessors. Justifiably, he deserves foremost rank as a founder of modern historical methodology and as the first historian to illuminate the institutional, legal, religious, and popular recesses of ancient and classical Roman history particularly. Unfortunately his writings are so densely detailed and he so lacked the gift of broad conceptualization that he was sharply criticized by Theodor Mommsen, Leopold von Ranke, and others of his more famous, if indebted, successors. Seldom read or cited by twentieth century historians in his field, he nevertheless was recognized as a major historian during the nineteenth century for his influence on the development of scientific history.

Bibliography

Barnes, Harry Elmer. *A History of Historical Writing.* 2d ed. New York: Dover, 1963. Written for nonspecialists, this is a clear general exposition of the evolution of modern historical craftsmanship. Niebuhr is appropriately cited in context but is not a principal subject. His influences, however are well noted. Contains a brief index.

Croce, Benedetto. *History: Its Theory and Practice.* New York: Harcourt Brace, 1921. Croce, a great Italian philosopher, presents a sophisticated synthesis of historical craftsmanship over the past two centuries, differentiating modern approaches to older, less evidential narrative, often fictional, styles. Niebuhr is briefly placed in context. Contains a brief index.

Fowler, W. Warde. *Roman Essays and Interpretations.* Oxford: Clarendon Press, 1920. An able, if sympathetic, scholarly narration of Niebuhr's career. This is a very useful and sound account. Clearly written for nonspecialists. Contains a few notes.

Gooch, G. P. *History and Historians in the Nineteenth Century.* London and New York: Longman, 1913. A clear and authoritative account, which in chapter 1 deals effectively with Niebuhr's minor predecessors and amply with Niebuhr's own critical contributions. Niebuhr is only cited in reference to other nineteenth century historians throughout Gooch's study. Contains footnotes.

Guilland, Antoine. *Modern Germany and Her Historians.* London: Jarrold, and New York: McBride, Nast, 1915. While there are minor errors, this work does an especially able job in chapter 1, "The Forerunners: Niebuhr." Contains footnotes and a useful, double-columned index.

Thompson, James Westfall. *A History of Historical Writing.* Vol. 2, *The Eighteenth and Nineteenth Centuries.* New York: Macmillan, 1942. Written brilliantly for both specialists and nonspecialists by a distinguished historian and historiographer, this extensive study is the best recent assessment of the subject. Footnotes are extensive and informative, and substitute for the lack of an overall bibliography. Contains a superb twenty-six-page double-columned index.

Clifton K. Yearley

NICÉPHORE NIÉPCE

Born: March 7, 1765; Chalon-sur-Saône, France
Died: July 5, 1833; Chalon-sur-Saône, France
Areas of Achievement: Invention and technology
Contribution: Niépce was a tenacious researcher who, despite rural isolation, succeeded in creating first a method of photomechanical reproduction and subsequently the earliest method of permanently recording the image of the camera obscura.

Early Life

Nicéphore Niépce was born in 1765 in Chalon-sur-Saône, a city located southeast of Paris, in the French department of Saône-et-Loire of the Burgundy region. His was a prosperous bourgeois family with several estates in the area. His father, Claude, was a lawyer who, suspected of sympathy for the king during the upheavals of the French Revolution, had to flee his home for a time. Four children were born to Claude and his wife. Their firstborn was a daughter and the second was a son, also named Claude, who was born in 1763. Though Claude was a lifelong friend and collaborator of his younger brother Nicéphore, a third brother, Bernhard, born in 1773, appears to have had no part in their photographic research.

Nicéphore and Claude were educated at a Catholic seminary in their hometown. Nicéphore is thought to have been intended by his father for the priesthood, and he taught briefly at the seminary following his studies there until the Revolution caused the religious order to be dispersed. In 1792, not long after the death of his father, Nicéphore joined an infantry regiment of Napoleon I's army, an act that may have been conceived partly as a way of allaying suspicions about his own political sympathies; in any case, military service was mandatory for a man of his age. Achieving the rank of lieutenant in May, 1793, he traveled to Italy and participated in the campaign there in the following year but soon fell victim to typhoid fever. Resigning his commission, he returned to France, living in the Mediterranean city of Nice, where he was employed by the district administration.

Nicéphore married in Nice in 1795, and two years later, while he pursued family business affairs in Cagliari, the capital of the island of Sardinia, a son, Isidore, was born to the young couple. Claude had accompanied his brother on this trip, and it appears that they had conducted some unsuc-

cessful experiments in an attempt to capture the image created in the camera obscura, an optical device consisting of a lens and a box, or chamber, within which an image could be viewed. The camera obscura had been used for centuries both as a technical aid for draftsmen and as a popular entertainment, but the Niépce brothers' experiment was perhaps the first such use of the apparatus. Only a few years later, Thomas Wedgwood and Sir Humphry Davy were to attempt a similar experiment in England, also without success.

Both brothers returned to their home in Chalon-sur-Saône in 1801. The family's remaining wealth allowed them to continue pursuing a variety of research. From their childhood, Claude and Nicéphore had shown a penchant for experimentation, making working-scale model machines together. In the next few years, they worked on an ambitious invention that they called the "Pyréolophore," an ancestor of the internal-combustion engine. Pyréolophore is a coinage based on Greek words that translates roughly as "producer of wind and fire." Air was mixed in a piston cylinder with lycopodium, a highly flammable plant spore, producing a controlled explosion powerful enough to propel a boat up the Saône River at twice the speed of the current. This invention, remarkable for its time, was patented by decree of Napoleon on July 20, 1807, from Dresden, Germany. The Niépce brothers continued to refine the Pyréolophore over the next twenty years with the hope of exploiting it commercially, but documentation does not suggest the importance of this endeavor relative to the work in photography, which occupied their attention during many of the same years.

It is known that the Niépce brothers conducted work in the cultivation of textile plants and the extraction of indigo dye but without creating successful business ventures based upon their efforts. Much of the work of Nicéphore and Claude seems to have been motivated more by curiosity than hope of financial gain. Nicéphore has been referred to by modern commentators as "a modest provincial amateur scientist" and as "a dilettante inventor (in the best sense of the word)," and it is certain that the prestige given to science and technology by the European Enlightenment exerted an influence upon him. Even the few existing published images of Nicéphore bear witness to his ties to the rational outlook of the eighteenth century, though they date from a much later period: His portrait is rendered in the neoclassical style, the reserved, formal kind of art typical of the latter half of the century, instead of in the more expressive and emotional Romantic style of the years of his maturity. These portraits, consisting of a sketch by his son, Isidore, a sculpture from 1853 by Jean August Barre based upon it, and a drawing from 1795 by C. Laguiche, depict Niépce as having a long but well-proportioned face and aquiline nose, and also possessing unmistakably gentle eyes that evoke a kindly personality.

Life's Work

Niépce conducted various researches at his country estate, Le Gras, in the village of Saint-Loup-de-Varennes, just south of Chalon-sur-Saône. Claude moved to Paris in 1816 to be better able to promote the Pyréolophore, but by then the brothers had begun to experiment in earnest with light-sensitive materials. The path to resuming the project that they had begun in 1797-1798 began with Nicéphore's interest in lithography, a new method of reproduction of drawings that had been introduced by Aloys Senefelder in 1798 in Munich, Germany. In 1812, a French nobleman had attempted to make the method better known in France, and by 1813, a craze for it had swept the nation. Nicéphore had begun by etching the stones drawn upon by his son, Isidore, but because the stones were of indifferent quality, he tried using pewter plates instead. Soon after father and son began this project, Isidore joined the army. Nicéphore, having little aptitude for drawing, turned from reproducing drawings to a search for a method of copying engravings onto his lithographic plates. The technique that he tried involved first oiling or waxing an engraving in order to make it transparent, then placing it atop a plate that had been coated with a light-sensitive material. These early experiments do not seem to have been successful, but in 1822, employing a form of asphaltum called bitumen of Judea as the light-sensitive coating, his efforts resulted in an effective method he named "heliography," derived from the Greek roots meaning "sun" and "drawing." In the early instances, these copies were made upon glass plates. The emulsion-coated plate was then exposed through the oiled engraving to the light of the sun for two or three hours. The areas of the asphaltum emulsion that had received ample exposure through the transparent paper alone were hardened by the action of light, but the areas of the emulsion lying under the dark areas of the print remained unhardened and were readily washed away by a solvent of lavender oil and turpentine.

Niépce's first attempts to record the image of a camera obscura began in April of 1816. A sheet of paper sensitized with silver chloride was exposed in one of three small cameras for an hour or more, resulting in a faint negative image. These negatives were treated in nitric acid in an attempt to fix them, but Niépce knew that the acid was bound to attack the image. A second problem with this method was the reversal of the values of the original scene, which he tried to solve by making a print using the camera negative in much the same way that he had used an engraving in his first attempts at photolithography. Some of these prints seem to have survived in a faded condition into the 1860's.

Two other approaches to recording the camera image were the use of substances that bleach in the presence of light and the attempt to capture an image on metal and lithographic stone in order to use it for printing plates, but neither of these was successful. In the next several years, Nicéphore experimented with other light-sensitive emulsions, communicating his research in guarded letters to Claude, who had moved to London in August of 1817. Little of Nicéphore's side of the correspondence survives, apparently because Claude destroyed the letters in order to forestall discovery of their line of inquiry.

As Nicéphore's method of heliography became more refined, the possibility of using it to record the camera obscura image presented itself. The first partial success in this endeavor dates from 1824 and is reported in an optimistic letter to Claude dated September 16, 1824, which mentions images captured on stone and glass. Nicéphore's attempt to etch the stones ended in failure, however, because the image was too faint. The following year, Nicéphore experimented with zinc and copper plates and in 1826 tried pewter. Aided by improved optics and by accumulated expertise in the preparation and handling of plates, in 1827—probably in June or July—Niépce produced the image that is today regarded as the first photograph, in the accepted sense of "a permanent image of a natural scene made with a camera." It is a view taken from an upper-story window at Le Gras, showing a courtyard of the estate with a wing of the main building on the left, some trees and a low building described as a bake house in the center, and a tower on the right. Judging from the somewhat contradictory lighting of the objects in the picture, the exposure probably lasted about eight hours. This $6\frac{1}{2}$-by-8-inch plate, which lay undiscovered in England until 1852, is part of the Gernsheim collection at the University of Texas, a legacy of the indefatigable historian who tracked it down. There is no conclusive proof that it is the first photograph, but since most of Nicéphore's trials were made from the same upper-story window of the house, it can be little different from other results achieved at this time that may have been lost; presumably, it is one of the best examples of his work, since it is one that he took to England with him in 1827 on a visit to see his ailing brother, Claude.

In early 1826, Niépce had ordered a camera obscura from the noted Paris opticians Charles and Vincent Chevalier, and he asked a cousin, who was to visit there, to buy the instrument for him. In conversation with Charles Chevalier, the cousin described the intended use of the specially equipped camera and even showed him an example of heliography. This unauthorized revelation soon reached another customer of the Chevaliers, the painter and scenic designer Jacques Daguerre, an ambitious man who was known principally as the proprietor of the diorama, a popular entertainment that simulated famous places and events by means of the manipulation of illusionistically painted scrims, lighting, auditory effects, and other theatrical devices. Daguerre had been conducting experiments toward fixing the image of the camera obscura—though without documented results—and upon hearing of the work of Niépce, wrote to him to gain information about his processes. Daguerre's first inquiries were all but rebuffed; Niépce was perhaps justifiably suspicious of a stranger whose motives he could not assess. After more than a year of correspondence, however, Daguerre won a response from Niépce by sending him a drawing. Niépce replied with a heliographic printing plate showing the Holy Family and a proof from it. The two men met for the first time in Paris in September, 1827, while Niépce was en route to London to visit his brother, and they met again in early 1828 on the return journey. During 1829, Daguerre slowly won Niépce's confidence, and when Niépce decided to write a handbook explaining his research, it was Daguerre's advice that Niépce should attempt to find a way of getting a large profit out of the invention before publication, apart from the honor it would gain for him. Niépce then

invited Daguerre to become a partner in perfecting heliography, and in December, 1929, they signed a ten-year contract to perfect and exploit the process.

The partnership was, in many ways, an unequal one, with Niépce supplying a far greater portion of the combined technical experience. Daguerre's potential contribution, however, was far from negligible; he was a man of great energy, a skilled entrepreneur who was perhaps perfectly suited to direct the commercial exploitation of a successful photographic process (although in this episode of photographic history, as in many later ones, the financial value of the technology was surprisingly elusive). Niépce had attempted to launch heliography in late 1827, during his visit to London. While staying at Kew, near the Royal Botanical Gardens, Niépce had become acquainted with Francis Bauer, a well-known botanical draftsman. Bauer, recognizing the importance of Niépce's experiments, suggested that Niépce address a meeting of the Royal Society on the topic of heliography. A notice on heliography, accompanied by several examples, was prepared but was never presented, ostensibly because Niépce was unwilling to disclose the entirety of his work and was himself disqualified by the society's rules from making a presentation.

Niépce returned to France in early 1828, disappointed by the lack of interest in his work and saddened by the death of his brother, who seems in his last months to have suffered from delusions, including one in which he regarded the Pyréolophore as a kind of perpetual-motion machine. These personal setbacks may well have helped pave the way for Niépce's partnership with Daguerre, to whom the burden of experimentation began to pass in the early 1830's. Little physical evidence remains of the work of either Niépce or Daguerre from these years. A glass plate picturing a still life of a table set for a meal, known only from a mediocre halftone reproduction of 1891, was smashed in 1909 by a demented professor who was supposed to conduct scientific tests on it. This object may have been the work of Niépce, of Daguerre, or even of Niépce's cousin Abel Niépce de Saint-Victor, who took up the heliographic process again in 1853.

By 1829, Niépce felt ready to write a book about his discoveries. Several drafts of an outline exist, and they are quite logical, showing that Niépce was putting his photographic experiences into useful form, perhaps with some thought of his posthumous reputation. Although his partnership with Daguerre remained valid, his productive contribution to it clearly appears to have diminished in the period immediately following its inception. On July 5, 1833, Niépce died of a stroke; he was sixty-eight years old.

Summary

Nicéphore Niépce was neither an artist nor a scientist but made a contribution to each field at a time when art and science were more naturally related than they became during the Industrial Revolution. His research was less systematic than that of the scientists of his day, and he appears not to have had productive contacts with specialists who could aid his experiments. Yet, as a generalist, he succeeded where better qualified people had failed. One reason for this may have been his determination, another is surely that he had the leisure and the resources, over a long period of time, to let his accumulated experiences coalesce into practical steps toward his goals.

It is interesting to speculate on how events might have developed if particular circumstances had differed. In the case of Niépce's inability to publish his notes in England during his sojourn there, there is strong justification for the view that, had he been successful in publicizing heliography in 1827, a series of communications between various noted individuals would almost certainly have resulted in the development, before 1830, of a photographic method based upon paper negatives. Not only would Daguerre's partnership with Niépce have been forestalled, along with the daguerreotype process that was its legacy, but also the great intellectual gifts of the Englishman William Henry Fox Talbot might not have been directed into photography. Whether this course of events would have had any truly lasting effect upon the art or technology of photography is, however, debatable, especially since both Niépce and Daguerre were cognizant of the possible advantages of emulsions coated upon glass plates, the method that was soon to triumph over both Daguerre's and Talbot's processes.

Though there is scant evidence of artistic intention in Niépce's research, his photograph from the window at Le Gras has assumed a monumental significance within the art of photography; as an item of photographic incunabula, it has taken on an aura that is more than sentimental. Technically primitive, it nevertheless announces the beginning of a new era in communication and a new dimension of artistic sensibility.

Bibliography

Braive, Michel F. *The Era of the Photograph: A Social History*. London: Thames and Hudson, 1966. In addition to a brief memoir of Niépce by his descendant, photographer Janine Niépce, this book offers several illustrations of Niépce memorabilia not found elsewhere.

Daval, Jean-Luc. *Photography: History of an Art*. New York: Rizzoli, 1982. This book treats Niépce only in passing, but it offers a rare reproduction of one of his heliographs that represents his experiments more accurately, perhaps, than the enhanced and even retouched illustrations available in other sources.

Fouque, Victor. *The Truth Concerning the Invention of Photography: Nicéphore Niépce, His Life and Works*. Translated by Edward Epstean. New York: Tennant and Ward, 1935. This difficult-to-find translation of a work originally published in 1867 contains the correspondence between Claude and Nicéphore Niépce, but the material is adequately available in the standard modern sources.

Gernsheim, Helmut. "The 150th Anniversary of Photography." *History of Photography: An International Quarterly* 1 (January, 1977): 3-8. An indication of Gernsheim's eminence in the study of the history of photography is given by the fact that this personal memoir is the lead item in the inaugural issue of this journal. The article is an account of his discovery in 1952, by scholarly instinct and luck, of the image now recognized as the first photograph.

Gernsheim, Helmut, and Alison Gernsheim. *The History of Photography from the Camera Obscura to the Beginning of the Modern Era.* Rev. ed. London: Thames and Hudson, and New York: McGraw-Hill, 1969. For years this was the standard detailed survey of the history of photography. This book displays both the authors' thoroughness and their affection for the subject. There are hundreds of excellent illustrations as well as notes, an index, and a bibliography meeting high scholarly standards.

——. *The Origins of Photography.* London and New York: Thames and Hudson, 1982. Essentially an adaptation of material from the Gernsheims' 1969 history of photography, this volume covers the photographic medium only until the end of the era of the calotype and daguerreotype. This book is better designed than its predecessor but contains fewer illustrations pertaining to Niépce.

Mullins, Justin. "Photography." *New Scientist* 155, no. 2099 (September 13, 1997). Describes the early photographic efforts of Niépce and includes information on how film operated, chemical film developing, and dyes used to produce colored images.

Newhall, Beaumont. *Latent Image: The Discovery of Photography.* New York: Doubleday, 1967. This is the best survey of the technical research pursued by Niépce, Daguerre, Talbot, and others. Written in an entertaining narrative style, this book by a leading historian of photography tells the human side of the story as well.

——, ed. *Photography: Essays and Images, Illustrated Readings in the History of Photography.* New York: Museum of Modern Art, 1980; London: Secker and Warburg, 1981. The rather dry documentation of material that survives from Niépce's experiments was understandably omitted from this collection, but the book vividly shows the cultural context of the search for a photographic technology. Indispensable to students of the early history of photography is the reprinting of the entire text of an 1857 article by Lady Elizabeth Eastlake, who affectionately calls Niépce the "philosopher of Chalon."

Scharf, Aaron. "The Mirror with a Memory." In *Pioneers of Photography: An Album of Pictures and Words.* London: British Broadcasting Corporation, 1975; New York: Abrams, 1976. This chapter contains generous excerpts from Niépce's diaries and correspondence as well as a highly amusing chart showing his linguistically oriented attempt in 1832 to derive a name for "photography" from Greek roots.

Whitmire, Vi. "Joseph Nicéphore Niépce 1765-1833." *PSA* 58, no. 10 (October, 1992). Short profile of Niépce.

C. S. McConnell

FRIEDRICH WILHELM NIETZSCHE

Born: October 15, 1844; Röcken, Prussian Saxony
Died: August 25, 1900; Weimar, Germany
Areas of Achievement: Philosophy and literature
Contribution: Though mostly ignored during his lifetime, Nietzsche's writings became a bellwether in the twentieth century for radical philosophical, psychological, linguistic, and literary critiques of Western culture. Through a series of remarkable works of German prose, Nietzsche sought to smash the idol of Christian morality and liberate a few who might follow after him into a triumphant and tragic this-worldly life.

Early Life

Friedrich Wilhelm Nietzsche—named for the reigning king of Prussia, Friedrich Wilhelm IV, whose birthday was also October 15—was born in a parsonage. His father, Karl Ludwig Nietzsche, was a Lutheran pastor; his mother, Franziska Nietzsche (née Oehler), was the daughter of a Lutheran pastor. (The union produced two other children, Elisabeth in 1846 and Joseph in 1848, who died shortly before his second birthday.)

With the death of his father in 1849, Friedrich would spend most of his early life surrounded by women: his mother, his sister, his paternal grandmother, and two maiden aunts. The family moved in 1850 to Naumburg, in Thuringia, where the young Nietzsche attended elementary school and a private preparatory school. In 1858, he entered Germany's most renowned Protestant boarding school, the Schulpforta, on a scholarship. There he met Paul Deussen, also a student, who became one of his few lifelong friends; Deussen found Nietzsche to be deeply serious, "inclined to corpulence and head congestions," and extremely myopic.

Nietzsche was graduated from the school at Pforta in 1864 with a classical education; that same year, he entered the University of Bonn to study theology and philology, the latter under Friedrich Wilhelm Ritschl. Unable to fit into the rowdiness of student life at Bonn—despite his entertaining students on the piano—Nietzsche abandoned any pretense of theological studies and transferred in 1865 to the University of Leipzig, where his friend Ritschl had gone. Writing to his sister Elisabeth about his abandonment of the Christian faith, Nietzsche told her that he had become a disciple of the truth, wherever it led; he could not be content with a religious happiness. That same year, the se-

rious Nietzsche told Deussen that a recently published "life of Christ" by David Strauss was disingenuous in its removal of the miraculous Christ from the Gospels while holding on to his precepts. "That can have serious consequences," said Nietzsche; "if you give up Christ you will have to give up God as well."

The year 1865 was remarkable for two other reasons. As Deussen later wrote, Nietzsche had told him that a street porter, asked to take him to a restaurant in Cologne, instead had delivered him to a brothel. Speechless, Nietzsche soon left. Deussen speculated that his friend remained a lifelong virgin. There is much scholarly debate on the subject, but it seems likely that Deussen was wrong. Since there is no indication in Nietzsche's correspondence that he ever had sexual relations with a woman of his own class, it is probable that in 1865 or later Nietzsche acquired syphilis at a brothel. Early in 1889, he would collapse into insanity.

It was in 1865 that Nietzsche encountered the works of the pessimistic philosopher Arthur Schopenhauer, and though Nietzsche was later to renounce his allegiance to Schopenhauer's perspective, and his anti-Semitism, by late in 1865 he had announced that he had become a follower. The Leipzig years, from 1865 to 1869, saw Nietzsche taken under Ritschl's wing as his protégé, the development of his friendship with Erwin Rohde, and the entrance of composer Richard Wagner into his life. After hearing Wagner's music in 1868, Nietzsche became a convert; meeting with the composer that same year, Nietzsche found that Wagner, too, loved Schopenhauer. Yet, as he would do with Schopenhauer, Nietzsche would one day reject Wagner.

Nietzsche entered into the cavalry company of an artillery regiment in October of 1867, but in March of the next year he suffered a serious chest injury while trying to mount a horse. On extended health leave from the military, Nietzsche resumed his studies in Leipzig; in 1869, the university (on Ritschl's recommendation) conferred a doctorate on Nietzsche on the strength of his published philological writings and without the customary examination and dissertation required for a German degree. That same year, Basel appointed Nietzsche to the chair of classical philology; he was twenty-four, no longer a citizen of Prussia, now a resident of Switzerland.

Life's Work

In the two decades of sanity that remained to Nietzsche, he would battle often against long periods of ill health, especially after 1870, when he fell victim to dysentery and diphtheria while serving as a medical orderly with the Prussian army in the Franco-Prussian War (1870-1871). On his return to Basel to resume his teaching chores in philology (he was an unsuccessful applicant to the chair of philosophy), Nietzsche was plagued with frequent bouts of nausea and exhaustion.

For a time, his one surcease was his friendship with Wagner. From 1869 until Wagner moved to Bayreuth in 1872, Nietzsche visited the composer and his wife, Cosima, some twenty-three times at the Wagner residence at Tribschen, near Lucerne. The composer welcomed a disciple; yet his increasing use of Christian images, especially in his last opera, *Parsifal*, sickened Nietzsche, as did Wagner's anti-Semitism. By 1878, their friendship had been sundered.

Nietzsche's first book broke with tradition. *Die Geburt der Tragödie aus dem Geiste der Musik* (1872; *The Birth of Tragedy Out of the Spirit of Music*, 1909) was far from being a classical philological study burdened by arcane footnotes. Instead, Nietzsche had written a speculative treatment of what he found to be two competing forces in ancient Greek life—the Dionysian, representing potentially destructive passion, and the Apollonian, representing reason and restraint. Greek tragedy had fused the two, but, with the triumph of Socrates, the Apollonian was in the ascendant. (Much later Nietzsche would redefine the Dionysian impulse as a sublimated or perfected "will to power" and would ally himself with Dionysus.)

Nietzsche was granted a leave of absence from Basel in 1876 because of ill health, but his continued headaches, vomiting, and deteriorating eyesight led to his resignation in May, 1879, with a pension of three thousand Swiss francs a year for six years. From that time onward, Nietzsche increasingly became an enigma to his friends. His publication of the aphoristic *Menschliches, Allzumenschliches: Ein Buch für freie Geister* (1878; *Human, All Too Human*, 1910, 1911) was characterized by Wagner as the beginning of Nietzsche's slide into madness. Nietzsche cut his intellectual mooring to Schopenhauer as well, writing a friend that he no longer believed what the philosopher had said.

In the decade beginning in 1879, Nietzsche, moving from boardinghouse to boardinghouse, always seeking new curatives, lived in the French Riviera, Italy, and Switzerland, a virtual recluse. His letter writing was a substitute for most human contact. Suffering almost ceaseless pain, Nietzsche turned within—as if the pain itself were a spur to creativity, or as if, through his project of revaluing traditional Christian values, his literary genius would master his physiology.

There was much emotional pain as well. His friendship with philosopher Paul Rée (who was investigating the psychological basis of religious belief), which had begun in 1873, was marred when in 1882 both men met Lou Salomé (later the wife of Orientalist F. C. Andreas, friend of Sigmund Freud, and mistress of the poet Rainer Maria Rilke) and both proposed—Nietzsche apparently through Rée. Declining both requests, Salomé counterproposed a platonic ménage à trois; Nietzsche's sister Elisabeth learned of the plan, took him to task for his immorality, and informed their mother of Nietzsche's behavior. The three continued in one another's company, but by November, with Salomé and Rée having departed, Nietzsche realized that he had been abandoned.

In January, 1883, in only ten days, Nietzsche penned the first part of what was to become his literary masterpiece, *Also sprach Zarathustra: Ein Buch für Alle und Keinen* (1883-1885; *Thus Spake Zarathustra*, 1896). His only work of fiction, the book (completed in 1885, the fourth and final part privately printed from Nietzsche's own funds) brings a biblical narrative style to parody the Socratic and Christian wisdom teachings, and to bring to "everyone and no one" (the subtitle) the teachings of the *Übermensch* (variously translated "superman" or "overman"). A more explicit elucidation of Nietzsche's philosophical orientation came in 1886 with *Jenseits von Gut und Böse: Vorspiel einer Philosophie der Zukunft* (*Beyond Good and Evil*, 1907), and, in 1887, *Zur Genealogie der Moral* (*On the Genealogy of Morals*, 1896). Books streamed from Nietzsche's pen. In the last year of his sanity, 1888, he wrote five of them, including *Der Antichrist* (1895; *The Antichrist*, 1896) and *Ecce Homo* (1908; English translation, 1911), the last a semiautobiographical overview of Nietzsche's published works.

Several months of euphoria preceded Nietzsche's descent into madness, but following his collapse in the Piazza Carlo Alberto, in Turin, Italy, on January 3, 1889—he had seen a cab driver beating his horse and had flung himself around the horse's neck—the darkness was complete. For the next eleven years, Nietzsche was variously cared for in a Basel asylum, by his mother in Naumburg (until she died in 1897), and by his sister in Weimar.

Elisabeth, married in 1885 to anti-Semite Bernhard Förster (who committed suicide in 1889), managed to gain control of Nietzsche's literary estate and began zealously to refashion her brother's image into that of a proto-Nazi. She withheld *Ecce Homo* from publication for twenty years after Nietzsche had written it, established a Nietzsche archive, and compiled and published a series of notes Nietzsche himself had never intended for publication. She edited it and titled it *Der Wille zur Macht* (1901; *The Will to Power*, 1910).

Only in the last year of his sanity did Nietzsche begin to receive important public notice, a result primarily of the philosophy lectures given by Georg Brandes at Copenhagen. It seems ironic that the first commercial successes of the man who wanted to be understood came at the hands of his sister, who carefully crafted a mythical Nietzsche. Poignantly, it was the ever-prescient Nietzsche who had written in *Ecce Homo*, "I have a terrible fear I shall one day be pronounced holy. . . ." Nietzsche died in Weimar on August 25, 1900, not yet fifty-six, his mane of hair and his shaggy mustache still dark brown.

Summary

There is much scholarly dispute over the nature of Friedrich Wilhelm Nietzsche's philosophy, and even over whether he intended to have one. In his mature works, from *Thus Spake Zarathustra* on, many themes seem important to Nietzsche, from the concept of the overman, the idea of eternal recurrence, of a man being in love with his own fate and thus triumphant in it, to the psychological origins of traditional morality, the nature of the will to power in human affairs, and the death of God, the last announced by a madman in section 125 of *Die fröhliche Wissenschaft* (1882, 1887; *The Joyful Wisdom*, 1910). Yet in Nietzsche's modified aphoristic style, his themes receive no systematic exploration; scholarly interpretations are legion.

Nietzsche's analysis of the psychology of the priest, and of Christian morality, anticipated Freud.

Traditional morality has quenched the instinct for life, and has pronounced sexuality, nobility of self, and intellect to be evil; the afterlife is promised only to those who submit to the priest, to the slave morality, the *ressentiment* of those who are weak. Nietzsche's message was that the sickness, the life-denying morality of the Church, must be replaced by the message of the overman; though perhaps an unachievable ideal, the overman is able to fall in love with every aspect of his fate and, without self-deception, to will the eternal repetition of every part of his life. God is dead—the new learning killed Him—but the late nineteenth century slumbered on in its nihilism, unaware of the consequences. Nietzsche's message of triumph and tragedy fell on deaf ears during his lifetime.

Yet his insights, often not fully developed, have been mined by twentieth century existentialists such as Albert Camus, deconstructionists such as Jacques Derrida and Michel Foucault, phenomenologists such as Martin Heidegger, religious thinkers such as Paul Tillich and Martin Buber, novelists such as Thomas Mann and Hermann Hesse, and playwright George Bernard Shaw; Sigmund Freud and Carl Jung also felt Nietzsche's influence. As a man "born posthumously," Nietzsche is a key to understanding the twentieth century's most influential and most deeply perplexing currents of thought.

Bibliography

Appel, Fredrick. *Nietzsche Contra Democracy.* Ithaca, N.Y.: Cornell University Press, 1999. In this volume, described as a jolt to historical scholars, Appel presents chapters on Nietzsche's views on issues such as friendship, family, solitude, and breeding along with analysis of Nietzsche's writings in favor of a political framework other than democracy.

Belliotti, Raymond Angelo. *Stalking Nietzsche.* Westport, Conn.: Greenwood Press, 1998; London: Greenwood Press, 1999. Interesting study of Nietzsche's thought designed for skeptical readers. Chapters are divided into themes in Nietzsche's work which are presented, then analyzed.

Gilman, Sander L., ed. *Conversations with Nietzsche: A Life in the Words of His Contemporaries.* Translated by David J. Parent. New York: Oxford University Press, 1987; Oxford: Oxford University Press, 1991. Fully aware of Elisabeth

Förster-Nietzsche's tendencies to mythologize her brother, this anthology draws carefully on her letters, and those from dozens of other correspondents and writers, to paint a picture of Nietzsche as others knew him. Accessible to the general reader, who will be struck by the varying impressions Nietzsche made on those around him.

Hayman, Ronald. *Nietzsche: A Critical Life*. London: Weidenfeld and Nicolson, and New York: Oxford University Press, 1980. A chronological account of Nietzsche's life and work. Includes a helpful timeline and a section of photographs. Hayman draws extensively upon Nietzsche's letters, especially in detailing Nietzsche's many illnesses. Attempts to integrate the man with his philosophy but is sometimes murky and cryptic.

Higgins, Kathleen. *Nietzsche's Zarathustra*. Philadelphia: Temple University Press, 1987. A cleanly written and accessible exploration of the book Nietzsche considered his best. Higgins finds thematic and structural unities when the book is considered from the literary standpoint. The first chapter draws on Nietzsche's life and letters during the time of the composition of *Thus Spake Zarathustra* to reveal Nietzsche's serious concerns behind the sometimes-mocking prophet. The twelve-page bibliography is useful.

Hollingdale, R. J. *Nietzsche: The Man and His Philosophy*. Baton Rouge: Louisiana State University Press, 1965. A sympathetic chronological and interpretive narrative, contending that, in the end, one is left with Nietzsche the man and not with some movement or philosophical system. A standard work by one of Nietzsche's English-language translators.

Kaufmann, Walter. *Nietzsche: Philosopher, Psychologist, Antichrist*. 4th ed. Princeton, N.J. and London: Princeton University Press, 1974. A standard and important account of Nietzsche's life and thought by one of his modern English-language translators. The extensive thirty-page annotated bibliography of primary and secondary sources is invaluable. Included are samples of Nietzsche's handwriting. Kaufmann attempts to smooth Nietzsche's rough edges even as he removes the onus of Elisabeth's manufactured image of her brother. Somewhat dated, as it takes issue with many works on Nietzsche published early in the twentieth century.

Roberts, Tyler T. *Contesting Spirit: Nietzsche, Affirmation, Religion*. Princeton, N.J.: Princeton University Press, 1998. Tyler focuses on the place of religion in Nietzsche's work arguing that although he denounces religion and mysticism, his works are filled with his own religious and mystic practices.

Solomon, Robert C., and Kathleen M. Higgins, eds. *Reading Nietzsche*. New York: Oxford University Press, 1988. Based on papers presented at a 1985 seminar on Nietzsche at the University of Texas at Austin. Twelve Nietzsche scholars in the Anglo-American tradition provide insightful interpretations of most of the Nietzsche canon. A ten-page bibliography of primary and secondary sources, including works on specific texts, is extremely valuable in directing first-time readers of Nietzsche into the mountain of Nietzsche studies. Works in the continental tradition are also cited in the bibliography.

Dan Barnett

FLORENCE NIGHTINGALE

Born: May 12, 1820; Florence, Italy

Died: August 13, 1910; London, England

Areas of Achievement: Nursing, hospital administration, and social reform

Contribution: Following a deeply rooted passion to serve God and combining it with a strong will and intellect, Nightingale revolutionized the nursing profession and the design and conditions of medical care and hospital facilities.

Early Life

On May 12, 1820, Florence Nightingale was born in and named for the romantic city of Florence, Italy. Her mother, Frances (Fanny) Nightingale, thirty-two, was a socially ambitious and strong-willed woman; her father, William Edward Nightingale, twenty-five, was a scholarly and liberal Cambridge man. Florence had one older sister, Parthe, and when the family returned to England, the sisters' education was first handled by governesses but soon taken over by their father. Thus, both girls received a broader and more liberal education than many women of their day. This early introduction to a competitive and intellectual world rather than a purely social and domestic one would be a great influence on Nightingale.

As a teenager, Nightingale was surrounded by relatives and friends, family visits and excursions to foreign countries, and the usual round of social events and gossip. Although she engaged in all the domestic and social obligations and was quite popular, she felt, as early as seventeen, a desire to do something more productive and useful with her life. She was expected to marry well and rear a family; still, Nightingale wanted more. In between social engagements, therefore, she would retreat into a private world of dreaming and writing what she later called her "private notes." Then, in 1837, she wrote in one of her diaries that God had called her to His service, but for what she was not sure. For the next sixteen years she would be tormented by this uncertainty. During these years, she unhappily continued to lead the social life that her mother prescribed, but she managed to find the time for isolated hours of self-reflection as well as visiting and nursing sick relatives.

In 1839, both Nightingale sisters were presented at court, and there Florence met Henry Nicholson, who wooed her for six years before she finally refused his marriage proposal. She could give no concrete reason other than her desire to do God's will, whatever that was. Again, she was overwhelmed by uncertainty about what her life's work should be, and her spells of quiet frustration and spiritual agony worried her mother. After all, Nightingale was attractive, if not beautiful, with dark reddish hair, gray eyes, a gay smile, and a sense of humor tempered with a sharp intellect and curiosity.

In 1842, another suitor presented himself: Richard Monckton Milnes, a Member of Parliament, a linguist, and a social reformer of sorts; in short, he seemed the perfect mate for Nightingale. Her feelings were nevertheless divided, for in that year she learned of the work being done at the Institute of Deaconesses at Kaiserwerth, Germany, regarding the training of nurses in hospital work. For two years, she kept this knowledge to herself; then one day she tentatively voiced a desire to devote her life to nursing. Her family, especially her mother, rejected the idea completely, and for the next six years Florence suffered from the denial both spiritually and physically. She believed that God had called her again, yet since she was unable to follow his calling, she thought she must be somehow unworthy. The best she could do was nurse sick relatives, friends, and villagers. By 1847, she had worked herself into a state of ill health, marked by migraines, chronic coughing, and a near breakdown.

She went to Rome in 1848 to regain her spirits and health. There, she met Sidney Herbert and his wife, Liz; her friendship with Sidney marked a turning point in her life. After this meeting, she soon rejected her long-waiting suitor Richard Milnes, again disappointing her family. Now alone and desperate for an answer to God's calling, she made her way (with the help of friends) to Kaiserwerth, Germany, but her family flatly refused to allow her to enter the school. By then, however, Nightingale was ill and suicidal; thus, she defied her family and in 1851, at the age of thirty-one, entered the questionable profession of nursing. Her rebellion did little good, however, for when she returned to England she found herself facing her mother's anger. Again, she was plunged into the social life and for the next two years suffered as she followed her mother's will, and, periodically, nursed the sick under the guidance of the Sisters of Charity in Paris. Then, in 1853, Liz Herbert made a decision on Florence's behalf; she recommended her as the new superintendent at the Institution for the Care of Sick Gentlewomen in London. At age thirty-seven, Florence's nursing career began in earnest.

Life's Work

As superintendent of the institution for the next fourteen months, Nightingale surprised the committee that appointed her in two respects. First, the "ministering angel" they had thought that they recruited proved to be a tough-minded and practical administrator who completely reorganized the hospital, from food to beds to medical supplies to sanitary conditions. Second, Nightingale insisted that any poor and ill woman should be admitted, not only those who were members of the Church of England. With a fight, she got most of what she wanted. She also wanted trained nurses, however, and this request was not easy to fulfill. Nightingale therefore began to formulate plans to establish a training school for nurses along the lines of Kaiserwerth. Her plans were interrupted, however, when England and France declared war on Russia in March, 1854. War reports in *The Times* stated that while England and France were victorious in battle, the casualty rate was alarmingly high. In October, Nightingale left England for the shores of the Black Sea with a handful of poorly trained nurses. As a result, she made her way into the annals of the Crimean War.

Once again, the Herberts, this time Sidney, opened the way for Nightingale by appointing her superintendent of the Female Nursing Establishment of the English General Hospitals in Turkey, a position never before held by a woman. It was a revolutionary step, and she took it gladly. Yet her initial enthusiasm was soon replaced by dogged determination, for what she found in the hospitals at Scutari was appalling. Despite assurances by the cabinet ministers in the War Office that everything was in order, Florence found the hospital and medical conditions deplorable. Besides a lack of basic medical supplies (bandages, splints, stretchers), nourishing food, adequate clothing, and clean water, the hospital was overrun with filth, vermin, and backed-up cesspools. In addition, the wounded, the diseased, and the dead were all crowded together in rooms with little or no ventilation. Foresight, luckily, had prompted Nightingale to bring supplies, equipment, and food with her, and while it was not nearly enough, it did help.

Lack of supplies, however, was not Nightingale's only obstacle. Even though her position was an official one, she met with stubborn resistance from the military doctors and staff in Scutari. War and women, even if they were nurses, did not mix. Slowly and steadily, however, Nightingale began her nurses on a cleanup campaign. The job was difficult, yet in time, the men were cleaned, clothed, and fed, and the hospital was scrubbed and emptied (as much as possible) of the overflowing dirt. Her next task was to request the rebuilding of the Barrack Hospital; again she met with opposition, but using her own money and influence, she managed to get the men better quarters.

Her final triumph came when the doctors (or at least most of them) relented and finally allowed Nightingale and her nurses actually to care for the patients and assist the doctors. Thus the "bird," as she was called, became more than merely a "ministering angel," a "lady with a lamp"; she used her official position and her passion to serve God and got things done, thus earning her title as administrative chief.

The struggle was long and slow, for Nightingale was battling men who were set in their ways; they not only objected to a woman coming that close to military matters but also stubbornly refused to admit that there was any sort of problem with the medical system. Yet Nightingale demanded change, and she had some powerful people on her side: Sidney Herbert, Dr. Sutherland, the Home government, *The Times*, public opinion, and the queen herself. Therefore, using whatever and whomever she could, Nightingale was able to reform the hospitals at Scutari, as well as some of the army's medical policies. Within a year after her arrival in the Crimea, the rate of mortality among soldiers dropped from forty-two percent to twenty-two percent per thousand men.

Nightingale not only was bent on improving the physical conditions of the men but also wanted to do something for their emotional state as well, for morale was extremely low. She set up, to the surprise and outrage of her opposition, reading and recreational rooms for the soldiers, assisted them in managing and saving some money from their salaries, and held classes and lectures for them; in short, she treated them like human beings. In the middle of all this change, she was still battling military and government officials and religious leaders who were upset by the lack of religious segregation among both the nurses and the patients. Nightingale refused, however, to let narrow-minded sectarian differences get in her way, and by July, 1856, a

few months after the declaration of peace, Nightingale considered her work in the Crimea complete. As she returned to England, news of her accomplishments preceded her, and the queen invited her to the court for the purpose of awarding her a brooch which bore a St. George's cross and the royal cipher encircled in diamonds surrounded by the words "Blessed are the merciful."

After her struggles and successes at Scutari, Nightingale's work was far from finished: For the next fifty years, she kept fighting for hospital reform. Doctors diagnosed a nervous condition and heart trouble, telling her that if she did not take an extended rest she could die. Nightingale refused flatly and continued her work, which had become both a passion and a mission. When she was ill and tired, she read and wrote letters or reports from her bed. When she felt well enough, she visited influential people and hospitals trying to implement her reforms. The army hospital at Scutari had been only the beginning; now she went after the Army Medical Department itself. Her supporters remained loyal and hardworking; in fact, they were joined by her Aunt Mai and Sir Harry Varney. Yet she also gained two formidable enemies—Lord Panmure, Secretary of State for War, and Dr. Andrew Smith, head of the Army Medical Department. Together, they either denied the need for reforms or managed to undermine her work. Nightingale had met resistance before, however, and their opposition did not stop her. As in the Crimea, so too in England she used her friends, her influence, and her social position to initiate change in medical procedures, sanitary conditions, hospital design, and patient care (both physical and emotional). She wrote an eight-hundred-page report, *Notes on Matters Affecting the Health, Efficiency, and Hospital Administration of the British Army* (1858), and *A Contribution to the Sanitary History of the British Army During the Late War with Russia* (1859), which was submitted to the Royal Commission. Members of the commission received the report favorably, and as a result, drastic changes were initiated according to Nightingale's recommendations between the years 1859 and 1861.

Nightingale was then contacted by the Sanitary Commission (an organization set up at her suggestion) and asked to investigate army medical conditions in India. By then, she had become quite a medical authority, and her reputation was spreading with the help of a published book entitled

Notes on Hospitals (1859), which completely revolutionized hospital construction and administrative practices. Then, in 1860, the Nightingale Training School for Nurses at St. Thomas's Hospital opened, and in the same year, Nightingale published *Notes on Nursing: What It Is, and What It Is Not.* Nightingale's establishment of a nursing hospital earned for her her reputation as the founder of modern nursing. Just when it seemed Nightingale was succeeding in all of her reforms, however, disaster struck. Sidney Herbert, her most powerful ally, became ill and soon died, and with his death her open door to the world of men and politics shut slightly. Still, for the next ten years, 1862-1872, she managed to initiate and enact many changes despite the hostility of the War Office.

By this time, however, Nightingale's health was again causing her problems, and she settled in a house on South Street, where she remained for the rest of her life, practically bedridden. Invalid she might be, but inactive and unproductive she was not. She had a constant stream of visitors (from friends to public officials both domestic and foreign) who came seeking her advice and expertise on hospital matters. Thus, from her bed, she dictated letters, reports, and policies regarding the construction of hospitals and the training of nurses; still she wanted to do more. Having devoted her life to the physical comfort of mankind, she now turned inward to her own metaphysical condition, reading everything that she could. As in her early adult years when she wrestled with religious questions and callings, she returned to a state of spiritual and intellectual turmoil.

Nightingale's last ten years, which she should have spent reveling in her accomplishments, were spent, instead, trying to satisfy unanswerable longings and questions. She became increasingly sentimental and senile. The once-thin, strong-minded woman had become a rather fat, simpleminded patient. The world had all but forgotten her. In 1907, sick and confused, she received the Royal Order of Merit; she was the first woman ever to be awarded this honor. It was presented to her in her bedroom, and her only reply was, "Too kind, too kind." Three years later, nearly blind, she died in her sleep on August 13, 1910.

Summary

Florence Nightingale has been pictured as a quiet, meek, self-sacrificing angel of mercy moving softly among dimly lit hospital corridors and beds filled with wounded soldiers. In short, she has been envisioned as the "lady with the lamp." Although she did spend many hours comforting the sick in this manner, this is only a partial and romanticized portrait of her. What is often not realized or remembered is that Nightingale was more than a nurse; she was a hospital reformer and administrator. Thus, although her role as nurse was a difficult task, both physically and emotionally, she also faced a more difficult task: She was a woman trying to do a man's job in a society that, generally speaking, opposed her. Luckily for Nightingale, she was also living in a time of great change. She was not alone in her passion and determination to change the health conditions of Great Britain; others, many of them women, were also fighting for changes in laws and customs, as well as social standards and attitudes. While she crusaded for more humane medical treatment and modern facilities, others were crusading for women's suffrage, the need for welfare for the poor and sick, and a general change in attitude toward education and status.

Although not outwardly concerned with these other changes, Nightingale must have been influenced by this growing climate, which challenged the Victorian status quo. While Nightingale's name may remain synonymous with nursing, her impact on hospital design, construction, and administration has remained strong even into the late twentieth century.

Bibliography

Calabria, Michael D. *Florence Nightingale in Egypt and Greece: Her Diary and "Visions."* Albany: State University of New York Press, 1997. A complete transcription of Florence Nightingale's previously unpublished diary kept during her travels in Egypt and Greece in 1850. It was during this time that she recognized her call to serve humanity.

Cook, Sir Edward. *The Life of Florence Nightingale.* 2 vols. London: Macmillan, 1913; New York: Macmillan, 1942. An exhaustive biography based on a comprehensive study of Nightingale's diaries and letters, in addition to material written about her in both government and medical reports, including those from the Crimean War. The study also includes a look at Nightingale from the point of view of friends and family,

based on their letters and memoirs. As a research tool, this is a valuable work.

Derieux, M. *One Hundred Great Lives.* Cleveland, Ohio: World Publishing, 1944; London: Odham Press, 1956. A short and concise chapter which refers briefly to Nightingale's early life, then moves on to describe the highlights of her career in the Crimea and her later work in hospital reform and nursing. Serves as a useful overview of her life and work.

Huxley, Elspeth. *Florence Nightingale.* London: Weidenfeld and Nicolson, and New York: Putnam, 1975. A well-written and readable biography exploring in great detail both Nightingale's personal history and her public life. It also includes a good overview of the historical and social world in which she moved. The book is well documented by excerpts from Nightingale's diaries and letters, as well as government publications. Huxley's approach is both thematic and novelistic.

Longford, Elizabeth. *Eminent Victorian Women.* London: Weidenfeld and Nicolson, and New York: Knopf, 1981. Longford's chapter on Nightingale is a clear and well-written chronology of her life and accomplishments. There is some editorializing regarding Nightingale's other biographers and her romanticized or exaggerated image. Longford's account is marred by her cryptic references to Nightingale's relationship with other women and her growing concern for matters intellectual and mystical.

Schnittkind, Henry Thomas, and Dana Lee Thomas. *Living Biographies of Famous Women.* New York: Book League of America, 1942. A brief and straightforward account of Nightingale's work during and after the Crimean War. The chapter mentions, in passing, her early and later years but concentrates primarily on the highlights of her career between the years 1856 and 1862. Contains little specific information or analysis.

Strachey, Lytton. *Eminent Victorians.* London: Chatto and Windus, and New York: Modern Library, 1918. Strachey devotes five chapters to Nightingale in this study of famous Victorians. (She is the only woman he includes.) These well-written and well-documented chapters concentrate not only on Nightingale's personal life and career but also on the social and political milieu in which she lived. The author's point of view is so close to the actual time in which Florence worked that Strachey's work has a tone and sense of familiarity with both his subject and the times.

Woodham-Smith, Cecil. *Florence Nightingale, 1820-1910.* New York: McGraw-Hill, 1951; London: Collins, 1964. Woodham-Smith's abridged edition concentrates primarily on Nightingale's early life and nursing career. Although well documented, it is aimed at a young adult audience and oftentimes borders on cliché. Nightingale's accomplishments as a hospital ad-ministrator and reformer are dealt with only briefly in the last few chapters.

Young, D. A. B. "Florence Nightingale's Fever." *British Medical Journal* 311, no. 7021 (December 23, 1995). Young offers evidence that Nightingale suffered from a bacterial infection contracted during the Crimean War. Identifies the condition as one that was often misdiagnosed.

Deborah Charlie

ALFRED NOBEL

Born: October 21, 1833; Stockholm, Sweden
Died: December 10, 1896; San Remo, Italy
Areas of Achievement: Invention, technology, and philanthropy
Contribution: Although Nobel is remembered for inventing dynamite and the blasting cap that ignites it, and although he held 355 patents for his inventions, he will be most remembered for the provision he made in his last will for the distribution of the income from the bulk of his estate to provide annual prizes to those who confer upon humankind the greatest benefits in the fields of physics, chemistry, physiology or medicine, literature, and peace.

Early Life

Alfred Bernhard Nobel spent his life in one sort of pursuit yet is enshrined in history for something quite different. Born in Stockholm to Immanuel and Andriette Nobel, Alfred was the fourth of their sons. His father was a visionary, an inventor whose fortunes swung from one extreme to another. When the family's fortunes were reduced, his mother operated a food shop to supplement their income.

Just before Alfred's birth, Immanuel's business in Sweden foundered. In 1837, Immanuel made an attempt to reestablish himself in Finland but failed. By 1842, however, he was a modestly successful manufacturer of mechanical devices in St. Petersburg, Russia. He flourished there until 1858, when the Russian government canceled its contracts, creating for him a new round of financial difficulties.

During his time in Russia, Immanuel had become fascinated with the explosive qualities of nitroglycerin, realizing that if the substance could be controlled it would have tremendous potential as military weaponry as well as for use in heavy industry and mining. Alfred, frail, colorless, and thin, was a sickly child with a spinal defect, who early shared this interest in nitroglycerin with his father. Often he was too ill to attend school, and, in Russia, he was taught exclusively by tutors. He showed a natural gift for languages, acquiring them as he traveled. He had lived in Finland and Russia, and he spoke Swedish at home. Between the ages of seventeen and nineteen, Nobel traveled in Germany, France, and the United States, learning languages as he went. Nobel, always dedicated to work, was a perfectionist, always demanding more of himself than more healthy people do.

Nobel and his brothers Ludvig and Robert worked in their father's plant in St. Petersburg. When it faced an impending financial disaster in 1858, Nobel, because of his fluency in English, was sent to England to try to negotiate financing for the business. He failed in this attempt, however, and his defeated father returned to Sweden. Nobel and his brothers remained in Russia, but in 1863, Nobel returned to Sweden to work with his father. Granted his first patent in 1857, Nobel was now on the way to discovering how to control nitroglycerin for commercial use. His invention of the blasting cap changed forever the way mining, massive construction, and war would be conducted.

Life's Work

Liquid nitroglycerin is among the world's most volatile substances. Nobel's device for igniting it, the blasting cap, consisted of a charge of gunpowder that could be ignited by a fuse and was attached to liquid nitroglycerin. This blasting cap gave workers who set the device time to seek shelter from the ensuing explosion. So revolutionary was this invention that Nobel gained fame in a matter of months, but his life was not free from sorrow, difficulty, and loneliness.

Just a year after the blasting cap was invented, Nobel's younger brother, Emil, a twenty-one-year-old student who worked in his brother's laboratory making detonators, was in the laboratory when it caught fire and exploded, killing five people who were working there, including Emil. The loss of this young son was so devastating to Immanuel that he soon suffered a paralytic stroke, from which he never recovered. Nothing, however—not even Emil's death—could shake Nobel's belief in what he was doing, and he proceeded to open explosives factories across Europe and in the United States.

So great was his confidence that Nobel yielded his patent rights when he opened foreign factories, agreeing that instead of receiving royalty payments he would receive a substantial share of the proceeds from each factory. It is this arrangement that caused him to be numbered among the world's wealthiest people by the time he died.

Nitroglycerin is a dangerous substance because it decomposes quickly; this decomposition inevitably leads to explosions. Few people realized in the 1860's and 1870's just how dangerous nitroglycerin was to work with. Two years after Nobel's laboratory exploded in 1864, a ship carrying nitroglycerin exploded and capsized near Panama, killing seventy-four people. Within months of that explosion, a San Francisco warehouse, in which liquid nitroglycerin was stored, exploded, killing another fourteen people. Nobel's factory near Hamburg, Germany, was completely destroyed by an explosion less than a year after it opened.

Continuing disasters impelled Nobel to find a safe way to store and ship nitroglycerin. Ever the inventor and thinker, Nobel knew that he had to find a way to turn nitroglycerin into a solid substance. He realized that he had to combine the liquid with something that could absorb it, and he finally settled on a siliconlike substance, kieselguhr, which was porous and would not add anything chemically to the substance with which it was mixed. Once nitroglycerin was mixed with kieselguhr, it could be formed into shapes, wrapped in paper, then transported or stored. The result was dynamite, so named by Nobel from the Greek word for power, *dunamis.*

With this advance in the latter part of the 1860's, Nobel was able to establish factories all over the world to mass-produce one of the world's most destructive substances. The production of his plants increased from a mere eleven tons in 1867 to more than three thousand tons in 1874, and to almost 67,000 tons produced by ninety-three factories—in all of which he had a financial interest—by the year of his death. Everyone connected with the production of dynamite was becoming rich; Nobel, however, because he shared in the profits of every dynamite factory in the world, was quickly gaining a financial position unheard of in Europe since the days of the Medicis.

Nobel's interest in invention never waned. After he invented dynamite, he invented an explosive gelatin more powerful than nitroglycerin, virtually impervious to shock and unaffected by moisture, which predated the sophisticated plastic explosives now available. Before Orville and Wilbur Wright flew their airplane at Kitty Hawk, North Carolina, in 1903, Nobel was experimenting with aerial photography as an expedient and accurate means of cartography, mounting his cameras on rockets. He was involved with experiments to find ways of synthesizing silk, rubber, and leather far in advance of the synthetic production of nylon, synthetic rubber, and vinyl a half century after his death. His smokeless gunpowder, *balliste,* first patented in 1887, was in great demand by armies throughout the world and added considerably to Nobel's coffers.

Through all this time, Nobel wandered from one place to another, buying houses in Paris, where he spent a considerable amount of time; at San Remo, Italy, where he bought the villa in which he eventually died; and in Sweden at Bofors, where he spent the last summer of his life. Nobel never married and his romantic involvements were never notably fulfilling, although he had a long, quite distant relationship with an Austrian, Sofie Hess, much his junior, to whom he wrote nearly daily and whom he supported during the later years of his life even though she had been married to someone else.

Summary
In his final years, Alfred Nobel speculated that he would die alone, unattended by anyone who loved him; his prediction was accurate. He spent the summer of 1896 at his home, Björkborn in Bofors, after which he went to his home in Paris, and then to San Remo. His health was failing, but he continued to work, write to his friends, and plan. On December 10, 1896, Nobel collapsed in his laboratory, and that evening, with only his servants present, Nobel died of heart failure.

On November 27, 1895, Nobel had drafted a holograph will, replacing one that left his vast fortune essentially to relatives, servants, and friends. The new will, for which Nobel will be forever remembered, substantially reduced his personal bequests. It directed that his residual estate be invested conservatively and that the income from these investments be used to establish annual prizes to be awarded with no reservations regarding nationality to those people whose activities are deemed to be of the greatest benefit to humankind in the fields of physics, chemistry, physiology or medicine, literature, and peace.

Nobel's will was contested and was in litigation for more than three years. Afterward, however, a system was established for the distribution of the income in the form of Nobel Prizes, the first set of which were awarded in 1901. As the income from the Nobel trust has increased, the size of each award has grown to the point that in 1985 the typical prize was worth over $350,000, ten times what the same award was worth thirty years earlier.

The list of Nobel laureates, which has now been expanded to include a sixth field, economics, contains the names of international giants in their fields: scientists of the stature of Albert Einstein,

Marie Curie, and Linus Pauling, writers such as William Faulkner and T. S. Eliot, physicians and physiologists such as Ivan Pavlov and Sir Alexander Fleming, and advocates of world peace such as Woodrow Wilson and Albert Schweitzer. The Nobel legacy is great because of the endowment he established to recognize those who contribute most to the benefit of humankind.

Bibliography

Barnard, Linda. "Alfred Nobel." *Cricket* 20, no. 4 (December, 1992). Profiles Nobel and includes information on his inventions, patents, and recipients of the Nobel Peace Prize.

Bergengren, Erik. *Alfred Nobel: The Man and His Work*. London and New York: Nelson, 1962. This brief overview of Nobel's life is supplemented by a list of Nobel institutions and of the awards that have been granted. It is particularly valuable for its discussion of Nobel's inventions and for its detail about the growing use and sales of dynamite. The research is extremely careful.

Evlanoff, Michael, and Marjorie Fluor. *Alfred Nobel: The Loneliest Millionaire*. New York: Ward Ritchie Press, 1969. This book is a study of Nobel's personal isolation and of his attempts to escape from his loneliness. It relates his establishing the Nobel Prizes to his guilt about the destructive effects of dynamite. Nobel is portrayed as a sensitive man with few roots, one whose intellect was a chief and isolating concern. Contains a list of all Nobel laureates from 1901 to 1968.

Fant, Kenne. *Alfred Nobel*. New York: Arcade, 1993. An interesting study of Nobel's life, this book includes letters between Nobel and Sophie Hess, a woman with whom he had a twenty-year affair.

Jackson, Donald Dale. "The Nobility of Alfred Nobel." *Smithsonian* 19 (November, 1988): 201-224. This substantial article, both meticulously researched and extremely well written, focuses on Nobel's pessimism and loneliness and on their causes, relating these conditions to his establishing the Nobel Prizes. Jackson has intriguing notions concerning Hess, the young woman in Nobel's life.

Nobelstiftelsen. *Nobel: The Man and His Prizes*. 3d ed. New York: Elsevier, 1972. This authorized biography has chapters by eminent representatives from the five fields in which the awards were originally granted as well as a biographical chapter by Henrick Schück and a chapter on Nobel and the Nobel Foundation by Ragnar Sohlman. This book is a good starting point for those wishing to know more about Alfred Nobel.

Pauli, Herta E. *Alfred Nobel: Dynamite King, Architect of Peace*. New York: Fischer, 1942; London: Nicolson and Watson, 1947. This early assessment of Nobel is outdated, although in its time it made a valuable contribution to Nobel scholarship. The book is strongest for its biographical information, including extensive materials on Nobel's business affairs as they expanded rapidly.

Sohlman, Ragnar. *The Legacy of Alfred Nobel: The Story Behind the Nobel Prizes*. Translated by Elspeth Harley Schubert. London: Bodley Head, 1983. This book was published originally in Swedish under the title *Ett Testamente* in 1950. Sohlman was Nobel's assistant in the last three years of his life and served as one of the executors of his will, giving him a significant role in establishing the Nobel award mechanism. Sohlman knew intimately the details of Nobel's business and life, and he presents these details clearly and directly in this excellent book, which also contains a copy of Nobel's will.

R. Baird Shuman

ANNIE OAKLEY

Born: August 13, 1860; Darke County, Ohio
Died: November 3, 1926; Greenville, Ohio
Area of Achievement: Sports
Contribution: An expert markswoman and consummate performer, Annie Oakley traveled throughout the United States and Europe demonstrating her expert shooting in an era when shooting was almost exclusively a man's sport.

Early Life

Phoebe Anne Moses, nicknamed Annie, was the fourth daughter born to the Quakers Jacob and Susan Moses of rural Darke County, Ohio. When Annie was still a young child, Jacob taught her to hunt and to trap. After Jacob's death from exposure in 1866, Susan and her eight children were left destitute. Young Annie was sent to the county poor farm, but she was soon chosen by a young farmer to be a companion for his wife and infant daughter. Although it was common for poor children to be farmed out, the ten-year-old Annie's fate was unusually cruel; she was overworked and physically abused by the farmer. For two years she was virtually a slave. In 1872, Annie fled, returning to the poorhouse, where she lived with the new superintendent and his wife as a member of their family. Under their care she attended school.

When Annie was fifteen, she returned to her mother. The enterprising young woman capitalized on her adroitness with firearms, entering into a business arrangement with a local merchant in which she supplied him with small game that was shipped to Cincinnati hotels. From that time forward, Annie earned her living with her shooting, proudly paying her mother's mortgage and boasting throughout her life that she had never had money other than what she personally had earned. From her early years of depredation Annie learned frugality. Throughout her life, she shrewdly managed and invested her earnings, thereby enabling Annie and her husband to live their retirement years in comfort.

Life's Work

Annie Moses—in 1882 she adopted the stage name Oakley—was twenty-one when she met her future husband, sharpshooter Frank Butler. Exhibition shooting was at its peak in popularity when Butler, who was traveling in Ohio with a variety show, competed in a contest against Annie Moses. Al-

though women sharpshooters were relatively common, Butler was surprised by the youthful, petite Annie Moses, who appeared to him to be a little girl. Moses outshot Butler that day, which marked the beginning of their courtship. The two married one year later.

During their early married years, Oakley and Butler toured variety theaters and skating rinks. It was at one such show that Oakley met the Sioux chief Sitting Bull, who became fond of her, naming her *Watanya Cicilla*, or "Little Sure Shot." The two would meet again when they both worked for Buffalo Bill Cody's Wild West Show. Butler soon realized he was outdistanced by Oakley's prowess and her showmanship; he retired from exhibition shooting to become Oakley's manager.

In 1884, after a short stint with the Sells Brothers Circus, the still relatively unknown Oakley applied to Buffalo Bill Cody for a sharpshooting position in his Wild West Show. Although he initially refused her, after the sudden departure of his star marksman, Captain Adam Bogardus, Cody gave Oakley a three-day trial. He was delighted with "Missie"—as he called her—and with only a brief interruption, Oakley remained with Cody's outfit until 1902.

Bursting into the arena sporting her trademark loose, dark, curly hair and her meticulously hand-sewn costumes of short skirts and leggings, Oakley was in constant motion during her ten-minute act. She leaped over a table to grasp her gun after a clay target had already been released, shot upside down, backwards while looking in a hand mirror, and occasionally from horseback and from a bicycle. She clowned with audiences by feigning horror over missed shots, which she did intentionally so that she would not be accused of cheating. She shot cigarettes from her husband's mouth and potatoes from her dogs' heads, and she split a playing card turned sideways. Athletic and quick, Oakley was one of the finest shots, and clearly the most engaging exhibition shooter, of her era.

At the height of its popularity in the 1880's, Buffalo Bill and his Wild West Show presented a spectacle of heroic cowboys and villainous horse-riding Plains Indians. Its massive cast of Indians, including for a year the famous Sitting Bull, and fancy-riding cowboys re-created shootouts, stagecoach attacks, and mock battles, thrilling audiences and generating an idealized image of the West in the minds of Americans and Europeans alike. Cody's outfit was the first and best of the numerous Wild West shows that became the inspiration for film Westerns of a later era. The youthful athlete Oakley became an audience favorite, attaining international superstar fame. Her life, along with Cody's, was mythologized.

After drawing record crowds at Staten Island and Madison Square Garden in 1886, the Wild West show traveled in 1887 to London, where Oakley was universally praised by audiences and reporters. In England, the once-poor country girl charmed royalty and traveled in upper-class social circles. Remarkably, Oakley was accepted at elite British gun clubs, where, despite being a woman, she was admired for her expert shooting. In London, she began teaching women to shoot, a tradition she continued for the rest of her life. Women were as capable of shooting as men, she believed, and she advocated the carrying of personal arms as a means of self-defense.

Oakley left Cody's show in 1887 for reasons that are obscured because neither Cody nor Oakley discussed the matter. During that year, she engaged in numerous exhibitions and matches, in which she had also participated when touring with the Wild West show in order to earn prize money and gain publicity. In 1885, for example, she attempted to shoot, after loading the guns herself, 5,000 glass balls in one day, scoring 4,722 and breaking a record for the last 1,000, of which she missed only 16. She set several other records, including one for American doubles scoring—two traps released simultaneously. During 1888, Oakley also traveled on the variety circuit performing trick shooting on stage, spent a short time with Pawnee Bill's Wild West Show, and starred in her first theatrical play, *Deadwood Dick: Or, The Sunbeam of the Sierras*. Although the critics despised the play, they wrote favorable reviews of Oakley. By early 1889, Oakley returned to Cody's show, where she remained as a star performer until she retired in 1902.

By 1892, Oakley's legend was firmly established; she had charmed London society, had become the darling of the newspapers, had achieved recognition at shooting clubs in England and the United States, and had even had clubs named for her. In 1889, she had extended her reputation to continental Europe when she traveled with Cody's Wild West Show to France, Italy, and Germany. In 1893, even the United States Army admitted her expertise by sending representatives to learn from her while she performed at the Chicago World's Fair.

Oakley's apparent youthfulness generated much of her stage appeal. Only five feet tall and weighing approximately 110 pounds, the petite Oakley astounded audiences with feats of endurance with heavy guns. In 1902, when her hair suddenly turned white, and she could no longer project the image of a young girl, Oakley and Butler retired from the Wild West show. She again tried acting, with a play called *The Western Girl*, written expressly for her and showcasing her marksmanship. This time, the play was successful with both critics and the public.

In 1903, Oakley's relationship with the press was abruptly shattered when newspapers throughout the country printed a story originating in Chicago with William Randolph Hearst's newsservice. Reportedly, Annie Oakley had been arrested stealing a man's pants to support her cocaine habit. She was represented as a destitute drug addict. A woman claiming to be Annie Oakley had indeed been arrested, but the newspapers had failed to confirm her identity, and she was, in fact, merely a burlesque impersonator of Oakley. In one of the largest libel suits ever initiated, Oakley sued and won settlements from newspapers throughout the country. Her battle to clear her reputation lasted for nearly five years and absorbed much of her energy. During that time, she performed some of her best trapshooting, establishing her reputation among the elite of the sport.

Oakley officially retired from show business in 1913, after having spent a brief time with the Young Buffalo Wild West Show. Butler and Oakley moved to an idyllic spot on the Eastern Shore of Maryland, but after a lifetime spent on the road, they could not easily reconcile themselves to a sedentary lifestyle. They soon resumed traveling. During World War I, Oakley toured army camps demonstrating her shooting. She also campaigned for the Red Cross. Amid plans to reenter show business in 1922, Oakley was partially paralyzed in a car accident, which ended her career. She died on November 3, 1926, and was followed eighteen days later by her husband, Frank Butler.

Summary

In an era when shooting was considered a men's sport, Annie Oakley advocated that all women be taught to shoot. She viewed guns as providing a form of independence for women, who, when armed and trained, would no longer be forced to rely on men for their protection. During her lifetime, Oakley estimated that she had trained more than fifteen thousand women and considered that women were as capable as men. She advocated providing shooting instructors and rifle ranges in schools for both boys and girls.

In other ways, Oakley was patently less iconoclastic. She jealously guarded her social reputation among upper-class Britons and Americans, bridling at challenges to her femininity, and when she was not performing, she functioned in what she deemed to be ladylike fashion: dressing conservatively, refraining from alcohol, and sharing a close monogamous relationship with her husband. During the suffragist movement, she condemned bloomers, which she considered unladylike, and "bloomer women." She did not advocate women's voting rights. She claimed that women should not "go in for sport so that they neglect their homes." After retiring to the Eastern Shore of Maryland, however, Oakley found herself to be a failure at homemaking. "I went all to pieces under the care of a home," she reported. Interestingly, in 1898, during the Spanish-American War, Oakley had written President William McKinley, requesting to be sent to the Cuban front. During World War I, she likewise wrote to the secretary of war, proposing the establishment of an armed women's regiment for home defense. Although her suggestions were never seriously entertained, her intent was genuine. Annie Oakley, according to her own definition of femininity, achieved fame and success in a predominantly male field that required strength, stamina, and great skill.

Bibliography

Blackstone, Sarah J. *Buckskins, Bullets, and Business: A History of Buffalo Bill's Wild West.* Westport, Conn.: Greenwood Press, 1986. A concise, detailed account of Cody's Wild West, describing the variety of acts and the logistics of moving the massive show from one engagement to another. Blackstone provides the best analysis of the impact of Cody's show on the development of the myth of the American West.

Broad, David B. "Annie Oakley: Woman, Legend and Myth." *Journal of the West* 37, no. 1 (January, 1998). Profile of Oakley, her years as a Wild West performer, and her performances with Buffalo Bill.

Flory, Claude R. "Annie Oakley in the South." *North Carolina Historical Review* 43 (1966): 333-343. Flory concentrates primarily on Oakley's years after her retirement from the Wild West Show during which she and Butler lived in Florida and North Carolina, giving shooting exhibitions and shooting lessons.

Kasper, Shirl. *Annie Oakley.* Norman: University of Oklahoma Press, 1992. Extensively utilizing newspapers and Annie Oakley's own scrapbooks, journalist Kasper has written an interesting and detailed biography of Oakley in which she has attempted to separate myths from documentable facts about Annie Oakley's life. Easily supplants earlier works as a definitive biography. Contains photographs, an index, and a bibliography.

Rosa, Joseph G., and Robin May. *Buffalo Bill and His Wild West: A Pictorial Biography.* Lawrence: University Press of Kansas, 1989. As its title indicates, this book is liberally illustrated. It contains a section summarizing Annie Oakley's career with, and apart from, Cody's Wild West Show. Contains a bibliography and an index.

Riley, Glenda. *The Life and Legacy of Annie Oakley.* Norman: University of Oklahoma Press, 1994. An interpretive biography of Oakley.

Russell, Don. *The Lives and Legends of Buffalo Bill.* Norman: University of Oklahoma Press, 1960. Russell's nearly five-hundred-page book on Buffalo Bill places Oakley's life in the context of Cody's Wild West Show. Russell provides the most detailed history available of Cody's outfit.

Mary E. Virginia

DANIEL O'CONNELL

Born: August 6, 1775; near Cahirciveen, County Kerry, Ireland

Died: May 15, 1847; Genoa, Italy

Areas of Achievement: Law, government, politics, and social reform

Contribution: Once the leader of the struggle for Catholic emancipation in the British Empire, O'Connell is identified with the principles of religious freedom and separation of church and state, nonviolent reform movements, early democratic organizations, and the upholding of the rule of law.

Early Life

Daniel O'Connell was born on August 6, 1775, on the southwest coast of Ireland near the small town of Cahirciveen (then a hamlet), in the barony of Iveragh and county of Kerry. Iveragh is situated at the western end of a mountainous peninsula running forty miles out into the Atlantic from the Lakes of Killarney. Its mountains and sea inlets afford beautiful scenery, and nowhere more so than at Derrynane, where O'Connell's family lived from the beginning of the eighteenth century (Derrynane is now preserved as a national monument). Iveragh had retained much of the Gaelic culture so that O'Connell was born into a society in which perhaps a majority of the people knew no English. Catholic landlords, the O'Connells were the principal family in Iveragh for some centuries before O'Connell was born in 1775. Fostered out at birth to a tenant of his father, in accordance with Gaelic custom, he returned to his parents' house at the age of four, knowing no English. He was the eldest son in a family of ten children. His father ran a general store in Cahirciveen and invested his profits in the purchase of land. His mother was a daughter of John O'Mullane, a Catholic small landlord of old family in County Cork. When still a boy, O'Connell was adopted as heir by his rich but childless uncle at Derrynane. Receiving his first schooling at Derrynane, he then proceeded to a boarding school near the city of Cork. In 1791, he was sent to France, first to the college of St. Omer and then to the English college at Douai. In January, 1793, Douai was closed by the French revolutionary government, and O'Connell left for England as virtually a refugee, a day or two after the execution of Louis XVI. He spent the next three years as a law student in London and then obtained his uncle's permission to complete his legal studies in Dublin, where he was called to the bar in 1798.

Moderately tall and broadly built, O'Connell looked impressive and distinguished rather than handsome, though his expressive blue eyes were commented upon. Having a powerful voice, he was one of the famous orators of his day, being able to appeal to more educated audiences as well as to great crowds. Although actively engaged in politics, he built up one of the largest practices of his day at the Irish bar. Because of his skill in defending great numbers of poor Catholics against charges they considered unjust, he early won widespread popular fame.

In 1802, O'Connell married his distant cousin, Mary O'Connell, one of the eleven penniless children of a County Kerry physician. For this impecunious marriage, he was disinherited by his uncle. Three years later, however, uncle and nephew were reconciled, and eventually O'Connell was bequeathed Derrynane and a third of his uncle's estate. The marriage was a very happy one, the only cause of distress being his extravagance, which left him always in debt. The charge that he was a womanizer is not supported by historical evidence. That it has been made can be explained by the fact that he was the last of the Gaelic folk heroes, and all these heroes from prehistory onward had a reputation for sexual energy—it was seen as part of their greatness—and O'Connell was no exception.

O'Connell entered politics in 1800, when he organized a meeting of Dublin Catholics to oppose the enactment of the Union between Great Britain and Ireland (whereby the Irish Parliament was abolished, and Ireland for the future elected representatives to the British Parliament). He seems to have been the only member of the Catholic-propertied classes to oppose the Union. By 1805, he was an energetic member of the Catholic Committee, a body of landlords, businessmen, and lawyers who sought full freedom and equality for Catholics so that they could enter Parliament and government service and not remain a subject people.

Life's Work

Politics in Great Britain and Ireland was at that time a matter for landlords and members of the upper-middle classes, for aristocratic dinner parties and, to a lesser extent, for committees and small public meetings. O'Connell was to alter this pattern when he founded the Catholic Association in 1823, which proved to be the first great popular democratic organization. In February, 1824, he introduced the penny-a-month plan, whereby tens of thousands of the poorer classes were enrolled and politically instructed. By the end of 1824, the whole country was roused, and for the next four years the Catholic Association exerted strong pressure on the British government. In 1828, there occurred a by-election for County Clare, and O'Connell was induced to contest it, the first Catholic to stand for Parliament since the seventeenth century.

It was realized from the start that the Clare election would be decisive. The contest was bitter, and O'Connell, who could be scurrilous, left nothing unsaid or undone to ensure victory. Special contingents of army and police stood by to deal with popular violence, but there was none. Instead, as great numbers gathered in and around the county town of Ennis, where the polling took place, the officials of the Catholic Association with the assistance of the clergy imposed strict discipline, even to the extent of banning the consumption of liquor. On the fifth day of the polling, when the count was two-to-one in O'Connell's favor, the Tory candidate conceded victory. Organized, disciplined, and instructed, the masses had shown their power. In the weeks that followed, the two chief members of the Tory cabinet, the Duke of Wellington as prime minister and Sir Robert Peel as home secretary (the minister in charge of Ireland), decided that Catholic emancipation must be enacted. Accordingly, in the spring of 1829, Peel introduced the bill which was passed by both houses without difficulty and received the royal assent in April.

The reasons for which the anti-Catholic Tory government conceded emancipation have frequently been misunderstood. The threat of civil war in Ireland is usually given as the reason, but that factor would not have been sufficient if the British body politic were united in defense of the Protestant establishment in Ireland. There was no such unity. The Whigs and their Radical supporters, who together made up half of the House of Commons, were sick of the long agitation for emancipation. Though not necessarily committed to any principle of religious freedom, they did respond to the Whig tradition of government by consent. Also, some of the more liberal of the Tories were prepared to concede. Should the Tory administration, by rejecting emancipation, provoke a civil war in Ireland, they

might find themselves voted out of office and replaced by a Whig government willing to enact the measure. There was the additional consideration that twenty or thirty Catholics might be returned for Irish constituencies at the next general election, and the Mother of Parliaments could look ridiculous if she refused them admission. In demanding emancipation for Catholics, O'Connell was careful to ask for it only on the general principle of freedom and equality for men of all religions. As early as 1807, he rested his case "on the new score of justice—of that justice which will emancipate the Protestant in Spain and Portugal, the Christian in Constantinople."

Once elected to Parliament, he applied his energies to a large number of causes. These included the extension of the parliamentary and local government suffrages; the Tolpuddle Martyrs; Poles persecuted by czarist Russia; Jewish emancipation; separation of church and state in Catholic as well as in Protestant countries, and even in the Papal States; free trade and especially the repeal of the Corn Laws; and the abolition of black slavery. In pursuing these aims, he was the leading Radical in the British Parliament in the 1830's.

With the passing of the emancipation bill, O'Connell hoped for great things for Irish Catholics, but his hopes were only partly realized. The Tories and the more conservative of the Whigs were determined to maintain Protestant dominance in Ireland and not to admit Catholics to office. In the general election of 1834, however, the Whigs lost their overall majority and were forced to come to terms with O'Connell if they wished to maintain a stable government. They negotiated an arrangement whereby O'Connell's party of some twenty-five Members of Parliament would support the Whigs and keep them in power provided they admitted Catholics to the Irish administration and sponsored certain reforms. As a consequence, the Protestant monopoly of power was broken, and Catholics were appointed to the civil service, the judiciary, and high posts in a modernized and expanded police force. The legislative reforms demanded by O'Connell were passed by the Commons but amended in an anti-Catholic direction by the House of Lords. Nevertheless, gains were made.

When the Tories returned to power in 1841 with a large majority in the House of Commons, O'Connell believed that he could look for no further reforms. When his year as lord mayor of Dub-

lin ended in October, 1842, he threw himself into the struggle for Repeal, that is the repeal of the Act of Union. British political opinion was determined to uphold the Union, seeing Repeal as involving sooner or later the breaking away of Ireland from the Empire. It was also considered that control of Ireland was essential to British military security. The question the historian must ask is: How could a perceptive politician such as O'Connell, with a long experience of British politics, believe that he could win Repeal? The only answer that makes sense is that he knew he could not; he was using the carrot of Repeal to rouse the Catholic masses so that, as in the case of Catholic emancipation, he could intimidate a British government into granting not Repeal but major reforms. Whatever his purpose, he had the Repeal Association hold great public gatherings known as monster meetings throughout the country, at which he made menacing speeches. Peel's nerve held, however, and in October of 1843, he called O'Connell's bluff by proclaiming the monster meeting announced for Clontarf outside Dublin. O'Connell called off the meeting.

Peel, however, was not the proverbial Bourbon. He realized that the Repeal movement was a response to real grievances, and in the years left to him as prime minister he enacted several reforms pleasing to the Catholic clergy and middle-class Catholics in general, and he planned to enact a measure giving tenant farmers a degree of legal security. Unfortunately for Irish Catholics, Peel was driven from office in 1846 by the Whigs (aided by O'Connell) and a majority of his own Tory Party, as soon as he had enacted the repeal of the Corn Laws.

The Repeal movement brought to the fore a group of idealistic young men who soon came to be known as the Young Irelanders. On the declared policy of Repeal, they were ostensibly at one with O'Connell, but there were fissures under the surface. Where he drew his political principles from the *philosophes* (excluding Jean-Jacques Rousseau) and the English Rationalists, such as Thomas Paine, William Godwin, and Jeremy Bentham (who though a zealous Catholic in his maturity had been a Deist as a young man), the Young Irelanders subscribed to Romantic Nationalism, the ideology then sweeping through Europe. O'Connell saw the nation as a collective unit, as the sum of all of its parts, whereas the young men of the movement realized that a nation is first and foremost a tradition; from that reality, they drew conclusions that bore little practical relevance to their own day but which would inspire later generations.

Unrealistic in the context of contemporary politics, the Young Irelanders demanded that the small Repeal Party should act independently of the Whig and Tory parties in the British Parliament and that O'Connell must not renew his "alliance" with the Whigs; they rightly suspected that, contrary to his declared policies, he intended to do just that. Though he tolerated much public criticism from the Young Irelanders, he often acted as if the Repeal Association were his private property and as if he were not bound by its decisions. The break between old and young came in July, 1846, on the question of violence. O'Connell insisted that all members of the Repeal Association must adhere to the principles of nonviolence and constitutionalism, on which the association had been founded and to which the members had pledged their allegiance repeatedly since then. The Young Irelanders insisted that these alleged principles were merely policies. They were constitutionalists by preference, but they considered that the use of violence might be necessary at some time in the future should constitutional methods fail. The two positions were mutually exclusive. The majority of the population sided with O'Connell, regardless of whether they understood the points at issue, but it was his last victory. Within months, the famine was ravaging the country, and by February, 1847, O'Connell knew himself to be dying. On the advice of his doctors, he set out on a pilgrimage to Rome but died on the way at Genoa on May 15, 1847.

Summary

Daniel O'Connell deserved the title "the Liberator," which was bestowed on him by his followers after Catholic emancipation. Though he had able Catholic lieutenants and received valuable cooperation from a number of Irish Protestants, he was the central figure in politically instructing and organizing a subject people. Catholic emancipation was the first political victory they knew after two centuries of discouragement and failure, and it was irreversible. The Catholic Association was the first popular democratic organization of the modern world. O'Connell was the first Catholic political leader and perhaps the first politician in any major Christian denomination in Europe to espouse the dual principles of religious freedom and separation of church and state. In the years from Catholic emancipation until his death, he was the outstanding European opponent of black slavery. As a practitioner of nonviolent reform, he ranks with Mahatma Gandhi and Martin Luther King. He embraced and expanded the British Whig tradition of government by consent which owed much to another Irishman, Edmund Burke. Future generations may well recognize him as the greatest upholder of the rule of law—not merely of law as made by one's own people but also of law as made by others—that Western civilization has produced.

Bibliography

Crimmins, James E. "Jeremy Bentham and Daniel O'Connell: Their Correspondence and Radical Alliance, 1828–1831." *The Historical Journal* 40, no. 2 (June, 1997). Crimmins reconstructs the relationship between O'Connell and Jeremy Bentham from their correspondence from 1828–1831. The author shows the progression from O'Connell's initial discipleship to their split occasioned by O'Connell's demands that Irish reforms be given first priority.

McCartney, Donal, ed. *The World of Daniel O'Connell*. Dublin: Mercier Press, 1980. Fourteen articles, mostly of high quality, describing O'Connell's image abroad, his role in the British Parliament, his attitude to black slavery, and his influence on the Liberal Catholic movement in Western Europe.

Moley, Raymond. *Daniel O'Connell: Nationalism Without Violence*. New York: Fordham University Press, 1974. A popular biography by a distinguished American political commentator.

Nowlan, Kevin B., and Maurice O'Connell, eds. *Daniel O'Connell: Portrait of a Radical*. New York: Fordham University Press, 1985. Eight articles on various aspects of O'Connell, notably his association with Gaelic Ireland, his social and economic ideas, and his role in British politics.

O'Connell, Daniel. *The Correspondence of Daniel O'Connell*. Edited by Maurice R. O'Connell. Dublin: Irish University Press, 1972-1980. Thirty-five hundred private letters to and from O'Connell.

O'Faoláin, Seán. *King of the Beggars: A Life of Daniel O'Connell, the Irish Liberator, in a Study of the Rise of the Modern Irish Democracy*. London: Nelson, and New York: Viking Press, 1938. Entertaining biographical study of O'Connell's personality. Intuitive rather than scholarly, it is the only work on O'Connell before 1960 that merits consideration.

O'Ferrall, Fergus. *Catholic Emancipation: Daniel O'Connell and the Rise of Irish Democracy, 1820-30*. Atlantic Highlands, N.J.: Humanities Press International, 1985. Comprehensive study of the Catholic Association as the modern world's first democratic mass movement. Both grass-roots organization and its effect on high politics are described.

Trench, Charles Chenevix. *The Great Dan: A Biography of Daniel O'Connell*. London: Cape, 1984. Historically sound and entertaining, this biography is written with wit and insight.

Maurice R. O'Connell

JACQUES OFFENBACH
Jacob Eberst

Born: June 20, 1819; Cologne, Prussia
Died: October 5, 1880; Paris, France
Area of Achievement: Music
Contribution: Over the course of one hundred operettas and a major opera, Offenbach virtually defined this form of musical theater through his characteristic mixture of gaiety, spontaneity, and infectious melody and thus became the first great influence in the process of internationalizing the operetta.

Early Life

Jacques Offenbach, one of the greatest figures in the history of operetta, was born Jacob Eberst, the second son of a peripatetic Jewish cantor and music teacher. Isaac Eberst, Jacob's father, was a poor man who, when not singing in the synagogue of his hometown, Offenbach-am-Main, Germany, supplemented his income as a music teacher by playing the fiddle in local cafés. Called "the Offenbacher" on his travels, Isaac thus adopted "Offenbach" as his legal surname.

Jacob clearly inherited more than his father's name, for the boy, along with his brother Julius, early showed a marked talent for music. Offenbach himself noted that he had learned to play the violin by the time he was seven, but by age ten he discovered the cello and it was with this instrument that the young man became a professional musician. Frail and thin throughout his life, Offenbach belied his appearance by playing the cello with the same high-spirited vivacity that was to characterize his music.

Offenbach's talent was in need of greater nourishment than that which could be obtained in Cologne, so in October, 1833, Isaac arranged for his son to go to Paris to enroll in the conservatoire, the pinnacle of musical opportunity. The story goes that Offenbach was at first denied admission on the grounds that he was not French, upon which he took up his cello and began playing a piece at first sight. The admissions committee did not let him finish but took his hand and welcomed him as a pupil. Offenbach began to study the violin, but within a year the young man left the conservatoire, probably from the need to earn a living. At fifteen, Jacob, now Jacques, Offenbach secured a job as cellist in the orchestra of the Opéra-Comique.

The business of music in Paris of the late 1830's was primarily a theatrical enterprise. Composers often conducted their own works and promoted them as well, and it was not uncommon for a composer of waltzes and social music to lead a sixty-piece orchestra in cafés along the boulevards. The young Offenbach submitted several of his waltzes to the leading composer-impresarios of the day, and one of his first, "Fleurs d'hiver" ("Winter Flowers"), was a popular success. By January, 1839, Offenbach, at age nineteen, gave his first public concert. Soon thereafter, he was asked to write the music for a vaudeville, *Pascal et Chambord*. Produced in March, 1839, the piece was a failure.

Undaunted, Offenbach continued to perform as virtuoso cellist and to teach. Over the next few years, he composed a number of cello works and performed in Germany and before the Queen of England. Thus, the salon and the drawing room—not the theater—dictated both the setting and the style for the compositions of Offenbach during the 1840's. His music was light, simple, generously diverting, and, above all, well crafted. The ballads and songs of this period are interesting in at least two respects. First, they often contain the melodic germs of his later work, for Offenbach had a lifelong practice of recasting earlier material. For another, they often contain elements of humor—such as the cello simulating a kazoo—that were to make his great operettas so distinctive.

It was, indeed, just this element of humor bordering on impertinence that—more than even the local musical politics—probably kept Offenbach from serious notice. Though he was known throughout the 1840's as a cellist and minor composer of songs and other salon pieces, his own ambition to write a musical work for the Opéra-Comique was spurned by the management of that theater. Meanwhile, Offenbach converted to Catholicism and married Herminie d'Alcain in 1844.

Life's Work

The Revolution of 1848 which made France, nominally at least, a republic, precipitated Offenbach's departure to Germany. The father of a young girl, he was as poor as a freelance composer of dance music could be, but he continued to pursue his ambition of writing for the musical stage and had his first work of this kind produced in Cologne. The work went virtually unnoticed. Now approaching thirty, Offenbach returned to Paris to see Louis Napoleon, nephew of Napoleon I, installed as Emperor of France. The so-called Second Empire had begun and with it the rising fortunes of Offenbach.

During his career as cellist and salon composer, he had met the director of the Théâtre-Français, the serious theater for all state-approved tragedies and comedies. In 1851, the director appointed Offenbach conductor of the house, hoping that the young cellist's musical abilities and vivacious personality would bring back the audiences lost to administrative and artistic chaos. As conductor, Offenbach presented not only the music of other composers but also, more pertinent to his own career, his own compositions. Before long, his own incidental music to plays and his *entr' actes* (music played during the intermissions) began to gain attention.

Now in a position to write the kind of light, witty theater music that he perceived as lacking on the French stage, he dedicated himself unceasingly to the task. From this period of the early 1850's, Offenbach began to compose an astonishing number of "little operas." In 1855 alone, he produced no less than twelve one-act operettas. This was the year in which he left his official post at the Théâtre-Français and opened his own theater, the Bouffes-Parisiens. Restricted now only by his own cleverness, Offenbach flourished. By his own admission, his major vice now and throughout the rest of his life was work. He wrote incessantly, steadily, and quickly. In 1856, eight operettas came from his fecund pen, and in 1857 seven more. These early operettas, such as *Ba-ta-clan* (1855), *La Bonne d'enfants* (1856), and *Les Deux Pêcheurs* (1857), possess a lyrical charm and freshness that characterize much of the composer's best music, but they fall victim to clumsy and dated librettos and are thus seldom heard or performed.

After producing almost thirty operettas in five years, Offenbach composed what was to be his first, and perhaps best-known, major work. Unlike his previous compositions, *Orphée aux enfers* (1858) is more ambitious in scope (two acts), more serious in the variety of musical types, and, above all, more witty in its parody of some of French society's most cherished traditions. Offenbach's chief librettist for the work was Ludovic Halévy, who, along with Henri Meilhac, was to write the book for Georges Bizet's *Carmen* (1875). Together, they

provided Offenbach with the librettos for his finest operettas. Offenbach's love of satire and parody infused the music of *Orphée aux enfers* with the sparkling wit and innocent naughtiness that became the composer's hallmark and a distinctive element of French operetta for the remainder of the century. Taking the Greek myth of Orpheus and Eurydice as its source, the operetta pokes fun at the pantheon of gods who talked not like Greek divinities but Second Empire boulevardiers, ladies and gentlemen of mid-nineteenth century French society. Along the way, there are musical parodies of Christoph Gluck, composer of the 1762 serious version of the Orpheus and Eurydice story, and of scenes from Italian opera. The finale consists of the famous cancan, during which the gods and goddesses cavort in a frenzied bacchanal.

Orphée aux enfers made Offenbach famous and rich, though money was never his constant companion. His generosity, love of luxury, and overall beneficent prodigality always kept the composer within view of his creditors. Still, his prodigality of money was at least equaled by his prodigality of genius as one after another operetta reached the stage. Between *Orphée aux enfers* in 1858 and his next great operetta, *La Belle Hélène* of 1864, Offenbach composed another twenty-eight works, including a ballet, *Le Papillon* (1860), and a three-act parody of medieval France, *Geneviève de Brabant* (1859). The latter contained a famous section that was later adapted by the United States Marine Corps for its well-known hymn.

When in 1860 the Opéra-Comique at last commissioned a work from him, Offenbach offered *Barkouf*. A ridiculous libretto about a dog that becomes head of state was coupled with music which the public, for once, did not understand. The work drew the disdain of music critics and composers such as Hector Berlioz, who attacked Offenbach's use of strange and awkward harmonies. *Barkouf* represents one of the few times Offenbach overextended himself and clearly illustrates the fatality of musical stage works in thralldom to a bad libretto. Offenbach was not to make the same mistake again. *La Belle Hélène* is regarded by many as his most brilliant operetta. For his source, the composer once again returned to Greek mythology, this time to the legend of Helen of Troy. Although conservative critics condemned the work for its blasphemy of Homer, the public knew better. With *La Belle Hélène*, Offenbach reached the zenith of his career. His orchestration now bore a richer chromatic harmony, evidence of Richard Wagner's influence, and the music sparkled with a brilliant libretto.

La Belle Hélène was followed by a series of witty and gently mocking operettas. Offenbach had become the darling of the Second Empire, even as he gaily laughed at it. With the Franco-Prussian War of 1870, however, the Second Empire tottered, and when it fell Offenbach's own success and the quality of his work soon also declined. He continued to write operettas, but he began imitating himself, revising earlier productions and depending increasingly on the spectacular and the impressive rather than on spontaneity.

Always pressed for money because of lavish spending, Offenbach accepted an offer to conduct concerts in the United States as part of the centennial celebration of 1876. During a three-month tour, he played excerpts from his work in New York, Philadelphia, and Chicago. Despite some critical reserve at the naughtiness of some of his operettas, Offenbach impressed many by his personality, and the tour was an ultimate success. His impressions of his American experience were published in Paris the following year.

By the late 1870's, however, two conditions had altered Offenbach's life, one physical, the other artistic. Afflicted by gout for a number of years, Offenbach was enduring more continuous pain as his ailment wracked his already frail body. Additionally, his dream of being taken seriously as a composer now manifested itself in his determination to write a masterwork of opera. He had been making sketches for a work based on stories by the German Romantic writer E. T. A. Hoffmann since 1875, but he wrote with uncharacteristic deliberation, signifying a more serious commitment rather than a decline in creative powers.

By 1880, Offenbach completed the score of his masterpiece, *Les Contes d'Hoffmann*. By October of that year, however, the disease precipitated heart failure, and Offenbach died on October 5, 1880. The orchestration of his great opera was completed by a family friend, Ernest Guiraud. Offenbach's masterpiece was thus performed in 1881, after his death, at the Opéra-Comique, the very theater in which he first dreamed of being recognized.

Summary

Though Jacques Offenbach did not actually invent the operetta, he did infuse the form with those elements of gaiety and good-natured fun that became the model for subsequent works of the kind. His influence on later masters such as W. S. Gilbert and Sir Arthur Sullivan and the Viennese composer Johann Strauss—whom Offenbach first urged to write operettas—is indelible; Offenbach must thus be regarded as a seminal figure in making operetta an international art form.

Gioacchino Rossini, himself an operatic master, referred to Offenbach as "the Mozart of the boulevards." The similitude is apt not only because Wolfgang Amadeus Mozart was Offenbach's idol—Offenbach kept a book of Mozart's music always by his bedside—but also because, like Mozart, Offenbach had a unique gift for melody and for lucidity of style. Like Mozart's, Offenbach's music is almost always perfectly suited to the context in which it is placed and which it thus defines. His melodies are among the most infectious ever written.

The connection with Rossini, who lived in Paris during Offenbach's greatest triumphs, is also pertinent in an artistic sense. Like Rossini, Offenbach understood the dramatic excitement generated at the end of a scene by the use of a galloping rhythm combined with a crescendo. His use of brass instruments particularly heightened the vitality of the melodic line. Finally, Offenbach's music epitomizes the saucy, high-spirited, and supremely confident atmosphere of Paris during the middle years of the nineteenth century.

Bibliography

Bordman, Gerald. *American Operetta: From "H.M.S. Pinafore" to "Sweeney Todd."* New York: Oxford University Press, 1981. Contains a brief history of the popularity of Offenbach in the United States, particularly citing his *La Grande-Duchesse de Gérolstein* (1867) as an influence on later American operetta formats.

De Almeida, Antonio. *Thematic Catalogue of the Works of Jacques Offenbach.* New York: Oxford University Press, 1999. The first comprehensive listing of the complete works of Offenbach including the author's twenty-five-year study of the primary sources. Covers in detail, 113 stage works, over 250 vocal works, and 253 instrumental pieces.

Faris, Alexander. *Jacques Offenbach.* London and Boston: Faber, 1980. This is probably the best biography in English. Himself a conductor, Faris presents a well-balanced, though often too minutely detailed, study. Includes liberal examples of musical notation and technique. Contains an excellent bibliography, including a complete chart of all Offenbach's work, published and unpublished.

Kracauer, Siegfried. *Offenbach and the Paris of His Time.* London: Constable, 1937; New York: Knopf, 1938. A sociological study of the theatrical and artistic traditions within which Offenbach lived and worked. Though accurate, the study tends to emphasize the political and revolutionary aspects of Offenbach's works.

Mordden, Ethan. *The Splendid Art of Opera: A Concise History.* New York: Methuen, 1980. Contains an excellent chapter on musical comedy that credits Offenbach with internationalizing operetta and examines the "remarkably innovative" *Les Contes d'Hoffmann.*

Offenbach, Jacques. *Orpheus in America: Offenbach's Diary of His Journey to the New World.* Translated by Lander MacLintock. Bloomington: Indiana University Press, 1957; London: Hamilton, 1958. Offenbach's memoirs about his American concert tour. His breezy prose serves as a revealing correlative to his musical style. Contains an excellent brief biographical introduction by the translator.

Revard, Stella P. "The Orpheus Strain." *Opera News* 57, no. 11 (February 13, 1993). Argues that Offenbach's Hoffmann character in the "Tales of Hoffmann" is patterned after the story of the mythological Greek poet, Orpheus.

Edward Fiorelli

BERNARDO O'HIGGINS

Born: August 20?, 1778; Chillán, Chile

Died: October, 1842; Peru

Areas of Achievement: The military and social reform

Contribution: Widely regarded by Latin Americans as the George Washington of Chile, O'Higgins, inspired by both the American and the French revolutions, followed the lead of the great Argentine general José de San Martín and helped Martín liberate Chile from Spanish colonial rule. Although he was not a political administrator, O'Higgins was able to inspire both the troops under his command and the Chilean civilian population to overthrow a long-detested regime.

Early Life

The illegitimate son of an Irish father, Ambrosio O'Higgins, who distinguished himself in the Spanish government's Chilean bureaucracy and as Viceroy of Peru, and a Chilean mother of impoverished background, Bernardo O'Higgins went to primary school in Lima, Peru, and London, England. The latter school was important because, while in London, O'Higgins, a bright and energetic student, met Latin American anti-Spanish revolutionaries whose liberation ideas stayed with him, greatly influencing his later military career.

When his father died, O'Higgins went back to Chile in order to oversee lands that his father had willed him. From all appearances, he was but one of many wealthy, ambitious young Chileans who, benefiting greatly from the hacienda system of landholding, would spend the rest of his life overseeing a large estate. Yet, perhaps as a result of the revolutionary contacts he had made in England, O'Higgins grew increasingly bitter about the ongoing Spanish occupation of Chile, resolving to help free the country from these bonds in a future struggle for independence.

Together with other patriotic, anti-Spanish aristocrats of liberal tendencies, O'Higgins in 1810 joined a group of delegates to Chile's congress, which was attempting to decide the country's political future. Unfortunately for all concerned, the congress was violently divided over which kind of governmental system Chile required. Some wanted a return to old ways of doing things, instituted centuries earlier by the conquering Spanish; others favored a republican form of government; still others hoped for a complete transformation of society which would do away with the past. Those who were not interested in the radical approach decided that working with others in the Santiago congress who failed to share their utopian vision of Chile was futile; thus, they left the congress, an act which allowed their political foes, calling themselves the Executive Power, to claim control of the Chilean government.

The rebels were ruthlessly defeated by José Carrera, who had fought against Napoleon I's army in Spain. Carrera, in a manner confusing to friend and enemy alike, supported constitutional reform while continuing allegiance to Spain's King Ferdinand, the latter action having been to camouflage true anti-Spanish intent.

The new constitution created a ruling triad, which included O'Higgins, who zealously believed in the reform of both society and government and in the creation of a benevolent state encouraging the betterment of the human condition. O'Higgins' first efforts were quashed by Peru's viceroy when the combined forces of O'Higgins' and Carrera's armies were routed in 1814, a rout that allowed the capture of Santiago, Chile, by Spanish forces and a setback to the budding revolution that resulted.

O'Higgins narrowly avoided being executed by the vengeful government forces; he took his army—what remained of it—over the Andes Mountains to Argentina, in itself a heroic feat. Discouraged by this untimely defeat, O'Higgins appeared to have become merely one more victim of the Spanish occupation, which was victoriously reasserting itself in the New World. In this defeat, Chile was joined by other countries elsewhere in Spanish America—Guatemala, Mexico, and Peru—that unsuccessfully battled oppression.

Life's Work

O'Higgins is often referred to as the liberator of Chile as well as a kind of George Washington figure. Like Washington, O'Higgins suffered early defeats, only to pull together his beaten forces and win the war. After the loss in 1814 to Spanish and loyalist troops, O'Higgins, like Washington, had the good fortune to have help from outside his nation. Argentina's San Martín, Governor of Cuyo Province, was able to give O'Higgins the right sort of assistance when he most needed it. Actually, without San Martín's expertise in military matters as well as his experienced army, the liberation of

Chile would most likely have remained a dream unfulfilled. This tall, handsome man was clearly a classic leader who, like O'Higgins, had the respect of his troops. San Martín became O'Higgins' mentor and friend.

The campaign for the independence of Chile began in 1817 at Mendoza, Argentina, where San Martín gathered together great amounts of ammunition and guns for the coming war. Buenos Aires was in the mood to supply what O'Higgins needed—another bit of good fortune.

In O'Higgins, San Martín recognized a strong, purposeful young leader, with whom he could share military leadership. Yet what faced them both was the daunting prospect of moving an army across Andean passes much more than three thousand meters in elevation. Nevertheless, supplies, including equipment designed for traversing gullies and ravines, were readied, though O'Higgins was not certain that they would take them where no army had gone.

Using the Los Patos and Uspollata passes in the Andes, the troops united under San Martín and O'Higgins met the Spanish and Chilean loyalists near Santiago at the town of Chacabuco. It was O'Higgins, however, who achieved the greatest triumph in that battle: He rose from relative obscurity that day to be numbered among Latin America's most illustrious liberators. San Martín also added to his already impressive reputation as a military genius.

Bravely, with little thought to his personal safety, O'Higgins led two sweeping cavalry charges into the Spanish ranks, causing the latter considerable losses and creating confusion in the ranks. These great attacks set the stage for San Martín's being offered the supreme directorship of Chile, as the new title was known. San Martín, however, graciously declined the position. The title was given to O'Higgins, an honor he happily accepted.

The independence of Chile was proclaimed by O'Higgins on February 12, 1818. Because of Spanish and loyalist entrenchment in the southern part of the country, however, the war was not over. It took San Martín's brilliant defense of Santiago and the repulse of counterforces at Maipu, near the capital on April 5 of that year, before O'Higgins could truly announce that Chile was free of its long Spanish occupation.

Deeply indebted to San Martín, who took over the Maipu battle after O'Higgins himself had fallen ill, O'Higgins returned the favor by assisting his friend in the battle to liberate Peru, the astute O'Higgins realizing that if the fledgling Chilean government were to survive, it would require that Peru and other neighboring states be free from Spanish enslavement. To this end, he joined San Martín once more, this time in acquiring a flotilla of ships, which were presented to a Scottish sailor, Thomas Cochrane, who created a Chilean fleet that was superior to anything operating in the Southern Pacific region. On August 20, 1820, the fleet left Valparaiso, and it included at least eight well-armed men-of-war and various other vessels. In September of 1820, the army under San Martín's command invaded Southern Peru while Cochrane blockaded the Peruvian coastline, attacking several Spanish ships in the process.

For O'Higgins, however, the main arena was no longer battle, but warfare of the political sort, wherein he would have to take charge of a newly free nation without any Latin American precedents to follow that would suit Chile's unique situation. To O'Higgins, the only workable way to govern a turbulent, newly freed country such as Chile was for him to declare himself a virtual dictator, which he did.

It was O'Higgins' and Chile's misfortune—since O'Higgins was a man of tremendous ability—that he could not be as successful a leader as he had been a soldier. It may have been that he lacked the skills that were needed to govern effectively, and it may have been the case that he simply was not interested in politics. Whatever the cause, history records that after trying to force various liberal social reforms on unwilling Chileans, O'Higgins was forced to resign as supreme director. In 1823, O'Higgins was deposed peacefully and sent into exile in Peru, where he stayed until he died.

O'Higgins was a true reformer by nature, his most pressing interest being in educational reform, for he believed that Chileans deserved to have widespread—even universal—public education. Thus, he re-created the once-defunct Instituto Nacional in Santiago and opened a number of schools for the people under the auspices of the English educator James Thompson.

Yet he also ordered that aristocratic titles and coats of arms be abolished and asked that estate entailment, the backbone of the hacienda system, be destroyed, measures that infuriated the rich landlords of Chile, who became convinced that O'Higgins was a threat to their pleasant, tradition-bound lifestyle. Other high-minded ideas of O'Higgins outraged more than the elite members of Chilean society, for he wanted to do away with cockfighting and bullfighting, both highly popular pursuits among the poor. The enslavement of black people, another popular institution, was also declared immoral by O'Higgins, much to the general consternation of the populace. To add to his problems, it was not only the rich who were angry but also the liberals and moderates from whose ranks O'Higgins himself had risen. Moreover, powerful military men found the director's ideas intolerable, and this turned out to be O'Higgins' undoing, for the military, under the leadership of Ramón Freire, led the revolt that ousted him in 1823 and sent him into Peruvian exile.

It was Chile's misfortune to lose one as capable as O'Higgins in its national infancy, when it needed a strong leader. After his departure, more than ten different directors came to and left office, each of them trying in his own way to keep Chile from disintegrating completely. Although stability did eventually come to Chilean government, it was a long time in coming.

Summary

Whatever ill might be said of Bernardo O'Higgins' last years in Chile, he remains that nation's greatest hero and its political benefactor supreme. Without him, Chile might have languished under Spanish rule for several more decades than it did. O'Higgins knew that the time had come for Latin American nations in general to rise up against their colonizers.

He, along with Simón Bolívar, San Martín, and, more recently, Fidel Castro, is one of the Latin American men of destiny who profited from a political and social climate in which revolutionary thought and action could flourish. The lessons drawn from France's bloody revolution and from the inspirational American experience in its war with England taught people of intellect and patriotism living after those revolutions had triumphed that it was possible to fight against and eventually conquer the most powerful of tyrannies. Notions also drawn from the French and American conflicts that became current in Latin America's revolutionary period—freedom, liberty, and self-direction—helped O'Higgins fight against Spanish oppressors, for older notions about being subservient to foreign masters seemed stale and lifeless. Although it

was not transformed immediately from a distant province of New Spain into a modern nation after O'Higgins and San Martín won the war of independence, Chile would eventually become known as one of Latin America's most reliably democratic nations. O'Higgins was shrewd enough and sufficiently visionary to realize that an opportunity had finally presented itself. He alone was able to take appropriate actions that would lead to the destruction of Spanish power in his part of the world. If he was not a dynamic politician or even a well-loved one, he created the new Chile almost single-handedly, and for that Chileans owe him much.

Bibliography

Collier, Simon. "The Story or Part of It at Least." In *From Cortes to Castro: An Introduction to the History of Latin America, 1492-1973*. London: Secker and Warburg, and New York: Macmillan, 1974. An insightful and reevaluative history of the political, social, religious, and economic currents shaping Latin American history over several centuries. A valuable account of the liberation movement led by O'Higgins and San Martín.

Eyzaguirre, Jaime. *O'Higgins*. 8th ed. Santiago, Chile: Editorial Zig Zag, 1972. An excellent biography that is very likely the finest one about O'Higgins. The author has at times an overinflated opinion of O'Higgins' attributes, yet the book does full justice to his seminal role in Chile's struggle for independence.

Kinsbruner, Jay. *Bernardo O'Higgins*. New York: Twayne, 1968. An invaluable contribution to O'Higgins scholarship that goes into considerable depth about O'Higgins' revolution and how he achieved all that he did in such a short time. Includes a selective bibliography.

Mehegan, John J. *O'Higgins of Chile: A Brief Sketch of His Life and Times*. London: Bennett, 1913. One of the better general introductions to the life and times of O'Higgins.

Worcester, Donald E., and Wendell G. Schaeffer. "The Wars of Independence in the South." In *The Growth and Culture of Latin America*. 2 vols. 2d ed. New York: Oxford University Press, 1970-1971. Discusses how Chilean society evolved during and after the revolution O'Higgins helped lead. Also good for placing O'Higgins in a historical context.

John D. Raymer

FREDERICK LAW OLMSTED

Born: April 26, 1822; Hartford, Connecticut
Died: August 28, 1903; Waverly, Massachusetts
Areas of Achievement: Social criticism and landscape architecture
Contribution: Olmsted traveled extensively in the antebellum South and wrote some of America's best critical descriptions of slavery on the eve of the Civil War. He designed Central Park in New York City and other urban parks across the country. Olmsted is considered the father of the profession of landscape architecture in the United States.

Early Life

Frederick Law Olmsted was born on April 26, 1822, in Hartford, Connecticut, the son of a prosperous dry-goods merchant. His family's material wealth and deep roots in the community gave Olmsted both the economic freedom and the personal confidence to pursue a leisurely course toward his major life works. On the other hand, he was physically frail and suffered from an eye problem that hampered his efforts at formal education. Olmsted was attracted to strenuous outdoor physical activity as compensation for his physical weakness and developed a keen appreciation of nature and the outdoors. During his early years, Olmsted acquired a taste for travel, and by the time he was in his midteens he had made several lengthy trips through various regions of the northeastern United States and Canada.

Olmsted matriculated at Yale, where he studied engineering, but his eye problem prevented regular study, and after practical training in surveying he worked briefly and unhappily for a dry-goods firm in New York City. This was followed by an extremely unpleasant year's experience as a sailor on a voyage to China. Returning to Yale, he studied agricultural science and engineering and then undertook practical training as a farmer on 130 Staten Island acres purchased by his father. As he became absorbed with scientific agriculture, Olmsted began to publish articles on rural subjects and drifted toward a career as a writer.

Life's Work

In the 1850's, Olmsted embarked upon his first noteworthy career as he traveled extensively and published accounts of his journeys. His first book, *Walks and Talks of an American Farmer in England* (1852), was well received and demonstrated his aptitude for keen social observation. It is also significant that Olmsted was quite favorably taken with the landscape and rural life of the country, reflecting his continuing interest in the scenic. With sectional tension between North and South escalating, he was commissioned by *The New York Times* to travel through Dixie and report on the region's social and economic conditions.

Olmsted was chosen because of his connections among rationalist intellectual circles, his moderate antislavery views, and his established literary reputation. Although the publisher of *The New York Times* was himself a moderate Free-Soiler, Olmsted was not chosen primarily because of his views on slavery but because of his reputation as a perceptive observer who could produce an objective report on the "peculiar institution."

Accordingly, in December of 1852, Olmsted began a fourteen-month tour that took him through much of the South and as far as Texas and across the Rio Grande. He sent back lengthy letters over the signature "Yeoman," which were published on the first page of the newspaper, beginning in February, 1853. These were followed by several volumes under various titles, which were finally distilled into his classic two-volume work, *The Cotton Kingdom* (1861). Olmsted's works were immediately hailed by contemporaries as the most important sources of objective information about the life and customs of the slaveholding states and became significant references as Europeans discussed the relative merits of the Northern and Southern causes in the American Civil War. Olmsted's works remain essential sources for modern historians, who regard them as classic contemporary portrayals and analyses of the plantation slavery system of the antebellum South. If Olmsted had done nothing else, his descriptions of slavery would have established his lasting reputation, but, remarkably, even as he was producing these works, he was embarking upon a second career for which he would become even better known.

In 1857, because of his continuing interest in landscape, Olmsted accepted the position of superintendent of the preparatory work on Central Park in New York City. Soon after, with his partner Calvert Vaux, Olmsted won the competition to provide a new design for the park. He signed his plans with the title "Landscape Architect" under his name, supposedly becoming the first to use this title formally. In 1858, he became the park's chief architect and began to implement his and Vaux's plan to make the park both materially and artistically successful. His work was interrupted by service during the Civil War as general secretary of the United States Sanitary Commission, the forerunner of the American Red Cross, but by this time his philosophy of landscape design was well established.

Olmsted started from the premise that it is essential for man to maintain a balance between civilization and nature in his life and that for the city dweller, particularly, it is imperative that places should be provided as a retreat from the pressures of overcrowded, overly civilized urban existence. While he had an appreciation for nature in the raw, "wilderness," Olmsted's real preference was for the pastoral, a natural environment which was ordered, designed, structured, but which provided the illusion of nature's own handiwork. Thus, the construction of Central Park would involve the movement of tons of dirt, the creation of lakes, sunken roads, bridges, and other features to manufacture the illusion of nature for the city dweller. Ironically, considering the fact that much of his later career was spent in the service of the wealthy and influential, Olmsted's interest in urban parks was shaped in part by a strong democratic impulse to provide facilities where all classes could find refuge and recreation.

In 1863, Olmsted left Washington to become superintendent of John C. Frémont's Mariposa mining estates in California, and while there he became a leading figure in the movement to set aside the Yosemite and Mariposa "big tree" reservations which culminated in the establishment of Yosemite Park. Yosemite eventually became part of the national park system. Olmsted was a consistent promoter of preserving scenic regions and often manufactured "wilderness" areas as part of his design scheme for urban parks.

After the Civil War was concluded, Olmsted returned to New York City and carried Central Park nearly to completion. When the project was begun, the site was an area containing pig farms and squatters' shacks which had no distinguishing physical features; twenty years and the labor of more than thirty-eight hundred workers were required to construct the hills, lakes, and paths which became so important to New Yorkers. Central Park established Olmsted's reputation and became the prototype for urban parks across the United States.

Olmsted's services were now much in demand, and he moved on to design additional parks for New York City and other cities across the nation, the Capitol grounds in Washington, D. C., a preservation plan for the Niagara Falls area, and numerous college campuses. Some consider his design for the system of lagoons, wooded islands, and plantings in Chicago's Jackson Park for the Columbian Exposition in 1893 his crowning achievement. He also became a fervent advocate of suburban living, balancing the features and values of both city and country in new planned communities on the borders of older urban centers. Olmsted and Vaux designed suburbs for several cities, the most famous being Chicago's Riverside, which opened in 1869.

Emotionally exhausted by the constant political maneuvering and compromise required for work in the public sector, in his later years Olmsted retreated to the service of precisely those wealthy plutocrats whose stranglehold on scenic outdoor areas his urban parks had helped to break. His clients included Andrew Carnegie, Leland Stanford, and George Vanderbilt, for whom he helped design the famous Biltmore estate in North Carolina. Olmsted suffered a mental collapse in 1893 and disappeared from public view until his death in 1903.

Summary

Frederick Law Olmsted was one of those amazingly talented individuals who was able to achieve striking success in several areas. He was a gifted social observer and writer who left some of America's best contemporary descriptions and analyses of the life and economy of the antebellum South. Shaped by an aesthetic appreciation for wilderness and the pastoral and by a strong democratic impulse, Olmsted became a passionate advocate of the need for balance between urban and natural experiences if one were to maintain a healthy existence. He thus became the first great proponent and designer of large urban parks which would be open to all people and allow city dwellers to maintain that necessary balance in their lives. His Central Park in New York City was the progenitor of the urban parks movement in the United States, and Olmsted fathered the profession of landscape architecture.

Bibliography

Fein, Albert. *Frederick Law Olmsted and the American Environmental Tradition*. New York: Braziller, 1972. Evaluates Olmsted's significance in the broad development of environmentalism.

Genovese, Eugene D. "Olmsted's Cracker Preacher." *Southern Cultures* 4, no. 3 (Fall 1998). Focuses on Olmsted's "Journey in the Seabound Slave States," which includes the character of a "Cracker" preacher in Georgia whose evangelical sermons denounced socialism and atheism.

Huth, Hans. *Nature and the American: Three Centuries of Changing Attitudes*. Berkeley: University of California Press, 1957. Discusses Olmsted's work as a landscape architect, as well as his efforts in the campaigns to preserve Yosemite and the area around Niagara Falls.

Newton, Norman T. *Design on the Land: The Development of Landscape Architecture*. Cambridge, Mass.: Belknap Press of Harvard University Press, 1971. Includes an assessment of Olmsted's role in the development of the profession.

Olmsted, Frederick Law. *The Slave States Before the Civil War*. Edited by Harvey Wish. New York: Putnam, 1959. Wish has written an excellent introduction discussing Olmsted's life and publications.

Roper, Laura Wood. *FLO: A Biography of Frederick Law Olmsted*. Baltimore and London: Johns Hopkins University Press, 1973. The definitive biography, combining social history with a nuanced portrait of its subject. Makes generous use of Olmsted's letters. Massively documented, though lacking a bibliography.

Runte, Alfred. *National Parks: The American Experience*. 3d ed. Lincoln and London: University of Nebraska Press, 1997. While the focus is upon cultural and economic influences in the creation and shaping of the American national park system, this work also discusses the contributions of Olmsted to park design, wilderness appreciation, and the Yosemite and Niagara Falls campaigns.

Tobey, George B. *A History of Landscape Architecture: The Relationship of People to Environment*. New York: American Elsevier, 1973. Includes considerable material dealing with Olmsted.

James E. Fickle

OSCEOLA

Born: c. 1804; Tallassee on the Tallapoosa River near present-day Tuskegee, Alabama

Died: Jan. 30, 1838; Fort Moultrie, Charleston, South Carolina

Areas of Achievement: Military affairs and Native American affairs

Contribution: Allegedly a participant in the First Seminole War, Osceola became a leader of the Seminoles, who refused to be moved west of the Mississippi; he initiated the Second Seminole War.

Early Life

Osceola later insisted, and some historians maintain, that both his father (name unknown) and mother (Polly Copinger) were Creeks and that his mother later married an Englishman, William Powell. A 1991 study by Patricia R. Wickman, however, provides impressive evidence that Powell was indeed Osceola's father, that Copinger's grandfather (James McQueen) and father were white, and that the boy also had black ancestors, as did many children who were born in the Upper Creek town of Tallassee. Nevertheless, Osceola was considered to be an Upper Creek, like his mother.

Osceola's mother's uncle, Peter McQueen, was chief of the village where Osceola was born and became a leader of the Red Sticks during the Creek War of 1813-1814. As that conflict escalated, many Creeks fled from Alabama into Florida. Among the refugees were Osceola and his mother, who followed McQueen and became separated from Powell during the migration. The young Osceola was captured by Andrew Jackson's troops during his 1818 campaign in Florida, but he was released because of his age. Allegedly he fought against Jackson in the First Seminole War.

Life's Work

Osceola settled in central Florida after Jackson's campaign and, like many dislocated Creeks, became known as a Seminole. He was never a hereditary chief, nor was he apparently ever elected to such a post; however, in the controversy surrounding the signing of the treaties of Payne's Landing in 1832 and of Fort Gibson in 1833, both of which provided for the relocation of the Seminoles to the West, he emerged as a leader of those who opposed removal.

A heated clash with Wiley Thompson, the federal Indian agent for central Florida, made Osceola an outlaw. Abolitionists later wrote that Thompson aided two slave catchers to capture one of Osceola's wives, who was a mulatto, but there is no evidence for this tale. Instead, the conflict apparently originated when Thompson called a council at Fort King to confirm the earlier treaties. Most of the Seminoles who were present silently refused to sign the documents placed before them, but Osceola allegedly plunged a knife through the agreement. Again, no contemporary account supports this story.

Other confrontations in the summer of 1835 led Thompson to have Osceola imprisoned in shackles, but Osceola was released when he agreed to support removal. Rather than abide by his agreement with Thompson, Osceola organized Seminole resistance and killed Charley Emathla, a chief who had supported emigration. Osceola and his followers then attacked a baggage train during December, 1835. Later that same month, he killed Thompson, while allies ambushed a force of more than one hundred regulars and killed all but three of them. On New Year's Eve, 1835, a large party led by Osceola attacked another detachment of regulars and punished them severely in the First Battle of the Withlacoochee, where Osceola was wounded slightly in the hand or arm but escaped capture.

This began the Second Seminole War, which would last until 1842. Until his capture in 1837, Osceola was the primary target of army operations because the U.S. military recognized his importance as a leader in the resistance. Participants in the campaigns against him noted that many of his followers were black. They would have supported him instead of the hereditary chiefs, and his desire to protect them may have been part of his motivation for continuing to fight long after his health began to fail. His evasion of army columns and bold attacks made him something of a folk hero in the United States, but it also earned him the hatred of military leaders, especially after he liberated more than seven hundred Indians held in a detention camp in June, 1837.

In October, 1837, General Thomas S. Jesup, frustrated by Osceola, treacherously accepted his request for a parley under a flag of truce. The Seminole leader, who was then suffering from malaria, and more than eighty of his followers were cap-

tured at their camp near Fort Peyton in a flagrant violation of the truce. Despite the public outcry, he was taken to Fort Mellon at St. Augustine, where two of his wives and two children, as well as his half sister and others, joined him. These two wives may have been the two sisters he had married in accordance with Creek custom, though there appear to have been others.

After several other Seminoles escaped, Osceola and his group were transferred on New Year's Eve, 1837, to Fort Moultrie at Charleston, South Carolina. There his health declined rapidly, and he died on January 30, 1838. Allegations vary as to the cause of his death, but most agree that his depression contributed to his rapid demise. Wickman says that quinsy, or tonsillitis complicated by an abscess, was the immediate cause of Osceola's death, and both malaria and recurring fevers were contributing factors in his declining health.

Summary

Osceola was buried outside Fort Moultrie on Sullivan Island with military honors, but before interment his head was removed by Frederick Weedon, the physician who had attended him during his fatal illness. It was displayed in a medical museum maintained by Valentine Mott of the Medical College of New York until the building was allegedly destroyed by fire in 1866.

The betrayal of Osceola destroyed any realistic hope of unity among the Seminoles. The war continued sporadically until 1842, when most of the surviving Seminoles moved West, as his family had after his death. Only a few remained in the swamps. The circumstances of Osceola's fight, capture, and death, which were often misrepresented, made him a folk hero to many. No fewer than twenty towns in the United States now bear his name, as do three counties, two townships, one borough, two lakes, two mountains, a state park, and a national forest.

Bibliography

Boyd, Mark F. "Asi-Yaholo, or Osceola." *Florida Historical Quarterly* 23 (January-April, 1955): 249-305. This is an overview of Osceola and the events of his life.

Covington, James W. *The Seminoles of Florida.* Gainesville: University Press of Florida, 1993. Covington covers the history of the Seminole Indians, their relations with the U.S. government, and the social conditions under which they lived during various periods.

Hartley, William, and Ellen Hartley. *Osceola: The Unconquered Indian.* New York: Hawthorn, 1973. This illustrated biography of Osceola includes bibliographic references.

Mahon, John K. *History of the Second Seminole War, 1835-1842.* Gainesville: University Press of Florida, 1967. Mahon's detailed study of the Second Seminole War includes illustrations, maps, and a bibliography.

Wickman, Patricia R. *Osceola's Legacy.* Tuscaloosa: University of Alabama Press, 1991. Wickman interweaves a biography of Osceola with the history of the Seminoles and considers the implications of the events of his lifetime for later interactions between Native Americans and the United States government. The book contains a bibliography and an index.

Richard B. McCaslin

SIR WILLIAM OSLER

Born: July 12, 1849; Bond Head, Ontario, Canada
Died: December 29, 1919; Oxford, England
Area of Achievement: Medicine
Contribution: Osler published the original *Principles and Practice of Medicine*, a classic text for many years, and he transformed medical education by extending it beyond the classroom to the patient's bedside.

Early Life

Any reading of the life of Sir William Osler quickly reveals an individual of widely varied interests and great vitality. He cared deeply for people and was loved in return by young and old alike. He had a special fondness for the young. Born in Bond Head, Ontario, near Lake Simcoe, on July 12, 1849, he was the youngest of nine children of an Anglican clergyman. Life on the frontier of Canada in the mid-nineteenth century was far from easy, and the earnings of a clergyman not great, yet what was lacking in material comfort was made up in the closeness and love of the family. A nurturing of intellect and an abundance of books instilled in the children the desire for education, and somehow from the meager funds available, Featherstone and Ellen Osler saw several sons through university and into professions.

Endowed with a fine mind as well as a small but wiry and healthy body, Osler excelled at both scholarship and sports. A sprightly sense of humor embroiled him in high jinks, a characteristic which would mark him throughout life. While at Weston School, one such prank ended with Osler, along with his fellows, in the Toronto jail. The Matron of Weston failed to appreciate their humor, of which she was the butt, and charged them with assault and battery.

Nevertheless, Osler pursued his studies with diligence. In this, he had the rare good fortune to cross the paths of not one, but two gentlemen who became his mentors and friends. They were friends to one another as well, and the available correspondence is indicative of the warm affection which the three shared. The first of these was the Reverend W. A. Johnson, who had opened Weston, the boarding school to which Osler was sent in preparation for university study. There, he came under Johnson's influence, and this good man became affectionately known as "Father" Johnson, not so much for his priestly calling as for his genuine caring for the students, especially Osler.

Father Johnson had a passion for botany, and young Osler became his companion and collaborator in this pursuit, an activity which helped to prepare him for the course he was to follow. The sharing of specimens and information went on for years, along with microscopic examination of specimens gathered on numerous forays into the woods and waters of the area.

The second individual to have significant impact upon the course of Osler's life was the physician Dr. William Bovell, in whose home Osler lived when he attended Toronto University. As a young man, Osler began preparation for the ministry, following his father's steps. Shortly, however, exposed to Bovell's remarkable mind as well as his vast library, Osler became interested in medicine. (Ironically, Bovell began theological studies and eventually took a charge in the West Indies, but the friendship continued.)

Transferring to McGill College, Osler completed his clinical study there in 1872. The faculty, upon his graduation, conferred a special award, remarking on the "originality and research" of his thesis which was illustrated with "33 microscopic and other preparations of morbid structure."

Life's Work

It was the custom of the time for young medical graduates to make a tour of medical facilities and schools in Europe. As his parents were not in a position to support such a venture financially, an older brother, himself bound for Scotland and pleased to have the company of his lively young brother, paid the cost of transportation. Osler continued his study in Vienna, in Berlin, and in London, allowing himself to expand his knowledge and experience.

Osler continued his microscopic studies, and a notation in his laboratory notebook records that on the fourteenth of June, 1873, he began studies of his own and others' blood as well as that of various animals, and there appear drawings of what he observed. Here was the beginning of his study of the circulatory system and the identification of platelets as a component of the blood. So passed two very frugal but rewarding years. Then, in 1874, a request came for Osler to return to McGill as a lecturer in the medical school. Acceptance of this offer inaugurated Osler's long and distinguished career as professor, clinician, scholar, and humanitarian.

Osler is said to have humanized the whole of medical practice. He was unusual not only for the respect he showed his students but also for the new collegial relationship that he established among physicians. More important still, the patient-physician relationship was revolutionized. Medical education was extended beyond the confines of the classroom and into the hospital, where patients rather than disease became the focus. If the situation appears to have changed in the late twentieth century, it may be that Osler's wisdom has been forgotten. "Don't ask the doctor; ask the patient" is a Yiddish proverb, but it could stand well as the motto of Osler's life and practice.

Another particular concern of Osler was his insistence that learning must be an ongoing process. Addressing young graduates in 1875, he exhorted them to "be students always" and to keep up their reading (as he himself never failed to do). In 1913, a few short years before his death, he greeted students at Yale as "fellow students." On another occasion, he urged the student body at McGill to seek as much truth as possible, stating:

> No human being is constituted to know . . . the whole truth. . . . The truth is the best you can get with your best endeavor [and] an earnest desire for an ever larger portion.

Looking at another facet of this exceptional human being, it appears that Osler never met a stranger. Harvey Cushing, in his superlative biography of the man, records one especially poignant yet characteristic event which illustrates this. In the autumn of 1875, Osler chanced to meet an English businessman in Montreal. The young man contracted smallpox and died. While attending the patient, Osler learned the address of his parents, and so he wrote to them, describing the illness and death of their son and conveying his sympathy. Many years later, he provided to the man's sister a photograph of the grave.

Osler's flair for jest, which belies his sober, even severe, countenance in surviving photographs, caused him to assume the pseudonym of Egerton Y. Davis, M.D. for purposes of satire and humor, addressing numerous issues in essays and letters. (Years later, he occasionally and affectionately referred to his son as "Egerton, Jr.") The byline surfaced from time to time over a number of years, gaining considerable attention.

In 1884, while in Leipzig, Osler was offered the Chair of Clinical Medicine at the University of Pennsylvania, which he is said to have accepted based on the flip of a coin. McGill's loss became Pennsylvania's gain. While in Philadelphia, Osler made significant contributions: He revived a faltering professional organization and founded and supported a student club, both of which he valued as a means of professional sharing and mutual support.

The Johns Hopkins University was developing a medical school, and in 1891, officials at the university invited Osler to Baltimore. While awaiting the opening of the school, he prepared his *Principles and Practice of Medicine* (1892), which became a standard text for many years. By 1930, in its eleventh edition, the book had been translated into at least four other languages. Later revisions, edited by others, never quite captured the style and flow of the original. Osler became, too, a part of the brilliant medical staff at Johns Hopkins, which was known as the "Big Four."

Osler returned to Philadelphia briefly in 1892 to marry Grace Revere Gross, the widow of a colleague and great-granddaughter of Paul Revere. Years later, in Oxford, their home was familiarly referred to as the "Open Arms." One of their children died in infancy and their son, Revere, grew to adulthood only to die in the trenches of France in 1917. It was a grief that Osler took to his own grave.

A request to accept the chair as Regius Professor of Medicine at Oxford took the Oslers to England in 1904. There William Osler was to spend his remaining years, serving with great distinction. On the occasion of the coronation of King George V in 1911, a baronetcy was bestowed, and Osler became Sir William—"much to the embarrassment of my democratic simplicity," he reported to a friend in a letter.

For some years Osler had been subject to episodes of bronchitis, and, in October of 1919, a severe cold developed into bronchitis and bronchopneumonia. Osler was unable to fend off this final illness, and he died on December 29, 1919.

Summary

When Sir William Osler died, he was widely known and admired in his profession and beyond. He brought freshness and humanity to the practice of medicine and humor to those around him. His example remains today and is acclaimed in his profession as unique. This fact was made apparent when, in 1951, a committee of his fellows republished those speeches and essays deemed to be his best in order to give medical students "a taste of Osler." These works show that his wide interests were not separate from medicine.

Osler believed profoundly, and proclaimed repeatedly to his students, that history, the classics, and an understanding of human behavior were essential to the holistic practice of medicine. An individual in need of medical care, he was convinced, seeks the attention and comfort of a fellow human being before drugs and treatment. Such wisdom is timeless, as fresh today as in Osler's own time.

Bibliography

Archives of Internal Medicine 84, no. 1 (1949). The entire issue is devoted to Osler on the occasion of the centenary of his birth.

Bryan, Charles S. *Osler: Inspirations from a Great Physician.* New York: Oxford University Press, 1997. The author resurrects the thoughts and work of Osler in contemporary terms.

Cushing, Harvey. *The Life of Sir William Osler.* 2 vols. Oxford: Clarendon Press, 1925; New York: Oxford University Press, 1940. This is the exhaustive biography from which the bulk of the information for this essay was drawn. It was written by one who knew medicine and surgery at first hand and who himself taught surgery at The Johns Hopkins University, where Osler had served on the first faculty. This work won the Pulitzer Prize.

Foucault, Michel. *The Birth of the Clinic.* Translated by A. M. Sheridan Smith. New York: Vintage Books, and London: Tavistock, 1973. Foucault describes this as "an archeology of medical perception." It examines the development of medical knowledge and practice, confirming that the modern entity of the teaching hospital was brought into being only in the nineteenth century. It was this forum which Osler introduced to the United States and in which he practiced as professor of medicine at Oxford.

Golden, Richard L. "Sir William Osler: Humanistic Thanatologist." *Omega - The Journal of Death and Dying (Farmingdale)* 36, no. 3 (May-June, 1998). Golden focuses on Osler's efforts to reduce the suffering of terminally-ill patients and his work in the areas of bereavement, euthanasia, and suicide. Includes Osler's reaction to the death of his son in World War I and his own illness and death.

Illich, Ivan. *Medical Nemesis: The Expropriation of Health.* London: Calder and Boyars, and New York: Pantheon, 1975. Illich explores twentieth century changes in health care: "the medicalization of life" and the intrusion of politics into health care in ways which Osler would have had difficulty reconciling with his philosophy of patient care.

Journal of the American Medical Association 210, no. 12 (1969). The entire issue is devoted to Osler. Published fifty years after his death.

Osler, William. *The Principles and Practice of Medicine.* New York: Appleton, and London: Pentland, 1892. This is a later edition of the textbook originally compiled by William Osler. It continues to be revised and updated by the faculty of The Johns Hopkins University for use as a text in the medical school.

———. *Science and Immortality.* London: Constable, and Boston: Houghton Mifflin, 1904. This is the publication of the lectures delivered by Osler at Harvard in 1904.

―――. *Selected Writings of Sir William Osler.* London: Oxford University Press, 1951; New York: Dover, 1958. This is a collection of essays and addresses by the author which span the adult years of his life. They demonstrate the breadth of his knowledge and interests as well as his fluency with the English language.

Mary Wilson Sage

NIKOLAUS AUGUST OTTO

Born: June 10, 1832; Holzhausen, Nassau
Died: January 26, 1891; Cologne, Germany
Areas of Achievement: Invention and technology
Contribution: Otto invented the first internal-combustion, four-stroke engine. His engine is the forerunner of modern gasoline automobile engines.

Early Life

Nikolaus August Otto was born in the small village of Holzhausen auf der Heide, on the Rhine. His father, postmaster and innkeeper in the village, died shortly after Nikolaus' birth. Nikolaus was a bright child who did well in school, and his mother wanted, at first, to enter her son in higher education. The unrest of 1848 changed her mind, however, and she decided that the business world would provide a better future for him. Accordingly, he gave up high school (where he had been a star student) and went to work.

Otto's first job was as a clerk in a small-town grocery store. From there he moved to a job as a clerk in Frankfurt, and eventually became a traveling salesman for a wholesale grocer, working out of Cologne. In 1860, still a traveling salesman, Otto read a newspaper account of a gas engine built by a Frenchman, Étienne Lenoir. The Lenoir engine was well known at this time, and Otto studied it carefully. As the piston of the Lenoir engine moved down the cylinder, it drew in a mixture of gas and air. An electric spark ignited the air/gas mixture halfway through the stroke, creating the power necessary to push the piston to the bottom of the cylinder. Each piston was doubled-sided, so the piston returned to its original position when the same steps were repeated on the opposite side. It is important to note that this engine did not compress the air/gas mixture and that it relied on illuminating gas (used in homes and street lamps) for its fuel. Lenoir had trouble getting it to run smoothly under a load.

Life's Work

With strong links to rural regions both in his boyhood and in his job, Otto was bothered by the fact that the Lenoir engine relied on a fuel which was available only through a system of pipelines found in the cities. He saw that the internal-combustion engine had the potential to become an important source of power in a wide variety of applications, and he determined to make an engine that could be used in city and village alike. He devised a carburetor for the Lenoir engine which enabled the engine to receive fuel from a tank rather than a pipeline. Although his patent application for the carburetor was rejected, he continued to work on the internal-combustion engine.

In 1861, Otto commissioned Michael Zons, an instrument maker and machine-shop owner in Cologne, to build a Lenoir engine. Otto studied this engine carefully in an attempt to make it run smoothly under a load. The main problem with the engine was the shock of detonation on the piston. While he was experimenting with this engine, Otto stumbled across a phenomenon which would later pay him great dividends. He drew in the air/gas charge and then, instead of allowing the piston to continue down the cylinder, he moved it back up toward the cylinder head, compressing the charge. Otto was surprised to find that the detonation was so violent as to turn the engine through several revolutions. This was the principle upon which he would later base the four-stroke cycle. After continued experimentation with the Lenoir engine, Otto decided that the difficulties were too great and turned to a new type of engine: the atmospheric engine.

The atmospheric engine resembled an upward-pointing cannon with gears and levers attached. As the motion of the flywheel pulled the piston up, air and gas were drawn in beneath the piston. At the same time, the piston pushed the air above it out of the cylinder and into a tank, where it was stored at above-atmospheric pressure. The combustion of the air/gas mixture pushed the piston up at high velocity to the top of the cylinder, creating a vacuum in the cylinder below the piston. The piston's own weight and the pressure difference between the air in the holding tank and the vacuum in the cylinder then returned the piston to the bottom of the cylinder.

Zons built a one-half horsepower model of the atmospheric engine for Otto in 1863. In order to develop the engine, Otto obtained financial backing from Eugen Langen, son of a wealthy industrialist, and they entered into a formal business agreement in March of 1864. With Langen's help, Otto refined the atmospheric engine. After three years of work, the Otto and Langen engine was shown at the 1867 Paris Exposition, winning the grand prize. Having built a successful engine, Otto and Langen now needed to manufacture and sell their product.

They found more capital, created the Gasmotorenfabrik Deutz corporation in 1872, and shortly thereafter were selling their engines around the world.

The Otto and Langen engine proved to be popular; five thousand were eventually built. The engine's reliance on atmospheric pressure (the final version did not have the holding tank for air) posed a serious limitation, however, by limiting its output to a maximum of three horsepower. Furthermore, it was extremely noisy and vibrated strongly when in operation. In response to these shortcomings, Otto began to think about a new type of engine (possibly reviewing his earliest experiments with the Lenoir engine) in which the air/gas mixture was compressed in the cylinder before ignition. The engine then used one stroke each for the intake, compression, ignition (and expansion), and exhaust functions. In such an engine there was only one power stroke for every four piston strokes, hence the name "four-stroke cycle." This was a bold step, considering that the double-acting steam engine— the dominant power technology of the time—used each stroke as a power stroke.

Otto was concerned that detonation of the compressed air/gas mixture would produce a violent explosion capable of damaging the engine. To lessen the shock of detonation, he devised a concept known as the "stratified charge," in which the richest mixture would be farthest from the piston, with successive layers of air and exhaust gases filling the remainder of the cylinder. Otto believed that this would create a gradual burning instead of a violent explosion. The stratified charge was so important to Otto that it constituted the main claim in his patent, rather than the four-stroke cycle or the compressed charge.

Otto built the first of these engines in 1876 at the Gasmotorenfabrik Deutz works. Even the rough prototype demonstrated the many advantages of the four-stroke engine to Otto and his partners. Compared to the atmospheric engine (and others of the time) the four-stroke engine produced, for the same displacement and engine weight, far more horsepower. In addition to erasing the three-horsepower ceiling of the atmospheric engine, the new engine operated with much less noise and vibration, earning the nickname "Silent Otto." Gasmotorenfabrik Deutz refined the prototype and eventually marketed the engine with great success. By the turn of the century, Otto's firm had built twenty-four thousand engines.

In 1882, the first of several claims against Otto's patent rights arose. He was to spend the rest of his life defending himself against these claims. The most damaging came from a competitor who wanted to void Otto's patent on the four-stroke cycle on the basis of an obscure pamphlet written in 1862 by the French engineer Alphonse-Eugène Beau de Rochas. Rochas had clearly stated the principles of the four-stroke cycle in his pamphlet, but apparently he never realized its significance and never built an engine operating on those principles. Nevertheless, in 1886 Otto lost his German patents on the four-stroke cycle. He considered the patent suits an attack upon his honor, and the defeat in 1886 left him an embittered man. The legal battle continued until 1890, when the last appeal ended. On January 26, 1891, Nikolaus Otto died of heart failure in Cologne.

Summary

Automobiles using Nikolaus August Otto's engine appeared on the roads of Europe only ten years after he built the prototype, and less than two decades later the Wright brothers' aircraft was propelled by a four-stroke engine. The predominant type of automobile engine today is a direct descendant of Otto's 1876 engine. One asset of Otto's engine is its flexibility, thanks to its small size, low weight, and the multitude of possible configurations (vertical, horizontal, single or multiple cylinders, ability to run on many kinds of fuels, and the like). Although Otto placed more faith in the stratified-charge concept than was probably warranted, he did, nevertheless, build the first successful engine to operate on the four-stroke cycle. For his persistence in solving the problems he encountered and for seeing them through to their respective solutions, he deserves the credit as that engine's inventor.

Bibliography

Bryant, Lynwood. "The Origin of the Automobile Engine." *Scientific American* 216 (March, 1967): 102-112. This article concentrates on the intellectual process by which Otto arrived at the 1876 engine. Bryant notes that Otto believed in the stratified charge to the end, although most other experts believed that the charge should be as homogeneous as possible. The many illustrations and photographs are a great help in understanding the technical details of Otto's engines. No documentation.

————. "The Origin of the Four-Stroke Cycle." *Technology and Culture* 8 (April, 1967): 178-198. Examines Otto's claim to inventing the four-stroke cycle. In a carefully documented and reasoned argument, Bryant shows that while others had the idea of a four-stroke cycle, credit for invention should go to Otto. The section on Rochas, the cause of much grief to Otto, is of special interest.

————. "The Silent Otto." *Technology and Culture* 7 (Spring, 1966): 184-200. Asks why Otto was successful after so many others had been trying to assemble an internal-combustion engine for seventy-five years. Traces his thought through fifteen years of development; points out that only in 1876, having gained much practical experience, was Otto ready to accept the four-stroke cycle he had discovered accidentally in 1862. In addition to the usual sources, Bryant has assembled evidence directly from the patent records.

Cummins, C. Lyle, Jr. *Internal Fire*. Lake Oswego, Oreg.: Carnot Press, 1976. Written by the son of the founder of the Cummins Engine Company, this book is an absorbing account of the internal-combustion engine from the seventeenth century to the present. While explaining each engine in this long tradition with plentiful technical detail (aided by line sketches and photographs), Cummins manages to place these developments in a broader context as well. Chapters 8 and 9 deal specifically with Otto. Cummins is not afraid to differ with other historians and generally provides good support for his argument. Despite sketchy footnotes, it is clear that he has consulted a wide range of sources.

Goldbeck, Gustav. "Nikolaus August Otto, Creator of the Internal-Combustion Engine." In *From Engines to Autos: Five Pioneers in Engine Development and Their Contributions to the Automotive Industry*, by Eugen Diesel, Gustav Goldbeck, and Friedrich Schilderberger. Chicago: Regnery, 1960. Goldbeck effectively puts together the highlights of Otto's life and his accomplishments in the development of his engine. Lacks documentation but appears reasonably accurate. Is less sterile than many sources in that Goldbeck tries to reveal a more human side to the successes and failures Otto experienced.

Brian J. Nichelson

SIR JAMES OUTRAM

Born: January 29, 1803; Butterley Hall, Derbyshire, England

Died: March 11, 1863; Pau, France

Areas of Achievement: The military and colonial administration

Contribution: Using a mixture of military force and sound administrative techniques, Outram helped to complete the construction of the British imperial system in India.

Early Life

James Outram was born January 29, 1803, at his home in Derbyshire, England. His father, Benjamin Outram, was a civil engineer who introduced iron rails to mining traffic; his mother, Margaret Anderson, was a Scottish agricultural writer's daughter. James's father died in June, 1805, leaving heavy debts, for he had been building an iron foundry. Margaret Outram returned with her children to her native Aberdeen, Scotland, where James was educated at the Marischal College. Outram was an indifferent-looking man with swarthy complexion and curly hair; Lady Canning, wife of one of India's governor-generals, said that he "was a very common looking little dark Jewish man, with a desponding slow hesitating manner." Although of puny build, Outram was athletic and adventurous; he enlisted as a cadet in the Indian army at the age of sixteen and arrived in Bombay in August, 1819, where he was posted for several years to various regiments, learning the military trade. Outram's generous nature was demonstrated early, when he stipulated that part of his pay be reserved for his mother. Outram also became a first-class outdoorsman: He was credited with more than half of the "first spears" thrown at tigers on hunting trips that he accompanied from 1822 to 1824, and he kept a lifelong interest in the hunt.

Life's Work

Outram's career as soldier and administrator assumed its shape in the middle and late 1820's. In April, 1825, he was made agent for the East India Company for much of Khandesh, a province north of Bombay which had recently devolved to the British. In that capacity, he pacified the Bhils—a race of nomads resisting British authority—and, gaining their admiration through his hunting prowess, succeeded in turning most of them into loyal subjects. This process, completed by 1835, rested on Outram's technique of converting the village *patels* (leaders) into officers of the government. After a Bombay interlude during which Outram married his cousin, Margaret Anderson, he carried out the same process of annexation by force and then pacification of Gujarat, a native state to the west of Khandesh (1835-1838).

In 1838, Outram became involved in the expanding British effort to bring order to the Sind, a region lying west of the Indus River. He was appointed aide-de-camp to Sir John Keane, the general in charge of trans-Indus operations. In August, 1839, Outram commanded an expedition across Afghanistan in pursuit of Dost Mohammed, whom the British had rejected as ruler of that country. Posing as an Afghan, Outram made an eight-day ride in November, 1839, through enemy territory to advise the Bombay government of Kalat's siege, an exploit which made him famous all over India. Despite Outram's audaciously successful raids against various Afghan and Baluchi tribesmen, the British were not victorious in the First Afghan War and eventually withdrew from the country, considerably humiliated.

Perhaps to compensate for recent disasters, the Indian government then determined to annex the Sind. Outram—who had been appointed political agent of Lower Sind in 1839 and of Upper Sind in 1841—was a noninterventionist, preferring to work with the local emirs to maintain the security of India's frontiers, but he could not stem the desire of the governor-general, Lord Ellenborough, for a cheap victory. General Sir Charles Napier was sent in June, 1842, to pacify the Sind, virtually superseding Outram in authority. Seeing that Outram could not protect them against Napier, the Sind leaders rebelled; Outram defended the British residency at Hyderabad, the Sind's capital, against eight thousand Baluchi tribesmen (February, 1843). Napier used this as an excuse to annex the Sind, cynically referring to his action as "a very advantageous, useful, humane piece of rascality." Although he liked Napier, Outram bitterly condemned the Sind annexation during a visit to England in May, 1843, as a breach of faith with the emirs and as "tyrannical—positive robbery." Such outspokenness angered many in the Indian government, even though Outram was made a brevet lieutenant colonel in July, 1843, in recognition of his past service in Afghanistan and the Sind.

Upon his return to India at the close of 1843, Outram was charged with conducting military operations against the Maratha rebels, south of Bombay toward Portuguese Goa. These having been successfully concluded, he was made resident of Satara in May, 1845, and then of Baroda in May, 1847—the highest civilian position possible within the Bombay administration. Baroda's government was corrupt, and with characteristic forthrightness, Outram criticized both Baroda's native ruler and local company officials in a report of October, 1851. The incensed Bombay administration removed Outram from his position in March, 1852; the company director in London upheld the removal while praising Outram's energy and honesty.

After another sojourn in England, Outram returned to India, where Lord Dalhousie (governor-general, 1848-1856) reappointed him resident at Baroda. Shortly afterward, Outram was transferred in April, 1854, to Aden, at the mouth of the Red Sea, as political agent and commandant of the garrison. The intense heat there weakened his health, and Outram was sent back to India and named resident at Oudh in December, 1854.

Oudh—last of the Muslim-ruled native kingdoms besides Hyderabad—lay strategically situated on the Ganges, between Delhi and Calcutta. Thus, it was a prime target of the East India Company's "doctrine of lapse," which called for annexation if native rule were considered incompetent. Oudh's rulers were undeniably bad; they had been previously warned that their maladministration would end in a British takeover. In March, 1855, Outram reported from Lucknow, the capital of Oudh, that conditions there were deplorable. The British could either run Oudh's affairs while leaving the king his title, or annex the state. Outram recommended the latter course, Dalhousie the former; the London authorities decided in Outram's favor. As the Oudhian ruler would not sign a treaty ending his sovereignty, Dalhousie proclaimed annexation on February 13, 1856, simultaneously naming Outram the chief commissioner.

Oudh's absorption helped bring on the Indian Mutiny of 1857, because many of the sepoys (soldiers employed by the East India Company) lived there. Already disaffected by the prohibition of wife-burning, by the use of bullets greased with taboo animals' fat, and by rumors of British intent to Christianize India, the sepoys decided to rebel, after the much-respected Outram left India in mid-1856 as a result of ill health. Lord Charles Canning, Dalhousie's successor as governor-general, wanted Outram back in Oudh, but Prime Minister Henry Palmerston sent the popular general to Persia instead, in early 1857, to lead a brief and successful war with that power. By the time Outram returned to Bombay, the Sepoy Mutiny had begun.

The stage was set for the central event of Outram's career—the relief of Lucknow, where the British garrison, some loyal sepoys, and several hundred dependents lay besieged in the British residency. Lord Canning intended him to raise the siege, but Outram waived his powers to Major General Sir Henry Havelock, an older officer whom he admired; unwisely, Outram continued to give "advice" freely, thus undercutting Havelock's authority. Nevertheless, with about 3,100 troops, both Havelock and Outram fought their way into Lucknow from Cawnpore fifty miles away on the Ganges, in only a week—September 19-25, 1857. Unfortunately, their force was too small to evacuate the residency, and they were besieged there in turn. Sir Colin Campbell, the British commander in India, finally relieved Outram on March 19, 1858, with an additional force of five thousand men. The garrison and dependents were then evacuated, although Havelock soon died of dysentery. Outram was left temporarily in charge of the Alambagh—a palace near Lucknow—to guard the city, while Campbell dealt with the rebellion in nearby Cawnpore.

As India passed under direct British rule following the mutiny's collapse, Outram became the toast of the country. He was appointed military member of the Governor-General's Council, received Parliament's thanks and a baronetcy, was made a lieutenant general in the Indian army, and received a large annual pension. Suffering from chronic asthma and bronchitis, Outram left India forever in July, 1860, returning to London to write his memoirs. He died while wintering at Pau, in southern France, on March 11, 1863, and was honored with burial in Westminster Abbey.

Summary

Sir James Outram was one of the most honorable and sensitive British officials in India during the years of evolution from rule by the East India Company to direct imperial domination. As a military man, he was always well liked by his officers and soldiers. Despite some of his questionable military decisions—notably his waiving of command to Havelock at Lucknow—no one ever questioned his integrity and bravery; Napier's characterization of Outram in November, 1842, as "the Bayard of India, without fear and reproach," was richly deserved. As a civil administrator, Outram was well respected, even loved, by the Indians and was known to be sympathetic toward them (for example, as the mutiny collapsed, he argued successfully with Canning to show clemency to sepoys who surrendered quickly). Rare among British officials of his time, Outram sensed the growth of Indian nationalism, saying of the Sepoy Mutiny, "It is absurd to call this a military rebellion." Although Outram's fame faded after his death, he should be remembered as a statesman who tried to soften the frequently oppressive process of British imperialism in India.

Bibliography

Edwardes, Michael. *Battles of the Indian Mutiny.* London: Batsford, and New York: Macmillan, 1963. A detailed military history of the Sepoy Mutiny. Outram's activities during the Lucknow campaign are exhaustively outlined, and criticized, in chapters 8-15. One of Batsford's British Battle series.

Gardner, Brian. *The East India Company.* London: Hart-Davis, 1971; New York: McCall, 1972. Outram's career is covered in the context of the institution that, at the end of its rule in 1858, controlled one-fifth of the world's population. The author stresses the strangeness of an entity which was neither company nor government.

Goldsmid, F.J. *James Outram: A Biography.* 2 vols. London: Smith, Elder, 1880. One of two full-length biographies of Outram. Heavily dependent on Outram's letters and other documents. There is no attempt to be evenhanded; the work is well written but overly adulatory.

Hibbert, Christopher. *The Great Mutiny: India 1857.* London: Allen Lane, and New York: Viking Press, 1978. A narrative history of the Sepoy Mutiny by a prolific historian and biographer. Hibbert draws on the memoirs of Outram and of practically every other major figure in the uprising. Good personal characterization of Outram.

Holmes, Thomas Rice Edward. *A History of the Indian Mutiny, and of the Disturbances Which Accompanied It Among the Civil Population.* 5th ed. London and New York: Macmillan, 1913. A good, but dated, treatment of the mutiny. Outram is prominently mentioned, and his personality and actions praised as knightly and chivalric. See especially chapter 9.

Trotter, Lionel J. *The Bayard of India: A Life of General Sir James Outram.* London: Dent, and New York: Dutton, 1909. A shorter biography than Goldsmid's, highly partial to Outram.

Woodruff, Philip. *The Men Who Ruled India: The Founders.* London: Cape, 1953; New York: St. Martin's Press, 1954. A study of the impact of the British on India. While admitting the faults of their rule, the author hoped that they would be remembered for their positive contributions. Outram is mentioned in passing, although positively.

Thomas John Thomson

ROBERT OWEN

Born: May 14, 1771; Newtown, Montgomeryshire, Wales

Died: November 17, 1858; Newtown, Montgomeryshire, Wales

Areas of Achievement: Industry and social reform

Contribution: Best known for his Utopian community of New Harmony in Indiana, Owen was both one of the leaders of the early Industrial Revolution and one of its greatest critics. He developed the cotton-spinning factory while demonstrating the efficiency and productivity which resulted from the benevolent treatment of workers. He pioneered in educational reform and became the chief spokesman for the cooperative movement.

Early Life

Born into a family of modest means in Newtown in Montgomeryshire, Wales, on May 14, 1771, Robert Owen attended a small local school only until the age of nine. His education was considerably advanced through his own determined reading. By his account, he read, during his youth, a book each day. At the age of ten, he left home to seek his fortune, working as a shop-boy in textile stores, eventually making his way to Manchester in 1786 just as the Industrial Revolution, centered on the textile industry in cities such as Manchester, was beginning.

Owen was fifteen when he arrived in Manchester, and his success came very early. He worked for three years as a shop assistant, but by early 1791 he had become a partner in a small cotton mill, and by the age of twenty he was the manager of a large, industrialized cotton-spinning factory. In this mill, Owen introduced the first use of American sea-island cotton, thus beginning the demand for that crop produced in the southern portion of the United States. The thread produced in Owen's spinning factory was generally recognized to be of superior quality, and he was regarded, at this early age, as the master of this new industry. By 1795, he was manager and co-owner of the large Chorlton Twist Company and was on his way to amassing an enormous fortune.

Through business connections, Owen met Miss Anne Caroline Dale, the daughter of David Dale, a wealthy textile industrialist in New Lanark, Scotland. Owen not only fell in love with Miss Dale, but also determined to buy her father's factories.

With the financial backing of his partners, the deal was made, and the New Lanark Twist Company formed, with Owen as sole manager and part owner. On September 30, 1799, he and Caroline were married, making their home in New Lanark. Given his later radical views on marriage, it would be impossible to term theirs a happy union.

As the new century opened, Owen approached his twenty-ninth birthday. He was a good-looking young man, whose sensitive mouth and eyes were checked by a furrowed brow and prominent nose. In his youth, he affected the hairstyle and dress of the romantic, and he looked almost poetic. As he grew older, however, and his utopian ideas caused heated attacks against him, Owen appeared more somber, dressing in black broadcloth which accented his rugged looks. Financial success came very early in Owen's life, and with the new century he looked forward to addressing a wide array of social problems, and with his enormous creditability as an industrialist he was confident he could change the world for the better.

Life's Work

As a cotton-mill owner and manager, Owen first achieved national, and even international, recognition as a result of the reforms he instituted for his workers. In those early days of the Industrial Revolution, working conditions were worse than poor; they were deplorable. Along with the long hours of dehumanizing drudgery in the dreary factories, the poor sanitation, the terrible overcrowding, and the absence of schools were the associated problems of drunkenness, theft, and other vices. Most notorious of all was child labor. Owen found that among his two thousand employees were some five hundred pauper children as young as the age of six.

Owen determined to improve these conditions and the lives of his workers. As early as 1806, when his factory and others closed as a result of the American embargo, Owen convinced his partners to take the extraordinary step of continuing to pay wages while his mills sat idle. With such an attitude, he won the loyalty and admiration of his employees, who surpassed all others in their productivity. He greatly improved housing, sanitation, and the physical plant in general. He provided free medical care, opened a company store where prices were very low, controlled the sale of whiskey, and docked the pay of public drunkards. This benevolence was not without the price of authoritarianism, and Owen ran New Lanark with a firm hand, even levying fines for sexual promiscuity. Nevertheless, these measures were remarkably successful in improving not only the lives of his employees but also the output of his mills. In the latter regard, Owen proved a superb manager in reorganizing the factory system and in evaluating individual production.

These reforms were expensive, and Owen was always at odds with his partners over the cost of his social experiments. In 1813, he formed a new company, this time with partners of a more kindred spirit, one of whom was Jeremy Bentham, the leader of the Utilitarians. This new arrangement allowed Owen to proceed with the enterprise which was closest to his heart: education. He believed, as he often said, that man's character was not made by him but for him; that is, environment played a greater role than heredity. Education was the answer to creating a proper environment and building good character. In 1814 at New Lanark, he began building an "institution for the formation of character," which included facilities for education, public meetings, and a nursery school, an idea new in Great Britain at the time.

Owen expressed virtually all of his philosophy in a pamphlet which appeared in 1813: *A New View of Society: Or, Essays on the Principle of the Formation of the Human Character*. This essay, coupled with the great success of his factory system, brought him international attention, and he was in contact with many of the great leaders of his world. Visitors flocked to see New Lanark, including the Grand Duke Nicholas, the future Czar of Russia. Owen was much admired, and his philanthropy was widely praised. He worked hard for legislation which would improve working conditions, and he was largely responsible for the Factory Act of 1819, although he was very disappointed with its limitations.

Unfortunately, Owen's early success went to his head, and he came to believe that he could solve all of society's problems. Within a few years, he declined from being a highly regarded industrialist to being dismissed as an eccentric crank. The first hint of his radical ideas came on January 1, 1816, when he gave the main address at the opening of his institute. On that occasion, he dismissed all existing institutions as false and based on erroneous principles. He claimed to have discovered new foundations which would allow the creation of a

perfect society, and he asserted that his ideas were supported by world leaders, philosophers, and educators. The following year, he proposed that the problem of the poor could be solved by having them live in small communal villages based on agriculture. Owen summarized this plan and its call for so-called Villages of Cooperation in the *Report to the County of Lanark, of a Plan for Relieving Public Distress and Removing Discontent, by Giving Permanent, Productive Employment to the Poor and Working Classes, Under Arrangements Which Will Essentially Improve Their Character, and Ameliorate Their Condition, Diminish the Expenses of Production and Consumption, and Create Markets Co-extensive with Production* (1820).

What really damaged Owen's reputation, however, was his deliberate and public assault on organized religion, a surprise attack which he delivered in a London address on August 21, 1817, and an attitude that doomed his other reform schemes by their association with atheism. Afterward, his continued baiting of the clergy compounded his notoriety. Yet Owen remained firmly unshaken in his purpose. Next he proposed that a community be founded where his principles could be tested. At his own expense, he created such a model at New Harmony in Indiana in 1825. The experiment lasted for three years and attracted a broad range of weird reformers and misfits as well as sincere adherents to Owen's principles of cooperation and association. The end was foreordained: New Harmony, after using up most of Owen's fortune, failed, and Owen returned to Great Britain in 1829.

In 1828, Owen had sold his share of the New Lanark Company. In 1831, his wife died, and all of his surviving children lived in the United States. Alone and no longer a wealthy industrialist, Owen became the chief spokesman for a movement which was later termed Utopian socialism (to distinguish it from Marxist socialism). Indeed, the actual term "socialism" seems to have become popular in meetings of the Association of All Classes of All Nations, which Owen founded in 1835. He worked tirelessly on behalf of his form of socialism, for cooperation, and against religion. He also openly opposed the institution of marriage and in his later life expressed a deep interest in spiritualism.

By the mid-1830's, Owen was actively involved in the trade union movement, establishing the Grand National Consolidated Trades Union, which for a time had a membership of more than half a million. His several organizations went through numerous name changes, and all were ultimately unsuccessful. In 1858, he became seriously ill and requested that he be taken back to his native village of Newtown. There, on November 17, 1858, he died. By his wish, he was buried in a churchyard next to the graves of his parents. His three sons did well in the United States. Robert became a member of Congress and a diplomat, David was a geologist, and Richard was a college professor.

Summary

Despite the controversy and failures which accompanied his life, Robert Owen left a remarkable set of legacies. In industry, he proved that high wages and good employee relations improve productivity. In education, his nursery school idea and the importance of environmental influences became standard concepts. His theories on cooperation gave birth to the cooperative movement, which demonstrated remarkable endurance. His attempt to build a model community was repeated numerous times in the nineteenth and twentieth centuries. The im-

petus he gave to the trade union movement was of particular historical significance. Despite the unfortunate personality traits which made him combative and difficult to deal with, he played a leading role in the attempt to resolve the social consequences of the early Industrial Revolution.

Bibliography

Cole, Margaret. *Robert Owen of New Lanark*. London: Batchworth, and New York: Oxford University Press, 1953. A brief and general but useful introduction.

Dean, Russell. "Owenism and the Malthusian Population: Questions, 1815-1835." *History of Political Economy* 27, no. 3 (Fall 1995). Discusses the debate between T. R. Malthus and Owen on theories of population.

Harvey, Rowland Hill. *Robert Owen, Social Idealist*. Berkeley: University of California Press, 1949. A more scholarly, yet highly readable, biography.

Holloway, Mark. *Heavens on Earth: Utopian Communities in America, 1680-1880*. 2d ed. New York: Dover, 1966. Properly includes Owen's New Harmony experiment and Owen's influence in America.

Jones, Lloyd. *The Life, Times, and Labours of Robert Owen*. 2 vols. 6th ed. London: Sonnenschein, and New York: Scribner, 1919. This early biography is useful because the author, born in 1811, was an adult during Owen's later years.

Kamau, Lucy Joyce. "Out of Harmony; Indiana Histories." *History Today* 47, no. 8 (August, 1997). Comparison of Owen's idea of a rural utopia, the open community concept versus the Harmony Society's vision in Posey County, Ind.

Noyes, John Humphrey. *History of American Socialisms*. Philadelphia: J. B. Lippincott, and London: Trubner, 1870. This work, by one of America's most famous Utopians, includes contemporary accounts of New Harmony and other Owenite communities.

Owen, Robert. *A New View of Society and Other Writings*. London: Dent, and New York: Dutton, 1927. One of the most important and the most generally available works by Owen.

Podmore, Frank. *Robert Owen: A Biography*. 2 vols. London: Hutchinson, 1906; New York: Appleton, 1907. This remains the standard biography of Owen.

Roy Talbert, Jr.

NICCOLÒ PAGANINI

Born: October 27, 1782; Genoa, Republic of
  Genoa (now Italy)
Died: May 27, 1840; Nice, Kingdom of Sardinia
  (now France)
Area of Achievement: Music
Contribution: From his own time to the present,
  Niccolò Paganini has been considered one of
  the greatest violinists the world has ever known.
  He was the father of the freelance virtuosi—
  master musicians who made their living by giving public concerts. His astonishing feats of
  skill on the violin, his uncanny dramatic flair,
  and the compelling rumors and legends
  spawned by his colorful lifestyle all combined
  to captivate the imagination of audiences
  throughout early nineteenth century Europe and
  distinguish him as one of the most intriguing
  figures in music history.

Early Life

The northern Italian culture into which Niccolò Paganini was born venerated musicians as much as
any other great musical culture in history. Considering the great deal of money available to musical
talent at that time, it was quite natural that a family
as poor as the Paganini's would raise a gifted child
such as Niccolò to no other end than the complete
development of his talents. Paganini's mother, Teresa, was a pious woman who claimed that while he
was being born, an angel came to her and told her
that the child would be the greatest violinist the
world had ever known. The young Niccolò grew up
under his mother's gentle yet constant prompting
to fulfill this divine commission. His father, Antonio, had a more direct and demanding influence on
the development of his talents. Antonio worked at
the Genoa harbor but was a gifted amateur musician. Although he spent most of his time drinking,
gambling, and scheming of ways to get rich, he
found time to teach Niccolò the mandolin at the
age of five and the violin at the age of seven.

Paganini claimed that within a few months of
learning the violin he could play anything on sight.
Antonio, recognizing his son's talents and willing
to exploit any financial prospect, forced Paganini
to practice from morning until night. When he
could teach Paganini no more, he arranged for his
son to take lessons with Giacomo Costa, the foremost violinist in Genoa. Paganini played in church
three times per week to help pay for his tuition, and

Antonio set up concerts throughout Genoa, where
Paganini played his own compositions and variations on standard pieces to great applause. At the
age of thirteen, Paganini went with his father to
Parma, where he studied composition for one year
and then made an extensive and successful concert
tour throughout northern Italy. Paganini constantly
chafed against Antonio's severity, and although he
did make a few concert tours between the ages of
fifteen and eighteen, he spent most of this time in
his room practicing and composing, as much to
avoid contact with his father as to attain perfection
in his art.

Life's Work

In September of 1801, at the age of eighteen, Paganini finally extracted himself from his father's control and set out on a path that was to make him the
talk of Europe. He pleaded to be allowed to go to a
festival in Lucca, Italy, where he would be able to
demonstrate his talents to travelers from all over
southern Europe. His father reluctantly consented
on the condition that he take his older brother. The
two set out for the festival, and Paganini met with
great success. When the festival ended in December, Niccolò, having tasted the sweet nectar of freedom, sent his brother home alone and decided to
remain in Lucca. For three years he lived the life of
a freelance artist and indulged the passions of
youth that had been long suppressed under his father's strict rule. His performances earned him a
great deal of money, which he gambled away and
then earned back at his next concert. Several times
he had to pawn his violin to pay a debt of honor.
Once while his violin was in hock he was in desperate need of an instrument with which to perform a concert. A wealthy businessman lent him a
Guarneri violin and was so moved by the performance that he insisted Paganini keep it. Although
he would later give up gambling altogether, it was
a major feature of his stay in Lucca and would
prove to be the source of a great financial failure
near the end of his life.

Paganini's amorous adventures during this period in Lucca and throughout his life were legendary. He was not an attractive man, but his genius
and magnetic personality gave him an appeal that
captured the hearts of women wherever he went.
The most important aspect of this period in Lucca,
however, was his development as a performer of

the first order. His early teachers had been closely associated with opera and the theater, which surely contributed to his sense of the dramatic and, combined with a financial opportunism he inherited from his father, gave him a keen sense of how to work an audience. His physical appearance also contributed to his popular appeal. His cadaverous presence was so alarming that it led to endless rumors of his associations with the devil, which he initially exploited for publicity but later regretted.

Paganini's programs were filled with music of his own composition—the works of other violinists and composers not being difficult enough for him—which emphasized his technical prowess and his ability to perform amazing tricks such as imitating the sound of farm animals and playing entire pieces on a single string that anyone else would find difficult playing on all four strings. This thrilled his audiences and earned him a great deal of money, but his propensity to pander to low tastes led critics to label him a charlatan. While this criticism is deserved to some extent, those who were most vocal in this regard had not heard him play, basing their judgments on reports of his performances and in reaction to the startling phenomena of Paganini that swept all of Europe. The most incredulous of critics had only to personally experience a performance to be disabused of the worst of this notion. Even while acknowledging dismay for his antics, the greatest composers and musicians of his day, including Franz Schubert, Franz Liszt, Gioacchino Rossini, Hector Berlioz, and Giacomo Meyerbeer, paid him homage as a master. He cut himself an enigmatic figure from those early days in Lucca and remained such throughout his life.

In 1805, Napoleon Bonaparte named his own sister, Elise, regent of Lucca. She appointed Paganini court conductor and solo violinist. Besides performing several times per week, his duties also included giving violin lessons to Elise's husband. After serving four years in this capacity, Paganini resumed his career as a freelance artist, delighting audiences all over the Lombardy region of Italy. In 1813, he gave a triumphant concert in Milan. He had considered following this performance with an international tour but was retained for thirty-six more concerts in Milan and then proceeded with an extensive tour of Italy. He would not leave his native land for another fifteen years.

By the time Paganini set out for Vienna in 1828, he was known throughout Europe, his fame having spread by travelers who returned home from Italy with reports of his amazing skills as well as fantastic rumors of his notorious lifestyle. After five months in Vienna, Paganini set out on a two and one-half year tour of Germany, Bohemia, and Poland. In 1831 he visited Paris, France, for the first time and later that year made the first of two tours of England. Everywhere he went, his concerts sold out even though he charged twice as much for tickets as any other performer. His performances invariably exceeded his reputation.

In 1834, Paganini returned to Italy and purchased an estate near Parma. For a brief time he took a post with Napoleon's second wife, Marie Louise, who was then the duchess of Parma. Paganini spent the remaining years of his life giving concerts and dabbling in the violin trade, buying and selling fine instruments as a hobby during his extensive travels. In 1836, he became enmeshed in a failed scheme to open a casino in Paris that was to bear the name Casino Paganini. An easy target because of his wealth and fame, Paganini was ruined by the lawsuits that followed this debacle. He left Paris in 1838 hoping to return to Genoa, but he was not to live much longer. He did not have a strong physical constitution, and his life had been filled with extended periods of illness. In 1840, still embroiled in litigation over the casino venture, his frail health, compounded by years of living on the road and the pressures of his recent financial setbacks, failed him. He died in Nice, unable to complete his journey home.

Summary

Public subscription concerts had been common for nearly one hundred years prior to Paganini's life, but only as a supplement to the support a musician received from wealthy patrons. With the rise of republican sentiment in Europe during the early nineteenth century, a new class of citizen emerged with new aesthetic demands that made public concerts a viable option for the musician who understood these demands. Paganini was the first to take advantage of these changing conditions. He defined the role of the freelance musician for generations to come, and his influence extended from the likes of Liszt to the modern rock band.

The legendary aspects of Paganini's colorful life and showmanship are fascinating, but it is his achievements as a composer and an artist that preserve his place in history. Although many of his compositions are flashy pieces of technical wizardry lacking musical substance, there are a few piec-

es that are premier works for the violin. His greatest compositions are his twenty-four caprices, a collection of violin studies exercising all the technical elements necessary to master the instrument. The ability to play this work remains a primary criteria for consideration as a master violinist. These caprices have also been the subject of transcriptions as well as theme and variations by numerous composers. His six violin concertos are highly regarded and are still a part of the standard concert repertoire.

Bibliography

Courcy, G. I. C. *Paganini: The Genoese*. Norman: University of Oklahoma Press, 1957. This book is one of two classic biographies on Paganini in English. The appendices include a genealogy of the Paganini family, two autobiographical sketches by Paganini himself, a list of compositions, a list of instruments owned by Paganini, and an extensive bibliography of pre-1950 works on Paganini.

Pulver, Jeffrey. *Paganini: The Romantic Virtuoso*. London: Joseph, 1936; New York: Da Capo Press, 1970. This book is a classic work on Paganini and includes an extensive bibliography compiled by Frederick Freedman.

Roth, Henry. *Violin Virtuosos: From Paganini to the 21st Century*. Los Angeles: California Classics Books, 1997. Roth traces the phenomenon of the violin virtuoso from Paganini to contemporary performers. Includes chapters on women violinists, American and Russian violinists, and the nature of the violin as art.

Sheppard, Leslie, and Dr. Herbert R. Axelrod. *Paganini*. Neptune City, N.J.: Paganiniana, 1979. A complete compendium of material related to the life and works of Paganini. This collaboration includes an engaging biography; hundreds of drawings and pictures of Paganini, his contemporaries, and modern performers of his compositions; reproductions of Paganini-related ephemera; stylistic samples and analysis of Paganini's music; a list of Paganini discography; and a facsimile of the twenty-four caprices.

Stratton, Steven S. *Nicolò Paganini: His Life and Work*. Westport, Conn.: Greenwood Press, 1971. The first half of this short book is a biography of Paganini, while the second half provides an in-depth analysis of his life, his artistic merit, and his significance as a composer.

Sugden, John. *Paganini*. London and New York: Omnibus Press, 1986. This book was originally published in 1980 as *Paganini: Supreme Violinist or Devil's Fiddler?* by Midas Books. It is a brief biography with many pictures and drawings. Appendices include a select bibliography, a discography, and a list of derivatives of Paganini's life and works in popular and serious culture.

Richard L. Mallery

ALICE FREEMAN PALMER

Born: February 21, 1855; Colesville, New York
Died: December 6, 1902; Paris, France
Area of Achievement: Education
Contribution: The second president of Wellesley College, Palmer championed the cause of educational reform for women, greatly influencing attitudes of educators and society at large concerning the need for quality education for women at every level.

Early Life

Alice Elvira Freeman was the oldest of four children born to James Warren Freeman and Elizabeth Josephine Higley Freeman on a farm in Colesville, New York. When Alice was nine years old, her father decided to pursue his interest in medicine in hope of improving the family economic situation. Elizabeth Freeman assumed full support of the children for two years and her husband received his degree from the Albany Medical College in 1864. Alice's early education came mostly from her parents. Her mother and grandmother had experience as schoolteachers, and her father was adventurous and inquisitive. The family was deeply religious and active in promoting moral and social causes. Alice was given household responsibilities that often included the care of younger siblings. She gained much practical knowledge and developed a deep love of nature which she carried into adulthood. At three years of age, Alice had taught herself to read; by the next year, she began to attend the village school. In the one-room school, however, educational stimulation was limited.

In 1865, Dr. Freeman moved his family to the nearby village of Windsor, New York, to begin his medical practice. Alice was enrolled at Windsor Academy, a coeducational preparatory school where she came into contact with formal, rigorous education for the first time. The academy's teachers came from prestigious institutions such as Harvard and Andover, and Alice excelled in her work. At age fourteen, she became engaged to a theology professor. She soon realized, however, that her own goals in life depended on her receiving adequate education. She viewed marriage as an equal partnership that would be impossible without an education equal to that of her mate. Six months after the young professor left for seminary at Yale, Alice broke the engagement.

The Freeman family lived in relative poverty to which the members responded with a certain resourcefulness and creativity. Although the parents valued education, for financial reasons it was decided that the funds available must go to Alice's brother, who would one day likely be in a position of supporting a family of his own. Alice had been preparing diligently at Windsor to enter college and was willing to sacrifice whatever was necessary to attend. She bargained with her parents that if they would even partially finance her higher education, she would take on no family responsibilities of her own until each of her three siblings had received the education they desired, and her father gave his consent.

Alice had thought of entering newly founded Vassar College, but was not satisfied that the college would offer women as rigorous an education as men received at the finest schools. Instead, she chose to travel far from home and take entrance examinations at the University of Michigan, one of the few universities in the country offering a coeducational program. Unfortunately, she failed the examinations. During her interview, however, she attracted the attention of the university president, who interceded on Alice's behalf. She was allowed six months to prove her suitability as a student. This she did admirably and, after years of financial hardship and sometimes ill health, graduated in 1876, with a bachelor of arts degree. Family finances had deemed it necessary for Alice to interrupt her studies in 1875 and take a temporary position as preceptress at a struggling high school in Ottawa, Illinois. From the outset, her skill as an administrator was evident. She negotiated smoothly with faculty and students and designed quality courses of study. Nevertheless, finishing her own education was her priority, and she returned as soon as possible to the university despite pleas from the community to remain.

Life's Work

After graduation from the University of Michigan, Alice Freeman embarked on a succession of difficult years as she fulfilled her resolution to help her family and educate her siblings. Jobs were low paying and not always of her choice; however, her record of achievements was no less than excellent in each situation. She taught in a girls' seminary in

Lake Geneva from 1876 to 1877 and from 1877 to 1879 at the high school of Saginaw, Michigan. In 1877, she received her first invitation to teach at Wellesley College as an instructor of mathematics, but refused for personal reasons. In 1878, Henry Fowle Durant, the founder of Wellesley, contacted her again with the offer of a position in the Greek department. Her sister Stella, to whom she was devoted, was ill and needed her care. Again, she declined. Stella died in 1879, and, although it was a time of deep sorrow for Alice, she was freed to go about her work with a more independent spirit. When Durant called for the third time, she accepted the chairmanship of the History department in 1879, and went to Wellesley.

The college had been founded by Durant and his wife in an effort to promote the same kind of education for women that was offered to men in the United States. The ideals were in close kinship with those that Freeman upheld, and she worked tirelessly with the young women whom she taught. The college was experimental and liberal in its program of studies, and Durant was insistent that research and laboratory work were more important than simply learning from a textbook. This placed a large demand on the faculty not only to lecture but also to prepare detailed reading lists from which the students worked. Shortly after Durant's death in 1881, Ada L. Howard, the president of Wellesley, resigned. Alice Freeman, whose work had shown dedication and consummate skill, was chosen at age twenty-six to be vice president of the college and acting president. In 1882, she became the second president of Wellesley, where her talent as an administrator and organizer of human resources found an ideal outlet.

During her six years as president, much of Freeman's time was spent stabilizing the academic and administrative structure while implementing goals Durant had set for the college. She organized the Academic Council composed of heads of the academic departments to which she turned often for advice and consultation in academic matters. Standing faculty committees were formed and a building program was begun which included a gymnasium and dormitories. Networks were created with feeder high schools in the country and the preparatory school was discontinued. Freeman's full energy then went into improving the collegiate program by raising academic standards and simplifying and standardizing the courses of study that were offered. Although tuition was increased,

Freeman also endeavored to make more scholarships available to students. Her contacts in the field and keen sense of people's abilities also culminated in successful efforts to build the faculty.

Alice Freeman's professional life was not restricted to the Wellesley campus, but extended to matters of general education. She was instrumental in establishing the Association of Collegiate Alumnae in 1882 (forerunner of the American Association of University Women), which brought together educated women nationwide who were interested in raising standards of education for women. She served two terms as president in 1885-1886 and 1889-1890. In 1884, she was one of three American delegates elected to attend the International Conference on Education in London.

In 1887, Alice Freeman's life took a new turn. A friendship with Harvard philosopher George Herbert Palmer developed into a romance, and the two were married on December 23. Having decided that her work at Wellesley was finished and the college was ready for a time of quiet growth and the watchful care of someone new, she resigned her position shortly before her marriage, much to the despair of the college and of her public, especially those who felt she had compromised her profession for marriage. Instead, she envisioned her future as an opportunity to continue to pursue her goals within the comfort of a lifestyle that for the first time included leisure. She was constantly available for public addresses and gave unselfishly of her time to any organization that supported the ideals of excellence in education, particularly that of women. She remained on the executive committee of the Board of Trustees at Wellesley until her death and was active as well in the founding of Radcliffe College as separate from, but affiliated with, Harvard. Her work was separate from that of her husband, but each received ample support and respect from the other. The couple spent several sabbaticals in Europe, where they traveled many miles on bicycle enjoying the countryside. Alice and her husband also spent many summers at the Palmer family farm in Boxford, Massachusetts, twenty-five miles north of Boston, where they enjoyed tranquility not possible in the city.

In 1891, Alice Palmer was one of five delegates from Massachusetts chosen to attend the World Columbian Exhibition in Chicago, an event that highlighted the work of international women in many professions, including education. In 1892, she received a Ph.D. degree from the University of

Michigan. In the same year, she was invited by the new University of Chicago to serve as their dean of women. Although Alice and her husband were both offered positions, they decided not to leave Boston. The university's president, William Rainey Harper, was determined to entice the most capable woman he knew in the field and persisted in modifying the conditions until she agreed to serve. She was required to spend only twelve weeks' residence in Chicago, allowed to elect her own sub-dean, and released from any teaching responsibilities. She stayed until 1895, having established policies on which others could build.

Her professional activity continued and included work with the Woman's Home Missionary Society of the Presbyterian Church and the Women's Educational Association, an organization founded in Boston in 1891 and of which she was president for nine years. The Massachusetts Board of Education appointed her to its membership in 1889, and she helped to raise levels of high school education in the state and ensure free high school education for every citizen. In 1902, while on sabbatical with her husband, Alice Palmer died in Paris of a heart attack at the age of forty-seven.

Summary

Alice Freeman Palmer was a true pioneer in the field of education for women. Her life was spent in preparation for her work and in professional endeavors that helped to drastically change the quality of academic opportunity offered to women in the United States. Her accomplishments were numerous, and, fortunately for society, came early in her brief life. She had a gift for working among people that called for the best from them and herself. Recognition included honorary degrees from Columbia University in 1887 and Union University in 1896. In 1920, she became the second youngest person to be named to the Hall of Fame at New York University, which recognizes professionals from a variety of fields. She left no writing for posterity other than a few articles and a book of romantic poems called *A Marriage Cycle* (1915). Her lasting mark was made, however, through her interaction with students and faculty and her willingness to involve herself fully with important causes in cooperation with others, thus bringing many worthwhile ideas to fruition. Her efforts made a difference for all women who have followed her as she opened the doors to educational and professional challenges never before possible.

Bibliography

Bordin, Ruth B. *Alice Freeman Palmer: The Evolution of a New Woman.* Ann Arbor: University of Michigan Press, 1993. The most recent biography of Palmer, Bordin's work gives an excellent account of Palmer's achievements, impact, and interaction with other prominent figures in the struggle for equal education for women.

Palmer, George Herbert. *The Life of Alice Freeman Palmer.* Boston: Houghton Mifflin, 1908. Written by her husband, this biography offers an intimate look at Alice Palmer's life and work. Some correspondence and poetry are included.

Palmieri, Patricia A. "Here Was Fellowship: A Social Portrait of Academic Women at Wellesley College, 1895-1920." *History of Education Quarterly* 23 (Summer, 1983): 195-214. A scholarly article that discusses the lives of various figures encountered by Palmer during her tenure as professor and then as president of the college.

Schwartz, Robert A. "Reconceptualizing the Leadership Roles of Women in Higher Education: A Brief History on the Importance of Deans of

Women." *Journal of Higher Education* 68, no. 5 (September-October, 1997). Schwartz resurrects the often neglected, but important role played by Deans of Women in the development of higher education including Palmer and others.

Storr, Richard J. *Harper's University: The Beginnings.* Chicago: University of Chicago Press, 1966. This history of the University of Chicago gives insight into Palmer's tenure as the first dean of women.

Weimann, Jeanne Madeline. *The Fair Women.* Chicago: Academy Chicago, 1981. This account of the Women's Building at the World Columbian Exposition discusses Palmer's involvement with the education exhibition.

Wein, Roberta. "Women's Colleges and Domesticity: 1875-1918." *History of Education Quarterly* 14 (Spring, 1974): 31-47. The article explores activity at Wellesley and Bryn Mawr at a time when decisions made had a major effect on whether female education would continue to perpetuate feminine passivity or foster independence.

Sandra C. McClain

LORD PALMERSTON
Henry John Temple

Born: October 20, 1784; Westminster, London, England

Died: October 18, 1865; Brocket Hall, Hertfordshire, England

Areas of Achievement: Politics and international relations

Contribution: Lord Palmerston made aggressive use of military and naval power to ensure security for British commerce, while attempting to work closely with France to avoid any risk of war.

Early Life

Though born at Westminster on October 20, 1784, Henry John Temple, the future Lord Palmerston, sprang from a long line of Anglican Irish aristocrats. His education at Harrow, Edinburgh University, and finally at St. John's College, Cambridge, earned for him a nobleman's degree, without examinations. He had no need, however, for such academic favors. His intelligence and talents would have ensured success even if he had been forced to compete for the prizes which the accident of noble birth thrust upon him.

Since the seventeenth century, the Temples had been Whigs. The reign of George III, however, had seen the emergence of the "king's party." Although under George I and George II (1714-1760) Toryism had been equated with treason, it enjoyed renewed respectability under George III (1760-1820). The road to any kind of patronage lay through personal loyalty to the king. He was determined to assert royal prerogative, as far as he could, without forgetting that since the Glorious Revolution of 1688-1689, British sovereigns had owed their crowns to Parliament rather than to divine right.

It is thus not a matter of an abandonment of Whig ideals, but a simple, pragmatic need to wear the king's colors which made the second Viscount Palmerston identify with what came to be called the "New Tory" Party, for forty years. At the death of the second Viscount on April 17, 1802, Henry John Temple succeeded to his father's title and estates as the third Viscount Palmerston. At the age of eighteen, he still had his university studies ahead of him. Appropriately, this scion of a Whig family was most profoundly influenced at Edinburgh by Professor Dugald Stewart, the leading Whig philosopher of the day.

It is, however, understandable that this bright, personable, and independently wealthy Irish peer chose to wear the Tory label when he first entered political life, in 1807. Whether as a Tory at the beginning of his career or as a Whig and a Liberal at the end, he was fundamentally an heir of the Glorious Revolution, mistrustful of royal power and devoted to a Parliament whose destinies were guided by educated and propertied aristocrats.

As an Irish peer, Lord Palmerston was eligible to seek election in the British House of Commons. At the age of twenty-two, he began his fifty-nine-year career in Parliament as the representative of a pocket borough whose voters had been bought by wealthy patrons on his behalf. It must be understood that no element of scandal attached to buying and selling votes in underpopulated boroughs. The rationale of the borough mongers asserted that only thus could able young politicians be recognized and helped to an early start in their careers.

Although almost immediately offered cabinet rank, Lord Palmerston contented himself with the noncabinet post of Secretary-at-War for twenty years, until 1828. He was apparently happy doing an efficient job at the War Office, showing no signs of ambition as he made his way through London society. He earned a name as a fashion setter, a womanizer, and a dilettante writer for political journals. He could have been dismissed as a brilliant young man who was wasting his talents and was destined to remain a second-rater. Although he made a few parliamentary addresses on foreign affairs, he took no real interest in diplomacy. It was to be the last thirty-five years of his long career which would earn for him the sobriquet "Most English Minister" and to identify him as the very embodiment of John Bull.

Lord Palmerston delayed matrimony until 1839, when he was married to the widow of Lord Cowper, Emily, née Lamb, sister of Prime Minister Lord Melbourne. The newlyweds had long been intimate during the lifetime of Lord Cowper, and gossip ascribed the paternity of Lady Cowper's younger children to Lord Palmerston. In any event, those children became his heirs.

Life's Work

Lord Palmerston owed his first attainment of cabinet rank to the prime ministership of that arch Tory, the Duke of Wellington. He resigned in 1828, in loyalty to his friend William Huskisson, who had been forced out of the cabinet after a major split with the Iron Duke. Thrown into opposition, Palmerston interested himself in diplomatic matters, for the first time. At last, the talented dabbler had found his forte. In June, 1829, he delivered one of the great parliamentary speeches of his career, establishing his reputation as a man who understood foreign affairs. Immediately, Lord Grey, the Whig leader, formed an alliance with the disaffected Tory. In September, 1830, Wellington invited Palmerston to return to the cabinet. The offer was refused, unless Wellington would include Lord Grey in a sort of Cabinet of National Unity. Wellington, quite predictably, declined the proposal. From that hour, most of Palmerston's biographers count him as having returned to his ancestral Whig origins.

When in 1830 Lord Grey attained the prime ministership after forming his own coalition of Whigs and disaffected Tories, Palmerston attained the office of Foreign Secretary at last. He held it until 1841 and again in 1846-1852.

Lord Grey's greatest achievement was the parliamentary Reform Bill of 1832. In Palmerston's domain at the Foreign Office, his accomplishments assumed a gigantic stature of their own. In France, the senior line of the House of Bourbon was overthrown and replaced by its cadet branch, the House of Orleans, personified by Louis Philippe, who reigned as King of France until overthrown in turn by the Revolution of 1848. Italian and Polish nationalists also made 1830 a revolutionary year, with suicidal results. Closer to Great Britain, however, a Belgian revolt against the King of the Netherlands required forceful British action, and it was the Belgian crisis which established Palmerston's reputation for brilliance in statecraft.

There was the gravest danger that Austria, Russia, and Prussia might intervene with armed force to assist the King of the Netherlands to regain Belgium. After all, the union of all the Low Countries under the Dutch sovereign had been one of the achievements of the Congress of Vienna, designed to prevent either French or Prussian aggression across that natural military highway formed by the flat Netherlands. Seen in that way, Lords Grey and Palmerston would have preferred to see the unity of the Netherlands preserved. As a realist, however, Palmerston perceived that there was no way of forcing French-speaking Walloons and Flemish Belgians, almost entirely Roman Catholic, to accept the sovereignty of the Calvinist Protestant Dutch House of Orange, which had unwisely treated the Belgian provinces as subordinate appendages rather than as fully participating states in a United Kingdom of the Netherlands.

Palmerston and Grey were ready to settle for an independent Belgium, provided that Louis Philippe did not regard it as a means to French aggrandizement. It took all Palmerston's skill, and a neat balance of conciliatory gentleness and bullying firmness, to get an adventuresome French army withdrawn from Belgium and to persuade Louis Philippe not to press the claims of one of his sons to be King of Belgium. At the same time, he had to restrain the Dutch from using force to repress the Belgian revolt, a repression which would have made it more difficult to control the French. Fortunately for Great Britain, France, and the Belgians, the Polish and Italian revolts of 1830 kept Austria, Prussia, and Russia so preoccupied that Palmerston was able to create an independent Belgium. As a crowning touch, the London Conference of 1831 obtained the consent of all the major powers to the erection of an independent Belgium. The king selected for the new state was Prince Leopold of Saxe-Coburg-Saalfeld, the widowed former son-in-law of Great Britain's King George IV. It was an incidental but significant bonus that Leopold was the uncle, both of the future Queen Victoria and her consort, Prince Albert. The queen selected for him, and imposed as an act of statecraft, was a daughter of Louis Philippe, King of France. Thus, everyone obtained something, the appearance of Anglo-French entente was maintained, the Belgians were freed, yet British security in the Low Countries seemed assured. Only the King of the Netherlands might complain of unrequited loss.

Palmerston took an aggressive role in setting disputed claims to the Spanish and Portuguese thrones, and in finding husbands for Donna Maria of Portugal and Isabella of Spain who would pose no threat to British interests. Although sympathetic to the Greek struggle for independence from Turkey, he devoted the last thirty years of his life to building and protecting a strong Ottoman Turkish barrier against Russian and French expansion.

He interested himself in active support for Protestant missionaries in the Levant and briefly toyed with the idea of a Jewish commonwealth in Palestine. Even after he had abandoned that idea, he continued to offer the most aggressive protection to the Jews of that area. Palmerston saw no contradiction between his drive to protect minorities on Turkish soil, whether Jews, Protestants, Druze, Samaritans, or Armenians, and his determination to save the Turkish Empire. After all, France used her role as protector of Roman Catholicism and Russia used her protectorate of Orthodox Christianity to build power bases in the East. Palmerston merely concluded that a strong British presence in the Levant was the best possible protection for Turkey against Russian or French ambitions.

When, from 1839 to 1841, Mehmet Ali, Viceroy of Egypt, threatened to rip Syria out of Turkish hands, in close alliance with Louis Philippe's France, Palmerston landed troops at Beirut and Acre, threatened to cut off the Egyptians, who were advancing against Turkey, and forced Egyptian retreat beyond the Sinai Desert. In the London Conference of 1841, he restored the sultan's authority in Syria, Palestine, and the Sinai, repulsed the French, and closed the Bosphorus and Dardanelles to warships in peacetime. As usual, however, he allowed a small prize even to the losers, awarding the title of Hereditary Viceroys of Egypt to Mehmet Ali and his heirs.

Making what can only be described as high-handed use of British power, Palmerston did not hesitate to bombard the Greek port of Piraeus in 1850 and to rip Hong Kong from China, all in the name of the right of British merchants and seamen to pursue trade without danger to their persons or property, even if the trade was in opium. Even imperial Great Britain threatened him with censure for going too far with gunboat diplomacy, but Palmerston always managed to rescue himself with an appeal to British pride, comparing anyone who carried a British passport to St. Paul who could say, *Civis Romanus sum*, or "I am a British subject," and be sure that he could travel where he willed.

Palmerston, like his longtime rival and ultimate partner Lord John Russell, did not hesitate to ignore Queen Victoria's clear constitutional right to be informed of all the details of foreign policy. Whether fearing that she would refuse her assent, or out of simple impetuosity, the great Liberal duet had no hesitation about showing the queen only as much as she might be expected to approve, and writing secret instructions to British envoys abroad on private stationery, bearing no indication of the writer's cabinet office. That Queen Victoria re-

ferred to Lords Palmerston and Russell as "those terrible old men" is scarcely surprising.

Most of Palmerston's biographers bemoan the fact that he was not Foreign Secretary during the disaster known as the Crimean War. At the very end of the war, when all that was left was to repair the damage as well as possible, he became prime minister at the age of seventy-one. He held that office for the first time in 1855-1858. His constant preoccupation for the rest of his life was to remain Napoleon III's confidant and collaborator to avert any possibility that Bonapartist adventurism might start anew the wars he remembered clearly from his youth.

Palmerston was an enthusiastic supporter of Italian unification. He was one of the original authors of the intervention in Mexico and was also the first to abandon any military role in that country in 1862, though he did recognize Emperor Maximilian during his short-lived empire.

He proclaimed his neutrality during the American Civil War, but his every gesture offered moral and material support to the Confederacy. To ardent Northerners such as the historian George Bancroft, Palmerston came to personify British hostility toward the United States.

His second and final tenure of the prime ministership, 1859-1865, witnessed British ineffectiveness during the Polish Revolt of 1863 as well as the German-Danish war of 1864. To the very end, however, Palmerston was in control of policy; on his very deathbed he was engaged in checking, line by line, the text of a new Belgian treaty. He died, two days before his eighty-first birthday, on October 18, 1865.

Summary

Lord Palmerston remained a man of the eighteenth century whose unconcern for the rigid conventions of Victorian Great Britain never alienated the public. Perhaps, in a perverse sort of way, he charmed a generation of Englishmen who could not imagine behaving privately as he behaved so nonchalantly in public. He was the delight of cartoonists, always the bully prizefighter with his shirt off, ready to knock the crowns off the heads of kings. He was adept at manipulating the press. Throughout his later career, his financial interests in newspapers which carried his "leaked news" and "authentic" copies of state papers, was a matter of debate. Above all else, this aristocrat, so hostile to democracy, understood the role of the printing press in exploiting public opinion.

It was his good fortune to live during Great Britain's era of Splendid Isolation, when safe behind her ocean wall, and guarded by the greatest navy in the world, London needed neither allies nor long-term treaties to feel secure. In the springtime of Free Trade, British goods could undersell competitors and no foreign products threatened British prosperity. Lord Palmerston dwelt in an age of optimism, fearless of the future.

Bibliography

Bell, Herbert C. F. *Lord Palmerston*. London and New York: Longman, 1936. A solid two-volume study, giving a splendid overview of the life of the third Viscount Palmerston.

Blumberg, Arnold. *The Diplomacy of the Mexican Empire, 1863-1867*. Philadelphia: American Philosophical Society, 1971. Makes use of British diplomatic correspondence which reveals Palmerston's original authorship of the London Convention of 1861, authorizing British, French, and Spanish military intervention in Mexico. It traces the British withdrawal of 1862 and the subsequent British diplomatic attitude toward Maximilian's empire.

Case, Lynn M., and Warren F. Spencer. *The United States and France: Civil War Diplomacy*. Philadelphia: University of Pennsylvania Press, 1970. Reveals the close Anglo-French entente maintained by Lords Palmerston and Russell concerning the policy pursued toward the Union and the Confederacy.

Ingle, Harold N. *Nesselrode and the Russian Rapprochement with Britain, 1836-1844*. Berkeley: University of California Press, 1976. Describes the brief period when Russia made a sincere effort to come to an amicable understanding with Great Britain for a division of the Near Eastern pie.

Kingston, Klari. "Gunboat Liberalism? Palmerston, Europe and 1848." *History Today* 47, no. 2 (February, 1997). Kingston describes Palmerston's views on Britain's use of power to maintain peace and suggests that he could have been instrumental in preventing the Crimean War had he acted differently.

Mange, Alyce Edythe. *The Near Eastern Policy of the Emperor Napoleon III*. Urbana: University of Illinois Press, 1940. A valuable study offering insight into the entente which was fostered by Palmerston with Napoleon III.

Partridge, Michael S. and Karen L. Partridge. *Lord Palmerston, 1784-1865: A Bibliography*. Westport, Conn.: Greenwood Press, 1994. The first comprehensive bibliography of Lord Palmerston's public and private life, this volume includes published and unpublished materials on his career, his speeches and published writings, and information on his years in government service.

Puryear, Vernon John. *England, Russia, and the Straits Question*. Berkeley: University of California Press, 1931. The definitive study of the means whereby British statesmen strove to keep Russian naval power out of the Mediterranean.

Southgate, Donald. *"The Most English Minister": The Policies and Politics of Palmerston*. London: Macmillan, and New York: St. Martin's Press, 1966. This readable study brings Palmerston to life and describes the impact of the man on British policy.

Thomas, Daniel H. *The Guarantee of Belgian Independence and Neutrality in European Diplomacy, 1830's-1930's*. Kingston, R.I.: Thomas, 1983. Palmerston's greatest accomplishment and his lifelong preoccupation were tied in with Belgian independence and neutrality. This massive volume is the best study of the subject.

Victoria, Queen of Great Britain. *Regina v Palmerston: The Correspondence Between Queen Victoria and Her Foreign and Prime Minister, 1837-1865*. Edited by Brian Connell. New York: Doubleday, 1961; London: Evans Brothers, 1962. Uses the letters exchanged to trace the gradual deterioration of their personal relationship. Connell allows the correspondents to speak for themselves but interlards his own comment, making the entire series understandable and entertaining for the amateur historian.

Webster, Sir Charles. *The Foreign Policy of Palmerston, 1830-1841: Britain, the Liberal Movement, and the Eastern Question*. London: Bell, 1951; New York: Humanities Press, 1969. This two-volume work deals only with Palmerston's first term as Foreign Secretary. It is, nevertheless, the key to understanding his philosophy on international relations, applicable to his entire career. Making extensive use of unpublished primary sources, including Palmerston's papers, this ambitious study is definitive.

Arnold Blumberg

MUNGO PARK

Born: September 10, 1771; near Selkirk, Scotland
Died: 1806; near Bussa on the Niger River
Area of Achievement: Exploration
Contribution: Combining great ambition with tremendous courage and stamina, Park discovered and died in his efforts to traverse the Niger River in Western Africa.

Early Life

Mungo Park was born on September 10, 1771, at Foulshiels Farm on the estate of the Duke of Buccleuch near Selkirk, Scotland. He was the seventh child of a well-to-do farmer, also called Mungo. Park received his early education at home and in the Selkirk grammar school. In 1786, he was placed as an apprentice to the Selkirk surgeon Dr. Thomas Anderson. This was a disappointment to his father, who wanted him to enter the ministry. With the help of Dr. Anderson, Park entered the medical school at Edinburgh University. He passed three sessions of medical studies and earned distinction in botanical studies. In 1791, after completing his medical studies, Park moved to London to seek employment.

Park's brother-in-law, James Dickson, a London botanist, introduced him to Sir Joseph Banks, President of the Royal Society, who secured for him an appointment as assistant medical officer on the East India Company ship, the *Worcester*. He sailed to the island of Sumatra in February, 1792, where he collected rare plants. Park's relationship with Banks continued to develop when he returned in 1793 with his specimens and data. After presenting several papers, Park, acting on the advice of Banks, offered his services to the African Association, an organization formed in 1788 to further geographical studies of Africa.

Banks was the most influential member of the Association, and he favored Park as the successor to Major Daniel Houghton, who had disappeared on the Association expedition in 1790 to locate the course of the Niger River. The Association was impressed by Park's medical, botanical, and geographic skills as well as his physical condition for such a demanding journey. Tall and handsome in a well-chiseled way, Park possessed remarkable stamina that permitted him to perform feats of physical endurance and survive illnesses that would prove fatal to lesser men. Women found him very attractive, which proved to be important because their kindness helped him several times on his expeditions. Park's reserved personality, religious fatalism, and driving desire for eminence made him the perfect explorer, capable of pursuing success with a single-minded ambition and a certain cold-bloodedness. Park's instructions from the Association were to explore the Niger River and to gather information about the nations that inhabited its banks. He received fifteen shillings for each day he spent in Africa and two hundred pounds for expenses.

Life's Work

Park sailed from Portsmouth on May 22, 1795, aboard the *Endeavor*, a brig bound for the Gambia River for ivory. He arrived at the British factory of Pisania on the Gambia on July 5 and resided at the home of Dr. John Laidley for five months while he studied the Mandingo language and recovered from his first bout with fever. Unable to travel with a caravan, Park set out on December 2 with an English-speaking Mandingo former slave, a young servant, and his equipment. He followed Houghton's earlier route and was forced to trade off most of his trafficable goods to gain the friendship of the petty chiefs.

Danger arose when Park entered the Islamic African kingdoms. He reached Jarra in the Moorish kingdom of Ludamar before Christmas and discovered that it was the village where Major Houghton had been murdered. As he crossed Ludamar, Park was constantly abused by the people he encountered, until he was seized by Moors and taken to the residence of King Ali of Ludamar. He was held prisoner for three months while suffering humiliating treatment from his captors. In July, 1796, Park escaped through the assistance of some native women who befriended him. With only his pocket compass and a horse, he endured incredible hardships before reaching Ségou on the Niger River on July 20. He described the Niger as being as broad as the Thames River at Westminster. From Ségou, he journeyed downriver to Silla, thus proving that the Niger flowed eastward; he was forced to turn back, though, because he could no longer obtain food.

Park started back from Silla on August 3 by another route farther south, where he was again ostracized or mistreated by the natives before, nearly dead, he reached Kamalia on foot on September

16. He spent seven months during the rainy season with a native slave-trader who took him on to Pisania in June, 1797. Park sailed from the Gambia on June 15 as ship surgeon on the *Charleston*, an American slave ship bound for the Carolinas. Switching ships at Antigua, Park arrived at Falmouth, England, on December 22.

Unannounced, Park arrived in London on Christmas morning and was warmly welcomed by Banks and the Africa Association. He had been gone for more than three years and was believed dead. His return was sensational in itself, but the news of his discovery of the Niger created a national excitement. Supported by a salary extension from the Association, Park wrote *Travels in the Interior of Africa* (1799), which rapidly sold out through several editions. The book was written in a dramatic and excellent literary style which made Park's name a household word and produced royalties in excess of one thousand pounds. He returned home to the Scottish countryside and soon married Alice Anderson, daughter of his old master, Dr. Anderson of Selkirk. After living at Foulshiels for nearly two years, Park established a medical practice in the village of Peebles in 1801. He refused an offer from Banks to lead an expedition to Australia because the salary was too small. In the end, however, Park's restlessness at Peebles, as well as Banks's persistence, led him to consider a new offer to return to Africa to lead an officially sponsored government expedition.

This new expedition was originally part of a larger plan by the British government to expel the French from the region of Senegambia and to establish a permanent British presence in that area. There were to be three wings to the operation—commercial, military, and naval—for the purpose of destroying French factories in Senegambia and replacing them with British factories at Wulli and Bondu. Park, as leader of the commercial wing, was to establish the new factories and negotiate trade agreements with the tribes he encountered during his exploration of the Niger. This plan was drastically altered by a change in the British government in 1804. Lord Hobart, who had approved the original plan, was replaced by Lord Camden as colonial secretary. The expeditionary force, including Park's command, was whittled down by Lord Camden.

When Park left for Africa aboard the *Crescent* on January 30, 1805, he held the rank and pay of captain and the privileges of a British envoy. He was to make treaties establishing British trading stations along the Niger while trying to discover the course of the Niger and ascertain if it were navigable from the sea. Park was accompanied by his brother-in-law, Alexander Anderson, as second-in-command, and George Scott, a Selkirk friend, as draftsman. In addition, five thousand pounds was placed at his disposal by the Treasury, and his wife and four children were guaranteed one hundred pounds a year if he failed to return.

Park's entourage, which included four carpenters and two sailors, arrived at Goree on March 28, 1805, where they were joined by Lieutenant John Martyn and thirty-five volunteers from the Royal Africa Corps. The carpenters were to build a forty-foot boat for the expedition when they reached the Niger. This expedition seemed to be efficiently organized, but it had been Park's single-minded determination and endurance that made his previous expedition a success. The size of his second expedition would become a hindrance that could not maintain the grueling pace that Park set.

So began Park's second and fatal expedition. He became impatient and against all advice led his columns into the West Africa bush during the rainy season. Sailing up the Gambia, Park reached Kayee, where he engaged a Mandingo guide named Isaaco. The overland march to Pisania taught Park that an expedition produced many different problems from traveling alone. The first rain fell on June 10, and the soldiers began to contract fevers. When possible, Park left them in villages, but occasionally they were abandoned where they fell. On August 19, when the expedition arrived at Bamako on the Niger, only eleven British members had survived. Park and the remnants of his expedition hired canoes which took them downstream to Sansanding, a little eastward of Ségou, where they remained for two months in preparation for the passage downriver. Scott had died during the march, and Anderson died on October 28. The expedition's survivors constructed a flat-bottomed boat from two native canoes which Park named HMS *Joliba*, the native name for the Niger. Only five of the British remained alive: Park, Lieutenant Martyn, and three soldiers. Isaaco was sent back with Park's final dispatches while the rest of the expedition sailed off down the Niger with many muskets and ample supplies.

In 1806, rumors about Park's death began to reach the coast. Isaaco was dispatched to the interior to find the truth, but all that he produced was Park's belt and a questionable account from Amadi Fatouma, who had guided Park downriver from Sansanding. Isaaco reported that Park had uncharacteristically shunned contact with the natives, offended the chiefs by refusing to pay their river customs, and fired upon anyone approaching the *Joliba*. Park sailed down the Niger past Timbukto to the village of Bussa (located in what would become Nigeria), where the natives attempted to stop his progress. During efforts to escape, the *Joliba* had capsized in the narrow Bussa Rapids, and Park and his companions had drowned. Although doubts about Park's death remained, later expeditions confirmed that he did die at the Bussa Rapids, but the manner of his death has always been subject to debate.

Summary

Mungo Park's second expedition was a tragic failure. Every European in his expedition perished, and despite the loss of life and the distance traversed, no new light had been cast on the termination of the Niger. Because of the uncertainty of distances, neither the coastward direction of the Niger nor the magnitude of Park's journey was immediately recognized. Park had commenced his last expedition erroneously believing that the Niger was the Congo River, and it is possible that he died holding that belief, despite having traveled more than three-fourths of the twenty-six-hundred-mile length of the river.

The supreme tragedy in the history of early African exploration was the loss of Park, one of the most respected explorers, in a expedition that added very little to geographical knowledge. His death was basically a result of two tragic errors in judgment: first, the decision to enter the bush country during the rainy season, and second, his avoidance of contact with the natives and his policy of firing on them. Park felt comfortable with the black Africans, but, by contrast, he feared the Moors. It must be remembered that Park left Sansanding a sick, desperate man who possibly lacked his normal clarity of judgment. Mungo Park created his own fame, and his achievements are remembered for the manner of his survival and for the death which made him and the Niger a single historical entity and inspired another generation of explorers.

Bibliography

Boahen, A. Adu. *Britain, the Sahara, and the Western Sudan, 1788-1861*. Oxford: Clarendon Press, 1964. General work on British exploration and trade in Africa. Boahen discusses Park's explorations in the context of British policy in Africa.

Brent, Peter. *Black Nile: Mungo Park and the Search for the Niger*. London: Gordon Cremonesi, 1977. An excellent biography, well-researched and handsomely illustrated.

Burns, Alan. *History of Nigeria*. 8th ed. London: Allen and Unwin, 1972; New York: Barnes and Noble, 1973. An excellent history of Nigeria with an emphasis on British influence. Includes a brief but valuable account of Park's explorations.

Craig, Simon. "Journey to the White Man's Grave." *Geographical Magazine* 69, no. 12 (December, 1997). Profile of Park covering his journey to the Niger River, his exploration of West Africa for the African Association, and his disappearance in Bussa in 1806. Includes stories from his book *Travels in the Interior Districts of Africa*.

Gramont, Sandre de. *The Strong Brown God: The Story of the Niger River*. Boston: Houghton Mifflin, and London: Gollancz, 1975. The best book on the European expeditions to the Niger River. Park's role and adventures are covered extensively and accurately.

Gwynn, Stephen L. *Mungo Park*. New York: Putnam, 1935. This is perhaps the best life of Park, but it is somewhat dated.

Langley, Michael. "The Last Journey of Mungo Park." *History Today* 21 (June, 1971): 426-432. A popular but well-written article on Park's fatal expedition of 1805-1806. Excellent illustrations and evaluation of Park's accomplishments.

Severin, Timothy. *The African Adventure*. London: Hamilton, and New York: Dutton, 1973. A brilliant survey of precolonial expeditions in Africa. Contains new material and excellent illustrations. Good coverage of Park's life.

Phillip E. Koerper

THEODORE PARKER

Born: April 24, 1810; Lexington, Massachusetts
Died: May 10, 1860; Florence, Italy
Areas of Achievement: Religion and reform
Contribution: A scholar with a strong social conscience, Parker was an influential Transcendentalist who helped shape American Unitarianism and was a leader in the abolitionist cause during the 1850's.

Early Life

Theodore Parker was born April 24, 1810, in Lexington, Massachusetts, into a family with a history of patriotic activity, including service at Lexington and Bunker Hill. Parker grew up on stories about this heritage and often referred to it when he was crusading for the liberty of black Americans. His parents John and Hannah (Segur Stearns) Parker inspired many aspects of his life. The youngest of eleven children, Parker was a bit spoiled by his mother, who often read the Bible to him and who encouraged the development of his strong conscience. Books were readily available in Parker's home as his father frequently purchased them and had access to a lending library. At school, although he could not attend full-time, Parker quickly showed his scholarly potential but was terrified by the theology of divine retribution found in the primers of that day; it was an interpretation he later rejected totally. The loss of his mother when Parker was thirteen years old left him with more and more work to do at home, and his formal secondary education ended three years later. Parker spent the next seven years teaching school and trying to accumulate enough money in order to attend the Harvard Divinity School.

In 1832, with the help of an uncle, Parker was able to open his own school at Watertown, Massachusetts. The school was quickly successful, so that, while he was still aiding his elderly father, Parker's financial situation improved. At his boardinghouse, he met Lydia Cabot, his future wife. She was the sort of woman he preferred: loving, cooperative, and supportive. Although he was often to work with strong-minded, intellectual women, Parker was never comfortable with them. Parker became friends with the Reverend Convers Francis, who provided books and scholarly guidance. Francis introduced the young Parker to the antislavery movement and to the idealistic philosophy of

scholars such as Immanuel Kant and G. W. F. Hegel, which strongly influenced his thought. He also began to explore modern biblical criticism. In 1834, Francis found a scholarship for him, and Parker sadly left Watertown for the Harvard Divinity School. Over the next two years he earned a degree and a reputation for frugal living, hard study, lightheartedness, and theological radicalism.

Life's Work

It took Parker a year to get a pulpit after he was graduated. Perhaps he was tainted with Transcendentalism or, as Unitarian ministers often were, perceived as too intellectual. Perhaps his awkward bearing, prematurely balding head, square frame, and large hands hardened by farm work resulted in a poor impression. Whatever the cause, Parker used the time to fill temporarily empty pulpits, to marry Lydia, and to begin his translation of and commentary on W. M. L. De Wette's *Beiträge zur Einleitung in das Alte Testament* (1806; *A Critical and Historical Introduction to the Canonical Scriptures of the Old Testament*, 1843). It was on this book that his scholarly reputation was grounded. Parker was among the first Americans to study and apply the higher biblical criticism that was being developed by German scholars.

In May, 1837, Parker accepted a call from a church in West Roxbury, Massachusetts. Over the next decade, Parker worked on developing his philosophical and theological ideas. He was already in the Transcendentalist school with Ralph Waldo Emerson and Henry David Thoreau, for he was convinced that sensory data confirmed only limited phenomena. The great moral truths, he believed, being self-evidently true, transcended such confirmation. These were known to the human conscience and depended on no outside authority. In May, 1841, he preached a sermon entitled "The Transient and Permanent in Christianity," arguing that all the supernatural trappings of the religion and even Jesus himself might be proven false or nonexistent without weakening the essential truth of Christianity. Each person must find the Kingdom of Heaven within himself, he argued.

Unitarianism, which was still largely a branch of Congregationalism, supposedly rejected creeds, but these ideas which Parker elaborated in subsequent years outraged many. After his 1841 sermon,

Parker could find few ministers who were willing to exchange pulpits with him, and the friends who did, including those who did not agree with him, faced congregational protests and even withdrawals. Undaunted, Parker criticized his colleagues freely, and eventually he was asked to resign from the Boston Association of Congregational ministers, a demand which he refused.

Convinced of God's enduring love—eternal damnation was, he believed, impossible, for it would make eternal life a curse—he renounced the religion of guilt and retribution that had tormented his childhood. A good man, a kind man, a just man, a loving man was a Christian regardless of whether he believed the traditional theology of that sect. Reason was a God-given tool, but in religion, as in Transcendentalist philosophy, intuition carried man to greater truths. With this emphasis on the individual's discovery of truth within himself, it should have been impossible for Parker to argue that anyone's beliefs were wrong. Yet he often did.

While becoming controversial among Boston's ministers, Parker was also becoming known as a Transcendentalist philosopher. His articles and reviews appeared in many journals and were a staple of the Transcendentalist organ *The Dial*, which first appeared in 1840. In this same period, Parker's friend George Ripley founded the Utopian community Brook Farm. Like Ralph Waldo Emerson, Parker chose not to join. Many who did also joined his West Roxbury congregation, and Parker often visited the farm. This exposure to intellectuals stimulated Parker's thought, which appeared as seven lectures which constituted the book *A Discourse on Matters Pertaining to Religion*, published in 1842. Writing—he had finished the two volumes on De Wette and another volume of collected articles—lecturing, preaching, parish duties, and disputes took their toll, and in September, 1843, he and Lydia left for a year in Europe. He spent this vacation visiting scholars and philosophers whom he admired.

Upon his return from Europe, Parker, more convinced than ever that Transcendentalism was the only viable form of religion, intended to prove his point. The demands of his congregation and calls for lectures which had to be written quickly always prevented him from doing the scholarly work he wanted. The old controversies were quickly renewed when, in December, 1844, he suggested the possibility that God might send man greater Christs in the future. His piety and respect for

Jesus were undeniable, yet he was willing neither to limit God's love and power nor to assume that the revelation of one age was adequate for another.

Yet more and more, he was heard with respect, and early the next year a Boston group created a church for him. Although sad to leave friends in West Roxbury, Parker was eager to be part of the intellectual ferment of the city, and the new Twenty-eighth Congregational Society, under his leadership, became the largest parish in Boston and possibly in the United States. Parker made many new friends, including such luminaries as William Lloyd Garrison, Charles Sumner, Julia Ward Howe, and Horace Mann, and became mentor of a few young Unitarian ministers such as Starr King.

In Boston, the childless Parker family was enlarged by the adoption of a young, distant cousin of Lydia. Parker also worked on his beloved library, which was becoming one of the largest private collections in New England, though increasingly in the 1850's lecture fees which had bought books were diverted to support the needs of fugitive slaves. From 1847 to 1850, Parker wrote for and helped edit *The Massachusetts Quarterly Review*, a new Transcendentalist journal. Although never the intellectual force that its founders intended it to be, the *Review* did give Transcendentalists, including Parker, an outlet for their ideas.

In the 1840's, Parker moved into the general social reform movement of the mid-nineteenth century. The cozy, self-satisfied, formulistic rut that even Unitarians had fallen into was not for him. He spoke of the virtues (though against the state imposition) of temperance, the importance of equality for women, the evils and unchristian nature of the Mexican War, and the need for penal reform as well as many other reforms.

Increasingly, however, justice for blacks came to dominate not only his reform impulse but virtually all of his efforts. In 1845, Parker joined Emerson and Charles Sumner in refusing to speak at the New Bedford Lyceum because blacks had been refused membership. He was driven by the memory of his forebears' fight to win liberty from Great Britain to make liberty a reality for all. While he did not know the peculiar institution at first hand, he recognized its transcendent evil quality just as he recognized the transcendent virtues of Christianity. He amassed a powerful statistical argument that slavery was not economical, but his true power as an abolitionist came from his fervor in invoking the higher law of morality in opposing slavery. Did the Bible accept slavery? he asked, and if the answer was affirmative, he insisted, then the Bible was wrong. On the issue of slavery, as on theological issues, the intuitive truth was not to be denied. Parker would do as he believed Jesus had done: reject statute in favor of what he knew to be right.

Galvanized to greater effort by the Fugitive Slave Law of 1850, Parker became a leader of the Boston Vigilance Committee organized to prevent return of escaped slaves to the South. He called for resistance in the same spirit that the Stamp Act had once been resisted. Men who came for William and Ellen Craft, runaway slaves who were parishioners of Parker, were driven from Boston by abuse and threats. When he married the Crafts, Parker, with an eye for the dramatic gesture, presented to William a Bible for the care of their souls and a sword for the care of his wife's freedom. It would be a sin to hate those who would reenslave them, he told the Crafts, but not to kill in order to preserve their freedom if no other means were available.

Parker's radicalism grew. When Thomas Sims was being taken back to Georgia in 1852, Parker eloquently denounced the "kidnaping" in public and urged the Vigilance Committee to attack the ship on which Sims was confined. The passage of the Kansas-Nebraska Act in 1854 only made matters worse, and Parker, in May of that year, helped organize an abortive raid on the courthouse where the recently arrested fugitive Anthony Burns was held. After Burns was taken away, Parker was indicted along with several others who had supported the raid. Parker was delighted with the idea of presenting his own defense and prepared quite a speech for that purpose. When the indictment was quashed on technical grounds, he had to be satisfied with publishing the defense.

Although he refused to attend a secessionist convention called by radical abolitionists, Parker was increasingly convinced that only war could eliminate slavery, and war was more acceptable to him than slavery. Although saddened by the violence of John Brown's antislavery victories in Kansas, he supported Brown and was a member of the secret Boston Committee of Six that provided moral and financial support for further efforts. He was out of the country at the time of the catastrophic raid on Harpers Ferry but wished he were home to defend the right.

As the 1850's passed, Parker's once-robust health declined, while his activities increased. In addition to his duties as minister of a congregation

formally numbering some seven thousand, he continued writing and antislavery activism. He was delivering approximately one hundred lectures each year all over the East and North. In 1856-1857, he was slowed by pleurisy and other respiratory problems to a mere seventy lectures, but after a vacation in the spring of 1858 and an operation for fistula, he seemed on the road to recovery. He was back to work too soon, and although he managed to preach for New Year's Day of 1859, the next Sunday the congregation gathered only to receive a note that because of a serious lung hemorrhage Parker would not be able to come. Parker was suffering from the greatest killer of the nineteenth century: tuberculosis. His congregation sent him overseas in the hope that better climates would help, but as was so often the case before antibiotics, the disease could not be stopped. He died May 10, 1860, in Florence, Italy.

Summary

Theodore Parker's life reflected much of the American spirit of reform and practicality. As a Transcendentalist, he was part of the first truly American school of philosophy, and his essays have been favorably compared with the work of Emerson. Parker never reached the poetic heights of Emerson, but he was better at clearly and systematically laying out the framework of his thought. He also injected a theme of empirical testing into the intuitive scheme of Transcendentalism. Parker was too good a scholar to accept the miraculous blithely. The less likely an event, the more proof he wanted before he would accept it.

Parker was also an important force in the development of liberal religion. His thought was critical and concrete rather than abstract and metaphysical. He rejected creeds and regarded atheism as impossible, except as the denial of the existence of higher law. Divorcing the essentials of Christianity from all authority but the individual's reason and conscience was clearly a step toward modernity and today's Unitarian-Universalist position that a sincere desire to find spiritual truth is the only requisite for membership.

Parker's reform efforts were also part of the reform tradition that has reappeared periodically throughout American history. His belief that the church should be a driving force in political reform might seem to defy the Jeffersonian tradition of separation of church and state, but Parker did not favor imposition of morality by legislation. The church was to lead by its example and show the society how much better it might be. Parker's reform spirit also had American democratic and egalitarian qualities. Even Abraham Lincoln seems to have learned from him, for Parker used a number of variations of the famous phrase about government of, by, and for the people. At least one example of this was communicated to Lincoln by his law partner, William Herndon, a friend of Parker. As he worked himself to death in the cause of abolitionism, Parker showed many of the finest characteristics of American reformers.

Bibliography

Albrecht, Robert C. *Theodore Parker*. New York: Twayne, 1971. A short but reasonably handled biography.

Castronovo, Russ. "Radical Configurations of History in the Era of American Slavery." *American Literature* 65, no. 3 (September, 1993). Discusses Parker's narrative on fugitive slaves as an example of literature's potential failings.

Chadwick, John W. *Theodore Parker: Preacher and Reformer*. Boston: Houghton Mifflin, 1900. Written by a Unitarian minister who knew and was inspired by Parker, this biography is rather uncritical but is important for its discussion of Parker's role in the development of Unitarianism.

Collins, Robert E. *Theodore Parker: American Transcendentalist: A Critical Essay and a Collection of His Writings*. Metuchen, N.J.: Scarecrow Press, 1973. After a long interpretive essay by Collins, selections from Parker's writings are included for comparison with works by Emerson on similar subjects. Collins' conclusion that Parker was a more important Transcendentalist than Emerson is an overstatement.

Commager, Henry Steele. *Theodore Parker*. Boston: Little Brown, 1936. Commager sometimes lets interpretive passages obscure the basic chronological structure of his book. He does a superb job, however, of setting Parker's life and work in context.

Fellman, Michael. "Theodore Parker and the Abolitionist Role in the 1850's." *Journal of American History* 61 (December, 1974): 666-684. An unusual interpretation portraying Parker as a thoroughgoing racist. Although the author has found some damning quotes, they come from rather scattered sources, and he ignores Parker's eloquent denunciations of black inequality. Parker did harbor some typical nineteenth century misconceptions about race, but this article overstates his views.

Parker, Theodore. *The Slave Power*. Edited by James K. Hosmer. Boston: American Unitarian Association, 1916. This is a collection of Parker's abolitionist writings and is the most convenient source in which to find the text of his most powerful antislavery orations.

Teed, Paul. "Racial Nationalism and Its Challengers: Theodore Parker, John Rock, and the Antislavery Movement." *Civil War History* 41, no. 2 (June, 1995). Focuses on the debate between Parker and Dr. John Rock concerning the fighting spirit exhibited by blacks.

Wilbur, Earl M. *A History of Unitarianism*. Cambridge, Mass.: Harvard University Press, 1945. A standard work on the subject; the section on American Unitarianism is very useful.

Fred R. van Hartesveldt

SIR HENRY PARKES

Born: May 27, 1815; Stoneleigh, Warwickshire, England

Died: April 27, 1896; North Annandale, New South Wales, Australia

Areas of Achievement: Government and politics

Contribution: As Premier of New South Wales for five terms, Parkes successfully promoted immigration to Australia, established public education, and sponsored the movement for federation.

Early Life

Henry Parkes was born in Stoneleigh, Warwickshire, on May 27, 1815. He was the youngest of seven children born to Thomas Parks (the spelling of the name at the time) and his wife Martha. Thomas Parks was a tenant farmer on a property the Parks family had worked for generations, but in 1823 he was forced by accumulated debts to leave, and the entire family went to Birmingham. In the city, all the children had to work, and Henry Parkes, at the age of eight, found employment first as a rope maker and then as a laborer in the brickyards and on the highways, where conditions were harsh and treatment often cruel. He later was able to apprentice himself to a bone and ivory turner.

Although his parents were both uneducated, Henry himself learned to read and write and, at an early age, came to love literature, especially the works of William Shakespeare. Part of his education during this period no doubt included exposure to the extensive political agitation for reform taking place in Birmingham, where impassioned orators addressed mass meetings. Parkes was soon contributing prose and poems to the *Chartist*, and apparently also attended classes at the Mechanic's Institute in Birmingham. Having completed his apprenticeship in 1836, he set up a trade of his own in bone and ivory turning, and was married to Clarinda Varney, the daughter of a well-established businessman who immediately disinherited her for the inappropriate marriage. Parkes, in his long career, was never successful in business, and his first venture failed within two years. The young couple then left Birmingham and moved to London, perhaps with some intention of emigrating, for after a few dire weeks of poverty, in which Parkes was again unable to establish himself, they announced in December of 1838 their decision to leave for Australia.

Parkes, his wife, and their two children sailed in March, 1839, as assisted immigrants on the *Strathfieldsaye*, arriving in Sydney in July of that year, along with a third child born during the voyage. The pastoral boom of the 1830's was in progress and employment was hard to find in the city, so Parkes went up to the Penrith area to work as a laborer on the estate of Sir John Jamison. The difficult and poorly paid work dissatisfied him, and six months later he was in Sydney working first as a salesman for an ironmonger, then as a hand in a brass foundry, and finally as a tide waiter for the Customs Department. The latter position lasted three years and enabled him to set his affairs upon a good enough foundation to try his hand again at his own trade. Subsequently, in 1845, he opened a business in ivory and toy manufacturing, and later he even tried branch shops in Maitland and Geelong, though they soon failed. It was during this period that Parkes put together his first volume of verse, entitled *Stolen Moments*, and found a hundred subscribers willing to finance it. The poems are conventional and didactic, but they do reveal the sincere and heartfelt thinking of a sensitive young man. From the first, however, it was clearly politics that absorbed Parkes's energies; upon his arrival in Australia, he quickly became conversant with the political issues and questions of the day. Gradually, as he became known in Sydney, he became acquainted with leading citizens, and in 1848 he acted as organizing secretary for Robert Lowe's campaign against William Charles Wentworth for the Sydney seat on the Legislative Council. In 1849, Parkes was active in the protest against England's renewal of convict transportation to Australia, becoming a prominent public organizer and speaker. Finally, in 1849, Parkes entered fully into his political career with the founding of a daily newspaper, the *Empire*, a venture backed by a few wealthy friends and encouraged by many others; Parkes was now in a position to command attention and respect.

Life's Work

Parkes worked diligently and with delight at his journalistic labors on the *Empire* from 1853 to 1858. During that period the Legislative Council drafted and adopted a conservative constitution, under the direction of Wentworth, which heavily favored squatters and landowners at the expense of the middle class and small settlers. The liberals opposed it vigorously and formed a constitution committee of their own, of which Parkes was an important member. Although the constitution came into operation in 1856, the liberals had organized themselves into an effective political force and were later able to mitigate some of the more regressive features of the new constitution through the passage of the Electoral Act of 1858 and the Land Acts of 1861. Parkes himself was elected to the new parliament's Legislative Assembly in 1856, having previously been a member of the old Legislative Council in 1854. He was thus able to use the *Empire* as an effective vehicle of liberal political opinion. By 1857, however, Parkes owed more than fifty thousand pounds to the paper's creditors and in 1858 was forced to cease publication of the *Empire*. This latest business failure was a bitter blow to Parkes, for he had invested his time, money, and hopes into the paper, and it led him to consider entering the legal profession at the age of forty-three as a way to secure his economic well-being. Nevertheless, Parkes could not resist politics for long, and between 1858 and 1861 he was alternately in and out of Parliament. Between 1861 and 1863, he was in Great Britain as one of two commissioners sent there by the Legislative Assembly to encourage immigration, his wife, Clarinda, and the children having been left behind in Sydney. During this lecture tour of Great Britain, Parkes met several prominent and influential people, in particular Thomas Carlyle and Richard Cobden, the great advocate of free trade who, Parkes claimed, won him over.

Upon his return to Australia in 1863, Parkes was once again active in politics, and in 1864 he was again elected to Parliament. By this time, Parkes had many supporters and admirers, both for his political views and for his personal qualities of leadership, pious idealism, and sheer energy. He was clearly a politician of promise and had quickly and astutely mastered the skills of the dubious art of manipulative politics. Parkes could be guileful and ruthless, but he was considered effective by all. In 1866, he obtained his first cabinet position as colonial secretary in the government of James Martin, and during that period Parkes was responsible for the passing of the Public Schools Act of 1866, which enlarged and unified the system of national schools and was generally recognized as a progressive piece of legislation. This act was a major accomplishment for Parkes, and his close identification with the bill (and his subsequent position as president of the Council of Education) accorded him considerable public attention. Parkes also convinced Florence Nightingale to send a contingent of trained nurses to Sydney to improve the hospitals in the colony, an achievement of which he was very proud. Although Parkes resigned from the government in 1870, having once again gone into bankruptcy, he returned the following year, and finally, in 1872 became premier at the age of fifty-seven. Thus began the ten-year period in which Parkes was premier three times, alternating with his chief rival, John Robertson (with whom he eventually forged a coalition lasting from 1878 to 1883). This was the summit of his political success, and his knighthood in 1877 seemed to confirm it.

Most of Parkes's accomplishments during this time were legislative and social: He helped reorganize the hospitals; he took an interest in the needs of delinquents and orphans and set up institutions for poor children; he continued to extend education reform; he sought to control the liquor trade more closely; he undertook numerous public works programs for roads, water systems, and railways; and he continued to encourage immigration to Australia from Great Britain. Parkes was well liked by the populace: His manner was dignified and his speech suitably platitudinous, his long white beard and white shock of hair gave him a masterful appearance, and his ministerial efforts appeared to be grounded in democratic principles. Parkes's views on matters were not always sharply distinct from those of his opposition—the 1880's and 1890's was a time of broad liberalism and reform, of widespread belief in "progress"—so his success was more often the result of his political skill and temperament than of his articulation of policy choices.

In 1881, Parkes became ill and was advised by his doctors to go abroad, which he did, while remaining premier, and spent eight months traveling in America and Great Britain. The trip turned into a triumphal procession in which he was hailed by politicians and entertained by eminent people on two continents, including several memorable days with Alfred, Lord Tennyson, who appears to have treated him as a fellow poet. Upon his return in late 1882, though, Parkes found that his political situation had eroded and his government was soon defeated. After a short period serving in the parliament, he once again departed for Great Britain in

1883, in part to find a way to improve his finances, and then returned to Australia in August of 1884. Back in Parliament briefly, he resigned over dissatisfaction with the state of politics, but stood for election again in 1885, when the government's action in sending troops to aid the British in the Sudan conflict angered Parkes. Then, in 1886, at the age of seventy-one, Parkes was once more premier. During the next two years, Parkes made some notable improvements, including the placing of the civil service and the railways under government commissions to avoid the abuses of political patronage. He also virtually banned the immigration of the Chinese, whose great numbers were considered a threat to the wage structure and economy of the country. In doing so, he may have averted serious racial conflicts that could have caused international repercussions.

These successes came at a difficult period for Parkes: Clarinda died in 1888, and his marriage in 1889 to Eleanor Dixon was not acceptable to polite society, or indeed to his own daughters. His financial problems continued: He once again declared bankruptcy in 1887 and assigned his estate to creditors. Yet Parkes, as the grand old man of Australian politics, was undeterred, and he continued to act with vigor and acumen; after a defeat in 1888 put him out of office, he came back within a few months and, as premier in 1889, formed his fifth and last ministry. Nevertheless, his powers of leadership were waning, for the younger generation of politicians was increasingly impatient with his views and his style, and Parkes had some difficulty in maintaining unity among his cabinet ministers. The boldest move Parkes made during this last period in power, and the one for which he is most often remembered, came as a complete surprise to his cabinet and seemed to reassert his capacity to lead. Returning from a trip to Queensland in 1889, he stopped at the town of Tenterfield and delivered a resounding speech advocating, in urgent and eloquent terms, the federation of the then separate Australian colonies. This was by no means a new idea, but Parkes had now thrown his weight behind it and moved rapidly and forcefully to gain his goal.

In 1891, he convened a federal convention in Sydney to draft a constitution. This was achieved, despite considerable difficulties and disagreements, in part because of the resolute efforts of Parkes and the persuasiveness of his impassioned oratory. Attempts were then made to have the new federal constitution ratified by all the colonies. Unfortunately, Parkes was unable to convince the people of New South Wales that this should be their primary concern, and without what he considered sufficient public support, he delayed in putting the measure before Parliament. In 1891, tired and suffering from the consequences of a serious accident, Parkes resigned from office, and the federation bill was not acted upon until after his death.

For the next three years, Parkes continued to serve in Parliament, but his effectiveness was finished. He retired in 1894, but in 1895 made an ill-advised attempt to unseat his old rival within his own party, George Houston Reid, and after an unusually bitter campaign, in which Parkes attacked his previous allies, the free traders and the federalists, he was defeated. During the campaign, Parkes's second wife died, and, left in penniless circumstances with many children, he married a third time, to a young woman named Julia Lynch. Parkes was soon seriously ill with pneumonia, and on April 27, 1896, he died of a heart attack.

Summary

Sir Henry Parkes spent almost half a century in public service, from the antitransportation movement in the 1840's to his last years in Parliament in the 1890's. His rise to prominence and power from humble beginnings is a testimony to the possibilities inherent in a democracy such as Australia's. His accomplishments were of a sort that may seem unglamorous and pedestrian, but they were instrumental in providing New South Wales (and later the whole of Australia) with the firm foundations of a responsive and responsible government. Matters of public education and welfare, of public amenities and works, are of the very fabric of social cohesiveness, and Parkes labored to that end. Not only was Parkes a politician in the sense of a man concerned with policy, but also he was one who understood the nature of party politics; as a leader he knew how to manipulate the machinery of government to his own advantage, and in a number of instances he revealed a certain pettiness and vindictiveness of character which suggests more the ruthless politician than the dignified statesman. Parkes saw himself as a man of the people, and often as the man of the hour, and this belief made him self-confident, though it also blinded him to his own worst defects and motives. The people may have laughed at his posturing and self-importance, at his chronic economic incompetence, but they were seldom scornful of Parkes. They accepted his foibles because they saw him as someone who had their interests at heart, and Parkes did much to repay that confidence.

Parkes is perhaps best remembered for his earliest accomplishment, the Education Act of 1866, and for his last accomplishment, the National Australian Convention for federation in 1891. The twenty-five years spanning these contributions were important years for the young colony, and Parkes did much to assist its growth and maturation. Although he did not live to see the advent of a federated Australia in 1901, he was surely a founding father of the new nation.

Bibliography

Bavin, Sir Thomas. *Sir Henry Parkes: His Life and Work*. Sydney: Angus and Robertson, 1941. This volume contains the John Murtagh Macrossan lectures given by Sir Thomas Bavin in 1940. It is a useful work, providing a generous and judicious overview of Parkes's career and his significant contributions to Australia. Bavin makes good use of contemporary accounts and draws upon Parkes's own autobiography (see below).

Lyne, Charles E. *Life of Sir Henry Parkes*. Sydney: Angus and Robertson, 1896; London: Unwin, 1897. This is a very early biography of Parkes and contains some interesting anecdotal information.

Martin, A. W. *Henry Parkes*. Melbourne: Oxford University Press, 1964. This small booklet is a fine introduction to Parkes. Martin gives a balanced account and, in a short space, is able to draw a sympathetic and incisive portrait of the man. Some well-chosen illustrations accompany the text.

Palmer, Vance. *National Portraits*. London: Angus and Robertson, 1940. This is a well-known collection of twenty-five brief lives of representative Australians. The chapter on Parkes, subtitled "The Politician," places his achievement within the context of the emerging nation. Stylishly written.

Parkes, Henry. *Fifty Years in the Making of Australian History*. London and New York: Longman, 1892. Written near the end of his life, this autobiography begins with Parkes's arrival in Australia in 1839 and ends with the federation controversy of 1892. It is very much an apologia but, despite its tendentiousness, gives an excellent picture of the period.

Tennyson, Charles, and Hope Dyson. *Tennyson, Lincolnshire, and Australia*. Lincoln: Lincolnshire Association and the Tennyson Society, 1974. This is a curious work, drawing upon the association of Parkes with the poet Tennyson. Contains some of their private correspondence.

Paul Kane

FRANCIS PARKMAN

Born: September 16, 1823; Boston, Massachusetts
Died: November 8, 1893; Jamaica Plain, Massachusetts
Area of Achievement: Historical scholarship
Contribution: Parkman was the greatest of the nineteenth century American patrician historians. He combined extensive research with an unparalleled literary artistry that continues to excite the imagination of readers. For many years, Parkman's seven-part series *France and England in North America* (1865-1892) was regarded as the definitive history of the three-sided struggle among the Indians, French, and English for dominion over the continent.

Early Life

Francis Parkman was born in Boston on September 16, 1823, the son of Francis and Caroline (Hall) Parkman. His paternal grandfather had been one of the city's wealthiest merchants; his father was pastor of the Old North Church and a pillar of Boston's Federalist-Unitarian establishment. On his mother's side, he traced his ancestry to the Puritan John Cotton. Because of his fragile health, Parkman was sent at the age of eight to live on his maternal grandfather's farm and attended school in nearby Medford. He returned to Boston at age thirteen, finished his preparatory work at the Chauncey Place School, and entered Harvard in 1840. He had acquired from his roamings on a stretch of untamed woodland at the edge of his grandfather's farm a romantic attachment to nature in the wild. His reading of the novels of James Fenimore Cooper sparked his interest in Indians, "the American forest," and the "Old French War." He was temperamentally a compulsively intense personality, driven by "passion" and "tenacious eagerness." During his sophomore year at Harvard, he appears to have decided upon what became his life's work: to write the dual story of the conquest of the Indians by the French and English and their struggle in turn for mastery. "The theme," he later recalled, "fascinated me, and I was haunted by wilderness images day and night."

At Harvard, Parkman was active in student extracurricular affairs, serving as president of the Hasty Pudding Club. He received sufficiently respectable grades in his course work for selection to Phi Beta Kappa. He spent his summer vacations tramping and canoeing in the forests of northern New En-

gland and the adjacent parts of Canada. Parkman hoped—in vain, as events turned out—that a strenuous regimen of outdoor living would strengthen his sickness-prone physique. He simultaneously took the opportunity to begin collecting material for his planned history project, filling his notebook with measurements of forts, descriptions of battle sites, reminiscences of survivors, and names and addresses of people in possession of old letters. In the autumn of 1843, he suffered a nervous illness and temporarily left Harvard for a tour of Europe to recuperate. He returned in time to be graduated with his class in August, 1844. At his father's behest, he went on to law school at Harvard. Although profiting from his exposure to the rules for the testing and use of evidence, he could not muster much enthusiasm for the law as such. His interests were primarily literary. His first appearance in print came in 1845, when he published in the *Knickerbocker Magazine* five sketches based upon his vacation trips. Although he was awarded his LL.B. in January, 1846, he never applied for admission to the bar.

After receiving his law degree, Parkman set out on what proved to be the formative experience of his life—a trip to the Western plains, partly in the hope of improving his health, partly to observe at first hand Indian life. Camping for several weeks with a band of Sioux Indians, he immersed himself in their habits, customs, and ways of thinking. During those weeks he contracted a mysterious ailment that left him a broken man physically on his return to Boston in October, 1846. His eyesight was so impaired that he could barely read, and he suffered from a nervous condition that made him unable to concentrate for longer than brief spurts. He still managed to dictate to a cousin who had accompanied him an account of their adventures that was serialized as "The Oregon Trail" in the *Knickerbocker Magazine* over a two-year span beginning in February, 1847. The account came out in book form in 1849 under the title *The California and Oregon Trail* (the shorter title was resumed with the 1872 edition). Parkman's experience with the Sioux shattered any illusions he may have gained from reading novels about the noble savage. "For the most part," he underlined, "a civilized white man can discover very few points of sympathy between his own nature and that of an Indian. With every disposition to do justice to their good qualities, he must be conscious that an impassable gulf lies between him and his red brethren. Nay, so alien to himself do they appear, that, after breathing the air of the prairie for a few months or weeks, he begins to look upon them as a troublesome and dangerous species of wild beast."

Life's Work

In 1848, Parkman began work on what became *History of the Conspiracy of Pontiac and the Indian War After the Conquest of Canada* (1851). He had a frame built of parallel wires to guide his hand while writing with his eyes closed in a dark room. For the most part, however, he relied upon others reading the source materials to him and transcribing his words. At first, his progress was painfully slow—the readings limited to a half-hour per sitting and his output averaging six lines a day. Gradually, however, he pushed himself to work for longer periods and successfully completed the two volumes within two and a half years. The work dealt with the Indian uprising in 1763-1765 against English occupation of the Western territories after the French surrender. His purpose, he explained, was "to portray the American forest and the American Indian at the period when both received their final doom." He divided his story into two distinct phases. During the first, the Indians triumphantly pushed the English back; in the second, the English turned the tide in a successful counterattack. Parkman's portrayal of Pontiac as the central figure on the Indian side was effective drama but inaccurate history. Later scholars have found that Pontiac was simply one Indian chief among many. The work's larger importance lies in how Parkman, in his introductory background chapters, sketched in outline the theme that he would develop more fully in his seven-part *France and England in North America*: the collision of rival cultures culminating in the English triumph on the Plains of Abraham in September, 1759.

History of the Conspiracy of Pontiac and the Indian War After the Conquest of Canada appeared in 1851. The first installment of *France and England in North America*, titled *Pioneers of France in the New World*, did not come out until 1865. The delay was partly a result of the amount of research involved. The major difficulty, however, was health problems and family tragedies that would have broken the spirit of a weaker personality. On May 13, 1850, Parkman married Catherine Scollay Big-

elow, the daughter of a Boston doctor. The couple had one son and two daughters. In 1853, however, he suffered a relapse in his nervous condition that forced him to give up his historical work temporarily. A man who always needed an interest, Parkman, during his enforced withdrawal from scholarship, wrote his only novel, *Vassall Morton* (1856). Its hero, reflecting Parkman's own image of himself, is a high-spirited, outdoors-loving young man of high social position who succeeds in overcoming melodramatic trials and tribulations. Unfortunately, Parkman himself was unable to cope with his own personal crises at that time. The death of his son in 1857, followed by that of his wife within a year, precipitated a severe breakdown in 1858. Although these health problems kept him out of the fighting, the Civil War had a major influence on his approach to the rivalry between the French and the English in the seventeenth and eighteenth centuries as a struggle, akin to the one under way in his own time, between "Liberty and Absolutism."

Pioneers of France in the New World focuses upon the founding of Quebec in the early seventeenth century under the leadership of Samuel de Champlain. The next volume in the series, *The Jesuits in North America in the Seventeenth Century* (1867), had as its major protagonists the Jesuit missionaries, such as Jean de Brébeuf, Charles Garnier, and Isaac Jogues, who tried to convert the Canadian Indians to Roman Catholicism. The third volume, which appeared in 1869 as *The Discovery of the Great West*, traces the explorations of Robert La Salle in the area of the Great Lakes and then down the Mississippi River and across what is now Texas and Arkansas in the 1670's and 1680's. Parkman's next two titles, *The Old Régime in Canada* (1874) and *Count Frontenac and New France Under Louis XIV* (1877), chronicle the political, social, and military history of New France during the last half of the seventeenth century. Their major theme is the corruption that came to pervade, and undermine, French colonial society despite the valiant, but unsuccessful, bid by Louis de Buade Frontenac to reverse the decay. Fearful lest he die before reaching the climax of his story, Parkman jumped ahead in the two volumes of *Montcalm and Wolfe* (1884) to deal with the final phase of the French-English struggle starting in the early 1750's and culminating in the surrender of Canada in 1763. In 1892, he filled in the gap with the two-volume *A Half-Century of Conflict*, in which he dealt with the fifty years of intermittent conflict from Frontenac's death in 1698 to the beginning of the French and Indian War in the 1750's.

The work rested upon painstaking research in primary sources. Parkman even boasted that the "statements of secondary writers have been accepted only when found to conform to the evidence of contemporaries, whose writings have been sifted and collated with the greatest care." His relied primarily upon the massive compilations of documents that had been published during the "documania" that had swept the United States in the aftermath of the War of 1812. At the same time, Parkman spent freely from the money he inherited from his father to purchase documents and have copies made of archival materials in this country and abroad. When formerly inaccessible La Salle documents became available, he rewrote *The Discovery of the Great West* to incorporate the new information. The revised version appeared in 1879 with the new title *La Salle and the Discovery of the Great West*.

Parkman never succumbed to the illusion of late nineteenth century scientific history that the facts spoke for themselves. "Faithfulness to the truth of history," he emphasized,

> involves far more than a research, however patient and scrupulous, into special facts. Such facts may be detailed with the most minute exactness, and yet the narrative, taken as a whole, may be unmeaning or untrue. The narrator must seek to imbue himself with the life and spirit of the time. He must study events in their bearings near and remote; in the character, habits, and manners of those who took part in them. He must himself be, as it were, a sharer or a spectator of the action he describes.

In pursuit of that goal, Parkman personally visited the sites about which he wrote. One of his major strengths was his feeling for the physical setting in which his story unfolded. His early writings occasionally suffered from labored prose and excessive detail. As time went on, however, his descriptions became terser, his imagery sharper. Parkman saw heroic leaders as the primary shapers of history. His own special forte was the delineation of personality. His technique was to build up a composite portrait by drawing upon his protagonist's own words and the accounts by contemporaries before assaying the individual himself. His appraisal of Frontenac strikingly illustrates his mastery of character portrayal.

What perhaps may be least forgiven him is the barbarity of the warfare that he waged, and the cruelties that he permitted. He had seen too many towns sacked to be much subject to the scruples of modern humanitarianism; yet he was no whit more ruthless than his times and his surroundings, and some of his contemporaries find fault with him for not allowing more Indian captives to be tortured. Many surpassed him in cruelty, none equalled him in capacity and vigor. When civilized enemies were once within his power, he treated them, according to their degree, with a chivalrous courtesy, or a gentle kindness. If he was a hot and pertinacious foe, he was also a fast friend; and he excited love and hatred in about equal measure. His attitude towards public enemies was always proud and peremptory, yet his courage was guided by so clear a sagacity that he never was forced to recede from the position he had taken.

Notwithstanding such attempts at evenhandedness when dealing with individuals, Parkman shared the prejudices of his time and class. He was a vocal opponent of woman's suffrage; his comments on what he called "the mazes of feminine psychology" were almost uniformly unflattering.

No democrat, he made no secret of his contempt for society's lower orders. He dismissed the hard-working German farmers of Pennsylvania as "a swarm of . . . peasants. . . who for the most part were dull and ignorant boors." He was no more enamored of the poorer whites of Colonial Virginia, considering them "of low origin," "vicious," and "as untaught as the warmest friend of popular ignorance could wish." He saw universal manhood suffrage as "the source of all the dangers which threaten the United States"; he pictured the immigrants of his own time as "barbarians . . . masses of imported ignorance and hereditary ineptitude." He was a social Darwinist before the publication of *On the Origin of Species* (1859). When describing in *The Oregon Trail* the "cannibal warfare" he witnessed among fishes in a pond, he ridiculed the dreams by softhearted philanthropists of a peaceful millennium. From minnows to men, he philosophized, life was incessant conflict, and he had no doubt that the outcome of the struggle for North America among the Indians, French, and English accorded with the "law of the survival of the fittest."

A thoroughgoing ethnocentrism marred Parkman's outlook. He pictured the Indians as barbarous savages: treacherous, deceitful, "a murder-loving race" filled with "insensate fury" and animated by "homicidal frenzy." "The Indians," he wrote in a typical descriptive passage, "howled like wolves, yelled like enraged cougars." Their white opponents "were much like the hunters of wolves, catamounts, and other dangerous beasts, except that the chase of this fierce and wily human game demanded far more hardihood and skill." As he put the matter bluntly in an 1886 public letter which dealt with contemporary white-Indian relations, "a few hordes of savages cannot be permitted to hold in perpetual barbarism the land which might sustain a hundred millions of civilized men." Despite his admiration for some individual Frenchmen, they were an inferior breed compared to the Anglo-Saxon. "The Germanic race, and especially the Anglo-Saxon branch of it," he wrote in his conclusion to *The Old Régime in Canada*, "is peculiarly masculine, and, therefore, peculiarly fitted for self-government. It submits its action habitually to the guidance of reason . . . . The French Celt is cast in a different mould. . . . he is impatient of delay, is impelled always to extremes, and does not readily sacrifice a present inclination to an ultimate good." That the English won and the French lost was no accident. "The cause lies chiefly in the vast advantage drawn by England from the historical training of her people in habits of reflection, forecast, industry, and self-reliance,—a training which enabled them to adopt and maintain an invigorating system of self-rule, totally inapplicable to their rivals."

Despite the almost constant pain he suffered, Parkman did not surrender to invalidism. He had a wide circle of friends and carried on an extensive correspondence. He had an excellent sense of humor, and his writings are dotted with sharp quips. He never lost his love for the outdoors and continued his camping trips as much as his health permitted. He took up flower-growing as a hobby during the 1850's, when incapacitated from pursuing his scholarly work, and grew so fascinated that the study of horticulture became a passion second only to history. His major achievement in this line was his development of a hybrid crimson lily named *Lilium Parkmanni* in his honor. His specialty, however, was roses, and his *The Book of Roses* (1866) was regarded for many years as the best guide to their cultivation. He served as a member of the Harvard Overseers (1868-1871 and 1874-1876) and as a fellow of the corporation (1875-1888), he was one of the founders of the Archeological Institute of America in 1879, and he played a leading role in the establishment of the American School of Classical Studies in Athens, Greece. Shortly after finishing *A Half-Century of Conflict*, he suffered an attack of pleurisy that proved almost fatal. He died November 8, 1893, of peritonitis at his home in Jamaica Plain (now part of Boston).

Summary

Commentators have differed about Parkman's place in American historiography. There are those who put him with the literary historians of the romantic school such as John L. Motley, William H. Prescott, and George Bancroft. Others see him as a forerunner of the late nineteenth century scientific historians. In a sense, both views are correct: Parkman had a foot in both camps. He attracted an immense readership during his lifetime. His friend Henry Adams summed up the predominant contemporary appraisal when he rated Parkman "in the front rank of living English historians." At the same time, Parkman enjoyed a higher reputation among professional academic historians than any other of his fellow amateurs except possibly Adams himself. Those who dealt with the same period not simply followed Parkman's chronological framework but also relied heavily upon his work for information. One scholar went so far as to state that "Parkman never makes a mistake, certainly never a glaring one." Even Vernon L. Parrington in his *Main Currents in American Thought* (1927-1930) acknowledged that the "Brahmin mind has contributed to American letters no more brilliant work." As late as 1953, the account in the standard *Literary History of the United States* (1948) concluded that "Parkman's whole method may be accurately summarized as an attempt to bring back the past just as it was."

More recently, Parkman's reputation has suffered an eclipse. Judged by modern standards, he had major shortcomings as a historian. The French-English rivalry in the New World was only a minor aspect of the worldwide struggle under way between those powers, but Parkman largely failed to explore the dynamics of that broader conflict. Even as regards its North American phase, Parkman's episodic, narrative approach focusing upon heroic personalities runs counter to the prevailing tendency to emphasize the role of larger social, economic, and cultural forces. The heaviest attack has come from ethnographers over Parkman's treatment of the Indians; he has even been accused of deliberately distorting evidence to put the Indians in the worst possible light. Such criticisms miss the point. As Frederick Jackson Turner rightly observed, Parkman was "the greatest painter of historical pictures that this country—perhaps it is not too much to say, that any country—has produced." The chorus of praise greeting the 1983 republication of *France and England in North America* in the Library of America series attests Parkman's "extraordinary power" as a literary artist. Notwithstanding its limitations, Parkman's history constitutes what a reviewer of the new edition aptly called "our great national epic."

Bibliography

Doughty, Howard. *Francis Parkman*. New York: Macmillan, 1962. Although biographical in format, this work is primarily an appraisal of Parkman's writings, focusing upon their literary and artistic qualities from the point of view of a layman rather than a professional historian.

Gale, Robert L. *Francis Parkman*. New York: Twayne, 1973. A rather pedestrian biographical survey followed by volume-by-volume summaries of the major works.

Jacobs, Wilbur R. "Lessons from the Master: Francis Parkman, Historian as Hero of the Early American West." *Journal of the West* 36, no. 4 (October, 1997). Jacobs provides an account of Parkman's development as a "hero-writer."

Jennings, Francis. "Francis Parkman: A Brahmin Among Untouchables." *William and Mary Quarterly* 42 (July, 1985): 305-328. An important attempt to debunk Parkman's reputation for accuracy and impartiality by exposing his racism and his distortion of the evidence in order to place the Indians in the worst possible light.

Parkman, Francis, Jr. *The Oregon Trail*. Edited by Bernard Rosenthal. Oxford and New York: Oxford University Press, 1996. This is Parkman's own detailed account of his journey west.

Pease, Otis A. *Parkman's History: The Historian as Literary Artist*. New Haven, Conn.: Yale University Press, 1953. A brief but perceptive analysis of "the preconceptions and interests" shaping Parkman's historical approach.

Van Tassel, David D. *Recording America's Past: An Interpretation of the Development of Historical Studies in America, 1607-1884*. Chicago: University of Chicago Press, and Cambridge: Cambridge University Press, 1960. Places Parkman in the context of the development of historical scholarship in the United States.

Vitzthum, Richard C. *The American Compromise: Theme and Method in the Histories of Bancroft, Parkman, and Adams*. Norman: University of Oklahoma Press, 1974. Primarily an exercise in "literary criticism" based upon detailed textual explication.

Wade, Mason. *Francis Parkman: Heroic Historian*. New York: Viking Press, 1942. The fullest and most detailed biography, based upon thorough research of Parkman's correspondence, journals, and notes. The work is marred only by the author's tendency toward hagiography.

John Braeman

CHARLES STEWART PARNELL

Born: June 27, 1846; Avondale, County Wicklow,
Ireland
Died: October 6, 1891; Brighton, Sussex, England
Area of Achievement: Politics
Contribution: Parnell fused disparate peoples and
organizations into a cohesive Irish Nationalist
party for the purpose of achieving home rule for
Ireland.

Early Life

Charles Stewart Parnell was born on June 27,
1846, at Avondale, the Parnell estate in County
Wicklow. He was the eighth child of John Henry
and Delia Stewart Parnell. His father's family was
Anglo-Irish, while his mother was of American ancestry, although not much should be made of this
fact. His heritage was Protestant, but he was to become more of an unbeliever than a believer. Parnell
was hardly serious about his education, even during his three and a half years at Cambridge. When
he left Cambridge, he returned to Avondale, which
he had inherited on his father's death in 1859.

Parnell was a tall, athletic-looking man. He wore
a beard and a mustache, but contemporaries regarded his eyes, which were a reddish-brown, as
his most distinctive feature. He possessed an iron
will, but was mild and gentle in personal inter-
course. A brother described him as having a "courteous but frigid exterior," and claimed that he became even more reserved as he matured. Parnell
also had a nervous temperament.

Life's Work

Parnell was first returned to the House of Commons in April, 1875, as a member for Meath. He
entered Parliament as a proponent of home rule for
Ireland, and it was as a member of Parliament that
he was to make his name, although his maiden
speech was uneventful except for the assertion that
Ireland was a nation, not a geographical fragment
of England. He was early recognized as one of the
more advanced "home rulers" and became a supporter of Joseph Biggar's policy of obstructing English legislation as a way to pressure England into
making concessions to Ireland. The most blatant
use of this procedure occurred on July 31 and August 1, 1877, when the House was kept in session
continuously for forty-five hours as seven Irishmen, including Parnell, thwarted the wishes of
three hundred Englishmen.

By 1879, Parnell was becoming the leader of the
nationalist movement. He was president of the
Home Rule Confederation of Great Britain and of
the recently formed Irish National Land League
but had not been chosen as Isaac Butt's successor
as leader of the Irish parliamentary party after
Butt's death. That honor had gone to an avowed
moderate, William Shaw, although his tenure was
short-lived. After the general election of 1880,
which saw Parnell begin to assert his authority over
the party and to emerge from the election with
twenty-four supporters out of sixty-three home rulers, Parnell was elected as chairman of the parliamentary party. One of his supporters for the leadership was William Henry O'Shea, and it was not
long before Parnell was addressing O'Shea's wife,
Katherine, as "My dearest love." This was an association that was to have momentous consequences.

Bringing Irishmen of different persuasions together was Parnell's great accomplishment. From
1879 to 1885, he devoted his energies in and out of
Parliament to promoting the national cause. In Parliament, he could be cooperative, as he was in enacting the Third Reform Bill, or he could be intransigent, as he and his supporters were in using the
tactic of obstruction. Out of Parliament, Parnell
was occupied with the development of tactics that
would demonstrate to the Irish people that he was
the leader who could deliver concessions that were
desired by both the extremists and the constitutionalists. He thus flirted with the Land League for a
time and partially initiated and then supported the
practice of making social lepers out of those Irishmen who dared to lease a property from which an
Irish tenant had been evicted, a practice that became known as boycotting. His association with
the extremists resulted in his being imprisoned in
Kilmainham jail from October 13, 1881, to May 2,
1882. This period of imprisonment only solidified
Parnell's hold on Ireland. By August, 1885, John
O'Leary, the Fenian leader and editor of the *Irish
People* was remarking that "Mr. Parnell is the undoubted choice of the Irish people just now, and as
long as that is so, and clearly so, I think it is the
duty of all Irishmen, even Irishmen of my way of
thinking, to take heed that they throw no obstacle
in the way of his carrying out the mandate with
which he has been intrusted."

Parnell's career was fast approaching its climax.
Parnell saw that climax as the grant of self-govern-

ment to Ireland. To that end, he proceeded to prepare for the general election of 1885 under the newly enlarged franchise of the reforms of 1884-1885. What he wanted to emerge from the election was a highly disciplined party of eighty or more members in the House of Commons that would hold the balance of power between the two English parties and would thereby be in a position to play one off against the other to see which would make the most concessions for Irish support. The elections produced the desired results. Parnell secured the election of eighty-six home rulers, a clear demonstration that he was the acknowledged leader of Ireland, and even of Ulster, for his party had secured a majority of one in that province. All home rulers had taken the pledge that they would vote as instructed by the leaders of the party. Furthermore, neither English party had emerged with a majority over its opponent and the Irish combined. Parnell could, therefore, keep either party in or out of power as he chose. He was, even more so than when Timothy M. Healy applied the term to him in 1880, "the uncrowned king of Ireland," a title that was to cling to his name to his death and beyond.

While circumstances looked promising for Parnell and the Irish, reality was to prove otherwise. The Conservatives concluded that there was no future for them in making concessions to Ireland, and the Liberals were not united in support of concessions. William Ewart Gladstone led those Liberals who were willing to concede home rule, but Joseph Chamberlain, leader of the Radical section, and Lord Hartington (Spencer Compton Cavendish, later eighth Duke of Devonshire), leader of the Whig section, were to split from the Liberal Party. Gladstone's Home Rule Bill was, therefore, defeated; ninety-three Liberals voted with the Conservatives against it. When a dissolution revealed that the country was even more anti-home rule than Parliament had been, the Conservatives were to come into office and remain in office, except for three years, for a twenty-year period. By the time the Liberals returned to office in 1892, Parnell was dead.

In the intervening years, Parnell's fortunes were to decline, rise to unprecedented heights, and then fall precipitously. Parnell and his party remained associated with the Liberals with the hope that once the Liberals were returned to office a new Home Rule Bill would be introduced and this time it would pass. Even before the First Home Rule Bill was introduced, however, Parnell's enemies were plotting his downfall. Their plan was to link him with criminal activities in Ireland, and they found a willing and naïve accomplice in the *Times*. A series of forged letters were sold to that paper and were printed in 1887 under the heading of "Parnellism and Crime," linking Parnell to the so-called Phoenix Park murders, the murder of the newly appointed chief secretary and the undersecretary in Phoenix Park in 1882.

The publication of the series coincided with the debate in Parliament on a new coercion bill. The timing of publication, along with the fact that the letters had been previously submitted to a distinguished lawyer, who was skeptical of their authenticity and who advised the *Times* against publication, has led some to speculate that the *Times* and the government were working together to discredit Parnell and Irish nationalism, thereby enabling the government to enact stringent coercive measures against Irish nationalists. Whatever the truth may be, Parnell's response to the accusations was one of outward indifference. In Parliament, he denied that he had written the letters, but he took no further immediate action. Parnell's inaction was partly a result of ill health. For some time he had been suffering from illness, about which the details are unknown, but which may have been Bright's disease.

When Parnell did take action, he asked for the appointment of a select committee to investigate the charges against him. The government refused a select committee but did enact legislation for the appointment of a special commission to investigate not only the charge that Parnell was implicated in the Phoenix Park murders but also the activities of the Land League, with which Parnell was no longer on the best of terms. In other words, the question of whether Parnell had written the letters which implicated him in the Phoenix Park murders was to be only a minor part of the investigation. The government had apparently become aware that the letters were suspect, and they did not want Parnell and Ireland to be regarded as injured parties when it was proven that Parnell had not written the letters attributed to him. Rather, the English government wanted to continue to rule Ireland with a strong hand under the new coercion law that had been enacted. The special commission legislation was passed, and the three judges conducted their investigation. The letters were proven to be forgeries, and the forger was revealed. The special commission also investigated the Land League, howev-

er, and when their report was debated in the Commons, government spokesmen and supporters dwelt upon the activities of the Land League rather than upon the fact that Parnell had been vindicated.

Parnell's vindication came in 1889, but almost immediately he had a new problem. Captain O'Shea sued his wife for divorce and named Parnell as corespondent. The divorce case ruined Parnell's political career and was partially responsible for his death. O'Shea secured his divorce and Parnell then married Katherine, but his party removed him as leader and the Catholic Church would no longer support him. With a segment of the party remaining loyal to him, he believed that he could recoup his position by demonstrating that he retained the support of the Irish people. Consequently he ran in by-elections, but this effort was too much of a strain for his already weakened constitution. He died in his wife's arms on October 6, 1891.

Summary

Charles Stewart Parnell was a remarkable man. A landowner and a Protestant, he became the leader of tenant farmers and Catholics in a nationalist movement that came close to achieving self-government for Ireland. He was also remarkable in that he was able to moderate between the constitutionalists and the extremists and to convince them to cooperate in a common objective. That he almost succeeded is a testimony to his ability, vision, and firmness of will. No other Irish leader, except perhaps Eamon de Valera, has since held such influence over the Irish people.

Bibliography

Abels, Jules. *The Parnell Tragedy*. London: Bodley Head, and New York: Macmillan, 1966. A popular account of the life of Parnell. It contains neither footnotes nor bibliography. The reader must use caution in separating fact from speculation.

Connell, Christopher. "Desire in the Classroom: The Lessons of Parnell." *Studies in Literary Imagination* 30, no. 2 (Fall 1997). Connell examines the treatment given Parnell in two Irish textbooks. In an attempt to remain neutral, the books deal with his achievements but ignore his private life, thereby missing the consequences his fall had on Irish society.

Foster, R. F. *Charles Stewart Parnell: The Man and His Family*. Hassocks: Harvester Press, and Atlantic Highlands, N.J.: Humanities Press, 1976. This is a supplement to the Lyons biography that deals more with the personal side of Parnell's life.

Jenkins, Roy. *Sir Charles Dilke: A Victorian Tragedy*. London: Collins, 1958; as *Victorian Scandal: A Biography of the Right Honourable Gentleman Sir Charles Dilke*, New York: Chilmark Press, 1965. While Parnell is not prominent in this work, it concerns a divorce case of another active politician; Jenkins speculates that the two cases have some things in common.

Larkin, Emmett. *The Roman Catholic Church in Ireland and the Fall of Parnell, 1888-1891*. Chapel Hill: University of North Carolina Press, 1979. This is a volume in Larkin's history of the Roman Catholic Church in Ireland and is especially useful for understanding Parnell's relations with the church.

Lyons, F. S. L. *Charles Stewart Parnell*. London: Collins, and New York: Oxford University Press, 1977. The best biography of Parnell by one of the best of Irish historians. A thoroughly scholarly work.

————. *The Fall of Parnell*. Toronto: University of Toronto Press, and London: Routledge, 1960. The best discussion of the divorce case and all its implications.

————. *Ireland Since the Famine*. London: Weidenfeld and Nicolson, and New York: Scribner, 1971. A good general history of Ireland for the period of Parnell's life.

O'Brien, R. Barry. *Life of Charles Stewart Parnell*. 2 vols. New York: Harper, and London: Nelson, 1898. A chronological life of Parnell by one of his contemporaries.

Oldstone-Moore, Christopher. "The Fall of Parnell: Hugh Price Hughes and the Nonconformist Conscience." *Eire-Ireland: A Journal of Irish Studies* 30, no. 4 (Winter 1996). Examination of Hugh Price Hughes' opposition to Parnell as a representative of Irish Home Rule interests. Hughes is often blamed for Parnell's downfall due to his criticism of Parnell's private life.

Albert A. Hayden

LOUIS PASTEUR

Born: December 27, 1822; Dôle, Jura, France
Died: September 28, 1895; Villenueve-l'Étang, near Saint Cloud, France
Areas of Achievement: Chemistry and biology
Contribution: Pasteur, by his pioneering work in crystallography, established the discipline of stereochemistry (left-handedness and right-handedness in organic structures). He spent the bulk of his career founding modern microbiology and making exciting discoveries in immunology.

Early Life

Louis Pasteur was born in Dôle on December 27, 1822, but he grew up in Arbois, a nearby and smaller town in which his father, Jean-Joseph, a veteran of Napoleon I's army, operated a tannery. His mother, Jeanne-Étiennette Roqui, was a gardener's daughter. The best portraits of his parents were done in pastels by young Louis himself, who was an excellent artist. He like them, was of medium height and dark-haired with a high forehead. His nearsightedness was said to have enhanced his ability to see small details close up. In his maturity, he wore the beard and mustache of most males of his time.

Louis was a late bloomer, and his grades in school were only slightly above average. He attended the Collège d'Arbois, and late in his career there, he became inspired and desired to enter the prestigious École Normale Supérieure in Paris. He left Arbois in 1838 and entered Barbet's preparatory school in Paris but became so homesick that his father had to bring him home. In 1839, Louis enrolled in the Collège Royal at Besançon, in his home province of Franche Comté. Away from home but not far from it, the young scholar partially supported himself with a student assistantship and received his bachelor of science degree in 1842. Although accepted to the École Normale Supérieure, Pasteur believed that he was not yet ready to enter, and thus he spent a year at Barbet's preparatory school before finally matriculating in the fall of 1843.

Pasteur did well at the École Normale Supérieure, passing high on the teachers' examination in 1845 and quite high in his comprehensive exams the following year. In 1847, he received his doctorate in chemistry and soon found employment as a professor, first at the University of Dijon, where he taught physics for a semester, and then at the University of Strasbourg, where in 1849 he obtained a position in the chemistry department. It was also in Strasbourg that Pasteur met Marie Laurent, the twenty-two-year-old woman whom he soon made his wife. Their marriage lasted a lifetime and produced five children, although three of the daughters died early from typhoid. Throughout his life, Pasteur was politically conservative except for a youthful involvement in the Revolution of 1848, and he was a thoroughgoing supporter of the Second Empire under Napoleon III. Indeed, he received considerable grants and recognition from the emperor and empress personally.

Life's Work

As early as 1848, Pasteur was publishing his work on crystals, which he had begun for his doctoral research. Working with tartaric acid, he searched for the solution as to why one form of the acid twisted to the right the light rays passing through it, while another form (paratartaric or racemic acid), did not rotate the plane of the light rays. The two forms of the acid were chemically identical, but Pasteur discovered that racemic acid had crystals which were either left-handed or right-handed—each the mirror image of the other. Using tweezers, he laboriously hand-separated the dried crystals into left and right piles. Then he dissolved each pile and found to his satisfaction that the left-handed crystal solution rotated light rays to the left and the right-handed to the right. When the two solutions were then mixed in equal amounts, no rotation occurred—the mixture was optically inactive. This breakthrough established Pasteur's reputation as a scientist, because it opened the door to stereochemistry, a new way of studying the molecular composition of substances. Pasteur had begun to understand dissymmetry, which characterizes not only organic forms but most inorganic forms as well.

Pasteur, as he continued his research on crystallography, moved to the University of Lille, where he served as a dean as well as a professor from 1854 to 1857. While at Lille, Pasteur was approached by a man seeking expert help in explaining why some of his vats of sugar-beet juice, which he was fermenting prior to distilling alcohol from the mash, had been going bad. Pasteur had been urged by his superiors to serve practical ends as well as pure science, and, as it happened, Pasteur's

own research into the composition of organic molecules had caused him to want to know how fermentation modified those molecules. Pasteur was eager to use the sugar-beet industry as a laboratory.

The scientist examined the vats and took samples. Under his vertically mounted microscope, Pasteur detected small, round globules of yeast from the "good" samples but found that the "bad" ones contained rodlike microorganisms, bacilli. He assumed that the yeasts, which he observed multiplying by budding, were the cause of fermenting beet sugar into the desired alcohol, but the rods were a mystery.

After considerable effort, he succeeded in formulating a soup in which he was able to culture the bacilli. After introducing only a few of the rods into the sterile solution, he saw them multiply into millions of vibrating germs. They were alive, and they were what crowded out the yeast and transformed the sugar into lactic acid—the acid of sour milk. Pasteur wrote a paper on his discovery entitled "Mémoire sur la fermentation appellée lactique" (memoir on the fermentation called lactic), which was published by the French Academy of Sciences in 1857. This paper was hailed as the initial proof that germs cause fermentation.

Pasteur's article of 1857 was the second great stride of his career, and as a result he was called to Paris and made director of scientific studies at the École Normale Supérieure. His elevated post, however, did not provide him with his own laboratory, so he created one for himself in two rooms in the attic. There he proceeded to demonstrate the extreme complexity of the processes involved in alcoholic fermentation. Chemists had previously expressed the conversion of sugar into ethyl alcohol and carbonic acid by means of a simple, inorganic formula, but Pasteur detailed the complex role of brewer's yeast in digesting the sugar into a number of compounds, of which alcohol was only the most important.

Continuing his work on microbes, Pasteur found that some bacteria required the absence of oxygen in order to survive, whereas others needed oxygen to live. The former he termed "anaerobic," and he named the latter "aerobic"—nomenclature used by science to the present day, as Pasteur was the first to bring to scientific and public attention the two different kinds of bacteria. Antoni van Leeuwenhoek and Lazzaro Spallanzani had earlier observed anaerobic bacteria but had failed to attract much notice to the discovery.

Pasteur then conducted a lengthy experiment on the canning of food, a process discovered by his fellow countryman François Appert in the time of Napoleon I. Pasteur showed conclusively that the heating of sealed containers killed the microbes that caused fermentation and putrefaction. That was the secret of food preservation. He explained that microbes are necessary for decomposition of organic matter into its inorganic components and that without such microbes all the plants and animals that had ever lived would have their dead remains choking the surface of the planet.

Pasteur also proved that microbes came only from other microbes, that life came from life, and that there was no spontaneous generation. Leeuwenhoek two hundred years earlier had disproved spontaneous generation, but few had been willing to listen. Pasteur was so insistent that he forced people to pay attention. To illustrate that microbes can be carried through the air, Pasteur and his assistants exposed many sterile cultures briefly to the air of a deep basement in Paris, the surface-level air in Paris, the air of a vineyard on a hill of the Jura Mountains, and finally the air high on the slopes of Mont Blanc. Pasteur found that the higher and more rural the area the lower the percentage of cultures that were contaminated. The only low-lying location that had pure air was the nearly draft-free deep cellar in Paris.

Next Pasteur and his chief assistant, Émile Duclaux, set up a makeshift field laboratory in Pasteur's hometown of Arbois. Wine producers in the area had been having difficulty, as their output was sometimes ropy, acid, oily, or bitter. Looking through his microscope, Pasteur startled the vintners by correctly pronouncing what was wrong with each sample without tasting it. To prevent the spoilage, Pasteur recommended a treatment that came to be known as "pasteurization"—heating the wine, once fermentation was complete, to a certain temperature below boiling and holding it there for a specified period of time. The temperature could be lower if the time were lengthened and vice versa. When farmers objected to cooking their wine, Pasteur explained that the natural acidity of their product made it less hospitable to germs and that the required temperature was really quite low. Milk, beer, cider, and other liquids could be similarly preserved, and Pasteur designed special equipment for commercial pasteurization.

One of Pasteur's former professors, J. B. Dumas, begged Pasteur to investigate a disease of silkworms, pébrine, a blight that was devastating a main industry in south central France. Between 1865 and 1870, Pasteur spent several months of each year in and around Alais (modern Alès), the center of the nation's silk culture. Pasteur's confusion about what ailed the silkworms was compounded, as he eventually discovered, by the fact that the worms were suffering not from a single disease but from two different microbial infections.

Before he attained a breakthrough in the silkworm diseases, however, Pasteur suffered a cerebral hemorrhage in October, 1868, at the age of forty-five. Many thought that he would surely die; his left side was completely paralyzed. Yet he regained partial use of his left side, and he walked, though with a severe limp. He depended on his assistants to do much of the manipulation required by his experiments, but his mind remained keen, and he never relinquished control over his laboratories. He had finished the rescue of the silk industry by 1870.

Pasteur, whose name was a household word in France and who had greatly assisted the French sugar-beet, wine, vinegar, silk, and beer industries, moved comparatively late in his career into the field of immunology. He confirmed the work of Robert Koch in Germany, who had discovered the complete life cycle of the anthrax bacillus, the cause of the animal (and sometimes human) disease anthrax, but he greatly desired to outdo the German. After considerable experimentation with animals, Pasteur announced that he had invented a vaccine, composed of weakened bacilli, which if injected into an animal would confer immunity against anthrax.

It was something Koch had never done. Skeptical French veterinarians in 1881 challenged Pasteur to a dramatic public experiment to test the immunization. Pasteur's assistants cautioned against accepting, as the vaccine had not been field-tested and a public failure could be devastating. Pasteur was adamant, however, and they caught the train for Pouilly-le-Fort, a village near Melun, southeast of Paris. Twenty-four sheep, one goat, and six cows were immunized, it was hoped, by Pasteur's assistant, the physician Émile Roux, with two injections of serum twelve days apart. Two weeks later, those animals and an equal-sized control group of animals were injected with a powerful culture of anthrax bacilli. All the immunized animals survived; all the others died; France went wild with the news.

Pasteur next turned to conquer rabies, probably motivated by childhood memories of an attack on his town by a rabid wolf. Sucking foam from the mouths of caged mad dogs, Pasteur and his men never found a responsible microbe, as hydrophobia is caused by a virus—something too small to be seen with a light microscope—but the scientists made a vaccine and used it successfully on animals. Then a mother brought in her son, bitten by a mad dog and sure to die. Pasteur ordered the child inoculated, and the child lived. Soon others came, even from distant Russia and the United States, and, except where too much time had elapsed, the cure was effective.

It was fitting climax to a brilliant career. On his seventieth birthday, a great celebration was held to honor Pasteur. Pasteur's son had to deliver his father's speech, in which Pasteur said that it gave him immense happiness to "have contributed in some way to the progress and good of humanity."

Summary

Louis Pasteur is best known for his work in bacteriology, a field which he virtually founded. His discoveries contributed greatly to the control and treatment of cholera, diphtheria, tetanus, tuberculosis, and other diseases. His studies of the transmission of infection also contributed to the development of antiseptic procedures in surgery. His discovery of vaccines to prevent anthrax and other diseases of animals had an enormous impact not only in France but also worldwide. Although less widely known than his contributions to immunology, Pasteur's pioneering researches in crystallography were of fundamental importance. Among the many great scientists of the nineteenth century, Pasteur stands in the first rank.

Bibliography

Compton, Piers. *The Genius of Louis Pasteur.* London and New York: Macmillan, 1932. A readable and thorough account of Pasteur's life and contributions, this book has several interesting photographs of people, places, and events in his life.

Cuny, Hilaire. *Louis Pasteur: The Man and His Theories.* Translated by Patrick Evans. London: Souvenir Press, and New York: Eriksson, 1963. This book provides detail without being overwhelming. Cuny's explanations of the technical aspects of Pasteur's work are readily comprehensible to the layperson.

Debre, P. *Louis Pasteur*. Translated by Elborg Forster. Baltimore: Johns Hopkins University Press, 1998. A fair and detailed account of Pasteur's public and private life. Heavily based on Pasteur's own notebooks and writings, Debre counters Geison's book *The Private Science of Louis Pasteur*, which accuses Pasteur of scientific misconduct.

De Kruif, Paul. *Microbe Hunters*. New York: Harcourt Brace, 1926; London: Cape, 1927. Although more superficial than the full-length biographies, this book has two exquisitely entertaining chapters on Pasteur that convey the excitement inherent in making scientific breakthroughs that result in saving lives and industries.

Dubos, René. *Louis Pasteur: Free Lance of Science*. Translated by Elizabeth Dussauze. New York: Scribner, 1976. This book is thorough and gives a good perspective on Pasteur. Includes a large photographic section.

Duclaux, Émile. *Pasteur: The History of a Mind*. Translated by Erwin Smith and Florence Hedges. Philadelphia and London: Saunders, 1920. Written by a man who studied and worked under Pasteur, this book provides many insights into Pasteur's thinking. Duclaux deals exclusively with Pasteur's professional life and not with his personal life, and gives a balanced treatment with proper credit to Pasteur's rival researchers.

Geison, Gerald L. *The Private Science of Louis Pasteur*. Princeton, N.J.: Princeton University Press, 1995. In this controversial biography based largely on Pasteur's laboratory notebooks, Geison studies aspects of the scientist's work which differ from the public record.

Vallery-Radot, René. *The Life of Pasteur*. Translated by R. L. Devonshire. London: Constable, and New York: McClure, Phillips, 1902. This is the standard biography of Pasteur and was written by Pasteur's son-in-law. The book provides many quotations from documentary sources and gives an inside look at Pasteur, his life and his work.

Allan D. Charles

WALTER PATER

Born: August 4, 1839; London, England
Died: July 30, 1894; Oxford, England
Areas of Achievement: Literature and art
Contribution: His emphasis upon the importance of sensibility and feeling made Pater a central figure in the "art for art's sake" movement that marked the transition from Victorian realism to twentieth century modernism.

Early Life

Walter Horatio Pater was born August 4, 1839, in London, England. His mother, née Maria Hill, came from a northern family and was a member of the Church of England; his father, Richard Pater, was a former Roman Catholic surgeon who died in 1842. According to family tradition, their most distinguished ancestor was the French painter Jean-Baptiste Pater (1695-1736), although the English branch of the Paters had become prominent merchants in the lace trade on the Norfolk-Suffolk coast. After his father's death, Pater's family moved to Enfield, from which he entered King's School, Canterbury, in 1853 and then matriculated at Oxford's Queen's College in 1858.

At Oxford, Pater studied Plato with the legendary professor of Greek Benjamin Jowett, became interested in German philosophy as the result of two visits to Germany, and was graduated with a degree in classics in 1862. He remained at Oxford and tutored private pupils until elected a Fellow of Brasenose College in 1865, the year in which he also made an extensive tour of Italy. His discovery of the achievements of the Italian Renaissance resulted in a series of essays on Leonardo da Vinci, Sandro Botticelli, Michelangelo, and other major figures, which were collected in his first book, *Studies in the History of the Renaissance* (1873).

Pater settled upon his major intellectual interests during a period of great aesthetic controversy. The "art for art's sake" philosophy espoused by the poets Dante Gabriel Rossetti and Algernon Charles Swinburne was in full bloom, as many of the era's creative talents rebelled against what they viewed as the crass materialism of Victorian society. Pater's dislike of any sort of unpleasantness kept him from engaging in the more partisan aspects of this conflict, but his stress upon the cultivation of aesthetic sensibilities made him an influential—if often reluctant—ally of those advocating greater freedom for the artistic temperament.

Although Pater's love of the fine arts was characterized by an almost religious fervor, his personal appearance often surprised those who knew him only from his writings. His clean-shaven cheeks and short, neat mustache were unusual in an age when extensive facial hair was the male norm, and in combination with his six-foot height and solid build often led to his being described as a dead ringer for a military officer. This impression was supported by his simple, precisely tailored clothes and the distinctive manner in which he walked—quickly and with a noticeable swing of his shoulders. A high, receding forehead and sparkling eyes set close together rounded out a public image that struck most contemporary commentators as quite at variance with the nature of his literary accomplishments.

Life's Work

The essays collected in *Studies in the History of the Renaissance* were adopted as a kind of manifesto by what became known as the "aesthetic movement," which included Rossetti, Swinburne, and such Pre-Raphaelite artists as John Everett Millais and W. Holman Hunt among its members. Pater's writing was lauded for having turned criticism into one of the fine arts, although those opposed to aestheticism attacked it as sterile, subjective, and dangerously hedonistic. Particularly controversial was the conclusion to *Studies in the History of the Renaissance*, in which Pater argued that those who would succeed in life must "burn always with this hard, gemlike flame." To many Victorian sensibilities this seemed a positively immoral basis for a philosophy of life: Thus, the conclusion was omitted from the book's second edition (*The Renaissance: Studies in Art and Poetry*, 1877) and only restored to its third edition (1888) in a revised and much less inflammatory version.

Pater's life at Oxford revolved around the home that he maintained with his two unmarried sisters, where a few friends and disciples served as a sounding board for his ideas on literature and art. He had little to do with the administrative affairs of his college, and on a typical day might well not leave the house except for a short evening walk. Despite his avoidance of publicity, Pater was held in very high regard by his colleagues: The Brasenose College chapel contains a memorial showing him in the center of a group consisting of Leonardo da Vinci, Michelangelo, Dante, and Plato.

Much of Pater's work was first published in periodicals such as *Fortnightly Review, Westminster Review, Pall Mall Gazette*, and *The Athenaeum*, and it was then collected in volumes such as *Imaginary Portraits* (1887), *Appreciations* (1889), and *Plato and Platonism: A Series of Lectures* (1893). As the title of the second of these suggests, Pater's critical faculties were directed toward the discovery of excellence rather than the detection of failure. He largely disregarded matters of technique, and instead sought to elucidate the qualities of temperament and the relevant aesthetic contexts which lay behind the actual work of art. For Pater, the artist has a valuable message for the informed, aware, and sympathetic audience, and it is the responsibility of the critic to respond to art in a manner that conveys its significant spiritual aspects.

As attacks upon his position mounted, among them an unflattering fictional caricature in William Hurrell Mallock's satire *The New Republic* (1877), Pater decided to write a major work which would demonstrate how his ideas enhanced the encounter with life's aesthetic elements. *Marius the Epicurean* (1885) is a loosely structured novel organized around the experiences of its protagonist, whose coming of age in second century Rome brings him into contact with a wide range of religious and philosophic ideals. At the end of the book, Marius is inclined toward but not yet fully convinced of the validity of Christianity, a conclusion that many critics found unsatisfactory in its tacit approval of heretical views. It nevertheless accurately reflected Pater's belief that it was openness to experience rather than the insistence upon dogmatic certainties which characterized the truly sensitive soul, and the book became one of the key texts for adherents of the aesthetic movement.

Pater's later years found him venturing a bit further into the social whirl. He rented a house in London, began to be seen in literary society, and even gave a few public lectures—in which his extreme nervousness was evident—on Renaissance art and literature. The year 1894 found him at the pinnacle of his success, an object of veneration by such young talents as Oscar Wilde and William Butler Yeats and the recipient of an honorary doctorate from the University of Glasgow. In June of that year, however, he was suddenly taken ill with rheumatic fever and then pleurisy, and on July 30, he died of heart failure occasioned by his long ill-

ness. Although he was deeply mourned by his many friends and disciples, it was in a sense appropriate that a life dedicated to the appreciation of beauty should cease at the apex rather than the nadir of its accomplishments.

Summary

Walter Pater's role in the sudden decline of the Victorian ethos and the equally rapid ascendancy of literary modernism was a crucial one. The fact that he was an extraordinarily shy, almost reclusive figure for much of his life meant that his influence rested upon his writings rather than a charismatic personality, and as a result he was taken seriously by the many intellectuals who viewed more flamboyant aesthetes—Wilde, most notoriously—as objects of ridicule rather than respect. Pater's solid academic background and early training in philosophy also helped to make his ideas palatable to many members of the educational establishment.

Pater's work also found many enthusiasts outside the ivory towers of England's great universities. His championing of the subjective approach to critical appreciation was immensely liberating to those reared in an atmosphere of Victorian deference to tradition and order, since it in effect substituted fresh individual responses for stale received opinions. Taking Pater as their guide, many people found the courage to express their own opinions without worrying about whether these were in line with the conventional wisdom.

In hindsight, Pater necessarily assumes the role of an early prophet in a revolution that has now been largely won. In addition to his historical importance as an advocate of the primacy of the developed aesthetic sense, however, Pater's elegant literary style can still be enjoyed by connoisseurs of fine writing, not least because it succeeds in exemplifying in prose what his heroes had achieved in the fine arts. Although the figures of such spiritual descendants as Wilde and Yeats now far overshadow that of Pater, it is important to remember that he was one of the first to oppose a dead and oppressive past with a vision of the capacity for enjoyment latent in everyone's endowments of feeling and sensibility.

Bibliography

Benson, Arthur Christopher. *Walter Pater*. London and New York: Macmillan, 1906. A typical example of Macmillan's English Men of Letters series, in which a light tone and the absence of scholarly apparatus conceal a thorough acquaintance with the subject. Although Benson got many of his facts wrong, his deft sketches of Pater's Oxford background and dominant personality traits still make the book worth consulting.

De Laura, David J. *Hebrew and Hellene in Victorian England: Newman, Arnold, and Pater.* Austin: University of Texas Press, 1969. A detailed investigation of the intellectual and personal relations maintained by three significant Victorian figures. The book is closely reasoned and not always easy to follow, but it is nevertheless a rewarding study that is particularly good on the history of the aesthetic movement.

Levey, Michael. *The Case of Walter Pater.* London: Thames and Hudson, 1978. Levey describes his work as a biography and includes an adequate account of Pater's early years, but his real focus is on his life as an Oxford don and the autobiographical nature of his writings. Levey often illuminates the connections between Pater's life and work, although he sometimes comes up with speculations that seem insufficiently grounded in historical fact.

Monsman, Gerald. *Walter Pater's Art of Autobiography.* New Haven, Conn.: Yale University Press, 1980. This attempt to abstract an autobiography from Pater's fiction theorizes that whatever the ostensible subject, he was in fact always meditating on the death of his parents. A Freudian interpretation expressed in the very latest modes of textual analysis; an interesting and provocative, if not always convincing, effort.

Pater, Walter. *Letters of Walter Pater.* Edited by Lawrence Evans. Oxford: Clarendon Press, 1970. Contains 272 of Pater's generally brief and uninformative letters. This material has been very well researched and annotated, and the reader does gain a good idea of what Pater's daily routine was like, if very little idea of what really engaged his more subtle thought processes.

Shuter, William F. *Rereading Walter Pater.* New York: Cambridge University Press, 1997. In this study of unpublished manuscript materials, Shuter argues that Pater's later work can provide an introduction to his earlier writings and change our understanding of his work.

Stein, Richard L. *The Ritual of Interpretation: The Fine Arts as Literature in Ruskin, Rossetti, and Pater.* Cambridge, Mass.: Harvard University Press, 1975. Stein argues that writing about art was a distinctive genre for the Victorians, and he discusses his three subjects in terms of their literary treatment of painting, sculpture, and architecture. The best elucidation of Pater's art criticism and its cultural antecedents.

Taylor, Benjamin. *Into the Open: Reflections on Genius and Modernity.* New York: New York University Press, 1995. Taylor considers the term "genius" from a philosophical and literary perspective using the writings of Pater, Paul Valry, and Sigmund Freud on the genius of Leonardo da Vinci as a basis. The writings of these men are then compared to Nietzsche's thoughts on genius.

Wright, Thomas. *The Life of Walter Pater.* 2 vols. New York: Putnam, and London: Everett, 1907. Wright is constantly pointing out mistakes in Benson's *Walter Pater*, and it must be admitted that Wright's documentation is much superior. Wright seems to have little feel, however, for Pater's elusive personality and is often an irritatingly clumsy writer. An essential but by no means polished resource.

Paul Stuewe

SIR ROBERT PEEL

Born: February 5, 1788; near Bury, Lancashire, England

Died: July 2, 1850; London, England

Areas of Achievement: Government and politics

Contribution: Peel was a Tory who broke with party doctrine to reform the criminal code, create an effective police force, legalize labor unions, and repeal the Corn Laws, thereby ensuring the success of free trade.

Early Life

Robert Peel was born February 5, 1788, in a cottage near Chamber Hall, his family's manor house near Bury in Lancashire. His father, Sir Robert Peel, and his mother, née Ellen Yates, were the children of partners who owned a successful cotton mill. The senior Peel's father had been a skilled craftsman who had founded the family fortune by manufacturing cotton textiles. The Peels thus were part of the new commercial aristocracy, only two generations removed from Yorkshire yeomen. The senior Peel, independently wealthy, had won a seat in Parliament, served in William Pitt's cabinet, and been rewarded with a baronetcy.

Young Robert Peel was educated at Marrow and at Christ Church, Oxford University, where he distinguished himself as a first-rate scholar in classics, history, and mathematics. He was a deeply religious High Church Anglican but was never interested in theological debate.

In 1809, at age twenty-two, Peel joined his father in the ranks of the Tory Party in Parliament. After brief periods in lesser offices, he accepted the post of secretary for Ireland. For five years, between 1812 and 1817, he stirred extreme reactions of hatred and admiration for his administration of Ireland. He pursued a repressive policy depending heavily on armed force to keep order. He earned a reputation as a thorough bigot for his opposition to Roman Catholic emancipation, which meant principally the right of Roman Catholics to hold public office. At the same time, Peel created the Irish Constabulary, an efficient police force which was to be a valuable model for his later work with the London police.

In 1817, Peel resigned the uncongenial Irish secretaryship and was rewarded by his party with a parliamentary seat representing Oxford University, his alma mater. His policies in Ireland had made him the natural spokesman for Oxford, which was known for its unyielding Anglican conservatism.

In 1820, Peel married. His wife, Julia, daughter of General Sir John Floyd, bore him five sons and two daughters. His devoted family formed a solid pillar of strength during the stormy years of his controversial political career.

Life's Work

From 1822 to 1827, Peel held the cabinet post of home secretary. With regard to Ireland and Catholic emancipation, he held to his old views. In other areas, however, his unyielding antireform Toryism showed signs of softening.

Peel took a leading role in convening a special parliamentary committee to investigate the condition of the working class. Francis Place, the former tailor who was to become the father of British labor unionism, selected representative workers, coached them carefully, and brought them to the committee to offer testimony, through the collusion of Joseph Hume, a brilliant parliamentary radical. Thus, Peel, whose own fortune rested on the factory system, became a willing aid to those seeking to legalize the formation of labor unions and strikes. In 1824, the Combination Acts and the Statutes of Apprentices, which had previously prevented strikes, were repealed.

Inspired by the earlier work of Sir Samuel Romilly and Sir James Mackintosh, Peel took the initiative in 1825-1826 in passing the Five Acts, a series of ordinances which reformed criminal law. By the end of the first quarter of the nineteenth century, it was no longer possible to get juries to bring in guilty verdicts that carried mandatory death sentences for such crimes as stealing a shilling's worth of merchandise or appearing on a highway masked or in blackface. The great object of the Five Acts was to fit punishment to crime. Peel accepted the dictate that the certainty of punishment is more important than the severity of penalty.

During a second term as home secretary, in 1829, Peel created the London Metropolitan Police, the source of the ultimately fabled Scotland Yard. That the police came to be called "Peelers" in Ireland and "Bobbies" in London constitutes a memorial to the same home secretary.

During his second term as home secretary, Peel entered the next phase in what his opponents termed a betrayal of old principles. In 1828, he joined in support of the repeal of the Test and Corporation Acts, which had previously ensured that only Anglicans and Presbyterians could hold office in the British Isles. In 1828, these rights were extended to nonconformist or dissenting Protestant denominations which had enjoyed freedom of religion since 1689 but whose members had been denied the right to hold office or to send their sons to Oxford or Cambridge Universities.

The full emancipation of Roman Catholics was another matter. In the popular mind, Roman Catholicism was still associated with the legends of "Bloody Mary Tudor," John Foxe's *The Book of Martyrs* (1559), and the alleged sinister intentions of King James II. The fact that most British Roman Catholics were Irish compounded theological and ethnic hatreds.

Nevertheless, a practical politician such as Peel found it easier to overcome old prejudices when he observed that the Irish had learned the fine art of political organization under the inspired leadership of the Protestant Irish nationalist Daniel O'Connell, who had founded the Catholic Association in 1823. O'Connell had proved that the Irish had the capacity to support and vote for Protestant parliamentary representatives pledged to Catholic emancipation and to do so in a disciplined and nonviolent fashion. Peel, who had a healthy respect for Irish violence, was perhaps more impressed with O'Connell's use of the electoral apparatus to attain his goals within the British system. Thus, it was Peel and the arch-Tory Arthur Wellesley, the Duke of Wellington, who persuaded King George IV to approve Catholic emancipation in 1829.

Peel's support of Catholic emancipation briefly cost him his seat in Parliament. He was too valuable for the Tories to lose, however, and he was back almost immediately. The firmness with which Peel opposed Charles Grey's parliamentary reform bill of 1832 regained for him many of the Tory allies he had lost over the issue of Catholic emancipation. It was Peel who rebuilt the Tory Party, which had fallen to a mere 150 members in Commons after Grey's Whig triumph.

In 1834, Peel became prime minister for the first time. His parliamentary majority was too precarious, however, and his cabinet fell. Interestingly, the issue which forced his resignation was a proposal to devote the surplus income of the Anglican church in Ireland to Irish nonsectarian education. He was thirty-four years premature with an idea

later passed into law by his great disciple, William Ewart Gladstone.

Peel's second and final tenure of the prime ministership occurred between 1841 and 1846. In foreign affairs, the ministry enjoyed two notable successes. An Afghan war was ended under honorable terms, and war was avoided with the United States by a settlement of the borders of Maine and Oregon. These years are chiefly remembered, however, for Peel's adoption of free trade. For twenty years, he had moved closer to the ideas of economists such as David Ricardo and pragmatic capitalists such as William Huskisson—after all, his own roots were not in the old aristocracy, which owed its wealth to agriculture, but in the new aristocracy, which had grown rich in the Industrial Revolution. In that sense, he had never been one with the country squires who made up the backbone of Toryism.

Thus, in 1842, Peel imposed an income tax to absorb a budget deficit. By the time that he left office, the Treasury boasted a surplus. Until the crucial year 1845, he managed to cut tariff rates on about 450 items, most of them raw materials not produced in Great Britain. Here again, Peel actually increased tariff income, as he approached free trade. His conversion to free trade raised criticism but did not precipitate party rebellion, because he did not speak of opening Great Britain to the free importation of foreign wheat. The Corn Laws protecting aristocratic landowners from the competition of foreign wheat were regarded as sacred. The aristocracy asserted that a financially secure gentry was the only class in society prepared by heredity, education, and tradition to serve their country in the armed forces and in government without regard to personal financial reward. Since 1836, however, under the leadership of Richard Cobden and John Bright, the Anti-Corn Law League had argued that eliminating the Corn Laws would reduce the price of bread, lower the cost of living, and permit foreign grain producers to sell agricultural produce in Great Britain, thereby increasing their purchases of British goods. Peel might have been content to refrain from touching the Corn Laws since they were so essential to maintaining Tory strength, rebuilt with such difficulty since 1832. Nature, however, intervened. An Irish potato famine plunged that island into starvation and despair in 1845. The price of food staples flew so high that only a repeal of the Corn Laws could solve the crisis of millions of people faced with penury, starvation, or emigration. Peel could no longer defend the Corn Laws and abandoned them. In 1846, he finally formed a cabinet which was committed to repeal of the Corn Laws. The parliamentary debate was bitter; the Tory Party split in two.

Benjamin Disraeli turned against his mentor, Sir Robert Peel, and led that large faction of the Tories who regarded the repeal of the Corn Laws as equivalent to social revolution and the destruction of the old aristocracy. Gladstone, by contrast, stood by his prime minister. The Tory ministry leading the fight for repeal knew that they were ending their own tenure of office because they could obtain repeal only with the help of Lord John Russell and the Whigs. In a magnificent gesture of self-sacrifice, Peel lost his own chance ever to be prime minister again and sent his party into twenty-eight years of eclipse. Nevertheless, by his adoption of a low revenue tariff system of free trade, he gave Great Britain forty years of unparalleled prosperity and that special brand of national optimism which historians refer to as mid-Victorian self-confidence.

Out of office, though still in Parliament, Peel lent his generous support to the Whig-Liberal cabinet in repealing the Navigation Acts in 1849. He also made a vain effort, in his last days, to obtain full civil rights for the Jews. On June 29, 1850, he suffered fatal injuries while horseback riding in a park near his London home. He died on July 2.

Summary

Sir Robert Peel must be remembered as the quintessential political pragmatist. An Anglican whose birth and education had infused him with a deep mistrust of Irish Catholics, he ended by doing more for them than any English leader had done before. He developed the Royal Irish Constabulary to carry out repressive measures, but ended by creating a London Metropolitan Police Force which became a model for maintaining order in a free society. By birth and education he belonged to the Tory gentry, but practical experience made him sympathetic to labor unions, legal strikes, and ultimately to laissez-faire capitalist free trade.

In a word, Peel held to no fixed position if experience proved him wrong. In the end, he enjoyed the respect and even the affection of those who at various times in his career had called him a renegade turncoat.

Bibliography

Cecil, Algernon. *Queen Victoria and Her Prime Ministers*. London: Eyre and Spottiswoode, and New York: Oxford University Press, 1953. A serious examination of Victoria's long reign and her view of the ministers who served her. In the examination of sixty-three years, Peel's role is retrospectively modest.

Conacher, J. B. *The Peelites and the Party System, 1846-1852*. Newton Abbot: David and Charles, 1972. Explores the fate of the Tories who followed Peel when he broke with Disraeli and the party loyalists in 1846. Some, like Gladstone, went on to become leaders in the Whig Party as it became the Liberal Party.

Cowie, Leonard W. *Sir Robert Peel, 1788-1850: A Bibliography*. Westport, Conn.: Greenwood Press, 1996. This bibliography is a comprehensive guide to the available information on Sir Robert Peel and includes manuscript collections and their locations, memoirs, diaries, and biographies. Also includes Peel's achievements as assessed by his contemporaries and later historians.

Gash, Norman. *Sir Robert Peel: The Life of Sir Robert Peel After 1830*. London: Longman, and Totowa, N.J.: Rowman and Littlefield, 1972. A very solid, well-written, meticulously documented biography which should be the first work consulted by anyone interested in Peel.

Jones, Wilbur Devereux. *The Peelites, 1846-1857*. Columbus: Ohio State University Press, 1972. Like the Conacher volume, this serious and well-documented work traces the impact of the disaffected Tories on the Whig-Liberal Party.

Marriott, Sir John Arthur Ransome. *Queen Victoria and Her Ministers*. London: Murray, 1933; New York: Dutton, 1934. The author is understandably an enthusiastic admirer of the uniqueness of the British unwritten constitution. He is at his best in explaining how a hereditary monarchy has managed to thrive within the framework of a society moving through liberalism to democracy. Only a small part of the work is devoted to any one prime minister, and Peel gets an appreciative but brief analysis.

Morrow, John. "The Paradox of Peel as Carlylean Hero." *The Historical Journal* 40, no. 1 (March, 1997). Morrow examines Carlyle's attitude toward Peel, his recognition of Peel's abilities, and how Peel's popularity was beneficial to Carlyle.

Parker, Charles Stuart, ed. *Sir Robert Peel, from His Private Papers*. 3 vols. London: Murray, 1891-1899; New York: Kraus, 1970. As the collection was published by the trustees of Peel's estate, and as Sir Robert's grandson George Peel wrote a eulogistic chapter, it may be assumed that this valuable source is accurate but selective and incomplete.

Peel, Sir Robert. *Memoirs by the Right Honourable Sir Robert Peel*. 2 vols. London: John Murray, 1856-1859; New York: Kraus, 1969. The memoirs were published by Earl Stanhope and Edward Cardwell on behalf of the trustees of the Peel estate, six years after Sir Robert's death. This valuable source reflects what the deceased hoped would be posterity's judgment of his work.

———. *The Speeches of the Late Right Honourable Sir Robert Peel, Bart., Delivered in the House of Commons, with a General Explanatory Index, and a Brief Chronological Summary of the Various Subjects on Which the Speeches Were Delivered*. 4 vols. London: Routledge, 1853; New York: Kraus, 1972. A valuable primary source.

Ramsay, Anna Augusta Whittal. *Sir Robert Peel*. London: Constable, and New York: Dodd, Mead, 1928. A solid, scholarly, and well-written study of Peel's life. It is particularly good for analyses of the political alignments which affected Peel's choices of policy.

Victoria, Queen of Great Britain. *The Letters of Queen Victoria: A Selection from Her Majesty's Correspondence Between the Years 1837 and 1861*. Edited by Arthur Christopher Benson and Viscount Esher. 3 vols. London and New York: Longman, 1907. Offers revealing comment by the queen on her benign relationship to Peel.

Arnold Blumberg

CHARLES SANDERS PEIRCE

Born: September 10, 1839; Cambridge, Massachusetts

Died: April 19, 1914; Milford, Pennsylvania

Area of Achievement: Philosophy

Contribution: Largely unrecognized by contemporaries, except for his contribution to pragmatism, Peirce developed a system of philosophy that attempted to reconcile the nineteenth century's faith in empirical science with its love of the metaphysical absolute. His difficult and often confusing ideas anticipated problems central to twentieth century philosophy.

Early Life

Charles Sanders Peirce, born on September 10, 1839, in Cambridge, Massachusetts, was the son of Benjamin Peirce, one of America's foremost mathematicians. During his childhood, Charles's mother, Sarah Hunt (Mills) Peirce, took second place to his dynamic father, who personally supervised the boy's education and provided a role model that inspired but also proved impossible to emulate. Convinced of his son's genius, Benjamin Peirce encouraged his precocious development. Charles began the study of chemistry at the age of eight, started an intense scrutiny of logic at twelve, and faced rigorous training in mathematics throughout his childhood. In the latter case, he was seldom given general principles or theorems. Instead, he was expected to work them out on his own.

At sixteen, Peirce entered Harvard, where his father was professor of mathematics. Contrary to expectations, Peirce proved a less than brilliant student, and he was graduated, in 1859, seventy-first out of a class of ninety-one. Probably too young and certainly too much the nonconformist to fit into the rigid educational system of nineteenth century Harvard, Peirce's inauspicious beginning in institutional academics was prophetic. Though he would continue his education, receiving an M.A. from Harvard in 1862 and a Sc.B. in chemistry the following year, his future did not lead to a distinguished career in academics or, indeed, in any conventional pursuit. His lot in life, in spite of so much promise, was frustration and apparent failure.

Peirce's difficulty in adjusting to the world of ordinary men was related to his unusual and often trying personality. Always his father's favorite, Peirce became convinced of his own genius and impatient with those who failed to recognize the obvious. Shielded and overindulged as a child, Peirce never developed the social skills required for practical affairs nor the self-discipline necessary to make his own grandiose vision a reality. Such problems were exaggerated by his passion for perfection and his abstract turn of mind. Peirce found real happiness only in the rarefied world of his own philosophical speculation.

As a youth, Peirce both attracted and repelled. Always prone to the dramatic gesture and, when he was inclined, a brilliant conversationalist, he could be an entertaining companion, but he could also use his rapier wit as a weapon. Of medium height, dark, swarthy, and fastidious in matters of dress, the handsome young Peirce reveled in his reputation as a lady's man and spent much energy in seeking the "good life." He actually paid an expert to train his palate so that he could become a connoisseur of fine wines. In 1862, Peirce married Harriet Melusina Fay, three years his senior and infinitely more mature and self-possessed. A feminist and intellectual in her own right, "Zina" worshiped her captive "genius" and labored for years to keep him out of serious trouble while restraining his extravagance. Yet she could also be jealous and possessive, and, though Peirce would experience some stability under Zina's influence, the marriage was doomed.

Life's Work

Upon his graduation from Harvard, Peirce went to work for the United States Coast and Geodetic Survey, a position acquired through his father's influence. Benjamin Peirce served as a consulting geometer for the organization and became its superintendent in 1867. Charles Peirce remained with the survey in various capacities until 1891, when he was asked to resign. This bureaucratic career, while terminated in less-than-desirable circumstances, was not without accomplishments. His deep commitment to the experimental method helped put the survey on a firm scientific basis, and Peirce himself became internationally known for his work on gravity research. He also continued an association with Harvard, once again through his father's influence, holding temporary lectureships in logic in 1865-1866 and 1869-1870 and from 1872 to 1875 serving as assistant at the Harvard Observatory. His observatory work on the measurement of light provided data for the only book he published during his lifetime *Photometric Researches* (1878). Peirce hoped for a permanent appointment at Harvard, but his lack of a Ph.D., his erratic life-style, and a typically personal quarrel with Harvard president Charles W. Eliot made the dream impossible.

More important than his actual work, the atmosphere and personal contacts at Harvard helped mold his philosophical outlook. Never idle, Peirce spent his spare time studying the work of Immanuel Kant, the ideas of the medieval scholastics, and various theories in logic and mathematics. The most useful forum for his developing ideas was the so-called Metaphysical Club. In the meetings of this unusual group, which included William James, Oliver Wendell Holmes, Jr., Francis E. Abbot, and Chauncey Wright, among others, Peirce had the opportunity to test his theories before a critical audience. It was there that he used the term "pragmatism" to describe the relationship between a conception and its effects which allows one to understand the actual meaning of the original conception by knowing its effects. While Peirce intended his idea as a theory of meaning, William James, more than twenty years later, would popularize the term and expand it far beyond the original intention. In fact, objecting to his friend's interpretation, Peirce, in 1905, coined the term "pragmaticism" to distinguish his thought from James's version.

In his Harvard years, Peirce began to write articles for *The Journal of Speculative Philosophy* and other scholarly publications, as well as more popular magazines such as *Popular Science Monthly*. Such articles, along with numerous book reviews, provided his major public outlet for the remainder of his life. Ignored by much of the philosophical community, these writings contained important contributions to logic, mathematics, and metaphysics.

Peirce finally got his chance to teach when he was hired as a part-time lecturer at The Johns Hopkins University in 1879. Apparently an effective teacher, he produced some of his best work in logic and scientific methodology at Johns Hopkins. Yet his erratic behavior, coupled with his divorce from his first wife and remarriage to a twenty-six-year-old French woman, the mysterious Mme Juliette Pourtalai, made it difficult for the authorities to accept him, no matter how brilliant, as part of the faculty. In 1884, Peirce was dismissed from his position because of unsuitable activities of a moral

nature, probably connected with his divorce and remarriage.

Peirce's second marriage began a phase of his life which would be philosophically productive but personally frustrating, ending in self-imposed exile. In 1887, his academic career hopelessly in shambles and his labors for the survey drawing to a conclusion, Peirce moved to Milford, Pennsylvania, a resort area on the Delaware river. With a small inheritance, he was able to purchase land and begin construction of an elaborately planned home he called "Arisbe." Though Peirce was able to live in his retreat for the remainder of his life, the mansion was never really completed. Typically, Peirce had overextended himself. When he lost his government salary in 1891 and suffered severe losses in the depression of 1893, he began a long slide into poverty. His closest and always tolerant friend, William James, tried to help as much as possible, arranging for a series of lectures in Boston in 1898 and finally convincing Harvard to allow the notorious philosopher to give a series of lectures at the university in 1903. No effort, however, even by America's most famous philosopher, would make Peirce acceptable to established society in the nineteenth century. Finally, James began collecting donations for a Peirce fund from interested and unnamed friends. From 1907 until his death in 1914, Peirce was largely supported by this fund, which amounted to about thirteen hundred dollars a year. Peirce, who had often been jealous of James and attacked his version of pragmatism with undisguised contempt, paid his friend a typical compliment by adopting Santiago (St. James) as part of his name in 1909.

Even in his last years, which were marred by illness, Peirce was productive. He continued to work in isolation, leaving behind a massive collection of papers. Ironically, Harvard, the institution which had so often rejected him, recognized his worth and purchased the manuscripts from his widow. Between 1931 and 1935, the six volumes of the *Collected Papers of Charles Sanders Peirce*, edited by Charles Hartshorne and Paul Weiss, were published by Harvard. This collection began what amounted to a revolution in American academic philosophy, making the ideas of Peirce a touchstone for twentieth century philosophical inquiry.

Unfortunately, the exact nature of Peirce's contribution to understanding is by no means clear. Numerous scholars have spent careers examining his writings, never reaching a consensus. The confusion is rooted in the nature of Peirce's work itself. Not satisfied with a contribution in a single area of inquiry, Peirce envisioned a vast architectonic system ending in a complete explanation of all human knowledge. In short, Peirce strove to be a modern Aristotle. While admirable, this goal ran up against a central dilemma in human thought, providing a source of tension within Peirce's system as well as within the world in which he lived.

Science, in the last years of the nineteenth century, revealed a limited vision of reality, of what could be known. The world, according to this view, consisted of matter and could be fully explained through the scientific method. Many thinkers, unable to accept this so-called positivistic version of reality, countered with an explanation based on the mind itself as the source of everything. Best represented in the idealism of Georg Wilhelm Friedrich Hegel, this view had spawned many variations. Peirce could not fully accept either position. Positivism seemed to deny the possibility of metaphysics or, perhaps better, a universe with meaning which could be understood by men. Idealism seemed hopelessly subjective, denying the possibility of actually knowing the physical universe.

Peirce set out to reconcile the irreconcilable by carefully examining immediate experience. Characteristically, this examination would be grounded on clear and precise thinking such as his famous "pragmatic maxim." He also rejected nominalism and accepted the position of the medieval scholastic Duns Scotus on the reality of Universals. Peirce insisted that cognition itself is reality, and everything that is real is knowable. The structure of experience is revealed in what he called "phaneroscopy." This term is typical of Peirce's obsession with the invention of new words to explain concepts, which is one of the reasons his ideas are so difficult. Phaneroscopy is roughly analogous to the modern concept of phenomenology. From his phenomenological basis, Peirce deduced three categories or qualities of experience which he termed Firstness, Secondness, and Thirdness. This division of experience allowed him to move from an essentially psychological analysis to logic itself through what he called the "semiotic," or the doctrine of signs. By signs, Peirce essentially meant those things in the mind which stand for the real things of the world. A word, for example, would be a sign but only one kind of sign. Peirce's analysis of signs and their relationships was a vast and complicated explanation of how human beings think

and provides the logical basis for his whole system.

A complete discussion of this difficult and obscure argument is not possible in this context, but most modern philosophers would agree that it constitutes Peirce's most important contribution to philosophy, particularly logic. Its obscurity, however, has led to many different interpretations. Phenomenologists, for example, find considerable comfort in his explanation of experience, while the logical positivists, who seldom agree with phenomenologists, also see their ideas reflected in Peirce's theory of signs. In fact, most philosophical systems in the twentieth century find some part of Peirce's ideas important in either a positive or a negative way.

Peirce's logic, however, was only the foundation of a broad system that included a complete theory of knowledge as well as cosmological speculations. This system, while not as widely accepted as his semiotic, includes a number of important concepts. For example, Peirce develops what he calls "tychism," or the doctrine of chance, which explains irregularities within nature. This idea should be balanced with "synechism," which is the doctrine that continuity is a basic feature of the world. Here again, Peirce reconciles the irreconcilable, and the result provides a reasonable picture of the actual condition of scientific inquiry. Synechism represents scientific law, which Peirce calls habit, without which one could not understand the operation of the natural world. Tychism, however, explains how change is possible and prevents a deterministic version of reality, which is the logical result of scientific law. Science then, while based on research which, if pursued to infinity, will result in "truth," must in the practical world be based on probability. Even in logic itself, one cannot be sure that all statements are correct. While not denying absolute truth, this concept, which Peirce called "fallibilism," provides a healthy corrective to those who are convinced that they have found the ultimate answer to reality.

Summary

Few can profess to understand all of Peirce's philosophy, and his work will probably never appeal to the average person unschooled in the mysteries of philosophical discourse. Yet his attack on the central dilemma of modern thought, created by scientific advance and its inevitable clash with human values, is the necessary starting point for many twentieth century philosophers and, through their work, has a profound influence on the way the world is viewed. It may be true that Peirce ultimately failed in his attempt to reconcile the "hard" world of science with cherished human values represented by the "soft" world of idealism, but, unlike his tragic personal life, his philosophy was certainly a glorious failure. Moreover, Peirce remained a true optimist who believed in the inevitability of human progress through reason. His system of thought, while far from perfect, did provide a view of reality that would make such progress possible. His first rule of reason demanded that the road to new knowledge always be left open. The greatest sin against reasoning, he believed, consisted in adopting a set of beliefs which would erect a barrier in the path of the search for truth.

Bibliography

Almeder, Robert F. *The Philosophy of Charles S. Peirce: A Critical Introduction.* Oxford: Blackwell, and Totowa, N.J.: Rowman and Littlefield, 1980. An analysis of Peirce's philosophy, stressing his epistemological realism, which contains a perceptive and detailed discussion of his theory of knowledge.

Brent, Joseph. *Charles Sanders Peirce: A Life.* 2d ed. Bloomington: Indiana University Press, 1998. In this updated biography, Brent has refined his interpretations of Peirce's work based on new research.

Conkin, Paul K. *Puritans and Pragmatists: Eight Eminent American Thinkers.* Bloomington: Indiana University Press, 1968. One of the finest overviews of American intellectual history. Places Peirce within the context of the development of American thought between Jonathan Edwards and George Santayana.

Goudge, Thomas A. *The Thought of C. S. Peirce.* Toronto: University of Toronto Press, 1950. One of the most perceptive studies of Peirce's thought. Sees Peirce's philosophy as resting on a conflict within his personality which produced tendencies toward both naturalism and Transcendentalism.

Moore, Edward C. *American Pragmatism: Peirce, James, and Dewey.* New York: Columbia University Press, 1961. An analysis of American pragmatism based on its three primary figures. Provides an excellent comparison of their different positions.

Ochs, Peter. *Peirce, Pragmatism, and the Logic of Scripture.* Cambridge and New York: Cambridge University Press, 1998. Ochs describes Peirce's pragmatism as the "logic of scripture" where the Bible's rules can be viewed logically as a means of repairing lives and societies.

Potter, Vincent G. *Charles S. Peirce: On Norms and Ideals.* Amherst: University of Massachusetts Press, 1967. An analysis of Peirce's attempt to establish aesthetics, ethics, and logic as the three normative sciences. The author places particular emphasis on the role of "habit" in the universe.

Reilly, Francis E. *Charles Peirce's Theory of Scientific Method.* New York: Fordham University Press, 1970. A discussion of Peirce's ideas concerning the method and the philosophy of science.

Skagestad, Peter. *The Road of Inquiry: Charles Peirce's Realism.* New York: Columbia University Press, 1981. Focuses on Peirce's theory of scientific method but also contains an introduction with considerable biographical information.

Thayer, H. S. *Meaning and Action: A Critical History of Pragmatism.* 2d ed. Indianapolis: Hackett, 1981. A comprehensive analysis of pragmatism, covering philosophers both in the United States and Europe.

David Warren Bowen

MATTHEW C. PERRY

Born: April 10, 1794; Newport, Rhode Island
Died: March 4, 1858; New York City
Areas of Achievement: The naval service and diplomacy
Contribution: In a naval career spanning almost half a century, Perry, besides commanding ships and fleets with distinction in peace and in war, proposed and accomplished reforms in naval architecture, ordnance, and organization, and through skillful negotiation introduced Japan into the modern community of nations.

Early Life

Matthew Calbraith Perry was born April 10, 1794, in Newport, Rhode Island. His father, Christopher Raymond Perry, was the descendant of original Quaker settlers of Rhode Island but served in privateers and Continental warships in the Revolution. The senior Perry met his Irish wife, Sarah Wallace Alexander, when he was a paroled prisoner in Ireland in 1781. Their eldest son, Oliver Hazard Perry (1785-1819), was the hero of the Battle of Lake Erie in 1813 and Matthew Perry's greatest hero.

In 1809, Matthew Perry was assigned as a midshipman to the schooner *Revenge*. A year later he transferred to the frigate *President*, in which he served in 1811 in the engagement with HMS *Little Belt* and in the War of 1812, when he was wounded slightly in the inconclusive fight with HMS *Belvidera*.

On December 24, 1814, he married Jane Slidell (1797-1879), daughter of a New York merchant, who bore him ten children. Their three sons and one of their sons-in-law were all navy or marine officers.

In 1815, Perry was assigned to the brig *Chippewa*, which was part of the Mediterranean Squadron, and at the end of this cruise he applied for furlough and commanded one, and perhaps more, of his father-in-law's merchant ships.

Life's Work

In 1819, Perry returned to naval service as first lieutenant in the corvette *Cyane*, which escorted the first settlers sent to Liberia by the American Colonization Society and patrolled the coast of West Africa to suppress the slave trade. Two years later, he was commanding the schooner *Shark* in African waters and the West Indies, where the navy was attempting to suppress piracy. Perry was of great assistance to the Liberian settlers in their efforts to establish their republic and was primarily responsible for the selection of the site of Monrovia.

From 1824 to 1827, Perry served as first lieutenant and later as acting commander in the battleship *North Carolina* in the Mediterranean Squadron. At this time the two responsibilities of the squadron, commanded by Commodore John Rodgers, were the protection of American shipping during the Greek war of independence and the implementation of a naval treaty with Turkey. Rodgers achieved both goals.

After service in the Charlestown naval yard, Perry was given command of the sloop-of-war *Concord* and in 1830 was responsible for conveying Minister John Randolph to St. Petersburg. This voyage was followed by two more years in the Mediterranean.

By this time Perry had developed all the skills which distinguished the rest of his naval career: total mastery of seamanship, a commanding presence, a great sense of duty and personal rectitude, negotiating skills of a high order, and a capacity for sympathy with people of diverse cultures. Much of this no doubt derived from his devout Episcopalianism, but it also was a product of high intelligence, which was reflected in a broad range of scholarly interests, particularly in history, ethnology, languages, and science.

When Perry was serving in the Mediterranean in this cruise, President Andrew Jackson was seeking agreements by which the European powers would agree to pay for spoliation of American commerce during the Napoleonic wars. In 1832, Perry commanded a squadron sent to Naples to support the efforts of American negotiators to collect payments from the Kingdom of the Two Sicilies. This show of strength apparently tipped the scales to produce the agreement of October, 1832.

The three greatest achievements of Perry's career were his efforts to modernize the navy, his service in the Mexican War, and his command of the expedition which first established formal relations with Japan.

From 1833, when he accepted command of the New York recruiting station, until 1843, when he ended his tenure as commander of the Brooklyn naval yard, Perry campaigned for naval reform. In an 1837 article, he outlined in detail the inadequacies of the United States Navy, which was eighth in the world, trailing even Turkey and Egypt and far behind Great Britain and France in naval architecture and ordnance. Perry is correctly considered the "father of the steam navy." He campaigned for construction of steam warships, and he initiated the action which led to the creation of the navy's Engineering Corps. He argued for the adoption of shell guns, invented the collapsible smokestack, advocated iron hulls for river gunboats, and recommended the creation of an independent Lighthouse Board. In addition, he was deeply involved in efforts to cure the old navy's problem of manpower procurement. In the early nineteenth century, crews were usually made up by robbing the merchant service and by recruiting foreigners and social misfits. Perry agitated for the creation of an apprentice system and for a school ship for their training. The attempted mutiny on the *Somers* in 1842 discredited this system, but that failure led to implementation of another of Perry's proposals: the creation of the Naval Academy.

In 1843, Perry was assigned to the command of the African Squadron, and in this capacity he negotiated a treaty with the local chiefs on the Ivory Coast, in which the chiefs agreed not to molest missionaries or plunder trading ships. He also was influential in settling differences between the immigrants and the native population of Liberia.

In the Mexican War, Perry first served as vice commodore of naval forces on the Mexican coast, subordinate to Commodore David Conner. He captured Frontera in October, 1846, and sailed fifty miles up the Rio Grijalva to attack Villahermosa and to capture nine enemy warships there. In November, he participated in the capture of Tampico, and the following month occupied Ciudad de Carmen. In March, 1847, he succeeded Conner as commodore and landed naval guns and gun-crews to support the troops Conner had landed to besiege Vera Cruz.

By the time Vera Cruz surrendered on March 29, 1847, Perry was commanding the largest American fleet up to that time—twenty-three vessels. In April, he attacked Tuxpan, destroying the forts and carrying off the guns captured by the Mexicans when an American brig ran aground.

His second attack on Villahermosa in June, 1847, was his greatest achievement in the war. He again advanced up the Grijalva to the underwater obstacles laid down by the enemy, then landed

eleven hundred men and led them personally on their three-mile march through Mexican defenses to capture Villahermosa.

The Japan expedition originated in Perry's memorandum to the secretary of the navy in the winter of 1851, in which he suggested that friendly relations could be achieved with Japan by a show of naval strength. He did not want command of the expedition, but he accepted it in January, 1852. His selection of ships and officers was careful, and his logistical planning was so effective that the colliers for refueling his steamers were in their assigned positions throughout the voyage. Before he could depart, however, he was ordered to investigate charges of British interference with American fishermen on the Canadian coast. His report on his findings led to the reciprocity treaty of 1854.

Perry's squadron arrived at Okinawa, then an independent kingdom, in May, 1853, and he established relations which enabled him to negotiate a treaty in the following year. After a side trip to the Bonin Islands, where, on Chichi Jima, he bought fifty acres as a possible coating station, the squadron reached Tokyo Bay on July 8, 1853.

Perry's behavior with the Japanese was remarkable for its combination of austere reserve, firmness, and cordiality. The Japanese sent minor officials to order the American ships away, but Perry dealt with them only through his subordinates, insisting on dealing with officials who could speak for the emperor. When Japanese guard boats attempted to ring his ships, he ordered them off under threat of opening fire. Finally, when it did not appear that the Japanese would accept President Fillmore's letter under any conditions, Perry informed them that if they would not accept it within a sufficient time he would land at Edo (Tokyo) in force and deliver it himself.

On July 14, Perry was invited to land with an armed retinue at Kurihama, near the mouth of Tokyo Bay, and, amid great formality on both sides, two Japanese officials accepted Fillmore's letter.

After wintering in Hong Kong, Perry returned to Japan in February, 1854, for further negotiations and landed in March. By the treaty of March 31, the Japanese granted two fueling ports, at Hakodate on Tsugaru Strait on southern Hokkaido and at Shimoda on the Izu Peninsula on Honshū. While the treaty did not make arrangements for trade, it did give Americans free access to the areas around the ports and arranged for shipwrecked American sailors to be sent to those ports for repatriation.

Perry examined the port of Shimoda and, after sailing to Hakodate to ensure that it was acceptable, he returned to Shimoda in June and reached further agreements with the Japanese on currency exchange, pilotage, and port dues. After sailing to Okinawa to negotiate the Treaty of Naha in July, 1854, he led his forces back to Hong Kong and with the treaty returned to the United States by commercial steamers.

In his last years, Perry enjoyed enormous public respect for his achievements in Japan. He devoted his time to service on the Naval Efficiency Board, which was engaged in weeding out overage naval officers, and concentrated much of his attention on the preparation of the official narrative of the Japan expedition and on writing several articles which revealed a great sense of the importance of the Pacific in future American naval and political strategy. He was convinced that Russia would be America's future Pacific rival and that it was crucially important to acquire coaling stations and naval bases in the western Pacific. Meanwhile, as a result of his achievements, the European powers were able to obtain treaties with Japan, and a trade agreement between the United States and Japan was achieved in 1858. Perry died in New York City on March 4, 1858.

Summary

Perry distinguished himself in his long naval career both as a commander and as a diplomat. Possessing not only the great skills in combat leadership that made him the most distinguished American naval officer of the Mexican War but also a remarkable combination of tact, firmness, patience, and empathy that enabled him to achieve great results as a negotiator, he succeeded both in founding the modern United States Navy and in using naval power to establish mutually productive relations with Japan. Perry's success in the latter case led him to the conclusion that the Pacific was to become his country's future arena of power and influence, and he made proposals for establishing naval bases in the Pacific which, if they had not disappeared in the domestic crisis in which the United States found itself in the 1850's, might well have prevented the rupture of Japanese-American relations in the 1930's. Perry recognized international political realities in the Pacific at a time when virtually every other American was concerned with the task of conquering and developing the continent and securing domestic harmony. When the

United States finally accepted international responsibility, it was obliged to fight a terrible war with the country with which Perry had established amicable relations and to maintain the presence in the Pacific which he had favored in the first place.

Bibliography

Barrows, Edward M. *The Great Commodore*. Indianapolis: Bobbs-Merrill, 1935. The best biography until it was superseded by that of Morison. Somewhat dated on the subject of the Japan expedition.

Fallows, James. "After Centuries of Japanese Isolation, a Fateful Meeting of East and West." *Smithsonian* 25, no. 4 (July, 1994). Examines Perry's career and voyage to Japan in 1853.

Griffis, William Elliott. *Matthew Calbraith Perry: A Typical American Naval Officer*. Boston: Cupples and Hurd, 1887. A friendly account, flawed by a misleading title and by occasional errors of fact. Provides most of the essential information on Perry's life.

Hawks, Francis L. *Narrative of the Expedition of an American Squadron to the China Seas and Japan*. Edited by Sidney Wallach. New York: Appleton, and London: Trubner, 1856. A convenient modern abridgement of the journals and reports of the Japan expedition. (The original was published in three volumes in 1856.)

Knox, Dudley. *A History of the United States Navy*. Rev. ed. New York: Putnam, 1948. A standard work which devotes a chapter to the Japan expedition and provides a good survey of the naval background of Perry's career.

Kuhn, Ferdinand. "Yankee Sailor Who Opened Japan." *National Geographic Magazine* 104 (July, 1953): 85-102. A general account of Perry's achievements in Japan, well illustrated with contemporary prints, many of them by Japanese artists.

Morison, Samuel Eliot. *"Old Bruin": Commodore Matthew Calbraith Perry, 1794-1858*. Boston: Little Brown, 1967; London: Oxford University Press, 1968. The definitive biography, by the most distinguished American naval historian. Full account of Perry's personal and professional life, with thorough treatment of social and political background, including the *Somers* affair and the achievements of Perry's father and brother.

Paullin, Charles Oscar. "The First American Treaty with Japan: 1851-1854." In *Diplomatic Negotiations of American Naval Officers, 1778-1883*, 244-281. Baltimore: Johns Hopkins University Press, 1912. Paullin was the outstanding student of this subject, and this chapter is a sound, basic account of Perry's accomplishments in Japan.

Pineau, Roger, ed. *The Japan Expedition, 1852-1854: The Personal Journal of Commodore Matthew C. Perry*. Washington, D.C.: Smithsonian Institution Press, 1968. A fine edition of Perry's journal, hitherto unpublished, with splendid color plates of watercolors and prints made during the voyage.

Walworth, Arthur. *Black Ships Off Japan*. New York: Knopf, 1946. A popular account of the Japan expedition, essentially accurate though its interpretation of Perry's character and behavior should be checked against that of Morison.

Yellin, Victor Fell. "Mrs. Belmont, Matthew Perry, and the 'Japanese Minstrels.'" *American Music* 14, no. 3 (Fall 1996). Discusses Perry's use of musicians on his mission to Japan and its impact on the Japanese.

Robert L. Berner

OLIVER HAZARD PERRY

Born: August 20, 1785; South Kingston, Rhode Island

Died: August 23, 1819; near Port of Spain, Trinidad

Area of Achievement: The naval service

Contribution: Perry's skillful seamanship and tactical tenacity in the War of 1812 provided an example of leadership and courage to the officers and crews of the young republic's fledgling navy.

Early Life

Born to a family of Rhode Island seamen, Perry's father, Christopher Raymond Perry, broke with the clan's tradition of Quaker pacifism to fight in the American Revolution. Four of Christopher's sons served in the United States Navy, one of whom was Matthew C. Perry, the famed naval commander and diplomat who opened Japan to Western commerce and thought. Reared in Newport, Rhode Island, and educated by his mother, Sarah Wallace Perry, Oliver signed on as a midshipman on his father's vessel, USS *General Greene*, at the age of fourteen. Four years later, he was a lieutenant on the twenty-eight-gun frigate USS *Adams*. Between 1803 and 1806, during the Tripolitan War, he served aboard the *Constellation*, captained the twelve-gun frigate *Nautilus*, and eventually transferred to the forty-four-gun frigate *Constitution* in Commodore John Rodgers' squadron. During the next six years, he directed the construction of various gunboats and commanded a schooner in American waters. In 1811, he married Elizabeth Champlin Mason of Newport. They eventually had five children, two of whom became military officers.

Life's Work

The outbreak of war found Perry commanding a gunboat flotilla at Newport, but in early 1813 he reported to Presque Isle (modern Erie), Pennsylvania, where he immediately began constructing vessels and organizing a crew in the midst of a wilderness. Captain Perry found himself engaged in a naval arms race with Captain Robert H. Barclay of the Royal Navy, who was patrolling Lake Erie and building his own vessels at a rapid pace. Perry's flotilla was under the overall command of Commodore Isaac Chauncey, stationed at Sackett's Harbor, New York, on the southeastern shore of Lake Ontario.

While the ship construction proceeded at Presque Isle, Perry joined Chauncey and General Henry Dearborn and superintended the naval gunfire and amphibious landing support of the attack on Fort George at the mouth of the Niagara River, May 27, 1813. Perry's conduct in this operation was a model of interservice cooperation. The success of the Fort George attack allowed Perry to move to Lake Erie five small vessels and fifty sailors.

At Presque Isle, Perry spent the spring and summer building, equipping, officering, and manning his small fleet of ten vessels, the largest of which were the USS *Lawrence* and the USS *Niagara*, each of 480 tons burden. To take his flotilla onto the lake, Perry had to cross the bar outside the harbor, a feat he could not accomplish in the presence of an enemy force since the shallow waters required that the guns and equipment of the vessels be removed before the ships could pass over. For inexplicable reasons, Captain Barclay relaxed his vigilance and allowed his foe the opportunity in early August to enter the lake unmolested. The battle for Lake Erie may well have been won at the Presque Isle bar, since crossing it allowed the Americans to achieve superior naval power on the lake.

Hoisting his flag on the *Lawrence* and with Lieutenant Jesse Duncan Elliott commanding the *Niagara*, Commodore Perry set out to fight Barclay's force and to cooperate with General William Henry Harrison's army, then encamped at Fort Meigs (west of modern Toledo, Ohio). Harrison could not advance toward Detroit unless Perry secured his lines of supply along the western shore of Lake Erie. After conferring with General Harrison, Perry located Barclay's fleet at Fort Malden, near the mouth of the Detroit River, but confrontation was delayed because of contrary winds and illness among Perry's crew. The Americans retired to Put-in-Bay in the Bass Islands, near modern Sandusky, where Perry received crew reinforcements from Harrison and awaited Barclay's decision to leave the protection of Fort Malden. Though outgunned, Barclay had to risk an engagement because Perry's dominance of the lake denied the British supplies for their troops in the Detroit vicinity.

The encounter, on September 10, 1813, should have been easily won by the Americans because Perry's two twenty-gun vessels gave a decided weight of metal advantage over the single twenty-gun HMS *Detroit* commanded by Barclay. Moreover, the initial wind advantage enjoyed by the British was lost because of a change in direction that allowed the Americans the power of initiative. Perry intended the *Lawrence* to engage the *Detroit* and the *Niagara* to attack HMS *Queen Charlotte*, the second largest of the British vessels. Not only did Elliott not engage the *Queen Charlotte*, but he also allowed that vessel to support the *Detroit* against the *Lawrence*. The result was that despite the heavy damage his flagship inflicted upon the *Detroit*, Perry found his vessel a wreck, her guns disabled, and most of her crew casualties. He transferred his flag to the undamaged *Niagara*, which he then took into action and quickly destroyed and captured the British vessels. His succinct message to General Harrison—"We have met the enemy and they are ours; two ships, two brigs, one schooner, and one sloop"—constitutes a model laconic after-action report. Elliott's conduct in this battle remains controversial and left a legacy of dispute with Perry that lasted long after the latter's death.

Perry's victory dramatically changed the military situation in the Middle West. Harrison quickly retook Detroit and pursued the British-Canadian-Indian forces eastward. Perry's vessels supported him, and when the two armies met at the Battle of the Thames on October 5, the naval captain acted as an aide to the general and assisted in the forming of the battle line.

Perry relinquished his command and made a triumphant tour to Newport. President James Madison promoted him to the permanent rank of captain, and Congress added five thousand dollars to the seventy-five hundred dollars in prize money that was his due and requested that the president give him a gold medal. In July, 1814, Perry took command of the newly commissioned USS *Java* at Baltimore but was unable to take the vessel to sea because of the British blockade and the ship's still uncompleted state. While in this capacity, he commanded a battery of seamen who harassed the British fleet as it withdrew down the Potomac after the raid on Washington.

On the return of peace with Britain in 1815, Perry took a squadron into the Mediterranean to assist Commodore Stephen Decatur in redressing American grievances against Algiers and Tripoli, whose cruisers had captured numerous American vessels and seamen since 1812. During this cruise, he engaged in a number of diplomatic efforts. He also became involved in a dispute with Marine Captain John Heath, which grew so embittered that, in a fit

of passion, Perry struck the *Java's* marine detachment commander. The incident resulted in a court-martial and a mild reprimand. Still unsatisfied, Heath would eventually engage Perry in a duel that ended with both unhurt and Perry not firing his weapon.

In 1819, Perry undertook a diplomatic mission to Venezuela. He conducted the delicate venture successfully but died of yellow fever contracted during the trip. Perry was buried on Trinidad. In a token of respect for his military prowess and post-battle humanitarianism, his funeral procession received full British honors. Seven years later, his body was returned to Newport for reburial and was marked with a granite obelisk erected by the state of Rhode Island.

Summary

The key to Oliver Hazard Perry's reputation is victory on Lake Erie. There, he demonstrated the elements of professionalism, presence, and determination that elicited the admiration of his officers and men. As he had done earlier at Fort George, in his support of General Harrison's ground force

Perry exhibited a degree of interservice cooperation uncharacteristic of many subsequent army-navy efforts. One of the few heroes in a war that was very divisive, his achievement of capturing a Royal Navy fleet was unprecedented in American history. Yet Perry was more than a distinguished warrior and seaman. His diplomatic efforts in North Africa and South America were typical naval endeavors of his day, and they set the tone for his younger brother's famous expedition to Japan. In the final analysis, his career, like that of John Paul Jones, Stephen Decatur, Thomas Macdonough, and James Lawrence, provided an example of valor, dedication, leadership, and patriotism that influenced American sailors for years to follow.

Bibliography

Dutton, Charles J. *Oliver Hazard Perry*. London and New York: Longman, 1935. The standard but undistinguished biographical study.

Forester, Cecil S. *The Age of Fighting Sail: The Story of the Naval War of 1812*. New York: Doubleday, 1956. A popular history by the author of the Horatio Hornblower stories, this is a good introduction to the problems confronted by Perry and his contemporaries.

Gilbert, Bil. "The Battle of Lake Erie." *Smithsonian* 25, no. 10 (January, 1995). Examines Perry, the Battle of Lake Erie, and the lack of U.S. preparedness for the War of 1812.

Hitsman, J. Mackay. *The Incredible War of 1812: A Military History*. Toronto: University of Toronto Press, 1965. Written from a Canadian perspective, this is a solid history with a strong focus on the war on the Great Lakes.

MacKenzie, Alexander Slidell. *The Life of Commodore Oliver Hazard Perry*. 2 vols. New York: Harper, 1840. A highly laudatory account by a naval officer who served under Perry, this study is notable for the numerous personal recollections that MacKenzie collected and for its defensive tone in the Perry-Elliott and Perry-Heath controversies.

Mahan, Alfred Thayer. *Sea Power in Its Relations to the War of 1812*. 2 vols. Boston: Little Brown, and London: Sampson Low, Marston, 1905. Volume 2 contains this distinguished naval historian's account of the Battle of Lake Erie; Mahan stoutly defends Perry's conduct.

Morison, Samuel Eliot. *"Old Bruin": Commodore Matthew Calbraith Perry, 1794-1858: The American Naval Officer Who Helped Found Liberia*. Boston: Little Brown, 1967; London: Oxford University Press, 1968. This account by a famous naval historian of the career of Perry's younger brother provides both family background and an analysis of the United States Navy in the early nineteenth century.

David Curtis Skaggs

JOHANN HEINRICH PESTALOZZI

Born: January 12, 1746; Zurich, Switzerland
Died: February 17, 1827; Brugg, Switzerland
Area of Achievement: Education
Contribution: Pestalozzi spent his life seeking ways to help students improve their learning skills so that they could develop into effective adults. His method was based upon imparting an awareness of and encouraging direct interaction with objects, progressing from simple steps to more complex ones in an orderly pattern, thereby achieving harmonious organic development.

Early Life

The Pestalozzis, Italians who immigrated to Switzerland from Locarno in the sixteenth century, settled in Zurich. By 1746, when Johann Heinrich Pestalozzi was born, the family had been in Zurich for two hundred years and had been accorded the full rights of citizens—a privilege in a city of 145,000, only 5,000 of whom were citizens. Heinrich was the youngest of Johann Baptist and Suzanne Hotz Pestalozzi's three children. Johann, a surgeon, died in 1751 at the age of thirty-three, leaving the family in straitened circumstances. Because Pestalozzi was a sickly child, his mother sheltered him, seldom allowing him to play with other children or to do chores. He was exposed to the poor when he visited his paternal grandfather, a clergyman near Zurich. The young Pestalozzi developed an interest in and sympathy for the poor.

At Zurich's Collegium Carolinum, Pestalozzi, an indifferent student, developed a consuming love for his country that led him to join the Helvetic Society and to write articles about the poor and suffering for its publication. Upon graduating from Collegium Carolinum, Pestalozzi entered the University of Zurich but abandoned his university studies soon after starting them. Having read Jean-Jacques Rousseau, Pestalozzi was particularly affected by *Émile: Ou, De l'éducation* (1762; *Emilius and Sophia: Or, A New System of Education*, 1762-1763). Rousseau's glorification of the natural life led Pestalozzi to spend the year 1767 studying agriculture. In 1768, he bought acreage near Birr and devoted himself to cultivating it. The failure of this venture in 1774 caused him to lose everything he owned except the house, Neuhof, which dominated his property, and a plot on which he raised food for his wife, Anna, whom he had married in

1769, and their son, Jean-Jacques, named for Rousseau.

By 1773, Pestalozzi had turned Neuhof into a school where he taught poor and unfit children to become cotton spinners. He taught them mathematics and catechism as they worked, and after work the boys gardened while the girls learned sewing and cooking. Pestalozzi also taught them the skills of basic literacy. The school attracted more than fifty unkempt students, ages six to eighteen. Pestalozzi, a slim, gentle man with a kind, understanding smile, reformed many of them, serving simultaneously as teacher and surrogate father. Nevertheless, in 1779 the school closed for lack of funds.

Life's Work

Pestalozzi was a dreamer, a true idealist, motivated primarily by his concern for those less fortunate than he and by his intense loyalty to Switzerland. He felt a deep personal commitment to make life better for his fellow humans, and he went through life seeking ways to bring about such an outcome as a way of improving society.

Pestalozzi's exposure to teaching during the five years at Neuhof suggested to him ways to create a better society and convinced him that social amelioration, his highest goal, proceeded from the bottom up by enabling the children of the poor to find a means of sustaining themselves, of gaining self-respect through productive work such as the cotton spinning that he taught them. He was not satisfied, however, for these students to be merely cotton spinners. He expected them to work with their minds, to elevate their thinking, and to imbue their lives with a dimension that typical workers lack. His ultimate aim was to make them functioning, effective members of the ideal democratic society that he envisioned for Switzerland. He thought education was society's obligation to all of its young. His ideas were precursors of the universal free education that was later widely accepted in developed nations.

Ruined financially by the failure of his school, Pestalozzi sought to make money by entering literary contests and thus began his career in writing. He first published *Abendstunde eines Einsiedlers* (1780; *Evening Hours of a Hermit*, 1912), which articulated his notion that human beings must work at developing their inner powers and that

such development can be accomplished best within a wholesome family environment supplemented by a well-designed educational program free to everyone.

The publication of *Lienhard und Gertrud: Ein Buch für das Volk* (1781; *Leonard and Gertrude: A Popular Story*, 1800), in which Gertrude reforms her heavy-drinking spouse and, aided by the local schoolmaster, saves her community from corruption, brought Pestalozzi great attention. With this book, Pestalozzi invented the biographical novel. Before 1787, the initial novel was followed by three sequels, the most important of which is *Christoph und Else lesen in den abendstunden das Buch "Lienhard und Gertrud"* (1782; Christopher and Elsa read the book *Leonard and Gertrude* in the evening), in which Pestalozzi attempts a less sentimental, more socially critical appeal than that in the earlier book, which a sentimental reading public had misinterpreted.

It was not until two decades later, however, that *Wie Gertrud ihre Kinder lehrt* (1801; *How Gertrude Teaches Her Children*, 1894), consisting of fourteen letters about education, appeared, making

its mark as the most coherent expression of Pestalozzi's educational tenets. If his books had brought him recognition, they brought him neither job offers nor money. He struggled to survive. He even made a desperate attempt to publish a newspaper, *Ein Schweizer-Blatt*, but this weekly soon failed. Nevertheless, the venture was important to Pestalozzi's development because, as editor, he wrote about how the state should deal with criminals, proposing the same sort of humane treatment for prisoners that he had accorded his students at Neuhof.

It was not until Pestalozzi was past fifty that he had another opportunity to work with children. The French invasion of Stans was a wholesale slaughter. When the French retreated, orphans had to be cared for. The Swiss government established a residential school for them, with Pestalozzi as head. Starting with fifty children, the school soon had eighty in residence. Pestalozzi worked with these students, assisted only by a housekeeper. The operation went reasonably well, even though the canton's dominant Catholic population viewed Pestalozzi, a Protestant, with suspicion.

After six months, the orphanage was taken over by the French, who again invaded the city, as a hospital. Pestalozzi, who was emotionally and physically spent, did not return to the orphanage when the facility was returned to that purpose. Instead, at age fifty-two, he became an assistant teacher in the poorest school in Burgdorf, where again he instituted his radical methods of discouraging rote learning, emphasizing understanding, and having students learn from observing and working with objects.

Not long after his initial assignment in Burgdorf, Pestalozzi was appointed sole teacher in a school of about sixty students from poor families. He could now implement the methods in which he most believed. Soon, the government helped him establish in Burgdorf Castle a school that attracted children from affluent families, not the kinds of students that most interested Pestalozzi. It was during this period that Pestalozzi published *How Gertrude Teaches Her Children*, the book that more than any other established his reputation.

When the government requisitioned Burgdorf, Pestalozzi was finally in a position to establish his own experimental school. After a brief, abortive attempt to work with Philipp Emanuel von Fellenberg at Hofwyl, Pestalozzi established his school at Yverdon in 1805. The school became important not only as an institution where children learned by novel methods that emphasized discovery, the understanding of concepts, and proceeding from the simple to the complex but also as a school that provided teacher training for hundreds of prospective teachers. Soon, governments from surrounding nations subsidized study at Yverdon for their most promising teachers.

Pestalozzi's methods were controversial throughout his lifetime. He was convinced that education is a growing and changing process, not a fixed one. At its best, education, thought Pestalozzi, could address and cure most social ills. He believed that education must be secular rather than religious. He valued the senses over the intellect, perhaps moving further in that direction than was prudent. Not all Pestalozzi's methods worked to the best advantage of students. For example, employing his idea that one should proceed from the simple to the complex, Pestalozzi had beginning readers learn small syllabic constituents of words before they read whole words. He had them memorize an imposingly large "syllabary" consisting of hundreds of items such as *am, em, im, om*, and *um* before they tackled words. Methods of this sort, although hypothetically interesting, proved counterproductive. In addition, the methods were applied to fields such as drawing, in which Pestalozzi had students draw constituent shapes—curves, lines, and circles—in isolation rather than drawing entities. His obsession with formal analysis limited his students and frustrated some teacher trainees at Yverdon, a number of whom, including Friedrich Froebel, became critical of Pestalozzi's method. When Yverdon closed in 1825, however, two years before its founder's death, it had made a significant impact upon education in the Western world. Objection to some of the specifics of Pestalozzi's pedagogy in no way diminishes the effect it had upon education, particularly at the elementary level.

Summary

Johann Heinrich Pestalozzi succeeded at little during his first fifty years. Had he not founded Yverdon, his books would document his social and educational philosophy. His influence, however, would be less far-ranging than it was after he gathered around him a coterie of disciples who would help propagate his work after Yverdon's closing and his death.

Had Pestalozzi died at fifty, he would not have had the opportunity to practice in any sustained way the pedagogy that he developed. Yverdon became his laboratory. If Pestalozzi had a salient shortcoming, it was that he refused to admit the ineffectiveness of some of the methods in which he believed. This shortcoming, however, was more than counterbalanced by his devotion to children and by the sincerity of his effort.

The Pestalozzi legacy points in several directions. His school at Yverdon became a model for laboratory schools and for teacher-training institutions throughout the world. The normal school in the United States is an outgrowth of Yverdon. Pestalozzi's emphasis on having children learn by doing rather than by reading or hearing about things leads directly to John Dewey and other progressive educators who came indirectly under Pestalozzi's influence.

Maria Montessori's object-centered education, which led to the establishment of Montessori schools throughout the world, employs the Pestalozzi method of learning through observing objects and arriving at generalizations from those observations. The notion of engaging the senses in learning activities can be traced to Pestalozzi and such contemporaries of his as Johann Bernhard Basedow, Froebel, and Rousseau.

Pestalozzi's idea that education is the right of all children, not widespread in his time, is a prevailing tenet in most countries today, as is the separation of schools from religious authority, a radical view in the early 1800's. Few educational theorists have had the diverse effect upon modern educational practices that Pestalozzi had, though much of his significant work came after he had experienced a lifetime of failure.

Bibliography

Downs, Robert B. *Heinrich Pestalozzi: Father of Modern Pedagogy.* Boston: Twayne, 1975. This brief biography is well researched and well written, although its bibliography of primary sources is slightly disappointing. The chronology at the beginning of the book is a helpful, ready resource.

Green, J. A. *The Educational Ideas of Pestalozzi.* London: Clive, 1904; New York: Greenwood Press, 1969. A small book that reproduces well-selected samples of Pestalozzi's most significant writing. Provides an excellent overview of the intellectual development of the man and his ideas.

Gutek, Gerald Lee. *Pestalozzi and Education.* New York: Random House, 1968. This fascinating book is the most comprehensive account of the development of Pestalozzi's educational philosophy. An indispensable source.

Mueller, Gustav E. "Heinrich Pestalozzi: His Life and Work." *Harvard Educational Review* 16 (1946): 141-159. A brilliant article that places Pestalozzi in a broad cultural context and demonstrates how his influence has pervaded most aspects of modern educational thought. Carefully researched and well reasoned.

Pestalozzianum and the Zentralbibliothek, Zürich, ed. *Pestalozzi and His Times: A Pictorial Record.* New York: Stechert, 1928. This hand-some book contains a fine introduction that goes deeply into Pestalozzi's background before presenting nearly one hundred pictures of the man, his family, places he lived and worked, and manuscript pages. An extraordinary book.

Silber, Käte. *Pestalozzi: The Man and His Work.* 4th ed. London: Routledge, 1976. A good treatment of Pestalozzi and the range of his ideas. This book supplants the earlier works and brings to light some of Pestalozzi's writing about topics other than education.

R. Baird Shuman

WENDELL PHILLIPS

Born: November 29, 1811; Boston, Massachusetts
Died: February 2, 1884; Boston, Massachusetts
Area of Achievement: Social reform
Contribution: Phillips was one of the foremost orators and writers in the American antislavery movement and other social movements from 1837 until 1884.

Early Life

Born in Boston on November 29, 1811, Wendell Phillips traced his American ancestry to the Reverend Mr. George Phillips, who came to Massachusetts with John Winthrop in 1630 on the *Arbella*. His father, John Phillips, was a prominent Boston politician, who served as a judge, as the presiding officer of the state senate, and as the first mayor of Boston under that city's corporate charter, as well as on the Harvard Board of Overseers. One of his relatives was the founder of Phillips Andover Academy, while another founded Phillips Exeter Academy. Wendell's mother, Sarah Walley, was the devoutly Calvinist daughter of a middle-class Boston merchant. Although Sarah came from a less distinguished family than her husband, she could trace her American ancestry to the early seventeenth century.

As a child, Phillips received the typical education of a Boston patrician. He attended Boston Latin School, where he won distinctions for his oratory, was graduated from Harvard College in 1831, and then studied at Harvard's new law school under Justice Joseph Story until 1834.

As a young lawyer, Phillips could look forward to what appeared to be a certain and successful future. Phillips was already financially secure from his inheritance. Politically, Phillips was fully in the tradition of conservative New England Federalists. He wrote in his Harvard class book of 1831, "I love the Puritans, honor Cromwell, idolize Chatham and Hurrah for Webster." He was connected by social class, and often by blood, to the most powerful and important families in Massachusetts. He was already noted as an unusually talented speaker and writer. In addition, he was healthy, physically fit, tall, handsome, and aristocratic in his bearing. Later in life, when proper Bostonians shunned him for his abolitionist activities, Phillips condescendingly retorted that his detractors were "men of no family."

By 1835, Phillips was on his way to building a successful and profitable law practice. Phillips was not particularly enthusiastic about law practice, but he probably would not have needed to continue in the field for very long. Like his father, Phillips could have looked forward to a successful career in politics, which would have been enhanced by his remarkable speaking ability, brilliant mind, and superb debating skills. In October, 1837, Phillips solidified his position in Boston society when he married Ann Terry Greene, the orphaned daughter of a wealthy and prominent Boston merchant. In that year, however, Phillips abandoned his law practice and society life for a fulltime career as an abolitionist agitator, social reformer, and professional orator.

Life's Work

In 1837, Phillips' life changed dramatically. In March, he gave a short speech supporting abolition at the Massachusetts Anti-Slavery Society. By the end of 1837, Phillips was a professional abolitionist speaker. This shift—from a socially prominent lawyer to a leading speaker for a despised group of radical reformers—was the result of his heritage, his marriage, and the events of the mid-1830's.

As an educated patrician, Phillips firmly believed in noblesse oblige. It was not inconsistent for him to champion the rights of an oppressed minority. Indeed, moderate opposition to slavery was part of his Federalist political background and his Puritan social and cultural heritage. Phillips was, in fact, a profoundly religious man whose Puritan background no doubt led him to a movement such as abolition, which sought to root out the United States' most sinful institution—slavery.

Phillips' relationship with Ann Terry Greene was critical to his development as an abolitionist. When he met Greene, she was already a committed abolitionist, active in the Boston Female Anti-Slavery Society. While courting Ann in 1836, Wendell met William Lloyd Garrison and the other abolitionists whom he soon would join. Although an invalid most of her life, Ann was actively involved in Wendell's career, giving him both intellectual and emotional support. Phillips claimed not only that Ann made him into an abolitionist but also that she was always ahead of him in analyzing the social issues of the movement. Throughout their marriage, Ann encouraged Phillips to remain uncompromising in his opposition to slavery, in his support of the free-men, and in support of the rights of women. Their only major political disagreement was over the rights of the Irish. Ann retained the anti-Irish bias of most Bostonians of her class; Wendell saw the Irish as an exploited class, much like blacks, and thus in need of an eloquent champion to further their search for social justice. When he met Ann in 1836, Phillips was not yet an abolitionist. Two events, one in 1835 and the other in 1837, coalesced with his relationship with Ann and his background to bring Phillips into the anti-slavery movement.

In 1835, a mob dragged the abolitionist editor William Lloyd Garrison through the streets of Boston with a rope around his body. Phillips witnessed the event with shock and outrage. At the time, Phillips was not sympathetic to abolition. Yet he considered himself to be fully a son of the American Revolution. As such, he believed in free speech for all, even radicals such as Garrison. The threatened lynching of Garrison violated Phillips' sense of order and constitutional rights. The young patrician lawyer now had a new view of the abolitionists—as protectors of civil liberties, because they were the victims of intolerance.

Phillips was even more profoundly affected by the death of Elijah Lovejoy, an abolitionist printer in Alton, Illinois. In 1837, Lovejoy was thrice attacked by mobs which threw his press into the Mississippi River. When a fourth press arrived in Alton, Lovejoy vowed to defend it. In the process, he was killed. At a meeting called to denounce this event, James T. Austin, Massachusetts' antiabolitionist attorney general, took the floor and gave an eloquent speech attacking Lovejoy. Austin compared Lovejoy's killers to the revolutionaries who organized the Boston Tea Party and declared that Lovejoy was "presumptuous and imprudent" for challenging the sentiments of the day. Phillips, still relatively unknown in Boston and not yet a committed abolitionist, immediately took the floor to answer Austin. His response electrified the crowd in Boston's Faneuil Hall; the printed version had a similar effect on those who read it. Pointing to the portraits of revolutionary leaders on the wall of Faneuil Hall, Phillips declared,

> Sir, when I heard the gentleman [Austin] lay down principles which place the murderers of Alton side by side with Otis and Hancock, with Quincy and Adams, I thought those pictured lips would have broken into voice to rebuke the recreant American, the slanderer of

the dead. . . . Sir, for the sentiment he has uttered, on soil consecrated by the prayers of Puritans and the blood of patriots, the earth should have yawned and swallowed him up.

Phillips then went on to defend the rights of free speech and of the press and to attack those who would deny it to abolitionists.

This speech was the beginning of Phillips' career as the greatest abolitionist speaker of the day. Indeed, in an age of great orators, Phillips may have been the best. Besides speaking on abolition, Phillips often gave lectures on artistic and cultural topics and on other political issues. He was in constant demand and made a good living from his speaking tours. Phillips gave one nonpolitical lecture, entitled "The Lost Arts," more than two thousand times in his career and earned more than $150,000 from it.

As an antislavery agitator, Phillips was noted for his "eloquence of abuse." Northern politicians who supported slavery risked the wrath of his wit. Edward Everett was "a whining spaniel," Senator Robert Winthrop "a bastard who has stolen the name Winthrop," and Daniel Webster "a great mass of dough." Abraham Lincoln, who had once represented a slaveowner in a fugitive slave case was "the slave hound from Illinois." When lecturing, Phillips could be abusively eloquent without even using words. During one speech, he mentioned the name of a United States attorney who was notorious for his support of the Fugitive Slave Law. Phillips then stopped his speech, asked for a glass of water, rinsed his mouth, spat the water out, and continued.

Besides his marvelous rhetoric, Phillips made important intellectual contributions to the antislavery movement. Phillips accepted Garrison's analysis that the Constitution was "a covenant with death and an agreement in Hell" that favored slavery. Since Phillips could not conscientiously support the Constitution, he ceased to practice law shortly after joining the abolitionist movement. Yet he applied his legal training and knowledge to his speeches, articles, and pamphlets. His analysis of the Constitutional Convention, *The Constitution a Pro-Slavery Compact: Or, Selections from the Madison Papers* (1844), was particularly important to the Garrisonian analysis of the American government.

More important than his antislavery theory was the role he developed as a professional agitator. Phillips was harsh, extreme, and unfair in his speeches and his pamphlets. His rhetoric, however, was purposeful. He sought to enrage the people of the North by dwelling on the horrors of slavery. In a speech on slavery, he would assert that "The South is one great brothel, where half a million women are flogged into prostitution." His goal was to force his audiences to contemplate the evil of slavery. Phillips succeeded far better than any of his contemporaries.

In 1860, Phillips opposed Lincoln, as he had almost all other politicians, because the latter was not sufficiently antislavery. During the Civil War, however, Phillips' agitation was sympathetic to Lincoln and the cause of the Union. He intuitively understood that the war would destroy slavery, and he supported the Emancipation Proclamation, even though it did not extend to all slaves in the nation.

Unlike many abolitionists, Phillips did not discontinue his work with the end of the war and the adoption of the Thirteenth Amendment. In 1865, he severed his relationship with his longtime associate Garrison because the latter wanted to dissolve his American Anti-Slavery Society. Phillips thought that the job of the abolitionists remained unfulfilled. Emancipation alone was insufficient; Phillips was farsighted enough to realize that freedom required granting full political and social equality to former slaves. Thus, Phillips remained a tireless supporter of equal rights for the freedmen throughout the 1870's.

With the Constitution no longer proslavery, Phillips felt free to participate in politics. In 1870, he ran for governor of Massachusetts on the Labor Reform ticket and received twenty thousand votes. By this time, Phillips divided his energies between caring for his invalid wife, agitating for the rights of the freedmen, and opposing the exploitation of workers in the emerging industrial economy. He agitated for an eight-hour day and a reorganization of the nation's economy to protect the poor and the working classes from the robber barons of the Gilded Age. By the time of his death in 1884, Phillips was a full-fledged labor radical, as indicated by his last major publication, *The Labor Question* (1884).

Summary

In 1881, Phillips was invited back to his alma mater to give the Phi Beta Kappa address. In his speech, entitled "The Scholar in a Republic," Phillips argued that the role of an educated man in a free society is "to help those less favored in life."

This had been the life of Phillips. In an age of great orators, he was among the best. Born to lead the elite, he led instead a movement which sought freedom for those at the bottom of society. He provided hard logic, brilliant rhetoric, and a measure of upper-class cachet for the antislavery movement. Phillips flourished on the fringes of American politics, consciously creating an "office" for himself as an agitator. Phillips never made policy. Yet, by helping to create an antislavery constituency, Phillips was able to influence politics and politicians throughout his career. In the process of opposing slavery, Phillips helped legitimize the professional agitator in American politics and society.

Bibliography

Bartlett, Irving H. *Wendell and Ann Phillips: The Community of Reform, 1840-1880.* New York: Norton, 1979. A brief biography of Phillips and his wife, based on a large collection of Phillips family letters discovered in the 1970's. Includes many letters written to and from Ann and Wendell Phillips. Focuses on the private life, as well as the public life, of the Phillipses.

————. *Wendell Phillips: Brahmin Radical*. Boston: Beacon Press, 1961. A sympathetic modern biography of Phillips. Covers his entire career, focusing almost entirely on his public life.

Filler, Louis, ed. *Wendell Phillips on Civil Rights and Freedom*. 2d ed. Lanham, Md.: University Press of America, 1982. A short collection of some of Phillips' greatest speeches. This volume begins with his brilliant defense of Elijah Lovejoy's right to publish an antislavery newspaper.

Hofstadter, Richard. "Wendell Phillips: The Patrician as Agitator." In *The American Political Tradition*. New York: Knopf, 1949; London: Cape, 1967. A superb essay on Phillips and his role as an agitator. One of the first modern reappraisals of Phillips.

Korngold, Ralph. *Two Friends of Man: The Story of William Lloyd Garrison and Wendell Phillips*. Boston: Little Brown, 1950. Study of the two leaders of the radical or Garrisonian wing of the abolitionist movement.

Phillips, Wendell. "Concerning the Impossibility of Union with Slaveholders." *Essential Documents in American History* (January, 1997). In this writing dated January 15, 1845, Phillips presents and discusses a resolution adopted by the American Anti-Slavery Society that called for abolitionists to cut ties with the present government, which supported slavery.

Stewart, James B. *Holy Warriors*. Rev. ed. New York: Hill and Wang, 1996. A superb short history of the antislavery movement which places Phillips in the context of other abolitionists. An excellent introduction to history of abolition.

Wiecek, William M. *The Sources of Antislavery Constitutionalism in America: 1760-1848*. Ithaca, N.Y.: Cornell University Press, 1977. Study of abolitionist thought, which places the ideas and theories of Phillips in context with other antislavery thinkers.

Paul Finkelman

FRANKLIN PIERCE

Born: November 23, 1804; Hillsborough, New Hampshire

Died: October 8, 1869; Concord, New Hampshire

Areas of Achievement: Government and politics

Contribution: After service in his state's legislature and in both houses of Congress, Pierce became the nation's fourteenth president, serving during the turbulent years between 1853 and 1857.

Early Life

Franklin Pierce was born on November 23, 1804, in Hillsborough, New Hampshire. His father, Benjamin, was an American Revolutionary War veteran and two-term state governor (1827-1828, 1829-1830). His mother, Anna Kendrick, was Benjamin's second wife. Frank, as family and friends called him, was the sixth of their eight children.

Frank attended local schools before enrolling in Bowdoin College. Overcoming homesickness and early academic nonchalance, he was graduated fifth in the class of 1824. Classmates there included John P. Hale, the 1852 Free-Soil Party's presidential candidate; Calvin Stowe, the husband of Harriet Beecher Stowe; and writers Henry Wadsworth Longfellow and Nathaniel Hawthorne. Pierce became close friends with Hawthorne, and the novelist later penned his campaign biography. Pierce taught school during semester breaks, but his major interest during his college years seemed to be the college battalion, in which he served as an officer.

After graduation, Pierce studied in several law offices including that of later United States Senator and Supreme Court Justice Levi Woodbury of Portsmouth. He was admitted to the bar in 1827 and immediately assisted in his father's successful bid for the governorship. When his father was reelected in 1829, he simultaneously gained a seat in the state legislature.

Life's Work

His political rise was steady. When first elected to the legislature, Pierce was named chairman of the Committee on Education. Later he served as chairman of the Committee on Towns and Parishes. In 1831, Governor Samuel Dinsmoor named him his military aide with the rank of colonel, and that same year and the next he served as Speaker of the House. In March, 1833, though he was not yet thirty years old, he was elected to the United States House of Representatives. By this time, his political course was already set. He had enjoyed rapid success because of his support for his father and the Democratic Party. From then on, he gave total loyalty to the party and to its experienced politicians.

Pierce served in the House from 1833 to 1837 before advancing to the Senate for one term (1837-1842). His service was undistinguished. He deferred to his elders (when he entered the Senate, he was its youngest member). He made no memorable speech and sponsored no key legislation. He served on several committees, eventually gaining the chairmanship of the Senate Pension Committee. He consistently accepted the Southern view on slavery, and was strongly antiabolitionist, a staunch defender of the Democratic Party, and a strong opponent of the Whig program. For example, he supported the Southern position on the Gag Rule and defended Andrew Jackson's opposition to internal improvements.

It was during these years that Pierce made the political contacts and created the impression that would result in his later nomination and election to the presidency. He came to be known as an accommodating person, fun loving, and always anxious to please. He seemed perfectly content to follow party policy, and he gave proper respect to his elders. He was a New Englander whom Southerners trusted. He formed a close friendship with Jefferson Davis during these years.

In 1834, Pierce married Jane Means Appleton, the daughter of a former Bowdoin College president and Congregational minister. Throughout their married life, she suffered from a variety of physical illnesses, anxiety, and depression; in addition, she held strict Calvinistic views on life. In contrast to her sociable husband, she felt very uncomfortable in social settings and consequently stayed away from Washington, D.C., as much as she could. Like many congressmen of that age, Pierce lived in a boardinghouse with several colleagues, and he joined them in drinking to try to compensate for the boredom of his existence. Pierce was no alcoholic, but he was incapable of holding any liquor. The smallest amount inebriated him. This problem, combined with his wife's unhappiness, which was exacerbated by the death of a newborn child, convinced Pierce in 1842 that he should go back to New Hampshire. There he prom-

ised his wife that he would never drink again or return to Washington.

In New Hampshire, Pierce became a successful lawyer. He did not spend much time analyzing legal principles because he was easily able to ingratiate himself with juries and win his cases that way. He was of medium height and military bearing, dark, handsome, and an excellent dresser. People who met him at social and political gatherings liked him immediately.

During these years, Pierce also played an active role in New Hampshire's Democratic politics. He was a driving force in most of the party's campaigns, achieving good success, though he lost out to college classmate Hale in a party dispute over Texas annexation. President James K. Polk offered him the attorney generalship, and his party wanted to return him to the Senate. He declined both offers.

When the Mexican War broke out, Pierce's long-held interest in military matters and his desire for more excitement than his Concord law practice provided caused him to volunteer as a private. Before he donned his uniform, he had gained the rank of brigadier general. He made many friends among the enlisted men, and General Winfield Scott named him one of the three commissioners who attempted to negotiate an unsuccessful truce. His combat record was much less sparkling. During his first combat in the Mexico City campaign, his horse stumbled, banging Pierce against the saddle horn and then falling on his leg. He fainted. Though still in pain when he was revived, he continued, only to twist his knee and faint again when he encountered the enemy. Later, he became bedridden with a severe case of diarrhea. He was happy when the conclusion of the war enabled him to return home.

Pierce resumed his legal and political pursuits. He supported the Compromise of 1850 and became president of the state constitutional convention. He helped rid the state party of an antislavery gubernatorial candidate and thereby improved his reputation in the South. When his former law tutor, Levi Woodbury, the state's choice for the 1852 Democratic presidential nomination, died in September, 1851, Pierce became New Hampshire's new favorite son. Remembering his promise to his wife, however, he said he would consider the nomination only in case the convention deadlocked. That was precisely what happened. None of the Democratic front-runners, James Buchanan, Lewis Cass, Stephen A. Douglas, and William L. Marcy, was able to obtain the necessary two-thirds of the convention ballots. On the thirty-fifth stalemated ballot, Pierce's name was introduced. He was a Northerner with Southern principles and a person everyone seemed to like. These characteristics carried the day. On the forty-ninth ballot, he gained the nomination. When his wife learned the news, she fainted from shock.

The 1852 presidential campaign between Pierce, Whig candidate Winfield Scott, and Free-Soiler Hale was issueless. Pierce made no formal speeches; according to the custom of the time, he allowed his supporters to campaign for him. Hawthorne quickly wrote a laudatory biography, and others worked to overcome the accusation that Pierce was a drunkard, a coward, and an anti-Catholic. (The latter accusation came from an anti-Catholic provision remaining in the revised New Hampshire constitution.) In a Boston speech the previous year, he had called for the enforcement of the Fugitive Slave Law yet voiced his belief that it was inhuman, so he had to work hard to repair damage in the South from that remark. He never denied the statement but insisted he had been misrepresented, and this seemed to satisfy his critics. He won the general election 254 to 42 in electoral votes, although he had a popular margin of only forty-four thousand.

At first, Pierce made good progress in organizing his administration. Then tragedy struck. He, his wife, and their eleven-year-old son, Benjamin, were riding the train from Boston to Concord when, without warning, their car toppled off the embankment. Benjamin was killed. Neither Pierce nor his wife was ever able to recover from the shock. They vainly sought to find meaning in the freak accident. Pierce wondered if his son's death was God's punishment for his sins. Jane Pierce concluded that God had taken the boy so her husband could give his undivided attention to the presidency.

Pierce thus entered office in a state of turmoil. The feeling of insecurity that caused him to want to please others and follow his party's line now received further reinforcement from the guilt and self-doubts resulting from his son's death.

His wife's reaction only added to his burdens. Quite by accident, she learned from a friend that her husband, far from not wanting to return to Washington as he had insisted, had actually worked hard to get the nomination. She had lost her son; now she learned that her husband had deceived her. She locked the bedroom door, seldom even appearing for public functions. Eventually she spent most of her time writing little notes to her dead son, apologizing for her lack of affection during his life.

Pierce became president determined to adhere to old-line Democratic policy, with a strong dose of expansionist ideas. Unfortunately, everything he tried seemed to fail. He attempted to broaden the base of support for his administration by giving patronage to all segments of the party, but loyal supporters, especially Southerners, became angry. He made decisions on what he considered to be principle but lost political support in the process. Most significantly, he did not seem to understand that slavery, especially its expansion into the territories, was a powder keg. He had always considered public opinion to be the stuff of demagogues, so he believed he could ignore the strong negative feelings about slavery which were gaining ground in the North.

Pierce seemed incapable of providing effective direction to his administration. His cabinet, the only one in history to remain intact for an entire term, was weak, but its members had to exert their authority since he did not. Jefferson Davis, the secretary of war, emerged as the most powerful of the group.

The tragedy of Franklin Pierce was that he was president during a time of major crisis and conflict. Pierce's presidency was dominated by controversy and even violence: the Kansas-Nebraska Act, Bleeding Kansas, Bloody Sumner, the Ostend Manifesto, the Gadsden Purchase, the destruction of the Whig Party and the birth of the Republican Party. The nation cried out for leadership, for some kind of direction, but Pierce was unable to provide it. Events seemed to provide their own impetus, and he seemed incapable of directing them. His pro-Southern and antiabolitionist attitudes, his desire to please, and his uncertainty about his own capabilities did not allow him to act effectively.

The Kansas-Nebraska Act demonstrated the problem quite clearly. Pierce believed that this law providing for popular sovereignty would effectively solve the controversy over slavery in the territories. He never understood why it resulted in violence instead. Increasingly, slavery was becoming a moral issue, but he continued to treat it as merely another solvable disagreement. He and the nation paid the price.

Despite the ever more obvious failure of his presidency, Pierce hoped for renomination, authoring his 1855 annual address as a campaign document. He excoriated the new Republican Party. He reminded Americans about the need for compromise and recognition of the concept of states' rights. He claimed that despite the South's longtime willingness to compromise, as, for example, in the Missouri Compromise, the North now refused to respond in kind. The Kansas-Nebraska Act was good legislation, Pierce argued, and it could solve the problem of slavery in the territories if it were allowed to; Republicans and other antislavery fanatics had to recognize that the South had rights, too. No one could arbitrarily limit slavery. Pierce believed that such fanaticism would result only in national disruption, and did anyone really want to destroy the interests of twenty-five million Americans for the benefit of a few Africans?

Pierce's battle cry brought down a torrent of criticism. When the Democratic National Convention met in 1856, it chose James Buchanan as its candidate, snubbing Pierce and making him the only sitting president who wanted to run for reelection not to receive his party's renomination for a second term. He was bitterly disappointed and went on a three-year tour of Europe. When the Civil War erupted, Pierce first supported the Union effort, but he quickly reverted to his pro-Southern position. In a July 4, 1863, Concord speech, he blasted Lincoln's policy on civil rights and emancipation and proclaimed the attempt to preserve the Union by force to be futile. While he spoke, word filtered through the crowd of the Union victory at Gettysburg. Once again events had passed Pierce by. He lived another six years, but he played no further public role. He died on October 8, 1869, in Concord, New Hampshire.

Summary

Franklin Pierce's life was filled with contradiction. He was an outgoing man who married a recluse. He was a Northerner, but he held Southern attitudes on the major issue of the day, slavery. He gained the presidency because he seemed to be what the nation wanted: an amiable man whom neither Northerners nor Southerners found offensive. Yet it was this appealing inoffensiveness, actually a lack of firm purposefulness, which doomed his presidency from the start. The nation's problems needed determination and skill of the highest order; in Franklin Pierce, the nation gained an irresolute man, overcome with personal problems, who did not understand the crisis swirling around him and was carried along by events instead of directing them.

Bibliography

Bisson, Wilfred J., comp., with assistance from Gerry Hayden. *Franklin Pierce: A Bibliography.* Westport, Conn.: Greenwood Press, 1993. This annotated bibliography provides sources on Pierce and his administration and includes a chronology, indices, and a biographical introduction.

Brown, Thomas J. "Franklin Pierce's Land Grant Veto and the Kansas-Nebraska Session of Congress." *Civil War History* 42, no. 2 (June, 1996). Examines Pierce's veto of Dorothea Dix's land grant bill and its affect on the relationships between Republicans and Democrats.

Freehling, William W. "Franklin Pierce." In *The Presidents: A Reference History*, edited by Henry F. Graff. 2d ed. New York: Scribner, and London: Simon and Schuster, 1996. A highly critical evaluation of Pierce. The New Hampshire politician is portrayed as a weak, vacillating individual whose mediocrity was the major reason why he was electable in 1852 and why he failed during his term.

Kane, Joseph N. *Facts About the Presidents: A Compilation of Biographical and Historical Data.* 6th ed. New York: Wilson, 1993. A compilation of basic factual information on all the American presidents. Unusual or unique aspects about each president's administration are included.

Nevins, Allen. *Ordeal of the Union: A House Dividing, 1852-1857.* Vol. 2. New York: Scribner, 1947. An excellent discussion of the Pierce years with insightful commentary on how his personality affected his policy. Nevins believes that Pierce's basic weaknesses doomed his presidency because they prevented him from taking the strong positions on national issues that the times required.

Nichols, Roy F. "The Causes of the Civil War." In *Interpreting American History: Conversations with Historians*, vol. 1, edited by John A. Garraty, 286-287. New York and London: Macmillan, 1970. A brief discussion of the White House relationship of Mr. and Mrs. Pierce. Nichols points out that Jane Pierce never recovered from the death of her son and became a virtual recluse in the White House.

————. *Franklin Pierce: Young Hickory of the Granite Hills.* 2d ed. Philadelphia: University of Pennsylvania Press, 1958. This is the standard biography of the fourteenth president, detailed yet appealingly written. It emphasizes that, rather than outstanding ability, Pierce's physical attractiveness, his Mexican War military reputation, his ability to convince people with his oratory, his party regularity, and his pro-South policy gained him the 1852 Democratic nomination and eventually the presidency.

Taylor, Lloyd C., Jr. "Jane Means Appleton Pierce." In *Notable American Women, 1607-1950*, vol. 3, edited by Edward T. James. Cambridge, Mass.: Belknap Press of Harvard University Press, 1971. A brief sketch of Pierce's wife which discusses how religious rigidity fostered a repressed personality which gave way under the strain of public life and the death of a young child.

John F. Marszalek

CAMILLE PISSARRO

Born: July 10, 1830; Charlotte Amalie, St. Thomas, Danish West Indies
Died: November 12, 1903; Paris, France
Area of Achievement: Art
Contribution: Pissarro contributed to the formation of Impressionist techniques and thus to the Impressionist movement in France in the last half of the nineteenth century. In addition, he played an instrumental role in establishing a series of exhibitions to promote the work of the Impressionist artists.

Early Life

Born in Charlotte Amalie, the capital of St. Thomas, Jacob Camille Pissarro was the third of four sons of Jewish parents, Frédéric Pissarro and Rachel Manzano-Ponie Petit. His father's family had left Bordeaux, France, in search of a better life and settled on St. Thomas, where they established a family-operated trading store. To his father's displeasure, Camille spent his youthful years roaming the luxurious paths of the island, preferring to sketch and paint rather than work in the family business. At the age of twelve, Camille was sent to school in Passy, a suburb of Paris.

In Passy, the young Pissarro was encouraged by his schoolmaster to nurture his obvious talent, despite explicit instructions from his father that he was to be educated in business. After five years in Passy, his father called him home. The time in France, however, had left its mark on Pissarro. For the next five years, Pissarro preferred to sit by the docks, drawing and sketching the ships, or to hike across the island in search of suitable motifs for his sketchbook. During one of these excursions, he encountered Fritz Melbye, a Danish marine and landscape artist who encouraged Pissarro in developing a method of working outside, "in the fresh air" (*en plein air*), which he continued throughout most of his career. In 1852, the two artists moved to Caracas, Venezuela, where Pissarro remained for two years, painting continuously and interacting with the energetic artistic community in the capital. The years in Venezuela awakened Pissarro to his own ignorance of technique and of new directions then being taken in art. He left for France in 1855, never to see his homeland again.

Pissarro was twenty-five when he arrived in Paris, enthusiastic but naïve and already sporting the full, Old Testament prophet beard for which he be-

came famous among his friends. While attending the Universal Exhibition, he discovered the work of Camille Corot, whose reputation, as both a painter and a teacher, was then at its height. Despite his youth and inexperience, Pissarro managed to show his work to the great master. Corot was favorably impressed, encouraging Pissarro to focus on developing what he termed values, or the harmony between two tones, in his work.

Life's Work

The meeting with Corot in 1855 set Pissarro on a path which he was to follow, with only occasional digressions, for the remainder of his artistic career. Heeding Corot's advice, he began to pay particular attention to the importance of tonal values in creating a truly harmonious work. He practiced a lifelong attention to the importance of drawing, to self-discipline manifested in daily exercising of his craft, to *pleinairisme* ("plain-airism"), to painting what he felt, and to painting not bit by bit but rather working on the whole canvas at once. In all of this he followed the tenets established by Corot. This focus on sensation ultimately became the basis of Pissarro's work.

In 1858, Pissarro moved to Montmorency in order to paint the landscape *en plein air*. This first move to the country announced Pissarro's lifelong struggle to reject the bourgeois oppressiveness of the city in favor of simpler, rural settings. Although later in life he was often to return to Paris, staying in various hotels and painting views of the city from his window, in his early years, he preferred the bucolic setting of the countryside to the bustle of urban life. During his frequent trips to the city, he developed friendships with most of the young avant-garde artists of the time, such as Paul Cézanne and Pierre-Auguste Renoir. Because of his natural ability to offer criticism and guidance without offending the delicate egos of his colleagues, Pissarro quickly became a trustworthy and articulate spokesman for the diverse group of artists soon to be known collectively as the Impressionists.

In 1871, Pissarro married Julie Vellay. Their first of seven children, Lucien, became an accomplished artist in his own right. Although much in love in the early years of their marriage, the couple's constant financial struggles turned Julie into a sharp-tongued, unsupportive partner in later years. From all accounts, except those of Julie, Pissarro was a loving father. Nevertheless, his financial responsibility to his children never deterred him from resolutely continuing his painting even in the worst of times.

Firmly established among the Impressionists in Paris by 1863, Pissarro exhibited three paintings at the Salon des Refusés, an exhibit organized for those artists whose work had been refused by the judges for the official Salon exhibit of that year. The system of exhibitions was tightly regulated at the time by official judges (under the auspices of the emperor himself), who sought to establish national, and thus conservative, tastes in art. The Salon des Refusés was approved by the emperor in response to the artistic outcry against the conservatism of the official Salon art. Here were presented the most revolutionary works of the day. The exhibition drew desultory remarks from critics, derision, and the laughter of incomprehension from the general public. Pissarro's works went virtually unnoticed as all attention was focused on Édouard Manet's scandalous masterpiece, *Luncheon on the Grass* (1863), which depicted a naked female model accompanied on a picnic by two clothed gentlemen.

Infuriated by the public's total disinterest in his work, Pissarro was nevertheless convinced of the rightness of the new direction he was taking with his compatriots. Unlike the realistic artists whose works were being shown in the grand Salons, Pissarro and the other Impressionists sought first to capture the fugitive effects of light on a subject at a particular moment in time. Through the use of bold colors, slashing brushstrokes, and motifs chosen from everyday life, these young iconoclasts attempted to transform on canvas an effect of an impression of reality into a visually more personal, thus in their view more realistic, representation of the world.

By 1874, Pissarro was one of the acknowledged leaders of the Impressionist movement and assisted in organizing an Exhibition of the Society of Painters, Sculptors, Engravers, etc., the first of eight Impressionist exhibitions. The show included the works of Edgar Degas, Claude Monet, Berthe Morisot, Renoir, Alfred Sisley, and Cézanne. Although his work elicited only negative reactions, during the late 1870's and early 1880's he continued to paint in the Impressionist mode, experimenting with colors and different brushstrokes. Gradually he developed a highly personal and easily identifiable style, known as "Pissarro's *trico-tage*" (knitting), consisting of parallel cross-hatchings of varying dimensions, which give his work of this period a distinctive sense of movement and textural unity.

Pissarro's art took a dramatic turn in October, 1885, after a meeting with the painter Georges Seurat. Influenced by then-current scientific theories of color and its perception by the human eye, Seurat departed from the Impressionists to develop a pointillist, or divisionist, style of painting using small dots of color rather than brushstrokes. Seurat's neo-Impressionist work announced a dramatically new intent to make visible the subjective rather than, as the Impressionists had sought to do, to make the objective world subjective. Pissarro exhibited his divisionist work alongside that of Seurat in May, 1887, but without success.

Pissarro's neo-Impressionist phase lasted about five years, although strictly pointillist technique distinguishes only part of his work of this period. While his works sold poorly, he made many new friends, particularly among the Symbolist poets and writers who regarded neo-Impressionism as a visual translation of their quest toward verbal fluidity and musicality. He was also developing a strong sense of the social function of art as a supportive statement of the need for societal change, as professed by the active group of anarchists in Paris with whom he was acquainted. Melding politics and aesthetics, his work contains numerous scenes of peasants working cooperatively and serenely in the fields, content in their distance from the harsh realities of industrialization. By the late 1880's, Pissarro had found the divisionist methods tedious and abandoned the technique.

A retrospective exhibit of his work in January, 1892, proved popular with critics and public, particularly a series of landscapes and landmarks painted during a trip to London. All seventy-one works exhibited were sold, finally establishing the artist's commercial success at the age of sixty-two. His continued association with various revolutionary groups resulted in his having to flee to Belgium in 1894. In his final years, however, Pissarro enjoyed the rewards of a lifetime of hard work. Financial security came with an exhibition in 1896 of a series of paintings of the Seine executed in Rouen. Two final series of works, one of the Parisian Grands Boulevards, the other of the Avenue de l'Opéra, capped his career with critical and public acclaim. Having rented in 1900 a small apartment in Paris, he spent his last years focusing his vision on urban motifs: views of the Louvre, the Pont-Neuf, and the Tuileries Gardens. At the age of seventy-three, he developed an abcess of the prostate gland. Having always believed in the country wisdom of homeopathic medicine, he refused the necessary operation and succumbed to septicemia in 1903.

Summary

Camille Pissarro never produced a signature painting which critics regard as his masterpiece. One may speak of a series of masterful works, yet no single work stands clearly above the rest. Perhaps this is true, as one critic has suggested, because Pissarro saw art as "a continual search after the eternally changing." His love of fall and winter scenes—for example, his fascination with light playing on snow-covered hills and streets—led him to paint dozens of canvases of Pontoise and its environs, each distinctive yet most effectively viewed as one part of a corporate vision of the village.

The internal coherence of each painting was supremely important for Pissarro. His son Lucien identified the dominant characteristic as a concern for *les valeurs rapprochées* (closely related values of color). Viewing Pissarro's work over a forty-year period from 1863 to 1903, one notes that while the artist often adjusted his style to his subject, he was always ruled by the immediacy of sensations brought into direct experience with his motif, sensations which he then struggled to order into an "idea of unity." Although his work was generally not appreciated in his own lifetime, critical consensus has established his rightful place among the giants of the Impressionist movement.

Bibliography

Adler, Kathleen. *Camille Pissarro: A Biography.* London: Batsford, and New York: St. Martin's Press, 1978. A short, 190-page biography, which was the first to reconstruct Pissarro's life for the English reader. The work contains numerous illustrations and photographs of the artist and his family. The useful combination of endnotes and bibliography into one document provide the reader with easy access to secondary sources, arranged chronologically.

Lloyd, Christopher, ed. *Studies on Camille Pissarro.* London and New York: Routledge, 1986. A series of essays covering diverse aspects of Pissarro's life and work, authored by some of the most imminent of modern Pissarro critics. Several previously unexplored aspects of Pissarro's work are examined, such as the link between his political philosophy and his art, and the possible influence of Rembrandt on Pissarro's etchings.

Rewald, John, ed. *Camille Pissarro.* London: Thames and Hudson, and New York: Abrams, 1963. Perhaps the best of the relatively few collections of Pissarro's work in print, included in the Library of Great Painters series. A short introduction highlights the principal events in the artist's life and identifies major influences. Historical and aesthetic commentaries accompany each color plate.

Shikes, Ralph E., and Paula Harper. *Pissarro: His Life and Work.* London: Quartet, and New York: Horizon Press, 1980. A thorough and sensitive rendering of Pissarro's life in the context of his artistic evolution. The work contains twenty-one color plates and black-and-white reproductions. Drawing from material previously unpublished, the authors seek to reveal the complex and contradictory character of the artist. A current bibliography and detailed index assist both the casual and serious reader.

Stone, Irving. *Depths of Glory: A Biographical Novel of Camille Pissarro.* London: Bodley Head, and New York: Doubleday, 1985. Although a biographical novel, Stone's work scrupulously follows the documented details and spirit of Pissarro's life. A splendid evocation of the times by the author of similar works on the lives of Vincent van Gogh and Michelangelo. The serious reader will not be deterred by the novel's six hundred compellingly written pages.

Ward, Martha. *Pissarro, Neo-Impressionism, and the Spaces of the Avant-Garde.* Chicago: University of Chicago Press, 1996. The author examines the rise of neo-impressionism, Pissarro's participation in the movement, and his relationships with different sectors of the Parisian art world.

William C. Griffin

PIUS IX
Giovanni Maria Mastai-Ferretti

Born: May 13, 1792; Sinigaglia, Papal States

Died: February 7, 1878; Rome

Area of Achievement: Religion

Contribution: Pius was elected pope in 1846, on the eve of the year of revolutions (1848). His was to be the longest papal reign in history. He led the Church through a difficult period into the era of Italian unity; in spite of the bitter conflict between church and state, he left the Church stronger at his death.

Early Life

Giovanni Maria Mastai-Ferretti was born into a family of lesser nobility in the Marches only a few years before Napoleon I marched into Italy. He studied at Viterbo and at a seminary in Rome, where he developed a vocation for the priesthood. He suffered from epilepsy in his youth and consequently his application for service in the Swiss Guard was refused. He later recovered and was ordained as a priest in 1819. He was sent on a papal mission to Chile (1823-1825), his only experience of foreign travel. He was director of a Roman orphanage, Tata Giovanni, from 1825 to 1827, thereafter serving in the Papal States as Archbishop of Spoleto (1827-1832) and Bishop of Imola (1832-1840). Gregory XVI elevated Mastai-Ferretti to cardinal in 1840. In these early years, Archbishop Mastai-Ferretti gained a deserved reputation as a devoted leader of his flock, and he was remembered with gratitude by his congregations as a man of sincere spiritual humility who set aside time to visit the poor and showed a special devotion to children. He also observed directly the consequences of the reactionary rule of Pope Gregory, and his recognition of the need for reform in the Papal States earned for him the reputation of a liberal.

At Imola, he formed a friendship with the liberal Count Giuseppe Pasolini, who introduced him to Vincenzo Gioberti's *Del primato morale e civile degli Italiani* (1843; of the civic and moral primacy of Italians). Gioberti was a Turinese priest whose earlier enthusiasm for Giuseppe Mazzini's ideas about Italian unity had raised suspicions about his orthodoxy. His thesis was that only the pope had the authority to bring unity to Italy, and the solution to the burning question of the Risorgimento was a federation of states under the presidency of the pope. At this period of Mastai-Ferretti's life, the reformist ideas of Gioberti were appealing, and he took a copy of the book with him when he was summoned to Rome for the conclave upon the death of Gregory XVI in 1846.

Life's Work

Mastai-Ferretti was elected pope on the fourth ballot, on June 16, 1846. He was the compromise candidate, between a liberal cardinal, to his left, and the former secretary of state to Gregory XVI, the reactionary Luigi Cardinal Lambruschini, to his right. He adopted the name of Pius for his revered Pius VII, once Napoleon's prisoner, who had helped the young Mastai-Ferretti enter the priesthood. Roman and European opinion was ecstatic. A liberal pope had been chosen, and it was widely believed that the days of absolute papal control of the Romagna were numbered.

One of Pius' first acts as pope was to grant amnesty to political prisoners and exiles. He granted freedom of the press, introduced street lighting to Rome, and established a new Roman Council (composed of an overwhelming majority of laymen, many of whom held openly republican views). He finally bent to the temper of the times and conceded a constitution in March, 1848. These reforms, however, were more the result of popular pressure than spontaneous concessions granted freely from above. The new pope was worried that he had unleashed forces beyond his control. When Venice and Milan, followed by Charles Albert of Piedmont, rose against the Austrian occupation, the pope refused to assume the symbolic leadership of the national struggle. In his allocution of April 29, 1848, he stated that, as the vicar of Christ on earth, he would not wage war on another Catholic power. That was the moment when the Papacy and the secular leaders of the Risorgimento parted company.

When the pope's prime minister, Count Pellegrino Rossi, was murdered on November 15, 1848, Pius was forced to flee Rome in disguise and seek asylum in Gaeta under the protection of King Ferdinand of Naples. A republic was declared in Rome, and Mazzini was summoned to lead it, with Giuseppe Garibaldi in charge of the defenses.

From Gaeta, the pope appealed to the Catholic powers to overthrow the insurgents, and the French government (under the republican president Louis Napoleon) found itself in the embarrassing position of sending a small force to challenge a sister republic. The Roman republic collapsed in July, 1849, but the pope did not return until the following April.

Henceforth all pretense at accommodation with secular reformers was abandoned. Under the stewardship of the astute secretary of state, Giacomo Cardinal Antonelli, the Papal States prepared for a return to paternalism. The groundwork was laid for a growing conflict between church and state as Charles Albert of Piedmont, under King Victor Emanuel II of Savoy and his chief minister Count Cavour, assumed the initiative in the final struggle for Italian unity. In Piedmont, the pope had to endure the spectacle of the sequestration of church property, the abolition of religious orders, and the assumption of all educational responsibilities by the state. In Cavour he found a far more formidable adversary than Mazzini and Garibaldi, for Cavour was a brilliant and occasionally unscrupulous politician prepared to impose his will. As the power of the secular state expanded, so papal territory shrank. As the Piedmontese drove the Austrians out of Lombardy in 1859, Cavour sent forces into the Romagna to wrest it from the rule of the Papacy. The loss of the Papal States was a heavy blow, for Pius considered this territory an essential part of the Church's patrimony, granted by God in perpetuity. For Cavour and most Western European leaders, however, the Papal States were a thorn in the side of modern progress, a medieval impediment in the path of the secular future.

In the two decades after 1850, the pope presided over a great international expansion and revival of the Catholic church and the spread of its teachings. In 1864, he published the encyclical *Quanta Cura* along with the Syllabus of Errors, denouncing virtually every social and moral belief that had achieved general acceptance since the French Revolution. The gesture was intended to be an assertion of papal authority in spite of the loss of the Romagna and adjoining territories. Between 1860 and 1870, Rome was defended by French troops provided by Napoleon III, who was acting under pressure from French Catholics; he found himself now in opposition to Charles Albert of Piedmont, whose ambitions he had earlier, as president of a republic rather than emperor, supported. The out-

break of the Franco-Prussian War in July, 1870, however, led to the withdrawal of the French occupational force and the collapse of papal resistance to the government of King Victor Emmanuel. The last obstacle to Italian unity was removed and the pope retreated to the Vatican Palace.

It was Pius who cast himself in the role of "the prisoner of the Vatican," but only after he rejected a generous offer of settlement from the government (the Law of Guarantees). He thus set the pattern for his successors by refusing to come to terms with the secular institutions of power and attempting to persuade Catholics not to participate in the political life of the state. It is not a coincidence that the Vatican Council summoned by Pius in 1869 proclaimed the pope infallible in all declarations on faith and morals in order to regain a hegemony in the spiritual sphere which had been lost in the temporal. Outbreaks of anticlericalism in Europe culminated in the abrogation of the concordat with Austria in 1874, followed by the aggressive anti-Catholic campaign (*Kulturkampf*) launched by Otto von Bismarck in Germany in 1875, which included the expulsion of Jesuits and a dissolution of

Catholic schools. In spite of his isolation and doctrinally intransigent stance toward the modern world, Pius retained until the end not only the affection of the faithful but also that of the Roman populace in general, as well as the esteem of his opponents. Pius died peacefully on February 7, 1878.

Summary

While Pius' reign may be viewed as a disaster politically, ecclesiastically it recorded some major successes. Since he was not a skillful diplomat or an experienced politician, these occurred in the area of doctrine. Three events above all stand out. In 1853, Pius set about defining the dogma of the Virginity of Mary. Demands for such a definition were initially received from the lower ranks of the religious orders and the Catholic laity. The pope then requested advice from his bishops, after which the doctrine was defined by a panel of experts. It was the pope himself (who had played an active role in all the proceedings) who read the proclamation at a ceremony in St. Peter's on December 8, 1854.

The Syllabus of Errors—published ten years to the day after the proclamation on Mary—is a trenchant expression of orthodoxy, setting the Church consciously at odds with a heterodox world which it deplores. Eighty propositions are listed and condemned in the syllabus, including pantheism, rationalism, liberalism, socialism, and communism. All the "principles of '89"—the heredity of the French Revolution—that had infiltrated themselves into the myriad struggles for reform in the nineteenth century and had contributed to the secularization of civic life are denounced by the syllabus. The document is above all remembered for its final condemnation of the hope that the Papacy can be reconciled to progress, liberalism, and modern civilization.

A similar theological conservatism is evident in the question of papal infallibility endorsed by the Vatican Council of 1869-1870. The pope was not well served by an unauthorized and imprudent article in a Jesuit publication suggesting that the doctrine would be presented in council and accepted without debate. This was by no means the intention, but it offered an opportunity to anti-Catholic forces to claim that the pope was in the hands of the Jesuits. The result was that the question was debated at inordinate length, but its ultimate ratifica-

tion by a vast majority of the assembled bishops was a personal triumph for Pius.

Taken together, these three questions of dogma illustrate the major concerns of Pius IX at a time when the Church, under fire from progressive and secular forces, sought to assert doctrinal unity behind the authority of God's appointed vicar on earth in order to keep a hold on the faith of its followers and to lead them into the modern era. Pius himself was not implacably opposed to every aspect of modern life; as pope, however, he saw his first duty as consolidating the power of the Church around the issue of faith and his second as securing a permanent place for the Church among the nation states of the new age.

Bibliography

Corrigan, Raymond. *The Church and The Nineteenth Century*. Milwaukee: Bruce, 1938. A propapal view by a Jesuit historian of Pius' career and his struggle with the major historical events of his reign, the challenge of republican and monarchical government. There are separate chapters on the unification of Italy, the doctrine of the Immaculate Conception, and the Syllabus of Errors.

Hales, E. E. Y. *The Catholic Church in the Modern World*. London: Eyre and Spottiswoode, and New York: Hanover House, 1958. Hales returns to the central episodes referred to in his biography, here treated with more specific historical detail and discussion. Chapter 7 through 11 deal with the major themes and struggles of Pius' reign, while his career as a whole is set in the broader history of the Church from the French Revolution to Italian fascism and the postwar democracy.

———. *Pio Nono*. London: Eyre and Spottiswoode, and New York: Kenedy, 1954. The fullest study of the pope's career in English and essential reading for the student or scholar. This is a political biography written as a defense of Pius' position vis-à-vis contemporary liberalism, the Roman republic, and Catholic progressives. Informative on his relations with Cavour, Victor Emanuel, and Napoleon III.

John, Eric, ed. *The Popes, a Concise Biographical History*. London: Burnes and Oates, and New York: Hawthorn, 1964. An encyclopedia of the lives of all the popes, each one written in all essential detail. The tone is pro-Catholic but not unctuous. The section on Pius IX is full, complete, and objective, while presenting an essentially sympathetic portrait of a troubled pontiff.

Kelly, John N. D. *The Oxford Dictionary of Popes.* Oxford and New York: Oxford University Press, 1986. The pages on Pius are concise and detailed, very clear on the major doctrinal contributions made by Pius to Catholic thinking. A useful introduction which will send students on to the complete biographies.

Mize, Sandra Yocum. "Defending Roman Loyalties and Republican Values: The 1848 Italian Revolution in American Catholic Apologetics." *Church History* 60, no. 4 (December, 1991). Discussion of Pope Pius IX's opposition to the unified Italian republic in 1848 and its affect on the views of U.S. Catholic apologists.

Rendina, Claudio. *I papi, storia e segreti.* Rome: Newton Compton, 1983. Another encyclopedia of papal biographies, this one written from a more skeptical point of view, underlining occasional scandals within the Papacy and those reactionary positions undertaken by all popes that aroused indignation in the opinion of non-Catholic Europe. Rendina's commentary on Pius IX, as in other cases, is enlivened by quotations from contemporary satirists in verse or prose.

Harry Lawton

FRANCIS PLACE

Born: November 3, 1771; London, England
Died: January 1, 1854; London, England
Areas of Achievement: Politics and social reform
Contribution: Place worked for the advancement of organizations and legislation for the betterment of the workingman.

Early Life

Francis Place was born on November 3, 1771, in a private debtors' prison near the Drury Lane Theatre Royal. His father, Simon Place, had in his early years been a baker; at the time of Francis' birth, he was bailiff to the Marshalsea Court and operator of a debtors' lockup house. Simon Place's propensity for gambling lost for him and his family their home and livelihood on at least three occasions. Still, though the elder Place was strict with his four children and often cuffed the boys rather than answer their questions, he saw to their education in the manner of the times. At four, young Francis was instructed by an old woman in Bell Street. After that, he and his brother attended boys' schools, where they were taught the rudiments of reading, writing, mathematics, and biblical studies. Place attributed his attainment of "right notions" and "power of reasoning" to the efforts of his last headmaster, who encouraged analytical thinking through regular discussion and rewards. Self-confidence, perseverance, industry, and a strong desire for learning were the result. From this time onward, Place read omnivorously, borrowing books and reading at bookstalls until he could afford a library of his own.

At fourteen, Place was apprenticed to a leather-breeches maker; he had chosen to learn a trade rather than read for the law. In the shop he enjoyed a fair amount of liberty, as long as he did his work, and by the age of eighteen he became a journeyman. Like most young men of his age, he ran with a street gang and frequented taverns. At the same time, though he was a conscientious worker and was steadily employed in various shops, he was never able to make a "respectable appearance," a goal dear to his heart.

With very little in the way of worldly goods but with high hopes of one day owning his own business, Place married Elizabeth Chadd, the daughter of servants, on March 17, 1791. He was nineteen years of age; she was seventeen. At that time, Place described himself as muscular and short (five feet, six inches), with black curly hair and beard.

The leather-breeches trade was in decline, but by taking assignments from several masters, in two years Place reached what seemed a secure position. It was during this year, 1793, that a strike by the Breeches Makers Benefit Society deprived him of his employment, even though he was not actually involved with the society. For eight months, he and his family nearly starved, but Place learned valuable lessons. He set up a system for making the strikers' money last and helped organize other trades. He also gained an intense appreciation of the plight of those who labored in abject poverty.

In June, 1794, Place joined the London Corresponding Society, a group of artisans and small shopkeepers who were concerned with "the unequal Representation of the People in Parliament." He became a member of the general committee and the executive committee, where he met aware, intelligent men who attended weekly readings and discussions. He also helped write their new constitution. Later that same year, Place was chosen to prepare the successful defense of several members accused of treason, Thomas Hardy, the founder, among them. Yet the tensions of the war years, resultant government restraints, the suspension of habeas corpus, and the Treasonable Practices Act and Seditious Meetings Act of 1795 caused a decline. Nevertheless, Place and his friend John Ashley worked to keep the group together and financially solvent. When many of their colleagues insisted on holding a public meeting (prohibited by the new law), Ashley and Place withdrew (June, 1797). A year later the whole committee was seized by Middlesex magistrates, and not long after, the organization dissolved. The society had served Place well, and he reciprocated by raising money for the families of the imprisoned.

During these years, Place had been working independently and, despite periods of hardship, refused to go back to journeyman status. Never again would he be dependent upon an employer. On April 8, 1799, he realized his dream. He and Richard Wild, his boarder and colleague, opened a tailor shop at 29 Charing Cross. Frugal habits and hard work earned for them the necessary creditors and customers, and their business flourished. A year and a half later, his scheming partner left Place with his wife and four children virtually penniless. Fortunately, his reputation had been made, lenders came to his aid, and he was able to set up a new business, first on Brydges Street, and by spring, at 16 Charing Cross. By 1816, his net profits exceeded three thousand pounds, and in 1817, he was able to turn his business over to his son and engage in public pursuits. By this time, there were ten living children of the fifteen born to him.

Life's Work

Place had become an elector for Westminster by virtue of his residence at Charing Cross in 1800. By the time of the 1805 and 1807 elections, his business well established, he became interested in the machinations of the election process whereby Whigs and Tories simply divided the two seats. The Duke of Northumberland's "beef, beer, and bread" purchase of votes sickened Place, and he worked to elect the Radical candidate, Sir Francis Burdett. The Westminster Committee was successful and became the key political unit in the district, with Place its chief organizer. His library became a meeting place for political discussion, and in time, leading political figures and their representatives gathered there to discuss and learn.

Place met and became friendly with many scholars, among them William Godwin, whose book *An Enquiry Concerning Political Justice, and Its Influence on General Virtue and Happiness* (1793) had provided the impetus for Place's venture into employer status. Unfortunately, his well-meant attempt to rescue Godwin from financial chaos was foiled by Godwin himself, and Place severed their relationship. His experiences with James Mill, whom he met in 1808, and Jeremy Bentham, whom he met in 1812, were happier. When Place joined them in their studies at Ford Abbey in Devon for several weeks in the summer of 1817, he became a devoted disciple of utilitarianism. Place later assisted Mill in copying, proofreading, and indexing his *History of British India* (1817). Place also aided Bentham in evaluating his *Rationale of Judicial Evidence* (1827) and in managing his business affairs. Along with other disciples, Place helped write Bentham's later books from his notes. Place believed in Bentham's practical approach to problems and shared his dedication to the principle that social policy should be determined according to "the greatest happiness of the greatest number."

When the Royal Lancastrian Association, a group dedicated to bringing education to the London poor through a system of student monitors, fell on hard times, Place and Mill both extended aid. Place served on the committee of its successor, the British and Foreign School Society, with the goal of organizing primary and secondary schools throughout London. Though the project failed, it became the prototype for later efforts. Place made a more lasting contribution in helping to found the London Mechanics Institute in 1823. He and Dr. George Birkbeck, who lectured to workingmen, saw to it that there was middle-class participation, that subject matter was mainly technical and scientific, and that orthodox political ideas were followed. As Birkbeck College, the school later became part of the University of London.

Place's interest in Thomas Robert Malthus' *An Essay on the Principle of Population as It Affects the Future Improvement of Society, with Remarks on the Speculations of M. Godwin, M. Condorcet, and Other Writers* (1798) led him to ponder the multiplying population and shrinking resources. While he could agree with Malthus' theory of population, that people multiply geometrically while food can only expand arithmetically, his own experiences militated against the abstinence and late marriage that Malthus advocated. In 1822, he published his only book, *Illustrations and Proofs of the Principle of Population*. In it, Place argued for conscientious contraception, although he is seldom credited with being the first to do so publicly.

Place's greatest triumph, according to his biographer, Graham Wallas, was his single-handed repeal of the Combination Laws. A law enacted in 1721 regulated the number of journeyman tailors; a second, enacted in 1799, prevented laborers from combining to change hours or wages. Place collected eight volumes of evidence illustrating the injustices suffered by workmen under these laws. Workers could be whipped or jailed for not accepting their masters' terms and even have their wages withheld if they banded together to demand money owed to them. At the same time, masters were demanding stiffer laws. Place began working to repeal these laws in 1814. Through writing articles and petitions and carefully instructing his protégé, the M.P. Joseph Hume, he finally won a parliamentary committee in 1824. Hume chaired the committee, and Place prepared endless instructions. Workers came to his home to give their stories, and he coached them to give their testimony. He set up questions for Hume to ask and rebuttals for objections. He reviewed each day's proceedings and set up outlines and indexes for Hume. He then drew up resolutions which were directly incorporated into the bill. Many setbacks followed, but the law passed both houses of Parliament in 1824, and a somewhat more restrictive law followed in 1825.

Place's wife, Elizabeth Chadd, died in 1824, and Place married a Mrs. Chatterly in 1830, from whom he was separated in 1851. In 1853, financial problems prompted his move to Brompton Square.

The reform spirit of England coincided with Place's period of peak performance. The July Revolution of 1830 in France, together with the death of King George IV and the accession of William IV, motivated the Radicals to pressure the Whigs for parliamentary reform. People everywhere held meetings in cities, towns, and parishes; artisans and workers met in their associations; farm workers carried on rick burning. Hard times made the situation tense, and even Place, a normally peaceful reformer, thought that violence might be necessary to bring about change. At the same time, he chaired meetings and helped organize the Parliamentary Candidates' Society and the National Political Union. When the first bill was rejected by the Lords on October 8, 1831, Place sponsored a peaceful procession, and urged Members of Parliament to propose a second bill. Tempers were running high when the Lords refused the second bill and the king refused to create new peers. Lord Grey resigned, and the Duke of Wellington set out to form a government of repression. The Birmingham Political Union threatened insurrection and contacted Place and the Parliament. At Place's connivance, it was decided that a run on the banks would thwart the duke. The scheme worked, Grey came back to power, and the third bill passed the Lords on June 4. Place had successfully steered a course between insurrection and stand-pat conservatism. He had advised workers and government leaders. The Reform Bill was only the beginning of the democratization of the English system, but Place was pleased that the people had asserted themselves and yet was satisfied that the bill did not grant the common people full power.

From 1834 to 1836, Place worked for the reorganization of local government through the Poor Law and the Municipal Corporation Act. He was enthusiastic about both and had unrequited hopes of becoming a Poor Law Commissioner. Place waged a campaign against the Newspaper Stamp Tax (enacted in 1819, it stipulated a four-penny duty on all periodicals under six pence) as a "Tax on Knowledge." In 1836, the tax was dropped to a penny; it was not abolished until 1855, the year after his death.

Disappointment with the Reform Bill and hard times led to a new drive for working-class solidarity in the mid-1830's. The Grand National Trades Union grew, and the home secretary, Lord Melbourne, talked of new combination laws. Place worked with laborers to apprise them of their rights and keep them within the law. In 1837, he helped William Lovett organize the Working Men's Association and in 1838 drafted the People's Charter. Chartism failed as a revolutionary movement, but five of its six goals (universal manhood suffrage, an abolition of property qualifications for M.P.'s, salaries for M.P.'s, equal electoral districts, and a secret ballot) later became part of the English system.

Place's involvement with the Anti-Corn Law League took him to Manchester in November of 1841 in cold and rainy weather. He never recovered from the resulting illness, and in 1844, he suffered a cerebral attack. Unable to read very much but still dedicated to the workers, Place spent his last years organizing clippings and pamphlets related to their history and assembling them into 181 volumes. He died in his sleep at the home of his two unmarried daughters on January 1, 1854.

Summary

It is difficult to assess the long-term influence of a man such as Francis Place. He has been criticized for lack of creativity, yet the time period in which he lived demanded just such characteristics as he possessed: a keen and receptive mind, analytical abilities, unflagging industry, and dogged persistence. His early experiences provided him with great understanding of and sympathy for workingmen. Though he never held an official position, he worked endlessly in their interest; that he sometimes pursued programs later rejected (for example, the Poor Law) is not surprising. It is a commentary on both his intellect and his character that he made friends and worked with many luminaries of the day and was consulted by men of all classes. Place foresaw the rise of the democratic system and the concomitant decline in both the aristocracy as a class and the House of Lords as an institution. That he worked diligently that workers might be prepared for the change through education and a gradual expansion of rights makes Place a key figure in the glorious history of England's peaceful change.

Bibliography

Cole, G.D.H., and Raymond Postgate. *The Common People, 1746-1946*. London: Methuen, 1938; New York: Knopf, 1939. Indispensable background reading for a broad understanding of the working-class movement and the conditions that fostered it. Place and his activities are well covered.

Johnson, Dorothy Catherine. *Pioneers of Reform: Cobbett, Owen, Place, Shaftsbury, Cobden, Bright*. London: Methuen, 1929; New York: Franklin, 1968. A brief and closely reasoned account of Place's life and career. Johnson sees her subject as without sympathy or emotion, a practical man of action. She traces the development of his philosophy through his contacts, especially with the utilitarians, and describes his political activities. Good brief rundown.

Place, Francis. *The Autobiography of Francis Place, 1771-1854*. Edited by Mary Thale. London: Cambridge University Press, 1972. Place traces his intellectual and political development together with his early economic fortunes. Unfortunately, his work with the Combination Laws is mentioned only briefly, and his later political activity, not at all. Letters to friends and relatives are included.

———. *Illustrations and Proofs of the Principle of Population*. London: Longman, 1822; Boston: Houghton Mifflin, 1930. Well-read and politically and socially aware, Place came to believe that Malthus' ideas of moral restraint for population control were completely impractical. They did not conform to experience or utility and were contrary to human nature. In this book, he reviews Malthus' ideas step by step and comes out unequivocally for early marriage as a prevention for promiscuity, and contraception as a remedy for its consequences.

———. *London Radicalism, 1830-1843: A Selection from the Papers of Francis Place*. Edited by D.J. Rowe. London: London Record Society, 1970. A unique collection, selected from Place's vast number of papers. Concentrates on the Reform Bill and the major organizations: The National Union of the Working Classes and the National Political Union. Limited coverage is given to the London Working Men's Association. Valuable for providing examples of Place's vast industry as well as of his lesser known ideas and activities.

Wallas, Graham. *The Life of Francis Place, 1771-1854*. London and New York: Longman, 1898. The only full-length biography of the subject. Wallas utilized all of Place's papers, except for the many volumes that he collected in his final years. Well written, this work incorporates the then unpublished autobiography, often in Place's own words, and provides a good picture of the subject and his development in the context of the times.

Ward, John Towers. *Chartism*. London: Batsford, and New York: Barnes and Noble, 1973. Beginning with a brief chapter, "The Antecedents," Ward traces the reform impulse through the Chartist years. He puts Place in historical context and relates his activities to those of his reformist contemporaries.

Marjorie Kratz

KONSTANTIN PETROVICH POBEDONOSTSEV

Born: May 21, 1829; Moscow, Russia
Died: March 23, 1907; St. Petersburg, Russia
Areas of Achievement: Government and politics
Contribution: As Director General of the Holy Synod and tutor to Czars Alexander III and Nicholas II, Pobedonostsev was a major contributor to the preservation of the autocratic governmental system in Russia against the forces of modernization.

Early Life

Konstantin Petrovich Pobedonostsev was born in Moscow, one of eleven children. His father, son of a Russian Orthodox priest and trained for the priesthood, became instead a professor of rhetoric and Russian literature at the University of Moscow. Little is known about Konstantin's mother, except that she was a descendant of an old-service noble family from near Kostroma. Konstantin, educated at home by his father, entered the School of Jurisprudence in St. Petersburg at thirteen; the school prepared him and others from gentry families for service in law courts and the judicial and legal branches of the imperial bureaucracy. Pobedonostsev spoke, read, and wrote in seven foreign languages and read widely throughout his life in the classics and in Russian and Western history and literature. While he believed that an educated Russia must give special attention to Western Europe and its achievements, there remained a basic tension in him throughout his life between a fascination with European ideas and a growing admiration for Russian traditions and institutions.

Upon graduation in 1846, Pobedonostsev returned to Moscow as a law clerk in the eighth department of the senate. Established by Peter the Great as the highest state institution to supervise all judicial, financial, and administrative affairs, by the nineteenth century the senate had evolved into the supreme court for judicial affairs and appeals against administrative acts of the government. Pobedonostsev's rise in senate employment was rapid and steady. By 1853, he was secretary of the seventh department; in 1857 he became secretary to both the seventh and eighth departments; and by 1863 he was named executive secretary of the eighth department.

His education and training in the senate, along with his numerous publications, singled him out as an unusually promising young scholar, teacher (he was appointed lecturer in Russian civil law at the University of Moscow in 1859), and administrator. As the government of Alexander II struggled with reforms following Russia's defeat in the Crimean War of 1853-1856, Pobedonostsev's work singled him out as one who could make an important contribution. The reforming decade of the 1860's was a turning point in both Pobedonostsev's career and his thinking.

Life's Work

In 1861, Pobedonostsev was appointed tutor in Russian history and law for the heir to the throne, Nicholas Alexandrovich. Upon the death of Nicholas from tuberculosis in 1865, Pobedonostsev continued as tutor for the new heir, the future Alexander III. This appointment was a key one in Pobedonostsev's life, removing him from the study and classroom and placing him in a position from which he would eventually exercise a profound influence on the course of late nineteenth century Russian history.

From 1866 to 1880, Pobedonostsev's rise through the bureaucracy continued to be steady and rapid. In 1868, he was named a senator, and in 1872 he was appointed a member of the Council of State, the major advisory body to the czar on projected laws and administration of the non-Russian areas of the empire. In April, 1880, he was appointed Director General of the Holy Synod. The synod, also established by Peter the Great, replaced the patriarch as head of the Russian Orthodox church and was one of the most important branches of the central government. As director general, a position he would hold for the next twenty-five years, Pobedonostsev was the czar's representative to this ruling body of the state church. Through this position, Pobedonostsev came to wield considerable influence over such aspects of government policy as education, access to information, social legislation, and civil rights.

The decade of the 1860's, associated with the Great Reforms of Alexander II, was an exhilarating time, but it proved to be the last time the autocratic system attempted to reform itself. While the reconstruction of society was concerned mainly with the emancipation of the serfs, most state institutions were subjected to intense scrutiny that resulted in various degrees of reorganization. Pobedonostsev's numerous studies advocating reform of the judicial system resulted in his appointment to work on the draft of the judicial reform of 1864.

While these early years might be termed his "liberal" period, the Polish uprising of 1863 and the resulting revolutionary unrest in Russia's major cities and towns came as a deep shock. Pobedonostsev began to turn against the introduction of new ideas and institutions, arguing instead that what Russia needed was more, not less, government control and supervision. His scholarly interests soon reflected this overall change in his outlook. Whereas up to 1864 his research reflected a certain criticism of some of Russia's central institutions, Pobedonostsev now devoted more time to the study of Russian civil law. His research resulted in the publication of his most important work, the three-volume *Kurs grazhdanskago prava* (1868-1880; course on civil law), which won for him high repute as a legal scholar. At the same time, Pobedonostsev became increasingly vocal in his belief that Russia must rely on its traditional values and institutions and reject the importation of alien ideas.

The rise of the revolutionary movement, culminating in the assassination of Alexander II in 1881, turned many in government and society against his policies of reform. Pobedonostsev was among those who saw liberalism as a fundamental threat to the principle of autocratic government and advised Alexander III that the czar's duty was to protect his people from the projects of constitutional reform associated with the last years of his father's reign. It was Pobedonostsev who drafted the famous manifesto of April 19, 1881, that ended all serious consideration of political reform in Russia for the next generation. From then on, the tall, thin, balding Pobedonostsev, peering out at the world from behind small, wire-rimmed glasses, was associated with the reactionary policies linked to the reign of Alexander III. His appointment as tutor to the future Nicholas II ensured that the autocratic system would not adjust itself to the new social and political movements of the day.

Pobedonostsev's political philosophy was spelled out coherently and succinctly in his most famous book, the collection of essays entitled *Moskovskii sbornik* (1896; *Reflections of a Russian Statesman*, 1898). Like many reactionary philosophers before and after him, Pobedonostsev vilified human nature as evil, worthless, and rebellious. Therefore, he believed that those who advocated reason instead of faith as the proper guide for hu-

man actions were fundamentally wrong. The enormous size of Russia, plus its complex national composition and the ignorance and economic backwardness of its peasantry, all pointed to the folly of introducing any concept of responsible government, freedom of the press, secular education, or laissez-faire economics. Instead, Pobedonostsev believed, society should be based on those traditional values and institutions that had shaped its character over the centuries. Thus Pobedonostsev, although widely read in European and American social and political literature, opposed any and all arguments for their application in the case of Russia.

There was a basic inconsistency in Pobedonostsev's thinking which can best be seen in his attitude toward Russia's minority peoples and religions. While he always insisted that the human being was a product of a historical tradition, Pobedonostsev refused to Russia's minorities the right to defend their cultural and historical form of life against the encroachments and bureaucratic enactments of the Russian state. In this case, he was more interested in the stability and extension of the autocratic system and argued continuously in support of those Russification policies that so alienated the minorities in the empire.

The revolution of 1905 overthrew autocratic government in Russia and established a constitutional monarchy with civil liberties and an extended franchise for a new legislative assembly. Pobedonostsev played no role in this crisis. The results of the revolution, by introducing institutions and values he had consistently resisted, merely confirmed his pessimism about human nature and the future of Russia. In October, 1905, he retired quietly from his position as Director General of the Holy Synod. While he remained on the Council of State, he no longer played a role in government. His last days, filled with illness, were passed quietly in his residence, working on his ongoing project of translating the Bible into Russian. It was there that he died in 1907. He was buried with little fanfare in the garden of Saint Vladimir's, a finishing school for young women planning to marry priests and work in parish schools.

Summary

Konstantin Petrovich Pobedonostsev is an excellent example of the conservative bureaucratic statesman associated with the reigns of the last two czars of Russia. Convinced as he was of the evil and weak nature of human beings, Pobedonostsev believed that the only institutions that might save the Russian people were the state, the Orthodox church, and the family. Of these he believed the state was central. These beliefs were used to justify his support for arbitrary and authoritarian government. Thus, in facing the momentous changes engulfing Western civilization in the late nineteenth century, Pobedonostsev set himself squarely against them all in the name of Russia's traditional values and institutions.

Since Pobedonostsev believed that a people's educational system reflected their society, it is not surprising that he had a deep interest in the educational policies of the empire. He believed that the educational system must remain firmly under the control of the autocratic system and the state church. The system he envisioned had as its first priority the instillation of a firm religious foundation in its students, along with an emphasis on patriotism and love of autocracy. Pobedonostsev bears considerable responsibility for the ruling that kept Russian higher education in shackles until the 1905 revolution restored some semblance of autonomy.

While he was suspicious of higher education as destabilizing for society, Pobedonostsev emphasized the role of the parish school as best suited to serve the interests of order. During his years as Director General of the Holy Synod, he was instrumental in allocating resources to develop the parish school system throughout the country. By 1900, half of all elementary schools were under the control of the synod, while slightly more than a third of all children receiving primary education were enrolled in parish schools, wherein they were taught the proper values of an autocratic society.

As tutor to the last two czars and as Director General of the Holy Synod for twenty-five years, Pobedonostsev was in a position to wield considerable influence on late imperial Russia. His opposition to all elements of liberalism and his support for the Russification of the national minorities made him, in the popular eye, the "grey eminence" behind the reign of Alexander III. Thus Pobedonostsev contributed to those policies that eventually caused a revolution that destroyed the entire imperial order.

Bibliography

Adams, Arthur E. "Pobedonostsev's Religious Politics." *Church History* 22 (1953): 314-326. Pobedonostsev subordinated the Orthodox church to the state in the name of political stability and state security. His efforts to strengthen and to extend Orthodoxy into the non-Russian provinces and among heretics and dissenters was motivated not by a desire to save souls but by a desire to preserve the Russian Empire.

———. "Pobedonostsev's Thought Control." *The Russian Review* 11 (1953): 241-246. In his effort to control Russia's thought, Pobedonostsev used his official position in the state and Church to persecute those whom he found dangerous to the stability of the system and to promote the careers of those whose views were in harmony with his own.

Basil, John D. "Konstantin Petrovich Pobedonostsev: An Argument for a Russian State Church." *Church History* 64, no. 1 (March, 1995). Profile of Pobedonostsev, his concept of a state church, and the changes in church and state issues in late Imperial Russia.

Byrnes, Robert F. "Dostoevsky and Pobedonostsev." In *Essays in Russian and Soviet History*, edited by John Shelton Curtiss. New York: Columbia University Press, 1962. Explores the close relationship between Pobedonostsev and Fyodor Dostoevski during the decade of the 1870's. While Soviet historians have argued that Dostoevski was influenced greatly by Pobedonostsev, especially in the writing of his later novels, evidence indicates this was not so.

———. *Pobedonostsev: His Life and Thought.* Bloomington: Indiana University Press, 1968. A standard biography, presenting an account of Pobedonostsev's life along with a discussion and analysis of his major writings and sociopolitical philosophy. Emphasizes his conservatism and his influence both at court and through the Holy Synod to maintain order and stability within the empire.

———. "Pobedonostsev on the Instruments of Russian Government." In *Continuity and Change in Russian and Soviet Thought*, edited by Ernest J. Simmons. Cambridge, Mass.: Harvard University Press, 1955. Analyzes Pobedonostsev's political philosophy, emphasizing his view that the duty of absolute government was to distinguish between right and wrong, good and evil, and to ensure social stability. The character of the state was formed by its national religious faith and its traditional political and social institutions.

Pobedonostsev, Konstantin P. *Reflections of a Russian Statesman.* Translated by Robert Crozier Long. London: Richards, 1898; Ann Arbor: University of Michigan Press, 1965. An eloquent and readable plea in support of the values and institutions of traditional Russia. Expounds Pobedonostsev's belief in the evil and perverse nature of the human being and his social philosophy of stability and order through autocratic government and the Orthodox church.

Thaden, Edward C. *Conservative Nationalism in Nineteenth Century Russia.* Seattle: University of Washington Press, 1964. Chapter 13, entitled "Bureaucratic Nationalism," discusses Pobedonostsev's thought and contribution to Russification policies toward the national and religious minorities in the empire. In support of these policies, Pobedonostsev was not averse to the use of the power of the state to educate and coerce or to the use of the parish schools to indoctrinate youth in the values of traditional Russia.

Jack M. Lauber

EDGAR ALLAN POE

Born: January 19, 1809; Boston, Massachusetts
Died: October 7, 1849; Baltimore, Maryland
Area of Achievement: Literature
Contribution: In addition to his achievements as one of the pioneering figures in American literature, Poe was influential in making magazine publishing an important force in the literary world of the nineteenth century.

Early Life

Edgar Allan Poe was born January 19, 1809, in Boston, Massachusetts. His mother, Elizabeth Arnold Poe, was a talented actress from an English theatrical family. Because Poe's father, David Poe, Jr., a traveling actor of Irish descent, was neither talented nor responsible, the family suffered financially. After apparently separating from David Poe, Elizabeth died in Richmond, Virginia, in 1811. The young Edgar, though not legally adopted, was taken in by a wealthy Scottish tobacco exporter, John Allan, from whom Poe took his middle name.

For most of his early life, Poe lived in Richmond with the Allans, with the exception of a five-year period between 1815 and 1820 which he spent in England, where he attended Manor House School, near London. Back in America, he attended an academy until 1826, when he entered the University of Virginia. He withdrew less than a year later, however, because of various debts, many of them from gambling; Poe did not have the money to pay, and his foster-father refused to help. After quarreling with Allan about these debts, Poe left for Boston in the spring of 1827; shortly thereafter, perhaps because he was short of money, he enrolled in the United States Army under the name "Edgar A. Perry."

In the summer of 1827, Poe's first book, *Tamerlane and Other Poems*, published under the anonym "A Bostonian," appeared, but it was little noticed by the reading public or by the critics. In January, 1829, he was promoted to the rank of sergeant major and was honorably discharged at his own request three months later. In December, 1829, Poe's second book, *Al Aaraaf, Tamerlane, and Minor Poems*, was published, and it was well received by the critics. Shortly thereafter, Poe entered West Point Military Academy, possibly as a way to get into his foster-father's good graces.

After less than a year in school, Poe was discharged from West Point by court-martial for ne-glecting his military duties. Most biographers agree that Poe deliberately provoked his discharge because he had tired of West Point. Others suggest that he could not stay because John Allan refused to pay Poe's bills any longer, although he would not permit Poe to resign. After West Point, Poe went to New York, where, with the help of some money raised by his West Point friends, he published *Poems by Edgar A. Poe, Second Edition*. After moving to Baltimore, where he lived at the home of his aunt, Mrs. Clemm, Poe entered five short stories in a contest sponsored by the *Philadelphia Saturday Courier*. Although he did not win the prize, the newspaper published all five of his pieces. In June, 1833, he entered another contest sponsored by the *Baltimore Saturday Visiter* and this time won the prize of fifty dollars for his story "Ms. Found in a Bottle." From this point until his death in 1849, Poe was very much involved in the world of American magazine publishing.

Life's Work

During the next two years, Poe continued writing stories and trying to get them published. Even with the help of a new and influential friend, John Pendleton Kennedy, a lawyer and writer, he was mostly unsuccessful. Poe's financial situation became even more desperate when, in 1834, John Allan died and left Poe out of his will. Kennedy finally persuaded the *Southern Literary Messenger* to publish several of Poe's stories and to offer Poe the job of editor, a position which he kept from 1835 to 1837. During this time, Poe published stories and poems in the *Messenger*, but it was with his extensive publication of criticism that he began to make his mark in American letters.

Although much of Poe's early criticism is routine review work, he began in his reviews to consider the basic nature of poetry and short fiction and to develop theoretical analyses of these two genres, drawing upon the criticism of A. W. Schlegel, in Germany, and Samuel Taylor Coleridge, in England. Poe's most important contribution to criticism is his discussion of the distinctive generic characteristics of short fiction, in a famous review of Nathaniel Hawthorne's *Twice-Told Tales* (1837). Poe makes such a convincing case for the organic unity of short fiction, argues so strongly for its dependence on a unified effect, and so clearly shows how the form is more closely allied to the poem

than to the novel that his ideas have influenced literary critics ever since.

In 1836, Poe married his thirteen-year-old cousin, Virginia Clemm, a decision which, because of her age and relationship to Poe, has made him the subject of much adverse criticism and psychological speculation. In 1837, after disagreements with the owner of the *Messenger*, Poe moved to New York to look for editorial work. There he completed the writing of *The Narrative of Arthur Gordon Pym* (1838), his only long fiction, a novella-length metaphysical adventure. Unable to find work in New York, Poe moved to Philadelphia and published his first important short story, a Platonic romance titled "Ligeia." In 1839, he joined the editorial staff of *Burton's Gentlemen's Magazine*, where he published two of his greatest stories, "The Fall of the House of Usher" and "William Wilson."

In 1840, Poe left *Burton's* and tried, unsuccessfully, to establish his own literary magazine. He did, however, publish a collection of his stories, *Tales of the Grotesque and Arabesque* (1840), as well as become an editor of *Graham's Magazine*, where he published his first tale of ratiocination, "The Murders in the Rue Morgue." In this landmark story, he created the famous detective Auguste Dupin, the forerunner of Sherlock Holmes and thus of countless other private detectives in literature and film. A biographical sketch published at that time described Poe as short, slender, and well-proportioned, with a fair complexion, gray eyes, black hair, and an extremely broad forehead.

In 1842, Poe left *Graham's* to try once again to establish his own literary magazine, but not before publishing two important pieces of criticism: a long review of the poet Henry Wadsworth Longfellow, in which he established his definition of poetry as being the "Rhythmical Creation of Beauty," and his review of Hawthorne, in which he defined the short tale as the creation of a unified effect. Between 1842 and 1844, after Poe moved to New York to join the editorial staff of the *New York Mirror*, he published many of his most important stories, including "The Masque of the Red Death," "The Pit and the Pendulum," "The Black Cat," and two more ratiocinative stories, "The Mystery of Marie Roget" and "The Gold Bug." It was with the publication of his most famous poem, "The Raven," in 1845, however, that he finally achieved popular success.

Poe left the *New York Mirror* to join a new weekly periodical, the *Broadway Journal*, in February of 1845, where he continued the literary war against Longfellow begun in a review written for the *Mirror*. The series of accusations, attacks, and counterattacks that ensued damaged Poe's reputation as a critic at the very point in his career when he had established his critical genius. Poe's collection of stories, *Tales*, was published in July, 1845, to good reviews. Soon after, Poe became the sole editor and then proprietor of the *Broadway Journal*. In November, he published his collection, *The Raven and Other Poems*.

The year 1846 marked the beginning of Poe's decline. In January, the *Broadway Journal* ceased publication, and soon after, Poe was involved in both a personal scandal with two female literary admirers and a bitter battle with the literary establishment. Moreover, Poe's wife was quite ill, a fact which necessitated Poe's moving his family some thirteen miles outside the city to a rural cottage at Fordham. When Virginia died on January 30, 1847, Poe collapsed. Although he never fully recovered from this series of assaults on his already nervous condition, in the following year he published what he considered to be the capstone of his career, *Eureka: A Prose Poem*, which he presented as an examination of the origin of all things.

In the summer of 1849, Poe left for Richmond, Virginia, in the hope, once more, of starting a literary magazine. On September 24, he delivered a lecture, "The Poetic Principle," at Richmond, in what was to be his last public appearance. From that time until he was found semiconscious on the streets of Baltimore, Maryland, little is known of his activities. He never recovered, and he died on Sunday morning, October 7, in Washington College Hospital.

Summary

Edgar Allan Poe is important in the history of American literature and American culture in two significant ways. First, he developed short fiction as a genre that was to have a major impact on American literature and publishing throughout the nineteenth century. His stories and criticism have been models and guides for writers in this characteristically American genre up to the present time. No one interested in the short-story form can afford to ignore his ideas or his fiction. Poe was influential in making American literature more philosophical and metaphysical than it had been before.

Second, and perhaps most important, Poe helped to make periodical publishing more important in

American literary culture. American writers in the mid-nineteenth century were often discouraged by the easy accessibility of British novels. Lack of copyright laws made the works of the great English writers readily available at low cost. Thus, American writers could not compete in this genre. Periodical publishing, and the short story as the favored genre of this medium, was the United States' way of fighting back. Poe was an important figure in this battle to make the United States a literary force in world culture.

The problem with Poe, however, is that he is too often thought of as the author of some vivid yet insignificant horror stories. Moreover, Poe's personality is often erroneously maligned: He has been called a drunk, a drug-addict, a hack, a sex pervert, and an exploiter. As a result of these errors, myths, and oversimplifications, it is often difficult for readers to take his works seriously. The truth is, however, that Edgar Allan Poe, both in his criticism and in his dark, metaphysically mysterious stories, helped create a literature that made America a cultural force not to be ignored.

Bibliography

Allen, Hervey. *Israfel: The Life and Times of Edgar Allan Poe*. 2 vols. New York: Doran, 1926; London: Bretano's, 1927. A romantic narrative of Poe's life, valuable for the information drawn from letters between Poe and John Allan.

Buranelli, Vincent. *Edgar Allan Poe*. 2d ed. Boston: Twayne, 1977. A somewhat sketchy study of Poe's fiction, poetry, and criticism, but still a good introduction to his work.

Carlson, Eric W., ed. *The Recognition of Edgar Allan Poe: Selected Criticism Since 1829*. Ann Arbor: University of Michigan Press, 1966. A valuable collection of some of the most influential critical remarks about Poe by artists, writers, and critics.

Elmer, Jonathan. *Reading at the Social Limit: Affect, Mass Culture, and Edgar Allan Poe*. Stanford, Calif.: Stanford University Press, 1995.

The author offers a new theory of mass culture and ideology based on analysis of four motifs in Poe's work.

Frank, Frederick S. and Anthony S. Magistrale. *The Poe Encyclopedia*. Westport, Conn.: Greenwood Press, 1997. Stunningly complete reference with over 1900 entries covering Poe's career, his responses to his contemporaries, those who affected Poe's writings, Poe's views on various subjects, and more.

Hoffman, Daniel. *Poe Poe Poe Poe Poe Poe Poe*. New York: Doubleday, 1972. An idiosyncratic and highly personal account of one critic's fascination with Poe that echoes the fascination of countless readers. Often Freudian and sometimes farfetched, the book provides stimulating reading and suggestive criticism.

Jacobs, Robert D. *Poe: Journalist and Critic*. Baton Rouge: Louisiana State University Press, 1969. An extensive study of Poe's career as editor, reviewer, and critic. Shows how Poe's critical ideas derived from and influenced periodical publishing in the mid-nineteenth century.

Moss, Sidney P. *Poe's Literary Battles: The Critic in the Context of His Literary Milieu*. Durham, N.C.: Duke University Press, 1963. A well-researched study of Poe's controversial battles with Longfellow and the many literary cliques of nineteenth century American publishing.

Quinn, Arthur Hobson. *Edgar Allan Poe: A Critical Biography*. New York and London: Appleton, 1941. Although this book is somewhat outdated in its critical analysis of Poe's works, it is the best and most complete biography, informed by Quinn's knowledge of Poe's literary milieu and his extensive research into Poe's correspondence.

Quinn, Patrick F. *The French Face of Edgar Poe*. Carbondale: Southern Illinois University Press, 1957. Ironically, Poe's fiction, poetry, and criticism had more influence on French literature in the nineteenth century than on American literature. Quinn's book explains why.

Charles E. May

HENRI POINCARÉ

Born: April 29, 1854; Nancy, France
Died: July 17, 1912; Paris, France
Areas of Achievement: Mathematics and physics
Contribution: Poincaré was one of the most important mathematicians of the late nineteenth century. He developed the theory of automorphic functions (a method for expressing functions in terms of parameters), did extensive work in celestial mechanics and mathematical physics, was a codiscoverer of the special theory of relativity, and his writing style was so clear that he wrote books about the philosophy of science that were read widely by the general public and translated into many languages.

Early Life

Henri Poincaré was born April 29, 1854, to one of the most distinguished families of Lorraine. His father, Leon, was a physician, and one of his cousins, Raymond, became President of the French Republic during World War I. Henri and his sister were adored by their mother, and she devoted herself to their education and rearing. When he was five, Henri contracted diphtheria, and the resulting weakness may have influenced his entire life. Since he was unable to join the other boys in their rough play, Henri was forced to entertain himself with intellectual pursuits. He developed a remarkable memory so that he could even cite page numbers for information in books that he had read many years earlier. In addition, because his eyesight was very poor, he learned most of his classwork by listening, since he could not see the blackboard. Thus, he was forced to develop the ability to see spatial relationships in his mind at an early age.

Although he was a good student in his early years, there was no indication of his impending greatness until he was a teenager. He won first prize in a French national competition and in 1873 entered the École Polytechnique, where he exhibited his brilliance in mathematics. Upon his graduation, Poincaré entered the École des Mines in 1875 to study engineering. Although he was a careful student, who did his work adequately, Poincaré spent much of his time pursuing mathematics as a recreation. He continued his practice of mathematics during his apprenticeship as a mining engineer.

Poincaré was not an extremely attractive man; he had thinning blond hair, wore glasses, and was short in stature; he was known for being absent-minded and clumsy. Nevertheless, he maintained a happy personal life. He married at age twenty-seven, fathered four children, whom he adored, and never wanted for friends, because he was by nature humble and interested in other people.

Life's Work

In 1879, Poincaré submitted the doctoral thesis in mathematics that he had written during his work as an engineer, and he received his degree that same year. The subject was the first of his great achievements: the theory of differential equations. His first appointment was as a lecturer of mathematical analysis at the University of Caen in 1879, and in 1881 he was invited to join the faculty at the University of Paris. He continued this appointment until his death in 1912, although by then his responsibilities had expanded to include mechanics and physics.

During his tenure, he was elected to the Académie des Sciences in 1887 and the Académie Française in 1908. this second appointment is most unusual for a mathematician, for it is given to honor literary achievements and is thus a sure indication of his lucid writing style. He was named President of the Académie des Sciences in 1906. Other awards included a Fellowship in the Royal Society in 1894, the Prix Poncelet, Prix Reynaud, and Prix Bolyai, and gold medals from the Lobachevsky Fund.

Much of Poincaré's early work was in differential equations, a branch of calculus which is linked directly to the physical world. It was natural, then, for him to turn his attention from pure mathematics to physics and celestial mechanics. Yet in his pursuit of solutions of physical and mechanical problems, he often created new tools of pure mathematics.

Poincaré was first drawn to celestial mechanics and astronomical physics by the classical three-body problem, which concerns the gravitational influence and distortions that three independent bodies in space would exert on one another; it held his interest throughout his life. Poincaré published partial results in his early years at the Sorbonne and later published work broadening the number of objects from three to any number. His results won for him a prize that had been offered by King Oscar II of Sweden.

In celestial mechanics, Poincaré was the first person to demand rigor in computations. That is, he found the approximations used commonly at the time to be unacceptable, since they introduced obvious errors into the work. Consequently, more powerful mathematics had to be developed. This work was not centered on any one branch of mathematics but instead included calculus, algebra, number theory, non-Euclidean geometry, and topology. In fact, the field of topology was begun in large part with Poincaré's study of orbits. He published much of this work in *Les Méthodes nouvelles de la mécanique céleste* (new methods in celestial mechanics), in three volumes between 1892 and 1899.

Poincaré's other early achievement was in the theory of automorphic functions, a study in mathematical analysis. These are functions which remain relatively unchanged though they are acted on by a series of transformations. He found that one class of these, which he called Fuchsian (for German mathematician Immanuel Fuchs), was related to non-Euclidean geometry, and this became an important insight. Indeed, there was some argument over priority in this development between Poincaré and German mathematician Christian Felix Klein; however, scientific historians agree that Poincaré was the developer of these theories.

It seems that all branches of mathematics held Poincaré's interest. Poincaré was essential to the development of algebraic geometry. Of particular importance is his development of a parametric representation of functions. For example, the general equation of a circle $x^2 + y^2 = r^2$ can be rewritten as two equations that describe the variables x and y in terms of some angle A. The equations $x = r$ sine A and $y = r$ cosine A are the equivalent of the original equation since $x^2 + y^2 = r^2$ sine$^2 A + r^2$ cosine$^2 A = r^2$ (sine$^2 A +$ cosine$^2 A$), which in turn equals r^2 since sine$^2 +$ cosine$^2 = 1$. Many problems can be solved using parameters that do not yield to any other methods.

Poincaré is equally important in physics. Although Albert Einstein is generally known for his theory of relativity, the special theory of relativity was discovered independently by Poincaré. He and Einstein arrived at the theory from completely different viewpoints, Einstein from light and Poincaré from electromagnetism, at about the same time (Einstein's first work was published in 1905, and Poincaré's was published in 1906). There can be no doubt that both men deserve a share of the credit. When Poincaré became aware of Einstein's work, he was quite enthusiastic and supportive of

the Swiss physicist even though most scientists were skeptical. Max Planck, who developed quantum theory, was another physicist who was recognized by Poincaré, while he was being scorned by others. In addition, Poincaré developed the mathematics required for countless physical discoveries in the early twentieth century. An example is the wireless telegraph. He also developed the theory of the equilibrium of fluid bodies rotating in space.

Poincaré had a rare gift for a mathematician: He was able to write clearly and to make mathematics and science exciting to people whose educations were directed toward other fields. One of his most widely known works in the philosophy of science, *Science et méthode* (1908; *Science and Method*, 1914), is devoted to a study of how scientists and mathematicians create. Poincaré believed that some things in mathematics are known intuitively rather than from observation or from classic logic. His articles and books in the philosophy of science were avidly read and translated into most of the European languages and even into Japanese.

Poincaré continued in relatively good health until 1908, and in 1912 he died of an embolism following minor surgery. The church Saint-Jacques-de-Haut-Pas, the site of his funeral several days later, was filled with eminent persons from all fields who had come to pay a last tribute to his greatness.

Summary

Henri Poincaré was clearly one of the great mathematicians of his time. In fact, some believe that he had no peer. He won virtually every mathematical prize available, and he also won several scientific awards. His work entered every field of mathematics at the time, and he created at least one new branch called algebraic topology. His discoveries inspired other mathematicians for years after his death. In addition, Poincaré did first-rate work in celestial mechanics and was a codiscoverer of the theory of relativity.

The more than thirty books and five hundred papers that Poincaré published are a testament to his prolific career, especially since he died during his productive years. In addition, his writings on the philosophy of science sparked public interest in mathematics and the physical sciences and foreshadowed the intuitionist school of philosophy. These works have helped define the way human beings think about mathematical and scientific creation and will continue to do so for years to come. The practical applications of Poincaré's work are numerous. Differential functions are the primary mathematics used in engineering and some of the physical sciences; his work in celestial mechanics was completely different from past works and altered the field's course. In addition, he offered many new ideas in pure mathematics.

Perhaps the most articulate tribute to Poincaré was given in the official report of the 1905 Bolyai Prize written by Gustave Rados: "Henri Poincaré is incontestably the first and most powerful investigator of the present time in the domain of mathematics and mathematical physics."

Bibliography

Bell, E. T. "The Last Universalist." In *Men of Mathematics*. London: Gollancz, and New York: Simon and Schuster, 1937. This book is a series of twenty-nine chapters, each introducing a different mathematician from the early Greeks to the early twentieth century. Its account of Poincaré focuses on three areas: the theory of automorphic functions, celestial mechanics and mathematical physics, and the philosophy of science. Biographical information is also included.

Gower, B. S. "Henri Poincare and Bruno de Finetti: Conventions and Scientific Reasoning." *Studies in History and Philosophy of Science* 28, no. 4 (December, 1997). Compares the thoughts of Poincare and de Finetti on scientific reasoning.

Miller, Arthur I. "Cultures of Creativity: Mathematics and Physics." *Diogenes*, no. 177 (Spring 1997). Examines the methods of creative thinking used by mathematician Poincare and physicist Albert Einstein, both of which mirror in some respects, the creative thought of artists.

Nordmann, Charles. "Henri Poincaré: His Scientific Work, His Philosophy." In *Annual Report of the Board of Regents of the Smithsonian Institution*. Washington, D.C.: Government Printing Office, 1913. Nordmann includes not only a summary of Poincaré's work and philosophy as the title indicates but also a considerable amount of biographical information.

Poincaré, Henri. *The Foundations of Science*. Translated by George Bruce Halsted. New York: Science Press, 1913. Contains a preface by Poincaré and an introduction by Josiah Royce. It argues Poincaré's philosophy of science.

———. "The Future of Mathematics." In *Annual Report of the Board of Regents of the Smithsonian Institution*. Washington, D.C.: Government Printing Office, 1910. This article represents Poincaré at his best. After a brief introduction, he guides the reader through most of the prominent fields of mathematics and predicts what he believed was to come. His explanations are excellent.

———. *Mathematics and Science: Last Essays*. Translated by John W. Balduc. New York: Dover, 1963. Another work in the philosophy of science.

Slosson, Edwin E. "Henri Poincaré." In *Major Prophets of To-day*. Boston: Little Brown, 1914. Slosson chose several representatives from the modern era whom he viewed as having lasting prominence. His article on Poincaré includes biographical information as well as a discussion of Poincaré's work in mathematics and philosophy.

Celeste Williams Brockington

JAMES K. POLK

Born: November 2, 1795; Mecklenburg County, North Carolina

Died: June 15, 1849; Nashville, Tennessee

Areas of Achievement: Government and politics

Contribution: A staunch nationalist, Polk used the authority of the presidency to bring about the expansion of the nation nearly to its continental limits. He added power as well as stature to the office.

Early Life

James Knox Polk was born in Mecklenburg County, North Carolina, on November 2, 1795. His parents, Samuel and Jane Knox Polk, were members of large Scotch-Irish families whose forebears began migrating to America late in the previous century. When James was eleven, Samuel moved the family westward to the Duck River Valley in middle Tennessee, where he became both a prosperous farmer and a prominent resident. The family was staunchly Jeffersonian in its politics, while Jane Polk was a rigid Presbyterian.

Young James was small in stature—of average height or less according to various accounts—and was never robust. At seventeen, he had a gallstone removed (without anesthesia), and thereafter his health improved somewhat. It became obvious early, however, that he would never be strong enough to farm, and contrary to his father's wish that he become a merchant, Polk decided on a law career with politics as his goal. For this goal, some education was necessary. He had been a studious youth but until the age of eighteen had had little formal schooling. Thereafter, he applied himself totally and entered the sophomore class at the University of North Carolina at the age of twenty. Two and a half years later, he was graduated with honors. Characteristically, he had worked diligently, but the drain on his physical reserves was so great that he was too ill to travel home for several months.

Upon his return to Columbia, Tennessee, Polk read law in the offices of one of the state's most prominent public figures, Felix Grundy. Through Grundy's sponsorship, Polk began his political career as clerk of the state senate in 1819 and was admitted to the bar the following year. Prospering as a lawyer, he was elected to the Tennessee legislature in 1823 and aligned himself with the supporters of the state's most famous citizen, Andrew Jackson. Soon he became friendly with Jackson, a presidential candidate in 1824, aided Old Hickory's election to the United States Senate, and thereafter was always associated with his fellow Tennessean.

On New Year's Day, 1824, Polk married Sarah Childress, a member of a prominent middle Tennessee family. Described as not particularly pretty, she was vivacious, friendly, and devoted, and the marriage, although childless, was apparently happy. By this time Polk's health had improved, but he remained slender, with an upright posture and a grim face below a broad forehead. According to contemporaries, he was always impeccably dressed, as befitted a promising young lawyer and sometime militia colonel on the governor's staff. Now nearly thirty, he was considered one of the state's rising Jacksonians.

Life's Work

Impressed with his legislative record and legal as well as martial success, in 1825 the Jackson faction supported Polk's bid for a seat in the House of Representatives against four opponents. His victory by a decisive plurality after a spirited campaign solidified his position among the followers of General Jackson. For the next four years, during the administration of President John Quincy Adams, Polk was in the forefront of the Jacksonians, who were determined to overturn the alleged "corrupt bargain" that had denied Jackson the presidency in 1824 and elect their man in 1828.

During the debates on the Adams program, considered too nationalistic by most congressmen, Polk seized numerous opportunities to express his opposition and to stand with the embryonic Democratic Party. He aided in reviving the "corrupt bargain" charge and spoke for economy, majority rule, and limited government. He embraced the party position against the protective tariff, internal improvements, and banks. Only on the question of slavery did he equivocate, as he would always do. Slavery was an evil, he believed, yet doing away with it was fraught with peril. It was best that all concerned recognize its existence and live with it as peacefully as possible.

The issues before Congress during the Adams term commanded less attention than the Jacksonians' primary goal—the election of Jackson. In this effort, Polk played an increasingly important part as his abilities and devotion to the cause be-

came more evident. In the bitter campaign of 1828, he constantly defended Jackson and carried on an extensive correspondence with him at his home in the Hermitage. Victory for Jackson followed and, despite interparty infighting for the position of successor to the new president, the future of the Jacksonian party looked promising.

In the next decade, Polk's rise in the party hierarchy was steady. He served as chairman of the House Ways and Means Committee in Jackson's first term and played a leading role in the president's victory in the Bank War. He enjoyed a growing reputation for speeches and reports showing much preparation, logic, and clarity. In 1835, he was elected Speaker of the House, and was reelected two years later. His four years in the chair, where he was the first to function as a party leader and to attempt to guide through a program, proved to be trying. The Whig Party was gaining strength while the slavery issue was intruding in the House, resulting in the passage of the infamous "gag rule." In the middle of his second term as Speaker, Polk decided to become a candidate for governor of Tennessee rather than risk probable defeat for re-

election. By now the recognized leader of the party forces in his home state, he won by a narrow margin in 1839.

Once again, Polk was the first incumbent to use an office for political purposes as a party leader. Yet since the governor had little real power and Whig opposition continued strong, Governor Polk was able to accomplish little in his single two-year term. When the victorious Whig presidential candidate, William Henry Harrison, easily carried Tennessee in 1840, Polk's chances for another gubernatorial term appeared to be slim. He was defeated for reelection in 1841 and failed again two years later. For the only time in his career, he was out of office.

On the national level, Polk's position in the party remained secure. In 1840, he was a leading candidate for the vice presidential nomination on the ticket with President Martin Van Buren but withdrew when the convention decided against making a nomination. Polk then began to work toward the nomination four years later, when it was expected that the former president would again contend for the top place. In the meantime, he repaired political fences and kept in touch with Van Buren and other party leaders.

Polk's comeback, which led to his nomination as the Democratic standard-bearer in 1844, is one of the best-known episodes in American political history. Expansionism, justified as "Manifest Destiny," was in the air as Texas clamored for admission to the Union while American eyes were on California and Oregon. It was expected that the presidential race would be between former president Van Buren and Whig Henry Clay. When both announced their opposition to the annexation of Texas, however, Van Buren's chances for the nomination faded. In the party convention in May, he withdrew when his cause looked hopeless, and on the ninth ballot delegates turned to Polk, who had declared for annexation weeks earlier. Although his nomination, recalled as the first "dark horse" selection, was a surprise to most voters, it was the result of much hard work and a correct recognition of the mood of the electorate.

In the ensuing campaign, Whig candidate Clay and his supporters obscured the issues by asking, "Who is James K. Polk?" Democrats responded by linking "Young Hickory" to the aged former president, vacillating on controversial matters such as the tariff and stressing annexation as a national, not sectional, question. After an exciting campaign,

Polk won a narrow victory brought about in part because a number of potential Clay voters cast ballots for an antislavery candidate. In his inaugural address, President Polk announced a brief but positive program. He called for settling the Oregon question (Congress had voted to annex Texas by joint resolution a few days earlier) by its "reoccupation" and for the acquisition of California. The tariff was to be reduced to a revenue level, and the Independent Treasury, killed by the Whigs, would be reestablished. Unique among American chief executives, Polk carried out his entire program.

The new president assumed his duties, determined to be in control. He appointed able cabinet members, many of whom were friends, and he consulted them and Congress frequently, although he made his own decisions. Seldom away from his desk, he was constantly besieged by office seekers who placed an added drain on his limited strength and energy. Not surprisingly, his appointments were largely "deserving" Democrats.

Foreign affairs immediately commanded Polk's attention. Oregon, occupied jointly with England since 1818, was rapidly filling up with Americans who anticipated eventual absorption by the United States. It was "clear and unquestionable," the president declared in his inaugural, that Oregon belonged to the United States. Yet he revealed to the British minister his willingness to compromise at the forty-ninth parallel. A negative response evoked from Polk a hint of war and a request in his first annual message for congressional sanction for termination of joint occupation. For the first time, there was a presidential reference to the Monroe Doctrine as justification for action, and war talk, including demands for "Fifty-four Forty or Fight," was heard. Neither nation wanted war, so the British countered with Polk's original suggestion, it was accepted, and a treaty was completed, setting the boundary at the forty-ninth parallel, where it has remained.

In the meantime, the Mexicans had not accepted the loss of Texas, and they now maintained that the southern boundary was the Nueces River, not the Rio Grande, as the Texans claimed. Polk agreed with the Texans and also feared that the British might interfere there, as well as in California and New Mexico. As tensions increased, he sent to Mexico City an offer of some thirty million dollars for the entire area. When the offer was refused, he ordered General Zachary Taylor to move his troops into the disputed section. A predictable clash took place, but before word reached Washington, Polk had decided to ask for war. Congress responded with a declaration on May 13, 1846. Although American forces were victorious from the beginning, the Mexican War, called "Mr. Polk's War," was among the most unpopular in the nation's history. Opposition to it was voiced in Congress, in the press, and among the people. Even though the two leading generals professed to be members of the party, Whigs led the protests, which tended to increase Polk's strongly partisan attitudes.

To a greater extent than any previous chief executive, Polk took his role as commander in chief seriously. His military experience was meager, yet he planned grand strategy, was personally involved in military appointments and promotions, and took the lead in peacemaking. His emissary (although technically recalled) completed with a defeated Mexico a satisfactory treaty which ceded California and New Mexico to the United States and recognized the annexation of Texas in return for some fifteen million dollars. Polk decided to accept the offer. The Senate narrowly approved the treaty on February 2, 1848, and the continental limits of the nation had almost been reached. Near the end of his term, Polk looked longingly at other areas, such as Cuba, but nothing further was done.

In Congress, the remainder of Polk's limited program was approved. The Independent Treasury was reestablished and remained in existence into the next century. In addition, the tariff was reduced considerably. Although these successes seemed to indicate party harmony, the Democrats actually were engaged in much interparty wrangling, adding to the president's many problems.

Of more lasting effect was the revival of antislavery agitation as a result of the possible addition of territory. In the midst of the war, as an appropriations measure was debated in Congress, Representative David Wilmot of Pennsylvania proposed an amendment banning slavery in any territory acquired from Mexico. This so-called Wilmot Proviso was never approved, yet it rekindled sectional animosities which finally led to secession some fifteen years later. Polk, a slaveholder who seldom thought of slavery in moral terms—he believed that the solution was the extension of the Missouri Compromise Line to the Pacific—was not directly involved in the ensuing agitation during the remainder of his term, yet the legacy of sectional bitterness continued to be linked to his administration.

In his acceptance letter in 1844, Polk declared that he would not be a candidate for a second time, the first nominee ever to do so. As his term drew to a close, he refused to reconsider. His health remained poor, and the split within his party was unsettling. Nor did his outlook improve with the election of one of the Mexican War generals, Zachary Taylor, as his successor.

Following Taylor's inauguration, the Polks slowly made their way home, often delayed by the poor health of the former president and well-meaning attempts by supporters to entertain them. Polk never fully recovered (his main complaint was chronic diarrhea) and he died June 15, 1849, slightly more than fourteen weeks after leaving office. His considerable estate, including a Mississippi plantation, was left to his widow, who lived until 1891, witnessing the tragic sectional split and devastating war brought about in part by the events associated with her husband's presidency.

Summary

The youngest presidential candidate elected up to that time and often called the strongest chief executive between Andrew Jackson and Abraham Lincoln, James K. Polk raised the presidency in public esteem. Although humorless, partisan, and totally without charisma, he was devoted to the office and impressed all those around him with his dedication and diligence. Nothing was allowed to interfere with the carrying out of his duties (except that no business was conducted on Sundays unless in an emergency). Unlike most occupants of the office, he seldom was away from the Capitol, absent a total of only six weeks in four years.

Under his leadership, a relatively brief, successful war was fought with Mexico, the annexation of Texas was completed, the most troublesome dispute with England was resolved, and the nation expanded almost to its continental limits. These accomplishments came about despite Polk's frail constitution and sharp political differences with the Whig Party and among his fellow Democrats. Unfortunately, his successes only added to the increasing sectional tensions which would soon tear the nation apart and cause a long, costly conflict.

Bibliography

Bassett, John Spencer, ed. *The Southern Plantation Overseer as Revealed in His Letters.* Northampton, Mass.: Smith College, 1925. Most of these letters, from the Polk papers, were written by overseers on Polk's plantations in Tennessee (sold in 1834) and Mississippi (sold by Mrs. Polk in 1860). The correspondence indicates that the Polks, who were apparently benevolent owners, derived much of their income from the labor of slaves.

Cutler, Wayne, et al., eds. *Correspondence of James K. Polk.* 6 vols. to date. Nashville, Tenn.: Vanderbilt University Press, 1969-1983. A well-edited, complete publication of all extant Polk papers. Also includes many letters to Polk. An indispensable source for the history of the period.

Haynes, Sam W. *James K. Polk and the Expansionist Impulse.* Edited by Oscar Handlin. New York: Longman, 1997. Haynes' biography goes beyond the customary treatment of Polk's expansionism to include accounts of the important issues and events that shaped America prior to the Civil War.

Johannsen, Robert W. *To the Halls of the Montezumas: The Mexican War in the American Imagination.* New York: Oxford University Press, 1985; Oxford: Oxford University Press, 1987. An interesting study of how the American people viewed the Mexican War and its effects on their lives. Reaches the usual conclusion that the war, although immediately successful, presaged great trouble.

McCormac, Eugene Irving. *James K. Polk: A Political Biography.* Berkeley: University of California Press, 1922. Somewhat dated, this was for many years the standard political biography of Polk. Still useful for an account of the political maneuvering in the Jackson years.

Polk, James K. *The Diary of James K. Polk.* 4 vols. Edited by Milo Milton Quaife. Chicago: McClurg, 1910. Only five hundred copies of the original diary were printed. Written between August 26, 1845, and June 2, 1849, it is highly personal and apparently was not written with an eye on future historians. As a result of a 1929 updated publication, in which selections of the earlier publication appeared, Polk's presidency was reassessed and his reputation considerably enhanced.

Schroeder, John H. *Mr. Polk's War: American Opposition and Dissent, 1846-1848.* Madison: University of Wisconsin Press, 1973. A provocative study of public opinion during the Mexican War. Conclusion is that Polk not only decided on the war before learning of the firing on American troops but also welcomed the conflict as a way to fulfill his expansionist plans.

Sellers, Charles Grier, Jr. *James K. Polk: Jacksonian, 1795-1843*. Princeton, N.J.: Princeton University Press, 1957.

———. *James K. Polk: Continentalist, 1843-1846*. Princeton, N.J.: Princeton University Press, 1966. These volumes constitute the best treatment of Polk and his times up to the introduction of the Wilmot Proviso, a portent of things to come. Well-balanced and thoroughly researched, the study established Polk's claim to be considered one of the "near great" presidents.

Shattan, Joseph. "One-Term Wonder." *The American Spectator* 29, no. 10 (October, 1996). Examines Polk's achievements during his short term as president including his territorial acquisitions.

Weems, John Edward. *To Conquer a Peace: The War Between the United States and Mexico*. New York: Doubleday, 1974. A popular treatment of the war. Largely undocumented but interesting and basically sound. Weems believes that Polk hoped to avoid war by making a show of force.

C. L. Grant

ALEKSANDR STEPANOVICH POPOV

Born: March 16, 1859; Turinskiye Rudniki, Perm, Russia

Died: January 13, 1906; St. Petersburg, Russia

Areas of Achievement: Invention and engineering

Contribution: A Russian pioneer in the invention of radio and its application, Popov also contributed to the development of X-ray photography. Outside Russia, he contributed to the development of radio in France.

Early Life

Aleksandr Stepanovich Popov was born in the village of Perm (modern Krasnoturinsk), located in a marshy area of northeastern Russia, just west of the Ural Mountains. Despite its relative isolation, Perm was an area of ancient Russian settlement, first made famous by Saint Stephen of Perm. Saint Stephen converted the pagan Permians after he proved incombustible when they attempted to burn him at the stake. For many generations, the clergy provided Perm's only intelligentsia. Popov was the fourth child in a priest's family of seven children. Though Popov left his village, he loved Perm and in later life took numerous photographs of his native landscape, which form an important collection.

By Popov's time, copper and iron mines, as well as a few factories, were in operation near his village. As a child, he is supposed to have built models of factory and mining equipment. He was educated in seminaries and seemed destined to enter the priesthood, but at the age of eighteen he decided instead to pursue his growing interest in mathematics and physics. He moved to St. Petersburg to attend the university, which was then nearing the apogee of its reputation in science. Among Popov's distinguished teachers were the chemist Dmitry Mendeleyev and the physicists Fyodor Petrushevsky and Orest Khvolson. The University of St. Petersburg was one of the first to offer courses on the physics of electricity and magnetism and had a fine physics laboratory run by Popov's mentor Vladimir Lermantov.

While a student from 1878 to 1882, Popov always worked, not only to support himself and to contribute to the support of his siblings but also to support his wife, Raisa Gorbunov, whom he married before graduating. Gorbunov pursued medical studies and eventually became a physician. Popov found most congenial employment with a newly founded St. Petersburg company, Elektrotekhnik, which built and maintained small electric stations around the city.

As a student, Popov took part in the world's very first electrical exhibition, in 1880, organized by a branch of the Russian Technical Society, which had just founded a new journal, *Elektrichestvo*. The exhibition was intended to raise money to fund the new publication and was a great success; it ran for a full month, attracting thousands of visitors. Popov worked as a guide throughout the exhibition, explaining the new marvels of technology to the public—a role that he was later to continue in public lectures and demonstrations, overcoming his initial shyness. A photograph of him from his student years shows a handsome, rather delicate-looking youth; later, he suffered from heart problems.

Popov was graduated from the faculty of mathematics and physics of the University of St. Petersburg with the degree of candidate (equivalent to a doctorate without a dissertation). His earliest research papers, published in *Elektrichestvo*, focused on the generation of electricity and the conversion of thermal energy into mechanical energy. He was trained in the spirit of concrete application of science, not for personal gain but for the good of others.

Upon graduation, Popov accepted a position at the Russian navy's most prestigious training institute, the Mine Officers' (or Torpedo) School in Kronstadt, on the Gulf of Finland, where he worked from 1883 to 1901. The Kronstadt facility had Russia's most advanced physics laboratory, and Popov was soon in charge of it. He also gave free public lectures, in which he shared his advanced knowledge, delighting in finding ways to make technology accessible to the average person. He had only the most limited funds at his disposal and learned cabinetmaking and glassblowing in order to construct innovative apparatuses himself. Every summer, he supplemented his income by running the electrical power plant for the annual fair at Nizhni-Novgorod (modern Gorky).

Life's Work

At the Mine Officers' School in 1889, Popov reproduced Heinrich Hertz's experiments with electromagnetic waves. In the same year, in order to popularize both the Hertz oscillator and the field of electrical engineering in general, Popov gave a series of public lectures on the recent research done on the relationship between light and electric phenomena. These lectures made him see the need for an apparatus to demonstrate, before a large audience, the presence of the waves generated by the Hertz oscillator.

Popov constructed a better detector of electromagnetic waves, which led to his invention of a lightning-storm detector and a radio in 1895. He began with the electromagnetic-wave detector (later called a coherer), invented by the French physicist Édouard Branly and improved it so that it could be used reliably outside laboratory conditions. By the beginning of 1895, Popov had evolved the primitive coherer into a complete radio receiver. By the spring of 1895, Popov had a radio transmitter ready to complement his receiver; it was based on a modified Hertz oscillator excited by an induction coil. Using the two devices, he conducted radio communication experiments in the physics laboratory and in the garden of the Mine Officers' School. In the course of these experiments, he added a new element of his own, the radio antenna.

Popov successfully demonstrated his system of wireless communication and presented a formal paper to an audience of scientists from the Russian Physics and Chemistry Society on May 7, 1895. A report on his demonstration appeared in the Russian press on May 12, 1895, followed by other reports in late 1895 and early 1896. It is on the basis of this work that Russia claims primacy for the invention of wireless radio communication, although the young Italian physicist Guglielmo Marconi secured a patent on his own radio in the summer of 1896, won the Nobel Prize in 1909, and superseded Popov's achievements.

Initially, the components of Marconi's radio, being tested by the British Telegraph Agency in 1896, were kept secret. When the structure of Marconi's radio was finally revealed in 1897, however, it was identical to Popov's: an enhanced coherer with antenna and Hertz oscillator excited by an induction coil. The detailed description of Marconi's invention was published in the British professional engineering journal, *The Electrician*, in 1897. Popov and other Russian engineers read it and were shocked by the coincidence. Popov declined to accuse Marconi of theft, saying in an address to the First All-Russian Electrotechnical Congress in 1900: "Was my instrument known to Marconi or not? The latter is very likely more probable. At any

rate my combination of the relay, tube, and electromagnetic tapper served as the basis of Marconi's first patent as a new combination of already known instruments."

Popov had no interest in a vainglorious contest for primacy but did wish his achievements to be acknowledged. In an 1897 article published in *The Electrician*, he took exception to a lengthy article just published by the British journal on the subject of the coherer and the radio, in which Popov's contribution was not even mentioned.

From May of 1895 onward, Popov continued to work with his wireless system, to lecture, and to give demonstrations. Noting that the device was sensitive to lightning discharges, he set it to record oscillations on paper, clearly indicating the approach of storms. From the summer of 1895, Popov's lightning-storm detector was put to effective, long-term use by the Russian Forestry Institute.

On March 24, 1896, Popov sent the world's first wireless message in Morse code across a distance of 250 meters, between two buildings. The message consisted of two words: "Heinrich Hertz." The witnesses were scientists of the St. Petersburg

Physics Society, holding a meeting at the University of St. Petersburg.

Unfortunately for his future fame outside Russia, Popov was distracted from his radio work by his curiosity about the latest scientific phenomenon, X rays, discovered by Wilhelm Röntgen late in 1895. Popov was drawn to investigate these in 1896 and was the first in Russia to take X-ray photographs of objects and human limbs.

Newspaper reports of Marconi's patent broke in the fall of 1896, spurring Popov to fresh efforts. Popov increased the distance of radio communication. He achieved ship-to-shore communication across six hundred meters in 1897; by 1901, he had expanded that to 150 kilometers. His work was simultaneously experimental and practical, being applied in rescue missions at sea almost immediately. He experimented with wavelengths lying on the boundary between the decimeter and meter ranges. He predicted the development of broadcasting and the possibility of detecting the directionality of radio waves.

Popov was energetic about making foreign contacts and broadening his expertise. In 1893, he attended the Chicago World's Fair, where he delivered a lecture; he witnessed the Third International Electrical Congress being held in Chicago at the same time. In a letter sent from the United States, he expressed a strong intention to visit Thomas Edison's laboratory, but it is not known whether he actually did so. He visited New York and Philadelphia. In the late 1890's, he made several trips to France and Germany to examine radio stations there. In Russia, he was much in demand as a consultant on the establishment of electrical power plants and civilian wireless telegraph stations.

In 1899, Popov built a headphone message receiver and then went to Paris to work with the French engineer Eugène Ducretet. As a result, Popov's headset (patented in 1901) was manufactured in Russia and France from 1901 to 1904 and was widely used. In 1900, he returned to Paris to collaborate with Lieutenant Tissot, one of the pioneers of French radio, on numerous improvements in radio design.

While civilian use of wireless radio was expanding, the Russian navy was slow to apply it. Because of Popov's on-site work, Russia's Baltic Fleet, harbored at Kronstadt, was supplied with both radios and trained personnel. Under the prodding of Vice Admiral Stepan Makarov, a commander based in Kronstadt who took an interest in

Popov's work, Popov began to receive modest funding. Unfortunately for Russia, there was no radio equipment aboard its Pacific fleet at the outbreak of the Russo-Japanese War of 1904-1905.

At this point, Popov was at last given a position worthy of his standing and achievement. Having been a professor at the St. Petersburg Electrotechnical Institute since 1901, he was unanimously elected rector in late 1905. Two weeks after his election, his entire faculty passed a resolution condemning "any forcible interference by the authorities in the life of the institute," referring chiefly to police searches of student dormitories and to student arrests.

Popov, who suffered from a weak heart and high blood pressure, was summoned to the office of the St. Petersburg governor for a stormy interview. He refused to back down and returned home in a shaken state. He died of cerebral hemorrhage a few days later, at the age of forty-six.

Summary

Aleksandr Stepanovich Popov belongs to the long line of Russian scientists not much appreciated by their government in their lifetimes. There is a consistent succession, from Paul von Schilling-Cannstadt, who in 1832 installed one of the world's first telegraph connections (which ran between the Communications Ministry and the czar's Winter Palace but was never used), to Dmitry Mendeleyev (who was dismissed from his university post under government pressure), to Andrei Sakharov (who wasted years in the closed city of Gorky for political reasons). While the rest of the world raced to master the wireless radio and its applications, funding teams of researchers, the Russian government—of which Popov was an employee—let Popov work alone, in his limited spare time. On two occasions, in 1925 and again in 1945, the Soviet government remembered Popov and effusively honored him. The regime had so little credibility on other fronts, however, that such honors added nothing to, and may have actually harmed Popov's international repute.

Popov—who did invent a wireless radio, the components and operating principles of which were in essence the same as those of the Marconi radio patented a year later—disparaged suggestions that he had been copied, modestly noting that he had simply put together components that individually were already known. In a time of intense scientific interest in electromagnetic waves, the hour was ripe for such an invention, whose appearance was perhaps inevitable. Popov was content to be part of the world of scientific discovery and to share his knowledge even with the nonscientific public.

He belonged to the first wave of what became the substantial, proud, and little-understood caste of Russia's early twentieth century engineers. Like the highly educated characters in the plays of his scientifically trained contemporary Anton Chekhov, Popov and other members of the technical intelligentsia looked forward to a humane, enlightened future that they did not expect personally to see.

Bibliography

Loffe, Khatskel A. "Popov: Russia's Marconi?" *Electronics World + Wireless World* 97, no. 1676 (July, 1992). Examines Popov's career as a physicist, his experiments, and his ultimate comparison to Marconi.

Popov, Alexander. "An Application of the Coherer." *The Electrician*, 1897. Popov's article translated into English, reflecting his precise mind and talent for educating.

Radovskii, M. *Alexander Popov: Inventor of Radio*. Translated by G. Yankovsky. Moscow: Foreign Languages, 1957. The most comprehensive study of the life and work of Popov. This work is intended for the general reader as part of the Men of Russian Science series. Contains abundant footnotes to sources but no bibliography. Photographs of persons, equipment, and sites are included.

Smith-Rose, R. L. "Marconi, Popov, and the Dawn of Radiocommunication." *Electronics and Power* 10 (1964): 76-79. This article presents the British view that Marconi should be given primacy.

Süsskind, Charles. "Popov and the Beginnings of Radiotelegraphy." *Proceedings of the Institute of Radio Engineers* 50 (1962): 2036-2047. Reprinted as a separate pamphlet by the San Francisco Press in 1962 and 1973, this article utilizes Soviet sources and is favorable to the Russian view of Popov's primacy.

D. Gosselin Nakeeb

JOHN WESLEY POWELL

Born: March 24, 1834; Mount Morris, New York
Died: September 23, 1902; Haven, Maine
Areas of Achievement: Exploration and science
Contribution: In 1869, Powell led the first party of
 exploration to descend the gorges of the Green
 and Colorado rivers by boat, stimulating interest
 in the geology and scenic wonders of the Grand
 Canyon. He also helped to establish the concepts
 of large-scale damming and irrigation projects as
 the keys to settlement and agricultural survival in
 the arid lands of the American West beyond the
 one hundredth meridian.

Early Life

John Wesley Powell was born on March 24, 1834,
at Mount Morris, New York, the son of a circuit-
riding Methodist minister who supplemented his
income by farming and tailoring. The family
moved to Ohio in 1841. The abolitionist views of
the Powell family were not well received in Ohio,
and John Wesley had such a difficult time at school
that he was eventually placed under the direction
of a private schoolmaster. This proved a significant
experience, for the young Powell accompanied his
tutor on biological field trips and developed a
strong interest in both biological and physical science. The family eventually moved on to Illinois,
where John Wesley grew to maturity. He spent several years combining a career as a teacher in Wisconsin and Illinois with sporadic attendance at several colleges, including Wheaton, Oberlin, and
Illinois College. During this period he undertook
extensive natural history excursions and ambitious
journeys by boat down the Illinois, Des Moines,
Ohio, and Mississippi rivers from St. Paul all the
way to New Orleans.

When the Civil War came, Powell immediately
enlisted as a private in an Illinois volunteer infantry
company. He rose quickly through the ranks and
became a student of military engineering and fortifications. He met and became a friend of General
Ulysses S. Grant and eventually commander of his
own battery in an Illinois artillery unit. He led his
battery into the fierce struggle at the Hornet's Nest
in the Battle of Shiloh, where he was hit by a Minié
ball, requiring the amputation of his right arm. Despite his injury he continued in service, seeing action and carrying out important duties in a number
of major campaigns and rising to the rank of brevet
lieutenant colonel.

After the war, Powell returned to Illinois and became professor of natural history at Illinois Wesleyan College, later moving to Illinois Normal University at Bloomington. By this time he had become
accustomed to taking his students into the field as
part of their training, but he was increasingly obsessed with the desire to reach further afield. He
was particularly drawn by the glamour and mystery
of the trans-Mississippi West and began to assemble the ingredients that would allow him to make
his first major expedition into that area.

Powell was instrumental in the establishment of a
state natural history museum in Bloomington, and
as its first curator he secured funding from several
governmental and private sources to undertake a
collecting expedition into the West. His friendship
with General Grant enabled him to arrange for low-
cost rations from army posts and for military protection for part of his trip. In 1867, the expedition,
including students, amateur naturalists, teachers,
and family members, set out from Council Bluffs
on the first of Powell's major expeditions. The summer was spent examining the country and collecting specimens in the Colorado Rockies, and Powell
remained after most of his party returned east and
journeyed along the Grand River in Colorado.

The following summer, Powell returned to the
Rockies with an expedition of twenty-five people,
sponsorship from various Illinois state institutions,
and encouragement from officials of the Smithsonian Institution, who were intrigued by his plans to
explore among the rivers and high peaks of Colorado. After time collecting specimens in the Middle
Park region, in late August Powell and six of his
party made the first ascent of Long's Peak. They
then moved into the White River basin, intending
to follow it down to the Green River and on to a
winter reconnaissance of the Colorado River. By
now Powell had become thoroughly captivated by
Western adventuring and scientific exploration and
was obsessed by the unknown mysteries and legends of the Colorado. He had actively promoted his
ideas and successfully publicized his activities and
plans and had something of a reputation as an explorer and scientist, as well as good connections in
the political and scientific communities. Although
this five-foot-six, bearded veteran with only one
arm hardly looked the part of the great explorer,
Major John Wesley Powell was on the threshold of
one of the great Western adventures.

Life's Work

The gorges of the Green and Colorado rivers were among the few remaining unexplored areas on the North American continent. The legends which had been constructed out of the tales of Indians, mountain men, and other sources told of a region of enormous waterfalls, vicious whirlpools and rapids, and enormous rock cliffs which offered no escape or refuge from the punishment of the river. Essentially Powell and his men would plunge into a river descent of nearly nine hundred miles with no real idea of what terrors and adventures lay before them. Back east, Powell made the best preparations he could. A Chicagoan built four small wooden boats, one sixteen feet long of pine, the other three twenty-one feet, of oak, with watertight compartments. Powell secured some financial support from a variety of public and private sources, although most of the meager financing came out of his own pocket. He assembled a varied group of nine companions, and on May 24, 1869, after several weeks of training, they set off down the Green River toward the Colorado.

They were on the river for ninety-two days. Their small vessels plunged through turbulent rapids, foaming cataracts, and towering canyon walls that at least matched most of the myths and legends. Two boats were lost, one expeditioner deserted early, three others were killed by Indians as they gave up on the river journey and attempted to climb out of the Grand Canyon. A confidence man surfaced who claimed that he was the only survivor of a wreck beneath a falls that had claimed the lives of the other members of the expedition, and newspapers across the country reported that Powell's party had been defeated by the river. By the time they in fact surfaced at a Mormon settlement below the canyon, Powell and his men had explored the Colorado River and the Grand Canyon and had discovered the last unknown river and mountain range in the American West. Powell's prodigious expedition marked him immediately as an American hero and one of the great explorers in the nation's history. It also meant that he could attract support and financing for further activities.

Powell returned to the Colorado two years later and retraced his original steps, now with the sponsorship of the Smithsonian Institution and the Department of the Interior. This expedition was a more determinedly scientific endeavor, operating as a survey group, the United States Geological and Geographical Survey of the Rocky Mountains, and they undertook a careful study, survey, and mapping of the canyon country. Powell became fascinated with the question not only of how the region—its canyons, plateaus, and mountains—looked but also of how they had been formed. He undertook additional Western expeditions and employed men who explored the high plateaus of Utah, the Colorado Plateau, Zion and Bryce canyons, and the Henry and Uinta mountains. The work of Powell and his associates introduced the idea of vast processes of uplift and erosion as responsible for the topography of the canyon and plateau country. They helped to popularize the geological concept of "base level of erosion." Powell's findings and ideas were published as *Explorations of the Colorado River of the West and Its Tributaries* (1875; revised and enlarged in 1895 under the title *Canyons of the Colorado*).

Powell's interest in the topography and geology of the Western regions led him naturally to a concern about the management of its lands. In 1878 he published *A Report on the Lands of the Arid Region of the United States*, which has been described as among the most important works ever produced by an American. Powell rejected both the concept of the inexhaustibility of natural resources and the idea that the West was the "Great American Desert" and not capable of supporting substantial settlement. Powell's familiarity with the West had convinced him that its lands and climate west of the one hundredth meridian were simply not suitable for development under policies that had been shaped by the conditions in the Eastern regions. The arid lands of the West required a different strategy, and the key was water management.

Powell argued that the arid regions would not support the traditional family farm on the eastern model and that the lands of the West should be categorized and utilized according to their most efficient uses for grazing, lumbering, mining, farming, and other purposes. Water should be considered a precious resource to be allocated by the community for the benefit of society in general rather than a privileged few. Government should undertake large-scale damming and irrigation projects so that the arid regions could be "reclaimed" and become productive. Powell's ideas represented a significant departure from the conventional wisdom regarding land use and the West, and his prestige as an explorer and scientist, coupled with his office as director of the United States Geological Survey from 1881 to 1894, put him in a position to be enormously influential in shaping the establishment in 1902 of the United States Bureau of Reclamation, which helped to make water management one of the major components of the early conservation movement.

During his Western expeditions, Powell had become fascinated by the cultures of the Indian tribes of the region, and it is characteristic of the man that he became a student of anthropology and headed the Bureau of Ethnology of the Smithsonian Institution during the same period that he led the Geological Survey. In 1880 he published his *Introduction to the Study of Indian Languages*.

Major Powell's retirement in 1894 was brought about partially because of physical ailments and partially because of his frustration in trying to get his ideas implemented. Ironically, his death in 1902 coincided with the passage of the Reclamation Act, which institutionalized many of his theories concerning land and water management.

Summary

Powell's career was significant on several fronts. As an explorer, his journey down the Colorado River through the Grand Canyon in 1869 ranks as one of the epic American adventures. His scientific background and interests prepared him for important accomplishments in mapping, surveying, and studying the geology of the plateau and canyon country, and for long service as director of the United States Geological Survey. During the same period, he headed the Bureau of Ethnology of the Smithsonian Institution. Powell became most interested in the problems of proper management and utilization of the lands in the arid West and was convinced that intelligent water management was the key to its development. He is one of the fathers of the concept of "reclamation" of arid lands through the construction of dams and irrigation projects.

Bibliography

Bartlett, Richard A. *Great Surveys of the American West*. Norman: University of Oklahoma Press, 1962. A comprehensive treatment that includes the work of Powell.

Childs, Elizabeth C. "Time's Profile: John Wesley Powell, Art, and Geology at the Grand Canyon." *American Art* 10, no. 1 (Spring 1996). Discusses the creation of Powell's surveys of the Grand Canyon.

Darrah, William C. *Powell of the Colorado*. Princeton, N.J.: Princeton University Press, 1951. A useful scholarly biography. Well researched, drawing on some unpublished sources, but rather colorless. Includes illustrations.

Dorman, Robert L. *A Word for Nature: Four Pioneering Environmental Advocates, 1845-1913*. Chapel Hill: University of North Carolina Press, 1998. The author offers profiles of Powell and three other noted American conservationists, emphasizing the effects of the economy, politics, culture, and society on their efforts and thought.

Exploring the American West, 1803-1879 (National Park Handbook no. 116). Washington, D.C.: Government Printing Office, 1982. This 128-page booklet is profusely illustrated and contains several photographs of Powell and his survey. The text is by William H. Goetzmann.

Fradkin, Philip L. *A River, No More: The Colorado River and the West*. New York: Knopf, 1981. Focusing upon the Colorado River and its tributaries, Fradkin discusses the federal land and water policies that shaped much of the West. Powell's role in the evolution of these developments is considered.

Goetzmann, William H. *Exploration and Empire: The Explorer and the Scientist in the Winning of the American West*. New York: Knopf, 1966. This Pulitzer Prize-winning book is the standard general treatment of the role of exploration in the American West. Contains a chapter dealing with Powell's life and career.

Savage, Henry, Jr. *Discovering America, 1700-1875*. New York: Harper, 1979. A very readable survey which is particularly good on the nineteenth century explorations.

Schwartz, Seymour I., and Ralph E. Ehrenberg. *The Mapping of America*. New York: Abrams, 1980. An enormously detailed and lavishly illustrated history.

Stegner, Wallace. *Beyond the Hundredth Meridian: John Wesley Powell and the Second Opening of the West*. Boston: Houghton Mifflin, 1954. The standard biography. Stegner brings a novelist's gifts to his compelling narrative. Illustrations juxtapose early artists' renderings of the Grand Canyon with some of the first photographs of the region.

Wild, Peter. *Pioneer Conservationists of Western America*. Missoula, Mont.: Mountain Press, 1979. A brief, breezy, superficial account which contains a chapter on Powell's explorations and theories.

James E. Fickle

WILLIAM HICKLING PRESCOTT

Born: May 4, 1796; Salem, Massachusetts
Died: January 28, 1859; Boston, Massachusetts
Area of Achievement: History
Contribution: Prescott proved that historical writing could achieve the permanence of literature; he introduced into American historiography all the methods of modern scholarship, and he remains the most distinguished historian of sixteenth century Spain and Spanish America in the English language.

Early Life

William Hickling Prescott was born in Salem, Massachusetts, on May 4, 1796. His father, William Prescott, a lawyer and judge who prospered in investments in industry, real estate, and the India trade, was the son of Colonel William Prescott, the hero of the Battle of Bunker Hill; Prescott's mother, Catherine Greene Hickling, was the daughter of another wealthy New England family. Prescott attended private schools in Salem and another in Boston when the family moved there in 1808. At Harvard, he suffered an injury to his left eye during a boyish fracas in the dining hall, which led to a lifetime of trouble with his eyesight. This event is the basis of the myth that he achieved literary fame in spite of blindness. Actually, he was never totally blind, but his eyesight and his general health were poor throughout his life.

When he was graduated from Harvard in 1814, Prescott's study of the law in preparation for joining his father's firm was cut short by impaired vision and rheumatic pains, and his parents sent him abroad for his health, first to the Azores, where his maternal grandfather was the American consul. He returned to Boston in 1817, after two years in England, France, and Italy, convinced that he would never be able to practice law. During the winter of 1817-1818, he was confined to a darkened room, where his sister read to him while he wrestled with the question of what career to pursue.

Prescott's first published work, an article on Lord Byron, appeared in the *North American Review* in 1821. By this time, he was determined to be a man of letters, a career made possible by the readers and secretaries whom he could afford to employ. In 1820, he married Susan Amory, the daughter of a wealthy Boston merchant, and he embarked on the systematic study of European literature. During the next nine years, he continued to publish essays on a variety of literary subjects while studying Italian and Spanish literature.

Life's Work

Prescott's study of the literature of Spain led to his determination to write a history of the reign of the fifteenth century monarchs Ferdinand and Isabella. Doubly isolated from documentary sources by his poor eyesight and his distance from Spanish libraries but blessed with sufficient wealth, Prescott employed full-time secretaries to read to him and to take dictation, and his many contacts in European libraries made possible a form of research that was remarkably complete, considering his difficulties. His friends in Europe found and made copies of often obscure documentary sources, and his remarkable memory gave him the ability to keep a large amount of historical information in mind as he organized his subject. *History of the Reign of Ferdinand and Isabella the Catholic* (1838), the result of eight years of writing, was, for a historical work, a remarkable success, both in the United States and

in England. Though later historians have charged that Prescott ignored the ordinary people of Spain in concentrating on the life of the Spanish court, it must be remembered that it was politics, diplomacy, and war, not "common life," that furnished subjects for historians in Prescott's time. This first work reveals high standards of objectivity, it is thoroughly documented, and Spanish historians have always considered it a basic contribution to fifteenth century historiography. All this is even more remarkable for being the achievement of a self-trained historian.

Prescott's success with his first book encouraged him to embark on the writing of the two works for which he is most famous, his accounts of the destruction of the Aztec and Inca empires by the conquistadors of Hernán Cortés and Francisco Pizarro. *History of the Conquest of Mexico* (1843) produced for Prescott a remarkable number of honors, including memberships in various historical societies in the United States and in Europe, honorary degrees, and, most significant, a membership in the Royal Academy of History in Madrid. This work, which has been issued in two hundred editions and has been his most translated book, is considered by most students of Prescott to be his masterpiece, admired particularly for its graceful style and overall design. It is a supreme example of the work of the first great generation of American historians—Prescott, Francis Parkman, and John Lothrop Motley—who, being unburdened by any philosophy of history, subordinated deep analyses of social background and lengthy explanations of the causes of events to simple narrative history written for both the edification and entertainment of the reader.

History of the Conquest of Peru (1847) was written in two years. The speed of its composition is an indication of the success of Prescott's mastery of the subject of sixteenth century Spain, his methods of research, and particularly the remarkable network of friends he had established in Spanish libraries. This work has not enjoyed the scholarly respect which *History of the Conquest of Mexico* has achieved, but this is less because of failing powers in its author than of the subject itself: Prescott found much less to admire in Pizarro than he had found in Cortés.

In 1850, he traveled in Europe, where he was a great social success and where, among other honors, he received a doctorate from Oxford University. The first two volumes of his fourth work, *History of the Reign of Philip the Second, King of Spain*, were published in 1855, and the final, third volume appeared in December, 1858, only a month before his death on January 28, 1859. This is the least of his four major works, probably because of the bad health that plagued him while he was writing it but also because he found so little to admire in his subject.

Prescott's four historical works are his primary claim to fame as a historian and man of letters. He also published "The Life of Charles V After His Abdication" (1856) as a supplement to William Robertson's *The History of the Reign of the Emperor Charles the Fifth* (1769), and what he called "some of my periodical trumpery" appeared as *Biographical and Critical Miscellanies* in 1845.

In spite of his physical ailments, Prescott's private life was serene. He was the father of four children, he enjoyed a wide circle of personal and professional friends, and he maintained a comfortable rhythm of the seasons as he worked in his library in Boston in the winter and spent his summers at Nahant or at the ancestral Prescott farm.

Prescott was in many ways a typical Boston Brahmin, a Unitarian in religion, a Federalist in politics and later a Whig, and a man with strong social concerns for his community and a belief that wealth confers obligations on the wealthy. Early in life, he was influential in the establishment in Massachusetts of an institution for the care of the blind, and he supported the Boston Atheneum all of his life. He earned the respect of many Mexican and Spanish friends by opposing the Mexican War and the Pierce Administration's designs on Cuba, and like most New England intellectuals, he opposed the Fugitive Slave Law and voted for John C. Frémont in 1856. He was a complex man who, in spite of his physical impairment, enjoyed social activity and gracious living, and he was a frequent help to other writers and researchers, but his ambition as a historian and man of letters triumphed over the double burden of ill health and social position while his wealth made possible research which no other American of his time could have achieved.

Summary

William Hickling Prescott combined thorough research and literary gifts to produce historical works which must be considered contributions both to historical knowledge and to American literature. Though he concentrated on the colorful aspects of his subjects and ignored the more prosaic and mundane life of common people, he produced remarkable examples of narrative and helped to raise historical writing in the United States from the often parochial concerns of his predecessors while avoiding the dullness which characterizes much of the admittedly fuller social and economic histories of later generations of historians. The fact that his work is eminently readable has obscured his importance as the first American historian to employ modern methods of historical research, an achievement that is even more remarkable when one takes account of the fact that he was completely self-trained and that he was burdened with ill health all of his life. Furthermore, at a time when American literary and historical interests, in the aftermath of revolution and nation-building, were inevitably turned inward, he made American readers conscious of cultures beyond their borders while helping to give American literature an international reputation.

Bibliography

Charvat, William, and Michael Kraus, eds. *William Hickling Prescott: Representative Selections*. New York: American Book Co., 1943. This selection of passages from Prescott's writing is supplemented by a brief account of his life and discussions of his literary style and the philosophical and political premises of his work.

Costeloe, Michael P. "Prescott's History of the Conquest and Calderon de la Barca's Life in Mexico." *The Americas: A Quarterly Review of Inter-American Cultural History* 47, no. 3 (January, 1991). An overview of nineteenth-century works in Mexican history by Prescott and Frances Calderon de la Barca.

Darnell, Donald G. *William Hickling Prescott*. Boston: Twayne, 1975. Primarily concerned with Prescott as a man of letters, Darnell provides a brief account of his life, a balanced assessment of his achievement as a historian, and lengthy examinations of each of his four major works.

Gardiner, C. Harvey. *William Hickling Prescott: A Biography*. Austin: University of Texas Press, 1969. The definitive biography by the most distinguished Prescott scholar, based on a thorough knowledge of primary sources and not likely to be superseded. A balanced assessment of Prescott's achievement as a historian and man of let-

ters and a full treatment of his complex personality and private life.

Kagan, Richard L. "Prescott's Paradigm: American Historical Scholarship and the Decline of Spain." *American Historical Review* 101, no. 2 (April, 1996). Compares historical views of Spain as a declining nation and Prescott's opposing thought which served as a model for later American historians.

Levin, David. *History as Romantic Art: Bancroft, Prescott, Motley, and Parkman*. Stanford, Calif.: Stanford University Press, 1959. A study of the first generation of American historians, their romanticism, and its effects on their writing, which Levin often considers unfortunate. His assessments of Prescott should be checked against Gardiner's.

Ogden, Rollo. *William Hickling Prescott*. Boston: Houghton Mifflin, 1904. Apparently intended to supplement George Ticknor's biography, it devotes more attention to Prescott as a person and takes greater account of his private papers. The best biography before Gardiner's.

Peck, Harry Thurston. *William Hickling Prescott*. New York: Macmillan, 1905. A brief biography which makes no use of primary sources but includes a useful discussion of Prescott's literary style.

Prescott, William H. *The Literary Memoranda*. Edited by C. Harvey Gardiner. 2 vols. Norman: University of Oklahoma Press, 1961. A collection of Prescott's private papers, which provide essential insight into his methods as a writer and researcher.

Ticknor, George. *Life of William Hickling Prescott*. Philadelphia: Lippincott, 1863; London: Routledge, 1864. Ticknor, himself the author of a major history of Spanish literature, knew Prescott intimately, but his biography provides no insight into his subject's personality and very little of his social and intellectual background. Includes useful appendices on the history of the Prescott family.

Williams, Stanley T. *The Spanish Background of American Literature*. 2 vols. New Haven, Conn.: Yale University Press, 1955. Includes a chapter on Prescott and provides insights into the sources of nineteenth century American interest in Spain and Spanish America.

Robert L. Berner

PIERRE-JOSEPH PROUDHON

Born: January 15, 1809; Besançon, France
Died: January 19, 1865; Paris, France
Areas of Achievement: Philosophy and economics
Contribution: Proudhon's greatest activity was as a journalist and pamphleteer. Hailed by his followers as the uncompromising champion of human liberty, Proudhon voiced the discontentment of the revolutionary period of nineteenth century France.

Early Life

Pierre-Joseph Proudhon was born on January 15, 1809, in the rural town of Besançon. Although the political and social climates were important influences on Proudhon's life, the experiences he had as a child growing up in a working-class family shaped his philosophical views in even more important ways. Proudhon's father, who was a brewer and, later, a cooper, went bankrupt because, unlike most brewers, he sold his measure of drink for a just price. Penniless after the loss of his business, Proudhon's father was forced to move his family to a small farm near Burgille. Between the ages of eight and twelve, Proudhon worked as a cowherd, an experience which forged in him a lifelong identity with the peasant class.

Proudhon's formal education began in 1820, when his mother arranged with the parish priest for him to attend the local college, which was the nineteenth century equivalent of high school. The stigma of poverty suddenly became very real to him when he contrasted his clothes with those of his wealthier comrades. Smarting from the insults of the other children, Proudhon protected himself from further pain by adopting a surly, sullen personality. During his fourth year at school, Proudhon read François Fénelon's *Démonstration de l'existence de Dieu* (1713; *A Demonstration of the Existence of God*, 1713), which introduced him to the tenets of atheism. Proudhon then ceased to practice religion at the age of sixteen and began his lifelong war against the Church.

Proudhon's life changed drastically on the eve of his graduation. Sensing that something was wrong when neither of his parents was present, Proudhon rushed home to find that his father, who had become a landless laborer, had lost everything in a last desperate lawsuit. Years later, Proudhon used his father's inability to own farmland as the basis for his belief that society excluded the poor from the ownership of property.

At the age of eighteen, Proudhon was forced to abandon his formal education and take up a trade. He was apprenticed to the Besançon firm of the Gauthier brothers, which specialized in general theological publications. Proudhon became proud of his trade as a proofreader because it made him independent. At home among the printers, who were men of his own class, he found that he had traded the isolation of the middle-class school for the comradely atmosphere of the workshop.

The printshop also enabled Proudhon to continue his studies, in an informal way, for it was there that he developed his first intellectual passions. His budding interest in language was cultivated by a young editor named Fallot, who was the first great personal influence on Proudhon's life. It was there too that Proudhon was introduced to the works of the utopian thinker Charles Fourier. Fourier's position that a more efficient economy can revolutionize society from within is reflected in the anarchical doctrines of Proudhon's greatest works.

Another lesson Proudhon learned at the printshop was that mastering a trade does not guarantee a living, as it would in a just society. His apprenticeship came to an end as a result of the Revolution of 1830, which overthrew the restored Bourbons. Although Proudhon hated to be out of work, he was infected with the spirit of revolution, which stayed with him throughout his life.

His friend Fallot persuaded Proudhon to move to Paris and apply for the Suard scholarship. During their visit to Paris, Fallot provided Proudhon with moral and financial support, because he was convinced that Proudhon had a great future ahead of him as a philosopher and a writer. When Fallot was stricken with cholera, however, Proudhon declined to accept his friend's generosity any longer and began seeking employment in the printing houses of Paris, but to no avail. Discouraged, Proudhon left Fallot to convalesce by himself in Paris.

Life's Work

A turning point for Proudhon came with the publication of his book *Qu'est-ce que la propriété?* (1840; *What Is Property?*, 1876). The book was actually a showcase for his answer to this question—

"Property is theft"—and it gained for Proudhon an immediate audience among those working-class citizens who had become disillusioned with Louis-Philippe, a king who clearly favored the privileged classes. Ironically, though, Proudhon was a defender of public property; he objected to the practice of drawing unearned income from rental property. This book represented a dramatic departure from the popular utopian theories embraced by most socialists of the day in that it employed economic, political, and social science as a means of viewing social problems.

Among the people who were attracted to Proudhon's theories was Karl Marx. In 1842, Marx praised *What Is Property?* and met Proudhon in Paris. Since Proudhon had studied economic science in more depth than Marx had, Marx probably learned more from their meeting than did Proudhon. Two years later, though, Marx became disenchanted with Proudhon after the publication in 1846 of Proudhon's first major work, *Système des contradictions économiques: Ou, Philosophie de la misère* (1846; *System of Economic Contradictions*, 1888).

Proudhon hoped that the Revolution of 1848 would bring his theories to fruition by deposing Louis-Philippe. He became the editor of a radical journal, *Le Représentant du peuple* (the representative of the people), in which he recorded one of the best eyewitness accounts of the Revolution. That same year, he was elected to the office of radical deputy. Surprisingly, Proudhon did not ally himself with the socialist Left. During his brief term in office, he voted against the resolution proclaiming the "right to work" and against the adoption of the constitution establishing the democratic Second Republic. His chief activity during his term in office was the founding of a "People's Bank," which would be a center of various workingmen's associations and would overcome the scarcity of money and credit by universalizing the rate of exchange.

The feasibility of such a bank will never be known, because it was closed after only two months of operation when Proudhon's career as a deputy came to an abrupt end. In 1849, Proudhon was arrested for writing violent articles attacking Napoleon III and was sentenced to three years in the Saint-Pelagie prison. Proudhon fled to Belgium but was promptly arrested when he returned to Paris under an assumed name to liquidate his bank, which had foundered in his absence.

Proudhon's imprisonment was actually a fortunate experience. It afforded him ample time to study and write; he also founded a newspaper, *Le Voix du peuple* (the voice of the people). In *Les Confessions d'un révolutionnaire* (1849; the confessions of a revolutionary), written while he was in prison, Proudhon traced the history of the revolutionary movement in France from 1789 to 1849. In *Idée générale de la révolution au XIXᵉ siècle* (1851; *The General Idea of the Revolution in the Nineteenth Century*, 1923), he appealed to the bourgeois to make their peace with the workers. *La Révolution sociale démontrée par le coup d'état du 2 décembre* (1852; the revolution demonstrated by the coup d'état), which was published a month after the release of Proudhon from prison, hailed the overthrow of the Second Republic as a giant step toward progress. Proudhon also proposed that anarchy was the true end of the social evolution of the nineteenth century. Because Proudhon suggested that Napoleon III should avoid making the same mistakes as Napoleon I, the book was banned by the minister of police. Still, the book created a sensation in France.

The most important event that occurred while Proudhon was in prison was his marriage to Euphrasie Piegard, an uneducated seamstress, whose management skills and resilience made her a suitable mate for a revolutionary. By marrying outside the Church, he indicated his contempt for the clergy. Marriage was good for Proudhon, and his happiness convinced him that marriage was an essential part of a just society.

The three years following Proudhon's release from prison were marked by uncertainty and fear. By the end of 1852, Napoleon III's reign was in crisis, and any writer who opposed him or the Crimean War was immediately ostracized. Proudhon's attempts to start a journal through which he could persuade the regime of Napoleon III to move to the Left against the Church was thwarted by the Jesuits. With his journalistic career at an end, Proudhon began a series of literary projects.

The year 1855 saw a significant shift in Proudhon's philosophical outlook. He arrived at the conclusion that what was needed was not a political system under which everyone benefited but a transformation of man's consciousness. Proudhon's new concern with ethics resulted in his *De la justice dans la révolution et dans l'église* (about the justice of the revolution and the church) in 1858. This three-volume work, which ranks as one of the greatest socialist studies of the nineteenth century, attacks the defenders of the status quo, including the Catholic church.

Although the book enjoyed great success, the anger that Proudhon had exhibited in this manifesto of defiance outraged the government and the Church. Once again, Proudhon was given a fine and a prison sentence. Proudhon submitted a petition to the senate, but to no avail; he was sentenced to three years' imprisonment and ordered to pay a fine of four thousand francs; his publisher received a fine as well. Proudhon again fled to Belgium, where he settled as a mathematics professor under the assumed name of Durfort.

Though Proudhon's publisher refused to accept any more of his political works, Proudhon continued to write. The last of Proudhon's great treatises, *La Guerre et la paix* (war and peace), appeared in 1861. This two-volume work explored Proudhon's view that only through war could man obtain justice and settle conflicts between nations. Proudhon also held that women must serve the state only as housewives and mothers in order to ensure a strong, virile nation. In response, Proudhon was branded a reactionary, a renegade, and a warmonger by both citizens and journalists.

Proudhon was forced to flee Belgium when his opposition to the nationalist movement, which he had expressed in various newspaper articles, created a furor. A large segment of readers objected to a statement in one of these articles that seemed to favor the annexation of Belgium by France.

After returning to France, Proudhon threw himself into his work, producing four books in only two years. This final burst of creativity was his last attempt to persuade the workers to abstain from political activity, while the imperial administration continued to distort the workings of universal suffrage. *La Fédération de l'unité en Italie* (1863; the federal principle and the unity of Italy) contains what is considered by many to be the best explanation of the federal principle that has ever been written. *De la capacité politique des classes ouvrières* (1863; of the political capacity of the working classes), inspired by the workers' refusal to support the candidates of the Second Empire in the legislative election of 1863, reflects Proudhon's new confidence in the proletariat. He now believed that the workers could be a viable force for achieving mutualism.

Although Proudhon's mental faculties remained sharp, his health deteriorated rapidly in the last two years of his life. He died of an undetermined illness on January 19, 1865.

Summary

Pierre-Joseph Proudhon was a radical thinker who was incapable of identifying completely with any single political ideology. Early in his career, Proudhon was a revolutionary who denounced the established political and economic institutions. As he grew older, he began to absorb some of those bourgeois values that he had scorned in his youth, such as the importance of the family and the inheritance of property. Thus, he is best described as a man of contradictions, a radical, a realist, and a moralist. In fact, he was viewed as a dissenter by other dissenters of the day: liberals, democrats, and republicans, as well as his fellow socialists.

Proudhon's influence on French politics extended well into the twentieth century. In the Paris Commune of 1871, Proudhon's political views carried more weight than did those of Marx. By the end of the nineteenth century, however, Proudhon's teachings seem to have been overshadowed by the Marxists. Through anarchism, Proudhon's influence was transferred to revolutionary syndicalism, which dominated French trade unionism into the twentieth century. The syndicalists favored a violent approach to the class struggle and employed the general strike as a weapon. Just before World War II, though, French trade unionism turned away from Proudhon as it began to cater to various political factions.

Bibliography

Brogan, D. W. *Proudhon*. London: Hamilton, 1934. A short but complete biography which includes summaries and critiques of Proudhon's work. The first half of the book does an excellent job of outlining those influences which shaped him as a writer and a thinker.

Dillard, Dudley. "Keynes and Proudhon." *Journal of Economic History*, May, 1942: 63-76. A fine introduction to Proudhon's economic and political philosophy. In his comparison between Proudhon and J. M. Keynes, who seems to have formulated his theories after Proudhon's, Dillard highlights the most important points in Proudhon's work, thereby clarifying some of Proudhon's more difficult concepts for the average reader.

Hall, Constance Margaret. *The Sociology of Pierre Joseph Proudhon, 1809-1865*. New York: Philosophical Library, 1971. A penetrating analysis of Proudhon's political philosophy and the effects it had on nineteenth century France. The brief biographical sketch in the beginning of the volume is an excellent introduction to Proudhon's life and times.

Ritter, Alan. *The Political Thought of Pierre-Joseph Proudhon*. Princeton, N.J.: Princeton University Press, 1969. An in-depth study of Proudhon's political views which explains the historical events that spawned his ideas and describes how Proudhon's theories have been interpreted in various times. Also demonstrates how Proudhon attempted to integrate revolutionary, realistic, and moral concepts into a cohesive political theory.

Schapiro, J. Salwyn. "Pierre Joseph Proudhon, Harbinger of Fascism." *American Historical Review*, July, 1945: 714-737. Theorizes that Proudhon was an intellectual forerunner of Fascism. Concentrates primarily on those radical elements of Proudhon's works which seem to have influenced National Socialism. Also contains a brief but useful sketch of Proudhon's life.

Vaughn, Gerald. "Dillard on Proudhon." *Journal of Economic Issues* 28, no. 3 (September, 1994). Short discussion of an article by economist Dudley Dillard published in 1942 on Proudhon's economic theories in the context of the French Revolution.

Woodcock, George. *Pierre-Joseph Proudhon*. London: Routledge, and New York: Macmillan, 1956. A standard biography of Proudhon's life, combining voluminous details of his personal life with a discussion and critique of his writings and philosophical views. Provides invaluable insights into the turbulent historical period of which Proudhon was a product and shows the role that he played as a catalyst in these events. Emphasizes Proudhon's willingness to suffer as a result of his devotion to his principles.

Alan Brown

AUGUSTUS WELBY NORTHMORE PUGIN

Born: March 1, 1812; London, England
Died: September 14, 1852; London, England
Area of Achievement: Architecture
Contribution: Pugin wrote treatises promoting the Gothic revival in church architecture and built more than one hundred distinctive buildings during his short career.

Early Life

The only son of a French immigrant architectural illustrator and his Calvinist wife, Catherine Welby, Augustus Welby Northmore Pugin was born on March 1, 1812. His father, Augustus Charles Pugin, who was fifty when Augustus was born, and Catherine were educators who ran a school for training architects and illustrators. In England, young Pugin attended class field trips and learned early to measure and draw buildings. He traveled with classes to France, absorbing the quiet grandeur of the medieval cathedrals. His memories of the crypts of the Continental cathedrals would later fire his interest in the Catholic faith.

When Pugin was twenty-three, his father died, leaving an unfinished manuscript, *Examples of Gothic Architecture* (1835). Pugin undertook to fulfill his father's contract for the book, demonstrating his skill and interest in architecture. His education in the field continued, without an apprenticeship. Pugin worked diligently to complete the manuscript, while traveling to study medieval art history and find clients.

Meanwhile, his domestic life inspired his building a home for his second wife, Louisa (his first wife, Anne, having died in childbirth). Saint Marie's Grange had a pleasing view and its own chapel, but it was soon too small for a growing family. When Pugin tried to sell the house, he found that his tastes were not average. The house did not imitate the fantastic castles and cottages of the day, and it took some time for his growing reputation to make the house salable.

Though reared as a Nonconformist, Pugin converted to Catholicism at the age of twenty-six, several years after the Catholic Emancipation Act. He found Catholic churches in England in poor condition after the Reformation years, their beauty and solemnity sadly diminished. His estimation of the state of the faith was further diminished by the performance of ceremonies without proper attention to details. Trompe l'oeil, artificial flowers, pagan symbols, and shabby upkeep he found incompatible with the aims of the faith. This grave dismay at the condition of his chosen church, and his sense of the Catholic church, specifically the English branch, manifested itself in a lifelong study of the Church in the medieval world, a time when church power was at its greatest. This scholarship would be the foundation of his building, decorating, and writing endeavors.

A look of serious contemplation is apparent in a portrait of Pugin by J. R. Herbert. Framed in an ecclesiastically styled piece decorated with quatrefoils and intertwined carved ribbons bearing the legend "En Avant," Pugin's face and hands seem to float above the dark background. Thin brows and a churlish mouth on a fleshy face seem loath to let the compass and pencil in hand remain still for posing. Pugin was always eager to attack his work—at a hare's pace.

Life's Work

As far as Pugin was concerned, the baroque London church St. Mary Woolnoth could keep the hours. Pugin designed churches with bell towers, rather than clock towers, to call the faithful. He believed that the proper concern of church architecture was not the temporal function of classical architectural forms. The influence of Greek and Roman forms Pugin could only regard with contempt as pagan creations, designed for the worship of idols. Not only was the spiritual inspiration defective, but also the current vogue for Roman designs, with the low slope to the roofs, according to Pugin was unsuitable to the severities of the English climate.

In the Gothic Pugin found the "only correct expression of the faith, wants and needs of our country." Pugin applied these principles by use of local materials, scrupulous attention to church liturgy, and study of medieval Gothic churches.

August, 1839, marked the opening of Pugin's first completed church, St. Mary's, Uttoxeter. Commissioned by John Talbot, the Earl of Shrewsbury, who would present Pugin with several additional commissions, the church was a monumental accomplishment for Pugin. He called it "the first Catholic structure erected in this country in strict accordance with the rules of ancient ecclesiastical architecture since the days of the pretended reformation."

Though this church earned his praise, it was not Pugin's ideal. Its success showed Pugin's ability to work gracefully within the constraints of a particular job. A simple church in comparison to his later works, it was mostly brick, though Pugin preferred stone, and it had no side aisles.

The inside was illuminated by Pugin's window of preference, a large round one over the door (usually he had to make do with the tall, pointed ones). The nave's high ceiling created a grand space separated from the chancel by a rood, or cross, which foreshadowed Pugin's use of rood screens. In the chancel, Pugin's reredos, or altar screen, featured eight angels in niches. Curtains to either side of the altar protected the clergy from breezes. To the right, Pugin included the three seats of the sedilia and sacrarium; to the left, a place for holding the consecrated hosts on Maundy Thursday.

This church, like his others, was not a mere copy of medieval designs. Pugin combined the Gothic design vocabulary, sometimes even adapting local medieval patterns, to available materials and the restraints of budget and location to create original solutions to the challenge of church building—with his particular ecclesiastical standards in mind.

For best achieving these standards in his own work, Pugin preferred St. Giles', Cheadle, another of his early churches commissioned by the Earl of Shrewsbury. Metalwork, vestments, and other accessories designed by Pugin and executed at the Hardman works in Birmingham furnished the interior. Begun in 1840 and completed six years later, the church was built from local stone, with local alabaster for the altar. Massive in scale with a two-hundred-foot spire, elaborate in decorations rich with symbolism, and sumptuous in colors all the way up the walls and over the ceiling, St. Giles' was immediately impressive and distinctively Pugin's.

Whereas St. Giles' had the tower in the center of the west side with the main entrance, Pugin's last churches advocated asymmetry, with the towers standing at the end of aisles or to the side of the nave.

While experimenting with tower location, Pugin was also developing his interior aesthetics. His Irish churches, which showed a remarkable respect for indigenous architecture and materials, contrasted with the ornamentation of St. Giles'. St. Mary's Cathedral, Killarney, begun in 1842 but completed after Pugin's death with altar and reredos by his son Edward, was designed as a huge cruciform

structure of stone crowned by a spire above the crossing. Irregular stones suggested a solid and immovable landmark, yet still drew the eye upward. Inside, the plain stone walls directed one to the detail in the pointed arches marching up the side aisles to the chancel.

Yet it was not in the innovative achievements of design that Pugin found the most satisfaction. Late in his short life, he commented that it was his writings which contributed the most to the advancement of Gothic principles. *Contrasts* (1836), his first book, subtitled "Or, A Parallel Between the Noble Edifices of the Fourteenth and Fifteenth Centuries, and Similar Buildings of the Present Day, Shewing the Present Decay of Taste," sarcastically examines the "advances" of the Reformation and finds them wanting. *The True Principles of Pointed or Christian Architecture: Set Forth in Two Lectures Delivered at St. Marie's, Oscott*, which followed in 1841, called for a rational examination of the Gothic to find it the form exclusively appropriate for ecclesiastical building. All upward design elements he found emblematic of the Resurrection, a further reason to complete spires on towers (the other being to shed precipitation). He also used the opportunity to strike another blow at classical design, "Greek temples are utterly inapplicable to the purpose of Christian churches . . . the architecture and arrangement of which have originated in their wants and purpose."

The Ecclesiological Society, later called the Cambridge Camden Society, a self-appointed hierarchy of judges on church design in England and abroad, found Pugin too broad-minded in his definition of good architecture. They contended that his principles were not exclusive to Gothic intention. In fact, a reader might be inclined to attribute Pugin's philosophy to the Bauhaus, nearly a century away: For Pugin, ". . . *there should be no features about a building which are not necessary for convenience, construction, or propriety.*" Further,

> In pure architecture the smallest detail should *have a meaning or serve a purpose;* and even the construction itself *should vary with the material employed*, and the designs should be adapted to the material in which they are executed.

Despite the subservience of form to function and the concern for truth to materials, Pugin would not build by the glass-box standard of the twentieth century. As a Victorian, he added the caveat that there should be ornament suitable to the purpose of the building. He backed the rhetoric with dictionaries of forms suitable for decorating: *Designs for Gold and Silversmiths* (1836), *Floriated Ornament: A Series of Thirty-one Designs* (1849), and *Glossary of Ecclesiastical Ornament and Costume* (1844, 1846, 1868).

For architects merely imitating a style, a group most offensive to Pugin, a little dictionary was a dangerous thing. Decoration, he believed, should be an integral part of the structure. His warning to the imitators was little short of a moral imperative: "The severity of Christian architecture requires a *reasonable purpose for the introduction of the smallest detail*, and daily experience proves that those who attempt this glorious style without any fixed idea of its unalterable rules, are certain to end in miserable failures."

Pugin's most famous commission, however, was not ecclesiastical. Sir Charles Barry had been impressed with Pugin's work, completing projects assigned to his father around the time of his death. When the competition for replacing the Houses of Parliament opened in 1835, Barry hired Pugin to draw his plans. Once awarded the commission, Barry hired Pugin to draw revisions, and later to design the innumerable details of decorating the interiors of the Houses. Under Barry's exacting standards, Pugin created a full range of secular furnishings with a distinctly Gothic flavor. Not only would Pugin create the design for a particular piece, but he would also detail the manufacturing specifications for John Hardman, in the case of metalwork, or other artisans for tile, wallpaper, furniture, or glass.

Summary

Though the Houses of Parliament remain intact, time has undone much of the Pugin gallery. Fashion, as well as official decree, has had its way with some of his designs. Decay and demolition have obliterated others. Larger congregations called for additions to his small parish churchs, often obscuring the original lines and intention of Pugin's work. Before the beginning of the twentieth century, many of Pugin's principles were declared obsolete. Within a century of the publishing of *The True Principles of Pointed or Christian Architecture* Pope Pius XII officially sanctioned removal of Pugin's beloved rood screens.

The Houses of Parliament and the churches that remain show Pugin's success in executing his intentions. His deep understanding of the Gothic style allowed him to transcend design by imitation. He analyzed the essence of design, participating in the canon ranging from Durandus to Charles-Édouard Le Corbusier.

The relentless pace of Pugin's life, a pace commensurate with the century after his own, combined with his pursuit of the ideals belonging to a time five centuries prior to his own left him mad in the end, and he died insane. He had, however, the final satisfaction of being buried in his own properly designed church, St. Augustine, Ramsgate.

Bibliography

Anson, Peter F. *Fashions in Church Furnishings, 1840-1940*. London: Faith Press, 1960. Begins with chapters on the early Victorian era and on Pugin. Very good source on the decoration of churches and altars in the context of the social and ecclesiastical ferment which these details sometimes stirred.

Atterbury, Paul, et al. *A. W. N. Pugin: Master of Gothic Revival*. New Haven, Conn.: Yale University Press, 1995. This book was written by ten Pugin scholars and presents an in-depth portrait of the man and his achievements.

Atterbury, Paul, and Clive Wainwright, eds. *Pugin: A Gothic Passion*. New Haven, Conn.: Yale University Press, 1994. One of the best modern profiles of Pugin with one hundred black and white and three hundred color illustrations.

Foster, Richard. *Discovering English Churches*. London: British Broadcasting Corporation, 1981; New York: Oxford University Press, 1982. Covering the architectural development of parish churches from the fourth century through the Gothic revival, this book presents the church-building heritage which Pugin researched for inspiration for his designs. Valuable for its glossary of architectural and ecclesiastical terms.

Pugin, A. Welby. *An Apology for the Revival of Christian Architecture in England*. London: Weale, 1843. This book is Pugin's argument for the revival of old forms and an explanation for the correct approach to employing the Gothic mode. Truly a delight as it castigates Christopher Wren and dismisses the sightseeing architects who brought back nonindigenous design from their travels.

———. *The True Principles of Pointed or Christian Architecture: Set Forth in Two Lectures Delivered at St. Marie's, Oscott*. London: Weale, 1841; New York: St. Martin's Press, 1973. Includes Pugin's engravings and his opinions on the proper manner of construction and ornamentation of buildings, especially churches.

Stanton, Phoebe. *The Gothic Revival and American Church Architecture*. Baltimore: Johns Hopkins University Press, 1968; London: Johns Hopkins University Press, 1997. Though the perspective is from "the Colonies," the Pugin influence in England and abroad permeates this account of nineteenth century church building. The history of the contentions between various ecclesiastical societies points out the superior achievement of a single individual who could rise above the ferment—not only in his architectural criticism but in the actual building as well.

———. *Pugin*. London: Thames and Hudson, 1971; New York: Viking Press, 1972. A well-organized, well-researched biography that benefits from an occasional look at Foster's glossary (see above). Nice balance between Pugin, the man, and Pugin, the author and architect. Stanton's bibliographies also recommend Sir Kenneth Clark's *The Gothic Revival* (1928), and Benjamin Ferrey's *Recollections of A. N. Welby Pugin and His Father Augustus Pugin* (1861).

Watkin, David. *Morality and Architecture*. Oxford: Clarendon Press, 1977; Chicago: University of Chicago Press, 1984. Examines the tradition of critics and designers who have aspired to the Platonic ideal in their architectural undertakings. An especially good book to consider in the light of Pugin's severe criticism of his own designs.

Ellen Clark

JOSEPH PULITZER

Born: April 10, 1847; Mako, Hungary
Died: October 29, 1911; Charleston, South Carolina
Area of Achievement: Journalism
Contribution: Combining a strong social conscience with a superb grasp of journalistic techniques, Pulitzer created with his *New York World* the prototype of the modern newspaper.

Early Life

Joseph Pulitzer was born April 10, 1847, in Mako, Hungary. His mother, née Louise Berger, was Austro-German and Catholic; his father, Philip Pulitzer, was Magyar-Jewish, a grain dealer affluent enough to retire by 1853, whereupon the family moved to Budapest. Pulitzer and his younger brother and sister (another brother died early) were educated by private tutors; he became fluent in German and French as well as his native Hungarian.

By the age of seventeen, Pulitzer was ready to make his own way. Brilliant, independent, and intensely ambitious, he first sought fame in the military. Having been rejected for enlistment by several European armies—his eyesight was very poor—he was approached by Union army recruiting agents, who were considerably less selective. Thus it was that Pulitzer came to the United States and, in September, 1864, enlisted in the Lincoln Cavalry. His military career was short, undistinguished, and unhappy; discharged in July, 1865, with very little money and no immediate prospects, he settled in St. Louis, Missouri, where there was a large German community.

Photographs of the beardless, bespectacled young Pulitzer show a profile seemingly tailor-made for the caricaturist: a prominent, beaky nose and an up-pointed, witchlike chin. At six feet two and a half inches, he was a tall man for his time, slender and ungainly. When he arrived in St. Louis, he spoke only the most rudimentary English. Nevertheless, his exceptional abilities and his capacity for hard work were soon noticed, and, after a series of subsistence jobs, he was hired as a reporter for the *Westliche Post*, an influential German-language paper with a strong reform bent. This association provided Pulitzer's entrée into politics, and he was elected to the Missouri state legislature in 1869. His financial acumen soon became evident as well, and by his mid-twenties he was able to enjoy a long vacation in Europe.

By the time of his marriage, in June, 1878 (his bride, the beautiful Kate Davis, was a distant cousin of the former president of the Confederacy), Pulitzer had achieved the kind of success that most immigrants could only dream of, but the direction which his life would take was not yet clear. Maintaining a desultory law practice, he continued to take an active interest in politics, but, impatient, imperious, he was ill suited to the demands of office. Later in 1878, however, he made what proved to be a decisive choice of vocation.

Life's Work

It was in December of 1878 that Pulitzer, acting through an intermediary, purchased at auction in St. Louis the bankrupt *Evening Dispatch*. The paper's sixteen-year history had been marked by failure, but it did possess a Western Associated Press franchise—a consideration which prompted the publisher of a recently established rival paper, the *Post*, to propose a merger exactly as Pulitzer had planned. For the first issue of the *Post and Dispatch* (soon to become simply the *Post-Dispatch*), Pulitzer wrote an editorial that ringingly asserted the paper's independence from special interests and its dedication to reform:

> The POST and DISPATCH will serve no party but the people; will be no organ of "Republicanisn," but the organ of truth; will follow no caucases [*sic*] but its own convictions; will not support the "Administration," but criticise it; will oppose all frauds and shams wherever and whatever they are; will advocate principles and ideas rather than prejudices and partisanship.

Although Pulitzer's great achievements are associated with New York, he laid the foundation for those achievements in St. Louis in the years from 1878 to 1883 with the *Post-Dispatch*. As publisher and editor, he was involved in every phase of the paper's operation. He was an editor of genius, as his memos to his staff attest: Even today, his notes could serve as a course in newspaper journalism. Always a shrewd judge of talent, he hired the gifted editor of the *Baltimore Gazette*, John A. Cockerill, to serve as managing editor of the *Post-Dispatch*; Cockerill later followed him to New York. Indeed, Pulitzer's ability to find good employees and treat them well played an integral part in his success: The average salary of the reporters for the *Post-Dispatch* was the highest of any paper in the country, and at a time when vacations were a luxury, every employee of the *Post-Dispatch* enjoyed a paid two-week vacation each summer. Pulitzer was, then, an inspiring leader and a relatively enlightened employer, but working for him was difficult: He had a pronounced dictatorial streak, which became much stronger as he grew older, and he could be ruthless in his judgments.

Having developed in St. Louis the brand of journalism that was to make him the most influential newspaperman of his time, Pulitzer was ready to move to New York—where, ironically, his brother Albert was prospering with the *Morning Journal*, which he had founded in 1882. (The arrival of another Pulitzer was not welcomed by Albert; never close, the brothers were permanently estranged thereafter.) The opportunity came in 1883, when Pulitzer bought the failing *New York World* from financier Jay Gould for $346,000; the deal was closed not long after Pulitzer's thirty-sixth birthday. Although a young man, he was in poor health: His eyesight was failing, and he suffered from a nervous disorder. (In a later age, he would probably have been diagnosed as manic depressive.) Moreover, the continuing profitability of the *Post-Dispatch* notwithstanding, in purchasing the *New York World* he had incurred an enormous debt. Such were the unpromising circumstances in which Pulitzer entered the arena of New York journalism, yet within a short time his *New York World* reigned supreme: The paper that sold fifteen thousand copies daily in 1883 sold almost fifteen million daily in 1898.

Great as his success was, Pulitzer was never fully able to savor it. In 1890, still in his early forties, he was compelled by blindness and the worsening condition of his nerves to give up firsthand supervision of the *New York World* although he kept in close touch with his editors, firing off innumerable memos. His mood swings and other manifestations of his illness made him a difficult companion for his wife and their children (four daughters, one of whom died in infancy and another of whom, her father's favorite, died at seventeen, and three sons, one of whom, Joseph Pulitzer, Jr., became a noted newspaperman in his own right, despite a conspicuous lack of paternal confidence in his abilities). Pulitzer spent much of the time in later years traveling; near the end of his life, his preferred residence was his magnificently appointed yacht *Liberty*, where, as was his custom, newspapers, magazines, and books were read to him in great abundance and where distractions and annoyances were minimized. It was on the *Liberty* that he died, on October 29, 1911. Among the provisions in his will was the establishment of the Pulitzer Prizes, annual awards in journalism and arts and letters; also included was a one-million-dollar bequest to the soon-to-be-opened Columbia School of Journalism, which he had endowed in 1903.

Summary

In countless ways, Pulitzer caught the democratic, egalitarian spirit of America, an achievement reflected in the enormous influence of his journalistic style. The *New York World* was a pioneer in increased sports coverage, especially of boxing and baseball. People from every walk of life—tradesmen and judges, firemen and Brooklyn belles—were featured in line-drawn portraits (photojournalism did not begin until the Spanish-American War), often accompanied by brief biographical sketches. That American institution, the Sunday funnies, can also be traced to the *New York World*, where, in 1894, the first colored comic strip appeared.

Pulitzer was able to accomplish so much because, to an extraordinary degree, his own character mirrored all the contradictions that distinguished late nineteenth century America. Genuinely idealistic, Pulitzer crusaded against widespread corruption and injustice, bringing to public attention, for example, the inhuman conditions in which many immigrants were forced to live and work. Certainly this sense of conscience was one key to the *New York World's* success. At the same time, however, Pulitzer was a master of sensationalism. Others before him had used lurid stories of crime, sex, and disaster to attract readers, but Pulitzer took this material and, with bold headlines, illustrations (diagrams of murder scenes were particularly popular), and first-rate reporting, made it both appealing and acceptable to a wide range of readers. Indeed, Pulitzer rarely challenged the essentially conservative values of his readers (values which he largely shared), whether the subject was women's rights or the plight of the unemployed.

Pulitzer's legacy is most visible in the prizes that bear his name, synonymous with excellence in journalism. Less obvious but more pervasive is his impact on the way in which Americans get the news, not only in the morning paper but also on

television, where sensationalism with a social conscience has enjoyed great success.

Bibliography

Barrett, James Wyman. *Joseph Pulitzer and His "World."* New York: Vanguard Press, 1941. An anecdotal biography by the last city editor of the *New York World*. Although the focus is on Pulitzer, the last three chapters follow the fate of the *New York World* after his death to the paper's last issue in 1931. Valuable for its insider's view but rambling and undocumented.

Juergens, George. *Joseph Pulitzer and the "New York World."* Princeton, N.J.: Princeton University Press, 1966. The best single book on Pulitzer's "new journalism." Concentrates on the crucial years from 1883 to 1885, though later developments are also noted. Juergens' approach is thematic rather than chronological; he provides a clear, objective, well-documented analysis of Pulitzer's journalistic techniques and their revolutionary impact.

King, Homer W. *Pulitzer's Prize Editor: A Biography of John A. Cockerill, 1845-1896.* Durham, N.C.: Duke University Press, 1965. A colorful account of Cockerill's career before, during, and after his tenure with Pulitzer. Perhaps exaggerates Cockerill's contributions to Pulitzer's success but offers a needed corrective to other accounts.

Lamb, Dianne. "Joseph Pulitzer and the Large Mass Communication Class." *Journalism Educator* 48, no. 4 (Winter 1994). Discusses the usefulness of Pulitzer's methods of increasing public awareness through dramatic news presentation in teaching journalism students. The author argues that objectivity and intellectualism cannot alone produce enthusiastic journalists.

Pfaff, Daniel W. *Joseph Pulitzer II and the Post-Dispatch: A Newspaperman's Life.* University Park: Pennsylvania State University Press, 1991. Pfaff, a professor of journalism at Penn State University, presents an exceptional biography of Pulitzer, focusing on his conflicts with his father and posing questions as to whether Pulitzer was a better newsman than his father.

Rammelkamp, Julian S. *Pulitzer's "Post-Dispatch," 1878-1883.* Princeton, N.J.: Princeton University Press, 1967. Stresses the significance of Pulitzer's St. Louis years, scanted in most studies. A valuable, well-documented study, as much social history (particularly concerned with the growth of the middle-class reform movement) as journalistic history.

Seitz, Don C. *Joseph Pulitzer: His Life and Letters.* New York: Simon and Schuster, 1924; London: Bles, 1989. Badly dated, this intimate portrait by Pulitzer's longtime business manager nevertheless remains indispensable; all subsequent biographers have drawn on it.

Swanberg, W. A. *Pulitzer.* New York: Scribner, 1967. Popular biography, marred by some irritating mannerisms, but the only full-scale life of Pulitzer since Barrett's book of 1941. Generally balanced and well-researched, drawing extensively on the Pulitzer papers at Columbia University and the Library of Congress.

Wittke, Carl. *The German-Language Press in America.* Lexington: University of Kentucky Press, 1957. Mentions Pulitzer only in passing but provides a detailed account of the milieu in which he made his beginning as a journalist and in which his political views were formed.

John Wilson

E. B. PUSEY

Born: August 22, 1800; Pusey, Berkshire, England
Died: September 16, 1882; Ascot Priory, Berkshire, England
Area of Achievement: Religion
Contribution: Pusey was a leader of the Oxford Movement to revive Anglo-Catholic doctrines and practices in the life of the Church of England, a defender of the Bible against attacks from higher criticism, and a distinguished scholar in Semitic languages.

Early Life

Edward Bouverie Pusey was born August 22, 1800, at Pusey, a village near Oxford, to a family with Huguenot roots. His father, Philip Bouverie, assumed the name Pusey when he succeeded to the Pusey manor in 1789. Edward's paternal grandfather was the first Viscount Folkestone.

Edward received his early education at a school in Mitchum, Surrey, operated by Anglican clergyman Richard Roberts. From there he went to Eton in 1812, where he studied under the tutorial guidance of Dr. Edward Maltby, who later became Bishop of Durham. In 1819, he enrolled at Christ Church College, Oxford, where he earned high distinction in classical studies. In 1824, Pusey obtained a fellowship at Oriel College, Oxford, evidently in recognition of his outstanding scholarship. His Latin-language essay on the colonial expansion of ancient Greece and Rome won for him a university award which enhanced his reputation for erudition.

Pusey received the B.A. in 1822 and the M.A. in 1825, and he spent the periods of June to September, 1825, and June, 1826, to July, 1827, in Germany at the universities of Göttingen, Berlin, and Bonn. While in that country he studied under some of Europe's most illustrious theologians, all but one of whom espoused the higher critical approach to the Bible and a rationalist interpretation of historic Christian doctrine. Pusey's exposure to this teaching came as a result of contacts with Friedrich Schleiermacher, Johann August Wilhelm Neander, Johann Gottfried Eichorn, and other noteworthy academicians.

Although Pusey established a cordial relationship with some of his German professors, and though he proved to be a brilliant student in their classes, he rejected higher criticism and became an outspoken defender of traditional Christian doctrines. The teaching of Ernst Wilhelm Hengstenberg, a professor at Berlin, seems to have encouraged Pusey to maintain his belief in the historical accuracy and divine authority of the Scriptures. Hengstenberg, once a rationalist himself, had begun moving toward pietism when Pusey met him, and both eventually became famous champions of orthodoxy, Hengstenberg in Lutheranism, his pupil in Anglicanism.

While in Germany Pusey mastered the Hebrew, Syriac, and Arabic languages, which equipped him well for work as an exegetical commentator on various books of the Old Testament.

Soon after returning to England, Pusey was married and was ordained a member of the clergy; he published *An Historical Enquiry into the Probable Causes of the Rationalist Character Lately Predominant in the Theology of Germany* in 1828. In this book the author sounded an alarm to fellow Anglicans to guard their church against German teachings which, he feared, might infect England and impair the religious health of her national church. Perhaps because of his awkward style, some readers misunderstood the book and contended mistakenly that Pusey was actually a rationalist himself. Pusey was never satisfied with this book, and later in life he took steps to prevent anyone from reprinting it.

Life's Work

The year 1828 was a turning point in Pusey's career, when the Duke of Wellington nominated him Regius Professor of Hebrew at Oxford, a position he retained until he died. By 1828, he had established his reputation through his studies in Germany and by his learned publications. As Regius Professor he continued the work of his celebrated predecessor, Alexander Nicoll, in collecting and editing Arabic manuscripts, and he taught Hebrew language classes with the devotion of a theologian dedicated to the exposition of the Old Testament. Pusey's students were numerous, and many were preparing for the ministry. He had a particular concern to convey to them his own confidence in the inspiration and reliability of the Bible.

In addition to his expert teaching, Pusey wrote extensively and published two profound commentaries on selected Old Testament books. *Daniel the*

Prophet appeared in 1864, and *The Minor Prophets with a Commentary Explanatory and Practical* was published between 1860 and 1877. Both of these works reflect the author's staunch conservatism in doctrine and his aggressive defense of the Scriptures against higher criticism.

Pusey defended the authenticity of Daniel against scholars who assigned the authorship of the book to the Maccabean era. He contended that it is the work of the sixth century B.C. prophet whose name it bears, and he related that he had selected this Old Testament book as a battleground on which he wanted to fight those who contended for the later date. In the course of stating his case, Pusey argued that the critical method of Bible study arose from the disbelief of its exponents. He wrote that he hoped to "shake the confidence of the young in their would-be misleaders. . . . Disbelief ha[s] been the parent, not the offspring of their criticism." In *The Minor Prophets*, he interpreted the bizarre experience of Jonah in the belly of a fish as literal history, and he accepted at face value Christ's claim that the entombment of Jonah in the sea monster prophesied his own burial and bodily resurrection.

The Hebrew Psalter was one of Pusey's favorite portions of the Bible. He studied the Psalms devotedly and entered numerous marginal notes, many of which are cross-references to other texts in the Bible. He intended to revise the King James Version, and for that purpose he used one special copy of the Scriptures in which he inserted corrections and emendations to the text. He completed the revisions in Job and Psalms and did extensive work on the Minor Prophets and the Pentateuch. Pusey did not, however, complete this project or publish what he had finished. In his will he expressed doubts about his textual revisions and directed that his work not be published. He began his effort to revise the King James Version in 1827, but after 1833 he directed his energies to other projects, principally to the Oxford Movement.

The Oxford Movement arose in response to the spread of skepticism which had originated in the eighteenth century and which had prompted considerable interest, especially among Liberal politicians, to reduce the wealth and privileges of the Church of England. Its adherents opposed liberalism—by which they meant materialism, rationalism, indifference to religious doctrines, and state control of the Anglican Church. Oxford Movement leaders decried Evangelicalism, Methodism, and those vigorous Protestants who vociferously denounced the Papacy.

The movement began formally in 1833, when John Keble, a renowned religious poet associated with Oriel College, preached a sermon subsequently published as *National Apostasy, Considered in a Sermon Preached in St. Mary's* (1833). Keble called fellow Anglicans to rise to the defense of their church and its rights which the Liberal government threatened to violate by reducing the number of bishops and exerting increasing control over ecclesiastical affairs. Soon able preachers and scholars from Oxford University began publishing *Tracts for the Times*, pamphlets designed to effect wide dissemination of their concerns. John Henry Newman became the most famous of these Tractarians, and Pusey adhered to the movement late in 1834 or early in 1835, probably at the urging of his friend Newman.

Pusey feared that the political victory which the Liberals had secured in 1832 would not only threaten the structure of the Anglican Church but also encourage the spread of indifference toward Christianity in general. His first written contribution to the Oxford Movement was a treatise on baptism, which appeared in three portions as tracts sixty-seven, sixty-eight, and sixty-nine. After the issuing of these compositions, the tracts became essays of great substance rather than simple pamphlets. Newman rejoiced at Pusey's contributions and hailed his adherence to the movement as greatly enhancing its credibility.

As a Tractarian, Pusey wrote extensively on theological themes. In *Scriptural Views of Holy Baptism* (1836), he argued that this sacrament unites one with Christ through regeneration, an interpretation widely held by High Church Anglicans but rejected by most members of the Evangelical wing of the Church of England. Although there was much criticism of his position, Pusey's teaching on baptism eventually gained broad acceptance within his church.

Ever since the Church of England had broken with the Papacy in the sixteenth century, its scholars had been divided in their understanding of the sacrament of the Eucharist. Pusey set forth an Anglo-Catholic view of this matter in a sermon preached at Oxford in May, 1843. He affirmed the Real Presence of Christ and portrayed the Eucharist as a means of comfort to penitents. Although he seems to have remained within the borders of Anglican doctrine, Dr. G. Fausett, Professor of Divinity, charged that the sermon contained heresy. The vice chancellor of the university then initiated proceedings against Pusey. A committee of six theologians examined the case, and Fausett was one of the six. The university statute governing such matters did not guarantee the accused a hearing, and Pusey did not receive one. The committee concluded that he had violated the doctrines of the Anglican Church, and the vice chancellor suspended him from preaching at the university for two years. Pusey received no formal notice about the identity of his accuser but learned it at second hand. University officials did not reveal exactly what were the offensive portions of the sermon, and even William Ewart Gladstone and Justice John Taylor Coleridge could not obtain an explanation on his behalf.

Pusey tried to show that his understanding of the Eucharist concurred with that of early church fathers, but his opponents dismissed that as advocacy of transubstantiation, which he really did not espouse. Pusey believed the presence of Christ in the sacrament to be a mystery beyond explanation.

Because High Church Anglicans in general and Oxford Movement leaders in particular believed that the Bible should be interpreted with reference to the fathers, ancient creeds, and liturgical traditions, Pusey initiated work on *Library of Fathers of the Holy Catholic Church Anterior to the Division of East and West* (1838-1885), a project which extended eventually to forty-eight volumes. Keble and Newman were joint editors. Although Pusey had full confidence in the truth of Scripture, he maintained that the Church must preserve ancient doctrines against modern private interpretations which, he believed, were the besetting sins of the Evangelicals both within and without the Church of England. He appreciated the Evangelicals' reverence for the Bible, but he disliked their rejection of Catholic sacramental teachings. Pusey, for example, accused them of rationalism in their denial of baptismal regeneration.

Because the Oxford Movement stressed the Catholicity of Anglican beliefs so vigorously, its leaders were often accused of being Roman Catholics at heart, as attacks on Pusey's view of the Eucharist attest. Suspicions about Romanist leanings were not entirely unfounded, for in 1845 John Henry Newman left the Oxford Movement to join the Papal Church. Pusey, however, despite his friend's efforts to woo him, remained a convinced Anglican.

Pusey disliked the great veneration for the Virgin Mary in Catholicism, and he regarded it as a major barrier to reunion between the Roman and Anglican churches. He tried to dissuade people from following Newman's example, claiming that the Church of England preserved the true doctrine of the sacraments and apostolic succession of bishops and genuine Catholic teachings. He published *The Doctrine of the Real Presence* (1855) and *The Real Presence* (1857) to support his contention.

Despite his defense of the Anglican Church against the claims of Rome, Pusey recognized that the two churches had much in common, and he wished that they could be reunited. He expressed this desire in *An Eirenicon* (1865-1876). There he cited Roman Catholic teachings about purgatory and indulgences, together with the position of the Virgin Mary, as chief obstacles to reunion. After Vatican Council I promulgated the dogma of papal infallibility in 1870, Pusey lost all hope for official reconciliation with Rome.

Although the Evangelicals often accused Pusey of Romanism, he maintained a remarkably generous attitude toward them. Whereas Newman and other spokesmen for the Oxford Movement strongly disdained the Protestant Reformers of the sixteenth century, Pusey was restrained in his criticisms of their teachings. When the Evangelicals proposed erecting a martyrs' memorial in Oxford to honor the reformers, he supported the effort, even though his colleagues in the movement regarded it as a device to embarrass them. Pusey's rather kindly disposition toward the Protestants is especially noteworthy when one realizes that he founded an order of Anglican nuns and composed the first manual to guide Anglican clergymen when hearing confessions.

The leaders of the Oxford Movement did not extol learning for its own sake but were scholar-zealots committed to a cause. They defended a definite body of doctrine which, they believed, constituted the very heart of Christianity, as the career of Pusey illustrates. Pusey was the most erudite advocate of this view. He seems never to have doubted what he believed, and he had little patience with Christians who lacked religious fervor. He did, however, sympathize with people who, because of intellectual problems, did not believe. He had great concern for the spiritual well-being of the wealthy, whom he often reminded of their obligation to aid the poor, and his order of nuns became famous for its ministry to the poverty-stricken residents of urban areas.

Summary

E. B. Pusey strove valiantly to combat secularism in a growingly materialist society. Among Oxford Movement leaders he was probably the most independent thinker. In contrast to Newman, who wanted the Anglican Church to elect its own bishops, Pusey appealed to the Crown to prevent unworthy men from becoming prelates. At first, he did not have episcopal approval for his plan to establish a religious order of nuns, but that did not deter him. Unlike others in the Oxford Movement who, because of subscription to apostolic succession, stressed obedience to bishops, he sometimes acted on his own without much regard for episcopal authority.

Although Pusey's resistance to higher criticism and his doctrinal conservatism did not prevail in the Church of England, his view of the sacraments, his order of nuns, and his espousal of Catholic traditions have remained potent influences in the worldwide Anglican communion.

Bibliography

Brilioth, Yngve. *The Anglican Revival: Studies in the Oxford Movement.* London and New York: Longman, 1925. This is still one of the most reliable surveys of the movement, one which no student of religion in the Victorian era can afford to ignore.

Brose, Olive. *Church and Parliament.* Stanford, Calif.: Stanford University Press, 1959. This basically political account helps one to place the Oxford Movement within the context of English Liberal reformist thinking and legislation.

Chadwick, Owen. *The Mind of the Oxford Movement.* London: Black, and Stanford, Calif.: Stanford University Press, 1960.

———. *The Victorian Church.* 2 vols. New York: Oxford University Press, 1966. Chadwick's two works are masterpieces of thorough scholarship and readable prose. They are invaluable for this subject.

Church, Richard William. *The Oxford Movement, Twelve Years, 1833-1845.* London and New York: Macmillan, 1891. This brings to modern readers the insights of one who participated in the movement and wrote the first account of its founding and early history. While the author wrote as an enthusiast, he was duly critical of his colleagues.

Fairweather, Eugene. *The Oxford Movement.* New York: Oxford University Press, 1964. A profound analysis by a skilled church historian.

Griffin, John R. "Dr. Pusey and the Oxford Movement." *Historical Magazine of the Protestant Episcopal Church* 42 (1973): 137-154. This unconventional interpretation attempts with little success to separate Pusey from other Oxford Movement leaders in beliefs and goals.

Liddon, H. P. *Life of Edward Bouverie Pusey.* Edited by John O. Johnston and Robert J. Wilson. 4 vols. London and New York: Longman, 1893-1897. Despite its age and the author's great devotion to Pusey, this remains the standard biography.

Livesley, A.G. "E. B. Pusey as Hebrew Scholar." *Expository Times* 94 (1982): 43-47. Rich in material about subject's methods and achievements in scholarship.

Newman, John Henry. *Apologia Pro Vita Sua.* Edited by Daniel M. O'Connell. Rev. ed. Chicago: Loyola University Press, 1930. An indispensable primary source for the careers of both Newman and Pusey.

Pusey, Edward Bouverie. *Daniel the Prophet.* London: John Henry and James Parker, 1864; New York: Pott, Young, 1876.

———. *Occasional Sermons Selected from Published Sermons of E. B. Pusey.* London: Walter Smith, 1884. Specimens of Pusey's pulpit work which show that he was a rather awkward preacher but one who proclaimed his message with great fervor.

———, comp. and ed. *The Minor Prophets with Commentary Explanatory and Practical.* 6 vols. Oxford: Parker and Co., 1860-1877; New York: Funk and Wagnalls, 1885. This effort offers the best evidence of the amazing erudition of Pusey, and they show his method as an apologist for traditional beliefs, theological and biblical.

James E. McGoldrick

ALEXANDER PUSHKIN

Born: June 6, 1799; Moscow, Russia
Died: February 10, 1837; St. Petersburg, Russia
Areas of Achievement: Literature and historiography
Contribution: Revered by generations of Russian writers, Pushkin's largest legacy is in poetry, and his literary memory is compounded by the fact that his works inspired internationally celebrated operas, ballets, and films.

Early Life

Alexander Pushkin was born in Moscow to a father who was a tenant of a ministerial steward and to a mother descended from the Abyssinian black who became the adopted godson and personal secretary of Peter the Great. Sergey Lvovich, Alexander's father, was more interested in drawing rooms and theaters than in his estate, which he left to the mismanagement of his wife, Nadezhda Osipovna Hannibal.

With curly, chestnut-colored hair, Alexander was a sallow, thick-lipped, and dreamy-eyed child. Neglected by his parents, who preferred his younger brother Leo and his elder sister Olga, he turned to his nanny, Arina Rodionovna, who regaled him with legends and songs about wizards, princesses, knights-errant, and elves. He also enjoyed the company of his maternal grandmother, Marya Hannibal, and it was at her country estate that Pushkin learned to love his native language.

As soon as he was old enough to read, he had a number of tutors, but he was a poor student. In 1811, he entered the lyceum in Tsarskoye Selo, a school instituted and sponsored by imperial decree, where he studied everything from religion and philosophy to swimming and horsemanship. At age fourteen, Pushkin published his first poem, "To a Poet-Friend," in the well-respected *European Herald*. His official entry into the literary world occurred on January 8, 1815, when, as part of his qualifying examination for the upper school, he recited his own poem "Recollections of Tsarskoye Selo" before distinguished guests. His remarkable use of language, rhythm, onomatopoeia, and references to myth established him as a prodigy.

During 1817, Pushkin's last year at school, he befriended hussars stationed at Tsarskoye Selo and joined them in bouts of drinking and gambling. After his graduation, he was appointed to the Ministry of Foreign Affairs, but in 1818 he joined the Society of the Green Lamp, a literary club with liberal political leanings. The next year, he was suspected of collaborating with revolutionaries. Further complications arose with the publication in 1820 of his long poem *Ruslan i Lyudmila* (English translation, 1936). This poem created enormous controversy, winning praise for its epic quality but drawing condemnation for, among other things, its atheism. Pushkin was forced into exile on Ascension Day, May 6, 1820. He spent the next few years in the south of Russia, especially in Yekaterinenshtadt, the Caucasus, and Kishinev.

Life's Work

Befriended by Nicholas Raevsky, the younger son of a general celebrated for his exploits in the Napoleonic Wars, Pushkin was invited to holiday with the Raevsky family in the Caucasus, which fueled his imagination for his poem *Kavkazskiy plennik* (1822; *The Prisoner of the Caucasus*, 1895). Raevsky's elder brother Alexander was the model for the poet's sneering Mephistophelean hero in "The Demon" of the same year.

As his literary fame increased, so did his social notoriety. He continued to be extravagant in misconduct, surviving a duel against an officer whom he had accused of cheating at baccarat and using the incident in his short story "Vystrel" (1831; "The Shot"). Pushkin finally resigned from the government in 1824, but the emperor transferred him to the Pushkin estate in the deserted province of Mikhailovka, near Pskov. There he lived in sparse, unheated quarters, without books or his customary amusements. He wrote to friends requesting copies of works by William Shakespeare, Friedrich Schiller, Johann Wolfgang von Goethe, Lord Byron, Miguel de Cervantes, Dante, Petrarch, John Milton, and Cornelius Tacitus.

Engrossed in his own idiosyncratic activities, he neglected the family farm. During this period, he completed *Tsygany* (1827; *The Gypsies*, 1957), a verse tale based on his experiences in Bessarabia, a story of defeated egotism. Strong on description, it had affected, bombastic dialogue. *Graf Nulin* (1827; *Count Nulin*, 1972), a thin, rather banal response to Shakespeare's *The Rape of Lucrece* (1594), shocked readers with its sexual frankness. Pushkin wrote many lyric poems in the same year, including "André Chenier," about the poet-martyr of the French Revolution. Its theme of heroic independence was regarded suspiciously by government censors, who deleted all references to the Revolution. Pushkin's political consciousness was further exercised in his drama *Boris Godunov* (1831; English translation, 1918), a powerful story of ambition, murder, and retribution. Never produced in Pushkin's own time, the play was savaged by critics, who thought it massively disorganized because it shifted focus from Czar Boris to the Impostor Dmitry.

This professional setback was coupled with trouble ensuing from Pushkin's friendship with several conspirators in the Decembrist Revolt on December 4, 1825, against Czar Nicholas I, who had ascended the throne after Alexander I had died suddenly in November. Sick with fury and shame for having had to plead for compassion over his friendship with a key conspirator, Pushkin was escorted to the emperor, who appointed himself the writer's censor and commanded the court to take note of the new, repentant Pushkin.

In Moscow, Pushkin lived with a friend and was invited to salons and parties of the famous, but the secret police watched him diligently. The czar wanted the poet supervised continually and tested Pushkin's loyalty and liberalism by both subtle and unsubtle means. Pushkin grew tired of Moscow and left for St. Petersburg, where he saw little of his parents. He was investigated rather belatedly for his authorship of *Gavriiliada* (1822; *Gabriel: A Poem*, 1926) and later was reprimanded for traveling without authorization.

His writing remained calm and controlled, though his life was not. In October, 1828, he began *Poltava* (1829; English translation, 1936), a poem on Peter the Great. Also that year, his beloved nanny Rodionovna died in St. Petersburg, and he met sixteen-year-old Natalya Goncharov in Moscow in the winter, falling victim to her youthful beauty. Natalya was to be his victimizing "madonna," for she was a vain, shallow creature. He became engaged to Natalya on May 6, 1830, but a cholera epidemic forced him to Boldino, where he composed *Povesti Belkina* (1831; *The Tales of Belkin*, 1947), his first sustained fictional work, and almost completed his master-piece *Evgeny Onegin* (1825-1833; *Eugene Onegin*, 1881), which he had started in 1823.

Written as a novel in sonnet sequences, *Eugene Onegin* was modern in its devastating sociological criticism amid the doomed Romanticism of the central characters. Technically, the story was in eight cantos, each stanza in four-foot iambics, alternating between masculine and feminine rhymes. It was the first occasion that Pushkin had used a regular stanzaic arrangement for a long poem, and the "Onegin" stanza with its final rhymed couplet was probably derived from Byron's *ottava rima*. It was the figure of Onegin, however, that sealed the importance of the work, for the melancholy Romantic had affinities with such figures as Goethe's Werner and Byron's Childe Harold, and he stands as the first hero of Russian realism.

Pushkin's marriage to Natalya in September, 1831, was followed by a move to St. Petersburg, where he served as historiographer and where his mounting debts compounded his anxieties. The next five years were solid successes as far as his literary achievements were concerned. In 1837, he was elected to the Russian Academy.

The final four years of Pushkin's life marked a transition from poetry to prose. In 1834, he produced *Skazka o zolotom petushke* (*The Tale of the Golden Cockerel*, 1918) in verse, but he found more renown with the novella *Pikovaya dama* (1834; *The Queen of Spades*, 1896), which bore comparison with *Eugene Onegin*. Its themes of destruction, death, and madness were underlined by subtle symbolism in a manner reminiscent of his great French contemporary Stendhal.

Pushkin's final masterpiece was *Kapitanskaya dochka* (1836; *The Captain's Daughter*, 1846), a historical novella set during the period of the Pugachev Rebellion. The hero is a young officer loyal to the queen, who runs the gamut of happiness, pain, and vindication both in love and in honor. In this work, Pushkin conjoins story and history, fashioning a thoroughly credible romance while also creating an interesting portrait of the rebel leader Emelyan Ivanovich Pugachev by presenting him through the sensitivities of less important characters. The alternation of scenes of love and domestic calm with scenes of battle and camp precedes Leo Tolstoy's orchestration of similar scenes in *Voyna i mir* (1865-1869; *War and Peace*, 1886), although Pushkin's scale is smaller.

Despite his literary prowess, Pushkin found himself caught up in a spiral of destructive passions. His wife, though by now the mother of his four children, was still a flirt. Besides being the emperor's special interest, she became the object of Baron Georges-Charles D'Anthès' admiration, the adopted godson of Baron Heckeren. On November 4, 1836, Pushkin received an anonymous "diplo-

mantic emotionalism and a cool intellect that moderates his tendency toward excess.

Although the tone of his writing varies almost as much as his inconstant temperament in life, the total body of his writing is charged with satirical humor and implicit sociological criticism. The most explicit evidence of this lies in works such as *Ruslan and Lyudmila, Gabriel, Count Nulin,* and *Eugene Onegin.* Versatile in everything from verse epistles to lyrics and narratives, from historical studies to Romantic tragedies, Pushkin was preeminently a poet and novella writer.

The paradox of Pushkin was that he was intensely Russian even when he was derivatively French. His landscape was thoroughly indigenous, as were his most memorable characters. His plays (of which only *Boris Godunov* has the scope and intensity of a major work) follow history's course even as they move into man's inner world of mind, spirit, and will. While at first there is little that is Slavic about Pushkin, his work evokes some of the most cherished memories of Russia's past and his own times.

ma," designating him a member of the "Order of Cuckolds." In response, Pushkin challenged D'Anthès to a duel, which was avoided by skillful manipulation on the part of Heckeren. On his friend's advice, D'Anthès married someone else and tried unsuccessfully to make peace with Pushkin. Matters came to a head with a duel on February 8, 1837, in which D'Anthès suffered a superficial rib injury while Pushkin was mortally wounded. Howling in agony, Pushkin turned to his wife to absolve her of any guilt for his death. He died on February 10.

Summary

There is no critical disagreement over Alexander Pushkin's legacy to succeeding generations of Russian writers in prose and poetry. His mature work drew on a variety of genres and influences, and he can no more be limited by the term "Romantic" than the term "realist." He was not a rebel by nature, so his Romanticism remained a force of circumstance. His most outstanding successes, *Eugene Onegin, The Queen of Spades,* and *The Captain's Daughter,* show a tension between a Ro-

Bibliography

Bloom, Harold, ed. *Alexander Pushkin.* New York: Chelsea House, 1987. Edited with an introduction by Harold Bloom, one of the major postmodernist critics, this is a representative selection of some of the best academic criticism on Pushkin. Opens with an introductory critical essay by Bloom and a note that comments on the eleven individual essays that follow. Includes discussions of Pushkin's poetry, prose, language, imagination, and image as a Russian national poet. Contains a chronology and a bibliography.

Debreczeny, Paul. *Social Functions of Literature: Alexander Pushkin and Russian Culture.* Stanford, Calif.: Stanford University Press, 1997. Study of the impact of literature on individuals and societal groups using Pushkin as a basis. Divided into three parts, Debreczeny's book looks at reader reaction to Pushkin's work, how social environments affect reader responses, and Pushkin's place in Russia's heart.

Lavine, Lumila Shleyfer. "Poetry, Prose, and Pushkin's 'Egyptian Nights.' " *Slavic and East European Journal* 42, no. 3 (Fall 1998). Discusses Pushkin's unfinished work "Egyptian Nights" and its poetic prose.

Mirsky, D. S. *Pushkin.* London: Routledge, and New York: Dutton, 1926. A critical biography that is sometimes unsatisfyingly brief in its treatment of many works, but it sheds light on Pushkin's psychology.

Simmons, Ernest J. *Pushkin*. Cambridge, Mass.: Harvard University Press, 1937. A well-documented account of Pushkin's life, but it contains no rigorous discussion of his work.

Troyat, Henri. *Pushkin*. Translated by Nancy Amphoux. London: Allen and Unwin, and New York: Doubleday, 1970. A massive but compelling biography that is richly evocative of Pushkin's life and times, while giving detailed analyses of all of his significant writing. While highly laudatory of the artist, it never forgets to present the man in all of his emotional mutations.

Vickery, Walter N. *Alexander Pushkin*. New York: Twayne, 1970. A useful guide for nonspecialist readers that conforms to a house style favoring much plot description and generalized comment. Its main focus is on Pushkin's themes and poetic personality.

Keith Garebian

SIR HENRY RAEBURN

Born: March 4, 1756; Stockbridge, Scotland
Died: July 8, 1823; Edinburgh, Scotland
Area of Achievement: Art
Contribution: For nearly forty years, Raeburn reigned as the leading portrait painter in his native Scotland, leaving a valuable pictorial record of many prominent and affluent personages of late eighteenth and early nineteenth century Scottish society.

Early Life

Henry Raeburn was born on March 4, 1756, in Stockbridge, then a suburb of the growing town of Edinburgh. He was the younger son of Robert and Ann Elder Raeburn. His family had long been associated with agriculture in the Scottish Lowlands, but his father had abandoned that life for a career in textile manufacturing, eventually becoming a successful mill owner. Both of his parents died when young Henry was only six, leaving him in the care of his elder brother, William.

In 1765, Raeburn enrolled at Heriot's Hospital, a prestigious private school in Edinburgh that provided its students with the classical education customary for a gentleman. Raeburn, who displayed a fondness for caricature while in school, received only a few years of formal education before being apprenticed at the age of fifteen to James Gilliland, a jeweler and goldsmith. Early in his apprenticeship, Raeburn began painting miniature portraits of his friends during his spare time. Gilliland, recognizing his potential, introduced his apprentice to the engraver David Deuchar. Raeburn received occasional drawing lessons from Deuchar and through him met David Martin, then considered Edinburgh's preeminent painter. Martin did not give Raeburn any formal instruction but permitted him to use his studio and allowed him to copy some of his works. Their budding friendship ended when Martin accused Raeburn of selling one of the copies he had made.

The aspiring young artist thus received remarkably little formal instruction. Nor was Edinburgh in the 1770's a city with either a public art gallery or frequent artistic exhibitions where he could study the works of acknowledged masters. Yet many middle- and upper-class homes contained portraits, which Raeburn undoubtedly examined; and reproductions of works by such established painters as George Romney and Sir Joshua Reynolds were also readily available. Raeburn was fortunate in that Edinburgh was an expanding and increasingly prosperous community in the late eighteenth century, creating a ready-made market for a determined and talented painter who could supply a steady stream of portraits to its citizens.

Raeburn's success in selling some of his miniatures, few of which survive, enabled him to negotiate a release from his apprenticeship and devote his energy to a full-time career as a portraitist. His earliest known full-size work in oil, *George Chalmers of Pittencrieff,* dates from 1776, but it is impossible to date accurately any of the other portraits from his early period, from 1776 to 1784.

Raeburn never endured the severe financial difficulties that plagued so many aspiring artists. His good friend John Clerk, a noted lawyer, introduced him to many prospective clients, and from his early twenties the artist had sufficient commissions to live comfortably. His financial future was secured by his 1778 marriage to Ann Edgar Leslie, a wealthy widow twelve years his senior and already the mother of three. Pleasant and supportive, Ann Raeburn proved to be an excellent wife. The couple had two sons, Peter and Henry, the elder of whom died as an adolescent.

Life's Work

In the late eighteenth century, it was still commonplace for aspiring artists to study abroad in order to observe the works of the great masters. In his late twenties and now comfortable financially, Raeburn decided to follow this tradition. He first traveled to London, where he met Reynolds, then president of the Royal Academy and the preeminent figure in the British art world. Reynolds permitted him to work in his studio for several weeks and was impressed by the young Scot's abilities. He strongly advised Raeburn to go to Rome and, not knowing of his financial situation, even offered him financial assistance. Raeburn declined the money but gratefully accepted the letters of introduction which Reynolds provided.

During his two years in Rome, Raeburn probably did not produce any full-scale portraits but instead devoted himself to the study of the great works of art that abounded in the city. He became friends with Pompeo Batoni, then a leading artist, who had painted many outdoor portraits of visiting Scots; Raeburn was also influenced by the antiquary and art dealer James Byrnes. Although his Italian sojourn did not radically transform Raeburn's style or subject matter, it undoubtedly had an effect on his use of poses, color, and tonality. After his return to Edinburgh in 1787, Raeburn rapidly replaced Martin as the city's leading portraitist, a status he maintained until his death. By 1795, Raeburn was able to move from his studio on George Street to more spacious accommodations at York Place, which he personally designed. In addition to his own studio, York Place also contained a large gallery where the public could view his works. He actively promoted artistic exhibitions in the city and freely lent his gallery for such purposes.

Described by contemporaries as a tall, robust man with a rather florid complexion, Raeburn enjoyed a prominent position in Edinburgh society, free from major rivals or controversies. An interesting conversationalist who was fond of anecdotes, the amiable portraitist became friends with many of the city's prominent citizens and achieved a social status denied to all but the most successful artists of the period.

Nothing was bohemian or unconventional about Raeburn's life-style. He enjoyed golf, fishing, and archery, as well as long walks in the country. He also retained a lifelong interest in architecture and had a passion for building miniature ships and models. As a painter, Raeburn was a diligent and dependable worker. Rising at seven, he was at work in his studio by nine and usually saw three or four sitters a day, keeping each of them between one and a half and two hours. He usually finished work by five and dined at six, thus freeing his evenings for time with family, friends, and hobbies.

When painting, Raeburn worked with much greater spontaneity than did most of his contemporaries. He never made preliminary sketches or drawings, but instead preferred to paint directly onto the canvas, starting with the forehead, chin, nose, and mouth. His free, bold brushwork resembled that of the Spanish master Diego Velázquez, examples of whose work Raeburn probably had studied in Rome. Raeburn believed that nothing should divert attention from the face, and his heads are more finely done than other parts of the body. His aim was always to capture the personality of the sitter, and many of his portraits have a delightful informality, with the subject relaxed in a chair.

Knowing that his portraits would be placed high on the walls of many homes, Raeburn preferred to paint his subjects from an angle similar to that from which they would eventually be viewed. He therefore placed them on a platform in his studio and, after studying them for some time, would

magically begin to capture their likeness, sometimes employing a brush up to a yard long.

Although he bowed to the tradition, popularized by such artists as Thomas Gainsborough and Reynolds, of including scenic settings as backgrounds for some of his portraits, Raeburn believed that such landscapes should not detract from the individuality of his sitter. In many of his portraits, he completely eliminated the background or reduced it to simple drapery. Raeburn's blunt, bold brushwork produced figures with squarish, solid countenances. His style changed remarkably little over the decades, although his tonality became lighter and his lighting less artificial in his later years. Contemporaries occasionally criticized his technique for being overly simplified and lacking in richness of color and refinement.

Despite Raeburn's prominence in Edinburgh, he long remained isolated from the center of the British artistic world and achieved a reputation in London only late in life; his visits to the capital were infrequent. In 1792, he sent his first three works to the city for the annual Royal Academy exhibition. The largest of these, a magnificent portrait of Sir John Clerk and his wife, arrived too late to be hung, but one of the aldermen, John Boydell, arranged for the portrait to be shown at the Shakespeare Gallery, where it attracted some favorable attention in the press.

Raeburn did not start regularly sending works to London until 1810, the year he seriously contemplated moving to the capital. John Hoppner, a fashionable London artist, had just died, and Raeburn considered taking over Hoppner's house and practice. It is possible that he considered the move because of recent difficulties caused by his son's financial failures. To recoup his losses, Raeburn had been forced to sell York Place and had even accepted commissions to copy portraits done by other artists—a rather unusual step for someone of his reputation. Ultimately, however, Raeburn abandoned the idea of relocating in London and decided to stay in his native city, where he had no serious competitors and his reputation was impregnable.

Gradually, the London establishment officially recognized the Scottish painter's abilities. He was elected an associate member of the Royal Academy in 1812 and, after failing to be elected to one of the two vacancies in 1814, was ultimately elevated to full membership in 1815. Further recognition came during the final years of his life. During George IV's visit to Edinburgh in 1822, Raeburn was knighted, thus earning the same social status achieved by Reynolds in the previous century. In May, 1823, Raeburn was appointed the king's painter in Scotland, but he did not live long enough to paint a planned portrait of the monarch in Highland dress. His last work was a portrait of Sir Walter Scott. Shortly after accompanying Scott and several others on an expedition to Ravensheugh Castle in Fife, Raeburn succumbed to a mysterious ailment and died, on July 8, 1823.

Summary

Often referred to as the "Scottish Reynolds," Sir Henry Raeburn left a valuable legacy of portraits of the Scottish society whose values and ideas he shared. Portraiture was the only type of painting he attempted, in part because it brought the most dependable and lucrative commissions. The exact number of Raeburn portraits remains unknown; he kept no record of his sitters, so neither an accurate chronology nor the exact quantity of his work is known. He produced at least seven hundred portraits during his long and productive career. Almost all of his famous Scottish contemporaries—such as Adam Smith, James Boswell, and David Hume—sat for Raeburn portraits, the main exception being Robert Burns. Raeburn's series of Highland chiefs in native garb, the most famous being *The Mac-Nab*, gained particular popularity. Yet the majority of his portraits were of various lawyers, academics, military officers, and others of the professional class who wished to have their likenesses preserved for posterity.

Raeburn's work remained relatively unknown outside Scotland until the twentieth century, in part because so much of it remained in private collections. By 1900, however, major galleries eagerly sought to acquire his portraits. Many critics now rank him as one of the most important figures in British art during the late eighteenth and early nineteenth centuries.

With his quiet, undramatic life-style hundreds of miles away from the turmoil of the London art world, Raeburn was long a rather obscure figure, and much less is known about the details of his life and work than is known about such contemporaries as Gainsborough, Reynolds, or Joseph Turner. Nevertheless, Raeburn's reputation as a superb portraitist seems secure. His diligent promotion of art in Scotland and his engrossing portraits undoubtedly provided a significant contribution to Great Britain's expanding role in the visual arts.

Bibliography

Armstrong, Sir Walter. *Sir Henry Raeburn*. London: Heinemann, and New York: Dodd, Mead, 1901. The standard biography, by a prominent art historian who also wrote works on Reynolds, Gainsborough, and Turner. Includes a catalog of Raeburn's paintings, prepared with the assistance of James L. Caw.

Arts Council of Great Britain, Scottish Committee. *Raeburn Bicentenary Exhibition*. Edinburgh: National Gallery of Scotland, 1956. Prepared as a catalog for the special Edinburgh exhibition celebrating the bicentennial of Raeburn's birth, this work includes an introductory biographical essay by David Baxandall and detailed explanatory notes about fifty-three of Raeburn's portraits.

Brotchie, Theodore C. F. *Henry Raeburn, 1756-1823*. London: Cassell, and New York: Funk and Wagnalls, 1924. Includes a brief bibliography, as well as a chart showing the prices paid for some of Raeburn's paintings between 1907 and 1922.

Caw, James L. *Raeburn*. London and New York: Jack, 1909. A brief study by the former director of the National Gallery of Scotland and leading authority on Scottish art history. Includes some original letters as well as eight color illustrations of Raeburn's portraits.

Greig, James. *Sir Henry Raeburn, R.A.* London: Connoisseur, 1911. Includes a fairly extensive catalog of Raeburn's paintings, selected correspondence, and numerous black and white reproductions.

Irwin, David, and Francina Irwin. *Scottish Painters at Home and Abroad, 1700-1900*. London: Faber, 1975. Takes advantage of the latest scholarly discoveries and contains a lively and well-written section on Raeburn and his influence, as well as making specific comments on many of his paintings. Contains a useful bibliography of books and articles.

Whitley, William T. *Art in England*. 2 vols. Cambridge: Cambridge University Press, and New York: Macmillan, 1928. A detailed account of the English art world of 1800-1837; proves useful for discussing Raeburn's relations with the Royal Academy. Corrects certain errors found in earlier studies. Includes numerous contemporary press reactions to Raeburn paintings exhibited in London during this period.

Tom L. Auffenberg

LEOPOLD VON RANKE

Born: December 21, 1795; Wiehe, Thuringia
Died: May 23, 1886; Berlin, Germany
Area of Achievement: Historiography
Contribution: Ranke is considered the father of modern historical scholarship and a founder of the German idea of history. His historical works rank as classics of modern historiography.

Early Life

Leopold von Ranke's father, Gottlob Israel Ranke, was a lawyer, but the Lutheran ministry was the traditional profession of the family. Ranke's parents expected him, the eldest of nine children, to follow a career in the Church. After an early education in local schools, he was sent to Schulpforta, a famous German public school known for the quality of its humanistic, classical curriculum. Ranke studied philology and theology at the University of Leipzig and received a doctoral degree in 1817 for a dissertation on the political ideas of Thucydides.

As a student, Ranke adopted the critical philological method of Barthold Niebuhr, a statesman and scholar whose *Römische Geschichte* (1811-1832; *History of Rome*, 1828-1842) reconstructed the historical origins of the Roman state. Ranke admired Niebuhr's history but not his clumsy prose. A master stylist himself, he was early influenced by the German of Martin Luther and Johann Wolfgang von Goethe. Although he remained a devout Lutheran, Ranke declined to enter the ministry. The classics and philology interested him more than dogma. In 1818, he became a master of classical languages in the *Gymnasium* in Frankfurt an der Oder. Entrusted with the teaching of history, Ranke was led to write his first book, *Geschichte der romanischen und germanischen Völker von 1494 bis 1514* (1824; *History of the Latin and Teutonic Nations from 1494 to 1514*, 1887), in which he applied his philological training to the field of modern history. Ranke was called in 1824 to the University of Berlin, where he taught until 1871.

Ranke's students left a vivid vignette of their master. He is described as a slight figure with dark, curly hair, a low voice, a lively speaking manner, penetrating blue eyes, and a serene temperament. He, in turn, took a paternalistic interest in his students, who eventually filled almost every chair of history in Germany. Surrounded by his children and grandchildren (he married Clara Graves, daughter of an Irish barrister, in 1843, and the cou-

ple had two sons and a daughter), he would say that he had another and older family, his pupils and their pupils.

Life's Work

In the programmatic preface to *History of the Latin and Teutonic Nations from 1494 to 1514*, Ranke gave a new direction to historical studies by declaring that it was not the duty of the historian to judge the past for the benefit of the present or the future. It was only "to show what actually occurred." This matter-of-fact statement was directed against the historiography of the Enlightenment, which had given history an abstractly defined end and viewed it as an ascending process in which a later age was superior to an earlier one. According to Ranke each age was unique, "each period is equally close to God."

In the appendix of his first book, Ranke added that he had found traditional histories untrustworthy; they did not correspond with the evidence he found in contemporary documents. For his history, he wrote, he had relied only on original sources, critically sifted and cross-examined. Ranke's ambition to use only "the purest, most immediate documents" led him to the Italian archives in 1827. In Italy, where he gratified his "archival obsession" for three years, Ranke became the first scholar to examine the famous *relazioni*, secret reports Venetian ambassadors had submitted to their government after diplomatic missions to the courts of Europe. In such materials, Ranke believed, the historian could divine the core and secret of human events. Upon his return to the University of Berlin, where he became a full professor in 1836, Ranke created the historical seminar and instructed advanced students in *Quellenkritik*, the critical study of the sources.

Ranke spurned the schematic history of the philosophers but he was, nevertheless, a generalist. Through the perception of the particular, the historian was to grasp the inner connection and complete whole of history. As a devout Christian, Ranke believed that the unity and tendency of the historical experience were an expression of divine purpose—the "hand of God" was evident in the particular and the universal.

Divine action in the historical world was largely realized through nations or states, Ranke contended, a theory he developed in "Political Dialogue"

(1836) and "The Great Powers" (1833), famous essays written while he was editor of the political journal *Historisch-politische Zeitschrift* (historical-political review) from 1832 to 1836. Ranke argued that there was no ideal political constitution. States developed their own genius and institutional forms: that was the task set them by God. Accordingly, power embodied in the nation-state was ethically good: It was an expression of God's will. This conception or idea of history, reflected in all of Ranke's historical studies, affirmed the importance of the great powers and identified the state as an ethical institution whose interests were in harmony with the general good.

While on his tour of the Italian archives, Ranke outlined the course of his future studies: first Italian, then French, English, and German studies. He turned to German history before the French and English, but otherwise the early outline of his life's work was followed faithfully. The national histories were capped by nine volumes of world history, *Weltgeschichte* (1881-1888; partial translation as *Universal History*, 1884), begun in his eighty-sixth year.

Ranke's Italian project, published from 1834 to 1836 in three volumes, was *Die römischen Päpste in den letzten 4 Jahrhunderten* (*The History of the Popes During the Last Four Centuries*, 1907), considered by many his finest work in form and matter. Ranke approached the popes as a historian fascinated by their role in world history, but they were also a subject in which he found the "thought of God." The history of the popes was followed by *Deutsche Geschichte im Zeitalter der Reformation* (1839-1847; *History of the Reformation in Germany*, 1845-1847), a six-volume history received in Germany as a national classic, although Ranke himself thought it inferior to his study of the popes. As the first of the Reformation volumes appeared, Frederick William IV recognized Ranke's eminence as a scholar and appointed him, in 1841, historiographer of the Prussian state. Ranke was ennobled, thereby adding "von" to his name, in 1865.

In the two decades after his study of the Reformation, Ranke wrote his massive histories of the great powers, all focusing on developments from the fifteenth to the eighteenth century. *Neun Bücher preussischer Geschichte* (nine books of Prussian history), a study later expanded to twelve books, appeared in 1847-1848, and *Englische Geschichte, vornehmlich im 16 and 17 Jahrhundert* (*A History of England Principally in the Seventeenth Century*, 1966) was issued in six volumes between 1859 and 1868.

In Ranke's opinion, the most important features of history between 1492 and 1789 were the creation of the modern state, the rise of the great powers, and the establishment of the state system. He appreciated the role of ideas in history and suggested that historians should pay attention to population, churches, agriculture, industry, and transportation. In practice, however, he was a political and diplomatic historian, and he focused almost exclusively on courts and chanceries. Later historians, with a greater interest in the evolution of society, assigned ideas and social and economic forces far more important roles in historiography. On the other hand, while he was the motive force behind the creation of an encyclopedia of German national biography, Ranke himself wrote little biography; exceptions were short biographical studies of Frederick the Great and Frederick William IV. For Ranke, the individual was important only when he played an active or leading role in general history.

It is not surprising that Ranke elected to spend his final years, although infirm and unable to read or write, preparing a world history. He was able to produce eight volumes, taking his story to the end of the fifteenth century, before his death in May, 1886, at the age of ninety-one. The universal history, although incomplete, was a fitting conclusion to Ranke's career: To comprehend the whole while obeying the dictates of exact research, he had written in the 1860's, was the ideal goal of the historian.

Summary

Leopold von Ranke is commonly identified as an empirical, nonphilosophical historian, the founder of the "scientific school" of history. This image is one-sided but not invalid. Ranke sought to write history as it actually happened, free of philosophical presuppositions, and he contributed a critical method which emphasized the use of documentary sources. He suggested that national cultures and periods of history should be examined on their own terms. German historians, however, also appreciated Ranke as a contemplative thinker, and most of his successors accepted his emphasis on the central role of the state and of foreign affairs in the European experience. Many, too, adopted his concept of the spiritual character of power, a theme that runs through Ranke's writings. It was only after World War II that leading German historians concluded that Ranke had been insufficiently pessimistic regarding power and the state.

Ranke's own works, and he published a large number of historical classics, are still valuable. They are largely free of bias and show an insight and style that make them profitable reading for modern students of history.

Bibliography

Gay, Peter. "Ranke: The Respectful Critic." In *Style in History*. New York: McGraw-Hill, 1974; London: Cape, 1975. A perceptive and gracefully written essay on Ranke as dramatist, scientist, and believer.

Geyl, Pieter. "Ranke in the Light of the Catastrophe." In *Debates with Historians*. London: Batsford, 1955; New York: Philosophical Library, 1956. A strong indictment of Ranke's idea that power was an expression of divine activity in the historical world.

Gilbert, Felix. *History: Politics or Culture? Reflections on Ranke and Burckhardt*. Princeton, N.J.: Princeton University Press, 1990. A selection of five essays by historian Felix Gilbert comparing the works of Rank and Jacob Burckhardt.

Gooch, G. P. "Ranke." In *History and Historians in the Nineteenth Century*. London: Longman, 1913.

———. "Ranke's Critics and Pupils." In *History and Historians in the Nineteenth Century*. London and New York: Longman, 1913. Two of the best brief studies in English on Ranke.

Higham, John, Leonard Krieger, and Felix Gilbert. *History*. Englewood Cliffs, N.J.: Prentice-Hall, 1965; London: Garland, 1985. A useful discussion of Ranke's influence in the professionalization of history in Europe and the United States.

Iggers, Georg G. *The German Conception of History: The National Tradition of Historical Thought from Herder to the Present*. Middletown, Conn.: Wesleyan University Press, 1968. A valuable interpretative survey of the theoretical presuppositions and political values of German historians. Ranke is identified as a founding father of a school that not only adopted the critical method but also viewed the state as an ethical good.

———. "The Image of Ranke in American and German Historical Thought." *History and Theory* 2 (1962): 17-40. A survey of divergent images of Ranke held by German and American historians.

Iggers, Georg G., and James M. Powell, eds. *Leopold von Ranke and the Shaping of Historical Discipline*. Syracuse, N.Y.: Syracuse University Press, 1990. This collection of essays produced as a result of a conference held in 1986 at Syracuse University, presents insight into the work of Ranke on several levels. Contributors include Donald R. Kelley, Peter Burke, and Felix Gilbert.

Von Laue, Theodore H. *Leopold Ranke: The Formative Years*. Princeton, N.J.: Princeton University Press, 1950. This book traces the development of Ranke's historical ideas in the context of contemporary Germany from 1795 to 1836. It includes Ranke's essays "Political Dialogue" and "The Great Powers" in translation as well as a useful bibliographical essay.

J. A. Thompson

GRIGORI YEFIMOVICH RASPUTIN

Born: c. 1870; Pokrovskoye, Siberia, Russian Empire

Died: December 30, 1916; Petrograd (now St. Petersburg), Russia

Areas of Achievement: Government and politics, and religion and theology

Contribution: Because of his mystic ability to improve the hemophilia of Alexei Nikolayevich, heir to the Russian throne, Rasputin ingratiated himself to Czar Nicholas II and Empress Alexandra. Rasputin's profligate ways and the refusal of the rulers to believe the scandal he consistently generated increased the estrangement between the rulers and their people, thus contributing to the Russian Revolution.

Early Life

Grigori Yefimovich Rasputin was born in the small Siberian village of Pokrovskoye. The exact date of his birth is unknown, as was true for most peasants at the time, but the most probable date was January 23, 1869 (January 10 on the Julian calendar used in prerevolutionary Russia).

Young Rasputin exhibited a remarkable ability to commune with and heal animals. Although illiterate, he liked to memorize scripture, and at age eighteen, he had a vision of the Virgin Mary. Legend claims that he also possessed gifts of precognition and clairvoyance, but villagers later remembered him primarily for his excessive drinking and proclivity toward sexual depravity. These apparently irreconcilable impressions were indicative of his whole life: Times of prayer and generosity coexisted with epic debauchery. He was variously viewed as a pious holy man and an insatiable satyr.

In 1889 Rasputin married Praskovya Fedorovna Dubrovina, who bore him three children. Rasputin became a farmer, but he was apparently unwilling to abandon his disorderly life; his drinking increased, and he was accused of petty thievery. He soon moved to a nearby monastery where he lived as a monk for three months. Some sources claim that the trouble he had stirred up in Pokrovskoye made temporarily vanishing a prudent idea. His time at the monastery proved to be a watershed. He permanently gave up tobacco and meat, and he temporarily gave up alcohol. He appeared nervous and restless, with moods swinging between severe depression and religious ecstasy. He prayed frequently, learned to read the Orthodox liturgy, and memorized huge segments of scripture. He also began to attract followers.

Within one month of his return from the monastery, Rasputin embarked on a series of long pilgrimages, traveling to holy shrines as a religious mendicant begging for food and lodging. Between pilgrimages, he awed his growing circle of admirers with descriptions of the holy places he had visited. Rasputin's physical endurance and self-confidence enabled him to spend the better part of a decade meandering throughout Siberia. He was welcomed into homes as a true holy man, perhaps because of his uncanny ability to recognize people with troubled minds and provide a calming peace.

His wanderings eventually brought him into contact with Russian aristocrats, many of whom were awed by his magnetic personality. In 1903 he visited Kazan, a religiously important city, where his piousness so impressed officials of the Russian Orthodox Church that he was welcomed as a true holy man. By ingratiating himself with progressively more important holy officers, he managed to gain valuable friends and allies. Rasputin's triumphant acceptance in Kazan paved the way for his welcome reception by the upper class society of St. Petersburg, the Russian Empire's capital city.

Life's Work

Rasputin, fortified by introductions to important religious and political personages, took up residence in St. Petersburg in 1905. The aristocratic citizens were fascinated by this unruly and unkempt peasant from the Siberian wasteland. His status as a religious teacher soon attracted a coterie of fawning disciples, mostly women. Rasputin expounded perverted twists to Christian doctrine, including the idea that salvation could be achieved only through repentance; therefore, one had to sin in order to have the opportunity to repent. His doctrine resolved the fundamental, seemingly irreconcilable conflict between religion and carnal appetites. He was always willing to help provide salvation through sexual sin for the many attractive, willing women who flocked to his apartment.

Alexandra Fedorovna, wife of Czar Nicholas II and empress of Russia, had given birth to four daughters before producing an heir to the Russian throne, Alexei, on July 30, 1904. Shortly after Alexei's birth, his parents learned that he was a hemophiliac; any bruise caused painful internal hem-

Rasputin (center) poses with some of his followers.

orrhaging, and the slightest injury could be fatal. Because hemophilia was incurable and because simple childhood accidents could lead to days of unrelenting agony, the czar and empress lived in a state of relentless distress. They sought solace through holy men, clairvoyants, and other dabblers in the occult arts whom they hoped could help relieve the sufferings of the heir apparent.

Rasputin's reputation for marvelous healing powers soon brought him to the attention of the royal couple. When he was introduced to them in October, 1905, they were convinced that this simple yet devout man was the very holy man for whom they were searching. Their faith was not entirely misplaced. When young Alexei next suffered from serious internal bleeding, Rasputin's bedside prayers caused an immediate improvement. The doctors had thought that Alexei would not survive, but he soon recovered. Over the next decade, Rasputin consistently alleviated the young heir's suffering. Whatever the explanation, there can be no doubt that his soothing presence or his prayers were effective. To the empress, Rasputin was a saint whom God used to effect miraculous cures.

Although Rasputin's debauchery continued to escalate, he always maintained a pious facade before the royal family. They trusted him implicitly and soon began to seek his council for appointments in the church hierarchy. Rasputin cleverly placed his cronies in important posts and had his enemies transferred to distant provinces. He soon began to meddle in civil appointments as well. His double life required supporters in key government posts and the dispatching of enemies. As his power grew, his spiritual demeanor eroded, and his ambition for political control was progressively magnified.

By accepting bribes to help people gain political offices or achieve their goals, Rasputin also accumulated considerable wealth, although his inherent generosity caused him to give much of it to needy people. Influential merchants flocked to Rasputin's sitting room, where the miracle-worker simplified business transactions by short-circuiting typical bureaucratic delays. He scribbled a few words to people whose help he needed, and his access to the czar assured that the simple sentence worked wonders.

As his political power grew, so did his number of enemies, including many former allies who had lost confidence in him. When drunk, he often boasted about his control over the czar and empress, causing ordinary citizens to lose faith in a monarch who would allow an ignorant lout of a peasant to be virtually omnipotent. Any incompetent fool who struck the fancy of this arrogant peasant could easily be assigned to an important ministerial post, while those best qualified were ignored. Nicholas and Alexandra lived in blissful ignorance of the escalating problems caused by Rasputin's political meddling. Harassed by perpetual fear for the heir and reassured by Rasputin's miraculous cures, they turned a deaf ear to all warnings.

As the number of Rasputin's enemies increased, so did the number of murder plots being hatched against him. In November of 1916, four noblemen formed a conspiracy to eliminate Rasputin. The conspirators, headed by Prince Felix Yusupov, lured Rasputin to Yusupov's palace during the late night of December 29 to poison him with potassium cyanide. Although Prince Yusupov later claimed that they murdered Rasputin for the idealistic and patriotic reasons of saving the Russian autocracy, the lofty aims were not justified by the hypocritical means and their cowardly denials when later accused of murder.

Rasputin had been told that he was being taken to meet Yusupov's beautiful wife, although she was not even in St. Petersburg at the time. Yusupov brought Rasputin into a basement room and served him poisoned cakes and poisoned wine while the others waited upstairs. Although enough poison had been used to kill a battalion, the lethal cakes and wine seemed to have no noticeable effect. A disconcerted Yusupov raced upstairs, retrieved a small revolver, and returned to shoot Rasputin. He appeared to die instantly, and Yusupov left. Returning later to examine the corpse, the prince noticed Rasputin's left eyelid trembling. Suddenly Rasputin's eyes popped open, and he jumped up and seized Yusupov by the neck. The prince ran up the stairs in horror; the others bound down the stairs just in time to see Rasputin sprinting across the courtyard toward an open gate. After taking two shoots in the back, Rasputin collapsed in the snow. The conspirators kicked him in the head to convince themselves that he was finally dead. They then bound the body with ropes and dumped it off a bridge over the Neva River through a hole in the ice.

The body was not found for several days, but when it was recovered it became apparent that Rasputin had still been alive when he was thrown into the water. One arm was half out of the rope, and his lungs were full of water, indicating that the actual cause of death was drowning. Rasputin was buried on the grounds of the czar's palace, but during the night of March 22-23, 1917, a crowd of rebel soldiers exhumed the grave and carried the coffin to a nearby forest, where the decomposing body was burned on an improvised pyre.

Summary

Because of Empress Alexandra's concern for young Alexei, she would believe no ill rumors about Rasputin. He had incredible power over her, and he misused it for his own nefarious purposes. Czar Nicholas II was a timid and vacillating man who consistently acquiesced to his wife's demands. If Rasputin wanted someone put into or out of office, he had only to mention it to the empress, who would request it of the czar.

The heavy casualties suffered by the Russian army during the first years of World War I caused the czar to take command of the troops at the front lines in 1915, effectively leaving Alexandra and Rasputin in charge of the country. Competent ministers were dismissed and replaced by Rasputin's unpopular and incompetent nominees. In just one year there were five interior ministers, three war ministers, four agriculture ministers, and three justice ministers. Economic conditions deteriorated, transportation was chaotic, and supplies for the military were chronically short.

Rasputin's constant meddling in political affairs had weakened an already weak government beyond the point of no return. By 1917 the czar had no credibility with his people or with government officials. Scarcely two months after Rasputin's murder, the czar was forced to abdicate, and a moderate provisional government took control. In October, 1917, the Bolsheviks seized power, and the country degenerated into a civil war that ultimately transformed the Communist regime into a dictatorship of terror. Although one cannot claim that Rasputin was responsible for the Russian Revolution, by fueling the rising tide of discontent against the monarchy, he was certainly a major contributing factor.

Bibliography

Fulop-Miller, René. *Rasputin: The Holy Devil*. New York: Garden City Publishing, and London: Putnam, 1928. This is one of the earliest accounts of Rasputin's life; the author succeeds in presenting the divergent facets of his personality in a well-researched and unbiased manner.

Fuhrmann, Joseph. *Rasputin: A Life*. New York: Praeger, 1990. This book is a well-researched history written from the perspective that there were always two Rasputins, the "real" one and the one who was said to exist. Furhmann consistently strives to disentangle these two.

Moynahan, Brian. *Rasputin: The Saint Who Sinned*. New York: Random House, 1997. This volume's meticulous attention to detail and historical accuracy does not render it any less readable.

Myles, Douglas. *Rasputin: Satyr, Saint, or Satan*. New York: McGraw-Hill, 1990. Myles provides a well-written and highly entertaining account of the Rasputin story. This work includes a glossary of foreign words with a guide to their pronunciation.

Rasputina, Maria, and Patte Barham. *Rasputin, The Man Behind the Myth: A Personal Memoir*. Englewood Cliffs, N.J.: Prentice-Hall, and London: Allen, 1977. These personal and favorably biased recollections were written by Rasputin's daughter six decades after his murder. Several of the accounts clash with other, less biased, evidence.

Youssoupov (Yusupov), Felix. *Rasputin: His Malignant Influence and His Assassination*. London: Cape, 1927; Salisbury, N.C.: Documentary Publications, 1976. This is an obviously biased apologia written by Rasputin's primary murderer ten years after the event. He maintains that Rasputin was the devil incarnate and that his murder was justified and necessary to save the Russian monarchy.

George R. Plitnik

RAMMOHAN RAY

Born: May 22, 1772; Rādhānagar, Bengal
Died: September 27, 1833; Bristol, England
Areas of Achievement: Religion and social reform
Contribution: Ray's writings have become the putative source for almost all India's social and religious reformist ideals. Known as "the father of modern India," Ray saw the Hinduism of his day as a debased form of a purer monotheism practiced in India during a prehistoric Golden Age. He also found many social customs of his own day—the forced suicide of widows and child marriage, for example—as decadent, medieval accretions on the noble patterns of the Vedic age.

Early Life

Among Bengalis of the eighteenth and early nineteenth centuries, priests (Brahmins) of the Kulin class ranked only slightly lower than the gods. Their inferiors customarily addressed them as "Lord" (*Thakur*). They also emulated the Kulin's dialect of Bengali and almost everything about their style. Kulin boys were much in demand as husbands and often had more than one wife. Rammohan Ray was born into a Kulin family and married twice while still in his early teens.

His father's ancestors had long before assimilated themselves into the culture of India's Muslim rulers and had served in many governmental posts. His father was a landowner (*zamindar*) who fell on hard times in later life. In 1800, his father was jailed for debt and died in poverty in 1803. Ray's mother's family had not moved so close to Indo-Islamic culture and supported themselves as ritual specialists.

As a boy, Ray studied Arabic and Persian and was sent to Patna in Bihar, which, as a center for Muslim learning, offered better instruction than his hometown school. That was a common practice among Hindus who adopted the cosmopolitan culture of Muslims. Ray acquired a knowledge of Islamic doctrine as well as an interest in the mystical teachings of the Sufis. These two philosophies may have been responsible for his lifelong iconoclasm. According to his own autobiographical notes, while still a teenager he criticized his father's devotion to images of the gods and was thrown out of the house. Ray seems to have romanticized his recollections of the next decade of his life, claiming a journey to Tibet to study Buddhism and a lengthy stay in Benares to learn Sanskrit. Because in later life he wanted to be considered an authority on ancient Hindu religious texts, he may have exaggerated his knowledge of the classical language.

Between 1797 and 1802, Ray seems to have spent much of his time in Calcutta, the burgeoning capital of Bengal and British India, where he acted as a moneylender. Many of his clients were young Englishmen employed by the East India Company. In this way his name became known in government circles, and he received an appointment in the Revenue Department. He eventually became a deputy district collector, the highest civil post an Indian could hold. During his active career, he invested in real estate, and by his early forties he had an ample fortune which allowed him to retire to Calcutta in 1815.

Life's Work

Beginning in the 1770's, a number of Englishmen began to expand their knowledge of India's non-Muslim traditions. Sir William Jones and Henry Colebrooke, among others, acquired a better-than-rudimentary knowledge of Sanskrit. As they discovered that an enormous body of literature existed in that tongue, they conceded to ancient Indian civilization a classical status analogous to that of Greece and Rome in Western tradition. Their efforts in the reconstruction of the history of India earned for them the sobriquet "Orientalist."

The work of the Orientalists had two institutional foci. The first was the Asiatic Society of Bengal, founded in 1784, and the second the College of Fort William, established in 1800. While the former was a typical learned society of the period which met regularly to hear papers by members on a variety of subjects published in the society's journal, the second was an unprecedented attempt to train the East India Company's servants in the languages of the peoples they expected to govern. Few of those young men proved to be able scholars, but the professors of the College of Fort William, with the help of numerous Indian assistants, kept extending their knowledge of Sanskrit and the texts written in it.

During his earlier stays in Calcutta, Ray had contacts with Englishmen active in the college. He began to learn English and became fluent in the language. He was not, however, alone in his interests and contacts with the British. A number of other Bengali intellectuals had similar connections and concerns. They imbibed a number of ideas which had originated with British scholars such as Jones and Colebrooke. One of the most important of these was the notion that Hindu civilization had enjoyed a Golden Age during which India produced a lofty and subtle religiophilosophical system every bit as valuable as that of the Greeks and Romans. They also believed that, in that halcyon time, India's society was well organized and featured a balance between the various classes.

For the Orientalists, as well as for such Indians as Ray who subscribed to their ideas, a major problem was explaining how the Golden Age had disappeared to be replaced by the polytheism, idolatry, and caste inequalities of their own day. Following the British lead, Ray and others saw Muslims as the cause of that decline. Despite a Muslim presence in the subcontinent of more than nine hundred years' duration, as well as the prominence of Hindus in Muslim governments from the very beginning of their rule, they began describing Muslims as foreign tyrants whose oppression brought on Hindu decadence. Since Ray maintained close personal ties to Muslims—in 1831, he became the Mughal emperor's first ambassador to the Court of Saint James—perhaps he espoused this opinion only as a way of inspiring his coreligionists, never thinking that the notion would have so long a life or such ultimately fatal consequences.

In 1815, Ray published *Translation of an Abridgment of the "Vedant": Or, Resolution of All the Veds, the Most Celebrated and Revised Work of Brahminical Theology*. In this book, he emphasized monotheist religious views, claiming that a pure monotheism was the true doctrine taught by Indian religious texts, especially the *Upanishads*, also known as the "End of the Vedas" (*Vedanta*). To reinforce these assertions, Ray translated several of the more than three hundred *Upanishads*. In his emphasis on monotheism—belief in a personal God—rather than monism—the assertion that all reality is an impersonal, featureless "One"—Ray seems to be reflecting his dependence not on the original Sanskrit texts but on Persian translations of them ordered by the Mughal prince Dara Shikoh. The *Upanishads* tended to stress monism, but as a Muslim Dara slanted his translations toward monotheism in order to make it seem that the texts were closer to Islam. Some of Ray's more perceptive critics pointed out that his interpretations proved that he did not have the Sanskrit learn-

ing required to give authoritative explanations of sacred literature. Ray's other concerns also provoked opposition.

As did most other religious critics in India's history, Ray soon became embroiled in controversies over social practices. He made the fate of Bengali women his special cause. At the time, women were uneducated, treated as weak creatures subject to the whims of their brutish husbands, and never allowed to leave their homes. Ray supported many measures to protect them. He championed attempts to outlaw the burning of widows on their husbands' funeral pyres. Though followed by only a few high-status families, the custom dictated that a woman volunteer for this fate, thus proving herself a "virtuous female" (*satī*). In practice, relatives used the occasion to avoid, through murder, having to support an unwanted female. He also opposed the practice of child marriage, which sometimes created widows who were eight or nine years old. Even though they were not consigned to the mortuary fires, these girls were forced to lead dreary lives either as the celibate servants of their in-laws or as unmarriageable burdens on their own parents and brothers.

Though many of his views derived ultimately from the Orientalists, Ray did not invariably support all of their schemes. For example, when some proposed the establishment of a Sanskrit college, he opposed the move, believing that it was better to teach English to Indians than to immerse them in an archaic language. In this instance, he seems to have anticipated the anti-Orientalist reaction which arose in the government of India in the 1840's and which dominated educational policy throughout the British period.

Ray's interest in religion blossomed in Calcutta. He became a defender of his purified version of Hinduism against attacks by missionaries. He found himself drawn closer to the teaching of the Unitarians, who were emerging in the 1820's as a distinct and, to the minds of most Christians, heretical sect. Their monotheism, iconoclasm, and refusal to assert the absolute superiority of Christian revelation attracted Ray. He began corresponding with leading Unitarians in England and the United States; at one point, he contemplated finishing his life in the United States in order to be close to William Ellery Channing. *The Precepts of Jesus, the Guide to Peace and Happiness*, published in 1820, displayed the Unitarian influence. In it, he selected only those passages of the *New Testament* that contained some moral injunction and ignored those mentioning miracles or that contained assertions of Jesus' divinity. Although Ray often said that his heart was with the Unitarians, he never formally joined their church, preferring always to be known as a Hindu.

In 1828, Ray and a few associates founded the Brahmo Sabha (later called the Brahmo Samaj), or "Society of God." In general, this church was supposed to promulgate reformed religious and social principles. The Brahmo Sabha had little time to evolve as an organization before Ray in 1831 accepted the post of Mughal ambassador to England and left Calcutta forever. After his departure, the organization became moribund until it was revived some nine years later. By the time he left the city, Ray's staunchest friends were either Muslims or British Unitarians. Most of his fellow Hindus either condemned or ignored him. In England, his health ebbed and his fortune dwindled. He became a much-revered figure among English Unitarians and died in one of their homes. A Unitarian minister preached his funeral sermon.

Summary

Though today universally acknowledged as the father of modern India, Rammohan Ray was not fully recognized while he lived. The work of providing him with this identity began in the years following his death. Debendranath Tagore revived the Brahmo Sabha (calling it the Brahmo Samaj) in the years 1840 through 1842 and realized that the society required a spiritual leader to give it cohesion. Tagore, whose family produced several of Bengal's leading intellectual and literary lights, began to edit Ray's Persian, English, and Bengali writings. After K. C. Mitra published a biography of Ray in the *Calcutta Review* of 1845, the practice of crediting Ray for the invention of everything modern and progressive became common. Ray's importance, however, may well have been in his being typical of an era when Indians of many faiths and Englishmen cooperated in securing European recognition of India's civilization as one of the world's most influential and important traditions.

Bibliography

Bhattacharya, Haridas, ed. *The Cultural Heritage of India.* Vol. 4, *Religions.* Calcutta, India: Ramakrishna Mission, 1969. The last volume in a series of books cataloging many aspects of the religious and social traditions of Indian life. Shows that Hinduism is a term loosely connecting a number of very different religious tendencies. The essay on the Brahmo Samaj describes Ray's influence on this group and its place in nineteenth and twentieth century India.

Basham, A. L., ed. *A Cultural History of India.* Oxford: Clarendon Press, 1975. Contains thirty-five essays discussing almost every aspect of India's history from ancient times to the present. By judicious reading, a beginner will be able to discover the broader intellectual and social context in which Ray and other reformist thinkers worked.

Farquhar, J. N. *Modern Religious Movements in India.* New York: Macmillan, 1915; London: Macmillan, 1924. Originally written by a sympathetic Christian missionary. The many reprintings of this book demonstrate its value as an introductory text. It has a clear style easily accessible to students. While a number of its views should be modified by reference to the work of modern scholars, notably David Kopf's books listed below, it remains a readable introduction to Ray and his era.

Hay, Stephen N., ed. *Sources of Indian Tradition.* Vol. 2, *Modern India and Pakistan.* 2d ed. New York: Columbia University Press, 1988. A valuable anthology of translations from primary sources, introductory essays, and comments on the sources. Places brief selections from Ray's writings in the context of his own time as well as relating them to the work of later generations of reformers.

Heimsath, Charles H. *Indian Nationalism and Hindu Social Reform.* Princeton, N.J.: Princeton University Press, 1964. Makes the vital connection between religious/social reform, its critics, and India's nationalist movement. The programs of both reformers and their critics must be understood as part of India's long drive for independence. Also has the merit of covering reformist movements in all the major cultural regions of the subcontinent.

Kopf, David. *The Brahmo Samaj and the Shaping of the Modern Indian Mind.* Princeton, N.J.: Princeton University Press, 1979. Together with the book cited below, this work provides a comprehensive and insightful history of Bengali intellectual life from the late eighteenth century to the early twentieth century. The first chapters give a succinct and penetrating appraisal of Ray's influence on modernizing Bengalis. Also describes Tagore's role in establishing Ray as the father of modern India.

―――. *British Orientalism and the Bengal Renaissance: The Dynamics of Indian Modernization, 1773-1835*. Berkeley: University of California Press, 1969. This valuable work demonstrates the complex interchanges between Englishmen and Indians which added a new dimension to Bengali intellectual life. Provides a history of the College of Fort William and places Ray's career in the context of Orientalist labors. Also charts the anti-Orientalist reaction of the 1830's and 1840's.

Ray, Raja Rammohan. *The Essential Writings of Raja Rammohan Ray*. Delhi: Oxford University Press, 1998. A collection of Ray's writings on social reform, education, women's rights, and more.

Robertson, Bruce Carlisle. *Raja Rammohan Ray: The Father of Modern India*. Delhi: Oxford University Press, 1995. This biography is valuable, but may be best used by those with a familiarity with Sanskrit due to the limitations of transliteration.

Gregory C. Kozlowski

RED CLOUD
Makhpíya-Lúta

Born: 1822; Blue Creek, near North Platte, Nebraska

Died: December 10, 1909; Pine Ridge, South Dakota

Areas of Achievement: The military and political leadership

Contribution: Red Cloud led the Dakota Sioux Indians through a difficult period, effectively resisting the onrush of American westward advance and later helping the Sioux make the transition to reservation life under American rule.

Early Life

In 1822, Red Cloud was born into the Oglala sub-tribe of the Teton branch of Dakotas (more popularly known as Sioux) on the high plains of what is now Nebraska. His father, a headman in the Brulé subtribe, was named Lone Man, and his mother was Walks-as-She-Thinks, a member of the Saone subtribe. There is disagreement over the origins of the name Red Cloud. Some sources contend that it was a family name used by his father and grandfather, while others claim that it was coined as a description of the way his scarlet-blanketed warriors covered the hills like a red cloud.

Very little is known about Red Cloud's early life. His father died when he was young, and he was reared in the camp of Chief Old Smoke, a maternal uncle. He undoubtedly spent his boyhood learning skills that were important to Sioux men at the time, including hunting, riding, and shooting. Plains Culture Indians sometimes conducted raids against enemies, and Red Cloud joined his first war party and took his first scalp at age sixteen. Thereafter, he was always quick to participate in expeditions against Pawnee, Crows, or Ute. Other Oglala frequently retold Red Cloud's colorful exploits in battle. During a raid against the Crows, he killed the warrior guarding the ponies and then ran off with fifty horses. This was a highly respected deed among Plains Indians, whose horses were central to their way of life. On an expedition against the Pawnee, Red Cloud killed four of the enemy—an unusually high number in a type of warfare in which casualties were normally low.

In the early 1840's, most Oglala bands camped around Fort Laramie on the North Platte River, where they could obtain a variety of goods from white traders. Red Cloud was part of a band known as the Bad Faces, or Smoke People, under the leadership of his uncle, Old Smoke. Another band in the area, the Koya, was led by Bull Bear, the most dominant headman among the Oglala and commonly recognized as their chief. The two groups frequently quarreled. One day in the fall of 1841, after young men of both sides had been drinking, a member of the Bad Faces stole a Koya woman. Bull Bear led a force to the Bad Face camp and shot the father of the young man who had taken the woman. The Bad Faces retaliated, and when a shot to the leg downed Bull Bear, Red Cloud rushed in and killed him. This event led to a split among the Oglala that lasted for many years. It also elevated Red Cloud's standing among the Bad Faces, and shortly after the incident he organized and led a war party of his own against the Pawnee.

Soon after recovering from wounds suffered in that raid, Red Cloud married a young Dakota woman named Pretty Owl. Sources disagree as to whether he thereafter remained monogamous or took multiple wives, a common practice among prominent Sioux. Nor is there agreement on how many children he fathered, although five is the number most accepted by scholars. Over the next two decades, Red Cloud's reputation and status continued to grow. By the mid-1860's, he was a ruggedly handsome man of medium stature with penetrating eyes and a confident and commanding presence. He was also a band headman and a leading warrior with an increasing following among the Bad Faces. Sioux social and political structure was very decentralized; no one person had authority over the whole group. Instead, certain leaders were recognized as chiefs on the basis of ability and achievement. An important member of his band, at this time Red Cloud was not yet a chief.

Life's Work

In the several decades before the Civil War, traders began operating in Sioux territory, followed by wagon trains, telegraph construction, and more. The Sioux welcomed most of the traders and at least tolerated most of the wagon trains, even though whites disrupted hunting by killing indiscriminately and chasing many animals away from traditional hunting grounds. By the closing years of the Civil War, American traffic across the northern plains increased even further. The discovery of gold in the mountains of Montana in late 1862 enticed more whites to cross Sioux land, leading to friction and occasional clashes. The final straw came when the government sent soldiers in to build forts and protect passage along a popular route known as the Bozeman Trail that linked Montana with the Oregon Trail.

In 1865, many Sioux, including Red Cloud, took up arms in resistance. Several Dakota leaders signed a treaty in the spring of 1866 that would open the Bozeman Trail, but Red Cloud and his many followers held out, insisting on a removal of soldiers. The government tried to ignore Red Cloud for a time, but the Sioux almost completely closed down travel and obstructed efforts to construct the forts. This was the high point in Red Cloud's career as a military strategist. He led his men to a number of victories, most notably the annihilation of Captain William J. Fetterman and eighty-two soldiers in an incident known to whites as the Fetterman Massacre and to Indians as the Battle of a Hundred Slain. In November of 1868, when, after negotiations, the army withdrew the troops and abandoned the forts, Red Cloud finally ended the war.

This victory increased Red Cloud's standing among his people, although he still was not the Sioux's exclusive leader. The United States government, however, assumed that he was the head chief and dealt with him as such. In the late 1860's, there was talk of creating a reservation for the Dakota, and Red Cloud surprised everyone by announcing that he would go to Washington, D.C., and talk about the idea. Some have argued that he was motivated by a desire to gain the status among the Sioux that he already enjoyed in the view of federal officials. On the other hand, he may have realized that since many white Westerners opposed a reservation and preferred the extermination of Indians, a reservation, combined with the withdrawal of troops from all Sioux lands, an important objective to Red Cloud, might be the best compromise he could achieve. He and twenty other Sioux leaders were escorted to the nation's capital in 1870 with great ceremony. Red Cloud did not win everything he wanted, but he clearly emerged as the most famous Native American of his time. He was applauded by many Easterners who sympathized

with Indians and saw Red Cloud as a symbol of justifiable response to white advance.

In 1871, Red Cloud settled on the newly created reservation, at the agency named after him. Then, only a few years later, gold was discovered in the Black Hills portion of the reserve, and the government pressured the Sioux to sell the area. When negotiations broke down, events quickly escalated into the Sioux War of 1876-1877. With one eye on the government, Red Cloud publicly opposed the armed action undertaken by some Dakota to stop the flood of prospectors onto their lands, but privately he seemed to sanction such moves. Red Cloud frequently became embroiled in political battles with federal agents on the reservation. He tried to win whatever provisions and concessions he could to ease his people's suffering, and he resisted government efforts to break down traditional cultural and political life. When many Sioux became involved in the controversial Ghost Dance in 1889-1890, Red Cloud avoided early commitment to or open encouragement of participation. Many dancers, however, believed that they indeed had his support. Red Cloud's frequent compromise position and his seeming cooperation with government agents sometimes made him suspect among some of his people, and, as a consequence, his influence steadily eroded. He died on the reservation on December 10, 1909.

Summary

Red Cloud emerged as a military and political leader at a dramatic and tragic time in the history of the Dakota Sioux Indians. Onetime powerful nomadic buffalo hunters, they were going through far-reaching changes. American westward advance constricted their land base, destroyed the buffalo upon which their economy depended, and ultimately brought about their impoverishment. Moreover, government attempts to destroy traditional Sioux ways of life on the reservation, while never completely successful, resulted in cultural shock.

For a time, Red Cloud resisted militarily as effectively as any Native American leader ever had. Then, when American domination became clear, he attempted delicately to balance the two worlds of Indian and white, hoping to win the best results possible for his people under the circumstances. This was a very difficult task, and he did not satisfy everyone. He was attacked from both sides—by whites for not doing more to encourage his follow-

ers to assimilate into the white world, and by some Sioux for being too willing to give in to government authorities.

Red Cloud stood as a symbol to many Indians (and some whites) of strong defense of homelands and culture, while to other whites he epitomized the worst in Indian treachery and savagery. For both sides, the name Red Cloud conveyed immense power and meaning. In the 1960's and 1970's, with the rise of the Red Power movement and a rejuvenation of Indian culture, he again became a symbol—this time to a generation of young Indian (and sometimes white) political activists who found inspiration in what they saw as his defiance in the face of unjust authority.

Bibliography

Cook, James H. *Fifty Years on the Old Frontier.* New Haven, Conn.: Yale University Press, 1923. Neither scholarly nor complete in its coverage of Red Cloud, it does contain some interesting, colorful, and firsthand descriptions of the Sioux leader and some of his exploits by a prominent frontiersman and close friend.

DeMallie, Raymond J., ed. *The Sixth Grandfather: Black Elk's Teachings Given to John G. Neihardt.* Lincoln: University of Nebraska Press, 1984. Does not focus on Red Cloud's life specifically but provides some direct accounts of various events in his life, especially surrounding the 1875-1876 Black Hills controversy, as told by Black Elk and other Sioux participants to poet John Neihardt.

Hyde, George E. *Red Cloud's Folk: A History of the Oglala Sioux Indians.* Norman: University of Oklahoma Press, 1937. Less complete and authoritative than the more recent book by James C. Olson, but generally well written and reliable. Focuses on the earliest period of which histori-

ans have any knowledge of Dakota history to about the end of the Sioux War of 1876-1877.

———. *A Sioux Chronicle.* Norman: University of Oklahoma Press, 1956. A continuation of *Red Cloud's Folk* that carries the story of the Oglala to the tragedy at Wounded Knee in 1890. Contains less information about Red Cloud, since his role was diminishing by the end of the 1800's. It does offer useful material on Red Cloud's part in Sioux history after the creation of the reservation in the 1870's.

Larson, Robert W. *Red Cloud: Warrior-Statesman of the Lakota Sioux.* Norman: University of Oklahoma Press, 1997. A well-researched, fair biography of Red Cloud with comprehensive documentation.

Olson, James C. *Red Cloud and the Sioux Problem.* Lincoln: University of Nebraska Press, 1965. The best and most complete account of Red Cloud. Except for some background information on the Dakota Sioux and Red Cloud's early life, it begins with the period immediately after the Civil War and ends with the death of Red Cloud in 1909.

Robinson, Doane. *A History of the Dakota or Sioux Indians.* Aberdeen, S.D.: News Printing, 1904. First printed by the South Dakota State Historical Society in 1904, this book bears the mark of scholarship in an earlier era in its attitude toward Indians. It is so factually solid and complete that it still stands as an important source for information on Red Cloud.

Utley, Robert M. *The Last Days of the Sioux Nation.* New Haven, Conn.: Yale University Press, 1963. An excellent history of the events surrounding the famous Massacre of Wounded Knee, including material about Red Cloud's participation in that event that reveals something about his role in Sioux society in 1890.

Larry W. Burt

ODILON REDON

Born: April 22, 1840; Bordeaux, France
Died: July 6, 1916; Paris, France
Area of Achievement: Art
Contribution: Through long years of artistic experimentation, Redon developed a mysterious, nostalgic, melancholy, and sometimes humorous fantasy world in his paintings, prints, and drawings. This world became his distinctive contribution to the allusive art movement of the end of the nineteenth century called Symbolism.

Early Life

Originally christened Bertrand-Jean, Odilon Redon was always known by his nickname, the masculine version of his mother's name, Marie-Odile. She was an American from New Orleans, Louisiana, where Redon's French father had established a lucrative business. Shortly before Redon's birth, his father brought the family permanently back to France. Redon was a sickly child; as a young boy, he was sent to live with an aged uncle at a rural family estate near Bordeaux. The boy lived a reclusive life close to nature, drawing the natural beauty around him and creating his own fantasy world. As an adult, he frequently returned to this home, which served as an unending source of inspiration. A nostalgia for this boyhood home never left him. From the age of eleven, he received professional art training. Originally, his goal was to become an architect, but it became clear that he did not possess the mathematical skills required for such a profession. At that point, his father allowed him to pursue training as an artist.

Redon was keenly interested in playing the violin and reading contemporary literature. His reading included works by Edgar Allan Poe, Charles Baudelaire, Gustave Flaubert, and, later, Stéphane Mallarmé. Both of these interests provided excellent background for his eventual artistic direction. The Symbolist style, with which Redon was allied, included musicians, writers, and visual artists. It favored an approach that suggested an emotional tone that was often pessimistic or melancholy, as well as mystical and fantastic, and certainly disturbing, which the viewer was encouraged to imaginatively embellish. Redon created prints, paintings, and drawings that developed these themes and often drew on the works of his favorite writers. Compared with the best-known works of the Symbolists, Redon's art had a benign cast to it that was more melancholy than disturbing.

Life's Work

At the age of twenty-five, Redon began studying painting in Paris under the Romantic-style artist Jean-Léon Gérôme. This was not a happy period for Redon. His teacher's philosophical attitude toward art was not agreeable to Redon, and he could not fit into the rigid studio regimen. He needed instruction that included a great deal of artistic freedom of expression. Gérôme's regimen emphasized the realistic reproduction of a subject, but realism was never a productive approach for Redon. Nature only provided a launchpad for his imagination.

In 1863, Redon returned to Bordeaux and continued a more productive period of work and study with his friend, the printmaker Rodolphe Bresdin, who taught him etching and engraving techniques. However, it was Bresdin's highly imaginative subject matter that really sparked Redon's interest. It was at this time that Redon immersed himself in the exploration of the graphic possibilities of black and white in both printmaking and drawing. The experimentation directed his work for the rest of his life. He readily understood the mysterious possibilities of shadowy, subtly graded darks that created an atmosphere of fantasy and otherworldliness. Redon studied the graphic works of German artist Albrecht Dürer and the dark-light contrasts of Rembrandt's etchings to learn technique. Francisco de Goya's etchings and engravings were also a strong influence on Redon, who was interested not only in Goya's graphic techniques but also in the psychological fantasy of such works as his *Caprichos* series (1799). Redon enjoyed creating other worlds that were less specific than those painted by Goya. In 1885, Redon created a lithographic series called *Hommage à Goya* to celebrate his enthusiasm for the Spanish artist.

Redon transferred the skill he had developed in rich dark-light effects to his charcoal drawings, which he called *noirs*, and then to lithography. Between 1879 and 1899, he produced twelve series in various graphic techniques, many of which had strong literary associations. The series were based on contemporary poems and novels but were not illustrations for them. Instead, literature provided the stimulus for his own independent interpretations, such as *À Edgar Poe* (1882). In the 1890's, Redon drew charcoals and lithographs as separate works based on Baudelaire's poetry collection, *Les Fleurs du mal* (1857; *Flowers of Evil*, 1931).

Two important nonartistic events shaped Redon's life. The first were the horrors that he experienced as a soldier in the Franco-Prussian War of 1870. The tragedies he witnessed affected what was already a pessimistic and imaginative mind. The other event was a happy one. In 1880, at the age of forty, Redon married. His wife, Camille, was an understanding spouse who competently handled the business side of their lives and raised their son.

Redon's many series of graphic works, along with charcoal drawings, dominated his output for many years. Around 1890, his numerous oil paintings and pastel drawings became more colorful, and the subject matter became more optimistic and less melancholy. This direction grew stronger when, in 1897, the rural family home in which he grew up was sold. It was as if a dark cloud had passed, and it allowed his work to develop in a more positive direction. Rich colors grew more dominant for the remainder of his career. This, too, was consonant with Symbolist theory, which promoted color for its emotional associations.

Redon created a range of imagery that he repeatedly used. A typical example of an image that he used in many different guises in which the context revealed its meaning was an independent eye. The eye first appeared in an 1878 charcoal drawing, *The Eye Balloon*. The floating eye looks up as it carries its basket above a featureless landscape. A silly element is injected into the scene by the addition of a fringe of eyelashes along the top of the balloon. The image invokes a freedom of consciousness sailing above the trials of daily cares, while the humor of the lashes leavens the seriousness. The combination of the deeply serious and a touch of humor was a frequent characteristic Redon's work. The eye balloon in a different guise can also mean a retreat into isolation. The eye sometimes appeared alone or as part of another object, such as at the center of an unfurling leaf or flower to anthropomorphize or humanize the consciousness of the plant.

A related but more complicated recurrent image was a severed head with (usually) closed eyes. This image had its acknowledged origin in the severed heads of murder victims, but Redon's usage, while it did suggest death, had less sinister connections.

The closed eyes suggested a dream world, reserve, separation from life, and a higher purpose in the transcendent. Multiple meanings were typical of Symbolist mystical suggestion. Flower imagery was another related symbol. A flower could be a human head with the previously mentioned multiple meanings attached to it. Flower or plant growth also suggested primordial themes that explored the concept of life-forms before the human race existed and related that to transcendent consciousness. The complexity of interrelated ideas had a basic appeal for Symbolist artists.

In 1903, Redon received official recognition from the French government when he was made a Chevalier of the Legion of Honor. Another honor followed in 1904, when the French government purchased one of his paintings. He was well enough known by then that an entire room was devoted to his works at the autumn art exhibition in Paris. By this time, his work displayed less tension and anxiety: He often painted portraits and flowers, explored mythological subjects, and used brilliant colors. In 1913, Redon's international fame grew when he was included in the controversial Armory Show in New York City. This exhibition introduced modern art in its various forms to the United States and was much discussed, praised, or damned depending on the critic.

Summary

Odilon Redon did not find his mature voice until he was forty years old. After that time, his works were exhibited widely in France and the United States. As a Symbolist artist, he developed the image of the eye balloon floating freely above the world as a personal and universal metaphor for the questing soul. This allusive image, which developed from Redon's identity as an outsider in society and the art world, eventually influenced the Surrealist art movement of the 1920's and 1930's, which delved into the dream and fantasy worlds explored by Freudian psychology. The Surrealists, in their turn, became an ever-present influence on the art of the twentieth century.

Bibliography

Bacou, Roseline. *Odilon Redon: Pastels*. Translated by Beatrice Rehl. London: Thames and Hudson, and New York: Braziller, 1987. This monograph on Redon's pastels includes seventy color reproductions with a short discussion of each. Bacou's introduction discusses the pastels by referring to quotations from figures in the Paris art world. Included are two short but very important documents about Redon's life: The first is made up of photographs of Redon, and the second is a twelve-page autobiography.

Delevoy, Robert L. *Symbolists and Symbolism.* New York: Rizzoli, and London: Macmillan, 1978. Delevoy defines Symbolism by discussing the various topics that constitute approaches to subject. This short work is profusely illustrated with examples by a large number of artists, including Redon.

Druick, Douglas W., ed. *Odilon Redon: Prince of Dreams 1840-1916.* Chicago: Art Institute of Chicago, and London: Abrams, 1994. This is a sizeable exhibition catalog (464 pages) celebrating the centennial of Redon's first retrospective exhibition. It contains the fullest treatment available in English of the artist's biography, extensive reproduction of his works, examples of artistic influences, and an analysis of his working techniques. The extensive bibliography contains all of Redon's published art criticism and personal journals.

Eisenman, Stephen F. *The Temptation of Saint Redon: Biography, Ideology, and Style in the "Noirs" of Odilon Redon.* Chicago: University of Chicago Press, 1992. This study investigates Redon's utopian subject matter, which the author sees as reconciling the artist's feelings of powerlessness that stemmed from a lonely childhood.

Keay, Carolyn, ed. *Odilon Redon.* London: Academy, and New York: Rizzoli, 1977. This short introduction to Redon's work contains sixty-six color and black-and-white reproductions.

Mathieu, Pierre-Louis. *The Symbolist Generation: 1870-1910.* New York: Rizzoli, 1990. Mathieu discusses the Symbolist style by defining the subgroups within the movement and identifying the differences created by geographical location.

Théberge, Pierre. *Lost Paradise: Symbolist Europe.* Montreal: Montreal Museum of Fine Arts, 1995. This 555-page exhibition catalog gives a comprehensive presentation of the Symbolist art movement. The discussion centers on the various topics that the style used as subjects.

Werner, Alfred. *The Graphic Works of Odilon Redon.* New York: Dover, 1969. This is the most complete overview of Redon's graphic works published with an English introduction. Two hundred nine lithographs, etchings, and engravings are included. The ten-page introduction is short but pithy.

Wilson, Michael. *Nature and Imagination: The Work of Odilon Redon.* Oxford: Phaidon Press, and New York: Dutton, 1978. Wilson provides a short but thorough discussion of the life and artistic career of Redon. The book contains seventy illustrations, many in color, with a few examples of works by artists who influenced Redon.

Ann Stewart Balakier

WALTER REED

Born: September 13, 1851; Belroi, Virginia
Died: November 22, 1902; Washington, D.C.
Area of Achievement: Medicine
Contribution: Reed served as the head of the commission that designed and conducted the experiments which revealed beyond a doubt that yellow fever was transmitted by the bite of an infected mosquito, thus making control of this terrible disease possible.

Early Life

Walter Reed was born September 13, 1851, in the small town of Belroi, Virginia, near Gloucester. He was the youngest of five children. His mother, Pharaba White, was the first wife of his father, Lemuel Sutton Reed, a Methodist minister. From the very first, it seemed as if Reed were destined to live a gypsylike existence. As an adult, he would reside in a nearly endless series of army camps; as a child, his family moved frequently as his father was sent to parish after parish in the regions of southeastern Virginia and eastern North Carolina. In 1865, however, the Reeds achieved some stability with a move to Charlottesville, Virginia, and Walter was able to attend school with some regularity. In 1866, he entered the University of Virginia, receiving the M.D. degree in 1869.

Feeling the need for more clinical experience, Reed next enrolled in the medical school of Bellevue Hospital in New York City, where, at the age of nineteen, he completed study for his second M.D. degree. A year's internship followed in New York's Infant's Hospital, after which he became a physician in two other hospitals in the New York area while also serving as a sanitary inspector for the Brooklyn Board of Health.

Life's Work

Unhappy with the insecurity of life as a public physician, yet having no good prospects for private practice, Reed decided upon a career in the military and, in 1875, passed the examinations which earned for him a commission as first lieutenant in the Army Medical Corps. He married Emilie Lawrence in 1876, and shortly afterward was transferred to Fort Lowell in Arizona. His wife soon joined him, and their son Lawrence was born in 1877. A daughter, Blossom, followed in 1883. The Reed children lived much the same restless life as their father had as a youngster as they followed

him in almost annual moves from army post to army post in Arizona, Nebraska, Minnesota, and Alabama.

These wanderings in the West were interrupted briefly in 1889, when Reed was appointed surgeon for army recruits in Baltimore. While stationed there, he sought and was given permission to work in The Johns Hopkins Hospital where he took courses in bacteriology and pathology. It was not, however, until 1893, when Reed returned to the East to stay, that his career finally began to flourish. In that year, he was promoted to the rank of major, assigned the position of professor of bacteriology and clinical microscopy at the recently established Army Medical School in Washington, D. C., and given the position of curator of the Army Medical Museum as well.

In 1896, Reed received his first real opportunity to demonstrate his ability as a medical investigator when he tracked down the cause of near-epidemic malaria among troops in the Washington barracks and in nearby Fort Myer, Virginia. In addition, in 1898, he chaired a committee that investigated the spread of typhoid fever in army camps. All this was excellent preparation for the task that Reed was about to undertake, and the task for which he is famous—that of resolving the riddle of yellow fever's transmission. The disease had been the scourge of the Caribbean Islands and the regions bordering on the Gulf of Mexico, as well as other port cities in North America and Brazil, for more than two centuries and had claimed hundreds of thousands of lives. Its abrupt but mysterious appearances and disappearances had long been the subject of controversy among physicians. Many believed the disease to be contagious, while many others were convinced that it was caused by local climatic conditions which created poisoned air (miasmata). By the end of the nineteenth century, much of the medical world had accepted the contagionists' view, believing that the disease was spread by fomites (items such as clothing or bedding used by a yellow fever victim).

Yet for at least a century, a few physicians had been skeptical of both explanations. Dr. John Crawford of Baltimore is sometimes credited with advancing a mosquito theory toward the end of the eighteenth century, as are Josiah Nott of Mobile, Alabama, and the French naturalist Louis Daniel Beauperthuy at about midpoint in the nineteenth

century. The real credit for a mosquito theory, however, belongs to the Cuban physician Carlos Juan Finlay, who, in 1881, not only suggested that mosquitos were responsible for the transmission of yellow fever but also narrowed the focus to the *Aëdes aegypti* (then called *Stegomyia fasciata*) mosquito. Finlay's difficulty was that he could not prove his theory.

In 1896, an Italian physician, Giuseppe Sanarelli, claimed to have isolated the causative agent of yellow fever and Reed, along with army physician James Carroll, was assigned the task of investigating that claim. They soon demonstrated it to be groundless, but this was only the beginning of Reed's work on yellow fever. He volunteered for duty during the war with Spain over the question of Cuban independence, but only got to Cuba after the war was over, arriving in Havana in 1899, to investigate a typhoid outbreak, and again in 1900, as the head of a commission sent to investigate the reasons for an outbreak of yellow fever among American troops still stationed on the island. Carroll, Aristides Agramonte, and Jesse Lazear made up the remainder of the commission.

At first, they made little progress with yellow fever, for their efforts were directed toward showing that the bacillus which Sanarelli believed to cause yellow fever was actually part of the group of hog cholera bacillus. It was only after Reed had investigated an outbreak of a disease originally thought to be malaria among soldiers in Pinar del Rio, that the commission settled down to its task. The disease in question turned out to be yellow fever, and the circumstances surrounding the death of one of the soldiers who had been a prisoner and locked in a cell particularly intrigued Reed because none of his cellmates had got yellow fever, not even the one who had taken his bunk and bedding. This fact seemed to discredit the fomite theory, and Reed wrote later that at this point he began to suspect that some insect was capable of transmitting the disease.

It was also at this point that several important findings began to converge. In 1894, Sir Patrick Manson had suggested that mosquitoes might be responsible for the transmission of malaria and in 1897, Sir Ronald Ross had proved it. On the other hand, malaria was a very different disease from yellow fever. One of the reasons why Finlay had been unable to prove that the *Aëdes aegypti* mosquito was responsible for spreading yellow fever was that he (and everyone else) was unaware of the long period (generally nine to sixteen days) of incubation the yellow fever virus requires in the stomach of a mosquito before that mosquito is capable of passing the disease along to a human host. In May of 1900, Henry Rose Carter of the United States Marine Hospital Service published his observations on outbreaks of the disease in Mississippi which for the first time revealed the lengthy incubation period.

Then, in the summer of 1900, the members of the commission met with Finlay, who placed the records of his experiments at their disposal. They had decided to test Finlay's theory using human subjects for the experiments.

Reed returned to Washington, but was back in Cuba in September, upon learning that Lazear, who had permitted himself to be bitten by an infected mosquito, was dead from yellow fever and that Carroll was seriously ill with the disease. It seemed that Finlay had indeed been correct, and Reed at this juncture designed and conducted the experiments that produced twenty-two more cases in soldier volunteers, proving once and for all that the female *Aëdes aegypti* mosquito was responsible for epidemic yellow fever. Armed with this knowledge, Major W. C. Gorgas was able to free Havana of the disease quickly and then eradicate it in Panama (making construction of the canal possible), while others wiped out yellow fever in urban centers elsewhere in the hemisphere. More than three decades would elapse before another form of the disease called jungle yellow fever would be discovered in some of the monkey populations of that area and in those of Africa. With this discovery came the realization that the disease could not be completely eradicated, but only controlled.

Unfortunately, Reed did not live long enough to see the whole of this triumph of man over yellow fever. After completing his experiments in Cuba, he returned, in 1901, to Washington, a hero and the recipient of many honors. He resumed his teaching duties but died in late 1902 of complications that developed following surgery on his ruptured appendix.

Summary

In no small part because of a sensationalist American press, Reed (as Cuban physicians and historians in particular have pointed out) has probably received too much credit for the solution of the age-old mystery of yellow fever's transmission. Yet Reed himself was always modest about his role in the matter and quick to pass along that credit to Finlay, and to his associates Carroll, Lazear, and Agramonte.

In truth, however, Reed was entitled to a lion's share of the credit. Finlay had not been able to prove the truth of his mosquito hypothesis, and Reed's colleagues were narrow specialists; Carroll was a bacteriologist, Lazear, a mosquito specialist, and Agramonte, a pathologist. Thus, it was Reed who successfully drew the work of these and others together and organized the experiments that made the final definitive breakthrough.

While his early career gives no hint of this kind of ability, his activities in investigating malaria and typhoid outbreaks during the years immediately prior to his yellow fever work surely prepared him well for that work. In all these undertakings, Reed revealed a fine scientific mind, and his success in the tropical medicine field, heretofore dominated by Europeans, brought much prestige to American science and American scientific education. Thus it is fitting that the small monument over his resting place in Arlington National Cemetery bears the in-scription, "He gave to man control over that dreadful scourge Yellow Fever."

Bibliography

Bean, William B. *Walter Reed: A Biography.* Charlottesville: University Press of Virginia, 1982. Despite its lack of documentation, it is clear that this study, by the leading authority on Reed, has been extensively researched, and as a full-length biography it has the virtue of providing a balanced account of Reed's life rather than concentrating excessively on his yellow fever work alone. Thus, it provides an excellent description of medicine and the military between the Civil War and the war with Spain.

———. "Walter Reed: He Gave Man Control of That Dreadful Scourge—Yellow Fever." *Archives of Internal Medicine* 89 (1952): 171-187. A succinct depiction of Reed's accomplishments.

Carmichael, Emmett B. "Walter Reed: Army Surgeon-Bacteriologist-Epidemiologist." *Alabama Journal of Medical Science* 8 (1971): 446-457. A brief biography of Reed that focuses on his work on yellow fever and the honors that he received for that work.

Carter, Henry Rose. *Yellow Fever: An Epidemiological and Historical Study of Its Place of Origin.* Edited by Laura Armistead Carter and Wade Hampton Frost. Baltimore: Williams and Wilkins, 1931. The author, himself one of the major actors in the drama of the conquest of yellow fever, provides the most thorough examination of the history of the disease as well as an account of its ultimate surrender to science.

Chappell, Gordon S. "Surgeon at Fort Sidney: Captain Walter Reed's Experiences, 1883-1884." *Nebraska History* 54 (1973): 419-443. Focuses on Reed's year of service as the chief medical officer at Fort Sidney, a Nebraska military post. An interesting glimpse of a slice of Reed's early career.

Gilmore, Hugh R. "Malaria at Washington Barracks and Fort Myer." *Bulletin of the History of Medicine* 29 (1955): 346-351. This is a brief description of the careful epidemiological investigation of a malaria outbreak among soldiers in the Washington, D.C., area carried out by Reed in 1896.

Kelly, Howard A. *Walter Reed and Yellow Fever.* 3d ed. Baltimore: Norman, Remington, 1923. The first scholarly and satisfactory biography of

Reed despite its uncritical nature. It traces his life from birth to death, but, as the title indicates, it places most of the emphasis on the work done by Reed and his associates on yellow fever.

Truby, Albert E. *Memoir of Walter Reed: The Yellow Fever Episode*. New York and London: Hoeber, 1943. This work, as the title indicates, is not biographical in nature but rather concentrates on the methods and techniques employed by Reed and his colleagues to demonstrate that the mosquito was indeed the carrier of yellow fever. In the process, the study also provides a fine background sketch of the Army Medical Corps and the conditions in Cuba with which Reed met upon his arrival.

Wood, Laura N. *Walter Reed: Doctor in Uniform*. New York: Messner, 1943. A biography for young people which, although fanciful at times, particularly in the words put in the mouths of the leading characters, is nevertheless well researched and well indexed.

Kenneth F. Kiple

FREDERIC REMINGTON

Born: October 4, 1861; Canton, New York
Died: December 26, 1909; Ridgefield, Connecticut
Areas of Achievement: Art and writing
Contribution: In his drawings and bronzes, Remington recorded the Old West before it vanished, thus preserving it for later generations.

Early Life

Born October 4, 1861, in Canton, New York, Frederic Sackrider Remington was the only child of Clara Bascomb Sackrider and Seth Pierrepont Remington, a newspaper editor and publisher. Remington's early childhood was marked by the four-year absence of his father, who was a lieutenant colonel in the Civil War. Upon his father's return, Remington eagerly listened to his tales of the cavalry and the West; perhaps Remington's lifelong fascination with the horse can be traced to this period. At any rate, Remington grew up sketching horses, cowboys, Indians, and soldiers. His artistic ability pleased his father, whom he idolized, but did not satisfy his practical mother, who envisioned for him a career in business. School never received much of his attention; instead, his childhood revolved around fishing, swimming and other outdoor activities.

In 1878, after two years at a military academy in Massachusetts, Remington entered Yale and its newly established School of Art and Architecture. In the college weekly, *Courant*, he published his first drawing, *College Riff-Raff* (1879), a cartoon of a bruised football player. Despite his interest in art, he was soon bored by the study of classical painting and sculpture, but he discovered a new diversion, football. Tall, robust, and burly, he was a natural football player and became a forward on the varsity team. In 1880, Remington's father died, leaving him a modest inheritance. Finding himself financially independent, at least momentarily, he left Yale against his mother's wishes, after having completed less than two years. In Canton, he tried several jobs, but none was to his liking. In the summer of 1880, upon meeting Eva Adele Caten of Gloversville, New York, he fell deeply in love and asked her father for her hand, but he was refused on the grounds that his future was not promising. Remington, dejected, left to find his fortune in the West. Working as a cowboy and a scout did not make him rich, but as a result of the trip he sold a sketch, *Cow-boys of Arizona: Roused by a Scout*

(1882), to *Harper's Weekly*, his first appearance in a major magazine, a milestone even if the sketch was redrawn by a staff artist.

In 1883, Remington bought a sheep ranch in Kansas. Yet the difficult and lonely work induced him to sell it in 1884. With the last of his inheritance, he invested in a saloon. Although the business was successful, his unscrupulous partners tricked him out of his share. After selling a few drawings to a Kansas City art dealer, he began seriously to consider an art career. In retrospect, he said of his interest in drawing, "I knew the wild riders and the vacant land were about to vanish forever. . . . Without knowing exactly how to do it, I began to record some facts around me and the more I looked the more the panorama unfolded." Thus, he began the task of chronicling the West before it disappeared.

Returning to New York, Remington again approached Eva's father, who relented, perhaps because Eva would have no other. After being married on October 1, 1884, he and his bride set out for Kansas City to establish their home. A steady income was not to be found, however, so after less than a year Eva returned to New York, and Remington resumed his travels through the West. At one time, he prospected for gold, at another, he rode with an army unit in search of Apaches, but always he sketched.

Realizing that New York City, with its many publishers, was the place for an aspiring illustrator, he returned in 1885 and, with Eva, set up a household in Brooklyn. The early days were difficult as he doggedly tried to sell his drawings, but the turning point came in 1886, when *Harper's Weekly* published on its cover his drawing *The Apache War: Indian Scouts on Geronimo's Trail* (1886). Soon Remington's work began to appear regularly in major magazines.

Life's Work

In the years following 1886, Remington became recognized as the foremost illustrator of his day. Over his lifetime, his drawings, numbering more than twenty-seven hundred, were published in forty-one different periodicals. His illustrations, with their Western themes, struck a responsive chord in the American public, whose curiosity had been aroused by the tales of gold and Indians, circulating out of the Wild West.

After 1886, Remington went West every summer to sketch and to collect Indian artifacts and cowboy paraphernalia. At other times, he traveled on assignment for magazines. In 1888, he covered the army campaign against the Apache. In 1890, he was in the Badlands of South Dakota, documenting the Plains Indian Wars. Traveling with the army, he experienced at first hand several brief skirmishes with the Sioux. The Wounded Knee Massacre, the last battle of the Indian Wars, took place a few miles from where he was situated.

When the Spanish-American War erupted, Remington, representing *Harper's Weekly* and William Randolph Hearst's New York *Journal*, went to Cuba. Arriving with the cavalry, he witnessed the assault of San Juan Hill. One of his paintings, *Charge of the Rough Riders of San Juan Hill* (1899), depicted Theodore Roosevelt, his friend of ten years, leading his men. Roosevelt's charge probably occurred more in Remington's imagination than in fact. Roosevelt, however, used the drawing to his advantage in creating his image as a

soldier and hero that would later prove useful to his political future.

Remington illustrated not only articles but also books, the first being *Mexico Today* (1886) by Solomon Buckley Griffin. In 1890, nearly thirty, he illustrated Henry Wadsworth Longfellow's *The Song of Hiawatha* (1855), the popularity of which can be attributed partly to Remington's drawings. He illustrated books by Owen Wister, the noted writer of Western tales, and, in 1892, he did the drawings for Francis Parkman's *The Oregon Trail* (1892). In all, he illustrated more than 140 books.

Remington also wrote about the West he loved. His first signed articles, published in 1888, concerned the Sioux uprising. In 1895, he published the first of his eight books, *Pony Tracks*, a collection of his articles concerning army life. In 1902, he wrote a novel *John Ermine of the Yellowstone*, a romantic Western, which, in 1903, he adapted for the stage. The drawings for the novel posed a problem: How was he to illustrate a love story when he rarely sketched women? He solved his dilemma when he hired the well-known illustrator Charles Dana Gibson to draw the female figures.

In addition to being known as a pen-and-ink illustrator, Remington was also a popular oil painter. Beginning in 1887, his work was accepted in major exhibitions, often receiving prizes. He was an associate member of the prestigious National Academy of Design and a member of the National Institute of Arts and Letters. Remington's favorite subject for his paintings as well as for his illustrations was the Old West, a world full of cowboys, Indians, and horses. His paintings typically emphasize action; the scene might be of riders and horses wildly racing for safety, as in *A Dash for Timber* (1889), or of men besieged, as in *The Fight for the Water Hole* (probably painted 1895-1902). His paintings tell the story of the taming of the West. The fur traders, scouts, and soldiers populating his canvases conquer the West through their determination and strength while the Indians, noble but also cruel, are shown in their losing struggle.

In 1895, after watching the sculptor Frederic W. Ruckstull at work, Remington tried the new medium; the result was *The Bronco Buster*, a casting of which was later presented to Theodore Roosevelt by the Rough Riders on their return from the Spanish-American War. Over the next fourteen years, he produced twenty-five sculptures, all except one focusing on a Western theme. His bronzes have the same focus on action and the same attentiveness to details that distinguish his drawings.

Remington was a disciplined artist: He would rise at six and draw until the early afternoon; later in the evening, he would return to his studio to plan his work for the next day. He was also a highly successful artist. First known as an illustrator, he also made his mark as a writer, painter, and sculptor. On December 26, 1909, at the age of forty-eight, he died of complications from an appendectomy. His art can be found at the Remington Art Memorial, in Ogdensburg, New York, and at the Amon Carter Museum of Western Art, in Fort Worth, Texas. The Thomas Gilcrease Institute of History and Art houses a large collection of Remington bronzes.

Summary

Through his illustrations, paintings, and bronzes, Remington created the image of the West held by most Americans. The lonely cowboy, the savage Indian, the limitless land, the noble horse, the brave soldiers who battle against overwhelming odds, and the pioneers who never question their right to settle the land are all in his paintings.

His illustrations and drawings have been valued as a documentary of the West. His rendering of the costumes of the Indian tribes, the different breeds of the horses, and the details of the soldier's dress have been praised for their authenticity. Some critics argue that Remington also romanticized the West, indicating the many buffalo skulls that litter his paintings, and others suggest that his work owes as much to his imagination as to fact, citing the historically inaccurate costumes of the Indians in *The Song of Hiawatha*. Both evaluations are correct. Remington was highly accurate in his early drawings, which were usually based on sketches done in the West, but the later paintings were often imagined reconstructions of fact and fantasy, portraying the spirit of the West rather than a particular moment. Yet whatever faults might be found in his paintings, they do not obscure the fact that Remington had a tremendous impact on how Americans view the West. Many would agree with Owen Wister, "Remington is not merely an artist; he is a national treasure."

Bibliography

Ainsworth, Ed. *The Cowboy in Art*. New York: World, 1968. A history of the cowboy and the artists who painted him. Charles M. Russell and Remington are recognized as the greatest of the cowboy artists, but they are not discussed any more fully than a host of minor artists. A glorification of the cowboy. Filled with Western lore.

Baigell, Matthew. *The Western Art of Frederic Remington*. New York: Ballantine, 1976. Contains a short introduction to Remington's life and work followed by color plates of Remington's paintings from 1887 to 1909. Baigell is critical of Remington's portrayal of the West, suggesting that it is a romanticized version.

Ewers, John C. *Artists of the Old West*. New York: Doubleday, 1973. Contains chapters devoted to the artists who popularized the West, including George Catlin, Albert Bierstadt, Frederic Remington, and Charles M. Russell. Discusses Remington's experiences during the Plains Indian War.

Jackson, Marta, ed. *The Illustrations of Frederic Remington*. New York: Bounty, 1970. A brief account of Remington's life, followed by drawings which are arranged by subject. Many of the drawings are not found in other books. Includes a brief commentary by Owen Wister on Remington's artistic contribution.

McCracken, Harold. *Frederic Remington: Artist of the Old West*. Philadelphia: Lippincott, 1947. A widely recognized biography. Contains colorful anecdotes gathered from Remington's friends and relatives. A glowing appraisal of Remington's artistic contribution. McCracken supplies a useful list of all of Remington's drawings, books, and bronzes. Included are forty-eight plates of paintings, pastels, and bronzes.

Richardson, E. P. *Painting in America: The Story of 450 Years*. New York: Crowell, and London: Constable, 1956. An authoritative study of American painting. Praises Remington as an illustrator who realistically recorded the West but criticizes the "crude and raw" color of his paintings.

Samuels, Peggy, and Harold Samuels. *Frederic Remington*. New York: Doubleday, 1982. This massive but readable biography is the most thorough, most balanced study of Remington to date. While the authors hold their subject in high regard, they do not fail to acknowledge his flaws. Their account emphasizes the influence of Impressionism on his later work.

Vorpahl, Ben Merchant. *Frederic Remington and the West: With the Eye of the Mind*. Austin: University of Texas Press, 1978. Traces how Remington was influenced by the West and how he, in turn, shaped the public's image of the frontier. An academic study, ranging widely in literature and social history.

Wear, Bruce. *The Bronze World of Frederic Remington.* Tulsa, Okla.: Gaylord, 1966. Discusses the bronzes, how they were cast, Remington's involvement with the production, and the problem of forgeries. The text is followed by plates of the bronzes and pertinent information about each work.

Barbara Wiedemann

ERNEST RENAN

Born: February 28, 1823; Tréguier, Côtes-du-Nord, France

Died: October 2, 1892; Paris, France

Areas of Achievement: Religious history and philosophical criticism

Contribution: Renan's writings encompass the areas of religion, history, science, and morality. His controversial biography of Jesus Christ illustrates Renan's ongoing theme of resolution of contradictions by emphasizing the problem of reconciling the historical and the spiritually divine Jesus.

Early Life

Joseph-Ernest Renan was born in Tréguier, a town in Britanny that was in many respects a religious center. His youth was shaded by a veil of devout Catholicism, to which he, in accordance with his mother's most intense wishes and his own strong inclinations, was committed. His father, Philibert, was a grocer and seaman. His mother, Magdelaine Féger, was widowed when Ernest was five years old, her husband having drowned—it has not been determined whether accidentally or otherwise—at sea. Ernest Renan had a brother, Alain, born in 1809, and a sister, Henriette, born in 1811. His sister was profoundly influential in his life, and his attachment to her is lyrically expressed in *Ma Sœur Henriette* (1895; *My Sister Henrietta*, 1895), which was initially published in a limited edition of one hundred copies in 1862 as *Henriette Renan: Souvenir pour ceux qui l'ont connue* (Henriette Renan: a remembrance for those who knew her) and reprinted posthumously.

From 1832 to 1838, Renan was a student at the Ecclesiastical School in Tréguier, while his sister, having failed to establish a private school for girls, accepted a teaching position in Paris. In 1838, Renan moved to Paris and studied rhetoric at the seminary of Saint-Nicolas du Chardonnet. After three years, he moved to the seminary of Issy-les-Moulineux outside Paris, where his study of philosophy began to bring about his wavering in religious faith. His sister, with whom he was to maintain an ongoing correspondence, had moved, during this time, to Poland, where she found employment as a governess. From Issy-les-Moulineux, he moved in 1849 to the parent seminary of Saint-Sulpice and entered upon his study of theology.

In his academic progression from rhetoric to philosophy to theology, the normal pattern of seminary education in France, Renan developed a devotion to literature, a skeptical turn of mind, and a sense of alienation in his separation, first, from Britanny and, later, from his mother. He remained firmly within his faith, however, and in 1844 became a tonsured cleric in evidence of his call to the priesthood. After a year, he came to realize that he lacked belief sufficient to this vocation, and his rationalism and scientific propensity led him to abandon the ecclesiastical for the secular life. His sister Henriette supported him in his decision and commended his firmness of purpose and strength of will.

He then set his life's course toward reconciling the two worlds which, as he assured his mother in her disappointment, were not, to his mind, separate. The world of Jesus (the world of religion) and the world of science contradicted each other but were not mutually exclusive. To his own way of thinking, he had departed from Jesus so as to be better able to follow Jesus.

Life's Work

In 1845, at the age of twenty-two, Renan, believing that his own emotions and his own thoughts were his God, became a tutor, an ultimately successful candidate for the *baccalauréat* and *licence* (roughly equivalent to the B.A. and M.A. degrees in the United States), a friend of the chemist Marcellin Berthelot, and a student of the Semitic languages (of which he was soon to become a professor). Two years later, he won the Volney Prize for his essay on the history of the Semitic languages. His friendship with the scientist, which proved to be lifelong, and his own predilection for science, along with his Semitic studies, adumbrated his major contributions to intellectual history and to the history of ideas; these are his *Historie des origines du christianisme* (1863-1882; *The History of the Origins of Christianity*, 1890) and *L'Avenir de la science* (1890; *The Future of Science*, 1890). Renan completed his work on *The Future of Science* in 1849, three years before the publication of his doctoral dissertation, *Averroès et l'Averroïsme* (1852). Segments of the text of *The Future of Science* appeared in journals, periodicals, and other of his books, but its full publication, with only minor revisions of the original, materialized only two years before his death.

One of the prime focuses of *The Future of Science* is criticism, a subject which he had initially expounded in his *Cahiers de jeunesse* (1845-1846; youthful notebooks). Renan's views on criticism as an intellectual activity anticipated much of the direction that was to be taken by post-World War II critical theorists. For him, true criticism was universal in character and was decidedly not to be limited to literary criticism and even more decidedly not to be identified with judgment and measurements against standards of form and composition. He believed that beauty was open-ended and not subject to the closure that is implied by the concept of an absolute. He saw criticism as a creative use of the powers of interpretation and a conceptual conjunction of history, topography, philosophy, and morality. Like the deconstructionists of the twentieth century, he disregarded the demarcations of disciplines and sought to reconcile the disciplines through comparativism, eclecticism, and synthesis; comparison served him in science, literature, and religion as the great tool of criticism. *The Future of Science* begins with the very simple statement, "Only one thing is necessary." The one thing proves to be, after all syntheses have been unified, science as that religion which comprises human feeling and human thought.

H. W. Wardman recognizes in *The Future of Science* the idea that "philosophy is a human science born of the union of philology and historical sympathy," and this prompts him effectively to conclude that Renan's philosopher is "a kind of seer fitted by his insight into human nature to take over from the Church the spiritual leadership of mankind." Philology, according to Renan, is "the science of the products of the human mind."

Renan's notion of history is an extension of Victor Cousin's concept of the three ages: a primary age informed by religion without science, a secondary age informed by science without religion, and a final age informed by both religion and science. The historical process is the development of the divine. In the final age, the development will have been concluded and God will be manifestly whole. The future of science, then, is the fulfillment of religion, that is to say, God.

Renan's masterwork was a seven-volume study, *The History of the Origins of Christianity*. The first of these volumes, *Vie de Jésus* (1863; *The Life of Jesus*, 1864), is the most famous and is the work for which Renan is best known. At the time of its publication, Renan had been married to Cornélie Scheffer for seven years, had become the father of two girls, the first having died eight months after birth, and had, in 1861, lost in death his sister Henriette, to whose soul he dedicated this work.

The life of Jesus, according to Renan, is the focal event of world history; it brought about the spiritual revolution that was the culmination of seven centuries of Jewish history and that in the subsequent three centuries would be established as a religion. This entire period of one thousand years is presented by Renan as embracing the origins of Christianity.

Renan depicts Jesus as a superior, indeed a sublime person but not as a god. His Jesus let his followers believe that He was God as He taught them the ways to fulfill their subjectivity. He holds that Jesus' immediate followers and their successors invented, in belief and desire, the Resurrection: "The life of Jesus ends, as far as the historian is concerned, with his last sigh. But so great was the mark he had made in the hearts of his disciples and several devoted women that for a few more weeks he was alive to them and he consoled them." This passage from chapter 26 is representative of the secular Jesus whom hosts of Renan's critics rejected and protested against. The whole of chapters 26 and 27 was, for example, among the exclusions from the French Book Club's ornately bound and illustrated 1970 abridgment of *The History of the Origins of Christianity*. The Christian clergy and laity assailed the book for its profanation and its author's apostasy. Literary critics frowned upon the idyllic and romantic Galilee that it painted and upon its overly genteel characterization of Jesus. The book became an international best-seller, however, going through eight printings in the first three months of its publication.

The second volume of *The History of the Origins of Christianity* appeared in 1866; it is a historiography of the Apostles, from A.D. 33 to 45, and an investigation into the continuing apotheosis of Jesus by way of visionary presumption, amplification of legend, and adaptation of mythical traditions. His third volume, *La Vie de saint Paul* (1869; *Saint Paul*, 1869), dedicated to his wife, who had accompanied him in his retracing of the travels of his subject, is replete with the topography and accoutrements of epic. Saint Paul is here reminiscent of the Homeric Odysseus: a man of action and purpose. The fourth volume (1873), following the

New Testament's book of Revelation as Renan's second and third volumes follow, respectively, the book of Acts and the Pauline Epistles, studies Emperor Nero as the Antichrist. The fifth volume (1877) expatiates upon the second Christian generation and the production of the first four books of the New Testament, the basis of his life of Jesus. He applauds Matthew and Mark as the genuinely divine increment of Christianity, berates Luke as special pleading, and sees John as fraudulent save for its recounting of various of Jesus' teachings. (Only nine of this volume's twenty-seven chapters are included in the above-mentioned French Book Club edition.) The sixth volume (1879) details the defeat of Gnosticism and Montanism and the establishment of the Orthodox Christian church. The concluding volume (1881) centers on Emperor Marcus Aurelius (161-180) and the end of the ancient world.

From 1888 to the year of his death, Renan published three of the five volumes of his last historical opus, *Histoire du peuple d'Israël* (*History of the People of Israel*, 1888-1895), the last two volumes of which were published posthumously in 1893. He looked upon this work as his completion of the history of Christianity's origins and as his exposition of the Jewish "subsoil" of Jesus' roots. The ten books of this work trace the development of Jewish monotheism, messianism, and religious mission—a development which entailed the sacrifice of nationalistic power to spiritual identity.

Renan died on October 2, 1892, from pneumonia and cardiac complications. Although his death was painful, it came after he had gained personal satisfaction from completing his life's work.

Summary

Ernest Renan's monuments are *The Future of Science, The History of the Origins of Christianity*, and *History of the People of Israel*. His other works are many, and they warrant careful study by anyone seriously interested in his contributions to modern thought. These include, apart from other works already mentioned, his correspondence, his *Souvenirs d'enfance et de jeunesse* (1876-1882; *Recollections of My Youth*, 1883), his *Discours et conférences* (1887; speeches and lectures), his philosophical dialogues, and his four philosophical dramas: *Caliban, suite de "La Tempête": Drama philosophique* (1878; *Caliban: A Philosophical Drama Continuing "The Tempest" of William Shakespeare*, 1896), *L'Eau de jouvence* (1881; the
fountain of youth), *Le Prêtre de Némi* (1886; the priest of Nemi), and *L'Abbesse de Jouarre* (1886; the abbess of Jouarre).

Renan is an outstanding example of the thinker whose crisis of spirit is resolved by his work. Like the English poet William Cowper (1731-1800), who adjusted to his unshakable belief that he was damned by engaging in constant literary effort, Renan overcame his loss of faith with a creative scholarship that brought him spiritual contentment.

In his spiritual secularism and his universal criticism, Renan was ahead of his time. His attitudes and ideas anticipated those of certain significant twentieth century theologians (for example, Hans Küng), literary artists (Miguel de Unamuno y Jugo), and critical theorists (Michel Foucault and René Girard), but his twentieth century successors not only found broader and more consistent readerships but also outdistanced him in depth and caliber of expression, though not in exquisiteness of prose.

Renan saw himself as a man of two worlds: religion and science. He belongs as well to two different temporal worlds: the nineteenth century, in which his ideas were uncommon and thereby largely unheeded, and the twentieth century, in which his ideas were largely unheeded because they had become commonplace.

Bibliography

Chadbourne, Richard M. *Ernest Renan*. New York: Twayne, 1968. An admirable and admiring account of the life and works of Renan, touching upon all the qualities that make Renan a "great historian, critic, and artist." This is one of the finest volumes in the Twayne's World Authors series; if one can find time for only one secondary work on Renan, this should be it.

———. *Ernest Renan as an Essayist*. Ithaca, N.Y.: Cornell University Press, 1957. An approach to Renan through his contribution to the tradition of essay-writing in France. Chadbourne stresses the seriousness of purpose that is to be found in the essays as against the author's propensity for irony, humor, and open-ended play. Considering that he may have made Renan appear overly serious, Chadbourne corrects the impression in his *Ernest Renan*.

Gore, Charles. Introduction to *The Life of Jesus*, by Ernest Renan. London: Dent, and New York: Dutton, 1927. Gore offers an excellent summary of the reception of Renan's *The Life of Jesus* by critics, liberals, and orthodox Christians. He also offers a vindication of Renan as a historian whose estimation of the historical value of the New Testament documents had come to be recognized as essentially correct. Gore's translation, the second into English and the first in international importance, should also be of interest to any reader seeking familiarity with Renan's most famous work.

Gore, Keith. "Ernest Renan: A Positive Ethics?" *French Studies* 41 (April, 1987): 141-154. A concise account of Renan's philosophical adjustment to his break with the Church and to the political situation in France (Second Empire, Franco-Prussian War, Third Republic). Gore claims that Renan's work comes closest to being "positive" in *Cahiers de jeunesse*. In a long footnote, Gore insists, contrary to assertions by H. W. Wardman (in a book written in 1979 in French), that in the ethical sphere, Renan was pragmatic, not metaphysical.

Neff, Emery. *The Poetry of History: The Contribution of Literature and Literary Scholarship to the Writing of History Since Voltaire*. New York: Columbia University Press, 1947. An appraisal of Renan's historiography as the work of a man of letters. Informative comparison of Renan's work to that of Jacob Burckhardt and John Richard Green. Neff states a cogent case for the long-term worth of Renan's distinctive and efficacious mode of historical inquiry. Helpful study of the fabric of historiography, to which Renan made a signal contribution.

Schweitzer, Albert. *The Quest of the Historical Jesus: A Critical Study of Its Progress from Reimarus to Wrede*. Translated by W. Montgomery. London: Black, and New York: Macmillan, 1910. Chapter 13 is devoted to Renan's *The Life of Jesus*. Schweitzer calls Renan's essay on the sources for the life of Jesus "a literary masterpiece" but finds the work inconsistent in its estimate and use of the Fourth Gospel and in its thoroughgoing "insincerity." Passing attention is accorded to Renan in other chapters.

Wardman, H. W. *Ernest Renan: A Critical Biography*. London: Athlone Press, 1964. The emphasis in this biography is upon Renan's life and work in the context of his times. Wardman offers a consistent characterization of Renan, noting, for example, Renan's fear of his work becoming outdated or being proved wrong by posterity, as well as Renan's metaphysical anxieties.

Wilson, Edmund. *To the Finland Station: A Study in the Writing and Acting of History*. New York: Harcourt Brace, and London: Secker and Warburg, 1940. Places Renan within the revolutionary tradition in Europe. Part 6 of chapter 1 discusses Renan in the context of the decline of the revolutionary tradition and praises *The History of the Origins of Christianity* as "a masterpiece—perhaps the greatest of all histories of ideas." Elsewhere in his text, Wilson suggests that Renan's moral force diminishes in proportion to his urbane tolerance of error and his diplomatic dissimulation.

Roy Arthur Swanson

PIERRE-AUGUSTE RENOIR

Born: February 25, 1841; Limoges, France
Died: December 3, 1919; Cagnes, France
Area of Achievement: Art
Contribution: One of the major French Impressionists, Renoir painted in the open air, handling the paint loosely, dissolving masses, and abandoning local colors. He differed, however, from most of the other Impressionists in his concentration on the human figure and in his strong interest in portraiture.

Early Life

Pierre-Auguste Renoir's father Léonard, a poor painter, moved his family from Limoges to Paris in 1845, when the painter-to-be was four years old. There the young Renoir, who displayed talent for music as well as for drawing, was enrolled in the choir school of the parish church of Saint-Roch. His elder sister Lisa first exposed him to painting at the age of nine by taking him to the Louvre. He would doodle in his exercise books in school, and he was later encouraged in art by Lisa's fiancé, the illustrator Charles Leray. At the age of thirteen, Renoir was apprenticed to the Lévy Frères firm of porcelain painters, for whom he painted decorative bouquets on dishware in an eighteenth century style. During his lunch periods, he hurried to the Louvre, where he practiced his drawing; later, in 1860, he was given official permission to copy there. After losing his job in the porcelain atelier in 1858, when the firm went bankrupt, he painted fans for a living, copying on them pictures of the rococo artists François Boucher, Jean-Honoré Fragonard, Nicolas Lancret, and Antoine Watteau. The sense of joy and gracefulness encapsulated in that phase of French painting would later be found in Renoir's own work.

Renoir enrolled in 1862 in the academically oriented studio of Charles Gleyre, a mediocre Swiss painter, where he met Jean Frédéric Bazille, Claude Monet, and Alfred Sisley. At gatherings at the home of a relative of Bazille, he met the painter Édouard Manet, the poet Charles Baudelaire, and the novelist Théophile Gautier. Leaving Gleyre's studio the next year, Renoir painted with his friends in the Fontainbleau Forest in order to sketch the landscape and move toward greater naturalism. They stayed at Chailly, near the encampment of the Barbizon painters, and Renoir met there the Barbizonist Narcisse Virgile Diaz de La

Peña. The major influence on Renoir's work from 1867 to 1870 was exerted by Gustave Courbet, whose heavy modeling, massive figures, and use of the palette knife can be seen reflected in Renoir's rendering of the nude in *Diane Chassereuse* (1867). In that picture there can be discerned, too, the influence of Manet in the use of an obviously contemporary figure to pose for a mythological scene.

Life's Work

In the spring of 1868, Renoir and Bazille moved to a studio in the rue de la Paix, where Monet would occasionally join them. In the evenings, they often went to the Café Guerbois, where there would be much talk of painting, with Manet as the presiding figure, the painter Paul Cézanne, the printmaker Félix Bracquemond, Henri Fantin-Latour, Constantin Guys, and Sisley, and the novelists Émile Zola and Gautier.

Renoir's leap into full-blown Impressionism occurred in 1869 with his paintings of *La Grenouillière*, the bathing place and floating restaurant at Bougival on the Seine. His intention was to combine the sense of poetry of the rococo with a motif from contemporary life. His strokes are broken. About half of the painted surface is given to the shimmering water, and light and atmosphere have become the unifying elements. Renoir and Monet painted side by side at that spot, and their compositions and placement of boats and figures on water-surrounded platforms are almost identical, except that Renoir gives somewhat more prominence to the figures.

During that time, as the supporter of his mistress Camille and her son Claude, Renoir struggled to make ends meet and often would borrow from Bazille. In 1870, he was drafted for the Franco-Prussian War. He believed that it was his duty to serve and was sent first to Bordeaux and later to Tarbes. Back in Paris by March 18, 1871, Renoir continued in the Impressionist manner through the 1870's. In his work he gave no indication of the political unrest of the times; his most ambitious paintings of the next years were of streets filled with leisurely strollers and of beautiful young people enjoying their carefree existence in the open air. *Dancing at the Moulin de la Galette, Montmarte* (1876) shows couples dancing at a popular open-air spot while other people converse and drink at the outdoor tables, a custom on Sunday afternoons. The crowd swirls about, with Renoir focusing on no single person or couple, giving a sense of randomness. Some figures are cut by the edge of the canvas. All seem to be enjoying themselves to the utmost, with no hint of anything troubling. Renoir once said, "The earth as the paradise of the gods, that is what I want to paint."

In 1874, Renoir took an active part in the organization of the Impressionist group and participated in some of the group's exhibitions. In spite of his adherence to what was then stylistically avant-garde, he also exhibited more conservative paintings at the salon and was commissioned to do portraits of prominent people. His portrait *Madame Charpentier and Her Children* (1878) was dignified and can be considered to be related to Impressionism mainly in the casual postures of the sitters. In the Charpentier circle he met Zola once again, as well as the author Alphonse Daudet, the critic Edmond de Goncourt, and the diplomat-banker Paul Bérard, who was to be a steadfast patron. From the mid-1870's, as Renoir began to obtain portrait commissions and as his pictures began to be collected, his circumstances improved.

In the spring of 1881, Renoir traveled to Algiers and then in the fall to Venice, Rome, and Naples, where he was impressed by the works of Raphael and by Pompeian frescoes. He became disaffected with his Impressionist involvement, convinced that he had lost much of his ability to draw. He said to the dealer Ambrose Vollard, "There is a greater variety of light outdoors than in the studio . . . because of this, light plays far too important a part, you have no time to work out the composition." Throughout the 1880's he gave figures a much firmer outline instead of partially dissolving them in light. He made preparatory drawings and grouped figures according to deliberate schemas, sometimes based on a specific monument of the past. The three sculpturesque nudes in *Les Grandes Baigneuses* (c. 1887) are based on a seventeenth century relief by François Girardon at Versailles. From 1888 on, his nudes became heavier, with broader hips, longer torsos, more-rounded legs, and smaller breasts, as he tried to capture something of the monumentality of the antique. In 1895, becoming interested in the plays of the ancient Greeks, he painted a series dealing with the Oedipus story.

Renoir, who so admired health, robustness, and joie de vivre, in later life had to cope with serious illness. In 1888, he visited Cézanne at Aix; Cézanne cared for him while he was ill. Arthritis combined with rheumatism became his chief affliction. In 1894, he began to walk with two canes. He traveled to various spas in the hope of finding a cure and wintered in the south. In 1913, he was confined to a wheelchair. Fortunately, after 1892 he had no financial worries, as a large one-man show that year at Durand-Ruel's proved a turning point. (Monet had introduced him to the dealer in the summer of 1872, and Durand-Ruel had done much in the 1880's to further the prices of Renoir's paintings.) Renoir also married rather late in life. His marriage with Aline Charigot in 1882 produced three sons: Pierre was born in 1885, Jean in 1893, and Claude in 1901.

In his children, Renoir found a new subject matter, yet he also continued to paint his radiant nudes, which in the 1890's were painted outside any environmental context and seemed to glow from within. Toward the end of Renoir's life, for example, as in the painting *Judgment of Paris* (1914), the nudes became bulbous and awkwardly heavy, perhaps reflecting the artist's own hampered mobility. Renoir also became engaged in sculpture from 1907. He was encouraged in this direction when he was visited that year by the sculptor Aristide Maillol, who did a bust of him. Renoir's sculptures are improvisations on his late paintings, with massive figures in slow movements. These include the *Judgment of Paris* (1916) and *Blacksmith (Fire)* (1916). As he was crippled and had little dexterity in his hands, Renoir made drawings for the design, and an assistant, adding and subtracting according to his directions, built up the model in clay. In 1918, Renoir because completely immobilized and had to be carried. Yet, before his death the next year, he made a last visit to the Louvre to see the old masters.

Summary

Although usually considered as one of the inner group of the French Impressionists, Renoir was in important ways atypical. Like the other painters, he portrayed (at first glance) the life of the times, but actually what he presented were young men and women in modern clothes acting as though they were in an arcadia devoid of the stresses of the day. In his evocation of a never-never land, he is as close, in spirit, to the rococo painters of the eighteenth century as he is to the Impressionists. Unlike the other Impressionists, Renoir makes little use of open spaces, sometimes expanding or con-

tracting to convey the tensions of modern life. Nor did he much explore flattenings, unusual perspectives, or cutting of figures (a device sometimes found in Renoir's paintings but seldom made much of). Renoir is perhaps best known for his paintings of figures rather than landscapes, unlike the other Impressionists. His paintings of nudes, especially, gained for him recognition, and his later nudes, with the unusual use of pigments providing a glowing, curiously weightless look, have provoked much interest.

Bibliography

Barnes, Albert C., and Violette De Mazia. *The Art of Renoir.* New York: Minton, Balch, 1935. By the noted and eccentric collector who amassed some two hundred paintings by Renoir. Barnes sees Renoir as an artist of the first rank. The text, however, is full of flowery phraseology and vague terminology. Barnes makes comparisons with Cézanne and others in his attempt to fit Renoir into a quasi-abstract mold.

Bent, Geoffrey. "Charm's Tenuous Truths." *The North American Review* 283, no. 3-4 (May-Au-gust, 1998). Short assessment of Renoir's career, his relationship with impressionism, and his need to please portrait clients.

Groom, Gloria. "Portraits by Renoir." *USA Today* 126, no. 2630 (November, 1997). Profile of Renoir and his career as a portrait painter.

Renoir, Auguste. *Pierre Auguste Renoir.* Introduction by Walter Pach. New York: Abrams, 1950; London: Idelhurst Press, 1951. Includes large, excellent color plates. Discusses Renoir's handling of his subjects, his use of color, and his composition.

Renoir, Jean. *Renoir, My Father.* Translated by Randolph Weaver and Dorothy Weaver. Boston: Little Brown, 1962. The artist's son, a film director, recounts his father's life, touching on the artist's friends, travels, tastes, and beliefs. The reproductions are few and in black and white, but the volume includes photographs of the artist and his family, and pictures of Manet, Camille Pissarro, and Cézanne.

"Special Section: A Renoir Symposium." *Art in America* 74 (March, 1986): 102-125. Includes the responses of various scholars to the 1986

Renoir retrospective held at the Grand Palais in Paris, the National Gallery in London, and the Museum of Fine Arts in Boston. Suggests that Renoir's reputation seems either to be on the wane or undergoing a major reassessment (with greater importance, for example, accorded the late glowing nudes).

Wadley, Nicholas, ed. *Renoir: A Retrospective.* New York: Levin, 1987. This authoritative work has contemporary accounts and evaluations.

Wheldon, Keith. *Renoir and His Art.* London and New York: Hamlyn, 1975. A brief but readable account of the life and development of Renoir's art. Includes comments from such scholars as John Rewald and Fritz Novotny. About half of the 102 plates are in color and some are full-page reproductions.

White, Barbara E. *Renoir: His Life, Art, and Letters.* New York: Abrams, 1984. White's work is useful because of its color illustrations, but its chief value lies in its use of Renoir's correspondence. White sees much of Renoir's work as derived from Monet and others.

Abraham A. Davidson

CECIL RHODES

Born: July 5, 1853; Bishop Stortford, Hertfordshire, England
Died: March 26, 1902; Muizenberg, Cape Colony,
South Africa
Areas of Achievement: Business and colonial administration
Contribution: Exponent of British colonization and
domination in the world, Rhodes was a business
tycoon who dominated the world's diamond supply and a benefactor who used wealth to establish the Rhodes scholarships.

Early Life

Cecil John Rhodes was born on July 5, 1853, at
Bishop Stortford, Hertfordshire, the fifth son of
the parish vicar, Francis William Rhodes, and his
second wife, Louisa Peacock. The family consisted of nine sons, four of whom entered the army,
and two daughters; none of the children was ever
wed. Cecil attended the local grammar school
from 1861 to 1869 but was not an outstanding student. At sixteen, his health failed, and, rather than
entering university, he was sent to South Africa.
Rhodes landed at Durban on October 1, 1870, and
proceeded to join his eldest brother, Herbert, who
had migrated to Natal and was seeking to grow
cotton there. Herbert was frequently absent from
the farm, and thus while still in his teens, Cecil
was made responsible for the management of the
operation.

Even at this early age, Rhodes indicated those
managerial skills that would make him a success in
the diamond and gold fields of southern Africa. In
his spare time he continued a private reading program, for Rhodes had made a decision: He would
one day return to England and pay his own way
through Oxford University. These dreams, however, were momentarily circumvented. Diamonds had
been discovered in the Orange Free State, in what
ultimately became known as the Kimberley Division. Herbert left cotton farming for diamond prospecting in January, 1871, and Cecil followed him
in October. In the fresh air of the high African
veldt, the younger Rhodes recovered his health.
The fear of tuberculosis that had originally taken
him to Africa was never to plague him again, as
long as he remained there, although he soon was to
manifest a heart condition that would ultimately
cost him his life. The next decade in Rhodes's life
was to be extraordinarily complex, alternating between managing the brothers' interests in diamonds and, after 1873, matriculating at Oxford.

In October, 1873, after modest success in the
Kimberley fields, Rhodes returned to Great Britain
to fulfill his ambition of attending Oxford. Although frustrated in his desire to attend University
College, he was recommended to and was able to
gain entry into Oriel. During this first term at Oxford, Rhodes caught a chill and was diagnosed as
having only six months to live; he therefore interrupted his education to return to Africa, where his
lungs were no longer a problem. Over the next several years, increasing involvement in business matters in Africa prevented his returning to Oxford full
time, but he kept terms whenever possible and as a
result of his determination was able to pass the
B.A. examination in 1881. As in his grammar
schooling, Rhodes was not a scholar, but these
years were significant in the formation of his outlook on life.

Rhodes devoured and absorbed books or ideas
that appealed to him. Three authors and their ideas
made a deep impression on the Oxford undergraduate: Aristotle's *Ethics* emphasized man developing his facilities to their fullest, Edward Gibbon's
*The History of the Decline and Fall of the Roman
Empire* (1776-1788) provided Rhodes with a creed
that the Roman imperium had fallen on nineteenth
century Great Britain's shoulders, and John
Ruskin's lectures outlined a gospel of public service. These ideas were absorbed at Oxford, and no
later experiences seem to have altered these impressions; in fact, experience seems to have
strengthened them in his faith, and their influence
is to be seen in the first of his wills, in 1877.

The young Rhodes is described by his contemporaries as a slender youth, retiring in nature and
with absolutely no interest in women. Maturity
was to increase his stature; he became a six-footer
with a broad chest and a massive head with wavy
brown hair that became white in his later years.
Rhodes was not what would normally be considered a good speaker, seeming to dream aloud, but
he was an effective one, as indicated by his ability
to persuade men to his way of thinking.

Life's Work

While pursuing his education, Rhodes's African
career made rapid progress, and he soon was to
identify completely with the subcontinent. From

1874 on, he was in partnership with Charles Dunell Rudd, and gradually these two increased their Kimberley holdings, concentrating their efforts on one of the two major mines, the De Beers mine. Rhodes quickly proved to be one of the shrewdest and ablest speculators in the district, with one major rival in Barney Barnato. The year 1874 was a difficult one in Kimberley; illness attacked the miners and problems in the mines forced many to give up, but Rhodes persevered and took advantage of others' problems to acquire their concessions. Both Rhodes and Barnato recognized the basic problem within the diamond industry: As long as individual miners produced diamonds and sold them on an unregulated market, no real progress was possible. Both saw in an amalgamation of the mines and regulation of supply (and thus of price) the solution to the industry's problems. To this end, on April 1, 1880, Rhodes and his associates formed the De Beers Mining Company, with £200,000 in capital.

This was not Rhodes's only dream. In 1875, he spent eight months traveling through Bechuanaland and the Transvaal on a trip that opened his eyes to the potential of central southern Africa and was to shape his vision of the African future. His dream was to secure this land for English occupation, to cooperate with the Dutch Boers inhabiting the Orange Free State and Transvaal, and ultimately, to create a federation of self-governing South African colonies under British rule—but not without the full assent and cooperation of the Boer population. Meanwhile, Rhodes had suffered his first serious heart attack and made his first will, dated September 19, 1877. Although several later wills would be drafted, Rhodes always adhered to the basic ideas expressed in this first one: his estate's assets were to be used to fund a society to promote

the extension of British rule throughout the world, the perfecting of a system of emigration from the United Kingdom and colonization by British subjects of all lands wherein the means of livelihood are attainable by energy, labour and enterprise, . . . the ultimate recovery of the United States of America as an integral part of the British Empire, the consolidation of the whole Empire, the inauguration of a system of Colonial Representation of the Imperial Parliament which may tend to weld together the disjointed members of the Empire, and finally the foundation of so great a power as to hereafter render wars impossible and promote the best interests of humanity.

These ideas were to dominate his life. Within this confession of faith may be seen his dream of a British-dominated South Africa, the nucleus of the Rhodes scholarships, and, fifty years before its realization, thinking that would produce the British Commonwealth of Nations.

Meanwhile, Rhodes had taken on another obligation. In 1880, Griqualand West was absorbed into Cape Colony, thus gaining representation in the Cape parliament. Cecil Rhodes was elected one of the two representatives for Barkly West in 1880, took his seat in the Cape legislature the following year, and was to represent that constituency for the remainder of his life. As a member of the Cape parliament, Rhodes sought to further his African dream, maintaining the widest degree of local self-government and simultaneously organizing and promoting British colonization as a means of extending British influence and domination over the land south of the central African lakes. He concentrated his initial efforts on obtaining British (or Cape) control over Bechuanaland, a vast inhospitable territory north of the Orange River through which ran the only practical route to the coveted northern lands—lands that were the object of German, Portuguese, and Transvaal Boer ambitions. An imperial protectorate was proclaimed over this region early in 1884, and a year later the southern portion of this territory became part of Cape Colony, with the northern portion remaining an imperial protectorate.

Within a year, new developments were to broaden Rhodes's horizons. In 1886, gold was discovered on the Rand in Transvaal, starting a gold rush which Rhodes was ultimately to join. Also, Rhodes was attracted to the vast expanse of territory north of the Limpopo River. This land, that of the Matabele under their king, Lobengula, became as Bechuanaland had been, the focus of attention for several powers, and on October 30, 1888, Lobengula signed a convention with the British granting them mineral rights to his land and promising to make no additional concessions. It became clear that the London government was not interested in additional costly colonial involvement, so Rhodes inquired if a chartered company would be acceptable. On this basis, the British South Africa Company was chartered July 13, 1889, with the right to develop land between the Limpopo and Zambesi Rivers, land which was soon named Rhodesia. Subsequently, this same company extended its interests beyond the Zambesi to the southern shore of Lake Tanganyika, in a further effort to bring all Africa from the Cape to Cairo under the British flag. These new acquisitions subsequently became Northern Rhodesia.

While these colonizing activities were being promoted, Rhodes was consolidating his position in the diamond mines. Gradually the De Beers Mining Company had been absorbing claims, as had Barnato at Kimberley, and it became obvious that sooner or later one of these entrepreneurs would have to absorb the other. In July, 1887, Rhodes bought out the assets of a French interest, and on March 13, 1888, Rhodes's and Barnato's interests were consolidated as the De Beers Consolidated Mines, with Rhodes as chairman. This company was not limited to producing and marketing diamonds; at Rhodes's insistence, it was authorized to acquire, settle, and exploit lands in Africa and to raise and maintain such military force as necessary in the pursuit of its objectives. It was Rhodes's companies, not the imperial or the Cape governments, that undertook the construction of a rail line into the interior as an initial step in Rhodes's dream of a Cape to Cairo railroad.

After less than a decade in the Cape parliament, Rhodes became prime minister in July, 1890, gaining and keeping power by the votes of both the British and the Boer. As prime minister, Rhodes sought to diminish as much as possible the interference of the British government in local affairs, but simultaneously he promoted the dream of an imperial federation. To this end he subscribed ten thousand pounds in 1888 to the Irish Home Rule movement; he believed Irish self-government was a necessary step on the road to imperial federation. The Cape prospered under Rhodes's leadership, but at the end of 1895 a decision was made and a course of action adopted that was to bring his downfall. Perhaps Rhodes believed that his heart condition doomed him to an early death and that to realize his dreams more impulsive steps had to be taken.

Rhodes had vainly sought the cooperation of Transvaal's president, Paul Kruger, to complete the South African federation. Relations were exacerbated by the Boer treatment of the foreign gold mine workers (the Uitlanders) of the Witwatersrand (at Johannesburg). Although these workers produced the wealth of the Transvaal, they were discriminated against and their needed mining supplies were heavily taxed. In December, 1895, the Uitlanders despaired of a peaceful resolution to their grievances and determined to seek reform by

violence; Rhodes was asked to support this endeavor and he agreed. A plan was worked out by which Uitlanders would rebel in Johannesburg and would ask for Cape assistance to make good their claims. Meanwhile, Rhodes had sent money and arms to the Uitlanders and simultaneously authorized Dr. Leander Starr Jameson to organize the force to respond to the Johannesburg appeal. Unfortunately, in the confusion, Jameson launched his invasion precipitously, on December 27, 1895, and his forces were defeated and captured by the Dutch within ten days. Although Rhodes had no direct responsibility for the raid, he resigned his premiership on January 6, 1896. A Cape investigation in the matter condemned Rhodes's actions, while absolving him of responsibility for the Jameson Raid; a British inquiry in 1897 found him guilty of grave breaches of duty as prime minister.

For the remainder of his life, Rhodes devoted himself to the development of Rhodesia and consolidating his loyal party in the Cape parliament. In 1896, he was personally involved in the pacification of the Matabele rebellion. With the outbreak of the South African War in October, 1899, Rhodes made his way to Kimberley and participated in the four-month siege of that city but emerged with his health broken. Business took him to Great Britain in 1901 and 1902, yet he returned to Africa to die in his adopted land at the age of forty-nine on March 26, 1902.

Summary

Cecil Rhodes's influence did not end with his death. His major legacy was the scholarships to Oxford that bear his name. Except for small personal bequests, the overwhelming bulk of his fortune of approximately six million pounds was left to public service. Part represents the Rhodes scholarships: two students from each state or territory in the United States, three from each of eighteen British colonies, and an additional fifteen from Germany were granted Oxford scholarships. This plan was the final result of that boyish dream outlined in the first will of 1877 to create a society to promote Great Britain's worldwide position. Additional sums were left to Oriel College, and land was bequeathed to provide for a university in Rhodesia.

Although Rhodes's hasty actions in 1895 doomed the immediate federation of the two English colonies and two Dutch republics, this scheme remained in the forefront of his mind. The restoration of responsible government and the federation of the four states into the Union of South Africa in 1909 represented a posthumous and partial fulfillment of Rhodes's dreams. Developments in South Africa since 1960 have deviated from his dreams. Rather than becoming part of a British-dominated Africa, Bechuanaland and the two Rhodesias have become independent: Northern Rhodesia as Zambia (1964), Bechuanaland as Botswana (1966), and Southern Rhodesia as Zimbabwe (1980). Even Rhodes's beloved Cape (as a component of the Union of South Africa) declared its status as an independent republic in 1961, thus severing ties with Great Britain. The most important piece of legislation enacted during Rhodes's premiership has influenced attitudes toward Africans ever since. This act, the Glen Grey Act of 1894, provided the blueprint for the modern apartheid system adopted officially in 1948. Rhodes believed that the African must be disciplined by work and must be relegated to his own districts where he would be allowed to own property. No matter how much they might prosper, Africans would never gain the Cape franchise and would be allowed to vote only for their local councils. Thus the native homeland (Bantustan) policy of the South African government also stems from a decision reached by Rhodes.

Bibliography

Flint, John. *Cecil Rhodes*. Boston: Little Brown, 1974; London: Hutchinson, 1976. A volume in the Library of World Biography. Flint approaches his protagonist as a fascinating case study of a self-made man who bartered wealth for political power and who manipulated British imperialism for his own ends. Critical, with a low regard for Rhodes's abilities.

Galbraith, John S. *Crown and Charter: Early Years of the British South African Company*. Berkeley: University of California Press, 1974. Example of the newer specialized studies regarding Rhodes and his activities; focuses on the internal policies and motives of the British South Africa Company and suggests deceitful dealings by the company and its agents with the natives.

Gross, Felix. *Rhodes of Africa*. London: Cassell, 1956; New York: Praeger, 1957. Written by a South African journalist, this book lacks the documentation needed to support its generally critical approach to Rhodes; views him as an unscrupulous adventurer and hints at shady financial dealings and homosexual tendencies.

Millin, Sarah Gertrude. *Cecil Rhodes*. New York and London: Harper, 1933. A fair and impressionistic biography appropriate for the chaotic life of the subject; written by one who loved Africa as much as Rhodes did. More concerned with Rhodes's personal side than Williams is.

Porter, Bernard. *The Lion's Share: A Short History of British Imperialism, 1850-1983*. 3d ed. London and New York: Longman, 1996. Brief, judicious general history of the British Empire during the age of the New Imperialism, allowing comparison of Rhodes's activities in Africa with events in other areas.

Tamarkin, M. *Cecil Rhodes and the Cape Afrikaners: The Imperial Colossus and the Colonial Parish Pump*. London and Portland, Oreg.: Frank Cass, 1996. The author examines a previously neglected area of Rhodes' life: his political relationship with the Dutch/Afrikaan-speaking community in the Cape Colony.

Williams, Basil. *Cecil Rhodes*. London: Constable, and New York: Holt, 1921. The first academic study of Rhodes, written by an author who was acquainted with Rhodes and most of the personalities figuring in the biography. The work is not uncritical, especially of the Jameson Raid, but is still largely an apologia for Rhodes and his work.

Wilson, Monica, and Leonard Thompson, eds. *The Oxford History of South Africa*. 2 vols. Oxford: Clarendon Press, 1969; New York: Oxford University Press, 1971. The second volume, dealing with the period after 1870, is useful in providing a more detailed background than Porter does for Rhodes's career and his impact on South Africa.

Ronald O. Moore

DAVID RICARDO

Born: April 18, 1772; London, England
Died: September 11, 1823; Gatcombe Park, Gloucestershire, England
Area of Achievement: Economics
Contribution: Ricardo was the most influential of the early nineteenth century thinkers who formalized the growing science of economics. His impact on economics continues today, and Ricardo has been acknowledged as the father of political economy.

Early Life

David Ricardo's Jewish-Spanish ancestors had migrated to Italy and then to Holland prior to 1700. His father, Abraham Israel Ricardo, left Holland in his early twenties to visit England, where he remained. He became a citizen, married Abigail Delvalle, from a well-to-do Jewish merchant family, and established himself as a successful merchant-banker with a broker's license. The family was important in the London Jewish community. David was the third child, and third son, of fifteen children.

Groomed to enter the family business, David received practical schooling in England and then was sent to Holland to continue his education in a commercial school under the care of an uncle. After two years in Holland he returned to England for a final year of schooling, after which he entered his father's business, at the age of fourteen.

Ricardo soon became involved in high-level financing of bills of exchange and public securities, quickly becoming a respected participant in the world of finance. His ability, however, led to conflict with his father over the latter's role as chief of the family. When Ricardo reached the age of twenty-one, he married a Quaker woman, Priscilla Ann Wilkinson, and was instantly ostracized by his family. Priscilla, too, was ostracized, but with less severity. David never again had any dealings with his mother; he was removed from his godfather's will as of the date of the wedding. By 1810, he was, however, fully reconciled with his father.

Ricardo was a small man and well proportioned. His skin appears to have been darker than the typical Englishman's; his eyes were reported to evince intelligence and thoughtfulness. His voice was high and squeaky, perhaps an advantage in Parliament, since that made it distinct. Although he was not robust or athletic, he enjoyed good health.

Life's Work

Ricardo, in 1793, was on his own. He and Priscilla leased a house in the Kennington Place area of London, followed by two more nearby in the next three years—each larger than the last. Having begun speculating in the stock market prior to his marriage, he was respected by private bankers, who provided him with a line of credit.

In 1796, Ricardo expanded his interests, becoming an avid amateur mineralogist. (In 1807, he would be one of the first members of the Geological Society.) In 1799, while he and Priscilla were in Bath for her health, David read Adam Smith's *The Wealth of Nations* (1776), the first work on capitalist economics. He immediately took an interest in political economy, the subject that would become his area of achievement.

During the years of the wars with revolutionary and Napoleonic France, Ricardo was active in war finance through purchase of government bonds and the creation of the professionalized stock exchange. He also served as an officer in volunteer military units. As one of a thousand originators of the London Institution, an organization to promote science, literature, and the arts, he made friends with the publisher of the *Morning Chronicle*, James Perry.

In 1797, the British government had suspended gold payments and issued paper bank notes. The effects of bank failures and inflation had created a long-standing controversy identified as "paper against gold." Perry asked Ricardo to write about the issue, which he did in 1809, publishing an essay entitled "The Price of Gold." The next year, he published *The High Price of Bullion: A Proof of the Depreciation of Banknotes* and became a public figure. His next publication was *A Reply to Mr. Bosanquet's Practical Observation on the Report of the Bullion Committee* (1811), considered the best controversial work on an economic topic to that date. His argument in both pieces was that government should control the supply of paper currency to reflect accurately the value of gold bullion. Ricardo, the successful man of finance, had become the public theorist.

By 1809, Ricardo was active in the Unitarian church. Priscilla and the children eventually became Anglicans, but David would not do so. He was attracted to Unitarianism for its respect for reasoned toleration.

With escalating costs as the war with France neared its end in 1815, Ricardo and others loyally continued to buy and deal in bonds. When Napoleon was finally defeated at Waterloo, the market soared, and Ricardo made a fortune. He purchased a grand London home—on land used for the American Embassy in the twentieth century—and the estate of Gatcombe in Gloucestershire, where as chief landholder he was expected to perform extensive community services. He also indulged in support of the arts, book collecting, educational reform, and intellectual discussions with such thinkers as Jeremy Bentham, James Mill (father of John Stuart Mill), and Thomas Malthus.

In 1815, Ricardo published his critique of the Corn Laws, *An Essay on the Influence of a Low Price of Corn on the Profits of Stock*. The Corn Laws were a means of guaranteeing English grain producers a high price for their products. Ricardo contended that they were an artificial interference with the workings of the market and thus benefited the landowner at the expense of everyone else.

By 1817, Ricardo had taken much of the profit from his war bonds and invested in other areas: in land, French bonds, and mortgages, which allowed him to retire from day-to-day business and devote time to other activities, including the writing of his *On the Principles of Political Economy and Taxation* (1817) and participation in Parliament.

On the Principles of Political Economy and Taxation was Ricardo's account of the growing discipline of economics. Ricardo propounded seven principles upon which an economy is based. First, the cost of production determines price. Second, the amount of labor required determines the value of an item. (This idea was based on Smith's "labor theory of value"; in the 1821 edition Ricardo conceded that the cost of production might also influence value.) The third principle described a rent theory based on Malthus' idea of population growth outstripping food production and wherein rent was the difference in price between the most and least productive acres. (Ricardo contended that this created permanent conflict between landowners and capitalists.) Further, for Ricardo there is a fixed supply of money for wages—the amount of capital in circulation—and as capital increases, population grows, more land is rented, capital profits shrink, and wages are lowered. Ricardo's fifth principle is that when wages fall below a minimum for survival, population drops as a result of war, pestilence, and disease (Malthus' contention). Ac-

cording to Ricardo's sixth principle, "diminishing returns" set in when capitalists must spend more on subsistence wages and therefore have less to invest and expand production. Ricardo's seventh and last principle is based on a quantity theory of money that projects rising prices resulting from an increased supply of gold, through domestic or foreign trade. These principles became the basis for economics as a scientific study, and some are at the heart of late twentieth century schools of thought.

In exchange for a four-thousand-pound fee and a large mortgage loan, Ricardo was given the House of Commons seat of Portarlington by the Earl of Portarlington. He took his seat in Parliament on February 26, 1819. His first speech, a month later, was on a bill to reform the Poor Laws. Not a great orator, Ricardo reluctantly joined in debate, but his wisdom on matters relating to economics was always in demand.

In 1820, Ricardo was reelected. He would retain his seat in the House of Commons until his death in 1823. His politics were decidedly those in support of tolerance, individual rights, and limits on the size of government. He attacked the Corn

Laws, usury laws, bounties, economic restrictions, and Robert Owen's pastoral Socialist schemes. He supported an annuity plan for the poor, the reduction of taxes, and the idea of paying off the national debt with a onetime tax on all land.

On July 12, 1822, Ricardo and family boarded a steamboat at the Tower of London steps and headed for the Continent for a five-month Grand Tour. The tour started in Amsterdam and extended to Leghorn, near Florence, Italy, where Spanish Jews had first migrated around 1600. In 1823, Ricardo was joined in Parliament by Joseph Hume, an advocate of the ideas of James Mill and Bentham. The two joined forces, voicing concern over the need for parliamentary reform. Ricardo began work on a plan to create a national bank (published after his death, in 1824). He also drew up plans for refurbishing Gatcombe. An earache, first noted in Italy, recurred early in September. Ricardo died of a mastoid infection near noon on September 11, 1823. He was buried in the churchyard at Hardenhuish.

Summary

David Ricardo managed in his lifetime to meld the world of finance with the life of the mind and the good of the body politic. Personally successful in business, he systematized the general principles of what would become the science of economics. Gifted in the practical, he contributed an original view on the theoretical. In the later years of his life, Ricardo expanded his interest to politics, tempering what he saw as the laws by which political economies worked with a concern for toleration, justice, and the public good.

Although his ideas have been superseded or modified by new theoretical approaches to economics, Ricardo managed to influence all positions on the economic spectrum, from the proponents of laissez-faire capitalism to those of socialism.

Bibliography

Grampp, William D. "Scots, Jews, and Subversives Among the Dismal Scientists." *Journal of Economic History* 36 (September, 1976): 543-571. An account of the abuse hurled at Ricardo and other political economists because they were Scots, Jews, or political radicals. Ricardo is shown to have been damned also for being a stockbroker.

Heilbroner, Robert L. *The Worldly Philosophers.* 6th ed. New York: Simon and Schuster, 1986. Chapter 4 is titled "The Gloomy Presentiments of Parson Malthus and David Ricardo." The gloom from Malthus concerns his theories on population. Ricardo is presented as a theorist dealing with abstractions—abstract workers, abstract capitalists. A good comparison of their ideas.

Henderson, John P., and John B. Davis. *The Life and Economics of David Ricardo.* Boston, Mass.: Kluwer, 1997. The first comprehensive intellectual biography of Ricardo. Henderson, an economist himself, examines Ricardo's life, his Sephardic background, his development and employment in the British financial markets, and his thoughts on rent and value.

Hollander, Jacob H. *David Ricardo: A Centenary Estimate.* Baltimore: Johns Hopkins University Press, 1910. From three lectures at Harvard University in 1910, Hollander's book is helpful in understanding the connection between later writings and his parliamentary activities.

Kuhn, W. E. *The Evolution of Economic Thought.* Cincinnati, Ohio: Southwestern, 1963. Includes a short sketch of Ricardo's life and contribution to economic ideas and public life. Also includes an analysis of Ricardo's monetary and banking theory in chapter 9.

Marshall, Alfred. *Principles of Economics.* 8th ed. London: Macmillan, 1920; Philadelphia: Porcupine Press, 1982. A discussion of the fundamental economic law of value. The human side of Ricardo is seen as a barrier to a clear exposition of his ideas. Marshall contends that Ricardo's unwillingness to repeat his ideas, to explain them in greater detail, led to errors of omission.

Minnis, A. J., et al, eds. *Essays on Ricardian Literature: In Honour of J. A. Burrow.* New York: Oxford University Press, and Oxford: Clarendon Press, 1997. A collection of essays that examines the influence of French culture on the Ricardian court, presents re-readings of familiar works, and relates the period's literature to the political and societal conditions of the time.

Ricardo, David. *The Works and Correspondence of David Ricardo.* Vol. 10, *Biographical Miscellany.* Edited by Piero Sraffa. Cambridge: Cambridge University Press, 1951; New York: Cambridge University Press, 1981. A collection of sketches and other personal data. The one source with some information about his physical appearance. A helpful volume of memorabilia. The most revealing personality glimpses, however, are in *Maria Edgeworth, Letters from England, 1813-1844*, edited by Christina Colvin (Oxford: Oxford University Press, 1971).

Weatherall, David. *David Ricardo: A Biography.* The Hague: Martinus Nijhoff, 1976. The most readable, human account. Particularly useful insights into the events that affected Ricardo and his times.

Lance Williams

HENRY HOBSON RICHARDSON

Born: September 29, 1838; Priestley plantation, St. James Parish, Louisiana

Died: April 27, 1886; Brookline, Massachusetts

Area of Achievement: Architecture

Contribution: By absorbing early medieval stylistic ideas, suffusing them with his own vision, and adapting them to the needs of his own time, Richardson earned his reputation as one of America's greatest architects.

Early Life

Henry Hobson Richardson had a distinguished ancestor, one of the founders of modern chemistry, Joseph Priestley, whose granddaughter Caroline married Henry Dickenson Richardson, a partner in a Louisiana cotton business, and gave birth to the future architect in 1838. The boy attended school in New Orleans and was destined for West Point, but the academy rejected him for stuttering. Having shown early promise in drawing and in mathematics, young Richardson entered Harvard College, with the goal of becoming a civil engineer. His academic work was unspectacular; his friendships, however, were constructive ones. He numbered among his friends Henry Adams, the future historian, and several young men who later helped him obtain commissions.

Richardson's Class of 1859 photograph shows wide-set eyes in a rather long, thin face with dark, wavy hair. Although he looked serious, his classmates found him buoyant and personable. Another photograph taken in Paris, where he decided to study architecture at the École des Beaux Arts upon his graduation, confirms contemporary accounts of him as tall, slim, and clean-shaven.

Returning to the United States at around the end of the Civil War, Richardson chose New York over his native Louisiana as the best location for a beginning architect. His first commission, in 1866, for a new Unitarian church in Springfield, Massachusetts, most likely arose from his college friendship with the son of an influential supporter of the project. In January of 1867, his career well launched, he married Julia Gorham Hayden, to whom he had been engaged since before his Parisian sojourn. The couple would have six children. Several factors—among them, early commissions in New England and the fact that his wife was a native of Cambridge, Massachusetts—suggested a move to the Boston area, and by 1874 the Richard-

sons had settled in Brookline, where he would continue to live and work.

Life's Work

The Romanesque qualities for which Richardson would become famous began to appear in the third church he designed, the Brattle Square Church in Boston's Back Bay, for which he won a competition in 1870. Taking advantage of local materials, he chose Roxbury puddingstone for this building, whose most original feature is its 176-foot corner tower, which has arches forming a carriageway at the bottom and smaller belfry arches above a frieze of sacramental figures, with a pyramidal roof. The tower is somewhat detached from the church, in the manner of the Italian campanile.

One indication of Richardson's spreading fame was a commission for the Buffalo State Hospital buildings, also in 1870. Another was his selection, two years later, as designer of Trinity Church in Boston's Copley Square, while the Brattle Square Church was still under construction nearby. Because this part of Boston is built on fill and is watery below the surface, the weight of the planned church required four thousand wooden piles beneath its foundation, and construction took more than three years. This elaborate project included a sanctuary and a parish house which Richardson connected to the church by an open cloister. Built of granite with brownstone trim from local quarries and topped with a red tile upper roof, the church forms a Greek cross with a central tower based on one in Salamanca, Spain, as adapted by Stanford White, then Richardson's assistant and later a noted architect. John La Farge, one of the premier artists of his time, designed the windows and interior decoration. It is an elaborate and colorful church, both inside and out, with elements of Gothic and high, round Romanesque arches, all of which exemplify Richardson's genius for combining and modifying different styles to produce a unique, self-expressive result. Although additions, many of them unfortunate, have altered the church since Richardson's time, it remains one of his most famous and admired structures.

Richardson enjoyed the opportunity to work at a time when small towns and cities in New England were seeking larger and more gracious public library buildings. Beginning in 1877, Richardson designed libraries for Woburn, North Easton, Quincy, and Malden, Massachusetts, as well as one for the University of Vermont. Although his fondness for massive structures ran counter to the American Library Association's standards for flexibility in library design, all of his library buildings remained in use more than a century later. The Thomas Crane Public Library in Quincy, of Quincy granite, again with brownstone trim, is the simplest and is generally considered his finest. It is a rectangular structure of three main parts: stack wing with tiered alcoves, central hall, and reading room. Its asymmetrical front entrance is a low, broad Syrian arch surmounted by a gable. To the left of the arch is a circular stair tower with a low, conical roof. Asymmetrical end gables mark both ends of the building, for which Richardson also designed the original furniture.

Richardson also designed two additions to his alma mater: Sever Hall (1878) and Austin Hall (1881). The former uses red brick to harmonize with the older architecture of Harvard Yard, while the latter, for Harvard Law School, is sandstone with an elaborately carved entry arch and interior fireplace. More than a century after its construction, Austin Hall continued to be used mainly for its original purpose. Most architectural historians date Richardson's maturity from the period in which these two educational buildings were designed, as well as the Crane Memorial Library (1880).

Richardson worked as a collaborator on the sprawling Albany, New York, capitol over a period of many years beginning in 1875, but his most personal monument in Albany is its City Hall, with a beautiful 202-foot corner tower, another design of 1880. In that year, construction began on a more unusual project, the Ames Monument in Wyoming, which commemorated two brothers' contributions to the completion and administration of the Union Pacific Railroad. It is a granite pyramid, sixty feet square at its base and sixty feet high, erected near the railroad's highest point above sea level. Medallions bearing busts of Oakes and Oliver Ames decorate the east and west faces, respectively. Twenty years after it was built, the railroad relocated to the south, and the nearby town of Sherman lost its economic base and disappeared. For most of the twentieth century, the monument has stood isolated and reachable only by secondary roads.

Other Richardsonian structures have fared worse. A number of his Massachusetts railroad stations have been demolished, others violently altered or allowed to fall into ruin; few continued as stations in the 1980's. His most celebrated commercial building, the Marshall Field Wholesale Store in Chicago, designed in 1885, was made of rock-faced red Missouri granite and red sandstone. Groups of windows were topped by arches at the fourth floor level of this seven-story building; narrower arches capped single rows of fifth-and sixth-story windows. The simplicity and harmonious proportions of this store can be admired today only in photographs, for, in 1930, the owner demolished it in favor of a parking lot.

Among his many other structures, Richardson designed a stone and a metal bridge in Boston's Fenway in the early 1880's, the Allegheny County courthouse and jail in Pittsburgh (1883-1884), and a considerable number of private residences, both of wood stone, large and small, from the East Coast to St. Louis. Two of the latter, the William Watts Sherman House in Newport, Rhode Island (1874), and the J. J. Glessner House in Chicago (1885), have, along with Trinity Church, Sever Hall, the Allegheny County buildings, and the New York State capitol, been designated National Historic Landmarks.

Like all prominent architects, Richardson had to face the problems of popularity. As his work expanded, so did his work force, and he found it necessary to delegate more authority and exercise less personal supervision over his projects. In the 1880's, he took on too much work, but he chose his assistants and construction firms carefully and would not tolerate shoddy work. Charles McKim and Stanford White of his office went on to renown in a firm of their own.

Richardson was a convivial man who enjoyed good company, good food, and good wine. Photographs of him in his maturity show the formerly slender architect to be a massive man with a full mustache and a bushy beard. One anecdote has three of his assistants standing together able to wrap themselves in one of his coats. Although his creative energy continued to flow, Bright's disease took its toll in his final years, increasingly limiting the mobility of a man whose work was frequently in progress in several scattered locations. In 1886, only a year after an *American Architect and Building News* poll rated five of his buildings among the ten finest in the United States, with Trinity Church first, and while his fame was finally reaching Europe, where American building had never been taken very seriously, Henry Hobson Richardson died at the age of forty-seven.

Summary

When Richardson began his work in the 1860's, civic buildings in the United States were likely to follow classical or Renaissance styles, churches often followed the Victorian Gothic, while commercial structures were most often mere utilitarian boxes. Thus, Richardson's boast that he would design anything from a chicken coop to a cathedral reflects no mere indiscriminate appetite for building but a rejection of outworn conventions and an affirmation that a developed architectural sensibility might apply itself to any sort of building. The more one studies the range of Richardson's work—public, commercial, religious, and private buildings—the more clearly they can be seen as the expression of his artistic vision. A suburban or village railroad station was to be taken as seriously as a church and was as worthy of beauty.

At the same time, Richardson did not neglect the requirements of the task at hand. He preserved his independence and would not yield to clients' notions that were inconsistent with his own ideas, but neither was he indifferent to their requirements. His buildings became more functional and less ornate as his career proceeded. His placement of windows, for example, was dictated not by formal requirements of the exterior façade only but by interior needs. Richardson was the first American architect to combine creativity of the highest order with receptiveness to the needs of contemporaries. In a period of divorce between aesthetic and utilitarian concerns, Richardson united them in his mature work.

His influence, powerful for several decades after his death, was not always beneficial. Certain features of his design—the arches, towers, and rough stone exteriors—were easy to imitate, but the Richardsonian integrity that fused these and other less obvious elements into an artistic whole was not. In the years following his death, some of the most notable architectural talents occupied themselves with the requirements of the skyscraper, which implied not great masses of masonry but skeletons of steel and lower floor windows on a scale incompatible with typical Richardsonian materials and designs. Although it is difficult to determine what contribution Richardson might have made had he lived longer, the work he left did not point toward the twentieth century. In large American cities, even Boston, which resisted it into the 1960's, the skyscraper became an economic inevitability. The glassy John Hancock Building now dwarfs nearby Trinity Church. Richardson's greatest commercial building, the Field Store, was wiped out as an anachronism as early as 1930 in downtown Chicago. Vast bland airports have supplanted Richardson's railroad stations as symbols of America on the move.

In recent decades, however, the value of Richardson buildings has been recognized more widely. The National Historic Landmark Program, which began in 1960, and the National Register of Historic Places Program, dating from 1966, offer substantial protection, the National Register including thirty-two of Richardson's works. The harmony and solid beauty of his best churches, libraries, and private homes continue to answer human needs left unsatisfied by the buildings which have come to dominate urban skylines.

Bibliography

Breisch, Kenneth A. *Henry Hobson Richardson and the Small Public Library in America: A Study in Typology.* Cambridge, Mass.: MIT Press, 1997. The author examines Richardson's designs for public libraries in Massachusetts and Michigan, the role of philanthropy in library construction, and the role of librarians in the development of library planning which often was in opposition to the desires of the architects.

Gill, Brendan. "A Fast Full Life." *The New Yorker* 73, no. 46 (February 9, 1998). A profile of Richardson and his career in architecture.

Hitchcock, Henry-Russell. *The Architecture of H. H. Richardson and His Times.* New York: Museum of Modern Art, 1936. The most thorough of the twentieth century studies of Richardson's work, this book contains some biographical facts and a learned, if often dogmatic, evaluation of his subject's significance.

———. *Richardson as a Victorian Architect.* Northampton, Mass.: Smith College Pamphlets, 1966. A lecture based on a seminar given at Harvard University in 1965. Hitchcock adroitly relates Richardson's work to the diverse strands that make up the complicated conception that is "Victorian architecture."

Mumford, Lewis. *The Brown Decades: A Study of the Arts in America 1865-1895.* New York: Harcourt Brace, 1931. Mumford argues that Richardson, in using metal skeletons in two of his late commercial buildings, laid the basis for bridging the gap between stone construction and the ensuing steel-and-glass age. An eloquent appreciation of Richardson's contribution to his profession.

Ochsner, Jeffrey Karl. *H. H. Richardson: Complete Architectural Works*. Cambridge, Mass.: MIT Press, 1982. This handsome book includes not only photographs and plans of proposed and completed Richardson projects but also views of the author and his studios which provide valuable insights into his working habits. Biographical information is restricted chiefly to the details of his business life. Extensive bibliographies and appendices showing the locations of his buildings and indicating their preservation status mark this meticulously researched volume.

O'Gorman, James F. *H. H. Richardson and His Office: Selected Drawings*. Cambridge, Mass.: Department of Printing and Graphic Arts, Harvard College Library, 1974. The thirty-page introductory essay by the most productive Richardsonian scholar since Hitchcock is particularly useful for its attention to the architect's working methods.

Roper, Laura Wood. *F. L. O.: A Biography of Frederick Law Olmsted*. Baltimore and London: Johns Hopkins University Press, 1974. Scattered references to Richardson and also a detailed account of the happy collaboration of Richardson with the greatest landscape architect of his time.

Russell, John. "Henry Hobson Richardson." *American Heritage* 32 (October, November, 1981): 48-59. A lively and beautifully illustrated essay by an art critic who sees Richardson as the transformer—even the creator—of the architectural profession in the United States.

Van Rensselaer, Marianna Griswold. *Henry Hobson Richardson and His Works*. Boston: Houghton Mifflin, 1888. All students of Richardson are heavily indebted to Van Rensselaer, who wrote the only true biography of a man whom she knew personally and whose work she understood thoroughly. Commissioned as a tribute to Richardson shortly after his death, the book remains a readable and valuable account of his works. Virtually all of the limited personal information to be had about its subject is to be found here.

Robert P. Ellis

ARTHUR RIMBAUD

Born: October 20, 1854; Charleville, France
Died: November 10, 1891; Marseilles, France
Area of Achievement: Literature
Contribution: Rimbaud became one of the most influential of the French Symbolist poets through his vigorous writings and his dramatic personal history.

Early Life

Jean-Nicholas-Arthur Rimbaud was born in Charleville, near the Belgian border, the family's second son. His parents were Frédéric Rimbaud, a career army officer, and Vitalie Cuif, an austerely devout and conscientious woman of peasant stock. Captain Rimbaud was seldom at the family home in Charleville. In September, 1860, after several violent clashes with his wife, he left the family forever.

Madame Rimbaud reared her children to be examples of propriety and devoted herself to the complete control of their thoughts and actions. The eldest child, Frédéric, was slow, but Arthur showed early promise. The boys entered school together in 1861. In 1865, they were transferred to the Collège de Charleville. Arthur soon outstripped his brother academically, met outstanding success in all studies but mathematics, and won an overwhelming list of year's end prizes.

The young Rimbaud is described as angelic, with blue eyes and round cheeks—an ideal schoolboy. Madame Rimbaud separated her sons from the other boys at school, but eventually they found a long-term friend in Ernest Delahaye, later to be Rimbaud's biographer. Rimbaud's skill in French prose composition and Latin verse won for him the respect of his classmates. The principal of the *collège* indulged him, lent books to his prodigy, and enjoyed Rimbaud's success in academic competitions.

By early 1870, Rimbaud was leading a double life. Outwardly obedient, he read voraciously in all periods and points of view and formed a global view based on revolution against middle-class norms. He hoped to become a journalist and escape his mother, with whom he identified all civil and religious restrictions. He shared long walks with Delahaye, with whom he read and discussed poetry. Several of his Latin poems had already been published when his first long piece of French verse appeared in January, 1870. In the same month,

Georges Izambard joined the faculty of the *collège* as a teacher of rhetoric. Izambard was very young, a political liberal, and a poet in his own right. He encouraged Rimbaud, lent him books, and discussed poetry with him. Through him, Rimbaud met Paul Bretagne, a friend of the famous poet Paul Verlaine. The boy was intoxicated by this link with Paris and found an outlet in poems celebrating nature and poetic aspirations as well as satires on the good bourgeois of Charleville.

On July 18, Napoleon III declared war on Prussia. When classes ended, Izambard left Charleville. Rimbaud's older brother ran away to follow the army. Delahaye was his only resource. Isolated, disgusted by bourgeois patriotism, and determined to rebel, Rimbaud ran away. On August 29, he made his first attempt, which ended with imprisonment in Paris for traveling without a ticket. Izambard posted bail and returned him to his mother. Between October, 1870, and April, 1871, he ran away three more times. Many poems written during this period are violent, revolutionary attacks on bourgeois society and the national government. The sixteen-year-old Rimbaud was probably in Paris in late April, 1871, during the last days of the Paris Commune, but left before the Thiers government retook the capital in the "bloody week" of May 7-14. During this stay, the runaway schoolboy witnessed wild scenes and possibly suffered homosexual rape. He also knew hunger and exposure and returned home ill and filthy. His personality and behavior had undergone a dramatic change. He was now determined to break his own ties to normal life.

Life's Work

On May 13 and 15, 1871, Rimbaud wrote his "Lettre du voyant" ("Seer Letter"), tumbling verses and exhortations as he described his ideal visionary poet. The Seer must reach new visions by a reasoned dismantling of all senses and create a new language, in which the senses join to shape material and poetic futures. No suffering or self-sacrifice is too great to reach this end, and other horrible workers will carry on after the individual's death. In a catalog of French poets of the past, Rimbaud heaps scorn on most but names Verlaine a Seer and true poet. Although Rimbaud had not yet met Verlaine, in September, 1871, he twice sent him poems and confided in him as an admired master. Verlaine, who was twenty-seven years old, married, and soon to be a father, was living with his in-laws. He took up a collection, sent for Rimbaud, and offered him temporary lodging with his wife's family. Rimbaud's single most famous poem, "Le Bateau ivre" ("The Drunken Boat"), was written as an introduction to Parisian poets before he left Charleville.

The inflexible young poet was immediately recognized by Verlaine's circle as a sort of evil angel and genius. He bent all of his energies to fulfilling his ideal of the Seer in his own life and Verlaine's. He provoked a series of violent confrontations with Verlaine's friends and family, moved from lodging to lodging, occasionally on the streets, returned to Charleville, but always urged the older man to free himself from his settled life. On July 7, 1872, the two poets left Paris for Belgium and continued to London, where they installed themselves and began to learn English. Their relationship was marked by frequent violent quarrels, separations, and Verlaine's illness. In the course of the year ending July, 1873, the older poet saw himself hopelessly alienated from his wife and the French literary world. In her suit for legal separation, Mathilde Verlaine accused him of homosexuality, a charge he always denied. Leaving Rimbaud penniless in London on July 3, 1873, Verlaine went to Brussels, with the plan either to reconcile with his wife or kill himself. He was joined in Belgium by his mother and Rimbaud. On July 10, Verlaine shot Rimbaud in the left arm. He was arrested on Rimbaud's complaint and spent eighteen months in Belgian prisons. He was released in January, 1875.

Most of Rimbaud's major verse works were written during the two years spent in close contact with Verlaine. Those years were spent in the hardest kind of living, supported by money from Verlaine's mother, with alcohol and hashish used as tools in a deliberate dismantling of his mind for poetry's sake. He had begun work on prose poems, which Verlaine would later publish as *Les Illuminations* (1886; *Illuminations*, 1932). He had written a major piece, "La Chasse Spirituelle" (the spiritual chase), now lost. During a period in Charleville, he had begun *Une Saison en enfer* (1873; *A Season in Hell*, 1932). Verlaine's arrest shook him, and he tried unsuccessfully to withdraw charges; he then retired to his mother's farm in Roche, where he finished *A Season in Hell*. This work, published in October, 1873, is the only book Rimbaud ever saw into print. He obtained at the print-

er's only a dozen copies; the rest of the printing was discovered in storage there in 1901. He left one copy at Verlaine's prison and embarked for Paris with the intention of distributing the rest in the hope of favorable reviews.

Although Verlaine was older and known as a violent drunk, Rimbaud was blamed for his imprisonment and was ostracized by Parisian literary circles. Their hostility led him to burn his copies of *A Season in Hell* when he returned to Roche. Many believe this to be the end of his literary life. Evidence suggests, however, that he continued working on prose poems after the publication of *A Season in Hell*, during a stay in London with the Provençal poet Germain Nouveau in the spring of 1874. This partnership ended abruptly when Nouveau realized the degree of ostracism awaiting Rimbaud's friends. Verlaine and Nouveau both were involved in copying Rimbaud's works, and it is almost entirely through Verlaine's efforts that Rimbaud's verse and *Illuminations* were published.

Sometime during the months following the departure of Nouveau, Rimbaud stopped writing literature. From 1875 to 1880, the former poet traveled. He studied German in Stuttgart, crossed the winter Alps on foot, visited Austria and Italy, and wandered with a Scandinavian circus. He went as far as Java in the Dutch colonial army, then deserted and worked his way to Europe on ship. Illness sent him home more than once. He studied piano and foreign languages, and even taught. He worked as an overseer for an engineering firm on Cyprus in 1878. In the end, he became a merchant working out of Aden and Harar in Africa, first as an agent for a French firm (beginning in 1880) and eventually on his own, trading in gold, coffee, skins, guns, and small goods for local consumption. He was one of the first white men to travel into the Shoa region of Ethiopia. The facts of his African years have less impact than the aura of adventure they lend his life. When he died of generalized carcinoma in Marseilles, the phenomenal spread of his literary reputation had just begun, and his absence from the scene enhanced public appreciation of his work.

Summary

Arthur Rimbaud's role as a literary meteor, a sort of fallen angel, was enough to guarantee for him a place as an icon of modern poetry. A large school of admirers, among them the great Christian poet Paul Claudel, saw him as a supreme example of spiritual adventure, a poet who pushed the quest for faith to its ultimate limits. An equally ardent school of thought sees the young poet as an unrepentant, Luciferian rebel. The study of Rimbaud's writings, with their shattering power of imagination, involves the reader in an absorbing enigma—the contemplation of language pursued into silence. Even though his work spanned barely five years, it can hardly be matched. Few walk away from Rimbaud in indifference.

Bibliography

Fowlie, Wallace. *Rimbaud*. Chicago: University of Chicago Press, 1965. This elegantly written work is especially focused on *Illuminations*. It gives an outline of Rimbaud's life, coupled with detailed literary and psychological analysis of key Rimbaud texts. Includes a selected bibliography.

Macklin, Gerald M. "Prayer and Parody in Rimbaud's 'Devotion.'" *French Studies* 51, no. 3 (July, 1997). The author analyzes Rimbaud's poem, "Devotion" including its structure, cadence, and themes.

Nunley, Charles. "Adieu, Arthur Rimbaud: A Future for Syntax in 'Le Parti pris des choses.'" *The Romantic Review* 87, no. 3 (May, 1996). Comparison of Frances Ponge's prose poetry and Rimbaud's work.

Petitfils, Pierre. *Rimbaud*. Translated by Alan Sheridan. Charlottesville: University Press of Virginia, 1987. The most complete of the Rimbaud biographies available in English. A thoroughly scholarly, yet accessible work which argues for an essential unity in Rimbaud's years as a poet and his mature life. The author does not analyze Rimbaud's writings as literature, but as evidence in the study of his life. An extensive bibliography is included.

Rimbaud, Arthur. *Complete Works, Selected Letters*. Translated with an introduction by Wallace Fowlie. Chicago: University of Chicago Press, 1966; London: University of Chicago Press, 1975. This is the translation of Rimbaud's poems used by Pierre Petitfils in his *Rimbaud*, reposing on the solid basis of Fowlie's long studies of the poet and his period.

St.-Aubyn, F. C. *Arthur Rimbaud*. Boston: Twayne, 1975. Part of Twayne's World Authors series, intended for undergraduate student research. Includes a chronology, a short biography, and an annotated bibliography.

Starkie, Enid. *Arthur Rimbaud*. Rev. ed. London: Faber, and New York: Norton, 1961. The standard English Rimbaud biographer for many years, Starkie writes from an intimate psychological viewpoint about the works and life of the poet. A short bibliography is included.

Wilson, Edmund. *Axel's Castle: A Study in the Imaginative Literature of 1870-1930*. New York and London: Scribner, 1936. The prominent American literary critic relates the life and work of Rimbaud to the literary movements of his day. The French poet is thus juxtaposed to William Butler Yeats, T. S. Eliot, and Gertrude Stein. Somewhat dated but still valuable.

Anne W. Sienkewicz

NIKOLAY RIMSKY-KORSAKOV

Born: March 18, 1844; Tikhvin, Russia
Died: June 21, 1908; Lyubensk, St. Petersburg, Russia
Area of Achievement: Music
Contribution: One of the greatest and most prolific of Russian composers, Rimsky-Korsakov embodied in his music the nationalist spirit which was so important an element in late nineteenth century Russian culture. He composed fifteen operas, in addition to symphonies, concerti, chamber music, and solo pieces for piano and voice.

Early Life

Nikolay Rimsky-Korsakov was born into a gentry family in the town of Tikhvin (then in the government of Novgorod) on March 18, 1844. Although he demonstrated an early aptitude for music, family tradition required that he pursue a service career, and in 1856 he entered the Imperial Russian Navy, remaining on active duty until 1865. Somehow, however, he managed to compose. He had early made the acquaintance of Mily Alekseyevich Balakirev and, in time, sent him the manuscript of a first symphony, for which the latter arranged a public performance in December, 1865.

From 1865 onward, Rimsky-Korsakov lived almost continuously in St. Petersburg, displaying an enviable ability to compose with an ease and rapidity which would characterize his entire career, for there was little of the artist's angst in him. He soon became one of the group known as "the Five" or "the Mighty Handful"—the others were Balakirev, Aleksandr Borodin, César Antonovich Cui, and Modest Mussorgsky—all of whom were dedicated to the creation of a distinctly Russian musical idiom. With the premiere of his first opera, *Pskovityanka* (1873; *The Maid of Pskov*), Rimsky-Korsakov's place among contemporary Russian composers was assured. Two years earlier, in 1871, he had been appointed the professor of composition and instrumentation at the St. Petersburg Conservatory, a position which he would occupy, except for a few months in 1905, for the remainder of his life. In 1874, he took over from Balakirev as director and conductor of the Free School Concerts, an arrangement which continued until 1881, and between 1886 and 1900 he was conductor of the newly established Russian Symphony concerts. By then, however, Rimsky-Korsakov had emerged as indubitably the most prolific of the Mighty Handful. He was blessed with a creative energy, a fluency of invention, and a melodic prodigality which, together with his devotion to traditional Russian folk song and folk melody, made him the embodiment of that phase of late nineteenth century Russian culture in which so many writers, artists, and musicians sought a return to a pre-Petrine Slavic heritage.

Rimsky-Korsakov experimented with most forms of musical composition, and although the bulk of his output was operatic, he wrote three symphonies, several symphonic suites, concerti for various instruments, a respectable corpus of chamber music (including three string quartets), solo pieces for the piano, choral works, and many songs. *Antar* (his second symphony, composed in 1868), *Skazka: A Fairy Tale* (1879-1880), *Capriccio espagnol* (1887), *Scheherazade* (1888), as well as the *Russian Easter Festival Overture* (1888) have remained perennial favorites. All exemplify Rimsky-Korsakov's qualities as a composer—me-

lodic inventiveness, strong rhythms, and brilliant orchestration.

Life's Work

It is primarily as a composer of operas that Rimsky-Korsakov occupies his prominent place in Russian music. He completed fifteen operas, and, of these, only three have non-Russian subject matter: *Mozart and Salieri*, based upon Alexander Pushkin's poem (first performed in Moscow in 1898); *Servilia*, based upon a Roman play by the popular contemporary dramatist Lev Mey (first performed in St. Petersburg in 1902); and *Pan Voyevoda*, with a Polish setting (first performed in St. Petersburg in 1904). His first opera, *The Maid of Pskov*, was also based upon a play by Mey. *The Maid of Pskov* is based upon a true episode, Ivan the Terrible's visitation upon the city in 1569, and the czar himself is one of Rimsky-Korsakov's most successful character roles. It was a favorite role with the famous bass Fyodor Chaliapin, and Rimsky-Korsakov thought him inimitable in it.

His second complete opera, *Maskaya noch* (*May Night*), based upon a story by Nikolai Gogol, was well received at its premiere at the Maryinsky in 1880. Two years later, in 1882, the Maryinsky witnessed the opening of what is perhaps his best-loved opera, *Snegurochka* (*The Snow Maiden*). Rimsky-Korsakov himself was extremely pleased with this work, in which he believed he had achieved for the first time a smooth-flowing recitative and in which the vocal writing as a whole constituted an advance upon his earlier work. *The Snow Maiden* was followed by *Mlada* (1892), *Christmas Eve* (1895), based upon a story by Gogol, and the magnificent, sprawling *Sadko* (1898), constructed from material taken from the *bylini*, the epic songs of medieval Russia, all three exemplifying his love of fantasy, folklore, and the fairy tale. In 1898, he returned to the subject matter of his first opera, *The Maid of Pskov*, and set to music Mey's original prologue, *Boyarinya Vera Sheloga*. It received its premiere in Moscow later that same year.

Rimsky-Korsakov now felt himself ready to fulfill a long-standing ambition, the composition of an opera based upon the subject matter of Mey's play, *Tsarskaya nevesta* (*The Tsar's Bride*). For this, he seems to have intended something rather different from his earlier operas. "The style of this opera," he declared, "was to be cantilena par excellence; the arias and soliloquies were planned for development within the limits of the dramatic situation; I had in mind vocal ensembles, genuine, finished and not at all in the form of any casual and fleeting linking of voices with others. . . ." *The Tsar's Bride* was given its premiere in Moscow in 1899. Moscow was also the location for the opening nights of *Skazka o tsare Saltane* (1900; *The Tale of Tsar Saltan*), based upon a poem by Pushkin, and the rarely performed *Kashchey bessmertny* (1902; *Kashchey the Immortal*). By then, however, Rimsky-Korsakov was absorbed in the composition of what is widely regarded as his greatest work, *Skazaniye o nevidimom grade kitezhe i deve Fevroniy* (1907; *The Legend of the Invisible City of Kitezh and the Maid Fevronia*), a story linking the thirteenth century Mongol invasion of Russia, the legend of Saint Fevronia of Murom, and the pagan animism of pre-Christian Russia on which he had previously drawn for *The Snow Maiden*. The result was a work of profound spirituality, which has been called, not inappropriately, the Russian *Parsifal*. It had its premiere at the Maryinsky in 1907, while the composer was at work upon his last opera, *Zolotoy petushok* (1909; *The Golden Cockerel*).

Among Soviet audiences, Rimsky-Korsakov's operas (of which *The Snow Maiden*, *Sadko*, *The Legend of the Invisible City of Kitezh and the Maid Fevronia*, and *The Golden Cockerel* may be regarded as the most original) enjoy enormous popularity. Outside the Soviet Union, they have not traveled well and are best known in the West through a series of brilliant orchestral suites (those of *Mlada*, *Christmas Eve*, *The Tale of Tsar Saltan*, and *The Golden Cockerel*).

Summary

Nikolay Rimsky-Korsakov's role in the development of Russian music was seminal, for in addition to his numerous compositions which now occupy a secure niche in the concert halls and opera houses of the Soviet Union and the world, he left his mark upon Russian music in two other ways. Because he possessed a temperament which did not feel threatened by creativity in others and because of his genuine interest in the work of fellow composers, he willingly undertook the completion of a number of important works by others left unfinished at the time of their deaths. No less significant for the future, his many years as a teacher at the St. Petersburg Conservatory meant that, for the last three decades of the nineteenth century and for the opening years of the twentieth, few young Russian instrumentalists or composers did not have firsthand exposure to him both as an instructor and as a generous, nurturing mentor.

A man of great personal integrity, a liberal, and a staunch opponent of the virulent anti-Semitism which flourished during the reigns of the last two czars, Rimsky-Korsakov found himself increasingly alienated from a regime in which reaction had replaced reform. In March, 1905, he sent a letter to the periodical *Rus* urging the case for the autonomy of the conservatory from the control of the Imperial Russian Musical Academy. He also sent an open letter to the director of the conservatory protesting police surveillance of the students. As a result of these actions, he was summarily dismissed from the professorship which he had held for thirty-four years. That was not the end of the matter, however, for his dismissal prompted the resignation from the faculty of, among others, Aleksandr Glazunov and Anatoly Lyadov. Before the end of the year, the conservatory attained sufficient independence to elect Glazunov its new director and, shortly thereafter, Rimsky-Korsakov was reinstated.

This episode does not seem to have interfered with Rimsky-Korsakov's habitually busy schedule. During the summer of 1905, he revised and supervised the printing of *The Legend of the Invisible City of Kitezh and the Maid Fevronia*, which had its premiere in 1907, and during 1906-1907 he worked on *The Golden Cockerel*. Then the censor intervened, ordering the omission of the entire introduction, the epilogue, and forty-five lines of the text. It has been suggested that the ban was motivated by the opera's subject matter, that the misadventures of the foolish King Dodon could be interpreted as a satire on the czar's court or his disastrous mismanagement of the Russo-Japanese War of 1905, but it is more likely that it was retribution for his publicly expressed liberal sentiments. Rimsky-Korsakov never saw *The Golden Cockerel* staged, for he died on June 21, 1908. Its first performance was given in Moscow in October, 1909.

Bibliography

Abraham, Gerald. *Essays in Russian and East European Music.* Oxford: Clarendon Press, and New York: Oxford University Press, 1985. The relevant essays in this collection are "*Pskovityanya*: The Original Version of Rimsky-Korsakov's First Opera," "Satire and Symbolism in *The Golden Cockerel*," and "Arab Melodies in Rimsky-Korsakov and Borodin."

———. *Studies in Russian Music.* London: Reeves, 1935; New York: Scribner, 1936. This earlier collection of Abraham's essays includes "Rimsky-Korsakov's First Opera," "Rimsky-Korsakov's Gogol Operas," "Snegurochka (Snow Maiden)," "Sadko," "The Tsar's Bride," "Kitezh," and "The Golden Cockerel."

Borovsky, Victor. *Chaliapin: A Critical Biography.* New York: Knopf, 1988. This definitive biography of the great Russian bass describes how Chaliapin interpreted the roles of Ivan the Terrible in *The Maid of Pskov* and Antonio Salieri in *Mozart and Salieri.*

Calvocoressi, Michel D., and Gerald Abraham. *Masters of Russian Music.* New York: Knopf, and London: Duckworth, 1936. The best general account of Rimsky-Korsakov's life and work. Both scholarly and readable.

Quraishi, Ibrahim. "'Kitezh' and the Russian Notion of Oriental Despotism." *The Opera Quarterly* 13, no. 2 (Winter 1996). Analysis of Rimsky-Korsakov's opera "The Legend of the Invisible City of Kitezh and the Maiden Fevronia," and its commentary on oriental despotism.

Ridenour, Robert C. *Nationalism, Modernism, and Personal Rivalry in Nineteenth-Century Russian Music.* Ann Arbor, Mich.: UMI Research Press, 1981. A scholarly investigation of Rimsky-Korsakov's circle and their critics to 1873.

Rimsky-Korsakov, Nikolay Andreyevich. *My Musical Life.* Translated by Judah A. Joffe. New York: Knopf, 1923; London: Secker, 1924. Essential reading for understanding the outlook and personality of the composer.

Seroff, Victor I. *The Mighty Five: The Cradle of Russian National Music.* New York: Allen, Towne, 1948. A popular account of Rimsky-Korsakov's circle of colleagues and friends.

Taruskin, Richard. "The Case for Rimsky-Korsakov (part 2)." *Opera News* 56, no. 16 (May, 1992). Profile of Rimsky-Korsokov's career as a composer of operas.

———. "The Case for Rimsky-Korsakov (part 2)." *Opera News* 56, no. 17 (June, 1992). The author defends Rimsky-Korsakov's works and argues that he became more creative after the death of Tchaikovsky.

———. *Opera and Drama in Russia as Preached and Practiced in the 1860's.* Ann Arbor, Mich.: UMI Research Press, and Epping: Bowker, 1981. An important study of the theatrical background to the theory and practice of opera as developed among the Mighty Handful.

Gavin R. G. Hambly

ALBRECHT RITSCHL

Born: March 25, 1822; Berlin, Prussia
Died: March 20, 1889; Göttingen, Germany
Area of Achievement: Religion
Contribution: Ritschl contributed to the liberalizing of nineteenth century Protestant theology by moving its concerns away from the speculative, neo-Scholastic abstractions that the faithful could not understand toward a renewal of a practical examination of the life of Jesus Christ as revealed in the New Testament. Since Christ was the perfect manifestation of the love of God, believers could have a model upon which to make proper value judgments.

Early Life

Albrecht Ritschl came from a solid religious background. His father, Carl Ritschl, was a bishop and general superintendent of the Lutheran church in Pomerania, and the boy grew up in the town of Stettin. He was an excellent student throughout his preuniversity career, excelling in languages and science. His mind welcomed complex information, because it gave him an opportunity to see how complexity grew and came together to formulate antithetical arguments that endlessly repeated the process. It was no doubt his penchant for synthesis that drew him early to the revolutionary work of Georg Wilhelm Friedrich Hegel, the leading professor at the University of Berlin during the first part of the nineteenth century.

Ritschl pursued his education at a number of prestigious universities during the years from 1839 to 1846. He studied at the University of Bonn and Halle, where he received his Ph.D. in 1843 and then pursued postdoctoral work at Heidelburg and Tübingen, where he studied church history with one of its leading scholars, Ferdinand Christian Baur. Baur became, for the next ten years or so, Ritschl's major mentor and influence. Ritschl's earliest scholarly works came out of the deep influence of Baur and his Tübingen school, which was an amalgamation of theologians and biblical scholars and historians that had been highly influenced by Hegel and his so-called conflict model of human history. This model proposed that history, like all other components of naturalistic process, works itself out in terms of the convergence of conflicting elements which then fall into necessary opposition and then form a new synthesis of meaning. History, like everything else in nature, operates within the laws of process, and Hegel had delineated the terms of those laws in his famous model of thesis, antithesis, and synthesis.

It was this Hegelian method of Baur and the Tübingen school that had informed Ritschl's first major scholarly work, *Das Evangelium Marcions und das Kanonische Evangelium des Lucas* (1846; the Gospel of Marcion and the canonical Gospel of Luke), and the success of this work established his career at the University of Bonn, where he became a full professor in 1859 at the age of thirty-seven. While this early work on the Gospel of Luke broke no new scholarly ground, it was an intelligently reasoned and lucidly written examination done within the mode of the Tübingen school of radical New Testament criticism.

It was Ritschl's next book, however, that broke all ties to Baur and his followers. During the years following the publication of his highly abstract book on the Gospel of Luke, Ritschl became increasingly disillusioned and disturbed at the intensified metaphysical approaches that theological and biblical studies were following. With each new theoretical-speculative volume emerging, the laity, the community of Christian believers, was being left behind, buried in the impossibly complex language and heady intellectualism of German scholarship.

Ritschl had found, however, an anchor and antidote to the cause of the increasing abstraction, Hegelian historical process, and he discovered it during the writing of his next book, which concerned the intellectual and spiritual ethos of the early Christianity of the first and second centuries. He performed a simple process of laying the emphasis on the first word, the adjective "historical" and removing it from the word "process." He found that the solid ground of history could save him from involvement in the endless speculative abstractions of the Hegelian dialectic. His next study was of the early Church Fathers and led him, historically, to the earliest forms of Christianity. He found that the closer Christianity came to the temporal and physical proximity of Jesus Christ—and to the earliest apostles and Church Fathers, the roots of the faith—the simpler and more pristine the message of Christianity became. History, then, stopped the Hegelian cyclic process and led him back linearly to the essential simplicity of the message of the Gospels. Once Ritschl disengaged himself from this cyclic model of history and attached himself to a linear model, he found relief in the bedrock of history.

In the second edition (1857) of his *Die Entstehung der altkatholischen Kirche* (1850; the rise of the old Catholic church), he announced the dramatic break, both personal and intellectual, with his mentor Ferdinand Baur. The move was a shattering blow to his former teacher. Two years later, Ritschl was appointed a full professor at the University of Bonn, rejecting similar offers from such prestigious schools as Strasbourg and Berlin. He became, then, the principal founder and exponent of what would be known as the liberal Protestant theological school that took root and flourished until just after World War I.

Life's Work

Ritschl's work after his major break with Baur proceeded with a serious redirection and reevaluation of the whole Christian enterprise. Once he found the anchor of hope in reinstating the historical Jesus Christ as the principal model for a Christian lifestyle and direction, a linearly sanctioned one at that, he was able to develop the major tenets of his revolutionary project. His basic working premise was the adaptation of a view regarding the moral nature of man that was new within the basic beliefs of Christianity: "In every religion what is sought, with the help of the superhuman spiritual power reverenced by man, is a solution of the contradiction in which man finds himself as both a part of nature and a spiritual personality claiming to dominate nature." Although this was his definitive statement of his views on man's moral nature made in his next work, the monumental three-volume study *Die christiliche Lehre von der Rechtfertigung und Versöhnuns* (1870-1874; *The Christian Doctrine of Justification and Reconciliation*, 1872-1900), his lectures and publications from 1857 through the 1860's thoroughly embodied this view.

What Ritschl had done, in effect, was to move Christianity away from its persistent and losing battles with two of its primary demons: the overly intellectualized speculations of natural philosophy on one hand, and the emotionalism of Pietism, on the other. Indeed, Ritschl's second major three-volume work was his definitive attack on such emotional subjectivism. Ritschl had to concede Immanuel Kant's proposition that man was unable to show evidence of or prove through any rational arguments the existence of God and, therefore, what

a Christian's duty is to God. Therefore, he was forced to discard the overly neat proofs of God's existence simply because they started from outside personal Christianity and built on general ideas unconnected either with biblical revelation or with a living Christian faith.

What was left for the sincere Christian was the other end of the philosophical spectrum: subjectivism and its expression, mysticism. Without rational proof of God's existence and influence in the world, the seeker after God is left with his own subjective responses and feelings about his experiences and, therefore, runs the risk of mistaking the knowledge of his own religious consciousness for some kind of valid knowledge of God. Ritschl, having found a way back to the authentic roots of Christianity via history, leaps over the mystical and rationalistic barriers and exhorts the Christian to return to the original message of the New Testament as it was presented by Martin Luther himself. The original message is available, he argued, in the life and revelation of Jesus Christ directly observed through a rigorously historical examination of the texts themselves.

In short, what Ritschl offered was an enfreshened vision of the very purpose of Christianity. Religion should stop engaging in fruitless searches for direct knowledge of God. Kant proved such efforts hopeless. Man must also admit that he is part of nature and, therefore, a divided being who must constantly war with his natural impulses. Yet he is also gifted with two qualities that lift him above mere beast consciousness: self-consciousness and the ability to assign value to his actions. He is capable of making moral and ethical choices which the lower animals are not. Those gifts qualify him, then, to assume moral domination in the world which, as a Christian, he is obliged to do.

In positing these enlightened views on the moral nature of man, Ritschl does away with several key Christian beliefs. He reveals unmistakably Romantic views when he dismisses the Calvinist view of man's innate depravity. Man, he believes, is basically good but must continually war with his animal impulses. With one dramatic gesture, Ritschl does away with Satan, original sin, and innate depravity. Man is, however, a divided being who needs the example of Jesus Christ, who bridged the gulf between his animal and spiritual impulses. Out of man's recognition of his plight, he derives his sense of obligation to rule over the natural world, to take dominion and stewardship over it, and to attempt to shape it into what he called the "Kingdom of God on earth."

Ritschl, in his magnum opus, *The Christian Doctrine of Justification and Reconciliation*, changed the older, guilt-laden term "justification," which had earlier meant the "forgiveness of sins," to mean the lifting of "guilt-consciousness" and a consequent bridging of the gulf between God and man. The second stage of the transforming operation he called "reconciliation," God's free act of mending the split between God and man through the life example and death of Jesus Christ. It was the original intention of the great Protestant Reformers, he claims, to restore "justification and reconciliation" to their previous central positions within early Christianity and to tap its infinitely vital energies and use them to renew the original force and meaning of Christianity.

The first volume of the work delineated the various propositions he used to make his points. The third volume lays out what the results and effects of the reorganization of the entire Christian enterprise will be. If Christianity returns to the early pragmatic interpretation of "justification and reconciliation" based upon replacing the knowledge about God with the practical revelations made in the life of Jesus Christ and recoverable through a historical study of the New Testament, the possibility of an ethical human community comes into being.

By 1864, Ritschl had moved to the University of Göttingen as a full professor, where he finished his two major works and taught not only biblical subjects but also dogmatics and ethics. His last twenty-five years at Göttingen brought forth his full powers as both a thinker and a writer. He died quietly there on March 20, 1889.

Summary

The achievement of Albrecht Ritschl was so significant in the late nineteenth and early twentieth centuries that theologians have invented a term called "Ritschlianism." Unquestionably, Ritschl became the most famous proponent of the new liberal Protestant theology during those years. His major works, *The Christian Doctrine of Justification and Reconciliation* and *Geschichte des Pietismus* (1880-1886; the history of Pietism), brought Protestant theology into the modern era by denying the validity of its endless oscillations between highly abstract, speculative debate over whether God can be known and how He can be known and the over-ly subjective, emotional, and mystical avenues into the divine mystery. Before Ritschl could approach these seemingly insurmountable projects, he first had to admit that Kant had been correct and that Christianity was forced to discard any remaining vestiges of natural philosophy. History must replace metaphysical speculation as an avenue to certainty, but a certainty only verified through action, not ideas. Jesus Christ's life and death immediately, simultaneously, and permanently effected justification and reconciliation and created the possibility of an ethical human community.

Bibliography

Barth, Karl. *Protestant Thought: From Rousseau to Ritschl*. Translated by Brian Cozens. New York: Harper, and London: SCM Press, 1959. Although renowned for a brutal attack on Ritschl and other liberal Protestant theologians, Barth nevertheless delivers a brilliant summary of all the various theological schools leading up to Ritschl and places him at the conclusion of a tradition that was summarily destroyed by World War I.

Heron, Alasdair I. C. *A Century of Protestant Theology*. London: Lutterworth, and Philadelphia: Westminster Press, 1980. In a chapter devoted to Friedrich Schleiermacher and Ritschl, the author clearly distinguishes their unique contributions but shows that Ritschl was forced to reject the older theologian's overemphasis on what came to be called "the theology of feeling." Succinct and highly informative.

Lotz, David W. *Ritschl and Luther: A Fresh Perspective on Albrecht Ritschl's Theology in the Light of His Luther Study*. Nashville: Abingdon Press, 1974. Lotz devoted much time and energy to shedding light on exactly what Ritschl derived from his own deep study of Martin Luther's major contributions to theology, particularly Luther's interpretations and explanations of the terms "justification and reconciliation."

Mackintosh, H. R. *Types of Modern Theology: Schleiermacher to Barth*. London: Nisbet, and New York: Scribner, 1937. The first and, perhaps, still the most comprehensive treatment of Ritschl that is not an entire book. Mackintosh clearly places Ritschl in a nineteenth century tradition and shows how he emerges from Schleiermacher, corrects him, and creates the way for other important theologians. There are many points in Ritschl's approach that clearly disturb

Mackintosh, but he explicates him with fairness and equanimity. Highly recommended.

Richmond, James. *Ritschl, a Reappraisal: A Study in Systematic Theology*. London and New York: Collins, 1978. Richmond shows how theologians are reviving Ritschl since he seems to have so closely adumbrated the more existential modern theologians. This is one of several correctives to certain Barthian neoorthodox criticisms.

Tillich, Paul. *Perspectives on Nineteenth and Twentieth Century Protestant Theology*. Edited with an introduction by Carl E. Braaten. New York: Harper, and London: SCM Press, 1967. Although he does not offer a comprehensive treatment of Ritschl, Tillich discusses Ritschl's influence on American theology long after it seemed dead in Germany. He credits the Ritschlians with introducing Kantianism into theology and labeling Kant the philosopher of Protestantism. Highly informative and intelligent.

Patrick Meanor

JOHN D. ROCKEFELLER

Born: July 8, 1839; Richford, New York
Died: May 23, 1937; Ormond Beach, Florida
Areas of Achievement: Industry and philanthropy
Contribution: One of the major industrialists and philanthropists in the history of the United States, Rockefeller pioneered in bringing a new scale to business organization through his phenomenally successful Standard Oil Company; he also brought a new scale to philanthropic giving.

Early Life

John Davison Rockefeller was born on July 8, 1839, in Richford, New York, to Eliza Davison and William Avery Rockefeller. His father owned a farm and traded commodities, such as salt and lumber. The family, which included John's older sister, two younger sisters, and two younger brothers, moved frequently: first to Moravia, New York; then to Owego, New York; and finally, to Cleveland, Ohio. John's education was irregular, but he studied hard and did have two years at Cleveland High School. His father, who by that time had become a wandering vendor of patent medicine, encouraged him to go into business. John especially liked mathematics, and he took a three-month course in bookkeeping at Folsom's Commercial College.

In selecting a job, Rockefeller was not as much interested in the salary as he was in the possibilities a position offered for learning about the business world. He selected a large and diversified merchant firm and started as a bookkeeper at a salary of $3.50 per week. After three and a half years, he left to form his own wholesale grain and grocery business with Maurice B. Clark. Together, the two had only four thousand dollars; during their first year, however, they grossed $450,000 and netted a fourteen-hundred-dollar profit. The following year, the Civil War began. The war gave Rockefeller, along with a number of other leading postwar industrialists, the opportunity to make his initial pile of money. Business at Cleveland-based Clark and Rockefeller boomed with major orders coming in from the army, other cities, and Europe. Rather than miss these business opportunities fighting in the Civil War, Rockefeller avoided the draft by paying for a substitute to fight in his place.

During these early business years, Rockefeller displayed the character traits and personal life-style that would be with him throughout his life. A devout Baptist, Rockefeller remained active in that church, even after becoming fabulously successful in business. For years, he taught Sunday school and served on church boards with streetcar conductors and other working-class people He also took seriously the biblical injunction to give away one-tenth of what he earned, even when starting out at a very low salary. He lived simply, had few pleasures, and was devoted to his family. In 1864, he married Laura Celestia Spelman, whose father was a prosperous businessman. Eventually, they had four children who lived to adulthood: three daughters, Bessie, Alta, and Edith, and a son, John D. Rockefeller II, of whom his father was quite proud. The family lived in a large, comfortable, but not ostentatious house in Cleveland until moving to New York in the 1880's. Rockefeller instilled a sense of industry and public responsibility in his offspring that extended down to the third and fourth generations, producing one vice president (Nelson) and three state governors (Nelson of New York, Winthrop of Arkansas, and John D. IV of West Virginia). Of all the leading American industrial families, the Rockefeller dynasty became the most remarkable.

Life's Work

It was possible for John D. Rockefeller to gain a monopolistic fortune in the oil business because of certain conditions that existed at that time. Oil was first used for medicinal purposes. Yet oil strikes in Pennsylvania in the 1850's greatly increased the supply. To find other uses for the product, the Pennsylvania Rock Oil Company hired Yale chemist Benjamin Silliman, Jr. Silliman discovered that oil could be distilled into kerosene for burning in lamps, and he also noted its lubricating qualities. At the time, oil was obtained by skimming off what floated on the surface of water-filled ditches and springs. With other uses, however, drilling quickly became economically viable. Independent oil wells and small-scale refineries sprang up in great profusion in northwestern Pennsylvania, and refineries also proliferated in Cleveland. The oil business was chaotic, with numerous small operators, overproduction, cutthroat competition, and alternating periods of boom and bust. Rockefeller perceived that whoever could bring order to this industry could make a fabulous fortune.

In 1863, Rockefeller began his involvement with the oil business. He and his wholesale grocery partners, along with refining expert Samuel Andrews, built a refinery in Cleveland. His wholesale grocery partners proved too cautious for Rockefeller's taste. In 1865, he decided to buy out the three Clark brothers, get entirely out of the wholesale grocery business, and devote himself to oil. By the end of the year, the firm of Rockefeller and Andrews had an oil refinery that was producing at least twice as much as any other single refinery of Cleveland's nearly thirty refineries.

Rockefeller prospered more than his competitors because of his foresight, attention to detail, emphasis on efficiency, lack of toleration for waste, and growing reputation as a successful businessman. These qualities allowed him to borrow heavily from bankers and to attract partners who brought additional capital to his firm. Henry M. Flagler joined Rockefeller in 1867, bringing with him a substantial amount of money and the ability to negotiate ever lower railroad shipping rates. Railroad rates were unregulated then, with railroads commonly giving favored shippers rebates on their publicly stated rates. The larger the shipper, the more favorable the rate. Rockefeller was able to play two railroads off against each other and water transportation off against the railroads. In turn, his lower shipping rates allowed him to undersell his competitors, steadily driving them out of business.

Meanwhile, Rockefeller implemented a policy of vertical integration. To cut his firm's dependence on related businesses, he began making his own barrels and then bought his own timber tracts to supply his cooperage plant. He owned his warehouses, bought his own tank cars, and, to the extent possible, owned or produced the raw materials and transportation he needed to operate. Finally, he fought waste by using kerosene by-products to become the oil industry's leading producer of paraffin and machine lubricants.

In 1870, to accommodate additional growth, Rockefeller converted his partnership into a joint-stock corporation, the Standard Oil Company of Ohio. Meanwhile, Thomas A. Scott of the Pennsylvania Railroad began organizing certain railroads, oil refiners, and well owners into the infamous South Improvement Company. The purpose was to form a monopoly and get rebates on their competitors' shipments. The public reaction was hostile, and the South Improvement Company quickly lost its charter. Rockefeller had been part of this

scheme, which badly tarnished his reputation. Yet, through the South Improvement Company, he acquired another wealthy partner, Cleveland refiner Oliver H. Payne.

Furthermore, Standard Oil decided to proceed on its own to create a monopoly in the oil business. Early in 1872, Rockefeller offered to buy out nearly all remaining Cleveland oil refineries. Owners could either accept a cash offer, take the offer in Standard Oil stock, or be driven out of business. With the South Improvement Company still a live entity and given the size of Standard Oil itself, most refiners sold out. Some claimed that they had been pressured into taking less than their businesses were worth, but those who acquired Standard stock did make small fortunes. Rockefeller accomplished this takeover of his Cleveland competitors in three months. From Cleveland, Standard then proceeded to acquire refineries in Pittsburgh, in Philadelphia, and on Long Island. By 1875, the firm was refining half of the oil products in the United States. Rockefeller's next step was to gain control of pipelines, oil terminals, kerosene distributors, and additional plants. He also attracted rival oilman John D. Archbold to his firm. By 1878, Rockefeller had secured his monopolistic position.

During the 1880's, Standard Oil continued to grow. The firm acquired new oil fields, built new refineries, and developed new refining methods. Under the direction of John's brother, William Rockefeller, the firm also expanded into the international market. Standard Oil products were a familiar sight in Asia, Africa, South America, and even Central Europe, where Standard encountered stiff competition from cheap Russian oil. Also, Standard Oil pioneered in corporate organization. Rockefeller employed the best legal talent to devise the concept of the trust. That meant that the stock of Standard's subsidiaries and related companies was combined with Standard's stock, new certificates were issued, and an executive committee with Rockefeller at the head assumed control. During 1883-1884, he transferred the corporate headquarters to New York City. Yet Standard Oil never took total control of the oil industry. While accounting for eighty to ninety percent of oil produced in the United States and making substantial profits, Standard did lower the price of its products. Rockefeller had stabilized a chaotic industry.

In the process, Rockefeller became very powerful and was feared and vilified. The lack of railroad rate regulation did much to make his monopoly possible. Unfair railroad rates upset many more people than Rockefeller's business competitors. The public began agitating for railroad rate regulation, first at the state level and then for the Interstate Commerce Act, passed in 1887. Since that law was largely ineffective, agitation continued until railroad rates were finally effectively regulated in the twentieth century. Throughout this agitation, the outstanding example of how unregulated railroad rates could lead to powerful monopolies was Standard Oil. The New York legislature investigated the company in 1879 and again in 1888. Henry Demarest Lloyd published an exposé in the *Atlantic Monthly* in March, 1881. Congress sought to dampen the public's concern with the Sherman Antitrust Act of 1890. When that law went initially unenforced, muckrakers again attacked. The best-known exposé was Ida M. Tarbell's *History of the Standard Oil Company* (1904). Rockefeller always refused to respond directly to these attacks. His attitude was that his products spoke for themselves. Not until 1905 did Standard Oil hire its first public relations expert. Nevertheless, the federal government proceeded to prosecute Standard Oil for violating the Sherman Antitrust Act. Under court order, the company broke into smaller, separate companies in 1911.

Rockefeller's wealth at one point approached $900,000,000. What to do with all this money posed a dilemma. He invested in the stock market and, in the 1890's, gained control of the Mesabi Range, the richest iron ore field in the United States. Within a few years, however, he sold his Range holdings to Andrew Carnegie. Increasingly, his interests were turning to philanthropy, where his impact was tremendous.

At first, Rockefeller's gifts to hospitals, colleges, and other institutions were haphazard, and his gifts were sometimes misused. Soon, however, he began to apply some of his principles for making money—of attention to detail and organization—to giving money away. He virtually made the University of Chicago with a founding gift in 1889 of $600,000 and later gifts (some from his son) totaling $80,000,000. He created the Rockefeller Institute for Medical Research in 1901 and the General Education Board in 1902. The latter helped to revolutionize medical education, fought the spread of hookworm, and worked to improve Southern agriculture. His philanthropy was further systematized with the creation of the Rockefeller Foundation in 1913. He gave away more than a half billion dollars, and the influence of his philanthropic institutions has continued to grow after his death. Rockefeller had turned over active leadership of the Standard Oil Company in 1897 but lived until 1937, dying at the age of ninety-seven.

Summary

John D. Rockefeller succeeded as a businessman and a philanthropist in part because of his personal qualities and in part because of his times. He had an uncanny ability to identify and secure leading executive talent. The extreme care with which he made decisions was accompanied by a boldness of action and accuracy of vision unmatched in his field. Furthermore, he had the steadiness to compete in a rough, competitive, "survival of the fittest" environment where there were few laws and regulations. Indeed, he turned this freewheeling environment to his advantage. He was able to build Standard Oil because of such conditions as the general absence of effective railroad rate regulation and lack of an income tax. He went into the oil business at a time when it was taking off, and good luck was with him when the gasoline-powered automobile came along to increase demand. He regarded himself as a trustee of his wealth and became, perhaps, the outstanding philanthropist in the United States. Finally, he instilled an obligation for public service in his descendants. Of all the "robber barons" of his generation, his long-range impact may have been the greatest.

Bibliography

Abels, Jules. *The Rockefeller Billions: The Story of the World's Most Stupendous Fortune.* New York: Macmillan, 1965; London: Muller, 1967. Scholarly, readable, with a good selection of photographs of Rockefeller, his family, business associates, and houses. Generally, Abels is favorably disposed toward Rockefeller.

Carr, Albert A. *John D. Rockefeller's Secret Weapon.* New York: McGraw-Hill, 1962. Focuses on the role that the Union Tank Car Company, established by Rockefeller and the key to his transportation system, played in the success of Standard Oil. In 1891, the company became a separate corporation from Standard Oil in response to the Sherman Antitrust Act. Carr covers the history of Union Tank Car up to 1961.

Chernow, Ron. "Blessed Barons." *Time* 152, no. 23 (December 7, 1998). Profiles three American business tycoons: Rockefeller, J. P. Morgan, and

Andrew Carnegie. Discusses the contributions of each toward U.S. industrial leadership and their well-known philanthropic efforts.

———. *Titan: The Life of John D. Rockefeller, Sr.* New York: Random House, and London: Little Brown, 1998. Chernow creates a winning biography of Rockefeller, a combination of "godliness and greed, passion and fiendish cunning." Chernow attributes Rockefeller's dichotomous personality to his parents.

Collier, Peter, and David Horowitz. *The Rockefellers: An American Dynasty.* New York: Holt Rinehart, and London: Cape, 1976. The bulk of this book is on John D. Rockefeller's descendants, down through his great-grandchildren, the impact his fortune has had on them, and their sense of public responsibility.

Hawke, David F. *John D.: The Founding Father of the Rockefellers.* New York: Harper, 1980. A chatty, popular account, this slim volume is not too extensively footnoted but is based on archival sources along with more detailed secondary sources, especially Nevins' 1940 biography.

Josephson, Matthew. *The Robber Barons: The Great American Capitalists, 1861-1901.* New York: Harcourt Brace, 1934; London: Eyre and Spottiswoode, 1962. In this critical account, Rockefeller is only one among many late-nineteenth century industrialists, but the book is excellent for setting him in the context of his time. Josephson is critical of the business practices and extensive power of Rockefeller and his associates.

Nevins, Allan. *John D. Rockefeller: The Heroic Age of American Enterprise.* New York: Scribner, 1940. Nevins is the scholarly authority on Rockefeller. This two-volume work was the most comprehensive, carefully researched, and balanced source on Rockefeller until Nevins' 1953 book appeared.

———. *Study in Power: John D. Rockefeller, Industrialist and Philanthropist.* New York: Scribner, 1953. More of a second biography of his subject than a revision, this book incorporates material based on a large amount of documents not available to Nevins in his earlier biography; it also reflects a maturing of Nevins' analysis. Both Nevins biographies can be profitably consulted.

Judith Ann Trolander

AUGUSTE RODIN

Born: November 12, 1840; Paris, France
Died: November 17, 1917; Paris, France
Area of Achievement: Art
Contribution: One of the greatest sculptors of all time, Rodin has been hailed for both the monumentality and the psychological penetration of his sculpture. Much of his work has a kinetic quality, a dynamism that takes over the solid material of his sculpture, transforming it into the expression of a towering personality.

Early Life

Born the youngest of two children in a working-class home, Auguste Rodin was educated with great care under the supervision of his uncle in a friar's school until he was fourteen. By the age of ten, he had already shown an interest in drawing, and it was thought that he would become an artisan. His teachers were impressed with his dedication and talent and encouraged him to believe that he would one day become a fine artist. Yet his early years were not full of success. Indeed, he failed three times to gain acceptance at the École des Beaux-Arts, where he had hoped to study sculpture.

Working as a craftsman, Rodin studied on his own the work of Antoine-Louis Bayre (1795-1875), who was famous for his lifelike depictions of animals. He also assisted Albert-Ernest Carrier-Belleuse (1824-1887) in his studio, beginning in 1864, and closely followed developments in the world of contemporary sculpture. His early sculptures, one of his father (c. 1860) and one of Father Pierre-Julien Eymard (1863), already exhibit his dexterous and precise sense for the human face. Father Eymard, the superior of the Societas Sanctissimi Sacramenti, profoundly impressed and touched Rodin, who had stayed briefly in a cloister before deciding that the religious life did not suit him.

Still largely unacknowledged, Rodin traveled to Italy in 1875 to study the sculpture of Donatello and Michelangelo. Not being able to afford a long trip, he soon returned to France with great enthusiasm for the Italian masters, which resulted in his sculpture, *The Age of Bronze*, a work that was so lifelike he was accused of having taken a mold of a live model. Other artists came to his defense in what was to be the first of many controversies concerning Rodin's techniques and choices of subject matter.

By the late 1870's, the state was acquiring sculptures such as *Saint John the Baptist Preaching*, which were every bit as realistic as *The Age of Bronze*, for by now the temper of the age was beginning to swing Rodin's way, valuing precisely his uncanny ability to render the human figure in bronze as if it were alive. Rather than accepting traditional sculpture with stereotypical gestures, Rodin had accustomed his contemporaries to a startling, almost photographic depiction of the individual, of a peasant-faced Saint John, for example, crooking one finger of his extended right arm while dropping his left arm, slightly flexed, to his side. This portrait of man in action, in mid-stride, with a body that reflected an inner psychological life and purposiveness, was a stunning achievement.

Life's Work

Now a figure of considerable influence, Rodin was courted and given many commissions, including one which involved the decoration of a door for the future Museum of Decorative Arts. Inspired by Dante's *Inferno*, Rodin chose to create *The Gates of Hell*, a work of enormous ambition which he never finished and perhaps never could, for as William Hale notes, the sculptor took as his subject the creation of chaos itself. Kept in his studio until his death, the work reflects the artist's constant experimentations with style and his engagement with all the inchoate human desires that are never quite fulfilled.

Seated atop this magnificent work is the world-famous statue *The Thinker*. He is at once a perfectly realized and enigmatic figure. With his chin resting on his bent right hand, and his upper body leaning forward in somber meditation, he is evocative of a powerful human intellect but also of a brooding, perhaps dissatisfied nature for whom thought itself does not suffice. Various commentators have noted that this powerfully muscled figure is out of proportion—a deliberate ploy to increase the tension of the pose, to use physical power to suggest mental strength. Behind the thinker, in the tympanum, are the vacant-faced figures of the damned, engaged in their ghastly dance of death while other falling figures suggest horror and the frustration of failed lives. On the twenty-one-foot-tall door (thirteen feet wide and three feet deep), the artist uses the size of human figures (ranging from six inches to four feet) to portray the differentiated scale of a world of human sufferers.

Rodin repeatedly flouted his society's notion of what was dignified and presentable. His commissioned sculpture of Victor Hugo was rejected because he produced a seated rather than a standing figure. Even more bitterness was occasioned by his monument to Honoré de Balzac, which many of his contemporaries considered to be grotesque, a violent and swollen piece that was called "an obscenity," "a toad in a sack," "this lump of plaster kicked together by a lunatic," and the like. Rodin was aiming, however, not for a faithful likeness of his subject but for a visceral rendering of his extraordinary imagination and body of work. The sculptor pursued his subjects like a biographer, and in the case of Balzac went so far as to visit the places where the novelist's fiction was set. Balzac had died at the age of fifty-one, his body exhausted from having produced his novels so intensely and rapidly. Rodin contacted Balzac's tailor to get a measure of his clothes, he checked accounts of the writer's physical appearance, and he exercised his conception of the writer by sculpting more than twenty studies of his head and body. Many of these preliminary efforts were realistic portraits, as though Rodin preferred to work with the outward facts and burrow more deeply into his subject's interior life. The result was a huge figure with a bull neck, a distorted face, and an immense torso—the point being that here was an artist whose very physical presence was magnificently marked by the lives he had imagined. The statue was like a thing of nature, with the figure's features erupting from the surface like volcanic life itself.

Rodin's work in marble—*The Kiss* (1886), for example—has been more accessible and a great favorite with the public. A highly erotic man and artist, Rodin has accentuated the effect of the embrace by the angle he has chosen, which has the woman's right leg thrusting forward while the man's fingers touch her thigh. There is an equality in the embrace, a mutuality (emphasized by the touching of their feet and the entwinement of their legs) that seems perfect.

By 1900, Rodin was recognized as the foremost sculptor of his period. Soon he would travel to do a bust of George Bernard Shaw (1906) and sculptures of English and American notables. In 1905, forty-two of his works were exhibited in the Luxembourg Museum. He continued to innovate, creating human figures which emphasize his interest in the motion and position of bodies. By fragmenting these sculptures, taking away certain physical features, expressions, and bodily parts, he accentuated his art. His *Walking Man* is headless, because nothing must distract from his study of the shift in weight, the rhythm of musculature, and the placement of the feet—all of which contribute to an appreciation of how a man walks. Rodin believed in the principle of leaving out something, of an understatement that allows other features or themes to be seen more clearly.

Summary

Auguste Rodin was both a great scholar and a creator of art. No artist of his stature has exceeded his ability to learn from his predecessors. He was also very much a man of the nineteenth century, taking a profound interest in individual lives, treating his preparations for portrait sculpture the way a modern psychological biographer does his or her research and writing, amassing evidence but also probing for the heart of the subject. He welcomed new tools—the camera, for example—not only to record his work, to help him in modeling and studying his subjects, but also to assist him in capturing reality from new points of view.

There are many accounts of Rodin working in his studio. The biography by Fredric V. Grunfeld contains many passages that show how carefully Rodin studied the nude human body—not simply to attain accuracy of presentation but also to use physical details, the tone and the play of different muscle groups, to suggest mental and spiritual life. Rodin knew that he had to imbue outward forms with a sense of inner life. His statues are not static. They have the dynamism of Renaissance forms, of the works by Donatello that Rodin admired so profusely, but Rodin's work has something more: the pulsing of muscles that reflect interior energies. It is as if the sculptor makes what is invisible visible.

Notoriously slow in executing his commissions, Rodin was known to keep works many years past their deadlines, half-finished, awaiting his inspiration and his maturing conception of what the work could yield to him. In some cases, as in his work on Victor Hugo, he never did find the right form, the appropriate means of expression for his subject. In others, as with his work on Balzac, he was determined to shape a figure that revealed all he had to say about this titanic figure of literature.

Perhaps more than any other sculptor, Rodin concerned himself with sculpture and its relation-

ship to nature. His pieces are renowned for the way they take the light, for the artist's realization that the meaning of form depends upon how it reacts with its environment. A work that has no context, or does not create a context for itself, is a work that is only half-realized. Few great artists have matched Rodin's exquisite sense of the wholeness of art, of the perfect work that creates its own standards, its own way of measuring itself and the world around it.

Bibliography

Butler, Ruth. *Rodin: The Shape of Genius.* New Haven, Conn.: Yale University Press, 1993. The first major reinterpretation of Rodin's life in many years. Butler, a Rodin scholar, uses protected archives and letters to separate fact from fiction. Well-illustrated.

Champigneulle, Bernard. *Rodin.* London: Thames and Hudson, and New York: Abrams, 1967. A sound biographical and critical study, with superb black-and-white and color plates, notes, and a list of illustrations. No bibliography and only an inadequate index.

Elsen, Albert E. *In Rodin's Studio: A Photographic Record of Sculpture in the Making.* Oxford: Phaidon Press, and Ithaca, N.Y.: Cornell University Press, 1980. A fascinating study of the way Rodin used and was influenced by photography in the creation of his work. Photographs of Rodin and his studio, as well as of his work in various stages of composition, make this an extraordinarily valuable study.

Grunfeld, Frederic V. *Rodin: A Biography.* London: Hutchinson, and New York: Holt, 1987. The first full-scale biography of Rodin to appear since 1936. Grunfeld has found and taken advantage of many new sources. His huge book is well written, copiously illustrated, and enhanced by a very full bibliography, extensive notes, and a comprehensive index. Written for both scholars and a larger, general audience, this biography is essential reading.

Hale, William Harlan. *The World of Rodin, 1840-1917.* New York: Time-Life, 1969. A copiously illustrated, life-and-times approach to the artist's life which includes a chronology of artists, a bibliography, a comprehensive index, and "A Guide to the Gates of Hell," detailing the architectural features and figures of this complex masterpiece.

Rodin, Auguste. *Auguste Rodin: Erotic Watercolors.* Introduction by Anne-Marie Bonnet. Michael Robertson, trans. New York: Stewart, Tabori, and Chang, 1995. A collection of 107 watercolors of female nudes done by Rodin between 1890 and 1917, many of which were considered scandalous when first exhibited. Appropriate for connoisseurs of erotic art.

———. *Rodin Sculptures.* Selected by Ludwig Goldscheider. London: Phaidon Press, and New York: Tudor, 1964. Large, handsome black-and-white reproductions of Rodin's most important works. This work is enhanced by detailed notes on plates and succinct introductions to the artist's life and work.

Carl Rollyson

JOHN AUGUSTUS ROEBLING

Born: June 12, 1806; Mühlhausen, Thüringen,
    Confederation of the Rhine
Died: July 22, 1869; Brooklyn Heights, New York
Area of Achievement: Civil engineering
Contribution: An academically trained civil engi-
    neer who worked in the middle decades of the
    nineteenth century when such talents were rare
    in the United States, Roebling fully exploited the
    potentialities of the suspension bridge, placing
    the United States in the forefront in construction
    of long-span, stable, heavy-load-bearing bridges
    for generations.

Early Life

John Augustus Roebling was born on June 12,
1806, in Mühlhausen, Thüringen, one of the German states of the Confederation of the Rhine, incorporated into Prussia in 1815. Prussia, the second largest of the German states, was in most
respects the most advanced. Roebling's parents
were respected citizens of the ancient walled town,
which was rich in Gothic architecture that later became one of the motifs in Roebling's work. Mühlhausen similarly enjoyed a rich cultural heritage,
Johann Sebastian Bach, among other noted figures,
having worked there. Because rapidly growing
Berlin was Prussia's political and cultural center,
Roebling was sent to Berlin's Royal Polytechnic
School in 1822. When he was graduated in 1826,
he had studied civil engineering, architecture,
mathematics, and philosophy (under Georg Wilhelm Frederick Hegel) and completed a senior thesis on suspension bridges.

Life's Work

Upon graduation, Roebling was employed for the
next three years as a civil engineer on both public
and military works for the Prussian government.
Prussia, however, was an autocratic state in which
the liberal, republican views that were to take root
in the German state until 1848, views Roebling
shared, withered. Because of such opinions, Roebling was officially listed as a subversive, and his
career accordingly ended. Seeking a freer reign for
his career and for his political convictions, he emigrated to Saxonburg in eastern Pennsylvania. For
the next six years, he unsuccessfully attempted
farming. With the craze for internal improvements,
particularly for canals and railroads, in full swing
and trained engineers rare, Roebling returned to

engineering in 1837, initially as a surveyor for the
Beaver River Canal, then shortly afterward for the
Pennsylvania Railroad. The enormous anthracite
deposits of northeastern Pennsylvania, the frenzy
to find economical means of getting the coal to
market as it increasingly became the nation's principal domestic and industrial fuel, ensured a demand for bridges. In 1844, at the age of thirty-
eight, Roebling earned his first commission, partly
on the strength of his invention, in 1840, of a method of manufacturing wire-rope cable, essential for
stable, heavy-duty suspension work. His first
project, built to carry the Pennsylvania State Canal
across the Allegheny River at Pittsburgh, was a
suspension aqueduct for canal boats. Its masonry
towers foreshadowed an Egyptian motif later to re-
appear in the Brooklyn Bridge. Roebling's next
four commissions, also aqueducts, were for the
Delaware and Hudson Canal, a company then rede-
signing its anthracite-carrying canals from the
coalfields of northeastern Pennsylvania to tidewa-
ter ports better able to compete with railroads. All
were multispan suspension structures. Convenient
for navigation, they were built without falsework—
one of the advantages of suspension construction.
Each consisted of troughlike flumes capable of carrying boats of sixty or more tons. The flumes were
solidly embanked with fitted timbers and into
transverse floor beams, all buttressed with sidewall
trusses. As on the famed Delaware Aqueduct,
which remained in use until the 1970's, the shore
piers and masonry spans were company built. All
the suspension work and its loads were designed
and built by Roebling. Indeed, the Delaware Aqueduct was a handsome, thousand-foot span hung on
eight-and-one-half-inch wrought-iron cables.
Aware of the cable's coming importance, Roebling, in fact, founded his own wire-cable factory
in Trenton, New Jersey, in 1849, just prior to completion of his Delaware and Hudson commissions.

In the meantime, a fire in Pittsburgh and the destruction of the Monongahela River's Smithfield
Bridge in 1846 brought him a commission for his
first vehicular suspension bridge. With two shore
abutments and six river spans, it stretched fifteen
hundred feet. The deck was carried by wrought-
iron rods hung from wire cables, which Roebling
spun onshore. Until traffic weights became too
great, the bridge was in all regards a success, resulting, late in the 1850's, in construction of an

identical bridge over the Allegheny River at Pittsburgh's Sixth Street. In this case, however, there were two differences: First, Roebling spun his wire cable on the bridge; second, his son, Washington, joined him, thus inaugurating his own career.

In 1851, John Roebling undertook his greatest challenge yet: construction of a railway suspension bridge across the Niagara River at Niagara Falls, New York. After a brilliant career, Charles Ellet, Roebling's predecessor, resigned his commission for the job, effectively ending his career. Moreover, leading engineers in both the United States and Europe considered the task impossible. Roebling designed a double-decked structure: the upper one carrying the mainline of the Grand Trunk Railway and the Great Western Railway of Canada; the lower one serving normal vehicular traffic. The Niagara gorge was deep; the river was deep and swift; the span to be covered on an absolute level was 821 feet from shore to shore. Roebling's design consisted of four ten-inch cables, each of 3,640 wires, hung from masonry towers. Characteristically, the load was carried by the cables and reticulations of radiating stays. Roebling completed this, the first of the world's railway suspension bridges, in 1855.

Meanwhile, Roebling rebuilt an Ellet bridge at Wheeling, West Virginia, and by 1856, he had embarked on ten years of frustrations—finances, ice, floods, and war—constructing a twelve-hundred-foot span across the Ohio River between Cincinnati and Covington, Kentucky. Since its opening in January, 1867, nevertheless, with its design unaltered, it continues in use, an even greater tribute to his engineering genius, tenacity, and industry than his remarkable Niagara Bridge.

Roebling's last and monumental work was begun in 1867, with his appointment as chief engineer for the New York Bridge Company, whose objective was bridging the East River between lower Manhattan and Brooklyn, then two separate cities. The growth of each dictated a need for the most efficient connections. River traffic was enormous; rail and shipping connections were awkward and inefficient; and, though a tidal river, the East River severed both cities and halted traffic by freezing over or being covered with ice floes periodically. Proposals for a bridge began at least by 1811, and, in 1857, Roebling made his own bid. The Civil War and objections from the United States Army Engineers shelved work until 1869. Roebling designed an unprecedented structure with a main span of 1,595 feet. Unfortunately, though built to Roe-

bling's specifications, the great bridge, which came to symbolize not only New York's greatness but also the aesthetic and structural abilities of American engineering, was completed by Washington Roebling fourteen years after his father's death. On his initial survey in July, 1869, John Roebling's toes were crushed against pilings by a ferry, and he died of a tetanus infection July 22, 1869, in Brooklyn Heights, New York.

Summary

Though Roebling has been popularly identified with the design of the magnificent Brooklyn Bridge, an American symbol as well as an example of artistic engineering, one of his major contributions lies elsewhere: He, along with a handful of others, demonstrated the necessity for, and the superiority of, professionally trained engineers and the passing of those who, however ingeniously, even brilliantly, worked by "guess and by God." This was especially true of bridge builders, who were increasingly confronted by the broad, swift rivers of America and by the vastly heavier burdens that had to be borne by their structures during rapid industrialization. Roebling did not invent the suspension bridge: As a simple form it was thousands of years old. On a modest scale and in modest circumstances, suspensions were being improved even as his career began. The precision of his designs, his mastery of wire-cable manufacture and use, and his mathematical assessment of loads and stresses that lend special character to all of his constructions, whether his aqueducts, his Wheeling, Pittsburgh, Cincinnati, or Niagara structures, however, made him the acknowledged master of suspension forms. By his boldness in adapting his designs to the peculiar needs of the American environment, he revolutionized bridge construction throughout the world. This was a legacy passed on not only by his son's completion of the Brooklyn Bridge but also by professional engineers everywhere.

Bibliography

Condit, Carl W. *American Building: Materials and Techniques from the Beginning of Colonial Settlements to the Present*. 2d ed. Chicago: University of Chicago Press, 1982. A standard study; chapters 8 and 12 are on Roebling. Excellent technical discussion of bridge construction, including the suspension work of Roebling, among others. Also strong on historical contexts of these developments. Readable and widely available.

————. *American Building Art: The Nineteenth Century*. New York: Oxford University Press, 1960. As excellent as all of Condit's studies. Concentration not only on building techniques but also on the aesthetics of structural architecture. Chapter 5 is particularly relevant to Roebling and suspension bridges.

Kirby, Richard S., and Philip G. Laurson. *The Early Years of Civil Engineering*. New Haven, Conn.: Yale University Press, and London: Oxford University Press, 1932. Standard and excellent. Includes portraits and very brief biographical sketches of Roebling and many other major civil engineers of national and international note. Chapter 5 is especially relevant.

Latimer, Margaret, Brooks Hindle, and Melvin Kranzberg. *Bridge to the Future: A Centennial Celebration of the Brooklyn Bridge*. New York: New York Academy of Sciences, 1984. A literary as well as a technical survey. Sound and accurate.

Steinman, David B., and Sara Ruth Watson. *Bridges and Their Builders*. New York: Putnam, 1941. Expertly done by engineering scholars. A fine survey.

Vogel, Robert M. *Roebling's Delaware and Hudson Canal Aqueducts*. Washington, D.C.: Smithsonian Institution Press, 1971. Fine monograph on Roebling's early work. Technically detailed with reproductions of Roebling's designs. Useful for understanding Roebling's later works.

Clifton K. Yearley
Kerrie L. MacPherson

SIR JAMES CLARK ROSS

Born: April 15, 1800; London, England
Died: April 3, 1862; Aylesbury, Buckinghamshire, England
Area of Achievement: Exploration
Contribution: Through determined and efficient leadership, Ross discovered the North Magnetic Pole, mapped hundreds of miles of coastline, and discovered scores of geographical features.

Early Life

James Clark Ross was born in London, England, of a Scottish family, but little is known of his boyhood until he joined the navy at the age of twelve under the guidance of his uncle, Sir John Ross, a commander in the Royal Navy. Probably fulfilling a family tradition, young Ross was taken onboard his uncle's ship as a first-class volunteer and was promoted rather quickly to midshipman and then to master's mate on the same vessel. He served with his uncle in the Baltic Sea, White Sea, and English Channel and on the west coast of Scotland. In 1818, when Ross was eighteen, he served as midshipman on the *Isabella* with his uncle, who commanded an Arctic expedition in a futile search for a northwest passage through the Canadian Arctic from the Atlantic to the Pacific Ocean.

The following year, Ross volunteered for service with William Edward Parry, who had been given command of the next Arctic voyage. Parry returned in 1820, having explored half the Northwest Passage and having accomplished far more than any previous explorer in that region. In the ensuing wave of public enthusiasm to finish the task of discovery, Parry was commissioned to command his second voyage to the Arctic. Ross was again assigned as midshipman on an expedition that consumed two years searching for an "Open Polar Sea." Ross functioned as naturalist, collecting birds, mammals, marine life, and plants. He frequently accompanied Parry onshore to make observations. Despite its scientific data and extensive natural history collection, however, the voyage, from the standpoint of its purpose, was a failure. Ross sailed with Parry on a third voyage to the Arctic (1824-1825), which was disastrous. During a storm, one of Parry's ships, the *Fury*, was driven hard into the ice, and Parry was forced to abandon it. This was Parry's last expedition in search of the Northwest Passage, but he and Ross made an over-

land assault on the North Pole. Traveling by sledge and dragging boats, they came within five hundred miles of the North Pole, a record unsurpassed for over fifty years.

Life's Work

In 1829, Ross, having been promoted to commander, sailed with his uncle, Commander John Ross, as his second-in-command on an Arctic exploration. James, seaman and scientist, and the active officer with the most Arctic experience in the Royal Navy, was the logical choice for a new try for the Northwest Passage. The expedition had fired the public imagination in that John had replaced the traditional sailing ship with a steam vessel, the *Victory*, thought to be superior for driving through ice. However, the machinery malfunctioned and progress was painfully slow; John, upon reaching Greenland, junked the engine and returned the *Victory* to a sailing vessel to the approval of all officers and crew.

James's wintering experiences with Parry proved invaluable. When the ship was snugged down for winter in Felix Harbor off Melville Island, he arranged exercise, activities, school instruction, and work for everyone. He instituted a new system of diet, patterned after the Eskimos, that ensured that the crew remain healthy. In the spring, James went on several hunting and fishing expeditions with Eskimo sledge parties and, with their help, mapped the coastlines.

During the second winter that they were trapped in the ice in Felix Harbor, James launched an expedition to the west coast of Boothia Peninsula (named for John's friend and benefactor, Felix Booth), where he discovered the North Magnetic Pole in 1831. After a third winter trapped in the ice, John determined to abandon the *Victory* and travel by sledge for Fury Beach. There, a canvas-covered house was constructed for living quarters, and supplies from Parry's abandoned ship, *Fury*, got them through the fourth Arctic winter. The following August, they were rescued by a whaler, and, after four and one-half years in the Arctic, they arrived in London in late September, 1833.

Beyond their miraculous return, the Rosses' expedition compiled results unequalled for many years. In addition to the discovery of the North Magnetic Pole, hundreds of miles of previously unknown coast were surveyed, and hundreds of miles of new shoreline were discovered. The Gulf of Boothia was discovered, and James had crossed the strait now named for him (Ross Strait).

In 1834, James Ross was promoted to post captain and, as a leading authority on terrestrial magnetism, was ordered to conduct the first systematic survey of the British Isles. This work was interrupted in 1836, when he was given command of the *Cove* and sent to the relief of eleven whalers containing about six hundred men who were frozen in the ice in Davis Strait, which separates Greenland from Baffin Island. Three hundred miles from Greenland, the *Cove* was struck by a tremendous storm, and only through the calm orders of Ross was the ship, although damaged, saved. Ross faced down a near mutiny of his crew to learn in Greenland that all vessels but one, which was never found, were safe.

Ross was the most experienced officer in Arctic navigation, having spent eight winters and fifteen navigable seasons in the Arctic region, and was also an expert in terrestrial magnetism. As the British Admiralty's choice to lead a proposed naval expedition to the Antarctic, Ross and his eminently qualified and carefully chosen crew departed on the afternoon of September 25, 1839. The two small but heavy ships, the *Erebus* and the *Terror*, which had been reinforced to withstand ice pressure, crossed the equator on December 3 and, after stopping at various points to set up observatories, reached Tasmania in August, 1840.

Cheered by the prospect of geographical discovery, Ross steered the *Erebus* and the *Terror* across the Antarctic Circle, breaking through the pack ice with ease. Heading for the South Magnetic Pole, Ross was disheartened to discover that the blink on the horizon was snow-covered mountain peaks. He sailed westerly in the sea that now bears his name (Ross Sea) and surveyed the magnificent mountain ranges, naming one of them the Admiralty Range, for the Lords Commissioners of the Admiralty, and the other for eminent members of the Royal Society and British Association. An active volcano, 12,400 feet high and belching flame and smoke, was named Mount Erebus, while a smaller, inactive volcano was named Mount Terror. Hopes of reaching the South Magnetic Pole were dashed when Ross encountered a perpendicular wall of ice between 150 and 200 feet high directly in front of him that stretched as far as the eye could see. Ross followed this barrier (his name for what was later named the Ross Ice Shelf) to the east for over two

hundred miles but, unable to move any farther south, reluctantly turned back to Tasmania for the winter.

Ross's second voyage into the Antarctic was disappointing, but the dangers were much greater. A terrific storm drove both ships into an ice pack that inflicted considerable damage and would have destroyed the vessels had they not been reinforced against ice. Ross managed to attain only a slightly higher latitude than the previous year before returning northward. On the way, a fierce gale caused a violent collision between the two ships, entangling the rigging and dashing the ships against each other. Gradually, the *Terror* forged past the *Erebus*, leaving the *Erebus* completely disabled. Rough weather continued as Ross called it a season and limped into the Falkland Islands. On his third cruise into the Antarctic, he was stopped again by the ice pack in March, 1843. As the season was too far advanced to attempt more, Ross signaled the *Terror* to turn back. He arrived in England in September of 1843 following an absence of four years and five months.

Ross's journey to Antarctica was one of the greatest voyages of discovery and exploration ever made. His geographical discoveries overshadowed the principal purpose of magnetic observation. Despite his disappointment at not reaching the South Magnetic Pole, his discoveries of Victoria Land, McMurdo Sound, Ross Sea, and the spectacular Ross Ice Shelf, among other geographical features, marked important advances in the knowledge of Antarctica.

On his return from Antarctica, Ross married Ann Coulman, but only after he contracted with her father never to go on any more long polar voyages. Long known as the "navy's handsomest man," he was eager to settle down on an estate he bought at Aylesbury. The terrible strain of long expeditions had taken its toll on his iron constitution, and he needed rest. He was given a knighthood and received an honorary degree from Oxford. He also wrote an account of his voyages and served as a consultant on Arctic matters.

In November, 1847, Lady Ross consented to allow her husband to command a rescue expedition in search of Commander John Franklin. The two-year voyage was a failure, for it was learned that Franklin and his crew had perished before Ross had left England. Ross returned exhausted and broken in health. Lady Ross died unexpectedly in 1857, and Ross died in 1862.

and covered with sand. Men were supplied with the best-quality warm clothing. Ross's insistence upon regular activity, work, and exercises for the men relieved boredom and supported morale. Unusually large stores of preserved meat and vegetables were laid in, reducing the chance of scurvy to a minimum. Frequent hunting and fishing expeditions also provided dietary supplements. Ross was one of the first Europeans to understand that increasing the quantity of food per man, especially the large use of oil and fat meats, was essential to successful Arctic living. Healthy men who returned from Ross's expeditions and the many others that followed owed their lives to his acumen.

Bibliography

Dodge, Ernest S. *The Polar Rosses: John and James Clark Ross and Their Explorations*. New York: Barnes and Noble, and London: Faber, 1973. Covers the explorations and related activities of both men. Gives detailed accounts of experiences that follow James Ross's log as well as insight into his working relationship with the British Admiralty.

King, H. G. R. *The Antarctic*. London: Blandford, 1969; New York: Arco Publishing, 1970. Provides an introduction to Antarctic science along with basic facts concerning Antarctic geography, natural history, and exploration. Contains a short but informative section on Ross.

Langley, Michael. *When the Pole Star Shone: A History of Exploration*. London: Harrap, 1972. Contains a history of exploration from ancient times to Neil Armstrong's landing on the moon. Includes chapters on polar navigators and the siege of the poles, with maps, sketches, and illustrations.

Mountfield, David. *A History of Polar Exploration*. London and New York: Hamlyn, 1974. Interesting focus on the experiences of men who explored polar regions and major obstacles they had to overcome. Contains an excellent section on Ross. Includes maps, illustrations, and sketches.

Sykes, Percy. *A History of Exploration: From the Earliest Times to the Present Day*. London: Routledge, 1933; New York: Macmillan, 1934. An extensive history of exploration from earliest to modern times with emphasis on more remote areas of the world. Includes a brief but informative section on Ross.

Mary Hurd

Summary

Sir James Clark Ross was a sailor's sailor, an officer whose skill in ice navigation and nerves of steel saved ships and men on various occasions. Patient and fearless, he endured the privation and suffering of the long sledge journeys by virtue of his own strength, stamina, and judgment.

Ross's enormous contributions to knowledge through magnetic observation, specimen collection, mapping, and discovery were largely possible because of his foresight and planning. By surrounding himself with men of scientific as well as Arctic experience, his expeditions were better equipped and therefore more successful than many of those of his contemporaries.

Ross, an introvert, developed techniques that made other explorers' tasks easier. One of his most significant contributions was his hard-won knowledge that successful exploration depends upon providing for the health, comfort, and safety of the men. Succeeding explorers benefitted from his wintering techniques in which the ship's deck, under the housing, was covered with two and one-half feet of snow, trod down to a solid mass of ice,

JOHN ROSS
Coowescoowe

Born: October 3, 1790; Turkey Town, Alabama

Died: August 1, 1866; Washington, D.C.

Area of Achievement: Statesmanship

Contribution: As a leader of the Cherokee nation during its ordeal of forced removal and civil war, Ross is the supreme example of nineteenth century Native American statesmanship.

Early Life

John Ross was born October 3, 1790, at Turkey Town, a Cherokee settlement near modern Center, Alabama. He was by blood only one-eighth Cherokee. His mother, Mollie McDonald, was the granddaughter of a Cherokee woman, but his father, the trader Daniel Ross, and all of his mother's other ancestors were Scottish. His father, while securing a tutor for his children and sending Ross to an academy near Kingston, Tennessee, did not want to stamp out his children's Cherokee identity, and his mother gave him a deep sense of loyalty to the tribe, to their ancient lands and traditions, and to the ideal of Cherokee unity. As a son of three generations of Scottish traders, Ross early showed an interest in business. In 1813, he formed a partnership with Timothy Meigs at Rossville, near modern Chattanooga, and two years later another with his brother Lewis Ross; during the Creek War of 1813-1814, when Cherokee warriors fought in Andrew Jackson's army, he did a lucrative business filling government contracts. During the Creek War, he served as adjutant in a company of Cherokee cavalry.

By the mid-1820's, his increasing involvement in the political affairs of the Cherokee nation caused him to abandon business. In 1827, he settled at Coosa, Georgia, thirty miles from the new Cherokee capital at New Echota, and established himself as a planter, with a substantial house, orchards and herds, quarters for his twenty slaves, and a lucrative ferry.

Ross served as a member of four Cherokee delegations to Washington between 1816 and 1825 and was president of the tribe's National Committee in 1818, when it resisted the attempt of Tennessee to persuade the tribe to surrender their lands in that state. In 1822, he was a cosigner of a resolution of the National Committee that the Cherokee would not recognize any treaty which surrendered Cherokee land. In 1823, Ross earned for himself the undying loyalty of the majority of the tribe when he rejected a bribe offered by federal commissioners and publicly denounced them in a meeting of the National Committee.

Life's Work

Ross was president of the convention which in 1827 produced the Cherokee constitution. This document, in its assignment of powers to three branches of government, its bicameral legislature, and its four-year term for the principal chief, was modeled on the Constitution of the United States. In 1828, he was elected principal chief, an office which he held until his death, and in 1829 he went to Washington on the first of many embassies which he undertook in that capacity.

The Cherokee established their republic within the context of an ongoing struggle to maintain their traditional claims against state governments, particularly that of Georgia. In 1802, Georgia had ceded to the United States its western territory (what later became Alabama and Mississippi) in exchange for a promise that all Native Americans would be removed from Georgia. A substantial number of Cherokee, accepting removal, surrendered their land rights and moved west. (One of them was the great Cherokee genius Sequoya, who gave his people a syllabary for their language.) With the inauguration of Andrew Jackson, who was determined to send the Cherokee west, and the discovery of gold on Cherokee land, it was clear that removal was inevitable. Ross was determined to exhaust every legal and political recourse, however, before submitting to the superior physical might of the United States government. Though Jackson was willing to assert the power of the federal government—even if it meant war—to put down any movement in South Carolina for "nullification" of the Constitution, he declared that in the Cherokee case he would not interfere with state sovereignty. As a result, his Indian Removal Bill of 1830 included the provision that any Native American who chose not to remove was subject to state law. Georgia therefore refused to recognize the legitimacy of the Cherokee republic and made no effort to prevent white squatters from moving into the Cherokee country. These official attitudes and the chaos caused by the gold rush produced a state of anarchy in which, on one occasion, Ross himself barely escaped assassination.

By 1833, pressure by the government of Georgia and by the Jackson Administration was producing dissension among the Cherokee themselves. John Ridge, son of an influential Cherokee family, and Elias Boudinot, editor of the *Cherokee Phoenix*, were both working for acceptance of removal and were thus undermining the efforts of Ross, who wanted the tribe to resist removal, and if it were inevitable, to accept it only on the best possible terms.

In 1835, returning from a trip to Washington, Ross found his land and house occupied by a white man, who was able to present a legal title granted by Georgia. In the same year, the Ridge faction signed the Treaty of New Echota, accepting removal. In spite of the fact that it was signed by only a handful of Cherokee, in spite of opposition by the Cherokee who had already settled in the West, in spite of a protest signed by fourteen thousand Cherokee, and in spite of Henry Clay's opposition in the Senate, it was approved by the Senate in May, 1836, and signed by Jackson.

Under the conditions of the treaty, the Cherokee were given two years to prepare for removal, and Ross spent that time in further hopeless efforts to persuade the government to give the entire Cherokee people opportunity to accept or reject the treaty. The removal itself was flawed by looting, arson, and even grave-robbing by white squatters; disease was inevitable in the stockades which served as holding pens; of the thirteen thousand who were removed, probably four thousand, including Ross's wife, died on the "Trail of Tears."

In his first years in Oklahoma, Ross devoted all of his energies to his efforts to unite three Cherokee factions: his own Nationalist followers, the Ridge-Boudinot faction which had accepted removal, and the Old Settlers, who had formed their own government and did not want to merge with the Easterners. In July, 1839, a convention wrote a new constitution, virtually the same as that of 1827, and passed the Act of Union, which was ratified by all parties. In spite of Ross's efforts for Cherokee unity, however, extremists in his own party exacted the traditional Cherokee penalty for selling tribal lands when they murdered Ridge and Boudinot. Ross was not involved in these crimes and did not condone them, but they were a source of disharmony in the tribe as long as he lived, and

they were the primary reason that he had difficulty negotiating a new treaty with the government in an attempt to guarantee Cherokee claims to their Oklahoma lands. Ross had opposed removal because he knew that if the government were allowed to confiscate the Georgia lands they could confiscate lands in Oklahoma later. The government refused to agree to guarantees, however, because the followers of Ridge and Boudinot claimed that Ross was responsible for the murders; finally, in 1846, the Polk Administration signed a treaty acceptable to all parties.

On September 2, 1844, Ross married Mary Bryan Stapler, daughter of a Delaware merchant, who bore him two children. The period from the 1846 treaty until the Civil War was a relatively happy time for Ross and for his people. He prospered as a merchant, raised livestock, and contributed much of his wealth to charities on behalf of poor Cherokee; under his guidance, seminaries and a Cherokee newspaper were established.

Though, by 1860, Ross owned fifty slaves, he opposed slavery on principle, and this issue in the 1850's was another source of tribal dissension, his full-blood followers opposing it and the mixed-bloods favoring it. When the war began and agents were working among the Oklahoma tribes on behalf of the Confederacy, Ross favored neutrality and adherence to the 1846 treaty. Only when the neighboring tribes accepted a Confederate alliance and the Cherokee nation was virtually surrounded was Ross willing to accept an alliance. Yet in June, 1862, when Union forces finally arrived from Kansas, he welcomed them, though he and his family were forced to leave the Cherokee country as refugees when the Union forces withdrew. His four sons by his first wife served in the Union Army, and one of them died in a Confederate prison.

For the next three years, Ross was in the East working to persuade the Lincoln Administration to send federal troops to the Cherokee country and to feed the six thousand pro-Union Cherokee who had taken refuge in Kansas. The last year of the war was a particularly unhappy time for him because of the illness of his wife, who died in July, 1865.

When Ross died on August 1, 1866, he was in Washington negotiating a peace treaty with the United States government and fighting the efforts of the Cherokee faction which had been pro-South in the war to get federal approval of a permanently divided tribe. The treaty which was proclaimed ten days after his death was his last contribution to the cause of Cherokee unity.

Summary

John Ross was passionately devoted to the ancestral homeland of the Cherokee and to their cultural traditions, but when he recognized that removal was inevitable he submitted to it in order to reestablish a unified Cherokee nation on the frontier; his people's achievement of a remarkable blend of tribal traditions and white man's political and economic methods was his greatest monument. Though he was "by blood" only one-eighth Cherokee, he grew up as a Cherokee, identified with the Cherokee people, and devoted his life to the great cause of tribal unity. The Cherokee tragedy, which remains permanently fixed as one of the most disgraceful acts of the American people, stands in contrast to the life of the man who was probably the most distinguished Native American political leader of the nineteenth century and who resembles Lincoln both in his political skills and in his vision of union as the only basis for peace and justice.

Bibliography

Eaton, Rachel Caroline. *John Ross and the Cherokee Indians*. Chicago: University of Chicago Press, 1921. A doctoral dissertation which concentrates on the political ordeal of the Cherokee during Ross's lifetime. Essentially accurate, though apparently written without access to all the early documents.

Meserve, John Bartlett. "Chief John Ross." *Chronicles of Oklahoma* 13 (December, 1935): 421-437. A brief but balanced account of Ross's life, though flawed by several errors in detail.

Moulton, Gary. *John Ross: Cherokee Chief*. Athens: University of Georgia Press, 1978. The best and most nearly definitive account of Ross's life and political struggles. Most useful because of its copious notes, which provide all the apparatus necessary for further study.

Starkey, Marion L. *The Cherokee Nation*. New York: Knopf, 1946. A semipopular account of Cherokee history from the beginnings to removal, with a final chapter devoted to later events. Written from the point of view of the missionaries to the Cherokee and perhaps overly sympathetic to the Treaty Party.

Wardell, Morris L. *A Political History of the Cherokee Nation, 1838-1907*. Norman: University of Oklahoma Press, 1938. A scholarly account of the Cherokee from removal to Oklahoma statehood. Refers to Ross in passing.

Woodward, Grace Steele. *The Cherokees*. Norman: University of Oklahoma Press, 1963. The best general account of the full range of Cherokee history, from first white contact to the late twentieth century. A fuller and much more balanced history than Starkey's book.

Robert L. Berner

GIOACCHINO ROSSINI

Born: February 29, 1792; Pesaro
Died: November 13, 1868; Passy, France
Area of Achievement: Music
Contribution: Rossini was one of the greatest composers of Italian opera in the nineteenth century. In almost forty works for the operatic stage, Rossini composed some of the last and finest specimens of the *opera buffa* and also numerous serious operas which laid the foundation for the ensuing generation of Italian Romantic composers. His brilliant overtures have enjoyed a separate life as concert pieces.

Early Life

Gioacchino Rossini was the son of musicians: His father, Giuseppe, was a hornist, and his mother, Anna (née Guidarini), was a soprano who, though musically untutored, sang minor roles in provincial theaters. Rossini's childhood coincided with Napoleon I's Italian campaigns, and his hometown of Pesaro on the Adriatic changed hands numerous times; the elder Rossini, an enthusiastic republican, was briefly imprisoned by papal authorities in 1800. Despite vicissitudes, Rossini's early life was not unhappy. Tradition has it that the young Rossini was unusually high-spirited and prankish, early manifestations no doubt of a drollery that was to remain with him in maturity.

The Rossini family settled in Bologna in 1804. For Rossini, this was a stroke of good fortune: He was able in 1806 to enter the Liceo Musicale, one of the finest music schools in Italy. That he had already acquired considerable prowess as a musician is attested by his election in the same year to the Accademia Filarmonica of Bologna, a remarkable honor for a fourteen year old. At the conservatory, Rossini's studies in counterpoint were directed by Padre Stanislao Mattei, a strict traditionalist whose rigorous method helped Rossini attain a well-regulated and fluent compositional technique.

Rossini's studies at the Liceo continued until 1810. By this time he had already completed his first opera, a serious work entitled *Demetrio e Polibio*, which would receive its first performance in 1812. Rossini's actual public debut as an opera composer was with a comic work, a one-act farce entitled *La cambiale di matrimonio* presented at the Teatro San Moisè in Venice in November, 1810. The opera was a triumph. Already the eighteen-year-old composer displayed evidence of the élan and wit which were to be the hallmarks of his later works. The success of *La cambiale di matrimonio* propelled Rossini into a mad whirl of opera composition: In the next twenty-six months, he composed six more comic works and established himself in the front rank of young composers. By age twenty-one, Rossini was a veteran of the operatic wars and a national celebrity; he was poised on the brink of international acclaim.

The larger-than-life Rossini personality had also begun to emerge. Witty and gregarious, Rossini cut a wide swath in society. Precocious in his interest in the opposite sex, he paid a price for his indulgences: Several venereal infections led to chronic urological problems in his middle years. Rossini was slender and attractive as a young man but soon fell prey to baldness and corpulence; all extant photographs show him well fleshed and bewigged.

Life's Work

Rossini emerged as a composer at a time when Italian opera was in transition. The *opera seria* (serious opera) as it had been cultivated in the eighteenth century was moribund; its rigidly conventionalized formality and its reliance on artificial mythological or classical plots caused it to wilt in the hotter artistic climate of the nineteenth century. *Opera buffa*, as it had been cultivated by Wolfgang Amadeus Mozart, was still a vital genre, but it had entered its final phase; it, too, was ultimately an expression of eighteenth century sensibilities. While Rossini remains most closely identified with *opera buffa* through the continuing appeal of works such as *The Barber of Seville* (1816), the clear majority of his operas after his apprentice phase were tragic or heroic works which may be viewed as attempts to recast the *opera seria* in nineteenth century terms. Ironically, Rossini himself remained ambivalent about the emerging Romantic style. Though he helped to shape the Romantic taste in librettos, and though he virtually invented the formal structure of the Romantic melodrama, he was reluctant to succumb fully to the wholesale emotional intensity of the Romantic style.

Nevertheless, the work which first brought Rossini international fame was the proto-Romantic *Tancredi*, a serious opera which was first performed at the Teatro La Fenice in Venice in February of 1813. The libretto, drawn from Voltaire and

Torquato Tasso, presents a costume drama of no particular distinction, but it afforded Rossini the opportunity to experiment with new methods of formal organization. Most of the formal conventions which sustained Rossini in later works are here present at least in embryonic state. These forms include the opening choral introduction interrupted by a solo, the multipart ensemble finale, and the extended *scena* for principal characters. A large measure of *Tancredi*'s success had to do, however, with its sheer tunefulness. *Tancredi*'s act 1 cavatina "Di tanti palpiti," for example, became an international hit by nineteenth century standards.

The decade following the premiere of *Tancredi* in 1813 marked the peak of Rossini's productivity as a composer of Italian opera. Rossini completed twenty-five operas in this span, including comic gems such as *L'italiani in Algeri* (1813), *The Barber of Seville, La cenerentola* (1817), and dramatic or tragic works such as *Otello* (1816), *Mosè in Egitto* (1818), *La donna del lago* (1819), and *Semiramide* (1823). As Rossini moved from triumph to triumph, he attained a celebrity that was virtually without precedent in the music world. Stendhal was guilty of only modest exaggeration when he wrote of Rossini in 1824: "Napoleon is dead; but a new conqueror has already shown himself to the world; and from Moscow to Naples, from London to Vienna, from Paris to Calcutta, his name is constantly on every tongue."

The Barber of Seville was undoubtedly Rossini's comic masterpiece. Although the work was first given under the title *Almaviva* in order to discourage comparison with a popular opera on the same subject by Giovanni Paisiello, Rossini's work soon eclipsed the older opera in popularity and has remained his most frequently given stage work. The opera stands in the older *opera buffa* tradition, but it has a quality of manic humor which is uniquely Rossinian.

From late 1815 until 1823, Rossini made Naples the base of his operations; ten of nineteen operas produced during this span were written for Neapolitan stages. At Naples, he became romantically involved with one of his prima donnas, the soprano Isabella Colbran. Rossini and Colbran were married in 1822, but the union was not enduring, and separation followed quickly.

The enormous and unbroken popularity of *The Barber of Seville* has obscured the fact that most of Rossini's operas in the Neapolitan period were serious. Of particular note were *Otello* and *La donna del lago*. The former was Rossini's only Shakespearean opera, and though the libretto lamentably perverts William Shakespeare's drama, the score is one of Rossini's most ambitious efforts to synthesize music and text. The entire last act presents itself as a musicodramatic unit rather than as a string of pieces; Rossini himself considered it to be one of his finest achievements. *La donna del lago*, based on Sir Walter Scott's *The Lady of the Lake*, demonstrates Rossini's interest in the literature of his day and was evidently the first of the many nineteenth century operas inspired by the writings of Scott.

In the final phase of his career, Rossini was drawn to Paris. While three of his four operas with French texts were in fact revisions of earlier Italian works, Rossini's last opera *Guillaume Tell* (1829), was newly composed and is his largest, and arguably his greatest, work. The tale of the Swiss patriot William Tell loosely follows Friedrich Schiller's play of that name and provided Rossini with a grand canvas on which to work. He responded with some of his finest music. The overture, whose electrifying gallop at the close has become a cliché, is nevertheless a superb inspiration.

After *Guillaume Tell* came the so-called great renunciation: Rossini simply ceased to compose operas. Numerous explanations have been adduced to account for his abrupt retirement: that he had said all that he had to say, that he was uncomfortable with the advent of unbridled Romanticism, that he deplored the decline of vocal standards, that he was suffering from ill health. In all probability, each of these factors contributed to Rossini's decision.

The early years of Rossini's retirement were plagued by ill health. During this period, he was nursed solicitously by his new mistress, the former courtesan Olympe Pélissier, whom he married in 1846. In the mid-1850's, Rossini settled permanently in Paris. For the remainder of his life, Rossini was treated like a *grand seigneur*; his salon was a magnet for young composers, and his pungent observations and jests were widely circulated.

Only a few compositions date from the long retirement. The two most impressive are sacred works: the highly dramatic *Stabat Mater* (1832) and the *Petite messe solennelle* (1853). Rossini also composed numerous epigrammatic and parodistic works for piano which he called *Péchés de vieillesse* (1835; sins of my old age).

Summary

Of the great nineteenth century Italian opera composers, only the mature Giuseppe Verdi surpassed Gioacchino Rossini in sheer compositional inspiration. In style, wit, originality, brio, and technical fluency, Rossini was abundantly endowed. Where Rossini was able to concentrate these gifts—in the comic operas and the overtures—he was able to achieve both critical and popular success. Ironically, Rossini did his most original work in a genre—the romantic *melodrama*—for which he was not fully suited by taste and temperament. In works such as *Otello*, *La donna del lago*, and *Guillaume Tell*, Rossini charted the course for the next generation of opera composers. Yet Rossini himself was reluctant to cross the threshold into the new age. His legacy is nevertheless substantial: His thirty-nine operas form a trove which has not yet been fully brought to light.

Bibliography

Gossett, Philip. "Gioacchino Rossini." In *The New Grove Masters of Italian Opera*. London: Macmillan, 1980; New York: Norton, 1983. Gossett's seventy-page essay, together with a full list of works, constitutes a reworking of his earlier entry for *The New Grove Dictionary* and is perhaps the most reliable and up-to-date account of Rossini generally available.

Mermelstein, David. "Getting Rossini Right." *Opera News* 62, no. 9 (January 17, 1998). Profile of Philip Gossett, Dean of Humanities at the University of Chicago and one of the world's authorities on Rossini. Gossett is the editor of the Rossini Edition whose goal it is to publish critical scores of all Rossini's works.

Rossini, Gioacchino. *Musique Anodine-Album Italiano: The Critical Edition of the Works of Gioachino Rossini*. Marvin Tartak, ed. Chicago: University of Chicago Press, 1997. This volume, which is based on Rossini's own manuscripts, includes earlier versions of six pieces, some of which have different text than the final versions.

Stendhal. *Life of Rossini*. Translated and annotated by Richard N. Coe. New York: Orion Press, 1970; London: Calder, 1985. Stendhal's famous biography has the merits of contemporaneity and literary brilliance. It was, however, a work of polemical journalism, not of scholarship, and it is marred by many inaccuracies.

Till, Nicolas. *Rossini: His Life and Times*. Tunbridge Wells, Kent: Midas, and New York: Hippocrene, 1983. This lavishly illustrated work is perhaps the best short introduction to Rossini's life and work for the general reader. Till provides excellent descriptions of Rossini's social and professional milieu and offers intelligent critical judgments couched in highly readable prose.

Toye, Francis. *Rossini: A Study in Tragi-comedy*. London: Heinemann, and New York: Knopf, 1934. First published in 1934, Toye's work engagingly championed Rossini and his works at a time when the composer's stock among music critics was low. Though perhaps overly reliant on the three-volume study by Giuseppe Radiciotti in Italian, this genial work remains valuable.

Weinstock, Herbert. *Rossini: A Biography*. London: Oxford University Press, and New York: Knopf, 1968. The most exhaustive account of Rossini's life in English, Weinstock's work is the product of impressive research and contains extensive notes, appendices, and a lengthy bibliography.

Steven W. Shrader

THE ROTHSCHILD FAMILY

Mayer Amschel Rothschild

Born: February 23, 1744; Frankfurt am Main   *Died:* September 19, 1812; Frankfurt am Main

Amschel Mayer Rothschild

Born: June 12, 1773; Frankfurt am Main   *Died:* December 6, 1855; Frankfurt am Main

Salomon Mayer Rothschild

Born: September 9, 1774; Frankfurt am Main   *Died:* July 27, 1855; Paris, France

Nathan Mayer Rothschild

Born: September 16, 1777; Frankfurt am Main   *Died:* July 28, 1836; Frankfurt am Main

Carl Mayer Rothschild

Born: April 24, 1788; Frankfurt am Main   *Died:* March 10, 1855; Naples, Kingdom of the Two Sicilies

James Mayer Rothschild

Born: May 15, 1792; Frankfurt am Main   *Died:* November 15, 1868; Paris, France

Area of Achievement: Business

Contribution: The Rothschild family developed one of the most successful banking and investment companies of all time. By locating branches in a number of major cities while keeping the business a family matter, they were able to coordinate international operations and provide services to clients and governments that were unavailable elsewhere.

Early Lives

Mayer Amschel Rothschild was born in the Frankfurt ghetto in 1744. His parents died only eleven years later of smallpox, but traveling with his peddler father had already had an impact on the boy. In the patchwork of principalities making up the eighteenth century Holy Roman Empire, even a minor trader might visit several countries in a day or two. Mayer Amschel was thus introduced at an early age to the mysteries of money exchanging. Although his parents had enrolled him in a Jewish religious school that prepared students to be scholars, after their deaths he was able to convince relatives that he would be better off in a business career. In 1757, an apprenticeship at the Oppenheimer Bank in Hannover was arranged. He returned to Frankfurt in 1763.

Mayer Amschel had become a dealer in rare coins, and in 1765 a connection made in Hannover arranged for him to display his wares for Prince William of Hesse, whose avarice was legendary. For four years, Mayer Amschel sold coins at bargain prices to the prince, getting little for his trou-ble. Later, however, he was able to buy the house the family had been renting, which became his home and office. He had an illustrated catalog printed. Most important, he married Gutle Schnapper in 1770. The union was fruitful: Five sons and five daughters grew to adulthood. The sons—Amschel, Salomon, Nathan, Carl, and James—would build the family business into a worldwide concern.

Mayer Amschel continued to court William, who was combining enterprises such as renting mercenaries to England for use in America and an inheritance to become enormously wealthy. His break came because of a friendship with Carl Buderus, William's chief financial adviser. Mayer Amschel had given Buderus a valuable coin, and, upon making a second visit to William in his new establishment in Kassel, Mayer Amschel got his first commission. This was the beginning of a relationship that proved extremely profitable to all concerned. By the 1790's, the family was comfortably well off and about to embark on the enterprise that would make it an international financial force.

Lives' Work

Annoyed by the haughtiness of an English cotton salesman, the twenty-one-year-old Nathan resolved to go to England and conduct business for the family; he would become the most successful of the entire clan. The stocky, powerful Nathan was round-headed with coarse features; his speech was crude, and he never lost his German accent. Interested in little but business, he was soon established as a major financier and trader in a variety of commodities, taking good advantage of the demands created by the French Revolutionary Wars. On the Continent, the Rothschilds were of enormous service in concealing valuables from the emperor's rapacious agents, but in England Nathan, at least at times, used the funds transferred for investment in bonds in more speculative investments. When he had to account for sums, he bought the requested bonds, making up the interest so that William of Hesse earned as much as if the bonds had been bought when ordered. This was all arranged in partnership with Carl Buderus, who helped hide the operation from William and became rich in the process.

The Rothschild firm was now extremely successful, thanks to its financial manipulations. Another factor was the increased business provoked in London and Frankfurt by the French blockade, which forced the opening of new markets as well as shifting old ones to Rothschild advantage. In 1810, the firm was renamed M. A. Rothschild and Sons, with Mayer Amschel and the four sons still in Frankfurt having shares—Nathan, in enemy territory, could get nothing legally but was promised his share when the political situation made it possible.

Nathan had, the year before, established his own bank in England and was beginning to be brought into government financial arrangements. In 1814, he had a hand in the very profitable process of collecting loans and transferring the funds to the Duke of Wellington in the Peninsula. In addition, he created an excellent system of couriers, carrier pigeons, and other means of communication, which usually meant that he had information about European events before his competitors and often was able to buy or sell government bonds to advantage. While Nathan was expanding the holdings of the English branch, his brothers were spreading family institutions around Europe. James had settled in Paris, where he had had some opportunity to help with Nathan's efforts to supply money to Wellington in Spain.

In 1819, a wave of liberal-nationalist feeling broke over the German Confederation, threatening the Rothschilds both as bankers who supported the conservative policies of Metternich and as Jews. The family was urged to abandon Frankfurt for Paris. Upon hearing of this, Metternich sent word that the Rothschilds would be welcome in Vienna, and subsequently he arranged for the Rothschild bank to raise an enormous loan for the Austrian government. Despite some troubling moments and charges of corruption, the bonds involved proved profitable for the bank and a good investment for purchasers. As the loan required much attention, Salomon opened a branch of the bank in Vienna. In 1821, Carl, the least forceful of the brothers, became the agent for the bank to raise a loan in Naples to help the Austrian government with the cost of maintaining an occupation to prevent revolution. His success not only improved the standing of the family in Vienna but also resulted in his remaining to open a new branch. In 1822, Metternich requested that the emperor bestow baronies on the five brothers.

Amschel, the only brother to be orthodox or slim, remained in Frankfurt, eventually becoming treasurer to the German Confederation and extremely influential in the financial policy-making of the Prussian government. The Rothschilds had become part of the economic and social elite.

Trouble arose when the Revolution of 1830 toppled the Bourbon government, for James Rothschild, deeply involved with government finance, did not believe the government was in trouble. Initial losses were serious, but the excellent communications system maintained by the family allowed Nathan and Salomon to sell French securities early and to rebuy at great profits. James's dependable, fiscally conservative management soon caught the attention of the July Monarch, Louis-Philippe, and James was brought back into a major role in French government finance.

The death of Nathan, while in Frankfurt to attend the 1836 wedding of his son Lionel, left James in Paris as the head of the family. Increasingly involved in the finances of both the government and Louis-Philippe personally, James's fortune approached fifty million pounds. His circle of friends included both aristocrats and intellectuals such as George Sand and Honoré de Balzac. Always pressed to support one cause or another, James gave generously only to be criticized for meanness by the rejected and unsatisfied.

In the middle of the century, the Rothschild business interest turned to railroads, resulting in much profit in Austria, Italy, and France. Efforts were also made to support international peace, as in 1840 when in Paris and Vienna the governments were soothed so that war would not destroy prosperity. In 1848, Carl persuaded the government of Naples to make liberal concessions to the revolu-

Mayer Amschel Rothschild.

tionaries and defuse the threat that in so many places led to violence.

In Paris, revolution again proved expensive. Not only was money invested in government securities at risk but also James's villa in the Bois de Boulogne was burned by the mob. In Vienna, Salomon had to abandon his house to the mob; Salomon went to Frankfurt, never returning to Vienna. James clung to his base in Paris and, by attaching himself to Eugène Cavaignac, Minister of War in the new revolutionary government, was soon back in the thick of politics and finance. Having been the bitter foes of Napoleon I, the Rothschilds were hardly eager for the advent of another. Their hopes were frustrated, however, when Louis-Napoleon Bonaparte was elected President of the Second Republic and then in 1852 declared himself Emperor Napoleon III.

In England, Lionel (1808-1879), already prominent in the business when his father died, became senior partner aided by his brothers, Mayer, Anthony, and Nathaniel. The second English generation began to move the family into traditional English upper-class patterns. Estates were purchased; Rothschilds were also becoming known for charity, art collecting, and hunting. Although the patriarch might not have approved of his sons' charitable impulses or artistic and sporting avocations, he would have been warmly in favor of their efforts to further the removal of civil and social disabilities from Jews. Although few Rothschilds felt much affinity for the outward forms of religion, they remained sensitive to their heritage.

Lionel, who devoted himself to the business, was urged by his friend, the great conservative politician Benjamin Disraeli, to seek a seat in the House of Commons. As members had to take an oath "on my true faith as a Christian," Jews were barred. In 1847, Lionel was elected to Parliament as a Liberal candidate for the City of London (the business district of the metropolis); although Commons passed a bill to allow him to take his seat, the bill was rejected by the House of Lords. Six times over the next eleven years, Lionel was reelected only to be turned away, despite the support of Disraeli. Finally in 1858, after a seventh electoral triumph, the Lords yielded, and Lionel became the first practicing Jew to be a Member of Parliament.

Membership in Parliament was only one element of becoming prominent in English society. The upper classes were tied together by relationships forged in public schools (the equivalent of private preparatory schools in the United States) and the two universities. As the University of Oxford had a religious test for graduation, the University of Cambridge was the institution for those of nonorthodox religious opinions; Cambridge did, however, require attendance at Anglican chapel. Although exceptions had been made for Lionel's brother Mayer and at least one other Jew, the requirement was not dropped by the university until 1856, and even then individual colleges could retain it. The change facilitated the matriculation of Lionel's son Nathan Mayer (called Natty) in 1859. Having distinguished himself socially at Cambridge and certainly having no lack of wealth, Natty made himself a force in Liberal politics and in 1885 became the first Jewish peer. His cousin Hannah married the Earl of Rosebery, a future prime minister, in 1878. Thus by the end of the nineteenth century, the Rothschilds were not only among the most wealthy of the English but also were firmly ensconced among the social and political elite.

On the Continent, Rothschild fortunes were more mixed during the middle years of the nineteenth century. In 1855, three of the original five brothers died: Carl of Naples, Salomon of Vienna, and Amschel of Frankfurt. The family was not quickly welcomed into the confidences of Napoleon III's government, although James's personal tie to the Empress Eugénie prevented complete ostracism. Although the French Rothschilds were frozen out of the organization of the Crédit Mobilier, a new French financial institution which, with government support, was enormously successful, Anselm, son of Salomon of Vienna, took the lead in developing the Kreditanstalt, a similar business in Vienna. By the late 1850's, a third generation—Alphonse of Paris (James lived until 1868), Anselm of Vienna, Lionel of London, and Mayer Carl of Frankfurt—were cooperating as well as the original brothers had. The Italian War of 1859-1860 strained the Credit Mobilier, resulting in a cosmetic reconciliation between the emperor and the Rothschilds. The same war began Italian unification, and, with the collapse of Naples as an independent state, the Rothschild Bank there was closed. It would not be reopened.

A growing public role was common for the family in the late nineteenth century. The Franco-Prussian War (1870-1871) did the Rothschild business no real harm and, since the bank managed the payment of the French indemnity, in the long run resulted in a profit. In England, Alfred Rothschild was appointed a director of the Bank of England in 1868, and, when Natty became a peer, his cousin Ferdinand replaced him in Parliament.

The end of the century found Rothschilds still running the family business but pursuing widely divergent nonbusiness interests. For example, Edmond devoted his time and money to supporting the establishment of colonies of poor Jews in Palestine; Lionel Walter (1868-1937) became well known as a naturalist; and Henri (1872-1947) was a successful physician and playwright.

Summary

The Rothschild family holds an extraordinary place in the world of international finance. In less than fifty years, the family went from poverty in the Frankfurt ghetto to control of one of the richest and most powerful banks in the world. Further, the family held its place throughout the turbulent nineteenth century. The Rothschild Bank was an early example of an international company with the twist that its branches were all controlled directly by family members and operated with an eye to the benefit of the entire clan. It is not surprising that, with their wealth and excellent communications system, the family was involved in the public financial operations in all the countries in which they had banks. More unusual is that, despite some use of bribery, the Rothschilds do not seem to have enriched themselves via corruption. The members of the family have generally been committed to serious public service as well as to profit-making.

Rothschilds have also done much to eliminate discrimination against Jews. Never stinting in the use of money and renown in the cause of coreligionists, they accomplished much. Elimination of restrictions on Jewish property holding in Habsburg territories, access to the Parliament, university, and peerage in England, and membership in the social elite of France are only some of their achievements. If noblesse oblige can be applied to the status of wealth, then it seems appropriate for the four generations of Rothschilds between 1758 and 1900.

Bibliography

Corti, Count Egon Caesar. *The Rise of the House of Rothschild*. Translated by Brian Lunn and Beatrix Lunn. London: Gollancz, and New York: Blue Ribbon, 1928. An account of the early years of the Rothschild rise to prominence and wealth. Its focus on the first generations makes it particularly useful, since the early years are generally less well known.

Cowles, Virginia. *The Rothschilds: A Family of Fortune*. London: Weidenfeld and Nicolson, and New York: Knopf, 1973. A popular family history recounting the story of the Rothschilds from their origins in eighteenth century Frankfurt to multinational prominence in the mid-twentieth century. The book is well written and corrects some of the most common myths about the Rothschilds, but it does leave other legends untouched.

Davis, Richard. *The English Rothschilds*. Chapel Hill: University of North Carolina Press, and London: Collins, 1983. The author, an excellent scholar, based this book on the Rothschild family papers and an in-depth knowledge of the period; the style makes it a volume for both the general reader and the serious student. For the English branch of the family, there is no better source of information or bibliography.

Elon, Amos. *Founder: A Portrait of the First Rothschild and His Time*. New York: Viking, 1996; as

Founder: Meyer Amschel Rothschild and His Time, London: Harper Collins, 1998. Elon examines the beginnings of the Rothschild empire amid the disturbing anti-Semitic culture of feudal Europe. Rothschild the man emerges from analysis of commercial documents and personal letters. Well-illustrated with photographs, paintings, maps, and city plans.

Ferguson, Niall. *The House of Rothschild: Money's Prophets, 1798–1848.* New York: Viking, 1998; as *The World's Banker: The History of the House of Rothschild,* London: Weidenfeld and Nicolson, 1998. Ferguson, the first historian to be given unrestricted access to the Rothschild archives, has produced a wonderful study of the Rothschild banking empire.

Morton, Frederic. *Rothschilds: A Family Portrait.* New York: Atheneum, and London: Secker and Warburg, 1962. Useful account of the family's history. The general focus makes it particularly desirable for the study of the family rather than of individual members.

Roth, Cecil. *The Magnificent Rothschilds.* London: Hale, 1939; New York: Pyramid, 1962. Long the standard general history of the family, this book, while still valuable, is dated. It is a complete, well-researched, and well-written account.

Fred R. van Hartesveldt

HENRI ROUSSEAU

Born: May 21, 1844; Laval, France
Died: September 2, 1910; Paris, France
Area of Achievement: Art
Contribution: Rousseau was the best known of the "naïve" artists of the late nineteenth century. His deceptively primitive paintings possessed a mysterious poetry that transcended their often banal subject matter and childlike technique to inspire such later artistic movements as Surrealism.

Early Life

When Henri-Julien-Félix Rousseau was born into the world in 1844, his father, Julien, worked as a tinsmith and lived in Beuchheresse Gate, a remnant of the old fortified wall that had once surrounded the town of Laval. Never financially well-off, Julien's debts grew to be so overwhelming that his creditors seized his house when Henri was only seven years old. The Rousseau family then left Laval, leaving young Henri as a boarder at the local school. He proved to be a below-average student but did win several medals for art and singing.

Rousseau left school when he was fifteen and obtained a job in a lawyer's office in Angers, where he worked for three years before signing up for a seven-year tour in the army in 1863. He later claimed that he had served with French forces in Mexico, but this seems to have been the product of his desire to promote himself rather than a historical fact. Rousseau married a young woman named Clémence from Saint-Germain-en-Laye in 1869 while still in the army, and the young couple settled in Paris after his discharge from the service in 1871. Although he initially resumed his premilitary occupation as a law clerk, Rousseau soon managed to obtain a position manning one of the toll booths that marked the entry into Paris. His nickname, *le douanier* (the customs collector), derived from this job with the Paris Municipal Toll Service.

Although Rousseau settled comfortably into his role as a minor functionary, his personal life contained a great deal of tragedy. Clémence bore nine children in rapid succession. Unfortunately, only one, a daughter named Julia, survived to adulthood. Seven of their other children died in infancy, and one son lived to be eighteen. Clémence died giving birth to the last of these ill-fated children. Rousseau would never marry again, although he would pursue a number of women throughout the rest of his life and unsuccessfully propose to many of them.

Rousseau later claimed that it was his lack of financial security that forced him to take the position as a toll booth collector and temporarily forsake his love of art. However, his undemanding job did provide him with ample time to pursue his hobby, and he frequently took time off work to paint. As he practiced, he grew increasingly confident in his talent and began thinking of making painting his full-time vocation. The death of Clémence appears to have pushed him to make his decision. Shortly after her death, he retired from the customs service in 1885, sent his two surviving children to live with relatives in Angers, and devoted himself exclusively to his art.

Life's Work

Rousseau marked his entry as a professional artist by exhibiting a number of his paintings at the official Salon des Artistes Français in 1885. He considered himself an "academic" painter at the time and had received advice and encouragement from two fairly prominent painters of this school, Gérôme and Félix Clément. However, his work received a very hostile reception at the salon. Spectators slashed two of his paintings with knives, and the judges had all of his work removed from the exhibition and declared that they were not up to the standards of the salon.

Most artists would have given up in the face of such universal condemnation of their work. However, if this hostile reception bothered Rousseau, he gave no indication in public. He did abandon his goal to exhibit at the official salon and instead began to show his work at the newly created Salon des Indépendants, an annual art exhibit that showcased the work of new artists. The new salon did not have a jury, so nearly all who wanted to exhibit their work were free to do so without fear of rejection. Rousseau took advantage of this "open door" policy and exhibited four of his paintings at the 1886 session of the Salon des Indépendants. Even though the public and critics still ignored his work, he sincerely believed that he was part of the artistic community since he had now shown his paintings in a public exhibit.

Rousseau's difficulty in gaining recognition for his work stemmed from the fact that it was difficult

to ascertain what he was trying to do. Although he claimed to be a painter in the classic academic style, his work did not adhere at all to the standards of this school. His paintings often demonstrated a childlike technique that included glaring disproportions in perspective and exaggerated characterizations. His subject matter was often banal, drawn frequently from book and catalog illustrations that attracted his eye. He often portrayed human characters in stiff, unnatural poses and simplified their facial expressions in an almost cartoonish manner. Even more disturbing for many of his contemporaries was the fact that it was never clear whether Rousseau's technique represented an intentional distortion of reality or merely reflected a severely limited talent.

Rousseau did not appear to have been upset by the criticism leveled at his work. Even though critics accused him of "painting with his feet" and viciously attacked every new painting that he presented at the annual shows of the Salon des Indépendants, he continued to remain completely oblivious to their barbs. Many scholars agree that his immunity to criticism was the product of his

naïve personality and have claimed that he frequently mistook sarcastic comments as praise.

The founders of the avant-garde movement in France, notably the playwright Alfred Jarry and the journalist Guillaume Apollinaire, took Rousseau under their wing and promoted his work. It was through their efforts that Rousseau met such innovative contemporary artists as Pablo Picasso, Paul Gauguin, and Camille Pissarro—all of whom admired aspects of his work. This acceptance by a segment of the avant-garde community buttressed Rousseau's own estimation of his work, but it brought him little financial success. His entry into this bohemian community also proved to be a mixed blessing. Many of his new "friends" exploited his childlike naïveté to pull a series of pranks on him. For example, Gauguin once told Rousseau that he had been awarded a government commission for a painting. Rousseau believed the story without question and promptly went to the Ministry of Fine Arts to receive his money and instructions. On another occasion, one of his friends sent him a phony letter from the president of France inviting him to dinner. Rousseau blithely went to the president's mansion at the appointed day and time, only to be turned away at the door. Rousseau would later claim that the invitation had been real but that he had forgotten to wear formal attire and had been asked to come back another day.

These pranks never caused Rousseau to reject his new friends. In fact, beginning in 1907, he began to hold "soirées familiales et artistiques"—parties to which he invited everyone whom he knew. These parties became celebrated events on the Left Bank in Paris and regularly attracted a large number of artists and intellectuals, including Georges Braque and Picasso. At the same time, Rousseau's reputation as a painter began to improve, thanks primarily to the efforts of Apollinaire, who tirelessly championed his work. Certain critics began to identify him with the fauvist movement (which also included Henri Matisse and Braque), and the young painters of this school also accepted Rousseau as one of their own. In fact, when a collection of fauvist paintings was organized for the 1905 Salon d'Automne, Rousseau's *The Hungry Lion* (1905) was accorded a place of honor next to the work of Matisse, Braque, Georges Roualt, and Raoul Dufy. This acceptance was highlighted by a huge banquet given by Picasso in Rousseau's honor in 1908. Although this event was partially put on in jest, it nonetheless reflected the warm feelings that the Parisian artistic community held for the eccentric and guileless *le douanier*.

Despite a growing appreciation of his work in certain sophisticated quarters, Rousseau still faced a great deal of scorn from mainstream critics and the general public during the last years of his life and found it very difficult to support himself through his art. When he died in 1910 from blood poisoning, he was buried in a pauper's grave in Paris. One year later, painter Robert Delaunay and Rousseau's former landlord collected enough money from Rousseau's former acquaintances to buy him a regular cemetery plot and a small tombstone. In 1924, his remains and tombstone were moved to the Parc de la Perrin in Laval.

Summary

After Rousseau's death, critics and the public alike finally realized the value of his work. His use of color, his attention to detail, and his unusual renderings of often banal subjects revealed a fresh artistic vision that is often stunning in its impact on the viewer. One is struck by the innocence and enthusiasm in his work, characteristics that would later gain the admiration of the Surrealists and expressionists. In his most famous paintings, such as *The Dream* (1910), *The Sleeping Gypsy* (1897), *The Football Players* (1908) and *Carnival Evening* (1886), an aura of mystery and wonder pervades the canvas, challenging the viewers' sense of reality and forcing them to acknowledge Rousseau's alternative interpretation of the world. Henri Rousseau viewed the world around him in a very original way, and his art, which embodied his unique view, still impresses viewers with its combination of simplicity, drama, and insight. His artistic legacy has outlasted the criticisms of his numerous contemporary detractors and continues to inspire generation after generation of painters. Rousseau always knew that he was a talented painter; it has just taken the rest of the world a little time to catch up with him.

Bibliography

Alley, Ronald. *Portrait of a Primitive: The Art of Henri Rousseau*. Oxford: Phaidon Press, and New York: Dutton, 1978. Alley provides a straightforward narrative of the life and work of Rousseau that emphasizes his contribution to the primitive art movement of the twentieth century.

Ehrlich, Doreen. *Henri Rousseau*. London: Bison, and New York: Smithmark, 1995. This work stresses that Rousseau's work had an important influence on future generations of artists despite his nonacceptance by the art establishment during his lifetime.

Keay, Carolyn. *Henri Rousseau, le douanier*. London: Academy, and New York: Rizzoli, 1976. This book is short on biographical details, concentrating instead on a very thorough examination of Rousseau's paintings and future influence.

Rich, Daniel. *Henri Rousseau*. New York: Museum of Modern Art, 1942. This is the first book in English to recognize the importance of Rousseau's work in shaping subsequent artistic movements in the twentieth century.

Schmalenbach, Werner. *Henri Rousseau: Dreams of the Jungle*. New York: Prestel, 1998. Schmalenbach examines the jungle paintings that Rousseau produced late in his career and investigates the issue of their inspiration and influence.

Shattuck, Roger. *The Banquet Years: The Origins of the Avant-Garde in France, 1885 to World*

War I. Rev. ed. New York: Random House, 1968; London: Cape, 1969. Shattuck argues that Rousseau, along with Guillaume Apollinaire, Erik Satie, and Alfred Jarry, personified the modernist movement in France during the late nineteenth century.

Vallier, Dora. *Henri Rousseau*. New York: Abrams, 1962; London: Thames and Hudson, 1964. This book offers a comprehensive analysis of Rousseau's painting. The text draws heavily on the artist's own writings about his work.

Christopher E. Guthrie

JOHN RUSKIN

Born: February 8, 1819; London, England
Died: January 20, 1900; Coniston, Lancashire, England
Areas of Achievement: Art and social reform
Contribution: Ruskin was the most influential critic of art and architecture in the nineteenth century, promoting the notion that art had a moral purpose; as a social critic, he worked to undercut notions of laissez-faire economics and utilitarianism, championing the dignity of individual workers and the need for national programs of education and welfare.

Early Life

John Ruskin's parents, wine merchant John James Ruskin and his wife Margaret, were convinced that their child was destined for greatness. With this future in mind, they reared him in sheltered comfort, keeping him from activities that might lead to injury, affording him few opportunities to play with children his own age. Young John read the Bible with his devout mother, who believed he would one day be a great divine, and listened to the works of Sir Walter Scott and other literary luminaries read by his father, who thought John destined for fame as a poet. In the isolation of his home, Herne Hill, outside London, Ruskin wrote poetry and sketched for amusement. There, too, he was privately tutored in preparation for entry into Oxford.

Business activities meant frequent trips for his father, and as a child Ruskin had ample opportunity to see both Great Britain and later the Continent in his parents' company. On a trip through France in 1835, he met Adèle Domecq, eldest daughter of his father's business partner; unaccustomed to the company of young females, Ruskin fell helplessly and confusedly in love. For several years he harbored deep feelings for Adèle, but he was eventually disappointed when she married a French nobleman in 1840.

Meanwhile, Ruskin was already writing on subjects that would occupy him for much of his adult life: art and architecture. He had published scientific papers when he was only fifteen, and had already published poetry before he enrolled at Oxford in 1837. While a student there, he began a series for *Architectural Magazine* titled "The Poetry of Architecture"; these essays stress the importance of landscape art as an expression of the artist's view of nature, not mere slavish imitation—a theme he would elaborate in his multivolume *Modern Painters* (1843-1860).

Ruskin's life at Oxford was by most standards unusual. Friends at Christ Church College knew him as a friendly sort, slender, with reddish hair, and pale blue eyes accentuated by the blue cravat he wore. Though he resided at the college, his mother had taken rooms nearby to oversee his education. For three years, Ruskin strove for the Newdigate Prize for poetry, largely at his father's insistence, winning the prize in 1839. Unfortunately, he found his preparation for Oxford insufficient in some areas and eventually had to take a leave of absence to recover from a stress-related illness. Not until 1842 did he receive a B.A., taking a double fourth in classics and mathematics.

Life's Work

Ruskin's emergence into the public forum came as a result of his passion for art. Long an admirer of the iconoclastic painter J. M. W. Turner, in 1842 Ruskin found himself compelled to undertake a systematic defense of the artist to rebut a savage review of Turner's work. At the same time, his family moved to Denmark Hill, which was to be Ruskin's home for three decades. There he wrote diligently what eventually became the first of a multivolume work explaining the principles that characterize great art: power, imitation, truth, beauty, and relation. The first volume of *Modern Painters* was published in 1843; Ruskin identified himself on the title page simply as "A Graduate of Oxford," ostensibly to mask the fact that he was so young to write so authoritatively.

Modern Painters was favorably received, and Ruskin set about immediately to continue his study. In 1845, he was allowed to travel to the Continent without his parents for the first time. In Italy he studied the works of antiquity and the Renaissance, a period for which Ruskin had great antipathy. He also spent considerable time studying the architecture of the cities through which he traveled. As a consequence, the second volume of *Modern Painters* did not follow slavishly the plan set out in the first volume and implied in its title; instead, Ruskin digressed to discuss the art he had observed during his more recent trips.

The success of his work made Ruskin popular socially, and his parents hoped he would eventually marry Charlotte Lockhart, granddaughter of Sir

Walter Scott. Ruskin, however, had other ideas; he fell in love with Euphemia ("Effie") Gray, daughter of a Perth businessman. After some months of awkward courtship, they were married, on April 10, 1848.

Marriage did not change Ruskin's life-style greatly; he continued his travels and writings, preparing studies of architecture that appeared in 1849 as *The Seven Lamps of Architecture*. Further investigations, and deeper thought about the relationship between great buildings and those who built them, resulted in the three volumes published in 1851-1853 as *The Stones of Venice*. In the work, Ruskin argues that one can read a city's history in its architecture, and make judgments about a society based on the kind of buildings it erects. During this same period, Ruskin began what was to be a lifelong defense of the Pre-Raphaelite painters and poets.

Meanwhile, relations between Ruskin and his wife deteriorated, as John's parents found their daughter-in-law an interloper in their close-knit family, a view their son came to share. By 1854, Effie could no longer stand the constant upbraiding and mental harassment; she fled back to her family, initiating a suit for annulment on the grounds that the marriage had never been consummated. Ruskin did not contest the suit. Two years later, Effie married the painter John Everett Millais, with whom she had a large family.

Freed from the constraints of married life, Ruskin returned to his parents' home and resumed work on *Modern Painters*. The third volume appeared in January, 1856; the fourth followed in April. In these books, Ruskin stated clearly his belief that great art can be produced only by men who feel acutely and nobly. At the same time, he began developing what was to become an important thesis in his later works: the inextricable relationship between art and the economy.

In 1857, Ruskin spent considerable time cataloging the nineteen thousand drawings that Turner had bequeathed to the nation upon his death in 1851. That same year, Ruskin delivered a series of lectures in Manchester. In them, he argued for public patronage of the arts, straying from strict commentary about art to remark on the status of Great Britain's economy and the ways in which the masses were being exploited and impoverished.

By 1860, Ruskin had finally finished *Modern Painters*. In the seventeen years during which he worked on this magnum opus, he had grown significantly in the appreciation of various artists, developed a moralistic theory of art and architecture, and suffered several personal setbacks. Never one to deal well with women, Ruskin found himself associating often with young ladies, even girls; his affiliation with Margaret Bell's girls' school at Winnington was one way in which he satisfied his psychological needs to share such company. A chance meeting in 1858 led to his infatuation with ten-year-old Rose La Touche. For more than a decade he pursued her affection, eventually proposing marriage when she turned eighteen (he was forty-seven at the time). Her continual rejection brought anguish to Ruskin, an anguish that found its way into his public writings through a series of private symbols and obscure autobiographical references.

Though he had spoken publicly and written often about the state of the economy for some time before 1860, in that year Ruskin emerged as a major critic of current economic and social programs. In the fifth volume of *Modern Painters*, he launched what would amount to a crusade, with himself cast in the role of Saint George against the dragon of a country obsessed with money and unwilling to recognize the dignity of its laborers. Meanwhile, Ruskin composed a series of essays on political economy for the new *Cornhill Magazine;* unfortunately, these were too controversial, and the editor, William Makepeace Thackeray, was forced to cancel them after several had appeared. Undaunted, Ruskin published the complete set in 1862 in a volume titled *Unto This Last*.

Ruskin's father objected to his son's new field of inquiry, and the early 1860's were difficult years. The senior Ruskin's death in 1864 freed Ruskin from constant criticisms but left him to care for his mother until she died in 1871. To help at Denmark Hill, Ruskin's cousin Joan Agnew came for a brief visit—and stayed almost constantly for the rest of the century, first assisting with Mrs. Ruskin, then serving as a younger companion and later nurse for Ruskin himself. Their relationship, which became quite intimate in its own way, survived Joan's marriage to Arthur Severn.

Throughout the 1860's Ruskin devoted himself to writing about economic issues, trying to relate the disparate branches of his studies into a coherent vision of human society. In 1867, he began writing "open letters" on a variety of social and economic issues. The first series he collected in 1872 as *Munera Pulveris*. A year earlier, he had initiated a monthly series of letters (which slowed in frequency after several years) addressed to the workingmen of Great Britain. Titling his series *Fors Clavigera* (1871-1884), a name he said implied "force" or "fortune" in the first word and "strength" or "patience" in the second, Ruskin wrote on a wide variety of topics, mingling autobiography and private symbology in tracts about art, politics, and economics. Many were considered incomprehensible by even the most astute Ruskin devotees; the intended audience was undoubtedly confused, even bewildered, by this strange mixture of personal narrative and public pronouncement.

His commitment to social issues did not keep Ruskin from pursuing his work in art. In 1870, he assumed the Slade Professorship of Art at Oxford, the first professor of art appointed in Great Britain. For several years, he used that forum to further his ideas concerning the relationship between art and religion, and art and morality. He also assembled a fine collection of works to illustrate his lectures, eventually bequeathing them to the university. In 1871, he funded a new school of art at Oxford, the Ruskin School of Drawing, still among the most prestigious of such institutions.

Meanwhile, Ruskin tried to implement some of the social theories about which he had written. In 1871, he officially founded the Guild of St. George, a Utopian society to promote humanistic living. Though the project eventually failed, Ruskin worked diligently to obtain land to establish ideal communities where men could share the products of their labors, and where they could enjoy the beauties of art (much of which Ruskin himself obtained for these planned communities).

The death of Rose La Touche in 1875 may have been responsible for the frenzy of work in which Ruskin engaged for the next several years. He continued to visit the Continent, to write new works or revise those which he thought required a change of focus, and to promote social causes. In the late 1870's, he began to suffer from intermittent fits of mental instability. Fighting the effects of this illness, Ruskin worked on a host of projects, including his autobiography, *Praeterita*, left unfinished in 1889 when his condition worsened to the point that he lost all capacity for work. In effect, he spent the last eleven years of his life totally incapacitated, simply existing at his home under the care of Joan Agnew Severn. He died in 1900 and was buried in the churchyard at Coniston.

Summary

Author of more than a hundred books and pamphlets on subjects ranging from art to politics, John Ruskin was one of the most influential writers of his age. To him is owed the recognition of the greatness of the painter Turner and the group of painters and poets known as the Pre-Raphaelite Brotherhood. More significant, Ruskin established principles for evaluating art that became touchstones for later critics and art historians. While his notion that all great art is inherently moral may have subsequently been discredited, his method of close reading of paintings and especially of architecture has had marked influence on the study of these art forms. Ironically, his imperative judgment that art has value for society, and is not simply ornament, led to the development of the art for art's sake movement, which also claimed an inherent value for art—but divorced from any utilitarian or moral value.

Like many other social commentators, Ruskin attracted a contemporary following, but subsequent generations have not sought his work as a model for their society. He was influential in bringing his countrymen to see the dangers of Benthamism and similar systems that treated people as ciphers.

Even though his direct influence on theories of art and economics has waned, Ruskin remains a significant figure in the living tradition of English literature. His best writings, laden with echoes of the Bible and literary classics, are often cited as models of the richness that can be achieved by one whose prose approaches poetry in style, allusion, and use of metaphor.

Bibliography

Abse, Joan. *John Ruskin: Passionate Moralist.* London: Quartet, 1980; New York: Knopf, 1981. Carefully researched biography focusing on Ruskin's efforts to promote various causes, and noting the importance that events in his personal life had in shaping his writings and public lectures. Includes a valuable bibliography of primary and secondary sources for those wishing to read more by or about Ruskin.

Beer, John. *Providence and Love: Studies in Wordsworth, Channing, Myers, George Eliot, and Ruskin.* New York: Oxford University Press, 1998. Beer compares Ruskin and four other writers based on common themes in their works including the idea of romantic love. Includes some manuscripts and letters published for the first time.

Burd, Van Akin, ed. *The Ruskin Family Letters: The Correspondence of John James Ruskin, His Wife, and Their Son, John, 1801-1843.* 2 vols. Ithaca, N.Y.: Cornell University Press, 1973. These important letters between Ruskin and his parents, covering the first forty years of Ruskin's life, provide valuable insight into the role his parents played in Ruskin's development as a critic. The letters also expand, or in some instances, correct, information provided in Ruskin's autobiography, *Praeterita.*

Cook, E. T. *The Life of John Ruskin.* 2 vols. London: Allen, and New York: Macmillan, 1911. The first detailed biography of Ruskin, written by one of the editors of the standard edition of Ruskin's works. Contains significant excerpts from letters and diaries, but omits details of Ruskin's decade-long relationship with Rose La Touche and his battle with mental instability.

Hewison, Robert. *Ruskin and Oxford: The Art of Education.* New York: Oxford University Press, and Oxford: Clarendon, 1996. Well-illustrated volume focusing on Ruskin's reasons for establishing the Ruskin School of Drawing at Oxford and his life as a critic of art, culture, and society.

Hilton, Tim. *John Ruskin.* 2 vols. New Haven, Conn., and London: Yale University Press, 1985. A scholarly biography based on a comprehensive study of available documents at the major Ruskin collections. Stresses the significance of Ruskin's later work, highlighting the writings on society and the economy, especially *Fors Clavigera.* Attempts to correct errors, lapses, and omissions in earlier biographies, especially those of Cook and other Victorian and Edwardian chroniclers.

Hunt, John Dixon. *The Wider Sea: A Life of John Ruskin.* London: Dent, and New York: Viking Press, 1982. Detailed, comprehensive biography that highlights the importance of travel in shaping Ruskin's ideas; concentrates on Ruskin's personal life, providing brief analyses of individual works.

Ruskin, John. *The Diaries of John Ruskin.* Edited by Joan Evan and J. H. Whitehouse. 3 vols. Oxford: Clarendon Press, 1956-1959. Though not a complete collation of such materials, these diaries are a key to understanding Ruskin's method of composition, and reveal much about the way his mind worked as an artist, a traveler, and an observer of life.

———. *Praeterita.* Oxford and New York: Oxford University Press, 1978. Ruskin's celebrated autobiography, highly selective in its presentation of details from the author's earlier life. Written between Ruskin's bouts with mental illness, it was intended to present those things that had given him enjoyment. Hence, stress is placed on travel and relationships with parents and mentors; there is no discussion, however, of his six-year marriage.

Laurence W. Mazzeno

LORD JOHN RUSSELL

Born: August 18, 1792; London, England

Died: May 28, 1878; Pembroke Lodge, Richmond Park, England

Areas of Achievement: Government and politics

Contribution: One of the leading Whig politicians of the nineteenth century, Russell held cabinet office for all but seven of the years between 1830 and 1866, and was twice prime minister.

Early Life

John Russell, a younger son of the fifth Duke of Bedford, came from a family that had historical ties with the English Reformation, the parliamentary cause in the Civil War, the opposition to the Catholic king, James II, the Glorious Revolution, and the Whig opposition to William Pitt the Younger's anti-French measures. Russell lived and breathed his family's history, and the events of the seventeenth and eighteenth centuries were as real to him as those of the nineteenth. His ancestor Lord William Russell was executed in 1683 for his part in the plot to exclude James II from the throne. Parliament over king, Whigs over Tories, Protestant truth over Roman Catholic obscurantism: These were the principles for which Russell believed his family stood.

Born two months premature, Russell, when fully grown, stood only about five feet, five inches tall and was frail of health. His size was a handicap in politics and a caricaturist's dream: His friends called him "Jack the Giantkiller"; his enemies drew him as a child. He married a widow, and the nickname "the widow's mite" followed. After study with tutors, Russell attended the University of Edinburgh; he also traveled in Portugal, Spain, and Italy, and he visited Napoleon at Elba. He enjoyed the title "Lord John" Russell as the younger son of a duke, and it is by this name that history knows him best.

Lord John entered the House of Commons in 1813 for the family pocket borough of Tavistock. He represented this area and several other constituencies until 1841, when he was returned for the City of London; he held that prestigious seat until 1861, when he was elevated to the peerage. His early political career, from 1813 to 1830, proved him to be an advanced Whig, supporting parliamentary reform, Dissenters' rights, and Roman Catholic Emancipation. Although not a great de-bater, he was able to hold the attention of the Commons through the force of his argument. This ability united with his family background to bring him to a position of leadership among the Whigs.

Life's Work

Russell was not immediately given a cabinet post when the Charles Grey ministry came to power in 1830. He served on the committee that drafted the Great Reform Bill, and he piloted it through the House of Commons. His great national popularity as a reformer dates from this period. He served as home secretary (1835-1839) and colonial secretary (1839-1841) under Lord Melbourne. During these years, Russell continued to express his advanced Whig views, supporting Dissenters' rights, reform of Irish grievances, the rationalization of the revenues of the Church of England, the Municipal Corporations Act, and other reforms in the areas of prisons, the Poor Law, and education. Although distasteful to the more conservative Whigs (Lord Stanley, the Earl of Ripon, and Sir James Graham resigned over Russell's proposal to confiscate revenues of the Irish church), Russell's proposals did not go far enough to suit the Philosophical Radicals, the Irish, and the militant Nonconformists. They had little choice but to support him, however, for the Conservatives were worse.

Lord John emerged as the leader of the Whig opposition during Robert Peel's ministry (1841-1846). When the Conservatives split over the questions of endowing the Irish Roman Catholic seminary at Maynooth and repealing the Corn Laws, Russell formed a government. He was prime minister from 1846 to 1852.

Russell's ministry continued the pattern of moderate Whig reforms set during the 1830's. The state's role in education, factories, and public health expanded. The Whigs supported representative and responsible government for the colonies. They persevered in their policies of free trade and laissez-faire economics, eliminating the last vestiges of protective tariffs. In the three areas of Ireland, foreign policy, and religious policy, however, the Russell ministry was unfortunate.

Russell's ministry coincided with the Irish Potato Famine. The government did not respond well to this disaster. Although it attempted to alleviate the famine with a large public works program, it believed that free-market economics would solve the problem of famine. Although free-market economics did not work, given the special circumstances of the Irish situation, the government, determined not to deviate from economic orthodoxy, refused to permit the direct relief necessary to prevent starvation. This policy promoted Irish discontent and terrorism, and created the myth, still held today, that the British had tried to starve the Irish.

In foreign policy, Russell came into conflict with Foreign Secretary Lord Palmerston. Russell imagined that the unification of Italy would both promote liberal political institutions and damage the Roman Catholic church. Palmerston, although himself a liberal, was an experienced diplomat concerned to promote international stability and British national interests. Moreover, Palmerston ran his foreign policy independent of his cabinet colleagues. This created conflicts that made it rather difficult for the government to respond effectively to the Revolution of 1848 and to the rise of Louis-Napoleon Bonaparte (Napoleon III) in France.

It was Russell's religious policy, however, that caused the loudest quarrels, that helped bring down his government in 1852, and that ultimately destroyed his career. As has been noted, his support of Dissenters' rights and of church reform alienated Anglicans and Conservatives; yet he did not go far enough to satisfy the more extreme Dissenters. When it came to Roman Catholics, his policies were so contradictory that they managed to alienate everyone. Russell supported the Maynooth endowment, and he proposed the concurrent endowment of Anglicans and Roman Catholics in Ireland. Yet he denounced Roman Catholicism as "superstitious" during the Papal Aggression crisis of 1850-1851 (when a papal hierarchy was created for Great Britain) and passed penal legislation against its bishops. His measures, offensive to Roman Catholics, were too weak to satisfy the anti-Catholics.

Russell was not blessed with a docile cabinet, and some of his ministers, especially Chancellor of the Exchequer Charles Wood and Lord Privy Seal the Earl of Minto, were inept. Russell was more liberal than most of his colleagues, who prevented him from introducing measures for further parliamentary reform.

All these factors combined to bring the Russell ministry to such a state of weakness by February, 1852, that Lord Palmerston (who had been fired from the cabinet the previous December) was able to bring it down.

Summary

It is the judgment of Lord John Russell's biographer, John Prest, that Russell ought to have retired from public life in 1852. Despite all the problems of his ministry, he stood in high public esteem as a reformer and as a man of honest and dedicated character. Russell, however, had not known when enough was enough. He continued in public office: foreign secretary, minister without portfolio, and Lord President of the Privy Council in the ill-fated Whig-Peelite Aberdeen Coalition (1852-1855), foreign secretary in the Palmerston ministry (1859-1865), and prime minister again (1865-1866) after Palmerston's death. His record in these offices was dismal, however, for he could not escape Palmerston's domination. During his tenure as foreign secretary, Russell directed most of his energies to domestic matters, especially abortive reform bills, and relied upon Palmerston and the rest of the cabinet to set foreign policy.

Russell was not the most successful of Queen Victoria's prime ministers. He issued public statements and committed his cabinet to policies without consulting his colleagues and without considering the consequences. Oftentimes, he announced a policy without having any idea of how to translate sentiment into practical legislation. He did not have a firm grasp of foreign policy and seemed to believe that foreign rulers were prepared to adopt without debate schemes that Lord Palmerston thought nonsensical. Russell was especially troubled when it came to religion, for he seemed unable or unwilling to devise programs that were politically feasible; he constructed schemes that were impracticable, unsystematic, and superficial.

The roots of Russell's muddle are to be found in his religious peculiarities. He was a Protestant insofar as he was hostile to Roman Catholicism, but he was no orthodox Christian. He believed that a religious establishment should be maintained to propagate rational religion and honest behavior, but he denied that Anglican clergymen were more than a species of civil servant. With respect to his personal faith, Russell had inherited eighteenth century skepticism, anticlericalism, rationalism, and latitudinarianism. His second wife, née Frances Elliot, daughter of the Earl of Minto, influenced his views. A Scots Calvinist of unusual scrupulosity, Lady John was an extreme anticlericalist who eventually gravitated to the Plymouth Brethren sect. She encouraged Russell to extremism in his views.

Russell's character and career reflect both the contributions of the Whig Party to Victorian politics and that party's limitations. He consistently supported measures that he thought would improve British institutions, but all too often he was unable to translate his ideas into programs that would work. He died on May 28, 1878, at Pembroke Lodge, a royal house in Richmond Park, placed by the queen at Russell's disposal.

Bibliography

Arnstein, Walter L. *A History of England.* Vol. 4. *Britain Yesterday and Today: 1830 to the Present.* 7th ed. Lexington, Mass.: Heath, 1996. A very readable survey of English history, useful for background.

Brown, Lucy M., and Ian R. Christie. *Bibliography of British History, 1789-1851.* Oxford: Clarendon Press, 1977. This bibliography of writings on British history for this period is organized by subject and is well indexed.

Ellens, J. P. "Lord John Russell and the Church Rate Conflict: The Struggle for a Broad Church, 1834-1868." *Journal of British Studies* 26 (1987): 232-257. A thoughtful and well-researched study of Russell's views and actions on an important issue connected with church-state relations.

Paz, D. G. "Another Look at Lord John Russell and the Papal Aggression, 1850." *Historian* 45 (1982): 47-64. Analyzes Russell's actions in an important religious controversy and argues that his anti-Catholicism stemmed from his unique religious views and his impetuous personality.

Prest, John. *Lord John Russell.* London: Macmillan, and Columbia: University of South Carolina Press, 1972. The definitive biography; integrates Russell's public career and quirks of personality.

Russell, First Earl. *The Early Correspondence of Lord John Russell, 1805-1840.* Edited by Rollo Russell. 2 vols. London: Unwin, 1913. More poorly edited than Gooch's work (see below), with errors of transcription, but it does make the documents available.

————. *The Later Correspondence of Lord John Russell, 1840-1878.* Edited by G.P. Gooch. 2 vols. London and New York: Longman, 1925. Not well edited, but useful.

————. *Recollections and Suggestions, 1813-1873.* Boston: Roberts, and London: Longman, 1875. Russell's own autobiography. Although Russell himself was not especially self-perceptive, this memoir reveals much about his character.

Walpole, Spencer. *The Life of Lord John Russell.* 2 vols. London and New York: Longman, 1889. A typical Victorian "double-decker" biography. Although replaced by Prest, its virtue lies in the documents that it prints, for Walpole was a good historian and careful transcriber.

D. G. Paz

SACAGAWEA

Born: c. 1788; central Idaho

Died: December 20, 1812; Fort Manuel, Dakota Territory

Area of Achievement: Exploration

Contribution: The only woman who accompanied the Lewis and Clark Expedition in exploring much of the territory acquired through the Louisiana Purchase, Sacagawea assisted as guide and interpreter.

Early Life

Sacagawea (also Sagagawea, Sakakawea) was born into a band of Northern Shoshone Indians, whose base was the Lemhi Valley of central Idaho. Her name translates as "Bird Woman" (Hidatsa) or "Boat Pusher" (Shoshonean). The Northern Shoshone, sometimes referred to as Snake Indians (a name given them by the French because of the use of painted snakes on sticks to frighten their enemies), were a wandering people, living by hunting, gathering, and fishing. As a child, Sacagawea traveled through the mountains and valleys of Idaho, northwest Wyoming, and western Montana. In 1800, at about age twelve, Sacagawea and her kin were encamped during a hunting foray at the Three Forks of the Missouri (between modern Butte and Bozeman, Montana) when they were attacked by a war party of Hidatsas (also called Minnetarees), a Siouan tribe; about ten Shoshone were killed and Sacagawea and several other children were made captives. Sacagawea was taken to reside with the Hidatsas at the village of Metaharta near the junction of the Knife and Missouri Rivers (in modern North Dakota).

Shortly after her capture, Sacagawea was sold as a wife to fur trader Toussaint Charbonneau. A French-Canadian who had developed skills as an interpreter, Charbonneau had been living with the Hidatsas for five years. At the time that Sacagawea became his squaw, Charbonneau had one or two other Indian wives.

All that is known of Sacagawea for certain is found in the journals and letters of Meriwether Lewis, William Clark, and several other participants in the expedition of the Corps of Discovery, 1804-1806, along with meager references in other sources. The Lewis and Clark party, commissioned by President Thomas Jefferson to find a route to the Pacific and to make scientific observations along the way, traveled on the first leg of their jour-

ney up the Missouri River to the mouth of the Knife River, near which they established Fort Mandan (near modern Bismarck, North Dakota) as their winter headquarters. The site was in the vicinity of Mandan and Hidasta villages. Here the expedition's leaders made preparations for the next leg of their journey and collected information on the Indians and topography of the far West.

Life's Work

Sacagawea's association with the Lewis and Clark Expedition began on November 4, 1804, when she accompanied her husband to Fort Mandan. She presented the officers with four buffalo robes. Charbonneau was willing to serve as interpreter, but only on condition that Sacagawea be permitted to go along on the journey. After agreeing to those terms, Lewis and Clark hired Charbonneau. At Fort Mandan on February 11, 1805, Sacagawea gave birth to Jean-Baptiste Charbonneau. Thus, along with the some thirty men, the "squaw woman" and baby became members of the exploring group.

The Lewis and Clark Expedition set out from Fort Mandan on April 7, 1805. Charbonneau and Sacagawea at different times were referred to in the journals as "interpreter and interpretess." Sacagawea's knowledge of Hidatsa and Shoshonean proved of great aid in communicating with the two tribes with which the expedition primarily had contact. Later, when the expedition made contact with Pacific Coast Indians, Sacagawea managed to assist in communicating with those peoples even though she did not speak their language. Her services as a guide were helpful only when the expedition sought out Shoshone Indians in the region of the Continental Divide in order to find direction and assistance in leaving the mountains westward. Carrying her baby on her back in cord netting, Sacagawea stayed with one or several of the main groups of explorers, never venturing out scouting on her own. Little Baptiste enlivened the camp circles, and Clark, unlike Lewis, became very fond of both baby and mother.

Several times on the westward journey Sacagawea was seriously ill, and once she and Baptiste were nearly swept away in a flash flood. In May of 1805, Sacagawea demonstrated her resourcefulness by retrieving many valuable articles that had washed out of a canoe during a rainstorm. Lewis and Clark named a stream "Sâh-câ-ger we-âh (*Sah ca gah we a*) or bird woman's River," which at a later time was renamed Crooked Creek. Not the least of Sacagawea's contributions was finding sustenance in the forests, identifying flora that Indians considered edible. She helped to gather berries, wild onions, beans, artichokes, and roots. She cooked and mended clothes.

Reaching the Three Forks of the Missouri, Sacagawea recognized landmarks and rightly conjectured where the Shoshone might be during the hunting season. A band of these Indians was found along the Lemhi River. Sacagawea began "to dance and show every mark of the most extravagant joy . . . sucking her fingers at the same time to indicate that they were of her native tribe." The tribe's leader, Cameahwait, turned out to be Sacagawea's brother (or possibly cousin). Lewis and Clark established a cordial relationship with Sacagawea's kinsmen, and were able to obtain twenty-nine horses and an Indian guide through the rest of the mountains. Coming down from the mountains, the exploring party made dugout canoes at the forks of the Clearwater River, and then followed an all-water route along that stream, the Snake River, and the Columbia River to the Pacific Coast. At the mouth of the Columbia River, just below present Astoria, Oregon, the adventurers built Fort Clatsop, where they spent the winter. Sacagawea was an important asset as the expedition covered the final phase of the journey. "The wife of Shabono our interpreter," wrote William Clark on October 13, 1805, "reconsiles all the Indians, as to our friendly intentions a woman with a party of men is a token of peace."

Besides her recognition of topography that aided in finding the Shoshones, Sacagawea's other contribution as guide occurred on the return trip. During the crossing of the eastern Rockies by Clark's party (Lewis took a more northerly route), Sacagawea showed the way from Three Forks through the mountains by way of the Bozeman Pass to the Yellowstone River. Lewis and Clark reunited near the junction of the Missouri and the Yellowstone. Sacagawea, Charbonneau, and infant Baptiste accompanied the expedition down the Missouri River only as far as the Hidatsa villages at the mouth of the Knife River. On April 17, 1806, they "took leave" of the exploring group. Clark offered to take Sacagawea's baby, whom Clark called "Pomp," with him to St. Louis to be reared and educated as his adopted son. Sacagawea, who consented to the proposal, insisted that the infant, then nineteen months old, be weaned first.

With the conclusion of the Lewis and Clark Expedition, details about Sacagawea's life become very sketchy. In the fall of 1809, the Charbonneau family visited St. Louis. Charbonneau purchased a small farm on the Missouri River just north of St. Louis from Clark, who had been named Indian superintendent for the Louisiana Territory. In 1811, Charbonneau sold back the tract to Clark. Sacagawea yearned to return to her homeland. Charbonneau enlisted in a fur trading expedition conducted by Manuel Lisa. In April of 1811, Sacagawea and Charbonneau headed up river in one of Lisa's boats. One observer on board at the time commented that Sacagawea appeared sickly.

Sacagawea left Jean Baptiste Charbonneau with Clark in St. Louis. On August 11, 1813, an orphan's court appointed Clark as the child's guardian. Sacagawea's son went on to have a far-ranging career. At age eighteen, he joined a western tour of the young Prince Paul Wilhelm of Württemberg, and afterward went to Europe, where he resided with the prince for six years. The two men returned to America in 1829, and again explored the western country. Jean Baptiste thereafter was employed as a fur trapper for fifteen years by the American Fur Company. He later served as an army guide during the Mexican War. Joining the gold rush of 1849, Jean Baptiste set up residence in Placer County, California. Traveling through Montana in May of 1866, he died of pneumonia.

There has been a lively controversy over the correct determination of the date and place of Sacagawea's death. Grace Raymond Hebard, a professor at the University of Wyoming, published the biography *Sacajawea* in 1933, in which she went to great lengths to prove that Sacagawea died April 9, 1884. Hebard traced the alleged wanderings of the "Bird Woman" to the time that she settled down on the Wind River Reservation in Wyoming. Hebard made a substantial case, based on oral testimony of persons who had known the "Bird Woman"; the hearsay related to known details of the Lewis and Clark expedition. Hebard also relied upon ethnological authorities. At the heart of the controversy is a journal entry of John Luttig, resident fur company clerk at Fort Manuel. On December 20, 1812, he recorded: "this Evening the Wife of Charbonneau, a Snake Squaw died of a putrid fever she was a good and the best Women in the fort, aged abt 25 years she left an infant girl." It is known that Sacagawea had given birth to a daughter, Lizette. The Luttig journal was not published until 1920. Hebard claimed that the death notice referred to Charbonneau's other Shoshone wife, Otter Woman. The issue, however, seems put to rest by the discovery in 1955 of a document in William Clark's journal dated to the years 1825 to 1828. Clark's list of the status of members of his expedition states: "Se car ja we au Dead." Nevertheless, the notion that Sacagawea lived until the 1880's continues to have support.

Summary

Sacagawea had a fourfold impact on the Lewis and Clark Expedition. Though she viewed much of the country the group traversed for the first time, her geographical knowledge was most important in locating the Shoshones in the Rocky Mountains and directing Clark's party through the Bozeman Pass. At crucial instances her services as a translator were essential, and she served as a contact agent. Perhaps, most of all, as an Indian mother with a young baby, she dispelled many of the fears of the Indians encountered on the journey, particularly the fear that the expedition might harm them. She may be credited as a primary factor in ensuring the success of the Lewis and Clark expedition. Sacagawea also contributed to the uplifting of morale. Throughout the venture she exhibited courage, resourcefulness, coolness, and congeniality. The presence of mother and baby encouraged a certain civilized restraint among the members of the party. Henry Brackenridge, who met Sacagawea in April of 1811, said that she was "a good creature, of a mild and gentle disposition." Clark expressed regrets at the end of the expedition that no special reward could be given to Sacagawea. In many ways she was more valuable to the expedition than her husband, who ultimately received compensation for their efforts.

Sacagawea's place in history was long neglected. Interest in her life, however, gained momentum with the centenary celebrations of the Lewis and Clark Expedition in the early 1900's and especially with the rise of the suffrage movement, which saw in Sacagawea a person of womanly virtues and independence. Eva Emery Dye's novel, *The Conquest: The True Story of Lewis and Clark* (1902), did much during the course of its ten editions to popularize an exaggerated role of Sacagawea on the famous journey of discovery.

Bibliography

Anderson, Irving. "A Charbonneau Family Portrait." *American West* 17 (Spring 1980): 4-13, 58-64. Written for a popular audience, this article provides a thorough and reliable account of the lives of Sacagawea, her husband Toussaint, and her son Jean-Baptiste.

————. "Probing the Riddle of the Bird Woman." *Montana: The Magazine of Western History* 23 (October, 1973): 2-17. A scholarly article that persuasively disputes the evidence gathered by Grace Hebard to argue that Sacagawea lived to be nearly one hundred years old.

Chuinard, E. G. "The Actual Role of the Bird Woman." *Montana: The Magazine of Western History* 26 (Summer 1976): 18-29. Emphasizes the role of Sacagawea as a guide and contact agent and challenges the exaggeration of her actual accomplishments.

Clark, Ella E., and Margot Edmonds. *Sacagawea of the Lewis and Clark Expedition.* Berkeley: University of California Press, 1979. Includes discussion of Sacagawea's life and the efforts made to popularize her legend. Although they provide a relatively accurate account, the authors choose to accept the discredited theory that Sacagawea lived until 1884.

Howard, Harold P. *Sacajawea.* Norman: University of Oklahoma Press, 1971. A balanced biography aimed at a general audience, this work attempts to sort out fact from legend in the life of Sacagawea.

Jackson, Donald, ed. *Letters of the Lewis and Clark Expedition, with Related Documents, 1783-1854.* 2 vols. 2d ed. Urbana: University of Illinois Press, 1978. Contains a variety of letters, journal entries, and other papers relevant to the activities of the expedition. Sheds some light on the contribution of the Charbonneau family.

Kidwell, Clara Sue. "Indian Women as Cultural Mediators." *Ethnohistory* 39, no. 2 (Spring 1992). Focuses on the role of Indian women in intercultural situations and includes information on Sacagawea, Pocahontas, and others.

Ronda, James P. *Lewis and Clark Among the Indians.* Lincoln: University of Nebraska Press, 1984. This scholarly study examines the contact made between the Lewis and Clark expedition and the Indians. Provides insights into Sacagawea's contributions to the success of the expedition. Includes an appendix that evaluates various books and articles about Sacagawea.

Weisbrod, Marie Webster. "Sacajawea: Native American Heroine." *Journal of the West* 37, no. 1 (January, 1998). Examines Sacagawea's role in the Lewis and Clark Expedition.

Harry M. Ward

SAIGŌ TAKAMORI

Born: January 23, 1828; Kagoshima, Kyūshū, Japan
Died: September 24, 1877; Kagoshima, Kyūshū, Japan
Areas of Achievement: Government and politics
Contribution: Saigō's military leadership and political support were instrumental in the events leading to the demise of Japan's last feudal government in 1868, while his championing of samurai ideals, culminating in the failed 1877 Satsuma Rebellion, during the early Meiji reform era earned for him the reputation as one of the last supporters of an honorable but outdated value system he ironically helped destroy.

Early Life

The Tokugawa Bakufu military government was a feudal polity controlling from its capital at Edo (modern Tokyo) about 260 hereditary *han* (domains) ruled by local daimyo lords. Former enemies of the Tokugawa clan were included in this arrangement as *tozama* (outside lords), and their lands were latent repositories of anti-Bakufu sentiments. Satsuma, on the southern island of Kyūshū, was a *tozama* domain ruled by the Shimazu clan. Saigō Takamori was born there in 1828 in the Kajimachi section of Kagoshima, the domain's castle town. Saigō was the eldest of seven children of a low-ranking samurai, serving as head of the Satsuma accounts department. Once proud fighting men, many samurai, as a result of the Pax Tokugawa, had become bureaucrats, assisting their lords in various administrative capacities. Saigō's father was such a retainer. Proud of his warrior heritage, yet reduced to the role of a fiscal manager, he struggled to supplement his low salary by farming.

Saigō, a heavyset boy with a thick neck, bushy eyebrows, and penetrating eyes, was reared among memories of his family's samurai heritage and his domain's proud history. During his youth, Saigō was trained in the fighting arts and had inculcated in him the principles of *Bushidō*, the code of samurai ethics. His formal learning occurred at the *Zōshikan*, the Satsuma clan school. There he received a traditional education grounded in neo-Confucian ethics, the activist moral philosophy of the Ming Chinese philosopher Wang Yang-ming, complemented by swordsmanship, Zen meditation, the nativist Shinto beliefs, and regular school subjects. He had a reputation for being a mischievous, headstrong, inarticulate, yet brave and charismatic young man. His burly stature and weight stood him well in sumo wrestling matches, but it also made him the butt of classmates' jokes. Upon finishing school at sixteen, he became an assistant clerk in the county magistrate's office.

Saigō became politically active when he became involved in a succession dispute within the domain's ruling family by siding with Shimazu Nariakira, who became daimyo in 1851, two years before Commodore Matthew C. Perry steamed into Uraga Bay near Edo with a squadron of "black ships" to demand an end to the self-imposed seclusion policy begun in the 1630's.

In recognition of his crucial support for his lord's rise to power, Saigō was taken into Nariakira's service. His presence at Nariakira's Kagoshima headquarters gave him entrée into the inner circle of Satsuma political discussions and policy-making. Saigō, from 1855 to 1858, traveled to Edo and Kyoto as Nariakira's private emissary in the complex political maneuvering among shogunate, imperial court, and daimyo over a commercial treaty that had been proposed by American consul general Townsend Harris and the naming of an heir to the childless shogun Takugawa Iesada.

Nariakira's political star eclipsed in 1858, when his preferred Hitotsubashi line candidate for shogun was rejected in favor of the Kii line. The victory of the Kii proponents brought to power Ii Naosuke, who became great elder in the summer of 1858. Ii signed the Harris treaty without court approval in July and launched the Ansei purge (1858-1860) to oust those opposing him and the shogunal policy of *kaikoku* (open the country).

Nariakira died in August, 1858. In despair at the loss of his patron and now on the political outside, Saigō resolved to commit suicide; he was dissuaded from doing so by Gesshō, a proimperialist Buddhist monk, who was also on Ii's purge list. Together they fled from Kyoto to Satsuma, where the authorities would not give them protection. They decided in a joint suicide pact to drown themselves in Kagoshima Bay. Gesshō succeeded; Saigō, however, was retrieved from the water and, after recovering, banished to Amami Oshima in the Ryukyu Islands.

Nariakira's half brother Hisamitsu had become regent for his son Tadayoshi, the new Lord of Satsuma. Hisamitsu, persuaded by Saigō's boyhood friend Ōkubo Toshimichi, decided to send troops to

Kyoto to support the emperor and then march on Edo to force reforms on the Bakufu. Ōkubo interceded with Hisamitsu for Saigō's return. On March 12, 1862, Saigō was recalled to Satsuma and soon consented to head an advance party of Satsuma troops to Kyoto. He irked Hisamitsu by holding discussions in Kyoto with radical *rōnin* (masterless samurai) wanting to overthrow the Bakufu. Consequently, he was ordered into a second exile (only six months after his pardon) to the islands south of Satsuma. Saigō spent his second banishment (1862-1864) brooding over his failure to avenge his honor through suicide, practicing his calligraphy, wrestling, writing poetry, and starting a family with a commoner, by whom he had two sons (he would take an official wife, Itoko, in 1865).

Life's Work

Again at the urging of Ōkubo, Saigō's second exile ended on April 4, 1864. After Ii Naosuke was assassinated by samurai extremists in March, 1860, the weakened shogunate tried to reach an accommodation with the proemperor, antiforeign forces in Kyoto. Given the title of war minister, Saigō was sent to Kyoto to serve as a Satsuma watchdog. There he faced plotters from the *tozama han* Chōshū (a Satsuma rival), maneuvering to overthrow the Bakufu elements at court. Saigō and his men helped pro-Bakufu Aizu samurai expel the Chōshū troops from Kyoto. Chōshū was declared rebellious, and a punitive expedition was authorized by the Bakufu to chastise this southwestern domain. Saigō was a leader of the December, 1864, Chōshū expedition that forced the domain to apologize, surrender some land, disband its militia, and have some leaders commit suicide. Saigō was instrumental in preventing a harsher treatment of Chōshū.

By 1865, however, Chōshū was rebuilding itself after an internal revolt by midrank samurai. Satsuma was now concerned that the Bakufu was becoming more powerful. Saigō and others began aiding loyalists such as Sakamoto Ryōma, a young Tosa (another outside domain) samurai, and certain Kyoto nobles allied with Iwakura Tomomi, an important court official. Saigō also met Great Britain's first envoy to Japan, Sir Harry Parkes, to try to persuade the English from wholeheartedly supporting the Bakufu. These efforts impressed Chōshū: the two *han*, burying differences in favor of a united front against the Bakufu, their common enemy, entered an alliance in March, 1866. A powerful

tozama coalition, soon augmented by Tosa, was in place to challenge the Tokugawa. When a second punitive Bakufu-led army (without Satsuma participation, at Saigō's insistence) was launched against Chōshū in the summer of 1866, the strengthened Chōshū domain had no trouble repelling them.

The ascendancy of Tokugawa Yoshinobu to the shogunate late in 1866 revived the central government; reforms were initiated and Western military matériel was secured. In the face of Satsuma opposition, however, the shogun had to agree in the fall of 1867 to a Tosa compromise requiring him to step down and join the daimyo ranks as the head of a power-sharing council. There was fear that the Tokugawa, still the strongest of the daimyo, might reassert its right to national rule; to counter this threat, Satsuma troops entered Kyoto, where Saigō and others, with the support of Iwakura, formulated a proclamation to be issued in the name of the fifteen-year-old emperor Mutsuhito, declaring the restoration of imperial rule.

On January 3, 1868, this proclamation was made in the context of a *coup d'état* in Kyoto led by Saigō. The office of shogun was officially ended; the Tokugawa were ordered to surrender all lands and titles, a demand that Yoshinobu refused. Saigō, a junior councillor in the new provisional government, led loyalist troops against holdout Bakufu forces, winning the Battle of Toba-Fushimi. His troops continued mop-up campaigns, which lasted until Edo castle was surrendered and the last Bakufu naval forces were defeated. Victorious in battle, Saigō spared most of his enemies, including the ousted shogun. The emperor, his reign title changed to Meiji (enlightened rule), was nominally restored in 1868, but the political future of the new government, transferred to the former Tokugawa seat of power, renamed Tokyo (eastern capital), was in the hands of a small coterie of young middle-and low-rank samurai from the domains of Satsuma, Chōshū, Tosa, and Hizen.

As the fighting diminished in 1868, Saigō returned to Kagoshima along with many of his soldiers. Whereas his colleague Ōkubo stayed in Tokyo to launch the Meiji regime, Saigō entered semiretirement, working as a clan councilor. He was a national military hero. The court offered him the third rank junior grade to recognize his contributions to the restoration, but he declined in self-deprecating tones, since such an honor would have put him at a rank higher than his daimyo. Realizing that Saigō's nonparticipation in the government and his influence at home could be troublesome, Iwakura, serving as an imperial messenger and accompanied by Ōkubo and Yamagata Aritomo, called on Saigō in January, 1871, with a direct order from the emperor, requiring his participation in the Tokyo government. Ever loyal, he acquiesced to the imperial command, becoming a chief counselor of state. He thus joined Ōkubo, Kido Koin (Chōshū), Itagaki Taisuke (Tosa), and Ōkuma Shigenobu (Hizen) in a coalition government representing the leading pre-Meiji restoration *han*.

In 1871, confident that their reforms had firmly established them in power, Iwakura led more than half of the government's leaders on a year-and-a-half-long trip to observe at first hand the United States and Europe and to convince the Western powers to revise the unequal treaties. Saigō, Itagaki, and Ōkuma were left in charge of a caretaker government bound by written promises not to initiate any new policies while the Iwakura Mission was abroad. In the area of foreign policy, however, independent action was contemplated. When Korea, under Chinese suzerainty, rejected Japanese overtures to recognize the Meiji government, Saigō wanted to go to Korea alone and provoke the Koreans to kill him, thus forcing Japan into war. Earlier, when fifty-four Ryukyuans were attacked by Taiwanese aborigines in 1871, he had called for a punitive expedition against Formosa. Saigō favored a foreign war to create a role for the many samurai who had been replaced by the new conscript army of commoners and who looked to him for leadership.

Before Saigō could have his permission to go to Korea confirmed by the emperor, Iwakura returned and persuaded Ōkubo to head the opposition to Saigō's plans. Ōkubo, the pragmatic realist, and Saigō, the romantic idealist, clashed over the *seikan* (conquer Korea) issue, ending their decades-long friendship. Iwakura followed Ōkubo's efforts by forcing Saigō and his pro-war partisans out of the government. To save face, it was announced that Saigō and many Satsuma supporters were leaving the government because of poor health. This was his irreversible break with the Meiji government, now dominated by the Ōkubo faction.

His retirement was outwardly peacefully spent romping in the Kagoshima woods with his dogs and composing poetry; there was, however, a political dimension to his retirement as well. He founded several private schools to train Satsuma youth in the fighting arts and traditional ethics. Elsewhere, as samurai were being stripped of their class privileges and becoming impoverished by the financially strapped government's reduction of their stipends, resentment turned into rebellion. In 1874, two thousand Saga samurai revolted unsuccessfully under Etō Shimpei, who had left the government when Saigō had. There were similar failed samurai uprisings in Kumamoto and Hagi two years later.

Wary of what Saigō might do, police informants watched for signs of disquiet in Kagoshima. The government decided to remove by ship a cache of arms from Kagoshima to prevent Saigō's followers from arming themselves. Hotheaded young samurai attacked the imperial arsenals to forestall the arms' removal, precipitating the 1877 Satsuma Rebellion. Saigō, probably aware of the futility of the rebellion, backed his followers, reaffirming his allegiance to the emperor while berating the evil politicians who surrounded him. Saigō's twenty-five thousand men faced at least three times as many government forces. A disastrous battle over Kumamoto castle depleted the rebel army, and its remnants were pursued throughout Kyūshū. In a cave at Shiroyama, Saigō rejected a request from Yamagata to surrender. As he was attempting to escape, he was wounded by a bullet. A samurai to the end, Saigō, to avoid capture and shame, committed ritual disembowelment on September 24, 1877.

Summary

Ending his life a traitor to the state he had helped to found, Saigō Takamori became a hero in death. In 1890, the Emperor Meiji pardoned him posthumously and restored his titles. This apotheosis, coming at a time when the Meiji oligarchy was secure in its power, reflected the popular verdict that Saigō had been a sincere, patriotic hero representative of samurai values nostalgically celebrated in a modernizing Japan that was struggling for an accommodation with its feudal past. The Satsuma Rebellion and Saigō's suicide for the cause were not only his but also the country's last backward glance at a consciously discarded tradition, the lofty virtues of which still resonated in the hearts—if not the minds—of many Japanese.

Saigō's life bracketed the sweeping changes that in a short period ended a feudal regime and established a centralized nation-state in its place. While the majority of the Meiji restoration leaders looked forward, Saigō clutched at a past symbolic of the pure samurai motives his political activism espoused. For later eras, Saigō's life and deeds would be a manipulatable legacy, often with altered facts, that would provide a model for jingoistic foreign adventurists, right-wing nationalists, and out-of-power political dissidents, who would claim him as their source of inspiration. Saigō's life was so complex that liberals, Westernizers, and other more progressive elements could similarly adopt the Satsuma warrior as their own.

Bibliography

Beasley, W. G. *The Meiji Restoration.* Stanford, Calif.: Stanford University Press, 1972; London: Oxford University Press, 1973. The most comprehensive treatment of the late Tokugawa to early Meiji period, with useful glossaries and a bibliography. Saigō's role in the important events of the time are woven into this factual and analytical narrative.

Buck, James H. "The Satsuma Rebellion of 1877." *Monumenta Nipponica* 28 (Winter 1973): 427-446. A thorough account of the samurai uprising and Saigō's participation, emphasizing the military and political maneuverings of the rebel and imperial forces.

Iwata, Masakazu. *Ōkubo Toshimichi: The Bismarck of Japan.* Berkeley: University of California Press, 1964. A biography of Saigō's Satsuma compatriot, with numerous references to Saigō's life where it intertwined with Ōkubo's. Provides an overall view of Satsuma politics and the domain's role in the restoration movement and early Meiji government.

Jansen, Marius B. *Sakamoto Ryōma and the Meiji Restoration.* Princeton, N.J.: Princeton University Press, 1961. Though focusing on this Tosa loyalist samurai, numerous references to Saigō are interlaced in this biographical narrative, describing the downfall of the Tokugawa shogunate.

Mayo, Marlene. "The Korean Crisis of 1873 and Early Meiji Foreign Policy." *Journal of Asian Studies* 31 (August, 1972): 793-819. An analysis of the background of and the reasons for the aborted Korean plan of Saigō and the political maneuvering which defeated it, placed in an overview of emerging Meiji diplomatic concerns.

Morris, Ivan. *The Nobility of Failure: Tragic Heroes in the History of Japan.* London: Secker and Warburg, and New York: Holt Rinehart, 1975. Chapter 9, "The Apotheosis of Saigō the Great," is an excellent English account of Saigō's life, analyzed as part of the Japanese fascination for failed heroes. Very useful notes contain additional biographical details.

Yates, Charles L. *Saigō Takamori: The Man Behind the Myth.* New York and London: Kegan Paul, 1995. An excellent biography that deals with the myths surrounding Saigō, about whom we know little in the way of hard fact. Examines his exiles, his simplistic political philosophy, and his health problems, and compares him with Ōkubo Toshimichi, a forceful post-Restoration figure and boyhood friend.

———. "Saigō Takamori in the Emergence of Meiji Japan." *Modern Asian Studies* 28, no. 3 (July, 1994). Yates attempts to disentangle the legends and truths about Saigō through an understanding of Meiji Japan.

William M. Zanella

AUGUSTUS SAINT-GAUDENS

Born: March 1, 1848; Dublin, Ireland
Died: August 3, 1907; Cornish, New Hampshire
Area of Achievement: Art
Contribution: Saint-Gaudens' memorial statues of America's greatest men and women are generally regarded as among the most beautiful and inspired examples of late nineteenth century artistic realism.

Early Life

Augustus Saint-Gaudens was born March 1, 1848, in Dublin, Ireland. His father was Bernard Paul Ernest Saint-Gaudens, formerly of the village of Aspet in southern France, a shoemaker who emigrated to London and then Dublin. It was in the latter city that he met and married Mary McGuiness, a handcrafter of slippers formerly from Bally Mahon, County Longford. Their first children, George and Louis, died in childhood; then Augustus was born in Dublin; finally, Andrew and another Louis were born in the United States.

Emigration from Ireland to the United States took place in 1848, during Augustus' infancy and the ruinous Potato Famine. The small family arrived at Boston but soon moved to New York City. Here the children were brought up in the Catholic faith and attended public schools.

A patron of the arts, Dr. Cornelius Rea Agnew, saw some pen-and-ink drawings by the child Augustus in his father's shop and recommended that he be apprenticed to an artist. Accordingly, in 1861, when he was thirteen, the boy began his apprenticeship under a stern taskmaster named Avet, a stone-cameo cutter.

The Civil War years and the personalities of that era impressed themselves upon the sensitive mind of the budding artist. Later, he would portray several of them in examples of his greatest works. He came to detest Avet, however, and almost turned his back on portraiture until he found employment with the shell-cameo artist Jules LeBrethon and was accepted as a student at the distinguished drawing school of the Cooper Institute. Before the war drew to a close in 1865, he was admitted to the still more prestigious National Academy of Design. His skills greatly heightened and his family's finances much improved by his earnings, Saint-Gaudens sailed for Europe at the age of nineteen.

Life's Work

In Paris, Saint-Gaudens obtained employment with an Italian cameo cutter and enrolled in a small art school and then in the world famous school of fine arts, L'École des Beaux-Arts. Here, Saint-Gaudens learned much of low relief and the special art of sculpture. In 1868, the American produced his first such work, a bronze bust of his father.

Several lifelong friendships were formed in the five years before Saint-Gaudens returned to the United States in 1872, one with Alfred Garnier, one with Paul Bion and another with the Portuguese Soares dos Reis. These accomplished young artists reinforced one another's desire to persevere in the face of brutal criticism and dwindling funds. Saint-Gaudens, with some of his friends from L'École des Beaux-Arts, lived for a while in Rome; there he completed several classic busts and his statues *Hiawatha* and *Silence*, later placed in Saratoga and New York City, respectively.

His brief return home, to New York, led to several commissioned works. During this time, his patrons included Senator William Evarts of New York, Edward Stoughton, Edward Pierrepont, Elihu Root, and L. H. Willard. Now a productive artist, he chose to live in Rome for the next three years, returning to the United States to stay in 1875. Before his return, he met and became engaged to an American girl in Rome, Augusta F. Homer.

The wedding took place at Roxbury, Massachusetts, on June 4, 1877. Both Augustus and Augusta were dark, average in height, and slim. She was considered by far the better-looking of the two, his chin and nose being long and angular. He also maintained a mustache and, generally, a beard of some kind. Their one child, Homer, was born in 1880. Back in New York, artist John La Farge helped Saint-Gaudens obtain such important assignments as the statue of Admiral David Farragut for placement in Madison Square, New York City, the St. Thomas (Episcopal) Church reliefs, also in New York, and those of the Edward King tomb in Newport, Rhode Island.

Early in the 1880's, Saint-Gaudens began a friendship which was to have a great impact on both his life and his work. A Swedish-born model, Alberta Hulgren or Hultgren, became his mistress; rechristened Davida (she later used the name Davida Johnson Clarke), she became his muse as well. The details of this relationship, long suppressed, remain sketchy. For many years, Saint-Gaudens maintained a separate household for Davida, by whom he had a son; her likeness is evident in a number of Saint-Gaudens' idealized female figures.

It was during this decade, too, that Saint-Gaudens fully established himself as an artist. By 1880, he had already completed the Morgan Tomb's *Angels*, the statue of Robert Richard Randall for Sailors' Snug Harbor, Staten Island, and several medallion and plaque low reliefs such as those of fellow artist Bastien-Lepage and friend Dr. Henry Shiff. A friend of whom he did caricatures was Charles Follen McKim. Another friend and patron, Stanford White, made valuable contacts on his behalf. In the years that followed, Saint-Gaudens added to his fame with statues or reliefs of Robert Louis Stevenson, William Dean Howells, the children of Jacob H. Schiff, Kenyon Cox, Peter Cooper, Princeton president James McCosh, Mrs. Grover Cleveland, General John A. Logan, General William T. Sherman, and Abraham Lincoln. The Lincoln statue was very highly regarded, and it came to rest, appropriately enough, in Lincoln Park in Chicago.

Other works included *The Puritan*, in Springfield, Massachusetts, a winged *Victory* on the Sherman Monument, *Silence, Amor Caritas*, caryatids, other glorified women, eagles for gold coins, horses, and angels. He taught courses at the Art Students' League in New York, accepted pupils readily at his studio on Thirty-sixth Street (most notably Frederick W. MacMonnies), and helped found the Society of American Artists and other groups to promote and advance the fine arts. His advice to aspiring artists was to "conceive an idea and then stick to it." Those who "hang on" will be "the only ones who amount to anything."

In 1891, Saint-Gaudens' most celebrated creation was unveiled: The slim nudity of his *Diana*, high on the tower of Stanford White's Madison Square Garden, provoked comment throughout the city of New York. (A second *Diana*, slightly altered and improved, later took the place of the first.) Many artists today, however, regard Saint-Gaudens' 1891 monument to Mrs. Henry Adams in Rock Creek Cemetery, Washington, D. C., and especially the relief he did there, commonly entitled *Grief*, as his greatest work.

Late in life, Saint-Gaudens suffered two great shocks: He lost his studio in a fire, and then he lost

his fast friend and patron White to a pistol bullet. The fire, in October, 1904, destroyed many small pieces of his life's work. The murder of White, a noted architect with a flamboyant life-style, was carried out by crazed playboy Harry K. Thaw in June, 1906, and was a scandalous affair. Saint-Gaudens died August 3, 1907, following a bout of poor health, in his beloved vacation site of Cornish, New Hampshire.

Summary

Realistic sculpture reached its zenith of popularity during the lifetime of Augustus Saint-Gaudens, and his own contributions helped to keep it popular. While many of his works, busts, reliefs, and complete statues are simply of wealthy patrons and their friends, his most memorable creations are largely associated with the great men and women of his lifetime, including Lincoln, Farragut, and Sherman.

His work is both inspired and inspirational, ideal for the dramatic memorial and the noble sentiment. It expresses feelings of passion, confidence, and courage; it is timely yet timeless.

Bibliography

Cortissoz, Royal. *Augustus Saint-Gaudens*. Boston: Houghton Mifflin, 1907. The author, a specialist in the field of American art and artists in the nineteenth century, has produced in this book an effective though somewhat rambling biography.

Cox, Kenyon. *Old Masters and New*. New York: Fox, Duffield, 1905. Cox was a close friend of Saint-Gaudens, and his insight into the subject's work is especially valuable. While dealing with such different artists as Michelangelo and James Whistler, he does set aside a chapter entitled "The Early Work of Saint-Gaudens," wherein the sculptor's Sherman is given particularly close inspection.

Greenthal, Kathryn. *Augustus Saint-Gaudens: Master Sculptor*. New York: Metropolitan Museum of Art, 1985. An excellent, thoroughly researched study. Among the 181 illustrations are twelve superb color plates. Includes an extensive bibliography.

Hind, Charles Lewis. *Augustus Saint-Gaudens*. New York: International Studio, John Lane, 1908. The author, a prolific biographer at the turn of the century, produced in this volume a very well illustrated if rather shallow biography.

Saint-Gaudens, August. *The Reminiscences of Augustus Saint-Gaudens*. 2 vols. Edited by Homer Saint-Gaudens. London: Melrose, and New York: Century, 1913. The son of the subject and himself a knowledgeable artist, Homer Saint-Gaudens speaks with authority. Inasmuch as he quotes his father extensively, Homer Saint-Gaudens is regarded as the editor, but he is generous with his own observations.

Taft, Lorado. *History of American Sculpture*. New York and London: Macmillan, 1903. This book is the best illustrated work available on the masterpieces of Saint-Gaudens and his contemporaries. Taft's lucid commentaries and beautiful full-page photogravures were so well received that this book went through several revisions and reprints.

Viladas, Pilar, and John Dominis. "Saint-Gaudens in New Hampshire: A Sculptor's Legacy." *Gourmet* 54, no. 10 (October, 1994). Discussion of the authors' visits to the New Hampshire home of sculptor Augustus Saint-Gaudens.

Wilkinson, Burke. *Uncommon Clay: The Life and Work of Augustus Saint Gaudens*. San Diego, Calif.: Harcourt Brace, 1985; Gerrards Cross, Bucks.: Smythe, 1992. The work of a novelist and popular biographer, this spirited account portrays Saint-Gaudens as part passionate romantic, part "Renaissance soldier of fortune." Provides information unavailable elsewhere, particularly concerning Davida Clarke, whose role in Saint-Gaudens' life is perhaps exaggerated by Wilkinson. Well documented; includes a useful section of illustrations.

Joseph E. Suppiger

THIRD MARQUESS OF SALISBURY
Robert Cecil

Born: February 3, 1830; Hatfield, Hertfordshire, England

Died: August 22, 1903; Hatfield, Hertfordshire, England

Areas of Achievement: Government and politics

Contribution: Serving as prime minister three times and foreign secretary four times, Salisbury guided Great Britain's domestic and foreign policies during the last quarter of the nineteenth century with a steady and firm hand.

Early Life

Robert Arthur Talbot Gascoyne-Cecil was born February 3, 1830, at the Cecil family estate at Hatfield, Hertfordshire. Cecil's father was James Brownlow Gascoyne-Cecil, second Marquess of Salisbury, and his mother was Frances Mary Gascoyne, an heiress to estates in Lancashire and Essex. Cecil, who was, according to his daughter Lady Gwendolen, "a nervous sensitive child in mind and body," suffered an irreparable loss when his mother died before he was ten.

After being taught by a local clergyman, Cecil spent a miserable period at a preparatory boarding school. When Cecil was ten, he was sent to Eton, where he did quite well in his academic subjects, but he despised his fellow Etonians for their constant bullying; his time there did nothing to improve his shy and withdrawn personality. When Cecil was fifteen, his father rescued him from his misery at Eton by removing him from the school. For the next two years, Cecil spent what he later called the happiest time of his childhood being tutored at his home at Hatfield. During this period, Cecil discovered an interest in botany, which he retained for the rest of his life; he also spent hours reading in the family library.

Just before he was eighteen, in 1848, Cecil went up to Christ Church, Oxford, to study mathematics. While at Oxford, he manifested his first interest in politics and became treasurer and secretary of the Oxford Union. His tenure at Oxford lasted only two years before he suffered a physical and mental breakdown; he was granted an honorary fourth-class degree.

After leaving Oxford, Cecil suffered a further breakdown of his health; on his doctor's orders, he was sent, in 1851, on a two-year journey to Austra-lia and New Zealand. During his travels, he regained his health although he was quite pessimistic about his future career; he did not want to practice law, and he saw little hope for securing a seat in the House of Commons. Cecil's pessimism soon faded when his father obtained for him the vacant seat of Stamford, Lincolnshire, the borough of Stamford being under the control of one of Cecil's cousins. In August, 1853, Cecil was elected, unopposed, as a Conservative Member of Parliament for Stamford; he remained unopposed for the next fifteen years. Cecil also competed for and was elected to a fellowship in All Souls College, Oxford, in 1853.

His first years in Parliament were of little inspiration, and he continued to have serious problems with his physical and mental health. At six feet, four inches, and with a thin, stooping figure, the poorly dressed Cecil was not impressive physically, but his spirits took a dramatic turn for the better with his introduction to Georgina Alderson, the daughter of a Norfolk judge. Despite his father's objection to the marriage (on the grounds that she lacked the necessary social and economic status), Cecil married Georgina in July, 1857. The outgoing and optimistic Georgina provided a solid counterbalance to her shy and pessimistic husband.

Because he needed to support his wife and a growing family, Cecil turned in the 1850's and 1860's to journalism as a way to supplement his precarious finances. He contributed a number of articles to the *Quarterly Review* and to the *Saturday Review*, which was owned by his brother-in-law. Cecil, who had entered Parliament in 1853 at the age of twenty-three, did not feel comfortable with the Tory leadership of the fourteenth Earl of Derby and Benjamin Disraeli, and he became gloomy about the character of the current political system. He acquired, during this period, a reputation as an independent thinker who was, both in his articles and in his speeches before the Commons, prepared to criticize his own party's policies and leaders.

Cecil's opposition to his party's leadership climaxed in the 1850's and 1860's with his determination to prevent any parliamentary reform of the British electoral system. He opposed any significant increase in the size of the British electorate, believing that any radical change in the electoral

system, such as the enfranchisement of the working classes, would irreparably harm the British system of checks and balances. When the Conservatives led by the Earl of Derby and Disraeli introduced, in early 1867, a reform bill which gave the franchise to all urban taxpayers, Cecil resigned his recently acquired seat in the cabinet.

During this period of debate over parliamentary reform, Cecil had assumed the courtesy title of Lord Cranborne and had become heir to the Salisbury title upon the death of his older brother. At his father's death in April, 1868, Cecil inherited the Hatfield estates and became the third Marquess of Salisbury. His achievements, which make him one of Great Britain's greatest statesmen, were to be attained while leading his party from the House of Lords.

Life's Work

The new Lord Salisbury's move to the House of Lords did not prevent him from criticizing the programs and policies of William Ewart Gladstone's Liberal government of 1868-1874. While politics occupied much of his time during this period, Sal-

isbury also found time to chair the Great Eastern Railway and was elected in 1869 as chancellor of Oxford University. He also spent much of his time at Hatfield with his growing family.

After the stunning victory of the Conservatives in the general election in 1874, Disraeli persuaded Salisbury to return to his former post as secretary of state for India in the new Conservative cabinet. It was during the Disraeli administration of 1874-1880 that Salisbury was propelled into prominence in foreign affairs and was established in his reputation as one of Great Britain's greatest diplomatic statesmen. After Russia invaded Turkey's possessions in 1877, both countries signed a peace treaty which forced the Turks to place their Balkan territories under Russian control. Disagreeing with the British cabinet's decision not to recognize the treaty, the fifteenth Earl of Derby resigned as foreign secretary, and Salisbury took his place in March, 1878. Salisbury successfully negotiated the terms of treaties with both Russia and Turkey, which paved the way for the famous Congress of Berlin, held in the summer of 1878. Although Disraeli commanded most of the attention at the congress, it was Salisbury's masterful diplomacy which succeeded in preserving the balance of power in the Balkans.

The Conservatives fell from power in the general election of spring, 1880, and Gladstone formed his second ministry (1880-1885); Salisbury was chosen to lead the Conservatives in the House of Lords when Lord Beaconsfield (Disraeli) died in April, 1881. Upon Gladstone's defeat in May, 1885, over a budget issue, Salisbury reluctantly became prime minister for the first time; during his administration, the question of Irish home rule dominated much of the debate. Salisbury, who served as his own foreign secretary, devoted much of his time during his brief ministry to Ireland and international problems, including the renewed tensions in the Balkans. After suffering defeat in the November, 1885, general election, Salisbury resigned as prime minister in January, 1886.

With the defeat of Gladstone's Irish Home Rule Bill in June, 1886, ninety-three Liberals (also known as Liberal Unionists) deserted the Liberal Party. Because of Salisbury's ability to persuade local Conservatives to give the Liberal Unionists free races in their constituencies, Salisbury and the Unionists triumphed in July, 1886, in the general election. He formed his second ministry, which would last until 1892.

The first months of Salisbury's second administration were dominated by the mercurial personality of Lord Randolph Churchill, who served as Leader of the Commons and Chancellor of the Exchequer. Churchill, who was constantly at odds with his fellow cabinet members, was allowed to resign over a budget issue in December, 1886; Salisbury, not Churchill, would run the 1886-1892 Conservative administration. The major domestic achievement of this administration was the passage of the Local Government Act of 1888, which created elected county councils in England and Wales. Other important pieces of domestic legislation included acts for mine regulation, working-class housing, and free education. Salisbury, who had taken over the Foreign Office in January, 1887, devoted much of his time and energy to international and colonial affairs. He made good use of his diplomatic skills in fending off the encroachments of France, Germany, and Portugal during the European partition of Africa. While by no means a crusading imperialist, Salisbury was determined to safeguard British interests in Africa.

With the Liberal victory at the polls in 1892, Salisbury lost control of the government for three years. Nevertheless, although Gladstone managed to pass an Irish Home Rule Bill through the Commons in 1893, Salisbury and others decisively defeated the bill in the upper chamber. Salisbury and the Conservatives returned to power with a convincing victory in the general election of summer, 1895; Salisbury would now serve as prime minister uninterrupted until his retirement in 1902.

Although heavily involved with foreign policy during his last administration, Salisbury did not ignore domestic and social issues. He pushed through acts concerned with workmen's compensation, vaccination, food and drugs, working-class housing, and Irish land purchase. In his foreign policy, all Salisbury's skillful diplomacy was needed to avert a war between Great Britain and France over the French intrusion into the Upper Nile. Salisbury was also involved in the successful negotiation between the United States and Great Britain over a boundary dispute between Venezuela and British Guiana. His diplomatic skills did not, however, prevent the outbreak of the South African (Boer) War from 1899 through 1902 between Great Britain and the Boer republics of Transvaal and the Orange Free State. Salisbury had supported the policy of achieving British control of the Transvaal, but he only re-luctantly supported Great Britain's entry into the Boer War.

Soon after the Conservative government was returned to power in the fall, 1900, election, the tired, seventy-year-old Salisbury gave up the Foreign Office. Now in declining health, he waited until the Boer War had been settled and a peace treaty signed before he handed his resignation to Edward VII on July 11, 1902. A little more than a year later, on August 22, 1903, Salisbury died at Hatfield.

Summary

Robert Cecil, Lord Salisbury, prime minister for nearly fourteen years, was one of Great Britain's most influential statesmen of the late Victorian period. While Disraeli and Gladstone dominated mid-Victorian politics, Salisbury overshadowed all of his rivals in foreign and domestic affairs. He was the last British statesman to head the government from the House of Lords and not from the House of Commons.

Salisbury is best known as one of Great Britain's great foreign policy statesmen. Although he was no jingoistic imperialist, the British Empire grew during his tenure as foreign secretary and prime minister. He did not actively promote the expansion of the British Empire but instead ensured that Great Britain's interests were protected abroad. Salisbury, who despised secret diplomacy, believed that foreign affairs should be conducted in the open and opposed interference in the internal affairs of other nations. He conducted his foreign policy in a very deliberate and methodical manner.

Although no diehard resister of change, Salisbury attempted in his domestic policies to reconcile individual liberties and freedoms with social and political stability. A firm believer in self-help in certain domestic areas, such as working-class housing reform, he was nevertheless willing to use the power of the state to address pressing problems which he believed threatened the entire fabric of British society.

Salisbury was in many ways the architect of the modern Conservative British Party; he made effective use of Gladstone's Irish home rule program to provide a secure base in the Conservative Party for moderate Liberals who had fled their own party over the home rule issue. Unlike many of his political contemporaries, he devoted considerable time and energy to managing party affairs. With his numerous speeches to Conservative associations, he was one of the first British politicians to make effective use of the stump speech to articulate his political opinions, and he also made effective use of Victorian periodicals to publicize his conservative views.

Salisbury was not the charismatic type of politician who needed society's adulation; he preferred to spend his time with his family at Hatfield or with his scientific experiments in his basement laboratory. Ironically, the shy and reserved Salisbury, who wanted to avoid publicity, served in the limelight for much of the last quarter of the nineteenth century as one of Great Britain's most famous and influential statesmen.

Bibliography

Brailey, N. "Sir Ernest Satow, Japan and Asia: The Trials of a Diplomat in the Age of High Imperialism." *Historical Journal* 35, no. 1 (March, 1992). Focuses on Lord Salisbury's time as foreign secretary and his problems with respect to a developing global foreign policy.

Cecil, Lady Gwendolen. *Life of Robert, Marquis of Salisbury.* 4 vols. London: Hodder and Stoughton, 1921-1932; New York: Kraus, 1971. Any study of Salisbury must begin with this definitive biography by his daughter; unfortunately, Lady Gwendolen's massive work follows her father only to the end of his second ministry in 1892.

Grenville, J. A. S. *Lord Salisbury and Foreign Policy: The Close of the Nineteenth Century.* London: Athlone Press, 1964. Salisbury's foreign policy has received much attention from scholars, and this study is a perceptive analysis of Salisbury's foreign policy between 1895 and 1902.

Kennedy, A. L. *Salisbury, 1830-1903: Portrait of a Statesman.* London: Murray, 1953; New York: Kraus, 1971. Kennedy offers a very readable portrait of Salisbury. Except for his coverage of the 1892-1903 period, however, he adds little which cannot be found in the more complete study of Salisbury by his daughter.

Marsh, Peter. *The Discipline of Popular Government: Lord Salisbury's Domestic Statecraft, 1881-1902.* London: Harvester Press, and Atlantic Highlands, N.J.: Humanities Press, 1978. While the majority of works on Salisbury have focused on Salisbury and his foreign policy, this well-researched and well-written book is a welcome addition to the growing body of literature concerned with the domestic and party leader.

Pinto-Duschinsky, Michael. *The Political Thought of Lord Salisbury, 1854-1868.* London: Constable, and New York: Archon, 1967. Through a detailed analysis of Salisbury's articles for the *Quarterly Review* and the *Saturday Review*, the author effectively examines the fundamental assumptions of Salisbury's political philosophy.

Salisbury, Third Marquess of. *Lord Salisbury on Politics: A Selection from His Articles in the Quarterly Review, 1860-1883.* Edited by Paul Smith. Cambridge: Cambridge University Press, 1972. Salisbury wrote thirty-three articles for the Tory *Quarterly Review* between 1860 and 1883; Smith presents a valuable analysis of Salisbury's ideas on politics in his introduction and skillful editing of seven of these articles.

Taylor, Robert. *Lord Salisbury.* New York: St. Martin's Press, and London: Lane, 1975. Taylor has written the best single-volume work on Salisbury; while others have concentrated on Salisbury's foreign policy, Taylor devotes most of his study to his subject's domestic record. The book also contains an excellent bibliography of the major primary and secondary sources.

Neil Kunze

JOSÉ DE SAN MARTÍN

Born: February 25, 1778; Yapeyú, La Plata
Died: August 17, 1850; Boulogne-sur-Mer, France
Area of Achievement: The military
Contribution: San Martín, against great odds, led the military forces that secured independence from Spain in Argentina, Chile, and Peru.

Early Life

José Francisco de San Martín was born on February 25, 1778, in the village at Yapeyú on the Uruguay River in what is modern northeastern Argentina, where his father, Juan, a career army officer, was administrator. José, the youngest of four sons, was educated in Madrid following his father's transfer there in 1785. Two years later, following in the footsteps of his father and older brothers, he requested a cadetship in the Spanish army.

His first military experience began at the age of fifteen in Morocco, against Algerian princes. He also fought in the French Revolution and the Napoleonic Wars. In 1808, Napoleon I sent French troops into Spain in order to reach Portugal, which had traded with France's archenemy Great Britain in defiance of Napoleon's wishes. This invasion, along with Napoleon's removal of the Spanish king, caused a furor among the Spanish, who mounted a guerrilla war against the French invaders. San Martín joined the fight against the French by enlisting in the service of the Spanish provisional government (junta), which had been established at Seville. San Martín distinguished himself in battle, receiving a medal and promotions.

For more than twenty years, San Martín served his king with faith and dedication. He had gained valuable experience and had received recognition for his distinguished service. It has been speculated that he did not believe that he had been adequately recognized and, for that reason, he decided to return to his native land and participate in revolutionary events there. San Martín was a Creole, a Spaniard born in the New World, and there was discrimination against Creoles in favor of Spanish-born Peninsulars. Also, in Spain, he had formed friendships with English officers who had imbued him with the revolutionary ideas of the Enlightenment. In 1812, he refused a promotion and returned to Buenos Aires to embark on an enterprise that would gain for him everlasting fame—the independence of South America.

Life's Work

The thirty-four-year-old San Martín returned to Buenos Aires, which in 1812 was in the middle of revolutionary activities. Creoles in Argentina had created a provisional government in the name of the deposed Spanish king Ferdinand VII. Realizing that San Martín would be a valuable member of their military forces because of his experience in Spain, the government gave him command of the army of Upper Peru, which had been defeated by Royalists and was recuperating in Tucumán. San Martín's military genius shone as he improved the soldiers, who lacked discipline and training.

Although not all biographers agree, many have asserted that San Martín founded a secret pseudo-Masonic society, the Lautaro Lodge, whose members dedicated themselves to the independence of South America from Spain. At any rate, San Martín was strongly dedicated to his native country's independence, and he believed that the provisional government should declare independence and abandon any pretense of loyalty to Ferdinand.

In 1814, San Martín asked to be relieved of his command, declaring that he was in poor health. He was then appointed governor-intendant of the province of Cuyo, which enjoyed a better climate than his previous residence in Tucumán. The real reason for this change, however, was San Martín's secret plan to defeat the Spanish in South America by attacking their stronghold in Peru, not through Upper Peru as the provisional government proposed but by creating a small, well-disciplined army in Mendoza, the capital of Cuyo, to cross the Andes Mountains and defeat the Royalists in Chile and then proceed to Lima, the capital of Peru, by sea. Mendoza was located at the eastern end of a strategic pass leading across the Andes to Chile. San Martín believed that independence would not be accomplished until the Spanish stronghold of Lima was captured.

For three years, San Martín devoted all of his considerable energy to his bold and daring plan—recruiting, training, and equipping his army of the Andes. The years in Cuyo were in many ways the happiest years of his life. Shortly after his arrival in Buenos Aires, he had married fifteen-year-old María de los Remedios Escalada, the daughter of a wealthy Creole merchant. Their only child, Mercedes, was born in 1816, during his governorship in Cuyo. San Martín was an efficient administrator,

accomplishing much for the people of Mendoza. He was very popular there, proving to be charming and persuasive with the people even though he never pretended to be a politician. He was a tall, broad-shouldered, handsome man with a large aquiline nose, thick black hair, and large, bushy whiskers. His complexion was dark, and he had dark, piercing eyes. He looked every inch the soldier, with a commanding presence.

In 1816, San Martín persuaded the Buenos Aires government to assist him in his bold scheme. Juan Martín Pueyrredón, head of the government, appointed him commander in chief of the army of the Andes. By January, 1817, San Martín's army of more than three thousand soldiers was ready to march across the snow-covered Andes and fulfill its mission. His soldiers successfully traversed the rugged mountains and, twenty-one days later, appeared before the astonished Spaniards on the Chilean side of the Andes. This amazing feat has been compared to Napoleon's march across the Alps in 1800 and Hannibal's similar march in the Punic Wars. San Martín's feat, however, had a greater effect on history, since it prepared the way

for the independence of Chile and Peru from Spain.

San Martín's forces inflicted a decisive blow against the Royalist army on February 12 at Chacabuco, which opened the way to Santiago, the Chilean capital. Two days later, his army jubilantly entered Santiago unopposed. Declining offices and promotions from the grateful Chileans, he continued with his plan to attack Lima by sea from some fifteen hundred miles away. To accomplish that, a navy was needed. There were still substantial Royalist forces in Chile, and another battle had to be fought to secure Chile's independence. This battle, fought in April, 1818, at Maipú, near Santiago, ended any further Royalist threat.

A year later, in preparation for his expedition against Peru, San Martín was appointed brigadier general of the Chilean army, projected to be some six thousand strong. In the meantime, a navy was being created in Chile for the upcoming invasion. The Chileans had enlisted the valuable assistance of Thomas, Lord Cochrane, a former English naval officer, who was made the commander of Chile's navy. San Martín's plans, however, were almost thwarted by events in Argentina, where political leaders were arguing over what form the government should take. Many favored a monarchy, as San Martín did, but agreement could not be reached. Amid this discord, the Argentine government ordered San Martín and his army to recross the Andes and return to Argentina. He refused but left his resignation up to his men, who insisted that he remain their commander. The Chilean government reinforced this revolutionary act by appointing San Martín commander in chief of liberation.

In August, 1820, the invasion of Peru, the last stronghold of Spanish power in South America, began. San Martín made it clear to his soldiers that their objective was to free, not to conquer, their Peruvian brothers. Upon his arrival in Peru, Spanish officials in Lima attempted to negotiate a compromise with San Martín, who insisted that Spain recognize the independence of Peru. San Martín proposed that a junta govern Peru for the time being; ultimately, he envisioned a constitutional monarchy for South America, with a king or emperor from the Spanish royal family. Soon, however, the negotiations broke down.

Peruvians in the north had been influenced by San Martín's writings and speeches calling for independence, and it was undoubtedly their demand for independence that caused the viceroy to evacuate the loyalist troops from Lima and the coast, leaving the way clear for San Martín to occupy the capital, which he quietly did on June 12, 1821. The independence of Peru was proclaimed officially on July 28, 1821, amid jubilation. Events, however, would soon turn against San Martín. In August, 1821, he announced that he would assume the title of protector of Peru, with full military and civil power, in order to deal with counterrevolutionary plots and the opposition of the powerful elite in Lima to San Martín's social reforms. Although he declared that he had no ambitious motives, many of his followers voiced criticism. There were also rumors that he wanted to be king. Matters were exacerbated when Lord Cochrane quarreled with San Martín and left Peru with his squadron of ships. San Martín was struck with a sudden illness which confined him to bed. Meanwhile, a large Royalist army gathered near Lima, challenging San Martín to a battle which he refused to join because of his smaller force.

Amid this unhappy state of affairs, San Martín announced that he would meet with Simón Bolívar, the liberator of Colombia, at Guayaquil to discuss plans for the complete liberation of Peru. The famous meeting of the two giants of South American independence took place on July 26 and 27, 1822. It has never been clear exactly what transpired at the meeting, but after it San Martín abruptly withdrew from public life. It is possible that San Martín withdrew because he saw that Bolívar possessed the greater resources necessary to win the final victory over the powerful Royalist army in Peru.

San Martín returned to Argentina, where he received the news of his wife's death. He left an indifferent and hostile Argentina with his young daughter and spent the remainder of his life in exile in Europe, where he suffered from poor health, poverty, and bitterness. He died in Boulogne-sur-Mer, France, on August 17, 1850, unaware that history would elevate him to legendary stature.

Summary

José de San Martín's claim to fame emanated from his bold and daring plan to cross the Andes, liberate Chile, and establish a base from which to attack Peru by sea and thus complete the liberation of southern South America. He was a great leader of men, inspiring them to great feats of endurance. He was a man of action rather than of reflection; he won battles and left other matters to statesmen. At the same time, it should be noted that he was a man who reflected the spirit of his age, since he was a believer in the ideals of the eighteenth century Enlightenment as evidenced in his ideas of independence and his strong support of education and social reforms. He was a rational man who correctly reasoned that South America was not ready for the republican type of government found in the United States. He supported monarchy as the solution to the chaos he saw emerging around him.

San Martín altered the course of history with his bold movements in Argentina, Chile, and Peru. A lesser man would never have accomplished what he did. He truly deserves to be remembered alongside other liberators in the New World, such as George Washington and Simón Bolívar.

Bibliography

Metford, J. C. J. *San Martín: The Liberator.* Oxford: Blackwell, and New York: Philosophical Library, 1950. A very readable, well-balanced, and scholarly account of San Martín's life. The author attempts to separate the man from the legend.

Mitre, Bartolomé. *The Emancipation of South America.* Translated by William Pilling. London: Chapman and Hall, 1893; New York: Cooper Square, 1969. A translation and condensation of Mitre's exhaustive multivolume *Historia de San Martín y de la emancipación sud-americana* (1887-1888), which is considered a classic. Poetically written. Combines a helpful index and a map.

Robertson, William Spence. *Rise of the Spanish-American Republics as Told in the Lives of Their Liberators.* New York and London: Appleton, 1918. Contains an excellent chapter on San Martín. Offers a well-written and well-researched summary of San Martín's role in the independence of Argentina, Chile, and Peru.

Rojas, Ricardo. *San Martin: Knight of the Andes.* Translated by Herschel Brickell and Carlos Videla. New York: Doubleday, 1945. A very sympathetic, very readable biography. The author believes that San Martín belongs to the "race of armed Saints" that includes Lohengrin and Parsifal. Helpful backnotes and an index.

Schoellkopf, Anna. *Don José de San Martín, 1778-1850: A Study of His Career.* New York: Boni and Liveright, 1924. A small volume, taken almost entirely from Mitre's works, including several verbatim quotations. Contains several illustrations and a helpful map of South America.

Tennant, Anne W. "The Glorious Renunciation." *Americas* (English Edition) 49, no. 4 (July-August, 1997). Focuses on South America between 1817 to 1822 when San Martín left for Peru rather than confront Bolivar in battle.

James E. Southerland

GEORGE SAND
Amandine-Aurore-Lucile Dupin, Baronne Dudevant

Born: July 1, 1804; Paris, France
Died: June 8, 1876; Nohant, France
Area of Achievement: Literature
Contribution: Sand contributed to nineteenth century French literature a prodigious number of important romantic novels, travel writings, and political essays.

Early Life

In many ways, George Sand's early life reads like one of her more improbable romantic novels, with her socially mismatched parents, her eccentric aristocratic grandmother, her unorthodox tutors, her flirtation with Catholicism, her unfortunate marriage, her idealistic quest for love, and her close proximity to the political upheavals of her age.

She was born Amandine-Aurore-Lucile Dupin, in Paris, in 1804, the year of Napoleon I's coronation. When Aurore was only four years old, her father, Maurice Dupin, a dashing officer in Napoleon's army, and a grandson of the illustrious Marshal of Saxe, was thrown from a Spanish stallion and died instantly. Aurore was left alternately in the care of her mother, Sophie, the lowborn daughter of a tavern keeper, and her fraternal grandmother, Mme Dupin de Francueil, a woman of aristocratic background and tastes.

Aurore endured the constant emotional and social friction between her two guardians until 1817, when she was sent to the Couvent des Anglaises in Paris to finish her education. At the convent, she was much appreciated by the nuns, despite her somewhat headstrong ways, and even felt the mystical attractions of a religious vocation. In 1820, to circumvent her taking the veil, Mme Dupin de Francueil brought Aurore home to the family estate at Nohant in Berry. There she learned to ride cross-saddle with her brother Hippolyte Chatiron, began to wear men's clothing for riding, and was taught to shoot by Stephane Ajasson de Grandsagne.

In the summer of 1821, Aurore's grandmother had a severe stroke, and Aurore nursed Mme Dupin de Francueil, an unusually difficult patient, until her death in December of the same year. Shortly afterward, in September of 1822, Aurore married Second Lieutenant Casimir Dudevant, bringing him a large estate of 400,000 francs. Her first child, Maurice Dudevant, was born in June of 1823. Her second child, Solange, probably fathered by Stephane Ajasson de Grandsagne, was born in September of 1828, and signaled the continued deterioration of her hasty marriage to the then-financially dependent and increasingly unpleasant Casimir.

In 1831, Aurore left her husband, and Nohant, for Paris, where she lived with her literary mentor, Jules Sandeau. Together, they coauthored articles for the French publication *Le Figaro* and, under the pen name Jules Sand, published an apprentice novel, *Rose et Blanche* (1831). In the early 1830's, Paris was in turmoil, in the aftermath of the July Revolution, and Aurore Dudevant was writing her first independent novel, to be published under the pseudonym George Sand.

Life's Work

In May of 1832, *Indiana* (English translation, 1833) was published. It was an immediate popular and critical success, launching a distinguished literary career which was to flourish unabated for forty-four prolific years. Sand followed up her first triumph rapidly, in only six short months, with an equally relished novel, *Valentine* (1832; English translation, 1902). This short period of time between novels was a good indication of the famous, almost notorious, fluency with which Sand was to write throughout her life. In 1832, she published *Lélia* (English translation, 1978), and these three early works, along with the ones that followed, *Jacques* (1834; English translation, 1847) and *Mauprat* (1837; English translation, 1870), were typical of Sand's characteristic concerns: the relationship between men and women, class differences in French society, marriage laws and conventions, and the romantic quest for passionate love. There is no question that Sand, when writing these early novels, was drawing on the experience of her own socially mixed parentage, her unhappy union with Casimir Dudevant, and her passionate but troublesome affair with the poet Alfred de Musset.

Critical interest in Sand's life and loves has always competed with interest in her works, and this is not surprising when one considers how much they are intertwined. It was, in fact, her ill-fated trip to Venice with Musset in 1833 that provided the material for her highly acclaimed *Lettres d'un voyageur* (1837; *Letters of a Traveller*, 1847), as well as the later novel *Elle et lui* (1859; *She and He*, 1902). *Consuelo* (1842-1843; English translation, 1846), the story of a charming prima donna, which evokes so beautifully the musical world of the eighteenth century, was written during her long liaison with Frédéric Chopin. With George Sand, life and art seem always to imitate each other.

The works of her second period, probably influenced by the socialist prophet Pierre Leroux, take a religious tone and concern for the common people, which were already present in Sand's earlier works. *Spiridion* (1839; English translation, 1842), which is a mystical story set in a monastery, and *Le Meunier d'Angibault* (1845; *The Miller of Angibault*, 1847), which has a man of the people for its hero, are typical of the novels of this political period, in which she was also establishing the socialist *Revue indépendante* (1841) with Pierre Leroux and gaining the reputation which would make her the unofficial minister of propaganda after the abdication of Louis-Philippe in 1848. As much as her heart was in the Revolution, and as hard as she worked for government reforms in her own province of Berry, she was sorely disillusioned by the reckless and often-irrational behavior of both the proletariat and the bourgeois participants. After the Coup of 1851, Sand focused her political work on interceding with Napoleon III on behalf of numerous imprisoned or exiled republicans. His fortunate admiration for her work made her an unusually successful advocate.

La Mare au diable (1846; *The Devil's Pool*, 1850), *François le champi* (1850; *Francis the Waif*, 1889), and *La Petite Fadette* (1848-1849; *Little Fadette*, 1850) are Rousseauesque paeans to the beauties of nature and the essential goodness of plain, simple peasants, no matter how hard their lives might be, or what difficulties circumstance might put in their way. These novels are a direct and startling contrast to her intense involvement in French politics, and are often considered her most beautiful and authentic works. The characters in these novels are clearly modeled on the Berrichon peasants, whom she had known from childhood.

In the 1850's, Sand's son Maurice had become fascinated with puppet theater, an interest that soon captivated Sand and eventually resulted in her writing a number of plays for the Paris theater. Her fluent, almost poetic, style was not suited to the theater of the day, however, and her plays did not bring her the popularity or the financial rewards of her earlier writings. In the last twenty-five years of

her life, Sand continued to publish novels with remarkable felicity, at least partly to support her estate at Nohant. The jewel of her later years is undoubtedly her autobiography, *Histoire de ma vie* (1854-1855; *History of My Life*, 1901), written to finance her daughter's dowry and to settle a number of pressing debts. This enormous work, of close to half a million words, first ran in 138 installments in the Parisian newspaper *La Presse*. It is not exactly an autobiography in the modern, or conventional, sense of the word: since more than one-third of the book is really about her editing of her father's correspondence with her grandmother; since it is quite restrained about the private details of her relationships with such interesting and renowned artists as Prosper Mérrimée, Jules Sandeau, Alfred de Musset, Frédéric Chopin, and Alexandre Manceau; since it was written fully twenty-one years before her death; and since it is full of seemingly unrelated digressions and didactic passages. Yet this amorphous tome is an unparalleled source of information about Sand's early life and fundamental ideas.

In her final two decades, Sand's literary output was primarily miscellaneous, with one of the outstanding features being a copious correspondence with other important writers, such as Gustave Flaubert. Sand was a diligent letter writer; more than twenty thousand of her letters are still extant.

George Sand died on June 8, 1876, of an intestinal occlusion, but not before she had seen the dawn of the republic in France, and not before she had spent her early morning hours writing as usual. She was buried at her beloved Nohant, and her funeral was attended by such notables as Prince Jérôme Bonaparte, Alexandre Dumas, *fils*, and Gustave Flaubert, as well as by the grief-stricken peasants of the district of Berry.

Summary

Ivan Turgenev said of George Sand, "What a brave man she was, and what a good woman!" Sand's androgyny, which expressed itself sometimes in her smoking and masculine clothing, and sometimes in the motherly solicitude with which she cared for her friends and lovers, is only one of the many dichotomies which are so characteristic of her life and work. It is important to remember that Sand was a woman with aristocratic blood and a family estate, who wrote socialist novels and worked for the republic. She was an idealistic, sometimes even mystical, novelist, who was, nevertheless, through-

out her life, the practical and financial center of her family. She was a famous Parisian and an avid traveler, who loved the quiet countryside of Berry with an almost spiritual devotion. She was a woman who had high respect for marriage but who also wrote some of the most damning criticism of the institution ever written. She was in all ways a woman, and a writer, who captured, in both her life and her works, the conflicted spirit of her age.

Bibliography

Barry, Joseph. *Infamous Woman: The Life of George Sand*. New York: Doubleday, 1976. An enthusiastic biography of George Sand by an author who sees her as "our existential contemporary." Especially useful for its long quotations from her correspondence, and for its well-chosen illustrations; for example, a manuscript page in Sand's own hand from her diary dated August 21, 1865.

Cate, Curtis. *George Sand: A Biography*. London: Hamilton, and Boston: Houghton Mifflin, 1975. This is the definitive biography of Sand for English-speaking readers. Cate follows the personal, literary, social, family, and economic life of Sand from her birth and the crowning of Napoleon in 1804, to her death and the rise of the republic in 1876.

Crecelius, Kathryn J. *Family Romances: George Sand's Early Novels*. Bloomington: Indiana University Press, 1987. A study of George Sand's early novels, with an emphasis on Sigmund Freud's concept of the Oedipal struggle.

Dickenson, Donna. *George Sand*. Oxford: Berg, and New York: St. Martin's Press, 1988. In this largely feminist analysis of Sand's life and work, Dickenson attempts to reinterpret some of the staples of the George Sand myth. She argues, for example, that Sand was a more professional and careful writer than critics, who look only at her prolific output, are usually willing to admit. She also combats the image of Sand as an omnivorous, devouring lover.

Glasgow, Janis, ed. *George Sand: Collected Essays*. Troy, N.Y.: Whitston, 1985. This collection of essays, in both French and English, is an unusual example of Franco-American scholarly cooperation.

Sand, George. *My Life*. Translated by Dan Hofstadter. London: Gollancz, and New York: Harper, 1979. Because the French original was exceedingly large and rambling, because it focused so much on Sand's family before her birth, because it was written long before Sand's career was completed, and because it was not especially frank about her liaisons with other famous artists, Hofstadter has wisely abridged his translation of Sand's autobiography for English readers.

———. *She and He*. Translated by George B. Ives. Philadelphia: Barrie, 1902. This clearly autobiographical novel is a fictionalized account of Sand's stormy affair with the artist Alfred de Musset. Thérèse's and Laurent's sojourn in Italy and Laurent's near-fatal illness closely resemble the events of Sand's life with Musset from 1833 to 1835.

Terzian, Debra L. "Feminism and Family Dysfunction in Sand's 'Valentine'." *Nineteenth-Century French Studies* 25, no. 3–4 (Spring-Summer 1997). Analysis of Sand's *Valentine* and its theme of social equality.

Thomson, Patricia. *George Sand and the Victorians: Her Influence and Reputation in Nineteenth Century England*. London: Macmillan, and New York: Columbia University Press, 1976. Thomson explores the connections between George Sand and Jane Carlyle, Elizabeth Barrett Browning, Charlotte and Emily Brontë, Matthew Arnold, George Eliot, Thomas Hardy, and Henry James. There is an especially good chapter entitled "George Sand and English Reviewers."

Wernick, Robert. "A Woman Writ Large in our History and Hearts." *Smithsonian* 27, no. 9 (December, 1996). Discusses Sand's literary career, her devotion to freedom, and how she was one of the most popular novelists of her time.

Cynthia Lee Katona

ANTONIO LÓPEZ DE SANTA ANNA

Born: February 21, 1794; Jalapa, Veracruz, Mexico
Died: June 21, 1876; Mexico City, Mexico
Areas of Achievement: Government and politics, and military affairs
Contribution: Santa Anna dominated Mexican life during the first forty years of its independence. While his many presidencies and other power struggles were endemic to his time, he bears the greatest responsibility for the loss of territory to the United States and for retarding the development of political maturity in Mexico.

Early Life

Antonio López de Santa Anna was born on the family estate in Jalapa, Veracruz, in eastern Mexico during the last decades of the Spanish Empire in the Americas. His family, of Spanish origin, had only been in Mexico for a few years before his birth. This made Santa Anna a *criollo* (born in America but of Spanish origin), which would be a factor in deciding his future alliances. He had little formal education and did not get along well with his classmates when he was obliged to go to school. His only real interests from an early age were things military. In 1810, after a brief, failed attempt at a career in commerce in the city of Veracruz, Santa Anna joined a local regiment of the Spanish army as a cadet. He soon transferred to a cavalry regiment and spent the next four years helping to subdue rebellions against Spain in what is now northeastern Mexico. He was promoted twice in 1812 for his service.

In 1813 Santa Anna saw action in Texas against both Mexican and American rebels. This first encounter with American rebels and the "war to the death" tactics that he witnessed Spain use against them would be important in his later dealings with Texas and the United States. After his return to Veracruz in 1814, he confined his military activities to putting down rebellions within the local region. He served as an aid to one of the last viceroys of Mexico in 1817, an assignment that took him briefly, and for the first time, to Mexico City. His spare time was spent furthering his education, particularly on military matters. It is important to note that Santa Anna did not like the pomp of Mexico City and preferred to spend his time in Veracruz. This would be a lifelong pattern in which his home province

would provide the requisite base of operations for his many rebellions.

In 1820 a revolt of Spanish troops in Spain forced the king to restore the earlier, radical constitution of 1812. When this news reached Mexico, it set in motion a number of rebellions by *criollo* military officers within the ranks of local Spanish forces. Lead by Agustín de Iturbide, these forces proclaimed an independent Mexico in 1821. Shortly after this proclamation, Santa Anna switched sides and declared his support for Iturbide and independence. This act was the first of a number of rebellions and changes of loyalty that characterized Santa Anna's future life; it also signaled his new role as a major public figure. The pattern of pronouncing against an existing government and the promulgation of a "plan" that set forth the rebel leader's concerns was the standard means of operation in Mexico during the first half of the nineteenth century. Therefore, Santa Anna's use of it was nothing unusual.

Life's Work

Santa Anna aided in securing the 1821 Treaty of Córdoba, in which Spain recognized Mexico's independence. For this and other revolutionary activity, Iturbide promoted him to brigadier general. Within one year, he broke with Iturbide and proclaimed a federal republic in 1822. He served briefly in the Yucatan, married in 1825, and generally remained out of the public eye until 1829, when he defeated Spanish forces at Tampico, bringing considerable glory to himself nationwide. In the light of this glory, he rebelled against the government in 1832 and was elected president in March, 1833. He immediately retired to his estates, leaving the daily government to his vice president and leaving the way open for a takeover of the government in 1834, when he proclaimed a centerist republic to replace the previous federal one. Given dictatorial powers, Santa Anna turned his attention to crushing anticenterist revolts in Texas and Zacatecas. He defeated Texan forces at the Alamo and Goliad in March, 1836. These two campaigns showed a brutal side of Santa Anna, one contradicted by his good treatment and even adoption of Texan prisoners in the 1840's. Within one month of these victories, he was captured at the San Jacinto River by Sam Houston, forced to sign treaties rec-

for his elaborate lifestyle were too high, and rebellions broke out in the north and in the Yucatan. By 1845, crowds were defacing his monuments. Amid all this, his first wife died, but he soon remarried. In May of 1845, rebels captured Santa Anna, put him in prison, and then exiled him to Cuba "for life."

Santa Anna returned triumphantly to Mexico on September 16, 1846, from his Cuban exile, having convinced U.S. diplomats that he alone could deliver more Mexican territory to the United States without a war. He then denounced negotiations and called for war with the United States. He was elected president on December 6, 1846. Santa Anna showed indecisiveness in the war with the United States. The Battle of Buena Vista was a stand-off, but Santa Anna retreated to Mexico City to quell political in-fighting. Within one year of his own return to Mexico, Santa Anna witnessed the American occupation of Mexico City. He fled to Jamaica.

From Jamaica, Santa Anna went to Colombia. From there, he was recalled to Mexico to save a nation in chaos that saw no solution to its problems. He was elected president in March of 1853 with dictatorial power and by December had assumed the title of "His Most Serene Highness." Faced with many of the same problems that existed in his previous tenure of office, Santa Anna sold the territory of the American southwest known as the Gadsden Purchase to the United States in an effort to refill the public coffers. Facing failure on all fronts, he sailed into exile again in 1855, first to Colombia and then to Saint Thomas in the modern U.S. Virgin Islands. This would be his last flight from power.

Despite his exile, Santa Anna could not avoid Mexican politics. He returned to his country in 1864 to support the French-backed emperor Maximillian. Within one month of his return, the French expelled him. In true fashion, Santa Anna turned his efforts to toppling Maximillian, spending considerable time in the United States propounding his ideas. While trying to enter Mexico in 1867, Santa Anna was imprisoned for nearly six months. Having lost most of his land and wealth and feeling the end at hand, he wrote his will. In November, 1867, he began his final exile, first in Cuba, then in the Bahamas. A broken Santa Anna returned to Mexico under an amnesty in 1874. Having returned home, he completed his memoirs and died on June 21, 1876. He was buried the next day near Guadalupe Hidalgo.

ognizing Texan independence, and sent to Washington, D.C., before returning to Mexico.

After spending the next year in relative disgrace and seclusion, Santa Anna returned to national attention with the loss of a leg during the Pastry Wars of 1838-1839. Riding this wave of glory, he now hurried to defend Anastasio Bustamante, the same president he had ousted in 1832. Santa Anna served as a dictator from March to July, 1839, while Bustamante was away. Economic and political collapse led Santa Anna to revolt and gain power in 1841. In December, 1842, he again assumed dictatorial powers by abolishing a short-lived republic. He was elected president by a hand-picked assembly in 1843.

Between 1842 and 1844, Santa Anna increased the size of the army, undertook works of urban renewal, and furthered his cult of personalism through statues, medals, and the military honors accorded the reburial of his lost leg. At this time he also revised Mexican public education and revitalized the Academia de San Carlos, the nation's premiere art institute. Decline began in 1844: Taxes

Summary

The period from the 1820's to the mid-1850's is often referred to as the Age of Santa Anna, for no other single force had such a constant and powerful effect on Mexico at this time. In many respects, Santa Anna's life was similar to that of many of his contemporaries, for these same years saw constant short-term governments that ranged the political spectrum from federal republic and central republic to dictatorship and monarchy. Few presidents served out their full terms of office, and military rebellions were the norm.

Santa Anna served five times as elected head of state and took power on several other occasions. When he ruled, he ruled absolutely, usually with a careful eye to clients' interests. When he was not in power, he made it difficult for strong opposition to develop. He represented the typical military leader of both his time in Mexico and in other areas of Spanish America by his cultivation of personalism, which substituted loyalty to and patronage from the person of the military leader rather than political institutions. This cult of personalism and the use of armed forces to propound and defend it effectively retarded the growth of politically viable institutions in Mexico. Santa Anna's alternate protection of and attacks on the Roman Catholic Church reflected the divided opinions of his day and presaged the Reform of 1857 and even the strong anticlericalism of the 1930's. Driven by personal ambition and lack of education, Santa Anna is best seen as an opportunist who could raise an army from nothing and turn disastrous defeats into resounding personal achievements through a timely preempting of rising popular or elite demands. He is best remembered as the one person who is most responsible for the alienation to the United States of roughly half of Mexico's territory.

Bibliography

Callcott, Wilfred H. *Santa Anna: The Story of an Enigma Who Once Was Mexico.* Norman: University of Oklahoma Press, 1936. This is the first major modern treatment of Santa Anna. It presents the contradictions present in Santa Anna's personality and the problems they posed for effective rule in Mexico.

Costeloe, Michael P. *The Central Republic in Mexico, 1835-1846: "hombres de bien" in the Age of Santa Anna.* Cambridge and New York: Cambridge University Press, 1993. Costeloe studies the men of position and wealth in Mexico as they interacted with Santa Anna as clients and opponents. The author presents Santa Anna as one of this group, explaining to some degree his move to a more autocratic government.

Jones, Oakah L. *Santa Anna.* New York: Twayne, 1968. Part of Twayne's Rulers and Statesmen of the World series, this is a very detailed account and remains one of the standard biographies of Santa Anna. Includes a very handy chronology.

Lynch, John. *Caudillos in Spanish America, 1800-1850.* Oxford: Clarendon Press, and New York: Oxford University Press, 1992. Lynch treats the origins, characteristics, and development of the *caudillo* (military-political leader) through the formative years of the Spanish-American republics. He then analyzes the careers of four *caudillos*, one of whom is Santa Anna, and finds him the least constructive of the figures studied.

O'Brien, Steven. *Antonio Lopez de Santa Anna.* New York: Chelsea House, 1992. Part of the Hispanics of Achievement series, this book, written for a younger audience, presents Santa Anna in a generally favorable light. Some illustrations included.

Olivera, Ruth R., and Liliane Crété. *Life in Mexico under Santa Anna, 1822-1855.* Norman: University of Oklahoma Press, 1991. Largely based on the observations and comments of visitors to Mexico and important residents there, this work presents an overview of daily life during the "Age of Santa Anna." Olivera covers the arts, industry, festivals, and social classes. This is one of the few studies to present Santa Anna in other than purely military or political activity.

Santa Anna, Antonio Lopez de. *The Eagle: The Autobiography of Santa Anna.* Austin, Tex.: Pemberton Press, 1967. This is a translation of Santa Anna's own account of his life and achievements. Although it is quite readable, Santa Anna generally presents himself as the victim of the conspiracies or incompetencies of others, which is very much in the style of Santa Anna's other publications.

St. John Robinson

LA SARAGOSSA
Maria Agustina

Born: 1786; Tortosa, Catalonia, Spain

Died: 1857; Saragossa, Spain

Area of Achievement: Military affairs

Contribution: By her legendary act of courage during the French siege of Saragossa, Maria Agustina (La Saragossa) symbolized Spanish resistance to Napoleon's forces during a crucial period of invasion in the Peninsular War.

Early Life

Maria Agustina Saragossa y Domenech was born in Tortosa, Catalonia, in Spain. While little is known of her childhood in Barcelona, she grew up in a period during which Franco-Spanish relations were frequently tense and, at times, openly hostile and belligerent. After the French Revolution of 1789 and the establishment of the revolutionary regime in France, Spain occupied a precarious international position. The revolutionary regime, having tried and executed the Bourbon monarchs in France, had no qualms about dissolving the Family Compact of 1761, which had allied the Bourbon monarchs throughout Europe, and attacking the Spanish monarchy.

In 1793 France officially declared war on Spain, causing a vicious anti-French fervor throughout the Iberian Peninsula as religious leaders and village volunteers rallied around military leaders to fight the French. Although peace was declared between the countries three years later, intense hatred continued to strain their relations, which soured irrevocably in 1808 when Napoleon Bonaparte and his officials refused to recognize Fernando VII, the newly crowned Bourbon monarch. Instead, Napoleon installed his elder brother, Joseph Bonaparte, upon the Spanish throne to make Spain obedient to France. A nationwide revolt ensued as Spain struggled against French domination. Before being assisted by the British in 1809, the Spanish fought alone for one year under circumstances that profoundly affected most Spaniards, including Maria Agustina.

Life's Work

Agustina gained her fame and legend by the heroic action she took when the French decided to besiege Saragossa, her native city. Napoleon's Iberian forces, after successfully conquering the Spanish cities of Tudela, Mallen, Alagon, and Epila, turned their attention towards Saragossa, the former Caesar Augusta of Roman Hispania and the capital of Aragon. The city occupied a fairly breachable position, being flanked only by the Ebro River on the north, an open plain to the south, and the Hueva stream to the east and southeast. Saragossa itself was in the wilderness of Aragon and had no access to the sea or communication with nearby cities. However, a twelve-foot wall surrounded the city, and many of the massive interior buildings, including several monasteries and the old Moorish stronghold, the Aljafería, had proved virtually impervious throughout centuries of warfare. The Spanish forces at Saragossa were not very sizable, numbering only one thousand regulars to be supplemented by five or six thousand civilians with little military training and few weapons. Nevertheless, pockets of resistance formed, particularly around different military leaders. José de Palafox, the leader of the Aragonese revolt and a native of Saragossa, helped form a junta made up of his friends and relatives.

When the French troops arrived on June 15, 1808, brigadier general Charles Lefebre-Desnoüettes pressed for Saragossa's surrender, anticipating a swift capitulation and a triumphant march into Aragon's capital. He did not want to lay traditional siege because he had few men and resources at his disposal after his other campaigns. The French general determined the weakest part of the city's defenses and successfully attacked the fortifications at one of the farthest external points, at Monte Torrero. Upon his order, some French soldiers managed to break through the Spanish defenses before the guns were in place, but most were slain while the remaining French forces retreated, which helped encourage the city's resistance. Incensed by the breach in security, Spanish leaders later ordered the officer in command to be tried and hanged publicly to instill fear and patriotic fervor into the town's inhabitants so they would work fervently to repel the French onslaught. The French general had completely underestimated the rebellious spirit of the Saragossans, who managed to repel the first French assault. At the end of the first day, the French army retired to an area one mile from the city's wall between the two rivers to await supplies and reinforcements. The French had lost almost seven hundred men in the fray, and Lefebre-Desnoüettes wanted to wait.

This reprieve from battle allowed Saragossa to form a more organized and deadly defense. Over the next several weeks, every inhabitant in the city worked in some capacity to fortify Saragossa's defense. Women and children made uniforms, while men fortified buildings, made ammunition, burned outlying houses, cut down trees, and readied weapons. Private homes became fortresses and bastions of defense. Everyone, including Agustina, prepared for a fierce and bloody battle.

On the morning of July 2, 1808, the French launched a full assault in six strategic areas: the cavalry barracks, the Aljafería Castle, and the gates of Portillo, Carmen, Sancho, and Santa Engracia. The Spanish, under the leadership of Palafox, sought to direct their defense from the centrally located monastery of San Francisco. The men worked the canons feverishly as their comrades died about them. Agustina gained her fame from a critical moment in the siege during which the French offense began to surmount the weakening defense at the strategically vital Portillo gate. The defensive position of the gate suddenly became vulnerable as artillery personnel serving the battery lay dying and defenders began to scatter. Rather than allow the French infantry to pour through an irreparably weakened stronghold, Agustina took a lit fuse from the hands of her dead fiancé or husband, an artilleryman, and touched it to a canon loaded with gunshot. Heedless of the carnage all about her, she shot the guns one after another, all the while, according to some accounts, deriding the cowardice of men fighting on both sides of the battle.

Agustina's actions instantly revived the Spanish defense and checked the French advance, which had moved to within one hundred meters of the guns. Although wounded in the battle, she fervently compelled her compatriots to arms. Men and women alike seemed to have admired and followed her example. She inspired at least one woman to take over the cannon from a dead soldier posted at the Santa Engracia battery and fire it at French infantry. Matching the patriotism of Agustina, Palafox refused to surrender, choosing instead to lead the city's inhabitants in a fight to the death. This proved unnecessary as the French soldiers broke ranks, many leaving their weapons behind in their flight. Until November, the Spanish successfully withstood the long-lasting siege.

After the first siege, the Saragossans were widely admired and honored throughout Spain. Every Spanish town produced plays such as *Los Patriotas de Aragon* (the patriots of Aragon) that depicted the Saragossans' defiance in the face of Napoleon's troops. Agustina earned the name "La Saragossa" and became famous in her own right throughout Spain and much of Europe. For her valiant and heroic actions, Agustina received a commendation from Palafox, the rank and salary of a gunner, and a shield of honor that was sewn to her sleeve.

Over the next several months, Saragossa's inhabitants worked to regain and fortify their defensive position, expecting that they would be able to again withstand a ferocious assault. The second siege began at the end of December, 1808, and seemed at first to follow the pattern of the first. Acting as an official gunner, Agustina was wounded in the defense of the city. Despite the best efforts of Agustina and the Saragossans, the siege lasted only until the middle of February, 1809. Although La Saragossa and the other city inhabitants fought gamely, even offensively at times, the French finally occupied the city. In those three months, Saragossa lost 54,000 people, with only 12,000 to 15,000 inhabitants remaining alive. Agustina miraculously survived the second siege and, along with all the inhabitants of Saragossa, was rounded up by the French before being dispersed throughout Aragon.

Little else is known of the woman heroically named La Saragossa. Occasional accounts of her actions surfaced in later years as French and Spanish soldiers alike bragged about having seen her in action at Saragossa or having met her in other skirmishes with the French. In each tale, her beauty, intelligence, and, most of all, her bravery in the face of adversity garnered her great honor, although few of these rumors can be substantiated or documented.

Agustina's legend and heroic reputation persist in poetry and art as well. The nineteenth century English Romantic poet Lord Byron saw La Saragossa in Seville wearing many medals and orders at the command of the Junta and was inspired to write a verse about her that was read throughout Europe. In *Childe Harold's Pilgrimage* (1812-1818, 1819), he wrote,

Her lover sinks—she sheds no ill-tim'd tear
Her chief is slain—she fills his fatal post
Her fellows flee—she checks their base career
The foe retires—she heads the sallying host:
Who can appease like her a lover's ghost?

Who can avenge so well a leader's fall?
What maid retrieve when man's flush'd hope is lost?
Who hang so fiercely on the flying Gaul,
Foil'd by a woman's hand, before a batter'd wall?

These verses illustrate how Lord Byron commemorated La Saragossa and helped vivify her legend in the imagination of his readers.

Francisco de Goya, a nineteenth century Spanish painter from Saragossa, further immortalized her legend in his series entitled *Los desastres de la guerra* (1810-1814; *The Disasters of War),* an expression of his disgust at the barbarity and bloodshed of the Peninsular War and his admiration of La Saragossa. One of his works, entitled *Qué Valor*, depicts Agustina standing at the canon amid the bodies of her fallen comrades ready to light the fuse and spur the Spanish defense to action. This painting was destroyed by the French in 1809. Two other painters, Juan Gálvez and Ferdinand Brambila, were commissioned by the restored Ferdinand VII to sketch scenes of Saragossa's heroics and devastation and produced an etching of Agustina and the canon in a series entitled *Las Ruinos de Zaragoza (The Ruins of Saragossa).*

When Agustina died in 1857, her body was returned to Saragossa and buried in the Portilla Church alongside the other heroes of Saragossa. A statue and cannon stand outside the church in honor of her memory.

Summary

Maria Agustina, as La Saragossa, clearly personified Spain's fierce resistance to Napoleon's incursions, not only at the sieges of Saragossa but also throughout the larger Peninsular War. Arguably, the prolonged defiance of the Saragossans wreaked havoc on Napoleon's campaigns in Spain and lowered the morale and fighting ability of his soldiers. Although the individual efforts of Agustina may not have had a permanent effect after the first siege and France was ultimately victorious, La Saragossa symbolized resistance, patriotism, and perseverance among the Spanish.

Bibliography

Esdaile, Charles J. *The Spanish Army in the Peninsular War.* Manchester: Manchester University Press, and New York: St. Martin's Press, 1988. Esdaile traces the history of the Spanish army from 1788 to 1814 and the impact of the French Revolution and the Napoleonic wars on Spain.

Gates, David. *The Spanish Ulcer: A History of the Peninsular War.* London: Allen and Unwin, 1985; New York: Norton, 1986. This book contains detailed sections on the first and second sieges of Saragossa within the context of the larger peninsular war.

Lovett, Gabriel H. *Napoleon and the Birth of Modern Spain.* New York: New York University Press, 1965. This two-volume set offers a comprehensive survey of Napoleon's wars in the Iberian Peninsula. A chapter on "Heroic Zaragoza" explains how Saragossa attempted to withstand the French forces and describes La Saragossa's patriotism.

Lynch, John. *Bourbon Spain 1700-1808.* Oxford and Cambridge, Mass.: Blackwell, 1989. Lynch provides an insightful and comprehensive overview of the crises facing the Bourbon monarchy in Spain. The book contains a bibliographic essay on different aspects of the Spanish Bourbon regime.

Rudorff, Raymond. *War to the Death: The Sieges of Saragossa, 1808-1809.* London: Hamilton, and New York: Macmillan, 1974. Rudorff offers one of the most comprehensive accounts of the two invasions of Saragossa. The book also contains several illustrations, including Goya's *Qué Valor* and other paintings concerning the sieges.

Tranie, J., and Juan Carlos Carmigniani. *Napoleon's War in Spain: French Peninsular Campaigns, 1807-1814.* London and Harrisburg, Pa.: Arms and Armour Press, 1982. This highly illustrated account of Napoleon's wars in Spain contains more description than analysis and includes a useful chronology of his military campaigns throughout Spain and Portugal.

Susanna Calkins

JOHN SINGER SARGENT

Born: January 12, 1856; Florence, Italy
Died: April 15, 1925; London, England
Area of Achievement: Art
Contribution: Sargent was renowned for his magnificent portraiture, which earned for him a reputation as a modern Van Dyck.

Early Life

Mary Newbold Singer Sargent, the artist's mother, was an incurable romantic. In 1854, she induced her husband, Dr. FitzWilliam Sargent, to abandon his medical practice and their comfortable, predictable bourgeois existence and move to Europe. Mary had recently come into a decent inheritance from her father, a wealthy fur merchant, and now saw no reason to live out her life among the dull, middle-class surroundings of Philadelphia. The transplanted Sargents usually spent their summers in northern France, Germany, or England, and headed to southern France or Italy during the winter, living in rented apartments. Florence, Italy, could be characterized as the family's "home base." There, the Sargents's eldest child, John, was born and attended school.

John Singer Sargent displayed a high degree of intellectual maturity, but his formal education was frequently interrupted by the family's travels. In addition to English, he spoke Italian, German, and French fluently; he became an accomplished pianist; he knew European literature, history, and art. His mother constantly hauled him around to museums and cathedrals; she was an enthusiastic watercolorist and encouraged him to make art his career, much to the dismay of her husband, who wanted his son to become a sailor. It was Mary Sargent who had her way, and John was allowed to attend the Academy of Fine Arts in Florence. The young student enthusiastically filled sketchbooks with drawings of classical monuments, copies of old master paintings, and still lifes; he drew people and scenes that he observed on his various travels. His parents showed his work to professional artists, and, when these experts confirmed John's talent, it was decided that he should be sent to Paris to further his studies.

Sargent arrived in the French capital in late spring of 1874 and was accepted by Charles Jurand Carolus-Duran, a famous academic portraitist, to join his atelier for advanced students; Sargent also passed the examinations for admission to the École des Beaux-Arts. He thus received one of the best formal art educations of his day. The Beaux Arts gave him a solid grounding in academism; Carolus-Duran taught him to paint in half-tones and trained him to eliminate all that was not essential from his composition. Sargent was also influenced by such artists as Édouard Manet and Eugène Boudin and some of the Impressionists; like them, he spent his summers in the French provinces painting outdoors. His progress was rapid. One of his paintings, *En route pour la pêche* (also known as *The Oyster Gatherers of Cancale*), which resulted from a summer in Brittany, won a second-class medal at the Salon of 1878, a great personal achievement for a young unknown artist. Carolus-Duran thought so highly of his pupil that he invited him to help paint the *Triumph of Marie de' Medici*, a large mural commissioned for the ceiling of the Luxembourg Palace. Sargent helped color the design but was also allowed to paint the two allegorical figures on either side of the principal portrait of Marie de' Medici; he also painted a bystander with the features of Carolus-Duran, who was so pleased that he allowed his pupil to paint a more formal portrait of him. The work, a remarkably perceptive representation done in half-tones and selective highlights, was artistically the culmination of the lessons Sargent had been taught. The portrait, both chronologically and artistically, marked the beginning of his professional career.

Life's Work

Sargent established his own studio (first on the rue Notre-Dame des Champs, later on the rue Berthier) and began to enjoy life as a rising young society artist. It was extremely difficult for a foreigner to break into the French market, however, and most of his commissions at that time came from wealthy foreigners living or visiting abroad. He did do an uncommissioned full-length portrait, *Madame Gautreau* (1884), which he hoped would open some doors, but the work was badly received at the Salon of 1884. Nevertheless, Sargent hardly suffered from lack of praise. According to Henry James, he was so talented that even on the threshold of his career he had nothing more to learn.

During this period, Sargent also did some subject paintings, such as the exotic *El Jaleo* (1882), a picture of a Gypsy dancer he saw while on a visit

to Spain. For the most part, however, he did not stray very far from his main source of income, although he became increasingly disenchanted with working in the French capital. His commissions had begun to decline, and he had not received the proper respect he thought he deserved. From time to time, his work had taken him to England as the wealthy British had less hesitation about having their portraits painted by foreigners than did the French.

Sargent passed the summer of 1885 at Broadway in the Cotswolds, where he did a number of landscapes. At that time, he apparently decided to make his residence in the British Isles more permanent; the following year, he closed down his Paris studio and moved to London, renting a studio previously occupied by James McNeill Whistler. The British capital would be his home for the rest of his life.

Commissions for portraits came slowly at first—some potential patrons, accustomed to the formalism of the Royal Academy, found his technique a bit too avant-garde—but gradually, he was commissioned for more and more work, until he had almost more than he could handle. Although the English art scene was not as exciting as the one he had left in Paris, Sargent's personal associations in the British capital were more congenial and fulfilling. Many of his clients were wealthy Americans, and one of these, Henry Marquand, invited him, in 1887, to come to the United States (to Newport, Rhode Island) to paint a portrait of his wife with the prospect of other commissions from Marquand's well-heeled friends.

Sargent's trip to the United States lasted eight months. He completed twelve formal portraits and had a one-man show in Boston in January, 1888, which received rave reviews. Everywhere he went, he was treated as a great artist and was appreciated in a way it seemed he had never been in Europe. Still, he returned to England; during the summer of 1888, he painted a series of pictures in the Impressionist style of Claude Monet, for whom he had an intense admiration. After this interlude, he returned to full-time portraiture. One of his most famous, *Ellen Terry as Lady Macbeth* (1889), he solicited himself. He returned to the United States in December, 1889, for another series of portraits, but he was also commissioned to decorate the upper landing of the Boston Public Library, a project that would occupy him intermittently for the next quarter of a century. As his theme, Sargent chose the development of religious thought from its pagan

origin, through Old Testament times, to Christianity. The actual painting was done in England on canvas and transported to Boston. Although Sargent considered the work to be one of his major contributions to contemporary art, the murals did not display his talent at its best.

Throughout the last years of the Victorian period and the following Edwardian period, Sargent was widely regarded as the greatest portrait painter in England, his status confirmed by the number of commissions he was now receiving from the British aristocracy and by his election to full membership in the Royal Academy in 1897. Yet the more famous he became and the greater the requests for his services, the more his interest in portraiture declined. He undoubtedly recognized that his work was suffering from repetition and a tendency toward formalism and artificiality. Consequently, from 1910 onward, he devoted the major part of his time to landscapes, journeying to Spain, the Holy Land, Egypt, Majorca, Corfu, and, especially, the Alpine region and Italy, for subject matter. He chose the subjects that pleased him, beginning his work early in the day, having plopped his easel down wherever the spirit moved him. Sargent continued to work in oils, but most of his production was now in watercolors.

Sargent was in the Austrian Tirol when World War I broke out. The local military authorities refused him permission to leave the country, and he remained in the village of Colfushg and continued to paint. He apparently took little interest in the course of hostilities, which he regarded as collective madness; he naïvely believed that fighting was suspended on Sundays. Finally, he managed to leave Austria and make it to Italy, through France, and back to England, where he resumed work on the mural for the Boston library.

He came again to the United States in 1916, and, on this trip, accepted another commission for a mural: for the rotunda of the Boston Museum of Fine Arts. When he returned to England in April, 1918, he was asked by the Ministry of Information's War Artists Committee to do a painting emphasizing wartime Anglo-American cooperation. He went to France to do research, staying there six months until October, one month before the armistice. The result was *Gassed*, painted in his London studio, which shows a line of Allied soldiers, eyes bandaged, being led one after the other toward a dressing station. The picture was displayed at the Royal Academy in 1919 and became an instant sensation, being judged one of the best paintings to come out that year.

Sargent now came more frequently to the United States, his work on his wall decorations monopolizing much of his time and energy. He was there from 1919 to 1920; he returned again in 1921 and in 1923, and he was planning to make a return trip to oversee the installation of his museum paintings. Just before he was scheduled to leave, on April 15, 1925, Sargent died of a heart attack, following a farewell party given by his sister. He was found with an open copy of Voltaire's *Philosophical Dictionary* (1764) beside him. His death drew national attention, marked by a memorial service in London's St. Paul's cathedral.

Summary

Like a great actor who devotes too much of his talent to soap operas instead of to the classics, Sargent for most of his productive life painted works lacking in spiritual depth and imaginative force, works that he was later to regret having done. "I *hate* to paint portraits! I hope I never paint another portrait in my life. . . . I want now to experiment in more imaginary fields," he said. Yet portraits were what he did best; when he was good, he was excellent; when he was bad, he was still extraordinary. For example, his portrait *Woodrow Wilson* (1917), not generally considered to be one of his best, is remarkable in the way it captures the humorless, messianic Wilsonian stare. Sargent's misfortune was to live at a time when painting the famous and haut-monde was increasingly looked on with derision.

Although he refused to accept any commissions in which he did not have complete artistic freedom, he remained acutely sensitive to the social and professional stature of his subjects, whom he frequently placed in his paintings in theatrical or symbolic surroundings. Sargent was a businessman who gave his sitters what they paid for. He posed them on Louis XV settees, in front of marble pillars, standing beside huge cloisonné vases, some wearing top hats and highly polished riding boots, as in *Lord Ribblesdale* (1902), or plumed bonnets, as in *Lady Sassoon* (1907), or adorned, as in *The Wyndham Sisters* (1899), in dresses worth small fortunes. Sargent was clearly an artist of *fin de siècle* conspicuous consumers, and he served them well.

The Americans claimed him as one of their own, but in training and performance he was completely European. Sargent based his style on Europe's traditional artistic values as expressed by the artists he admired. He never tired of going to museums to learn from the great artists of the past, such as Diego Velázquez, Titian, Tintoretto, Peter Paul Rubens, and, above all, Frans Hals, whose loose brushwork became Sargent's own trademark. Sargent's painterly style was enlivened with splashes of clear color that attested the lessons he had learned from the Impressionists. He was never able to adapt his palette completely to theirs, however, and sometimes he became too garish or somber. "One day the American painter Sargent came here to paint with me," Monet recalled. "I gave him my colors and he wanted black, and I told him: 'But I haven't any.' 'Then I can't paint,' he cried and added, 'How do you do it!'" Sargent came the closest to Impressionism in his watercolors, especially those he did in Venice, which also reveal him at his spontaneous and individualistic best. Yet, if Sargent had failings as a painter, they were failings of theme, not of expertise, for his was overpowering and could rival that of the finest painters of any age.

Bibliography

Charteris, Evan Edward. *John Sargent*. London: Heinemann, and New York: Scribner, 1927. This official biography is built largely from quotations, letters, and anecdotes. The author, who was a personal friend of Sargent, was too close to his subject to be truly objective, and the painter's personality remains elusive. Sargent is revealed as tremendously dedicated, hardworking, and self-critical, but such traits alone are hardly the stuff of drama.

Kilmurray, Elaine, and Richard Ormond, eds. *John Singer Sargent*. Princeton, N.J.: Princeton University Press and London: Tate Gallery, 1998. This book evaluates Sargent's work, which included portraits, landscapes, watercolors, and murals. Published in conjunction with an international exhibition, it includes 150 color reproductions of his works and insightful essays and biographical material.

Lubin, David M. *Act of Portrayal: Eakins, Sargent, James*. New Haven, Conn.: Yale University Press, 1985. Contains extensive sexual-sociological analysis of Sargent's famous portrait of the Boit children, *The Daughters of Edward Boit* (1882). Essentially an exercise in speculation and provocation, showing that what is not known about a painting need not stand in the way of intellectualizing about its meaning.

McSpadden, J. Walker. *Famous Painters of America*. New York: Crowell, 1907. A brief description of Sargent's life and work, written during his lifetime in obvious recognition and appreciation of his genius. Argues that, despite Sargent's thoroughly European training and formation, "Americans may rightfully claim Sargent."

Memorial Exhibition of the Works of the Late John Singer Sargent. Boston: Museum of Fine Arts, 1925. A catalog of some of Sargent's most famous works, shown to commemorate the unveiling of his mural decorations in the Boston Public Library. The works on display came almost exclusively from American collections and thereby help to reinforce the artist's image as a native son.

Mount, Charles Merril. *John Singer Sargent*. New York: Norton, 1955; London: Cresset Press, 1957. A complete, well-researched, and lavishly documented account in which even the most insignificant aspects of Sargent's life seem worthy of inclusion. Mount, who is also a portraitist, offers intelligent and perceptive commentary about his subject's style and techniques.

Olson, Stanley. *John Singer Sargent: His Portrait*. London: Macmillan, and New York: St. Martin's Press, 1986. A literate, sympathetic, but objective biography, particularly strong in its portrayal of the varied figures who played a part in Sargent's life. Includes a small selection of illustrations.

Ormond, Richard. *John Singer Sargent: Paintings, Drawings, Watercolors*. London: Phaidon Press, and New York: Harper, 1970. An oversized book with many plates of Sargent's principal works, too many, unfortunately, reproduced in black and white. The commentary on each is informative and incisive, however, as is the biography, highlighting the major periods of the artist's life.

Simpson, Marc. *Uncanny Spectacle: The Public Career of the Young John Singer Sargent*. New Haven, Conn.: Yale University Press, 1997. Using the artist's correspondence with friends and family and several contemporary critical works, Simpson examines all of Sargent's work exhibited through 1887.

Wm. Laird Kleine-Ahlbrandt

FRIEDRICH KARL VON SAVIGNY

Born: February 21, 1779; Frankfurt am Main
Died: October 25, 1861; Berlin, Prussia
Area of Achievement: Law
Contribution: Savigny was a leading historian of Roman law. In the field of legal philosophy, he is considered generally to be either the founder or the leading exponent of the so-called historical or Romantic school of jurisprudence, which means that the content of a given body of law can only be understood through a process of historical research.

Early Life

Friedrich Karl von Savigny, who was thin, with thick dark hair and a kind and generous face, descended from a wealthy Protestant noble family which had emigrated from Lorraine to Frankfurt. Savigny, whose family name came from the castle of Savigny near Charmes in the Moselle valley, was educated at the Universities of Göttingen, Jena, Leipzig, Halle, and Marburg; at Marburg, he studied under Philipp Friedrich Weiss, a specialist in medieval jurisprudence, and Anton Bauer, whose reputation was gained in activities keyed toward the reform of German criminal law. Receiving his degree in 1800, Savigny determined to spend his life in scholarly pursuits. Personally wealthy, he was probably the first of the ruling classes to take up teaching as a career, a field that, because of its low pay and accordingly poor social standing, had hitherto largely drawn its members from the lower-middle classes. As privatdocent at Marburg, where he lectured in criminal law and on the Pandects of the Roman law, he published *Das Recht des Besitzes* (1803; *Treatise on Possession: Or, The Jus Possessionis of the Civil Law*, 6th ed. 1848), which he allegedly wrote in seven months and which gained for him offers of two chairs, one at Greifswald and one at Heidelberg. Savigny also published in 1803 a brief article in a short-lived English periodical, *The Monthly Register*, in which, after an assessment of German universities at that time, he declared that only four of almost forty universities in Germany were of more than local importance. In 1804 Savigny married Kunigunde Brentano, so he declined both university offers in favor of a honeymoon that included searching the libraries of France and Germany for manuscripts that would aid him in writing a proposed history of Roman law in the Middle Ages.

Savigny did, however, advise the government of Baden, one of the many independent German states, on the reorganization of the University of Heidelberg, which helped to make Heidelberg one of the important seats of learning in Europe. In 1808, Savigny went to the University of Landshut in Bavaria as professor of Roman law, and, in 1810, he not only took a significant share in the foundation of the University of Berlin but also was the first to be elected rector, or vice chancellor. He helped to organize the university on lines similar to those employed at Heidelberg, but with perhaps greater success. Savigny remained at the University of Berlin until March of 1842.

Life's Work

In 1817, Savigny became a member of the Department of Justice in the Prussian Privy Council and, in that same year, a member of a commission for organizing the Prussian provincial estates. In 1819, he became a member of the Berlin Court of Appeal and Cassation for the Rhine Provinces, in 1826 a member of the commission for revising the Prussian code, and in 1842 chairman of the newly established department for revision of statutes. In 1842, he was also appointed *Grosskanzler* (high chancellor), or head of the juridical system in Prussia, a post he held until the Revolution of 1848, after which he devoted himself to his writing and research, holding no more government positions.

In 1806, Napoleon I promulgated the Code Napoleon, which provided a uniform body of rules for the French nation; many Germans looked upon this code enviously as an example of what should and could be done for the German people. In 1814, a professor of civil law at the University of Heidelberg, Anton Friedrich Justus Thibaut, wrote an article arguing that the law of the German people be codified both as a means of unifying the German states and as a means of applying a universally held logic or rule of reason to the law. Savigny objected strenuously in his famous pamphlet *Vom Beruf unserer Zeit für Gesetzgebung und Rechtswissenschaft* (1814; *Of the Vocation of Our Age for Legislation and Jurisprudence*, 1831), theorizing that law, like language, arises out of the customs, traditions, needs, and spirit of a particular people or community (*Volkgeist*) and that law cannot be imposed on a people or community arbitrarily. Something that is logical and reasonable for the French or English mind may be entirely illogical for the German. Rather than arbitrarily impose a mass of legislation upon a people, one must research the particular history of that people to determine the law that suits it best. This exaltation of customary law, as distinguished from law as a universal rule of reason, was derived from the worldview of the Romantics. It proved, whether intended so by Savigny, to be not only the glorification of things German but also a recognition of distinctions between one German state and another. Furthermore, this concept of Savigny argued against the codification of the law of any particular people at any particular time, because, according to Savigny, the law, wherever located, was always in the process of evolving and neither could nor should reach a point where codification was possible. In 1815, with Karl Friedrich Eichorn and Johann Friedrich Ludwig Göschen, he founded the *Zeitschrift für geschichtliche Rechtswissenschaft* (journal of historical jurisprudence), a periodical voicing the ideas of the historical school.

Savigny's theories, therefore, were the heart of the Romantic branch of the historical school of jurisprudence, which tended to dominate the German universities until his death and which were powerful enough to delay until 1900 the codification of German law—well after German unification in 1871. Nevertheless, despite Savigny's emphasis on the historical approach, he was not an advocate of natural law. In his *Juristische Methodenlehre, nach der Ausarbeitung des Jakob Grimm* (wr. 1802-1803, pb. 1951; legal methodology as elaborated by Jakob Grimm), delivered as a lecture at Marburg, Savigny voiced the view that the historical approach should be systematic, so that the result contributes to a clearly defined system of legal science.

A second aspect of Savigny's work dealt with the study and research of Roman law. His *Geschichte des römischen Rechts im Mittelalter* (1815-1831, 1834-1851; partial translation as *The History of Roman Law During the Middle Ages*, 1829) remains the definitive work on the subject. Although Roman law, which he admired, had been codified, Savigny tried to demonstrate that, despite the codifications, Roman law was actually administered as customary law, bringing it into conformity with the historical school of thought. Apart from this, Savigny's scholarship eliminated much of the incongruity that had clouded the understanding of Roman law during the period from the fall of the

Roman Empire until A.D. 1100. *System des heutigen römischen Rechts* (1840-1849) presents in its eighth volume Savigny's theories of private international law and the first modern systematic presentation of this phase of the law. The eighth volume also shows that Savigny was acquainted with the work of Joseph Story, an associate justice of the United States Supreme Court. In 1850, Savigny published *Vermischte Schriften* (miscellaneous writings), a collection of various pieces on the law. *Das Obligationenrecht* (1851-1853; the law of contracts), which is a furtherance of *System des heutigen römischen Rechts*, emphasizes freedom of contract, which proved of great use after the unification of Germany in the rise of industrial capitalism prior to World War I.

Although Savigny opposed a codification of German law, he nevertheless approved the application of the Roman law code to Germany, avoiding this contradiction by stating that Roman law during the Middle Ages had been so generally applied to and used by the German people that it had become in many respects part of the German customary law and thereby reflective of the German *Volkgeist*.

Savigny's thinking is weak in that codification is not necessarily an imposition of arbitrary law upon an unwilling people; it may be a mere memorial of a people's customary law, and codification may thus be a plateau in the natural evolution of a people's customary law. Further, as Julius Stone has noted, the *Volkgeist* doctrine "probably exaggerated the role in legal development of popular consciousness as distinct from the consciousness of small groups, either of specialists or of a dominant class," as well as "the element of conscious attitudes . . . which lies behind a people's relation with its law."

Summary

Friedrich Karl von Savigny's contribution to law lies in his objection to codifications and in his scholarship in Roman law. He connected these two aspects of his work by maintaining that there had never really been a codification of Roman law but merely a development of customary law by an evolutionary process natural to the Roman people and the Roman Empire. This spirit of nationhood in the law was contrary to the nineteenth century efforts of the codifiers to press upon the German people an arbitrary set of laws unnatural to it. At the time of his writing, Savigny was very popular; those who wanted greater democracy were delighted with the concept that the people and not the nobility were the real makers of the law, and the nobility or aristocracy was happy to have found a way to avoid needed reforms. In the end, the results were not entirely salutary, for Savigny's emphasis on the *Volkgeist* tended to strengthen the concept of German mysticism, to glorify the superiority of German law, to stifle reforms, to inhibit the development of a badly needed code for a unified people, and perhaps even to set another stone in the edifice of corrupt nationalism. Savigny's major contribution to the law, it would appear, remains his scholarly work in laying open the field of Roman law, his insistence that the practice and theory of jurisprudence must be one and the same, his recognition of the evolutionary process in law, and his elevation of the profession of teaching and scholarship.

Bibliography

Allgemeine Deutsche Biographie. Leipzig, Germany: Duncker and Humblot, 1875-1912. The article on Savigny, in this fifty-six-volume biography of prominent Germans, presents a clear and sometimes provocative presentation of Savigny's life and doctrines. In German.

Jones, J. Walter. *Historical Introduction to the Theory of Law.* Oxford: Clarendon Press, 1940; New York: Kelley, 1969. Chapter 2 discusses the legal codes in France and Germany, Thibaut, and Savigny's criticism of the codes, together with excellent material on the pros and cons of the historical school of legal thought. The concepts of other legal historians of the period are brought to bear upon the historical school so that the reader obtains a fair view of the thinking on the subject during the nineteenth century.

Kantorowicz, Hermann U. "Savigny and the Historical School of Law." *Law Quarterly Review* 53 (July, 1937): 326-343. Presents some of the facts of Savigny's life but largely deals with the meaning of the historical school. Kantorowicz believes that it is Savigny's scholarship and research in Roman law that constitute his real contribution to legal science. The article, however, is difficult reading for the layperson.

Montmorency, James E. G. de. "Friedrich Karl von Savigny." In *Great Jurists of the World*, edited by John Macdonell and Edward Manson, vol. 2. London: Murray, 1913; Boston: Little Brown, 1914. Deals with biographies of great jurists from Gaius through Rudolph von Ihering. In the selection on Savigny, Montmorency gives a general picture of Savigny's concepts of the historical school of law. Montmorency does not discuss the essential contradiction between Savigny's glorification of the evolutionary law of a particular people and his desire to impress Roman law upon the Germans, a point that is well discussed in the work by Stone, cited below.

Stone, Julius. *The Province and Function of Law.* London: Stevens, 1947; Cambridge, Mass.: Harvard University Press, 1950. Chapter 18 is probably the best brief study of Savigny's ideas. Concisely presents Savigny's opposition to a code for Germany and gives a fine overview of his work in the Roman law of the Middle Ages in Europe and as applied to Europe in his own time. Also treats the essential conflict between Savigny's insistence on an evolutionary customary law, his demand for an acceptance of the codified Roman law, and his attempt to resolve the conflict.

Robert M. Spector

GERHARD JOHANN DAVID VON SCHARNHORST

Born: November 12, 1755; Bordenau, Lippe

Died: June 28, 1813; Prague, Bohemia, Austrian Empire

Area of Achievement: The military

Contribution: Scharnhorst's modernization of the Prussian army made it the model for the armies of the nineteenth century. Among the reforms which he either initiated or helped to push through were the development of the general staff, the abolition of army corporal punishment, a scheme for training large numbers of recruits, and the overhaul of Prussian tactical training.

Early Life

On November 12, 1755, Gerhard Johann David von Scharnhorst was born in Bordenau, a small town in the principality of Lippe, one of the sleepy, minor German states of the time. The son of an independent small farmer, Scharnhorst was born a commoner whose connections to the aristocracy were limited to two uncles who sold fish and other supplies to the kitchen of the Elector of Hanover. Nevertheless, Scharnhorst's father had served in the artillery of the Hanoverian army as a sergeant major, and it was a military career that the young boy would pursue.

Scharnhorst had the good fortune to be enrolled at the Military Academy of the Count of Schaumburg-Lippe, a cadet school which provided an education far above what was commonly taught at such provincial institutions. Commissioned as an officer-cadet in 1778 and made second lieutenant in the artillery in 1784, Scharnhorst, like Napoleon I, took advantage of new openings in the military for men of the middle class. Recent inventions had made the artillery technologically the most advanced arm of the European armies, and its officers were necessarily chosen on a basis of proficiency rather than of noble birth.

Despite its incorporation of technological progress in its military hardware, the army in which Scharnhorst served was still grounded in the military philosophy of the era which effectively ended with the American War of Independence in 1776 and the advance of the armies of the French Revolution after 1792. In both campaigns, the old European armies, which relied on a small, perfectly drilled body of professional soldiers able to move with mathematical precision to the orders of its commander, were beaten by an ill-trained but highly motivated mass army which replaced chessboard strategies with a revolutionizing reliance on open fire and massive offensive punches.

Since the European aristocrats had decided to fight revolutionary France, Scharnhorst first fought on the battlefields of Belgium and distinguished himself both as a courageous tactical leader and as a valuable chief of staff. In order to share his new insights into modern warfare, Scharnhorst took on the editorship of an influential military journal and began his lifelong career as a military writer. The Hanoverian army, however, was not an adequate vehicle for Scharnhorst's ambitions, and the forty-five-year-old major began to look for advancement elsewhere.

Life's Work

In 1801, Scharnhorst offered his services to King Frederick William III of Prussia; however, he attached three conditions to his coming: He asked to be made lieutenant-colonel, to be raised to the nobility, and to be allowed to transform the Prussian army into a modern fighting force which could therefore withstand the onslaught of France. As further proof of his qualifications, the Hanoverian officer attached three essays on military topics.

In December, 1802, when Scharnhorst was actually ennobled, the Prussian king had answered all of the young man's requests and had made him director of the War Academy in Berlin. Physically, Scharnhorst did not quite fit one's idea of a Prussian staff officer: A portrait by Friedrich Bury shows an intelligent face framed by soft brown hair; Scharnhorst's expressive eyes gaze over a long, fleshy nose, and his mouth seems to be trying to suppress an ironic smile. His contemporaries noted an absence of stiffness in Scharnhorst, and, on the parade ground, his was not an impressive figure; when he addressed the troops, his voice failed to inspire them. On the other hand, his writings were exceptionally clear, witty, and persuasive. All in all, the Prussian king had obtained an officer who stood out of the crowd of his mostly noble and aging colleagues.

From his very first year in Prussian service, Scharnhorst gathered around him an impressive body of students, among whom was the young Carl von Clausewitz, whose ideas would later revolutionize military thought. At the same time, Scharnhorst communicated actively with fellow reformers in and out of the military; to create a forum where the reform of the army could be discussed, he founded the Military Society of Berlin in July, 1801. Soon, young and enlightened officers joined to express their ideas and to put them on paper in the society's publications.

Meanwhile, the triumphs of Napoleon began to draw the eyes of the Prussian reformers to his military machine. The movement and organization of large masses of soldiers required immense organizational support, and the French had designated that task to a still-rudimentary general staff. The idea caught on with the Prussians, and in 1803 the old quartermaster-general's staff was enlarged and reorganized. As a result, Scharnhorst was made general quartermaster-lieutenant for Western Germany (the Prussian possessions west of the river Elbe) and at once began to order such revolutionary activities as field trips for staff officers and peacetime reconnaissance and mapping of potential grounds of conflict.

War came in 1806, and Scharnhorst tested his theories of modern military leadership when he served as a staff aide to the charismatic General Gebhard Leberecht von Blücher; however, the two men could not save the generally poorly led Prussian army. Captured with Blücher and released later, Scharnhorst fought valiantly at Preussisch Eylau in the East, but his superiors failed to use this tactical gain in order to engineer a strategic reversal. In 1807, Prussia had to admit defeat and sign the Peace of Tilsit.

In the aftermath of defeat, the king appointed an Army Reform Commission, which, headed by Scharnhorst, would examine the wartime conduct of every Prussian officer. As a final result of these examinations, only two of the generals who had served in 1806-1807 would still be on active duty in 1813. Furthermore, the king ordered the institution of a Ministry of War. Scharnhorst was appointed head of its General War Department and thus was put in charge of overseeing the army as a whole.

In his new position, Scharnhorst began to draft energetic proposals for reform. Central to his thoughts was the idea of a standing army in which all male citizens would serve their nation for a certain time. An important step toward this goal was taken on October 9, 1807, when Scharnhorst's civilian counterpart, the great reformer Baron Heinrich vom und zum Stein, moved the king to proclaim the abolition of serfdom in Prussia as of November 11, 1810. By this, the people of Prussia were freed to serve the state rather than their landowners.

The French limit on Prussia's army, however, which was to be kept to forty-two thousand men, prohibited the building of a larger force of conscripts and volunteers. Here, Scharnhorst found an ingenious way out when he proposed his famous *Kruempersystem*, or "shrinkage system." According to this scheme, regular soldiers of a regiment were sent on leave, while fresh recruits took their place and received a quick but thorough training. Although the effect of this system has been overestimated, Prussia had at hand about sixty-five thousand trained soldiers in 1813, and some of the surplus came from the *Kruempersystem*.

Before the suspicious French effected his removal from the General War Department in 1810, Scharnhorst had also worked on the opening of the officer corps to members of the middle class. Meanwhile, for the common soldier, Scharnhorst was coinstrumental in abolishing humiliating forms of corporal punishment, such as scourging or "running the gauntlet." While he stayed with the emerging general staff, Scharnhorst gave the Prussian army its modern organization into brigades and divisions which would each consist of a combination of infantry, cavalry, and artillery. The need for modernized tactical training did not escape his view; the army training regulations of 1812 bear witness to his influence in their placing of a new emphasis on operational flexibility and common sense, fire power, and the formation of a strong attacking force. Soldiers were increasingly trained in the field and on the rifle range, while the parade ground became less important.

When France forced Prussia into war against Russia in 1811, Scharnhorst removed himself to a remote outpost in Silesia until fortunes changed and Prussia, now an ally of Russia, declared war on France on March 16, 1813. The new war brought to fruition all the reforms for which Scharnhorst and his colleagues had struggled. Universal service was proclaimed on February 9, and the idea of a militia was realized with the formation of the *Landwehr* and *Landsturm*. Volunteers rushed to the Prussian recruitment centers, and Scharnhorst found himself appointed chief of staff to General Blücher. Together, they engaged the French in two battles. At Grossgörschen, Scharnhorst received a foot wound which developed gangrene and ultimately killed him on June 28, 1813, while he was waiting in Prague on a mission to win Austria's entry into the war against France.

Summary

At a crucial moment in Prussian history, Gerhard Johann David von Scharnhorst succeeded as a leading military reformer who laid the foundations for the survival and ultimate triumph of the Prussian army in the war with France after 1813. His idea of a well-organized citizen army backed by the logistical help of a general staff would find its ultimate expression in the victories of the Prussian armies in 1866 and 1871. Scharnhorst's ideas thus proved essential for the creation of the German Empire by Otto Bismarck and Kaiser William I.

Throughout his years in the service of the Prussian state, Scharnhorst stressed the importance of education and individual dignity and responsibility for all reforms. This emphasis links Scharnhorst's military work to the struggles of his civilian counterparts, reformers such as Stein and Prince Karl von Hardenberg; it also makes him exemplary of the zeitgeist of a new era in Prussia and Germany, which drew inspiration from thinkers such as Immanuel Kant and Georg Wilhelm Friedrich Hegel.

In his reforms, Scharnhorst was always led by a deep humanism as well as a sincere appreciation of the individual soldier. As a practicing Christian, Scharnhorst also rejected the idea that army and warfare fell completely within the private sphere of the ruler. Like his pupil Clausewitz, the great reformer firmly believed in a political, rather than a personal, purpose of a nation's defense forces.

Bibliography

Dupuy, T. N. *A Genius for War: The German Army and General Staff, 1807-1945*. London: Macdonald, and Englewood Cliffs, N.J.: Prentice-Hall, 1977. Dupuy, a retired air force colonel, views Scharnhorst as a brilliant thinker who, together with an influential group of reformers, laid the groundwork for Prussia's emerging superiority in army organization and operational leadership. Very readable and richly illustrated. Contains useful maps.

Feuchtwanger, E. J. *Prussia: Myth and Reality*. London: Wolff, and Chicago: Regnery, 1970. Covers the Prussian state from its origins to its abolition in 1947 and contains a valuable chapter on the reform era. Describes Scharnhorst's accomplishments in detail and places them in the context of a broad reform movement. Depicts the obstacles which were laid in the path of the reformers by opposing elements of the old establishment. Readable, with four maps.

Goerlitz, Walter. *History of the German General Staff, 1657-1945*. Edited and translated by Brian Battershaw. London: Hollis and Carter, and New York: Praeger, 1953. An extremely useful look at Scharnhorst in his role as a military reformer who would prove crucial to the development of the German war machine. Contains a personal view of the man, his general environment, and his supporters, friends, students, and opponents. Very readable; illustrated.

Kitchen, Martin. *A Military History of Germany from the Eighteenth Century to the Present Day*. London: Weidenfeld and Nicolson, and Bloomington: Indiana University Press, 1975. Centers on the democratic aspects of Scharnhorst's reform work. Places him in the framework of Germany's military history. Gives some background information on the Prussian state and its army. Well written and persuasive.

Koch, H. W. *A History of Prussia*. London and New York: Longman, 1978. A detailed account of Scharnhorst's struggles with the Prussian establishment. Contains valuable extracts of Scharnhorst's writings in translation that are not generally available in English. Contains maps and tables. Somewhat scholarly and dry in its approach but useful for further studies.

Reinhart Lutz

FRIEDRICH WILHELM JOSEPH SCHELLING

Born: January 27, 1775; Leonberg in Württemberg
Died: August 20, 1854; Bad Ragaz, Switzerland
Area of Achievement: Philosophy
Contribution: Schelling contributed to the development of German Idealism and to the rise of German Romanticism. His later ontological and mythological speculations, though unpopular among his contemporaries such as G. W. F. Hegel, have influenced modern existentialism and philosophical anthropology.

Early Life

Friedrich Wilhelm Joseph Schelling was born in Leonberg, Württemberg, where his father, Joseph Friedrich Schelling, was an erudite Lutheran pastor. In 1777, his family moved to Bebenhausen near Tübingen, where his father became a professor of Oriental languages at the theological seminary. Schelling was educated at the cloister school of Bebenhausen, apparently destined for the ministry by family tradition. A gifted child, he learned the classical languages by the age of eight. From 1790 to 1792, he attended the theological seminary at Tübingen, where he met Hegel and Friedrich Hölderlin, the great Romantic poet. The Tübingen Evangelical Theological Seminary, located in the buildings of an old Augustinian monastery, is idyllically set over the Neckar River on a cliff, ensconced in green hills, with a view of the snow-topped craggy Alps in the distance. Good friends while students at Tübingen, Schelling, Hegel, and Hölderlin were partisans of the French Revolution and spent many hours discussing philosophy: the pantheism of Baruch Spinoza, the pure concepts of Immanuel Kant, and the Idealist system of Johann Gottlieb Fichte.

For several years after finishing at Tübingen, Schelling was a tutor for the sons of a noble family in Leipzig. He was a precocious and passionate thinker and progressed more quickly in his career than the older Hegel. His first published philosophical work was *Über die Möglichkeit einer Form der Philosophie überhaupt* (1795; on the possibility and form of philosophy in general). This text was followed by *Vom Ich als Prinzip der Philosophie* (1795; of the ego as principle of philosophy) and the article "Philosophische Briefe über Dogmatismus und Kritizismus" (1796; philosophical letters on dogmatism and criticism). The basic theme of these works is the Absolute, which

Schelling interpreted not as God but as the Absolute ego. This ego is transcendental and eternal and can be experienced through direct intuition, which Schelling defined as an intellectual process. In 1798, at the exceptionally young age of twenty-three, Schelling became a professor of philosophy at the University of Jena, where Hegel taught as an unsalaried lecturer between 1801 and 1807, and where in October, 1806, Napoleon I defeated the Prussian army and thus conquered Prussia, the most powerful state in Germany.

Life's Work

Schelling's life's work as a philosopher and teacher began at the University of Jena, the academic center of Germany. At Jena, he became a colleague and friend of the famous Fichte, at the time Germany's leading philosopher. Fichte, who had been one of Schelling's idols, had read and strongly approved of Schelling's early philosophical work. Schelling and Hegel, both Idealist philosophers, coedited the *Kritisches Journal der Philosophie.* Even though Hegel was five years older than Schelling, he at this time was thought of as Schelling's disciple; his first book compared the philosophies of Schelling and Fichte.

Jena at this time was also the center of German Romanticism, and in nearby Weimar Friedrich Schiller and Johann Wolfgang von Goethe, German dramatists and poets, were at the height of their careers. Schelling knew both and was profoundly influenced by the Romantic movement. German Romanticism, in turn, was influenced by Schelling's philosophy, which emphasized the importance of the individual and the values of art. German Romanticism and Schelling's Idealist philosophy are both characterized by the "inward path" to truth, the quest for the totality of experience, and the desire for unity and infinity. Schelling's career falls into two periods: the first, from 1795 to 1809, and the second, which was less productive but no less significant, from 1809 to 1854.

Schelling's peers at Jena—Goethe, Schiller, the Romanticists Friedrich and August Wilhelm Schlegel, the writer/critic Ludwig Tiech, and Hegel—constituted a close group of friends who strongly influenced one another's work. For convenience, Schelling's philosophy can be divided into four stages: the subjective Idealism or his work before Jena; the philosophy of nature; the philosophy of identity; and the philosophy of opposition between negative and positive. The two middle stages belong to his first period of productivity, while the fourth stage belongs to his final period. The second stage, his most famous and influential, began with his *Ideen zu einer Philosophie der Nature* (1797; partial translation as *Introduction to the Philosophy of Nature*, 1871). In opposition to Fichte's idea of the world as a product of ego, Schelling on the one hand argues that the world of nature is as important as the ego and on the other finds a common ground between the two in the essence of matter, which he defines as force. In his *Von der Weltseele, eine Hypothese der höheren Physik zur Erklärung des allgemeinen Organismus* (1798; on the world soul, a hypothesis of advanced physics for the interpretation of the general organism), Schelling argues that the interpretation of the unity of nature was the basic aim of science and thus that the object of scientific study was force, of which mechanical, chemical, electrical, and vital forces were merely different manifestations. This theory is similar to the unified field theory sought by Albert Einstein and now being convincingly proposed by modern physicists such as John Hagelin. In 1799, Schelling published another book on natural philosophy, defining force as pure activity. He believed that nature realized itself in finite matter through an infinite self-referral that never reached completion. This theory he considered parallel to Kant's idea of reason forever striving toward an unattainable absolute.

While in Jena, Schelling became engaged and eventually married under bizarre circumstances. Through his friendship with August Schlegel and his charming wife, Caroline, the daughter of a professor in Göttingen and one of the most intellectually gifted women in German Romanticism, Schelling became informally engaged to Auguste Böhmer, Caroline's sixteen-year-old daughter by a previous marriage. Auguste, however, died in 1800, and Schelling was later held partly responsible for having treated her illness on the basis of his amateur medical knowledge and his impetuous self-confidence—a common trait among the Romantics. This tragedy created a bond between Schelling and Caroline, who had already felt a mutual attraction. In 1803, through the aid of Goethe, Caroline obtained a divorce from Schlegel and married Schelling. The three remained friends in true Romantic style, but the intrigue surrounding the marriage renewed allegations of Schelling's

role in Auguste's death, causing him to leave Jena and join the faculty at the University of Würzburg.

At the height of his second stage, Schelling published *System des transzendentalen Idealismus* (1800; *Introduction to Idealism*, 1871), his most mature and systematic philosophical statement, in which he attempts to unite his theory of nature with the theory of knowledge developed by Kant and Fichte. In defining human consciousness as pure self-activity in opposition to the not-self, Schelling built a theory involving three stages: a movement from sensation to perception, perception to reflection, and reflection to will. This movement connected knowledge and its object. Schelling believed that since concepts cannot exist without their objects, knowledge consists of a meeting of self, object, and process, or of knower, known, and process of knowing—a view also espoused by the Vedic philosophy of India. The transcendental idealism of this book was the one area in which Schelling influenced the mature philosophy of Hegel, especially his theory of the dialectic.

In 1806, Schelling was called to Munich to be an associate for the Academy of Sciences and the secretary of the Academy of Arts. Later, he became the secretary of the philosophical branch of the Academy of Sciences. These were government sinecure positions that gave Schelling extra time for research and allowed him to lecture in Stuttgart. Around this time, he became increasingly interested in aesthetic theory and lectures on the philosophy of art. He believed art to be an organic whole that was served by its parts and moved teleologically toward a specific purpose. This purpose was not pleasure, utility, knowledge, or morality but rather beauty, which Schelling defined as the infinite actualized within the finite. He held that human intelligence in philosophy is abstract and limited, whereas in art it awakens to itself and realizes its unbounded potential. Because it reconciles nature and history and is the aim of all intelligence, art is the highest philosophy.

Schelling's third stage of thought, the philosophy of identity, proposes that the production of reality arises not from the opposition of intelligence to nature but rather from the identity of all objects in the Absolute. The identity of nature and intelligence has its source in reason, defined as an infinite field. In describing Schelling's absolute theory of unity between subject and object, Hegel wittily compared it to the night, "in which all cows are black." Schelling's theory of absolute identity was a type of pantheism, holding nature to be inseparable, even if distinguishable, from God. Here Schelling derives from the mystic Jakob Böhme. Since the essence of God is will, He can be apprehended only by means of will—that is, in action—and not by means of mere rational comprehension.

During this period, Schelling published *Philosophische Untersuchungen über das Wesen der menschlichen Frieheit* (1809; *Of Human Freedom*, 1936), in which he distinguishes between two aspects of God: perfection and the ground of being. Evil is the ground which teaches mankind the difference between good and evil, and which is therefore a necessary stage in the development toward perfection.

In 1809, Caroline died prematurely. Schelling was so distraught he did not publish another book for the rest of his life and entered the final, existential phase of his career. He first propounded his positive philosophy of this period in *Die Weltalter* (1913, written in 1811-1813; partial translation as *The Ages of the World*, 1942), a work that consisted of three volumes, one of which is *Philosophie der Mythologie* (philosophy of mythology). In *The Ages of the World*, Schelling describes the history of God as the divine principle expressed in human history, especially in religion and myth. God is the eternal nothing, the ungrounded basis necessary for the ground to exist. By alienating Himself from Himself through His own oppositional nature, God the Absolute creates the possibility of His relative opposite, which Schelling defined as freedom. Freedom is both the cause of the fall from the Absolute and the trace of the Absolute after the fall. Whereas a negative philosophy developed the idea of God by means of reason alone, Schelling's positive philosophy developed this idea by reasoning backward from the existence of the created world to the existence of God as its creator.

Summary

The two phases of Friedrich Wilhelm Joseph Schelling's career were distinctly different. His second, more despondent, phase consisted of his last philosophical period, stretching across forty-five years from 1809 to 1854, in which he saw his significance as a German Idealist decline. Failing to revive his influence against Hegelianism in Berlin in 1841, he became melancholic and pessimistic, a condition he tried to surmount by developing a system of metaphysics based on Christian revelation and a personal God. Hegel's great philosophical influence was denied to Schelling, whose early and middle periods—his philosophy of nature and philosophy of identity—fell between Fichte's Idealism and Hegel's system of the Absolute spirit.

Nevertheless, over the past century Schelling's independence and importance to philosophy have become more apparent. In its concern not only with the nature of reality but also with the fact of its very existence, Schelling's philosophy bears a strong, if suggestive, resemblance to modern existentialism. In *Philosophie der Mythologie*, Schelling ventures into the field of philosophical anthropology by arguing that humanity, as the embodiment of freedom and creative intelligence, is the essence of the world, which finds expression in mythmaking and religion, humanity's most profound activities. He explored the moods of sadness associated with humanity's being in the world. Like Søren Kierkegaard, Friedrich Nietzsche, Martin Heidegger, and Jean-Paul Sartre, Schelling sought to express the ineffable poignancy of human existence, anticipating the notions of existential anxiety and psychoanalytic resistance to cure. Schelling, however, was convinced that despair was denied the last word on human existence by the revelation of God.

Bibliography

Beach, Edward A. *The Potencies of God(s): Schelling's Philosophy of Mythology*. Albany: State University of New York Press, 1994. Beach examines Schelling's views of religion as a complex theory of spiritual powers residing in the unconscious of a society's collective mind.

Brown, Robert F. *The Later Philosophy of Schelling: The Influence of Boehme on the Works of 1809-1815*. London: Associated University Presses, and Lewisburg, Pa.: Bucknell University Press, 1977. A comprehensive analysis of Schelling's ontology and doctrine of God as influenced by Jakob Böhme's mysticism. Deals with philosophical and theological problems, such as the immutability of God, and the stages in which Schelling incorporates Böhme's ideas. Contains bibliography of German and English secondary texts.

Esposito, Joseph L. *Schelling's Idealism and Philosophy of Nature*. London: Associated University Presses, and Lewisburg, Pa.: Bucknell University Press, 1977. Analysis of Schelling's philosophy of nature and its influence on nineteenth century science. Also traces the influence of Schelling's idealism in America and provides a modern vindication of objective idealism against those who criticize Schelling for the lack of a guiding vision. Contains selected bibliography of secondary sources, mainly in German.

Marx, Werner. *The Philosophy of F. W. J. Schelling: History, System, and Freedom*. Translated by Thomas Nenon, with a foreword by A. Hofstadter. Bloomington: Indiana University Press, 1984. Explores Schelling's conception of history as the relationship between freedom and necessity, then compares this conception with the contemporary theory of history developed by J. Habermas, showing how the latter first renounces and then proceeds to incorporate the categories of the former. Also treats Schelling's self-intuition compared to Hegel's phenomenology and interprets Schelling's notion of human freedom.

Schelling, F. W. J. *The Ages of the World*. Translated with an introduction by Frederick de Wolfe Bolman. New York: AMS Press, 1942. Schelling's text is preceded by a seventy-nine-page introduction, in which Bolman analyzes the twofold nature of Schelling's philosophy, discusses reality and nature in his development through 1812 and his interests after 1812, and then interprets *The Ages of the World*. Ends with a synoptic outline taken from the original manuscript.

———. *System of Transcendental Idealism*. Translated by Peter Heath, with an introduction by M. Vater. Charlottesville: University Press of Virginia, 1978. Schelling's most mature and complete philosophical statements and one of his few works translated into English. Concerns the relation between self and object in his transcendental idealism. Good introduction that compares Schelling to Fichte, Hegel, and other philosophers and discusses the relationship between the self and consciousness.

Snow, Dale E. *Schelling and the End of Idealism*. Albany: State University of New York Press, 1996. A comprehensive introduction to Schelling's philosophy. The author argues that Schelling was instrumental in the development of German idealism.

White, Alan. *Schelling: An Introduction to the System of Freedom*. New Haven, Conn.: Yale University Press, 1983. White covers Schelling's entire fifty-year career in terms of the history of modern philosophy, lucidly arguing that Schelling attempts to produce a system of freedom. Schelling is shown to identify problems with freedom and evil not treated by Hegel. Contains selected annotated bibliography.

William S. Haney II

FRIEDRICH SCHLEIERMACHER

Born: November 21, 1768; Breslau, Silesia
Died: February 12, 1834; Berlin, Prussia
Areas of Achievement: Theology and philosophy
Contribution: Schleiermacher helped Christian theology address the challenges and opportunities that were offered theological thought by modern historical consciousness. His most lasting contribution has been his theological system.

Early Life

Friedrich Daniel Ernst Schleiermacher was born in Breslau, Silesia. His parents entrusted his education to the Moravian Brethren at Niesky. This Moravian community espoused a form of Lutheran piety associated with Count Nikolaus Ludwig von Zinzendorf. They respected the primacy of the devotional life and particularly urged a devotion to Jesus over theological formulations. They also appreciated the disciplined life.

At Niesky, where the young Schleiermacher studied from 1783 to 1785, he followed a pietistic curriculum and also had his first taste of a humanistic education. First at Niesky and then at the Moravian theological school in Barby, he was engaged in the study of Latin and Greek. This Greek study was to prove to be the beginning of classical studies and eventually led to his great German translation of Plato. In these years, he came into contact with an impressive style of piety which continued to inform his life and thought. He withdrew from the seminary at Barby because he found little understanding among his teachers for his own honest struggles and doubts. His horizons were expanded beyond Moravian piety and his previous classical studies when, in 1787, he transferred to the University of Halle.

In Berlin in 1790, Schleiermacher passed his first theological examination, and shortly thereafter he accepted a position as a private tutor in the household of Count Dohna, in West Prussia. In 1793, he became a teacher in Berlin, and the following year he completed his second theological examination. In 1794, he also received ordination in the Reformed Church and entered its service as the assistant pastor in Landsberg. The tradition of Moravian piety, his classical studies, and his ordination for ministry in the Reformed Church all serve as the backdrop for Schleiermacher's life's work.

Life's Work

Schleiermacher's two most celebrated literary works are *Über die Religion: Reden an die Gebildten unter ihren Verächtern* (1799; *On Religion: Speeches to Its Cultured Despisers,* 1892) and *Der christliche Glaube nach den Grundsätzen der evangelischen Kirche im Zusammenhange dargestellt* (1821-1822; *The Christian Faith,* 1928). Both works have their geographic place of origin in Berlin, yet they were written in two different periods of Schleiermacher's life and are separated by two decades.

On Religion was written after several years' experience as a preacher and after having worked on several philosophical treatises. The Reformed clergyman had been called to the Charité Hospital in Berlin as a chaplain and preacher. Close to the turn of the century, Schleiermacher was enjoying the cultural milieu of the new Berlin society and a circle of Berlin's Romantics, to whom he had been introduced through his friendship with the poet Friedrich Schlegel. This was the beginning of the first creative period in his career. It was especially the speeches collected in *On Religion* which first made Schleiermacher famous. His audience was a circle of nontheological friends, the cultured despisers of religion, the literary and philosophical circles of society in the capital city. For them, piety had been displaced by aesthetic intuition.

In the first speech, which Schleiermacher calls an apology or a defense, he draws the distinction between religion's trappings and religion itself. The young chaplain asks his friends why they have only been concerned with shells of religion rather than going to the kernel of the matter. That kernel concerns the "pious exaltation of the mind [*Gemüt*] in which . . . the whole world is dissolved in an immediate feeling of the Infinite and the Eternal." The second and longest speech develops the nature or essence of religion. His concern was that religion be certain of its own roots and its independence in its relationship to philosophy and to morality. Religion is not only knowing or rationalism. It is not simply doing or moralism. Religion starts and ends with history. History is the most general and the most profound revelation of the deepest and the most holy. What is the finest and dearest in history can only be received in the feeling of the religious mind. Religion has to do with receptivity; it has its life in gaining perspective or intuition and feeling

(*Anschauung und Gefühl*). Perspective is oriented toward the *Universum*, which has to do not only with the universe of space but also with the spiritual or intellectual world and with the historical context of relationships.

The third speech collected in *On Religion* is about the cultivation or formation of religion. Piety lies beyond teaching. A teachable religion itself would be absurd. Yet teaching can awaken piety in others. The fourth speech presents the relationship of religion and society and speaks of religious community, communication, and the church. The final speech discusses the God who became flesh, providing an overview of the phenomenological world of religion.

Following these speeches, in 1800 Schleiermacher published an ethical companion piece, *Monologen: Eine Neujahrsgabe* (*Schleiermacher's Soliloquies*, 1926). Taken together, *On Religion* and *Schleiermacher's Soliloquies* brought forth charges of pantheism. These charges, together with some concern about the young Schleiermacher's circle of friends in Berlin, led his elder and friend Friedrich Samuel Gottfried Sack to encourage a stay some distance from Berlin in Stolp. Schleiermacher thus left Berlin to serve as a court chaplain in Stolp from 1802 to 1804. He later accepted a call to Halle as preacher to the university, which included academic duties in a special appointment, which eventually became a regular appointment as professor. Schleiermacher's appointment made the theological faculty the first in Prussia to include both Lutheran and Reformed theologians.

When Schleiermacher returned to Berlin, he was a mature thinker, theologian, and philosopher. In 1809, he became preacher at Trinity Church, and in the same year he married Henriette von Willich, the widow of a friend who had died two years earlier. She brought two children into the marriage, and four other children issued from their union. By this time, the first edition of his translation of Plato's dialogues had appeared. The following fall he became a professor at the new university in Berlin, where he was to remain almost a quarter of a century. He was the first dean of the university's theological faculty, a position he occupied several times. He lectured in Christian ethics, church history, dogmatics, New Testament studies, and practical theology, as well as aesthetics, dialectics, ethics, hermeneutics, pedagogy, and psychology.

It was in the milieu of Berlin and his several responsibilities there that he conceived, composed,

and published his major work, *The Christian Faith*. The two-volume work has a significant title, which translated reads, "the Christian faith systematically set forth according to the principles of the Evangelical church." The last part of the title suggests that Schleiermacher was a church theologian who took history seriously. In his introduction to his magnum opus, Schleiermacher gives an explanation of dogmatics and its methods. After the introduction, he divided his work into two major parts. The first concerns the development of religious self-consciousness as it is presupposed by but also contained in Christian piety. It treats creation and preservation and also the attributes of God and the states of the world which correspond to creation and preservation. The original divine attributes are God's eternity, omnipresence, omnipotence, and omniscience.

The second part of *The Christian Faith* develops self-consciousness as it is determined by the antithesis of sin and grace. This part appears to move from an understanding of sin to christology, through soteriology (theology dealing with salvation), ecclesiology, and eschatology (theology dealing with the Second Coming and Last Judgment). The theologies discussed in the second part are both more dialectical and more unified or coordinated than this simplified schema would suggest. For Schleiermacher, pious self-consciousness is determined by the consciousness of sin and grace. The consciousness of each person is developed within a system of three coordinates: the human being, the world, and God. Sin, both original and actual, is understood as the human condition. The state of the world is thus evil, while God's attributes are holiness and righteousness. The Christian is conscious of God's grace. The Holy Spirit is the means of grace, which arises out of God's love and wisdom.

Schleiermacher by and large held to the traditional dogmatic sequence of salvation history moving from creation to the Last Judgment. His one departure from this traditional order comes in his treatment of the doctrine of God. Along with the doctrine of God's attributes (love, wisdom, omniscience, and the like), the doctrine of God usually appears at the beginning of dogmatics. In Schleiermacher's dogmatics, the doctrine of God's attributes is treated in three sections over the whole of the work, but there appears to be no doctrine of God. The human experience of reality is thus called to serve in characterizing God's attributes. Rather than being omitted in Schleiermacher's dogmatics, God is described in relation to man's experience of reality.

According to Schleiermacher's method, each part of *The Christian Faith* consists of an ingenious tripartite arrangement which discusses pious self-consciousness, theology or divinity, and cosmology or the world; yet, in each section, the sequence of these topics is different. The self, God, and the world are therefore treated three times before Schleiermacher comes to the conclusion of his work. For the conclusion of the work, Schleiermacher transposed the doctrine of the Trinity, traditionally in dogmatic literature at the beginning with the doctrine of God, to the climax of his dogmatics.

Summary

Friedrich Schleiermacher is without a peer among modern theologians in the originality of his attempt to reconstruct the doctrine of God. His theology respects the fundamental distinctions between God and the world and between divinity and humanity, while affirming the interrelatedness of God, the self, and the world. In his life and thought, both piety and culture remained constant themes. He has rightly been recognized as the "father of modern theology."

Schleiermacher was not a theologian who disassociated himself from the preaching office of the church. Karl Barth has noted that Schleiermacher actively sought to present the most exposed, the most difficult and decisive theological position in the pulpit. That was true throughout his creative and mature life. Like Martin Luther and John Calvin before him, Schleiermacher gave himself year after year to the demands of both preaching and academic work.

Bibliography

Barth, Karl. "Schleiermacher." In *Protestant Theology in the Nineteenth Century: Its Background and History*. London: SCM Press, 1972; Valley Forge, Pa.: Judson Press, 1973. An appreciation and critique of Schleiermacher's theology from Barth's own perspective as a theologian who provides an alternative to Schleiermacher. Contains a modest index of names.

Gadamer, Hans-Georg. *Truth and Method*. Edited and translated by Garrett Barden and John Cummings. 2d ed. London: Sheed and Ward, and New York: Crossroad, 1989. This substantial work contains an analysis of Schleiermacher's hermeneutics and the questionableness of Romantic hermeneutics. Gadamer was a student of Martin Heidegger. Includes a helpful subject and name index.

Gerrish, B. A. "Continuity and Change: Friedrich Schleiermacher on the Task of Theology." In *Tradition and the Modern World: Reformed Theology in the Nineteenth Century*. Chicago: University of Chicago Press, 1978. Schleiermacher is discussed in the context of the Reformed tradition. Includes a good treatment of Emil Brunner's early work on Schleiermacher, which has never been translated.

————. *A Prince of the Church: Schleiermacher and the Beginnings of Modern Theology*. London: SCM Press, and Philadelphia: Fortress Press, 1984. A very brief introductory study that places Schleiermacher's theology in a broad context.

Keesee, Neal K. "The Divine Purpose in 'On Religion'." *The Journal of Religion* 78, no. 3 (July, 1998). Discussion of Schleiermacher's "On Religion." Schleiermacher influenced Protestant theology through his belief that God's love provides believers with creative thoughts.

Niebuhr, Richard R. *Schleiermacher on Christ and Religion: A New Introduction*. New York: Scribner, 1964; London: SCM Press, 1965. Treats the elements of Schleiermacher's style with fine discussions of his hermeneutical and historical background.

Redeker, Martin. *Schleiermacher: Life and Thought*. Translated by John Wallhausser. Philadelphia: Fortress Press, 1973. An excellent introduction by the editor of the German critical edition of *The Christian Faith*. Contains a good bibliography and a brief index of persons.

Thandeka. *The Embodied Self: Friedrich Schleiermacher's Solution to Kant's Problem of the Empirical Self*. Albany: State University of New York Press, 1995. Thandeka examines the theory of self-consciousness found in the works of philosophers such a Kant, Schelling, and Schleiermacher, focusing on Schleiermacher's *Dialektik*, a series of lectures delivered between 1811 and 1831.

Authur B. Holmes

HEINRICH SCHLIEMANN

Born: January 6, 1822; Neu Bockow, Mecklenburg-Schwerin

Died: December 26, 1890; Naples, Italy

Area of Achievement: Archaeology

Contribution: A stunningly successful merchant in his early years, Schliemann began a new career in his middle age as an archaeologist. Relying on an unwavering faith in Homer, he found and excavated Troy and unearthed the riches of Mycenae, and thus singlehandedly brought the splendors of the Greek Bronze Age to the attention of both amateurs and professionals.

Early Life

Heinrich Schliemann was born, the fifth of many children, in the small village of Neu Bockow, in Mecklenburg-Schwerin. His christened name was Julius, but he soon took the name of an older brother who had died ten weeks before Schliemann was born. Schliemann reports that by age seven he had already decided to find Troy upon seeing a woodcut of it in a history book that he received as a present from his father for Christmas in 1829. When Schliemann was nine years old, his mother died. It was also about this time that his father, Ernest, was disgraced for an affair with a maid and was temporarily suspended from his post as a Protestant clergyman. The scandal was an embarrassment and this, in addition to his mother's death, caused the family to break up.

Schliemann entered school, but in 1836 he was forced to leave to serve as an apprentice in a grocer's shop. It was during this period that he met a drunken miller, a former student, who recited Greek for Schliemann and intensified his love of Homer. Manual labor was difficult for Schliemann, who was of slight build and pale complexion. He soon departed to make his fortune in Venezuela, but a shipwreck caused him to land in Amsterdam, where he took a series of menial jobs. During this period, he began his lifelong habit of language study, based on a method of his own devising. He eventually learned some eighteen languages and claimed to learn them in periods ranging from six weeks to six months. In 1844, he joined a mercantile firm, and in 1846, his hard work and newly acquired fluency in Russian convinced the firm to send him as its representative to Russia. There, Schliemann flourished, trading many items, but especially indigo, from his base in St. Petersburg, where he quickly established his own business.

He was soon a millionaire, and in 1851 embarked for the United States, ostensibly to help settle the affairs of his dead brother Ludwig but also to make investments in the booming West. He established a bank dealing in gold dust in Sacramento and earned large profits. By 1852, he was back in St. Petersburg, where he married Ekaterina Petrovna Lyschin. He was to have two children, Sergei and Nadezhda, but little happiness from this union. He profited greatly from the Crimean War and the American Civil War, and in 1863, in his early forties and at a stage at which most men look forward to settling down, he liquidated his business and began the second phase of his life.

Life's Work

In 1866, after a two-year world tour which included the Far East and resulted in the first of his eleven books, Schliemann enrolled in the Sorbonne, finally able to complete his education. He soon traveled again and once more visited the southern United States; yet most important for his future work were visits to several Greek sites that he would later excavate, including Ithaca, Mycenae, Tiryns, and Troy. He even dug, without permission, in the area of Troy in 1868, trying to disprove the theory that Burnarbashi held the remains of Homer's Troy. Schliemann was convinced that his choice, Hissarlik, was the true site of Troy.

Upon returning to St. Petersburg to find his estranged wife gone, along with their children, Schliemann left that city, never to return. In 1869, he received a doctorate from the University of Rostock for his publications to date and then returned to the United States to divorce under the state of Indiana's liberal laws. It was during this trip that Schliemann received American citizenship, and not in 1850 as he often related. He was proud of his citizenship and often signed himself "Henry Schliemann."

Even before Schliemann left the United States, he wrote a former tutor, now a Greek archbishop, asking him to find a wife suitable to help him pursue his dream of finding Troy. The archbishop suggested his cousin, Sophia Engastromenos, whom Schliemann courted cautiously. Impressed by her beauty and love of ancient learning, he married her on September 23, 1869. She, along with Troy, was to be an overriding passion in his life. The couple had two children, Andromache and Agamemnon.

In 1870, Schliemann began to dig at Hissarlik, again illegally, as his permit from the Turks was slow in coming. By 1871, he began legal excavations, but his excavation techniques were unquestionably inferior. He chose speed over care and eliminated higher strata without proper documentation in his zeal to get to the lowest levels. At times, he employed up to 150 men, and his equipment included jackscrews, chains, and windlasses to tear down walls that hindered his progress. In 1873, he found the famed "gold of Troy," a hoard of gold jewelry, which he smuggled out of the country. One crown alone was said to consist of 16,353 individual pieces. Widely displayed in a photograph of Sophia wearing them, the jewels were lost when Allied forces invaded Berlin at the end of World War II. Schliemann ended excavations in 1873 and published *Troja und seine Ruinen* (1875; *Troy and Its Remains*, 1875), whose bold claims of having found Priam's city brought strong criticism. Denied a permit for Troy by Turkish officials bristling at the loss of the treasure, he turned his sights elsewhere.

In 1874, Schliemann was already at Mycenae, where he dug illegally for five days before being stopped. There, he hoped to find Homer's "Mycenae rich in gold," the home of Agamemnon, Greek leader at Troy. As he waited for permission from the Greeks, however, he was well occupied. He first settled a suit by the Turks for the loss of the treasure and then traveled again, as he always did when between projects. In 1876, he began at Mycenae and, with naïve faith in the ancient author Pausanias, excavated within the walls of the city, looking for the tombs of Agamemnon and Clytemnestra. He soon found five shaft graves that contained vast wealth (the gold alone weighed some thirty-three pounds). He was wrong in his dates, for these graves antedate the supposed dates of Agamemnon by some 250 to 300 years, but the excitement he caused was immense. Schliemann announced his finds in the media, and the public's imagination was immediately stirred. His subsequent book *Mycenæ* (1878) did not receive unanimous praise, since his tendency to make hasty judgments on incomplete evidence was antithetical to the staid approach of most classical scholars.

Never one to rest for long, Schliemann was off again for Troy, where he dug from 1879 to 1880.

His book *Ilios* (1880) is more reasoned and careful than his previous works and shows a greater respect for proper archaeological technique. It also contains the autobiographical essay that is the sole source for information on Schliemann's early life. In 1881, he excavated at Orchomenus, another city important in Homer's writings, and visited the ongoing excavations by the Germans at Olympia, where he was impressed by the modern and careful techniques being used.

In 1882, Schliemann was back at Troy, trying to understand its confusing stratigraphy, this time with the help of Wilhelm Dörpfeld, a young architect whom Schliemann had met at the Olympia excavations. The publication that resulted from this dig, *Troja* (1884), was a great improvement on his earlier works.

At this time Schliemann began to take an interest in the island of Crete, where he was convinced that he would find further prehistoric remains. With his astonishing skill for finding the right places to dig, he located the future site of Knossos, home of the Minoan civilization. The businessman in him prevailed, however, as he never could agree to pay the asking price for the site. Later, this civilization would be unearthed by Sir Arthur Evans, a man who was much influenced by Schliemann and his finds.

Schliemann next turned to another site indicated by Homer, Tiryns. Just a few miles from Mycenae and the fabled home of Heracles, Tiryns was a strong citadel whose stone walls continue to be impressive. The publication of *Tiryns* (1885) served further to convince the world of the vibrancy of Bronze Age, or Mycenaean, culture. Schliemann traveled in 1886 and 1887, partly to rest and partly to recover his health which, never sound, had begun to deteriorate. In December of 1889, he returned to Troy in order to silence some of his critics. In 1890, on his way home to spend Christmas with his family in Greece, Schliemann's chronic earaches became worse. He underwent surgery in Halle in November, but in his haste to return to his family he left bed early, only to collapse on Christmas Day in Naples. Temporarily denied access to a hospital because of a lack of identification, Schliemann was taken instead to a police station. He died the next day, December 26, 1890, apparently as a result of the infection's spreading to his brain.

Summary

Heinrich Schliemann was an uncompromising businessman. He was also a passionate romantic who believed in Homer as others would believe in the Bible and who put a copy of Homer's *Iliad* to his son Agamemnon's forehead shortly after the child's birth. Schliemann was cold and arrogant with his critics but could be tender to his wife and children. His early excavation techniques were undoubtedly appalling, and he destroyed much that was of value. Yet it was he who found what others had failed to find, and he strove to improve his technique as he went along, often bringing experts such as Dörpfeld to his later excavations.

In some respects, it is Schliemann's energy that most impresses. He did not begin his archaeological career until he was in his forties, and he was largely self-taught. He financed his excavations himself, using profits from investments, which he continued to manage while he excavated and wrote ceaselessly.

While other scholars produced theories from behind their desks, Schliemann went to Asia Minor with Homer in hand and found the site generally accepted today as Troy. While others read Pausanias on Mycenae, Schliemann used his writings to unearth a civilization that had lain beneath the surface of the Greek soil for three thousand years. In the end, this was Schliemann's greatest accomplishment, for through his energy and excavations he changed forever the way the Western world viewed Homer and its own heritage.

Bibliography

Brackman, Arnold C. *The Dream of Troy*. New York: Mason and Lipscomb, 1974. A novelistic biography recounting Schliemann's discovery of Troy. Vivid but not scholarly. Poorly reproduced illustrations.

Calder, William M., and David A. Traill, eds. *Myth, Scandal, and History*. Detroit, Mich.: Wayne State University Press, 1986. Consists of five essays demythologizing Schliemann through critical examination of his record. Also includes an edition of his Mycenaean diary.

Cottrell, Leonard. *The Bull of Minos*. London: Evans, 1953; New York: Facts on File, 1958. A general book on Bronze Age Greece, with significant space devoted to Schliemann and his works. A good introduction for the reader who wants to learn something of the actual remains Schliemann unearthed as well as something about the man himself. Somewhat uncritical in its acceptance of Schliemann's versions of events.

Deuel, Leo. *Memoirs of Heinrich Schliemann*. New York: Harper, 1977; London: Hutchinson, 1978. Thorough analysis of Schliemann's life, with generous selections from his own works, letters, and diaries. Balanced, with careful criticism and analytical sections, full notes, and a bibliography.

Moorehead, Caroline. *The Lost Treasures of Troy*. London: Weidenfeld and Nicolson, 1994; as *Lost and Found: The 9,000 Treasures of Troy-Heinrich Schliemann and the Gold That Got Away*. New York: Viking, 1996. Although primarily a biography of Schliemann, there are good chapters on the post-World War II period when Nazis turned over Schliemann's treasure to Soviet officials, who kept it hidden until 1993.

Payne, Robert. *The Gold of Troy: The Story of Heinrich Schliemann and the Buried Cities of Ancient Greece*. London: Hale, and New York: Funk and Wagnalls, 1959. A readable and enjoyable biography, flawed only by its tendency to accept much of what Schliemann wrote at face value.

Poole, Lynn, and Gray Poole. *One Passion, Two Loves: The Story of Heinrich and Sophia Schliemann, Discoverers of Troy.* New York: Crowell, 1966; London: Gollancz, 1967. A very enjoyable study of the later part of Schliemann's life, using previously unpublished letters.

Rose, Mark. "What Did Schliemann Find—and Where, When, and How Did he Find it?" *Archaeology* 46, no. 6 (November-December, 1993). Examines the inconsistencies in Schliemann's accounting of his discoveries at Troy, which have raised questions as to the original objects found, who was there at the time of the discovery, and the circumstances surrounding Schliemann's transport of the treasure to Turkey.

Stone, Irvine. *The Greek Treasure: A Biographical Novel of Henry and Sophia Schliemann.* London: Cassell, and New York: Doubleday, 1975. A biographical novel, based on careful study of the available Schliemann material, some of it used here for the first time.

Kenneth F. Kitchell, Jr.

ARTHUR SCHOPENHAUER

Born: February 22, 1788; Danzig, Poland
Died: September 21, 1860; Frankfurt am Main
Area of Achievement: Philosophy
Contribution: In the tradition of Immanuel Kant, Schopenhauer developed a pessimistic system of philosophy based upon the primacy of will.

Early Life

Arthur Schopenhauer was born on February 22, 1788, in the Hanseatic city of Danzig (modern Gdańsk), then under nominal control of Poland. His father, Heinrich, was an affluent merchant of Dutch aristocratic lineage, cosmopolitan in outlook and republican in politics. After Danzig lost its freedom to Prussia in 1793, he moved his family and business to Hamburg. Schopenhauer's mother, Johanna, also of Dutch descent, later became a successful romantic novelist.

Since Heinrich Schopenhauer planned a mercantile career for his son, Arthur's education emphasized modern languages, which came easily to him. At age nine, he was sent to Le Havre to learn French, the first of six foreign languages he mastered. In return for agreeing to enter a merchant firm as an apprentice, his father rewarded him with an extended tour—lasting nearly a year and a half—of England, Scotland, France, Switzerland, Austria, and Germany, an experience that strengthened his own cosmopolitan perspective and further developed his facility with languages.

As an apprentice and later a clerk, Schopenhauer found the work tedious and boring, and after the death of his father by drowning, presumed a suicide, in 1805, he altered his life's goals. With an inheritance adequate to assure independence and with encouragement from his mother, he entered grammar school at Gotha and then studied under tutors in Weimar, mastering Latin and Greek. At age twenty-one, he enrolled as a medical student in the University of Göttingen, changing to philosophy in his second year. His first influential teacher, G. E. Schulze, advised him to concentrate on Plato and Kant—the two thinkers who would exert the strongest impact on his philosophy.

In 1811, Schopenhauer attended lectures at the University of Berlin by Johann Gottlieb Fichte and Friedrich Schleiermacher; scathing responses in his notes set the tone of his lifelong contempt for German academic philosophy. When revolution against Napoleonic rule flared in Berlin, Schopen-hauer fled to the village of Rudolstadt, where he wrote his dissertation for a doctorate from the University of Jena. In *Über die vierfache Wurzel des Satzes vom zureichende Grunde* (1813; *On the Fourfold Root of the Principle of Sufficient Reason*, 1889), he explores types of causation—physical, logical, mathematical, and moral.

After receiving his doctorate, Schopenhauer returned to Weimar to live in his mother's house, but the two could not agree. She found him moody, surly, and sarcastic; he found her vain and shallow. Disagreements and quarrels led her to dismiss him, and he left to establish his residence in Dresden in 1814, there to begin his major philosophical work. For the remaining twenty-four years of Johanna Schopenhauer's life, mother and son did not meet.

Life's Work

In Dresden, after completing a brief treatise on the nature of color, Schopenhauer was ready to begin serious preparation of his greatest philosophical work, *Die Welt als Wille und Vorstellung* (1818; *The World as Will and Idea*, 1883-1886). Its four books, with an appendix on Kantian philosophy, include the conceptual ideas that Schopenhauer developed and elaborated throughout his career as an independent philosopher. Book I explains the world, everything that the mind perceives, as representation, a mental construct of the subject. Through perception, reasoning, and reflection and by placing external reality within the mental categories of time, space, and causality, one understands how the world operates. Yet one never understands reality as it exists, for the subjective remains an essential element of all perception.

The fundamental reality that eludes understanding is, as book 2 makes plain, the will, that Kantian thing-in-itself. Understood in its broadest sense, will exists in everything—as a life force and much more. In plants, it drives growth, change, and reproduction. In animals, it includes all of these as well as sensation, instinct, and limited intelligence. Only in man does the will become self-conscious, through reflection and analysis, though the will is by no means free in the usual sense. Every action is determined by motives—to Schopenhauer another name for causes—that predetermine one's choices. Thus, one may will to choose but not will to will. With its conscious and unconscious drives, will presses each person toward egoistic individualism;

yet demands of the will, far from bringing peace, well-being, and gratification, lead only to additional struggle and exertion. As a consequence, unhappiness in life inevitably exceeds happiness.

As a respite from the imperious demands of the will, man finds solace in the beauty that exists in nature and art, and the awakening of the aesthetic sense serves to tame the will by leading it toward disinterested contemplation. To enter a room and discover a table filled with food is to anticipate involvement, consumption, and interaction with others. To look at a painting of the same scene invites simply reflection and appreciation, removing any practical considerations from the will, thereby suspending its feverish activity.

Yet the solace afforded by beauty is only temporary; in book 4, Schopenhauer explores saintliness, which implies denial and permanent taming of the will. By recognizing that others experience the same unrelenting strife that the will brings to himself, a person can develop compassion. Through the power of reflection, one can recognize one's own motives and, through studying motives, become aware of those previously unknown and unacknowledged. Thus, while he cannot achieve freedom of choice, man may acquire a negative capability of rejecting and taming the will. Renunciation, denial of the will, represents for Schopenhauer the path to Nirvana. The best attainable life is that followed by the Hindu *sanyasas* and the ascetic saints of early Christendom.

After publishing his magnum opus, Schopenhauer left for a vacation in Italy, confident that his work would be recognized as a true account of the philosophy foreshadowed by Kant and accepted as a solution to all outstanding problems of philosophy. Instead, the work was ignored both by the reading public and by academic philosophers. From Dresden, he moved to Berlin, where he expected to become a university professor. Appointed to lecture on philosophy at the university, he selected a schedule that competed with lectures by G. W. F. Hegel, then at the height of his popularity, whose optimistic system was the antithesis of Schopenhauer's. Unable to attract students, Schopenhauer spent more than a decade in reading and desultory wandering, though with Berlin as his primary residence. In 1833, he settled in Frankfurt, where he remained for the final years of his life.

There his life assumed a measure of regularity and simplicity. His modest wants were easily met on his inherited income. Although he gave serious

consideration to marriage more than once during his lifetime, he rejected the idea, choosing casual relationships instead. He lived in a boardinghouse, took regular walks for exercise, and dined in company at the Englische Hof Hotel. His day began with work in the morning, followed by a brief diversion through playing the flute. In the afternoons, he stopped by the public library for reading and study; an omnivorous reader, he was widely knowledgeable in the arts and sciences and, like his father, read the London *Times* almost every day of his adult life. He was short of stature, with a thick neck—characteristics, he thought, of genius. His portraits show penetrating blue eyes; a lined, intelligent face; a prominent, forceful nose; and, in old age, two curled locks of white hair on either side of a bald head.

Schopenhauer produced a series of minor works as further elaboration of his system—an attack on academic philosophy, *Über den Willen in der Natur* (1836; *On the Will in Nature*, 1888), and *Die beiden Grundprobleme der Ethik* (1841; *The Basis of Morality*, 1903). After issuing a much-expanded second edition of his major work in 1844, he completed two volumes of essays and miscellaneous writings on a wide variety of subjects, *Parerga und Paralipomena* (1851; *Parerga and Paralipomena*, 1974). With its graceful if sometimes barbed style and its combination of brilliant insights and freely indulged speculation, it expanded the philosopher's reading public.

During his final decade, Schopenhauer experienced the fame and adulation he had long anticipated. A third edition of *The World as Will and Idea* appeared in 1859, this time owing to popular demand. His work was widely discussed and became the subject of university lectures throughout Europe. He began to attract followers, some drawn more by his lucid, jargon-free prose than by his ideas, and on his birthdays tributes poured in from admirers. Shortly before his death, he began to experience recurring chest pains; on the morning of September 21, 1860, he sat down to breakfast at his usual time. An hour later, his doctor, stopping by to check on him, found him still seated in the chair, dead.

Summary

A philosopher in the tradition of Kant, Arthur Schopenhauer modified Kantian terms and categories to accord primacy to will, regarding it as the inscrutable thing-in-itself. Far from an optimistic view, his alteration implies a largely blind force striving for individual advancement and doomed to frustration and defeat. Confronted with this pessimistic reality, the reflective person seeks to tame the will through asceticism. In the *Upanishads*, his favorite bedtime reading, Schopenhauer discovered that Eastern religious thinkers had anticipated important ideas of his system, and he himself helped popularize Hindu and Buddhist thought in Europe.

Schopenhauer's successors have generally accepted portions of his system while rejecting others, and his influence has been almost as varied as his system. Friedrich Nietzsche followed him in granting primacy to the will but envisioned will as a constructive force for progress. Eduard von Hartmann attempted a synthesis of Schopenhauer and Hegel in his *Philosophie des Unbewussten* (1869; *Philosophy of the Unconscious*, 1931). Scholars have discovered a profound debt to Schopenhauer in Hans Vaihinger's *Die Philosophie des Als-Ob* (1911; *The Philosophy of "As If*," 1924); Ludwig Wittgenstein was influenced by Schopenhauer as well. Sigmund Freud acknowledged that, in large measure, his theory of the unconscious was anticipated by the philosopher.

Since Schopenhauer gives aesthetics a prominent and honorable place in his system, it is not surprising to discover that he has influenced artistic creation significantly. Richard Wagner enthusiastically embraced Schopenhauer's speculations on music, in part because he accorded music first place among the arts. Writers such as Leo Tolstoy in Russia; Thomas Mann in Germany; Guy de Maupassant, Émile Zola, and Marcel Proust in France; and Thomas Hardy, Joseph Conrad, and W. Somerset Maugham in Great Britain are, in varying degrees, indebted to Schopenhauer for their world view and for their pessimistic depiction of human life and character. One should note, however, that the enthusiasm for blind will at the base of twentieth century Fascism is a perversion of Schopenhauer's thought. Passages in Schopenhauer that reflect racism, anti-Semitism, and misogyny, attitudes undeniably present in his work, should be placed within the context of his overall pessimism concerning human nature.

Bibliography

Copleston, Frederick. *Arthur Schopenhauer, Philosopher of Pessimism*. 2d ed. London: Search Press, and New York: Barnes and Noble, 1975. Examines Schopenhauer's system in the light of Roman Catholic and religious thought. Calls attention to inconsistencies and contradictions but at the same time provides insightful summary and analysis of Schopenhauer's major ideas.

Fox, Michael, ed. *Schopenhauer: His Philosophical Achievement*. Brighton: Harvester Press, and Totowa, N.J.: Barnes and Noble, 1980. A collection of essays by distinguished scholars. The book is divided into three sections: general articles, giving overviews of Schopenhauer, articles dealing with basic philosophical issues, and comparative studies that relate Schopenhauer's philosophy to others' and explore intellectual debts.

Gardiner, Patrick. *Schopenhauer*. Baltimore: Penguin, 1963; London: Penguin, 1967. A general but penetrating analysis of Schopenhauer's life and philosophy. Gardiner offers a balanced assessment of the philosopher's strengths and weaknesses, clarifying the intellectual debt to

Kant but providing only brief consideration of Schopenhauer's influence on others.

Hamlyn, D. W. *Schopenhauer.* London and Boston: Routledge, 1980. A general survey of Schopenhauer's philosophy. Clarifies his terms, explains his epistemology, and offers extensive analysis of his philosophical debt to Kant.

Jacquette, Dale, ed. *Schopenhauer, Philosophy and the Arts.* Cambridge and New York: Cambridge University Press, 1996. A collection of thirteen new essays by Schopenhauer scholars examining his theory of aesthetics from a number of philosophical perspectives.

Magee, Bryan. *The Philosophy of Schopenhauer.* Rev. ed. Oxford: Clarendon Press, and New York: Oxford University Press, 1997. A scholarly introduction to Schopenhauer's philosophical system. Explores the effects of his early life on his system and places his ideas in their philosophical tradition. Numerous appendices trace his influence on others.

Wallace, William. *Life of Arthur Schopenhauer.* London: Scott, and New York: Lovell, 1890. A comprehensive overview of Schopenhauer's life, philosophical system, and influence. Biographical information draws heavily upon previous studies in Germany and offers an illuminating account of his daily life.

White, F. C. *Schopenhauer's Early Fourfold Root: Translation and Commentary.* Aldershot, Hampshire, and Brookfield, Vt.: Avebury, 1997. The first translation for the English-speaking world of Schopenhauer's doctoral thesis, originally published in 1813. The translation is accompanied by commentary that makes Schopenhauer's thought accessible to both scholars and students.

Stanley Archer

FRANZ SCHUBERT

Born: January 31, 1797; Himmelpfortgrund, near Vienna, Austria

Died: November 19, 1828; Vienna, Austro-Hungarian Empire

Area of Achievement: Music

Contribution: Schubert created the *Lied* (art song) and set models for subsequent ones in his more than six hundred *Lieder*. His larger instrumental works, in their freedom of form and enhanced key relationships, became models for the lyrical Romantic sonatas and symphonies of the later nineteenth century. The expressively songful character of his shorter piano pieces was equally influential.

Early Life

Franz Schubert was born in a suburb of Vienna, the son of a schoolmaster and one of the five of his fourteen children to survive infancy. Though the Schubert family were in humble circumstances, they were highly musical, and Franz as a child learned violin from his father, piano from his older brother Ignaz, and singing and basic music theory from Michael Holzer, choirmaster of the parish church of Liechtenthal. At the age of nine, Franz was engaged as a boy soprano in the Imperial Chapel and was enrolled in its school, the Imperial and Royal Stadt-Konvikt (boarding school), where he was also a violinist in the student orchestra.

His earliest surviving compositions date from 1810. In 1811, he began keyboard studies with the court organist, Wenzel Ruzicka, and in the following year began studies in composition with Antonio Salieri, who had been Wolfgang Amadeus Mozart's rival and one of Ludwig van Beethoven's teachers. This year was critical in other ways for Schubert: His voice changed, thus preventing him from continuing in the chapel choir as a boy soprano, and his mother died. His father remarried in the following year.

Though Schubert's voice had changed, he remained a scholarship student at the Imperial and Royal Stadt-Konvikt. In 1813, he renounced his scholarship, probably because he would be required to devote his time to academic studies rather than to music, and instead entered the teacher training program at the St. Anna Normal School in 1814. He continued to participate in the Imperial and Royal Stadt-Konvikt's musical life and played in its orchestra, for which his first three symphonies were written. In 1814, he wrote string quartets for his family ensemble, in which he played viola, and his first major compositions. He set to music the poem "Gretchen am Spinnrade" (Gretchen at the spinning wheel) from Johann Wolfgang von Goethe's *Faust: Eine Tragödie* (1808; *The Tragedy of Faust*, 1823). He also wrote the Mass in F Major for the parish church in Liechtenthal.

After passing the examination for teacher certification in 1814, Schubert was a part-time assistant in his father's school, preferring to devote most of his time to composition. He was exempted from military service because he was barely five feet tall (thus below the army's minimum height requirement); his friends called him *Schwammerl* (little mushroom) because of his stocky build and short stature.

Schubert met Therese Grob, a skilled amateur soprano, in 1814 and fell in love with her. In 1816, the relationship was ended, since Schubert could not afford to marry her after he was rejected for a post as music teacher at the Normal School in Laibach (modern Ljubljana, in Yugoslavia). From then on he was indifferent to women, seeking rather the company of congenial friends, many of whom he had known since his days at the Imperial and Royal Stadt-Konvikt and who were extremely helpful in getting his music performed or in writing texts which he set as songs. From the year 1816 come the fourth and fifth symphonies, a string quartet, the Mass in C Major, and more than one hundred songs. The following two years were relatively fallow.

Life's Work

Two works from 1819 mark Schubert's full musical maturity: the Piano Quintet in A Major (called *Trout* because the fourth movement is a set of variations on his song "Die Forelle," which means "trout") and a remarkably concise three-movement Piano Sonata in A Major. He also finished the first of his operas, *Die Zwillingsbrüder* (the twin brothers), which received six performances in the following year. Schubert made several ventures into opera during the following four years, all of which were unsuccessful because of the lack of dramatic interest in the librettos.

The year 1823 was critical for Schubert in other respects. He became seriously ill; most writers consider the ailment to have been syphilis, from which he recovered although the secondary symptoms, especially headaches and gastritis, plagued him through the remainder of his life. Yet he completed *Die Schöne Müllerin* (the fair maid of the mill), his first song cycle, so called because he set to music a group of poems by the same author, Wilhelm Müller, which were written around the central theme of a miller's apprentice who falls in love with his employer's daughter when she prefers a huntsman.

Next, Schubert concentrated on writing chamber music and songs. His main chamber works of this period are two great string quartets, in A minor and D minor; an octet for clarinet, bassoon, French horn, string quartet, and string bass in six movements; and several piano duets, written for the daughters of the Esterházy family when he spent the summer as a music teacher on their country estate of Zselis in Hungary (he had been there earlier in 1818). Schubert's immediately succeeding works include the Symphony in C Major, finished in 1826; a large-scale String Quartet in G Major, also completed in that year; and a large-scale Concert Rondo in B Minor for violin and piano. The year 1827 saw two piano trios and the gloomy song cycle *Winterreise* (winter journey), in which Schubert again used poems by Müller. In *Winterreise*, a young man, rejected by his beloved, undertakes a journey on foot in midwinter in a vain effort to forget her and risks losing his sanity. From this cycle comes one of Schubert's best-loved songs, "Der Lindenbaum" (the linden tree), which is virtually a folksong in German-speaking countries. The central theme of isolation and alienation displayed in this song cycle was a favorite one in Romantic literature.

The year 1828 saw Schubert's greatest achievement. Foreign journals were reviewing his music favorably, and foreign publishers were interested in his music. His public concert devoted entirely to his music was a great success. Many of his best compositions—the Fantasy in F Minor for piano duet, the String Quintet in C Major, the last three piano sonatas, the Mass in E-flat Major, and the group of songs published after his death as *Schwanengesang* (swan song)—stem from this, his final, year. He had even begun lessons in counterpoint with Simon Sechter, later to be the teacher of Anton Bruckner. In November, his health suddenly deteriorated; in slightly more than a week, he lapsed into a coma and died. His illness was diagnosed by his doctors as "nervous fever"; most modern scholars consider his fatal illness to have been typhoid fever, brought on by the unsanitary conditions of the suburb of Vienna where he was then living.

Many legends that have evolved about Schubert have been demolished by subsequent research. He was a prolific composer, but his supposed spontaneity was the result of much forethought and revision. For example, one of his most famous early songs, "Erlkönig" (the elf king), with a text by Goethe, was supposed to have been written in a single afternoon in 1815 and performed that evening. Schubert, however, revised "Erlkönig" six times before its publication as his Opus 1 in 1821. One of the tragedies of music is Schubert's abandonment of several major compositions before their completion. The most famous of these incomplete works is the "Unfinished" Symphony in B Minor (1822), in which Schubert wrote two outstanding symphonic movements and sketched a third movement as a scherzo, but not even sketches have survived for a finale.

Schubert's life of poverty has also been misunderstood. He rejected positions with regular hours, seeking one that would enable him to devote full time to composing. Such positions were bestowed on those with many years of musical achievement, and Schubert was passed over in favor of much older and more experienced men. He was relatively well paid by his publishers, but he spent money lavishly when he had it, not so much on himself as on the circle of friends with whom he lived and whom he accompanied on summer vacations in the mountains, where he did much of his composing. Social conditions had changed: The nobility, ruined by the Napoleonic Wars, could not support a composer in the manner that Joseph Haydn or Ludwig van Beethoven had been aided, and the middle-class public could not provide a steady income. Schubert's main audience consisted of the friends who attended the so-called Schubertiads—evenings when Schubert and others played the piano and sang for a mostly male audience, who did much drinking and stayed as late as 3:00 A.M. He was beginning to achieve a wide reputation as a composer of merit during the last year of his life.

Summary

Only a small amount of Franz Schubert's music was published during his lifetime—several songs and piano duets, but only one string quartet, four piano sonatas, and no orchestral music. His music

was aimed more toward the middle-class drawing room than the concert hall, and Schubert himself was not a charismatic virtuoso performer such as Niccolò Paganini or Franz Liszt, who were able to attract well-paying crowds.

Schubert changed the course of music in many ways. Before him, composers who wrote songs undertook to provide a simple setting for a poem, with an almost rudimentary piano accompaniment that often was intended to be played by the singer, rather than to create an independent musical composition that would utilize the full resources of the piano and all the techniques of harmonic color and melodic expression in the way that Schubert did. In the sphere of the large instrumental work, Schubert provided an alternative to Beethoven, writing movements that were lyric and epic rather than heroic and dramatic. Schubert used the possibilities inherent in the widening of the tonal spectrum to expand the forms of his movements. The short, spontaneous piano piece was not original with Schubert, but he set the standard for subsequent works in this genre.

Schubert's influence on subsequent composers was not immediate but was especially strong on those who played major roles in making his music known throughout the nineteenth century: Robert Schumann, Franz Liszt, and Johannes Brahms. The full range of Schubert's genius has become appreciated only in modern times with the performance and recording of many of his large-scale works.

Bibliography

Brown, Maurice J. E. "Schubert." In *The New Grove Dictionary of Music and Musicians*, edited by Stanley Sadie. Washington, D.C.: Grove's Dictionaries of Music, and London: Macmillan, 1980. Brown's critical studies of Schubert's music are distilled in this comprehensive article embracing both the composer's life and music.

————. *Schubert: A Critical Biography.* London: Macmillan, and New York: St. Martin's Press, 1958. This is the standard scholarly study of Schubert's work, with the focus on his music. Written for the person with musical understanding.

Deutsch, Otto Erich, ed. *Schubert: Memoirs by His Friends.* Translated by Rosamond Ley and John Nowell. London: Black, and New York: Macmillan, 1958. This volume contains many first-hand accounts by those who knew Schubert personally and intimately.

Deutsch, Otto Erich, with Donald R. Wakeling.

The Schubert Reader: A Life of Franz Schubert in Letters and Documents. New York: Norton, 1947. This documentary biography consists of English translations of the documents directly pertaining to Schubert, thus providing direct insight into the composer's life and the circumstances surrounding his work.

Einstein, Alfred. *Schubert: A Musical Portrait.* New York: Oxford University Press, 1951. This sensitive appreciation of Schubert's music by one of the giants of early twentieth century musical scholarship is well worth reading because of its valuable and penetrating insights into Schubert's music.

Kramer, Lawrence. *Franz Schubert: Sexuality, Subjectivity, Song.* Cambridge and New York: Cambridge University Press, 1998. Analysis of Schubert's ability to convey a wide range of human and sexual types through song.

Newbould, Brian, ed. *Schubert Studies.* Aldershot, Hampshire, and Brookfield, Vt.: Ashgate, 1998. A collection of eleven essays by Schubert scholars and performers covering neglected topics such as analysis of tempo conventions, Schubert's influence on later composers, his biographical information, and his relationships with women.

Osborne, Charles. *Schubert and His Vienna.* London: Weidenfeld and Nicolson, and New York: Knopf, 1985. This is a book on Schubert for the general reader, with the emphasis on his life and environment rather than on his music. Provides a very readable introduction to Schubert, though the musical information is mostly praise rather than critical analysis.

Reed, John. *Schubert.* London: Dent, 1987; New York: Oxford University Press, 1997. Provides excellent discussion of Schubert's life, with the music important though subordinate. Written in a style suited more for the general music lover than for the specialist scholar. Some musical background is necessary for a full appreciation of this volume.

Solomon, Maynard. "Franz Schubert and the Peacocks of Benvenuto Cellini." *Nineteenth-Century Music* 12 (1989): 193-206. The author strives to show that Shubert and his circle of friends were part of Vienna's homosexual underground. In the absence of any direct evidence, he relies heavily on gossip, inference, implication, and code words in use 170 years ago.

Rey M. Longyear

ROBERT SCHUMANN

Born: June 8, 1810; Zwickau, Saxony
Died: July 29, 1856; Endenich, near Bonn, Prussia
Area of Achievement: Music
Contribution: Schumann was important not only as a composer of music during the Romantic period but also as an editor of *Neue Zeitschrift für Musik*, which did much to establish standards of musical criticism.

Early Life

Robert Alexander Schumann was born on June 8, 1810, at Zwickau in Saxony. His father was a publisher of scholarly books, and his mother was the daughter of a surgeon. Robert was the youngest of five children, four sons and one daughter. August Schumann's publishing business was successful enough that Robert was able to enter a private preparatory school for his early education. Already, at his father's instigation, he was studying the piano, the instrument that would remain his favorite throughout his life. After the preparatory school, Schumann attended the Zwickau Lyceum, where he studied the classics as well as the piano. Literature and music, then, were both strong interests of the young Schumann and remained so throughout his life.

At the lyceum, Schumann played the piano in concerts, read widely in classical Greek and Roman authors, and studied such German writers as Friedrich von Schiller and Johann Wolfgang von Goethe. He even wrote some poetry, although when he attempted to recite from memory one of his poems before the student body, his mind went blank, and he stood in silent embarrassment on the stage. This incident may have contributed significantly to Schumann's aversion to public speaking throughout his life.

Schumann spent his formative years if not in affluence at least at a comfortable material level. In 1826, however, tragedy struck when his elder sister Emilie, who was afflicted with typhus fever and a terrible skin disease, committed suicide. August Schumann was crushed by this event and himself died a few weeks later. Schumann, too, was deeply affected by his sister's death and from that time forward could never bring himself to attend a funeral, not even his mother's. Schumann's mother, Johanna, and Gottlob Rudel, the guardian appointed to look after Robert's share of August's estate,

agreed that the boy should pursue a legal career. With no one to support his own desires, Schumann acquiesced, although he knew that he would never lose his love of music. In an 1828 letter to a friend describing his feelings upon leaving the lyceum, he wrote, "Now the true inner man must come forward and show who he is."

Enrolling first at the University of Leipzig, Schumann found the study of law even more boring than he had feared. Influenced by a friend at Heidelberg, who wrote of the exciting university life there, Schumann persuaded his mother and Rudel that he should go to Heidelberg to continue his study. He was, however, anything but the model student, spending his time in taverns and restaurants instead of in the pursuit of his legal studies. He also spent much time with Anton Thibaut, a law professor much interested in music. Schumann spent many hours at Thibaut's home, making and enjoying music.

On July 30, 1830, Schumann wrote what he called the most important letter in his life: one to his mother, pleading that he be permitted to give up his legal studies and journey to Leipzig to study piano with Friedrich Wieck, who promised to turn the young Schumann into a great pianist. Johanna Schumann agreed, and at age twenty Robert Schumann began his musical career.

Life's Work

Schumann had met Wieck in Leipzig. A kind of self-made man, the latter's early life was the opposite of Schumann's. Poor, and often forced to rely on charity for food and for money to cover his education, he developed into an autocrat with a violent temper. Following his own system of instruction, he set himself up as a piano teacher. He saw the clear relationship between playing the piano and singing and trained his students to strive for a "singing touch" at the keyboard. His prize student was his own daughter Clara. Viewing her almost as an extension of himself, Wieck carefully molded and developed her talent to a level that made her something of a sensation across Europe. In 1832, when Schumann came to study with Wieck, Clara was thirteen years old. The relationship between them grew over the next several years from one of elder brother and younger sister to one of love.

On one occasion, when Wieck had taken Clara on a performing tour, Schumann, perhaps in an effort to find a technique to help him catch up with the talented Clara, fashioned a sling of sorts to keep one finger out of the way while the others were being exercised. Exactly what happened to his hand is not clear. Schumann himself only said that it was lamed. Some scholars suggest that no injury actually occurred and that Schumann may have suffered motor damage from an overdose of mercury, a substance then widely prescribed for syphilis. Whatever the cause, the effect was devastating to the young pianist. He tried numerous cures to no avail.

When Wieck discovered that the relationship between Schumann and Clara was becoming more than simply friendship, he flew into a rage, vowing that his daughter was destined to be a concert pianist, not a hausfrau. Love, however, was not to be daunted, and the two young people applied to the courts for permission to marry. The wedding took place on September 12, 1840, and the couple settled in Leipzig, an important musical center of the time.

An ardent admirer of Franz Schubert's piano music, Schumann, up to the time of his marriage, had written only for the piano. In 1840, however, he turned his creative efforts to *Lieder* (art songs), many of which were in celebration of his love for Clara. These *Lieder* show clearly Schumann's attention to form and reflect the same power of emotion and flow of melody as do Schubert's, although the harmonics are more complex. Schumann probably realized that such art songs gave him the opportunity to blend his feeling for poetry and his genius for melody. In these songs, as one might expect, the piano has a more significant role than it does in those of other composers of *Lieder*.

Schumann's gift with words was evidenced also in his editorship of *Neue Zeitschrift für Musik* (new journal for music), a magazine that served as an outlet for the writings of young Romantic musicians in Germany. Indeed, when Schumann first met Felix Mendelssohn in 1835, he was more noted for his work with this magazine than for his music, a situation that led Mendelssohn to see him first as a kind of dilettante. Schumann, on the other hand, had only the highest regard for Mendelssohn as a composer.

If 1840 could be called Schumann's year of songs, the next year could certainly be called the year of symphonies. Although he had flirted earlier with the idea of a symphony, he had never completed one. In 1841, he completed two. The First Symphony, whose initial idea came to Schumann from a poem about spring by Adolf Böttger, was completed in the remarkably short period of one month. Called the *Spring Symphony*, it is buoyant and fresh in its mood and is marked by a driving rhythmic energy. The Symphony in D Minor was also written in 1841, although it was not published until ten years later and is referred to as the Fourth Symphony. It was performed once in 1841, but because of the cold reception it received, Schumann withdrew it and put it aside until 1851, when he revised it. Schumann left no word as to what meaning lay behind the music of this symphony. It was no doubt Schumann's intention, according to Brian Schlotel, that it be received as absolute music.

Schumann spent the year 1842 working primarily on string quartets, three of which he dedicated to Mendelssohn. This same year, he accompanied Clara on a concert tour to Hamburg. Although her marriage no doubt limited her career as a concert pianist, Clara was ever ready to play her husband's compositions and to interpret them faithfully to her audiences. It was in a sense a perfect combination—Schumann's talent as a composer complemented by his wife's talent as a pianist.

In 1843, Schumann turned his efforts toward composing choral works, the most important of which was "Paradise and the Peri," a work for solo voices, chorus, and orchestra. Schumann conducted it himself December 4, 1843. Encouraged by the reception of this work, he composed a musical setting for Goethe's *Faust* (1790-1831). Also at about this time, Schumann suffered a second physical breakdown, the first, less serious, having occurred in 1842. This second breakdown was marked by constant trembling, a number of phobias, and auricular delusions, and it made serious work impossible. Hoping that a total change of scene would be helpful, the Schumanns moved to Dresden.

While at Dresden, Schumann completed the Piano Concerto in A Minor (1845), the famous C Major Symphony (1846), and his only opera, *Genoveva* (1848). The latter was an unsuccessful attempt to emulate Richard Wagner's German operas. In addition to composing, Schumann directed the Liedertafel, a male choral society. Neither of the Schumanns was particularly happy with the music scene in Dresden, and when the opportunity to become municipal director of music at Düssel-

dorf arrived, Schumann accepted. Unfortunately, Schumann did not exhibit the same level of talent in conducting as he did in composing, and he was encouraged in 1852 to resign. After some argument, he finally left in 1853.

In 1850, Schumann completed his Symphony No. 3, the *Rhenish*, and also his Concerto for Cello and Orchestra. In the former, Schumann attempted to put into music his feelings about the Rhine, a river rich in scenery and legend. The full score of the symphony was completed in somewhat more than one month, and Schumann himself conducted it in Düsseldorf on February 6, 1851. Although his artistic talents and creative powers are apparent in this symphony, time for Schumann was running out. Within three years, in a period of utter depression, he attempted suicide by jumping into the river that had stimulated his imagination to compose the *Rhenish*. Although the suicide attempt was thwarted by some fishermen, death came soon enough. Schumann's last years were spent at Endenich, a hospital for the insane. With his limbs in terrible convulsions and with the sounds of music filling his head, Schumann died on July 29, 1856.

Summary

Along with Frédéric Chopin, Felix Mendelssohn, Johannes Brahms, and Anton Bruckner, Robert Schumann composed works that reflect the artistic energies of the Romantic movement in music. Schumann was also instrumental in developing critical standards for music. His periodical *Neue Zeitschrift für Musik* served as an outlet for musical criticism and as a support for struggling composers of the time, including Chopin and Brahms.

Schumann's music itself reflects clearly the strong emotions and individualistic values of the Romantic period. Focusing early in his career on miniature pieces, Schumann exemplified the desire of Romantic composers to communicate directly and intensely with the listener. The year 1840 may be called Schumann's year of songs, many of which were inspired by his wife Clara. These beautiful flowing melodies testify to Schumann's love of poetry and his desire to meld the literary with the musical.

Alternating periods of intense creative productivity with periods of deep depression, Schumann moved from miniatures and songs to larger works—symphonies, choral works, chamber music, piano concerti, and an opera. His four symphonies are generally considered the most significant contributions to that genre since Ludwig van Beethoven's works. Although sometimes criticized for their somewhat heavy and unimaginative orchestrations, Schumann's symphonies show his desire to experiment with both themes and form.

In his chamber music, Schumann made great use of the piano, sometimes to the consternation of some musicologists. Nevertheless, as John Gardner and others have pointed out, Schumann's influence ranged widely among his contemporaries and successors in that genre. Once the piano took over from the harpsichord in the late eighteenth century, the door was open for a Schumann to give the former its deserved place in chamber music.

Except for the Piano Concerto in A Minor, some musicologists view Schumann's concerti as representing a falling off of his creativity. Others argue, however, that Schumann, like other composers of the period, faced the challenge of "getting out from under" Beethoven and that his concerti are justified efforts in new directions of form and theme. He saw the concerto as a great art form, one that was to be treated not casually but nobly—but one which had to evolve if it were to remain vital.

Schumann completed his first symphony at the age of thirty, after having heard Schubert's Symphony in C Major in 1839. Certainly influenced by Beethoven's work in the symphony, Schumann nevertheless sought new forms in his own symphonies. Not generally considered a giant of symphonic composition, Schumann must still be viewed as having considerable importance in symphonic history. The same may be said for his choral music. Often neglected, this music came late in Schumann's life, when his mental problems increasingly interfered with his creative powers. Still, as Louis Halsey has argued, much of this music is of high quality. A man of restless personality and strong creative spirit, Schumann has been called the typical Romantic. Not a revolutionary to the same degree as Beethoven, he nevertheless made a significant contribution to music of the Romantic period.

Bibliography

Bedford, Herbert. *Robert Schumann: His Life and Work*. New York and London: Harper, 1925. A readable biography that traces Schumann's career. Focuses on cities in which Schumann lived and worked. Somewhat dated.

Brion, Marcel. *Schumann and the Romantic Age*. Translated by Geoffrey Sainsbury. London: Collins, and New York: Macmillan, 1956. Places Schumann in the German Romantic tradition and examines his work against the background that influenced him. A good basic book on Schumann.

Daverio, John. *Robert Schumann: Herald of a "New Poetic Age."* New York: Oxford University Press, 1997. This book was chosen as an Outstanding Academic Book of 1997 by Choice. It is the first comprehensive study of Schumann's work and life in almost one hundred years and includes information on the impact of Schumann's mental illness on his creativity, analysis of later works, and his influence on other composers.

Krebs, Harald. *Fantasy Pieces: Metrical Dissonance in the Music of Robert Schumann*. New York: Oxford University Press, 1999. Analysis of Schumann's metrical style based on a theory of metrical conflict presented by the author.

Niecks, Frederick. *Robert Schumann*. London: Dent, and New York: Dutton, 1925. A standard biography that presents a meticulous and exhaustive record of Schumann as a man and as a composer.

Ostwald, Peter. *Schumann: The Inner Voices of a Musical Genius*. Boston: Northeastern University Press, 1985. Written by a psychiatrist, a fascinating study of the degenerative forces that brought Schumann to his death in a mental hospital. Relates Schumann's music to his states of mind.

Schumann, Robert. *The Musical World of Robert Schumann*. Edited and translated by Henry Pleasants. London: Gollancz, and New York: St. Martin's Press, 1965. Presents a chronological arrangement of Schumann's own writings on various composers of his time. A good view of Schumann the critic. Good for insights into various composers and their music.

Walker, Alan, ed. *Robert Schumann: The Man and His Music*. London: Barrie and Jenkins, and New York: Barnes and Noble, 1972. A study of Schumann through thirteen essays by music scholars. Covers Schumann's background as well as the various kinds of music he composed.

Wilton Eckley

CARL SCHURZ

Born: March 2, 1829; Liblar, Prussia
Died: May 14, 1906; New York, New York
Areas of Achievement: Government and politics
Contribution: Recognized as a leader of the German-American community in the United States, this partisan of liberty fled Germany after the revolutions of 1848 and made a career as a journalist and politician, serving as a Union general in the Civil War, a senator from Missouri, and a secretary of the interior.

Early Life

Carl Schurz was born to Christian and Marianne (Jüssen) Schurz on March 2, 1829, in one of the outbuildings of a moated castle in the Prussian Rhineland (modern West Germany), where his grandfather worked for Baron Wolf von Metternich. His family was of humble origin but was respected in the local context of village life; his grandfather was the count's estate manager, one uncle was the mayor of a neighboring village, and his father was the Liblar schoolmaster. Schurz was reared a Roman Catholic, but with a strong dose of Enlightenment skepticism; as an adult, he considered himself a "freethinker." As a boy, he enjoyed the run of Metternich's estate, its formal gardens, its forests, and its farmlands. His parents noted his unusual intelligence and his musical skill and resolved to make sacrifices to give him a higher education. Thus he left his father's school in the village, going to preparatory school at neighboring Brühl and then at Cologne, several miles away. When he was seventeen, the family moved to the nearest university town, Bonn, so that the boy could study there, even though his parents had suffered financial reverses which temporarily put his father in debtors' prison.

At Bonn, Schurz began to make a name for himself both in the politically liberal fraternal organizations and as a budding scholar, under the tutelage of the young Romantic, Gottfried Kinkel. Then came the revolutionary fervor of 1848. Immediately, Schurz interrupted his formal education and turned to a life of political activity. Like many young men of his generation, he saw 1848 as the opportunity to achieve a unified German state with a liberal-democratic constitution. Too young to stand for election himself, he turned to journalism and popular agitation to support his goals. His zeal

for freedom and justice, his skills as a writer and speaker, and his tireless and combative commitment to his cause were characteristics that would distinguish him as a prominent American statesman years later. He joined the revolutionary army which fought against the old monarchies and barely escaped with his life when it was forced to surrender. In 1850, he returned to Prussia from exile in France and Switzerland in disguise and rescued Professor Kinkel from the prison to which the Prussians had condemned him. After spending a brief time in Paris and London, where he wooed and married Margarethe Meyer, daughter of a well-to-do Hamburg mercantile family, he decided to leave the Old World for America. If he could not be a citizen of a free Germany, he concluded, he would become a free citizen of the United States.

The tall, slim young man with thick glasses affected the flowing hair and mustache of a Romantic liberal in 1848; as he matured, he was recognizable for his bushy beard and sharp features, so often caricatured by Thomas Nast.

Life's Work

Schurz and his young wife arrived in the United States in 1852, staying first in Philadelphia and eventually settling in Watertown, Wisconsin, in 1855. As an immigrant, he was neither tired nor poor. His wife's dowry was enough to set him up in business. His fame as a daring fighter for freedom in Germany, his solid education, his gifts as a writer and speaker, and his political ambition combined to make him a well-known figure almost immediately. Although he rarely stood for election himself, his persuasiveness with German-American voters made him a force to be reckoned with in the ethnic politics of that age.

He led the Wisconsin delegation to the Republican National Convention in 1860. Though originally pledged to William H. Seward, he became an avid supporter of Abraham Lincoln once he had received the nomination. Schurz traveled more than twenty-one thousand miles campaigning for Lincoln, speaking in both English and German, and was credited with swinging much of the German-American vote away from its traditional inclination for the Democratic Party and into Lincoln's camp. In gratitude, Lincoln appointed him minister to Spain and, after the onset of the Civil War, brigadier and then major general in the Union army. Schurz's military career did little to enhance his reputation. He was only in his early thirties, and his high rank was clearly a result of political influence rather than demonstrated military skills. Schurz did his best, however, to contribute to the Union cause, seeing action at the Second Battle of Bull Run, Gettysburg, and Chancellorsville. Lincoln invited Schurz to report directly to him on the wartime situation, which Schurz did with great energy, pressing the president to emancipate the slaves.

After the war, Schurz settled in St. Louis as part owner and editor of the German language *Westliche Post*. His wife never liked the American Midwest, however, and so she spent much of her time in Europe. While visiting his family in Germany in 1868, Schurz made a widely reported visit to Berlin, where the onetime revolutionary was warmly received by Otto von Bismarck, now prime minister of Prussia and chancellor of the emerging German Empire.

Schurz was critical of President Andrew Johnson but enthusiastically supported Ulysses S. Grant in the 1868 elections. German-American forces were influential in Missouri politics, and the state legislature sent him to Washington, D.C., as a senator. Once there, he became disillusioned with the apparent corruption in the spoils system, and he turned his polemical skills to the issue of civil service reform. This challenge to the status quo alienated many of his party allies, and he was not returned to office in 1874. The Senate provided a platform for Schurz's oratorical skills, and he gained a national reputation as a spokesman for reform and for the German-American community. Because of his criticisms of United States politicians, some alleged that he was not a patriotic American. He responded with a turn of phrase which has become famous: "My country right or wrong: if right, to be kept right; and if wrong, to be set right."

No partisan loyalist, Schurz was active in founding the Liberal Republican Party, which supported Horace Greeley for president over Grant in 1872. With the election of 1876, however, he returned to the Republican Party, supporting Rutherford B. Hayes, and after Hayes's victory, Schurz was made secretary of the interior. He attempted to initiate environmental controls, particularly over forest lands, and to follow a humanitarian policy with respect to the Indians. Inevitably, his liberal idealism was unable to overcome deep-seated interests which opposed his policies. He left government office in 1881, never to serve again, and pursued his career as a journalist, author, and lecturer. He made New York his home, where he became editor in chief of the *Evening Post* and, eventually, *Harper's Weekly*.

As an independent, he found himself among the "Mugwumps," who were more committed to his liberal ideals, especially civil service reform, than to any political party. Looking at his record, one sees a man who supported James A. Garfield (Republican) in 1880, Grover Cleveland (Democrat) in 1884, 1888, and 1892, William McKinley (Republican) in 1896, William Jennings Bryan (Democrat) in 1900, and Alton B. Parker (Democrat) in 1904. In an age when corruption was often an accepted part of the political process, Schurz remained free of its taint. His nineteenth century liberalism has been criticized as being narrow and doctrinaire, a *laissez-faire* philosophy which had little room for labor unions and social programs. Yet his concepts of personal liberty, due process of law, and clean government surely put him in the mainstream of American political thought and action. He favored suffrage for blacks (but not for women) and spoke out strongly against anti-Semitism. In the 1890's, he looked with dismay upon American diplomatic and military expansion and, polemically as ever, crusaded as an anti-imperialist. The onetime general loathed war and its accompanying atrocities; moreover, he seemed to fear that an active policy overseas by the United States might at some time lead to a conflict with the land of his birth, Germany. As a man in his sixties and seventies, he traveled and spoke as avidly against an American empire as he had once fought for Lincoln's election and freedom for the slaves. Though he no longer was alleged to be able to swing the German-American vote in major elections, he was widely praised as that community's leader and was showered with honors. He died peacefully at his home in New York City at the age of seventy-seven.

Summary

Schurz saw himself as "the main intermediary between German and American culture." He continued to be equally fluent in German and English, writing his widely read memoirs in both languages. He traveled back and forth many times between the United States and the old country, filled with pride

Bibliography

Easum, Chester V. *The Americanization of Carl Schurz.* Chicago: University of Chicago Press, 1929. A brief, older work, upon which further scholarship on Schurz has depended.

Fuess, Claude M. *Carl Schurz, Reformer: 1829-1906.* Edited by Allan Nevins. New York: Dodd, Mead, 1932. A gentlemanly biography by a scholar of German-American parentage.

Holden, Walter. "Confusion on the Road to Wauhatchie." *Military History* 13, no. 5 (December, 1996). Focuses on the blame placed on Schurz and the late arrival of his troops for the failure of General John Geary's unit at Wauhatchie.

Schurz, Carl. *Intimate Letters of Carl Schurz: 1841-1869.* Edited and translated by Joseph Schafer. Madison: State Historical Society of Wisconsin, 1928. Hitherto unpublished letters, mostly to members of his family, which shed light on Schurz's career and personal life beyond that shown in the six-volume set cited below.

———. "The Need for a Rational Forest Policy." *Essential Documents in American History* (January, 1997). This is the text of Schurz's speech to the American and Pennsylvania Forestry Associations in 1889 calling for rational use of American forests.

———. *The Reminiscences of Carl Schurz.* 3 vols. New York: Doubleday, 1907-1908; London: Murray, 1909. An entertaining and enlightening view of Schurz as he saw himself, with insightful sketches of the great men he knew, especially Lincoln, Bismarck, and a long list of American political figures. A modern abridgment by Wayne Andrews (New York: Scribners, 1961) is available, with an introduction by Allan Nevins.

———. *Speeches, Correspondence and Political Papers of Carl Schurz.* Edited by Frederic Bancroft. 6 vols. New York: Putnam, 1913. The vast array of Schurz's political output is set forth in this old, but well-edited, collection of his works.

Trefousse, Hans L. *Carl Schurz: A Biography.* Knoxville: University of Tennessee Press, 1982. A scholarly study of Schurz, based on exhaustive study of the printed and manuscript sources, in the United States and in Europe, including some private letters to his companion in later life, Fanny Chapman. Excellent notes and bibliography.

Gordon R. Mork

for both. When accused of mixed loyalties, he responded that he loved equally his "old mother" and his "new bride." Stalwart and eloquent, he vigorously defended the cause of freedom, as he saw it, in Germany and in the United States. His stubborn dedication to his principles and his combative temperament sometimes earned for him the enmity of political opponents. Surely not even all German-Americans supported him on every issue. As a group, however, they were proud of his accomplishments, the most impressive of any German immigrant at that time, and they agreed with him that fondness for their country of origin did not diminish their patriotism as Americans. Schurz would have been deeply saddened by the political and diplomatic events of the first half of the twentieth century which brought the United States and Germany into conflict, but much heartened by the development of a firm alliance between America and a liberal-democratic Germany after 1945.

DRED SCOTT

Born: c. 1795; Virginia
Died: September 17, 1858; St. Louis, Missouri
Area of Achievement: Civil rights
Contribution: Scott instigated a legal challenge to the definition of "citizenship" for black people in the United States. His challenge led to the Supreme Court's 1857 *Dred Scott v. Sandford* decision, which became a step toward Civil War and the end of slavery.

Early Life

Dred Scott was most likely born sometime around 1795 in Virginia, although no actual documents remain to substantiate this. He was born a slave, and little information about him exists in the official record until he reached adulthood. Scott probably arrived in St. Louis, Missouri, in 1830 from Virginia and Alabama, accompanying his owner, Peter Blow, Blow's wife Elizabeth, and their children. The Blows had been farmers in Virginia and Alabama, but when they arrived in Missouri, they tried their hand as owners of a boarding house, which was only barely successful.

Scott is described in the record as being about 5 feet tall and very dark skinned. He was illiterate. It is likely that Scott had been a slave to the Blows since his adolescence, if not his childhood, and the emotional connections Scott made with the sons of Peter and Elizabeth proved to be helpful to the Scott family later. During the series of trials that began with Scott's suit to be recognized as a citizen of the United States, a St. Louis newspaper reporter interviewed Scott and reported that, although he was illiterate, he was "not ignorant" and that it was clear that he had learned much from his travels. Scott had most likely led a life of hard work and little else. By 1832, however, both Peter and Elizabeth had died; thereafter, Scott entered the history books.

Life's Work

After Peter Blow's death, Scott was purchased by an army officer named John Emerson. Scott traveled with Emerson to Illinois when Emerson was transferred to an army base there in 1833. There is almost no written record of what Scott actually thought or felt about this major change in his life since neither Scott nor Emerson spoke or wrote about their experiences or their relationship with each other. Emerson had been born in Pennsylvania and had studied medicine there, and the two men were approximately the same age. Scott's primary duties centered on being Emerson's personal servant, but part of Scott's work also included clearing a parcel of land that Emerson had purchased in Iowa (then part of the Wisconsin Territory). Sometime in 1836, Scott went with Emerson to Fort Snelling in an area that later became St. Paul, Minnesota, a region where slavery was prohibited by the Missouri Compromise. While he was in Minnesota, Scott married a woman named Harriet who was about half his age and who was also a slave in the territory. Scott's wife may have been purchased for him by Emerson, or she may have been given to him as a gift by a man who ran a trading post or worked as a liaison to American Indians in the territory. During their twenty-year marriage, Dred and Harriet Scott had four children: two sons who died in infancy and two daughters.

In 1837, Emerson transferred back to St. Louis, but he left the Scotts in Minnesota. Emerson had expected to send for the Scotts shortly after his return to Missouri, but he was almost immediately transferred again to Louisiana, where he married Eliza Irene Sandford, a woman about fifteen years his junior. Emerson then sent for the Scotts, who traveled to Louisiana unchaperoned and arrived as they had agreed by riverboat. By the time Scott and his wife packed and moved out of Minnesota to be reunited with Emerson, they had lived for one year or more on their own in free territory. This would eventually become the basis of their case in the Supreme Court.

About six months after their journey down the Mississippi River to Louisiana, the Scotts and the Emersons returned to Minnesota. The Scotts' first daughter was born during this trip, while they were still in free territory. They named her Eliza, after Emerson's wife. In December, 1843, Emerson died about one month after the birth of his own daughter. The chain of events ignited by his death changed the lives of Scott and his family and, perhaps, changed the course of American history as well.

In his will, Emerson bequeathed his earthly goods to his wife and, after her death, to his daughter. The will allowed Eliza to sell whatever she needed from the estate in order to support herself and her daughter. Eliza's brother, John Sandford, was named an executor for Emerson's will, although Eliza's father, Alexander Sandford, was administrator of record for the will in the state of Missouri. When her father died in 1848, Eliza took over the details of handling her husband's will. During the few years between the death of Emerson and the first court case brought by Dred and Harriet Scott, the couple traveled to Texas to work for Eliza's brother-in-law, who was also in military service. The Scotts returned to St. Louis in 1846, and shortly after their return, they put in motion the process that would eventually affect race, law, and politics in the United States.

Having lived as free people, the Scotts were no longer content to quietly accept their status as slaves. On April 6, 1846, they filed individual requests in the Missouri court to bring suit for their freedom based upon their long residence in free territory. These first requests were granted, and the Scotts then filed suit against Eliza for damages for "ill-treatment" and "false imprisonment" based upon the Scotts' contention that they were, in fact, free people. Because Scott was barely literate and a man of insubstantial means, it has been suggested that antislavery activists were at the bottom of this seminal case in an effort to mount a test case that would ignite the antislavery movement. However, the Scotts had observed the changing times and were also aware from their conversations with Peter Blow's son Taylor that other former slaves who had brought similar suits had been declared free based on the finding that taking a slave into free territory to reside amounted to an act of emancipation.

The basis of the case seemed clear-cut: Dred sued based on his long residence in Illinois and the Wisconsin Territory, while Harriet based her claim on her residence in the Wisconsin Territory. The cases filed later by the Scotts' daughters were based on the fact that the first daughter was actually born in free territory and the second daughter was born to a free mother. The Missouri court in St. Louis, following well-established precedent, found that the Scotts, based on their long residence in free territory, were indeed free.

In 1852, the Missouri Supreme Court disagreed and reversed the lower court's decision. The sons of Scott's former owner, Peter Blow, were sympathetic and helped Scott by contributing the fee for a new lawyer to represent the Scotts' appeal before the United States Circuit Court of Missouri. The motive for the Blows' long and steady support of

Scott and his family seems to have been based on fond recollections of growing up with Scott, since Taylor Blow and his brother were strongly pro-Southern in their politics. In any event, in 1854, the U.S. Circuit Court upheld the Missouri Supreme Court's finding that Dred and Harriet Scott should, and would, remain slaves. It was a remarkable coincidence of historical timing that brought the Scott case to the stage of national events; ultimately, the case had a significant impact on the hearts and minds of people around the world.

In 1855, Americans were concerned with the events in "Bloody Kansas" as settlers on both sides of the slavery question attempted to decide by violent means whether the Kansas-Nebraska Territory would be free or slave. Because of this, the *Dred Scott* case moved up on the docket of the Supreme Court. In early 1856, the matter of *Dred Scott v. Sandford* finally came up for argument in the Supreme Court, but jurisdictional and other technical matters were not resolved until December. After several months of debate, the Supreme Court voted 7 to 2 that Dred Scott was not a citizen of the United States. The language of Chief Justice Roger B. Taney's finding in the *Dred Scott* decision was clear:

> Can a negro, whose ancestors were imported . . . and sold as slaves, become a member of the political community . . . brought into existence by the Constitution of the United States, and as such become entitled to all the rights, and privileges . . . guaranteed by that instrument to the citizen?

The Taney Court's answer was a resounding "no," because they found that black people

> were not intended to be included, under the word "citizen" in the Constitution, can therefore claim none of the rights and privileges . . . that instrument provides . . . On the contrary, they [are] . . . considered as a subordinate and inferior class of beings, who have been subjugated by the dominant race, and, whether emancipated or not, yet remained subject to their authority . . . [and were] so far inferior that they had no rights which the white man was bound to respect.

The response to the decision, delivered by Chief Justice Roger Taney and his associate justices to a standing-room-only crowd of newspaper writers and many others interested in the outcome of the case, was swift and divided along regional and political lines. Antislavery activists centered in the North denounced the finding as immoral, while

many Southerners expressed satisfaction with the decision.

The sons of Peter Blow refused to accept the judgment of the court and purchased Scott and his family, then freed them almost immediately. Dred and Harriet Scott continued to live and work in St. Louis, although the state required that they post a bond in the amount of $1000 to ensure their good behavior. Again, Taylor stepped in to help, using his property as security for the Scotts' bonds. However, Scott's free status was short-lived: he died on February 17, 1858, and was buried in Calvary Cemetery in St. Louis.

Summary

The life of Dred Scott had an ordinary beginning, and yet the flash point of pre-Civil War politics was the 1857 Supreme Court finding in *Dred Scott v. Sandford*, instigated by an illiterate, middle-aged black man who refused to accept slavery as his obligatory status in life. The Supreme Court found in *Dred Scott v. Sandford* that black people were not citizens of the United States and thus had no rights that white citizens were bound to respect. After the Civil War, in 1868, the Fourteenth Amendment to the Constitution, which ensured citizenship rights for black Americans, directly reversed this finding. Dred Scott, the man whose case against the Supreme Court was undoubtedly the catalyst to an organized fight against slavery, died in St. Louis, Missouri, before the citizenship of black Americans was clearly set out in the Constitution.

Bibliography

Asim, Jabari. "Dred Scott Square." *Obsidian II: Black Literature in Review* 3 (Winter 1988). Asim provides a poet's perspective on Scott.

Erlich, Walter. *They Have No Rights: Dred Scott's Struggle for Freedom*. Westport, Conn.: Greenwood Press, 1979. Erlich provides an overview of Scott's difficult battle for freedom.

Fehrenbacher, Don E. *Slavery, Law, & Politics: The Dred Scott Case in Historical Perspective*. Oxford and New York: Oxford University Press, 1981. Fehrenbacher places the Scott case in the context of U.S. history in general and explores the ongoing implications of the Supreme Court's 1857 decision.

Finkelman, Paul. *Dred Scott v. Sandford: A Brief History with Documents*. Boston: Bedford, 1997. Finkelman's book contains detailed and useful documentation of the Scott case.

Dale Edwyna Smith

SIR GEORGE GILBERT SCOTT

Born: July 13, 1811; Gawcott, Buckinghamshire, England

Died: March 27, 1878; London, England

Area of Achievement: Architecture

Contribution: Because of his designs for the Foreign Office, St. Pancras Hotel, and the Albert Memorial, as well as his restoration of many important medieval buildings throughout Great Britain, Scott became one of the most highly regarded architects in nineteenth century England.

Early Life

George Gilbert Scott was born on July 13, 1811, at Gawcott, Buckinghamshire, the fourth son of Thomas and Euphemia (née Lynch) Scott. Both his father, a curate at the church in Gawcott, and his mother, from a family with strong Wesleyan connections, held severe religious views and reared their large family in a very strict and pious manner. Because of their mistrust of local High Church schools, Scott never received a formal education. Until the age of fifteen, he was taught at home by his father. Scott then demonstrated an interest in architecture, so his father sent him to an uncle for a year of preparatory schooling. In 1827, Scott was apprenticed to James Edmeston, a local architect with religious views similar to those of the Scott family. Scott always considered himself uneducated and regretted this lack of formal schooling throughout his life.

Scott's interest in medieval churches surfaced during this period under Edmeston, but the latter attempted to redirect his energies toward more practical designs and condemned Gothic architecture as too expensive and wasteful of building materials. In fact, Edmeston went so far as to write to Scott's father several times complaining that the young man wasted too much time sketching medieval buildings. In any case, Scott successfully completed his apprenticeship in 1831 and, after a two-month visit home, he moved to London and joined the firm of Grissell and Peto.

The next year, 1832, he moved to the firm of Henry Roberts, where he worked under the direction of Sir Robert Smirke. Scott would later look back at this period as unproductive and barren, years in which the emphasis on practical designs stifled his natural inclinations and originality. In 1834, following the death of his father, he associated himself with an architect who was drawing designs for workhouses that would be constructed under the New Poor Law. Scott saw this as an opportunity to break free from the various practical masters who had thus far controlled the content of his work, and, in violation of certain rules of professional etiquette, he personally visited Poor Law boards throughout the country and pushed his own plans for the new workhouses. As a result, he obtained four contracts for workhouse construction, and, to handle this new work, he formed a partnership with W. B. Moffat, another former apprentice of Edmeston. Scott was finally on his own, and the famous firm of Scott and Moffat had been born.

On June 5, 1838, Scott was married to Caroline Oldrid, his second cousin. During their long marriage, they produced five sons, two of whom would later also pursue careers in architecture. Balding and stocky, Scott affected the long, bushy sideburns that were popular among Victorian men. Acquaintances noted that he was careless about his appearance and often arrived at important business meetings in rumpled and mismatched suits. Yet behind this slightly eccentric façade lurked the clear, intelligent eyes and determined mouth of a young man who knew what he wanted and how to get it.

Life's Work

The partnership of Scott and Moffat endured until 1845, and, during its existence, the two men produced nearly fifty workhouses and orphanages. Scott also accepted commissions to construct churches in the towns of Birmingham, Shaftesbury, Hanwell, Turnham, Bridlington Quay, and Norbiton. Although church architecture would later become Scott's specialty, these early designs suffered from his concentration on workhouse construction and were generally undistinguished and rather clumsy.

In the early 1840's, Scott's latent talent for Gothic architecture was stimulated through his friendship with Augustus Northmore Pugin, a noted architect and a pioneer in the nineteenth century Gothic revival. Responding to Pugin's encouragement, Scott designed his first Gothic building, St. Giles in Camberwell, in 1840. Public response to this church was very favorable and convinced Scott to abandon his "practical" work in favor of more imaginative and romantic Gothic designs.

Scott's growing reputation as a Gothic architect received a tremendous boost in 1844 when he won an open competition to design the Lutheran church of St. Nicholas in Hamburg, Germany. The success of this mock-fourteenth century structure led, in 1847, to an important commission to restore the Anglican cathedral in Ely. In preparation for this assignment, Scott visited France in order to observe the Gothic cathedrals at Amiens, Chartres, and elsewhere. This habit of visiting Gothic monuments on the Continent for inspiration for his work in Great Britain would become a regular feature of Scott's career.

Between 1845 and 1862, commissions literally poured into Scott's office. The design of new, and the restoration of old, churches constituted the vast majority of these assignments and included such excellent examples of neo-Gothic architecture as his creation of the cathedral of St. John in Newfoundland, Canada, and his restorations of cathedrals in Ripon, Salisbury, Lichfield, and Hereford. Perhaps his most famous work during this period was his restoration of the chapter house and monuments of Westminster Abbey in 1849. His careful research for this important project would later be incorporated into a book, *Gleanings from Westminster Abbey*, which Scott published in 1861. As a result of his growing fame, Scott was made an associate member of the Royal Academy in 1855 and was promoted to full membership in 1861.

In 1856, Scott entered a competition for the contract to rebuild the Foreign Office buildings. He proposed a French-inspired Gothic design for the buildings, and, in 1858, he was awarded the position of chief architect for the reconstruction project. Proponents of classical architecture, however, opposed his Gothic design and received support from such notable parliamentary leaders as Lord Palmerston. As a result, the House of Commons, after heated debates between supporters of the two architectural schools, ordered that an Italian classical design also be drawn up so that it could be compared with Scott's original Gothic proposal. Scott tried his best to maneuver around the order, but in 1861 he was forced to submit an Italian influenced design that satisfied both Palmerston and the House of Commons. Advocates of the Gothic school accused Scott of treason for this compromise, but the finished buildings nevertheless proved to be among the best in his career.

Scott's most prestigious commission came in 1864, when he won a court-sponsored competition to design a monument in memory of Queen Victoria's recently deceased husband, Prince Albert. The success of this memorial, a shrine containing a seated statue of the prince consort, led to other royal commissions, such as the restoration of Thomas, Cardinal Wolsey's chapel in Windsor Castle in 1869. In 1872, Scott was knighted as a reward for all of his work for the royal family.

A year after the Albert Memorial commission, in 1865, Scott designed perhaps his best work, St. Pancras Station in London. He regarded the completed building as the culmination of his search to achieve a Gothic style that would serve modern structural and aesthetic purposes. The station still stands as a monument to the Victorian Gothic revival that Scott did so much to launch and promote.

Although Scott worked busily until the end of his life, none of his work after 1865 equaled the quality of that of the 1850's and early 1860's. As befit his status as one of Great Britain's best-known architects, he spent much of his time during the late 1860's and 1870's engaging in honorary and educational activities. From 1873 to 1876, he served as president of the Royal Institute of British Architects. He also occupied the prestigious post of professor of architecture at the Royal Academy from 1868 to 1878. His lectures were published in 1879 as a two-volume work entitled *Lectures on the Rise and Development of Medieval Architecture*. In addition to these activities, Scott also devoted much time and energy to promoting the establishment of an Architectural Museum in London, a project that was realized shortly after his death. He died of a heart attack on March 27, 1878, at the age of sixty-six, and was buried in Westminster Abbey.

Summary

Sir George Gilbert Scott had a very prolific career. From 1847 until his death in 1878 he completed 732 projects, including twenty-nine cathedrals, 476 churches, twenty-five schools, twenty-three parsonages, fifty-eight monuments of varying size, twenty-five college chapels, twenty-six public buildings, forty-three mansions, and assorted other designs. He was the best known and most successful British architect during the mid-nineteenth century, and much of his work remains standing today.

Yet, even before his death, a growing number of critics questioned both Scott's neo-Gothic style and the manner in which he conducted his restorations. His Gothic designs, as exemplified by his work on Westminster Abbey, are often eclectic and overblown. Scott all too frequently took the unique traits of medieval French, Italian, and German architecture and mixed them together in an apparently random fashion to produce his own "Gothic" designs. The result of this practice struck some contemporaries, and most modern students, as a rather gaudy and incoherent jumble, one that critics claim typified the Victorian Gothic revival.

Scott also remodeled buildings as he restored them. Rather than trying to recapture the original design, he frequently altered structural components, added ornamentation, and even changed the building materials. In many ways, he did not restore buildings at all; instead, he reconstructed them to conform with his vision of what Gothic architecture should be like. This practice, in fact, led to the formation in 1878 of the Society for the Protection of Ancient Buildings, an organization dedicated to preserving old structures from the revisionism of architects such as Scott.

Scott's reputation has suffered a tremendous decline since his death. He will always be recognized as one of the foremost advocates of the Gothic architectural revival of the mid-nineteenth century. Nevertheless, as the aesthetic quality and the historical integrity of this revival has been severely questioned by successive generations, Scott's place in the history of British architecture has steadily diminished.

Bibliography

Clarke, B. F. L. *Church Builders of the Nineteenth Century*. London: SPCK, and New York: Macmillan, 1938. Scott figures prominently in this generally positive assessment of the British Gothic revival.

Cole, David. *The Work of Sir Gilbert Scott*. London: Architectural Press, and Westfield, N.J.: Eastview, 1980. The most complete work in print on Scott and his contribution to British architecture. The author's approach is generally sympathetic, and he stresses that an accurate appreciation of Scott's work can only be obtained by comparing it with that of his contemporaries, not by judging it by modern standards.

Ferriday, Peter, ed. *Victorian Architecture*. London: Cape, 1963; Philadelphia: Lippincott, 1964. A collection of essays, most written by the editor. The essay on the Gothic revival correctly emphasizes Scott's contribution but provides little in the way of biographical information.

Goodhart-Rendel, H. S. *English Architecture Since the Regency: An Interpretation*. London: Constable, 1953; St. Clair Shores, Mich.: Scholarly Press, 1977. This book includes only a few pages on Scott and his work, but it does provide an excellent summary of the various objections to the architect and the Gothic revival in general.

Hitchcock, Henry Russell. *Architecture: Nineteenth and Twentieth Centuries*. London and Baltimore: Penguin, 1958. This book includes a section on the British Gothic revival of the mid-Victorian period and provides a concise, though negative, interpretation of Scott's contribution to it.

Jordan, W. J. "Sir George Gilbert Scott R.A.: Surveyor to Westminster Abbey, 1849-1878." *Architectural History* 23 (1980): 60-85. An excellent summary of Scott's career from midcentury until his death. In spite of the article's title, it goes beyond his work on Westminster Abbey and discusses his general role in the Gothic revival.

Scott, Sir George Gilbert. *Personal and Professional Recollections*. London: Sampson Low, Marston, 1879; New York: Da Capo Press, 1977. A long, rambling autobiography which includes some insights into Scott's personal beliefs and an explanation of what he was trying to achieve. This book is also full of biographical details that are not available elsewhere.

Christopher E. Guthrie

SIR WALTER SCOTT

Born: August 15, 1771; Edinburgh, Scotland
Died: September 21, 1832; Abbotsford, Scotland
Area of Achievement: Literature
Contribution: Scott's narrative poems about the stirring events in Scottish and medieval history were immensely popular in the nineteenth century, and in fiction he created the genre of the historical novel.

Early Life

Walter Scott counted among his ancestors many notable and colorful figures from Scottish history, and during his early years, after an attack of polio crippled his right leg, he spent hours listening to family stories and songs about their exploits. Even as a young boy, he collected these ballads and folktales, which vividly presented the past. He would later use this knowledge in the poems and novels which won great acclaim during his lifetime, and which endure to this day as classics of English literature.

After being educated at home, Scott was sent in 1778 to high school in Edinburgh. He impressed both his teachers and his peers with his intelligence, his good nature, and his ability to tell stories; he was less accomplished in his scholarship. In 1783, he entered the Old College, but his interest remained the study and pursuit of ballads. In 1786, he joined his father, who was a lawyer, as an apprentice and was called to the bar in July of 1792.

Scott made a competent though not outstanding lawyer, and his main interest continued to be literature, although he seemed to regard the writing profession as not quite suitable for a gentleman. Despite his doubts, however, he could not refrain from seeking out, collecting, and reciting the poetry of his native land. Inevitably, he tried his hand at composition.

In 1797, Scott visited the Lake Country, where he met Charlotte Mary Carpenter, daughter of a deceased French refugee. After a brief courtship, Scott's suit was approved by Charlotte's guardian, the Marquess of Downshire, and the couple were married on Christmas Eve, 1797. Their union, comfortable rather than passionate, produced four children.

Through exercise to overcome his infirmity, Scott developed a powerful and robust physique; he was an avid horseman and walker, and graceful, despite his lameness. Scott's many portraits show a man of regular, rather than handsome, features, with keen, bright eyes. They also reveal the intelligence, good humor and compassion for which he was well-known. Scott's contemporaries were universal in their admiration for him.

Life's Work

Scott's entry into the literary world was almost casual. After collecting the ballads of others, he began to compose some of his own. A government appointment with few duties gave him time to collect and write, and some of his earlier attempts were published in 1802 and 1803 in *The Minstrelsy of the Scottish Border.* Encouraged by the favorable attentions of friends and critics, Scott next wrote the *The Lay of the Last Minstrel,* which was published in early 1805.

This work was immediately popular and established Scott as a major contemporary literary figure. Unfortunately, at this same time Scott entered into a long, complicated, and ultimately ruinous relationship with the printers and publishers John and James Ballantyne. Scott began loaning money to the Ballantynes in 1802; by 1805, he was a silent financial partner in the firm. This connection would eventually lead to fiscal disaster.

In the meantime, Scott continued his industrious and successful efforts. He edited a complete collection of John Dryden's poetry, wrote for the *Edinburgh Review,* and started writing *Waverley: Or, 'Tis Sixty Years Since* (1814). Putting aside the novel, however, he turned to another narrative poem, *Marmion: A Tale of Flodden Field,* which was published in 1808 with great success. In 1810, *The Lady of the Lake* followed and was equally well received.

In 1809, Scott joined with the Ballantynes in a publishing firm, John Ballantyne and Company. Scott advanced half of the capital himself, and perhaps provided the Ballantynes' portion as well. The unequal nature of this arrangement was to continue throughout the short life of the company. In 1813, the firm narrowly endured a serious crisis, surviving only through Scott's intercession with another publisher, Archibald Constable, whom he persuaded to purchase large amounts of debt-laden Ballantyne stock. Part of the problem lay in Scott's enthusiastic but injudicious support of other, less talented, authors, and part in the Ballantynes' business misadventures. By 1810, all the considerable income from Scott's writing was going to meet outstanding obligations.

Unfortunately, a threat appeared to that income. His next two books, *Rokeby* (1812) and *The Bridal of Triermain* (1813), sold reasonably well, but by no means as well as Scott's earlier works. Scott had probably exhausted himself in this particular genre and was faced with the growing competition from younger poets, such as Lord Byron. Scott's final attempts in historical narrative verse were *The Lord of the Isles* (1815) and *Harold the Dauntless* (1817). Neither poem was a major success, but by then Scott had found success in a genre of his own creation, the historical novel.

According to tradition, Scott rediscovered his manuscript of *Waverley* while looking for some fishing tackle and decided to finish it. It was published in July of 1814; six editions were printed the first year. Scott published this, and subsequent novels, anonymously; not until 1827 did he admit authorship, although it was widely known almost from the first.

Waverley was a new departure in British literature, a work that mingled fiction with historical fact, placing its imagined characters in the middle of real, dramatic events. Scott drew largely from the tales he had heard as a child, and *Waverley*, like the best of his novels, has an immediate, energetic quality that engages and excites the reader.

Scott now began a ten-year period of intense, almost unparalleled creativity; nine novels were finished within a five-year time span. *Guy Mannering* and *The Antiquary* appeared in 1815 and 1816, respectively, then the Tales of My Landlord series commenced in 1816 with the dual publication of *The Black Dwarf* and *Old Mortality*. *Rob Roy* (1818) and *The Heart of Midlothian* (1818) proved that the works were growing increasingly popular, as did another double publication, *The Bride of Lammermoor* and *A Legend of Montrose* (1819).

In 1819, Scott tried a new setting for his fiction, the Middle Ages. *Ivanhoe* (1819) was the first of a line of novels which drew, not on Scott's knowledge of his native land, but on his reading. The vivid characters, and the forward, exciting thrust of the narrative made *Ivanhoe* immediately, and permanently, popular.

These were Scott's most successful years as a writer. His works were widely read and were bringing him a considerable income. He was constantly enlarging and expanding his home, Abbots-

ford, where he received many illustrious visitors and entertained the countryside in a fashion worthy of a Scots laird. He received a baronetcy from George IV in 1820, and the next year was active in the reception of the king in Edinburgh.

Scott continued to write, working the new vein of medieval romance. *The Monastery* (1820) and *The Abbot* (1820) fell short of the power and popular reception of *Ivanhoe*, but *Kenilworth* (1821) and *The Pirate* (1821) regained much of his earlier audience. In quick succession appeared *The Fortunes of Nigel* (1822), *Peveril of the Peak, Quentin Durward* (both published in 1823) and *St. Ronan's Well* (1824). The skill and ability Scott showed in these works varied considerably; he was clearly out of his element in tales of the gothic (*The Abbot*) or in the novel of society (*St. Ronan's Well*), but was adept at accounts of action and descriptions of the picturesque.

With the publication of *Redgauntlet* in 1824, however, Scott returned to the Scottish themes he knew so well. The novel is one of his finest, with memorable characters drawn from Scott's family and friends. In 1825, Scott brought out the dual set *Tales of the Crusaders*, containing the rather weak *The Bethrothed*, and the much more successful *The Talisman*.

Scott's complicated relationship with the Ballantynes now brought about financial disaster. He had changed publishing houses from Ballantyne to Constable and Cadell, but considerable obligations were shared between his former publishers and Scott himself. Scott's continued expenses from Abbotsford further weakened his position. In 1826, after a long period of increasingly frantic negotiations, and amid general economic crisis, Scott and his publishers found that they faced bankruptcy. Scott declared himself personally responsible for the continuation of business and the settlement of all debts. The creditors' faith in Scott as an author and a man was shown by their prompt agreement to an arrangement which would permit Scott to take care of the debt without personal ruin or disgrace. Even as he returned to his writing desk, to work on a multivolume biography of Napoleon Bonaparte, fresh misfortunes dogged him. On May 15, 1826, his wife died. Although the couple had not been especially close, the loss was still keenly felt by Scott.

The Life of Napoleon Buonaparte was published in 1827, and Scott immediately began a new project, *Tales of a Grandfather*, which was to be a history of Scotland for children. It appeared in the winter of 1827 and was so successful that two more volumes appeared in 1828 and 1829. Plans were made for a uniform edition of the Waverley novels, with autobiographical prefaces by Scott; the edition proved a considerable success, and gave proof that Scott's better work remained popular with readers.

Such was not the case, however, with his later efforts. *The Fair Maid of Perth* (1828) and *Anne of Geierstein* (1829) showed an unmistakable decline in his abilities. His physical condition also declined, and in February, 1830, he suffered a stroke; another followed in November. During this time, he continued to work on a new novel, *Count Robert of Paris*, which was interrupted by a third, yet more serious attack in April of 1831. Upon his recovery, he completed *Count Robert of Paris* and his last novel, *Castle Dangerous;* these were published together in the fall of 1831.

Scott's friends now prevailed upon him to take a tour for his health. The government placed a naval frigate at his disposal to carry him to the Mediterranean. He toured Malta and Italy, where he viewed the tomb of the last of the Stuarts. He was traveling down the Rhine River when, on June 9, a severe attack left him paralyzed; he was carried back to Great Britain semiconscious. Upon his return to his beloved Abbotsford, he rallied briefly, but died on September 21, 1832.

Summary

Sir Walter Scott's enduring contributions to literature fall into three categories: his narrative poems, his Scottish novels, and his novels of chivalric romance. In each of these three genres he produced works which not only delighted his contemporaries but also have shown themselves to be of lasting significance.

Scott himself was modest about the narrative poems, and there is much in them that is more narrative than poetic. Still, at their best, works such as *The Lay of the Last Minstrel* or *The Lady of the Lake* have an undeniable power in rhythm and expression that makes them excellent examples of their particular genre.

Scott's gift for narrative best served him in his prose works, especially in the Scottish novels. In these books, he drew upon his own memories and experiences in the Scottish countryside, and from the tales and stories he had heard since his youth. Many readers find in *Waverley* or *Redgauntlet* merely exciting adventures, skillfully told, but Scott put more into his novels than that.

A passionate believer in community and tradition, Scott looked back on the Scottish past with sympathy and upon the present without illusion. He seems to have been acutely aware that the heroic age had passed, and that it had been replaced by one that was more prosaic. It is the tension between these two ideals, and the elegiac sadness for the older society that yet lingered in parts of the Highlands, that give additional resonance and power to the best of Scott's works.

As the virtual creator of the historical novel, Scott was responsible for an entirely new genre. While some may point to anachronisms of detail or perspective in works such as *Ivanhoe*, more attention should be paid to Scott's renovation of history as a suitable topic for fiction. The historical novels have characters who lived in earlier times yet were understandable to contemporary readers. This was a new and often difficult task, and Scott succeeded in it more often than not.

Scott's place within the pantheon of English literature remains disputed. Some critics believe that he wrote too much and too hastily, and that his work suffered as a result. There is certainly some truth to this view, especially with Scott's later work, composed while he was in declining health and under intense pressure. Nevertheless, Scott's finest work can withstand this criticism, for his characters are vivid, his plots compelling, and his style vigorous. His work has weathered time and changes in critical fashions, and remains an essential part of our literary heritage.

Bibliography

Daiches, David. *Sir Walter Scott and His World.* London: Thames and Hudson, and New York: Viking Press, 1971. A well-written and extensively illustrated survey of Scott and his time. Daiches brings a considerable amount of knowledge to the reader in a clear, easily understood fashion.

Johnson, Edgar. *Sir Walter Scott: The Great Unknown.* 2 vols. New York: Macmillan, and London: Hamilton, 1970. A comprehensive biography of Scott that has become the modern definitive life. Johnson makes good use of the many sources and resources available and has an accurate perception of Scott's writings.

Lauber, John. *Sir Walter Scott.* New York: Twayne, 1966. A brief, introductory survey that concentrates on the work rather than the man. This study is excellent for the beginning student and helpful for the new reader of Scott's works. Contains a good basic bibliography.

Lockhart, John Gibson. *Memoirs of the Life of Sir Walter Scott.* 5 vols. Philadelphia: Carey, Lea, and Blanchard, 1837-1838; London: Murray, 1839. Lockhart was Scott's son-in-law, and this work is the seminal biography of Scott, containing much important information and almost as much mythology. Its firsthand material and documents make it essential for the serious student of Scott, but it must be read in conjunction with more recent, and less uncritical, studies.

Pearson, Hesketh. *Sir Walter Scott: His Life and Personality.* London: Methuen, and New York: Harper, 1954. A brisk and readable work, but more in the nature of a popular biography than a serious study. The literary views are sometimes misleading.

Sutherland, John. *The Life of Walter Scott: A Critical Biography.* Oxford and Cambridge, Mass.: Blackwell, 1995. In a masterful biography, Sutherland attempts to disentangle the mythical Scott from the real.

Michael Witkoski

WINFIELD SCOTT

Born: June 13, 1786; Petersburg, Virginia
Died: May 29, 1866; West Point, New York
Area of Achievement: The military
Contribution: Scott, whose military career spanned more than fifty years, left his mark by showing the power of volunteer troops fighting in a republican army.

Early Life

Winfield Mason Scott was born June 13, 1786, near the tobacco market town of Petersburg, Virginia. His father William, a captain on the patriot side in the American Revolution, died in 1791, leaving only a modest inheritance and little in the way of a memory for the young boy. His mother, Ann Mason, was descended from an important Virginia family, and she spent her widowhood teaching her son the ways of the Virginia gentry until her death in 1803.

Young Scott was educated by private tutors in Petersburg and at the new capital at Richmond. At age nineteen, he enrolled at the College of William and Mary. He showed little aptitude for college work and left the Williamsburg school after a year without earning a degree. The young man decided on a career in the law, and in accordance with the custom of the day, studied law with an established attorney. When a war scare after 1807, however, caused Congress to vote funds to enlarge the United States Army in anticipation of war with Great Britain, Scott abandoned a legal career for the sword. In May, 1808, Scott became a captain in the regular army.

Scott was exceedingly tall by the standards of his day—six feet, five inches—and in his younger years, muscular but not fat. Photographs of the elderly Scott showing his three-hundred-pound bulk do not give an accurate picture of the young captain. Along with a striking figure, Winfield Scott bore a somewhat haughty manner. This was characteristic of many Virginia gentlemen of the time, but Scott was both especially quick to take offense at perceived snubs and insults and not shy about voicing his own opinions. Indeed, his lack of tact got him court-martialed during his first tour of duty at Natchez in the Mississippi Territory in 1810. Captain Scott openly proclaimed the former commanding officer General James Wilkinson a traitor in league with former vice president Aaron Burr. For this affront, Wilkinson had the young man disciplined for disrespect to a superior officer. Scott postponed marriage until the age of thirty; when he did wed, he chose Maria Mayo, the daughter of an important Richmond editor, for his bride.

Life's Work

The War of 1812 brought a host of young officers forward into national prominence. At the start of the war, the United States Army was commanded by men who had learned their military skills back in the Revolutionary War. Most of the commanders of the first year of the war were simply incompetent to fight a war on the offensive as called for by the leaders in Washington, and not until they were replaced by younger men did the war go more favorably for the Americans. The two great young generals who emerged in 1813 and 1814 were Andrew Jackson and Winfield Scott, a pair of men who later became bitter rivals.

The great task for an American commander in the War of 1812 (as in the Revolution) was to solve the problem of making raw American troops stand up in the field to trained British regulars. Much of the American force consisted of state militiamen serving limited terms with little training. Too often in battle, the militia ran or refused to fight. Scott, more than any other commander on the Canadian front, managed to shape an army of militiamen and regulars into an effective fighting force. A measure of the success of his efforts may be seen by looking at the first and last battles on the Niagara Frontier, the stretch of land connecting Lake Erie to Lake Ontario and separating the United States from British North America. In October, 1812, shortly after gaining the rank of lieutenant colonel in the United States Army, Scott participated in the Battle of Queenstown on the west bank of the Niagara River. The attack was a disaster for the Americans, as a large body of American militia refused to cross the river, claiming that their mission included only defense of New York and not the invasion of Canada. Scott's party, outnumbered and badly outfought, was captured by the British, and the young Virginian had to spend an enforced stretch in British captivity until he could be exchanged.

During the summer campaign of 1813 on the lakes, Scott distinguished himself by leading a successful assault on the British Fort George on the Niagara River and, later, by aiding in the burning

of York (modern Toronto). The next spring—May, 1814—Scott was promoted to brigadier general and was given responsibility for training the men under the command of General Henry Dearborn for a campaign to clear the Niagara Frontier of British forces. In July, Scott led American troops, both regulars and state militiamen, in the fierce battles of Chippewa (opposite Buffalo) and Lundy's Lane (near Niagara Falls). The latter battle was perhaps the bloodiest of the war, with four hundred killed on both sides. The effect of the July fighting was to establish American control of the Niagara region and to show that Americans could stand up to British veterans who had fought successfully against Napoleon. At Lundy's Lane, Scott himself showed extraordinary personal courage: He had several horses shot from under him and was hit twice by bullets, in the ribs and shoulder. He spent a month recovering in Buffalo before journeying to Philadelphia for further treatment, and at war's end Major General Scott was still recovering from his wounds.

In 1816, Scott journeyed to Europe not so much to sightsee as to interview veterans of the Napole-

onic Wars. He came back filled with new ideas about how to train and lead a new American army and over the next thirty years put his ideas into practice. In 1817, he was called to New York City to head the Eastern Military District, a command he held until 1831. During these years, the general devoted himself to improving the training of troops, an effort that first saw print in his 1821 publication *General Regulations for the Army: Or, Military Institutes*. This writing consisted of rules for camp life and drill and reflected Scott's experiences in the War of 1812 and his European interviews. He later amplified his ideas on the use of the foot soldier in his *Infantry Tactics* (1835), a manual used by the army until the Civil War.

The 1830's were an extraordinarily busy time for the middle-aged Scott. He did more hard riding during this decade than any other. In the summer of 1832, President Jackson ordered him to take a regiment west to help in the suppression of the Sac rebellion led by Black Hawk. This was only one of a series of wars between Native Americans and white Americans prompted by Jackson's "Removal" policy. The Sac were defeated by Illinois and Wisconsin militiamen before Scott reached the Upper Mississippi country; unfortunately, the regiment was badly decimated by a cholera epidemic. Scott remained long enough to negotiate Black Hawk's surrender and the removal of the Indians west of the Mississippi. Next, the general traveled to Charleston, South Carolina, on a confidential mission for the president to survey the state of federal installations in the city and harbor in light of the threats made by the "nullifiers" in the Palmetto State. Scott made sure the hotheads in South Carolina knew that the federal government stood prepared to defend its property and the right to collect tariff duties.

After the successful defusing of the Tariff showdown, Scott's next field assignment came in early 1836, when President Jackson sent him to Florida to put down the Seminole rebellion (again in response to Jackson's removal policy) led by Osceola. After six months with little success against the Indians, Scott was recalled to Washington and there faced a "court of inquiry" about his conduct in prosecuting the Florida war. Scott was enraged at this insult from the President but still managed to convince the court that his strategy of fortifying outposts in the swamps to launch small raids against the Indians was preferable to marching columns of hundreds of men back and forth in search of the Indians. The court cleared Scott of any mal-feasance, and in the end, his strategy of counter-guerrilla warfare against the Seminoles proved successful.

Almost as soon as the Washington charges were settled, Scott had to deal with a series of frontier crises. First, in January, 1838, he traveled to Buffalo to prevent the smuggling of American arms to Canada after the famous Caroline Affair. His apt diplomacy, surprising to some in a military man, helped ease a potential *causus belli* between the United States and Great Britain. Then, in May, Scott traveled to Tennessee to organize the army's handling of the removal of fifteen thousand Cherokee westward to the trans-Mississippi Indian Territory. Again, the army was needed to enforce a Jackson removal treaty, but the results were especially horrible as thousands of Indians suffered on what became known as the Trail of Tears. By the time the march was actually under way, however, Scott was otherwise engaged in more frontier diplomacy, this time at Detroit where he sought to prevent a new border skirmish between the Americans and the British across the river. That task accomplished, the general ventured in winter across the northern United States to the Maine-New Brunswick border to prevent yet another border flare-up from exploding into war, this time in March, 1839, the so-called Aroostook War over the proper boundary along the St. John's River. While Scott was engaged in his journeys for peace, leaders of the Whig Party mentioned his name as a candidate to run for the presidency in 1840. Though he never became president, Winfield Scott hoped for the next twenty years to achieve that goal, and in 1852 he did get the Whig nomination but failed to convince the electorate.

In 1841, Scott finally became the senior officer in the United States Army and alternated his attention between military affairs and his political ambitions. His job was made harder in 1845 when a Democratic administration, hostile to Scott, came into office determined to engage in a war with Mexico. Scott was thought too old to command in the field the American detachment sent to acquire the Rio Grande territory in 1845 and 1846, and when this force did provoke a war, Scott's subordinate Zachary Taylor earned the glory at Monterrey and Buena Vista. President Polk found winning a peace harder than winning battles, however, and in the late fall of 1846 had to turn to Scott to lead a campaign to bring the Mexicans to surrender.

From March through September of 1847, Scott led one of the most brilliant campaigns in the history of the United States Army. Against a larger enemy fighting to defend its own capital, Scott captured Mexico City despite disease, despite the forces of Mexican General Antonio López de Santa Anna, and despite the sniping of various Democratic politicians (one of whom was on his staff by presidential order). The campaign began at Vera Cruz with an amphibious landing, the first such coordination between the army and navy in United States history. Scott laid siege to Vera Cruz for a week, bombarding the city daily and earning a reputation among the Mexicans as a barbarian because of the hundreds of women and children killed in the shelling. Scott then began his march to Mexico City, first defeating the Mexican Army at the mountain heights of Cerro Gordo where the enemy had hoped to bottle up the Americans. From April 19, 1847, through mid-May of the same year, Scott and his army advanced along the National Road toward Mexico City. When he got within fighting distance, the Mexicans asked to begin peace negotiations. Scott's army had decreased to five thousand men because of disease, and he used the summer months of negotiation to rebuild his army to fourteen thousand well-drilled men. In August, when negotiations collapsed, Scott made his famous daring march south along Lake Chalco and flanked the Mexican forces, attacking Mexico City by the back door along the road from Acapulco. On August 20, Scott's men captured the mountain pass at Cherabusco, just four miles south of the capital. Again, the Mexicans asked to negotiate, and again the talks led nowhere. From September 8 through September 13, Scott carried out a series of feints against the Mexican forces and, at the climactic battle of Chapultepec, stormed into the city. His smaller army defeated the Mexican army of thirty thousand men.

The peace that followed was anticlimactic, and Scott became embroiled in charges and counter-charges with Democratic officers in the army and politicians back in Washington. While he was the acknowledged conqueror of Mexico, he was not universally seen as a hero, and he had to watch the junior Zachary Taylor receive the Whig nomination for the presidency in 1848. The difference in popular estimation between the two generals may be seen in their nicknames: Taylor was "Old Rough and Ready," Scott "Old Fuss and Feathers." When Scott did finally run for the White House in 1852, his opponent (and former subordinate in Mexico) Franklin Pierce trounced him, mainly because Scott's Whig Party had self-destructed over a number of issues. Scott was honored for his services in 1853 and became lieutenant general of the army, a post he held until his retirement in October, 1861. He distinguished himself when the Civil War broke out, first by not succumbing to rebel blandishments to join the Confederacy and second by devising a plan that ultimately was carried out in defeating the rebels, the so-called Anaconda Plan. The plan bore that name because Scott envisioned a slow, squeezing attack against the South, first down the Mississippi, then a gradual frontal attack in Virgina, combined with a naval blockade to cut off the South's commerce. The strategy worked, though at a terrible cost that Scott could not foresee: 600,000 died. The old man spent much of the war working on his memoirs and, when he felt the end near, asked to be carried to West Point so that he could die at the Military Academy. Scott's death came on May 29, 1866.

Summary

Winfield Scott came into the army when it was a tiny force and the nation was still a small, self-conscious republic; when he left the United States Army, it was on the verge of becoming the army of the "Coming of the Lord," the Union Army of two million soldiers that destroyed slavery and the rebel republic. The problem with which he wrestled as a military man was the same on the Niagara Frontier as in Mexico and would be, too, for the Union Army at the Battle of Bull Run: how to take an army of raw volunteers and make them an army capable of fighting European regulars. In other words, how could one ask amateurs to kill and be killed? This was a task at which George Washington had failed until the last year of the Revolution, and it is to Scott's credit that he succeeded in 1814 and in 1847. Indeed, most European observers had expected the Mexicans to win the war in 1846 precisely because Mexico had an army trained by Europeans and the Americans were still the same amalgamation of volunteers and militia that had performed so poorly in the War of 1812. Scott's solution to the problem of how to make obedient but innovative soldiers out of the manpower of a democratic society was to emphasize drill as well as humane treatment. During his commands after 1817, he sought to make the life of the common soldier more comfortable and less harsh, on the theory that men fought better when not brutalized by their own officers. The outcome at Lundy's Lane and Chapultepec shows that Scott indeed did adjust the hierarchical organization of military life to the democracy of the new republic.

Bibliography

Bauer, Jack K. *The Mexican War: 1846-1848*. New York: Macmillan, 1974. This volume in the "Wars of the United States" series is useful for those interested in Scott as a strategist. It contains a very good account of the Vera Cruz to Mexico City campaign, along with fine maps.

Eisenhower, John S. D. *Agent of Destiny: The Life and Times of General Winfield Scott*. New York: Free Press, 1997. This biography is based on published sources as well as secondary materials and covers Scott's military abilities, his ego and temper, and his desire to be president.

Johannsen, Robert. *To the Halls of the Montezumas: The Mexican War in the American Imagination*. New York: Oxford University Press, 1985; Oxford: Oxford University Press, 1987. This work discusses how contemporaries saw the Mexican War and is especially perceptive about why Zachary Taylor became a hero and Scott did not.

Mahon, John K. *The War of 1812*. Gainesville: University of Florida Press, 1972. This book gives Scott his due as part of the new generation of commanders who emerged in 1813. Helpful maps show the battles along the Niagara Frontier.

Potter, David M. *The Impending Crisis: 1848-1861*. New York: Harper, 1976. This political history of the coming of the Civil War treats Scott's election campaign of 1852 in the context of the breakup of the Whig Party. The author finds Scott a better general than a politician.

Schwartz, Frederic D. "Great Scott." *American Heritage* 48, no. 2 (April, 1997). Discussion of Scott's actions and victory against Mexico in the Mexican-American War of 1847.

Scott, Winfield M. *Memoirs of Lieut.-General Scott*. 2 vols. New York: Sheldon, 1864. This is the essential starting point for Scott students. It is long-winded and touchy about points of honor, but Scott does get the final say against his critics. Scott's *Memoirs* are thin with regard to the subject's political career, emphasizing instead his military exploits.

Victor, Orville James. *Life and Military and Civic Services of Lieutenant General Winfield Scott.* New York and London: Beadle, 1861. All the 1852 "campaign biographies" are inaccessible except in a few research libraries; the Victor book appears in a popular microfilm series and gives a straightforward account of the details of Scott's military career.

Weigley, Russell F. *History of the United States Army.* New York: Macmillan, 1967; London: Batsford, 1968. The author evaluates Scott both as a strategist in war and as a molder of the army. He sees Scott as an excessively vainglorious man, but still the builder of the professional officer corps.

James W. Oberly

EDWARD WYLLIS SCRIPPS

Born: June 18, 1854; near Rushville, Illinois

Died: March 12, 1926; at sea, off the coast of Monrovia, Liberia

Areas of Achievement: Journalism and publishing

Contribution: Through delegating responsibility but maintaining control of his holdings, Scripps established a publishing empire that eventually included newspapers, the United Press Association, Acme Newsphotos, and the United Feature Syndicate. Late in life he founded, with his half-sister Ellen, the Scripps Institute of Oceanography, the Scripps Foundation for Research in Population Problems, and the Science News Service.

Early Life

Edward Wyllis Scripps was born on a farm near Rushville, Illinois, on June 18, 1854, the son of James Mogg Scripps and Julia Osborne Scripps. He was the youngest of thirteen children in his father's three families (his father had been married three times). In a sense, Scripps was destined for a publishing career because his ancestors had been active in the field: William Armiger Scripps, his grandfather, had been the publisher of the *True Briton* and part owner of the *London Literary Gazette* in England, and his father had been a bookbinder in London, England, before he emigrated to the United States in 1844.

Because his mother, who was forty when he was born, disciplined him harshly and criticized him, Scripps became bitter toward her and turned to his half-sister Ellen, who was eighteen years older than he, for affection, acceptance, and guidance. She became a surrogate mother and lifelong confidant, financial backer, and supporter. Her aversion to publicity, love of solitude, sense of responsibility, freedom from tradition and dogma, and range of intellectual interests all influenced Scripps. A loner and relative failure at school, he was, with Ellen's encouragement, a voracious early reader of the many books in his father's extensive library.

His half-brother George, fifteen years his senior, was another ally who, despite the prevailing family notion that Scripps would amount to nothing, defended him. When George later joined Scripps and his brother James in the newspaper business, he usually sided with Scripps against James. James's relationship with Scripps was ambivalent. While he recognized his half-brother's talent, he was also

jealous, more conservative than Scripps, and fearful of losing control. Squabbles, which sometimes became legal battles, were common in the Scripps family.

Before he joined James in Detroit, Michigan, in 1872, Scripps worked on his father's farm. Although he was a sickly child, he became quite healthy, probably because of the physical labor on the farm; however, he never liked the work and enjoyed his reputation as the "laziest boy in the county." Scripps was not really lazy. He hired boys his own age, rather than adults, to work on the farm, thereby saving money, and then increased their efficiency by encouraging them to race each other. This ability to seize an opportunity and get others to work efficiently for him also characterized his career in publishing and explained his willingness to hire good editors and then give them responsibility and incentives. Scripps did not believe in doing anything he could get someone else to do.

In 1872, when he was eighteen, Scripps had to decide what to do with his life. Because he had read so widely, he was drawn to a literary career, but the family newspaper tradition also attracted him. Since James was editor of the *Detroit Tribune*, he should have been assured of a place on his paper, but James, who remembered him as a sickly, argumentative youngster, refused to hire him. The only other career option for him was teaching, but when he met some of his pupils, a tough-looking group, he gave up his teaching plans.

Life's Work

Scripps's publishing career began in Detroit, where he was supposed to take a job in a drugstore that was being opened by one of his cousins. Scripps, however, went directly to the *Detroit Tribune*, where his half-brother William, foreman of the job shop, employed him as an office boy in the counting room. When James and William left the *Detroit Tribune* and started a job-printing plant, Scripps went with them and gradually learned the printing business. When the *Detroit Tribune* burned to the ground, Scripps salvaged the lead from the type and earned about one thousand dollars.

Shortly afterward, James decided to found an old dream of his, a small, cheap (two cents), condensed newspaper rather than the large, conventional five-cent papers. The *Detroit Evening News* succeeded despite widespread predictions of failure. Instead of being a reporter, a job he was not qualified for, Scripps was a carrier boy, initially selling papers but quickly hiring others to do his job at less money until he had two thousand subscribers. He used a similar strategy, picking the right people as carrier boys, when he was put in charge of increasing circulation in outlying areas.

Not content with the business part of publishing, Scripps turned to writing. Because his brother would not give him a reporter's job, he had to offer his services for no pay. Through hard work and persistence he gradually, by rewriting other reporters' stories, honed his writing skills and became city editor. In this position he stressed "personal journalism," or exposé writing. When libel suits ensued, the family incorporated the paper in 1877, and Scripps used his one stock share (out of the fifty issued) to borrow money from family members to start other newspapers, which produced the stock to fund still more papers.

In 1879 Scripps traveled to Europe with George, and the trip became a pivotal point in Scripps's life. While abroad he decided that he would become wealthy, that environment and circumstances determined one's fate, and that he would establish his own paper in Cleveland, Ohio. While in the Colosseum in Rome, he also decided to create his own journalistic empire. Over James's protests, he became editor of the *Cleveland Penny Press*, a position from which he controlled the business manager, ostensibly equal in power. (In the future, Scripps editors would control the newspapers, while business managers sold advertising and subscriptions.) Despite some financial problems, the *Cleveland Penny Press* was as successful as the *Detroit Evening News*. With the *Cleveland Penny Press* Scripps established a policy that applied to all of his later papers: Report all the news and support the workers and the underdogs.

In Cleveland he defeated another giant in American newspaper publishing, Edwin Cowles, but when he started the *St. Louis Chronicle* in 1880, he was not as successful with Joseph Pulitzer, owner of the *St. Louis Post-Dispatch*. When Scripps returned to Cleveland, he was accused of libel but won a "not guilty" verdict. Shaken by recent events, he went to Europe with Ellen and again resolved to take charge of his life, which had been marked by heavy drinking and womanizing. Upon his return to the United States in 1883, he focused his energies on the *Cincinnati Penny Post*, which became a voice against the corruption in Cincin-

nati, Ohio. By 1884 the *Cincinnati Penny Post* was in the black, and by 1885 its circulation exceeded that of the *Detroit Evening News*.

Following his secret marriage to Nackie Holtsinger on October 7, 1885, Scripps overcame the faults that had plagued him in the past. At this point he had also achieved his European resolutions of 1883. He was worth about $250,000 and had an annual income of $20,000. From his country home in West Chester, Ohio, he began to practice remote-control management. In 1887, during James's absence, Scripps was caught in a power struggle with John Sweeney, a favorite of James. Scripps won with the backing of George and a reluctant James and assumed, at the age of thirty-five, control of the four Scripps papers that became the Scripps League.

Scripps also established the New York Advertising Bureau to obtain national advertising for all four newspapers and the New York News Bureau to get news coverage in Washington, D.C., and abroad. However, once again there was trouble between James and Scripps, who lost the battle when George sided with James. Scripps was left with only the *Cincinnati Penny Post* and the *St. Louis Chronicle* under his control. Leaving Milton McRae (he called his two papers the Scripps-McRae League) in charge, he retreated to Southern California, where he built Miramar, a large estate near San Diego. His fortunes turned in 1892 when George switched sides and added his *Cleveland Penny Press* to the Scripps-McRae League. When George died in 1900, James contested the will, which gave Scripps George's stock. When the dispute was settled, mostly in Scripps's favor, Scripps was able to expand the Scripps-McRae League and two other chains Scripps controlled. When he retired in 1908, his newspaper holdings included about two dozen papers. In addition, in 1907 he had created the United Press, which provided an alternative source of news to the Associated Press.

During his retirement, Scripps oversaw his journalistic empire, though he left the day-to-day operations to his editors and to McRae. By 1907, however, a growing rift between Scripps and McRae led to McRae's removal from the business. Scripps's son Jim subsequently became the business manager of the firm and served in that capacity until he, too, became the target of Scripps's displeasure and was removed from power in 1919, when Scripps came out of retirement. In 1922 Scripps put his son Robert and Roy Howard in charge of a new newspaper conglomerate, Scripps-Howard, which added still more newspapers. Scripps then retired again and retreated to the *Ohio*, his yacht, on which he died on March 14, 1926.

Summary

Scripps was one of the giants of the newspaper industry. Like William Randolph Hearst, Pulitzer, and Cowles, he established a journalistic empire that endured. With his "penny" newspapers he helped bring all the news to the lower classes, and his papers were independent rather than public-relations organs for political parties. Despite his own capitalistic success, his sympathies were with the workers, the underdogs, and the forces that opposed political corruption. He believed in the right of labor to organize and bargain collectively, even though his own profit margins were diminished by such activities. In fact, Scripps was more than willing, especially after 1908, to disclose his values and beliefs; in his "disquisitions" and letters, usually dictated, he commented on a wide range of topics, including biographical anecdotes (although not always reliable) and newspaper policies.

It was these policies that accounted for his success. From the beginning, he was an idea person who started things, found able people and gave them the freedom to finish what he had started, and then moved on to new projects. That is why his editors rather than his business managers ran the papers. If their papers, which were owned by Scripps, were successful, the editors could acquire stock in them, thus providing them with real financial incentives. Scripps always insisted on keeping at least 51 percent of each paper, however, and thereby retained control of the entire chain. It was this desire for autocratic rule, even if exercised by remote control from Miramar or one of his yachts, that brought him into conflict with members of his family, especially James and Jim, and with his trusted associates when their ideas clashed with his. Seldom has a man so indelibly put his stamp on a business enterprise he founded.

Bibliography

Casserly, Jack. *Scripps: The Divided Dynasty*. New York: Fine, 1993. After an initial chapter on Scripps, the remainder of the book is devoted to Scripps family squabbles and the life and career of Edward Scripps, Scripps's grandson. Contains the Scripps family tree.

Cochran, Negley D. *E. W. Scripps*. New York: Harcourt Brace, 1933. An early appreciative biography of Scripps, including many details about the newspapers he founded.

Gilson, Gardner. *Lusty Scripps: The Life of E. W. Scripps (1854-1926)*. New York: Vanguard Press, 1932. Extensive early biography of Scripps, including material on Scripps's publishing ancestors.

Knight, Oliver, ed. *I Protest: Selected Disquisitions of E. W. Scripps*. Madison: University of Wisconsin Press, 1966. Contains comments on the nature of the "disquisitions," a succinct but helpful biography, and many well-edited disquisitions arranged in thematic groups, including several on journalism.

McCabe, Charles R., ed. *Damned Old Crank: A Self-Portrait of E. W. Scripps Drawn from His Unpublished Writings*. New York: Harper, 1951. A series of Scripps's writings, arranged chronologically, that span his life; the essays concern his "bad habits," business anecdotes, family quarrels, and journalistic insights. The selections were chosen by a family member.

Trimble, Vance H. *The Astonishing Mr. Scripps: The Turbulent Life of America's Penny Press Lord*. Ames: Iowa State University Press, 1992. The most complete biography of Scripps. Trimble had access to Scripps's voluminous correspondence and his disquisitions; consequently, much of the biography is in Scripps's own words.

Thomas L. Erskine

RICHARD JOHN SEDDON

Born: June 22, 1845; Eccleston, St. Helens, Lancashire, England

Died: June 10, 1906; on board SS *Oswestry Grange*, off Sydney, Australia

Areas of Achievement: Politics and government

Contribution: The first New Zealand prime minister who was not a "gentleman," Seddon completely dominated politics between 1893 and 1906. Astute, domineering, and incredibly popular, Seddon laid the foundation of the first social democratic, egalitarian welfare state in the world.

Early Life

Richard John Seddon was born June 22, 1845, at Eccleston, St. Helens, Lancashire, England, the second son of Thomas Seddon, the headmaster of Eccleston Hill Grammar School, and his Scottish wife, Jane Lindsay of Annan, Dumfriesshire. Jane, who had lost a leg as a child and whose willpower and intellect Richard inherited along with his father's powerful physique and stentorian voice, was schoolmistress of the local denominational school. Seddon's school record was undistinguished. Unmanageable, unruly, and disinterested, he was sent at the age of twelve to his grandfather's farm at Bickerstaffe. This was a disaster, and in 1859, when he was fourteen, he was apprenticed to a firm of engineers at St. Helens. Although a competent workman, Seddon was sacked for agitating for better pay; he then moved to the Vauxhall works at Liverpool, where he obtained his Board of Trade engineer's certificate. Trade depression and restlessness compelled him to emigrate to the goldfields of Australia in 1863. He worked first at the government railway workshops at Williamstown, Melbourne, and returned to that job after he failed to find gold at Bendigo. In Williamstown, Seddon became a corporal in the local Volunteer Artillery Corps and a noted boxer and athlete. Already, he was a young man of great strength, on one occasion walking the length of a two-hundred-foot-long workshop with fifty-six-pound weights attached to each foot and two others strapped to each hand. A further twenty-eight-pound weight he held in his teeth.

Seddon became engaged to Louisa Jane Spotswood, the daughter of a former Geelong ferryman whose family, after distinguished service in the East India Company, had gone down in the world. On hearing that alluvial gold had been discovered on the west coast of New Zealand, Seddon joined the rush and arrived at Hokitika on March 1, 1866. A diligent prospector and member of mining parties, he put his Australian experience to work in constructing Californian-type water races, dams, and sluices. By 1866, he was a storekeeper and butcher at Big Dam, Waimea, where in 1872 he opened a saloon, adjacent to his store. Seddon walked around the diggings with a five-gallon keg of beer strapped on his back, refreshing miners and expounding his political views. He knew most people on the goldfields and never lost his great political talent for remembering names and distributing patronage. At this stage, he was a huge, broad-shouldered man with heavy features, fair hair, and piercing blue eyes—an unmistakable personality in a small world of rough-and-ready miners. He had already returned to Geelong and married Louisa, by whom he had three sons and six daughters. His family life was contented, simple, and loving. One son later became a Member of Parliament and another was killed in action in France in 1918.

Seddon began his political career in 1870, when he was elected to the Arahura Road Board. Service on the Westland Provincial Council followed. He obtained a growing reputation as a miners' advocate whose intimate knowledge of mining legislation and of local needs carried him into the New Zealand Parliament in 1879. In 1876, he had shifted his Queen's Hotel and store to the Kumara goldfields, was bankrupted but recovered, and was regarded as a clever, loquacious local politician. In the New Zealand Parliament, he joined a small band of radicals who unswervingly supported Sir George Grey, his political mentor. Seddon's early career in the New Zealand Parliament was relatively undistinguished, although he did, after seven years, manage to get the gold duty abolished. It was in Parliament that he developed his great capacity for stonewalling, his antipathy to Chinese miners (which he shared with his Australian and Californian brethren), and his complete mastery of parliamentary procedures and tactics. A rough diamond, the like of whom the New Zealand Parliament had seldom seen, a man whose aitches were misplaced or not used at all, Seddon was nevertheless the complete, new, working individual's politician, giving long speeches packed with detail in which "his words came in a full flood, rushing along with a great sound like many waters."

In 1890, this humanist, radical, vigorous bush lawyer and complete politician was returned as a member of a group which in 1891, as the new Liberal-Labour government, embarked on the most thorough series of social democratic reforms in New Zealand history.

Life's Work

Seddon became minister for public works, mines, and defense in the John Ballance ministry. Working nearly eighteen hours a day, he quickly mastered the routines of his department and, after establishing a new system of railways and roads construction on the cooperative principle, embarked, as the "Jolly Minister," on a continuous series of travels throughout New Zealand. This developed into a royal progress, during which Seddon attended countless banquets, saw innumerable delegations, and distributed largess in the form of patronage, roads, and railways. At the same time, the Liberal ministry was embarking on the greatest program of reforms in New Zealand history. Under the lands minister John Mackenzie, large estates were acquired for settlement and distribution to small farmers on favorable terms and cheap loans from the state. Under W. P. Reeves, the minister for labor and education, the world's first Industrial Conciliation and Arbitration Act, designed to avoid clashes between capital and labor and to regulate every aspect of labor relations, was introduced. A redistributive land and income tax was introduced and the ability of the Legislative Council to reject radical legislation was smashed when the colonial secretary acknowledged the right of Ballance to nominate enough councillors to allow the passage of his legislation.

Ballance was already a dying man when Seddon became acting premier and leader of the House in 1892. He had no special claims to succeed Ballance, especially as Sir Robert Stout was the acknowledged leader of the radical Liberals and Reeves the most creative and intelligent member of the cabinet. Seddon, believing that possession was nine-tenths of the law, completely outmaneuvered them both and became premier on May 1, 1893, after New Zealand's most extreme cabinet crisis. As Seddon himself said, "When the Captain was called away, the First Mate took his place." From then until his death, Seddon reigned supreme in New Zealand politics. Indeed, after 1900, he se-

cured increasing majorities at the elections, although his dominance over mediocre cabinet colleagues created a vacuum which the Liberals could not fill after his death.

While Seddon never matched the great range of reforms of 1891-1893, his speedy response in saving the Bank of New Zealand during the financial crisis of 1894, by giving it a state guarantee and making the government supreme in public finance, laid the foundation for monetary policies more in tune with his humane feelings. In restraining those who wanted to prohibit the sale of liquor by introducing local option polls, he outflanked the most powerful social protest movement of the time. Though an early enemy of women's suffrage, he facilitated the measures by which New Zealand became the first nation in the world (after the American states of Wyoming and Utah) to grant the vote to women.

His great triumph came with the passing of the world's first Old Age Pensions Act in 1898. This guaranteed New Zealand's preeminence as the world's social democratic laboratory. The act was extended in 1905 and further measures safeguarded women's and children's lives while at the same time access to state secondary and technical education was granted. The state involved itself in virtually all aspects of New Zealand life.

Fabian Socialists Sidney and Beatrice Webb visited New Zealand in 1898 and, with a combination of English condescension and fascination, observed Seddon at the height of his power. They had seen him in England at the Jubilee as "a gross, illiterate and forceful man . . . incurably rough in manner and sometimes rather the worse for liquor." Yet, on his native ground, the New Zealand Parliament, he was a gentleman with tremendous courage and unbelievable industry; he kept three secretaries busy at dictation at once, and was "shrewd, quick, genial—but intensely vulgar—tolerant and blunt." Devoted almost entirely to politics and politicians, he was a great practical "doer" whom the common people adored as he responded, "like a player upon a pianner," to their every need and wish. In short, the Webbs compared him with a successful American city boss, which was rather unfair. Their further assessment that he resembled a talented popular senator from the Western United States was nearer the mark.

While maintaining his complete grip on New Zealand politics and his place in the hearts of the people whose material circumstances rose as New

Zealand recovered from the ravages of the world Depression, Seddon, after attending Queen Victoria's Diamond Jubilee celebrations in London in 1897, took up the imperial mantle that Grey had worn. Already, on September 15, 1893, Grey had telegraphed Seddon that his "position is a capital training for higher things—all the great questions between England and her colonies, and the United States are coming on in the greatest way the world has ever known." Seddon visited Great Britain again for the coronation of King Edward VII in 1902. He became a privy councillor of Great Britain and pressed for more formal ties between the various parts of the empire. His visits reinforced his horror at the evils of industrialism, and he constantly reiterated his creed that New Zealand was "God's own country." He attempted to annex Samoa, New Caledonia, Fiji, and the Cook Islands, but only succeeded in persuading the British Colonial Office to allow New Zealand to control the latter. Seddon even saw President William McKinley but got short shrift when he requested that the United States allow New Zealand to control the Hawaiian Islands.

Under Seddon's leadership, New Zealand became in 1899 an enthusiastic participant in the Boer War in South Africa, sending six thousand troops and much unsolicited and bombastic advice. Seddon visited South Africa on his way to the coronation and renewed his unsuccessful attempts to make the British Empire economically and militarily self-sufficient and contained. Indeed, it was after a hectic visit to Australia seeking preference for New Zealand goods after New Zealand had declined to join the Australian Federation that the 280-pound Seddon clutched his heart and died with his head resting on his wife's shoulder. He died on board the SS *Oswestry Grange* on June 10, 1906. His body was embalmed, and he was buried at Wellington, New Zealand, amid scenes of mourning and a sense of loss that was both genuine and universal.

Summary
Through his long career, Richard John Seddon displayed political skills of a very high order. A tremendously hardworking premier, he carried a load of additional portfolios ranging from treasury to Maori affairs that would have killed lesser men. He never faltered; indeed, his popularity increased with his tenure of office. He placed New Zealand on the map with his social legislation, and his re-

forms lasted. He managed prosperity well; as a conservative said, "I would sooner have Seddon with prosperity than anyone else without." He left his country prosperous and contented and for a brief time strutted on the imperial stage during the glittering height of the British Empire. Above all, he left the lot of the common people much improved. He divined and reflected their aspirations for modest property and for economic security. As he said, soon before his death

> All legislation which I have brought to bear upon the human side of life is the legislation which counts most with me. . . . There is much talk of men being Radicals, Conservatives, Socialists, and Liberals. I am none of these. I am a humanist. I desire to improve the conditions of the people, to inspire them with hope, to provide for their comfort, and to improve them socially, morally, and politically.

Bibliography
Burdon, Randal Mathews. *King Dick: A Biography of Richard John Seddon*. Christchurch: Whitcombe and Tombs, 1955. Although more than thirty years old, this thorough, vigorous, and critical biography remains the standard reference. It should be supplemented by more recent interpretations summarized in the relevant chapters of *The Oxford History of New Zealand*. Burdon also wrote the entry for Seddon in A. H. McLintock's *The Encyclopaedia of New Zealand, Vol. III*. Wellington: Government Printer, 1966.

Drummond, James. *The Life and Work of Richard John Seddon*. Christchurch: Whitcombe and Tombs, 1906. Completed by a journalist soon after Seddon's death, this eulogistic panegyric nevertheless conveys some of the spirit of the times and the popular (and populist) appeal of "King Dick."

Reeves, William Pember. *State Experiments in Australia and New Zealand*. 2 vols. London: Alexander Moring, 1902; New York: Dutton, 1903. The classic account, still not superseded, of the state initiatives taken by reforming liberal governments in Australia and New Zealand. Particularly useful on the Ballance and Seddon administrations. Reeves, a Fabian Socialist, was Seddon's minister for labor and education until 1896, when he became agent-general for New Zealand in London after failing to stop the Seddon surge to political dominance. His history of New Zealand, *The Long White Cloud* (3d ed.

London: Allen and Unwin, 1924), is still worth consulting for its cool appraisal of Seddon and his ministry. Reeves himself coined the sobriquet "King Dick," the title of chapter 24, still the most lively and perceptive profile of Seddon.

Ross, Angus. *New Zealand Aspirations in the Pacific in the Nineteenth Century.* Oxford: Clarendon Press, 1964. Chapters 14 and 15, "Seddon's Imperialism I and II," analyze in a scholarly and seminal fashion Seddon's attempts to fulfill New Zealand's imperial dream of a "mini-empire" in the Southwest Pacific.

Siegfried, André. *Democracy in New Zealand.* Translated by E. V. Burns. London: Bell, 1914. The Tocqueville of the Antipodes, Siegfried's shrewd and rational French insights encapsulate Seddon's colonial milieu.

Sinclair, Sir Keith. *William Pember Reeves: New Zealand Fabian.* Oxford: Clarendon Press, 1965. An intriguing biography of one of the few intellectuals in New Zealand politics. Chapter 11, "The Captain Called Away," is especially useful, as are the numerous quotations and descriptions of Seddon from Reeves's unpublished papers.

Webb, Beatrice, and Sidney Webb. *Visit to New Zealand in 1898: Beatrice Webb's Diary with Entries by Sidney Webb.* Wellington: Price, Milburn, 1959. A valuable portrait of Seddon in political action by two English Fabians.

Duncan Waterson

IGNAZ PHILIPP SEMMELWEIS

Born: July 1, 1818; Buda, Hungary, Austrian Empire

Died: August 13, 1865; Vienna, Austrian Empire

Area of Achievement: Medicine

Contribution: Semmelweis, a Hungarian physician, was the first to recognize the infectious nature of puerperal fever (childbed fever). His use of antiseptic techniques in obstetric practice greatly reduced deaths from the fever and paved the way for the development of modern surgery.

Early Life

Ignaz Philipp Semmelweis was born in 1818 in Buda, Hungary, the fifth of ten children born to József Semmelweis, a prosperous grocer, and Terézia Müller, the daughter of a coach manufacturer, one of the richest men in Buda. Semmelweis' father belonged to a German ethnic group and had moved to Buda from Kismarton, becoming a citizen in 1806. In the early nineteenth century, the influence of the German and Serbian elements was so great in Buda that the busy center of commerce had lost much of its Hungarian, Magyar, character. The trading class, including the Semmelweis family, spoke a German dialect, Buda Swabian, at home and in commerce. Although most people in this class spoke Hungarian fluently, few were able to read and write it correctly. The teaching of Hungarian was compulsory in the secondary schools, but formal instruction was still, for the most part, in Latin and German. Consequently, Semmelweis experienced language difficulties throughout his lifetime. His clumsy German dialect made him the butt of jokes in Vienna, where he was to spend the most important part of his life, and his confessed antipathy to writing made him reluctant to publish his discoveries and respond to his critics.

Little is known about Semmelweis' childhood. Described by his contemporaries as a happy, honest, and industrious child, Semmelweis attended the Royal University Catholic Grammar School, one of the best schools in Hungary, where he placed second in a class of sixty. After a two-year arts course at the University of Pest, he began the study of law in 1837 in Vienna. The University of Vienna and its affiliating general hospital, the Allegemeines Krankenhaus, were world centers for the study of medicine. After attending an autopsy with friends who were medical students, Semmelweis abandoned the study of law for medicine. He studied medicine in Vienna for a year, continued his studies from 1839 to 1840 at the University of Pest, and returned to Vienna to complete his studies and receive his medical degree in 1844 at the age of twenty-six.

Three rising young professors who were to make medical history befriended and influenced Semmelweis: Josef Škoda, professor of internal medicine, Karl von Rokitansky, the pathologist who directed the Institute for Pathological Anatomy of the medical school, and Ferdinand von Hebra, the first professor of dermatology at the University of Vienna. Under these professors, the carefree young Semmelweis became a serious and disciplined doctor.

Life's Work

Semmelweis decided to specialize in obstetrics and gynecology, working in the obstetric and surgical clinics of the Allgemeines Krankenhaus. During the two years he had to wait for the position that he had been promised, he obtained his master's degree in obstetrics and doctor's degree in surgery, visited the obstetric clinic daily, frequented Škoda's lectures, and dissected with Rokitansky. Semmelweis was appointed first assistant lecturer to Professor Johann Klein in July of 1846.

The obstetric clinic was divided into ward 1, where medical students were instructed, and ward 2, where midwives were taught. Semmelweis was assigned to ward 1, where Klein was in charge. Before going to the clinic each day, Semmelweis performed autopsies on obstetric and gynecological cases. Postmortem dissection followed every death in the hospital. Ward duties included examining every patient in labor, conducting daily teaching rounds, assisting with operations, and instructing the medical students through autopsies and clinical practice.

Sensitive and compassionate by nature, Semmelweis was appalled by the mortality rate from childbed fever, or puerperal fever (from puerperium, the six weeks following childbirth), which ranged as high as 25 to 30 percent. Although the disease had been known since ancient times, it did not become a scourge until the beginning of the seventeenth century, when lying-in hospitals were established to care for the poor. It rarely occurred outside the hospitals. Between 1653 and 1863, there were two hundred so-called epidemics of puerperal fever in Europe.

The disease was variously attributed to atmospheric influences, overcrowding, poor ventilation, the onset of lactation, anxiety, bowel inflammation, deterioration of the blood, suppression of the discharge from the uterus, and a host of other causes. By the end of the eighteenth century, many English physicians had come to believe it was a specific acute infectious disease peculiar to pregnant women, transmitted in the same way as smallpox or scarlet fever, through direct or indirect contact. To prevent epidemics, doctors isolated the patient, used disinfectants, and maintained clean and well-ventilated wards. Thus, they were able to prevent the spread of the disease, while not completely understanding its nature. Oliver Wendell Holmes, Harvard anatomist and professor, subscribed to this contagion theory and in 1843 was the first to discuss the danger of attending women in labor after performing autopsies.

Although most obstetricians in Europe believed that puerperal fever was unpreventable, Semmelweis was obsessed by the desire to discover the cause of the disease. He systematically eliminated each hypothesis. Except for the fact that medical

students were taught in ward 1 and midwifery students were taught in ward 2, the two wards were identical; they were both filthy, poorly ventilated, and crowded. Admissions to each ward occurred on alternate days. Yet the death rate in ward 1 was two to three times higher than in ward 2. Semmelweis concluded that puerperal fever could not be an epidemic of infectious disease because an epidemic would affect the two wards indiscriminately, occur outside the hospital, and exhibit seasonal variations. Through careful analysis of statistical data from 1789 on, he determined that the fatality rate was lower during periods when there was less interference with the birth process, fewer examinations, or fewer dissections. Gradually he came to suspect a connection between puerperal fever and the students' common practice of examining patients without careful handwashing after dissection. Unfortunately, his preoccupation with a problem that Klein considered inevitable and the collection of statistics which put the clinic in a bad light, alienated his superior, and on October 20, 1846, Semmelweis' appointment was discontinued.

Semmelweis was reinstated in his position on March 20, 1847, and returned to work from a holiday, only to learn that his friend Jakob Kolletschka had died in his absence from blood poisoning from a septic wound incurred during an autopsy. The findings at Kolletschka's autopsy were identical to those of the puerperal patients and their babies. By May, 1847, Semmelweis was sure that matter from the cadavers caused puerperal fever. The mortality in the second ward was low because midwifery students did not do postmortem examinations. Semmelweis decided that hands could only be considered clean if they no longer smelled of the cadavers. He instituted a strict policy of handwashing in chlorinated lime and using a nailbrush before each examination. Mortality rates in his ward dropped from 18.27 in April, 1847, to 0.19 by the end of the year. There were no deaths in March and August of 1848, but mortality rates increased when students were careless and when a woman with cancer of the uterus and another woman with an infected knee were admitted. Semmelweis now realized that infection could be airborne and transmitted from any infected source as well as from the examining hand soiled from cadavers. He prescribed handwashing between examination of individual patients.

Semmelweis encountered resistance to his methods. Klein did not understand him, resented his innovations, and became his bitter enemy. Medical students and nurses resented having to wash their hands. The rest of the world misunderstood his theory. Since he refused to publish, his friend Hebra published an editorial in December, 1847, in the journal of the Medical Society of Vienna about Semmelweis' discovery. Hebra clearly indicated that discharge from living organisms as well as cadaveric infection could cause puerperal fever but, unfortunately, called it an epidemic disease. A second article by Hebra, stressing the spread of puerperal infection from postmortem dissection, appeared in the journal in April, 1848, but this time he failed to allude to Semmelweis' discovery that the disease could be transmitted by material from living bodies as well as from cadavers. This created a serious misunderstanding of Semmelweis' theory. Physicians who did not practice postmortem dissection rejected the theory outright.

Meanwhile, Europe was in political turmoil and Semmelweis' Hungarian patriotism further offended Klein. When his appointment ended in March, 1849, Klein refused to renew it. Semmelweis tried to regain his post. When it was finally offered to him, there were restrictions he believed too degrading to accept. Before leaving Vienna for the last time, in May, 1850, he presented his discovery to the Medical Society of Vienna in a lecture, "The Origin of Puerperal Fever."

For the following six years, Semmelweis was in charge of the obstetrics department at the St. Rochus Hospital in Pest. There, he reduced the mortality rate from puerperal fever to less than 1 percent, compared with 10 to 15 percent in Vienna during the same period. He became professor of obstetrics at the University of Pest in 1855, developed a successful private practice, married in 1857, and had five children. His theory was accepted in Budapest, but the hostility of Vienna and the world community of obstetricians filled him with agony and bitterness.

In 1861, he finally published his life's work, *Die Ätiologie, der Begriff, und die Prophylaxis des Kindbettfiebers* (*The Cause, Concept, and Prophylaxis of Childbed Fever*, 1941). Prominent obstetricians and medical societies ignored or rejected his work, and he responded in scathing open letters which alienated even his friends. In 1865, fifteen years after leaving Vienna, Semmelweis developed signs of mental illness, and on August 13, died in a mental home in Vienna. Ironically, the cause of death was blood poisoning from an injury sustained during an operation he had performed. The truth of his doctrine was not accepted in Europe for at least two decades after his death.

Summary

It is difficult to appreciate Ignaz Philipp Semmelweis' contribution to medical science from the perspective of the twentieth century. So many advances have become commonplace; so many truths that were bitterly resisted have become self-evident. Working before Louis Pasteur's research in 1857 led to the germ theory and laid the foundation for advances in modern medicine, Semmelweis recognized the infectious nature of puerperal fever and realized that it was not a specific disease per se but could be caused by contact with any infected material through either direct or indirect means. Many physicians of his day working in different countries recognized aspects of the truth about puerperal fever. There are similarities in the work of Semmelweis, Holmes, and Joseph Lister, so the debate about who deserves the most credit in the history of antisepsis may never be resolved. Semmelweis, however, was the first to recognize that the disease was a form of blood poisoning, and he applied antisepsis in surgery as well as in obstetrics fifteen years before Lister.

Semmelweis was a great scientist who combined the powers of clinical observation, expert knowledge of pathology and obstetrics, and scientific honesty. He refused to accept the prevailing dogma of his day but persevered in his determination to understand the cause of the disease and the means of preventing it. He developed a theory about the cause of puerperal fever, tested it, and developed a means of preventing the disease. He was the first person in medical science to prove his theory using statistics.

It was Semmelweis' great misfortune that all but a few of his contemporaries rejected his theory, which resulted in the needless sacrifice of countless lives. Great discoveries have seldom been accepted without a struggle, but there can be no doubt that he contributed to his own tragedy. He antagonized his critics by his abrasive manner, and he refused to publish. If he had published when he was in Vienna with the help of Škoda and Hebra, his ideas might have been received more favorably.

Bibliography

Antall, József, and Géza Szebellédy. *Pictures from the History of Medicine: The Semmelweis Medi-*

cal Historical Museum, Budapest. Budapest, Hungary: Corvina Press, 1973. A collection of color photographs of portraits and artifacts from the Semmelweis Museum. Narrative includes a brief overview of Semmelweis' life and contributions and a history of the museum, which is the house where he was born.

Carter, K. Codell, and Barbara R. Carter. Childbed Fever: A Scientific Biography of Ignaz Semmelweis. Westport, Conn.: Greenwood Press, 1994. Interesting account of Semmelweis' discovery of the cause of maternal deaths from childbed fever and the conflicts his assertions created with senior physicians. He was ultimately confined to an insane asylum where he died at forty-two.

Céline, Louis-Ferdinand. Mea Culpa and The Life and Work of Semmelweis. Translated by Robert Allerton Parker. London: Allen and Unwin, and Boston: Little Brown, 1937. A subjective, romantic, and passionate tribute to Semmelweis, written by a French novelist.

Gortvay, György, and Imre Zoltán. Semmelweis: His Life and Work. Translated by Eva Rona. Budapest, Hungary: Akademiai Kiadó, 1968. A comprehensive and definitive biography, translated from Hungarian for the Federation of Hungarian Medical Societies' celebration of Semmelweis' birth. Incorporates the latest research to correct errors in previous biographies and includes a chronological list of events in the life of Semmelweis, along with numerous illustrations.

Semmelweis, Ignaz. The Etiology, Concept, and Prophylaxis of Childbed Fever. Translated by K. Codell Carter. Madison: University of Wisconsin Press, 1983. Semmelweis' classic contribution to medical literature. Includes statistical proofs and logical arguments. Redundant, awkward style.

Slaughter, Frank G. Semmelweis, the Conqueror of Childbed Fever. New York: Schuman, 1950. The most readily available and beautifully written biography of Semmelweis, with imaginative speculations. Helpful orientation to historical and scientific context of Semmelweis' life and work. Contains a few insignificant errors from previous biographers.

Thompson, Morton. The Cry and the Covenant. New York: Doubleday, 1949; London: Heinemann, 1951. A moving, dramatic, fictional biography, more concerned with fact than fiction. Contains both graphic details and a description of the broad social and cultural context in which Semmelweis conducted his research.

Weissmann, Gerald. "Puerperal Priority." The Lancet 349, no. 9045 (January 11, 1997). A historical look at Semmelweis and other physicians involved in conquering childbed fever.

Edna B. Quinn

SEQUOYAH

Born: c.1770; Taskigi, near Fort Loudon, Tennessee

Died: August, 1843; near San Fernando, Tamaulipas, Mexico

Areas of Achievement: Language and linguistics, and Native American affairs

Contribution: Sequoyah single-handedly devised a Cherokee syllabary that allowed his tribal nation to become literate in their own indigenous language—a first for American Indian cultures located north of the advanced pre-Columbian civilizations of Mexico and Central America.

Early Life

Solid factual information on the life of Sequoyah is rather sparse, and some anecdotes tend toward myth making. Uncertainty exists as to his date of birth, usually cited as 1760 or 1770, and even the time and circumstances of his death. Various sources also render his American Indian name as Sikwaji, Siwayi, or Sogwili, meaning "sparrow" or "principal bird." Furthermore, his Euro-American name is cited as George Gist, Guess, or Guest. However, standard accounts generally adhere to the following sketch of Sequoyah's early life and later accomplishments.

Sequoyah was born in the Cherokee village of Taskigi near the Tennessee River. The original Cherokee homeland was a large and scenic mountainous region encompassing northern Georgia, southern Tennessee, northern Alabama, and corners of the Carolinas. Most sources assert that his father was a white trader named Nathanial Gist who deserted Sequoyah's mother, Wurteh, a full-blooded Cherokee. The youngster and his mother moved to near Williston, Alabama, when he was twelve years old. Later he pursued various occupations or trades, working as a farmer, a blacksmith, a silversmith, a hunter, and a fur trader. Moreover, he also displayed considerable artistic talent in sketching animals and nature scenes.

Along with other Cherokee volunteers, Sequoyah served for several months during 1813 and 1814 under the command of General Andrew Jackson in a war against a rebellious faction of Muskogee Creek traditionalists. In 1815, he married a woman known as Sally, the first of five wives. Sometime before this period, his name began to appear in documentary sources as George Guess, probably a misspelling of Gist. In spite of his mixed heritage and assumed name, he neither spoke nor read English, having grown up in a traditional Cherokee community with no formal education. In 1818, Sequoyah moved westward with a group of over two hundred Cherokees who settled in northwestern Arkansas. About one thousand of their countrymen had preceded them to the area a few years earlier. These groups, known as the Western Cherokees or Old Settlers, increased in numbers and later moved into adjacent areas of present-day Texas and Oklahoma.

Life's Work

Sequoyah is internationally acclaimed as a Native American genius who succeeded in creating a system of writing for Cherokee speakers. Work on this great task began almost one decade before his westward migration. Contact with white people and observation of their customs led to his fascination with the uses of writing. The letters and notes that he saw white people using ("the talking leaves") represented an advanced means of communication with such obvious advantages as transmission of knowledge and information over long distances. Convinced that he could produce a written Cherokee language, he threw himself into what would become a twelve-year obsession. Another contributing factor may have been a hunting accident or war wound that left him lame in one leg. Forced to assume a less active lifestyle, the former hunter and warrior now devoted nearly all of his time and energy to the ambitious project.

At first scratching symbols on bark and wood and later using pen, ink, and paper, Sequoyah experimented by trial and error with various methods of developing a script. His initial efforts centered on using symbols or pictures for every word in the language. After creating about two thousand characters, he rejected this approach as too cumbersome and difficult to memorize. Following other futile attempts, he finally seized on the idea of breaking up words into the various syllables or sounds that formed them. This involved the very rigorous and patient task of identifying all sounds used in Cherokee speech, then assigning a symbol to each. Since certain sounds or syllables in one word are repeated in many others, the number of required characters was greatly reduced. Constant refinement eventually lessened the number of symbols in his emerging syllabary to eighty-six. Se-

quoyah created some of these characters himself. Others were Greek and Roman letters copied at random from written materials that he could not understand.

Sequoyah faced ridicule from some Cherokees who viewed his obsession as a foolish waste of time and violent opposition from others who linked it with sorcery. In 1821, after having taught his system to a daughter and a few family friends, he temporarily returned to the East, where he put finishing touches to his work and met with the Cherokee National Council, which officially approved the new syllabary.

The simple and ingenuous nature of this remarkable discovery was soon evident. This syllabary of sounds was different from an alphabet of letters used in spelling words. Although it contained many more characters than the twenty-six-letter English alphabet, the syllabary could rapidly be mastered. By memorizing the eighty-six characters for every sound in their native speech, Cherokees could become literate within days or weeks. In contrast, it took three to four years for Cherokee pupils to learn to read and write English in the schools established by missionaries. Furthermore, with a completely phonetic system, spelling was not a problem. Soon thousands mastered the syllabary without the use of schools or textbooks. In a few years, nearly all members of this Native American tribal nation were literate in their own language.

The Cherokee national leadership, which was struggling to retain possession of the homeland in the face of increasing pressure by avaricious local white settlers to dispossess the tribe, took advantage of this transformation to mass literacy. Tribal leaders who adopted a constitution and legal system similar to that of the United States believed that by appropriating many features of the dominant Euro-American culture, the Cherokees would be accorded the right to remain on their lands. The nation soon acquired a printing press with typeset in the new Cherokee script. Publications included Christian literature and a tribal newspaper, *The Cherokee Phoenix*. Cherokee laws were codified, legislative acts were printed, and business transactions were recorded in ledger books. Literacy also bound the Eastern and Western Cherokees closer together.

Sequoyah's accomplishments were not limited to his miraculous syllabary. He is also credited with creating a new Cherokee numbering system. Heretofore, the Cherokees had used "mental" numbers up to one hundred without means of adding, subtracting, multiplying, or dividing. The new process provided for nearly infinite totals and employed signs and formulas for calculating.

Now a prominent figure among the Cherokees, Sequoyah returned to Arkansas in late 1822 and served as diplomat and mediator. In 1827, he accompanied a delegation of Western Cherokees to Washington, D.C., for the purpose of securing their land, personal property, and treaty rights from the illegal activities of white settlers. The result was the 1828 treaty that exchanged Cherokee holdings in Arkansas for new lands a little farther west. Thereafter, Sequoyah resided in the Indian Territory. His cabin was located near Salisaw in what is now Sequoyah County of eastern Oklahoma.

The spring of 1839 witnessed the traumatic arrival of over thirteen thousand Eastern Cherokees. The newcomers were victims of a controversial removal policy that forced over seventy thousand Native Americans of the "Five Civilized Tribes" (Cherokees, Chickasaws, Choctaws, Creeks, and Seminoles) from their sacred homelands in the South. The genocidal Cherokee experience, known as the Trail of Tears, cost about four thousand lives. Outnumbered two to one, the Old Settlers did not wish to relinquish any governing control to the eastern faction. Especially dangerous was the intense ill feeling between the newcomers and a small group that had arrived around 1836 after signing a controversial removal treaty with the United States in defiance of the legitimate Cherokee government and 90 percent of their countrymen. Sequoyah took a more flexible position in opposition to that of many other Western Cherokees and assisted in obtaining a unified Cherokee government in the summer of 1839. At this same time, he also persuaded about fifteen hundred Cherokee refugees from Texas, survivors of a murderous assault by a Texan military unit, to forego revenge and settle permanently with their countrymen in Indian Territory.

Sequoyah's intellectually curious nature persisted into old age. In 1842, he left on an expedition to trace the location of a mysterious group of Cherokees who were believed to have migrated to the Southwest around the time of the Revolutionary War. He was never heard from again. In 1845, a party sent to look for him reported that Sequoyah had died in August, 1843, and was buried near the village of San Fernando in the northern Mexican state of Tamaulipas. The account, however, remained unconfirmed, and his body was never found.

Because of his international fame, Sequoyah received various honors during his lifetime and after his death. In 1841, the Cherokee National Council awarded him a silver medallion and granted him a small life pension. In 1911, the state of Oklahoma had the famous Cherokee's statue placed in Statuary Hall of the Capitol Building in Washington, D.C. Finally, the species of towering giant redwood trees along the northern California coast is named Sequoia in his honor.

Summary

If the story of Sequoyah is accurate, he stands alone as the only person in world history to single-handedly create a complete alphabet, a process that took other cultures, including the white races, centuries to develop in a collaborative effort. It should also be noted that Cherokee is one of the most complex Native American languages. For this reason, the Moravians and other missionary groups failed in earlier attempts to create a Cherokee alphabet. Although the astounding and difficult nature of this breakthrough by an uneducated individual has prompted some to doubt the truth of his discovery, no one has disproved it.

The scarcity of solid sources on this interesting American Indian intellectual, as well as the political-ideological bias of his biographers, has contributed to widely differing interpretations and speculation about his role and significance. Sequoyah is a cultural hero to both Caucasians and his own people. White supporters of past government policies to assimilate tribal people proclaim his great accomplishment as that of uplifting a tribal nation to the Euro-American level of civilization. On the other hand, Cherokees used the syllabary to record and thereby preserve many ancient tribal traditions and rites that the U.S. government policy sought to eradicate in the name of civilization and progress. These include medical lore, healing ceremonies, ball games, and the use of magic. Regardless of differing interpretations, many agree that Sequoyah's remarkable creation aided the beleaguered Cherokee people by stimulating national pride and providing another means to fight injustice, and later to rebound from defeat, during this difficult period of their history.

Bibliography

Bird, Traveler. *Tell Them They Lie: The Sequoyah Myth*. Los Angeles: Westernlore, 1971. This revisionist account is by a descendent of Sequoyah who argues that a Cherokee alphabet predated Sequoyah. The book depicts him as representative of an old tradition of warrior-scribes, a fiery traditionalist, and resistance leader against U.S. cultural imperialism rather than one who sought to facilitate assimilation.

Foreman, Grant. *Sequoyah*. Norman: University of Oklahoma Press, 1938; London: University of Oklahoma Press, 1987. Foreman's book is regarded by some as the standard biography of this creative and famous Cherokee. It relies heavily on archival records and descriptive views of individuals who encountered Sequoyah.

Foster, George E. *Se-quo-yah: The American Cadmus and Modern Moses*. Philadelphia: Office of the Indian Rights Association, 1885. This is a classic example of the late nineteenth century assimilationist outlook of Christian reformers who influenced federal American Indian policy. Foster glorifies Sequoyah as the great educator of his nation who led the Cherokees to the promised land of U.S. civilization.

Kilpatrick, Jack F. *Sequoyah: Of Earth and Intellect*. Austin, Tex.: Encino Press, 1965. The author, a Cherokee whose wife is a descendent of Sequoyah, presents a fairly standard account of his subject's impressive life and accomplishments. The book employs a few documentary sources not found in Foreman's book.

Waters, Frank. *Brave Are My People: Indian Heroes Not Forgotten*. Santa Fe, N.M.: Clear Light, 1993. This book contains a brief biographical sketch of Sequoyah based on secondary sources that provides a standard heroic treatment of the subject.

Woodward, Grace Steele. *The Cherokees*. Norman: University of Oklahoma Press, 1963. Woodward focuses largely on the early nineteenth century period during which Sequoyah was an active force in Cherokee history. The book is useful for grasping the relevant background events, but the interesting and readable narrative account sometimes becomes polemical in its advocacy of the Cherokee national cause.

David A. Crain

SAINT ELIZABETH ANN BAYLEY SETON

Born: August 28, 1774; New York, New York
Died: January 4, 1821; Emmitsburg, Maryland
Areas of Achievement: Religion and education
Contribution: Through her resourceful, independent, and pioneering spirit, Elizabeth Seton had a profound influence on nineteenth century American education, laying the foundations of the Catholic parochial school system.

Early Life

Elizabeth Bayley Seton was born August 28, 1774, in New York City. Her father, Dr. Richard Bayley, was an eminent surgeon and professor of anatomy at King's College (later Columbia University). Her mother, Catherine Charlton Bayley, was the daughter of the rector of an Episcopalian church in New York. Little else is known of her, and she died when Elizabeth was three. Bayley remarried, but Elizabeth never formed a close bond with her stepmother. As a child, Elizabeth was a lively, exuberant girl. She was educated at a private school, excelling in French and enjoying dancing and music. She also had a strong introspective tendency and a profoundly religious temperament. Her early upbringing was unsettled; her father was dedicated to his work and gave her little close attention (although there is no doubt of his love for her), and she and her seven half brothers and half sisters were frequently sent to stay with relatives in New Rochelle.

As a young woman, Elizabeth was under medium height, but she was well proportioned and graceful; her features had a pleasing symmetry, and her dark, lively eyes attracted attention. She radiated intelligence and charm. In 1794, at the age of nineteen, she married William Magee Seton, the son of a prominent New York businessman. It was by all accounts a successful and happy marriage, and between 1795 and 1802, Elizabeth Seton gave birth to two sons and three daughters.

She was not, however, to have a conventionally serene and prosperous life. Forced by circumstances to mature early, responsibility for the welfare of others became a constant feature of her life. The death of her father-in-law in 1798 left her in charge of six more young children, and the death of her own father in 1801 was another severe blow. In the meantime, William Seton's business affairs had foundered, and the family was faced with a financial crisis, which was complicated by a steady deterioration in her husband's health. Doctors recommended a sea voyage, and in 1803 William, Elizabeth, and their eldest daughter, Anna, sailed for Italy. William survived the voyage but died in Pisa, Italy, just after the family had been released from quarantine at Leghorn.

It was while in Italy, where Seton stayed for three months following her husband's death, that she first came into contact with Roman Catholicism. This contact was through her friendship with the Filicchi family, particularly the two brothers, Philip and Antonio. Her interest in religion, which had never been far from the surface, had earlier been stimulated by Henry Hobart, the gifted Episcopalian minister who preached at Trinity Church in New York. Now she felt the attraction of Catholicism, and her stay in Italy initiated a period of intense inner turbulence, the issue of which was to have momentous consequences.

Life's Work

On her return to New York in 1804, she was torn between the Catholic faith which she now wished to embrace and the innumerable ties which held her to the Protestant religion into which she had been born. For a year, she struggled to make a decision, corresponding with the Filicchis, John Carroll, Bishop of Baltimore, and Bishop John Cheverus of Boston, while also receiving the opposite counsel of Henry Hobart. Finally, on March 14, 1805, she publicly professed her allegiance to the Roman Catholic faith and began to attend St. Peter's Church, the only Catholic church in New York City. Thus began a period of three years in which her new faith was tested to its utmost. She had exchanged social position and respectability, the security of being in the majority, for a minority faith composed mainly of poor immigrants. Her family and friends reacted with coolness to her decision, turning to dismay when Seton's sister-in-law, Cecilia Seton, became a convert to Catholicism in 1806.

Seton's most pressing need at this time was to establish a secure home for her young family. She took part in a scheme to establish a small school at which she would be an assistant teacher, but the enterprise failed. Following this failure, with financial support from her friend John Wilkes, Seton established a boardinghouse for boys. This, however, was also a short-lived venture.

By 1808, at the instigation of Father William Dubourg, the president of St. Mary's College at Baltimore, she had left New York for Baltimore to take charge of a boarding school for girls located in Paca Street, next to St. Mary's Chapel. The school got off to a slow start, with only two pupils, rising to ten by the end of the year. During this period of one year, Elizabeth's vocation was becoming clear to her; she wanted to form a religious community. By March of the following year, in consultation with her friends and advisers, she had agreed to move to the village of Emmitsburg, about fifty miles from Baltimore. The new settlement was to be financed by Samuel Cooper, a Catholic convert. Seton took vows of poverty, chastity, and obedience, was adopted as the head of the community, and became known as Mother Seton.

On June 21, 1809, accompanied by her eldest daughter and three other women, she traveled to Emmitsburg. The Sisters of Charity of St. Joseph had been formed. Father Dubourg became the first superior, and the new community adopted a slightly modified version of the constitution and rules of the French community, the Daughters of Charity of St. Vincent de Paul. By December, sixteen women were living in a simple cottage known as the Stone House, which was the community's first home. There were only five rooms, one of which was set aside as a temporary chapel, and it was with some relief that the sisters moved into their more spacious permanent home, known as the White House, in February, 1810.

From this point onward, growth was rapid. By the summer, there were forty pupils at the school, many from well-to-do families, and by 1813, the number of sisters had increased to eighteen. The curriculum consisted mainly of reading, writing, spelling, grammar, geography, and arithmetic. Music, language, and needlework were also taught. Mother Seton played some part in teaching, but as the school became established, she spent more time in administration and supervision. The success of the school was a result of the effective inculcation of piety and strict morality, reinforced by firm but compassionate discipline. It is through her work at Emmitsburg that Mother Seton is rightly known as the founder of the Catholic parochial school system in the United States. She worked indefatigably—encouraging, consoling, admonishing, mothering, and organizing. She translated religious texts from the French, prepared meditations, gave spiritual instruction, kept a journal, and still had time to carry on a lively correspondence.

Mother Seton continued to be surrounded by the illnesses and deaths of those she loved. Her half sister Harriet died in 1809, and Cecilia Seton followed four months later. The death of her eldest daughter, Anna Maria, in 1812, affected her more deeply than any other. Yet her strength of character, serenity, and resilience were never more apparent than in adversity. Her ability to rise above sorrows and maintain her devotion to her calling ensured the survival and growth of the community in the difficult early years.

Within a short period, the community was expanding. By 1814, the St. Joseph orphanage in Philadelphia had applied to the Sisters of Charity for the services of a matron and two sisters, and in the following year, four other sisters were sent to Mount Saint Mary's College in Emmitsburg. In 1817, the first establishment of the Sisters of Charity was founded in New York City, originally as an orphanage, but like the earlier community in Philadelphia, quickly expanding into a school. Plans were made for schools in Baltimore, and the first of these was established in 1821. Mother Seton, however, did not live to see it. After several years of declining health, she died on January 4, 1821, at the age of forty-six.

Summary

Born two years before the declaration of the Republic, Elizabeth Seton grew up in a land which was alive with a newfound sense of freedom, of its own vast potential. She, too, was an American pioneer, although her expertise was not in the claiming and cultivation of land but in the edification and training of the young and in the schooling of souls. In addition to her profound contribution to nineteenth century education, she offered comfort, support, and hope to an untold number of people who came under her care. She combined the American virtues of innovation, self-sufficiency, and independence with the spiritual values of humility and service. Neither mystic nor theologian, she was a practical woman who emphasized simplicity and efficiency in daily affairs, both spiritual and material.

It had always been clear to those who came into contact with her that she was a woman of exceptional spiritual stature. Some recognized, with prophetic accuracy, that she would make her mark on history. As early as 1809, before Seton had even moved to Baltimore, Bishop John Cheverus envisaged "numerous choirs" of her order spreading throughout the United States, and she herself expected "to be the mother of many daughters." At her death, her confessor, Father Simon Bruté, instructed the Sisters of Charity to preserve every scrap of her writing for posterity. After her death, her communities quickly spread across the land: to Cincinnati, Ohio, in 1829; to Halifax, Nova Scotia, in 1849. By 1859, a community had been formed in Newark, New Jersey, and by 1870, Greensburg, Pennsylvania, had been added to the list.

It was not until 1907, however, that the cause for her canonization was introduced. In 1959, her life was declared heroic, and she received the title of Venerable. Two miraculous cures, which had taken place in 1935 and 1952, were attributed to her intercession, and Beatification followed in 1963. In 1975, Pope Paul VI proclaimed her a saint. The poor widow who had endured many trials, the convert who had founded a holy order, had become, 154 years after her death, the first American-born saint of the Catholic Church.

Bibliography

Dirvin, Joseph I, C. M. *The Soul of Elizabeth Seton: A Spiritual Portrait.* San Francisco: Ignatius Press, 1990. Father Dirvin, an authority on Saint Elizabeth Seton, makes use of her writings, correspondence, and recollections to create an inspiring biography and spiritual look at this important saint.

———. *Mrs. Seton: Foundress of the American Sisters of Charity.* Rev. ed. New York: Farrar, Straus, 1962. One of the three biographies which were reissued to mark the occasion of Mother Seton's canonization. Strongly Catholic in tone yet also scholarly and well documented, it presents a warm, sympathetic portrait which captures the essential, simple goodness of the woman as she went about her daily affairs.

Feeney, Leonard. *Mother Seton: Saint Elizabeth of New York.* Rev. ed. Cambridge, Mass.: Ravengate Press, 1975. Concise biography which will appeal to Catholic readers. Others may find themselves alienated by the author's stylistic eccentricities and his conservative religious point of view, which tends to intrude upon his subject.

Heidish, Marcy. *Miracles: A Novel About Mother Seton, the First American Saint.* New York: New American Library, 1984. Notable for the ingenious device of using as narrator a fictionalized version of a priest who sat on the tribunal investigating one of the miraculous cures attributed to Mother Seton. His job is to be devil's advocate. The flaw in the novel is that the down-to-earth, skeptical priest, full of doubt and wry humor, becomes far more interesting than the heroine.

Hoare, Sister Mary Regis. *Virgin Soil.* Boston: Christopher Publishing House, 1942. Detailed examination of the American Catholic parochial school system, and convincing argument for Elizabeth Seton as its founder.

Kelly, Ellin M., ed. *Numerous Choirs: A Chronicle of Elizabeth Bayley Seton and Her Spiritual Daughters.* Vol. 1, *The Seton Years, 1774-1821.* Evansville, Ind.: Mater Dei Provincialate, 1981. Useful primarily for the long extracts from Seton's letters and journals, which form the core of the narrative and give vivid insight into her mind. Arranged in strict chronological order, with as little editorial comment as clarity permits.

McCann, Sister Mary Agnes. *The History of Mother Seton's Daughters: The Sisters of Charity of Cincinnati, Ohio, 1809-1917.* 3 vols. New York:

Longman, 1917. The story of the first ninety years of the Cincinnati community. The chief interest centers on the stormy episode in 1850, when the Cincinnati Sisters refused to join the other communities in affiliating themselves to the French Sisters of Charity of St. Vincent de Paul (see volume 2).

Melville, Annabelle M. *Elizabeth Bayley Seton: 1774-1821*. New York: Scribner, 1951. Definitive biography, scholarly and objective, free of the hagiographic tone of many other biographies.

Bryan Aubrey

GEORGES SEURAT

Born: December 2, 1859; Paris, France
Died: March 29, 1891; Paris, France
Area of Achievement: Art
Contribution: Seurat became one of the most perceptive imagists of the modern city and its inhabitants in the late nineteenth century. His great curiosity about new developments in technology and the sciences transformed his art into one based increasingly upon scientific and pseudo-scientific theories, something valued highly by twentieth century modern movements. His work may be seen also as a prophecy of surface abstraction and grand decoration.

Early Life

Georges Seurat was born in Paris in 1859. His father, Chrysostome-Antoine Seurat, a legal official, retired at age forty-two and lived apart from his wife, Ernestine, and their three children. Seurat saw his father each week at dinner at his mother's apartment on the boulevard de Magenta in Paris. His parents' marriage has been described as advantageous, respectably bourgeois, and comfortable but dreary.

Seurat shared his mother's strong and regular features as well as the precision and diligence with which she applied herself undemonstratively to tasks at hand. With his father, Seurat shared a quiet, serious, even distant mien. Very little is known of Seurat's childhood, and he was difficult to get to know as a man. Most reminiscences from his friends or colleagues are consistent in their inability to penetrate the artist's personality. It is debatable, however, whether Seurat's private nature was abnormal. In his dedication to work, he was serious to the point of humorlessness, touchy, and even irritable.

Seurat, who drew well as a child, was encouraged in art especially by a maternal uncle, Paul Hausmonte-Faivre. The novice artist drew objects from his environment that caught his interest; by age fifteen, Seurat's interest in art had become an obsession, and he withdrew from a regular school to enroll in a local drawing school. At this municipal school from 1875 to 1877, he moved through a demanding and classically based curriculum, which stressed endless hours of drawing human anatomy from engravings, from casts of antique sculpture, and from live models. Seurat's academy drawings reveal that he apparently preferred disciplined and sober images from symmetrically ordered compositions with a minimum of gesture and dramatic movement. He thus studied the work of Jean-Auguste-Dominique Ingres and Hans Holbein, the Younger.

Seurat's next stage of training came on entering the prestigious École des Beaux Arts in 1878; he was admitted to the painting class of Henri Lehmann, a disciple of Ingres. Seurat may have appreciated Lehmann's disciplined drawings more than his paintings, and Seurat's academic training may have failed to stimulate a healthy interest in color. The years 1875-1879 witnessed Seurat's growth primarily in draftsmanship, careful techniques, sophisticated design, and an identification with imagery carrying moral overtones, all lessons carried over into his mature work.

Life's Work

Following a year of compulsory military service, Seurat returned to Paris in November of 1880 and in a short time settled into a studio not far from the site where he had studied with Lehmann. Seurat left the École des Beaux Arts after barely a year for reasons still unclear, but by 1880-1883 he was again submitting work to the salon. During this same period, Seurat devoted himself to challenges in drawing and in so doing developed a mature style. His drawing and painting methods became parallel manifestations of a desire to regularize Impressionist painting methods and record everyday urban life with the nobility of classical art in the museums. With Impressionism as a starting point, Seurat restricted himself to drawing in black and white, usually with charcoal, chalk, or conte crayons, moving away from an emphasis on line and contour toward softer, broader marks that acknowledged mass, the subtleties of atmosphere, and a concentration upon light. This approach yielded effects both academic and vanguard. The drawings reveal by 1883 a strong traditional handling of form through tonal contrast. Yet the regularized all-over treatment, the neutral stance toward imagery, and the increasing concern with scientific theory had little in common with accepted academic practices at the time.

A masterful approach was evident by 1883 in Seurat's drawings; at that time, he felt sufficiently confident to develop a major painting, one upon which he hoped to establish a reputation. His con-

fidence was based upon intense practice in drawing over three years plus much exploration in painting methods and in color theory. A thorough familiarity with Eugène Chevreul's theories of simultaneous complementary contrasts of colors and a reading of Ogden Rood's *Modern Chromatics* (1879) helped him immeasurably to realize optical mixing in both painting studies and finished drawings.

The first painting to benefit from this theoretical and technical input was the large work *A Bathing Place, Asnieres* (1883-1884). In the preparatory works and the final painting, French citizens swim, go boating, or rest as they enjoy a noon-hour break from work in the industries of a northern Paris suburb. Here the artist calculated and toiled to synthesize the variables and immediacy of Impressionist works by Claude Monet, Pierre-Auguste Renoir, and others.

The salon jury of 1884 did not find *A Bathing Place, Asnieres* museum-worthy, but fortunately for Seurat a number of other rejected artists that year formed the Société des Artistes Indépendants, which sponsored uncensored, unjuried shows and accepted Seurat's painting. Seurat was encouraged but remained frustrated and threw himself into an even more ambitious painting, *A Sunday on the Grand Jatte*, painted 1884-1886, and with dimensions nearly the same as *A Bathing Place, Asnieres*.

The monumental painting depicts nearly life-size middle-class Parisians enjoying a work-free day on a slender island in the river Seine, where, dressed in current fashions, many promenade or sit quietly. Compositionally speaking, the lengthening shadows of mid-afternoon help unify the complex placement of figures. Many of the strollers are arranged in silhouetted profile and almost no figures venture a spontaneous movement. Thus, there is a sense of the illogical leisure of mannequins instead of humans occupying a charmed environment. This mechanical aesthetic was no accident. In *A Sunday on the Grande Jatte*, Seurat methodically constructed a painting which extends the Impressionist treatment of subject but does not emulate the Impressionists' pursuit of transitory effects. It became a landmark work because it necessitated a new critical language and, as it happened, a new movement. Upon viewing the painting at the last Impressionist group show in 1886, art critic and friend to Seurat Félix Fénéon proposed the term Neo-impressionism.

Furthermore, *A Sunday on the Grande Jatte* possessed a radical appearance, composed as it was of thousands and perhaps millions of tiny dots painted with impressive control and evenness. The technique employed became known as pointillism because of the use of points or dots of unmixed pigments. Yet pointillism, arresting in its own right, was not the most important part of Seurat's program. The artist was investigating new quasi-scientific painting theories devised by critics Chevreul, Charles Blanc, and John Ruskin, as well as developments in commercial printing. That intense study resulted in the concept of divisionism, a theory that advocated breaking down colors into separate components and applying them almost mechanically to a primed canvas in almost microscopic amounts, whereupon an optical mix occurred for spectators. The resultant optical mix was thought to be superior in luminosity to effects possible from traditional palettes wherein colors were mixed as tints or hues before application to a canvas. The immediate difference for Seurat was a painted approximation of the vibrating subtleties of reflected light, for example, as found in the partial tones of shadows in nature.

Not to be overlooked too was a concurrent advancement in color printings—the chromotypogravure, which intrigued Seurat, already fascinated by technology. The chromotypogravure replicated colors via screens or regular systems of dots and, as in Seurat's pointillism, produced an atmospheric mass and subtle gradations instead of lines or sharp contrasts of form.

Pointillism and divisionism, which regularized the painted effects of Impressionism, would have been satisfying accomplishments in themselves for some progressive painters of the 1880's, but not for Seurat. Upon finishing *A Sunday on the Grande Jatte*, which was also rejected at the Paris Salon, he took up a different challenge, that of systematizing the means of expressing emotional effects in paintings through carefully predetermined amounts of colors and types of light. Regularizing emotions in paintings was not new in France. There were plenty of precedents from Nicolas Poussin in the 1600's to Jacques-Louis David in the late 1700's. Seurat's new preoccupation, though, was based mostly on the publications of Charles Henry, a contemporary psychologist and aesthetician. Henry sought a scientific way to regularize connections between the formal elements of painting—colors, tones, or lines—and their impact upon viewers' emotional responses.

Such formulas appeared in Seurat's next well-planned painting, *Une Parade de cirque* of 1888. Known generally as *La Parade* (the side show), it focused on the midway of an urban circus. The scene, lit by gas jets, may be a nocturne, but more is dark in *La Parade* than the atmosphere. This entertainment scene is not joyous, despite a milling crowd and performing musicians. Solemnity and dutiful actions seem the rule and are reinforced by a muted surface system of dark blue and red dots. The painting is a balanced geometrical artifice underscored by the application of the ancient Greek guide, called the golden section, believed to establish beautiful proportions.

A number of marine subjects painted at or near Honfleur, Grandcamp, Port-en-Bessin, and Gravelines represent the artist's other painting interests from 1885 to 1891. These paintings parallel the works discussed in this essay technically and compositionally, and, though perhaps less provocative, they are no less brilliant in conception or execution.

Only days before the Salon des Indépendants opened in 1891, Seurat became ill, possibly from infectious angina or acute meningitis. Quickly moved from inadequate lodging to his mother's apartment, also in Paris, he lapsed into delirium and died there on March 29.

Summary

Precocious as a youth, Georges Seurat was the master of his intentions for art by 1880. He could not know it at the time, but his career would be over in only eleven years. Deliberate in technique and a theoretician besides, his mature oeuvre included fewer than twenty major paintings, yet Seurat is considered one of the most influential of the late nineteenth century painters in France.

He modernized classical configurations and exhausted orthodox formulas, after which he ventured into uncharted waters and speculated upon radical approaches to picture-making. Indeed, art viewers during his life and since usually imagine that technique or process was his dominant concern. Yet much of Seurat's conceptual direction was governed by careful reading of art theory, literature, physics, and pioneering works in psychology. Furthermore, despite the appearance of Cartesian order and asymmetrical balance invoked through the golden section of the ancient Greeks, Seurat's paintings by 1886 reflect an exploration of the new Symbolist movement, a movement decidedly subjective.

Seurat's primary subject, interwoven among fields of dots, was the modern city and the activities of its various classes of people, in particular the middle-class at its leisure. In so doing, he transformed pedestrian information into a dignified and clarified expression, befitting the traditional art of the museums while simultaneously reflecting an enthusiasm for science and technology.

Bibliography

Broude, Norma. "New Light on Seurat's 'Dot': Its Relation to Photomechanical Color Printing in France in the 1880's." *Art Bulletin* 56 (December, 1974): 581-589. In a valuable piece of scholarship, Broude explores the parameters of the pointillist technique. In doing so, she draws quite helpful connections between Seurat's method, begun about 1885, and a new commercial printing technique involving chromotypogravure. There are also connections to an equally new attempt at color photography called the autochrome process. Those technologies fascinated

Seurat because he was searching for an optically induced half-tone value system.

Dorra, Henri, and John Rewald. *Seurat*. Paris: Les Beaux-arts, 1959. Noteworthy are letters between Seurat and the Symbolist art theorist Fénéon, a perceptive and well-documented chapter titled "The Evolution of Seurat's Style," a chronological list of exhibitions in which Seurat's paintings have been shown, a lengthy bibliography, plus indexes of patrons and collectors as well as Seurat's art listed by title and subject.

Goldwater, Robert J. "Some Aspects of the Development of Seurat's Style." *Art Bulletin* 23 (March, 1941): 117-130. Concentrates upon stylistic developments in the last five years of the artist's career, plus relationships between Seurat's career and those of his contemporaries. Goldwater emphasizes that Seurat was highly interested in various currents of his time, both in art and in other professions to the degree that he was as much influenced by contemporary developments as he influenced others.

Leighton, John and Richard Thomson. *Seurat and the Bathers*. New Haven, Conn.: Yale University Press, and London: National Gallery, 1997. The authors focus on Seurat's painting "The Bathers," discussing the format, subject, and techniques used.

Nochlin, Linda. "Body Politics: Seurat's Poseuses." *Art in America* 82, no. 3 (March, 1994). Examines Seurat's paintings of female nudes.

Prak, Niels Luning. "Seurat's Surface Pattern and Subject Matter." *Art Bulletin* 53 (September, 1971): 367-378. This fine article addresses some of Seurat's intentions for the surface characteristics of his mature style, chief among which were the transformation of observed fact into rigorous abstract pattern. That, according to Prak, was achieved eventually by the painter through continual simplification of figures, continuity of forms (either defined or suggested), and the application of Blanc's theories to painting.

Thomson, Richard. *Seurat*. Oxford: Phaidon Press, and Salem, N.H.: Salem House, 1985. A good monograph which benefits from international research. Its standard chronological approach is enriched by rarely seen drawings and painted studies and a penetrating text, which correctly explores Seurat's absorption in current art and scientific theory.

Tom Dewey II

WILLIAM H. SEWARD

Born: May 16, 1801; Florida, New York
Died: October 10, 1872; Auburn, New York
Areas of Achievement: Diplomacy and politics
Contribution: As an antislavery leader who helped to found the Republican Party during the 1850's, Seward, who contested Lincoln for the presidential nomination in 1860, went on to become one of the United States' greatest secretaries of state.

Early Life

The ancestors of William Henry Seward came to America from England during the early eighteenth century. His parents, Samuel and Mary Seward, reared five children. Young Seward was influenced mainly by his father, who valued discipline and wealth. At age fifteen, Seward left home for Union College in Schenectady, New York. A financial dispute with his father led him to leave Union College for Georgia, where he taught school (and observed slavery at first hand) for a short time. Returning to New York State, he completed his studies at Union College. He then worked for two law firms before being admitted to the bar in 1822. The following year, Seward moved to Auburn, near Syracuse, where he joined the law firm of Judge Elijah Miller. Judge Miller provided him not only a job but also a bride, for Seward married the judge's daughter, Frances, in 1824.

For men such as Seward, Auburn proved to be a great source of political opportunity. By the mid-1820's, Seward had already become very active in the National Republican Party, which supported John Quincy Adams, and he then became active in the Antimasonic Party, which not only challenged the "secret government" of the Masons but also advocated protective tariffs and government support for the construction of roads, canals, and railroads. It was as an Antimason that Seward launched his public career. He won a seat in the state senate, and he increasingly became a favorite of the leading political organizer of his party, Thurlow Weed (also of Auburn). The two men became close friends and established a lifelong political relationship which soon brought Seward to national prominence. Weed first carried Seward into the new Whig Party as it emerged during the winter of 1833-1834, then engineered Seward's nomination for governor. Although Seward lost when he first ran for the office in 1834, he triumphed four years later.

By the time he became governor, Seward had proven himself to be highly ambitious, often unprincipled, and tough. He stood for the Whig economic program of tariffs, internal improvements, and the national bank, and took a daring position in support of temperance, prison reform, and the abolition of jail sentences for debtors. On race issues, however, he was inconsistent. Although he detested slavery, he opposed, with equal vehemence, granting the right to vote to blacks. Yet he recognized that the controversy over slavery might offer him political opportunities, and he grabbed them during the next twenty-five years.

Life's Work

Portraits of Seward show a handsome man about five feet, six inches tall, with a graceful, thin face marked by an aquiline nose, a ruddy complexion, and wavy, red hair. Early photographs of Seward are not as flattering: The lines in his face are less graceful, his look less direct. This discrepancy can be observed also in his political career, for Seward often offered less than met the eye. As governor, he became well-known for his opposition to slavery and his support for the education of Catholic immigrant children in the face of nativist Protestant objections, and he continued to advocate high tariffs and internal improvements. Yet he took none of these positions without first having carefully assessed their potential impact on his career. When the Whigs in New York suffered reverses during the mid- and late-1840's, they turned to Seward as their best chance to regain a seat in the United States Senate. Their plan succeeded. In 1849, the Auburn lawyer moved to Washington, D.C.

The next twenty years witnessed the zenith of Seward's political career. Opposing the Compromise of 1850 because it did not end the expansion of slavery, Seward delivered his most famous speech. He argued before the Senate that there existed "a higher law than the Constitution" that prohibited the movement of slavery into free territory. This speech, which was reprinted thousands of times during the following decade, turned Seward into one of the leading symbols of the antislavery movement, a hero to Northerners, a demagogue to Southerners. Moreover, Seward's "higher law" speech guaranteed that when the Whig Party disintegrated during the period between 1852 and 1854, Seward would be called upon to lead the Republican Party, which replaced it. Seward in New York, Abraham Lincoln in Illinois, and Salmon Chase in Ohio all came to lead the new party that was both sectional (not national) and fundamentally opposed to the expansion of slavery into the territory acquired by the United States following the Mexican War.

Yet both Seward's friends and his foes exaggerated his opposition to slavery, for he was first and foremost a nationalist—and, as such, hardly a radical within the abolitionist cause. Slavery, he believed, would impede national development, but he was against so rapid and wrenching a transition away from slavery as might lead to war and destroy the Union. Seward favored gradual, not immediate, abolition. He advocated compensation for slaveholders who freed their slaves. A conservative and traditionalist, unlike many abolitionists, he continued to praise the Constitution. That Seward was a nationalist also explains his support of federal funding of internal improvements, tariffs, and development of the West. He remained suspicious of executive power, although not when it was used to assert the national interest against foreign competitors. Seward believed that, eventually, the United States would extend its boundaries from coast to coast and would encompass Canada and Mexico and Alaska (which he helped to purchase from Russia in 1867). As a nationalist, he believed, as did his hero John Quincy Adams, that Providence intended for the United States to dominate the Western Hemisphere. He believed that the political and moral contradictions of slavery would discredit this mission.

Seward viewed the systems of the nation's free and slave states and territories incompatible. This incompatibility would, he claimed in an 1858 speech, lead to "an irrepressible conflict," meaning that the United States would eventually have to extend either the free or the slave system to all of its borders. Lincoln shared this conviction, and the likelihood that either Lincoln or Seward would become the Republican Party nominee for president in 1860 led many influential Southerners to advocate secession.

Seward desperately wanted to become president, but, for a number of reasons, he failed to receive his party's nomination. The "irrepressible conflict" speech had become so notorious that many Republicans feared that its author could not win the election. Furthermore, Seward's long-standing support for Catholic education, stemming back to the New York education quarrels of the 1840's, left nativists in his party dissatisfied. (As for Thurlow Weed, another likely candidate that year of 1860, he was simply outmaneuvered by the opposition—a rare but important occurrence in his political career.) Thus, the Republican Party named Abraham Lincoln its candidate for the presidency. Seward's defeat was a bitter blow, yet—although he genuinely believed Lincoln to be less qualified than himself—Seward loyally supported Lincoln in the general election. Lincoln rewarded this loyalty, offering Seward the post of secretary of state following his electoral victory.

During the next eight years, Seward proved himself to be among the nation's most outstanding State Department chiefs, though it was not immediately apparent. He began his work in a provocative manner. He proposed that Lincoln, in effect, serve as a figurehead president while Seward assume the real powers of the presidency. He threatened war against England and France in order to motivate the South to return to the Union in a burst of nationalistic fervor. He insulted the British at a moment when the Union needed foreign support against the challenge of the Confederacy.

If his early diplomacy appeared belligerent, however, he quickly mended his ways. From the beginning of the Civil War in 1861, Seward's major task was to minimize foreign support for the Confederacy. The South not only sought diplomatic recognition from the Europeans; it also sought military aid in the form of loans and equipment, especially naval craft that could challenge the Union blockade of Southern ports.

Preoccupied with military and political matters, Lincoln gave Seward a free hand in the diplomatic arena. Seward played it well. When a Union naval captain plucked two Confederate officials off the *Trent*, a British frigate, officials in London threatened war. Seward avoided conflict in a very adroit maneuver in which the British, for the first time since the American Revolution, accepted the American view of neutral rights on the high seas. In like manner, Seward, through a combination of bluff, public appeal, and skillful negotiation, discouraged both the British and the French from aiding the Confederacy either diplomatically or materially.

Seward's skill was evident in more than simply wartime diplomacy. He shrewdly unveiled the Monroe Doctrine when the French installed a puppet regime in Mexico, and he effectively laid the foundation for American financial claims against

London stemming from damage inflicted on Union shipping by a Confederate cruiser, the *Alabama*, constructed in Great Britain. More important, his vision of an American continental empire culminated in his imaginative purchase of Alaska in 1867. "Seward's Folly," his critics called the acquisition, but even an unfriendly Congress recognized its potential value.

The plot to kill Lincoln also targeted Seward, who was severely wounded. He recovered to serve President Andrew Johnson as secretary of state, generally endorsing Johnson's Reconstruction policy. The fact is that Seward remained willing to subordinate black rights to what he believed to be the main task, that of the reconciliation of the North and the South.

Nevertheless, it was foreign policy, not Reconstruction politics, for which he would be remembered. Retiring from public life in 1869 and returning to Auburn, he died three years later, October 10, 1872.

Summary

William Seward's career touched upon virtually all the major issues of the pre-Civil War era. He became one of the country's leading Whig (and later Republican) leaders in part because he thoroughly supported the main Whig principles: nationalism, a limit on executive power, strict support for the Constitution, a high tariff to fund internal improvements, and low land prices in order to stimulate westward expansion. Yet it was antislavery that, above all, shaped his career. Seward became a leading opponent of the expansion of slavery, and he nearly rode this issue into the presidency.

What Seward lacked, however, was conviction. Seward never conveyed Lincoln's sense that slavery was a genuine American tragedy. To an extent, Seward was victimized by his evident ambition. He was not fully trusted, in large measure because he was not fully trustworthy. Too often he subordinated political principle to personal interest, a weakness which limited his effectiveness with allies and foes alike.

Nevertheless, his skepticism about principle allowed him to compromise where compromise was necessary and made him a particularly effective diplomat. Next to John Quincy Adams, he had the broadest vision of any secretary of state in American history. He was a practical man, a man of action rather than an intellectual. Whatever the flaws in his character, his record speaks for itself.

Bibliography

Adams, Ephraim D. *Great Britain and the American Civil War*. 2 vols. London and New York: Longman, 1925. Adams, while very sympathetic toward the British, nevertheless provides a fair and detailed account of Seward's first four years as secretary of state.

Case, Lynn M., and Warren F. Spencer. *The United States and France: Civil War Diplomacy*. Philadelphia: University of Pennsylvania Press, 1970. An excellent survey of Seward's foreign policy from a Continental perspective. Seward is viewed with grudging respect.

Ferris, Norman B. *Desperate Diplomacy: William H. Seward's Foreign Policy, 1861*. Knoxville: University of Tennessee Press, 1976. A sympathetic account of Seward's diplomacy, with a focus on the *Trent* affair.

———. *The Trent Affair: A Diplomatic Crisis*. Knoxville: University of Tennessee Press, 1975. A thorough but dull account of the crisis that nearly brought Great Britain and the United States to war in 1861.

Paolino, Ernest N. *The Foundations of American Empire: William Henry Seward and U.S. Foreign Policy.* Ithaca, N.Y.: Cornell University Press, 1973. The author views Seward as defining a commercial imperial mission for the United States. Curiously, the book ignores the Civil War.

Seward, William H. "Hampton Roads Conference." *Essential Documents in American History* (January, 1997). Seward's own account of the Hampton Roads Conference attended by Abraham Lincoln; includes meeting agreements and Lincoln's announcements.

————. *William H. Seward: An Autobiography from 1801-1834, With a Memoir of His Life, and Selections from His Letters.* 3 vols. Edited by Frederick Seward. New York: Derby and Miller, 1877. The editor was Seward's son. This volume provides a look at Seward's entire life from his own perspective.

Valone, Stephen J. "'Weakness Offers Temptation': William H. Seward and the Reassertion of the Monroe Doctrine." *Diplomatic History* 19, no. 4 (Fall 1995). Examination of Seward's policy for addressing France's violation of the Monroe doctrine.

Van Deusen, Glyndon G. *William Henry Seward.* New York: Oxford University Press, 1967. The best one-volume biography. Van Deusen is sympathetic to but rarely uncritical of Seward, whom he views as a man both unprincipled and practical.

Warren, Gordon H. *Fountain of Discontent: The Trent Affair and Freedom of the Seas.* Boston: Northeastern University Press, 1981. This work is less kind to Seward than the work of Ferriss. It is very helpful in clarifying the complex legal issues of the affair.

Gary B. Ostrower

SHAKA

Born: c. 1787; Mtetwa Empire
Died: September 22, 1828; Zulu Empire
Areas of Achievement: Monarchy and the military
Contribution: Shaka revolutionized the military and political organization of the Zulus and their neighboring peoples, transforming the systems from the traditional to what might have developed into a modern nation-state, had not colonialism intervened. His achievements enabled the Zulus to resist European conquest until the late nineteenth century and preserved Zulu national identity.

Early Life

Shaka was the illegitimate child of a young Zulu chieftain and a woman from a clan with whom his father ordinarily could not have chosen a wife because of kinship restrictions. His parents attempted unsuccessfully a contrived marriage, but Shaka and his mother were shortly exiled from his father's *kraal* (homestead). They went to live with his mother's clan, a branch of Mtetwa people, but there Shaka found himself ostracized and humiliated by the boys in his age group.

Even before attaining puberty, Shaka displayed the personality that was to mold his career. He was a reclusive, brooding child, deeply attached to his mother, prone to outbursts of consuming violence. It has been reported that he once nearly killed two older boys who had taunted him. When his father's *kraal* offered reconciliation and membership in his adolescent age group, Shaka angrily rejected the offer in public, embarrassing his father and deepening the feud between the two clans of Shaka's parents.

There is nothing to indicate that Shaka received any more than the traditional education provided for all Zulu youths in adolescence. That would have amounted to indoctrination into tribal customs and pragmatic knowledge of the environment. Oral tradition depicts Shaka as a youth driven to reckless bravery, a superior athlete and warrior whose talents only fed the jealousy of his peers.

Life's Work

At the age of twenty-one, Shaka joined the fighting ranks of the great Mtetwa chief, Dingiswayo. A remarkable leader in his own right, Dingiswayo had conquered some thirty tribes, including the Zulu, and had attempted to discourage the incessant feuding among his subjects, much of it caused by the food and land shortages resulting from a prolonged drought in the region in the late eighteenth century. Dingiswayo organized trading expeditions to the tiny European outpost on the coast of southern Africa and formulated the beginnings of a centralized kingdom.

Life as a soldier offered Shaka the opportunity to display his genius for military innovation. Traditionally, combat in southern Africa had been decided by the two opposing groups deploying themselves some fifty yards apart and hurling javelins and spears across the intervening distance until one side or the other retired. Shaka, dissatisfied with these tactics, adopted the *assegai*, a short stabbing sword, as his weapon, thus requiring hand-to-hand combat with enemies. There is some evidence that Shaka was familiar enough with advanced forms of iron-smelting technology to comprehend that, properly forged, these blades could be made much harder and more destructive than the less elaborate iron weapons normally used by his people.

Shaka also developed more disciplined tactics than previously used in the region. He disdained the loose array of warriors characteristic of javelin combat in favor of a close-order deployment, wherein a solid line of animal-skin shields confronted the enemy. Two "horns" of infantry extended from this central formation to outflank enemy forces. Reserves to the rear of the formation stood ready to rush into any weakness created in the enemy lines. Shaka's regiment won victory after victory against confused opponents. His new tactics changed warfare from limited skirmishing to a modern bloodletting that often terrorized potential opponents into submission.

Shaka's father, meanwhile, had maneuvered himself into the Zulu chieftancy. Upon his death in 1816, a grateful Dingiswayo had Shaka installed as the Zulu leader. Two years later, Zwide, the chief of a rival tribe and would-be usurper, assassinated Dingiswayo, Shaka set out to wreak vengeance. Luring Zwide's much larger force into a valley where no provisions could be found and foregoing the final battle until his opponents were weak from hunger, Shaka's men devastated Zwide's forces.

Shaka now displayed an insight even more remarkable than those which punctuated his military career. He dispatched the survivors of Zwide's army to his rear guard and, following their retraining in Zulu military tactics, incorporated them into his army. The lands vacated by Zwide's fighters and their families were colonized by Zulu. Shaka evidently perceived that, in order to build a large army and empire, the tribal structure of southern Africa had to be broken down. The notion of awarding land to successful and loyal soldiers, in a country where most land had been held more or less in common, carried the seeds of social and economic revolution.

Within six years after the death of Dingiswayo, Shaka's empire embraced tens of thousands of square miles. He could muster an army of 100,000 men. From the giant *kraal* at Bulawayo, Shaka ruled over an entity without precedent in southern Africa. European traders and diplomats made their way to Bulawayo to seek alliances and privileges.

It was a fleeting moment. Shaka's military regimen was harsh beyond reason, a product of his own troubled mind. He demanded celibacy of his troops, granting the right to marry only to those who excelled in battle. His officers clubbed to death any recruit too faint-hearted to bear the pain and deprivation of forced marches and ordeals. His new military tactics were like a plague loosed on the land, virtually depopulating the country around Bulawayo and forcing his columns to march hundreds of miles for new recruits and conquests. Shaka ruled as an absolute monarch, and a tyrannical one at that. His periodic fits of rage often led to the execution of hundreds of innocent bystanders. Soldiers who were only suspected of cowardice were killed at once. European guests at Bulawayo reported that Shaka almost daily chose soldiers or courtiers, at whim, for execution.

Throughout Shaka's career, his penchant for violence seems to have been most pronounced in connection with the original injustice meted out to his mother. Shortly after becoming chief of the Zulus, Shaka hunted down those who had ostracized him and his mother and had them impaled on stakes. The occasion of his mother's death—by natural causes—caused a violent outburst. In Bulawayo alone, seven thousand people were killed over the next two days. Shaka's officers summarily butchered anyone who did not meet arbitrary standards for adequate display of grief. Shaka ordered his empire into a bizarre year of mourning for his mother. Under pain of death, married couples were to abstain from sexual relations. No cows or goats were to be milked, no crops planted. Shaka's army

embarked on a new round of conquests, in some cases hundreds of miles from Bulawayo.

Such demands pushed even the most loyal of Shaka's followers beyond their limits. Food shortages and disease quickly began to take their toll. In 1828, when Shaka ordered his army to attack the Portuguese settlement at Delagoa Bay, his brothers, Dingane and Mhlangane, assassinated him. Dingane then killed Mhlangane, assumed the throne, recalled the exhausted army, and revoked Shaka's irrational edicts.

Summary

Given Shaka's extraordinary behavior, especially in the last years of his life, historians have been prone to characterize him in psychological terms. Shaka has been labeled a psychotic and a manic-depressive. Because he left no male heir—he often observed that a son would try to kill him for the throne—and because he demanded nudity and celibacy among his soldiers, some historians suspect latent homosexuality. Perhaps any leader of Shaka's dimensions might be cast in psychological types. Preferably, however, one should understand Shaka as a true innovator, perhaps a genius, let loose in a society and environment typified by violence, natural upheaval, and the beginnings of contact with the outside world.

Most historians concur that Shaka lived in a South Africa wherein the population was approaching the limits of agricultural productivity; land, therefore, was already coming to be viewed as a scarce resource and a basis of political power. The great droughts and famines which seem to have ravaged south Africa in the eighteenth century, together with the more limited but still novel sociopolitical achievements of his predecessor Dingiswayo, made Shaka's world one of turbulence and frayed traditions. As is evident from the frequent appearance of potential usurpers and ambitious chiefs among Shaka's opponents, there were many who might have undertaken the task of building an empire. Shaka succeeded because of his unique mentality.

Shaka's achievement also passes a crucial historical test: It survived and flourished long after the death of its creator. Despite the level of violence which seems to have attended it, Shaka created a Zulu protostate which remained intact for the rest of the nineteenth century. Only the British, using the latest in automatic weapons, finally managed to subdue the Zulus in 1879. Consciousness of a Zulu national identity remains a strong mobilizing force in the struggle for authority and land in the modern Republic of South Africa.

Bibliography

Ballard, Charles. "Drought and Economic Distress: South Africa in the 1800's." *Journal of Interdisciplinary History* 17 (1986): 359-378. Discusses how favorable conditions in the eighteenth century fostered growth of Nguni population and herds, while drought in the early nineteenth century forced rapid migration and accelerated development of the absolutist state of Shaka by forcing Zulus into military service.

Gluckman, Max. "The Rise of a Zulu Empire." *Scientific American* 202 (April, 1960): 157-168. Gives an excellent summary of major events, and speculates on Shaka's possible psychological condition.

Golan, Daphna. *Inventing Shaka: Using History in the Construction of Zulu Nationalism.* London and Boulder, Colo.: Rienner, 1994. A stunningly comprehensive study of Zulu history.

Guy, J.J. "A Note on Firearms in the Zulu Kingdom with Special Reference to the Anglo-Zulu War, 1879." *Journal of African History* 12 (1971): 557-570. Although it deals with events later than the Shaka period, this valuable study criticizes both British and Zulu use of firearms and their frequent failure to deploy them to full advantage.

Hamilton, Carolyn. *Terrific Majesty: The Power of Shaka Zulu and the Limits of Historical Invention.* Cambridge, Mass.: Harvard University Press, 1998. Hamilton examines the continued influence of Shaka Zulu and how it has changed over time.

Inskeep, R. R. *The Peopling of Southern Africa.* London: Global, 1978; New York: Barnes and Noble, 1979. A study of the factors influencing population movements in southern Africa and methods of reconstructing these patterns.

Lamar, Howard, and Leonard Thompson, eds. *The Frontier in History: North America and South Africa Compared.* New Haven, Conn.: Yale University Press, 1981. Demonstrates how comparative frontier studies can lead to hypotheses concerning the emergence of military leadership in such diverse cultures as North American Indians and southern African tribes. An important methodological experiment.

Marks, Shula. "Firearms in Southern Africa: A Survey." *Journal of African History* 12 (1971): 517-530. Suggests that, although the Zulus acquired firearms early in the eighteenth century, they were little used for military purposes until it became necessary to defend against the British. Underscores the importance of Shaka's military innovations in using indigenous weapons and tactics.

Ogunbesan, K. "A King for All Seasons: Chaka in African Literature." *Présence Africaine* 88 (1973): 197-217. Examines the role of Shaka as a pan-African cultural hero and his exemplary role as seen by writers and intellectuals.

Ritter, E. A. *Shaka Zulu: The Rise of the Zulu Empire.* London and New York: Longman, 1955. A classic account of the career of Shaka. Some passages take the style of a historical novel, but the work is essentially accurate.

Roberts, Brian. *The Zulu Kings.* London: Hamilton, 1974; New York: Scribner, 1975. A popular but useful and innovative account of the rise of Shaka. Stresses Shaka's concept of a territorial power base as a revolutionary development in African political thought.

Selby, John. *Shaka's Heirs.* London: Allen and Unwin, 1971. Provides an extended discussion of Shaka's career and of those who attempted to emulate him in the Zulu environment which the warrior king had altered forever.

Ronald W. Davis

ANNA HOWARD SHAW

Born: February 14, 1847; Newcastle upon Tyne, Northumberland, England

Died: July 2, 1919; Moylan, Pennsylvania

Area of Achievement: Women's rights

Contribution: The first American woman to hold divinity and medical degrees simultaneously, the Reverend Shaw was a central figure in the crusades for political equality and women's rights.

Early Life

Anna Howard Shaw was born on Valentine's Day, 1847, in Newcastle upon Tyne, England. As the sixth child of a fragile and despondent mother and a restless and irresponsible father, Anna was not a likely prospect for fame or fortune. At age four, Anna moved with her family to the United States, settling in New Bedford, Massachusetts. Shortly before the Civil War, the Shaw family moved to the Michigan frontier. Anna spent her early teens cutting firewood, digging wells, caring for her sickly mother, and generally overseeing the Shaw household while her father and older brothers were away at war.

Anna pitied her mother, viewing her as a weak, lonely woman, overburdened with meaningless household chores, embittered by her plight yet unwilling or unable to escape her oppression. As a youth, Anna dreamed that she would be different. After years of indecision, Anna marshaled the courage to defy family tradition and pursue a formal education. At the age of twenty-four, despite the protests of her father, she left home to attend a high school in Big Rapids.

While in Big Rapids, Shaw met the Reverend Marianna Thompson. Inspired by this new and unusual role model, Shaw decided that she also would prepare for the ministry. Embarrassed at her decision, yet knowing that his disapproval would not stop her, her father attempted to dissuade Anna by offering to send her to the University of Michigan if she agreed to abandon her ministerial ambitions. By now a young woman with growing self-confidence, Shaw rejected her father's offer, secured a Methodist preaching license, and enrolled at Albion College, a Methodist school in southern Michigan.

Without financial or emotional backing from her family, Shaw supported herself during her two years at Albion with occasional preaching and public temperance speaking. Buoyed by her success,

Shaw left Michigan for the School of Theology of Boston University, becoming only the second female to enroll at the institution. After being graduated in 1878, she secured a pastorate in East Dennis, Massachusetts. In 1880, Shaw pursued full ordination within the Methodist Episcopal Church. Denied such ordination, she entered into fellowship with the smaller Methodist Protestant denomination, and, amid great controversy, she was ordained as an elder in October of 1880.

Having successfully entered one profession dominated by men, Shaw embarked in 1883 on a second "for men only" profession. Without giving up her pastorate, Shaw began part-time work toward a medical degree. After completing her studies in 1886, Shaw became the first American woman to hold divinity and medical degrees simultaneously.

Despite her accomplishments, Shaw in the 1880's was undergoing a midlife crisis. Sympathetic from her youth to the plight of the disadvantaged, Shaw had entered the ministry in hopes of elevating the discouraged from their spiritual poverty. Convinced later that she must do more to relieve human suffering, she returned to medical school, and, after her graduation, requested a temporary leave from the pastoral ministry in order to serve as a paramedic in the slums of South Boston. While ministering to the emotional and physical needs of women prostitutes, Shaw concluded that the solutions to many of their problems were political. Ministers and physicians could treat the symptoms, but legislatures responding to the demands of an enlightened electorate were needed to eliminate the root causes of social injustice, poverty, and sickness.

Life's Work

At age thirty-nine, Anna Howard Shaw left the preaching and healing ministry for another career. Joining first the Massachusetts Suffrage Association and later the American Woman Suffrage Association (AWSA), Shaw became a full-time organizer and lecturer for the causes of suffrage and temperance. At the urging of Frances Willard, a fellow Methodist preacher and president of the Woman Christian's Temperance Union (WCTU), Shaw accepted the chair of the Franchise Department of the WCTU. Her task was to work for woman suffrage and then to use the ballot to gain "home protection" and temperance legislation.

In 1888, Shaw was selected as a delegate to represent both the WCTU and the AWSA at the first meeting of the International Council of Women. While at the gathering in Washington, D.C., Shaw met Susan B. Anthony, the renowned leader of the more radical National Woman Suffrage Association (NWSA). Anthony, who at this time was looking for recruits to groom for leadership within the NWSA, was immediately impressed with Shaw's potential. As a sturdy, spunky young woman, Shaw had the stamina for travel; as a single person, Shaw had total control of her time; as an extemporaneous preacher, Shaw had impressive oratorical skills; and as a respected religious figure, Shaw had a reputation that would soften the NWSA's "irreligious and radical" public image.

During the convention, Anthony made Shaw her special project, flattering her and reprimanding her for not efficiently using her gifts for the cause. Unlike Willard and other "social feminists," Anthony viewed suffrage less as a means to an end than as a fundamental right that must not be denied. As a single-issue woman, Anthony challenged Shaw not to waste her talents on temperance, but to commit herself totally to full suffrage. In response to Anthony's challenge, Shaw shifted her allegiance from the AWSA to the NWSA and promised Anthony that suffrage would become her consuming goal.

The emerging Anthony-Shaw friendship had a profound impact on the suffrage movement. In 1889, Shaw helped to persuade the AWSA to merge with Anthony's and Elizabeth Cady Stanton's NWSA, creating for the first time in two decades a semblance of organizational unity within the movement. Three years later, Anthony accepted the presidency of the unified National-American Woman Suffrage Association (NAWSA) and secured for Shaw the vice presidency.

The Anthony-Shaw tandem was inseparable—collaborating, traveling, even living together. An odd-looking couple, good-naturedly called by friends "the ruler and the rubber-ball," Anthony and Shaw were strikingly different in appearance, style, and talent: Anthony was tall and thin, an unconventional, religious agnostic and organizational genius; Shaw, a roly-poly Methodist preacher with a quick wit and golden tongue. Despite, or perhaps because of their differences, they were able to extend each other's outreach and effectiveness. Shaw, exploiting her religious reputation and church con-

tacts, introduced Anthony into mainline Protestant circles previous closed to Anthony and "her girls." Anthony, in return, taught the inexperienced Shaw how to devise and execute a strategy for suffrage victory. Grooming Shaw for executive leadership, Anthony prodded Shaw to follow a strategy of moderate agitation, always pressing forward the cause of suffrage, yet never alienating the masses with unnecessary conflict. More traditional than Anthony, Shaw accepted her master teacher's pragmatism. By the time of Anthony's death in 1906, Shaw had learned her lessons well.

Between 1904 and 1915, Shaw served as president of the NAWSA. During this era, the organization grew from 17,000 to 200,000 members and superintended suffrage victories in eight additional states. As the organization grew, however, it also became more divided. The success of the militant suffragettes in England pressured Shaw to abandon the methods she had learned under Anthony for more militant tactics such as campaigning against the political party in power rather than individual candidates unfriendly to suffrage, picketing the White House, calling hunger strikes, and pressing for immediate suffrage elections, even if there was no prospect for victory. Although Shaw grew to accept "passive resistance," she refused to abandon her mentor's game plan. "I am, and always have been," Shaw asserted in 1914, "unalterably opposed to militancy, believing that nothing of permanent value has ever been secured by it that could not have been more easily obtained by peaceful methods."

Although Shaw's policy of moderation raised her stature among the rank and file of the NAWSA, it also cost her respect among the more aggressive members within her executive committee. In December, 1915, at age 68, Shaw stepped down as president of the NAWSA, a position she had held longer than any other woman, and accepted the lifetime honorary position of president emeritus. Although official NAWSA publications attempted to cover up the internal feud, and most members never realized the depth of the disharmony, Shaw's resignation was not voluntary. Leaving the administrative details to the returning president, Carrie Chapman Catt, Shaw began working full-time at what she did best—traveling, lecturing, and evangelizing for the suffrage cause.

In May, 1917, President Woodrow Wilson asked Shaw to head the Woman's Committee of the Council of National Defense. Always an American patriot, and, like Wilson, mesmerized by the prospect of making the world safe for democracy, Shaw left the suffrage circuit to accept the appointment. For two years, she worked to mobilize American women to contribute to the war effort. Following victory in Europe, Shaw resigned as chair of the Woman's Committee. In appreciation for her war service, President Wilson awarded her the Distinguished Service Medal of Honor, an award never before bestowed upon an American woman.

Shaw's retirement from public service, however, was short-lived, for soon she returned to the lecture circuit—this time to win support for the League of Nations. Although her spirit was willing, the ailing Shaw was unable to withstand the strain of another campaign. Succumbing to pneumonia, Shaw died in her home in Moylan, Pennsylvania, on July 2, 1919.

Summary

A Methodist clergywoman who was persuaded that Jesus Christ embodied the best attributes of both man and woman, that in Christ there was neither male nor female, and that full suffrage would adorn the coming millennial Kingdom, Anna Howard Shaw was an eternal optimist who never doubted that suffrage victory would be won. Claiming the motto "Truth loses many battles, but always wins the war," Shaw spoke and acted as if the impossible was already a reality. For Shaw, full suffrage, like the coming Kingdom, could be delayed but not denied.

Shaw's religious reputation and noted nonmilitancy made her an ideal candidate to lead the counterattack against those who opposed suffrage rights for women. In virtually every address, Shaw hammered at the "ridiculous" arguments of those who insisted that woman's suffrage would destroy the home, the church, and the nation. Early in the campaign, her opponents often challenged Shaw to public debates. By 1913, however, the National Anti-Suffrage Association adopted a policy of prohibiting any of its speakers from debating Shaw. Their cause, they believed, was better served by ignoring rather than challenging the Methodist suffrage evangelist.

Following her death, newspaper editors, regardless of their stand on the woman question, united in their testimonials to Shaw. The *New Haven Register* eulogized Shaw as "the best beloved and most versatile of the suffrage leaders"; *The Nation* labeled her as "the ideal type of reformer. . . . the despair of the anti-suffragists because she was so normal and sane, so sound and so effective"; the *Philadelphia Press* praised the "sense, moderation and dignity in her methods which won and held respect even of those who opposed her cause"; and the more conservative *Atlanta Constitution* characterized Shaw as follows: "Though an ardent suffragist, her sense of justice was so impressed upon her records that anti-suffragists and suffragists alike trusted her." Such tributes from both suffrage friends and foes suggest that the woman widely known as the "Demosthenes of the suffrage movement" had become by the time of her death a national heroine. Despite these accolades, however, Shaw has been largely neglected by historians, and she remains the only central leader of the suffrage movement without a full-length biography.

Bibliography

Flexner, Eleanor. *Century of Struggle: The Woman's Rights Movement in the United States*. Rev. ed. Cambridge, Mass.: Belknap Press of Harvard University, 1975; London: Harvard University Press, 1976. A revision of an original 1959 publication, this overview remains the standard text-book on the women's rights movement.

Linkugel, Wil A. *Anna Howard Shaw: Suffrage Orator and Social Reformer.* New York: Greenwood Press, 1991. This introduction to Shaw includes a collection of her speeches and is an extension of Linkugel's 1960 Ph.D. dissertation "The Speeches of Anna Howard Shaw."

Pellauer, Mary D. *Toward a Tradition of Feminist Theology: The Religious Thought of Elizabeth Cady Stanton, Susan B. Anthony, and Anna H. Shaw.* Brooklyn, N.Y.: Carlson, 1991. A monograph within the Chicago Studies in the History of American Women series, this volume analyzes Shaw's feminist theology and compares it with the theologies of other leading feminists of the period.

Shaw, Anna Howard. *The Story of a Pioneer.* New York and London: Harper, 1915. In the absence of a full-length biography, this readable autobiography remains the best general introduction to the life of this suffrage crusader.

Spencer, Ralph W. "Anna Howard Shaw." *Methodist History* 13, no. 2 (January, 1975). This article, which is derived from Spencer's 1972 Ph.D. dissertation, sketches Shaw's career, emphasizing her Methodist contacts and experiences.

Terry D. Bilhartz

MARY WOLLSTONECRAFT SHELLEY

Born: August 30, 1797; London, England
Died: February 1, 1851; London, England
Area of Achievement: Literature
Contribution: As an innovative and politically subversive writer of novels, tales, and stories, Shelley was a significant contributor to the history of women's writing and the development of prose fiction.

Early Life

Mary Wollstonecraft Shelley was born in London on August 30, 1797, to the celebrated feminist writer Mary Wollstonecraft and the radical philosopher William Godwin. Ten days later, Wollstonecraft died of puerperal fever, and for four years William raised his daughter and her half-sister Fanny (Wollstonecraft's daughter with Gilbert Imlay) alone. From infancy, Mary was in the company not only of her philosopher father but also of his friends, among them the poet Samuel Taylor Coleridge and the essayists Charles and Mary Lamb.

William apparently felt unfit to raise his daughters alone, and when he married Mary Jane Clairmont in 1801, he cited as one motivation his need for assistance with educating Mary and Fanny. Mary seems to have disliked her new stepmother, and whatever the truth of Clairmont's feelings about her stepdaughter, Mary certainly believed that her stepmother—who tended to privilege her own daughter, Jane—resented the bond between William and his daughter. As Mary grew into adolescence, she turned to a study of her mother's writings, often reading in the solitude of Wollstonecraft's grave in Saint Pancras churchyard. She read and absorbed not only Wollstonecraft's works but also William's 1798 memoir of his late wife; thus, before she reached adulthood, Mary was immersed in her parents' radical political beliefs and became aware that society frowned on those who espoused such views.

In 1812, English poet Percy Shelley introduced himself to William, whom he admired; before long, Percy was a regular visitor at the Godwin establishment. Percy's frequent visits notwithstanding, Mary probably met him briefly only once or twice before 1814, when she returned from a lengthy visit to Scotland. Percy was a married man, but he and young Mary were drawn to each other. Within months of their first real meeting, and despite the disapproval of the Godwins, Mary and Percy eloped to France. With them was Jane Clairmont. The trio travelled through Europe for six weeks, after which they returned to England. The Godwins and the Shelleys were hostile to the irregular relationship that had developed between Mary and Percy, so the couple had to live on their own in a series of lodgings, often moving to evade their creditors.

Life's Work

Mary and Percy were together for nearly eight years, but they were unable to marry until 1816, when Percy's first wife, Harriet, committed suicide. That year was important to Mary Shelley for another reason: In June she began to write *Frankenstein*, which she completed the next year. The Shelleys' unconventional lifestyle left them vulnerable to criticism and social ostracism, and eventually, in 1818, they left England once again to escape the hostility and settled in Italy. For Mary, the Italian years were eventful. She studied Italian and Spanish with her husband and learned Greek with the help of an aristocratic émigré. Percy also tutored Mary in Latin, and within two years she was collaborating with him on translations. Mary's efforts were not limited to the acquisition of language skills. She completed two works of fiction— the novella *Mathilda* (1818), the historical novel *Valperga: Or, The Life of Castruccio, Prince of Lucca* (written between 1818 and 1821), and possibly the short piece, "Valerius: The Reanimated Roman." During those years, she also wrote two mythological dramas—*Proserpine* (1922) and *Midas* (1922)—in blank verse.

The Shelley marriage was not without problems. Although heir to a fortune, Percy only had an allowance while his father lived, and the young couple's financial worries followed them to Italy. Two of their four children died (their first child lived only eleven days). In addition, Mary succumbed to bouts of depression, possibly exacerbated by her husband's infatuations with other women, including Jane Clairmont—now called Claire—whose presence in the Shelley home was problematic. Having given up her daughter by Lord Byron, Claire embroiled the Shelleys in her quarrels with Byron about custody of the child. During the Shelleys' last year together, the marriage was in trouble, and the two were virtually estranged from one another. To compound their difficulties, in June, 1822, Mary suffered a miscarriage and nearly died, and her depression deepened.

Percy drowned in July, 1822, in a storm off the Italian coast, leaving Mary a penniless widow at twenty-four with a two-year-old son, Percy Florence. The poetry that she wrote in the months after her husband's death reveals the depth of her grief and her feelings of guilt about their estrangement in the year before the accident. After remaining in Italy for one year after her husband's death, Mary was forced to return to England by her financial difficulties and by the need to ensure her son's future as the Shelley heir. She spent the remaining twenty-nine years of her life working as a professional writer to support herself, her son, and her aging father and stepmother.

When Mary, having buried her husband's ashes in Rome, returned to England in 1823 to begin her professional writing career, she was already a published author. In addition to *Mounseer Nongtong-paw* (a satiric poem published in 1812 when she was fifteen) and *Frankenstein* (1818), she and Percy had published *History of a Six Weeks' Tour through a Part of France, Switzerland, Germany, and Holland* (1817). *Valperga* (1823) was published shortly after her arrival in England.

During a forty-year writing career, Mary produced a considerable body of literary work in a number of different genres: six novels and one novella; nineteen pieces of short fiction; travel narratives; short nonfiction articles in a variety of periodicals and other publications; biographies of scientific and literary figures in France, Italy, Spain, and Portugal; poetry; and drama. In addition, she edited and wrote introductions for two editions of Percy's poems as well as a collection of his essays and letters. She also published translations of works originally written in German and Italian. In the context of literary history, Mary's most important works are her novels and her nonfiction prose works.

Mary Shelley's most significant contribution to the history of the English novel are *Frankenstein* (1818), *The Last Man* (1826), and possibly *Valperga*. Her three other novels—*The Fortunes of Perkin Warbeck* (1830), *Lodore* (1835), and *Falkner* (1837)—were written much later, during the years when her literary efforts were focused on making money, and they are not as polished; nevertheless, these later novels are important elements of Shelley's oeuvre and should not be discounted.

Frankenstein, Shelley's best and most famous novel, was published when its author was only twenty-one. According to Shelley's journal, the novel was inspired by two 1816 events—a ghost-story-writing contest and a discussion of the possibility of employing electricity to "galvanize" a manufactured humanoid—that culminated in a nightmare from which Shelley awoke to begin *Frankenstein*. Although frequently classified as "horror fiction," *Frankenstein* is a more serious work than the popular label suggests. The novel is not only a provocative interrogation of scientific method, but it is also an exploration of the nature of loneliness and the role of environment in shaping an individual's psyche.

Shelley's short fiction exists in the form of one novella—*Mathilda*—and several short stories, many of which were published in *The Keepsake*, a popular annual publication with silk or leather covers, gilt edges, engravings, and poetry and stories from popular authors. Much has been said about the autobiographical elements that appear in Shelley's short fiction, but her novella and tales can also be read as explorations of narrative form or as treatments of the tensions between the domestic sphere and the public sphere.

Although many agree that Shelley's most significant works are her novels, she also produced an important body of nonfiction of three distinct types: travel narrative, biography, and literary criticism and review. Between 1823 and 1844, she contributed to several major periodicals, including the *Westminster Review*, *The Liberal*, and *London Magazine*, and completed several books. Her travel writing, which includes several short essays as well as *Six Weeks' Tour* and *Rambles in Germany and Italy* (1844), explores several ideas, including the distinction between a tourist and a traveler and the nature and manifestation of taste. Shelley's biographical work includes the three-volume *Lives of the Most Eminent Literary and Scientific Men of Italy, Spain, and Portugal* (1835-1837) and the two-volume *Lives of the Most Eminent Literary and Scientific Men of France* (1839), and some shorter pieces, including *Memoirs of William Godwin* in the 1831 edition of Godwin's *Caleb Williams*.

While not strictly biography, Mary Shelley's prefaces and notes to the editions of Percy Shelley's work are key elements in the development of the Percy Shelley legend. Through her careful selection and arrangement of the works to be included in the editions, she constructs a distinctive ver-

sion of Percy, one that privileges his talents and virtues and glosses over his radicalism. At the same time, Mary's prefaces and notes comprise part of her literary criticism in that her commentary on Percy's poetry incorporates her ideas on the nature and functions of poetry and on poetic genres. Like Mary's annotations for the editions of her husband's poetry, her book reviews and essays on literary subjects are significant for their influence on the substance and shape of literary taste in nineteenth century England.

Summary

Although known primarily as a novelist and founding mother of the science fiction genre, Mary Shelley's literary contributions are much more extensive than her popular reputation suggests. As a book reviewer and author of short prose for various literary journals and periodicals, she was one of the first modern professional literary critics. In her role as an early arbiter of popular literary taste, she and her fellow critics were influential in creating a literary canon that privileged English literary works.

Throughout her life, Shelley was conscious of her heritage as the daughter not only of William Godwin but also, and more especially, of Mary Wollstonecraft; Percy Shelley encouraged her to prove herself worthy of her family history. From her study of her mother's work, Mary Shelley absorbed ideas about independence and sexual freedom for women; from her father she received a progressive education embodying the ideals of the French Revolution. However, Mary Shelley was also very much a product of her culture and time, and her work reflects the tensions she must have felt as she attempted to negotiate a compromise between the ideals of her early education and the conventions of nineteenth century English society.

Bibliography

Fisch, Audrey A., Anne K. Mellor, and Esther H. Schor, eds. *The Other Mary Shelley: Beyond Frankenstein*. New York: Oxford University Press, 1993. This is a valuable collection of critical essays that illuminate Shelley's major and less well-known works. The essays by Corbett, Favret, Paley, and Schor are particularly recommended.

Mellor, Anne K. *Mary Shelley: Her Life, Her Fiction, Her Monsters*. London and New York: Routledge, 1988. Mellor discusses Shelley's major works. Among other things, the book provides a discussion of *Frankenstein* in the context of early nineteenth century science and illuminates Percy Shelley's contributions to his wife's novel.

Poovey, Mary. *The Proper Lady and the Woman Writer: Ideology as Style in the Works of Mary Wollstonecraft, Mary Shelley, and Jane Austen*. Chicago: University of Chicago Press, 1984. Poovey places Shelley in the context of her contemporaries in late eighteenth and early nineteenth century England. Includes a particularly valuable discussion of Shelley's revisions of *Frankenstein* for the 1831 edition of that novel.

Smith, Johanna. *Mary Shelley*. New York: Twayne, and London: Prentice-Hall, 1996. Smith provides an excellent and detailed overview of Shelley's writings arranged by genre and focusing on the political and cultural milieu in which Shelley lived and wrote.

Spark, Muriel. *Mary Shelley: A Biography*. New York: Dutton, 1987; London: Constable, 1988. Considered by many to be one of the best short biographies of Shelley, this crucial book reestablished Shelley as a serious writer whose work is worthy of critical attention.

St. Clair, William. *The Godwins and the Shelleys: A Biography of a Family*. London and Boston: Faber, 1989. A useful introduction to the radical tradition that shaped Shelley's life and career. Although the book provides a great deal more information on William Godwin than on the other principals, his life and activities provide the context for his daughter's development as a writer.

Sunstein, Emily. *Mary Shelley: Romance and Reality*. Boston: Little Brown, 1989; London: Johns Hopkins University Press, 1991. Sunstein's book is the most complete biography of Shelley. The appendix provides detailed listings of works definitively identified as Shelley's as well as works that might be attributed to her; chapter notes explicitly identify key primary sources of information about Shelley's life and work.

E. D. Huntley

PERCY BYSSHE SHELLEY

Born: August 4, 1792; Field Place, near Horsham,
  Sussex, England
Died: July 8, 1822; At sea off Leghorn, Italy
Area of Achievement: Literature
Contribution: In his zeal to renew the human spirit
  and to reform society, Shelley produced an im-
  passioned, philosophically complex poetry suf-
  fused with prophetic vision.

Early Life

The eldest child of seven, Percy Bysshe Shelley
was born at Field Place near Horsham, England, on
August 4, 1792, to Timothy Shelley, a socially
prominent country squire and sometime Member
of Parliament, and the former Elizabeth Pilford.
Although there were eventually problems between
the politically radical poet and his comparatively
conventional father, Shelley's early homelife was
both emotionally and physically comfortable.
Shelley received an excellent education, first with a
local clergyman, the Reverend Evan Edwards, and
later at Sion House Academy (1802-1804), Eton
(1804-1810), and, for a short time, Oxford (1810-
1811). Supplementing this formal instruction with
omnivorous reading, Shelley was rivaled for erudition among the English Romantic poets only by
Samuel Taylor Coleridge. In addition to his extensive knowledge of literature, philosophy, and science, young Shelley purportedly dabbled in the occult, attempting on at least one occasion, according
to some biographers, to communicate with the
Devil. The attempt was unsuccessful.

With abundant curly hair and facial features
which might more accurately be described as pretty than handsome, the bookish Shelley was the object of much adolescent bullying during his days at
Sion House and Eton, a circumstance which helps
to explain his lifelong hatred of oppression. Part of
this persecution was the result of the traditional
hazing of underclassmen by upperclassmen and
part an expression of the scorn directed against apparent weakness and actual eccentricity by the
strong and the conventional. Because of the victim-
ization he experienced directly and because of the
more serious social and political inequities which
he read about and witnessed, Shelley was a rebel
against irresponsible power and unreflecting obedience to authority from early in his life, seeing in
selfish strength and mindless conformity twin
props to injustice.

Despite his zeal to change the world, Shelley's
first publications were not manifestations of his rebelliousness but of his fascination with gothic horror. While still in his teens, he wrote and published
a pair of gothic novels, *Zastrozzi: A Romance*
(1810) and *St. Irvyne: Or, The Rosicrucian* (1810),
neither of which made an impression on the reading public. A collaboration with his sister Elizabeth, *Original Poetry by Victor and Cazire* (1810),
also contained much gothic material, including
several pages plagiarized from the anonymous ballad collection, *Tales of Terror* (1801).

After his matriculation at Oxford in April of
1810 and his acquaintance with fellow undergraduate Thomas Jefferson Hogg, Shelley's gothic urge
gave way to iconoclasm, with dire consequences
for his future. Having worked together on a handful of trifling compositions, Shelley and Hogg delivered to the printer toward the end of 1810 an unsigned tract entitled *The Necessity of Atheism*.
Shelley sent copies to various English ecclesiastics
and to virtually all the Oxford faculty, and after
their authorship had been discovered, he and Hogg
were expelled from the university, still largely a
theological institution, on March 25, 1811.

Shelley moved about restlessly during the next
few months, spending part of his time in London,
where he renewed his acquaintance with sixteen-
year-old Harriet Westbrook, a friend of his sister.
Convinced that Harriet was a victim of authoritarian persecution, the impulsive Shelley fled with her
to Edinburgh, where the two were married on August 28, 1811. Although the marriage was one of
the great mistakes of Shelley's life, it was, at first,
reasonably happy despite the inevitable disapproval of Shelley's father, already furious over the Oxford fiasco. Harriet accompanied the peripatetic
Shelley from Edinburgh to York to Keswick to
Dublin. When his pamphleteering and speechmaking among the Irish failed to stir their zeal for freedom, Shelley and Harriet moved temporarily to
Wales and then to Lynmouth, Devon, where his political agitation brought him under government surveillance. In September of 1812, after a short return to Wales, Shelley, just turned twenty, traveled
with his young wife back to London.

Life's Work

Shelley's purpose in going to London was to raise
funds for a Welsh land-reclamation project, but its

more important consequence was the formation of friendships with the publisher Thomas Hookham, who would soon print Shelley's first important poem, *Queen Mab: A Philosophical Poem* (1813), the poet Thomas Love Peacock, who would eventually inspire the brilliant "A Defence of Poetry," and the political philosopher William Godwin. Godwin, with whom Shelley had been corresponding since January, was the writer of *An Inquiry Concerning the Principles of Political Justice* (1793), the primary source of Shelley's egalitarian political thought.

After another short stay in Wales, during which much of *Queen Mab* was written and an attempt made on Shelley's life by a mysterious assailant, the Shelleys moved again to Ireland and from there back to London, where *Queen Mab* was printed—for private circulation among England's political radicals—in May of 1813. Heavily influenced by Godwinism, the poem attacks monarchy, capitalism, marriage, and other aspects of European civilization as Shelley knew it with a fervor which discouraged public distribution of the poem in reactionary England. In fact, when an unauthorized edition of the poem was released in 1821, its publisher was quickly imprisoned for his temerity.

The years immediately following the printing of *Queen Mab* were a period of chaos in Shelley's personal life, and for this reason, they were comparatively less productive than the extraordinary times still to come. Gradually realizing his incompatibility with Harriet, who had borne him a daughter in June of 1813 and would bear him a son in November of 1814, Shelley fell in love with the brilliant young Mary Godwin, much to the consternation of her generally freethinking father. The couple fled to France in July of 1814, returning to England in September. The scandal inspired by their elopement and by the birth of their daughter in February of 1815, a child who died within a month, increased their ostracism from respectable English society.

Sir Bysshe Shelley, the poet's grandfather, died in early January of 1815, and in June, Timothy Shelley, almost certainly to minimize complications in the transfer of estate properties, granted the wayward Percy a one-thousand-pound yearly allowance, twenty percent of which was to go to Harriet. Freed at last from severe financial problems, Percy and Mary rented accommodations in the vicinity of Bishopsgate, where Shelley worked intensely on *Alastor: Or The Spirit of Solitude, and*

Other Poems. When it appeared in February of 1816, a few days after the birth to Mary of William Shelley, the book included its author's name, the first of Shelley's works to do so. Its title poem is a symbolic narrative of a young poet's destruction when he undertakes an impossible quest for a self-generated ideal. The poem seems at least partially to be a warning to the idealistic Shelley himself.

Mary and Percy, along with Mary's half sister Claire Clairmont, began their second trip to the Continent in May of 1816. They arrived at Lake Geneva soon thereafter, where they hoped to encounter Lord Byron, with whom Claire had recently become involved and whose daughter, Allegra, she would bear in the following year. Despite the clash between Byron's dark cynicism and Shelley's customary idealism, the two poets got on well together, and while the Alps were inspiring Byron's gloomy *The Prisoner of Chillon* and portions of *Childe Harold's Pilgrimage* (1812-1818), Shelley was composing the "Hymn to Intellectual Beauty" and *Mont Blanc* (1817). Suggesting a transformed Wordsworthianism, Shelley's two poems imply a nonanthropomorphic something whose power lies behind all things but who can be known only indirectly through one's own power of creative intellect.

Following the Shelleys' return to England on September 8, 1816, two tragedies occurred which haunted the poet for the remainder of his life. On October 9, Fanny Imlay, another of Mary's half sisters, took a fatal dose of laudanum, and on November 9, Harriet jumped into the Serpentine. Her body was recovered on December 10. Percy and Mary were married on December 30, but this attempt to make their relationship socially acceptable failed. Shelley was declared an unsuitable father for his two children, and their care was entrusted to a Dr. and Mrs. Hume.

Despite the emotional trauma of this period, Shelley became acquainted with Leigh Hunt, liberal editor of *The Examiner*, literary parodist Horace Smith, essayist Charles Lamb, critic William Hazlitt, and poet John Keats. He also achieved a reconciliation of sorts with his father-in-law, Godwin. His London friends, new and old, provided ample companionship for the Shelleys during visits to their latest home, this time in Great Marlowe, where they lived from February of 1817 until February of the following year and where their daughter Clara was born on September 2. Nor did they neglect their writing. While Mary completed *Frankenstein* (1818), inspired by an evening of ghost stories at Byron's villa on Lake Geneva the previous August, Percy wrote two political tracts, *A Proposal for Putting Reform to the Vote Throughout the Kingdom* (1817) and *An Address to the People on the Death of the Princess Charlotte* (1817?), as well as the longest of his poems, *The Revolt of Islam* (1818). Originally published as *Laon and Cynthia* (1817), *The Revolt of Islam* tells the story of a revolution carried out without malice and eventually defeated by the ruthless reactionary forces of oppression. The poem implies, as does much of Shelley's work, that the task of reforming the world will meet with many temporary defeats before its final triumph and that true revolutionaries must operate out of a spirit of love rather than a spirit of hatred, even if death is the reward of such virtue.

On March 11, 1818, the Shelleys left England for the third time, an exile from which the poet would never return. After traveling overland to Milan, Shelley corresponded tactfully with Lord Byron about Byron's infant daughter Allegra, but the aristocratic poet, involved in a period of monumental debauchery in Venice and wanting to avoid

Claire at all costs, refused to claim his daughter. He eventually agreed to take her from the hands of her nurse Elise, but the hopes of Claire and the Shelleys that Allegra would win her father over and become a beloved member of the Byron family were never realized. She would die of typhus on April 20, 1822, in a convent nursery near Ravenna, Italy, where Byron had placed her.

After leaving Milan, the Shelleys took up residence in Leghorn for a month, followed by a two-month stay in the Appenines. Percy was working on a translation of Plato's *Symposium* at about this time and was completing *Rosalind and Helen* (1819), a poetic narrative of the trials and triumphs of love. A reunion of Shelley and Byron at Venice in late summer provided material for *Julian and Maddalo: A Conversation* (1824), primarily a poetic dialogue between a Shelleyan idealist and a Byronic cynic. Most of the poem was written at a villa in Este lent to the Shelleys by Byron, as were much of the "Lines Written Among the Euganean Hills," a topographic poem about personal and social regeneration, and the first act of Shelley's great poetic drama *Prometheus Unbound* (1820). *Prometheus Unbound* was ultimately to become Shelley's deepest statement on the transforming power of love and forgiveness in a world dominated by vengeful hatred.

Shelley himself was in need of forgiveness during the Este period. Having been forced by a lie to Byron to ask Mary to make a precipitate journey to Este, Shelley inadvertently caused the death of his frail daughter Clara, barely a year old. Under the stress of travel, Clara developed dysentery and died at Venice on September 24, 1818. The grief-stricken Mary never entirely forgot this apparent lapse in her husband's concern for his family's welfare.

On November 5, 1818, the Shelleys left Este and, after visiting Rome, lived for several weeks in Naples. They then returned to Rome, where Shelley wrote the second and third acts of *Prometheus Unbound* and began *The Cenci* (1819), which he finished in August at Leghorn. If *Prometheus Unbound* is Shelley's profoundest statement on the power of love to save and purify, *The Cenci*, a drama influenced by Jacobean tragedy, is his strongest delineation of the power of hatred to corrupt. The play narrates the downfall of Beatrice Cenci, whose participation in a plot to kill the father who has raped her destroys her soul in a way that her father's crime alone could never have done.

The move to Leghorn during the composition of *The Cenci*, at least partially a reaction to the latest unhappy episode in the Shelleys' lives, the death of their son William in Rome on June 7, 1819, also produced *The Masque of Anarchy*, an allegory of political oppression inspired by the slaughter of peaceful demonstrators for reform in Manchester on August 16, 1819, the infamous Peterloo Massacre. Although intended for quick publication in Leigh Hunt's *The Examiner*, the poem was so volatile that it was not presented to the public until 1832.

From Leghorn, the restless Shelleys moved to Florence, settling in during October of 1819. On November 12, Mary gave birth to Percy Florence Shelley, her only child to survive to adulthood. Also at Florence, Percy finished *Peter Bell the Third*, a Wordsworthian parody which remained unpublished until 1839, and the final act of *Prometheus Unbound*. Eventually published in the *Prometheus Unbound* volume was another of the poems of the Florence period, the magnificent "Ode to the West Wind," Shelley's visionary statement of the revolutionary's faith that a new and better world will arise when a corrupt world falls into ruin.

The Shelleys' next move was to Pisa, where they lived during much of the first half of 1820. They then spent several weeks of the summer at Leghorn, moving from there to the Baths of San Giuliano and returning to Pisa on October 31. The poems of this period include several more of those which appeared in the *Prometheus Unbound* volume, among them "The Sensitive Plant," "The Cloud," and "To a Skylark." All three poems explore man's mingled compatibility and incompatibility with the sublunary natural world. Two other products of 1820 were *Oedipus Tyrannus: Or, Swellfoot the Tyrant*, a farcical drama satirizing contemporary English politics, and *The Witch of Atlas*, a seriocomic allegory of the presence of divine beauty in the realm of mutability. *Oedipus Tyrannus* was anonymously published in 1820 and was immediately suppressed, while *The Witch of Atlas* appeared in the *Posthumous Poems of Percy Bysshe Shelley* (1824).

The last two years of Shelley's life, spent mainly at Pisa, were among his most productive. Buoyed by the companionship of such friends as Thomas Medwin, Edward and Jane Williams, Lord Byron, and Edward Trelawny, all members at one time or another of the famous Pisan Circle, Shelley wrote both inspired poetry and inspired prose. In January and February of 1821, after visiting Teresa Viviani in the Convent of St. Anna, where her father had sent her until he could find her an appropriate husband, Shelley composed *Epipsychidion* (1821), a poem of the psyche's yearning for its ideal mate. The poem was published anonymously in May of 1821. In February and March of the same year, in answer to Thomas Love Peacock's "The Four Ages of Poetry," Shelley wrote "A Defence of Poetry," an eloquent essay on the poet's function as prophetic visionary, a work which unfortunately did not appear in print until 1840. In May and June, after hearing of the death of Keats, he produced *Adonais: An Elegy on the Death of John Keats* (1821), among the finest of all English elegies and a passionate affirmation of the immortality of artistic genius. In October, he wrote *Hellas: A Lyrical Drama*, a poetic drama inspired by the War of Greek Independence and dedicated to Prince Alexander Mavrocordato, a Pisan friend who had left to fight on the side of the revolutionaries. Published in February of 1822, *Hellas* was the last of Shelley's works to appear during his lifetime.

In the final months before his death, Shelley was working on the drama *Charles the First* (1824) and on the dark dream vision *The Triumph of Life* (1824). He finished neither. Occupying many of his hours during this period, too, was a daredevil fascination with sailing. Many of his poems include comparisons of the imaginative soul to a boat moving across an expansive sea, and though Shelley had never learned to swim, the dangerous freedom of the open ocean possessed an irresistible appeal for him. With a cabin boy, Charles Vivian, and his friend Edward Williams, Shelley set sail during threatening weather on July 8, 1822, for San Terenzo from Leghorn in his new boat the *Don Juan*. The bodies of the three washed ashore several days later. Shelley was not yet thirty years old.

Summary

Shelley was a poet for whom the millennial promise of the French Revolution had not been realized but might still be achieved. He despised the reactionary politics of the postrevolutionary period and worked tirelessly to inspire that transformation of the human soul which might prepare the way for the era of freedom, peace, and love which he so deeply desired. He saw the poet as reforming prophet, capable of energizing the human spirit by giving it glimpses of perfect, eternal truth. He yearned for the ideal and desperately hoped for the salvation of the mundane. Since his death in Italy at age twenty-nine, he has been the symbolic embodiment of youthful rebellion and unvanquished benevolence for generations of liberal reformers, and though they have not produced a world equal to his vision of a new Golden Age, they have achieved, often under his direct influence, some of his most cherished goals.

Bibliography

Baker, Carlos. *Shelley's Major Poetry: The Fabric of a Vision*. London: Oxford University Press, and Princeton, N.J.: Princeton University Press, 1948. A pioneering and eminently successful attempt to present a unified reading of Shelley's most important poems. Weaving intellectual biography together with extensive analyses of individual works, Baker treats Shelley as a philosophical visionary.

Blunden, Edmund. *Shelley: A Life Story*. London: Collins, 1946; New York: Viking Press, 1947. A readable, intelligent biography of medium length. Excellent for gaining an understanding of the historical context of Shelley's life and work.

Bonca, Terri C. *Shelley's Mirrors of Love: Narcissism, Sacrifice and Sorority*. Albany: State University of New York Press, 1998. A comprehensive, psychobiographical analysis of Shelley's problems with gender identity and narcissism.

Curran, Stuart. "Percy Bysshe Shelley." In *The English Romantic Poets: A Review of Research and Criticism*, edited by Frank Jordan. 4th ed. New York: Modern Language Association of America, 1985. A description and evaluation of scholarly work on Shelley. A standard source for any serious student of the poet.

————. *Shelley's Annus Mirabilis: The Maturing of an Epic Vision*. San Marino, Calif.: Huntington Library, 1975. A discussion by one of the century's foremost Shelley scholars of the writings produced from late 1818 to early 1820. Curran's premise is that Shelley fully embraced the vocation of poet during this key period and dedicated himself to the arduous task of creating a poetic vision worthy of standing beside those of the epic visionaries of the past. The breadth of Shelley's sources is voluminously documented.

Reiman, Donald H. *Percy Bysshe Shelley*. London: Macmillan, and New York: Twayne, 1969. An excellent condensed analysis of Shelley's life and writings. Includes a useful three-page chronology of major events and a six-page selected bibliography. Especially worthwhile for the beginning student.

Shelley, Percy Bysshe. *Shelley's Poetry and Prose: Authoritative Texts and Criticism*. Edited by Donald H. Reiman and Sharon B. Powers. New York: Norton, 1977. Authoritatively edited texts of nearly all Shelley's important works, with informative notes and a generous selection of essays by the critics.

Wasserman, Earl R. *Shelley: A Critical Reading*. Baltimore: Johns Hopkins University Press, 1971. A book of uneven brilliance which lacks the unity and consistency of Baker's volume but is highly original and strongly recommended for the advanced student looking for intellectual challenge.

White, Newman Ivey. *Shelley*. 2 vols. New York: Knopf, 1940; London: Secker and Warburg, 1947. Despite its date of publication, this compendiously detailed study remains the standard scholarly biography. Extensively endnoted and indexed.

Robert H. O'Connor

WILLIAM TECUMSEH SHERMAN

Born: February 8, 1820; Lancaster, Ohio
Died: February 14, 1891; New York, New York
Area of Achievement: The military
Contribution: One of the architects of the Union victory in the Civil War and a father of modern warfare, Sherman was also a leader in the nation's late nineteenth century Indian wars in the West.

Early Life

Tecumseh Sherman was born February 8, 1820, in Lancaster, Ohio. His father, Charles R. Sherman, was a lawyer and Ohio Supreme Court justice. His mother, Mary Hoyt, was a graduate of an Eastern school for women. They migrated from Connecticut to Ohio in 1811 and produced there a family of eleven children, including later senator and cabinet member, John Sherman. Tecumseh (Cump) was their sixth child.

When Tecumseh was nine years old, his father died suddenly, and his family was broken up. He was taken up the street to live with the family of Thomas Ewing, later United States senator and cabinet member. There he was baptized in the Catholic Church and received the Christian name, William, to go with his Indian one. From then onward, he was William Tecumseh Sherman. Ewing never adopted him, but he always treated him like a son.

Sherman had a happy childhood, enjoying his friends and relatives and often participating in innocent pranks. He received the best education Lancaster had to offer and, at the age of sixteen, Ewing arranged a West Point appointment for him. Sherman endured the military academy boredom and was graduated sixth in his 1840 class.

During these early years, Sherman came to admire his foster father and adopt many of his Whig Party attitudes. At the same time, he always felt a need to prove himself capable of survival without Ewing's help. At West Point, he accepted the aristocratic concept of the superiority of the professional soldier over the volunteer. Sherman came to view his military friends as his family and throughout his life always felt most comfortable around them.

Upon graduation, Sherman received a commission in the artillery and assignment to Florida, where he participated in the Second Seminole War. Though combat was rare, he came to see the Indi-

ans at first hand and developed the mixture of admiration and repugnance toward them that he was to hold all of his life. In March, 1842, he was sent to Fort Morgan, in Mobile Bay, where he first experienced the pleasures of polite society. His June 1, 1842, transfer to Fort Moultrie, near Charleston, allowed him to continue his socializing, of which he soon tired. For four years, he lived a boring existence, brightened only by his passion for painting, a furlough back to Ohio highlighted by his first trip down the Mississippi River, and investigative duty in the area of his later march on Atlanta. He also became engaged to Ellen Ewing, his foster sister, with whom he had corresponded since his 1836 departure for West Point. Sherman never painted much after he left Fort Moultrie in South Carolina, but all these other experiences were to have a profound effect on his later life.

When the Mexican War erupted, Sherman hoped to participate in the fighting. He was instead sent to Pittsburgh on recruiting duty. He chafed under his bad luck and jumped at the chance to travel around the Horn to California. By the time he arrived, however, the war there was over, and he found himself adjutant to Colonel Richard B. Mason, spending long hours battling correspondence, not Mexicans. He became very depressed. The 1849 discovery of gold provided him with new excitement, and he absorbed all he could of the gold fever, though the inflation almost ruined him. In 1850, he was sent East with messages for General Winfield Scott, and on May 1 he married Ellen Ewing. Their wedding was an important Washington social event, as Thomas Ewing was then a member of President Zachary Taylor's cabinet.

During the decade of the 1850's, Sherman fathered six children and tried unsuccessfully to support them. From 1850 to 1853, he served in the Army Commissary Service in St. Louis and New Orleans, at which time he resigned his commission to open a branch bank in San Francisco for some St. Louis friends. The pressures of banking in the boom and bust California economy, his chronic asthma, and a homesick wife who wanted to return to her father's house caused Sherman to spend the years from 1853 to 1857 in recurring depression. When the bank closed in 1857, he took on as personal debts the unsuccessful investments he had made for army friends. He carried that financial burden to New York, where he opened another

branch bank only to see it fail during the Panic of 1857. He was crushed; no matter what he tried, he met failure. Instead of establishing independence from his foster father, he repeatedly had to look to him for support. Thomas Ewing continued to hope that Sherman would agree to manage his salt interests in Ohio, but Sherman refused. Instead, he went to Kansas as part of a law and real estate business, along with two Ewing sons.

The business failed, and Sherman desperately tried to return to the army for his economic (and psychological) salvation. There were no openings, but an officer friend told him about a new Louisiana military seminary looking for a superintendent. Sherman applied and became founding father of what became modern Louisiana State University. When secession came, duty convinced him he had to leave the job and the people he had come to love. He believed that he had to sacrifice his economic well-being for the sake of the Union.

Life's Work

After leaving Louisiana in February, 1861, Sherman became angry over alleged Northern nonchalance toward Southern secession. He found a position with a St. Louis street railway company, determined to remain aloof from the national crisis until he could see a change. Thomas Ewing and John Sherman urged him to reenter the Union army, and, through their efforts, he was named a colonel of the Thirteenth Infantry Regiment in May, 1861. He stood over six feet tall, with long legs and arms, piercing blue eyes, sandy red hair that seemed always to be mussed, a grizzly reddish beard, and a generally unkempt appearance. He spoke rapidly and often, his mind able to reach conclusions before his charmed listeners understood his premises.

Before he could serve with the Thirteenth Infantry, he was appointed to a staff position under Winfield Scott and, in July, 1861, commanded a brigade at Bull Run. He saw that fiasco as further proof that the North was not taking the war seriously enough.

He was happy to leave chaotic Washington for Kentucky to help Fort Sumter hero Robert Anderson organize the Union war effort there. Upon arrival, he quickly convinced himself that the Confederate forces were much larger than his were and that it was only a matter of time before they would overrun him. He sank into depression and lashed out at newspaper reporters for allegedly publicizing his weaknesses. At his own request, he was transferred to Missouri in November, 1861, where his outspoken negativity convinced many that he was unbalanced. He took a twenty-day leave in December, 1861, and was mortified to see his sanity unfairly questioned in the press. When he returned to duty and was given command over a training facility in Missouri, his depression deepened and he even contemplated suicide. The Union war effort and his own career seemed hopeless.

His transfer to Paducah, Kentucky, in February, 1862, and his association with the successful Ulysses S. Grant slowly lifted his spirits. He distinguished himself as a division commander in the bloody battle of Shiloh in April, 1862, and he then defended Grant and other generals against press and political criticism of their roles in the battle. When he was promoted to major general of volunteers and took part in Henry W. Halleck's capture of Corinth in May, 1862, he began to believe that the Union effort had hope and he could play an important role in any success.

In July, 1862, Grant appointed Sherman to the post of military governor of recently captured Memphis. Sherman was able to use both his banking and military experience to govern that hotbed of secession sentiment. It was there that the activities of Confederate guerrillas caused him to see at first hand that the war was not simply a contest between professional soldiers. The general populace had to be controlled if the Union effort was to be successful. When guerrillas fired on a boat in the Mississippi River, Sherman leveled a nearby town. He had long recognized the determination of the Southern populace, and he now began to see that only a destruction of this stubborn intensity would resolve the conflict in the Union's favor. He would utilize this insight at the appropriate time.

In December, 1862, Sherman led an unsuccessful assault on the heights above Vicksburg. When the press resuscitated the insanity charge against him, he court-martialed a reporter, the only such event in American history. The trial, though it might have been an excellent exposition of the inevitable conflict between the military and the press in wartime, proved to be little more than a conflict of personality. It settled little.

Sherman was part of Grant's enormous army which captured Vicksburg in July, 1863, and he was made brigadier general in the regular army as a reward. He became commander of the Army of Tennessee when Grant became supreme commander in the West; he participated in the successful November lifting of the Confederate siege at Chattanooga. In January, 1864, he commanded the Meridian, Mississippi, expedition, which showed him yet again the effectiveness of the destructive activity he was later to use during his March to the Sea.

In the spring of 1864, Grant moved East to become general-in-chief of all Union armies, and Sherman took command over Western forces. On May 5, 1864, Grant attacked Lee in Virginia, and Sherman took on Joseph E. Johnston in Georgia. After first organizing railroads to supply his troops, Sherman battled Johnston throughout the spring and summer of 1864, slowly but inexorably pushing the Confederates from the Chattanooga region toward Atlanta. Jefferson Davis became nervous at Johnston's constant retreat and replaced him with offensive-minded John Bell Hood. The new Confederate commander attacked Sherman and was defeated. Atlanta fell in September, in time to influence the reelection of Abraham Lincoln that November.

Sherman then showed the Confederates that war had indeed become total. He ordered the civilian evacuation of Atlanta. When his order was met with shocked protests, he responded: "War is cruelty, and you cannot refine it." He did not: In November, he began his March to the Sea, revolutionizing warfare by cutting himself off from his base of supplies, living off the countryside, and destroying goods and property. His aim was to convince the Confederates that their war effort was doomed. He became the father of psychological warfare. On December 21, 1864, his army reached Savannah and made contact with the Atlantic fleet. His presentation of the Georgia city to Lincoln as a Christmas present electrified the North.

On February 1, 1865, Sherman began his march through the Carolinas. On April 17, Johnston and his Confederate forces surrendered at Durham Station, North Carolina. Sherman, who had retained his affection for Southerners throughout the war and had only conducted his total warfare as the most efficient way to end the hostilities quickly, demonstrated his feelings in the peace agreement he made with Johnston. He negotiated political matters, neglected to insist that slavery was over, and, in general, wrote an agreement very favorable to the South. In Washington, the Administration, just then reeling from the assassination of Lincoln, was shocked. Secretary of War Edwin Stanton and

General Henry W. Halleck led the opposition to the agreement, and Sherman was forced to change it, suffering sharp criticism from both the public and the press.

With the war over, Sherman became commander of troops in the West. He fought the Indians and helped construct the transcontinental railroad. When Grant became president in 1869, Sherman became commanding general, a position he held until his retirement in 1883. His tenure was filled with controversy as he battled secretaries of war and Congress over his authority, his salary, and sufficient appropriation for the troops. When he published his memoirs in 1875, the blunt directness of those two volumes created a controversy, including a bitter exchange with Jefferson Davis.

From his retirement in 1883 until his death in 1891, Sherman kept busy attending veterans' reunions and the theater, while also becoming a popular after-dinner speaker. In 1884, he categorically refused to run for the presidency, establishing a standard which allegedly reluctant office seekers have been measured against ever since. In 1886, he and his family moved from St. Louis to New York. On February 14, 1891, he died from pneumonia.

Summary

William Tecumseh Sherman was one of the leaders of the successful Union war effort that prevented the disruption of the United States. He helped introduce the nation and the world to the concept of total war, his Civil War activities serving as a harbinger of the kind of conflict to be fought in the twentieth century. He devised his mode of warfare as a way to end the hostilities quickly, but it helped prolong Southern animosity toward the North into the twentieth century. Still, when Sherman toured the South in 1879, he received a friendly greeting.

Sherman's life, apart from his Civil War years, is important in itself. Before the war, he attended West Point with many of the other military leaders of the Mexican and Civil wars. He served in the army in Florida during the Second Seminole War. In California, he composed a report to President James K. Polk which announced the discovery of gold and helped set off the famous Gold Rush of 1849. During the 1850's, as a banker, he was one of San Francisco's leading businessmen during its formative years. In 1860, he helped found what is modern Louisiana State University. After the war, Sherman's tenure as general-in-chief of the United States Army from 1869 to

1883 allowed him to influence the direction of such events as the Indian Wars, Reconstruction, and the disputed election of 1876. Thus, Sherman influenced the development of American society throughout his life. He was one of the major figures of the nineteenth century.

Bibliography

Athearn, Robert G. *William Tecumseh Sherman and the Settlement of the West*. Norman: University of Oklahoma Press, 1956. A thorough study of Sherman's participation in the postwar Indian troubles and his role in the construction of the transcontinental railroad. Sherman was neither as harsh toward the Indians as the West desired nor as lenient as the East wished. He believed that the completion of the railroad would force the hostile Indians onto reservations.

Barrett, John G. *Sherman's March Through the Carolinas*. Chapel Hill: University of North Carolina Press, 1956. A detailed military history of Sherman's final campaign through North and South Carolina. Sherman reluctantly put his concept of total war into practice during this march from Savannah, Georgia, to Raleigh, North Carolina. His army inflicted special punishment on South Carolina because the soldiers blamed the Palmetto State for starting the war.

Castel, Albert. "Prevaricating through Georgia: Sherman's 'Memoirs' as a Source on the Atlanta Campaign." *Civil War History* 40, no. 1 (March, 1994). Discusses the major and minor discrepancies between Sherman's personal memoirs (his 1875 book about his service in the Civil War) and the "Official Records of the Union and Confederate Armies."

Glatthaar, Joseph T. *The March to the Sea and Beyond: Sherman's Troops in the Savannah and Carolinas Campaigns*. New York: New York University Press, 1985. An excellent analysis of the makeup and attitudes of the common soldier in Sherman's army during his marches. The author analyzes the soldiers' views about their cause, black Southerners, white Southerners, camp life, and pillaging.

Hirshson, Stanley P. *The White Tecumseh: A Biography of General William T. Sherman*. New York: Wiley, 1997. In the first Sherman biography to employ regimental histories, Hirshson provides a view of Sherman from the perspective of the men who served under him. The book presents Sherman in a sympathetic light and places more emphasis on Sherman's battles than previous biographies.

Lewis, Lloyd. *Sherman: Fighting Prophet*. New York: Harcourt Brace, 1932. Though dated and written without the benefit of all the now available Sherman documentation, this is still a valuable and very readable biography. It puts special emphasis on Thomas Ewing's influence on his foster son. The vast bulk of the book details the Civil War years, and coverage of the postwar years is unfortunately brief.

Liddell Hart, Basil H. *Sherman: Soldier, Realist, American*. New York: Dodd, Mead, 1929; London: Stevens, 1959. A fine study of Sherman's Civil War military activities by a leading military historian. The author states that Sherman was far ahead of his time and that later generations of military men might have profited from his example had they paid attention.

Marszalek, John F. "Celebrity in Dixie: Sherman Tours the South, 1879." *The Georgia Historical Quarterly* 46 (Fall, 1982): 368-383. An account of Sherman's postwar tour through most of the sites of his Civil War battles. The author finds that Sherman received a warm response in Atlanta, New Orleans, and everywhere else he went in the South.

————. *Sherman's Other War: The General and the Civil War Press*. Rev. ed. Kent, Ohio: Kent State University Press, 1998. A thorough account of Sherman's battles with reporters during the war, this study also contains an extended analysis of his personality during this period. Argues that Sherman fought the press in a constitutional battle formed more by personality than by First Amendment principles.

Merrill, James M. *William Tecumseh Sherman*. Chicago: Rand McNally, 1971. A detailed popular biography which has the benefit of the major Sherman manuscript collections. It discusses all aspects of Sherman's life but is especially valuable for its coverage of his postwar years.

Sherman, William T. *Memoirs of General William T. Sherman*, 2 vols. New York: Appleton, and London: King, 1875. Sherman's controversial and absorbing account of his life from 1846 to the end of the Civil War. This is an essential source for gaining an understanding of Sherman's perception of the battles in which he participated and the leaders with and against whom he fought.

John F. Marszalek

HENRY SIDGWICK

Born: May 31, 1838; Skipton, Yorkshire, England

Died: August 28, 1900; Cambridge, Cambridgeshire, England

Areas of Achievement: Philosophy and education

Contribution: A proponent of higher education for women and an advocate of research into paranormal phenomena, Sidgwick attempted in philosophy to reconcile an intuitive approach to morality with that of utilitarianism. His reasoned defense of the resulting ethical method produced one of the most significant works on ethics in English, the capstone of nineteenth century British moral philosophy.

Early Life

Henry Sidgwick was born on May 31, 1838, the son of William and Mary (Crofts) Sidgwick, both from northern England. His father, an Anglican clergyman and headmaster of the Skipton, Yorkshire, grammar school, died in 1841. Henry's early life was characterized by frequent moves (which apparently brought on a kind of stammer which never left him), but in 1852 Henry was sent to Rugby School; the rest of the family, his mother and three other surviving children, settled in Rugby the following year.

Sidgwick was strongly influenced in his early life by one of his Rugby masters, Edward White Benson, a cousin nine years older than he. Benson soon joined the Sidgwick household; he would later marry Sidgwick's sister, Mary, and would be the Archbishop of Canterbury from 1883 until the year of his death. The precocious Henry came to idolize his cousin and followed his advice by enrolling at Trinity College, Cambridge, after his graduation from Rugby in 1855. Cambridge was to be his home for the rest of his life.

Sidgwick's early university experience brought a host of academic awards, and as an undergraduate he was elected to the Apostles Society. The Apostles were dedicated to the pursuit of truth, wherever it might be found, and Sidgwick found himself taken by the spirit of honest inquiry into religion, society, and philosophy. He would devote his life to the great philosophical questions, seeking always for honesty and truth to triumph over rhetoric. Indeed, Sidgwick's writing is characterized by a kind of zealous balance, the author being at pains to give each aspect of an argument or counterargument its due.

Some readers of Sidgwick have taken this balancing effort as a fault and have yearned for the simple dogmatic statement which Sidgwick was loathe to make. He was not a system builder in philosophy; his was the task of honest elucidation and tentative judgment.

In curious contrast to the stodgy feel of his major works, Sidgwick the man was a witty conversationalist (using his stammer at times as a dramatic device) and a lover of poetry. Small in stature, his large silken beard flapping in the breeze as he ran along the streets of Cambridge to his lectures, he was vigorous, sturdy, and good-humored. The academic life suited him perfectly.

Life's Work

Sidgwick was twenty-one in 1859. In that year, his sister married Edward Benson; Henry himself was elected a fellow of Trinity and appointed to an assistant tutorship in classics and thus began his career as a teacher and writer. It was a time of ferment in the intellectual world; that same year, *On the Origin of Species* by Charles Darwin first saw publication, as did *On Liberty* by John Stuart Mill. Mill became a major influence on Sidgwick, though the two often took differing philosophical positions. Through his contact with the Apostles, Sidgwick became convinced that the truth of Christianity was an open question. The influence of Benson's Anglican orthodoxy had begun to wane.

Sidgwick did not lightly dismiss the Christian story, yet even an intense study of the ancient Semitic texts left him unsatisfied. He realized that he was dealing with philosophical issues: If the miracle stories from the Scriptures were true, then reports of miracles from all ages must be considered, but then the accuracy of science itself (which admits of no supernatural interventions in its descriptions of the regularities of the world) is called into question. It appeared to Sidgwick that the probability of a real miracle was much less than the likelihood that witnesses were erroneous, untruthful, or credulous. "I still hunger and thirst after orthodoxy," he wrote, "but I am, I trust, firm not to barter my intellectual birthright for a mess of mystical pottage." Yet Sidgwick, never given to fanaticism, produced no anti-Christian propaganda. He recognized the value of the faith for others, but honesty compelled him to a skeptical view of

Christianity. He would wrestle with the idea of theism for the rest of his life.

Sidgwick's honesty became a cause célèbre in 1869 when he resigned his Fellowship at Cambridge rather than continue to subscribe to the Thirty-nine Articles of the Church of England, which was required by law for the post. Though by 1869 affirmation of the Anglican doctrines was an empty formality in academic circles, it is characteristic of Sidgwick that he took the matter seriously. It is further a recognition of his abilities as an instructor that, far from being relieved of his duties, Sidgwick was appointed to a special post at Cambridge that did not require doctrinal subscription and reappointed as a fellow when such tests were abolished in 1871. In 1872, he was passed over for the Knightsbridge Professorship of Moral Philosophy but was elected to the post in 1883 after the death of the incumbent. Sidgwick continued teaching at Cambridge, in one post or another, until his death, with only occasional lectures elsewhere. (Several collections of his lectures were published posthumously.)

Sidgwick began his academic duties as a lecturer in the classics, but his interests soon encompassed moral and political philosophy, economics, and epistemology. His most enduring contribution came in *The Methods of Ethics*, first published in 1874, which ran to seven editions (the last, published after his death, came in 1907).

The Methods of Ethics does not seek to build a theoretical system of ethics but rather to discover if some coherence can be brought to the moral judgments actually made by men and women and if two apparently conflicting sources of moral imperatives can be reconciled. One source, intuitionism, was exemplified by the "common sense" philosophy of Thomas Reid, who made conscience the self-evident supreme authority in moral choices, and William Whewell, who allowed for a progressive intuition of moral concepts. Ethics must be based on principles derived by reason (the so-called moral faculty) and not on some calculation of the consequences of an action. This, the second source, is utilitarianism (or "universal hedonism"), which calls those actions right which produce the greatest happiness for the greatest number. Its varied exemplars included William Paley, who disavowed some inherent moral sense, Jeremy Bentham, associated with political reform movements and a secular approach to ethics, and John Stuart Mill, who depre-

cated intuitionism as merely the consecration of deep-seated prejudices.

Sidgwick agreed with the intuitionists that the common moral judgments of mankind could only be ordered by some self-evident first principle, but he attempted to demonstrate that this first principle was none other than the utilitarian dictum. Thus, moral choices are actually made on the basis of the self-evident principle of maximizing the good. Yet there were really two kinds of utilitarianism: universal hedonism (or rational benevolence), which strived to maximize the universal, or societal, good, and egoism (or prudence), which strived for maximizing the agent's good. When these two forms of utilitarianism are in conflict (when, for example, an agent must choose to save either himself or his fellows), can a rational choice be made between them? Is it possible to determine the cases in which egoism should take precedence over altruism?

For Sidgwick the answer was no. Without bringing in additional assumptions (for example, that God exists and will ultimately reward the altruistic choice), it is impossible to pronounce egoism or altruism the more rational way. Sidgwick was left with a kind of fundamental dualism of the practical reason, needing some cosmic postulate in which to ground ethical choice. Yet God's existence is far from self-evident, and the mere desire that virtue be rewarded is not proof that it will be. Here *The Methods of Ethics* concludes, leaving for others the task of placing ethics in a larger context and so avoiding Sidgwick's dilemma.

Sidgwick's interest in psychic phenomena paralleled his quest for some evidence that might justify belief in another realm of existence and so provide the "cosmic postulate" for practical ethics. He had become interested in the paranormal when he was twenty-one; in 1882, in response to a sustained fascination with the subject, Sidgwick became the first president of the newly formed Society for Psychical Research. Though he would often observe purported mind readers or those with "second sight," Sidgwick's greatest contribution was in validating the very existence of such an organization. As he put it, "My highest ambition in psychical research is to produce evidence which will drive my opponents to doubt my honesty or veracity."

Sidgwick married Eleanor Mildred Balfour, the sister of Arthur James Balfour, in 1876; as a couple, they became deeply involved in probing supposed psychic events. Eleanor was perhaps the more credulous; she was convinced that telepathy was a reality, while her husband was never quite certain.

Sidgwick was certain that speculative philosophy did not excuse him from practical responsibilities. He had long been interested in the education of women and, after reading *On the Subjection of Women* (1869) by Mill, laid plans for giving university lectures to women. Victorian thought generally assumed women were by nature unable to reach higher learning, but Sidgwick eventually saw the opening of Newnham Hall for Women, as part of Cambridge, in the year of his marriage. In 1892, Eleanor Sidgwick became president of the college. Childless, the Sidgwicks lived there the rest of their lives.

Sidgwick was a prolific writer. An essay for the *Encyclopaedia Britannica* in 1878 was issued in 1886 as *Outline of the History of Ethics*. In 1883, he published *Principles of Political Economy*; *Elements of Politics* followed in 1891. His life was terminated by cancer on August 28, 1900. He had requested that these words should accompany the simple burial service: "Let us commend to the love of God with silent prayer the soul of a sinful man who partly tried to do his duty."

Summary

Henry Sidgwick believed he had failed to develop a coherent ethics without reliance on some cosmic postulate that would guarantee a reward for the selfless. Others would attempt to place ethics within the context of evolutionary thought, and still others would ground ethics on metaphysics (idealism, for example). Nevertheless, Sidgwick's masterwork, *The Methods of Ethics*, was a hallmark in Victorian philosophy not for its originality but for its clarity and exquisitely precise exploration of reason in ethical decision making. Sidgwick concluded that reason alone could not resolve the conflict facing beings who had an ego life and at the same time a life in community. He had shown in his history of ethics that the Greek idea of the Good involved both pleasure and virtue (or duty); now the two had become separated, with reason powerless to mediate between individual pleasure and one's duty to society.

Sidgwick has been characterized as the last of the classical utilitarians; in his work he prepared the way for new approaches to ethics by marshaling the data of common sense and articulating how far the principle of universal hedonism could be

taken. He embodied in his life, as well as in his writing, the qualities of caution, good sense, an irenic spirit, balance, and the conviction of the supreme importance of moral choices.

Bibliography

Blanshard, Brand. "Henry Sidgwick." In *Four Reasonable Men*. Middletown, Conn.: Wesleyan University Press, 1984. Popular study of Sidgwick, bordering at times on hagiography, by a rationalist philosopher. Blanshard is impressed by Sidgwick's quiet reasonableness on the printed page and in life.

James, D. G. *Henry Sidgwick: Science and Faith in Victorian England*. London and New York: Oxford University Press, 1971. A short study of Sidgwick, full of prickly observations about his constant uncertainty and incurable irresolution. Part of the Riddell Memorial Lectures series, the volume remains unfinished because of the untimely death of James, formerly the vice chancellor of the University of Southampton. An entire lecture is devoted to Sidgwick and the poet Arthur Hugh Clough.

Schneewind, J. B. *Sidgwick's Ethics and Victorian Moral Philosophy*. Oxford and New York: Clarendon Press, 1977. A major technical study of *The Methods of Ethics*, attempting to place it in the context of Victorian philosophical movements. This volume, which has extensive bibliographies, is useful as a guide to each section of *The Methods of Ethics*. Clearly written, for the most part.

Schultz, Bart, ed. *Essays on Henry Sidgwick*. Cambridge and New York: Cambridge University Press, 1992. A collection of essays by distinguished philosophers reassessing Sidgwick's work as an ethical and political theorist, a historian, and a reformer.

Sidgwick, Arthur, and Eleanor M. Sidgwick. *Henry Sidgwick: A Memoir*. London: Macmillan, 1906. The standard reference for Sidgwick's life, compiled by his brother and Henry's widow. Arranged chronologically, the book contains excerpts from correspondence and diaries and includes a comprehensive bibliography of Sidgwick's writings. The section on Sidgwick as a teacher contains numerous appreciations.

Sidgwick, Henry. *The Methods of Ethics*. 7th ed. London: Macmillan, 1907; Indianapolis, Ind.: Hackett, 1981. Sidgwick's masterwork, complete with analytical table of contents, comprehensive index, and an autobiographical fragment written by Sidgwick later in his life. Difficult to follow for the uninitiated.

————. *Outline of the History of Ethics for English Readers.* London and New York: Macmillan, 1886. The book contains the enlarged text of Sidgwick's original article for the *Encyclopaedia Britannica.* A final chapter on the work of Sidgwick himself has been added by Alban Widgery of Duke University.

Dan Barnett

THE SIEMENS FAMILY

Ernst Werner von Siemens

Born: December 13, 1816; Lenthe, Prussia   *Died:* December 6, 1892; Berlin, Germany

Karl Wilhelm (*later* Sir Charles William) Siemens

Born: April 4, 1823; Lenthe, Prussia   *Died:* November 19, 1883; London, England

Friedrich Siemens

Born: December 8, 1826; Lübeck, Prussia   *Died:* May 24, 1904; Berlin, Germany

Karl von Siemens

Born: March 3, 1829; Lübeck, Prussia   *Died:* March 21, 1906; St. Petersburg, Russia

Areas of Achievement: Invention and technology

Contribution: The four Siemens brothers were notable for their many contributions to applied technology in nineteenth century electrical and steel industries, including telegraphy, the electric dynamo, and the open-hearth steel furnace.

Early Lives

Four brothers among the thirteen children of Christian Ferdinand and Eleonore Deichmann Siemens and many of the brothers' sons became famous as inventors, scientists, and engineers, whose applied technology led to the creation of significant advances in electrical and steel industries, especially in telegraphy, the dynamo, the electric railways, and in the open-hearth steel furnace. Their father was a farm manager of large Prussian estates; he died in 1840, only a year after their mother had died.

The eldest son, Ernst Werner, while serving in the Prussian artillery at the age of twenty-three, assumed the guardianship of his seven younger brothers and successfully guided them into technological schools and profitable positions across nineteenth century Europe. Two brothers and one sister died in childhood; one brother became a farmer; and another became a glass manufacturer. Werner, William (earlier named Karl Wilhelm), Friedrich, and Karl were all born in Prussia (modern West Germany). These four made enormous contributions to modern technology and manufacturing in their lifetimes.

Werner and some of his brothers attended St. Catherine's School in Lübeck. Upon completion of grammar school there, Werner enlisted in the Prussian army in order to enter the Berlin Artillery and Engineering School. Upon graduation in 1837, he was promoted from ensign to second lieutenant in the Third Artillery Brigade and was stationed at Magdeburg. He took William along to study at the Trade and Commerce School there while he continued in the military service. Transferred to Wittenberg in 1840, Werner experimented with electrolysis and succeeded in developing a process for gold plating by galvanic current and was granted a five-year patent for it in 1842. By selling his rights to a jewelry firm, he began a lifelong income from his inventions.

William Siemens emigrated to England in 1843 and became a naturalized citizen in 1859. A prolific inventor, he was granted 113 English patents; as a shrewd businessman, moreover, he accumulated a large fortune. Karl Siemens had studied at Lübeck and at Berlin before joining his brother Werner in his endeavors. He became the most cultivated and diplomatic member of the family, having a keen sense of business management. Werner wrote of him: "Karl was the true connecting link between us four brothers, who indeed differed radically from one another, but were bound together for lifelong common work by an all-abiding fraternal love." Friedrich Siemens had gone to sea from Lübeck in sailing ships but returned to work with Werner and then with William in England. Werner declared him "the born inventor" with a "characteristic of steady, spontaneous, uninfluenced thinking and self-training [which] gave him a peculiarly meditative air and his performances a pronounced originality."

Lives' Work

One of the great technological achievements of the Siemens brothers was the development of instruments and the establishment of international firms under their control for the European and Asian telegraph systems. First to utilize the substance called gutta-percha for covering underground telegraph wires, Werner created a screw press that extruded the substance around the wire while hot and cooled it into a seamless insulated covering that could carry electrical current underground or underwater. Then, he joined forces with a young physical mechanic, Johann Georg Halske, forming the firm of Siemens and Halske in Berlin, to perfect his invention of a self-interrupting dial telegraph instrument. Werner resigned from the military service in 1847, the year of his dial invention, and began manufacturing telegraph cable and equipment to fulfill contracts from Prussia and Russia to lay long lines between key cities, which soon outmoded all optical semaphore systems along military or railroad routes.

By the 1850's, Werner's firm had constructed the line from Berlin to Frankfurt am Main, and that success led to contracts with his brother William to lay submarine cables across the Atlantic, with his brother Karl to lay lines out of St. Petersburg for Russia and to connect the famous London to Calcutta, or Indo-European, telegraph line that opened in 1870. The rare combination of inventive skill, manufacturing capability, and useful diplomatic-political connections enriched the firms of the Siemens brothers and their shareholders.

As the London agent for his brothers' European firm of Siemens and Halske, William spent much of his career advancing the realm of the electric telegraph. In 1874, he laid the first Atlantic cable from England to the United States from a special ship he designed, the *Faraday*. For his distinguished achievements, he won medals at industrial exhibitions and the presidency of many English engineering and metals associations. In 1862, he was elected a Fellow of the Royal Society of London, the oldest scientific society, founded in 1662. In 1883, seven months before his death, he was knighted by Queen Victoria for his services. He had married Anna Gordon in 1859; they had no children, and she died in 1901.

Karl developed the Russian branch of the German firm and directed most of the construction of the international telegraph lines and cables that the family firms won contracts to build. Later, he became a Finnish-Russian citizen in order to do business in Russia; he married and lived in St. Petersburg for many years and was raised to the hereditary Russian nobility in 1895. After Werner's death, Karl became head of Siemens and Halske (Johann Georg Halske withdrew from the partnership in 1867).

Perhaps the most significant invention of the Siemens brothers was the construction of the regener-

Ernst Werner von Siemens

ative furnace for the emerging steel industry. Friedrich pioneered the work of the firm on the application of the regenerative principle into the smelting of steel in conjunction with the French engineer Pierre-Émile Martin to create the famous Siemens-Martin open-hearth furnace. In England in 1856, Sir Henry Bessemer had patented a forced-air process for the smelting of steel; in the United States, William Kelly had devised a "pneumatic process" as early as 1849 but belatedly received an American patent in 1857. Friedrich and William applied their regenerative principle to the smelting furnaces with much larger capacities for molten metal, glass, and special materials. In 1864, in cooperation with Martin, they developed the so-called Siemens-Martin process, which works on the heat-storage principle.

In conventional furnaces, air and the combustible gases are introduced cold into the furnace, and the hot waste gases escape via smokestacks. In the regenerative process, the heat of the waste gases is captured for use in preheating the air and the com-

Sir Charles William Siemens

First adopted for commercial steel manufacture in 1865, by 1896 the tonnage of steel from England's Siemens-Martin furnaces had surpassed the production of all Bessemer furnaces.

A third field of invention and manufacture evolved from Werner's invention of the "dynamo-electric machine," which he demonstrated in 1866. Almost at the same time, Charles Wheatstone in England and Samuel Alfred Varley in France had exhibited similar apparatuses and contested the priority of Werner's claim. Eventually Werner gained recognition when he demonstrated his invention and published an account of the principle behind it. Again, it was the firm of Siemens and Halske that was quickly able to apply the new dynamo into practical applications and then manufacture the electrical apparatus.

Nearly 250 dynamos were manufactured each year by Siemens and Halske in the 1880's. The number reached five hundred by 1892, as street and home lighting came of age, as did electrical motors for streetcars, railways, and factories. Siemens and Halske proceeded to develop the first electric tramway in 1881 in Lichterfelde with an overhead bow collector touching the trolley line. Siemens' arc lamps illuminated the Berlin Potsdamer Platz in 1882; the brothers demonstrated their first electric lift or elevator at the Mannheim Industrial Exhibition in 1880 and in 1892 produced their first electricity meter, called a "saber meter."

Summary

Werner and Sir William Siemens were the outstanding geniuses among the Siemens brothers; Friedrich and Karl Siemens extended the technology developed by the firm of Siemens and Halske into telegraph and electric systems sold, installed, and maintained by the company across the Western world. The family was instrumental in advancing the theoretical and technological fields of nineteenth century electronics with hundreds of patents granted to them and to members of their pioneering firm.

The Siemens brothers were significant leaders in German, English, and Russian enterprises of telegraphy, telephones, and electrical systems that served to promote the advancement of knowledge, the speedy transmission of information, and the shipment of people and material via electrical railways across Europe and Asia. Their several contributions to the manufacturing of steel, copper, and glass into less expensive materials for modern life

bustible gases. Two or four refractory brick chambers are next to the smelting unit, and, in alternating fashion, the hot waste gases are passed through the chambers, which have large thermal storage capacity. Then, valves close and new air and gases are preheated as they are introduced through the hot chambers and fed into the furnace. This process creates much higher temperatures for smelting, permits the use of low-grade gases, and saves on fuel costs.

For twelve years, from 1847 to 1859, William, in England, had tried unsuccessfully to apply this regenerative principle to steam engines. In 1856, Friedrich obtained a patent for the idea of using a waste heat condenser for industrial furnaces. In France, Martin had made steel by wrought iron, or cast iron, in a similar regenerative open-hearth furnace. Martin and the Siemenses combined their efforts in the Siemens-Martin process, which utilized iron ore directly from the mines. Eventually, the open-hearth process became immensely profitable as the recycling of scrap iron was implemented.

immensely contributed to the Industrial Revolution after the great Crystal Palace Exposition of London in 1851, when Siemens and Halske were awarded the Council Medal, the first of hundreds to be won by the brothers.

Bibliography

Derry, T. K., and Trevor I. Williams. *A Short History of Technology from the Earliest Times to A.D. 1900*. Oxford: Clarendon Press, 1960; New York: Oxford University Press, 1961. This text is a sequel to the five-volume *A History of Technology*, begun by Charles Singer. Good coverage of the Industrial Revolution. A chapter entitled "Coal and the Metals" covers developments in the making of inexpensive steel. Comparative tables showing the chronological events of technological achievements in Great Britain, Europe, and the United States along with bibliographies for each chapter enhance this introductory study.

Pole, William. *The Life of Sir William Siemens*. London: Murray, 1888. The authorized biographer of the Siemens brother who had made England his home. It was produced by a popular biography of that era with the help of family and friends, who provided personal papers and recollections.

Siemens, Charles William. *The Scientific Works of C. William Siemens*. 3 vols. Edited by E. F. Bamber. London: Murray, 1889. These papers, including his addresses, lectures, and papers read before scientific societies provide closer detail of his inventions and business ventures.

Siemens, Georg. *History of the House of Siemens*. 2 vols. New York: Arno Press, 1977. This set describes the development of inventions by the various Siemens brothers and the practical applications of them via the business enterprises in Europe and elsewhere. Much of the business story relates the efforts of William and Werner (volume 1). The tragic chapters on the two world wars include the technological advancements in telephony, telegraphy, and electrical fields to the year 1945 (volume 2).

Siemens, Werner von. *Inventor and Entrepreneur: Recollections of Werner von Siemens*. Translated by W. C. Coupland. 2d ed. London: Lund Humphries, 1966; New York: Kelley, 1968. This autobiographical work provides one of the best stories of the gifted Siemens family and modestly relates Werner's own great achievements as inventor and businessman. His story centers on the telegraph and electrical systems that his firm, Siemens and Halske, had established in many nations.

Singer, Charles, et al., eds. *A History of Technology*. Vol. 5, *The Late Nineteenth Century, 1850 to 1900*. Oxford: Clarendon Press, 1954-1958. Although the Bessemer process had pioneered the making of steel, the Siemens-Martin open-hearth method ultimately outproduced it in the twentieth century. This volume presents the most readable introduction of both means of steel manufacturing.

Paul F. Erwin

SITTING BULL
Tatanka Iyotake

Born: March, 1831; near the banks of the Grand River, Dakota Territory

Died: December 15, 1890; Standing Rock Agency, South Dakota

Area of Achievement: American Indian leadership

Contribution: Sitting Bull led his people from their zenith in the middle of the nineteenth century to the decline of their culture in the face of the superior technology and numbers of the whites.

Early Life

Sitting Bull (Tatanka Iyotake) was born in March, 1831, a few miles below the modern town of Bullhead, South Dakota. During his first fourteen years, his Sioux friends called him Slow, a name he earned because of his deliberate manner and the awkward movement of his sturdy body. The youth grew to manhood as a member of the Hunkpapa tribe, one of seven among the Teton Sioux, the westernmost division of the Sioux Confederation. His people thrived as a nomadic hunter-warrior society. As an infant strapped to a baby-board, he was carried by his mother, as the tribe roamed the northern Plains hunting buffalo. At five years, he rode behind his mother on her horse and helped as best he could around the camp. By the age of ten, he rode his own pony, wrapping his legs around the curved belly of the animal (a practice which caused him to be slightly bowlegged for the remainder of his years). He learned to hunt small game with bow and arrows and to gather berries. He reveled in the games and races, swimming and wrestling with the other boys. His was an active and vigorous life, and he loved it.

The warrior dimension of Sioux male life came more into focus as the boy grew. The Tetons concentrated most of their wrath on the Crow and Assiniboin Indians, at first, and the whites, at a later time. The hub of Sioux society centered on gaining prestige through heroic acts in battle. Counting coups by touching an enemy with a highly decorated stick was top priority. The Sioux lad learned his lessons well, and, at age fourteen, he joined a mounted war party. He picked out one of the enemy, and, with a burst of enthusiasm and courage, he charged the rival warrior and struck him with his coup stick. After the battle, word of this heroic deed spread throughout the Hunkpapa village. The

boy had reached a milestone in his development; for the remainder of his life, he enjoyed telling the story of his first coup. Around the campfire that night, his proud father, Jumping Bull, gave his son a new name. He called him Sitting Bull after the beast that the Sioux respected so much for its tenacity. A buffalo bull was the essence of strength, and a "sitting bull" was one that held his ground and could not be pushed aside.

In 1857, Sitting Bull became a chief of the Hunkpapa. He had ably demonstrated his abilities as a warrior, and his common sense and his leadership traits showed promise of a bright future for him. While his physical appearance was commonplace, he was convincing in argument, stubborn, and quick to grasp a situation. These traits gained for him the respect of his people as a warrior and as a statesman.

Life's Work

Sitting Bull's leadership qualities were often put to the test in his dealings with the whites. During the 1860's, he skirmished with the whites along the Powder River in Wyoming. He learned of their method of fighting, and he was impressed with their weapons. In 1867, white commissioners journeyed to Sioux country to forge a peace treaty. They also hoped to gain Sioux agreement to limit their living area to present-day western South Dakota. While his Jesuit friend Father Pierre De Smet worked to gain peace, Sitting Bull refused to give up his cherished hunting lands to the west and south and declined to sign the Treaty of 1868. Other Sioux, however, made their marks on the "white man's paper," and the treaty became official.

Developments in the 1870's confirmed Sitting Bull's distrust of the white men's motives. Railroad officials surveyed the northern Plains in the early 1870's in preparation for building a transcontinental railroad that would disrupt Sioux hunting lands. In 1874, the army surveyed the Black Hills, part of the Great Sioux Reservation as set up by the treaty, and, in the next year, thousands of miners invaded this sacred part of the Sioux reserve when they learned of the discovery of gold there. The tree-covered hills and sparkling streams and lakes were the home of Sioux gods and a sacred place in their scheme of life. The whites had violated the treaty

and disregarded the rights of the Sioux. Sitting Bull refused to remain on the assigned reservation any longer and led his followers west, into Montana, where there were still buffalo to hunt and the opportunity remained to live by the old traditions. As many other Sioux became disgruntled with white treatment, they, too, looked to Sitting Bull's camp to the west as a haven from the greedy whites. In this sense, he became the symbol of Sioux freedom and resistance to the whites, and his camp grew with increasing numbers of angry Sioux.

The showdown between Sioux and whites came in 1876. The United States government had ordered the Sioux to return to their reservations by February of 1876, but few Indians abided by this order. The government thus turned the "Sioux problem" over to the army with instructions to force the natives back to the agencies. In the summer of 1876, General Alfred H. Terry led a strong expedition against Sitting Bull's camp. The Indian chief had a premonition of things to come when he dreamed of blue-clad men falling into his camp. Soon, he would learn the significance of this portent. A detachment of cavalry from Terry's column under the command of Lieutenant Colonel George A. Custer attacked Sitting Bull's camp. The forty-five-year-old chief rallied his men, and they defeated Custer, killing more than three hundred soldiers, including their leader.

While the Sioux had won the battle of the Little Big Horn River, they decided that it was time to leave the area and divide up into smaller groups in order to avoid capture. Many additional soldiers were ordered into the northern Plains, and they spent the remainder of the summer and fall chasing and harassing the fleeing Sioux. While other groups of Sioux eventually returned to their agencies, Sitting Bull led his people to Canada, where they resided until 1881. Even though the Canadian officials refused to feed the Sioux, the natives were able to subsist in their usual manner of hunting and gathering until 1881, when the buffalo were almost gone. Because of homesickness and a lack of food, Sitting Bull finally surrendered to United States officials, who kept him prisoner at Fort Randall for two years.

By 1883, Sitting Bull had returned to his people at Standing Rock Agency in Dakota Territory and soon became involved in unexpected activities. In that same year, the Northern Pacific Railroad sponsored a last great buffalo hunt for various dignitar-

ies, and Sitting Bull participated. In the next year, he agreed to tour fifteen cities with Colonel Alvaren Allen's Western show. Sitting Bull was portrayed as the Slayer of General Custer, but the stubborn Indian chief found this label inaccurate and distasteful. In 1885, Sitting Bull signed with Buffalo Bill Cody's Wild West Show and traveled in the Eastern United States and Canada during the summer. He sold autographed photographs of himself and eventually gave away most of the money he made to poor white children who begged for money in order to eat. At the end of the season, the popular Buffalo Bill gave his Indian friend a gray circus horse and large white sombrero as a remembrance of their summer together.

During the latter part of the decade, Sitting Bull returned to Standing Rock, where he settled into reservation life. The Hunkpapa still cherished him as their leader, much to the dismay of agent James McLaughlin, who sought to break the old chief's hold over his people.

In 1890, Wovoka, a Paiute Indian prophet from Nevada, began to preach a message that most Indians prayed was true. He dreamed that he had died and gone to Heaven. There, he found all the deceased Indians, thousands of buffalo, and no whites. The Indian prophet taught that, in order to achieve a return to the old ways of life, the Indians had only to dance the Ghost Dance regularly until the second coming of the Messiah, who would be in the form of an Indian. The Ghost Dance spread rapidly throughout much of the West, and soon Sioux were following Wovoka's teachings. Sitting Bull had his doubts about the new religion, but he realized that it disturbed the whites and in particular agent McLaughlin, and so he encouraged his people to dance.

The events that followed brought about the death of Sitting Bull as well as the military and psychological defeat of the Sioux. Cautious Indian officials deplored the fact that the natives were dancing again. Sitting Bull, the symbol of the old culture, was still their leader, and they decided to arrest him. McLaughlin chose Sioux Indians who served in the Agency Police Force to apprehend Sitting Bull. They came to his hut to seize him during the night of December 15, 1890, and a scuffle broke out. The fifty-nine-year-old chief was one of the first to be killed. In the dust and confusion of the struggle, fourteen others died. Several days later, other Sioux who had left their reservation were stopped at Wounded Knee Creek, and a scuffle again broke out with the white soldiers, who were trying to disarm them and to force them back to the agency. When the fighting was over on that cold December day, 153 Sioux had died and the dream of a return to the old way of life was lost forever.

Summary

Sitting Bull, the proud leader of the Hunkpapa, had died along with many of his people. He had served his people well as a feared warrior and respected chief. He had fought against Indians and whites, including sixty-three coups against unfortunate natives. The whites had suffered their worst defeat when they attacked his village. Although the old chief was unable to fight, he proved his inspirational mettle to the people. During his last years, he continued to serve as a model for his followers, although in a losing cause. Technology and the overwhelming white population were forces that even the stubborn Sioux leader could not subdue. Gone were the days of nomadic camp life, horseback riding, and buffalo hunting. Also gone were the memories of courtships and polygamous marriages: White Americans hoped to convert the Sioux tribesmen into Christian yeoman farmers. By 1890, the frontier phase of American history had passed, and citizens confronted the problems of immigration from southern and eastern Europe, the growing urbanization, and the massive industrialization which would make the United States a world leader. The Sioux life that was so well adapted to the plains environment was gone forever.

Bibliography

Adams, Alexander B. *Sitting Bull: An Epic of the Plains*. New York: Putnam, 1973; London: New English Library, 1975. A richly detailed popular account of Sitting Bull's life, with a good description of the various divisions and tribes of the Sioux.

Anderson, Ian. "Sitting Bull and the Mounties." *Wild West* 10, no. 5 (February, 1998). Profile of Sitting Bull focusing on his meeting with Northwest Mounted Police Major James Walsh, his warnings to Walsh, and the circumstances of his death.

Bailey, John W. *Pacifying the Plains: General Alfred Terry and the Decline of the Sioux, 1866-1890*. Westport, Conn.: Greenwood Press, 1979. Follows Sitting Bull's career in the period after the Civil War, with particular emphasis on his role as the leader of the nonreservation Sioux and their conflict with the military in the 1870's.

Johnson, Dorothy M. *Warrior for a Lost Nation: A Biography of Sitting Bull*. Philadelphia: Westminster Press, 1969. A readable book based upon limited research. Includes Sitting Bull's pictographs or calendar of winter counts which recorded his feats in battle.

Rosenberg, Marvin, and Dorothy Rosenberg. "There Are No Indians Left but Me." *American Heritage* 15 (June, 1964): 18-23. The story of Sitting Bull's last ten years and his bitterness regarding the reduction of the Great Sioux Reservation in 1889.

Utley, Robert Marshall. *The Lance and the Shield: The Life and Times of Sitting Bull*. New York: Henry Holt, 1993; London: Pimilico, 1998. True to his reputation as a superb storyteller, Robert Utley creates the tale of Sitting Bull set in the context of Sioux history and culture. Excellent re-creation of the battle against Custer's Seventh Cavalry and emphasis on Sitting Bull's life afterwards, including his life as a refugee in Canada, his return to the United States, and his death in 1890.

————. *The Last Days of the Sioux Nation*. New Haven, Conn.: Yale University Press, 1963. An excellent book that focuses on the death of Sitting Bull and the Wounded Knee battle of 1890. The author illustrates how the Sioux suffered a military and psychological conquest that saw their demise after the failure of the Ghost Dance.

Vestal, Stanley. *Sitting Bull: Champion of the Sioux, a Biography*. Boston: Houghton Mifflin, 1932. The most reliable biography of Sitting Bull, based upon oral and documentary research. The author was closely associated with the Plains Indians since his boyhood and proved to be a careful student of their culture.

John W. Bailey

SAMUEL SLATER

Born: June 9, 1768; near Belper, England
Died: April 21, 1835; Webster, Massachusetts
Area of Achievement: Industry
Contribution: In the early years of America's modern economic history, Slater almost single-handedly established the basis upon which the country's industrial development would be built by effectively founding textile manufacturing in New England.

Early Life

Samuel Slater was born June 9, 1768, near Belper in Derbyshire, England, the fifth child and second son of William Slater, a yeoman farmer, and Elizabeth Fox Slater, and was educated in the nearby school of Master Thomas Jackson. When he was fourteen, his father was killed in a farming accident, and Slater apprenticed himself to Jedediah Strutt, one of the early English textile manufacturers and a collaborator with Richard Arkwright in the development of textile-manufacturing machinery. Strutt was like a second father to Slater, and he rewarded the boy for the design of a device for distributing yarn more effectively on the spindle.

In the later eighteenth century, England enjoyed a virtual monopoly in advanced textile manufacturing technology. This monopoly was guarded by laws which prescribed heavy penalties for exporting technical information or for emigration of textile workers. At the same time, state governments in the United States were offering substantial incentives for the development of technology for the industrial exploitation of American cotton and wool, and while Slater was still indentured, Pennsylvania granted a bounty of a hundred pounds for a carding machine, even though it was only partially successful.

Slater therefore was determined to go to America. Before he was twenty-one he was given responsibility for assembling the equipment at one of Strutt's new mills, and this experience and the memorized details of everything he had learned in his apprenticeship were the only assets he carried to the newly formed United States when he emigrated in September, 1789, disguised as a farm laborer to escape detection as a textile worker breaking the laws of England.

Arriving in November, 1789, Slater found work for a brief time in New York City in the very small factory of the New York Manufacturing Company, which was producing yarn with inferior equipment. Meanwhile, he made contact with Moses Brown of Providence, whose mill was machine-spinning cotton with defective equipment, and offered to duplicate the machinery of Richard Arkwright. Brown introduced him to his kinsman, Sylvanus Brown, and Slater agreed to build yarn-making equipment at the latter's mill in Pawtucket, Rhode Island. He was only twenty-one.

Life's Work

Establishing a partnership with William Almy and Smith Brown, two kinsmen of Moses Brown, Slater, at a wage of a dollar a day, built the first efficient yarn-making equipment in the United States, duplicating the basic elements of Arkwright's system—the carder and the water-frame spinner—and the Almy-Brown mill began using it to spin yarn on December 20, 1790, producing relatively small quantities because Slater was forced to use Surinam cotton, which was finer and more carefully

cleaned than cotton from the American South. Three years later, however, Eli Whitney's invention of the cotton gin made possible the mass-production of cotton thread and cloth from domestic supplies. In staffing the mill, Slater followed the practice, which apparently had proven efficient in England, of employing children under the age of twelve to operate the machinery. This machinery was built of oak and iron parts forged by Oziel Wilkinson, whose daughter Hannah became Slater's wife on October 2, 1791.

In 1793, the firm of Almy, Brown and Slater built what came to be called the Old Slater Mill in Pawtucket, and spinning began there on July 12, 1793. Slater continued his partnership with Almy and Brown, even though they opened another mill on their own in 1799 and ran it in competition with Slater, using without compensation the methods he had perfected. Then, forming a partnership with relatives of his wife, he built at Rehobath the first mill in Massachusetts to use the Arkwright system, the so-called White Mill, which began production in 1801.

By this time, Slater was using power looms and was hiring experienced English textile workers to tend them, including his brother John, who arrived in America in 1803 with plans for the "mule," invented in 1779 by Samuel Crompton for making muslin. Slater was still employing children, but he had established a reputation for fair dealing. He lent new employees money to establish themselves, and from the very beginning he provided a Sunday school which taught his juvenile employees reading, writing, and arithmetic. In fact, Slater for a time taught in this school himself, and ultimately he created a day school for mill children, usually paying the teachers' salaries himself.

In 1806, the town of Slaterville, Rhode Island, was established, built around a mill which Slater had built there in partnership with Almy, Brown, and John Slater. By the time that American industry was suffering a recession because of the Embargo Act of 1807 and the Non-Intercourse Act of 1809, Slater's mills were surviving because of careful domestic marketing of yarn, and in 1812 he built yet another mill at Oxford, Massachusetts. When the New England mills suffered a severe depression in the aftermath of the Napoleonic Wars because of the flood of cheap English goods into American markets, Slater suffered severe losses, but the Protective Tariff of 1816 soon restored the industry.

On October 2, 1812, Hannah Slater died, leaving her husband with six small sons to rear. In November, 1817, he married a widow, Esther Parkinson. He involved his sons, if they were interested, in the operation of his mills, even in their adolescence. For example, his son John at the age of thirteen was his father's representative at the Oxford mill. Only one of the four sons who survived their father, Horatio Nelson Slater, lived to old age.

In 1814, in partnership with Edward Howard, Slater established a second mill at Oxford for the manufacture of woolen cloth, and when Howard sold his interest to Slater in 1829, the latter established Slater and Sons with his sons George, John, and Nelson. In time, this firm became the Dudley Manufacturing Company, and the company towns of Oxford and Dudley were merged in 1832 as the town of Webster, which Slater so named because of his admiration of Daniel Webster. Webster, Massachusetts, was home to Slater for the rest of his life.

Slater's establishment of mills continued through the prosperity of the 1820's. In 1823 at Jewett City, Connecticut, he formed S. and J. Slater with his brother, selling out his share to John in 1831. In 1825, with five partners, he acquired a mill at Amoskeag, near Manchester, New Hampshire. There he built a second mill, a sawmill, a cornmill, and a dam for water power, and established the Amoskeag Manufacturing Company. Up to this time, all of Slater's mills had been powered by water, but in 1827 he built at Providence the first steam-power textile factory in Rhode Island and one of the first in the country. In all, between 1790, when he formed his first partnership with Almy and Brown, and 1827, Slater formed thirteen partnerships. In addition, he maintained a farm, engaged in a variety of philanthropic enterprises, and helped to incorporate and was for fifteen years president of the Manufacturers' Bank of Pawtucket.

The economic slump which began in 1829 was accompanied by the onset of the ill health which plagued Slater's last years. He once said that in his first thirty years in America he worked sixteen hours a day. In his last years, in ill health, he was struggling to maintain his industrial enterprises in the face of poor economic conditions. He died at Webster, Massachusetts, on April 21, 1835, recognized throughout the country as what President Andrew Jackson called him when he greeted him at Pawtucket in 1833: the father of American manufactures.

Summary

At a remarkably young age, Samuel Slater, almost single-handedly, created the American textile industry and established the basis of American industrialism. Less an inventor than a man who built upon the inventions of others, he possessed considerable mechanical aptitude; his commercial success, however, derived mostly from his great cleverness in establishing factories, organizing production, taking advantage of the latest mechanical developments, and discovering the most effective methods of marketing his product. His single most important contribution to the growth of American industry was his establishment of a system of manufacture broken down into steps so simple that even children could perform them. This was of crucial importance during the early development of American industry because of the chronic shortage of skilled manpower in that period. With Eli Whitney, who inaugurated the system of manufacturing interchangeable parts rather than complete, custom-made assemblies, Slater stands as one of the two most influential figures in the first years of America's industrial revolution.

Bibliography

Bagnall, William R. *Samuel Slater and the Early Development of Cotton Manufacturing in the United States*. Middletown, Conn.: Steward, 1890. Except for an obscure biography published in the year following Slater's death, this is the only nineteenth century biography. Superseded by Cameron.

Blake, John. "Samuel Slater." In *Lives of American Merchants*, by Freeman Hunt, 451-472. New York: Hunt's Merchant's Magazine, 1856. A brief nineteenth century account of Slater's life and achievements.

Burlingame, Roger. "The Spinning Hero: Samuel Slater." *North American Review* 246 (Autumn, 1938): 150-161. A brief and somewhat superficial tribute to Slater's achievements by a distinguished historian of American industry.

Cameron, E. H. *Samuel Slater, Father of American Manufacturers*. Freeport, Maine: Wheelwright, 1960. The only modern full-length biography, written with the assistance of H. N. Slater, Samuel Slater's great-grandson, and based in part on the research and unpublished manuscript of Frederick L. Lewton.

Conrad, James L., Jr. " 'Drive That Branch': Samuel Salter, the Power Loom, and the Writing of America's Textile History." *Technology and Culture* 36, no. 1 (January, 1995). Conrad provides a detailed account of Samuel Slater's contributions to the textile industry.

Gustaitis, J. "Samuel Slater: Father of the American Industrial Revolution." *American History Illustrated* (May, 1989). Discusses how Slater revolutionized the textile industry by reconstructing the cotton spinning machines he had used in England.

Lewton, Frederick L. "Samuel Slater and the Oldest Cotton Machinery in America." In *Smithsonian Report for 1936*. Washington, D.C.: Smithsonian Institution Press, 1936. Lewton devoted a large part of his life to research on Slater and was the primary modern authority on the technical aspects of Slater's equipment. Cameron based his biography on Lewton's unpublished manuscript. The oldest Slater machinery is in the Smithsonian museum. This is a semitechnical description of it.

Tucker, Barbara M. *Samuel Slater and the Origins of the American Textile Industry*. Ithaca, N.Y.: Cornell University Press, 1984. Largely a case study of Slater's factory system from 1790 to 1860. Examines Slater's management methods in relation to the English system in which he was trained and the innovations made necessary by American conditions. Valuable for an understanding of Slater as a factory master, but thin on biographical detail.

Welles, Arnold. "Father of Our Factory System." *American Heritage* 9 (April, 1958): 34-39, 90-92. A brief account of Slater's life and accomplishments, with useful and enlightening illustrations from the prints of the period.

Robert L. Berner

JEDEDIAH STRONG SMITH

Born: January 6, 1799; Jericho (Bainbridge), New York

Died: May 27, 1831; near Cimmaron River en route to Santa Fe, New Mexico

Area of Achievement: Exploration

Contribution: The most adventurous of the nineteenth century mountain men, Smith charted trails through the Rockies that opened the American West to settlement by the pioneers who followed the fur traders.

Early Life

Jedediah Strong Smith, possibly the greatest of the American mountain men, was born January 6, 1799, in New York State. Like many other American families, the Smiths moved a number of times as the frontier pushed farther west.

Smith's family appears to have been thoroughly middle class and respectable. Smith received a good education and was well read. Family tradition, in fact, credits a book, the 1814 publication by Nicholas Biddle of *History of the Expedition of Captains Lewis and Clark*, with firing the young Smith's imagination and making him determined to see the places Merriwether Lewis and William Clark described in their journals. By 1822 he and his family had made their way to Missouri. There he signed on with the Rocky Mountain Fur Company, recently organized by William Ashley and Andrew Henry. Smith became one of the original Ashley Men, the individual fur trappers and traders that set off into the wilderness under Ashley's command.

Life's Work

Ashley, a Missouri businessman, and Henry, an experienced fur trapper, originated the annual trappers' rendezvous in the intermountain regions of the West. The Rocky Mountain Fur Company would pack supplies and trade goods for the mountain men in to a central location, such as a site on the Green River in Wyoming, and pack the furs out, eliminating the lengthy trek to St. Louis for individual trappers and traders. Ashley's plan met resistance from the Arikara, a Native American tribe whose members had become accustomed to serving as the middlemen between white fur traders and other tribes on the upper Missouri, but Ashley simply relocated his base of operations and effectively cut the Arikara out of the fur business. Other

trading companies quickly copied the idea and, before overtrapping ended the fur trade, hundreds of mountain men would gather for the midsummer rendezvous to dispose of the furs taken in the previous year and to stock up on supplies for the coming winter.

Unlike the stereotypical image of the uncouth mountain man, generally portrayed in popular culture as hard-drinking and vulgar in language and behavior, Smith was a devout Christian, neither drank nor smoked, and was consistently serious in his demeanor. Even when personally in danger or in pain, he remained calm, never allowing his men to see his concern or fear. On his second expedition, a grizzly bear attacked and mauled Smith. The bear smashed Smith's ribs and tore at his scalp. The bear left Smith alive, but with his scalp literally dangling by an ear. He coolly instructed one of his companions, Jim Clyman, to reattach the loose skin using needle and thread. Clyman stitched the scalp back in place as best he could but was convinced that repairing the ear was hopeless. Smith told him to try anyway. Clyman did. After a two-week convalescence, Smith resumed command of the party.

Contemporaries of Smith described him both as highly respectable and as an inspiration to those around him. When called upon to say a few words over the grave of John Gardner, a recently deceased fellow fur trader, Smith's eulogy moved observers to comment that Smith left no doubt in anyone's mind that their friend had found salvation. Coupled with his legendary physical courage, it is not surprising Smith quickly established himself both as a leader and as an explorer.

Smith spent his first winter in the mountains along the Musselshell River in present-day Montana. The following summer, 1823, Ashley directed Smith to take a group of men and find a Native American tribe known as the Crow with the object of establishing trade relations with them. Smith's party succeeded in making contact with the Crow people and spent the winter with them. Members of the Crow tribe described to Smith the Green River area in what is now the state of Wyoming. The Green was reputed to be an area rich in furs and thus far unexploited by other traders, and Smith and his men resolved to explore the region. In the spring of 1824 Smith and his party rediscovered South Pass, a passageway through the Rocky

Mountains, and successfully traversed it with both wagons and livestock, proving that such travel was possible. Previous parties had relied completely on pack animals to carry supplies and trade goods. South Pass had been utilized before by white men, in 1814, but the route had been forgotten. Other trails, such as the one over Lemhi Pass used by the Lewis and Clark Expedition, were impassable with wagons and were just barely passable with horses and mules. The trail that Smith blazed through Wyoming in 1824 later became an integral part of the Oregon Trail, the path that thousands of pioneers would take to reach the Pacific Northwest.

Smith and the men with him spent the following year trapping and trading in Wyoming and Idaho. Following the first trappers' rendezvous, he returned to St. Louis with William Ashley and the company's furs. Andrew Henry had decided to retire from the fur trade, so Ashley asked Smith to replace Henry as his partner.

Smith returned to the mountains ahead of Ashley and his main party the following spring to arrange for the trappers' rendezvous. At the rendezvous, Ashley negotiated the sale of his share of the company to Smith and two new partners, David Jackson and William Sublette. Ashley—in exchange for a promissory note signed July 18, 1826, which committed Jackson, Smith, and Sublette to pay "not less than seven thousand dollars nor more than fifteen thousand dollars" for merchadise— agreed to arrange for the shipment of trade goods to the location of the following year's rendezvous. After the rendezvous ended, Ashley returned to St. Louis while Smith, Jackson, and Sublette divided their party into smaller groups for the fall hunt.

Smith, accompanied by seventeen men, decided to explore the region south of the Great Salt Lake and to assess its potential for the fur trade. Smith and his men traveled the length of Utah, following first a tributary of the Colorado River and then Colorado itself, pushed on into what is present-day northern Arizona, and then crossed the Mojave Desert into California, eventually reaching the Spanish mission at San Gabriel near present-day San Diego. The 1776 Spanish Dominguez-Escalante Expedition had attempted this route across the desert but had failed to complete it. The bulk of Smith's party remained on the Stanislaus River in California in the spring of 1827 while Smith and two men attempted to find a route back to northern Utah through the Sierra Nevada. They succeeded and, striking northeast across Nevada, became the

first white men to cross the Great Salt Lake Desert as they returned to Utah for the trappers' rendezvous at Sweet (now Bear) Lake.

Smith, as was common practice among many American explorers, fur traders, and mountain men, kept extensive journals. His harrowing description of the journey across the Salt Lake Desert—replete with phrases such as "I durst not tell my men of the desolate prospect ahead" and "We dug holes in the sand and laid down in them for the purpose of cooling our heated bodies"— makes it clear that even Smith had his doubts regarding their survival. Nonetheless, having survived the trek across not merely one but several arid deserts, Smith continued his explorations. He arrived at the rendezvous July 3, having traveled through most of the American Southwest during the previous year, only two days later than he had promised Ashley in 1826 that he would be there. Scarcely two weeks after completing his harrowing journey from California, he was again heading south and west, motivated, as he said in his journal, "by the love of novelty."

Having left a significant number of his men in California in the spring of 1827, Smith retraced his route to the Pacific Ocean in the fall of that year. Highly suspicious of Smith's motives, the Spanish governor threatened the Americans with jail. Officials softened their stance and did allow Smith and his men to spend the winter of 1827-1828 in the San Francisco Bay area, but they made it clear that they did not want the Americans to linger any longer than necessary. In the spring they proceeded north to present-day Oregon, and Smith became the first white man to travel from California to Oregon by an overland route. The Kelawatset Indians of the region proved hostile, however, and killed the majority of Smith's men in an attack. Smith and three other survivors managed to reach Fort Vancouver, where they were aided by British trappers. After spending the winter of 1828-1829 at Fort Vancouver, Smith returned to the Flathead region for the 1829 trappers' rendezvous. Briefly reunited with his partners, Jackson and Sublette, Smith then led a large force of men into the Blackfoot country of Montana and Wyoming for the fall hunt.

The Indians of the northwest were becoming increasingly unfriendly, worsening the risks to both trappers and traders, so in 1830 Sublette, Smith, and Jackson decided to sell their trapping interests to the Rocky Mountain Fur Company. They returned to St. Louis and became involved in the growing trade with Santa Fe. Smith himself planned to give up the wandering life and settle down in St. Louis. His mother had died recently, and he felt a strong sense of obligation to his family. By 1830 he had spent eight years in almost constant travel and exploration. Perhaps the novelty of new places was finally losing some of its allure. He purchased both a farmhouse and a town house, hired servants, and talked about preparing his complete journals and maps for publication. Still, he allowed himself to be persuaded to make one last trip. In the spring of 1831 he agreed to lead a trading expedition to Santa Fe to help the buyers of his fur company procure supplies. A band of Comanches apparently surprised and killed Smith while he was scouting ahead of the main party in search of drinking water near the Cimmaron River along the Santa Fe Trail. The planned editing and publication of his complete journals never took place, and most of his papers were lost following his death.

Summary

Although numerous American explorers charted sections of the continent, few covered as much territory or saw as wide a variety of terrain as Smith, nor did their travels have as significant an impact on later settlement. Smith's journal, written on his trek from the Green River in Wyoming to Arizona and then on to the Pacific coast, contains the first descriptions by Americans of both the wonders of the Grand Canyon and the magnificent redwood groves of California. His trek across the South Pass of the Rockies, a five-hundred-mile journey with pack wagons and livestock, opened a trail that would be utilized by thousands of pioneers en route to Oregon. Similarly, his trek across the Great Salt Lake Desert and Nevada blazed a more direct route to California. It later served as the route first for the Pony Express and then for U.S. Highway 50.

Bibliography

Allen, John Logan. *Jedediah Smith and the Mountain Men of the American West*. Introduction by Michael Collins. New York: Chelsea House, 1991. This biography written for a juvenile audience chronicles the exploits of the early nineteenth century mountain men who opened trails through the American West. Bibliographical references and index.

Brooks, George R., ed. *Southwest Expedition of Jedediah S. Smith: His Personal Account of the Journey to California, 1826-1827*. Glendale, Calif.: Clark, 1977. Smith's journey across the Mojave and the Great Salt Lake Desert, in his own words.

Dale, Harrison Clifford. *The Explorations of William H. Ashley and Jedediah Smith, 1822-1829*. Lincoln: University of Nebraska Press, 1991. Originally published as *The Ashley-Smith Explorations and the Discovery of a Central Route to the Pacific, 1822-1829*, in 1941. Includes original journals edited by Dale. Excellent history that summarizes the travels of both Ashley and Smith and sets them in a historical context.

Davis, Lee. "Tracking Jedediah Smith Through Hupa Territory." *The American Indian Quarterly* 13 (Fall, 1989): 369. Provides vivid details about one segment of Smith's travels. Davis, by looking at one aspect of Smith's explorations in detail, helps to flesh out the more general accounts of his travels.

Morgan, Dale L. *Jedediah Smith and the Opening of the West*. Lincoln: University of Nebraska Press, 1953. A good basic biography of Smith, containing a portrait.

Neihardt, John Gneisenau. *The Splendid Wayfaring: Jedediah Smith and the Ashley-Henry Men, 1822-1831*. New York: Macmillan, 1920. Fascinating examination of Smith and his fellow fur traders and trappers and their mythic status in American history.

Smith, Jedediah Strong. *The Southwest Expedition of Jedediah S. Smith: His Personal Account of the Journey to California, 1826-1827*. Edited by George R. Brooks. Glendale, Calif.: Clark, 1977. These accounts, by the explorer himself, are supplemented by a bibliography and an index.

Sullivan, Maurice S. *The Travels of Jedediah Smith*. Santa Ana, Calif.: Fine Arts Press, 1934. Using materials from Smith's surviving journals, this book has long been considered the definitive reference on Smith's life and travels.

Nancy Farm Mannikko

JOSEPH SMITH

Born: December 23, 1805; Sharon, Vermont
Died: June 27, 1844; Carthage, Illinois
Area of Achievement: Religion
Contribution: Smith founded the first indigenous American religion, the Church of Jesus Christ of Latter-day Saints. He developed a novel exegesis of the traditional Protestant Bible and provided new scriptures, including the Book of Mormon.

Early Life

Joseph Smith was born December 23, 1805, in Sharon, Vermont, the third son of Joseph Smith, Sr., and Lucy Mack Smith. The Smiths were a hardworking but impoverished farm family of New England stock. For the first ten years of his life, Joseph's family moved from one rocky New England farm to another, unable to achieve the financial success that would enable them to settle and become established members of the community. In 1816, the Smiths joined the stream of migrants leaving New England for the trans-Appalachian West. They settled in upstate New York, eventually purchasing a farm near Palmyra.

The Smiths, in moving to Palmyra, had arrived at one of the focal points for the religious revivals which convulsed the nation during the first three decades of the nineteenth century. In the fervor of religious controversy, mainstream denominations splintered and sects multiplied, especially in upstate New York, which was known as the "burnt over district," because it had been repeatedly scorched by the fires of the spirit. There, shouting evangelists from the mainstream denominations competed with prophets of a forth-coming millennium and communitarian groups such as the Shakers. Others, disgusted by revivalism and competition between denominations, longed for Christian unity through a restoration of the primitive Church of apostolic times.

The Smiths, like other poor farmers in the 1820's, suffered from the precarious conditions caused by the developing American economy. Young Smith, with only limited schooling, worked as a laborer on his father's mortgaged farm. Upstate New York was dotted with Indian mounds. Like many others in the area, Joseph sometimes searched for buried treasure. In 1826, he was brought to trial as a disorderly person and impostor in connection with these "money-digging" activities.

Life's Work

Smith's outward life was that of any other farmer's son. In 1827, he married Emma Hale and seemed to have embarked upon an ordinary life, marred only by his lack of financial security. Yet Smith's life was far from ordinary. In 1830, he emerged as a prophet and began to build the Church of Jesus Christ of Latter-day Saints.

The series of extraordinary events which transformed Smith into the Mormon prophet began when he was fourteen. As he later told his followers, he had gone into the forest to pray for guidance as to which of the competing denominations and sects he should join. The Lord and Christ Jesus appeared to him and told him that all the denominations were in error.

The revelations which led to the formation of the Mormon Church began in 1823, when, according to Smith, he was visited by the Angel Moroni. The angel guided Smith to a buried stone box, which contained a book written on gold plates and a set of spectaclelike stones which, when worn, enabled Smith to read the book. In September, 1827, Smith was allowed to take the plates home and began translating the book, dictating the text to various scribes from behind a curtain. When the translation was completed, the plates were given back to the angel. In 1830, the Book of Mormon was published.

The Book of Mormon tells the story of a pre-Columbian settlement of Hebrews in America. They are visited by Christ after his crucifixion. He establishes his church in America. After two hundred years, this church and the Hebrew civilization in America are destroyed in a war between the Hebrew tribes, the Nephites and the Lamanites. One of the Nephite survivors, Moroni, buries golden plates containing a history of his people in a hill in upstate New York, where they could be recovered and used to restore Christ's church in America.

With the publication of the Book of Mormon, Smith, then twenty-four, began to attract a nucleus of believers. In 1834, the Church of Jesus Christ of Latter-day Saints was organized. Believers were to be guided by the Bible, the Book of Mormon, and subsequent revelations announced by Smith. The new church grew rapidly, and the Saints gathered into communities to be near their prophet, who promised that a Mormon city, a new Zion, would soon be built on the western frontier in Missouri.

Mormons moved into Missouri to prepare the way, while Smith and the Church's leadership moved from New York to a Mormon community in Kirtland, Ohio.

The Mormons' clannishness and religious unorthodoxy aroused hostility among the old settlers in Missouri. In addition, the Mormons were non-slave-holding Yankees, moving into a slave state. A small-scale war broke out between the old settlers and the Mormons. Smith himself was arrested in 1838 and convicted of treason by a Missouri court. Sentenced to death, he managed to escape to Illinois.

There, Smith and the other Mormon refugees, joined by new converts from Great Britain, began to build a model city on the banks of the Mississippi. Incorporated in 1840, Nauvoo became one of the wonders of the American West. Mormons moved there by the thousands, and construction began on a massive temple.

Smith was the acknowledged leader of the city's spiritual and political life. He was prophet and "lieutenant general" of a Mormon legion of two thousand troops. Still a young man in his thirties, Smith impressed visitors with his vibrant personality. Tall, handsome, with light-brown hair, blue eyes, and a sharp, prominent nose, Smith was a commanding presence in Nauvoo. He also wielded considerable political power in Illinois. Nauvoo's city charter made it almost independent of state authority. Yet the Mormons, by voting as a block, could swing Illinois state elections. The Mormons' power made their neighbors suspicious and afraid; their fears were not allayed when, in 1844, Smith announced his intention to run for the presidency, hoping to focus the public's attention on the injustices to which his people had been subjected.

Smith's control over the Church also made some of his followers uneasy, as did the rumors (later proven true) that the prophet had privately authorized plural marriage, or polygamy. In 1844, Mormon dissidents set up a press, intending to publicize their discontent. Smith ordered the press destroyed. He was arrested by the state of Illinois, charged with treason, and incarcerated in the Carthage, Illinois, jail. On June 27, 1844, a mob attacked the jail, and Smith was killed.

In death, Smith became a martyr. His church continued to grow and prosper, establishing a center in Utah and eventually becoming a respected American denomination with millions of converts throughout the world.

Summary

Historians have argued that Smith founded the only truly native American religion, and that his theology reflected both the optimism and the anxiety of early nineteenth century United States. The new church was especially appealing to Americans who were tired of sectarian squabbles, because it offered a restoration of apostolic and priestly authority. The Latter-day Saints could cut through endless debates as to which church was right and promise Christian unity. The Church also appealed to those offended by the emotionalism of the revivals. Finally, the new church tapped into the stream of millennialism then current in American religious thought, promising the establishment of the kingdom of God on earth, the building of the new Zion in the United States.

Smith's church also appealed to Americans who disliked the intensely competitive economy and society characteristic of the United States in the 1830's. For every individual who achieved success, there were thousands like the Smiths who barely scraped by, lacking money and status. The early Mormons experimented with communally held property; although these experiments were not successful, the Church continued to offer a ready-made community which promised economic security to all members. In addition, the structure of the Church itself provided positions of authority and respect for all male believers.

Smith's views on the afterlife can be seen as the quintessence of American optimism. After a life spent progressing in the service of the Church, Mormon men could continue to progress after death and would themselves become gods. Non-Mormons would be relegated to a lesser Heaven, but very few people would actually be doomed.

Smith thus founded a highly successful church which offered stability and security as well as progress to people living in an era of rapid change. For his followers, he was also an inspired prophet who had provided them with new scriptures authenticated by divine revelation.

Bibliography

Arrington, Leonard J., and Davis Bitton. *The Mormon Experience: A History of the Latter-day Saints*. 2d ed. Urbana: University of Illinois Press, 1992. A sympathetic but objective church history by two Mormon historians, placing Smith in the context of his times. The first section deals with Smith and the early days of the Church.

Bailyn, Bernard, et al. "Dissent: The Mormons as a Test Case." In *The Great Republic: A History of the American People*, edited by David Brion Davis, 326-331. Lexington, Mass.: Heath, 1977. A brief but highly informative analysis of the Mormons as dissenters from the economic, social, and sexual norms of nineteenth century America.

Barrett, Ivan J. *Joseph Smith and the Restoration: A History of the Church to 1846*. Provo, Utah: Brigham Young University Press, 1967. Written for Mormons and published by the press of a Mormon university, this book is hardly objective but does offer an interesting and detailed chronicle of Smith's life as seen by his followers.

Brodie, Fawn M. *No Man Knows My History: The Life of Joseph Smith, the Mormon Prophet*. 2d ed. New York: Knopf, 1971. The most famous biography of Joseph Smith. According to Brodie, Smith was a likable phony who made up the Book of Mormon as part of a money-making scheme. In later life, surrounded by people who believed in him as a prophet, he became what he had pretended to be. A later edition of the work contains a psychoanalytic interpretation of Smith's actions, concluding that he may not have been a deliberate fraud, but rather an impostor, using fantasy to resolve his own identity conflict.

Bushman, Richard L. *Joseph Smith and the Beginnings of Mormonism*. Urbana: University of Illinois Press, 1984. Mormon historian Bushman recounts the history of the Mormon movement prior to 1831, focusing on Smith and his family and describing events as participants perceived them.

Compton, Todd. *In Sacred Loneliness: The Plural Wives of Joseph Smith*. Salt Lake City, Utah: Signature, 1997. Well-researched study of Joseph Smith's 33 wives, each presented individually with citations of each wife's private documents. Includes an impressive bibliography and photographs of the women. Shows polygamy to be a lonely existence for the women involved.

Flanders, Robert B. *Nauvoo: Kingdom on the Mississippi*. Urbana: University of Illinois Press, 1965. This history of the Mormon model city explores Smith's role as city planner and town leader.

Hansen, Klaus J. *Mormonism and the American Experience*. Chicago: University of Chicago Press, 1981. In this volume in the University of Chicago's History of American Religion series, Hansen discusses the origins of the Mormon Church, summarizing most of the theories historians and psychologists have propounded about Smith, and analyzes Smith's theology and its applications in the history of the Latter-day Saints.

Smith, George D. "Mormon Plural Marriage." *Free Inquiry* 12, no. 3 (Summer 1992). Discusses Smith and the practice of polygamy in the Mormon community.

Jeanette Keith

JOHN HANNING SPEKE

Born: May 4, 1827; Orleigh Court, Devon, England

Died: September 15, 1864; Neston Park, near Bath, England

Area of Achievement: Exploration

Contribution: Speke traveled extensively in East and Central Africa and during the course of his explorations discovered Lake Victoria, the source of the Nile River.

Early Life

John Hanning Speke was born May 4, 1827, at Orleigh Court in southwestern England. He was the son of William and Georgiana Hanning Elizabeth Speke. His father was a retired army officer, and his mother came from a family of wealthy merchants. Relatively little is known of Speke's early years. He showed an interest in zoology from a tender age but was a restless boy who cared little for school. Whenever possible, he was out in the fields and woods, and it is from these youthful days that a lifelong interest in natural history and sport dates.

In 1844, the same year his father came into possession of the family estate at Jordans (many sources wrongly suggest that this was Speke's birthplace), he received assignment as a second lieutenant in the Forty-sixth Bengal Native Infantry Regiment, in the Indian Army. This assignment followed completion of his studies at Blackheath New Preparatory School in London.

April 24, 1844, may be said to be the day when Speke was vested with the responsibilities of manhood. On this day the seventeen-year-old lad was examined and passed as an entering officer cadet for Indian army service. Speke's preferment was in all likelihood largely a result of his mother's influence with the Duke of Wellington. He had already passed the required medical examinations prior to his final application, so he was able to begin active service almost immediately. On May 3, 1844, he boarded ship and four months later was in India. The Asian subcontinent and its life apparently suited him well. He demonstrated some facility with languages, and by the end of his second year of service, he had passed an examination in Hindustani. He also had ample opportunity to indulge his love of hunting and made many forays into the plains and the Himalaya Mountains in search of sport.

Speke saw active service in the Second Sikh War when he served as a subaltern officer in the "fighting brigade" of General Colin Campbell's division, and on October 8, 1850, he was promoted to the rank of lieutenant. It was also at this point that he first began to think of African exploration, although at the time collecting specimens of the continent's animal life weighed more heavily in his mind than geographical discovery. For the time, though, any such journey was only a dream. He still had five years' service remaining before he would become eligible for an extended furlough.

Meanwhile, he scrupulously saved his money and underwent conscious training in preparation for African exploration. Each year he made excursions into the mountains of Tibet, he developed his skills as a surveyor and cartographer, and he became an excellent hunter and marksman. Speke actually cared little for the dull routine of army life, as he later confessed, and he clearly was a man in search of adventure. This obsession would drive him all of his life, as he constantly sought to conquer that which was mysterious or unknown. This trait, coupled with his interest in nature, was vital in his choosing the arduous life of an explorer.

Thanks to the favor of his superiors, he was able to obtain regular extended leaves, and late in 1854, he had the opportunity for which he had so long waited. He was to join a fellow Indian army officer, Richard Francis Burton, in exploring Somaliland. He and Burton had met on shooting outings in India, and their common interest in Africa had drawn them together. From this juncture onward, for the remaining ten years of his life, Speke would be almost completely preoccupied with African discovery.

Life's Work

The Somaliland undertaking proved an abortive one. While camped on the coast, the party was attacked, with Speke being badly wounded and briefly held captive. The attack also planted the seeds of discord between Burton and Speke, for in the confusion Burton believed that his companion had not responded to the native attack as readily or bravely as he should. Yet realizing that Speke had "suffered in person and purse," Burton invited him to join another expedition. This journey began in December, 1856, with its primary objective being the discovery of the mysterious sources of the Nile River.

*John Speke (left) with fellow explorer
Captain Grant*

The pair, rather than taking the standard approach of moving upriver along the Nile, traveled overland from the East African coast opposite Zanzibar. Together they discovered Lake Tanganyika, which would ultimately prove to be the source of the Congo (today's Zaire) River, although Burton thought it might be their objective. On the return journey, while Burton remained in camp at Kazeh (modern Tabora, Tanzania) investigating some of the social and sexual customs which so fascinated him, Speke made a flying march to the north.

His objective was a lake which local reports said stretched to the ends of the earth, and on July 30, 1858, he first sighted the vast body of water which he instinctively knew was the Nile's source. He named it Lake Victoria, after his sovereign, but because of time considerations and the fact that he was nearly blind from ophthalmia, Speke had no opportunity for a proper reconnaissance of the lake. Nevertheless, he returned to Kazeh proclaiming that he had discovered the Nile's source, a conclusion which Burton ridiculed. Henceforth there

would be bitter discord between the two, although they had little choice but to retain at least the vestiges of friendship during the perilous return journey to Zanzibar.

Once back in England, however, Speke immediately claimed credit as the discoverer of the Nile's source, and his theories attracted widespread attention. He had preceded Burton back to England, and when the leader of the East African Expedition returned a few weeks later, he found, to his regret, that Speke was the "lion of the day." The Royal Geographical Society, with the encouragement of Sir Roderick I. Murchison, had decided to finance a new expedition for the purpose of obtaining proof of Speke's claims. Accompanied by James Augustus Grant, another acquaintance from his Indian army days, Speke returned to East Africa in 1860.

Despite facing an incredible variety of obstacles, ranging from incipient warfare among tribes living along the route to recurrent demands for *hongo* (passage fees), the expedition made its way to the important lake kingdoms of Buganda and Karagwe. While Grant stayed behind at the latter location (ostensibly because of a leg injury but probably owing to Speke's egotistical reluctance to share any fame which might come from his discoveries), Speke marched eastward to the Nile. On July 21, 1862, he reached the river and followed it upstream until he reached the falls at the north end of Lake Victoria. This massive outflow of water he named the Ripon Falls, in honor of the president of the Royal Geographical Society, Lord Ripon.

At this juncture, his task seemed simple enough. All that remained was to collect Grant and proceed downriver until the expedition reached a known point on the Nile. This proved impossible though, thanks to objections raised by tribes living along the river. The necessity of taking a detour away from the Nile as he moved downriver left Speke's claims open to dispute, and it would not be until 1890, long after his death, that his contentions would be proved completely correct. Nevertheless, after overcoming a series of vexing impediments placed in their way by African chieftains, Speke and Grant managed to resume their travels downriver. Falling in with a company of Arab slave and ivory traders, they reached Gondokoro, the last outpost of European civilization, on February 15, 1863.

There they met Samuel White Baker and his mistress (later to become his wife) Florence von

Sass. After a few days with this extraordinary couple, they proceeded onward in their journey back to England. Once home, Speke and Grant were welcomed in tumultuous fashion, although challenges from Burton and others regarding the accuracy of Speke's geography produced considerable controversy. The matter occasioned widespread debate in newspapers, learned circles, and among the general public. Eventually, it was agreed that Burton and Speke would debate on the subject before a meeting of the British Association for the Advancement of Science, with the noted missionary/explorer, Dr. David Livingstone, acting as moderator.

The debate was scheduled for September 16, 1864, but it never took place. As a packed house listened in shocked silence, it was announced that Speke had shot himself while out hunting partridges the previous afternoon. The dramatic nature of his death added to the controversy surrounding the entire matter of the Nile's source, and the subject would be one of contention and uncertainty in Africanist and geographical circles for another generation. The nature of Speke's death, which was officially ruled accidental but which many believed, with some justice, was suicide, simply added a further element of poignancy. Only in 1890, after the travels of Baker, Henry Morton Stanley, and others had added to knowledge of the Nile's headwaters, was the problem completely solved. In the end, Speke's claim to precedence as discoverer of the Nile's source was fully vindicated.

Summary

John Hanning Speke's fame rests entirely on his African travels, and his discovery of Lake Victoria was, as another African explorer, Sir Harry H. Johnston, has said, the greatest geographical discovery since North America. His work, along with that of Livingstone, Burton, Stanley, and other African explorers, excited great public interest in Africa and thereby eventually fueled the flames of imperialism. In a sense, African discovery provided the foundation upon which the scramble for colonial possessions on the continent was built, and Speke did much to create the widespread interest in all things African which characterized the mid-Victorian era.

There can be no doubt that Speke was a contentious individual, but his single-minded mania for discovery loomed large in his success as an explorer. His legacy is one of having solved an age-old mystery and in so doing directing European attention to Africa in an unprecedented fashion. He remains in many ways an elusive figure, thanks to a paucity of surviving personal papers and a rather secretive nature, but recent research suggests that his was a complex personality, as was indeed generally the case with African explorers.

Bibliography

Bridges, Roy C. "Negotiating a Way to the Nile." In *Africa and Its Explorers*, edited by Robert I. Rotberg. Cambridge, Mass.: Harvard University Press, 1970. A useful overview of Speke's explorations set against the wider scope of nineteenth century African discovery.

Hanbury-Tenison, Robin. "The Search for the Source." *Geographical Magazine* 67, no. 7 (July, 1995). Discusses the centuries-long search for the source of the Nile River and Speke's 1858 theory that its source was Lake Victoria.

Maitland, Alexander. *Speke*. London: Constable, 1971. The only full-length biography of Speke yet written, this work is flawed by inadequate research and an overemphasis on psychoanalysis. Nevertheless, it is the best available account of Speke's life.

Speke, John Hanning. *Journal of the Discovery of the Source of the Nile*. Edinburgh: Blackwood, 1863; New York: Harper, 1864. Speke's personal account of his final African journey.

James A. Casada

HERBERT SPENCER

Born: April 27, 1820; Derby, England
Died: December 8, 1903; Brighton, England
Area of Achievement: Philosophy
Contribution: Best known as the leading Social Darwinist of the nineteenth century, Spencer was a broad-ranging thinker who epitomized the scientific mentality of his age. He coined the phrase "survival of the fittest" and attempted to build a comprehensive philosophical synthesis based on evolution.

Early Life

Herbert Spencer was born on April 27, 1820, in Derby, England. An only child, he was educated until the age of ten by his father, a private tutor. His unorthodox father, a Dissenter, and the lack of peers molded the young Spencer into an intellectual introvert. He was reared amid discussions of the great political and philosophical issues of the day, and his father's associates consisted primarily of Quakers and Unitarians. Spencer received further education, mostly in mathematics and mechanics, from his uncle, Thomas Spencer, who headed a school near Bath. The enormous learning which he later demonstrated was acquired principally through his own efforts.

Declining an offer from his uncle to send him to Cambridge, in 1837 Spencer took a job as a civil engineer with the London and Birmingham railway company. He worked for a number of different railways, traveled widely, introduced several technical innovations, and advanced in his career. He had, however, developed a deep interest in politics, and in 1841 he left his engineering career and returned to Derby to live on his savings while writing political commentary.

Initially, Spencer dabbled in radical politics rather unselectively, but some of his early pieces in the *Nonconformist* reveal that his narrow view of the role of the state had already developed. In 1843, he moved to London, where he believed he could advance his literary career He did very poorly, selling only a few items, most of them on phrenology. Soon, his funds depleted, he returned to his engineering work. He quickly became disillusioned with the world of business, and he left it in 1846, exposing railway fraud in an essay in the *Edinburgh Review.*

At the age of twenty-six, Spencer had largely failed in engineering, politics, and journalism. He was both lonely and alone in his increasingly deep meditations. His dedication to philosophical inquiry and his serious reading precluded a social life, and he never married. His dark brown hair was beginning to recede, and in later life he was partially bald, a feature he sought to counter by wearing his hair long on the sides, with bushy sideburns. His face was calm, but pale, and in general his slight figure suggested frailness and delicacy. He was an excellent conversationalist but somewhat abrupt and quite fixed in his opinions.

Life's Work

In 1848, Spencer's career took a turn for the better when his schoolmaster uncle assisted him in securing a position in London as subeditor of *The Economist.* With this position, Spencer had not only a modest level of financial security but also the spare time to work on the great philosophical project he had been contemplating. At *The Economist* Spencer found like-minded individualists, and his laissez-faire attitude hardened into the rigidness for which he would become famous.

The serious writing effort on which Spencer had been working for some time was completed in the summer of 1850 and published the following year under the title *Social Statics.* With his job and his book, Spencer enjoyed a wider social life, but he continued his father's traditions of nonconformity and he enjoyed being something of an eccentric who flaunted convention. In 1853, the death of his uncle, who had aided him so greatly, brought him a legacy, which was small but sufficient for him to leave *The Economist* and live independently as an author. That same year, however, he suffered the first of a series of physical and nervous ailments which plagued him for the rest of his life. He traveled widely in search of better health, argued with his friends, remained lonely and unhappy, and became a confirmed hypochondriac.

Spencer continued, however, to write prolifically. In 1855, he published *The Principles of Psychology,* and in 1860 he announced his plan to produce a ten-volume work with the general title *The Synthetic Philosophy.* He suffered a serious nervous breakdown and treated himself with opium, but the work was finally completed in 1896. He financed his work by selling subscriptions, with the subscribers receiving installments of about ninety pages every three months. Some interest in the work was expressed in Great Britain, but it was support from the United States that actually gave Spencer the financial wherewithal to complete his work. An inheritance from his father, along with the proceeds from the sale of his books, allowed him to live comfortably for the rest of his life. He died on December 8, 1903, and the remains of his cremation are at Highgate Cemetery.

At the basis of Spencer's philosophy lay two fundamentals: first, the tremendous importance given to science that was characteristic of his age; second, the sanctity of political and economic laissez-faire that he acquired from his Dissenter and radical background. In fact, Spencer combined these two to make laissez-faire a natural law. He was not, however, the only one to do this. Both science and the idea of laissez-faire were dominant in the mid-nineteenth century, as was the idea of progress, also very important to him. Spencer, however, was the foremost spokesman of these ideas, and he set them forth in his volumes in a way that convinced his contemporaries.

Spencer was, moreover, the only one of his time to attempt a synthesis of all thought, based on science and especially evolution, and which included philosophies of education, biology, psychology, sociology, and ethics, as well as politics. Such a comprehensive system was possible only to the nineteenth century mind, which embraced science in such an enthusiastic and general fashion. Most of Spencer's proofs rested on mere analogies, usually biological, and by the time of his death such generalizations were outdated in a world which had become highly technical and specialized. Having been the most popular thinker of his time, especially in the United States, Spencer fell from favor as rapidly as he had risen, and by the early years of the twentieth century he was largely forgotten, dismissed by philosophers as not being sufficiently philosophical and by scientists as being too much the generalist. Spencerian thought, however, remains well worth studying, not only for what it suggests about the nineteenth century mind but also for what it reveals about the origins of the modern social sciences.

Spencer is always linked, and rightly so, to Darwinian evolution, but it is not merely as a disciple of Charles Darwin that he is important. The evolutionary perspective was current before Darwin produced his famous *On the Origin of Species* in 1859. Geological evidence supported evolution, and Spencer was aware of these investigations and

had been moved to that view by his own observations during excavations for railways. Moreover, his own writings on competition in business influenced Darwin, and while Darwin's work revolutionized Spencer's thinking, as it did that of so many others, it was Spencer who coined the term "survival of the fittest." Spencer, it should be noted, never became a complete Darwinist; for example, he continued to hold to the pre-Darwinian notion of the inheritability of acquired characteristics. It was Spencer, though, who was the most energetic in applying the principles of evolution and natural selection to society, and in doing so he became the archetypal Social Darwinist.

The great work, *The Synthetic Philosophy*, that Spencer announced in 1860 took nearly forty years to complete and is divided into several separately titled parts. *First Principles* appeared in 1862 and is typically metaphysical with its insistence on the existence of an ultimate Unknowable, which could be appreciated but never understood, and typically scientific with its assertion on evolution as the motor of all development, change, and progress. *The Principles of Biology*, a work of two volumes published in 1864 and 1867, was both a survey of developmental physiology and an assertion of the iron law of evolution in the movement from lower to higher forms. He followed his evolutionary theme in the reworking of *The Principles of Psychology* (originally published in 1855), which appeared in a second edition in 1870 and 1872, by insisting that consciousness, too, had gone through successive stages.

Spencer's most influential thesis came in *The Principles of Sociology*, which appeared in three volumes from 1876 to 1896. Here, he provided his organic view of society, that is, that a society is like an organism. In making this analogy, Spencer introduced the study of structure and function into the field of sociology, as well as proving the value of comparative analysis. He also stated in the strongest terms his extreme individualism and negative view of government. From such attitudes has come the tradition that Spencer was rather brutal and pessimistic. In fact, he viewed progress as a natural process, but progress involved the elimination of the weak and unfit. The last portion of the great synthesis was *The Principles of Ethics*, of which one volume was published in 1892 and the other in 1893, and here he took the lessons from nature to create a moral code. In the preface to the last volume of *The Principles of Ethics*, he included a note indicating that evolution had not been the absolute principle, at least in ethics, that he had hoped. In addition to these works, he completed an autobiography in 1889 (published in 1904), and in 1902, a year before his death, he was nominated for the Nobel Prize for Literature.

Summary

Enormously popular in his day, by the middle of the twentieth century Herbert Spencer was entirely neglected by serious scholars, except to be mentioned as the classic proponent of Social Darwinism, an honor which served only to strengthen his negative image. Nevertheless, Spencer made important contributions in the study of society, particularly in the areas of social evolution and the problem of the individual versus the state. If nothing else, his version of natural selection, which he expressed in the phrase "surival of the fittest," has secured for him a permanent historical significance.

Bibliography

Duncan, David. *The Life and Letters of Herbert Spencer*. London: Methuen, and New York: Appleton, 1908. Useful because of the primary sources included.

Elliot, Hugh. *Herbert Spencer*. London: Constable, and New York: Holt, 1917. Interesting because of the early date and because it clearly shows that Spencer's decline had already begun.

Gray, Tim. *The Political Philosophy of Herbert Spencer: Individualism and Organicism*. Aldershot, Hampshire, and Brookfield, Vt.: Avebury, 1996. The author argues that the historical criticisms leveled at contradictions in Spencer's political philosophy are actually due to a fundamental misunderstanding of the foundation of Spencer's thought. Gray concludes that perhaps "individualism" and "organicism" are not contradictory ideas, as is historically assumed.

Hofstadter, Richard. *Social Darwinism in American Thought*. Rev. ed. Boston: Beacon Press, 1955. An excellent examination of Spencer's considerable influence in the United States.

Kennedy, James G. *Herbert Spencer*. Boston: Twayne, 1978. A brief but useful and available survey of Spencer's life and thought.

MacRae, Donald G., ed. *The Man Versus the State*. London and Baltimore: Penguin, 1969. An excellent essay assessing Spencer's importance regarding individualism vis-à-vis big government; introduces eight pieces by Spencer.

Peel, J. D. Y. *Herbert Spencer: The Evolution of a Sociologist*. London: Heinemann, and New York: Basic Books, 1971. Excellent on Spencer's contributions to sociology.

Spencer, Herbert. *An Autobiography*. 2 vols. London: Williams and Norgate, and New York: Appleton, 1904.

———. *Herbert Spencer on Education*. Edited by Andreas M. Kazamias. New York: Columbia University Press, 1966. With a lengthy introduction, these selections from Spencer's writings focus on one of his least-known areas of concern.

Turner, Jonathan H. *Herbert Spencer: A Renewed Appreciation*. Beverly Hills, Calif.: Sage, 1985. A sympathetic view, citing Spencer's contributions to modern sociological methodology and theory.

Weinstein, D. *Equal Freedom and Utility: Herbert Spencer's Liberal Utilitarianism*. Cambridge and New York: Cambridge University Press, 1998. The author reexamines Spencer's thoughts on liberal utilitarianism.

Wiltshire, David. *The Social and Political Thought of Herbert Spencer*. Oxford and New York: Oxford University Press, 1978. A good biographical overview, which concentrates on political theory.

Roy Talbert, Jr.

MIKHAIL MIKHAYLOVICH SPERANSKY

Born: January 12, 1772; Cherkutino, Russia
Died: February 23, 1839; St. Petersburg, Russia
Areas of Achievement: Government and law
Contribution: A career bureaucrat, Speransky sought to liberalize and modernize the Russian government by limiting the power of the autocracy, reforming local government, and codifying Russian law.

Early Life

Mikhail Mikhaylovich Speransky was born on January 12, 1772, of peasant origins, in Cherkutino, a small provincial village to the northeast of Moscow. His family was impoverished and poorly educated and lacked even a family surname. In fact, Speransky did not acquire his name until he began his formal education at the age of twelve, when he entered the ecclesiastical academy at the provincial capital of Vladimir. He was already a promising student, and his intellectual skills and academic accomplishments brought him immediate recognition. In 1790, Speransky was accepted for advanced study at the prestigious Alexander-Nevsky Seminary in St. Petersburg, once more distinguishing himself in his academic pursuits. In addition to the traditional seminary curriculum, Speransky acquired a thorough foundation in the rationalist and materialist thought of the Enlightenment and philosophe writers, which would influence him for the rest of his life. Following his graduation in 1792, Speransky was offered a part-time teaching post at the academy, and in 1795 he was appointed instructor of philosophy and prefect (dean). After rejecting the proffered appointment, Speransky entered the service of Prince A. B. Kuratin, an influential member of the imperial court. For the next year, Speransky continued his study of French Enlightenment thought and encountered the philosophy of Immanuel Kant as well. In 1796, Kuratin was appointed by Emperor Paul I as procurator-general of the senate, which was similar to being prime minister of the government. Kuratin then used his influence to secure for Speransky a position in the government bureaucracy at the beginning of 1797.

By the end of 1798, Speransky had ascended into the upper levels of the bureaucratic Table of Ranks. In the process, he acquired increased responsibilities and hereditary noble status, both of which reflected his growing importance and influence within the bureaucracy and St. Petersburg society. He became acquainted with the concepts of English political philosophy and its emphasis on conservative social corporateness and institutional reform, which now attracted the previously Francophile nobility following the excesses of the French Revolution. It was at one of these encounters that Speransky met his future wife, Elizabeth Stephens. They were married in 1798 and in 1799 produced a daughter, also Elizabeth. His wife died shortly after their daughter's birth. Speransky, already aloof and introverted by nature, became even more withdrawn as he used his career as a means to overcome his personal grief.

Life's Work

In 1801, a new czar, Alexander I, ascended the Russian throne. With him came the hope on the part of many younger Russians that his vague sympathies toward liberalism and reform could be translated into reality. For Speransky, it brought the notice of the new czar and his appointment to the newly formed Ministry of Interior. Attaching himself to the fringes of the "unofficial committee," Speransky spent the years between 1802 and 1808 creating the intellectual foundations required for the restructuring of the Russian political and social order. In his deliberations, he drew upon the philosophical ideals of the Enlightenment, the political concepts of the English system, and his own understanding of Russian historical development.

From the outset, Speransky recognized that the key to any broad reform within Russia was the reform of the autocracy itself. As constituted by the reforms of Peter I and consolidated by Catherine II in the previous century, the autocracy was the only legitimate source of authority within the Russian political system and could not be prevented from exercising that authority in a capricious and arbitrary manner. To Speransky, this represented the epitome of political lawlessness, which could not be tolerated in a rational and enlightened society. Not only was such lawlessness destructive to the stability, cohesion, and order of the society in general, but also in Russia's case it was the primary cause of her political, economic, and social backwardness. Moreover, it prevented Russia from throwing off the burdens of that backwardness by obstructing modernization through meaningful reforms. The only enlightened means to overcome this lawlessness on the part of the ruler, Speransky argued, was the establishment of the rule of law to which all within the society were subject. In this way, rules could be established to govern the relationship between the ruler and the ruled, while also formulating the context in which authority would be exercised by the ruler.

Although Speransky formulated the essential elements of his rule of law concept in 1801-1802 and 1803 for "Mémoire sur la legislation fondamentale en général," summarized by V. I. Semevskii as "Pervi politicheskii traktat Speranskogo" (1907; on the fundamental laws of the state) and "Zapiska ob ustroistve sudebnykhi i pravitel' stvennykh uchrezhdenii v Rossii" (1905; report on the establishment of judiciary and government institutions in Russia), the opportunity to present his formulations to Alexander did not occur until 1809. By the time it did, Alexander's earlier sympathies had dissipated. He rejected Speransky's constitutional plan (known also as the Plan of 1809) as an unacceptable limitation of authority of the autocracy. Speransky's influence at the imperial court began to wane. By 1812, a variety of factors conspired to drive him from power. The cruelest blow, however, came from Alexander himself, who sent his former administrative secretary and assistant into exile, first at Nizhni Novgorod on the upper Volga River and then to Perm in western Siberia near the Ural Mountains. He remained there in disgrace until 1816.

In 1816, the exiled Speransky was permitted to return to government service as a provincial official in the remote province of Penza, near Perm. There he began the difficult task of reforming the chaotic Siberian local government. Pleased with his success, Alexander then appointed Speransky governor-general of Penza in 1819 so that he could implement his Penza reforms throughout Siberia. In 1821, Alexander recalled Speransky to St. Petersburg and appointed him to the State Council for the purpose of reorganizing the system of local government in Russia along the Siberian model. By 1825, Speransky succeeded in establishing a system that would serve Russia for the remainder of the nineteenth century.

Speransky now turned his attention to judicial and legal reform. All agreed that the Russian judicial system, like that of local government previously, was in shambles. The obvious solution was a new codification of Russian laws to replace the Sobornoye Ulozheniye 1649 (code of 1649), which had never been effectively updated. By 1832, Speransky published the *Plonoye sobraniye zakanov Rossiyskoy imperii* or PSZ (1830; complete collection of the laws of the Russian Empire), which represented the codification of all laws enacted between 1649 and 1832. Speransky also compiled and published the *Svod Zakanov* (1832-1839; digest of laws), incorporating all legislation still in force in 1832. Together they served as the ultimate source of legal authority in Russia until 1917. When Speransky died in 1839, he was a much honored and respected statesman.

Summary

Ironically, the impact of Mikhail Mikhaylovich Speransky's career as a reformer is twofold. His early reforms demonstrated that there were individuals in Russia who were concerned about the direction of Russian development during the first half of the nineteenth century. Many of them, like Speransky, concluded that Russia's only hope for future salvation was through the dissolution of the autocracy and the establishment of some form of constitutional government. The fact that Speransky's own constitutional proposals foundered on the rock of autocracy and were thus stillborn did not alter that outlook. Others soon emerged to assume the mantle of leadership in the struggle against the autocracy. One such group, the Decembrists, incorporated many of the ideas from Speransky's Plan of 1809 into their political programs for reform in 1825. While they also failed in the attainment of their goals, it became very clear that the struggle against the autocracy would continue until it accepted the end of its absolutism. Had the autocracy been willing to implement the constitutional reforms put forth by Speransky in 1809, limited as they were, it might have survived the challenges against it after 1870. That it did not do so only postponed the fate which it suffered in 1917.

This leads to the second aspect of Speransky's reforms that must be considered. For the most part, it involves the nature of his work after 1816, which significantly enhanced the efficiency and effectiveness of government administration in Russia. The great irony is that while Speransky's earlier reforms contributed to efforts to reform the autocracy, his later reforms made it possible for the autocracy to resist those efforts and to survive during the remainder of the nineteenth century.

Bibliography

Christian, David. "The Political Ideals of Michael Speransky." *The Slavonic and East European Review* 54 (1976): 192-213. A scholarly and historiographical examination of Speransky's political ideals. Belongs to the school of interpretation which argues that Speransky was a radical liberal reformer and thus rejects Marc Raeff's *Rechtstadt* interpretation (see below). Excellent footnotes incorporating considerable bibliographical material.

Gooding, John. "The Liberalism of Michael Speransky." *The Slavonic and East European Review* 64 (1986): 401-424. Through criticism of Speransky's writings, Gooding supports the conclusions of Christian's article. Includes extensive footnotes which encompass a wide range of bibliographical materials.

Jenkins, Michael. "Mikhail Speransky." *History Today* 20 (1970): 404-409. A short and popularized account of Speransky's career designed primarily for high school students.

Raeff, Marc. *Michael Speransky: Statesman of Imperial Russia, 1772-1839.* 2d ed. The Hague: Martinus Nijhoff, 1969. The most comprehensive, analytic, and scholarly biographical treatment of Speransky in the English language. Contains exhaustive notes, a bibliography, and indexes that guide the student into every facet of Speransky's life and activities as well as that of general Russian history between 1772 and 1839.

———. *Plans for Political Reform in Imperial Russia, 1730-1905.* Englewood Cliffs, N.J.: Prentice-Hall, 1966. This collection of original sources includes documents on government reform (1802) and the codification of state law by Speransky (1809).

———. *Siberia and the Reforms of 1822.* Seattle: University of Washington Press, 1956. A comprehensive and scholarly treatment of Speransky's Siberian reforms of 1816-1821 and their impact on the shaping of his reform of local government in Russia after 1822. Extensive notes, a bibliography, and indexes.

David K. McQuilkin

MADAME DE STAËL

Born: April 22, 1766; Paris, France
Died: July 14, 1817; Paris, France
Areas of Achievement: Literature, philosophy, government, and politics
Contribution: Madame de Staël publicly articulated the liberal, rational opposition to the injustices and corruption of the French government during the Revolution and under Napoleon I. Her social and literary criticism, as well as her colorful personal life, placed her in the vanguard of the Romantic movement, and her two major novels constitute early treatments of the concerns of women.

Early Life

Madame de Staël was born Anne-Louise-Germaine Necker in Paris on April 22, 1766, the only child of Suzanne Curchod Necker, the beautiful and highly educated daughter of a Swiss clergyman, and the Genevese financier Jacques Necker, who was to achieve fame as minister to Louis XVI. Despite her learning, Madame Necker was considered a rather narrow woman by the urbane Parisians, and her relations with her daughter were always rigid and distant. Though not without critics of his own, the stodgy Jacques Necker was widely esteemed as a man of public and private virtue. Germaine's natural love for her father was intensified by her childhood awareness of the public acclaim he enjoyed. As an adult, Germaine's consciousness of her place in the prominent Necker family helped to form her notions of social criticism and political activism and her sense of personal destiny.

A precocious child, Germaine was educated at home in imagined accordance with *Émile: Ou, De l'éducation* (1762; *Emilius and Sophia: Or, A New System of Education*, 1762-1763), Jean-Jacques Rousseau's radical exposition on childhood education. Madame Necker stalwartly maintained one of the literary salons for which Paris was celebrated during the eighteenth century, and Germaine grew up on familiar terms with such people as Denis Diderot, Jean Le Rond d'Alembert, Comte de Buffon, and Abbé Raynal. In this rarefied environment, she absorbed the liberal politics and morals of the Enlightenment.

On January 14, 1786, after years of negotiation, Germaine Necker married a Swedish aristocrat, Eric Magnus, Baron de Staël-Holstein, a favorite of Gustav III and—in accordance with the mar-

riage negotiations—Swedish ambassador to the French court. De Staël may have felt some affection for Germaine (and some, certainly, for her dowry of 650,000 pounds), but she apparently felt none for him, and their first child, Edwige-Gustavine, was probably the only one of their four children actually fathered by de Staël. More important, however, Germaine gained a measure of social and economic independence from the marriage. In the embassy residence in Paris, she established a salon of her own, which soon became the gathering place for such liberal members of the aristocracy as Mathieu de Montmorency, Talleyrand, and Louis, Vicomte de Narbonne Lara. In the early days of her marriage, she used her husband's court connections to try to advance the position of her father, and she took advantage of de Staël's frequent absences to lead the relatively independent life that was possible for women of her station in eighteenth century Paris.

Life's Work

Madame de Staël's residence at the Swedish embassy in Paris was one of the more attractive features of her marriage agreement, for Jacques Necker had been dismissed by Louis XVI in 1781 and had moved his family to Saint-Ouen, where Germaine had sorely missed the intellectual life of Paris. Necker was recalled by Louis XVI in 1788, and was then dismissed and recalled once again at the fall of the Bastille. He continued at his post through the march on Versailles in September, 1789, and the massive nationalization effected by the Assembly under Comte de Mirabeau. Necker finally resigned in September, 1790, and repaired to the family estate of Coppet, near Geneva.

During her father's interrupted tenure at court, Germaine attempted to elicit support among her influential friends of the liberal aristocracy for a constitution and a bicameral government, as a compromise between the continued abuses of the Bourbon dynasty and the inevitable triumph of the Third Estate. On August 31, 1790, she gave birth to a son, Auguste, fathered by Narbonne, with whom she had been involved for about a year and a half. Determined that Narbonne should be the leader of the new government, Madame de Staël became further embroiled in intrigues at court until Narbonne was appointed war minister at the request of Marie Antoinette; he was dismissed, however, in March,

1792. At about the same time, de Staël was recalled to Sweden when Louis and Marie Antoinette were arrested attempting to escape Paris in a maneuver arranged by Gustav III. Gustav was assassinated in March, 1792, however, and de Staël returned to Paris, where Madame de Staël continued to encourage the constitutionalists and agitated for the restoration of Narbonne. She finally fled Paris for Coppet the day before the September massacres began in 1793.

Madame de Staël's relationship with Narbonne—which followed a similar liaison with Talleyrand and coincided with a profound friendship with Montmorency—was characteristic of her lifelong attraction to the heroes of her political and intellectual causes. Much of her own appeal resided in her power as a fascinating conversationalist, and even those who were prepared to be intimidated by her were often won over by her exuberance and lack of pretension. Possessing none of her mother's conventional beauty, she was nevertheless a woman of imposing physical appearance. Her wide, luminous eyes were considered her most attractive feature. A woman of Junoesque proportions, Madame de Staël continued to dress in the revealing diaphanous fabrics and décolleté lines of empire fashion even after she had grown heavy in middle age. Her frank display of her ample bosom and legs, and her continuance of the eighteenth century custom of the *levée*, amazed younger, more conservative Parisians and provoked the derision of her enemies. She customarily wore a turban, which undoubtedly lent a Byronic dash to her overall appearance.

During the Terror, Madame de Staël lived much of the time at Coppet, spending considerable money and energy smuggling refugees from the liberal aristocracy out of Paris. She gave birth to her son Albert, also the child of Narbonne, on November 20, 1792, and left shortly thereafter for England, where Narbonne had sought refuge from the Terror. Rumors of her complicity in the Revolution and in the Terror were circulated by aristocratic French émigrés living in England until she was no longer received by members of the upper class. Disappointed by the conservatism of the British, her relationship with Narbonne strained, she returned in June, 1793, to her husband near Coppet, where Narbonne finally joined her in August, 1794.

In 1794, the year of her mother's death, Madame de Staël met Benjamin Constant, with whom she would be involved in a passionate and embattled relationship for the next fourteen years. With the fall of Robespierre in 1794, she returned to Paris and reopened her salon. At this time, she worked to encourage support for the positive changes wrought by the Revolution; the degree of influence she wielded is measured by the fact that she was expelled from the city alternately by both royalists and republicans. Her only daughter, Albertine, probably the child of Constant, was born in Paris on June 8, 1796. In 1797, Madame de Staël formally separated from her husband; debilitated by a stroke suffered in 1801, he died the following year en route to Coppet.

In 1795, Madame de Staël published *Essai sur les fictions (Essay on Fiction*, 1795), in 1796, *De l'influence des passions sur le bonheur des individus et des nations (A Treatise on the Influence of the Passions upon the Happiness of Individuals and Nations*, 1798), and, in 1800, *De la littérature considérée dans ses rapports avec les institutions sociales (A Treatise on Ancient and Modern Literature*, 1803). In these and later writings, her examination of the concept of perfectibility—the idea that scientific progress would lead humankind toward moral perfection—and her contention that critical judgment must be relative and historically oriented earned for her a place near Chateaubriand as a precursor of Romanticism. In 1802, she published the novel *Delphine* (English translation, 1803), which explores the role of the intellectual woman.

One of the most significant factors in Madame de Staël's life was her relationship with Napoleon, whom she first met in 1797. She early admired him as a republican hero: His successful coup of 18 Brumaire seemed to actualize the liberal abstractions of revolutionary politics. Nepoleon, thoroughly conventional in his attitude toward women, however, could not approve of the highly vocal, public role that Madame de Staël had assumed; moreover, he resented the free discussion of his government that was encouraged at her salon, to which even his own brothers were frequent visitors. As he became more tyrannical, she became increasingly critical, eventually labeling him an "ideophobe." He expelled her from France in 1803 and crowned himself emperor the following year.

Her eleven years in exile from France during the reign of Napoleon seemed a spiritual and intellectual death sentence to Madame de Staël. Immediately upon her expulsion, she visited Germany, where she was welcomed as the author of *Del-*

phine. She met with the great thinkers and writers of Weimar and Berlin, including Johann Wolfgang von Goethe, Friedrich Schiller, and August Wilhelm von Schlegel, with whom she formed a long-lasting attachment. In April, 1804, Constant brought her news of her father's death. Prostrate with grief, she returned to Coppet.

From 1804 to 1810, Madame de Staël officially resided at Coppet, where she gathered around her a group of loyal and intellectually stimulating friends, including Schlegel and Jeanne Récamier. She spent much of her time away from the estate, however, venturing into France and traveling to Italy until she was confined to Coppet as a result of the machinations of the French and Genevese police. The Romantic and feminist concerns of her 1807 novel *Corinne: Ou L'Italie* (*Corinne: Or, Italy,* 1807) brought her renewed fame, and in 1810 she completed *De l'Allemagne* (*Germany,* 1813), a thinly disguised critique of contemporary France, which was suppressed by Napoleon; it was published in England in 1813.

In 1811, she took another lover, John Rocca, a young Genevese sportsman who had been wounded in military action and was now tubercular. Rocca fathered her last child, Alphonse, and in 1816 they were married. Shortly after the birth of Alphonse, she fled Coppet and traveled throughout Europe, involving herself in Russian and Swedish political intrigues directed toward overthrowing Napoleon. Napoleon's abdication in 1814 brought Madame de Staël the freedom to reestablish herself in Paris, where she died on Bastille Day, in 1817.

Summary

Madame de Staël was a brilliant and unconventional woman whose circumstances of birth allowed her to witness some of the most significant events of Western history and whose intelligence and moral courage led her to participate. In the face of serious opposition, she lived with great enthusiasm and energy, balancing the exercise of intellect and creativity with the pursuit of a passionate personal life.

Madame de Staël tended the flame of the Enlightenment through the darkest days following the French Revolution. The rational tenor of her criticism of oppression and her defense of freedom provided a constant corrective not only to political tyranny but also to the social and cultural constraints that bound her as a woman. In her nonfictional prose, she sought support for her philosophical stance in the individualistic spirit of English and German Romanticism and in the cultural relativism afforded by her experiences in Germany, Italy, and Russia. Her examination, in *Delphine* and *Corinne,* of the difficulties encountered in the personal lives of gifted and creative women has gained new attention from feminist critics. Madame de Staël thus continues to assert her vivacious presence.

Bibliography

Gutwirth, Madelyn. *Madame de Staël, Novelist: The Emergence of the Artist as Woman.* Urbana: University of Illinois Press, 1978. This book is a feminist analysis of the biographical, cultural, and social sources of the novels *Corinne* and *Delphine,* especially in their focus on the complications created by talent and love in women's lives. Includes notes, a bibliography, and an index.

———. "Madame de Staël, Rousseau, and the Woman Question." *PMLA* 86 (January, 1971): 100-109. Gutwirth discusses Madame de Staël's attempted resolution of the conflict between the conservative ideals of feminine behavior endorsed by Rousseau and the more radical example of achievement provided by her own life.

Herold, J. Christopher. *Mistress to an Age: A Life of Madame de Staël.* Indianapolis, Ind.: Bobbs-Merrill, 1958; London: Hamilton, 1959. This standard biography is eminently readable and sympathetic, although slightly ironic in tone. Herold treats Madame de Staël's life in its entirety, emphasizing the effects of her relationship with her parents and focusing on her prodigious literary accomplishment and her unconventional personal life. Informed by an easy familiarity with French politics and culture, the book includes illustrations, an extensive annotated bibliography, and an index.

Hogsett, Charlotte. *The Literary Existence of Germaine de Staël.* Carbondale: Southern Illinois University Press, 1987. Writing from a feminist standpoint, Hogsett provides a critical analysis of Madame de Staël's writings as they reveal her development as a woman writer struggling to define herself in a male-dominated tradition. Contains notes, a bibliography, and an index.

Isabell, John. "The Painful Birth of the Romantic Heroine: Staël as Political Animal, 1786–1818." *The Romantic Review* 87, no. 1 (January, 1996). Discusses Staël's desire to participate in the politics of her day and her creation of the romantic heroine as a substitute.

Levaillant, Maurice. *The Passionate Exiles: Madame de Staël and Madame Récamier.* Translated by Malcolm Barnes. London: Allen and Unwin, and New York: Farrar, Straus, 1958. Levaillant examines Madame de Staël's life in exile at Coppet, with particular focus on her friendship with Jeanne Récamier. The book quotes extensively from the two women's correspondence.

Moers, Ellen. "Madame de Staël and the Woman of Genius." *American Scholar* 44 (Spring, 1975): 225-241. A discussion of Madame de Staël's view of the gifted woman in terms of the cultural liberation provided by the Italian setting of *Corinne.*

Smith, Bonnie G. "History and Genius: The Narcotic, Erotic, and Baroque Life of Germaine de Staël." *French Historical Studies* 19, no. 4 (Fall 1996). Smith studies the many facets of Staël's approach to history.

West, Rebecca. "Madame de Staël." *Encounter* 13 (July, 1959): 66-73. This article is a perceptive review of Herold's biography, supplementing his depiction of Madame de Staël with an intelligent assessment of circumstances mitigating some of the more eccentric aspects of her life.

Diane Prenatt Stevens

LELAND STANFORD

Born: March 9, 1824; Watervliet, New York
Died: June 20, 1893; Palo Alto, California
Areas of Achievement: Business, politics, and education
Contribution: As president of the Central Pacific Railroad, Stanford guided the project which produced the nation's first transcontinental railroad; he also founded Stanford University, in Palo Alto, California.

Early Life

Amasa Leland Stanford was born on March 9, 1824, in Watervliet, New York, located on the western side of the Hudson River opposite Troy. His father, Josiah, was a versatile Yankee who combined farming, innkeeping, and contracting on local road and canal projects. In 1836, Josiah Stanford moved the family to a farm on the Albany-Schenectady turnpike, where the young Stanford and his five brothers observed the westward migration pass directly in front of their home. This Western exodus and his father's contracting business greatly influenced Stanford and helped to inspire him in his later railroad pioneering ventures.

Educated in local public schools and by itinerant tutors, Stanford enrolled, at the age of seventeen, in the small and racially integrated Institute of Science and Industry in Whitesborough, New York. Unhappy with its limited curriculum, he soon transferred to another school near Utica, New York, before settling at the Methodist Cazenovia Seminary near Syracuse. There, he became an active member of the debate society; became interested in the Whig politics of his hero, Henry Clay, the spokesman of a national program of internal improvements; and kept up a steady correspondence with his father on the latter's newfound interest in railroads. By the spring of 1845, Stanford quit school to apprentice at an Albany law firm and was admitted to the bar in 1848.

In the same year and with his law credentials now established, Stanford left Albany and traveled West, first to Chicago and then, by year's end, to Port Washington, Wisconsin, almost twenty miles due north of Milwaukee. In the nation's newest state, Stanford prospered and earned more than a thousand dollars in his first year on the frontier. He continued his earlier political interests and ran unsuccessfully as a Whig candidate for county district attorney. He then returned to Albany briefly in 1850 to marry Jane Lathrop, the daughter of a substantial Albany merchant, whom he had met in his law apprentice days. They returned to Port Washington, where he practiced law for another two years before becoming restless and dissatisfied with his profession.

In 1852, Stanford left Wisconsin, determined to start again in gold rush California. Again returning to Albany before the journey West, he encountered unrelenting opposition from his wife's father, who forbade her from accompanying her husband to the wilds of California. Bowing to his father-in-law's demands, Stanford sailed from New York City without his wife in June, 1852. Thirty-eight days later, after a passage through the Nicaraguan isthmus, Stanford arrived in San Francisco on July 12 and quickly moved on to Sacramento, the gateway to the gold country.

All five of the Stanford brothers had already preceded him to California and had established themselves in a loose-knit network of mercantile ventures. The Stanford clan understood early that more gold could be extracted through storekeeping than through gold-panning. Indeed, one of the brothers, Charles, had returned to Albany to serve as purchasing agent for the Stanford family's expanding commercial enterprises in California. Stanford soon opened a store of his own, first in the town of Cold Springs, then in the boomtown of Michigan Bluff, which, in 1853, had grown from a population of thirty to two thousand. Because of his previous law experience, Stanford was soon elected the town's justice of the peace, his only elective office until his 1861 gubernatorial victory.

In 1855, upon the death of his father-in-law, Stanford was finally able to bring his wife to California. In the fall of that year, they relocated to Sacramento and built a store valued at fourteen thousand dollars. Now fond of the substantial, he had quit the gold fields for good. He was no longer a storekeeper but a prosperous merchant who was supplementing his income by numerous profitable investments in mining ventures.

As a gentleman of property and standing, Stanford next turned to politics. In the 1856 presidential election year, Stanford became an active organizer for the infant Republican Party. As a delegate to the party's first statewide convention, he endorsed its demand for the building of a Pacific transcontinental railroad. In the spring of 1857, he was an unsuccessful candidate for Sacramento city alderman and in the fall lost a race for state treasurer. Despite these defeats, Stanford had firmly established himself in Republican Party circles and was nominated for governor in 1859. The Democratic Party dominated California politics, and Stanford won less than ten percent of the votes. National events, however, were rapidly changing the state's political picture. By 1861, the California Republican Convention, now greatly encouraged by Abraham Lincoln's election, nominated Stanford again. The fall gubernatorial election closely paralleled the presidential race of the previous year, and Stanford was elected by defeating a badly divided Democratic Party.

Life's Work

Inaugurated governor in January, 1862, Stanford began to merge his two new careers, politics and railroading. Since June of the previous year, Stanford had been president of the newly formed Central Pacific Railroad of California. Indeed, while he discharged his gubernatorial duties faithfully and ably throughout his two-year term, he remained, by his own definition, a businessman who was primarily committed to the transcontinental railroad enterprise which became his life's work. He may have worn two hats, but railroading was his overarching passion.

Stanford's association with the Central Pacific Railroad can be traced to his Whig political roots and his longtime interest in internal improvements. It took Theodore Dehone Judah, however, a Connecticut-born engineer, to help transform Stanford's dreams into tangible realities. Judah had already built New York's Niagara Gorge Railroad, and by the late 1850's he had devoted his life to the building of a transcontinental railroad. When San Francisco investors turned him down, he was given an enthusiastic reception by Sacramento businessmen, including Stanford. In addition to Stanford, Judah recruited three other principal investors: Charles Crocker, Mark Hopkins, and Collis Huntington. Each of the associates was a prosperous Sacramento merchant; all were about the same age; all but Huntington were native New Yorkers; and all had been active in the California Republican Party. In June, 1861, these four (soon known as the Big Four) became the railroad's directors, with Stanford the president.

The Big Four's first priority was electing Stanford governor. As Judah advised, "a good deal depends upon the election of Stanford, for the prestige of electing a Republican ticket will go a great way toward getting what we want." With Stanford as governor, it became easier to attract potential investors and to secure favorable action from the state legislature. According to Huntington, the company's vice president, "President Stanford promoted, the California legislature passed, and Governor Stanford signed seven acts of benevolence toward the Central Pacific"—one of which was a $500,000 subsidy, which was passed in the wake of some personal lobbying on the floor of the legislature by the governor. Stanford was equally successful in his dealings with Washington. Regarding California gold as central to the financial health of the nation in the midst of the Civil War, Congress and President Lincoln probably needed little persuasion in aiding Stanford's transcontinental railroad. On July 1, 1862, only six months after he had become governor, a federal bill to float loans to the Central Pacific became law. The terms provided both outright land grants and mortgage bonds in the form of long-term loans.

Stanford's venture began on a shoestring. On paper, the Central Pacific Railroad was capitalized at $8,500,000, with each share selling at one hundred dollars. The reality, however, was far different. Only fifteen hundred shares were actually sold, and the associates purchased forty percent of the stock for a mere ten percent down. Stanford, then, began his meteoric rise to fortune, fame, and philanthropy with a fifteen-hundred-dollar investment.

Finally, in October, 1863, the Central Pacific began to lay its first tracks, and Stanford had already resolved not to seek reelection but to devote his entire energy to the building of the railroad. His most important contribution during this period involved the creation of a separate "dummy" company, the so-called Contract and Finance Company, which, in turn, "sold" its construction services and its equipment back to itself under the name of the Central Pacific Railroad. This financial sleight-of-hand allowed the associates to juggle the books successfully and to transfer funds from one account to the other, as well as to hide their own personal profits. As the sole owners of the "Contract and Finance Company," the Big Four reaped huge profits which far exceeded comparable investments by the other investors, who could only purchase stock in the railroad.

Stanford, however, frequently found time to travel into the field and to rough it with the workers. He proposed that snowsheds be constructed in the Sierra to protect the tracks and the work crews. By 1869, thirty-nine miles of sheds had been built at a cost of two million dollars, a vivid demonstration of the massive undertaking that Stanford was leading. Finally, with a reliable and sufficient source of funding secured and a steady supply of materials guaranteed, Stanford's Central Pacific Rairoad cut through and over the Sierra Nevada, raced through the high desert of the state of Nevada, and joined the Union Pacific Railroad at Promontory Point (near Ogden), Utah, on May 10, 1869. With Stanford (the only member of the Big Four present) to drive (and to miss) the ceremonial golden spike, the nation's first transcontinental railroad had been completed.

This was not the end for Stanford and his associates, but rather the beginning of a comprehensive and near-monopolistic railroad system in California and the Southwest. In 1867, Stanford engineered the buy out of the Western Pacific, a pro-spective competitor. This was soon followed by a successful raid on the Southern Pacific Railway, which had received a charter to run from San Francisco south to San Diego and on to New Orleans. Before the Southern Pacific could begin to operate as an independent entity, however, Stanford and the Central Pacific acquired control of it, probably sometime between March and September, 1868. By 1884, twenty separate lines had been consolidated and reorganized into the Southern Pacific Corporation. Stanford and the associates had knitted together a system which managed five thousand miles of track and controlled eighty-five percent of California's railroads.

Presiding over the empire, however, did take an increasing toll on Stanford. In May, 1880, near Hanford, eight men were killed in the Battle Mussel Slough in the course of eviction proceedings. Despite public opinion to the contrary, Stanford took the hard line and helped to precipitate the bloody confrontation. Ever more defensive in the next few years, Stanford lashed out against the reformers who called for railroad regulation and adamantly refused to answer questions which touched on bribery and influence-peddling posed by the state's railroad commissioners, whom he abhorred. Moreover, the Southern Pacific was incorporated in the state of Kentucky to protect the company from the ever-increasing hostility of California juries.

The financial complexities of the Central Pacific-Southern Pacific combine have always been shrouded in mystery. Nobody who knew of the inside workings would ever talk; nobody on the outside could ever get in. From an initial investment of fifteen hundred dollars in cash, each of the associates earned thirteen million dollars from the Central Pacific alone. When he died in 1893, Stanford, who had already given away money lavishly, was still worth at least thirty million dollars and was one of the richest men in the United States.

With such an immense fortune, Stanford did not stint on the good life. His sumptuously decorated fifty-room mansion atop San Francisco's Nob Hill, with its precious wood paneling, was palatial. As befit a man of means, Stanford was able to live the life of a country squire. He purchased nearly eight thousand acres of land south of San Francisco that he called the Palo Alto Farm. He raised championship trotters there and became an international expert on their breeding and training. His farm was universally considered the best of its kind in the world. Stanford's interest in horses also led to the world's first motion-picture experiments at the Palo Alto estate. In hopes of discovering whether a trotter had all four feet off the ground at some point during its gait, Stanford hired the noted English photographer, Eadweard Muybridge, and planned much of the experiment himself. Stanford was a pioneer in the California vinoculture, and his Vina Winery, set amid an immense fifty-five-thousand-acre spread, was the largest and most modern in the world. For all the money and attention he lavished on this endeavor, however, the results were little better than mediocre.

By the 1880's, travel became a way of life with the Stanfords, who frequently took the grand tours of Europe. On one such excursion, their only (indeed, almost revered) child, Leland, Jr., died of typhoid fever in March, 1884, in Florence, Italy. Grief-stricken, the Stanfords resolved to build a university in memory of their son on their Palo Alto property. Active from the beginning in every phase of the establishment of the university, from architecture to curriculum, Stanford was a solicitous and affectionate overseer of the enterprise. Stanford University, one of the few private coeducational universities, was opened on October 1, 1891, and in some ways, Stanford considered it his most significant achievement.

While still active in planning the university and continuing as president of the Southern Pacific system, Stanford unexpectedly entered politics when the Republican-dominated California legislature elected him to the United States Senate in January, 1885. He served a relatively undistinguished eight years in that body and was a conservative spokesman for an unregulated economy. On occasion, however, Stanford demonstrated that he could transcend the limitations of his Darwinistic philosophy. He introduced a radical federal loan program for debt-ridden farmers and supported an innovative national funding proposal for education. In the last decade of his life, Stanford was, by far, the most popular of the Big Four. He died at his Palo Alto home on the evening of June 20, 1893.

Summary

Stanford was quintessentially an American "type." Born of pure Yankee stock, he joined the Western migration to the frontier and rose to become a millionaire and the richest man in the Senate. He did not possess an extraordinarily brilliant or analytical mind, like an Andrew Carnegie, for example, but he did possess a wealth of diligence and patience, and an unerring eye for the main chance. He was productively restless and was adroit enough to seize opportunities that were wide open in California. In its early days, the state broke far more men than it made, and it is a tribute to Stanford that he survived the test.

Stanford was not wholly of the Central Pacific-Southern Pacific system, but he was the paramount leader of the Big Four. Of all the associates, he was the one best able to work with all segments of the population. He was the glue that kept this hard-driving clique together. His single-mindedness during his two-year gubernatorial term probably saved the endeavor. At the same time, and for the same reason, this unswerving commitment to his transcontinental railroad interrupted his political career. As governor, Stanford did exercise undue influence on the California legislature, and throughout the years, his railroad system did exercise an octopuslike grip on the entire state. At a time when a transcontinental system was a national imperative, beyond the means of any individual or private group, Stanford helped to discover how to harness the financial resources of government. In the process, he did, indeed, become wealthy, but the public gained, too. Certainly, San Francisco became and remained the hub of the West, because it was at the center of Stanford's transportation network. For all of its rapaciousness, the system did offer reliable service. This enriched California agriculture, the state's source of wealth after the gold rush had played out.

Stanford was not quite a robber baron. His workers were loyal and were well paid. He was a collector of things (houses, horses, jewels, art), but he did not flaunt them. He was a man of great wealth, but also a man of philanthropy. He was, finally, a new kind of American capitalist, who, in the absence of regulatory legislation and income tax, tested the outer limits of private enterprise. Stanford both lived in and helped define an age. Rules had not been made to temper the acquisitive men of his generation. His life was proof that he made the most of all of his opportunities; his life was also proof that more legislation was needed to hold men of business more accountable to the general public.

Bibliography

Bancroft, Hubert Howe. *History of the Life of Leland Stanford: A Character Study.* Oakland, Calif.: Biobooks, 1952. Published posthumously, this work is valuable because it was written by the dean of Western historians, who knew Stanford personally. Valuable primary sources, especially on the founding of Stanford University.

Bean, Walton E. *California: An Interpretive History.* 7th ed. New York: McGraw-Hill, 1998. A magnificent study of California which skillfully combines narrative and interpretation. Provides the context in which to place Stanford.

Beebe, Lucius Morris. *The Central Pacific and Southern Pacific Railroads.* Berkeley, Calif.: Howell-North, 1963. A large picture book, with rare photos, good maps, a lively text, and superlative captions.

Brown, Dee. *Hear the Lonesome Whistle Blow: Railroads in the West.* New York: Holt Rinehart, and London: Chatto and Windus, 1977. Good analysis of the effects the transcontinentals had on Native Americans and on the ecology of the West. Very strong on how the various systems helped to transform life and society in the West.

Clark, George T. *Leland Stanford: War Governor of California, Railroad Builder and Founder of Stanford University.* Stanford, Calif.: Stanford University Press, and Oxford: Oxford University Press, 1931. Written by the director emeritus of the Stanford library, the work is an adulatory biography. Very strong on the founding of the university.

Griswold, Wesley S. *A Work of Giants: Building the First Transcontinental Railroad.* New York: McGraw-Hill, 1962; London: Muller, 1963. A gripping popular account, especially strong on the engineering marvels; also, helpful in comparing the Union Pacific with the Central Pacific. Strong, also, on the personalities of both systems.

Holliday, J. S. *The World Rushed In: The California Gold Rush Experience.* New York: Simon and Schuster, 1981; London: Gollancz, 1983. An extraordinary account from a wealth of primary sources by a historian who re-creates the world of the gold camps that Stanford knew well. Does not mention Stanford, but tells the reader much of what a man such as Stanford observed, thought, and felt.

Lewis, Oscar. *The Big Four: The Story of Huntington, Stanford, Hopkins, and Crocker.* New York and London: Knopf, 1938. Written with verve, this is a generally critical account of Stanford and associates; contains excellent character sketches of each of the partners and Theodore Judah.

Norris, Frank. *The Octopus: A Story of California.* New York: Doubleday, and London: Richards, 1901. The first of a projected trilogy on the growing, selling, and use of wheat, this novel is an account of the struggle between the wheat growers of California and Stanford's Southern Pacific.

Tutorow, Norman E. *Leland Stanford: Man of Many Careers.* Menlo Park, Calif.: Pacific Coast, 1971. The definitive Stanford biography, at times turgidly written, but most impressive in research and evenhanded in its analysis. Clearly, this account is indispensable for any extensive consideration of Leland Stanford.

LeRoy J. Votto

HENRY MORTON STANLEY

Born: January 28, 1841; Denbigh, Denbighshire, Wales

Died: May 10, 1904; London, England

Area of Achievement: Exploration

Contribution: Best known for finding and resupplying Dr. David Livingstone in 1871, Stanley was the first white man to chart a number of the great lakes in central Africa and follow the Congo River to its mouth. His exploration opened much of Africa to European commerce and colonization.

Early Life

Henry Morton Stanley, the illegitimate child of nineteen-year-old Elizabeth Perry, was born in Denbigh, Denbighshire, Wales, on January 28, 1841. He was christened John Rowlands, thus receiving the same name as his probable father, a twenty-six-year-old farmer. At the age of four, he entered the local grammar school, but two years later he was placed in St. Asaph Union Workhouse, where he received most of his formal education.

Stanley applied himself diligently to his studies, exhibiting a trait that would endure throughout his life. Though he was a man of action who could act impetuously, his successes in Africa owed much to the care with which he prepared his expeditions. A journalist who visited Stanley's apartment in 1874 noted that "the chairs, tables, sofas and settees, nay even the very floor itself—are laden with books, newspapers, manuscripts and maps" over which Stanley pored until late every night, making careful notes about weather, topography, and needed supplies.

Stanley also demonstrated his penchant for rashness at St. Asaph, for, according to his autobiography (1909), he ran away at the age of fifteen after knocking his teacher unconscious. He fled first to a cousin, Moses Owen, for whom he worked briefly as a teacher while receiving the last of his own classroom instruction. Owen's mother disliked her nephew, so after nine months Stanley had to leave his post as student-tutor. Instead, he earned a precarious living as a shepherd and bartender at Treneirchion, Wales, before crossing the border to Liverpool. From this port, in December, 1858, he sailed as a cabin boy aboard the *Windermere*, bound for New Orleans.

Once in the United States, Stanley again ran away from a desperate situation, jumping ship even though he was a stranger without prospects for employment. Luck favored him, though, and he was adopted by a generous cotton broker, Henry Hope Stanley, whose name he took; the "Morton" was a later addition. After clerking in New Orleans and Cypress Bend, Arkansas, Stanley enlisted in the Arkansas Greys when the Civil War began. Captured by Union forces at the Battle of Shiloh in April, 1862, he shifted his allegiance rather than languish in a prison camp. This phase of his military career ended quickly when he received a medical discharge less than a month after joining an Illinois regiment. He would make one further attempt to serve, signing with the federal navy on July 19, 1864. After seeing action off the coast of North Carolina, he jumped ship on February 10, 1865; Stanley was apparently born to command but not to serve.

A perpetual victim of wanderlust, in June, 1865, Stanley agreed to work as a free-lance writer for the Missouri *Democrat* (in St. Louis) to report on the Colorado gold rush. Over the next two years, this love of travel would carry him from the American West to the Middle East and back to his native Denbigh before he returned to Missouri.

Life's Work

Shortly after returning to the United States, Stanley seized an opportunity to travel once more. England was preparing to invade Abyssinia, and Stanley offered to cover the story for the New York *Herald*. Its owner, James Gordon Bennett, agreed—provided that Stanley would pay all of his own expenses. Stanley accepted these terms. Through bribery, skill, and luck, he was the first to report the British victory at the Battle of Magdala, thus securing a permanent spot on the staff of Bennett's paper.

Two years later, Bennett selected his young European correspondent for the mission that would make Stanley's name a household word and forever change the map of Africa. Dr. David Livingstone, missionary and geographer, had first gone to Africa in 1841. In 1866, he set out to find the source of the Nile River but soon disappeared. As concern for his safety mounted, Bennett asked Stanley to find and resupply the missing explorer.

Bennett's concern, though, was more journalistic than humanitarian; he recognized what Stanley's story would do for the circulation of the *Herald*. To be sure that the newspaper would have good copy regardless of the outcome of the rescue effort, Bennett first sent Stanley to cover the opening of the Suez Canal, on November 17, 1869, and to file a series of reports on the Middle East. Thus, Stanley could not begin his search for Livingstone until early 1871. On November 10, 1871, after overcoming bad weather, disease, and hostile tribesmen, Stanley found the man he was seeking, greeting him with the words that would soon echo throughout Europe and America: "Dr. Livingstone, I presume?" Stanley had given the *Herald* its story, and he had saved Livingstone, whose supplies were almost exhausted and who was suffering from dysentery. Livingstone tried to persuade Stanley to join him in his quest for the source of the Nile, while Stanley argued that Livingstone should return to England. Neither convinced the other, but Stanley was clearly captivated by the missionary and by Africa. Even though he was eager to tell his story to the Western world, Stanley tarried at Ujiji on Lake Tanganyika until March 14, 1872.

Back in London, Stanley described his life as a "whirl of cabs, soirées, dinners, dress-clothes and gloves." He was added to Madame Tussaud's waxworks; Queen Victoria sent him a jeweled snuffbox bearing the inscription, "Presented by Her Majesty, Queen Victoria to Henry Morton Stanley, Esq. in recognition of the prudence and zeal displayed by him in opening communication with Doctor Livingstone and thus relieving the general anxiety felt in regard to the fate of that distinguished Traveller." She also granted him an audience at Dunrobin Castle.

Not everyone was equally enthusiastic over Stanley's achievement, particularly since he pointed out that neither the Royal Geographical Society nor the British government had done much to help Livingstone. Stanley was accused of fabricating the whole account and of forging the Livingstone letters and diary he brought back with him. In August, 1872, he bitterly described the treatment he had received from the Royal Geographical Society and the British upper classes:

> First they would sneer at the fact of an American having gone to Central Africa—then they sneered at the idea of his being successful. . . . My story is called "sensational" and unreal etc. I assure you that I think after decently burying Livingstone in forgetfulness they hate to be told he is yet alive.

When Stanley offered to accompany the belatedly organized relief expedition under the auspices of the Royal Geographical Society, he was rebuffed. Nevertheless, the society could not ignore the general sentiment concerning Stanley's success, and on October 31, 1872, it reluctantly awarded him its highest honor, the Victoria Gold Medal.

In the midst of speeches, dinners, honors, and receptions, Stanley found time to write two books about his recent adventures, *How I Found Livingstone* (1872) and *My Kalulu* (1873). The latter, a fictionalized adventure tale for youngsters, did not do well, but *How I Found Livingstone* was an immense success, selling more than seventy thousand copies.

Finding and resupplying Livingstone had captured the popular imagination; as Sir Clement Robert Markham observed, however, "The fellow has done no geography." The same could not be said of Stanley's next expedition. On November 17, 1874, he plunged into the African jungle again, determined to cross the continent from east to west, locate the source of the Nile, and chart the unknown equatorial regions.

Such a feat offered great rewards and equally large challenges. The weather could be oppressively hot, and torrential rains could quickly turn a campsite into a sea of mud. The natives who carried the supplies often proved unreliable; they would desert or, worse, mutiny. Dysentery, malaria, and typhus took a heavy toll: Stanley was the only white man in the party to survive the journey. Hostile tribes posed yet another danger; in a single battle at Vinyata, twenty-one people were killed by Nyaturu warriors. Within three months, Stanley had lost more than half of his original caravan.

The jungle exacted a price from Stanley himself also. In 1874 in London, he had weighed 178 pounds; since he was only five feet, five inches tall, his figure was portly. Yet he carried himself with military erectness, and photographs show arching brows above clear, gray eyes, a firm mouth, and flowing mustache. By the time he reached Ujiji on Lake Tanganyika early in 1876, he weighed only 118 pounds, and his black, wavy hair was streaked with gray.

Already, though, he had become the first white man to navigate and chart Lake Victoria, and he had discovered Lake George. Still greater achievements lay ahead. From Lake Tanganyika, he headed north along the Lualaba River, taking a route no European had ever followed and one that even natives feared, for the river was lined with cannibals. By choosing to go north rather than south, Stanley was to "do" geography indeed, for he not only discovered Stanley Falls and Stanley Pool, but also was to demonstrate conclusively that the Lualaba was part of the Congo rather than the Nile. Moreover, he would become the first European to travel the length of the Congo, for waterfalls and rapids blocked the way from the west, and previously the jungle had denied access from the east.

Again Stanley's feats aroused the interest of the Western world. Gold medals flowed in from learned societies in Europe and the United States; both houses of Congress gave Stanley a unanimous vote of thanks. Léon Gambetta of France summarized the popular sentiment of the day when he declared, "Not only, sir, have you opened up a new continent to our view, but you have given an impulse to scientific and philanthropic enterprise which will have a material effect on the progress of the world."

Such, in fact, were Stanley's aims. He hoped to end the slave trade in central Africa, Christianize the natives, and improve their material lot through commerce with the West. Events were to prove these plans illusory, for Stanley's explorations were to open the western half of the continent to Arab slave traders and equally exploitative European empire builders.

Stanley was still largely unaware of this perversion of his dreams when he agreed to return to the Congo for the Comité d'Études du Haut Congo, organized by King Leopold II of Belgium. He would have preferred British support, but England was not interested. When Lieutenant Verney Lovett Cameron attempted to annex part of the Congo for the British Empire, Parliament refused the offer. Working for Leopold, Stanley earned his nickname, Bula Matari, "smasher of stones." Between 1879 and 1882, he surpassed the king's expectations, founding Leopoldville, building a three-hundred-mile wagon road from the Atlantic to Stanley Pool, and creating a small fleet to navigate the upper Congo River beyond. Because of these efforts, Belgium would receive 900,000 square miles in the center of the continent.

In November, 1886, Stanley began a lecture tour in the United States to recount his recent adventures, about which he had also written a book, *The Congo and the Founding of Its Free State* (1885). The work was sufficiently popular to be translated into seventeen languages. He was quickly recalled for his final trip to Africa, though, this time to rescue Emin Pasha (born Eduard Carl Schmitzev), a

German posing as a Turk. This mysterious figure had been appointed governor of the Equatorial Province in Southern Sudan and had remained loyal to England after the followers of Muhammed Ahmed (the Mahdi) had overrun Khartoum and killed General Charles George Gordon, the British governor (1885).

For some reason, Stanley chose to approach Emin Pasha from the west. If he expected that the roads, stations, and fleet he had set up along the Congo would speed his journey, he was mistaken, for much of what he had established was already reverting to jungle. The march was in many ways a disaster. More than half the members of the expedition died along the way, and rumors of Stanley's death also circulated. On December 21, 1887, however, Parliament learned that Stanley had accomplished his mission of resupplying Emin, and the House of Commons rose in a body to give him an ovation in absentia.

Of all Stanley's forays into Africa, this last had the least enduring significance. Emin was better supplied than Stanley with everything but ammunition, and even this relief was not sufficient to prevent his being forced to flee shortly afterward. Yet Stanley was again the hero of the day. Already in Zanzibar, Stanley found piles of telegrams from world leaders. He had promised his publisher a book about the expedition, so he stayed in Cairo because he knew that in Europe he would be kept too busy to complete it. Meanwhile, in Berlin audiences watched a play about his adventures in Africa. In Reykjavík, people sang "Aurora Borealis" about his feats. Mugs and plates bearing Stanley's picture appeared in London shops, as did song sheets with titles such as "Stanley's Rescue" and "The Victor's Return." A lecture tour in the United States brought Stanley sixty thousand dollars; a similar round of talks in England added another ten thousand dollars.

The workhouse boy from Wales had become rich. He also finally found a wife. Twice before, he had been jilted, and in 1886, Dorothy Tennant had rejected his proposal. Now she changed her mind, and on July 12, 1890, they were married in Westminster Abbey. The ceremony assumed the scale of a coronation. The Abbey was filled with the prominent and the powerful, including William Ewart Gladstone, the Lord Chancellor, and the Speaker of the House of Commons. So popular was the event that five thousand people had to be turned away from the overcrowded church.

At his wife's urging, in 1892 Stanley gave up his American citizenship, which he had taken in 1885 to protect his royalties from piracy. Shortly afterward, he stood for Parliament; though he lost his first bid, he succeeded in 1895 and served for five years. To a man of action, the House of Commons held little fascination, however, and he complained of its "asphyxiating atmosphere." Honors continued to pour in; in 1899, he was awarded the Grand Cross of the Bath, thus becoming Sir Henry Morton Stanley, and the Atheneum, the most prestigious club in London, elected him a member.

Stanley still longed for action and Africa, but his four expeditions had aged him. In 1900, he retired to Surrey, where his wife named a local stream the Congo and a small lake Stanley Pool. These were the closest he would come to the places that had made him famous. He died in London on May 10, 1904.

Summary

Henry Morton Stanley had hoped to be buried in Westminster Abbey near Livingstone, with whom his name had been so closely linked. Although his funeral did occur there, he was denied burial in the historical shrine because by 1904 his name had also become associated with the Congo Free State, a synonym for atrocities.

"I was sent for a special work," Stanley had written in his autobiography, a work he had defined as "the redemption of the splendid central basin of the continent by sound and legitimate commerce." Through his explorations and his writings, he had opened up that area to reveal its richness to the Western world. His call for missionaries in the 1870's had brought such a response from England that Uganda became a British colony. He not only drew up the borders of the Congo Free State, later to become the Belgian Congo, but also ensured British involvement in the Sudan and eastern Africa through his various expeditions. As a journalist and explorer, he never failed to accomplish the missions on which he was sent. Whether he thereby effected Africa's redemption or damnation, though, remains an open question more than a century after he shed the first rays of light on Africa's heart of darkness.

Bibliography

Anstruther, Ian. *Dr. Livingstone, I Presume?* New York: Dutton, 1957. A detailed account of Stanley's early years and his rescue of Dr. Livingstone. Though the book touches briefly on Stanley's later achievements, it essentially ends in 1874.

Bierman, John. *Dark Safari: The Life Behind the Legend of Henry Morton Stanley.* New York: Knopf, 1990; London: Hodder and Stoughton, 1991. A fascinating biography that follows Stanley's evolution from abandoned illegitimate child to journalist, to explorer.

Farwell, Byron. *Man Who Presumed: A Biography of Henry M. Stanley.* New York: Holt Rinehart, 1957; London: Longman, 1958. A good biography for the general reader. Farwell adds no new information, but his account is clearly written and entertaining.

Hall, Richard. *Stanley: An Adventurer Explored.* London: Collins, 1974; Boston: Houghton Mifflin, 1975. The most detailed biography, revealing many previously unknown details about Stanley's early life. Maps and photographs supplement the well-written text.

Hamshee, C. E. "Stanley's Second African Journey." *History Today* 18 (October, 1968): 713-721. An account of the organization, problems, and accomplishments of Stanley's journey across Africa from 1874 to 1877.

Severin, Timothy. "The Making of an American Lion." *American Heritage* 25 (February, 1974): 4-11, 82-85. Stanley was passing himself off as an American two decades before he assumed United States citizenship. Severin tells Stanley's story from the American perspective, concentrating on his early life in this country and the ecstatic American response to his achievements.

Smith, Ian R. *The Emin Pasha Relief Expedition, 1886-1890*. Oxford: Clarendon Press, 1972. A scholarly examination of Stanley's last African adventure. Draws on previously unpublished material to place the expedition in the context of European imperialism. Also recounts the harrowing experiences of both the Advance and Rear Columns trying to reach Emin Pasha.

Tames, Richard Lawrence Ames. *Henry Morton Stanley*. Aylesbury, England: Shire, 1973. In less than fifty pages, Tames provides a good overview of Stanley's career. The brief text is richly illustrated to reveal both the man and his milieu.

Joseph Rosenblum

EDWIN M. STANTON

Born: December 19, 1814; Steubenville, Ohio
Died: December 24, 1869; Washington, D.C.
Areas of Achievement: Government and military affairs
Contribution: Combining excellent administrative skills with attention to detail, Stanton as secretary of war made a major contribution to Union victory during the Civil War.

Early Life

Edwin McMasters Stanton, born on December 19, 1814, in Steubenville, Ohio, was the eldest child of a physician descended from a Quaker family. When Stanton's father died, the thirteen-year-old had to leave school to help support his family. He worked in a local bookstore and continued his education during his spare time.

His guardian and mother's attorney, Daniel L. Collier, impressed by the young man's ambition, loaned him money in 1831 so that he could attend Kenyon College at Gambier, Ohio. A year later, however, worsening family finances forced Stanton to withdraw from school. His former employer contracted with Stanton to manage a bookstore in Columbus, Ohio. After a disagreement with his employer, Stanton asked Collier for loans to study law in Columbus. Collier, however, suggested that Stanton return to Steubenville to study with him. Stanton passed the bar in 1836 and practiced in Cadiz, Ohio, as a partner of an established attorney and also formed an association with Judge Benjamin Tappan. In 1838, Stanton returned to Steubenville to oversee the practice of Senator-elect Tappan.

Stanton proved to be an extremely hardworking attorney. He spent hours preparing cases and consequently was often better prepared than his colleagues. By 1840, Stanton had established himself as a lawyer, had managed to repay all of his debts to Collier, and for the first time was providing a financially secure environment for his family. He married Mary Lamson of Columbus on December 31, 1836. Stanton and his wife shared a love for contemporary literature and often spent evenings reading aloud and discussing current events. The Stantons had two children, Lucy Lamson and Edwin Lamson. The death of Lucy was a terrible blow to the Stantons, and in March, 1844, the death of his wife nearly drove Stanton insane. In

1846, his brother Darwin, whom Stanton had put through medical school, committed suicide.

These personal tragedies completely changed Stanton's personality. He had been sickly as a child and, because of his health and his need to work, was isolated from others. Even so, he had a pleasant demeanor and enjoyed socializing, but now he became withdrawn and suffered from a deep depression. He disliked social events and was often rude and quarrelsome. He exhibited these traits for the remainder of his life.

Lonely and unhappy, Stanton decided to seek new opportunities in Pittsburgh, Pennsylvania, in the fall of 1847. He maintained residency in Ohio, however, and kept in touch with state affairs. His law practice bloomed in Pittsburgh, and he achieved national recognition. He represented the state of Pennsylvania against the Wheeling and Belmont Bridge Company, a company in Wheeling, Virginia, which had obtained permission from the state of Ohio to build a suspension bridge across the Ohio River. The proposed bridge, too low to permit existing steamboats to cross under the structure, would cut off Pittsburgh from river commerce. Pennsylvania sued either to stop construction of the bridge or to force the company to build a higher bridge. Stanton proved his point when he hired a steamboat to run at full speed under the bridge. When the steamboat's smokestack and superstructure were destroyed, Stanton won a favorable judgment.

The bridge case brought Stanton numerous clients, and he also worked as a junior counsel in the patent infringement case of *McCormick v. Manny.* Stanton's client, John H. Manny, lost, but Stanton performed ably in the case. During the trial, he met Abraham Lincoln briefly for the first time.

On June 25, 1856, Stanton married Ellen Hutchinson of Pittsburgh, and moved to Washington, D.C., to devote his time to practicing before the United States Supreme Court. Stanton found happiness with his new wife, and they had four children, but he never recovered the more congenial demeanor so manifest during earlier days. The ambitious attorney did well in the new environment. In 1858, Stanton was selected as a special United States attorney to represent the government in numerous fraudulent land claims in California arising from land deeded to individuals before the Mexican war. He spent most of the year in California laboring to reconstruct the necessary records. Stanton's attention to detail allowed him to win a number of victories and saved the government millions of dollars.

Although Stanton devoted his energies to civil law, he also proved himself to be an able criminal lawyer. Daniel E. Sickles, a New York congressman, scandalized the country in February, 1859, when he murdered Philip B. Key. United States Attorney for the District of Columbia and son of Francis Scott Key, best-known as the author of "The Star-Spangled Banner," Key had been carrying on an affair with Sickles' wife, and the congressman acted while in a rage. Stanton and his associates used the plea of temporary insanity for the first time in the United States. The jury acquitted Sickles, and Stanton's fame grew.

Life's Work

Stanton had not been actively engaged in politics before the Civil War. He was a Jacksonian Democrat who opposed slavery. He accepted the Dred Scott decision, however, and believed that constitutional provisions regarding slavery had to be enforced. He disliked Southern Democrats and fervently supported the Union as the crisis atmosphere grew in 1859 and 1860. After Lincoln's election in November, 1860, the nation faced a crisis of immense magnitude. Stanton believed in the Union and on December 20 agreed to serve in President James Buchanan's cabinet as attorney general for the short time before Lincoln assumed office. Stanton worked hard to preserve the Union and to stiffen Buchanan's resolve to keep the country together. Stanton joined others in the cabinet in opposing the abandonment of Fort Sumter, South Carolina, and kept an eye on individuals he believed were plotting against the government.

Stanton distrusted Lincoln's administration during the early months of the Civil War. Highly critical of Lincoln, Stanton became a friend and adviser of Major General George B. McClellan after he took command of the Army of the Potomac and then became general in chief.

Lincoln needed a new manager for the War Department capable of handling the massive mobilization of men and resources needed to fight to preserve the fractured Union. Secretary of War Simon Cameron, however, had turned out to be both inept and corrupt. It is not clear why Lincoln decided to appoint Stanton, but the Republican president needed support from War Democrats. For whatever reason, on January 15, 1862, Stanton was confirmed as secretary of war; the War Department and the United States Army had found a master.

Stanton acted immediately by reorganizing the War Department, hiring new and better qualified personnel, and carefully investigating existing contracts. Contractors were pressured to deliver needed supplies, but supplies had to arrive on time and be of proper quality. He often worked far into the night, and he expected the same of his subordinates. Stanton efficiently managed a large-scale enterprise, and the Union armies never lost a battle for lack of supplies or equipment.

The war secretary also understood the importance of communications and transportation. Acting through Congress, he took over telegraph and railroad lines essential to carrying on the war. Stanton created a military telegraph system operated by the civilian-controlled War Department, not the army. Consequently, all information flowed through Stanton's office, enabling him to manage the flow of news and to censor anything of value to the South. The press criticized Stanton for censorship, but his actions were a sound and necessary wartime measure.

The railroad was equally important to the war effort. On one occasion, Stanton moved two army corps from the Eastern theater to Chattanooga, Tennessee, complete with arms, equipment, and supplies, in less than a week. Government control of the railroads in military areas proved to be a key factor in the war. Stanton established a railroad building program to repair and build new rail lines at an unprecedented rate. The war secretary clearly understood the technology of modern war.

In his early months as secretary, Stanton maintained a close relationship with McClellan. The general and Lincoln, however, had never agreed on strategy. Stanton soon realized that McClellan was a brilliant organizer but no fighter. The secretary's views may also have been colored by his improving relationship with Lincoln. The president wanted a fighting general who understood the political and military realities of the war. In August, 1862, Stanton worked to remove McClellan from command, although the general was briefly returned to duty during the fall.

Both Stanton and Lincoln sought a general who acted rather than one who simply asked for more men and supplies. Consequently, both often inter-

fered with military operations early in the war when they thought generals were not doing enough. They maintained civilian control of the war effort in the face of a real danger that armies and generals might become too powerful and gain the upper hand in government.

In 1863, Major General Ulysses S. Grant, with his victories at Vicksburg and Chattanooga, emerged as the general both Lincoln and Stanton had sought. In March, 1864, Lincoln appointed Grant to the newly created rank of lieutenant general and gave him command of the entire one-million-man Union army. Grant found no cause to complain about Stanton. Stanton did all in his power to procure what Grant needed, but Grant never asked for more than could be realistically delivered. The combination of Stanton, Lincoln, and Grant brought Union victory when General Robert E. Lee surrendered to Grant at Appomattox Court House on April 9, 1865.

Stanton was shattered by Lincoln's assassination on April 14. The two men had developed a close working relationship, making it possible to wage an immense war. Stanton's anger never really abat-

ed, and he sought and prosecuted the assassins with a vengeance.

Grant's terms to Lee had been generous, but within political limits set by Lincoln. Major General William Tecumseh Sherman, however, fearing a bloodbath in the wake of Lincoln's death, negotiated a much broader surrender agreement with Confederate General Joseph E. Johnston in North Carolina two weeks after Appomattox. Sherman's terms enraged Stanton, who leaked them in garbled terms to the press and who privately accused Sherman of disloyalty. Sherman had certainly exceeded his authority, and after a cabinet meeting, Grant went to North Carolina and quietly supervised new terms. Sherman never forgave Stanton for his behavior. Ironically, both men probably acted out of grief over Lincoln's death.

President Andrew Johnson asked Stanton to stay in his cabinet. During the war he had left the Democratic Party, and by 1865 he fully sympathized with the Radical Republicans. Johnson's view of Reconstruction turned out to be far different from that of the Radical Republicans and of Stanton. The war secretary from the summer of 1865 onward differed with the president, wanting harsher terms imposed on the South. He approved of the Freedmen's Bureau and the Civil Rights Act of 1866, although both were enacted over Johnson's veto. He supported the Military Reconstruction Act, which passed over Johnson's veto on March 2, 1867, and assisted Radicals in formulating additional Reconstruction legislation that summer.

Johnson decided to remove Stanton from office early in August and demanded Stanton's resignation. The war secretary refused, however, on the grounds that the Tenure of Office Act gave Congress control over his removal. He used this pretext even though he himself believed that the act was unconstitutional. Johnson then suspended Stanton, making Grant secretary of war *ad interim*, until Congress could act. When the Senate refused Johnson's request, Stanton returned to office, and Johnson decided to remove him anyway. Impeachment proceedings against the president followed, failing by one vote on May 26, 1868. At that point, Stanton stepped down.

The tension-filled years had damaged his health, and he never fully recovered. Stanton had abandoned his law practice to serve his country and, without the energy to reestablish it, faced serious financial difficulties. When Grant assumed the presidency, he gave Stanton an appointment to the

United States Supreme Court, which was quickly confirmed by the Senate. Stanton, however, died before taking office, on December 24, 1869.

Summary

Stanton faced many adversities early in life. He struggled to get an education because of his family responsibilities. Even so, he appears to have been a cheerful and congenial youth with a taste for literature and political discussion.

His great ability as an attorney gave him national prominence. By 1859, Stanton was on the road to great wealth with an annual income in excess of forty thousand dollars. Personal tragedies, however, altered Stanton's personality. The death of his first child followed by the death of his first wife and the suicide of his younger brother had a profound effect on the man. He had always been demanding, but with personal tragedy he became rude and quarrelsome, and his relations with others remained cold and distant.

He gave up wealth and security for public office, apparently with patriotic motives. A Democrat who opposed slavery, he fervently supported the Union. He joined Buchanan's cabinet in its waning months to help keep the nation together. With the onset of the Civil War, while critical of the Republican Party, he supported the Union.

Stanton proved to be an able secretary of war and thus a key to Union victory. The ability to act quickly while at the same time paying attention to the smallest detail made him a good administrator. He expected the best from subordinates and replaced those who did not measure up. Along with Lincoln, he ensured the maintenance of civilian control over an enormous army during a revolutionary time.

After the war, Stanton opposed readmission of the South to the Union without guarantee of full freedom to the former slaves. Stanton disagreed with Johnson's lenient Reconstruction policy. He fought hard to retain his position in the government for the simple reason that he believed himself to be right and Johnson to be wrong. Too much blood had been shed for him to do otherwise. A truly remarkable man, Stanton certainly deserves to be remembered as one of the great war secretaries, perhaps even the greatest.

Bibliography

Flower, Frank Abial. *Edwin McMasters Stanton: The Autocrat of Rebellion, Emancipation, and Reconstruction.* New York: Wilson, 1905. A laudatory biography that has some value because of the author's access to papers no longer available.

Gorham, George C. *Life and Public Service of Edwin M. Stanton.* 2 vols. Boston: Houghton Mifflin, 1899. Gorham was commissioned by Stanton's family to prepare this biography. The author also had access to family papers that have since been scattered.

Hyman, Harold M. "Johnson, Stanton, and Grant: A Reconsideration of the Army's Role in the Events Leading to Impeachment." *American Historical Review* 66 (October, 1960): 85-100. This is an excellent discussion of the clash between Stanton and Johnson.

Pratt, Fletcher. *Stanton: Lincoln's Secretary of War.* New York: Norton, 1953. A readable treatment of Stanton, but unequal to Thomas and Hyman.

Thomas, Benjamin P., and Harold M. Hyman. *Stanton: The Life and Times of Lincoln's Secretary of War.* New York: Knopf, 1962. A beautifully written biography based on massive research. It is unlikely that a more balanced treatment will appear.

United States War Department. *The War of the Rebellion: A Compilation of the Official Records of the Union and Confederate Armies.* 128 vols. Washington, D.C.: Government Printing Office, 1880-1901. These volumes contain the essential documents covering Stanton's work in wartime.

David L. Wilson

ELIZABETH CADY STANTON

Born: November 12, 1815; Johnstown, New York
Died: October 26, 1902; New York, New York
Areas of Achievement: Women's rights and politics
Contribution: Stanton was one of the founders of the organized women's rights movement in the United States, and she served as one of its chief leaders during the second half of the nineteenth century.

Early Life

Elizabeth Cady was born November 12, 1815, in Johnstown, New York. She was the fourth of six children born to Daniel and Margaret Cady who survived childhood. Through her mother she was descended from a wealthy family, the Livingstons, who were part of the political elite of New York. Her mother's father, James Livingston, was an officer in George Washington's army during the American Revolution and a member of the New York state legislature. Elizabeth's father, Daniel Cady, was a successful lawyer who served in the New York state legislature and the United States House of Representatives, and, after 1847, he was a member of the New York State Supreme Court. Daniel Cady was a conservative in his political views and became an active member of the Federalist Party. Elizabeth's parents were very strict Presbyterians who held firmly to traditional Calvinist doctrines of predestination and the depravity of human nature. As a child, Elizabeth found this version of religion frightening, even to the point of having nightmares that the Devil was attempting to possess her.

Several events in Elizabeth's childhood helped awaken her to the realization that women held a subordinate position in American society. Her father wanted very much to have a son, but each of Elizabeth's three brothers died young. At the death of his third son, Daniel Cady openly lamented to Elizabeth that she was not a boy. Part of the impetus for Elizabeth's refusal to accept a traditional female sex role may have stemmed from her attempt to be the son her father so fervently desired. A second instance which brought a new awareness of the disadvantage of being female occurred in her father's law office. Hearing of a case in which a female friend sought unsuccessfully to reclaim property she had purchased with her own money, but of which she had been deprived because of a state law transferring a woman's property to her husband

when she married, Elizabeth became so upset that she attempted to cut the relevant pages out of her father's law books.

Even as a child, Elizabeth displayed intellectual ability considerably beyond that of the average youth. Believing that becoming a learned person was essential if she were to be equal to boys, she began the study of Greek at age eleven, later winning a prize at the Johnstown Academy for her achievements in this area. In spite of her outstanding academic record, she was not allowed to enroll at Union College, which admitted only boys, and had to be content with a girls' boarding school, Troy Female Seminary, which she attended from 1830 to 1833. Although most girls' boarding schools at this time were primarily finishing schools, concentrating on developing their students' social skills, Troy was unusual in that it attempted to provide academic training comparable to that which colleges provided men. The seminary encouraged its students to be self-reliant and provided careful training in writing skills, which Elizabeth later believed to have contributed to her success as an author.

After graduation from Troy Female Seminary, Elizabeth did not seek a career and at this point displayed little evidence that she would become a reformer. Even in this period, however, she occasionally displayed those qualities of independence and a militant opposition to efforts to place women in a subordinate position which marked her later life. She became the head of a young women's association which raised funds to enable an aspiring minister to attend seminary. When the recipient of their funds was invited to deliver a special sermon and chose to speak on women's inferiority, Elizabeth rose from her seat in the front pew and led the other young women out of the church in a gesture of protest.

During the 1830's, Elizabeth was increasingly drawn into the abolitionist reform effort by her cousin Gerrit Smith. His home was a station on the Underground Railway, and the accounts of their experiences by fugitive slaves made a lasting impression on Elizabeth. It was while attending an anti-slavery meeting that Elizabeth met the man who eventually became her husband. Henry Stanton was a member of the executive committee which directed the activities of the American Anti-Slavery Society. He was a gifted public speaker who had risked his life on several occasions by speaking against slavery to hostile crowds. When he proposed marriage to Elizabeth, her parents were totally opposed, because they considered abolitionists to be fanatics. Marriage to Henry was an important turning point in Elizabeth's life, for he was not wealthy, and she knew that the social elite of New York would never accept them as long as he remained an abolitionist. Nevertheless—and even though her parents remained opposed and did not attend her wedding—Elizabeth married Henry in May, 1840. In two important respects, the marriage ceremony reflected her emerging feminist consciousness: At her request, the traditional bride's promise to obey her husband was deleted from the wedding vows, and, while adding her husband's name, she retained her own name.

Life's Work

Almost immediately after their marriage, Elizabeth and Henry left for London to attend an international antislavery convention. This proved to be a very traumatic experience for her. Many male delegates feared that association with feminism would harm the abolitionist cause and opposed allowing women to be delegates. The first major issue discussed at the conference was whether women delegates should be allowed to participate on an equal basis with men. It was eventually decided that women should not be allowed to sit on the convention floor with men and should not be permitted to speak at the conference. Cady Stanton was deeply angered by the treatment accorded women and resolved to organize a women's rights convention when she returned to the United States. Although eight years passed before that conference was held, her treatment at the London convention was directly responsible for convincing her that women must join together in an organized effort if they were to progress toward equality.

After their return to New York, Cady Stanton became immersed in domestic activities. She had seven children between 1842 and 1859, and her husband considered it her responsibility to rear them. Partly because Henry was often away from home, sometimes for as long as eight months, Cady Stanton was frequently depressed and resented the burdens of housework and child rearing. In her speeches and writings in later years, she often stressed birth control as of central importance in improving the position of married women; it is

likely that her remarks at least partially reflected her own experiences.

After discovering that other women shared her sense of discontent, Cady Stanton organized a women's rights convention at Seneca Falls, New York, at which women's grievances could be expressed. It was intended to be a local event, and she did not expect a large turnout. Nevertheless, more than three hundred persons came for the convention, including a number of prominent reformers from nearby Rochester. Cady Stanton wrote the key document discussed by the convention, a list of women's grievances which she called the Declaration of Sentiments. It was modeled after the Declaration of Independence and drew upon the same natural-rights arguments to justify an end to discrimination based on sex. The list of grievances was lengthy and covered a wide spectrum: the admission of women to institutions of higher education, the right to enter professions such as law and medicine, the right of employed married women to retain their earnings, and an end to the double standard of sexual morality. Resolutions on these points received the unanimous support of those at the convention. A resolution proposing women's suffrage, however, proved far more controversial and passed by only a bare majority. Even Cady Stanton's husband, Henry, opposed the suffrage resolution. After the convention, Cady Stanton's father attempted to persuade her to remove her name from the list of those who had signed the Declaration of Sentiments, but she refused to do so. Her decision to persevere was an important turning point in her emergence as a nationally prominent feminist reformer.

During the years after the Seneca Falls convention, Cady Stanton continued her activities on behalf of women's rights but was also active in other reform movements. In 1852, angry because the New York State temperance organization discriminated against women, she helped found the Women's State Temperance Society of New York. Her advocacy of temperance reflected a belief that excessive drinking by men often had serious consequences for women. Because of the brutality often exhibited by drunken men toward their wives, Cady Stanton urged that the grounds for divorce be expanded to include consistent heavy drinking. The majority of the women members were too conservative to consider Cady Stanton's suggestion that the grounds for divorce be liberalized, and when they refused to reelect her as president, she

withdrew from the organization. She also remained active in the abolitionist movement, urging the immediate emancipation of slaves, and opposed Abraham Lincoln's candidacy for the presidency in 1860 on the grounds that he was too moderate on the slavery issue and might compromise with the South. When, after the war, constitutional amendments were proposed extending the suffrage and civil rights to blacks, Cady Stanton campaigned to have the amendments extended to women. Opposition to this step by her abolitionist friends contributed to its failure and drove a wedge between them; this was widened when she, in turn, argued against the Fourteenth and Fifteenth amendments because she feared the newly enfranchised blacks would be hostile to women's suffrage.

In 1851, Cady Stanton met Susan B. Anthony and initiated a friendship which had an important influence on the American feminist movement in the second half of the nineteenth century. Cady Stanton persuaded Anthony to become involved in the campaign for women's rights, and the two worked closely on behalf of that cause for the next forty years. Cady Stanton was a talented writer and

public speaker but disliked the administrative work necessary to conduct a major campaign. Anthony excelled at such work, however, and thus the two formed an effective team. Although Anthony later received more public recognition for her role in bringing about women's suffrage, she was the junior partner in the relationship and acknowledged that Cady Stanton was the true founder of the organized women's rights movement in the United States.

With the assistance of Anthony, Cady Stanton promoted the cause of women's suffrage in a variety of ways. In 1866, she ran for Congress as an independent in order to test the constitutional right of a woman to hold public office. In the following year, she conducted an extensive campaign in Kansas, speaking throughout the state on behalf of a state constitutional amendment on women's suffrage. In 1871, Cady Stanton and Anthony made a speaking tour around the West, seeking to stimulate support for women's suffrage. In 1878, Cady Stanton was responsible for the introduction of a women's suffrage amendment to the Constitution in Congress, a measure which was reintroduced in each subsequent Congress until it was passed in 1920. She appeared in Congress almost every year until late in her life to speak on behalf of the women's suffrage amendment. Perhaps her most important contribution to that movement was the major part she played in establishing and directing the National Woman Suffrage Association. Cady Stanton and Anthony formed the NWSA in 1869, and Cady Stanton served as its president until 1890, when it merged with the rival American Woman Suffrage Association. A prolific writer, Cady Stanton joined with Anthony in coauthoring three volumes of *History of Woman Suffrage* (1881-1886), an invaluable source on the American women's suffrage movement.

Although women's suffrage was her major concern, Cady Stanton never restricted her reforming efforts to one issue. She frequently shocked female audiences by her ideas on marriage and divorce. This caused friction between her and Anthony, who maintained that the cause of women's suffrage was being harmed by associating it with radical proposals for easier divorce. Cady Stanton also alarmed Anthony with her criticisms of the Church. She believed that the Church was a major force maintaining the subordinate position of women, and from 1878, Cady Stanton endeavored to persuade the NWSA to take a public stand against this. Unsuccessful in this effort, Cady Stanton then attempted to establish a committee of women to prepare a revised version of the Bible which would eliminate its sexist language. Eventually she proceeded on her own to write an extensive commentary on the biblical passages which directly discussed the status of women. Published in 1895 as *The Woman's Bible*, it defended women against the claim that they were responsible for Original Sin because of Eve's behavior in the Garden of Eden. Cady Stanton was deeply hurt when the work was repudiated by other women's suffrage leaders, who feared that it would lead the public to dismiss the suffrage movement as irreligious.

Although her eyes began to fail during the last years of her life (she was completely blind by the time of her death), Cady Stanton continued to write on women's issues until her death, on October 26, 1902, in New York City. She continued to enjoy life during old age, but her last years were marred by the breakdown of her friendship with Anthony and the efforts of women's suffrage leaders to distance themselves from her because of their belief that *The Woman's Bible* would prove harmful to their cause.

Summary

The position of women in American society has changed considerably since the mid-nineteenth century, and Cady Stanton was one of the central figures helping to bring about that change. As the founder of the organized women's rights movement in the United States and its recognized leader during the second half of the nineteenth century, she was a vital figure in an important and continuing reform movement. Although often remembered primarily in connection with the women's suffrage issue, she viewed suffrage as a means by which reforms could be instituted in other areas affecting women rather than an end in itself. While she held important offices in women's organizations, Cady Stanton was equally important as a publicist whose writings articulated the reasons that feminists wished to alter relationships between the sexes. Her writings on these issues were so extensive that it would be appropriate to consider her the chief theorist or intellectual of the late nineteenth century women's rights movement.

Since her death, Cady Stanton's contribution to the American women's suffrage movement has been overshadowed by that of Anthony. This is in part because many of the women's suffrage activists in the generation immediately after Cady Stanton's death did not share her views on issues other than suffrage. The revival of feminism in the United States since 1960, however, has brought a renewed interest in her life and work, partly because she did emphasize that the nonpolitical forces which kept women in a subordinate position were as important as those which were political.

Bibliography

Banner, Lois. *Elizabeth Cady Stanton: A Radical for Women's Rights.* Boston: Little Brown, 1980. The best single volume on Cady Stanton's life and thought. It presents her as the philosopher of the feminist movement and is especially helpful on her theories.

DuBois, Ellen Carol, ed. *Elizabeth Cady Stanton, Susan B. Anthony: Correspondence, Writings, Speeches.* New York: Shocken, 1981. This is an excellent collection of the correspondence between Cady Stanton and Anthony, which also includes many of Cady Stanton's more important speeches and articles. The critical commentary by DuBois is very helpful in placing the documents in context.

Flexner, Eleanor. *Century of Struggle: The Woman's Rights Movement in the United States.* Rev. ed. Cambridge, Mass.: Harvard University Press, 1975. Widely regarded as the best history of the campaign for women's suffrage. It includes some references to Cady Stanton but focuses on the movement itself rather than on its leaders.

Forster, Margaret. "Elizabeth Cady Stanton, 1815-1902." In *Significant Sisters.* New York: Oxford University Press, and London: Secker and Warburg, 1984. A well-written chapter in a book about prominent feminists. It makes extensive use of Cady Stanton's letters and other original sources in conveying a vivid sense of her personality.

Griffith, Elisabeth. *In Her Own Right: The Life of Elizabeth Cady Stanton.* New York: Oxford University Press, 1984; Oxford: Oxford University Press, 1985. A very detailed account of Cady Stanton's life based upon extensive research in primary sources. It is a psychological study which excels in discussing Cady Stanton's private life.

Lutz, Alma. *Created Equal: A Biography of Elizabeth Cady Stanton.* New York: John Day, 1940. This was the first scholarly biography of Cady

Stanton. It is a clear, objective, narrative account which concentrates more on her political activities than on her thought.

Murphy, Cullen. "The Gospel According to Eve." *American Heritage* 49, no. 5 (September, 1998). Discusses Stanton's publication of *The Woman's Bible* and the criticism she sustained from those in the women's suffrage movement.

Stanton, Elizabeth Cady. *Eighty Years and More: Reminiscences, 1815-1897.* London: Unwin, and New York: European Publishing, 1898. Written near the end of her life, Cady Stanton's autobiography provides the fullest account of her life from her own point of view. Although invaluable for its firsthand information, it is very brief on some events in her life and omits others entirely, and thus must be supplemented by other sources.

Stanton, Elizabeth Cady and Susan B. Anthony. *The Selected Papers of Elizabeth Cady Stanton and Susan B. Anthony,* vol. 1: *In the School of Anti-Slavery, 1840–1866.* Ann D. Gordon, ed. New Brunswick, N.J.: Rutgers University Press, 1997. First in a planned six-volume set documenting the interface between Stanton and Anthony. This volume covers their early interests in temperance, women's rights, and abolition. Useful primary source for those interested in nineteenth century reform movements.

Harold L. Smith

FREIHERR VOM STEIN

Born: October 26, 1757; Nassau, Holy Roman Empire

Died: June 29, 1831; Cappenberg, Prussia

Areas of Achievement: Government, politics, and social reform

Contribution: Stein was the architect of the reform movement in Prussia, during the period from 1806 to 1808, that altered the authoritarian nature of the Prussian state in the direction of modern liberalism and resulted in fundamental changes in Prussian institutions.

Early Life

Heinrich Friedrich Karl, Freiherr vom und zum Stein was the ninth of ten children born to Karl Philipp Freiherr vom Stein and Langwerth vom Stein (née von Simmern). The vom Stein family was of the Imperial Knighthood and had been independent proprietors within the Holy Roman Empire for more than seven hundred years when Karl (as he was called by his family and friends) was born in his ancestral home at Nassau on October 26, 1757. His father had entered the bureaucracy of the neighboring state of Mainz, where he eventually rose to the rank of privy councillor.

Stein's parents impressed upon him that as a representative of his caste he had the patriotic duty to devote his life to the service of the community. With that end in mind, he was matriculated at age sixteen at the University of Göttingen to study law and political science preparatory to entering government service. Although Göttingen was experiencing perhaps its most dynamic era of literary ferment during Stein's stay there, he was relatively unaffected by it. He concentrated on the study of history and of constitutional and legal theory, which apparently deepened the patriotic feelings imbued in him by his parents and strengthened his determination to enter government service.

Stein's original inclination was to enter the still-extant but ineffective government machinery of the Holy Roman Empire. After leaving Göttingen, he traveled to the Imperial Chamber at Wetzlar, the Imperial Court Council in Vienna, and the Imperial Diet at Regensburg in order to gain an understanding of the political and administrative structure of the empire.

Apparently disillusioned by the largely figurehead nature of imperial administration, Stein accepted an appointment to the Prussian bureaucracy under Frederick William II in 1780 at the age of twenty-three. Some of his biographers have suggested that even at this early age, Stein had already concluded that the best hope of unifying all the German people into a strong political entity, with liberal institutions and a constitution, lay with Prussia.

Life's Work

For the next sixteen years, Stein held progressively more responsible positions within the Prussian government, primarily in mining operations and in the provincial administration in Prussian Westphalia. This experience gave him an intimate knowledge of the workings of local government and led to his appointment in 1796 as head of all the Prussian Rhenish and Westphalian administrative districts. His success in this capacity and other endeavors resulted in his appointment in 1804 as minister of economic affairs for the royal government in Berlin. There Stein rapidly developed the conviction that the Prussian governmental and social systems would have to be drastically reformed and modernized if Prussia were to survive what Stein perceived as an inevitable clash with the burgeoning Napoleonic empire. Stein's vocal insistence on reform resulted, in 1807, in his dismissal by Frederick William III shortly after the disastrous Prussian defeat by Napoleon I at the Battles of Jena and Auerstedt.

Stein's forced retirement to his family estate at Nassau gave him time to systematize and set down on paper his ideas concerning the reforms necessary to modernize and rejuvenate the Prussian state. In his famous *Nassauer Denkschrift* (1807; Nassau memorandum), Stein argued that if the Prussian state was to survive, its citizens must be allowed to participate in the management of its affairs. He further suggested in his memorandum that only self-government could instill into the Prussian people the patriotism and community spirit which would allow Prussia to survive in an increasingly dangerous world. Stein's lifelong study of British history and his admiration for the British parliamentary system undoubtedly contributed to his advocacy of the establishment of a similar system in Prussia.

During Stein's unwilling retirement, Napoleon forced Frederick William to sign the Treaty of Tilsit. The terms of the treaty considerably diminished the size and autonomy of the Prussian state and convinced many Prussians in the bureaucracy and the army of the necessity of sweeping reforms in the governmental apparatus. Napoleon insisted on the dismissal of Frederick William's foreign minister, Karl von Hardenberg, and the appointment of Stein in his place. Frederick William confirmed Stein as Prime Minister of Prussia on October 4, 1807.

Stein took advantage of a wave of patriotism and widespread demand for reform engendered by the twin debacles of Jena and Tilsit to force Frederick William to accede to the first of the great changes in Prussian government, administration, and society later known collectively as the Prussian Reform movement. The first, and in many ways the most far-reaching, of the reforms was promulgated on October 19, 1807, as the Law Concerning the Emancipated Possession and the Free Use of Landed Property and the Personal Relationships of the Inhabitants of the Land. This law emancipated the Prussian serfs from feudal obligations and enabled the Prussian aristocracy to sell their land to non-nobles. In addition, the law enabled all Prussians to follow the vocation of their choice. The law was a decisive step toward the destruction of the old caste relationships of Prussian society and the creation of civic and legal equality.

One year later, Stein was responsible for the creation of effective local self-government for the towns and cities of Germany through the issuance of the *Städteordnung* (municipal ordinances). He then turned his attention to modernizing the national government. He replaced the old, secretive councillor administration with departmental ministries of foreign affairs, internal affairs, finance, justice, and war, each with responsibility and authority for the whole of the Prussian kingdom. He also reorganized provincial administration along more efficient lines. Whether Stein would have succeeded in introducing in Prussia the national parliament, which he so admired in the English system, will never be known. Napoleon forced Frederick William to dismiss him from office on November 24, 1808, after French spies intercepted a letter Stein sent to a friend criticizing the French emperor and his policies toward Prussia.

Stein took refuge until 1812 in Austria, where he continued to correspond with his successor Hardenberg and with other men in the bureaucracy and the army of Prussia who were carrying the banner of reform. In 1812, he answered a summons by Al-exander I of Russia to come to St. Petersburg as a political adviser. He was instrumental in that capacity in negotiating the Russo-Prussian alliance in 1813, after Napoleon's 1812 invasion of Russia ended in catastrophe. He then provided moral leadership for the German states during the war of liberation, which ended with Napoleon's final defeat and exile in 1815. During that period, Stein also continued to influence those men in Prussia who pursued progressive reform, men such as Johann Gottlieb Fichte, August von Gneisenau, Ernst Arndt, Heinrich von Kleist, and Wilhelm and Alexander von Humboldt. At the Congress of Vienna, Stein championed the cause of the political unification of the German states but was not satisfied with the final form that unification took. He regarded the Germanic Confederation that resulted from the deliberations at Vienna as little more than the ghost of the recently deceased Holy Roman Empire.

After the Congress of Vienna, Stein retired to his estate of Cappenberg, Westphalia, where he devoted the remainder of his life to the writing of history and to the publication of the works of other historians on the subject of German history. He died in his home on June 29, 1831.

Summary

Freiherr vom Stein was a pivotal figure in the transformation of Prussian government from an absolute monarchy toward liberalism and constitutionalism. He was, along with Hardenberg, one of the champions of the concept that such changes must be instituted peacefully and slowly from above, or else they will be brought about violently and quickly, and with unforeseeable consequences, from below, as in the French Revolution. His conviction that the reforms must be made was based less on a concern for individual liberty and human rights than on a desire to prevent German institutions from being overwhelmed by the French. He realized that the powerful forces of nationalism and liberalism unleashed by the French Revolution of 1789 could not be withstood without unleashing similar forces in Germany. He hoped to control those forces while retaining the virtues of older Prussian society.

The unfinished nature of his reforms had far-reaching consequences for the development of Prussian and German society: The serfs were freed, but without land; the former serfs were reduced to the status of migrant agricultural laborers, many of whom migrated to the cities and became the nucleus of the proletariat, which turned to Marxism and trade-unionism in later decades and caused much turmoil in imperial Germany. Equality before the law was established, but without constitutional guarantees; the widespread and unsatisfied desire among the Prussian intellectual community and the bourgeoisie for a constitution and a parliament culminated with the Revolution of 1848. The principle of participatory government was established, but without a medium through which it could be practiced. The essentially conservative approach to reform adopted by Stein created a tradition in Prussia of expecting the government to effect necessary reform in societal institutions that prevailed into the twentieth century.

Bibliography

Gray, M. W. "Prussia in Transition—Society and Politics Under the Stein Reform Ministry of 1808." *Transactions of the American Philosophical Society* 76 (1986): 1-175. Gray's article is primarily concerned with the milieu in which Stein's reforms took place and the effects of the reforms on Prussian society, rather than with Stein himself. An excellent introduction to the era of the Prussian Reform movement.

Holborn, Hajo. *A History of Modern Germany, 1648-1840*. New York: Knopf, 1964; London: Eyre and Spottiswoode, 1965. Holborn's book contains several chapters on the Prussian Reform movement and provides sketches of the most important of the leaders of the movement, including Stein. The book places the reform movement and the reformers in their proper perspective in German history.

Meinecke, Friedrich. *The Age of German Liberation, 1795-1815*. Translated by Peter Peret and Helmuth Fischer. Berkeley: University of California Press, 1977. One of the best accounts of the period, Meinecke's book provides a good account of Stein's life and work. Meinecke argues that Stein and the other reformers successfully provided the transition between absolutism and representative government that made possible the unification of Germany half a century later.

Seeley, John Robert. *Life and Times of Stein: Or, Germany and Prussia in the Napoleonic Age*. Boston: Roberts, 1879. Seeley's book is the only full-length biography of Stein in English. It is perhaps overly laudatory. In the main, it agrees with Meinecke's evaluation of Stein and his reforms.

Simon, Walter. *The Failure of the Prussian Reform Movement*. Ithaca, N.Y.: Cornell University Press, 1955. Simon is critical of both the reforms and the reformers, including Stein, of whom he writes at great length. Simon argues that the failure of the reforms to establish a unified German state with a constitutional, parliamentary form of government led directly to the development of the authoritarianism of the German empire after 1871 and ultimately to the Third Reich.

Paul Madden

JAKOB STEINER

Born: March 18, 1796; near Utzendorf, Canton of
Bern, Switzerland
Died: April 1, 1863; Bern, Switzerland
Area of Achievement: Mathematics
Contribution: Steiner was one of the greatest geometers of the first half of the nineteenth century. His major geometrical books and dozens of
articles established him as a chief authority on
isoperimetric geometry and as the founder of
modern synthetic geometry in Germany.

Early Life

Jakob Steiner was born into a family of thrifty,
humble, and hardworking Swiss farmers, near the
village of Utzendorf, Canton of Bern, Switzerland, on March 18, 1796. Though the youngest of
five children, he contributed from a very early age
to the family income, the family expecting nothing more than the most modest intellectual development. Consequently, he remained illiterate until
he was fourteen and continued farmwork until he
was nineteen. According to his later recollections,
before he had any formal education he developed
an astounding capacity for spatial conceptualization. Contrary to the desires of his father, Jakob
entered the school of the Swiss educational reformer Johann Pestalozzi at Yverdon. Out of conformity with Swiss educational precepts, Pestalozzi continued stressing the pedagogical
importance of individual training and direct experience for his students. Before Pestalozzi's institution failed, Steiner had become a teaching assistant. Thereafter, Steiner entered Heidelberg
University, where he pursued numerical perceptions in connection with imaginative spatial concepts. From 1818 until 1821, while earning a living as a teacher, Steiner worked with one of the
institution's leading geometers, whose lectures
and ideas he profoundly disdained. Notwithstanding, Steiner obtained his doctorate from Heidelberg, thereafter accepting a teaching position as a
tutor at a private school.

Fortunately, the eldest son of the famed German
statesman and philologist Wilhelm von Humboldt
was one of his pupils. Steiner's acquaintance with
the distinguished Humboldt family altered his fortunes. The Humboldts introduced him to Berlin's
premier mathematicians, and Steiner was encouraged to accept a teaching post at a Berlin vocational institution during the next decade.

Eventually the University of Berlin created an
endowed chair, which Steiner was to fill—indeed,
he had, since 1834, been a member of the Berlin
Academy on the basis of his previous mathematical, or geometrical, writings.

Life's Work

Steiner's mathematical publications commenced in
1826, while he still tutored at his vocational
school. This creative production coincided with the
founding by August Leopold Crelle of what became one of the nineteenth century's most famous
mathematical publications, *Journal für die reine
und angewandte Mathematik* (the journal for pure
and applied mathematics). Professionally, Steiner
expanded his reputation in 1832 with his *System-
atische Entwicklung der Abhängigkeit Geome-
trischer Gestalten* (systematic evolution of the mutual dependence of geometrical forms), a planned
introduction to a five-part series never to be completed.

Steiner's work does not readily reduce to layman's terms. It is projective geometry, built upon
synthetic constructions. Geometry's basic forms
are based on planes. Projective geometry moves
from the fundamental plane to lines, planar pencils
of lines to pencils of planes, bundles of lines, bundles of planes—and then into space itself, steadily
generating higher geometric forms. For Steiner,
one form in this projective hierarchy related with
the others.

It was not the originality of Steiner's work that
was dominant, although the questions he raised
were then novel considering geometers' principal
preoccupations. Steiner's own view was that "the
writings of the present day have tried to reveal the
organism by which the sundry phenomena of the
external world are bound to one another." What he
sought to determine was how "order enters into
chaos," how all parts of the external world fit naturally into one another, and how related parts join
to form well-defined groups. Specifically, it was
the brilliantly stated and systematic treatment
Steiner lent to his inquiries that gained for him his
reputation.

The unique and justly famed French École Polytechnique, with its unparalleled training of
France's intellectual elite and special concentration
of intensive mathematical training had long before
Steiner's day divided geometry into two branches:

the analytical and the synthetic, or projective. In the early seventeenth century, René Descartes had explained how numbers could be utilized to describe points in a plane or in space algebraically. Steiner, however, concentrated on the other branch: projective geometry, which did not usually resort to the measurements or lengths of angles.

Steiner learned something from Johann Pestalozzi and his eccentric preoccupation with right triangles, and as a pedagogue Steiner, like Pestalozzi, encouraged his students' independent and rigorously logical search for learning. As might be expected, Steiner avoided figures to illustrate his lectures. His own intuitions were so much a part of his character, he sought both in teaching and writing to use them. Nor did he neglect his own disciplined scholarship. He read exhaustively the works of his European counterparts, staying on the cutting edge of his investigations.

Mathematical authorities agree that in midcareer Steiner still fell short of his goals by rejecting the achievements of some of his predecessors and contemporaries. For example, he lost the chance to employ signs drawn from Karl August Möbius' synthetic geometry and therefore the opportunity for the full deployment of his imagination. It is small wonder that Steiner sometimes wrote of "the shadow land of geometry."

Steiner's practical ambitions, related to, but lying near or on the margin of his geometrical scholarship, were not as shadowy. Perhaps this was understandable, for in class-conscious Berlin and the German academic world, his social origins were not advantageous. His special professorship or chair created for him at Berlin University was partly an effort to avoid this implicit embarrassment. Moreover, the timing of his publications was partly calculated to advance him toward the directorship of Berlin's planned Polytechnic Institute. Hence, in 1833 he published a short work, *Die geometrischen Konstructionen, ausgeführt mittelst der geraden Linie und eines festen Kreises* (*Geometrical Constructions with a Ruler, Given a Fixed Circle with Its Center*, 1950), which was intended for high schools and for practical purposes. Indeed, following his appointment to his Berlin chair, he never completed what he promised would be a comprehensive work.

Steiner apparently was not surprised when analytical geometricians discovered that his own results could often be verified analytically. It was not so much that Steiner disdained others' analyses.

Rather, he was headed in a different direction of inquiry, and he believed that analysis prevented geometricians from seeing things as they actually are. Like other projective geometers, he thought that because projective geometry could advance so swiftly from a few fundamental concepts to significant statements, he, like them, eschewed the formidable axiomatic studies that were the hallmark of Euclidean geometry. Most mathematicians argued against him, however, that despite Steiner's disclaimers, there was no royal road to a new geometry. No matter how logical, clear, and intuitive Steiner's projective geometry was, most geometricians actually wanted to see—metrically and analytically—what the projectivists were describing. Geometry was, for its nineteenth century scholars, simply too full of irrationals to make its results completely tenable.

Summary

Jakob Steiner was not the originator of projective or synthetic geometry. Nevertheless, his contributions were substantial and significant in the revival and advancement of synthetic geometry. This was the result of his clearly presented intuitions and his marvelous systematization of his projections. Before the close of his career, moreover, he had both trained others through the clarity of his lectures and writings and encouraged other geometricians such as Julius Plücker, Karl Weierstrass, and Karl von Staudt to resolve problems which had eluded or defeated him. These geometricians, through their own citations and references to his work, spread his name further throughout the European mathematical community. In addition, Steiner left a substantial body of published works.

By the 1850's, his health declined and the eccentricities of an always contentious character increased. He journeyed from spa to spa seeking the rejuvenation of his health. He died on April 1, 1863, at such a spa in Bern, Switzerland. Yet his repute and the respect of geometricians for his revitalization of synthetic geometry and its conundrums outlasted him.

Bibliography

Klein, Felix. *Development of Mathematics in the Nineteenth Century*. Translated by M. Ackerman. Brookline, Mass.: Math-Sci Press, 1979. Klein's work is indispensable, as very little of Steiner's writing has been translated into English. Filled with technical mathematical signs, symbols, and equations, it nevertheless contains much that is understandable by laymen. His expositions include biographical material on all mathematicians treated, with Steiner prominently among them, as well as good contextual explanations of their objectives, problems, and results. Contains ample illustrations.

Kline, Morris. *Mathematical Thought from Ancient to Modern Times*. New York: Oxford University Press, 1972. A layman's survey, which while largely ignoring Steiner, nevertheless places his work in a broad comprehensible framework. Contains illustrations, a good select bibliography, and an index.

Newman, James R., ed. *The World of Mathematics: A Small Library of the Literature of Mathematics from A'h-mosé, the Scribe, to Albert Einstein*. 4 vols. New York: Simon and Schuster, and London: Allen and Unwin, 1956. Volume 2 of this work is pertinent to Steiner's context and to defining aspects of his work. Illustrations help nonspecialists appreciate the nature of some synthetic, isoperimetric geometrical problems and their attempted solutions. A fine explication of certain projective geometrical investigations. There are bibliographical citations scattered throughout and a select bibliography and usable index at the end of the second volume.

Porter, Thomas Isaac. "A History of the Classical Isoperimetric Problem." In *Contributions to the Calculus of Variations, 1931-1932: Theses Submitted to the Department of Mathematics of the University of Chicago*. Chicago: University of Chicago Press, 1933. Rather than a raw thesis, this essay is an excellent survey of the synthetic geometrical problems Steiner, among others, tackled. Illustrated and readily understandable for those lacking special math training. Includes a substantial, if somewhat dated, bibliography.

Torretti, Roberto. *Philosophy of Geometry from Riemann to Poincaré*. Boston: Reidel, 1978. This important study is critical for a sound understanding by specialists as well as nonspecialists of a creative period in the development of both German and French mathematics, once again placing Steiner in a somewhat different historical context from that of the works cited above. It has some illustrations, a select bibliography, and an index.

Clifton K. Yearley

CHARLES PROTEUS STEINMETZ

Born: April 9, 1865; Breslau, Germany
Died: October 16, 1923; Schenectady, New York
Areas of Achievement: Engineering and education
Contribution: Steinmetz helped lay the engineering foundations for the large-scale use of electric power through his technical achievements, his role as an educator and inspirer of other engineers, and his creation of research and engineering institutions. In the process, he came to personify electrical engineering to a public that understood little of its technical details.

Early Life

Charles Proteus Steinmetz was born Carl August Steinmetz in 1865, in Breslau, Germany (modern Wroclaw, Poland). His father, Carl Heinrich Steinmetz, son of a German Lutheran father and Polish Catholic mother, worked as a clerk and lithographer with the state railways and was a congenital hunchback who passed that disability on to his only son. His mother, born Caroline Neubert, was the daughter of a well-to-do Breslau family of German Lutherans. She died when Carl August was only a few months old.

Reared mainly by his grandmother, Steinmetz had a pleasant and comfortable childhood. His combination of strong intelligence and a weak body directed him to a university education. He enrolled at the University of Breslau as a student of philosophy, specializing in mathematics. The friend who drew him into mathematics, Henry Lux, also drew him into socialism. Steinmetz joined a group of Social Democrats espousing the ideal of Ferdinand LaSalle, who opposed Karl Marx by arguing that socialism could be achieved without revolution, a theme that Steinmetz would develop throughout his life.

Steinmetz's involvement in both mathematical study and socialism came to a critical point in 1888. Still without a degree, Steinmetz was completing a dissertation based on the geometrical ideas of the German mathematician Bernhard Riemann when he assumed the editorship of the local Social Democratic newspaper. It had already drawn the attention of the police with its antigovernment, though nonviolent, editorial policy. According to Steinmetz's later recollections, he left the country in 1888 with the police looking for him and the threat of possible prosecution hanging over him.

He spent a year in Zurich, Switzerland, where he took the only engineering courses of his career at Federal University but again departed without a degree. He had begun writing technical articles about the new field of electricity; the most promising place to make a career in that field was the United States, where capital and opportunities for electrification were abundant and engineering talent was scarce. With a prosperous friend, Oscar Asmussen, he sailed to New York.

Life's Work

Steinmetz's entry into New York Harbor in June, 1889, past the new Statue of Liberty, was in the best Emma Lazarus tradition: Tired and weak (Steinmetz was suffering from a bad cold in addition to his disability), a member of a huddled mass yearning to breathe free, he was still a Socialist on the lam, penniless and in shabby clothes, and he spent two days at Ellis Island, where he was nearly rejected for entry into the country. Fortunately, he also had assets: the friendship of the wealthy Asmussen and a letter of introduction to an earlier political refugee, Rudolf Eickemeyer, who had long since established himself at Yonkers, New York, as a successful manufacturer of hat machinery and Civil War revolvers. Steinmetz was set with a job as the one-man research and development staff supporting Eickemeyer's efforts to diversify into the new business of electric motors.

Within only two years, Steinmetz rose to the top of the American electrical engineering profession. His distinctive appearance—his twisted form, less than five feet tall, his neat if grizzled beard and ever-present cigar—became well-known first among engineers and soon among that segment of the public that was interested in science and technology. He then changed his name to Charles Proteus Steinmetz, reflecting his confidence in his own powers and his sense that he had made a new life for himself in America. In 1890, he introduced to engineers his law of hysteresis, a formula for predicting the energy lost through magnetizing and demagnetizing the electromagnets used in electrical equipment. This was no academic exercise but a crucial tool for designing generators, motors, and transformers. His accomplishment was repeated in 1893 with his second major contribution to electrical engineering, the use of "imaginary" numbers in electrical calculations, which made it possible to determine the characteristics of complex electrical machines by calculation rather than trial and error.

The unexpectedness of Steinmetz's rise and the importance of his purely technical work, however, should not be overrated. His patron, Eickemeyer, was a fine inventor who had developed an important new type of electric motor before Steinmetz came along as well as instruments that made it easy for Steinmetz to study hysteresis. The "law" was actually an empirical special case of more general findings arrived at earlier by a British physicist; the imaginary number applications had been anticipated by a Harvard professor. Steinmetz's greatness lay in communicating these ideas, educating a generation of engineers about them, and inspiring others to use mathematics to solve practical problems. Meanwhile, the electrical inventions of Eickemeyer's company caught the eye of a giant company created in 1892 to dominate the electrical manufacturing business, the General Electric Company. It followed its consistent policy of buying up competing companies and absorbing good engineers in the bargain by purchasing Eickemeyer's company and rights to Steinmetz's services in 1893.

General Electric sent Steinmetz to its second biggest plant, in Lynn, Massachusetts, to serve as a calculator of the electrical characteristics of its products and systems. He was unhappy there, but a reorganization in 1893 sent him to a more congenial setting in Schenectady, New York, where there were plenty of German immigrants and trained engineers. Soon, he was Schenectady's best-known citizen. Defying his physical weakness, he rode a bicycle, skied, and paddled a canoe. He filled his home laboratory with sparking and glowing electrical apparatus as well as a crow and collections of orchids, cacti, and lizards. His weekly poker games drew General Electric executives and engineers, and his summer cabin drew young protégés. He befriended in particular a young engineer, Joseph Hayden, whom he adopted, and his family. On the job, he moved beyond engineering calculations to consulting.

As General Electric's chief consulting engineer, he provided problem solving and advice for all of the company's departments. He gained fame as an oracle, but a closer look shows that he was not particularly adept at putting his finger on key trends. For example, he did not recognize the system of polyphase alternating current as the key to modern electrification, and he badly underestimated the industry's ability to develop high-voltage transmission systems. He made some two hundred patented inventions, but only one of them, a new type of street light, had any substantial commercial success. In the narrow realms of invention and consulting, his impact on the electrical art was not as great as that of such now-obscure contemporaries as his General Electric colleagues William LeRoy Emmet and Ernst Alexanderson, his Westinghouse rival Benjamin Garver Lamme, or the independents Nikola Tesla and William Stanley.

It was as educator and inspirational motivator that he truly shone. He wrote twelve books, including the classic *Theory and Calculation of Alternating Current Phenomena* (1897), an often-reprinted textbook. He published more than two hundred articles, in everything from mass periodicals to the *Physical Review*. While still an employee at General Electric, he accepted a professorship in electrical engineering at Schenectady's Union College and created a first-rate department that he then turned over to one of his protégés, Ernest Berg.

Steinmetz received an honorary degree from Harvard in 1899, and its accompanying citation for him as "the foremost expert in applied electricity of this country and therefore the world" captures in its hyperbole and chauvinism some of the reasons for which America embraced Steinmetz as a public figure. He enjoyed and used the publicity. For example, he used his eminence to sponsor within General Electric the first industrial laboratory devoted in part to true scientific research (1900) and one of industry's best engineering laboratories (1907).

Steinmetz had completed his major technical work by 1910 (a later and highly publicized experiment in making lightning in the laboratory was a useful engineering exercise that does not rank with his earlier work). His interest in socialism, dormant since the 1890's, revived. He became a leader of the local Socialist Party that took over Schenectady's city government in 1912. In the posts as head of the Board of Education, head of the Parks Commission, and president of the Common Council, he led efforts to build schools and parks that greatly improved the quality of life in that city.

Steinmetz still espoused evolutionary socialism, but now it was colored by his industrial experience. His major statement of that view, the book *America and the New Epoch* (1916), emphasized cooperation and organization as the keys to socialism. The large corporation and its methods would gradually

blend with the state and turn it into a cooperative commonwealth run by experts who were above politics.

This brand of corporate socialism may have disappointed his more doctrinaire colleagues. He and other members of the reformist wing were briefly expelled from the party, though he was taken back and ran in 1922, unsuccessfully, on the Socialist ticket for the post of state engineer. Steinmetz showed that he had not adopted reform socialism out of cowardice or a need to conform. From the sinking of the *Lusitania* in 1915 until the United States' entry into World War I in 1917, he argued the proneutrality case with a vigor dangerous for one so obviously of German descent. After the war, he also voiced a number of unpopular or extreme positions in newspaper articles and interviews. His predictions and advocacies ranged over electric vehicles, the capabilities of the varied European "races," the coming energy crises and biological revolutions, and a widely publicized exchange of letters with Vladimir Ilich Lenin about the electrification of the Soviet Union. Never of strong constitution, he died after a brief illness in Schenectady in 1923.

Summary

Steinmetz was a brilliant engineer and inventor, but his emergence as the individual embodying the profession of electrical engineering for the American public in the early twentieth century was attributable to more than his brilliance. Electricity was a glamorous new technology with a theory inaccessible to the public. People needed to personify it, and the novelty of a small, misshapen man commanding the lightning caught their fancy. He was indeed a leader in the application to electrical engineering of new methods of applied mathematics and organized research, but the same could be said of a half-dozen contemporaries whose names remained unknown. His true greatness was as an educator, explainer, and motivator. Those strengths, along with his distinctive appearance, an immigrant background personifying the melting-pot myth, an adherence to a personal and nonradical brand of socialism, and (especially posthumously) the support of the publicity machine of his long-time employer, the General Electric Company, won for him renown that went far beyond technology.

Bibliography

Alger, Philip, and Ernest Caldecott, eds. *Steinmetz the Philosopher*. Schenectady, N.Y.: Mohawk, 1965. A valuable collection of Steinmetz's essays on political, social, and educational topics. Perhaps best summed up by one essay's title: "The Bolsheviks *Won't* Get You if You *Do* Watch Out."

Hammond, John Winthrop. *Charles Proteus Steinmetz: A Biography*. New York and London: Century, 1924. The most comprehensive summary of Steinmetz's life, written by a General Electric publicity writer who worked with him at Schenectady. Uncritical in its admiration for the subject. Makes little attempt to put either the technical work or the political and social ideas in perspective. A combination of useful primary material and mythmaking.

Kline, Ronald. *Steinmetz: Engineer and Socialist*. Baltimore: Johns Hopkins University Press, 1992. The author examines Steinmetz's contemporary reputation.

Lavine, Sigmund A. *Steinmetz: Maker of Lighting*. New York: Dodd, Mead, 1955. Another recycling of the Hammond Material.

Leonard, Jonathan Norton. *Loki: The Life of Charles Proteus Steinmetz*. New York: Doubleday, 1929. This account by a science journalist is somewhat livelier than Hammond's book, but it contains little additional information, beyond puncturing one or two myths. (Steinmetz worked for a salary, not as myth would have it, in exchange for a checkbook given him by General Electric.)

Miller, John Anderson. *Modern Jupiter*. New York: American Society of Mechanical Engineers, 1958. Again, the Hammond material and approach, but supplemented somewhat by material made available by the Steinmetz heirs and a former assistant. Though the author is an engineer, he does little to clarify Steinmetz's technical role. Perhaps because he is an engineer, he does little to clarify Steinmetz's socialism.

Steinmetz, Charles Proteus. *America and the New Epoch*. New York and London: Harper, 1916. Steinmetz made here his fullest exposition of his brand of socialism. Argues that the era of competition is dead and that the era of cooperation has succeeded it. Corporations and government must blend together to form a corporatist state ruled by large organizations where the distinction between public and private has vanished.

George Wise

STENDHAL
Marie-Henri Beyle

Born: January 23, 1783; Grenoble, France
Died: March 23, 1842; Paris, France
Area of Achievement: Literature
Contribution: Stendhal combined the themes of Romanticism with the style of realism. His insistence on telling the truth about emotions in simple, stark terms resulted in novels that, although not very popular during his lifetime, have become classics.

Early Life

Information about the life of Marie-Henri Beyle (who wrote as Stendhal) is voluminous and almost all suspect. Too much of it comes from his own autobiographical works—*Vie de Henry Brulard* (1890, 1949; *The Life of Henry Brulard*, 1925) and *Souvenirs d'égotisme* (1892, 1950; *Memoirs of Egotism*, 1949)—which are faithful accounts of Stendhal's feelings about the events of his life but not necessarily faithful accounts of the events themselves. His father, Chérubin Beyle, was a lawyer and, according to Stendhal, acquisitive and stern. His mother, Henriette Gagnon Beyle, to whom he was exceptionally close, was gay and urbane. The loss of his mother in 1790 was a devastating blow. His Aunt Séraphie Gagnon took over the task of rearing the seven-year-old Marie-Henri, but he found her a sour-tempered disciplinarian. Their relationship was never warm. His grandfather, Henri Gagnon, provided not only a cheerful refuge from his father and Aunt Séraphie but also an introduction to the intellectual world of the Enlightenment. The young Marie-Henri found little companionship outside his family. He was kept away from the other children of the community, whom his father and aunt regarded as common. His tutor, the Abbé Jean-François Raillane, was cold and old-fashioned. One of the many things Beyle liked about the French Revolution was that in 1794 Raillane had to flee from it.

One of the many reforms generated by the Revolution was the creation of local schools. Such an institution opened in Grenoble in 1796, and Beyle was enrolled. It was his first opportunity to mix freely with people his own age. His performance was poor during his first year. He soon fell head over heels in love with a theater performer, Virginie Kubly, and although they never actually met, she was his first passion. Romantic turmoil would never again be long absent from his life. By 1799, he had the opportunity to study mathematics at the École Polytechnique in Paris.

Beyle, however, never enrolled at the school. With the fascination of a small-town boy in the big city, he began to explore Paris. Within a month, he was seriously ill and was rescued by cousins named Daru, who gave him a place to stay and an introduction to society. Later, they obtained for him a position as clerk at the Ministry of War. Although Beyle's health returned, his illness caused him to lose much of his hair. From this time on, he wore a wig, and as he was stout, with short legs and a large head, he always felt physically inadequate. His luminous eyes were his only striking feature.

His position as a clerk proved depressing, but in May, 1800, Beyle was invited to join his cousins in Italy. En route, he visited Jean-Jacques Rousseau's birthplace in Geneva and then joined Napoleon I's army, which was passing through the St. Bernard Pass to surprise the Austrians. Milan entranced Beyle. He began learning Italian and was smitten by Angela Pietragrua, whose bureaucrat husband tolerated her many liaisons. Sexually uninitiated and still very shy, he was unsuccessful with Angela but contracted syphilis from a prostitute. Symptoms, apparently from this disease, recurred for the remainder of his life. In September, Pierre Daru was able to get his young cousin a provisional commission as sublieutenant in the cavalry. His posts in small rural villages proved boring, and Beyle soon finagled a staff position. Daru was angered because his name was used without his permission, and after a few months Beyle was ordered back to his regiment. He returned on October 26, 1801, only to fall ill; taking a medical leave, he set out for Grenoble.

He enjoyed his new status in his hometown and prolonged his leave, occupying his time by studying the philosophy of the Sensationalists. Beyle came to deny that man was rational, but although he rejected free will, he did conclude that the self-aware human could change his fate by living deliberately. Intellectually, he was growing up, and his long yearning for action was giving way to analysis. He resigned his commission and resolved to pursue a career of letters. Following yet another unrequited infatuation, he set off for Paris in April, 1802, to become a playwright.

Life's Work

For the next two years Beyle lived the life of a scholar in Paris, reading William Shakespeare, John Locke, Thomas Hobbes, and especially Antoine Destutt de Tracy, whose rationalism he found appealing. He tried unsuccessfully to write drama in verse and lived on a small allowance from his father, who was glad to have his son out of the army.

While taking acting lessons, Beyle fell in love with Mélanie Guilbert, a starlet of twenty-four and an unwed mother. In April, 1805, he agreed to accompany her to Marseilles, where she had a job and he had an opportunity to go into business with his friend Fortuné Mante. These plans soon fell apart. In the spring of 1806, he returned to Grenoble and began to seek the favor of Pierre Daru again. In October, he went to Brunswick with Pierre's brother Martial, who was to be intendant there. Beyle spent the next two years as a civil servant in Brunswick, bored but successful.

Beyle was now a favorite of Pierre Daru and a good friend of his wife, Alexandrine, who with good grace and no ill will rebuffed a clumsy effort at seduction. On August 1, 1810, Beyle was appointed auditor of the Council of State. He was soon living sumptuously and beyond his means. He also began an affair with Angélina Bereyter, a member of the Opéra-Bouffe of the Théâtre Italien. Although the two remained together until 1814, the attraction for him was essentially physical.

After a leave in 1811, during which he toured his beloved Italy and renewed his courtship of Angélina Bereyter—successfully this time—Beyle asked to be reassigned to active military duty. He was sent off as a courier in the summer of 1812 and found himself following the army to Moscow. When Napoleon ordered retreat, Beyle was appointed commissioner of war supplies and ordered to organize supplies at Smolensk, Mohilar, and Vitebsk. With the retreat becoming little more than a rout, he could not continue his mission beyond the first city, and after much hardship and danger as he joined the flight, he got back to Paris on January 31, 1813. He was justly proud of his conduct but ready to be done with war.

In the spring, however, he was ordered back to duty and, surprisingly revitalized, was a witness to the Battle of Bautzen in May. He then fell ill, probably from typhus, but recuperated and was back in Milan in early September. His military experiences proved invaluable for later writing, when he became one of the first to portray battle realistically from the individual's perspective. At the end of the year, he returned to Paris, hoping to write comic plays and find a permanent situation in Italy. Instead, he was ordered to help prepare for the defense of Dauphiné. The strain was too much, and he was soon ill again. He took leave but, lacking income, had to give up his luxurious life-style. Eager to establish himself as an author, he published, at his own expense, a biographical study of the composers Joseph Haydn, Wolfgang Amadeus Mozart, and Pietro Metastasio in 1814, but the book was mostly plagiarized. He was fortunate that his love of secrecy and aliases had led him not to use his own name.

Unable to find a job, Beyle returned to Milan, where he tried to live on his army pension and renewed his relationship with Angela Pietragrua. Needing money, he devoted himself to writing, publishing two books in 1817, *Histoire de la peinture de Italie* (1817) and *Rome, Naples, et Florence en 1817* (1817, 1826; *Rome, Naples, and Florence in 1817*, 1818). The former was in part plagiarized, and the original parts were personal, emotional reactions to the work of various painters. The latter was a sort of travelog with commentary and was a minor success. It was also his first use of the name "Stendhal," taken from a small German town and used to obscure the identity of an author critical of the handling of Italy at the Congress of Vienna. It was to become Beyle's most common pseudonym and the one under which he became famous. Pleased by having had some success, Stendhal started the first of two efforts to write a study of Napoleon. Neither of these was ever finished, and the manuscripts were published only after his death. They do make clear the author's view of the young Napoleon as the heir of the Revolution, of the Empire as a betrayal of the revolutionary ideals, and of the restored Bourbon government as contemptible.

On March 4, 1818, Stendhal met Mathilde, Viscontini Dembowski, whom he always called Métilde. Wildly in love, he pursued her for three years, only to be repeatedly rejected. In 1821, penniless and again suffering from venereal disease, he returned to Paris. The relationship with Métilde resulted in *De l'amour* (1822; *Maxims of Love*, 1906), in which he offered a combination of objective analysis and confession. He was developing his characteristic style, combining the rationalism of the Enlightenment with the emotional outpourings of the Romantics.

Stendhal made his home in Paris for the next decade, visiting England twice and Italy once during those years. In 1823, he published part 1 of *Racine et Shakespare* (1823, 1825; *Racine and Shakespeare*, 1962). This work catapulted Stendhal from the rank of minor author into a prominent place among those battling over aesthetic standards. Stendhal's firm assertion that there are no permanent criteria for beauty put him clearly in the ranks of the Romantics. Shakespeare was his example of a playwright who rejected the traditions and took his art into glorious new realms. Stendhal continued his role of Romanticism's champion with *Vie de Rossini* (1823; *Memoirs of Rossini*, 1924), which defends Romantic music. As Stendhal's fame grew, so did his acquaintances among the literati of Paris; among his associates were Honoré de Balzac, Benjamin Constant, Alfred de Musset, Alphonse de Lamartine, and Adolphe Thiers. His love in the mid-1820's was Countess Clémentine (Menti) Curial, but though they remained friends, she ended the affair in 1826. Stendhal responded by writing *Armance* (1827; English translation, 1928), his first novel. Although generally regarded as a failure, *Armance*, which concerned the frustrations of love dampened by impotence, allowed Stendhal to express his sense of alienation and launched him on a career of writing fiction.

At the end of the decade, Stendhal, realizing that his greatest success had come with travel books, added *Promenades dans Rome* (1829; *A Roman Journal*, 1957), which became a popular guidebook to the city. He also had several brief love affairs. Suddenly, in 1830, Stendhal's years of struggle culminated in a work of genius. *Le Rouge et le noir* (*The Red and the Black*, 1898) was a brilliant blending of styles: first- and third-person perspectives, Romantic self-revelation, and classical external analysis. Stendhal achieved a remarkable shifting of perspectives among characters and narrator without losing simplicity or sacrificing the clarity of the story.

Even as Stendhal was producing *The Red and the Black*, France was undergoing the July Revolution, and with the establishment of the more liberal government of Louis-Philippe, the author hoped that he might again find a place in government service. He requested a job as consul in Italy and was

posted to Trieste, only to be rejected by the Austrian government, which controlled that city, as a radical—his political comments in his travel books had not been forgotten. In February, 1831, he was named consul at Civitavecchia on the Tyrrhenian Sea, near Rome.

During his service at Civitavecchia, Stendhal wrote his two previously mentioned autobiographical pieces and the unfinished novel *Lucien Leuwen* (1855, 1894, 1926-1927; English translation, 1950). His writing was interrupted by intermittent ill health, and in March, 1836, he returned to Paris, where he remained for three very productive years. His most important work of this period was *La Chartreuse de Parme* (1839; *The Charterhouse of Parma*, 1895), which he expanded from one of his Italian short stories in about two months. The hero, Fabrice del Dongo, is more like the youthful Stendhal in being innocent and idealistic than was Julien Sorel of *The Red and the Black*, who is crafty and self-serving. Both characters, however, are examples of men who rise from relatively obscure beginnings and whose careers conclude on the executioner's scaffold.

In June of 1839, Stendhal reluctantly began his return to Civitavecchia, taking three months to make the trip. In the fall, he began a new novel, *Lamiel* (1889, 1971; English translation, 1950). Although typically Stendhalian in describing the struggle of an ambitious youth to find success and love, it is unusual in that the youth is, in this case, female. As a result of increasing problems with vertigo and, in March, 1841, an attack of apoplexy, Stendhal could not complete this novel. On October 21, 1841, he left for France, where, after attending a rally, he died of a stroke during a walk on March 23, 1842.

Summary

As a novelist, Stendhal broke new ground by his skillful combination of classical style and Romantic themes. All of his important works are consciously autobiographical, though they are much more concerned with accurate descriptions of feeling than of events. Despite the emphasis on the personal, the prose style remains simple and analytical, much more like that of the philosophes than the Romantics. With his ability to tell a story from shifting points of view, displaying the emotions of various characters, Stendhal was establishing a new novel form that would be a hallmark of the twentieth century.

Stendhal also contributed to social history. His travel works, such as *Mémoires d'un touriste* (1838; partial translation in *Memoirs of a Tourist*, 1962), offer not only travel notes but also social and political commentary. Such eyewitness accounts are always valuable, but when the witness has the sensitivity of a Stendhal, their value is much enhanced. Thus, his writings are still read as both history and literature.

Bibliography

Alter, Robert, with Carol Cosman. *A Lion for Love: A Critical Biography of Stendhal.* New York: Basic Books, 1979. The emphasis of this volume is criticism, and its authors do an excellent job of presenting their analysis of Stendhal in a historical context. Not the book to read, however, for a clear chronological description of his life.

Atherton, John. *Stendhal.* London: Bowes and Bowes, and New York: Hillary House, 1965. A short but effectively done biography. Atherton's comments are insightful and well grounded in research.

Bell, Sheila M. "Stendahl's 'Vie de Henry Brulard': The Engravings—a Public or Private Matter?" *Modern Language Review* 93, no. 2 (April, 1998). Discusses the possible significance of the engravings included by Stendhal with his "Vie de Henry Brulard," which appear to be unrelated to the text or the art mentioned therein.

Brombert, Victor H. *Stendhal: Fiction and the Themes of Freedom.* New York: Random House, 1968. Although a work of criticism, this book contains much biographical information, and it gives a useful analysis of the themes in Stendhal's fiction. Ties his work into what is known of the nineteenth century novel.

Cremin, Joan. *Selfhood, Fiction, and Desire in Stendhal's "Vie de Henry Brulard" and "Armance."* New York: Lang, 1998. Cremin examines the themes of selfhood, desire, and fiction in two representative texts by Stendhal.

May, Gita. *Stendhal and the Age of Napoleon.* New York: Columbia University Press, 1977. An excellent, full biography that provides a detailed chronological account of Stendhal's life. The best straightforward biography available.

Strickland, Geoffrey. *Stendhal: The Education of a Novelist.* London and New York: Cambridge University Press, 1974. An attempt to analyze the forces that shaped Stendhal and to show how those forces influenced his work. It is both biographical and critical, and although it could not replace a traditional biography, it does provide much useful analysis with a biographical foundation.

Fred R. van Hartesveldt

ALEXANDER H. STEPHENS

Born: February 11, 1812; Wilkes County, Georgia

Died: March 4, 1883; Atlanta, Georgia

Areas of Achievement: Government and politics

Contribution: Stephens, called "Little Aleck" by his colleagues because he only weighed one hundred pounds, was a member of the United States Congress from 1843 to 1859 and vice president of the Confederate States of America during the Civil War. Following the war, he again served in Congress and as governor of Georgia.

Early Life

Alexander Hamilton Stephens was born in the Georgia Piedmont about fifteen miles southwest of Washington, Georgia. He was the third child of Andrew B. and Mary Stephens. Soon after his birth, Alexander's mother died. Alexander inherited his mother's poor health and was plagued by illnesses throughout his life.

In 1813 his father married Matilda Lindsey, the daughter of a Revolutionary War veteran. Alexander did not get along well with his stepmother, but he was very close to his father, who was a skilled craftsman and teacher. From 1820 through 1824, Alexander attended his father's school. In 1826, Andrew Stephens died at the age of forty-four, and Alexander was sent to Warren County, Georgia, to live with his uncle, Aaron Grier. At first he attended a Roman Catholic school, but in 1827 he entered an academy in Washington, Georgia, to study Latin and Geography. While there he lived at the home of Alexander Hamilton Webster, a Presbyterian minister. Alexander's admiration of Webster led to his adoption of Hamilton as his own middle name. In 1828 he entered Franklin College in Athens, Georgia, and graduated first in his class in 1832 at the age of twenty.

Following his graduation from college, Stephens took a teaching position in Madison, Georgia; however, he left that position after only four months. He then worked as a tutor for the children of a doctor in Liberty County in southeastern Georgia. In January, 1834, he moved to Crawfordville, Georgia, and began to study law. In July of that year he passed the bar and, at the age of twenty-two, began to practice law in Crawfordville.

Life's Work

In 1836 Stephens began his political career in Taliaferro County, Georgia, when he was elected by a two-to-one margin to the Georgia House of Representatives. He served in that position until 1841. He then left politics to concentrate on his law practice but returned two years later and was elected to the state senate, where he served for two years. During his six years in the Georgia legislature, Stephens learned how to respond to his constituents and mastered the skills of legislative tactics, parliamentary procedure, and party strategy.

In 1843 Stephens was selected by the Whig Party to run against the Democratic candidate, James H. Starke, for the United States House of Representatives. In a statewide campaign, Stephens, defending the Whig program of tariffs, distribution, and a national bank, defeated Starke 38,051 votes to 35,001 votes. He then began a political career in the U.S. House of Representatives that lasted until 1859. In Congress, Stephens supported the annexation of Texas in 1845, not solely for the purpose of extending slavery but to increase southern political power in the Union. However, while Stephens condemned the slave trade, he defended slavery by arguing that it would always be necessary wherever whites and blacks lived together in comparable numbers. Stephens supported both the Compromise of 1850 and the Kansas-Nebraska Act of 1854, both of which attempted to establish a criteria for the extension of slavery into the territories.

After the Whig Party disintegrated in the 1850's, Stephens reluctantly joined the Democratic Party. During intraparty battles between 1857 and 1860, Stephens defended Senator Stephen A. Douglas and popular sovereignty and consistently opposed secession. In 1859 Stephens made a speech in which he advocated reopening the African slave trade, a position that few Southerners supported. His argument was based on the idea that if there was an expansion of the slave states admitted to the Union, it would be necessary to secure more slaves to occupy these new states. If the prohibition against the slave trade continued, the South would have to abandon its race with the North for colonizing new states.

Following the election of Abraham Lincoln to president in 1860, Stephens argued in a speech before the Georgia legislature that Georgia should remain loyal to the Union. He believed that Lincoln's election had been constitutional and that there was not sufficient grounds to secede from the Union. Furthermore, if the South seceded it would be committing the aggression. He argued that the

South should wait for the North to commit an act of aggression against the region before trying to secede. Stephens' position, however, was largely rejected.

On January 16, 1861, a convention was held in Milledgeville, Georgia, to consider the question of secession. Stephens was offered the presidency of the convention, but he declined. He argued against secession once again, saying that the point of resistance should be the point of aggression. He felt that a united South could obtain a redress of grievances in the Union and said that he would vote against secession because no existing cause warranted it. Despite Stephens' plea, the ordinance of secession passed by an overwhelming majority.

Shortly thereafter, Stephens was selected as a delegate from Georgia to go to Montgomery, Alabama, for a convention of the seceded states, where he served on a committee that drafted the Constitution for the Confederacy. The document was remarkably similar to the U.S. Constitution except for the provisions that recognized and protected slavery. Included in the document was a provision supported by Stephens and his moderate allies that would allow the admission of nonslave states to the Confederacy.

The convention also chose former U.S. senator Jefferson Davis of Mississippi as president of the Confederacy and Stephens as vice president. On February 11, 1861, Stephens took the oath of office as vice president of the Confederacy on his forty-ninth birthday. Soon thereafter, Davis asked Stephens to lead a Confederate commission to go to Washington, D.C., to negotiate with the United States for the transfer of forts at Charleston, South Carolina, and Pensacola, Florida. Stephens refused since he saw such efforts as futile.

Despite the fact that they held the top two positions in the Confederacy, the relationship between Davis and Stephens quickly cooled. Two measures passed by the first Confederate Congress, a conscription law and an act authorizing the suspension of the writ of habeas corpus in the Confederacy, were strongly opposed by Stephens. He argued that such measures were despotic and threatened constitutional liberty. In February, 1865, Stephens headed the Confederate commission to a peace conference at Hampton Roads, Virginia. This effort failed.

Following the end of the Civil War, Stephens was arrested in Crawfordville. On May 25, 1865, he was sent to prison at Fort Warren in Boston Harbor. One month after he was imprisoned, Stephens applied directly to President Andrew Johnson for a pardon. In his letter to President Johnson, he reviewed his political career, his support of states' rights and the Constitution, and his opposition to secession. Johnson felt it was important that Stephens and other moderates who would support Johnson's plan for Reconstruction should be at home instead of in jail. In October, 1865, Johnson granted Stephens a pardon. Stephens met with Johnson in Washington, D.C., after his release and pledged support for Johnson's policy for Reconstruction. He then returned home to Crawfordville, Georgia, and became involved in politics.

In 1866 Stephens was elected to the U.S. Senate; however, he was denied his seat because Georgia had not properly reconstructed according to congressional guidelines. Stephens then wrote a two-volume work entitled *A Constitutional View of the Late War Between the States* (1868-1870) in which he presented the South's position on states' rights and secession. He argued that the South had failed in its efforts in part because of the Confederacy's attempt to centralize power.

During this period Stephens also argued that the Democratic Party should oppose Reconstruction, the Fourteenth and Fifteenth Amendments, and test oaths to determine eligibility for office in the post-Civil War South. To accept these things would be a repudiation of secession and states' rights. However, between 1868 and 1870, Georgia was subject to Radical Reconstruction. During this era, the Ku Klux Klan was organized in Georgia, and the Klan functioned as the military arm of the Democratic Party, attacking the freedmen and their white supporters. Despite Stephens' states' rights beliefs, he rejected the activities of the Ku Klux Klan because it went outside the law.

Stevens' view of the role of African Americans also changed after the Civil War. He proposed a system of representation for the new Georgia Constitution based on class. He argued that at first the freedmen should have their franchise restricted or should be required to have white representatives; however, he felt that political rights ought to be granted to them for the South's own future good, that provisions for the education of African Americans should be granted immediately, and that school attendance should be compulsory.

In December, 1868, Stephens was offered the position of chair of history and political science at the University of Georgia, but he declined it because of poor health. He returned to political life in 1873 when he was elected to the U.S. Congress, where he remained until 1882; however, his focus on constitutional issues had ceased to be relevant to a country that was concerned with economic growth. He returned to Georgia in 1882 and ran for governor despite his poor health. On October 4, 1882, Stephens was elected governor by over sixty thousand votes, carrying 130 out of 137 counties. In February, 1883, Stephens went to Savannah, Georgia, to speak at the city's sesquicentennial celebration. Exposure to the cold and damp air, however, resulted in his final illness. On March 4, 1883, Stephens, the Georgia statesman and political leader, died after serving only 119 days as governor.

Summary

Alexander Stephens, despite his small stature and poor health, was one of the dominant figures in Georgia politics in the nineteenth century. His political life seemed to be a series of contradictions. Politically, he went from being a Whig to a Democrat. He was a strong supporter of states' rights, but, as the South moved toward secession, Stephens stressed the virtues of the Union and became a reluctant supporter of the Confederacy. While he served as vice president of the Confederacy, Stephens found himself in conflict with President Jefferson Davis over the relationship between the Confederacy and its members. He strongly opposed the centralization of power even though the Confederacy was involved in a war. Some historians view Stephens as an impractical idealist; others view him as a man who lived by his principles. Despite the contradictions in his life, Stephens remained enormously popular in the state of Georgia throughout his life. His election as governor in 1882, with over 60 percent of the vote, illustrated that Little Aleck's popularity with the people of Georgia was a constant in a personal life filled with contradictions.

Bibliography

Brumgardt, John A. "The Confederate Career of Alexander H. Stephens." *Civil War History* 28 (March, 1981): 64-81. A sympathetic analysis of Stephens' philosophy and conflicts with Jefferson Davis during the Civil War.

Rabun, James Z. "Alexander Stephens and Jefferson Davis." *American Historical Review* 58 (January, 1953): 290-321. An analysis of the two major leaders of the Confederacy. This article analyzes the differences and conflicts between the two men and how they symbolized the differences that existed in the Confederacy itself.

Richardson, E. Ramsey. *Little Aleck: A Life of Alexander H. Stephens, The Fighting Vice-President of the Confederacy.* Indianapolis: Bobbs-Merrill, 1932. A biography of Stephens that presents a sympathetic interpretation of his life and accomplishments.

Schott, Thomas E. *Alexander H. Stephens of Georgia.* Baton Rouge: Louisiana State University Press, 1988. The most comprehensive biography of Stephens' personal and political career.

Stephens, Alexander H. *Recollections of Alexander H. Stephens: His Diary Kept When a Prisoner at Fort Warren, Boston Harbor, 1865.* New York: Doubleday, 1910. This volume includes reflections on his prison life and reminiscences.

William V. Moore

GEORGE STEPHENSON

Born: June 9, 1781; Wylam, Northumberland, England

Died: August 12, 1848; Chesterfield, Derbyshire, England

Area of Achievement: Civil engineering

Contribution: By constructing and equipping the Stockton and Darlington and the Liverpool and Manchester railways, Stephenson demonstrated the economic viability of the steam railway, guaranteeing its rapid development as Great Britain's basic transportation system.

Early Life

George Stephenson was born at Wylam, Northumberland, near Newcastle on the bank of the River Tyne, on June 9, 1781. Because the economy of his native Tyneside was based on coal, he grew up surrounded by technological elements used extensively in coal mining which were later to be brought together in the railway industry. Coal from the mines often reached the coal-carrying ships on the Tyne by means of tramways, where wagons rolled on wooden rails. On the level, horses were used to pull the wagons. On the downgrade, gravity sufficed. Large stationary steam engines pumped water from the mines and operated the winding gear which lifted coal and miners from the depths. Steam engines had been introduced into England by Thomas Savery and Thomas Newcomen toward the beginning of the eighteenth century and had been greatly improved by James Watt in the 1760's.

Stephenson's father worked as an engineer with steam machinery at a succession of Tyneside pits. Young Stephenson embarked on a similar career when, barely out of childhood, he joined his father as an assistant fireman. He received no formal schooling and was still illiterate at age eighteen. Educational credentials were of no concern, however, to the miners and mine owners of the Tyneside. Their interests were in the extraction and shipment of coal, efficiently and, if possible, safely. Stephenson rapidly proved to have the skills and instincts of a natural mechanic. Engaged as a maintenance man for the Grand Allies, a consortium of Northumbrian mine owners, Stephenson quickly earned a reputation as one who could fix or improve a machine after briefly watching its operation, absorbing its principles in his own mind even though he was generally unable to ex-

plain those principles adequately to others. At age thirty, in 1811, his success in refining a hitherto unsuccessful steam pump, so that a constantly flooded coal pit could for the first time be worked, attracted more than local attention. Four years later, in the autumn of 1815, a brief spate of experimentation led to Stephenson's creation of a safety lamp for use by coal miners, a lamp which would not ignite mine gases and cause disastrous underground explosions. Stephenson's lamp emerged almost simultaneously with that of Sir Humphry Davy. Apparently, the unschooled Northumbrian and the respected scientist had independently hit upon the same principle at the same time. Stephenson's work for the mines led also to his participation in improvements in the transport of coal. In 1814, Stephenson's first locomotive, the Blucher, went into operation, a cumbersome, slow, and inefficient machine, not a major improvement on other Northumbrian locomotives, which had begun to supplement horses and fixed engines in the Tyneside coal fields. Stephenson's older brother was driver of the Blucher and—indicative of the still-early stage of locomotive evolution—his sister-in-law was once called upon to push the Blucher when it stalled. In 1816, Stephenson patented a new type of rail assembly for use on coal tramways, because as motive power became heavier, the permanent way required analogous improvement.

Life's Work

Stephenson might have remained a locally respected but obscure mechanical jack-of-all-trades on the Tyneside had he not attracted the attention of Edward Pease, the Quaker proprietor of coal mines in County Durham, thirty-five miles south of Stephenson's Tyneside. The County Durham coalfield had suffered historically, as contrasted with that of the Tyneside, because of its inadequate access to deep water. Pease and his circle hoped to overcome that handicap by constructing a canal or tramway connecting the mines west of Darlington with tidal water at Stockton. On April 19, 1821, Pease and Stephenson met at Darlington, and from that consultation came Stephenson's appointment as engineer of the Stockton and Darlington Railway. Stephenson surveyed the twenty-five-mile line and supervised its construction. His son Robert, born in 1803, assisted in the survey and in

June, 1823, was put in charge of Robert Stephenson and Company, of Newcastle, a firm established by the two Stephensons and the Pease family to build locomotives which would supply some of the power for the Stockton and Darlington. The new railway, opened on September 27, 1825, was a hybrid operation. Horses pulled some trains, locomotives others. Although there was some passenger traffic, the road was designed primarily for coal, and several inclined planes sped the coal wagons on their way toward the sea by gravity. The Stockton and Darlington was an immediate success, financially as well as mechanically. Investors, engineers, and journalists from throughout Great Britain and the Continent as well made tours of inspection, returning home to spread the news of Stephenson's triumph.

Even before the opening of the Stockton and Darlington, Stephenson had been engaged by Liverpool investors as engineer of the Liverpool and Manchester. Heavy traffic in that vital corridor, raw cotton from America passing through the port of Liverpool to the textile factories at Manchester, and manufactured cloth making the return journey from Manchester had been monopolized by the Bridgewater Canal, which supplied service that shippers considered both unreliable and expensive. Plans for a rival means of transport had been around for years, but it took the evident progress on the Stockton and Darlington to convert talk into action. Stephenson, working from earlier surveys and relatively cursory fieldwork of his own, presented plans to a parliamentary committee in March, 1825, only to discover, for the first time in his life, the existence of substantial opposition to his plans. The canal interests joined with local landowners to contest the Liverpool and Manchester's application for permission to acquire land by eminent domain, and opposing counsel found it easy to make Stephenson sound incompetent and his plans inadequate. Stephenson's engineering genius lay in his ability to get things built and operating and in his confidence in that ability. His paper plans were faulty—to the consternation of conventionally trained engineers—because he fully intended to resolve real problems on the ground when construction was under way. That had always been his method and, with Stephenson, it worked. Speaking in a heavy Northumbrian dialect almost incomprehensible to the parliamentarians in London, and saddled with admittedly defective specifications, Stephenson was unable to defend his

project, and it was rejected by the parliamentary committee.

The Liverpool promoters reacted to Stephenson's humiliation by engaging three professionally trained engineers, George and John Rennie and Charles Vignoles. It was they who won parliamentary approval for the Liverpool and Manchester in the parliamentary session of 1826. Men of that stripe, with the right accents and paper qualifications, including membership in the Institute of Civil Engineers, presented a striking contrast to Stephenson. Intellectually insecure, Stephenson throughout his career remained defensively hostile toward his better-connected competitors. Even physically, the contrast between Stephenson and men such as the Rennies was obvious. Tall, muscular, and ruddy-cheeked, Stephenson looked like a man accustomed to hard labor out-of-doors. The proprietors, well aware of the contrasts, had nevertheless not lost their basic faith in Stephenson, who was again put in charge of the project once the parliamentary hurdle had been surmounted. The Liverpool and Manchester was built under Stephenson's close personal supervision. Not only was

Stephenson the engineer of the thirty-mile line, which included the massive cut at Olive Mount at the Liverpool end and the difficult construction across the unstable bog at Chat Moss toward Manchester, but also the Stephensons supplied the company's motive power. Before trials held on the line at Rainhill in 1829, there had been some question as to whether the line would be operated by horse or by locomotive. The development, primarily by Robert Stephenson, of a much speedier and more efficient locomotive, the Rocket, which won the Rainhill competition against four other machines, settled the question of railway power definitively in favor of the steam locomotive. When the Liverpool and Manchester was opened on September 15, 1830, the railway had come of age, and Stephenson was the man most prominently associated with it in the public mind.

Even before the completion and striking financial success of the Liverpool and Manchester, serious plans for its extension were in hand. Stephenson was appointed engineer of the southern portion of the Grand Junction, a line designed to connect the Liverpool and Manchester with Birmingham, but once again sloppy paperwork revealed deficiencies in his survey and the Grand Junction passed out of his control. He supervised construction of the Manchester and Leeds, which made the first rail crossing of the Pennines by means of a tunnel more than a mile and a half long, and of the lines which were to become the core of the giant Midland Railway: the Birmingham and Derby, the North Midland, and the York and North Midland. Their completion, in 1840, resulted in a complete although circuitous connection between London and York. It fell to his son, Robert, to direct construction of the London and Birmingham, completed in 1838, and the routes north from York. With the opening of Robert Stephenson's Royal Border Bridge at Berwick in 1850, two years after George Stephenson's death, a through route was established between London and Edinburgh, only twenty years after the opening of the Liverpool and Manchester.

Summary

Dr. Dionysius Lardner, a publicist sometimes more addicted to rhetoric than to facts, awarded to George Stephenson in 1836 the title "Father of the Locomotive," a title impossible to defend. Locomotives, in common with many other important inventions, were not the product of one mind. If anyone deserved that title, it is probably Richard Trevithick, the Cornish mining engineer. In the Stephenson family, Robert's contribution to development of the locomotive is greater than that of his father. Stephenson's achievements in mechanical engineering, although certainly not minimal, are greatly surpassed by his contributions in civil engineering, the survey and construction of economically viable railway lines without which there would have been no scope for the locomotive. Stephenson strove always to construct a nearly level line in order to enable the locomotive to use its power for speed rather than for climbing. Consequently, a Stephenson line is marked by cuts, great earthen fills, tunnels, and occasional circuitry—anything to avoid grades. Although some of Stephenson's successors were less willing to sacrifice directness for levelness, Stephenson's designs established a norm for subsequent British railway-building practice.

An even greater contribution is tied to Stephenson's insistence on use everywhere of a "standard" gauge between parallel rails, although the question of gauge also points to limitations characteristics of Stephenson. He adopted his "standard" gauge (four feet, eight and a half inches) without apparent calculation, merely using the gauge customarily found on Northumbrian tramroads. There was no technological justification for selection of the basic measurement which governed all future construction of railway lines and rolling stock. When first identified by Stephenson, his gauge was four feet, eight inches. The extra half inch appears to have crept in through usage, an indication of Stephenson's rough-and-ready methods. Still, his insistence on a standard gauge was central to his early recognition of the potential of a unified national railway system. Only with a standard gauge would it be possible for railway equipment to run freely throughout Great Britain. By contrast, Isambard Kingdom Brunel, engineer of the Great Western Railway, a man of greater technological brilliance, used a seven-foot gauge, indicative of Brunel's lack of concern about the significance of the resultant inability to interchange traffic with other lines. Fixed firmly in Stephenson's mind was a vision of the kind of integrated national rail network which in fact emerged, and which to Victorian Britain became as vital and basic as the automobile was to become for the late twentieth century world.

Bibliography

Carlson, Robert E. *The Liverpool and Manchester Railway Project, 1821-1831*. Newton Abbot: David and Charles, and New York: Kelley, 1969. A detailed study of the project through which Stephenson gained and held the public eye.

Jeaffreson, J. C., and William Pole. *The Life of Robert Stephenson*. 2 vols. London: Longman, 1864. The standard nineteenth century biography of Robert Stephenson, carefully composed but less readable, and therefore less influential, than Samuel Smiles's work on George Stephenson.

Perkin, Harold. *The Age of the Railway*. London: Panther, 1970; New York: Drake, 1973. This is a well-documented study, by a social historian, of the impact of the railway on Victorian society. Chapter 3, "The Men Who Made the Railways," contains material on Stephenson.

Rees, Gareth. *Early Railway Prints: British Railways from 1825 to 1850*. Oxford: Phaidon Press, and Ithaca, N.Y.: Cornell University Press, 1980. Contains ninety-five contemporary plates, thirty-one in color, offering a vivid visual impression of British railways in the period of Stephenson. Included are sixteen views of the Liverpool and Manchester Railway.

Robbins, Michael. *The Railway Age in Britain and Its Impact on the World*. Baltimore: Penguin, 1965. A highly readable short account of the building of the British railways and their place in the Victorian scene. Chapter 3 is entitled "George Stephenson and the Great Builders."

Rolt, L.T.C. *The Railway Revolution: George and Robert Stephenson*. London: Longman, 1960; New York: St. Martin's Press, 1962. The major modern biography, working from the premise that the two Stephensons were complementary figures, neither of whom can be adequately understood in isolation from the other. Based on both published and manuscript materials and including maps of Stephenson lines and drawings of Stephenson locomotives.

Simmons, Jack. *The Railway in England and Wales, 1830-1914: The System and Its Working*. Leicester: Leicester University Press, and Atlantic Highlands, N.J.: Humanities Press, 1978. An excellent modern introduction to the English railway, containing numerous references to Stephenson's contributions.

Smiles, Samuel. *Life of George Stephenson*. London: Murray, and New York: Harper, 1864. The classic biography, of major importance in solidifying Stephenson's reputation as a Victorian hero. Occasionally attributes to George Stephenson work which was in fact that of his son.

John Ranlett

THADDEUS STEVENS

Born: April 4, 1792; Danville, Vermont
Died: August 11, 1868; Washington, D.C.
Areas of Achievement: Civil rights and politics
Contribution: Although greatly disliked during his lifetime and by some later historians, Stevens was the leading advocate of a just policy for former slaves; his program was only a part of his larger commitment to equality for all people.

Early Life

Thaddeus Stevens was born April 4, 1792, in Danville, Vermont, to Sally and Joshua Stevens. His mother, who had the greatest influence on Thaddeus' personality, was a Baptist. Her Calvinism, evangelism, and piety contributed to his later devotion to principle and duty. Born with a club foot, Thaddeus was the last child in a family of four children. Sally worked, saved money, and taught young Stevens; she wanted him to have the finest available education, and she succeeded. Joshua, his father, was a generally unsuccessful shoemaker. The family was poor. Thaddeus was close to his mother since she provided most of his elementary education. She discouraged him from playing or associating with the local boys because of his physical handicap. Under her guidance, at a very young age Thaddeus learned to read the Bible.

Intellectually, Thaddeus was not disadvantaged. Although he had various run-ins with those in authority, at the age of twenty-two he was graduated from Dartmouth College. He was a shy young man who nevertheless often spoke his mind on issues and situations throughout his long life. Undoubtedly, his verbal skills were compensation for his physical disability; his wit and scorn became legendary.

In 1814, Stevens moved to York, Pennsylvania, to begin his law practice. He soon moved to the village of Gettysburg and became a leading lawyer in the area and a partner in the James D. Paxton Iron Works. Stevens served on the Gettysburg town council. His earlier political activity was with the Federalist Party, but as that party declined, Stevens became a leader in the Anti-Masonic movement because he distrusted the influence of secret societies in a republic. He believed that secret societies were elitist and created aristocracies of special privilege for their membership. Though the Anti-Masons generally became Whigs, Stevens was never popular with that party's leadership despite his strong opposition to Andrew Jackson and his policies. From his first political experience, Stevens was a strong nationalist whose program included the belief that government could create opportunities for all men. He never retreated from that general belief.

In 1833, Stevens was elected to the Pennsylvania house of representatives. During the next ten years, Stevens was politically active. He opposed any propositions based on class distinctions or any discrimination based on race or color. For example, Stevens in 1835 saved the principle of free public schools for all in Pennsylvania by defeating a proposed charity or pauper-school law. He also supported state aid to higher education. Stevens was a member of the Board of Canal Commissions, a powerful state planning agency. Unfortunately, his party, the Whigs, greatly influenced by Stevens' leadership, lost the dispute over control of the state house of representatives known as the Buckshot War. Discouraged, after another election, Stevens retired from party politics. He also needed to repair his personal fortune; his iron works had put Stevens more than $200,000 in debt. By 1842, Stevens was practicing law in Lancaster, Pennsylvania. He was fifty years old, and his prospects appeared to be limited; he was, however, on the eve of his greatest contribution to American history.

Life's Work

From 1848 to 1853, Stevens served in the House of Representatives as a Whig. His strong opposition to the Fugitive Slave Law, as part of the Compromise of 1850, contributed to his defeat. He returned to Lancaster, working to save his failing iron business. An important figure in the creation of the Republican Party in Pennsylvania, he was returned to the House in 1858, where he served until his death ten years later.

Despite his age and poor health, Stevens played a major role in the dramatic Civil War decade. He opposed any concession to the threat of secession from the Southern states. Early in the war, Stevens clearly stated his belief that the rebel states, by their behavior, had placed themselves beyond the pale of the Constitution; therefore Congress would determine their future status in any program of reconstruction.

In 1861, he became the chairman of the Ways and Means Committee and helped formulate the government's fiscal policy during the war, supporting the distribution of greenbacks, for example. Unlike many of his fellow Americans, Stevens recognized that slavery and the Union's fate were intermingled. He argued that any slave used in any military capacity should be freed, and he urged confiscation of all property used for insurrectionary purposes. Despite his contemporary and historical reputation for harshness, he never advocated execution for any rebel leaders. In fact, he opposed capital punishment. Nevertheless, he pushed for a punitive program against the Confederacy.

On March 28, 1864, he introduced the Thirteenth Amendment in Congress. As chairman of the House group of the Joint Committee on Reconstruction, he was a key member of the Radical Republicans. He contributed to the writing of the Fourteenth Amendment, and he supported it as part of the Reconstruction Act. He broke with President Andrew Johnson over his veto of the Freedmen's Bureau Bill. The alienation increased as Johnson pardoned more and more Confederates. On March 19, 1867, Stevens introduced a bill to confiscate all public land in the South, including individual rebel property. He wanted "forty acres and a mule" for every freedman and planned to use the money from the sale of rebel lands to finance military pensions and to retire the national debt. The bill was not passed. A milder form of Reconstruction prevailed.

Although he personally doubted its success, Thaddeus Stevens introduced the resolution for the impeachment of President Andrew Johnson. He was chairman of the managers who argued for impeachment before the Senate, but his failing health limited his contribution to the proceedings. The vote for removal failed by one vote. As a practical matter, the president now controlled Reconstruction.

Exhausted by his age and his activities, Stevens died on August 11, 1868, in Washington, D.C. As a matter of honor, the Republicans in his district kept his name on the ballot in the fall election.

Summary

Praised and cursed during his lifetime and after, Stevens nevertheless was one of the few politicians to see how slavery and the Union were combined. A strong abolitionist, Stevens believed that the federal government should ensure civil rights and just economic opportunities for freedmen. Although in the minority during his lifetime because of prevalent racism and because of his contemporaries' belief in limited government, Stevens' ideas were later vindicated by historical developments. Without any reservation, Thaddeus Stevens was an egalitarian. He recognized that class and class origins were key elements in determining a person's chances in life. He believed that government could balance the equitable opportunities between the rich and the poor. In his own way, Stevens' ideas anticipated the creation of the modern welfare state. Because the cemeteries of Lancaster were for whites only, Stevens, on his deathbed, ordered that he be buried in a black graveyard. In death as in life, Thaddeus Stevens continued questioning the status quo and thereby became one of America's greatest reformers.

Bibliography

Belz, Herman. *Emancipation and Equal Rights: Politics and Constitutionalism in the Civil War Era*. New York: Norton, 1978. Good overview of the complex issues facing the United States during the Civil War.

Brodie, Fawn M. *Thaddeus Stevens, Scourge of the South*. New York: Norton, 1966. The most balanced biography. The author still views Stevens' motivation in terms of punishment and hostility.

Current, Richard N. *Old Thad Stevens: A Story of Ambition*. Madison: University of Wisconsin Press, 1942. Highly critical. Stevens is depicted as ambitious for power and is held responsible for many evils, including the rise of big business.

Foner, Eric. *Free Soil, Free Labor, Free Men: The Ideology of the Republican Party Before the Civil War*. New York: Oxford University Press, 1970; London: Oxford University Press, 1971. A basic study for understanding the varied ideologies that influenced Stevens' life and thought.

Korngold, Ralph. *Thaddeus Stevens: A Being Darkly Wise and Rudely Great*. New York: Harcourt Brace, 1955. In this biography, Stevens is heroic in stature, pure in motive. Tends to overstate his many achievements.

McCall, Samuel W. *Thaddeus Stevens*. Boston: Houghton Mifflin, 1899. The best of the biographies written in the nineteenth century. It dwells on the public life of Stevens.

McPherson, James M. *Ordeal by Fire: The Civil War and Reconstruction*. 2d ed. New York: McGraw-Hill, 1992. With a massive bibliography, broad chronological scope, and illuminating details, this book is the best available volume on the subject.

Pickens, Donald K. "The Republican Synthesis and Thaddeus Stevens." *Civil War History* 31 (March, 1985): 57-73. Places Stevens' ideas in the context of recent historiographic developments.

Stevens, Thaddeus. *The Selected Papers of Thaddeus Stevens,* vol. 1, *January 1814-March 1865.* Edited by Beverly Wilson Palmer and Holly Byers Ochoa. Pittsburgh: University of Pittsburgh Press, 1997. Includes the collected, but limited papers left by Stevens. Basis for Hans Trefousse's biography, *Thaddeus Stevens: Nineteenth-Century Egalitarian.*

Trefousse, Hans L. *The Radical Republicans: Lincoln's Vanguard for Racial Justice.* New York: Knopf, 1968. In a revision of the traditional argument, this book claims that Radicals led Lincoln to positions which he was inclined to take in the first place but had regarded as politically risky.

———. *Thaddeus Stevens: Nineteenth-Century Egalitarian.* Chapel Hill: University of North Carolina Press, 1997. Recommended for all libraries, Trefousse's biography is the first of Stevens in over fifty years. Presenting Stevens as an orator, opponent of slavery, and egalitarian, this is a significant addition to Civil War literature, which has not always been kind to Stevens.

Vaughn, William P. *The Antimasonic Party in the United States: 1826-1843.* Lexington: University Press of Kentucky, 1983. An insightful history of political Anti-Masonry. Balanced. Explains why an egalitarian such as Stevens could be attracted to such a cause.

Donald K. Pickens

ROBERT LOUIS STEVENSON

Born: November 13, 1850; Edinburgh, Scotland
Died: December 3, 1894; Vailima, near Apia, Samoa
Area of Achievement: Literature
Contribution: The author of thirty-two books during his brief lifetime, Stevenson created various classics in the field of children's literature as well as several popular adult works, including *The Strange Case of Dr. Jekyll and Mr. Hyde*, which has exerted a powerful influence on Western cultural imagination.

Early Life

Scotland was not only the country of Robert Louis Balfour Stevenson's birth, but it was also the history-laden nation he later often revisited in both his nomadic life and his adventure romances. As the son and only child of Thomas Stevenson, a lighthouse engineer in Edinburgh, Robert was expected to adopt his father's profession. However, he was more interested in the sea and travel in general than in the coast. In fact, from his teenage years until his death, Stevenson's travels were so extensive that no biographer has been able to give a full account of them. His journeys began when his mother took him, as a young man, on periodic visits to the European continent for the sake of his health, which was compromised throughout his life by lingering pulmonary disorders. Despite a lackluster performance as a student and numerous interruptions in his education caused by illness, Stevenson eventually completed a law degree at the University of Edinburgh in 1875. Nevertheless, his heart was set on travel and writing. Although Stevenson was sincere in these avocations, they also expressed resistance to his Scottish family's expectations in particular and to Victorian respectability in general.

This implicit rebellion against convention informed his early substitution of "Louis" for his baptismal name "Lewis," his agnosticism, his profligate behavior as a university student, and his flamboyant adult public image. To his disapproving parents and friends, rebelliousness seemed at first to account for Stevenson's sudden departure for California, where on May 19, 1880, he married Fanny Van de Grift Osbourne, a divorcée ten years his senior who had two children. This sensational marriage was a good match for Stevenson, who subsequently created his most enduring work. Up to this point he had published various discursive travelogues such as *An Inland Voyage* (1878), a record of a canoe journey in Belgium and France; *Edinburgh: Picturesque Notes* (1878), a book of prose and pictorial sketches of his quaint birthplace; and *Travels with a Donkey in the Cévennes* (1879), an account of a ten-day French mountain walking tour taken with a donkey named Modestine. These books attracted some interest when they first appeared, but none of them could have established Stevenson's reputation.

Life's Work

Treasure Island (1881-1882) and *The Strange Case of Dr. Jekyll and Mr. Hyde* (1886) are Stevenson's most enduring books. *Treasure Island*, based on a watercolor map created to amuse Stevenson's stepson Lloyd Osbourne, was not an immediate success when it was serialized in *Young Folks* between July, 1881, and June, 1882. It became a best-seller as a book one year later. This morally ambiguous, dreamlike romance, with its larger-than-life villain Long John Silver as observed by young Jim Hawkins, was popular with juvenile and adult readers alike, including Stevenson's father. As a classic of children's literature, *Treasure Island* has not been out of print since its publication and has often been exploited in sequels by later authors as well as retold in stage, film, radio, comic-book, and television versions.

The Strange Case of Dr. Jekyll and Mr. Hyde has likewise remained in print for more than one century and has been similarly adapted to various media. A morally ambiguous, nightmarish romance of a dual personality divided against itself between base desires and noble ideals, this book was at first undertaken by Stevenson as a shilling shocker, a sensational type of fiction to be marketed cheaply for mass readership. With his wife's advice, however, Stevenson reshaped the work into a stunning Hawthornian allegory of good and evil that became an instant best-seller in Britain and the United States (where pirated editions were prevalent). That the two main character types in this romance have made an indelible impression on Western cultural imagination is evident in the frequency of allusions to Jekyll and Hyde in both ordinary and professional speech.

These two books of absent or equivocated moral message reflect the psychological terrain established during Stevenson's early life, during which

he personally challenged familial and social expectations. If *Treasure Island* is a boy's daydream and *The Strange Case of Dr. Jekyll and Mr. Hyde* is a man's nightmare, both share a rebellious fantasy of gratifying the self's desires without guilt. Jim Hawkin's flight to a pirate world of vicious self-indulgence is related to Hyde's relish for wanton dissipation and violence. Such an observation provides a glimpse into an underground motive behind Stevenson's creativity, not his conscious intention. Concerning intention, Stevenson's expressed primary goal was to entertain and, on occasion, to instruct. *The Strange Case of Dr. Jekyll and Mr. Hyde*, it could be reasonably argued in terms of Stevenson's intentional allegorical design, therapeutically urges its readers to embrace community as the cornerstone of a healthy personal identity.

Stevenson's physical health lapsed in the interval between these two books. Confined to bed in a dark room as a result of a bronchial hemorrhage, he wrote most of *A Child's Garden of Verses* (1885), an enormously popular work of poetry that satisfied his immediate financial exigencies. Stevenson, who uncomfortably depended upon the largess of his father, always felt harassed by the need for money. As a result and in spite of being an invalid, Stevenson maintained an extraordinary productivity even from his sickbed. While ill, he wrote, among other books, *Kidnapped* (1886), a historical romance featuring an adolescent Scottish Lowlander; *The Black Arrow* (1888), a juvenile novel set during the War of the Roses; and *The Master of Ballantrae* (1889), a psychological tale of a fatal rivalry between two Scottish brothers.

Concern for his relentlessly precarious health led Stevenson to accept an offer by Scribners, his American publisher, to write a book about the Pacific islands. Setting sail in June, 1888, he and his family visited, among other places, Tahiti, Oahu, and the Hawaiian Islands. Within the next two years, they voyaged to Australia, the Gilbert and Marshall Islands, and Samoa, where he built a home on a four-hundred-acre estate he named Vailima. The welfare of the Samoans, particularly a concern over their economic exploitation by colonists, became a fervid cause for Stevenson, who in turn was fondly nicknamed *Tusitala* (storyteller) by the islanders.

Stevenson delighted in narrating original tales to his admiring Samoan audience, such as the clever "The Isle of Voices." This tale, with a moral about living life as if it were a work of art, is included with the well-known "The Bottle Imp" and the critically acclaimed "The Beach of Falesá" in *Island Nights' Entertainments* (1893). Stevenson also rapidly completed *Catriona* (1893), also known as *David Balfour*, as a sequel to *Kidnapped*, which some readers thought needed such a conclusion. *Catriona* contains Stevenson's most ambitious attempt to depict female characters, and he spoke of it as his best book. It was, however, never as popular as several of his earlier writings, and later critics preferred two nonjuvenile works (written in collaboration with his Lloyd Osbourne) composed during this late period of his brief career: *The Wrecker* (1892), a suspenseful tale involving a shipwreck, massacre, and treasure; and *The Ebb-Tide* (1894), a dark account of three island outcasts that anticipated Joseph Conrad's early fiction.

Weir of Hermiston (1896), a posthumously published work left as an incomplete manuscript when Stevenson died of a cerebral hemorrhage on December 3, 1894, at the age of forty-four, was soon acclaimed as Stevenson's potential masterpiece. The novel, dictated to his stepdaughter Isabel Osbourne Strong, combines Stevenson's most effective characterization and his inveterate affection for Scottish history. Whether Stevenson had finally matched or surpassed the achievement of his predecessor Sir Walter Scott, the writer to whom he had been compared throughout his career, did not matter to his friends in Samoa. In honor of their beloved *Tusitala*, grieving Samoans cut, with extreme difficulty, a steep pathway to the summit of Mount Vaea, where Stevenson was buried as he had requested.

Summary

Since his death, as during his lifetime, Stevenson's reputation as a writer has been as divided in sentiment as his books are divided between an insistence on disciplined conscience and a celebration of uninhibited imagination—in other words, between Victorian mores and amoral aesthetics, austere realism and carefree romance. Whereas his poetry, travelogues, and essays have little currency, Stevenson's fiction endures among a wide audience. His contemporary reviewers, anticipating later literary critics, may have found much to fault in his fiction, but for over one century, general readers, young and old, have found much to admire.

The romance form of the novel preferred by Stevenson and other writers of his time has fallen into disfavor and is often regarded as escapist literature suitable for children. *Treasure Island* and *Kidnapped* indeed remain classics of children's literature despite their lack of a clear moral center. *The Strange Case of Dr. Jekyll and Mr. Hyde* endures as a widely recognized fixture in Western culture despite Stevenson's low estimation of it. *The Ebb Tide* and "The Beach of Falesá" have been favored with increased attention in literary studies, whereas "The Suicide Club" (from *The New Arabian Nights*, 1882), "The Body Snatcher" and "Markheim" (from *The Merry Men and Other Tales and Fables*, 1887), and "The Bottle Imp" prevail as perennial choices for anthologies marketed to a general audience. The compass of Stevenson's influence on other writers is as extensive as were his many travels. To observe the impact of *Treasure Island* on H. Rider Haggard's *King Solomon's Mines* (1885) and J. M. Barrie's *Peter Pan* (1904), and of *Kidnapped* on John Buchan's *The Thirty-nine Steps* (1915) is merely to single out three phenomenal best-sellers indebted to Stevenson's work. That Stevenson's fiction continues to entertain countless readers is ample testimony to his achievement.

Bibliography

Bell, Ian. *Robert Louis Stevenson: Dreams of Exile.* New York: Holt, and London: Headline, 1993. Interprets Stevenson's life as an ongoing effort to reconcile various opposite inclinations, including his ambivalent attitude toward Scotland.

Daiches, David. *Robert Louis Stevenson and His World.* London: Thames and Hudson, 1973. A profusely illustrated overview of Stevenson's life and work that is especially suitable for young adults.

Eigner, Edwin M. *Robert Louis Stevenson and the Romantic Tradition.* Princeton, N.J.: Princeton University Press, 1966. A reliable, accessible discussion of the sources and implications of the Romantic features of Stevenson's writings.

Furnas, J. C. *Voyage to Windward: The Life of Robert Louis Stevenson.* New York: Sloane, 1951; London: Faber, 1952. Presents a highly readable and authentic account of Stevenson's life with particular sensitivity to the positive role of his wife in his career.

Maixner, Paul, ed. *Robert Louis Stevenson: The Critical Heritage.* London and Boston: Routledge, 1981. A valuable collection of reviews of Stevenson's books published between 1878 and 1894.

Nollen, Scott Allen. *Robert Louis Stevenson: Life, Literature and the Silver Screen.* Jefferson, N.C.: McFarland, 1994. Documents and analyzes the history of radio, film, and television adaptations of Stevenson's stories.

Pope-Hennessy, James. *Robert Louis Stevenson.* London: Cape, and New York: Simon and Schuster, 1974. A dramatic retelling of Stevenson's life with particular attention devoted to details of human interest.

Stevenson, Robert Louis. *The Letters of Robert Louis Stevenson.* Edited by Bradford A. Booth and Ernest Mehew. New Haven, Conn., and London: Yale University Press, 1994-1995. 8 vols. Offers a treasure trove of Stevenson's opinions that in general tell the story of Stevenson's life better than any biographer.

Swearingen, Roger G. *The Prose Writings of Robert Louis Stevenson: A Guide.* London: Macmillan, and Hamden, Conn.: Archon Books, 1980. A remarkable resource for data pertaining to the biographical, publication, and source histories of Stevenson's prose works.

William J. Scheick

LUCY STONE

Born: August 13, 1818; Coy's Hill, near West
Brookfield, Massachusetts
Died: October 18, 1893; Dorchester, near Boston,
Massachusetts
Areas of Achievement: Social reform and women's
rights
Contribution: Stone committed her life to the
struggle for woman suffrage and equal rights.

Early Life

Lucy Stone was born near West Brookfield, Massachusetts, on August 13, 1818, into a family whose
ancestors were among New England's first settlers.
Lucy's father, Francis Stone, tanned hides and
served as the community's teacher until her birth, at
which time he settled into farming. At home he commanded absolute authority, and discipline was swift,
marked with severe whippings and humiliation.

Hannah Matthews Stone, Lucy's mother, was an
obedient, hard-working housewife. Despite this
outward docility, Lucy saw in her mother a quiet
anger and resentment against male domination as
prescribed by fundamental Christian ideology. Her
father's control and her mother's grudging submission were such powerful influences that as a child
Lucy swore never to marry or accept such a contemptible station in life.

Her developing objection to the status of women
compelled Lucy to pursue a solid education and, in
the process, to learn Greek so that she could verify
the accuracy of biblical translations regarding a
woman's position in society. At the age of sixteen,
she was hired to teach at a local school with a salary of four dollars per month. The salary itself enraged Lucy because male teachers with the same
credentials earned four times the money.

When not teaching, Lucy continued her studies
at the local seminary for girls until 1843, when, at
the age of twenty-five, she entered Oberlin college
in Ohio, the only college that admitted female students and one that also supported the emancipation
of slaves. Abolitionism was not new to Lucy. She
had avidly read William Lloyd Garrison's *The Liberator* since it began publication, and she considered herself a "Garrisonian"—supporting a more
radical antislavery stance than Oberlin College itself. While a student at Oberlin, Lucy taught
former slaves, worked in the school cafeteria,
learned Greek, founded the college's first women's
debating society, and delivered her first public

speech on women's rights and slave emancipation.
Considered too radical by her peers and a potential
troublemaker by the college, she nevertheless
earned respect for her determination, intelligence,
and ability to argue an issue soundly and convincingly. Following her graduation in 1847, she was
hired by the Massachusetts Anti-Slave Society as a
public speaker—a position considered socially improper for a woman.

Life's Work

Against her parents' wishes, Lucy Stone delivered
her first public address on slave emancipation and
women's rights in the summer of 1847. Stone possessed strong conviction, sound logic, and an eloquence in oratory which compelled even the most
ardent opponent of women's rights to listen respectfully. Stone made frequent public lectures
during that year, and most of these speeches concentrated on issues of women's rights.

By the end of the decade, New England had become the center of a growing social reform movement in the nation, and Stone was quickly emerging as one of the movement's most competent and
committed proponents. She advocated the strict
control of alcoholic beverages, arguing that liquor
destroyed the fabric of the home and emboldened
men to abuse their wives. She criticized Christianity for relegating women to a position of social inferiority and for not taking a stronger antislave position. She championed a woman's right to own
property, to receive an advanced education, and to
be granted equal status before the law. Without
doubt, her arguments were sharply criticized by the
male-dominated social order of the era, but the
women who filled her lecture halls and whispered
encouragement strengthened Stone's resolve to
continue speaking for equality. She made women's
rights her principal topic and was noted as the first
woman speaker to do so. For her near solitary public position, she became known as the "morning
star" of the women's rights movement.

Lucy Stone was the primary organizer of the
First National Woman's Rights Convention, held in
Worcester, Massachusetts, on October 23, 1850.
More than one thousand participants listened to
speakers such as Sojourner Truth, Sarah Tyndall,
Frederick Douglass, and Stone present their calls
for woman's equality. Although the Seneca Falls
Convention of 1848 was the first such gathering, it

had drawn a limited local audience of reformers. The 1850 convention, however, placed the issue of women's rights before a national audience and set into motion an annual conference largely directed by Stone who, at her own expense, published a report of the conference proceedings.

Stone's hectic lecture schedule took her across much of the nation pressing state assemblies for equal rights for women. In 1853, she endorsed a woman suffrage petition presented to the Massachusetts Constitutional Convention in Boston. From there, she spoke in Cincinnati, Pittsburgh, St. Louis, Louisville, and several other cities. Her presentations included specific points regarding women's equality in marriage—perhaps because of her developing relationship with Henry Blackwell, to whom she was married in May, 1855.

Symbolic of her expectations and demands for equality in marriage, Stone retained her maiden name and never did she refer to herself as Mrs. Blackwell, preferring instead Lucy Stone, wife of Henry Blackwell. Taking the husband's name amounted to the loss of a woman's identity, she argued. She further insisted that once married, a woman's property should remain hers, and the same should be true for the product of her labor and the guardianship of the children. According to Stone, a husband's control over a wife's property amounted to nothing short of legal theft. Moreover, nonconsensual sex was the equivalent of marital rape, she stated. She further demanded the abolition of the entire system of legal codes and customs that placed women under the care, protection, and exclusive control of their husbands. Personal independence and equal human rights, she maintained, could never be relinquished by a woman because of marriage, and the law should recognize the institution as an equal partnership.

Stone's arguments were certainly advanced for the era in which she lived. More often than not she was considered too extreme in her views. Typically, male listeners were outraged by Stone's speeches, and women found her ideas correct but impossible to attain. Despite the cool, and sometimes even hostile, response given her by the general public, Stone persisted in demanding equal rights in marriage.

The Civil War interrupted Stone's public lecturing. Also, the birth of her daughter refocused Stone's attention to child rearing and would have taken her from the lecture circuit even if the war had not erupted. Moreover, she started having severe headaches that occasionally confined her to bed for days.

Despite these interruptions, Stone resumed her active public life following the war. Increasingly, she emphasized woman's suffrage in her speeches—a right she believed was central to women's equality. She argued for suffrage in a series of lectures throughout New England and New York, coauthored a petition for Congress to consider women's right to vote, and helped organize a convention that led to the founding of the American Equal Rights Association. In March, 1867, Stone argued for black and woman suffrage before the New Jersey legislature stating that every person capable of rational choice was entitled to the right to vote. Democracy required equal suffrage. When a woman is denied the vote, she added, the very principle of democracy itself is violated. If women were indeed the natural possessors of morality, she concluded, then extension of the franchise would automatically bring a humane attitude to legislation. She spread her views throughout the North and again lobbied Congress, was instrumental in the formation of the New England Suffrage Association, and helped organize the New Jersey Woman Suffrage Association.

That women were not included in the Fifteenth Amendment only intensified Stone's battle for equal rights. Throughout 1869, she labored to publish *Woman's Journal*, with seven thousands copies of the first edition sold in early January, 1870. Voting rights was the primary focus of each edition, and this first issue highlighted Wyoming's new woman suffrage law. The *Journal* also addressed a variety of women's issues and concerns such as education, health, marriage, work, and the rearing of children.

Stone took residence on the floor above the *Journal*'s office and from there worked to gain advertisers, subscribers, and news stories. She spent hours managing the office, handling financial matters, and arranging for printing and distribution. Despite the hectic and consuming work, she maintained a lecture schedule that took her into Pennsylvania, Vermont, New York, and throughout Massachusetts. At the same time, she continued her active involvement in the American Equal Rights Association and in the creation of an amendment to grant woman suffrage nationally.

The 1870's were no less busy for Stone. Persons who could not vote, she consistently argued, were defenseless in society. Power rested in the ballot box, and once women received the franchise the ills of society would be remedied. To bring added pressure on state legislatures, Stone looked for untapped sources of support. The suffrage movement had relied upon a minority of women—those who were well educated, skilled at public speaking and organization, and not intimidated by the male population or by accepted norms for proper female behavior. In the late 1870's, Stone sought to include middle-class women by making the push for suffrage a socially acceptable position among women themselves. The formation of women's clubs in communities across the nation would afford women the opportunity to discuss the issue of suffrage and to chart a course of action locally to advance the cause. With clubs becoming fashionable outlets for middle-class women, Stone believed suffrage specifically, and the demand for equal rights in general, could be pressed forcefully by a new body of supporters. She imagined the widespread effect of such political action in every town and anticipated the strength such clubs could use in lobbying state legislatures. In one month she recruited almost 1,100 women into local clubs.

At the same time, Stone criticized government efforts to provide protective legislation for women in the workplace arguing that gender-based laws guaranteed unequal treatment for women, even if the intention of the legislation was positive. In addition, through the *Woman's Journal*, she championed better working conditions for all individuals, an end to inhumane conditions in reform schools, the elimination of government and business corruption, and she protested vigorously existing federal policy regarding American Indians. Before the decade ended, *Woman's Journal* was distributed in every state and in thirty-nine foreign countries.

Despite declining health throughout the 1880's, Stone remained as active as possible. In May, 1893, she attended the World's Congress of Representative Women at the World Columbian Exposition in Chicago. More than 150,000 people from twenty-seven nations assembled for a week-long convention. Among the slated speakers was Lucy Stone. Weak and frail, she took the podium and delivered her address entitled "The Progress of Fifty Years." She traced the course of the women's rights movement over five decades, praised the women who had unselfishly devoted themselves to the struggle, and clearly detailed the much improved status of women in contemporary America. She ended the speech with a reminder—much more work was needed, and the movement must continue until full equality was achieved.

Stone's speech in Chicago was her last. Five months later, on October 18, she died with her daughter Alice at her side. In commemoration of her life's work, university dormitories, city parks, and public schools were named in her honor. The suffrage movement persisted until passage of the twentieth amendment in 1919 which granted woman suffrage. The *Woman's Journal* continued publication until 1931, and, with each issue, echoed Lucy Stone's demand for gender equality.

Bibliography

Blackwell, Alice Stone. *Lucy Stone: Pioneer of Woman's Rights*. 2d ed. Boston: Little Brown, 1930. Alice Stone Blackwell, Lucy Stone's daughter, presents an insightful and personal view of her mother's personal and public life.

Gring-Pemble, Lisa M. "Writing Themselves into Consciousness: Creating a Rhetorical Bridge between the Public and Private Spheres." *Quarterly Journal of Speech* 84, no. 1 (February, 1998). Examines the development of a shared consciousness among nineteenth century women through letter-writing, using as a basis the letters between Stone and Antoinette Brown Blackwell.

Hays, Elinor Rice. *Morning Star: A Biography of Lucy Stone, 1818-1893*. New York: Harcourt Brace, 1961. Hays portrays Stone as a solid, committed champion of women's rights and the emancipation of slaves—a model for contemporary feminists and reformers.

Kerr, Andrea Moore. *Lucy Stone: Speaking Out for Equality*. New Brunswick, N.J.: Rutgers University Press, 1992. Kerr attempts to create Stone as an individual as influential and important a suffragist as Elizabeth Cady Stanton or Susan B. Anthony.

Lasser, Carol, and Marlene Merrill, eds. *Friends and Sisters: Letters Between Lucy Stone and Antoinette Brown Blackwell, 1846-93*. Urbana: University of Illinois Press, 1987. Lucy Stone's personal thoughts, views on women's rights, and half-century friendship with Antoinette Brown Blackwell, the first woman ordained into the Protestant ministry, is revealed through their private letters to each other.

Woloch, Nancy. *Women and the American Experience*. 2d ed. New York: McGraw-Hill, 1994. This publication surveys the history of women in America from the early seventeenth century through the late 1970's and places Lucy Stone in the broader context of the suffrage movement.

Kenneth William Townsend

JOSEPH STORY

Born: September 18, 1779; Marblehead, Massachusetts

Died: September 10, 1845; Cambridge, Massachusetts

Area of Achievement: Law

Contribution: Story's collaboration with Chief Justice John Marshall on the United States Supreme Court set the nationalistic tone of decision-making and established the legal foundations for the growth of the American economy.

Early Life

Joseph Story was born in Marblehead, Massachusetts, on September 18, 1779, the first son of Mehitable Pedrick and Elisha Story. His father, a physician, had participated in the Boston Tea Party, had joined the Sons of Liberty, and had confronted the British at Lexington, Concord, and Bunker Hill. Brought up in a family that was profoundly religious but inclined to liberal theological doctrine, firmly patriotic and Republican, Story was prepared for Harvard at the Marblehead Academy, a private school, where he learned the rudiments of a classical education.

In 1794, Story entered the Cambridge institution. He was ambitious, studious, articulate, and committed to intellectual pursuit. Working his way through a curriculum that included the obligatory Greek and Latin, Euclidian geometry and trigonometry, history and theology, there was yet time to read the works of William Shakespeare, Johann Wolfgang von Goethe in translation, and Jean-Jacques Rousseau; to converse with his classmate, William Ellery Channing, the later founder of New England Unitarianism; and to write poetry. He was graduated from Harvard, second to Channing, in 1798 and immediately became a law apprentice to Samuel Sewall, a Federalist congressman and later a Massachusetts Supreme Court justice, and, for a short time, to Samuel Putnam in Salem, Massachusetts.

Story was twenty-two years old when he was admitted to the Essex County bar; three years later, he married Mary Lynd Oliver, only to be temporarily traumatized by her death in June, 1805 (he remarried in 1808), and the subsequent demise of his father two months later. Yet he rapidly became the leading practitioner before the Essex County Court of Common Pleas, derived a lucrative income from his legal talents and associations, was

elected as a Jeffersonian Republican to the Massachusetts legislature, and found time to write the first of a plethora of law volumes. In the Massachusetts General Court (the technical name for the state assembly), he sponsored new legislation to structure and increase judicial salaries, to enhance the authority of the courts, and to create an equity tribunal. His brief career as a congressman in 1808 earned for him the enmity of President Thomas Jefferson, for although he defended the Embargo Act at its inception, Story later urged its repeal, convinced that the prohibition on international trade would destroy New England's commercial economy.

Story's most important case was *Fletcher v. Peck*. In February, 1810, he argued the position of Massachusetts speculators in Georgia lands before the United States Supreme Court. Although there was no doubt that the 1795 grant by the state legislature was stained with widespread corruption, and although Chief Justice John Marshall deplored the circumstances of the land deal, he held for the Court that the rescinding act of the Georgia assembly offended the contract clause of the Constitution. It was the first time that the Supreme Court exercised judicial review over state legislation.

Life's Work

Story was soon to become a colleague of the justices before whom he appeared in the Georgia litigation. On November 11, 1811, two months after his thirty-second birthday, despite Jefferson's misgivings, he was appointed by President James Madison as an associate justice of the United States Supreme Court. He was the youngest man ever to be seated on the high tribunal.

Throughout his long career on the Supreme Court, serving for thirty-three years, he justified the confidence that Madison had bestowed upon him. He witnessed the War of 1812, the controversy over Missouri's entrance to the Union as a slave state, the emergence of an industrial economy, the election of Andrew Jackson, and, in 1835, the appointment of Marshall's successor, Roger B. Taney. His opinions were almost uniformly learned, closely argued, and logically consistent. Along with Marshall, his friend and colleague, he was strongly nationalistic and intent on energizing and facilitating the development of a national economy. In *Martin v. Hunter's Lessee* in 1816, he

responded to Virginia's challenge to the Supreme Court's appellate jurisdiction by arguing that uniformity of decisions and of application of the constitutional imperatives necessitated review of state laws and judicial opinions. He collaborated with Marshall in framing the great nationalistic rulings in *McCulloch v. Maryland* (1819) and *Gibbons v. Ogden* (1824). In his concurring opinion in *Dartmouth College v. Woodward* (1819), he explicitly extended the immunity of charters from legislative annulment to business corporations. Later, in 1837, in *Charles River Bridge v. Warren Bridge*, he wrote a measured but trenchant dissent to Taney's opinion that public charters were to be interpreted narrowly in favor of the state.

Story was persuaded that economic investment would decline if American businessmen came to the conclusion that state grants and charters were at the mercy of legislative whim and that debts could easily be dissolved by retroactive bankruptcy acts. He strove to create a climate in which individual entrepreneurs could use their skills and inventive genius to exploit the vast economic potential of the American continent. He pursued this objec-

tive not only in more prominent cases but also in some forty legal opinions relating to patents, favoring inventors and promoting technological advancement.

At the same time, there were others on the Marshall and Taney courts who believed that bankruptcy laws cushioned the danger of making financial mistakes and encouraged risk-taking. They contended that state-granted monopolies would breed complacency, discourage technological innovation, and slow economic progress. Their differences with Marshall and Story were not over the goals of economic policy but over the strategies of achievement.

The Marshall Court was committed to the protection of private property rights. On the surface, it maintained an aura of unanimity in cases involving slavery and the foreign slave trade. Yet underneath, the justices' personal views of the South's "peculiar institution" diverged from Story's hatred of slavery to Bushrod Washington's public defense of his ownership of human beings. In December, 1819, in the midst of the Missouri Controversy, Story made a long and passionate address at the Salem town meeting, denouncing the extension of slavery as contrary to the spirit of the Declaration of Independence and the Constitution. In the case of *La Jeune Eugénie* (1822), which he heard and decided while acting as a circuit judge in Boston, he depicted the nightmarish slave trade, and although he remanded the ship to the French consul, he declared that the nefarious traffic was against international law. Later, in 1841, in *The Amistad* case, he ruled that the captive blacks who had mutinied on board the ship, killed its officers, and attempted to sail back to Africa were free men who were justified in taking extraordinary measures to regain their liberty.

Story's most difficult opinion on slavery came a year later, in *Prigg v. Pennsylvania*. The case involved the constitutional right of slaveholders to recapture fugitives escaping across state lines. Committed to the supremacy of federal law and torn by his personal antipathy toward slavery, the associate justice effected a compromise, upholding the constitutionality of the Fugitive Slave Act of 1793 but at the same time declaring that individual states had no legal obligation to assist in its enforcement.

The *Prigg v. Pennsylvania* decision was excoriated by abolitionists, applauded by Southerners, and criticized in dissent by Chief Justice Taney as rendering the Fugitive Slave Act inoperative. Although Story was deeply aggrieved by the abolitionist reaction, he was no stranger to popular and legal controversy. In *Cherokee Nation v. Georgia* in 1831, in a rare instance in which he parted company with Marshall and joined with Smith Thompson in dissent, he argued that the Southwestern tribe was entitled to federal protection from state oppression. A year later, in *Worchester v. Georgia* (1832), he saw his views vindicated as the chief justice decided that Georgia law interfered with Cherokee treaty rights and could not withstand constitutional scrutiny.

Story's record on slavery and the American Indian in part manifested an empathy with oppressed minorities. Yet he was fearful of the democratic spirit of the Jacksonians. He was concerned that the excess and disorder of unruly majorities threatened the fabric of the Union. He became increasingly isolated on a court dominated by Jacksonian appointment; although he respected Taney and was a personal friend of the Ohioan, John McLean, he was dismayed by the political atmosphere of the Court and by his perceived defects in its legal scholarship. His dissent rate on major constitutional issues relating to slavery, the commerce clause, and the status of corporations rose to fifty percent; in no important case did he produce an opinion favoring Southern interests.

Story believed that law was a science. Along with his erudite opinions, from 1805 to 1845, he published eleven law digests, treatises, and commentaries on such varied subjects as equity jurisprudence, agency, and conflict of laws. Perhaps the most important was the *Commentaries* (1832-1845). Dedicated to Marshall, the *Commentaries* reviewed the legal history of the United States, beginning with the Colonial charters, covering the Articles of Confederation, and concluding with a close examination of the Constitution. The book is nationalistic in perspective, sometimes combative in tone, and almost always elaborate in style. Story's history was biased; his strictures on Jefferson and other exponents of states' rights were polemical. Yet the work was popular, went through several editions, was cited in later Supreme Court decisions, and was still in use at the end of the nineteenth century.

The *Commentaries* reflected an effort to educate the American people. From the judicial bench and the author's desk, Story also went into the classroom to teach a generation of aspiring lawyers. Appointed as Dane Professor of Law at Harvard in

1829, he was in part responsible for the development of its legal reputation; he sold at below cost his own library to enhance its holdings and brought prominent politicians and lawyers such as Daniel Webster and John Quincy Adams to his classes. His lectures, sprinkled with personal experience and vivid digressions, combined case law and legal history, comparative jurisprudence, and treatise literature; they were intended to produce a system geared to the needs of American society. His students included the abolitionist Wendell Phillips, the writer Richard Henry Dana, and the senator Charles P. Sumner.

Although the law was his passion, Story planned to resign his seat on the Supreme Court in the fall of 1845. He had been ill in 1842, ill again until the spring of 1843. He felt alienated from his colleagues on the Court; he was shocked and disgruntled by the defeat of Henry Clay and the election of yet another Democrat, James K. Polk, to the presidency in 1844. He wanted to devote his efforts to full-time teaching at Harvard Law School, to write his memoirs and a tenth commentary on admiralty. He died on September 10, 1845, probably the victim of a heart attack, his last circuit court opinion lying on his desk.

Summary

In 1828, a portrait of the associate justice depicts Story in judicial robes, given to baldness, with magnetic blue eyes and a round face radiating firmness and energy. It was an appropriate characterization. Story, as had Marshall and his other colleagues, had a unique opportunity to shape American law and to interpret the language of the Constitution. There were few precedents; the English common law was often too rigid to meet the exigencies of the new American environment of bustling commerce and incipient industrialization. Story seized the opportunity to strengthen the federal government by expanding its powers at the expense of the states and by furthering an economic policy that would protect and promote the activities of American entrepreneurs.

His heroes were George Washington and John Marshall; his villains, Thomas Jefferson and Andrew Jackson. His predilections were conservative and antidemocratic. Although his influence and reputation waned in a nation of rapid change and later egalitarian orientation, his contributions to American nationalism, to the rational study of law, and to legal education are incalculable.

Bibliography

Baxter, Maurice G. *The Steamboat Monopoly: Gibbons v. Ogden, 1824*. New York: Knopf, 1972. A narrative and assessment of the case in which the Marshall Court had its first opportunity to interpret the commerce clause of the Constitution.

Beveridge, Albert J. *The Life of John Marshall*. 4 vols. Boston: Houghton Mifflin, 1916-1919. The classic biography of the chief justice, in four volumes, elegantly written, but marred by a consistent anti-Jefferson and pro-Marshall bias. The last two volumes go beyond Marshall's life and constitute a history of the Court over which Marshall presided.

Cable, Mary. *Black Odyssey: The Case of the Slaveship Amistad*. New York: Viking Press, 1971. A short history of the Supreme Court's slave-trade opinion, known by contemporaries as the Case of the African Captives. The book focuses on the background and incarceration of the kidnapped blacks in a Boston jail and the arguments before the Supreme Court of Francis Scott Key for the Spanish claimants and John Quincy Adams for the detained Africans and on their subsequent return home.

Dunne, Gerald T. *Justice Joseph Story and the Rise of the Supreme Court*. New York: Simon and Schuster, 1970. A nontechnical and well-written introduction to the life of the associate justice and to the cases and decisions in which he participated.

Finkelman, Paul. "Story Telling on the Supreme Court: Prigg v. Pennsylvania and Justice Joseph Story's Judicial Nationalism." *Supreme Court Review* (Annual 1994). Examines Story's pro-slavery decision written in the case of *Prigg v. Pennsylvania.*

Newmyer, R. Kent. *Supreme Court Justice Joseph Story: Statesman of the Old Republic*. Chapel Hill: University of North Carolina Press, 1985. The most comprehensive and analytic review of Story's public life. Argues that his judicial record and his roles as legal educator and publicist can best be understood in the context of a Republican culture originating with the American Revolution.

————. *The Supreme Court Under Marshall and Taney*. New York: Crowell, 1968. A survey of the pre-Civil War Supreme Court which emphasizes the continuity of decisions under the leadership of Marshall and that of his successor.

Swisher, Carl Brent. *Roger B. Taney*. New York: Macmillan, 1935. The standard analysis of the judicial philosophy of Taney and his court. In part, attempts to refurbish Taney's reputation in relation to the notorious 1857 *Dred Scott v. Sandford* decision.

Zobel, Hiller B. "Naming a Justice: It has Always Been Politics as Usual." *American Heritage* 42, no. 6 (October, 1991). Examines the politically based appointments of justices to the Supreme Court including Story, Oliver Wendell Holmes, and others.

David L. Sterling

HARRIET BEECHER STOWE

Born: June 14, 1811; Litchfield, Connecticut
Died: July 1, 1896; Hartford, Connecticut
Areas of Achievement: Social reform and women's rights
Contribution: Stowe's popular novel *Uncle Tom's Cabin* attacked slavery as a threat to the Christian family and helped to end this institution in the United States. In this and later novels, Stowe wrote as an early advocate for women—one who wished to help them by creating a "women's sphere" in the home.

Early Life

Lyman Beecher, Harriet Beecher's father, was a stern New England Calvinist preacher whose image of a God who predestined humans to heaven or hell left a mark on his children. The fact that Harriet's mother died when she was four made Harriet's father's influence even more important. By the age of six and a half, the young "Hattie," as she was known to her family, had memorized more than two dozen hymns and several long chapters in the Bible. As an adult, however, Harriet Beecher would substitute for her father's dogmas a religion of hope that stressed the love and compassion of Christ rather than the divine judgment that her father preached. Some people hold that she "feminized" her father's religion. Throughout her life, she retained a strong sense of religious mission and zeal for social improvement.

At age twelve, Harriet moved to Hartford to live with her older sister Catharine, a purposeful woman who had started the Hartford Female Seminary. Harriet attended Catharine's school and stayed on as a teacher and guardian of young children. In 1832, she moved with her family to Cincinnati, Ohio, where her father had been offered the post as president of the new Lane Theological Seminary. Three years after arriving in Cincinnati (in January, 1836), Harriet Beecher married Calvin Stowe, a Lane professor.

These years in the West prepared Stowe for her later career. She had eight children between 1836 and 1850, and if she and Calvin had not alternated taking "rest cures" in Vermont over the years, she might have had more. In 1834, Harriet won a fifty-dollar prize for "A New England Sketch," which was published in the *Western Monthly Magazine.* From that point on, the members of her family saw

her as a person of literary promise, even though she claimed that this activity was only a way of supplementing the always meager family income. In 1842, Calvin wrote to his wife, "[My] dear, you must be a literary woman. It is written in the book of fate."

While in Cincinnati, Harriet also experienced the intense emotions aroused by the slavery issue during these years. On one visit to a Kentucky plantation, she saw slaves whom she later used as models for some of the characters in *Uncle Tom's Cabin.* In 1836, a local mob attacked the print shop of an abolitionist in the city, and the struggle between the abolitionists and the moderates at Lane eventually drove her father to retire and her husband to take a job at Bowdoin College in Maine in 1850.

Life's Work

When President Abraham Lincoln met Harriet Beecher Stowe in the fall of 1862, he greeted her as "the little lady who made this big war." He was not alone in believing that Stowe's *Uncle Tom's Cabin* (1852) had been a crucial event in arousing the antislavery sentiments that led to the outbreak of the American Civil War in 1861. Although *Uncle Tom's Cabin* was not the best novel of the nineteenth century, it certainly had the greatest impact. *Uncle Tom's Cabin* sold 300,000 copies the year it was published, and Stowe's great work helped to end slavery by personalizing that "peculiar institution." Slavery was wrong, the novel argued, because it was un-Christian. More specifically, slavery tore children from their mothers and thus threatened the existence of the Christian family. It has been said that *Uncle Tom's Cabin* was "a great revival sermon," more effective than those of her father. Harriet herself later wrote that the book was written by "the Lord Himself. . . . I was but an instrument in his hands."

Each of the main characters in this melodramatic novel displayed virtues and vices that were important to Stowe. The main character, Tom, was sold by a kind master, Mr. Shelby, to a second one, Augustine St. Clare, who had ambiguous feelings about slavery and planned to free Tom. Before he could do so, St. Clare was killed and Tom was sold to a singularly evil man, Simon Legree, who finally beat Tom to death when the slave refused to tell him the hiding place of two slaves who were planning to escape.

Aside from Tom, the strongest characters in the novel were female. The slave Eliza, also sold by Mr. Shelby, escaped with her son (who would have been taken from her) by jumping across ice floes on the Ohio River. She and her husband George were finally reunited in Canada. Little Eva, the saintly and sickly child of Augustine St. Clare, was a Christ-like figure who persuaded her father to free Tom before she herself died. Mary Bird, the wife of an Ohio senator, shamed her husband into helping Eliza when she sought comfort at their home. Senator Bird violated the Fugitive Slave Law of 1850—which he had helped to pass and which required Northerners to return escaped slaves—by helping Eliza. Ophelia, a cousin of Augustine St. Clare who came from Vermont to help him care for his invalid wife and child, was the model of a well-organized homemaker who was especially proud of her neat kitchen. Another courageous female was the slave Cassy, who quietly poisoned her newborn with opium after she had had two other children sold away from her.

It was no accident that so many of the heroes in *Uncle Tom's Cabin* were women motivated by a Christian love of neighbor or that the most dramatic events in the novel focused on the way slavery destroyed families. *Uncle Tom's Cabin* was particularly effective in arousing antislavery sentiment and particularly infuriating to Southern defenders of slavery, precisely because it dramatically attacked one of the strongest arguments of slaveholders, the religious one that saw slavery as an essential part of the patriarchal system of authority established by God and sanctioned by Scripture. For Stowe, Christianity began at home with a strong family. Any institution that undermined the family was necessarily unchristian.

In many ways, Harriet Beecher Stowe was a lay preacher whose writings were sermons. Like some other nineteenth century advocates of women's rights, Stowe believed that women were morally superior to men. She did not believe that women should govern the country or replace men in the world of business, but rather that they should set a moral example for society through their control of the "domestic sphere," where they could influence society by shaping the lives of their children. Stowe advocated greater equality between the men's sphere and the women's sphere. Women deserved greater respect because most of them—

slave or free—were mothers, and therefore they had a greater understanding of both love and the "sacredness of the family" than men did.

In some of her later novels, especially *Pink and White Tyranny: A Society Novel, My Wife and I* (both 1871) and *We and Our Neighbors* (1875), Stowe continued to argue that women could improve the world by being guardians of morals in the home. She was not a "radical" advocate of full social equality for women, and she was critical of reformers such as Elizabeth Cady Stanton and Susan B. Anthony. Yet, despite her active professional career as a writer, which made her the principal wage earner in the family after 1853, Stowe continued to maintain that she wrote only to supplement the family income. She also continued to write novels in which strong women—for example, Mary Scudder in *The Minister's Wooing* (1859) and Mara in *The Pearl of Orr's Island* (1862)—acted as female ministers who taught their families the path to salvation from the well-ordered kitchen that was, in effect, a domestic pulpit.

This complex woman continued to publish until she was nearly seventy. Although *Uncle Tom's Cabin* had a greater impact on American history than any other single novel, Harriet Beecher Stowe's literary reputation rests on those novels that portrayed life in the New England villages of her youth: *The Pearl of Orr's Island, Oldtown Folks* (1869), and *Poganuc People: Their Loves and Lives* (1878). Although peopled by stern Calvinist ministers and wise, compassionate women, these works were not consciously written to correct a social injustice, as was *Uncle Tom's Cabin*. In 1873, Stowe used some of her income to buy a large home in Hartford, Connecticut, where she and Calvin spent their last years. Calvin died in 1886, ten years before his sometimes controversial wife.

Summary

Harriet Beecher Stowe will always be remembered primarily as the author of *Uncle Tom's Cabin*, which helped to end slavery in the United States and to spark the bloodiest war in American history. In the 1850's and 1860's, she remained one of America's most popular writers. Many of her works were first serialized in *The Atlantic Monthly* and then published as books, which earned her a steady and comfortable income.

Historians now recognize that Harriet Beecher Stowe's contribution to American history goes be-

yond these accomplishments. Although one cannot view this traditionally religious woman as a modern feminist, she did play an important role in women's history. Writing was one of the few "respectable" careers open to women in nineteenth century America, since women could write at home and legitimately argue that their work was necessary to supplement family income. It is somewhat ironic that Stowe's fiction, which powerfully affected the course of events outside the "domestic sphere," was written to earn greater respect for women as leaders of the home and family. It is also interesting that a century after Stowe's reputation was at its peak, Betty Friedan's pathbreaking book *The Feminine Mystique* (1963) would attack the central idea of Harriet Beecher Stowe: that women's primary role should be to lead and shape the home and family.

It is a tribute to Harriet Beecher Stowe that Friedan's work was necessary. Stowe softened the harsh Calvinism of her father by emphasizing a religion of love more congenial to women; she also defended a separate "sphere" for female activity in American life. It can be argued that both of these things were necessary to raise the status of women in America. That, in turn, made it easier for other women to demand later the greater freedom that women enjoy in the United States a century after Stowe's death.

Bibliography

Adams, John R. *Harriet Beecher Stowe*. New York: Twayne, 1963. This short biography emphasizes the connection between Stowe's personality and her writings. Adams sees Stowe as a subservient person who finally declared her independence from domestic restrictions by writing *Uncle Tom's Cabin*.

Ammons, Elizabeth, ed. *Critical Essays on Harriet Beecher Stowe*. Boston: Hall, 1980. This useful collection contains essays on Stowe by literary critics and modern feminist scholars. Dorothy Berkson's essay "Millennial Politics and the Feminine Fiction of Harriet Beecher Stowe" is particularly good.

Braker, Regina. *Weapons of Women Writers: Bertha Von Suttner's "Die Waffen Nieder!" As Political Literature in the Tradition of Harriet Beecher Stowe's "Uncle Tom's Cabin."* New York: Lang, 1995. Comparison of Stowe's *Uncle Tom's Cabin* and Bertha von Suttner's *Die Waffen Nieder! (Lay Down Your Arms!)* based on Tolstoy's theory of art.

Crozier, Alice. *The Novels of Harriet Beecher Stowe*. New York: Oxford University Press, 1969. This study provides the best synopses of Stowe's works. The author stresses Stowe's religious motivation and notes that most of her novels were widely read and respected by educated readers of her day.

Degler, Carl N. *At Odds: Women and the Family in America from the Revolution to the Present*. New York: Oxford University Press, 1980; Oxford: Oxford University Press, 1981. The passages on Stowe show a self-reliant woman who was equal to her husband in many ways. She managed her own financial affairs, was more interested in her writing than in routine domestic chores, and even gave her husband advice on how to control his sexual urges.

Douglas, Ann. *The Feminization of American Culture*. New York: Knopf, 1977; London: Papermac, 1996. The introduction to this work and a later section on Stowe show how she feminized the religion of the Calvinist preachers of her father's generation. Douglas sees Stowe's contribution to American life as an ambiguous one that both helped and hindered her twentieth century sisters.

Hedrick, Joan D. *Harriet Beecher Stowe: A Life*. New York: Oxford University Press, 1994. In the first full-scale biography of Stowe in over fifty years, Hedrick presents her successes, personal hardships, and accomplishments in a perceptive addition to the literature.

Stowe, Harriet Beecher. *Uncle Tom's Cabin*. Boston: Jewett, and London: Clarke, 1852. This famous work, always mentioned in textbooks but less often read, offers the best way to acquire an understanding of what was important to Stowe—and to many of her female readers in nineteenth century America. Many editions are available.

Wilson, Robert Forrest. *Crusader in Crinoline: The Life of Harriet Beecher Stowe*. Philadelphia: Lippincott, 1941; London: Hutchinson, 1942. This lengthy biography remains the best single source for a full account of Stowe's life. It must be supplemented with some of the newer studies cited previously.

Ken Wolf

JOHANN STRAUSS

Born: October 25, 1825; Vienna, Austria
Died: June 3, 1899; Vienna, Austria
Area of Achievement: Music
Contribution: Strauss built upon the musical achievements of his father and Austrian dance composer Joseph Lanner to raise the waltz to its highest level of development, a point at which it passed from dance music to symphonic music. His achievements in the operetta were less dramatic, for only two of his operettas have received lasting acclaim.

Early Life

Johann Strauss was born in Vienna, Austria, the eldest child of Johann and Anna (Streim) Strauss, both of whom were musically accomplished. Indeed, the father's reputation as a composer, performer, and conductor of waltzes was already established when the younger Strauss was born. The younger Strauss early demonstrated his musical gift when, at the age of six, he played a waltz tune on the piano. Despite the considerable musical talent of all of his sons, the elder Strauss forbade them to pursue their interests, allowing them to play only the piano, not the violin, the instrument essential to waltz composition. Strauss's mother, however, not only preserved his first composition but also successfully circumvented her husband's prohibition against the violin lessons. The conspiracy between son and mother, who provided one of her husband's violins and the money for the lessons, was eventually discovered by the elder Strauss, who destroyed the violin and beat his son.

Although his father had enrolled him in the prestigious Schottengymnasium for four years and the Polytechnikum, where he studied business, for an additional two years, Strauss was able to escape the banking career that his father intended for him when the elder Strauss left his family for Emily Trampusch in 1842. Strauss had secretly studied the violin under Franz Amon, whose position as conductor of one of the Strauss orchestras made him familiar with the elder Strauss's gestures and mannerisms, which the younger Strauss imitated. When Strauss could openly pursue his musical career, he continued his violin studies with Anton Kohlmann, ballet master and violinist at the Kärnthnertortheater, and studied music theory with Jo-

seph Drechsler, organist and composer of church music. Under Drechsler's tutelage and prodding, Strauss composed a church cantata, though Strauss's real interest was in waltz composition.

Because of his father's stubborn opposition, Strauss encountered many obstacles when he attempted to stage his first concert. The elder Strauss, by suggesting that he would musically boycott any ballroom allowing his son to perform, effectively closed the Viennese musical world to his son. Strauss accordingly went outside the inner city and staged his first concert at Dommayer's Casino at Heitzing, a suburb of Vienna, on October 15, 1844. Despite the somewhat hostile crowd—his father's business manager, Carl Hirsche, had provided tickets to rowdies to disrupt the concert, which consisted of Strauss's own waltz compositions—the *Sinngedichte* (poems of the senses) earned nineteen encores. One reviewer wrote, "Good evening, Father Strauss! Good morning to you, Strauss Junior!"

After his son's triumphant debut, the elder Strauss offered his son a position as concertmaster and assistant conductor, but the offer was refused. The two men effected a reconciliation of sorts, but their essential differences surfaced in 1848, when civil war erupted. The conservative elder Strauss sided with the Royalists, and his son sided with the rebels. Though neither Strauss's political commitment was strong, the change from waltzes to marches did produce some notable music. When the revolt was brutally crushed and Francis Joseph became emperor, the younger Strauss incurred royal displeasure, but his father's fate was worse: a decline in personal popularity, unprofitable tours, depression, and in 1849 death from scarlet fever. With his father's death, the son began a career that would establish him as "the Waltz King."

Life's Work

After his father's death, Strauss assumed control of his father's orchestra and at his first concert, October 11, 1849, played Mozart's *Requiem*, thereby winning the loyalty of the Viennese, some of whom had resented his challenge to his father. He also partly atoned for his political "error" of 1848 by his 1854 performance of his popular *Annen-Polka* at the ball prior to Francis Joseph's marriage to Elisabeth von Wittelsbach. In the 1850's, the waltz craze captivated Vienna, and the prolific Strauss produced scores of new waltzes to meet the increasing demand. While many of the compositions were named for professional associations and societies—the astute Strauss knew how to market his product—only one, the *Acceleration Waltz* (written for the students of the Vienna engineering school), involved a marriage of title and music.

So popular were Strauss's waltzes and so exhausting was his conducting schedule (he conducted daily, and often more than one of his orchestras) that in 1853 he had to convalesce in the Alps. It was this hectic pace that resulted in his drafting his brother Joseph, who was an engineer, as a conductor. (Strauss later persuaded his brother Eduard to assume a similar role.) Because he had been freed from sole responsibility for the family business, Strauss could tour and perform abroad as his father had done. In 1854, he signed a contract to perform yearly in Russia at the resort of Pavlovsk, and he toured Europe with an orchestra between 1856 and 1886.

Aside from his abortive relationship with Olga Smirnitzki, whom he had met in Pavlovsk, Strauss had only casual liaisons with women until 1862, when he met and married Jetty Treffz, an older woman who had been mistress to Baron Moritz Todesco. In a sense, Jetty replaced Anna Strauss. Released in 1864 from all contractual obligations as conductor of the family orchestral business, Strauss turned to composition at the mansion he and Jetty had bought at Heitzing. The 1860's were marked by Strauss's greatest waltzes, *Tales from the Vienna Woods* and *The Blue Danube*, though the latter, which was originally written for performance with a choral group, was initially a failure, primarily because of the lyrics. When it was later played in Paris as a purely orchestral performance, it was so well received that it became the musical motif of the International Exhibition of 1867.

Strauss's triumph in Paris resulted in an invitation to England in 1867, where he won more critical acclaim. His most notable tour, however, occurred in 1872, when he was paid $100,000 to appear at the World's Peace Jubilee in Boston. There, before an outdoor audience of 100,000 people, he conducted, with the help of many assistant conductors, an orchestra of 1,087 instruments. This musical extravaganza, later repeated on a more modest scale in New York, appalled Strauss, who nevertheless thereby became the richest musician of his time.

Even though the waltz was virtually synonymous with Strauss and Vienna, another musical form began gaining favor among the Viennese. Jacques Offenbach had popularized the operetta, a kind of parodic opera with a socially subversive message. Jetty and Maximilian Steiner, impresario of the Theatre an der Wien, convinced Strauss to apply his talent to the operetta. Had he remembered the fate of *The Blue Danube*, Strauss might well have foreseen that music without a suitable libretto was doomed to failure. In addition, Strauss seemed an unlikely composer for operetta because he had had practically no exposure to theater and consequently knew little about dramatic composition; he was simply more comfortable with music than with language. On the other hand, he already had found the constraints of the waltz formats incompatible with his developing symphonic interests.

The first operetta was not staged because of casting problems; the next two, with mediocre librettos, were comparative failures with brief runs. Yet *Die Fledermaus* (1874; the bat), his third effort, proved to be an enormous success, though its farcical content was at odds with a depressed Vienna, which had just suffered a stock market crash. The operetta, involving a masked ball and a confusion of characters, was adapted from a play and had a good plot; the libretto by Richard Genée and Karl Hafner was exceptional. In fact, *Die Fledermaus* marked the zenith of Strauss's career in operetta, and, though he wrote several more, he did not return to the form until 1885, when *Der Zigeunerbaron* (the gypsy baron) was staged. Like *Die Fledermaus*, *Der Zigeunerbaron* succeeded because the music and the libretto, which was by Ignaz Schnitzer, were complementary rather than at odds.

During the eleven years between his operetta successes, Strauss's life changed dramatically. Jetty, the inspiration for his more serious music and his operetta efforts, died in 1877. After a disastrous five-year marriage to Angelica Dietrich, who was thirty-three years his junior, he married in 1887 Adele Deutsch Strauss, a young widow, with whom he spent his remaining years. In order to divorce Angelica and marry Adele, he had to become a Protestant, surrender his Austrian citizenship, and become a citizen of the Duchy of Saxe-Coburg-Gotha.

His marriage and his developing friendship with Johannes Brahms made Strauss's last years con-

tented ones. He continued to write operettas, as well as some orchestral waltzes. One of his most notable waltzes was the *Kaiserwaltzer* (1888; emperor waltz), written in celebration of Francis Joseph's forty-year reign. This piece is both waltz and march, suggesting the emperor's glory, and has been regarded as more tone poem than dance. Such was the identification between "the Waltz King" and Francis Joseph that Strauss's death on June 3, 1899, was regarded as the end of a political as well as a musical era.

Summary

The Strauss family's virtual control of the music business in Vienna paralleled the dominance of the Habsburg dynasty, which in the nineteenth century enjoyed one of its most opulent and successful periods. The waltz and the beauty and harmony it represented became a kind of opium of the people, and the Habsburg prosperity created a mood receptive to it. The acknowledged "Waltz King" was the younger Johann Strauss, arguably one of the most Viennese of composers.

Strauss found in the waltz the almost perfect vehicle for his own personality, which had its dark side. Beneath the sweeping vitality and lush sweetness of the waltz was a wistful melancholy especially suited to Strauss. The waltz, however, became a prison for him as he attempted to force his musical inspiration into the tyranny of monotonous three-quarter time. As he developed, absorbing not only the waltz influence from his father and Joseph Lanner but also the more liberating influence of Franz Liszt and Richard Wagner, he was inevitably drawn toward the symphonic and away from the demands of the dance industry. His waltzes accordingly changed; the introduction and coda became almost as long as the waltz proper.

For his operettas, Strauss used the work of Jacques Offenbach and Franz von Suppé as the foundation for his own efforts. In his *Der Zigeunerbaron*, however, he transcended his predecessors and actually gave the operetta a new direction that was followed by others, including Franz Lehár. Strauss, in effect, brought both nineteenth century music forms to their artistic heights, but neither form was to survive the cultural and political upheaval that also accounted for the Habsburgs' demise. Strauss embodied the nineteenth century, and his grave, opposite Schubert's and next to Brahms's in the Central Cemetery in Vienna, testifies to his stature not only in Austria but also in the universal world of music.

Bibliography

Fantel, Hans. *The Waltz Kings: Johann Strauss, Father and Son, and Their Romantic Age*. New York: Morrow, 1972. While Fantel provides biographies of the two Strausses, he stresses the relationship of music to politics so that the reader has a broad cultural and political context for tracing the evolution of the waltz. The well-written, informal text is well indexed, and Fantel provides a good bibliography, particularly of the extramusical context, and a list of the compositions of father and son.

Gartenberg, Egon. *Johann Strauss: The End of an Era*. University Park: Pennsylvania State University Press, 1974. Places Austria in a broader European political context and provides an interesting account of the predecessors of the waltz. Gartenberg analyzes *Die Fledermaus* in detail and explains why Strauss's operettas, with two exceptions, did not succeed critically. Profusely illustrated, well indexed, and documented—contains bibliographies concerning the Strauss family, as well as the literature and music of the period, the Habsburg dynasty, and the political context.

Jacob, Heinrich E. *Johann Strauss, Father and Son: A Century of Light Music*. New York: Crown, 1939. Jacob stresses the conditions in Vienna that facilitated the development of the waltz, relates Strauss's waltzes to other contemporary music, and devotes much attention to the operettas. Although the focus is on the Strauss family, Jacob does discuss the heirs, notably Franz Lehár, to the Strauss tradition.

Pastene, Jerome. *Three-Quarter Time: The Life and Music of the Strauss Family of Vienna*. New York: Abelard Press, 1951. Pastene divides his book into three parts: Johann Strauss, the father; Johann Strauss, the son; and the other Strauss sons and Lehár. Pastene, himself a conductor, provides lengthy analyses of several major works and also includes a catalog by opus numbers and the works by the four members of the Strauss musical dynasty.

Wechsberg, Joseph. *The Waltz Emperors: The Life and Times and Music of the Strauss Family*. London: Weidenfeld and Nicolson, and New York: Putnam, 1973. Wechsberg discusses the origins of the waltz, defines the era of the waltz as beginning with Joseph Lanner and ending with Strauss's death in 1899, finds Strauss's best waltzes really symphonic music, and explores the psychological side of his subject.

The book is profusely illustrated (many of the illustrations are in color) with memorabilia and lithographs.

Thomas L. Erskine

GEORGE EDMUND STREET

Born: June 20, 1824; Woodford, England
Died: December 18, 1881; London, England
Area of Achievement: Architecture
Contribution: Street designed and built the Law
   Courts in London, and he was a leading builder
   of churches in England and Europe during the
   Gothic Revival.

Early Life

George Edmund Street was born on June 20, 1824,
in Woodford, Essex, England. He was his father's
third son; Thomas Street was a solicitor in London
with an office in Philpot Lane. His forebears came
from the Worcestershire area of England. George's
mother was Mary Anne Millington, Mr. Street's
second wife.

In 1830, Thomas Street moved his family from
London to Camberwell. There, George attended a
local school at Mitcham and went on to the Camberwell Collegiate School, from which he was
graduated in 1839. Shortly thereafter, in 1840,
George went to work for his father at the Philpot
Lane office. George did not seem suited for a solicitor's work, however, and he was unhappy there. A
few months later, Thomas Street died suddenly,
and his office was closed.

George, then unemployed, in the next few
months came under the influence of his older
brother Thomas, who was an avid sketcher. George
began to take up drawing himself and found that he
had some talent for it. For a short time he took
drawing lessons from Thomas Haseler, a painter,
and through this teacher's influence and his mother's encouragement, in 1841 George became a pupil under the architect Owen B. Carter of Winchester. Since formal schools of architecture were in
short supply in Victorian England, most future architects learned their profession by apprenticing
themselves to an established architect, as George
Street did.

In 1844, young Street, having shown enthusiasm
for ecclesiastical building, moved to the office of
George Gilbert Scott as an assistant. Scott kept
Street in his employ for five years but, seeing the
young man's potential, also let him begin to work
for his own clients, although still from Scott's office.

Life's Work

By 1849, Street had completed architectural work
on several churches, including the restoration of St.
Peter's in Plymouth. He was now fully prepared to
open his own architect's office. Early in his new career, Street, through his church restorations, came
to know Samuel Wilberforce, Bishop of Oxford.
The bishop was so impressed with Street's hard
work and careful planning that he appointed him
the diocesan architect. As a result, Street moved to a
new home at Wantage, from which he could conduct his work on churches in Oxfordshire.

Street was also a frequent traveler at this time.
He first roamed the English countryside with his
brother Thomas, sketching church buildings. In
1850 and 1851, he made the first of his foreign
tours and especially studied the famous churches
of France and Germany.

In May of 1852, Street moved his practice to a
larger office in Oxford and acquired two pupils,
Edmund Sedding and Philip Webb, both of whom
would later become noted architects. In 1853,
Street was awarded two large contracts: one for a
theological college at Cuddesdon for the Anglican
church, and the other for the East Grinstead Sisters' institution. The latter work he did without financial compensation, since his sympathy with the
sisters' work was very strong.

In 1853, Street completed a very important tour
on the Continent. He visited northern Italy, especially to study ancient church architecture. While
on all of his tours, Street was a hard worker; he was
determined to examine as many buildings as possible each day. In order to achieve this goal, he
would tour and sketch all day and then board a
train where he would sleep at night while en route
to his next destination. All the hours of research
that Street expended in Italy paid off well. Besides
finding some inspiration for his own architecture,
he collected notes for his influential book *Brick
and Marble in the Middle Ages: Notes of a Tour in
the North of Italy* (1855). Similarly, in 1854, Street
toured the churches of northern Germany and
wrote several papers on his research there.

When French churchmen planned to build a new
cathedral at Lille in 1855, they held an open competition to find the best architect for the work. Such
competitions were frequent in Victorian England
and Europe. They encouraged many architects to
submit designs for new buildings; then the best design was awarded the commission for the project.
Runners-up were sometimes given awards as well.
Street placed second in the contest at Lille, France.

In 1856, when the British government held an architects' competition for the planning of a new government office building, more than two hundred architects took part. Street's design was one of only seventeen that won premiums. His design was in the Gothic style, of which he was an enthusiastic advocate. England, in the middle of the nineteenth century, was experiencing a Gothic revival, in which the most favored architectural style was to copy and adapt thirteenth century designs for current buildings. Most of Street's work was done in the Gothic style, and he is considered, along with his mentor Sir George Gilbert Scott, to be one of the greatest Gothicists of Victorian England.

According to one estimate, about eighty percent of Street's completed buildings are churches or church-related structures. Some of Street's most powerful and memorable churches include St. Mary Magdalene's in Paddington, St. John's in Torquay, All Saints' in Clifton, and St. James the Less in Westminster. A review of these buildings helps to explain Street's style and his success. St. Mary Magdalene's shows some details of design that point to an influence from Northern Italian Gothic. An innovation by Street at All Saints' was the wide nave with its aisles being narrower than usual in the English tradition of church building; these elements were incorporated by the architect to benefit large congregations. Of this group of churches by Street, the most famous, however, is St. James the Less.

St. James the Less was basically a Gothic-style church, but it also had picturesque aspects. The picturesque style of architecture emphasized the harmony of buildings with their surroundings (which was especially popular in England in the early nineteenth century). This particular church also shows Street's Continental influences at work. In 1862, when St. James the Less was completed, architectural critics especially noted its foreign aspects. The touches on this church reflect designs from northern Italy and were appreciated by the critics, who believed that they enhanced the beauty of the building. A tower 134 feet in height is the most breathtaking aspect of St. James the Less. It is of Italian design and a departure from the slender steeples of previous Victorian English churches. Street also personally designed the interior of St. James; he planned the tile work that appeared in the aisles, as well as the pillar carvings that depict Christ's miracles. In this area of fine design in ar-

chitecture, Street was considered a master with an artist's touch. He also was effective in blending various architectural styles.

Despite a considerable amount of church work throughout the 1860's, Street found time to continue his tours in Europe. Between 1861 and 1863, he completed three study trips to Spain. The result was his fine book *Some Account of Gothic Architecture in Spain* (1865); in addition to writing this text, Street also provided his own drawings for its illustrations.

In 1866, Street entered a famous and controversial competition for a new public building in London. This was the contest to design the new Law Courts to be located on the Strand. This particular architectural competition provoked controversy because Street was awarded the contract even though he did not officially win the competition. A committee of lawyers, for whose use the Law Courts was intended, liked best the designs of Alfred Waterhouse. The assigned architectural judges thought that Street should design the building itself and that Edward M. Barry should do the interior decoration (a split contract). Finally, in June of 1868, Street alone was commissioned to build the Law Courts, only after much discussion.

Unfortunately, Street had some obstacles to surmount in finishing the Law Courts. He was dealing with government officials who kept a strict and parsimonious budget; he was not the favorite architect of the lawyers; and the building itself was an enormously large project. Street would draft in ink and by hand some three thousand designs for the exterior and the interior of the Law Courts. He was also still heavily involved in ecclesiastical building all through the 1860's and 1870's, while work on the courts progressed.

The Law Courts, completed the year after Street died, received some harsh criticism from the lawyers who used them, as well as from Street's fellow architects. Although the building's complex yet enriching exterior designs form an exquisite picturesque grouping along the Strand, some critics believed that the exterior was too diverse, appearing as several buildings rather than as one unit. Also, lawyers complained that the acoustics inside were of poor quality, making their work more difficult. One feature almost everyone admired was the majestic great vaulted hall of 230 feet by 82 feet that Street made the focal point of the building's interior. This dignified hall was an example of the Victorian Gothic style at its best.

Street worked for the dioceses of York, Winchester, and Ripon during the 1860's and 1870's, in addition to the Oxford diocese. Street undertook many church restorations, most notably the cathedral at Bristol, where he rebuilt the nave. In 1871, he also restored York Minster and Carlisle churches; at the latter he was required to rehabilitate a fratry that dated to the fifteenth century. After Street built his own home in 1873 at Holmbury in Surrey, he became active in the local parish. As a result, he designed and built, at his own expense, the church of St. Mary in Holmbury.

Along with all this very strenuous work, Street also suffered from personal tragedies in the 1870's. His wife, Mariquita Proctor Street, to whom he had been married on June 17, 1852, died in 1874. Their marriage had produced a son in 1855, Augustus Edmund Street, who worked with and later succeeded his father in their architectural office. On January 11, 1876, Street married Jessie Holland, but sadly, she died that same year. He remained a widower for the rest of his life. After suffering two paralyzing strokes, Street died in London on December 18, 1881, at the age of fifty-seven.

Summary

George Edmund Street enjoyed a highly productive and influential career as an architect. He was an innovator in church design and made a strong impression in English Victorian architectural circles. He was a forceful member of the Ecclesiological Society, a frequent contributor to their journal, *The Ecclesiologist*, and a celebrated lecturer on matters of decoration, style, and taste in architecture. He was elected to the prestigious Royal Society in 1871 and served as its president during the year before his death.

Street also enjoyed a career as a church builder throughout Europe. He designed and constructed churches for American communities in Paris and in Rome and for English communities in Genoa, Lausanne, Mürren, and Rome. In 1878, in recognition of his outstanding designs on display at the Paris Exhibition, Street was awarded the Knighthood of the Legion of Honor in France. He was also given membership in the Royal Academy at Vienna, Austria.

Only one year before his death, Street had the honor of being appointed as professor of architecture at the Royal Academy in England. He also made a lasting impact on the several students he had trained in his office; the group included Philip Webb, J. D. and Edmund Sedding (brothers), Norman Shaw, and William Morris (the founder of the Arts and Crafts movement in England).

For all of his many accomplishments in building and his lasting contributions to English architecture and decoration, George Edmund Street is immortalized in a statue by H. H. Armstead in the Law Courts. He is depicted as a long-legged craftsman, seated, engaged in supervising a task. Street here has a long face with a high forehead, further highlighted by his baldness. He also sports a long, full beard. He gazes down, engrossed in his work as he was in life.

Bibliography

Dixon, Roger, and Stefan Muthesius. *Victorian Architecture*. 2d ed. London: Thames and Hudson, 1985. A good survey of Victorian architecture. Street is covered in detail in a section on church building. The 250 illustrations include many building plans and photographs from the Victorian era. An appendix lists the individual works of more than three hundred architects.

Eastlake, Charles. *A History of the Gothic Revival in England*. London: Longman, and New York:

Scribner, 1872. Eastlake discusses in detail the phenomenon of the Gothic architectural style in Victorian England. He reviews Street's place in the revival and his churches at length. An appendix contains a chart of famous buildings (and their outstanding features) by several architects, including Street. A very useful book.

Fergusson, James. *History of the Modern Styles of Architecture*. London: Murray, 1862; New York: Dodd, Mead, 1891. Fergusson was a contemporary of Street and a harsh critic of the design of the Law Courts. The information on Street is found in the second volume of this two-volume set. Street's fine work on churches is also highlighted.

Richards, J. M. *The National Trust Book of English Architecture*. New York: Norton, and London: National Trust, 1981. In this handsome volume intended for the general reader, Richards discusses Street's church designs to some extent but focuses more attention on the Law Courts competition. Includes many black-and-white photographs, as well as color plates, all of excellent quality. A glossary is included.

Street, Arthur Edmund. *Memoir of George Edmund Street, R.A., 1824-1881*. London: Murray, 1888; New York: Blom, 1972. The author was the architect's son; this account provides both a discussion of his father's career and a list of his works. Six lectures that George Street gave as a professor form an appendix.

Summerson, John. *Victorian Architecture: Four Studies in Evaluation*. New York: Columbia University Press, 1970. This volume is based on a series of four lectures delivered in 1968. By way of introduction, Summerson describes the nature of Victorian architecture in general. He analyzes in detail the style and design of St. James the Less, Street's famous church in London. Includes many black-and-white photographs, featuring interiors as well as exteriors.

Watkin, David. *English Architecture: A Concise History*. London: Thames and Hudson, and New York: Oxford University Press, 1979. A well-illustrated text, in which Watkin gives a precise account of Street's career and buildings. He also explains the various architectural influences found in Street's works. Watkin places Street in perspective as a major British church builder. A good bibliography is included.

Patricia E. Sweeney

ANTONIO JOSÉ DE SUCRE

Born: February 3, 1795; Cumaná, New Granada
(now Venezuela)
Died: June 4, 1830; in the Berruecos Mountains,
near Venta Quemada, Ecuador
Area of Achievement: Military affairs
Contribution: Sucre was a leading military and political leader in the struggle of South American
patriots to achieve independence from Spain.
The republics of Venezuela, Colombia, Ecuador,
Peru, and Bolivia were created as a result of this
conflict.

Early Life
Antonio José de Sucre was the fourth generation of
his family to reside in Cumaná, a port city located
on the far eastern coast of present-day Venezuela.
His great grandfather, Carlos de Sucre, reestablished the family in northern South America after
having served as an official of the Spanish crown in
Cartagena and Havana. Carlos' son, Antonio, married a descendant of a conquistador family and
served as a colonel in the royal Spanish infantry.
Vicente, son of Antonio, served first as a lieutenant
of the Spanish army and, after the independence
movement began, as a colonel in the newly formed
revolutionary army. Vicente fathered a large family. Antonio José, born in Cumaná on February 3,
1795, was his seventh son.

The Spanish Empire collapsed in 1808, a victim
of French emperor Napoleon Bonaparte's expansionist policies. This event accelerated the aspirations of independence that had developed among
the Creole element within the Spanish colonies.
The Creoles were the Spaniards born in the Americas. They felt that they had been relegated to a
second-class status by the Spanish crown. Positions of power and importance were reserved for
the *Peninsulares*—those Spaniards born in the
mother country.

Young Sucre supported this movement for liberation and subsequently devoted his entire life to its
service. As early as his sixteenth birthday, he followed the tradition of his family and became a soldier. After a brief stint at a Caracas military school,
he returned home, joined the rebel army, and was
given command of a company of engineers. From
1813 to 1817, he fought in a series of campaigns
against royalist forces. Sucre's military accomplishments earned him the rank of general in the
rebel army at the early age of twenty-three.

Life's Work
In 1819, Sucre met Simón Bolívar, a fellow Venezuelan who would go down in the annals of Latin
American history as the "Liberator." The two
formed a lifelong friendship, and Sucre would
prove to be Bolívar's most loyal and trusted supporter in the many military campaigns that followed in Colombia, Venezuela, Ecuador, Peru, and
Bolivia.

Sucre had earned a good reputation as a military
leader in the liberation of both Venezuela and Colombia from the Spanish crown. The struggle
against the royalist forces had been bloody, with
both sides killing prisoners even after surrender.
Two of Sucre's own brothers were shot while being
held as prisoners of war, and a third was assassinated while a patient in a hospital. Moreover, the campaigns were made doubly difficult by fratricidal
fights within the ranks of the rebels themselves, a
situation that would continue throughout the struggle for independence.

However, it was for his accomplishments under
the direction of Bolívar in the emancipation of Ecuador, Peru, and Bolivia that he acquired his greatest fame. Bolívar sent his young charge into Ecuador to emancipate that country, which was no small
compliment to Sucre, since Bolívar had planned to
lead the campaign himself. Sucre proved his military ability. Although he was operating in unfamiliar territory—the mountains of the Andes—and
commanding an army of his own for the first time,
he defeated the royalist forces, first at Yaguachi and
then at Mount Pichincha on the outskirts of Quito.
He broke the pattern of killing prisoners by offering the royalists free passage from the area if they
surrendered the city itself. The Spaniards accepted
the offer and left Quito. The power of the Spaniards in Ecuador had ended. Bolívar promoted Sucre to major general and made him governor of
Quito.

Hardly had Sucre commenced the task of organizing Ecuador when Bolívar sent him on a new
assignment to Lima to command the Colombian
forces in the area and to protect the newly won territory from reconquest by a new Spanish army. The
task was further complicated by infighting among
the Peruvian officials themselves, as well as by Peruvian, Chilean, and Argentine military commanders who failed to achieve agreement on how to
meet the new threat.

Nevertheless, Sucre persisted despite the problems within the rebel camp. On December 7, 1824, he met the opposing Spanish commander, Viceroy José de La Serna, in a battle on the Plain of Ayacucho, some 11,000 feet above sea level. This would be the deciding battle for control of Peru. La Serna, thinking that he had the patriot forces trapped, launched what turned out to be a disastrous attack on Sucre's well-positioned forces. Despite a royalist force that was one and one-half times as large as his own, Sucre's superior battlefield tactics won the day. He accomplished this goal in just one hour of intense fighting. The royalists lost twice as many men in the battle as did Sucre. The Spanish prisoners that were taken, including Viceroy La Serna himself, outnumbered the patriots' own total forces. Ayacucho was to be Sucre's greatest military victory. He was named grand marshal of Ayacucho as a result. The Spanish hold on South America was broken forever.

Sucre's next task involved securing the independence of Upper Peru. He marched into the province in January of 1825. Bolívar charged him with restoring order to an area that was in a state of virtual anarchy. Sucre had to assume the role of governor and establish a framework for a viable political structure. The new grand marshal had protested to Bolívar on more than one occasion that such a task was beyond him, that he was a soldier and lacked the necessary formal education to carry on such work. Nevertheless, Bolívar completely trusted his loyal subordinate and prevailed upon him to undertake the task.

The hero of Ayacucho faced an initial problem in the matter of jurisdiction of the area that he had entered. Upper Peru had been assigned to Buenos Aires, not Peru, so he had, technically at least, entered foreign territory. Nevertheless, Sucre took up the task of organizing the newly acquired territory. He issued a decree that dictated the formation of a representative assembly of local citizens to adopt a form of government satisfactory to the constituency, including a guarantee of provincial autonomy if they desired it. Bolívar criticized his old comrade-in-arms for this action, stating that it inferred the right to sovereignty by the Upper Peruvians rather than simply provincial status. Sucre refused to back down in the matter and proceeded with plans to create a truly representative democracy rather than one dominated solely by the upper class. Bolívar reluctantly sanctioned the formation of the assembly and

placed Upper Peru under Sucre's political authority on a temporary basis.

The assembly convened, named the new country Bolivia in honor of Bolívar, and called on Sucre to assume the role of supreme ruler in Bolívar's absence. Sucre agreed with some hesitation. As he had so often stated publicly, he did not like political life. Shortly thereafter, Bolívar himself visited the new country and promised to use his influence with the Peruvian legislature to promote Bolivian independence. He recommended a series of democratic reforms as well, leaving their implementation to Sucre after his departure.

Sucre then began the challenging process of developing an administrative structure for the country. He introduced a tentative constitution, established ministries, laid out boundaries for departments, and secured, by treaty with Peru, an outlet for Bolivia to the Pacific Ocean. This vital corridor was seized by Chile later during the subsequent War of the Pacific.

Sucre organized a judicial system separate from the political establishment. He introduced a merit system for government employees and a postal program with regular communications to both Lima and Buenos Aires. The marshal also encouraged private enterprise by setting up a favorable economic climate for the country's mining industry.

After completing this initial labor for the new country, Sucre sought to be relieved from further responsibility. Instead, the new congress prevailed on him to accept the office of the country's first president, in spite of Sucre's personal preferences to the contrary. On October 9, 1826, he took the oath of office. Sucre's two-year term turned out to be a difficult one. Bolivia proved very hard to govern, given the continuous unrest that was generated among its various political factions. Sucre himself suffered a serious wound to his right arm in quelling an incipient revolt launched by a group of discontented soldiers stationed at Chuquisaca. The damage was so severe that Bolivia's first president remained crippled throughout the remainder of his life. He was required, at one point, to defend the new country against an incursion by his former allies, the Peruvians. Sucre left office in 1828 with evident relief.

Now both an ex-soldier and an ex-politician, Sucre returned to Quito, Ecuador, married Doña Mariana Carcelón y Larrea, marquise of Solanda, and entered into private life. His new spouse, a wealthy heiress, owned substantial estates in and around Quito. Sucre contented himself with their management. His daughter, Teresa, was born the following year. He continued to maintain regular correspondence with his old Venezuelan comrade Bolívar, expressing sorrow at the political turmoil that existed throughout the countries that they had played such a major role in liberating.

The fratricide that plagued the independence movement throughout the campaigns against the Spaniards continued into the period of nation-building that followed. Sucre himself turned out to be a victim of this tragedy when, on June 4, 1830, while on his way through the Berruecos Mountains of Ecuador bound for Quito, the thirty-five-year-old grand marshal of Ayacucho was ambushed and assassinated. His death was charged to a political rival, José María Obando, commander of the army in nearby Pasto, although the latter never paid for the crime. Sucre lies buried today in the cathedral at Quito, Ecuador.

Summary

Although Antonio José de Sucre played a subordinate role to the more famous liberator, Simón Bolívar, he was instrumental in the accomplishment of many of Bolívar's military successes. He was a talented soldier who lacked the charisma of his famous leader, but he accomplished much with his quiet, determined, and skilled leadership. His tenure as the first president of Bolivia gave that new country a set of laws and a political structure that launched it on the road to permanent statehood.

Bibliography

Hoover, John P. *Admirable Warrior: Marshal Sucre, Fighter for South American Independence.* Detroit, Mich.: Blaine-Ethridge, 1977. This is a well-written, uncomplicated biography of Sucre by an author who saw his subject as an unselfish patriot in the cause of the South American liberation from Spain.

Lopez Contreras, Eleazar. *Synopsis of the Military Life of Sucre.* New York: Elliot, 1942. This brief biography by a former fellow Venezuelan general emphasizes the military aspects of Sucre's career.

Lynch, John. *The Spanish American Revolutions 1808-1826.* 2d ed. New York: Norton, 1986. Lynch gives an overview of all the South American battles for independence, providing a background for the independence movement to which Sucre committed his life.

Robertson, William Spence. *Rise of the Spanish-American Republics.* New York and London: Appleton, 1928. Chapter 8 is devoted solely to a detailed biography of Sucre.

Sherwell, Guillermo A. *Antonio José Sucre, Hero and Martyr of American Independence.* Washington, D.C.: Byron and Adams, 1924. Sherwell's flattering biography emphasizes the positive characteristics of Sucre: his honesty, fairness, and humility, even when he led armies of thousands and held a country's presidency.

Carl Henry Marcoux

LOUIS SULLIVAN

Born: September 3, 1856; Boston, Massachusetts
Died: April 14, 1924; Chicago, Illinois
Area of Achievement: Architecture
Contribution: Known as the father of the skyscraper, Sullivan was a pioneer in the artful design of the tall building and in the development of distinctly American architecture.

Early Life

Louis Henry Sullivan was born September 3, 1856, in Boston, Massachusetts. His mother, né Adrienne List, was born in Geneva, Switzerland, to a Swiss mother and a German father. Her family emigrated to Boston in 1851, where she met the man who was to become Louis' father, an Irish immigrant dancing master named Patrick Sullivan. During his infancy, Louis and his parents shared a house with his mother's family, in part from financial necessity. Louis formed a strong attachment to his grandparents, particularly to his grandfather, a former teacher.

When the two families separated in 1861, the Sullivans took up residence briefly at the seaside in Folly Cove, Massachusetts. There, Sullivan developed a great love of the sea that would remain with him into maturity. Louis was reluctant to leave the life of rambling on the rocky coast to start school in Boston in 1862, and there is some evidence that it was his strong rebellion against first grade at the Brimmer School which prompted his parents to send him to live again with his grandparents, who had since moved to the country themselves. There, Louis continued to find classroom learning tedious but enjoyed wandering the countryside and learning from his grandfather, who was tolerant of his questions and of absenteeism from school.

Rebelliousness toward formal education, faith in his own interests and instincts, and a conviction that learning was better accomplished through observation of nature and close interaction with a master would characterize the rest of Sullivan's educational career. By the age of twelve, he was already so fixed in his ambition to become an architect that he chose not to accompany his parents when they moved to Chicago, but rather to live with his grandparents near Boston, where he believed he could get a superior education. Without completing high school, he gained admission to the Massachusetts Institute of Technology at sixteen, but within the year became disillusioned with the rigidity and classicism of the architecture program there and sought more practical training, working for the Philadelphia architect Frank Furness. Sullivan's later work showed the influence of both Furness, who was noted for his ability to subsume detail into an overall composition, and the Philadelphia Functionalists, architects of commercial buildings who emphasized structure and height; nevertheless, Sullivan moved on quickly to Chicago, where he worked in the office of another prominent architectural master of the day, William Le Baron Jenney.

In 1874, Sullivan made another, characteristically brief, attempt to gain academic training in architecture. Against stiff competition, he won admission to the prestigious École des Beaux Arts in Paris, only to remain enrolled for less than a year. Despite its brevity, this experience shaped his method of working throughout his life; it was at the École des Beaux Arts that Sullivan learned the "esquisse," or sketch, method of design, whereby the architect, after carefully considering a problem, prepares a rapid drawing which becomes the fixed basis for all future work on the project. Sullivan used this technique throughout his career, on one occasion completing the initial sketch for one of his most famous works, the Wainwright Building, in less than three minutes.

Life's Work

The period of Sullivan's most important contributions to American architecture began in 1883 when he formed a partnership with the German-born Dankmar Adler, a structural engineer. Sullivan had begun collaborating with Adler on a free-lance basis after his return to Chicago in 1875. Only four years earlier, Chicago had been devastated by the great fire, so there was much architectural work to be had. The partners concurred in their preference for designing public buildings, and as the men gained fame, these became an ever-increasing proportion of their commissions, ultimately adding up to at least two-thirds of their completed works.

Adler, who had both technical genius and the ability to work with clients, was the perfect complement to the artistic and sometimes temperamental Sullivan. The most illustrious product of their collaboration was the massive Auditorium Building, erected between 1886 and 1890 at a cost of three million dollars to house the Chicago Opera

Festival. The building took up an entire city block and rose to seventeen stories in a massive tower. When the building was completed, Adler and Sullivan took up offices in the top two floors of the tower, and it was there that the young Frank Lloyd Wright worked as personal assistant to Sullivan until 1893, at which time the two men had a falling out over Wright's taking on free-lance design work, in defiance of the terms of his contract with Adler and Sullivan. Despite the ill-will on which they parted, Wright acknowledged Sullivan as his master in his autobiography.

Adler and Sullivan's success with the Auditorium Building led to other commissions, and in increasing numbers, these were outside Chicago. Adler, because of his expertise in acoustics, was invited to consult on the design of Carnegie Hall in New York City, and the firm was hired to build a new Opera House in Pueblo, Colorado. In 1890, they were asked to design the Wainwright Building in St. Louis, an office tower that first illustrated Sullivan's ability to give the tall building an artful and coherent structure.

In 1895, the firm dissolved with Adler's retirement from architecture to work for an elevator company and earn a regular salary, a step necessitated by a period of economic depression in the country which left Sullivan and Adler with few design commissions. The two men parted with some hard feelings which were intensified by Sullivan's claiming sole credit for the last building they designed, perhaps the most magnificent of their skyscrapers, the Guaranty Building in Buffalo, New York.

The last twenty years of Sullivan's life were spent in increasing hardship, isolation, and embitterment; his marriage at age forty-two to a much younger woman ended after ten years. In the midst of another national depression which left him with little work, Sullivan was forced to sell most of his possessions in order to make a settlement with his estranged wife. Included in the sale was the vacation home he had designed for himself on the sea at Ocean Springs, Mississippi; the house was revolutionary in its simple, horizontal design that took maximum advantage of the ocean setting, while offering protection from summer heat. At this retreat, Sullivan had designed elaborate rose gardens and again displayed the love of nature and the sea that he had first manifested as a boy.

In his last years, Sullivan's only commissions were for a series of eight small banks in Midwestern cities. Although they were not immediately recognized as masterpieces, these structures display the balance of contradictory impulses which is characteristic of Sullivan's genius. They are brick structures whose simple mass is offset by intricate decoration, concentrated at points of interest, either highlighting the entrance or the flat roof line. At this time, Sullivan also expressed his aesthetic philosophy in writing, completing his *The Autobiography of an Idea* only days before his death on April 14, 1924.

Summary

Sullivan worked in a period of aesthetic ferment, at a time when American artists were attempting to discover a national style and to break free from European tradition. Sullivan, who believed that the architect should be "a poet and an interpreter of the national life of his time," expressed his democratic convictions in his preference for designing public buildings, in his inviting and encompassing entrances—most notably the famous golden doors of the Transportation Building which he designed for the Columbian Exposition—and in his use of humble native plants such as corn husks, weeds, and grasses in his design motifs.

The development of steel frame construction and of the elevator made the construction of skyscrapers a possibility and introduced a range of new design difficulties, notably how to make such buildings light and how to organize their facades so as to create aesthetic wholes rather than agglomerations, which Sullivan was the first to master. He pioneered in the treatment of the exterior of such buildings as a skin through which their structure could be perceived, and he applied his famous principle, "form follows function," to the design of the facade of the skyscraper, arguing that it should reflect the functional tripartite division of such buildings into an entry level or base, a stack of office tiers, and an attic which would house machinery. Sullivan's theory of the skyscraper was articulated not only in his most successful buildings, such as the Guaranty Building in Buffalo, but also in his influential essay, "The Tall Office Building Artistically Considered."

During the first half of the twentieth century, Sullivan was largely respected for his modernism. The increasing simplicity of his overall designs was praised, while his profuse surface ornamentation was largely ignored, or was considered to be a regrettable remnant of nineteenth century taste.

In the 1970's, however, with the reawakening of interest in Art Nouveau and the contemporary British Arts and Crafts Movement, reassessment of Sullivan's contribution also began, and an appreciation for the contradictory elements of his work arose.

Bibliography

Bush-Brown, Albert. *Louis Sullivan.* New York: Braziller, 1960. A brief but informative overview of Sullivan's life and work containing many excellent illustrations, showing the interiors as well as exterior views of most of his most famous buildings.

Connely, Willard. *Louis Sullivan as He Lived: The Shaping of American Architecture.* New York: Horizon Press, 1960. A sometimes unreliable biography which focuses on Sullivan's professional influence.

Kaufmann, Edgar, Jr., ed. *Louis Sullivan and the Architecture of Free Enterprise.* Chicago: Art Institute of Chicago, 1956. The exhibition catalog includes illustrations and discussion of many of Sullivan's major works.

Menocal, Narciso G. *Architecture as Nature: The Transcendental Idea of Louis Sullivan.* Madison: University of Wisconsin Press, 1981. This study of the ideas underlying Sullivan's design work, which was written by a historian, emphasizes his connections to nineteenth century American thought.

Morrison, Hugh. *Louis Sullivan: Prophet of Modern Architecture.* New York: Norton, 1935. A pathbreaking work, this was the first full-length biography of Sullivan to appear. It focuses on the historical and intellectual context in which Sullivan's work was done.

Sears, Barry. "On the trail of . . . Louis Sullivan Banks." *Antiques and Collecting Magazine* 98, no. 9 (November, 1993). Examines a number of banks designed by Sullivan, including examples in Minnesota, Iowa, and elsewhere.

Sprague, Paul E. *The Drawings of Louis Henry Sullivan: A Catalogue of the Frank Lloyd Wright Collection at the Avery Architectural Library.* Princeton, N.J. and Guildford: Princeton University Press, 1978. This catalog emphasizes Sullivan's skill as a draftsman and facilitates study of his design methods.

Sullivan, Louis Henry. *The Autobiography of an Idea.* New York: American Institute of Architects, 1924. This embittered intellectual autobiography, written in the third person late in the artist's life, is as revealing in its omissions as it is in its often unreliable narrative of events.

————. *Kindergarten Chats.* In *The Interstate Architect and Builder,* 2-3 (February 16, 1901-February 8, 1902). New York: Wittenborn, Schultz, 1947. This extended Socratic dialogue on architecture, conducted with a younger colleague, reputedly modeled on Frank Lloyd Wright, was originally published in fifty-two installments.

Twombly, Robert. *Louis Sullivan: His Life and Work.* New York: Viking Press, 1986. This well-researched study corrects misinformation provided both by Sullivan, in his autobiography, and by other writers. It emphasizes Sullivan's achievements in the context of American architectural history.

Wiseman, Carter. "The Rise of the Skyscraper and the Fall of Louis Sullivan." *American Heritage* 49, no. 1 (February-March, 1998). Profile of Sullivan that includes his work on the concept of the skyscraper.

Wright, Frank Lloyd. *An Autobiography.* London and New York: Longman, 1932. In chapter 2, Wright recounts his experiences working as Sullivan's assistant.

Patricia Sharpe

CHARLES SUMNER

Born: January 6, 1811; Boston, Massachusetts
Died: March 11, 1874; Washington, D.C.
Areas of Achievement: Civil rights and politics
Contribution: For a quarter of a century, Sumner was the most significant proponent in high public office of equal rights and equal opportunities for black Americans.

Early Life

In youth, Charles Sumner received little affection from his puritanical father, a Boston lawyer and politician, and his severe, distant mother, who was preoccupied with rearing his eight younger brothers and sisters. Shy and inhibited, young Sumner avoided outdoor games in favor of solitude and books. After studying at the Boston Latin School in the early 1820's, he attended Harvard College, from which he was graduated in 1830 at age nineteen. At six feet, two inches in height, weighing only 120 pounds, Sumner was ungainly, amiable, studious, humorless, and nervous near women.

Sumner was graduated from the Harvard Law School in 1834, but, temperamentally unsuited to his father's profession, he was unable to establish a successful practice. In December, 1837, he abruptly left Boston for Europe, where he spent three years in travel, living mostly on borrowed money. Letters of introduction from friends of his father procured for him invitations to visit eminent jurists, writers, and political leaders in Great Britain and France, many of whom were favorably impressed by the young New Englander's good manners and eager idealism.

Arriving home in May, 1840, Sumner gloried in his sudden prominence as one of the few Americans during that era who had enjoyed social success in Europe. He volubly recapitulated his triumphs in Boston drawing rooms while his law practice languished. As his celebrity diminished during the early 1840's, however, Sumner became increasingly moody, suspicious, and sensitive. In 1844, he suffered a physical breakdown.

Life's Work

The crisis eventually passed. Ardent involvement in social reform movements was Sumner's therapy for recovering from his depression. Embracing the cause of prison reform, he soon divided the local penal improvement society into warring factions when he tried to replace its longtime secretary with his friend Francis Lieber. As a member of the Peace Society, he used an Independence Day address in 1845 not only to denounce all wars but also to attack personally the uniformed militia members in his audience. Such exhibitions of tactless self-righteousness soon made Sumner a social outcast in Boston. Nevertheless, the pugnacious eloquence with which he assailed established institutions brought him many admirers outside his immediate circle.

In time, Sumner confined his attempts at social regeneration almost exclusively to the antislavery movement. By the mid-1840's, he had begun to give speeches and publish articles condemning the South's peculiar institution as a national evil, which Congress ought eventually to abolish. Following the admission of Texas to the Union in 1845, Sumner joined a group of "Young Whigs" in Massachusetts, including Charles F. Adams, Richard H. Dana, Jr., John G. Palfrey, and Henry Wilson, who challenged the Boston Whig oligarchy, led by Congressman Robert Winthrop and Senator Daniel Webster, for collaborating in the aggrandizements of Southern slaveholders. Joining for the first time in party politics, Sumner helped to edit the antislavery newspaper published by this group. His bitter denunciations of the Mexican War further alienated the Boston Brahmins but drew praise from Northern abolitionists and peace advocates, who characterized their new spokesman's relentless vituperation as high moral courage.

After the Mexican War, Sumner became a candidate for Congress on the ticket of the Free-Soil Party, but he lost the 1848 election to Winthrop by a large margin. Two years later, running for the same office, he received less than five hundred votes. Once again, he seemed a failure.

Early in 1851, however, a coalition of Democrats and Free-Soil Party members in the Massachusetts legislature elected Sumner to the United States Senate. Cautious at first, he did not make the first of many Senate speeches against slavery until August 26, 1852. Soon, however, he was trading denunciations and insults with spokesmen for the slaveholding aristocracy, while other Northern senators spoke circumspectly or remained silent. His combativeness produced a surge of sentiment in his favor throughout the North, while he became a hated symbol of radical abolitionism in the South. In

1855, seeking political allies, he joined the Massachusetts Republican Party, recently established.

Sumner's most famous Senate speech, which was delivered on May 19, 1856, was entitled "The Crime Against Kansas." For three hours, he denounced what he called Stephen Douglas' swindle, the Kansas-Nebraska Act of 1854, and berated both its author and his former Senate seatmate, Andrew P. Butler of South Carolina. Continuing his indictment on the following day, he labeled Douglas a loathsome animal, and he called Butler a liar and a madman. On May 22, South Carolina congressman Preston Brooks, avenging the wrong to his kinsman Butler, used his cane to beat Sumner senseless on the Senate floor.

Rendered an invalid by his wounds, Sumner became a martyr in the North, his empty seat in the Senate a convenient symbol for Massachusetts Republicans in the 1856 presidential election campaign. John C. Frémont led their ticket to a statewide sweep, and Sumner was overwhelmingly reelected to the United States Senate in January, 1857.

For the next three years, Sumner made only rare appearances in the halls of Congress. Most of that time he spent in Europe, alternating between ineffectual treatments by physicians and extensive touring and social engagements. Not until June 4, 1860, did he feel well enough to deliver a substantial speech in the Senate. Entitled the "Barbarism of Slavery," it was his main contribution to Abraham Lincoln's successful presidential campaign, an effusion of vituperation against the slaveholders whom Sumner held responsible for his difficulties, both physical and emotional.

To the Southern threat of secession, Sumner retorted that there could be no compromise with slavery. For a time he hoped that the withdrawal of Southerners from Congress would make possible the acquisition by the United States of Canada. As for the cotton states, he was quite willing to let them depart. As his former friends and benefactors Senator William H. Seward of New York and Congressman Charles F. Adams of Massachusetts struggled along with others to construct a principled compromise designed to avert civil war, Sumner accused them of obliquity and labeled them Ishmaelites. He was willing to relinquish territory, he said, but he would never barter principle. He tried to prevent the appointment of Adams as Lincoln's minister to Great Britain and to undermine Seward's direction of United States foreign policy

as secretary of state. Indeed, he worked covertly for the next two years to cause Seward's ouster from the cabinet in order to obtain the State Department for himself, but Lincoln greatly valued the services of the New Yorker and refused to give him up.

For the next eleven years, Sumner served as chairman of the Senate Foreign Relations Committee. He believed that his should be the decisive voice on United States foreign policy. Using spies in the State Department such as the eccentric Adam Gurowski, denouncing Seward to foreign diplomats and journalists in Washington, and criticizing him to highly placed correspondents abroad, Sumner worked surreptitiously to appease the antidemocratic governments of European nations. His object was to avoid foreign complications, but his methods actually exacerbated them.

An example of this was the *Trent* affair. When the British government, in December, 1861, sent an ultimatum requiring the release of four Confederate envoys seized by a federal naval captain from a British mail steamer, the *Trent*, Sumner pleaded with President Lincoln to hold out for international arbitration of the question, an approach which would probably have brought Great Britain and France into the Civil War on the side of the slave states. Lincoln, following Seward's counsel, instead authorized the release of the captives.

Trying to rouse support in Massachusetts during 1862 for his reelection to a third term in the Senate, Sumner continually pressed the President to proclaim the entire abolition of slavery. Lincoln, trying to hold the border slave states in the Union, insisted that the object of the war was to restore the Union, not to free the slaves. Nevertheless, in February, 1862, Sumner publicly propounded the doctrine of state suicide, asserting that the seceding states had forfeited their sovereignty within the Union and must become conquered provinces. It was past time, he declared, for the confiscation of Southern property, especially of slaves, by the federal military authorities. When Lincoln issued his preliminary emancipation proclamation in September, Sumner claimed that the president was finally following his lead.

In the Senate during the last two years of the Civil War, Sumner was increasingly isolated even from the other radicals of his own party. In relentless pursuit of freedom and equal rights for black Americans, he regularly castigated rather than attempted to cajole his colleagues, and despite being cultivated assiduously by both the president and Mrs. Lincoln, he regularly criticized the chief executive in his conversations and correspondence for being lethargic, disorganized, and ineffectual. He refused to support Lincoln for renomination in 1864 and only reluctantly campaigned for him against General George B. McClellan, the Democratic nominee, as the least of two evils.

Because of his alienation from most of the other senators, Sumner played a minor role in constructing the apparatus of postwar reconstruction, including the passage of the Thirteenth, Fourteenth, and Fifteenth amendments to the Constitution. He was kept off the Joint Committee on Reconstruction and was barred from the committee set up to supervise the Freedman's Bureau and the enforcement of civil rights legislation in the South. He continually exasperated his fellow radicals by carping at their efforts but rarely suggesting practical alternatives. As always, he stressed principles, not means.

In October, 1866, four months after the death of his mother, Sumner married Alice Mason Hooper, the widowed daughter-in-law of a Massachusetts congressman. The senator was fifty-five; his new wife was still in her twenties. The marriage soon foundered. Mrs. Sumner sought younger male companionship and humiliated her husband by flaunting her liaison. Eight months after the wedding, the couple separated, and the senator never spoke to his wife again. In 1873, he divorced her.

Almost from the start of Andrew Johnson's presidency, Sumner excoriated him as a disgrace to the office. By early 1868, the Massachusetts senator was a determined exponent of impeachment, accusing Johnson of treason against the United States. When the effort to remove the chief executive from office fell short by a single vote in the Senate, Sumner bitterly denounced those who cast ballots against Johnson's deposition. Soon thereafter, he began campaigning for Ulysses S. Grant for president, in the process successfully seeking his own reelection to a fourth term.

While Johnson was still president, Sumner supported ratification of the Alaska purchase treaty negotiated by Secretary of State Seward. His opposition would have been fatal to that project, as it was to Seward's treaties to annex the Danish West Indies (later known as the Virgin Islands) and to purchase territory in the Dominican Republic for an American naval base. Sumner's committee also rejected the Johnson-Clarendon convention with Great Britain, negotiated on Seward's instructions in an attempt to ease dangerous tensions growing out of the Fenian crisis and out of the refusal of the British government thus far to arbitrate American claims for damages incurred at the hands of Her Majesty's subjects during the Civil War. Sumner declared in a Senate speech on April 13, 1869, that because British aid to the Confederates had caused the war to be doubled in duration, the English owed the American people damages of two billion dollars.

For a while, Sumner was able to dictate United States foreign policy to Seward's successor, the inexperienced Hamilton Fish. As the senator with the longest continuous service, he even exercised influence, for the first time, over domestic legislation. This stopped, however, after he repeatedly blocked bills and appointments favored by Grant, culminating his obstructiveness by getting the Senate to kill a treaty to annex the Dominican Republic (the president's principal foreign policy objective). The angry chief executive retaliated by dismissing Sumner's friend John L. Motley as minister to England. When Sumner threatened a peaceful settlement of the Civil War Alabama claims by calling for the transfer of Canada to the United States as his price for support of an arbitration award, Fish and Grant were able to get him ousted as chairman of the Foreign Relations Committee.

On May 31, 1872, a vitriolic Sumner delivered a four-hour speech, "Republicanism Versus Grantism," charging the president with nepotism and corruption, hoping thereby to help block Grant's renomination for a second term. The Republican National Convention at Philadelphia nevertheless endorsed the president by acclamation. Sumner then backed Horace Greeley, the Democratic and liberal Republican candidate for the presidency. Grant's easy victory, accompanied by the rise of the venal Benjamin F. Butler to political supremacy in Massachusetts, signaled the nadir of Sumner's influence in his home state. His health declined rapidly. Facing an uphill battle for reelection in 1874, virtually isolated and widely ridiculed in the Senate, having through many years driven away most of his friends and political allies by egotistical outbursts against them, and worried about heavy debts incurred during buying binges, Sumner lived his final months as a solitary invalid, his attacks of angina pectoris increasing in frequency and intensity, until on March 11, 1874, his heart finally stopped.

Summary

Sumner served in the United States Senate for more than twenty-three years. Yet he was never a universally respected leader in that body, nor is his name attached to any portion of the landmark legislation of his epoch. Whether his party was in or out of power, his role was invariably that of obstructionist. For this he was well suited: His diligence in preparing elaborate, didactic assaults on the purposes and programs of others, his power of invective, and his uncompromising adherence to his own ideas brought him a strong following among reformers of the North, who admired his fidelity to principles of human rights and who were not subjected personally to his vehemence. The widely repeated story, the main author of which was Sumner himself, that he played a decisive role in keeping the United States from armed conflict with Great Britain and France during the Civil War is untrue. His greatest service to the nation was that of keeping relentless pressure on other politicians for almost a quarter of a century to include black Americans under the protection of the Bill of Rights.

Bibliography

Donald, David. *Charles Sumner and the Coming of the Civil War*. New York: Knopf, 1960. Based on extensive research, this is the most thorough treatment of Sumner's life prior to the inception of the Civil War. While Donald is appreciative of his subject, he is more objective than most earlier writers.

————. *Charles Sumner and the Rights of Man*. New York: Knopf, 1970. The fullest account available of Sumner's career during the period of the Civil War and Reconstruction, this is the concluding volume of Donald's highly praised modern biography.

Nason, Elias. *The Life and Times of Charles Sumner*. Boston: Russell, 1874. A biography rushed out with little time for serious research or reflection.

Pierce, Edward L. *Memoir and Letters of Charles Sumner*. 4 vols. London: Sampson Low, Marston, and Boston: Roberts Brothers, 1877-1893. Typically Victorian, this study comprises extracts from documents held together with uncritical commentary and reminiscences of the subject by people disposed to speak only well of him.

Pierson, Michael D. "'All Southern Society Is Assailed by the Foulest Charges': Charles Sumner's 'The Crime Against Kansas' and the Escalation of Republican Anti-Slavery Rhetoric." *New England Quarterly* 68, no. 4 (December, 1995). Examines a Senate address on anti-slavery given by Sumner in 1856, which is considered by many as an example of his minimal political savvy due to its personal attacks on prominent Democrats. The author argues to the contrary, using Sumner's campaign against slavery as evidence of his political acumen.

Ruchames, Louis. "Charles Sumner and American Historiography." *Journal of Negro History* 38 (1953): 139-160. Here is found the assessment that all of Sumner's biographers before Donald were uncritical and superficial.

Schurz, Carl. *Charles Sumner: An Essay*. Edited by Arthur Reed Hogue. Urbana: University of Illinois Press, 1951. This long eulogy of Sumner by a younger contemporary should be read skeptically but with appreciation of some shrewd insights.

Storey, Moorfield. *Charles Sumner*. Boston: Houghton Mifflin, 1900. A brief laudatory account in the famous "American Statesman" series. Though biased and not always factually reliable, it is probably the best introduction to Sumner's life available.

Sumner, Charles. *Charles Sumner: His Complete Works*. Boston: Lee and Shepard, 1900. This is a collection of speeches carefully edited in later years by their author. To obtain a closer approximation of what Sumner actually said, a careful researcher will consult contemporary newspapers, the *Congressional Globe*, and, if possible, Sumner's manuscripts.

———. "Sumner's Resolutions on the Theory of Secession." *Essential Documents in American History* (January, 1997). Text of Sumner's resolutions concerning government relations with rebellious states.

Norman B. Ferris

BERTHA VON SUTTNER

Born: June 9, 1843; Prague, Austro-Hungarian Empire

Died: June 21, 1914; Vienna, Austro-Hungarian Empire

Areas of Achievement: Literature and social reform

Contribution: Suttner inspired and organized peace movements and was instrumental in persuading Alfred Nobel to establish the Peace Prize named for him. Her novel *Die Waffen nieder!* (1889; *Lay Down Your Arms*, 1892) was a clarion call for disarmament.

Early Life

Bertha von Suttner, née Countess Kinsky, was born in Prague into an old noble family with a long and distinguished military tradition. Her father, Field Marshal Count Joseph Kinsky, died before she was born. On her mother's side, Kinsky was related to the poet Joseph von Korner. In her teens, she dreamed of a career as an opera singer; she was encouraged in this, but, after a short while, she realized that her talent was insufficient. A precocious child, she read Plato's works and those of Alexander von Humboldt, a great German scientist, before she was sixteen. From her governesses she learned French and English. Later, she taught herself Italian. Kinsky must have been a beautiful girl. When she was only thirteen years old, a prince wanted to marry her, and in letters she is invariably mentioned as a very lovely girl. She was an only and very lonely child, and until the age of twelve she had no playmates. This experience reinforced her inclination to live in a world of dreams and fantasies.

After her father's death, her mother was left with a modest income, but the expenses of Kinsky's singing lessons and her mother's compulsive gambling at the fashionable casinos diminished their limited funds. At the age of thirty, Kinsky took a job as a governess with the family of Baron and Baroness von Suttner. Though their youngest son, Arthur, at twenty-three years of age, was seven years younger than Kinsky, the two fell in love. Their romance was eagerly fostered by the girls of the family; they were very fond of Bertha and were fascinated by the development of romantic love. It was quite otherwise with the parents. When the romance was discovered the highly incensed baroness did not lose any time in finding a new, distant position for Kinsky.

This new position was with Alfred Nobel, the inventor of dynamite, who lived, at the time, in Paris. A bachelor at age forty-three, he was looking for a secretary-housekeeper who was also familiar with languages. In his advertisement he wrote, "A very wealthy, cultured, elderly gentleman, living in Paris, desires to find a lady, also of mature years, familiar with languages, as secretary and manager of his household." Despite her youth, Kinsky undoubtedly fit all the other requirements, for she was hired right away. A week later Nobel had to return to Sweden; the king had summoned him. Kinsky too was called away from Paris. Upon receipt of a telegram from Arthur confessing that he could not live without her, Kinsky hurried to Vienna. There, in great secrecy, they married.

For their honeymoon, which according to Kinsky lasted nine years, they went to the Caucasus in Russia. The invitation had come from a prince, who was one of their friends. Their stay was a curious blend of being both guests and employees of their hosts. At first the prince had hopes of finding employment for Arthur. When that failed, Arthur was employed as an architect and overseer while Bertha gave music and language lessons. When the day's work was done, they changed their work-clothes for evening dresses and tuxedos and mingled on equal footing with the local aristocracy. Arthur started to write articles that were published in the Austrian newspapers. Whether out of envy or the desire to imitate—she herself wrote that she could not decide which—Bertha too began to write. Her first published work was a light piece, an essay of the type known as a feuilleton, and it was signed with a pseudonym, but still it gave her confidence. Filled with the assurance that they could make a living as writers, they were ready to return home. In May, 1885, after nine years, they said farewell to the Caucasus.

Life's Work

Upon their return, Bertha and Arthur were forgiven for their secret marriage, and they rejoined Arthur's family. Published two years before their return, Bertha's book *Inventarium einer Seele* (1883; inventory of a soul) gave her entrée into literary circles. She soon added two important works to her oeuvre. *Daniela Dormes* (1886) and *Das Maschinenzeitalter: Zukunftsvorlesungen über unsere Zeit* (1889). *Daniela Dormes* in many ways is

more a discussion than a novel. In it, however, one can discern Suttner's philosophical and moral views: She is sympathetic to the plight of the Jews, and she believes in Darwinism as a social force. *Das Maschinenzeitalter* is a look into the future. Suttner commented that she wrote the book to rid herself of the gloom with which the present filled her. The book was replete with scientific and philosophical themes; in scientific circles there was so much prejudice against the capacity of women as thinkers that a book signed with a woman's name would not have been read, so Suttner used the pseudonym "Jemand" (anyone).

The turning point of Suttner's life was approaching. With the money earned by *Das Maschinenzeitalter*, she and her husband decided to go to Paris. There they again met Nobel, and through him they also met the intellectual and social elite of the city. It was in Paris that Suttner first heard about the existence in London of a society called the International Peace and Arbitration Society. From that moment, she decided to promote it with all her efforts. She realized that her talent lay in writing; she also realized that in order to reach as many people as possible, the novel form would be best. As a published author, she assumed that the publication of *Lay Down Your Arms* would not be a problem. The topic, however, was considered so dangerous that many publishers refused it. Suttner would have liked to have had the book run as a serial in a periodical, but this was refused. A publisher finally accepted the work but demanded that certain parts be cut and others be rewritten. The publisher also wanted to change the title to a less provocative one. Suttner refused. To the astonishment of the publisher, *Lay Down Your Arms* became a best-seller; it was translated into dozens of languages. She received plaudits from Nobel and Leo Tolstoy, among others. Tolstoy compared the book to Harriet Beecher Stowe's *Uncle Tom's Cabin* (1852) and commented that he hoped that just as Stowe's work had influenced the abolition of slavery so should *Lay Down Your Arms* influence the abolition of war.

The success of the book soon engulfed Suttner in a series of peace activities. In 1891, she was elected president of the Austrian Peace Society, and she represented her country at a congress of international peace movements in Rome. The same year, she met a journalist, Alfred Hermann Fried, who also was later to receive a Nobel Peace Prize. The two founded a monthly periodical that bore the same title as that of Suttner's book. During the next eight years, this monthly was a powerful instrument in keeping the peace movement before the eyes of the world. Suttner also was occupied with the preparations for the First Hague Peace Conference. The conference aroused great expectations. The Czar of Russia, Nicholas II, had called upon world leaders to discuss efforts toward universal peace. This call was hailed by the champions of peace as a gigantic step toward its achievement. Until that time, pacifists had been considered as dreamers and utopians. This condescending attitude hurt their cause as much as the hostile attitude of the militarists. Jean-Henri Dunant, the founder of the Red Cross, commented that now, "whatever may happen, the world will not shriek, 'Utopia!'" "Utopians," as Suttner noted, was the favorite circumlocution for "crazy fellows." At the conference, France was represented by a former prime minister and Great Britain by Julian Pauncefote, the British ambassador to the United States. One of the honorary presidents of the conference was Andrew D. White, the American ambassador to Germany. Among all these glittering personalities, Suttner was feted, admired, and listened to. Ivan Bloch, a Russian journalist, was instrumental in the endeavor to change world opinion to accept disarmament and peace as a real possibility and not merely as a utopian dream. Bloch's book *Budushchaia voina* (1898; partial translation as *The Future of War, in Its Technical, Economic, and Political Relations*, 1899) was widely regarded as being partially responsible for the idea of a peace conference. His thesis was that with the advanced technology of arms and armies the idea that one could wage war without destroying society was "utopian." Before going to the conference, Bloch had a long interview with the czar.

Suttner also fought against anti-Semitism. Her husband perhaps played a more important role in this fight, but she was his coworker. Anti-Semitism was virulent in the Austro-Hungarian Empire. Indeed, one of Adolf Hitler's chief idols was the anti-Semitic mayor of Vienna. Arthur founded the Union to Combat Anti-Semitism.

In December, 1902, Arthur died. In order to bear her grief, Suttner threw herself into furthering the cause of peace. She wrote, she attended meetings, and she went to conferences. In 1904, she went on a speaking tour in the United States. She met President Theodore Roosevelt, who assured her that universal peace was coming. She was impressed by Philadelphia and its Quaker inhabitants, friends of peace. On her return to Europe, she was greatly encouraged by the way many dominions of the British Empire were about to be given Commonwealth status. She saw a promising future for other states, particularly for her homeland, where the old age of the emperor made people aware of inevitable changes that would follow his death. In 1905, she received the Nobel Peace Prize.

In the summer of 1914, an International Peace Conference was scheduled to be held in Vienna. In the last week of June of that year, however, a shot rang in a provincial city in an obscure province of the Austro-Hungarian Empire. It killed the heir to the throne of the Empire as well as his wife. Soon there were millions and millions of other victims; World War I had erupted. Suttner was spared the knowledge of war—she died of stomach cancer a week before the assassinations in Sarajevo.

Summary

Bertha von Suttner united in herself two traits that are rarely found together: idealism and realism. It was her idealism that led to her faith in a world without war. Hundreds before her had that same dream, but Suttner also had the clear-sightedness, the practical sense, and the knowledge of the way the world is directed by statesmen and leaders. In her work she was helped by her husband, who shared her ideas and was also a writer of some note. Even greater help came to her in the form of the zeitgeist. At the turn of the century, a host of great writers, philosophers, and statesmen were advocating the idea of a peaceful world. The idea was there—in search of a leader. Suttner took the role. The peace conferences she organized, the speaking tours she embarked upon, her book with its noble challenge, and the periodical she helped found all had the effect of making and keeping the world aware that the fight for peace can be as vigorous as its opposite. When Suttner was received by the crowned heads of Great Britain, Sweden, Norway, and the Netherlands, when she conferred with a former president and the President of the United States, it was not only a personal triumph, but also a victory for the cause of peace. The Nobel Peace Prize and the annual peace conferences that followed the First Hague Peace Conference are testimony to her influence.

Bibliography

Braker, Regina. *Weapons of Women Writers: Bertha Von Suttner's "Die Waffen Nieder!" As Political Literature in the Tradition of Harriet Beecher Stowe's "Uncle Tom's Cabin."* New York: Lang, 1995. Comparison of Suttner's *Die Waffen Nieder! (Lay Down Your Arms!),* based on Tolstoy's theory of art, and Harriet Beecher Stowe's *Uncle Tom's Cabin.*

Davis, Calvin DeArmond. *The United States and the First Hague Peace Conference.* Ithaca, N.Y.: Cornell University Press, 1962. An excellent account of the First Hague Peace Conference with particular emphasis on the American role in it. Offers a scholarly, lucid presentation of the problems of establishing a Permanent Court of Arbitration.

Kempf, Beatrix. *Woman for Peace: The Life of Bertha von Suttner.* Translated by R. W. Last. London: Oswald Wolff, 1972; Park Ridge, N.J.: Noyes Press, 1973. Kempf had access to the Library of the United Nations in Geneva, where most of the material pertaining to Suttner's work is now collected. Occasionally laudatory, this nevertheless critical work provides an illuminating look at Suttner's life and work. Except for Suttner's own memoirs, it is the best work about her. The accounts of her lecture tours and the text of her speech in San Francisco in 1912 are valuable. Complete bibliography and index.

Playne, Caroline E. *Bertha von Suttner and the Struggle to Avert the World War.* London: Allen and Unwin, 1936. The author knew Suttner personally and participated with her in two International Peace Conferences. Contains good anecdotal material. The style is somewhat pedestrian, but the eyewitness accounts are useful. Index, no bibliography.

Suttner, Bertha von. *Memoirs of Bertha von Suttner: The Records of an Eventful Life.* Boston and London: Ginn, 1910. Because Suttner kept a diary, her memoirs are quite detailed. She gives outstanding sketches of statesmen, writers, and leaders of nations. Index.

Wiener, P. B. "Bertha von Suttner and the Political Novel." In *Essays in German Language, Culture, and Society,* edited by Siegbert S. Prawer et al. London: University of London, 1969. A useful and enlightening essay on the essence of the political novel, with special regard to the difference between the political novel and the social novel. Provides a good analysis of Suttner's main work, *Lay Down Your Arms,* and compares it to other antiwar novels. The notes following the articles are alone more valuable than many a longer article.

George Javor

JOSEPH WILSON SWAN

Born: October 31, 1828; Sunderland, Durham, England

Died: May 27, 1914; Warlingham, Surrey, England

Areas of Achievement: Invention and technology

Contribution: Swan's invention and business leadership helped launch the electric lighting industry. He pioneered in artificial fibers. His technical contributions enriched a wide range of other fields, from photography to batteries to tanning.

Early Life

Joseph Wilson Swan was born on October 31, 1828, in Sunderland, Durham, England. His parents, John and Isabella Cameron Swan, were both descended from Scottish families that had settled in England in the middle of the eighteenth century. John Swan built up a comfortable business selling iron fittings for ships, such as anchors and chains. He was, however, easy-going, generous, and unbusinesslike and lost much of his wealth by backing his own unsuccessful ventures and inventions.

While the money lasted, Joseph was educated at a dame school and a local boarding school, but his real education came from everyday life in the bustling Tyneside region of England, then one of the world's leading centers for the iron industry, shipbuilding, the mining and use of coal, and a wide range of supporting industries. Highlights of this education included some excursions to an uncle's rope works and a demonstration by a family friend of a static-electricity machine.

Departure from school at age fourteen served to further Swan's education. He was apprenticed to two Sunderland druggists, both of whom died before three years of his six-year term were up. He then moved on to work as a full-fledged chemist for a friend, John Mawson, a chemist and druggist, first in Sunderland and later in Newcastle. While working there, Swan found enough spare time to experiment, improvising equipment using the flasks and bottles in the pharmacy. He made coils and condensers and tried out simple electrical experiments. "He was a great enthusiast," a coworker recalled. "It was only after the day's work was over that he was able to experiment, for he had no proper laboratory. . . . His experiments were always carried out not only with skill and forethought, but with the least possible risk of failure."

Life's Work

This low-risk, incremental approach to invention characterized Swan's life's work. He later concluded that his particular strength as an inventor was not in conceiving wholly new things but in "looking at anything being done in the nature of a handicraft or process and finding a better way of doing it." At age seventeen, he began to apply this strength to the electric light, an invention already more than thirty years old but not yet in practical use. By 1848, he had developed his own version of one of the principal types already proposed, an incandescent carbon conductor glowing in a glass-enclosed vacuum. Swan's main improvement was to use a strip of carbonized paper in place of a graphite rod for the conductor. Electricity, however, was too expensive to make the lamp economical, and the vacuum he could produce was not good enough to give it a long life, so he turned to other areas.

Swan's employer, Mawson, a prosperous businessman, devout Methodist, and public servant, ushered Swan into Newcastle's inner circle of religious dissenters and political liberals. Swan also became a leader of the local literary and philosophical society. His associations thus brought Swan local business, public, and scientific backing as he emerged as an inventor.

The first photograph he saw, in a Sunderland shop window in about 1850, launched him on a series of photography inventions. By 1856, he had improved the formula for making collodion, a key ingredient in photographic plates, and Mawson built a factory to manufacture it. By 1864, Swan had improved the process of photographic printing, taken up the manufacture of specialty chemicals, and earned one of the world's first patents on the process of chrome tanning.

Swan's chemical inventions won for him prizes at the Paris Exposition of 1867. In that year, however, he was to suffer two personal tragedies. First Mawson died in an explosion. Then Frances White Swan, whom he had married in 1862 and who had borne him four children, died suddenly of a fever contracted in childbirth. It was well into the 1870's before Swan had stabilized his family and business life. He was married to his late wife's sister, Hannah White, who bore him five more children, and found new partners for the pharmaceutical and chemical firm of Swan and Mawson. In 1877, elec-

tricity generation and vacuum technology had advanced far enough to justify another attempt at the electric light. Swan hired Charles Stearn, a bank clerk turned vacuum experimenter, to assist him in experiments on producing light by the incandescence of carbon.

By February, 1878, he was probably closer to this goal than any of his several worldwide rivals when he demonstrated publicly at Newcastle a light based on the now-familiar combination of carbon conductor and evacuated glass bulb. At that time, his great American rival, Thomas Edison, was still concentrating on unworkable schemes involving platinum conductors turned on and off frequently by thermostats.

Yet Swan's was not yet a practical lamp. He stalled at this point for the next several months. Meanwhile, Edison made two crucial decisions: to return to carbon, perhaps inspired in part by Swan's success, which was reported in the technical press, and to use a hair-thin, high-resistance filament as his conductor, rather than the thicker, lower-resistance rods or strips used by Swan and others. Early in 1880, after Edison had publicly un-

veiled his filament, Swan followed with a similar design. He proceeded to make several improvements to filament manufacture. The judgment of historians is that he emerged a close but distinct second to Edison as inventor of the practical incandescent lamp.

In 1881, backed by Newcastle investors, Swan incorporated the Swan Electric Light Company, a successful venture for the manufacture and sale of incandescent lamps. This led to a patent suit by Edison, in which, if brought to trial, Swan foresaw, "the word 'filament' [would be] strongly insisted on." Forestalling a trial, the parties compromised, and in 1884 the Edison and Swan United Electric Company was formed. For several years thereafter, it dominated Great Britain's electric light manufacturing business.

Swan moved on to other areas of invention, developing an improved form of the lead acid storage battery and carrying out work on copper brazing and the fuel cell. The best known of his later inventions were spin-offs of his light bulb work. Seeking to perfect the filament in the mid-1880's, he decided that best results would come from making a carbon structure with uniform properties. Assisted by Leigh S. Powell, Swan found a practical solvent for gun-cotton (nitrocellulose) and squeezed the resulting paste through a die to make fine, uniform threads. Swan soon recognized that they had possibilities as fabrics as well as filaments. Hannah Swan knitted some into lace, which was exhibited in 1885 under the name "artificial silk." This was a milestone on the path to the invention of rayon and the development of the artificial fiber industry. Swan himself, however, left the exploitation of this invention to others.

In the late 1880's, he widened his interest to carry out scientific researches on the electrodeposition of copper and the stress in materials produced by high electric fields. The quality of his research won for him election as a Fellow of the Royal Society in 1894. He earned many other honors, including the presidencies of the Institution of Electrical Engineers, the Society for Chemical Industry, and the Faraday Society. Swan was knighted in 1904. In 1908, he retired to Warlingham on the North Downs of Surrey.

The leisure of his later years allowed full expression of the personal qualities that he had displayed throughout his life: fairness, an open mind, modesty, gentleness, and courtesy. Yet all rested, an associate recalled, on "a tranquil undercurrent of dignity and power." Dark, slim, and serious in his youth, he matured into a plump patriarch with a long white beard and sparkling eyes, a writer of lively letters with occasional bursts of poetic imagination. He was a rigid teetotaler, an optimist, a liberal in politics, and a great believer in the progressive influence of science, always emphasizing that the value of science was greater than any material improvement. He died peacefully at Warlingham on May 27, 1914.

Summary

Joseph Wilson Swan was born into the nineteenth century world of the heroic inventor-craftsmen immortalized by Samuel Smiles. He survived to see a world of giant corporations and government- and industry-sponsored laboratories. His own work linked the two eras. His inventing showed a sure sense for picking the field that was ripe for a major step and a sure hand at experiment and improvement. His efforts in electric lighting and artificial fibers stopped just short of total success, but placed him among the top few major contributors in each area. Unlike his great rival Edison, he was not a footloose independent entrepreneur and self-promoter. Instead, he invented from a secure base in an established industrial community. As a man welcome in the university laboratory, the scientific society's meeting hall, the government hearing room, or the businessman's office, Swan's activities foreshadowed the formalizing of such ties into the academic-industrial-government science-and-technology complex of today. Yet Swan operated with a nineteenth century optimist's independence and dignity that inventors of any era could well emulate.

Bibliography

Chirnside, R. C. "Sir Joseph Swan and the Invention of the Electric Lamp." *Electronics and Power* (February, 1979): 95-100. Discusses Swan's contribution to electric lighting technology, and the Edison-Swan rivalry.

————. *Sir Joseph Wilson Swan, FRS, Pharmacist, Chemist, Electrical Engineer.* Newcastle-on-Tyne: Newcastle-on-Tyne Philosophical Society, 1979. Discussion by a chemist of Swan's work in the context of Newcastle science and technology, adding technical background not available in the inventor's biography.

Clouth, Diane. *Joseph Wilson Swan, 1828-1914.* Gateshead: Tyne-and-Wear Archives, 1979. Well-illustrated history of Swan's achievements and local developments; gives a good sense of the context of Swan's life and work.

Swan, Mary E., and Kenneth R. Swan. *Sir Joseph Wilson Swan, FRS, Inventor and Scientist.* London: Benn, 1928. Well-written biography by two of Swan's children. Contains many valuable personal details and clear, nontechnical descriptions of his major inventions.

Wise, George. "Swan's Way." *IEEE Spectrum* 19 (April, 1982): 66-72. Describes Swan's inventive style, especially in contrast with that of his rival Edison, and indicates how those differences in style led to Edison's victory in the electric lamp race, but also to Swan's harmonious and productive total career.

George Wise

HIPPOLYTE-ADOLPHE TAINE

Born: April 21, 1828; Vouziers, France

Died: March 5, 1893; Paris, France

Areas of Achievement: Art, literature, historiography, and philosophy

Contribution: As a critic and historian of the arts and society, Taine dominated much of the intellectual life in France in the last half of the nineteenth century. Influential in England and the United States, much of his history and literary theory has fallen into disrepute in this century. Yet his method and his appreciation of literary works continue to engage critics and historians.

Early Life

Hippolyte-Adolphe Taine was twelve years old when his father, an established attorney, died. Left with a modest inheritance and scholarly inclinations, the young man was sent to a boarding school in Paris. He loved learning and soon revealed a mind superior to both his fellow students and his teachers. Deeply influenced by the philosopher Baruch Spinoza, Taine had lost his religious faith by the age of fifteen. He took a naturalistic view of the world, in which the human intellect and nature are viewed as parts of a single process. History, if it was examined carefully, revealed a total structure that functioned on the same principles as nature. Consequently, societies grew and declined in an organic manner as did natural phenomena, and the historian or philosopher could find the laws of society, history, literature, or any human endeavor in the same way that scientists found such laws to operate in nature.

It was Taine's devotion to Spinoza that led to his failing the *agrégation* (a series of examinations at the École Normale Supérieure) in 1851. His conservative examiners found his elucidation of Spinoza's moral system to be "absurd." In effect, Taine was flouting their most fundamental conceptions about free will and morality, for he argued that human beings were largely the products of their race, their time, and their environment. Taine seemed to attack the concept of individuality and of moral responsibility, apparently abandoning the notion that human beings created their own world in favor of a belief in determinism.

If Taine's early academic career was hampered by his unorthodox views, his lectures on literature and art soon brought him attention both in France and abroad. He was the harbinger of the great naturalistic novelists of the nineteenth century such as Émile Zola, who took as their subject matter the way a culture shapes human character. Taine was one of the first men of letters to study science rigorously and to develop a human psychology based on his courses in physiology, botany, zoology, and anatomy. His work was greeted with enormous enthusiasm, since it promised to put the study of history, literature, and culture as a whole on an objective basis and free it from the arbitrary prejudices of the critic.

Life's Work

The publication of Taine's *Histoire de la littérature anglaise* (1863-1864; *History of English Literature*, 1871) solidified his reputation as the leading philosophical critic of his age. Rather than simply present summary descriptions of the great English authors' lives and works, Taine propounded the notion that English literary history was not solely the record of individual achievements. Rather, it had a shape and a structure that could be elucidated, so that each author became a part of a tradition and could be seen as the product of his environment and his age. Literature was no more an accident, or merely the manifestation of an individual mind, than were the elements of nature.

In collections of essays and lectures in the next ten years and in his travels across Europe, Taine promoted a methodology based, he believed, on the rigor of scientific principles. In a lecture on the nature of art (first given in Paris in 1864 and published in English translation in 1875), Taine established the rules of his method. According to Taine, one must first study the artist's body of work and become familiar with the artist's characteristic themes and techniques. Then one must examine the artistic tradition out of which the artist develops, taking note of how his work is illustrative of that tradition. Finally, it is necessary to explore the social climate, the intellectual influences, the race, the language, and the customs of the world the artist inhabits. Taken in total, this method, in Taine's view, yields a comprehensive, unbiased view of art.

Taine's view of art is historical: "Arts appear and disappear along with certain accompanying social and intellectual conditions," he asserts in his lecture on the nature of art. The implication of his argument is that artistic genius is an intensified example of environmental influences. The artist is the finest expression of the whole culture but not a creation unto himself. All that makes William Shakespeare distinctive can be found in his contemporaries, Taine argues, but only Shakespeare expresses the exquisite combination and modulation of those elements that make a great artist. Returning to science as his guiding principle, Taine concludes: "The productions of the human mind, like those of animated nature, can only be explained by their *milieu*." Such a statement, in his estimation, was a law he had discovered in his study of art, not an idea he foisted upon it. He offers his readers "facts," for science "imposes no precepts, but ascertains and verifies laws."

It must be remembered that Taine was writing at a time when eminent Victorian figures such as Thomas Carlyle were advancing a great man theory of history. The legacy of Romanticism had been to exult in individualism and to see society coalescing about the figures of extraordinary men. On the contrary, Taine contends, a writer such as Honoré de Balzac is great precisely because he creates a literature of characters who typify their times, their culture, and their race. Balzac's *La Comédie humaine* (1829-1848; *The Human Comedy*, 1885-1893, 1896), his series of novels on French life, are the best history of his era because he is so attuned to the way in which his characters are manifestations of their society. Similarly, Stendhal repays study because he is so intimately aware of how individual psychology is linked to the history of his times. His characters are motivated by historical conditions; there is a logic to their imaginations that springs from their milieu.

In the last twenty years of his life, Taine shifted from an interest in art and philosophy to the writing of a history of contemporary France. Never deeply engaged by political issues, he nevertheless felt the need (given his historical frame of mind) to discover the roots of his culture. Because he believed that societies grow organically, and thus that individuals and events are all connected to one another, he devised a multivolume history beginning with the *ancien régime* (the era before the Revolution) and ending in his own day.

The French Revolution bothered Taine because it seemed more like a disruption than a continuation of history. The year 1789 was when France was radically changed from a society that evolved from a tradition to a new country that established a government according to universal, abstract principles. Taine did not believe that such principles existed,

except insofar as they might be seen evolving in history. His profoundly conservative cast of mind could not allow for a catastrophic event that suddenly transforms the structure of a society. In his view, such an upheaval is doomed to failure.

Taine is not nostalgic about the past. Indeed his history of France documents the desperate situation of the people in the twenty-five years preceding the Revolution. He does not deny the need for change, but he deplores the anarchy and violence of the Revolution. Napoleon I restored order but at the cost of destroying liberty among various social classes. Having to deal with the failed revolutions of his own time (the upheaval of 1848, the Paris Commune of 1871), Taine was not sanguine about the way his countrymen effected change. His rather vague solution was to counsel a sympathetic understanding of the place of all classes and elements of society.

Summary

Except for his literary essays, Hippolyte-Adolphe Taine is not read much today. His notions of science are outdated and suspect, and he is unable to see that the vaunted objectivity of his methodology is no such thing. When Taine's history of France is examined, it is clear that it is as subjective and determined by his biases as any other history would be. Taine would not have been very surprised by this judgment, since he believed that human beings were the products of their times. Yet he did fail to see the contradictions in his own methodology, that his brand of conservatism was temperamental and could not be explained only in terms of his time, place, and tradition.

It has been noted that Taine's reputation since his death has steadily declined. Yet subsequent critics and historians owe Taine an enormous debt. For example, Taine reversed the excesses of Romanticism, with its lionizing of the individual, and perceived important facts about the relationship between the individual and society that naturalistic novelists explored with considerable brilliance. Nearly every critic who has covered the subjects and the periods that were at Taine's command has felt compelled to deal with his ideas—if only to refute them. Finally, Taine merits study as one of the last men of letters who tried to integrate his insights into many different fields of study: psychology, literary criticism, aesthetics, art, philosophy, and history. In an era of specialization, his work is still an admirable example of the effort to grasp intellectual life in its entirety.

Bibliography

Eustis, Alvin A. *Hippolyte Taine and the Classical Genius*. Berkeley: University of California Press, 1951. A well-written scholarly monograph that concentrates on Taine's debt to classical writers and scholarship. Information is presented succinctly and judiciously. The bibliography is still useful.

Gargan, Edward T., ed. *The Origins of Contemporary France*, by Hippolyte-Adolphe Taine. New York: Holt, 1878. Gargan's long introduction provides important biographical information on Taine and a shrewd analysis of his position as a historian.

Kahn, Sholom J. *Science and Aesthetic Judgment: A Study in Taine's Critical Method*. London: Routledge, and New York: Columbia University Press, 1953. An important monograph for specialists, this book will prove somewhat difficult for students not already familiar with several of Taine's texts. Nevertheless, this is an essential study of Taine's philosophy and methodology.

Weinstein, Leo. *Hippolyte Taine*. New York: Twayne, 1972. The only comprehensive introduction in English to Taine's life and work. Chapters on his life, philosophy, method, and psychology, career as a literary and art critic, and role as a historian of France give a thorough summary and critique of Taine's achievements and influence. Notes, an annotated bibliography, and an index make this an indispensable study.

Wellek, René. *A History of Modern Criticism, 1750-1950*. Vol. 4. London: Cape, and New Haven, Conn.: Yale University Press, 1955. One of the most important sources for tracing the history of literary criticism and Taine's place within it. Wellek discusses the significance of Taine's *History of English Literature* and the way the critic deals with matters of style.

Carl Rollyson

TALLEYRAND

Born: February 2, 1754; Paris, France
Died: May 17, 1838; Paris, France
Area of Achievement: Politics
Contribution: Talleyrand directed the foreign relations of his country in a time of changing principles and changing regimes—the Directory, the Consulate, the Empire, and the Restoration Monarchy—trying to adjust his French patriotism with the establishment of a viable balance of power that formed the basis of European relations for a century.

Early Life

Talleyrand's family came from an old and highly distinguished line of sovereign counts, but at the time he was born the family had lost a considerable amount of its former importance. His parents were courtiers whose business, attending the offspring of Louis XV, gave them little time to spend with their most recent addition. Talleyrand was sent to a wet nurse, a poor woman who lived in the Saint-Jacques district. Although such surrogate mothering was a common practice, with Talleyrand it was excessive: The parents did not see their son for the next four years. While in his nurse's care only several months, he fell from a chest of drawers, breaking his right foot. The injury did not receive proper medical attention and the bones knit badly, leaving him with a club foot. For the rest of his life he was unable to walk without a cane or a brace.

When Talleyrand was three, his older brother died, leaving him heir to the family title and estates. He would have become a soldier, but his injury made this impossible. The family therefore decided to have him forfeit his rights in favor of his younger brother, Archambaud, and become a churchman. After elementary school, he attended the seminary of Saint Sulpice. From there, he went to the Sorbonne receiving, in 1774, a degree in theology. He took his first vows in April, 1775. Several months later, as the Abbé de Périgord, he attended the royal coronation of Louis XVI at the Cathedral of Rheims.

Talleyrand's noble lineage gave him entrée to the court and its opportunities. In September, 1775, he was confirmed as the Abbot of Saint-Rémy in Rheims, a sinecure that paid him eighteen thousand livres a year. Henceforth, his rise in the church hierarchy was rapid: In 1779, he became a deacon and a priest; in 1880, he became an agent-general of the Assembly of the Clergy to manage ecclesiastical property; in 1789, he became the Bishop of Autun. He also managed to pick up other properties in Champagne and Poitou. All of his benefices combined gave the thirty-four-year-old prelate a personal income of about 100,000 livres a year. With such resources he could now live the good life, far from ecclesiastical duties in provincial cities.

In church matters he had a reputation as a defender of tradition and privilege, but his private life was otherwise. He preferred to spend his time in Paris, frequenting the salons, conversing with such men as Voltaire, Comte de Mirabeau, and Charles Alexandre de Calonne, and seducing women. His sexual successes were the subject of much gossip, admiration, and amusement. Despite absenteeism from his official obligations—he only visited his bishopric once for a period of thirty days—he became Autun's clerical delegate to the meeting of the Estates-General held at Versailles in May, 1789. The petition of grievance, or cahier, which he brought with him, and which he helped to write, called for the establishment of local representative government, for the abolition of feudal privilege, and for the creation of a national assembly to curb the power of royal despotism. He favored putting the estates of the Church at the disposition of the nation; when the time came, he provided the rationale for reconciling such expropriation with the sacredness of private property. Talleyrand argued that these church lands had been the property of the nation all along, maintaining the entire body of the faithful in a Catholic land could be the nation itself. His knowledge of Church administration was invaluable in helping to destroy the organization's power.

He also gave legitimacy to the civil constitution of the clergy by celebrating Mass on the Feast of the Federation, July 14, 1790, at the Champ de Mars on the first anniversary of the taking of the Bastille. He helped consecrate recently elected bishops to replace those who had refused to pledge their loyalty to the new order. Shortly afterward, in February, 1791, he renounced his priestly vows and returned to the status of layman, whereupon he was excommunicated by the pope.

Life's Work

Talleyrand's first attempt at national diplomacy, a métier that became his main profession the rest of

his life, came in 1792. Because of the self-denying ordinance, he was unable to run for election to the new parliament created by the old constituent assembly. Instead, he managed to be sent on a mission to London to try to secure British neutrality in the event of the outbreak of hostilities between France and Austria. The mission was not succesful; the British wanted to maintain their free hand as the holder of the balance of power and rejected any commitments. Talleyrand nevertheless continued his diplomatic efforts. He returned to London on two other occasions—in January and May of 1792—but the results were equally disappointing.

At home Talleyrand watched with dismay the increasingly radical direction of politics. During his third visit to the British capital, France was at war with both Austria and Prussia. The early defeats led to the outbreak of domestic violence which led to the September Massacres, which made life dangerous for all men of Talleyrand's antecedents. With the coming of the Reign of Terror, he fled to Great Britain then was forced to leave for the United States, where for a time he lived in Philadelphia. He did not like American

hospitality. In his opinion the climate was too hot or too cold, there was a dreadful lack of culture, and the food was inedible.

Not until 1796 did he return to France, the new government of the Directory giving him permission. He found that in his absence he had been elected to the newly formed Institute of Arts and Sciences. He renewed old acquaintances through which he came to the attention of the powerful director, Vicomte Paul de Barras, who had him named minister of foreign affairs in July, 1797. At this time France was in an expansionist mood, believing its destiny lay in extending its boundaries to the Alps and the Rhine and in liberating Europe's suppressed peoples from the yoke of feudalism and despotism. Its mission was to carry out a crusade for universal freedom.

Such ambitions did not seem unreasonable to nationalists, even though, as long as France was committed to such goals, there would be constant war. None who held high office at this time could have publicly believed otherwise, least of all a minister of foreign affairs. Talleyrand wanted to make France respected and feared, but he believed war to be wasteful and absurd. He wanted to end the current hostilities with Austria and Great Britain, but the victory had to contribute to the stabilization of Europe by not destroying the balance of power. It must also contribute to French prosperity.

To these ends Talleyrand put forth a scheme to establish French preponderance in the eastern Mediterranean by mounting an expedition to Egypt. The Turkish Empire was in dissolution and, by seizing its choicest parts, France could expand its commercial interests and hold bargaining counters to bring about peace with the British. Ever mindful of his own interests, Talleyrand began cultivating a friendship with Napoleon I, who also favored the Egyptian campaign. Both were contemptuous of the current political system which they believed was contributing to French defeat and weakness.

In July, 1799, sensing that the end of the Directory was near, Talleyrand resigned his post and retired to private life. When Napoleon returned from Egypt in October of that year, Talleyrand joined a conspiracy to bring the general to power. For his support, Napoleon made Talleyrand foreign minister. The two seemed to agree on the essentials of French foreign policy and upon the necessity of creating a European equilibrium which could assure the security and prestige of France.

Talleyrand presided over the reorganization of Germany. He helped to arrange compensation for princes dispossessed of their territories on the west bank of the Rhine by giving them church lands in other parts of Germany. These transactions satisfied the time-honored principle of compensations, but they also made Talleyrand tremendously wealthy. In fact, the foreign minister was one of the greediest men of France in an age renowned for corruption. He saw nothing wrong in demanding kickbacks for his services to enable him to live in the style befitting his station. Such venality often made it difficult to ascertain the dividing line between personal and public advantage.

The height of his professionalism undoubtedly came with the signature of the Peace of Amiens, on March 25, 1802. In this treaty the British had to acknowledge effective French control of the Netherlands, Belgium, the left bank of the Rhine, and northern Italy. The British, especially in recognizing French power in the lowlands, abandoned a policy which they once regarded as essential for their security. Thus, after a decade of wars, France emerged as the most powerful state in Europe. Talleyrand boasted that his country now enjoyed such power, glory, and influence that even the most ambitious person could desire nothing more for his country.

Napoleon, however, was not the sort of master ever to be satisfied. While his foreign minister struggled to make the Peace of Amiens the basis of a new European equilibrium, Napoleon was planning ever larger conquests. Relations between the two men began to chill, but Talleyrand continued to share in Napoleon's glory. He could be an embarrassingly servile sycophant when it suited his purposes. When it at last became obvious that Talleyrand could no longer reconcile his sense of moderation and longing for personal survival with such a willful conqueror, he resigned. This event occurred in 1807, after the signing of the Treaty of Tilsit with Russia that recognized the division of Europe into two spheres: the Russian in the East and the French in the West. Talleyrand, having accumulated sufficient worldly goods to live in royal style—he was the master of the vast feudal estate of Valençay and of a superb townhouse in Paris on the Place de la Concorde—became the reigning prince of Benevento but again left before the inevitable fall of a regime.

Napoleon was vexed at his minister's desertion but continued to use him for special tasks. In these tasks Talleyrand proved less than reliable. At the summit conference at Erfurt with Alexander I, Talleyrand secretly urged the Russian czar to stand firm and not let Napoleon destroy Austria. After helping Napoleon arrange the overthrow of the Spanish Bourbons, Talleyrand turned against the venture and conspired with Police Minister Joseph Fouché to have Napoleon overthrown, replacing him with Napoleon's brother-in-law, Joachim Murat. Napoleon discovered who was behind the scheme and denounced Talleyrand, on January 28, 1809, before a restricted meeting of the council of state.

Talleyrand lived in retirement until 1814, when, with the Napoleonic Empire in ruins, he helped arrange the Bourbon Restoration. Talleyrand insisted that this be conditional upon the establishment of constitutional government. Talleyrand again became minister of foreign affairs. He was largely responsible for the Treaty of Paris, which concluded peace between France and the allies. He was also the principal French representative at the Congress of Vienna—arranged by the British, Russians, Prussians, and Austrians—which restored an equilibrium to a Europe ravaged by a quarter of a century of war.

Talleyrand retired once more, this time unwillingly, in September, 1815. Fifteen years later, however, with the advent of the July Monarchy, he was again offered the foreign ministry. He chose instead to go to London as an ambassador. He stayed in this post the next four years, participating in the negotiations which established an independent Belgium. In his long career he had served under seven different regimes and had intrigued against more than half of them; as he later noted, however, these betrayals had the support of a majority of his fellow countrymen. Upon his deathbed, he insisted that he receive extreme unction on the knuckles of his clenched fists rather than on his palms as befitting a bishop of the Roman Catholic church.

Summary

Talleyrand embraced the assumptions existent since the Treaty of Westphalia (1648) that foreign policy was essentially nonideological and that states could preserve their independence by preserving a proper balance of power. This moderate approach made him favor creating an entente with the entrenched powers against the revisionist powers, which meant assisting Great Britain and Austria curb Russia and Prussia, as he did at the Congress of Vienna. He characteristically exaggerated his role at that summit meeting, but his performance there was consistent with the principles by which he believed the affairs of nations should be conducted. "The first need of Europe," he told the representatives of the great powers, "is to banish forever the opinion that right can be acquired by conquest alone, and to cause the revival of that sacred principle of legitimacy from which all order and stability spring." Through skillful exploitation of the differences between the allies, he managed to put France on a more equal footing with them, helping to increase the respectability of the French monarchy as a force for order, moderation, and conservatism.

Although frequently vilified for his material and sexual avarice—he is a Freudian's delight with his loveless mother, his disinheritance, and his love-hate relationship with Catholicism—Talleyrand stands forth as the quintessential diplomat—one who realized that international politics is the art of the possible. He realized, too, that national security is not dependent on the survival of the fittest but on the mutual acceptance by great powers of their limitations and on the need to temper their rivalries and ambitions to preserve the security of one another.

Bibliography

Brinton, Crane. *The Lives of Talleyrand*. New York: Norton, 1936; London: Allen and Unwin, 1937. If Brinton's biography were not so engaging, intelligent, and analytically erudite, it would be dismissed as a rank apology. Indeed, Brinton seems to go out of his way to make allowances for Talleyrand, but his presentation of Talleyrand as the consummate moderate diplomat is nevertheless convincing.

Cooper, Duff. *Talleyrand*. London: Cape, and New York: Harper, 1932. This Tory politician makes no great discourse on Talleyrand's skills or vices, presenting him simply as an eminently sensible Frenchman, a practical, peace-loving man free from the vice of nationalism and horrified by the spirit of conquest. In a sense one of the first Europeans.

Dwyer, Philip G., comp. *Charles-Maurice de Talleyrand, 1754-1838: A Bibliography*. Westport, Conn.: Greenwood Press, 1996. This is the first bibliography devoted to Napoleon's foreign minister, Talleyrand. It includes a chronology and a summary of his career, archived sources and their locations, Talleyrand's own writings, and writings about him.

Ferrero, Guglielmo. *The Reconstruction of Europe: Talleyrand and the Congress of Vienna, 1814-1815*. Translated by Theodore R. Jaeckel. New York: Putnam, 1941. Ferrero credits three men with the creation of a new and stable order out of the ruins of the Napoleonic Empire: Czar Alexander I, King Louis XVIII, and Talleyrand, who "seems to have the right of precedence over all the statesmen who have appeared in the Western world since the Revolution." Ferrero attributes Talleyrand's predisposition to revolt against all regimes and powers to the childhood accident that left him a cripple.

Greenbaum, Louis S. *Talleyrand, Statesman-Priest: The Agent-General of the Clergy and the Church of France at the End of the Old Regime*. Washington, D.C.: Catholic University of America Press, 1970. Primarily an examination of the administrative history of the French Catholic church in the last third of the eighteenth century. Greenbaum also shows how such an organization became the school for statesmanship in forging the political career of Talleyrand.

Orieux, Jean. *Talleyrand: The Art of Survival*. Translated by Patricia Wolf. London: Secker and Warburg, and New York: Knopf, 1974. Comprehensive treatment which borrows heavily from the definitive biography by Georges Lacour-Gayet. Written in a catechistic style, the work portrays Talleyrand as a great custodian and transmitter of civilization, one "ever willing to meet the demands of the future for the sake of survival and the preservation of mankind's achievement."

Talleyrand-Périgord, Charles Maurice de. *Memoirs of the Prince de Talleyrand*. Edited by the Duc de Broglie. Translated by Raphaël Ledos de Beaufort and Mrs. Angus Hall. 5 vols. New York and London: Putnam, 1891-1892. A standard primary source. The first two volumes are somewhat sketchy in documentation. There is some compensation in the fullness of the official correspondence concerning the Congress of Vienna and the London Conference.

Wm. Laird Kleine-Ahlbrandt

ROGER BROOKE TANEY

Born: March 17, 1777; Calvert County, Maryland
Died: October 12, 1864; Washington, D.C.
Area of Achievement: Law
Contribution: During his tenure as Chief Justice of the United States for twenty-eight years, Taney successfully used his considerable talents to adjust the law to the new egalitarian political and economic currents and states' rights concerns of Jacksonian democracy, while preserving the essentials of both property rights and the authority of the federal government. In dealing with the volatile issue of the expansion of slavery in the territories, Taney also sought moderation until the *Dred Scott* case, when he unsuccessfully attempted to resolve judicially what Congress and the president were unable to decide legislatively.

Early Life

Roger Brooke Taney, third of seven children, was born in Calvert County in southern Maryland on the Patuxent River, March 17, 1777. His father, Michael Taney, was from an old Maryland planter family of some wealth and had been educated in Europe. His mother, née Monica Brooke, was the daughter of another distinguished Maryland planter family. Michael Taney, though hot-tempered and impatient, loved his children and took great interest in their upbringing. Monica Taney was a pious and gentle person of little education, always willing to give help to anyone in need, including slaves. Roger Taney apparently learned from her solicitude for American blacks.

Taney attended a local school, a boarding school, and then for several years he and the other Taney children studied at home under David English, a tutor and graduate of Princeton hired by their father. At age fifteen, Taney was sent off to Dickinson College in Carlisle, Pennsylvania, where he studied and lived with the difficult but brilliant Dr. Charles Nisbit, president of the college. In the spring of 1795, Taney passed the oral examination required for graduation and was voted valedictorian by his classmates. It was an honor he had wanted but did not relish achieving. Public speaking was difficult for Taney throughout his life, upsetting his somewhat delicate health and often leaving him worn out and ill for days. Taney was a thin, flat-chested youth with thick black hair, solemn eyes, and a face that showed much character but

was not handsome. Like his mother, he was painfully shy, but those who learned to know him found a warm and friendly personality with an engaging and penetrating intellect. Taney had a gift for stating the difficult in clear, simple language, which served him well in his profession.

From 1796 to 1799, Taney clerked in the office of a prominent Annapolis judge. During this time, he made friends with Francis Scott Key, later famous for his poem "The Star-Spangled Banner." After being admitted to the bar in 1799, Taney tried practicing in several locations, but because of insufficient business, he moved to Frederick, Maryland, in March of 1801, where he remained for the next twenty years. Frederick was a small town of three thousand, but there were old family friends and relatives in the vicinity. Taney accepted all types of cases and was soon the most prominent lawyer in the area. In 1803, he was a candidate for the Maryland state legislature, but lost. During this time, he courted Anne Key, sister of his friend Francis Scott Key, who lived nearby at Terra Ruba, the Key family estate. By 1805, he was secure enough financially to propose, and they were married, January 6, 1806. Anne Taney was a kind and tranquil person who soothed Taney when his nerves were frayed, nursed him when his health was bad, and was a great comfort to him all their married life. Six daughters and a son, who died in infancy, were born to the Taneys.

Although a respectable stalwart in Maryland Federalist circles, Taney leaned toward more flexible democratic ideals, a tendency that the War of 1812 accentuated. Taney led a dissenting prowar faction nicknamed the "Coodies." His popularity with the voters increased as a result, and he was elected to the Maryland senate in 1816, where he served until 1821. During these years, partly as a result of his Southern plantation heritage, Taney opposed the second Bank of the United States, particularly after the economic slump of 1819, which was widely blamed on the bank. He welcomed the bank's power to provide regulation of state banks but opposed what he perceived as its excessive power and privilege. Taney also became involved in projects to aid American blacks. He was no abolitionist but did believe that slavery was an unfortunate institution and should be ended someday. He supported the African colonization movement for free blacks and measures to protect free blacks

from unscrupulous slavers who would kidnap them for sale as slaves in the lower South, freed his own slaves, and was always kind and attentive to their interests. Yet while he agreed that slavery must be ended, he believed that it must be done slowly and solely by the actions of the individual states. He was deeply concerned all his life that the federal government would intrude and end slavery abruptly and destroy the South.

By 1823, when Taney was forty-six, he had acquired a statewide legal reputation and an increasing amount of business requiring him to be in Baltimore. To advance his career, he sold his practice and home and moved to Baltimore. Taney's success, however, was atypical. In an era in which public speaking was judged by style and the ability to quote from great literature, he spoke without gestures or emphasis, in a low voice, simply, earnestly, and without apparent artfulness. The effect, coming from the frail, stooped figure in black, ill-fitting clothes, with a long solemn face, was considerable. He had many wealthy clients, and by 1827, he was so well-known that the governor selected him for the prestigious post of state attorney

general. He held the post and continued his private practice until 1831.

Life's Work

After the collapse of the Federalist Party and the adoption of many Federalist ideas by the Jeffersonians during the Era of Good Feelings, Taney drifted into the Democratic Party. In 1824, he supported the election of Andrew Jackson but was not active in the campaign. His former Federalist associates, who had not forgiven Taney for leading the Coodies, generally supported John Quincy Adams and his program, which favored commercial and financial interests over agriculture. Taney could not agree with them and by 1826 headed the Maryland Central Committee to elect Jackson in the 1828 election. When the Peggy Eaton Affair made the split in Jackson's cabinet impossible, Secretary of State Martin Van Buren maneuvered to get the entire cabinet to resign and President Jackson to appoint a new one. The United States attorney generalship was offered to Taney, who accepted. It did not pay well, and Taney had not wanted a position with the government, but he decided that he should accept.

Taney gained national prominence and notoriety in Jackson's cabinet over his role in the Bank War. When a law was passed in Congress renewing the charter of the second Bank of the United States, Taney recommended that Jackson veto it; Jackson agreed, and Taney wrote the constitutional portion of Jackson's veto message. Taney was convinced that the bank meant to put state banks out of business and dominate the American economy. Jackson had similar suspicions. The probank interests in Congress, which were primarily members of the Whig Party, were furious with Taney and in June of 1834 refused to confirm him as secretary of the treasury when Jackson appointed him to that post.

Taney returned to Baltimore to resume his law practice. Jackson kept seeking his advice and offering him various official positions, which Taney refused until he was offered an associate justice position on the Supreme Court. In January of 1835, the Whigs in the Senate once again blocked Taney's confirmation. In July of 1835, Chief Justice John Marshall died, and President Jackson, determined to find a place in government for Taney, nominated him as Marshall's successor. After the fall election, a new, more favorable Congress was sitting, and this time Taney was confirmed, on March 15, 1836.

As Chief Justice of the United States, Taney brought change to the Supreme Court. When riding circuit, he ended the custom of giving long lectures to grand juries on the philosophy of American law and government. Federalist judges had often turned such lectures into political speeches against the Democratic Party. He also ended the custom of wearing small clothes (knee breeches) under judicial robes and wore ordinary trousers instead. In *Charles River Bridge v. Warren Bridge* (1837), his first important constitutional case, Taney gave notice of a change of emphasis from the supremacy of national law toward states' rights. The case involved the constitutional provision barring states from altering the obligations in a contract. The Marshall court had interpreted this clause strictly to protect property rights, including even implied obligations. Taney was not hostile to property rights or the contract clause of the Constitution but thought Marshall's interpretation too extreme and believed that an implied obligation should not prohibit state legislatures from exercising their best judgment on behalf of the general welfare and to promote progress. In other cases, Taney made it clear that the Marshall doctrine on the supremacy of national law to control interstate commerce would not be destroyed, only amended to allow some state involvement. While Taney distrusted the power of great aggregations of wealth in corporate form and believed that the state needed some authority to police such power, he also recognized the advantages to the American economy of the corporations' success and the need for the Court to protect their interests in the American economic system.

Taney was not the dominating figure on the Court that Marshall had been. It was not because he lacked the brilliance, but because he chose to operate in a more collegial fashion and because the Taney court had a greater diversity of political philosophy than did Marshall's. It sometimes proved impossible for the Court to arrive at a consensus. It is perhaps the mark of his ability that he achieved agreement as often as he did in times that were racked by sectionalism and the changes brought by the beginnings of the industrial revolution.

The most troublesome issue for the Court was slavery. The issue reached the Court in the form of questions concerning nonpayment for slaves brought illegally into a state, whether slaves who had overpowered a ship's crew and sailed to a Northern port were free men or still slaves to be returned to their owners, and free black sailors on English ships who were locked up while their ship was docked in Charleston. These cases were slowly dragging the Supreme Court into the sectional conflicts over slavery when the case of *Prigg v. Pennsylvania* (1842) came before the Court and sped up the process. Justice Joseph Story, writing for the majority, which did not include Taney, declared a Pennsylvania law unconstitutional because it interfered with a federal power. The state law would make free persons of slaves who could reach the state's territory, which conflicted with the national government's responsibility to see fugitive slaves returned to their proper owners. Story went on, however, to declare that federal power over the matter was exclusive. Taney disagreed because he did not want to discourage those states willing to help, nor did he like the implications for Congress. Soon, many Northern states made it illegal for their state and local officials to give any aid to federal officers attempting to enforce the federal Fugitive Slave Law. The Southern states then asked Congress to consider the problem and enact a stronger law, the very action Taney had feared. Any congressional attempt to cope with the problem could only increase North-South friction. Taney was aware that if the friction increased too much, the South would be likely to attempt secession. He believed that if slavery remained strictly a state issue, a North-South confrontation could be avoided, and the South would then have the time necessary to end it slowly, without massive disruption. This appears to be the motivation behind his generally misunderstood and infamous *Dred Scott* decision.

There had been several attempts to get the Supreme Court to rule on the federal government's power to prohibit the expansion of slavery into the territories. The issue came squarely before the Court in 1857 in the *Dred Scott* case. The specific issue was whether Dred Scott, a slave, had been made a free man when his master took him first to a free state and then to a territory free of slavery because of the Missouri Compromise. There was enormous political pressure put on the Court to resolve what neither the president nor Congress wanted to touch. At first, the Court tried to dodge the issue and decide the case on the narrow grounds that in returning voluntarily with his master to Missouri, Dred Scott reconfirmed his status as a slave, and, since slaves had no right to sue in court, the Supreme Court had no jurisdiction. This would have meant a low key opinion. Justice Louis McLean, however, hoping to be nominated by the newly formed Republican Party for president, insisted on writing a dissenting opinion to advertise his position that Congress had the authority to decide whether slavery could exist in a territory and that the Missouri Compromise was constitutional.

Taney felt impelled by McLean's improvident action to answer for the Court's majority. Taney reasoned that the South's and the Union's security required that the Court declare that slaves were property and not persons, that property could not sue in court, that Congress had no authority to allow a kind of property—in this case slaves—in one part of the American territories while making it illegal in the rest of the territories, that this meant the Missouri Compromise was unconstitutional, and that Congress was obliged by the Constitution to protect all forms of property in all parts of the territories equally. Because the Constitution recognized the institution of slavery and the Court was bound by the Constitution, no other decision on these issues was possible.

The uproar in the North over the Court's decision, however, was enormous. The seven majority justices were bitterly vilified as the vicious minions of slavocracy, especially Taney. The abolitionists, the Free-Soilers, and the Republicans perceived the Missouri Compromise as a proof of the power of Congress over slavery in the territories, and its constitutionality was central to their case against the expansion of slavery in the territories. The *Dred Scott* decision left their whole political platform in a constitutional shambles. Taney did not reply to his critics, and his friends were unable and unequal to the task. The prestige of the Court collapsed and the federal government was now virtually helpless to resolve the conflict over slavery in a manner acceptable to both North and South. Taney was impressed and encouraged by President Abraham Lincoln's conciliatory inaugural address, but the South greeted it with secession.

Taney was an old, sick man when the Civil War began, and his last years were difficult; his wife had died in 1855, few members of the Lincoln Administration had anything but scorn for him, and the press continued to vilify his decisions. He continued, though, to insist that the Constitution be honored even in war. When he issued a writ of *habeas corpus* to force the army to release John Merryman, a prominent Marylander arrested for suspected secessionist activities, he was in fact declaring President Lincoln's suspension of the writ unconstitutional. When the matter was finally decided by a Republican Court after Taney's death, Taney was fully vindicated and an important new rule of law was established. There were other attempts by Taney to restrain the federal government's exercise of arbitrary power, and each time, Taney was attacked by the press and rebuffed by the executive branch of the government. Yet he continued and also drafted opinions on important constitutional principles likely to come up in cases before the Court. In the fall of 1864, a chronic intestinal disorder from which he had suffered for some years became acute and violently painful. With his mind clear until the end and two of his daughters by him, he died October 12, at 10:00 P.M. As he had requested, the funeral service was a quiet and modest affair, all the more so because most Republican cabinet officers refused to attend.

Summary

Taney was a man of modest tastes, but his intellect and strength of character made of him a judicial statesman of the highest order. Before *Dred Scott*, even his critics respected him, and some, such as Henry Clay, even came to admire him. As chief justice, he first dedicated himself to restraining the concentrations of financial, commercial, and industrial power that threatened to dominate and plunder the agricultural majority. He was neither radical nor doctrinaire in his judicial philosophy. The Marshall Court's doctrines protecting inalienable rights were not destroyed and even became stronger in being adapted to the changing economic conditions of the industrial revolution.

As the sectional conflict over slavery increased, Taney perceived its potential threat to the South and to the Union. He hoped to keep Congress from assuming any authority over slavery to avoid tempting the North to force its views on the South. Should the North attempt coercion, Taney could conceive of only two possible results: Either the North would succeed and the South be destroyed, or the South would choose secession and rupture with the Union. Both alternatives could be avoided if the slave states were allowed the time necessary to find their own means of ending their peculiar institution, a development to which he was sympathetic and that he considered inevitable. The *Dred Scott* decision became the means by which Taney attempted to carry out these ideas, but only after Justice McLean insisted on publishing his contrary beliefs. Here Taney may have made an error in strategy. It might have been better for the Court to ignore McLean and keep to the original narrowly based decision. It is unlikely, however, that it would have made any difference. The political moderates who had achieved the compromises of 1820 and 1850 had been too far reduced in number by 1857 to support the Court's solution.

Bibliography

Baxter, Maurice G. *One and Inseparable: Daniel Webster and the Union*. Cambridge, Mass.: Harvard University Press, 1984. A superb, in-depth biography of one of Taney's most formidable political opponents, who frequently argued cases before the Supreme Court during much of Taney's time as chief justice. Provides a different view of the Taney years on the Court.

Crane, Gregg D. "The Lexicon of Rights, Power, and Community in 'Blake': Martin R. Delaney's Dissent from 'Dred Scott.' " *American Literature* 68, no. 3 (September, 1996). Crane discusses Delaney's dissenting opinion on Chief Justice Taney's *Dred Scott* decision, including the conflict between Delaney's denunciation of Taney's racist views and his agreement on the issue of rights as an entitlement of power.

Fehrenbacher, Don E. *The Dred Scott Case: Its Significance in American Law and Politics*. New York: Oxford University Press, 1978. This excellent example of historical writing is a serious and detailed scholarly account of the *Dred Scott* case, with considerable attention given to the whole range of issues facing the United States on the eve of the Civil War.

Friedman, Lawrence M. *A History of American Law*. 2d ed. New York: Simon and Schuster, 1985. A readable yet scholarly history of American law from Colonial times to 1900, with a short epilogue on the twentieth century. Mentions the impact of the Taney Court, but there is very little about Taney personally.

Horwitz, Morton J. *The Transformation of American Law, 1780-1860*. Cambridge, Mass.: Harvard University Press, 1977. Probably the best single volume on the history of American law of the era yet written. Emphasis is on the transformation of English law in the Colonies into a modern national legal system and how this transformation aided economic development. Mentions Taney only briefly.

Hyman, Harold M., and William Wiecek. *Equal Justice Under Law: Constitutional Development, 1835-1875*. New York: Harper, 1982. A thorough and scholarly treatment of constitutional history from 1835 to 1875. The early chapters include discussions of the decisions of the Taney Court.

Kelly, Alfred H., Winfred A. Harbison, and Herman Belz. *The American Constitution: Its Origins and Development*. 7th ed. New York and London: Norton, 1991. An excellent single-volume constitutional history of the United States. Emphasis on cultural and historical influences. Includes mention of Taney and the Supreme Court's decisions during his tenure as chief justice, but covers little of his personal life.

Kutler, Stanley I. *Privilege and Creative Destruction: The Charles River Bridge Case*. Philadelphia: Lippincott, 1971. An excellent short discussion of the *Charles River Bridge* case, its background, and Taney's reasons for the decision. Little concern for Taney's personal life.

Newmyer, R. Kent. *The Supreme Court Under Marshall and Taney*. New York: Crowell, 1968. A succinct but thorough and perceptive study of the Taney Court in the context of the people and events of the times. The Taney chapters concentrate on his tenure as chief justice.

Swisher, Carl Brent. *Roger B. Taney*. New York: Macmillan, 1935. This is the only scholarly biography of Taney, and, although dated, it is very well done and useful. The author explains Taney's constitutional principles within the context of his experience and heritage.

Richard L. Hillard

ZACHARY TAYLOR

Born: November 24, 1784; Orange County, Virginia
Died: July 9, 1850; Washington, D.C.
Areas of Achievement: Government and military affairs
Contribution: Climaxing a military career of nearly forty years with major victories in the Mexican War, Taylor used his popularity as a war hero to win office as twelfth president of the United States.

Early Life

Zachary Taylor was born November 24, 1784, at Montebello, a kinsman's country home in Orange County, Virginia. He was the third of eight children born to Richard and Sarah Dabney Strother Taylor, both members of prominent Virginia families. Richard Taylor was a lieutenant colonel in a Virginia regiment during the American Revolution; his father, also named Zachary Taylor, was a wealthy planter and surveyor general of Virginia.

During 1769 and 1770, Richard Taylor surveyed land in central Kentucky and around the Falls of the Ohio at the modern city of Louisville. In the spring of 1785, shortly after Zachary's birth, Richard Taylor moved his family to Jefferson County, Kentucky, where he carved out a farm known as Springfield, near Louisville. As a youth, Zachary studied under Kean O'Hara, who would become one of Kentucky's leading early nineteenth century educators, and Elisha Ayer, an itinerant Connecticut teacher. He also assisted his father with farm work.

In 1806, possessing a youthful passion for a military career, Taylor got a brief taste of army life as a volunteer in the Kentuckian militia. His long career as an officer did not commence until June, 1808, however, when he received a commission as first lieutenant in the United States Army from Secretary of War Henry Dearborn. Appointed to the Seventh Infantry Regiment, he spent several months on recruiting duty in Kentucky, followed by temporary command of Fort Pickering, near modern Memphis, Tennessee, before reporting to General James Wilkinson at New Orleans in June, 1809. A short time later, he contracted yellow fever and returned to Louisville to recover. While at home, he met Margaret Mackall Smith, whom he married on June 21, 1810. They had six children, four of whom lived to maturity. Their daughter Sarah Knox Taylor was the first wife of Confederate president Jefferson Davis. Richard Taylor, their only son, became a lieutenant general in the Confederate army.

After his recovery and marriage, Taylor was promoted to captain and assigned to General William Henry Harrison, territorial governor of Indiana. In April, 1812, just before the War of 1812, Captain Taylor assumed command of Fort Harrison, near Terre Haute, which he successfully defended against an attack by some four hundred Indians the following September. Promoted to the rank of brevet major, he commanded several frontier posts during the second war with England.

In early 1815, Taylor won promotion to the full rank of major, but when the army was disbanded, he was reduced to his prewar rank of captain. Deciding to pursue private business, he declined reassignment, resigned his commission, and returned to his family's Kentucky farm.

Now thirty years old, Taylor epitomized neither the country gentleman nor the military hero. Five feet, eight inches in height, he was muscular and broad-shouldered with disproportionately long arms. He had a full-shaped head with an oval face, a wide, somewhat slanting brow, and prominent cheekbones. His long nose and hazel eyes gave him an eaglelike appearance.

Life's Work

Zachary Taylor was devoted to the soil, but his passion for military service was even stronger. Thus, in 1816, when President James Madison offered to reinstate him at his previous rank of major, Taylor accepted. His initial assignment was command of Fort Howard, near Green Bay, Wisconsin, where he remained for two years. After a furlough in Kentucky, he received a promotion to lieutenant colonel in 1819 and was assigned to the Fourth Infantry at New Orleans. A series of commands and special assignments followed over the next twelve years. In 1822, he built Fort Jesup, Louisiana, and the following year, he served as commandant of Baton Rouge. In 1824, he was appointed superintendent general of the recruiting service at Cincinnati and Louisville and served until 1826, when he reported to Washington, D.C., to serve on a board chaired by General Winfield Scott to study militia organization. In May, 1828, Taylor assumed command of Fort Snelling, in the unorganized Minnesota territory. Fourteen months later, he took command of

Fort Crawford at Prairie du Chien in the Michigan Territory, now part of Wisconsin. There he remained until mid-1830.

In April, 1832, Taylor was promoted to colonel. Meanwhile, the Black Hawk War had erupted in Illinois. Colonel Taylor, on leave in Kentucky after recovering from an illness, sped to Galena, Illinois, and in May took charge of the First Infantry Regiment, under command of General Henry Atkinson. Three months later, Taylor participated in the decisive Battle of Bad Axe on the Mississippi River, north of Prairie du Chien. Black Hawk escaped the battlefield but was captured in late August. Taylor received custody of the defeated war chief and turned him over to Second Lieutenant Jefferson Davis, who escorted Black Hawk to Jefferson Barracks, Missouri.

With the end of the Black Hawk War, Taylor resumed command of Fort Crawford, where he remained until November, 1836. During this duty, he demonstrated a strong interest in the education of both white and Indian children and attempted to control the harsh practices of whiskey merchants and fur traders in their dealings with the tribes in the region. Upon relinquishing his command at Fort Crawford, the colonel reported to Jefferson Barracks and took charge of the right wing of the army's Western Department under General Edmund P. Gaines. In this capacity, Taylor exercised military authority over the entire Northwest.

His new command lasted less than eight months. In July, 1837, Taylor received instructions to take elements of the First Infantry from Forts Snelling and Crawford to Tampa Bay, Florida, where General Thomas S. Jesup was bogged down in the Second Seminole War. While the colonel was en route, Jesup violated a temporary truce and captured Seminole leader Osceola and about two hundred of his followers—but hundreds more waited deep in the Everglades.

Taylor and his troops arrived in Florida in the fall, and the colonel took command in the field. In early December, 1837, after weeks of preparation, Taylor left Fort Gardiner with a force of more than one thousand regular and volunteer troops. Pursuing the Seminoles into the vicinity of Lake Okeechobee, Taylor made contact with a large force on Christmas Day. In a fierce battle that cost the lives of several of his top officers, Taylor routed the Seminoles and drove them from the field. The victory won for Taylor a promotion to brevet brigadier general, and a short time later, he re-

placed General Jesup as commander of the Florida theater.

General Taylor remained in Florida for two more years before assuming command at Baton Rouge. The following year, Taylor succeeded General Matthew Arbuckle as commander of the Second Department, Western Division, headquartered at Fort Smith, Arkansas. There, he remained until May, 1844, when he returned to Fort Jesup to assume command of the First Department. In June, 1845, after the United States annexed Texas, he received orders to move his troops to Corpus Christi, on the Nueces River, to protect the new state in case of attack by Mexico. The following January, President James K. Polk ordered Taylor to move to the Rio Grande, occupying territory whose possession was a source of dispute. In late March, Taylor established a position opposite the Mexican town of Matamoros. A month later, several American soldiers were killed in a skirmish with Mexican troops. On May 13, 1846, Congress declared war on Mexico.

Taylor, however, did not wait for the declaration of war. On May 8, he engaged and defeated a much larger Mexican force at Palo Alto. The next day, he defeated the Mexicans again at Resaca de la Palma. As a result, Polk promoted him to major general and gave him command of the Army of the Rio Grande. More victories followed as he captured Monterrey in September and crushed a force under General Antonio Lopez de Santa Anna at Buena Vista in February, 1847.

With the end of the Mexican War, Taylor returned to the United States, receiving a hero's welcome at New Orleans in December, 1847. A short time later, he retired to his home in Baton Rouge and began tending to the affairs of Cypress Grove, the Mississippi plantation he had acquired a few years earlier. His retirement was brief. In 1848, the Whig Party, starved for victory, nominated the military hero for president and secured his election over Democrat Lewis Cass and Free-Soiler Martin Van Buren.

Although a slaveholder, President Taylor was a staunch Unionist. Faced with the volatile issue of slavery in the territories acquired from Mexico, he supported California's admission as a free state in 1849 and the organization of New Mexico and Utah without consideration of the slavery issue. When Congress convened in January, 1850, Senator Henry Clay proposed a series of compromise resolutions designed to defuse these and related issues, including a Texas-New Mexico border dispute, the fugitive slave question, and the future of the slave trade in Washington, D.C. While Congress debated the Compromise of 1850, delegates from nine Southern states met in Nashville in June to consider the defense of Southern rights and their section's future within the Union. Moderate voices prevailed, but more radical "Fire-eaters" raised the specter of secession. Taylor, however, continued to resist any compromise that would promote the expansion of slavery and promised to meet disunionist threats with force.

The political deadlock remained on July 4, when Taylor attended a ceremony related to construction of the Washington Monument. He became overheated and, according to tradition, tried to cool off by consuming large quantities of cherries and iced milk. That evening he contracted gastroenteritis, from which he died on July 9.

Summary

In many respects, Zachary Taylor symbolized both the aspirations and the anxieties of the American people during the mid-nineteenth century. In a period pervaded by the spirit of Manifest Destiny, his victories in the Mexican War contributed to the nation's acquisition of a vast new territory, including the future states of California, New Mexico, Arizona, Nevada, and Utah. Only four days before his death, President Taylor signed the Clayton-Bulwer Treaty with England, the first diplomatic step toward construction of the Panama Canal.

As president, however, the victor of Buena Vista had to deal with the practical consequences of Manifest Destiny. As both a Unionist and a plantation owner with more than one hundred slaves, he embodied the conflicting social and economic forces which confronted the nation during the decade before the Civil War, especially citizens of the border states and Upper South. In Taylor's case, Unionist sentiments formed during four decades in the nation's military service triumphed over his own economic interests. During the decade that followed his death, however, a growing number of his fellow Southerners resolved the conflict between slavery and Union in the opposite direction. When the election of Abraham Lincoln as president in 1860 convinced many Southerners that they no longer could protect their "peculiar institution" within the Union, they chose secession. They elected as their president Zachary Taylor's friend and former son-in-law, Jefferson Davis.

Bibliography

Bauer, K. Jack. *Zachary Taylor: Soldier, Planter, Statesman of the Old Southwest.* Baton Rouge: Louisiana State University Press, 1985. This well-researched, well-written volume is the first account of Taylor's life to appear since 1951. Particularly useful for the general reader, Bauer's work gives a balanced view of Taylor's early life, military career, and brief presidency.

De Voto, Bernard A. *The Year of Decision, 1846.* Boston: Little Brown, 1943; London: Eyre and Spottiswoode, 1957. Taylor fares poorly in this spectacular, almost theatrical saga of America's westward march. From the Mexican War to the Mormon emigration to Utah, De Voto captures the profound national emotions that undergirded Manifest Destiny.

Hamilton, Holman. *Zachary Taylor: Soldier of the Republic.* Indianapolis, Ind.: Bobbs-Merrill, 1941. Volume 1 of Hamilton's magisterial biography, this remains the best single book on Taylor's early life and military career. Thoroughly researched and highly readable, it is sympathetic yet balanced, especially in regard to Taylor's dealings with his military and political rivals.

———. *Zachary Taylor: Soldier in the White House*. Indianapolis, Ind.: Bobbs-Merrill, 1951. A worthy companion to the preceding volume, this book explores the brief but important tenure of the nation's last slaveholding president. Thoroughly researched, it demonstrates that Taylor was a much more active president than is commonly believed.

Heard, Alex. "Exhumed Innocent: The Grave-Digging Craze." *The New Republic* 205, no. 6 (August 5, 1991). Examines the trend involving the exhumation of famous figures, the circumstances of whose deaths have been questioned. Includes Taylor and others proposed.

Jackson, Jack. "General Taylor's 'Astonishing' Map of Northeastern Mexico." *Southwestern Historical Quarterly* 101, no. 2 (October, 1997). Discusses how the miltary value of maps was discovered by Taylor in his successful military campaign during the U.S.-Mexican War of 1845-1848.

Potter, David M. *The Impending Crisis, 1848-1861*. Completed and edited by Don E. Fehrenbacher. New York: Harper, 1976. Taylor is one of the many important figures who appear in this excellent narrative of the political events leading from the Mexican War to the outbreak of the Civil War. An outstanding contextual volume, it synthesizes the vast literature dealing with the complex issues of slavery, expansionism, and sectional politics.

Singletary, Otis A. *The Mexican War*. Chicago: University of Chicago Press, 1960. This concise treatment of the war which climaxed American continental expansion is both historically sound and quite readable. Its emphasis is on military events and political intrigues at the expense of diplomatic relations between the United States and Mexico.

Weinberg, Albert K. *Manifest Destiny: A Study of Nationalist Expansionism in American History*. Baltimore: John Hopkins University Press, 1935. Zachary Taylor's name does not appear in this analytical study of American expansion from the Louisiana Purchase to the Spanish-American War, but the book is essential to understanding the policy motives behind the military ventures in which he participated.

Carl E. Kramer

PETER ILICH TCHAIKOVSKY

Born: May 7, 1840; Votkinsk (Vyatka district), Russia
Died: November 6, 1893; St. Petersburg, Russia
Area of Achievement: Music
Contribution: Tchaikovsky is one of the most popular Western composers. His soaring melodies, expressive supporting harmonies, and lush orchestration have made his concertos and later symphonies the epitome of late Romantic musical opulence.

Early Life

Peter Ilich Tchaikovsky, the son of a mining engineer, received a good education as a child through his French governess, Fanny Dürbach, and his piano teacher, Mariya Palchikova. In 1848, his father retired and moved to St. Petersburg, where Tchaikovsky entered the preparatory program of the School of Jurisprudence in 1850, graduating nine years later. His mother, from whom he inherited his sensitivity, died in 1854. Tchaikovsky remained close to his father and siblings, five brothers and a sister, especially to his younger twin brothers, Anatoly and Modest.

Tchaikovsky accepted a position as a clerk in the Ministry of Justice in 1859, and in 1861 he began studies at the Russian Musical Society, which was transformed into the St. Petersburg Conservatory in 1862 under Anton Rubinstein. Tchaikovsky resigned his government position in the following year to become a full-time student at the conservatory, studying composition and orchestration with Rubinstein. He was graduated, with a silver medal in composition, in 1865. In the following year, he began his duties as a teacher of harmony at the newly founded conservatory in Moscow, headed by Anton Rubinstein's brother Nikolay.

Life's Work

Tchaikovsky's musical development was late in comparison to that of such composers as Ludwig van Beethoven, Franz Schubert, Robert Schumann, or Frédéric Chopin: The main compositions from his twenties are the song "None but the Lonely Heart," which contains the quintessential Tchaikovskyan melody in accompaniment to a text written by Johann Wolfgang von Goethe, and the uneven First Symphony in G Minor, subtitled *Winter Daydreams*. The first version of *Romeo and Juliet,* a fantasy overture based on William Shakespeare's tragedy, was finished in 1869, although the final version was not completed until 1880; this is the first of his orchestral works to be part of the standard repertory.

The works of Tchaikovsky's thirties include the second, third, and fourth symphonies; three string quartets (the first contains the famous "Andante cantabile," based on a Ukranian folk song that Tchaikovsky collected on a summer holiday in Kamenka in 1865); the first piano concerto (the introduction to the first movement is perhaps Tchaikovsky's best-known melody); and a violin concerto. The piano concerto received its premiere in the United States. Also from these years is his finest opera, *Yevgeny Onyegin* (Eugene Onegin), based on the poem by Alexander Pushkin; it is a psychological drama rather than a grand opera or mythological drama and showed that there was an alternative path to Richard Wagner's music dramas in the serious musical theater. Other major works include his orchestral fantasy *Francesca da Rimini* and the ballet *Swan Lake*.

The 1870's were the years in which Tchaikovsky began to establish his international musical reputation, but they were tragic for him personally. In 1868, he met the Belgian soprano Désirée Artôt, four years his senior, and began a courtship which was terminated first by his doubts about marriage and then by her sudden marriage to another singer in the touring opera company of which she was a member. In 1877, he married Antonina Milyukova, a young woman whom he scarcely knew; biographers have speculated that his real reason for his marriage was to quiet the rumors of homosexuality, which may have been manifested during his student days at the School of Jurisprudence. The marriage to Milyukova was a disaster, never consummated, and it eventually ended in divorce in 1881 after she bore another man an illegitimate child.

Further rumors about homosexual affairs at the Moscow Conservatory may have caused Tchaikovsky to resign his professorship there at the end of 1878. A more likely explanation is that Tchaikovsky came increasingly to resent the demands that teaching made on the time he wished to devote to composition. The advent of a mysterious patroness, Nadezhda von Meck, who provided him with a generous subsidy on the condition that they never meet (although they exchanged a voluminous cor-

respondence), gave Tchaikovsky financial independence for twelve years.

The six years afterward were less productive ones for the composer. The main works of this relatively fallow period were the opera *Orleanskaya Dyeva*, after Friedrich Schiller's drama *Die Jungfrau von Orleans* (1801; *The Maid of Orleans*, 1835), a fanciful historical drama about Joan of Arc; the Piano Trio in A Minor, an elegy for Nikolay Rubinstein; and the serenade for string orchestra.

Tchaikovsky was not a member of the circle of composers around Mili Balakirev, the *Moguchkaya Kuchka* (mighty handful), which included Modest Mussorgsky and Nikolay Rimsky-Korsakov, but he did receive advice from Balakirev on *Romeo and Juliet* and on the work marking Tchaikovsky's creative renewal, the program symphony *Manfred*, based on a poem by George Gordon, Lord Byron, featuring the wanderings and unfulfilled love of an alienated outsider. Tchaikovsky finished the work in 1885; it belongs to that small group of literary program symphonies that includes Hector Berlioz's *Symphonie fantastique* and *Harold in Italy* and Franz Liszt's *Faust Symphony*. The four movements depict, respectively, Manfred's wanderings and his memories of his beloved Astarte; Manfred's encounter with the witch of the Alps; a pastoral slow movement where Manfred encounters the inhabitants of the Swiss mountains; and a final movement first depicting the court of the demon Ahriman, then featuring Manfred's forgiveness by Astarte and his peaceful death. The work is Tchaikovsky's orchestral masterpiece, but it is not performed frequently because of its length and technical difficulty.

Among the other works marking Tchaikovsky's creative renewal are the Fifth Symphony, his most popular work, in which he follows the technique of *Manfred* in having a "motto theme" appear in all four movements of the work in various transformations; the pleasant string sextet "Souvenir of Florence"; and his other major opera, *Pikovaya Dama* (*The Queen of Spades*), based on a story by Alexander Pushkin as adapted by Tchaikovsky's brother Modest. Despite its macabre topic, the opera has been one of Tchaikovsky's most popular.

Tchaikovsky's last few years were marked by outward success and constant travel, but deep inner conflicts. He was the first major composer to visit the United States, conducting his music in April and May of 1891 (especially the first piano concer-

to) in New York, Baltimore, and Philadelphia and visiting Washington, D.C., and Niagara Falls. He was very pleased at the acclaim and hospitality he received, but he was torn with homesickness for Russia. In the following year, he received an honorary doctor of music degree from the University of Cambridge in England. His outward honors were canceled in his mind by fits of despair, fears that his creativity was exhausted and that he was repeating himself musically, and compulsive travel marked by spells of homesickness during which he would cancel concerts to return to Russia. His two main last works, however, reveal the disparity in his creative impulses: the Sixth Symphony (called, after his death, the *Pathétique* by his brother Modest), with its unusual form, ends with a despairing slow movement; while the ballet *Shchelkunchik* (*The Nutcracker*, based on a tale by E. T. A. Hoffmann), has delighted children at Christmas for decades—the suite extracted from the ballet is Tchaikovsky's most frequently performed composition.

The circumstances of Tchaikovsky's death in November, 1893, shortly after the first performance of the Sixth Symphony, are still a matter of controversy. The traditional account is that either by accident or by design (if one accepts the "suicidal" thoughts expressed in the last movement of the Sixth Symphony) the composer drank a glass of unboiled water during a cholera epidemic in St. Petersburg in late 1893. Alexandra Orlova brought to the West the story that she had heard from an elderly member of the Russian Museum staff, who claimed that the drink was actually poison and was taken to escape the possibility of a scandal brought on by a homosexual encounter. More recently a less lurid theory has been advanced: Tchaikovsky did ingest contaminated food or water during the cholera epidemic, but his doctor misdiagnosed his ailment until it was too late to institute a regimen of proper treatment.

Summary

Tchaikovsky composed effectively in virtually every musical genre of the late nineteenth century: symphony, opera, ballet, art song, concerto, chamber music, and even church music (his Russian Orthodox church music, especially the Vespers of 1882, includes some of the finest examples of the genre), though his solo piano music is the least effective of his works. He worshiped Wolfgang Amadeus Mozart's music and esteemed his French contemporaries—such as Georges Bizet, Léo Delibes, and Camille Saint-Saëns—over such German composers as Richard Wagner and Johannes Brahms, whose music he particularly disliked (Brahms reciprocated this feeling).

Tchaikovsky's musical development is more comparable to the spiral (as his brother Modest suggested) than to the straight-line development of a Beethoven or Schubert. Particularly striking elements of his style are his soaring melodies, his effective use of the orchestra, his rich supporting harmony (which in many respects recalls the devices of Liszt), and his experiments with musical form. Though not particularly close to the Russian nationalist composers, he could use Russian folk songs as effectively as any of them, as best seen in the finale of his Second Symphony.

His extensive travels in the West and his formal training in Western compositional techniques at the St. Petersburg Conservatory have given rise to the mistaken idea that he was Western rather than Russian in his musical orientation; yet he considered himself Russian above all, and he is still honored as a national treasure in the Soviet Union. Tchaikovsky has been faulted by critics for his piling of climax upon climax in an almost frenzied and hysterical manner (the development section of the first movement of the Fourth Symphony, for example), his compositional technique of seeming to stitch blocks of music together, and an almost blatant vulgarity (the finale of the Fifth Symphony), but Beethoven, Giuseppe Verdi, and Gustav Mahler have been accused of vulgarity also.

Tchaikovsky set the standard for the large-scale epic symphony, bravura concerto, and dramatic ballet among Russian and Soviet composers, and he is often the composer through whom many young persons are first attracted to art music. He remains one of the few composers for whom programs devoted entirely to his music attract a sizable audience. His popularity among the general musical audience shows no sign of waning, and recent critical studies have elevated his stature to that of one of the major composers of the late nineteenth century.

Bibliography

Abraham, Gerald, ed. *The Music of Tchaikovsky.* New York: Norton, 1946. A series of ten essays by specialists on various aspects of Tchaikovsky's life and work. Edward Lockspeiser's account of "Tchaikovsky the Man" is of special interest for the general reader, though all the essays are oriented more toward music lovers than musical scholars.

Brown, David. "Pyotr Il'yich Tchaikovsky." In *Russian Masters 1: Glinka, Borodin, Balakirev, Musorgsky, Tchaikovsky.* London: Macmillan, and New York: Norton, 1986. The entry is essentially Brown's article on Tchaikovsky's life and works in *The New Grove* dictionary with additions. The article provides the best short survey of the composer's life and works, though it is flawed by the author's uncritical acceptance of Orlova's lurid account of Tchaikovsky's suicide. The list of works and bibliography are especially complete.

———. *Tchaikovsky: A Biographical and Critical Study.* Vol. 1, *The Early Years (1840-1874).* London: Gollancz, and New York: Norton, 1978. The most complete account of the composer's boyhood and youth, with critical discussions of his works of the period. The graphic analyses provide easy-to-grasp diagrams of the musical structure of these compositions.

———. *Tchaikovsky: A Biographical and Critical Study.* Vol. 2, *The Crisis Years (1874-1878).* London: Gollancz, and New York: Norton, 1983. The turbulent years of the composer's first compositions to gain international acceptance, coupled with the crucial events of his life during this period, are extensively discussed. The analyses of his music are not quite as detailed in Brown's other works and are flawed by some forced and unconvincing attempts to find thematic interrelationships. Two additional volumes are in preparation.

Kearney, Leslie, ed. *Tchaikovsky and His World.* Princeton, N.J.: Princeton University Press, 1998. A collection of essays emphasizing Tchaikovsky's later life and influence. Included are a number of the composer's own writings about music, published here for the first time in English.

Orlova, Alexandra. "Tchaikovsky: The Last Chapter." *Music and Letters* 62 (1981): 125. This article contains the basic statement (though the author has since modified some of her arguments) of the sensational account of Tchaikovsky's supposed suicide after his trial by a court of honor composed of alumni of the School of Jurisprudence.

Poznansky, Alexander. *Tchaikovsky's Last Days: A Documentary Study.* Oxford: Clarendon Press, and New York: Oxford University Press, 1996. The official account of Tchaikovsky's death from cholera has been disputed by those who claim he committed suicide to avoid having his homosexuality discovered. Poznansky, privy to the Tchaikovsky archives in Klin, Russia, provides an accurate account of the composer's last weeks and death, finding no evidence of a cause other than cholera.

———. "Tchaikovsky's Suicide: Myth and Reality." *Nineteenth-Century Music* 11 (1988). In an extensively documented study, the author refutes Orlova's argument that Tchaikovsky committed suicide and posits the thesis that the composer's death was the result of his doctor's misdiagnosis and that proper treatment was begun too late.

Wiley, Roland John. *Tchaikovsky's Ballets*. Oxford: Clarendon Press, and New York: Oxford University Press, 1985. This study examines the music of Tchaikovsky's three grand ballets—*Swan Lake*, *Sleeping Beauty*, and *The Nutcracker*—and also investigates the circumstances surrounding their composition, their original and subsequent productions, and the audiences for these ballets.

Yoffe, Elkhonon, ed. *Tchaikovsky in America: The Composer's Visit in 1891*. Translated by Lidya Yoffe. New York: Oxford University Press, 1986. Copious excerpts from Tchaikovsky's diaries, correspondence, and news accounts of the time of Tchaikovsky's visits to New York, Baltimore, and Philadelphia in 1891, and the abortive ventures to bring him to the United States for subsequent tours.

Rey M. Longyear

TECUMSEH

Born: c. 1768; Old Piqua, western Ohio

Died: October 5, 1813; Thames River, southeastern Canada

Area of Achievement: Native American leadership

Contribution: Leading Indians of the Old Northwest in a united defense against the intrusion of white settlers, Tecumseh contributed significantly to the development of pan-Indianism in American history.

Early Life

In the Shawnee village of Old Piqua on the Mad River of what is modern western Ohio, Tecumseh was born to Methoataske, a Creek Indian woman. Her Shawnee husband, Puckeshinwa, had met her earlier, while staying with Creek Indians in Alabama. When Tecumseh was still a very young boy, Virginians began pushing into Kentucky onto lands used extensively for hunting by the Shawnee. The Indians resisted, and in 1774, Virginia Governor Lord John Dunmore led troops into the area. Puckeshinwa died in one of the subsequent battles, leaving support of his family in the hands of relatives and in those of a war chief named Blackfish from a nearby village.

During the American Revolution, the Shawnee again went to war against whites. In 1779, local Kentuckians wrongly accused several Shawnee, including a popular leader known as Cornstalk, of some recent killings and senselessly killed them. The intense fighting that followed eventually led about a thousand members of the tribe to move for a time to southeastern Missouri. Methoataske was one of the migrants, but Tecumseh and his seven brothers and sisters did not accompany their mother. Instead, other family members took the children. Tecumseh moved in with his sister Tecumpease and her husband and eventually developed a very close relationship with his older sibling. The muscular young Shawnee also became popular among his peers, distinguishing himself in games and in shooting skills. At age fifteen, Tecumseh experienced his first battle. American pioneers again started flooding onto Shawnee lands near the end of the Revolution, many of them crossing the Appalachian Mountains and then descending the Ohio River in flatboats. In 1783, the young warrior accompanied his brother Chiksika on a war party in an effort to stop the flatboat traffic.

After winning independence, Americans considered themselves the owners of lands formerly claimed by Great Britain, including the Old Northwest (the area bordered by the Appalachian Mountains on the east, the Mississippi River on the west, the Ohio River on the south, and Canada on the north, comprising the modern states of Ohio, Indiana, Illinois, Wisconsin, and Michigan). Kentuckians attacked Shawnee villages in 1786 after blaming that group for raids actually launched by the Mingoes and Cherokee in opposition to settlement west of the Appalachians. The Shawnee hit back, with Tecumseh frequently taking part in the fighting. In 1787, he joined a war party led by his brother that went south and helped Cherokee attack settlements in Tennessee and southern Kentucky. Chiksika was killed in the action. The death of his brother greatly intensified Tecumseh's hatred for the expansionistic whites, and he stayed in the area for the next two years, seeking vengeance.

With Chiksika no longer in a position of leadership, Tecumseh was able to assert himself. Five feet, ten inches tall, with a powerful physical presence and a dynamic speaking ability, he quickly gained a large following, especially among the younger, more antiwhite members of his tribe. By the time the group of Shawnee warriors returned to the Old Northwest in 1790, Tecumseh had emerged as a popular war chief. In addition to his outstanding skills in warfare, however, he also gained a reputation for being kind and good-humored. He frequently demonstrated compassion for those who were weakest or least privileged and an aversion to the torture or murder of prisoners. These qualities made him exceptional at a time when indiscriminate brutality was common on both sides in frontier warfare.

Life's Work

Upon his return to the Old Northwest, Tecumseh found his antiwhite sentiments increasingly in tune with those of many Indians in the region. Settlers had been pouring into the southeastern Ohio River valley, and the frontier again erupted into violence. In the early 1790's, the United States government sent armies in on two occasions in attempts to counter Indian resistance, but in both cases, tribes united to hand the whites embarrassing defeats. Together with the prodding of the British to the north in Canada, these victories encouraged tribes to join in a common political front to negotiate a permanent Indian state in the Old Northwest. Differences among the groups, however, prevented success in the effort. The United States then tried a third time for a military solution, sending an army under Major General Anthony Wayne. This time the results were different, with the Americans claiming victory in the 1794 Battle of Fallen Timbers. The next year, some of the defeated Indians signed the Treaty of Greenville, giving up more than two-thirds of what became Ohio.

Tecumseh fought well in the last two of the three famous battles for control of the Old Northwest and thus added to his growing reputation. He refused to accept the outcome of the Treaty of Greenville, however, and soon was recognized as the dominant leader of those Indians who resolved to put an end to any further white incursions into the region. Over the next decade, Tecumseh and his followers traveled and lived throughout Ohio and Indiana. Then, in 1805, one of his brothers, who had failed at nearly everything he had attempted, claimed to have died, to have been taken to the Master of Life, and to have been appointed to lead his people to salvation. He renounced liquor and launched a fundamentalist spiritual movement that encouraged Indians to reject white influence and return to traditional values. He promised believers that the happier times of the past would be restored. He was known as Tenskwatawa, or the Prophet, and after Tecumseh's conversion to the new faith, the two brothers moved first to Greenville in western Ohio and eventually to Tippecanoe Creek in Indiana. There, in a village that would be named Prophet's Town, Indians from throughout the Old Northwest came to live and join the movement, including Wyandot, Kickapoo, Potawatomi, Miami, Wea, and Delaware.

American officials such as William Henry Harrison, governor of the Indiana Territory, watched events with apprehension. Harrison was well-known for making treaties with individual tribes and winning much land for the government at low prices and through means that were not always ethical. In fact, his practices had deepened the anti-white attitudes of many younger Indians who resented the loss of homelands and led them to join the Prophet's movement. Then, in 1809, Harrison gathered chiefs friendly to the government and convinced them to cede more than three million acres of land in the Treaty of Fort Wayne. This event quickly elevated the status and position of

Tecumseh, who had been developing a position that rejected the legitimacy of recent controversial treaties. Land was commonly owned by all tribes, according to the Shawnee war chief, and could not be sold individually.

Tecumseh traveled throughout the Old Northwest and even into the South, trying to win support for a political and military confederacy that would join many tribes under his leadership to stop white expansion. Then, just as Tecumseh was experiencing some success, Governor Harrison took advantage of his absence from Prophet's Town and in November of 1811 marched an army to within two miles of the Indian village. Tenskwatawa had been left in charge and decided to take the initiative and attack first. The subsequent Battle of Tippecanoe was not a dramatic Indian defeat, but the defenders withdrew and allowed the whites to destroy Prophet's Town. Tecumseh returned, broke with his brother in anger over the way he had handled the situation, and struggled to put his broken movement back together. The coordinated attack that Tecumseh had hoped would stop the onrush of settlers became a series of random raids across the frontier. Many Americans blamed the British for the violence because they supplied the Indians with arms. This became one of several events that contributed to the outbreak of the War of 1812 against Great Britain. Tecumseh and many of his followers joined the British because the former mother country had tried several times to control American expansion and thus offered Indians the best hope for retaining their homelands. Tecumseh fought in a number of battles and was eventually killed in Canada on October 5, 1813, at the Battle of the Thames.

Summary

In the last half of the eighteenth century, white expansion undermined the livelihood and life-style of Indians in the Old Northwest. Settlers destroyed game, treaties (many of them fraudulent or at least questionable) eroded the Indian land base, and alcohol disrupted social arrangements. Tribes grew dependent on European trade goods and eventually were used as pawns in the rivalries between the European superpowers over dominance in North America. The result was an almost constant state of war. This, in turn, elevated the importance of war chiefs among groups such as the Shawnee, who traditionally had separate political leadership for war and for peace.

As a war chief, Tecumseh emerged into a position of leadership in this environment. The movement that he would lead started as a primarily spiritual one under his brother, the Prophet. Tecumseh secularized and politicized the movement as Indians, under intense pressure to give up their lands, were increasingly attracted to his vision for stemming the tide of white advance. He encouraged Native American groups to forget their traditional hostilities toward one another and join in a common military and political effort. This position is referred to as Indian nationalism, or pan-Indianism, and has been one of the most significant developments in the long term of Indian history. Identification on the basis of being Indian with less emphasis on tribal divisions remains a strong force in Native American affairs in the late twentieth century. Other Indian leaders before Tecumseh had attempted intertribal alliances but on more limited scales and without much success. Even though he was a brilliant strategist, Tecumseh's movement ultimately failed in its immediate objectives as well. Yet he undoubtedly contributed as much toward the evolution of pan-Indianism as any other single historical figure.

Tecumseh has enjoyed more admiration and respect, even among his contemporary foes, than any other Native American leader. As a result, he has attained an unparalleled status in legend and mythology. Evidence of this can be seen not only in the many biographies written about him but also in the many spurious or exaggerated stories about his life that have gained popularity and fooled even some of the best historians who have written about him.

Bibliography

Eckert, Allan W. *A Sorrow in Our Heart: The Life of Tecumseh*. New York: Bantam, 1992. In a wonderfully written tale based on historical fact, Eckert, a six-time Pulitzer nominee, creates a vivid picture of this soldier, hunter, and crusader. Includes a thirty-page bibliography, maps, and 115 pages of notes.

Edmunds, R. David. *The Shawnee Prophet*. Lincoln: University of Nebraska Press, 1983. Focuses on Tenskwatawa but contains much information on Tecumseh. Demonstrates how the stories of the two famous brothers are intertwined and have to be considered together and also describes the social and political milieu in which their movement thrived.

———. *Tecumseh and the Quest for Indian Leadership*. Boston: Little Brown, 1984. The best complete biography of Tecumseh. Up-to-date and scholarly, yet relatively brief and very readable. It is also the most balanced account, discussing in a concluding chapter many of the myths surrounding the Shawnee leader's life to which other historians have fallen victim.

Josephy, Alvin M., Jr. "Tecumseh, the Greatest Indian." In *The Patriot Chiefs*. New York: Penguin Books, 1961; London: Eyre and Spottiswoode, 1962. Reliable and well written, this stands as the best short summary of Tecumseh and his importance in history, although the author presents a slightly more romanticized version of the leader's life than most of the good later scholarship.

Klinck, Carl F., ed. *Tecumseh: Fact and Fiction in Early Records*. Englewood Cliffs, N.J.: Prentice-Hall, 1961. This useful anthology presents a variety of perspectives on Tecumseh's significance and on some of the controversies about his life through selections of both primary and secondary resource materials.

Oskison, John M. *Tecumseh and His Times: The Story of a Great Indian*. New York: Putnam, 1938. One of the best of the many earlier biographies of Tecumseh. It is more popular than scholarly and sometimes suffers from a style that is too romantic and ornate. Nevertheless, it is complete and generally solid.

Sugden, John. *Tecumseh: A Life*. New York: Henry Holt, 1998. The definitive biography of Tecumseh.

———. *Tecumseh's Last Stand*. Norman: University of Oklahoma Press, 1985. A very good treatment of a narrow range of Tecumseh's life. It begins in the summer of 1813 and discusses in great detail his role in the War of 1812. It also deals with some of the later controversies such as who actually killed Tecumseh and where he was buried.

Tucker, Glenn. *Tecumseh: Vision of Glory*. Indianapolis: Bobbs-Merrill, 1956. A long and basically reliable biography, but it stands as perhaps the best example of the common tendency to overromanticize Tecumseh and accept too many of the questionable myths that shroud his life.

Larry W. Burt

THOMAS TELFORD

Born: August 9, 1757; Glendinning, Scotland
Died: September 2, 1834; London, England
Area of Achievement: Civil engineering
Contribution: By building an extraordinary number of bridges, canals, harbors, roads, and waterways, Telford became one of the great engineers of his day and helped to establish the profession of civil engineering in Great Britain.

Early Life

Thomas Telford was born on August 9, 1757, in a thatched cottage, in the border country of Scotland. His father died several months later. Twenty-three years later, his only child would commemorate him with a gravestone inscribed: "In Memory of John Telford who, after living thirty three years an unblameable shepherd, died at Glendinning, November, 1757."

The shepherd's wife was soon put out of the cottage that had been provided as part of her deceased husband's salary, and she moved to a small cottage where she and her son occupied one of the two rooms. She was devoted to her son, although she did not have the means to support him. Fortunately, her brother paid the fee for Thomas to attend the parish school in Westerkirk. There the boy received some rudimentary education and made several lifelong friends.

As a very young child, Thomas helped to support himself by bird scaring, cow herding, and sheepherding. The latter took him away from home for weeks at a time. While spending long nights in the countryside, his intense love for nature and his native country grew. Before leaving the Eskdale Valley in his early twenties, he wrote a poem in its honor in which he referred to feeling "Nature's love" and rejected the "artificial joy" of urban life.

In Telford's day the primary education received by a boy was through an apprenticeship to a master of a craft. At age fourteen, his formal schooling complete, Telford was apprenticed to a stonemason who mistreated him. "Laughing Tam" was good-natured, but also well able to protect himself, and after several months he left his apprenticeship rather than stay with a cruel master. A cousin came to the rescue by arranging for an apprenticeship with another stonemason. Although he worked in a country village, a large-scale program of improvement was under way there which afforded him op-

portunities to learn his craft well as both apprentice and journeyman mason.

Telford informally continued his education throughout this period. A woman heard of his eagerness to learn and opened her small library to him. He reveled in reading John Milton's *Paradise Lost* (1667, 1674) and any other available books. Poetry and prose remained the loves of his life, to which he turned after long, hard days of labor. Many of Telford's poems were published anonymously, including one in memory of Robert Burns.

Thomas Telford was a tall, well-built man with brown, curly hair and lively, twinkling brown eyes. He was among the most sociable of men and was always quick to laugh and make others laugh with his anecdotes. Despite the ready laugh, however, little is known of this private man, who never married or shared himself freely with others.

Opportunities for work and career advancement in eighteenth century Scotland were extremely limited, so many Scots flocked to England, the British Empire, and America. After working for a year in Edinburgh, Telford joined the exodus. In January, 1782, at age twenty-four, with a borrowed pair of breeches and a horse which was to be delivered, he set out for London.

Life's Work

In London, the newcomer was soon at work building Somerset House at the end of Waterloo Bridge. Forty years later, as the world-renowned resident of the Institution of Civil Engineers, he would proudly point out the masonry that he had laid with his own hands. While laying these stones, he wrote of his ambition to a friend back in Eskdale:

> At present I am laying schemes [plans] of a pretty extensive kind. . . . My innate vanity is too apt to say when looking on the Common drudges—as well as other places—Born to command ten thousand slaves like you.

Thus, while still a stonemason, Telford already thought as a master. He formed a friendship with the best workman among his fellow workers and thought of ways for the two of them to make their fortunes. At night he read books on architecture and wrote his friend that

> knowledge is my most ardent pursuit, a thousand things occur that would pass unnoticed by good, easy people who are contented with drudging on in the

beaten path, but I am not contented unless I can reason every particular.

Although his original business plans fell through, Telford continued his hard work and studies and found other opportunities. At his next job, he assumed the role of supervisor.

The great patron of Telford's early career was Sir William Pulteney, who had originally come from the stonemason's home country. When Pulteney began a significant building program in Shrewsbury he entrusted Thomas with much of the work. Telford was soon called "young Pulteney" by the local inhabitants and greatly enhanced his reputation by defying public opinion when he predicted the collapse of a medieval church several days before it occurred. Though Telford had only good things to say about Pulteney, this very wealthy man was also extraordinarily frugal and could not have been an easy employer. The only breach between the two men occurred in 1791 when, under the reformist influence of the French Revolution, Telford occasioned a riot in Scotland by sending a copy of Thomas Paine's *The Rights of Man* (1791-1792) under Pulteney's postage frank. Telford, who sub-

sequently had little concern for politics except as they affected his projects, lost his interest in radical political change after this unsettling experience. He joined the secret, fraternal society of the Freemasons, which provided a safe outlet for his rationalistic inclinations.

Telford's first great project was the Ellesmere Canal, which connected the Mersey, Dee, and Severn rivers. The aqueduct at Pont Cysyllte was an unprecedented engineering triumph which Sir Walter Scott described as a magnificent work of art. Telford's innovative spirit is reflected in his pioneering the use of iron in the building of bridges. Although others built the first iron bridges, Telford gained public acceptance for them.

During this same period, he did a significant amount of dock, harbor, and pier building and was soon involved in building an enormous number of roads and bridges in the Highlands of Scotland. This region was suffering from the decline of the clan system and severe depopulation as sheep replaced men on the hillsides. The government was alarmed, since it feared that this great source of military recruits would soon dry up and that much of Scotland would become an economic desert. Another problem was that the sea-lanes around Scotland were so treacherous that when two ships left Newcastle on the same day, one bound for India via the English Channel and the other for Liverpool via the Scottish seas, Bombay was reached before Liverpool. Thus was born Telford's greatest challenge: the Caledonian Canal.

This extraordinary engineering triumph had been envisioned by James Watt and John Rennie but was completed by Telford. The construction went on from 1803 to 1822 and beyond, at great cost and in the face of enormous obstacles. Regrettably, the canal was not an economic success, as it cost twice as much as predicted, the size of ships increased beyond the capacity of its locks, governmental tariff policies destroyed its economic base, and the steamship and steam railroads made it obsolete.

At age fifty-one, Telford took his first sea voyage in 1808 when he traveled to Sweden to begin work on the Gotha Canal. This remarkable canal was built between 1809 and 1833 in the most inclement weather. It was primarily the work of Count Baltzar Bogislaus von Platen, who relied heavily on Telford and who honored him with a Swedish grant of nobility which the Scot, characteristically, failed to use in England. Telford returned to Britain soon after completing the canal and devoted much of his enormous energy to building roads and bridges in the North of Wales. The Menai suspension bridge was one of his greatest achievements. Another was the setting of concrete under water.

Robert Southey, the poet laureate, after taking a six-week trip with the engineer in 1819, wrote "Telford's is a happy life, everywhere making roads, building bridges, forming canals, and creating harbours [sic]." It was a nomadic existence; Telford traveled so often and widely that he did not have a permanent residence until late in his life. Wherever he went, he enjoyed warm and friendly relationships. Part of the secret of his success was his intimate knowledge of the capabilities and habits of common workers. He had a great disdain for theoretical engineers and chose his very able assistants from among his workers. He was an excellent judge of men and had a marked preference for hiring Lowland Scots. His administrative skills were excellent, as witnessed by his ability to oversee a large variety of complex, long-term projects simultaneously. His reputation for fairness, honesty, and good judgment was such that he served as the final arbiter in disputes.

Telford's ability to deal effectively with people is evident in his maintaining support for long-term, costly projects, despite the difficulties of dealing with governmental bureaucrats, to whom he referred as "insects." He was one of a number of men bringing a heightened respect to the emerging profession of civil engineering. Road building, which his great rival John Rennie disdained, was accepted by him as a worthy area of activity. Indeed, the "Colossus of Roads," unlike his contemporary John McAdams, built in the Roman manner, which lasts for centuries and even millennia. His status with engineers was such that when he joined the struggling Institution of Civil Engineers in 1820 as its first president, it became the center of the profession in Great Britain. Telford was honored with membership in the Royal Society, and in 1828 a royal charter was granted to the society he headed. He raised its intellectual level by establishing the rule that all members give an annual professional paper.

Thomas Telford's final years brought difficulties as well as honors. He was alone, having never married; in declining health; and increasingly deaf. Furthermore, the railroad mania was breeding a new group of engineers who could not understand the Scot's lack of enthusiasm for this revolutionizing mode of transportation. Though he saw the steam engine as a viable mode of transportation, Telford believed too strongly in the principle of the open road not to have doubts about the monopolistic practice of building private railroads. Though he was associated with the building of some railroads, his loyalty to canal owners also deterred him from active participation. As a result, a railroad-obsessed generation of engineers unjustly remembered him as a reactionary opponent of the technology of the future.

Telford's lifelong love of literature was reflected in his generous bequests to the English poet Southey, to the Scottish poet Thomas Campbell, and to the establishment of several libraries in Scotland. His beloved Institution for Civil Engineering and other friends received the rest of his worldly goods.

Summary

Thomas Telford epitomized the ideal of the self-made man who helped to create the economic infrastructure of industrial society. He considered the poverty of his birth to be an advantage as he worked his own way up from humble stonemason in rural Scotland to the greatest engineer of his day in London. His jovial public personality hid both his enormous professional ambition and the complexity of his private self.

Telford was a driven man. His contemporaries saw him as the "Colossus of Roads" who relentlessly built bridges, canals, harbors, roads, and waterways. The importance of the improved transportation and communications that he wrought cannot be exaggerated. Britons, especially the Scottish and Welsh, were brought within a single cultural and economic network.

The Menai Bridge in Wales and the Caledonian Canal in Scotland were monuments to his art and dedication as an engineer. The economic failure of the Caledonian Canal was caused by factors well beyond his control, since no one could foresee the manner in which the steamship and steam railroad would transform transportation. The engineer's reputation suffered severely because of his lack of enthusiasm for the railroad.

Telford made a great contribution to the rise of the profession of civil engineer. He did this in a number of ways. He set an extraordinary example, in Rickman's words, "as a soldier, always in active service," and in the enormous volume of his work and its importance for Great Britain's development. Finally, he lent his name to the presidency of the Institution of Civil Engineers and his considerable efforts to make the association a success.

Telford's legacy is visible in the numerous roads and bridges that he built that are still in service, withstanding loads that were unimaginable two centuries ago, when he designed them. It is also present in the viability of the Institution of Civil Engineers. In 1968, Telford's special contributions were recognized when an entire industrial district was named Telford in his honor.

Bibliography

Fergusson, James. "The Telford Centenary: Scotland's Debt to the Eskdale Mason." *Scots Magazine* 21 (September, 1934): 422-436. This article surveys the accomplishments, place in history, and character of this Lowland Scot. Though the conclusion that Telford was not a complex person is not borne out by the evidence, the essay is worth reading. A brief companion article on Telford's literary qualities and friendship is also noteworthy.

Gibb, Alexander. *The Story of Telford: The Rise of Civil Engineering*. London: MacLehose, 1935. This volume provides a fairly complete, chronological record of Telford's work. Though the diversity of his projects is hard to follow at times, the book is still an invaluable source. The list of Telford's engineering works at the end is most helpful.

Karwatka, Dennis. "Technology's Past." *Tech Directions* 54, no. 7 (February, 1995). Profile of Telford that includes his career, achievements, and family background.

Meynell, Laurence. *Thomas Telford: The Life Story of a Great Engineer*. London: Bodley Head, 1957. This schoolboy's account is part of the Men of the Modern Age series. The author also cowrote a biography with James Brindley in 1956 using the same materials.

Pearce, Rhoda M. *Thomas Telford: An Illustrated Life of Thomas Telford, 1757-1834*. Aylesbury: Shire Publications, 1973. This forty-eight-page survey is worth examining.

Petroski, Henry. "The Public Profession." *American Scientist* 82, no. 6 (November-December, 1994). Petroski offers a balanced look at Telford and Isambard Kingdom Brunel, British engineers whose failures and false starts are rarely discussed.

Rolt, L.T.C. *Thomas Telford*. London and New York: Longman, 1958. This is a short, readable, and comprehensive biography of the father of civil engineering. Readers should begin their study with this volume, unless Telford's autobiography is available to them.

Smiles, Samuel. *Lives of the Engineers*. Vol. 2, *Thomas Telford*. London: Murray, 1862; New York: Kelley, 1968. This Victorian biographer loved to record the history of the self-made man. Telford was a perfect subject for him, and though the book is marred by a worshipful approach and a failure to examine some of the oral history it recorded, it is still readable and of value.

Telford, Thomas. *Life of Thomas Telford, Civil Engineer, Written by Himself*. Edited by John Rickman. London: Payne and Foss, 1838. Telford's longtime friend compiled this lengthy account of his labors and the beautiful companion atlas of his works. Unfortunately, it offers no real insight into Telford the man. There is little published material on his private life.

Paul H. Elovitz

ALFRED, LORD TENNYSON

Born: August 6, 1809; Somersby, Lincolnshire, England

Died: October 6, 1892; Alderworth, near Haslemere, Sussex, England

Area of Achievement: Literature

Contribution: Generally considered to be the quintessential Victorian poet, Tennyson grappled with grief in the midst of the most profound theological crisis in the history of the modern world, caused by the emergent theory of evolution. Tennyson's poetry of spiritual struggle and affirmation captured the soul of his generation.

Early Life

Alfred Tennyson was born on August 6, 1809, the fourth of George Tennyson's twelve children. His mother, née Elizabeth Fytche, was an easy-going and indulgent woman who encouraged her children's literary efforts. At the rectory, young Alfred had access to his father's twenty-five-hundred-volume scholarly library, which included books on theology, philosophy, history, classical and Oriental literature, and science. Although Tennyson was educated formally first at a village school and later at a boys' school in Louth, the majority of his pre-university instruction was received at home under his father's supervision. George Tennyson was an intellectually gifted and well-educated man whose intelligence and learning were undermined by his emotional instability. Alfred Tennyson's tempestuous and insecure home life during childhood fostered periods of despondency that were severe enough to affect adversely his physical health throughout his lifetime. Yet despite having to undertake numerous water cures for a variety of ailments which were indiscriminately identified as gout, Tennyson lived a long and productive life. Although the instability of his early years contributed to his unhappiness, it also deepened his sensitivity to the spiritual turmoil of his generation.

Six months before Tennyson commenced his studies at Cambridge University in 1827, a volume entitled *Poems by Two Brothers* was published by a Lincolnshire bookseller. It was in fact a collection by three brothers; half of the poems it contained were written by Alfred Tennyson, while the other poems were contributed by his elder brothers Frederick and Charles. The volume received little notice, but it did allow Tennyson to enter university with some confidence in his poetic ability. His physical appearance, as it was described upon his arrival at Cambridge, communicated a greater confidence than he felt. Standing more than six feet tall, he towered above his fellows, and his broad chest and massive head were imposing. His swarthy handsomeness, deep brown eyes, and long, dark, unkempt hair gave him a mysterious, romantic air. Severe shortsightedness lent him a remote gaze which was often mistaken for aloofness. His poor eyesight also contributed to his social ineptness on occasions when he would either scrutinize his companions at an awkwardly close range or else, insecure without visual cues, withdraw from general conversation entirely.

At Cambridge, in 1829, Tennyson made the most important acquaintance of his life. Arthur Henry Hallam, who had been a fellow competitor for the Chancellor's gold medal for English verse, which Tennyson won with his poem "Timbuctoo," became not only his closest friend but also his literary advocate. He encouraged Tennyson to publish his first notable collection of poetry, *Poems, Chiefly Lyrical*, in 1830 and anonymously gave it a favorable commentary in *The Englishman's Magazine* in 1831. In his review, Hallam defined Tennyson's style in terms which modern critics have described as an anticipation of Symbolist poetics. Tennyson's enduring dislike of magazine criticism began with a scathing review of *Poems, Chiefly Lyrical* in *Blackwood's Magazine* in 1832. Because of his fear of poor reviews, Tennyson was hesitant to publish new poems, a tendency which remained with him throughout his career. Yet this fear also drove him to scrupulous revision, which often improved his work.

Life's Work

Tennyson was recalled to Somersby immediately before his father's death in March, 1831, and he never returned to the university to complete his degree. The following year, at Hallam's urging, he assembled the manuscript of a volume entitled *Poems* (1832). It included a number of pieces often found in modern anthologies: "The Lady of Shalott," "Œnone," "The Palace of Art," and "The Lotos-Eaters." *Poems* was unfavorably received when it was first published, but in 1835, the philosopher John Stuart Mill wrote a review praising Tennyson's use of scenery to symbolize feeling. Mill's encouragement arrived too late, however, to offer

much comfort; when it appeared, Tennyson was still grieving Hallam's untimely death in the summer of 1833.

Tennyson composed some of his finest poems in the period following his friend's death, particularly the exquisite elegiac stanzas that were to make up the commemorative poem *In Memoriam* (1850). Lacking Hallam's energetic support, the young poet failed to publish a new volume of poetry until 1842. Between Hallam's death in 1833 and the publication of *In Memoriam* in 1850, only two books appeared: *Poems* (1842) and *The Princess* (1847). The 1842 volume incorporated revised versions of the best work he had published in 1833 along with some new poems including "Ulysses," "Break, Break, Break," and his early Arthurian piece, "Morte d'Arthur." *The Princess*, a long narrative poem, presents a rather superficial treatment of the serious Victorian issue of women's education. The conflict between a prince and a princess, whose engagement is broken when the princess decides to found a women's university, dissolves when she sees the error of her politics and returns to fulfill her promise of marriage. The resolution is achieved principally through the songs, which focus on the personal rather than the political implications of the couple's relationship. Despite its poetic imperfections, *The Princess* was a popular success.

In Memoriam established Tennyson's growing reputation as a lyric poet. The volume's short poems, in the distinctive *abba* stanza form, are arranged not by date of composition but by their place in the psychological pattern of grieving. The tone of the poems moves from frustration and anger at the indifference of Nature to man's fate toward a celebration of human love. The publication of *In Memoriam* opened new opportunities in Tennyson's personal life. The trial edition that he sent to Emily Selwood in 1849 helped to revive their broken engagement, and in 1850, after fourteen years' delay, they were married. The success of *In Memoriam* also brought royal recognition; at the end of the year, Queen Victoria made Tennyson poet laureate. Shortly before his death, the monarch awarded him a barony.

After 1850, Tennyson published many short poems, which appeared first in literary magazines and later in collected volumes. He also wrote several unsuccessful plays. His major works in this period were two long poems, *Maud and Other Poems* (1855) and *Idylls of the King* (1859-1885). Tenny-

son's first attempt at a narratively conceived poem since *The Princess, Maud* tells of a young man driven mad by thwarted love who kills his lover's brother in a duel. His act of murder and Maud's subsequent death plunge the hero into even greater despair until he redeems himself through self-sacrifice in a patriotic war. The story unfolds not in a conventional narrative but in a series of lyrics which express the hero's subjective responses to external events. The innovative style perplexed the critics, whose reviews were generally hostile. Tennyson forever maintained that *Maud* was his favorite poem, despite its miserable reception, and he became notorious for reading it aloud to company at every opportunity.

Idylls of the King is based on Sir Thomas Malory's medieval account of the Arthurian knights in his *Le Morte D'Arthur* (1485). Tennyson had first dealt with the topic in his own "Morte d'Arthur," published in *Poems*. Revised and renamed "The Passing of Arthur," it eventually appeared as the conclusion of twelve "idylls" which make up Tennyson's complete Arthurian cycle. *Idylls of the King* is a complex and occasionally brilliant narrative poem which has stimulated a remarkable amount of scholarly criticism since the mid-1960's. Although the contemporary critical response was ambivalent at best, *Idylls of the King* met with wide popular acclaim.

Summary

The self-absorbed lyricism of Alfred, Lord Tennyson's early poems, tempered by the conservative fears of social upheaval which preoccupied the poet later in life, evolved into a poetry which dealt with the important issues of his time by drawing them into a personal focus. What John Stuart Mill discussed in a philosophical treatise, *On the Subjection of Women* (1869), for example, Tennyson explored through the relations between a prince and his intellectually ambitious princess. While Tennyson's emphasis in *The Princess* on an ideal of domestic harmony that ignores the complex socioeconomic forces that shape political reality may seem myopic and naïve to a modern reader, the use of an intimate focus in *In Memoriam* is very effective. It was in personal terms that nineteenth century individuals were best able to comprehend the chaos that scientific discovery and growing industrialization had made of their worldview.

The Princess, Tennyson's first serious attempt to reconcile the social and didactic with the personal and emotive claims of poetry, earned for him not only popularity but also the financial security to proceed with his long-postponed marriage. The stellar success of *In Memoriam* three years later thrust Tennyson into a degree of fame and fortune which swelled with the interest of an increasingly literate middle-class population at home and the growing enthusiasm of his audience in the United States.

In the wake of two equally hostile poetic sensibilities (*fin de siècle* aestheticism, which denigrated the moral dimension of art, and early twentieth century modernism, which abhorred subjectivity), Tennyson's reputation suffered an unfortunate reversal. Not until the middle of the twentieth century, when modern American scholars such as W. D. Paden and Edgar F. Shannon reevaluated Tennyson's achievement, did the great Victorian begin to regain literary respectability. Since the publication of Jerome H. Buckley's seminal study in 1960, excellent modern editions have appeared along with a host of scholarly, biographical, and critical works that have reclaimed Tennyson for the twentieth century.

Bibliography

Buckley, Jerome H. *Tennyson: The Growth of a Poet.* Cambridge, Mass.: Harvard University Press, 1960. Buckley examines the external influences of the Victorian moral, social, intellectual, and scientific climate in the light of the personal details of the poet's biography to chart the growth of Tennyson's poetic sensibility.

Jump, John D., ed. *Lord Alfred Tennyson: The Critical Heritage.* New York: Barnes and Noble, 1967; London: Routledge, 1996. A significant source of criticism emphasizing contemporary responses to Tennyson's work.

Martin, Robert Bernard. *Tennyson: The Unquiet Heart.* New York: Oxford University Press, 1980. Martin's readable study draws on a wealth of published Tennyson biographies and criticism as well as unpublished letters and manuscripts.

Page, Norman. *Tennyson: Selected Poetry.* London and New York: Routledge, 1995. The author presents Tennyson as a voice for his time through examination of sixty years of his poetry. Includes a comprehensive introduction, bibliography, and extensive notes.

Palmer, D. J., ed. *Tennyson.* London: Bell, and Athens: Ohio University Press, 1973. A collection of essays, three of which are particularly interesting; "Tennyson: A Reader's Guide" gives a historical bibliographic survey of Tennyson scholarship and criticism; "Tennyson and His Public 1827-59" and "Tennyson and Victorian Social Values" provide social and literary context.

Ricks, Christopher. *Tennyson.* 2d ed. Berkeley: University of California, and London: Macmillan, 1989. The modern editor of Tennyson's poems offers a critical biography that makes use of previously inaccessible manuscripts and biographical material.

Shannon, Edgar F. *Tennyson and the Reviewers: A Study of His Literary Reputation and of the Influence of the Critics upon His Poetry, 1827-51.* Cambridge, Mass.: Harvard University Press, 1952. An examination of the dynamic relationship between Tennyson's poetry and the reviews.

Shaw, W. D. *Tennyson's Style.* Ithaca, N.Y.: Cornell University Press, 1976. An excellent study of Tennyson's poetry in the context of literary tradition in general and of Romantic and Victorian poetic theory and practice in particular.

Tennyson, Alfred. *The Poems of Tennyson.* Edited by Christopher Ricks. London and New York: Longman, 1969. The most complete and scholarly edition of Tennyson's poems. It includes one early play, *The Devil and the Lady* (wr. c. 1823), but excludes the later plays. Ricks draws on the Eversley edition, which contains Tennyson's own annotations, and on numerous unpublished manuscripts.

Tennyson, Sir Charles. *Alfred Tennyson.* London and New York: Macmillan, 1949. Written by Tennyson's grandson, this is the first authoritative formal biography of Tennyson. In addition to Tennyson's life and personality, the book deals with the poet's social, political, intellectual, and religious milieu.

Tennyson, Hallam, Lord. *Alfred Lord Tennyson: A Memoir.* 2 vols. London and New York: Macmillan, 1897. A rather biased and overprotective biography by the poet's eldest son. Despite its lack of objectivity, it is an excellent biographical sourcebook. All subsequent biographers have relied on its materials.

Beverley Allix

ELLEN TERRY

Born: February 27, 1847; Coventry, Warwickshire,
England
Died: July 21, 1928; Smallhythe, Kent, England
Area of Achievement: Theater
Contribution: As the leading Shakespearean ac-
tress and one of the most liberated women of her
time, Terry left an indelible impression on the ar-
tistic and social worlds of Victorian England.

Early Life

Alice Ellen Terry was, as the theatrical cliché has
it, very nearly "born in a costume trunk." One of
eleven children born to the roving players Ben and
Sarah Terry, she was delivered in a theatrical room-
ing house in Coventry, Warwickshire, England, on
February 27, 1847, while her parents were on tour.
Her early years were spent in the then only margin-
ally respectable world of the theater. She literally
grew up backstage, and, since she never received
any serious formal education, the theater served as
her schoolroom. From the beginning, young Ellen
was overshadowed by her older sister Kate, whose
promise as an actress won for her a contract with
the legendary actor-manager Edmund Kean in
1852. It was at Kean's Princess's Theatre in London that the nine-year-old Ellen made her theatrical debut in the role of Prince Mamillius in William Shakespeare's *The Winter's Tale*. The Keans,
especially the disciplinarian Mrs. Kean, were an
important influence on Ellen, teaching her lessons
about acting and about theatrical protocol that
would serve her well in later years.

Though Kate was clearly the burgeoning star of
the family, Ellen had gained considerable exposure
during her family's years with the prestigious Kean
troupe, and in 1861 she joined the London-based
troupe of Albina de Rhona, under whose auspices
she appeared in some ten plays, most of them forgotten melodramas. In 1862, Ellen joined the Bristol stock company that employed Kate, and the
Terry sisters quickly became local celebrities, attracting the attention of fans and critics alike.
Among the latter was Edward William Godwin, an
aspiring architect and theatrical designer. Ellen
was strongly attracted to the married, twenty-eight-
year-old Godwin, and to what he represented: culture, sophistication, and bohemianism.

Still, she was a very busy actress who, still in her
teens, was methodically learning her trade and attracting favorable attention. In the space of a year

she appeared in Shakespeare's *Othello* and *Much
Ado About Nothing*, in Richard Brinsley Sheridan's
The Rivals, and in Tom Taylor's *Our American
Cousin* (which was to achieve notoriety as the play
Abraham Lincoln was watching when he was assassinated in 1865). It was playwright Taylor who
introduced Ellen to the painter George Frederick
Watts, a temperamental and talented portraitist and
a member of the increasingly important Pre-
Raphaelite school of poets and painters. Struck by
the picturesqueness of the Terry sisters, Watts used
them as models for his beautiful *The Sisters*. He
was the first painter to immortalize Ellen Terry, and
she later served as a model for some of his best
paintings, including *Choosing, Ellen Terry*, and
Ophelia, Ellen posing as Shakespeare's doomed
heroine in the latter.

On February 20, 1864, the sixteen-year-old Terry married the forty-six-year-old Watts, and the
marriage seems to have been disastrous from the
first. Terry's desire for stability and respectability
in what had been a peripatetic and uncertain life is
somewhat understandable; less understandable is
Watts's motivation for marrying a girl thirty years
his junior. An inept lover and a hopeless neurotic,
Watts immediately tried to educate Terry in the
ways of polite society, and the formerly carefree,
high-spirited girl was miserable. The constant
stream of celebrities through the Watts home—including the poets Robert Browning and Alfred,
Lord Tennyson, and the politicians Benjamin Disraeli and William Ewart Gladstone—only slightly
alleviated Terry's boredom and frustration at being
seen and not heard.

After ten months, Terry left Watts and returned
to her parents, a social outcast. Reluctantly, she began to act again, though for two years she was still
overshadowed by her sister's now undisputed star-
dom. In 1867, Terry joined the acting company at
the New Queen's Theatre, where she met a young
actor named Henry Irving and played opposite him
in a bastardization of Shakespeare's *The Taming of
the Shrew*. Somewhere along the line, however, Edward Godwin reentered her life, and in October,
1868, Terry ran off with him, leaving no word of
her whereabouts with her family and leading them
to believe that she had met with foul play. The
mystery was soon solved, and it was discovered
that she and Godwin had taken up residence together in the village of Wheathampstead, thirty-

five miles from London. She stayed with Godwin for some seven years and bore him two children: Edith in December, 1869, and Edward in January, 1872. The world would later know the boy as Gordon Craig.

Life's Work

Little is known of Terry's years with Godwin, though for a time, at least, they seem to have been very happy. This was the most settled and domestic period that Terry would ever know, and she took great pleasure in keeping the house, tending the children, and welcoming her lover home after his daily commute from London. Terry and Godwin shared many interests, the most important of which was the theater. Terry learned to aid Godwin in his stage designs, and together they read the works of Shakespeare. In time, Godwin designed and built a house for his family, and together he and Terry planted and tended a garden. Their rural idyll came to an end, however, when finances forced Terry to return to the stage. Though undeniably a major architectural and artistic talent, Godwin had no head for business, and by the winter of 1873-1874 the

bill collectors were pounding at the door. The playwright Charles Reade, an old family friend, offered Terry a part in his current play, *The Wandering Heir*, and in February, 1874, Terry returned to the stage after an absence of some five years.

Bolstered both by favorable reviews and by the need for money, Terry performed in several more plays with Reade before accepting an offer from a Mrs. Bancroft, the actress-manager of the Prince of Wales Theatre, to play Portia in Shakespeare's *The Merchant of Venice*. Though her career was straining her relationship with Godwin, he was enlisted to supervise the scenery and costumes for the production, and the results were magnificent. Godwin's design work, however, was dominated by Terry's performance: When the play opened in April, 1875, Terry became an overnight sensation. Her first major Shakespearean role had made her a major star, and she had acquired a legion of fans who came to see her perform even in the less distinguished plays that followed the closing of *The Merchant of Venice*.

Terry's relationship with Godwin, however, could not bear the strain. In March, 1876, he was married to one of his students. Terry, in turn, was married to the actor Charles Wardell in November, 1877, soon after her divorce from Watts became final.

That same year, Terry moved to the Royal Court Theatre, where she scored a huge success in *Olivia*, an adaptation of Oliver Goldsmith's novel *The Vicar of Wakefield* (1764) written especially for her by W. G. Wills. In 1878, theatrical history was made when the same Henry Irving with whom Terry had acted eleven years before invited her to play opposite him in a new production of *Hamlet* at the Lyceum Theatre. This was the great age of the theatrical actor-manager who not only acted in plays but also oversaw nearly every facet of their production, from costume design to music to provincial tours. With his closest rival, Sir Herbert Beerbohm Tree, Irving reigned over this era, combining artistic sensibility with an unparalleled flair for public relations. He and Terry were to remain together for some twenty years, during which they undertook nearly every major Shakespearean play and transformed the Lyceum into a theatrical legend.

During those years, Terry maintained a schedule that would fell most modern performers. Besides performing at the Lyceum in London, she and Irving regularly toured the British provinces and together made seven grueling but profitable tours of the United States. In addition, she still had family responsibilities. By 1881, she and Charles Wardell had legally separated, and Terry acted as both mother and father to her children. Her correspondence shows that she was a caring parent to both "Edy" and "Teddy," but it is clear that her son was the love of her life.

From early childhood, he displayed the talent and temperament of the born artist, often appearing in plays with his mother but possessing in greater measure his father's talent for the graphic arts. As Gordon Craig, he would change the history of theatrical design, but his personal life was always a shambles. Financially and personally irresponsible, he was forever relying on his mother's name and on her money to establish him in one business venture after another, and to extricate him from a lifetime of trouble. Though he often neglected her, Terry adored him to the end of her life, acting as a doting grandmother to his many illegitimate children, including one by the dancer Isadora Duncan.

In spite of a short-lived third marriage late in her life, Terry's only other enduring professional and personal commitment was to Irving, though whether the two were ever really romantically involved is unknown. Certainly she spent more time with him than with anyone else, both onstage and offstage. Besides the plays of Shakespeare, the two scored major triumphs in Wills's adaptation of Johann Wolfgang von Goethe's *Faust*, in Tennyson's *The Cup*, and in revivals of *Olivia*. As famous in the United States as in their native England, the pair became the stuff of myth, anticipating such great twentieth century acting duos as Alfred Lunt and Lynn Fontanne and Hume Cronyn and Jessica Tandy. Unlike modern performers, however, who characteristically star in a play for a Broadway season and then, perhaps, tour with it for a year, Terry and Irving never abandoned their great roles. Less haughty than modern theater, the theater of the Victorian Age demanded that actors maintain a repertoire of tried and true hits that, in the event of another play's failure, could be revived at short notice and with a minimum of rehearsal. Such performers as Terry, Irving, and their great contemporaries Sarah Bernhardt, Eleanora Duse, Edwin Booth, and Joseph Jefferson carried around in their heads dozens of parts, ranging from the English and Continental classics to long-forgotten popular melodramas. Irving had just finished an engagement with one of these latter, *The Bells*, when he died on October 13, 1905.

The reverence and dignity accorded Irving at the time of his death bespoke the respectability that he had brought to the profession of acting, a lower-class business when he and Terry had first begun. Terry, too, garnered honors late in her career. In 1906, her friends and admirers staged a benefit to celebrate her fiftieth anniversary on the stage, and among the participants were actresses Mrs. Patrick Campbell and Lillie Langtry, opera star Enrico Caruso, composer Sir Arthur Sullivan, mystery writer Sir Arthur Conan Doyle, and poet and novelist Rudyard Kipling. From 1910 to 1921, she undertook a series of lecture tours and was everywhere received as a royal personage. In 1925, she was accorded the honor that had long eluded her: She was created Dame Grand Cross of the Most Excellent Order of the British Empire by King George V and Queen Mary. Ever open to new experiences, the elderly Terry appeared in several silent films, though the cinema was clearly not her medium. She died of a stroke on July 21, 1928, in her beloved cottage at Smallhythe.

Summary

During her long life, Ellen Terry attracted the attention of many celebrities. While yet an obscure young bride, she befriended Great Britain's poet laureate, Alfred, Lord Tennyson, and was photographed by Lewis Carroll, the author of *Alice's Adventures in Wonderland* (1865), who adored her. She was painted not only by her husband, G. F. Watts, but also by John Singer Sargent, the most acclaimed portraitist of his age. The painter William Holman Hunt designed her first bridal gown. She counted among her fans painter James McNeill Whistler and poet Algernon Charles Swinburne. Poet, playwright, and novelist Oscar Wilde wrote sonnets for her, and J. M. Barrie, the author of *Peter Pan*, wrote a play for her. For many years she carried on an intimate correspondence with George Bernard Shaw, who also wrote a play for her. Isadora Duncan confided in her as she would have in a mother, and her women friends included the legendary actresses Lillie Langtry, Sarah Bernhardt, and Eleanora Duse.

Little wonder, then, that Ellen Terry is credited with helping to create the modern star system, in which performers are lauded not only for their performances but also for their personalities. She was one of the first actresses to endorse a commercial product, and one of the first to start a fashion trend when she appeared in *Olivia* for the first time in the

1870's. In her unaffected and "natural" style of acting and in her unconventional personal life, Terry was in every way an original, representing as she did a sharp departure from the histrionics of the early nineteenth century stage and from the restrictive morals of Victorian England.

Bibliography

Auerbach, Nina. *Ellen Terry, Player in Her Time.* New York: Norton, and London: Phoenix House, 1987. A sensitive biography of Terry, her difficult life, and the people who influenced her.

Craig, Edward Gordon. *Ellen Terry and Her Secret Self.* London: Sampson Low, Marston, 1931; New York: Dutton, 1932. Terry's son's reminiscences of his mother tell as much about him as they do about her, but they are continually interesting, providing anecdotes and impressions that one can find nowhere else. A colorful memoir by a spoiled child who became an important personage in his own right.

Irving, Laurence. *Henry Irving: The Actor and His World.* London: Faber, 1951. Any study of Terry must include a biography of Irving and this one, though written by the great actor-manager's grandson, is surprisingly thorough and well documented. A definitive biography.

Manvell, Roger. *Ellen Terry.* London: Heinemann, and New York: Putnam, 1968. The closest thing to a definitive biography, this study is exhaustive and carefully researched.

Prideaux, Tom. *Love or Nothing: The Life and Times of Ellen Terry.* New York: Scribner, 1975; London: Millington, 1976. Written by a distinguished popular journalist, this book is chatty, personal, and interpretive. Recommended for the general reader.

Saintsbury, H. A., and Cecil Palmer, eds. *We Saw Him Act: A Symposium on the Art of Sir Henry Irving.* London: Hurst and Blackett, 1939; New York: Blom, 1969. This eccentric and lively collection of essays on Irving's stage career contains innumerable references to Terry. Essential to understanding the chemistry between Terry and Irving.

Terry, Ellen. *Ellen Terry and Bernard Shaw: A Correspondence.* Edited by Christopher St. John. New York: Putnam, 1932. A fascinating record of the relationship between two luminaries. These letters show Terry's private side to have been as compelling and charismatic as her stage performances.

―――. *Ellen Terry's Memoirs.* New York: Putnam, 1932; London: Gollancz, 1933. First published as *The Story of My Life* in 1908. Like any autobiography, this book is not to be trusted as fact, but it provides otherwise unattainable insights into Terry's dedication, humor, and humanity.

J. D. Daubs

NIKOLA TESLA

Born: July 9, 1856; Smiljan, Croatia
Died: January 7, 1943; New York, New York
Area of Achievement: Electrical engineering
Contribution: With his brilliant, intuitive insight and endless creative imagination, Telsa laid the foundations for many of the technological developments of the twentieth century.

Early Life

Nikola Tesla was born on July 9, 1856, in the village of Smiljan, Croatia, in what is now Yugoslavia. His father was an Orthodox priest, and his mother, in spite of her lack of formal education, was a remarkably capable woman who invented numerous household devices and developed a prodigious memory for epic poetry. Tesla was later to attribute his own powers to her influence. When Tesla was six, the family moved to the city of Gospic, and Tesla excelled at the local school, particularly in languages and mathematics. From his earliest years he showed a remarkable aptitude for solving mechanical problems and the rigid self-discipline and unshakeable self-confidence which were to lead him to success. As a boy, he also possessed a delicate constitution and frequently suffered from ill health.

In 1875, Tesla entered the Austrian Polytechnic School in Graz, where he studied compulsively, sometimes for twenty hours a day. Even at this young age he was occupied with the problem of the feasibility of using alternating current for the distribution of electrical energy. His solution, when it came, was to revolutionize the world of electrical engineering.

Financial difficulties forced Tesla to leave the Polytechnic at the end of his second year. His mother raised the money for him to travel to Prague, where he continued his studies, although he was not officially enrolled in any university. For the most part, Tesla was self-taught.

In 1881, he traveled to Budapest and found a lowly position in the Central Telegraph Office. While in Hungary he suffered from one of the nervous disorders which were to be a regular feature of his life, but following his recovery came a significant moment. One evening he was walking toward the sunset reciting a passage from Johann Wolfgang von Goethe's *Faust*, when the principle of the rotating magnetic field came to him in a sudden flash of realization, and he knew that he had the solution to the problem of the alternating current system. At this time, however, he had neither time nor means to build the machine he could see so clearly in his mind.

In 1882, he moved to Paris, where he secured a job with the Continental Edison Company. Two years later, in 1884, armed with a splendid recommendation from the manager of the company, a former associate of Thomas Alva Edison, Tesla sailed for the richer pastures of America, arriving in New York in June of that year. The stage was set for Tesla's brilliant and extraordinary career.

Life's Work

Edison was impressed by Tesla and offered him a job. The two great inventors were vastly different in method and personality, however, and were not destined to have a long working relationship. Tesla resigned over a disagreement about financial compensation for his redesign of Edison's dynamos. Tesla's reputation had been growing, however, and a group of financiers offered him a company under his own name, for which Tesla developed an improved and more economical arc lamp. Yet he was given little control over the company, and there was no scope for his large ambitions. He soon resigned. For the next year, his life was difficult, and he was forced to take any job that came along in order to stay alive.

By 1887, his luck changed, and so began a decade of high achievement and recognition. A. K. Brown, of the Western Union Telegraph Company, became interested in Tesla's ideas concerning alternating current, and this quickly led to the formation of the Tesla Electric Company. In the same year Tesla filed his first alternating current patents, and in 1888 he was invited to address the American Institute of Electrical Engineers. He made such an impact that another inventor and industrialist, George Westinghouse, showed keen interest. Westinghouse soon negotiated a contract with Tesla for his polyphase system of alternating current dynamos, a system which would allow power to be economically distributed over large distances. This gave rise to a bitter rivalry between Westinghouse, armed with Tesla's system, and Edison, whose company was committed to using the direct current system; it became known as the "battle of the currents."

By the early 1890's, Tesla had developed a worldwide reputation as a brilliant inventor. He was invited to Europe, where he lectured to prestigious scientific societies, including the Royal Society of Great Britain. He made an impressive figure. Standing six and a half feet tall, of slender build, with blue eyes and black hair, and always immaculately dressed, he was the complete showman. During his lectures he would conduct spectacular electrical demonstrations, keeping his audience enthralled with his almost unlimited vision of the possibilities of electrical power.

By 1893, the battle of the currents was all but over. Tesla's system had provided the power for the spectacular Chicago World's Fair in 1893, the first electrical fair in history, and in the same year the Niagara Falls Commission announced that they had awarded a contract to build three generators at Niagara Falls to Westinghouse's firm. The project proved to be one of the great engineering feats of the age.

These were highly productive years for Tesla; he worked on a variety of different projects at once and also led a lively social life in New York alongside the wealthy and famous. He built the Tesla coil, an air-core transformer designed to produce high voltages at high frequencies; he discovered the healing possibilities in high-frequency currents applied to the human body; he invented the carbon button lamp, the shadowgraph (forerunner of X-ray), and a new reciprocating dynamo, which proved to be the inspiration for the modern electric clock. In a lecture in 1893, he described the principle of radio broadcasting; a number of years before Guglielmo Marconi's practical demonstrations; in 1898 he demonstrated the first radio-controlled robot boat. In many of his ideas, Tesla was ahead of his time. He pioneered the basic principles of radar, which were not to be developed for another thirty years. He wanted to create artificial lightning to control the world's weather, and he developed a new science called telegeodynamics, which he said could be used to locate ore deposits.

Restlessly spinning new ideas, he then entered on a major project, the building of a laboratory at Colorado Springs, which was to develop his vision of a worldwide broadcasting system. There he built the largest Tesla coil ever, a twelve-million-volt machine capable of producing artificial lightning which soared up to 135 feet in the air. His spectacular experiments aroused a great deal of local curiosity, and his much-publicized belief that he had received signals from another planet earned for him considerable ridicule.

In 1900, Tesla closed the laboratory and returned to New York. By the following year he had obtained the backing of the financier J. Pierpont Morgan, for the construction of a transmitter for the world broadcasting system on a site Tesla named Wardenclyffe, on Long Island, New York. The combination of labor troubles and Morgan's withdrawal of financial support, however, resulted in the failure of the project.

After the failure of Wardenclyffe, Tesla's scientific reputation came under attack. His opponents portrayed him as an impractical dreamer, and the high point of his career was over. Despite the criticism, Tesla's inventive spirit remained undimmed. In 1906, he turned to designing a new turbine, which he thought could drive an ocean liner across the Atlantic in three days, but he lacked funds to translate the theory into practice.

In 1915, it was rumored that he and Edison had won the Nobel Prize, but in what appears to have been a last-minute change of mind by the Nobel committee, the prize was awarded elsewhere. Tesla's disappointment was only partially allayed when in 1917 he was awarded the prestigious Edison Medal from the American Institute of Electrical Engineers.

In his last years Tesla was increasingly afflicted by phobias and neuroses and lived virtually as a recluse. He had never accumulated wealth from his inventions, and he was now saved from poverty only by an honorarium of seven thousand dollars per annum from the Tesla Institute in Belgrade, which had been founded in 1935.

He died alone, on January 7, 1943, at the age of eighty-six, in his hotel room in New York. At his funeral in the Cathedral of St. John the Divine in New York, two thousand people were in attendance, and tributes from many of the world's great scientists poured in to honor the man who had, so to speak, set the world alight.

Summary

The last quarter of the nineteenth century was the great age of invention and industrial expansion in the United States. Circumstances were highly favorable for growth. There were wide markets, and labor, raw materials, and capital were freely available. There were few political or social barriers to free enterprise, and far-sighted entrepreneurs were quick to see commercial possibilities in the breakthroughs being made in science and technology. The rewards were great for those who were pre-

pared to take the risks. Machines and mass production revolutionized home, factory, and office: electric lighting, telephones, cameras, adding machines, and typewriters all became commonplace.

Circumstances were particularly favorable for the growth of the electrical manufacturing industry. Tesla, who was one of the estimated fourteen million European immigrants who arrived in America in the last two generations of the nineteenth century, arrived at the right place at the right time. There is no doubt that he had found his natural home. Although a Serb by birth, he was perfectly attuned to the American spirit. He was, he said, "at heart an American before I thought of coming here to live." All of his life he prized the American citizenship he had been awarded in 1891.

His legacy is everywhere apparent. His greatest discovery, the alternating current motor, laid the foundation for the power system used throughout the industrialized world. The Tesla coil is widely used in television and radio sets, and scientists still eagerly explore Teslian concepts. The Tesla turbine, for example, was still being investigated and developed nearly half a century after his death. The publication in 1978 of Tesla's research notes from Colorado Springs aroused a fresh wave of interest, although because Tesla could always visualize his designs and possessed a photographic memory, his written records are usually incomplete.

In 1975, Tesla was inducted into the National Inventors Hall of Fame, a fitting honor for the man whose brilliant skill and indefatigable labor harnessed the basic forces of nature for the betterment of the human condition.

Bibliography

Cathie, Bruce. "Tesla: The Forgotten Genius." In *The Pulse of the Universe—Harmonic 288*. London: Reed, 1978. Enthusiastic account of Tesla's life. Claims that Tesla's installations at Colorado Springs and Wardenclyffe fall on earth grid lines.

Cheney, Margaret. *Tesla: Man Out of Time*. Englewood Cliffs, N.J.: Prentice-Hall, 1981. Admiring, competent, readable biography. Especially good on the numerous ways in which Tesla anticipated modern technologies. Interesting chapter on the fate of Tesla's papers after his death.

Colladay, Morrison and John J. O'Neill. *Nikola Tesla: Incredible Scientist and Prodigal Genius and the Life of Nikola Tesla*. Kila, Mont.: Kessinger, 1996. This profile of Tesla includes information on his patents, writings, a bibliography, and illustrations.

Hall, Stephen H. "Tesla: A Scientific Saint, Wizard or Carnival Sideman?" *Smithsonian* 17 (June, 1986): 120-134. Lively article, ranging over Tesla's achievements, his eccentricities, and the controversies which surround the extent of his contributions to science.

Hunt, Inez, and Wanetta W. Draper. *Lightning in His Hand: The Life Story of Nikola Tesla*. Denver, Colo.: Sage, 1964. Not as detailed as Cheney, above, but soundly researched, sympathetic to Tesla's achievements. Uses Tesla correspondence not available to O'Neill, below.

O'Neill, John J. *Prodigal Genius: The Life of Nikola Tesla*. New York: Ives Washburn, 1944; London: Spearman, 1968. Earliest biography. O'Neill was science editor of the New York *Herald Tribune* and Tesla's friend. Lively and anecdotal; presents a fascinating portrait of the man. Has been partially superseded by the greater information available to later biographers.

Passer, Harold C. *The Electrical Manufacturers, 1875-1900*. Cambridge, Mass.: Harvard University Press, 1953. Mentions Tesla only briefly but gives a scholarly account of the social, economic, technical, and entrepreneurial factors which produced the rapid expansion of the electrical industry.

Seifer, Marc. *Wizard: The Life and Times of Nikola Tesla, Biography of a Genius*. Secaucus, N.J.: Carol, 1996. Resurrects Tesla, the often-ignored genius who created remote control, wireless communication, fluorescent lighting, and cheap electric power.

Tesla, Nikola. *Nikola Tesla: Lectures, Patents, Articles*. Edited by Vojin Popović, Radoslav Horvat, and Nikola Nikolić. Belgrade, Yugoslavia: Nikola Tesla Museum, 1956. Contains five of the most important of Tesla's lectures, including an explanation of the induction motor. Also includes more than eighty patents, scientific and technical articles, and Tesla's views about how electricity will solve world problems.

Bryan Aubrey

SYLVANUS THAYER

Born: June 9, 1785; Braintree, Massachusetts

Died: September 7, 1872; South Braintree, Massachusetts

Areas of Achievement: Education, engineering, and military affairs

Contribution: Thayer, known as the "Father of West Point," is remembered for reorganizing the administration and curriculum of the U.S. Military Academy at West Point and for firmly establishing a scientific and theory-based system of engineering education in the United States.

Early Life

The son of a wealthy Massachusetts farmer, Sylvanus Thayer initially embarked on a classical education at Dartmouth College in Hanover, New Hampshire, which he attended from 1803 to 1807. While at Dartmouth, however, Thayer became an avid student of Napoleon Bonaparte and his campaigns and developed such a strong interest in a military vocation that he sought and obtained an appointment as a cadet to the U.S. Military Academy at West Point, New York, in 1807. Graduated from the academy in 1808 after only one year of attendance, he was commissioned a second lieutenant of the Army Corps of Engineers. Although the threat of war with England after the Chesapeake Affair undoubtedly accelerated his graduation, Thayer had impressed his instructors as being a capable student who took his chosen profession of military engineering very seriously.

Still stationed at West Point upon graduation, Thayer spent the next four years engineering coastal fortifications in New York and New England, a reflection of the poor condition of the United States' coastal defenses and of the sudden importance of the academy and its engineer graduates to the defense of the nation. While at West Point during this period, Thayer was additionally assigned as an instructor of mathematics at the academy, an indication of his interest in education. He also continued his professional development as a military engineer through active membership in the U.S. Military Philosophical Society, demonstrating what would become a lifelong commitment to military engineering and engineering education.

With the advent of the War of 1812, Thayer, now a first lieutenant, left West Point and began active campaigning first as chief engineer to General Henry Dearborn on the Niagara frontier in 1812

and then as engineer to General Wade Hampton along Lake Champlain in 1813. Promoted to captain of engineers in October, 1813, Thayer was assigned to improve the harbor defenses of Norfolk, Virginia, during 1814 under the command of General Moses Porter. From his wartime service, Thayer gained an appreciation of the U.S. Army's great need for professionally educated and disciplined officers.

At the war's end, Thayer, holding the rank of brevet major for his service at Norfolk, again found himself stationed at West Point and once again able to pursue his study of military and civil engineering. With Napoleon's escape from Elba and the beginning of the Hundred Days, the final campaign of the Napoleonic Wars in Europe, Thayer requested a furlough in order to study military developments in France. However, Brigadier General Gardner Swift, chief of engineers, instead ordered Thayer to Europe on active duty on a trip that historian Todd Shallat has termed "a crucial event in American engineering."

Life's Work

Recognizing in the aftermath of the War of 1812 that it was imperative for the U.S. Army and its academy to stay abreast of contemporary European military theory and practice, Thayer and Colonel William McRee, a fellow West Point graduate and engineer, left for France in the spring of 1815. They spent the next two years observing allied military operations, studying French fortifications, studying procedures at the French artillery school at Metz, and, most important, conferring with instructors at France's premier military engineering school, the École Polytechnique. When Thayer and McRee were recalled to the United States in early 1817 to assume other duties, they brought with them campaign maps, engineering charts, scientific instruments, and nearly one thousand military, scientific, and engineering texts for use at the academy.

On July 17, 1817, Major Thayer became the U.S. Military Academy's third superintendent, a post that he would hold for sixteen years and one for which he would become known as the "Father of West Point." Although the academy had formally been in existence since 1802, there were still no definitive systems of administration or instruction in place, deficiencies recognized by both the civil-

ian and the military leadership. With poor discipline rampant in the corps of cadets, a lack of consistent academic instruction and supervision, and meager technical facilities, little had actually changed at West Point since Thayer had been a cadet. Thayer, who had a thorough knowledge and an appreciation of French engineering and methods of instruction and who was highly regarded for his keen analytical mind and organizing abilities, was the perfect choice for superintendent. With a strong commitment to the Army and to military engineering, and with the complete support of both Brigadier General Swift and the new secretary of war, John C. Calhoun, Thayer began an institutional reform of the U.S. Military Academy that has endured essentially unchanged to the present day.

Thayer's comprehensive reforms of the academy were both administrative and curricular in nature. With regard to the former, the "Thayer System," as it came to be known, bore the strong imprint of the French École Polytechnique and embodied a reorganization of academy life that included weekly examinations, weekly recitations, the ranking of cadets according to their academic performance, the institution of small-group instruction in sections composed of students with similar academic rankings, and the assignment of cadets to branches of the service according to their academic performance. The rigor of the new curriculum became renowned among American educators. George Ticknor, a Dartmouth College classmate of Thayer and a future president of Harvard University, was not alone when he voiced the opinion that the cadets at the academy were "a body of *Students*, constantly devoted to an intellectual discipline much more severe than their military discipline—who are much more thoroughly taught . . . than any of the young men, who are sent to any of our colleges."

Like the academy's new administrative procedures, the technical curriculum that Thayer established borrowed a great deal from French military education. First and foremost, French became a mandatory subject at the academy because Thayer felt it to be the language of military science and engineering and because the majority of the academy's textbooks were in French. In addition, four of the seven professors actually were French. However, the true substance of Thayer's academic reforms lay in the science and mathematics courses that became the foundation of the academic curriculum.

By adding regular offerings of engineering, natural philosophy (science), and mathematics to the curriculum and then weighting them more than traditional subjects such as military tactics and French, Thayer established a science- and theory-based system of education at the academy. The technical education received by academy graduates was so comprehensive that it remained unmatched by any other college or university in North America until after the Civil War. The prominence of army engineers in civil engineering projects, particularly railroad and canal building, was so great that it is clear that academy-trained engineers were at least as important to the antebellum United States as the professional officer corps it provided to ensure the nation's defense (the primary reason for the academy's existence).

Although Thayer resigned as superintendent of the U.S. Military Academy in 1833 after a dispute with President Andrew Jackson over Jackson's interference with Thayer's disciplining of cadets, the academy continued to bear Thayer's imprint long afterward. Part of Thayer's success as superintendent was based on his being an able administrator and his talent for picking the right people for the right jobs. Several professors who were handpicked by Thayer in the 1820's and 1830's continued their professorships well into the 1870's, lending a definite continuity of Thayer's vision of West Point and of military service to successive generations of army officers.

Thayer himself returned to field duty with the Army Corps of Engineers and was primarily responsible for the harbor defenses of Boston, Massachusetts. He later served as the president of the Army's Board of Engineers. After taking a medical leave because of failing health in 1858, Thayer finally retired from the Army as a colonel of engineers and a brevet brigadier general in 1863. Even then, he continued his interests in education and engineering by endowing a private academy and founding a library in his hometown of Braintree, Massachusetts, and contributing to the establishment of a school of architecture and civil engineering (now known as the Thayer School of Engineering) at his first alma mater, Dartmouth College.

Summary

During the sixteen years that Sylvanus Thayer presided as superintendent of the U.S. Military Academy at West Point, he instituted reforms that caused the academy to graduate disciplined, well-educated officers for the U.S. Army. The small corps of West Point graduates performed well during the mass mobilizations of the Mexican and Civil Wars and in leading and administering a tiny peacetime army spread across a constantly expanding United States. While the Army still had organizational problems throughout the nineteenth century, Thayer's reforms at West Point helped prevent the military disasters of the War of 1812 from reoccurring. After 1817, academy graduates proved to be true professional soldiers, putting the U.S. Military Academy at West Point on an equal footing with its European counterparts.

Thayer's establishment of a rigorous, scientific curriculum at the U.S. Military Academy also contributed to the creation of a technical institution that was unequaled during the antebellum period. West Point-trained civil, railroad, and mining engineers, on active duty and as civilians, were commonly regarded as the premier builders and technical advisors of the early republic and made substantial contributions to the economic growth and technological expansion of the United States during the nineteenth century. Academy graduates proved to have an impact on the social, cultural, and technical life of the United States in far greater proportion than their numbers would suggest. Ultimately, the "Thayer System" at West Point helped standardize engineering and scientific education in the United States by providing a model for other academic institutions to emulate.

Bibliography

Ambrose, Steven A. *Duty, Honor, Country: A History of West Point.* Baltimore: Johns Hopkins University Press, 1966. A history of the U.S. Military Academy at West Point that concentrates on the service of famous graduates. Thayer's importance as the "Father of West Point" is emphasized.

Hill, Forest G. *Roads, Rails & Waterways: The Army Engineers and Early Transportation.* Norman: University of Oklahoma Press, 1957. Covers the importance of army civil engineers to the internal improvement of the antebellum United States. The first chapter covers the formation of the U.S. Military Academy at West Point and the development of the "Thayer System."

Morrison, James L., Jr. *The Best School in the World: West Point: The Pre-Civil War Years, 1833-1866.* Akron, Ohio: Kent State University Press, 1986. Morrison covers the history of the U.S. Military Academy from Thayer's resignation as superintendent in 1833 to the removal of the academy from the Army Corps of Engineers' jurisdiction in 1866. Several chapters highlight the legacy of Thayer's educational and administrative reforms.

Shallat, Todd A. *Structures in the Stream: Water, Science, and the Rise of the U.S. Army Corps of Engineers.* Austin: University of Texas Press, 1994. Though intended as a broader social history of the Army Corps of Engineers and its management of water projects, chapters highlight the impact of European engineering traditions on the development of scientific engineering in the United States and Thayer's persistent advocacy of the French system of education at the École Polytechnique.

Tyack, David. *George Ticknor and the Boston Brahmins.* Cambridge, Mass.: Harvard University Press, 1967. Tyack focuses on George Ticknor and his educational reforms at Harvard University but briefly describes Thayer's reforms at the U.S. Military Academy from the perspective of a civilian and a humanist. Ticknor, a Dartmouth classmate of Thayer, regarded the academy at West Point under Thayer's tutelage as a model for collegiate education in the United States.

J. C. Larrabee

ADOLPHE THIERS

Born: April 15, 1797; Marseilles, France
Died: September 3, 1877; Saint-Germaine-en-
Laye, near Paris, France
Areas of Achievement: Government, politics, and
historiography
Contribution: Thiers was a central figure among
the moderate politicians who in the early nineteenth century created the July Monarchy and,
forty years later, the Third Republic. He also
wrote important multivolume histories of the
revolutionary and Napoleonic eras.

Early Life

Marie-Joseph-Louis-Adolphe Thiers was born a
month before his parents married. Four months later his ne'er-do-well father, Louis, disappeared and
was not heard from again until his son was successful enough to provide financial support. Adolphe was reared in poverty by his mother, Marie-
Madeleine (née Amic), and her mother. The experience left him with a lifelong inclination to seek
some support and approval of his actions from older women.

With the help of relatives, Thiers received a
proper education, and in November, 1815, he began a three-year tenure in law school at Aix-en-
Provence. Thiers became a member of the bar in
November, 1818, but times were hard for young
lawyers. Thiers, short, almost gnomish, with a
reedy voice, lacked the presence to get even his
share of cases. He filled his time and pockets by
competing for literary prizes offered by regional
academies, but his real livelihood was provided by
his mother. Prospects were few, and, urged by his
friend François Mignet, Thiers decided to try his
hand as a writer in Paris. He left his family and a
woman who seems to have expected marriage.

In November, 1821, after a brief stint in a secre-
tarial position, Thiers joined the staff of the liberal
newspaper the *Constitutionnel;* three months later,
he signed a contract to write a history of the French
Revolution. Bourbon Royalism was in the political
ascendancy, and the liberals were happy to have
new recruits, so Thiers rose quickly.

By the mid-1820's, Thiers's reputation as a journalist was established, and the ten-volume *Histoire de la révolution française* (1823-1827; *The
History of the French Revolution*, 1838) proved
him to be a historian of note. He was moving in
prominent circles, such as that of the banker

Jacques Laffitte, where, along with his future rival
François Guizot, he met the legendary Talleyrand.
Political discussion was intense, and Thiers's hostility to the Bourbons and the aristocracy was
growing. Although, like most liberals of the era,
Thiers embraced the Enlightenment's faith in reason, commitment to civil rights, and religious
skepticism, he still favored constitutional monarchy rather than a republic.

Life's Work

In January, 1830, Thiers, Mignet, and Armand Car-
rel inaugurated the *National*, which became Thiers's chief organ of persuasion for a number of
years. The paper was a leading voice in the criticisms of the government of Charles X, and when
the king's efforts to strengthen royal authority provoked open resistance in July, its offices were a
center of revolutionary activity. Although he had
spoken for moderation, faced with revolt, Thiers
helped to write a proclamation claiming credit for
the *National* in calling France to arms. He worked
diligently to get a constitutional monarchy created
under Louis-Philippe, the Duke of Orléans. That
was formally accomplished on August 9.

In the first month of the new regime, Thiers was
given several senior-level government appointments and resigned from his journalistic connections. He would serve in six governments over the
next decade. Thiers, however, had too little property to qualify. The Dosne family sold him a house in
Paris on good terms, and Thiers was elected deputy
for Aix-en-Provence and appointed Parliamentary
Undersecretary for the Ministry of Finance.

Practical experience influenced Thiers's views of
government, and by the spring of 1832 he had
shifted from the Party of Movement to the Party of
Resistance. The death of the premier, Casimir Péri-
er, led to a new government with Thiers as minister
of the interior. His delicate task was to control the
Duchess of Berry, who was leading efforts for a le-
gitimist uprising in the name of her dead husband.
She was interned without trial and, conveniently
for Thiers, proved to be illegitimately pregnant.
The duchess was allowed to leave the country quietly. In January, 1833, Thiers shifted to the Ministry of Commerce and Public Works, and in June he
was elected to the French Academy.

The next November, the thirty-six-year-old Thiers married Élise Dosne, who had turned fifteen

the day before the wedding. The dowry was 300,000 francs plus, unofficially, the money remaining due on his house, which was simply never paid. The relationship between Thiers and Élise was never very close, but Thiers became part of his wife's family, who gained political and economic influence from the connection. Madame Dosne, Thiers's mother-in-law, served for many years as the older woman Thiers needed for emotional support.

Thiers's political influence continued to grow, and by early 1834 he and Guizot were the dominant figures in the government. In the spring, unrest among workers, encouraged by the left-wing press, led to efforts at censorship and arrests for union activities. On April 13, barricades were erected in Paris, and Thiers, as minister of the interior, sent troops that crushed the uprising. Thiers's reputation was marred for the rest of his career, however, because of deaths that became known as the Massacre in the Rue Transnonain. The Left never forgot Thiers's involvement.

Elections in June resulted in extended political infighting among the leading politicians, but Thiers remained at the Ministry of the Interior. In February, 1836, the government, then under the Duke of Broglie, was defeated, and on February 22 Thiers became the premier. Knowing that his majority was undependable, he kept the chamber busy with noncontroversial internal improvements, while he pursued an active foreign policy in hopes of boosting his standing. After clashing with the king about support for a pro-French liberal government in Spain, Thiers was out of office in September.

Thiers was active in opposition until January, 1840, when, having organized the defeat of the current government, he left Louis-Philippe little choice but to ask him to form a government. Drawing in the Left with patronage and winning the support of the moderate conservatives who were eager for stability, Thiers had what appeared to be a solid administration. He had, however, inherited Middle Eastern trouble. A territorial dispute dating to the Greek revolt of the 1820's had been simmering between Muhammad 'Alī of Egypt and his overlord, the sultan. Thiers, the historian, tied Egypt's troubles to Napoleon I and also was interested in French expansion in North Africa. Thiers backed the Egyptian against all the other powers, believing that Mehemet could get hereditary possession of Egypt and life possession of Syria as a minimum concession. Eventually, the other powers acted

without consulting France, and the Egyptians collapsed in the face of a token force. Anti-French feeling spread all over Europe, and by October, 1840, Louis-Philippe, who had never been willing to do more than talk to help Mehemet, replaced Thiers with a government run by Guizot. Although he did not suspect it at the time, Thiers was beginning thirty years as a member of the opposition.

Although he remained active in the chamber, Thiers devoted much time to writing. In 1839, he had signed a contract for a history of the consulate and the empire, receiving 500,000 francs for the first ten volumes. He traveled to Napoleonic battle sites and worked in French archives as he began to write this history. In December of 1840, he was elected to the Académie des Sciences, Morales, et Politiques.

In 1842 and 1846, Guizot was reelected, but there was more and more unrest. In February, 1848, a campaign of protest banquets came to a head when the government attempted to block one scheduled for a working-class district in Paris. Frightened by the ensuing demonstration, Guizot resigned. Frantic maneuvering to reestablish government led to a brief attempt by Thiers to take control, but, when told he was too unpopular, he stepped aside. In the end, the king abdicated in favor of his grandson. That proved unacceptable—Thiers made no effort to support the arrangement—and the Second Republic emerged. Openly reluctant about participating, Thiers was defeated in the first series of elections for the new National Assembly. In May, however, he won in four separate by-elections.

Once in office, Thiers began to fight for a bicameral legislature, which was rejected, and in opposition to the right to work. He argued that the country could not afford the national workshops, employing 1.5 to 2 million workers, started by the revolutionaries. He established his economic ideas in *Du droit de propriété* (1848). He grudgingly approved the election of Louis-Napoleon Bonaparte as president, but refused, out of loyalty to the Orleanist family and reluctance to face the many problems of the new government, to preside at the first cabinet. In the next few years, he devoted himself to conservative party politics, helping with a successful election campaign in the spring of 1849. He helped develop the very conservative Falloux Law, reforming education and a new electoral law reducing the electorate by almost one-third. In debating the latter, he spoke of the dangers of the

"vile mob," a phrase that would haunt him. Thiers openly broke with Louis-Napoleon in 1851 over control of the military, but a prosperous economy and a reputation for stable government kept the prince-president's popularity high. When in December, 1851, Louis-Napoleon made himself Emperor Napoleon III, Thiers and seventeen other deputies were among ten thousand opponents exiled or transported. Thiers settled in Switzerland until August, 1852, when the exile was lifted, and worked on his history of the consulate and empire. Over his life, Thiers produced some thirty volumes of political history. He also wrote his memoirs.

By 1863, Thiers had finished the last volume of his twenty-volume *Histoire du consulat et de l'empire* (1845-1862; *History of the Consulate and the Empire of France Under Napoleon*, 1845-1862) and was open for new employment. Napoleon's popularity was in decline and the republicans were gaining popularity. Thiers was persuaded to run in the following year's elections. He won a Parisian seat, getting workers' votes despite his anti-Left reputation. He promptly embarked on a campaign, championing individual freedoms. With the emper-

or seeking to regain lost support, liberalization was steadily achieved.

The July, 1870, confrontation with Prussia over the question of a Hohenzollern (a royal German family) candidate for the Spanish throne found Thiers arguing for peace. Although he was the subject of jeers when the Franco-Prussian War erupted, the rapid and overwhelming Prussian victory—Napoleon was captured at Sedan, and Paris was besieged by mid-September—vindicated him. Thiers refused to be in the government of national defense, but he accepted a diplomatic mission, visiting London, St. Petersburg, Vienna, and Florence in a vain quest for support. He did manage to arrange for armistice talks.

Thiers's goal was to hold elections and, having established a new government, to make peace on the best possible terms, though France was not in a very good bargaining position. He was opposed by Léon Gambetta, leader of the republican Left. Thiers prevailed, and elections were held February 8, 1871, with Thiers's supporters winning a clear victory. The new assembly elected Thiers, almost unanimously, as chief of the executive power of the French republic. In the peace treaty with Prussia, France lost Alsace-Lorraine and was saddled with a 5,000-million-franc indemnity. One of Thiers's biggest successes as head of the new Third Republic was raising two large loans and getting that indemnity paid without undermining the national economy.

The withdrawal of the Prussians had left leftwing militants in control of Paris. When the new national government tried to assert control, civil war erupted. Thiers had to raise an army and defeat the Paris Commune, keep the Prussians from taking advantage of the trouble, and hold public support. Although the city had to be shelled and brutality was common, the city was recaptured, and, because the action was prompt and uncompromising, the Prussians found little opportunity to fish in troubled waters. There was leftwing sentiment especially in the cities, but few were willing to chance a renewal of the horrors of 1793. In the end, Thiers triumphed.

In August, 1871, Thiers was appointed President of the Republic, a post he held until May, 1873. During his tenure, he presided over the establishment of a conservative republic. He fought unsuccessfully for protectionism and blocked efforts to establish an income tax. He also resisted the adoption of the Prussian system of universal military service. Thiers had become convinced that a republic was the only workable system for a conservative France. His loss of power was largely the result of urging the right to abandon its dream of monarchy and accept the republic. This cost him support, and he was unable to control a confrontation between conservatives and radicals. He had to resign. Thiers spent his last four years active in opposition politics and, on September 3, 1877, after a choking fit at lunch, lapsed into a coma and died.

Summary

Adolphe Thiers's life can hardly be separated from nineteenth century French politics. He devoted his energies to public service, political journalism, and political history. His biography is really the political history of nineteenth century France, for he was intimately involved in all the major changes of that century. He had made his name in time to influence the Revolution of 1830—he produced more than one hundred articles for the *National* in the first six months of that year—and became part of the new government. Thiers's skills, however, were most effective in opposition—as practical politician, journalist, or historian. Thiers spent almost his entire career out of power. The conversational debating style he developed to overcome his naturally weak voice was very effective, and he was a formidable parliamentary foe.

During the middle of the century, Thiers wrote history and championed political moderation in the chambers, his reputation for knowledge and stability growing. In retrospect, his rise to power in the crisis of 1870 seems almost inevitable. Not only was he already respected, but also his resistance to the wave of nationalism that led to the war won for him even more kudos. Not only did he deal effectively with making peace but also he proceeded to oversee the creation of a conservative republican regime that lasted until it was destroyed by the Nazi conquest of World War II.

Bibliography

Albrecht-Carrié, Rene. *Adolphe Thiers: Or, The Triumph of the Bourgeoisie.* Boston: Twayne, 1977. A short, straightforward biography by a very good historian. Does a good job of showing Thiers to be a part of the rise of the middle class to dominance during the nineteenth century.

Allison, John M. S. *Thiers and the French Monarchy.* London: Constable, and Boston: Houghton Mifflin, 1926. A major study involving Thiers's career. The main theme is the monarchy, but, given Thiers's intimate involvement with that institution, he plays a major part in the book.

Bury, J. P. T. *France, 1814-1940.* 5th ed. London and New York: Methuen, 1985. A classic survey introduction to French political history. An excellent source for brief accounts of Thiers's activities, but more important for providing context in which those activities must be seen to be understood.

Bury, J. P. T., and R. P. Tombs. *Thiers, 1797-1877: A Political Life.* London and Boston: Allen and Unwin, 1986. Excellent biography with the emphasis on Thiers's public life. The authors portray their subject as a centrist who evolved from constitutional monarchist to republican over the course of his career.

Dallas, G. "An Exercise in Terror? The Paris Commune, 1871." *History Today* 38, no. 7 (February, 1989). Examines the Commune of Paris, created in 1871 under Thiers, focusing on possible terrorism practices and use of hostages.

Horne, Alistair. *The Fall of Paris: The Siege and the Commune, 1870-71.* London: Macmillan, 1965; New York: St. Martin's Press, 1966. A superbly written account of the collapse of the Second Empire and the emergence of the Third Republic. The author's treatment of these events as part of the same larger development is effective and informative. Both the style and the approach lend themselves to the nonspecialist.

Fred R. van Hartesveldt

THEODORE THOMAS

Born: October 11, 1835; Esens, East Friesland,
  Germany
Died: January 4, 1905; Chicago, Illinois
Area of Achievement: Music
Contribution: A professional musician from childhood, Thomas pioneered the then new role of
  virtuoso conductor, markedly raising standards
  of orchestral performance both in light and in serious works. With the Chicago Orchestra, he also
  perfected the means of supporting and maintaining ensembles of the highest quality. He was virtually the father of the modern American
  symphony orchestra.

Early Life

Johann August Thomas, the future conductor's father, was master of music for the town of Esens.
Young Theodore Christian Friedrich Thomas, surrounded by music and musicians from birth, quickly established himself as a prodigy. As a child he
could read any music set before him by the town's
musicians and was an accomplished violinist by
the time the family emigrated to New York City in
1845.

At first, the Thomas family scarcely prospered;
son as well as father found it necessary to play in a
variety of theater orchestras, dancing schools, and
even saloons to support the household. In 1848,
they traveled to Portsmouth, Virginia, for steady
employment; Theodore, thirteen years old, was
nominally in the United States Navy, in whose
band he was playing second horn. A year later,
Theodore resigned; he would reminisce at the end
of his life that his father had so increased his income that the son's contribution was no longer
needed. The fourteen-year-old fiddler then took off
by himself on a tour of the American South, playing concerts wherever he could drum up an audience and attending to every detail, from putting up
posters to selling tickets. It should not be imagined
that he did nothing but play unaccompanied violin,
however, for whenever the materials presented
themselves, he formed ad hoc ensembles. His wanderlust satisfied for the time being, he returned to
New York City in 1850.

Thomas had virtually no formal schooling in the
United States. His performing jobs usually kept
him up well past midnight, and there were no laws
either forbidding child labor or compelling attendance at school. Yet he grew up to be not only cul-

tivated but also a genuine intellectual. In part, this
achievement reflected the high culture of his parents, as well as his keen receptivity to the many
plays, poems, and librettos he encountered in his
many musical jobs. What he did not pick up from
the orchestra pit, he supplied by self-directed reading. Between 1850 and 1860, he established himself as one of the finest violinists in the booming
cultural milieu of New York City. In 1854, the New
York Philharmonic Society elected him to membership; in the same year, he accepted a position in
a small orchestra, touring the United States with
what surely was the leading concert attraction of
the season, Adelina Patti, soprano; Maurice Strako-
sch, piano; and Ole Bull, violin. It should be pointed out that orchestras were then ephemeral things,
summoned into being by managers of theaters, opera houses, choral societies, or concert tours. National and international concert circuits were also
relatively new, especially in the United States.
Even the most famous musical celebrities normally
toured in groups, to provide their audiences with
the greatest possible variety of musical delights.

In 1855, at the age of twenty, Thomas accepted
the invitation of William Mason to play first violin
in his string quartet. Mason, the son of the pioneering New England musician, Lowell Mason,
had recently returned from studying music in Europe, culminating in piano lessons with Franz
Liszt in Weimar. He and the quartet became the
nucleus for a series of chamber-music concerts
which would last until 1870. Thomas soon assumed so much responsibility and radiated so
much leadership that the series became known as
the Mason-Thomas concerts. In the early years,
guest artists, especially vocalists, abounded, and
each program would contain a single weighty
work otherwise surrounded by short, melodious,
and popular numbers. Within the first year, however, the quartet was playing Ludwig van
Beethoven's Opus 130, a work which can daunt all
but the most serious audiences. In their later years,
however, Mason and Thomas offered nothing but
major works by major composers.

Thomas first led an orchestra in 1860, taking
over an opera performance on short notice because
the regular conductor was unhappy about his pay
being in arrears. In 1862, the Brooklyn Philharmonic hired Thomas as coconductor. He was sole
conductor there from 1866, and that proved to be

his longest employment, ending only in 1891, when he moved to Chicago. More significant for the future, however, were the concerts of 1862 which Thomas organized and conducted himself in New York City. He had long since determined that most conductors merely kept time, that most orchestras had such shifting and unreliable personnel and so very little rehearsal time, that no really fine performances could possibly be drawn from them. Furthermore, the musicians themselves, needing to pursue jobs whenever and wherever they could, were unable to enforce standards of quality even when they planned concerts through their own guilds or unions. The Philharmonic Society, founded in 1842, was such a guild and retained that organization into the early twentieth century. The orchestra hired its conductors, usually from among the membership; such conductors were always fine musicians, but they had no disciplinary powers whatever. Thomas was determined to change all this; in the course of his lifetime, he succeeded. By 1864, established both as a virtuoso violinist and a rising conductor, Thomas married Minna Rhodes; in subsequent years, they had three sons and two daughters, the marriage ending with Minna's death in 1889. As a young man, he was strikingly handsome, slender, and of medium height, with a well-trimmed dark mustache, penetrating eyes, and the look of a sensitive artist. As an older man, he was no longer slender, and the mustache became bushy, while his aura of authority continued to grow.

Life's Work

In 1864, Thomas began his series of Symphony Soirees, in competition with the New York Philharmonic Concerts, but since each organization presented only six programs a year, the small but growing concert audience in New York City was hardly overtaxed. Seeking more work for himself and his players, he began, in 1865, his long series of "summer garden" concerts, chiefly in New York, but also on tour and, from 1877 onward, often in Chicago. The touring began in 1869 and, in conjunction with the popular summer concerts, gave the Theodore Thomas Orchestra something like full-time employment. This was unique in the United States at the time; indeed, only the remaining court and church orchestras of Europe then provided full-time work for classically trained players.

The Theodore Thomas Orchestra grew from thirty to sixty players in its years of touring and sum-

mer concerts; it was never of the size and force of modern virtuoso orchestras, and it played chiefly the sort of light concert music which survives in the programs of the Boston Pops and its imitators. Yet Thomas was still preparing the way for the future great orchestras of the United States by the quality of his ensemble, which profited from his devoted leadership and from the unprecedented advantage of staying together, month after month and year after year. While his programming assumed an unsophisticated audience, he managed to include at least one serious work in each concert, thereby gradually educating the public.

In 1873, Thomas began a new phase of his career by taking his orchestra to the first Cincinnati May Festival. He was musical director of the whole undertaking and continued as such through the sixteenth festival in 1904, just before his death. The United States had seen several music festivals already, but they had tended mainly toward massive accumulations of singers, players, and fireworks, rather than aiming at the highest possible expressions of musical art. The idea of concentrating large ensembles and audiences for a few intense days of music-making, especially when the weather is neither paralyzingly cold nor suffocatingly hot, has always made sense. While Thomas' music festivals had plenty of symphonies, concertos, and concert arias, they were built around large-scale works for soloists, chorus, and orchestra. The oratorio, perfected by George Frideric Handel in eighteenth century England, became one of the most popular musical forms in nineteenth century Germany, Britain, and the United States. The music festival gave Thomas an unprecedented opportunity to raise public taste, so he tried to promote similar festivals in other leading cities. He succeeded in several, including Pittsburgh, San Francisco, St. Louis, Chicago, and New York, but after one or two festivals these cities failed to maintain the required level of commitment; only the Cincinnati Festival became permanent.

The exposition held in Philadelphia in 1876 proved that Thomas had become the most celebrated musician in the United States, for he was chosen to direct its music. In the end, he overreached himself, planning more concerts than the public could support, but even with cancellations and unpaid debts, the Centennial Exposition advanced both Thomas' career and his sacred cause of serious music. He commissioned several works by such American composers as John Knowles Paine and

Dudley Buck and invited leading performers from all over the world. Yet there was one more source of discord. Thomas encouraged the Women's Committee to raise the unprecedented sum of five thousand dollars for an original piece of music by the great Richard Wagner. That curious genius applied more energy to getting himself paid than to executing his commission; the work he submitted was inferior in quality to the contribution of the Americans, or indeed, to anything Wagner himself had composed since his student days.

In 1877, Thomas accepted the post of conductor of the New York Philharmonic, on the understanding that he would continue to give a separate series of concerts with his own orchestra. This appointment also continued, with brief interruptions, until his move to Chicago. He tried a permanent move in 1878, accepting the leadership of the Cincinnati Conservatory of Music. Autocrat that he was, however, he soon resigned: The trustees of the organization would not grant him the power he deemed necessary to produce good musicians. Based again in New York, with increasingly long guest appearances elsewhere, he continued strengthening his

position through the 1880's, though he barely survived the collapse of the American Opera Company. That was an attempt to present modern operas in English translation with American-trained singers; altogether worthy in plan, it was inadequately financed and poorly managed. It was also in competition with the new Metropolitan Opera, where young Walter Damrosch was successfully presenting the music dramas of Richard Wagner with European-trained singers.

Still the best-known and most widely respected conductor in the United States and financially secure after the final liquidation of the opera company, Thomas nevertheless suffered from severe depression in 1889. Minna died after a long and painful illness. Losing the resiliency of youth, he disbanded the orchestra, which depended on touring for most of its engagements. Artistically, he was exasperated with what he called scratch orchestras, by which he meant ensembles whose personnel he could not choose and shape to his own high standards.

In May, 1890, Thomas married Rose Fay, a woman of great musical and literary culture. Her brother, Charles Norman Fay, a utilities executive in Chicago, then organized what Thomas most desired: a permanent association, underwritten by wealthy citizens, to guarantee the budget of an orchestra over which he would have absolute artistic control. Here was the model for virtually all the major orchestras of the United States. The New York Philharmonic had typically played six concerts each season; the Chicago Orchestra (later the Chicago Symphony Orchestra) played twenty.

Yet problems remained. Chicago's great World's Fair of 1893 tempted Thomas, its music director, to another surfeit of newly commissioned works, guest orchestras and choruses, and famous soloists. After some unpleasant carping caused by merely allowing Ignacy Jan Paderewski to play his own Steinway piano (technically barred from the fairgrounds because Steinway and Sons had declined to exhibit in Chicago), Thomas resigned. Yet, as in 1876, the programs of classical music in Chicago set new standards of scope and virtuosity.

Thomas led the Chicago Orchestra through fourteen seasons; only the Boston Symphony Orchestra, founded in 1881 by Henry Lee Higginson and run on idealistic and autocratic principles similar to those of Thomas, could rival it for the quality of programs and execution. The conductor, however, had one more goal to accomplish. The Auditorium

Theater, that landmark of American architecture, was far too vast and cavernous for Thomas' taste. Also, he had to share it with several other organizations. With the help of his friend Daniel Hudson Burnham, he planned and built Orchestra Hall. Tragically, Thomas died after a brief illness in January, 1905, within a month of playing his first concert, with his own orchestra, in his own hall.

Summary

When Theodore Thomas began his conducting career in the 1860's, there was no such thing as a famous orchestral conductor in the United States and scarcely a permanent symphony orchestra. Through tours, festivals, considerate programming, persistence, and even through writing essays on the appreciation of good music he contributed more than anyone else to the emergence of virtuoso orchestras in the United States. Entirely trained in this country, he was a genuine cosmopolite, eager to promote genius wherever it appeared. He was a great musician, and he helped make music a great force for cooperation and civility.

Bibliography

Burg, David F. *Chicago's White City of 1893*. Lexington: University Press of Kentucky, 1976. Discusses Thomas' second venture in planning music for a world's fair.

Davis, Ronald L. *A History of Music in American Life*. 3 vols. Huntington, N.Y.: Krieger, 1980-1982. Presents a balanced view of all aspects of American musical life. The second volume treats the era of Theodore Thomas.

Mueller, John H. *The American Symphony Orchestra: A Social History of Musical Taste*. Bloomington: Indiana University Press, 1951; London: Calder, 1958. Takes a broad, detailed, and scholarly view of its subject.

Otis, Philo Adams. *The Chicago Symphony Orchestra: Its Organization, Growth and Development, 1891-1924*. Chicago: Clayton, 1924. A valuable compendium of facts by a long-term participant in the musical life of Chicago.

Petteys, Leslie. "Theodore Thomas's 'March to the Sea.' " *American Music* 10, no. 2 (Summer 1992). Follows conductor Thomas' 1883 American tour, which covered thirty cities and included seventy-three concerts.

Russell, Charles Edward. *The American Orchestra and Theodore Thomas*. New York: Doubleday, 1927. Entertainingly traces Thomas' role in the development of major orchestras and star conductors.

Thomas, Rose Ray. *Memoirs of Theodore Thomas*. New York: Moffat, Yard, 1911. Contains the fullest treatment of the conductor's life. Written by his second wife, it is reverent and idealistic in tone.

Thomas, Theodore. *Theodore Thomas: A Musical Autobiography*. Edited by George P. Upton. 2 vols. Chicago: McClurg, 1906. Falls into several sections. Thomas avoided personal anecdotes and any form of gossip; his essay in the autobiography chiefly outlines his career and expresses his musical ideals. His friend and longtime admirer, George P. Upton, partly makes up the want of personal details in his appreciative essay. The second volume, lovingly gathered from Thomas' papers by the editor, sets forth the concert programs of more than forty years; it is uniquely valuable as a record of musical performances. Unfortunately, the reprint (New York: Da Capo Press, 1965) omits this second volume.

Upton, George P. *Musical Memories: My Recollections of Celebrities of the Half Century, 1850-1900*. Chicago: McClurg, 1908. Contains many reminiscences of Thomas while re-creating the artistic world in which he played so significant a part. Upton was music critic of the *Chicago Tribune* for more than forty years.

Robert McColley

HENRY DAVID THOREAU

Born: July 12, 1817; Concord, Massachusetts
Died: May 6, 1862; Concord, Massachusetts
Area of Achievement: Literature
Contribution: As essayist, naturalist, social critic, and editor, Thoreau has come to be recognized as a major figure in the Transcendentalist movement.

Early Life

David Henry Thoreau, who, characteristically, chose to reverse the order of his first and middle names, was born on July 12, 1817, in Concord, Massachusetts. Though he traveled widely in his imagination, he spent most of his forty-four years in that remarkable New England town. His mother, née Cynthia Dunbar, was a forceful, socially conscious woman of Scottish ancestry. His father, John Thoreau, came of French Huguenot stock; a reticent man, he was not very successful in business until he became a pioneer manufacturer of lead pencils. Henry was very close to his older brother John, whose death in 1842 affected him deeply. His sister Helen died in 1849, but his other sister, Sophia, survived him to serve as the guardian of his reputation.

After his graduation from Harvard, Thoreau taught briefly in a Concord school, but he resigned rather than be required to flog his pupils. From 1838 to 1841, he ran his own, relatively progressive, school in Concord, teaching Latin, Greek, and science. He spent 1843 in Staten Island, as a tutor in the household of Ralph Waldo Emerson's brother William. He also worked at various times as a house painter, carpenter, mason, surveyor, and pencil maker. During the years he lived with Ralph Waldo Emerson and his wife, Thoreau served as a kind of handyman. He also helped Emerson edit the Transcendentalist magazine *The Dial*.

Thoreau gave his first public lecture in the Concord Lyceum in 1838, and he continued intermittently as a lecturer for the remainder of his life. He was uncompromising toward his audience, particularly on the subject of slavery, and the reaction to his presentations was mixed. At Emerson's instigation, Thoreau began to keep a journal, which, published posthumously, serves as a valuable source for his experiences, observations, and reflections.

At five foot seven, he was slightly taller than average for his time, with longish hair and a prominent nose. He was striking, though not especially handsome, in appearance, and he made no effort to dress stylishly. Thoreau's only proposal of marriage, to a seventeen-year-old woman in 1840, was rejected, and he recoiled in horror from another woman's offer to him. He died, an equable bachelor, of the tuberculosis that first struck him in 1836 and that afflicted several members of his family.

Life's Work

From August 31 to September 13, 1839, during a break from their school, Thoreau and his brother John traveled by canoe along the Concord and Merrimack rivers. Over the course of a decade, Thoreau transformed their experiences into *A Week on the Concord and Merrimack Rivers* (1849), one of only two Thoreau books published during his lifetime. A short work, *A Week on the Concord and Merrimack Rivers* reshapes a fourteen-day excursion into a Saturday-Friday rhythm. In addition to recording the flora, fauna, and people that Thoreau encountered along the way, the book is a miscellany of poems and essays on a variety of topics, including friendship, local history, fishing, Christianity, Oriental religion, quackery, and Geoffrey Chaucer. Thoreau published one thousand copies of the work at his own expense, and he noted in his journal that 706 of them remained unsold in his attic.

On July 4, 1845, Thoreau moved into a cabin which he had built on land belonging to Emerson, along the shores of Walden Pond, two miles from Concord. He lived there, alone, for more than two years, until September 6, 1847, but in his account of his stay, the experience is translated into the natural cycle of a single year. Because of the indifferent response to *A Week on the Concord and Merrimack Rivers*, Thoreau did not rush into print with his second book. Instead, between 1846, when he first began writing it, and 1854, when he finally published it, Thoreau reshaped his material through journal entries, essays, poems, lectures, and more than half a dozen successive manuscript drafts. The result, *Walden: Or, Life in the Woods* (1854), is Thoreau's supreme achievement and one of the most accomplished works in American literature. Written in a baroque, epigrammatic style, *Walden* is not simply the record of one man's eccentric sojourn in a sylvan setting; it is an allegory of the deliberate life, a crafty provocation to its readers to awaken from the torpor and the quiet desperation of their lives. Thoreau describes his solitary existence beside Walden Pond as an experiment, and so, too, is his prose reenactment.

> I went to the woods because I wished to live deliberately, to front only the essential facts of life, and see if I could not learn what it had to teach, and not, when I came to die, discover that I had not lived. . . . I wanted to live deep and suck out all the marrow of life, to live so sturdily and Spartan-like as to put to rout all that was not life, to cut a broad swath and shave close, to drive life into a corner, and reduce it to its lowest terms, and, if it proved to be mean, why then to get the whole and genuine meanness of it, and publish its meanness to the world; or if it were sublime, to know it by experience, and be able to give a true account of it in my next excursion.

Thoreau is intent on clearing his life of the unnecessary encumbrances that materialism and a lack of self-reliance encourage. His book, which concludes with the exuberance of spring revivifying the pond, would have readers undergo a similar process of purifying enlightenment. *Walden* demands a careful reader, one alert enough not to dismiss it as a naïve effusion over nature, one sensitive to its author's extravagant, incendiary wit compounded of puns, paradoxes, and hyperboles.

In July, 1846, Thoreau spent one night in the Concord jail because of his refusal to pay a local poll tax. In a lecture first delivered in January, 1848, he explained his actions as a refusal to collaborate in the injustices of a government whose conduct of the Mexican War and whose perpetuation of the institution of slavery he stubbornly opposed. First published under the title "Resistance to Civil Government," the essay into which it evolved is best known as "Civil Disobedience" and is Thoreau's best-known essay. It proclaims the primacy of the individual and insists that if governmental policy cannot pass the muster of conscience, it ought to be resisted.

In 1857, Thoreau met abolitionist John Brown and was enormously impressed. He had earlier lectured in opposition to slavery, but Brown's arrest, following his raid on Harpers Ferry, Virginia, to incite a slave insurrection, inspired Thoreau to write his impassioned "A Plea for Captain John Brown." Though Thoreau's strenuous defense of Brown's actions did not save Brown from execution, the essay was probably the most widely read Thoreau work during his lifetime. "Slavery in Massachusetts," which he had written in 1854, calls for the state to secede from the nation and the individual

from the state rather than acquiesce in an oppressive system. Published in William Lloyd Garrison's *The Liberator*, "Slavery in Massachusetts" also had a relatively large readership.

Though he was more closely tied to Concord than were any of its other major authors, Thoreau undertook a few brief excursions elsewhere—to Maine, Cape Cod, New Hampshire, Quebec, and Minnesota. These trips provided material for several works that were not published in their entireties until after his death. *Cape Cod* (1865), for example, is a cheerful report on the environment and the local lore of what was then an exotic region. *The Maine Woods* (1864) is a fairly straightforward and perceptive description of the people, plants, and animals in the northeastern frontier of the United States. Thoreau's final excursion came on May 6, 1862, in the family home in Concord; according to his sister Sophia, his last sentence was: "Now comes good sailing."

Summary

Thoreau was a friend of several of the most important New England authors of the mid-nineteenth century, among them Ralph Waldo Emerson, Nathaniel Hawthorne, and Bronson Alcott. He was not widely known outside the Concord circle, however, and within it he was generally condescended to as someone who had never accomplished anything beyond a local interest. Both *A Week on the Concord and Merrimack Rivers* and *Walden* were out of print by the time of his final illness. Yet those two books were reprinted within weeks of his death, and five volumes of Thoreau's unpublished writings were brought out during the early 1860's. His reputation began to expand, first as a nature writer. Despite his crusty insistence, in *Walden* and in the pugnacious essay "Life Without Principle," that he refused to be exemplary of anything but fierce independence, he even attracted disciples.

Late in the nineteenth century, Thoreau attracted the admiration of British critics, particularly Laborites, as a social critic. Early in the twentieth century, Mohandas Gandhi was so impressed by "Civil Disobedience" that he published it as a pamphlet. Gandhi credited Thoreau's ideas on nonviolent resistance to illegitimate authority as being a principal inspiration behind the movement for Indian independence. In the United States, Martin Luther King, Jr., was a fervent champion of Thoreau's political ideas. "Civil Disobedience" has continued to be invoked not only by opponents of

racism but also by those objecting to nuclear armaments and nuclear power. More than one protestor has spent more than one night in jail, convinced that he or she was a genuine Thoreauvian.

The ascendancy of Thoreau's literary reputation was more gradual, but, with more than two hundred editions of *Walden* in existence and his face on a postage stamp, the recluse of Walden Pond is now one of the foremost celebrities of American literature, as widely studied, read, and respected as any other author of his time. He has even eclipsed his Transcendentalist mentor Emerson in popularity. *Walden* is acknowledged as Thoreau's masterpiece, and it is read not as a series of naïve nature descriptions but as a complex and sophisticated literary performance. The delights of its dazzling style have drawn attention to the craftsmanship of many of his other writings.

Despite Thoreau's posthumous apotheosis as master of observation, of political principles, and of the English language, he remains a difficult writer. His rich prose is elusively allusive and often deliberately abrasive. Those who would keep pace with the brisk movement of his prickly mind are those who have learned, and earned, the serenity of self-reliance.

Bibliography

Glick, Wendell, ed. *The Recognition of Henry David Thoreau: Selected Criticism Since 1848*. Ann Arbor: University of Michigan Press, 1969. An anthology of historical commentaries documenting the growth in Thoreau's reputation—from obscurity and condescension to veneration.

Harding, Walter. *The Days of Henry Thoreau: A Biography*. New York: Knopf, 1965. The standard full-scale biography by the most respected specialist in the field.

———, ed. *Thoreau: Man of Concord*. New York: Holt Rinehart, 1960. A compilation of recollections of Thoreau by dozens of his contemporaries, it provides testimony to the life within its nineteenth century contexts.

Lebeaux, Richard. *Thoreau's Seasons*. Amherst: University of Massachusetts Press, 1984. An application of psychologist Erik Erikson's theory of personality development to Thoreau's life from his Walden Pond experiment until his death.

Matthiessen, Francis O. *American Renaissance: Art and Expression in the Age of Emerson and Whitman*. London and New York: Oxford University Press, 1941. With extensive chapters on each of its major figures, this is the pioneering study of the Transcendentalist movement, the one that set the agenda for future studies of the period.

Richardson, Robert D., Jr. *Henry Thoreau: A Life of the Mind*. Berkeley: University of California Press, 1986. A recent biography, concentrating on Thoreau's intellectual development from age twenty until his death.

Shanley, J. Lyndon. *The Making of Walden*. Chicago: University of Chicago Press, 1957. A fascinating analysis of the stages in the composition of Thoreau's most celebrated work; it demonstrates that, far from a spontaneous record of actual experiences, *Walden* was in fact a carefully contrived work of art.

Van Anglen, Kevin P., ed. *Simplify, Simplify: and Other Quotations from Henry David Thoreau*. New York: Columbia University Press, 1996. Presents 750 of Thoreau's most important thoughts on a range of subjects.

Wagenknecht, Edward. *Henry David Thoreau: What Manner of Man?* Amherst: University of Massachusetts Press, 1981. A brief, literate overview of the life and its major themes. Wagenknecht proceeds topically rather than chronologically.

Steven G. Kellman

ALEXIS DE TOCQUEVILLE

Born: July 29, 1805; Paris, France
Died: April 16, 1859; Cannes, France
Areas of Achievement: Political science and sociology
Contribution: A political and social analyst, Tocqueville was the earliest, the greatest, and surely the most percipient observer of the initial growth and increasing persuasiveness of democracy in all areas of American culture.

Early Life

Alexis-Henri-Charles-Maurice Clérel, Comte de Tocqueville, was born in the Paris suburb of Verneuil on July 29, 1805, a few years after his aristocratic parents had been released from their imprisonment by revolutionary forces for their close relations with the collapsed monarchy of Louis XVI and for their outspoken support of it before revolutionary tribunals. Alexis' father, Hervé, subsequently became a prefect (governor) in various states under the restored monarchy of Charles X. His mother never fully recovered from her treatment during the Revolution. Living on family properties at Verneuil, Tocqueville was first tutored by Abbé Lesueur, the Catholic priest who had taught his father and a man whom Tocqueville would remember affectionately for having instilled in him a belief in the Christian principles that he would abandon for a time but would return to in later life.

In his adolescence, the young Tocqueville spent six years in Metz and completed his studies brilliantly at the local *lycée*. A perceptive, if not an omnivorous, reader profoundly impressed by the writings of René Descartes, Tocqueville gave up his strict Catholicism for a more critical Christian Deism, that is, a belief in human reason, rather than God, as the operative force in man's affairs. Emotionally and intellectually more at ease with tangible matters that were susceptible to precise analysis than with theories, Tocqueville embarked on law studies, which he completed in 1825. Almost immediately, he and his brother Edward took an extended tour of Italy and Sicily, the importance of which emerged in the voluminous and detailed journals he kept. What he perceived was not so much the invariable landscapes as evidences of social structure, the shape of which he deduced by the structure of the applicable political systems and laws. Perhaps because he was only twenty-two years old, he imaginatively compared his keen observations on the Italian scene with his knowledge of French and British institutions.

Meanwhile, in 1827, he was offered a career which both his family background and his own predilections seemed to favor. By royal patent from Charles X, Tocqueville was appointed to a Versailles judgeship in the department of Seine and Oise, literally within the shadow of the king's residence. Fearful that the routines of his office might render him incapable of judging great movements or of guiding great undertakings, Tocqueville, nevertheless, devoted himself to his duties. Later, Charles X, the king who had appointed him, chose abdication in the face of the Revolution of 1830. At war with himself for having to swear allegiance to the new monarch, Louis-Philippe, whose values he repudiated, Tocqueville still remained in service long enough to request from the minister of interior in 1831 leave to investigate the penal system in the United States.

Life's Work

Accompanied by another French magistrate who was both a colleague and a friend, Gustave de Beaumont, a man who later served as a deputy to the National Assembly and as the French ambassador to London and Vienna and was a writer-scholar of distinction in his own right, Tocqueville invented the pretext of studying the American penal system in order to tackle the larger task that he had set for himself—a thorough, on-site investigation of what then was the world's first and only completely democratic society: the United States. Only twenty-six years old, Tocqueville appeared less robust than the country that would absorb his attention. Portraits accent long arms and a short, thin, and frail body. Beneath locks of brown hair, his delicate, aristocratic face was dominated by large, intelligent brown eyes. He and Beaumont embarked for New York in April, 1831.

Returning to France in 1832, Tocqueville and Beaumont finished their study of the American penal system. It was published in 1833 as *Du système pénitentiaire aux États-Unis et de son application en France* (*On the Penitentiary System in the United States and Its Application in France*, 1833). This official obligation resolved, Tocqueville left his judicial post, moved into a modest Paris apartment, and began what he later described as the happiest two years of his life, writing his two-volume *De la démocratie en Amérique* (1835, 1840; *Democracy in America*, 1835, 1840). This work was proclaimed the classic treatment of its subject throughout the Western world and assured Tocqueville's fame as a political observer and political philosopher, and, later, as a sociologist.

While writing the third volume of *Democracy in America*, Tocqueville in 1837 sought election as a deputy from his native constituency, La Manche. Failing in 1837, he succeeded in 1839, serving in the Chamber of Deputies continuously until 1851 and almost always in opposition to the government of Louis-Philippe. From 1842 to 1848, practicing his belief that a healthy state was founded upon vigorous local government, he served on the local general council. Although he never perceived himself as a political leader, he nevertheless reinforced his convictions by public service.

Meanwhile, he was among the few who prophesied the coming of the Revolution of 1848, which ended the Second Republic, replacing it with the plebiscite government of Louis Napoleon, who was soon to proclaim the Second Empire and his rule as Napoleon III. Though he had voted against Napoleon, Tocqueville was reelected to a new national assembly and on June 2, 1849, was appointed France's foreign minister. Once again, his acceptance of the post was intended to keep the republican spirit alive, certain as he was that Napoleon intended to bury it. Over the next few months as foreign minister—he resigned on October 31, 1849—he dealt with the Austrian-Piedmontese conflict, the Turkish question, problems with the Roman Catholic church, and Swiss rights of asylum, each an important problem at the time.

Exhausted when he left office, he served on yet another parliamentary commission studying the question of Napoleon's reeligibility as president—an issue resolved dramatically by the president's own *coup d'état* of December 2, 1851. It was amid such events, the latter of which shocked Tocqueville as well as most of Europe's informed opinion, that he began writing *Souvenirs de Alexis de Tocqueville* (1893; *The Recollections of Alexis de Tocqueville*, 1896, 1949) in June, 1850. Although many scholars regard it as his greatest book, a classic historical, sociological, and political analysis of the antecedents, personalities, and events of the Revolution of 1848 in France, Tocqueville had not intended it for publication.

With the completion of *The Recollections of Alexis de Tocqueville*, Tocqueville was already embarked on his *L'Ancien Régime et la révolution* (1856; *The Old Régime and the Revolution*, 1856), in which, after five years of exhaustive archival research, he demonstrated that the centralization of power in France was not a consequence of the Revolution of 1789 but rather had been proceeding for centuries. This extension of power, pursued by an alienated and obsolete aristocracy and running counter to gains in popular power and popular enthusiasm for equality and freedom, helped make revolution inevitable. This was Tocqueville's last work. Lying ill for several weeks at his family estate at Cannes, he confessed, regretted that he had not been a more ardent disciple of Catholicism, and died on April 16, 1859.

Summary

Alexis de Tocqueville's principal moral and intellectual concern was with freedom. He was not a liberal, however, any more than he was a democrat. Liberalism skirted on unbridled individualism, democracy on an egalitarian reductionism, a tendency to put everyone on an equal, but low level. Rather, in Tocqueville's view, all freedom begins with recognition that man is the creature of a larger collectivity, a creature of God. Lacking this appreciation, no one can really call himself free. From that basic premise—and it suffuses all of Tocqueville's major works—he strove through his extraordinary powers of observation and research to develop a political philosophy that struck a balance between men's rights and their duties. While capable of dealing in abstractions in these matters, he nevertheless felt comfortable only when fitting them into historical and substantive cultural contexts, whether his immediate interests were structural, that is, sociological, or lay in the measurement and movement of power, that is, political.

Being neither a liberal nor a democrat but a French aristocrat who recognized that the authority of aristocracies in France and Great Britain had been shattered—and in the United States, he believed, had never existed—lent Tocqueville's work its much-admired objectivity. His major studies were offered primarily for the consideration of Frenchmen. While democratization had proceeded much further in the United States, France, he believed, also confronted the same conditions. While manifested dramatically in political upheavals and revolutions, both historical tendencies (toward popular power and toward centralized power), he believed, were centuries in the making. The question for his day was, Would the age-old centralizing process that he discerned, when joined with the inevitable centralizing power of majoritarian and egalitarian democracy, lead to tyranny—though a tyranny of, or in the name of, the masses? Tocqueville sensed what the twentieth century has proved—most authoritarian states have justified themselves as being democratic, as governing in the name of the people. Democrats, it seemed on his evidence, were assuming the political and administrative roles of aristocracies. In the face of the egalitarian surge, however, the centralization of power was broadening, not declining, hence the interference of the state increasingly menaced the integrity of the individual's freedom.

Thirteen years older than Karl Marx, Tocqueville wrote of the importance of classes in history, while utterly rejecting what later became Marx's determinism respecting their roles. Unearthing the interrelations among a people's perceived and historical experiences, their manners and mores, and the configuration of their political institutions, his works place him among the other great men who analyzed the nature of society, beginning with Aristotle and proceeding through modern times.

Bibliography

Herr, Richard. *Tocqueville and the Old Regime.* Princeton, N.J.: Princeton University Press, 1962. The author, a specialist in modern French history, deals with the incompleteness and apparent inconsistencies of Tocqueville's *The Old Régime and the Revolution.* An informative and well-written work with a selective bibliography and a useful index.

Jardin, Andre. *Tocqueville: A Biography.* Lydia Davis, trans. New York: Farrar Straus Giroux, and London: Halban, 1988. Comprehensive examination of the factors in Tocqueville's private and public life that affected his writing, opinions, and political career.

Laski, Harold J. "Alexis de Tocqueville and Democracy." In *The Social and Political Ideas of Some Representative Thinkers of the Victorian Age,* edited by F. J. C. Hearnshaw. London: Harrap, 1933; New York: Barnes and Noble, 1967. Laski, a distinguished British liberal-left political analyst and a force behind the extension of the British welfare state, cogently examines Toc-

queville's views on social democracy and their relevance to modern democracies. No notes, bibliography, or index. Generally available.

Mayer, Jacob Peter. *Alexis de Tocqueville: A Biographical Study in Political Science.* New York: Harper, 1960. Mayer is one of the foremost authorities on Tocqueville, having researched, translated, revised, and completed many of Tocqueville's works. This is a delightfully informative and clearly written overview intended for general readers. There is one portrait, an appendix assessing Tocqueville's influences after a century, endnotes, a useful bibliography, and a reliable index. Generally available.

Mitchell, Harvey. *Individual Choice and the Structures of History: Alexis de Tocqueville As Historian Reappraised.* Cambridge and New York: Cambridge University Press, 1996. In a new study, Mitchell provides valuable insight into Tocqueville's works and his philosophy of history.

Pierson, George W. *Tocqueville and Beaumont in America.* New York: Oxford University Press, 1938. This remains the definitive study of Tocqueville's months in the United States. A thorough evaluation of the settings through which these two friends passed, of the people they met, and of the sources that they employed for their study of the American penal system and, in Tocqueville's case, for his great study of democracy. Traces Tocqueville's intellectual development with an eye to clarifying all of his writings. Clearly written and understandable by general readers. There are footnotes, a good bibliography, and a valuable index.

Tocqueville, Alexis de. *Democracy in America by Alexis de Tocqueville.* Edited by Phillips Bradley. 2 vols. New York: Knopf, 1945. This is a revised version of the first English translation and includes informative notes, historical essays, useful bibliographies, and extensive indexes in each volume. The author claims that Tocqueville's work remains one of the most magisterial analyses ever produced on the principle of the sovereignty of the people, its cultural roots, and its evolving political effects.

_____. *Recollections.* Edited by Jacob Peter Mayer and A. P. Kerr. Translated by George Lawrence. New York: Doubleday, 1970. This is the best edition of what many regard as Tocqueville's finest work. Mayer and Kerr, experts on Tocqueville, provide an informative introductory essay, many footnotes, a select bibliography, and an extensive index. Available in good bookstores as well as major college and university libraries.

Zetterbaum, Marvin. *Tocqueville and the Problem of Democracy*. Stanford, Calif.: Stanford University Press, 1967. An examination of Tocqueville's proposition that democracy was inevitable and therefore that democracy had to be made safe for the world. The author's view is that the "inevitability thesis" distracted readers from Tocqueville's central concern about perfecting democracy and of harmonizing the demands of justice with those of excellence. However brief, this is an enlightening study, clearly written and intended for the general reader. There are footnotes throughout, a useful bibliography, and a valuable index.

Clifton K. Yearley

LEO TOLSTOY

Born: September 9, 1828; Yasnaya Polyana, Russia
Died: November 20, 1910; Astapovo, Russia
Areas of Achievement: Literature and social reform
Contribution: During the first half of his long and active life, Tolstoy brought universal fame to Russian literature through his fiction. In later years, he achieved worldwide renown as a pacifist, social activist, and moralist. He is equally significant as a novelist and moral philosopher.

Early Life

Leo Tolstoy traces his aristocratic origins back to the founding of the Russian state in the ninth century. His ancestors, at times faithful servants, at times opponents of the Crown, amassed fame as well as respectable wealth over the centuries. Thus Tolstoy, though orphaned at age eight, grew up in comfort under the care of relatives at the various Tolstoy residences. He subsequently shaped a vague memory of his mother, who died when he was two, into an idealized portrait of the perfect woman and featured such a paragon in many of his major works. His first published narrative, *Detstvo* (1852; *Childhood*, 1862), re-creates a boy's tender relationship with and painful loss of his mother.

A flamboyant lifestyle, filled with carousing and gambling, prevented Tolstoy from completing university study, but he revealed an early talent for writing and meticulously recorded daily details, from purest thoughts to debauched acts, in his diaries. He continued keeping such journals until old age, providing future literary historians with rich source material for every stage of his life. His elder siblings and relations, dismayed at the young count's irresolution and wantonness, sent him in 1851 to the Caucasus, where Russia was engaged in sporadic military operations with hostile natives.

Tolstoy's subsequent participation in the Crimean War put an end to the unstable years of his youth. Active service during the siege of Sevastopol motivated him to set down his impressions of the carnage in a series of sketches, "Sevastopol v dekabre," "Sevastopol v maye," and "Sevastopol v avguste" (1854-1856; collected in translation as *Sebastopol*, 1887). His original and above all truthful accounts pleased a public that had grown tired of the prevailing vainglorious, deceitful war reports. So convincingly did Tolstoy chronicle the horror of battlefield life and communicate his disillusionment with war that czarist censors moved to alter his exposés. Tolstoy's later devotion to nonviolence stems from these experiences. His perceptions about the ineptitude of military commanders juxtaposed to the courage and common sense of foot soldiers resurface in his major work, *Voyna i mir* (1865-1869; *War and Peace*, 1886). Moreover, his dispute with the authorities over his forthright reporting set the stage for a lifelong confrontation with the imperial autocracy.

Life's Work

Tolstoy's long literary career followed several distinct directions. The labors of his younger years belong to the field of aesthetic literature, though he embarked on that course only after lengthy deliberation. When he returned to St. Petersburg in 1855 following military service, high society lionized the young hero and for a time drew him back into the swirl of its carefree amusements. His strong didactic bent and quarrelsome nature did not, however, endear him to the literary establishment. He soon antagonized writers on all sides of the social and political spectrum and in the end thought it best to develop his talents without the help of contemporaries. The deaths of two brothers and an execution witnessed in Paris in 1857 led him to approach life in a more serious vein. He opened and directed a school for peasant children on his estate, using pedagogical methods which he himself established, and entered into lively journalistic polemics with other educators over his scheme of placing moral teachings above the acquisition of knowledge. These and other controversial public exchanges brought renewed government interference which impelled Tolstoy to turn to less antagonistic activity. In 1862, he married Sophia Behrs, sixteen years his junior, became a country gentleman, and settled down to a life of writing.

The 1860's were almost wholly devoted to the composition of the epic *War and Peace*, which went through so many revisions and changes of focus, even as it was being serialized, that no clearly definitive version of the novel exists. Among the diverse issues embedded in the finished product are Tolstoy's own interpretation of the Napoleonic Wars, a richly drawn panorama of early nineteenth century Russian upper-class society supplemented by many biographical details, a firm conviction that the values of close-knit family life are far superior to social rituals, and a wealth of sundry philosophical observations. *War and Peace* owes its immense success to the author's vast descriptive talents, which manage to neutralize his lifelong tendency to sermonize.

Reflections on the importance of stable domestic existence also dominate Tolstoy's second major work, *Anna Karenina* (1875-1878; English translation, 1886), in which he chronicles the fates of three aristocratic families and demonstrates that the title figure's insistence on personal happiness to the detriment of family duty engenders tragedy for all concerned. The novel also develops Tolstoy's pet notion that Russian peasant mores are morally superior to high society's ideals. Ideas about the meaning of death and the validity of suicide also represent an important strain in *Anna Karenina*, reflecting Tolstoy's own frequent contact with death, as he lost several children and other close relatives in the 1870's during the composition of the novel. The themes of these two major works are echoed in the many shorter pieces produced by the prolific Tolstoy during the same period.

The late 1870's represent a watershed for Tolstoy, a time when a prolonged spiritual crisis forced him to evaluate both his privileged life and his literary endeavors. A drastic reorientation evolved from this period of introspection. No longer able to justify his considerable wealth in the face of millions of illiterate, destitute peasants and laborers, Tolstoy resolved to make amends by placing his talent and means at the disposal of the poor. In consequence, he actively challenged what he perceived to be the hypocrisy of Russia's ruling institutions. Since the Russian Orthodox church worked closely with the conservative czarist government to maintain the status quo, it too became a target of Tolstoy's dissatisfactions. After publication of the strongly anticlerical *Voskreseniye* (1899; *Resurrection*, 1899), Tolstoy found himself excommunicated, an action he dismissed lightly, having over the years developed a personal Christianity which became the basis of much of his nonfictional writing. His spiritual anxieties and search for an acceptable faith are chronicled in *Ispoved* (1884; *A Confession*, 1885). Both Tolstoy's literary style and his subject matter underwent extreme changes during this time. The works became shorter, using more succinct and simpler language, and became decidedly more opinionated. Fiction largely gave way to social and philosophical commentary, and even the remaining fic-tional pieces were intricately shaped to transmit Tolstoy's moral messages. Thus, *Smert Ivana Ilicha* (1886; *The Death of Ivan Ilich*, 1887) presents Tolstoy's view of the proper attitude toward death and dying, and the play *Vlast tmy* (1887; *The Power of Darkness*, 1888) warns of the grim consequences engendered by evil thoughts and deeds. Tolstoy justified the political nature of this type of fiction by challenging the very morality of aesthetic detachment. Since even his polemical commentaries adhered to respectable literary standards, he never lost his readership. On the contrary, people of all persuasions debated his works with interest, even fascination.

Tolstoy's efforts to use his name and fortune in support of favorite causes gave rise to severe disharmony within the Tolstoy family. For long years, the spouses battled over property and copyright privileges. These quarrels led Tolstoy to replace his earlier emphasis on family unity with issues of personal salvation and questions of ethics. He returned to the theme of family in one of his most controversial narratives, *Kreytserova sonata* (1889; *The Kreutzer Sonata*, 1890). In this work he denies that marriage is a valid social institution by defining its main purpose as the gratification of lust, detrimental to women and destructive of personal integrity. The major character, Pozdnyshev, murders his wife in a bout of jealousy and proposes the abolition of all sexual acts, even at the expense of humanity's extinction.

Not all Tolstoy's later views express such absolute negatives, but most of his mature output was disputations in nature. For example, his treatise *Chto takoye iskusstvo?* (1898; *What Is Art?*, 1898) sets forth his revised opinion on the nature and role of literature. He dismisses most art, including his own earlier writings, as immoral and undemocratic, suggesting instead that all art forms be morally instructive and executed in simple, guileless fashion accessible to the multitudes.

Throughout his long life, Tolstoy continued to espouse peaceful settlement of international conflicts. In time, his advocacy of nonresistance made him into a prominent spokesman against war and the death penalty. His regard for the impoverished masses and his many controversial stands brought him worldwide fame. The image of the revered, bearded, aged "repentant nobleman," holding court and expounding his position on national and global topics while dressed in homemade rural attire, drew diverse crowds from far and wide. His very

renown prevented an angry czarist government from treating him harshly. To prevent the total dissolution of his domestic bonds, Tolstoy permitted the family to remain at the imposing country estate, but he himself withdrew to a humble corner of it to observe a rigorously modest life-style. At the age of eighty-two, he decided to cut even these ties and secretly left home to live henceforth entirely according to his convictions. Illness almost immediately forced him to abandon the train journey, and he died at the stationmaster's house a week later, surrounded by dignitaries and reporters. He lies buried in a distant corner of his estate. His simple, unadorned grave and the mansion, converted into a Tolstoy museum after the Russian Revolution, are a favorite stop for countless visitors and tourists.

Summary

Leo Tolstoy's impact as both artist and moralist continues undiminished. His fictional works, especially his earlier ones, retain a charm that is proof of his enormous descriptive powers. Yet even these works express personal preferences and values, which the author elucidates at every opportunity. Thus it is, in the final analysis, Tolstoy the teacher, moralist, and public commentator who dominates. Through his doctrine of nonresistance, which he based on the words of Jesus and through which he resisted many inequities of the state, he set examples for similar movements in India under Mohandas Gandhi and the United States under Martin Luther King, Jr. While his pronouncements on behalf of the poor often assume an overly shrill tone, he backed these convictions with solid action. Not only did his income and efforts facilitate great humanitarian projects, from famine relief to resettlement of religious dissenters, but also he himself found no peace until he had adjusted his life-style to fit the humblest. His deliberations on death and ideas on how to cope with it cut through the stilted social conventions of his time to find universal appreciation and application in the twentieth century.

Closely linked to Tolstoy's thoughts about death and dying was his quest for a new religious attitude. By examining the doctrines and practices of the Russian Orthodox church as well as other religions and finding them incompatible with Jesus' words, he pointed to alternative approaches, advocating a way of life based on the Gospels, not church dogma. In this, too, he anticipated certain twentieth century movements toward a personal fundamentalism.

Tolstoy also generated opposition. His dogmatic and frequently cantankerous method of conveying his beliefs alienated many potential adherents. In the manner of all prophets, he brooked no contradiction of his scheme of universal ethical improvement. Even so, his many achievements and contributions as major writer, social activist, and moral philosopher remain universally acknowledged.

Bibliography

Benson, Ruth Crego. *Women in Tolstoy: The Ideal and the Erotic.* Urbana: University of Illinois Press, 1973. Concentrates on Tolstoy's changing vision of the role and importance of family life. Suggests that Tolstoy struggled most of his life with a dichotomous view of women, regarding them in strictly black-and-white terms, as saints or sinners. Analyzes the female characters in the major and several minor works in terms of such a double view. An interesting and provocative piece of feminist criticism.

Bloom, Harold, ed. *Leo Tolstoy.* New York: Chelsea House, 1986. A collection of critical essays, encompassing the years 1920-1983. The views expressed give a very good sampling of the wide range of opinions about Tolstoy prevalent among Western critics. Many of these critics assign a prominent place in literary history to Tolstoy, comparing him to, among others, Homer and Johann Wolfgang von Goethe. Some of the articles deal with specific works; others define Tolstoy's contributions to nineteenth century European intellectual movements. Limited bibliography.

De Courcel, Martine, *Tolstoy: The Ultimate Reconciliation.* Translated by Peter Levi. New York: Scribner, and London: Macmillan, 1987. A detailed biography, annotated with selected bibliography, which relies heavily on the notebooks and diaries of Tolstoy and those of his wife, Sophia. Concentrates on Tolstoy's domestic life but has extensive references to his general public activity. Posits the unique notion that Tolstoy left home at the end of his life in order to return to aesthetic literature.

Greenwood, E. B. *Tolstoy: The Comprehensive Vision.* London: Dent, and New York: St. Martin's Press, 1975. For Greenwood, Tolstoy's diverse strivings were attributable to his belief that art and life could be brought together under one philosophical tenet. Greenwood detects a search for such a unified vision in most of the major writings. Stresses Tolstoy's contribution to philosophy and religion.

Rancour-Laferriere, Daniel. *Tolstoy on the Couch: Misogyny, Masochism, and the Absent Mother.* New York: New York University Press, and Basingstoke, Hampshire: Macmillan, 1998. Fascinating psychoanalytical study of Tolstoy's papers and diaries, focusing on his feelings about women and celibacy, and describing the childhood events that shaped his views.

Rowe, William W. *Leo Tolstoy.* Boston: Twayne, 1986. Concise introduction to Tolstoy's life and work, with special emphasis on the major novels and later didactic writings. Discusses, briefly, most of Tolstoy's major concerns. Excellent treatment of individual characters in the major novels. Selected bibliography.

Sankovitch, Natasha. *Creating and Recovering Experience: Repetition in Tolstoy.* Stanford, Calif.: Stanford University Press, 1998. The author argues that repetition is a recurring theme in Tolstoy's work and provides examples demonstrating this device as a means of shaping of characters and relationships.

Simmons, Ernest J. *Tolstoy.* London and Boston: Routledge, 1973. Extensive chronological account of Tolstoy's public activities. Includes social and cultural background on Russia during Tolstoy's time and discusses the importance of Tolstoy's theories on religion, society, morality, and literature. Adds comments on Tolstoy's relevance to the twentieth century and on his international stature. Selected bibliography.

Tolstaia, Andreevna S. *The Diaries of Sophia Tolstoy.* Edited by O. A. Golinenko et al. Translated by Cathy Porter with an introduction by R. F. Christian. New York: Random House, 1985. Illustrated. This massive personal record of Tolstoy's wife, detailing their life together, spans the years 1862-1910. Sophia Tolstoy kept an almost daily account of her husband's opinions, doubts, and plans concerning his literary activity and social ventures as well as of her relationship with other writers and thinkers. The diaries often portray Tolstoy in an unfavorable light, since the spouses were temperamentally incompatible, and she chafed under his domination. She collaborated closely with Tolstoy for many decades, however, and her notes give a fascinating and intimate view of the Tolstoy family and of the extent to which this family served as background for many of the literary episodes.

Wilson, A. N. *Tolstoy.* London: Hamilton, and New York: Norton, 1988. A long but immensely readable biography, breezy, insightful, and opinionated, by a prolific and highly regarded British novelist. Illustrated; includes a useful chronology of Tolstoy's life and times as well as notes, bibliography, and index.

Margot K. Frank

HENRI DE TOULOUSE-LAUTREC

Born: November 24, 1864; Albi, France
Died: September 9, 1901; Château de Malromé, France
Area of Achievement: Art
Contribution: By means of more than seven hundred paintings, sketches, lithographs, and posters, Toulouse-Lautrec recorded vividly the people and activities of Paris in the last decades of the nineteenth century. He elevated color lithography and the poster to major art forms.

Early Life

Henri Marie Raymond de Toulouse-Lautrec Monfa was born into an aristocratic family whose lineage went back to the time of Charlemagne. In separate falls in 1878 and 1879, he broke the femurs of both legs. Throughout his life his legs remained small, while his upper body grew normally. He always required a cane to support his four-foot, six-inch frame. After these accidents, he was not able to dance or to ride, the usual activities of his social class. During his convalesence, his mother and a family friend, René Princeteau, a deaf-mute artist of equestrian scenes, encouraged him to paint.

Though tentative in technique, his early pictures, *Soldier Saddling His Horse, Trotting Horseman, Amazon,* and *White Horse Gazelle,* are full of life and quite accomplished. They manifest an unfiltered naïveté and are all the more striking for their deliberate use of bold color combinations.

In 1882, Toulouse-Lautrec became a pupil of Léon-Joseph-Florentin Bonnat and, in 1883-1887, of Fernand Cormon. Both academicists, they taught Toulouse-Lautrec the principles of composition. His work was thenceforth more controlled. A visit home in 1883 produced the somewhat Impressionistic oil *The Artist's Mother at Breakfast.*

In 1885, twenty-one years of age and financially independent, Toulouse-Lautrec opened a studio in Montmarte in the building where Edgar Degas had his studio. Degas became his artistic idol, though in 1894 Degas would harshly accuse Toulouse-Lautrec of imitation. His first lithograph was a song-sheet cover in 1887 for Aristide Bruant, who gave Toulouse-Lautrec his first public showing on the walls of his café, Le Mirliton. Toulouse-Lautrec's pastel portrait of Vincent van Gogh, whom he had met at Cormon's in 1886, belongs to the same year.

In 1887, Toulouse-Lautrec painted *Portrait of the Artist's Mother Reading.* At first it seems Impressionistic, but, in fact, the subject is not treated as the focus of light; thrust in the foreground, her presence dominates the painting. For Toulouse-Lautrec, "Nothing exists but the figure. . . . Landscape is only accessory."

Life's Work

Toulouse-Lautrec's art is set against the period known as *fin de siècle* or *la belle époque.* Toulouse-Lautrec, who saw beauty in the ugly and heroism in the underside of Paris, reflects both terms. He called himself a historian of life, which he viewed without pity, false moralizing, or self-righteousness. His pictures are precious historical documents and rival novels and histories in describing the life and moral outlook of his generation.

Impressionism influenced Toulouse-Lautrec's work; yet he more precisely falls in the French drawing tradition of Jacques-Louis David, Jean August Dominique Ingres, and Degas. He did not use shimmering, all-enveloping light as did the Impressionists. He emphasized line, pattern, and pure, unmodeled color without chiaroscuro, as in Japanese art and the then-current Nabi movement. His colors, as are his subjects, are theatrical and often harsh. In his love of line, he differed from other Postimpressionists, such as van Gogh and Paul Gauguin, who stressed mass and solidity. By a few deft strokes of line, he penetrated his subjects' essential character. Toulouse-Lautrec's gift, as was Degas', was to capture figures from contemporary scenes in characteristic poses at unguarded moments, always with some caricature. As his friends noted, he would passionately pursue his subjects in the prime of their careers, then drop them.

In 1888, under the spell of Degas, Toulouse-Lautrec began to illustrate the lowlife of Paris. Montmartre was its focus since the opening of the café Le Chat Noir in 1881. His first important painting was *Le Cirque Fernando: Circus Rider,* done in the flat style of the Japanese prints he collected. Like Gauguin, whom he had recently met, he preferred a bold distortion of perspective to the Impressionists' sense of light.

By this time, Toulouse-Lautrec drew for the leading illustrated journals, *Courrier Français, Paris Illustré, Figaro Illustré,* and *Rire.* He did this

not for money—Toulouse-Lautrec never needed art to make a living—but for recognition. In 1888, too, Toulouse-Lautrec first submitted work for the annual Brussels exhibition of the avant garde XX (the twenty) group. The next year saw his major oils, *Au bal du Moulin de la Galette* and *The Girl with Red Hair.* The Moulin de la Galette was one of Toulouse-Lautrec's café haunts.

The Moulin Rouge's opening ushered the gay nineties into Paris. This café became the in place for Paris society, including Toulouse-Lautrec and his cousin and companion, Gabriel Tapié de Céleyran. It was the venue of his best-known pieces. His painting, *Au Moulin Rouge: La Danse* (1890), graced the foyer of the café. It is his first depiction of the dancer La Goulue (the glutton: the stage name of Louise Weber) and her partner, Valentin le Désossé. In 1891, the Moulin Rouge commissioned Toulouse-Lautrec's first poster to advertise the same dancers. He created a sensation by flaunting La Goulue's scandalous white muslim drawers. The poster both launched her career and gave the artist wider recognition. Désossé dominates the foreground in stark profile, while Toulouse-Lautrec and his friends are silhouetted in back. In the same

year, *La Goulue au Moulin Rouge* featured her famous deep décolletage.

Toulouse-Lautrec's thirty-one posters are consciously flat, asymmetrical, and decorative; figures are often cropped at the border. His "line, flair, and daring layout" were immediately praised in the press. Jules Chéret, the greatest poster artist of his day, named Toulouse-Lautrec as his successor. Toulouse-Lautrec's prints were better for his painting skills, but the fluidity and economy of stroke of the lithographic medium added to the descriptive capability of his paintings. He did many identical pictures in both mediums.

Toulouse-Lautrec's friendship with the rising star Jane Avril is marked by numerous representations of her over several years. Avril admired his art and may have been in love with him. *Jane Avril Entering Moulin Rouge*, *Jane Avril Leaving Moulin Rouge*, and *Jane Avril Dancing at Moulin Rouge* appeared in 1892. In the last, Toulouse-Lautrec used oils in a sketchy manner to render the dancer's movements. Avril is absorbed in her dancing, her isolation emphasized by the couple in the background who pay her no attention.

In 1892 came a masterpiece, *Au Moulin Rouge.* In a framework of diagonals appear the artist himself, his cousin Tapié de Céleyran, La Goulue, other friends at the table in the foreground, and the mysterious green-faced lady partially cropped off at the right. In 1892, two posters of Bruant in his familiar black coat and red scarf made the entrepreneur's profile known throughout Paris.

A Corner of the Moulin de la Galette of the same year is a minor masterpiece. Human forms are set in overlapping planes. The isolation of these denizens of the demimonde is established by the fact that no one's gaze engages that of another person.

In 1893, Toulouse-Lautrec's poster *Jane Avril at the Jardin de Paris* again "put her in the limelight," said the journal *Fin de Siècle* on September 3. Another poster, *Jane Avril at Divan Japonais*, announced a new café which opened auspiciously, attracting crowds to hear the songs of Yvette Guilbert, but closed soon after. Avril is in the foreground while Guilbert is shown performing but with her head cropped out of the frame. Toulouse-Lautrec's frequent use of cropping as well as his ability to focus on one area, allowing all else to appear marginal or distorted, reflects his awareness of the new medium of photography, which was then influencing the art world. On the psychological level, too, Toulouse-Lautrec recorded his subjects as a camera, with emotional detachment.

Also in 1893, Toulouse-Lautrec did a painting and poster, *Loie Fuller at the Folies Bergère*, of an American to whom he was briefly attracted for her whirling, serpentine "fire dance." His paintings won the approval of Degas and an invitation to join and exhibit for the Independents, a prestigious society of engravers.

Around 1893, Toulouse-Lautrec's interest turned to faces, especially as highlighted by the gas-flares of theaters, rather than the human form as a whole (now often merely sketched in). In this year, his theater prints for *L'Escarmouche* appeared as did eleven litho-portraits of Paris show-people for a *Café-Concert* album and a poster for the book *Au pied de l'échafaud* (1893; at the foot of the scaffold), which was the memoir of Abbé Jean-Baptiste Faure, the chaplain to thirty-eight condemned men. The silhouetted spectators behind the condemned man's harshly lit face are reminiscent of the first Moulin Rouge poster.

Already in 1892, Toulouse-Lautrec had painted prostitutes, most notably *Woman with Black Boa*, whose hard smile betrayed a calculating coldness. Two years later, he set up his studio in the newest and finest brothel, remained there for several months, and produced fifty oils and hundreds of drawings. The last and unquestioned masterpiece of this group names the brothel: *The Salon des Moulins*. Early in that year, Toulouse-Lautrec's poster for a new book, *Babylone d'Allemagne*, "papered every wall in Paris," according to *Fin de Siècle* of February 18, 1894. He also did lithographs for the *Revue Blanche*. His chief occupation for nine months, however, was the album of sixteen lithographs of Guilbert performing her risqué half-spoken chansons. The album had caused a scandal for its deification of a mere café diva. Critics called Guilbert the ugly made uglier. She herself complained at Toulouse-Lautrec's unflattering caricatures of her red hair, uptilted nose, and thin lips but still autographed the hundred copies. In addition, a charcoal and an oil of Guilbert displayed her odd, angular appearance and her trademarks: a low-cut gown and long black gloves.

In London in 1895, Toulouse-Lautrec sketched Oscar Wilde at his celebrated trial. In Paris, his large (five-foot square) oil entitled *Marcelle Lender Dancing the Boléro in "Chilperic"* and several drawings of her back reveal his then current female interest. An album, *Thirty Lithographs*, contained bust-only studies of Jeanne Granier, Lucien Guitry, Jeanne Hading, Sarah Bernhardt, and other stars of the stage. In this same year came his oil of *La Clownesse, Cha-U-Kao*, whose name derives from *chahut-chaos*, a wild dance popular at the Moulin Rouge; *La Danse de La Goulue*; and a portrait of cabaret singer May Belfort. The girl in *La Toilette* (1896) may have belonged to the dancers at Les Moulins. Herein Toulouse-Lautrec returned to a more modeled style. Important works in this year include an oil and a poster *Mademoiselle Eglantine's Troupe* dancing the can-can. Eleven prints of life in the brothels appeared in the women's journal *Elles*. Toulouse-Lautrec showed that these girls, portrayed conversing with clients and serving them camomile tea, were not uniformly lewd but had "exquisite feelings unknown to virtuous women."

An exhibition of lithographs at Maurice Joyant's Paris gallery first engendered a still-prevalent pejorative interpretation of Toulouse-Lautrec's life and art. The critic A. Hepp wrote, "The odd, deformed and limping man was evident in the works." Edmond Goncourt added, "All his drawings seem to reflect his own caricature-like deformity."

Certainly, Toulouse-Lautrec's deformity inevitably affected his outlook. An alternative view, however, recognizes that Honoré Daumier, Édouard Manet, Degas, and others had already established the lowlife as a subject of art. Thus, though Toulouse-Lautrec often joked about his appearance, was sensitive to others' comments, and felt less exceptional in the rough society which he portrayed, he was not morbidly alone in drawing on that society for his work. Rather, he was accepted in that company for his coarse wit and generosity as a congenial, nonthreatening presence.

Toulouse-Lautrec's drawings of lesbians in 1897 raised the forbidden to the level of art by their compassionate detachment. He was drinking heavily and reached a nadir early in 1899. On March 17, an alcoholic and suffering from venereal disease, he entered St. James Clinic at Neuilly-sur-Seine, on the outskirts of Paris, where he remained until May 20. While in the clinic, he nevertheless contributed twenty-two animal prints to the *Histoires Naturelles* of his friend Jules Renard and did a series of circus scenes from memory. After his release he recuperated by the sea, traveled, and painted *The Englishwoman at the "Star," Le Havre* in 1899. There then followed (1899-1901) a series of lithographs on the world of the racetracks, of which the best known is *The Jockey*, in color. He painted *La Modiste* in 1900.

After seven months with his mother at Malromé in 1900, he returned to Paris in 1901. His last painting is the unfinished *Examination Board*, in which the figures are not outlined but solidly modeled. The examinee is his cousin Tapié de Céleyran. His last months were spent at Malromé, where he died in September, 1901.

Summary

Henri de Toulouse-Lautrec was a post-Impressionist who, in altering what he saw in order to increase its impact on the observer, presaged the more subjective twentieth century German expressionism. His influence can be seen in the work of Edvard Munch, Pablo Picasso, and Henri Matisse. Amid the emergence of new movements in art such as pointillism, symbolism, and primitivism, he ascribed to no school. His most original achievements were in color lithography and poster art. Toulouse-Lautrec preeminently lived the French writers' slogan, that an artist must be of his time.

Bibliography

Canaday, John. *Mainstreams of Modern Art.* 2d ed. New York: Holt Rinehart, 1981. Chapter 22 contains a brilliant appreciation of Toulouse-Lautrec, placing him in the larger context of *fin de siècle* art.

Cooper, Douglas. *Henri de Toulouse-Lautrec.* New York: Beechhurst Press, 1952; London: Thames and Hudson, 1955. A short biography. Includes twenty-six illustrations, ten in color; available in most museum shops.

Fermigier, André. *Toulouse-Lautrec.* Translated by Paul Stevenson. London: Pall Mall, and New York: Praeger, 1969. The best and most accessible biography; includes more than two hundred illustrations.

Frey, Julia Bloch. *Toulouse-Lautrec: A Life.* London: Weidenfeld and Nicolson, and New York: Viking, 1994. Well-written, sensitive biography by a trained artist that follows Toulouse-Lautrec's journey from sickly child to radical artist.

Pollock, Griselda. "Fathers of Modern Art, Mothers of Invention." *Differences: A Journal of Feminist Cultural Studies* 4, no. 3 (Fall 1992). Discusses symbolism in Toulouse-Lautrec's popular nineteenth century advertising posters

Toulouse-Lautrec, Henri de. *The Posters of Toulouse-Lautrec.* Edited with an introduction by Edouard Julien. Boston: Boston Book and Art Shop, 1966. A short text, but fine color copies of all thirty-one posters.

―――. *Toulouse-Lautrec.* Text by John Nash. New York: Funk and Wagnalls, 1978. A volume in the Great Artists series, this concise biography rebuts the theory that Toulouse-Lautrec's deformity embittered his life and influenced his choice of subjects. Sixteen color illustrations with excellent commentaries.

―――. *Toulouse-Lautrec: His Complete Lithographs and Dry Points.* Edited by Jean Adhémar. London: Thames and Hudson, and New York: Abrams, 1965. A thorough biography emphasizing his lithography and posters. Complete in its reproduction of 350 lithographs.

Daniel C. Scavone

RICHARD TREVITHICK

Born: April 13, 1771; Illogan, Cornwall, England
Died: April 22, 1833; Dartford, Kent, England
Area of Achievement: Civil engineering
Contribution: Trevithick developed the high-pressure steam engine. The importance of his invention was not merely its efficiency—it made steam engines applicable for many uses. Trevithick is known as "the father of the locomotive engine," as his engines were used for road and rail locomotives, for powering dredgers and steam ships, and in agricultural threshing machines.

Early Life

Richard Trevithick was born April 13, 1771, in one of the most remote parts of England. Cornwall is the most westerly county in the country, more than 250 miles from London. The Cornish were a fiercely independent group, unrelated racially to the English, and with a language of their own similar to Gaelic, Welsh, and Breton. Although it had gone out of general use about one hundred years before Trevithick's birth, there remained heavy remnants of Cornish in the everyday language of the miners among whom he grew up. The countryside of west Cornwall around Illogan is wild and poor. In the 1770's, there were only two occupations that could sustain a family—fishing and mining—a harsh factor that is immortalized in the county's coat of arms. Until 1870, Cornwall was the world's greatest source of copper and tin but subject to frequent periods of boom and depression.

Richard Trevithick was the only son of Richard Trevithick, manager of several mines until his death in 1797. The elder Trevithick was a friend of the preacher John Wesley and himself became a Methodist class leader. The young Trevithick did not enjoy his encounter with formal education at Camborne School. He often played the truant. He was, however, an impressive athlete. At six feet, two inches tall, with prodigious strength, he became one of the most powerful Cornish wrestlers of his day, and stories abound concerning his lifting strength. In addition, after growing up listening to his father, who was a noted pumping engineer; to William Murdock, James Watt's chief assistant and a resident at Redruth from 1780 to 1799; and to William Bull, the leading exponent of a rival Cornish school of engineers, Trevithick developed

an inventive genius. As early as 1795, the young Cornishman received payments for improvements he made in steam-engine fuel consumption. By 1797, he was engineer at Ding Dong mine near Penzance. That same year, Trevithick married Jane Harvey, the daughter of John Harvey, who was the owner of the famous Hayle foundry.

Trevithick was in many respects a most impressive man. With his broad shoulders, great height, massive head, and bright blue eyes, he was imposing indeed. In his ideas and projects, he was courageous and ingenious. By all accounts, he could be fierce but was also tenderhearted, impetuous but too easily discouraged. He constantly worked facing a shortage of capital. Trevithick was essentially an experimenter, not a businessman, and for this he was to pay dearly.

Life's Work

Cornish mines were often old and very deep. From the early part of the eighteenth century, steam engines were used to pump out the water collecting in the bottom of the shafts. The old Newcomen engines were modified by Cornish engineers, but the appearance, in 1777, of the new engine developed by Matthew Boulton and James Watt soon made the Cornish among the firm's first and best customers. There were, however, two problems. The first was that the Watt engine was under patent, which made its purchase expensive. The second was that to power the engine, one needed coal. Cornwall had no coal deposits and thus had to import, again at great expense. By 1800, Cornish engineers were engaged in a bitter fight with Boulton and Watt, evading patent rights with minor improvements and trying to come up with an alternative, more efficient engine of their own.

In this, Trevithick succeeded. He invented a high-pressure steam engine which could pump water at a level of forty to fifty pounds per square inch, in contrast to the five to ten pounds of the Watt engine, and which he later developed to work at 145 pounds per square inch. Naturally, Watt disliked this rival, more efficient development and tried all he could to get a law passed in Parliament banning Trevithick's engine as a danger to the public. In addition to this large engine for pumping water from the mines, Trevithick, in the same year, designed and built a small steam-winding engine for the Wheal Hope mine to power the transit of miners between surface and mine galleries and to raise ore and refuse. It was known as the "Puffer Whim," after the noise it made. It was this engine, the first man-made compact and portable source of power, that Trevithick patented in 1802 and which formed the basis of his efforts in road and rail loco-motion. By 1804, Trevithick had made and sold fifty such engines.

As early as 1796 and 1798, Trevithick had made models of a steam locomotive. After his invention of the Puffer Whim, he set about designing and building a steam carriage for road use. On Christmas Eve, 1801, at Beacon Hill near Camborne, the first road test was carried out. Trevithick's steam carriage carried several passengers up the hill at four miles per hour and sped along at eight to nine miles per hour along the flat. It was Great Britain's earliest self-propelled road vehicle. The following month, January, 1802, Trevithick and his cousin Andrew Vivian, who supplied the money, set off for London to exhibit the machine and to solicit interest. Trevithick was interviewed by the president of the Royal Society and the famous scientist Sir Humphry Davy, both Cornishmen, and at least two trips of several miles each were undertaken by the steam carriage around suburban London in heavy traffic. The results were mixed. On the second trip, a pothole momentarily wrested control of the vehicle from its inexperienced driver and it plowed into a wall. Trevithick suddenly canceled the public exhibitions, upset by the lack of publicity and, no doubt, discouraged by the fact that the roads of Great Britain were so bad that general adoption of his vehicle was impractical.

Not completely daunted, Trevithick took a job at the Pen-y-darran ironworks in South Wales. There, in 1803, he invented a rail locomotive. It later pulled ten tons of iron, seventy men, and five wagons at five miles per hour for nine and a half miles. Yet again, misfortune prevented Trevithick's triumph from achieving national recognition. The locomotive and its load proved to be too heavy for the tramway. Many of the tramplates broke under the strain, as did several of the hooks linking the wagons. After a few runs, the owners, not wanting the expense of replacing the track, converted the locomotive into a stationary pump. In 1805, Trevithick applied his engine for use in a dredger in the Thames estuary. By 1808, he designed a lighter, simpler locomotive, the "Catch-Me-Who-Can," which ran on an oval track near the site of Euston Square in north London. Passengers rode for one

shilling each. Once again, bad luck dogged him, and, after a rail broke and the locomotive left the track, the venture, which had never been a financial success, was aborted.

The next year, 1809, Trevithick was consulted on the practicality of a tunnel under the Thames. His experimental driftway was three-quarters complete when he seems to have tunneled too near the river bed. The passage was flooded and his efforts abandoned.

In 1811, Trevithick went bankrupt. The same year saw him collaborate with the London engineer Matthew Murray on a high-pressure steam engine and boiler for *L'Actif*, a captured French privateer which was being outfitted as a packet boat. The engine was later used on the *Courier*, which made one of the first sea voyages by steam along the English coast. The following year, 1812, Trevithick turned his attention to agriculture. He experimented with a steam plow and constructed a powered threshing machine which proved an unqualified success but was not adopted. In the same year, he developed a cylindrical boiler which was widely used as a steam-supplier for stationary engines until 1844.

By 1814, Trevithick became absorbed with a plan to engineer the famous mines of Peru on Cornish principles. Nine of his engines were shipped out to Lima with several of his associates as engineers. It was a complete success, and in 1816, Trevithick himself gave up all of his prospects in England and set sail. He arrived in Lima in early 1817 and was received royally. After he surmounted countless difficulties and had made and lost several fortunes, Peru's war of independence broke out. His machines were destroyed, and he was pressed into the army. He invented a new gun. Forced by all the upheavals to leave Peru, Trevithick reached Cartagena on the Isthmus of Panama after several mishaps, nearly drowning, nearly starving, having done some prospecting in Costa Rica, and having lost everything. There, in 1827, he chanced to meet Robert Stephenson, the young railway engineer who was returning home from the mines of Colombia to help his father, George, save his business. Stephenson lent Trevithick fifty pounds to get home. They were shipwrecked before they reached New York.

Back in England, Trevithick lived the remainder of his life in poverty, constantly inventing. His last patent, for the use of superheated steam, was granted in 1832. The previous year, he had been invited to speak before a parliamentary committee which was investigating the use of steam vehicles on roads. He made a sad picture. As the historian of early British motorcars wrote,

> One gets the feeling that Trevithick, old, ill, *passé*, and concerned mainly with talking about his latest steam engine design, was trundled in as a polite gesture to an ancient and revered national monument, who could hardly be ignored on such an occasion—certainly he was little questioned.

Trevithick died a pauper in Dartford, Kent. No stone marks his grave. He was outlived by his wife and six children. Two of his sons themselves became notable engineers.

Summary

Richard Trevithick's life was dogged by misfortune and his lack of commercial incentive. He was much more concerned with finding new and better ways to apply his inventions than with developing a business around them. He constantly ran out of money and, mainly for that reason, the value of his inventions was often not widely known or appreciated.

It was often several years after his inventions were made that they were taken up by others who were accorded the credit. The Cornish Engine, which gained a worldwide reputation in the nineteenth century, was developed from Trevithick's high-pressure steam engine of 1800 and his cylindrical boiler of 1812. His work on a road locomotive was rediscovered in the 1820's and 1830's by several engineers. The rail locomotive he built in 1804 at Pen-y-darran was reproduced by his assistant, John Steele, the following year at Wylam Colliery near Newcastle and served as a basis for George Stephenson's experiments a decade and more later.

Later in the nineteenth century, Trevithick was acclaimed "the real inventor of the locomotive" and "one of the greatest mechanical benefactors of our country." In 1888, a memorial window to Trevithick was erected in Westminster Abbey, a Trevithick medal was enacted by the Institution of Civil Engineers, and an engineering scholarship was endowed in his name at Manchester. Trevithick, the wayward inventor, still suffers from lack of recognition when compared with Watt or the Stephensons. In inventive genius, he was every bit their equal.

Bibliography

Dickinson, H., and A. Titley. *Richard Trevithick: The Engineer and the Man.* Cambridge: Cambridge University Press, 1934. A good account of the man and his importance in the history of engineering. Sober, but sometimes overly critical of the man's personal faults. An excellent starting place.

Hall, Basil. *Extracts from a Journal Written on the Coasts of Chili, Peru, and Mexico, in the Years 1820, 1821, 1822.* 2 vols. Boston: Wells and Lilly, and London: Hurst, 1824. This is an eyewitness account of the country, people, and events in Peru during the period of revolutionary and military upheaval. Trevithick does not appear in these pages, but he was stranded in the middle of these same events.

Landes, David S. *The Unbound Prometheus: Technological Change and Industrial Development in Western Europe from 1750 to the Present.* London: Cambridge University Press, 1969. Widely regarded as a classic explanation of how and why Europe industrialized.

Leifchild, J. R. *Cornwall: Its Mines and Miners.* London: Longman, Brown, Green, and Longman, 1855; New York: Kelley, 1968. The author reports on the Cornwall of the 1830's and 1840's, though it has some value for the period of Trevithick's youth and early career. It comments on scenery, the districts where Trevithick grew up and worked, all aspects of the working of the Cornish mines, and Cornish culture.

Mantoux, Paul. *The Industrial Revolution in the Eighteenth Century.* Rev. ed. New York: Harcourt Brace, 1927; London: Cape, 1928. A brilliant, clearly written, comprehensive account by a famous French historian, it provides the background necessary to understanding why England was the first country to witness an industrial revolution.

Nicholson, T. R. *The Birth of the British Motor Car, 1769-1897.* 3 vols. London: Macmillan, 1982. Contains much material on Trevithick either missing elsewhere or lightly passed over. Very useful for a sense of the scope of Trevithick's genius.

Pike, Fredrick B. *The Modern History of Peru.* London: Weidenfeld and Nicolson, and New York: Praeger, 1967. Chapters 2 and 3 explain the troubled times in which Trevithick chose to work in Peru, providing a good description of the intricacies of revolutionary upheaval.

Rolt, R. T. C. *Victorian Engineering*. London: Lane, 1970; Baltimore: Penguin, 1974. Excellent in establishing the place in engineering history held by Cornwall, the bitter rivalry that developed between the Cornish engineers and the Boulton and Watt Company, and Trevithick's most influential role in the development of steam engines.

Smiles, Samuel. *Lives of the Engineers*. Vol. 5, *The Locomotive: George and Robert Stephenson*. London: Murray, 1879; New York: Scribner, 1905. By the famous author of *Self-Help* (1859), the book contains much valuable information on the early attempts at road locomotives, including much of interest on Trevithick, including his penniless meeting with Robert Stephenson in a Central American seaport in 1827 and their subsequent shipwreck.

Turner, R., and S. L. Goulden. *Great Engineers and Pioneers in Technology*. Vol. 1. New York: St. Martin's Press, 1981. While the biographical entry devoted to Trevithick is necessarily short, a perusal of those of his contemporaries and of the next generation of engineers reveals the man's outstanding importance.

Stephen Burwood

SOJOURNER TRUTH

Born: c. 1797; Hurley, Ulster County, New York
Died: November 26, 1883, Battle Creek, Michigan
Area of Achievement: Social reform
Contribution: A featured speaker at abolitionist meetings before the Civil War, Truth worked initially to expose the immorality of the practice of slavery and later to ensure to welfare of emancipated African Americans.

Early Life

Sojourner Truth, originally Isabella Baumfree, was born into slavery in Hurley, Ulster County, New York, around 1797. Her parents were slaves owned by Colonel Johannes Hardenbergh, a prosperous farmer of Dutch descent. Her father, James, a tall man said to be "straight as a tree" (for which he received the Dutch surname of "Baumfree"), was of African and possibly American Indian descent. Her mother, Betsey, also known as "Mau Mau Bett," was of African lineage; through family and biblical stories, she instilled in Isabella and her ten siblings the value of family and spirituality. She assured Isabella she could always talk to God when there was no one else to turn to. Formal education was not available, but Isabella developed a self-reliance and strength in her young years that would preserve her through severe testing and make her work in social reform possible. Her childhood also provided the background from which the vivid and memorable anecdotes used in her lectures would later spring.

Isabella herself was sold at the age of nine. Although she was a diligent worker, she was beaten for her inability to communicate with her owners, the Neelys (Isabella spoke a Dutch dialect). Next, she was sold to the Schryvers, who owned a tavern. During her time with the Schryvers, her mother died, and her father soon followed. Eventually, Isabella was sold to the Dumonts, where she worked part-time as a field hand and helped in the kitchen. At this time, Isabella's greatest wish was to please; sometimes, she would stay up half the night working to gain favor with her master.

When grown, Isabella fell in love with Robert, a slave from a neighboring farm, but they were forbidden to marry because Robert's master disapproved of the match. After the couple continued to met secretly, Robert was severely beaten and made to marry another woman. Isabella, in turn, was given in marriage to another Dumont slave named Tom. She still had the youngest two of their five children with her as the date for her emancipation approached in 1827 (New York legislators had decreed that all slaves above the age of twenty-eight in that year would be emancipated; previous laws had freed slaves born after 1799).

The year 1827 marked a turning point in the life of Isabella Baumfree. Dumont had promised Isabella and her husband their freedom in 1826 and a log cabin in which to live in exchange for her hard work and faithfulness as a slave. Despite sustaining an injury to her hand, Isabella worked harder than ever for that year in order to fulfill her part of the bargain. When the time came for Dumont to deliver, however, he refused, knowing that he needed her labor in order to overcome losses from crop failure. Furthermore, he illegally sold Isabella's son Peter out of state after she escaped his farm.

Isabella sought help after her escape. Quaker friends sent her to live with Isaac and Maria Van Wagener. It was during this period that Isabella took her first successful political action, suing for the recovery of her son by entering a plea before the Grand Jury of Kingston, and winning; Quakers helped Isabella raise money to retrieve Peter and they were reunited. The fact that the Van Wageners insisted on being called by their names, rather than by "master," impressed Isabella, since she had always perceived slave holders as being innately better than slaves.

Isabella's religious conversion followed, as did the beginning of her life as Sojourner Truth. Truth recounts her conversion as suddenly being overcome by the feeling she was loved, and feeling love for everyone else—even people who had abused her. She also sensed the presence of someone between her and God (Jesus), and realized her mission in life was to preach the injustice of slavery until it had disappeared for good.

Truth moved to New York City in 1829 and worked there as a maid until 1843, when she left to begin her career as a lecturer for the abolition of slavery and human rights. Truth, who said she conversed with God as with another person, claimed that God himself had now given her the name of "Sojourner" because she was to be a traveler and "Truth" because that was what she was to spread throughout the land. This name change signaled Truth's break with her former identity as a laborer, a slave bearing her master's name, and marked the

Sojourner Truth with Abraham Lincoln

beginning of her lifelong dedication to the fight to recognize the rights of all human beings.

Life's Work

During the twenty-five years that followed, Sojourner Truth traveled thousands of miles, lecturing in twenty-one states and in the District of Columbia. She would routinely set up the white sash given to her by abolitionist women with texts written across it "proclaiming liberty throughout the land," begin singing, then preach about the injustice of slavery as people gathered around her. By the 1840's, Truth had become a popular figure and known to be an impressive speaker, six feet tall, clad in gray dress with a turbanlike scarf covering her head, and armed with a mind quick and courageous enough to adapt to, disarm, and delight audiences that were especially hostile to African Americans and women who supported abolition or women's rights. Many lecturers left the United States at this time, rather than face proslavery mobs who frequently threatened lives and broke up meetings. Truth also inspired a famous work of art by the American sculptor, William Wetmore Story, entitled "The Libyan Sibyl"; the statue, of marble, resulted in part from the description given to the sculptor by Harriet Beecher Stowe, and was known for its majesty and mysterious quality.

Truth lived for many years in Northampton, Massachusetts, where she had happened onto the Garrisonian abolitionists during her travels. The Garrisonians held the brotherhood and sisterhood of all people sacred; thus, slavery was a violation against God, and the fight against it became a holy war. The group was resolved to overthrow the system of slavery through education and persuasion, and Truth demonstrated this after Frederick Douglass' declaration in a public meeting that the only way for African Americans to gain their freedom was by force, when she asked, "Frederick, is God dead?"

The Garrisonians believed that women were men's equals, and in this way were allied with the women's movement. In 1850, Truth attended the Worcester, Massachusetts, Woman's Rights Convention and participated in the Woman's Rights Convention in Ohio in May of 1851. In the refrain (also the title) of her famous speech, "Ain't I a Woman?" Truth addressed the white women present who wanted rights for women, but at the same time believed African American women to be inferior because of their race. Truth also related her own lifelong history of back-breaking labor, refuting the conventional ideal of women as being unaccustomed to labor or confrontation. Most notably, she addressed biblically based claims of the natural intellectual inferiority of women, countering them with biblical facts. For example, she noted that while men based their claims of superiority upon the fact that Christ was a man, Christ himself was the product of God and a woman, leaving men out of the picture altogether.

Truth's narrative was first written down in 1850 by Olive Gilbert, a white abolitionist. Gilbert's rendering offers vivid stories of Truth's early life and transformation into revivalist and abolitionist, including humorous anecdotes and instances of Truth's effective handling of audiences, but also masks much of her renowned enthusiasm and directness—especially where this directness clashes with the ideal of womanhood during her time. An example of Truth's direct approach which is not included in Gilbert's text is Truth's response to male hecklers who asked if she were a man or a woman; she bared her breasts in proof—not to her own embarrassment, but rather to their collective shame.

A second edition of Truth's narrative, published in 1878, included news articles and correspondence regarding Truth, as well as samples from her "Book of Life"—a book she carried with her, filled with signatures of authors, senators, politicians, and friends—including President Abraham Lincoln, whom she visited in Washington, D.C., in 1864. During the Civil War, Truth nursed soldiers, bringing them food and gifts, funding her work by lecturing, singing, and selling her own photograph on which was written: "I sell the shadow to support the substance." She also became a freedom rider on the street cars which she rode to take care of the soldiers. On one occasion after successfully fighting to remove the Jim Crow cars (cars reserved for African Americans, but often used by whites), Truth drew a crowd while voicing her desire for a ride, which was at last granted, and rode further than she needed to make her point definite.

After the Emancipation Proclamation was signed, in 1863, Truth stayed in Washington, D.C., to work with newly freed slaves whose children were being kidnapped and taken to Maryland— still a slave state—organizing posses and persuading mothers to swear out warrants, as she once had done, finding homes and jobs in the northern states for many others. Truth also produced fifty petitions at her own expense in 1870 (when she was nearly eighty years old) asking Congress for land in the western United States that could be used to resettle freed people who were elderly, homeless, or unemployed.

Truth believed strongly that unemployment robbed people of dignity and humanity; crime was becoming a problem among the homeless and unemployed. Truth endorsed a general plan to Christianize, educate, and provide land for freedmen, as well as prohibit the drinking of rum, another source of demoralization. Truth attempted to convince politicians that since the future of her people was at stake, money used to imprison vagabond children could be better used to give them homes, churches, and schools. Truth also believed that children would fare better if women were allowed political rights.

Truth died in Battle Creek, Michigan, in November of 1883, after almost a century of struggle for social reform. Her funeral was attended by more than a thousand people, and a marble monument was erected there in her honor in 1947.

Summary

At a time when the cooperation between white abolitionists and African Americans was limited, as was the alliance between the woman suffrage movement and the abolitionists, Sojourner Truth was a figure that brought all factions together by her skills as a public speaker and by her common sense. She worked with acumen to claim and actively gain rights for all human beings, starting with those who were enslaved, but not excluding women, the poor, the homeless, and the unemployed. Truth believed that all people could be enlightened about their actions and choose to behave better if they were educated by others, and persistently acted upon these beliefs.

Truth's written narrative is one of many narratives presented to the public by abolitionists as proof against proslavery advocates' claims that African Americans were content with slavery and incapable of caring for themselves. Her speeches were also an effective weapon against slavery and were especially successful in drawing crowds to antislavery meetings and opening eyes to the injustice and irrationality of slavery. Like other freed slaves, Truth was a primary witness who could testify to the real suffering of slaves as well as demonstrate to proslavery crowds that, contrary to popular belief, African Americans were thinking, feeling human beings. Sojourner Truth is considered, along with Harriet Tubman, to be one of the two most influential African American women of the nineteenth century. W. E. B. Du Bois conveyed the importance of her contribution best when he described Truth as "one of the seven who made American slavery impossible."

Bibliography

Campbell, Karlyn Kohrs. "Style and Content in the Rhetoric of Early Afro-American Feminists." *Quarterly Journal of Speech* 72 (November, 1986): 434-445. Campbell discusses the difficulties African American women abolitionists faced as public speakers, which Truth was successful in combating through the power of metaphor and personal experience in speaking.

Dick, Robert C. *Black Protest: Issues and Tactics.* Westport, Conn.: Greenwood Press, 1974. Dick describes Truth's work as an African American antislavery lecturer, demonstrating her charisma, humor, and strength, as well as discussing the significance of slave narratives, both written and oral, in the antislavery movement.

Fauset, Arthur Huff. *Sojourner Truth: God's Faithful Pilgrim.* Chapel Hill: University of North Carolina Press, 1938. This is yet another rendition of the narrative of Sojourner Truth as told to Olive Gilbert, made into factual fiction by Fauset. The narrator focuses on Truth's religious devotion and strength, as does Gilbert.

Gilbert, Olive. *Narrative of Sojourner Truth.* Edited by Margaret Washington. New York: Vintage, 1993. In the introduction to this edition of the *Narrative of Sojourner Truth*, editor Margaret Washington explores the Dutch culture in relation to slavery, the elements of culture and community in interpreting the effects of slavery upon African Americans, and the issue of gender in relation to the authorship of the narrative.

———. *Narrative of Sojourner Truth, a Bondswoman of Olden Time: With a History of Her Labors and Correspondence Drawn from Her "Book of Life."* New York: Oxford University Press, 1991. Introduced by Jeffrey C. Stewart, the prefacing material to Olive Gilbert's rendering (originally published in 1850) outlines Truth's contribution to African American women's literature beginning with Phillis Wheatley. This book is part of a series aiming to resurrect the literature of African American women by uncovering the genre's nineteenth century roots.

McKissack, Patricia C., and Fredrick McKissack. *Sojourner Truth: Ain't I a Woman?* New York: Scholastic, 1992. This juvenile biography provides a straightforward introduction to Sojourner Truth, clarifying the details of her early life in slavery, explaining her connection with early abolitionists, and providing insights into her efforts on behalf of women's rights. Includes a bibliography of sources for further study.

Painter, Nell Irvin. *Sojourner Truth: A Life, a Symbol.* New York: Norton, 1996. A fascinating biography that challenges the authenticity of historical sources on the life of Truth. Painter places Truth's life in the proper social context by creating a clear picture of African American life in New York City and uses her own brand of analysis employing a psychological framework to expand our understanding of Truth's life.

Samra, Matthew K. "Shadow and Substance: The Two Narratives of Sojourner Truth." *Midwest Quarterly* 38, no. 2 (Winter 1997). The author argues that a clearer picture of Truth can be created through analysis of her own speeches and letters than from the biography written by Truth's friend Olive Gilbert.

Jennifer McLeod

Born: November 26, 1811; Hsiang-hsiang, Hunan, China

Died: March 12, 1872; Nanking, China

Areas of Achievement: Politics and the military

Contribution: Tseng directed the Ch'ing Dynasty's extraordinary suppression of the Taiping Rebellion. His strategy used locally recruited but professional armies and required twelve years to succeed. He continued to serve in high office and is recognized as a key figure in the Ch'ing restoration that began in the 1860's. Renowned for his probity, Tseng recruited men who became the dynasty's chief ministers after his death, but few approached his talents or his upright character.

Early Life

Tseng Kuo-fan came from a large landowning family striving to become part of the scholar-official elite. In 1838, he passed the highest imperial examination and became a member of the prestigious Hanlin Academy, where he had considerable leisure to develop his theories of government. In 1849, he was appointed to an important post in the central civil bureaucracy. Over the next three years, he acquired broad experience in the upper echelons of government.

The teachings of T'ang Chien, a scholar-official who adhered to the orthodox school of Neo-Confucianism associated with Chu Hsi, had great influence on Tseng. T'ang advocated a combination of Neo-Confucian self-cultivation and active service to the state. Chu Hsi had followed that pattern; it was also to characterize Tseng's life.

Tseng was a thin, stern-looking man with a long beard, whose whole demeanor reflected his lifelong practice of Puritan self-denial. Tseng is famous for having kept a daily diary reflecting his moral concerns and for his regular practice of self-examination and self-improvement in the Neo-Confucian mode.

Tseng's father and his four younger brothers all gained distinction in service against the Taipings. Following Chinese social practice, Tseng was married at age sixteen to a woman chosen by his parents. Tseng had a typically large family, two sons and five daughters. One son became a distinguished diplomat and his daughters married prominent men. Tseng's family life was exemplary in terms of Neo-Confucian morality, because he avoided personal corruption and family favoritism

while still harnessing his family's talents to the dynasty's service.

Tseng should be counted among Peking's intellectual elite before 1852. His own ideas were eclectic and focused on questions of practical administration or statecraft. He believed that the Ch'ing Dynasty had been harmed by too much autocratic power. His solutions stressed practical measures that would decrease centralization while maintaining the emperor's role in the system. Thus, he was not a reformer but sought the regular practice of Neo-Confucian principles of good government by morally upright men. Tseng believed that if good officials, on the emperor's behalf, emphasized three matters—recruiting able subordinates, conducting careful financial management, and maintaining appropriate military strength—then the dynasty's future would be assured. These principles became the hallmarks of his career.

Life's Work

In 1852, Tseng returned to his home district as the tide of the Taiping Rebellion swept out of south China and across the Hunan Province in the central Yangtze valley region. Tseng Kuo-fan was in retirement to observe the proper mourning following his mother's death, but he nevertheless accepted an imperial appointment to lead local defense efforts. The Taiping siege of the Hunan provincial capital of Changsha had not succeeded, but the rebel forces, swollen to more than half a million, had taken other cities and were preparing to attack eastward into the richer economic regions along the lower Yangtze River. In April, 1853, the city of Nanking in Kiangsu Province fell to the Taipings, who ruled from there until July, 1864.

Using the somewhat vague authority of his post, Tseng raised a new-style military force, the Hunan Army. This command, which became the model for other regional armies, combined bands of mercenary fighters with local self-defense forces under the leadership of an officer corps dominated initially by local literati. Tseng insisted upon sound organization, professional fighting skills, and absolute loyalty to the Ch'ing Dynasty. He believed that the Hunan Army had transcended its origins as a local militia and often stressed the differences between it and the many unruly militia units that flourished in the 1850's and 1860's. His army numbered as many as 130,000 and contained both land and naval fighting forces, but it was not large in terms of the period. Such locally organized and led military units were anathema to the dynasty, which feared that they might turn upon the throne, but Tseng's loyal service in Peking and his reputation as a staunch orthodox Neo-Confucian won important backers at the court for his experiment.

Initially the Hunan Army operated as an adjunct to the regular Ch'ing armies. Although the Hunan Army had only limited success in the mid-1850's, it took pressure off the hard-pressed regular Ch'ing armies and became accepted as a part of the anti-Taiping forces. Command of the Ch'ing forces remained in the hands of regular generals, many of whom were Manchus or Mongols. They made their headquarters at the so-called Great Camp of Kiangnan near Nanking. In 1856, the Taiping movement underwent an internal crisis which weakened their cause for more than three years. During this time, the Ch'ing regular military could not subdue the rebellion; then, in 1859, a new prime minister revived the Taipings. A spring offensive by the Taiping armies overran the Ch'ing headquarters at the Great Camp of Kiangnan in May, 1860, killing several top Ch'ing generals and destroying their units.

This Taiping offensive of 1860 became the turning point of the war. At this juncture, the dynasty turned to Tseng, who was elevated to the position of viceroy in the lower Yangtze region and given overall command of the efforts against the Taipings. Tseng initiated a plan to capture the Yangtze river city of Anking, above Nanking, which he saw as the key to control of the whole region. He placed his brother Tseng Kuo-ch'uan in command and, after a carefully prepared siege, Anking fell in September, 1861, with a slaughter of most of the city's inhabitants.

Tseng's next move was to advance his protégés, Li Hung-chang and Tso Tsung-t'ang, to be governors of key provinces in the lower Yangtze valley. They led their own provincial armies and pressed inward from the coastal region toward Nanking, while Tseng's forces deployed eastward from Anking. By mid-1862, Tseng's combined forces had hemmed in the Taipings. Another two years of bloody fighting ensued before the Taiping emperor was killed and most of his forces were slaughtered or captured. Tseng had accomplished a great victory that revived the Ch'ing Dynasty's rule of China.

Tseng's victory marked a shift that gave increased power and importance to Han Chinese offi-

cials in the Ch'ing system. Also, Tseng's success realized some changes that he had advocated in Peking prior to 1852. The creation of provincial armies, still loyal to the dynasty, and their leadership by Han Chinese modified the autocratic, centralized rule that he had criticized. The armies themselves, partly armed with Western weapons, embodied his concern with appropriate military strength. The civil war was financed by new taxes which embodied both innovation and prudent fiscal measures. The most notable was an internal transit tax on shipments of goods known as *likin*. This tax itself produced a more decentralized financial administration, thus also lessening central control, but avoided a fiscal crisis for the dynasty. Finally, Tseng made every effort to select the best men to serve in his own headquarters. He did not initiate each of these measures, but they all fit into his approach to statecraft.

Tseng maintained his Neo-Confucian reliance on achieving good government through men of moral character, rather than upon laws or formal discipline. Yet he sometimes despaired at the corruption among his own military and civilian subordinates. He lived with their failings, but he was extremely severe toward the Taipings. On the battlefield or in defeat, soldiers and civilians alike received little mercy from Tseng or his armies.

Tseng began the task of reconstruction while still fighting. Again, his approach stressed careful plans and administration. As always, he looked to the matters of prudent defense measures, recruiting able officials, and sound fiscal management. Within months of defeating the Taipings, he began disbanding most of the Hunan Army, searched carefully for the men of highest character to fill official posts, and tried to return the tax system to a peacetime basis so that both farmers and the dynasty could prosper.

As the reconstruction was beginning, the court again called on Tseng for help against a major rebellion, the Nien. These rebels had operated from nests or lairs in Anhwei and Honan provinces since the early 1850's. Remnants of the Taiping forces joined the Nien in late 1864, and then in May, 1865, Nien cavalry killed the Ch'ing commander, the Mongol general Senggerinchin. Within days, the frightened court, which had no effective armies between themselves and the Nien, assigned Tseng to take command. Tseng's own forces were already disbanded, so he relied upon the available Ch'ing and local forces, stiffened by Li Hung-chang's Anhwei army. Tseng led the anti-Nien efforts until December, 1866, during which time he penetrated the Nien's home territory and broke up their links to the villages. Tseng's strategy then called for his armies, stationed at key points in large encampments, to attack the columns of Nien cavalry as they moved outward from their former base areas. After Li Hung-chang assumed command in 1867, he followed a variation of this strategy and defeated the Nien within a year.

In addition to his role in the suppression of the Taiping Rebellion, Tseng played a part in the so-called self-strengthening movement, which promoted the use of Western technology. His association with this movement began in 1861, when he and his subordinates began employing foreign units, especially foreign artillery and ships, against the Taipings. These foreign-equipped and foreign-led units were mercenaries. The most famous was the "Ever Victorious Army," which was led after 1862 by Charles "Chinese" Gordon, a British Victorian adventurer and hero. The battlefield effectiveness of these foreign units was undeniable, and Tseng accepted the suggestions that the Ch'ing forces should acquire new foreign equipment. Tseng remained an advocate of such borrowing until the end of his life, but he always saw Westernization as a secondary element in making China strong. Western weapons and technology had practical uses, but for matters of principle Tseng never wavered in his Neo-Confucian orientation.

In 1867, Tseng was appointed to a top position in Peking, and in 1868 he became viceroy of the metropolitan region around Peking. There is evidence that Tseng's health was already in serious decline at this time, but he remained a hard-working administrator. In 1870, he was called upon to settle the difficult diplomatic situation arising out of the Tientsin massacre, when Catholic missionaries were murdered by mobs who believed that Catholic sisters were killing the foundling babies they took in. Tseng took a conciliatory approach to the foreign demands, which angered some belligerent officials, so his protégé Li Hung-chang again relieved him. Tseng was transferred to the viceroy's post in Nanking and died in March, 1872, shortly after arriving there.

Summary

The dynasty granted Tseng Kuo-fan the hereditary title of marquis for his extraordinary service, and this unprecedented honor for a Han Chinese official was fully deserved. Without his leadership, the Manchu rule of the Chinese Empire would have fallen to the mid-nineteenth century internal peasant rebellions.

Tseng, although never the most powerful or influential official during his lifetime, has come to symbolize the revival of Ch'ing fortunes in the mid-nineteenth century. He became a model particularly to those who wanted to find in recent history a Chinese figure who upheld the highest virtues of traditional Neo-Confucianism. Tseng's austere, frugal, serious life of self-improvement and service to the state was invoked by Chiang Kai-shek, in particular, between 1928 and 1949.

Tseng's legacy also has its detractors. His own high principles proved insufficient to wean others away from self-aggrandizement and personal enrichment while in government service. Self-strengthening began the difficult business of matching the burgeoning power of the Western industrial nations, but it stopped far short of the adaptations China needed to ensure its own territorial integrity and military strength. The T'ung-chih restoration was real, but the institutional and personal weaknesses that Tseng found rampant survived under the Kuang-hsu emperor and produced a great crisis following the dynasty's defeat in the First Sino-Japanese War. Ultimately, Tseng's approach rested on the service of upright men as loyal officials to the state. The standards of duty, sacrifice, and service that Tseng himself embodied proved, however, too lofty for even his most able followers to achieve. With their lesser stuff the dynasty's slide resumed after Tseng's death.

Bibliography

Kuhn, Philip A. "The Taiping Rebellion." In *The Cambridge History of China*, edited by John K. Fairbank, vol. 10. Cambridge and New York: Cambridge University Press, 1978. An excellent summary of Tseng's career and his ideas; places him in the historical context of his times. For more detailed treatment see Kuhn's *Rebellion and Its Enemies in Late Imperial China: Militarization and Social Structure, 1796-1864* (Cambridge, Mass.: Harvard University Press, 1970).

Kuo, Ting-yee, and Kwang-ching Liu. "Self-strengthening: The Pursuit of Western Technology." In *The Cambridge History of China*, edited by John K. Fairbank, vol. 10. Cambridge and New York: Cambridge University Press, 1978. A description of the late nineteenth century effort at modernization which explains Tseng's influence without overemphasis on his role.

Liu, Kwang-ching. "The Ch'ing Restoration." In *The Cambridge History of China*, edited by John K. Fairbank, vol. 10. Cambridge and New York: Cambridge University Press, 1978. A reconsideration of the T'ung-chih restoration and Tseng's place in it.

Shen, Han-yin Chen. "Tseng Kuo-fan in Peking, 1840-1852: His Ideas on Statecraft and Reform." *Journal of Asian Studies* 27 (November, 1967): 61-80. A discussion of Tseng before he became famous, with attention to his place in the intellectual milieu of mid-nineteenth century China.

Wright, Mary C. *The Last Stand of Chinese Conservatism: The T'ung-chih Restoration, 1862-1874*. Stanford, Calif.: Stanford University Press, 1957. This is the strongest presentation of the case for a mid-nineteenth century restoration inspired by Tseng's ideal.

David D. Buck

HARRIET TUBMAN

Born: c. 1820; Bucktown, Dorchester County, Maryland

Died: March 10, 1913; Auburn, New York

Areas of Achievement: Civil rights and nursing

Contribution: A fugitive slave herself, Tubman was called the "Moses" of her people for rescuing numerous slaves from bondage and leading them to freedom.

Early Life

Harriet Tubman was born into slavery in 1820 in the small community of Bucktown, Dorchester County, on the eastern shore of Maryland. She was the daughter of two slaves, Benjamin Ross and Harriet Green, one of ten or eleven of the couple's children. Her ancestors had been brought to the United States from Africa sometime in the early eighteenth century. Her master, Edward Brodas, named her Araminta, but she quickly took on her mother's name and came to be known as Harriet.

Her slave status quickly became obvious to her. As a young child, she saw two of her sisters carried away in chains. She received no schooling, and by the age of five she was already at work as a baby-sitter and maid. Her mistress worked her as a maid during the day and then demanded that she remain alert to the baby's cries at night. Once when Harriet dozed off and the baby's crying awakened the mistress, the woman pummeled the young slave about her face and neck.

At six, Harriet was hired out to a new master who taught her how to trap muskrats and how to weave. Once, he caught her taking a sugar cube from his table, and she had to run away to avoid punishment. When she returned, tired and hungry, after several days' absence, she was whipped.

The remainder of her childhood was spent in various other occupations. She worked again as a nursemaid and later split and hauled wood, part of the time working with her father. She was also a field hand. None of her various masters seemed happy with her work, and she was frequently in trouble.

When she was twelve or thirteen, she suffered an accident that was to affect her for the rest of her life. An overseer became angry at another slave for leaving his work and demanded that Harriet help in his whipping. She refused and instead tried to help the man escape. In his anger, the overseer picked up a two-pound weight and threw it at the fleeing slave. His aim proved faulty, however, and he struck Harriet on the head, knocking her unconscious. For the rest of her life, she suffered a form of sleeping sickness brought on by the blow, often falling asleep involuntarily. These spells only increased her reputation as a poor worker.

In 1844, her mother forced her to marry a free black man named John Tubman, with whom she lived for five years. They had no children. While discussing his free status, Tubman became curious about her own background. In 1845, her inquiries turned up the fact that her mother had actually been emancipated some years previously, but a former master had hidden this fact from her. This revelation caused Tubman to look at her enslavement in an even more critical light.

The year 1849 proved to be the turning point in her life. Her master at this time was a young, sickly white man who was under the care of an adult guardian. When the young man died in 1849, the rumor spread that the guardian planned to sell all of his slaves. Tubman decided to run away. Her husband refused to join her, but two of her brothers went along. They quickly lost their nerve, however, and she was forced to travel the one hundred miles or so out of Maryland, through Delaware, to Philadelphia on her own. Along the way, she found aid from sympathetic blacks and whites. When she reached free soil, she had mixed feelings. She was excited about reaching freedom, but she was sad that her family members were still chattel. She determined somehow to free them. Her life of slavery was over; a new career was soon to begin.

Life's Work

When she reached Philadelphia, she met William Still, a black man reputed to be the chief "conductor" on what was referred to as the Underground Railroad. This collection of abolitionists, Quakers, and other sympathetic blacks and whites had established a series of houses, barns, caves, passageways, and the like for fugitive slaves to use as they made their way north to freedom. This so-called Underground Railroad was not nearly as well organized as myth would have it, but there is no denying that numerous individuals helped the fugitives escape. Tubman had already experienced some of this help during her own escape, and now she learned more about the system from Still and another close ally, the Quaker Thomas Garrett of Wilmington, Delaware.

Tubman first had to find work in a hotel to earn a livelihood, and thus she began the pattern she was to follow from then on. She was never a paid agent, so she had to do manual labor of various sorts to pay her own way and help finance her slave-rescuing activities. (Sometimes, abolitionists did give her some financial support for particular excursions.)

In December, 1850, she made the first of some twenty trips back into slavery. She went to Baltimore and brought out her sister and two children. In 1851, she rescued a brother and his family. When she returned for her husband in the fall of that year, she found him remarried and uninterested in joining her.

For the rest of the 1850's Tubman engaged in her slave-stealing activities, rescuing somewhere between sixty and three hundred people. Her work was complicated by the recently enacted Fugitive Slave Law of the Compromise of 1850, which made it no longer safe for runaways to remain in the North. She began to take her fugitives into Canada, from 1851 to 1857 considering St. Catharines, Ontario, her home. From there, she made eleven trips into slave territory. Her most spectacular rescue, and the most personally satisfying one, was her success in bringing out her parents in 1857 in a specially contrived wagon. Her raids were so successful, in fact, that frightened Maryland slaveholders held a meeting in 1858 and put a price of forty thousand dollars on her head.

Her success was the result of intelligence, planning, determination, a mystical faith in God, and courage. She carried drugs to anesthetize babies. She used a pistol to embolden fugitives on the verge of losing their nerve, giving them the choice of continuing or dying on the spot. She used cryptic messages to announce her arrival and sang songs with hidden messages to implement her plans. Once, she and her fugitives boarded a southbound train on the supposition that no slave hunter would suspect blacks traveling in that direction. Another time, she saw a former master approaching her and loosed some chickens as a diversionary tactic to get by unnoticed. She sometimes physically carried fugitives; she encouraged; she prayed; she bullied. As she later explained: "I never ran my train off the track and I never lost a passenger." She was convinced that God had chosen her for her work and protected her in its execution.

During the 1850's, her fame spread among the abolitionists. She traveled to New England, where she came to know Ralph Waldo Emerson, Frederick Douglass, Gerrit Smith, and Thomas W. Higginson. William Henry Seward, though hardly an abolitionist, befriended her also and in 1857 sold her a house in his hometown, Auburn, New York, where she took up residence with her aged parents.

In 1859, when she spoke to the Fourth of July meeting of the Massachusetts Anti-Slavery Society, she so mesmerized its secretary that he forgot to take notes and had to apologize to the membership for the lapse. Fortunately, others whom she met during these years left descriptions of her. She was short, of very dark color, medium build, with missing upper front teeth. She dressed simply, reminding one observer of her slave past and another of her Quaker acquaintances. She was not an attractive woman, and the fact that she often fell asleep as soon as she sat down gave the impression of fragility rather than the strength that she actually possessed.

In the late 1850's, she met John Brown when he was touring black communities in Canada looking for recruits to join in his attempt to capture the federal arsenal at Harpers Ferry and begin a massive slave uprising. Tubman approved of his slave-insurrection plan, and only an unknown illness at a crucial time prevented her from completing her recruiting mission. She considered him the personification of Jesus Christ because of his willingness to die for black people in slavery. Brown was similarly impressed with her, introducing her to Wendell Phillips as "General" Tubman. At another time, he offered the quintessential nineteenth century sexist praise, referring to her repeatedly as a man.

In the spring of 1860, on her way to an anti-slavery meeting in Boston, Tubman passed through Troy, New York. She found to her dismay that federal marshals had discovered a fugitive and were preparing to take him back to slavery. Tubman helped lead the city's opposition. She grabbed hold of the fugitive and, though her clothes were nearly ripped from her, she held on. After further struggle and several near misses, she successfully gained for the fugitive his freedom. Later that year she made her last trip into Maryland, but by that time the nation was on the verge of war and her abolitionist friends were concerned for her safety. They now escorted her into Canada, where she had led so many fugitives previously. Her slave-rescuing days were over.

She remained in St. Catharines only briefly. In the spring of 1861, she returned to the United States and apparently followed General Benjamin Butler's Massachusetts troops as they marched southward to defend Washington. In May, 1862, armed with a letter from the governor of Massachusetts, she went to General David Hunter's command in South Carolina to help in the war effort. At first she served as a nurse, gaining renown for her ability to cure disease among those under her care. Later she became a spy, given authority to organize and command a black scout and spy unit. She participated in several raids, leading the successful July, 1863, Combahee River expedition. Later she watched black troops attack Fort Wagner near Charleston. In 1864, she became concerned over the health of her parents and traveled to Auburn, returning to Virginia near the end of the war to work briefly at a hospital in Fortress Monroe.

On her way home from Virginia, Tubman learned that slavery's end had not created a promised land for the newly freed people. The conductor on the railroad refused to honor her nurse's pass and called her a racist name. Despite her strenuous protests, he and three other men threw her bodily into the baggage car.

Tubman returned to Auburn, where she spent the rest of her life. She began a home for aged blacks in her own house, married Civil War veteran Nelson Davis in 1869 (John Tubman having died several years previously), and helped Sarah Bradford write an autobiographical book entitled *Scenes in the Life of Harriet Tubman* (1869). The publication of this book allowed her to complete the purchase of her house, but she remained in difficult financial straits all of her life. Beginning in the late 1860's, with Seward's support, she requested federal payment for her Civil War service. Nothing happened until 1897, when she received a pension of twenty dollars a month.

During these post-Civil War years, she was also active in the temperance and the women's rights movements, working with Susan B. Anthony and other feminists. Her fame had early spread overseas, and upon the publication of her autobiography, Queen Victoria sent her a gift and invited her to visit England.

Harriet Tubman died in Auburn on March 10, 1913. She received a full military funeral conducted by the Grand Army of the Republic. The following year, the city of Auburn dedicated a memorial to her on the county courthouse lawn. Booker T. Washington was the main speaker for the event. In 1978, when the United States Postal Service inaugurated its "Black Heritage U.S.A." stamp series, Tubman was the first person honored.

Summary

In a world which saw the slaveholder as dominant and the slave powerless, in a society which believed in white superiority and black inferiority, in a time when man was mover and a woman's place was in the home, Tubman was a contradiction. She showed the slaveholder that he was not all-powerful; she told the slave that enslavement might not have to be permanent. She demonstrated to a racist and sexist age the truth of black and female capability. She was a "Moses" leading people from slavery into freedom.

Though her symbolic effect was significant, her actual success was limited. She affected slaves only in a border area and no more than sixty to three hundred of them. She did not rescue any slaves in the Deep South, their chances of running away made impossible by the simple fact of distance. Yet even there she had an effect. If slavery was insecure anywhere, it was threatened everywhere. Runaways in Maryland were perceived to be a threat to Mississippi slaveholders as they were to those in Maryland. The bounty for her capture demonstrated better than any words just how upsetting her activities were.

Tubman represented the ideals of freedom and the willingness to endanger one's life for others. This small woman, who never learned to read and write and thus never read the Declaration of Independence, nevertheless exemplified this document in a most profound way.

Bibliography

Bennett, Lerone, Jr. "Free for Christmas." *Ebony* 50, no. 2 (December, 1994). Discusses Tubman's efforts in transporting seven slaves to freedom at Christmas 1854.

Bradford, Sarah E. H. *Harriet Tubman: The Moses of Her People.* Introduction by Butler A. Jones. New York: Lockwood, 1886. An expanded version of the 1869 original book, this is the basic source for information on Harriet Tubman's life. Bradford interviewed Tubman and also included comments about her by a number of leading nineteenth century Americans. In many ways, this is Tubman's autobiography.

Conrad, Earl. *Harriet Tubman.* Washington, D.C.: Associated Publishers, 1943. This is the best biography available and is much more detailed than the Bradford book because Conrad added data not included in the earlier account. This book concentrates on the ten-year period from 1849 to 1859 and cites Tubman as a symbol of the many other nameless fugitives who fled to freedom.

Heidish, Marcy. *A Woman Called Moses.* Boston: Houghton Mifflin, 1976. A historical novel grounded firmly in historical fact. The reader receives an accurate feeling for Tubman, particularly because the book is written in the first person and emphasis is placed on the forces that shaped and directed her.

Petry, Ann. *Harriet Tubman: Conductor on the Underground Railroad.* New York: Crowell, 1955. A well-written, carefully researched juvenile biography which emphasizes the childhood influences that fired Tubman's hatred of slavery. This book is longer and more interpretive than the Sterling book.

Sterling, Dorothy. *Freedom Train: The Story of Harriet Tubman.* New York: Doubleday, 1954. A fictionalized, generally accurate biography aimed at the teenage reader. There are some fine illustrations. It is a good introduction into the subject for the young reader looking for an easily read basic account of Tubman's life.

John F. Marszalek

IVAN TURGENEV

Born: November 9, 1818; Orel, Russia
Died: September 3, 1883; Bougival, France
Area of Achievement: Literature
Contribution: Turgenev combined the lyrical with the realistic in fiction that had a powerful influence on social conditions in his own time and on later writers such as Anton Chekhov and Henry James, who truly ushered in the modern period in literature.

Early Life

Ivan Turgenev was born November 9, 1818, in Orel, Russia, to Varvara Petrovna, a wealthy landowner, and Sergey Turgenev, a cavalry officer. According to Turgenev's own comments, he was an enthusiastic reader at an early age, reading not only the fiction and poetry of Russian writers but also the English fiction of Charles Dickens.

His family moved to Moscow in 1827, and in 1833 Turgenev entered the University of Moscow, which he attended for one year, when, upon another family move to St. Petersburg, he entered the university there. He was graduated in 1837 and went to Berlin, where he was enrolled at the University of Berlin, studying philosophy for three years. Upon returning to St. Petersburg in 1841 and failing to find an academic position, he secured a minor post with the Ministry of the Interior. While traveling in Europe in 1843, he met Pauline Viardot, a French singer, who became his lifelong love and inspiration.

Turgenev retired from the civil service in 1845 and began to devote himself full-time to writing poetry. Because his mother disapproved of this decision as well as of his infatuation with Viardot, a married woman, she cut off his allowance. Turgenev followed Viardot, who tolerated his infatuation, to Europe to be near her. He returned to Russia in 1850 because of his mother's serious illness. When she died, he was left the heir of a substantial fortune and was thus able to follow his literary interests, which at this time he very successfully shifted from poetry to fiction. In 1847, he had begun the writing of the short stories which, in 1852, were to be published as one of his greatest works, *Zapiski okhotnika* (*Russian Life in the Interior*, 1855; better known as *A Sportsman's Sketches*, 1932).

Life's Work

When *A Sportsman's Sketches* were being published in periodical form, they created a social uproar in Russia, for they presented the serf as more than a mere slave and, in fact, as often more human and genuine than the landowners themselves. Because the stories were seen as a protest against the serf system, the authorities began to watch Turgenev closely. In 1852, when he wrote an enthusiastic obituary notice on the death of his fellow writer Nikolai Gogol, he met further disapproval; the authorities banished him to his country estate, where he was forced to stay for a year and a half.

When he returned to St. Petersburg, after the publication of *A Sportsman's Sketches* in book form, he found himself to be the leading light of St. Petersburg literary culture. *A Sportsman's Sketches* has often been considered historically important for the influence it had on the abolition of the serf system in Russia; in fact, the book has even been compared in this regard to Harriet Beecher Stowe's *Uncle Tom's Cabin: Or, Life Among the Lowly* (1852). Yet the aesthetic and critical importance of the stories, the reason many of them continue to be read, lies in their unique blend of the lyrical and the realistic. Such stories as "Bezhin Meadow" and "The Country Doctor," two of the most familiar in the collection, create a dreamlike and sometimes surrealistic world, even as they manage to remain solidly grounded in phenomenal experience. As a short-story writer, Turgenev historically stands somewhere between the folktale fantasy of Nikolai Gogol and the nightmare reality of Franz Kafka.

For the next few years after the success of *A Sportsman's Sketches*, Turgenev, who felt inspired by travel, was forced to stay at home because of the Crimean War. Moreover, many biographers suggest that he was in a deep depression because of the impossibility of his tireless love for Viardot. As a result, he published little during this period, with the exception of his short novel *Rudin* (*Dmitri Roudine*, 1873; better known as *Rudin*, 1947), which appeared in 1856. In a drastic shift—which may have resulted partly from his freedom to travel and partly from his acceptance of the Viardot situation—within the next five years Turgenev alternated between traveling on the Continent and writing some of his most respected works, including the novels *Dvoryanskoye gnezdo* (1859; *Liza*, 1869;

better known as *A House of Gentlefolk*, 1894) and *Nakanune* (1860; *On the Eve*, 1871), the novella *Pervaya lyubov* (1860; *First Love*, 1884), and the essay "Gamlet i Don Kikhot" (1860; "Hamlet and Don Quixote," 1930). He also finished his best-known novel, *Ottsy i deti* (*Fathers and Sons*, 1867), in 1861 and had it published the following year.

Fathers and Sons is built around what Turgenev perceived as an emerging type of man in Russia, a type which he named "nihilist," a term to which Turgenev's novel gave great currency at mid-century. The character Bazarov in Turgenev's novel is one who rejects religion, art, and the Russian class system and emphasizes instead scientific empiricism. Turgenev was vilified by Russian intellectuals and praised by the Russian secret police for this depiction, for the novel was misinterpreted as supporting the conservative "fathers," while casting doubt on the radical "sons." Turgenev, in a defense of his work, argued that by "nihilist" he really meant "revolutionary," and that his work was directed against the gentry as the leading class. As a result, Russian critics began to see the work as the herald of the coming revolution.

In addition to frequently coming in conflict with either the authorities or the radical dissenters, Turgenev's life was also often plagued by conflict with his literary relationships. He was friends with such great Russian writers as Ivan Goncharov and Leo Tolstoy but had bitter quarrels with both of them. Goncharov accused him of plagiarizing from an unpublished manuscript, and Tolstoy accused him of moral illness because of his liaison with Viardot. The quarrel with Tolstoy, which occurred at a dinner party and involved a disagreement about helping the poor, almost resulted in a duel and lasted for seventeen years. A few years later, he also had quarrels with Fyodor Dostoevski because of a debt Dostoevski owed Turgenev.

In 1863, when the Viardots went to live in Baden-Baden, Germany, Turgenev visited them there, where he was received as an old family friend, a role he seemed willing to play, if only for the opportunity to be near Pauline. Indeed, his desire to be near her was so great that he also moved to Baden-Baden. From all indications, his life there was happy and his health was good, in spite of the fact that his relationship with the beloved Pauline was less than he desired. Enjoying a life of hunting and social leisure, however, Turgenev did little

work; *Dym* (1867; *Smoke*, 1868) is the only novel that he wrote during his eight years in the German resort.

Turgenev's life always seemed dominated by his attachment to Viardot; when she moved once again, Turgenev followed, first to London and then to Bougival, France, where Turgenev and the Viardots bought a summer home jointly in 1874. In France, Turgenev began a close relationship with several prominent writers, including Gustave Flaubert, George Sand, Émile Zola, Edmond de Goncourt, and others. Once more, Turgenev seemed preoccupied with matters that kept him from his writing. The only important works he published during this period were two novellas, one of which was *Veshniye vody* (1872; *Spring Floods*, 1874; better known as *The Torrents of Spring*, 1897).

Turgenev began working on his last, and his longest, novel, *Nov* (*Virgin Soil*, 1877), in 1876. This story of love and revolution, published in 1877, was not well received by Russian critics; conservative commentators thought it criticized

Russia too much, while radical critics thought the revolutionary characters were not true-to-life. Yet the work was enthusiastically read outside Russia, being immediately translated into many different languages and receiving rave reviews from influential critics.

Turgenev fell ill in early 1882 and moved to the summer home he owned with the Viardots in Bougival in June of that year. Although he was in much pain, his illness was not properly diagnosed as spinal cancer, and Turgenev did not believe his life was in danger. On September 3, 1883, after having dictated a story critical of the Russian aristocracy, Turgenev died surrounded by his family and friends. In a funeral that amounted to national mourning, he was buried in St. Petersburg in Volkov cemetery.

Summary

Ivan Turgenev always declared himself a realist whose every line was inspired by something that he actually observed. When his works were published, their importance lay less in their artistic and aesthetic qualities than in their documentation of the social realities of Russian life. Indeed, such works as *A Sportsman's Sketches* were said to have been at least a partial cause for the abolition of the serf system, much as *Uncle Tom's Cabin* had an effect on the abolition of the system of slavery in the United States. Turgenev's later works are also remembered for their depiction of a world that was doomed to die with the Russian Revolution.

Yet when Turgenev is most studied today, it is not for his social realism, but rather for what has been termed his poetic realism. It is his stories and his novellas, in which reality is presented as often lyrical and dreamlike, rather than his novels, in which he sought to present reality concretely and socially, that have won for him a permanent place in the history of modern literature. The influence of his short-story style on those writers who ushered in the modern period, such as Anton Chekhov, Henry James, and later Sherwood Anderson and others, is his most important literary legacy.

Bibliography

Freeborn, Richard. *Turgenev: The Novelist's Novelist*. London and New York: Oxford University Press, 1960. A general study of Turgenev's novels, both in terms of their place in nineteenth century Russian literature and culture and in terms of Henry James's view that Turgenev was a "novelist's novelist." Freeborn primarily discusses Turgenev's four major novels: *Rudin*, *A House of Gentlefolk*, *On the Eve*, and *Fathers and Sons*.

Frost, Edgar L. "Hidden Traits: The Subtle Imagery of 'Living Relics'." *Slavic and East European Journal* 36, no. 1 (Spring 1992). Frost examines Turgenev's story "The Relics," a little-noticed piece that is rich in imagery and deserving of more attention.

Magarshack, David. *Turgenev: A Life*. London: Faber, and New York: Grove Press, 1954. A detailed but highly readable account of Turgenev's life. Along with Yarmolinsky's biography cited below, it is the most frequently referred work on Turgenev. The work attempts to account for the relationship of Turgenev's art to his life and is particularly helpful in discussing the role that Turgenev's dramas played in the development of his art.

Pritchett, V. S. *The Gentle Barbarian: The Life and Work of Turgenev*. London: Chatto and Windus, and New York: Random House, 1977. This popular study is quite accessible to the general reader, but it is largely based on the previous biographies of Magarshack and Yarmolinsky. Although little is new here, it is characterized by Pritchett's lucid style and his critical understanding of Turgenev's fiction. Pritchett's approach is to use details from Turgenev's life to increase the reader's understanding of his novels and short stories.

Ripp, Victor. *Turgenev's Russia: From "Notes of a Hunter" to "Fathers and Sons."* Ithaca, N.Y.: Cornell University Press, 1980. This critical study deals only with Turgenev's fiction between *A Sportsman's Sketches* and *Fathers and Sons* and therefore does not deal with his drama. It is valuable, however, in clarifying Turgenev's place in nineteenth century Russian literature and thought and in delineating the important cultural issues which inform his fiction.

Schapiro, Leonard. *Turgenev: His Life and Times*. Oxford and New York: Oxford University Press, 1978. This biography makes use of materials about Turgenev's life and work previously available only in Russian and materials about his relationship with Viardot previously available only in French. This is purely a biographical study and makes no efforts to analyze Turgenev's work.

Wilson, Reuel K. "Ivan Turgenev's 'Rudin' and Joseph Conrad's 'Heart of Darkness': A Parallel Interpretation." *Comparative Literature Series* 32, no. 1 (Winter 1995). Compares writings by Turgenev and Joseph Conrad, finding similarities in theme and structure. Both involve the death of the main character on foreign soil.

Yarmolinsky, Avrahm. *Turgenev: The Man, His Art, and His Age*. London: Hodder and Stoughton, and New York: Macmillan, 1926. Not only is this book valuable in providing a detailed account of Turgenev's life and artistic development but also it discusses his intellectual and artistic development and his contribution to an understanding of nineteenth century Russian culture.

Charles E. May

J. M. W. TURNER

Born: April 23, 1775; London, England
Died: December 19, 1851; London, England
Area of Achievement: Art
Contribution: Turner, the outstanding revolutionary painter of landscapes, was a Romantic. With the vast complexity of his work, he has been called the Shakespeare of English art. An artist far ahead of his time, he is without equal in depicting the sea in all of its moods.

Early Life

Joseph Mallord William Turner was born in Covent Garden to a barber and a wigmaker. His mother, Mary Marshall, was some six years older than his father, William ("Joseph Mallord" are names from his mother's family). While he is said to have been the eldest son, there are no extant references to other children, except for a sister three years younger, Mary Ann, who died when Turner was eleven.

His mother, apparently subject to fits of manic rage, was committed to Bethlehem Hospital for the Insane in December, 1800—by neighbors, not family members—and died there in April, 1804, in her early sixties. Biographers have frequently attributed Turner's problems with women and his fascination with nature in its most violent phases to his mother's influence. As he left no journals or autobiography, Turner's own thoughts on this subject, as on others, remain unknown. Only his words in reported conversations are available.

His father, who, Turner said, never praised him except for saving a shilling, exhibited his son's drawings in the shopwindow and boasted that his son would become a painter. After the death of Mary Turner, William Turner served as his son's factotum until his death in 1829 at the age of eighty-five.

From childhood, Turner was completely absorbed with capturing on paper what his eye saw and his mind perceived and imagined. His relations considered him inarticulate and found him ungrateful because he failed to write thank you notes. As a child, he knew the urban life of London, the shipping on the Thames, the open sea at Margate (the subject of some of his earliest and last drawings), and the rural scene at Brentford, where he stayed with an uncle and attended the Free School as a day boarder in 1786.

He took lessons from Thomas Malton, a watercolor painter of architectural studies, and in December of 1789, he was admitted as a student at the Royal Academy school where he studied for four years. His first exhibit at the Royal Academy was a watercolor in 1790, and in March, 1793, he was awarded the "Greater Silver Pallet" for landscape painting by the Society of Arts. He was employed by Dr. Thomas Monro to copy drawings by John Robert Cozens and other artists during the evenings. He exhibited his first oil painting—*Fishermen at Sea*—at the Royal Academy in 1796. In 1799, Turner was elected an Associate of the school and left his parents' home, taking lodgings in Harley Street. In 1802, Turner was elected a full member of the Royal Academy at the youngest age possible.

Turner was a very short man, so short that when walking and holding a presumably not large fish by its gills, its tail dragged on the ground, as did the bottom of Turner's frock coat. When prevailed upon to paint his self-portrait, Turner worried that his work would be devalued because of his appearance. He was a man of phenomenal energy and industry, routinely hiking twenty-five miles a day to sketch; who carried secrecy to extremes; and who was devoted to a small number of friends, including W. F. Wells and Walter Fawkes.

In 1799, Turner met Sarah Danby, a young widow with four children; although they were never married, they had two daughters, Evelina and Georgianna. Because Turner never spoke of his relationships with women— his mother; his sister; Sarah Danby; her niece, Hannah Danby; Sophia Booth, the second widow with whom he lived (1834 until his death)—his personal life is subject to much speculation. Nothing is known of Sarah Danby's death, but it is likely that Turner's relationship with her lasted into the 1820's. In Turner's will of 1829, he provided for each of his two daughters, for Sarah Danby and for Hannah Danby. Assumptions abound, but probably names disappear from his subsequent wills simply because Turner outlived those individuals.

The only contemporary biography—by G. W. Thornbury, recognized as quite unreliable—portrayed Turner as a miser and accused him of "wallowing in Wapping" (the brothel district). While Turner was indeed concerned with money—which he saw as his only means of pursuing his artistic ambition—there is evidence that he was frequently generous and in no way meanspirited, much less vulgar, despite his cockney accent. He did go to Wapping to collect rents. If his figure drawings came from Wapping, this will never be known for certain, since his champion, John Ruskin, destroyed these drawings, which he pronounced obscene, after Turner's death.

Life's Work

Turner's life's work, his art, was his life: No separation is possible. If his relationships with women remain a mystery, it is nevertheless clear that his life was consumed by his practice of his art. When he died, he left to his nation, on condition that a gallery be built to house his work, three hundred oil paintings and twenty thousand watercolors and drawings, which did not include the hundreds of oils and watercolors already in private collections. There are also more than two hundred bound sketchbooks in the British Museum.

Turner became an expert architectural and topographical draftsman, and there is an underlying sense of structure even in his late abstract work. He sketched from nature all of his life and intently studied the work of others. It was as if he had to conquer the artistic method and achievement of every previous artist in order to find his own mode of expression. After his election to membership in the Royal Academy, Turner made his first trip to France and Switzerland (he had already made many sketching tours in England and Wales). His paintings have been cataloged in terms of his trips to Europe which he continued up to the age of seventy.

There are 318 oil paintings in the Turner bequest and more than two hundred in private collections. Martin Butlin and Evelyn Joll divide his paintings into five periods: 1793-1802, before Turner went abroad; 1803-1819, before he made his first trip to Italy; 1819-1829, before he made his second trip to Italy; works painted in Rome, 1828-29; and 1829-1851, his later works—with the second and fifth the largest groups. Turner's work was viewed with increasing bewilderment. *The Fifth Plague of Egypt* was Turner's first historical subject and was very well received. *Calais Pier, Sun Rising Through Vapour,* and *The Battle of Trafalgar* elicited negative comment. *Snow Storm: Hannibal and His Army Crossing the Alps* was well received and exemplifies Turner's very different approach to historical painting with nature playing the dominant role. *Dido Building Carthage* and *Sun Rising Through Vapour* were finally offered to the Nation-

al Gallery in Turner's will, on condition that they be hung permanently next to two of Claude Lorrain's paintings.

Turner remained ever cognizant of his duty to the Royal Academy, which he viewed as the mother of all British artists. He put aside his inclination to withdraw into his work to meet all of his responsibilities as a member. He was very proud of his appointment as a professor of perspective in 1807—frequently signing his work RA, PP. He did not, however, deliver any lectures until 1811, when he had completed lengthy study and nearly two hundred large drawings and diagrams to demonstrate his points. His lectures were unintelligible; often he seemed to be laughing at some private joke. He did not resign his position until 1837, although his last lectures were in 1828. His work sold consistently, much of it on commission, first at the Royal Academy and later in his own galleries.

Turner valued poetry and read widely, appending words from James Thomson, Mark Akenside, Edward Young, and John Milton to his paintings. Beginning in 1812, he used lines from his own unpublished poem, "Fallacies of Hope," which are of interest only because they are Turner's. He did illustrations for Sir Walter Scott, and in 1834, his illustrations of Lord Byron's poems were exhibited. Yet with all of his travel on the Continent, he never learned French, German, or Italian, for words were never his medium. He was apparently completely unaware of the political upheaval around him, but he knew the conditions of the roads.

The *Liber Studiorum* (1807-1819) constitutes a text without words on the expressive power and scope inherent in landscape art. W. F. Wells, one of Turner's best friends, persuaded him to begin these engravings in 1806; the first volume was published in 1807 and the last in 1819. Turner published these engravings at his own expense and marked each of the seventy-one plates in one of six ways: as pastoral, epic or elevated pastoral, marine, architectural, mountainous, or historical. These engravings are in mezzotint on copper and printed in dark brown. The *Liber Studiorum* is an unequaled compendium of landscape styles.

Turner was sufficiently self-reliant that the harsh, sometimes venomous, criticism of his work did not deter him. Sir George Beaumont and *Blackwood's Magazine* remained hostile, and Turner was accused of having an optical disease and was frequently pronounced insane. He rarely said anything critical about his fellow artists and never made any attempt to respond to negative criticism. When the young middle-class John Ruskin met the sixty-year-old bohemian artist for the first time and called him the Great Angel of the Apocalypse, Turner was considerably taken aback.

Turner was no purist in method, but would use any means to achieve the truth he sought. While he used constant sketches as a basis for his drawings, watercolors, engravings, and paintings, his finished works were not intended to represent the optical truth of the moment in terms of light or weather (Claude Monet found Turner antipathetic), but rather his own inspiration. His two oils of the fire in 1834 at the Houses of Parliament are visionary, not realistic. Turner placed his Juliet in Venice rather than Verona because he was in love with the former city (*Juliet and Her Nurse*). In *The Fighting Téméraire' Tugged to Her Last Berth to Be Broken Up* and *Rain, Steam, and Speed—The Great Western Railway*, Turner shows his fascination with man's battle to control nature, however pessimistic he might have been about the future of humanity. The imagery in *Slavers Throwing Overboard the Dead and Dying*, *Peace: Burial at Sea*, and *Death on a Pale Horse* is indubitably powerful and without equal in British art.

Toward the end of Turner's life, when he was living with Sophia Booth in a house he had purchased in her name (and was letting people in the area call him Puggy or Admiral Booth), he lost his teeth, and a false set would not help. He subsisted on two quarts of milk and an equal amount of rum a day.

In his will, Turner bequeathed his finished work to the nation on condition that a gallery be built and gave most of his large fortune to what was to be a charity to support poor male artists of legitimate British issue. Because his father's relatives contested the will and his executors failed to protest, the latter never happened. Nor was any distinction made between his finished and his unfinished work—which he might not have wanted anyone to see—and the National Gallery received all of his work. Turner did want his work to be seen as a whole, so the meaning would be clear, but it was not until 1987 that the Turner Gallery next to the Tate opened its doors.

Summary

J. M. W. Turner may indeed be likened to William Shakespeare, for the richness of his exploration of man's relationship with the environment is beyond measure. Only by mastering the difficulties of landscape could he free himself of society's views and express himself. He was a poetic, not a scientific, painter. He was seeking a reality of his imagination, even though he drew from nature. After Turner, landscape painting could never again be regarded as inferior. In his late and abstract oils of an estate, Petworth, which he never exhibited, he had completely merged his technique in watercolor with his technique in oil. He perceived reality as constantly changing, as light and energy, and he saw light as color.

While his landscapes have people, they are not the most prominent part of the works: He presents his human figures as he draws his viewers into his work, by his vortices. In attempting to present a comprehensive view of the world, he involved in his art the interaction of nature and humanity. He drew from mythology, history, poetry, contemporary events, and his own private poetry, the subjects for his work. The apocryphal best he could say about art was that it was "a rum business." While he took enormous artistic license, his grasp of water, land, trees, mountains, masonry, ships, leaves, and fish, was exact. Yet only in Turner's time is his

The Angel Standing in the Sun even conceivable. What he offers finally is a vision of enchantment.

Because of his scope, Turner is difficult to comprehend as an artist; the label Romantic does not suffice any more than Elizabethan suffices for Shakespeare. It has been said that no other artist captured the landscape of Switzerland as Turner did. It has also been said, more remarkably in view of Italian art, that no other artist captured the light of Venice as Turner did. Elizabeth Rigby wrote that Turner "does what he will—others do what they can." If Turner country is not to be located in any one geographical place, surely it is because Turner's artistic vision is both rare and universal.

Bibliography

Butlin, Martin, and Evelyn Joll. *The Paintings of J. M. W. Turner.* 2 vols. New Haven, Conn.: Yale University Press, 1977. Discusses each of Turner's oil paintings—its origin, exhibition history, contemporary reviews, providing rare reproductions. Invaluable.

Heffernan, James A. W. *The Re-Creation of Landscape: A Study of Wordsworth, Coleridge, Constable, and Turner.* Hanover, N.H.: University Press of New England, 1985. Argues that the literature of the two poets is not definable in terms of dynamic temporality nor the work of the two artists in terms of spatial fixity. Cogent and important.

Herrmann, Luke. *Turner: Paintings, Watercolors, Prints and Drawings.* London: Phaidon Press, and Boston: New York Graphic Society, 1975. Valuable data on the artist and his work, with reproductions and notes by a Turner scholar.

Hill, David. *Turner in the North.* New Haven, Conn.: Yale University Press, 1996. In a comprehensive study of Turner's work, Hill presents photographs of many of the actual sites used by Turner in creating his sketches. Includes the sketches, many published here for the first time, and the finished oils and watercolors.

———. *Turner on the Thames: River Journeys in the Year 1805.* New Haven, Conn.: Yale University Press, 1993. Hill follows Turner's trail on the Thames river and presents photographs of the sites, Turner's original sketches, and the finished watercolors and oils.

Lindsay, Jack. *Turner: The Man and His Art.* New York: Watts, and London: Granada, 1985. Provides valuable data on Turner's life and place in English landscape art.

Paulson, Ronald. *Literary Landscape: Turner and Constable.* New Haven, Conn.: Yale University Press, 1982. A valuable discussion of the relation between landscape images and literary texts and Turner's use of literary references, as opposed to John Constable's suppression of same.

Rosenblum, Robert. *Modern Painting and the Northern Romantic Tradition: Friedrich to Rothko.* New York: Harper, and London: Thames and Hudson, 1975. Traces a tradition from Romantics, such as Turner, to Vincent Van Gogh and Edvard Much in the late nineteenth century, to German Expressionism, to twentieth century abstract painters, such as Piet Mondrain.

Turner, J. M. W. *Collected Correspondence of J. M. W. Turner.* Edited by John Gage. Oxford: Clarendon Press, and New York: Oxford University Press, 1980. A thorough presentation of 342 generally brief letters, significant because they are Turner's. Biographical index.

Walker, John. *Joseph Mallord William Turner.* New York: Abrams, 1976; London: Thames and Hudson, 1989. The most complete single volume on Turner, essential to any study of this artist.

Carol Bishop

Born: October 2, 1800; Southampton County, Virginia

Died: November 11, 1831; Jerusalem, Virginia

Areas of Achievement: Civil rights; and religion and theology

Contribution: Turner led the largest slave revolt in the history of the United States. As a slave preacher, he linked religion, liberation, and black militancy, thus providing a model for many future black liberation movements.

Early Life

Nat Turner was born as a slave on the Benjamin Turner plantation in Southampton, Virginia. His mother was African born, and his father escaped from slavery to the North when Turner was a young child. From the beginning, Turner was perceived as a remarkable child by both his family and his white owner. Born into a slave culture that mixed elements of African tradition with Christianity, Turner exhibited birthmarks that, according to African custom, marked him as a person with spiritual gifts and power. He was treated accordingly by his relatives and the local slave community. His owner saw his early intelligence and encouraged Turner to learn to read and write. His paternal grandmother was extremely religious and provided religious education. He attended services and received religious education at Benjamin Turner's Methodist meeting house, where the slaves were encouraged to worship with their master and his family. Turner, from his childhood, read the Bible regularly and engaged in prayer and meditation, coming to believe that he had a special calling. His religious study and his visions convinced him that Christianity affirmed the equality and dignity of all people and that slavery was a sin against God and his teachings.

By the 1820's, Turner had already acquired a reputation among other slaves in terms of his intelligence and spiritual gifts. He also began to have regular religious visions. Most important was his report of an encounter with a spirit that approached him and spoke the Biblical verse, "Seek ye the Kingdom of Heaven and all this shall be added unto you" (Luke 12:31). Turner interpreted this as a sign that he had a special religious mission. Later, in 1821, he escaped after a dispute with his master; however, after thirty days and another vision, he returned to his enslavement. He believed that personal escape was an evasion of the greater mission to which he had been called. After this, his mystical experiences increased in number and intensity as he began to find signs in the heavens and in hieroglyphic figures that he discovered on leaves. During this time, he took on the role of a Baptist preacher. His reputation as a preacher spread, and he was allowed some freedom in traveling about, reportedly journeying as far as Hartford County, North Carolina, in 1828. His power as a preacher was so great that even some white people were impressed by his message, including a plantation overseer, Ethelred T. Brantley, who, despite disapproval from the white community, was baptized by Turner.

During this time period, Turner had a vision that was to shape future events. He saw a battle in the air between black and white spirits in which streams of blood flowed. Later, in May of 1828, he was informed by the spirit that, like Christ, he was to wage a "fight against the Serpent" and that he would receive the appropriate sign when the battle was to begin. Drawing heavily on the judgment motifs of the Old Testament prophets and the biblical apocalyptic visions of a battle that is described as the final war between good and evil, Turner came to understand himself as a messianic figure who was called to initiate an upcoming battle between good and evil that would end with the freeing of the slaves.

Life's Work

The sign that Turner was seeking and the events that gained Turner historical notoriety began with a solar eclipse in February, 1831. Turner saw this as the sign that the battle would soon begin. He began planning a slave revolt with four other slaves—Henry Porter, Hank Travis, Nelson Williams, and Sam Francis—that was to begin on July 4. The plan was to kill local slave owners, seize their weapons, rally other slaves to their cause, and then march on the county seat, Jerusalem, Virginia, and seize weapons from an armory. The hope was that by then, a well-armed slave army would be formed to engage in a final battle to end slavery. On July 4, however, Turner fell ill, and the attack was postponed.

Turner waited for another sign. It came in August, 1831. For three days—the "Three Blue Days of 1831"—the sun over North Carolina and Virgin-

THE NINETEENTH CENTURY: NAT TURNER / 2277

ia had a strange blue cast. In response, on August 21 Turner called together his group of followers, which now numbered eight. They gathered for an evening meal, finalized their plans, and then, just after midnight on August 22, put the plan into action. They first went to the house of Turner's current owner, John Travis, and, armed with a hatchet and broadax, killed Travis, his wife, and their children—six people in all. They gathered some guns and ammunition and moved from farm to farm in the region. By Tuesday morning, August 23, the group with Turner numbered about seventy, and they had killed fifty-seven white people, over half of which were women and children, in the twenty-mile area of the Boykins district of Southampton. As they moved down the road from Cross Keys to Jerusalem, they met their first resistance in the form of a white militia under the command of Captains Alexander Peete and James Bryant. After some initial success, Turner's group was subsequently scattered. Soldiers from Fort Monroe and white militia from surrounding areas were dispatched to put down the rebellion. Many of the slave insurgents were quickly captured. White people retaliated with a terrorist campaign against black people in the area, both slave and free. As many as two hundred black people may have been murdered; many of them were lynched, and many were tortured. The massacre would have become worse had not General Eppes intervened and dismissed the militia groups.

Turner escaped and lived in the woods near Cabin Pond, eluding capture for six weeks. He was discovered by a white man, Benjamin Phipps, on Sunday, October 30, hiding in a hole he had dug under a fallen tree. He was taken to Jerusalem on November 1, convicted during a five-day trial, and hanged on November 11. During the time he was in prison, he made lengthy verbal confessions to his attorney, Thomas R. Gray, which were subsequently published and became the primary source of information about Turner and his planned revolt. When asked at his sentencing whether he had more to say, Turner showed no remorse, but only replied, "Was not Christ crucified?" Fifty-three black people, including Turner, were arrested. Twenty-one were acquitted, twelve were transported out of state, and nineteen others, in addition to Turner, were hanged.

At the time of Turner's revolt, antislavery sentiment had become strong in the North and some parts of the South. David Walker's *Appeal to the*

Coloured Citizens of the World, which advocated the violent overthrow of slavery, had been published in 1829, and William Lloyd Garrison was already actively involved in advocating the abolition of slavery through political action. The Southampton rebellion intensified the debate and tended to harden positions on both sides. As a response to the revolt, legislation was passed throughout the South that set new penalties for teaching slaves to read, limited the rights of slaves to preach, and placed limits on the rights of slaves to gather for religious services. The education of free black people was also severely limited as many of the informal black schools were closed. Many free black people were pressured to move North.

The debate surrounding the rebellion emerged again in the 1960's with the publication of William Styron's fictionalized account of the life of Turner, *The Confessions of Nat Turner* (1966). According to African American critics, the book portrays Turner as a crazed fanatic and a precursor of the black militants who were gaining prominence in the 1960's and thus is a veiled criticism of black radicalism. African American scholars responded to the book with a period of intense historical research and inquiry to present a more accurate portrayal of Turner.

Summary

Nat Turner's notoriety came as a result of his leading the largest slave revolt in the history of the United States. More important, however, Turner was a black religious leader who embodied a central theme of the black religious tradition in the United States. Like those who would follow, including Martin Luther King, Jr., and Malcolm X, he proclaimed that the God of the Old Testament was a god that set slaves free and demanded social justice, a god who exacted judgment on societies that were not just and who required people to take action to rectify social injustice. Turner's actions also highlight the fact that slaves did not passively accept slavery but acted to obtain their freedom and equal rights. Turner's confessions have been an important historical source that demonstrates the continued influence of African traditions on slave culture and African American religion.

The historical debates surrounding the portrayal of Turner are significant in understanding the racial divide that exists in the United States. The focus on the brutality of Turner's revolt in the debate following the rebellion and in later portrayals by people such as Styron shows the refusal of white America to understand the context of black radicalism. Turner's revolt was a demand for freedom and rights, a response to a system that bought and sold people, separated families, and arbitrarily tortured and executed slaves. To understand the violence of some forms of black radicalism, it is necessary to understand the violence of the system to which it is a response.

Bibliography

Aptheker, Herbert. *American Negro Slave Revolts*. New York and London: Columbia University Press, 1943. Aptheker places Turner's revolt in the historical context of other slave revolts during this time period.

Clarke, John Henry, ed. *William Styron's Nat Turner: Ten Black Writers Respond*. Boston: Beacon Press, 1968. This book is a response to Styron's novel by a variety of black scholars who are attempting to counteract what they see as a distorted portrayal of Turner.

Duff, John B., ed. *The Nat Turner Rebellion: The Historical Event and the Modern Debate*. New York: Harper, 1971. This work is a recounting of the ongoing debate about the interpretation of Turner and his rebellion.

Foner, Eric, ed. *Great Lives Observed: Nat Turner*. Englewood Cliffs, N.J.: Prentice-Hall, 1971. This collection of historical documents represents reactions to and changing interpretations of Turner in a variety of historical time periods.

Greenberg, Kenneth S., ed. *The Confessions of Nat Turner and Related Documents*. New York: Saint Martin's Press, 1996. Greenberg's book includes the text of Turner's confessions to Thomas R. Gray and some other historical documents from the time period.

Oates, Stephen B. *The Fires of Jubilee: Nat Turner's Fierce Rebellion*. New York: Harper, 1975. Oates provides a detailed historical account of the life of Turner, the rebellion, and the debates and legislation that ensued.

Styron, William. *The Confessions of Nat Turner: A Novel*. New York: Random House, 1966; London: Panther, 1967. This is a very controversial but popular fictionalized account of Turner's life and the rebellion by a white Southern author.

Tragle, Henry Irving, ed. *The Southampton Slave Revolt of 1831: A Compilation of Source Material*. Amherst: University of Massachusetts Press, 1971. This book contains a comprehensive collection of historical reports and accounts of the revolt and the ensuing debate.

Wilmore, Gayraud. *Black Religion and Black Radicalism: An Interpretation of the Religious History of Afro-American People*. 3d ed. Maryknoll, N.Y.: Orbis, 1998. Wilmore places Turner's life and self-understanding in the context of African American religious traditions.

Charles L. Kammer

MARK TWAIN
Samuel Langhorne Clemens

Born: November 30, 1835; Florida, Missouri
Died: April 21, 1910; Redding, Connecticut
Area of Achievement: Literature
Contribution: In *The Adventures of Huckleberry Finn* (1884), Twain gave America the prototypical initiation novel, but his humor and nostalgia for the past increasingly gave way to his pessimism about man's technological "progress."

Early Life

Samuel Langhorne Clemens was born November 30, 1835, in Florida, Missouri. The ancestors of his mother, née Jane Lampton, and his father, John Marshall Clemens, were mostly English and Irish and had lived in Virginia and Kentucky. While both sides of his family claimed distinguished English ancestors, those aristocratic ties were never clearly identified, and the Clemens family was hardly affluent when Samuel was born. Nevertheless, Samuel's father was a cultivated, educated man (he had studied law) who was determined to be successful financially. Consequently, because there appeared to be more opportunity, in 1839 the elder Clemens moved his family to Hannibal, located on the banks of the Mississippi. Unfortunately, John's financial dreams did not materialize, and he died in 1847, when Samuel was eleven. Partly by default and partly because of her personality, Jane Clemens became a central influence in Samuel's life. In fact, the similarities between his mother and Olivia Langdon, his wife, were so pronounced that one could speculate that his mother's influence subconsciously affected his choice of a wife.

Shortly after his father's death, Samuel, probably for financial reasons, was apprenticed to a local printer, and his newspaper career was launched. In 1850, he went to work for his older brother, Orion, on the Hannibal *Western Union*, and until 1857, he worked as a typesetter for various newspapers. During this period, he also wrote sketches and published his first story. His newspaper career was fortuitously interrupted in 1857, when he learned to be a steamboat pilot on the Mississippi. Those experiences formed the basis for his *Life on the Mississippi* (1883) and also deepened the influence that the Mississippi had on the body of his work. In 1862, he first used the pen name "Mark Twain," taken from the river boatmen's cry to indicate two fathoms of safe water. When the outbreak of the Civil War brought his piloting career to an end, Twain served briefly with some Confederate "irregulars," but he gladly accepted Orion's offer to accompany him to Nevada, where Orion served as "secretary" to that territory.

During his Nevada years, Twain unsuccessfully prospected for gold and silver and successfully returned to the newspaper world, writing for the *Virginia City Territorial Enterprise*, where he developed, partly through emulating humorist Artemus Ward, his lecturing persona. In 1864, he moved to San Francisco, where he continued his newspaper work on the *Morning Call* and also contributed work to the *Californian*, a literary magazine. Among his California works was "The Celebrated Jumping Frog of Calaveras County," a short story that catapulted him to national prominence and established him as a spokesman for the vanishing American frontier. After a trip to Hawaii, about which he wrote and lectured, he left California in 1866 and went East to New York City.

Life's Work

Twain's decision to go east was a significant one. Despite his "frontier" humor and Southern speech, he became an Easterner who looked nostalgically to the South for his literary landscape and to the West for his values. In effect, Twain was split between the progressive, materialistic East of the future and the reactionary, individualistic Southwest of the past. Even Twain's appearance seemed a contradiction: A handsome man given to elegant clothes (white suits became his trademark in his later years), he was also a cigar-smoker and whiskey-drinker who never became "genteel" in manner. Far from subscribing to the notion of "art for art's sake," he made writing his business and was ambitious both financially and socially. In fact, it was the split between art and business that produced works that appear inconsistent, contradictory, and careless. The pressure to make money did cause him to produce inferior work, as Twain himself acknowledged.

Shortly after moving to New York, Twain met Henry Ward Beecher, a prominent preacher and brother to Harriet Beecher Stowe, the author of *Uncle Tom's Cabin* (1852). When he learned that

Beecher's congregation was planning a Mediterranean steamboat excursion to Europe and the Holy Land, he persuaded the *Alta California* to finance his trip in exchange for providing the newspaper with travel letters, which were popular at the time. The revised travel accounts eventually became *The Innocents Abroad* (1869), a book that enabled him to abandon his newspaper work and to devote his full attention to writing. The trip was also significant because it resulted in his marriage, in 1870, to Olivia Langdon, whose brother had met Twain on the voyage and had showed the author Olivia's picture. During their thirty-three years of marriage, Olivia was the ideal wife and confidante, but she also served as an unofficial "editor" whose moral views tempered Twain's writing.

After his marriage, Twain embarked on what was to become a typical divided course of action: He began to write *Roughing It* (1872), and he acquired part ownership of the Buffalo *Express*, the first of a series of unsuccessful business ventures. Another pattern was also established during the early years of the marriage: depression caused by sickness and death. Olivia's father died in 1870; Olivia herself was sick and gave birth prematurely to their first child, Langdon, who died in 1872. Despite these setbacks, Twain moved his family to Hartford, Connecticut, where he built an impressive mansion, a symbol of his ambition and materialism.

Twain's Hartford years were his most productive artistically and financially. In 1873, he published, in collaboration with his Hartford neighbor, Charles Dudley Warner, *The Gilded Age*, his first attempt at an extended work of fiction. After successfully adapting the novel to the stage (1874), he published *The Adventures of Tom Sawyer* in 1876 and, in 1880, published another travel book, *A Tramp Abroad*. In 1882, *The Prince and the Pauper* appeared, and in 1884, *The Adventures of Huckleberry Finn*, his most artistic and significant novel, was published. Within a month, *The Adventures of Huckleberry Finn* was embroiled in censorship problems that continued to plague the novel, but the novel also quickly became a best-seller and has become one of the most widely read and taught novels in American literature.

The Adventures of Huckleberry Finn was the first publication of the Charles L. Webster Publication Company, which Twain formed after having problems with his previous publishers. Like his father, Twain believed that he had business acumen,

and the financial success of *The Adventures of Huckleberry Finn* and *The Personal Memoirs of U. S. Grant* (1885-1886), which Twain published in his publishing company, Charles L. Webster and Company, confirmed his belief that he was both a financial and artistic genius. In 1886, an overconfident Twain, who optimistically believed in technology and in the promise of a typesetting machine, acquired half ownership of the Paige Typesetter; in 1889, he purchased all rights to the machine. By the time Twain ended his futile speculation in the ill-fated invention, he had accumulated debts of $100,000. In an effort to economize, he closed his Hartford house in 1891 and moved to Europe, but he was bankrupt by 1894. Even his substantial earnings from the publication of *A Connecticut Yankee in King Arthur's Court* (1889) and *Tom Sawyer Abroad* (1894) could not compensate for the financial strain caused by his obsession with the typesetting machine.

Twain, to his credit, did not attempt to take advantage of bankruptcy laws and instead set about paying off his debts by undertaking an exhausting round-the-world lecture tour in 1895 and by continuing to publish books: *Personal Recollections of Joan of Arc* (1896), *Tom Sawyer, Detective* (1896), and *Following the Equator* (1897), a travel account prompted by his 1895 lecture tour. These sales, coupled with a lucrative contract with Harper and Row for rights to his collected works, enabled Twain to pay off his debts in full by January of 1898. Although he recovered financially, Twain suffered several setbacks from which he never fully recovered. While he was in England in 1896, his favorite daughter died of meningitis; his already frail wife died in 1904, after suffering from physical and mental problems; his daughter Clara married and settled in Europe in 1909; Jean, his other daughter, died scarcely two months after Clara's marriage.

Despite the misfortunes that plagued him after 1898, Twain continued to write prolifically, but most of this material, because of its nihilistic philosophy, was not published until after his death. Olivia, who was concerned about his image and who served as his literary editor/censor, opposed the publication of the deterministic tract *What Is Man?* (1906). *The Mysterious Stranger*, which occupied Twain for several years and which existed in various versions, was not published until 1916, when Albert Bigelow Paine, Twain's official biographer, conflated the versions and published his reconstruction as Twain's own work. Twain, who had been left quite alone by Clara's marriage and the deaths of his wife and other children, died April 21, 1910, long before the American public had been made aware of the "literary Lincoln's" darker side.

Summary

In many ways, Mark Twain was as contradictory a person as his real name and pen name suggest. The adoption of the pen name indicates, to some extent, a person not content with himself but determined to forge a new personality, to create a new person—in effect, not unlike James Gatz/Jay Gatsby, to be both creator and creature. Like Gatsby, too, Twain was caught up in the American dream of material success, social ascent, and technological progress; unlike Gatsby, however, he came to satirize and scorn many of the values to which he subscribed.

For most Americans, Mark Twain is indelibly associated with Huckleberry Finn, the youthful protagonist who "lights out for the territory" rather than return to the "civilization" represented by Aunt Sally. Yet *The Adventures of Huckleberry Finn* contains another juvenile persona who only "plays" at nonconformity and rebellion: Tom Sawyer. There is as much Tom Sawyer in Twain as there is Huckleberry Finn. Even *The Adventures of Huckleberry Finn* is more than it appears to be, juvenile fiction in the vein of *The Adventures of Tom Sawyer;* it is also an initiation novel which depicts a boy's adventures and his inner growth, presents the conflict between appearance and reality, and satirizes Southern gentility and aristocratic pretension. Because *The Adventures of Huckleberry Finn* is such an enjoyable story, however, many readers ignored the Colonel Sherburn incident, with its scathing indictment of mankind. For many readers, Mark Twain was the lecturer-writer of juvenile fiction and travel books, a humorous teller of frontier tales.

Twain's humor was considerably blacker than the general public, which lionized him, believed. In some ways, his humor was similar to Ambrose Bierce's, but that similarity was overlooked by a public which dubbed the latter "Bitter Bierce." As his ambitious entrepreneurial schemes failed and his loved ones died, Twain became increasingly pessimistic about men and about institutions, and his later works are marked by pessimism, determinism, and nihilism. Although Twain was nostalgic about the innocence of children, the children in *The Mysterious Stranger* are light-years away from Tom and Huck. *A Connecticut Yankee in King Arthur's Court* provides yet another example of public unwillingness to confront the complexity that was Twain. Twain's novel satirizes the institutions, particularly chivalry and the Church, of medieval England, which is juxtaposed to turn-of-the-century America, represented by Hank Morgan, a believer in progress and technology. Morgan's well-intentioned technology, however, ultimately produces only death. When Twain's novel was adapted to film, it was bowdlerized into a musical starring Bing Crosby.

Twain was very much a product of his age. As a spokesman for an already vanishing frontier, he lampooned the pretense and the institutions of the East while he yearned for the lost values of youth and individualism. These nineteenth century values were in conflict with the twentieth century technology he first embraced and then, like Henry Adams, came to despise.

Bibliography

Brooks, Van Wyck. *The Ordeal of Mark Twain.* New York: Dutton, 1920; London: Heinemann, 1922. A seminal book on Mark Twain in which Twain is seen as a victim of his environment. Brooks's book criticizes the role that Eastern respectability had in neutering Twain's work and discusses the frontier as a negative influence.

De Voto, Bernard. *Mark Twain's America.* Boston: Little Brown, 1932. De Voto's book attacks the thesis espoused by Brooks and insists that the frontier, particularly frontier humor, actually made Twain a better writer. De Voto's book is seen as a healthy corrective to Brooks's book.

Ferguson, John De Lancey. *Mark Twain: Man and Legend.* Indianapolis, Ind.: Bobbs-Merrill, 1943. A well-written study that takes into account previous Twain scholarship. Contains some particularly interesting commentary on the significance of the river in Twain's fiction.

Fishkin, Shelley F. *Lighting Out for the Territory: Reflections on Mark Twain and American Culture.* New York: Oxford University Press, 1996; Oxford, Oxford University Press, 1997. Examination of Twain from a new perspective—an analysis of his racial attitudes and how his works have been used and abused.

Geismar, Maxwell. *Mark Twain: An American Prophet.* Boston: Houghton Mifflin, 1970. Geismar opposes the view that commercial interests and censorship weakened Twain's work and claims that Twain's greatness was partly a result of his lifelong interest in the past and in childhood.

Howe, Lawrence. *Mark Twain and the Novel: The Double-Cross of Authority.* Cambridge and New York: Cambridge University Press, 1998. Howe looks at Twain's fascination with and suspicion of authority that is represented in his books as a fight between personal freedom and social control.

Lynn, Kenneth S. *Mark Twain and Southwestern Humor.* Boston: Little Brown, 1959. A sympathetic treatment of Twain's use of Southwestern folk humor in which Lynn discusses Twain's artistic use of that humor.

Miller, Robert K. *Mark Twain.* New York: Ungar, 1983. Miller's book contains a biography and helpful critical analyses of Twain's major works.

Salomon, Roger B. *Twain and the Image of History.* New Haven, Conn.: Yale University Press, 1961. One of the best treatments of Twain's conceptions of history and of human nature, Salomon's book explores the role of the dream as a means of escaping the implications of Twain's nihilism.

Smith, Henry Nash. *Mark Twain: The Development of a Writer.* Cambridge, Mass.: Harvard University Press, 1962. Smith traces Twain's problems with style and structure in several of his novels, examines his ethical ideas, and discusses the conflict between contemporary culture and native American humor.

Tenney, Thomas Asa. *Mark Twain: A Reference Guide.* Boston: Hall, 1977. The most comprehensive bibliography of Mark Twain scholarship, the book is indispensable to the Twain scholar.

Wagenknecht, Edward. *Mark Twain: The Man and His Work.* New Haven, Conn.: Yale University Press, and Oxford: Oxford University Press, 1935. A good overview of Twain and his work.

Thomas L. Erskine

WILLIAM MARCY TWEED

Born: April 3, 1823; New York City

Died: April 12, 1878; New York City

Area of Achievement: Goverment and politics

Contribution: William Marcy "Boss" Tweed's name is synonymous with corruption and dishonesty in urban government. Through the power waged by Tweed's Tammany Hall political machine, New York City and its citizens were systematically bilked of millions of dollars in taxes meant for civic projects. Tweed was eventually brought down by his own greed and the combined efforts of a reform coalition of prominent citizens, ordinary people, *The New York Times,* and political cartoonist Thomas Nast.

Early Life

William Marcy Tweed was born April 3, 1823, in lower Manhattan, New York City, the son of Richard and Eliza Tweed. Tweed's great-grandfather, a blacksmith, had emigrated to America from Scotland around 1750. His father was a maker of chairs, and William left school at eleven to apprentice in that trade. At thirteen, he apprenticed with a saddler, leaving to spend a brief stint at a private school in New Jersey to learn bookkeeping. He became a junior clerk at a New York mercantile firm before advancing to a position as head bookkeeper at the small brush manufactory in which his father had invested. At nineteen, he became an officer in the company, and at twenty-one, he married Mary Jane Skaden, the daughter of the factory's principal investor.

The young Tweed, an energetic, powerfully built, ruddy-faced, jovial man, six feet tall and a robust three hundred pounds, may have found the business of making brushes a dull undertaking, for he soon discovered an outlet much more to his liking: volunteer firefighting. By 1850, he had become foreman of a company he had helped to organize, the celebrated Americus No. 611. He was then twenty-seven years old. In the latter half of the nineteenth century in America, volunteer firefighting organizations were one of the ways for ambitious young men to get ahead in politics. Powerful "Big 611," easily identified by the Bengal tiger symbol painted on the company's fire engine, propelled its leader into the public eye; he was soon running for the position of alderman in his home ward under the auspices of the Democratic Party. He lost by a small margin, but he won his next race

easily owing to a split in the Whig vote engendered by a third candidate—a friend of Tweed who was persuaded to do him a favor. The year was 1852, and Tweed was learning how to succeed in politics.

Life's Work

He was learning fast and from the best—the New York City Common Council was widely and cynically known at that time as The Forty Thieves—and the brush factory was soon abandoned for more lucrative pastures. He was an urban political animal, in his element in city politics, a truth realized when he served for two unmemorable years (1853-1855) in the U.S. House of Representatives in Washington, D.C., something he would not repeat again. From then on, he would stick to running for the state senate and city aldermanic positions. In 1856, however, he lost his next race for alderman. Undaunted, and now drawn into the Tammany faction with Peter B. Sweeny and Richard B. Connolly in opposition to Mayor Fernando Wood, he was picked to be head of a new, bipartisan, popularly elected board of supervisors formed to check election fraud. It became, instead, another opportunity for graft and corruption.

Other appointed and elected offices beckoned in quick succession, and Tweed became commissioner of schools, deputy street commissioner, a New York state senator (1867-1871), and chairman of the New York state finance committee. On the Tammany Hall front, he was elected sachem in 1857 and by 1859 was clearly the most influential man in the organization. (He appropriated the Bengal tiger from the volunteer fire company to stand as a symbol of the society, alongside the head of Tammany, a Native American.) He dominated the 1860 state Democratic convention and was thus able to secure several choice spots for his friends and allies. Owing to his influence, Sweeny was elected district attorney in 1857 and Connolly county clerk; George G. Barnard was elected to the office of recorder and later to the New York State Supreme Court. Another crony, A. Oakley Hall, succeeded Sweeny as district attorney in 1860. Although Tweed himself was defeated in a run for the office of sheriff in 1861, the election was not a total loss, as his enemy Fernando Wood was also defeated in the mayoral race.

Undeterred by his lack of legal expertise, Tweed had himself certified by his friend Barnard as a lawyer, and he further enriched his coffers by opening a law office in 1860. He extorted large payoffs for his services from companies desirous of doing business with New York such as the Erie Railroad. In 1864, he bought control of the New York Printing Company, which shortly thereafter became the official printer for the city; other businesses were also coerced into having to deal with the company. His next acquisition, the manufacturing Stationers' Company, was a way for him to sell supplies to the city at graft-inflated prices. The greatest boondoggle of all, the new county courthouse (later to be known as the Tweed Courthouse), was built with stone and marble from a Massachusetts quarry owned by Tweed. The courthouse, expected to cost half a million dollars, wound up costing the city's taxpayers approximately $13 million, most of it winding up in Tweed's capacious pockets.

Now a millionaire as well as a sachem of Tammany Hall, Tweed began to move in much more exalted circles. In 1867, he bought a large residence uptown in Murray Hill, off Fifth Avenue. He was now hobnobbing with neighbors such as the banker J. P. Morgan. He became a partner of the notorious financier/robber barons Jay Gould and James Fisk and became a director of several important utility companies and financial institutions. Gould and Fisk paid him off handsomely, in stock and a board directorship, for enabling them to get the Erie Classification Bill through the state legislature in order to legalize fraudulent railroad stock issued by their firm.

By the time Tweed secured the post of grand sachem of Tammany Hall in 1868, his power in New York was absolute. The "Tweed Ring," a confederation of like-minded crooks and ward heelers with whom "Boss" Tweed surrounded himself, were the rulers of all they surveyed. The ebullient Tweed shared his ill-gotten gains with his ring, increasing the proportion of their graft intake from 50 percent of all bills rendered to the city in 1869 to an astounding 85 percent shortly thereafter. Proceeds were divided by Tweed, the city comptroller, the county chairman, and the mayor. They also had a separate fund used exclusively for bribery.

Tweed moved into an even larger house on 43rd Street and Fifth Avenue and maintained a stable and carriage house an 40th Street. By the early 1870's, he had been named to the boards of the Harlem Gas Company, the Brooklyn Bridge Company, and the Third Avenue Railway Company

and was president of the Guardian Savings Bank. He also organized the Tenth National Bank to control city monies and his ever-increasing personal fortune.

Incredibly, a number of New York City's respected leaders were duped for a long period as to Tweed's criminal character. The city charter of 1870, which further cemented the Tweed Ring's hold on New York, was actually supported by honest and upstanding luminaries such as philanthropist Peter Cooper and newspaper publisher Horace Greeley. Retribution, however, was on its way. The talented Austrian-born political cartoonist Thomas Nast launched the first volley against the Tweed Ring in 1869 with a series of caricatures that ran in *Harper's Weekly*—among them the memorable "Let Us Prey," which depicted Tweed and his cronies as fat vultures feeding off the city. The Tammany Tiger became a familiar symbol in Nast's drawings; he did not let up his barrage until 1872. In the fall of 1870, *The New York Times* ran an editorial concerning the massive cost overruns on the county courthouse. Some months later, in the spring of 1871, whistleblowers within the Tammany organization supplied hard proofs of widespread swindling and corruption to George Jones, publisher of *The New York Times*. Though the Tweed Ring attempted to bribe the newspaper so that the story would not see print, it appeared in July of that year; soon thereafter, an indignant group of citizens met at the Cooper Union to form a committee to take back their city. Democratic state chairman Samuel Jones Tilden filed an affidavit citing Tweed and his ring's misdeeds, and the affidavit became the basis of a civil suit for recovery of the city's money.

Despite this notoriety, the serious threat of imminent arrest, and his summary expulsion from the Tammany Society, Tweed was reelected to the state Senate. By December, 1871, however, his astonishing luck had run out, and he was arrested in a criminal action. (Others in his ring, taking no chances, had already fled abroad.) It took two trials to convict Tweed; in late 1873, he was fined $12,750 and sentenced to twelve years in prison. He nevertheless managed to get his sentence reduced on appeals to one year and paid only $250 in fines. He was rearrested in early 1875 in a civil action brought by New York state to recover $6 million of what had been stolen. Unable to secure the $3 million in bail set by the state, he escaped from his prison cell later that year, fleeing first to Florida,

then Cuba, and from there to Spain. A Nast cartoon printed in *Harper's Weekly* on July 1, 1876, led to his arrest in Spain, and he was returned to the United States in the late fall of that year. The warrant issued in New York for his arrest described him thus at the end of his career:

> [F]ifty-five years of age, about five-feet eleven inches high, will weigh about two hundred and eighty pounds, very portly, ruddy complexion, has rather large, coarse, prominent features and large prominent nose; rather small blue or grey eyes, grey hair, from originally auburn color, head nearly bald on top from forehead back to crown, and bare part of ruddy color; head projecting toward the crown. His beard may be removed or dyed, and he may wear a wig or be otherwise disguised. . . .

Unable to pay the judgment that had been levied against him in the civil action, in which he was convicted in absentia of 204 out of 240 counts, he was confined to jail. His subsequent lengthy and detailed testimony confessing his guilt, an attempt to be pardoned for his crimes, did not work. He died of pneumonia in the Ludlow Street prison on April 12, 1878. At his side

was his manservant, who had opted to accompany him to jail; everyone else, including his family, had long since deserted him.

Summary

William Marcy Tweed has come to stand for all that is bad in American urban politics. He helped to spawn a particularly grotesque breed of individual—the bloated, powerful political boss—whose like has appeared again and again on the local and national scene; few such successors, however, have even begun to approach the phenomenal levels of graft achieved by the Tweed Ring and its leader. In the twentieth century, Mayor Richard Daley of Chicago and Carmine De Sapio of New York City were old-time political bosses in the spirit—if not the intense corruption—of Boss Tweed. Modern historians estimate that the Tweed Ring stole between $30 million and $200 million from the city of New York, but a final, definitive figure will probably never be known.

The tragedy of William Marcy Tweed, though, was that he had tremendous leadership and organizational skills, which, combined with a genial personality, could have served him well and long if he had chosen to follow an honest career in government. He did have good instincts when it came to running a municipal government, and some of what he did was positive and humanitarian. He was responsible for the widening of Broadway and for the preservation of the Central Park site that became the Metropolitan Museum of Art; he helped new immigrants to the city—at a time when they were disdained and overlooked by most New Yorkers—by seeing to it that they had food, clothing, and shelter. He helped set up the Manhattan Eye and Ear Hospital, opened orphanages, almshouses, and public baths, sought funding for parochial schools, and worked to increase state aid to private charities. He also was behind the effort to obtain a greater degree of home rule for New York City. Although it has been argued that these public services were mere sops granted to the poor in an attempt to gain even more political power, some scholars do not agree with such an assessment.

The scope of the corruption, fraud, and graft of Tweed and the Tweed Ring, however, remains unparalleled in urban government, and their unrestrained feeding at the public trough is what history most vividly remembers. For his years of systematically cheating the city and manipulating public trust, Tweed has continued to be vilified as one of the nineteenth century's most reprehensible men. On his death, New York City mayor Smith Ely refused to fly the City Hall flag at half-staff; that verdict still stands.

Bibliography

Allen, Oliver E. *The Tiger: The Rise and Fall of Tammany Hall*. Reading, Mass.: Addison-Wesley, 1993. A look at the times and political machine that spawned Boss Tweed.

Bales, William A. *Tiger in the Streets*. New York: Dodd, Mead, 1962. A straightforward account of Tweed's life and career.

Callow, Alexander B., Jr. *The Tweed Ring*. New York: Oxford University Press, 1966. Detailed, thoroughly documented history of Tweed and the men he handpicked to defraud the city of New York.

Hershkowitz, Lao. *Tweed's New York: Another Look*. New York: Doubleday, 1977. A reevaluation of Tweed's impact on New York City.

Mandelbaum, Seymour J. *Boss Tweed's New York*. New York: J. Wiley, 1965. Gives credit to Tweed for exerting strong leadership at a time of chaos and change in the growing metropolis of New York City.

Werner, Morris R. *Tammany Hall*. New York: Doubleday, 1928. Sets Tweed against the background of the Democratic political machine.

Zink, Harold. *City Bosses in the United States: A Study of Twenty Municipal Bosses*. Durham, N.C.: Duke University Press, 1930. Excellent chapter on Tweed, with good references.

Jo Manning

JOHN TYLER

Born: March 29, 1790; Greenway, Charles City County, Virginia
Died: January 18, 1862; Richmond, Virginia
Areas of Achievement: Government and politics
Contribution: Upon the death of President William Henry Harrison, Tyler became the first vice president to succeed to the presidency following the death of a chief executive. Tyler established the precedent that in such circumstances the new president holds the office in both fact and name.

Early Life

John Tyler was born on March 29, 1790, near Richmond, Virginia. His father was a distinguished Virginian who served as governor, as speaker of the state House of Delegates, and as a judge. Tyler was reared in an atmosphere of aristocratic privilege and refinement and imbued with a sense of responsibility and commitment to public service. He attended the College of William and Mary and excelled academically, while his interest in political theory and practice grew. He shared the strict constructionist Jeffersonian Republican views of his father, under whom he began to read law at the age of seventeen. Tyler was admitted to the Virginia bar in 1809, and at the age of twenty-one, he was elected to the Virginia House of Delegates. After brief military service in the War of 1812, Tyler returned to civilian life as a public servant. His striking physical appearance was a considerable political asset. He was six feet tall, slender, with a high forehead, aquiline nose, fair complexion, brilliant eyes, and a ready smile.

Life's Work

Tyler first achieved national office with his election to the United States House of Representatives in 1816. As a congressman, Tyler was dedicated to the principles of his family and section. He was a strict constructionist in his view of the Constitution and favored limitation of the powers of the federal government. These views led Tyler to oppose nationally financed internal improvements projects because they might extend the power of the federal government. He opposed creation of the first Bank of the United States for the same reason, as well as on constitutional grounds. While Tyler was consistent in his opposition to the slave trade, he nevertheless voted against the Missouri Compromise in 1820, believing that the "peculiar institution"

would perish for lack of suitable geographical areas for its expansion. Tyler was defeated in a United States Senate race in 1820 and retired briefly from politics to serve as chancellor of the College of William and Mary. He was elected governor of Virginia in 1825, won a seat in the United States Senate in 1827, and began to move toward national prominence.

Tyler supported William H. Crawford for the presidency in 1824 and was elected to the Senate as an anti-Jacksonian. As the Republican Party split into factions and began the process of dividing into National Republicans and Democratic Republicans, Tyler was offended by the rising tide of mass politics that came to be known as "Jacksonian Democracy." While the aristocratic Virginian was very cordial and effective when dealing with members of his own class, the common folk and their heroes made him uncomfortable. Tyler was especially critical of what he termed the barking of newspapers and the brawling of demagogues. Nevertheless, in 1828, the Virginia senator supported Jackson's successful presidential bid as the candidate of the Democratic Republicans. While Tyler agreed with Jackson's views on some matters, he was repulsed by what he perceived as the new president's authoritarianism, and soon his principles caused Tyler to split from the Tennessean and the Democratic Party.

Even when Tyler agreed with the president's positions on key issues, he often disapproved of his methods. Prime examples were nullification and the bank. Nullification became an issue during Jackson's presidency because of two developments affecting the South. The first was the tariff: In 1828, Congress passed a high protective tariff which Southern planters, dependent on an export economy, strongly opposed. Tyler was among the Southern senators who spoke and voted against this "Tariff of Abominations." The second development was the unification of the Northeast and Northwest into a national political force, relegating the South to minority status among the sections. Southern extremists were beginning to talk about separation from the Union in order to rescue the South from the tyranny of the majority. Vice President John C. Calhoun understood and empathized with the growing fear and frustration of the South yet wanted desperately to preserve the Union. Calhoun developed the theory of Nullification as a means of protecting the interests of the minority section within the Union.

Nullification and the tariff were linked when South Carolina threatened to declare the tariff null and void within its borders if it was not repealed by Congress. Despite an effort by Congress to avoid confrontation by passing a new compromise tariff, Calhoun decided the time had come to test his doctrine, and South Carolina began the process of Nullification. President Jackson issued an extremely strong proclamation rejecting South Carolina's constitutional position and threatened personally to lead a military force into the state to enforce the tariff and the will of the federal government. Congress passed the Force Act authorizing the president to use force to ensure that federal laws were obeyed. Tyler found himself in a troubling and ambiguous situation. On one hand, he shared South Carolina's opposition to high tariffs, but on the other, he did not accept the doctrine of Nullification. He also considered, however, Jackson's Nullification proclamation to be a violation of the Constitution, and he was the only senator to vote against the Force Act. Furthermore, Tyler objected to the forcefulness of Jackson's reaction to South Carolina's challenge.

The bank question created similar contradictions and ambivalence. Tyler opposed the attempt to recharter the Bank of the United States on economic and constitutional grounds. When President Jackson attempted to destroy the bank, however, by removing the government's deposits from its coffers, Tyler was among the senators supporting resolutions condemning Jackson's actions. When the Virginia legislature ordered him to recant and vote for a motion to expunge the resolutions, Tyler resigned from the Senate and left the Democratic Party.

The Virginian now found himself drifting into uncharted political territory. He was among those Southerners who were moving toward the new Whig Party, which was emerging in opposition to the executive tyranny of "King Andrew." Yet Tyler was somewhat out of step with his new political companions. His political and constitutional views were not consistent with those of most other Whigs. Tyler had left Jackson and the Democrats largely as a result of methodology rather than constitutional differences. He had remained true to his original views and philosophy, while the Whig Party seemed a loose coalition of diverse groups with room for considerable philosophical latitude. Nevertheless, although he was defeated in a Senate

election in 1839, Tyler was nominated for the vice presidency on the Harrison ticket the following year as the Whigs attempted to win the votes of other former Southern Democrats.

By now the Virginia politician who featured in one of the most famous campaign slogans in American political history had matured into a dignified and appealing figure. He continued to be somewhat distant in dealing with the masses and was sometimes accused of vanity, but most considered him friendly and considerate. He was unfailingly good-humored and patient and scrupulously honest. Even Tyler's political enemies found him difficult to dislike, and they respected his ability as a campaigner, for he had become a polished and effective orator. Tyler was nominated not because of his character or abilities, however, but because he appealed to disaffected Southern Democrats. Ironically, within a few short months the entire political structure was in turmoil, and Tyler was thrust onto center stage.

The Harrison and Tyler ticket won the election of 1840 easily, but within a month of his inauguration, Old Tippecanoe was dead. Supposedly, the dying chief executive's last words were a request that his vice president carry out the true principles of government. Ironically, the leaders of the Whig Party were soon to learn that Tyler did not share their concept of what constituted those true principles. Their chagrin and apparent amazement upon learning about the Virginian's views were somewhat surprising, for throughout his long political career, Tyler had demonstrated a philosophical and constitutional consistency that is unusual among politicians.

The marriage of Harrison and Tyler was strictly one of convenience. The Virginian had scarcely known, and was not favorably impressed by, Old Tippecanoe. The Whigs, however, expected that the actual leadership in a Harrison Administration would emanate from Congress, and Tyler was a close friend of Senator Henry Clay of Kentucky. Clay probably believed that Tyler would support the Whig programs that the Kentuckian planned to introduce in Congress, including plans for a new national bank. Tyler's oratory in the presidential campaign was sufficiently vague to provide substance for such a view, but within a few months, Clay would be a bitter political enemy, attacking the Virginian as a traitor to the Whig Party.

The first question faced by Tyler and the nation was fundamental: What was his status upon Harri-

son's death? Was he president in fact or only in name? Whether he was simply to attempt to carry out Harrison's views and programs or operate just as though he had been elected to the office was unclear. This was the first time that a vice president had ascended to the presidency upon the death of a chief executive, and the Constitution is rather vague concerning the succession. It says simply that if the president is removed from office, dies, resigns, or is unable to discharge his duties, the office will devolve on the vice president. This phrase could imply that the vice president inherits the office itself or, equally plausible, that the vice president simply performs the duties of the office. Tyler, usually the strict constructionist, interpreted the Constitution very broadly and claimed all the rights and privileges of the presidency. There was some contemporary criticism of his position, but the practice has been accepted and followed since that time.

Tyler retained the Harrison Cabinet members, reinforcing the impression that he would follow in the dead president's footsteps. Clay and the Whig leadership quickly and confidently submitted their legislative program, which called for a higher tariff and the creation of a new Bank of the United States. Congress enacted legislation for both the bank and the tariff, but the Whigs soon discovered that they had misread the situation. Tyler vetoed both measures with language that was highly reminiscent of Andrew Jackson. Some Whigs angrily charged that Tyler was a traitor, others that he was jealous of Clay. In actuality, Tyler was neither. He was simply acting in accord with the strict constructionist, agrarian views which he had absorbed from his father and had held since his youth. He stood his ground in the face of tremendous pressure, which included recriminations from Clay, blandishments from majoritarian Whigs, and a rock-throwing mob that attacked the White House.

Tyler argued that the legislation creating the new bank was unconstitutional and that the proposed institution posed the threat of an economic monopoly. He suggested a modified "exchequer" system as a compromise, but the Whig leaders forged ahead and again attempted to created a new bank, this time thinly disguised as a "fiscal corporation." Tyler vetoed that too, and the situation deteriorated into open warfare between the Whig president and his party. Tyler also struck down Clay's distribution program and other Whig legislation, and the Kentuckian resigned from the Senate in frustration and disgust.

Clay's resignation was followed by that of most of Tyler's cabinet members. The president replaced them with men of his own stripe, former Democrats who shared his views. There were public demonstrations against Tyler, he was burned in effigy, and in January, 1843, the Whigs brought impeachment charges against the man they now called "His Accidency." He was not convicted, but the Whigs formally expelled him from the party, as it disintegrated into shambles.

Tyler was now a man without a party, but he continued to perform his duties in accordance with his principles and in apparent good humor. During his presidency, he signed the Pre-emption Act, which made land more accessible and stimulated settlement in the Northwest, he helped end the Seminole War, and he was involved in the resolution of the Canadian boundary dispute with Great Britain. By 1844, he hoped for election to the presidency as an independent candidate but failed to generate significant support. Tyler then withdrew from the race and endorsed the Democrat, James K. Polk of Tennessee, who ran and won on an expansionist platform. During his last days in the presidency, the Virginian signed measures annexing Texas and admitting Florida to statehood.

John Tyler retired to his James River plantation in Virginia, a man without a party. He continued to be interested in public affairs and his graciousness, character, and obvious goodwill won the affection of his neighbors. He became an honored citizen and was an influential Southern leader as sectional turmoil increased during the 1850's. Tyler remained loyal to the Union and attempted to promote compromise on sectional issues but finally voted in favor of secession as a delegate to the Virginia secession convention. He served in the provisional Congress of the Confederacy and was elected to the Confederate House of Representatives but died in January, 1862, before taking his seat. He was buried in Richmond.

Summary

John Tyler was the first vice president to inherit the presidency upon the death of a chief executive, the first president to face impeachment charges, and the only one to be officially expelled from his party. He is remembered today primarily as a historical footnote, but he deserves better. He was a man of great integrity and considerable ability who remained steadfast in his views and true to his principles. Despite the turmoil of his presidency he achieved some positive accomplishments and significantly shaped the theory of vice presidential succession under the United States Constitution.

Bibliography

Chitwood, Oliver Perry. *John Tyler: Champion of the Old South*. New York and London: Appleton, 1939. Though dated, this book remains the standard biography of Tyler.

Crapol, Edward P. "John Tyler and the Pursuit of National Destiny." *Journal of the Early Republic* 17, no. 3 (Fall 1997). Explores Tyler's vision of national destiny, its importance in the history of the early republic, and its shortcomings.

Fraser, Hugh Russell. *Democracy in the Making: The Jackson-Tyler Era*. Indianapolis, Ind.: Bobbs-Merrill, 1938. A dated but useful account.

Gunderson, Robert G. *The Log-Cabin Campaign*. Lexington: University of Kentucky Press, 1957. This work discusses Tyler's role in the 1840 presidential campaign.

Howe, Daniel Walker. *The Political Culture of the American Whigs*. Chicago and London: University of Chicago Press, 1980. Howe analyzes the anti-Jackson movement which helped to create the Whig Party.

Lambert, Oscar Doane. *Presidential Politics in the United States, 1841-1844*. Durham, N.C.: Duke University Press, 1936. This is a dated but useful treatment.

Morgan, Robert J. *A Whig Embattled: The Presidency Under John Tyler*. Lincoln: University of Nebraska Press, 1954. Morgan's work focuses on Tyler's presidency.

Peterson, Norma Lois. *The Presidencies of William Henry Harrison and John Tyler*. Lawrence: University Press of Kansas, 1989.

Seager, Robert. *And Tyler Too*. New York: McGraw-Hill, 1963. This is a joint biography of Tyler and his second wife, Julia Gardiner Tyler.

James E. Fickle

MARTIN VAN BUREN

Born: December 5, 1782; Kinderhook, New York
Died: July 24, 1862; Kinderhook, New York
Areas of Achievement: Government and law
Contribution: Van Buren played a central role in the development of the modern party system. As president from 1837 to 1841, he kept the peace, eased sectional tensions over slavery, and formally separated the Treasury from private banks.

Early Life

An early example of a self-made man, Martin Van Buren began his career in Kinderhook, a small village on the post road to New York City about twenty miles south of Albany. There, on December 5, 1782, he was born into the family of Abraham and Hannah Van Buren, both of respectable if undistinguished Dutch stock, going back to early Colonial days. After an apparently happy childhood, the young Van Buren ended formal schooling at fourteen and spent the next seven years in law offices, first at Kinderhook and then in New York. Admitted to the bar in 1803, he began practice in his home village, soon moved to Hudson, and, in 1816, settled in Albany, where he continued practice for twelve more years. Each move marked a new level of success in the law and could be measured by the growing respect of his fellows and by an income, derived largely from small clients, which laid the basis for an estate later estimated at $200,000. In 1807, he married a childhood playmate and distant cousin, Hannah Hoes, and sired four sons—Abraham, John, Martin, and Smith Thompson—before Hannah's death in 1819. There were later flirtations and rumors of a second marriage, but Van Buren remained a widower.

Politics as well as the law engaged the ambitious Van Buren and opened a career leading from the state senate in 1812 to the White House twenty-five years later. Time spent in his father's tavern—a gathering place for Republicans in the exciting decade of the 1790's—had sparked his interest and had begun to draw out an uncommon aptitude which was to make him one of the first and best politicians in the nation's history. Foes ascribed his success to the arts of management and intrigue, calling him the Little Magician. Such epithets as "sly fox" and "noncommittalism" were also associated with his name. Friends, by contrast, appreciated his uncanny ability to "read men," to fathom the motives of opponents and conciliate the interests of

followers. Moving into the political arena once dominated by upper class gentlemen, Van Buren cultivated the needed qualities of prudence, compromise, and self-control. Elements of style also signaled the ambitions of a lower-class person in the period of transition to a more democratic society and found symbolic expression in the care which the young legal apprentice gave to his wardrobe. On borrowed funds, he replaced his simple Republican attire with the knee breeches, buckled shoes, and tricornered hat of his Federalist mentor. Along with fine clothes would come a taste for good wine, suavity of manners, and great conversational gifts.

Personal appearance enhanced his style and image. Crowned with curly hair of sandy red and graced with ease of movement, the young Van Buren commanded attention in spite of his thin and smallish five-foot, six-inch frame. In later years, he gained a large amount of weight and lost most of his hair, but thick sideburns of reddish gray framed an imposing brow. Lending further distinction to his countenance were big, blue, penetrating eyes and the ever-present trace of a smile, suggesting benign contentment to some and calculating guile to others. Here was a man, one bemused Virginia aristocrat observed, who might row to his object with muffled oars.

Life's Work

Van Buren's career in public office was a mix of personal ambition and a statesman's sensitivity to the needs of a rapidly changing society. In 1812, he began an eight-year tenure in the state senate, and for four of those years he also held the office of attorney general. The first part of his senate service was distinguished by unswerving support of the War of 1812 at a time when Federalists voiced bitter opposition; by the end of the war he attracted national attention with his proposal for conscripting troops. In 1817, he gave belated but indispensable support for digging the Erie Canal, a project closely linked to his political foe, DeWitt Clinton. At the same time, Van Buren opposed most applications for new bank charters, for he wished to moderate the forces of change which were transforming an agrarian society into one featuring manufacture, commerce, and the spirit of enterprise. He also played a central role in the state convention which made the old state constitution of

1777 more conformable to the new democratic age. More offices were opened to the elective principle, and the number of adult, white male voters was more than doubled.

It was also during his senate years that Van Buren and his associates developed a disciplined party organization along modern lines. Nurtured by spoils and animated with an ethic of loyalty to the will of the majority expressed in caucuses and conventions, the party apparatus reached out from Albany to all parts of the state. Techniques of mass appeal and a style of campaigning not unlike religious revivals generated excitement and drew the people into the political process. While rank-and-file party workers were attracted to spoils, "new men" such as Van Buren saw the party as a means of access to the power of government once reserved for the elite. Through its democratic organization and appeal, Van Buren and his party were normally able to outmatch the old style of elite politics followed by Clinton and, by the mid-1820's, gained control of the state.

Supported by his party, Van Buren won election to the United States Senate in 1821 and remained in that post for the next seven years. His reputation had preceded him to the Senate, where he soon enjoyed great influence and claimed the chair of the Judiciary Committee. A central concern was to revive two-party competition, which had ended, with the rapid decline of the Federalists, in the so-called "era of good feelings." Van Buren saw it as an era of bad feelings: Political conflict did not cease but turned inward, shattering the unity of the Republican Party into personal and sectional factions. The Missouri Controversy was one result; another was the disputed election of 1824, resolved at last by the House of Representatives in favor of John Quincy Adams—a neo-Federalist in Van Buren's eyes. Van Buren then assumed leadership of the opposition to the new administration with the object of reestablishing the political base of the old Republican Party which had reposed in Virginia and New York. To attract Southern support, he spoke out for states' rights against the idea of strong national government advocated by Adams. Working closely with others, he fashioned a North-South coalition behind Andrew Jackson in 1828, and he pictured the presidential contest with Adams as a rerun of the old battles between Republicans and Federalists. To aid the cause, Van Buren ran for governor of New York and, as he hoped, his election contributed to Jackson's triumph. After

three months at Albany, Van Buren resigned as governor and joined Jackson in Washington.

During Jackson's presidency, from 1829 to 1837, Van Buren served in turn as secretary of state, minister to England, and vice president. At the State Department, he gained by treaty the long-standing goal of opening trade with the British West Indies. His tenure as minister in 1831-1832 was cut short when political foes in the Senate refused to confirm his recess appointment. Happily for his career, however, the Senate action created a backlash of sentiment which enabled Jackson to choose him, through the party's first national convention, as vice president for the second term. In whatever position he held, Van Buren enjoyed great influence with Jackson. Except for the issue of internal improvements, he had little impact on the formulation of specific policies. His influence was of a more general kind, namely, that of helping shape Jackson's perception of the presidency in party terms. All earlier presidents, no matter how partisan their actions, had identified with the eighteenth century ideal of a "patriotic chief" above party. Yet Jackson set a new pattern by acting both as a president of the party and a president of the whole country. With Jackson's support, Van Buren received the party's nomination for president and, thanks to the divided state of the Whig Party, he won the election of 1836.

During his own presidency, from 1837 to 1841, Van Buren addressed three key matters. First, as a party president, he worked to contain sectional tensions over slavery. He enlisted the support of Northern Democrats to sustain the House "gag" on abolitionist petitions and to complete Jackson's timetable for removing Indians from the Old Southwest. In return for this support, he prevailed on Southern Democrats to surrender for the time their desire for bringing slaveholding Texas into the Union. Second, Van Buren kept the peace with Great Britain. The aid many Americans gave to the rebels in Canada created great tensions, but the president held firmly to the policy that citizens violating Canada's neutrality could expect no protection from the government. An even greater crisis arose over the disputed boundary with New Brunswick, leading by early 1839 to an impending confrontation between British forces and the Maine state militia. With bipartisan support, the president restrained further movements by the militia and worked out a truce arrangement with the British minister in Washington. The treaty resolving the boundary dispute came in the following administration, but Van Buren rightly claimed a "peace with honor."

At great political cost, finally, Van Buren pushed through Congress his central domestic measure for an independent Treasury. As his basic response to the Panic of 1837, it would separate Treasury operations from all private banks. Jackson had severed the connection with the national bank and deposited government revenues in selected state banks. Unhappily, these funds added to the momentum of other forces which, by 1835, generated a speculative mania and then the collapse two years later. Van Buren's plan would have the Treasury keep and disburse its own funds and use only specie or government paper, but no bank notes, in all its operations. The effect on the general currency of the country would be deflationary to some degree, yet the clear need of a depressed economy would seem to be for some degree of currency inflation. While fully aware of this fact, Van Buren held to the view that, over the long term, a deflationary policy would assure a sound recovery and work against any future cycle of boom and bust. Whig foes, by

contrast, skillfully exploited the short-term need for some form of currency inflation, rightly sensing its popularity in a nation increasingly committed to enterprise. The Whigs also put their political house in order as they looked to the election of 1840. Ending their earlier divisions, they nominated a military hero of sorts, General William Henry Harrison, and conducted a "log cabin" campaign that utilized to the fullest extent those techniques of mass appeal which Democrats had developed earlier. As a result, Van Buren was soundly defeated in his bid for reelection.

Van Buren was never able to avenge his stunning defeat. Principled opposition to the issue of Texas annexation four years later denied him the party nomination, which went instead to James K. Polk. For a number of reasons—among them a sense of betrayal by his party and a genuine concern for its increasingly pro-Southern tilt—he agreed to stand as the candidate of the Free-Soil Party in 1848 on a platform of opposing the spread of slavery. Within two years, however, he returned to his old party. Even though it remained strongly pro-Southern throughout the 1850's, he still believed that its states' rights doctrine and its appeal in both sections made it indispensable for preserving the Union. After the Civil War broke out, he supported President Abraham Lincoln, but before his death in July, 1862, it was clear that the war was in the process of transforming the federative Union of states into a more consolidated nation.

Summary

Historians for the next half century generally tended to echo the epithets fashioned by Van Buren's foes and to underrate the Little Magician's contribution to the nation's history. His idea of disciplined party organization, two-party competition, and a party presidency survived the Civil War and helped shape political life ever since. As president, he served the nation well by keeping peace with Great Britain at a time when war might have brought disaster to the young country. To his credit, some other depression president might have welcomed war as a diversion from domestic problems. Van Buren also merits good marks for his courage and consistency on the issue of an independent Treasury, for many expected him to follow a more popular course. His central measure also lasted a long time. Repealed by triumphant Whigs in 1841 and then restored by President Polk, the independent Treasury measure remained in operation until the Federal Reserve System was established. It did not end the cycle of boom and bust—as the panics of 1857, 1873, and 1893 show—but it is doubtful if any other plan would have worked much better in a country so fully committed to free enterprise. Along with his modest but real acts of statesmanship, in sum, Van Buren should also be remembered as an authentic expression of the American Dream, a genuine example of the self-made man.

Bibliography

Alexander, Holmes. *The American Talleyrand: The Career and Contemporaries of Martin Van Buren*. New York and London: Harper, 1935. The most hostile biography of Van Buren. It elaborates Whig charges against the spoilsman politician, opportunist, and schemer but is lively and well written.

Cole, Donald B. *Martin Van Buren and the American Political System*. Princeton, N.J.: Princeton University Press, 1984. The best of the biographies. Thorough, balanced in assessment, and well researched, it does an especially good job placing Van Buren in the context of economic and political development.

Curtis, James C. *The Fox at Bay: Martin Van Buren and the Presidency, 1837-1841*. Lexington: University Press of Kentucky, 1970. The first full-length work on the presidential years. Light on analysis of the economic background but good on the intraparty politics in Van Buren's party.

Lynch, Denis Tilden. *An Epoch and a Man: Martin Van Buren and His Times*. New York: Liveright, 1929; London: Kennikat Press, 1971. Dated but the most balanced of the older biographies. Contains much useful material on the personal life of Van Buren but fails to put his public career in context.

Morrison, Michael A. "Martin Van Buren, the Democracy, and the Partisan Politics of Texas Annexation." *Journal of Southern History* 61, no. 4 (November, 1995). Discusses Van Buren and the Texas annexation issue.

Niven, John. *Martin Van Buren: The Romantic Age of American Politics*. New York: Oxford University Press, 1983. The first biography on Van Buren in nearly fifty years. Well written, good on his private life, and good in synthesizing works which assess him in a favorable light. Too brief, however, on the presidential years.

Remini, Robert V. *Martin Van Buren and the Making of the Democratic Party*. New York: Columbia University Press, 1959. The best single volume on Van Buren's work in party organization. If he is pictured as a "politician," Van Buren is also pictured as a Jeffersonian ideologue and man of principle.

Shade, William G. " 'The Most Delicate and Exciting Topics': Martin Van Buren, Slavery, and the Election of 1836." *Journal of the Early Republic* 18, no. 3 (Fall 1998). Shade examines the 1836 presidential election, an election often ignored by historians, and Van Buren's management of the slavery issue.

Shepard, Edward M. *Martin Van Buren*. Boston: Houghton Mifflin, 1888. Part of the "American Statesman" series and the most sympathetic of the older biographies. It shares the Whig judgment against spoils but praises Van Buren for his Jeffersonian ideals and hard-money policy.

Wilson, Major L. *The Presidency of Martin Van Buren*. Lawrence: University Press of Kansas, 1984. Part of the Kansas presidential series. Thorough on the economic background of the Panic of 1837, the currency implications of the independent Treasury, and the party debate leading to Whig victory in 1840.

Major L. Wilson

CORNELIUS VANDERBILT

Born: May 27, 1794; Port Richmond, Staten Island, New York

Died: January 4, 1877; New York, New York

Areas of Achievement: Steamship and railroad industries

Contribution: Vanderbilt created a worldwide shipping and railroad business that was both efficient and profitable. Vanderbilt endowed Central University (later renamed Vanderbilt University) with one million dollars.

Early Life

Cornelius Vanderbilt, one of nine children of Cornelius and Phebe Vanderbilt, was born on May 27, 1794, in Port Richmond, Staten Island, New York. The Vanderbilts had difficulty supporting their huge household, yet the family managed, for the most part because of Mrs. Vanderbilt's careful monitoring of finances.

Mrs. Vanderbilt came from a family of New Jersey farmers. She tempered her husband's visionary schemes to get rich quick, and her strength and fortitude were the backbone of the family. Young Cornelius' father was of the third generation of a family that had migrated to America from Holland in search of the freedom to practice their Moravian religion; like the family of Mrs. Vanderbilt, they were farmers.

Thus, young Cornelius Vanderbilt was born into a situation which was not very promising. Vanderbilt hated school, preferring to spend his time outside involved in sports and even work. He was tall and strong for his age and was an excellent swimmer, an unsurpassed climber, and a wrestler whom few could beat. Despite his distaste for school lessons, he had a vigorous mind and quickly learned to sail and to use tools.

Vanderbilt took to the water, and it became his substitute for the schoolhouse. He spent entire afternoons watching craft navigate upon the beauty of New York Bay. It was alleged that in time he knew by sight every ship that used the port, and that he had learned the rig and outline of every fishing boat or coaster that navigated on the rivers.

Vanderbilt became adept at sailing the clumsy family boat, and he became the one who was trusted to take farm produce into New York. At sixteen, his attraction for the sea became so strong that he announced to his mother he was running away from home to become a sailor. His mother inter-

vened, and the two reached an agreement. Vanderbilt would be paid one hundred dollars to plough some hard, rough family land, and his earnings would be used to purchase a boat.

Vanderbilt quickly closed his first "contract." Like a crafty Tom Sawyer, he enlisted help from the neighborhood boys, promising his workers rides in his new boat. Vanderbilt put his new boat to work immediately and spent sixteen hours a day ferrying passengers for eighteen cents a trip. At the end of the first year, he repaid his mother the one hundred dollars and earned an additional one thousand dollars as well. At the end of the second year, he gave her one thousand dollars and bought partial interest in several other boats. Thus, he had devised on a small scale the system that would one day make him one of the wealthiest men in the world.

At nineteen, Vanderbilt fell in love with Sophia Johnson, the attractive daughter of his father's sister Eleanor. Both his parents objected, yet Vanderbilt married Sophia without their blessing on December 19, 1813.

Life's Work

To support his family, Vanderbilt set up a ferry system, and with his good reputation for delivery he obtained a contract to supply six forts around New York. The work was hard since it took a full day to supply one fort and that left Sunday as his only day off. Yet profits were large, and new schooners were added to a growing fleet.

When Robert Fulton launched the *Clermont*, Vanderbilt was not alone in realizing that the steamboat was the future of sea travel. For several years, Vanderbilt worked for Thomas Gibbons, commanding boats and streamlining procedures. During this period, the two men fought the state-granted monopoly Fulton enjoyed. The Supreme Court of the United States, after a wait of seven years, finally heard the case and declared that such monopolies were unconstitutional.

Because of his independent spirit and vision of the future, Vanderbilt resigned from his position with Gibbons and moved his family from New Brunswick back to New York in 1829. In the spring of 1830, with forty thousand dollars in savings, he entered the New York steamboat business. He constructed better boats than his competition and delivered services that were cheaper and more efficient. For the first five years, he made thirty thousand dollars a year and then his income in 1836 rose to sixty thousand. None of his more than one hundred vessels was ever burned, wrecked, or destroyed. He chose only the best captains and carried no insurance.

By age forty, Vanderbilt was worth $500,000. The Vanderbilts had twelve children (one son died in infancy) and lived at No. 10 Washington Place in New York City. Vanderbilt was all but brutal to his family, running it with more sternness than the captain of a vessel, and brooked no disobedience or contradiction. He educated all of his children, and George Washington Vanderbilt, his favorite, was sent to West Point. The sons were expected to earn their own living rather than count on their father's wealth. William Henry Vanderbilt, who was especially distasteful to his father, married against Vanderbilt's wishes and lived with his wife on nineteen dollars a week.

It is ironic that this man, who will forever be associated with the railroad industry, was nearly killed in a train accident. In 1833, Vanderbilt was thrown from a train, dragged along the track, and flung down an embankment. He broke several ribs which punctured his lungs but survived despite archaic medical treatment.

As Vanderbilt aged, he looked more and more aristocratic, as if he had been born to be wealthy and handsome throughout his life. Time had caused the top of his head to go bald, but the sides of his head still sported the white, bushy sideburns that created a look of distinction.

By 1864, Vanderbilt had sold his steamships to Daniel B. Allen and Cornelius K. Garrison for three million dollars. He then began to shift his investments into the railroad industry. He was nearly seventy and was worth not less than twenty million dollars.

Vanderbilt's success in the railroad industry must be credited in some small part to his son William, whom Vanderbilt had treated so harshly in his youth. Without his father's help, William was soon quite wealthy himself, owning a house, a farm, and land, with the farm yielding twelve thousand dollars a year.

Vanderbilt, noticing William's success, decided to test him by placing him in charge of the failed Staten Island Railroad. William knew next to nothing about railroads but sold his farm and accepted the challenge. In two years, almost miraculously, he took the railroad from bankruptcy and no credit

to solvency. His astonished father looked on in the background as William was made president of the Staten Island Railroad.

After some resistance, Vanderbilt entered the railroad industry on a larger scale in the winter of 1862-1863 by buying heavily the stock of the Harlem Railroad. The stock doubled and kept rising based on the magic name of the owner. Vanderbilt continued buying. The stock had sold for three dollars a share in 1857; on April 22, 1860, it sold for seventy-five dollars.

Vanderbilt was president of Harlem Railroad. His son William was made vice president and again implemented the procedures he had learned when he turned around the Staten Island Railroad. Within time, William created a second success.

Vanderbilt began adding more railroads to his empire, beginning with stock in the Hudson River Railroad. He was not interested in speculation but rather in making the railroads profitable. Soon he had full control of the Hudson and, as the Harlem Railroad began to show profits, Vanderbilt rewarded William by naming him vice president of the Hudson.

Next, Vanderbilt began to buy the stock of the New York Central, using two million dollars he had made off Harlem, thus repeating his practices in the steamship business. At the age of seventy-three, he took over the New York Central, and the massive improvements that took place on the Harlem and the Hudson River railroads were repeated, this time with an even tougher overhauling, and the connections were multiplied.

Vanderbilt consolidated his New York railroads into the New York Central, thereby maximizing efficiency. He made William vice president, and the railroad profited quickly under his now experienced leadership.

On August 17, 1868, Sophia Vanderbilt died. Within a year, Vanderbilt married Miss Frank A. Crawford, a much younger woman who was a distant relative of Vanderbilt's mother.

Vanderbilt continued to add railroad lines to his holdings like so many toys in a child's closet. In time he owned Canada Southern, Michigan Central, and Great Western. The combined railroad was 978 miles long and worth $150 million, half of which he owned. Yet this was the man who had fought against monopolies.

At eighty-one, Vanderbilt remained in good physical and mental health. He had accumulated one of the world's great fortunes, and, despite his tyranny and ruthlessness, he had created remarkable transportation systems for the United States. On January 4, 1877, Vanderbilt died at his home in New York.

Summary

Cornelius Vanderbilt must be labeled one of the great capitalist successes of all time. Throughout his life, he fought for the principle of free enterprise as guaranteed by the Constitution. From his mother, he learned to be frugal and to save money; from his father, he learned that get-rich-quick schemes rarely worked and that, instead, one could make money through hard work and wise investment, delivering a good product for a fair price. Many of his business practices continue to be standards in the American trade world.

Vanderbilt was born with no privileges, yet his story could not exactly be called rags to riches. He did literally start with a one-hundred-dollar boat which in a lifetime of eighty-two years he turned into 100 million dollars. During his youth, he was an archetypal American child, a Huck Finn who loathed education and spent his time dreaming on the banks of New York's waterways learning obsessively all that he could about boating.

After his death, some of his heirs continued the family empire until its dissolution in the twentieth century. The family homes in Newport, Rhode Island, and Asheville, North Carolina, would become museums. The Vanderbilt name would be kept alive through its association with railroads no longer owned by the family and, with true irony, through Vanderbilt University.

Bibliography

Andrews, Wayne. *The Vanderbilt Legend: The Story of the Vanderbilt Family, 1794-1940*. New York: Harcourt Brace, 1941. Only the first two chapters center on Cornelius Vanderbilt. Because of its span, the book fails to cover much in detail. Includes a family tree, photographs, footnotes, a bibliography, and an index.

Croffut, William A. *The Vanderbilts and the Story of Their Fortune*. Chicago and London: Belford, Clark, 1886. Croffut received help from the Vanderbilts until a disagreement severed the connection. A balanced analysis of the story, although the prose is turgid and the book is dated. Presents Vanderbilt with his rough edges.

Dunne, Dominick. "The Vanderbilt Century." *Vanity Fair* 58, no. 1 (January, 1995). Examines the Vanderbilt family, including background on Cornelius.

Hoyt, Edwin P. *The Vanderbilts and Their Fortunes*. New York: Doubleday, 1962; London: Muller, 1963. Emphasis on money and power. Well researched. Tells how the fourth generation lost the empire. Contains a bibliography.

Jennings, Walter Wilson. "Cornelius Vanderbilt: Illiterate Giant of Transportation." In *Twenty Giants of American Business*. New York: Exposition Press, 1952. Summarizes well the high points of Vanderbilt's life. Author extracts from a variety of sources. A good starting point.

Klein, Maury. "The First Tycoon." *Forbes* 146, no. 9 (October 22, 1990). Profile of Vanderbilt and his logical yet ruthless business practices.

Stoddard, William O. "Cornelius Vanderbilt: Competition." In *Men of Business*. New York: Scribner, 1893. Short overview in dated language, written to inspire careers in business. Overly positive.

John Harty

GIUSEPPE VERDI

Born: October 10, 1813; Le Roncole, Duchy of
   Parma
Died: January 27, 1901; Milan, Italy
Area of Achievement: Music
Contribution: Verdi, one of the giants of nineteenth
   century opera, was an innovator who during a
   long career evolved his own form of music drama and contributed at least half a dozen of the
   most enduringly popular operas in the international repertory.

Early Life

Giuseppe Verdi was born on October 10, 1813, in
Le Roncole, a village in the Duchy of Parma. He
was the son of Carlo Verdi and his wife, Luigia,
who together eked out a modest living as owners of
a wine and grocery store. Verdi's musical talent revealed itself early, and his father bought him an old
spinet when Giuseppe was eight. When he was ten,
he played the organ at the village church. His talent
was noticed by Antonio Barezzi, a wealthy merchant in nearby Busseto, who arranged for Verdi to
be tutored by Ferdinando Provesi, the director of
the music school in Busseto. Provesi taught him to
play the flute, the bass clarinet, the horn, and the
piano. After finishing high school in Busseto, Verdi
became Provesi's assistant. In 1833, Verdi traveled
to Milan, hoping to win a place at the conservatory,
but his application was refused because he was
over the age limit.

Barezzi provided for him to stay in Milan and
take private lessons from Vincenzo Lavigna, a conductor at La Scala. Verdi proved to be a diligent
student, sometimes working fourteen hours a day.
In 1834, Verdi returned to Busseto, hoping to fill
the vacancy left by the death of Provesi. The post,
however, had already gone to another candidate,
and the slight to Verdi caused a storm in the small
town. Eventually, after a public competition, Verdi
was appointed Busseto Master of Music. This was
in April, 1836; the next month, Verdi married Mar-
gherita Barezzi, the daughter of his benefactor.

Verdi began teaching, composing, and conducting, and his first opera, *Oberto, conte di San Boni-
facio,* was performed at La Scala in November,
1839. It ran for only fourteen performances, but
Verdi received a contract for three more operas. He
began working on *Un giorno di regno,* which was
performed in September, 1840, but it was withdrawn after the premiere. Shocked by this failure

and the death of his wife in the same year—as well
as the loss of his infant son the previous year—
Verdi decided never to compose again. After some
months, the director of La Scala persuaded him to
read a libretto based on the biblical story of Neb-
uchadnezzar. As a result, Verdi wrote *Nabucco,* his
first major work. Premiered at La Scala in March,
1842, it was an immediate success, and Verdi
found himself being hailed throughout Italy as the
successor to his fellow countrymen, Vincenzo
Bellini and Gaetano Donizetti.

Life's Work

Verdi often referred to the next nine years of his
life, during which he wrote fourteen operas, as his
period "in the galleys." The Italian operagoing
public was accustomed to a regular supply of new
works, and Verdi gave them what they wanted. After *Nabucco* came *I Lombardi alla prima crociata*
(1843); audiences were quick to apply the story,
about the struggle of the Lombards to free Jerusalem from the Saracens, to the contemporary Italian
struggle to throw off Austrian rule, and Verdi's music became a symbol of Italian nationalism. *I Lombardi all prima crociata* was followed by *Ernani*
(1844), *I due Foscari* (1844), and *Giovanna d'
Arco* (1845). In 1845, dissatisfied with standards of
production, Verdi broke his connection with La
Scala and was not to return until 1869. His next
two operas, *Alzira* (1845) and *Attila* (1846), were
performed in Naples and Venice, respectively.
Then came what is probably the best opera of his
early period, *Macbeth,* based on William Shakespeare's tragedy. It premiered in Florence in March,
1847.

Verdi had by now gained an international reputation, and later in 1847 he was in London, producing *I masnadieri.* The successful premiere was attended by Queen Victoria. Verdi returned home via
Paris, where he renewed his friendship with
Giuseppina Strepponi, who had sung in the premiere of *Nabucco.* They began living together, in
defiance of the rigid conventions of the period, and
married twelve years later. In 1848, political events
became more important than artistic ones in Verdi's life. It was a year of revolutions throughout
Europe, and the Austrians were driven out of Milan. When Verdi, who was an enthusiastic patriot,
heard the news in Paris, he left immediately for
Milan. The freedom and unification of Italy was

still in the future; republicans and monarchists quarreled among themselves, and in May Verdi returned to Paris. Milan was occupied by Austrian troops once more in August; the failure of the nationalist revolt depressed Verdi.

In 1849, Verdi and Strepponi moved back to Busseto, scandalizing the local people by their illicit liaison. Four operas followed over the next four years, including the patriotic *La battaglia di Legnano* (1849) and *Luisa Miller* (1849). Then within two years came three masterpieces. *Rigoletto*, first performed in March, 1851, and based on a play by Victor Hugo, was Verdi's first worldwide success. The heartbreaking story of the hunchback Rigoletto and his beautiful daughter Gilda includes one of Verdi's most popular melodies, "La donna e mobile," and the brilliant quartet "Bella figlia dell' amore." Over the next four years, *Rigoletto* was performed all over Europe and in the United States.

After Verdi and Strepponi moved to a new home in Sant' Agata, close to Busseto, Verdi began working simultaneously on *Il trovatore* and *La traviata*. *Il trovatore*, based on a drama by the Spanish playwright Antonio Garcia Gutiérrez, premiered in January, 1853, in Rome. It was an immediate and brilliant success, its superb melodies weaving a compelling tale of passion and vengeance, tenderness and melancholy. Less than two months later came the premiere of *La traviata*, based on a novel by Alexandre Dumas, *père*. For several reasons, however, the first performance was a failure: Verdi had discarded some old conventions, and the opera was performed in contemporary dress; it also featured a courtesan as heroine, which offended public taste. In 1854, the opera was performed again, this time successfully, at a different theater in Venice.

Verdi was now famous and wealthy, although he was not immune to failure: *Simone Boccanegra* (1857), which followed *Les Vêpres siciliennes* (1855), was not well received. Verdi was to revise it twenty-four years later. His next opera, *Un ballo in maschera*, which concerns the assassination of Gustavus III Adolphus of Sweden, premiered in Rome in 1859. Like a number of Verdi's previous operas, it was subject to censorship—the authorities were wary of having an assassination depicted on the stage.

In 1859, political events once more came to the fore. To Verdi's delight, Milan was liberated, and after Parma voted to join neighboring Modena, Verdi was elected as deputy to the new assembly.

He led a delegation to Vittorio Emanuele, King of Piedmont, to request the union of Parma with Piedmont. In 1861, Verdi was reluctantly persuaded to stand for election to Italy's new national parliament, and he remained a member until 1865. He did not care for the day-to-day business of politics. In the 1860's Verdi wrote only two operas: *La forza del destino* (1862), which was first performed in St. Petersburg in the presence of Czar Alexander II, and *Don Carlos* (1867). The latter was based on Friedrich Schiller's verse drama of the same name, and the libretto was in French.

In the last twenty-two years of his life, Verdi entered yet another creative phase. *Aïda*, commissioned by the Khedive of Egypt to mark the opening of the Suez Canal, was first performed in Cairo in December, 1871. Verdi stayed in Italy preparing for the performance in Milan, which followed shortly afterward. Full of pageantry and spectacle, *Aïda* was his greatest success. It has been called the last grand opera, and yet in spite of its vastness—a performance can use up to five hundred extras—the tender emotions of the three main characters, caught in a love triangle, are intimately conveyed. After the success of *Aïda*, Verdi seemed to have reached the summit of his career. Yet three great works were still to come. The first of these was the *Messa da requiem* (1874), in memory of the Italian poet and patriot Alessandro Manzoni, which is notable for the dramatic rather than devotional quality of the music.

For more than a decade following this work, Verdi lived in virtual retirement on his estate at Sant' Agata. He only reluctantly agreed to write *Otello* when he was shown the outstanding libretto, based on Shakespeare's play and written by the Italian poet Arrigo Boito. *Otello* was first performed at La Scala in February, 1887. It was another triumph: the musical event of the decade and Verdi's finest tragic opera. Verdi's final great work, *Falstaff* (1893), was an astonishing feat for a man in his eightieth year. It was his first comic opera in fifty years, and the libretto was again written by Arrigo Boito, based on Shakespeare's *The Merry Wives of Windsor*, with some material from *Henry IV*. Full of warm humor, fast-paced, and subtle, *Falstaff* was first performed at La Scala, in February, 1893. Verdi's last works were religious and included *Te Deum* (1896) and *Stabat Mater* (1897). In 1897, his wife died, and in January, 1901, while in Milan, Verdi suffered a stroke. He died six days later, on January 27, at the age of eighty-seven.

Summary

In spite of the fact that a large number of Giuseppe Verdi's twenty-six operas were hugely successful in his lifetime and that many of them quickly became part of the international repertory, full critical appreciation of his work was slow in coming. For some years after his death, only *Otello* and *Falstaff* were considered worthy of serious praise. The situation began to change first in Germany in the 1920's, with the Verdi Renaissance. This was partly a reaction against Verdi's great contemporary, Richard Wagner; indeed, during this period, there were almost as many performances of Verdi's operas in Germany as there were of Wagner's and far more than those of any other composer. Since then Verdi's reputation has steadily grown throughout the world. At least six of his operas, *Rigoletto*, *Il trovatore*, *La traviata*, *Aïda*, *Otello*, and *Falstaff*, are universally acknowledged as masterpieces and are among the most frequently performed, and best loved, of all operas. In addition, the *Messa da requiem* has power to rouse those who do not normally respond to religious music.

Verdi revolutionized nineteenth century opera. As an innovator, he was second only to Wagner. He quickly outgrew the operatic conventions of the period, which valued beautiful melodies and demonstrations of vocal agility more than dramatic action. Particularly from *Aïda* onward, Verdi perfected a form of continuous music drama, quite distinct from that of Wagner, in which the music served as an expression of character and dramatic situation. In this he proved himself equal to the daunting task of putting Shakespeare, the dramatist he most revered, into operatic form. These final works of Verdi reveal his technical mastery, psychological insight, and that deep sympathy for humanity—its passions, sufferings, follies, and nobility—that pervades his work as a whole.

Bibliography

Budden, Julian. *The Operas of Verdi*. 3 vols. Rev. ed. Oxford and New York: Clarendon Press, 1992. Three of the most impressive volumes ever written on Verdi. Volume 1 covers Verdi's first seventeen operas and includes plot summaries and biographical background. Shows how Verdi outgrew the conventions of nineteenth century Italian opera. Volume 2 covers *Il trovatore* to *La forza del destino* and includes details of Verdi's revisions and alterations. Volume 3 analyzes the composition, structure, and first performances of *Don Carlos*, *Aïda*, *Otello*, and *Falstaff*. Also discusses the creative process, the relationship between composer and librettist, and Verdi's relationship to contemporary Italian composers.

Chusid, Martin. *Verdi's Middle Period 1849-1859: Source Studies, Analysis, and Performance Practice*. Chicago: University of Chicago Press, 1997. This collection of essays by noted and new Verdian scholars focuses on the operas written between 1849 to 1859.

Conati, Marcello, ed. *Encounters with Verdi*. Translated by Richard Stokes. Ithaca, N.Y.: Cornell University Press, 1984. A major contribution to Verdi studies. Contains fifty eyewitness accounts written by Verdi's contemporaries who knew him, including composers, artists, musicians, critics, and journalists. Covers the period 1845-1900. Much of the material is previously unpublished. Conati's excellent introductions and extensive notes further illuminate Verdi's life and music. Also includes bibliography and index.

Gatti, Carlo. *Verdi: The Man and His Music*. Translated by Elisabeth Abbott. London: Gollancz, and New York: Putnam, 1955. One of the most important and enjoyable biographies. Originally published in 1931. Gatti, who as a young man knew Verdi, writes tenderly and affectionately about the man he admired.

Parker, Roger. *Leonora's Last Act: Essays in Verdian Discourse*. Princeton, N.J.: Princeton University Press, 1997. A collection of essays by the author on analysis and criticism of Verdi, including contemporary multidisciplinary concerns such as feminist theory. Autograph scores are included, inviting further interpretation.

Toye, Francis. *Giuseppe Verdi: His Life and Works*. London: Heinemann, and New York: Random House, 1931. One of the first comprehensive studies of Verdi in English. Divided into two parts. The first is intended for the general reader and surveys Verdi's life and music; the second is more specialized, treating each opera in detail, including an account of the librettos and their origins.

Verdi, Giuseppe. *Letters of Giuseppe Verdi*. Edited, compiled, and translated by Charles Osborne. London: Gollancz, 1971; New York: Holt Rinehart, 1972. Contains nearly three hundred letters written by Verdi between the ages of thirty and eighty-seven. Verdi did not expect these candid, down-to-earth, pithy letters to be published; they reveal his immense care for every detail of his craft and give insight into his dealings with theater directors, publishers, and librettists. Contains a biographical introduction.

Weaver, William, and Martin Chusid, eds. *The Verdi Companion*. New York: Norton, 1979; London: Gollancz, 1980. Ten short essays on various topics, including Verdi's relationship with the Risorgimento, with the city of Milan, and with librettists, as well as his attitude to operatic texts and his relationship to contemporary Italian opera. Includes a critical bibliography, a seventy-page chronological timetable of his life, and a list of major works by date of first performance.

Bryan Aubrey

JULES VERNE

Born: February 8, 1828; Nantes, France
Died: March 24, 1905; Amiens, France
Area of Achievement: Literature
Contribution: Verne was a popular and prolific French novelist whose works were immediately translated into other major languages. He is credited with being the father of the literary genre now known as science fiction.

Early Life

Jules Verne was born on February 8, 1828, in the French seaport of Nantes, the first son (and one of five children) born to Pierre and Sophie Verne. Descended from a long line of merchants, seamen, and lawyers, it was expected that Verne would practice law. That wish conflicted with his nature. The adventuresome Verne ran away from home at age eleven and attempted to set sail from Nantes on a departing ship. Caught and punished by his parents, Verne promised his mother that "from now on I'll travel only in my imagination." Only an average student, Verne was obedient to his father's hopes, studied law, and tried his luck as an attorney. For him it was a boring and frustrating profession.

While studying in Paris, Verne had met and befriended the famed writer Alexandre Dumas, *père,* author of *Les Trois Mousquetaires* (1844; *The Three Muskateers,* 1846) and the "father of the historical romance." Verne recalled his childhood fascination with "the literature of adventure," such as Daniel DeFoe's *Robinson Crusoe* (1719) and Johann Wyss's *Der schwietzerische Robinson* (1812-1827; *The Swiss Family Robinson,* 1814, 1818, 1820). With the encouragement of Dumas, Verne left the security of his law practice to write. His initial play, *Les Pailles rompues* (1850; the broken straws), was successful at Dumas's Théâtre Historique. Between 1851 and 1861, Verne penned some fifteen plays, most of which were never produced. For a short time, however, he was the secretary of the Théâtre Lyrique.

In 1856, while attending a wedding, Verne met Honorine Fraysee, a rich young widow with two children. It was a case of love at first sight. They were married on January 10, 1857, in a simple ceremony. In 1861, their son, Michel, was born. A happy union, the marriage lasted for forty-eight years.

By 1860 Verne began to regard himself as a professional failure. His writings were not earning much income, and he was accused of living off the income of a wealthy wife. Attempts to supplement his income by selling stocks failed. Because he had written some scientific articles, Verne attempted a piece on aeronautics and exploration. Africa was a popular subject because of the discoveries of adventurers such as Richard Francis Burton and John Speke. Verne proposed exploring the Dark Continent by balloon. This scientific text was repeatedly rejected by publishers. P. J. Hetzel (who wrote under the pseudonym P. J. Stahl) advised Verne to rewrite it as fiction, suggesting that Verne could do for science what Dumas had done for history. Verne acted on the advice, and the firm of Hetzel and Company published Verne's *voyages extraordinaires* (fantastic voyages) beginning with *Cinq Semaines en ballon* (1863; *Five Weeks in a Balloon,* 1876). The work was an immediate success, and Hetzel gave Verne a lifetime contract. His career as the creator of what would be called "science fiction" had begun.

Life's Work

At age thirty-five, Verne had found his life's work. In his remaining forty-two years, he would write more than sixty "scientific romances," averaging two books per year and winning the reputation of "the father of science fiction." Verne drew on two of his major loves in the writing of science fiction: geography and science.

Though he seldom traveled, Verne was an avid reader of travel books and was recognized as an accomplished amateur geographer. Early in his career, he wrote a popular history of geographical exploration from the Phoenicians to the nineteenth century, *La Decouverte de la terre* (1878; *The Discovery of the Earth,* 1878), while he also collaborated on an illustrated geography of France. This fascination with a sense of place gave Verne the ability to provide intimate and convincing details in his novels, even those set in remote places in the Americas and the Pacific. Of seafaring stock and as an accomplished yachtsman, Verne filled his novels that were set on the oceans with compelling data that would normally only be known to a sailor. Verne's feeling for locale was consistently persuasive.

Though he was not an inventor, Verne was an avid reader of scientific literature, and he had the gift to see the technological application of many of the great discoveries of the nineteenth century. Verne's writing anticipated that of science fiction author Arthur C. Clarke in this respect, for there is always a hard core of scientific fact inside his fantastic tales. Late in his life, when someone dared to compare his writing to that of the British author H. G. Wells, Verne protested, insisting, "I do not see the possibility of comparison between his work and mine . . . his stories do not repose on very scientific bases. . . . I make use of physics. He invents." Verne's novels were predictive of twentieth century realities such as helicopters in the skies, submarines under the seas, and space travel beyond the earth. In *Les Cinq Cents Millions de la Bégum* (1878; *The Begum's Fortune*, 1880), Verne foretold both poison gases and rocket-propelled missiles, while in *Face au drapeau* (1896; *For the Flag*, 1897), he anticipated the use of high explosives (atomic energy) to terrorize international trade. Verne, in fact, helped create what he described in fiction. Simon Lake, one of the developers of the

modern submarine, stated in his autobiography that "Jules Verne was in a sense the director-general of my life." I. O. Evans, an authority on the history of science fiction, felt that "Verne and Wells may have done far more than to foretell such developments; they may actually have helped to bring them about."

To Verne's passion for geography and science, one must add his skill as a masterful storyteller. Though his characters could sometimes lecture the readers on science, the excitement of the tale being told prevented one from feeling that the novel was pedantic. In an early story, Verne took his readers through an Icelandic volcano deep into the heart of the planet in *Voyage au centre de la terre* (1864; *A Journey to the Centre of the Earth*, 1872). That novel had a German hero, Professor Hardwigg, who encountered water-dwelling dinosaurs—the plesiosaurus and the ichthyosaurus—at the earth's core. Phileas Fogg, a proper English gentleman, was featured accomplishing a feat that many in the nineteenth century felt to be impossible, *Le Tour du monde en quatre-vingts jours* (1873; *Around the World in Eighty Days*, 1873). Fogg won his wager that he could circumnavigate the planet in less than two and one-half months, and soon Verne's fiction was being turned into fact by American and European reporters who attempted the task.

If one could go into the earth and around the earth, then why not leave the earth? An American hero designed a giant bullet-shaped projectile to be sent into space by the use of ordinary gunpowder from a site in Florida (coincidentally close to Cape Canaveral) in Verne's classic *De la terre à la lune* (1865; *From the Earth to the Moon*, 1873), which was followed by the sequel *Autour de la lune* (1870; *From the Earth to the Moon . . . and a Trip Around It*, 1873). From the depths of space, Verne took his fans to the depths of the ocean with the mysterious hero (whose nationality is still disputed) Captain Nemo (which means "No Name"), the captain of the *Nautilus*, earth's "first undersea ship," in *Vingt mille lieues sous les mers* (1869-1870; *Twenty Thousand Leagues Under the Sea*, 1873). This successful volume invited a sequel, *L'Île mystérieuse* (1874-1875; *The Mysterious Island*, 1875).

The influences on Verne's writing were many and complex. He was a devoted Roman Catholic and an avid reader of scientific literature, but he was especially indebted to the American author Edgar Allan Poe. Poe's short story "Hans Phfall," which described a balloon trip from the earth to the moon, inspired several of Verne's aerial adventures. Verne's novel *Le Sphinx des glaces* (1897; *An Antarctic Mystery*, 1898) was, in effect, an effort to try to complete Poe's unfinished *Narrative of Arthur Gordon Pym*. From Poe, Verne learned about the power of plot and the necessity of fascination in effective writing. His indebtedness to Dumas was obvious, for both encouragement and insight into the development of character. Verne, in turn, was to impact many of the major writers of science fiction in the twentieth century, from H. G. Wells to Isaac Asimov.

Though Verne wrote during Victorian times, his attitude toward the role of science in the human future was not one of uncritical optimism. At times science was viewed as a source of liberation. In *Twenty Thousand Leagues Under the Sea*, Captain Nemo informed Professor Aronnax that under the seas "there only is independence. . . . There I recognize no masters! There I am free." In *Maître du monde* (1904; *Master of the World*, 1914), Robur ("the conqueror") haunted the skies in his new machine, a combination helicopter-submarine called the Terror, which would enable him to rule the world. By poetic justice, Robur's Terror is destroyed by an act of nature, a thunderbolt. In later novels, Verne predicted that science would be used to produce instruments of mass destruction. As J. Kagarlitski noted, "Jules Verne, at the end of his life, arrived at the idea of the possible catastrophic consequences of the progress of science."

Summary

As an author, Verne was a world celebrity within his own lifetime. As a French citizen, he was awarded the Légion d'Honneur in 1870. As a resident of Amiens, he was active in municipal government. As a lover of the sea, he was a skilled yatchsman who sailed to Britain, Scandinavia, the Baltic Sea, and the Mediterranean Sea until that activity was prevented in 1886 through a wound inflicted by a madman, his nephew Gaston, who shot Verne in the foot at point-blank range. Later in life, Verne, an authentic workaholic, suffered from arthritis, blindness in one eye caused by a cataract, and increasing struggles with depression. His death on March 24, 1905, deprived the planet of a prophet and master storyteller, but Verne's ability to entertain continued, for a number of successful motion pictures have been based on his movies, including *Twenty Thousand Leagues Under the Sea* (1916 and 1954), *The Mysterious Island* (1929 and 1961), *From the Earth to the Moon* (1958), *Journey to the Center of the Earth* (1959), and, perhaps the most popular of all, *Around the World in Eighty Days* (1956).

Bibliography

Born, Franz. *Jules Verne: The Man Who Invented the Future*. Translated by Juliana Biro. Englewood Cliffs, N.J.: Prentice-Hall, 1964. This is a readable and reliable account of the novelist that presents him as a "secular prophet" who anticipated the life-altering inventions of the twentieth century.

Chesneaux, Jean. *The Political and Social Ideas of Jules Verne*. Translated by Thomas Wikeley. London: Thames and Hudson, 1972. Concise and beautifully illustrated, this work attempts to analyze the "world view" of "the prophet of Amiens." In some ways dated, it needs to be supplemented by more recent critiques of Verne's thought.

Costello, Peter. *Jules Verne: Inventor of Science Fiction*. London: Hodder and Stoughton, and New York: Scribner, 1978. This brief study relates Verne to the literary genre that he is credited with inventing and perfecting, though Verne regarded himself simply as an author of "scientific romances," not "scientific fiction."

Evans, Idrisyn Oliver. *Jules Verne and His Work*. London: Arco, 1965; New York: Twayne, 1966. This solid introduction to the "fictional futurist" and his writings by a respected Verne scholar of the post-World War II era is concise and nicely illustrated.

Lottman, Herbert R. *Jules Verne: An Exploratory Biography*. New York: St. Martin's Press, 1996. This scholarly examination of Verne is thoroughly researched and will remain definitive for some time. The exposition is lengthy and is enriched with an extensive bibliography.

Taves, Brian, Stephen Michaluk, Jr., and Edward Baxter. *The Jules Verne Encyclopedia*. Lanham, Md.: Scarecrow Press, 1996. This is a must. In spite of the brevity, the reader is introduced to the key facts, figures, and events of the Jules Verne corpus. Used in conjunction with a good biography while reading Verne's works, it will prove invaluable.

Teeters, Peggy. *Jules Verne: The Man Who Invented Tomorrow*. New York: Walker, 1992. This work is popular, fast-paced, concise, and readable, and it provides a good starting point for the reader who needs a quick introduction "to the father of science fiction."

Verne, Jean Jules. *Jules Verne: A Biography.* Translated and abridged by Roger Greaves. New York: Taplinger, 1976. It is not often that one is afforded a view of an author from within his own family. Verne's grandson, a distinguished judge, insisted that his grandfather's philosophy was that "the world needed not new science, but new morals." Insightful and succinct.

C. George Fry

QUEEN VICTORIA

Born: May 24, 1819; Kensington Palace, London, England

Died: January 22, 1901; Osborne House, Osborne, England

Areas of Achievement: Government and monarchy

Contribution: While striving to assert a greater role for the sovereign in British constitutional government, Queen Victoria accepted a gradually diminishing role. Her personal moral force lent such prestige to the Crown, however, that she made it possible for her successors to play a creative part in the continuity of government.

Early Life

On November 6, 1817, Princess Charlotte, the only child of George, Prince of Wales, died in childbirth, her infant son dying with her. That meant that of the twelve surviving children of King George III, not one could claim legitimate offspring. Stained by debauchery, the monarchy had lost its prestige. Consequently, 1818 became the year in which three of King George III's unmarried sons were called upon to marry and beget royal progeny.

Leopold of Saxe Coburg Saalfeld, the widower husband of the late Princess Charlotte, served as matchmaker, presenting his sister Victoria as a bride for Edward, Duke of Kent. Victoria was thirty years old, the widow of Prince Emich Charles of Leiningen, and unquestionably fertile, having borne her late husband a son, Charles, and a daughter, Feodore. The prospective parents of an heir to the British throne were married on July 11, 1818. On May 24, 1819, their daughter was born. The child was christened Alexandrina Victoria, the first name ultimately abandoned, being a tribute to Czar Alexander I of Russia, the infant's godfather. The Duke of Kent died of pneumonia on January 23, 1820, but he had already served his country by producing the heiress presumptive to the throne.

Thus, the Princess Victoria grew to womanhood under the smothering watchfulness of her mother. Victoria of Leiningen shielded her daughter from too much contact with her uncles, King George IV and William IV, regarding their courts as hopelessly dissolute. Closeted at Kensington Palace, the two Princesses Victoria shared a chaste bedroom every night until the daughter became queen and could command her mother to give her some privacy. The young Victoria entered adolescence almost entirely deprived of the companionship of children her own age and surrounded by adults maneuvering to advance their own self-interest. Under these abnormal conditions, observers may perceive the sources of three seemingly contradictory lifelong attitudes of Queen Victoria: She had a strong aversion to the physical aspect of sexuality, she overidealized male perfection, and she desperately needed a series of strong male figures whom she could dominate even as she was dominated by them. Understanding these elements is the key to grasping her complex relationship with her Uncle Leopold, who became King of the Belgians in 1831, with Baron Ernest Stockmar, with Prime Minister William Lamb, Viscount Melbourne, with her husband, Prince Consort Albert, with Prime Minister Benjamin Disraeli, and with her Scots servant John Brown. In reverse, those men who did not choose to master the fine art of simultaneously dominating and being dominated ended in very stormy relationships with the queen. One need only remember Prime Ministers Henry Temple, Viscount Palmerston, Lord John Russell, William Ewart Gladstone, and most tragically, her son and heir the future King Edward VII.

Life's Work

At six o'clock on the morning of June 20, 1837, the eighteen-year-old Princess Victoria received word that she was queen, at the death of her uncle, William IV. She was fortunate in two ways. As she was past her eighteenth birthday, no regency council was required. Her first prime minister, Lord Melbourne, established an excellent rapport with her from the start, training her unobtrusively in the delicate matter of understanding the limits placed on royal power under the unwritten British constitution.

Understanding British constitutional limits, always difficult, was particularly challenging in 1837. Until the onset of George III's final, nightmarish, ten-year illness in 1810, the old king had personally controlled patronage and appointments. This meant that through the disposition of thousands of lucrative posts and sinecures, Victoria's grandfather had been able to create a political machine which ensured that he could choose his own ministers. The king had no need to dirty his hands with the purchase of parliamentary seats. That could be left to borough mongers who owed the king their positions in society and government. Consequently, the king did not ordinarily have to fear a confrontation with his ministers, since nothing was likely to get through Parliament unless it had royal approval beforehand. From 1810 to 1837, all that had changed. George IV and William IV, Queen Victoria's uncles, had allowed power to slip from their hands. Ambitious politicians had taken over the all-important power of patronage, though the sovereign was consulted, and usually heeded, if he chose to assert his will. The fact is that Victoria's two predecessors lacked the skill and the will to operate such a delicate mechanism. By the time that Victoria came to the throne, it would have taken such enormous strength to retrieve what had been squandered in the previous twenty-seven years that the politicians would not have tolerated it. A constitutional crisis would have resulted. In the low state of royal prestige following the reigns of three sick, debauched, or ineffective kings, the British might have toppled the throne itself, rather than allow an eighteen-year-old queen to assume powers last exercised by her grandfather in 1810.

Working to press Queen Victoria toward her proper constitutional role was her Uncle Leopold, King of the Belgians, and his confidential agent Baron Ernest Stockmar, a physician turned political philosopher. These two very able men began to inculcate in the young monarch their own view of the British constitution as seen through German binoculars. On February 10, 1840, a third and much more important Saxe Coburg ally entered Victoria's life. Her marriage to Prince Albert meant that a very strong view of royal powers would prevail for the next twenty-one years until the Prince Consort died in 1861. The match might never have been made if Uncle Leopold had not conspired to lead his brother's son, and his sister's daughter to the altar. Nevertheless, the political alliance proved to be a love match.

While Albert lived, he was the gray eminence behind the throne. He read and made comments on all ministerial correspondence. It was Albert who saw to it that no important diplomatic dispatches left England until the queen had read and initialed them. Albert took care to allow Victoria to conduct interviews with ministers by herself, but she was the faithful conduit for his ideas and attitudes.

Even Albert, however, could not recover for Victoria what the royal uncles had thrown away. Parliament chose its own leaders. The chief of the ma-

jority party was almost always accepted as prime minister by the queen. As late as 1880, Queen Victoria tried to install a prime minister other than William Ewart Gladstone, whom she detested. Yet she was beaten, had to accept Gladstone, and never attempted to assert her will in the choice of a prime minister again.

Precisely because the queen read all major foreign office correspondence, Lord John Russell and Lord Palmerston sent controversial orders to envoys on their own personal stationery, without showing them to the queen. By that technique, Palmerston was able to recognize Napoleon III's seizure of power and to encourage the unification of Italy without gaining the royal assent. It was little wonder, then, that the queen referred to Lords Russell and Palmerston as "those terrible old men." Nevertheless, Albert acting as royal watchdog certainly placed restraints on the behavior of ministers acting irresponsibly. It is very probable that the prince, by his editing of one of Lord Russell's ultimata to the United States in 1861, played a major role in preventing the Trent Affair from dragging Great Britain into the American Civil War.

The death of Prince Albert in 1861 brought the queen into the second phase of her sixty-three-year reign. At Albert's death, Victoria fell into such a pathologically deep mourning that her behavior bordered on psychotic. Two forces kept her in contact with reality.

One was the obsessive need to control the lives of her nine children and, ultimately, her grandchildren and great grandchildren. The enormous volume of her correspondence with her descendants reflects an energy which is essentially healthy. The second element drawing her to reality was her continued interest in all aspects of government. A prime minister such as Benjamin Disraeli, who needed a mother figure in his life as badly as the queen needed a father figure, enjoyed what can only be described as a perfect platonic love. Disraeli was always able to persuade the queen that a given measure would have pleased Prince Albert. Disraeli could dispense flattery with a neat blend of sincere devotion and theatrical art. Granting the queen the title Empress of India in 1876 and staging a durbar at Windsor Castle, at which she wore the jewelry of the Moguls and received the homage of Indian princes, did not add one iota to royal power. It did, however, enhance Victoria's self-image to sign her letters, thenceforth, Victoria R[egina] and I[mperatrix]. The creation of an imperial

monarchy encouraged the queen, to the very end, to hold close to her heart every shred of the royal prerogative which had survived.

Nevertheless, the very fact that Victoria enjoyed the longest reign in British history meant that an eighty-one-year-old woman, at the end of her long career, could no longer keep her hand on all the strands of government. Even the railroad, the telegraph, and ultimately the telephone did not suffice to keep the queen entirely *au courant* on the fine details of events at London, when she was summering at Balmoral in Scotland, at Osborne on the south coast, or enjoying a winter visit to France or Germany. After every cabinet meeting, the queen's prime ministers dashed off reports of the minutes for the queen, but nothing replaced face-to-face discussions held at Buckingham Palace or Windsor Castle. The queen was too seldom in residence near London.

To almost the very end, the queen remained free of serious illness. As late as January 15, 1901, she was prepared to go out for a drive at Osborne. Her final illness and confinement to bed lasted only six days. Surrounded by her family, she died peacefully on January 22.

Summary

At the end of her life, Queen Victoria was the grandmother of an Emperor of Germany, an Empress of Russia, a Queen of Spain, and of a vast concourse of lesser royal personages. In her person, she was the only link binding independent dominions such as Canada, Australia, and New Zealand to the United Kingdom of Great Britain. In 1837, she had inherited the throne of an oligarchic aristocracy dominated by a few hundred families. When she died in 1901, she found herself the beloved mother of a great industrial democracy in which any man of talent might rise in society and government. The early death of Prince Albert had been a great blow to the revival of royal power, but it may have been the greatest contribution possible to the survival of monarchy in Great Britain.

The historian Walter Bagehot defined the sovereign's rights as "to be consulted, to encourage and to warn." It is probable that Victoria never heard that definition. It is certain that she would not have accepted it as accurate. Nevertheless, the British monarchy has survived precisely because it is exactly what Bagehot said that it should be. Depending upon the intelligence and personality of individuals, British monarchs may still play a role in shaping policy, as King Edward VII certainly affected foreign affairs. Fundamentally, however, it was Victoria at the end of her career who captured the essence of a modern sovereign's role. She had become neutral in politics, elevated above national debates. She alone knew all the state secrets and could serve as a link, uniting all the administrations of her reign, a symbol of the eternity of the state itself.

Bibliography

Benson, Edward Frederic. *Queen Victoria*. London and New York: Longman, 1935. An excellent early study of the reign by one of the first scholars to have access to a full range of primary sources.

Bolitho, Hector. *The Reign of Queen Victoria*. New York: Macmillan, 1948; London: Collins, 1949. Because of the author's experience as a biographer of several generations of the British royal family, this treatment of the queen is more intimate than most.

Cecil, Algernon. *Queen Victoria and Her Prime Ministers*. London: Eyre and Spottiswoode, and New York: Oxford University Press, 1953. A solid survey of the long series of ministers who shaped the course of the reign, 1837-1901.

Eyck, Frank. *The Prince Consort: A Political Biography*. London: Chatto and Windus, and Boston: Houghton Mifflin, 1959. A particularly valuable book because it downplays the role of the prince as a husband and emphasizes his role as a royalist political leader interested in restoring the queen's prerogative rights.

Homans, Margaret and Adrienne Munich, eds. *Remaking Queen Victoria*. Cambridge and New York: Cambridge University Press, 1997. A collection of essays by scholars in art, cultural studies, women's issues, and literature that focuses on the ways in which Victoria was viewed by her subjects and by those outside her realm.

Longford, Elizabeth. *Queen Victoria: Born to Succeed*. New York: Harper, 1964. An exceptionally well-written, scholarly, and detailed account of the reign.

Marriott, Sir John Arthur Ransome. *Queen Victoria and Her Ministers*. London: Murray, 1933; New York: Dutton, 1934. This relatively short book cannot do full justice to all the prime ministers who served Victoria from 1837 to 1901. It is very valuable, however, in two contexts. It gives great emphasis to such noteworthy relationships as those of the queen with the great political rivals, Disraeli and Gladstone; it also offers particularly valuable insights drawn from analyses of the changing role of the monarchy.

Monypenny, William Flavelle, and George Earle Buckle, eds. *The Life of Benjamin Disraeli, Earl of Beaconsfield*. 6 vols. New York: Macmillan, and London: Murray, 1913-1920. This six-volume work is rich in selections from the correspondence of Disraeli, containing candid references to the queen. As Disraeli enjoyed a more confidential relationship with Victoria than did any of her other ministers, his comments are revealing.

Munich, Adrienne. *Queen Victoria's Secrets*. New York: Columbia University Press, 1996. Munich looks at the many faces of Queen Victoria.

Victoria, Queen of Great Britain. *The Letters of Queen Victoria: A Selection from Her Majesty's Correspondence Between the Years 1837 and 1901*. Edited by Arthur C. Benson, et al. 3 series in 9 vols. London: Murray, and New York: Longman, 1907-1930. This is the largest published collection of the queen's correspondence, but there are numerous other collections of letters, particularly to and from her family. See Roger Fulford's *Dearest Child* (1964) and Sir Frederick Ponsonby's *Letters of the Empress Frederick* (1928).

————. *Regina v. Palmerston: The Correspondence Between Queen Victoria and Her Foreign and Prime Minister, 1837-1865*. Edited by Brian Connell. New York: Doubleday, 1961; London: Evans, 1962. Traces the gradually deteriorating relationship between the queen and one of her least liked ministers.

Arnold Blumberg

RUDOLF VIRCHOW

Born: October 13, 1821; Schivelbein, Pomerania
Died: September 5, 1902; Berlin, Germany
Areas of Achievement: Medicine, politics, and anthropology
Contribution: Virchow received worldwide recognition for his contribution to medical science, anthropology, archaeology, and public health. His greatest contribution to medical science was in establishing the principles of cellular pathology.

Early Life

Rudolf Ludwig Karl Virchow was born in the small eastern Pomeranian city of Schivelbein, the only child of a minor city official and farmer. He began his formal education in the *Gymnasium* at Coslin, where he distinguished himself by his linguistic abilities; he soon mastered Latin, learned Greek, English, and French, and was a good Hebrew scholar. In October, 1839, he entered the medical school of the Friedrich-Wilhelms-Institut, in Berlin. Johannes Müller, a physiologist, anatomist, and pathologist, and Johann Lucas Schönlein, an outstanding German clinician, influenced Virchow as he began his research activities while still an undergraduate. In 1843, he presented his thesis "De rheumate praesertim corneae" (rheumatic disease, particularly of the cornea), received his doctorate in medicine, and was given the position of assistant at the Charité Hospital. In the following year, he obtained the post of prosector of anatomy to the Charité Hospital, acting as assistant to Robert Froriep, whom he eventually succeeded only three years later, in 1846.

Froriep assigned to his young assistant, as a theme for independent investigation, the study of phlebitis. Virchow's thorough and brilliant studies outlining the principles of thrombosis and embolism formed a new chapter in pathology. In addition, his observations on leukemia opened new points of view on the origin and nature of white blood corpuscles. In 1847, at the age of twenty-six, with Benno Reinhardt he started the *Archiv für pathologische Anatomie und Physiologie, und für klinische Medizin* (archives for pathological anatomy and physiology and clinical medicine), a journal he continued to edit alone after his colleague's death in 1852.

In 1848, a singular event occurred which Virchow, in later life, regarded as the most decisive in his life. Sent on an official mission to study an epidemic of "hunger typhus" (relapsing fever) in famine-ridden Upper Silesia, a Prussian province occupied by a Polish minority, he published a scathing report indicting the government, insisting that the causes of the epidemic were social as much as—if not more than—medical. His antigovernment stance, coupled with the fact that, on his return, he had allied himself with the ultraradical party and founded a medico-political journal, *Die medizinische Reforme* (medical reform), resulted in his dismissal from all professional posts in Berlin. His fame as a pathologist had spread, and the University of Würzburg seized the opportunity and offered Virchow the professorship of pathology and the directorship of the newly founded Pathological Institute, where Virchow dedicated himself to research work.

As a young man, Virchow presented a small professorial figure. He was short, thin, blond, dark-eyed, and was accorded the nickname *Der Kleine Doktor* (the little doctor). He was quick in mind and body, often transfixing inattention or incompetence with a flash of sarcasm. Yet he was approachable, hospitable, and particularly warm and friendly to the sick and poor.

Life's Work

As professor of pathology at the University of Würzburg, Virchow entered the most creative period of his life. For the next seven years, his systematic and methodical research culminated in outlining the fundamental principles of cellular pathology. For centuries before Virchow, the origin of life and the seat of disease were the subjects of many theories and controversies. Medieval anatomists localized disease to one of the larger regions or cavities of the body, such as the head, chest, or abdomen. In the mid- to late eighteenth century, anatomists, led by Giovanni Battista Morgagni, attempted to find the actual diseased organ, and Marie François Xavier Bichat showed that in the same organ, sometimes one and sometimes another tissue might be the seat of disease. In the third decade of the nineteenth century, the microscope had disclosed the existence of cells, and in the next decade the study of pathological anatomy was directed to their study. Research in this area was faced with two major hurdles: First, cells could not be demonstrated in several tissues, even in their most developed state; second, the origin of new cells was completely unknown. The answer to the latter question was heavily prejudiced by the so-called cell theory of Theodor Schwann, who asserted that new cells arose from unformed, amorphous matter, which he termed "cytoblastema."

When Virchow arrived at the University of Würzburg in 1849, he had already brought with him some ideas about the principles of cellular pathology. Here, he proceeded to demonstrate the existence of cells in bone and in connective tissue, where their existence had hitherto been doubtful. This discovery of cells of connective and other allied tissues offered him the possibility of finding a cellular matrix for many new growths. These studies led to his coining the aphorism *omnis cellula e cellula* (each cell stems from another cell), which became the recognized hallmark of the biological cell theory. Virchow's conception of disease rested on four main hypotheses: first, that all diseases are in essence active or passive disturbances of living cells; second, that all cells arise from parent cells; third, that functional capacities of the cells depended on intracellular physicochemical processes; and finally, that all pathological formations are degenerations, transformations, or repetitions of normal structures.

Internationally famous for his research and teaching at Würzburg, Virchow was called back to the University of Berlin in 1856. Virchow agreed to return on the condition that a pathological institute be founded. The government agreed, and Virchow arrived to continue work with indefatigable zeal and published his *Die cellular Pathologie in ihrer Begründung auf physiologische und pathologische Gewebelehre* (1858; *Cellular Pathology as Based upon Physiological and Pathological Histology*, 1860), describing his work on the subject. Virchow's own aphorism *omnis cellula e cellula* is the basis for his work on tumors during 1863-1867, which treats these formations as physiologically independent new growths of cellular structure. He continued to write and edit his medical journal and enjoyed the satisfaction of celebrating its jubilee in December, 1897. Under his direction, the department of pathology at the Charité Hospital became a model for other institutions. He personally supervised the establishment of one of the best pathology museums in the world. In addition, he delivered lectures regularly, which were attended by an international audience. He was not a great orator; his voice was weak and his speech simple, but once on the platform the small man with the sharp dark eyes commanded attention.

He once again entered politics and was elected member of the municipal council; in 1862, he took his seat in the Prussian Diet, and by his sheer ability was recognized as leader of the opposition Radical Party. He led a desperate fight against Otto von Bismarck's dictatorship, and it is said that Bismarck became so annoyed with Virchow that he challenged him to a duel, which was averted by behind-the-scenes negotiations through Bismarck's intermediaries, who were determined to prevent it.

Virchow was also president of the German Geographical Society and the Society of Anthropology and Ethnology. He even had his own anthropological collection, mainly consisting of crania of the different human races. An accidental shelling of the Museum of Natural History in Paris during the war prompted the publication of an indignant pamphlet stating that the Prussians were not a Germanic but a barbaric race. That stirred Virchow's patriotism to the extent that he instigated a colossal public census of the color of the hair and eyes in six million German schoolchildren, concluding that there was no evidence of a predominant "German type" among them. He was interested in archaeology and worked in excavation sites of ancient Troy in Greece and Egypt; he also conducted his own fieldwork in the Caucasus in 1894.

Virchow remained at the forefront of international medicine and was showered with honors from scientific academies in Germany, France, and England. In 1891, his seventieth birthday was celebrated and a gold medal was presented to him by the emperor in recognition of the immense services Virchow had rendered to science. On January 5, 1902, he fell when exiting a tram car but, although he fractured a leg in the accident, recovered and was able to move about on crutches. He then went to Harzburg to recuperate, but he became weaker. Three weeks prior to his death, his friends decided to take him back to Berlin; Virchow did not tolerate the journey well, lapsed into a coma from which he never recovered, and died on September 5, 1902. Virchow was given a public funeral with honors and laid to rest in the cemetery of St. Matthew.

Summary

Rudolf Virchow, one of the founders of modern biomedicine, was also a proponent of social re-

form. According to Virchow, medicine was to be reformed on the basis of four principles: First, the health of the people is a matter of direct social concern; second, social and economic conditions have important effects on health and disease; third, the measures taken to promote health and to combat disease must be social as well as medical; and fourth, medical statistics should be the standard of measurement. Virchow's contribution to the improvement of public health was monumental; his discovery of the pathophysiology of the parasitic disease trichinosis led a successful ten-year campaign to establish compulsory meat inspection in Germany. At the request of the Berlin city council, he designed and supervised a sewage-disposal system that set the pattern for similar systems in Germany and elsewhere. He organized the ambulance service for the army; and, recognizing the importance of nurses to medical care, he opened a nursing school.

While Virchow made significant contributions in many fields, he became world-famous for his work in cellular pathology. The fundamental principles of cellular pathology outlined by him, particularly the dictum *omnis cellula e cellula*, forever closed the last loophole for opponents of this system and secured a position of great importance in physiology. Virchow was the first to systematize the theory of cellular pathology and to give medicine a common denominator for all diseases. Virchow's success may be attributed to the quality of his research, his prolific publications, his single-minded determination, and the growth of his influence on medicine. His work on cellular pathology had far-reaching consequences, contributing to progress in medicine and in surgery. It is therefore a fitting tribute that cellular pathology has been hailed as one of the great events in the history of medicine.

Bibliography

Ackerknecht, Erwin H. *Rudolf Virchow: Doctor, Statesman, Anthropologist*. Madison: University of Wisconsin Press, 1953. This is the first full-length study of Virchow, covering 240 pages. Although the author introduces the book with a brief life history, this is primarily an analysis of Virchow's work in medicine, politics, and anthropology. An extensive bibliography, strictly confined to items quoted in the text, is supplemented by an exhaustive biographical glossary. This book contains one sketch and two portraits of Virchow, including the first published portrait of Virchow as a septuagenarian.

Carr, James G. *Rudolph Virchow*. Chicago, Ill.: Northwestern University Bulletin, 1938. This concise twenty-three-page biography of Virchow contains translated excerpts of letters from Virchow to his parents that shed light on his early years, family life, and customs. No bibliography or illustrations are provided.

Jacobi, Abraham. *Rudolf Virchow*. New York: Trow, 1881. This thirty-five-page booklet is packed with information. Emphasizes Virchow's work in pathology and the work leading to the establishment of the principles of cellular pathology. Bibliography is not provided.

Virchow, Rudolf. *Disease, Life, and Man: Selected Essays*. Translated by Lelland Rather. Stanford, Calif.: Stanford University Press, 1958. This book contains selected essays by Virchow on a range of subjects, including cellular pathology, scientific medicine, and philosophy. An excellent introduction by the translator covers Virchow's place in history, and explores his role in the establishment of the principles of cellular pathology and the foundations of modern medicine. An appendix contains the German titles and sources of articles translated, including an extensive biographical glossary.

————. *Thrombosis and Emboli, (1846-1856).* Translated by Axel C. Matzdorff and William R. Bell. Canton, Mass.: Science History Publications, 1998. Another recently translated work by Virchow, this volume deals with his work on pulmonary embolism.

Welch, Henry. "Rudolph Virchow, Pathologist." *Boston Medical and Surgical Journal* 125 (1891): 453-457. An article written on the occasion of Virchow's seventieth birthday celebrations at Johns Hopkins University. This essay gives a thorough and scholarly review of Virchow's work in the field of pathology.

Anand Karnad
Abraham Verghese

RICHARD WAGNER

Born: May 22, 1813; Leipzig, Saxony

Died: February 13, 1883; Venice, Italy

Areas of Achievement: Music and theater

Contribution: Wagner wrote the librettos and scores of some of the world's greatest operas, most notably *Tristan und Isolde* (1859) and the tetralogy *Der Ring des Nibelungen* (1874; *The Ring of the Nibelungs*). A conductor, musical director, and writer as well as a composer, he raised standards for musical performances and developed the aesthetic of the *Gesamtkunstwerk* (total work of art), using compositional techniques based on chromaticism, variable meter, the leitmotif (a musical phrase with dramatic import), and an "infinite melody" of continuous expressiveness and significance.

Early Life

Richard Wagner was born in the German cultural and commercial center of Leipzig. Legally the son of police actuary Friedrich Wagner and his wife, Johanna, the young Wagner was never certain whether his father was actually Ludwig Geyer, the painter, actor, and poet whom his mother wed nine months after the death of Friedrich in November, 1813. Geyer died when Wagner was eight years old, but the child was called Richard Geyer until his middle teens.

While Wagner never mastered score-reading or an instrument, he was an autodidact with ever-expanding interests in music, theater, and culture. His initial schooling took place during his family's stay in Dresden, where he took piano lessons and explored ancient Greek mythology. He spent his late adolescence in Leipzig, beginning lessons in harmonic theory in 1828 and briefly studying violin with a member of the Gewandhaus Orchestra in 1830. The following year, he dabbled in musical studies at the University of Leipzig and became a pupil of Christian Theodor Weinlig.

A survey of Wagner's earliest successes and failures during the ensuing years indicates the wide range of his ambitions. By the end of 1833, he had composed his Polonaise in D for Piano (1832), conducted his Concert Symphony in C Major (1832) in Prague and Leipzig, started and abandoned work on an opera, and secured employment at the Würzburg city theater. In 1834, he became music director of Heinrich Bethmann's theatrical company in Magdeburg, completed his opera *Die Feen*

(The Fairies), published an essay for Robert Schumann's *Die Neue Zeitschrift für Musik*, made his debut as an opera conductor in Lauchstadt, and completed a libretto for *Das Liebesverbot* (1836; *The Ban on Love*). After first attempting to have this opera presented in Leipzig, Berlin, and Paris, Wagner conducted one performance of it in 1836 in Magdeburg, before the company there disbanded.

Also in 1836, Wagner wed Christine Wilhelmina ("Minna") Planer, an actress whom he first met in Lauchstadt. During the first years of this troubled marriage, Wagner experienced a decline in productivity. In 1837, he wrote an overture based on *Rule, Britannia!* (originally by Thomas Arne) and soon afterward assumed the post of music director of the city theater in Riga, where he sparked controversy (as he had in Magdeburg) by proposing numerous reforms, including plans for a subscription series.

When his contract in Riga was not renewed, Wagner traveled with Minna to Paris via the Norwegian coast, arriving in September, 1839. There he intensified his literary activity, received the support of Giacomo Meyerbeer, and became exposed to the work of Hector Berlioz. Initially occupying himself with such piecemeal work as composition for vaudevilles, he soon completed the first versions of the *Faust Overture* (1840), the grand tragic opera *Rienzi* (1840), and the Romantic opera *Der fliegende Holländer* (1841; *The Flying Dutchman*). By early 1843, the premieres of the latter two works had established Wagner as a composer and conductor of note.

Life's Work

In February, 1843, Wagner assumed the position of royal *Kapellmeister* left vacant after the death of Francesco Morlacchi. During his stay in Dresden, Wagner again antagonized his colleagues. Rigorous rehearsal schedules, a rearrangement of the traditional seating arrangement, and the eradication of the seniority system were among the improvements suggested by Wagner, who rarely succeeded in having his ideas enacted.

Wagner's brilliant but unorthodox approach to conducting, eliciting an impressive range of dynamic nuance, called upon orchestra and audience members to follow an idiosyncratic series of tempo changes that fully indulged the maestro's subjectivism. To retain his office, Wagner was forced to promise to interpret only new operas in this manner and to conform to tradition in conducting the old ones.

His talent as a creative administrator enabled Wagner to mount spectacles such as the 1843 choral festival, for which he hastily composed *Das Liebesmahl der Apostel* (1843; *The Love Feast of the Apostles)* for more than thirteen hundred performers. He was, however, dissatisfied with this performance as well as with the premiere two years later of his grand Romantic opera *Tannhäuser* (1845), which he revised extensively over the years.

Wagner, who met the Russian anarchist Mikhail Bakunin in 1848, supported the Dresden Revolution of 1849. He fled Germany in the wake of its failure, staying briefly in Weimar, the home of his friend Franz Liszt, before settling in Zurich. Following a discouraging January, 1850, excursion to Paris, Wagner wrote the anti-Semitic essay "Das Judentum in der Musik" (1850; "Jewishness and Music"). Wagner was also frustrated with circumstances surrounding the 1850 premiere of *Lohengrin*, directed by Liszt. In this Romantic opera, Elsa of Brabant loses the mysterious knight Lohengrin after the machinations of her enemies and her own curiosity compel her to ask him forbidden questions about his origin. Wagner's distance from the production (he did not hear a complete performance of the work until 1861) prompted him to ponder the creation of a theater designed to showcase his own works.

While in exile, Wagner completed his aesthetic treatise *Oper und Drama* (1852; *Opera and Drama*, 1913) and finished *Das Rheingold* (1854; *The Rhinegold)* and *Die Walküre* (1856; *The Valkyrie),* the first half of *Der Ring des Nibelungen* cycle. Among his financial supporters in Zurich was his neighbor Otto Wesendonck, whose wife, Mathilde, was an object of Wagner's romantic interest; his settings of her poems are known as the *Wesendonck Lieder* (1858). When the tension between the Wesendoncks and the Wagners reached a point of crisis, Wagner left Zurich for Venice, where he finished the full score of the second act to *Tristan und Isolde* in 1859. Intervention of the Saxon police forced him to complete the work in Lucerne.

By the end of the year, Wagner had returned to Paris, where successful concerts in 1860 resulted in an order from Napoleon III for a production of *Tannhäuser* at the Opéra; this support from the French government helped Wagner secure a partial amnesty, allowing travel through any part of Ger-

many except Saxony. The 1861 Opéra performances occasioned the famous anti-Austrian Jockey Club protests that forced *Tannhäuser* to close.

In 1862, a sickly Minna visited her husband in Biebrich before retiring to Dresden, where she died in 1866. Wagner, who soon received a full amnesty, dabbled in romantic affairs and conducted his own music throughout Europe, offering a profitable series of concerts in St. Petersburg and Moscow in 1863. Final relief from financial woes came in 1864 in the person of King Ludwig II of Bavaria, who provided the artist with generous political as well as monetary support. The mid-1860's also saw the intensification of Wagner's relationship with Cosima, the daughter of Liszt and the wife of conductor/pianist Hans von Bülow, for a time one of Wagner's staunchest supporters.

Supported by Ludwig, Wagner established a luxurious home in Munich, where *Tristan und Isolde* was first performed in 1865. A tragic love story colored by Wagner's relationship with Mathilde as well as his readings of Schopenhauerian and Buddhist philosophy, this opera is perhaps his most successful attempt at creating the sustained music drama that he proposed in his writings. Opening with the ambiguous "Tristan chord" (F-B-D-sharp-G-sharp), his score is characterized by an extreme chromaticism of melody and harmony that borders on atonality, and his verse is characterized by the deft employment of alliteration, rhyme, and assonance. Together with his sensuous phrasing and evocative manipulation of leitmotifs, these elements effectively evoke an atmosphere of intensifying yearning. The strenuous title roles were performed by Ludwig Schnorr von Carolsfeld (whose death three weeks after the fourth performance fueled rumors that the vocal parts were unperformable) and his wife, Malvina.

Later in 1865, local hostility toward Wagner led to his departure to Switzerland, where he and Cosima established their home, Tribschen. For the next two years, the two strenuously tried to hide their relationship from King Ludwig, who slowly awakened to what their enemies—including an unbalanced Malvina—were as strenuously trying to point out to him. Cosima and Bülow finally dissolved their marriage in July, 1870; Cosima married Wagner the following month, by which time she was already the mother of Wagner's children Isolde, Eva, and Siegfried.

In 1868, Wagner saw the successful premiere of his most comic opera, *Die Meistersinger von*

Nürnberg (1867; *The Mastersingers of Nuremberg*). The story of an untrained singer who wins his beloved by outsinging members of a conservative songster's guild was in part a scarcely concealed attack on Eduard Hanslick, one of the composer's harshest critics. At the end of the year, Wagner met Friedrich Wilhelm Nietzsche, whose move from fervid support to chilly hostility can be traced through his writings.

Dominating Wagner's musical activities through the 1860's and the 1870's was his vision of mounting a full Ring cycle in a festival theater dedicated to his works. After plans to build such a house in Munich were abandoned in 1868, Wagner's discouragement turned to outrage when Ludwig commanded that performances of *Das Rheingold* and *Die Walküre* be given in 1869 and 1870, respectively; Wagner went so far as to deceive the king to forestall a similarly decreed performance of *Siegfried* (1871), the third part of the tetralogy.

By 1872, Wagner had chosen the town of Bayreuth as the site of his festival. Leaving Tribschen, he spent the next four years supervising the construction of the Festspielhaus and engaging in fund-raising and the recruiting of personnel. He also completed the cycle's final installment, *Götterdämmerung* (1874; *The Twilight of the Gods*), and arranged the tetralogy's publication for performance.

The August, 1876, premiere of the Ring cycle in Bayreuth represented the triumphant culmination of twenty-eight years of labor. Prominent figures from around the world flocked to this four-day forerunner of modern festivals, where they were immersed in an epic of gods, Valkyries, and giants told through Wagner's alliterative *Stabreim* verse and massive orchestration. The only disappointments associated with the festival were its large deficit and Nietzsche's departure before its conclusion.

Wagner, however, was now secure enough to spend his later years riding the crest of his popularity, his operas receiving performances throughout Europe. He dedicated much of his time to writing essays on sundry topics, completing the fourth volume of his unreliable but revealing autobiography *Mein Leben* (1911; *My Life*). Months prior to his death of a heart attack, his final opera, *Parsifal* (1882), received its premiere under the direction of Hermann Levi at Bayreuth. Considered by Wagner and his followers as a sacred work, this tale of miraculous redemption is traditionally offered during the Christian holiday of Easter.

Summary

Notwithstanding his tremendous talent as a composer, conductor, and artistic manager, Richard Wagner's sheer force of will seems to have permitted him to emerge triumphant from a career haunted by scandal and indebtedness. A combination of creativity, charisma, and controversy attracted followers to him, the cultish phenomenon of Wagnerism testifying to the magnetism of his personality. In the decades after his death, Wagner's stature as a musician mushroomed. Through the end of the nineteenth century, a significant portion of the creative world was influenced to some degree by his work, and composers past the turn of the century felt compelled to refer to his works in measuring the value of their own.

Considered in tandem with his musical achievements, Wagner's nationalism and anti-Semitism made him a cultural hero of the Fascist regime of Adolf Hitler, who closely identified Wagner's thought with his own policies. As a result of this association, works by Wagner were not programmed in Israel until Zubin Mehta led the Israel Philharmonic in a 1974 concert that was disturbed by catcalls and fistfights.

Besides being performed regularly at the world's principal opera houses (Bayreuth remains a shrine for present-day Wagnerians and music lovers in general), Wagner's music has been preserved in numerous video and audio recordings. Outstanding among the latter is a 1965 recording of *Der Ring des Nibelungen*, a legendary performance by Sir Georg Solti and the Vienna Philharmonic Orchestra, featuring vocalists Dietrich Fischer-Dieskau, Kirsten Flagstad, Christa Ludwig, and Birgit Nilsson. Wagner's music has penetrated into many aspects of popular culture, most notably as the familiar melody "Here Comes the Bride," which may be heard in act 3 of *Lohengrin*. Other settings in which excerpts from Wagner's works are heard outside their original context include Bugs Bunny cartoons, films by surrealist Luis Buñuel, works by composer John Cage, and Francis Ford Coppola's film *Apocalypse Now* (1979).

Bibliography

Burbidge, Peter, and Richard Sutton, eds. *The Wagner Companion*. New York: Cambridge University Press, and London: Faber, 1979. This collection of essays covers a broad range of Wagner-related subjects.

Cicora, Mary A. *Mythology As Metaphor: Romantic Irony, Critical Theory and Wagner's Ring.* Westport, Conn.: Greenwood Press, 1998. An original interpretation of Wagner's "Ring" operas from a literary and critical perspective. Of interest to Wagner scholars, musicologists, literary scholars, and those interested in German cultural history.

————. *Wagner's Ring and German Drama: Comparative Studies in Mythology and History in Drama.* Westport, Conn.: Greenwood Press, 1999. Cicora examines Wagner's "Ring" series and its place in the traditions of German drama. By comparing the "Ring" operas with dramas by Schiller, Hebbel, and others, the multifaceted nature of Wagner's work is revealed.

Deathridge, John, and Carl Dahlhaus. *The New Grove Wagner.* Edited by Stanley Sadie. London: Macmillan, and New York: Norton, 1984. Highly recommended as a supplement for serious research, this concise scholarly treatment of Wagner's life, thought, and music includes critical analyses of potentially misleading sources of information, particularly *My Life.*

Donington, Robert. *Wagner's "Ring" and Its Symbols.* London: Faber, and New York: St. Martin's Press, 1963. An expert presents a thorough investigation of Wagner's most complex work.

McGlathery, James M. *Wagner's Operas and Desire.* New York: Lang, 1998. McGlathery studies ten of Wagner's most performed operas, focusing on the role of erotic passion in them.

Millington, Barry. *Wagner.* London: Dent, 1984; New York: Vintage, 1987. A brief and well-organized biography including a useful chronology and bibliography. Also includes guides to Wagner's musical compositions and a biographical listing of significant personalities in his life.

Newman, Ernest. *The Life of Richard Wagner.* New York: Knopf, and London: Cassell, 1933-1946. This four-volume biography remains the most comprehensive English-language account of Wagner's life.

Schonberg, Harold C. "Colossus of Germany." In *The Lives of the Great Composers.* 3d ed. New York: Norton, 1997. In this book, the highly popular music journalist surveys Wagner's life and most lasting contributions.

————. "Richard Wagner." In *The Great Conductors.* New York: Simon and Schuster, 1967; London: Gollancz, 1968. A major music critic of *The New York Times* engagingly outlines Wagner's contributions to the art of conducting.

Shaw, George Bernard. *The Perfect Wagnerite.* London: Richards, and New York: Bretano's, 1898. The witty dramatist discusses the Ring cycle and other aspects of Wagner's legacy.

Shelton, Geoffrey. *Richard and Cosima Wagner.* London: Gollancz, and Boston: Houghton Mifflin, 1982. The translator of Cosima's diaries explores the famous couple's love affair and marriage.

Westernhagen, Curt von. *Wagner: A Biography.* Cambridge and New York: Cambridge University Press, 1978. This major study supplements Newman's biography with more recent scholarship.

David Marc Fischer

EDWARD GIBBON WAKEFIELD

Born: March 20, 1796; London, England
Died: May 16, 1862; Wellington, New Zealand
Areas of Achievement: Politics, government, and social reform
Contribution: An enthusiastic champion of the British Empire and colonization during the early Victorian decades, when such enthusiasm was out of general favor in many circles in and out of Parliament, Wakefield promoted emigration and anticipated notions of self-government that had significance for the development of the later British Commonwealth.

Early Life

Edward Gibbon Wakefield was born in London on March 20, 1796, the eldest son and second child of Susanna Crash and Edward Wakefield. The Wakefields were a well-established merchant and manufacturing family with prominent Quaker connections, while the Crash family were successful farmers, but certainly more socially obscure than the Wakefields. Though prominent evangelical humanitarians such as Hannah Buxton, wife of the emancipator of the slaves, Thomas Fowell Buxton, and Elizabeth Fry of prison reform fame were numbered among Edward Gibbon Wakefield's cousins, his father cultivated friendships in Radical and Benthamite circles, and Wakefield's own penchants ran definitely toward the latter.

Portrait paintings from his youth and middle years and a photograph taken late in life convey a determined face with a square chin, a straight nose, a broad forehead, and the eyes of a visionary.

Married somewhat impetuously to Eliza Anne Frances Pattle, at the age of twenty, Edward Gibbon Wakefield enjoyed a brief but apparently happy four years, ended by his wife's death following the birth of the couple's second child. Six years later, the still-young widower, with greater impetuosity and little judgment, abducted a young heiress, Ellen Turner, whom he spirited to Gretna Green for a hasty marriage before fleeing to the Continent. This ill-conceived venture, which led to his trial and imprisonment at Newgate, was quite widely publicized at the time. It was not the last episode to generate controversy or entangle his life and reputation in conflict. Nevertheless, his incarceration focused his attention and undoubted energies on prison reform—only the first of numerous causes to which he was to give himself with singular intensity.

Life's Work

While serving his term in Newgate, Wakefield not only developed a keen awareness of the atrocious conditions of the penal system but also became acquainted with convicts awaiting transportation to Australia, as well as some who had previously been there. This seems to have quickened his interest in the antipodes, about which he proceeded to learn all that he could. While still languishing in prison, he produced a series of letters purportedly written by an Australian colonist, which appeared first in the *Morning Chronicle* and then in a volume entitled *Letters from Sydney* (1829). These letters contained the germ of what was to become his famous theory of "scientific colonization," and they testify to his fertile imagination and power of description, since he had at that time been nowhere near the lands he described with apparent believability.

Released from prison in 1830, Wakefield turned his attention immediately toward colonization projects, particularly in Australia. Subsequently, Wakefield was to play a highly controversial role in settlement schemes in both Australia and New Zealand. Gleaning the elements of his plan from varied sources in the vast literature available on the subject, he proposed a means of promoting the speedy, but orderly, establishment of colonies down under.

The Wakefield program called for subsidized emigration, financed through the sale of colonial lands at a "sufficient price." This price was to be high enough to prevent unbridled land grabbing and uncontrolled settlement, but not so high as to make the acquiring of land an unattainable goal for hardworking and worthy pioneers. New settlers would first provide the colony a reliable labor supply, but with diligence, the newcomers would themselves save enough to purchase their own land in time. The orderly sale of land would provide an ongoing source of revenue to finance future emigration in the same manner. Thus, Wakefield envisioned a virtually self-regulating method whereby English society could be transplanted to the far reaches of the globe.

Opinions vary widely on the soundness of Wakefield's attempts to grapple with the economic problems of colonization, but in the 1830's, his concept of "sufficient price" provoked lively discussion among leading figures within the school of classical economics. In a narrow but important way, Wakefield's name belongs in the history of economic thought.

Wakefield has been portrayed by his supporters as a great champion of overseas empire when enthusiasm for it had declined significantly in London. His was reputedly the superior vision of a positive, ordered extension of Great Britain overseas, while men of lesser vision saw colonies at best as a destination for the "shoveling out of paupers." To future generations of admirers, this commitment made Wakefield a key to the future evolution of the Commonwealth—even its founder—in an age when the skeptics greatly outnumbered the champions of Great Britain's worldwide involvements, often gloomily forecasting the separation of maturing colonies from the mother country like "ripe fruit." Commonly dubbed "imperial radicals" or "colonial reformers," Wakefield and his followers conveyed an alternate message of a growing empire of transplanted Britons, staunchly loyal to the Crown.

Among the prominent converts to his plan were Lord Durham, Charles Bullet, and Sir William Molesworth, young political radicals of the day. Durham, perhaps the most important of his group, found Wakefield impressive enough to engage him as a member of his staff during his famous mission to Canada, resulting in the Durham Report of 1839. In this venture also, Wakefield's role generated controversy, but his commitment to "responsible government," for the colonies of white settlement became, along with his land schemes, the basis of his ideas about the Empire. "Responsible government," in the parlance of the times, meant control of the colonial executive by the colonial legislature, particularly the lower chamber, in a manner analogous to the Parliament in London. It implied colonial control of matters relating to the colony alone, and thus proposed a divided sovereignty—a very dubious notion to many politicians in England.

Wakefield may be said to have reached the highpoint of his influence in persuading the House of Commons to convene a Select Committee on the Disposal of Colonial Lands in 1836. Here, in a relatively receptive atmosphere, he appeared as the chief witness, lobbying vigorously for his program, particularly promoting his New Zealand

scheme. Earlier settlement programs in Australia having fallen short of the scientific colonization ideal, New Zealand was Wakefield's greatest hope for fulfillment of his design. For some observers, Wakefield is recognized as New Zealand's founder. Yet here, as elsewhere, his role and his contribution are subject to widely differing assessments.

Wakefield's interest group, reorganizing the New Zealand Company (already in existence but previously quite unsuccessful in promoting emigration), did manage to send settlers and obtain land in 1839 and 1840. The British presence was confirmed by Maori consent—though the chieftains had little understanding of their actions—in the Treaty of Waitangi. French designs on the territory were discouraged, and British claims established.

Despite Colonial Office reticence, the New Zealand Company did proceed with its program, but settlement was far less systematic and less speedily accomplished than Wakefield intended, and he himself ultimately forsook his own colonization principles. Considerable animosity developed between the New Zealand Company and many of the settlers, and even his bid to promote "responsible government" was mired in factional dispute. It has been suggested that a very basic miscalculation on Wakefield's part was his penchant for agriculture at the expense of pastoralism, to which the country was then better suited. At any rate, the fulfillment of his ideas proved increasingly elusive. The political leadership to which he aspired evaded him. The last decade of his life was a twilight of alienation and growing obscurity. On May 16, 1862, Wakefield died in Wellington, one of the centers of New Zealand settlement upon which Wakefield had staked so much of his dream of empire.

Summary

Whatever have been recent assessments of Edward Gibbon Wakefield as an economic theorist, it is worth noting that Karl Marx found his writings on colonial land exploitation significant enough to dedicate a chapter of *Das Kapital* (1867-1894) to them. Primarily, however, Wakefield's name will always be linked with scientific colonization, despite the fact that nowhere in the British Empire were his principles translated into practice in any more than very fragmentary fashion. To preserve and enlarge Great Britain overseas was the goal he espoused, along with an enthusiasm for the virtues of capitalism and the prospects of personal gain that such grand schemes might produce. Patriotism and profits were apparently closely associated in his mind. Admirers stress the former; detractors, then and now, often point accusingly to the latter.

Bibliography

Bloomfield, Paul. *Edward Gibbon Wakefield: Builder of the British Commonwealth.* London: Longman, 1961. A highly laudatory biography, the tone of which is quite at odds with the widespread criticism of imperialism that has generally characterized the postcolonial era.

Carrington, C. E. *The British Overseas: Exploits of a Nation of Shopkeepers.* Cambridge: Cambridge University Press, 1950. Chapter 7, "The Colonial Reformers, 1830-1846," is a clear and succinct overview of Wakefield and his movement, surveying his activities throughout the Empire.

Kittrell, Edward R. "Wakefield's Scheme of Systematic Colonization and Classical Economics." *American Journal of Economics and Sociology* 32 (January, 1973): 87-111. Maintaining that Wakefield's influence on classical economics was "of a very little, albeit important nature," the author surveys his ideas, particularly the notion of "sufficient price."

Manning, Helen Taft. "The Present State of Wakefield Studies." *Historical Studies: Australia and New Zealand* 16 (1974): 277-285. This distinguished scholar gives a brief and very useful summary of recent work on Wakefield, noting both the continuing traditions of pro-Wakefieldian writings and the growing literature critical of the man, his following, and his ideas.

Norman, John. *Edward Gibbon Wakefield: A Political Appraisal.* Fairfield, Conn.: New Frontiers of Fairfield University, 1963. One of the more favorable treatments of Wakefield, portraying him as "one of the truly great founders of the new British Empire."

Philipp, June. "Wakefieldian Influence and New South Wales, 1830-1832." *Historical Studies: Australia and New Zealand* 9 (1960): 173-178. This brief study of Wakefield's role in this Australian colony minimizes the role of scientific colonization, though generally the author is more favorably inclined toward Wakefield than many recent writers.

Stuart, Peter. *Edward Gibbon Wakefield in New Zealand.* Wellington: Price Milburn for Victoria University, 1971. A very important treatment of Wakefield's career in New Zealand; based on rigorous research, it explodes many legends and myths relating to the founding of New Zealand. The subject is portrayed in an uncomplimentary fashion.

Raymond M. Cooke

JOHN WALTER II

Born: February 23, 1776; London, England
Died: July 28, 1847; London, England
Areas of Achievement: Publishing and journalism
Contribution: The son of John Walter I, founder of *The Times* of London, John Walter II fought to establish some of the principles and practices that are fundamental to modern journalism, above all the freedom to report and interpret the news independent of financial sponsorship or government pressure. Under his leadership, *The Times* became the leading newspaper of Europe and created a body of informed public opinion that had the power to move government.

Early Life

John Walter II was born on February 23, 1776, the fifth child and second son of John Walter and his wife, Frances Landen. His father, a London businessman who turned to printing in middle age after losing his shipping business in the American Revolution, had started *The Daily Universal Register* in 1784 as a way of publicizing a new printing technique, "logography." The newspaper prospered more than the process: By 1792, the paper—by then renamed *The Times*—had one of the largest circulations among English morning papers. "Logography" had been abandoned.

Walter attended Merchant Taylor's School in 1787. At the age of fourteen, he was apprenticed to the London printer Thomas Longman but soon transferred to work under his father in Printing House Square. In 1796, he went to Oxford with the intention, apparently, of studying for the church but was recalled by his father the following year to work in the printing house. Walter's father had handed over the management of his business and newspapers to his eldest son, William, in 1795, but this arrangement was evidently not a success. On Walter's return, he was made an equal partner with his father in the printing end of the business, while William remained editor of the papers. In 1801, at the age of twenty-five, Walter was given a sixteenth share of profits from *The Times* and from his father's other paper, *The Evening Mail*. From 1803, he became sole manager and editor of *The Times*. His father, though still principal shareholder, did not interfere with his management of the paper. Indeed, he had been contemplating closing it down because the circulation had again dropped.

Life's Work

Walter quickly put his stamp on *The Times*. At this time, newspapers were assumed to be venal, and journalism was considered hardly a respectable profession. It was customary for newspaper printers to cover some of their printing costs through political favors of one sort or another, whether to politicians or to customers. The elder Walter allied himself with William Pitt the Younger, newly in office, and sang his praises in the paper. He also sought and won the post of printer to the customs in 1787, accepted from the Treasury three hundred pounds a year as "reward for the politics of the paper" from 1789 to 1799, routinely took payment for printing corrections and retractions to unflattering news reports, and as regularly accepted payment for theatrical puffs written by theater management (masquerading as impartial reviews). His son took every opportunity to break with this practice, struggling doggedly with the authorities and others whose interests were vested in the existing system. After some years, he succeeded in shaping a paper whose reputation for integrity brought it a circulation large enough to give financial independence, and thus political freedom. In a remarkable statement of principle in a leading article of *The Times* (February 11, 1810), Walter spelled out his objectives and his experience in trying to reach them.

An early opportunity to take a stand concerned the position of printer to the Customs, which his father had lost in 1799 after printing words critical of the House of Commons. In 1806, Walter was invited to petition for return of the post. It was understood that its return would be considered a favor of government, to be repaid in due course. Though Walter certainly had hoped to recover the position, he refused the terms on the grounds that he did not want *The Times* to carry an obligation to any office of government.

For most London newspapers foreign news was derived from foreign journals which were sent to the English Post Office, translated there, and distributed at a price to the newspaper offices. From 1805, Walter began building his own foreign news service. The apparatus included dispatch agents and foreign correspondents and translators, and was on a scale unheard of at that time. The service, however, was unacceptable to the postal officials, and Walter found that dispatches addressed to him were being held up at ports, on orders of the Home Office. He protested, but to no avail: He was told that the delays would cease if he wrote in support of the government. He had his mail sent undercover to other offices in London, and with the Napoleonic blockade of English ports Walter hired smugglers to bring his packages to Great Britain. At this point, however, the government had the same difficulties as Walter, so he made a deal: His own blockade-runners, unmolested, would supply foreign journals to the government also.

Walter himself was described as proud, reserved, and high-principled: an able businessman who was hard on himself and strict with others. He believed in hard work, thrift, and self-reliance; thus, he never allowed "combinations" of his workmen, and in 1810 broke a strike among his men by helping at the press and case himself. His friends contrasted him with his father, a man who "never did an honest act in his life." A family man, he had few close friends and little liking for social or political circles. Walter established among the writers at *The Times* a system of anonymity in keeping with his own character, and which was said to have something of the quality of a secret society. Contributions to the paper were unsigned; positions on the staff of the paper were strictly confidential. Even within the organization writers might not know one another's names. The result was a degree of unity and protection that was important for a paper which had put itself at war with entrenched elements of authority. It also protected the reputation of writers who had some social standing, and who would not want their association with a newspaper to be known.

In 1812, John Walter I died. His will made John II sole owner of the premises at Printing House Square, sole and salaried manager and editor of *The Times*, and holder of a share in its ownership. This will has been interpreted variously as an expression of faith in his son's ability, and an act of revenge for the loss of the Customs Office.

With his father's death, Walter's work took a different direction. *The Times* had by now a reputation for serious news and comment, as well as a solid financial footing. Walter gradually withdrew from direct management of the editorial side of the paper and turned his attention to running the printing business. His greatest contributions to journalism over the next decade were in two areas: pioneering the use of steam in the newspaper printing

house, and separating the work of newspaper editing from management.

Walter's first encounter with improved printing presses was in 1804, when he underwrote the cost of developing a new "self-acting" printing system consisting of four presses driven by a single machine. After spending fourteen hundred pounds on the idea Walter abandoned it: He realized that, like his father's "logography," the invention would not work. In 1808, and again in 1812, he was approached by a German engineer, Friedrich Koenig, who was attempting to harness steam power to presses. The demonstration of 1812 was convincing: Walter ordered two double cylinder presses and two steam engines at a total cost of twenty-eight hundred pounds. In 1814, the presses were assembled and installed in the printing office in complete secrecy, for fear that the regular employees would see them as a threat to their jobs and destroy them. The old presses were capable of printing about 240 sheets an hour; the new ones could print eleven hundred. There were also savings in composition costs, for with the old presses Walter had been obliged to set type in duplicate for any edition of over forty-five hundred in order to get the daily papers out in time. *The Times* (combined with Walter's thrice-weekly *The Evening Mail*) was for some years the only paper with a circulation large enough to justify the cost of Koenig's machines.

Once the new machines were installed, Walter looked for someone to take over the responsibility of editing the papers. His first appointment was John Stoddart, but Stoddart proved too inflexibly Tory for either Walter or his readers. Later, he promoted one of his own writers, Thomas Barnes, and this choice was most successful. With Walter as editor *The Times* had been known for the high quality of its foreign, legal, and parliamentary reporting. Under Barnes, its domestic news and forceful leading articles became equally famous. During this period, the paper earned its popular name, "The Thunderer."

With Barnes in the editor's seat, Walter was developing a life for himself outside the newspaper business. His first wife died within a year; in 1818, he married again and his son John Walter III was born. He had bought land and built a house at Bear Wood in Berkshire. Over the next ten years, Walter gradually removed himself from direct responsibility for *The Times*. This retreat probably had to do with his new ambition to sit in Parliament: Journal-

ism was not yet considered a gentlemanly pursuit, and association with a particular paper would cast doubt on the impartiality of a man's judgment. Walter gave up the salary of one thousand pounds allowed him by his father's will and sold most of his shares in the paper to employees. In 1832, he was returned as the Whig member for Berkshire, a seat he held until 1837. He was known as a plain speaker and reluctant debater, but a vehement opponent of the Whig Party's oppressive Poor Laws: a better representative of the people than of his party. In 1841, changing to the Tory Party, Walter sat briefly as the member for Nottingham.

Walter did not interfere with Barnes's editorial policy, though he never gave up his ultimate responsibility for the management of *The Times* or for the hiring and firing of his staff. In 1841, Barnes died and Walter appointed John Thaddeus Delane his successor. Delane, the second great editor of the paper, held the position until 1879.

John Walter died of cancer in London on July 28, 1847. His son, John Walter III, who had worked alongside the father for the last years of his life, succeeded him as proprietor of *The Times*.

Summary

John Walter II's outstanding achievement was to establish an honest daily paper at a time when such a thing was almost inconceivable. Not only was bribery commonplace, but also most printers assumed that there was no other way to cover costs. Walter met and overcame each aspect of venality in his trade and finally demonstrated that a truly independent newspaper could indeed be supported by no more than advertising and the subscriptions of its readers.

Walter was not alone in his beliefs. His success in building the paper's circulation showed that the public was ready to pay for serious reporting. When he refused to print theatrical puffs and printed candid theater reviews instead, Walter found allies among the young liberal writers of weekly and quarterly journals. When he found himself wrestling with the Post Office he published, on behalf of all newspapers, an account of the existing system whereby editors were obliged to pay the Post Office for foreign news. He was sued and lost the case, but the penalty was minimal and it was generally considered that *The Times*, and journalism, had won a moral victory.

The principle of editorial independence that Walter introduced is by no means invulnerable and has been tested again in many new circumstances. Yet Walter demonstrated that a truly independent paper is a force with which government must reckon: a force that had not been seen before.

Bibliography

The scarcity of published material dealing with the early years of *The Times* can be explained by Walter's own reserve and the rule of anonymity that he imposed on his writers: *The Times* has proved to be a tough nut for historians to crack. Yet there are good original records of legal and financial transactions in the archives of *The Times*.

Evans, Harold. *Good Times, Bad Times*. London: Weidenfeld and Nicolson, 1983; New York: Atheneum, 1984. A personal and angry account of Evans' career as editor, first at *The Sunday Times* and then, for one stormy year, at *The Times*. Walter himself figures little, but the principles of editorial responsibility that he established become central to the tale and are reexamined in the modern context. Includes a bibliography, but it is mostly for the twentieth century.

Thursfield, James Richard. "John Walter." In *Dictionary of National Biography*. Edited by Sir Leslie Stephen and Sir Sidney Lee, vol. 20. London: Oxford University Press, and New York: Macmillan, 1885-1901. Informative entries by Thursfield on each of the three proprietors of *The Times:* John Walter I, II, and III.

The Times of London. February 11, 1810: leading article. John Walter's manifesto and statement of principle.

————. *The History of "The Times."* 4 vols. London: Times, 1935. A work in four volumes of which the first, subtitled "The 'Thunderer' in the Making, 1785-1841," deals extensively with Walter and his two great editors, Delane and Barnes. This, the "authorized" history, was written by staff of *The Times* (anonymously, in their own tradition). It is thoroughly researched, indexed, and documented and supplies a list of published and unpublished sources. Remains the best published source available on its subject

————. *A Newspaper History, 1785-1935: Reprinted from the 150th Anniversary Number of The Times, January 1, 1935.* London: Times, 1935. A companion of sorts to *The History of "The Times"* and published on the same day, but by no means the same material. This book consists of a series of thirty-three studies of different aspects of *The Times* and journalism over 150 years: readership, reporting, the "agony" column, London newspapers, presses, type, and many other subjects. Walter has only a few pages to himself, but his work and era play a part in many of the essays. Illustrated and indexed but without bibliography or footnote references.

Elizabeth Harris

LESTER FRANK WARD

Born: June 18, 1841; Joliet, Illinois
Died: April 18, 1913; Washington, D.C.
Area of Achievement: Sociology
Contribution: Ward's concern for the enduring features of social life caused him to become one of the founders of the discipline of sociology. As a result of his contributions, the first systematic examinations of the complexities of the market economy, the social role of women, social and intrapersonal conflict, and social planning became core parts of social explanation.

Early Life

Lester Frank Ward was born in Joliet, Illinois, on June 18, 1841. He was the tenth and last child of Justus and Silence (Rolph) Ward. Lester Ward's father was an itinerant mechanic who worked at a host of jobs but never seemed to settle down into any one of them. He had been a fife major during the War of 1812 and received a warrant to 160 acres of virgin land in Iowa for his services. He did not take advantage of this grant until 1855, when the Wards homesteaded in Buchanan County, Iowa. There, Justus Ward died. Silence Ward outlived her husband by twenty-two years. The daughter of a clergyman, she was a refined and scholarly woman who had a flair for literature which ten children did not take away from her. Much of the physical strength Lester Ward possessed and most of his indomitable will were derived from his mother.

Of his early years, little is known. They were spent in relative hardship, poverty, and hard work. Quarrying rock, tending a sawmill, and breaking the virgin prairie are among the activities in which his family engaged. His much-traveled family and the frontier region where most of his adolescence was spent provided little opportunity for formal educational experience. He was briefly enrolled in elementary school in Cass, Illinois, until 1855, when the family moved to the rolling prairies of Iowa. No schools were near the Buchanan County farm. When Justus Ward died, Silence Ward returned to St. Charles, Illinois, with the two youngest children, Erastus and Lester. There, Lester Ward returned to school; to earn their tuition, he and his brother performed farm chores and assisted in the corn and wheat harvests of the area. Ward proved to be an avid and exceedingly able student. He read everything available, including what he would term

"yellow covered literature"—the pulp books of that era. Indeed, so taken was he by them that he tried his own hand at writing romantic fiction; several of his pieces were published in the St. Charles *Argus*.

Ward's intellectual curiosity ranged well beyond the confines of the classroom into such areas as botany, zoology, and biology. He taught himself French, Latin, and Greek, and had a working knowledge of several other languages as well.

In 1858, Ward moved with his brother Erastus to Myersburg, Pennsylvania, to join another brother, Cyrenus Osborne Ward, in a wheel-hub factory. There, he met his future wife Elizabeth (Lizzie) Caroline Vought, the daughter of a poor shoemaker. Ward enrolled at Susquehanna Collegiate Institute in Towanda, Pennsylvania, where he again excelled as a student. In 1862, he responded to the call for volunteers and enlisted at Myersburg in the 141st Regiment of Pennsylvania Volunteers. He married Elizabeth Vought on August 13 and reported for duty on August 26. Ward saw action at Chancellorsville, where he was wounded three times and captured by Confederate forces. He was exchanged for a wounded Confederate lieutenant colonel and spent the remainder of his enlistment in the Veteran's Reserves Corps, which guarded Washington and handled army supply. Ever mindful of educational opportunities, Ward also tutored the wounded in French and Latin while he himself was convalescing. Ward was discharged in November, 1864, and early the following year he took a job as a clerk in the Treasury Department; he would remain a government employee for more than forty years. His wife joined him in early 1865. Their only child, Roy Fontaine, was born on June 14; unfortunately, the baby died in May, 1866.

While employed by the government, Ward enrolled in night school at Columbian College (now George Washington University), where he would be graduated with a bachelor of arts degree in 1869 and a master of arts in 1872; he also earned a law degree in 1871. His educational achievements led to several promotions and many added responsibilities. Quickly recognized for his expertise in the natural sciences, he undertook countless field trips into the West, eventually rising to the position of chief paleontologist in the United States Geological Survey. Ward was a prolific writer, and his scientific treatises range from *A Guide to the Flora of Washington, District of Columbia and Vicinity*

(1882), *The Cretaceous Formation of the Black Hills as Indicated by the Fossil Plants* (1889), to *Status of the Mesozoic Floras of the United States* (1904), with many others in between. Ward resigned from governmental service in 1905. Following a summer in Europe, he took a professorship of sociology at Brown University. The remainder of his life was spent in higher education.

Life's Work

Lester Frank Ward is remembered today as one of the primary founders of sociology as a distinct discipline. He helped create the American Sociology Society, of which he was president in 1906, and served as advisory editor of his fledgling *American Journal of Sociology* in 1896. Ward's intellectual significance and the justification for the study of his life and thought lie in his efforts to reconcile mid-nineteenth century democratic assumptions and ideas with late nineteenth century developments resulting from scientific work in biology and from the urban-industrial transformation of American life. This intellectual and social revolution began a period of rapid change—an era which, late in the twentieth century, shows no signs of ending—and Ward's attempts to explain intellectual and social environments in transformation retain a profound relevance.

Ward championed a belief in the potential of the common man—a faith inspired by his own background and experiences. Early he became convinced that the differences between the upper and lower classes in American society were a matter of neither luck nor heredity but mainly one of education. He believed that universal public education operating within a framework of democratic political institutions could generate the human talent necessary for the exploitation of scientific knowledge for humanistic ends. As such, Ward believed that it was possible for the American public to remain true to its historical values in the midst of a world of rapid change—both physical and social. To Ward, man was not the captive of deterministic natural laws, as many scientists and social philosophers of the late nineteenth century claimed. Man, Ward taught, had the intellectual powers to control the forces of nature in the direction he chose.

Ward wrote that sociology is the science of human achievement. As such, he was not particularly concerned with method. He thought the main method of science was that of generalization—interpreting and reasoning about facts. While Ward assumed that the social world was bound by the same scientific laws as all cosmic evolution, his work in botany, biology, and zoology forced him to argue that such forces were controllable by man. He used intuition and keen observation to arrive at some of his sociological generalizations. He believed that the social "laws" thus gained should be applied to improve human society. Ward held that man, because of his intellect, had the ability to use social laws, if not change them. Ward offered a caution in this application. The tragedies of history, he believed, derived as much from false application as from false ideas. Thus, education must be universal, and government must become an agent of the people. The ideal government was a democratic one, which would channel its energies into producing the positive social changes benefiting the entire welfare of all classes.

While sociological thought and modes of analysis have changed greatly since Ward's day, his concerns with the enduring features of social life are very similar to the substantive interests of current sociologists. Such questions as the role of women in society; intellectual, scientific, and artistic creativity; social and intrapersonal conflicts; social welfare and social planning; the role of deception and ruse in social affairs and especially in political life; and the social consequences of professionalization, crime, and deviancy still provoke interest. Ward dealt with all of these issues.

Lester Ward's most significant writings are *Dynamic Sociology* (1883), on which he toiled for fourteen years, and *The Psychic Factors of Civilization* (1893). Those portions of his work which are most significant today reveal a passionate concern for social reform and the promotion of a liberal ideology. He believed that humans could shape their own destinies through the perfection of social mechanisms and institutions. While he recognized evil and folly, he was not overawed by them. Reasoning man, he said, could overcome them. Thus, he rejected the notions held by some sociologists that an authoritarian order needed to be imposed upon society. He denied Spencerian logic's conclusion that man can only react to the impersonal forces of nature. He provided the reasonable alternative to both.

Although Ward's professional career as a sociologist was relatively brief, his contributions to the discipline were significant. He died on April 18, 1913, in Washington, D.C.

Summary

It is impossible to sum up in a brief fashion the thought of Lester Ward. His learning was vast, his interests broad, his impact upon American thought far-reaching. He was the first American sociologist to bring his learning and experiences in peace and war to bear upon the problems raised by Auguste Comte and Herbert Spencer. Ward destroyed forever the naïve Manchesterism which Spencer claimed represented the ultimate design of the universe and restored humanism to sociology. Ward recognized the role of women in civilization. He made a plea for humanity. Despite his vagaries, Ward stands among the giants of the nineteenth century.

Bibliography

Chugerman, Samuel. *Lester F. Ward, the American Aristotle: A Summary and Interpretation of His Sociology*. Durham, N.C.: Duke University Press, 1939. The definitive biography of Ward. Must be consulted by anyone seeking to understand Lester Ward the man as well as his thought.

Scott, Clifford H. *Lester Frank Ward*. Boston: Twayne, 1976. This introductory study combines a brief account of Ward's life with an analysis of his thought. Includes an assessment of Ward's impact on his contemporaries.

Timasheff, Nicholas S. *Sociological Theory: Its Nature and Growth*. 4th ed. New York: Random House, 1976. Places Ward in perspective as a social theorist.

Ward, Lester Frank. *Lester Frank Ward: Selections from His Work*. Edited by Israel Gerver. New York: Crowell, 1963. Excellent, brief presentation of key positions Ward espoused. Contains a good evaluation of Ward's impact upon the discipline of sociology.

———. *Lester Frank Ward and the Welfare State*. Edited by Henry Steele Commager. Indianapolis, Ind.: Bobbs-Merrill, 1967. Contains a brief autobiographical sketch that reveals much about Ward. Commager does a masterful job of explaining Ward's theories—especially those involving the need for governmental involvement. Indispensable for the serious student.

———. *Young Ward's Diary*. Edited by Berhard J. Stern. New York: Putnam, 1935. This diary, kept by Ward between 1860 and 1870, is a valuable source for discovering the origin of many of his explanations of social organization and social interaction.

Richard J. Amundson

MONTGOMERY WARD

Born: February 17, 1844; Chatham, New Jersey
Died: December 7, 1913; Highland Park, Illinois
Areas of Achievement: Business and environmentalism
Contribution: Combining extraordinary business foresight with innovative technical methods and a genuine concern for his fellow citizens, Ward revolutionized the history of trade by founding the first mail-order business and introduced the concept of environmental protection by beautifying the Chicago lakefront.

Early Life

Aaron Montgomery Ward was the son of Sylvester A. Ward and Julia Laura (Green) Ward. His great-grandfather, Israel Ward, served as a captain in the French and Indian War under George Washington at Springfield, New York, in 1772. His great-grandfather on his mother's side, Zeptha Squire, was an officer in the Revolutionary War. There were seven children in the Ward family, Aaron Montgomery being the third born. To his family and friends, he was known as Monty.

In 1853, when Ward was eight years old, the Ward family, beset by financial difficulties, moved to Niles, Michigan. Ward attended public school until he was fourteen years old; at that time, he decided to abandon his studies in order to help his father support the family. His first job was that of an apprentice cobbler. After that, he did odd jobs for one year at a barrel factory. Next, he worked in a brickyard, where he loaded bricks on scows for shipment down the river; yet Ward had ambition, and he was unwilling to remain in an unskilled position such as that one for very long. After two years, he was offered employment as a clerk in a general store in the port city of St. Joseph by the man who owned the scows that carried the bricks. Thus, at the age of nineteen, Ward left Niles to begin his business training in St. Joseph. Within three years, Ward rose to head clerk and then general manager of the store. In 1861, the Civil War broke out. Ward decided to stay at the job, and he continued to send money home to help his family, thus abandoning any dreams of carrying on the family tradition of military service and glory. He learned about small-town retailing, became a first-rate bookkeeper, and improved his writing of business letters and the grammatical accuracy of his everyday speech.

It was at this general store that Ward first became aware of the plight of the farmers and the discrimination they faced in the marketplace. The farm trade had always been an outlet for damaged or unfit stock. Through Ward's efforts, however, there was a notable change in the merchandise offered to the farmer. Ward insisted on receiving the perfect merchandise he ordered and was willing to pay for. The quality of merchandise did indeed improve, and the farmers grew to depend on it. Although the exchange of goods was done by barter, Ward instituted the price tag system, whereby each farmer was given a due bill which stated the amount of money his goods were worth and with which he was, for the first time, given a choice of articles he could purchase from the store. The farmers were gratified to see a cash value equated with their hard labor.

Even at this young age, Ward always thought of his customers' convenience. For example, he made a picnic grove complete with tables and benches on the land adjacent to the store so that the farm families could eat lunch and their children could play safely.

In 1865, at the age of twenty-one, Ward left the general store and Michigan to work as a clerk for two years in a wholesale house in Chicago called Field, Palmer and Leiter, the forerunner of Marshall Field and Company. Since there was no possibility for advancement, he took another job for another wholesale dry-goods house in Chicago. Unfortunately, this firm failed, and he became a traveling salesman for a similar firm based in St. Louis. Traveling and selling to the rural market, he acquired a deeper knowledge of the problems of the farmers and thus conceived the idea with which he would make his distinctive contribution to America.

The farmers had to pay extremely high prices for a small selection of inferior goods at retail prices compared with the money they earned in crop production at wholesale prices. Rural consumers wanted to enjoy the same comforts as city dwellers but were often the victims of monopolists and the numerous middlemen required to bring manufactured commodities to rural locations. Ward conceived a solution to the problem which revolutionized the business world: He envisioned a mail-order business to serve the rural trade, buying in large quantities for cash direct from the manufacturers and selling for cash directly to the farmer at low markups. Eliminating the middlemen, Ward reasoned, would allow him to market merchandise directly to the farmers at reduced prices. Prices could be reduced even further by offering customers additional savings accumulated through bulk orders from suppliers.

To execute his idea, Ward needed more experience in merchandising. Consequently, he found employment as a buyer for a wholesale dry-goods house in Chicago. This position introduced him to a new dimension of merchandising, for he was required to buy merchandise from the manufacturers for his firm to resell.

With his savings, Ward began to accumulate a small inventory with which he planned to launch his business. In 1871, he lost everything in the Great Chicago Fire, but this proved to be only a temporary setback, for he had ambition, tenacity, and a strong will to succeed. He lowered his standard of living in order to begin saving again. Even during these times of personal misfortune, he was always sympathetic to the problems of the less fortunate and gave whatever he could to them. Also during this time, Ward—tall, slim and square-shouldered, with thick brown hair and a well-kept mustache—married Elizabeth Cobb of Kalamazoo, Michigan, with whom he later had a daughter, Marjorie. In August of 1872, with the full support of the National Grange, he and his brother-in-law, George R. Thorne, founded Montgomery Ward and Company.

Life's Work

Ward and Thorne began their operations in the loft of a livery stable in Chicago. Ward chose the city of Chicago as the place to establish his business because he believed that it was the real capital of the United States, a country of farmers and ranchers who saw themselves as excluded from the commercial life and comforts of the prosperous and sophisticated East. There was a single desk among the stock, which was piled to the ceiling. The only employee was a teenage boy who wrapped packages and carried them to the post office.

The partners sent the first Montgomery Ward and Company catalog out to National Grange members in the spring of 1872. It was a single eight-by-twelve-inch printed sheet, with no pictures and very little descriptive matter. It listed 163 articles, the most expensive of which was a lady's gold-plated watch selling for eight dollars. Nothing was priced below one dollar.

Ward was a keen judge of merchandise and bought at prices which enabled him to sell to the rural consumer at prices he could afford. He believed that his first duty was to his customers, and he sincerely wanted to meet the needs of the farmers. Thus, he often enclosed a friendly handwritten letter along with his catalog asking the farmer what his wishes and wants were. If their replies indicated that there was a large demand for an item, he would negotiate with the manufacturer; such was the case with the sewing machines. He concluded a deal with a sewing-machine manufacturer which enabled him to offer it at thirty dollars, twenty dollars under the retail price. If he received requests for isolated items, he bought them and sent them at only five percent over what it cost him, thus becoming the purchasing agent for rural America.

Ward's wife Elizabeth was invaluable in his endeavor. She suggested that he offer more variety in his catalog and that he expand to include gift items and other amenities. She also selected articles that were of interest to women and saw to it that only the most current fashions were listed in the catalog. As a result, the farm women were offered a selection of merchandise as stylish and modern as that of Marshall Field and Company.

In 1873-1874, the purchasing agencies of the National Grange bought merchandise through the Montgomery Ward and Company catalog to stock their cooperative retail stores, thus reinforcing the goodwill of the farmers and causing the line of merchandise to expand greatly. Since the business was conducted on a cash basis, it survived the Panic of 1873. By 1874, the firm had made several moves. The catalog was now a twenty-four-page booklet. In 1875, the catalog contained seventy-two pages and the first pictures of the articles. During that year, Ward adopted the first consumer protection policy: satisfaction guaranteed or your money back. This was a powerful inducement for distant customers. By 1876, the catalog had 150 pages with illustrations.

In 1878, the catalog created a sensation by offering ready-to-wear dresses for women. Previously, ready-to-wear merchandise was confined to men's suits and men's and women's overcoats. Orders from the National Grange ladies began to pour in.

During the first few years, Montgomery Ward and Company served only National Grange families. As more requests came in from outsiders,

Ward consulted with Grange officials and, with their full approval, opened his field to the general public.

By 1888, annual sales had reached one million dollars. Local retail merchants felt threatened and reacted with hostile anti-Ward slogans and organized campaigns to burn Ward catalogs. The local newspapers, dependent upon the advertising of these town merchants, joined in attacking the mail-order houses. Ward and his company were often the butt of journalistic jokes, but Ward persevered and his firm expanded and flourished under his guidance and leadership, rooted in the conviction that business should be conducted for the benefit of the consumer. Ward believed that he was offering a service to farmers which local stores had failed to render; he left freedom of choice to the farmer.

The year 1899 was a peak for Montgomery Ward and Company. The catalog contained more than one thousand pages and featured a cover illustration of the new Ward Tower, the final headquarters of the company and the showplace of Michigan Avenue in Chicago. It had twenty-five stories, which made it the tallest commercial building in the world. It contained six steam elevators and a marble lobby. Sightseers were encouraged to visit and were given a tour of the warehouse, with its assortment of twenty-five thousand items, and the mailroom, where thirty clerks did nothing but open letters all day long.

Ward retired from active management of the company in 1901, although he still retained the title of president. At that time, it was the largest company in its field; it would eventually expand to include six hundred retail stores and enjoy many years of billion-dollar sales. Since Ward had no sons, the management of the business passed into the hands of his five nephews, the sons of his partner, Thorne. All became vice presidents in charge of various departments. At the time of Ward's death in 1913, annual sales amounted to forty billion dollars, customers were served in all parts of the world, and the staff of employees numbered six thousand.

Ward's conviction that business should be conducted for the benefit of the consumer was mirrored in his personal life. Court documents indicate that by 1890, long before pollution in lakes and parks was accorded any importance, Ward had begun a long legal battle that was to cost him a personal fortune and the friendship of some of Chicago's most influential citizens. It was in this year

that he sued the city of Chicago for littering the lakefront with street debris, refuse, livery stables, and squatters' shacks. He fought against the erection of any man-made municipal structures on the lakefront, basing his suit on the original titles on maps of the area which prohibited buildings of any kind when it was acquired from the federal government. Ward was severely criticized, accused of obstructing progress and dubbed the Watchdog of the Water Front. He responded by saying that he was the one who was most concerned about Chicago's progress and that he would continue his fight in the name of the poor people of Chicago. He envisioned a park which would not be the heritage of the elite but of the masses, about whom he genuinely cared. It would be a place where they could repose and refresh their spirits during the noon hour. It took four court trials and twenty years of waiting before Ward would win the battle. By the late twentieth century, Grant Park, as it came to be called, was the envy of every waterside city.

Summary

Aaron Montgomery Ward was single-handedly responsible for the most significant breakthrough in the history of trade. He made it possible for many people scattered over wide areas to buy a variety of high-quality goods at fixed and fair prices.

Ward's great success was the combination of three factors. First, he persevered until his firm was named the official supply house for the National Grange. He started his company with the intention of eradicating the economic and social discrimination directed at farmers, and he worked very hard to cater to their interests and wants. Second, he introduced the idea of a money-back guarantee, which was one of the earliest landmarks in consumerism. This policy set a standard of excellence in consumer relations and conditioned the American public to expect high-quality merchandise and service as well as fair play from every business enterprise. Ward adamantly abided by his policy that the sacrifice of quality to the point of not giving satisfaction made an article worthless, however low the price. Finally, he developed the homey style of writing that became a trademark of his catalogs, contributing significantly to his success.

Yet Ward contributed more than techniques to American business. He contributed a philosophy as well, an attitude of commitment and devotion to customer service that was just as revolutionary in its time as the idea of selling goods by mail.

As a result of the success of the new concept of mail-order business and the subsequent war that followed between the mail-order houses and the retail merchants, the town stores were forced to change their attitudes. They had no choice but to offer a larger variety of stock, improve the quality of their merchandise, and establish fair prices. Competition with Montgomery Ward and Company put an end to the previously accepted notion that anything is good enough for the farmer. The shopkeepers found, much to their astonishment, that the farm market was worth cultivating.

The creation of this new industry and its subsequent success was only part of the impact made by Ward. Material, social, and cultural aspects of American life were altered by catalog merchandising. The change was so evident that in 1946 the Montgomery Ward and Company catalog was selected among one hundred American books chosen for their bearing on the life and culture of the people.

Ward's interest in the American consumer was matched by his concern for the environment of his fellow citizens. For this reason, he undertook a lengthy battle with his personal resources so that the ordinary citizens of Chicago could one day enjoy the blue waters of Lake Michigan from a clean and beautiful park.

Ward had always been interested in the plight of the poor and the victimized. Even before he started his mail-order business, with which he sought to alleviate the problems of the farmers, he always gave of his time and whatever money he could to help the less fortunate. After he made his fortune, his philanthropic acts continued on a larger scale;

he donated coal to heat homes and gave generously to hospitals. After his death, his wife carried on his spirit of generosity. Her largest donation was that of eight million dollars to Northwestern University to establish a medical and dental center in her husband's name.

Bibliography

Baker, Nina Brown. *Big Catalogue: The Life of Aaron Montgomery Ward*. New York: Harcourt Brace, 1956. The story of the life and times of Aaron Montgomery Ward. Details the making of the company, Ward's views concerning consumerism, environmentalism, and philanthropy, and his methods and accomplishments.

Herndon, Booton. *Satisfaction Guaranteed: An Unconventional Report to Today's Consumers*. New York: McGraw-Hill, 1972. Presents the problem of how to maintain the guarantee of satisfaction, first offered to consumers by Ward, in today's complex world.

Montgomery Ward and Co. *Aaron Montgomery Ward, Entrepreneur, Environmentalist, Consumerist*. Chicago: Author, 1971. A series of pamphlets and illustrations of the life of Aaron Montgomery Ward, pages of his catalog, and the Chicago lakefront.

Weil, Gordon L. *Sears Roebuck, USA: The Great American Store and How It Grew*. New York: Stein and Day, 1977. Discusses the American catalog business and how it grew. Some of the men most responsible for its success were former Montgomery Ward employees.

Anne Laura Mattrella

BOOKER T. WASHINGTON

Born: April 5, 1856; near Hale's Ford, Virginia
Died: November 14, 1915; Tuskegee, Alabama
Area of Achievement: Social reform
Contribution: Combining an optimistic outlook with a spirit of accommodation in race relations, Washington provided leadership and a program to American blacks during an era of segregation.

Early Life

Booker Taliaferro Washington was born April 5, 1856, on a farm near Hale's Ford, Virginia. His mother, Jane Ferguson, was a slave and a cook for James Burroughs; his father was a white man whose identity is unknown. Washington had a brother John, four years his senior, also a mulatto, and a sister who died in infancy. When the family was emancipated, it settled in Malden, West Virginia, five miles from Charleston.

From 1865 to 1871, Booker worked in the local coal and salt mines, attending school between early morning and later afternoon stints of labor. For a year and a half, he was a houseboy for the wife of the mine owner; in this capacity, he learned demanding standards of performance, attention to detail, and the virtues of hard work, cleanliness, and thrift.

Having heard of a new school in eastern Virginia where blacks received vocational training, Washington entered Hampton Normal and Agricultural Institute in the fall of 1872. Founded by an idealistic Civil War general, Samuel C. Armstrong, the school reinforced the influences of his houseboy experience and pointed him toward his future. "At Hampton," he later said, "I found the opportunities . . . to learn thrift, economy and push. I was surrounded by an atmosphere of business, Christian influences, and the spirit of self-help, that seemed to have awakened every faculty in me." Armstrong, with his emphasis on industrial education for blacks and the virtues of hard work and self-discipline, was perhaps the major influence in molding young Washington.

During the four years after his graduation in 1875, he taught school at Malden, West Virginia, and briefly attended Wayland Seminary in Washington, D.C. In 1879, he was called to Hampton Normal and Agricultural Institute to supervise instruction of Indian students whom Armstrong had recruited in the West. During his second year, he taught night classes for youths who worked for the institute during the day.

In 1881, he eagerly grasped the opportunity to start his own school at Tuskegee, Alabama. His model was Hampton, and he established in the Deep South an institution which expressed his by then mature social values. The Civil War and Reconstruction had brought freedom, citizenship, and suffrage to blacks, yet little had been done to prepare blacks to live as citizens, voters, and independent workers. What was needed, Washington believed, was to give blacks industrial education and moral training by which they could become economically self-sufficient and able to partake of the blessings of liberty and citizenship. The exercise of political rights and entrance into the professions could be deferred. "Let us give the black man so much skill and brains that he can cut oats like the white man; then he can compete with him," he affirmed. The liberal arts were not to be neglected, but they were not foremost.

Now twenty-five years of age and in good health, a persuasive speaker, he stood tall, an energetic figure with striking features—gray eyes, full lips, broad nose, reddish hair, and brown skin. Throwing himself vigorously into his challenging responsibilities, he recruited students from the countryside and secured an abandoned plantation for a campus. In 1882, he married a childhood friend, Fannie N. Smith, who bore him a daughter and died in 1884. When the number of pupils grew to fifty, he employed another black teacher, Olivia A. Davidson, who became his second wife and gave birth to two sons. She died in 1889; a third marriage was to Margaret James Murray, "lady principal" at Tuskegee, who survived him.

Meager legislative appropriations and growing enrollments impelled Washington to solicit funds in the North and Midwest. Beginning in 1883, he secured assistance from the Slater and Peabody funds, the money from the first being used to build a carpenter shop and make other improvements. Fund-raising became a fixed part of his activities; in the course of time he was garnering $100,000 a year, gaining support from John D. Rockefeller, Andrew Carnegie, Julius Rosenwald, and others. By the end of his career, Tuskegee Institute owned an endowment of nearly two million dollars.

Washington quickly emerged as a national spokesman for his race. In the summer of 1884, he

was invited to address the annual meeting of the National Education Association in Madison, Wisconsin. He spoke on "the broad question of the relations of the races," foretelling the views for which he became famous eleven years later. Meanwhile, the address won for him recognition among educators and helped his fund-raising efforts.

It was the address he delivered in 1895 at the Cotton States and International Exposition in Atlanta that made him a national figure and the leading spokesman for black Americans. In this address, Washington rejected ideas of return to Africa or migration to the North. "Cast down your bucket where you are," he exhorted. Blacks must begin at the bottom of life and not at the top, as Reconstruction policy had attempted; the leap from slavery to freedom had been too quick. Life at the bottom meant labor in agriculture, mechanics, commerce, and domestic service. Blacks must "learn to dignify and glorify common labour and put brains and skill into the common occupations of life."

Seeking to allay Southern white apprehensions about the potential advance of blacks within the region, Washington gave an assurance, "In all things that are purely social we can be as separate as the fingers, yet one as the hand in all things essential to mutual progress." Progress, he went on, is inevitable, and nearly eight million blacks—one third of the South—would help in marching forward.

Blacks and whites listened while he warned against agitation on questions of social equality. Not artificial forces but production for the world's markets would bring blacks the full privileges of the law. "The opportunity to earn a dollar in a factory just now is worth infinitely more than the opportunity to spend a dollar in an opera-house." Pledging the patient, sympathetic help of blacks, he looked forward to a time of material benefits to the South, followed by "a blotting out of sectional differences and racial animosities . . . and a willing obedience among all classes to the mandates of law."

Washington's Atlanta address came at a time of increasing discrimination against blacks. The United States Supreme Court in the Civil Rights cases had opened the door to segregation; a year after the Atlanta address, the Court gave positive sanction to separate-but-equal facilities for blacks. A movement to strip blacks of the right of suffrage had begun in Mississippi in 1890, and emboldened by Washington's subordination of political privileges to economic opportunity, Southern white leaders pushed forward with segregation and disenfranchisement. Lynching of black men in the South, especially on the allegation of raping white women, was on the rise.

Pushing his idea of equal economic opportunity that he thought in time would blot out racial animosities, Washington advocated a policy of black accommodation to the oppressive climate. His policy won immediate favor with Southern whites, who welcomed the renunciation of political privilege and equality as well as the prospect of a harmonious section prospering through the labor of skilled, contented blacks. Northern whites, who had turned away from notions of intervention in the South, applauded Washington's giant step down the road toward reunion and his vision of a Southern economy where Northern capital might profitably be invested. Blacks, in the main, were proud of the recognition Washington won and looked to the Tuskegee educator as their principal leader for the next score of years. Washington's national influence grew quickly after the "Atlanta compromise." He had already made friends with powerful figures in the North, philanthropists who were contributing to Tuskegee; he came to exert control over giving to black colleges, and his favor was necessary to secure aid.

With the accession of Theodore Roosevelt to the presidency, Washington gained control of black appointments to federal office. His influence continued under William H. Taft, and Washington's secretary claimed that "During the administrations of both President Roosevelt and Taft hardly an office of consequence was conferred upon a Negro without first consulting Mr. Washington." He lost his influence in politics when Woodrow Wilson, a Southern-born leader of a party with its base in the South, became president and ordered segregated facilities for blacks in federal service.

Besides philanthropy and politics, Washington exerted influence in the black press. Backed by most of the black press in the nation, Washington dispatched reams of releases publicizing Tuskegee and his ideas. He fed unsigned editorials to receptive editors and on occasion made financial contributions to black editors. He secretly purchased the *New York Age*, which he believed to be "the strongest and most widely circulated Negro paper in the country," and after he sold it, continued to advise its editor.

Yet it must not be supposed that Washington fully acquiesced in segregation and disfranchisement.

His Atlanta speech was ambiguous, and if, for example, he declared that "the agitation of questions of social quality is the extremest folly," he did not intend racial inequality to be permanent. He believed in gradual evolutionary progress under which blacks, enjoying material prosperity, would gain complete equality in the South.

To this end and without fanfare, he exerted his influence to stem the tide of disenfranchisement. He wrote a public letter in 1895, urging the South Carolina convention to allow blacks to qualify for the vote by education, and he made similar attempts to allow a degree of black voting and strengthen black education in other Southern states.

He was less open and vocal in his opposition to segregation. Behind the scenes, he worked against the passage of laws segregating Pullman cars, though he himself was rarely accorded separate facilities. He also fought laws to segregate housing, usually in private letters and through other persons. Lynching, however, impelled him to be active; the burning alive of a Georgia black for alleged rape and murder elicited from him a letter appealing to both blacks and whites to maintain law and order. In later years, he continued to speak out against lynching and periodically compiled lists of lynchings in the United States which he cited in speeches and correspondence.

His public stance of accommodation, however, incurred criticism and opposition. The challenge sprang in part from a contrasting figure: a Northern-born scholar who was the first black to receive a Ph.D. from Harvard University. He was W. E. B. Du Bois, historian and sociologist, who at first supported Washington's work and toyed with the notion of teaching at Tuskegee.

Du Bois held a set of ideas that stood in contrast to those of Washington. He believed that Washington's emphasis on industrial training was too narrow, his accommodation to segregation and disenfranchisement an acceptance of injustice, his protests too moderate, his faith in the white South's cooperation with black progress misplaced. Blacks should acquire a broad education; the best minds, whom he called the Talented Tenth, should be prepared for leadership of the black race; caste distinctions found in segregation and disenfranchisement should be ended; blacks should not allow their faith to repose in Southern whites but feel free to migrate northward; and they should not rely heavily on self-help but seek external support. In

keeping with this last idea, Du Bois helped organize a movement that in 1910 produced the National Association for the Advancement of Colored People (NAACP). A biracial movement, heavily dependent upon Northern white support and leadership, the NAACP took up the fight for full legal and political rights for blacks, employing litigation as a principal weapon.

The NAACP presented a challenge which Washington met by stressing two alternatives. One was the National Negro Business League which he had founded in 1900, drawing together black business leaders from three hundred cities; the other was the Urban League, organized in 1911 to foster economic opportunities for blacks in cities. These activities strengthened and complemented his strategy for achieving equality for blacks.

Summary

Though he remained the preeminent leader of his race until his death on November 14, 1915, Washington saw his influence decline with the election of Wilson and the emergence of the NAACP. By 1915, his philosophy was becoming obsolete as the nation was rapidly urbanizing and industrializing, and blacks were migrating to Northern cities.

In many ways, Washington had caught the spirit of his age, with its stress on material advancement, faith in progress, self-help, and individualism. Living and working in the South, he probably necessarily accepted white-imposed restraints on black rights and favored white and black cooperation. Tuskegee Institute could not have existed under the administration of a militant black leader. For a generation of black Americans, Washington did much to inspire pride in race, point to a means of progress, and urge sharecroppers and tenants to become owners of farms and skilled workers.

Bibliography

Du Bois, W. E. B. *The Souls of Black Folk: Essays and Sketches*. Chicago: McClurg, 1903; London: Constable, 1905. Written by Washington's leading critic, this book contains an early critique of the Tuskegee educator and his philosophy. It offers a useful contemporary perspective.

Erhagbe, Edward O. "African-Americans and the Defense of African States against European Imperial Conquest: Booker T. Washington's Diplomatic Efforts to Guarantee Liberia's Independence 1907-1911." *African Studies Review* 39, no. 1 (April, 1996). Erhagbe examines

Washington's efforts to obtain U.S. aid for Liberia and its eventual independence.

Ferguson, Karen. "Caught in 'No Man's Land': The Negro Cooperative Demonstration Service and the Ideology of Booker T. Washington, 1900-1918." *Agricultural History* 72, no. 1 (Winter 1998). Examines the Negro Cooperative Demonstration Service, Washington's efforts and commitment to black progress, and the ironic failure of the program in many cases.

Harlan, Louis R. *Booker T. Washington: The Making of a Black Leader, 1856-1901*. New York: Oxford University Press, 1972; London: Oxford University Press, 1975. The first volume of the best biography, based upon profound scholarship, this work is written in a clear style and with good judgment.

———. *Booker T. Washington: The Wizard of Tuskegee, 1901-1915*. New York: Oxford University Press, 1983; Oxford: Oxford University Press, 1986. The second and final volume of the prizewinning definitive life, this work fulfills the promise of the first volume.

Harlan, Louis R., et al., eds. *The Booker T. Washington Papers*. 13 vols. Urbana: University of Illinois Press, 1972-1984. These volumes bring together the voluminous papers of Washington, comprising his speeches, telegrams, letters, and miscellany. Edited with scholarly notes, the papers are invaluable for an understanding of the man and his activities.

Scott, Emmett, and Lyman Beecher Stowe. *Booker T. Washington: Builder of a Civilization*. New York: Doubleday, and London: Unwin, 1916. Written by Washington's secretary and a descendant of abolitionists, this book is valuable for its inside vantage point. Sympathetic in tone, it is nevertheless frank and revealing.

Spencer, Samuel R., Jr. *Booker T. Washington and the Negro's Place in American Life*. Boston: Little Brown, 1955. A short, reliable, and readable biography, with ample interpretation and balanced judgment.

Washington, Booker T. *Up from Slavery: An Autobiography*. New York: Doubleday, 1901; London: Morning, 1904. The author's account of his early years, this work also contains a straightforward description of Tuskegee Institute. It has enjoyed a wide readership and stands as a classic.

James A. Rawley

CARL MARIA VON WEBER

Born: November 18, 1786; Eutin, Oldenburg
Died: June 5, 1826; London, England
Area of Achievement: Music
Contribution: Weber was the principal founder of German Romantic music. Best known as an opera composer, he made many significant contributions to piano music and wrote some of the staples of the wind instrument player's repertoire.

Early Life

Carl Maria von Weber was born in the small town of Eutin, the son of Franz Anton Weber, who directed a touring theatrical troupe, and Genovefa Brenner, an actress and singer. Weber's earliest memories were of playing among the theatrical scenery of his father's troupe. Sickly, and with a damaged right hipbone, he did not have an active childhood, and his early education was haphazard. Weber's father was the uncle of Wolfgang Amadeus Mozart's wife and hoped that the boy would become a musician.

When the theatrical company was trapped in Salzburg in 1797 by Napoleon I's invading army, Carl was enrolled in the choir school at the cathedral and received his first systematic instruction in music from Michael Haydn, the younger brother of the famous composer Franz Joseph Haydn. His first compositions, a set of six fughettas, were published in 1798 and favorably reviewed in the *Allgemeine musikalische Zeitung*, Germany's leading music periodical, for which Weber was later to write. After more travels, Weber returned to Salzburg to revise an early mass (now lost) and his first surviving opera, *Peter Schmoll und seine Nachbarn* (1803), of which the overture is still performed.

Weber then traveled extensively, and he studied most profitably with the composer-priest Georg Joseph Vogler in Vienna in 1803 and 1804. Vogler helped him obtain an appointment as music director in Breslau (modern Wrocław, Poland), where, at the age of seventeen, he was unable to cope with the intrigues of the musicians and singers and resigned. While in Breslau, he had a near-fatal accident, drinking by mistake engraving acid, which his father had carelessly stored in a wine bottle; though Weber recovered, his fine tenor singing voice was destroyed. After his resignation from Breslau, he stayed briefly in nearby Karlsruhe, where he wrote his only two symphonies and the first version of his Concertino for French Horn for the orchestra of the Duke of Württemberg-Öls.

Life's Work

The reasons for Weber's departure from Karlsruhe are unclear, but he left Breslau hurriedly when recognized by a creditor and, after a concert tour, accepted a post as secretary to the brother of the Duke of Württemberg in Stuttgart in 1807. Weber went through a dissolute period when he was socially in great demand for his improvisations on the piano or guitar but was in disfavor with the tyrannical duke. Among his few Stuttgart works are piano pieces and his opera *Silvana* (1810).

Weber lost his position in Stuttgart in 1810. One account is that he was involved in selling a deferment from Napoleon's army; another is that the duke's brother entrusted Weber with money to buy horses but Weber's father, who was visiting at the time, used it to settle his own debts and left his son to get into financial trouble to cover the loss. In any case, Weber was imprisoned and banished from Württemberg.

Weber then embarked on a series of tours, including a visit to his teacher Vogler in Darmstadt, and resumed composing, with his first piano concerto, his first piano sonata with its perpetual-motion finale, and his sparkling one-act comic opera *Abu Hassan* (1811) as the main results. He began a fruitful association with the clarinetist Heinrich Baermann, for whom he wrote a successful clarinet concertino, which is still frequently performed. Weber later wrote a number of major works featuring the clarinet, including two concerti for that instrument and the *Grand Duo Concertant* for clarinet and piano. He also suffered several misadventures, including a string of unsuccessful love affairs and, while crossing Württemberg territory on his way to Switzerland, of being recognized, arrested, and briefly imprisoned before being allowed to proceed on his journey.

Weber's first really stable position was in Prague, where he accepted a three-year contract as director of the opera in 1813. He not only reorganized the musical establishment but also paid careful attention to the acting, to the scenic designs, and to the costumes in order to create a musical-dramatic whole. The repertoire was composed mainly of French operas of the time in

German translation. One of the many new singers he engaged was Caroline Brandt, who was later to become his wife. During his stay in Prague, the first symptoms of the tuberculosis, of which he was to die, became evident. He resigned in 1816, ostensibly because of the damp winter weather, and, after visits to Berlin, accepted the post as director of the German opera in Dresden.

During the brief interval between Prague and Dresden, Weber wrote some of his most characteristic piano music, especially the second and third sonatas. Weber's piano music is quite unusual, because he had unusually long fingers and especially extended thumbs, which permitted him to execute extremely wide leaps or span large chords that are physically beyond the reach of most pianists. These characteristics account for the brilliant sonority of his piano music and for its neglect by most pianists, who lack the physical ability to do this music justice.

The capstones of Weber's piano works, the *Konzertstück* (concert piece) in F Minor (1821) and the fourth sonata (1819-1822), were written later. The freedom of form in the *Konzertstück* influenced Felix Mendelssohn and Robert Schumann in their piano concerti; the programmatic character and deep expression of the fourth sonata influenced Schumann and Franz Liszt, who were champions of Weber's music.

Weber's position in Dresden, though it became permanent after 1818, was nevertheless difficult. He was director of the newly organized German opera (part of the movement of national consciousness that swept the German states during and after the wars with Napoleon), but the principal court opera was Italian, under the direction of Francesco Morlacchi. The Italian opera was able to hire the better singers and had the larger budget. Weber sought to resign to move to Berlin, but the opera house there was destroyed by fire. Weber's patron, Count Vitzthum, was able to obtain for Weber a permanent appointment in Dresden, enabling him to marry Caroline Brandt, whom he had courted for four years.

In Dresden, Weber extended his concern about producing operas in a manner that would ensure their dramatic as well as musical effect by insisting that the singers and chorus be able to act as well as sing, by strengthening the orchestra, and by improving the set designs. His ideal was to create a whole that would be greater than the sum of its individual parts and thus paved the way for such later

reformers of operatic production as Richard Wagner and Gustav Mahler. He was a pioneer in the conducting of operas; instead of directing the performance from the piano, he stood in front of the stage, conducting with a thick baton, which he held in the middle, and rearranged the seating of the orchestra so that all the players could see his gestures. In addition, he published introductory summaries of the new operas before their performance in the local press to explain the works and thus educate his audience.

The work that occupied most of Weber's free time was the opera *Der Freischütz*, which was finished in 1820 and first performed in Berlin in the following year. The title is best translated as "the charmed bullet," although it is usually literally rendered as "the free shooter"; the libretto came from a popular ghost story adapted by Weber's poet friend in Dresden, Johann Friedrich Kind. In the opera, the huntsman Max is unable to hit anything at which he shoots and thus is certain to lose the shooting contest at which the hand of his beloved Agathe is to be bestowed. In reality he is under a curse set by his colleague Caspar, who offers Max the chance to obtain charmed bullets from the devil Samiel. The climactic scene is the second act finale, laid in a desolate ravine in the forest, where Caspar and Max cast the magic bullets amid a host of various apparitions. Unknown to Max, the last bullet is Caspar's to direct; he plans to kill Agathe with it. At the shooting contest, however, the bullet kills Caspar; Max then confesses what he has done and is sentenced to temporary banishment, but Agathe will wait for him. The work's popularity in German-speaking countries is owing not as much to the plot as to the musical numbers, the arsenal of Romantic horror effects in the Wolf's glen scene, the depictions of a smiling nature in the arias of the main protagonists, and the choruses composed in a popular vein.

Weber's opera was so popular so quickly that he was invited to write an opera for Vienna. He chose a medieval topic, *Euryanthe* (1823), for which Helmine von Chezy, a poet in Dresden, wrote an extremely convoluted libretto. The numerous inconsistencies of the plot and its stilted verse have been accused of having adversely affected an experimental opera with continuous music that contains some of Weber's best writing; attempts have been made to rewrite the libretto, but none has been successful.

During Weber's stay in Vienna, the symptoms of tuberculosis recurred, causing Weber to depart for Dresden. He had to abandon his writing about music (he had even drafted a semiautobiographical musical novel) and writing for piano in order to concentrate on a commission from London for a musical-dramatic work, which took shape as *Oberon* (1826), his last composition. With this work and his appearance as conductor in London, Weber hoped to amass enough money to support his wife and two sons after his death, which he sensed would be soon, since his illness was becoming worse. Weber even learned English in order to set the text appropriately.

Oberon can best be described as a multimedia work, a series of elaborate stage tableaux with vocal and instrumental music, as shown by the original playbill indicating the "order of the scenery," which includes Oberon's bower with an apparition of the Baghdad of Harun al-Rashid at the opening, and the hall of arms in the palace of Charlemagne at the end. Huon of Brabant is assigned the task of rescuing Rezia and her friends from the Emir of Tunis and bringing them before Charlemagne. Weber was thus given the opportunity to write in his chivalresque vein as well as to write exotic music for the Arabs and nature music in Rezia's grand air "Ocean, Thou Mighty Monster" and in the subsequent chorus of mermaids. Weber had planned to rewrite the work as an opera with recitatives rather than spoken dialogue upon his return to Germany, but his death in London of tuberculosis and an ulcerated windpipe on June 5 brought an end to this project. Subsequent attempts have been made, mostly in Germany, to complete Weber's project or to perform the individual numbers linked together with spoken dialogue, as in the original production.

Summary

Carl Maria von Weber is known today chiefly through the overtures to his operas, his clarinet works, and Berlioz's arrangement for orchestra of his piano piece "Invitation to the Dance," a brilliant waltz. In German-speaking countries, the opera *Der Freischütz* is a national tradition, but it has resisted translation into other repertoires. Weber's extensive use of the orchestra to underscore the drama, his freedom of form, and his occasional use of leading motives and transforming their musical contexts influenced Wagner as well as several other composers. In *Der Freischütz*, Weber had given a model of what a true national opera should be, with its use of popular idioms and with common people rather than kings and lords as principal characters. In this work and in *Oberon*, he furnished models for musically depicting both nature and the supernatural spirit world, as he provided examples for portraying the world of chivalry in *Euryanthe* and later in *Oberon*. Though Weber's reach often exceeded his grasp, and his development as a composer was cut short by an early death, he remains one of the most influential composers of the early nineteenth century.

Bibliography

Finscher, Ludwig. "Weber's *Freischütz:* Conceptions and Misconceptions." *Proceedings of the Royal Musical Association* 40 (1983/1984): 79-90. The author examines the assumptions that the first performance of Weber's *Der Freischütz* was the birthday of German Romantic opera. The libretto is based on the trivial aspects of "dark" Romanticism and has little to do with German Romantic poetry; the work's success was owing not to folk melodies but to Weber's success in composing in a popular vein.

Grout, Donald Jay, with Hermine Williams. "The Romantic Opera in Germany." In *A Short History of Opera*, 3d ed. New York: Columbia University Press, 1987. Presents the different characteristics of eighteenth and nineteenth century opera and the traits of German opera in particular before discussing Weber's last three operas. Weber was the real founder of German Romantic opera and the most important composer in that genre before Wagner.

Mercer-Taylor, Peter. "Unification and Tonal Absolution in 'Der Freischütz.'" *Music and Letters* 78, no. 2 (May, 1997). Analysis of von Weber's "Der Freischütz," including tonal aspects, plot, and musical technique.

Tusa, Michael C. "Richard Wagner and Weber's *Euryanthe*." *Nineteenth Century Music* 9 (Spring 1986): 206-221. Many writers have commented on the strong influence and resemblances between Weber's *Euryanthe* of 1823 and Wagner's *Lohengrin* of 1847. The author identifies the various similarities between the two works in detail and shows the strong influence of Weber's opera on Wagner's *Tannhäuser* (1845).

Warrack, John. *Carl Maria von Weber*. 2d ed. Cambridge and New York: Cambridge University Press, 1976. The standard biography of Weber in any language. The author presents careful discussion of the composer's life and music, with special attention to the operas. General readers will be grateful for the extensive plot summaries of each opera.

———. "Carl Maria von Weber." In *The New Grove Dictionary of Music and Musicians*, edited by Stanley Sadie, vol. 20. London: Macmillan, 1980; Washington, D.C.: Grove's Dictionaries of Music, 1981. A shorter version of the biography, with an updated bibliography, presented in a concise form but without the detail and operatic plot summaries of his full-length biography.

Weber, Carl Maria von. *Writings on Music*. Edited by John Warrack. Translated by Martin Cooper. Cambridge and New York: Cambridge University Press, 1981. The volume contains Weber's fragmentary autobiographical novel as well as his reviews for various papers and journals and his introductions to the operas he conducted in Prague and Dresden. Each entry is given an extensive preface and is thoroughly annotated. The introduction shows that Weber's alleged attacks on Ludwig van Beethoven's music are unfounded; rather, he generally praised Beethoven's works. Weber's reviews illustrate the immense amount of music that was performed then but is completely forgotten today.

Weber, Max Maria von. *Carl Maria von Weber: The Life of an Artist*. Translated by J. Palgrave Simpson. London: Chapman and Hall, and Boston: Ditson, 1865. 2 vols. Though this biography by Weber's son—based on the letters and documents saved by Weber's widow and the recollections of Weber's family—is extremely partisan and chauvinistic with reliance on obsolete information, it nevertheless presents a lively account of the petty intrigues and frustrations of court life, especially in Dresden, that Weber underwent.

Rey M. Longyear

DANIEL WEBSTER

Born: January 18, 1782; Salisbury, New Hampshire

Died: October 24, 1852; Marshfield, Massachusetts

Areas of Achievement: Law, oratory, politics, and diplomacy

Contribution: The greatest orator of his time, Webster, more than any other individual, articulated a near-mystical devotion to the Union which would define Northern patriotism during the Civil War.

Early Life

Daniel Webster was born January 18, 1782, in Salisbury, New Hampshire. His father, Ebenezer, a veteran of the French and Indian War and of the American Revolution, was a tavern keeper, farmer, and local politician. Webster's mother, Abigail Eastman, was a second wife, who, like her predecessor, bore Ebenezer five children; Daniel was the youngest except for one girl. The teamsters who put up at his father's tavern nicknamed him "Black Dan" because of his dark complexion, jet-black hair, and black eyes.

Slight of stature for his age, although with an unusually large head, Daniel was often spared the heavier chores which his brothers and sisters shared on the farm. As a boy he cultivated his precocious mind and strongly emotional nature. Books were hard to come by, but he read everything he found and, blessed with almost total recall, remembered what he read. His father, with whom he had a close relationship, hoped Daniel would get the kind of education he had missed, and in May, 1796, enrolled him in the Phillips Academy in Exeter. Tile boy was shy and sensitive about his homespun clothing, clumsy cowhide boots, and awkward manners, but he made "tolerable progress" with his studies. Only in declamation was he unable to match his fellows; at the public exhibitions, despite careful preparation, he could never command sufficient resolution to rise from his seat and present his speeches.

In December, 1796, Webster returned to Salisbury without having completed his course. A brief period of country schoolteaching ended with an arrangement for him to study with a minister in the neighboring community of Boscawen, who had offered to prepare him for Dartmouth College. At Dartmouth, Webster pursued his studies with ener-

gy, was graduated near the top of his class, and was elected to Phi Beta Kappa. In contrast to his failure at Exeter, he was outstanding in his college literary society and developed a reputation as a public speaker. While only a junior, he was invited to deliver a Fourth of July address at Hanover.

Following graduation, Webster spent several years in rather desultory preparation for a legal career. He read law with a Salisbury attorney, taught in the academy in Fryeburg, Maine, and finally went to Boston, Massachusetts, in July, 1804, where he was accepted as a clerk in the law office of a leading New England Federalist, Christopher Gore. After completing his studies and being admitted to the bar in March, 1805, he began to practice law in Boscawen, where he could be near his family In September, 1807, his father having died the previous year, Webster moved to Portsmouth, New Hampshire, where he remained for nine very happy years. In May, 1808, he married Grace Fletcher, a clergyman's daughter. In August, 1816, he moved with his wife and two children to Boston, a rising metropolis.

Life's Work

Webster entered politics as a strict constructionist and an antinationlist. During two terms in the House of Representatives as a Federalist, 1813-1817, Webster opposed the War of 1812. Although he did not advocate secession, he kept up his obstructionist activities in Congress, while the Republican administration grew increasingly desperate. As a spokesman for the dominant merchants and shippers of New England, he vigorously opposed protective tariffs as probably unconstitutional and certainly inexpedient; in later years, as a protectionist, he was hard put to refute himself.

What national reputation Webster enjoyed prior to 1830 was largely derived from his appearances before the United States Supreme Court. He joined with Chief Justice John Marshall in giving a nationalistic, Hamiltonian interpretation to the Constitution. His skillful arguments in the *Dartmouth College* case (1819), *McCulloch v. Maryland* (1819), and *Gibbons v. Ogden* (1824) brought him recognition as the nation's leading constitutional lawyer.

In 1822, Webster won the Boston district seat in the House of Representatives. He shortly transcended his early sectionalism to become an outstanding nationalist, favoring a national bank, federal appropriations for internal improvements, and, reflecting New England's shift from commerce to manufacturing, a protective tariff. He became known as one of the chief exponents of the "cause of humanity" because of his advocacy of American support for Greek independence from the Ottoman Empire. In June, 1827, the Massachusetts legislature elected the ex-Federalist as a National Republican to the United States Senate. After the death of his wife, he was married in December, 1829, to Caroline Le Roy, the daughter of a wealthy New York merchant.

Webster's second reply to South Carolina senator Robert Y. Hayne, delivered in the Senate on January 26-27, 1830, answered Hayne's defense of John C. Calhoun's Nullification doctrine with a powerful defense of national sovereignty. It gave Webster a reputation as one of the leading statesmen of the nation. His new stature made Webster a potential presidential candidate, and thereafter the hope of reaching the White House was constantly in the back of his mind and influenced many of his actions.

Webster's support for President Andrew Jackson during the Nullification crisis of 1832-1833 brought rumors of a rapprochement between the two antagonists. Webster thought of uniting Jacksonians and Websterites in an anti-Nullification "Constitution and Union" Party that would secure his own election to the presidency in 1836. He made overtures to Jackson, only to be rebuffed, and had no choice but to join the emerging Whig Party and to seek the presidency through that organization. His candidacy for 1836 ended when most Northern Whigs and Anti-Masons supported General William Henry Harrison, a hero of the War of 1812. Webster received only the fourteen electoral votes of Massachusetts.

In the "log-cabin-hard cider" election of 1840, Webster campaigned for Harrison; and the victorious candidate made him secretary of state. The elderly Harrison died on April 4, 1841, only one month after his inauguration. Webster continued in office under Harrison's successor, John Tyler. His effort to settle the Northeastern boundary dispute with Great Britain was successfully concluded with the signing of the Webster-Ashburton Treaty of 1842. Webster's decision to remain in the Tyler Cabinet after all of his fellow Whigs had resigned severely strained his party ties and threatened his political future. Tyler's desire to annex Texas gave

Webster the excuse he needed to give up his office in May, 1843.

Webster went back to the Senate in 1845. Mindful of the lasting harm that his opposition to the War of 1812 had done to his presidential ambitions, he reluctantly supported the Mexican War, but he never believed it to be justified. The election of 1848 brought him the usual fourth year frustration as the Whigs nominated General Zachary Taylor, the victor of Buena Vista, who was elected. Webster's Seventh of March speech in support of the Compromise of 1850 was his final effort to eliminate the slavery issue from national politics; it enraged New England antislavery men, who likened him to a fallen angel. Webster became, after Taylor's death in July, 1850, secretary of state in Millard Fillmore's administration. His presidential ambitions were again revived in 1852, but the Whigs nominated General Winfield Scott. Sick in mind and body, Webster repudiated Scott's candidacy and correctly prophesied the downfall of the Whig Party. He died at his farm, Marshfield, on October 24, 1852, murmuring, "I still live!" Reflecting no more than his mental confusion about experiencing death, these final words would later take on a much broader symbolic meaning to many people.

Summary

Webster was a highly flawed yet fascinating human being, the stuff of which legends are made. He drank and ate to excess, spent money recklessly, and was chronically dependent on powerful creditors such as the National Bank. Combined with his political ambition, these weaknesses in his character constituted the "Black Dan" alter ego of his patriotic, disinterested, "Godlike Daniel" self. The Democrats never tired of reminding the voters that the champion of the Constitution and the Union had been a partisan Federalist congressman during the War of 1812. A perennial presidential candidate after 1830, Webster had to transcend New England's regional interests, while continuing to serve them. Intoning hymns to the Union was an obvious solution, and Webster's high point was his great debate with Hayne. Generations of Northern schoolchildren would memorize his ringing appeal: "Liberty *and* Union, now and forever, one and inseparable!" Webster believed that the United States had a special destiny and that Americans had a unique character with which to fulfill it. The last hopes of mankind, he said at Bunker Hill in 1825, rested on the success of the Union, the American experiment in popular government. Webster was less successful in trying to get the federal government to adopt a policy of economic nationalism, helping business in an age of economic growth through high tariffs, bank charters, and transportation subsidies. In his various roles as constitutional lawyer, orator, politician, and diplomat, he strengthened the sense of American nationalism. President Abraham Lincoln would echo Webster's Union theme in his Civil War addresses, such as the one at Gettysburg on November 19, 1863.

Bibliography

Bartlett, Irving H. *Daniel Webster.* New York: Norton, 1978. This gracefully written, psychologically insightful biography is an attempt to understand the Black Dan-Godlike Man paradox along with the enigmatic inner man behind the dual images.

Baxter, Maurice G. *Daniel Webster and the Supreme Court.* Amherst: University of Massachusetts Press, 1966. Webster exerted a particularly strong influence on the bench in its application of the commerce and contract clauses. Baxter's handling of Webster's legal career, and especially his many appearances before the Supreme Court, is masterful.

————. *One and Inseparable: Daniel Webster and the Union.* Cambridge, Mass.: Harvard University Press, 1984. Benefiting from the Webster Papers project at Dartmouth College, this is the long-awaited full-scale scholarly biography. Webster is portrayed as an ardent patriot, an advocate of American nationality, and a champion of peace and Union—who was at the same time a self-promoting politician who changed his principles to meet the interests of his constituents and who was sometimes insensitive to the great moral issues of the day.

Brown, Norman D. *Daniel Webster and the Politics of Availability.* Athens: University of Georgia Press, 1969. An account of Webster's presidential ambitions during the years in which a second American party system of National Republican-Whig and Democratic parties emerged out of the superficial Republican unity of the so-called Era of Good Feelings. General Andrew Jackson's tremendous popular success influenced Whig strategists to pass over Webster in 1836, 1840, 1848, and 1852, in favor of military heroes for the presidency.

Collison, Gary. " 'This Flagitious Offense': Daniel Webster and the Shadrach Rescue Cases, 1851–1852." *New England Quarterly* 68, no. 4 (December, 1995). Discusses how Webster's political ambitions and his desire to enforce the Fugitive Slave Law backfired when returned slaves were never convicted.

Current, Richard N. *Daniel Webster and the Rise of National Conservatism.* Boston: Little Brown, 1955. This excellent brief biography emphasizes Webster's advocacy of a national conservatism for the United States as his response to the needs of the business community. The elements of his political philosophy were an expansive but peaceful Americanism, self-discipline, Constitution worship, beneficent technology, the harmony of group interests, and power tied to property.

Dalzell, Robert F., Jr. *Daniel Webster and the Trial of American Nationalism: 1843-1852.* Boston: Houghton Mifflin, 1973. Dalzell explains better than any previous study Webster's actions during his tragic last years, when the pressures on him to confirm, modify, or abandon his nationalism were the greatest.

Nathans, Sydney. *Daniel Webster and Jacksonian Democracy*. Baltimore: Johns Hopkins University Press, 1973. This study explores Webster's responses, as a man and as a type of political leader, to the organized, systematic, and continued party strife that took firm root in the era of Andrew Jackson.

Remini, Robert V. *Daniel Webster: The Man and His Time*. New York: Norton, 1997. This new biography reveals Webster to be an important influence in American politics between the War of 1812 and the Civil War, concerned about his family, his land, and above all, his place in history.

Norman D. Brown

AUGUST WEISMANN

Born: January 17, 1834; Frankfurt am Main
Died: November 5, 1914; Freiburg im Breisgau, Germany
Areas of Achievement: Biology, natural history, zoology, and genetics
Contribution: Weismann is most noted for his development and refinement of the theory of the continuity of the germ plasm, for his devout support of Darwinism and the principle of natural selection, and for his discrediting the idea of the inheritance of acquired characteristics.

Early Life

August Friedrich Leopold Weismann was born in Frankfurt am Main on January 17, 1834, to Johann Konrad August Weismann, a classics teacher at the *Gymnasium* in Frankfurt, and Elise Eleanore Lübbren Weismann, a musician and painter. He was the eldest of four children, and his home life was simple and happy. As a young boy, Weismann showed an active interest in nature. He collected butterflies, caterpillars, beetles, and plants, and he assembled a herbarium. He was a lover of art, literature, and music (especially that of Ludwig van Beethoven). These interests continued throughout his life. He became an accomplished pianist. He attended and did well at the *Gymnasium* where his father was a teacher.

Weismann was interested in chemistry and physics as a young adult and wanted to pursue studies in that direction. His father and friends of the family, however, suggested that he pursue medicine, since a career in medicine would be more lucrative. To this end, he entered the University of Göttingen in 1852, where he studied with Friedrich Henle and Friedrich Wöhler in an atmosphere that emphasized research rather than broader problems. He received his medical degree in 1856.

Life's Work

Following graduation, Weismann continued his research while working as an assistant in the medical clinic at Rostock. In 1857, he transferred to the Chemical Institute so that he could pursue his interest in chemistry. This was followed by a tour of four German universities and a more extensive stay in Vienna.

Weismann entered private medical practice in Frankfurt in 1858. His practice allowed him sufficient time to pursue studies on heart muscle fibers.

His private practice was interrupted in 1859 by the war between Austria and Italy, at which time he entered the German army and served as a surgeon at the field hospital in Italy. He resumed private practice in 1860.

In 1861, Weismann abandoned medicine to pursue what had become his main interest, the biological sciences. He attended the University of Giessen for two months in 1861 and was profoundly influenced by Rudolf Leuckart, under whom he began his studies in insect embryology. He considered the two months he spent with Leuckart to be the most important and inspiring time of his career.

Following his stay at Giessen, Weismann became the private physician of Archduke Stephan of Austria. While in this position, from 1861 to 1863, Weismann had ample time to pursue his interest in insect development and completed his first major work, *Die Entwicklung der Dipteren* (on the development of the diptera in the egg), in 1864. He also had time to read Charles Darwin's *On the Origin of Species* (1859). Like so many scientists of the time, Weismann was profoundly influenced by Darwin's book. Along with Ernst Haeckel and Fritz Müller, Weismann became one of Germany's staunchest supporters of Darwinian theory.

In 1863, Weismann became a privatdocent at the University of Freiburg and taught zoology and comparative anatomy. In 1866, he was appointed extraordinary professor and, in 1874, professor. He was the first to occupy the chair of zoology at Freiburg. He soon became director of the Zoological Institute at the university. He was a well-respected teacher, who always attracted large numbers of students.

Weismann's first research papers examined insect histology and embryology. Several papers on these subjects were published between 1862 and 1866. One important discovery he made was that, during metamorphosis, tissues completely dedifferentiate and then redifferentiate during the formation of the adult. Weismann was also interested in the origin and fate of the germ cells of hydrozoans. The germ cells of multicellular organisms such as hydrozoans are set aside from the somatic cells early in development and provide for the continuity of the organism through the sperm and the egg. The somatic cells will eventually die, but the germ cells live on in a new individual. Only the reproductive cells have the capacity to form a complete, new individual. From these observations, Weismann developed the theory for which he is most noted, of the continuity of the germ plasm.

In 1864, Weismann's eyesight failed, and he had to cease work on the microscope. Although he turned to more general problems, his microscopic work was continued by his students, his assistants, and Marie Dorothea Gruber, whom he married in 1867. His wife read to him constantly so that he could keep abreast of the latest scientific developments. His eyesight became so poor that he took a leave of absence from his teaching position from 1869 to 1871. During that time, his eyesight improved, and he resumed lecturing in 1871 and active research in 1874. His eyesight again failed in 1884.

Work on the theory of the continuity of the germ plasm occupied the last thirty years of Weismann's life as an active scientist. The theory encompassed many areas but primarily focused on heredity and evolution. He first published on these topics in 1883. Although he was not the first to suggest the principle of the continuity of the germ plasm, he did develop the idea to its fullest. He contended that the germ plasm was to be found on the chromatin threads, the "idants" (chromosomes) in the nucleus of the cell. He hypothesized that the idants were composed of smaller units, the "ids," which in turn were composed of the "determinants," the individual hereditary units, which he correctly envisioned as being linearly arranged. The determinants, he thought, were composed of still smaller, more basic units, the "biophors."

Based only on a priori knowledge, Weismann reasoned that the chromosome number must be halved during the formation of the reproductive cells and hypothesized that a "reduction division" must occur during the process. This, he thought, was to prevent doubling of the germ plasm at each generation. This is considered by many to be his most significant and effective scientific contribution. Weismann believed that during fertilization individual ancestral germ plasms, each carrying variations, were combined. He thought that, as well as introducing new variations, this process created new combinations of variations.

Weismann's ideas on the continuity of the germ plasm put him in direct conflict with many other scientists of the time, since many had come to discredit natural selection as a mechanism of evolution and advocated Lamarckism, the inheritance of acquired traits, as an alternative. Even Charles Dar-

win proposed the theory of pangenesis, where each body part was thought to produce a gemmule, which could be modified by the environment and eventually passed to the germ cells. Weismann investigated many cases of reported inheritance of acquired characteristics and could find no authenticated instance of such inheritance. His own classic experiments, in which he cut off the tails of mice over several generations but found no tendency for the tail to shorten in succeeding generations, were instrumental in challenging Lamarckism. Weismann thought that the only way acquired characteristics could be passed to the offspring was if the germ cells were affected. He became more devoted to the theory of natural selection than did Darwin. Weismann did not believe that the environment in any way affected heredity.

Weismann extended Darwin's theory of natural selection to the germ cells in a new theory called germinal selection. He thought that the determinants struggled with one another for nutriment and that the stronger ones would triumph and eliminate the weaker ones. Thus, only the stronger ones would survive in the germ plasm and be passed to the offspring. This, he thought, could account for the loss of organs during evolution. Later work failed to support his idea of germinal selection. Weismann extended his germ plasm theory to development. He correctly thought that the determinants directed differentiation in individual cells but incorrectly envisioned that this was a result of the distribution of different determinants to different cells during cell division. He therefore thought that mitosis could be qualitatively unequal while being quantitatively equal.

Weismann's main works on heredity and evolution were published in *Studien zur Descendenztheorie* (1875-1876; *Studies in the Theory of Descent*, 1882), *Essays upon Heredity and Kindred Biological Problems* (1889-1892), *Das Keimplasma: Eine Theorie der Vererbung* (1892; *The Germ-Plasm: A Theory of Heredity*, 1893), *On Germinal Selection as a Source of Definite Variation* (1896), and *Vorträge über Descendenztheorie* (1902; *The Evolution Theory*, 1904). *The Evolution Theory* became an important and widely read book. It has been said that since Weismann's theoretical contributions to science were so important, his experimental and observational work was often overshadowed.

Weismann retired from the faculty of the University of Freiburg in 1912. He died peacefully at Freiburg im Breisgau, Germany, on November 5, 1914, at the age of eighty.

Summary

August Weismann was one of the most respected biologists of the latter part of the nineteenth century and the early part of the twentieth century. His ideas stimulated considerable discussion and research. His theories on heredity and development were far-reaching. He correctly recognized that the hereditary material was contained within the nucleus of the sperm and egg and that the hereditary material of the germ cells is reduced to one-half during the maturation of the sperm and egg. In a single theory, the germ plasm theory, he explained the meiotic reduction division, sexual reproduction, development, and natural selection. It has been said that Weismann's "ingenious synthesis helped prepare the way for twentieth-century genetics." Weismann was elected to the Bavarian Academy of Sciences and, as a foreign member, to the Linnean Society, the American Philosophical Society, and the Royal Society of London. He received numerous honorary degrees and medals, including the Darwin/Wallace Medal of the Linnean Society and the Darwin Medal of the Royal Society.

Bibliography

Churchill, Frederick B. "August Weismann and a Break from Tradition." *Journal of the History of Biology* (1968): 91-112. This brief article discusses Weismann's most significant contribution, the theory of the continuity of the germ plasm. Also shows how his work related to that of Ernst Haeckel and others and how it influenced the development of modern biological thought.

―――. "Life before Model Systems: General Zoology at August Weismann's Institute." *American Zoologist* 37, no. 3 (June, 1997). The author traces the metamorphosis of General Zoology into Model Systems Research, which began in the late nineteenth century.

Coleman, William. "The Cell, Nucleus and Inheritance: An Historical Study." *Proceedings of the American Philosophical Society* 109 (1965): 126, 149-154. Like the articles by Churchill, this article analyzes the impact of the work of Weismann and others on modern biological thought. It is one of the few modern works that analyzes Weismann in this light.

Conklin, Edwin. "August Weismann." *Proceedings of the American Philosophical Society* 54 (1915): iii-xii. This is a brief summary of Weismann's contribution to science, written by a friend on the occasion of Weismann's death.

Weismann, August. *Essays upon Heredity and Kindred Biological Problems.* 2 vols. Oxford: Clarendon Press, 1891-1892; Oceanside, N.Y.: Dabor, 1977. This collection contains some of Weismann's most important theoretical contributions on heredity, the continuity of the germ plasma, sexual reproduction, and evolution.

―――. *The Germ-Plasm: A Theory of Heredity.* London: Scott, and New York: Scribner, 1893. This is the most significant book written by Weismann. It addresses the most important theoretical contributions Weismann was to make to science.

Charles L. Vigue

DUKE OF WELLINGTON
Arthur Wellesley

Born: May 1, 1769; Dublin, Ireland
Died: September 14, 1852; Walmer Castle, near Dover, Kent, England
Areas of Achievement: The military and politics
Contribution: One of Great Britain's finest military leaders, Wellington, through victories in the Peninsular War and at Waterloo, hastened the downfall of Napoleon and the end of the Napoleonic Wars.

Early Life

Arthur Wesley (after 1798, Wellesley) was born on May 1, 1769, in Dublin, Ireland, to an Anglo-Irish family. His father was Garret Wesley, first Earl of Mornington, and his mother was Anne Hill, daughter of Viscount Dungannon. The family attached little importance to Arthur's education. He attended a preparatory school before going to Eton for two years. After his father's death in 1781, his mother decided that young Wellesley should pursue a military career and sent him to a French riding school at Angers, where he learned French tactics and language.

In 1787, Wellesley obtained a commission in the army but did little, if any, military duty as he was also an aide to the Lord Lieutenant of Ireland and a member of the Irish Parliament. By his first military engagement in 1794 in Flanders, Wellesley was a lieutenant colonel in the Thirty-third Regiment of Foot.

Life's Work

In 1796, Wellesley went to India with his regiment. The appointment of his brother Richard, Lord Mornington (later Marquess Wellesley), as Governor-General of India helped his prospects. After the fall of Seringapatam in 1799, he became governor of Mysore. He became chief political and military agent in the Southern Mahratha States and the Decan in 1803. War broke out, and Wellesley led his troops into a fierce battle near the village of Assaye. The British lost a third of their strength before the enemy broke. Wellesley would forever compare battle losses to those at Assaye. In December, 1803, the fortress of Gawilghur surrendered to his forces. For his Indian service, he received thanks from Parliament, a sword from the people of Calcutta, and the Order of the Bath. He resigned his Indian appointments early in 1805 and arrived in England on September 10, 1805, after eight years' service in India.

Sir Arthur Wellesley, as he was then known, was a handsome figure upon his return to England. He was of medium height and slim build, with closely cropped brown hair (defying both fashion and military regulations), piercing light-blue eyes, and an aquiline nose. He dressed simply and neatly, wearing military dress only when necessary. He was a man of honor and integrity and expected the same of others. He always did his duty regardless of his personal feelings.

Upon his return from India, Wellesley commanded an infantry brigade sent to reinforce British troops on the Elbe. There he learned of French emperor Napoleon I's victory at Austerlitz, which left Great Britain alone against France. Upon his return to England, Wellesley married the Honorable Catherine Dorothea Sarah (Kitty) Pakenham (daughter of Edward Pakenham, second Baron Longford) on April 10, 1806, in Dublin. They had two sons: Arthur Richard, born on February 3, 1807, and Charles, born on January 16, 1808. Wellesley became Chief Secretary of Ireland in 1807, a difficult and frustrating position which made him welcome the opportunity to join a military expedition to Denmark.

Foreign Secretary George Canning believed that Napoleon might use the fleet of neutral Denmark against England and demanded that it be placed in British custody until the end of the war. When Denmark refused, Canning sent the British navy to Copenhagen in July, 1807, with a small land force including a brigade commanded by Wellesley. He played a small, but key, role in the successful British operation there.

In May, 1808, revolt broke out in Spain against Napoleon when he placed his brother, Joseph Bonaparte, on the Spanish throne. Delegations from Spain and Portugal urged English intervention in the Iberian Peninsula, and in July, Wellesley (now a lieutenant general) was given temporary command of an expeditionary force to Portugal. The British army landed in Mondego Bay and moved toward Lisbon. Wellesley's force fought the French on August 14 at Roliça, where he salvaged a desperate situation. Nevertheless, the French es-

caped. Wellesley moved to Vimeiro to cover British troop landings and was surprised by French forces. After heavy fighting, the French withdrew, leaving the road to Lisbon open. One senior officer prevented Wellesley from pursuing the French, while a second negotiated and persuaded him to sign an armistice. Published in London as the Convention of Sintra, it was extremely unpopular, and the three generals faced a Court of Inquiry, which approved the convention.

Meanwhile, Spanish resistance to the French collapsed and British forces were driven from Spain in December, 1808. By the end of March, 1809, the French were in Oporto and the Portuguese were demanding British aid. Wellesley, in command of a force to defend Portugal, arrived there April 22, 1809. On May 12, the British forces crossed the Douro River, captured Oporto, and then marched for Spain. On July 27 and 28, they defeated French forces in a fierce battle at Talavera. Wellesley (after September, 1809, Viscount Wellington of Talavera) retreated in the face of French reinforcements. Because of inadequate supplies and transport, Wellington's army wintered in

Portugal, where he ordered the secret construction of the Lines of Torres Vedras, defensive hill fortifications connected by natural escarpments. In 1810, the French took the key border fortresses of Ciudad-Rodrigo (Spain) and Almeida (Portugal). Wellington again withdrew his forces to Portugal, luring the French into the wasted countryside only to repel them on September 27 at Bussaco, where the French sustained heavy losses. By October, Wellington had the allied army inside the Lines of Torres Vedras.

Early in 1811, Wellington forced the French from Portugal, overextending his supply lines in the process. The French attempt to strengthen the garrison at Almeida ended with the Battle of Fuentes de Oñoro (May 3-5). Wellington's army took Almeida, but the garrison escaped. Increased French strength again caused Wellington's withdrawal to Portugal, where his army could be supplied by sea. In 1812, Wellington took the vital fortresses of Ciudad-Rodrigo (January 19) and Badajoz (April 16), liberated Salamanca (June 17), defeated the French at the Battle of Salamanca (July 22), and entered Madrid (August 12). Although the 1812 campaign had been his most successful to date, Wellington abandoned the siege of Burgos and retreated to Portugal to correct the deficiencies of the previous campaign.

In 1813, the French began withdrawing from Spain. Wellington's forces moved quickly north; a major victory at Vitoria (June 21) liberated Spain and opened France to invasion. On July 25, French forces crossed the Pyrenees but were stopped at Sorauren on July 28. On October 7, Wellington's forces were victorious at the Bidassoa and crossed into France. British victories followed at the Nivelle and the Nive. On February 27, 1814, Wellington bested the French at the Battle of Orthez. In April, he took Toulouse just before learning that the allies were in Paris and Napoleon had abdicated.

Wellington (now a duke) went to Paris and then to Madrid for twelve days, trying to prevent civil war. He bade farewell to his troops at Bordeaux and on June 23, after an absence of five years, arrived in England to a tumultuous reception. He served as British ambassador to France and then as delegate to the Congress of Vienna.

When news of Napoleon's escape from Elba reached Vienna, Wellington was given command of the joint allied force. He took command in Brussels on April 15, 1815, and began training his polyglot army. On June 15, Napoleon led the French army into Belgium. On June 18, Wellington deployed his forces near the village of Waterloo, where, in a hard-fought battle with heavy losses, the allies prevailed. Napoleon withdrew to France. Wellington led the allied armies in pursuit, crossing into France on June 21. Napoleon abdicated on June 22, the same day that Wellington became commander of the army of occupation. Wellington remained in France most of the time until the occupation ended in August, 1818.

Upon his return to England in 1818, Wellington's involvement in politics and public life seemed inevitable. After he joined the cabinet in December, he held several offices, including prime minister (January, 1828, to November, 1829). He was Lord High Constable at the coronations of George IV, William IV, and Victoria. He represented Great Britain at the Congress of Verona in 1822 and in Russia in 1826. He was commander in chief of the British army periodically from 1827 until his death. Though his career as a party politician ended in 1846, he was a close adviser to Queen Victoria and godfather to her third son. Wellington died at Walmer Castle on September 14, 1852, and was buried at St. Paul's, London, after a magnificent funeral.

Summary

The Duke of Wellington became for many the symbol of British success in the Napoleonic Wars. Ironically, during the war, his cautious military strategy drew much criticism. Wellington knew that his was the only army England had and that, if he lost it, it could not be replaced. He never lost a military battle, although he often retreated to avoid untenable situations. Until Waterloo, many people believed that he was unbeaten only because he had never faced Napoleon.

Wellington's success was based on learning from his mistakes. A disastrous night attack in India made him reluctant to attack at night without previous daylight reconnaissance. Problems with Spanish and Portuguese allies in the Peninsula made him distrust allies and avoid relying on them. The disasters of his first military engagement in Flanders made him realize the importance of keeping supply lines open and taking care of the men. Leaked information about his movements and plans appeared in British newspapers, making him reluctant to confide in anyone. Blunders by his staff officers made him attend to every detail himself.

Wellington was a gentleman and an officer. He always did his duty regardless of his personal feelings. As an officer he saw to the well-being of his men because it was his duty. His men had no affection for him, but they respected him because he took care of them. In battle he rode among them, calm and cool, always where fighting was thickest. He insisted upon strong discipline, using the lash and the gallows if necessary (and advocating corporal punishment for the army throughout his life). He recommended the Waterloo medal for all ranks, but he showed little gratitude to or interest in his men after the war.

Wellington was a die-hard aristocrat and fought change. In spite of difficulties with incompetent officers who bought commissions and promotions, he defended the system because it ensured that officers would come from the upper classes. He spent much of his early manhood outside England and never really understood the cares and concerns of the English people. He opposed reform in parliamentary representation despite gross inequities. His unwillingness to compromise on this made him the symbol of conservatism and the target of the mob. On several occasions, mobs surrounded Apsley House (his London home), throwing stones at the windows, which he had covered with iron shutters. He cared nothing for the opinions of his generation or of history.

Wellington's immediate legacy to the British military was a tragic one. In the years after Waterloo, the British army modeled itself on Wellington's army. It neglected training staff officers because Wellington considered the public school and the regiment the best training. Wellington did his own staff work, not trusting his officers. Later commanders did not have his ability or attention to detail. It took the British disasters in the Crimean War to change this system.

Bibliography

Bryant, Arthur. *The Great Duke: Or, The Invincible General.* London: Collins, 1971; New York: Morrow, 1972. Objective, thorough account of Wellington's military career. Gives attention to often-neglected Indian period of his career.

Cooper, Leonard. *The Age of Wellington: The Life and Times of the Duke of Wellington, 1769-1852.* London: Macmillan, and New York: Dodd, Mead, 1963. Popular treatment without documentation. Places Wellington's life in context with contemporaneous events.

Davies, Godfrey. *Wellington and His Army*. Oxford: Blackwell, 1954; Westport, Conn.: Greenwood Press, 1974. Brief account of the military aspects of Wellington's career (especially the Peninsula and Belgium). Generally uncritical of Wellington and harsh on his critics.

Guedalla, Philip. *The Duke*. London: Hodder and Stoughton, and New York: Harper, 1931. Classic, literary biography. Guedalla believes that Wellington's later unpopularity with the British people came not from his opposition to reform but from his success as a soldier, as the British prefer heroes to be slightly unsuccessful.

Hibbert, Christopher. *Wellington: A Personal History*. Reading, Mass.: Addison Wesley, and London: Harper Collins, 1997. Hibbert, a noted historian, produces another winning biography full of new insight into Wellington's life and character.

Longford, Elizabeth. *Wellington: The Pillar of State*. London: Weidenfeld and Nicolson, and New York: Harper, 1972. Excellent and useful account of Wellington's life after Waterloo, a period often slighted.

————. *Wellington: The Years of the Sword*. London: Weidenfeld and Nicolson, and New York: Harper, 1969. Detailed, factual account of Wellington's life from 1769 to 1815. The most useful and thorough of recent works.

Philips, C. H. *The Young Wellington in India*. London: Athlone Press, 1973. Originally given as the Creighton Lectures in History in 1972. Philips focuses on Wellington's years in India and how they contributed to his military leadership.

Veve, Thomas D. *The Duke of Wellington and the British Army of Occupation in France, 1815-1818*. Westport, Conn.: Greenwood Press, 1992. Full, detailed account of Wellington's last active military assignment—the command of the occupation army in France from 1815 to 1818.

Judith A. Parsons

W. C. WENTWORTH

Born: Probably August 7, 1790; probably at sea, between Sydney and Norfolk Island, Australia

Died: March 20, 1872; Wimborne, Dorset, England

Areas of Achievement: Government and politics

Contribution: Wentworth contributed both to egalitarian and conservative forces in Australian life.

Early Life

William Charles Wentworth was the son of Catherine (née Crowley) and D'Arcy Wentworth. Catherine was transported to Australia for seven years after being convicted at the Stafford assizes on July 30, 1788. She arrived at Sydney on June 28, 1790, and was then sent to Norfolk Island, where she arrived on August 7, 1790. D'Arcy was a medical practitioner who was charged with highway robbery on four occasions. He was acquitted each time, and before the last case was over he had obtained an appointment as an assistant surgeon on the Second Fleet. D'Arcy and Catherine sailed to Sydney on the same ship, and their son was probably born at sea as they sailed from Sydney to Norfolk Island.

For his first five years, Wentworth lived on Norfolk Island. The family returned to Sydney in February, 1796, and moved to Parramatta, where D'Arcy served in the medical center and where Catherine died in 1800.

Wentworth was educated in Great Britain. He returned to Sydney in 1810 but left for London in 1816, where he entered the Middle Temple in February, 1817, to prepare himself, as he wrote, to be "the instrument of procuring a free constitution for my country." He finished his legal studies in 1823, returning to Sydney in 1824, where he married Sarah Cox, the daughter of an emancipist blacksmith, in 1829. More than six feet tall, with auburn hair, Wentworth had a Roman head and massive form. He was also known for his slovenly dress and the disrespectful bearing he frequently adopted during his speeches. He had a harsh voice but was admired for his forceful speaking.

Life's Work

Upon returning from Great Britain in 1810, Wentworth was appointed acting provost marshal by Governor Lachlan Macquarie in October, 1811, and was granted 1,750 acres on the Nepean. Two years later, with William Lawson, Gregory Blax-

land, and four servants, he set out to cross the Blue Mountains. After twenty-one days, as Wentworth wrote, "the boundless champaign burst upon our sight." They had found abundant pasture land and knew that animals could be transported to it on foot. Their discovery further stimulated the pastoral industry, and Wentworth was rewarded with an additional thousand acres.

Two years after this exploratory trip across the Blue Mountains, Wentworth went to Great Britain to continue his education. When he returned to Sydney in 1824, he brought with him a printing press and with it started a newspaper, *The Australian.* In that paper he took up the cause of the "emancipists," those persons who had served the sentence for which they had been transported. Before this time, he had reacted against the attempt by those with no convict heritage—the "exclusives"—to force the emancipists to remain inferior citizens. In *A Statistical, Historical, and Political Description of the Colony of New South Wales and Its Dependent Settlements in Van Dieman's Land* (1819), he commented that "the covert aim of these men is to convert the ignominy of the great body of the people into a hereditary deformity. They would hand it down from father to son, and raise an eternal barrier of separation between their offspring, and the offspring of the unfortunate convict."

Wentworth used his newspaper to promote the rights of the emancipists and to advance his own political career. He criticized the pretensions of the exclusives and agitated for jury trial and political representation for both emancipists and the free-born children of convicts. As free immigration increased and transportation to New South Wales ended, however, the emancipists decreased as a percentage of the population, with the result that by 1840 the emancipist issue was no longer as significant as it had been. In addition, trial by jury had been adopted in 1830, by which time Wentworth had sold his shares in the paper. He continued to agitate and to petition for self-government, and in 1835 he joined with others to found the Australian Patriotic Association to work for representative government in New South Wales.

During this period of agitation for self-government, his father died in 1827. Wentworth's inheritance added to his already considerable holdings, and he continued to acquire property. He purchased Vaucluse in 1827, where he proceeded to build a stately mansion which he made the center of his activities. The property was later increased to five hundred acres, making his home a substantial estate. He also acquired several sheep stations, possessing at least fifteen at one time. With these large holdings, his pastoral interests occupied much of his time, and he gave up his legal practice. At the time of his death, his properties in Australia were assessed at 96,000 pounds and those in London at 70,000 pounds.

Wentworth had prospered economically; politically, his success was slower. In the late 1820's and early 1830's, he was popular with the poorer people of Sydney and with the emancipists. While he had deep feelings for the emancipists, he was no democrat. His own inclinations were to remove social barriers to advancement but to permit only people of wealth to have political rights. As he developed his pastoral holdings and acquired more and more wealth, these inclinations became more pronounced. When he defended the old land system, attempted to prevent the abolition of transportation, and gave his approval to the importation of Asiatic labor, many former supporters deserted him, and his former newspaper asserted that he had betrayed the native-born of New South Wales and that his day was over. In reality, while his day as the leader of the emancipists was indeed over, his day as the leader of the pastoralists was only beginning.

The pastoral industry was the leading one in Australia, but the change in land policy in 1831 had irritated the pastoralists. Now they must buy or lease their holdings, rather than receive free grants. Since this new policy came from London, pastoralists more than ever wanted the colony to be given more control over its own affairs. Already, there had been the gradual concession of rights to the colony. An advisory legislative council of between five and seven official members had been established in 1823, and that council had been increased to fifteen members in 1828, with seven of the fifteen being unofficial members. With the diminution of the convict percentage of the population and the abolition of land grants, there was a reorientation from social and political concerns to economic and political matters. This new focus brought Wentworth, the former emancipist leader, into alliance with his exclusivist antagonist, James Macarthur. The exclusives had previously desired a nominated Legislative Council but were willing to accept an elective one in order to win over the wealthy emancipists. In addition, the emancipists

moderated their desire for a liberal franchise, recognizing that such a franchise might be a threat to their wealth. In other words, the emancipists and exclusives now found a common enemy in the Colonial Office, with James Macarthur and William Charles Wentworth leading the agitation for representative government and autonomy.

With the cessation of transportation to New South Wales in 1840, even more rights were conceded to the colony. The Constitution Act of 1842 enlarged the Legislative Council to thirty-six members, twenty-four of whom were elected. Wentworth became one of these twenty-four when he was elected to the council in 1843. In the council, Wentworth led the pastoralists in their struggle for a change in land policy. He and his fellow squatters wanted to protect their interests in the land, which they proposed to do by maintaining control of the Legislative Council and having control of crown lands transferred to the council.

The council remained Wentworth's forum of activity for the rest of his time in Australia. He remained popular with the pastoralists, but his standing with the majority of New South Welshmen declined. Determined to protect their economic interests, the pastoralists continued to control the Legislative Council. When the colony was authorized to draw up its own constitution in the early 1850's, Wentworth became the chairman of the select committee that drafted the constitution. In that document, the pastoralists attempted to maintain their control over affairs by a restrictive franchise and by requiring a two-thirds majority to amend the constitution. Wentworth wanted to go even further and establish a hereditary peerage, which would serve as the upper house of the bicameral legislature. This proposed aristocracy did not survive the debates in the Legislative Council, and the British government struck out the two-thirds provision. Nevertheless, Wentworth and his colleagues had given to New South Wales a constitution which provided for control over their own domestic affairs. Wentworth had accomplished his goal of giving a free constitution to his country. Having done so, he retired from active affairs and spent the rest of his life in Great Britain, where he died in 1872. His body was returned to Australia, where it was interred on his estate at Vaucluse.

Summary

On the surface, it appears that William Charles Wentworth changed his principles in mid-life; in reality, he was consistent. He was never a democrat, although his support of the emancipists caused many to look upon him as a believer in equality. He did not believe in distinctions made on the basis of birth, but he actively promoted distinctions made on the basis of ability. His support of the emancipists and then of the pastoralists is not, therefore, contradictory but rather consistent. The pastoralists had demonstrated their ability, and not all of them had come from the respectable class. The true measure of a person was not birth but what a person accomplished in life.

In keeping with Wentworth's support of ability was his commitment to education. If people were to develop to their fullest potential, and if New South Welshmen were to make free institutions work, education was essential. Wentworth was at least partly responsible for the establishment of the first real system of primary education in New South Wales. He was also a leader in the establishment of the University of Sydney and served on its original senate.

Bibliography

Byrnes, John V. "William Charles Wentworth and the Continuity of Australian Literature." *Australian Letters* (April, 1963): 10-18. A discussion of Wentworth's role in the origin of Australian literature.

Clark, C. M. H. *A History of Australia.* 4 vols. Melbourne: Melbourne University Press, 1962-1978. Aside from being a detailed account of Australian history covering the period of Wentworth's political career, this volume provides almost the equivalent of a biography of Wentworth.

Green, H. M. "Wentworth as Orator." *Journal of the Royal Australian Historical Society* 21 (1935): 337-360. A sympathetic presentation of Wentworth as politician and speaker.

Hughes, Robert. *The Fatal Shore: The Epic of Australia's Founding.* New York: Knopf, and London: Collins, 1987. A delightful book which gives a thorough account of convict life in Australia. Particularly useful for the discussion of the emancipist-exclusive controversy.

Jose, Arthur. *Builders and Pioneers of Australia.* London: Dent, 1928; Freeport, N.Y.: Books for Libraries Press, 1970. Jose's sketch of Wentworth is a useful account of his life and work. Jose explicitly states that D'Arcy Wentworth was probably guilty of highway robbery and that friends arranged for him to leave Great Britain.

Melbourne, A. C. V. *Early Constitutional Development in Australia: New South Wales, 1788-1856.* London: Oxford University Press, 1934. The standard work dealing with constitutional agitation and the grant of responsible government.

———. *William Charles Wentworth.* Brisbane: Biggs, 1934. This is an expansion of the John Murtagh Macrossan Lectures for 1932. The book has to be used with caution, particularly with regard to Wentworth's birth. The interpretation of Wentworth presented by Melbourne is, however, the basis of all later interpretations.

Ward, John Manning. *James Macarthur: Colonial Conservative, 1798-1867.* Sydney: Sydney University Press, 1981. A biography by a sound scholar. Because of the relations, both unfriendly and friendly, between Macarthur and Wentworth, the references to Wentworth, which are based on research in the Wentworth papers, are extremely useful.

Wood, F. L. "Some Early Educational Problems, and W. C. Wentworth's Work for Higher Education." *Journal of Royal Australian Historical Society* 17 (1931): 368-394. A discussion of the impact of religion on education and of Wentworth's contribution to the founding of Sydney University.

Albert A. Hayden

GEORGE WESTINGHOUSE

Born: October 6, 1846; Central Bridge, New York
Died: March 12, 1914; New York, New York
Area of Achievement: Technology
Contribution: Both an ingenious inventor and a shrewd entrepreneur, Westinghouse developed both mechanical and electrical inventions that permitted America to emerge as a major industrial nation in the late nineteenth century. As an inventor, he designed the air brake, signaling systems, and other key inventions for railroads, and as an entrepreneur he supported the creation of electric light and power systems, using alternating current.

Early Life

George Westinghouse was born October 6, 1846, in Central Bridge, New York, the eighth child in a family of ten. His mother, Emaline Vedder, was of Dutch-English stock, while his father, George Westinghouse, Sr., was German. A mechanic and an inventor, George, Sr., operated a machine shop in Schenectady, New York, where he manufactured agricultural equipment, mill machinery, and small steam engines. Along with his brothers, young George received most of his education by working in his father's shop. Although he briefly attended Union College in Schenectady in 1865, he soon decided that he preferred to learn by experimenting with machines rather than by reading books. Throughout his career, Westinghouse perfected his many inventions by drawing more on his mechanical skills than on any formal training in science or engineering.

At the outbreak of the Civil War, Westinghouse was anxious to set out on his own and win glory as a soldier. Though only fourteen, he attempted to run away and join the army, only to be stopped by his stern father. Two years later, he overcame his father's opposition and enlisted as a private. After passing a competitive examination in 1864, he transferred to the United States Navy and became an engineering officer. While serving on board ship, Westinghouse installed a small lathe, which he used to fashion various gadgets.

After the war, Westinghouse returned to work for his father but devoted his free time to invention. In 1865, he received his first patent, for a rotary steam engine which was an improvement over the common reciprocating (up and down) engines then in use. Rather than put this invention into production, however, Westinghouse was soon attracted by the challenges of improving railroad technology. Because of their scale of operations and importance to American business, railroads offered the greatest technological challenges and, consequently, attracted creative and ambitious Americans in the late nineteenth century. After witnessing a train accident in which a number of cars were derailed, Westinghouse designed a car replacer which permitted repair crews to use a special set of rails to slide derailed cars back onto the main tracks. Joining with two local businessmen, he began manufacturing his car replacer in Schenectady. Hoping that this new enterprise would succeed, Westinghouse married Marguerite Erskine Walker in 1867. Unfortunately, Westinghouse did not prosper in Schenectady and his partners succeeded in pushing him out of the business. Disgusted, Westinghouse moved in 1868 to Pittsburgh, where he found a more cooperative group of business associates.

Life's Work

From the 1870's to the 1900's, Westinghouse was a major figure in Pittsburgh industry, designing numerous new products and establishing more than sixty different companies. Of his many inventions, perhaps the most original was the air brake. Shortly after he had perfected the car replacer, Westinghouse began giving serious thought to preventing accidents by developing better brakes for trains. At that time, trains were stopped by the engineer shutting off the locomotive and by brakemen in individual train cars applying mechanical brakes. With this arrangement, it was possible to bring a train to a scheduled stop at a station but it was impossible to stop in case of a sudden emergency. To remedy this, Westinghouse explored various mechanical and electrical schemes, all of which he found unreliable. By chance, he happened to read a magazine article about how compressed air was being used in boring the Mount Cenis tunnel in the Italian Alps. Inspired by this article, Westinghouse designed a brake system consisting of a series of brakes in each individual car, all of which were powered by an air compressor in the locomotive. By opening or closing a single valve, the engineer could apply the brakes throughout the train and bring the train to a quick stop. Westinghouse patented this device in 1869 and established the Westinghouse Air Brake Company. For the next two decades, Westinghouse

continued to improve this invention, so that by 1890 it was the standard braking system used on all American trains. Not satisfied with the national market, Westinghouse went on to establish factories worldwide, and soon his air brakes were to be found on trains in Europe, Australia, and Russia.

Experience with the air brake led Westinghouse to develop other inventions for the railroad industry. To keep train cars from crashing into one another when the train was stopped, he perfected friction draft gear. To help coordinate the movement of numerous trains on railroad networks, Westinghouse designed an improved signaling system in which electricity and compressed air were used to control signals along the track. To manufacture his signaling system, Westinghouse organized the Union Switch and Signal Company in 1881 and hired a number of talented engineers.

Drawing on this team of engineers, Westinghouse decided in 1884 to plunge into the newly emerging field of electric lighting. At this time, the electrical industry was dominated by Thomas Edison, who had perfected the incandescent lamp and a distribution system using direct current (DC). To compete with Edison, Westinghouse bought up the patents of other inventors and had his engineering staff convert the patents into successful products. Following this strategy, Westinghouse purchased the patents for an incandescent lamp and dynamo from William Stanley, an alternating current (AC) transformer from Lucien Gaulard and John Gibbs in Europe, and an AC motor from Nikola Tesla. Working with Stanley and Tesla, Westinghouse engineers combined these individual inventions into a coherent system of light and power using AC. Perceiving this new system as a threat to his DC technology, Edison attacked the Westinghouse system, claiming that the high voltages used with AC would lead to unnecessary accidents and death by electrocution. In response to this attack, Westinghouse steadfastly maintained that his system was safe; to demonstrate its great potential, he undertook an impressive installation at the 1893 Chicago World's Fair. At the fair, twenty-four giant AC generators delivered power safely to one hundred thousand lamps, which lit up the fair buildings in a spectacular fashion. While the Chicago installation impressed the general public, Westinghouse convinced professional engineers of the value of his system by using AC to harness and transmit the tremendous power of Niagara Falls in 1896. Largely as a consequence of Westinghouse's entrepreneur-

ial vision and the skill of his engineers, America came to enjoy the benefits of AC power.

The success of the Chicago and Niagara installations ensured that the Westinghouse Electric Company (organized in 1886) would grow and prosper. Rather than manufacture only AC equipment, however, Westinghouse encouraged this company to introduce new products. Drawing on his extensive experience with the railroads, he and his engineers developed both electric streetcars and locomotives. This work led the Westinghouse Company to build large-scale generating equipment and special motors for the New York subway system and to undertake the electrification of the New York, New Haven, and Hartford railroads in 1906.

Still fascinated by steam engines, Westinghouse purchased the patent rights to the steam turbine perfected by the English inventor Charles A. Parsons. Under his direction, the horizontal steam turbine was adapted first for use in electric generating stations in 1900 and then to power ships in 1912. Much more efficient than the reciprocating engine, the steam turbine has been used extensively in both nuclear power plants and steamships. Westinghouse acquired some 360 patents for these many inventions.

In developing his inventions, Westinghouse moved easily from the machine shop, where he often worked with his hands, to the boardroom, where he met with financiers and businessmen from around the world. In both contexts, his physical appearance and intellectual power commanded immediate attention. Photographs taken at the height of his career reveal a tall, portly man with a strong face and a walrus mustache. Generally soft-spoken and patient, he expressed dissatisfaction by raising his large right hand and quietly saying, "But you don't understand"; such an admonition from Westinghouse was usually enough to change the mind of any opponent.

From his earliest days as a manufacturer, Westinghouse took a special interest in the welfare of his employees. He was among the first major employers in the United States to give his men a half day off on Saturday. In 1889, when the Westinghouse Air Brake Company moved to Wilmerding, fourteen miles east of Pittsburgh, Westinghouse built a new town, complete with houses, churches, schools, and parks. With regard to his professional staff, Westinghouse advised his executive vice president, "I want you to employ none but gentlemen." In general, he succeeded in hiring only honest and hardworking young engineers, and many of the technical achievements of the Westinghouse organization can be attributed to Westinghouse's ability to hire, supervise, and motivate a strong engineering staff.

Although Westinghouse amassed a large fortune from his many inventions and enterprises, he generally regarded money as a resource for future projects and invested much of his money back into his companies. Throughout his career, he was always at work and seldom indulged in luxuries such as vacations. In 1913, however, at the first signs of a heart condition, his physician prescribed rest, and the great inventor reluctantly retired to his estate in Lenox, Massachusetts. To occupy himself, Westinghouse occasionally went fishing in a nearby pond. One day, his rowboat capsized and he was thrown into the chilly water. In the course of this accident, he strained his heart and caught a severe cold from which he never recovered. He died quietly in New York City on March 12, 1914. Curious and creative to the end, he spent his last days designing an electrically operated wheelchair, which he intended to use during his convalescence.

Summary

As an inventor and entrepreneur, Westinghouse helped bring about a series of profound changes in American business and technology. When he began his career in the late 1860's, most American business firms were small-scale partnerships or family enterprises, employing at most a few hundred people. With the exception of the railroads, most technology was personal and familiar, developed and used by average Americans in small workshops and on family farms. By the time Westinghouse died in 1914, American industry was dominated by huge corporations with thousands of workers. By then, American technology was characterized by gigantic plants using complex machines and large amounts of electric power. Based on science, this new technology was essential yet incomprehensible to most Americans.

Westinghouse contributed to these fundamental changes in American business and technology by combining the strengths of the nineteenth century with the opportunities of the twentieth century. From his father's generation, he had learned about technology by working with his hands, and he used his skills as a machinist to perfect remarkable new devices such as the air brake and the steam turbine. From the past, he also carried forward a personal

and fatherly concern for his workers, which translated into a policy of decent working conditions and which elicited deep respect from his employees. Finally, he was one of the last heroic entrepreneurs who insisted on presiding over all aspects of business. Westinghouse refused to specialize or delegate authority and took a lively interest not only in invention but also in finance, manufacture, and marketing.

Yet Westinghouse was not simply a nineteenth century figure: He was also a visionary who vigorously shaped the business and technology of the twentieth century. He correctly perceived that as American industry expanded rapidly, it would require a better transportation network as well as new sources of power; consequently, he concentrated on improving railroad technology and introducing AC power. While a craftsman himself, he saw clearly that new technology would be continually improved through the application of science and he did not hesitate to hire college-trained engineers and scientists. Finally, like other twentieth century industrialists, Westinghouse realized that American business must serve both national and international markets, leading him to create several large, well-organized corporations with branches worldwide.

Thus, in the broadest sense, Westinghouse was a transitional figure in American business and technology. Through his personality and career, one can see how traditional nineteenth century values and practices were used to shape the modern industrial world of twentieth century America.

Bibliography

American Society of Mechanical Engineers. *George Westinghouse Commemoration.* New York: Author, 1937. Consists of papers given by leading engineers on the occasion of the ninetieth anniversary of the birth of Westinghouse. Although the papers are anecdotal, they do provide valuable details about Westinghouse's personality and accomplishments.

Chandler, Alfred D., Jr. *The Visible Hand: The Managerial Revolution in American Business.* Cambridge, Mass.: Harvard University Press, 1977. Provides a broad overview of the changes occurring in American business and technology during the period in which Westinghouse was active.

Hughes, Thomas P. *Networks of Power: Electrification in Western Society, 1880-1930.* Baltimore: Johns Hopkins University Press, 1983; London: Johns Hopkins University Press, 1993. Discusses the role of Westinghouse in developing AC for use in electrical utilities.

Leupp, Francis E. *George Westinghouse: His Life and Achievements*. London: Murray, and Boston: Little Brown, 1918. Though lively and entertaining, this biography contains many conversations made up by the author. While accurate for general information, it should be used cautiously.

Passer, Harold C. *The Electrical Manufacturers: 1875-1900*. Cambridge, Mass.: Harvard University Press, 1953. Includes a full history of the Westinghouse Electric Company and its efforts to develop and promote AC.

Prout, Henry G. *A Life of George Westinghouse*. New York: Harper, 1921; London: Benn, 1922. Commissioned by the American Society of Mechanical Engineers, this biography includes detailed descriptions of Westinghouse's inventions as well as a list of his patents. A business associate of Westinghouse, Prout provides insight into Westinghouse as financier and manufacturer. This is generally regarded as the standard biography of Westinghouse.

Usselman, Steven W. "Air Brakes for Freight Trains: Technological Innovation in the American Railroad Industry, 1869-1900." *Business History Review* 58 (Spring 1984): 30-50. The best single source available on how Westinghouse developed and promoted the air brake.

————. "From Novelty to Utility: George Westinghouse and the Business of Innovation during the Age of Edison." *Business History Review* 66, no. 2 (Summer 1992). Compares Westinghouse and Thomas Edison with respect to their priorities in the areas of business and innovation.

Wicks, Frank. "How George Westinghouse Changed the World." *Mechanical Engineering* 118, no. 10 (October, 1996). Profile of Westinghouse, including personal background, inventions, railroad modernization, and anecdotes.

W. Bernard Carlson

JAMES McNEILL WHISTLER

Born: July 10, 1834; Lowell, Massachusetts
Died: July 17, 1903; London, England
Areas of Achievement: Arts and letters
Contribution: Aside from producing one of the most popular and best-known paintings in the world, Whistler developed an artistic style and ideas about the role of the artist which were to influence art and art criticism throughout the world.

Early Life

In 1878, at the libel trial in London in which James Abbott McNeill Whistler sued the famous art critic John Ruskin, Whistler thought to add glamour to his case by claiming that he had been born in St. Petersburg, Russia; on other occasions, because of family ties to the American South, he claimed Baltimore as his birthplace. He was, however mundane it might have seemed to him, actually born in Lowell, Massachusetts, the son of George Whistler, a respected and successful engineer of Irish-English descent who had been educated at West Point and who built railroads in the United States and in Russia for the czar. Anna McNeill, George Whistler's second wife (his first died young), a member of a North Carolina family of Scottish lineage, was James's mother and was to be the subject of his famous painting.

It was while living in Russia with his family that young Whistler first showed artistic leanings; he took drawing lessons at the Imperial Academy of Science. The Whistler family, at the height of its prosperity, traveled well and extensively in Europe. For extended periods, most of the family lived in England, while George Whistler was occupied with his work in Russia, where he died in his late forties.

Whistler's family, now somewhat limited financially, returned to the United States, and Whistler, by then a young man, entered the United States Military Academy at West Point in 1851. A charming but willful and mischievous teenager, he made little attempt to conform to the disciplines of the academy and, in 1854, he was asked to leave. Through family connections, he was hired as a draftsman by the Winans Locomotive Works in Baltimore, but he was too eccentric in his working habits and had to withdraw. He moved on to a job with the United States Coast Survey in Washington, where he again fell afoul of the system and

was forced to resign. He did, however, gain valuable experience in etching at the survey office, and it was to be one of his strengths as an artist.

At the age of twenty-one, Whistler left the United States to study in Paris. He was supposed to study at the respectable, conservative École des Beaux-Arts, but he became a student in the more informal *atelier* system, in which pupils worked with individual artists. He entered the raucous, improper world of the Parisian art students with enthusiasm and was soon a close friend of Gustave Courbet and Henri Fantin-Latour. He met and associated with all the young painters who were to become the leaders in the Impressionist movement.

In 1859, having finished his education as a student artist, Whistler moved from Paris to London, where he was determined to make his career and where he was to live, save for occasional absences, for the rest his life.

Life's Work

In 1890, Whistler published a collection of his letters under the title *The Gentle Art of Making Enemies.* The title was no exaggeration, since his career had been one battle after another. England always had a difficult time with this upstart from the United States.

The English public had an established and confident taste for narrative pictures, usually of a very high technical quality, when Whistler arrived in London. From the beginning, Whistler, influenced partly by his French experience and partly by his own natural gifts and inclinations, refused to paint moral tales of middle-class life or to follow the Pre-Raphaelites in creating an idealized medieval dreamworld, and he was not reluctant to make fun of painters who did so. Witty, acerbic, always saucily inclined to quarrel, he was not above punching his enemies. He fought in the streets, in the courts, and always in the newspapers and magazines, and he became one of the great "characters" of the world of English arts and letters.

What made him even more difficult to deal with, if one tried to do so, was his undependability as an artist, his maddening slowness, his too-common failure to deliver work, often long-since paid for. Smartly, if eccentrically, dressed, a neat slip of a man sporting a monocle, known for his series of mistresses and for never getting anything done, he had a very difficult time financially. Influential figures such as Gabriel Rossetti befriended him, but he gained more enemies than friends.

If his personality was wildly improper, his art was quite the contrary. His work was low-keyed, lacking in definition, often unrealistically flat, and he tended to use few colors. In France, he might have had an easier time of it as he might have been seen in the context of his associations with Courbet, Hilaire Degas, and Édouard Manet. He was not, however, really an Impressionist, since he was interested in rendering not reality but the artist's reaction to it. His paintings were, as the critics complained, meaningless, and Whistler happily agreed with that comment. The French influence and his longtime interest in Japanese and Chinese art fused with his own talent for seeing a work of art as independent of its source, as an arrangement of mass and color. He was trying to achieve pattern, tonality, feeling. His landscapes, often night scenes, puzzled the British, who could not accept the lack of detail, the muzzy, muted colors, the seemingly sloppy draftsmanship. Even his portraits looked fuzzy, and he often quarreled with his sitters since he would not give them an idealized mirror image. What things really looked like, or ideally looked like, was irrelevant to Whistler.

His famous work, which everyone knows as "Whistler's Mother," was, in fact, called *Arrangement in Grey and Black, No. 1: The Artist's Mother*. As conservative as it seems, this painting was originally rejected by the Royal Academy in 1872, was accepted only by special arrangement, and was roundly derided by the critics. His titles for his paintings, which he called "nocturnes" and "arrangements" and numbered according to color groups, were original and confusing. When he did something well, he would do it in irritating ways. His famous *Harmony in Blue and Gold: The Peacock Room* (1867-1877) was a masterpiece of interior decoration, but Whistler produced it in a way which permanently alienated his patron. Savaged unfairly by Ruskin in print, Whistler sued the critic and won, but the jury would give him only a farthing, and the case forced him into bankruptcy.

The Ruskin case did produce one of Whistler's most famous comments upon the plight of the artist. He admitted that the painting commented upon by Ruskin had taken only a short time to paint. The lawyer questioning him suggested that the price which he had asked for it was high, given the time it took to produce. Whistler's rejoinder was to be-come famous: "I ask it for the knowledge of a lifetime."

This capacity to talk wittily about his art was to become an important part of Whistler's reputation, and he was to defend himself and his ideas of art and the artists in print as well. His pamphlet *Whistler v. Ruskin: Art and Art Critics* (1878), based in part on his experiences in the Ruskin trial, was a great success, and during the 1880's, still very much an outsider and still a magnet for financial and legal trouble, he gradually became accepted by the British intelligentsia. In 1881, the famous painting of his mother was shown in Philadelphia and New York, although no major gallery in the United States or Europe owned a Whistler.

A following of young British artists started to develop around the painter in the mid-1880's, and he often spoke in public in London with some considerable success. Even the students at the Royal Academy invited him to address them, and he was asked to speak at Cambridge University.

In 1891, the tide turned. The Corporation of the City of Glasgow purchased his very fine portrait of the Scottish man of letters Thomas Carlyle, and more telling, the Louvre purchased his *Arrangement in Grey and Black, No. 1*, and France made him an Officer of the Legion of Honor. For the first time in his life, there was a sustained demand for his work at prices which allowed him to settle his debts and buy a home in Paris. In Great Britain, there was criticism of the fact that Whistler, that most estimable representative of British contemporary art, was not represented in the major galleries; art society in the United States also started to take him seriously.

Charles Freer, the Detroit locomotive manufacturer, became a friend of Whistler in the 1890's and used his considerable fortune to collect slowly the works which were to be the basis for the finest collection of Whistler in the world, housed in an elegant gallery on the Mall in Washington and bearing Freer's name, but holding the treasures of Whistler's vision.

Financially secure, his reputation and popularity as a painter and as a spokesman for the artist growing, Whistler continued to work sporadically through the decade, moving back and forth between London and Paris. He was no less inclined to quarrel than he had been when everyone rejected him in his youth, and he was continually in and out of the law courts and the gossip columns. For a time, he was involved, if only slightly, in an art

school in Paris, and he never fully gave up working and sometimes finishing small portraits (sold at very high prices). To the end, his charm and wit were in nervous balance with his zest for vindictive confrontation. He died in his studio in London one afternoon, in 1903, while waiting for Charles Freer to take him for a drive.

Summary

It is, perhaps, best to consider Whistler as a cultural phenomenon whose work and influence went far beyond his skills as a painter. His fierce independence and his determination to do things his way in the face of sometimes damaging artistic, financial, and personal consequences may be seen as an example of the American abroad, a man refusing to be either patronized or instructed by his European betters. It is, however, unwise to put too much emphasis upon his American personality, since he himself was so little interested in his native country and spent most of his life fighting his way into the European artistic community. He was proud of his American birth, his Southern family connections, and even his West Point education (he seemed conveniently to forget that he had been virtually expelled), but his world was European.

In that world, however, he showed eventually that it was unwise to take him for granted intellectually or artistically as the poor American cousin, and he made major contributions to the way in which the public was to look at art, producing in his own work and in his public statements ideas which were to undermine the proposition that art's function was merely to mirror reality. He was, also, an important influence on the idea of "art for art's sake," and he showed that the artist had rights as well as obligations and was ready to fight for them.

Whistler's interest in and use of French and Oriental influences in his own work were to lead many young English artists out of the insularity of the British tradition in art. In literature, the Symbolist poets, many of whom he knew personally, were influenced by him, and aspects of his style can be seen later in the work of T. S. Eliot and Ezra Pound, both American poets who chose to live and work in Europe in much the same way that Whistler had done. His use of musical terms as titles for his paintings came full circle in Claude Debussy, who admired him and whose style was in some ways a musical version of what Whistler was trying to achieve pictorially. The idea of "tone," the attempt to express the deepest, most delicate emotional ambiguities, a concept which became so common in art at the end of the nineteenth century, owed much to Whistler's quiet, dimly glowing paintings and to his combative declamations in the salons and law courts of London.

George du Maurier, an early friend, tried to include him as a character in the novel *Trilby* (1894), and Whistler enlisted the courts to get him out, but he lives on in novels by Henry James and Marcel Proust, who hardly had to fictionalize him.

Bibliography

Fleming, Gordon. *The Young Whistler, 1834-66.* London and Boston: Allen and Unwin, 1978. An exploration of the early years, with considerable use of French materials, letters, critiques, and journals. Whistler was a proficient linguist, and his letters to and from French friends, including Fantin-Latour, are used extensively.

Gregory, Horace. *The World of James McNeill Whistler.* New York: Nelson, 1959; London: Hutchinson, 1961. Whistler is best understood in the labyrinthine context of his artistic and social connections. Gregory modestly eschews any attempt to be definitive, but he makes some sensitive points of connection between Whistler's art and his peculiar personality. A lively account.

MacDonald, Margaret F. *James McNeill Whistler: Watercolors, Pastels, and Drawings: A Catalogue Raisonne.* New Haven, Conn.: Yale University Press, 1995. This catalog of Whistler's pastels, watercolors, and drawings includes 1,400 black-and-white and 200 color illustrations.

Merrill, Linda. *The Peacock Room: A Cultural Biography.* New Haven, Conn.: Yale University Press, 1998. Merrill examines the celebrated, yet controversial Peacock Room, decorated for London shipowner Frederick Leyland by Whistler between 1876 to 1877. Includes a history of the room, descriptions of the porcelain collection housed there, accounts of parties held there, and 150 black-and-white and 105 color illustrations.

Pennell, E. R., and Joseph Pennell. *The Life of James McNeill Whistler.* London: Heinemann, and Philadelphia: Lippincott, 1908. The monumental, two-volume biography by the husband and wife who became camp followers of Whistler in his last years. Essential reading, but highly prejudiced in Whistler's favor. Good selection of pictures in monochrome.

Pocock, Tom. *Chelsea Reach: The Brutal Friendship of Whistler and Walter Greaves*. London: Routledge, 1969. Whistler's most bizarre disciples were the Greaves brothers, who followed him about and could do startling imitations of his work. An example of the kind of black comedy Whistler was inclined to encourage and then regret.

Spalding, Frances. *Whistler*. Oxford: Phaidon Press, and New York: Dutton, 1979. A short, handy study with good photographs and excellent reproductions.

Sutton, Denys. *Nocturne: The Art of James McNeill Whistler*. London: Country Life, 1963; Philadelphia: Lippincott, 1964. A good study of the development of his art, placing it and his ideas in the contemporary world.

Weintraub, Stanley. *Whistler: A Biography*. London: Collins, and New York: Weybright and Talley, 1974. A graceful and entertaining retelling of the lunatic life of Whistler; as good as any novel.

Charles H. Pullen

WALT WHITMAN

Born: May 31, 1819; West Hills, New York
Died: March 26, 1892; Camden, New Jersey
Area of Achievement: Literature
Contribution: The first real poet of American English, Whitman created a language to express the spirit of American democracy and used that language to shape a vision of a new continent that still fires the American imagination.

Early Life

Walt Whitman was born in a two-story, cedar-shingled house that his father had built about thirty miles east of New York City on Long Island. He was born in the same year as his fellow writers Herman Melville and James Russell Lowell and was also the exact contemporary of Queen Victoria of England. His father's family, as Whitman recalled them, "appear to have been always of democratic and heretical tendencies." Walter Whitman, Sr., had been born on the day of the storming of the Bastille in 1789 and trained his sons as radical democrats, identifying with independent farmers and laborers and regarding financiers and power brokers as "the enemy." His mother's family were of Dutch ancestry, inclined to the freethinking tradition of the Quakers, and Whitman ascribed his creative impulses to her non-bookish sense of practical learning. He felt that her combination of the "practical and the materialistic" with the "transcendental and cloudy" might be the source of his own contradictory instincts.

The family moved from the rural regions of Long Island to Brooklyn in 1823. Already a bustling market town, Brooklyn was the third largest city in the United States by 1855 with a population of 200,000. The elder Whitman hoped to make a fortune in real estate, but he lacked the shrewdness to prosper in a speculative arena, and the Whitman family moved about once every year for the next decade. A mediocre student but an avid reader, young Walt went to work for the *Long Island Patriot*, a local newspaper, at the age of twelve in 1831. He became a journeyman printer, but a fire in the printing district forced him out of work, and a quarrel with his father ended the possibility of any work on the family farm. He took a series of jobs as a country schoolteacher between 1836 and 1841, but only a few of his quarter-year appointments were renewed. He established a warm relationship with many of his students, but his explo-

sive temper and stubborn insistence on the validity of his ideas led to frequent clashes with the school authorities. Whitman moved back to New York City in 1841, but continued arguments with his father impelled him to take lodgings in a boardinghouse in lower Manhattan. Between school assignments, he had published his earliest known writing, an item entitled "Effects of Lightning," in the August 8, 1838, issue of the *Long Island Democrat*. The rather rough and motley group of people he met in the boardinghouse district became the models for some of the characters in his first novel, *Franklin Evans* (1842), the story of a farmer's apprentice from Long Island who comes to New York. Whitman also published about a dozen short stories—mostly in the manner of Edgar Allan Poe or Nathaniel Hawthorne—between 1841 and 1845, and while the stories are derivative and very sentimental, his work during this time convinced him that he could be a writer.

While he continued to maintain close contact with his family, often acting as a third "parent" with his younger siblings, Whitman was now an independent young man making his way in the world. He stood nearly six feet tall, weighed about 180 pounds, had large hands and feet, a broad nose, full lips, and in later life, a bristling beard. He walked with a confident stride, could leap easily aboard a moving Broadway stage, and appeared at ease with the rugged, masculine presence he projected. As his close friend John Burroughs observed, however, there was also "a curious feminine undertone in him which revealed itself in the quality of his voice, the delicate texture of his skin, the gentleness of his touch and ways." By 1848, he had worked for ten different newspapers, most prominently as the editor of the Brooklyn *Daily Eagle*, and was an active citizen in Brooklyn political affairs, even writing lumbering patriotic verse when the occasion required it. His involvement with the Democratic Party in Brooklyn drew him into the rapidly developing debate over slavery in the 1840's, and his stand on the explosive issue of Free Soil led to his firing in 1848 from the *Daily Eagle*. Through his contacts in the field of journalism, he was able to work briefly as an editor of the New Orleans *Crescent* while that paper was reorganized in the early part of 1848, his first trip to the South. Upon his return to New York, he rented a storefront in lower Manhattan with the plan of set-

ting himself up as a kind of lecturer and "universal authority," a "Professor of Things in General" like the hero of Thomas Carlyle's *Sartor Resartus* (1833-1834), a book he found fascinating. Apparently, there was no public demand for his wisdom.

During the late 1840's and the early 1850's, he continued with real estate work, renovating buildings with his family, including considerable carpentry work. He enjoyed the swirl of intellectual life in New York, counting young painters, actors, and writers among his friends. He attended numerous lectures (including Ralph Waldo Emerson's famous address "The Poet"), kept up with original theories in the sciences (phrenology, hydrology), studied archaeology as an interested layman and would-be Egyptologist, debated new philosophical constructs (Fourierism), and listened enthusiastically to music of all sorts, from American folk music to the celebrated "Swedish Nightingale" Jenny Lind. He recalled these times as "days of preparation; the gathering of the forces"; the preparation he referred to was for the creation and publication of his masterpiece, *Leaves of Grass* (1855-1892).

Life's Work

Whitman claimed that he had begun "elaborating the plan of my poems . . . experimenting much, writing and abandoning much" in 1847, but his assertion that he began "definitely" writing the poems down in 1854 seems closest to the actual facts. The first "notes" that Whitman made for the poems usually consisted of flashes of illumination, revelations of the self and its relationship to the world. He had no guide for the form of these poems, regarding most of the prominent poets of his day as negative examples. Henry Wadsworth Longfellow's enormously popular *The Song of Hiawatha* (1855) he thought had, at best, a "pleasing ripply" effect. Whitman invented a style which was appropriate for his subject, demonstrating that form is an extension of content or an expression of content, and proving the wisdom of Henry David Thoreau's contention that American poetry is nothing but "healthy speech."

On May 15, 1855, just before his thirty-sixth birthday, Whitman registered the title *Leaves of Grass* and brought the copyright notice to the printing office of Thomas and Joseph Rome. He had been working steadily there throughout that spring, continuing to write and revise while he helped to set type and read the proofs. He not only

wrote but also designed, produced, published, and eventually promoted the book which, as Justin Kaplan says, "for nearly forty years [he] made the center of his life, the instrument of health and survival itself." There were 795 copies of the first edition, and two hundred were bound in cloth at a unit cost to Whitman of thirty-two cents, while the remaining copies were given a cheaper binding. The manuscript remained in the Rome brothers' print shop until it was burned accidently in 1858 "to kindle the fire" as Whitman remarked laconically. On the frontispiece, there was a portrait, uncaptioned, of a bearded man, hand on his hip, hat rakishly askew. Ten pages of prose were followed by eighty-three of poetry, and on page 29, the anonymous author revealed himself:

Walt Whitman, an American, one of the roughs,
   a kosmos,
Disorderly, fleshy and sensual . . . eating and drinking
   and breeding,
No sentimentalist . . . no stander above men and
   women or
apart from them . . . no more modest than immodest.

Whitman was a tireless champion of his own work, but of all of his acts of self-promotion, his most successful and in some senses his most audacious was his gift of *Leaves of Grass* to Ralph Waldo Emerson, the philosopher-poet king of American letters. Emerson replied from Concord, Massachusetts, on July 21, 1855, in a five-page tribute, in which he expressed his enthusiasm for the poetry and saluted the poet "at the beginning of a great career." Many other reviews were less generous, some extremely negative ("a mass of stupid filth"), but praise from people such as Henry David Thoreau, Charles Eliot Norton, and others was sufficient encouragement for the poet. Whitman was already preparing the second edition in 1855 and 1856, composing the first draft of his great poem "Crossing Brooklyn Ferry" (then known as "Sundown Poem") during this time. He continued to supply friendly journals with information about and anonymous reviews of his work, and supplemented his income by writing and selling articles to various newspapers. At Christmas, 1859, he published "Out of the Cradle Endlessly Rocking," then titled "A Child's Reminiscence," which was one of the new poems included in the 1860 edition.

Perhaps because of Emerson's compliments, a Boston publisher, Thayer and Eldridge, offered to produce the second edition of *Leaves of Grass*, and although Emerson cautioned Whitman about some of the sexually suggestive poetry (arguing that unimpeded sales of the book depended on public acceptance), Whitman felt that the book would have to stand as it was. "I have not lived to regret my Emerson no," he stated. He did discard the prose preface, retitled some of the poems, revised several and added 124 new ones, producing a thick volume of 456 pages, bound in orange cloth and stamped with symbolic devices. Now, he thought that *Leaves of Grass* was being "really published" for the first time. This time, the frontispiece was a portrait by a friend which presented Whitman wearing a coat, wide collar, expansive tie, and a grave, intent expression. The book's reception was important to Whitman, but events of a larger magnitude captured his attention.

In February, 1861, Whitman saw Abraham Lincoln, already a protoheroic image for him of the New Man of the West, when the president traveled up Broadway to stay at the Astor. In April of that year, 250,000 people filled the streets to welcome Major Robert Anderson, a soldier at Fort Sumter. The nation was moving toward the War Between the States, and Whitman's admiration for Lincoln and his cause, plus his brother George's rather impetuous enlistment, tempted the poet himself momentarily to consider military service. But at forty-two, he recognized that he had neither the qualifications nor the disposition to be a soldier. Instead, his instinct for involvement in the great anguish of the Union, and his instinct to offer comfort to young men suffering, led him to New York hospitals, where he worked as a nurse (eighty percent of the nurses were male). When his brother was wounded, he traveled to Virginia and shared mess and tent with George for a week. He was trying to earn a living by publishing occasional articles at this time, but when he returned to Washington, he wrote to Emerson that he had ended his "New York stagnation," and he began to try to find a government job. He spent the war years tending the wounded and casually seeking a political appointment, and in 1864, after a lifetime of exceptional health, he suffered a collapse as a result of stress, hypertension, and depression. He was never quite as vigorous again. He succeeded in obtaining a job as a government clerk in 1865, but after Lincoln's death, the new administration swept his friends out and he lost his job.

In October, 1865, Whitman published *Drum Taps*, including the poem "O Captain! My Cap-

tain!" his most successful poem during his lifetime, and the superb "When Lilacs Last in the Dooryard Bloom'd," the one poem not included in an anthology celebrating Lincoln a few years later. He was rehired by the government to work in the attorney general's office in 1866 and saw his good friend William O'Connor offer strong support for his work in a sixty-page pamphlet, *The Good Gray Poet* (1866), and in a very positive review in *The New York Times*. His work was beginning to develop a favorable reputation in Europe that surpassed the public estimate of his accomplishments in the United States. As a kind of rejoinder to his old intellectual antagonist Carlyle, he published *Democratic Vistas* in 1871, agreeing with Carlyle's pessimistic view of the "present" but envisioning a positive future for his country. As a kind of poetic counterpart to *Democratic Vistas*, he also completed *Passage to India* (1871), in which he described materialistic concerns giving way to spiritual enlightenment.

Whitman suffered a stroke in January, 1873. His mother died in May of that year, a severe blow, and he was discharged from his government job in July. Another stroke occurred in February, 1875, but it did not keep Whitman from his enthusiastic plans for a centennial edition of *Leaves of Grass*, as well as readings and essays commemorating the event. His recollections of his wartime experiences were published in *Specimen Days and Collect* in 1882 and 1883, which also contained his thoughts on the natural world. In 1884, Whitman bought a house on Mickle Street in Camden, New Jersey, and slept under his own roof for the first time in his life. He lived there for eight years, remaining true to the emblem on his writing table, "Make the Works," through that time. In January, 1892, only two months before his death, he had prepared an announcement for what has become known as the "Death-Bed" edition of *Leaves of Grass*, and in his last years, he became, in the words of Allen Ginsberg, "lonely old courage teacher" to his friends and admirers.

Summary

According to Justin Kaplan, *Leaves of Grass* contained "the most brilliant and original poetry yet written in the New World, at once the fulfillment of American literary romanticism and the beginnings of American literary modernism." As much as he contributed to American literature, however, Whitman's contributions to American cultural life were equally great. At a time when the arts in the United States were still held in a kind of patronizing thrall by European antecedents, Whitman claimed equality for American experience and demonstrated the dominion of singularly American creation. He liberated poetry from its narrow British inclination toward narrative and ode and closed the gap between poetry and its audience.

Similarly, he resisted the tyranny of fashion by his insistence on the beauty of ordinary citizens of the republic and gave Americans a sense of the finest aspects of their own character through his definitive admiration for the open, easy, accepting nature of American life and social commerce. He celebrated the individual, saw the strength of the singular amid the surging crowds of America's cities, and at the same time, caught the spirit of America's pride in its growing industrial and technological might.

He was reared a quasi-Quaker and followed no standard doctrine or specified religion, but his poetry is based on the best precepts of Christianity—a sympathy whose scope is universal and inclusive, stemming from a predisposition to love and understand. Nevertheless, he was also a kind of pagan, a lover of many gods, ecumenical and free of prejudice and bigotry in his writings, a feature all the more impressive for his personal struggle to overcome some of the more ingrained cultural assumptions of his day.

When the bridge near Camden was named for him, objections from self-designated "Christians" and "Patriots" that Whitman's books were not properly moral echoed the criticism of his own time. His unabashed expressions of erotic ardor, especially the images of love emphasizing handsome young men, confounded the noxious Puritan strain still virulent in American life, but his sense of love, like his sense of religion, was not limited by any sectarian preference. Rather, his emphasis on social liberty, individual freedom, and artistic integrity, culminating in his archetypal image of the American nation always on the entrance of an open road, stands as a reminder of American strength as a country. As Guy Davenport says, Whitman has been woven into Americans' myth of themselves as their "greatest invention in literature" and as their "lyric voice." As his life and time fade into the glories of a heroic past, his poetry remains as an emblem of his country's beautiful innocence at the dawn of its creation.

Bibliography

Allen, Gay Wilson. *The Solitary Singer: A Critical Biography of Walt Whitman*. New York: Grove Press, and London: Calder, 1967. A good critical biography, the first one to connect the poet's life to his work. Comprehensive, if not exceptionally penetrating, it provides a sound overview of Whitman's life and his range as a poet.

Brasher, Thomas L. *Whitman as Editor of the Brooklyn "Daily Eagle."* Detroit, Mich.: Wayne State University Press, 1970. A thorough account of Whitman's work as a journalist, connecting his newspaper work to the social and political conditions of New York City and the country at large.

Davenport, Guy. "Whitman." In *The Geography of the Imagination*, edited by Guy Davenport. Berkeley, Calif.: North Point Press, 1981; London: Picador, 1984. An exceptionally imaginative and unusually empathetic essay which captures the sensibility of the poet and sets it amid the cultural context of Whitman's times.

Erkkila, Betsy and Jay Grossman. *Breaking Bounds: Whitman and American Cultural Studies*. New York: Oxford University Press, 1996. A collection of essays from cultural critics in literature; gay/lesbian studies; American, European, and Latin American studies; and art history. Provides original thought on Whitman and his central place in cultural studies.

Folsom, Ed. *Walt Whitman's Native Representations*. Cambridge and New York: Cambridge University Press, 1994. Folsom looks at four areas of American culture that gave Whitman material for his writings: the destruction of American Indian culture, baseball, photography, and dictionaries.

Kaplan, Justin. *Walt Whitman: A Life*. New York: Simon and Schuster, 1980. An excellent biography, combining solid historic research with perceptive, revealing commentary, this is undoubtedly the definitive biography in the twentieth century. A Pulitzer Prize and National Book Award recipient, crucial for an understanding of Whitman's life and art.

Miller, James E., Jr., ed. *Walt Whitman's "Song of Myself": Origin, Growth, Meaning*. New York: Dodd, Mead, 1964. Detailed, competently academic interpretation of *Song of Myself*, demonstrating Whitman's interest in the development of the mystical tradition.

Price, Kenneth M., ed. *Walt Whitman: The Contemporary Reviews*. Cambridge and New York: Cambridge University Press, 1996. A collection of contemporary commentary on Whitman's work, this volume includes reviews by Henry James, Oscar Wilde, and Whitman himself, writing anonymously.

Traubel, Horace. *With Walt Whitman in Camden*. Vol. 1. London: Gay and Bird, and Boston: Small, Maynard, 1906.

———. *With Walt Whitman in Camden*. Vol. 2. New York: Appleton, 1908.

———. *With Walt Whitman in Camden*. Vol. 3. New York: Kennerly, 1914.

———. *With Walt Whitman in Camden*. Vol. 4. Philadelphia: University of Pennsylvania Press, 1953.

———. *With Walt Whitman in Camden*. Vol. 5. Carbondale: Southern Illinois University Press, 1964. An account in five volumes (each published separately by a different company) by a close friend and companion of the poet's last years.

Whitman, Walt. *The Correspondence*. Edited by Edwin Haviland Miller. 6 vols. New York: New York University Press, 1961-1977. All the letters Whitman wrote that are available, plus solid scholarship which sets the context and explains the situation of their writing.

Zweig, Paul. *Walt Whitman: The Making of the Poet*. New York: Basic Books, 1984; London: Viking Press, 1985. Thoroughly researched and quite knowledgeable coverage of the period in Whitman's life between his employment with the Brooklyn *Daily Eagle* and the first publication of *Leaves of Grass*. An incisive tracing of the genesis of the poem.

Leon Lewis

JOHN GREENLEAF WHITTIER

Born: December 17, 1807; Haverhill, Massachusetts

Died: September 7, 1892; Hampton Falls, New Hampshire

Area of Achievement: Literature

Contribution: Over a career spanning more than sixty years, Whittier produced a large body of poetry that was not only extremely popular in its own day but also reflected with remarkable clarity and consistency some of the cultural and social attitudes of nineteenth century America.

Early Life

The record of John Greenleaf Whittier's early life is almost a paradigm of the American myth about the country boy who, through talent and diligence, comes to take his place among the leaders of his generation. The second of four children born to John and Abigail Whittier, John Greenleaf was reared on the family farm in northern Massachusetts. A secluded, lonely tract surrounded by low, rolling hills and forests, the farm sat amid the fertile Merrimack Valley, where the young poet spent his youth helping his father, uncle, and younger brother work the land.

Farm life had its moments of quiet, peaceful beauty, and, as the son of devout Quakers, young Whittier came to appreciate the emotional and religious security instilled by his rural surroundings. By fifteen, he was almost six feet tall and slender with dark, piercing eyes. A quiet boy, he enjoyed reading beside the kitchen fireplace, even dabbling in verses of his own. Besides the Bible, his favorite author was Robert Burns, the Scottish balladeer of the late eighteenth century.

The influence of Burns on Whittier's poetic taste and technique was to be indelible, from Whittier's early narrative and legendary poems of New England folklore to the later poetic reminiscences of his mature years. He later recalled, in numerous letters and essays, those early years on the farm when a Yankee peddler would arrive with dry goods for the family and a tale or two for the future poet.

In 1826, at the age of nineteen, Whittier published his first poem. "The Exile's Departure" appeared in *The Newberryport Free Press.* Generally regarded as a bad poem, it was Whittier's first venture into the two worlds that were to occupy him for most of his creative life: politics and poetry.

The editor of *The Free Press* was William Lloyd Garrison, who was already establishing himself as an early opponent of slavery. Garrison recognized Whittier's literary talent and, in 1828, invited the young man to Boston, Massachusetts, to write for *The American Manufacturer.* These early efforts were mostly political editorials addressed to the laboring man and his fight for fair working conditions.

Over the next two years, Whittier produced a significant body of work—political editorials, book reviews, poems, sketches—and was gaining a reputation as an honest, fearless journalist. Whittier's Quaker heritage, in fact, played a crucial role in his development as a writer. Well liked, gentle, and dedicated, he was a lifelong pacifist and a conscientious supporter of social justice. By the early 1830's, the rumblings of the slavery issue were already being felt. Though he returned to the farm in 1829 and remained there to take care of the family after the death of his father in 1830, Whittier continued to write and work. His health, always brittle, broke down from the strain of overwork—he suffered continually from migraine headaches—but by 1832 he was writing regularly and had decided that politics were to be his serious calling, having concluded that political activity was the way to achieve moral and social reform.

Life's Work

Though Whittier's first book, *Legends of New-England,* was published in 1831, it was merely a hodgepodge of trite verse and light prose that added little to his reputation. Throughout the 1830's, Whittier's main focus was on the growing national concern with the issue of slavery. As early as 1833, he produced one of the earliest manifestos on the cause of abolition. *Justice and Expediency,* a prose pamphlet, took the nation by storm, and Whittier became more famous as a propagandist in the cause of antislavery than as a poet. In December, 1833, he was elected to serve as a delegate to the National Anti-Slavery Convention in Philadelphia, Pennsylvania, a position that eventually led to his election to the Massachusetts legislature in 1835.

Amid his political life as a propagandist and legislator, he continued to produce poetry in support of his political ideals. The mid-1830's saw such antislavery poems as "Toussaint L'Ouverture," a brief account of a black revolutionary in Haiti who suffered treachery by Napoleon Bonaparte and died in chains. "The Slave Ships" of 1834 commemorated the drowning of dozens of African slaves who were thrown overboard from a French ship during an outbreak of contagion. "The Farewell of a Virginia Slave Mother" appeared in 1838 and anticipated, in some of its melodramatic images, the famous passages from Harriet Beecher Stowe's *Uncle Tom's Cabin* (1851).

The 1840's literally signalled a new era for Whittier. By faith (a Quaker), if not by disposition, he had been a zealous reformer and an active intellectual in the abolitionist cause, but with the growing "gentrification" of the country—a burgeoning middle class and a more literate public seeking "polite" literature—Whittier became more interested in celebrating the local and regional beauties of his own New England. However, he still wrote poems and essays in support of the antislavery movement. "Massachusetts to Virginia" (1843), for example, was a rebuke to "the Old Dominion" for coercing the state of Massachusetts to extradite an escaped slave. "The Christian Slave" of the same year was an angry denouncement of the hypocrisy involved in selling a slave who was considered more valuable for being a Christian. Alongside these indictments, whose bitter tone clearly shows the moral outrage of the poet, Whittier produced dozens of quiet, sunny poems of New England places, scenes, and characters. *Lays of My Home and Other Poems* appeared in 1843. A collection of ballads, New England legends, and nature poems, the book included the kind of work that was to establish Whittier as a major poet of his generation. "The Merrimack" was a reminiscence of the river that ran by his boyhood farm. "The Bridal of Pennacock" retold the American Indian legend about the fidelity of a wife, and "The New Wife and the Old" was a "Yankee Faust" tale that Whittier remembered being told as a boy.

He continued to earn a living as an editor and major contributor to a number of newspapers and magazines, most notably *The National Era*, to which he contributed more than one hundred poems and hundreds of essays between 1847 and the late 1850's. This was a most prolific period in Whittier's career, during which many of his best-known poems appeared. One of his most famous, "Ichabod," was published in 1850. Whittier had read a speech by statesman Daniel Webster, who had called for a compromise on the slavery issue and who supported the Fugitive Slave Law, by

which escaped slaves were to be returned to their masters. Surprised and infuriated, Whittier wrote about Webster as "Ichabod," a forlorn, fallen creature who was spiritually dead because his faith and honor were gone. The poem is among his best, effectively fusing the reformer's fervid abolitionist ideals with the poet's restrained, allusive control of his material.

Another poem to catch the popular imagination was "The Barefoot Boy," which appeared in 1856. Often quoted in its day, the poem was an idyll of youth, a celebration of the country boy whose simple innocence was a source of joy to the poet, himself once a country boy. Though it echoed in sentiment some of the Romantic theories of childhood immortalized by the poet William Wordsworth, Whittier's poem was unashamedly sentimental, positive, and sunny. Its clarity and charm made it an instant success.

The founding of *The Atlantic Monthly* in 1857 opened a wider opportunity for Whittier as a poet. His reputation had already become secure with the publication of several volumes, including the so-called Blue and Gold edition of his work in the same year. Now, at age fifty, Whittier felt the financial security and creative freedom that his work as an editor and journalist had never afforded him. The years immediately before and after the Civil War saw the culmination of his achievement as a poet. In "Skipper Ireson's Ride" (1857), Whittier produced a classic American ballad about the disgrace of Captain Floyd Ireson, who abandoned his sinking vessel and was tarred and feathered by the women of Marblehead. It was a poem of wit, irony, and narrative verve. In 1860, Whittier produced *Home Ballads and Other Poems.* "Telling the Bees," one of the thirty-six poems in the collection, was a notable example of the poet's mature work. Written to commemorate the death of his sister, Mary, this quiet elegy recorded the poet's feelings through the symbol of the beehives draped in black. It was controlled, concise, and moving.

Whittier's finest work was published in 1866. *Snow-Bound: A Winter Idyl* was a long reminiscence of the poet's boyhood. In sharply pictorial details, the poem recorded the Whittier family's physical and emotional security within the house while a snow storm raged. In a series of vignettes, the poet presented the half-dozen or so members of the household, including the visiting schoolmaster, who passed the time before the fire with stories and incidents of character. The poem was notable as well for its structure. Physical details of the approaching storm and its aftermath were contrasted with the warm, peaceful life inside. The poet skillfully expressed the theme of familial love, not through bald statement, but through contrasting and precise imagery. With *Snow-Bound,* Whittier achieved national recognition. His seventieth birthday in 1877 was celebrated in New England with a festive dinner in his honor. When he died in 1892, he was one of America's most beloved poets.

Summary

John Greenleaf Whittier is an interesting poet for several reasons. He can be seen as an example of the kind of poet nineteenth century America considered important. His work was often dogmatic, trite, moralistic, even excessive; but in his use of native material such as New England history, legend, and landscape, Whittier made poetry accessible to the general reading public. Never obscure,

he thus served as the poetic spokesman of his age. His work was a kind of cultural mirror that reflected the conventional middle-class attitudes of the period.

Whittier can also be appreciated on his own terms as a genuine poet. Over a span of sixty years, he evolved from a political versifier to a disciplined, learned artist who produced a handful of American ballads, moving elegies, and sensitive, nature poems. His best work was honest and distinctively American.

Bibliography

Kribbs, Jayne K. *Critical Essays on John Greenleaf Whittier.* Boston: Hall, 1980. This is a collection of book reviews and critical assessments from Whittier's contemporaries, especially James Russell Lowell. It also includes articles by twentieth century critics and biographers.

Leary, Lewis. *John Greenleaf Whittier.* New York: Twayne, 1961. This is a good, short introduction to the poet's life and work that offers a brief review of Whittier's significant poetry in light of the poet's Quaker heritage.

Pickard, John. *John Greenleaf Whittier: An Introduction and Interpretation.* American Authors and Critics Series. New York: Holt Rinehart, 1961. Pickard provides a largely sympathetic treatment of Whittier, whose best work is examined in light of the poet's religious humanism. The book emphasizes the evolution of the poet's work from the political and mundane to the sensitive and personal.

Pickard, Samuel T. *Life and Letters of John Greenleaf Whittier.* Boston: Houghton Mifflin, 1894; London: Samson Low, 1895. This standard biography of the poet was written by his nephew. It is valuable for the contemporary accounts of the poet's life and work and presents Whittier as an honest reformer with genuine poetic gifts.

Wagenknecht, Edward. *John Greenleaf Whittier: A Portrait in Paradox.* New York: Oxford University Press, 1967. Wagenknecht concentrates on the conflicts in Whittier's life, particularly the paradox between his celibate lifestyle and his attraction to women, between his moral conscience and his quest for fame.

Edward Fiorelli

OSCAR WILDE

Born: October 16, 1854; Dublin, Ireland

Died: November 30, 1900; Paris, France

Areas of Achievement: Literature; and theater and entertainment

Contribution: Wilde's comedies, including such masterpieces as *The Importance of Being Earnest*, were the finest seen on the English stage for many years and have endured as witty testaments to his artistic credo that art is superior to life.

Early Life

Oscar Fingal O'Flahertie Wills Wilde was born in Dublin, Ireland, the second son of Sir William Wilde, a prominent surgeon, and Jane Wilde (née Elgee), a poet and Irish nationalist. He was raised in an affluent, successful, and intellectually stimulating home. From an early age, Oscar and his brother Willie were allowed to sit at the foot of the adults' dinner table and listen to the conversations of the Wildes and their guests, many of whom were prominent in Irish social and literary circles.

At ten, Oscar was sent to the Portora Royal School in Enniskillen. Physically, he was a tall and awkward boy, but he had already revealed signs of the sharp wit that would later fascinate the literary world. He was also noted for his fast reading, once claiming to have read a three-volume novel in thirty minutes. He excelled in Latin and Greek and won a scholarship to Trinity College, Dublin, which he entered in October, 1871.

At Trinity, Wilde won several academic prizes, including the Berkeley Gold Medal for Greek. Strongly influenced by his tutor, the Reverend John Mahaffy, a professor of ancient history, Wilde continued to excel at classics and won a scholarship worth ninety-five pounds per year at Magdalen College, Oxford, which he entered in October, 1874. It was at Oxford that Wilde encountered two men who were to influence his thought. The first was art critic and writer John Ruskin, who was at the time a professor of fine arts. Ruskin believed that art should have a moral component, and as Wilde worked with him on a road-building project, Wilde found the idea that art might promote the improvement of society to be an attractive one. Wilde was also exposed to a contrary, and more important, influence in the form of Walter Pater, fellow of Brasenose College. According to Pater, what mattered in life and art were not moral or social concerns, but the intense appreciation of sensual beauty, especially that produced by works of art. While under Pater's spell, Wilde took to referring to Pater's *Studies in the History of the Renaissance* (1873) as "my golden book."

Wilde flourished during his time at Oxford, living a flamboyant lifestyle and dressing as a dandy. He also excelled in academics, winning the Oxford Newdigate Prize for Poetry with "Ravenna," a poem that describes his response to his first sight of the Italian city. After receiving his bachelor of arts degree in November, 1878, Wilde went to London to pursue his career, unsure of what that career might be.

Life's Work

It did not take Wilde long to set himself up in London. He shared rooms off the Strand with his Oxford friend Frank Miles. Wilde cultivated a wide circle of acquaintances, and after his mother arrived in London, he was the chief attraction at the literary salon that she presided over at her Chelsea home. With his witty conversation, outrageous opinions, and outlandish, colorful taste in clothes, Wilde was soon the talk of London. He became the clear leader of the art-for-art's-sake school of aesthetics, a school of thought that had been introduced to England by Pater and emphasized that art need serve no utilitarian end; its mere existence as a thing of perfection and beauty was sufficient.

In 1881 Wilde published his first work, *Poems*, a collection of lyrical poems that are mainly derivative in style from poets such as John Keats, Alfred Tennyson, and Dante Gabriel Rossetti. The book quickly went through five editions but was badly reviewed by critics. However, such critical dismissal hardly made a dent in Wilde's growing celebrity, and the following year he visited the United States for a highly successful lecture tour. Upon arriving in New York on January 3, 1882, Wilde told a custom's officer, in one of most famous bons mots, "I have nothing to declare but my genius." In the course of twelve months, Wilde delivered more than eighty lectures, and he arrived back in England more sought after than ever before. He promptly spent the next three months in Paris, where he made the acquaintance of many leading literary and artistic figures, including Stéphan Mallarmé, Paul Verlaine, and Edgar Degas.

In the fall of 1883, Wilde became engaged to Constance Lloyd, the daughter of an Irish barrister, whom he had met two years earlier. They married in May of the following year and, within just over two years, gave birth to two sons, Cyril and Vyvyan. The growth of his family put Wilde under financial strain; although he was well known and celebrated, he was without a reliable income. After another lecture tour and taking on some literary journalism, he became editor of *The Woman's World* in 1887, a position he retained until 1889.

In 1888, Wilde entered the seven-year period of his greatest success, during which he published almost all the work—as novelist, short story writer, dramatist, and social and literary critic—on which his reputation rests. The first such work was *The Happy Prince and Other Tales* (1888), a collection of fairy tales that one reviewer compared to those of Hans Christian Andersen.

In 1890, the abbreviated serial version of Wilde's novel *The Picture of Dorian Gray* appeared in *Lippincott's Monthly Magazine*; it was published in book form the following year and made an immediate impact on the reading public. The story tells of a young man of great beauty who pursues a selfish, hedonistic life, apparently without any consequences. However, a mysterious portrait of him slowly changes in a way that reveals how his soul has been corrupted. When he finally decides to reform his life, he stabs the portrait in a rage; when others arrive on the scene, they find the portrait restored to one of youth and beauty, while Dorian Gray himself lies dead—old, wrinkled, and disgusting.

In 1891, Wilde also published *Intentions*, a collection of essays that expressed his ideas about the relationship between life and art; two more collections of short stories; and an essay called "The Soul of Man Under Socialism," a somewhat misleading title to a piece that is mainly about individualism and art. In addition, Wilde's play *The Duchess of Padua* was produced in New York under the title *Guido Ferranti*.

From 1892 to 1895, Wilde's career reached its zenith with London and New York productions of his witty comedies *Lady Windermere's Fan* (1892), *A Woman of No Importance* (1893), *An Ideal Husband* (1895), and his masterpiece, *The Importance of Being Earnest* (1895), which ran for eighty-six performances to popular and critical acclaim. With its brilliant wordplay (including extensive use of paradoxes and epigrams) and its farcical plot (which includes such stock devices as intercepted letters and mistaken identities), the play embodies a perfect fantasy world that has little relation to life as it is really lived. Describing his overall aim in the play, Wilde explained that he wished to treat all the trivial things of life seriously and the serious things with a studied triviality.

However, the year of Wilde's greatest success, during which three of his plays were playing simultaneously in London, was also the year of his downfall. In May, 1895, Wilde was tried and found guilty of "gross indecency," a euphemism for homosexual activity, which at the time was a criminal offense. He was sentenced to two years in prison with hard labor. The seeds of Wilde's tragic fall had been sown in 1891 when he had met Lord Alfred Douglas, a young poet with whom he formed an intimate friendship. Douglas' father, the Marquis of Queensberry, accused Wilde of homosexuality. In March, 1895, Wilde recklessly sued Queensberry for criminal libel, but he lost the case and was immediately arrested and put on trial. The trial ended with the jury unable to reach a verdict, but Wilde was retried almost immediately, and this time there was to be no reprieve.

Wilde was imprisoned under harsh conditions. Confined to his cell for twenty-three hours per day, he was at first denied all books except a Bible, a prayer book, and a hymn book. His hard labor consisted of picking oakum in his cell. Conditions improved later, and he was able to obtain more books. While in prison, Wilde wrote a confessional letter to Douglas called *De Profundis* (1905) and a collection of poetry titled *The Ballad of Reading Gaol* (1898). On his release from prison in May, 1897, Wilde emigrated to France, never to return to England. Divorced and financially ruined, he had to rely on friends for support. His health deteriorated, and he died in 1900 in the Hotel d'Alsace in Paris.

Summary

Oscar Wilde's greatest achievement was the way he used language to create what has been called a form of comedy as pure as the music of Wolfgang Amadeus Mozart. Demolishing the complacency of Victorian social, moral, and artistic assumptions with the weapons of wit, Wilde delighted in turning stuffy platitudes upside down and then turning to the audience for applause. It was a brilliant performance that ensured that during his life, Wilde would be both greatly admired and maliciously mocked. Although his enemies eventually found satisfaction in his disgrace, it is Wilde, if literary history is the judge, who has had the last laugh. This is not only because he was an important influence on a variety of twentieth century writers and literary forms—from the Symbolist dramas of William Butler Yeats to the stylish comedies of Somerset Maugham and Noël Coward, and perhaps even the absurdist plays of Eugène Ionesco and Samuel Beckett—but also because of the fact that of those artists in the 1890's who worked in the literary forms known as aestheticism and Decadence, it is Wilde who has remained enduringly popular. Indeed, in the late 1990's, as the centenary of his death approached, interest in Wilde underwent a kind of renaissance. There was an outpouring of scholarly studies, and plays such as the Off-Broadway *Gross Indecency: The Three Trials of Oscar Wilde* (1997), by Moisés Kaufman, and David Hare's *The Judas Kiss* (1997), which played in London and New York, further imprinted Wilde's name on the popular imagination.

Bibliography

Ellmann, Richard. *Oscar Wilde*. London: Hamilton, 1987; New York: Knopf, 1988. This is the definitive biography, a prodigious work of scholarship that is elegantly written and sympathetic to Wilde. Ellmann argues from circumstantial evidence that Wilde died of complications from syphilis that he picked up while at Oxford and also disputes the commonly held notion that Wilde converted to Catholicism on his deathbed.

Ericksen, Donald H. *Oscar Wilde*. Boston: Twayne, 1977. This useful, concise introduction to Wilde's life and career emphasizes the analysis of individual works and includes an annotated bibliography.

Foldy, Michael S. *The Trials of Oscar Wilde: Deviance, Morality, and Late-Victorian Society*. New Haven; Conn.: Yale University Press, 1997. By analyzing the trial testimony and press coverage, Foldy argues cogently that the prosecution of Wilde was not solely based on matters of morality but was directly linked to wider social, cultural, and political issues.

Harris, Frank. *Oscar Wilde: Including My Memories of Oscar Wilde by George Bernard Shaw*. East Lansing: Michigan State University Press, 1959. Harris was one of the few friends who remained loyal to Wilde after his downfall. His biography, although highly readable and full of interesting anecdotes, is not always reliable. Shaw's afterward is a shrewd assessment of Wilde.

Holland, Merlin. *The Wilde Album*. London: Fourth Estate, 1997; New York: Holt, 1998. This is a useful complement to the weightier biography by Ellmann. Holland, Wilde's grandson, supplements his biographical narrative with various artifacts—including photographs, press clippings, and political cartoons—that document Wilde's emergence as a media celebrity and show how Wilde consciously created his own fame. The book includes rare family photos and all twenty-eight publicity portraits made for Wilde's 1882 U.S. tour.

Pearson, Hesketh. *Oscar Wilde: His Life and Wit*. New York and London: Harper, 1946. Although superseded by the massive research and detail contained in Ellmann, this remains a full and engaging account of Wilde's life.

Bryan Aubrey

CHARLES WILKES

Born: April 3, 1798; New York, New York
Died: February 8, 1877; Washington, D.C.
Area of Achievement: Exploration
Contribution: Wilkes's determination and leadership as commander of the United States Exploring Expedition of 1838-1842 ensured the success of this major step in the emergence of the United States as a naval and scientific power.

Early Life

Born April 3, 1798, in New York City, Charles Wilkes was the youngest child of John Deponthieu Wilkes, who had immigrated to the United States from Great Britain during the Revolutionary War, and Mary Seton, whose father was her husband's business partner. Because of John D. Wilkes's success in business, the family was relatively affluent.

Wilkes's life was disrupted before his third birthday by the death of his mother. Thereafter, he was reared by various female relatives and friends, including his aunt, Elizabeth Seton (the first American saint, canonized in 1974). Subsequently educated at boarding and preparatory schools, Wilkes rejected Columbia College or a career in business for a life in the army. After three cruises on merchant ships during the years 1815-1817, Wilkes obtained his commission as a midshipman in the United States Navy in 1818.

His decision to pursue a naval career despite the objections of his father may have been an early indication of two of Wilkes's most enduring characteristics; his determination to do things his way and his self-assuredness. Once he had decided that a particular course of action was correct, he never wavered, no matter who criticized or objected. Add to this a bluntness in word and manner and a self-righteous attitude, and the result was a man in constant conflict with superiors, peers, and subordinates.

Life's Work

Wilkes served on a number of ships during the early years of his career. There were also extensive stretches of land duty and periods of leave while awaiting orders. The time during which he was not at sea was spent studying mathematics and the naval sciences: hydrography, geodesy, and astronomy. He studied with Ferdinand Hassler, the first superintendent of the United States Coast Survey, and gained experience in surveying. (During one of

these periods on land, in April, 1826, just prior to his promotion to lieutenant, Wilkes married Jane Renwick, whom he had known since childhood.) In February, 1833, he became superintendent of the Depot of Charts and Instruments (the forerunner of the Navy Hydrographic Office and the Naval Observatory). By the mid-1830's, it was clear that he was one of the leading scientific minds in the United States Navy.

It was his scientific reputation, relatively minor among civilian scientists but outstanding compared to his fellow naval officers, which led to Wilkes's orders in March, 1838, to command the United States Exploring Expedition, despite his junior rank (he was thirty-ninth of forty lieutenants). It was not Wilkes's first contact with the Expedition, which would occupy more than two decades of his life. When the Expedition was first authorized in 1828, Wilkes had volunteered for duty with it; the idea of such an expedition was shelved a year later. In 1836, it was again authorized, and Wilkes was selected to travel to Europe to purchase the neces-

sary scientific apparatus. When he returned in January, 1837, he found the Expedition in disarray and still far from ready for sailing. After rejecting subordinate positions with the Expedition, he accepted the responsibility as commander.

On August 18, 1838, the United States Exploring Expedition, usually known as the Wilkes Expedition, set sail from Norfolk, Virginia. Among its objectives were the surveying and charting of portions of the Pacific Ocean for the benefit of the American shipping industry, the establishment of good relations with the native populations of the region, and scientific observations and collecting in a number of disciplines. There were six ships, five hundred sailors, and nine civilian scientists under the command of the clean-shaven lieutenant whose hair always appeared disobedient. In a typical act of audacity, Wilkes assumed the rank of acting captain upon leaving port, despite the fact that the secretary of the navy had denied him that appointment.

The Expedition returned to New York in the summer of 1842, having circumnavigated the earth and cruised more than eighty-seven thousand miles. Only two of the original ships survived the entire cruise; two had sunk, one was sent back early, and one was sold, while another ship had been added in 1841 to replace one of the lost ships. The Expedition had explored, surveyed, charted, and mapped the Pacific Ocean basin from Oregon to Australia. Its exploration of the coast of Antarctica confirmed that the great ice mass was in fact a continent. More than four thousand zoological, fifty thousand botanical, and thousands of ethnographical specimens were brought back by the explorers. Most of these scientific specimens were eventually deposited in the Smithsonian Institution in 1858.

The first order of business, however, were courts-martial. Wilkes brought charges against a number of his junior officers, and in turn, a number were brought against him. He was found guilty on only one charge, excessive punishment of sailors, and sentenced to a public reprimand. Characteristically, in his autobiography (1979), Wilkes dismisses his court-martial as a vendetta on the part of the secretary of the navy.

With the courts-martial out of the way, Wilkes focused his energy on ensuring that the fruits of the Expedition would not be lost. In the summer of 1843, he was promoted to commander and given the responsibility for the Expedition's collections and reports. Except for survey duty in 1858, the

Expedition remained his only official concern until the outbreak of the Civil War (he was promoted to captain in 1855). He published the five-volume *Narrative of the United States Exploring Expedition* in 1844, taking credit for authorship, although in fact he functioned more as an editor. He lobbied Congress for the funding for, and oversaw the publication of, nineteen scientific reports, authoring those on meteorology and hydrography himself.

Wilkes's personal life changed during these years. In 1848, his wife, Jane, who had borne him four children, died. Six years later, he married Mary Lynch Bolton, who bore him two additional children, although one, born when Wilkes was sixty-seven, did not survive infancy.

During the Civil War, Wilkes held a number of successful commands and was promoted to commodore. There was, however, controversy during this time as well. While captain of the *San Jacinto* in November, 1861, he removed two Confederate agents from the British mail packet *Trent*. Although he was hailed as a hero by the American public and government, members of the latter changed their attitude when it was realized that Wilkes's action could precipitate a war with Great Britain. The agents were freed. A subsequent clash with Secretary of the Navy Gideon Welles led to a second court-martial of Wilkes in 1864 for disobedience of orders, a finding of guilty, and suspension from the navy.

In 1866, Wilkes was promoted to rear admiral on the retired list. He continued working for the publication of the final volumes of the Expedition reports, although Congress ceased their funding in 1873 with a number of reports unpublished. Wilkes died in his home in Washington on February 8, 1877. In 1909, his remains were placed in Arlington National Cemetery.

Summary

In the 1830's, American science was just beginning to step upon the international stage. Although scientific exploration, a common enough activity among the great European powers, had been attempted with some success by the United States Army, the United States Exploring Expedition represented an effort on a scale far larger than the republic had ever attempted. The possibility of failure was high.

Despite the odds, the Expedition succeeded. Not only did the Expedition meet its military objectives, but also its scientific achievements placed the

United States in a position of intellectual respectability. A model was provided for subsequent naval exploratory expeditions. To a very large extent, credit for that success must go to Wilkes. He was a difficult man to get along with, could not tolerate opposition or criticism, and knew far less about the world, especially science, than he thought he did. Yet, when energy, drive, and determination were needed, whether aboard ship or in the halls of Congress, Wilkes met the challenge. James Dwight Dana, the young geologist on the Expedition, thought that no other naval officer could have done better. Combining a dedication to duty with a sympathy for science, Wilkes left the world a legacy of scientific and geographical knowledge.

Bibliography

Henderson, Daniel M. *The Hidden Coasts: A Biography of Admiral Charles Wilkes.* New York: Sloane, 1953. The first full-length biography of Wilkes, this is an example of the pro-Wilkes partisan literature. It handles the scientific activities of the Wilkes Expedition very poorly and is of questionable accuracy.

Ponko, Vincent, Jr. *Ships, Seas, and Scientists: U.S. Naval Exploration and Discovery in the Nineteenth Century.* Annapolis: Naval Institute Press, 1974. Surveys the naval exploring expeditions of the antebellum period. Places the Wilkes Expedition in its larger context.

Smith, Geoffrey Sutton. "The Navy Before Darwinism: Science, Exploration, and Diplomacy in Antebellum America." *American Quarterly* 28 (1976): 41-55. Treats antebellum naval exploration as part of the diplomatic efforts of the United States to secure a commercial empire.

Stanton, William. *The Great United States Exploring Expedition of 1838-1842.* Berkeley: University of California Press, 1975. Provides an analysis of the scientific contributions of the Wilkes Expedition. Stanton argues that the Expedition gained international respect for the American scientific community.

Tyler, David B. *The Wilkes Expedition: The First United States Exploring Expedition, 1838-1842.* Philadelphia: American Philosophical Society, 1968. Concentrates on the exploring and surveying aspects of the Expedition rather than the scientific. This history focuses on the performance of Wilkes as a commander and his relationship with his officer corps and civilian scientists.

Viola, Herman J., and Carolyn Margolis, eds. *Magnificent Voyagers: The U.S. Exploring Expedition, 1838-1842.* Washington, D.C.: Smithsonian Institution Press, 1985. A collection of articles by scientists and historians. This represents the latest and most balanced account of Wilkes and his expedition.

Wilkes, Charles. *Autobiography of Rear Admiral Charles Wilkes, U.S. Navy: 1798-1877.* Edited by William James Morgan, David B. Tyler, Joye L. Leonhart, and Mary F. Loughlin. Washington, D.C.: Naval History Division, 1979. A massive defense of his career, this autobiography provides unique insight into the mind of the man. Both the positive and the negative aspects of his character shine through.

Marc Rothenberg

EMMA WILLARD

Born: February 23, 1787; Berlin, Connecticut
Died: April 15, 1870; Troy, New York
Area of Achievement: Education
Contribution: A strong belief in the need for women to be properly educated influenced Willard to develop new methods of training teachers and to work for the professionalization of teaching.

Early Life

Emma Hart Willard was the ninth of the ten children her mother, née Lydia Hinsdale, bore as Samuel Hart's second wife. Her paternal forefathers included Stephen Hart and Thomas Hooker, a clergyman who left England in 1633 and founded the towns of Hartford and Farmington, Connecticut. Robert Hinsdale, a maternal forefather, settled in Dedham, Massachusetts, in 1637 and later became a founder of Deerfield, Massachusetts.

Life in the simple farmhouse where Willard was born was anything but routine. Her home was a center of intellectual curiosity that encouraged learning. Evenings were spent listening to Samuel Hart speak of the founding of the Republic, or discussing John Locke, Bishop George Berkeley, and other philosophers. Lydia Hart frequently read aloud and taught the children about Geoffrey Chaucer, John Milton, and William Shakespeare.

Willard, eager for learning and a voracious reader, taught herself geometry at the age of thirteen. At fifteen she enrolled at the Berlin Academy. Two years later, she began teaching the younger children of Berlin in the district school. When Willard taught, she made her subjects interesting, allowed recreation periods, and gave much deserved praise to her students. In 1805 she conducted classes for older boys and girls in her father's house. A year later she took charge of the Berlin Academy during the winter term. During the spring and fall of these years, she also attended classes at two private female schools in Hartford.

Her reputation as a teacher grew. She was offered a position at three schools: in Middlebury, Vermont; Westfield, Massachusetts; and Hudson, New York. Willard accepted the position as an assistant at the academy in Westfield because it was close to her parents' home. She was not, however, given full authority to direct the school. Disappointed with her limited duties, she left after only a few months, to take charge of the girls' academy in Middlebury, Vermont. A pretty blue-eyed girl with fair hair and a well-proportioned figure, she spent her free time studying science, writing poetry, and visiting friends. While in Middlebury she fell in love with Dr. John Willard, a twice-widowed physician, who had given up medical practice to accept the position of Marshal of Vermont offered by President Jefferson. They were married on August 10, 1809, when Emma was twenty-two and Dr. Willard, fifty. John Hart Willard, their only child, was born a year later.

With her husband's encouragement, Willard began to study his medical books. His nephew, John Willard, lived with them while attending Middlebury College. John freely shared his class notes and texts with Emma and patiently answered all questions as she taught herself the knowledge that formal education had denied her. This experience opened Willard's eyes to the inequities between male and female education. Never before had she fully realized that women were deprived of educational opportunities.

Dr. Willard was on the Board of Directors when the State Bank of Vermont was robbed in 1812. The board members were suspected and made to pay restitution. To aid her husband and ease his financial burdens, Willard opened the Middlebury Female Seminary in her own home during the spring of 1814. Her second goal was to create a better school than those in existence. Willard pioneered new fields of study for women. She was careful, however, also to satisfy those of conventional mind. Gradually adding mathematics, history, and modern languages to the curriculum, Willard showed that women could pursue subjects traditionally reserved for men. From the outset, she encouraged her students to consider teaching. Those interested became assistant teachers while continuing their studies. She personally conducted examinations of students and invited Middlebury College teachers to attend and witness the strength and development of the students' minds.

Willard knew she needed more teachers to teach additional subjects, but she had no money. When negotiations with Vermont officials failed to result in the establishment of a female seminary located at Burlington, she chose to seek the support of Governor DeWitt Clinton and the New York legislature for a program of state-aided schools for girls. In February, 1818, she sent Clinton a completed copy of *An Address to the Public; Particularly to the Members of the Legislature of New-York, Proposing a Plan for Improving Female Education* (1819). The *Plan* contained four sections detailing the existing inadequacies in female education, outlining both the proper facilities and the curriculum needed, and carefully listing the benefits of such an education to society. Emphasized were the facts that there would be better trained teachers for the common schools and that women would be willing to work for less pay. This last statement would come to haunt Emma. The following year, a determined Emma went to Albany to lobby for her *Plan*. Almost fearless in the face of prejudice against female education, she personally met with, and presented her proposal to, members of the New York legislature. The legislature chartered the Waterford Academy for Young Ladies and passed legislation authorizing a share of the Literary Fund to be given to female seminaries.

Life's Work

In anticipation of state funding, the seminary was relocated to Waterford, New York, where Willard could make her work more visible to the legislature. No money was allocated, however, and none was received for sixteen years. Within a short time, she received an offer of financial aid from the Common Council of Troy, New York. The Council agreed to raise four thousand dollars by means of a special tax to purchase a female academy. In September, 1821, the Troy Female Seminary opened. The city was an ideal location. Because the seminary was situated in an inland port on the Hudson, students from distant areas could easily come to the school, and its newly trained teachers could easily travel westward. At her new school, Willard continued to develop the methods she had initiated at Middlebury. Workdays of twelve to fifteen hours were not uncommon for her. To illustrate and supplement her teaching methods, she began to write the first of numerous textbooks on geography and history. A collection of her poems was also published.

The seminary was successful; within ten years it had an enrollment of more than three hundred, including more than one hundred boarding students. The school was designed to prepare students for life. Willard initiated a system of self-government with monitors and demerits. She emphasized good manners and personal appearance, not fancy dress. To make the girls feel more at home, Willard of-

fered each student a small room with a roommate. Willard held weekly talks with the girls stressing manners and behavior. She was their role model, just as the school became a model for future American boarding schools. The curriculum included classical and domestic subjects and introduced advanced science courses. Willard held public examinations of individual students at the end of each term. She gave financial aid to those students interested in teaching, providing free tuition, board, and even clothes, if needed. Repayment was to be made after graduation when the student secured a teaching position. Willard did not believe in the same education for boys and girls. She adhered to the ideology of woman's domestic role, and she discouraged any interest in politics.

As her students began careers in teaching across the United States, Willard founded the Willard Association for Mutual Improvement of Female Teachers. She kept in touch with her former students, providing news about alumnae, constantly advising them about teaching methods, and exhorting them to continue to learn new subjects throughout life.

When Dr. Willard, who had been school physician and business manager, died in 1825, Willard took full charge of the school. Thirteen years later, royalties from her numerous books made it possible for Willard to give control of the seminary to her son John and his wife, Sara Lucretia (née Hudson). Following retirement, she married Christopher Yates, an Albany physician, on September 17, 1838. The marriage was a disaster, and after nine months she left him to live in Berlin, Connecticut, with her sister Mary. (A divorce was granted in 1843 by the legislature of Connecticut.) While she lived there, Willard began to assist Henry Barnard, secretary of the State Board of Commissioners, in his campaign to improve the common schools, and later that same year, 1840, she was elected superintendent of four district schools for Kensington, Connecticut.

Four years later, at her son's urging, she returned to Troy and lived in a small house on the school grounds. Willard continued to write and publish poems, as well as *A Treatise on the Motive Powers Which Produce the Circulation of the Blood* (1846). She gained recognition for her work in physiology and was one of the few women admitted to the Association for the Advancement of Science.

In 1845-1846, Willard conducted a series of teacher institutes throughout southern New York State and Southern and Western states as far as Texas. In her later years, in addition to revising her textbooks, Willard studied both Greek and Hebrew because she wanted to read books in their original language. Willard also began to work for different causes. She exhorted the French government to consult women as it drafted a new constitution. She worked to preserve the Union and peace. She published *Universal Peace* (1864), which proposed an international organization, similar to what later became the League of Nations, to settle international problems. Willard remained active until her death in 1870, at eighty-three. She was buried in Oakwood Cemetery outside Troy, New York. The Troy Female Seminary was renamed the Emma Willard School in 1895.

Summary

Before 1820, women's place was in the home. All intellectual pursuit was discouraged because it was thought that it would harm the female. The little education available to females was obtained either at "dame" schools, usually conducted by poorly trained women in their own homes, or during summer months when some district schools would admit girls. After 1790, female seminaries began to develop. Because of tuition and other costs, poor girls were automatically excluded.

As Willard grew to adulthood and developed into a teacher, she began to realize how limited female education was. Later, when she established her own school, she worked vigorously to free women from ignorance. Willard was interested in developing thinkers, scholarship, and high ideals and encouraged self-respect and self-support.

Her aim had been to advance the cause of female education as the only base that could support the advancement of women. She believed that women had much to give to their country. Willard proved that women could do serious study without harm to themselves. While Willard did not work for women's rights as such, she served as a bridge between traditional supportive women and the Victorian suffragists by being willing and able to challenge conservative notions.

The Troy Female Seminary predated the establishment of girls' schools in Boston and New York. It was a pioneer normal school established some eighteen years before the founding of Horace Mann's normal school. Willard was the first to think seriously about the problems and methods of teaching, the first to encourage the professionalization of teaching. She was the first woman to write textbooks on advanced subjects and may have been the first female lobbyist. She recognized the virtue of continuing education throughout one's life. Willard's contribution to female education was a major element in the development of women's colleges and coeducational universities into a permanent part of national life in the United States.

Bibliography

Anticaglia, Elizabeth. *Twelve American Women*. Chicago: Nelson-Hall, 1975. Presents good biographical sketches of twelve women, ranging from Anne Hutchinson to Margaret Mead, selected for their significant contributions to American civilization. One chapter is devoted to Willard.

Beadie, Nancy. "Emma Willard's Idea Put to the Test: The Consequences of State Support of Female Education." *History of Education Quarterly* 33, no. 4 (Winter 1993). Discusses state support of education for females in New York between 1819 and 1867 and Willard's arguments and analyses.

Cott, Nancy F. *The Bonds of Womanhood: "Woman's Sphere" in New England, 1780-1835.* 2d ed. New Haven, Conn.: Yale University Press, 1997. Tries to explain the duality of the "bond" which tied New England women together as well as to their station in life. Of particular interest is the third chapter, which offers a cohesive rationale for schooling women beyond the level of minimal literacy.

Cremin, Lawrence A., and R. Freeman Butts. *A History of Education in American Culture.* New York: Holt Rinehart, 1953. Provides a sound historical background on the development of American education. One of the leading works in recent times.

Flexner, Eleanor. *Century of Struggle: The Woman's Rights Movement in the United States.* Rev. ed. Cambridge, Mass.: Harvard University Press, 1975. Covers the women's rights movement from the Mayflower to 1920, when women won the vote. Flexner provides significant information about the many smaller movements within the larger one. The first two chapters cover the position of women up to 1800 and the early steps taken to secure equal education.

Goodsell, Willystine, ed. *Pioneers of Women's Education in the U.S.: E. Willard, C. Beecher, M. Lyon.* New York and London: McGraw-Hill, 1931. Following a brief introduction to women's education, part 1 presents a brief biography of Willard. Excerpts from her *Plan* and three selections from the prefaces of her texts are included.

Hoffman, Nancy. *Women's "True" Profession: Voices from the History of Teaching.* Old Westbury, N.Y.: Feminist Press, 1981. Presents the experience of teaching from the viewpoint of the teacher and highlights critical themes which defined teaching as woman's work. Representative teachers are chosen, Willard among them. A brief biography of Willard is included along with a facsimile of the handwritten letter she sent to Governor Clinton.

Lutz, Alma. *Emma Willard: Daughter of Democracy.* Boston: Houghton Mifflin, 1929. Written in the style of Willard's *Letters and Journals*, this dated portrait, written by an alumna of the school, remains the definitive work on Willard. All subsequent biographers have drawn from it.

————. *Emma Willard, Pioneer Educator of Women.* Boston: Beacon Press, 1964. Written in honor of the sesquicentennial of the Emma Willard School, it borrows much from Lutz's earlier work, which contains more complete information.

Rudolph, Frederick. "Emma Willard." In *Notable American Women, 1607-1950: A Biographical Dictionary*, vol. 3, edited by Edward T. James, Janet W. James, and Paul S. Boyer, 610-613. Cambridge, Mass.: Belknap Press of Harvard University Press, 1971. A good biographical sketch.

Scott, Anne Firor. "The Ever Widening Circle: The Diffusion of Feminist Values from the Troy Female Seminary, 1822-1872." *History of Education Quarterly* 19 (Spring 1979): 3-25. Presents an analysis of the alumnae of the Troy Female Seminary and attempts to show the decisive influence Willard had not only on the students but also on every part of the country to which they went. Valuable, well-documented study that concludes that higher education played an important part in the diffusion of feminist values.

Townsend, L.F., and B. Wiley. "Ever the Teacher, Even when Honeymooning: Emma Willard's Lost Geography Lesson." *New England Quarterly* 64, no. 2 (June, 1991). Discussion of a geography tutorial written by Willard while on her honeymoon.

Willard, Emma. "Education and the Weaker Sex." *Essential Documents in American History* (January, 1997). This is the text of Willard's address to the New York legislature supporting reform in female education.

Rita E. Loos

FRANCES WILLARD

Born: September 28, 1839; Churchville, New York
Died: February 18, 1898; New York, New York
Areas of Achievement: Education, temperance, and women's rights
Contribution: Advocating a "do everything" policy for reformers in the late nineteenth century, Willard helped advance the causes of temperance and women's rights as president and the most famous and symbolic leader of the Woman's Christian Temperance Union.

Early Life

Frances Elizabeth Caroline Willard, born on September 28, 1839, in Churchville, New York, was the fourth of five children, three of whom survived infancy. Her mother, Mary Thompson (Hill) Willard, traced her ancestry back to early New Englanders of English origin. Her father, Josiah Flint Willard, came from a long line of New England and New York farmers.

When Frances was two, her family moved to Ohio and then migrated to the Janesville, Wisconsin, area, where she grew up. Her mother provided her first schooling. A young tutor and a visiting aunt continued her schooling until Frances was fifteen. After attending a district school and a school for girls, she enrolled in the Milwaukee Female College and thereafter transferred to Northwestern Female College in Evanston, Illinois. Frances was graduated in 1859 with a laureate of science degree. She held a number of teaching positions in Illinois during the next few years and moved to Genesee Wesleyan Seminary in Lima, New York, to hold a job as a preceptress during the 1866-1867 academic year. Frances returned to Evanston in the winter of 1867-1868 and nursed her father until he died in January, 1868.

Shortly after her father's death, Willard departed for two years of travel throughout Europe, including Russia and Greece, and to Egypt, Palestine, and Turkey, with her friend Kate Jackson. Jackson's wealthy father paid for the travel. Willard attended lectures and studied languages, art, and music in Berlin, Paris, and Rome, thus expanding her intellectual capacity and heightening her desire to achieve.

In 1871, Willard was appointed president of Evanston College for Ladies. In 1873, when Northwestern University totally absorbed Evanston College, she was made dean of women and professor of English and art at Northwestern. That same year, Willard helped found the Association for the Advancement of Women. In 1874, after suffering academic frustration and experiencing personal difficulties with Charles Fowler, the president of Northwestern and her former fiancé, she resigned, never again to hold a formal academic position. Her stately physical presence, kindly face, and penetrating eyes belied the fact that this attractive and highly motivated thirty-five-year-old woman was unhappy and, at that point in her life, lacking clear direction.

Life's Work

In the midst of rising temperance fervor and expanding antisaloon activity throughout the country, Willard was soon able to realize her ambitions. In October, 1874, she was chosen secretary of a newly formed women's temperance organization in Chicago. The next month, she attended the organizing convention of the National Woman's Christian Temperance Union (WCTU) and was chosen national corresponding secretary. She immediately advocated that the WCTU should dedicate itself to numerous other reforms. Annie Wittenmyer, the first president of the WCTU, opposed broadening the organization's perspective beyond temperance and was shocked by Willard's 1876 national convention speech in support of a women's suffrage resolution.

In early 1877, Willard resigned her Chicago WCTU position to become the director of women's meetings for the evangelist Dwight L. Moody. Moody's orthodoxy, however, was too restraining; hence, she resigned in September and returned to Evanston with Anna A. Gordon, whom she had met in the Boston Moody Crusade and who thereafter became her lifelong secretary, aide, and confidante. In 1877, when her relationship with Wittenmyer became even more strained, Willard resigned as WCTU national corresponding secretary and began lecturing nationwide on women's rights and suffrage.

After being elected president of the Illinois WCTU in 1878, Willard campaigned vigorously for new temperance laws. She initiated and directed a petition campaign to induce state legislators to pass a law allowing women in Illinois to vote on the liquor question. Although the petition died in committee, its effect was evident in the state's spring election as a majority of Illinois towns adopted local option. This petition campaign served as a model for subsequent and similar actions for the WCTU in other states.

Although the internal organizational fight over political activity continued, Willard steadily won new adherents. In 1879, she was elected president of the National WCTU and held that position for the remaining years of her life. Under her leadership, the WCTU expanded from a religious group primarily dedicated to temperance to a strong women's organization. She effected many internal changes in the organization and molded the annual conventions into well-publicized, smooth-running, and inspiring affairs. She sought and acquired for the WCTU working relationships with other religious and reform groups.

As National WCTU president, Willard, already highly regarded, became a well-traveled and effective speaker who could and did move audiences. Her speaking fees were her only source of income until 1886, when the WCTU presented her with an annual salary of eighteen hundred dollars, later raised to twenty-four hundred dollars. Supporting herself, her mother, and Gordon, Willard remained in constant financial need throughout the 1880's. The sales of her autobiography, *Glimpses of Fifty Years: An Autobiography of an American Woman,* published in 1889, provided sufficient additional income to allow her barely to meet her needs.

After becoming national president, Willard continued to speak out for women's suffrage. Responding to her urging, delegates to the national convention in 1880 endorsed the ballot for women; in 1882, a new WCTU department of franchise was established to distribute suffrage literature and to encourage members to work for the vote. A member of the American Woman Suffrage Association, Willard worked closely with numerous suffrage organizations and introduced leading suffrage leaders to WCTU national conventions.

Willard carefully led the WCTU and her followers into various other reform causes. She pinpointed her strategy well in her handbook *Do Everything,* published in 1895. She argued that almost all reforms had temperance aspects. By 1889, thirtynine WCTU departments of work existed, each of which was designed to educate the public and be a group to bring pressure in order to secure reform legislation. The areas of reform, in addition to temperance, included prostitution, health and hygiene, city welfare, prison reform, labor reform, and

rights for blacks. Attempting to do so much meant that at times the work was superficial. Many WCTU members, moreover, continued to concern themselves only with the liquor problem.

Beginning in 1883, Willard led the WCTU into international work. She convinced the WCTU to send temperance missionaries abroad to establish unions and to convince women in other countries to oppose the traffic in alcohol and narcotic drugs. The World's WCTU was established in 1891; Willard was elected president. By 1897, the World's WCTU represented more than two million women.

In attempting to bring the WCTU into party politics, Willard encountered her greatest internal organizational difficulties. After endorsing James A. Garfield for the presidency in 1880 and then being disappointed by his repudiation of his pledge to support prohibition and women's suffrage, Willard established the Home Protection Party and attempted in 1882 to combine it with the Prohibition Party. Many members opposed involving their organization in party politics. In the early 1890's, Willard tried to get prohibition and women's suffrage planks inserted into the 1892

Populist Party platform and attempted to bring the Prohibition Party into the Populist Party. She regarded her failure to accomplish these results as a personal defeat.

Affected by her political failure and by the death of her mother, Willard went to England in the summer of 1892 to rest and to spend time with a friend, Lady Henry Somerset. From then until the end of 1896, she stayed mostly in England, spending only sixteen months in the United States. During this time, she attempted with but little success to garner support from British women for her "do everything" policy. She also changed both her thinking and advocacy. She espoused socialism, argued that poverty was the major cause of intemperance, and spoke out on her belief that education rather than prohibition was the best way to solve the liquor problem.

Dissatisfaction with Willard among WCTU leaders grew between 1892 and 1896. Her unorthodox views, continued emphasis upon politics, extended absences, and lack of attention to developing organizational problems finally caused an eruption of opposition at the 1897 national convention. Her rank-and-file followers held the line, however, re-electing her by an overwhelming vote of 387 to nineteen. Chronic anemia took its toll the next year as Willard's health declined dramatically. She died in New York City on February 18, 1898.

Summary

Although she did not wholly realize her dream of creating an all-inclusive women's reform organization, Willard, stressing the familiar themes of home, family, and temperance, successfully convinced many women, who had previously been indifferent to reforms, to broaden their perspective and to engage in numerous reform activities. During her twenty years as National WCTU president, she retained the backing of the great majority of WCTU members. After her death, the WCTU moved away from the "do everything" policy and emphasized the issues of prohibition and total abstinence. Willard nevertheless remained the most illustrious and idealized symbol of the WCTU woman.

In many ways, Willard's story is the story of the WCTU, the largest organization of women in nineteenth century America. Led by Willard, the WCTU fought not only for temperance but also for women's suffrage, prison reform, facilities for dependent and neglected children, federal aid to education, and legislation to help laborers. During the Willard presidency, 1879 to 1898, the WCTU dominated the entire women's movement in the United States. In addition to molding the WCTU into the model for future women's organizations, Willard, more than any of her contemporaries, instilled the vision of feminist goals in the consciousness of great numbers of American women.

Bibliography

Bordin, Ruth. *Woman and Temperance*. Philadelphia: Temple University Press, 1981. The best book on the WCTU and one of the two best analyses of Willard. A well-documented, well-written, and careful study that places both the WCTU and Willard in historical perspective.

Earhart, Mary. *Frances Willard: From Prayers to Politics*. Chicago: University of Chicago, 1944. The best overall biography and one of the two best analyses of Willard. Well documented and objective. Contains listing of all writings by Willard.

Gordon, Anna A. *The Beautiful Life of Frances Willard*. Chicago: Woman's Temperance Publishing Association, 1898. Uncritical, but typifies those books that have produced an idealized myth of the life and work of Willard.

Gordon, Elizabeth Putnam. *Women Torch-bearers: The Story of the Woman's Christian Temperance Union*. Evanston, Ill.: National Woman's Christian Temperance Union Publishing House, 1924. Although mostly uncritical and apologetic, this history of the WCTU presents a unified sketch of activity influenced by Willard. Not nearly as good as, but should be compared to, Borden.

Gusfield, Joseph. *Symbolic Crusade: Status Politics and the American Temperance Movement*. 2d ed. Urbana: University of Illinois Press, 1986. A sociological study of what the author calls status politics and the American temperance movement. The book contains some insights into the leadership of Willard and data on the WCTU and the temperance movement.

Ivy, James D. " 'The Lone Star State Surrenders to a Lone Woman': Frances Willard's Forgotten 1882 Texas Temperance Tour." *Southwestern Historical Quarterly* 102, no. 1 (July, 1998). Discusses Willard's career as a prohibitionist and her contributions to the cause.

Leeman, Richard W. *"Do Everything" Reform: The Oratory of Frances E. Willard*. New York: Greenwood Press, 1992. Leeman's is the first study of the oratory of Willard. Includes texts of representative speeches, a chronology of significant addresses, and a bibliography.

Willard, Frances. *Glimpses of Fifty Years: An Autobiography of an American Woman.* Chicago: Woman's Temperance Publishing Association, 1889. Contains detail about Willard and about other WCTU leaders. Tends to be apologetic and spotty in coverage but does give a flavor of Willard.

―――. *Woman and Temperance: Or, The Work and Wonders of the Woman's Christian Temperance Union.* Hartford, Conn.: Park, 1883. Contains "field notes" of Willard but is badly organized and apologetic. Has considerable information about some WCTU leaders and their activities. First biographical sketch, praiseworthy but uncritical, is of Willard and is written by Mary A. Lathbury.

Norton Mezvinsky

WILLIAM IV

Born: August 21, 1765; Buckingham House, London, England
Died: June 20, 1837; Windsor Castle, near London, England
Area of Achievement: Government
Contribution: The Reform Bill of 1832, which may well have averted a revolution, could not have been passed without King William IV's support. His reign also witnessed the continued increase of the House of Commons' power and the continued erosion of the power of the Crown.

Early Life

The third son of George III and his queen, Charlotte of Mecklenberg-Streilitz, Prince William Henry was born at Buckingham House (Buckingham Palace after its expansion in the 1820's) on August 21, 1765. His eldest brother, George, Prince of Wales, was to be educated as heir to the throne; his older brother Frederick, later the Duke of York, was slated for an army career. George III decided that William should have a naval career. Accordingly, after being tutored at Kew Palace from 1772, William, accompanied by his tutor, joined the navy in June, 1779. He was on active service for nine of the next eleven years and served on vessels that cruised to America and the West Indies, his voyages punctuated by brief visits to Kew or Windsor. When in New York in the last year of the American Revolution, he was the subject of an abortive kidnapping plot. He was on the Continent from 1783 to 1785, primarily in the family court of Hanover. Elevated to the rank of captain in 1786, William was given command of his own ship and posted to the maritime provinces of Canada. Summoned home by the Prince of Wales during their father's fit of madness in 1788, he returned to England via the West Indies. To his surprise and perhaps to his disappointment, he found that the king had recovered and resumed authority. Some months thereafter, in May, 1789, William was created Duke of Clarence.

The duke had few apparent talents and lacked a commanding presence. Even flattering portraits reveal the pear-shaped head that provided an irresistible feature for caricaturists. Moreover, he was often boorish, insensitive, and vulgar and offended the strict king by leading a profligate life, having engaged in a series of affairs. A capable junior officer and captain, he was judged by both the Admiralty and the king to be lacking the abilities necessary for command of a fleet. Denied that promotion, his naval career was effectively ended. For decades, William remained unemployed, subsisting on the parliamentary grant provided him as a royal duke. Given his situation, perhaps it was inevitable that he drift into the filial opposition that characterized royal relations in eighteenth century England and associate himself, briefly, with the social circle that formed around the Prince of Wales.

Life's Work

In 1790, the Duke of Clarence established a liaison with the actress Dorothea Jordan. The relationship lasted some two decades. The couple had ten illegitimate children, all surnamed FitzClarence, and lived with their brood near Hampton Court, the duke having been appointed Ranger of Bushy Park, which gave him the use of that property. Mrs. Jordan continued her acting career, thereby supplementing the duke's parliamentary grant. Most likely it was boredom as well as mounting debts that impelled Clarence to end their connection and search for a younger and more well-endowed consort who would meet with the approval of the monarch as required by the Royal Marriages Act of 1772. That quest soon became an affair of state, all the more important after Princess Charlotte, the Prince Regent's only child, died in 1817. After his overtures had been spurned by several English heiresses and foreign princesses, William finally secured the engagement of Adelaide, Princess of Saxe-Meiningen. The prospective marriage allowed the duke to negotiate a significantly larger parliamentary grant, and the couple was married in July, 1818. Each of their two children, both girls, died in infancy.

When George III died in 1820, the Prince of Wales, Prince Regent since 1812, succeeded to the throne in his own right as George IV. In 1827, the Duke of York died, which made the Duke of Clarence heir presumptive. The new prime minister, George Canning, thereupon appointed him Lord High Admiral, an office which had been unfilled for more than a century. The duke launched into naval business with alacrity. He soon overstepped the bounds of the restored but restricted office, however, and was compelled to resign in August, 1828. He had, however, emerged from a lifetime of relative obscurity.

The Duke of Clarence succeeded to the throne as William IV in June, 1830, at the age of sixty-four. The unpopularity of his predecessor coupled with William's breezy informality resulted in his succession being welcomed by the populace. He also had ample opportunity to indulge an idiosyncratic penchant for speechmaking in the early months of his reign. The elections of July, 1830, resulted in no immediate change of government, but the Duke of Wellington some months later remained intransigent about parliamentary reform, lost the confidence of the House of Commons, and resigned. William called upon the second Earl Grey, leader of the Whig Party now pledged to reform, to form a government.

In his capacity as a peer since 1789, William had publicly discussed only a few issues. He had unabashedly denounced the evils of adultery; he cited his West Indian experience in supporting the slave trade and slavery; he supported his brother's divorce from Queen Caroline; and he supported the Wellington government's bill for Catholic emancipation. Despite little political involvement, he had been imbued with traditional ideas about the English constitution which he thought validated a government comprising Kings, Lords, and Commons; presumably there was an equilibrium or balance among these three estates of the realm. William recognized, however, that the powers of the House of Commons had increased and that the monarch's powers were not as great as they once had been, but certain functions, he knew, still belonged to the king as part of the royal prerogative. Above all, he retained the increasingly anachronistic view that the ministers were still the king's ministers in fact as well as in theory.

Although he consented to Grey's selection of each minister, William reposed his confidence in Lord Grey personally, not in the cabinet collectively. Grey, moreover, was most responsible for reassuring the king about the essentially conservative intentions of the government and in persuading him that the alternative to parliamentary reform was a revolution which would destroy both the monarchy and the aristocracy. Impressing the king with these views, Grey had to counter the overwhelmingly Tory sentiments of Queen Adelaide, the FitzClarences, and the Duke of Cumberland, the king's younger brother. The court's opposition to reform was all the more shrill given the looting and riots that occurred in the countryside and the agitation of political unions in some of the towns.

The government's Reform Bill was far more extensive than had been anticipated, but the king's reservations were overcome by Lord Grey. When the government was reversed on an amendment in the House of Commons, however, it called upon the king to dissolve Parliament and hold new elections. Despite his fear of violence accompanying elections, William agreed, persuading himself that the Lords' imminent address requesting that he refuse a dissolution constituted an infringement on the royal prerogative. The elections of 1831, virtually a plebiscite on reform, resulted in securing the House of Commons for the Reform Bill. The king became enormously popular, since his name was associated with the reform cause, a development he resented. The Lords, however, rejected the bill on its second reading in October, 1831.

The months that followed witnessed a few concessions to the peers, but none on what ministers considered to constitute the principles of the bill— abolition of rotten boroughs, a uniform franchise in the boroughs, and extension of parliamentary representation to the unrepresented towns. William sought to have the government make some concession on the last point, but to no avail. He could do little more than encourage Grey to negotiate with a few moderate peers, but those negotiations were fruitless. It became increasingly evident even to the most conservative ministers that the Reform Bill could only be passed if the government were armed with the king's promise to create sufficient new peers to force the bill through the House of Lords. The king first consented to a token creation and then to sufficient peers to carry the bill, but the prospect of a mass creation of peers—even if preference were given, as he stipulated, to eldest sons of existing peers, collateral heirs, and Scottish and Irish peers—caused him to renege. Consequently, when the government resigned in May, 1832, the king recruited Wellington to form a coalition administration that could produce a bill acceptable to the Lords. Wellington was unable to do so. William, therefore, had to recall Grey and formally submit to his government's demand for a creation of peers if necessary. It proved to be unnecessary only when William's pledge became known. The Reform Bill became law in June, 1832, though the king declined a personal appearance in Parliament to give the royal assent.

Other important legislation was promulgated by the Whig governments of the 1830's, much of it distasteful to the king. Such was the case with the abolition of slavery in 1833, to which he consented but which he still considered objectionable. He was most upset with the ministers' treatment of the Irish question, which occupied much of Parliament's time during the remainder of his reign. In particular, he opposed the intended appropriation of Irish Church revenues to secular purposes, considering it an erosion of established institutions.

The controversy about the matter resulted in the resignation of four conservative ministers in 1834. William accepted their resignations only on condition that Grey accept them, once again demonstrating his reliance upon his prime minister. He construed the subsequent resignation of Lords Grey and Althorp in July, 1834, on a related Irish matter, to be tantamount to the resignation of the entire cabinet. Once again, he attempted to establish a coalition government of all parties, which he thought was necessary to stem encroachment upon the powers of both the Crown and the House of Lords by the newly reformed House of Commons. Again, none of the leading politicians seriously considered a coalition viable or desirable. William then select-

ed the Whig the second Viscount Melbourne as his prime minister.

William's most dramatic attempt to restore the Crown's power was his dismissal of the Whig government in November, 1834, ostensibly because Lord Althorp had to leave the Commons for the Lords to succeed his father. It proved to be the last time that a king dismissed a ministry that had the support of a majority of the House of Commons. While the constitutionality of the king's action was not seriously questioned at the time, it was ineffective politically. The House of Commons refused to support the succeeding Tory government. When Grey declined a plea that he abandon retirement and lead a coalition, the king was forced to submit again to Melbourne and the Whigs in April, 1835. His suggestion that Melbourne submit the matter of appropriation of Irish church revenues to a board of judges as a judicial question was rejected out of hand. Nor would Melbourne formally accept the king's right to exclude specific politicians from his cabinet.

William continued to feel besieged during the last two years of his reign. He was dismayed by some legislation, such as the Municipal Corporations Bill of 1835, but was relieved that the government was unable to enact the legislation for diverting surplus Irish church revenues to secular purposes. He died at Windsor Castle on June 20, 1837, and was succeeded by his niece, Victoria.

Summary

William IV's brief reign remains of considerable importance in English constitutional history. While the power of the Crown had been declining steadily for decades, in the early nineteenth century the king to some extent still ruled as well as reigned. Far more than a figurehead, the monarch had real power. In William IV's reign, that was most evident in the need to have the king's support to pass the Reform Bill. William's views on foreign affairs also had to be considered, especially since he was the last king of England who was also King of Hanover. The Reform Bill that required the king's support to pass, however, further eroded the Crown's power. It gave even greater power to the electorate, now augmented in numbers, and thereby reinforced the House of Commons as the dominant part of government as defined by the English constitution. Therefore, William IV's old-fashioned views about a balance of power between

King, Lords, and Commons were no longer appropriate. He was compelled in 1835 to recall the Whigs after dismissing them because the cabinet was far more responsible to the House of Commons than to the king. The cabinet may have remained the king's ministers in theory, but they were no longer the king's ministers in fact. William IV had also expressed concern about the erosion of the House of Lords' power and the conflict between the two houses of Parliament. That conflict would continue throughout the nineteenth century, until the power of the Lords was drastically reduced by the Parliament Act of 1911.

Bibliography

Brock, Michael. *The Great Reform Act.* London: Hutchinson, 1973. Now the standard account of the struggle for the Reform Bill. William's dependence on Grey is emphasized.

Butler, J. R. M. *The Passing of the Great Reform Bill.* London and New York: Longman, 1914. This book is an old but still valuable account in which the king is somewhat more at center stage than in Brock (above).

Fulford, Roger. *From Hanover to Windsor.* London: Batsford, 1960. The first chapter of this volume on the monarchy contains an elegant essay on William IV, who is favorably evaluated.

Gash, Norman. *Reaction and Reconstruction in English Politics, 1832-1852.* Oxford: Clarendon Press, 1965. A judicious interpretation of the constitution and political parties by a distinguished scholar. The first chapter discusses the decline of the Crown's power during William IV's reign.

Kriegel, Abraham D., ed. *The Holland House Diaries, 1831-1840.* London and Boston: Routledge, 1977. The introductory essay discusses the legislation of the Whig governments of the 1830's, the functions of the cabinet, and its relations with the king.

Somerset, Anne. *The Life and Times of William IV.* London: Weidenfeld and Nicolson, 1980. A popular biography, recommended mainly for the lavish reproductions of contemporary paintings and political cartoons.

Thompson, Grace E. *The Patriot King: The Life of William IV.* London: Hutchinson, 1932; New York: Dutton, 1933. An old, well-written, popular biography, out of date in its interpretation of politics but good in its portrait of William.

Ziegler, Philip. *King William IV.* London: Collins, and New York: Harper, 1971. The best biography. Ziegler goes a bit too far in claiming that William was England's first constitutional monarch.

Abraham D. Kriegel

GEORGE WASHINGTON WILLIAMS

Born: October 16, 1849; Bedford Springs, Pennsylvania

Died: August 2, 1891; Blackpool, England

Areas of Achievement: History and politics

Contribution: As the author of the first reliable history of black Americans and a prominent political spokesman and observer, Williams contributed to the development of African American identity and racial pride.

Early Life

George Washington Williams was born in Bedford Springs, Pennsylvania, on October 16, 1849. His father, a free black named Thomas Williams, is believed to have been the son of a white Virginia planter and a slave woman. Sometime during the 1840's, the elder Williams moved to Bedford Springs, where he met and married Ellen Rouse, a light-skinned local black woman. George was the second of five children born to the couple. His childhood was a difficult one, plagued by frequent moves, family instability, a scant education, and Thomas Williams' heavy drinking. Although the elder Williams eventually tempered his life-style enough to serve as the minister of a black church in Newcastle, Pennsylvania, George became incorrigible and was placed in a refuge house for delinquent juveniles. There, he discovered literature and religion, interests that were to permeate his adult life.

Drawn by a sense of adventure, Williams went off to fight in the Civil War at age fourteen. By falsifying his age and using an assumed name, he was able to enlist in a black Union army regiment in August, 1864. He saw action in the closing battles in Virginia, including the campaigns against Petersburg and Richmond. After the war, his unit was transferred to Texas, but he soon left it and joined the revolutionary forces that were fighting to overthrow Emperor Maximilian, an Austrian interloper on the Mexican throne. Shortly before Maximilian's capture and execution in 1867, Williams returned to the United States and reenlisted. He served for more than a year as a cavalry sergeant at military posts in Kansas and Indian Territory (modern Oklahoma) until discharged in 1868.

Although untrained and barely literate, Williams was licensed as a Baptist preacher shortly after his military career ended. In September, 1870, he enrolled at the Newton Theological Institution, a Baptist school and seminary near Boston, Massachusetts. Williams completed both his general studies and his theological training in an astonishingly brief four years and was recognized as a good student. In June, 1874, he was graduated from Newton, was ordained in the Baptist clergy, and married Sarah A. Sterrett. A prominent member of Boston's black community during his Newton years, Williams was named pastor of the city's historic, black Twelfth Baptist Church in 1873. While in that position, he joined other black leaders in working for passage of a national civil rights bill, publicly voiced his concerns about the course of Reconstruction, and penned a history of the local congregation. When he resigned his pastorate in October, 1875, it was to pursue these two emerging interests—politics and history.

Life's Work

One month before resigning his Boston pastorate, Williams went with his wife and infant son to Washington, D.C., which had become a gathering place for many of the nation's black leaders. With their assistance, he soon inaugurated a new weekly newspaper called *The Commoner*, which he hoped would reach beyond the "chilling shadow of slavery" and become "a powerful agent for reorganizing the race." Although he believed that it would attract a national audience, few subscribed and he was unable to sustain it beyond eight issues. The brevity of his encounter with the national political scene merely heightened Williams' interest in politics.

In February, 1876, Williams was called to the pastorate of the Union Baptist Church in Cincinnati, Ohio. He quickly made his mark on the local black community as an energetic pastor, an articulate spokesman and imaginative leader in racial affairs, and a regular contributor to the *Commercial*—a leading local newspaper—on a variety of local and national issues. He also became active in local Republican Party circles, rapidly gaining control of the party machinery in the city's black precincts. Nominated as a candidate for the Ohio legislature in 1877, Williams proved a strong campaigner, but he was overwhelmingly defeated as many white voters openly refused to cast their ballot for a black man. After this taste of politics, he left the ministry and briefly published a newspaper called *The Southwestern Review* (1877-1878).

When it folded, the peripatetic Williams embarked upon the study of law with Alphonso Taft, the father of President William Howard Taft and a politician of national prominence in his own right. He later attended lectures at the Cincinnati Law School.

Continuing to campaign extensively for Republican candidates, Williams proved to be particularly adept at "waving the bloody shirt"—linking the Democratic Party with the Confederacy, slavery, and responsibility for starting the Civil War. In 1879, he was again nominated as a candidate for the Ohio legislature. Despite widespread criticism, he campaigned hard, openly courted white support, and was narrowly elected. Williams distinguished himself as an active legislator, sponsoring several reform measures, including legislation to control the use of alcoholic beverages. On occasion he became the center of controversy, as when he called for a civil rights resolution after encountering racist treatment in Columbus restaurants, hotels, and newspapers. He also unsuccessfully sought the repeal of a state law prohibiting interracial marriages.

In 1881, Williams refused to seek a second term in the Ohio legislature. His announced reason was the desire to devote his time to historical research and writing. The centennial celebrations of American independence in 1876 had heightened his early interest in history. Moving to Columbus, he began work on a general history of African Americans. A diligent and thorough researcher, he succeeded in completing a massive, two-volume study of his race from its African origins through the end of Reconstruction. This work, entitled *History of the Negro Race in America from 1619 to 1880* (1883), established Williams as a capable historian and was well received by leading Eastern magazines and newspapers. The New York *Independent* called it "an epoch-making book."

Although sales of his first book were disappointing, Williams began work on a second, which was eventually published as *History of the Negro Troops in the War of the Rebellion, 1861-1865* (1888). The work proved to be much broader than the title, examining the role of black soldiers in the American Revolution, the War of 1812, the Haitian Revolution, and other conflicts. This work was widely heralded, but the subsequent appearance of Joseph T. Wilson's *Black Phalanx* (1888), another history of black participation in the Civil War, limited sales and publicity for the volume. Williams

also researched a two-volume history of Reconstruction, but it was never published. He experimented with other literary forms, penning a play on the African slave trade and a novel on the subject of interracial marriage. Although the novel was rejected by numerous publishers, its first eight chapters were eventually published in the Indianapolis *World* (1888), a black newspaper.

Shortly after the publication of his *History*, Williams returned to Massachusetts to live. Although he practiced law and stumped the state for Republican candidates, he derived most of his income from lecturing on black history, Africa, and general literature. Delivering hundreds of lectures throughout the Northeast, he soon gained a reputation as an eloquent speaker, and the handsome, mustached Williams must have cut a striking figure for his audiences.

Williams maintained his interest in politics. On March 2, 1885, two days before leaving office, President Chester A. Arthur, a Republican, nominated him to serve as minister resident and consul general to Haiti. Although the Senate immediately confirmed him, and he was sworn in, the incoming

Democratic administration of President Grover Cleveland refused him the post. He challenged the action in federal court but was denied redress. He abandoned the effort in 1889 after the newly inaugurated Republican president, Benjamin Harrison, appointed black leader Frederick Douglass to the post.

Depressed by his inability to obtain a diplomatic position, Williams turned his attention to Africa. In 1884, he had written articles on African geography, and, in testimony before the Senate Committee on Foreign Relations, he had urged American recognition of the Congo Free State. In the years that followed, he visited Europe several times to attend conferences on the African slave trade and African missions. In 1889, he interviewed King Leopold II of Belgium about his efforts to bring commerce and Christianity to the Congo (modern Zaire). When S. S. McClure of the Associated Literary Press commissioned him to write a series of articles on the Congo, and railroad magnate Collis P. Huntington asked him to report on the progress of the Congo railway being built by the Belgians, he visited the African continent.

Although King Leopold attempted to discourage him, Williams sailed for Africa in January, 1890. He spent four months exploring the Congo from the mouth of the Congo River to its headwaters at Stanley Falls. The trip revealed the Belgians' inhuman exploitation of black Africans. Williams responded by publishing *An Open Letter to His Serene Majesty, Leopold II, King of the Belgians* (1890), which extensively criticized Belgian colonial policy in the Congo. After visiting Portuguese and British possessions in East Africa, Williams went to Egypt, where he contracted tuberculosis. By the spring of 1891, he had improved enough to return to England, where he intended to write a full report of the European colonial impact on Africa. Concerned for his health, he hurried to the coastal city of Blackpool, where he hoped that the Irish Sea air and the curative powers of a local spa would restore his health. They did not. Williams died of tuberculosis and pleurisy on August 2, 1891.

Summary

George Washington Williams contributed many "firsts" to the African American experience. He was one of only a few blacks outside the South to serve in a state legislature during the nineteenth century. Representing Hamilton County, Ohio, he distinguished himself during a single term in the Ohio legislature.

Williams is best remembered for his contributions to the writing of African American history. His books were the first reliable studies of the black role in America's past. On the cutting edge of historical research, Williams gathered information from thousands of volumes, but also employed church minutes, school statistics, newspapers, and oral interviews in compiling his works. This took him on an extensive tour of Western military posts, where he interviewed numerous black veterans of the Civil War. Williams explored beyond the stereotypes and prejudices in his research on the war and thus reclaimed a place for blacks in the history of the American Revolution, the antislavery movement, and the Civil War. He also delved into African history and was among the first historians to provide a realistic portrayal of the African kingdoms of Benin, Dahomey, Yoruba, and Ashanti. The epic quality of his work brought it attention in major magazines and newspapers, which was highly unusual for black research at that time. In researching his history of black soldiers in the Civil War, Williams became one of the first students of that conflict to use the official records of the Union and Confederate armies. Although he eventually moved away from historical studies, he left his mark on future investigations of the African American experience. Twentieth century black leader W. E. B. Du Bois called Williams "the greatest historian of the race."

Williams was the first African American to investigate extensively European colonialism in Africa. His criticism at first stirred controversy in the United States and abroad, but later colonial observers substantiated his claims. As a result, the Congo Reform Association was founded in 1904 to crusade against conditions in the Congo Free State. In 1890, these accomplishments prompted readers of the *Indianapolis Freeman* to vote Williams one of the ten greatest African Americans in history.

Bibliography

Franklin, John Hope. *George Washington Williams: A Biography.* Chicago: University of Chicago Press, 1985. The only reliable biography of Williams, this well-documented and balanced study is based on years of extensive research in a wide variety of obscure sources.

Gerber, David A. *Black Ohio and the Color Line: 1860-1915*. Urbana: University of Illinois Press, 1976. This valuable, well-documented work provides a context for understanding Williams' Ohio years. It includes a lengthy discussion of black institutions, politics, and race relations in Ohio during the 1870's and 1880's.

Slade, Ruth. *King Leopold's Congo: Aspects of the Development of Race Relations in the Congo Independent State*. London and New York: Oxford University Press, 1962. Examines King Leopold II's policies in the Congo Free State. It credits Williams as one of the first critics of colonialism to demonstrate that Belgian officials in the Congo violated international trading practices established by European diplomats.

Thorpe, Earl E. *Black Historians: A Critique*. New York: Morrow, 1971. A general overview of African American historians from 1836 to the present. It critically analyzes Williams' historical writings and compares him with Joseph T. Wilson and other black historians of his time.

Williams, George Washington. *History of the Negro Race in America from 1619 to 1880*. 2 vols. New York and London: Putnam, 1883. The best way to understand Williams' historical contribution is to pursue this massive, two-volume study of African Americans from colonial days through Reconstruction. It has been conveniently reprinted in a single volume by Arno Press and *The New York Times*.

Roy E. Finkenbine

ISAAC MAYER WISE

Born: March 29, 1819; Steingrub, Bohemia
Died: March 26, 1900; Cincinnati, Ohio
Areas of Achievement: Religion and education
Contribution: As a pioneering Reform rabbi with the avowed goal of uniting American Jewry, Wise became the greatest organizer of Reform Jewish institutions. He was the architect of and prime mover in the establishment of the Union of American Hebrew Congregations (1873), Hebrew Union College (1875), and the Central Conference of American Rabbis (1889), and he served as the first president of each of those three organizations.

Early Life

Isaac Mayer Wise, born on March 29, 1819, in Steingrub, Bohemia (in modern Czechoslovakia), was the oldest surviving son of Regina and Leo Weiss. At the age of four, he began his studies under the direction of his father, a poor teacher, who had his own primary school. By the age of six, Isaac Mayer, an obvious prodigy, was studying the Bible and the Talmud. By the age of nine, after having learned everything his father could teach him, he went to study with his grandfather, a physician well steeped in Jewish learning. In 1831, when twelve and after the death of his grandfather, he went to Prague to study in a school famous for instruction in the Talmud. He then became an outstanding student in Prague. In 1835, Wise journeyed to Jenikau and enrolled in Bohemia's most famous rabbinical school, headed by Rabbi Aaron Kornfield. At Kornfield's school, Isaac Mayer studied secular as well as religious topics. He completed his formal education by attending the University of Prague for two years and the University of Vienna for one year, during which time he also worked as a tutor.

After officially becoming a rabbi in 1842, at the age of twenty-three, Wise accepted a rabbinical position in Radnitz, Bohemia. In May, 1844, he married Theresa Bloch, a former student, with whom he had ten children during thirty years of happy marriage. Continuing to study and to advance intellectually, he was greatly influenced by Gabriel Kiesser, the great jurist and parliamentarian, who heightened his awareness of nature and the need for political liberalism. He was also greatly influenced in religious liberalism by Samuel Hirsch. Attending a rabbinical conference in Frankfurt in 1845, Wise met, spoke with, and listened to four noted religious thinkers, Abraham Geiger, Samuel Adler, Zacharias Frankel, and David Einhorn, all of whom severely questioned many aspects of traditional Judaism and laid the basis for Reform.

Wise soon realized that Radnitz was too small and isolated for him. Believing the United States to be a place where Jews would be receptive to the idea of Judaism as an evolving faith open to liberal and rational thinking consistent with the Enlightenment, he decided to emigrate to the New World. With his wife and young daughters, he began a sixty-three-day voyage in May, 1846, arriving in New York on July 23.

Life's Work

Isaac Mayer Wise served as rabbi of Congregation Beth-E1 in Albany, New York, for four years. In his desire to improve public worship, he introduced numerous reforms, including mixed pews for men and women, the full inclusion of women in the synagogue, choral singing, and confirmation as a replacement for the Bar Mitzvah. Although continually facing opposition from the more traditionally oriented, Orthodox element in his congregation, Wise continued to advocate and pursue changes and reforms in both faith and practice. In 1847, he originated the idea of a single ritual for the American Jewish community. In 1848, he called for a rabbinical meeting the next year to establish a union of congregations; this first call for a meeting failed. Having become a regular contributor to two American Jewish publications, Wise continued writing as well as arguing orally the merits of this union proposal.

Wise, in 1850, accepted an offer to become the rabbi of Beth Elohim in Charleston, South Carolina, an avowedly Reform congregation. He changed his mind, however, and finally refused the offer. Opposition to his Reform ideas increased at Congregation Beth-El. On the morning of the eve of Rosh Hashanah (the beginning of the High Holy Days) in 1850, he was dismissed as rabbi at a rump meeting of the board of directors. At services the next day, a riot broke out. Shortly thereafter, a minority of the Beth-El congregation left with Wise and established a new synagogue, Anshe Emet (men of truth). Anshe Emet was a congregation committed to Reform, the fourth such in the United States; the other Reform congregations were in Charleston, Baltimore, and New York.

In 1854, Wise accepted the post of rabbi of Congregation B'nai Jeshuran in Cincinnati and stayed there the rest of his life. Soon after arriving in Cincinnati, he began to publish a weekly, *The Israelite*, which was later renamed *The American Israelite*, and a German supplement, *Die Deborah*. In both publications, he advocated the centralization of Jewish institutions. He also established Zion College, which combined Judaic and secular studies. In 1855, Wise called for a rabbinical synod that, he hoped, would unite American Jewry by developing an overall authority for Judaism in the United States. His call prompted the convening of a rabbinical conference in Cleveland, at which an intense debate between Orthodox and Reform rabbis erupted. Desiring to avoid conference failure, Wise sought agreement for a public declaration that would meet the minimal requirements of Orthodoxy but not violate the spirit of Reform. Wise's carefully worded declaration was finally accepted by the Orthodox and moderate Reform representatives in attendance. In the declaration, Wise stated that the Bible was "of immediate divine origin and the standard of our religion." He referred to the Talmud as containing the traditional, legal, and logical exposition of the biblical laws which must be expounded upon and practiced "according to the comments of the Talmud."

Wise, who presided at the conference, was overjoyed with the affirmative vote for the declaration. For him, this signaled a forthcoming union of all congregations in the United States. He believed that Orthodoxy would ultimately bow to a Reform emphasis attached to Jewish tradition. Wise's joy, however, was short-lived. Orthodox rabbis, at first satisfied, became suspicious of Wise's intentions. Radical Reform rabbis, led by David Einhorn in Baltimore, violently attacked the declaration as betraying Reform. Wise engaged in vigorous debate with both sides, but the synod idea quickly collapsed from lack of support.

Despite numerous setbacks, Wise continued to advocate a union of congregations, a common prayer book, and a college to train American rabbis. In 1856, he published *Minhag America*, a modified curtailment of the traditional Hebrew ritual. He wrote extensively and discussed his ideas orally in repeated visits to Jewish communities throughout the United States.

The coming of the Civil War not only deferred Wise's activities somewhat but also seemed to spark within him a desire to seek a career in national politics. He showed little sympathy for the abolitionist agitation preceding the Civil War and was willing to tolerate slavery rather than risk dissolution of the Union. During the Civil War, he joined the so-called Copperhead Democrats; in 1863, he accepted nomination for election to the Ohio State Senate, but he withdrew from the race because of his congregation's opposition to his candidacy.

After the Civil War, Wise agitated again for a union of congregations. He attended the 1869 Reform rabbinical conference in Philadelphia and assented to the resolutions adopted there. Soon thereafter, however, he moved away from the substance of those resolutions, realizing that his identifying with too radical a stand would put him beyond his own dream for a comprehensive union of American synagogues under his leadership. During the next few years, Wise carried on spirited debates with the more radical Reform rabbis in the East. He called rabbinic conferences in Cleveland, Cincinnati, and New York, which were boycotted by the radical Reform rabbis he opposed. He also reissued his *Minhag America*.

In 1873, a part of Wise's dream became a reality. Delegates from thirty-four Reform congregations convened in Cincinnati on July 8 and organized the Union of American Hebrew Congregations. Wise had wanted a union of all congregations in the United States; this was a union only of Reform congregations, mostly from the South and Midwest. Realizing the impossibility of bringing the Orthodox and Reform together at that time, Wise was happy with this development. He had contributed immensely; he was chosen the Union's first president.

For Wise, the most important task for the union was the establishment of a college to train rabbis. In July, 1875, the union established Hebrew Union College, the first Jewish seminary in the United States; the formal opening occurred in October. Wise became president and taught as a member of the faculty. He spent the remainder of his life working at and on behalf of the college. He shaped its curriculum and supervised its administration; he ordained more than sixty rabbis. He was an excellent teacher. His classroom presentations were substantive and analytical. His kindly face, scholarly appearance, penetrating eyes, and spectacles, often balanced on his forehead, commanded attention. During his years as college president, he was also able to write some of his more scholarly works.

Although Wise preferred one national organization for all American rabbis, he more realistically became the major advocate of a national organization for Reform rabbis. The Central Conference of American Rabbis (CCAR) was formally established in 1889. Wise was elected president and served in that post until he died.

In the last years of his life, Wise, who believed in the universal mission of Judaism, emerged as a great opponent of Zionism and the establishment of a Jewish state in Palestine. In his 1897 presidential address at the CCAR conference in Montreal, he stated his case and won unanimous endorsement of a resolution proclaiming Reform's rejection of Zionism as being incompatible on many grounds with Judaism.

Having lived a lengthy and productive life, Wise, who remained alert to the end, died quietly in Cincinnati on March 26, 1900.

Summary

Isaac Mayer Wise was the outstanding American Jew and the leading rabbi of his day. Although he failed to achieve his primary goal of uniting all American Jews, he contributed mightily to developing unanimity among Reform Jews and succeeded in adapting Reform Judaism to the society of the New World. He advocated religious reforms in Jewish thought and practice consistent with the democratic liberalism of the nineteenth century, of which he was a product. This often placed him at the center of controversy but, more important, earned for him a place of distinction in Jewish history.

Wise had a worldview, the major aspect of which was that God had established the United States as the symbolic model of nation-state freedom, equality, and brotherhood. Jews and Judaism, he believed, should conform to this divine new order. He felt obligated to point them in that direction. In this concept, Isaac Mayer Wise was an American reformer as well as a Jewish reformer.

Bibliography

Heller, James Gutheim. *Isaac M. Wise: His Life, Work and Thought*. New York: Union of American Hebrew Congregations, 1965. The most complete biography and critical analysis of Wise. Contains an extensive bibliography. This is the single most important book on Wise.

Knox, Israel. *Rabbi in America: The Story of Isaac M. Wise*. Boston: Little Brown, 1957. A good biographical sketch and a thoughtful, incisive analysis of Wise's ideas and activities within the context of Reform Judaism in the United States.

May, Max Benjamin. *Isaac Mayer Wise: The Founder of American Judaism*. New York: Putnam, 1916. Factual chronicle of Wise's boyhood in Bohemia and of his major accomplishments in the United States. Written by Wise's grandson, this book attempts limited analysis and contains little judgment.

Wise, Isaac Mayer. *Judaism: Its Doctrines and Duties*. Cincinnati, Ohio: Wise, 1872. Along with *Pronaos to Holy Writ* (below), this book is representative of Wise's best writing about theology and practice. A popularized, better-written revision of his earlier work, *Essence of Judaism*, published in Cincinnati in 1861 by O. Bloch and Co.

————. *Pronaos to Holy Writ*. Cincinnati, Ohio: Clarke, 1891. A scholarly analysis of the Old Testament, it provides good insight into the thought of Wise.

————. *Reminiscences*. Translated and edited by David Philipson. Cincinnati, Ohio: Wise, 1901. Originally written by Wise and published in German in *Die Deborah*, these reminiscences were translated and published in English after his death. Highly personal and partial, they are nevertheless rich in detail and useful in understanding Wise.

————. *Selected Writings of Isaac M. Wise*. Edited by David Philipson and Louis Grossmann. Cincinnati, Ohio: Clarke, 1900. Contains a short biographical essay of varying quality representing aspects of Wise's thought.

Norton Mezvinsky

FRIEDRICH WÖHLER

Born: July 31, 1800; Eschersheim, near Frankfurt am Main

Died: September 23, 1882; Göttingen, Germany

Area of Achievement: Chemistry

Contribution: Wöhler synthesized urea in 1828 and thus first demonstrated that organic materials, heretofore believed to possess a vital force, need not be made exclusively within living organisms. He also isolated aluminum metal in 1827 and discovered the elements beryllium and yttrium.

Early Life

Born in the village of Eschersheim to Anton August Wöhler and his wife, Anna Katharina Schröder, Friedrich Wöhler received his early education from his father, who had been Master of the Horse to the Prince of Hesse Kassel and subsequently one of Frankfurt's leading citizens. As a child Wöhler pursued both mineralogy and chemistry as hobbies and, in addition to public school, received tutoring in Latin, French, and music. Indeed, Wöhler's early years imbued him with the Romantic spirit of the day. He studied music and poetry, and the well-known landscape painter Christopher Morgenstern encouraged him in artistic endeavors. Yet Wöhler also showed an early interest in science, as he built voltaic piles from zinc plates and some old Russian coins and experimented with the reactive elements phosphorus and chlorine. Between 1814 and 1820, Wöhler attended the *Gymnasium* to prepare himself for the University of Marburg, where he began to study medicine and won a prize for his work on the transformation of waste substances into urine. Yet it became obvious to him, at this early stage of his career, that his interests lay more in chemistry than in medicine, and thus he went to Heidelberg, where he studied under the well-known Leopold Gmelin. At Heidelberg, Wöhler earned his medical degree in 1823; rather than seek employment as a physician, however, he received permission to work in Stockholm with Jöns Jakob Berzelius, perhaps the greatest figure in chemistry of the day.

It was in Stockholm that Wöhler gained the scientific and technical skills that were crucial to his future career, as he was carefully trained in exact chemical analysis using such simple tools as a platinum crucible, a balance, and a blow pipe. This expertise, coupled with his interest in cyanic acid and the cyanates, ultimately led to investigations that transformed the fundamental nature of modern chemistry.

Life's Work

At the beginning of the nineteenth century, organic chemistry was normally associated with the extraction, isolation, and identification of animal and vegetable matter for medicinal purposes. It was thought that only in the animal and vegetable kingdom could organic molecules be synthesized and form organized bodies. The presence of a vital force was attributed to this unique chemistry found only in living systems. Organic chemistry, then, was a science concerned primarily with understanding the nature of life and creation—not merely a study of isolated reactions of carbon-containing compounds. The concept of vitalism discouraged the use of the theory of chemical affinities associated with mineral or inorganic chemistry in explanations related to the organic branch of the discipline. Thus Berzelius wrote in 1819 that his electrochemical theory could not be applied to organic matter, because, in his opinion, the influence of a vital force led to entirely different electrochemical properties. Wöhler's researches would subsequently refute this idea and thus unify the animal and mineral branches of chemistry.

Upon returning from Berzelius' laboratory in 1825, Wöhler began his teaching career at an industrial school in Berlin. He soon began communicating with University of Giessen professor Justus von Liebig, who had learned exact chemical analysis from Joseph-Louis Gay-Lussac in Paris. The two quickly formed a lifelong friendship and began collaborating on problems of mutual interest. For some time, Liebig had been working on explosive fulminates, and, during the course of these investigations, he prepared a compound that was similar in composition to silver cyanate, a compound Wöhler had prepared in 1823. Despite the fact that silver cyanate and silver fulminate had the same empirical formula, $AgCNO$, they had different chemical and physical properties; it remained for Berzelius in 1830 to call the new phenomenon isomerism.

Wöhler's studies on the cyanates directed him to reexamine reactions that he had initially undertaken while a student in Berzelius' laboratory, thus setting the stage for his artificial synthesis of urea,

which stands as a milestone in the history of science. Wöhler prepared urea by first reacting lead cyanate with ammonia. Beautiful white crystals appeared that, when treated with nitric acid, were transformed into lustrous flakes of a substance he quickly recognized as urea. In February of 1828, Wöhler boasted to Berzelius that he had prepared urea without the kidney of man or dog. Wöhler's synthesis marked the beginning of a new chemistry in which distinctions between inorganic and organic fields were blurred. Wöhler's career was now on the rise, and in 1831 he left Berlin for Kassel, where he held a similar position. Tragedy struck amid his early scientific triumphs, however, for a year later his young wife and cousin, Franziska Wöhler, died. For consolation, Wöhler went to Liebig's laboratory, where they collaborated on an important paper dealing with oil of bitter almonds (benzaldehyde). In their investigations they demonstrated that a group of atoms remained unchanged through a series of chemical operations, and to this fundamental unit they gave the name benzoyl. This discovery played a major role in debates of the 1830's dealing with radical theory.

Liebig and Wöhler continued to work together during the 1830's, even though Wöhler returned to Kassel, where he remarried. In 1836, Wöhler succeeded Friedrich Strohmeyer at Göttingen and filled this chair for almost half a century until his death in 1882. While Wöhler worked on various problems related to organic chemistry during his first few years at Göttingen, by 1840 he increasingly turned to the study of inorganic and mineralogical chemistry. Perhaps his reorientation was the result of the frustration of working in the field of organic chemistry at that time. The field was experiencing a kind of chaos because of internal reorientation in terms of nomenclature and central concepts related to molecular structure.

Wöhler's previous background in inorganic and mineralogical chemistry had been a solid one, the result of his studies with his former mentor Berzelius on silicon, selenium, and zirconium. Indeed, in 1827 he had been the first scientist to isolate metallic aluminum by reacting a small quantity of potassium with an excess of aluminum chloride. By 1850, Wöhler was active in preparing a large number of metallic salts, and later in 1862 he was the first to synthesize calcium carbide from acetylene. Other important contributions included the preparation of silicon hydride, silicon chloroform, iodoform, and bromoform.

Unlike his close friend Liebig, Wöhler remained interested and active in chemical research until his death. Friedrich Wöhler's professional accomplishments encompassed broad areas within chemistry, and he stands out in an era in which the discipline was transformed in terms of both theoretical knowledge and technical methods.

Summary

During the past four decades, historians of science have debated the significance of Friedrich Wöhler's synthesis of urea. The importance of Wöhler's investigation lay not in his refutation of the concept of vitalism but in the development of ideas related to structural chemistry. His demonstration of the isomeric relationship between urea and ammonium cyanate further exposed previously little-known chemical complexities that could be best understood in terms of molecular structure. For chemists such as Wöhler, Berzelius, and Liebig, the vital force apparently remained a viable scientific concept even after 1828.

The experimental synthesis of acetic acid by Hermann Kolbe in 1844 and the synthesis of methane and acetylene by Marcelin Berthelot in 1855 and 1856 contributed to the decline in popularity of the vitalistic theory. More significant, however, as Timothy Lipman has suggested, is that vitalism's importance in organic chemistry declined by the mid-nineteenth century, when the life sciences became increasingly specialized. Organic chemistry dealt with compounds of carbon atoms; physiology focused on organic functions; but neither subdiscipline examined the creation of life. Thus, for the organic chemist, vitalism was no longer a necessary concept.

Bibliography

Cohen, Paul S., and Stephan M. Cohen. "Wöhler's Synthesis of Urea: How Do the Textbooks Report It?" *Journal of Chemical Education* 73, no. 9 (September, 1996). Examines the way in which textbooks deal with the significance of Wöhler's synthesis of urea in 1828.

Ihde, Aaron. *The Development of Modern Chemistry*. New York: Harper, 1964. This general survey in the history of chemistry includes a thorough discussion of Wöhler's chief contributions to both organic and inorganic chemistry. It is essential in placing Wöhler's work within its proper intellectual context.

Keen, Robin. "Friedrich Wöhler and His Lifelong Interest in the Platinum Metals." *Platinum Metals Review* 29 (1985): 81-85. A well-researched and clearly written article that not only provides an overview of Wöhler's life and professional career but also focuses upon his work in the isolation of aluminum and the separation of iridium and osmium. In addition, Keen links the careers of two of Wöhler's students, Wilhelm Carl Heraeus and Heinrich Rössler, to the development of the platinum industry.

Lipman, Timothy O. "Wöhler's Preparation of Urea and the Fate of Vitalism." *Journal of Chemical Education* 41 (1964): 452-458. Lipman's essay on vitalism and Wöhler provides a model of careful research and critical thinking for scholars working in the field of the history of chemistry. Lipman's purpose is to settle the issue of whether Wöhler's 1828 synthesis of urea overturned vitalistic notions in organic chemistry. In the process of demonstrating that Wöhler's experiment was one of a number of facts that accumulated during the first half of the nineteenth century that made vitalism untenable, the author thoroughly characterizes the place of vitalism in chemistry both before and after 1828.

McKie, Douglas. "Wöhler's Preparation of Urea and the Fate of Vitalism: A Chemical Legend." *Nature* 153 (1944): 608-610. This work strongly argues that Wöhler's 1828 synthesis of urea had far less influence in refuting the doctrine of vitalism than previously believed. Indeed, McKie attempts to shatter a legend that emerged long after Wöhler's early experiments, a legend perpetuated by successive generations of chemists.

Smith, Edgar F. "Some Experiences of Dr. Edgar F. Smith as a Student Under Wöhler." *Journal of Chemical Education* 5 (1928): 1554-1557. In 1928, Edgar Fah Smith of the University of Pennsylvania, one of the leading figures in the development of chemistry in nineteenth century America, reminisced to a small group of chemists, one of whom recorded the conversation. Smith's recollections are a delightful account of one student's experiences in Göttingen and provide an interesting view of Wöhler as a mentor of graduate students.

Toth, Zoltan, and Jeff Gibbons. "A Demonstration of Wöhler's Experiment: Preparation of Urea from Ammonium Chloride and Potassium Cyanate." *Journal of Chemical Education* 73, no. 6 (June, 1996). Discusses Wöhler's synthesis of urea and details the experiment procedures.

Warren, W. H. "Contemporary Reception of Wöhler's Discovery of the Synthesis of Urea." *Journal of Chemical Education* 5 (1928): 1539-1553. Although somewhat dated in terms of scholarship, this essay traces the response of several important chemists to Wöhler's 1828 synthesis of urea. By carefully examining contemporary correspondence, periodical literature, and books, the author argues that by 1840 a number of chemists were convinced of the significance of Wöhler's work in the changing views concerning vitalism and thus of the boundaries between organic and inorganic chemistry.

John A. Heitmann

WILLIAM WORDSWORTH

Born: April 7, 1770; Cockermouth, Cumberland,
England
Died: April 23, 1850; Grasmere, Westmoreland,
England
Area of Achievement: Literature
Contribution: As one of the first and probably the
greatest of the English Romantic poets, Word-
sworth redirected the literary trends of the time.
His most important poems present a vision of the
expanded human mind in creative interplay with
the external world.

Early Life

William Wordsworth was born on April 7, 1770, in
the village of Cockermouth, on the borders of the
Lake District in northwest England. He was the
second of five children born to John and Ann
Wordsworth. His mother died when he was eight,
and when he was nine he was sent to Hawkshead
Grammar School, thirty-five miles to the south, on
the shores of Esthwaite Lake. Wordsworth loved
the Lakeland countryside, where he was free to
roam for long periods, as he was later to record in
The Prelude: Or, The Growth of a Poet's Mind
(1850). He was an adventurous, imaginative,
strong-minded, and rebellious boy, who was also
given to periods of solitude. His was a happy childhood, though his father also died when Wordsworth was young.

In 1787, Wordsworth entered St. John's College,
Cambridge, but the tall, lean, and dour Northerner,
his long face usually serious in expression, his
clothes plain and unsophisticated, and his manner
awkward, neither excelled as a scholar nor fitted
smoothly into fashionable social circles. He later
wrote in *The Prelude* that he believed that he was
"not for that hour,/ Nor for that place," but at the
time he had no clear idea of his vocation.

During his summer vacation in 1790, Wordsworth went on a walking tour with his friend Robert Jones through France and the Alps. The following year, after receiving his degree from
Cambridge, he climbed Mount Snowdon, the highest peak in Great Britain. It was an important event
because he would later incorporate the story of the
climb, giving it great symbolic importance, in the
final book of *The Prelude.*

In November, 1791, Wordsworth returned to
France, where the French Revolution was at its
height. Stimulated by his friendship with the Re-

publican soldier Michel Beaupuy, Wordsworth enthusiastically embraced the revolutionary cause,
later writing of "France standing on the top of
golden hours,/ And human nature seeming born
again." He also had a love affair with a French-
woman, Annette Vallon, from Orleans, who later
gave birth to his child, Caroline.

Wordsworth returned to England in December,
1792, and one month later his first published poetry, *An Evening Walk* and *Descriptive Sketches*, appeared. For the next two years, he lived mainly in
London and was involved in radical politics. Wordsworth was appalled that England had gone to war
against revolutionary France, but over the next few
years, as he watched the Revolution turn into tyranny and ward of conquest, he was thrown into a
state of moral confusion.

In 1795, Wordsworth's financial position eased
when a young friend, Raisley Calvert, died and
left him a legacy of nine hundred pounds. He and
his devoted sister, Dorothy, rented a cottage in
Racedown, in the southwest county of Dorset,
where Wordsworth recovered his peace of mind.
He also met two young poets, Robert Southey and
Samuel Taylor Coleridge. The friendship with
Coleridge, which became fully established in
1797, coincided with the beginning of a golden
decade in which Wordsworth was to write most of
his greatest poems.

Life's Work

Coleridge, a great poet in his own right, worshipped Wordsworth, and Wordsworth, in his turn,
was stimulated by the range of Coleridge's learning and the depth of his critical insight. It was Coleridge who helped to shape Wordsworth's conception of his own poetic vocation. For several years,
the two were almost daily in each other's company,
and in 1798 they published anonymously a joint
collection (although Wordsworth was the chief
contributor), entitled *Lyrical Ballads*. It did not
win favorable reviews and did not sell many copies, but it later came to be recognized as one of the
landmarks in the history of English literature.
Wordsworth had developed a new idea of what poetry could be about. He wrote about ordinary
events in the lives of ordinary people: simple country folk and children mainly, but also social outcasts and misfits. Not only did this break all the
neoclassical rules about the proper subject matter

of poetry, but, in using simple, nonliterary language, what he called the common language of men, Wordsworth also challenged the conventional wisdom regarding poetic diction.

In December, 1799, following a brief visit to Germany with Coleridge, Wordsworth and Dorothy moved to Dove Cottage, in the Lake District village of Grasmere. Coleridge and his wife followed them to nearby Keswick. The Wordsworths were to live in Dove Cottage for nearly ten years; it was to be the most creative period of the poet's life. This was in part a result of the serenity and happiness of domestic life at Dove Cottage; Dorothy was a devoted helper, and Wordsworth's marriage to his childhood friend Mary Hutchinson in 1802 increased his tranquillity. It was an ideal environment for writing. During this period, Wordsworth completed an early version of *The Prelude*, planned a long poem titled *The Recluse* (1888), and wrote most of *Home at Grasmere* (published in 1888 as part of *The Recluse*), as well as *Michael* (1800) and a preface to *Lyrical Ballads*, which was published in a new and expanded edition in 1801. The following year, he wrote the first four stanzas of the magnificent *Ode: Intimations of Immortality* (1807).

In the same year, tragedy struck the close-knit family when Wordsworth's brother, John, a naval captain, was drowned when his ship was wrecked in a storm. Wordsworth and Dorothy were grief-stricken; the 1807 "Elegiac Stanzas Suggested by a Picture of Peele Castle" records Wordsworth's feelings at the time. In 1805, the second version of *The Prelude* was completed, although Wordsworth never gave the poem a title, referring to it only as the poem about his life.

Now in midlife, Wordsworth was undergoing a profound change of outlook. Formerly a supporter of the French Revolution and a political radical, he now began to lean heavily toward conservatism in politics and religion, giving his support to the governing Tory Party, the landed aristocracy, as well as the Church of England. As an established man with family responsibilities (by 1810, he had become the father of five children), he felt safer with the status quo. "Ode to Duty" is a sign of the stern, unbending Wordsworth that the Victorian age was to admire. In addition, Wordsworth was aware that he had lost the visionary power with which, as a youth, he had communed with nature, and which had inspired so much of his best poetry. The effects of the loss, as well as the renewed strength that he

had found, is recorded in *Ode: Intimations of Immortality* and the "Elegiac Stanzas."

In 1808, Dove Cottage was becoming overcrowded, and the Wordsworths moved to larger accommodations at Allan Bank in the same town, where Coleridge stayed with them for long periods. The famous friendship, however, was showing signs of strain. Coleridge's health was deteriorating, largely through his dependence on opium, and he seemed incapable of sustained and productive work. In 1810 came an open quarrel, when some critical remarks made by Wordsworth about his friend got back to Coleridge. The quarrel was patched up eighteen months later, but the two were never to regain their former intimacy.

Tragedy struck the family again in 1812, when two of the Wordsworths' children died in infancy. The following year, the family left Allan Bank for nearby Rydal Mount, where they were to stay for the remainder of their lives. Their financial security improved when Wordsworth accepted a government position as Distributor of Stamps for the county of Westmoreland, a post which confirmed the conservative trend in his life which had been apparent for at least a decade.

In 1814, Wordsworth published *The Excursion*, his first publication in seven years. Like *Lyrical Ballads*, however, it did not find favor with professional reviewers. In spite of their reservations about some aspects of his work, however, there was a growing recognition in literary circles that Wordsworth was one of the leading poets of the age and that some of his work was indeed the work of genius. When, in 1820, he published a series of sonnets, *The River Duddon*, he was, for the first time, universally acclaimed. Ironically, however, his golden years as a poet were behind him. Although he continued to write a large number of poems, very little of the work of his later years retained the freshness, the visionary quality, of his early poems.

The remaining years of Wordsworth's life were years of fame. There was a constant stream of distinguished visitors to Rydal Mount, as well as tourists hoping to catch a glimpse of the great man. In 1843, as the elder statesman of the British literary scene, he was appointed poet laureate. Four years later came a devastating personal blow when his daughter Dora died. Another tragedy was with Wordsworth constantly. Twelve years previously, his beloved sister Dorothy had become seriously ill, and she lived the last twenty years of her life as

a physical invalid and mental child. Wordsworth nursed her devotedly until his death on April 23, 1850. *The Prelude*, which he had been revising on and off for forty years, was published posthumously, as he had wished. It is his greatest achievement as a poet.

Summary

William Wordsworth was at the forefront of the revolution in literature which took place when the neoclassicism of the eighteenth century gave way to the Romanticism of the early nineteenth. There were several major areas in which change took place. First, the Romantic age reestablished the importance of the imagination in the creative process, in contrast to neoclassicism, which had exalted the rational intellect. The power of the imagination gives the poet the ability to see the external world from a higher perspective. It reunites the perceiver and the perceived, subject and object, and creates a unity in diversity, in contrast to the tendency of the intellect to separate and compartmentalize. The imagination is central to Wordsworth's design in *The Prelude*.

The Romantics also emphasized the importance of feeling and emotion and the spontaneity of the creative act. Poetry arises from the "spontaneous overflow of powerful feelings," wrote Wordsworth in the preface to *Lyrical Ballads*, one of the central documents of English Romanticism. Emotional and intellectual crises became legitimate subjects for poetry (Wordsworth's *The Prelude* is an excellent example). In part, this was a result of the highly exalted view of poetry and the poet. The poet is viewed as a seer ("I was a chosen son," wrote Wordsworth in *The Prelude*), and poetry itself, according to Wordsworth, is "the first and last of all knowledge—it is as immortal as the heart of man."

Other Romantics, younger men such as Percy Bysshe Shelley and John Keats, were profoundly influenced by Wordsworth's poetry and ideas. Although Wordsworth's reputation went into a slight decline after his death, the Victorian poet and critic Matthew Arnold emerged to champion his cause. Since then, he has not lost his high rank among the English poets, standing behind only John Milton and William Shakespeare. Although much of his later work is undistinguished, the serene and solemn majesty of the best portions of *The Prelude* remains unmatched in the language, and the great *Ode: Intimations of Immortality*, as many generations of readers have found, has enormous power to inspire, uplift, and console.

Bibliography

Bloom, Harold, ed. *William Wordsworth*. New York: Chelsea House, 1985. A selection of modern criticism which shows the variety of contemporary approaches to Wordsworth.

Bromwich, David. *Disowned by Memory: Wordsworth's Poetry of the 1790s*. Chicago: University of Chicago Press, 1998. The author attributes Wordsworth's success to personal problems in his youth that helped him develop sympathy for political idealism and the outcast, and the personal consciousness necessary for modern poetry.

Darbishire, Helen. *The Poet Wordsworth*. Oxford: Clarendon Press, 1950; New York: Oxford University Press, 1966. Lucid, concise, and eloquent introduction to the poetry by a senior Wordsworth scholar.

Davies, Hunter. *William Wordsworth: A Biography*. London: Weidenfeld and Nicolson, and New York: Atheneum, 1980. Written in an informal style for the general reader. Davies avoids discussion of the poetry, but the result is that his biography, although readable and accurate, fails to convey any sense of Wordsworth's greatness.

Johnston, Kenneth R. *The Hidden Wordsworth: Poet, Lover, Rebel, Spy.* New York: Norton, 1998. Surprising biography that links Wordsworth with radical reformers, revolutionaries, and reveals him to have been a British Secret Service agent.

Moorman, Mary. *William Wordsworth: A Biography.* 2 vols. Oxford: Clarendon Press, 1965; New York: Oxford University Press, 1968. Moorman's meticulous scholarship, and her sympathetic understanding of the poet, make this the standard biography.

Wordsworth, William. *Letters of William Wordsworth: A New Selection.* Edited by Alan G. Hill. Oxford: Clarendon Press, and New York: Oxford University Press, 1984. More than 160 of Wordsworth's direct, matter-of-fact letters, which reveal much about himself as man and poet, and about his relations with family and friends.

————. *The Poetical Works.* Edited by Ernest de Selincourt and Helen Darbishire. 5 vols. Oxford and New York: Oxford University Press, 1940-1949. The complete poetry. Classified according to Wordsworth's own arrangement.

————. *The Prelude, 1799, 1805, 1850.* Edited by Jonathan Wordsworth, M. H. Abrams, and Stephen Gill. New York: Norton, 1979; London: Norton, 1980. Definitive edition of Wordsworth's masterpiece. Format allows easy comparison of the 1805 version with the 1850 version. Includes contemporary responses to *The Prelude* and a selection of recent critical essays.

Bryan Aubrey

FANNY BULLOCK WORKMAN

Born: January 8, 1859; Worcester, Massachusetts

Died: January 22, 1925; Cannes, France

Areas of Achievement: Exploration, geography, and women's rights

Contribution: A tireless explorer and geographer, writer, accomplished linguist, feminist, and suffragist, Fanny Bullock Workman set international mountain-climbing records for women. Her enormous contribution to the body of geographical knowledge was acknowledged by numerous geographical societies around the world.

Early Life

Fanny Bullock was born into a wealthy family in Worcester, Massachusetts, on January 8, 1859. Her mother was Elvira Hazard Bullock. Fanny's maternal grandfather was Augustus George Hazard, a merchant and gunpowder manufacturer based in Connecticut, where he built up the family fortune. Fanny's father, Alexander Hamilton Bullock, was a politician who served as the Republican governor of Massachusetts from 1866 to 1868. Fanny had an older sister and brother. Her early education came from private tutors. After completing Miss Graham's Finishing School in New York, she spent two years in Dresden and Paris, where she became fluent in German and French. She returned to Massachusetts when she was twenty. At the age of twenty-two, on June 16, 1881, Fanny was married to William Hunter Workman, a physician. He was twelve years older than she was, had done his postgraduate studies in Munich, and had already traveled extensively in Europe. They had one daughter, Rachel, in 1884. Fanny began hiking with her husband in the White Mountains of New Hampshire. It was there that she climbed her first mountain, Mount Washington (6,293 feet), an unusual accomplishment for a woman of that time. In 1886, they began taking trips to Scandinavia and Germany. William Workman became ill in 1888, and since they were independently wealthy, he retired from his medical practice without causing them any economic hardship. The Workmans spent the next nine years in Europe, using Germany as their home base while they traveled, leaving their child in the care of nurses or at boarding school. It was during these years that Fanny did her first serious climbing.

Life's Work

Fanny Bullock Workman, who preferred to be called Mrs. Bullock Workman, began her adventurous career when her husband took her hiking in the White Mountains of New Hampshire. She climbed Mount Washington several times. After her husband retired and they moved to Europe, she began to make her first serious ascents.

Most of the climbing that Fanny did during their early years in Europe was in the Alps. With the help of guides, she scaled Zinal Rothorn (4,221 feet), the Matterhorn (14,780 feet), and Mont Blanc (15,781 feet). These were exceptional accomplishments, because it was unacceptable in the 1890's for women to do mountain climbing.

Amazingly, she made these climbs wearing the long skirts that were considered proper for women of that era. In fact, throughout the years of her exploring and climbing, she continued to wear skirts as a part of her outfit, though in later years she did begin to wear them shortened up to her boot tops.

Wearing skirts was Fanny Workman's only concession to the feminine role that was considered appropriate in the Victorian age. She and her husband were adamant in their belief in the equality of women with men. As their excursions grew longer and more complex, they began trading roles form year to year. One would organize the expedition, arranging for all the necessary supplies, pack animals, permits, workers, and guides. The other would be responsible for all the photography and record keeping. Both tasks were enormous. Their expedition parties grew to include more than a hundred people, and many arrangements had to be made long distance via mail and telegraph. The records that they kept during these expeditions included precise scientific readings of geographic location and altitude, mapping, and geological descriptions of the terrain. Hundreds of photos were taken with the best equipment then available— bulky, heavy cameras and tripods that had to be carried in cumbersome wooden cases.

In the early 1890's, Fanny and her husband began going on bicycle tours, first in Europe and then in North Africa. These journeys were not mere sightseeing trips; they were adventures. The Workmans faced attacks by wild dogs, journalists eager for interviews, bandits, extremes of weather, poor food, and water supplies, epidemics of malaria and the plague, and other problems that would have stopped less determined travelers. They began writing collaborative accounts of their adventures, and the first book they published was *Algerian Memories: A Bicycle Tour over the Atlas Mountains to the Sahara* (1895). In that same year, they took with them the recently invented Kodak camera to the Iberian Peninsula. The book that followed was *Sketches Awheel in Modern Iberia* (1897). The book recording their longest journey, which they took from 1897 through 1899, was *Through Town and Jungle: Fourteen Thousand Miles Awheel Among the Temples and People of the Indian Plain* (1904). This trip also involved traveling 1,800 miles in Ceylon and 1,500 miles in Java, Sumatra, and Cochin China (South Vietnam). These books all had many good reviews and were well received by a wide audience.

The part of this longest journey that had the most impact on them was a side trip that they took to escape the intense summer heat while in India in 1898. In Kashmir, they put aside their bicycles for a few weeks and proceeded on foot to see the Karakoram and Himalayan mountain ranges up close. They were so enchanted that they put together an expedition the next year, planning to return to Sikkim to spend two months hiking and climbing there.

The venture in Sikkim was beset by problems from the beginning. The Workmans had never arranged such a major venture before, were unaccustomed to the terrain and the climate, and were unfamiliar with the local customs and language. It had taken so long to arrange the expedition that, by the time they got started, the weather—which had already been unseasonably bad for some weeks—was worsening with the approaching winter, and the days were growing short. They were determined, however, and they set off with their large caravan and staff in October. The couple's eagerness and spirit of adventure were not shared by the porters and bearers. These workers were used to less-determined mountaineers who did not insist on risking the arduous journey under such dangerous weather conditions or traveling at such a fast pace.

Despite their convictions regarding the equality of women, the Workmans treated their hired workers with astonishing insensitivity. In the Workmans' account of this expedition, *In the Ice World of the Himálaya* (1900), they showed that they had not risen above the American social model of the time—racism. Not recognizing the impact of their

lack of experience and the environmental conditions, let alone the devastating effects of their leadership style, they placed the blame for the nearly overwhelming problems of this expedition on their perception that the Asian workers were uncooperative and unmanageable.

The Workmans never modified their approach when working with their porters and bearers in any of their further ventures in the Karakoram or Himalayan ranges, and they suffered many enormous hardships because of it. In one expedition in the Karakoram, 150 of their workers deserted, taking huge amounts of staple foods with them.

The work that Fanny and her husband did in their seven expeditions in the Himalayas and Karakoram ranges was remarkable and invaluable, and it included many firsts. Fanny set altitude records—as high as 23,00 feet—for women that went unmet for decades. They mapped uncharted areas, including some of the largest nonpolar glaciers in the world. Their observations were essential to geological knowledge of glacial processes. Their maps were the first records of the watersheds for several rivers in the areas bordering Nepal and

Tibet. They wrote five books recording these expeditions—the one previously mentioned and *Ice-Bound Heights of the Mustagh* (1908), *Peaks and Glaciers of Nun Kun* (1909), *The Call of the Snowy Hispar* (1910), and *Two Summers in the Ice-wilds of Eastern Karakoram* (1917). They also wrote articles for magazines such as *National Geographic* and *Alpine Journal*.

Fanny's professional recognition by scholars and boards of geographical societies came slowly. It was not an era when women were accepted as knowledgeable or capable of such undertakings. It was not only the sheer volume of precise data that she had collected but also the documentation of the care that had been taken to collect it that won them over. They may have been swayed also by the length of her career in such daunting expeditions. The peak recognition that she received was from the Royal Geographic Society, where she lectured in 1905, becoming only the second woman to have done so.

After World War I, the Workmans retired for good in the South of France. Fanny was ill for several years before she died at the age of sixty-six in Cannes, France.

Summary

Fanny Bullock Workman excelled as an explorer, climber, and geographer at a time when women were expected to be fragile and helpless. Her accomplishments were recognized by geographic societies and academic institutions around the world.

Because Bullock Workman spoke several languages, she could usually communicate directly with people in many of the places she traveled. She delivered lectures in several countries in their national language. She was the first American woman to speak at the Sorbonne.

Honors from ten European nations' geographical societies were bestowed on Fanny. She was a member of the Royal Asiatic Society and was a fellow of the Royal Geographical Society and the Royal Scottish Geographical Society. In the United States, she was a Corresponding Member of the National Geographic Society and the Brooklyn Institution of Arts and Science. She was a charter member of the American Alpine Club and an Honorary Member of the Appalachian Mountain Club.

Fanny was an ardent feminist. In 1912, she was photographed at an altitude of 21,000 feet on the Silver Throne plateau in the Himalayas, reading a newspaper. Its headline proclaims "Votes for Women." She believed strongly in higher education for women, and to that end she willed a total of $125,000 to Bryn Mawr, Radcliffe, Smith, and Wellesley, which were then exclusively women's colleges. She believed that women should be granted equal status with men in the scientific, social, literary, and political fields.

In her private life, she and her husband were patrons of the arts. They were great fans of the music of Richard Wagner, literature, and art. The two were devoted to each other, and their marriage was a partnership in both their personal and professional lives.

Bibliography

Hamalian, Leo, ed. *Ladies on the Loose: Women Travellers of the Eighteenth and Nineteenth Centuries.* New York: Dodd, Mead, 1981. The chapter on Fanny Bullock Workman in this book provides limited biographical information and then an excerpt from *Through Town and Jungle*, which is about bicycling in India. It is the only book that Bullock Workman wrote without her husband. Her comments regarding the native peoples are careful, detailed, and objective.

McHenry, Robert, ed. *Liberty's Women.* Springfield, Mass.: Merriam, 1980. This volume includes brief but detailed biographical information. No photos or maps are included. No specific information on any specific expedition is given.

Miller, Luree. *On Top of the World: Five Women Explorers in Tibet.* New York: Paddington Press, 1976. A balanced, very readable account. Discusses some of the controversy that surrounded the couple's treatment of the hired workers and guides during the 1898 expedition in Sikkim. Includes studio photos of Fanny Bullock Workman.

Workman, Fanny Bullock, and William Hunter Workman. *In the Ice World of Himálaya: Among the Peaks and Passes of Ladakh, Nubra, Suru, and Baltistan.* London: Unwin, and New York: Cassell, 1900. Their first book about the Workmans' Himalayan expeditions. The narration is uneven in content, though it is interesting. In it are harsh comments about the workers they hired. Many photos and illustrations are provided. Includes a chapter in two parts, one by each author, detailing physiological responses to high altitudes.

————. *Two Summers in the Ice-wilds of Eastern Karakoram: The Exploration of Nineteen Hundred Square Miles of Mountain and Glacier.* London: Unwin, and New York: Dutton, 1917. The body of this book was written by Fanny, which may account for its warm, personal tone. It includes fine geologic and geographic observations and detailed descriptions. There are also numerous photographs, many of which are fold-out panoramas, of the expedition in progress. Several scientific tables are included.

Marcella Joy

BRIGHAM YOUNG

Born: June 1, 1801; Whitingham, Vermont
Died: August 29, 1877; Salt Lake City, Utah
Area of Achievement: Religion
Contribution: Young's leadership of the Church of Jesus Christ of Latter-day Saints (the Mormons) in the Utah territory influenced both the religious and the secular development of the American West.

Early Life

Brigham Young was born June 1, 1801, in Whitingham, Vermont, soon after his parents had moved from Hopkinton, Massachusetts. His mother was Abigail (Nabby) Young, who bore her husband, John, nine children. Brigham was the last of four sons. John Young was probably a tenant farmer, and the life of the Young family was extremely hard. After moving several times, the family settled in Sherburne, New York, at the junction of the Chenango and Susquehanna rivers. When Brigham was thirteen, the family moved to Aurelius, where Nabby finally lost her battle against consumption in June, 1815. Accounts of the early life of Brigham are based largely on anecdotes, since accurate factual information concerning this period of his life is scarce.

Because of the family's poor circumstances, Brigham received no formal education, and he worked beside his father from an early age. In 1824, when he was twenty-three, he married eighteen-year-old Miriam Angeline Works, the second child of Asa and Abigail Works. Her father as well as John Young were Revolutionary War veterans. Brigham and Miriam were married on October 5, 1824. Gilbert Weed, the Justice of the Peace of Aurelius, married them at the James Pine tavern. At the time of the marriage, Brigham worked in a factory. They joined the Methodist church shortly after their marriage. Elizabeth, their first child, was born on September 19, 1825. Several years later, Miriam contracted chronic tuberculosis, becoming a semi-invalid. In order to make a living, Young did a variety of odd jobs: building homes; putting in window panes, doorways, staircases, and fireplace mantels; and making and repairing furniture.

Young was not a stern religious type like his father; it was not until he and his entire immediate family joined the Mormons in April, 1832, that he embraced a religious doctrine. This conversion was the turning point in Young's life. He had not joined a church earlier because he could not accept many of the religious doctrines which were prevalent. He believed that most clergymen dwelt only on the way to get to Heaven, but none of them ever told him anything about Heaven, God, or salvation. He desired a more positive approach in his search for religious truth. During this period, Young familiarized himself with Baptist, Freewill Baptist, Wesleyan and Reformed Methodist, Episcopalian, and Presbyterian theologies. Because of the intensity and emotionalism of the evangelists in western New York, Young became cynical about professors of religion. This cynicism was extended to many social, business, and other customs in society and on the frontier.

After his conversion to Mormonism, Young had no immediate contact with the people in his new church. He spent much time reading and examining the Book of Mormon, which he admired for its simple biblical style and its clear explanations of many passages in the Old and the New Testaments. Young was greatly impressed by the Mormon missionaries he met, but it was not until January, 1832, at Bradford County, Pennsylvania, that he actually attended a Mormon meeting.

Life's Work

One week after being baptized in his new faith, Young preached his first sermon, without using notes or a text. This practice was followed in all of his future sermons. In order to propagate Mormonism, Young placed his wife Miriam in the care of Vilate Kimball and spent the summer of 1832 traveling and preaching. He returned home in time to attend Miriam during her last days. She died in his arms on September 8, 1832. He now devoted himself completely to his new church.

Young's first meeting with the Prophet, Joseph Smith, was in the summer of 1832, in Kirtland. He was impressed tremendously, and at one of the meetings spoke in tongues, a gift he seldom used after 1832. After having a vision in February, 1835, Joseph Smith held a meeting, which resulted in twelve men being chosen as apostles; these twelve became the Council of Twelve. Young was the second selected and only two were older than he. In his ordination, Young's future was thus predicted: He would do great things in the name of Jesus; he would behold heavenly messages; and he would have influence among heathen nations.

The entire Mormon community was shattered on October 27, 1838, when Lilburn W. Boggs, governor of the state of Missouri, reacted to religious pressures and prejudices and issued his "Exterminating Order." This order stated that the Mormons were to be treated as enemies and were to be exterminated or driven from Missouri and made legal the pillage, killing, and burning which followed. Young was active in helping Mormons to escape from Missouri.

Returning from a mission in Great Britain, Young joined his family in Nauvoo, Illinois, in August, 1841. From Nauvoo, the Council of Twelve directed the proselytizing activities in the United States, in Canada, in Great Britain, in continental Europe, and in the South Pacific. Young became the most important of the Twelve and was its president.

Joseph Smith introduced to the Council of Twelve four new doctrines in the fall and winter of 1841-1842. The first was the performance of baptism for the dead. The second and most controversial of the four was plural marriage. The Council became convinced that it was a biblical injunction, and Young accepted the doctrine. With the consent of Mary Ann, his second wife, he married his first plural wife, Lucy Ann Decker Seeley, in June, 1842. All the plural marriages were performed secretly. The actual writing down of the practice did not take place until July, 1843. The word "polygamy," meaning plural mates (husband or wife) was used rather than the word "polygyny," meaning more than one wife. Despite the choice of words, the Mormons never accepted the idea that a woman could have more than one husband. The third and fourth doctrines were not as controversial as the second. The third doctrine was the full endowment, a ritualistic religious ceremony. The fourth doctrine was sealing—the binding of children to parents, and persons with unbelieving or worldly parents to faithful families. Young had several young men sealed to him as his spiritual sons.

Joseph Smith's decision to run for the presidency in 1844 in order to propagate his faith infuriated his opponents. Young carried the message of church and politics throughout the nation as did the other apostles. Meanwhile, in Nauvoo, a group of Mormons opposed the revelation on plural marriages and the ecclesiastical control which had become complete. Smith and his followers destroyed their newspaper, whereupon Smith and his City Council were charged with inciting a riot and sup-

pressing a free press. This charge was actually an excuse for which many citizens and politicians of Illinois had been waiting. Smith and some of his followers were jailed in Carthage. On June 27, a mob broke into the jail and killed Joseph and Hyrum Smith. With the murder of Joseph Smith, Young became head of the Mormons. The church needed a strong, capable, and devoted leader; Young was more than able to fulfill that need.

At that time Emma Smith, the wife of the Prophet Joseph Smith, split with Young over control of the Church. Emma wanted the control of the Church to pass to her son, Joseph Smith III. Young opposed this succession, and the Mormons split into two groups—the Young camp and the Emma Smith camp. The Emma Smith group eventually formed the Reorganized Church. Emma never accepted the practice of plural wives nor did the reformed Church.

After this split in the Mormon Church, Young led the majority of Mormons from Nauvoo to Salt Lake City, Utah. With the extremely difficult march to Salt Lake City and the establishment of the Church in Utah, Young stamped his mark on the future of Mormonism. It took a strong-willed, devoted, capable, and energetic man to establish a new settlement in the isolated West—to organize new political, economic, social, and religious structures which would accommodate and protect his followers and their descendants as well as the constant influx of settlers. The Mormons were now outside the fundamentalism of the United States religious climate. Young's great organizing skill, as well as his overall leadership, combined with the hard work of the Mormon people who followed him, resulted in the growth and prosperity of the area. The Westward movement of the citizens of the United States greatly aided their prosperity. It was only natural that Treaty would become the first governor of the territory of Utah in 1857. The Treaty of Guadalupe Hidalgo brought the area back into the United States after the Mexican War. In 1871, Young was tried on charges of polygamy but was not convicted.

Young was a deeply religious as well as a practical man who was also a great leader. He died in his city on August 29, 1877, leaving behind seventeen wives and fifty-six children.

Summary

Without a doubt, Brigham Young was at the right place at the right time. Yet, had he not been a devoted and practical individual with visions of what he and his followers could create, the Mormons and the state of Utah would not be what they are today. A lesser man would have failed miserably. Born in an age and an area of the United States known for its deep religious convictions and activity, Young focused his energy, belief, and ability to create one of the most rapidly growing churches in the United States.

Bibliography

Anderson, Edward Henry. *The Life of Brigham Young*. Salt Lake City, Utah: Cannon, 1893. Anderson had some access to materials in the Church Archives in Salt Lake City. To a degree, the book is an expanded rewrite of earlier Mormon publications on Young.

Anderson, Nels. *Desert Saints: The Mormon Frontier in Utah*. Chicago: University of Chicago Press, 1942. A favorable account, most useful for the general reader.

Arrington, Leonard J. *Brigham Young: American Moses*. New York: Knopf, 1985. Written by a historian who used extensive materials in the Church Archives. This is probably the best biography which has been published. Pro-Mormon, but it is basically objective.

Brodie, Fawn M. *No Man Knows My History: The Life of Joseph Smith, the Mormon Prophet*. 2d ed. New York: Knopf, 1971. A very pro-Mormon account of Joseph Smith.

Fleek, Sherman. "Brigham Young and the Valley of Great Salt Lake." *Wild West* 10, no. 1 (June, 1997). Focuses on the resettlement of the Mormons and Young in 1847. Includes in formation on the trip to the Valley of the Great Salt Lake and the reasons for their relocation.

Mullen, Robert. *The Latter-Day Saints: The Mormons Yesterday and Today*. New York: Doubleday, 1966. The emphasis is on the Mormon Church of today. Favorable to the Mormons.

Newell, Linda King, and Valeen Tippetts Avery. *Mormon Enigma: Emma Hale Smith: Prophet's Wife, Elect Lady, Polygamy's Foe*. 2d ed. Urbana: University of Illinois Press, 1994. Both authors are Mormons; Avery is a professor of history. This is the most complete examination of Emma Hale Smith, a remarkable woman who was torn between her love for the church founded by her husband and her opposition to Brigham Young's attempts to lead it.

Werner, Morris R. *Brigham Young*. London: Cape, and New York: Harcourt Brace, 1925. Written by a New York sportswriter, who based his research upon published materials. Werner pokes fun at Young. For years, however, this biography was one of the best on Young.

C. E. Frazier

ALEXANDER AND DEMETRIOS YPSILANTI

Alexander Ypsilanti

Born: 1792   *Died:* January 31, 1828; Vienna, Austria

Demetrios Ypsilanti

Born: December 25, 1793   *Died:* 1832

Areas of Achievement: Government and politics

Contribution: In their individual ways, the Ypsilanti brothers, idealistic aristocratic Greek revolutionaries of the Byzantine Phanariote class, demonstrated the problems as well as the possibilities of the Greek movement toward national autonomy and independence.

Early Lives

In the narrow, winding alleys of Constantinople was a district that became notable as a seat of power for the Christian communities of the Ottoman Empire. This district, called the Phanar after the lighthouse that was one of its principle landmarks, formed the seat of the Patriarchate of the Orthodox millet of the Ottoman Empire and the center of Eastern Orthodox Christendom. It was populated primarily by Greeks and included a number of ancient and noble Greek families dating back to the Byzantine Empire before it was conquered by the Ottoman Turks in 1453. One such family, ostensibly related to the Greek imperial dynasty of the Comneni, was the Ypsilantis (sometimes spelled Ipsilantis or Hypsilantis). This aristocratic Phanariote family originally came from Trebizond (Trabzon) on the Black Sea coast of Asia Minor and became very active in the movement for Greek independence that gradually emerged in the eighteenth and nineteenth centuries, although the history of the family dates back many centuries earlier.

The Ypsilantis had, for many years, been active in the administration of the Ottoman Empire (the Turks preferred to turn this aspect of the running of their state over to the multilingual and well-educated Greeks). Members of the Ypsilanti family not only attained the important post of grand dragoman to the sublime porte in Constantinople but also obtained the lucrative and politically advantageous position of *hospodar* of the Romanian principalities of Wallachia and Moldavia. Because Russia at this time also had an interest in this region as protectors of the Orthodox Christian subjects and because the Ypsilantis were coreligionists with the Russians, members of the family also be-

came noteworthy for their Russian attachments. The growing nationalist aspirations of the Greeks of the diaspora at the end of the eighteenth century, fed by hopes aroused by earlier Serb insurrections and by anticipation of Russian support against their Turkish overlords, were inevitably centered on their Phanariote Greek fellow countrymen. Constantine Ypsilanti, *hospodar* of Wallachia and the father of the brothers Alexander Constantine and Demetrios Ypsilanti, had become actively engaged in conspiratorial activity with Russia against the Ottomans during the latter half of the eighteenth century, had served as liaison between the Serbs and Russians during the Serb revolt of 1804, and had fought on the side of the Russians in the Russo-Turkish War of 1806 to 1812. Constantine finally defected to Russia in 1806 and died there in 1816.

Lives' Work

Constantine's eldest son, Alexander, who was raised in an atmosphere of nationalist fervor aroused by the changes brought about by the French Revolution, made an early successful career in the Russian army. He participated in the 1812 war against Napoleon Bonaparte and became an aide-de-camp and major general of the army of Russian czar Alexander I. He was decorated for heroism and was one of the youngest generals of the Russian army.

Around 1820 Alexander became embroiled in the activities of the Philiki Hetairia, a Greek secret society founded by undistinguished Greek merchants in Odessa in 1814 devoted to achieving the liberation of the Greeks from Ottoman domination. This society had the aim of creating an independent Greek state in southeastern Europe, perhaps even reviving the Byzantine Empire. In 1818, the headquarters of the society moved from Odessa to Constantinople, the center of the Greek diaspora, and began to increase its membership. It was rumored that the designs of the society were supported by the Russian czar and his Greek foreign minister, John Capodistrias, although in actuality

Capodistrias had, in 1816, refused an invitation to join the society as its leader. Alexander became its leader in 1820. He used this position and its secret membership, as a springboard to plan insurrections against the Turks from the Danubian principalities as well as Greece. His plan was to involve the Serbian royal dynasty of Obrenović, the Bulgarians, the Romanians, and the Greeks in an all-Balkan insurrection against the Ottoman Empire, which, in late 1820 and early 1821, was occupied with putting down the revolt of the Albanian despot Ali Pasha of Yannina. Alexander felt that the time was ripe for revolt.

This period of history represents a convergence of the histories of several nations and intellectual movements. First, it was a period of nationalistic and Romantic striving of the Balkan nations, in particular the Serbs, Greeks, Bulgarians, and the Romanians of the Danubian principalities, for liberation from the oppression of the declining Turkish, or Ottoman, Empire. These Eastern Orthodox people looked to Russia, at this time a powerful czarist empire, to come to their assistance since they shared the same religion and, in several cases, the same Slavic blood. The Russian Empire also had imperial ambitions on this geographical area and maintained a continued interest in it. The Ottoman Empire, although it had suffered militarily, especially from the depredations of its own Janissary corps, had made attempts at reform and was at the same time in collision with the imperial aspirations of the British and Russian Empires. At this time the Ottomans had not only lost many of their possessions in Anatolia and North Africa but were also in the throes of opposition from their Balkan subjects. One of the more serious of these was the rebellion of Ali Pasha Tepelenë, the Albanian warlord and brigand who had become the despot of Yannina in Epirus. He had created a small state for himself in Epirus and was quickly becoming a powerful force to be reckoned with. In 1804 the Serbs, under their leader Karadjordje Petrović, had revolted against the intolerable conditions created by the Turkish Janissaries and were, by 1807, demanding independence from Turkey itself. The question as to the ultimate fate of the Ottoman Empire was at this time a complex foreign policy issue, since the allocation of power in Europe hung in the balance. It was an age of intrigue, secret societies, freemasonry, and committed revolutionaries whose patriotic aspirations did not always spring from strategic calculation or common sense. It was an age of in-

cipient nationalism and quest for freedom inspired by the ideas of the French Revolution and the Enlightenment.

In 1820 the Turks turned their forces against the troublesome Ali Pasha of Yannina. The Greeks saw this as an opportunity to make their own bid for autonomy. Alexander had been waiting for just such an opportunity. He planned to personally lead a revolt that would restore to the Greeks their state and the freedom to recover the great empire of the Byzantines. Although there were a number of Hetairists in the principalities who might support him, he felt that he needed to act expeditiously before the Turks could raise a counterrevolutionary force.

The first Greek insurrection broke out in the Romanian Principalities when Alexander led a group of Greek officers of the Russian army and other supporters into Moldavia in March of 1821. He issued a call for Greek and Romanian popular support, intimating that he already had the support of the Russian czar. He did not succeed in gaining peasant adherence, however, or that of fellow Romanian insurrectionists, in particular that of Tudor Vladimirescu, mainly because of mistrust of the Phanariotes because of their past injustices. He also appealed to the czar to come to his aid, but to no avail. The czar disclaimed any responsibility for the insurrection, expressed his extreme displeasure, and dismissed Alexander and his brothers from the Russian army henceforth. In June, 1821, Alexander and his Sacred Battalion were thoroughly defeated by the Turks at the Battle of Dragasani. Alexander, his brother Nicholas, and a few supporters escaped into Austria only to be captured later. Alexander was tried and imprisoned in Bohemia, only to be released shortly before his death in 1828.

Although initially unsuccessful, this marked the beginning of the pathway to the independence of Greece, since Alexander's ill-fated attempt coincided with another uprising that was taking place in the Peloponnese with the involvement of his brother Demetrios, and with better fortune. Demetrios had also joined the Russian army and in 1821 fought in the Peloponnese on the side of the Greeks. He later achieved a career in Greek politics. He had been appointed by his brother Alexander as the representative of the revolutionary secret society, the Philiki Hetairia, in Greece. He first attempted to organize the Greek islanders from Hydra and then went to the Peloponnese, where he put forth his plan for organizing the Greek Morea into a sort of parliament. He encountered opposition, however, from the more entrenched local notables, most of whom did not wish to submit to a central authority. He became president of the national assembly that met at Argos in December, 1821, partly because he, too, was presumed to have Russian support. However, he became disillusioned by the internal squabbling of the Greeks and instead went to Corinth to organize its siege against the Turks.

This insurrection captured the popular imagination, attracting philhellenes from all over Europe along with material and financial support. Although beset with internal factionalism, the Greek revolt was saved through foreign intervention after Great Britain, France, and Russia combined against the Ottoman Empire at the Battle of Navarino on October 20, 1827. This victory was followed by the Russo-Turkish War of 1828-1829. By 1832 the sultan had acknowledged the independence of Greece. As later dissension arose among the Greeks, Demetrios withdrew from politics. His ideas were in advance of his time since he envisioned a rule of law in which Greeks and Turks could live together.

Summary

Alexander and Demetrios Ypsilanti both continued the revolutionary tradition begun by their illustrious family, including the attainment of high office, attachment and loyalty to Russia, distinguished military service, and active involvement in revolts against the forces of oppression. They both put misguided faith in secret societies and intrigue and misled their followers concerning the level of their support from Russia, but both were natural leaders who were able to find a following. Although both saw their dreams and aspirations fail during their lifetimes, the ultimate goals of both brothers were vindicated by history.

Bibliography

Campbell, John, and Philip Sherrard. *Modern Greece*. New York: Praeger, and London: Benn, 1968. This book contains considerable discussion of the Philiki Hetairia and its import.

Clogg, Richard, ed. *The Struggle for Greek Independence: Essays to Mark the 150th Anniversary of the Greek War of Independence*. London: Macmillan, and Hamden, Conn.: Archon, 1973. This book covers the Phanariotes, Philiki Hetairia, the independence movement, insurrections, and the philhellenic movement.

Dakin, Douglas. *The Unification of Greece, 1770-1923*. London: Benn, and New York: St. Martin's Press, 1972. Dakin focuses on the constitutional and state formation questions that followed the independence movement.

Djordjevic, Dimitrije, and Stephen Fischer-Galati. *The Balkan Revolutionary Tradition*. New York: Columbia University Press, 1981. Djordjevic discusses the revolutionary movements of the seventeenth through the nineteenth centuries and the formation of states in the Balkans.

Woodhouse, C. M. *The Greek War of Independence: Its Historical Setting*. London: Hutchinson's University Library, 1952; New York: Russell, 1975. Woodhouse discusses the effect of Ypsilanti's abortive insurrection and its effect of the *megali idea* of a greater Greece.

Zakythenos, D. A. *The Making of Modern Greece: From Byzantium to Independence*. Oxford: Blackwell, and Totowa, N.J.: Rowman and Littlefield, 1976. Zakythenos discusses the social and political background of Greece and the Greeks during the Ottoman period.

Gloria Fulton

ÉMILE ZOLA

Born: April 2, 1840; Paris, France
Died: September 28, 1902; Paris, France
Area of Achievement: Literature
Contribution: Zola's major contributions were in three areas: literature, as a writer of poetry, drama, novels, and essays; literary theory, as one of the major forces in defining naturalism as a literary school; and human rights, as a defender of Alfred Dreyfus, who was falsely accused of treason and sentenced to Devil's Island.

Early Life

Born in Paris on April 2, 1840, Émile Zola spent his first eighteen years in Aix-en-Provence. Zola's father, Francesco Zola, was a high-spirited Venetian, bursting with grandiose ideas for engineering projects. With a doctorate in engineering from the University of Padua, Francesco helped plan the first public railway in Europe, served in the French foreign legion, and, in 1839, married Émilie-Aurélie Aubert. Twenty thousand francs in debt, he nevertheless installed Émilie in an expensive Paris apartment, where Émile, their only child, was born.

Francesco's fortunes improved when Aix accepted his plan to build a canal to bring water to the municipality. The family moved to Provence, where work on the canal proceeded. During construction, Francesco caught cold and succumbed to pneumonia, leaving his family not only destitute but also ninety thousand francs in debt. Émilie moved with her son to smaller quarters, bringing her parents to live with them. Émilie's parents looked after the grieving Émile while Émilie did housework for other people, supplementing that modest income by gradually selling most of her furniture.

The family tried to protect the delicate Émile. Dark-haired and dark-eyed, he had his father's broad face and protruding brow, on which worry lines, lines of conscience, developed early. A speech defect caused Émile's classmates to taunt him. His mother used her dead husband's connections to obtain for the boy a scholarship to Collège Bourbon, where he emphasized scientific studies but developed his passion for literature. Here began his friendship with his classmate Paul Cézanne.

When he was eighteen, Zola moved to Paris, where his mother had relocated to increase her earnings. Isolated and lonely, he lived in squalid surroundings, first with his mother, then alone. Poverty was ever-present. Émile enrolled in the Lycée Saint-Louis, but twice he failed the baccalaureate examinations, partly because his use of French was judged limited and defective. He took menial jobs and at twenty-four published his first collection of stories, *Contes à Ninon* (1864; *Stories for Ninon*, 1895), which was encouragingly reviewed but brought him little money.

Life's Work

Stories for Ninon, although a promising beginning for a young author, shows little of the combination of careful observation, practiced objectivity, and scientific method that characterized Zola's most celebrated works. The stories are modeled on medieval fables, quite a different focus from that of the naturalistic themes for which Zola is best known. Zola's first novel, *La Confession de Claude* (1865; *Claude's Confession*, 1882), failed to employ the close, objective techniques of observation Zola demanded in his naturalistic credo, *Le Roman expérimental* (1880; *The Experimental Novel*, 1893), a theoretical work that significantly changed the course of writing in Europe, Great Britain, and the United States. His second and third novels, *Thérèse Raquin* (1867; English translation, 1881) and *Madeleine Férat* (1868; English translation, 1880), moved toward the realism practiced by Honoré de Balzac, Gustave Flaubert, and the brothers Edmond and Jules de Goncourt, whose writings attracted Zola, a voracious reader.

When Zola was writing these novels, however, he had not yet been exposed to Claude Bernard's *Introduction à l'étude de la médecine expérimentale* (1865; *Introduction to the Study of Experimental Medicine*, 1927), a book from a nonliterary field on which Zola was to model his formal approach to literature, which catapulted him to the forefront of an emerging school of literature that took writing well beyond the realism then prevalent in French literature.

Almost a decade before Zola read Bernard's influential book in 1878, the year of its author's death, he had begun the daunting literary task of writing *Les Rougon-Macquart* (1871-1893; *The Rougon-Macquart Novels*, 1885-1907), designed to examine in minute detail two generations of a family, considering especially the roles that both heredity and environment played in the lives of its members. This work is an interconnected series of twenty novels. Three books of the ambitious cycle, *L'Assommoir* (1877; English translation, 1879), *Nana* (1880; English translation, 1880), and *Germinal* (1885; English translation, 1885), are considered Zola's finest.

Before Zola began work on this cycle, however, he had stirred controversy in literary circles with *Claude's Confession*, in which his forthright and nonjudgmental presentation of a prostitute created legal problems for him in a France that very strongly controlled language and the arts. If his early work was considered notorious, by the time he was writing the Rougon-Macquart cycle, the bourgeoisie viewed him as completely outrageous, a threat to public decency.

Not until *L'Assommoir*, the seventh book of the Rougon-Macquart series, was published in 1877 did Zola's writing bring him much money. He had eked out a living before that time writing essays and doing a variety of journalistic jobs. Income from *L'Assommoir*, however, enabled him to buy a summer home at Médan. He had already attracted an enthusiastic following, especially among notable writers and artists who took very seriously Zola's writing in defense of the Impressionistic artists of his day.

A significant turning point in Zola's life came in 1880, the year in which his mother died and in which *Nana* and *The Experimental Novel* were published. In this year, also, Zola's theory of literary naturalism was exemplified with the publication of the anthology *Les Soirées de Médan* (1880). This work grew out of regular weekly soirées Zola held in both Médan and Paris. In these soirées, the participants, under Zola's staunch guidance, defined literary naturalism categorically, and the regular attendees, including Guy de Maupassant, Joris-Karl Huysmans, and Henri Céard, each contributed a story to the anthology.

If *The Experimental Novel* was the handbook for literary naturalists, *Les Soirées de Médan* became their manifesto. The naturalism Zola espoused moved beyond realism in that realism attempts to present life as it really is, whereas naturalism applies a scientific method to presenting reality, with the intention of identifying social ills and, through experimentation, reaching an understanding of those ills in ways that will enable society to remedy them.

Bernard wrote of the "vital circulus," the symbiosis between the muscular and nervous activities that preserve the blood-producing organs and the blood that nourishes the organs manufacturing it. Zola transformed this concept into his "social circulus." When an organ of society becomes infected, novelists, according to Zola, must proceed scientifically as physicians do. They must discover the simple initial cause that explains the indisposition. By exposing the cause, they then make it amenable to remedy.

Naturalistic writers, then, observe, record faithfully and in detail as a laboratory scientist would, and present their findings in literary form. Naturalistic authors remain detached from their material, presenting consistently exact records of their observations rather than observations colored by personal predilections. They show how heredity and environment act upon the human organism in the social setting to create human behavior. Few literary naturalist, including Zola, remained wholly faithful to the tenets of naturalism. Nevertheless, these tenets profoundly affected the writings of future generations of authors. The positive aspects of society were treated only as they contributed to causes of social ills. Just as medicine deals with physical pathologies, so did Zola's naturalism explore social pathologies.

From his earliest days, Zola had a great zeal for reform. He sought to change a society he considered imperfect. He was fearless and, when necessary, autocratic in working to bring about social changes he deemed imperative. He was incredibly hardworking, ever planning literary projects huge in scope, not unlike the grandiose engineering projects his father had planned a generation earlier. By 1893, Zola had, quite remarkably, completed the twenty novels of the Rougon-Macquart cycle and in the same year began work on the trilogy *Les Trois Villes* (1894-1898; *The Three Cities*, 1894-1898), consisting of *Lourdes* (1894; English translation, 1894), *Rome* (1896; English translation, 1896), and *Paris* (1898; English translation, 1898).

As his work on the trilogy neared its end, Zola, incensed at what he considered the wrongful conviction for treason and sentencing to Devil's Island of Captain Alfred Dreyfus in 1894, took a public stand in support of Dreyfus and published his stirring letter "J'accuse" (1898; "The Dreyfus Case," 1898), which led to a reopening of the case and to the eventual acquittal of the defendant. Zola, however, as a result of his stand, was found guilty on

two charges of libel, fined three thousand francs, and sentenced to a year in prison.

Before the execution of his sentence, Zola fled to England, where he remained until France's president, Émile-François Loubet, pardoned him in 1899, whereupon Zola returned to France. There, he continued work on another massive project, *Les Quatre Évangiles* (1899-1903; English translation, 1900-1903), to consist of four novels, three of which, *Fécondité* (1899; *Fruitfulness*, 1900), *Travail* (1901; *Work*, 1901), and *Vérité* (1903; *Truth*, 1903), he completed before his death by coal gas asphyxiation in his Paris apartment on September 28, 1902. The death, first thought to be accidental, was likely a murder committed by elements who opposed his participation in the Dreyfus case.

Summary

Émile Zola was a man with exuberant plans, a man of enormous energy and courage. He lived a life guided by principles he arrived at consciously and intelligently. In addition to his prolific literary career, Zola's involvement in public affairs, always guided by his intellect and his immutable conscience, distinguished him throughout his life.

Zola's support of Impressionist artists in the 1860's forced him into an unpopular public stand well before his own future was assured. He supported what he believed without regard to personal consequences. He was equally stalwart in the 1870's and 1880's, as he was developing his own literary credo, which, in its final formulation as literary naturalism, became a publicly unpopular movement. Zola spent the last years of his life preoccupied with the Dreyfus affair, and on his death it was this stand that seemed best to exemplify to his countrymen his spirit of social reform, as Anatole France noted in his oration at Zola's funeral.

Zola's literary theories directly affected scores of authors, among whom some direct inheritors were Gerhart Hauptmann, Hermann Sudermann, Arthur Schnitzler, August Strindberg, Henrik Ibsen, Thomas Hardy, D. H. Lawrence, Eugene O'Neill, Frank Norris, Upton Sinclair, and Thomas Mann. Indirectly, his literary theories affected even those authors who rebelled against naturalism and went on to found such important countermovements as literary expressionism.

Bibliography

Baguley, David. *Critical Essays on Émile Zola.* Boston: Hall, 1986. The twenty essays in this book, some written especially for this volume, others drawn from previously published sources, present a balanced view of Zola criticism, ranging from such early critics as Algernon Swinburne, Henry Havelock Ellis, and Heinrich Mann to such later ones as Roland Barthes, Irving Howe, and Naomi Schor.

Brown, Frederick. *Zola: A Life.* New York: Farrar Straus Giroux, 1995; London: Macmillan, 1996. A detailed biography of Zola, whose life was as exciting as those of the characters in his books.

Knapp, Bettina L. *Émile Zola.* New York: Ungar, 1980. A brief, direct presentation, accurate and highly appropriate for those just beginning to explore Zola. The chronological table is especially useful.

Lowe, Romana N. *The Fictional Female: Sacrificial Rituals and Spectacles of Writing in Baudelaire, Zola, and Cocteau.* New York: Lang, 1997. Lowe studies the ultimate demise of female characters in late nineteenth and twentieth century text through analysis of writings by Zola, Baudelaire, and Cocteau.

Richardson, Joanna. *Zola.* London: Weidenfeld and Nicolson, and New York: St. Martin's Press, 1978. Richardson succeeds in showing how what she considers Zola's contentiousness relates to the impact of his work, which overall is excellent more as a reflection of a well-defined literary credo than as an artistic contribution. Especially valuable for its clear exposition of the Dreyfus affair.

Schom, Alan. *Émile Zola: A Biography.* London: Macdonald, 1987; New York: Henry Holt, 1988. The excellence of its prose style and the carefully chosen illustrations make this book a reading delight. The research is exhaustive, and the revelations that point to Zola's death's being a well-planned assassination made to look like an accident raise fascinating questions for the modern reader.

Schor, Naomi. *Zola's Crowds.* Baltimore: Johns Hopkins University Press, 1978. Schor is concerned with Zola's remarkable ability to control the huge numbers of people who populate a work as massive as the Rougon-Macquart series, in which each novel is at once independent from but interconnected with the others. An interesting thesis in the light of Gustave Le Bon's theory of the crowd.

Walker, Philip. *Zola.* London and Boston: Routledge, 1985. This thoughtful book is meticulous in its research although somewhat pedestrian in its organization. The most valuable chapter in it is "Full Summer," which explores fruitfully Zola's necrophobia, a matter that had significant bearing on his writing.

R. Baird Shuman

Dictionary of World Biography

The 19th Century

Indices

AREA OF ACHIEVEMENT

HISTORIOGRAPHY. *See also* **EDUCATION**

HORTICULTURE. *See also* **BOTANY; LANDSCAPE ARCHITECTURE**

INDIAN AFFAIRS. *See* **NATIVE AMERICAN AFFAIRS**

INDUSTRY. *See* **BUSINESS AND INDUSTRY**

INVENTION AND TECHNOLOGY. *See also* **AVIATION AND SPACE EXPLORATION; COMPUTER SCIENCE; ENGINEERING**

JOURNALISM. *See also* **PUBLISHING**

MANUFACTURING. *See* BUSINESS AND INDUSTRY; ENGINEERING; INVENTION AND TECHNOLOGY

MATHEMATICS. *See also* STATISTICS

MEDICINE. *See also* NURSING; PHYSIOLOGY

METALLURGY

METEOROLOGY

MICROBIOLOGY. *See* BIOLOGY

MILITARY AFFAIRS. *See also* GOVERNMENT AND POLITICS

GEOGRAPHICAL LOCATION

ESTONIA. *See* GERMANY

ETHIOPIA

FRANCE

NAME INDEX

PHOTO CREDITS

All photos in this volume are courtesy of the Library of Congress except for the following:

American Stock/Archive Photos: 391

Archive France/TAL/Archive Photos: 260

Archive Photos: 333, 527, 552, 598, 684, 760, 889, 944, 1108, 1168, 1305, 1465, 1493, 1549, 1652, 1753, 1967, 1994, 2034, 2039, 2248

Archive Photos/Frank Driggs Collection: 1239

Associated Publishers: 2336, 2397

Hawaii State Archives: 1373

Institute of Texan Cultures: 1251

Missouri Historical Society: 498

National Archives: 323, 590, 916, 1696, 1852, 2123, 2359

National Library of Medicine: 110, 1659, 1981

The Nobel Foundation: 183, 711, 1289, 1298, 1553, 1675

Smithsonian Institution: 593, 1343, 1703, 2180

Sommer Collection/Archive Photos: 668